Dictionary *of* BIBLICAL IMAGERY

General Editors

Leland Ryken

James C. Wilhoit

Tremper Longman III

Consulting Editors

Colin Duriez

Douglas Penney

Daniel G. Reid

InterVarsity Press

Downers Grove, Illinois, USA

Leicester, England

InterVarsity Press, USA
P.O. Box 1400, Downers Grove, IL 60515, USA
World Wide Web: www.ivpress.com
E-mail: mail@ivpress.com

Inter-Varsity Press, England
38 De Montfort Street, Leicester LE1 7GP, England

InterVarsity Press®, U.S.A., is the book-publishing division of InterVarsity Christian Fellowship/USA®, a student movement active on campus at hundreds of universities, colleges and schools of nursing in the United States of America, and a member movement of the International Fellowship of Evangelical Students. For information about local and regional activities, write Public Relations Dept., InterVarsity Christian Fellowship/USA, 6400 Schroeder Rd., P.O. Box 7895, Madison, WI 53707-7895.

Inter-Varsity Press, England, is the book-publishing division of the Universities and Colleges Christian Fellowship (formerly the Inter-Varsity Fellowship), a student movement linking Christian Unions in universities and colleges throughout the United Kingdom and the Republic of Ireland, and a member movement of the International Fellowship of Evangelical Students. For information about local and national activities write to UCCF, 38 De Montfort Street, Leicester LE1 7GP.

Cover Photography: Lilies of the Valley by Lefever/Grushow from Great Britain. Altar/lamb photographs by Daniel Blatt.

Interior Illustrations: Roberta Polfus

USA ISBN 0-8308-1451-5

UK ISBN 0-85111-753-8

Printed in the United States of America ∞

Library of Congress Cataloging-in-Publication Data

Dictionary of biblical imagery/general editors: Leland Ryken, James
  C. Wilhoit, Tremper Longman III; consulting editors: Colin Duriez,
  Douglas Penney, Daniel G. Reid.
     p.   cm.
  Includes bibliographical references and indexes.
  ISBN 0-8308-1451-5 (cloth: alk. paper)
  1. Bible—Language, style—Dictionaries.   2. Symbolism in the
Bible—Dictionaries.   I. Ryken, Leland.   II. Wilhoit, Jim.
III. Longman, Tremper.   IV. Duriez, Colin.   V. Penney, Douglas,
1956- .   VI. Reid, Daniel G., 1949- .
BS537.D48   1998
220.3—dc21
                                          98-16945
                                             CIP

British Library Cataloguing in Publication Data

A catalogue record for this book is available from the British Library.

26	25	24	23	22	21	20	19	18	17	16	15	14	13	12	11	10	9	8	7	6	5	4	3	2	1
20	19	18	17	16	15	14	13	12	11	10	09	08	07	06	05	04	03	02	01	00	99	98

Contents

InterVarsity Press

Executive Director
Robert Fryling

Editorial Staff

Editorial Director
Andrew T. Le Peau

Managing Editor
James Hoover

Reference Book Editor
Daniel G. Reid

Copyeditors
Ruth Goring
Elizabeth G. Yoder

Proofreader
Drew Blankman

Editorial Assistants
Eric Romero
David Zimmerman

Editorial Interns
Anita Genzink
Kay Kleinjan

Production Staff

Production Manager
Nancy Fox

Production Coordinator
James Erhart

Design
Kathy Lay Burrows

Design Assistant
Andrew Craft

Interior Illustrations
Roberta Polfus

Typesetters
Gail Munroe
Audrey I. Smith

Programming Consultant
Andy Shermer

Preface

This *Dictionary of Biblical Imagery* was conceived as a reference book that would assist readers, students and communicators of the Bible in exploring the fascinating and varied world of the imagery, metaphors and archetypes of the Bible. It appeared that conventional Bible dictionaries and encyclopedias provided little help in this area. For those whose Bible's were pencil-marked with cross-references to images, motifs and other literary features, the lack of such a reference work seemed like a crime—or a publisher's opportunity!

From there the vision of the *Dictionary* grew to include articles on character types, plot motifs, type scenes, rhetorical devices, literary genres and the individual books of the Bible. In the end, some articles have sprawled across broad subject areas (such as "Animals" or "Legal Images") and others are tightly focused (such as "Harp" or "Mustard Seed"). Many articles are innovative and clearly distinguish this work from other Bible dictionaries (such as "Well, Meeting at the" or "Cheat the Oracle"). And even where articles entitled "Wall" or "Tower" arouse a right-brained reader's distaste for archaeological description and detail, the emphasis is decidedly on the evocative dimensions of these subjects.

Despite approximately 850 articles, this *Dictionary* is not comprehensive. This acknowledgment is a testimony to the vast and varied sea of biblical imagery, and to the limited time and energy of both editors and publisher. It is always a challenge to create a reference work in a field where no predecessor has established a "canon" of entries. It can also be a delightful adventure as the editors repeatedly encounter new vistas and angles of vision along the way—and try to help others see them too. But after seven years of planning and labor—and a work much longer than originally projected—the time has come to cease and desist and publish. We console ourselves in the generous thought that future revisers can learn from our efforts and build on this foundation. We also believe that our readers, as they work with this *Dictionary*, will see that they can launch out on their own and explore other facets of biblical imagery.

From the first, the editors sought to bring together the talents and perspectives of both literary and biblical scholars in a complementary marriage of expertise. But it quickly became apparent that in order to produce a satisfying volume, the claims of individual authorship would need to be subsumed under the editorial vision. So the decision was made in favor of a policy that would allow a free editorial hand in shaping, rewriting and augmenting the articles. Experience in creating reference works of this type has shown that as the work progresses, the editors themselves gain an ever deeper and broader view of the subject. Lateral connections and new insights flourish as articles and pages compound. A policy was created to allow this editorial vision to be fed back into the work. Thus the articles are unsigned (a list of contributors may be found at the beginning of the book). Although some articles appear much as they were originally authored, the vast majority of them have been worked over by several editorial hands, and they are frequently lengthier than the originals. As a result, this *Dictionary* has become a highly collaborative effort in which individual claims to authorship (not least those of the individual editors) have been set aside in the interest of what we trust will be a valuable contribution to understanding and enjoying the Bible. We offer our sincere thanks and appreciation to the approximately 150 contributors who have labored to make this work a reality. But we also accept full responsibility for any deficiencies in the final product.

The primary audience for this *Dictionary* is not scholars but laypeople. We have tried to create a readable and interesting work, one that will not only serve as an indispensable reference tool that augments conventional Bible dictionaries but will also open up new avenues of reading and appreciating the Bible. This book, we hope, will unfold new perspectives for all students of the Bible, new approaches for communicators of the Bible—including those in the fine arts—and heart-warming insights for devotional readers of the Bible. If readers capture some measure of the joy we have experienced even in the midst of our reading the proofs of this emerging book, we will have achieved our goal.

The Editors

How to Use this Dictionary

Abbreviations
Comprehensive tables of abbreviations for general matters as well as for scholarly and biblical literature may found on pages ix-x.

Authorship of Articles
The articles are unsigned (see preface), but a full list of contributors may be found on pages xi-xii, in alphabetical order of their last name.

Bibliographies
A bibliography has been appended to some articles. The bibliographies include works cited in the articles and other significant related works. Bibliographical entries are listed in alphabetical order by the author's last name, and where an author has more than one work cited, they are listed alphabetically by title. Abbreviations used in the bibliographies appear in the tables of abbreviations.

Cross-references
The *Dictionary* has been extensively cross-referenced in order to aid readers in making the most of material appearing throughout the volume. Five types of cross-referencing will be found:
    1. One-line entries appearing in alphabetical order throughout the *Dictionary* direct readers to articles where a topic is discussed:
    Enameled Imagery. See Hard, Harden, Hardness; Jewels and Precious Stones; Permanence.
    2. An asterisk before a single word in the body of an article indicates that an article by that title appears in the *Dictionary.* For example, *"angel" directs the reader to an article entitled **Angel.**
    3. A cross-reference appearing within parentheses in the body of an article also directs the reader to an article by that title. For example, (*see* Lightning) directs the reader to an article entitled **Lightning.** Such cross-references are most frequently used either to direct the readers attention to an article of related interest.
    4. Cross-references have been appended to the end of articles, immediately preceding the bibliography, to direct readers to articles significantly related to the subject:
    See also BANQUET; BLESSING, BLESSEDNESS; FILL, FULLNESS; HARVEST; LAND FLOWING WITH MILK AND HONEY; PARADISE; STOREHOUSE.

Indexes
A *Scripture Index* is provided to assist readers in gaining access to information related to various biblical texts.
    The *Subject Index* is intended to assist readers in finding relevant information on topics that have not been assigned a separate article or are taken up in more than one place.

Transliteration
Hebrew and Greek words have been transliterated according to a system set out in the front matter. Greek verbs appear in their lexical form (rather than infinitive) in order to assist those with little or no knowledge of the language in using other reference works.

Abbreviations

General Abbreviations

cf.	compare
chap(s).	chapter(s)
DSS	Dead Sea Scrolls
e.g.	for example
ed.	edition; editor(s); edited by
esp.	especially
Gk	Greek
Heb	Hebrew
i.e.	that is
LXX	Septuagint (Greek translation of the Old Testament)
mg.	margin
n.d.	no date
n.s.	new series
NT	New Testament
OT	Old Testament
par.	parallel passage in another/other Gospel(s)
repr.	reprint
rev.	revised (edition)

v. or vv.	verse or verses
vol.	volume

Translations of the Bible

JB	Jerusalem Bible
KJV	King James Version (Authorized Version)
NASB	New American Standard Bible
NEB	New English Bible
NIV	New International Version
NLB	New Living Bible
NRSV	New Revised Standard Version
RSV	Revised Standard Version

Apocrypha and Septuagint

4 Ezra	4 Ezra
1-4 Macc	1-4 Maccabees
Sir	Sirach (or Ecclesiasticus)
Wis	Wisdom of Solomon

Books of the Bible

Old Testament			*New Testament*	
Gen	Ezra	Dan	Mal	Phil
Ex	Neh	Hos		Col
Lev	Esther	Joel	*New Testament*	1-2 Thess
Num	Job	Amos	Mt	1-2 Tim
Deut	Ps	Obad	Mk	Tit
Josh	Prov	Jon	Lk	Philem
Judg	Eccles	Mic	Jn	Heb
Ruth	Song	Nahum	Acts	Jas
1-2 Sam	Is	Hab	Rom	1-2 Pet
1-2 Kings	Jer	Zeph	1-2 Cor	1-2-3 Jn
1-2 Chron	Lam	Hag	Gal	Jude
	Ezek	Zech	Eph	Rev

Periodicals, Reference Works and Serials

AB	Anchor Bible
ABD	*Anchor Bible Dictionary*
ANEP	*Ancient Near East in Pictures*
ANET	*Ancient Near Eastern Texts*
BASOR	*Bulletin of the American Schools of Oriental Research*
BibSac	*Bibliotheca Sacra*
CBQ	*Catholic Biblical Quarterly*
DBTEL	*Dictionary of Biblical Tradition in English Literature*

DJG	*Dictionary of Jesus and the Gospels*
DLNTD	*Dictionary of the Later New Testament and Its Developments*
DPL	*Dictionary of Paul and His Letters*
ExpT	*Expository Times*
IDB	*Interpreter's Dictionary of the Bible*
IntC	Interpretation Commentary
ISBE	*The International Standard Bible Encyclopedia* (revised)
JBL	*Journal of Biblical Literature*

Transliteration of Hebrew and Greek

HEBREW

Consonants

א = '	י = y	שׁ = š		*Short Vowels*	
בּ = b	כּ = k	תּ = t		_ = a	
ב = b̲	כ = k̲	ת = t̲		ֶ = e	
ג = g	ל = l			ִ = i	
ג = g̲	מ = m	*Long Vowels*		ֳ = o	
ד = d	נ = n	(ה)ָ = â		ֻ = u	
ד = d̲	ס = s	ֵ֯ = ê			
ה = h	ע = '	ִי = î		*Very Short Vowels*	
ו = w	פּ = p	וֹ = ô		ֲ = ᵃ	
ז = z	פ = p̄	וּ = û		ֱ = ᵉ	
ח = ḥ	צ = ṣ	ָ = ā		ְ = ᵉ (if vocal)	
ט = ṭ	ק = q	ֵ = ē		ֳ = ᵒ	
	ר = r	= ō			
	שׂ = ś				

GREEK

A = A	Θ = Th	o = o	Ψ = Ps
α = a	θ = th	Π = P	ψ = ps̄
B = B	I = I	π = p	Ω = Ō
β = b	ι = i	P = R	ω = ō
Γ = G	K = K	ρ = r	‘P = Rh
γ = g	κ = k	Σ = S	ῥ = rh
Δ = D	Λ = L	σ/ς = s	‘ = h
δ = d	λ = l	T = T	γξ = nx
E = E	M = M	τ = t	γγ = ng
ε = e	μ = m	Y = Y	αυ = au
Z = Z	N = N	υ = y	ευ = eu
ζ = z	ν = n	Φ = Ph	ου = ou
H = Ē	Ξ = X	φ = ph	υι = yi
η = ē	ξ = x	X = Ch	
	O = O	χ = ch	

Contributors

Alexander, T. Desmond. The Queen's University of Belfast, Belfast, Northern Ireland.

Allen, Erick, Kintnersville, Pennsylvania, USA.

Allison, Dale C., Jr. Pittsburgh Theological Seminary, Pittsburgh, Pennsylvania, USA.

Apkera, Jacob. Nigeria.

Arnold, Clinton E. Talbot School of Theology, La Mirada, California, USA.

Balchin, John F. Purley, Surrey, England.

Baldwin, Joyce. (Deceased) Formerly, Eastwood, Nottinghamshire, England.

Bancroft, RoseLee. Alice Lloyd College, Pippa Passes, Kentucky, USA.

Banks, Robert. Fuller Theological Seminary, Pasadena, California, USA.

Barker, David G. Heritage Theological Seminary, London, Ontario, Canada.

Barratt, David J. Chester, England.

Bauckham, Richard J. University of St. Andrews, St. Andrews, Fife, Scotland.

Bell, Richard H. University of Nottingham, Nottingham, England.

Bennett, David. Mountain Park Church, Lake Oswego, Oregon, USA.

Bible, Jesse J. Willow Grove, Pennsylvania, USA.

Birdsall, Brent. Huntington, Indiana, USA.

Boda, Mark J. Canadian Bible College/Canadian Theological Seminary, Regina, Saskatchewan, Canada.

Braddock, Matthew. Quincy, Massachusetts, USA.

Brown, Ann. Cardiff, Wales.

Burke, Donald E. Catherine Booth Bible College, Winnipeg, Manitoba, Canada.

Burns, Lanier. Dallas Theological Seminary, Dallas, Texas, USA.

Carroll R., M. Daniel. Denver Seminary, Denver, Colorado, USA.

Chan, Frank. Glenside, Pennsylvania, USA.

Chisholm, Robert B., Jr. Dallas Theological Seminary, Dallas, Texas, USA.

Claass, Stefan. Mainz, Germany.

Colwell, Jerry D. Heritage Baptist College, London, Ontario, Canada.

Dawn, Marva J. Christians Equipped for Ministry, Vancouver, Washington, USA.

Duguid, Iain. Westminster Theological Seminary in California, Escondido, California, USA.

Du Mont Brown, Sarah. Trinity Christian Academy, Addison, Texas, USA.

Duriez, Colin. Inter-Varsity Press, Leicester, England.

Eckman, James. Grace College of the Bible, Omaha, Nebraska, USA.

Elrod, Eileen Razzari. Santa Clara University, Santa Clara, California, USA.

Enns, Peter. Westminster Theological Seminary, Philadelphia, Pennsylvania, USA.

Esler, Philip F. University of St. Andrews, St. Andrews, Fife, Scotland.

Etchells, Ruth. University of Durham, Durham, England.

Evans, Craig A. Trinity Western University, Langley, British Columbia, Canada.

Evans, Mary J. London Bible College, Northwood, Middlesex, England.

Felch, Douglas A. Grand Rapids, Michigan, USA.

Felch, Susan M. Calvin College, Grand Rapids, Michigan, USA.

Fink, Larry E. Hardin Simmons University, Abilene, Texas, USA.

Gentrup, William F. Arizona State University, Tempe, Arizona, USA.

Gledhill, Thomas D. Evangelical Theological College of Wales, Mid-Glamorgan, Wales.

Glodo, Michael J. Reformed Theological Seminary, Orlando, Florida, USA.

Graham, Lowell B. Providence Christian Academy, St. Louis, Missouri, USA.

Green, Douglas. Westminster Theological Seminary, Philadelphia, Pennsylvania, USA.

Green, Joel B. Asbury Theological Seminary, Wilmore, Kentucky, USA.

Groves, Alan J. Westminster Theological Seminary, Philadelphia, Pennsylvania, USA.

Habermas, Ronald T. John Brown University, Siloam Springs, Arkansas, USA.

Hallett, David. Ardsley, Pennsylva-

nia, USA.

Harmon, William B. Vancouver, Washington, USA.

Harvey, Jo Ann. Immanuel Presbyterian Church, Warrenville, Illinois, USA.

Harvey, Robert W. Immanuel Presbyterian Church, Warrenville, Illinois, USA.

Hasenclever, Frauke. Taunusstein, Germany.

Hatina, Thomas R. London, England.

Heller, Jack. Kenner, Louisiana, USA.

Hepper, Nigel. Richmond, Surrey, England.

Hess, Richard S. Denver Seminary, Denver, Colorado, USA.

Hill, Andrew E. Wheaton College, Wheaton, Illinois, USA.

Hong, In-Gyu. Reformed Theological Seminary, Seoul, South Korea.

Horine, Steven C. Harleysville, Pennsylvania, USA.

Howard, David M., Jr. New Orleans Baptist Theological Seminary, New Orleans, Louisiana, USA.

Howe, Bonnie G. T. Berkeley, California, USA.

Hudson, Don M. Western Seminary Seattle Campus, Kirkland, Washington, USA.

Hughes, Frederick E. Cheltenham & Gloucester College of Higher Education, Gloucestershire, England.

Hughes, Kent. College Church, Wheaton, Illinois, USA.

Huttar, Charles A. Hope College, Holland, Michigan, USA.

Huttar, David K. Nyack College, Nyack, New York, USA.

Ibach, Robert. Dallas Theological Seminary, Dallas, Texas, USA.

Jobes, Karen H. Westmont College, Santa Barbara, California, USA.

Kaufmann, U. Milo. University of Illinois at Urbana-Champaign, Urbana, Illinois, USA.

Keener, Craig S. Eastern Baptist Theological Seminary, Philadelphia, Pennsylvania, USA.

Kellegrew, Marsh. Mercer Island, Washington, USA.

Kelly, Michael B. Philadelphia, Pennsylvania, USA.

Kingdon, David. Glas Bryntirion Press, Bridgend, Wales.

Klein, William W. Denver Seminary, Denver, Colorado, USA.

Klem, John F. Central Baptist Theological Seminary, Virginia Beach, Virginia, USA.

Kojecky, Roger F. Northwood, Middlesex, England.

Konkel, August H. Providence Theological Seminary, Otterburne, Manitoba, Canada.

Lamport, Mark A. Gordon College, Wenham, Massachusetts, USA.

Lindsey, Victor. East Central University, Ada, Oklahoma, USA.

Littledale, Richard J. Purley Baptist Church, Purley, Surrey, England.

Longman, Tremper, III. Westmont College, Santa Barbara, California, USA.

Lucas, Ernest C. Bristol Baptist College, Bristol, England.

Ludwick, Robert D., II. Ballwin, Missouri, USA.

Lyall, Francis. University of Aberdeen, Aberdeen, Scotland.

Lynn, Robyn D. Westmont College, Santa Barbara, California, USA.

Lyons, Michael A. Glenview, Illinois, USA.

McCartney, Dan G. Westminster Theological Seminary, Philadelphia, Pennsylvania, USA.

McClarty, Wilma. Southern College, Collegedale, Tennessee, USA.

McKeever, Michael C. Fresno, California, USA.

Makujina, John. Philadelphia, Pennsylvania, USA.

Mawhinney, Allen. Reformed Theological Seminary, Orlando, Florida, USA.

Meier, Samuel A. Ohio State University, Columbus, Ohio, USA.

Miller, Daniel R. Deerfield, Illinois, USA.

Miller, David G. Mississippi College, Clinton, Mississippi, USA.

Mills, Don. Central Baptist Theological Seminary, Virginia Beach, Virginia, USA.

Moore, Erika. Worthington, Pennsylvania, USA.

Moore, James J. Worthington, Pennsylvania, USA.

Motyer, Stephen. London Bible College, Northwood, Middlesex, England.

Neale, David A. Canadian Nazarene College, Winnipeg, Manitoba, Canada.

Newman, Carey C. Louisville, Kentucky, USA.

Nielson, Kathleen Buswell. Wheaton College, Wheaton, Illinois, USA.

Olson, Dennis T. Princeton Theological Seminary, Princeton, New Jersey, USA.

Parker, Margaret. (Deceased) Formerly Walnut Creek, California, USA.

Patterson, Richard D. Forest, Virginia, USA.

Penney, Douglas. Wheaton College, Wheaton, Illinois, USA.

Perrin, Nicholas. Aurora, Illinois, USA.

Pocock, Michael. Dallas Theological Seminary, Dallas, Texas, USA.

Porter, Stanley E. Roehampton Institute, London, England.

Pratt, Richard L., Jr. Reformed Theological Seminary, Orlando, Florida, USA.

Provan, Iain. Regent College, Vancouver, British Columbia, Canada.

Ragen, Brian Abel. Southern Illinois University at Edwardsville, Ewardsville, Illinois, USA.

Read, Peter. Monmouth, Gwent, South Wales.

Reid, Daniel G. InterVarsity Press, Westmont, Illinois, USA.

Reid, Debra K. Spurgeon's College, London, England.

Riso, Mary T. South Hamilton, Massachusetts, USA.

Ritchie, Daniel E. Bethel College, St. Paul, Minnesota, USA.

Roberts, D. Phillip. Temple Terrace, Florida, USA.

Robertson, George W. St. Louis, Missouri, USA.

Ryken, Leland. Wheaton College, Wheaton, Illinois, USA.

Ryken, Lisa. Tenth Presbyterian Church, Philadelphia, Pennsylvania, USA.

Ryken, Philip G. Tenth Presbyterian Church, Philadelphia, Pennsylvania, USA.

Sandy, Brent. Salem, Virginia, USA.

Schumann, Anne. Mainz, Germany.

Schuurman, John F. Wheaton Christian Reformed Church, Wheaton, Illinois, USA.

Schwab, George M., Sr. Fort Washington, Pennsylvania, USA.

Sider, J. Philip W. Carlsbad, California, USA.

Siebald, Manfred. Johannes Gutenberg-Universität Mainz, Mainz, Germany.

Sims, James H. The University of Southern Mississippi, Hattiesburg, Mississippi, USA.

Sohn, Seock-Tae. Reformed Theological Seminary, Seoul, South Korea.

Spencer, Aida Besançon. Gordon-Conwell Theological Seminary, South Hamilton, Massachusetts, USA.

Stabnow, David. Melrose Park, Pennsylvania, USA.

Stallman, Robert C. Central Bible College, Springfield, Missouri, USA.

Stone, David A. London, England.

Stroup, William L., Jr. Collingdale, Pennsylvania, USA.

Thatcher, Thomas W. Cincinnati Bible Seminary, Cincinnati, Ohio, USA.

Thiselton, Anthony C. The University of Nottingham, Nottingham, England.

Tidball, Derek J. London Bible College, Northwood, Middlesex, England.

Tischler, Nancy M. The Pennsylvania State University, University Park, Pennsylvania, USA.

Travers, Michael E. Mississippi College, Clinton, Mississippi, USA.

Vanhoozer, Kevin J. Trinity Evangelical Divinity School, Deerfield, Illinois, USA.

Walley, Christopher D. Leamington, England.

Walters, James. John Brown University, Siloam Springs, Arkansas, USA.

Watson, Duane F. Malone College, Canton, Ohio, USA.

Wendler, Linda. Northwestern College, St. Paul, Minnesota, USA.

Whittle, Amberys R. Georgia Southern University, Statesboro, Georgia, USA.

Wilhoit, James C. Wheaton College, Wheaton, Illinois, USA.

Williams, Derek L. Northampton, England.

Williams, Michael J. Calvin Theological Seminary, Grand Rapids, Michigan, USA.

Willoughby, Robert. London Bible College, Northwood, Middlesex, England.

Wood, Derek R. W. Waddington, Lincolnshire, England.

Woodard, Branson L., Jr. Liberty University, Lynchburg, Virginia, USA.

Wheaton College Student Assistants:

Christopher Bunn

Matthew Erickson

Bill Kerschbaum

Clay Spurlock

Introduction

"Light dawns for the righteous."

"The Lord raised up for them a deliverer, a left-handed man."

"Lot was sitting in the gate of Sodom."

The Bible is more than a book of ideas: it is also a book of images and motifs. Everywhere we turn we find concrete pictures and recurrent patterns. Some of these, like the image of light, are universal. Others, like the motif of left-handedness, are unexpressive until we have been alerted to their significance. The meaning of others, such as the image of sitting in the gate, is lost on modern readers until they are initiated into what the motif meant in other places at other times.

In all three instances, we will understand the Bible better with the aid of a dictionary that helps us to *see* what is literally in the biblical text and to understand its *significance* and *meaning*. Stated another way, we will miss a lot of what the Bible contains if we do not see and understand the literal and symbolic meanings of the Bible's images.

How Does the Bible Communicate Truth?

Because of the predominantly theological and devotional purposes to which Christians put the Bible, it is almost impossible not to slip into the error of looking upon the Bible as a theological outline with prooftexts attached. Yet the Bible is much more a book of images and motifs than of abstractions and propositions. This is obscured by the way in which preachers and theologians gravitate so naturally to the epistles. A biblical scholar has correctly said that the Bible speaks

> largely in images. . . . The stories, the parables, the sermons of the prophets, the reflections of the wise men, the pictures of the age to come, the interpretations of past events all tend to be expressed in images which arise out of experience. They do not often arise out of abstract technical language.[1]

This dictionary accepts this as a working premise.

The Bible is a book that *images* the truth as well as stating it in abstract propositions. Correspondingly, the truth that the Bible expresses is often a matter of truthfulness to human experience, as distinct from ideas that are true rather than false. The Bible here follows a common pattern. A noted theologian has stated it thus:

> We are far more image-making and image-using creatures than we usually think ourselves to be and . . . are guided and formed by images in our minds. . . . Man . . . is a being who grasps and shapes reality . . . with the aid of great images, metaphors, and analogies.[2]

These images, in turn, are important to a person's world view, which consists of images and stories as well as ideas.

Recent brain research has given us a new slant on this.[3] Research has found that the two sides of the human brain respond differently to different types of stimuli. The left hemisphere's forte is analysis, reason and logic. The right hemisphere is dominant in visual and other sensory processes, as well as in the exercise of emotion and the recognition of humor and metaphor. Conceptual and emotionally neutral words activate the left hemisphere, while words that name images and are emotionally laden activate the right hemisphere. The focus of this dictionary is on the aspects of the Bible that make it right-brain discourse.

Defining Terms: Image, Symbol, Metaphor, Simile

The key terms that underlie this dictionary carry their common meanings. The most foundational term is *image*. An image is any word that names a concrete thing (such as tree or house) or action (such as running or threshing). Any object or action that we can picture is an image.

Images require two activities from us as readers of the Bible. The first is to experience the image as literally and in as fully a sensory way as possible. The second is to be sensitive to the connotations or overtones of the image. When we stop to reflect on the image of water, for example, we find that it connotes such qualities as refreshment, sustenance and life. The most elementary form of connotation is simply whether an image is positive or negative in association in the context in which it appears.

When we encounter an image in the Bible, therefore, we need to learn to ask two questions: (1) What is the literal picture? (2) What does this image evoke? Answering the first question will insure that we have allowed the Bible to speak to our "right brain"—that part of us that responds to the concrete realities that the Bible records. Answering the second question will lead to an awareness of connotations, associations and significance. If either of these levels of response is missing, our experience of the Bible is impoverished.

A *symbol* is an image that stands for something in addition to its literal meaning. It is more laden with meaning than simply the connotations of the straight image. In the overwhelming majority of cases, symbolism emerges as a shared language in a culture. In other words, it will be extremely rare that a biblical writer will create a symbol for a single occasion.

The image of water will illuminate how image and symbol work and how they differ from each other. In the narrative of the exodus, water functions as a full-fledged image when we read that "there was no water for the people to drink," followed by the account of how Moses struck the rock to make water flow "that the people may drink" (Ex 17:1-7, RSV). The connotations of water spring from its literal properties and include refreshment and retrieving life from the threat of death. Water moves beyond image and assumes the status of a symbol when Jesus tells the woman at the well, "Whoever drinks of the water that I shall give him will never thirst; the water that I shall give him will become in him a spring of water welling up to eternal life" (Jn 4:14 RSV). Whereas with the *image* the literal properties of water are of primary importance, in Jesus' *symbol* it is the second level of meaning—salvation—that is primary. Of course, water would never have become a symbol of salvation if it did not possess the physical properties that it does, so even with a biblical symbol we will impoverish the impact of an utterance if we do not pause to experience the literal side of the symbol.

Metaphor and *simile* function much like symbol, and nothing much is lost if these terms are used interchangeably. A *metaphor* is an implied comparison. For example, when Paul writes that "I planted, Apollos watered" (1 Cor 3:6), he is not speaking of a literal plant. He refers to a figurative planting and watering in the form of proclaiming the Gospel to produce conversion and the teaching of the truth to produce Christian nurture. A *simile* also compares one thing to another, but it makes the comparison explicit by using the formula *like* or *as*. An example is the proverb "Like cold water to a thirsty soul, / so is good news from a far country" (Prov 25:25).

Metaphor and simile are bifocal utterances that require us to look at both the literal and figurative levels. The literal meaning of the word *metaphor* speaks volumes in this regard. It is based on two Greek words that together mean "to carry over." *First* we need to relive the literal experience of water; *then* we need to carry over that meaning to such realities as Christian nurture and good news from a far country. The connection between the halves of the comparison is not arbitrary but logical. To perceive the logic of the connections that a metaphor or simile makes, we need to do justice to the literal qualities of the image, remembering that metaphors and similes are images first and comparisons secondly.

Bible dictionaries and commentaries commonly err in one of two directions, and it is the aim of this dictionary to achieve a balance. On the one hand, some resources channel all their energies into uncovering the original context of an image, making sure that we get the literal picture but never asking what feelings or meanings are elicited by the image. Images call for interpretation, and to leave biblical imagery uninterpreted is a great waste. The images of the Bible exist to *tell* us something about the godly life, something they will not do if they are allowed to remain as physical phenomena only. In short, a common failing of commentaries and dictionaries is that they do not adequately speak to the issue of *significance* (what an image signifies by way of meaning).

But the opposite failing of ignoring the literal level of imagery in a scramble to tell us what an image *means* is even more common. Here, for example, is what some standard sources did with an image that occurs at least seven times in the psalms—the horn that God raises up: (1) "the power and the stability of the kingship"; (2) "the [term] scarcely needs comment, with the evident implications of strength"; (3) "*horn* here symbolizes strong one, that is, king"; (4) "figurative for granting victory or bestowing prosperity." All of these pieces of commentary lavish their attention on what the image of the horn *means,* without ever telling us what kind of literal horn we should picture. Some back issues of *National Geographic* will give us more help than the commentaries, with their pictures of rams butting each other with their horns or a deer warding off an attacking cougar with its antlers. The time is ripe for some bold new commentaries and dictionaries with pictorial accompaniment to make the literal images come alive.

Motifs and Conventions

A *motif* is a pattern that appears in a written text. At its most rudimentary, such a pattern is something that we notice in an individual biblical text. For example, as we read the story of Jacob's meeting Rebekah at a well (Gen 29:4-12), we can identify a pattern unfolding: the arrival of the man from a foreign land, the appearance of the woman at the well to fetch water, a dialogue between the man and woman, the drawing of water from the well by either the man or the woman as a gesture of thoughtfulness toward the other, the woman's running home to tell her family, and inviting the stranger into the home of the future betrothed in an act of hospitality and welcome.

Even though a single instance of such a pattern warrants the application of the term *motif,* it is more customary to apply the term to repeated instances of the same pattern. In the Bible, for example, the motif of meeting one's future betrothed at the well appears several times—not only with Jacob and Rebekah but also with the servant of Abraham who is sent to bring back a bride for Isaac (Gen 24:10-33) and with Moses upon his arrival in Midian (Exod 2:16-21). The literary term currently in vogue to designate the recurrence of common ingredients in a story is *type scene.* Robert Alter, who popularized the concept, defines a type scene as "an elaborate set of tacit agreements between artist and audience about the ordering of the art work," and a "grid of conventions" that readers come to recognize and expect.[4]

A motif is thus made up of a set of *conventions*— ingredients that recur so often in similar situations that they become expectations in the minds of writers and readers alike. The idea of conventions seems most natural when we are dealing with narratives. To put the protagonist of the story in a situation that tests him or her, for example, is a convention that most stories follow. Equally pervasive is the tendency of stories to be structured as a conflict that reaches resolution, often accompanied by a moment of epiphany (insight, revelation) near the end of the story. Again, it is a rare story that does not end with the convention of poetic justice (virtue rewarded, vice punished).

But conventions are not limited to the stories of the Bible. It is a convention of lament psalms, for example, to include a reversal or recantation: after crying to God, defining a crisis that seems hopeless and asking God to deliver, the poet reverses himself by expressing his confidence in God and vowing to praise God for deliverance. The motif of reversal is equally common in biblical prophecy, where the prophet often pictures a future era when the present situation is reversed—where the wicked now in power will be put down, for example, or when the misery of human history will give way to a millennium of perfection.

While this dictionary is not intended as a comprehensive guide to literary conventions in the Bible, its entries dealing with motifs will in effect be an exploration of the conventions upon which both writer and reader have implicitly agreed. The practical benefit of having these conventions brought to our awareness is that as we read and teach the Bible we will see a great deal more than we would otherwise see. Instead of experiencing every text as a new event that needs to be puzzled over, we will begin to experience various types of biblical texts as a journey through a familiar landscape. Conventions like those that operate in the story of meeting one's future betrothed at a well will also enable us to apply to one story what we have learned from other texts. Furthermore, because some of the motifs and conventions of the Bible have dropped out of circulation since ancient times, having them identified will enable us to see patterns and meanings in the Bible that would otherwise remain obscure.

Although motifs are more likely to revolve around plot or action than around images, we should pause to note that motifs often incorporate images. Earlier we noted instances of water as an image, symbol, metaphor and simile. Water figures as a *motif* in an ancient practice known as ordeal by water. In this motif, ability to survive being submerged in water was regarded as a sign of innocence, while drowning signalled that a person was evil. In the Old Testament, for example, the flood and the Red Sea crossing were trials by water in which God's judgment against evil people was manifested in their drowning while the righteous were preserved. Several Psalms (e.g., 69:12-15 and 124:1-5) likewise picture ordeal as a flood from which the speaker must be rescued.

Do Literary Conventions Mean That the Bible Is Fictional?

It is fair to ask at this point how all this talk about literary conventions relates to the question of the historicity or fictionality of the Bible. The answer, in brief, is that the presence of conventions and literary artifice in the Bible does not by itself say anything at all about historicity or fictionality.

It is true that scholars like Robert Alter tend to regard the presence of conventions and type scenes as a sign of fictionality. But this assumption is unwarranted. Underlying the assumption that the presence of literary artifice in the Bible signals fictionality is the unstated belief that events like this do not happen in real life. But real life is full of "type scenes." Real life stories of meeting one's future spouse at college would be as filled with repeated ingredients as Old Testament stories of meeting one's spouse at a well.

In real life, and not just in literature, we constantly impose patterns on the flow of events. It is not a matter of making things up but of "packaging" them—in other words, of selectivity and arrangement. Consider the conventions of the television sports report or interview. The reporter is filmed with a sports arena in the background. During the course of the report the reporter either interviews an athlete or is momentarily replaced by a film clip of sports action. It is a rule of the sports interview that the conversation consist only of clichés and that it be devoid of anything approaching intellectual substance. The syntax of the athlete being interviewed is expected to be rudimentary or even nonexistent in the usual sense. It is a rule that at some point the athlete mumbles something to the effect of "just trying to go out there and do my job." A look of false modesty is expected to accompany this world-changing announcement. At the end of the report, the reporter stares into the camera and utters a catchy, impressive-sounding one-liner.

The artifice of such conventions is obvious. Yet the artifice and high degree of conventionality do not make the interview anything other than a factual event that really happened. What such conventions *do* signal is the degree to which communication, whether on television or in the Bible, is based on shared assumptions or expectations between writer and audience about how certain things are communicated or composed.

To take an instance that relates to the Bible, we can consider the conventions of a love story, whether in literature or real life. It is easy to produce a list of conventions that make up a love story: an eligible hero and heroine who are worthy of each other, initial unawareness on the part of the lovers that they are meant for each other, obstacles to the romance that must be overcome, asking friends about the eligible "other," a memorable first meeting or a first date, report of the first date to Mom or a roommate, courtship (including wooing of both the bride-to-be and her mother), goodbye moments, a matchmaker, meetings in a country or natural setting, bestowing of favors, secret meetings, a rival, background observers, betrothal and marriage. Now it so happens the Old Testament story of Ruth contains all of these ingredients. Does that make the story fictional? How could it necessarily make it fictional when the ingredients are equally present in real life romances?

Underlying this dictionary is an editorial bias that runs counter to the tendency of some to find fiction in the Bible, namely, a conviction that the very presence of such universal elements in the Bible makes it more lifelike, not less lifelike. There can be no doubt that the writers of the Bible carefully selected and arranged their material. The result is that the accounts we find in the Bible are more highly structured than real life is ordinarily felt to be, with the result that we see things more clearly in the Bible than we usually do in real life. A comment by the poet T. S. Eliot will clarify the matter. "It is the function of all art," wrote Eliot, "to give us some perception of an order in life, by imposing an order upon it."[5] This dictionary explores the patterns that the biblical writers have imposed on life, with a view toward understanding what those patterns clarify about life.

Archetypes

A final term that requires definition for purposes of this dictionary is the word *archetype*. An archetype is an image or pattern that recurs throughout literature and life. Archetypes are the universal elements of human experience. More specifically, an archetype falls into one of three categories: it is either an image or symbol (such as the mountaintop or evil city), or a plot motif (such as crime and punishment or the quest), or a character type (such as the trickster or jealous sibling).

Many of the images and motifs discussed in this dictionary are archetypes. They recur not only throughout the Bible but in literature generally, and in life. Being aware of them will help us draw connections—between parts of the Bible, between the Bible and other things we have read, between the Bible and life.

Archetypes are a universal language. We know what they mean simply by virtue of being humans in this world. We all know the experiences of hunger and thirst, garden and wilderness. Ideas and customs vary widely from one time and place to another, but archetypes are the elemental stuff of life. In the words of literary scholar Northrop Frye (noted archetypal critic), "Some symbols are images of things common to all men, and therefore have a communicable power which is potentially unlimited."[6] Another literary scholar defines the master images of the imagination as "any of the immemorial patterns of response to the human situation in its permanent aspects."[7] A study of the images and motifs of the Bible will confirm one scholar's comment that "the Biblical vocabulary is compact of the primal stuff of our common humanity—of its universal emotional, sensory experiences."[8]

Such elemental images are primal in the sense of being rooted in essential humanity, independent of civilized trappings and complexity. One effect of reading this dictionary will be to uncover the primal roots of the Bible. Someone has said that

> the themes of the Bible are simple and primary. Life is reduced to a few basic activities. . . . We confront basic virtues and primitive vices. . . . The world these persons inhabit is stripped and elemental—sea, desert, the stars, the wind, storm, sun, clouds, and moon, seedtime and harvest. . . . Occupation has this elementary quality also.[9]

The entries in this dictionary will confirm this view of the Bible as a primal and elemental book.

There are also psychological overtones to an exploration of these elemental images of human life. The modern study of archetypes began with psychologists (though archetypes have long since been separated from that source). Part of the psychological dimension is that there is wisdom and strength to be found in being put in touch with bedrock humanity in this way. Carl Jung wrote that archetypes "make up the groundwork of the human psyche. It is only possible to live the fullest life when we are in harmony with these symbols; wisdom is a return to them."[10] One of the benefits of exploring the territory charted in this dictionary is to see anew that while the Bible is more than a human book, it is also a book rich in recognizable human experience.

A further useful thing to know about images and archetypes is that when we begin to categorize them, we find good and bad, desirable and undesirable, ideal and unideal versions of the various categories. Kings can be benevolent or tyrannical, for example. Lions are usually a negative archetype, but they can also symbolize power and rulership in the hands of the good. Here is a beginning list of the archetypes of the Bible, arranged by categories:

Category of Experience	The Archetypes of Ideal Experience	The Archetypes of Unideal Experience
Supernatural agents and settings	God; angels; the heavenly society; heaven; Abraham's bosom	Satan; demons, evil spirits; evil beasts and monsters (such as those in the book of Revelation); pagan idols; the witch; hell
Human characters	The hero or heroine; the virtuous wife/husband/mother/father; the bride or groom; the godly and benevolent king or ruler; the innocent or obedient child; the loyal friend, servant, or disciple; the wiseman; the true shepherd; the pilgrim; the godly priest; the teacher of truth or seeker after truth; the heroic and innocent martyr; the guide, protector, or watchman; the chaste virgin; the helpful matchmaker; the temperate person; the triumphant warrior; masters of a vocation (the good farmer, craftsman, etc.); the saint, penitent, convert; the just judge; the deliverer	The villain; the tempter or temptress the harlot, prostitute or adulterer; the taskmaster, tyrant or oppressor (usually a foreign oppressor); the wanderer, outcast or exile; the traitor; the traitor; the sluggard or lazy person; the hypocrite; the false religious teacher or priest; the hireling or unreliable shepherd; the fool; the drunkard; the thief; the the domineering spouse or parent; the deceiver; the dupe; the meddling eavesdropper; the seducer or seductress; the glutton; the unjust judge; the wayward child or vicious sibling; the beggar; the sinner; the rebel; the robber; the prodigal; the murderer; the persecutor
Human Relationships	The community, city, tribe or nation; images of communion, order, unity, hospitality, friendship, love; the wedding or marriage; the feast, meal or supper; the harmonious family; freedom; covenant, contract or treaty; loyalty; adoption; images of legitimate power or authority (scepter, rod, crown); chastity and virginity	Tyranny or anarchy; isolation among people; images of torture (the cross, take, scaffold, gallows, stocks, prison, etc.); slavery or bondage; images of war, riot or feud; family discord or sibling rivalry; treason; abandonment; images of punishment, like the rod; adultery and sexual perversion
Clothing	Any stately garment that shows legitimate position or success; festal garments such as wedding clothes; fine clothing given as a gift of hospitality; white or lightcolored clothing; clothing of adornment (such as jewels); protective clothing (such as a warrior's armor or shoes for one's feet)	Ill-fitting garments (often symbolic of a position that is usurped or not held legitimately); garments of mourning (such as sackcloth and rent garments); dark clothes; tattered, dirty or coarse clothing; any clothing that suggests poverty or bondage; a conspicuous excess of clothing or lack of clothing (including barefootedness and nakedness)
The human body	Images of health, strength, vitality potency, sexual fertility (including the womb and seed); feats of strength, dexterity or conquest; images of sleep and rest; happy dreams; rituals of festivity (such as an anointed head); birth; cleansing and cleanliness; the hand, right arm, eye and head; healing	Images of disease, deformity, barrenness, injury or mutilation; physical ineptness (e.g., stumbling or falling); acts leading to defeat; sleeplessness or nightmare, perhaps related to guilt of conscience; death; blindness and deafness; filthiness; physical effects of guilt

Food	Staples such as bread, milk, meat, manna, oil; abundance of a harvest of grain; luxuries (such as wine and honey); olive; grapes	Hunger, drought, famine, starvation, cannibalism; poison; drunkenness;
Animals	A community of domesticated animals (usually a flock of sheep or herd of cattle); the lamb; a gentle bird (such as the dove); any animal friendly to people; singing birds; animals or birds noted for their strength (such as the lion, horse or eagle); fish	Monsters or beasts of prey; the wolf (enemy of sheep), tiger, dragon, vulture, owl or hawk; the cold and earthbound snake; any wild animal harmful to people; the goat; the unclean animals of Old Testament ceremonial law; wild dogs; ignorant mules
Landscape	A garden, grove or park; the mountaintop or hill; the fertile plain or valley; pastoral settings or farms; the safe pathway or easily traveled road; places of natural refuge or defense (such as a rock, hill or hiding place)	The dark forest; the wilderness or wasteland (which is either too hot or too cold); the dark and dangerous valley; the tomb; the labyrinth; the dangerous or evil pathway; the cave (associated with barbarism) or pit (confinement, imprisonment)
Plants	Green grass; the rose; the vineyard; the tree of life; any productive tree, vine or plant; the lily; evergreen plants (symbolic of immortality); herbs or plants of healing; engrafting; grain (especially wheat and barley)	The thorn or thistle; weeds; dead or dying plants; unproductive plants; the willow tree (symbolic of death or mourning); chaff; pruning of dead branches
Buildings	The city; the palace or court; the military stronghold; the tabernacle, temple or church; the altar; the house or home; the tower of contemplation or watchfulness; the capital city, center of the nation; the storehouse; well-built foundations and pillars; the inn; the door or gate of entry and protection; the city wall; the boat or ark of saftey or rescue; the marketplace; the threshing floor	The prison or dungeon; the wicked city of violence, sexual perversion or crime; the tower of imprisonment or wicked aspiration (such as the tower of Babel); pagan temples and altars; buildings without solid foundations; the wastehouse (empty, vacuous and decaying building)
The inorganic world	Jewels and precious stones (often glowing and fiery); fire and brilliant light; burning that purifies and refines; rocks of refuge; gold, silver and pearl; durable metals (like iron and bronze)	The uncivilized world in its unworked form of deserts, rocks and wilderness; dry dust or ashes; fire that destroys and tortures (instead of purifying); rust and decay; ashes
Water	A tranquil, lifegiving river, stream stream or pool; a spring or fountain; showers of rain; flowing water (as opposed to stagnant water); water used for cleansing	The overflowing river or stream; the sea and its monsters; stagnant pools or cisterns

Forces of nature	The breeze or wind; the sprint and summer seasons; calm after storm; the sun or the lesser light of the moon and stars; light, sunrise, day; the the rainbow	The storm or tempest; the autumn and winter seasons; sunset, darkness, night; earthquakes, flood or hail; images of mutability (faded rose, dried grass, vapor); lightning and thunder; whirlwind
Sounds	Musical harmony; singing; laughter	Discordant sounds, cacophony, weeping, wailing, sighing
Direction and motion	Images of ascent, rising, height (especially the mountaintop) or motion (as opposed to stagnation); straight; right (as opposed left)	Images of descent, lowness, stagnation or immobility; suffocation; confinement; crooked (as opposed to straight); left (as opposed to right)
Actions	The quest or journey; positive transformations, (such as the death-rebirth movement, conversion, or the rite of baptism); acts of worship (sacrifice, offering, burning of incense, festal processions); fullness; the overcoming of obstacles (enroute to a happy ending); virtue rewarded; escape or liberation; rescue; reform; reunion, reconciliation, forgiveness; homecoming; reward; pilgrimage; being found	The antiquest (such as Jonah's attempt to flee from God); capture; decline of fortune or degradation of character; crime and punishment; fall from innocence; emptiness; murder; temptation; the punishment of vice; suffering; terror or danger; exile or banishment; cataclysmic destruction; being lost

This chart of archetypes is one of the chief patterns that the human imagination imposes on reality. We might say that archetypes are among the chief building blocks for writers of the Bible. Of course they impose these patterns on life as a way of clarifying life.

What Is the Practical Usefulness of This Dictionary?

This is a practical book, in a number of ways. One of its uses is to provide a biblical reader with an improved grasp of the literal level of the Bible. In the thirteenth century Roger Bacon argued that the church had done a good job of communicating the theological content of the Bible but had failed to make the literal level of the biblical text come alive in people's imagination. We are in a similar situation today. One of the goals of this dictionary is to provide a corrective. This dictionary will show that concrete images lie behind many of the abstractions in modern English translations of the Bible.

In addition to enhancing our awareness of the Bible as a work of imagination (our image-making and image-perceiving capacity), this dictionary is designed to enrich a reader's affective response to the Bible. Pictures affect us emotionally in ways that abstractions do not (which is not to say, of course, that abstractions necessarily leave us unmoved).

If this book improves our awareness of the literal level of meaning of the Bible, paradoxically it also improves our ability to interpret the figurative level of meaning. Many entries in this dictionary are divided into an analysis of the concrete, literal properties of a biblical image or motif, and of the symbolic meanings that gather around the literal level. In these instances, our understanding of the figurative meanings is enriched by the context provided by the concrete or literal level of meaning.

A systematic treatment of images and motifs in the Bible also allows us to see the unity and progression of the Bible. Unity emerges when we see that many of the master images of the Bible pervade it from beginning to end. Some of these motifs, moreover, show a discernible progression, especially (but not only) in the New Testament fulfillment of Old Testament foreshadowings. The motif of the annunciation of the birth of a son to a barren mother, for example, can be traced from Sarah through the story of Gideon's mother and Hannah, and thence to the nativity stories of John the Baptist and Jesus.

This dictionary also suggests a strategy for preaching and teaching the Bible. One area of application is theological. Tracing a master image or motif through the Bible from beginning to end sooner or later touches upon most major areas of biblical theology and is therefore a fresh way to view the theological content of the Bible. Furthermore, a study of biblical images and motifs shows that the Bible is both a timeless book and a timebound book (in the sense of being rooted in cultural contexts that change as history unfolds). Such a study therefore provides a way of achieving a major task of preaching and teaching—that of bridging the gap between the biblical world and our own world by first journeying to the ancient world and then making a return trip to our own place and time. An important part of the return trip consists of seeing how much universal human experience is present in the Bible.

To sum up, this is a book with many uses. It is a book to be browsed, packed as it is with new information and insights about the content of the Bible. It is equally a reference book—for exegetes, interpreters, preachers, teachers and lay readers of the Bible.

Who Wrote This Dictionary?

The study of images and motifs is an interdisciplinary enterprise, and this dictionary is accordingly the product of both biblical and literary scholars. Individual entries were written and/or edited by both groups of scholars. Biblical scholars are adept at placing biblical images and motifs in their ancient setting and in recognizing ancient patterns that a modern reader is unlikely to have encountered. Literary critics can bring to bear on the Bible their knowledge of literary motifs that literature has exhibited through the centuries. Both disciplines can help to interpret the meanings and nuances of biblical images and motifs.

Notes

[1] James A. Fischer, *How to Read the Bible* (Englewood Cliffs, N.J.: Prentice-Hall, 1981), p. 39.

[2] H. Richard Niebuhr, *The Responsible Self* (New York: Harper & Row, 1963), pp. 151-52, 161.

[3] For summaries of research, see these sources: Michael C. Corballis and Ivan L. Beale, *The Ambivalent Mind: The Neuropsychology of Left and Right* (Chicago: Nelson-Hall, 1983); Sid J. Segalowitz, *Two Sides of the Brain* (Englewood Cliffs, N.J.: Prentice-Hall, 1983); Sally P. Springer and Georg Deutsch, *Left Brain, Right Brain,* rev. ed. (New York: W. H. Freeman, 1985).

[4] Robert Alter, *The Art of Biblical Narrative* (New York: Basic Books, 1981), p. 47.

[5] T. S. Eliot, *On Poetry and Poets* (New York: Farrar, Strauss & Cudahy, 1957), p. 93.

[6] Northrop Frye, *Anatomy of Criticism* (Princeton: Princeton University Press, 1957), p. 99.

[7] Leslie Fiedler, "Archetype and Signature," reprinted in *Myths and Motifs in Literature,* ed. David J. Burrows et al. (New York: Free Press, 1973), p. 28.

[8] John Livingston Lowes, "The Noblest Monument of English Prose," in *Literary Style of the Old Bible and the New,* ed. D. G. Kehl (Indianapolis: Bobbs-Merrill, 1970), p. 9.

[9] Howard Mumford Jones, "The Bible from a Literary Point of View," in *Five Essays on the Bible* (New York: American Council of Learned Societies, 1960), pp. 52-53.

[10] Carl Jung, *Psychological Reflections,* ed. Jolande Jacobi (Princeton: Princeton University Press, 1953), p. 47.

A

AARON'S ROD

Aaron's rod appears almost exclusively in the story of the *exodus, where it emerges as a master image and where it may merge with references to the *rod of Moses and even the rod of God (Ex 4:20; 17:9). The significance of the rod was kept alive in the Hebrew consciousness by virtue of its being stored as a memorial in the Holy of Holies after it had miraculously blossomed (Num 17:10; Heb 9:4).

The Bible itself does not tell us exactly what kind of rod or staff it was. It might have been a shepherd's rod used for protecting and rescuing sheep or a traveler's walking stick or a weapon. The prosaic, commonplace nature of this unspecified staff may itself be part of its significance, making it a foil to the supernatural power that the rod displays in the story of the exodus.

The rod linked specifically with Aaron appears first when Moses and Aaron have their first meeting with Pharaoh. On this occasion the rod assumes miraculous powers by being transformed into a *serpent when Aaron throws it on the ground, and then swallowing the serpents that had been called forth by the Egyptian magicians' rods (Ex 7:8-12). Later the rod effected three of the ten *plagues—turning the water of the Nile into blood (Ex 7:14-23), calling forth frogs (Ex 8:1-5) and bringing gnats (Ex 8:16-19).

Even more impressive is the subsequent blossoming of Aaron's rod. Following the rebellion of Korah, Dathan and Abiram against the authority of Moses and Aaron, Moses collected a rod from the leaders of each of the twelve tribes, plus Aaron's rod for the tribe of Levi. In the evocative account of the biblical narrative, "On the morrow Moses went into the tent of the testimony; and, behold, the rod of Aaron for the house of Levi was budded and brought forth buds, and bloomed blossoms, and yielded almonds" (Num 17:8 KJV). In a tragic let-down, the final reference to the rod occurs when Moses doomed himself by striking the rock instead of speaking to it. Here we read that "Moses took the rod from before the LORD," apparently linking it with Aaron's rod kept as a memorial in the Holy of Holies (Num 20:9).

What does Aaron's rod signify in the Bible? Throughout its history it has associations of miraculous power, especially the power to transform physical reality. As a symbol of supernatural power

working through human agencies, the rod also evokes a sense of authority, both political (it helped the nation's leaders win its conflicts) and priestly (its blossoming coincided with the establishment of the house of Aaron and tribe of Levi in a priestly role). Although this ordinary rod was far from being a royal *scepter, it nonetheless seems scepter-like in our imaginations as we read of its miraculous powers.

By being linked specifically with Aaron (and perhaps with Moses as well), this particular rod is also an index to the exalted status of Aaron and Moses. It reminds us of magical talismans that signal the uniqueness and heroic status of such heroes of ancient literature as Odysseus and Aeneas. Furthermore, the association of Aaron's rod with the Holy of Holies gives it a sacral significance, making it a visible memorial to God's sacred presence and power. Finally, the springing of life from an inanimate object is an archetypal rebirth image, connoting passage from death to life.

See also ROD, STAFF; SCEPTER.

ABANDON, ABANDONED. *See* FORSAKE, FORSAKEN.

ABEL

*Cain and Abel, the most famous *brothers in biblical literature, were perhaps even twins, since the Bible never mentions that *Eve conceived twice before their birth. But no matter. They might as well have been Siamese twins, so closely are the two associated. Allusions to either feed off the other in symbiotic style.

The story unfolds in Genesis 4, where Abel, the model child, obedient and righteous, becomes a brother slain. Seven times in eleven verses (Gen 4:2-11 NASB) the fact is stressed that the two are brothers, thus indelibly emphasizing the depravity of Cain—jealous enough to commit even fratricide. Within the story itself, Abel is a decidedly secondary character, providing the occasion for the main action.

In the NT Abel gets brief but significant mention, first by Christ himself. In parallel passages from Matthew 23:35 and Luke 11:51, Jesus draws on the Abel story to strengthen his diatribe against the scribes and Pharisees: "You serpents, you brood of vipers, how shall you escape the sentence of hell? . . . [U]pon you may fall *the guilt* of all the righteous blood shed on earth, from the blood of righteous Abel to the blood of Zechariah" (Mt 23:33-35 NASB). Abel thus becomes forever Exhibit A, an eternal symbol of the *martyred righteous, slain by someone who hated him because his deeds were righteous and the murderer's were evil (1 Jn 3:12).

The author of Hebrews contrasts the faith-oriented Abel with his works-oriented brother: "By faith Abel offered to God a better sacrifice than Cain" (Heb 11:4 NASB). In Hebrews 12 the author uses another allusion to Abel, this time contrasting him not with Cain but with Jesus himself: "And to Jesus, the mediator of a new covenant, and to the sprinkled blood, which speaks better than the blood of Abel" (Heb 12:24 NASB). The writer is obviously alluding to the Genesis account of the Lord's asking, "What have you done? The voice of your brother's blood is crying to Me from the ground" (Gen 4:10). Abel's blood called for *vengeance, but Jesus' blood spoke for forgiveness.

Close analysis of the Abel narrative emphasizes how prophetic are the words of Hebrews 11, with their assurance that "through faith, though he [Abel] is dead, he still speaks" (Heb 11:4 NASB). Abel endures through the centuries as a symbol of obedience coupled with a righteousness-by-faith religion. Likewise, he represents those killed simply because they performed a righteous deed, innocent martyrs for God's cause. Abel's blood still cries from the ground, a cry of warning for whose who oppose God's people, a cry of hope for the slain righteous seeking vindication.

See also CAIN.

ABHOR, LOATHE

The English words *abhor* and *loathe* translate biblical terms that connote the image of turning away from something because of extreme dislike or intolerance. These words are used in reference to both people and God. The primary actor where such language is involved is God, who loathes things of which fallen humans tend to be tolerant.

From the divine vantage point God is nauseated by any human activity that is not in accordance with his law (Lev 26:11; Prov 11:1; Ezek 23:18). *Sin and *idolatry are common targets of God's abhorrence (Deut 7:25; 12:3). His *disgust with them grows to the point where he cannot bear them any longer. God warns fledgling Israel to avoid adopting the customs of the Canaanites, whom he is about to drive out because he "abhorred them" (Lev 20:23 NRSV; cf. Deut 18:9, 12). He later warns his people that if they ignore his warnings and follow the surrounding nations in their idolatry, they too will be the recipients of his disgust (Lev 26:30).

Specific practices that God finds abhorrent include eating unclean *animals (Deut 14:3), sacrificing flawed animals (Deut 17:1), cross-dressing (Deut 22:5), using a *prostitute's fee as a religious offering (Deut 23:18), a husband's resuming relations with a wife whom he has divorced (Deut 24:4), dishonesty (Deut 25:16), lying (Ps 5:6), the religious ceremonies of unrepentant people (Amos 5:21) and nationalistic pride (Amos 6:8). In the book of Revelation Christ's spewing the lukewarm Laodiceans out his mouth is a gesture of disgust (3:16). While people apart from God often fail to perceive his judgments, redeemed humanity can learn to abhor—and thereby turn away from—those things God loathes (cf. Ps 31:6; 97:10; 119:104; Amos 5:15; Rom 12:9).

People too loathe things in the Bible. After *raping his sister Tamar, Amnon abhors her (2 Sam 13:15). The sores of Job are loathsome (Job 2:7), and the suffering Job finds both food (6:7) and life (7:16; 9:21; 10:1) loathsome. His family and friends, in turn, find Job loathsome (Job 19:17, 19). People under stress loathe food (Ps 107:18). In Amos's picture of a society that has lost its moral bearings, people actually "abhor the one who speaks the truth" (Amos 5:10), and in a similar picture Micah pictures a nation of people "who abhor justice and pervert all equity" (Mic 3:9 RSV). In contrast, Ezekiel paints pictures of penitents who loathe themselves for their evil deeds (Ezek 20:43; 36:31).

See also DISGUST, REVULSION; HOLINESS; IDOL, IDOLATRY.

ABOMINATION

From the broadest perspective an abomination is something loathsome and repulsive according to one's cultural and religious values. For the Egyptians the Israelites were an abomination because they were *shepherds, an occupation they despised (Gen 46:33-34). For the Israelites an abomination was ritually unclean food (Deut 14:3). For the fool it is turning away from evil (Prov 13:19); and for the wicked and righteous it is each other (Prov 29:27).

From the biblical perspective an abomination callously disregards and actively disdains the values God has established. It affronts God's holiness, sovereignty as Creator and purposes expressed in the Law. There is an irony in the image of abomination. It is not chosen in brazen rebellion against God, but is perceived within the values of the offender as the good and right thing to do. Thus the sacrifice of the wicked (Prov 15:8), the prayer of the lawbreaker (Prov 28:9) and blemished sacrifice (Deut 17:1) are abominations, although their practitioners do not perceive themselves as committing an abomination. Idolatry and its related immorality (Deut 27:15; Jer 13:27; Rev 17:4-5) and witchcraft and sorcery (Deut 18:10-12) characterize dismissal of God's sovereignty. Failures of God's people to separate from pagan practices that are in conflict with the Law (Ezra 9:1) are abominable, as are such practices as lying, arrogance, evil plans, murder (Prov 6:16-19; Rev 21:27) and sexual aberrations (Lev 18:6-23). Images of peril accompany abomination, for those committing abominations are subject to the wrath and judgment of God (Ezek 7:1-4).

The ultimate image of abomination is the Abomination of Desolation, an image of horror from 167

B.C. when Antiochus IV Epiphanes placed an altar to Zeus on the altar of God in the Jerusalem temple (Dan 9:27; 11:31; 12:11; 1 Macc 1:54, 59; 2 Macc 6:1-2). For Judaism and Christianity this abomination was paradigmatic and prophetic of an evil, pagan individual or force arrayed against God and his people and usurping God's rightful worship by desecrating the temple. In the Gospels, Rome's destruction of Jerusalem and the temple (Mt 24:15; Mk 13:14; Lk 21:20) was just such an abomination. This abomination underlies the eschatological images of the man of lawlessness (2 Thess 2:3-4), the antichrist (1 Jn 2:18; 4:3), the great whore (Rev 17:4) and the beast (Rev 13).

See also ABHOR, LOATHE; ANTICHRIST; DISGUST, REVULSION; HOLINESS; IDOL, IDOLATRY; TEMPLE.

BIBLIOGRAPHY. D. Ford, *The Abomination of Desolation in Biblical Eschatology* (Washington, DC: University Press of America, 1979).

ABRAHAM

To biblical writers Abraham has more than historical status. He captures their imagination as an image of various spiritual themes in both Old and New Testaments. The character of Abraham has multiple dimensions that can be plotted in terms of the rhetorical or persuasive purposes of the biblical writers.

The Portrait in Genesis. In Genesis, Abraham is presented as the important forefather to whom God gives promises and with whom God makes a *covenant. At times the content of this promise or covenant is not specified. On most occasions it is linked to a specific element: either the promise of land (Gen 12:7; 13:14-15, 17; 15:7, 18; 17:8); the promise of seed (Gen 12:2; 13:16; 15:5, 18-21; 17:2, 4-7, 16, 19; 22:17); or the promise of covenant (Gen 17:7, 19, 21). Abraham is also promised blessing for all the nations (Gen 12:3; 18:18; 22:18; 26:4; 28:14).

The second most frequent image for Abraham in the book of Genesis is as an example of *obedience (Gen 12:1-4; 17:1, 23; 18:19; 22:16-18; 26:4-5). Abraham is portrayed as one whose obedience was essential to his relationship with Yahweh and to the relationship of his descendants to Yahweh. This does not mean that Abraham is presented as perfect, for on two occasions his deceit is highlighted (Gen 12:10-20; 20:1-18). Although the faith of Abraham is assumed in his obedient response to Yahweh's call to Palestine, this is emphasized only in Genesis 15:6. However, later in the Bible it becomes a major part of the imagery surrounding Abraham.

The blessing of all nations through Abraham is highlighted not only in general statements in the book of Genesis but also in his role as intercessor for his nephew Lot. This intercession is first seen in Genesis 14, where he saves Lot from the hands of foreign kings. It reaches a height in Genesis 18 as he pleads with Yahweh on behalf of Lot, leading to Lot's rescue from the city of Sodom. This role of intercession for the nations is founded on the fact that

Yahweh considers Abraham his confidante (Gen 18:17).

Complementing the more spiritual side of Abraham—as the recipient of divine promise, as example of obedience and faith, as intercessor—is the social dimension of this patriarch. Abraham is a domestic *hero in Genesis. As in Homer, "home" means possessions as well as family. Abraham is consistently shown in his domestic roles—as husband, uncle, father, clan leader and possessor of flocks and herds. As clan leader Abraham is diplomat to a series of august figures, including kings and the priest Melchizedek. As owner of goods Abraham is linked with the images of *sheep and goats, *flocks and herds.

There are, finally, the literal images that dominate the story of Abraham in Genesis. The backbone of the plot is the *journey motif, which in turn produces the specific images of desert, *water/wells, camels and donkeys, physical movement, *tents and a proliferation of specific place names (either geographic locales or towns, both of which give the story an international flavor). The story is also a *quest story, as the hero from start to finish is in quest for a son, descendants and a land. The progressive revelation of the covenant is likewise a major plot motif, and this quest generates a conflict within Abraham between faith in God's promises and a tendency toward expediency.

The extravagance of God's covenant promises is linked to images of the stars of the sky, the sand of the seashore and the dust of the earth. Abraham's religious devotion to God is most consistently linked with images of *altar and sacrifice and, in the climactic episode (Abraham's offering of Isaac to God), with a *mountaintop. The contractual language of obligation and reward permeates the passages in which God renews his covenant with Abraham. Related to the covenant motif is the importance of characters' *names (and changes in those names) in the story. Finally, the divine-human encounter is a central motif in the story, and close scrutiny of the text shows how much of the action is embodied in conversations between God and Abraham instead of through direct narration of events.

Other Old Testament Images. Elsewhere in the OT, Abraham retains the motifs of Genesis, but the imagery surrounding him expands. As in Genesis, the rest of the OT portrays Abraham most often in association with the promises of the covenant. This connection is rarely to the promises in unspecified terms (Ex 2:24; 2 Kings 13:23) or linked to the covenant (Deut 29:13). The majority of references are linked to the promise of land (Ex 3:16; 6:3, 8; 32:13; 33:1; Lev 26:42; Num 32:11; Deut 1:8; 6:10; 9:5; 30:20; 34:4; 1 Chron 16:15-18; 2 Chron 20:7; Neh 9:7-8; Ps 105:8-11, 42-44; cf. Is 51:2; Ezek 33:24) and a few to the promise of seed (Ex 32:13; Lev 26:42; Josh 24:2-3; cf. Neh 9:23; Is 51:2; Ezek 33:24). As can be seen in both Isaiah 51:2 and Ezekiel 33:24, the Abrahamic covenant of seed was very comforting to those who had experienced the pain of exile. The blessing of all nations through Abraham receives little notice (Ps 47:9).

Abraham as obedient forefather is rarely highlighted in the rest of the OT. An exception is the prayer in Nehemiah 9:7-8, which claims that God found Abraham's heart faithful, a term for a good covenant partner (cf. Deut 7:9; Is 49:7; cf. Ps 78:8, 37). This faithfulness of Abraham becomes the basis on which the promise of the land is secured.

Alone and in series with the other patriarchs, Abraham's name is used to identify the God of Israel: God of Abraham (Ps 47:9; cf. Is 29:22); God of Abraham, Isaac, and Jacob (Ex 3:6, 15; 4:5; 6:3); God of Abraham, Isaac, and Israel (1 Kings 18:36; 1 Chron 29:18; 2 Chron 30:6). This connection of Abraham with the name of God accentuates the foundational role that Abraham plays in the establishment of the covenant between God and Israel.

Abraham is presented at times as progenitor of the Israelites (1 Chron 1:27, 28, 34; Ps 105:6; Is 41:8; 51:2; Jer 33:26). This connection is not merely biological but also has spiritual implications and connects the Israelites with the promises and covenant established between God and Abraham.

Because of his role in the establishment of covenant and promise for Israel, Abraham's name appears on many occasions as the foundation for mercy to Israel. When requests for deliverance are made, the appeal is grounded in Abraham (Ex 32:13; Deut 9:27; 2 Chron 20:7; 30:6; Neh 9:7; Ps 105:42). When prophecies or promises are given announcing salvation, Abraham is mentioned (Lev 26:42; Is 29:22; 41:8; 51:2; Jer 33:26; Ezek 33:24; Mic 7:20). When historical events are recounted where God brought salvation, Abraham is highlighted (Ex 2:24; 3:16; 6:3; 2 Kings 13:23). Abraham thus serves an important role in the ongoing relevance of the promises and covenant in the life of the nation. He becomes an indispensable image for deliverance for Israel. Only once is Abraham mentioned in the context of judgment: in Numbers 32:11, where those who disobeyed at Kadesh Barnea are banned from seeing the promised land. Even in this context, Caleb and Joshua are mentioned as receiving the promise.

Abraham played a role as intercessor for the nations, and this was traced in Genesis 18 to his status as confidante of God. This status, afforded to only one other individual in the history of Israel (Moses, in Ex 33:11), may be reflected in two instances outside of Genesis in which Abraham is called "the friend of God" (2 Chron 20:7; Is 41:8).

Abraham in the Writings of Paul. Hansen (158-60) has surveyed the use of the image of Abraham in Paul by highlighting three purposes: soteriological, ecclesiological and missiological. Paul uses Abraham at the service of his soteriology by citing him as a scriptural argument for justification by faith. At the same time, Paul also uses Abraham to defend the inclusion of the Gentiles among the people of God (ecclesiological) and for his own mission to the Gentiles (missiological). The second two are so interrelated that they can be covered together. The keynotes of Paul's references to Abraham are the motifs of *faith and promise.

Faith, which is largely implicit in Genesis and absent in the rest of the OT, forms the cornerstone of Paul's use of Abraham as an image of faith in contrast to the law and circumcision, with special focus on Genesis 15:6 (Rom 4:2-5; Rom 6—12). Circumcision serves merely as a "seal" of the righteousness of faith (Rom 4:11).

In Paul the promise of *land, so important in OT passages, is left to the side, while the promise of *seed is focused not only on the nation of Israel but expanded to include the Gentiles. Although Abraham is considered the physical progenitor of the Hebrew people (Rom 4:1; 9:7; 11:1; 2 Cor 11:22), this aspect is set aside by Paul in favor of a focus on Abraham as spiritual progenitor of a spiritual race. The seed of Abraham (Gal 3:29) consists of those who are of the faith mediated through the one seed, Christ (Gal 3:15-18). This seed is not the children of the slave girl but rather of the free woman (Gal 4:21-31), a contrast between biological and spiritual seed (Rom 9:6-9). The promised blessing of all nations is seen as fulfilled in the Christian church as the Spirit received by the Gentiles by faith (Gal 4:13). Thus the Abrahamic promises and covenant are used by Paul to include the Gentiles among the people of God.

Other New Testament References. The rest of the NT shares some of the emphasis of Paul. Though lacking the Pauline focus on the Gentiles, several passages share with Paul the thought that the physical seed of Abraham does not equal spiritual seed (Mt 3:8-9; Lk 3:8; Jn 8:33-58). Similarly, Hebrews 11:8-19 gives us a picture of Abraham as a hero of faith in a manner similar to passages in Romans and Galatians.

Elsewhere the NT expands the image of Abraham beyond Pauline limits. While Hebrews 11 expresses Abraham's faith similar to Pauline passages, James 2:18-26 is distinct. As with Hebrews 11, the focus is on the sacrifice of Isaac on Moriah, and as with Paul there is a particular interest in Gen 15:6; but the faithful obedience of Abraham is inseparable from his faith and is seen as the expression of it. In fact, as James relentlessly pursues his theme that faith without works is dead, he actually reaches the conclusion that Abraham was justified by works as well as faith.

As in the OT the NT uses Abraham in epithets that identify God (Mt 22:32; Mk 12:26; Lk 20:37; Acts 3:13; 7:32), and Abraham is pictured as the progenitor of the Hebrew race (Mt 1:1, 2, 17; Lk 3:34; Acts 7:2-8, 16, 17; 13:26; 19:9; Heb 2:16). Additionally, Abraham is viewed in Luke 1:54-55, 67-79 as the foundation for benefits on his descendants.

In the Gospels the promise of seed is defined as spiritual seed. This promise is important to the picture of Abraham as the father of faith in Hebrews (Heb 6:13-15; 11:11-12, 17-19), as is the promise of land (Heb 11:8-10, 13-16), which is also seen as spiritual in fulfillment. Christ as the ultimate seed of

Abraham is legitimized by his connection to the patriarch (Mt 1:1, 17; Lk 3:34) although Christ is seen as transcending Abraham (Jn 8:39-58).

The blessing of the Gentiles is highlighted in Acts 3:25. But in contrast to Paul, Peter is citing Genesis 22:18 rather than Genesis 12:3, and his speech is focused more on the privileged position of the Jews in Jerusalem on that day than the result on the Gentiles.

Finally, some minor uses of Abraham include Peter's mention of Sarah's obedience to Abraham (1 Pet 3:6), Jesus' reference to Abraham as an eschatological figure in whose bosom the righteous dead rest (Mt 8:11; Lk 13:28; 16:22-25, 29-30) and the connection with Melchizedek in Hebrews 7:1-9 to argue for the superiority of Christ to Aaron.

See also COVENANT; GENESIS; SEED.

BIBLIOGRAPHY. G. W. Hansen, *Abraham in Galatians: Epistolary and Rhetorical Contexts* (Sheffield: JSOT, 1989); R. A. Harrisville, *The Figure of Abraham in the Epistles of St. Paul: In the Footsteps of Abraham* (San Francisco: Mellen Research University Press, 1992); G. E. Mendenhall, "The Nature and Purpose of the Abraham Narrative," in *Ancient Israelite Religion: Essays in Honor of Frank Moore Cross*, ed. P. D. Miller, P. D. Hanson and S. D. McBride (Philadelphia: Fortress Press, 1987) 337-56; A. T. Lincoln, "Abraham Goes to Rome: Paul's Treatment of Abraham in Romans 4," in *Worship, Theology and Ministry in the Early Church*, ed. M. J. Wilkins and T. Paige (Sheffield: JSOT, 1992); S. Sandmel, *Philo's Place in Judaism: A Study of Conceptions of Abraham in Jewish Literature* (augmented edition) (New York: KTAV, 1971); J. Van Seters, *Abraham in History and Tradition* (New Haven, CT: Yale University Press, 1975).

ABRAHAM'S BOSOM

The term *bosom* (sometimes also rendered "lap" or "side") translates several Hebrew words and one Greek word. In most cases in both languages the image connoted is of a warm, secure place in which one lies or is carried (e.g., Num 11:12; Ruth 4:16; Is 40:11; 49:22; Mic 7:5; Jn 1:18; 13:23). Occasionally it represents the seat of internal thought or emotion (e.g., Job 19:27; Eccles 7:9; Ps 79:12; Prov 21:14).

The more specific phrase "Abraham's bosom" occurs only twice in the Bible, both in Jesus' parable about the rich man and Lazarus (Lk 16:19-31). Abraham's bosom is the warm, secure place of high honor—since Abraham was the father of the Jews—where the poor beggar Lazarus is taken by the angels at his death, in contrast to the rich man who had ignored Lazarus in life, who ended up in "Hades" (Lk 16:23 RSV). The two places are distinguished from each other, and there is a great gulf that cannot be crossed between the two (Lk 16:23, 26).

The origin of the imagery is much discussed, but it probably combines the idea of John 13:23 of a guest's place of honor at a banquet, where the guest would recline next to the table with his head near or touching the host (cf. Jn 21:20) with the idea of a child lying in a parent's bosom or lap (see Jn 1:18, where Jesus is in his Father's bosom).

Because of the distinction in Jesus' parable between Abraham's bosom and Hades (or *hell), the term has been understood as a synonym for paradise or *heaven, and it has been used as such in Western literature (Jeffrey, 11). The image also found its way into a well-known spiritual, "Rocka My Soul in the Bosom of Abraham," with essentially the same meaning.

See also AFTERLIFE; HEAVEN.

BIBLIOGRAPHY. "Abraham's Bosom," *DBTEL* 11.

ABSALOM

Although we may not remember his name or deeds, most of us will never forget the astonishing picture of Absalom: arms flailing, mule slipping out from under him, long hair held fast in the unrelenting clutches of a great oak. Absalom has his hair cut annually, each haircut yielding 200 shekels (about 5 pounds) of *hair (2 Sam 14:26).

Absalom was King *David's third son. Scripture records two main incidents from his life. In the first his half-brother Amnon (David's first-born) *rapes his sister Tamar and then throws her out of his chamber in utter humiliation and *shame. This double offense leads to Absalom's killing Amnon before all their brothers two years later. The second event is Absalom's conspiracy and unsuccessful attempt to usurp David's throne. When this conflict culminates in battle, Absalom meets his end "hanging between heaven and earth." Technically, he is caught by his head, not his hair (2 Sam 18:9), and is killed by Joab's spears, not the tree (2 Sam 18:14).

From these accounts Absalom emerges as a ruthless and calculating individual. His essences are vengeance, greed and power fixation. (Ironically, his name means "the father of peace"). His crimes of murder and conspiracy were long premeditated—years in each case. Yet David's affection for Absalom was so great that in his grief he wailed, "If only I had died instead of you—O Absalom, my son, my son!" (2 Sam 18:33).

ABUNDANCE

Abundance in the Bible is of two types—physical, or earthly, and spiritual. The two are interrelated, for earthly abundance is consistently portrayed as a *blessing from God, who gives it as a reward for covenant keeping or simply out of grace. On a spiritual level the vocabulary of abundance is related to such large and overriding issues as salvation, miracles, reward, evil and honor to God. References are found in both Testaments, and some images recur as themes in both. Overall, images of abundance are used in the Bible primarily as a means of inspiring worship or of encouraging obedience to God.

Physical Abundance. We could predict that images of abundance in an agrarian society would lean heavily in the direction of nature, crops, weather, livestock, produce and food. The Bible confirms this.

At a physical level, abundance is associated with *grain (Gen 41:49), *water (Num 24:7; Deut 28:47), *cattle and *sheep (1 Kings 1:19), produce (1 Chron 12:40; Neh 9:25), food (Job 36:31; Ps 78:25), *rain (Pss 65:10; 104:16) and crops (Prov 14:4). At a more commercial level, abundance is associated with building materials (2 Chron 11:23), money (2 Chron 24:11), riches (Ps 49:6; 52:7), *jewels (Prov 20:15) and mercantile goods (Ezek 27:16). In the martial world of the OT, the spoils of war (2 Chron 20:25) and a supply of *weapons (2 Chron 32:5) can be abundant. The OT counterpart of the American dream of a car in every garage and a chicken in every pot is inviting a neighbor to sit under one's own *vine and fig tree (Zech 3:10).

In keeping with the whole orientation of the Bible to place human and earthly life against a backdrop of spiritual reality, images of physical abundance are often linked to God's blessing on righteousness. In Deuteronomy God promises abundant blessings to the children of Israel if they obey, but punishment if they disobey. He brings the nation to the "good and spacious land" of Canaan, "a *land flowing with milk and honey" (Ex 3:8 NRSV) where if they please God, "the LORD will open . . . his rich storehouse, the heavens" to give blessings to them (Deut 28:12 NRSV). However, if they do not return thanks by serving "the LORD [their] God joyfully and with gladness of heart for the abundance of everything," God will give this abundant blessing to be enjoyed by other peoples (Deut 28:47-68).

Such a thing happened when both the Babylonians and the Persians took over Israel after Israel's disobedience. To King Nebuchadnezzar of Babylon, Israel's conqueror, God gave great power, providing him with "the kingdom, the power, the strength, and the glory," so that "wherever the sons of men dwell, or the beasts of the field, or the birds of the sky, he has given them into your hand and has caused you to rule over them all" (Dan 2:37-38 NASB). Similar power and luxury were given to King Xerxes of Persia, who threw a lavish party to display "the riches of his royal glory and the splendor of his great majesty." The *banquet is described as being held on "couches of gold and silver on a mosaic pavement of porphyry, marble, mother-of-pearl, and colored stones," where drinks in golden vessels served vast amounts of wine (Esther 1:4-7 NRSV).

However, before the children of Israel disobeyed, God did bless them abundantly, especially through Solomon, the son of David who had pleased God so much with his heart for God. It pleased God greatly that Solomon asked for wisdom instead of riches, so God promised to bless him. He "gave Solomon wisdom, discernment, and breadth of mind as vast as the sand that is on the seashore" (1 Kings 4:29 NRSV). In addition, however, God promised to also give him what he did not ask for, namely, "both riches and honor all your life; no other king shall compare with you" (1 Kings 3:13 NRSV). The country itself also had a share in that blessing, becoming "as numerous as the sand by the sea; they ate and drank and were happy" (1 Kings 4:20 NRSV).

In response to God's great blessings, Solomon responded properly by giving back to God as abundantly as he had received. Following his father's covenant with God that his son would build a house for God, Solomon constructed an elaborate *temple in which nearly every article was overlaid with *gold (1 Kings 6:21-22). The riches with which the temple was decorated were so elaborate that "Solomon left all the utensils unweighed, because there were so many of them; the weight of the bronze was not determined" (1 Kings 7:47 NRSV). Then the temple was dedicated with an elaborate ceremony in which many people gathered to witness the sacrificing of so many sheep and oxen that "they could not be counted or numbered" (1 Kings 8:5). God responded faithfully, expressing his pleasure by filling the house of the Lord with such an intense cloud of his presence that the priests could not stand to minister because of the cloud, "for the glory of the LORD filled the house of the LORD" (1 Kings 8:10-11 NRSV). Thus, God demonstrated that he rewarded obedience with abundant blessing.

God's Abundant Kingdom. One of the chief uses of images of abundance occurs in God's references to his chosen people and all that he promises them. Although images of abundance occur in reference to how God's people will be blessed if they obey, they also occur in reference to the numbers of God's chosen people. When God promises Abraham that he will make him the father of many nations, he explains the number of his descendants in terms of plenty. God declares, "Count the stars, if you are able to count them. . . . So shall your descendants be" (Gen 15:5 NRSV). The beginning of this proliferation of Israelite people happens in Egypt, when the *seventy people who followed Joseph into Egypt became a large number because they were "fruitful, and increased greatly, and multiplied, and became exceedingly mighty, so that the land was filled with them" (Ex 1:7 RSV). Thus, God begins to fulfill his promise to make Abraham's descendants abundant in number.

In the NT, God promises similarly that many are waiting to be saved. Looking out at the multitudes of people who were longingly seeking truth, Jesus commented to his disciples, "The harvest is plentiful, but the workers are few. Therefore beseech the Lord of the harvest to send out workers into His harvest" (Mt 9:37-8 NASB). In John, Jesus observes similarly that the fields "are white for harvest" (Jn 4:35). Therefore, God promises the believer hoping to evangelize that there are an abundance of people waiting to become children of God.

Spiritual Meanings. The imagery of an abundant *harvest also appears in the Bible as a metaphor for spiritual realities. On the negative side the great wickedness of the earth is sometimes portrayed with the imagery of abundance. In the time of Noah "the wickedness of humankind was great in the earth"

(Gen 6:5 NRSV). Joel speaks of wickedness as ripening the human race for the last judgment: "Put in the sickle for the harvest is ripe. Go in, tread, for the wine press is full. The vats overflow, for their wickedness is great" (Joel 3:13 NRSV). The picture of Babylon in Revelation 18:11-13 is couched in the imagery of abundance symbolic of the fullness of evil on the earth, and the sins of Babylon are "heaped high as heaven" (Rev 18:5).

More often, though, the imagery of abundance is reserved for spiritual goodness. God's steadfast *love (Ps 5:7; 69:13) and goodness (Ps 31:19; 145:7) are both abundant. So is his mercy (Ps 51:1; 69:16) and power (Ps 147:5). Isaiah speaks rapturously of the abundance of God's "salvation, wisdom, and knowledge" (Is 33:6). In the spiritualized world of the NT we are not surprised to read about "abundance of grace" (Rom 5:17), abundant consolation through Christ (2 Cor 1:5), an apostle's "abundant love" for one of his churches (1 Cor 2:4), "abundant joy" (2 Cor 8:2), faith that "is growing abundantly" (2 Thess 1:3), and such Christian virtues as grace, *peace, *mercy and love that exist "in abundance" (2 Pet 1:2; Jude 2).

Jesus and the Abundant Life. The imagery of abundance is also a special feature of the earthly life and ministry and teaching of Jesus, who says, "I am come that they might have life, and that they might have it more abundantly" (Jn 10:10 KJV). We find the imagery of abundance in the miracles Jesus performed, symbolic of the magnitude of the promised blessings that Jesus was able to provide. When confronted with a hungry multitude of people, Jesus transformed five loaves and two fishes into enough food to feed five thousand men along with additional women and children (Mt 14:15-21). In fact, there was such abundance that afterward *twelve baskets of leftovers were collected. Similarly, when the disciples could catch no *fish on their own, Jesus commanded them to put their nets down into deep water, where they surprisingly caught so many fish that their nets began to break, and they filled two boats "so that they began to sink" (Lk 5:4-7).

In his parables, too, Jesus was fond of images of abundance—a hundredfold harvest, a *mustard seed that becomes a *tree reaching into heaven and providing habitation for birds, a messianic *banquet, stewards who double their master's investment.

Heavenly Abundance. The crowning example of abundance appears in Revelation 21:9-27, where John describes the city of New *Jerusalem that God has prepared for those who know him. The great glory of God gives her a brilliance "like a very costly stone, as a stone of crystal-clear jasper" (Rev 21:11; see Jewels and Precious Stones). It is 1500 miles long and appears like "pure gold, like clear glass" (Rev 21:16, 18). The foundation of the city wall is equally beautiful, being "adorned with every kind of precious stone": jasper, sapphire, chalcedony, emerald, sardonyx, sardius, chrysolite, beryl, topaz, chrysoprase, jacinth, amethyst (Rev 21:19-20). Thus this

passage predicts the consummation of the many promises of the Bible: abundant blessings await those who have faithfully obeyed God.

See also BANQUET; BLESSING, BLESSEDNESS; FILL, FULLNESS; HARVEST; LAND FLOWING WITH MILK AND HONEY; PARADISE; STOREHOUSE.

ACTS OF THE APOSTLES

The book of the Acts of the Apostles is a tale of two cities—*Jerusalem and *Rome (and we can note in passing that the world of the book of Acts is a largely urban world, in contrast to the prevailing agrarian world of the Bible up to this point). The narrative begins with Peter and the disciples in an upper room in Jerusalem on the day of *Pentecost and ends with Paul under house arrest in Rome. Of course these cities are symbolic as well as literal: Jerusalem symbolizes the Jewish context for the genesis of Christianity; Rome, the Gentile world to which the gospel would be taken. The geographical transfer is also a theological transfer from Hebraism to Christianity. As the narrative moves from Jerusalem to Rome, simultaneous antithetical impulses are at work. The story begins with a group of people (Peter and the disciples) but ends with one individual (Paul), while at the same time the number of converts increases from few to many. The effect is one of simultaneous contraction (in the number of protagonists) and expansion (in the number of converts).

In this narrative that connects Jerusalem and Rome, Luke characteristically patterns his story with care and artistry. Like its antecedent the Gospel of *Luke, the book of Acts is structured as a *quest. In the prologue Luke characterizes the ensuing story as a teleological journey that will make the disciples "witnesses in Jerusalem and in all Judea and Samaria and to the end of the earth" (Acts 1:8 RSV). Within the framework of the book of Acts itself, "the end of the earth" is Rome; from there, the gospel is taken to the far reaches of the Roman Empire and eventually beyond. In fact, the story of the early church is the logical sequel to the story of Christ's earthly life and ministry in the Gospels (Acts 1:1-2). In keeping with the conventions of a quest story, the book of Acts is permeated with the image of the *journey. Once the missionary journeys of Paul take center stage in chapter 13, the conventions of the *travel story take over, including the familiar emphasis on geography and specific places.

Yet this archetypal quest narrative appears unusual to modern eyes in at least two ways. There is first the overwhelming multiplicity of self-contained incidents and protagonists between the beginning and the end. There is also an apparent lack of resolution and closure in Paul's lingering imprisonment at the story's end. The narrative lacks the obvious unity of a single protagonist and the classical sense of "beginning, middle and end" that characterize most traditional narratives. Still, the story is purposeful and unified.

The outward movement of the church is structured as a succession of waves. The broadest scheme is a *threefold one: events in Jerusalem (Acts 1—5), the church's mission in Palestine and Syria (Acts 6—12), and the mission and imprisonment of Paul (Acts 13—28). The outward expansion of the church is also structured as an ever-widening spiral built around the following pattern: Christian leaders arise and preach the gospel; God performs mighty acts through them; listeners are converted and added to the church; opponents (usually Jewish) begin to persecute the Christian leaders; God intervenes to rescue the leaders or otherwise protect the church.

Another source of unity and purpose in Acts is the foils that Luke employs so effectively. One pair of foils is Stephen and Saul (Acts 7:1—8:1). After Stephen recounts the history of the Jews' rejection of God's messengers culminating in their crucifixion of Jesus, the text records that "the witnesses laid down their garments at the feet of a young man named Saul," who "was consenting to his death" (Acts 7:58; 8:1 RSV). With consummate artistry Luke focuses on Stephen and Saul, the believer and the persecutor. The foil is made even more poignant in retrospect when, on his way to Damascus, Saul, like Stephen before him, has a vision of the resurrected Christ (Acts 9:1-6). The characters of Stephen, the Jewish convert, and Saul, the later apostle to the Gentiles, parallel the larger structure of Acts, looking back to Jerusalem and forward to Rome.

Peter and Paul are also foils. Peter is the protagonist in the first twelve chapters; Paul, in the remaining chapters. Peter is the inspired but "uneducated" (Acts 4:13) preacher at Pentecost and speaker at the Jerusalem Council; Paul, the masterful orator of many sermons delivered across the Mediterranean world and finally in Rome. Peter is a bridge to Paul, whose conversion is reported well before Peter's departure from the narrative. In addition, Peter comes to understand that the gospel is for Gentiles too (Acts 10:11-35), while Paul is the Apostle to the Gentiles. Luke thus transfers the mantle of protagonist from Peter to Paul, who will take the gospel from Jerusalem to Rome.

Within the larger bimodal framework of Jerusalem/Rome and Peter/Paul, Luke unifies Acts with a series of images. The most obvious image in the early portions of the narrative is *light and its variant *fire (about ten references). The church is initiated by the "tongues of fire that separated and came to rest on each of [the disciples]" (Acts 2:3 NIV). Presumably this phenomenon was one flame that subsequently divided into separate flames to rest on each disciple's head. The fire symbolized the Holy Spirit (Acts 2:4). The image of light reappears at the martyrdom of Stephen when he gazes into heaven and sees "the glory of God, and Jesus standing at the right hand of God" (Acts 7:55 NIV). It is likely that, as elsewhere in the Scriptures, the glory of God is represented in part by radiant light, and that Stephen has a beatific vision dominated by light.

Even more dramatic than the light at Stephen's death is the blinding light that struck Saul to the ground when he was on his way to Damascus (Acts 9:3; cf. 22:6). Paul later described it as "a light from heaven, brighter than the sun, shining round me" (Acts 26:13 RSV). As at Pentecost this use of light is a beginning—at Pentecost, of the church, and here, of Paul's conversion and subsequent apostolic ministry. Other instances of light, such as that on the night of Peter's escape from prison (Acts 12:7), further unify the narrative in Acts.

A second image pattern is *prisons and jails, so frequent as to become one of the prominent visual images in Acts. In fact, the last eight chapters, apart from the travel interlude, are set entirely in prisons and courthouses; even on board ship Paul is a prisoner. There are approximately twenty references to prisons and ten each to *gates, *doors and *guards. In several prison incidents Luke gives us dramatic, even ironic images of open and closed doors. In one incident the Sadducees arrest the apostles and put them in jail in Jerusalem; but overnight an angel opens the prison doors and takes them out, giving them an "open door" to preach the next morning at the temple courts (Acts 5:18-23).

An even more dramatic incident is Peter's miraculous rescue from prison, where despite being guarded by four squads of soldiers, Peter is led past an iron gate that opens of its own accord (Acts 12:1-11). In the sequel to the rescue from prison—Peter's difficulty in joining a home prayer meeting—Rhoda, in her surprise, ironically leaves Peter standing at a closed door (Acts 12:12-16). In one of Paul's imprisonments a violent earthquake shakes the prisons and opens the doors, leading the Philippian jailer to think that suicide is his only recourse (Acts 16:20-39). But the open door of the gospel proves to be more important to the jailer than the open doors of the prison. While prison scenes recur with some frequency in Acts, it is the irony of the open doors that the reader remembers—open prison doors and opportunities for Peter and Paul to preach the gospel. The only prison door that does not open is Paul's in Rome; however, Paul's witness while under house arrest in Rome spreads the gospel throughout the Roman Empire—another "open door," this one at the end of the book of Acts.

Some of the motifs that unify the book of Acts are the conventional ones in an *adventure story. These include danger, narrow escapes, voyages, shipwrecks, rescues, riots, imprisonments, escapes, martyrdoms. Adventure stories stress variety, and Acts runs true to form with its variety of urban settings (a virtual roll call of the major cities of the ancient Mediterranean world) and physical places (temples, prisons, courts, deserts, ships, seas, barracks, theaters).

The forensic imagery of trial and defense, as well as oratorical situations, are master images in the book of Acts. They are accompanied by elaborate attention to dramatic effects—descriptions of settings, direct quotation of speeches, and stationing and gesturing of characters. Nearly 75 percent of the book is devoted to dramatized speeches, most of them having the character of a defense. The metaphoric overtone of the trials and defenses that pervade the book is that the gospel itself is being tried and defended.

While a first reading of the book of Acts may give the impression of a loose narrative that lacks the control of Luke's Gospel, a more careful reading suggests that Luke is very much in control of his material. Acts does not come to a complete conclusion with all of the loose ends neatly tied; rather we are left with the "inconclusive conclusion" of Paul's imprisonment and the knowledge that the gospel will go forth from that place despite Paul's incarceration. In a sense the book of Acts never ends. It has much in common with the serial story that ends with the formula "To be continued." In another sense, however, Luke writes a very tight narrative. He provides structure and order for the narrative in the unifying motifs of light and prisons, journeys and defenses. He patterns events in the form of a quest with a specific goal. Perhaps most dramatically, he sets the world of Acts between two cities. Peter begins the narrative in Jerusalem, and Paul carries it to Rome. This tight, bimodal pattern may well suggest God's providential oversight, with the inconclusive ending suggesting the ongoing responsibility of God's witnesses to carry on the task others have started.

See also DOOR; LUKE, GOSPEL OF; PENTECOST; QUEST; TRAVEL STORY.

ADAM

Adam is a leading figure in the Western literary and theological imagination, and he is a paradox, being both the original innocent and the archetypal sinner. In the Bible's story of creation, fall and redemption, he is the prototypical human figure. His biblical stature far exceeds the dimensions suggested by the relatively few times his name appears as a proper name in the Bible (between one and two dozen, depending on the English translation), for his presence is frequently evoked in imagery, motifs and allusions.

The principal features of Adam the archetype are shaped from the rich textual soil of Genesis 1—5. The common Hebrew word *'ā dā m*, which becomes the proper name *Adam*, is used within these chapters in its generic sense of "human," or with the definite article as "the human," prior to its emergence in the text as a proper name for the first male human. The point at which *'ā dā m* should be treated as a proper name is not agreed upon by translators, and English translations will vary in where they shift from "man"/"human" to "Adam." But the fact that the final Hebrew text of these chapters identifies Adam as a specific person allows some justification for our grouping all of these references under the imagery of Adam.

Adam as Divine Image. Adam is first and foremost related to God. In the spare and schematized language of Genesis 1, Adam is the fleshly distillation of the creative and divine word, stamped with the divine image. In the concrete portrayal of Genesis 2, Adam's form is shaped by the Divine Potter's hands, animated by the divine breath blown into his nostrils. Against the canopy of space and the topography of earth—beating, swarming and lumbering with fertile and fantastic life—Adam stands in unique relationship with God. The divine image in man and woman (Gen 1:27) simultaneously evokes and deconstructs the role of an idol in the ancient world. No stone or wood chiseled into a godling's image, "the Adam" in two—male and female—is an animated, walking, talking and relating mediation of the essence, will and work of the sovereign creator God. As living image of the living God, Adam bears a relationship to God like that of child to parent. He is made for intimate, reciprocal relationship with God, designed for relationship with his created others and born to the divine and creative vocation of earth-care and earth-filling (Gen 1:28).

With Adam's privilege comes responsibility. The image of Adam as one who receives divine commandments is a significant feature of the Genesis account. The divine command "not to eat" has as its corollary the universal human responsibility before God in the specific commandments given to Israel at Sinai.

Earthy Adam. Adam is shaped from the dust of the ground. This relation to the earth is subtly reinforced for the Hebrew ear in the assonance of *'ā dā m* "human" and *'ª dā mâ* "ground" (Gen 2:7). It is then sealed in the tragic epitaph, "dust thou art, and unto dust shalt thou return" (Gen 3:19 KJV). The narrative offers no overt physical description of this man (we are left to assume he bears the features of everyman), but again the Hebrew *'ā dā m/'ª dā mâ* word play resonates with *'dm,* "to be red," suggesting a rusty shade of soil. This relation of Adam to earth, soil and field is one aspect of Adam's relation to the entire created order.

While Genesis clearly speaks of Adam's "rule" over the creation, it is a theme set in the context of dependence. Adam is a dependent consumer, an aspect brought out in two images: seeing and eating. God provides him with trees pleasant to the sight and good for food. Adam partakes of creation through eye and mouth and shares in the pleasure of God by seeing the creation and calling it good. Clearly he is dependent on the creation for his own physical sustenance, but there is also a sense that Adam without a creation that is a "delight to the eye" is an Adam somehow diminished.

In the Genesis 1 creation account, Adam emerges as "the human" (*hā 'ā dā m,* Gen 1:26-27), differentiated as male and female in gender and sexual identity (Gen 1:27). As the apex of the unfolding creative activity of God, both man and woman are commanded to "fill the earth," "subdue it" and "rule" over every living thing. For these image bearers of the sovereign Creator, a principal expression of that image is an active rule that represents the loving dominion and care of God over the wonders of creation. Adam, true archetype of humankind, is appointed vice-regent in the territorial dominion of God. Male and female are regal figures, empowered, anointed and charged with exercising the benevolent rule of their cosmic Creator Lord. With a mere handful of deftly ordered words, the lofty bearing, stature and commission of ancient oriental kingship is breathtakingly disassembled and the royal crown placed on the sturdy heads of everyman and everywoman.

In the narrative of Genesis 2 the Adamic rule is expressed in three concrete activities: (1) cultivating or "serving" *('ābad)* the garden; (2) keeping, or "guarding" *(šāmar)* the garden; and (3) naming *(qārā' . . . šēm)* his fellows in the community of animate life. We enter the world of a splendid royal garden of grand proportions, stunning in design and irresistible in appeal, over which a king has set his vice-regent to till, to protect and to explore by naming.

In his "tilling" or "serving" (the Hebrew word *'ābad* can mean either), we see Adam entering into the ongoing divine work of maintaining the fertility and productivity of the garden. It is an agricultural image in which Adam's relation with the land is portrayed from a farmer's or game warden's standpoint, a complement to the divine "planting" (Gen 2:8) and "shaping" of beast and bird (Gen 2:19). But Adam is not just a laborer; he is an "eater," a consumer of the fruitful trees. Nor is Adam simply a consumer; he is one whose eye delights in the beauty of the trees as living signatures of the benevolent and creative artistry of God (Gen 2:9). A priestly overtone to this work also emerges—a double meaning of *'ābad* is probably intended, as we will see—with Adam mediating God's care for the creation. Adam is also a protector of the garden, one who "keeps" or "guards" *(šāmar)* by watching over its welfare and integrity and defending it from any harmful and destructive forces, whether lurking within or intruding from without.

Adam's commission to "name" engages him in what we have come to call science but what the ancients knew as wisdom. To know is to name; to name is to know and express the essential nature of someone or something. The divine Creator falls silent and observes as the creatures parade past Adam and as Adam perceives and orders this world of wonders into a relational taxonomy radiating from his personal point of reference. Adam is the true prototype of the royal wisdom of Solomon, who "would speak of trees, . . . of animals, and birds, and reptiles, and fish" (1 Kings 4:33 NRSV). But in all of Adam's naming of birds and cattle and creatures, which too are formed "out of the ground" (Gen 2:19), he does not find a true other, "a helper as his partner" (Gen 2:18, 20) in life and royal mission.

Adam as Husband. Of Adam's actual naming the creatures, the text is silent. But when he finds his "help meet" (KJV), "one like unto him," Adam turns from namer and taxonomist to poet, shaping simple words of delightful discovery into parallel verse:

This at last is bone of my bones
    and flesh of my flesh;
this one shall be called Woman,
    for from Man this one was taken.
    (Gen 2:23 NRSV)

This exclamation is affirmed and universalized in the narrator's voice: "Therefore a man leaves his father and his mother and clings to his wife, and they become one flesh" (Gen 2:24 NRSV). From the one human is formed another, their differentiation and deep relationship reflected in two new names set side by side: *'iš* "man" and *'iššâ* "woman." As two genders they reunite as "one flesh." In some deep and mysterious sense Adam truly finds himself in relationship with Eve. Together, same bone and flesh, they form and generate community in their fruitfulness and multiplication (Gen 1:28). This archetypal image of union—man and woman as one flesh—is the cell structure out of which the organism of human society and culture is built.

Father Adam. Adam is imaged as the father of us all, the progenitor of all humanity. From the union of Adam and Eve, "the mother of all living" (Gen 3:20), comes Cain, then Abel, then Seth and then other sons and daughters. This proliferation of "seed" is in keeping with the divine commandment for Adam to "be fruitful and multiply and fill the earth" (Gen 1:28). Throughout the early chapters of Genesis we find the seed of Adam multiplying, then nearly exterminated in the Flood, and then multiplying again to fill out the roll call of nations in Genesis 11. But Adam's fatherhood is a blessing dulled by pain as Cain murders Abel and becomes a "wanderer on the earth" (Gen 4:14). Fresh hope is found in the birth of Adam's son Seth (Gen 4:25-26), who is happily dubbed "a son in his likeness, according to his image" (Gen 5:3). Here, perhaps, is the first aspirant to that "offspring of the woman" who will crush the head of the serpent (Gen 3:15).

The fatherhood of Adam, a relationship of the one to the many, is a hallmark of his biblical stature. At key points the biblical story will depict a "one" related to the "many," whether Abraham to his seed, corporate Israel to the nations, or Christ to Jews and Gentiles; and it is the archetype of Adam that foreshadows the relationship and stamps its imprint on the text of the story.

Tragic Adam. Adam defines the nature of tragedy for the biblical story. He is the model of a man blessed with peace and intimacy with God. Fertile land bursting with life, water flowing fresh from its springs, trees laden with good fruit and pleasant to the eye, animal life fantastic in form and coexisting in neighborly peace, and a woman created for fulfilling union as "one flesh"—all of these gifts image the goodness of God and his love for Adam and the rest of creation. But Adam's reaching for the forbidden fruit epitomizes the irrationality and recklessness of the alien power of sin, as well as its seeming irreversibility. By taking and eating, an avalanche of consequences is set in motion. Adam's relationships with God, Eve, himself, earth and creatures are all fractured.

The image is not so much of "fall" as of exile and alienation. Eden is not abolished, but Adam is banished. He is exiled from the divine presence, the *tree of life, and the *garden of paradise. A shadow of alienation hovers over his relationship with God, with Eve and with his son Cain. The three principal relationships of Eden that compose the core of the imagery of blessing—his relationship with God, with other humans and with the creation—each come to bear the sign of an indelible curse. What Adam thinks or feels can only be teased from his minimal speech and actions. But there are no more words of delight, only words that distill fear ("I was afraid, . . . I was naked, . . . I hid myself," Gen 3:10) and evasion ("the woman whom you gave . . . she gave," Gen 3:12). However the resolution of this story is to be worked out, it must pass through the pain of suffering and of death.

Adam and Israel. Adam is Scripture's archetypal human through whom we are to see and measure the human predicament. But the human predicament and hope is more finely delineated in the figure and story of Israel, and the archetype of Adam is implied in a variety of images and aspects of Israel's story. The story of Adam provides a lens through which to view Israel.

The image of Adam is passed on to his son Seth (Gen 5:3), but Adam as the archetypal man of the biblical story also projects his image on subsequent figures and narratives that unfold in the generations of Scripture. The Adamic motifs in the story of Noah have frequently been noted. Noah is memorably set in relationship with God, the creation and his surviving community. Stepping forth from the ark, Noah, a new progenitor of humanity after the great judgment, is commanded, as was Adam, to "be fruitful and multiply, and fill the earth." Even his sovereign relationship with the animals is reminiscent of Adam's, though now marked by "fear and dread" (Gen 9:1-4).

But the scriptural imprint of Adam's image does not stop with Noah. Emerging from the primeval history (Gen 1–11), the text's eye scans the multitude of nations and singles out one individual with a peculiarly Adamic stature. From the east, the direction of Adam's exile (Gen 3:24), *Abraham moves west toward a land of promise, a land for the moment ironically desolated by severe famine (Gen 12:10) and somewhat less than Eden. Abraham hears the word of God and obeys. He lives in memorable relationship with a woman, Sarah, and together they struggle to "be fruitful and multiply," to produce descendants as numerous as the sand of the shore and the stars of the sky. The promise that Abraham and his *seed will be fruitful, multiply and inherit the land is repeated at strategic moments in the Genesis ancestral narrative (Gen 12:2-3; 17:2, 6, 8; 22:16-18; 26:3-4, 24; 28:3; 35:11-12; 47:27; 48:3-4). In Abraham's response to God's word rests the future bless-

ing of the nations. These Adamic motifs subtly adorning the story of Abraham set up overtones of recapitulation in this overture of redemption.

As Abraham's progeny generates Israel, so Israel's story and symbols also evoke Adamic motifs. Most notable are the concentrated correlations between Eden and Israel's sanctuary. The *gold and onyx of Eden reappear in the *tabernacle, where gold is found in abundance and onyx stones are now engraved with the names of the sons of Israel (Ex 28:9-12; cf. 25:7). The tree of life is symbolized in the branched and flowering lampstand (Ex 25:31-40). Plants are carved into the wooden walls and doors of Solomon's temple—palms, flowers and gourds (1 Kings 6:29-35)—their profusion evoking a garden setting in which the priests serve (cf. Ps 52:8; 92:12-14). And in the outer court the pillars and "sea" are decorated with lilies, pomegranates and gourds (1 Kings 7:18-22, 24, 26).

There are no animals on the carvings of the inner chambers, but in the outer court real animals are abundant as sacrifices, and the archetypal figures of bulls and lions are represented in art (1 Kings 7:25, 29, 36). Cherubim are found amid the palms and flowers in the inner chambers, on the curtains and veil of the tabernacle (Ex 26:1, 31; 36:8, 35), and on top and outstretched above the ark of the covenant (Ex 25:18-22; 1 Kings 6:23-28). Their presence evokes the guardians stationed at Eden's east entrance (Gen 3:24; cf. Ezek 28:14), and their features, suggested by other texts (Ezek 10) and ancient Near Eastern art, are a composite of beast (lion, sometimes the bull), bird (eagle) and human images.

The fount of water that arises in Eden and feeds four major rivers is thought by some to be symbolized in Solomon's massive "sea" of water (1 Kings 7:23-26). Though this bronze basin clearly served a practical purpose in temple service, there is good reason to believe that against the backdrop of ancient Near Eastern mythology it symbolizes the waters of chaos that Yahweh has subdued and now channels to nourish the earth (see Keel, 136-138, 142-43).

This, together with the ritual significance of the spring of Gihon at the foot of Mount *Zion (cf. Gen 2:13; 1 Kings 1:33, 38, 45; 2 Chron 32:30; 33:14), inspires the *river imagery of the Psalms (Ps 46:4; 74:13-15) that is associated with Zion and temple. It is this river imagery that once again erupts in Ezekiel's vision of the eschatological temple, where a mighty tree-lined river now originates from beneath the temple threshold (Ezek 47:1-12; cf. Zech 14:8; Rev 22:1-2), nourishing trees and aquatic life along its eastward flow. Finally, the entrance to the Jerusalem temple and its inner courts and chambers are oriented toward the east, recalling the situation of Eden's gate.

The commission of Adam to till, or serve (*'ābad*), and to protect, or guard (*šāmar*), the garden are functions also associated with levitical and priestly duty (for guarding the sanctuary, cf. Num 1:53); and Adam's ordering of the animal world by naming corresponds with the priestly assignment of distinguishing clean from unclean animals and judging what is appropriate for sacrifice. The cultic representation of Israel that culminates in the actions of one purified and holy man, the high priest, who enters the Holy of Holies once a year, is replete with Adamic symbolism. The adornment of the high priest symbolizes the regal glory of Adam (cf. Ezek 28:13), whom later Judaism could describe as clothed in light. The sanctuary of the Lord, God's symbolic dwelling place within Israel, among whom he will "walk" (Lev 26:12; cf. Gen 3:8), images the hope and promise that Israel as a new Adam will return to Eden. This biblical correlation between priest and Adam has an afterlife of imagery in the pseudepigraphal Jewish text (c. 250 B.C.), the *Testament of Levi* 18:10, where the "new priest" will "open the gates of paradise," "remove the sword that has threatened since Adam" and "grant to the saints to eat of the tree of life." The OT sanctuary symbolism of the high priest as Adam, serving in the presence of plants and animals, suggests a poignant backdrop to Paul's declaration that "the creation waits in eager expectation for the sons of God to be revealed" (Rom 8:19 NIV).

The imagery of Adam in Eden, focused and articulated in the sanctuary symbolism, may be observed in the broader patterns of Israel's life as a corporate Adam before God. Israel is given in trust a fertile land, its edenic fruitfulness (cf. Joel 2:3) imaged in pomegranates, grapes and figs, and "flowing with milk and honey" (Num 13:23, 27). As he did for Adam, God offers to Israel blessings, but he also commands "thou shalt not" (Gen 2:17; Ex 20:1-17) in the memorable form of *law. The theme of divine commandment finds its corollary in the edenic commandment not to eat of the tree of the knowledge of good and evil. As in Eden, so in Israel: obedience to God's commandments, including a right and wholesome relationship with the land, will bring blessings epitomized as *life* in a peaceful community, a prosperous land and the presence of God (Lev 26:3-13; Deut 28:1-14). Disobedience will lead to a curse, summed up as *death* and precipitating in broken community, exile (to the east) from the good land and loss of the glorious presence of God from Israel's midst (Lev 26:14-33; Deut 28:15-68).

Adam Restored. Israel's understanding of Adam as the progenitor of all humanity is clearly explicated in the Genesis text, and it forms the background of Psalm 8's reflective wonder at humanity's place in the created universe:

When I consider your heavens,
   the work of your fingers,
the moon and the stars,
   which you have set in place,
what is man that you are mindful of him,
   the son of man that you care for him?
   (Ps 8:3-4 NIV)

But the "man"/"son of man" of this psalm is not simply universal and abstract humanity. A particu-larism is implied as the psalmist speaks on behalf of a specific community that confesses allegiance to "our Lord" in contrast to its Lord's "enemies," "foe" and "avenger" (Ps 8:1-2). For the psalmist the most prominent embodiment of "man"/"son of man" is Israel, the chosen people from amidst the nations, whose preeminence is represented and symbolized in the Davidic king of the psalm's superscription. The Adamic imagery of glory, honor and creational rule is cut to fit the figure of Israel before it is released to any other nation, people or community.

A similar understanding informs *Daniel's vision of four composite and horrible beasts, representing Israel's enemy empires who arise from the primordial sea. They are vanquished by "one like a son of man," a heavenly human figure who represents or embodies Israel, God's true humanity (Dan 7). The corollary of Adam ruling over the beasts is Israel subduing and ruling over the nations. This understanding of Israel's elect Adamic role is amply testified in the literature of Second-Temple Judaism (see Wright, 23-26) and is well illustrated by texts from the Dead Sea Scrolls, where the sectarian Jewish community, regarding itself as the true Israel within Israel, expects to receive the blessed restoration of Adam's glory (1QS 4:23; CD 3:20; 1QH 17:15; 4Q171 3:1).

The prophets, in speaking of the eschatological renewal of Israel's land and of the entire creation, unfurl lavish imagery of a renewed paradise with Israel as God's redeemed Adam, the true humanity, exalted over the nations. Isaiah presents us with striking images of this renewal:

The wolf will live with the lamb, . . . The cow will feed with the bear, . . . and the young child put his hand into the viper's nest. They will neither harm nor destroy on all my holy mountain. (Is 11:6-9; cf. 65:25 NIV)

I will open rivers on the bare heights,
   and fountains in the midst of the valleys. . . .
I will put in the wilderness the cedar,
   the acacia, the myrtle, and the olive;
I will set in the desert the cypress,
   the plane and the pine together.
   (Is 41:18-19 NRSV)

The LORD will surely comfort Zion . . .
he will make her desert like Eden,
   her wastelands like the garden of the LORD.
   (Is 51:3 NIV)

Like Adam, redeemed Israel is not truly and fully itself apart from paradise.

Adam and Christ. In the NT the comparison of Adam and Christ and the imagery of Christ as a new Adam play a prominent role, particularly in Paul's letters. But it is not limited to Paul. Luke, for example, traces the genealogy of Jesus back to Adam, "son of God" (3:38) and draws us to consider the correlation between Adam and Christ. Adam as son of God is the father of the human race, and Jesus, whose divine sonship has just been declared at his baptism (Lk 3:22), is the progenitor of a new people that grows to include members from all nations (Lk 24:46-47). Mark also suggests Adamic imagery in his brief and teasing snapshot of Jesus in the wilderness "with the wild beasts" (Mk 1:13). Other Adamic allusions in the Gospels have been suggested, but it is Paul who rightly occupies our focus, for he most clearly develops the image in his christological typology of salvation.

Paul's use of Adamic imagery is well developed in Romans. When Paul says that "all have sinned and fallen short of the glory of God" (Rom 3:23), he echoes Psalm 8:5, where the human figure is crowned with glory and honor, as well as Genesis 1:28. And when Paul speaks of people who have "exchanged the glory of the immortal God" for images of mortal humans and beasts (cf. Ps 106:20), he is again informed by the figure of Adam. Humans are created to worship God, in whose image they are created and should ever grow in likeness. The entire creation has lost its original radiant glory and has been subjected to futility and decay (Rom 8:20-21).

In Romans 5:12-21 Paul develops a run of Adamic typology. The reign of sin and death is contrasted with the reign of grace, righteousness and eternal life. "Sin entered the world through one man, and death through sin, and in this way death came to all men because all sinned" (Rom 5:12 NIV). Adam is portrayed as a figure whose actions, as the father of all humanity, have an ongoing effect through subsequent generations. It is as if his disobedience allowed the entrance of an alien and hostile force into God's world, which all his descendants serve by their misdeeds. But if Adam's disobedience is the pattern and undoing of the many, Adam is also "a pattern of the one to come" (Rom 5:14), "the one man, Jesus Christ" (Rom 5:15) who will redeem the many.

If the story of the first Adam was a human one in relationship with God, the story of the second Adam is infused with divine grace and regenerative power as God uniquely embodies himself in the human story and transforms it. The legacy of sin, judgment and condemnation unleashed by the transgression of the first Adam is counteracted by the one act of righteousness, the obedience of Christ, the second Adam. Whereas death reigned through the first Adam, through the second Adam the many will themselves reign in life (Rom 5:17). Through the disobedience of the first Adam, many were made sinners; through the obedience of the second, many will be made righteous (5:19). The dark and degenerative rule of death is overthrown by the radiant and generative rule of life.

Adam, and Israel likewise, appears more covertly beneath the argument of Romans 7:7-12. Here the picture is of sinful passions aroused by the law and bearing fruit for death. The law said, "You shall not covet." But sin seized its opportunity in the commandment and "produced in me all kinds of covetousness" (Rom 7:8 NRSV). An echo of Eden captured in this voice of Israel (for it is possible that Israel is individualized and speaking as "I" in Rom 7), whose experience with the law followed precisely this pattern. Rabbinic interpretation, in fact, understood the law to have existed prior to creation; thus the commandment to Adam not to eat of the tree (Gen 2:17) was viewed as an expression of Torah. When Adam ate, the consequence was death and exclusion from the tree of life, the same pattern of action and consequence laid out by the law and enacted by Israel in its tragic history.

In a redemptive vein Paul speaks of the emergence of a new humanity through the work of Christ: "our old man [Adam] is crucified together with Christ" (Rom 6:6). The corporate nature of this image is probably what informs the metaphor of the community as one body consisting of many members with complementary gifts and functions (Rom 12:4-8).

In 1 Corinthians 15 Paul uses Adamic imagery to speak of the resurrected Christ. The point of comparison begins with death and life: "For as in Adam all die, so in Christ all will be made alive" (1 Cor 15:22 NIV). But it does not end there. Christ is resurrected and exalted, and through him the spiritual dominions, authorities and powers will be destroyed:. "For he must reign until he has put all his enemies under his feet. The last enemy to be destroyed is death. For he 'has put everything under his feet' " (1 Cor 15:25-27 NIV). With the imagery "under his feet," Paul first alludes to Psalm 8:5 and then cites the text. Christ as the last Adam is enthroned as cosmic Lord of the new creation. Thus not only are beasts and other creatures in submission under his feet but also the very cosmic powers and the "last enemy," death.

The figure of Adam reappears several verses later as Paul is explaining the concept of a resurrection body. Quoting Genesis 2:7 he reminds readers that "the first man Adam became a living being," but the "last Adam," became "a life-giving spirit" (1 Cor 15:45 NIV). Again, the first man was "natural," "of the dust of the earth" and "earthly," as are his descendants "who are of the earth" (vv. 46-48). The last Adam, however, is "spiritual" and "from heaven." Those who share the life of the last Adam will be "of heaven," for "just as we have borne the likeness of the earthly man, so shall we bear the likeness of the man from heaven" (v. 49). The human life of the old and the new creation shares in the qualities of its respective "Adamic" progenitors.

Paul frequently employs Adamic imagery in conjunction with glory imagery and the motif of transformation. In 2 Corinthians 3, he speaks of the fading glory of the old covenant under Moses in contrast with the surpassing glory of the new. Here the contrast is between Moses and Christ, but it seems evident that Adamic imagery lies behind the comparison, with Moses as the singular representative of Israel's stature as a "new" Adamic people. In contrast with the radiance that faded from Moses' face after his encounters with God, those who now reflect the Lord's glory "are being transformed into his likeness with ever-increasing glory, which comes from the Lord, who is the Spirit" (2 Cor 3:18). They are on the true trajectory toward redemptive Adamic glory that radiantly reflects the image of God.

That image of God is first and foremost found in "the glory of Christ, who is the image of God" (2 Cor 4:4). The typology of old and new creation clearly surfaces in 2 Corinthians 4:6: "For God, who said, 'Let light shine out of darkness,' made his light shine in our hearts to give us the light of the knowledge of the glory of God in the face of Christ" (NIV). Christ, the last Adam, is the human image of the glory of God, the prototype of the new humanity that will inhabit the new creation. In view of this, the afflictions borne by the believing community are only "light" and "momentary," the divine process of building a renewed and "eternal weight of glory" (2 Cor 4:17). While the "outer man" *(anthrōpos)* is "wasting away," the emergent "inner man" is "being renewed day by day" (2 Cor 4:16). Thus Paul can say: "if anyone is in Christ—behold, a new creation! The old has gone, the new has come!" (2 Cor 5:17).

The theme of a new humanity shaped for a new creation emerges in Paul's bold statements of unity. In Colossians 3:9-11 Paul speaks of believers having "stripped off the old man *[palaion anthrōpon]*" and "put on the new [man]" "which is being renewed in knowledge according to the image of its creator." The two Adams clearly inform this language. The image is a corporate one, and in this new Adamic humanity, the divisions of the old Adamic family are overcome: "there is no longer Greek and Jew, circumcised and uncircumcised, barbarian, Scythian, slave and free" (cf. Gal 3:28, "neither male nor female"). A variation on this theme is found in Ephesians 2:14-15, where the division between Jew and Gentile is in view. Christ (i.e., the last Adam) has created "in himself one new man *[kainon anthrōpon]* out of the two" (NIV).

Paul's portrayals of the preincarnate and "cosmic" Christ also employ Adamic imagery. In Colossians 1:15 Christ is "the image of the invisible God, the firstborn over all creation." He is the heavenly, preexistent Adam, the prototypical image of God that finds its reflection in the human Adam. Likewise, in his redemptive work, Christ is "the head of the body, the church," the community of the new creation, and "he is the beginning and the firstborn from among the dead" (Col 1:18 NIV). While the old Adam failed to fulfill his God-given dominion over the creation, Christ brings cosmic reconciliation and peace (Col 1:20). In a similar vein Philippians Paul 2:6 speaks of Christ being in the "form" *(morphē)* of God, a term probably intended as synonymous with the Adamic "image" *(eikōn)*. Some interpreters of Philippians 2:6-11 have seen further allusions to Adam informing this versified story of Christ. Whereas Christ was in the form/image of God, he did not regard "equality" with God ("you will be like God," Gen 3:5) as something to be grasped or exploited. In counterpoint to the Adam of Genesis 2—3, the preexistent Christ took the path of obedience. This entailed death on a cross, a death that reversed the consequences of the tragic death of Adam. Therefore Christ was "highly exalted" to a position of cosmic rule, with every power "in heaven and on earth and under the earth" in submission to him.

For Paul the biblical imagery of the first Adam and the creation finds a correspondence in the last Adam and a new creation. Christ as Adam is leading his people back to a renewed Eden. Nowhere is this biblical relationship more poignantly evoked than in Romans 8:19-23. The creation, subjected to futility and decay, "waits with eager longing for the revealing of the children of God" (v. 19 NRSV). The children of the last Adam are the harbinger and hope of the new creation. The "groanings" and birth pangs of an emergent new humanity find their echo in the groanings of the whole creation, and the Spirit himself utters "groans" that words cannot express. This new creative work of God progresses through pain and affliction as God's chosen ones are "conformed to the likeness" of the Son and eventually "glorified" (Rom 8:29-30).

See also CREATION; EVE; GARDEN; GENESIS; TEMPLE; TREE OF LIFE.

BIBLIOGRAPHY. O. Keel, *The Symbolism of the Biblical World: Ancient Near Eastern Iconography and the Book of Psalms* (Winona Lake, IN: Eisenbrauns, 1997); J. Levison, *Portraits of Adam in Early Judaism* (JSPSup 1; Sheffield: Academic Press, 1988); G. Wenham, *Genesis 1-15* (WBC: Waco, TX: Word, 1987); N. T. Wright, "Adam, Israel and the Messiah" in *The Climax of the Covenant* (Minneapolis: Fortress, 1991) 18-55.

ADOPTION

The Greek word *hyiothesia* ("adoption") occurs only five times in the NT, all in the Pauline corpus (Rom 8:15, 23; 9:4; Gal 4:5; Eph 1:5), but its significance is great because of its conceptual and emotive power and its relationship to many other familial ideas. It never refers to a literal adoption but always to the blessing of God's people by their heavenly Father. Adoption carries many associations in modern Western culture—both negative and positive—that may or may not have analogies in ancient cultures. Thus it is particularly important that we grasp the cultural and social context of adoption in the ancient world.

The background of the metaphor has been much debated. There are no instances of *hyiothesia* in the LXX, and neither the OT nor later Judaism reports adoption legislation. In part this was because other customs such as polygamy, legitimate heirs by female slaves (Gen 16:1-5), "levirate marriage" (Deut 25:5-10) and *apothrōpos* ("guardianship") in later Judaism met some of the same social needs. There seem to be a few instances of adoption in the OT, but these are always based on the laws of foreign peoples with whom the Israelites had contact (Gen 15:2-3; Gen 30:3; 50:23; Ex 2:10; Esther 2:7). The issue of adopting orphaned or unwanted children, particularly those unrelated by blood kinship, is not addressed.

Despite the lack of a formal adoption law, there was a clear sense of God adopting the king. Psalm 2 conveys the adoption of Israel's king: "I [the Lord] have installed my king on Zion. . . . He said to me, 'You are my Son; today I have become your Father' " (vv. 6-7 NIV). The adoption of the king as a representative of Israel may very well lie behind Paul's use of the adoption language. This motif is made even more universal in the covenant language of 2 Samuel 7:14: "I will be his [the king of the Davidic line] father, and he will be my son." J. M. Scott shows that this adoption was later applied by Judaism not only to the Davidic Messiah but to the eschatological people of God.

Another influence on the development of the metaphor is the well-defined and frequently used adoption legislation of Greece and Rome. It is clear, however, that the sociolegal practice does not fully explain the Pauline usage. An equally powerful shaper of the image was the OT and later Jewish belief that God was a Father who had called and redeemed, and who would bless, his children (Deut 32:6; 2 Sam 7:14; Ps 68:5; 89:26; 103:13; Is 63:16, 64:8; Mal 2:10). For Christians, Jesus' experience of (Lk 2:49; 3:22; 22:42; 23:46) and teaching about (Mt 5:45; 6:4-5, 8-9, 14-15, 18) his Father in heaven is pivotal. Those who are "in Christ" have been "adopted" as God's people in much the same sense as God redeemed Israel and made this people his "Son" (Hos 11:1).

In the ancient world family membership was the primary context of social, religious, economic and political security and fulfillment. To move from one family system to another was an event of life-changing importance. In this social context adoption is used in the NT to communicate a whole set of nuances of God's blessing on his people. Adoption is listed among the greatest blessings of God upon Israel (Rom 9:4, "to them belong the adoption," NRSV) and in the triumphant doxology of Ephesians 1:5, "adoption as his children" is named as a chief blessing of the gospel.

The sociolegal customs and the OT notion of the authority of God as Father combine to stress the authority of God as the adopter. Adoption is an expression of the electing love of God (Eph 1:5; Rom 8:29), which transfers the adopted child from the family of disobedience (Eph 2:2-3, where the NIV translation unfortunately obscures the metaphor) to the family of God. Adoption is an image of redemption, not of creation. The adopted one has been graciously and marvelously freed from bondage and made God's child (Hos 11:1; Gal 4:5).

A major focus of the adoption texts is that the believer is adopted by virtue of union with Christ, the Son of God (Eph 1:5). This notion has no antecedent in the sociolegal practices of Rome or the OT world, though this has frequently been maintained. Rather, it derives from the central themes of Jesus' life and message (Jn 1:12,18; 8:42-44). Life-changing Christian adoption is through Christ, the Son of God, the Messiah of Israel, who makes the last days' familial promises of God (Jer 3:19; Hos 1:10; 2 Cor 6: 18) a present reality.

The presence of these blessings is witnessed to by the eschatological spirit of adoption, who assures God's children of their adoption. The child of God, confident of Father's care, cries out with the same words Jesus used, "*Abba,* father" (Lk 22:42; Rom 8:15). The use of the Aramaic *abba* is probably due to liturgical influences and indicates its centrality in the piety and worship of the earliest congregations. Family membership in the ancient world included not only the benefits of security but also the derivative benefit of liberty within the family. Using this powerful image, Paul proclaimed that God's child was free from the pursuit of righteousness through the law (Gal 3:16-24).

Ancient as well as modern adoption brings benefits as well as responsibilities of family membership. Similarly, Paul stressed the ethical obligations of the adopted child of God (Rom 8:11-15; Eph 1:4-5). The adopted child has inherited a new family narrative, Israel's story, and is expected to live and act in accordance with that story and its ancestral exemplars like Abraham. This responsibility involves God's child in a life of faith and a struggle with sin. It is not, however, a battle fought in fear. It is fought in the liberated confidence (Rom 8:15-16) of the coming victory in the consummation of adoption (Rom 8:23). This same assurance also carries God's children through the agonies of suffering toward their glorious future when adoption blessing will reach its fullness (Rom 8:18-23, 28-30).

See also DAUGHTER; FATHER; MOTHER, MOTHERHOOD; ORPHAN; SON.

BIBLIOGRAPHY. J. M. Scott, "Adoption, Sonship," *DPL* 15-18.

ADULTERY

Both Old and New Testaments agree that adultery is sin. In the OT any married woman who has intercourse with a man other than her husband is guilty of adultery, as is any man who has sex with another man's wife. But it is sometimes acceptable for a man to have multiple wives or concubines. Jesus holds up a more consistent standard in the NT, with both men and women called to be faithful to their one spouse (see Mt 19:3-9), and the Epistles set a high standard for sexual purity (1 Cor 6:18-20 and Heb 13:4).

The Bible's most graphic teachings against adultery come in Proverbs 5:1-23 and 6:20—7:27, where images of injury, entrapment and death are used to underline the dangers and the sheer folly of adultery: "Can a man walk on hot coals without his feet being scorched? So is he who sleeps with another man's wife" (Prov 6:28-29 NIV). "He followed her like an ox going to the slaughter, like a deer stepping into a noose. . . . Her house is a highway to the grave" (7:22, 27 NIV). Adultery in the wisdom literature comes to picture hidden deeds, which are done in secret because the perpetrator senses they are wrong, and which inevitably are found out: "The eye of the adulterer watches for dusk; he thinks, 'No eye will see me,' and he keeps his face concealed" (Job 24:15 NIV).

The most striking example of adultery in the Bible is the story of David and Bathsheba (2 Sam 11:1-5), which has reverberated throughout literature and art and which remains the archetype for the respected religious or civil leader falling from favor through sexual sin. For all its brevity, the story is richly imaged, with pictures of a springtime setting, an afternoon stroll on the roof, the viewing of a beautiful woman bathing, the secret visit and the subsequent message that the woman is pregnant.

Equally evocative is Jesus' internalizing of the principle of adultery with his comment in the Sermon on the Mount that "anyone who looks at a woman lustfully has already committed adultery with her in his heart" (Mt 5:28 NIV). Jesus' teaching develops the concern clearly expressed in the OT over one's internal disposition. The words of Proverbs 6:25, "Do not lust in your heart after her beauty or let her captivate you with her eyes" (NIV), make this concern clear.

The NT continues the figurative use of adultery when those who reject Jesus (Mt 16:1-4), those who choose friendship with the world (Jas 4:4) and those who follow false teaching (Rev 2:20-22) are called adulterous. A major image for *apostasy in the OT is adultery. Finally, the book of Revelation symbolizes the ultimate end of all opposition to God when angels announce the fall of Babylon, "the great prostitute who corrupted the earth by her adulteries" (Rev 19:2 NIV).

See also APOSTASY; MARRIAGE; PROSTITUTE, PROSTITUTION; SEX.

BIBLIOGRAPHY. R. C. Ortlund Jr., *Whoredom: God's Unfaithful Wife in Biblical Theology* (Grand Rapids: Eerdmans, 1997).

ADVENTURE STORY

The designation "adventure story" is a loose one that denotes a story having stock ingredients that evoke a certain atmosphere. The distinguishing feature of an adventure story is that it strikes a reader as extraordinary—beyond the commonplace routine. Adventure is synonymous with excitement. Variety of action and remoteness of setting are staples, as is the marvelous or miraculous. Conflict and danger are heightened, and spectacular feats are a regular feature. Surprise is a common element. *Storms, disguises, *shipwrecks, *battles, *journeys through dangerous landscapes, chases, *hiding, arrests and *escapes are frequent story material.

Elements of the adventure story are continuously present in the Bible. The quality of the marvelous and supernatural is present from start to finish by virtue of the fact that God is a continuous actor in the stories of the Bible. Miracles and larger-than-life events are the norm. The resulting world is one in which streams stop their flow, food miraculously appears, the earth opens up to swallow evil people and the dead are raised to life. Action is heightened in such a world. We are continuously surprised by events. Diverse types of story material are juxtaposed—for example, home versus battlefield, or a conversation with a spouse versus an encounter with God. Things keep changing as we turn the pages of the Bible. Life often seems like a continuous narrow escape in books such as the epic of *Exodus, the OT historical chronicles, the *Gospels and the book of *Acts. Settings familiar to the original audience are remote from the experience of a modern reader, making the action seem all the more adventurous.

Cataloging specific adventure stories in the Bible is superfluous. The elements noted above are common in biblical narrative, and the general quality of adventure is present as well. Most stories in the Bible have an affinity to the adventure story.

See also QUEST; TRAVEL STORY.

ADVOCATE. *See* HOLY SPIRIT; LEGAL IMAGES.

AFFLICTION

Affliction is understood in modern parlance as persistent suffering or anguish. So defined, it provides helpful insight into the varied biblical images of affliction. In the most fundamental sense, affliction is the mirror of fallenness within the creation. Although God created the world good (Gen 1—2), sin intruded after the Fall (Gen 3; Rom 8:20). Through *Adam and *Eve's rebellion (Rom 5:12, 19) humanity inherited a permanent state of affliction—sin—which is the cause of recurring suffering and sorrow. The general human condition is thus one of affliction. In addition the Bible contains more pointed images of affliction, specific manifestations of a fallen condition.

Scriptural images of affliction fall into three categories—physical, emotional and spiritual. While the Bible abounds in stories and pictures of affliction, we can get to the heart of the idea by examining the experience of two familiar characters': *David in the OT and Paul in the NT.

While many of the psalms (9; 36; 72; 107) speak of affliction, David's laments in Psalms 25 and 51 graphically portray his struggles with these difficulties. On the physical level the psalmist faces affliction as illness and distress (25:16-18, 20). He also fears the physical threat of his enemies (25:2). Emotionally, affliction is seen in David's contrite sinner's prayer in Psalm 51. His existential wrestling with sin captures the emotional component of affliction. Again the threat of enemies' unkind words or deeds have an impact and remain on David's mind (25:19). Spiritually, the psalmist seeks forgiveness of his sins (Ps 25: 7, 11, 18) as relief for his afflicted condition (25:16-18; 51:1-4).

In the NT six Pauline "catalogs of affliction" (Rom 8:35; 1 Co 4:9-13; 2 Co 4:8-9; 6:4-5; 11:23-29; 12:10) give a comprehensive overview of the difficulties the apostle faced. Each of these catalogs portrays a wide variety of physical dangers, emotional barriers and spiritual handicaps, ranging from "trouble" (Rom 8:35) to *"hunger" (1 Cor 4:11), *"persecution" (2 Cor 4:8) to "imprisonment" (2 Cor 6:5) and *"shipwrecks" (2 Cor 11:25) to "hardships" (2 Cor 12:10). These catalogs of affliction give images of the range of human affliction in the Bible.

The Bible relates three purposes for affliction. One is discipline. Since God is a Father, he disciplines his children when they rebel (Prov 3; Heb 12). Such discipline may be preventive, as in the case of Paul who was given a "*thorn in the flesh" to prevent him from pride (2 Cor 12). However, the Bible clarifies that this discipline is not punitive. David was assured that though his son would die, David's *adultery was forgiven (2 Sam 12:13-14; cf. 2 Cor 12:9-10). Therefore, disciplinary affliction reveals God's love for his people.

Another purpose for affliction is *sanctification. David's affliction restored him to *obedience (Ps 119:67), taught him God's decrees (Ps 119:71), proved the power of Scripture (Ps 119:50, 92) and demonstrated God's faithfulness (Ps 119:75). The Christian's sufferings follow the pattern of Christ's and thus confirm that one is united with him (Mk 10:39; Rom 8:17; 2 Cor 1:5; Phil 1:29; 3:10; 1 Pet 1:6-7; 4:1-2, 13). Paul indicates that suffering is necessary in the life of the Christian (Col 1:24). Affliction also increases a Christian's capacity to know and enjoy Christ (Phil 4:12-13; Jas 1:2-5).

Some affliction is simply for God's *glory. Job's affliction is the classic illustration. When *Satan accused Job of only serving God because of his creature comforts, God allowed Satan to destroy them (Job 1:6-12). In the end Job got only questions from God, no explanation for why he allowed Satan to afflict him (Job 38–41). It was purely for God's glory.

Affliction is not a one way street, for the Bible also presents a God who suffers. God is in anguish when his people sin (Gen 6:6-7; Jer 9:1-2). He is distressed when his people are *oppressed (Judg 10:16; Is 63:9; Acts 9:4-5). In Christ he saved his people through *suffering, identifying with their brokenness by himself taking on affliction (Is 53:1-4; Heb 4:14-16) and intercepting God's wrath against their sin (Is 53:5-12).

To summarize, the Bible speaks of humans suffering affliction because of their iniquities (Ps 107:17). However, God "does not ignore the cry of the afflicted" (Ps 9:12); "he will defend the afflicted" (Ps 72:4). Ultimately, it is a privilege to suffer affliction (Phil 1:29) because the afflicted can take confidence in God's promise that his "power is made perfect in [our] weakness" (2 Cor 12:9).

See also OPPRESSION; PERSECUTION; SUFFERING.

AFTERLIFE

The afterlife is a central image of the Christian faith. All human beings are destined to partake in the afterlife: *heaven (*paradise) for those who are in Christ, *hell (*punishment, absence from God) for the unregenerate. The final goal and reward for all Christians is eternity in the Lord's presence. Moreover, the NT (especially Paul) envisions the Christian life as one that already participates in the heavenly realities that are to be experienced fully only with the return of Christ and the resurrection of the body.

Old Testament Premonitions. OT images of the afterlife are impoverished compared to those of the NT. The OT picture of an afterlife is only modestly developed. Instead, the focus in the OT is more on God's care for his people in terms of earthly *blessing, particularly *land and offspring, and God's punishment of both unfaithful Israelites and pagan nations by *exile or *death.

Land and offspring are the content of God's promised blessings to his people as far back as Abraham (Gen 12:1-3). This two-fold promise to Abraham is reiterated throughout the patriarchal narratives and is a regular refrain throughout the history of the monarchy, including the prophetic literature: Israel's obedience insures her presence in the land, whereas her disobedience brings outside attack and eventual exile. Some have considered the land/offspring promise to Abraham as an implicit reference to an afterlife blessing for Abraham, since these promises were not fully realized until many generations after his death, but this is really quite removed from the more developed sense of the afterlife we find in the NT. Whatever scant reference to the afterlife there might be in the OT, one must at least conclude that it does not play the primary role that it does in the NT. Furthermore, what little there is of the afterlife in the OT is of a varied and ambiguous nature. There are passages that suggest that death is the end, a few that seem to imply that consciousness continues after death and many others that are simply difficult to pin down precisely.

A common understanding of death in the OT is that it signifies final separation from the land of the living and even from God as well. We see this quite clearly in such passages as Psalms 6:5; 30:9; 31:18; Isaiah 14:11; 38:18-19 and Job 3:13-19. The key word used here is the Hebrew šᵉʾôl which, at least in these passages, refers to the unconscious, decaying (or sleeping, cf. Job 3:13) state of the body in the *grave. The psalmist wishes not to go there, since no one remembers or praises God from the grave (Ps 6:5). For Job, as for Homer, the afterlife is a shadowy oblivion—a place where "the wicked cease from turmoil" and "the weary are at rest" (Job 3:17 NIV), "a land of gloom and deep shadow," of "deepest night, of deep shadow and disorder" (Job 10:21-22 NIV). The best that can be said in this vision of the afterlife is that the troubles of life have ceased: "Captives . . . no longer hear the slave driver's shout. . . . [A]nd the slave is freed from his master" (Job 3:18-19 NIV). Other passages reinforce the relative paleness of OT images of the afterlife, which picture the afterlife as something one would wish to avoid rather than look forward to (Ps 16:10; 86:13; 102:26). There is a sense in which the OT imagery of afterlife is gripping precisely by virtue of its absence. Since there is no afterlife, these texts enjoin the readers to focus on their relationship to God in the here-and-now.

It would be wrong, though, to suppress the images of a positive afterlife that emerge occasionally in the OT. The writer of Ecclesiastes, in describing the moment of human death, differentiates between the dust returning to the ground and the spirit returning to God who gave it (Eccles 12:7). The accounts of how Enoch (Gen 5:24; cf. Heb 11:5) and Elijah (2 Kings 2:1-18) are taken to heaven after their earthly lives seem to suggest some notion of conscious existence in a transcendent world. Some commentators argue on the basis of the imagery of the Psalms for a clearer belief in an afterlife than is sometimes granted. Psalm 1:3 compares the godly person to a *tree whose leaves never wither, an archetypal symbol of immortality. Psalm 49:15 claims that "God will redeem my life from the grave; he will surely take me to himself" (NIV); while in Psalm 73:24 the poet predicts, "Afterward you will take me into glory" (NIV). Psalm 16:10-11 claims that God "will not abandon me to the grave" but will instead "fill me with joy in your presence, with eternal pleasures at your right hand" (NIV); Psalm 139:24 speaks of being led "in the way everlasting" (cf. Prov 12:28, which claims that "in the way of righteousness there is life; along that path is immortality"). The closest OT approximation to the NT confidence and ecstasy about the afterlife is Job's eschatological confidence that his *Redeemer lives and that, after his skin has been destroyed, in his flesh he will yet see God (Job 19:24-27).

Several other OT passages hint at consciousness in the afterlife. In 1 Samuel 28:1-24 the witch of Endor calls up Samuel's spirit at Saul's request. (The condemnation of "a medium or spiritist who calls up the dead" in Deut 18:11 also seems to assume, but by no means clearly, the existence of an afterlife of some sort.) Saul requests Samuel to be called up so that he can ask him how he might defeat the Philistines, since God has turned his back on him (1 Sam 28:15). Samuel's reply is one of judgment: Saul and his army will be defeated because he previously disobeyed God (cf. 1 Sam 13:1-15; 15:1-35). Here we see the imagery of the afterlife closely associated with judgment. A similar notion is found in Daniel 12:1-4, perhaps the clearest statement of the afterlife in the OT, especially verse 2: "Multitudes who sleep in the dust of the earth will awake: some to everlasting life, others to shame and everlasting contempt" (NIV). This imagery ties in somewhat with the passages cited above that speak of death as the end: death represents in some sense separation from God, either by non-existence or "shame and everlasting contempt," the latter clearly implying an after*life*.

Daniel 12:1-4 does not simply speak of judgment, however. Some of the dead will "awake" to "everlasting life." The context of these verses is God's end-time deliverance of his people, whether dead or alive. It is difficult to be precise about what it means for the dead to "awake" (i.e., a spiritual or physical existence), but it does seem clear that this afterlife deliverance is a "resurrection" of some sort. This imagery is equally prominent in Isaiah 26:19: "But your dead will live; their bodies will rise. You who dwell in the dust, wake up and shout for joy. Your dew is like the dew of the morning; the earth will give birth to her dead" (NIV). This may, however, refer to Israel's restoration as a nation rather than to a personal bodily resurrection. The passage parallels Ezekiel 37:12: "O my people, I am going to open your graves and bring you up from them; I will bring you back from the land of Israel" (NIV). The language of death and resurrection is employed to speak of Israel's return to the land after exile. Hence, afterlife describes the actual state of deliverance, in this case possession of the land. In Ezekiel and Isaiah we therefore have the juxtaposition of the here-and-now reward of land, so prominent throughout much of the OT, and the hereafter reward of the afterlife.

New Testament Certainties. The imagery of afterlife as deliverance is developed more fully in the NT, so much so that it forms one of the central foci of NT soteriology. Imagery of the afterlife in the NT is both a future certainty and, for the believer, a present reality.

The future certainty of the afterlife for believer and unbeliever alike is a central NT fixture. This afterlife is presented in two stages. The first stage concerns the state of the individual after death, what is sometimes referred to as the "intermediate" state. The NT does not seem to present us with any sort of a complete image of the unbeliever during this stage, but it does point us in certain directions with respect to the believer's state upon death. Luke 16:17-31, for example, presents the enigmatic picture of Lazarus after death at Abraham's side (Lk 16:22), while the rich man is tormented in hell (Lk 16:23). Although the NT does not fill in the gaps for us, "Abraham's side" is presented in rabbinic literature as the temporary abode of the righteous preceding their final vindication. It also seems from this parable that the unbeliever's intermediate state is in hell, but the details simply are not given to round out the picture fully (*see* Abraham's Bosom).

Paul gives a clearer picture of the state of the believer after death (Phil 1:21-24). Apparently, once Paul "departs" he is "with Christ" (v. 23). The context of this passage, however, is not really to expound on the precise nature of the afterlife but on Paul's firm conviction that he will remain in this life for the sake of the Philippian church. Hence it is difficult to make many firm pronouncements on the nature of the afterlife on the basis of this text. On the other hand it does seem clear that, at least for the believer, the intermediate state is one of blessing in Christ's presence.

Whatever ambiguity there might be surrounding the intermediate state is more than made up for when the topic turns to the final state of believer and unbeliever after Christ's return. The *Second Coming of Christ is a regular refrain in the NT (e.g., Mt 24:1-35 and parallel passages; Jn 14:1-4; 2 Thess 2:1; 2 Tim 4:8; Tit 2:13), and with his coming is ushered in the full flowering of his kingdom, or in the language of Revelation 21:21 "a new heaven and a new earth."

Nowhere does the Bible encourage the common picture of the afterlife as one of robed creatures, listlessly playing harps while seated on clouds. Rather, the afterlife is pictured as the final and complete return of God's people to the land, which was such a prominent mark of blessing in the OT. It is, according to Revelation 22:1-6, a return of sorts to the Garden of Eden, the original land of blessing. We see here the redemptive story of the Bible come full circle: deliverance in Christ is for the ultimate purpose of returning to God's people the original Edenic blessedness. The promise of land in the OT was merely prelude to the heightened realization of the fulfillment of this promise of the afterlife in Revelation 21 and 22.

The actual pictures of the afterlife for believers stress six motifs. One is that the future blessed state of the redeemed is a state of *triumph, usually pictured by the image of the *crown (1 Cor 9:25; 2 Tim 2:5; 4:8; Jas 1:12; 1 Pet 5:4; Rev 3:11; 6:2) but also drawing on the imagery of reigning (Rev 2:26-27; 3:21) and judging (1 Cor 6:2-3). A second image is of the afterlife as a reward for endurance in the faith in the present life—a state that Jesus calls "the joy of your master" (Mt 25:21, 23 RSV) and that is elsewhere called simply a *"reward" (1 Cor 3:14; Rev 22:12) or "prize" (Col 2:18). Third, the *glory that believers receive in the afterlife is permanent or unfading (1 Cor 9:25; 15:42-57; 1 Pet 1:4; 5:4). Fourth, the glory of the afterlife already exists in heaven—it is a mansion that Jesus has gone to prepare (Jn 14:1-3) and a state that is "reserved" for believers (1 Pet 1:4 KJV). Fifth, a person is transformed into a higher state of being while retaining his or her personal and even bodily identity (1 Cor 15; Rev 2:17, which states that each saint in heaven is given "a new *name" known only to that person and Christ). Finally, the future life of the saints in heaven is a condition of ongoing activity in a definite place, with emphasis on the experience of worship of God (Rev 4; 19:1-9).

There is still one more sense in which the NT authors, particularly Paul, present a picture of the afterlife not simply as a future hope but as a present reality for those who are in Christ. Since Christ's first coming the realities of the *kingdom of God have begun to be realized in a heightened manner not known to the OT saints (1 Pet 1:10-12; Heb 1:1-4). The coming of the kingdom, not merely in the future sense but as a present reality, is central to the gospel. To put the matter more concretely, the present reality of the kingdom is nothing less than the realities of the future kingdom breaking into the present world order. The manner in which the future afterlife is present in the lives of believers is made explicit in several Pauline passages. For example, the reality of our *resurrection to a new life is so certain that Paul speaks of that resurrection in the past tense (Col 3:1-4). Paul's point seems to be that when one becomes united with Christ (Rom 6:5) that union has immediate implications. Since Christ has been raised from the dead, so also have those who are united to him. It is not that the believer's resurrection is solely a past event, but believers, by virtue of their union with Christ, participate now in that future reality. Likewise, Paul can assert in Ephesians 2:6 that believers are so united to Christ that "God has raised us up with Christ and seated us with him in the heavenly realms" (NIV). The believer's union with Christ is so intimate that he or she is, in some mysterious sense, already raised from the dead and sitting with Christ in heaven.

In keeping with the more detailed pictures of the afterlife in the NT, a definite understanding of *hell as the afterlife of unbelievers also emerges. Mainly hell gives us reversed versions of the motifs already noted for the blessed in the afterlife. If heaven is a place "reserved" for believers (1 Pet 1:4 KJV), blackest *darkness is reserved for the reprobate (1 Pet 2:17; Jude 13). If bliss awaits the faithful, punishment awaits the faithless (Mt 10:28; Rom 2:8-9; 22:13; Rev 14:10). *Light dominates heaven, but *fire (Mt 5:22; 13:42; 18:9; Rev 20:14-15) and darkness (Mt 8:12; 2 Pet 2:17; Jude 13) prevail in hell. While the blessedness of heaven is unending, in hell it is *torment that continues without respite (Mt 3:12; 25:41; 2 Thess 1:9; Jude 7; Rev 14:11).

Summary. Like many other motifs in the Bible, images of the afterlife show a distinct progression from the OT to the NT. In regard to the afterlife that awaits the redeemed of the Lord, this progression is a glorious illumination, as the OT preoccupation of the finality of the grave (with only occasional flashes of an immortal hope) gives way to rapturous pictures of a heavenly destination that itself becomes the goal of human exertion in this life. Added to this is the way the NT views the afterlife as not only a future certainty but also a present reality. It is the vital, concrete presence of the afterlife in this life that shapes the very heart of Christian life and conduct for those who labor to enter the life to come.

The inverse of this is that the progression of the shadowy gloom of the grave in the OT develops into an even darker NT picture of hell as the place of punishment for unbelievers. On balance, then, biblical images of the afterlife partake of both hope and warning, and in both cases the pictures carry the force of a promise of what is to come.

See also ABRAHAM'S BOSOM; APOCALYPTIC VISIONS OF THE FUTURE; BLESSING; END TIMES; HEAVEN; HELL; JUDGMENT; PARADISE; RESURRECTION.

AGE. *See* WORLD.

AGRICULTURE. *See* FARMING.

ALIEN. *See* FOREIGNER; LEGAL IMAGES; PILGRIM, PILGRIMAGE; WANDERED, WANDERING.

ALPHA AND OMEGA. *See* JESUS, IMAGES OF.

ALTAR

Nothing is more prominent as a biblical image for worship and religious allegiance than the altar. It is no exaggeration to say that the most visible sign of one's devotion to the true God in the worship of the old covenant is the building of altars or traveling to them for acts of sacrifice or offering.

Altars in the Old Testament. An altar in the Bible is always "built" or "made," whether of earthen *brick, undressed *rock, or *wood perhaps overlaid with precious metal. It is a raised platform (three cubits, or about five feet high, in the *tabernacle design of Ex 27:1; ten cubits, or about seventeen feet high in Solomon's *temple, 2 Chron 4:1) on which *fire is kindled. The very form suggests a *table or brazier (Is 29:2). The top four corners of many Israelite and Canaanite altars rose to points called *"horns." They were set beneath the open sky, whether in a field, a high place or a temple court, where their smoke could ascend unhindered to heaven. Their deliberate construction is indicated by verbs associated with them: they are "established," "set up," "placed" and "arranged"; and in their repair they are "healed," "renewed" and "purified." In fact, from Sinai on, their design is specific (Ex 27:1-8). Thus Ahaz goes afoul of divine holy order in commanding that an altar be built according to his sketch of one he saw in Damascus (2 Kings 16:10), and Solomon's brazen altar has outgrown the Sinai specifications.

The story of altars in Israel's *worship inclines toward one altar in one place of worship: the central sanctuary of the Jerusalem temple (2 Sam 24:18-25; 1 Chron 18:21-30). An altar built at Bethel (1 Kings 12:33) or another holy place is, in the run of the biblical narrative, bound for destruction (1 Kings 13:1-3; 2 Kings 23:15). Thus it is no surprise to find in the biblical text that the plural *altars* is nearly synonymous with pagan influence and is frequently accompanied by verbs of destruction. Although an altar may be built by *Abraham or Joshua or *David or *Solomon, it is always the "altar of the LORD," dedicated to his worship alone. We get the sense of the altar as a focal point of life lived in covenant allegiance. Although Abraham erects a series of altars where he "called on the name of the LORD" and marked out the *land of promise,

the establishment of a central sanctuary defines a center in Israel's map of holy space. Other sanctuaries and their altars, sacred places and ancient traditions competing for the title of "center" are implicitly or explicitly destined for destruction and ultimately cannot stand.

Biblical altars convey a number of meanings, but the central one is always the place of slaughter, the place of *blood *sacrifice. The Hebrew word for altar *(mizbēaḥ)* comes from the word for slaughter *(zāḇaḥ)*. Yet, there are biblical altars on which other sorts of offerings are made. Besides the central altar of sacrifice in the courtyard, the temple also contained two altars in the sanctuary: a gold altar for the offerings of *incense, which represented the prayers of the people ascending to the Lord, and a table for the perpetual offering of the "bread of the presence." But those altars and the sacrifices presented on them were secondary in significance and location.

The chief officiants at the altar are the *priests, who are assisted by the Levites. As holy representatives of Israel, they maintain the altar and its appliances, protecting its purity and the holy order of sacrifices. What is offered on this altar moves from Israelite family to male head to priest and to God. It is a place of holy interchange.

Israelite males present themselves, their offerings and their sacrifices by "going up" or "before" the altar, but the psalmist can speak of a joyous thanksgiving that takes them "around" the altar (Ps 26:6). "Going up" is particularly evocative of the ideal attitude for approaching an altar. In the spatial orientation of Scripture we can no more imagine "going down" to sacrifice (as if to a chthonic deity) than "going down" to Jerusalem. Biblical altars clearly lift our eyes upward. They follow the model of temples in the ancient Near East, which were constructed on high places, whether Mount *Zion of Yahweh or the mythical Mount Zaphon of Baal. Whether constructed at five-foot height or on a raised platform, the altar thrusts the acts of worship upward toward the threshold of *heaven. So in Ezekiel's visionary temple (Ezek 43:17) the altar reaches by gradations to the height of eleven cubits, or about nineteen feet. It is mounted by steps facing east, and the offerer moves from east to west, as if to reenter the gates of Eden (*see* Adam; Garden).

The central purpose of the altar is the blood sacrifice. In the OT the required sacrifice consisted of the blood of *animals, which was either sprinkled against the altar or smeared on its horns, and the daily offering of *lambs and *doves at the altar continued into NT times.

The first altar mentioned in the OT is the one Noah builds after the waters of the *flood have receded (although the first offering to God is made by *Cain and *Abel, Gen 4:3-4). On it Noah offers a burnt offering, and the Lord, pleased with the sacrifice, makes his *covenant with Noah, giving him and his descendants the right to eat the flesh of animals (Gen 8:20). From that point on, the eating of meat and the forming of covenants are nearly always associated with altars. The covenant between the Lord and the children of Israel is ratified when Moses sprinkles blood against the altar and the people (Gen 24:4-6), and the continuing covenant between the Lord and Israel is marked by the ongoing sacrifices at his altar.

Before the centralization of worship at the Jerusalem temple, there were many local altars. These were made either of earth or of unhewn stone in deliberate contrast to the golden *idols of other nations (Ex 20:24-25). It is likely that every slaughtered animal was presented at some kind of altar. Later, when sacrifice was restricted to the single altar in the Jerusalem temple, that altar for burnt offering became the focus of Israelite worship. The bronze-covered acacia altar described in Exodus and the larger altars erected later were the scenes of the great moments in Israelite worship: the burnt offering every morning and evening, and the sin

An altar found at Megiddo with "horns" at its four corners.

offerings and guilt offerings that removed impurity or made reparation for misdeeds. With the destruction of the temple and the loss of the altar of sacrifice, a great part of Israelite worship was made impossible.

Altars have several meanings beyond their association with blood sacrifice:

Monuments. In Genesis monuments are often made in the presence of God. Abraham and Isaac mark their encounters with the Lord by building altars (Gen 12:8; 26:25). In Joshua the Reubenites erect an altar on which no sacrifice will be offered as a sign of the unity of Israel (22:21-29).

*Places of *refuge.* By clinging to the "horns of the altar," a fugitive might gain asylum unless his crime was willful murder (Ex 21:14). Joab, for example, seeks sanctuary at the altar, although Solomon does not respect it. The horns of the altar were symbols of both power and protection.

Table for a deity. The altar as a *table for a deity is clearly evoked in only a few contexts, but these might simply reveal a significance that was broadly

assumed. Ezekiel 41:22 speaks of the altar as "the table that is before the LORD," and the association is repeated in Malachi 1:7: "You place defiled food on my altar. But you ask, 'How have we defiled you?' By saying that the LORD's table is contemptible." In this vein we can understand the effect of Noah's sacrifice to the Lord on his newly built altar: the *smell of burnt offerings was pleasing to the Lord (Gen 8:21).

New Testament Usage. In the NT the altar remains the place of sacrifice, but the sacrifice presented at the altar changes radically. "A pair of turtledoves or two young pigeons" are offered when Jesus is presented as an infant at the temple (Lk 2:24), but after that point the NT sees the altar as the scene of a very different sort of sacrifice.

Jesus invokes the altar and the Holy of Holies in the sanctuary as the two principal features of the holy place—a place that has been profaned. His focus is not on the animals offered according to the law but on the blood of those *martyrs whose sacrifices prefigure his own, "from the blood of Abel to the blood of Zechariah, who perished between the altar and the sanctuary" (Lk 11:51; Mt 23:35). In Revelation the slaughter offered before the altar is again that of the suffering witnesses, not of the sacrificial beast. The souls of the martyrs "who had been slaughtered for the word of God" speak from under the altar (6:9). There seems, however, to be no altar in the New *Jerusalem, just as there is no temple, for the *Lamb is enthroned, and there is no need for a place of sacrifice.

In Hebrews, Jesus himself is identified with the altar, and his single sacrifice is contrasted with the repeated offerings at earlier altars: "We have an altar from which those who officiate in the tabernacle have no right to eat" (13:10). This passage is the culmination of the NT tendency to merge all the images of sacrifice into one in Jesus, who is the great high priest, the lamb of sacrifice, and here the altar as well. As altar, priest and sacrifice, Jesus unites all the images associated with biblical altars. He becomes the memorial of the new covenant, the place of sacrifice, and the place of asylum.

See also SACRIFICE; TABLE; WORSHIP.

AMBASSADOR. *See* AUTHORITY, HUMAN.

AMOS, BOOK OF

The dominant theme threading through the variegated fabric of Amos is that of impending judgment, balanced by a vision of *restoration at the end. The reader is immediately introduced to Amos's several oracles of *judgment with a striking metaphor: the God who served as Israel's shepherd has now become a roaring *lion (Amos 1:2; 3:8). He is pictured as a God of judgment who threatens to do bad things to his disobedient people, while also exhorting them to corrective action. Throughout his *satiric book Amos shows a dramatic flare for parody (echoing familiar formulas while inverting their effect). Accordingly, Amos proves to be a master of informal satire, a strategy that allows this untrained prophet from Tekoa to be the spokesman for social and spiritual protest.

Amos's prophecies are structured into four groups of collected oracles. The announced theme is followed by a series of eight oracles of judgment against the nations of Syro-Palestine (Amos 1:3—2:16). Using the common prophetic pattern of geographical orientation, Amos announces judgment on the nations surrounding Israel (including Judah), tracing a circle on the map before zeroing in on the northern kingdom, the main target of his prophetic ministry. A second group of three collections of oracles denouncing the many sins of Israel (Amos 3:1—6:14) follows, each composed with standard opening (Amos 3:1; 4:1; 5:1) and closing (Amos 3:11; 4:12; 6:7) formulas, and the whole unit terminated with a judgment oracle underscoring the certainty of Israel's invasion. A third group of oracles is cast in the form of five visions of coming judgment (Amos 7:1—9:10), each of which contains standard opening formulas (Amos 7:1, 4, 7; 8:1; 9:1). An interesting literary device within this group of visions is the insertion of a biographical notice (Amos 7:10-17) that serves as a hinge between the first three visions, detailing Israel's hopeless spiritual condition, and the last two visions, which predict Israel's imminent and certain judgment. A final section is a salvation oracle promising a future hope of restoration and everlasting blessings through the establishment of the kingdom in accordance with the promises in the Davidic covenant (Amos 9:11-15). The last two oracles of judgment from the preceding section are stitched to the closing salvation oracle via the repetition of such phrases as "in that day" (Amos 8:3, 9, 13; 9:11) and "the days are coming" (Amos 8:11; 9:13).

Additional examples of structural sophistication can be discerned within the individual collections. The opening series of oracles against the nations follow a common pattern: (1) an opening formula ("thus says the LORD" RSV); (2) a balanced pair of clauses ("for three transgressions . . . and for four"); (3) a set formula for judgment ("I will not revoke the punishment"); (4) a statement of indictment (in each case Amos lists only one of the announced four sins); (5) a list of judgments (beginning with the statement, "So I will send fire upon . . ."). Again the judgment oracle of Amos 5:1-17 is given in chiastic format: announcements of judgment (Amos 5:1-3, 16-17), call to repentance (Amos 5:4-6, 14-15), accusation and announcement of judgment (Amos 5:7-13) and two woe oracles containing the usual elements of invective, criticism and threat (Amos 5:18-26; 6:1-17).

In keeping with his posture as the plain-spoken prophet of informal satire, Amos (like *Micah) uses the language and imagery of common speech. His judgment oracles are permeated with a pastoral tone filled with the sights and sounds of everyday life drawn from the natural and agrarian worlds, as we would expect from someone who was "among the shepherds of Tekoa (Amos 1:1) and who identifies himself as "a herdsman, and a dresser of sycamore trees," whom God took "from following the flock" (Amos 7:14-15). Accordingly we find references to *threshing (Amos 1:3), *lions (Amos 1:2; 3:4-5, 8, 12), a cart loaded with *grain (Amos 2:13), a *bird in the *trap (Amos 3:5-6), the *shepherd and his *pasture (Amos 1:2; 3:12; 7:14-15), threshing (Amos 1:3), a shepherd's rescue of a sheep (Amos 3:12), *rain and *harvest (Amos 4:7; 7:1), *gardens and *vineyards (Amos 4:9; 5:11, 17; 9:13, 14), the sycamore *tree (Amos 7:14), blight and mildew (Amos 4:9), *locusts (Amos 4:9; 7:1), ripe *fruit (Amos 8:1-2), and *horses and plowing (Amos 6:12).

His observations on life are far-ranging. In the social sphere he warns the idle rich concerning their greed and ill-gotten luxuries (Amos 3:10, 12, 15; 5:11; 6:4-6; 8:5), their *drunkenness (Amos 2:8, 12; 4:1) and immorality (Amos 2:7), and above all, their injustice toward the oppressed poor (Amos 2:7, 8; 3:9; 4:1; 5:7, 10-12; 6:12; 8:4-6; see Poverty). Spiritually, Israel is guilty of false religion (Amos 5:5, 21-27; 8:10) and outright *idolatry (Amos 3:14; 4:4-5) by which it has forsaken God, the Creator of all (Amos 4:13; 5:8-9, 26-27; 9:2-6).

In the political arena Amos often tells of *war and its attendant ills: besieged cities with their battered *gates (Amos 1:5), *walls (Amos 1:7, 10, 14) and *fortresses (Amos 1:7, 10, 12; 2:2, 5), swinging *swords (Amos 1:11; 7:17; 9:4), and ravished women (Amos 1:13). He warns the populace of the impending sounding of the *trumpet (Amos 3:6), announcing the coming of the horrors of war to Israel (Amos 2:14-16; 4:2-3, 10; 5:1-2, 5; 7:16-18; 9:1, 4). The time is near when *famine (Amos 4:6) and thirst (Amos 4:8; 8:13) and then the silence of *death (Amos 6:9; 8:3) will overtake them. Those who are fortunate enough to survive will be led away with hooks into captivity (Amos 4:2), and even there they will face the threat of death (Amos 9:4). The sins for which the surrounding nations are indicted in the oracles against the nations (Amos 1:3—2:3) are all atrocities in warfare.

Although Amos is the prophet of informal satire, his messages are presented in a variety of genres and literary devices. In addition to the repeated oracles of judgment and the concluding salvation oracle, one encounters poetic ladder parallelism (Amos 1:3, 6, 9, 11, 13; 2:1, 4, 6), a pure narrative episode (Amos 7:10-17), vision reports (Amos 7:1—9:10), occasional *wisdom sayings (e.g., Amos 5:19; 6:12; 9:2-4, 13) and a *proverb cluster (Amos 3:3-6). Amos's artistry may be seen in his use of colorful literary features such as metaphor (Amos 2:7; 3:8-10; 4:1; 5:2, 18, 20; 8:11) and simile (Amos 2:9, 13; 3:12; 4:2, 11; 5:24; 8:10; 9:9). Also to be noted are synecdoche (Amos 2:14-16; 8:13), irony (Amos 4:4) and anthropomorphism (Amos 9:8).

Amos makes use of a number of themes and motifs in presenting his oracles. God's judgment is portrayed as *wind (Amos 1:14) and *fire (Amos 1:4, 7, 10, 12, 14; 2:4, 5; 4:11; 5:6, 9). Especially to be noted is the *Day of the Lord (Amos 3:14; 5:18; 8:3, 9, 11, 13; 9:11, 13) and the resultant feature of a *mourning populace (Amos 5:16; 8:3, 8, 10). Accordingly Amos often holds the threat of *exile before his hearers (Amos 5:27; 6:7; 7:17; 9:4, 14). In keeping with his basic denunciation of Israel, the prophet proclaims the need of justice so as to correct the prevailing social injustice (Amos 3:10; 4:1; 5:10-11, 13, 15, 24; 6:12; 8:4-6). Israel's *Redeemer, who delivered Israel out of Egypt (Amos 2:10; 3:1-2; 9:7), advises Israel to "seek me and live" (Amos 5:4-6:14).

Noticeable throughout the book of Amos is an underlying theme of *reversal. Israelites are warned that false (Amos 4:4) and purely ritualistic religion (Amos 5:21-22) will only serve to turn the anticipated day of the Lord's deliverance into one of disaster (Amos 5:18-20). The rich who are at ease (Amos 6:1) and who mercilessly oppress the poor (Amos 8:4-6) will find their situation reversed as they are led away with hooks into exile (Amos 4:1-3). In that sad hour songs of mirth (Amos 6:5) and worship (Amos 5:23) will be turned into wailing (Amos 8:3), and *festival will be replaced by mourning (Amos 8:10). Not even the strongest, swiftest or bravest can hope for escape (Amos 2:14-16; cf. 5:19).

Yet there is hope that this too can be reversed. As a shepherd saves but a few items of a dismembered sheep from the ravages of a lion, so there is veiled hope that a mutilated Israel will be rescued by its shepherd (Amos 3:12). For although the present kingdom will be destroyed, a remnant will be saved (Amos 9:8). Israel's humbled people will be restored to their land, the demolished cities will be rebuilt, and the devastated lands will once again flourish (cf. Amos 4:6-11; with 9:11-15).

A final point of unity is the prevailing tone of angry denunciation. Amos is unapologetic and relentless. As we read his book, we are consistently assaulted with evidence of human misconduct, predictions of destruction and commands to reform.

Despite its brevity the book of Amos is a rich repository of memorable images. The images fall into three main categories. One is the imagery of *evil practices* currently occurring: selling the needy for a pair of shoes and trampling the head of the poor into the dust (Amos 2:6-7), making Nazirites drink *wine (Amos 2:12), houses of ivory financed through exploitation (Amos 3:15), empty religious observance (Amos 5:21-22). The second is the imagery of *divine judgment and disaster:* a person's being pressed down as a cart full of sheaves presses down (Amos 2:13), women being led into slavery with fishhooks through their flesh (Amos 4:2), drought that destroys crops (Amos 4:6-9), houses being smitten into fragments (Amos 6:11), feasts turned into mourning (Amos 8:10). Third is an image pattern of *ideal*

godliness and its blessing that reaches its climax in the final oracle of redemption: justice rolling down like waters and righteousness like an everflowing stream (Amos 5:24), the mountains dripping sweet wine (Amos 9:13), people planting gardens and eating their fruit (Amos 9:14).

See also PROPHECY, GENRE OF.

ANCESTORS. *See* GENERATION(S)

ANCESTRESS. *See* ENDANGERED ANCESTRESS.

ANGEL

From the *Garden of Eden to the renewed *heaven and earth, angels are found repeatedly throughout the Bible. These beings are also spoken of as spirits, cherubim, seraphim, sons of God, the heavenly host, or in a few instances, even referred to by their proper names, such as Michael and Gabriel.

In the biblical text, angels are real living beings. They are supernatural and nonphysical, but may assume a corporeal appearance for a period of time. Angels are therefore not symbols of another reality. In one sense, however, an angel is an image—an image of the invisible God. Even their names, ending in "-'*el*" (the Hebrew expression for God), as in Gabri*el,* suggests their close connection to the deity. On many occasions God chose to mediate his presence to his people through angels. When he revealed himself to Moses on Mount Sinai, the Lord said, "no one may see me and live" (Ex 33:20 NIV). Thus, in reality, it was the "angel of the LORD" that appeared to Moses in the form of a *burning bush when God disclosed himself as the "I am," or YHWH (Ex 3:2).

The ultimate revelation of God was not through an angelic mediator figure, but through his "Word" (the *logos*), the *Son of God (Jn 1:1-18). The author of *Hebrews makes an eloquent case for the superiority of Jesus to angels by pointing to his sonship, his position at the *right hand of the Father, his more excellent name and the fact that he is worthy of the *worship and adoration of the angels (Heb 1:1-13). Throughout the history of the church, however, many have interpreted the OT appearances of the "angel of the LORD" as preincarnate manifestations of the second person of the Trinity, the Lord Jesus Christ.

One of the primary activities of the angels is their continual offering of praise and worship to the one seated on the *throne. This may have been the only role of the class of angels known as *seraphim,* the six-winged beings Isaiah saw in his visionary experience. As they flew around the Lord seated on his throne, they proclaimed: "Holy, holy, holy is the LORD Almighty; the whole earth is full of his glory" (Is 6:3). In John's heavenly vision he saw innumerable angels ("thousands upon thousands" and "ten thousand times ten thousand") encircling the throne worshipping not only the Father, but also Jesus, here represented by the figure of the *lamb. He is said to be worthy of this angelic worship because he was slain as a sacrificial lamb (Rev 5:12), which has made it possible for his people to be freed from their sins and to become "a kingdom and priests to serve his God and Father" (Rev 1:6).

Not all angels are benevolent and constantly ascribing *glory and praise to the Father. There are a large number of who have engaged in grievous rebellion against God. They struggle with the good angels and work to bring about the demise of the people of God. Some of these original transgressors are imprisoned in a place called Tartarus and await their divine judgment (2 Pet 2:4; Jude 6). The rest act out their hostile intentions under the leadership of *Satan, whose fall may be figuratively narrated in Ezekiel 28 and Isaiah 14. Ultimately they will not succeed in their evil plots. The angelic war in heaven depicted in Revelation 12:7-12 portrays the dragon as "not strong enough." They are consequently defeated by Michael and his angels. Their final doom is certain when God works to utterly eradicate every form of evil from his new creation (Rev 20:7-10).

The angels of the Lord were frequently involved in announcing and raising up deliverers for the people of God when they were trapped in various forms of bondage. The angel of the Lord thus appears to *Moses, calling on him to free the Israelites from their plight in Egypt (Ex 3). Manifesting himself in human-like form, the angel of the Lord "came and sat down under the oak in Ophrah" where he met Gideon and commissioned him to deliver Israel from Midian (Judg 6:11-17). In the case of *Samson the angel of the Lord appeared to both of his parents, announcing his impending miraculous birth to the *barren woman (see Birth Story). He then instructed the couple on how to raise him under a Nazirite vow and revealed that he would deliver Israel from the hands of the Philistines (Judg 13).

Angels were also deeply involved in proclaiming the birth of God's end-time deliver, the Lord Jesus Christ. An angel of the Lord announced his miraculous birth to Joseph (Mt 1:20); Gabriel explained the wonderful news to *Mary (Lk 1:26-38); and an angel of the Lord, accompanied by a multitude of the heavenly host, proclaimed the event to a group of shepherds near Bethlehem (Lk 2:8-20).

Throughout biblical history, angels provided guidance, help and encouragement to God's people. This is perhaps why they can be referred to as "ministering spirits sent to serve those who will inherit salvation" (Heb 1:14). It was the angel of the Lord who intervened to prevent *Abraham from sacrificing his only son Isaac in obedience to God and provided the patriarch with a suitable substitute for the offering (Gen 22:9-14). Subsequently an angel even guided Abraham's servant to find a wife for Isaac (Gen 24:7, 40). After their deliverance from slavery, and as they began their wilderness wanderings, God assured Israel by saying, "I am sending an angel ahead of you to guard you along the way and to bring you to the place I have prepared" (Ex

23:20). The psalmist exclaims God's benevolent protective power toward his people at all times: "The angel of the LORD encamps around those who fear him, and he delivers them" (Ps 34:7) and "He will command his angels concerning you to guard you in all your ways" (Ps 91:11). Certainly Daniel and his companions were aware of this protection after their experience of angelic protection through the intense heat and flames of a furnace (Dan 3:28) and then later when "God sent his angel, and he shut the mouths of the lions" (Dan 6:22).

Angelic watchfulness and protection even extends to little *children. Jesus said that "their angels in heaven always see the face of my Father in heaven" (Mt 18:10), thus giving rise to the Christian concept of "guardian angels." In the early days of the church, angels twice intervened and miraculously released apostles from *prison (Acts 5:19-20; 12:7-11). They also provided guidance at many crucial junctures, such as for Philip when an angel of the Lord directed him to the Ethiopian official (Acts 8:26) and for the Gentile Cornelius, who was directed by "a holy angel" to visit the apostle Peter (Acts 10:22).

Angels have served, and will continue to serve, as God's agents for dispensing his judgment. This is one of the primary functions of the angels as they are revealed in the Apocalypse (see Revelation, Book of). Seven angels sound the seven trumpet judgments of God (Rev 8–9); seven angels carry the seven last plagues (Rev 15); and four angels bound at the Euphrates are released and kill a third of humanity (Rev 9:14-15). This terrifying and destructive work of angels in meting out God's wrath was also characteristic of certain OT events. In the time of Abraham two angels carried out God's retribution against the cities of *Sodom and Gomorrah (Gen 19:1-29). When the Assyrian king Sennacherib threatened Israel, "an angel of the LORD went out and put to death a hundred and eighty-five thousand men in the Assyrian camp" (2 Kings 19:35; 2 Chron 32:21; Is 37:36).

Angels will accompany Jesus when he returns (Mt 16:27; Mk 8:38; Lk 9:26; 2 Thess 1:7). They will be Christ's special envoys to "gather his elect from the four winds, from one end of the heavens to the other" (Mt 24:31). They will also assist the Son in separating evil ones from the righteous and executing the divine *judgment (Mt 13:37-43).

Primarily, then, angels are supernatural beings closely linked with the work of God himself. They are surrounded by an aura of the numinous. A human encounter with an angel is in some sense an encounter with the divine. Angels are known to us not as individualized characters but as agents. Their primary activities are praise and worship of God in his heavenly court, making announcements and carrying messages on behalf of God to humans, intervening with guidance and protection in the lives of people, and dispensing the judgments of God.

See also ANNUNCIATION; ASSEMBLY, DIVINE; HEAVENLY ARMIES/HOST.

BIBLIOGRAPHY. S. Noll, *Angels of Light, Powers of*

Darkness (Downers Grove, IL: InterVarsity Press, 1998).

ANGER

In the Bible, anger is attributed both to people and to God. Anger or wrath is an emotion, a response growing out of an interpretation of certain stimuli. It may produce a desire to respond, but agents (people or God) determine if, how and when they will respond. The idiom of anger is the imagery of *fire. Both humans and God are said to "burn with anger" (Gen 39:19; Ex 4:14). Anger might flare up like a flame (2 Sam 11:20), be stirred up like a fire (1 Kings 14:22) or smolder (Ps 80:4). Anger's similarity to fire may be observed in its spontaneity, in the difficulty with which it is contained and in its destructive power.

Old Testament. The pages of the Scriptures present numerous examples of both human and divine anger and the responses to it. Human anger is usually depicted as a loss of self-control that results in evil behavior. The sage expresses his assessment of such anger: "Anger resides in the lap of fools" (Eccles 7:9 NIV). Jacob rebuked his sons Simeon and Levi for their murderous anger; he cursed their fierce and cruel anger (Gen 49:6-7). David warns his readers to avoid anger (Ps 37:8; cf. Job 36:13). Several proverbs speak of the wisdom of not provoking others to anger (Prov 15:1; 19:11; 20:2) or how restraining anger keeps one out of worse trouble (Prov 15:18; 16:32).

There are examples of seemingly appropriate ways to express anger. When Jacob's wife Rachel was jealous of her sister and blamed him for her inability to have children, Jacob was angry, but he responded with wise words (Gen 30:1-2). Pharaoh's adamant refusal to allow the Israelites to leave Egypt caused Moses to be very angry, but the text says he simply left Pharaoh's presence taking no immediate action (Ex 11:8). The Psalms present numerous examples of anger directed toward the injustice of cruel people (Ps 59:11; 69:28) as well as toward God himself (Ps 77:6-9; 90:7-12). The key seems to be keeping anger in control—adopting a measured response (e.g., Judg 9:30; 2 Sam 12:5; Neh 5:6).

The overwhelming majority of instances of anger in the OT speak of God's anger both against his chosen people and against pagan nations. God's anger differs, however, from most examples of human anger. Expressions of God's anger exhibit no loss of control. Rather, as an act of God's will, his anger results in deliberate *judgments against sin—actions appropriate to the situation and in keeping with his own character as holy and just. When Moses protested at the prospect of being God's spokesman before Pharaoh, the Lord's anger burned against Moses, but he allowed Aaron to be the replacement speaker (Ex 4:13-15). Yet in other places God's anger does not appear to have such favorable outcomes. When the wandering Israelites complained about their hardships, God's anger was aroused, and his fire consumed some of the outskirts of the camp (Num 11:1). When the people wailed at their limited diet of *manna, in his anger God threatened to force them to eat quail until they detested it (Num 11:10, 18-20). In his anger God instructed Moses to put to death all those who worshipped the Baal of Peor (Num 25:3-4). In anger God prevented the entire generation of unbelieving adults from entering the Promised *Land, forcing them to experience forty more years of wandering in the desert (Num 32:10-13; cf. Heb 3:11; 4:3). Moses warned the Israelites to fear God alone, "for the LORD your God, who is among you, is a jealous God and his anger will burn against you, and he will destroy you from the face of the land" (Deut 6:15).

When a king or the nation rejected God in favor of other deities, his anger burned hot (e.g., Deut 7:4; 9:19; 29:20, 23-24, 27-28; 1 Kings 14:9-11, 15). The book of Judges details Israel's "on again–off again" trust in God. When they abandoned God and provoked him to anger, God allowed their enemies to overwhelm them (e.g., Judg 2:11-15). His anger often resulted in Israel's domination by foreign powers (e.g., 2 Kings 13:3), in *plagues or in other devastation. Perhaps worst of all, he removed his presence from the nation (e.g., Num 12:9; 31:17; Deut 32:16, 21-22; Josh 23:16; 2 Kings 17:18). Eventually God repudiated the entire nation, saying, "I will remove Judah also from my presence as I removed Israel, and I will reject Jerusalem, the city I chose, and this temple, about which I said, 'There shall my Name be'" (2 Kings 23:26-27).

The prophets from Isaiah to Malachi multiply examples of expressions of God's anger against his people. When God's people fail to trust him—they literally serve other gods, disobey his commands or fail to walk in his ways—his consistent response is anger, and that anger often leads in the most serious way to judgment.

Despite this catalog of awful displays of God's anger, the other side of the picture is equally striking. When God's people repent from sin and place their trust in him, God turns aside his anger and brings *mercy, compassion and *blessing (Deut 13:17-18). David expresses confidence that God's anger against his people is only a momentary experience in contrast to a lifetime of God's favor (Ps 30:5). The psalmists believe that God often restrained his anger and did not give full vent to the judgment Israel deserved (Ps 78:38; 103:8-9). He characteristically terminates his wrath and *forgives people's sins (Ps 85:3-5). The prophets concur, convinced that God will turn aside his anger when his people return to him (e.g., Is 12:1; 48:9; Jer 3:12-13; Hos 14:4; Joel 2:13; Jon 4:2; Mic 7:18). Perhaps the prophet Nahum best puts both truths together: "The LORD is a jealous and avenging God; the LORD takes vengeance and is filled with wrath. . . . The LORD is slow to anger and great in power" (Nahum 1:2-3; cf. 1:6-7).

It appears that God's anger is not automatic or predictable, nor is God ever "out of control." The Psalmists expect that God may exercise or withhold his anger in response to prayer. They implore God not to rebuke or discipline in anger (Ps 6:1; 27:9). Yet they also implore God to rise up in anger against his enemies (Ps 7:6). Common in the psalms is the theme of imprecation against God's enemies, sometimes termed "the nations": "In his wrath the LORD will swallow them up" (Ps 21:9; cf. 56:7; 69:24).

New Testament. When Jesus confronted people's *hardness of *heart and failure to acknowledge his message, he sometimes responded in anger (Mk 3:5). The classic instance of Jesus' expression of anger occurred when he confronted the abuses he found within the temple precincts (Mt 21:12-13; Jn 2:14-16). Instead of the temple being a place for true worship and service of God, the Sadducees had turned it into a place of business where money was exchanged and animals were sold. In Jesus' parable of the wedding feast, the king's anger is certainly justified (Mt 22:7; cf. Lk 14:21).

On the other hand, when Jesus attacked the hard-heartedness of many of his hearers, they responded to him with anger (Lk 4:28). Paul experienced similar reactions to his preaching at Ephesus (Acts 19:28). Paul saw anger as a basic element of the sinful nature. So he explained that displays of anger characterize unbelievers and not Christians (Gal 5:20). Yet the NT writers acknowledge the presence of anger in a Christian's life. Paul's counsel is to avoid sin when angry (Eph 4:26). Yet he shortly urges the readers to avoid anger, among other vices (Eph 4:31; Col 3:8). Jesus instructs his followers to avoid anger against a fellow disciple (Mt 5:22). Parents ought not provoke anger in their children (Eph 6:4; Col 3:21). Proper prayers by the men at Ephesus implied their avoidance of anger (1 Tim 2:8). Believers should be slow to anger (Jas 1:19) since it does not accomplish righteousness in a person's life (Jas 1:20). They are not to avenge themselves but leave vengeance to the wrath of God (Rom 12:19; cf. Lev 19:18).

The NT speaks of God's anger in both present and future terms. As in the OT, God's anger is represented as his actions or responses to human sinfulness. Several texts explain God's anger in the present. John affirmed that God's wrath now rests on those who fail to believe in Jesus (Jn 3:36). Paul asserted that God presently reveals his anger against those who suppress the truth of the gospel (Rom 1:18; 1 Thess 2:16). He taught that governmental authorities serve as agents of God's anger to punish criminals (Rom 13:4). God's anger comes on the disobedient, though it is not easy to say whether the author intended this to refer to present or future expressions of God's anger (Eph 5:6).

As to future anger, John the Baptist affirmed that there was "the wrath to come" (Mt 3:7; Lk 3:7). Jesus predicted a time of God's judgment on Israel (Lk 21:23). Paul spoke of a coming day of God's anger when his righteous judgment will be revealed against unrepentant sinners (Rom 2:5, 8; cf. 9:22; Col 3:6; 1 Thess 1:10). Left to their own attempts to keep God's law, people will face God's anger (Rom

4:15). Only through justification on the basis of Jesus' atonement can people find *salvation and escape from God's coming wrath (Rom 5:9; 1 Thess 5:9). Thus Christians were formerly "children of wrath"—that is, their only prospect was to encounter God's angry judgment against their sin—but this is no longer their state (Eph 2:3). The Apocalypse speaks several times of God's anger. Those who experience the great day of the wrath of the Lamb would rather be dead, so awesome is its destructive force (Rev 6:16-17). The plagues of the Apocalypse display God's anger against his enemies (Rev 14:10, 19; 15:1, 7; 16:1, 19; 19:15). Wrath describes the day of judgment when the wicked are destroyed and the saints rewarded (Rev 11:8).

See also DAY OF THE LORD; HELL; JUDGMENT.

ANIMALS

The Hebrew and Aramaic of the OT uses about 180 words, the Greek NT about 50 words, to name a total of about 70 types (not species) of animals. The many distinctions as to class, gender and age of domesticated animals account for the seeming discrepancy: eleven Hebrew and Aramaic words for sheep; eight Hebrew words for goat; eight Hebrew words for cow or ox, along with seven Greek words; eight Hebrew words translated "lion"; ten kinds of locust or grasshopper in Hebrew; ten Hebrew and four Greek varieties of snake; five words for horse and so forth. All this duplication contrasts with the many animal names whose exact meaning is still uncertain (*see* Birds).

The Hebrews' need to identify animals stemmed not from a desire for thorough scientific understanding but from a pragmatic need to answer basic questions about them: Can they be eaten? Do they pose a danger to people? Do they harm crops? Animals that were undomesticated but nevertheless tolerant of human presence were more likely to be noted and named consistently. If an animal had a low tolerance for human presence or was nocturnal, it stood a good chance of carrying a large mythical burden. While these cultural differences produced an outlook on animals understandably quite distinct from ours, the incongruities are exaggerated by the view that animals are players, both agents and pawns, in the cosmic struggle delineated in the Bible. This view lends additional significance to the imagery of various animals. In addition, the biblical imagination participates in a universal tendency to equate certain animals with specific traits, as when horses and mules are equated with ignorance (Ps 32:9) or doves with being easily deceived and senseless (Hos 7:11).

Animals as Unclean. A large portion of the animals mentioned in Scripture occurs in lists of unclean animals (Lev 11; Deut 14) that make little use of imagery themselves and contribute little information helpful to the identification of the animals listed. While some have sought health reasons for prohibitions about food (e.g., diseases transmitted through pork), the majority if not all the taboos about which animals may be eaten probably arise from several causes. The Israelites' long past as agricultural nomads would naturally give rise to customs expressing their dependence on domesticated stock. Mythological associations of certain animals or superstitions about them make eating them unthinkable (*see* Mythical Animals).

A disdain for protein in some forms may arise from common sense (e.g., vultures eat carrion, so don't eat vultures) or from a rudimentary natural philosophy (e.g., juicy caterpillars do not breathe and so do not share the breath of God; therefore they belong to the same category as worms and are allied with the evil forces of decay. Do not eat them.) There is some evidence that the Israelites had correlated disease agents, unclean animals such as flies and rodents (1 Sam 6), with the plagues they carried. They could not, however, articulate the cause or mechanism. The Israelite outlook was similar to that of their neighbors, who sought healing through the symbolic methods of sympathetic magic, offering golden figures of the affected body part and the unclean visitant in an attempt to propitiate the responsible deity, be it their own or a foreign one (*see* Magic; Disease and Healing).

Animals as Signs of Desolation. As is true in some cultures today, the appearance of certain animals is regarded as an omen. Frequently these animals are ones whose nighttime calls seem to be messages from the spirit world (owls, hyenas, frogs) or who themselves seem to be acting as messengers (crows, ravens, bats) or animals that by habit already possess negative associations with death (snakes, vultures). Such passages as Isaiah 34:11-15 and Habakkuk 2:14, in describing the desolation of once inhabited cities, sometimes include among "real" animals reference to mythological creatures that frolic and cry in the ruins (satyrs, night hags or liliths [Is 34:14]). Our post-Enlightenment cultural outlook requires us to distinguish between real and mythical animals; however the ancient poets were under no such constraint. To them some animals held evil or even demonic associations. Some demons appeared as animals, as when frogs represent unclean spirits (Rev 16:13). The variation in translation of some animal names reflects the difficulty of identifying these creatures—consider the various translations of *lilith* as "night hag" or "screech owl" in Isaiah 34:14—but generally their symbolic import is clear enough from the context, and parallelism provides additional hints as well.

Animals as Servants. The Genesis account lays out the moral implications of humanity's relationship to animals by establishing parallels to humanity's relationship to God. God delegates the dominion of animals to people (Gen 1:28) just as God is their *dominus* (Lord). The man works for God tending garden, and the beasts work for man. Although all kinds of animals can be "tamed" (Jas 3:7), domestication is practical only with animals that are willing to live in high densities (herds or packs), provide

some harvestable resource and can be easily maintained (herbivores, since carnivores are hard to feed). Also, it would be pointless to domesticate unclean animals. By these criteria most beasts worth domesticating had been domesticated by biblical times. As reliable, ungrudging workers, livestock provided metaphors for loyalty and trainability, but also occasions for moral generalizations. The idea of pets probably arose through the interaction of children with young animals, but it is almost absent from ancient literature. The parable of the one ewe lamb of the poor man hints that (as on some farms today) not all animals were treated as mere produce (2 Sam 12:3, cf. Tobit's dog, Tobit 5:16; 11:4).

Cattle. *Cattle are mentioned primarily as an indicator of wealth (Gen 13:2; Ezek 38:12; 1 Chron 5:9). In dreams or in poetry, well-fed cows serve as metaphors of wealthy people or nations (Amos 4:1; Jer 46:20); starving cows, of lean years (Gen 41:26). Cattle produced many of the good things in life: *butter or cheese (Deut 32:14; Prov 30:33; 1 Sam 17:17; 2 Sam 17:29), *dung for fuel (Ezek 4:12) or fertilizer (Lk 13:8). Some cattle were raised specifically to be eaten, "calves of the stall" (1 Kings 4:23; Mal 4:2), and were a luxury that marked special occasions (Lk 15:30). They also contributed as beasts of burden, either laden (Gen 45:17, 1 Chron 12:40) or pulling (1 Sam 6, 2 Sam 6).

As an important link in the economy, animals deserved to be well treated. A number of ethical laws regarding their treatment seem to arise as extensions of the Golden Rule. The *ox and *donkey are personified: they know their owner (Is 1:3). The rights of animals are discussed along with those of other property (slaves and wives) in Exodus 21 and 22. Like people, animals deserve rest (Ex 23:12; Deut 5:14) and water (Lk 13:15). It is too cruel to make an ox work with grain while withholding it (Deut 25:4), and similar courtesy applies to people (1 Cor 9:9; 1 Tim 5:18). You must help an ox in trouble (Deut 22:4), even if it is your enemy's (Ex 23:4). Likewise, Jesus heals a woman on the Sabbath because any decent person would help an animal on that day (Lk 14:5).

Sheep. As with cattle, the long history of Israelite nomadic dependence on *sheep surfaces in the imagery associated with them. The *horn of the sheep finds ritual use as a ceremonial instrument (Josh 6:4) or *oil container (1 Sam 16:1). Whole economies were based on *wool (2 Kings 3:4). Both the wool and the animals themselves (Ezek 27:18) stood for wealth and could serve as tribute (2 Chron 17:11). The purity of wool (probably its cleanness close to the skin when parted or sheared) served as a symbol of sinlessness (Is 1:18). Prohibitions against weaving wool with *linen also stemmed from extensions about the purity of wool (or perhaps a reluctance to become dependent on sedentary farming methods and produce, i.e., flax production [Lev 19:19]). The care of sheep also taught responsibility (Lk 15:4) and accountability (Gen 31:39).

27

Most of all, however, sheep served as simple models of people. People are sociable, lost without a herd to belong to. A "vagabond" cannot survive (Gen 4:12). People are creatures of habit, easily led astray (Is 53:6), defenseless against marauding *wolves (Zeph 3:3; Jn 10:12) or lions (Jer 50:17) and desperately in need of a shepherd (Zech 10:2). If we follow in God's paths, we become his sheep (Ps 23; 95:7; 100:3). Jesus is our Good Shepherd (Jn 10:11-14) or Great Shepherd (Heb 13:20). The shepherd knows his sheep by name, and they know his voice (Jn 10:3-4). He calls them "my sheep" (Ezek 34; Jn 21:16-17).

The obvious similarities between humans and sheep, as well as the parallel hierarchy of God to mortal and mortal to sheep, commended the mystical substitution of a *lamb as redemptive offering for the firstborn male (Ex 13:2, 13) for the yearly atonement (Ex 12) and the eternally efficacious *Passover (Rev 5:6) that rescues us from ourselves (Jn 1:29, 36). Christ is a lamb because he is "obedient unto death" (Phil 2:8), "silent before his shearers" (Is 53:7), innocent (Heb 4:15) and acceptable as "without blemish" (Num 28:3).

Goat. In contrast to sheep, *goats are savvy, self-reliant, an image of the worldly-wise. Goats are those who don't need God. He will have no need for them, but will separate them from his sheep (Mt 25:32). The head-butting typical of goats serves as prophetic metaphor for political clashes (Dan 8:6). The wilder associations of goats, especially with unspecified evils of the wilderness, fed the image of goat-like spirits or satyrs (Is 13:21, 34:14; Lev 17:7, 2 Chron 11:15). The "scapegoat" was sent away to Azazel, perhaps a demon of the wilderness (Lev 16:9).

Camel. The legendary abilities of the camel to survive in the desert made possible transdesert commerce and nomadism. Genesis 24 records their necessary care. Other passages allude to their large numbers as a sign of wealth or might (Judg 6:5, 8:26; 1 Chron 5:21; 1 Kings 10:2). David kept camels (1 Chron 27:30).

Ass or Donkey. The *donkey was a low-maintenance, multipurpose agricultural asset. Its strong ties to agriculture can be seen in the phrase "ox and ass" used as a term for domestic animals in general (Lk 13:15). The donkey demanded lower quality and less forage than the horse, which only the wealthy could afford. Donkeys, consequently, far outnumbered horses or camels (Ezra 2:66; Neh 7:68). The counterpart to modern tractors, donkeys were required for serious farming. Those who drove away "the ass of the fatherless" were cruelly sending them into sure bankruptcy (Job 24:3). In addition to being laden, donkeys were often ridden, either saddled (2 Sam 16:1) or with a garment as cushion (Ezek 27:20; cf. Mt 21:7). A donkey could be stubborn (Num 22:29), but even so it "knows its master's crib," which is more than Isaiah could say for Israel (Is 1:3). A donkey was the traditional mount of nobility (Judg 12:14) and later of kings (Zech 9:9).

Mule. The mule (usually the offspring from a donkey stallion and horse mare) is a practical and literal compromise between the efficiency of the donkey and the strength of the horse. Mules functioned as mounts for David's sons (2 Sam 13:29). Absalom was killed when he failed to stay on his mule (2 Sam 18:9). As a sign of Solomon's impending ascension, David mounted him on his own mule (1 Kings 1:33).

Jesus orchestrates his triumphal entry around a mule, still regarded as a mark of kingship in Palestine. (A war horse would not have symbolized the arrival of the Prince of Peace.) Matthew explicitly mentions both the mare and the colt as fulfillment of prophecy (Mt 21:2; Zech 9:9). The mule was illegal to breed because it was a hybrid (Lev 19:19) and also infertile. Mules therefore had to be replenished by importing (cf. Ezek 27:14). Mules faithfully performed the agricultural side of their dual role. As a beast of burden a mule load became a unit of measure (2 Kings 5:17), and a millstone was literally a "donkey mill" (Mt 18:6; Mk 9:42). The mule's reputation for stubbornness invited the inevitable comparison to human behavior (Ps 32:9).

Horse. Unlike the donkey and the mule, the *horse was impractical for peaceful uses. For 3,500 years people constantly adapted the horse and improved their use of it to serve as the ultimate military weapon (until the tank). Historically, peoples who mastered the horse (Trojans, Mitannians, Hurrians, Mongols, etc.) rose to dominate their neighbors. The neighing of horses and the tramping of hooves sounded the prelude to war (Jer 8:16; 47:3). The prohibition against amassing horses is directed against self-sufficient political power (Deut 17:16; cf. 1 Sam 8:11).

Mounted cavalry and *chariots gave overwhelming superiority in battle, especially on the plains (1 Kings 20:23). But it was central to Israelite history that this advantage did not apply to hill country, and even on the plains it could be neutralized or rendered a disadvantage by unexpected events such as rain and mud (Ex 14:25; Judg 5:4; Josh 11:5). When it rained, Elijah outran Ahab's chariot (1 Kings 18:45-46). David kept enough horses and chariots to be safe (2 Sam 8:4); however his sons later relied on them in their political coups (Absalom, 2 Sam 15:1; Adonijah, 1 Kings 1:15). Solomon's power rested on unprecedented numbers of horses (four thousand in 2 Chron 9:25 or forty thousand in 1 Kings 4:26; 10:26-29). Such confidence in animal might was as impious as relying on foreign political alliances (Ps 33:17; Hos 1:7; Is 31:1).

The difficulty of controlling such a large, powerful animal when driven by its hormones made the horse a potent symbol of raw desire, meanings still attached to English words like *stud* or *stallion*. The prophet invoked such similes to characterize the people's wanton idolatry (Jer 5:8; 50:11). The prophet resorts to barnyard images, probably being intentionally crude to emphasize God's disdain when he compares the people's lust for foreign countries to a harlot desiring a stud with a donkey-sized penis or with emissions as copious as a horse's (Ezek 23:20). That an animal as large as a horse could be controlled at all was astonishing (Jas 3:3). Since the horse epitomized power, both military and reproductive, it is not surprising that some occupants of Palestine buried their horses with honor or that images of horses were worshiped even in Jerusalem (2 Kings 23:11).

Pig. The pig, domestic (Lk 15; Mt 8:30) or wild, was forbidden to Jews. This made it not only useless, but a nuisance as a threat to agriculture. "The boar from the forest" ravages the neglected *vineyard (Ps 80:13). The taboo against pork was shared by the ancient Egyptians and probably derived from the pig's omnivorous habits that occasionally led it to feed on carrion. Dogs (see below) and pigs have much in common. Their behavior exposes their true natures. They are paired as wild, street animals, tolerated, but belonging to no one (Is 66:3; Mt 7:6). The dog will eat its *vomit and the pig must have its wallow (2 Pet 2:22). Like a harlot, the pig cannot be cleaned up; it returns to its old ways (Prov 11:22). The ring in a pig's snout is not for decoration (cf. Is 3:21). It has no values and but acts unreasonably (Mt 7:6). Swine (and dogs) are symbols of filth and paganism (Is 65:4; 66:3, 17). The prodigal was no doubt horrified to be reduced to feeding pigs, but it was worse to covet their food, the very source of their uncleanness (Lk 15:15-16).

Dog. The Bible invokes the image of the *dog often, but rarely in a positive light. The Israelites were familiar with dogs, not as a cherished pets, but as members of packs that fed at the town dump and roamed the streets at night howling (Ps 59:6). Because of their scavenging function, dogs became synonymous with garbage. "Do not give what is holy to the dogs" (Mt 7:6) means do not throw it out. Cattle killed by wild animals shall be "thrown out for the dogs" (Ex 22:31). The practice of dishonoring foes by denying burial made dogs, among other animals (1 Sam 17:44; Jer 8:2; 16:4), the de facto undertakers who "licked the blood" of many (Naboth, 1 Kings 21:19; Ahab, 1 Kings 21:24; 22:38; Jeroboam, 1 Kings 14:11; Baasha, 1 Kings 16:4). To fulfill the prophecy, Jezebel's body does become dung on the face of the field, but only after the dogs have digested it (2 Kings 9:10, 36). The dogs may lick Lazarus' wounds as a foreshadowing of his death and interment in them (Lk 16:21). The dog's regurgitation reflex, useful for transporting food to their pups in their former wild state, served to cement their label as unclean (Prov 26:11). The logical connection between a dog's diet of refuse and its unclean habits further supported the belief that what enters in through the mouth does defile one.

The struggle for survival at the town dump and a semi-wild existence did not produce friendly dogs. Dogs seemed to know nothing of obedience and were dangerous to pet (Prov 26:17). The fear of

being eaten by such dogs is real (Ps 22:16-17). In return for a begrudging toleration they provided watchmen services, and they were even believed to sense spiritual dangers. The absence of a dog bark during Israel's exodus indicates that God miraculously silenced either the departure of the Israelites or the dogs so that they did not alert the Egyptians (Ex 11:7). The prophet likens his defenseless nation to a pack of lazy watchdogs that could not bark anyway (Is 56:10).

Dogs were the object as well as the source of routine insults. Goliath believes facing David in single combat is beneath his dignity: "Am I a dog?" (1 Sam 17:43, cf. 2 Sam 3:8). Evidence suggests that the transparently subservient behaviors of dogs—groveling, fawning, bowing—were actually practiced before superiors. Haza'el reacts to Elisha's prediction of his ascension to the throne of Syria saying, "What is your servant, who is but a dog, that he should do this great thing?" (2 Kings 8:13 RSV).

The marginal existence of a dog was a given. Its death was not mourned, but expected. Groveling subordinates repeatedly identify themselves to superiors as "dead dogs": "What is your servant that you should look on such a dead dog as I?" (2 Sam 9:8). A dead dog is a cheap life: "Why should this dead dog curse my lord the king?" (2 Sam 16:9). David's comparison of Saul's pursuit to hunting "after a dead dog" (1 Sam 24:14) craftily combines two meanings. David is not worth hunting, and doing so is an act of cowardice.

As bad as a dog's life was, "a living dog is better than a dead lion" (Eccles 9:4). A few passages hint that not all dogs led a dog's life. Job laments that he is scorned by young upstarts whose fathers were not good enough to work alongside the dogs guarding his flock (Job 30:1). The dog that accompanies Tobias on his long, dangerous journey is probably more than a mere pet (Tobit 5:16; 11:4). Jesus chides the Syrophoenician woman by saying that it would be unkind to toss out to scavenging dogs food that the children were still eating. She salvages his metaphor, reminding him that some doggies (probably young or small ones brought into the house by children) actually do receive table scraps (Mk 7:28).

In spite of these few hints of the positive image the dog would later have, the term is overwhelmingly negative and serves as a label for anyone beneath contempt. Paul warns Gentile Christians to watch out for dogs, the Judaizers (Phil 3:2). Hebrew law uses the term *dog* for male prostitute (Deut 23:18), perhaps referring to the position assumed in male-male intercourse, and it reappears in a list of apocalyptic evildoers: dogs, sorcerers, prostitutes, murderers, idolaters, lovers of the false (Rev 22:15).

Animals as Dangerous. The Bible names many animals simply because the mere mention of them evokes fear. Their fierce behavior is likened to the dealings of God, enemies or wicked individuals. The predatory armies of Babylon resemble frightful animals. They are swifter than cheetahs, fiercer than wolves. Their horsemen fly from afar like vultures and are as swift as *eagles (Hab 1:7-8). The imagery implies that the victims of war are as prey.

Lion. The twelve Hebrew words for *lion testify to deep concern about it. As top predator, raider of livestock (1 Sam 17; Amos 3:12) and foe with legendary strength, the lion has always been surrounded by myth. The many references to its roar suggest that it was heard more often than seen, but even its voice was cause for concern (Amos 3:8). Because when the lion is on the hunt something is going to die, it symbolizes the absolute power of kings and even of God. There is no way to prepare for its attack. It lurks secretly (Ps 10:9), bursts from hiding, emerging from thicket (Jer 49:19; 50:44; 25:38; Job 38:40) or forest (Jer 5:6, 12:8). When someone turns the tables on the lion, it is newsworthy (2 Sam 23:20). But even the strength and self-sufficiency of the lion does not exempt it from providential care (Ps 34:10).

Malicious in action, premeditated in harm, ruthlessly efficient in killing, the lion metaphorically embodies evil. The wicked are like lions "eager to tear . . . lurking in ambush (Ps 17:12 RSV; cf. Ps 7:2; 22:13, 21). The devil behaves like a lion (1 Pet 5:8). The righteous can only emulate the boldness of the lion (Prov 28:1). Even God is a lion who metes out punishment: "I will be to them like a lion" (Hos 13:7 RSV). Balaam's oracle employs the lion as an image of the inexorable rise of Israel (Num 23:24), echoing Jacob's deathbed metaphor, "Judah is a lion's whelp" (Gen 49:9 RSV). Eventually recognized as a messianic prophecy, the idea is recast in the apocalyptic title "Lion of the tribe of Judah" (Rev 5:5).

Leopard. This solitary cat was known for its habit of surveying its territory from high lookouts (Song 4:8). Unlike the lion it seldom betrayed its location by calling and so seemed all the more sinister (Hos 13:7). As a lurking danger "a leopard will lie in wait near their towns" (Jer 5:6 NIV). In visions it symbolizes yet another rapacious predator (Dan 7:6; Rev 13:2). As with the lion the leopard's quintessentially carnivorous nature will be recreated as a vegetarian (Is 11:6). Although Habakkuk envisions horses "swifter than leopards," the emphasis on speed suggests that the Hebrew word for leopard may also designate the cheetah (Hab 1:8). Egyptian royalty were already keeping cheetahs by this period.

Bear. To judge from the dozen references to the bear, the Israelites knew it as a dangerous animal. It points to violence and power, usually in conjunction with the lion (1 Sam 17:34, 36-37; 2 Sam 17:8, 10; Amos 5:19; Is 11:7; Hos 13:8; Prov 28:15; Lam 3:10). Amos characterizes the people's predicament with the Hebrew proverb "as if a man fled from a lion, and a bear met him" (Amos 5:19)—equivalent of our "out the frying pan, into the fire." They also recognized that "a bear robbed of its cubs" was violent because of human provocation (Prov 17:11; Hos 13:8). The she-bears that attacked Elisha's mockers may well have been aggravated by a perceived threat to their cubs (2 Kings 2:24). Unlike the

lion's growl, which intimidates, the bear's growl sounded plaintive to the Hebrews (Is 59:11). The bear inflicts most of its damage with its paws and claws. With its reputation for heavy-handedness, the bear personifies a "wicked ruler over a poor people" (Rev 13:2).

Wolf. The wolf is bold, opportunistic and ruthless in contrast to its victim, the sheep, which is naive, trusting and vulnerable (Mt 10:16). The name *wolf* identifies an inner nature that, even if covered in sheep's clothing, shows itself in behavior (Mt 7:15). The tribe of Benjamin was characterized as a wolf because of its opportunistic misadventures within the pack of twelve tribes. The wolf figures consistently as a metaphor for the wicked who prey on God's flock, whether spiritually (Jn 10:12) or politically and morally (princes, Ezek 22:27; judges, Zeph 3:3). The Messianic kingdom will be as different from this world as a noncarnivorous wolf is from the familiar wolf of legend (Is 65:25).

Fox or Jackal. Experts debate whether the fox and jackal are strictly separated in the mind of the inhabitants of Palestine in antiquity or now; however their imagery is quite separate. The words rendered "jackal" are consistently used to conjure images of ruin and desolation, of crying in the night. When a city becomes abandoned, the harbingers of doom that have lurked on the outskirts move in. It becomes the haunt of the jackal along with ominous birds, evil spirits, satyrs and liliths (Hazor, Jer 49:33; Jerusalem, Jer 9:11; Nineveh, Zeph 2:13-15; Babylon, Is 13:22; Rev 18:2).

The fox (as traditionally rendered, but which may also be a jackal) is not an omen of desolation, but a very small and light carnivore. It has the temerity to associate with lions at the kill, take what it can and dodge the consequences. Herod plays the crafty fox to Caesar's lion (Lk 13:32). He is a political nuisance, but not worth bothering with. In early Jewish literature the fox portrays a lesser person as opposed to the truly powerful, who are lions. Sanballat mocks that even the light-footed fox couldn't step on Nehemiah's wall without toppling its stones (Neh 4:3). Given the common metaphor of vineyard to refer to sexual pleasures, the foxes in Song of Songs 2:15 seem to point to some unidentified, yet regrettable negative—opportunists that are difficult to catch and punish.

Animals as Wild. Wildness points to an independence from human interference or even knowledge. The Bible frequently evokes wild animals as a prodding reminder of human ignorance or of the breadth of divine knowledge. The poet deliberately chooses the hippopotamus (Behemoth) and the crocodile (Leviathan) because they are exotic and unfamiliar to his audience. They summoned awe and reverence the way stories of man-eating plants do for children. They help us imagine a fiercely unpredictable Creator. Who else could conceive a grass-eating monster (Job 40:15)?

The wildness and variety of nature, like the pageant of creatures that portrays it, praise the Creator. The wild ox is untamable (Job 39:9-12). Leviathan is gloriously wild and uncapturable (Job 41:1-8). The ways and habits of wild creatures are inscrutable (Job 39), as mysterious and unfathomable as the cosmos (Job 38). Mythological animals and genuine brutes evoke the splendor and majesty of creation, pointing directly to the exuberant creativity of their maker. Job thinks God made sea monsters just for the fun of it. Animals and seasons obediently follow God's laws, but humanity does not (Jer 8:7). One cannot tame oneself or even as small a part as one's own tongue (Jas 3:7-8). Who, after all, is the real brute, the "irrational creature" (2 Pet 2:12)? The real dragon, the serpent, the primordial enemy lives within.

Novelty is a luxury the wealthy can afford, so Solomon imports exotic creatures from eastern and southern kingdoms. Apes, peacocks and perhaps elephants appeared as curiosities (1 Kings 10:22 par. 2 Chron 9:21). Elephants, recently extinct in western Asia, were still known by their tusks (ivory tusks are mentioned in Ezek 27:15; cf. 1 Macc 6:30).

Animals as a Source of Wisdom. Some animals just seem proud: the strutting cock, the he-goat, the lion (Prov 30:29). The term "sons of pride" seems to refer to lions (Job 28:8) or perhaps underground snakes, but elsewhere to unspecified animals (Job 41:34).

Some tiny animals have notable accomplishments. Lazy people could learn and improve themselves by watching ants (Prov 6:6-8), which are organized without a bureaucracy and which plan ahead admirably (Prov 30:24-25). Badgers are small and few, but wisely live in impenetrable rock fortresses (Prov 30:26). *Locusts swarm inexorably forward without visible leadership (Prov 30:27). Lizards are easily caught and frail, but live like kings in palaces (Prov 30:28). Nor does small necessarily mean insignificant. David discounts his potential to succeed Saul by calling himself a flea (1 Sam 24:14). A small political state pestering large, grain-fed Egypt is like gadfly tormenting a fat cow (Jer 46:20). Even the worm (see below) accomplishes God's ends.

Nature also harbors some nasty creatures and some negative lessons. Those who ignore God are placing confidence in a spider's web (Prov 8:14). The wicked build a house as insubstantial as a spider's web (Prov 27:18). The unjust weave a web of mischief. It appears overnight like a spider's web. Their plots are viper's eggs, much worse after they hatch (Is 59:5).

Animals as Divine Agents. Since all events are under God's control, animals function as divine agents. Some fulfill God's mission. Others are co-opted by evil and permitted to harm. Behavior considered abnormal for an animal suggests that it is filling such a role. A normal lion would have eaten the donkey or the prophet in 1 Kings 13:25-26. Its unexpected behavior betrays its divine mission (1 Kings 13:28). Other lions punish a disobedient prophet (1 Kings 20:35-36) or idolatrous Samaritans (2 Kings 17:25-26). The bears Elisha summons to

punish the disrespectful lads tear them open, but no mention is made of eating (2 Kings 2:24). At the advice of diviners the Philistines load the ark on a cart pulled by two milk cows, which unnaturally walk away from their bawling calves to return the cart to Israel, a sign that the God of Israel "has done us this great harm" (1 Sam 6:7-9). Ravens would not naturally feed humans, but they fed Elijah at God's command (1 Kings 17:4). The bite of a snake, coming as a surprise (Gen 49:17; Amos 5:19), must have seemed unprovoked and unnatural, giving the serpent a permanent role in the spirit world.

Locusts, though individually insignificant and crushable (Ps 109:23; Num 13:33), in swarms are like armies on the march (Prov 30:27), and armies are compared to locusts (Judg 6:5; 7:12). They pounce like despoilers (Is 33:4). A bewildering array of kinds of locusts (Joel 1:4) with numberless mouths "consume the years" (Joel 2:25; Deut 28:38). The masses of locusts quickly exhaust the standing crops and move on. They signify a brief existence (Jer 46:23; 51:14; Nahum 3:15-17; 4 Ezra 4:24). People, like gnats, will die in huge numbers (Is 51:6). Real enemies swarm like bees (Deut 1:44; Ps 108:12), but real hornets act as God's allies and shock troops (Ex 23:28; Deut 7:20; Josh 24:12).

The *worm, as an agent of destruction, belonged in God's arsenal too. Like its overgrown relative the serpent, the worm is part of the forces of decay. Before people had an understanding of worms as the larva of insects, nature seemed to spontaneously decay into worms, as did the old manna (Ex 16:20). Worms (including maggots and moth larva) were agents of ruin and corruption (Deut 28:39; Is 14:11; 51:8), offering the living a foretaste of hell, a personal preview of death. Luke vividly narrates that Herod became a worm-feast (Acts 12:23) as punishment for his hubris (cf. 2 Mac 9:9; 1 Mac 2:62-63). Less severely, a God-appointed worm makes a didactic dinner of Jonah's beloved shade vine (Jonah 4:7).

In a fallen world locked in cosmic conflict, harm is a two-way street. Animals may administer suffering to help punish the behavior of humanity, but as part of creation they suffer in turn as a consequence of human sin (Jer 12:4; Joel 1:18, 20). In fact all creation groans under the burden of the Fall (Rom 8:22). The coming Messianic kingdom, with the absence of "natural" evils like decay, will be unrecognizable by biological criteria of this age (Is 65:25).

Fish. Although not traditionally a sea-faring people, the Israelites did enjoy many varieties of *fish as food (Deut 14:9). The abundance of fish in Egypt was one of the pleasant memories (Num 11:5). The desire for fresh fish caused some to ignore Sabbath regulations and buy from the men of Tyre (Neh 13:16).

The relative ease with which unsuspecting game is taken by fishing allows an efficient and ruthless enemy to be characterized as fishers and hunters (Jer 16:16). People were hooked and dragged like fish (Hab 1:15; Amos 4:2). The oppressed or victims of the wicked are like fish or game trapped in nets (Mic 7:2; Ezek 32:3; Ps 66:11). (In addition to fishing, nets were used widely for hunting and war.) The same image has a positive twist in Jesus' expression "fishers of men" (Mt 4:18). Like the winnowing after harvest or the separation of the flock, the sorting of the catch serves as a metaphor for the final judgment (Mt 13:47).

Paul argues by analogy from the difference in flesh of beast, fowl and fish (1 Cor 15:39), a distinction that allowed centuries of believers to eat protein on Fridays even when "meat" was banned. The fish became a special symbol for early Christians because the letters of the Greek word *IXTHUS* formed an acrostic for the initials of several common names for Jesus: *Iēsous, Xristos, Theou Hyios, Sōtēr* (Jesus, Christ, Son of God, Savior). In an age where words were regarded not as merely arbitrary symbols, but as repositories of deeper, secret sense, discernible by the learned, acrostics held special significance and revealed deeper meanings. In this case it also pointed to other symbolic links: loaves and fishes, the trade of many apostles, the breakfast by the sea and so forth.

See also BIRDS; CATTLE; DOG; DONKEY, ASS; DOVE; EAGLE; FISH, FISHERMAN; FLOCK; GOAT; HORSE; HUNTING; LAMB; LION; MYTHICAL ANIMALS; OX, OXEN; PLANTS; SCAPEGOAT; SHEEP, SHEPHERD; SWINE; TRAP, TRAPPING; WOLF.

BIBLIOGRAPHY. G. S. Cansdale, *All the Animals of the Bible Lands* (Grand Rapids: Zondervan, 1970); E. Firmage, "Zoology," *ABD* 6:1109-67; B. L. Goddard, *Animals and Birds of the Bible* (Grand Rapids: Associated Publishers and Authors [n. d.]); *Fauna and Flora of the Bible* (New York: United Bible Societies, 1972).

ANNUNCIATION

Although technically a general term referring to the announcement of some impending event, in modern English *annunciation* has come to be associated almost exclusively with the *angel Gabriel's announcement to *Mary that she is to be the mother of Jesus. The image of the young girl receiving such an unexpected and disturbing message has caught the imagination of artists through the centuries so completely that it comes as a surprise to many to realize that the story is told only once, in Luke's Gospel, and is not referred to, either directly or indirectly, anywhere else in the NT. However, there are many associated stories and ideas, and the simple, brief record in Luke 1:26-38 is packed with images and concepts that are picked up elsewhere in the NT and given great significance.

The angel Gabriel, Daniel's instructor (Dan 8:16; 9:21) and well known in intertestamental literature as a senior spiritual messenger, is sent by God, who is clearly portrayed as the prime director in this situation. The angel is acting solely and entirely on his behalf. The recipient of his message is Mary, an engaged *virgin, signifying both purity and preparedness. The picture is not one of mere objective transfer of information. Mary is spoken to by name and recognized as a person. She herself, noted as already being aware of God and his presence, has been specifically chosen not simply to receive the message of the impending arrival of "the Son of the Most High" (Lk 1:32 NRSV) but actually to be his mother. Her natural fear and perplexity are noted and dealt with. She and her reactions are taken seriously.

Thus the story has more than christological significance. It reinforces the OT teaching that God relates to individuals and is personally involved with human beings. It confirms that women are significant to him in their own right. It recognizes the importance of response, in Mary's case, dependence and freely accepted obedience: "Here I am, the servant of the Lord; let it be with me according to your word" (Lk 1:38). It majors on purpose and on hope. God's involvement with individual human beings comes in a context of concern for humankind as a whole. This story clearly conveys the fact that God has purposes for the world and will take action to ensure that these purposes are carried out. This in itself brings a strong sense of hope, reinforced by the picture of impending new birth—there is something to which Mary, and humankind as a whole, can look forward.

But clearly the christological significance is there and is important. The baby to be born will be a human being with a human name, Jesus, which indicates a task of redemption (Mt 1:21). But this particular human baby will also be "the Son of the Most High." The Holy Spirit himself will provide the power that will make his birth possible. His greatness, his rule and the eternal nature of his task are all indicated: "The child to be born will be holy; he will be called Son of God" (Lk 1:35). The specialness of Mary, favored by God, pales into insignificance when compared with the specialness of her son.

John Macquarrie regards the annunciation to Mary as a helpful illustration in the understanding of the church. He sees a parallel between the original bringing to birth of Christ and the responsibility of the church to, as it were, bring Christ to birth in the world. "Just as she was the bearer of the Christ, so the Church his body, brings christhood into the world. But this takes place through the action of the Spirit in the Church which again is the community of the Spirit" (Macquarrie, 354). Thus the annunciation reminds us of the involvement of God in providing his power and his grace, of the way in which he comes to human beings, conveying to them his purposes and allowing or calling them to have a part in carrying out those purposes.

Other Annunciation Stories. There are related annunciations to Joseph (Mt 1:18-25) and to Zechariah (Lk 1:5-20). Both of these also capture the sense of God's involvement with human history, the reality of communication and relationship, the care for human feelings and human reactions, and the awareness of both purpose and hope. But there are a number of OT stories that are brought to mind by the annunciation to Mary in Luke 1:26-38 and the following verses where Mary and Elizabeth reflect together on what has happened to them and how it affects the history of God's people.

The narratives in Genesis 15:4-5, 17:15-21 and 18:9-15 describe Sarah and *Abraham receiving the specific announcement that within the year they will have their own child. That the connection with Luke 1 is more than just incidental is shown by Gabriel, as he tells Mary of the pregnancy of the older Elizabeth, picking up as a statement the question that faced Sarah and Abraham, "Is anything too hard for the LORD?" Where God is involved, the concept of impossibility has to be completely reconsidered.

The predicted birth in Isaiah 7:14, which comes to initial fulfillment in Isaiah 8:3, is directly related in Matthew 1:22-23 to the announcement to Joseph of Jesus' birth. Perhaps it is the elements of hope and a transformed future that provide the greatest link at that point. The announcement of the impending birth of *Samson to Manoah's wife in Judges 13 and the story of Samuel's birth in 1 Samuel 1—2 (not strictly an annunciation but with many connection to the accounts in Luke 1) both bring out the way in which God relates directly to women as actors in, not just observers of, the ongoing program that God has set before his people. The cooperation between God and his servants seems to be a key concept in the annunciation image.

In summary, the annunciation is one of the incremental motifs in the Bible that keeps amplifying until it reaches its culmination in the example of Christ. The stories that make up the "canon" of this genre are those involving Abraham and Sarah; Samson's mother, Hannah; Zechariah; and finally, Mary.

See also ANGEL; BARRENNESS; BIRTH; BIRTH STORY; MARY THE MOTHER OF JESUS.

BIBLIOGRAPHY. R. Alter, "How Convention Helps us Read: The Case of the Bible's Annunciation Type-Scene," *Proof* 3 (1983) 115-30; R. E. Brown, *The Birth of the Messiah* (2d ed.; New York: Doubleday, 1993); J. Macquarrie, *Principles of Christian Theology,* (London: SCM, 1966).

ANOINTING

To anoint literally means to pour or rub *oil on a person or thing. Rooted in OT culture the practice of anointing in the Bible symbolizes various kinds of special recognition shown to places (Gen 28:18); *temple and its furnishings (Ex 40:9-10); garments (Lev 8:30); *kings (1 Kings 1:39; 2 Kings 9:6); religious leaders (Ex 28:41; Lev 8:12, *priests; 1 Kings 19:16, *prophets); heavenly beings (Ezek 28:14); or simply honored *guests (Ps 23:5; cf. Lk 7:46; Jn 11:2). Anointing usually means two things: it sets a person or thing apart as holy and consecrated, and it confers authority on a person who is anointed. In the Bible the *holiness and *authority that reside in ritual anointing are considered to be conferred by

God, though mediated through a person acting on God's behalf.

In the ancient Near East, anointing with oil was used to ratify and solemnize commitment in diplomatic relations, business contracts, nuptial rites and the liberation of slaves. It did not necessarily have religious significance. Some of these aspects are reflected in OT passages such as Genesis 28:18-22, where the anointing rite is a symbol of contractual relations between Jacob and God, or Hosea 12:1 and 1 Kings 5:11, where oil is used as an expression of *friendship. In addition, Mesopotamian anointing rites included the idea of people being permeated by divine activity and supernatural power.

In OT religious rituals, anointing signifies consecration for priestly (Ex 30:30; Lev 4:3, 5) and royal service (1 Sam 2:10). It symbolizes God's choice and appointment and therefore involves divine action in preparation for service (1 Sam 10:1). The powerful symbolism of this rite accounts for the preservation of Saul's life in 1 Samuel 26:9-23—to kill Saul would show disregard for the king's special status as God's anointed (see 2 Sam 1:16; 2 Sam 19:21). In this respect, anointing involves God's blessing and preservation (Ps 18:50; Hab 3:13). After *Solomon's anointing, words of blessing are declared on him (1 Kings 1:39), and warnings come to kings themselves not to harm God's anointed prophets (1 Chron 16:22; cf. Ps 105:15).

The theme of blessing is further associated with the anointing rite in Psalm 133:2, where precious oil is used as a metaphor for God's bountiful provision for priestly leaders. A similar emphasis occurs in Psalm 45:7, where the anointing of a royal figure is described as an anointing of joy. In 1 Samuel 10:6-9 God's role in anointing is associated with the receiving of God's Spirit, the change of *heart and the promise of God's presence. The same emphasis occurs in 1 Samuel 16:13, where David's anointing immediately precedes his receipt of "the Spirit of the LORD . . . in power." Thus the anointing of OT kings is a special symbol of God's provision through the gift of his Spirit.

It is appropriate, therefore, that in the OT the title "anointed one" becomes a synonym for individuals chosen, appointed, consecrated and equipped for office. The title is restricted to royal figures (Ps 2:2; 89:38; 132:10) except for Daniel 9:25-26, where it refers to a future ruler. Hence, in the NT it is appropriate that the title, in its Greek form "Christ" *(Christos),* is applied to Jesus (Jn 1:41; 4:25; Acts 4:24-27).

In the NT the rite of anointing is not used for consecration or worship. Instead, anointing is often thought of in figurative terms to describe the spiritual basis of Jesus' ministry (Lk 4:18; Acts 10:38; Heb 1:9) and the spiritual work God performs in believers' lives (2 Cor 1:21-22; 1 Jn 2:20, 27). The emphasis is not on the act of anointing but on the *Holy Spirit with whom one is anointed.

The NT also refers to the social use of anointing

for embalming and cosmetic purposes (Mt 6:17; Mk 16:1; Lk 7:38, 46; Jn 11:2; 12:3). These instances also suggest that anointing symbolizes the giving of recognition, a concept with its basis in the OT (see above). The NT draws on the cultural use of olive oil for medicinal/healing (see Disease and Healing) purposes in NT times (cf. Mk 6:13; Lk 10:34; Jas 5:14).

See also HOLY SPIRIT; OIL.

ANTICHRIST

Surprisingly, given the highly developed portraits attending the figure of the antichrist throughout Christian history, the term itself appears a mere four times in the Bible—only in 1 and 2 John, never in Revelation. We find comparable figures, however, in Mark 13:22 and parallels ("false christs"), 2 Thessalonians 2:3 ("the lawless one"), and Revelation 13, 17 (the sea beast). These are all related to false *prophets: deceivers who steer people from the ways of the Lord (e.g., Deut 13).

2 John 7-11 warns of the coming of deceivers/antichrists, while 1 John 2:18-22; 4:1-6 advises that they are already active. Such people go beyond the teaching of *Christ. Their behavior is unloving and immoral. They disavow Jesus' incarnation and messiahship. The presence of these "*enemies of Christ" intimates the advent of "the last days."

Revelation 13 paints a similar, if more startling, picture. Empowered by the dragon (*Satan, cf. Rev 12:9), the sea beast (see Monster) is Christ's negative image: he mimics Jesus' *crowns (Rev 13:1; 19:12), his honorable titles (Rev 13:1; 19:11-16), his exercise of divine power (Rev 13:2; 12:5, 10), his promotion of divine *worship (Rev 13:4; 1:6) and his death and resurrection (Rev 13:3; 1:18; 5:6). The beast is a counterfeit christ, who through his flashy signs competes with Christ for allegiance and worship (cf. Mk 13:22; 2 Thess 2:3-4; Rev 13:13-14). Importantly, his power is limited and will be overcome by Christ (2 Thess 2:3; 1 Jn 4:4; Rev 19:20).

John, who wrote to warn Christians against the blasphemous power wielded by the empire, identifies this beast as Rome ("the city on seven hills," cf. Rev 17:9). But his images reveal that the power of antichrist residing in the beast is far bigger than Rome. It lives on beyond the first century, to the present and to the eschaton, wherever the nature and message of Christ are refuted in the service of fraudulent demands for absolute loyalty.

See also CHRIST; ENEMY; MONSTER, MONSTERS; SATAN.

BIBLIOGRAPHY. W. Bousset, The Antichrist Legend (London: Hutchinson, 1896); B. McGinn, Antichrist: Two Thousand Years of the Human Fascination with Evil (San Francisco: HarperCollins, 1994).

ANTIHERO

The antihero is a familiar archetype in modern literature—the protagonist characterized by an absence of the traits or roles that conventionally qualify a person to be considered heroic. It is no surprise that we find antiheroes in a book that subverts worldly standards of success as often as the Bible does. The key text is 1 Corinthians 1:26-31, where Paul asserts regarding those who came to faith in Christ that "not many of you were wise according to worldly standards, not many were powerful, not many were of noble birth" (RSV). Biblical narrative gives us numerous examples of the pattern.

The *younger child who supplants the elder is so frequent in the OT that it can be called a biblical archetype, and in it we can see an inversion of an important conventional heroic norm that was especially important in the ancient world. Joseph and David were both youngest sons chosen by God for a heroic destiny rather than other family members. Moses lacked the eloquence that ordinarily accompanied heroism in the ancient world (Ex 3—4); Jeremiah felt similarly inadequate (Jer 1:4-10). Several OT characters rose to heroic prominence in foreign cultures when their status as exiles might have seemed to disqualify them—Joseph, Ruth, Daniel, Esther. Even a *prostitute (Rahab) makes it into the roll call of faith (Heb 11:31). The antihero motif also finds its way in latent form into the *hero stories of the Bible, where the list of wholly idealized characters is exceedingly brief and where even the most heroic characters are usually portrayed as having flaws.

Gideon is perhaps the most fully drawn antihero in biblical narrative (Judg 6—8). He begins as a classic case of low self-esteem. Instead of being of royal blood, he comes from the weakest clan in his tribe and describes himself as being the least in his family (Judg 6:15). Whereas the conventional hero story celebrates deliverance brought about by great and strong warriors, the story of Gideon shows the small part that human effort plays in the conquest of the enemy. Instead of accepting the conventional reward for military victory—kingship—Gideon declines on the ground that God is the real deliverer (Judg 8:22-23). As in many of the OT narratives, God is given the honor that is usually accorded a human hero. Gideon, in short, is an antihero in his lack of self-reliance and of any achievement that he can call his own, and in his unwillingness to aggrandize himself by assuming political rulership.

The NT counterpart is Paul, whose heroic status is built largely on an absence of the traits and achievements that would ordinarily be considered heroic. Paul's heroism stemmed from God-given authority rather than from his natural abilities. The Corinthian congregation found Paul's letters "weighty and strong, but his bodily presence . . . weak, and his speech of no account" (2 Cor 10:10 RSV). He was afflicted by "a thorn in the flesh" (2 Cor 12:7), and it was only by God's grace that his weakness did not hinder his effectiveness (v. 9). Externally, Paul's career is a litany of failures—"beatings, imprisonments, tumults, labors, watching, hunger" (2 Cor 6:5 RSV).

The motif of the antihero enters nonnarrative

passages as well. Psalm 18:31-42 follows a conventional motif of martial literature—the arming of the hero and the warrior's boast—but here the arming of the hero is ascribed to God, who is also the subject of the warrior's *boast. The songs of Hannah (1 Sam 2:1-10) and Mary (Lk 1:46-55) celebrate God's "deheroizing" of the exalted figures in society and elevation of those without heroic claim. The beatitudes of Christ's Sermon on the Mount paint a portrait of a person whose salient traits reverse what the human race has usually regarded as heroic behavior. A prophet like Amos is heroic only in the strength of God's call; he himself is "no prophet, nor a prophet's son; but . . . a herdsman, and a dresser of sycamore trees" (Amos 7:14 RSV).

The apotheosis of the antihero comes in the song of the *suffering servant in Isaiah 52:13—53:12. We might say that if we use conventional heroic norms as a standard, this servant is praised for all the wrong reasons. He is without distinguished ancestry or impressive appearance. In fact, he is mutilated and executed instead of winning a battle against enemies. He is silent instead of assertive, he wins rewards for others instead of himself, and he dies condemned as an ordinary criminal, making "his grave with the wicked" (Is 53:9). Even the conventional picture of dividing "the spoil with the strong" (Is 43:10) is atypical, inasmuch as the "spoil" is spiritual rather than physical, achieved for others rather than himself. This portrait of the Messiah is elaborated in the Gospels, where we read about Jesus' humble origins and the failure of his career when judged by conventional standards of success.

See also HERO, HEROINE; YOUNGER CHILD.

ANTLER. *See* HORN.

APOCALYPSE, GENRE OF

Apocalypse was a literary genre that flourished in the period between the OT and NT (though apocalpytic visions of the future can be found in the OT as well as the NT). When read aloud an apocalypse held ancient listeners spellbound with special effects and promise of better days ahead. Visions of heaven and the future, featuring extraordinary creatures and events, focused attention on a whole new world. Natural catastrophes ravaging the earth portrayed God's final judgment on the evil in the world. Cosmic fireworks ushering in the new age suggested how revolutionary God's decisive triumph would be. These previews of God's will being "done on earth as it is in heaven" drew the attention of hearers away from the crises of everyday life. They caught glimpses of another time and another world where, devoid of the vice of the present global order, the virtue of God's universal order prevailed.

But today's readers are often puzzled and frustrated by this genre. The unexpected imagery and out-of-this-world experiences seem bizarre and out of sync with most of Scripture. Taking this literature at face value leaves many readers scrambling to determine "what will happen when," thus missing the intent of the apocalyptic message. Yet apocalypticism, the perspective that informs apocalyptic literature, is in some ways very modern: current science fiction and space fantasy in both literature and movies use graphic and disturbing images similar to those in the genre of apocalypse.

Characteristics. Apocalypse as a genre is exceptional for its underlying feeling of hopelessness: evil seems to have the upper hand. The conclusion is that things will definitely get worse before they get better. Yet glimpses of heaven and the future make it clear that God is on the throne and in control. And those glimpses reveal how totally opposite are our world and God's. Fortunately, God will soon start the processes to make our world like his world. But the predicament is so critical that God himself must visit this earth again. The only solution is catastrophic judgment against all forms of evil and the establishment of a completely new order that will last forever.

Taking its name from the Greek word for "revelation" *(apokalypsis)*, apocalypse is the genre primarily identified with the book of *Daniel in the OT and the book of *Revelation in the NT. But it is difficult to set clear boundaries around the genre of apocalypse, because apocalypticism is a way of thinking that emerges in various contexts. Several passages in the OT employ apocalyptic content and technique (Is 24—27, 56—66, Ezek 38-39, Joel 2:28—3:21, Zech 1—6 and 12—14), suggesting that a shift from prophecy to apocalyptic was underway toward the close of the OT.

The majority of extant apocalypses were written after the OT period. They are included in the group of writings now known as the Jewish pseudepigrapha. *1* and *2 Enoch, Jubilees, 2* and *3 Baruch, 4 Ezra,* and the *Apocalypse of Abraham*—all apparently written between the third century B.C. and the second century A.D.—are representative of Jewish apocalyptic. Among the Dead Sea Scrolls, fragments of *1 Enoch* have survived; and in some of the literature of the Qumran sect, apocalyptic influence is prominent. During the first few centuries of the church apocalyptic fervor continued, resulting in a variety of Christian apocalypses.

In the NT, in addition to the book of Revelation, apocalypticism is especially evident in Jesus' Olivet discourse (Mk 13), in some portions of Paul's letters (1 Thess 4:13—5:11; 2 Thess 2:1-12), and in 2 Pet 3:1-13. Early Christianity had numerous similarities with the apocalyptic movement in Judaism.

Though apocalypse may be considered a subgenre of prophecy, the two literary styles are sufficiently different to merit calling them separate genres. Prophecy speaks to those who have backslidden and begs them to repent; apocalyptic speaks to the faithful and urges them to persevere. Prophecy announces God's judgment of sin on a local scale using natural means; apocalyptic announces a coming cataclysm when the whole earth will be destroyed. Prophecy records its message in poetry; apocalyptic in narrative accounts of visions and heavenly journeys full of mystery. Prophecy promises restoration and future blessing; apocalyptic an unexpected divine visitation that will result in a new heaven and new earth.

Themes and Motifs. Apocalyptic literature has a number of common themes and motifs:

Hopelessness. Evil is intensifying and conditions are deteriorating (Is 57:3-13). The earth is being trampled and crushed by wickedness (Dan 7:23). *Famines, *earthquakes and *wars are increasing (Mk 13:7-8). *Persecution is escalating (Mt 24:9-12, 15-22).

God's sovereignty. The Lord can be trusted no matter how bad the situation (Is 26:1-4). Heaven and earth may be destroyed, but God's words will never pass away (Mt 24:35). God is on his *throne and takes care of those whose robes have been washed in the blood of the *Lamb (Rev 7:14-16).

Catastrophic judgment. Earthquakes will cause walls to fall down, cliffs to crumble and mountains to be turned upside down; *hailstones and burning sulfur will fall from the sky (Ezek 38:19-22). The *sun will turn black, the *moon will turn red, *stars will fall on the earth, the elements will be destroyed by *fire, and the earth will become bare (Mt 24:29; 2 Pet 3:10; Rev 6:12). *Birds will eat the flesh of the rulers of this world (Rev 19:17-18, 21). The perpetrators of evil will be thrown into a lake of burning sulfur (Rev 19:20; *see* Hell).

Celestial visions. In God's presence, purity is required (Zech 3:3-7). Heavenly creatures are so bright that they appear to be on fire (Dan 10:5-6; Rev 1:12-16). The splendor of heaven is so stunning that it is like a room of precious stones and crystal (Rev 4:2-6; *see* Jewels and Precious Stones). The new *Jerusalem descending from heaven will have *twelve *gates, each fashioned from a single *pearl. It will have transparent *gold streets, and it will shine with God's *glory (Rev 21:10-27).

Ethical teaching. "Show mercy and compassion to one another . . . do not think evil of each other" (Zech 7:9-10 NIV). "He who stands firm to the end will be saved" (Mt 24:13). Since the master is returning, faithfulness is required of servants (Mt 24:45-51; 25:14-30). "Since everything will be destroyed in this way, what kind of people ought you to be?" (2 Pet 3:11). "This calls for patient endurance and faithfulness on the part of the saints" (Rev 13:10; 14:12).

Divine visitation. The Lord will appear on the Mount of Olives (Zech 14:4). "Then suddenly the Lord you are seeking will come to his temple" (Mal 3:1). "For as *lightning that comes from the east is visible even in the west, so will be the coming of the Son of Man" (Mt 24:27, 30, 36-44; cf. 25:1-13). "For the Lord himself will come down from heaven" (1 Thess 4:16). "Look, he is coming with the *clouds, and every eye will see him" (Rev 1:7). "But if you do not wake up, I will come like a *thief, and

you will not know at what time I will come to you" (Rev 3:3; 16:15). "I saw heaven standing open and there before me was a white *horse, whose rider is called Faithful and True" (Rev 19:11).

The new age. Peace will be restored (Zech 8:3-8). People will enjoy what God intended from the beginning (Mt 25:34). The new heaven and new earth will be a home of righteousness (2 Pet 3:13). A resurrection will bring back to life all those who died unjustly (Rev 20:4-6) as well as all those who have ever lived (Rev 20:12-15). *Pain, *death, *tears and impurity will be removed forever (Rev 21:4, 27). Healing will be provided for everyone (Rev 21:2-3).

The themes of apocalyptic are most often expressed in bold and graphic imagery. This imagery may be allusions to earlier biblical phrases, though the phrases may be reinterpreted in the present context. For example, the *"Son of Man" motif in Mark 13:26 draws on Daniel 7, but the meaning is not the same in both places. The imagery in the book of Revelation has many parallels with the books of Ezekiel and Daniel, but individual images cannot be assumed to mean the same in both contexts. The imagery of apocalyptic is very fluid and is dependent on the immediate context.

Understanding Apocalyptic. The imagery of the genre of apocalypse has probably been subjected to more incorrect interpretation than any other aspect of Scripture. The problem is primarily a matter of distance between the ancient audience and modern interpreters. To bridge that distance the following guidelines are necessary: (1) Read with the ear of an ancient listener. Apocalyptic forms of expression were very common outside the Bible, and contemporary readers need to become familiar with that mindset to understand biblical apocalyptic literature and symbolism. (2) Be sensitive to the setting of crisis. Apocalyptic authors wrote with a flair for the spectacular in an attempt to lift the sights of despairing listeners from their current problems to God's striking solutions. (3) Expect symbolic language. The events described in apocalyptic literature are often presented with literary techniques found more commonly in poetry: metaphor, hyperbole, personification, irony, numerical patterns and so forth. These special effects allowed apocalyptic to describe heaven and the future with captivating imagery. (4) Consider the oral nature of ancient society. Literature was written to be read aloud or quoted from memory. Listeners came away with an overall impression more like an impressionistic painting than like a photograph in high resolution. Individual details remained a puzzle, but the big picture was clear. (5) Recognize the function of apocalypse. It was a message of hope for the oppressed, a warning to the oppressors and a call to commitment for those unsure of their loyalties.

See also DANIEL; END, IMAGES OF THE; EZEKIEL; PROPHECY, GENRE OF; REVELATION, BOOK OF.

BIBLIOGRAPHY. G. B. Caird, *The Language and Imagery of the Bible* (2d ed.; Grand Rapids: Eerdmans, 1997); J. J. Collins, *The Apocalyptic Imagina-*

tion (New York: Crossroads, 1989); D. Hellholm, ed., *Apocalypticism in the Mediterranean World and the Near East* (Tübingen: J. C. B. Mohr, 1983); C. C. Rowland, *The Open Heaven* (London: SPCK, 1982); D. S. Russell, *The Method and Message of Jewish Apocalyptic* (Philadelphia: Westminster, 1964).

APOCALYPTIC VISIONS OF THE FUTURE

More perhaps than any other parts of the Bible, the apocalyptic visions of the end of history and life in the eternal realm are a language of images. Many of these images are fantastic, transcending anything known in empirical reality.

It is possible to get a preliminary view of the territory by dividing the Bible's images of the future into three broad categories. First, there is a neutral category of images that simply portray future events as neither good nor bad in themselves, with their status depending on one's state of soul. Included in this group are the *Day of the Lord, the Last *Judgment, the appearing of Christ and the *resurrection of the dead. Second, there is a category of decidedly negative images, including cosmic collapse, moral degeneration (including the spirit of *antichrist and "the lawless one"), a great tribulation and signs preceding the return of Christ. A third category is images of bliss: the millennium, new heavens and a new earth, new *Jerusalem, and the wedding feast of the *Lamb. Overall, we can generalize about the Bible's images of the future that they combine mingled hope and pessimism.

General Traits. The imagery of these visions is dialectical, dividing the cosmos and the human race into categories of good and evil, *light and *darkness, redemption and judgment, *reward and punishment. The world of the Bible's apocalyptic visions is claimed by God and counterclaimed by forces of evil. There is no neutral ground. Although the good is ultimately victorious, the imagery of terror probably dominates most people's experience of apocalyptic writing.

Apocalyptic imagery is otherworldly or fantastic. Its aim is to suggest a world that transcends ordinary reality. In these visions we move in a world of such fantastic images as "living creatures" with "six wings and . . . covered with eyes all around" (Rev 4:8 RSV), two flying women with *wings like those of a stork (Zech 5:9) and a beast that "was like a lion, and it had the wings of an eagle" and that had its wings plucked off and then stood "on two feet like a man" (Dan 7:4 RSV; *see* Mythical Animals). The imagery of strangeness is a staple in apocalyptic visions, which are often surrealistic in effect. The characters in this apocalyptic realm are part of its strangeness. Animal characters are common, as are *angels and *demons.

The imagery of apocalypse is cosmic, extending to the whole universe. The elemental forces of nature—*sun, *moon, *stars, *sea, *mountain—are part of the cosmic sweep. Often these elemental cosmic forces become actors in the story—falling from the sky, refusing to give their light, being removed from their familiar places, suddenly protecting or attacking human characters.

Symbolic *colors and *numbers form image patterns in apocalyptic visions. White is the color of purity; red, of either evil or warfare; black, of death. The *numbers *three, *seven, ten and *twelve (and their multiples) signify perfection, completeness, fulfillment, victory. Six is a sinister number—approaching seven but falling fatally short.

The imagery of *suffering and *terror is prominent in apocalyptic visions. We enter a world of heightened terror—of *earthquakes and *famines, of *persecution and *war, of people fleeing to the mountains, of fearsome *locusts that hurt people with their scorpion-like tails, of *plagues. A feeling of helplessness accompanies these visions, inasmuch as the terror is visited upon humanity by forces of superior power, usually supernatural in nature.

For all its apparent concreteness and vividness, the imagery of apocalyptic writing is essentially nonvisual and nonpictorial. While this literature *seems* to paint specific pictures, the images are almost impossible to put into composite pictorial form. Ezekiel's vision of the divine *chariot and its attendants (Ezek 1) can stand as a test case. Corresponding to the prevailing nonvisual nature of these visions, oral/aural imagery naming sounds is prominent.

Apocalyptic imagery is inherently symbolic. It uses specific images to stand for something or someone else. In the book of *Revelation the dragon is *Satan, the Lamb, Christ. When Isaiah pictures a *river overflowing a nation (8:5-8), it is actually a prediction of invasion by Assyria. Daniel's vision of a statue composed of various minerals is a symbolic picture of successive empires (Dan 2:31-45). We can call this mode "symbolic reality," meaning that it portrays events that really happen in history and at its consummation, but that it does so by means of symbolism. Much of this imagery is like that of our familiar political cartoons in which caricatures and symbolic figures or objects represent people and events on the current scene.

The element of strangeness in apocalyptic imagery can easily lead to the misconception that such writing is esoteric. Yet the word *apocalypse* means "to unveil." In significant ways apocalyptic writing is folk literature. Its images are those of our waking and sleeping dreams—*blood, lamb, dragon, *monster, *water, sea, sun, war, *harvest, *bride, *throne, *jewels. The second half of the book of Revelation is a spiritualized version of familiar folktale motifs: a woman in distress who is marvelously rescued, a hero on a white *horse who kills a dragon, a wicked *prostitute who is finally exposed, the marriage of the triumphant hero to his bride, the celebration of the *wedding with a *feast, and a palace glittering with jewels in which the *hero and his bride live happily ever after. What apocalyptic imagery most requires of us is a keen eye for the obvious and a childlike receptivity to folktale patterns.

Leading Motifs. Apocalyptic images of the future congregate around five main motifs: (1) the immediacy of the end, (2) the cataclysmic character of the end, (3) spiritual conflict, (4) the transformation of the cosmos and (5) divine provision in the new epoch of salvation. Apocalyptic visions of the future typically emphasize the coming of God to crush evil, destroy the enemies of God's people and vindicate the faithful.

Immediacy of the end. In the NT the immediacy of the end is conveyed by a variety of images, including the *thief who comes in the night (Mt 24:43; Lk 12:39; 1 Thess 5:2, 4; 2 Pet 3:10; Rev 3:3; 16:15), the master who returns after a long *journey (Mk 13:34-36; Lk 12:35-38, 42-48) and the *bridegroom who arrives in the middle of the night (Mt 25:1-13). In Isaiah 43:19 the "new thing" that God is doing "springs forth" so quickly that God asks, "Do you not perceive it?" The visions of Revelation are an account of "what must soon take place" (Rev 1:1), and the final testimony from Christ in the book is, "Surely I am coming soon" (Rev 22:20).

Cataclysmic end. Apocalyptic visions typically include a stereotyped list of catastrophes that will precede final judgment. These include famine, earthquakes, wars, betrayal, plagues and signs in the heavens (e.g., Joel 2; Mk 13; Rev). Some writings also speak of the coming of a time of great tribulation (Dan 12:1; Mk 13:24; Rev 7:14), an unprecedented time of affliction numbered among the many woes that accompany the end. 2 Peter 3:10 summarizes this direction of thought with its statement that "the heavens will pass away with a loud noise, and the elements will be dissolved with fire, and the earth and the works that are upon it will be burned up" (RSV). While in this picture sudden cataclysm is the dominant motif, we should note in passing that the visions of Revelation present a complementary pattern of slow deterioration of the elements—gradual pollution of streams and the ocean, loss of vegetation, and intensifying heat.

The imagery of cataclysm tells us at least two things. First, it underscores the power of evil. Human agency will never be enough to overcome the forces of evil. Only God can do so, and he will do it decisively at the end of time. Second, this imagery emphasizes the need for faithful and holy living in the midst of affliction and in anticipation of the age of salvation.

Spiritual battle. Good and evil are engaged in a final combat to the death. Battle imagery is prominent—for example, Michael and his angels are fighting against the dragon (Rev 12:7). In apocalyptic realms, beasts arise from the sea to make war on the saints (Rev 13:1-10), the kings of the earth gather to make war against Christ (Rev 19:19) and Satan's hosts surround the camp of the saints (Rev 20:9). All of this battle imagery is unsettling, of course, but our anxiety as we read is kept in check by the consistency with which the forces of evil are finally punished for the havoc they have either threatened or achieved. The battle motif is resolved by the imagery of punishment for evil—the *winepress of the wrath of God (Rev 14:19-20), plagues visited on the followers of the beast (Rev 16:1-11), the burning of the harlot of Babylon (Rev 18:9-10), the throwing of Satan into the lake of fire (Rev 20:10).

Transformation of the cosmos. At the end, things will be reversed from what has prevailed in fallen history. There are two aspects to this reversal—the defeat of evil, and the triumph of the good. Jeremiah 4:23-28 portrays the "un-creation" of the world that reverses the creation story of Genesis 1. 2 Peter gives us a vision of complete dissolution followed by the assertion, "But according to his promise we wait for new heavens and a new earth in which righteousness dwells" (2 Pet 3:13 RSV). Revelation 21 uses similarly imagery, drawing explicit attention to the absence of death, mourning, crying and pain, "for the former things have passed away" (Rev 21:4; cf. Is 33:24; 65:20). In the new universe there will be no more *sea (Rev 21:1), a reference to the final triumph over evil and chaos, which is often pictured in the Bible as a sea *monster: the dragon (Job 7:12; Ps 74:13), Leviathan (Job 40:15-24; Ps 74:13-14; 104:26; Is 27:1), Rahab (Job 9:13; Ps 89:10; Is 51:9-11) and the serpent (Job 26:13; Is 27:1).

Divine provision in the new epoch of salvation. The apocalyptic vision is not all one of gloom and doom. Though apocalyptic visions may appear to be pessimistic, they actually move toward a vision of good triumphant. It is true that these visions offer little hope of recovery in the present age; but even in the tumultuous history of the world, God is working a redemptive purpose. Even more importantly, though, apocalyptic visions are emphatic that good will ultimately and completely defeat evil. Hence, they picture a new order in which all human needs are satisfied, including the longing for evil to be eradicated from human life. The "golden age" prophecies of the OT prophets (e.g., Is 60—66; Jer 30—33; Amos 9:11-15), as well as the interspersed visions of heavenly bliss in the book of Revelation, offer assurances at the level of imagery that all will be well and all manner of things will be well.

See also AFTERLIFE; ANTICHRIST; APOCALYPSE, GENRE OF; DAY, DAY OF THE LORD; END TIMES; MILLENNIUM; PROPHECY, GENRE OF; REVELATION, BOOK OF; SECOND COMING.

BIBLIOGRAPHY. D. E. Aune, "Apocalypticism," *DPL* 25-35; G. B. Caird, *The Language and Imagery of the Bible* (Grand Rapids: Eerdmans, 1997 [1980]); L. J. Kreitzer, "Apocalyptic, Apocalypticism," *DLNTD* 55-68.

APOSTASY

The images used to portray apostasy generally show a gradual and self-willed movement away from God. Such apostasy is pictured as a *seed planted on thorny ground and choked by *thorns (cares of the world, Lk 8:14), the heart hardened by the deceit of *sin

(Heb 3:12-15), "crucifying again the Son of God and holding him up to contempt" (Heb 6:6 NRSV) and having "spurned the Son of God, profaned the blood of the covenant . . . and outraged the Spirit of grace" (Heb 10:29). There are at least four distinct images in Scripture of the concept of apostasy. All connote an intentional defection from the faith. The four images are *rebellion, backsliding or turning away, falling away, and *adultery.

Rebellion. In classical literature *apostasia* was used to denote a coup or defection. By extension the LXX always uses it to portray a rebellion against God (Josh 22:22; 2 Chron 29:19). The defining image is the rebellion of *Satan ("adversary") against God. The picture is one of seemingly loyal followers turning against their leader. The thorny theological issues are not addressed by this image, which is content to portray seemingly loyal followers who, generally through a crisis, become rebels against God's reign. Paul predicted that a serious apostasy ("day of rebellion") would occur before the end of the age as a result of the *antichrist's work (2 Thess 2:3).

Turning away. Apostasy is also pictured as the heart turning away from God (Jer 17:5-6) and righteousness (Ezek 3:20). In the OT it centers on Israel's breaking covenant relationship with God through disobedience to the law (Jer 2:19), especially following other *gods (Judg 2:19) and practicing their immorality (Dan 9:9-11). Through the KJV the term *backsliding* (Jer 2:19, 5:6) has become a common phrase for certain forms of apostasy.

The image of backsliding should be powerful because following the Lord or journeying with him is one of the chief images of faithfulness in the Scriptures. Leaders are the ones that troops and disciples literally follow. Abigail referred to *David's troops as "the men who follow you" (1 Sam 25:27). In the image system of Scripture, what one follows reflects one's values. On the mundane level, when David was a shepherd, his routine was set by the *sheep so much that it can be said, "Now then, tell my servant David, 'This is what the LORD Almighty says: I took you from the pasture and from following the flock to be ruler over my people Israel' " (2 Sam 7:8 NIV).

In another context, Peter can allude to a path not taken. He declares, "We did not follow cleverly invented stories when we told you about the power and coming of our Lord Jesus" (2 Pet 1:16 NIV). The same Hebrew root *(swr)* is used to picture those who have turned away and ceased to follow God ("I am grieved that I have made Saul king, because he has turned away from me," 1 Sam 15:11) as well as those who repent ("But in their distress they turned to the LORD, the God of Israel, and sought him, and he was found by them," 2 Chron 15:4). The image of turning away from the Lord, who is the rightful leader, and following behind false gods is the dominant image for apostasy in the OT.

Falling. The image of falling, with the sense of going to eternal destruction, is particularly evident in the New Testament. Underlying this image is the association of falling with physical injury and disability (Prov 24:16; Jer 8:4) and with destruction when structures collapse as did the walls of Jericho (Josh 6:20) or the tent in the Midianite soldier's vision (Judg 7:13).

While slipping and falling are part of our universal human experience, their use in the NT was undoubtedly furthered by Jesus' effective use of this image. In his parable of the wise and foolish builders, in which the house built on sand falls with a crash in the midst of a *storm (Mt 7:24-27), and of the *blind leading the blind, in which both fall into a *pit (Lk 6:39), he painted a highly memorable image of the dangers of falling spiritually. The image of falling takes a different shape when Jesus is spoken of as "destined for the falling and the rising of many in Israel" (Lk 2:34 NRSV). Jesus speaks of himself as a *stone rejected by the builders that causes some to fall and break in pieces (Lk 20:18). The author to the Hebrews graphically describes the effects of falling away for those "who have once been enlightened, who have tasted the heavenly gift, who have shared in the Holy Spirit, who have tasted the goodness of the word of God and the powers of the coming age." They cannot be restored because they are "crucifying the Son of God all over again and subjecting him to public disgrace" (Heb 6:4-6 NIV).

Adultery. *Adultery is the most common concrete image for apostasy in the OT. Apostasy is symbolized as Israel the faithless spouse turning away from Yahweh her *marriage partner to pursue the advances of other gods (Jer 2:1-3; Ezek 16; *see* Prostitute). These images from Jeremiah and Ezekiel suggest how intensely God loves his people and how hurt he is by their betrayal: "Your children have forsaken me and sworn by gods that are not gods. I supplied all their needs, yet they committed adultery and thronged to the houses of prostitutes" (Jer 5:7 NIV). Adultery is used most often to graphically name the horror of the betrayal and covenant breaking involved in idolatry. Like literal adultery it does include the idea of someone blinded by infatuation, in this case for an *idol: "How I have been grieved by their adulterous hearts . . . which have lusted after their idols" (Ezek 6:9).

The association of idolatry and adultery is a powerful and multifaceted metaphor for the biblical writers, perhaps reflecting the ritual practices of Canaanite fertility religion. Idolatry, like an illicit love affair, could cause one to forget about important relationships: "[they] did not remember the LORD their God, who had rescued them from the hands of all their enemies on every side" (Judg 8:34). Israel's engagement with idolatry, particularly with Baal, elicits descriptions such as, "No sooner had Gideon died than the Israelites again prostituted themselves to the Baals" (Judg 8:33). The erotic appeal of Baal is conveyed in the Lord's word to Elijah: "Yet I reserve seven thousand in Israel—all whose knees have not bowed down to Baal and all whose mouths have not kissed him" (1 Kings 19:18). The idea of secrecy, which is a prominent aspect of sexual adultery, is alluded to in Job 31:27: "My heart was secretly enticed and my hand offered them [the sun and moon as deities] a kiss of homage." In general, idol worship was so brazen that this secretive element is not an explicit part of the imagery of adultery as apostasy.

Other images. Israel the apostate is pictured in a variety of other colorful images: a rebellious *ox, a *prostitute, a wild *vine, a stain that will not wash off, a camel in heat and a *thief caught in thievery (Jer 2:19-28). Images of peril accompany apostasy, for to have forsaken God is to be subject to his judgment (Ex 22:20; Deut 6:14-15; 17:2-7). The prophetic proclamation of Israel is basically a call to repent of apostasy or be destroyed by foreign powers.

The NT contains a host of images of apostasy, including a plant taking *root among the rocks but withering under the hot sun of testing (Mk 4:5-6, 17 par.), or those who fall prey to the wiles of false teachers (Mt 24:11), heretical beliefs (1 Tim 4:1; 2 Tim 4:3-4), worldliness and its defilement (2 Pet 2:20-22), and *persecution (Mt 24:9-10; Rev 3:8). The Christian apostate is pictured as a *branch that does not abide in the vine of Christ and thus withers and is cast into the fire (Jn 15:6). Animal behavior is evoked in a *dog returning to its vomit or a clean pig (*see* Swine) returning to the mire (2 Pet 2:22).

Jewish *apocalyptic contains the image of the great apostasy that precedes the coming of the Messiah (*1 Enoch* 93:9), which in Christian thought accompanies the antichrist or "man of lawlessness" and precedes the *second coming of Christ (2 Thess 2:3). It depicts the final and all-out attempt of rebellious evil to usurp the claims of God and gain the allegiance of humankind.

See also ADULTERY; PROSTITUTE, PROSTITUTION; REBELLION; SIN.

BIBLIOGRAPHY. I. H. Marshall, *Kept by the Power of God: A Study of Perseverance and Falling Away* (London: Epworth, 1969; repr., Minneapolis: Bethany Fellowship, 1975); M. Gundry-Volf, *Paul and Perseverance: Staying In and Falling Away* (Louisville, KY: Westminster John Knox, 1990).

APOSTLE. *See* AUTHORITY, HUMAN.

APPETITE

Spiritual *hunger and *thirst are recurring concepts in both the Old and New Testaments. Physical sensations associated with hunger and thirst are linked repeatedly with the felt need for spiritual resources, goodness or communion with God himself. The physical sensation of hunger is a natural figure for man's spiritual longing. As Alexander Schmemann writes, "In the biblical story of creation man is presented, first of all, as a hungry being, and the whole world as his food" (Schmemann, 11). And again, "Behind all the hunger of our life is God. All desire is finally for Him" (Schmemann, 14). *Food

and *eating images constitute a major motif of the Bible and help deliver one of its major themes: humanity lives in daily, hourly, dependence—both physical and spiritual—on God the providential Creator. So it is not surprising that appetite is an important figure as well.

From the beginning, people have failed to seek satisfaction in the right place; they have sought to satisfy spiritual hunger and thirst with literal food, sex, knowledge, wealth or political power of one kind or another. Spiritual appetite has one ultimate and proper object, God himself. The psalmist affirms God as the appetite's proper object in a fine, food-related image: "Taste and see that the LORD is good; blessed is the man that takes refuge in him" (Ps 34:8 NIV). Another familiar passage implicitly points to God as the proper object of spiritual appetite: "As the deer pants for streams of water, so my soul pants for you, O God. My soul thirsts for God, for the living God" (Ps 42:1-3 NIV). Two more examples will suffice to illustrate this image pattern: "For he satisfies the thirsty and fills the hungry with good things" (Ps 107:9 NIV); "I spread out my hands to you; my soul thirsts for you like a parched land" (Ps 143:6).

The most obvious improper object of spiritual appetite, not surprisingly, is literal food and drink in excess. When these objects are consumed intemperately, the behavior is called gluttony. While *Adam and *Eve's eating of the fruit of the knowledge of good and evil was an act of disobedience and pride, it was also an act of misdirected appetite. (The poet Milton saw the embodiment of all sins in Adam and Eve's act, including gluttony.) In the wilderness God provided *manna; however, "some of them paid no attention to Moses; they kept part of it until morning, but it was full of maggots and began to smell" (Ex 16:20 NIV). Interestingly, Jesus notes that the manna eaten in the wilderness was not the true *bread from heaven, but that rather he is the true bread, the proper object of spiritual appetite. Gluttony and *drunkenness are often linked as essentially the same sin (e.g., Deut 21:20; Prov 23:21).

Jesus explicitly warns against the displacement of the spiritual appetite by literal food, drink and worldly cares: "Be careful, or your *hearts* will be weighed down with dissipation, drunkenness and the anxieties of life, and that day will close on you unexpectedly like a trap" (Lk 21:34 NIV; emphasis added). With Jesus also comes the promise of living *water, an expression associated with both the indwelling Spirit and with general spiritual fulfillment. In the Sermon on the Mount we find the best-known hunger-and-thirst passage: "Blessed are those who hunger and thirst for righteousness, for they will be filled" (Mt 5:6; see also Lk 6:21). Jesus' use of water imagery related to thirst appears in John 4, 6, and 7. When the Samaritan woman marvels that he, a Jew, would ask her for water, he answers: "If you knew the gift of God and who it is that asks you for a drink, you would have asked him and he would have given you living water." And, "whoever drinks the water I give him will never thirst. Indeed, the water I give him will become in him a spring of water welling up to eternal life" (Jn 4:10, 14 NIV). But she, mistaking his meaning, expresses her hope that she will not have to come to the well anymore to draw.

In Capernaum, Jesus used similar images, declaring himself to be the bread of life to the crowd he miraculously fed the day before: "I am the bread of life. He who comes to me will never go hungry, and he who believes in me will never be thirsty" (Jn 6:35). And in Jerusalem, at the Feast of Tabernacles, "Jesus stood and said in a loud voice, 'If anyone is thirsty, let him come to me and drink. Whoever believes in me, as the Scripture has said, streams of living water will flow from within him.' By this he meant the Spirit, whom those who believed in him were later to receive. Up to that time the Spirit had not been given, since Jesus had not yet been glorified" (Jn 7:37-9). Clearly the image of living water is associated with the indwelling Spirit's work in the life of the God-hungry, God-sustained individual—the spiritual, as opposed to the carnal, being. Jesus' imagery echoes several OT passages and anticipates the images of his revelation to John: "The words of man's mouth are as deep waters, and the wellspring of wisdom as a flowing brook" (Prov 18:4 KJV; see also Ps 36:9; Is 12:3; Jer 2:13). In Revelation 7:16-17 we are reminded of the shepherd of Psalm 23, leading his flock beside the still waters: Never again will they hunger; never again will they thirst. The sun will not beat upon them, nor any scorching heat. For the Lamb at the center of the throne will be their shepherd; he will lead them to springs of living water. And God will wipe away every tear from their eyes (NIV). In this neat reversal the *Lamb leads the saved to "living fountains of waters." Finally, at the close of Revelation, we read: "The Spirit and the bride say, 'Come!' And let him who hears say, 'Come!' Whoever is thirsty, let him come; and whoever wishes, let him take the free gift of the water of life" (Rev 22:17 NIV).

In addition to directing the heart's appetite toward its true object, Jesus clearly states that the mind and body's uncontrolled appetites are enemies to spiritual growth: "The worries of this life, the deceitfulness of wealth and the desires for other things come in and choke the word, making it unfruitful" (Mk 4:19 NIV). Paul and Peter each insist on personal discipline regarding the appetites: "Let us behave decently, as in the daytime, not in orgies and drunkenness, not in sexual immorality and debauchery, not in dissension and jealousy. Rather, clothe yourselves with the Lord Jesus Christ, and do not think about how to gratify the desires of the sinful nature" (Rom 13:13 NIV). "For you have spent enough time in the past doing what pagans choose to do— living in debauchery, lust, drunkenness, orgies, carousing and detestable idolatry" (1 Pet 4:3).

In summary, as portrayed in the Bible, people are creatures of appetite. They were created as such by God. On a physical level, appetite itself is good, and one of the things that makes the *Song of Songs so refreshing is that the voice of satisfied appetite is strong (Song 2:3; 4:16; 5:1). But the attempt to find satisfaction on a purely earthly and physical level is futile, as the book of *Ecclesiastes shows with its repeated pictures of unsatisfied appetite (see especially Eccl 6:7, with its assertion that "all the labor of man is for his mouth, and yet the appetite is not filled" KJV). Human appetite is ultimately filled by God—by tasting and seeing that the Lord is good— and the person who trusts in God is blessed (Ps 34:8).

See also DRINK; DRUNKENNESS; EATING; FOOD.

BIBLIOGRAPHY. A. Schmemann, *For the Life of the World: Sacraments and Orthodoxy* (Crestwood, NY: St. Vladimir's University Press, 1973).

APSU. *See* COSMOLOGY.

ARCHANGEL. *See* ANGEL.

ARCHERY

The use of the bow and *arrow, for which there is evidence from 1900 B.C., is referred to from Genesis (21:20, 27:3) to Revelation (6:2). Although occasionally mentioned in reference to *hunting or in harmless activities, it is primarily viewed as an effective *weapon of *war and instrument of execution (Gen 48:22; 1 Sam 31:3; 2 Sam 11:24; 2 Kings 9:24; 2 Chron 35:23). Archers were foremost in the heat of the battle. It is the sense of its penetrating and deadly accuracy that lies behind its imagery. Archers were part of the warfare of ancient Israel, but most of the archers mentioned in the Bible are from foreign armies. Archers killed Uriah the Hititte (2 Sam 11:24); a Syrian archer killed Ahab (1 Kings 22:34); Egyptian archers killed Josiah (2 Chron 24:23).

Job complained that his suffering made him feel that God was using him for target practice. He felt cornered by God's archers and vividly describes being stalked and pitilessly attacked: "His archers surround me. Without pity, he pierces my kidneys and spills my gall on the ground" (Job 16:13 NIV; cf. 7:20; 16:12). This complaint was echoed by Jeremiah in Lamentations (2:4; 3:12-13). Habakkuk (3:9) similarly resorted to the image of archery as a symbol of God's anger. The unleashing of skilled archers to attack *Babylon without restraint is also said to be the means by which God would mete out his judgment on her for her wickedness (Jer 50:9, 14, 29; cf. 51:3). The ability of an arrow to find a chink in one's armor and thereby deliver the judgment of God (e.g., Ahab in 1 Kings 22) makes the arrow and archer a symbol for the vulnerability of all humans, no matter how powerful or protected, and the inevitability of God's judgment.

The piercing destructiveness of the arrow becomes a fitting picture of other destructive elements, from the conspiratorial or deceptive tongue on the personal level (Ps 64:3; Jer 9:8) to the onset of famine on a national level (Ezek 5:16). In the NT Paul adopts the imagery of arrows with heads set on fire to warn believers of the attacks of the devil and to encourage them to seek protection by taking up the *shield of faith (Eph 6:16).

Consistent with its military usage, peace is symbolized by broken bows and the removal of bows and arrows (Ps 46:9; Hos 2:18; Zech 9:10). On one occasion, Hosea 1:5, the broken bow is used less happily to signal Israel's defeat. Bows can fail, and God's people are encouraged not to substitute their trust in him for trust in the bow (Ps 44:6-7; Hos 1:7). The image of the faulty bow is also developed differently as a picture of unreliable people in whom God cannot place his trust (Ps 78:57; Hos 7:16).

Archery is also used as the basis for more positive images. Psalm 18, a song of victory that celebrates a warrior's victory on the battlefield, paints a vivid picture of the skill and muscular strength required in an archer's hands and arms to wield a bow (v. 34), attributing the training in that skill to God. The psalms also compare the blessing of many sons to the happiness of an archer having a quiver full of arrows (127:3-5). This passage may also indicate that the archer had become a symbol not only for skill and terror but for of virility and manliness.

Isaiah speaks of the servant of the Lord as made into a "polished arrow" and concealed in God's quiver (49:2). As such the servant, free from unevenness or roughness that might deflect the flight, will accurately penetrate the distant target by being a light to the Gentiles. But the servant would be protected until the time was right for advance (Is 49:1-7).

One point popularly made by preachers does not work on closer examination. "Falling short of the glory of God" (Rom 3:23) is often spoken of as missing the mark, that is, failing to hit the target, let alone the bull's- eye, or the arrow dropping short. But *hystereo,* the word Paul uses here, simply means "absent" or "lacking."

See also ARMOR; ARROW, ARROW OF GOD; DIVINE WARRIOR; HUNTING; SHIELD; WEAPONS, HUMAN AND DIVINE.

ARK

The Bible tells about two arks—the ark of Noah and the ark of *Moses. While the building of Noah's ark was no doubt a prophetic sign and warning to neighbors who saw its gradual erection, the primary meaning of both of thesse arks in the Bible is preservation and rescue.

The ark that Noah builds (Gen 6–8) is a huge construction, symbolic of the magnitude of the task God entrusted to the one person of virtue in this day, "a righteous man, blameless in his generation" (Gen 6:9, RSV). The ark was approximately 450 feet long and 75 feet wide and was divided into three stories of about 15 feet each. An image not only of magnitude but also of sturdiness and careful planning, the ark was made of gopher wood covered inside with waterproof pitch and was divided into separate rooms. By the time

we add a roof and a window to the structure, it emerges in our imagination as a floating home, a place of safety for the remnant of the human race and the animal kingdom that survived the *flood. The ark singles out its inhabitants as special, the lone survivors of their respective species.

Above all, this ark represents the preservation and rebirth of human life. It preserves life from death as God sends a *flood that undoes his creative work in an act of judgment against sinful humanity (Gen 6:5-7). In contrast to the destruction of the world outside the ark, "God remembered Noah and all the beasts and all the cattle that were with him in the ark" (Gen 8:1). Here the ark is the object of God's mercy toward his creation. Associations of rebirth are indelibly part of our experience of ark through the image of the olive leaf that the *dove finally brings back to the ark as the waters subside. Noah steps out of the ark as a second *Adam, witnessing a new beginning, as Genesis 9:1 repeats the language of the original creation story: "Be fruitful and multiply, and fill the earth" (cf. also Gen 9:2-3).

There is also a second, lesser-known ark in the OT in the story of the preservation of the infant Moses as he is entrusted to the Nile River (Ex 2:1-3). The word usually translated as "basket" is actually the same word as is translated as "ark" in the story of Noah. The word for ark, *tē bâ,* appears in the Hebrew Bible only in these two places; and in both, the person the ark is to serve is similarly indicated (*lᵉkâ,* "for yourself"; *lô,* "for him"). As the rabbis recognized (cf. *Exod. Rab.* 1:20), Moses is a second Noah, who stands at another beginning (cf. Ex 1:7 and Gen 1:28, and note that according to Ex 2:2, when Moses was born, his mother "saw that he was a goodly child," words that recall the refrain of Gen 1). As Noah, the savior of all living things, is preserved upon the waters in an ark, so it is with Moses, the savior of Israel.

The discussion of Jesus' death in 1 Peter 3:18-22 refers to Noah's ark as the author discerns a parallel with baptism: the church borne to safety by baptism recalls Noah's family on the ark, snatching life from certain death through God's rescue of them. The comparison is especially apt, for as in both Genesis and Exodus the ark is associated with creation imagery, Christians have always thought of baptism as being a new creation.

See also ARK OF THE COVENANT; FLOOD; MOSES.

ARK OF THE COVENANT

The ark of the covenant was a wooden box, covered with *gold and fitted with rings through which carrying rods could be placed. The wood was expensive acacia wood, and the gold, of course, was precious. But the physical size of the ark was not impressive, being only about three and three-quarters feet long and two and one-quarter feet wide and high (see Ex 25:10-22).

The functional purpose of the ark was as a simple container for holy objects. The various names of the ark, "ark of the covenant" (e.g., Josh 3:11) and "ark of the testimony" (e.g., Ex 25:16), are references to the fact that the tablets containing the Ten Commandments were placed inside it (Deut 10:1-5). Other notable items included in the ark were a sample of the *manna of the wilderness and Aaron's budding staff (see Heb 9:4-5; *see* Aaron's Rod).

Though small, this box-like container was one of the most potent images of God's presence during the early OT period. The materials used (acacia wood and pure gold) were also used in the construction of the *tabernacle, God's symbolic home on earth. Indeed, the ark was an integral part of the tabernacle structure and was normally kept in the most holy place (Ex 40:3).

In the tabernacle the ark was understood to be the *throne or the footstool to the throne of God (2 Kings 19:15). Above the ark were placed two cherubim with outstretched wings and downcast eyes. God was envisioned as enthroned on the *wings. The ark was the symbol of God's very presence on earth.

Being small and provided with carrying poles, the ark was mobile. Thus the ark served two important purposes during the history of early Israel. During the *wilderness *wanderings, when the people of God were on the march, the tabernacle was packed away and the ark led the way, representing God's leadership of the tribes as they made their way toward the *land of promise (Num 10:35-36). This use of the ark is closely tied with the second purpose. The ark was often taken by the army as it engaged in battle with foreign foes. It represented the presence of the *divine warrior with the army. The famous battle of Jericho is one of the more notable examples of the ark symbolizing God's presence and power with the army of Israel (Josh 6).

The ark is rarely mentioned in the literature of later Israel, leading to speculation that the original ark was captured or destroyed sometime soon after Solomon's reign (possibly during Shishak's invasion, cf. 1 Kings 14:25-29). However, the ark appears twice in the NT. In Hebrews 9:4-5 the ark is mentioned in a description of the OT cult, which is marvelously replaced by Jesus Christ who fulfills it. We no longer need a tabernacle or ark because Jesus Christ "tabernacles" among us (Jn 1:14) and is the very presence of God. In Revelation 11:15-19 the events surrounding the blowing of the seventh trumpet are given. This is the time for the "judging of the dead" (v. 18). At the climactic moment God's heavenly temple appears, and within it is seen the ark of the covenant, God's mobile battle standard. This vision is accompanied by convulsions of nature associated with the appearance of the divine warrior.

See also DIVINE WARRIOR; TABERNACLE.

BIBLIOGRAPHY. C. L. Seow, "Ark of the Covenant," *ABD* 1:386-93; M. H. Woudstra, *The Ark of the Covenant from Conquest to Kingship* (Phillipsburg, NJ: Presbyterian and Reformed, 1965).

ARM

Both the arm and the *hand are biblical images of power. Typically such images suggest power toward a purpose, although the agent may be either divine or human. For example, the psalmist praises the Lord, whose "arm is endued with power" (Ps 89:13 NIV); but elsewhere he pleads with God to "break the arm of the wicked and evil man" (Ps 10:15) who preys upon the weak. Depending on context the images of the arm or hand can represent power in action, either good or evil.

Dominating all else is the epithet "outstretched arm" (nearly twenty references, e.g., Ex 6:6 and 15:16; Deut 4:34). Whenever this formulaic phrase appears, it is always in reference to the power of God. This image can apply to God's power in creation, in the deliverance of his people or in his judgment.

In Jeremiah such imagery carries the theme of God as Creator. It is "by great power and outstretched arm" (Jer 32:17) that the Lord creates the heavens and the earth; when God speaks to the nations surrounding Israel, he uses the same image to describe his creation of the earth and its creatures (Jer 27:5).

In Deuteronomy the outstretched arm of God appears repeatedly as an image of God's power to redeem Israel from slavery in Egypt. Here the image is especially vivid: God stretches forth his arm, reaching his people where they are and saving them from their distress. Such an event is a unique attestation of God's power; nothing like it has ever been seen before (Deut 4:34). In reference to God's deliverance of Israel, Moses describes God's "mighty hand and outstretched arm" in a synonymous parallel "with great terror and with miraculous signs and wonders" (Deut 26:8). Israel's deliverance and all the miraculous events accompanying it are contained in the image of God's outstretched arm.

But God's outstretched arm also functions as a picture of divine judgment. In response to Israel's idolatry, God allows the Babylonians to take Jerusalem, proclaiming, "I myself will fight against you with an outstretched hand and a mighty arm in anger and fury and great wrath" (Jer 21:5). The image is powerfully ironic: the very power of God that brought Israel into being is now allied with Babylon toward her defeat.

Isaiah is the most creative with the image of God's arm. Although never using the expression *outstretched arm*, Isaiah speaks of God's arm in fourteen different contexts. Clearly reflecting on the arm of the Lord as God's power to deliver in the *exodus, Isaiah looks ahead to show that the same arm will bring God's people out a second time, in a new exodus, from the *exile they have experienced among the nations.

One of the more comforting images in the Bible is that communicated by the symbolic use of the plural *arms:* God carrying his people. The *divine warrior, whose arm so threatens his enemy, joins his arms together to carry his people: "The eternal God is your refuge, and underneath are the everlasting arms" (Deut 33:27). Isaiah 40:11 pictures God as a *shepherd, leading his flock and carrying the lambs in his arms.

The arm image is used only twice in the NT. Both occurrences are in the Gospels (Lk 1:51 and Jn 12:38 [Is 53:1]), and both quote or allude directly to an OT passage. John 12:38 links the miracles of Jesus to the arm of the Lord precisely in the way the book of Deuteronomy linked God's miracles to the action of his arm. Though the NT never explicitly links them, it was the same arm that stretched out to deliver Israel from bondage in Egypt that was outstretched on the *cross to deliver believers from bondage to death.

See also HAND; FINGER; STRENGTH, STRONG.

ARMIES OF HEAVEN. *See* HEAVENLY ARMIES/HOST.

ARMOR

In ancient warfare a soldier's body was vulnerable at many points to fatal or disabling wounds, whether by piercing *arrow, thrusting *sword or swinging battle ax. Field warfare and hand-to-hand combat required a maximum of protection without compromising mobility and agility. For the period of roughly two thousand years, stretching from Abraham to Paul, two pieces of armor were well known in the biblical world: the helmet and the *shield. The breastplate was common in the Greco-Roman period, though a type of scaled armor was in use by the middle of the second millennium B.C. Greaves, or shin guards, were used by some armies and warriors. In the OT we find many references to armor in narrative accounts of Israel's history as well as an abundance of armor imagery. Most notably armor serves as a metaphor for God's protection of the righteous. 2 Chronicles 26:14 (cf. Jer 46:4) indicates that a helmet, along with a shield and coat of armor, was a regular part of a soldier's outfit during the period of Israel's kings.

Armor as Image. Putting on armor symbolizes preparation for war and its hazards (Jer 46:4), against which even armor is no sure protection. Thus in 1 Kings 20:11 the king of Israel sends a message to his confident enemy, "One who puts on his armor should not boast like one who takes it off." The proof of a warrior's prowess is in his successful return from battle. In 1 Kings 22 Ahab, the king of Israel, attempts to *cheat the prophet who has prophesied his death in battle. As he battled in disguise, "someone drew his bow at random and hit the king of Israel between the sections of his armor" (1 Kings 22:34 NIV). God's judgment is sure and finds gaps in human armor as surely as it exposes gaps in a theology of defiance.

The most striking biblical picture of an armored warrior is Goliath, the monstrously intimidating Philistine champion of war: "He was over nine feet tall. He had a bronze helmet on his head and wore a coat of scale armor of bronze weighing five thousand shekels; on his legs he wore bronze greaves, and a bronze javelin was slung on his back" (1 Sam 17:5-6 NIV). Goliath's challenger, the young David, stands before him, vulnerably clad in the thin clothing of a shepherd and carrying a slingshot. David has tried on king Saul's armor (Israel's champion of war who has fearfully retired to his camp) but found it ill fitting, clumsy and not suited for the task at hand. The story of David's unarmored victory over Goliath forms a vivid image of the biblical theme of power in *weakness, of faith exercised in the face of insurmountable odds, of divine protection and victory given to one who, in contrast with Saul, utterly trusts in God's deliverance (cf. 1 Sam 17:37).

The armor of a defeated warrior symbolizes *shame for the vanquished and *honor for the victor. David takes Goliath's weapons into his own tent, and his sword will be held as a treasure in the sanctuary at Nob (1 Sam 21:9). When the Philistines found the body of Saul on the battlefield, they "put his armor in the temple of the Ashtoreths and fastened his body to the wall of Beth Shan" (1 Sam 31:10). The public display of Saul's unarmored body reinforces the shame of defeat, and the armor placed in the temple is a trophy of the gods, a symbol of their victory over Israel and, so they think, over Israel's God. The "anointed" instrument of God, Cyrus, will "subdue nations before him" and "strip kings of their armor" (Is 45:1). And in Luke's version of Jesus' parable of binding the strong man, a stronger one attacks, overpowers him, and "takes away the armor in which the man trusted and divides up the spoils" (Lk 11:22 NIV). Jesus is the "stronger one," who is defeating Satan and stripping Satan's armor (cf. Is 49:24-26). The imagery of stripping a spiritual enemy of weapons and armor may lie behind Colossians 2:15, where some interpreters see Christ disarming the powers and authorities in his death on the cross (see commentaries for the disputed sense of *apekdysamenos* in Col 2:15). Jesus, the *naked, shamed, unarmed and unarmored warrior on the cross is the real victor over the vaunted powers of this age.

Christians are to follow their victorious Christ by putting on spiritual armor and engaging in the battle where power is found in weakness, victory in Christian virtues and the armaments of faith. Christ's death and resurrection has placed his followers at the turning point of the ages: "The night is nearly over; the day is almost here. So let us put aside the deeds of darkness and put on the armor of light" (Rom 13:12 NIV). The crucial battle in the warfare against *Satan has been won and his fate determined, but the war continues. Paul urges the church, the army of Christ, to "put on the full armor of God so that you can take your stand against the devil's schemes" (Eph 6:11, 13; cf. 1 Thess 5:8). The helmet, shield and breastplate, or scaled armor, form a panoply of spiritual armor calling for individual attention.

Helmet. The *head is the first point of bodily protection in battle. A blow that would be merely painful or partially disabling to another portion of the body, when taken in the head can leave a soldier unconscious, permanently disabled or dead. The helmet was usually, and ideally, made of metal, though it could also be constructed of leather. We read that Goliath and King Saul had helmets of bronze (1 Sam 17:5; 17:38). Paul speaks of the Christian helmet as the "hope of salvation" (1 Thess 5:8) or simply *"salvation" (Eph 6:17). Here he borrows the image of Isaiah 59:17, where God, the *divine warrior, dresses himself for battle and puts the "helmet of salvation on his head" (cf. "Impartial justice as a helmet" in Wis 5:18). From Paul's standpoint the climactic divine victory of salvation has been won and its reality, or sure "hope" of its final outcome, are the primary protection for the church as it carries out its life in the midst of the conflicts of this age.

Shield. The shield is a portable and maneuverable protection device capable of absorbing the impact of an enemy's weapons, whether they are wielded by hand or launched through the air. Behind a shield, a person is protected from the aimed assault of an enemy. The deadliest arrow is absorbed, the fiercest blow deflected, and the shielded soldier is enabled to advance against the enemy or quickly return a fatal wound.

Shields were a framework of wood, wicker or metal covered with thick leather. They were generally two types (cf. Jer 46:3): the smaller shield (variously shaped) used to defend against the sword, spear and battle ax, and the large shield (which reached from the ground to a man's chin) used to protect a soldier while besieging a city (cf. Is 37:33; Ezek 26:8). In the OT we read of shield bearers, trusted soldiers who would carry and position the shield for a king or mighty warrior (Goliath, 1 Sam 17:7, 41), defending him, for example, while he fired arrows at the enemy.

The shield was so basic to a soldier's outfit that "shield and spear" or "shield and sword" symbolized a warrior trained and ready for battle (Judg 5:8; 1 Chron 5:18; 12:8, 24), and the image of uncovering the shield signified preparation for battle (Is 22:6; cf. Jer 51:11). Nahum portrays the fearsome armor of the army of the Lord marshaled against Nineveh: "The shields of his soldiers are red; the warriors are clad in scarlet" (Nahum 2:3).

The image of a shield is frequently used in the OT to speak of God's protection from an enemy. In some cases the image is used in parallel with the image of God as a *"rock": "my God is my rock, in whom I take *refuge, my shield and the horn of my salvation." (2 Sam 22:3 NIV; par. Ps 18:2; cf. 2 Sam 22:31; Ps 18:30). The circumstances of life often lend themselves to battlefield imagery. In the face of his enemies the psalmist confesses, "you are a shield around me, O LORD" (Ps 3:3 NIV) or "The LORD is my strength and my shield; my heart trusts in him, and I am helped." (Ps 28:7; cf. Ps 7:10; 91:4). This sense of protection is joined with God's favor, blessing and help in time of need (cf. Ps 5:12; 7:10;

33:20). The image of the Lord as a "help and shield," a symbol of Israel's trust, is thrice repeated in Psalm 115:9-11, and "refuge" and "shield" are aligned in Psalm 119:114. In Proverbs the seemingly abstract notion that "every word of God is flawless" is set side by side with the militaristic image of God as "a shield to those who take refuge in him" (Prov 30:5), thus leading us to consider the ways in which God's words offer protection amidst the assaults of life.

*Jerusalem, a city laden with symbolic value in the Bible, is the focus of images of divine destruction and of protection. Isaiah presents an image of divine protection of the city: "Like birds hovering overhead, the LORD Almighty will shield Jerusalem; he will shield it and deliver it, he will 'pass over' it and will rescue it (Is 31:5 NIV). And Zechariah

A warrior with helmet, shield, breastplate and greaves.

molds the shield into an eschatological image in speaking of the *day when the Lord will "shield those who live in Jerusalem" (Zech 12:8), and under his protection "the feeblest among them will be like David, and the house of David will be like God" (Zech 12:8 NIV).

Closely associated with the idea of protection is the biblical motif of God as a divine warrior. In some instances the shield or a weapon can evoke the broader motif of the divine warrior: "Blessed are you, O Israel! Who is like you, a people saved by the LORD? He is your shield and helper and your glorious sword. (Deut 33:29 NIV).

> Contend, O LORD, with those who contend
> with me;
> fight against those who fight against me.
> Take up shield and buckler;
> arise and come to my aid.
> Brandish spear and javelin
> against those who pursue me.
> (Ps 35:1-2 NIV; see Ps 140:7; Zech 9:15)

In Psalm 144:2 the imagery of divine warrior and shield are placed in parallel with *fortress/stronghold imagery:

> He is my loving God and my fortress,
> my stronghold and my deliverer,
> my shield, in whom I take refuge,

who subdues peoples under me. (Ps 144:2 NIV) It is as if the biblical motif of the divine warrior follows a trajectory leading to the universal establishment of the *kingdom of God and of peace. The psalmist glimpses this goal and speaks of God making wars to cease, breaking the bow, shattering the spear and burning shields with fire (Ps 46:9; cf. 76:3).

Although the shield can speak plainly of protection, in some instances it evokes divine favor. When God speaks to Abram after his routing a coalition of kings, we hear reassuring words:

Do not be afraid, Abram.

I am your shield,

your very great reward (Gen 15:1 NIV).

God is Abram's defender, and Abram, who took no spoils from battle, is assured that God's special favor is his *reward.

We sometimes find the shield symbolizing the *glory of a warrior. In the case of Saul's tragic death in battle, "the shield of the mighty was defiled, the shield of Saul—no longer rubbed with oil" (2 Sam 1:21 NIV). The *oil may refer to the warrior's preparing his shield for battle (cf. Is 21:5), both to enhance its beauty and its deflective power. But this is an instance of metonymy, where the shield is an image of Saul: Saul was defiled by death in battle and no longer the anointed one of Israel. The metonymy of shield and king appears also in the psalms. When the psalmist asks God to "Look upon our shield, . . . look with favor on your anointed one" (Ps 84:9), he has in mind the king of Israel. This meaning is more transparent in Psalm 89:18: "Indeed, our shield belongs to the LORD, our king to the Holy One of Israel" (NIV). The metonymy of shield and royalty was a natural one, evoking not only the king's responsibility to protect his people but also the theme of the king as warrior, "commander in chief" of Israel's army.

The parallel images of "sun and shield" attributed to God in Psalm 84:11 might be a biblical echo of the solar disk imagery found in some ancient Near Eastern religions, with the circular shape of the *sun, an image of power and protection, joined with an image of warfare, a circular shield.

The description of the woman in Song of Songs 4:4 provides a striking instance of shield imagery:

Your neck is like the tower of David,

built with elegance;

on it hang a thousand shields,

all of them shields of warriors. (Song 4:4 NIV)

The familiar joining of fortress and shield imagery in this case suggests the woman's regal beauty and inaccessibility to all but her lover. Behind the image of "a thousand shields" may lie a "literal" picture of layers of beaded necklace worn around the woman's neck. The image of shields hung on fortress walls is also found in Ezekiel 27:10-11, where the shields and helmets of Tyre's mercenary soldiers are depicted as hanging on the city's walls and are said to bring Tyre's "beauty to perfection" (NIV).

The potent symbolism of the shield is evident

when we read of the two hundred large shields of hammered gold and three hundred small shields of hammered gold that were created for Solomon (1 Kings 10:16-17; 2 Chron 9:15-16). These were ceremonial shields, used perhaps on ceremonial occasions, but otherwise hung within Solomon's Palace of the Forest of *Lebanon. Though we may not understand their full significance, they surely evoke the impregnable splendor and strength of the Solomonic empire. The fate of these shields provides commentary on national decline: the gold shields of Solomon were looted by King Shishak of Egypt, and then replaced by Rehoboam with bronze shields (1 Kings 14:26-27).

Perhaps the best known instance of shield imagery is in Ephesians 6:16: "take up the shield of faith, with which you can extinguish all the flaming arrows of the evil one." Here we find various strands of OT shield imagery converging (as well as Wis 5:19, where God is depicted as taking "holiness as an invincible shield" [NRSV]). Faith in God, now focused in his saving work in Christ, protects believers from the chief of all enemies, "the evil one," or *"Satan." In the field of spiritual warfare, faith in the Divine Warrior who has defeated Satan in a climactic victory at the cross and resurrection will offer protection from Satan's flaming missiles. Like soldiers, the church must prepare for battle by "taking up" the *thyron*, the word for a large shield covered with thick leather and extensive enough to protect the entire body. Its spiritual ability to extinguish flaming arrows may be based on the properties and preparation of actual shields or simply refer to the supernatural quality of the shield of faith. A living faith in the God and Father of our Lord Jesus Christ is a sure protection from the assaults of the Evil One in the most vital warfare of all.

Breastplate or Scaled Armor. Armor covering the warrior's thorax, abdomen and back would protect his vital organs from deadly wounds. Scaled armor, consisting of small, interlocking rings of metal or metal "scales" bound together by thongs appears to have been in use in the ancient Near East from the middle of the second millennium B.C. Another type of protection was a thick leather jacket. We do not find many instances where this category of armor is mentioned in the Bible, though its use by "professional" warriors seems to be broadly assumed. Goliath and Saul, both notable warriors, have coats of armor (1 Sam 17:5, 38). King Uzziah provides his entire army with coats of armor along with shields, spears, helmets, bows and slingstones (2 Chron 26:14). We have already seen that this armor was not invincible, for the random Aramean arrow found the gap in Ahab's no doubt carefully constructed armor (1 Kings 22:34; 2 Chron 18:33), apparently piercing between his breastplate and scaled armor.

The prophet Isaiah fashions the breastplate into an image as he envisions God as a warrior who puts on "righteousness as his breastplate" (Is 59:17; cf.

Wis 5:18). Ephesians 6:14 carries forward this image, crafting the breastplace of righteousness into a piece of armor for the church. The Isaiah passage is clearly in view, and so the armor of righteousness is received from God ("the full armor of God") but "put on" by the church for conflict in "the evil day," both in the present moment and in the final assault of the Evil One. In 1 Thessalonians 5:8, however, the Christian virtues of faith, hope and love are in view, with "faith and love" put on as a breastplate, along with the "hope of salvation" as a helmet (cf. Is 59:17). Faith and love in the lives of the "sons of light" not only serve to build up the community but form a vital protective armor in a world of darkness. The early history of loving and faith-filled Christian communities in the midst of pagan society was to demonstrate the truth of this imagery.

See also DIVINE WARRIOR; ENEMY; SHIELD; WEAPONS, HUMAN AND DIVINE.

ARMY, ARMIES

The vast majority of the nearly three hundred uses of the word *army* in the Bible refer to a literal, physical army, either of Israel or of Israel's enemies. But a network of powerful images gathers around these literal references.

The starting point is Exodus 15:3, where the Lord is described as a *warrior (literally, "man of war"). As a warrior the Lord has just defeated the armies of Pharaoh by drowning them in the Red Sea, while Israel stood and watched. This conception of God as a God who fights is something that Israel had in common with her neighbors, who all had lively traditions of "holy war." The essence of holy war ideology was the close association between earthly and heavenly forces—an association often made clear literally by taking the gods into battle. When the *ark of the covenant arrived in the camp of Israel's army, the Philistines were terrified: "Who will deliver us from the hand of these mighty gods? They are the gods who struck the Egyptians with all kinds of plagues in the desert. Be strong, Philistines!" (1 Sam 4:8-9 NIV).

This story reveals that the OT does not adopt holy war ideology uncritically. The presence of the ark did not protect Israel, and it was captured amid wholesale slaughter. On the other hand, the Israelites learned to expect that the Lord would fight their battles for them, so three times in the Psalms we meet the lament, "the Lord no longer goes out with our armies" (Ps 44:9; 60:10; 108:11). Such experiences produced heart searching: For what sin was God punishing the people by his absence from the battlefield (cf. Josh 7; 1 Sam 3:11-14)? But even these psalms express the confident expectation that "through you we push back our enemies; through your name we trample our foes" (Ps 44:5; cf. 60:12; 108:13).

The armies of Israel, therefore, were literally "the armies of the living God" (1 Sam 17:36); so that when Goliath taunted the Israelite army, he actually "defied the armies of the living God" (1 Sam 17:45; cf. 2 Sam 1:12). This is why the armies of Israel could

be the direct agents of God's punishment (e.g., 1 Sam 15:3).

Further dimensions of this identification are revealed by the title "Lord of Hosts." This title is used some 267 times in the OT, and its military connotations are well revealed by David's words to Goliath: "I come against you in the name of the LORD of hosts, the God of the armies of Israel"(1 Sam 17:45). The word *hosts (ṣᵉbāʾôt)* is the plural form of a common word for "army" (e.g., Judg 8:6; 9:29; Ps 44:9; 60:10; 108:11), so "God of armies" would not be an inappropriate translation. In the exchange between David and Goliath, these hosts are clearly the armies of Israel. But this is not so clear in Joshua 5:13-15, when the angelic "commander of the LORD's host" appears to Joshua. Since Joshua himself is the commander of the literal army, which host does this angel command?

The answer is not hard to find. When Deborah and Barak celebrate their famous victory over Sisera, they sing that "from heaven the stars fought, from their courses they fought against Sisera" (Judg 5:20). They believed that another army had fought alongside theirs—an army that caused a massive downpour (5:21) so that Sisera lost his strategic military advantage, the use of his chariots (4:15). In calling this hidden army "the stars," they are employing one of the conventional ancient identifications of this hidden angelic host (*see* Heavenly Armies/Host). We encounter this host also in 1 Kings 22:19 (notice that military strategy is being discussed) in Deuteronomy 32:8 (where they are called "sons of God"), in Psalm 82 (where they are called "gods" and "sons of the Most High"), in Job 38:7 (where they are "sons of God" and "morning stars") and of course in Luke 2:13 (where they are "a great company of the heavenly host"). In Isaiah 37:36 it is the singular "angel of the LORD" who fights. This army of God encamps around Elisha in 2 Kings 6:17 (cf. Ps 34:7) and marches audibly into battle ahead of David in 1 Chronicles 14:15 (cf. Ezek 1:24).

The reason it was so wrong for David to take a census of Israel's fighting capacity (2 Sam 24, 1 Chron 21) was probably that it faithlessly ignored the vital presence of this heavenly force, which could not be counted. The ideal battles are those where the human forces are minimal so that it is obvious that "the battle is the LORD's!" (1 Sam 17:47; 2 Chron 20:15; cf. Judg 7; 1 Sam 14:1-14), for it is the Lord alone who is "mighty in battle" (Ps 24:8). The prophets were charged with the awful responsibility of announcing to Israel that the Lord had changed sides and was using the armies of other nations as his own army against Israel (Is 10:5-19; Jer 1:14-16; Hab 1:5-11; Joel 2:1-11).

The OT therefore leaves us with a clear perspective on the ontology of armed force in human society: it only exercises destructive or dominating power insofar as that power is given to it and is actually exerted by the Lord and his hosts. It is God who overthrows or establishes kingdoms (Amos 9:7; Jer 1:10; Is 13:4, 19; Dan 4:25), using human armies if he wills, but not dependent on them. This interaction between divine and human power is especially clear in Daniel and forms the essential background to Jesus' proclamation of the kingdom of God.

Fed by this OT perspective, Jesus' hearers would inevitably have ascribed direct political significance to his message. In Daniel the *kingdom of God means the violent overthrow of earthly kingdoms (e.g., Dan 2:44; 7:23-27). So it is highly significant that the "heavenly host" in Luke 2:14 announces peace on earth, that Jesus consistently resists the use of force as a sign of the kingdom (e.g,. Mt 10:7-10, cf. Lk 22:49-51) and that military imagery is not used extensively of the church in the NT. Victorian hymn writers and missionaries loved to picture the church marching into battle with banners waving, but this is unlike Paul. Only once does he pictures discipleship as warfare, and there he explicitly safeguards the metaphor from misunderstanding: "we do not wage war as the world does" (2 Cor 10:3-5).

But this does not mean that the OT understanding of human and heavenly armies and their relationship is rejected in the NT. As in OT holy war thinking, the advance of the kingdom signals a spiritual battle played out in the heavenly arena. But it is exorcisms and healings that mean the fall of *Satan from heaven (Lk 10:9-20); and it is at the end of the age that the heavenly forces will be sent out to purge the world of evil (Mt 13:40-43). If the Christian must be armed with "the strength of God's power," then it is in order to be defended against "the spiritual forces of evil in the heavenly realms" (Eph 6:10). The offensive *weapon is simply the gospel, spoken for instance by a defeated (imprisoned) apostle (Eph 6:17-20).

In Revelation the church is pictured as an army, but it is an army that is numbered in order to be protected, not to fight (Rev 7:3-8), which follows a *Lamb singing and playing harps (Rev 14:1-4) and which goes into battle like a *bride wearing wedding garments rather than armor (Rev 19:7-8, 14). The heavenly armies appear, throwing Satan out of heaven (Rev 12:7-9) and supplying the various angels who play key roles in judgment and victory, following the crucial victory won by the Lamb. Holy war takes place, but at no point does it become part of the political ideology of the followers of Christ.

See also ARCHERY; ARMOR; ARROW, ARROW OF GOD; DIVINE WARRIOR; HEAVENLY ARMIES/HOST; SHIELD; SWORD; WEAPONS, HUMAN AND DIVINE.

BIBLIOGRAPHY. T. Longman III and D. G. Reid, *God Is a Warrior* (SOTB; Grand Rapids: Zondervan, 1995); G. von Rad, *Holy War in Ancient Israel* (Grand Rapids: Eerdmans, 1991); Y. Yadin, *The Art of Warfare in Biblical Lands* (London: Weidenfeld and Nicolson, 1963).

ARROW, ARROW OF GOD

In ancient Near Eastern literature, nearly every *weapon available for human use had a divine counterpart. From Mesopotamia to Greece the arrow figures prominently in this arsenal. The Bible, with its many references to the arrow of God, is no exception.

The prescientific worldview understood otherwise inexplicable phenomena in terms of an unseen reality that paralleled the visible one. The just person participated in a spiritual warfare fought by greater powers with unseen weapons whose results spilled over into the visible universe. In such a framework, separating literary metaphor from authentic belief proves difficult, if not fruitless. We may more profitably ask why the arrow functioned as such a fitting image of divine intervention in the physical world.

In contrast to most other weapons, the arrow strikes from afar (Gen 21:16). While one may defend against many other weapons, the arrow strikes suddenly (Ps 64:7), so swiftly that time stands still (Hab 3:11). The bowman may let his arrow fly from ambush (Jer 9:8). The arrow may wound randomly (1 Kings 22:34). These qualities—long range, lightning quick, unseen, perhaps even random—made the bow and arrow not only a weapon to be feared in the visible world but also the prime symbol of divine justice meted out. Homer regularly attributes a man's premature, nonviolent death from unknown cause to "the gentle shafts of Apollo," a woman's to the arrows of the goddess Artemis.

Arrow of God. God's arrow deals death in many forms. Perhaps due to the natural pairing of *thunder and *lightning, the image of God's arrows is commonly preceded by mention of thundering wrath. While arrow frequently refers to lightning, either implicitly or explicitly (2 Sam 22:15; Ps 18:4, 144:6, Zech 9:14; Hab 3:11), the bow of God may also smite with arrows of war (Deut 32:42); flood (Ps 77:17, but note also Gen 9:13, 14, 16 where "bow" becomes *"rainbow" in some translations, masking the concrete imagery of God's promise to "hang up his bow"); *famine (Ezek 5:16); calamity and pestilence (2 Esdras 16:16-19, cf. 1 Chron 21:12, 27); *plague (Deut 32:23-24; Hab 3:5) or individual sickness brought on by "spiritual" poisoning (Job 6:4, 16:13; Ps 38:2-3); and perhaps other natural disasters, such as *earthquake (Hab 3:9). Almost any act of God could be accomplished by his arrows with many other weapons in reserve. Scripture labels the recipients of God's punishment as his "targets" (Lam 3:12).

Arrow of Evil. The devil and his minions and human accomplices also employ the arrow. The devil's fiery darts (Eph 6:16) find their inspiration in the flaming arrows of Psalm 7:13 (note that the Hebrew is difficult; NIV interprets these as "God's arrows"). In Ps 91:5 arrow parallels terror, pestilence and plague, read by some as demonic afflictions.

Arrows as Speech. Among many negative images, one isolated positive figure likens a prophet (or perhaps his words) to a polished (purified) arrow (Is 49:2, cf. Jer 51:11). In keeping with the devil's title of slanderer, "arrows of the wicked" typically refers to false speech (Ps 57:4; 64:3; 120:2-4; Prov 25:18;

26:18; Jer 9:8; Sir 19:12). The ancients imagined that words flew toward their mark with the speed of arrows. Neither words nor arrows left any trace of their flight path (Wis 5:12). Awe at the swift, untraceable flight of speech lies behind Homer's recurrent metaphor, "winged words."

Arrows as Oracles. The magic of arrows further allowed the ancients to divine with them. Ezekiel 21:21 records that Nebuchadnezzar consulted his oracle by casting lots with (lit. "shaking") arrows. (Akkadian literature and early Arabic sources attest similar practices, cf. also Hos 4:12.) In a parallel with a twist, when Jehoash seeks advice from the ailing Elisha, the prophet commands the king to beat the ground with the arrows and then interprets the future for the king based on the action of the arrows (2 Kings 13:18). In yet another message drawn from arrows, Jonathan's warning to David hinges on the interpretation of the actions of arrows (1 Sam 20:21).

See also ARCHERY; ARMOR; DIVINE WARRIOR; HUNTING; SHIELD; WEAPONS, HUMAN AND DIVINE.

ARTEMIS. *See* GOD, GODDESSES.

ASCENSION

The ascension of Jesus into *heaven is narrated only by Luke—in brief form in Luke 24:51 ("While he blessed them, he parted from them, and was carried up into heaven" RSV) and in an extended version in Acts 1:6-11. The main image pattern associated with the event is the imagery of transcendence: Jesus ascended from earth to heaven, indicating a movement from one sphere of reality to another. Ephesians 4:8 describes Jesus' ascending "on *high," while Colossians 3:1-2 surrounds the ascended Christ with references to "things that are above" as contrasted to "things that are on earth." Luke tells us that "a cloud took him out of their sight" (Acts 1:9), and the disciples responded by "gazing into heaven" and "looking into heaven" (Acts 1:10-11). The event is also accompanied by images of supernatural mystery—a disappearing person, a *cloud that veils and two *angelic messengers who instruct the baffled disciples.

Much is connoted by the ascension in addition to the physical images that surround it. First, the event is a boundary and a transition: it brings Jesus' earthly existence to a close (hence its positioning at the end of Luke's Gospel) and marks the beginning of the Holy Spirit's replacement of Jesus on earth (hence its positioning at the opening of the book of Acts). The ascension also completes the cyclic U-shaped life of the incarnate Christ—a descent followed by an ascent, with an obvious sense of completeness and closure. In John 6:62 Jesus speaks of "the Son of man ascending where he was before," while Ephesians 4:10 states that "he who descended is he who also ascended far above all the heavens, that he might fill all things" (RSV).

Secondly, the ascension is the ultimate example of the generally positive meanings of the archetype of ascending (*see* Ascent). Its main meaning is exaltation. Along with the *resurrection the ascension of Jesus vindicated his divine identity and the efficacy of his redemptive work. In the brief catalog of Christ-exalting events in the hymn printed in 1 Timothy 3:14, the climactic event is that Christ "was taken up in glory." Other imagery associated with Christ's ascension into heaven reinforces the sense of exaltation. When Jesus ascended, for example, he took a position of honor at the *right hand of God the *Father (Eph 1:20; Col 3:1; Heb 1:3; 8:1; 10:12; 12:2). The ascended Christ is "far above all rule and authority and power and dominion, and above every name that is named" (Eph 1:21 RSV).

Closely linked to the exaltation of Christ in the ascension is the motif of kingly *triumph over the forces of evil and *enemies of God. This is anticipated in Psalm 68:18, with its picture of a victorious king ascending "the high mount, leading captives in thy train." Ephesians 4:8 applies the motif to Christ. In the cosmic conflict between good and evil, the ascension of Christ "has put all things under his feet and has made him head over all things for the church" (Eph 1:22 RSV).

Finally, the ascension of Jesus into heaven, while marking the end to his earthly life, is also associated with the motif of preparation for a brief return visit to earth. Jesus ascended into heaven in order to prepare a place to which his disciples can follow him (Jn 14:1-4). The ascended Christ will reappear "in glory" (Col 3:4; *see* Second Coming).

The Bible also draws an application for believers. By virtue of their faith in Christ, believers have actually been "raised up" to sit with Christ "in the heavenly places" (Eph 2:6), and they are exhorted to "seek the things that are above, where Christ is, seated at the right hand of God" (Col 3:1 RSV).

See also ASCENT; EXALTATION, ENTHRONEMENT; HEAVEN; HIGH, HEIGHT, HIGH PLACE; PENTECOST.

ASCENT

In directional symbolism to be high is good, and to be low is bad. *Heaven is high; *hell is low. Emotional ecstasy is portrayed as being on a height; depression is a *valley. The imagery of ascent names the movement from a lower place to a higher place, and it accordingly partakes of the generally positive associations of being high.

Some of the imagery of ascent takes its place within the two-tiered picture of the universe that the Bible everywhere assumes. Heaven is above earth, and creatures who move from earth to heaven do so by ascending. Thus *angels ascend back to heaven after completing an earthly assignment (Judg 13:20; cf. Gen 28:12; Jn 1:51), and Elijah ascends to heaven in a *whirlwind when he is translated (2 Kings 2:11). The psalmist makes vivid his claim that he cannot escape from God's presence by picturing an antiquest (*see* Quest) in which he tries to evade God. One of the possibilities that he pictures is ascending to heaven, only to find that God is there (Ps 139:8). Isaiah's taunt against the proud king of Babylon pictures the king as aspiring to ascend to heaven (Is 14:13-14).

Another cluster of references uses the imagery of ascent metaphorically to denote a person's rise in status or position. Thus a king might ascend the *throne of his predecessor (2 Chron 21:4). Sometimes this ascent is ascribed to God in his role as conqueror. Psalm 68:18 pictures a *Divine Warrior ascending "the high mount" in a *triumphal procession (NRSV). Christ too is pictured in John's Gospel as ascending to heaven (Jn 3:13; 6:62; 10:17), as he is in later NT references as well (Acts 2:34; Eph 4:8-10).

A third family of references occurs in contexts of worship and is rooted in the physical position of the *temple on a high place in Jerusalem. To worship God at the temple is accordingly described as ascending "the hill of the LORD" (Ps 24:3). A group of fifteen pilgrim psalms (Ps 120—134) bears the repeated heading "a song of ascents," implying that the psalms were sung en route as the pilgrims "went up" to the temple in Jerusalem.

See also ASCENSION; EXALTATION, ENTHRONEMENT; HIGH, HEIGHT, HIGH PLACE.

ASHES

The Bible makes use of ashes in both narrative and prophetic descriptions of cities and peoples under God's wrath. In the background lies the ancient military practice of burning enemy cities, so that the association of ashes with death is common, as in Jeremiah's picture of a "whole valley of the dead bodies and the ashes" (Jer 31:40 RSV).

In keeping with the biblical motif of God as *warrior, the prophetic visions sometimes picture God's fire as consuming a wicked person or nation. Examples include the prophecy against Tyre, where God's fire turned it "to ashes upon the earth" (Ezek 28:18), and the destruction of Sodom and Gomorrah, which God "condemned to extinction" by turning them "to ashes" (2 Pet 2:6). In an apocalyptic passage those who fear God "shall tread down the wicked, for they will be ashes under the soles of your feet, on the day when I act, says the LORD of hosts" (Mal 4:3).

Since the word *ashes* is literally an image of complete waste, it also lends itself to use as a metaphor for *weakness, ephemerality and emptiness: "your maxims are proverbs of ashes" (Job 13:12; also Ps 142:6; Is 44:20). This same connotation underlies the use of ashes in expressions of intense grief and loss. The often repeated phrase "in sackcloth and ashes" paints a vivid picture of mourning women and men in torn clothing, lying or kneeling on the ground as they heap ashes and dust upon themselves (2 Sam 13:19; Esther 4:1, 3; Is 58:5, 61:3; Jer 6:26, 25:34; Ezek 27:30). In addition to this visible, physical ritual, the psalmist speaks figuratively of eating "ashes like bread" to symbolize his suffering (Ps 102:9; compare Ps 80:2). The theme of reversal in

Lamentations 4:5 effectively contrasts the royal purple with ashes: "Those nurtured in purple now lie on ash heaps."

Perhaps the most familiar biblical use of ashes imagery is in expressions of *repentance. The association of ashes with images of destruction and *grief makes it an appropriate symbol of human mortality and consequently of the humility required of human beings before their Creator and Judge. Job's initial cry of mourning, "I have become like dust and ashes," later becomes a prayer of confession, "I repent in dust and ashes" (Job 30:19; 42:6). In other biblical prayers of both confession in "sackcloth and ashes" (Dan 9:3-5; Jn 3:6; Mt 11:21; Lk 10:13) and petition (Gen 18:27), the image of ashes is a moving reminder of the human position before God. It is no coincidence that the marking of foreheads with ashes in Ash Wednesday services is accompanied by the words "Remember, man, that thou art dust and to dust thou shalt return."

In this context the ceremonial use of ashes in the OT has great significance. Having been swept from the *altar and taken to "a clean place" (Ex 27:3; Lev 1:16, 4:12, 6:10-11; Num 4:13; 2 Kings 23:3), the ashes from the burned sacrifices are later used under certain circumstances in purification rituals to wash those who are unclean (Num 19:9-10, 17; Heb 9:13). "How much more," explains the author of Hebrews, "shall the blood of Christ . . . purify your conscience from dead works to serve the living God?" (Heb 9:14). Though the biblical use of ashes imagery centers primarily on the fragility of life, this aspect of sacrificial cleansing transforms that emphasis from one of potential pessimism into one of humble hope.

See also ALTAR; FIRE; MOURN, MOURNING.

ASHTORETH. *See* GODS, GODDESSES.

ASS. *See* DONKEY, ASS.

ASSEMBLY, DIVINE

The Bible presents us with an earthly world and a heavenly world, two interconnected—and sometimes indistinguishable—stages on which the biblical drama takes place. The view of the heavenly world focuses primarily on the divine *throne room and related elements of divine royalty. This is the imagery of transcendence adapted by the Bible from its cultural environment. The gods of the ancient Near East were not spoken of in abstract terms—as theologians today might speak of divine sovereignty, omnipotence, omnipresence or aseity—they were vividly imaged in the language of *kingship and warfare, love and fertility, house building and banqueting. And so also for Israel, to "do" theology was to tell God's story and to fashion images and metaphors that both rightly described their subject and engaged the imagination. The theologians of the Bible—its poets and prophets, chroniclers and sages—borrowed, refashioned and subverted the images and symbols of the gods of their neighboring cultures. Their audiences expected to be offered glimpses of the heavenly court as a means of understanding the ways of God.

The Divine Assembly in its Cultural Setting. In Mesopotamian and Canaanite religion it was customary to speak of the high gods as kingly figures. Such a god was imagined to be enthroned in a heavenly palace (on which his earthly temple was modeled). The god had a heavenly assembly, or council, a deliberative body invested with the task of guiding the fate of the cosmos (*see* Cosmology). In the Mesopotamian myth of Enuma Elish, the gods are presided over by the high god Anu. In a Canaanite texts from Ugarit, we find the high god El presiding over the major and minor gods and addressing them as "gods" or "my sons." Israel speaks of Yahweh as a heavenly king who presides over his council. But in the OT we find the status of the "gods" subverted, for they are demoted to subservient figures, frequently called *angels or spirits.

The dwelling place of God is imaged as a cosmic *mountain, which in Canaanite mythology is Mount Zaphon in north Syria, the dwelling place of the gods. Isaiah condemns the hubris of the king of *Babylon as he deigns to set his throne "on the mount of assembly in the far north" and make himself "like the Most High" (Is 14:13 RSV). In the OT, God has chosen *Zion as the site for his temple-palace. As the earthly counterpart to his heavenly dwelling place, Zion is called the "holy mountain of God" (Ezek 28:14, 16). It is "beautiful in elevation, . . . the joy of all the earth, Mount Zion, in the far north, the city of the great King" (Ps 48:2 RSV; cf. Ps 46:4). Thus in the biblical imagination the Canaanite mountain of the gods is displaced and the status of "holy mountain" and "mount of the assembly" is transferred to Zion. If Zion's present elevation is admittedly not as grand as Mount Hermon and other mountains to the north, in the last days "the mountain of the house of the LORD shall be established as the highest of the mountains" (Is 2:2-4; Mic 4:1-3 RSV). Since it is the seat of the divine assembly, "out of Zion shall go forth the law, and the word of the LORD from Jerusalem" and from there God "shall judge between the nations" (Is 2:3-4; Mic 4:2-3 RSV).

The divine assembly is the celestial counterpart to the social institution of the "elders in the gate" (e.g., Deut 21:19; Ruth 4:1-11; Ps 107:32; Prov 31:23). It is a board of advisors or counselors with whom the supreme deity consults, an "assembly of the holy ones" (Ps 98:5). In context of war, its members can be called the "hosts," or "army" of heaven, who engage in divine warfare under the "Lord of Hosts" (*see* Divine Warrior). Psalm 82 evokes the scene of the divine assembly: "God has taken his place in the divine council; in the midst of the gods he holds judgment" (Ps 82:1 RSV). But in this case God is displeased with the members of the divine assembly. The assembly cowers as God hauls them onto the royal carpet: "How long will you judge unjustly and show partiality to the wicked?" (Ps 82:2 RSV). For

their heedlessness toward the weak and needy as well as their other shortcomings, God pronounces *judgment on them: "I said, 'You are "gods"; you are all sons of the Most High.' But you will die like mere men; you will fall like every other ruler" (Ps 82:6-7 NIV).

Divine Assembly and Prophetic Messengers. The story of the prophet Micaiah ben Imlah in 1 Kings 22 offers a fascinating glimpse of deliberation within the heavenly council. On the earthly plane, Ahab, the king of Israel, is deliberating with Jehoshaphat, the king of Judah, over whether they should attack Ramoth Gilead. They inquire of the fawning court prophets, who heartily agree that they should attack. But then they inquire of Micaiah, who is always heedless of the party line, Micaiah speaks of his vision of the divine council:

> "I saw the LORD sitting on his throne, and all the host of heaven standing beside him on his right hand and on his left; and the LORD said, 'Who will entice Ahab, that he may go up and fall at Ramoth-Gilead?' And one said one thing, and another said another. Then a spirit came forward and stood before the LORD, saying, 'I will entice him.' And the LORD said to him, 'By what means?' And he said, 'I will go forth, and will be a lying spirit in the mouth of all his prophets.' And he said, 'You are to entice him, and you shall succeed; go forth and do so.' "
> (1 Kings 22:19-22 RSV)

This imagery of the prophet having access to the divine council—and being a messenger for the council—clarifies the "call" scene of the prophet Isaiah. In Isaiah 6 the prophet has a vision of "the LORD sitting upon a throne, high and lifted up; and his train filled the temple" (Is 6:1 RSV). Here the earthly *temple provides entrance to the heavenly temple (complete with marvelous creatures attending the throne), and the heavenly kingship of Yahweh is juxtaposed with the earthly kingship of Uzziah (Is 6:1). Struck by the wondrous sight of Yahweh the king and overcome with a sense of personal and corporate sin, Isaiah receives *forgiveness. He then hears the Lord deliberating before his council: "Whom shall I send, and who will go for us?" The response comes not from a "god" within the divine assembly but from Isaiah himself, "Here I am! Send me." And the Lord responds, "Go, and say to this people . . ." (Is 6:8-9 RSV). Likewise we should perhaps understand Isaiah 40:1-2—"Comfort, comfort my people, says your God. Speak tenderly to Jerusalem" (RSV)—as words uttered by Yahweh to the heralds assembled in divine council. The voice of the heavenly herald then cries out, "In the wilderness prepare the way of the LORD" (Is 40:3 RSV).

The Assembly of Gods and Angels. It is clear that the Bible does not regard the "gods" of the divine assembly as peers of God: "There is none like thee among the gods, O Lord" (Ps 86:8 RSV; cf. Ps 135:5). "For who in the skies can be compared to the LORD? Who among the heavenly beings is like the

LORD, a God feared in the council of the holy ones, great and terrible above all that are round about him?" (Ps 89:6-7 RSV; cf. Ps 29:1; 97:7; 138:1). Although among Israel's neighbors these gods were clearly regarded as deities, later Judaism came to speak of them as high-ranking *angels. In keeping with this view, the LXX often translates these "sons of God" or even "gods" as angels (Deut 32:8; Ps 8:5; 138:1 [LXX 137:1]). The NT often follows the LXX, so that "thou hast made him a little less than God" (or "gods," Ps 8:5) appears as "a little lower than the angels" in Hebrews 2:7.

In the book of Job the divine assembly plays a role near the outset. It provides the background for understanding "the Satan" who enters on "a day when the sons of God came to present themselves before the LORD" (Job 1:6 RSV). In Job, *Satan is not presented as the evil spiritual being we come to know in the NT but as one who plays a legal role in the heavenly court as "the accuser." Even though he is not loyal to God, Satan, by virtue of his rank as a divine being, is permitted to appear at meetings of the council on a day when "the sons of God" come to present themselves before the Lord (Job 1:6; 2:1). Satan's role as "accuser" requires this (Zech 3:1; Rev 12:10).

Another picture of the divine council is offered in Daniel 7. Here the scene is more highly developed. The council assembles for judgment of the great empires of the earth, depicted as dreadful monsters. As Daniel "looks" in his vision, he sees "thrones" placed and the "ancient of days," with raiment "white as snow" and hair "like pure wool" taking his seat on a throne of "fiery flames, its wheels . . . burning with fire" and issuing forth "a stream of fire" (Dan 7:9-10 RSV). The council is attended by a stunning myriad of heavenly beings: "a thousand thousands served him, and ten thousand times ten thousand stood before him" (Dan 7:10 RSV). Their business is to render judgment, and the books are opened. The result is that the dominion of the beasts is taken away, with the final beast causing a great commotion and then being executed (Dan 7:11). Then, on a *cloud *chariot, "one like a son of man" arrives at the assembly. This being, representing the "saints of the Most High" (Dan 7:27 RSV), is honored by the council with universal and eternal sovereignty (Dan 7:14). When the scene concludes, Daniel, his head spinning from the spectacle, approaches one of those standing in the assembly and inquires about the meaning of this event. A full explanation ensues (Dan 7:15-28). This fully elaborated vision of the divine assembly is a prototype for many later scenes of divine assembly and throne room in Jewish apocalyptic literature.

The Divine Assembly in the New Testament. In the NT the inner circle of the divine assembly consists of angels who surround the heavenly throne. The primary theme is *worship, and there is an implied understanding that the worship of the church mirrors the worship of heaven. In Colossians 2:18 Paul exhorts the Colossian believers not to be influenced by those who place heavy demands on their access to the "worship of angels," that is, the heavenly worship conducted by angels within the heavenly assembly (this meaning is more likely than "worship directed toward angels"). Paul warns against those who advocate a rigorous asceticism that purports to offer access to this heavenly worship (Col 2:20-23). Instead, Paul uses the imagery of believers being "raised with Christ" and setting their hearts on "things above, where Christ is seated at the right hand of God" (Col 3:1 NIV). Paul reminds the Philippians of their heavenly citizenship (Phil 3:20) and the Ephesians are blessed "in the heavenly realms" (Eph 1:3), for "God raised us up with Christ and seated us with him in the heavenly realms in Christ Jesus" (Eph 2:6 NIV).

But the divine assembly is most fully developed in the book of Revelation. In Revelation 4—5 the seer enters the heavenly throne room where he first observes God the Father seated on a throne and attended by four living creatures who ceaselessly sing his praise (Rev 4:6-8). In a further circle around the throne are twenty-four thrones (Rev 4:4) on which are seated twenty-four elders, angelic figures who fall down in reverence and cast their *crowns before the throne, singing of the glory and majesty of God. In the hand of the one seated on the throne is a scroll that no one is worthy to open except for a *Lamb "as though it had been slain" (RSV), standing between the throne and the circle of four living creatures (Rev 5:5-7).

The Lamb receives the same worship from the heavenly assembly as does the one on the throne, and the assembly enlarges to include angels "numbering myriads of myriads and thousands of thousands" and then to encompass the entire cosmos as "every creature in heaven and on earth and under the earth and in the sea, and all therein" join in the heavenly praise (Rev 5:11, 13 RSV). In a further scene we find 144,000 martyrs "who have come through the great tribulation" (Rev 7:14 RSV) joining the heavenly praise as they stand before the throne and the Lamb, praising God and the Lamb (Rev 7:9-12). In Revelation 14:1-5 the 144,000 appear again as a great army of saints accompanying the Lamb on Mount Zion.

The divine assembly in Revelation 4—5 is highly developed and transformed in comparison with the scenes we find in the OT, with its closest point of contact being Daniel 7. The emphasis on heavenly worship, is recapitulated in Revelation 19:1-8, though the motif of deliberation is present with the question of who will open the *scroll (Rev 5:2-5) and takes more prominence in the judgment scene of Revelation 20. There we learn of "thrones on which were seated those who had been given authority to judge" (Rev 20:4 NIV) and of a judgment that takes place before a "great white throne" (Rev 20:11-15). These heavenly assemblies are intimately linked to the destiny of the earth, its inhabitants and the spiritual world. Here, as in the OT, what transpires in the heavenly council has great consequences for the course of cosmic events.

See also ANGEL; ASSEMBLY, HUMAN; DIVINE WARRIOR; GODS, GODDESSES; JUDGMENT; PROPHET, PROPHETESS; ROYAL COURT; WORSHIP.

BIBLIOGRAPHY. E. T. Mullen Jr., "Divine Assembly," *ABD* 2:214-17; idem, *The Divine Council in Canaanite and Early Hebrew Literature* (Chico, CA: Scholars Press, 1980).

ASSEMBLY, HUMAN

Because stories (including those in the Bible) are typically structured around a single protagonist, most readers tend to think of the Bible as presenting stories about individuals. Yet only a relatively small minority of biblical stories are devoid of what we might call assemblies of people. Assemblies range on a continuum from the formal assembly on one end to informal, ad hoc and even extemporaneous collections of people who happen to be on the scene.

While the focus of this article will be on the more formal assembly as a biblical image, we should not overlook categories of informal assemblies that greatly expand the importance of the image in the Bible. Informal assemblages of people occur in such categories as *travel stories, *street scenes, courtroom scenes (*see* Legal Images), *battle scenes, *harvest scenes, communal work projects, crowd scenes, *judgment scenes of public exposure and punishment (including stoning), and such like. Once we are alerted to these categories, the Bible emerges in our imaginations as typically involving not isolated individuals but individuals performing actions in a social environment that includes groups of people.

The image of the assembly reaches far beyond occurrences where the word *assembly* appears, but some preliminary generalizations are possible if we pause to note the usages of the word. The word assembly appears 164 times in the NIV, and all but ten of these occur in the OT. The overwhelming majority of these occurrences, moreover, refer to a religious assembly, as we might deduce from the sections where they cluster (sixty-eight references in Exodus through Deuteronomy, thirty-six in 1 Kings through 2 Chronicles, thirteen in Psalms).

The major spiritual events of the Bible are public events and consequently human assemblies are part of the biblical story from start to finish. Generally these assemblies are quite nonformal gatherings without clearly defined legal, political or religious authority. The image of the crowd is very important for the Gospel writers, not only to give the sense of the public nature of Jesus ministry but also to show his willingness to share his message with the unwashed masses who at times are more receptive than the religious establishment (Mt 7:29) and can be quite positive so that the leaders fear arresting Jesus in public (Mk 12:12). But the crowd is also (as is the crowd in Shakespeare's plays) fickle and cries out, "Crucify him, Crucify him" (Jn 19:15).

One of the chief roles for assemblies in the Bible is to supply witnesses to an event. The NT writers use numerous *witnesses to show that the events of the Gospels were not just private revelations. The crowd sees the raising of Lazarus (Jn 12:17) and the disciples will "bear witness of [Jesus]" because they have seen Jesus' entire ministry (Jn 15:26-27). Paul uses the idea of the assembly as a witness at several points. He tells Timothy, "the things which you heard from me in the presence of many witnesses, these entrust to faithful men, who will be able to teach others also" (2 Tim 2:2 NASB), Paul also cites as evidence for the reality of Christ's resurrection that Jesus "was seen by more than five hundred of his followers" (1 Cor 15:6 NLB).

To the biblical writers, human assemblies are brought forth as premiere evidence in their arguments. Because so many major events in salvation history occurred in the public eye, writers call their audience to act as witnesses to well-known events: " 'I have revealed and saved and proclaimed—I, and not some foreign God among you. You are my witnesses', declares the LORD, 'that I am God' " (Is. 43:12 NIV; cf. Is 44:8, 55:4). Here the thought is that Israel bears automatic testimony to the power and reality of the Lord.

In a similar way, the "great assembly" becomes an important place for *worship. The psalmist declares, "I will give you thanks in the great assembly; among throngs of people I will praise you" (Ps 35:18 NIV). Here the image is of staking oneself in front of others by clearly declaring faith in God both in front of witnesses and as a ministry and encouragement to others (Ps 26:12; 40:9; 68:26). The image in Psalm 1 of sinners unable to stand "in the assembly of the righteous" (Ps 1:5, NASB) points to the status of the religious assembly as a community of believers who share a common faith.

Groups of people often take on a quasi-legal status in the Bible. An example is stoning as a form of ritual execution that was to be carried out by the congregation (Lev 24:14; Num 15:32). According to the law, stoning was only to be carried out for a delineated set of offenses and with proper witnesses. Uncovering Achan's theft was a public event, and when the verdict was reached, "all the Israelites stoned Achan" (Josh 7:25 NLB). Such an execution carried out by a public assembly is not to be construed as an act of mob violence. Its alternative of mob violence does indeed occur in the Bible. The Israelites were so distraught that they wanted to stone *Moses (Num 14:10). Rehoboam's emissary to the Northern Kingdom, Adoram, was stoned (1 Kings 12:18). In Luke the religious leaders are portrayed as fearing that the people would stone them if they denied that John the Baptist was a prophet (Lk 20:6). The release of Barabbas rather than Jesus illustrates how assemblies can be swayed to make incorrect decisions (Mk 15:6-14).

Whereas OT judicial assemblies seem rather occasional and ad hoc, with people called together whenever an offense seems to require action, in the NT we move in a more familiar world of regularly constituted courts of justice. Often these are Jewish assemblies (chiefly the Sanhedrin) that wield civil power (alarmingly so in the Gospels and Acts) on the basis of religious authority. One thinks of the sequence of assemblies before which Jesus is hauled in the circumstances leading to his execution, and the numerous times that the apostles and Paul were tried by Jewish authorities in the book of Acts.

In the OT milieu a common form of assembly was the *marketplace. *Authority of a democratic sort was exercised in the marketplace, where assemblies sometimes have the character of a mob scene. Mobs form quickly in any people-filled area. When Paul and Silas cast a demon from a slave girl, they are dragged to the market "to face the authorities" (Acts 16:19). The market was a barometer of spiritual as well as political affairs. Observance of the *sabbath in the marketplace indicated renewed commitment to God (Neh 10:31) and frustrated wicked men (Amos 8:5). In the same way, disregard for God's provision was signaled by busy sabbath commerce and continually troubled the righteous (Neh 13:15-19). Also, oppression and fraud in the marketplace were metaphors for public iniquity (Ps 55:11). We should note in passing that if the marketplace was sometimes the scene for mob action in the Bible, most mob scenes are street scenes.

In addition to the marketplace as a place where groups naturally assemble in the social world of the Bible, there is the *well and the city *gate. Numerous important meetings occur at the well because it is the place where townspeople regularly assemble and where travelers make an entry into a *village. The connotations of "sitting in the gate" (or its variant "sitting in the seat") are more *legal, inasmuch as the place where the elders of the town (an early-day version of the town council) met, and where civil actions transpired.

Human assemblies are prominent in the book of Revelation. Here the church is pictured as an *army and as a group of battle-weary martyrs waiting for justice to be established. It is an army which is numbered in order to be protected, not to fight (Rev 7:3-8), which follows a *Lamb singing and playing *harps (Rev 14:1-4), and which goes into battle like a *bride wearing *wedding garments rather than armor (Rev 19:7-8, 14). The heavenly armies appear, throwing *Satan out of heaven (Rev 12:7-9), and supplying the various angels who play key roles in judgment and victory, following the crucial victory won by the Lamb. Whereas the Bible begins with a couple in a garden, it ends with the grandest assembly of all—the complete company of the redeemed, forever secure in *heaven, which is portrayed as an endless worship assembly.

See also ASSEMBLY, DIVINE; GATE; LEGAL IMAGES; MARKETPLACE; ROYAL COURT; STREET; WORSHIP.

ASTROLOGY. *See* ORACLE.

ATHLETICS
Although some type of athletic activity seems to be implied in a few OT passages (Gen 32:24-26; 2 Sam 2:12-17; Ps 3:7; 19:5), most of the references to athletics occur in the NT, particularly in the writings of Paul. Paul demonstrates thorough acquaintance with the sporting events of his day as seen in his references to *running (Gal 2:2), boxing (1 Cor 9:26), *wrestling (Eph 6:12), gladiatorial contests (1 Cor 4:9; 15:32) and (possibly) chariot races (Phil 3:13-14).

Athletic images conjure up a number of stimulating associations, including rigorous training or exercise (1 Cor 9:25; 1 Tim 4:7-8), singleness of purpose (1 Cor 9:26), delayed gratification (1 Cor 9:25), streamlining for maximum performance (Heb 12:1), self-control (1 Cor 9:27), *perseverance (Heb 12:2) and endurance (1 Tim 4:8). Athletic endeavor also involves intense competition with lofty objectives (1 Cor 9:24) and high stakes (Eph 6:12), and it requires faithful adherence to a prescribed set of rules to avoid disqualification (2 Tim 2:5; 1 Cor 9:27). In spite of all the hard work, the end result is transitory fame. But for the Christian the *crown to be won is imperishable (1 Tim 4:8; 1 Cor 9:25).

See also RACE; RUNNING; WRESTLING.

ATONEMENT
The English word *atonement* is derived from the two words "at onement" and denotes a state of togetherness and agreement between two people. Atonement presupposes two parties that are estranged, with the act of atonement being the reconciliation of them into a state of harmony. The theological meaning is the reconciliation between God and his fallen creation, especially between God and sinful human beings. Atonement is thus a solution to the main problem of the human race—its estrangement from God stemming from the fall of *Adam and *Eve. A range of biblical images portrays this central event of the religious faith of the Bible.

The Sacrificial Imagery of the Old Testament. The imagery of animal *sacrifice, especially *blood sacrifice, is the dominant OT image for atonement, based on the principle that "under the [OT] law almost everything is purified with blood, and without the shedding of blood there is no forgiveness of sins" (Heb 9:22 RSV). The OT sacrificial laws are a series of variations on that theme. The imagery of atoning sacrifice may be summed up in this manner: the *sins of humanity violated the *holiness of the Creator and brought the sentence of *death, a sentence that can be averted only by the *substitution of a sacrifice of death. Through the blood of sacrifice, sinful people are able to receive the blessing of God instead of his judgment.

From the earliest times of human history, animal sacrifices were designed to establish atonement between God and his sinful image bearer. Some interpreters have even understood the animal-skin clothing given to Adam and Eve as symbolic of blood sacrifice (Gen 3:21). The importance of animal sacrifices is clearly displayed in the practices of *Abel (Gen 4:2-4; cf. Heb 11:4), Noah (Gen 8:20) and the Patriarchs (Gen 13:18; 26:25; 33:20; 35:7), though little meaning is assigned to these animal sacrifices prior to Moses. One clue, however, appears outside the Pentateuch in the retrospective account of Job 1:5. Here Job sacrifices on behalf of his children to protect them from divine judgment against their sins. Animal sacrifices are thus portrayed as a way of atonement, a means of securing divine favor for sinful people.

The law of Moses brings extensive development to the imagery of sacrificial atonement. At the first *Passover (Ex 12:1-30) the blood of the sacrificed *lamb on the doorways of Israelite homes protects the faithful from the judgment of death. When the Lord sees the blood he does not harm those within the home. Leviticus 1—7 describes a variety of sacrifice rituals to be practiced at the tabernacle. The detailed ritual instructions regarding whole burnt *offerings (Lev 1:1-17), guilt offerings (Lev 5:14—6:7) and sin offerings (Lev 4:1—5:13) indicate that the problem of sin before the holy God of Israel is a chief concern. The people are unable to approach God enthroned in his holy place without following the prescribed arrangements and offering the appropriate sacrifices.

The clearest expression of the imagery of atoning sacrifice appears in the legislation for the Day of Atonement (Lev 16:1-34; 23:27-32; cf. Heb 9:7-12). An intricate series of rituals is assigned to the tenth day of the seventh month of Tishri to atone for the sins of the entire nation. The sacrificial ritual itself involves three main steps (Lev 16:11-22). First, Aaron sacrifices for himself and his house so he can continue the ceremony without fear of judgment (Lev 16:11-14). Second, he offers the sin-offering of a *goat for the congregation of Israel (Lev 16:15-19). Third, Aaron lays his hands on a second goat (a *scapegoat) and sends it outside the camp to die (Lev 16:20-22).

All of these actions and the rituals surrounding them have important symbolic value that expresses various aspects of the imagery of atonement. The use of two goats in the ritual of atonement clearly reveals the two sides of atonement. The first goat is sacrificed, and its blood sprinkled on top of the *ark of the covenant ("atonement cover" [NIV], "mercy seat" [KJV], "mercy seat" [RSV], Lev 16:15, 27). This act symbolizes the divine side of atonement: God's holy justice is satisfied by the sprinkling of blood before him. The second goat represents the human side of atonement. The sins of the people are transferred to the goat by Aaron's hands. The goat is then escorted outside the camp to "carry on itself all their sins" (Lev 16:21-22 NIV). By means of this transfer the people are cleansed of the defilement sin has brought on them.

This twofold imagery helps to resolve a long-standing theological controversy over the imagery of atonement. Two viewpoints on atonement have come to expression in the terms *expiation* and *propitiation*. Expiatory views of atonement focus on sacrifices as the way to free people of sin and its defilement. Propitiatory understandings of atonement present sacrifices as the appeasement of divine wrath. The symbolism of two goats on the Day of Atonement indicates that both concepts are essential in the OT imagery of atonement. The sacrificial system of the OT is presented as God's design for satisfying the just judgment of God but also for removing the guilt of sin from those for whom sacrifices are made.

It is important to note that the OT imagery of atonement through sacrifice is not a matter of mere ritual. Unfortunately, as the OT relates, Israel from time to time reduces the symbols of atonement to outward practice, as if merely performing the rites of sacrifice will bring them atonement. The OT prophets, however, make it clear that sacrifices are ineffectual without sincere repentance and faith. In fact the practice of sacrifice apart from appropriate inward commitments stirs the judgment of God. For instance Isaiah reports God's rebuke: "I have had enough of burnt offerings; . . . I do not delight in the blood of bulls. . . . Bring no more vain offerings" (Is 1:11, 13 RSV). Other prophets respond to Israel's hypocrisy in much the same way (e.g., Amos 4:4, 5; Jer 7:21). Put simply, sacrificial rituals atone for those who have genuinely turned from sin and humbled themselves before God. Nothing less than such inward sincerity accompanying sacrifice will bring about reconciliation between God and sinful humanity.

Through the course of the OT story, it becomes clear that the system of animal sacrifice is inadequate. While the prophets announce that Israel will suffer the judgment of exile, they also proclaim that a greater way of atonement is on the horizon. The restoration of God's people from exile will be accomplished not by animal sacrifice but by human sacrifice. The clearest expression of this expectation appears in Isaiah 52:13—53:12. Isaiah speaks of God's "servant" (Is 52:13), the son of David who will be "wounded for our transgressions" and "bruised for our iniquities" (Is 53:5). "The LORD has laid on him the iniquity of us all " (Is 53:6). In fact, this servant will become "a guilt offering" for the people of God (Is 53:10).

The New Testament Imagery of Christ's Sacrifice. The NT rests its doctrine of atonement on this prophetic concept of the *suffering servant. Thirty-four times we find various NT writers refering to Isaiah's proclamation as fulfilled in Jesus (e.g., Acts 8:32-35; 1 Pet 2:22-25). Jesus' death is the substitutionary suffering of the Son of David that brings appeasement of divine wrath and sets God's people free from the guilt of sin.

The Gospels elaborate on the atoning nature of Christ's death in a number of ways. Matthew explains that Jesus is the promised child who saves his people from their sins (Mt 1:21). Matthew 8:17 links Jesus to the *suffering servant of Isaiah 53 and offers the image of substitution. John the Baptist calls Jesus "the *lamb of God who takes away the sin of the world" (Jn 1:29). Mark claims that Christ's death is the payment of a *ransom (Mk 10:45). Luke depicts the atonement of Christ as the escape from God's wrath (Lk 3:7). In John's Gospel, Jesus uses a number of images to explain the atoning significance of his death. He will be lifted up as Moses lifted the *serpent (Jn 3:14). He is the *bread of heaven and eternal life can be found by eating his flesh and blood (Jn 6:33). He is the good *shepherd who will die for his sheep (Jn 10:11).

The Pauline epistles also offer a number of images to capture the various facets of the richness of Christ's atoning work. One of Paul's favorite images for describing humankind's plight under sin is slavery. Paul writes that Christ's atonement has set us free from our enslavement (Gal 5:1). Paul also describes our "natural" death as the *"wages" earned from our sin. But the justice due us is absorbed by Christ and replaced by the "gift" of eternal life (Rom 6:23; 5:17). Reiterating prominent OT images, Paul describes Christ's atoning work in terms of the offering of a sacrifice (Eph 5:2). At least two images of atonement having to do with obligation to the law emerge in Paul's writings. First, though sinners are held captive to the law of sin (Rom 7:23), they are released from the law of death and bondage and are justified by the righteousness of Christ alone (Rom 3:20-26). Second, because of people's inability to keep the law, they bear the *"curse" of the law, but Christ has borne the curse in their place (Gal 3:12).

Paul also portrays atonement in legal terms (see Legal Images). With courtroom imagery the sinner is pronounced as the object of divine judgment both now and at the end of the age (Rom 1:24, 26, 28; 2:16). Yet because of Christ's atoning work there is no condemnation (Rom 8:1). In similar terms, fallen humanity is described as the object of God's holy wrath, but in Christ's sacrifice there is escape from the coming wrath (1 Thess 1:10; 5:9). Another important Pauline image of atonement is that of reconciliation. Though we were once *enemies, we now have become reconciled through the blood of Christ (Rom 5:10-11). The hostility between God and his creation is abolished for those who benefit from the atoning work of Christ. The scope of this reconciliation reaches cosmological proportions: through Christ, God will "reconcile to himself all things, whether on earth or in heaven, making peace by the blood of his cross" (Col 1:20 RSV).

No NT book is richer in the imagery of atonement that the epistle to the Hebrews. Unfolding the ultimate meaning of the priestly activity in the OT tabernacle, the author explains that Jesus is not only the great high *priest but the sacrifice as well (Heb 9:6-13). The OT ceremonial sacrifices and practices were only "external regulations, applying until the time of the new order" (Heb 9:10 NIV). The imagery of animal blood is emphasized in Hebrews as a "shadow" of the effectual cleansing of the blood of Christ (Heb 9:13-14). Hebrews also highlights the finality of Christ's sacrifice, thereby making the work of Christ the climactic image of atonement. Though the priest "stands daily at his service, offering repeatedly the same sacrifices," Christ has "[offered] for all time a single sacrifice for sins" (Heb 10:11-14 RSV). What the blood of animals could have never accomplished, Jesus accomplished once and for all. But this redemption included great suffering. The author of Hebrews frequently employs images of suffering surrounding the atoning work of Christ to impress upon the imaginations of Christians the great cost of salvation (Heb 2:10; 5:7; 13:12).

Images of the atonement fill the *Revelation of John. Christ is often designated as the *lamb who was slain but *triumphed (Rev 5:6, 12; 17:14). The redeemed "have *washed their robes and made them white in the blood of the Lamb" (Rev 7:14 RSV). The atonement is celebrated by the living creatures and elders surrounding the throne of heaven (Rev 5:11-12). This great song of redemption becomes the chorus of every believer. In Revelation 19:9 the imagery of the sacrificial lamb is joined with the imagery of the final *wedding *feast. This great celebration of salvation symbolizes that atonement will be fully accomplished when the redeemed in Christ enter their final destiny of eternal life in the new heaven and new earth.

Summary. The imagery surrounding the Bible's teaching on atonement threatens to overwhelm us by its very abundance and multiplicity. Much of the biblical data can be summed up under five master images or controlling motifs. One is the *bearing away of sins* so that sinners can be freed from a penalty they have incurred (the OT scapegoat escorted into the wilderness, 1 Pet 2:24; Heb 9:28). Second is the financial image of a *ransom* that is paid in exchange for sinners (Mt 20:28; Mk 10:45; 1 Tim 2:6; Rev 5:9). A third motif is the *substitute* who takes the place of sinners, suffering the punishment that stems from God's justice in their place (Is 53:4-6; Rom 5:12-21, with its emphasis on Christ as the second *Adam, the representative of the human race who effects redemption for it; 2 Cor 5:14; Gal 3:12). Fourth, the OT sacrifices and Christ as the fulfillment of those sacrifices are a *satisfaction* (not simply a waiving) of the offense that the human race has committed against God by virtue of its sinfulness, and an *appeasement* of the just anger of God against the human race for its offense (Rom 3:24-26; Heb 2:17; 1 Jn 2:1-2). And fifth, atonement is a *legal* and *juridical* meeting of the requirements of the law so that sinful people can stand acquitted before God the judge (Rom 3:7; 5:18-19; 8:1; 2 Cor 5:19). The result of all these transactions, finally, is *reconciliation* between an offended, holy God and a sinful, rebellious humanity (Rom 5:7-11; 2 Cor 5:18-20; Col 1:20).

See also BLOOD; CLEANSING; CROSS; CURSE; GUILT; JESUS, IMAGES OF; LAMB; LEGAL IMAGES; OFFERING; PASSOVER; PRIEST; SACRIFICE; SIN; SUFFERING SERVANT; TRIUMPH.

BIBLIOGRAPHY. L. Morris, *The Atonement: Its Meaning and Significance* (Downers Grove, IL: InterVarsity Press, 1983).

ATROCITY. *See* TORTURE.

AUTHORITY, DIVINE AND ANGELIC

It is helpful to distinguish between biblical images of authority that speak of the heavenly, or spiritual, realm and those that speak of the human realm. In the biblical scheme of the cosmos, all authority is derived from God. And within the heavenly, or spiritual, realm there is a delegated authority that is granted to the angels. But a malignancy of rebellion has infected even the spiritual order of things, and so a distinction must be drawn between the authority of "good" and "bad" (or demonic) angelic powers.

Divine Authority. Biblical images of authority prove Israel's God revealed in Jesus to be the only true God. False *gods like Baal or Mammon exert great power but are usurpers without legitimacy. The true value of Mammon, for example, is symbolized by figures of *nakedness and poverty for the Laodiceans' supposed riches in contrast to *white *garments and *fire-refined *gold given by God (Rev 3:17-18).

The image of four horsemen (Rev 6:1-8) illustrates the difference between power and authority. Forces of war, economic disorder and death, symbolized by red, black and pale *horses, influence history but have no ultimate sovereignty. Only Christ, rider of the white horse, returns later and wears the name "King of kings and Lord of lords" (Rev 19:11-16; cf. Rev 17:14; Dan 2:47; 1 Tim 6:15).

Sovereign kingship. The most prevalent figure of divine authority in both testaments is the *kingship of God. The Israelites are warned that human kings will lead them into the world's economic, political and warring practices and away from serving the heavenly King who rightly claims their obedience because he brought them out of Egypt (1 Sam 8:7-18). Symbols of kingship, such as a *throne or *scepter, also image God's authority to *judge and rule (Ps 9:7; 45:6; 47:8; Is 6; Ezek 1; Heb 1:8; Rev 4—5, 7).

Daniel's vision of God is particularly vivid in its depiction of divine authority. God's authority is evoked in his title Ancient of Days, and his great age, a symbol of authority in the ancient world, is imaged in his hair which is "white like wool" (Dan 7:9). The awesome picture of his wheeled throne, ablaze and sending forth a river of fire, is fittingly framed by the myriad throngs that attend him. He has authority over the empires of the earth, and displaces the monstrous fourth beast (Dan 7:10). Then to the "one like a son of man" he grants "authority, glory and sovereign power," the worship of all peoples and nations, and "an everlasting dominion that will not pass away" (Dan 7:13-14 NIV). This is a picture of sovereign and heavenly authority that will not be surpassed until the John the Seer unfurls his vision of the heavenly throne room in Revelation 4 and 5. These images are the ancient textual equivalents of a modern day epic film, complete with spectacular effects and a cast of thousands. They press the borders of the audience's imagination and compel them to join in the heavenly *worship of the One who reigns in cosmic authority.

The symbols of sovereignty are also invoked to image the authority of the *Son. Following his incarnation and obedience to the point of death on a *cross, Christ is "highly exalted" and given the throne name of Lord. This is "the name that is above every name, so that at the name of Jesus every knee should bend, in heaven and on earth and under the earth, and every tongue confess that Jesus Christ is Lord" (Phil 2:9-11 NRSV). This universal image is similarly imaged in 1 Corinthians 15:24-28, where Christ's authority extends over the spiritual powers whom he will subdue: "God has put all things in subjection under his feet" (1 Cor 15:27 NRSV; *see* Under the Feet). But Christ's eschatological authority is rooted in his protological authority: "in him all things in heaven and on earth were created, things visible and invisible, whether thrones or dominions or rulers or powers—all things have been created through him and for him" (Col 1:16 NRSV).

He is the image of the heavenly Father, whose authority derives from the fact that he is the one Creator God who is also actively engaged in the redemption of his *creation. The God of the Bible is no remote deity of deism; he is actively engaged in sustaining his creation. Images derived from his creative and redemptive work rightly speak of his sovereignty. The Lord declares, "Woe to him who quarrels with his Maker." To enter into dispute with God is like *clay arguing with the potter or like a *child asking her parents why they have begotten her (Is 45:9-13). Similarly, the image of Jesus as "author and perfecter" portrays his mastery over faith because he is its source (Heb 12:2).

Authoritative word. Perhaps the most comprehensive image for God's authority is the "word of God." Control over creation is pictured by God's speaking and the creation coming into being (Gen 1); sovereignty over history is figured by God's declaring new things before they spring into being (Is 42:9). The word from God always is effective (Is 55).

The NT images the authoritative word of God by repeatedly announcing that events in Jesus' life are fulfillments of prophecy. The prophets themselves are images for God's authority in their legitimizing phrase, "Thus saith the LORD." And that word, having gone out from the mouth of God, has run its effective course in history and brought it fulfillment to birth.

*Jesus claims his own divine authority by building on this prophetic image. Repeatedly the Gospels record his saying, "Truly I say to you," thus going beyond the prophets' phrase to picture his own authority as the living Word. His teaching is imbued with an authority that is "not as the scribes" (Mk 1:22 NRSV). Healing and exorcism is also an image displaying Jesus' authority. When religious leaders protest that he blasphemes by *forgiving sins, Jesus effectively commands the paralytic to get up (Mk 2:1-12). The crowds recognize the image of his authority when he successfully commands unclean spirits to come out (Lk 4:36; Mk 1:27). And when he commands the raging *sea to "be still," his authoritative word echoes the divine word that subdues the forces of *chaos (Mk 4:39; cf. Job 26:12; Ps 65:7; 89:9). In his memorable action in the *temple (Mk 11:15-17), he enacts the coming destruction of the temple and later suggests that he is the cornerstone of a new temple (Mk 12:10-11; cf. Mk 14:58). Jesus' posture toward the temple, the center of Israel's *sacred space and the touchpoint of *heaven and *earth, signifies an implied authority over all that is sacred to Israel.

The name *lord* and the authority of the master's word is used as an image by the centurion at Capernaum who seeks Jesus' healing for his servant (Mt 8:5-13). The title and idea of lordship always represent Christ's authority (especially as multiplied through the phrase, "Lord of lords," noted above). In the Hebrew Scriptures the term *adonai* ("lord") is not often used alone for God, but is usually coupled with the personal name of God (*Yahweh*) when it is intended to convey his authority. When coupled with the phrase "of hosts," the name Yahweh, generally translated "Lord," delineates God's authority over various entities, such as the *stars (Is 40:26, 45:12). It is part of the field of imagery associated with Yahweh the *divine warrior. At his command the hosts of heaven fight from their heavenly courses (Judg 5:20). Similarly, when the Lord refers to *locust hordes invading Israel as his "army," the figure represents his commanding control (Joel 1:4-7; 2:1-11, 25). The people of Israel are called "the hosts of the Lord," and the picture of their departing Egypt in Exodus 12:41 suggests God's authority also over *Egypt, *Pharaoh and the gods of this great superpower. Jeremiah underscores this sovereignty over Israel by using the image of "the Lord of hosts, the God of Israel" more than thirty times.

Often the meaning of "hosts" is ambiguous. Zechariah uses the term frequently in association with an angelic visit concerning God's plan for *Jerusalem, so the image might represent God's authority over the heavenly hosts as well as over Israel's history. Psalm 103 places the phrase "his hosts" between the angels "obeying the voice of his word," and all his works in all places of his dominion (Ps 103:20-22); likewise, Psalm 148 offers the image of "hosts" between angels and the *sun, *moon and *stars (Ps 148:2-3). All these figures are important

because the title "Lord of hosts" occurs hundreds of times to picture God's authority over everything imaginable (see especially Isaiah, Jeremiah, Haggai and Zechariah). In Malachi, the phrase "says the Lord of hosts," combines more than twenty times the images of God's authoritative word with all the hosts he commands.

Many of God's names serve as images of his authority. Isaiah 44:6 mingles "Lord of hosts" with "King of Israel," "Redeemer" and "first and last" to confirm that there is no other true God. Isaiah 48:12 connects the idea of "first and last" with the authority God wields over creation, whereas in Revelation that image expresses more his sovereignty over *history (Rev 1:8, 11; 21:6; 22:13). Though the figure of Father connotes many meanings, it symbolizes God's authority, especially in connection with disciplining children, as Hebrews 12:7-12 makes clear.

Psalm 29 brings together many images to ascribe to the Lord the "glory due his name." That phrase, the coupling of *"glory" with *"strength," and the Psalm's contents combine to imply that the word *glory* is itself an image for divine authority. Seven times "the voice of the Lord" is described to portray God's sovereign creation and rescue of Israel. The poem culminates in the image of God as king over all, sitting enthroned over the primordial flood—a picture representing authority over both nature and history.

Angelic Authority. The authority of good *angels is a derived legitimacy, pictured by "the glory of the Lord" that accompanies angelic visitation (Lk 2:9). Hebrews 9:5 underscores angels' representation of God's authority by declaring that above the ark of the covenant were "the cherubim of the Glory" (cf. 2 Sam 6:2). Similarly, the seraphim of Isaiah 6:2 proclaim antiphonally the authority of "the Lord of hosts" portrayed in the glory which fills the earth. Though angels serve primarily as images for God's authority, they also wield it with various objects also symbolizing it, such as the cherubim's flaming swords at the *Garden of Eden (Gen 3:24), the seraphim's burning coal (Is 6:6-7) and the *trumpets, *seals and *bowls of Revelation.

Demonic Authority. That the powers of evil exercise only a usurped authority is portrayed by the image of the dragon (whose seven heads symbolize "perfect" authority; *see* Monster) being thrown down from heaven in the war with archangel Michael and his angels (Rev 12:3, 7-9). Just as God the Father passed on his authority to the Son and the Son to the *Holy Spirit (Jn 5:26-27; 16:7-15), so *Satan's imitation of God and of his authority is represented by the figures of the dragon giving authority to the first beast and of the second beast exercising the authority of the first (Rev 13:2-12). The images of the "prince of devils" (Mt 9:34; 12:24), of this world (Jn 12:31; 14:30; 16:11) and "of the power of the air" (Eph 2:2) all show Satan's authority to be falsely derivative and less than the divine authority of the King.

The NT somewhat ambiguously uses several terms as images for Satan's minions. Under the general title of "methods of the devil," Ephesians 6:11-12 names four agents—principalities (*archē*), authorities (*exousiai*), world rulers of this darkness and spiritual forces of wickedness in the heavenlies. When the first two terms are used in connection with human entities, their meaning is clearly that of governments and public officials (e.g., Tit 3:1), but how the supernatural powers employing Satan's authority should be conceived is left unexplained (1 Cor 15:24; Rom 8:38; Col 1:16; 2:10; 15; Eph 1:21; 3:10; 6:12). Other images include *stoicheia* ("elements," Gal 4:3, 9; Col 2:8, 20) and *angeloi* ("angels," Rom 8:38; 2 Thess 1:7; 1 Cor 4:9; 6:3; 11:10; 13:1; Gal 3:19; Col 2:18). Though the exact meaning of these terms is widely debated, their significance as images is that evil supernatural forces exploit authority in many forms. Certain is the assurance that at the end of time all evil angels and authorities will be subjected to Jesus (Mt 28:18), who sits at God's right hand (also a figure for authority, Mk 14:62; 1 Pet 3:22; 1 Cor 15:24). The triumph of God's ultimate authority is vividly portrayed by the image of the devil and his minions being thrown into the lake of *fire and *brimstone (Rev 20:10).

See also ANGEL; ASSEMBLY, DIVINE; AUTHORITY, HUMAN; DEMONS; DIVINE WARRIOR; GOD; KING, KINGSHIP; ROYAL COURT.

AUTHORITY, HUMAN

Authority is legitimate power. It implies freedom as well as permission to decide and to act. In the human community people in authority provide leadership, direction and discipline. Within the various social structures of the biblical world, we observe many different positions of authority, including parents with *children, masters with *slaves, elders with tribes and *cities, *priests within the *temple, and judges, *prophets and *kings whose sphere of authority extended to an entire nation and even beyond the borders of Israel. The Greco-Roman world provided additional examples of authority drawn from the extended household, the workplace, the city-state and the imperial government. Some of these authority roles supply images and illustrations for spiritual leadership within the nation of Israel and later the community of followers of Jesus.

Images From The Extended Family. *Father/ Mother.* In the ancient world the *father held absolute authority as ruler of the household, but was also expected to guard, support and help the family members. In the OT we find the term *father* used of Naaman by his servant (2 Kings 5:13), of the prophet Elisha by two kings of Israel (2 Kings 5:21; 13:14) and of a young Levite invited by different Israelites to be their priest (Judg 17:10; 18:19). In each case it is a title of *honor given to one who has a role of spiritual leadership.

Although Jesus teaches his *disciples to see *God as their Father, and warns them not to call any human leader their "father" (Mt 23:9), senior leaders in the apostolic community often refer to younger believers as their children (e.g., Peter with Mark, 1 Pet 5:13; Paul with Timothy, 1 Cor 4:17; the apostle John with his readers, 1 Jn 2:28). In 2 Corinthians 12:14 Paul speaks of his readiness to sacrifice with *joy for the Corinthian believers, as a parent saves up for the children. In a beautifully tender passage in 1 Thessalonians, Paul describes himself and his ministry team as a *nursing mother (1 Thess 2:7) as well as an encouraging father providing individualized care (1 Thess 2:1-12). As a spiritual mother, Paul agonizes in giving birth to new believers (Gal 4:19), but as a father, he is also prepared to discipline his children (1 Cor 4:15, 21).

Elder. The term *elder* is used most frequently for leaders of the NT congregations. Its basic meaning is "someone who is older." In the Jewish community the elders were part of the patriarchal clan system. As heads of families they held basically unchallenged authority and were responsible for judicial, political and military decisions. The elders in the Jerusalem church receive the gift for famine relief from the church at Antioch (Acts 11:30) and help decide the basis on which *Gentiles should be received into the church (Acts 15). Paul and Barnabas appoint elders for each of the churches they establish on their first missionary journey (Acts 14:23). Peter refers to himself as a "fellow-elder" (1 Pet 5:1-3), and John the apostle calls himself "the elder" in his second and third letters (2 Jn 1; 3 Jn 1).

Guardian/Pedagogue. In Greco-Roman households of means, the guardian, or pedagogue *(paidagōgos)*, acted as the guardian, disciplinarian or guide for children, conducting them to and from school and overseeing their education until they reached maturity. Sometimes regarded fondly, more often the pedagogue was remembered as a harsh figure, ready to punish with the rod any infraction of his discipline ("heirs, as long as they are minors, are no better than slaves," Gal 4:1). The guardian was to be given respect, as was the father. In Galatians 3:24-25 and 4:1-2 Paul describes the Sinai covenant as a pedagogue that leads Israel to Christ. The law pointed out and punished sin and brought its charges to their age of majority ("the date set by the Father," Gal 4:2), the epoch of Christ. In 1 Corinthians 4:15-16 Paul says that even though the Corinthians have many who assist them and watch over them in their Christian life like guardians, he alone is their spiritual father.

Steward/Manager. Two of the favorite images used by Jesus and the apostles are *"servant" *(diakonos)* and *"slave" *(doulos)*. Although the emphasis is usually on the authority of the Lord as master, there is one kind of household servant who has authority over the property and over the other servants, that is the "steward" or "manager" *(oikonomos)*. In Matthew 24:45-51 (cf. Lk 12:42-48) Jesus tells a parable contrasting the faithful and wise servant, who provides food at the proper time for the household, with the wicked servant who mistreats his fellow-servants. Paul describes the church leader as a steward entrusted with God's work, who must be blameless (Tit 1:7) and faithful (1 Cor 4:2-4). Peter exhorts all Christians to use their spiritual gifts as good stewards of God's grace (1 Pet 4:10).

Images from the Workplace. *Expert builder.* In 1 Corinthians 3:10 Paul compares himself to an expert *builder *(architekton)* who lays the foundation at Corinth upon which others are building. In secular Greek a *tekton* was a craftsman in *wood, *stone or metal, and the *architekton* was the head builder, or contractor or director of works, who oversaw the entire project (cf. Is 3:3, where the master craftsmen is among those who will be removed through God's judgment on the nation).

Pilot. A very colorful leadership word, used only once in the NT (1 Cor 12:28), is *kybernēsis* (administration), based on the word *kybernētēs,* which means the captain, pilot or steersman of a *ship. In the LXX *kybernēsis* is given as the function of rulers (Prov 1:5; 11:14). The term *kybernētēs* is used literally of sailors in Ezekiel 27:8, 27-28 (LXX) and of the pilot of a ship in Acts 27:11 and Revelation 18:17. Acts 27:11 makes clear that the owner of the ship and the pilot are two different people. The owner of the ship determines where it is to go, but the pilot determines the best route and method to get there. In the same way the overall goal of the church is defined by the Lord, the "owner," but the role of the administrator is to establish the specific direction and to coordinate the activities of the other members toward that end.

Shepherd. One of the most familiar and best-loved images of spiritual leadership is the shepherd (*see* Sheep, Shepherd), familiar from passages like Psalm 23 and Ezekiel 34. Although Jesus clearly describes himself in shepherd terminology in John 10, he applies this term only indirectly to his disciples (sending the Twelve to the "lost sheep of Israel" in Mt 10:6 and telling Peter to feed and care for his sheep in Jn 21:15-17). However, after the ascension, when Jesus is no longer present to give personal leadership to his flock, the shepherd metaphor becomes more prominent. Paul exhorts the leaders of the Ephesian church in Acts 20:28: "Take heed to yourselves and to all the flock" (RSV). Also speaking to elders, Peter says, "Tend the flock of God that is your charge" (1 Pet 5:2 RSV). Notice that in both cases the flock belongs to God, not to the shepherd; the shepherd is a servant, assigned the task of caring for God's people (*see* Flock).

The shepherd image conveys ideas of tenderness, nurture and devotion; but it also implies discipline (the *rod and the staff), the setting of limits (*protection against *wolves) and the right to establish direction (leading to *pasture). In fact, the verb *poimanō* is sometimes translated as "rule" (Rev 2:27; 12:5; 19;15; cf. Ps 2:9).

Images from the Larger Community. *Ambassador.* The ambassador was an authorized repre-

sentative who represented the people who sent him and negotiated for them. More than simply the deliverer of a message, the ambassador was authorized to act on behalf of the sender. The status of the ambassador was generally related to the status of the ruler that he represented. In 2 Corinthians 5:20 Paul, speaking of his apostolic role, says, "We are therefore Christ's ambassadors, as though God were making his appeal through us" (NIV). In Ephesians 6:20 he invites the Christians to pray that he will be able to proclaim boldly the gospel, "for which I am an ambassador in chains" (NIV)

Apostle. The apostle is one who is sent by another. The verb *apostellō* appears frequently in the Gospels, in reference to the sending of Jesus by the Father (e.g., Mt 15:24) and the sending of the apostles by Jesus (e.g., Jn 17:18). Jesus uses the word often in his parables to describe servants sent on assignments by their masters (e.g., Mt 20:2; Mk 12:1-6). In Mark 3:13-19 (cf. Lk 6:12-16) Jesus calls his *disciples together and designates twelve of them to be his apostles. The "sent ones" will have two basic responsibilities. First, they are called together to be with Jesus, that is to share a common life. In the second place, they are called to share in a task, to announce a message and to exercise authority over the powers of darkness. They will share in Jesus' own authority, speaking and taking action as representatives of the Messiah. Others who are called apostles in the NT include Paul (Rom 1:1), Barnabas (Acts 14:4,14), Silas and Timothy (1 Thess 1:1; 2:6-7), and possibly Andronicus and Junias (Rom 16:7).

Herald. In classical Greek the "herald" *(keryx)* was commissioned by a ruler or by the state to call out some item of news or to announce a judicial verdict. The word implies a binding and commanding proclamation. Paul calls himself a herald in 1 Timothy 2:7 and 2 Timothy 1:11.

Leader. Two different Greek words are translated as *"leader." The word *hēgoumenos,* which means leader in the sense of a guide, is used of kings of Israel (Ezek 43:7), military commanders (1 Macc 9:30; 2 Macc 14:6), rulers of Judah (Mt 2:6) and Joseph's position as ruler of Egypt (Acts 7:10). Thus it is used for broad and authoritative leadership roles. In Acts 15:22 Judas and Silas are called "leaders among the brothers." The author of Hebrews exhorts his readers to remember their leaders, to imitate them, to obey them and to submit to them (Heb 13:7, 17).

Another word for leader, *prohistamenos,* was used in secular Greek for leadership in an army, a state or a party. The basic meaning is "to set before or over someone or something." It implied guarding, protecting and taking responsibility, combining presiding with personal care. Paul uses this word for church leaders in 1 Thessalonians 5:12, 13 and 1 Timothy 5:17 and cites leadership as a spiritual gift in Romans 12:8.

Overseer. In secular Greek the word *overseer (episkopos)* was used of men with responsible positions with the state and of officials in religious communities. It implied overall supervising, ordering, evaluating and setting direction. This term is used interchangeably with "elder" for leaders in the local congregations (Phil 1:1; 1 Tim 3:1; Tit 1:5, 7; Acts 20:17; 1 Pet 5:1, 2).

Royal priest. At the foot of Mount *Sinai, before the giving of the Ten Commandments, God says to his people, "You will be for me a kingdom of priests and a holy nation" (Ex 19:6 NIV). The same idea of the corporate priesthood of the entire nation of Israel is contained in the promise of Isaiah for Israel regathered by the Messiah in the year of Jubilee: "You will be called priests of the Lord" (Is 61:6 NIV). The image of priest is not used in the NT for individual believers, but for the community as whole. Peter calls believers a "holy priesthood" (1 Pet 2:5) and a "royal priesthood" (1 Pet 2:9). The privileges of leading in *worship and of *offering *sacrifice, formerly reserved for the priests, now belong to all God's people.

The book of Revelation employs the image of priest several times to describe the privileged position made available to Christians. In Revelation 1:6 John describes Jesus Christ as the one who has made believers to be "a kingdom and priests to serve his God and Father" (NIV). In Revelation 5:9-10 the four living creatures and the twenty-four elders sing praise to the *Lamb, who made believers from every nation to be "a kingdom and priests" who will "reign on the earth." Revelation 20:6 says that believer-priests will reign with Christ for a thousand years. These verses highlight another aspect of the priestly function: to share in God's rule, just as the priests taught the law to God's people and helped them to order the life of the community accordingly.

Prophet. The OT *prophet was one who proclaimed the word of God and was called by God to warn, to encourage, to comfort and to teach. The prophet was responsible directly to God and did not receive authority from any human appointment. Jesus was popularly acclaimed as a prophet by his contemporaries (Lk 24:19; Jn 4:19; 6:17; 7:40; 9:17) and seemed to regard himself as a prophet (Lk 4:24; Mk 6:4; Mt 13:57), though he was, like John, "more than a prophet" (Mt 12:38-41; Lk 11:29-32). Very early in the history of the church, people known as prophets are recognized and given leadership in the believing community. We find some prophets having an itinerant ministry (Acts 11:27-28; 21:10) while others function as part of the ongoing leadership of the congregation (Acts 13:1; 15:22, 32). The functions of prophets specifically detailed in the NT include warning the Christian community of impending difficulties (Acts 11:28; 21:10-11); speaking to encourage, strengthen, comfort and instruct believers (Acts 15:32; 1 Cor 14:24-25); and preparing God's people for works of service (Eph 4:11-12). Prophets are often mentioned together with apostles as playing the foundational leadership roles in the church (1 Cor 12:28; Eph 2:20; 4:11),

Teacher. In secular Greek the word *teacher (di-

daskalos) was widely used and covered all those who were engaged in the formal transfer of knowledge and skills. The word occurs only twice in the LXX, probably because the OT emphasis is more on obedience than on imparting information. Yet in the NT we see that within the Christian community as well, the task of the teacher is not only to communicate the facts of the Christian faith but also to be concerned for changes in attitude and behavior.

In Acts the leadership of the Antioch church consists of prophets and teachers (Acts 13:1). In the list of spiritual gifts in 1 Corinthians 12:28, teachers are cited third, grouped with apostles and prophets. In Ephesians 4:11 "teachers" appear after apostles, prophets and evangelists, in a sort of hyphenated form with "pastors," thus "pastor-teachers," who share in the work of equipping other believers for ministry.

Another word used for teaching in the Christian community is *katecheō*, which means to pass on information about something. In Galatians 6:6 Paul says that the community should provide support for its teachers.

Missing Images. It is significant to note that in their images for life and leadership within the believing community, Jesus and the apostles avoided the numerous words compounded from the root *arch-*, which have to do with rule, and which carry a strong tone of authority. At least sixteen of these words occur in the NT, but none of them are ever applied to the disciple of Jesus, with the exception of Paul's reference to himself in 1 Corinthians 3:10 as an "expert builder" *(architekton)* who laid the foundation for others to build upon. Jesus often refers to his followers as "servants" and as "brothers," encouraging them to think of themselves as those who were "under" and "among" rather than "over." Jesus places far more emphasis in the development of his disciples on their following than on their leading. He warns his disciples against the rulers of the Gentiles, who lord it over their followers and exercise authority over them. Instead, Jesus tells them: "Whoever wants to be great among you must be your servant, and whoever wants to be first must be your slave" (Lk 20:25-27 NIV).

The image of the servant remains a central motif in the NT letters. Even the apostles, who exercise the highest human authority within the church, describe themselves as servants of Christ (1 Cor 3:5). Their ministry is called *diakonia,* the service of a table waiter. Whatever authority each one has, he or she possesses it by the call of God and by the grace of God. The authority is not to be used to domineer but to serve and to *build.

Portraits of Authority and Attitudes Toward Authority. *Attitudes toward civil authority.* The young *David, even though he is recently anointed (1 Sam 16:13), enters the service of King Saul, giving him the proper devotion and honor due a *king (1 Sam 16:21-23) and remaining in his service despite Saul's occasional attempts to kill him (1 Sam 18:11).

Here we have an odd picture of a subject who knows that he will be king but still renders honor to the incumbent Saul—despite the necessity of dodging Saul's spears. This regard for the king's authority is continued in a later incident when David has an opportunity to kill Saul, but out of honor for the Lord's anointed, he does not (1 Sam 24:10).

A sorry example of a subject in relationship to his king is the case of King David and Joab, his army commander. David instructs Joab to make sure that Uriah the Hittite will die in battle (2 Sam 11:14-15). Joab automatically obeys, and in giving blind obedience to his lord, Joab disobeys a higher, superseding relational authority: his own obedience to God and the laws of God.

An incident of pure and simple respect for kings, perhaps a healthy fear, comes from the time of Zechariah and the rebuilding of the *temple in Jerusalem. King Darius issues an edict concerning the Jews and the temple construction. He decrees that the local authorities, namely, Tattenai, the governor of Trans-Euphrates, should give all necessary support to the project. Darius concludes his edict by explaining that those who do not obey will be impaled on a piece of wood pulled from their own house. Needless to say, the Jews are given enthusiastic support by Tattenai and his peers (Ezra 6:6-13).

In the Gospels we find the Pharisees raising for Jesus the subject of taxes (Mt 22:17). Is it right to pay taxes to Caesar? The answer given by Jesus is suitably ambiguous—give to Caesar what is Caesar's (Mt 22:21)—and suitably damning, for the Pharisees produce from their own pockets the coin bearing the blasphemous image of Caesar.

In Paul's instructions that believers should pay taxes to Caesar and submit to his authority (Rom 13:1-6; Tit 3:1; 1 Pet 2:13), we find a godly respect for the authority structures that God has ordained (Rom 13:1; cf. Dan 2:21). The righteous should not fear the government. Only those citizens who do wrong should. (Rom 13:4; 1 Pet 2:14). On the other hand, a fear not unlike the fear that is proper toward God—attitudes such as awe, devotion, respect, etc.—is to be rendered to the king (Prov 24:21). These principles inform the narrative portrait in Acts when Paul appeals to Caesar, throwing himself on the mercy of Rome (Acts 25:10-11). We see a display of a Christian's attitude toward civil authority, in this case a Roman citizen toward Caesar, with the expectation that justice will be done. Paul manifests the attitude that he had articulated in Romans 13:3-4: a citizen who has done only good should have nothing to fear from his government.

Attitudes toward people by civil authorities. Various degrees of incompetence are displayed by the kings of Israel. Rehoboam, the son of Solomon, shows an affinity for incompetence in that he declares to his people that his rule will be characterized by scourging people with scorpions (1 Kings 12:14). Here is an example of a ruler refusing to listen to his own people (1 Kings 12:15).

Cyrus, king of Persia, deals with the people of Israel with great mercy. This is, no doubt, due to God moving his heart. However, the fact is that Cyrus chose to obey the dictate of God, resulting in his attitude of encouragement, charity and generosity; he provides for the people of Israel to return and rebuild the temple in Jerusalem (Ezra 1:2-11).

A quisling, toady attitude toward the people is displayed by Pontius Pilate in the matter of Jesus' sentencing. Though Pilate is fully aware of Jesus' innocence, he is more interested in the people's favor. Pilate is willing to murder an innocent man and release a murderer simply to enjoy the good will of the people (Lk 23:23-25).

Attitudes toward priests. The relationship between the first high priest, Aaron, and the people of Israel is indicative of the long and tumultuous affair of priest and people that runs jaggedly through biblical history. Though the people have every reason to fear and reverence Aaron as the channel of God's power—from the days of the plagues and his serpentine rod (Ex 7:8-13)—they demonstrate a recurring tendency to forget the potency of his office. Thus we have such incidents as the golden *calf, where the people approach Aaron the high priest and, in effect, demand that he participate with them—no, lead them into sin (Ex 32). In contrast, we later find the people of Israel eagerly standing before Aaron, waiting for his blessing and for the completion of the sin offering, ready to fall on the ground in joy with no memory of the golden calf (Lev 9:22-24).

Paul's trial before the Sanhedrin demonstrates the automatic honor and respect that a priest engenders in the people. Before Paul knows who Ananias is, he speaks rudely to him; but after he is told that Ananias is the high priest, Paul immediately backs down, saying that one should not speak evil of a ruler (Acts 23:3-5).

A fine disregard is shown by the apostles for priests in Jerusalem. Even though the priests repeatedly command them not to preach the gospel, throw them into jail and have them flogged, the apostles do not pay attention to them (Acts 5:40-42). Such incidents as these illustrate the dynamic that earthly authorities can be righteously superseded if those authorities overstep their God-given boundaries, in this case the proclamation of the gospel.

Attitudes by priests toward the people. Hophni and Phineas, the two sons of Eli, are two examples of priests who misuse and abuse their positions of trust as priests (1 Sam 2:12-17). They are contemptuous of their fellow Israelites as they steal from the people's offerings and sleep with the women who serve at the Tent of Meeting (1 Sam 2:22).

The grief and sorrow of Ezra the priest when he hears that the people of Israel have been intermarrying with neighboring people portrays a man who feels the weight of responsibility for his people, regarding them as if they are his children. When he hears the news, Ezra tears his clothes and rips hair from his head and beard (Ezra 9:3). Then he fell on his knees before God and prays—a priest confessing before God on behalf of the people.

Annas, Caiaphas and the rest of their priestly entourage do not punish Peter and John for fear of displeasing the people (Acts 4:21). We recognize that they are doing the right thing, even though it is for the wrong reason. However, the more fundamental dynamic of priests ordering their behavior according to the whim of the people harks back to the relationship of Aaron with the people of Israel and Aaron's tendency to conform to the desires of the people (e.g., the golden calf).

Attitudes of children toward parents. In the biblical perspective, the beginning of a *child's regard for his or her parents begins with honor. The commandment concerning the parent-child relationship, "Honor your father and your mother" (Deut 5:16 NIV), is the first commandment given that speaks directly to a horizontal, human-to-human relationship. It sets the biblical standard of all children's behavior toward their parents. According to Mosaic law, if a child curses his father and mother, he will receive the punishment of death (Ex 21:17). Such apparent severity serves to underscore the honor given to the child-parent relationship.

The God-based authority and value of the position of the father is highlighted in the idea of the paternal blessing, a *blessing sought after and coveted by any son. The story of Jacob and Esau illustrates the worth placed upon a father's spoken words of blessing. Jacob is willing to go to extraordinary lengths to obtain the blessing, even if it means incurring the wrath of his brother (Gen 27).

The three sons of Noah display two different attitudes toward their father, resulting in markedly disparate effects. Ham, the youngest son, does not honor Noah in his drunken and naked state. Shem and Japheth, however, demonstrate decorous filial respect by covering their father's nakedness while, at the same time, being careful not to look upon him (Gen 9:20-23). The practical outcome of all of this is that Ham is cursed and his two older brothers are blessed (Gen 9:25-27).

The honor that Isaac accords Abraham in allowing his father to choose a wife for him is emblematic of the time and culture. The idea is perhaps surprising for a modern society (Gen 24), a surprise that only serves to delineate the immense chasm between images of child-parent relations of modern times and those of the Bible.

A stark, though perhaps macabre, example of a daughter honoring her father is found in the story of Jephthah's daughter. She respects the oath that her father has taken, even though his impetuous words have condemned her to death (Judg 11:30-39).

The story of Esther affords another curious picture of a child honoring her father—in this case, a father figure. Though Mordecai is only the cousin of Esther, he raises the young orphan as if she were his daughter (Esther 2:7). Esther is obedient to Mordecai before and after she becomes queen (Esther 2:10,

20). Even though in all practicality she is in social authority over Mordecai, the bonds of fatherhood compel her to give honor and obedience to him.

An interesting event in Jesus' own childhood underscores the biblical ideal of the obedience and honor a child should give to his parents. When Joseph and Mary reproach him for staying behind in Jerusalem, Jesus protests mildly that he has to be in his Father's house. However, he then returns home and is obedient to them (Lk 2:49-51). Later, Jesus exemplifies child-parent honor toward his mother at the wedding at Cana (Jn 2:1-11).

Attitudes toward children by parents. Genesis portrays *Abraham loving his son Isaac greatly, perhaps more than he loved his own life. However, such fatherly affection does not cause him to waver before the request of God: "Take your son, your only son, Isaac, whom you love . . . sacrifice him there as a burnt offering" (Gen 22:1-3 NIV). The love that *Jacob has for his son *Joseph comes at the expense of his other sons, for Jacob loves Joseph more than the others, resulting in enmity among the brothers (Gen 37:3-4).

King David's love for his son *Absalom is maintained despite Absalom's rebellion and attempt to wrest the kingdom from David. When Absalom is finally killed, David weeps and bemoans the fact that he himself had not died in his son's place (2 Sam 18:33).

Even though Jesus seems to be separating himself from his earthly parents, intent on beginning his ministry, he still demonstrates a filial responsibility and obedience toward his mother when she requests a miracle of him at Cana (Jn 2:1-8).

See also AUTHORITY, DIVINE AND ANGELIC; CHILD, CHILDREN; CIVIL DISOBEDIENCE; FATHER, FATHERHOOD; KING, KINGSHIP; LEADERSHIP; MOTHER, MOTHERHOOD; PRIEST; PROPHET.

AVENGER

The word *avenger* evokes the notion of revenge or of setting matters right. It appears in the Bible in both a *legal or civil sense as a code that governs human behavior, and in a theological sense as a picture of God's *judgment and *salvation. To a *guilty person being pursued, the avenger is a figure of terror; to the person who has been wronged, the avenger is a figure of justice and therefore consolation—a silencer of the human protest against unpunished wrong. In both cases there is something awe-inspiring and fearful about the avenger.

On a human and civil plane the institution of the avenger existed within an ancient or primitive society that had not yet evolved our system of courtroom trial. In such a milieu exacting justice was a family duty, with the primary responsibility resting on the male who was next of kin to the aggrieved party. The avenger was the designated and impartial agent of justice—the one who exacted satisfaction for a wrong by punishing the wrongdoer in kind (hence the "eye for an eye" law that reverberates throughout the Mosaic code). Of course the possibility always existed that an avenger might exceed a just retribution, as in the sinister figure of Lamech, who boasted to his wives that he had exacted vengeance *sevenfold (Gen 4:23-24).

The concept of the avenger finds its most concrete expression with respect to blood revenge. This reflects an ancient Near Eastern practice by which the avenger of blood avenged the death of a blood relative. Limits were placed on this practice in Israel: *murderers were executed, but persons guilty of unintentional manslaughter could seek *refuge at the *altar (Ex 21:13) or in certain designated cities (Num 35:11-28; Deut 4:41-43; Josh 20:1-9), where they were exempt from blood vengeance.

There may be a reference to the desert code of vengeance in Psalm 23:5, with its picture of a *table prepared in the presence of enemies. According to this code, which is intertwined with the desert law of *hospitality, someone fleeing from avengers was exempt from vengeance for a span of two days and the intervening night ("so long as the food is in this bowels") if he or she could touch the ropes of a tent or throw himself within the entrance. When the period of immunity ended the guilty person had to go forth and face the bloody assize.

In the OT various leaders fill the role of avenger in a range of situations. *Samson avenged the burning of his wife and her father (Judg 15:6-7) and the loss of his eyesight at the hands of the Philistines (Judg 16:28). Saul spoke of avenging himself on his enemies (1 Sam 14:24; 18:25). Joab was judged blameworthy by *David for having avenged the death of his brother during a time of truce (1 Kings 2:5). Elsewhere the nation of Israel assumed the role of avenger, as in their defeat of the Midianites (Num 31:2) and of those who plotted their murder during the time of *Esther (Esther 8:13).

In the Bible the avenger ($g\bar{o}$'$\bar{e}l$ $hadd\bar{a}m$) is actually a "redeemer" or "restorer" of the *blood (= life) that was taken. The killing of a relative was understood by the remaining family members as stealing blood that belonged to the entire clan and therefore must be returned. This concept is associated with the *Passover celebration in which the destroyer exacts the blood (lives) of the Egyptians, who had subjected the lives (blood) of the Lord's people to *bondage. Here the avenger is satisfied only after he sees the lamb's blood on the doorposts.

The image of the avenger finds its fullest expression with respect to God, since it is to God that vengeance ('$ekdik\bar{e}sis$) ultimately belongs (Rom 12:19; Heb 10:30). The earliest appearance of the image of the avenger occurs in Genesis 3, where the flaming swords of God's cherubim protect God's holy garden from intrusion by fallen mortals.

God acts as avenger in a range of situations. Sometimes he acts as avenger on behalf of individuals against their enemies (Judg 11:36; 1 Sam 24:12; 25:39; 2 Sam 4:8; 16:8). He protects the nation of Israel against its enemies (Joel 3:21; Nahum 1:2; Is 1:24; Jer 46:10).

But God also acts as avenger *against* Israel: he promises to avenge the blood of his servants and prophets against those who slay or oppress them (Deut 32:43; 2 Kings 9:7; Ps 9:10), and he avenges himself against his people when they break his covenant (Lev 26:25; Ps 99:8). Also important is the motif of God's "day of vengeance" (Is 34:8; 61:2; 63:4).

In the NT too God functions as avenger (*ekdikos*) in all matters among his people (1 Thess 4:6). Jesus asked rhetorically, "And shall not God avenge his own elect, which cry day and night unto him?" (Luke 18:7 KJV). Christ is portrayed as avenger in the ultimate sense. As the slain Lamb he avenges his own blood (Rev 5:6-9) as he wages holy *warfare on his *enemies (Rev 19:11-15). During this time of unrestrained *violence (Rev 19:15), the uniquely qualified avenger completely vanquishes himself of his archenemy *Satan and his followers (Rev 20:10-14; see also the parable of the landowner, Mt 21:33-45).

With God's role as avenger so prominent in the Bible, it is not surprising that a subordinate motif is the prayers that his persecuted followers pray to him as avenger. We find such prayers in the individual and corporate *lament psalms (e.g., Ps 7:6; 79:10; 94:1-2). In the apocalyptic vision of the *martyrs under the altar, the martyrs cry out, "O Sovereign Lord, holy and true, how long before thou wilt judge and avenge our blood on those who dwell upon the earth?" (Rev 6:10 RSV). These passages form the biblical subtext for John Milton's moving sonnet occasioned by the massacre of the Waldensians, which begins with the line, "Avenge, O Lord, thy slaughtered saints."

See also BLOOD; GUILT; MURDER STORIES; LEGAL IMAGES; VIOLENCE.

AWAKENING

The general concept of "awakening" captures the notion of either rousing oneself or being aroused in order to take action, as in the call to Deborah to "wake up" in song (Judg 5:12 NIV). Such calls to action are usually accompanied by urgency and intensity, as seen in the emphatic repetition "wake up, wake up!" (Judg 5:12; cf. Is 52:1). It suggests an arousal from the passivity and vulnerability of sleep in order to seize the initiative, to take aggressive action (Judg 16:14, 20). Although the Scriptures frequently employ the motif in its usual sense of awaking from physical sleep (e.g., Gen 41:4; Acts 16:27), this meaning is enriched in a number of significant ways.

Among its most fascinating usages are instances where the biblical poet issues urgent appeals to God to "wake up," to respond to pleas for *justice (Ps 7:6), vindication (Ps 35:23), *triumph (Ps 44:23), *salvation (Ps 80:2) and deliverance (Is 51:9). Jesus' awakening from his peaceful slumber in the stern of the boat by his fearful disciples is an enactment of this biblical motif of "divine sleep" (Mk 4:38-40). The language of the petitioner is such that his prayer forms an expression of acute anguish and impatience over God's apparent unresponsiveness to great need, as in the case of oppression (Ps 7:6) or defeat (Ps 44:23). It is the psalmist's prayer that the silence of God be broken by swift intervention. But God's silence must never be mistaken for sleep (121:3-4)! God is ever to be contrasted with "sleeping Baal" and lifeless idols (1 Kings 18:27; cf. Hab 2:19). God's swift judgment is likened to a person who "wakes from the stupor of wine" (Ps 78:65; cf. Joel 1:5). In a most vivid way it captures the idea of a sudden and dramatic turn of events.

In the human arena moral slumber is likened to wickedness and debauchery (1 Thess 5:6-7). Believers are exhorted to wake up from this sleep and remain alert, given the lateness of the eschatological hour (Rom 13:11-14; 1 Thess 4:6) and the approaching dawn of deliverance (Ps 57:8), the early rays of which are already beginning to appear. God's people are to "come to their senses" (1 Cor 15:34) or "wake to righteousness" (KJV). Such a spirit of wakefulness is extolled as a virtue (Prov 20:13) in part because it signifies an attentive ear to God's word (Is 50:4)—an indispensable element of spiritual wakefulness. Failure to wake up leads to discipline for believers (Rev 3:2) or (in the case of unbelievers) judgment (1 Thess 5:4ff) and shame (Rev 16:15).

"Wakefulness" is used in the Scriptures in a number of other ways: (1) to depict bodily (Jn 11:11; Dan 12:2) and spiritual (Eph 5:14) resurrection in contrast to the sleep of physical and spiritual death; (2) to signify a troubled spirit (Ps 102:7); or (3) to serve as evidence of trust in the Lord's protection (Ps 3:5). Finally, the Scriptures use awakening in poetic ways, as when the wind is exhorted to blow (Song 4:15) or a musical instrument to "awake the dawn" (Ps 108:2), when a sword strikes (Zech 13:17), or when latent passions are ignited (Song 2:7).

Ultimately the believer can rejoice in the truth that "he died for us so that, whether we are awake or asleep, we may live together with him" (1 Thess 5:10).

See also SLEEP.

B

BAAL. *See* GODS, GODDESSES.

BABEL, TOWER OF

The image of the Tower of Babel has a hold on the Western imagination that is out of proportion to its actual importance in the Bible. The story is told in just nine short verses (Gen 11:1-9) and is not mentioned again. Yet it is one of the most evocative images in the entire Bible—a spectacle of creaturely aspiration toward deity that finds its counterpart in the mythological story of the Titans who tried to supplant Zeus and were punished by being hurled into Tartarus.

Artists have imagined the tower as a physical and architectural phenomenon reaching massively into the sky. More recent biblical commentary entertains the possibility that the tower was a ziggurat—an astronomical observatory for use in divination and occult mastery of the universe. The meaning of the image remains the same in either case. Although in the popular mind Babel denotes confusion and discord, the image encompasses much more than this.

In the biblical text the Tower of Babel begins as a venture in human autonomy: "Come, let us build ourselves a city; . . . let us make a name for ourselves" (Gen 11:4 RSV). As we overhear the excited talk, we catch the hints of the timeless human urge for fame and permanent achievement, as well as for independence and self-sufficiency. The tower is thus an image of human aspiration and pride, accompanied by a spirit of boasting in human achievement. Lurking in the background is the classical notion of *hubris*—overweening human *pride that leads people to think themselves godlike, as hinted by the desire of the builders to include within their city "a tower with its top in the heavens" (Gen 11:4 RSV). Since *heaven is the abode of God, we can interpret the venture as an attempt to storm God's dwelling place. We should note also that in the ancient Near East temples to the gods were built on *high places, with the human city surrounding the dwelling place of a deity.

The fact that the builders conceive of their enterprise as a *city awakens a whole further set of associations. The city is par excellence an image of human community—an image of the universal human dream of unity with other people (in the story the people speak "to one another," Gen 11:2), combined with a desire for sedentary permanence ("lest

we be scattered abroad upon the face of the whole earth," Gen 11:4). We should note that this collective pride is mingled with *fear, so that the city becomes a *quest for safety as well as achievement. The dream of unity is enhanced by Babel's being a unilingual city: "Now the whole earth had one language and few words" (Gen 11:1 RSV).

Babel, of course, is also a symbol of human inventiveness and ingenuity—a triumph of both reason (as the people calculate their needs and consider the means of meeting those needs) and imagination (as the people create a brand new vision of how things might be). It is a place of language and communication: "they said to one another" (Gen 11:3).

The city, moreover, is a picture of human ability to control and master the world. The Genesis narrative hints at this by emphasizing the specific building materials: " 'Come, let us make bricks, and burn them thoroughly.' And they had brick for stone, and bitumen for mortar" (Gen 11:3 RSV). This is a picture of technology (note that the people make *bricks instead of mining *stone), of material power, of monumental architectural ability, of culture and civilization, of forethought and planning. *Fire is a universal symbol of civilization, art and craft; while bricks are the symbol of permanence and stability. But bitumen or asphalt is hardly an adequate mortar, so already we sense a flaw in the blueprint.

Babel symbolizes the dream of human civilization. It is an attempt to meet human means by the peaceful means of invention, language, utopian plan-

A Babylonian ziggurat, or step temple, perhaps like the tower of Babel.

ning, social cooperation, creativity, culture and technology. Yet God declares the dream a nightmare in a story that to this day represents a primal act of divine *judgment.

Halfway through the story the focus shifts from the human perspective to God's perspective: "And the LORD came down to see the city and the tower, which the sons of men had built" (Gen 11:5 RSV). We can see in this reaching down a counterpoint to the human aspiration upward, with an implicit irony in the fact that whereas the human builders envisioned their architectural feat as a skyscraper, from a more transcendent viewpoint it is so small that God must come down to catch a glimpse of the tower. The story is thus "a remarkable satire on man's doing" (von Rad). God disapproves of the dream of limitless human achievement: "Behold, they are one people, and they have all one language; and this is only the beginning of what they will do; and nothing that they propose to do will now be impossible for them" (Gen 10:6). God therefore thwarts the attempt at unity by diversifying human language, with the result that "the LORD scattered them abroad over the face of all the earth" (Gen 10:9).

Behind this statement by God we can infer retrospectively that the dream pursued with so much zeal and with such apparently innocent motives was really a picture of *idolatry—an attempt to make people and civilization the basis of security and the object of ultimate allegiance. The Tower of Babel as envisioned was implicitly a substitute deity, and it carries the same divine scorn that idolatry carries everywhere in the Bible. In God's view, division of the human race is preferable to collective *apostasy, and the experiment in human initiative apart from God ends in judgment. What began as a stunning example of unity (one language) ends in dispersal, a motif inverted on *Pentecost (Acts 2) when a *multiplicity* of spoken languages in the *city* of Jerusalem produces the new *unity* of the Christian community.

What a wealth of human meanings converge in the single image of Babel! It is an ambivalent image, evoking powerful feelings of a wide range. On one side we can see the human longings for community, achievement, civilization, culture, technology, safety, security, permanence and fame. But countering these aspirations we sense the moral judgment against idolatry, pride, self-reliance, the urge of material power and the human illusion of infinite achievement. It is a picture of misguided human aspirations ending in confusion—in literary terms an episode of epic proportions that follows the downward arc of tragedy. Acting as a single entity the human race reached for everything and ended only with division. The concluding picture of a half-built tower and city is a monument to human aspiration gone awry and to divine judgment against human illusions of infinity. The very etymology of the word *Babel* suggests the two aspects of the story: the Akkadian word *Bab-ili* means 'gate of God,' while the Hebrew *balal* means 'to stir up, to confound.'

See also BABYLON; BRICKS; CITY; HIGH, HEIGHT, HIGH PLACE; IDOLATRY; JUDGMENT; PRIDE.

BIBLIOGRAPHY. G. von Rad, *Genesis: A Commentary* (Philadelphia: Westminster, 1972) 148-152; L. R. Kass, "What's Wrong with Babel?" *The American Scholar* 58 (1989-90) 41-60.

BABY

"It's a boy!" "It's a girl!" This is (almost) always good news in the Bible, especially when the baby fulfills a divine promise. Babies in the Bible are an image of (a) the mystery of life created (in some sense a miracle from God), (b) God's provision for parents (especially mothers), (c) the removal of the stigma of *barrenness, (d) the potential for either good or evil, and (e) inconsolable grief when an infant dies or is executed.

Isaac (Gen 21:1-7), Jacob (Gen 25:21-26), Joseph (Gen 29:22-24), Samson (Judg 13) and Samuel (1 Sam 1) are all special babies because their *births confirm the promise of salvation. Their births also come as something of a surprise, since they were delivered by women stigmatized by *barren wombs. The element of surprise highlights the divine origin of life and heightens the joy of birth. Sarah laughed to see her baby boy (Gen 21:6); Hannah sang for joy (1 Sam 2:1-10). Naomi was barren too, but the grandson she cradled in her lap was her kinsman-*redeemer: Obed, grandfather of King *David (Ruth 4:13-17). Although not in the patriarchal line, the story surrounding the birth of a promised *son as a reward for godliness to the barren Shunammite woman also fits the biblical archetype (2 Kings 4:11-17).

The context within which we can understand the value and joy that OT people placed on babies is the stigma that attached to women who bore no children. The barren wife is an object of pity, an archetype of the outcast in Hebrew society (e.g., Sarah [Gen 16:1-6], Rachel [Gen 29:31—30:24] and Hannah [1 Sam 1:1-11]). In such a cultural milieu "the fruit of the womb" is regarded as a "heritage" and *"reward" from God (Ps 127:3 RSV).

The general biblical pattern is thus that babies are very nearly the highest earthly *joy that a person can expect to experience. The stories of *Cain (Gen 4:1), Ishmael (16:1-6) and Esau (25:24-5) are the exceptions that prove the rule: babies are bad news when they grow up to be enemies of the people of God.

The best-known birth stories in the Bible focus on miracle babies. Isaac and *Samson at once come to mind, both of them offspring whose birth was announced to a barren wife. *Moses was another miracle baby, not because his mother was barren but because his life was forfeit to the Egyptians (Ex 2:1-10; cf. Acts 7:19). His mother put him in a papyrus basket (*see* Ark), along the banks of the Nile, where his cries evoked pity even from Pharoah's daughter. The birth of John the Baptist followed the patriarchal pattern. Elizabeth was as old as Sarah and as barren as Rachel (Lk 1:5-25), but she gave birth to a baby boy. When her baby leaped in her womb, he proved that a fetus is a person (Lk 1:41; cf. Jer 1:5, Ps 51:5).

The nativity of Jesus is the climax of the Bible's attention to babies. The infant *Jesus shared a common humanity with the other babies of promise, but the difference made all the difference in the world. The reason for Mary's inability to bear a son—*virginity—proved that her baby was God as well as human (Mt 1:18-25). Mary gave birth to a baby for every human to celebrate: the Savior of the world, Jesus Christ.

Having a baby brings joy to a house, but infant mortality brings inconsolable *grief. Pharaoh killed all the Hebrew baby boys (Ex 1:15-22), and David grieved over the mortal illness of Bathsheba's son (2 Sam 12:15-25). When Solomon judged between two women who were fighting over the life and death of a child, the mere prospect of having her son divided led the real mother to prefer giving the baby to the rival claimant (1 Kings 3:16-28). The Shunammite woman is "in bitter distress" when her son dies after heatstroke in the harvest field (2 Kings 4:27). Jeremiah's sad prophecy captures a mother's grief: "A voice is heard in Ramah, weeping and great mourning, Rachel weeping for her children and refusing to be comforted because they are no more" (Jer 31:15 NIV; cf. 6:26). Rachel's *sorrow without succor found its fulfillment when Herod slaughtered the baby boys of Judea (Mt 2:16-18).

Rachel and her sisters will not grieve in the eternal *kingdom of God. According to Isaiah, "never again will there be in [that kingdom] an infant who lives but a few days" (Is 65:20). Nor will parents worry about the safety of their precious babies, for "the infant will play near the hole of the cobra, and the young child will put his hand in the viper's nest" (Is 11:8-9). Jesus says, "The kingdom of God belongs to such as these" (Lk 18:16).

Biblical writers are often keen observers of the intimate relationship between a baby and her mother. God can no more forget to care for his people than a mother can "forget the baby at her breast" (Is 49:15). The psalmist compares his rest in God to a weaned child with his mother (131:2; cf. 1 Sam 1:22-24, Is 28:9), no longer squirming in agitation for his mother's *milk. The theme of the maturing infant is echoed in the NT, where believers are taught to be like hungry newborns who "crave pure spiritual milk" (1 Pet 2:2). But like all babies, they are also supposed to grow up. "Anyone who lives on milk, being still an infant, is not acquainted with the teaching about righteousness" (Heb 5:13).

See also BARRENNESS; BIRTH; BIRTH STORY; DAUGHTER; FATHER, FATHERHOOD; FAVORED CHILD, SLIGHTED CHILD; MILK; MOTHER, MOTHERHOOD; SON; WOMB.

BABYLON

Babylon is one of the dread images of the Bible,

stretching from OT history to the apocalyptic vision of *Revelation. Like its equally famous counterpart *Nineveh, the origins of Babylon (=Babel) lie with Nimrod, "the first on earth to be a mighty man" (Gen 10:8-10). Certainly Babylon herself is portrayed throughout the Bible as the mightiest of *cities, often used by God to bring crushing judgment on other nations (e.g., Jer 21:2-10; 25:8-11). She is his tenant farmer, driving the nations as *oxen under her yoke (Is 47:6; Jer 27:1-12; 28:1-17); his war club, used in their destruction (Jer. 51:20-23); a golden *cup of wrath in his hand, making all the earth *drunk and mad (Jer 51:7; cf. 25:15-38); a zoo keeper, keeping custody of dangerous Judean *lions (Ezek 19:9); Judah, the *prostitute's spurned lover, taking his terrible retribution (Ezek 23:11-35); a *fire set under the cooking pot of Jerusalem, "cooking" her inhabitants in siege and simultaneously burning off the pot's impurities (Ezek 24:1-14); Israel's captor, tormentor, devastator and the location of her *exile (Ps 137:1, 8).

Used by God in his providence, Babylon herself is not immune from judgment at his hands for her impiety, *idolatry and *pride—things for which the inhabitants of the region early gained a reputation (Gen 11:1-9). Her king is pictured as the god of a non-Israelite myth who aspired to ascend the *mountain of the gods and make himself equal to God (Is 14:12-14; cf. Jer 51:53 and especially Dan 3—5 for a narrative exploration of the theme); as a gentle and refined *virgin, unravished and unconquered by any nation (Is 47:1); as mistress of all the kingdoms (Is 47:5), proud and secure as she sits *enthroned like a *goddess (Is 47:7-11; cf. 45:5, 18, 21 for her language as the language of God). Yet the king who sought to ascend to heaven is brought down to the *pit (Is 14:13-15); an axman relieved of his duties (Is 14:4-6); a corpse slain in *battle, yet shamefully unburied (Is 14:18-20).

Queen Babylon, the glory of the Chaldeans, becomes *Sodom and Gomorrah (13:19; cf. Jer 51:39-40). She exchanges her throne for the dust, her pampered existence for the drudgery of grinding *grain; she is deprived of veil and *garments that guard her noble dignity (Is 47:1-3). She knows the pain of a *woman in travail, the insecurity of the hunted gazelle or the defenseless *flock from which *lambs can easily be taken (Is 13:8, 14; Jer 50:44-45). She is both *widow and bereaved *mother (Is 47:8-9), disgraced by the behavior of her *children and rendered infertile (Jer 50:11-13); a wasted ruin inhabited by wild beasts and *flooded with water (Is 13:20-22; 14:23; Jer 51:37). She is the proud opponent of God now *hunted down by his *archers (Jer 50:13-14, 29-30); a field about to be *harvested in judgment, a *threshing floor awaiting the winnowers to separate the *wheat from the *chaff (Jer 51:1-5, 33); *lions made drunk with *wine and slaughtered while asleep, as if they were *sheep and *goats (51:38-40). God's war club now lies broken and shattered (Jer 50:23); the destroying mountain is now destroyed by God (Jer 51:25-26); the *monster who has swallowed up God's people is now forced to regurgitate them (Jer 51:34, 44).

Already in the OT (cf. Is 13:1-22, esp. the ultimacy of the language in Is 13:9-13; 14:3-23) and certainly in the NT (e.g., 1 Pet 5:13; cf. 1:1; 2:11), Babylon stands not for a specific power but more generally for world power in opposition to God—the empire where God's people live in *exile. This is particularly clear in *Revelation, which draws heavily on OT imagery in portraying the end times. Here stands Babylon the great, the mother of *prostitutes. She is the harlot, drunk on the blood of the *martyrs, making others drunk with the wine of fornication (Rev 17:1-6), forced by God to drink a double draught of judgment in her own *cup (18:3-6). She is the arrogant and secure queen of the whole earth, now smitten suddenly and decisively with pestilence, mourning and famine (17:15-18, 18:7-8); desolate, *naked and destroyed (17:16); deprived of all her previous luxuries (18:11-19). She is the ruin inhabited by *demons and *birds (18:2). The force of the imagery is the more strongly felt in Revelation because of the deliberate contrast drawn toward the end of the book between Babylon and the new *Jerusalem, which is presented as the *Bride of Christ (19:6-9; 21:1-27).

See also BABEL, TOWER OF; CITY; EXILE; EZEKIEL; ISAIAH; JEREMIAH; PRIDE; REVELATION; ROME.

BACK SIDE

The "back side" is a spatial or positioning image of being behind or in back of a person. It ranges from an evocative image of divine glory to an equally evocative image of rejection.

The image of God's "back side" (*'āḥôr*) is employed in the passage in which *Moses, on Mount *Sinai, requests to see God's *glory (Ex 33:18—34:8). But God tells the lawgiver that no one can see his face (or "front") and live (Ex 33:20). Moses is nevertheless permitted to see God's back side (Ex 33:23), at which time the Lord declares that he is "full of grace and truth" (Ex 34:6). God's "back side" is here a veiling image, distancing the full glory of God from human view, but paradoxically revealing a very full sense of God's glory even as it is partly concealed.

The prologue to *John's Gospel (Jn 1:1-18) alludes to this OT image of glory. According to the last verse, "No one has ever seen God; the only *Son, who was in the bosom of the Father, he has made him known" (Jn 1:18 RSV). The fourth evangelist contrasts Moses, through whom the *law was given, with Jesus, through whom came *grace and truth (Jn 1:17). Whereas Moses could not see God's *face (i.e., look fully upon his grace), the incarnation permits humankind to view God's grace (Jn 1:14), as revealed by the one who had existed from eternity in a face-to-face relationship with God (Jn 1:18, and 1:1: "and the Word was with [lit. facing] God").

An understanding of the biblical imagery of being "cast behind" depends on our awareness that the face is the source of personal contact with another. Hence to face someone implies attention or awareness and often connotes a loving gaze or empowerment. To be cast "behind" (*'aḥar*), therefore, is to be removed from someone's sight or presence. Sometimes in the Bible this is a negative image of rejection of a person or of God. Thus Ahijah pronounces God's *judgment against Jeroboam because he had cast God behind his back (1 Kings 14:9). Elsewhere, Israel faces judgment because the nation has forgotten God and has cast him behind its back (Ezek 23:35). Equally ignominious is the way the Israelites "cast thy law behind their back and slew thy prophets" (Neh 9:26 KJV).

The most famous instance of such rejection occurs in the NT. Following Jesus' first passion prediction, Peter rebukes Jesus (Mk 8:32). Jesus rebukes Peter in turn: "Get behind [*opisō*] me, Satan! For you are not on the side of God, but of men" (Mk 8:33 RSV). Getting "behind" Jesus conjures up this image of rejection. Peter's opposition to Jesus' passion is to be banished from the thinking of the disciples.

As an image of removal, being cast behind can also have a positive connotation when it signifies God's *forgiveness of sin. The repentant Hezekiah prays, "You have cast all my sins behind Your back" (Is 38:17 NKJV). The image here is not just of something placed behind someone where it could be seen by turning around but instead placed where it can never be seen. The same image appears in Paul's statement, "forgetting what lies behind and straining forward to what lies ahead, I press on toward the goal for the prize of the upward call of God in Christ Jesus" (Phil 3:13-14 RSV).

See also BEHIND; FACE, FACIAL EXPRESSIONS; GLORY.

BIBLIOGRAPHY. E. Dinkler, "Peter's Confession and the 'Satan' Saying: The Problem of Jesus' Messiahship," in *The Future of Our Religious Past*, ed., J. M. Robinson (London: SCM Press; New York: Harper & Row, 1971) 169-202; A. T. Hanson, "John 1:14-18 and Exodus 34," in *The New Testament Interpretation of Scripture* (London: SPCK, 1980) 97-109.

BAKING

Baking is one of the commonplace household routines in the Bible that keeps us rooted in the everyday world. It assumes symbolic meanings when it is part of *hospitality and worship practices, and it also becomes a full-fledged metaphor.

Good baking is an indispensable element of biblical hospitality. "Quick!" said Abraham to Sarah, "get three seahs of fine flour and knead it and bake some bread" (Gen 18:6 NIV). The provision of baked goods is a sign of welcome to the servants of the Lord. Abigail brought two hundred loaves of *bread to David (1 Sam 25:18). Both Elijah and Elisha were fed by women, whether they had few resources or many with which to bake (1 Kings 17:13-14; 2 Kings 4:8). Through their willingness to serve others by the work of their hands, these women demonstrated that common household tasks are not merely secular but sacred. The Lord himself provides the ingredients for such service, for the widow of Zarephath found that "the jar of flour was not used up and the jug of oil did not run dry" until the Lord sent rain again (1 Kings 17:16). By contrast, one of the *curses for disobeying the covenant is the withholding of the supplies needed to make bread, so that "ten women will be able to bake your bread in one oven" (Lev 26:26).

If baking is an image of ideal hospitality to others, it can also be perverted to a selfish use. Two biblical deceptions are made all the more reprehensible by their use of baking. Jacob used baked bread and lentil stew to entice his brother Esau to despise his *birthright (Gen 25:34). Tamar baked bread to cheer an ailing brother, but Amnon violated her charity and *raped her (2 Sam 13:1-22).

The details of baking take on religious significance in the context of worship. In their haste to leave Egypt, "the people took their dough before the yeast was added" (Ex 12:34). In remembrance of this act, the Israelites were instructed to make bread for the *Passover meal without yeast (Ex 12:8; see Leaven). Similarly, the instructions for making offerings to the Lord in the temple often describe cakes and breads made without yeast (e.g., Lev 2:4: "If you bring a grain offering baked in an oven, it is to consist of fine flour: cakes made without yeast and mixed with oil"). Here the prohibition against yeast hints at the freedom from the taint of sin that God demands of his people.

Yet the offering for the Feast of Weeks was to include two loaves baked with yeast "as a wave offering of firstfruits to the LORD," (Lev 23:17).The fullness of the yeast breads perhaps symbolized the fullness of the harvest. Indeed, the baking of bread used for temple worship was considered so important that a particular Levite "was entrusted with the responsibility for baking the offering bread" (1 Chron 9:31).

While the NT has less to say about baking, it has nearly as much to say about yeast. Jesus occasionally puts yeast in a positive light, teaching that "the kingdom of heaven is like yeast that a woman mixed into a large amount of flour until it worked all through the dough" (Mt 13:33). This parable turns on the gradual, abundant expansion of yeast-filled dough; in the same way, the *kingdom of God grows slowly and surely.

On other occasions the connotation of yeast is entirely negative: "Be on your guard against the yeast of the Pharisees and Sadducees" (Mt 16:5-12). The property of yeast in view here is its ability to work its way throughout the dough. Unsound teaching is like yeast in its ability to infect the community of faith. There is at least an echo here of the demand for holiness that the OT injunctions against yeast were intended to convey. In the NT Paul calls us to "keep the Festival, not with the old yeast, the yeast of malice and wickedness, but with bread without yeast, the

bread of sincerity and truth" (1 Cor 5:8).

See also BREAD; FOOD; GRAIN; HOSPITALITY; LEAVEN, LEAVENING.

BALDNESS

"In all Israel there was not a man so highly praised for his handsome appearance as *Absalom" (2 Sam 14:25 NIV). The next verse shows that one of the chief reasons he was so admired was his luxuriant head of hair. Similarly, white hair is a significant characteristic shared by the Ancient of Days (Dan 7:9) and the risen Christ (Rev 1:14).

By contrast, the absence of hair was a cause for shame. For the prophet Elisha to be jeered at and described as "you baldhead" (2 Kings 2:23) was obviously an insult, though whether his baldness was due to natural hair loss or a shaved tonsure is not clear. Apart from this the Bible views the shaving of the head as a mark of *mourning (e.g., Jer 16:6) and as evidence of God's judgment, both on his own people (e.g., Is 3:17, 24; 7:20; 22:12; Ezek 7:18; Amos 8:10; Mic 1:16) and on their enemies (e.g., Is 15:2; Jer 47:5; 48:37; Ezek 27:31; 29:18). The reference in Micah evokes the image of the vulture, whose pale, down-covered head contrasts with the well-feathered heads of other birds.

To shave the head as a sign of mourning is forbidden for priests on the grounds that it would compromise their holy calling and "profane the name of their God" (Lev 21:5; Ezek 44:20). The same reason lies behind the prohibition in Deuteronomy 14:1 against any of God's holy people shaving the front of their heads "for the dead."

Letting the hair grow was one of the conditions attached to the *vow made by a Nazirite (Num 6:5). Such hair was seen as dedicated to the Lord (Num 6:9) and was to be shaved off when the period of the vow came to an end (Num 6:18) or if accidentally defiled (e.g., if someone suddenly died in the Nazirite's presence). The phenomenal strength of *Samson, the most famous Nazirite in the Bible, is linked with the length of his hair (Judg 16:17-22). The apostle Paul and his companions are recorded as having shaved their heads for ritual purposes (Acts 18:18; 21:24).

See also HAIR.

BANISHMENT. *See* EXILE.

BANNER

Banners are identifying flags or streamers attached to the end of a standard. Throughout history they have served three main purposes: to identify a group, to claim possession of a space or territory and to lend festivity to a celebration. Banners are rallying points, physically and/or emotionally.

The Bible contains fewer than a dozen direct references to banners, and the context is almost entirely military. More often than not the banner of victory is ascribed to God. The earliest example is Exodus 17:15, where Moses celebrates the victory of the Amalekites by building an *altar, calling the name of it "the LORD is my banner" and saying, "a hand upon the banner of the LORD" (RSV). In the Psalms too it is God who sets up a banner for his people (Ps 60:4), who for their part ascribe their *triumph to God by setting up banners "in the name of our God" (Ps 20:5). Jeremiah's prediction of Babylon's destruction is prefaced by the statement, "Declare among the nations and proclaim, set up a banner and proclaim, conceal it not" (Jer 50:2 RSV), along the lines of a warrior boldly planting a banner as a sign of taking possession.

The remaining instances of the word *banner* are in the *Song of Songs. In the Shulamite woman's picture of Solomon's taking her into the court harem, the climactic note of triumph is that "he brought me to the banqueting house, and his banner over me was love" (Song 2:4). Here the banner is an image of both festivity or celebration and claiming possession. In a courtly and military world, one of the supreme images of exhilaration is the sight of an army advancing with its banners unfurled. This supplies the emotional context for the lover's declaration that his beloved's beauty is as "terrible as an army with banners" (Song 6:4, 10).

BANQUET

Banquets are special meals celebrating important events. Unlike Jewish cultic *feasts, they are not official *worship events, but neither should banquets held among God's people be regarded as "secular" events, since such banquets can mark God's intervention and display his abundant provision.

Banquets are never mere mealtimes or only celebrations of the occasion that give rise to the banquet. They are loaded with messages about who is up and who is down in status; who is in and who is out of the social or political circle. Invitations signify being "in." Proximity to the host and the amount and quality of the food and drink offered indicate status (Gen 43:31-34; Lk 14:7-12; Jn 2:10). Refusal to attend a banquet is a powerful negative social message defying the authority and honor of the host (e.g., Esther 1:12, 16-20; Mt 22:1-14).

Occasional Banquets. Many biblical banquets are held in royal courts. They display royal *honor and power (Esther 1:3-12; 5:4-6, 8, 12, 14, 6:14; 7:8; Dan 5:1, 10; and the coronation banquets of David, 1 Chron 12:38-40, and Solomon, 1 Kings 1:39-41). Banquets are venues for political and social discourse and dealing. An invitation to attend is a distinct honor implying power, trust and insider status. Military or political treaties and victories are also celebrated with banquets (Gen 26:30; 31:54). When the victor is a king, the banquet is also "royal" (2 Sam 3:20).

Communities hold banquets to celebrate and give thanks for God's provision (e.g., sheep shearing, 1 Sam 25:11; 2 Sam 13:23-27; harvest, Judg 9:27). Other banquets mark long-awaited events like the completion of Solomon's *temple (2 Chron 7:8) or

unexpected blessings (1 Kings 3:15; Lk 15).

Rites of passage—birthdays and weanings, *weddings and *funerals—are also celebrated with banquets, though all the birthday banquets recorded in the Bible are royal ones (Pharaoh, Gen 40:20; Herod, Mk 6:21). *Abraham "made a great feast" on the occasion of Isaac's weaning (Gen 21:8). Several wedding banquets are recorded (Gen 29: 22; Judg 14: 10, 17; Jn 2: 8-9). There is inferential evidence of rites of mourning including banquets held in honor of the deceased and for the comfort of the family (2 Sam 3:35; 2 Sam 12:16-17; Jer 16:5-9; Ezek 24:16-17, 22-3; Hos 9:4).

Finally, *hospitality sometimes takes the form of a banquet. *Guests may be entertained and welcomed with lavish banquets.

Banquet imagery draws from the varieties of literal banquets; the significance of the allusion varies according to the sort of banquet the writer has in mind. Matthew combines different types when he records Jesus' parable of a king who holds a wedding banquet for his son (Mt 22:2-9; cf. Mt 25:10). Often a literal banquet bears figurative significance, as when the royal banquet to which the nations come bearing gifts in tribute to King David becomes messianic (1 Chron 12:38-40).

Victory Banquets. Ancient Near Eastern mythology of the *gods follows a general pattern of warfare, victory, kingship, house (temple/palace) building and celebration/banqueting. The order of events follows a logical progression and is heavenly mirror of a human pattern. Celebration following victory on the battlefield is an archetypal image, and banqueting is its centerpiece. We first capture a glimpse of it in a tiny vignette following the first battle in the Bible: After Abraham's defeat of Kedorlaomer and his allies, "King Melchizedek of Salem brought out bread and wine" (NRSV) and blessed Abraham and God (Gen 14:18-19). Elsewhere the psalmist alludes to a victory banquet: "You prepare a table before me in the presence of my enemies; you anoint my head with oil; my cup overflows" (Ps 23:5 NRSV). This banquet displays God's "goodness and mercy" (Ps 23:6). Jeremiah pictures the plight of Israel in an image of *Babylon banqueting on Zion's delicacies, a devouring that will be disgorged when God defeats Babylon (Jer 51:34-44). Isaiah's picture of the eschatological banquet of God is especially memorable (Is 25:6, see below). The ultimate victory and final defeat of evil are marked with a victory-wedding banquet in John's eschatological vision (Rev 19:9, 17-18).

Messianic Banquet. Closely related to the victory banquet motif is the vision of an eschatological banquet. Isaiah 25:6 provides the benchmark image of this banquet: "On this mountain the LORD Almighty will prepare a feast of rich food for all peoples, a banquet of aged wine—the best of meats and the finest of wines" (NIV). The stories of *Jesus' table fellowship with a variety of people and his reputation as "a glutton and a drunkard, a friend of tax collectors and sinners" (Mt 11:19 NRSV) point out the extraordinary place of eating and banqueting in his ministry. Jesus is one who "welcomes sinners and eats with them" (Lk 15:1-2 NRSV) and thereby enacts God's welcome to sinners to enter the kingdom of God. Dining with him, however, is no guarantee of entrance into the kingdom (Lk 13:26-27), for to some he will say "I do not know where you come from" (Lk 13:27 NRSV). But in the future "people will come from east and west, from north and south, and will eat in the kingdom of God" (Lk 13:29 NRSV; cf. Mt 8:11-12). At the Last Supper, Jesus alludes to the coming eschatological banquet when he says, "I will never again drink of this fruit of the vine until that day when I drink it new with you in my Father's kingdom" (Mt 26:29 NRSV; Mk 14:25; Lk 22:18; cf. Lk 22:28-30).

Symposium Banquet. The motif of banqueting is particularly prominent in Luke's Gospel. Here the banquet scenes are imaged as a Greco-Roman symposium, a formal banquet followed by a drinking and engaging conversation where serious topics of mutual interest are addressed. Diners recline on couches arranged in a U-shape around a central table, and a guest's position at the table is an indication of relative honor. Luke 14:1-24 is a formal banquet scene at the home of a Pharisee, and Jesus tells several parables about banqueting, including one about seeking honor at a dinner (Lk 14:7-11). Jesus sows the seed of transformation within these dinners. Rather than displays of relative honor and exculsiveness, the dining of the kingdom is to be open and inclusive (cf. Lk 7:36-50).

Wedding Banquets. Figurative uses of the wedding banquet occur in the Gospels (Lk 12: 36; Mt 22:4; 25:10; and see Song 2:4) and the Apocalypse (Rev 19:9). These banquets have the flavor of a wedding's hopeful, joyful celebration of love and harmonious relationship. In answer to the question of why the Pharisees' and John the Baptist's disciples fast and Jesus' disciples do not, Jesus responds, "How can the guests of the bridegroom mourn while he is with them? The time will come when the bridegroom will be taken from them; then they will fast" (Mt 9:15 NIV). In other words, now is a time for celebration, for banqueting and not fasting.

Bad Banquets. Banquets sometimes become signs of decadence and defeat, markers of judgment for idolatry and injustice, and foretastes of final judgment, doom and woe. Those who answer to the seductive call of the "foolish woman" will be "her guests . . . in the depths of Sheol" (Prov 9:13-18 NRSV). A proverb well sums up wisdom in dining: "Better is a dinner of vegetables where love is than a fatted ox and hatred with it" (Prov 15:17 NRSV). Jobs sons and daughters engage in ceaseless rounds of banqueting, and Job the righteous father offers burnt offerings on their behalf, lest during their festivities his children "have sinned, and cursed God in their hearts" (Job 1: 4-5 NRSV). The churlish Nabal, oblivious to the judgment about to come

upon him, holds a feast in his house, "like the feast of a king," and his "heart was merry within him, for he was very drunk" (1 Sam 25:36 NRSV). Isaiah captures the apostasy of Israel as a people who "rise early in the morning in pursuit of strong drink, . . . whose feasts consist of lyre and harp, tambourine and flute and wine, but who do not regard the deeds of the Lord" (Is 5:11-12 NRSV; cf. Jer 51: 39; Amos 6: 4-6). Finally, in Revelation 19:17-18 the judgment of God is gruesomely depicted as a "great supper of God" in which carrion birds are invited to feast on the flesh of the kings of the earth and their armies.

But on the whole, banquets in the Bible imply and display blessing, prosperity, abundance, wealth, victory and joy. As signs of God's faithfulness and human righteousness, as markers of God-anointed and ordained power, they become a foretaste of heavenly blessing and honor.

See also FEAST, FEASTING; GUEST; HOSPITALITY; MEAL; SUPPER.

BIBLIOGRAPHY. S. S. Bartchy, "Table Fellowship," *DJG* 796-800.

BAPTISM

Because *water rituals were more common in antiquity than they are today, ancient people would have understood the symbolism of baptism more readily than most modern readers do. The Egyptians, Mesopotamians, Hittites and Hebrews used water in purification rituals (e.g., Lev 13:8-9). In NT times, when Greek cultural influences on Christianity were more direct than ancient Near Eastern cultures, most temples had rules concerning ritual *purity. Many Greek philosophers (e.g., Stoics and Pythagoreans, but not Cynics) valued ritual purification, and some mystery cults employed ritual washings before their initiation rites.

Jewish Background. Jewish people in Jesus' day were generally meticulous about the ritual *washings commanded in the Hebrew Bible and had added other ritual washings as well. Well-to-do people in the wealthy neighborhoods of Jerusalem even had their own ritual immersion pools. The Essenes of the Qumran community (the people who wrote the Dead Sea Scrolls) were among the most meticulous; besides the initial washing required to join the sect, they were always washing themselves subsequently to insure ritual purity. Ceremonial washing became part of Jewish piety in the Hellenistic period, and in the two centuries before the time of Jesus, Jewish people were immersing themselves at appropriate times. Pharisees began to apply the priestly practice of hand washing.

Jewish people practiced one particular kind of once-for-all ritual washing, however. This was the baptism administered to Gentiles when they wished to convert to Judaism and wash away their former impurity. Baptism was so characteristic of Jewish conversion rituals, next to the more painful accompanying practice of male *circumcision, that even pagan writers like Epictetus mention it. According to later Jewish regulations concerning private baptisms, the immersion must be so complete that even if a person were otherwise naked, the immersion would be invalidated if so much as the string of a bean covered the space between two teeth. But full immersion, coupled with circumcision (for males) and a sincere heart, meant conversion. Some later Jewish teachers insisted that a Gentile converted in this manner became "like a newborn child," completely separated from his or her Gentile past.

John the Baptist. John the Baptist obviously did not have Jewish people strip naked for public baptisms in the *Jordan, but he probably did insist that they bend forward and submerge completely under the water, according to standard Jewish practice. The term *baptism* could indicate dipping, sprinkling or immersion, but the Jewish custom was immersion. John proclaimed this as a "baptism of repentance," a once-for-all sort of act, purifying a person from their former ways in view of the coming *kingdom. Quite in contrast to the sort of once-for-all baptism of Gentiles mentioned above, however, John demanded that Jewish people also undergo this rite. He regarded Jewish people as in need of conversion to God's way as much as *Gentiles (Mt 3:9; Lk 3:8).

Jordan River and Wilderness. For the Gospel writers, John's baptizing in the Jordan and his ministry in the *wilderness evoke the *exodus-conquest tradition of Israel's beginnings as it is seen through the subsequent Elijah tradition. John calls Israel back to the wilderness and the Jordan. Israel is being prepared for a *restoration or reconstitution, their repentance being signified by a renewed encounter with the waters crossed by their ancestors. (The problem for this perspective is that Israel originally crossed on dry ground; however, note in Josh 3:15 and 4:18 that the Jordan was at flood stage at the time). But Josephus tells us that at least one other Jewish prophetic figure, Theudas, thought that the way to signify a moment of deliverance was to take his followers out to the wilderness for a reenactment of the Jordan crossing and the conquest of the *land. John is much like Elijah and Elisha, who are associated with the Jordan River. Elijah parts the waters, and Elisha has the Gentile Naaman wash in the Jordan for his healing. The question put to the Baptist in John 1:24-25, "Why then do you baptize if you are not the Christ, nor Elijah, nor the Prophet?" (NIV), implies that the religious leaders of the day took seriously the symbolism of the Jordan/wilderness, which hearkened back to Elijah and symbolized cataclysmic change.

Images Associated with Christian Baptism.
An initiation event. When Jesus commanded disciples to baptize subsequent disciples, he was not just alluding to regular washings from frequent impurities. Jesus, like John, was using baptism to signify what once-for-all baptisms normally signified to his Jewish hearers: an act of conversion, a public way of breaking with one's past life and beginning a new one. Baptism was to conversion something like what

the engagement ring is to many engaged couples in modern Western society: the official, public declaration of the commitment. Because this was a specific kind of conversion—not conversion to any form of Jewish faith but specifically to faith in Christ—Christians designated baptism "in the name of the Father, Son, and Holy Spirit" (Mt 28:19) or "in the name of Jesus" (Acts 2:38, referring to the baptized person's confession of faith in Christ—2:21; 22:16).

Symbolism of death, burial and resurrection. The image of being covered by water is linked almost intuitively by Christians to the death, burial and resurrection of Jesus and hence to our own experience of redemption. The baptism with which Jesus will be baptized (Mk 10:38), referring to his coming death (cf. Lk 12:50), forms a link with Paul's references to being baptized into the *death of Jesus (Rom 6:4; Col 2:12).

Inner transformation and empowerment. In the case of Spirit baptism the image of an act symbolizing conversion has been taken one step further as a declaration of inner transformation and empowerment by the *Holy Spirit. Because baptism was such a powerful image among John's and Jesus' first followers, John the Baptist and Jesus could use this image when they recalled earlier prophets' promises of the Spirit's coming (Mk 1:8; Acts 1:5; 11:16). The prophets had already described the Spirit in terms of water in their promises concerning the last days, and Jesus takes up this image—in this case not one of immersion by stepping into water but rather of water being poured out upon people (Is 44:3; Ezek 39:29; Joel 2:28).

The Hebrew Bible, contemporary Judaism and various NT writers associate the Spirit with both spiritual purification (e.g., Jn 3:5, where the phrase may be a hendiadys meaning "water of the Spirit," cf. Jn 7:37-39) and prophetic empowerment (e.g., Acts 1:8; 2:4, 17-18). Different NT writers thus apply the image with different emphases. Thus, for example, John the Baptist, who contrasts Spirit baptism with a *fire baptism that contextually means judgment (Mt 3:10-12; Lk 3:9, 16-17), emphasizes the eschatological salvation aspect of the Spirit's coming. John 3:5 likewise may be using Jewish proselyte baptism as a symbol for the true conversion of Spirit baptism.

Overwhelmed. Part of the image of baptism is being overwhelmed by water, the Holy Spirit or difficulties. When James and John ask to sit at Jesus' right hand in *paradise, he asks, "Can you drink the cup I drink or be baptized with the baptism I am baptized with?" (Mk 10:38). Here Jesus uses baptism as a picture of being overwhelmed with the pain and anguish of his last days (see Lk 12:50). The picture of baptism as being immersed and overwhelmed comes through clearly in 1 Peter 3. There is an easy movement between baptism that saves and the salvation of Noah and his family from/through deluge. By contrast Luke, who generally emphasizes the prophetic empowerment dimension of the Spirit (e.g., Lk 1:67; 2:26; Acts 2:17-18; 4:8; 10:45-46; 13:9; 19:6), focuses on that aspect of the Spirit's work. His narratives thus present more postconversion in believers' lives (e.g., Acts 4:8; 8:16-17) than one might guess from most NT writers' theological statements, including his own (Acts 2:38-39).

See also FLOOD; PURITY; WASH, WASHING; WATER.

BIBLIOGRAPHY. G. R. Beasley-Murray, *Baptism in the New Testament* (Grand Rapids: Eerdmans, 1962); J. D. G. Dunn, *Baptism in the Holy Spirit: A Re-examination of the New Testament Teaching on the Gift of the Spirit in Relation to Pentecostalism Today* (London: SCM Press, 1970).

BAREFOOT

In the Bible being barefoot means more than simply having no shoes on one's feet. Thus in different biblical contexts being barefoot can symbolize humility, high status or reverence for God.

Humiliation. Bare feet symbolize one's inner state, serving as an image of spiritual poverty. This association stems from the custom of humiliating and despoiling the vanquished (2 Chron 28:15). Making the prisoners go barefoot served the practical purpose of preventing escape and of providing loot for the victors. This routine practice allows the word "stripped" to imply being stripped of both clothes and shoes (Job 12:17, 19; Mic 1:8). The prophets wandered about barefooted, vividly acting out the inevitable fate of those destined for captivity (Is 20:2-4; Mic 1:8).

The self-imposed "captivity" of *mourning also required the removal of shoes (Ezek 24:23). On the other hand, restoration of shoes (and clothing) clearly signified reinstatement of social standing (Ezek 16:10; 2 Chron 28:15; Lk 15:22). That David flees barefooted alludes to the temporary captivity of his kingdom at the hands of Absalom (2 Sam 15:30) as well as the haste of his departure (2 Sam 15:14). By contrast, however, being shod emphasizes preparation and readiness to perform the Lord's bidding (Is 5:27; Mk 6:9; Eph 6:15).

Status. In the context of foot washing, the baring of feet signifies the status of an honored guest. The ancient Near Eastern code of *hospitality required washing the feet of one's guests (Gen 18:4; 19:2; Judg 19:21), implicitly acknowledging the elevated status of the barefoot one (1 Sam 25:41). John the Baptist extends this image further by confessing that he was unworthy even to remove Jesus' sandals (Mt 3:11). In turn, Jesus dramatically subverts this symbolism when he washes the bare feet of his disciples, using the occasion to teach that service, rather than social standing, determines greatness in the kingdom of heaven (Jn 13:1-20).

Shoes serve as a mark of civility for animals as well as humans. Jeremiah describes Israel's idolatrous ways using an image of an unshod (undomesticated) donkey out of control, likening the nation's fickle religious behavior to that of a brute in heat, driven by hormones rather than reason (Jer. 2:25).

Reverence. In two instances God explicitly requires barefootedness of his servants: *Moses at the burning bush (Ex 3:5), and the confirmation of Joshua as the new Moses (Josh 5:15). In both cases the text gives as the reason, "The ground where you stand is holy." It is true that only the priests with ceremonially washed bare feet could enter God's presence (Ex 30:19). However, because the ground is cursed since the Fall (Gen 3:17), these instances may signify that this curse no longer obtains where God's glory is present. Furthermore, some ancient societies regard nakedness as the natural and acceptable condition of a pure worshipper. The OT hints at such a view (Gen 2:25). In addition, shoes were almost certainly made of the skin of dead animals and difficult to cleanse of accumulated filth. The connection between nakedness and cleanliness surfaces frequently in many cultures and probably finds support in the widespread belief that the deity is best approached *au naturel* (1 Sam 19:24), in the condition of one's birth (Job 1:21; Eccles 5:15). There is no shame in sinless nakedness (Gen 2:25).

See also FEET; HOLINESS; WASH, WASHING.

BARN

Barns dot the landscape of our countryside and are the focal point of most farms. Today barns come in various sizes and designs but essentially have the function of providing shelter for livestock, equipment and crops. In Scripture barns refer primarily to granaries and typically would have been lined underground pits or silos, or rooms or storage houses. Barn is an image of *abundance. It suggests storage and safety for one's food. When the king of an agrarian nation prays for national prosperity, his prayer includes the image of "our barns . . . filled with every kind of provision" (Ps 144:14 NIV), and the wise man believes that the reward that will come from honoring God with one's wealth is that "then your barns will be filled to overflowing" (Prov 3:10 NIV).

Barns symbolize an accumulation of wealth. It is the best attempt humans make to survive, control or master their world. Although this hoarding mentality may be instinctual, it smacks of self-sufficiency and misplaced confidence. Yet even barns can burn or be sacked. Jeremiah reports that in the tumultuous days surrounding the Babylonian invasion, people had "wheat and barley, oil and honey, hidden in a field" (Jer 41:8 NIV). They had most likely placed these staples in buried pots for fear that barns or granaries would be sacked.

Jesus commonly used agrarian examples in his teaching. What did he mean when he spoke of barns? Primarily barns contrast human security with divine provision. Barns are the focal point of a satiric parable in which an enterprising farmer's building project becomes an index of his worldlymindedness and misplaced values (Lk 12:13-21). Perhaps the most familiar reference is Luke 12:24: "Consider the ravens: They do not sow or reap, they have no storeroom or barn; yet God feeds them. And how much more valuable you are than birds!" (NIV). This is an ancient religious tension: preparing for the future may suggest lack of trust in God (cf. the exemplary storehousing of the ant, Prov 6:6-8; 30:25).

In addition, barns connote divine *rescue from judgment. "His winnowing fork is in his hand, and he will clear his threshing floor, gathering his wheat into the barn and burning up the chaff with unquenchable fire" (Mt 3:12 NIV; 13:30; Lk 3:17). Judgment is inevitable. The barn embodies safety in the face of ultimate danger. The *wheat left on the *threshing floor will be consumed; the grain in the barn will not. "Barn" represents the sovereign protection of God.

See also ABUNDANCE; FARMING; GRAIN; STOREHOUSE; WHEAT.

BARRENNESS

Barrenness in the Bible is an image of lifelessness, where God's redemptive blessing is absent. In the beginning the verdant fecundity of the *Garden of Eden and the splendor of male and female *sexuality promised a fertility that glorified all life as originally created by God.

When *Adam and *Eve sinned, God *cursed the blessed fertility of his creation. The soil of the garden thereafter produced *thorns and thistles, requiring laborious toil to yield food. Human fertility was cursed as childbearing became a painful and life-threatening event. In the Bible fruitful *land and fertile women are images of the blessedness of life as God had originally intended it. The opposite of these, desolate land and barren women, are biblical images of the consequences of *sin.

The image of the barren wife is one of the Bible's strongest images of desolation and rejection. We find this first in *Genesis, where the examples include Sarah (11:30), Rebekah (25:21) and Rachel (29:31). The classic case of barrenness is Hannah (1 Sam 1). A NT example is Elizabeth. In wisdom literature one of four things that are never satisfied is "the barren womb" (Prov 30:16 NIV).

Conversely, few images of *joy can match that of the barren wife who becomes pregnant. To the psalmist a supreme blessing of God is his settling "the barren woman in her home as a happy mother of children. Praise the LORD" (Ps 113:9). In Isaiah's oracle of *redemption the barren woman is enjoined to "burst into song, shout for joy" at the prospect of bearing children (54:1). Both Hannah and Elizabeth are examples of barren women who are made to rejoice when they finally bear a child.

In the *covenant with ancient Israel, God pronounced blessing for covenant obedience in terms of fertility, and curse for covenant disobedience in terms of barrenness:

> If you fully obey the LORD your God and carefully follow all his commands I give you today, . . . The fruit of your womb will be blessed, and the crops of your land and the young of your livestock. . . . However, if you do not obey the LORD your God

> . . . The fruit of your womb will be cursed, and the crops of your land, and the calves of your herds and the lambs of your flocks.
> (Deut 28:1-4, 15-18 NIV)

The prophets later use the imagery of barrenness to indict God's people for their sin of disobeying the covenant. Prophetic images of unfruitful and desolate land predict the judgment God would send through drought, insect infestations and the ravages of war (Is 5:1-10; Joel 1:1-12; Hab 3:17). The unfaithfulness of God's people is personified by images of *Zion as a barren woman who *prostitutes her sexuality, thus frustrating her fertility (Jer 3:1-3; Ezek 23; Hos 9:11, 12).

In Isaiah's prophecy the promise that God will restore the blessedness of life is expressed through transforming the imagery of the barren land and the barren woman. In the day of restoration the desolate land will burst into bloom (Is 35:1-7) and the barren woman will sing and rejoice because of an unexpected and abundant fertility (Is 54:1).

Jesus Christ is the consummation of God's plan to resurrect humanity from the lifelessness of sin. His lineage is traced through unexpected births to barren women, starting with Sarah; through a wanton woman, Rahab; through the adulterous relationship of *Bathsheba and *David; and finally from the innocent barrenness of his *virgin mother, Mary (Mt 1:1-16). Throughout redemptive history God transforms barrenness and frustrated fertility into the fruit of eternal life.

The book of Revelation ends the story of earthly history with images of a *garden perpetually bearing fruit in the New *Jerusalem (Rev 22:1-6) and of a pure *bride coming to meet her bridegroom (Rev 21:1-5). Scripture ends as it begins with images of verdant fecundity and of male and female sexuality signifying the blessing of eternal life with God that, because of Jesus Christ, could not be miscarried by sin.

See also ABUNDANCE; BIRTH; CHILD, CHILDREN; CURSE; FRUIT, FRUITFULNESS; WOMAN, BIBLICAL IMAGES OF; WOMB.

BASIN. See BOWL.

BATHSHEBA

Of all of *David's wives, Bathsheba is the most remembered. This is surprising because her character seems to be defined mainly by passive behavior and relationships with her husbands, son and stepson rather than by outstanding individual qualities or actions. Her beauty was apparently her primary asset. It was also David's downfall, for when he saw her from his palace roof, he desired her, summoned her and exercised his *droit du seigneur.* (It's possible that she seduced him; the text is unclear about why she was bathing where he might see her.) Bathsheba became pregnant. Her husband, Uriah the Hittite, an honorable and distinguished soldier, paid with his life for David's moment of weakness, as did the baby. Later Bathsheba bore *Solomon, heir to David's throne.

Two later incidents involving Bathsheba appear in 1 Kings. When David's son Adonijah seeks to take the aging David's *throne, Bathsheba secures it for Solomon. Later, in a curious irony, she agrees to use her motherly influence on Solomon and carries to him Adonijah's request to have David's private nurse, Abishag, for himself. It's unclear from the account why Bathsheba decides to help Adonijah. Perhaps she has been deceived, or she wants to test her power over Solomon. (Or perhaps she knows the request is so irregular that Adonijah, Solomon's nemesis, is sure to be executed because of it.) The venture ends in Adonijah's death, and the reader finds no further mention of Bathsheba.

For the Bible overall, Bathsheba is probably most significant as object rather than subject. She is the "forbidden fruit" that David can't resist: a beautiful woman, another man's wife, a symbol of David's own laziness and self-indulgence during the season "when kings go out to battle" (2 Sam 11:1 RSV). Like the forbidden fruit in Eden, Bathsheba is also a figure of judgment, for David's union with her results in repeated death, violence and humiliation within his own family (prophesied in 2 Sam 12:10-12). Because her inner motivations are never given, readers of the Bible must accept her character ambiguity and can only guess whether she was vamp or victim or something in between.

See also ADULTERY; DAVID; WOMAN, BIBLICAL IMAGES OF.

BATTLE STORIES

The Bible is a book of human and divine battles (*see* Warrior, Divine). In regard to both it is impossible to overstate the degree to which the world of the OT was (like other ancient societies) a warrior culture. Warfare was a way of life in the sense that it occurred more or less continuously.

The main repository of battle stories in the Bible are the books of Numbers, Joshua, Judges, Kings and Chronicles, though the psalms and prophetic books often allude to the rituals of warfare as well. The discussion that follows is a roadmap to the motifs and conventions that make up the composite battle story in the Bible.

Prelude to Battle. The initial action of battle stories in the Bible varies. In the case of holy warfare, which we encounter in the narratives of Israel's conquest of the promised land, Israel is directed by God to move forward and take the land (e.g., Num 13:1-2; 14:1-9; Josh 1; 5:13—6:5). Because God is giving the land to Israel, God is the one who initiates the action, directs Israel into battle and brings the victory. If Israel transgresses the commands of God, the result is tragic defeat (Num 14:41-45) or subsequent judgment (Josh 7). Before attacking a city that is located outside of the land God is giving Israel, an offer of peace is to be extended. If the offer is accepted by the city, Israel is to subject the enemy to forced labor (Deut 20:10-11). If the offer is rejected, they are to be engaged in battle, the men subjected

to the sword but the women, children, livestock and everything else taken as plunder (Deut 20:12-15).

In numerous other stories of warfare the initial action is *provocation* by one nation against another. Such provocation might consist of ongoing antagonism toward a neighboring nation or a raid designed to yield spoils of war, but the main pattern in the period of Israel's kings is an invasion from a superpower like Assyria or Babylon designed to conquer and assimilate a nation.

Sometimes the invasion comes swiftly and terribly. On other occasions a preliminary protocol is followed. The king of an army intent on invasion might send emissaries who threaten an enemy nation and attempt to coerce subjection without fighting. In Israel it is expected that the leader will inquire of the Lord, perhaps by consulting a prophet or priest, and so receive the word to proceed or not to proceed into battle (cf. 1 Sam 23:1-6; 30:7-8; 1 Kings 22:1-28).

Once battle becomes inevitable, the mustering of an army is the next step. In the wilderness Israel moves and camps according to tribes, and a militarism pervades this organization. The census of tribes in Numbers 1 is clearly a military census, and the pattern of Israel's encampment in the wilderness is styled as a military encampment with God, the divine commander-in-chief, dwelling at the center of the encampment (Num 2). Israel, while not a professional army, is a people divinely prepared to enter and conquer the land of Canaan.

During the period of the judges, professional armies are still unknown in Israel. Armies consist of volunteers. The law for Israel's warfare even calls for officers to announce that those who have built a new house, planted a new vineyard or pledged themselves to marriage to return home (Deut 20:5-7). In addition, those who are afraid or fainthearted should return home (Deut 20:8). This volunteerism in early Israel is evident as Deborah and Barak lead the battle against Sisera: "not a shield or spear was seen among forty thousand in Israel" and "willing volunteers" follow the princes of Israel into battle (Judg 5:8-9 NIV). Gideon summons soldiers with a sounding trumpet and messengers (Judg 6:34-35), and then releases most of them. Once the battle is joined against the Midianites, he experiences difficulty in enlisting the support of towns on the path of flight and pursuit (Judg 8:1-7; cf. Judg 5:15-17). We find an unusual and grisly summons to battle in the story of the Levite whose concubine is ravaged and killed by the Benjaminites; the Levite summons Israel to vengeance against the Benjaminites by cutting his concubine into twelve pieces and sending them throughout Israel (Judg 19—20). And even king Saul leaves his farming behind for the moment and sends a summons to battle, producing what must have been a somewhat rag-tag army.

In a battle against the Midianites, one thousand gather from each of the twelve tribes (Num 31:5); the ambush at Ai is carried out by thirty thousand fighting men (Josh 8:3). Battle lines are drawn, and men are divided into "units of hundreds and of thousands" (2 Sam 18:4). In several battles Israel's army is much smaller and weaker than their enemies, but God grants victory. Against the Arameans the Israelites were "like two small flocks of goats while the Arameans covered the countryside" (1 Kings 20:27 NIV); nonetheless, because of God's help the Israelites "inflicted a hundred thousand casualties on Aramean foot soldiers in one day" (1 Kings 20:29 NIV).

Warfare in Israel is ideally a sacred event. Nowhere is this more clear than in the holy warfare in which Israel conquers the land of promise. It is warfare undertaken at God's command and in his presence. For this reason Israel approaches battles much like it approaches worship in the sanctuary. Sacrifices are made to God (1 Sam 13), soldiers "consecrate" themselves (Josh 3:5) and abstain from sexual intercourse (1 Sam 21:5; and Uriah's refusal to have relations with his wife in 2 Sam 11:11), and the war camp is maintained in a state of ritual cleanliness (Deut 23:9-14). When Israel marches against Jericho, the procession of priests and the *ark of the covenant (the footstool or portable throne of God) preceding the army symbolize God's presence and leadership in the battle. This is symbolized as Israel marches through the wilderness. When the ark sets out in front of Israel, Moses says,

Rise up, O LORD!
May your enemies be scattered;
may your foes flee before you.
(Num 10:35 NIV)

Another preliminary to battle is planning the strategy. In the case of holy warfare in the OT, the leader of the Israelite army will expect to be instructed by God regarding how to conduct the impending battle (Judg 20:28). If God has answered positively to the inquiry of the leader, a cry will go out, "Shout! For the LORD has given you the city" (Josh 6:16; cf. Josh 8:1, 18; 10:8, 19; Judg 3:28; 4:7, 14; etc.). The reports of spies, memorialized in *spy stories, might enter prominently into the strategy for battle (Num 13; Josh 2; Judg 18:9-10). A favorable report from a scouting expedition might send an army into battle confident of victory (Josh 2), while a prediction of defeat might actually lead an army not to engage in battle at all (Num 13).

Once the armies are arrayed for battle, the final rituals unfold with a grim march toward inexorable conflict. Foremost among these rituals is the taunting of the enemy (see Taunt), which might be accompanied by a challenge to single combat by a champion warrior, such as Goliath, in a prebattle attempt to establish dominance. Psychological warfare in the days or hours before battle is important. Another prebattle ritual is that of the leader encouraging his troops on the night before battle and rallying them with a battle cry (Josh 10:19; Judg 7:20; 1 Sam 17:20, 52) on the day of the battle. Finally, in ancient epic literature the arming of the warrior for battle is a major ritual (cf. 1 Sam 17:38-39), and *armor itself

is considered an extension of the character and prowess of the warrior. We catch hints of the convention in the Bible (Judg 3:16; Ps 18:31-35; 84:9; 89:18).

Battle. While the Bible contains few extended narratives of how a battle unfolds, it is possible to discern common motifs. The essential action is attack and defense, offense and defense. Attacks were normally conducted at dawn (see Ps 46:5 for an implied reference). The imagery of *flight and pursuit is an inevitable part of battlefield action. On other occasions the capture of prisoners of war resolves the conflict (Num 21:1). Of course the best scenario of all is when no opponents survive (Num 21:3, 35; 1 Sam 15:3).

Surprise attacks are always a possibility in warfare, and they are favorites of those who tell the stories of battle, especially when they result in the unexpected victory of an underdog. On one occasion an all-night march results in Israelite victory over five cities who had joined against Israel (Josh 10:9-10). Another surprise attack leads to victory against troops, horses and chariots, an army "as numerous as the sand on the seashore" (Josh 11:4 NIV). Gideon surprises the Midianites with the sound of *trumpets and three hundred breaking jars (Judg 7:16-22). In another battle, men hide in fields overnight and then creep toward the city in such number that an unsuspecting guard said to those who warned him of the approaching army: "You mistake the shadows of the mountains for men" (Judg 9:36).

A variation on the motif of surprise is *ambush*. The noise of pursuit and of victory is described in the conquest of Jericho (Josh 6:16), when an ambush is suddenly created by the walls collapsing. Joshua lures the people of Ai out of their city after directing 30,000 men to hide on the other side of the city and flood it when the warriors of Ai left the city to pursue the the Israelites; the plan works perfectly (Josh 8). Jeroboam attempts to ambush Judah by sneaking soldiers behind them as he gives a long speech; but the hand of God is against him, so he fails and Israel is routed (2 Chron 13:1-20). When Jeroboam obeys God's command to praise him, "the LORD set ambushes against the men of Amnon" (2 Chron 20:22 NIV).

Hand-to-hand combat is a staple of ancient battle stories. David confronts Goliath in the name of the Lord with a slingshot and defeats the nine-foot man (1 Sam 17:1-51); a second generation of Philistine giants is likewise defeated by courageous individuals (2 Sam 21:15-22). Jonathan says "Nothing can hinder the LORD from saving, whether by many or by few" just before he had his armor-bearer climb up a cliff bare-handed to meet waiting Philistines at the top and kill twenty between the two of them in "an area of about half an acre" (1 Sam 14:1-15 NIV). Fighting between Judah and Israel includes a poolside scene where each group presents twelve young men who fight in hand-to-hand combat. All twenty-four die when each unceremoniously "grabbed his opponent by the head and thrust his dagger into his opponent's side" (2 Sam 2:13-17 NIV).

Another important convention of battle stories is the *siege*. Mighty armies might conduct combat by laying siege, camping around the city, preventing trade and forcing famine on its inhabitants until a battle was engaged or the city yielded. Nebuchadnezzar besieges Jerusalem during Zedekiah's reign (2 King 25:1-12). Jeremiah prophetically describes the siege's end (Jer 37:1-10; 39:1-10; 46—51:64; 52:12-23). Sennacherib attempts the same, but Hezekiah develops a strategy against it: he stops the water flow out of the city, repairs the wall and builds additional reinforcements from the inside, stockpiles additional weapons, organizes military officers, and encourages the people that God is with them. The siege fails, and Sennacherib is killed by his own people (2 Chron 32:1-22).

Accounts of *direct attack* but only partial victory are also common (1 Sam 4:1-2; 1 Sam 31:1-10; 2 Sam 10:6-19; 2 Chron 14:9:15; 2 Chron 18:29-34—chariot battle). David's mighty battle feats are catalogued by chronology and by the magnitude of the victory (1 Chron 18). Routing the enemy was the goal—an image of complete, overwhelming defeat.

In holy warfare Israel was not to fear the enemy but believe that God would deliver the enemy into their hand. "Fear not" is the watchword (Exod 14:13-14; Josh 8:1; 10:8, 25; 11:6; Judg 7:3; 1 Sam 23:16-17) and courage is a virtue of faith. By contrast, the enemy loses courage and is overwhelmed by a divine terror, dread and panic (Exod 23:27-28; Deut 2:25; 7:23; Josh 10:10; Judg 4:15; 7:22; 1 Sam 5:11).

After the Battle. The rituals enacted by the victorious army after the battle are even more elaborate than those that precede and accompany the battle. The keynote is exultation, and it takes multiple forms. One is the formal recording of the number of casualties, especially on the side of the vanquished. Here, one senses, is proof of the superiority of the conquering army. A recurring motif in ancient battle stories is that the leader of the victorious army is offered kingship as a reward (Judg 8:22).

Also important is the verbalizing of the victory in an act of celebration and thanksgiving. We read, for example, about shouts of victory (Ex 32:17-18). A conventional lyric form of the OT is the song of victory—a poem exulting in the success in battle and rehearsing the details, perhaps as a way of prolonging the ecstasy (Ex 15:1-18; Judg 5; Ps 18). The song of victory is sometimes called a "new song" to designate that it is an occasional poem celebrating the latest victory (Ps 98). Elsewhere we catch hints of a formal announcement and recognition of victory (Ps 98:2; Is 52:7-10) and of songs sung in triumph in public settings (Judg 5:10-11).

The victorious army might also perform religious rites of thanksgiving and sacrifice to their deity. In the days or hours following the battle, the conquering army and its leader might undertake a *triumphal procession (Ps 68:24-27). Feasting and celebration might ensue (Is 25:6).

Dominating everything else is the ritual of plundering and taking of spoils (Is 53:12; Ps 68:12; Judg 5:30). The taking of a trophy from the enemy has a ceremonial significance. It might consist of armor or a head or even the living leader of the rival army brought back for public display. Thus Saul spares Agag as part of his general orientation of bolstering his public image with his people instead of relying on God. Plunder is a primary benefit of successful combat, but nobility of purpose and dedication to God might be exhibited in not taking any spoils of battle (Gen 14:22-23). In Israel's holy warfare the taking of spoils is expressly forbidden. It is God's battle and all of the spoils belong to him. Thus we find instances where everything is "devoted" to the Lord in a sacrificial slaughter and burning (e.g., Josh 6:24). Even when the war booty is distributed evenly, such as in 1 Samuel 30:23-25, it is done so on the basis that the plunder belongs to the Lord.

In 1 Samuel 30 David and his men fight to regain their town that was plundered by an Amalekite raiding party. Because the Amalekites are drunk on the wine they have plundered, David easily defeats them (1 Sam 30:15-19). Scenes of plunder are often detailed (2 Kings 14:11-14; 2 Chron 14:13). Plunder can include land, and king Uzziah develops such lands to the enhancement of his power (2 Chron 26:6).

In the days of Israel's volunteer militias, soldiers were finally dismissed to return home, probably with the cry, "To your tents, O Israel!" (2 Sam 20:1; 1 Kings 12:16; cf. Judg 20:8; 1 Sam 4:10; 2 Sam 18:17; 19:8; 20:22).

The defeated army also experiences postbattle rituals. If defeated soldiers survive, they cower in fear and trembling (Ps 2:10-11). Judgment and *vengeance might be exacted from them, either in such a brutal form as having their eyes gouged out or cutting off thumbs and big toes (Judg 1:6, 7) or in the milder form of their having tribute exacted from them (Ps 72:9-10) or gifts expected from them (Gen 14:18). Shame and humiliation of the defeated is symbolized in such motifs as the victor's foot on the vanquished's neck (Josh 10:24), treading on the enemy (Ps 60:12; 108:13) and the defeated as the footstool of the victorious (Ps 110:1; 1 Kings 5:3; 2 Sam 22:39; Ps 18:38).

Because men fought the battles, ancient battle stories are largely a man's world—but not entirely. In the background of every battle story is the specter of the women—wives and mothers—back at the city, awaiting their fate in terrible anxiety. Their moments of waiting are an all-or-nothing prospect: either they will be carried off into slavery or worse, or they will enjoy a nice addition to their domicile and wardrobe in the form or plunder from the vanquished enemy. The moment of waiting is captured by a familiar motif of the woman at the window, looking out for the return of her man (Judg 5:28; 2 Kings 9:30;

2 Sam 6:12). The ecstasy of knowing that one's husband or army has won the battle is captured by the ritual of women's going out to meet the triumphant warriors as they return, either with *music and *dancing (Ex 15:20-21; 1 Sam 18:6) or with chants, as in the famous (and ominous) refrain that arouses Saul's paranoia, "Saul has slain his thousands, and David his ten thousands" (1 Sam 18:7).

Character Types. In addition to the plot motifs noted above, battle stories also contribute a gallery of recurring character types. Stock characters who usually play no more than functional roles in battle stories include watchmen (*see* Watch, Watchman), spies (*see* Spy Stories) and *eavesdroppers, all of whom contribute to an atmosphere of mystery, intrigue, danger and suspense. Sometimes a king's preparation for battle includes consulting a *prophet to ascertain the oracles from God. Couriers carry diplomatic messages between the rival sides or announcements of the outcome of a battle (Jer 51:31).

The primary character type in battle stories, though, is the warrior. In warrior cultures, warriors are the dominant *heroes. The archetypal warrior is more than a soldier, surpassing the latter in stature, physical prowess and skill, qualities equally useful and sometimes exemplified in dangerous encounters with wild beasts (Samson, Judg 14:5-6; David, 1 Sam 17:34-37; Benaiah, 2 Sam 23:20/1 Chron 11:22; *see* Hunting). Above all, the archetypal warrior is a paragon of physical strength, agility and courage. In a culture that determined status by military prowess, warriors are the heroes of Israel. Fighting for kings and for God himself, the warrior is esteemed for leadership, skill and personalized weapons. They are few in number and great in might, fame, responsibility and reward. With their fierce courage and skill, warriors make an army successful; but like all human feats or features, they must humbly bow before God or be judged.

God calls some of the OT warriors to their posts. David explains (Ps 89:19) and exemplifies the pattern. With confidence in God born of previous successes with wild *animals, he offers to fight Goliath and becomes a warrior who surpasses all others (1 Sam 16:18; 2 Sam 17:8, 10). Because of his lifestyle of bloodshed leading a band of men in flight from Saul, David is told by God that Solomon, rather than he, will build the temple (1 Chron 28:3).

Other warriors are also called by God. While farming, Gideon is addressed by the angel who says, "The LORD is with you, mighty warrior" (Judg 6:12 NIV) and so his career begins. Jephthah, the illegitimate son of a Gilead and a prostitute, is driven away from the family in adulthood by his legitimate half-brothers; later, his warrior prowess prompts them to request that he return to lead them against the Ammonites (Judges 11:1-11). Some warriors were men whom God decreed should carry out his wrath (Judg 5:11, Is 13:3). Jehu, commander of Ahab's army, is anointed king and told to destroy the entire house of Ahab (2 King 9). He fulfills the word of the Lord, killing even his close friends and his priests with whom he had served (2 King 10:11).

As evidenced by the humble beginnings of Joshua, Jehu and David, the difference between warriors called by God and others is that they are called to serve from a position of weakness. God clearly enables those not accustomed to war to fight for him, commanding, "Beat your plowshares into swords and your pruning hooks into spears. Let the weakling say, I am strong!" (Joel 3:10 NIV). In promises of vengeance, he likens Judah to a bow, Ephraim to an arrow and Zion to a warrior's sword (Zech 9:13).

Other warriors are simply skilled. Most of these are grouped following explanations of their collective exploits, but a few are specifically named. Those with the general epithet of mighty warrior include Nimrod (Gen 10:8-9; 1 Chron 1:10); Zadok and his officers (1 Chron 12:28); Zicri, an Ephraimite warrior who killed Maaseiah, the king's son (2 Chron 28:7); Eliada, "a valiant soldier" (2 Chron 17:17); *Samson (Judg 15-17) and Naaman (2 Kings 5:1). Special exploits, such as Elisha's stint as military strategist (1 Kings 18), are highlighted. The Gadites are mentioned twenty-nine times. Defecting from Saul's army to David's, they "were army commanders; the least was a match for a hundred, and the greatest for a thousand" (1 Chron 12:14). Another famous group were David's Thirty (2 Sam 23:24-39) with whom Uriah the Hittite served.

Though a king's overdependence on warriors often signaled his demise (Ps 33:16; Hos 10:13), many kings retained their posts because of the mighty warriors who supported them. David's success in Israel was due in part to the massive band of warriors that defected to his side from Saul's (1 Chron 12-13, esp. 12:1, 8, 21). We know most of the many warriors in Scripture from the lists of those who were under one of David's commanders like Joab (2 Sam 20:7).

Warriors for kings were in the noble class, included among the officials of Israel: army officers, powerful palace administrators (1 Chron 28:1), judges and prophets (Is 3:2). Comparable to the top military officers in our day, they were considered "famous men" (1 Chron 5:24), "outstanding leaders" (1 Chron 7:40); and they often represented their respective clans (Judg 18:2; 1 Chron 5:24; 1 Chron 7:40, 12:30). They also escorted the king's travel (Song 3:7).

Warriors were talented with special skills in battle. Some could handle a bow (1 Chron 8:40; 12:2), others a shield and spear (1 Chron 12:25). One group could "sling a stone at a hair and never miss" (Judg 20:16); another group was able to shoot arrows or sling stones right-handed or left-handed (1 Chron 12:2). David's Gadites had "the faces of lions, and they were as swift as gazelles in the mountains" (1 Chron 12:8 NIV). Their fame stemmed from their military and physical prowess. Likewise, the armies of God are pictured with complete power, organization and ability. Joel's depiction of an "army" of locusts destroying the land is particularly evocative: "They charge like warriors; they scale walls like soldiers. They all march in line, not swerving from their course. They do not jostle each other; each marches straight ahead. They plunge through defenses without breaking ranks. They rush upon the city; they run along the wall. They climb into the houses; like thieves they enter through the windows" (Joel 2:7-9 NIV).

Warriors were among the best-dressed of Israel. To heighten the threat of their image, unusual detail is devoted to describing their battle gear. They have special belts (2 Sam 18:11), some with dagger sheaths (2 Sam 20:8), specific boots and garments (Is 9:5). Some are even clad in scarlet (Nahum 2:3). They are armed with unusually sharp arrows (Ps 120:4), with quivers "like an open grave" (Jer 5:16) and with spears of pine (Nahum 2:3). The "shields of warriors" are above the rest (Song 4:4), and "the warrior's sword" like no other (Zech 9:13).

Like other supreme images in Scriptures, warriors pale in comparison to God. In both imagery and event, God is the divine *warrior (Ex 15:3; Judg 6:12; Job 16:14; Is 42:13; Jer 14:9; 20:11; Zeph 1:14). The demise of warriors signals God's judgment for their pride. His disabling of their strength is depicted in images of broken bows, not only arrows (1 Sam 2:4; Jer 51:56), of limp arms (Ps 76:5) and bodies exhausted of strength, unable to move (Jer 51:30). He makes them stumble over each other (Jer 46:12), uses their own weapons to kill them (Hab 3:14) and sends "a wasting disease" to infect their sturdy physical frame (Is 10:16). In instances of prideful rebellion, groups of warriors are specifically judged (1 Chron 5:24- 25; Is 21:16-17).

In God's presence warriors are terrorized, with hearts like women in labor (Jer 48:41; 49:22; 50:36; 51:30). Images of brave warriors fleeing naked punctuate the utter terror before God of those who usually terrorize (Amos 2:16; Jer 46:5; Hab 3:13). The psalmist accurately states: "No king is saved by the size of his army; no warrior escapes by his great strength" (Ps 33:16 NIV; cf. Amos 2:14).

Summary: David and Goliath. The story of David and Goliath (1 Sam 17) is not the only full-fledged battle story in the Bible, but it is the prototypical one that best sums up the genre itself. The story opens with the rival armies stationed within view of each other. Geography is important to the battle, with mountains the preferred site for stationing an army prior to battle and a valley the place where the fighting would actually occur. Goliath is the archetypal champion whose armor is detailed and who utters taunts and challenges to his enemy. In keeping with the holy war context of much OT warfare, the homespun boy hero David also utters a taunt; but his taunt is charged with religious significance, as opposed to the self-reliant boast of Goliath (1 Sam 17:45-47).

In order to get a hearing with the king, David must boast of his past prowess (1 Sam 17:34-37).

David is armed for battle with the king's armor, which proves unwieldy for him (1 Sam 17:38-39). David's preparations for battle are unconventional, but they fit the convention of the warrior's equipping for battle by choosing his preferred weapons. Most full-fledged battle stories begin and end with group scenes, but their tendency is to focus central attention on single combat and on the main feat of the victor's defeat of his rival. The story of David and Goliath runs true to form.

Postbattle rituals also appear. The Philistines flee when they see that their champion is dead, showing how single combat before battle is viewed as important in ancient warfare. The Israelite army shouts (1 Sam 17:52) and pursues the Philistine army. The ritual of claiming a trophy consists of David's beheading the giant and carrying the head into camp and of putting Goliath's armor in his tent (1 Sam 17:54). Although David has to wait to claim the usual reward of kingship, he does marry the king's daughter (1 Sam 18:17-27). Overall, this specimen battle story from the OT does not so much praise David as a great warrior, as it declares God as a great deliverer.

See also ARCHERY; ARMOR; ARMY, ARMIES; ARROW, ARROW OF GOD; DIVINE WARRIOR; HUNTING; SHIELD; SWORD; WEAPONS, HUMAN AND DIVINE.

BIBLIOGRAPHY. T. Longman III and D. G. Reid, *God Is a Warrior* (SOTB; Grand Rapids: Zondervan, 1995); G. von Rad, *Holy War in Ancient Israel* (Grand Rapids: Eerdmans, 1991); Y. Yadin, *The Art of Warfare in Biblical Lands* (London: Weidenfeld and Nicolson, 1963).

BEAR. *See* ANIMALS.

BEARD

The full, rounded beard was a sign of manhood and a source of pride to Hebrew men. It was considered an ornament, and much care was given to its maintenance. In fact, the wealthy and important made a ceremony of caring for their beards. Custom did not allow the beard to be shaved, only trimmed (Lev 19:27; 21:5), except in special circumstances. For example, shaving the beard was a requirement for the man cleansed of an infectious skin disease (Lev 14:9), and people in mourning would often shave or pull out their beards (Ezra 9:3; Is 15:2; Jer 41:5; 48:37). Ezekiel was told by God to shave off his beard as a symbol of coming destruction (Ezek 5:1).

The beard was also an object of salutation (2 Sam 20:9), the focus of oaths (Mt 5:36) or blessings (Ps 133:2) and even the focus of shame or curses. An attack on the beard is an attack on the person. Because the beard was a symbol of manhood, it was a great insult to degrade someone's beard. Thus David's men suffer grave humiliation when they return from a diplomatic mission with half of each man's beard shaven by the Ammonites. In fact, they did not return to Jerusalem until their beards had grown back (2 Sam 10:4-5). Similarly, Isaiah warns Israel that they will suffer a figurative emasculation at the hand of the king of Assyria who will "shave your head and the hair of your legs, and . . . take off your beards also" (Is 7:20 NIV). The messianic figure in Isaiah 50 is not only abused as his beard is pulled out, but suffers great humiliation and shame (Is 50:6).

See also BALDNESS; HAIR.

BEASTS. *See* ANIMALS; MONSTERS; MYTHICAL ANIMALS.

BEAT, BEATING

The nearly eighty references to beating fall into distinct clusters. *Harvesting accounts for several of these. One is the process of separating the useful nutritional parts of a harvested crop from its waste. Thus olives are beaten for *oil (Ex 29:40; Lev 24:2; Deut 24:20) and *wheat is beaten for its *grain kernels (Judg 6:11; Ruth 2:17). Olive trees are also beaten to shake loose the olives (Is 17:6; 24:13). The Israelites beat *manna in mortars before boiling or baking it (Num 11:8). Turning this to metaphoric use, military songs of victory in the OT use the image of beating enemies "fine like the dust of the earth" (2 Sam 22:43 NRSV) and "fine, like dust before the wind" (Ps 18:42 NRSV).

A similarly positive cluster deals with the processes of metallurgy. *Gold was beaten to form shields (1 Kings 10:16-17; 2 Chron 9:15-16). In the millennial age, *swords will be beaten into plowshares and spears into pruning hooks (Is 2:4; Joel 3:10; Mic 4:3). *Silver is likewise said to be beaten (Jer 10:9).

Negatively, the forces of nature can beat down upon vulnerable people. Thus the *sun "beat down upon the head of Jonah so that he was faint" (Jon 4:8 NRSV), *rain and *wind beat upon the houses in Jesus' parable of the two houses (Mt 7:25, 27) and the waves "beat into the boat" of Jesus and the disciples, threatening to swamp it (Mk 4:37)). According to Proverbs 28:3, "A ruler who oppresses the poor is a beating rain that leaves no food" (NRSV).

Beating the *breast was a familiar image of sorrow, dismay and contrition in the ancient world. Biblical people are portrayed as engaging in the practice (Is 32:12; Nahum 2:7; Lk 18:13; 23:27, 48).

Beating an object to pieces sometimes figures as an image of destroying something offensive, especially pagan *idols. Josiah beat a pagan idol to dust (2 Kings 23:6), as well as altars and sacred poles (2 Chron 34:7). The prophet Micah envisions Samaria's images "beaten to pieces" (Mic 1:7).

By far the largest category is inflicting bodily pain or punishment on a subjected person or group. Several distinct subcategories emerge. At its most positive, beating with the rod is an image for the discipline of children (Prov 23:13-14) and metaphoric blows and "beatings" are said to cleanse a person from evil (Prov 20:30).

We also find beating as an image of legitimate and legal punishment for misbehavior. Thus it is legiti-mate to beat a thief who is found breaking in (Ex 22:2), and the Mosaic law allowed for a judge to oversee the beating of a guilty party with lashes (Deut 25:2). Nehemiah beat some of the people who have intermarried with pagans (Neh 13:25).

Some of the images of beating are military in nature. The Amorites "beat down" the Israelites (Deut 1:44), and the people of Israel were beaten by the servants of David (2 Sam 2:17). Jeremiah envisions warriors beaten down and fleeing in haste (Jer 46:5).

The biggest single category is beating as part of the motif of *martyrdom—godly people subjected and oppressed by godless bullies. The motif begins with the Egyptians' oppression of the Hebrews (Ex 2:11; 5:14, 16). Jeremiah was beaten and imprisoned by enraged officials (Jer 37:15). Jesus predicted that in the future his disciples would be persecuted with beatings (Mk 13:9). The motif reaches its climax in the beatings endured by Jesus during his *passion (Mk 14:65; Lk 22:63) and the missionary career of Paul (Acts 16:22, 37; 18:17; 21:32; 1 Cor 4:11; 2 Cor 6:5; 11:25).

See also THRESHING, THRESHING FLOOR.

BEATITUDE

A beatitude is a pronouncement of blessing, phrased in a formula that begins with the phrase "blessed is" or "blessed are." The word *blessed* has connotations of happiness, felicity, satisfaction and well-being. To pronounce a blessing in the formal rhetoric of a beatitude is to do more than express a wish—it is in some sense to confer the quality of blessedness on a person or group, or to declare the reality of something that is perceived in the person or group.

Beatitudes in the Bible usually confer happiness on a general character type, but sometimes they appear in a narrative context and are directed to a specific person. While a beatitude usually expresses a wish for future well-being, it is sometimes a statement of response for something that a person has already done. Naomi responds to Ruth's account of Boaz's generosity with the statement, "Blessed be he by the LORD" (Ruth 2:20 NRSV). Although we customarily think of a beatitude as expressing blessing on humans, an important OT motif is the pronouncement of blessing on God. Taking all of these types into account, the number of beatitudes expressed in the Bible is well over a hundred. Wherever they appear, they are evocative—high points of positive sentiment toward someone and expressive of an ideal toward which others should aspire.

One avenue toward understanding the beatitudes of the Bible is to note the qualities of character that lead to a pronouncement of blessing or happiness in the formulaic rhetoric of the beatitude. When we do so, we find a distinction between the OT and NT beatitude. Who is pronounced blessed in the OT? The person who by discretion prevents an impulsive person from *vengeance (1 Sam 25:33 RSV); the *wives and *servants of a wise king (1 Kings 10:8;

2 Chron 9:7); people who take *refuge in God (Ps 2:12; 34:8) and whose sins are *forgiven (Ps 32:1-2); the nation whose God is the Lord (Ps 33:12; 144:15); people who consider the poor (Ps 41:1; Prov 14:21), who worship God in the temple (Ps 65:4; 84:4), who keep God's commands (Ps 119:1-2) and who have many *children (Ps 127:3-5). If we are looking for an OT counterpart to the beatitudes of the Sermon on the Mount, with their composite portrait of the blessed person, Psalm 1 will suffice: it is an extended picture of the blessedness of the godly person, beginning with the evocative beatitude, "Blessed is the man," and including the summary that "in all that he does, he prospers" (Ps 1:3 RSV).

What all these OT beatitudes express is the blessedness of the godly and moral person in this life. They arise from a religious community that values God supremely and views everyday life as a quest to secure God's *covenant blessing, including, but not limited to, its material benefits. OT beatitudes extol the results of trusting in God and praise the prudent person who lives in conformity to God's rules for living. They confirm rather than challenge conventional wisdom.

By contrast, the overwhelming preponderance of NT beatitudes are revolutionary in their rhetoric and sentiment, and apocalyptic in their vision. They pronounce blessing on the person who will share the coming *kingdom, and they reverse conventional values by calling people to a radical lifestyle. The blessed person is now not the person living the moral life and prospering as a result of it, but rather the person whom Christ will find *awake when he comes (Lk 12:37-38, 43) and who will eat *bread in the kingdom of God (Lk 14:15). The blessed person is the one "who endures trial, for when he has stood the test he will receive the crown of life which God has promised to those who love him" (James 1:12 RSV). These beatitudes of the kingdom are also christocentric, pronouncing blessing on "the King who comes in the name of the Lord" (Lk 19:38) and on the disciples whose eyes have seen Christ (Lk 10:23).

The beatitudes of Matthew 5:1-11 can be taken as normative of NT beatitudes. Together they give us a portrait of the ideal follower of Christ, and they consistently conceive of blessing in unconventional ways. The person who is declared blessed is not the earthly success story but those who are poor in spirit, who mourn and are meek, who are merciful and pure in *heart, and so forth. Furthermore, the rewards that are promised to these people are spiritual and apocalyptic—receiving the kingdom of heaven, inheriting the earth, seeing God, obtaining a great reward in heaven. Climaxing the NT apocalyptic beatitudes are seven beatitudes scattered throughout the book of Revelation (Rev 1:3; 14:13; 16:15; 19:9; 20:6; 22:7, 14).

While always retaining its immensely positive effect, the biblical beatitude reflects in microcosm the progression from OT to NT, with the goal of godly well-being in the covenant present giving way to a christocentric and *apocalyptic focus on the arrival and future consummation of a radical spiritual kingdom that reverses conventional ways of thinking, even among the godly.

See also BLESSING, BLESSEDNESS; CURSE.

BIBLIOGRAPHY R. A. Guelich, *The Sermon on the Mount* (Waco, TX: Word, 1982) 62-118.

BEAUTY

Beauty is first of all an aesthetic quality that names what we find attractive, satisfying and excellent in an object or person. With visual art and music, this beauty is perceived through the senses. With a work of literature, beauty is perceived by the mind and imagination. While it is possible to define the specific ingredients of artistic beauty—such as unity, balance, symmetry and harmony of parts—the references to beauty in the Bible do not take us in this analytic direction. Instead the biblical writers are content with beauty as a general artistic quality denoting the positive response of a person to nature, a person or an artifact.

Although beauty begins as a specifically artistic response, by extension we use it to indicate a generalized positive response to something. Thus when Jesus commends Mary's anointing of his feet, he does so with the statement that "she has done a beautiful thing to me" (Mt 26:10; Mk 14:6 RSV). Isaiah does not have physical appearance in mind when he asserts, "How beautiful upon the mountains are the feet of him who brings good tidings" (Is 52:7 RSV). In a similar way, some of the references to the beauty of men, women and children noted below suggest not only external physical beauty but also an inner beauty of character and personality. We move even further from an artistic use of the term to a more metaphoric use when beauty is attributed to character of God. Here the positive qualities of artistic beauty provide a language for identifying the perfection of God and the pleasure that a believer finds in the perfection.

Modern English translations give us approximately a hundred biblical references to *beauty* and *beautiful,* and the overwhelming majority of these references are positive. Beyond the appearance of the word itself are pictures of things or persons that biblical characters and writers find beautiful. The impression that these references leave is that beauty is something of great value in human and spiritual experience.

Biblical Images of Beauty. What then do biblical writers find beautiful? The answer is an ever-expanding list. Houses can be beautiful (Is 5:9), *crowns can be beautiful (Is 28:5; 62:3; Ezek 16:12; 23:42), *garments can be beautiful (Josh 7:21; Is 52:1) and *flocks can be beautiful (Jer 13:20). So can ornaments (Ezek 7:20), a person's *voice (Ezek 33:32), a *city (Lam 2:15), whitewashed tombs (Mt 23:27) and a clay vessel (Rom 9:21). The elevation of a *mountain can be beautiful (Ps 48:2). As we consider the very range of things that appear beautiful to the biblical writers' imaginations, we find evidence for the claim that God "has made everything beautiful in its time" (Eccles 3:11 RSV).

If artifacts can be beautiful, so can people. Within the Bible, *women are said to be beautiful no fewer than twenty times (RSV). *Men also possess beauty (1 Sam 25:3; 2 Sam 14:25; Is 44:13), as did the child *Moses (Acts 7:20; Heb 11:23). The ultimate objectifying of the beauty of the human form is found in Isaiah 44:13, where the prophet speaks of the fashioning of an idol that has "the figure of a man, with the beauty of a man" (RSV). Outer and inner beauty combine in the proverb: "The glory of young men is their strength, but the beauty of old men is their gray hair" (Prov 20:29 RSV), where gray *hair is both physically attractive and a sign of mature wisdom.

Romantic *love has always been closely aligned with the experience of beauty, and the Bible gives us examples. In the *Song of Songs when the lovers meet, they are delighted with what they see: "Behold, you are beautiful my love; behold, you are beautiful; your eyes are doves. Behold, you are beautiful, my beloved, truly lovely" (Song 1:15-16 RSV). The pastoral setting for this idealized love, a royal bower, is an extension of the beauty of the couple (Song 1:17); and this same setting provides images to express the beauty of the lovers, who are (for example) a rose of Sharon, a lily of the valley and an apple tree (Song 2:1, 3). In fact virtually every object that the poet names in the Song of Songs is an image of beauty. In love poetry like this, the lovers' perception of beauty is inspired by love. The same may be said of Abraham's perception of his wife Sarah: "I know that you are a woman beautiful to behold" (Gen 12:11 RSV). Yet Sarah's beauty is clearly attested as fact in the story that follows. In Psalm 45 (like the Song of Songs a royal epithalamium or wedding poem), the poet predicts regarding the bride that "the king will desire your beauty" (v. 11); and in the picture of the *wedding festivities that follows, we read that "the princess is decked in her chamber with gold-woven robes; in many-colored robes she is led to the king" (vv. 13-14 RSV).

Although the biblical view of nature tends to value *nature first of all for its utilitarianism (Ps 104), occasionally we see nature praised for its beauty. Sunrise has the qualities of a "bridegroom leaving his chamber" (Ps 19:1). The *flower is a biblical touchstone of beauty (Is 28:1, 4; 40:6; Jas 1:11), a motif climaxed in Jesus' picture of "the lilies of the field" that are so resplendent that "even Solomon in all his glory was not arrayed like one of these" (Mt 6:28-29). Elsewhere the olive *tree is said to be beautiful (Hos 14:6), and when God planted his *paradisal garden, he "made to grow every tree that is pleasant to the sight" (Gen 2:9). The Song of Songs is a small anthology of the beauties of nature, with images of flowers appearing on the earth (Song 2:12), *vines blossoming (Song 2:13) and mandrakes giving forth fragrance (Song 7:13).

Balancing nature as a locus of beauty for OT believers was the *temple, next to nature their most vivid experience of aesthetic beauty. We catch a glimpse of how beautiful the temple appeared to Hebrew eyes when one of the disciples, coming out of the temple with Jesus, exclaims, "Look, Teacher, what wonderful stones and what wonderful buildings!" (Mk 13:1 RSV). This accords with the OT worshiper's claim regarding God that "strength and beauty are in his sanctuary" (Ps 96:6). When the temple was rebuilt, God himself put "into the heart of the king, to beautify the house of the LORD" (Ezra 7:27 RSV). The holy garments of Aaron and his sons were "for glory and for beauty" (Ex 28:2, 40). It was when worshipers were surrounded by such artistic and architectural beauty that they could "behold the beauty of the LORD" (Ps 27:4) and could enjoin others to "worship the LORD in the beauty of holiness" (1 Chron 16:29 KJV; cf. Ps 29:2; 96:9). Aesthetic pleasure is part of the meaning of the pilgrim's exclamation upon catching sight of the temple, "How lovely is thy dwelling place, O LORD of hosts!" (Ps 84:1 RSV).

The beauty of the *tabernacle and temple are known to us mainly in the biblical accounts of the materials and fashioning that went into them (Ex 25—30, 35—39; 1 Kings 6—7; 1 Chron 22—27; 2 Chron 2—4). This seemingly endless catalog of materials and plans pulsates with an artist's delight in the physical materials and artistic design used in the process of artistic creation. Together these chapters are a heightened image of artistic beauty—a celebration of human artistry. The divine sanction for this artistry is not only that God gave the plans for the construction; he also inspired the artists who did the work (Ex 31:26; 35:30—36:1). The arts in general are a biblical image of beauty. References to *music in the psalms confirm one of the psalmists' claims that the sound of the *harp is "sweet" (82:1 RSV; "pleasant" KJV). The prevailingly literary nature of the Bible is yet another biblical image of beauty. One of the authors explicitly states that beauty of style was important to his enterprise: "the Preacher sought to find pleasing words" (Eccles 12:10 RSV).

The Beauty of God. The move from beauty as an aesthetic quality to a spiritual response that we can see in the references to the beauty associated with worship in the temple reaches its culmination in biblical references to the beauty of God. These can hardly be an aesthetic response, though we should not dismiss the way the language of aesthetics becomes the best way for the believer to express the delight and satisfaction that he or she finds in God. When David asserts that the "one thing" that he will seek after is "to behold the beauty of the LORD" in the temple (Ps 27:4), the experience of beauty expresses his longing to see God face to face. It is really God that he seeks, not a beautiful image. This beauty of the Lord represents one of the many paradoxes of Christianity, for it is clear from the Scriptures that the beauty of God refers at one and the same time to literal appearance and to that invisible quality that makes God the definition of beauty. Somehow in God beauty of spirit and beauty of appearance are perfected, as captured in the evocative picture of "the perfection of beauty" that "shines forth" from Zion (Ps 50:2).

The explicit references to beauty in relation to God seem to be an attempt to express the inexpressible, to describe the "immortal, invisible, the only God" (1 Tim 1:17). Hence the following verses: "Honor and majesty are before him; strength and beauty in his sanctuary" (Ps 96:6 RSV); "In that day the LORD of hosts will be a crown of glory, and a diadem of beauty to the remnant of his people" (Is 28:5 RSV). Here beauty is related to the majesty and *glory, the kingship and sovereignty of God—words full of mystery that will only take on their full meaning when, as David longed to do, we "behold the beauty of the LORD" (Ps 27:4). Yet the beauty of God is linked with solid and tangible objects and real places—a crown, a diadem and the sanctuary of the Lord. Isaiah promises that "your eyes will see the king in his beauty, they will behold a land that stretches afar" (Is 33:17 RSV), a verse that exquisitely combines the visual image and the unsearchable depth of the beauty of the Lord. When *Moses descended from Mount Sinai, his *face was shining simply from being in the presence of the Lord.

Although the word *beauty* is not used, it is overwhelmingly implied by those few persons in the Bible who look upon God. It is as though beauty does not define God, but God defines beauty. The descriptions of the Lord tell us what beauty is. For example:

> In the year that King Uzziah died I saw the LORD sitting upon a throne, high and lifted up; and his train filled the temple. Above him stood the seraphim; each had six wings: with two he covered his face, and with two he covered his feet, and with two he flew. And one called to another and said: "Holy, holy, holy is the LORD of hosts; the whole earth is full of his glory." And the foundations of the thresholds shook at the voice of him who called, and the house was filled with smoke. (Is 6:1-4 RSV)

Similarly, John's vision of the risen and ascended Son of God:

> In the midst of the lampstands one like a son of man, clothed with a long robe and with a golden girdle round his breast; his head and his hair were white as white wool, white as snow; his eyes were like a flame of fire, his feet were like burnished bronze, refined as in a furnace, and his voice was like the sound of many waters; in his right hand he held seven stars, from his mouth issued a sharp two-edged sword, and his face was like the sun shining in full strength. When I saw him, I fell at his feet as though dead. But he laid his right hand upon me, saying, "Fear not, I am the first and the last, and the living one; I died, and behold I am alive forevermore, and I have the keys of Death and Hades." (Rev 1:13-18 RSV)

Here, surely, are images of transcendent beauty.

An extension of the beauty of God is the beauty of *heaven, which the book of Revelation portrays as a place of transcending and transcendent beauty. This is especially evident in the detailed picture of the New *Jerusalem in Revelation 21—22:5, where the imagery of adornment, *jewels, *light, *glory and *paradise creates a dazzling impression of a beauty that far surpasses anything earthly.

The Limits of Beauty. For all its endorsement of earthly and heavenly beauty, the Bible also cautions its readers about beauty. First, earthly beauty (in contrast to heavenly beauty) is temporary, as is made clear in references to the "glorious beauty" of "the fading flower" (Is 28:1; cf. Is 40:6-8). Second, beauty is powerless to protect itself from physical destruction (Is 64:11; Jer 4:30). Third, beauty can seduce a person into morally harmful actions like *adultery (Prov 6:25). Fourth, physical beauty is only skin deep and is no guarantee of godly character: "Charm is deceitful, and beauty is vain, but a woman who fears the LORD is to be praised" (Prov 31:30 RSV; cf. Prov 11:22, with its picture of a "a beautiful woman without discretion"). Fifth, even when beauty does not conceal a defective inner character, it is of lesser value than inner spiritual character. This critique of external beauty is present in the apparently undistinguished physical appearance of Jesus. In Isaiah's prophecy about the coming of God's *suffering servant, we read that he will have "no beauty or majesty to attract us to him, nothing in his appearance that we should desire him" (Is 53:2 NIV). In fact this suffering servant "was despised and rejected by men" and "as one from whom men hide their faces he was despised, and we esteemed him not" (Is 53:3 RSV).

The most extended critique of human and earthly beauty occurs in Ezekiel 16, an oracle of judgment against Jerusalem (see also the parallel indictment of Tyre in Ezek 27—28). The case against beauty is *idolatry—a worship of and trust in one's own beauty. God pictures himself as having decked his chosen nation (a personified Jerusalem) with jewelry, so that she "grew exceedingly beautiful" (Ezek 16:13), with her renown going "forth among the nations because of [her] beauty, for it was perfect through the splendor which I had bestowed upon [her]" (Ezek 16:14). What could go wrong with such a positive picture of beauty? The answer: "You trusted in your beauty" (Ezek 16:15) and "prostituted your beauty" (Ezek 16:25). It is not beauty that is indicted in this vision; beauty itself is a gift conferred by God. What is condemned is the perversion of beauty in pride, self-absorption and self-worship.

Summary. The imagery of beauty is extensive in the Bible, ranging from the paradise in which God planted every *tree that is pleasant, to the sight of the resplendent heavenly Jerusalem that dazzles our sight in the closing pages of the Bible. We can infer from the biblical images of beauty that the longing for beauty, along with an ability to recognize and experience it, exists within every human being. Although the Bible does not state it explicitly, it is a fair inference that experiences of earthly beauty awaken a longing for a beauty that is more permanent and transcendent than anything this life can give—a longing for the beauty of God. Certainly the beauty of the holy city (and its forerunner, the *Zion of the temple) is inseparable from the glory of God, who is himself its source, its temple and its light. In heaven all God's servants will see his face as David longed to do: "There shall no more be anything accursed, but the throne of God and of the Lamb shall be in it, and his servants shall worship him; they shall see his face, and his name shall be on their foreheads" (Rev 22:3-4 RSV). And in seeing God they will see beauty in its pure form for the first time.

See also ADAM; FLOWERS; GARDEN; GLORY; JERUSALEM; JEWELS AND PRECIOUS STONES; LIGHT; LOVE STORY; MAN; SONG OF SOLOMON; TEMPLE; TREE, TREES; WOMAN; ZION.

BIBLIOGRAPHY. W. A. Dyrness, "Aesthetics in the Old Testament: Beauty in Context," *JETS* 28 (1985) 421-32; P. Sherry, *Spirit and Beauty: An Introduction to Theological Aesthetics* (Oxford: Oxford University Press, 1992).

BED, BEDROOM

Beds are mentioned throughout Scripture, the most famous bed probably being that of Og of Bashan, the last of the giant Rephaites, whose iron bed was "more than thirteen feet long and six feet wide" (Deut 3:11 NIV). In the Bible, beds also serve to picture various aspects and conditions of the people who lie in them. Specifically, beds portray comfortable *rest, sloth, *pain, permanent residence (even death), the privacy of the soul and *purity or impurity, especially relating to *sexual activity.

The state of comfortable rest associated with beds seems almost a part of the literal meaning. When the psalmist recalls David's oath not to enter his house, go to his bed or allow sleep to his eyes until he has found "a place for the LORD," we clearly understand that David means not to rest or take his ease until he has seen to the job of building the temple (Ps 132:1-5). Job, in his torment, looks to his bed for "comfort" and "ease," but even there, he says, God disturbs him with frightening *dreams and visions, so that he can find no rest (Job 7:13-14). Isaiah gives Israel a vivid picture of coming punishment: God's people think they are secure and comfortable, but because of their disobedience soon they will find "the bed is too short to stretch out on, the blanket too narrow to wrap around you" (Is 28:20).

Sometimes the comfortable rest of a bed appears not as desirable, but as slothful or even evil, as when Ahab, unable to procure Naboth's vineyard for himself, "lay on his bed sulking" (1 Kings 21:4). Proverbs 26:14 pictures a *sluggard as one who "turns on his bed" like "a door turns on its hinges." Amos condemns the comfortable, corrupt Israelites who "sit in Samaria / on the edge of their beds" and who "lie on beds inlaid with ivory / and lounge on your couches" (Amos 3:12; 6:4). In such passages beds picture slothful and decadent ease.

In some cases the inactivity of a bed connects not with rest or sloth but with pain, as in Job 33:19, in which we read of one "chastened on a bed of pain." The "sickbed" and "bed of illness" (Ps 41:3) become at times symbols of pain and even punishment: pagan Jezebel, as the representative of sexual immorality and pagan idolatry, is "cast on a bed of suffering" (Rev 2:22).

Beds can themselves represent one's home. When David speaks of making his bed in the depths, he means making the depths his dwelling place—taking up residence there (Ps 139:8). Making one's bed sometimes offers an image of that most permanent dwelling, death. Ezekel calls the grave of Elam "a bed . . . among the slain" (Ezek 32:25). In his despair Job asks whether the grave is the only home for which he can hope, and in the following parallel line he pictures himself in that grave, spreading out his bed in darkness (Job 17:13).

Although beds can picture external and even eternal dwelling places, they more commonly offer a picture of that private, internal place where a person ponders, meditates or plots. The bedroom is the place of the most personal, secret thoughts. So when Solomon advises his hearers not to curse the rich in their bedrooms, he is urging them to take care for their most private thoughts and words (Eccles 10:20). The psalms contain multiple pictures of people on their beds, opening their hearts before God (e.g., Ps 4:4; 63:6). In the Song of Songs, the beloved tells how "all night long on my bed / I looked for the one my heart loves," meaning that both in her literal bed and in her most private thoughts and dreams she has been focusing her desires on her lover (Song 3:1).

In Hosea 7:14, God's disobedient people "do not cry out to me from their hearts / but wail upon their beds." The picture of them on their beds shows their slothful inactivity, but it also exposes their hearts, which are hopelessly turned in on themselves rather than crying out to God, as the verse's first line mentions by contrast. Periodic mentions of evildoers plotting evil on their beds reveal the sinful interiors of people's houses and hearts (e.g., Ps 36:4; Mic 2:1).

In general, beds tell the story of the purity or impurity of a person's life, especially in relation to sexual activity. The bed often functions as a direct symbol of *sexual activity. When Potiphar's wife back in ancient Egypt says, "Come to bed with me," we understand the nature of this invitation (Gen 39:7, 12). Throughout Scripture, for a son to defile a father's bed means for that son to have sexual relations with his mother or with his father's wife, and any such activity is condemned as vile and sinful (Gen 49:4; 1 Chron 5:1; Deut 22:30; 27:20).

Two kinds of women make their appearance in the book of Proverbs: the pure and the impure. The impure is a *prostitute who lures the innocent youth, enticing him with descriptions of her bed, which is covered with colored linens from Egypt and perfumed with exotic spices (Prov 7:16-17). The pure woman is a wise wife who herself makes the coverings for her bed, keeping her eyes and her hands busy in her own home rather than setting them on foreign goods—whether fabric or flesh (Prov 31:22). Their different beds offer pictures of their contrasting pure and impure sexual activity as well as their pure and impure hearts.

The bed as a picture of sexual impurity becomes a symbol, on another level, of spiritual impurity and *adultery. For example Isaiah, condemning God's people for idolatry, accuses them of making their beds in the high places where they go to offer their pagan sacrifices. God himself accuses his people of uncovering their beds, opening them wide, making pacts and experiencing intimacy with those idolaters "whose beds you love" (Is 57:7-8). Similarly Ezekiel pictures the wrongful military alliances of Judah and Israel with surrounding pagan nations in terms of prostitution: Israel becomes the prostitute who defiles herself and invites the Babylonians, among others, to her "bed of love" (Ezek 23:17).

One of the most delightful contrasts to the beds of impure sexual activity appears in Song of Songs, as the pure-hearted lovers in that book celebrate their "verdant bed," using all the richness and fertility of nature to picture the rich pleasure of their sexual intimacy (Song 1:16). From the woman's perspective, her lover's cheeks "are like beds of spice." Such images, ripe with sensuous enjoyment, cluster throughout the book and communicate the delight of pure hearts and bodies joining together.

Throughout Scripture beds reveal in various ways the intimate conditions and relationships of those to whom they belong. From the biblical perspective, what human beings do in their beds offers a telling picture of what they are doing with their lives: beds can gauge rest, sloth, pain, true residence and the privacy and purity of the human heart.

See also ADULTERY; HOME, HOUSE; MARRIAGE; REST; SEX; SLUGGARD; SONG OF SONGS.

BEGGAR, BEGGING

In the Bible begging is seen as an extreme condition. The OT spells out careful rules for how the children of Israel are to deal with those who are reduced to begging for their livelihood. While the rules are often designed to protect the poverty stricken from oppression and harm (e.g., Prov 22:22), the OT also sees the need to beg as an image of the curse on the wicked (Ps 109:10). The psalmist notes that he has never seen the children of the righteous "begging bread" (Ps 37:25 NASB). Proverbs notes that the *sluggard "does not plow after the autumn, so he begs during the harvest and has nothing" (Prov 20:4). Those that beg are stigmatized by the extent of their need and the causes for that need; the need to beg is a sign of disfavor on beggars even while they

are being cared for under the laws of charity and *hospitality.

Charity for the poor may be behind some of Jesus' own actions on behalf of beggars. But the image of begging is also transformed in the NT record. In the Gospels beggars become an important image of how the grace of God extends beyond human ability. Both Mark and Luke record the story of Blind Bartimaeus, reduced to begging because of his physical handicap. When he stops Jesus, requesting mercy, Jesus not only extends the required courtesy to the blind beggar but also heals him physically and restores him spiritually (Mk 10:46-52; Lk 18:35-43).

In at least two *parables Jesus uses people who beg as examples of the righteous. In Luke, Jesus tells the story of a judge "who did not fear God, and did not respect man" (Lk 18:2). But the judge is finally moved by a woman whose appeals for *justice resemble the intensity and endurance of a beggar. In the parable the intensity and repetition of the woman are set up as an example of how *prayer, even without that effort, moves God, who unlike this judge is just.

The most significant transformation of a beggar, however, occurs in Jesus' parable of the rich man and Lazarus (Lk 16:19-31), based on the motif of the reversal of fortune in the *afterlife. In this parable the beggar becomes the honored one, showing that the grace of God is no respecter of persons. In fact the story suggests that those who lack here on earth will be rewarded spiritually.

The image does not suggest, however, that God needs to be begged in order to open the supplies of the *kingdom. Instead it reassures those who are reduced to begging that their cries will be heard, their dignity will be restored and their desires will be answered. The stories of Bartimaeus, the persistent *widow, and Lazarus remind hearers of the gospel that, far from being a reason for rejection, poverty symbolically becomes an opportunity for miracle and grace. Begging, as a symbol of need acknowledged, becomes the means by which God can meet need.

These concrete examples help to illustrate Christ's metaphorical use of poverty in the *beatitudes of theSermon on the Mount, where he informed his followers that the "poor in spirit" were blessed, for they would receive "the kingdom of heaven" (Mt 5:3).

See also ABUNDANCE; BEATITUDES; POVERTY; REWARD; WEAK, WEAKNESS.

BEHIND. *See* BACK SIDE.

BELLY

In addition to its straightforward meaning, the Bible uses the belly to summon images of beauty, greed, the inner self and the life-giving womb.

Belly as Anatomy. Part of the curse meted out to the serpent who deceived Eve was that it would have to crawl on its belly and, as a consequence, be forced to eat dust (Gen 3:14). The psalmist echoes this image to emphasize the fallenness of God's people as they complain of misery and oppression bringing them down to the dust so that their bodies "cling to the ground" (Ps 44:25).

The lover draws admiring attention to the 'belly' (translated "waist" in NIV and NRSV), among other well shaped features of his beloved (Song 7:2). The wealthy and opulent, unaccustomed to want, have large bellies (Judg 3:17; Jer 5:27) in contrast to the lean belly of the poor (Is 17:4). The term "cows of Bashan" to refer to rich women implies corpulence (Amos 4:1). The large belly of Behemoth is a sign of his strength (Job 40:16). The belly with its direct connection to the necessities of physical life occasionally stands in contrast to the spiritual, so that the psalmist by the phrase "soul and belly" means "body and soul" (Ps 31:10; 44:26).

Belly as Greed. The wants and appetites of the belly serve as both metaphor and motivation for the wicked and make it the seat of avarice and passion (Job 20:20). The cravings of the belly are a picture of the life of the flesh (i.e., the self) which is in opposition to the life of the Spirit. The parables of the Rich Fool (Lk 12:13-21) and the Rich Man and Lazarus (Lk 16:19-31) pivot around the imagery of the satisfied appetite and underline the foolishness of thinking that the good life is a full belly (cf. Deut 32:15; Job 20; Rom 16:18). Paul contrasts those "whose god is their belly" and "whose mind is on earthly things" with those "whose citizenship is in heaven" (Phil 3:19-20). The link between sin and the stomach is obvious and strong, but Jesus explicitly denies that Jewish food laws, that regulate the categories of food that go into the body, play any role in corrupting the desires and action of people (Mt 15:17; Mk 7:19).

Belly as Mind or Soul. The Bible records fatal injuries to the belly for several characters (Eglon, Judg 3:21; Amasa, 2 Sam 20:10; Judas, Acts 1:18). Since the belly is a vulnerable area of the body, it shelters one's essence. The Hebrew and Greek terms for "belly," variously translated, occur repeatedly to designate the "inmost being" (Prov 18:8 = 26:22; 20:27, 30; 22:18; Job 15:2, 35; 32:18; Jn 7:38). The belly also senses emotions, gut feelings, such as anguish (Jer 4:19) compassion (Lk 10:33; cf. "bowels and mercies" AV Phil 2:1) and affection (2 Cor 6:12).

Belly as Womb. The belly appears poetically parallel to "womb" (Job 10:18; Is 48:8; 49:1, 5). Swelling of the abdomen is, of course, associated with pregnancy, though it was also diagnostic of an adulteress (Num 5:11-31). Belly by itself can signify birth (Hos 9:11), but also occurs frequently in idioms meaning womb: "son of my belly" (Job 19:17); "fruit of the belly" (Micah 6:7); "from the belly," i.e., "since birth" (Judg 13:5). The womb, if life fails to emerge from it, is a grave. Jonah, despairing of escape from the great fish, says, "out of the belly of Sheol I cried" (Jon 2:2).

See also ABRAHAM'S BOSOM; APPETITE; BREAST; STOMACH.

BEND THE KNEE. *See* BOW, BOWING; KNEE, KNEEL.

BENEATH. *See* UNDER.

BENEDICTION

Whereas a *beatitude is a blessing pronounced by a person on either another person or on God, a benediction is God's blessing conferred on a person or group by God's designated human agent. Although benedictions are not limited to worship settings (e.g., Gen 9:26-27; 14:19-20; 27:27-29), they are especially associated with them. In the OT the formal benediction was pronounced by the Aaronic priests (Num 6:24-26; 2 Chron 30:27), while NT benedictions are pronounced by the apostles in their epistles. The Aaronic blessing is perhaps the most memorable biblical benediction:

"The LORD bless you and keep you;
the LORD make his face shine upon you
 and be gracious to you;
the LORD turn his face toward you
 and give you peace." (Num 6:24-26 NIV)

If we look at the Aaronic and apostolic benedictions most commonly associated with worship occasions (Num 6:24-26; Rom 15:13; 2 Cor 13:14; Heb 13:20-21), we note the following motifs: (1) God-centeredness, in the sense that God is the one whose blessing is invoked and who is understood to be the source of the blessings of grace and peace; (2) a solemn tone and exalted imagery embedded in language polished by liturgical use; (3) an aura of authority, so that the pronouncing of them by God's qualified and special agents not only expresses a wish but actually confers God's blessing on the recipient.

The benedictions have a distinctive rhetorical flavor, sonorous in their tone and formally embellished. The Aaronic benediction, for example, consists of three pairs of verbs, each having "the LORD" as the subject of the action. The NT benedictions feature similar parallelism of phrases and syntax, owing to their roots in the Jewish liturgical heritage.

See also BEATITUDE; BLESSING.

BENJAMIN

The name Benjamin means "son of my *right hand." This itself points to Benjamin's role in biblical narrative: he is a favored son of Jacob, the latest to be born to a prolific patriarch, born of the favored wife Rachel (who died in Benjamin's childbirth).

In the Joseph narratives, Benjamin becomes a substitute when Joseph, Jacob's *very* favorite son, is sold into slavery and presumed to be dead. Jacob says that Benjamin's death will bring down his gray hair to Sheol, exactly as he had said of Joseph (Gen 42:38). Benjamin goes to Egypt by caravan as had Joseph (Gen 43:15); he receives the same favored treatment as Joseph (Gen 43:34); and eventually the attitude of the brothers toward Joseph is revealed in their attitude toward Benjamin. Appropriately to this substitute role, Benjamin is entirely passive, never speaking a word.

As the last to be born, Benjamin also represents the completion of the family of Israel in Genesis. Yet no sooner is he born and the family completed than the family starts to break apart with the death of his mother (Gen 35:16-20), followed by further family disruptions culminating in the sale of Joseph. But here as well, Benjamin represents the reconciliation of the complete family by his role in reuniting Joseph and his brothers.

In Judges the role of the tribe of Benjamin is reversed from the passive and positive role of the individual in Genesis. Now active, this "son of the right hand" (cf. Gen 35:18) has become an aggressive *left-handed warrior. No longer a stand-in for Joseph, Benjamin now stands in contrast to Judah. The first judge, Othniel, is from the tribe of Judah (Judg 3:9-10). But the second, the left-handed and deceptive Ehud, for whom there is no mention of the Spirit, is from Benjamin (Judg 3:12-30). Later the *hospitality of the Judahite father of the Levite's concubine contrasts with the lack of hospitality shown in Gibeah of the region of Benjamin (Judg 19:4-9, 15-21). The subsequent *rape of the concubine marks that Benjaminite city as another *Sodom (Judg 19:22-24), while the cutting of her body into twelve pieces to summon the tribes to avenge this atrocity is itself a grotesque and ambiguous act (Judg 19:29). On the surface the nation is being called together; in deep structure it is being cut apart. The contrast is further apparent when Benjamin sides with Gibeah, while Judah leads the assault against the town (Judg 20:12-13, 18). When Gibeah is finally taken by ambush, the reader is reminded of the use of the same deception in the original conquest of that territory, so that Benjamin symbolizes a reversal in the direction of the nation (Judg 20:29-47, cf. Josh 8:4-25). By the end of Judges the brother who once was the reconciliation of his family has become the beginning of its dissolution.

In Samuel the choice of Saul of Gibeah as the first king is an ominous sign. An initial emphasis on the "least of the tribes" theme suggests connections with the positive "younger brother" theme in Genesis (1 Sam 9:21). But when Saul cuts a yoke of oxen into pieces to summon the nation to war (1 Sam 11:7), the reader knows that he is not the favored brother of Genesis, but the divisive and warlike Benjamin of Judges. Benjamin continues to represent divisive forces in the nation, especially in persons such as Sheba and Shemei (2 Sam 16:5-7; 20:1). Yet the ambiguity of Benjamin is aptly portrayed in the fact that David, while hiding from Saul at Ziklag, was joined by six hundred Benjaminites who, interestingly, could sling a stone with either their right hand or their left (1 Chron 12:1-2). It may be this legacy of zeal that Paul proudly claims when he reminds the Philippians that he is "of the tribe of Benjamin, a Hebrew of Hebrews" (Phil 3:5).

During the divided monarchy Benjamin was often reckoned with Judah (e.g., 1 Kings 12:21). But Benjamin, now a divided tribe and the very ground on which Judah and Israel fought (1 Kings 15:16-22), was flanked on its southern border (its right hand) by Jerusalem (which originally belonged to Benjamin, cf. Judg 1:21) with its temple of Yahweh, and on its northern border (its left hand) by Bethel (which also originally belonged to Benjamin, cf. Josh 18:22) with its sanctuary for one of the golden calves. Is the tribe right-handed or left-handed? In either case, this youngest brother again reveals the heart of the rest of the brothers, and it is now a divided heart, in accordance with the seemingly contradictory blessings of Jacob and Moses (Gen 49:27; Deut 32:12).

See also RIGHT, RIGHT HAND.

BIBLIOGRAPHY. J. Ackerman, "Joseph, Judah, and Jacob," in *Literary Interpretations of Biblical Narratives* (Nashville: Abingdon, 1982) 2:85-113; L. Klein, *The Triumph of Irony in the Book of Judges* (Sheffield: JSOT Press, 1988) 161-92; D. Steinmetz, *From Father to Son* (Louisville, KY: Westminster John Knox, 1991) 120-27; B. Webb, *The Book of Judges* (Sheffield: JSOT Press, 1987) 188-97.

BET, DARE

The most obvious example of the archetypal bet or dare is the story of Elijah on Mt. Carmel (1 Kings 18), where the prophet summons the prophets of Baal to a showdown in which both he and the prophets prepare a *sacrifice and call down *fire from heaven. The silence of Baal and the display of God's power in burning up both the *altar and the *water around it make up one of the most rousing stories in the Bible.

The bet or dare motif is present in obvious ways in other stories. The trial of Job begins with a pair of "double dares." God in effect dares *Satan to find fault with his "blameless and upright" servant (Job 1:8; 2:3). Satan in turn bets that Job will turn on God if he is afflicted (Job 1:9-11; 2:4-5), and God accepts the terms of the dare (Job 1:12; 2:6). In Job's subsequent career of finding fault with God, Satan initially seems to win the dare; but in the end he is defeated, not even appearing in the final chapter of the book as he is banished from the scene.

Daniel and his three friends take a chance on God's vindicating them when they propose to refuse the king's food and drink for ten days on the supposition that they will outperform the students who accept the king's fare (Dan 1:5-16). *Samson bets thirty sets of garments that the Philistine young men attending his *wedding feast cannot guess his riddle (Judg 14:12-19), and his losing of the bet through his inability to resist the pleas of a pagan wife foreshadows the tragic shape of his life to come. More positively, Gideon challenges the angel of God in the celebrated fleece tests (Judg 6:36-40).

Goliath dares the Israelite army to send forth a soldier to engage in single combat and loses the challenge when God strengthens the boy *David for the task (1 Sam 17; *see* Battle Stories). When *Abraham undertakes a delicate negotiation with God over the fate of *Sodom, he subjects himself to a latent dare, inasmuch as he does not *know* how many "righteous" there are in Sodom (Gen 18:22-33). As Jesus hangs on the cross, his tormentors dare him to come down from the cross (Mt 27:42; Lk 23:37).

God is sometimes the one to present the challenge. In Malachi 3:10 God issues a challenge regarding the tithe: "Bring the full tithes into the storehouse; . . . and thereby put me to the test, says the LORD of hosts, if I will not open the windows of heaven for you and pour down for you an overflowing blessing" (RSV). In the NT incident of the woman caught in *adultery accused by the scribes and Pharisees, Jesus dares anyone who is without sin to cast the first stone (Jn 8:1-11).

See also VOW, OATH.

BETHLEHEM

The Bethlehem in Zebulun (Josh 19:15), the home of the judge Ibzan (Judg 12:8, 10), is not an important place in the Bible; but the Bethlehem in Judah (cf. Judg 17:7), just a few miles south-southwest of Jerusalem, is remembered for several reasons. According to Genesis 35:16-20 and 48:7, Rachel was buried near there. Thus Matthew 2:17-18 can associate Jeremiah 31:15 ("A voice was heard in Ramah, lamentation and bitter weeping, Rachel weeping for her children; she refused to be consoled, because they were no more" [RSV]) with Herod's slaughter of the infants even though Jeremiah 31:15 names not Bethlehem but Ramah (cf. 2 Sam 10:2).

Tragedy is linked to the small village in Judges 19, where a concubine from Bethlehem is ravished by Benjaminites until dead—a deed that leads Israel to war with *Benjamin. Much later, Ezra 2:21 and Nehemiah 7:26 refer to Bethlehemites returning from the Babylonian captivity, and Jeremiah 41:17 mentions Israelites who stay near Bethlehem when they flee from the Babylonian king to Egypt.

If Bethlehem is regularly a setting for tragedy and sadness, it is equally the city of *David the king, "the village where David was" (Jn 7:42; cf. 1 Sam 17:12, 58). David herds sheep outside Bethlehem (1 Sam 17:15). There he has dealings with a Philistine garrison (1 Chron 11:15-19). And there Samuel anoints him king (1 Sam 16:1-13). Because of David's descent from *Ruth and Boaz, the setting in Bethlehem of the story of Ruth is emphasized (Ruth 1:1-2). Bethlehem literally means "house of bread," and the grain fields so prominent in Ruth reinforce the aptness of this title. Furthermore, David's association with Bethlehem illumines the prophecy of Micah 5:2, which looks forward to a Davidic ruler from Bethlehem (cf. Jn 7:42).

In Matthew and Luke the tragic and royal associations of Bethlehem meet as the messianic Son of David, in accordance with Micah 5:2, is born in Bethlehem (Mt 2:1-6; Lk 2:4). His birth, however, is met by hostility: Herod orders the slaughter of all the male children in Bethlehem two years and under. Again Bethlehem witnesses death.

If Micah 5:2 makes Bethlehem "little among the clans of Judah," in Matthew 2:6 this text is quoted as affirming that Bethlehem is "by no means least among the rulers of Judah." Whether or not Matthew's line attests a textual variant, the change can only mean that by coming into the world at Bethlehem, the Messiah has brought the city greatness. Here as elsewhere, the last becomes first.

See also BENJAMIN; DAVID.

BETRAY, BETRAYAL

Betrayal is the stuff of which dramas are made. The Bible has its share of such stories, including Delilah's betrayal of *Samson's secret (Judg 16) and Judas's betrayal of Jesus (Mt 26:48-50). Such actions are not given simple pejorative labels, however, as they might have been in modern media. Rather, the writers use expressive words, which can have a variety of positive and negative meanings, to evoke the true nature of the dark deeds.

The chief OT image of betrayal is wrongful exposure of what should remain hidden (Heb *gālâ*). Thus the gossip who "betrays a confidence" (Prov 20:19 NIV) is literally "revealing" the information wrongly. However, God rightly reveals (*gālâ*) his secrets to the prophets (Amos 3:7). The same word also describes unlawful sexual relations (Lev 18:6, literally "to uncover" nakedness), suggesting that any wrongful exposure of private matters strikes at the very root of a person's identity. Thus tabloid journalism exposés of private lives would qualify as betrayal in OT terms. So too would character assassination by gossips, whom wise people avoid (Prov 20:19). By contrast, when David's *adultery was exposed, it was by private challenge from a prophet, not by public headlining (1 Sam 12).

A secondary OT image of betrayal is that of deceit, especially "breaking faith" with God or another person (Heb *bāgad*); that is, disloyalty. This is a powerful image in a culture that prized close solidarity and trust. Jeremiah's bitterness stems partly from the fact that his own family has betrayed him (Jer 12:6) in just the same way as the nation has been unfaithful to God by acting like an adulterous spouse (Hos 5:7). Betrayal in this sense rips relationships apart and cuts the threads that hold a community together.

The NT image of betrayal, mostly restricted to the actions of Judas, is quite different. It is that of "handing over" one person to another (Gk *paradidōmi*), as in Pilate's quasilegal handing over of Jesus to the executioners (Mt 27:26). Judas Iscariot, dubbed "the betrayer" in most versions, in the Greek is literally "the one who handed [Jesus] over."

This puts his action firmly in the realm of human power play, whatever his motives were. For one awesome moment in history, Judas the mortal had

Christ the eternal in his power. Judas could force Jesus to conform to his own confused plans. He played God and became the archetype of all who exert their wills over others.

By extension, Judas was therefore betraying much more than Jesus' whereabouts (Lk 22:3-6) or even his friendship and trust (Jn 13:26-30). He was also betraying the basic principles of Christian conduct: denial of self-will, trust in God's providence, and love for others that refuses to manipulate them. Far from enabling Christians to explain away Judas's act as pure greed or satanic inspiration, the NT forces them to regard as betrayal any self-willed use of power against another, whether it be physical, litigious, emotional or spiritual. Like the OT "uncovering," such acts betray a person's essential humanity, identity and freedom. And yet Judas's betrayal is itself caught up into God's transcendent plan, so that the words of Joseph to his brothers are strangely recalled: "You meant evil against me; but God meant it for good" (Gen 50:20).

See also DECEPTION, STORIES OF.

BIBLE

In considering the Bible as a whole, two aspects are relevant: images *about* the Bible, including how the Bible pictures itself, and unifying motifs *in* the Bible as a whole.

Images of the Bible. The most prevalent image by which biblical writers refer to the collection of words that became our Bible is *word*. The Bible is "the word," specifically the Word of God. The implication is that the Bible exists through the medium of language, whether oral or written. It is further implied that this word is a communication, inasmuch as the purpose of words is to convey meaning to the understanding of the listener or reader. Finally, to speak of the Bible as the Word of God (as the Bible itself does repeatedly) is to imply that the Bible carries authority for a person's life because of the authority of its human authors as spokespersons of God and because of the *authority of the ultimate author, God himself.

Another common term for the Bible is *Scripture* or *scriptures,* used in the NT only (and there fifty times). The word *scripture* is a generic term referring to something that is written. The OT counterparts to this NT designation are the words *book* and *scroll,* used several dozen times to call attention to the physical form in which the biblical writings were preserved and handed on.

A common OT image for the Bible is *law,* on the premise that the first parts of the Bible that were recorded were the Pentateuch, much of which is devoted to delineating the Mosaic law. Thus when the psalmist says that the godly person meditates day and night on God's law (Ps 1:2), he speaks of the equivalent of our Bible. So too in Psalm 119, where the assertions made about God's law (and its synonyms) are equally true of the entire Bible. To speak of the Bible as the law also points to the Bible as

containing God's guidelines for living, which people are under obligation to obey.

Additional terms that we commonly use for the Bible, even though they do not appear within the Bible, are nonetheless helpful images for naming features that the Bible possesses and claims for itself. The word *Bible,* based on the Latin *biblia,* means "little books," calling attention to the fact that the Bible is an anthology of collected writings, written by numerous authors over many centuries and encompassing the usual range of genres and styles that we expect in an anthology. The word *canon* means "standard" or "rule" (literally "reed" or "measuring rod") and denotes the status of the Bible as an authoritative and inspired book, unlike other books. When Peter refers to "the other scriptures" (2 Pet 3:16 RSV), we can infer the existence in his day of a canonical standard for some parts of the Bible. In a secondary way too, these canonical writings are a standard for belief and conduct—God's expectations for what people should believe and his moral prescriptions for life.

The designations *Old Testament* and *New Testament* are postbiblical, but they too are true to the spirit of the Bible. Literally, a testament is a will, but when applied to the two parts of the Bible, the term is synonymous with covenant. Inherent in the terms *old* and *new* is the idea of both change and continuity. The old covenant points forward to something beyond itself; the new covenant is the fulfillment of the old. Together these two comprise an organic whole; neither can be fully understood by itself. Many formulas have been suggested as further ways of understanding the relationship between the two Testaments. The NT reveals what is concealed in the OT. The OT tells us *what* Christ is; the NT shows us *who* he is.

Two additional images for the Bible may be noted. The NT refers to the OT (or parts of it) as "oracles" from God (Acts 7:38; Rom 3:2), thereby designating the Bible as a direct pronouncement from God and a message to be heeded as divinely inspired. Parts of the Bible are also designated as a "revelation" from God (e.g., Rom 16:26; Eph 3:5), implying that the Bible is something that had to be revealed from God, as being something beyond human origin or attainment.

How the Bible Pictures Itself. With the foregoing terms as a backdrop, it is obvious that the Bible's comment on itself is a major biblical motif. Even when such self-designations refer to only a part of the Bible, their meaning can be extended to the Bible as a whole when they accurately apply.

Some of the Bible's self-designations refer to its special status as God's revelation. Here we find references to "the sacred writings" (2 Tim 3:15 RSV), to the Bible as a "prophecy" that did not come "by the impulse of man" but as a result of authors being carried along by the Holy Spirit as they "spoke from God" (2 Pet 1:21 RSV), and to the fact that the Bible is "not . . . the word of men but . . . the word of God"

(1 Thess 2:13 RSV).

Other passages paint a picture of the qualities of the Bible, which is variously a *lamp to illuminate a person's pathway (Ps 119:105), "a lamp shining in a dark place" (2 Pet 1:19 RSV), something so durable that it "abides for ever" (1 Pet 1:25 RSV), something that "is living and active, sharper than any two-edged *sword" (Heb 4:12 RSV), something that warns a person (Ps 19:11), something essential to life (Mt 4:4), a *mirror in which a person can see himself or herself (Jas 1:22-25). One of the rare biblical writers to state his method of composition calls attention to the selfconscious artistry evident in the Bible: "Besides being wise, the Preacher also taught the people knowledge, weighing and studying and arranging proverbs with great care. The Preacher sought to find pleasing words, and uprightly he wrote words of truth" (Eccles 12:9-10 RSV; cf. Lk 1:1-4).

Other passages give a many-sided picture of how people should use this Word from God: they should *meditate on* it (Ps 1:2 and numerous passages), *be instructed* by it for salvation (1 Tim 3:15), *obey* it (Lk 11:28), *continue in* it (Jn 8:31), *keep* it (2 Chron 34:21; Ps 119:67; Jn 14:23), *hear* it (Jer 31:10; Eph 1:13), *receive* it (1 Thess 2:13), *read* it (Mt 21:42; 2 Cor 3:15), *dwell in* it (Eph 3:17), *believe* it (Jn 2:22), *search* it (Jn 5:39), *praise* it (Acts 13:48) and *hide* it within their hearts (Ps 119:11 KJV). The Word is also something that *abides in* believers (Jn 5:38; 1 Jn 2:14), that *goes forth* (Is 2:3; 55:11) and that is *implanted in* those who believe it (Jas 1:21). We read dozens of times that the word of the Lord *came to* someone (especially prophets). As so often with biblical images and motifs, the image of the Word comes to focus on Christ, who is the eternal Word of God (Jn 1:1) that "became flesh" (Jn 1:14).

Unifying Themes in the Bible. The main subjects covered in the Bible are the nature of God and the nature of people. Dominating everything else is the character of God, a topic that underlies more passages of the Bible than any other concern. The Bible mainly answers the question of what God is like by narrating what he has done, but not to the exclusion of direct statements about God's character. The theme of God's self-revelation is so pervasive that nearly every page of the Bible will provide an answer to the question of what God is like.

Balancing this preoccupation is the nature of people. Repeated themes under that rubric include the significance of the individual, the importance of the individual's relationship to God and society, the dual nature of people (who are both physical and moral/spiritual beings), moral responsibility, and the human capacity to make moral and spiritual choices.

Usually the twin topics of God and people appear together, resulting in the motif of the divine-human relationship. The Bible explores people's inescapable connections with God and God's unrelenting interest in what people do. The most customary biblical way of portraying this relationship is the *covenant motif. Throughout the Bible it is clear that people cannot be considered apart from their relationship to God and further that this relationship has been disrupted by sin and is in need of repair.

The problem of *evil and the *suffering that it causes are likewise major themes of the Bible. The authentic note of human suffering is pervasive. Some of this suffering is simply the result of the fall of the human race and the cosmos from original innocence. Some of it is the result of self-destructive evil that individuals bring on themselves; some of it is inflicted by other people and even by groups or nations.

The acts of God are another major motif of the Bible. The acts of God fall mainly into the categories of creation and providence, redemption or salvation, and judgment. The actions of people accompany this history of God's acts. Human actions fall into a dual pattern of good and evil, virtue and vice, as the Bible presents models of virtue for the reader to emulate and examples of vice to avoid. If we combine the divine and human stories that make up the Bible, we find an overarching narrative consisting of the following sequence: *creation, *fall, *covenant (the promises of God to the patriarchs and the nation of Israel), *exodus (including the revelation at Mt. *Sinai and the conquest of Canaan), Israelite monarchy, *exile and return, the life and teaching of Jesus, *salvation, the beginnings of the Christian church and the consummation of history.

A unity of faith emerges from the foregoing content of the Bible. The Bible is an organic whole, based partly on the premise that the NT fulfills what is foreshadowed in the OT. Throughout the Bible the same God is portrayed. The view of people is constant. The big ideas of the Bible are present throughout—God, human nature, creation, providence, good and evil, salvation, eschatology.

Narrative Unity in the Bible. In addition to being unified by a system of ideas, the Bible is unified by its overarching narrative. The Bible as a whole tells a story. It is a series of events having a beginning, a middle and an end (Aristotle's definition of plot). The shape of the Bible as a whole confirms this: it begins with the creation of all things, it takes a plunge into evil (Gen 3), it meanders through fallen human history, and it winds its way slowly and painfully back to the consummation of history, with the final defeat of evil and triumph of good. This is obviously the archetypal U-shaped comic plot (*see* Comedy as Plot Motif).

A central plot conflict between good and evil organizes the story. A host of details makes up the system of conflicts: God versus Satan, God versus sinful humanity, good people versus evil people, inner human impulses toward good and evil within the same person. Almost every story, poem and proverb in the Bible fits into this ongoing plot conflict between good and evil. Every human act or attitude shows people engaged in some movement, whether slight or momentous, toward or away from God in this story of the soul's choice.

Related to the plot conflict is the necessity of

choice on the part of people. Every area of life is claimed by God and counterclaimed by forces of evil. There is no neutral ground. Every human event shows an allegiance to God or rebellion against him. People are always at the crossroads in this momentous story. The Bible is a series of great moral and spiritual dilemmas and choices made by people who are morally responsible. The crucial action, moreover, consists of an individual's or nation's *response* to external situations. Outside circumstances do not coerce people to choose as they do; these circumstances only provide the *occasion* for human choice.

In the master story that unifies the Bible as a whole, *God is the chief actor, the protagonist. Not even the most seemingly insignificant human actions can be understood apart from the characterization of God. God's unfolding purposes in history are the "meta-narrative" of the Bible, which is often called "salvation history." This history focuses on God's great plan to save people from their sin and its eternal consequences. Human history in the Bible unfolds within the providential framework of God's acts of redemption and judgment, as God deals with evil in the universe.

Summary. For all its diversity the Bible is a unified book. The terms by which we call it, as well as the Bible's comments on itself, call attention to the Bible as a single book and as a sacred book that makes a claim on our beliefs and lives in a way that no other book does. A unified system of beliefs lends further unity to this book, as does the overriding story that it tells.

BINARY PATTERNS. *See* RHETORICAL PATTERNS.

BIND, BOUND
With well over a hundred occurrences the imagery of binding pervades the Bible. Many of the images of literal, physical binding keep us rooted in the real world of Bible times. Sheaves of *grain are bound (Gen 37:7; Ps 129:7), *donkeys are bound to stationary points like a *vine (Gen 49:11), a waistcloth is bound (Job 12:18), and carpets are bound with cords (Ezek 27:24). Here we are simply in touch with the physical realities of the ancient world.

The imagery of binding can also have a *legal or contractual force of obligation. Thus a servant is "bound or hired" (Ex 12:45; Lev 22:10 NRSV), laborers are bound (Lev 25:6, 40), a person who makes a *vow is bound to keep it (Num 30:4-13), a person who gives a pledge to a neighbor is bound to another (Prov 6:1), and spouses are bound to each other (1 Cor 7:27, 39). The essential idea is that of being joined to a person by contractual means. By metaphoric extension, binding becomes an image for other types of joining, as when love binds other virtues together in perfect harmony (Col 3:14) or Jerusalem is declared to be "a city that is bound firmly together" (Ps 122:3) or folly is said to be "bound up in the heart of a child" (Prov 22:15 RSV).

The most graphic cluster of images concerns the physical subduing of someone by force, usually (though not always) in military contexts. *Abraham bound Isaac before placing him on the *altar (Gen 22:9). Not surprisingly the vocabulary of binding appears a dozen times in the story of *Samson. Kings carried into *exile are bound (2 Chron 25:7; 33:11; 36:6; Nahum 3:10). The three friends of *Daniel are bound before being thrown into the furnace (Dan 3:23). The imagery of binding permeates the story of the *passion of Christ, as well as the missionary career of Paul.

A further cluster focuses on the binding of wounds, where a majority of the references describe what God does metaphorically in his compassion for the human race (Ps 147:3; Is 30:26; 61:1; Ezek 34:4, 16).

The most mysterious and overtly theological references are Jesus' use of the imagery of binding to show the efficacy of earthly decisions in spiritual matters in the heavenly realm. In giving the metaphoric "*keys of the kingdom" to Peter, Jesus claimed that "whatever you bind on earth shall be bound in heaven" (Mt 16:19 RSV). Jesus used the same formula in his discourse outlining the process to be followed in disputes among believers (Mt 18:18).

Binding also appears in eschatological contexts. In one of Jesus' parables, the *wedding guest without a suitable garment is bound hand and foot and thrown into outer darkness (Mt 22:13). At the advent of the millennium the dragon (*Satan) is bound in chains and cast into a pit (Rev 20:1-3).

See also LOOSE, LOOSING.

BIRDS
A cursory comparison of almost any mention of specific birds in English translations of the Scriptures, especially of the OT, will convince the reader that identifying individual species with Hebrew names is not an exact science (see Holmgren's tabulation of various English equivalents for Hebrew bird names). This problem stems from several causes: (1) Hebrew bird names are often onomatopoetic (see Driver), frustrating classification. Who could identify accurately which bird is labeled "chirper" or "twitterer" by such a generic description? (2) Names often describe some habit of the animal. Unfortunately some rather different animals may exhibit similar habits. For example, the *tinšemet* (which may mean "hisser") is both an unclean bird (Lev 11:18) and a lizard (Lev 11:30). (3) Some names occur seldom and/or in lists with few contextual clues as guides (Lev 11; Deut 14). (4) At times names that appear in corrupted portions of the text and the versions (LXX, Vulgate, etc.) provide nebulous or conflicting testimony, suggesting confusion even in antiquity.

Taxonomy and Myth. Fortunately taxonomy is not the goal, nor is it essential to the imagery evoked by the mention of birds. The context often provides hints regarding (or even direct mention of) the mythology associated with a bird, although its specific identity may remain open to debate. These clues usually narrow the type of bird sufficiently for translation and interpretation even without a secure identification of the species.

The author's reference to the habits or mythology surrounding a creature is a shortcut, a parabolic and oversimplified but useful means of conjuring in the hearers' minds the qualities associated with a particular animal. The scientific accuracy of the caricature is in no way germane. For example, the cruelty of the ostrich (Lam 4:3) or its greedy witlessness (Job 39:13-18), perhaps motivated by misunderstood habits, derive their meaning from the Hebrew cultural mythology of the ostrich and so serve the author's illustrative purpose regardless of the actual natural history of the bird. The Hebrew name for the ostrich, literally "violent one," reflected and perpetuated negative opinions about the bird. In short, ancient views of animals and birds differ fundamentally from our own. It is unquestionably their view that must inform the text and interpret its imagery.

By and large the similes constructed around birds refer to their characteristic habits. The habits of birds group them into types, which naturally serve as metaphors.

Unclean Birds. Myth, folklore and superstition dominated peoples' thinking about animals in a world lit only by fire. Nocturnal creatures were spirits on errands of evil in a dark realm where human perception failed. Animals or birds that cried out at night were in collusion with sinister forces. Night or day, creatures that hissed or spit proved that they contained evil spirits or were poisonous and were to be avoided. Birds that frequented ruins (which marked places obviously cursed) betrayed their association with dark supernatural forces (Is 13:20-23; 34:11-14; Zeph 2:13-15; Rev 18:2).

Objectionable habits also contribute. Eating corpses not only made buzzards, vultures and such birds unclean but also linked them symbolically (and perhaps even in belief) with the realm of the dead, identifying them as agents of the supernatural. To make one's *grave in a vulture's gut indicated abandonment by one's fellows and one's deity (2 Sam 21:10; Jer 7:33). With this in mind, Goliath incorporated in his taunt the threat to give David's flesh to the birds of the air (1 Sam 17:44). As the expected aftermath of war, vultures pick over the stripped corpses of the fallen (Job 39:30; Mt 24:28; Lk 17:37; Rev 19:17, 21). The plainly ruthless ways of the *eagle resemble those of invading *armies (Jer 49:22). The "eagle that hastens to eat" symbolizes swift carnage of war (Deut 28:49; Jer 4:12; Hab 1:8). Just as armies, *famines, *plagues and beasts were agents of divine punishment, so too were birds of prey (Jer 12:9). They even served as ominous signs of impending *judgment (Hos 8:1). Proverbs links an ignominious death with sins in life by vivid description of bird behavior: "The eye that mocks a father and scorns to obey a mother will be picked out by the ravens of the valley and eaten by the vultures" (Prov 30:17 RSV).

Birds as Food. Birds represented food, easily kept alive and fresh. Both Solomon and Nehemiah list birds among the provisions of their tables (1 Kings 4:23; Neh 5:18). That the lists in Leviticus 11 and Deuteronomy 14 contain forbidden birds implies the existence of many more edible birds. The enumeration of young birds among *sacrifices testifies to their edibility, for what is acceptable to God is licit for his people (Gen 15:9; 9 times in Leviticus). If birds were a poor person's sacrifice (Lev 12:8; Lk 2:24), they were also a poor person's meat, selling at "two sparrows for a farthing" (Mt 10:29-31) or "five for two farthings" (Lk 12:6-7). The depletion of bird populations from egg and nest robbing required limitations as part of the mandated stewardship of creation (Deut 22:6).

Birds as Quarry. Everyday encounters with birds, torn from their natural place and used for trade and food, familiarized the image of birds as victims. David laments that Saul pursues him "like one who hunts partridge in the mountains," deliberately comparing himself to a common quarry, but especially to the kind of bird that prefers to escape by running rather than by flying (1 Sam 26:20). The ancients seem to have invested much time, energy and ingenuity in capturing birds (see Hunting). The great medley of Hebrew words for net, snare, gin, *trap, toils, terrors and so forth exhausts the range of English synonyms (Job 18:8-9) and points to an elaborate industry with a wide variety of methods. Some methods of capture employed stealth, for "in vain is the net spread in the sight of any bird" (Prov 1:17). Others used hostage birds to lure their own kind (Sirach 11:30).

The sinister overtones of the "snare of the fowler" resonate even in the modern imagination (Ps 91:4). Some birds must have been easily duped, hence the simple person rushes headlong as a bird into a snare (Prov 7:23). Even so, the devices sometimes failed, allowing the psalmist to say, "Our soul has escaped like a bird out of the snare" (Ps 124:7 NASB). In stark contrast to human frustrations at controlling birds, when Daniel suggests that God has given the birds of the air into Nebuchadnezzar's hand, he engages in hyperbole or hints that the king has usurped divine prerogatives (Dan 2:38).

Birds as Symbols of Escape and Safety. Familiarity with the ability of birds to escape shows itself in the many references to their flight as well as in religious symbolism. The impurity of a "leprous" house is cleansed by the death of one bird and carried away (symbolically or magically) by a second bird released alive (Lev 14:52-53, cf. Lev 16:22). The psalmist asserts that God is inescapable even "if I take the wings of the morning" (Ps 139:9). He wishes that he had "wings like a dove, for then I would fly away and be at rest." (Ps 55:6). The poet also wonders if his soul should "flee like a bird" (Ps 11:1). The metaphor of soul or spirit as a bird, common in ancient literature and art, finds its culmination in the

*Holy Spirit descending as a *dove (Mt 3:16; Mk 1:10; Lk 3:22; Jn 1:32).

The enviable flying ability of birds and the constancy of their day-to-day foraging, "neither sowing nor reaping," have long suggested an idyllic, worry-free existence (Lk 12:24). With minds unencumbered by the modern mechanistic view of nature, the biblical authors repeatedly invoke the trust of birds in the daily bread supplied by Providence as an example of piety (Ps 147:9; Job 38:41). God, who regularly provides birds with *food, can, in an ironic twist, use birds to provision humans (1 Kings 17:4).

The obvious parallels between bird nests and human houses resulted in still more analogies to God's provision. Sparrows and swallows, with exemplary wisdom, built their nests in the Lord's house and sought the protection of his altar (Ps 84:3). Other birds, such as the stork, find safety high in the fir trees (Ps 104:17). God's reward for this trust and simple faith appears in the fact that all birds have nests, but not all humans have homes (Lk 9:58). Conspicuous, yet inaccessible, nests stand as symbols of heaven-ordained security (Song 2:14; Jer 48:28). Nations trust in their mountain strongholds just as nesting eagles do, but their aerie is not inaccessible to the Lord (Jer 49:16; Obad 1:4).

Wings as Shelter. While *wings suggest swiftness (2 Sam 1:23) or soaring strength (Is 40:31; Obad 1:4), they also recall the protective parenting habits of birds (Ex 19:4; Deut 32:11). Jesus mixes the image of tender care under sheltering wings with the implied rebuke at those "dumb clucks" who would shun safety, repeating the prophetic theme of people as the least obedient of God's creatures (Mt 23:37; cf. Jer 8:7). The wings of God offer divine protection (Ps 17:8; 36:7; 57:1; 61:4; 63:7; 91:4; Ruth 2:12), even healing (Mal 4:2). In contrast to the comfort provided by God's wings, malevolent spirits (Heb *rûaḥ,* rendered "wind" in many translations) were often pictured with wings and could use them to oppress those seduced into idol worship (Hos 4:19).

Rhythms of Bird Life as Faithfulness and Trust. Birds served as an obvious indicator of the seasonal cycles, rhythms to which the ancients tuned their lives. The geography of the Middle East funnels all migratory birds from Europe and Asia, raptors and song birds alike, through Palestine on their way to winter in Africa. This twice yearly event, impressive even now, was undoubtedly more so in antiquity. Any witness to such a spectacle saw the hand of Providence orchestrating the relocation of a vast portion of creation to "dwell in the uttermost parts of the sea" (Ps 139:9). In response to the wonder of migration, William Cullen Bryant penned the words "There is a Power whose care teaches thy way along that pathless coast" ("To a Waterfowl"). The Lord asks Job, "Does the hawk fly by thy wisdom?" (Job 39:26). For Jeremiah the obedience of nature served as a reprimand to recalcitrant humanity. "Even the stork in the heavens knows her times; and the turtle-dove, swallow, and crane keep the time of their coming; but my people know not the ordinance of the LORD" (Jer 8:7 RSV).

In addition to seasonal activity, the daily habits of birds governed those of people. Jesus' allusion to the "cock's crow" may refer to a watch of the night so named (esp. Mk 13:35, but also Mt 26:34; Mk 14:30; Lk 22:34; Jn 13:38; Pliny, *Nat. Hist.,* IX.46). The preacher observes that the elderly wake early, accompanied by the predawn twittering of birds: "And the doors shall be shut in the streets, when the sound of the grinding is low, and he shall rise up at the voice of the bird" (Eccles 12:4 KJV).

Birds as Moral Examples for Humans. The universal tendency toward anthropomorphic interpretations of bird behavior generates many images. The *dove earns its amorous reputation from its soft voice and its habit of continually renewing its pair bond. No wonder it is mentioned six times in Song of Songs (1:15; 2:14; 4:1; 5:2, 12; 6:9). The sparrow, known for its gregarious habits, is unnatural and out of place when alone, a symbol of isolation and loneliness (Ps 102:7). Other solitary birds, like the pelican *(qe'āt)* and the owl, also evoke barren, desolate and forsaken pictures. The cries of several birds (probably owls *[bᵉnôt yaʿᵃnâ],* Mic 1:8; swift *[šûs],* crane *['āgûr]* or dove *[yônâ],* Is 38:14) strike the human ear as mournful. The Hebrew word for dove, the same as the name of the prophet Jonah, may mean "mourner" as an integral part of his story.

Some bird behaviors lend themselves directly to moral lessons. The ceaseless unresting flight of the swallow is likened to a *curse that cannot alight on its undeserving target (Pr 26:2). Ephraim is likened to a dove, "easily deceived and senseless" (Hos 7:11 NIV). The supposed exemplary family life of the stork earned it the designation "pious" (Heb *ḥᵃsîdâh,* Jer 8:7; cf. the Latin *pietaticultrix).* (In Aesop's fable *The Stork and the Farmer,* the stork argues he should be set free because he cares for his parents in their old age. Cf. Pliny, *Nat. Hist.,* X.63.)

Still other behaviors were deemed so strange as to be unnatural, and yet the proper simile restores the right perspective. The seeming indifference of the ostrich to its young, although ordained by God and compensated with speed (Job 39:13-18) is not an acceptable model for human parenting (Lam 4:3). One who unlawfully collects possessions and wealth is like the partridge who raises chicks she did not hatch; in the end they will be gone (Jer 17:11). (The opinion that partridges raise the chicks of others probably stems from the occasional practice of some pairs which lay a second clutch before the first has hatched and combine them after hatching. The older chicks which became independent sooner were not believed to be the pair's own.)

Birds as Beautiful. The beauty of birds has been a universal source of their attraction. Solomon undoubtedly collected peacocks for their exotic beauty (1 Kings 10:22; 2 Chron 9:21). The psalmist evokes the delicate, shimmering beauty of a bird's wing in

Psalm 68:13, and a woman admires her lover's raven-black hair in Song of Songs 5:11.

See also ANIMALS; DOVE; EAGLE; HUNTING; WING.

BIBLIOGRAPHY. G. S. Cansdale, *All the Animals of the Bible Land* (Grand Rapids: Zondervan, 1970); G. R. Driver, "Birds in the Old Testament," *Palestine Exploration Quarterly* (1955) 5-20; 129-140; P. Farb, *The Land, Wildlife and Peoples of the Bible* (New York: Harper & Row, 1976); V. C. Holmgren, *Bird Walk Through the Bible* (New York: Seabury, 1972); A. Parmelee, *All the Birds of the Bible* (London: Lutterworth, 1960).

BIRTH

A number of images are woven around the natural and supernatural events of birth in the Bible. In narrative, birth stories often emphasize the fact that the great saviors of Israel are gifts from God. The births of Isaac, *Jacob, *Moses, *Samson, and Samuel involve either the opening of a closed womb or the overcoming of a threat, showing that these individuals, who continue the promised line or provide *rescue for the people of God, are not the result of human efforts, but of divine initiative. Of course Jesus' birth from a *virgin *womb is the ultimate supernatural gift, showing that this Savior of saviors is from God, not the result of natural procreation.

Birth imagery is also employed in both the Old and New Testaments to interpret the relationship between God and his people. Moses, in his song to the assembly of Israel, declares that the nation has behaved unnaturally: "You deserted the Rock, who fathered you; you forgot the God who gave you birth"(Deut 32:18 NIV). The psalmist celebrates that "glorious things are said of you, O city of God: I will record Rahab and Babylon among those who acknowledge me—Philistia too, and Tyre, along with Cush—and will say, 'This one was born in Zion' " (Ps 87:3). In other words those who acknowledge God are considered to have been born in *Zion, the city of God.

Salvation. In the NT birth is used more explicitly as a *salvation image. For example, John wrote in the prologue to his Gospel, "Yet to all who received him [Jesus], to those who believed in his name, he gave the right to become children of God—children born not of natural descent, nor of human decision or a husband's will, but born of God" (Jn1:12-13). Jesus explained to Nicodemus, "Flesh gives birth to flesh, but the Spirit gives birth to spirit. You should not be surprised at my saying, 'You must be born again' [or 'born from above']" (Jn 3:6-7). Jesus continued with the analogy that "the wind blows where ever it pleases. You hear its sound, but you cannot tell where it comes from or where it is going. So, it is with everyone born of the Spirit" (Jn 3:8). Spiritual birth, like the *wind, cannot be controlled by human action; but the effects of radical inner renewal can be clearly seen in an individual. James extends the new birth imagery by picturing those who have been born again as "a kind of firstfruits of all he created" (Jas 1:18). Believers are the firstfruits, and in the future the regeneration or renewal will extend to all things (Mt 19:28).

The antithesis of being born of God is portrayed very graphically. Isaiah remonstrates with those who "conceive trouble and give birth to evil. They hatch the eggs of vipers" (Is 59:4-5). The psalmist grieves that "he who is pregnant with evil and conceives trouble gives birth to disillusionment" (Ps 7:14). "Sin," wrote James, "gives birth to death" (Jas 1:15).

Suffering and Deliverance. In sentencing *Adam and *Eve after their act of rebellion, God said to the woman, "I will greatly increase your pains in childbearing; with pain you will give birth to children" (Gen 3:16). From this time on, pain in childbirth is inevitable and inescapable. The powerful image of the anguished woman giving birth recurs in the prophecies of Isaiah and Jeremiah (Is 21:2-3; 26:16-21; 66:7-14; Jer 13:21; 22:23; 30:6; 49:24; 50:43). Both prophets liken the pangs of the nations, confronted with God's judgment, to the *terror and *pain that grips a woman in childbirth. Isaiah's prophecy against *Babylon predicts, "Terror will seize them, pain and anguish will grip them; they will writhe like a woman in labor" (Is 13:8). Jeremiah, announcing the disaster that is to fall on Israel records, "I hear a cry as of a woman in labor, a groan as of one bearing her first child—the cry of the Daughter of Zion gasping for breath, stretching out her hands and saying, 'Alas! I am fainting; my life is given over to murderers' " (Jer 4:31).

Sometimes the image of the *woman suffering intensely in childbirth is juxtaposed with the promise of deliverance. Isaiah combines the figure of the woman Israel, in great distress before the Lord, with the promise of *resurrection and Israel's deliverance: "But your dead will live; their bodies will rise . . . the earth will give birth to her dead" (Is 26:16-19). God's impatience to deliver his people is likened to the impatience of a woman to be delivered of a child (Is 42:14).

The image of travail is also applied to the whole creation, which "has been groaning as in the pains of childbirth" as it waits to be "liberated from its bondage to decay" (Rom 8:21-22). The sudden, unexpected and unavoidable onset of labor is a vivid eschatological image: "Destruction will come on them suddenly, as labor pains on a pregnant woman, and they will not escape" (1 Thess 5:2-3). Prior to his *ascension, as he is about to leave the disciples, Jesus uses the image of the woman giving birth to teach them about his final return. He illustrates the way anguish and suffering may be dramatically forgotten and turned to joy: "A woman giving birth to a child has pain because her time has come; but when her baby is born she forgets the anguish because of her joy that a child is born into the world. So with you. Now is your time of grief, but I will see you again and you will rejoice, and no one will take away your joy" (Jn 16:21-22).

See also BABY; BARRENNESS; BIRTH STORY; BIRTH-

RIGHT; CHILD, CHILDREN; WOMAN, IMAGES OF; WOMB.

BIRTH STORY

*Birth is the earliest miracle of human life. At the creation, *Adam and *Eve were commanded to be *fruitful and multiply (Gen 1:28). Throughout the OT the birth of *babies is an important element in the story of God's work in history. Such passages as the lists of "begats" in Genesis and Chronicles and the promise to Abraham of the blessing on his *"seed" point to the importance of human fertility. In early history, before the physical facts of birth such as fertilization and gestation were fully understood, birth was seen as a miracle, a blessing from God. This spirit is heightened in the birth stories of the Bible.

Given the importance of birth in the Bible, it is not surprising that the birth story is an identifiable narrative genre in the Bible. In general, birth stories are reserved for extraordinary rather than routine births, which are briefly chronicled instead of receiving a full-fledged birth story. The more extended biblical birth narratives tend loosely to follow a general pattern:

1. A *barren wife or couple desire a child.

2. An angel appears to announce the promise of a son.

3. The birth occurs, accompanied by miracles or extraordinary events.

4. Hostile forces threaten the newborn baby.

5. God protects the child so that he or she may grow to maturity.

6. The grown person becomes a hero, saint or savior.

Of course not every ingredient is present in every birth story.

The first full-fledged birth story in the Bible is that of *Abraham's child of promise, Isaac (Gen 12—21:7). Its most salient features are the repeated promise of God that he would give Abraham and Sarah a son after their childbearing years were over and the status of Isaac as part of the fulfillment of a *covenant promise. The birth of *Moses, future deliverer of a nation, appropriately focuses on the *rescue of the infant from what appears to be certain death (Ex 2:1-10; see Ark). *Samson's birth (Judg 13) occurs to a barren mother, is accompanied by a double annunciation from an angel and produces a Nazirite from birth. Samuel is born to a barren mother in answer to her prayer (2 Sam 1—2), and the special features of his birth include his dedication to God's service from childhood and the song of Hannah praising God for his blessing to an outcast. The genre of the birth story continues in the NT with the birth of John the Baptist (Lk 1), whose birth is foretold to the husband of a barren wife and is accompanied by the song of his father, Zechariah.

Underlying these birth stories of the Bible is an incremental principle, with the whole series moving toward its ultimate example in the birth of *Jesus. The nativity of the Messiah is the most elaborate birth story in the Bible (Mt 1—2 and Lk 1—2). Highlights include the annunciation, the song of *Mary (known as the Magnificat and closely resembling the song of Hannah), conception by the *Holy Spirit, a *virgin birth and the nativity itself, which is accompanied by such miracles as the angelic chorus, the songs of Anna and Simeon, providential guidance of the adoring wisemen, and the warning vision resulting in the flight into Egypt. A visionary account of this birth story can be found in Revelation 12:1-6, where a woman in travail (Israel) gives birth to a son who is to rule all nations (Christ), who thwarts the dragon's (*Satan's) attempt to destroy him by ascending into heaven as mother and child are miraculously protected by God.

We can also find a metaphoric birth story in the Bible. In the OT, Israel as a spiritual entity is portrayed as the child of a woman in travail (Is 26:17-18; 66:5-14). God had from the beginning predicted that he would father such a child, starting as early as God's promise to Eve in the *Garden (Gen 3:16) and continuing in the patriarchal promises to establish a "seed" that would become a nation. Israel's coming into being was accompanied by miracles at every turn, most notably during the *exodus from Egypt.

The biblical use of birth narratives moves from the physical need for continuity to the spiritual need for renewal. The OT, with its host of genealogies, emphasizes the physical lineage, combined with the sense of Israel's being a covenant people. The NT focuses on the new covenant, an expansion of the concepts of *family and birth. The family is transformed into a spiritual community of those who follow Christ. Birth is now the new birth of the true believer, as in Jesus' comment about being "born anew" by the Spirit (Jn 3:6-7). When a woman cried out to Christ, "Blessed is the womb that bore you," Jesus responded, "Blessed rather are those who hear the word of God and keep it" (Lk 11:27-28 RSV), implying that the greatest of all birth images is the image of being born again as a child of God.

See also BARRENNESS; BIRTH; BIRTHRIGHT; MARY THE MOTHER OF JESUS; VIRGIN; WOMAN, IMAGES OF; WOMB.

BIBLIOGRAPHY. R. E. Brown, *The Birth of the Messiah* (Updated Ed.; New York: Doubleday, 1993).

BIRTHRIGHT

The concept of birthright is expressed in the OT by the noun $b^e\underline{k}\hat{o}r/b^e\underline{k}\hat{o}r\hat{a}$. It is inseparably linked to the notion of "firstborn" through their common Hebrew root $b\underline{k}r$. Of the 158 occurrences of this root, only four are in a verbal form, which indicates that the nominal form is foundational for other nuances. The concept of birthright alludes to the privileges and expectations of primogeniture. The noun always occurs in the singular with the special meaning of the legal claims of the eldest *son to a double portion of the inheritance and the right to bear the family's *name and other privileges.

Literal Usages. *Jacob's appropriation of Esau's birthright is the most important illustrative use of the term (Gen 25:29-34). Jacob is thereby entitled to *covenantal blessings and mediation of *Abraham's lineage under God. The blessings in context are prosperity and dominion (Gen 27:27-8, cf. 39-40 for Esau's corresponding curse). Covenantal mediation entitles the firstborn to a double share of the family's inheritance (Deut 21:15-17). Although the concept and attendant customs were common in the ancient Near East, the rank and favor of primogeniture in the OT is seen as more than customary and is regarded as being graciously bestowed by God. Thus in spite of Rebecca and Jacob's respective deceptions and Esau's godlessness (Gen 25:34), the elder son is to serve his younger brother (Gen 25:23, cf. 44:12-20) according to the sovereign will of the Lord (cf. Mal 1:2-3 with Rom 9:3).

The choicest of *sacrifices, firstborn and firstfruits (see First), are to be dedicated to God (cf. Gen 4:4 and legal contexts such as Lev 27:26). Within a long line of sons, birthright privileges are further divided according to age and moral qualifications. Because of his incest, Reuben as eldest son is deprived of his usual rights (Gen 49:3-4). The blessings of birthright are given to his nephews, the sons of Joseph (1 Chron 5:1) as firstborn of Jacob's beloved Rachel.

Although the figure of the firstborn and his birthright is used commonly in the OT (e.g., 2 Chron 21:3; Jer 31:9, in the NT *prōtotokeia* ("birthright") appears only once in an allusion to the "godlessness" of Esau (Heb 12:16). Esau's faithlessness valued temporary relief over lasting blessings (Heb 12:17); therefore, readers should not compromise their faith to get relief from persecution, lest they forfeit blessings as joint heirs with Christ (Heb 12:1-3).

Figurative Meanings. An important use of the word firstborn in a figurative sense is Exodus 4:21-23, where the Lord calls Moses to deliver *Israel, "my firstborn son," with a warning of *plague on Pharaoh's firstborn son (cf. Jer 31:9 for the Lord's commitment to his collective firstborn, Ephraim). The parallel of firstborns leaves no doubt about its meaning; the "house of Jacob" is Yahweh's honored heir who has been called to be a kingdom of priests and a holy nation, establishing worship and dominion in the chosen land (Ex 19:3-6; Deut 4:5-8; cf. 1 Pet 2:10 for similar language regarding the church).

Israel's birthright as a young nation is contingent on the favor of the sovereign Creator, the Most High, rather than on any power of conquest, as proven by the *Passover and passage through the *sea. By the same token, the Lord's curse on Egypt's firstborn is celebrated as a consummate vindication of his firstborn people (e.g., Ps 78:51; 105:36).

The figure of nation as firstborn emerges when Israel becomes its representative son under the Father, the *Davidic king, who is promised perpetual divine favor and dominion (2 Sam 7:14-17). The Davidic son, in turn, previews the ideal *king in messianic prophecy who will establish the Father's rightful dominion over the earth and its kings (Ex 19:5; Ps 2; 89:20-29; 110; etc.). There is also a shift in emphasis from primogeniture to adoption of the "anointed one" (Ps 2:2; 89:20, 27), so that God's rightful claim to the earth is expressed as the inheritance of David's sons (Mt 1:l, 20; Lk l:32-33). The supreme dominion, as noted above, is traced to his position as the anointed of the Most High Father to the exclusion of all other kings.

In the LXX and the NT *prōtótokos* ("first-born") is used rather than the classical *prōtotókos* ("bearing for the first time"). Thus preeminence and privilege are emphasized rather than birth. The singular *prōtótokos* in the NT always refers to Christ, whether literal (Mt 1:25; Lk. 2:7, Heb 1:6) or figurative.

NT authors develop the term's imagery with reference to Christ's rule and salvific deliverance or eschatological inheritance. Christ is the "firstborn over all creation" (Col 1:15 NIV), which in context means ultimate supremacy or preeminence in everything. Inheritance is also in view in the phrase "first-born from the dead" (Col 1:18; Rev 1:5), for in an imperial metaphor, the *Lamb alone is worthy to break the *seals of the *scroll of creation. That is, he alone can rightfully claim the estate of creation as his *inheritance (Col l :20; Rev 5:6-7; 6: 1). The breaking of the seals marks the structural progression of the Revelation from the fallen world to the new creation. In receiving creation, Christ as Lamb will also receive "his brethren" as coheirs of glorious dominion (Col 1:18; Rom 8:29-30; Heb 12:23). Nevertheless, as firstborn his "birthright" is absolute supremacy in rank.

See also BIRTH; BIRTH STORY; FIRST; SON.

BITTER. *See* GALL.

BLACK

The number of actual references to black are far less than one might expect (16 times in the NIV). Generally black is used as a descriptive *color with some overtones of foreboding. However *darkness, which is the absence of light, is far more associated with judgment and punishment.

The metaphoric contrast of *white and black, so common in Western culture, is not prevalent in the Bible. It is only found in Matthew 5:36 where our inability to order the details of our lives is pictured by not being able to change our hair color ("you cannot make even one hair white or black"). Likewise the modern association of black = sin is not part of biblical imagery. Most frequently black simply describes an object's color.

As a color, black describes *birds (e.g., "the red kite, any kind of black kite" [Lev 11:14 NIV]), hair color in examinations of leprosy ("it does not seem to be more than skin deep and there is no black hair in it" [Lev 13:31]) and the hair of the lover in Song of Songs ("wavy and black as a raven" [Song 5:11]). In two passages people suffering various diseases and deprivation are described as having their skin turn black. Job declared: "My skin grows black and peels" (Job 30:30). Similarly, Jeremiah describes those who remain after the destruction of *Jerusalem as being "blacker than soot" (Lam 4:8). Here the connotation is the dramatic change that illness and famine brought more than a symbol of *judgment.

Black is used to describe the *horses pulling the northbound chariots the prophet Zechariah sees in his vision (Zech 6:2, 6). The specific colors of the horses seem to have no obvious symbolism, but are used to distinguish each of the four from the others. A black horse also appears in Revelation when the third seal of judgment is opened (Rev 6:5). In both scenes the horses are going out from the presence of the Lord into the world, symbolizing the intervention of God's judgment in the events of history.

The horses and chariots seen in the visions of Zechariah and Revelation are implements of ancient *warfare. Coming from the presence of God, they are images that form part of the biblical theme of God as the *divine warrior who righteously fights and ultimately destroys sin and evil. The dominant hue of this warfare imagery throughout the Bible is blackness or darkness. In these scenes God is portrayed as a threatening presence who descends in darkness to destroy his enemies, and his judgment is symbolized by blackness.

The Bible describes God both as living in unapproachable light (1 Tim 6:16) and as dwelling in thick darkness (Ps 97:2; cf. Ps 104:2). While the people of ancient Israel remained at a distance, Moses approached the thick darkness of Mount *Sinai where God was (Ex 20:21).

Throughout the OT the coming of God in judgment is painted in shades of black. In anger God parts the heavens and comes down with dark *clouds under his feet; he makes darkness his covering when he shoots his *arrows and rebukes his *enemies (Ps 18:9,11). The prophets described a coming judgment on sin as "a day of darkness and gloom, a day of clouds and blackness" (Zeph 1:15; Joel 2:2).

Blackness or darkness appears less frequently in the NT. Jude describes false teachers, who license immorality and deny Jesus Christ, as "wandering stars, for whom blackest darkness has been reserved forever" (Jude 13).

The contrast of *light and darkness is a major motif of John's Gospel, where Jesus is portrayed as the light of the world who disperses the darkness of divine judgment. All three Synoptic Gospels poignantly report that as Jesus died on the cross, darkness fell over the whole land (Mt 27:45; Mk 15:33; Lk 23:44). At the crucifixion God descended in judgment, the divine warrior fighting the final and ultimate battle that destroyed sin and evil.

See also COLORS; DARKNESS; LIGHT.

BLEMISH. *See* SPOT.

BLESSING, BLESSEDNESS

The Bible abounds in pictures of blessing—blessing sought, blessing promised, blessing conferred, blessing received. Blessing presupposes a benefactor and

a recipient, and not infrequently there is a mediator who pronounces or confers the prospect of blessing from God to a human recipient. In the Bible, blessing is ultimately from God, though people often pronounce a wish for blessing on fellow humans. The quest to attain a state of blessedness is a universal human longing, and the Bible differentiates the way that will lead to blessedness from things that lead away from it. In the Bible the things that make for blessedness range from the physical to the spiritual, from the earthly to the heavenly.

The first sphere of blessing that we read about in the Bible is the creation. When God created the earth's *animals, "he blessed them" and commanded them to multiply (Gen 1:22 RSV). After the *flood, God's blessing on Noah and his sons included their dominion over the creation and its provision for human life (Gen 9:1-7). Thereafter in the biblical account, nature is a continuous arena of God's blessing; his blessing rests *on* creation and he blesses various aspects of creation *through* or *by means of* the creation.

God's blessing is continuously seen both on creation and through creation to the human race (Ps 104). Natural *abundance is thus one of the leading images of divine blessing in the Bible. It is a universal blessing, not limited to believers in God; as Jesus noted, God "makes his sun rise on the evil and on the good, and sends rain on the just and on the unjust" (Mt 5:45 RSV).

A second picture of blessing is the blessing of OT fathers on their sons as they approached their time of death. The best known examples occur in *Genesis, especially Isaac's blessing on Jacob and Esau (Gen 27) and Jacob's blessing on his sons (Gen 48—49). Such blessings were more than good wishes; in some sense they were efficacious in bringing about what the patriarch conferred. As an extension of family blessings, Moses blessed his nation on the eve of his death (Deut 33).

A third image of blessing is the blessing tied to the *covenant. Such blessing is already introduced when God calls Abraham: "I will bless those who bless you, and . . . by you all the families of the earth shall bless themselves" (Gen 12:3 RSV). Thereafter the very idea of the covenant is connected to blessing. Five motifs permeate these references. One is promise, as God promises to bless those who keep his covenant. A second is the conditional nature of the blessing, or blessing as part of a test of the obedience of people. Whether the context is an inauguration of a future era (as when Moses prepares the Israelites for settlement in Canaan in Deut 28—30 or when Samuel institutes Saul as king in 1 Sam 12) or a prophetic *oracle of *judgment for a nation's failure to obey God's covenant obligations, the premise is that the covenant blessing is conditional. Third, therefore, blessing is conceived as being in some sense a *reward for obedience. Balancing this, fourth, is the theme of grace: although God rewards obedience, it his grace that leads him to do so.

Human merit is never assumed: as Moses delineates the special status of Israel, he makes it clear that God's blessing is solely a result of his love (Deut 7:6-16). Finally, the opposite of blessing resulting from obedience to God is always assumed to be a curse resulting from disobedience. Blessing and curse are opposite sides of a coin in the divine economy (see esp. Deut 28).

Building upon OT motifs of blessing, blessing in the NT is the spiritual state of those who belong to Christ's *kingdom. A chosen nation is no longer the locus of God's blessing, but individual believers are. Whereas blessing in the OT always retains a heavy (though not exclusive) emphasis on physical prosperity, blessing in the NT era finds very little place for material prosperity. Blessing is overwhelmingly conceived as a spiritual inheritance reserved in heaven for the believer. In fact, in the Beatitudes Jesus pronounces blessing on those who suffer deprivation in this life. Paul likewise sounds the keynote when he writes, "To the weak I became weak . . . I do it all for the sake of the gospel, that I may share in its blessings" (1 Cor 9:22-23 RSV).

See also ABUNDANCE; BEATITUDE; BENEDICTION; CURSE.

BLIND, BLINDNESS

Some of the most vivid pictures of the Bible center on blindness, including the *Sodomites' groping about Lot's house, the dim-eyed Isaac tricked by his son, *Samson's eyes gouged out, a troupe of blinded Syrian warriors being led from their intended destination to Samaria, the drama of the man born blind healed by Jesus to the consternation of the Pharisees, the blind *beggars who cried out pathetically to Jesus as he passed by and the temporary blindness of Paul at his conversion. The characters in the Bible who are physically blind are a moving spectacle of human misfortune. However, in a spiritual sense, blindness is congenital for all humans, who inherit the tendency simply by virtue of belonging to the human race. In both physical and spiritual instances, blindness is an image of *terror, helplessness and despair unless reversed by God's miraculous intervention.

The physical blindness referred to in the Bible is either congenital (Jn 9:1) or acquired. In a region of dust and bright sunlight, ophthalmic diseases were common, as attested by the frequency with which blindness is referred to in Scripture (Lev 19:14; Job 29:15; Mt 9:27; Lk 14:13). Blindness is one of the several disabilities that prevented someone born into a priestly family from exercising his ministry (Lev 21:18); and although blind people deserve special consideration according to the law (Lev 19:14), blindness could be a synonym for *weakness and helplessness (2 Sam 5:6; Is 59:10; Lam 4:14).

Blinding is a punishment for wrongdoing in neighboring nations (2 Kings 25:7), but never in Israel. On occasion, in order to promote his own purposes, God temporarily blinds individuals or groups of people, either totally or in regard to some-

thing they attempt to see (Gen 19:11; 2 Kings 6:18; Acts 9:9; 13:11). Physical blindness is regarded by some of Jesus' contemporaries as evidence of divine punishment, something Jesus strongly denies (Jn 9:1-3).

Figuratively, blindness refers to an inability to recognize the truth, usually a culpable condition. As such, it describes judges whose judgment is perverted because of bribes (Ex 23:8; Deut 16:19; Job 9:24), *idolaters whose worship is illogical as well as wrong (Is 44:9-10) and people who simply do not want to know (Is 43:8). Such blindness to the truth and mental confusion could actually be the result of God's judgment on those who did not want to admit the truth and who therefore forfeit the ability to perceive it at their cost (Deut 28:28-29; Is 6:9-10; 29:9-10). This is true of the Israelites, both leaders (Is 56:10) and followers (Is 42:18-19). Only God in his mercy can reverse this condition (Is 29:18; 35:5; 42:16). Paul describes gradual blindness when he writes of those whose "foolish hearts were darkened" (Rom 1:21). In another vein he talks of seeing poorly now in contrast to seeing perfectly in the life to come (1 Cor 13:12).

The imagery of sight and blindness is especially prominent in the account of Jesus' earthly ministry. The high incidence of physical blindness in the world of the Gospels is attested by the frequency with which Jesus performed miracles of giving sight to the blind. It is, in fact, one of the most vivid signs of Jesus' supernatural power. Spiritual blindness is no less prominent in the Gospels. Jesus described the religious leaders and teachers of his own generation in terms of blindness (Mt 15:14; 23:16-17, 19, 24, 26). The irony of their situation is that in their spiritual ignorance they assumed that they understand perfectly. Jesus remedied spiritual as well as physical blindness (Mt 13:17; Jn 9:39). Those who rejected Jesus' words came under a judgment similar to that of Israel—a state of permanent blindness (Jn 12:40; cf. Rom 11:7-10).

Although metaphorically blindness may describe mere ignorance (Rom 2:19), it usually carries the overtones of an unwillingness to face up to the truth (Jas 1:23-24); and in the case of those who do not believe in Christ, this is the work of Satan (2 Cor 4:4). As such it requires a miracle in order to become aware of the significance of Christ. Similarly, Christian believers who revert to their pre-Christian ways are described as blind, not perceiving the contradiction expressed in their behavior (2 Pet 1:9; 1 Jn 2:11). Blindness describes the fact that they are unaware of the gravity of their condition (Rev 3:17).

See also DEAF, DEAFNESS; DISEASE AND HEALING; MAIMED, HALT AND BLIND.

BLIND GUIDES. *See* PHARISEE.

BLOOD

The appearance of blood is never a good sign. While blood is natural, the sight of it is not. To the ancients its red *color, along with its mystical connection with life and *death, made it a powerful and ominous symbol of *violence and wrong, *guilt and coming punishment. Only in the framework of sacrifice could blood portend good news.

Blood as Human Life. Blood, often in the pair "flesh and blood," stands for humanity (Jn 1:13; Gal 1:16; 1 Cor 15:50). Without blood humans return to dust. The dust of a decaying corpse and the absence of blood are signs of our perishable, corruptible nature (1 Cor 15:49). The pair "blood and water" carries similar symbolism (Jn 19:34; 1 Jn 5:6). Blood is so much a sign of human mortality that the disciples (and we with them) struggle to fathom that the resurrected Christ still has flesh and *bones (Lk 24:39).

Blood as Death. Because the life is in the blood (Lev 17:11, see below), the mention of blood connotes life imperiled (2 Sam 23:17; 1 Chron 11:19), life passing out of the body. Since the blood contains the life-breath *(neeš)* of God, the spirit returns to God who gave it (Eccles 12:7) and reports to the Creator each case of bloodshed (Gen 4:10). Job pleads, "O earth, cover not my blood and let my cry find no resting place" (Job 16:18 RSV). The mere mention of blood points to the stark fact of death without drawing attention to the manner. Blood marks death by unnamed violence (Ezek 5:17; Hab 2:17), child *sacrifice (Ezek 23:37, 45), envy and jealousy (Ezek 16:38), covetous *murder (1 Kings 21:19; 2 Kings 9:26), even suicide (Mt 27:8; Acts 1:18-19). As if it were the firstfruits of death, the blood ebbs away into the ground before the body decays into dust (Is 63:6).

Blood as Guilt. Blood as guilt stems from blood as a sign of death due to violence. In many passages the mere mention of blood assigns *guilt. Biblical authors use phrases such as "the blood of Jezreel" (Hos 1:4), "city tracked with blood" (Hos 6:8 RSV), "hands full of blood" (Is 1:15). The psalmist fears "men of blood" (Ps 139:19 RSV). Furthermore, the blood of the slain not only cries out to God but pursues the murderer (Ezek 35:6). Shed blood weighed like a burden to be carried until death (Prov 28:17). *Cain objects that his punishment (or guilt) is too great to bear (Gen 4:13). The blood and the attendant guilt are pictured as resting on the hands and head (Mt 27:24-25, see Hands, Washing of). Deeds of blood awaited repayment (2 Sam 16:8).

Blood as Impurity. While blood inside the body could be ignored, outside the body it could not. Just as blood flowed from torn bodies, it likewise symbolized a rupture in the fabric of life. Blood, whether due to violence or other ills, destroyed the *cleanness of creation. Animal blood was handled according to strict ritual. It was not to be left on the ground uncovered by dust (Lev 17:13). Human blood had even more power to defile (Ps 106:38; Is 59:3; Lam 4:14). Even the predictable bleeding of *women required strict purity laws (Lev 12). Chronic conditions left sufferers virtually ostracized (Lk 8:43).

Wanting to contrast God's righteousness with human attempts at purity, Isaiah can find no image more abhorrent than comparing all our righteous deeds to menstrual rags (Is 64:6).

Blood as Omen. The vivid red color of fresh blood still strikes the viewer with almost unnatural force. Other elements whose color change unnaturally to red were said to have become blood. Just as human blood is proof of torn flesh, so the appearance of cosmic blood points to a hemorrhaging universe and causes wide spread fear. As an omen for Egypt the Nile river changed to blood (Ex 4:9; 7:17). A sunrise turns the water blood-red against Moab (2 Kings 3:22). The Apocalypse borrows the image of *water turning to blood (Rev 9:8; 16:4). Joel warns of portents—blood in the sky and the moon turned to blood (Joel 2:30-31). Peter cites these signs of the *Day of the Lord (Acts 2:19), and they figure again in John's vision (Rev 6:12).

Blood as Sacrifice and Propitiation. The shedding of human blood in the OT is treated as a capital offense: "Whoever sheds the blood of a human, by a human shall that person's blood be shed" (Gen 9:6 NRSV). The shedding of animal blood is allowed in OT law, but only through ritual slaughter. This blood is treated with great respect. It may not be consumed (Lev 17:10), and it plays an essential element in the sacrificial cult. The blood of the animal is not only shed, but it is also brought into contact with the holy that is symbolized, for example, by the *altar or the mercy seat in the Holy of Holies (see Temple).

The ritual release of blood is seen as the release of the individual's life, his *nepeš* (Ex 12:23; Heb 11:28). Leviticus summarizes the crucial idea: "For the life [*nepeš*] of the flesh is in the blood; and I [God] have given it to you for making atonement for your lives [plural of *nepeš*] on the altar; for the blood atones through the life [*nepeš*]" (Lev 17:11 NRSV). The *nepeš* of the one making the offering is identified with the *nepeš* of the sacrificial animal. The shedding of blood symbolizes the surrender of life. Furthermore, it is a surrender of life to the holy as seen, for example, in the sprinkling of blood on the mercy seat on the Day of Atonement (Lev 16:15).

This OT backdrop is the proper setting for understanding certain verses in the NT about the blood of Christ. In Romans 3:25 the blood of Christ is not the blood of a *martyr but blood of his sacrifice for sins. God publicly set forth Christ as a mercy seat. The presence of God and the place of the atonement are to be found in Golgotha, not behind the veil in the Holy of Holies. Christ's blood atones for our sins and achieves our justification (Rom 5:9; see Legal Images). The letter to the Hebrews further develops the significance of sacrificial blood. The blood of bulls and goats effects a purification of the flesh, but the blood of Jesus does much more: it purifies our consciences from dead works to worship the living God (Heb 9:13-14; 10:4; cf. 4 Macc 6:29).

At the Last Supper, Jesus equated his blood with the new covenant. Taking a cup of *wine, Jesus said:

"This is my blood of the covenant, which is poured out for many" (Mk 14:24 NRSV). This may be compared to Exodus 24:3-8, where Moses, taking the blood of *oxen, threw half of it against the altar and half over the people of Israel. In both cases, blood seals a covenant (Heb 9:18; cf. Zech 9:11 and Gen 15:9-18, where animals were killed to seal *Abraham's covenant with God).

John expresses Christ's divinity in blood imagery. Christ's blood contained life from God in a way that normal human blood did not. To experience eternal life, the believer must drink his blood (Jn 6:53-54). When his disciples struggled to understand, he explained that "the spirit gives life, the flesh is of no avail" (Jn 6:63 RSV).

As the early Christians came to grasp that atonement is reached through the blood of Christ and not through the blood of bulls and goats (Heb 10:4), some saw, probably on the basis of Leviticus 17:10-11, that the law forbidding the consumption of animal blood was no longer binding.

Blood as Wine. In the OT *wine is the "blood of grapes" treaded out (Gen 49:11). The prophet envisions God's triumphant army treading down their foes and drinking their blood like wine (Zech 9:15). Violent oppressors will be drunk with their own blood as with wine. By using this familiar imagery equating blood with wine, Christ empowers the symbolism of the old covenant to serve also the new covenant. The history of redemption comes full circle in the Eucharist. When the NT replaces the blood of sacrifice with wine, the offering of the fruit of the ground, which had been ineffective and unacceptable (Gen 4:3-4), now becomes a remembrance (Lk 22:19) that the sacrifice has been made once for all (Heb 10:10).

See also DEATH; GUILT; PURITY; SACRIFICE; WINE.

BLOOM. *See* FLOWERS.

BLOSSOM. *See* FLOWERS.

BLUE. See COLORS.

BOAST

As creator, redeemer and provider for a chosen people, God is the only appropriate source for boasting. In the OT boasting in God and God's provision symbolizes humanity's proper posture before the Almighty, whether boasting of protection (Ps 5:11), deliverance from enemies (Ps 44:4-8) or righteousness and favor (Ps 89:15-17). Such boasting consists of confession, thanksgiving and worship (Ps 34:3; 44:8), and stills all false boasting based on pride and self-righteousness (1 Sam 2:2-3).

Boasting was in important motif in martial literature (including ancient epic), and a formal boast was a standard ritual of warfare (cf. Ex 15:9; 1 Kings 20:11). We catch a hint of this convention in Psalm 18:31-42, a psalm of thanksgiving that celebrates victory on the battlefield. But here the overall tone is *parody as David attributes his strength in battle to God.

Boasting in anything other than God affronts God with arrogant self-sufficiency. Such boasting symbolizes fallen humanity's natural inclination to trust in human wisdom, might and wealth rather than understanding and knowing God (Jer 9:23-24). Scripture depicts the rich and powerful who assume they are more clever and powerful than God and who boast in their affliction of the righteous and poor (Ps 52:1; 94:1-7). Their arrogant claims will dissolve in *shame and *judgment. There is an ironic twist in the interface of boasting and judgment: the nations God employs to destroy Israel because of her boasting (Is 9:8-12) are in turn destroyed by God for their boasting of being the sole authority in the world (Is 10:12-19; Zeph 2:8-15). The Bible shows the foolishness of boasting about tomorrow when as finite beings we do not know what it will bring (Prov 27:1). Uses such as these and Paul's use of *kauchaomai* suggest an underlying meaning of failure to acknowledge God or his divine role in history.

In the NT boasting in God's work of redemption through Christ symbolizes the proper stance of redeemed humanity toward God (Rom 5:11; 1 Cor 1:31; 2 Cor 10:17). Such boasting indicates a lack of confidence in the flesh (Phil 3:3), a trust in the *cross (Gal 6:14) and participation in Christian hope (Rom 5:2; Heb 3:6). Boasting in what God has given to or is doing in the Christian is also commended. Paul can boast of his authority (2 Cor 10:8), churches he founded (Phil 2:16; 1 Thess 2:19), his *suffering (Rom 5:3), a good conscience (2 Cor 1:12), work for God (Rom 15:17) and even his *weakness in which God's strength is demonstrated (2 Cor 12:5-10).

Since justification is a gift of God through faith in Christ, no one—not even *Abraham (Rom 4:1-3)—can boast in works in the hope of justification (Rom 3:27; Eph 2:8-9). Boasting in the flesh is excluded (2 Cor 11:18), whether in the *law (Rom 2:23), *circumcision (Gal 6:13), *wisdom (1 Cor 1:26-31), comparison with others (2 Cor 10:12, 18) or outward appearance (2 Cor 5:12). No benefits of the flesh can provide the grounds for boasting, because they are ultimately gifts of God (1 Cor 4:7). Such boasting symbolizes the shameful and foolish inclinations of sinful humanity to trust in its own accomplishments (2 Cor 11:16-21).

See also HONOR; PRIDE.

BIBLIOGRAPHY. C. Forbes, "Comparison, Self-Praise and Irony: Paul's Boasting and the Conventions of Hellenistic Rhetoric," *NTS* 32 (1986) 1-30.

BOAT

The boats of the Bible are tossed about on dark and stormy *seas. In them God provides shelter from life-threatening danger. A boat is first found in Genesis 8 when God kept Noah, his family and the animals safe from the *flood that destroyed all life in a boat called an *ark. The safety Noah's ark provided is highlighted in the three references to it in the NT (Mt 24:38; Lk 17:27; 1 Pet 3:20). In Exodus 2:5 the little basket that kept baby Moses safe from drowning in the Nile is called by the same Hebrew word used for Noah's ark.

The boat is a life-saving shelter throughout Scripture. In the Gospels, Jesus keeps his disciples safe in a boat, though they fear for their lives in a storm on the Sea of Galilee (Mt 8:23-27; Mk 4:35-41; Lk 8:22-25). On his sea-voyage to Rome, Paul commands the sailors to stay aboard the ship when caught in a storm of hurricane force. Although the ship was destroyed, everyone aboard safely reached land (Acts 27:31, 44).

In the Gospels, Jesus frequently enters a boat on the Sea of Galilee in order to escape the crowds (Mk 3:9, 4:1) or be conveyed from one place to another. Sailing is labor intensive, and only once is Jesus possibly in a boat alone (Mk 4:1). Generally he is accompanied by multiple followers when he was in a boat.

Because the Bible uses the sea as an image of danger, chaos and death, the boat portrays the safety God provides for his people from life's most threatening evils. Consequently the ship has been seen as a fitting image of the *church, especially when it is the setting for Jesus' miracles. Two miracles stories set in boats convey this picture: the stilling of the *storm (Mk 4:35-41 par. Mt 8:23-27; Lk 8:22-25) and walking on water (Mk 6:45-52 par. Mt 14:22-33; Jn 6:16-21). In addition, the miraculous catch of *fish (Lk 5:4-11; Jn 21:4-8) may picture the spiritual sustenance provided for the church. The parallel is never directly made in the NT, but the image of Jesus' power over the *demonic powers, symbolized by the *wind and waves, the boat providing a means to gather in the harvest of fish, the boat as a symbol of safety and the sense of it carrying people to a destination have been sufficient for many to virtually equate church and boat/ship.

Israel was never the seafaring equal to some of its neighbors. So the sailors and captains who benefited from Rome's commercial success and lament her fall (Rev 18:17-19) are assumed to be pagans. Jehoshaphat tried to revive sea trade on the Red Sea (1 Kings 22:48-49), but his fleet foundered. The chronicler viewed this as a divine judgment on the unholy alliance that lay behind the venture (2 Chron 20:35-37). Commercial shipping was owned by foreign powers, and Isaiah uses this to paint a vivid picture for an eschatological gathering of faithful Israel in Jerusalem: "Surely the islands look to me; in the lead are the ships of Tarshish, bringing your sons from afar, with their silver and gold, to the honor of the LORD your God, the Holy One of Israel, for he has endowed you with splendor" (Is 60:9).

See also FISHING; SEA; SHIP, SHIPWRECK.

BIBLIOGRAPHY. S. Wachsmann, *The Sea of Galilee Boat* (New York: Plenum, 1995).

BODILY ANGUISH. *See* TREMBLING, SHAKING, BODILY ANGUISH.

BODY

The body is a highly significant and complex image in the Bible. Human images and experiences of the body, though undergirded by important continuities, are also socially constructed. Ideals of *beauty, for example, vary from culture to culture. And the image of the body is deeply tied to particular worldviews, in which the body is viewed as a microcosm of the cosmos. The manner in which a culture regards boundaries of the body, defined first by *skin and then, by extension, by *garments and *hair, reflect the way in which that culture views the boundaries of its social body. The gateway orifices of the body—the *eyes, *ears, *mouth and genitals—may be guarded against pollution in a manner analogous to the way that a nation's ports of entry must be guarded and maintained by checkpoints. Jesus subverts the Pharisaic view of the body, with its purity laws that carefully guard what enters the body through the mouth. He maintains that "nothing outside a man can make him 'unclean' by going into him. Rather, it is what comes out of a man that makes him 'unclean.' " For food "doesn't go into his heart but into his stomach, and then out of his body" (Mk 7:15, 19 NIV). Or Jesus can speak of the eye as "the lamp of your body. When your eyes are good, your whole body also is full of light. But when they are bad, your body also is full of darkness" (Lk 11:34 NIV).

The Bible, particularly the OT with its laws and stories regarding ritual purity, has provided a casebook for anthropological investigation. These factors are well kept in mind when reflecting on biblical imagery of the body, but they will not be considered in any detail here. This article deals primarily with the image of the body as a whole or as an organic unity of parts. Separate articles focus on the limbs and other parts of the body.

The Body Created and Recreative. The first human body in the Bible is a creation of God. *Adam's body is shaped by the divine potter's hands, animated by the divine *breath breathed into his *nostrils. Against the backdrop of the created order, Adam is a bodily image of the living God. But this first body also bears a relationship to the *earth, and this is subtly reinforced in the Hebrew assonance of 'ādām "human" and 'ªdāmâ "ground" (Gen 2:7). The earthly nature of the body is then sealed in the tragic epitaph, "dust thou art, and unto dust shalt thou return" (Gen 3:19 KJV). Though the Genesis narrative offers no overt physical description of this first human body, the Hebrew word-play resonates with the Hebrew word 'dm, "to be red," and suggests a body of the rusty shade of soil. The distinction between the human body and the beasts, and the fact that the man can find none "like unto him" among the beasts, differentiates the human body from other living beings (but cf. Dan 4:33; 5:20-21). The creation of the woman from the side of man, using his rib, is an image of bodily differentiation based in equality. The relation between the male and female body is set out in balanced poetry:

This at last is bone of my bones
and flesh of my flesh;
this one shall be called Woman
for from Man this one was taken.
(Gen 2:23 NRSV)

From the one human body is formed another, and their differentiation and deep relationship is reflected in two new names set side by side: *'iš* "man" and *'iššâ* "woman." As two genders they reunite as "one flesh." In *marriage union, Adam's body finds its perfect counterpart in the body of the woman. Together, as same *bone and flesh, they form and generate community in their fruitfulness and multiplication (Gen 1:28). This archetypal image of union—man and woman as one flesh—holds an allusion to the generative power from which the body of human society will unfold. From these two bodies, fitly joined, new bodies emerge (cf. Gen 15:4; 35:11; 2 Sam 7:12), "the fruit" of the body (Mic 6:7). The author of Hebrews uses the image of descendants coming from the bodies of their progenitors when arguing for the priority of the priesthood of Melchizedek over the priesthood of Levi, "because when Melchizedek met Abraham, Levi was still in the body of his ancestor" (Heb 7:10 NIV).

The Bible's insistence that the human body is created by God, not evolved by chance from lower forms of life or a byproduct of the romances or wars of the *gods, places a high value on the body. It is the work of a divine artisan, an intricate and fleshly distillation of divine wisdom, a creation "a little lower than the heavenly beings" but capable of bearing the crown of honor and glory (Ps 8:5). This high regard for the human body is summed up in the psalmist's wonder at the work of the Creator. The one who created the cosmos has done a work no less wonderful and mysterious in shaping the human frame:

For you created my inmost being;
you knit me together in my mother's womb.
I praise you because I am fearfully and wonderfully
made;
your works are wonderful,
I know that full well.

My frame was not hidden from you
when I was made in the secret place.
When I was woven together in the depths
of the earth,
your eyes saw my unformed body.
(Ps 139:13-16 NIV; cf. Eccles 11:5)

Job in his suffering forms a series of three metaphors of God creating the body human. He is a potter, or one who makes *clay figurines, he is cheese maker and he is a tailor, or a leatherworker:

Your hands shaped me and made me.
Will you now turn and destroy me?
Remember that you molded me like clay.
Will you now turn me to dust again?
Did you not pour me out like milk
and curdle me like cheese,
clothe me with skin and flesh
and knit me together with bones and sinews?
(Job 10:8-11 NIV)

God has created the body, and the body is created to be in relationship with God. Those who earnestly seek God can say, "my soul thirsts for you, my body longs for you" (Ps 63:1 NIV). A right relationship with the Creator, the "fear of the Lord," "will bring health to your body and nourishment to your bones" (Prov 3:8 NIV; cf. Prov 4:22). And those who rely on their good Creator are instructed not to worry "about your life, what you will eat; or about your body, what you will wear. Life is more than food, and the body more than clothes" (Lk 12:22-23 NIV).

The goodness of the body as a creation of God is powerfully confirmed by the incarnation. This is memorably imaged by John as he writes, "The Word became flesh and dwelt among us" (Jn 1:14 RSV), or when the author of Hebrews has Jesus declare when he comes into the world, "Sacrifice and offering you did not desire, but a body you prepared for me" (Heb 10:5 NIV; cf. Ps 40:6 LXX).

The Body Covered and Uncovered. The Bible disapproves of the public *nakedness of man and woman outside the original state of the first man and woman in the *Garden (Gen 2:25). The human need to cover the body is associated with the first couple's eating of the *fruit of the knowledge of good and evil: "Then the eyes of both were opened, and they knew that they were naked; and they sewed fig leaves together and made loincloths for themselves" (Gen 3:7 NRSV). A publicly naked body is shameful and is associated with a certain self-consciousness that disrupts the original perfect state (Gen 3:9-11).

The human body also needs protection from the elements (Ex 22:27), and clothing offers this. Paul asks Timothy to bring his cloak from Troas (2 Tim 4:13) as he anticipates the coming winter (2 Tim 4:21). He has experienced being "cold and naked" (2 Cor 11:27). A body unclothed is not only cold, a body stripped of clothing and *jewelry (Ezek 16:39) is a body bereft of the insignia of social standing and identity. A naked body is not a sign of freedom from society's constraints but of incalculable loss of place and *honor. When the naked Gerasene demoniac is delivered by Jesus and restored to his community, he is found "clothed and in his right mind" (Mk 8:27, 35 RSV). For these reasons, nakedness can be a fitting image of *judgment, as when Jeremiah says of Israel, "it is because of your many sins that your skirts have been torn off and your body mistreated" (Jer 13:22 NIV). The central biblical image of public shame and judgment is the naked Jesus hanging on the *cross.

The Body of Stature. Humans in general are impressed with bodies of grand stature. The OT has an expression for sizing up the full stature of a human: "from the sole of his foot to the crown of his head" (2 Sam 14:25 RSV; Deut 28:35; Job 2:7; Is 1:6). Bodies of gigantic stature can strike fear, such as that of Goliath, who was "over nine feet tall" (1 Sam 17:4 NIV). (Most Israelite men probably did not exceed five and a half feet in height.) The Israelite spies report that the Canaanites are "stronger and taller than we are" (Deut 1:28 NIV). "All the people we saw there are of great size. . . . We seemed like grasshoppers in our own eyes, and we looked the same to them" (Num 13:32-33 NIV). Amos speaks of the Amorites as being as "tall as the cedars and strong as the oaks" (Amos 2:9 NIV). Enemies of great bodily stature and strength are challenges to faith.

Bodily stature, when it does not reach grotesque proportions, may be attractive. Saul's stature is an important ingredient in his attractiveness. He is described as "a handsome young man. There was not a man among the people of Israel more handsome than he; from his shoulders upward he was taller than any of the people" (1 Sam 9:2 RSV; 10:23). And Samuel says that "there is none like him among all the people" (1 Sam 10:24 RSV). But when Samuel goes "head hunting" for a new king to fill Israel's executive office, the LORD's warning about David's brother Eliab will echo throughout the Bible as a caution against outward measures of a person: "Do not look on his appearance or on the height of his stature, because I have rejected him; for the LORD does not see as morals see; they look on the outward appearance, but the LORD looks on the heart" (1 Sam 16:7 NRSV).

The Body Beautiful and Odd. The *beautiful body is not overlooked by the Bible, though we find it noted more frequently in the OT than in the NT. The ancestresses Sarah (Gen 12:11, 14), Rebekah (Gen 24:16) and Rachel ("lovely in form" Gen 29:17 NIV) are all described as beautiful. Joseph, David and Absalom are singled out as examples of male beauty. Joseph is "well built and handsome" (Gen 39:6 NIV). The description of David evokes a picture of a strong lad who combines genetic fortune with the natural beauty endowed by life in the outdoors: "he was ruddy, with a fine appearance and handsome features . . . a fine-looking man . . . ruddy and handsome" (1 Sam 16:12, 18; 17:42 NIV). Absalom is given closer description: "In all Israel there was not a man so highly praised for his handsome appearance as Absalom. From the top of his head to the sole of his foot there was no blemish in him. Whenever he cut the hair of his head, . . . its weight was two hundred shekels" (i.e., over 5 lbs.; 2 Sam 14:25-26 NIV). Absalom's freedom from blemish or defect is shared by the noble young Israelite men who are selected for service to the king of Babylon. They are described as being "without any physical defect, handsome" and possessing equally admirable intellects (Dan 1:4 NIV).

Occasionally the Bible gives us a glimpse of the distinctive characteristics of a man's body, but these details are rare. *Esau, for example, is said to be "a hairy man" in contrast with *Jacob who is "a smooth man" (Gen 27:11 NIV). In fact, when Esau is born it is said that he was "red, and his whole body was like a hairy garment" (Gen 25:25 NIV). This physical characteristic plays into the profile of Esau within the larger narrative of the brothers, for he is a rustic character, a man of the open country and a hunter. Another distinct figure of a man is the enemy defeated by David's men at Gath: "a huge man with six fingers on each hand and six toes on each foot— twenty-four in all" (2 Sam 22:11 NIV).

The richest descriptions of male and female bodies are given in the *Song of Songs. Here we see the male body described through the eyes of the woman (or, more likely, a male writer taking on the perspective of a woman). The poetic description in Song of Songs 5:10-16 focuses on the head, hair, eyes, cheeks, lips, mouth, arms, legs and torso. The description is sensuous and luxuriant, rich in *nature imagery, from *animal to *plant life, and abundant in imagery of wealth, from *jewels to precious *metals and ivory. Movement and solidity, taste and smell, softness and hardness are all evoked. Set within the larger context of the Song, the beauty of this male body refracts moral virtue. Likewise the description of the woman in Song of Songs 6:5-7 and 7:1-5 wanders over her anatomy—the feet and thighs, the belly, navel and breasts, the neck, eyes, nose, head and hair. Whereas the male torso and appendages are celebrated for their solidity verging on angularity, the female parts evoke curvaceousness and roundness complemented by images of fertility. But above the shoulders she is statuesque and well defended, with a neck like an ivory tower, a nose like the tower of *Lebanon and a head crowning her like Mount Carmel.

Ideals of bodily beauty may vary from time to time and from culture to culture, but the Song of Songs leaves no doubt that the human body can be beautiful and is a thing to be enjoyed and celebrated in the presence of God its Creator. But the voice of wisdom abruptly draws us back to the practical and spiritual realities of beauty:

"Like a gold ring in a pig's snout is a beautiful woman who shows no discretion" (Prov 11:22 NIV). "Charm is deceptive, and beauty is fleeting; but a woman who fears the LORD is to be praised" (Prov 31:30 NIV). And the prophet Isaiah places the beauty of the human body in proper perspective: "All flesh is grass, and all its beauty is like the flower of the field. . . . The grass withers, the flower fades; but the word of our God will stand for ever" (Is 40:6-8 RSV; cf. Ps 78:39).

The body—male or female—is ultimately regarded in the Bible as a physical form with the mysterious capability of emanating virtue and godliness. 1 Peter contrasts outward adornment and beauty with the cultivation of the "inner self, the unfading beauty of a gentle and quiet spirit, which is of great worth in God's sight" (1 Pet 3:4 NIV). Although the focus here is on women, the same principle certainly applies to men.

The Body of the Wealthy, the Poor and the Wicked. Wealth and poverty, godliness and wickedness, are frequently imaged in the condition of the body. The bodies of the wealthy are stylized as *fat, sleek and radiant in skin. Fatness can be an image of rich *abundance, and so Job speaks of the wicked whose "face is covered with fat and his waist bulges with flesh" (Job 15:27 NIV). On the other hand, to say that "the fat of his body will waste away" (Is 17:4 NIV) is to portray a person who has enjoyed God's blessings but is undergoing divine judgment.

The bodies of the wicked may be viewed from two perspectives. One psalmist considers that they often seem to be "healthy and strong, . . . free from the burdens common to man; they are not plagued by human ills" (Ps 73:4-5). But then the psalmist realizes that this is all a fantasy; their final destiny is nothing but ruin and destruction (Ps 73:17-19). In reality, the wicked, who love to pronounce their curses and take no pleasure in blessing, are treading on the verge of death, for their curses return to them and invade the body: "He wore cursing as his garment; it entered into his body like water, into his bones like oil. (Ps 109:18 NIV). The godly are reminded of the ill effects of a life divorced from wisdom: "A heart at peace gives life to the body, but envy rots the bones" (Prov 14:30 NIV). Perhaps the most grotesque imagery of bodies under divine judgment comes from Zechariah's prophecy against the nations that have fought against Jerusalem: "Their flesh will rot while they are still standing on their feet, their eyes will rot in their sockets, and their tongues will rot in their mouths" (Zech 14:12 NIV).

The Body of Bone, Flesh and Blood. The Bible sometimes images the body in its hard, soft and fluid parts, its *bone, flesh and *blood. A frequent expression of kinship in the OT is "bone and flesh" (translated "flesh and blood" by the NIV). The expression first occurs in an emphatic form in Adam's exclamation that Eve is "bone of my bones and flesh of my flesh" (Gen 2:23 NIV). When all Israel gathers before David at Hebron, they declare in one voice, "we are your own bone and flesh" (2 Sam 5:1; 1 Chron 11:1). This expression, in which two opposite parts of the human body—hard structure and soft substance—stand for the whole, evokes a rudimentary picture of the body and a recognition of what we would call a "genetic" relationship between kin.

The image of "flesh and blood" evokes something quite different. An *enemy's body, slain on a battlefield, is "flesh and blood." The *divine warrior will make his *arrows "drunk with blood" while his "sword devours flesh" (Deut 32:42). Or in the words of Ezekiel's prophecy against Egypt, the land will flow with their blood and the ravines will be filled with their bodies (Ezek 32:6). Human flesh and blood are the food of scavenging birds and animals after battle (Ezek 39:17-18; cf. Rev 19:18, 21). Perhaps this sheds a harsh but interpretive light on Jesus's words to his disciples when he tells them that they will gain eternal life by eating his flesh and

drinking his blood (Jn 6:53-56). His death is both judgment and sacrifice, and his body, rendered into the two parts associated with brutal death and slaughter, will paradoxically give life to those who consume it as a sacrificial meal. But in the NT, "flesh and blood" is also an image of human bodily existence in this age, incompatible by its nature with the age to come: "flesh and blood cannot inherit the kingdom of God" (1 Cor 15:50 NIV). The image can also be used to distinguish between human enemies and spiritual ones, for Ephesians reminds us that we do not struggle "against flesh and blood" but against spiritual powers (Eph 6:12)

The incarnation is variously expressed in the NT, but the image of "flesh" is one means of underscoring its bodily reality. In the Gospel of John we read that "the Word became flesh and made his dwelling among us" (Jn 1:14 NIV), and in Hebrews we find that Jesus shares "flesh and blood" with humanity (Heb 2:14). John, distinguishing between those of true faith and those who are false teachers, declares that "every spirit that acknowledges that Jesus Christ has come in the flesh is from God" (1 Jn 4:2; cf. 2 Jn 7). After the resurrection, Jesus demonstrates that his body is real: "Touch me and see; a ghost does not have flesh and bones, as you see I have" (Lk 24:39 NIV). Nevertheless, the NT acknowledges that the *resurrection body is different from the body of our present human existence, and Paul explains this by falling back on an analogous distinction between different types of flesh: "Not all flesh is alike, but there is one flesh for human beings, another for animals, another for birds, and another for fish" (1 Cor 15:39 NRSV).

Flesh is sometimes an image of the soft body parts. As the most perishable part of the body, it "rots" (Zech 14:12), "wastes away" (Job 33:21 NIV), is "eaten away" (Num 12:12 NIV), devoured by dogs and enemies (2 Kings 9:36; Ps 27:2) or torn by thorns and briers (Judg 8:7). The flesh can also serve as an image of human *weakness and impermanence, as when the flesh and heart fail (Ps 73:26) or God remembers that Israel is "but flesh, a passing breeze that does not return" (Ps 78:39 NIV) or an enemy's mere "arm of flesh" is contrasted with the power of Israel's divine warrior (2 Chron 32:8). Job hurls a protest of faith against the apparent transience of human flesh and bodily existence: "After my skin has been destroyed, yet in my flesh I will see God" (Job 19:26 NIV).

The softness of flesh is a positive image in the context of spiritual renewal. Ezekiel speaks of God creating in his people a "new heart," of replacing their "heart of stone" with a "heart of flesh" (Ezek 36:26). Here the *heart as the center of thought and consciousness, deadened and congealed by *sin and *rebellion, is brought back to vital spiritual life. But within this context of spiritual life, the flesh can also be an image of the outward and superficial as opposed to the inner and real. Jeremiah declaims God's coming judgment against those who are "circumcised only in the flesh" (Jer 9:25 NIV), and for Ezekiel, those who are not circumcised in "heart and flesh" must not enter the Lord's sanctuary (Ezek 44:7, 9).

Most, if not all, occurrences of the word *flesh* in English translations of the NT represent the Greek word *sarx*. In certain contexts the NIV has translated *sarx* as "sinful nature" (e.g., Rom 7:5, 18, 25; 8:3-9, 12-13). Although Paul can speak of *sarx* as the physical matter of living bodies (1 Cor 15:39), as a part of the human body that represents the whole (synecdoche, 1 Cor 6:16), as a human person or even the human race (Gal 2:16; Rom 3:20), or simply as the sphere of human relationships and kinship based on natural birth (Rom 9:3, 5, 8), it is the morally negative image that dominates the horizon for many readers of Paul.

Sarx, "flesh," is Paul's common metaphor for inherent human sinfulness. But as one among several Pauline uses of the term, it should not cloud our understanding of the body as the good creation of God that will be redeemed. The image of *sarx* as rebellious human nature occurs most frequently in Romans and Galatians. Particularly in Galatians the image seems to be gauged to subvert the ideology of those who are promoting the circumcision of the "flesh." Against these Judaizers, who wish to boast in the Galatians' circumcised flesh, Paul produces this counter-image of flesh as opposed to the "Spirit" (Gal 3:3) and its fruits (Gal 5:16-17). In this dualistic imagery, gauged for particular effect, the age of the new creation (Gal 6:15) is contrasted with this "present evil age" (Gal 1:3) which exercises its control over the "flesh" and even over religious rites (*circumcision) associated with the flesh (*see* Galatians). The picture is further refined in Romans, where "flesh" is a member of a trilateral alliance of spiritual powers: sin, flesh and death (Rom 6—8; *see* Romans).

The Body Strong and Weak. The Bible presents numerous images of bodily strength, particularly that of warriors. *Samson is the most memorable. Samson's bodily strength is a special God-given strength, to be sure, but one can hardly read the stories of Samson and imagine him to be slight in physique. His legendary feats include slaying a *lion with his bare hands (Judg 14:5-7), killing great numbers of *Philistines (Judg 14:19-20; 15:8, 14-17), carrying off the city *gates of Gaza (Judg 16:3), breaking his bonds as if they were charred flax or string (Judg 15:14; 16:7-9, 11-12, 13-14) and finally bringing down the temple of Dagon on the Philistine worshipers as well as on himself (Judg 16:23-20). Goliath is a warrior champion of hideous size and strength (1 Sam 17:4-7), and though his young opponent David is no physical match, David too is strong enough to slay a lion and a bear (1 Sam 17:34-37). To slay a lion, the strongest of Palestine's predatory animals, is a high mark of bodily strength. David's mighty warrior Benaiah counted among his memorable feats the slaying of a lion in a pit on a snowy day (2 Sam 23:20). Even the prophet Elijah proves to be a strong runner when the power of the Lord comes upon him and he outruns Ahab's chariot all the from Carmel to Jezreel (1 Kings 18:46). On the opposite side of the coin is the Gerasene demoniac, possessed by a militaristic "legion" of demons, whose spirit-driven strength breaks the chains that bind him (Mk 5:29).

It is assumed that warriors will have strong bodies, but the Preacher injects a note of counter-wisdom drawn from long observation: "The race is not to the swift or the battle to the strong" (Eccles 9:11 NIV). Under judgment, even "the lovely young women and strong young men will faint because of thirst" (Amos 8:13 NIV). The strength of the human body, however, is more often assumed than noted in the Bible. In a culture where much of daily life consisted of bodily exertion—hauling water, grinding meal, weaving cloth, planting and harvesting crops, managing domestic animals, traveling on foot—the fleeting picture of the virtuous wife who has arms that are "strong for her tasks" (Prov 31:17 NIV) surely notes the rule rather than the exception. When the Bible does praise the strength of the male body, it is presented in images of hardness: "His arms are rods of gold set with chrysolite. . . . His legs are pillars of marble" (Song 5:14-15 NIV).

The prevailing tone of the Bible is that bodily strength is a gift from God, and in its most exceptional instances—such as Samson and Elijah—it is an empowerment of the Spirit of God. Those who boast in their strength (e.g., 1 Sam 17:42-44) are setting themselves up for a fall. The only one who is truly strong is the Lord, and in contrast human bodily strength is puny: "the Egyptians are men and not God; their horses are flesh and not spirit" (Is 31:3 NIV). Those who directly encounter the power of God find their bodies *trembling, *melting and dissolving in anguish. The recognition that the strength of the body is a fragile thing, even when compared with the human will, is summed up in the well-known words of Jesus in Gethsemane: "the spirit is willing, but the body is weak" (Mk 14:38 NIV).

The Body Impaired, Diminished and Restored. Frequently in the Bible we find mention of bodies that are not whole, whose faculties are impaired from birth or by accident or by age. Leviticus presents us with a catalogue of bodily conditions that call for purification or exclude one from full engagement in the life of Israel. Various infectious skin diseases afflict the body and call for cleansing measures (Lev 13—14). A woman's body after childbirth is judged ceremonially unclean (Lev 12), and so is a woman in menstruation or a man or woman with any bodily discharge (Lev 15). These are conditions that break the boundaries of bodily wholeness.

Bodily wholeness is one of the prerequisites for the sons of Aaron to offer sacrifices in the house of God, and the list of disqualifying defects is a brief catalog of unacceptable bodily deformity or impairment of the male body: "no man who is blind or lame, disfigured or deformed; no man with a crippled foot or hand, or who is hunchbacked or dwarfed, or who has any eye defect, or who has festering or running sores or damaged testicles" (Lev 21:18-20 NIV).

These restrictions on bodies deviating from the norm are due to the *holiness of God, who may only be approached by representatives of Israel who are whole in body and who offer animal sacrifices that are likewise whole in body (Lev 22:19-22). As undesirable as bodily impairment may be, Jesus suggests that the loss of an offending body part—an eye or a hand—is better than having the whole body thrown into hell (Mt 5:29-30).

The *skin is the protective boundary of the body as well as an outward indicator of the inner condition of the body. Consequently skin diseases or conditions that affect the integrity of the skin instill a particular horror. Job gives voice to his despair as his body suffers decay at its outer limits: "My body is clothed with worms and scabs, my skin is broken and festering. . . . I prefer strangling and death, rather than this body of mine" (Job 7:5, 15 NIV). "My skin grows black and peels; my body burns with fever (Job 30:30 NIV). But even this condition of the body is not without hope: "Yet if there is an angel on his side as a mediator, one out of a thousand, . . . then his flesh is renewed like a child's; it is restored as in the days of his youth" (Job 33:23-25 NIV).

Suffering, sin, guilt and divine wrath manifest themselves in bodily anguish. It can be as if the body is on the threshold of death. The psalmist says,

Because of your wrath there is no health in my body;
    my bones have no soundness because of my sin.
My guilt has overwhelmed me
    like a burden too heavy to bear. . . .
My wounds fester and are loathsome
    because of my sinful folly.
I am bowed down and brought very low;
    all day long I go about mourning.
My back is filled with searing pain;
    there is no health in my body.
I am feeble and utterly crushed;
    I groan in anguish of heart. (Ps 38:3, 5-8 NIV)

Even an oracle of judgment may affect the body of the prophet: "At this my body is racked with pain, pangs seize me, like those of a woman in labor" (Is 21:3 NIV). The psalmist confesses before God that "my flesh trembles in fear of you" (Ps 119:120 NIV). And intellectual exercise is no escape from the toll that work takes on the body: "Of making many books there is no end, and much study wearies the body" (Eccles 12:12 NIV).

Within the OT we find a notable member of the royal family who has a bodily impairment. Mephibosheth, son of Jonathan, is lame in both feet, a condition inflicted when he was dropped by his nurse as she was running in flight (2 Sam 4:4). He receives special consideration from David and is given a place at the king's table "like one of the king's sons" (2 Sam 9:1-13; 19:26-30). It is notable that Jesus, the Son of David, heals those who are lame or have other bodily infirmities or defects and associates with them in table fellowship (e.g., Mt 26:6; Mk 14:3). In his miracles of healing, Jesus restores bodies to wholeness and so brings estranged Israelites into the full privileges of being the people of God. In this he inaugurates the messianic age:

Then will the eyes of the blind be opened
    and the ears of the deaf unstopped.
Then will the lame leap like a deer,
    and the mute tongue shout for joy.
    (Is 35:5-6 NIV)

This text from Isaiah is brightly illustrated in the NT story of the man crippled since birth who begs outside the temple gate. When he is healed through the ministry of Peter, his feet and ankles become strong, and he enters the temple courts, walking and leaping and praising God (Acts 3:1-10).

The Body Inhabited by Spiritual Powers. The Bible sometimes speaks of human bodies inhabited by nonhuman spiritual powers. These powers are either good or evil, the Spirit of God or the malevolent spirits of darkness. Although this imagery comes into its own in the NT, it is foreshadowed in the OT where the Spirit or "power" of God comes upon various prophetic figures such as Saul (1 Sam 19:23-24), Elijah (1 Kings 18:46), Elisha (2 Kings 3:15) and Micah (Mic 3:8). More specifically, Bezalel son of Uri is "filled . . . with the Spirit of God" and with the assorted skills of craftsmanship necessary for building the *tabernacle (Ex 31:3; 35:31 NIV), and Joshua is "filled with the spirit of wisdom" (Deut 34:9 NIV). It is to Luke that we owe the most vivid images of individuals being filled with the Spirit. John the Baptist is "filled with the Holy Spirit even from birth" (Lk 1:15 NIV); his mother is filled with the Spirit as she utters her blessing on Mary (Lk 1:41); and his father, Zechariah, is filled with the Spirit and prophesies (Lk 1:67). At *Pentecost all of the gathered believers are filled with the Spirit and speak in tongues (Acts 2:4), and later Peter (Acts 4:8) and Paul (Acts 9:17; 13:9) and other disciples (Acts 4:31; 13:52) will be filled with the Spirit. And in Ephesians the metaphor of "filling" is set in contrast with being filled, or drunk, with wine (Eph 5:18).

Elsewhere the metaphor of "dwelling" can be used to speak of life guided by the Spirit of God: "You, however, are controlled not by the sinful nature but by the Spirit, if the Spirit of God lives in you. . . . But if the Spirit of him who raised Jesus from the dead is living in you, he who raised Christ from the dead will also give life to your mortal bodies through his Spirit, who lives in you" (Rom 8:9-11). Finally, and most dramatically, Paul reminds the Corinthians that "your body is a temple of the Holy Spirit within you" (1 Cor 6:19 NRSV).

But the fearsome counterpart to a body being "filled" with the Holy Spirit is a body inhabited by demons, or "unclean spirits." The Gerasene demoniac has a "legion" of spirits who come out of him and enter a herd of swine (Mk 5:9-13; Lk 8:30-32). Mary Magdalene is identified as one from whom "seven demons had come out" (Lk 8:2 NIV; Mk 16:9). And in many other instances we read of demons "coming out" of individuals, with the implication that these spirits somehow inhabit these human bodies. Jesus even speaks of an evil spirit going out of a man and seeking but not finding rest. The spirit will then return to his former "house," now "swept clean and put in order," and bring "seven other spirits more wicked than itself" (Lk 11:24-26 NIV). It is as if to say that a body vacated but not inhabited by the Spirit of God is a body with its "vacancy" sign turned on.

The Body in Decline. Job speaks of the wealthy person who dies in "full vigor" with the "body well nourished" and "bones rich with marrow" (Job 21:23-24 NIV). And Lamentations intones the lament of Jerusalem under the hand of God's judgment: "He has made my skin and my flesh grow old and has broken my bones" (Lam 3:4 NIV). But the prevailing view in the Bible is the straightforward reality of *death as the terminal point of a gradual decline. The physical body achieves its fullest potential in youth and then seems to slide toward the *grave. The imagery of bodily decline presented in Ecclesiastes 12:1-7 is unsurpassed: The body's posture and carriage decline "when the keepers of the house tremble, and the strong men stoop"; *eating grows difficult as "the grinders cease because they are few"; eyesight is impaired as "those looking through the windows grow dim"; *sleep is fragile and yet hearing fails as "men rise up at the sound of birds, but all their songs grow faint"; and finally, the body fails as "man goes to his eternal home and mourners go about the streets. . . . [A]nd the dust returns to the ground it came from, and the spirit returns to God who gave it" (NIV).

Old age brings a decline in the body's vitality and warmth in sharp contrast with the body of one's youth. Thus David in his old age "could not keep warm even when they put covers over him," and he required the services of a "young virgin" to attend to him and lie beside him "that our lord the king may keep warm" (1 Kings 1:1-4 NIV; cf. 2 Kings 4:34).

The aging of the body is also an opportunity for faith. Abraham's strikes a remarkable image of faith when he believes God's promise of a son from his body and Sarah's womb, even when they are both old. As Paul puts it, "Without weakening in his faith, he faced the fact that his body was as good as dead—since he was about a hundred years old—and that Sarah's womb was also dead" (Rom 4:19 NIV).

The Body of Death. In the OT when life leaves a body, the body immediately becomes ceremonially unclean (Lev 21:11; Num 9:6-7). Death is a powerful contaminant. A living body that comes in contact with a dead body must go through rituals of *cleansing prior to being reinstated into full membership among the "clean" (Num 5:2; Hag 2:13). In the book of Numbers the uncleanness of dead bodies is a notable motif, for this book relates the death of an entire generation of Israelites in the *wilderness.

How are those who come in contact with dead bodies to be restored fully to life within Israel's camp? A cleansing agent of water combined with the ashes of a red heifer plays an important role in purifying the body of a person made unclean by contact with death (Num 19). The image of an unclean dead body is not simply explainable on the grounds of a modern understanding of sanitation, though the analogy is apt. It is an image that draws our attention to the boundary between the realm of the living and the realm of the dead. In the schema of Israel's holy camp within the wilderness, where God dwells in its midst (Num 5:2-4; cf. 9:13), death is associated with the wilderness, the world outside the camp. Dead bodies are transported outside the camp, and those who come in contact with dead bodies remain unclean for a period of seven days while they undergo purification. If they fail to do so, they will be "cut off from Israel" (Num 19:13). The "body" of Israel (represented by the camp with its boundaries) is to be pure, living and undefiled by death in much the same manner that individual Israelite bodies are to be undefiled by death.

Dead bodies are to be *buried. They are to be returned to the earth from which they came: "for dust thou art, and unto dust shalt thou return" (Gen 3:19 KJV). It is easy to understand why the OT portrays the realm of the dead, sheol, as the "underworld" (Is 14:9-11). One goes "down" to death, or the grave (Job 21:13; Ps 55:15; Is 14:15; Ezek 31:15-17). And there the body is consumed by *worms, maggots and *decay (Job 21:26; Is 14:11). In contrast, a body left exposed is a shameful thing (Jer 36:30). And a body treated like refuse and eaten by wild beasts is the ultimate shame (2 Kings 9:34-37). Even the dead body of a criminal or an enemy that is hung on a tree is to be buried by nightfall (Deut 21:22-23; Josh 8:29; 10:26-27). Failing to keep this law brings desecration on the land the Lord gives Israel, for a body subjected to hanging is a body cursed, and a cursed thing has the power to defile (Deut 21:23; cf. 1 Sam 31:10).

Some dead bodies are brought back to life. Elisha brings to life the dead body of the Shunnamite woman's son (2 Kings 4:32-35). A dead body thrown into Elisha's tomb springs to life as it touches Elisha's bones (2 Kings 13:21). But these are only resuscitated bodies. Job speaks with confidence of a true resurrection (Job 19:26 NIV), and Christ's body is the first to be raised from among the dead in the resurrection of the last days. Peter speaks eloquently of the resurrection of Christ, summoning up the reversal of bodily decline: "he was not abandoned to the grave, nor did his body see decay" (Acts 2:31 NIV; cf. Acts 13:36).

The Body of Christ. The primary use of the word *body* as an image in the NT is the Pauline "body [Gk sōma] of Christ" as an image of the *church. This understanding of "body" as an image for the Christian community of faith is rooted in the Hebraic rejection we see also in the OT of any distinction between the body and the spirit. "Body" in both OT and NT refers to the whole human being, with corporeal substance being the very expression of the person. Hence, such an image as we find addressed to the church in Corinth, "Now you are the body of Christ and each one of you is a part of it" (1 Cor 12:27), rests on the idea of the body as the essential expression of the whole person: in this case the crucified and risen Christ. This is the key to a right understanding of the NT image of the church as "the body."

The primary use of "body" (of Christ) as an image for the church can never be separated from the words with which Christ institutes the Last Supper and the sacrifice they describe: "This is my body[—whole person—broken] for you" (Mk 14:22; 1 Cor 11:24). So the liturgical, eucharistic image of "this is my body" lies behind Paul's use of "Christ's body, the church." Just as it was both a metaphor—as Jesus held and broke the *bread, saying "this is my body"—and also an actuality, in that his body was literally to be given, so the church as the body of Christ is both a metaphor and an actuality (e.g., Rom 12:4). The church, being the present corporeal, earthly manifestation of the saving act of Christ, is not just "like" a body, it "is" a body. But the special nature of this body is that the "being a body" is effected by Christ.

In Colossians we see this double meaning strongly emphasized. In Colossians 1:22 the body is the crucified body of the Lord Jesus. Yet in Colossians 1:18 and 1:24, Paul is clearly using the same term for the Christian community ("He is the head of the body, the church. . . . For the sake of his body, that is, the church"). Likewise when Paul has his vision on the Damascus Road, Jesus confronts him with the question "Saul, Saul, why do you persecute me?" (Acts 9:4 NIV). It is clear in the narrative that Paul had not directly persecuted Jesus but rather has attacked the church. Christ is so closely identifies with the church that to persecute the church is to persecute Christ.

The crucified body of Jesus and the ecclesial body, the church, therefore cannot be separated. Several consequences for the meaning of the image flow from this. First, though, we must note that in the earlier epistles, particularly Corinthians and Romans, the emphasis is on the local church as expressing in its unity the crucified and living Christ. But in the later epistles, Colossians and Ephesians, the image has moved outward to embrace the universal church (Col 1:18; 2:19; Eph 1:22-23; 4:16). Christ is the "head" of a body which is more than the local community of faith, and this change in the image is of the greatest importance, because it marks through its shift a vision of a church "producing fruit and growing . . . all over the world" (Col 1:6 NIV), a calling to mission which is at least as imperative as the call to build up the life of the local faith community.

This missionary dimension of the "growing body" image is in part a response by Paul, particularly in Colossians, to a preoccupation of the Greek world to which the gospel was preached. That is, Paul is addressing the so-called cosmic anxiety of the Hellenic culture: the fear that the cosmos was separated from God and so subject to powers and demons. (Though we would express our fears differently, the issue of the cosmos and the sovereignty of God over it has a peculiarly contemporary note.) In Colossians, Paul asserts in the context of the image of the church as the body of Christ that the universe is subject to the lordship of Christ (Col 1:15-17). He is head—in the sense of having dominion over—the defeated powers of the cosmos as he is head ecclesiologically over the reconciled (Col 1:22) community, the church. The form of this dominion is in the preaching and spread of the gospel through all the world, permeating the cosmos.

The saving power of this preaching to all creatures is emphasized in the nature of the reconciled community as it is presented as the "body of Christ" in Ephesians. In Ephesians 2:13-16 those reconciled to God "in one body through the cross" are the once irreconcilable Jews and Gentiles. The "one body" is both the crucified body of Christ but also, indivisibly, the "one new man" of Ephesians 2:15, which Christ, "abolishing in his flesh the law with its commandments" (NIV), has created "in himself" out of the two, Jew and Gentile. The mission to all non-Jews is furthering the growth in unity of "the body" in a way which is a paradigm for all divided humanity (Eph 2:12-16). It has been well said that this too has a cosmic dimension, since all growth of the body, the church, through the preaching of the gospel, is but bringing to light what already is. So the "demons," who may seem to control the separation of the world from God, are powerless against "the fullness of him that fills everything in every way" (Eph 1:23 NIV) in the subjection of all things to Christ "not only in the present age but also in the one to come" (Eph 1:21 NIV).

The force of the body as image of the church thus becomes very challenging. For the body of Christ, crucified and risen, creating unity and service in his followers is a given fact, not a dream of potential. It is the believers' unity with Christ which creates the fellowship, not the fellowship which creates the unity with Christ. Both in the local church and in the church universal, unity and service are properly the spontaneous expression of being the "body of Christ." It is a service which therefore all Christians offer not only to each other but, like their Lord, beyond, for Christ is (so they must be) "the body for the world."

The Body Redeemed. The holistic view of "body" as the whole person, which permeates the Bible, makes for certain other implications for "body" as image. For it means that body becomes the place where we meet God and live out our service to him. It is the expression of our divinely given creatureliness, where obedience is practiced. And it is seen always therefore in relationship, with God and the fellow creatures with whom we share our corporeality, our "bodiness."

It follows that redemption must be understood not as "from" the body but "of" it (Rom 8:23). Therefore even the future life is a bodily one. "In the body" in Paul's writing usually means "earthly," but there will be a God-given "heavenly" body (1 Cor 15:35-44; cf. Rom 8:11). Nonbodily resurrection is inconceivable to Paul. Equally, nonresurrection is inconceivable, since it is a participation in the resurrection body of the Lord Jesus. In 2 Corinthians 5:1-10 Paul makes a distinction not between "soul" and "body" but between our future resurrection bodies and the present mortal ones. In these present mortal bodies we will be questioned in the judgment, for it is where we do our living, believing, serving. Life after death is dependent on the gracious will and act of God through Christ Jesus, and our human appropriating of it. The reality of that appropriation is expressed by our life in the body (Rom 8:11; 1 Cor 6:14).

Hence the body image attracts the theme of sovereignty over the body, the sovereignty of God versus the sovereignty of sin. In Romans 6:12 Paul writes, "Therefore do not let sin reign in your mortal body" (NIV). God has broken the sovereignty of sin in our bodies because he has bought them back as his own possession, for they are now, through his sacrifice, Christ's. Because Christ has given his own "body," his total person, for them, they belong to him and he to them (1 Cor 6:13).

Hence, too, these same bodies will be made like Jesus' "body of glory" (Phil 3:21), so the body, the total person, will itself be transformed. (This neither assumes nor denies the regrouping of the material substance of our bodies). The form of this body of *"glory" cannot be surmised. What is certain is that it is in some way "like," empowered by, the resurrection body of Christ.

There are implications here for the church as the "body of Christ." In its earthly body it is called to identify itself with the incarnate and crucified Christ, offering itself (both in its individual members and corporately) as a sacrifice to God, so that it is no longer its own: "present your bodies as a living sacrifice, holy and acceptable to God" (Rom 12:1 RSV). It can do this only through Christ's body, given for us. But the promise that this lowly body will be made like his exalted body is a promise also that the church itself shall be transformed into a body of glory. For the church as the body of Christ participates not only in the crucified but also the resurrected body of the Lord.

The Body Disciplined. A further aspect of the NT body image grows from the original Hebraic understanding. If, for Christians, the body is where one is redeemed and lives out the redeemed earthly life, it follows that an over-spiritualized piety is inappropriate (2 Cor 7:1). Hence in his Corinthian letters Paul insists that it is in his body that he brings the life of Christ into effect for the community. What we do

with our bodies (whether corporately as a community or as individual members) is a part of the totality of both obedience to Christ and proclamation of him. So the suffering which is visible in Paul's body lends conviction to his preaching (2 Cor 1:3-7), for the *wounds he bears in his body are also the wounds of Jesus (Gal. 6:17), and he bears about in his body constantly the dying of Jesus: "so that his life may be revealed in our mortal body" (2 Cor 4:11 NIV). For the life of Jesus can only be shown forth in the body. So, while rejecting asceticism as a way of salvation (Col 2:3), Paul finds it necessary to take steps to discipline and control his body (1 Cor 9:27).

All this lies behind his specific words on the *sexual activity of the body (1 Cor 6:18). It is not possible for the Christian, who is united in the body with Christ, to enact in that same body sexual immorality (1 Cor 6:13, 15). Behind this lies the view that in the sexual act the body—the whole person—belongs wholly to the "other" (it is a holistic view of sexual activity) so it cannot belong to both Christ and a prostitute (1 Cor 6:16-18). All of this is implicit in one of Paul's most mysterious and powerful images involving both body and flesh: in Ephesians 5:23-32 Paul likens the relationship of Christ and his church to that between husband and wife. Christ loves the church as his own body, and "in this same way, husbands ought to love their wives as their own bodies . . . for we are members of his body" (Eph 5:28, 30). And so we are a part of the same "profound mystery" in relationship with Christ as that within which *husband and *wife "become one flesh" (Eph 5:31, 32). There are implications here for both the corporate life of the church—which in its earthly "body" must never be "joined with" that which dishonors the body of Christ—and for the personal lives of its individual members.

The obverse of this sexual image is that the body, while being a morally neutral context in which we make our choices (one can be "in the body" and also "in the Lord," 2 Cor 12:1-3), is yet also vulnerable: physically, to hurt and mortality; spiritually, to limitations of spiritual discernment (Mat 16:17); and morally, to sin (Rom 6:12). Hence the reiterated insistence on the body's purchase by Christ, that it may be under his sovereignty. Hence, too, the use of the term *flesh*, on occasion, to indicate a state of sin. Romans 8:13 warns against living "according to the flesh" (translated in NIV as "sinful nature," but the word is *sarx*), for that means certain death. Therefore one must "by the Spirit" put to death "the misdeeds of the body." And the whole argument culminating in Romans 6:12 suggests that "the body" once belonged to sin and by nature, but for the grace of Christ, would easily revert to sin (cf. 1 Cor 6:20).

The Body Discerned. This vulnerability to sin is focused in the Last Supper references within the image of the church as body. Paul issues a sharp warning about anyone who participates in the Eucharist "without discerning the body" and thus eats and drinks "judgment against themselves" (1 Cor 11:29

NRSV). The lack of discernment has two aspects. First, it refers to the failure to recognize the power of Christ's act of self-giving in the incarnation and supremely on the cross. It is not the actuality of flesh within the sacrament that is in view but the actuality of Christ's effective act of redemption. This is the "true body," the "real presence" of the holy table.

The second aspect of sinning in "not recognizing the body" flows from this, for it is the failure to recognize the unity within which the partaker actually stands. Since the bread we break is "a sharing in the body of Christ, . . . we who are many are one body, for we all partake of the one bread" (1 Cor 10:16-17 NRSV). Hence it is not a potential unity which goes unrecognized but an actual one, made so by the actuality of Christ's gracious action. "Discerning" this involves living out in the church, bodily, this unity, what it already is, in and through Christ.

The sin of not discerning is in the end only to be overcome through Christ's grace operating in our life. Then our own will and longing is offered wholly to him. Hence the last word on the image of the body and its concomitant, flesh, for both the local and the universal church and for its individual "members," is perhaps that of Paul in Galatians 2:20: "I no longer live, but Christ lives in me. The life I live in the body, I live by faith in the Son of God, who loved me and gave himself for me".

See also ARM; BELLY; BREAST; EAR, HEARING; EYE, SIGHT; FAT, FATNESS; FEET; FINGER; HAIR; HAND; HEAD; HEART; INNER PARTS, BOWELS; LEG; LIPS; MOUTH; NAKED, NAKEDNESS; NECK; NOSE, NOSTRILS; SEX; STOMACH; THIGH; TOE.

BIBLIOGRAPHY. J. H. Neyrey, *Paul, In Other Words* (Louisville: Westminster John Knox, 1990); H. W. Wolff, *Anthropology of the Old Testament* (Philadelphia: Fortress, 1974).

BODY OF CHRIST. *See* BODY.

BOLDNESS

Boldness is a biblical motif associated with those whose *courage is born out of their trust in God; it is a trait of the righteous, who are "as bold as a *lion" (Prov 28:1 NIV). Many *heroes of the biblical narratives convey this image of boldness; often it is a single bold act that reveals a character's trust in God. One example is Abraham's bargaining with God on behalf of Sodom. Although he admits to being no more than "dust and ashes," *Abraham engages the Lord like a vendor in the marketplace, convincing him to spare Sodom for the sake of at first fifty, then forty-five, forty, thirty, twenty, and finally only ten righteous people within the city (Gen 18:23-32). God keeps to his bargain but destroys *Sodom and Gomorrah anyway, because there is no one righteous left to be found there (Gen 18:25). While his boldness in haggling with God seems perilous, it reveals that Abraham knows God and trusts him to act justly.

In a similar episode, when God resolves to destroy Israel for their idolatry with the golden calf, *Moses entreats him to relent so that the Egyptians should not speak ill of the Lord because of Israel's fate (Ex 32:12). Moses then appeals to the promise that God swore to Abraham to produce a nation from his descendants, and at this the Lord agrees to spare Israel (Ex 32:13,14). Here it is Moses's boldness that secures a future for Israel. Moreover, Moses has grounds to speak boldly before God, because he knows that God is faithful and will keep his promises.

The motif of boldness also serves a pivotal and declarative purpose. Often a character's bold act is key to the further unfolding of the story, which culminates in the indisputable victory of God and a declaration of his power. For example, it is the boldness of *Daniel, who insists on praying to God despite the danger, that makes possible God's subsequent delivery of him from the lions. This proves to be such a compelling testimony to the power of Daniel's God that king Darius proclaims, "He is the living God and he endures forever" (Dan 6:26). It is likewise with Shadrach, Meshach and Abednego, who are bold enough to face the furnace and accept death rather than worship idols. Consequently God has the opportunity to save them from the flames, thus demonstrating the degree of his might to Nebuchadnezzar (Dan 3:16-28). In both cases it is the boldness of the characters that moves the story forward and makes known the power of God to preserve those who trust him.

The same is true of those who exhibit boldness in the NT: God's purposes and the revelation of his power depend on the bold acts of those who put their trust in him. Thus John the Baptist preaches the coming of Jesus the Messiah (Jn 1:29-31); and at the risk of being stoned, Jesus declares to the Jews, "before Abraham was born, I am" (Jn 8:58). Peter preaches that Jesus is the Christ before the Jews at Pentecost (Acts 3:12-26), and Paul proclaims the gospel before Festus and Agrippa (Acts 26:4-23). In each case it is a boldness founded on trust in God that carries forward and reveals God's purposes.

An important characteristic of these bold biblical figures is that they act with the knowledge that whatever they do is subject to God's authority. They may act boldly, sometimes to the point of appearing to challenge God, but always with the understanding that it is God who is in control of the events they are helping to unfold. It is this submissive feature of biblical boldness that distinguishes it from *brashness, which does not acknowledge God. One example of brashness is King Ahab, who is heedless of God and utterly brazen in his idolatry (1 Kings 16:30-33). Because Ahab does not acknowledge God even after repeated warnings, his actions are not bold but rather display the brashness of a fool, as God's eventual judgment of him confirms (1 Kings 22:37, 38). In contrast the biblical motif of boldness finds expression in those who acknowledge God and whose courage is tempered and instructed by their complete trust in him.

See also BRASHNESS; COURAGE; HERO, HEROINE.

BONDAGE AND FREEDOM

The connected images of bondage and freedom are employed with great power and significance in the Bible. A word study alone will not reveal the full extent of the imagery, which underlies some of the greatest biblical themes, including *sin, *redemption, flesh and spirit, *law, and truth. Two literal images of bondage prevail in the Bible—the political state of a nation and the condition of *slavery. The image of the prison is also important. Freedom is defined simply as the release from these types of bondage. Metaphoric uses turn these into spiritual conditions.

Political Bondage and Freedom: Egypt. The leading image of political bondage in the Bible is the four hundred years of slavery the nation of Israel endured in *Egypt, which was rendered famous to readers of the English Bible by the evocative epithet "house of bondage" in the KJV. Behind this expression lie the Exodus stories of the enslavement of Israel in Egypt, in which Israel "groaned under their bondage, and cried out for help, and their cry under bondage came up to God" (Ex 2:23 RSV).

If the slavery of the nation in Egypt is the master image of political bondage, the *exodus from Egypt is correspondingly the major image of political freedom. The whole exodus story is told as a liberation from political bondage, described by the great language of redemption in Deuteronomy: "The LORD has brought you out with a mighty hand, and redeemed you from the house of bondage" (Deut 7:8 RSV; cf. 9:26, 13:5). The description of this deliverance as a redemption introduces the idea of new ownership. Israel has been bought by its deliverer and now belongs to him: "I bore you on eagles' wings and brought you to myself" (Ex 19:4 RSV). This freedom does not mean autonomy. Israel no longer belongs to *Pharaoh and to Pharaoh's gods, but to God. Thus the story of the exodus introduces a spiritual dimension into both the bondage and the deliverance: leaving bondage to the anti-God powers of Egypt, Israel is brought into a new relationship with the Lord.

The tragedy of Jewish history in the OT is that the freedom secured by God at the exodus was only temporary. Moses in Deuteronomy already envisions a sad future when the process of deliverance will be reversed because Israel will fail to maintain the covenantal relationship with its Deliverer. When Moses lists the *curses that will befall the nation if it fails to obey God's commands (Deut 28), he paints an ever-expanding picture of bondage, including political bondage (Deut 28:64-68). Moses himself predicts that the nation will rebel against God and "do what is evil in the sight of the LORD, provoking him to anger through the work of your hands" (Deut 31:29 RSV).

Bondage and Freedom in Later Old Testament History. This fall back into bondage is a leading motif in the history that follows. We see the cycle in *Judges, where in response to Israel's sin, the

Lord repeatedly "sold them into the power of their enemies round about" (Judg 2:14; cf. 3:7, 12; 4:2; 6:1; 10:7; 13:1). The process reaches a climax in 2 Kings 17, when Israel is finally deported to political bondage in Assyria. The prophets comment on the spiritual causes underlying this renewed enslavement, which was a political reality for many of them. Thus Jeremiah warns Judah in the Lord's name: "Through your own fault you will lose the inheritance I gave you. I will enslave you to your enemies in a land you do not know" (Jer 17:4 NIV). In the OT political bondage is tied to the spiritual state of the nation, having disobedience to covenant obligations as its clearly announced cause.

If the *exile is the later counterpart to bondage in Egypt, the liberation counterpart to the earlier exodus is the restoration of Israel after exile. Some of the prophetic pictures of freedom refer to the literal return of a remnant to the Promised *Land, but in the visions of the *millennium the vision seems to broaden in scope beyond that. In both cases the return to the land is a return to God, and freedom is the result. In the coming golden age, captive Jerusalem will "loose the bonds from her neck" (Is 52:2). God himself will "break the yoke from off their neck, and . . . burst their bonds" (Jer 30:8 RSV; see also Nahum 1:13). God will "bring out the prisoners from the dungeon" (Is 42:7 RSV; see also Is 49:9; 61:1).

Slaves and Prisoners. The political bondage of nations is supplemented by two other main categories—slavery (*see* Slave, Slavery) and imprisonment (*see* Prison). The more than 250 references to slaves and slavery picture the social world of Bible times—a world in which household slaves or servants were an accepted part of the socioeconomic structure. No matter how accepted the practice was, it was nonetheless a form of bondage in which slaves were under the complete control of their masters. Freedom was the condition toward which slaves aspired; a stipulation in the Mosaic law prescribed that Hebrew slaves must be freed after six years of labor for a master (Ex 21:2). One of the reasons God sent Judah into exile was its failure to keep its promises to free slaves (Jer 34). A stock antithesis (especially in the NT) is "slave and free."

Over a hundred biblical references to prisons and prisoners show it to be a major image of bondage as well. The Bible gives us instances of both just imprisonment (2 Kings 17:4; Ezra 7:26) and unjust incarceration (Gen 39:20; Jer 37:18), but in either case imprisonment is a uniformly negative experience that takes away a person's freedom. Accordingly, release from prison is one of the most evocative images of freedom in the Bible—one that focuses on the moment of transition from bondage to freedom. One of four mini-rescue stories in Psalm 107 is of the prisoners who had "sat in darkness and in gloom, . . . in affliction and in irons," whose hearts "were bowed down with hard labor." When they cried to the Lord, "he delivered them from their distress; he brought them out of darkness and gloom, and broke their bonds asunder" (Ps 107:10-14 RSV).

Jesus and Paul. While the literal versions of bondage and freedom in the OT often shade off into metaphoric and spiritual meanings, with Jesus the primary frame of reference is spiritual. Since Jesus started no liberation movement to free slaves, his famous statement in this vein must be metaphorically intended when he claims that God "has sent me to proclaim release to the captives and recovering of sight to the blind, to set at liberty those who are oppressed" (Lk 4:18 RSV). So too in John 8:31-32: "If you continue in my word, you are truly my disciples, and you will know the truth, and the truth will make you free" (RSV). And again, "Every one who commits sin is a slave to sin. . . . So if the Son makes you free, you will be free indeed" (Jn 8:34, 36 RSV).

The motif of bondage and freedom is central to the teaching of Paul, and it takes two forms: bondage to law and bondage to sin and death.

The first Pauline motif sees the OT ceremonial law—and indeed also the moral law if it is viewed as the means for attaining salvation by purely human merit—as a bondage from which the Christian gospel of grace as God's gift frees a person through faith. The classic text is the epistle to the *Galatians, written to dissuade Christian converts from succumbing to the attempts of Judaizers to get them to adhere again to the OT ceremonial law as a necessary part of salvation. "For freedom Christ has set us free," writes Paul; "stand fast therefore, and do not submit again to a yoke of slavery" (Gal 5:1 RSV). Christ was "born under the law, to redeem those who were under the law" (Gal 4:4-5). To "rely on works of the law" for salvation is to be "under a curse" (3:10). Similarly, to place oneself under the OT law is "slavery," while choosing "the Jerusalem above is free" (Gal 4:24-25 RSV).

The customary motif of bondage to sin and death is also present in Paul. This is implied, for example, when Paul writes, "You were called to freedom, brethren; only do not use your freedom as an opportunity for the flesh," which is an implied bondage (Gal 5:13 RSV; see also 1 Pet 2:16). So too in *Romans, Paul equates sin and bondage: "You are slaves of the one whom you obey," and to obey sin "leads to death" (Rom 6:16; see also Rom 6:20 and 2 Pet 2:19, which asserts that "you are a slave to whatever has mastered you" NIV). Correspondingly, a Christian can give "thanks . . . to God, that you who were once slaves of sin have . . . been set free from sin" (Rom 6:17-18 RSV). There is an eschatological side to this as well: a day is coming when "the creation itself will be set free from its bondage to decay and obtain the glorious liberty of the children of God" (Rom 8:21 RSV).

Paul's love of paradox and metaphor leads to a further motif—that of believers in bondage or imprisonment to Christ. People "who were once slaves of sin . . . have become slaves of righteousness" (Rom 6:17 RSV). Again, "you have been set free from sin and have become slaves of God" (Rom 6:22 RSV). Elsewhere Paul pictures himself as a willing "prisoner for Christ Jesus" (Eph 3:1) and "prisoner for the Lord" (Eph 4:1). This equals the boldness of an evocative OT reference to the people of the coming restoration as "prisoners of hope" (Zech 9:12).

See also BABYLON; CURSE; DEATH; EGYPT; EXILE; EXODUS, SECOND EXODUS; PHARAOH; PRISON; REDEEM, REDEEMER; SIN; SLAVE, SLAVERY.

BONE

The Hebrews knew that the bones supported the body and that great bones meant great strength (Job 40:18). The articulations of the skeleton also provided natural divisions for sacrificial animals, whose bones should not be broken, so bone occasionally designated the severed limbs (Judg 19:29) or a "cut" of meat (Ezek 24:4). The bulk of the more than one hundred mentions of bone, however, refers not to actual bones, but to the bones as the essence of the individual, the repository of physical (Job 20:11; 30:17, 30, psychological (Ezek 37:11) and spiritual health (Prov 3:8), even of life itself. It is beyond human understanding "how the spirit comes to the bones in the womb of a woman with child" (Eccl 11:5).

Other uses of the Hebrew word for bone, 'esem, offer a wider insight into its range of meaning. Occasionally it means "essence" or "self" as in the expressions (literally rendered) "the bone of the heavens" meaning "the sky itself" (Ex 24:10) or the common idiom "in the bone of this day" meaning "on the very same day" (e.g., Gen 7:13). In keeping with this figure of speech, individuals refer to their bones when describing the deepest aspects of their lives, the core of their being, their very selves. The sensation of pain in the bones is used to express the depth of anguish (e.g. Job 30:17; Ps 6:2) and is linked with unforgiven sin and divine judgment (e.g. Ps 32:3; 38:3; 51:8; Lam 1:13; 3:4).

*Adam's description of *Eve as "bone of my bones and flesh of my flesh" (Gen 2:23 NIV) conveys his sense of the fact that, unlike the animals he has named, this new individual is profoundly and essentially him. The OT uses "bone and blood" (e.g., Judg 9:2; 2 Sam 5:1 AV; Job 2:5; cf. "flesh and bone," Lk 24:39) in the same sense that we refer to relatives as "our flesh and blood."

That a lifeless body, upon touching Elisha's bones, should receive its spirit again and stand upright underscores the importance and power associated with the bones (2 Kings 13:21; cf. 1 Kings 13:31). As the last part of the human body to decay, the bones enshrined and preserved the essence of an individual. The bones are the remains (Amos 6:10; Gen 50:25; Ex 13:19) and symbolize the fate of the individual. The bones of the wicked lie "strewn at the mouth of Sheol" (Ps 141:7). The poets often use bones to picture what remains of God's people (Ps 22:15; 31:11; 102:4; Lam 1:13; Hab 3:16). Ezekiel's

Valley of Dry Bones, like the nation (Jer 50:17; Micah 3:2-3), lacks only the Spirit of God to come to life (Ezek 37). To destroy the bones is to remove all hope of return (Ezek 37:11). Crushed bones signify utter destruction (Num 24:8; Is 38:13; Dan 6:24). The *Passover regulations prohibited breaking any of the bones of the sacrificial *lamb to preserve the integrity of its essence (Ex 12:46; Num 9:12). John, presenting Christ as the complete Lamb of God (John 19:33-36), records that his bones were not broken at the crucifixion, in fulfillment of the OT prophecy (Ps 34:20).

As the last surviving part of an individual, bones were to be treated with respect (Sir 49:15; 1 Macc 13:25). Burning the bones had serious consequences (Ezek 24:10; Amos 2:1). Joseph took care to ensure that his bones would be brought back to the Promised Land (Gen 50:25; Ex 13:19; Heb 11:22). Not to be buried but to have one's bones exposed was a sign of particular disgrace (2 Sam 21:1-15), the ignominy of which served as a common battlefield *taunt (1 Sam 17:44; 1 Kings 14:11; 16:4; 21:24) and evidence of divine *judgment (Ps 53:5; Jer 8:1-3).

To touch human bones or the graves in which they were buried resulted in ceremonial uncleanness (e.g. Num 19:16) and so tombs would be whitewashed as a warning to keep away (Mt 23:27). Bones which remained unburied led to the defilement of the land (Ezek 39:15). Contact with human bones rendered an *altar deconsecrated (1 Kings 13:2; 2 Kings 23:14-20; Ezek 6:5).

See also BODY; BURIAL, FUNERAL; DEATH.

BOOK

The Hebrew term translated "book" actually refers to anything that is written, whether it is a letter, certificate of divorce, indictment, genealogical record or volume. Several types of materials were used in ancient writing. Clay tablets were the first writing material. Animal skins were used early as well. The skins were sewn together to form a roll, which was then wound around either one or two rods to form a scroll. Papyrus rolls were used in Egypt by about 3000 B.C. and were used by the Jews to record the law of Moses. Eventually the codex, or book form, replaced the scrolls, but this was not until at least the second century A.D.

References to "book" or "books" in English translations number well over a hundred (NIV 128, NRSV 140). The majority of these references are to either the Book of the Law (also called the Book of the Covenant) or to OT court chronicles. Beyond these references the two most important and evocative "books" in the Bible are metaphoric books. One is the heavenly record of the deeds of every living person. Another is the list of names of those who will dwell in the eternal city. In Revelation this book is called the book of life (Rev 20:15). In the background is the practice in biblical times of keeping an official register of the names of citizens of a given town or kingdom. If citizenship was forfeited, the name would be blotted from the register.

The books of God's record of a person's deeds and his register of heavenly citizenship are intertwined, since a person's actions are the basis of judgment. This combination can be traced all the way back to Exodus 32:32, where Moses asks that his name be blotted out of God's book if God will not forgive Israel's sin. On the day of final judgment the book of deeds will be opened, and each person will be judged according to what he or she has done. But another book, the book of life written from the foundation of the world, will also be opened at that time (Rev 17:8; 20:12). Jesus will acknowledge before the Father and the angels those whose names are written there (Rev 3:5). Everyone will be judged from the books of deeds, but those whose names appear in the book of life will enter the eternal city (Rev 21:27). Those whose names are not written in the *Lamb's book of life will be cast into the lake of fire (Rev 20:15).

A variation of the book of a person's life occurs in Psalm 139:16, where the events that are preordained to happen in a person's life are said to be written in God's book "before one of them came to be" (NIV).

*Scroll imagery is sometimes used in prophesy as a symbol of God's revelation to the prophet. In Ezekiel 2:9—3:3 Ezekiel receives a scroll from God, written on both sides. He is told to eat the scroll, a symbol of his acceptance of God's call and revelation to him. "So I ate it, and it tasted as sweet as honey in my mouth" (3:3). Similarly John receives a scroll in Revelation (10:8-11). "Take it and eat it," he is told. "It will turn your stomach sour, but in your mouth it will be as sweet as honey" (Rev 10:9). Here the prophesy is good news to the saints, but with it comes distress, hence John's stomach turns sour. Another scroll appears in Revelation, also with writing on both sides. Here, only the Lamb that was slain is worthy to break its seven seals. Each seal brings wrath, and the scroll is opened, revealing God's judgment.

Certainly for the Jew the most important book was Scripture, even though it is rarely called that in the Bible itself. Jealously guarded by the scribes (transcribers of the OT), the meticulous and accurate preservation of the holy writings are amazing when compared to other human writings of the time that have been lost.

See also BIBLE; SCROLL.

BORN AGAIN. *See* REBIRTH.

BORROW, BORROWING. *See* LEND, LENDING.

BOSOM. *See* ABRAHAM'S BOSOM; BREAST.

BOUND. *See* BIND, BOUND.

BOW, BOWING

Bowing is one of the most basic acts of showing deference in the Scripture. The image of bowing or prostrating oneself is contained in several of the key biblical words for worship (*see* Lying Prostrate).

The most common use of bowing is to portray appropriate respect and deference. This use is found throughout the biblical narratives. Examples include Abraham bowing low before the three visitors (Gen 19:2), Abraham bowing as part of the land transaction (Gen 23:7), Ruth bowing to Boaz (Rev 2:10) and Mephibosheth bowing before his benefactor, David (2 Sam 9:8). By and large ordinary bowing is simply a detail that helps carry along the story being told. Not so for the other categories of bowing.

The first is bowing to an illegitimate object. In the Decalogue bowing to idols is used in the prescription against *idolatry: "You shall not bow down to them or worship them" (Ex 20:5 NRSV). A typical assessment of Israel during the monarchy was that "they forsook all the commands of the LORD their God and made for themselves two idols cast in the shape of calves, and an Asherah pole. They bowed

An Egyptian woman bows down with one leg drawn up beneath her to allow her to rise easily.

down to all the starry hosts, and they worshipped Baal" (2 Kings 17:16 NIV). The habitual nature of this false worship is described thus: "He walked in all the ways of his father; he worshipped the idols his father had worshipped, and bowed down to them" (2 Kings 21:21 NIV). With biting irony Isaiah describes how a person fashions an idol with his own hands and then bows down to it: "From the rest he makes a god, his idol; he bows down to it and worships. He prays to it and says, Save me; you are my god" (Is 44:17 NIV).

Another sense is bowing against or apart from one's will. In Psalm 72 one of the results of the king ordering his ways after those stipulated by God is that "the desert tribes will bow before him and his enemies will lick the dust" and that "all kings will bow down to him and all nations will serve him" (Ps 72:9, 11 NIV). Examples of this include when Israel is going to have to bow before its enemies: "Kings will see you and rise up, princes will see and bow down, because of the LORD, who is faithful, the Holy One of Israel, who has chosen you" (Is 49:7 NIV); "They will bow down before you with their faces to the

ground; they will lick the dust at your feet. Then you will know that I am the LORD; those who hope in me will not be disappointed" (Is 49:23 NIV).

See also LYING PROSTRATE.

BOW. *See* ARCHERY; ARROW, ARROW OF GOD.

BOWELS. *See* INNER PARTS, BOWELS.

BOWL

A bowl is a container, usually rounded in shape, that contains either liquids or solids. Often the word is found in a culinary context, though not exclusively. It is related to other types of containers like jars, *cups and basins. Although there is overlap between these containers, the bowl might be differentiated from the jar by shape and the basin by size.

The Bible often mentions the bowl in its literal sense, but frequently the word will have symbolic overtones. For instance, as a container a bowl can symbolize fullness and completion. In Zechariah 9:14-17 the prophet describes an appearance of the *divine warrior with the result that they will be saved from their enemies. Metaphorically the people of God are described here as "full like a bowl used for sprinkling the corners of the altar" (Zech 9:15 NIV; see Num 7:13, 19, etc., for reference to the bowls used in temple service).

The bowl has symbolic value not only in the light of its essential nature as a container but also by virtue of what it contains. A notable example of this occurs in Revelation 16 where seven angels carrying "the seven bowls of God's wrath" (Rev 16:1) pour out their contents on the earth, resulting in punishments on its inhabitants.

The bowl can also have symbolic value in the light of its use. In the OT, for instance, bowls play a major role in the worship of Israel and are closely connected to the sanctuary (Ex 24:6; 25:29; 27:3 37:16; 38:3). As such, the bowls, which surely had a literal function, also come, by virtue of their association with the holy place, to connote the presence of God and his holiness.

Furthermore in Matthew 5:15 (Mk 4:21; Lk 11:33), Jesus teaches his followers that they must be the *light of the world and that they should not obscure their responsibility by putting their light under a bowl. Such an unnatural use of a bowl over a *lamp illustrates how strange it would be to hide one's "good deeds and praise" (v. 16). In another Gospel context (Mt 26:23) Judas and Jesus have used a common bowl in their meal together. This then becomes a pointer to the one who will betray him. The irony is that a bowl shared at mealtime is a symbol of intimacy and trust. The one who betrays Jesus is one who is close to him.

The image of the bowl also appears in the famous portrait at the end of Ecclesiastes of the physiological symptoms of old age, followed by death. At the end of his speech the teacher concludes his comments on death with the image of household objects that are destroyed and rendered useless. Among other objects, we read of a "golden bowl" (Eccles 12:6). Life is like a precious and useful object that is ultimately rendered useless.

See also CUP.

BRANCH

Branches in the Bible refer either to *trees or *vines. While the overwhelming preponderance of references is symbolic, the symbol, as always, is rooted in the physical properties of the thing itself. At a literal, physical level, branches are a picture of a healthy and productive tree or vine. The branch is linked to either the solid trunk or main stock that nurtures and anchors it or the leafy outgrowth that springs from it. In the butler's dream that *Joseph interpreted, a vine's three branches *leaf out miraculously into clusters of ripened *grapes, an image of fertility and *abundance (Gen 40:10). In the exuberant picture of nature's provision in Psalm 104, the *birds are pictured as living and singing in the branches of the trees that grow by streams (Ps 104:12). The evocativeness of the branches of a healthy tree is captured by the reference in Ezekiel 19:10 to a vineyard "fruitful and full of branches by reason of abundant water" (RSV).

Mainly, though, branches provide a rich array of symbols in the Bible. In a land with regions where trees were a relative rarity, a healthy tree with strong branches readily became a symbol of strength and prosperity. If leafy, fruit-bearing branches indicate a prospering olive, vine or *fig tree, they readily become a symbol for a human family: "Joseph is a fruitful bough, a fruitful bough by a spring; his branches run over the wall" (Gen 49:22 RSV). Nations too, and especially their rulers, are referred to as trees. *Pharaoh, king of Egypt, is told to consider Assyria like "a cedar in Lebanon, with fair branches and forest shade. . . . All the birds of the air made their nests in its boughs; under its branches all the beasts of the field brought forth their young" (Ezek 31:3, 6 RSV). But because the tree became proud of its towering height, "its branches will fall, and its boughs will lie broken" (Ezek 31:12). Psalm 80 pictures Israel as a vine brought by God out of Egypt, whose mighty branches covered mountains (Ps 80:10). Tragically the vine had been cut down and burned.

Just as the branch full of leaves and fruit is an archetype of abundance and *blessing, so the broken or fruitless branch is an emblem of ruin and God's disfavor. When one of Job's counselors paints a portrait of the fate of an evil person, one of the details is that "his branch will not be green" (Job 15:32), while another counselor asserts regarding the wicked that "his branches wither above" (Job 18:16). Nebuchadnezzar's downfall is pictured as a tree that is hewn down, with its branches cut off and with birds fleeing from its branches (Dan 4:14). Extended to a national level, the image yields a picture of the Lord cutting off "palm branch and reed in one day" (Is 9:14) and hewing away "the spreading branches" of

trees (Is 18:5; see also Jer 11:16 and Ezek 15), while a nation in decline is compared to four or five pieces of fruit on the branches of a fruit tree (Is 17:6). Again the day is coming when God will burn up evildoers and "leave them neither root nor branch" (Mal 4:1).

But if branches figure prominently in the oracles of judgment, they are also present in the OT visions of coming *restoration. The day will come when "the branch of the LORD shall be beautiful and glorious, and the fruit of the land shall be the pride and glory of the survivors of Israel" (Is 4:2). Israel restored will be like a transplanted cedar that brings forth boughs and bears *fruit (Ezek 15:22-23). Within the visions of a coming golden age, the image of the branch receives special focus as a symbol of the Messiah. Thus "there shall come forth a shoot from the stump of Jesse, and a branch shall grow out of his roots" (Is 11:1 RSV). Again, "the days are coming, says the LORD, when I will raise up for David a righteous Branch" (Jer 23:5 RSV; see also Jer 33:15). Zechariah has prophecies about "my servant the Branch" (Zech 3:8 RSV) and "the man whose name is the Branch" (Zech 6:12 RSV). In these messianic prophecies the image of the branch becomes a title for God's coming leader, who will be both king and priest.

A cluster of branch images might be termed ceremonial. The OT Feast of Booths included the ritual of residing for seven days in makeshift booths made from the branches of leafy trees (Lev 23:40; Neh 8:15). The mysterious "two anointed who stand by the Lord of the whole earth" are pictured as the "two branches of the olive trees" on the right and left of a lampstand (Zech 4:12-14 RSV). *Palm branches were cut down and spread on the road in front of Jesus during the triumphal entry into Jerusalem (Mt 21:8; Mk 11:8; Jn 12:13) as part of a victory ritual.

The ability of a branch to sprout from the stumps of some types of tree makes it a symbol of *rebirth. In Job 14:7-9 the case is put that "there is hope for a tree, if it be cut down, that it will sprout again" and "put forth branches like a young plant" (RSV). As noted above, this rhythm underlies the references to the branch in the prophetic visions, where the tearing down of branches is regularly balanced with visions of branches restored or planted in the oracles that predict a coming messianic age.

When we come to the NT images of the branch, we move in quite a different world. Here the focus is on the functional side of branches and what that can tell us about *salvation. Most famous of all is Jesus' discourse about his being the true vine (Jn 15:1-6). Drawing on familiar practices of husbandry, Jesus pictures himself as the true vine and his followers as branches dependent on the main vine. Bearing fruit depends on remaining united to the main vine. Any branch that does not bear fruit is *pruned so that it may bear fruit. Anyone who does not abide in the true vine withers and is cast onto a pile of branches destined for burning.

Romans 11:16-24 elaborates the image in a similarly extended way, this time to picture the relationship of the salvation of Gentiles to the Jewish religion. The unbelief of the Jews is likened to branches that are broken from an olive tree. Gentile belief is portrayed as branches *grafted onto the existing tree. Jews who come to belief will likewise be grafted onto the tree.

We may note, finally, Jesus' parable in which he pictures a *mustard plant that becomes a tree, "so that the birds of the air come and make nests in its branches" (Mt 13:32; cf. Mk 4:32; Lk 13:19). The fantastic size of the mustard "tree" is offered as a picture of the expansive promise of the kingdom of heaven.

As we survey the image of the branch in Scripture, it is obvious that it appears most often in the prophetic visions, as an oracle either of judgment or of coming salvation. In the Bible the image inherently tends toward symbolism, and its treatment is often imaginative and fantastic, with branches being given qualities and a magnitude that literal branches do not possess.

See also FIG, FIG TREE; GRAFTING; LEAF; PALM TREE; PRUNING; TREE, TREES; VINE, VINEYARD.

BRASHNESS

Brashness (or rashness) is characteristic of those who speak or act hastily or impulsively. Although things said or done brashly are not always sinful, they generally show a lack of wisdom and need a reasoned correction. In Psalm 31:22 David confesses, "For I said in my haste, 'I am cut off from before Your eyes'; Nevertheless You heard the voice of my supplications when I cried out to You" (NKJV). In Psalm 116:11 he notes, "I said in my haste, 'All men are liars'" (NKJV).

Impulsive brashness is a preoccupation in the wisdom literature of the Bible, which offers repeated warnings against it. It shows a lack of knowledge (Prov 19:2) and is common to fools (Prov 14:29; 29:20; Eccles 7:9; *see* Folly). Impulsive haste is linked with foolish quickness to *anger (Prov 14:29; Eccles 7:9). It is an open invitation to end up being shamed (Prov 25:8) and can lead to poverty (Prov 21:5). It is even possible to be brash in one's zeal before God: "Do not be rash with your mouth, and let not your heart utter anything hastily before God. For God is in heaven, and you on earth; therefore let your words be few" (Eccles 5:2 NKJV). In the epistle of James, perhaps the clearest NT example of wisdom literature, we find the famous injunction, "Be swift to hear, slow to speak, slow to wrath" (Jas 1:19 NKJV).

The narratives of the Bible give us actual examples of the self-destructiveness of brashness. Thoughtless and impulsive zeal seized Jephthah when he made his vow to sacrifice the first thing he saw coming out of his house to meet him (Judg 11:31-39) and Uzzah when he reached out to steady the *ark of the covenant (2 Sam 6:6-7). Personal anger motivated *Moses to strike the *rock (Num 20:10-12), James and John to call for fire against the Samaritans (Lk 9:54-56) and Peter to cut off Malchus's ear (Mt 26:51-53; Jn 18:10).

Impulsive brashness may seem like a minor vice, but Psalm 106:33 links Moses' brash words with rebellion against the Spirit of God, and 2 Timothy 3:4 (NIV) puts it in a list of truly ignominious vices. Isaiah prophesies that in the future kingdom, "The heart of the rash will understand knowledge" (Is 32:4 NKJV).

See also ANGER; FOLLY.

BREAD

Bread, made of either *wheat or barley, was a staple of the biblical diet. Its importance—Sirach 29:21 calls it "essential"—appears from the phrase "staff of bread" (Lev 26:26; Ezek 5:16; 14:13 RSV), implying that bread enables one to walk. This is so much the case that bread often just means *"food" and is so translated in English versions. The phrase "by bread alone" (Deut 8:3), means "by food alone" (cf. Gen 3:19; Num 21:5; Lk 15:17).

In addition to being food for human beings, bread belongs to religious ritual. It is one of the things to be *sacrificed to the Lord (Ex 29:2; Lev 2:4-16). Legislation also directs that twelve fresh loaves (the so-called "showbread" or "bread of the presence") be always arranged on a table before the Holy of Holies (Ex 25:30; 1 Chron 9:32; Heb 9:1-5); and OT law commands that unleavened bread be part of the *Passover ritual (Ex 12:1-28).

Bread as Gift. Bread is often a gift of *hospitality (Gen 14:18). This is so much so that Jesus, when he sends his missionaries out, can tell them to take no bread for the journey (Mk 6:8). The presumption is that bread will be happily supplied to them by those who accept their message.

But bread is even more a divine gift. For it is God who fills the *hungry with good things (Lk 1:53). This is why one gives thanks for bread (Lk 9:16). Although bread is a human product—dough is made with human hands (Mt 13:33) and *baked (Is 44:19)—there is no dough without grain, and there is no grain without the *rain, which God sends (Mt 5:45). Biblical thought is appropriately captured by the traditional Jewish prayer, "Blessed art thou, O Lord our God, king of the universe, who creates the fruit of the earth."

That God is quite literally the giver of bread appears in several remarkable miracle stories. When the Israelites wander in the desert and become hungry, they find on the ground *manna, which is "the bread which the LORD has given you to eat" (Ex 16:15; cf. Ps 78:25). When Elisha is faced with a hundred hungry men and not enough bread to feed them, the Lord nonetheless says, "They shall eat and have some left." In the event all are fed and some food is left (2 Kings 4:42-44). Twice when Jesus is with exceedingly large crowds, he takes only a few loaves of bread and some fish and miraculously distributes them to everyone (Mk 6:30-44; 8:1-10)—acts of divine provision and hospitality on a grand scale.

The bread of the Eucharist is also conceived as a

divine gift. At the Last *Supper, Jesus takes bread, says a *blessing, breaks the bread and shares it with his disciples (Mk 14:22). Here the act of giving bread means that Jesus gives himself up on behalf of others; that is, under the figure of the bread, the Son of God is revealed as a sacrificial offering.

Eschatological Bread. If bread is a divine gift in the present, it will also be a divine gift when God's kingdom comes in its fullness. The occasion for Jesus recounting the parable of the *banquet (Lk 14:16-24) is a man's declaration "Blessed is he who shall eat bread in the kingdom of heaven" (Lk 14:15). This is a reference to the eschatological banquet (Is 25:6-8; Rev 19:9), as are Jesus' words at the end of the Last Supper: "I shall not drink again of the fruit of the vine until that day when I drink it new in the kingdom of God" (Mk 14:25 RSV).

Related to this is the intriguing promise in Revelation 2:17: "To the one who conquers I [Jesus] will give some of the hidden manna." Whether the image is of manna again descending from on high (as in *2 Apoc. Bar.* 29:8) or of the recovery of the golden urn of manna that was kept in the temple (Heb 9:4)—in Jewish legend the vessels of the temple were not carried off but miraculously hidden (*2 Apoc. Bar.* 6:1-10)—we cannot be sure. In either case, the eschatological promise is that the saints will be given "bread from heaven" (Neh 9:15). God will meet the needs of his people.

The Lord's Prayer. Jesus teaches his followers to pray for their "daily *(epiousios)* bread." The expression is pregnant with meaning. The (presumably) Aramaic original no doubt alluded to Exodus 16:4, where it is said regarding the manna that "each day the people shall go out and gather enough for that day." If so, then the prayer asks God to feed his people now (*epiousios* means "for the coming day" in the sense of "today") just as in the past. But given that (a) "the coming day" can be given eschatological sense (cf. "the day of the Lord"), (b) manna was thought of as bread, and (c) there was an expectation that God would send manna in the end as at the beginning, many have taken Jesus' words to refer to the bread of the eschaton (so already the *Gospel of the Hebrews,* according to Jerome).

There is no need to set the two interpretations against one another. Jesus and his first followers undoubtedly thought of the bread of his *table fellowship as being both the present gift of God and a token of God's eschatological provision for the saints. The same may be said of the bread of the Last Supper, and it is wholly appropriate that exegetical history has regularly connected the fourth line of the Lord's Prayer with the Eucharist. So "give us this days our daily bread" can call to mind four things at once—the manna in the wilderness, God's beneficent sovereignty in the present, the Eucharist, and the eschatological future.

Bread as Metaphor. Bread is sometimes used metaphorically. In Numbers 14:9 Joshua exhorts Israel not to "fear the people of the land, for they are no more than bread for us; their protection is removed from them, and the LORD is with us; do not fear them." In other words, it will be as easy to defeat the Canaanites as it is to eat bread. In Isaiah 55:2 listening to the word of the Lord is likened to eating bread. The same image lies behind Proverbs 9:5, where Wisdom invites the wise to "come, eat of my bread." It is understandable that in later Jewish tradition bread and manna become symbols of Torah (*Mek.* on Ex 13:17).

The Bible's most striking metaphorical use of bread appears in John 6. Here Jesus declares that he is "the bread of life" (v. 35; cf. vv. 33, 41, 48, 51). The image is appropriate because John 6 brings together all the major biblical themes associated with bread. The bread from heaven is said to be a gift from above—"my Father gives you the true bread from heaven" (v. 32). Jesus' multiplication of loaves and *fish recalls Elisha's similar miracle (2 Kings 4:42-44) and is explicitly compared with the provision of manna in the wilderness (vv. 31-34, 49-51). The bread that is Jesus gives life in the present (vv. 35, 47) but also means eternal life (vv. 27, 40). Finally, Jesus associates himself as the true bread with the Eucharist: "Unless you eat the flesh of the Son of man and drink his blood, you have no life in you" (v. 53).

Mention should be made, finally, of the name *Bethlehem, which literally means "house of bread, city of bread." There is obvious symbolism here: God, who provided bread in the wilderness and sent his Son as the salvific bread from heaven, ordained that Christ would be born in the city of bread.

Summary. Bread is one of many biblical images that, if traced through the canon, yields a picture of salvation history and biblical doctrine in microcosm. Salient points on the chart include bread as a staple of life that comes to all people from God's providence, miraculous sustenance of life for God's chosen people in their wilderness wanderings at the time of the Exodus, the spiritual reality of faith in Christ and his atoning death, and the participation in the coming eschatological messianic banquet.

See also ABUNDANCE; EATING; FOOD; GRAIN; HOSPITALITY; MANNA; SUPPER; TABLE; WHEAT.

BIBLIOGRAPHY. E. M. Yamauchi, "The 'Daily Bread' Motif in Antiquity," *WTJ* 27 (1964-65) 145-56.

BREADTH. *See* WIDE, WIDENESS.

BREAST

Like many other body parts, the breast has strong symbolic significance in Scripture. The breast is used as an image of female *sexuality. The picture of the *mother feeding her child at the breast is widely used as a symbol of both comfort and security. The concept of security is also picked up in the protection afforded to the exposed and vulnerable breast by the use of the breastplate as body *armor. Almost all uses of the term in Scripture relate directly or indirectly to one of these three concepts.

Solomon extols the qualities of the breasts of the

beloved woman (Song 4:5; 7:3; 8:10). Proverbs encourages the young man to restrict his sexual activities to his own wife: "May her breasts satisfy you at all times" (Prov 5:19). On the one hand, the images convey a very positive attitude toward the pleasures and comforts of sex as God-given; and on the other hand, a clear condemnation of promiscuous behavior as a misuse of sex. Hosea longs for his wife to "put away . . . her adultery from between her breasts" (Hos 2:2 NRSV).

The picture of a little *baby comforted and nourished at the mother's breast is evocative for all people and particularly significant for both the mother and the child. For the mother, having children at the breast provides both fulfillment and status: "Who would ever have said . . . that Sarah would nurse children?" (Gen 21:7 NRSV); "Blessed [are] . . . the breasts that nursed you" (Lk 11:27). But two images present the extremes: dry breasts are synonymous with childlessness (Hos 9:13; see Barrenness) and the proverb "The leech has two daughters; 'Give, give,' they cry" may allude to the frustration of nursing twins (Prov 30:15 NRSV).

For the child there is safety ("safe on my mother's breast" [Ps 22:9]), security ("Can a woman forget her nursing child?" [Is 49:15]) and consolation at the mother's breast. It may be that for the adult, the hug provides a similar comfort. Perhaps it is not stretching the imagination too much to see John's reclining on the breast of Jesus at the Last Supper in those terms (Jn 13:25, 21:20).

*Jerusalem, like all large cities, was viewed as a mother to her inhabitants, who were encouraged to "rejoice with Jerusalem . . . that you may nurse and be satisfied from her consoling breast; that you may drink deeply from her glorious bosom" (Is 66:10-11 NRSV). Even the comfort of God is appropriately pictured as that of a nursing mother (Is 49:15; 66:13). The same picture is occasionally used positively to emphasize success: "You shall suck the *milk of nations, you shall suck the breasts of kings" (Is 60:16 NRSV; cf. 49:23) and negatively to represent danger or lack of security: "Blessed are . . . the breasts that never nursed" (Lk 23:29 NRSV; cf. Job 3:12; 24:9; Mt 24:19). Beating the breast graphically symbolizes loss of security, or lack of peace of (Nahum 2:7; Is 32:12; Lk 18:13; 23:48).

The breast shelters the emotions and the breath of life. For the soldier a breastplate offered some security (see Armor). Metaphorically, the believer is encouraged to find spiritual security by wearing the breastplate of righteousness (Is 59:17; Eph 6:14), or of "faith and love" (1 Thess 5:8).

See also MILK; MOTHER, MOTHERHOOD; NURSE; SEX.

BREASTPLATE. See ARMOR.

BREATH

Breath is part of a group of words, including *wind and *spirit, that evoke a wide range of dynamic relationships between God, humanity and creation. The two main Hebrew words for this group (rûaḥ and nᵉšāmâ) are often used in parallel form, which enriches the OT images for breath immeasurably. Hebrew rûaḥ can mean "breath," "wind" or "spirit," allowing more than one interpretation of many OT passages and obscuring the outlook of the original language. For example, does an *idol have no breath in it or no spirit in it? Does the absence of breath prove that no spirit lives there (Jer 10:14)? Or the poetic observation translated as "who makes winds his messengers" (Ps 104:4 NIV) can also be translated as "who makes his angels spirits" (Heb 1:7 NKJV). Does a spirit or a breeze brush the poet's face in Job 4:15? English forces a choice between the two meanings, impoverishing the original imagery.

Like Hebrew rûaḥ, Greek pneuma can mean either "wind" or "spirit." Jesus explains the spiritual nature of God's activity by recourse to the wind (Jn 3:8). The NT usually employs separate words for "breath" and "spirit," although the ideas occasionally merge. The risen Christ breathes on the disciples and says, "Receive the Holy Spirit" (Jn 20:22).

Breath is an image that links God with humanity in creation, salvation, prophecy, faith and judgment. At the creation of Adam, "the LORD God formed man of dust from the ground, and breathed into his nostrils the breath of life; and man became a living being" (Gen 2:7 NASB). Human breath, equated with the divine breath, is an allotment of life, a portion of the divine spark and a gift (Job 27:3). The necessity of breathing becomes an image for total dependence upon God. Referring to all creation, the psalmist writes, "When you take away their breath, they die and return to the dust" (Ps 104:29 NIV; cf. Job 34:14-15). At the flood, human rejection of God is punished by the destruction of everything "in whose nostrils was the breath of the spirit of life" (Gen 7:22 NASB).

While the OT affirms that the breath of life is given by God to all humans (Dan 5:23), his breath also has a particular role in the salvation of his people. At the exodus a "strong east wind" drives back the Red Sea, after which a blast of God's breath unleashes the sea again and covers Pharaoh's army (Ex 14:21; 15:10). In describing his escape from Saul, David broadens the image of God's driving back the waters with a "blast of the breath of thy nostrils" (Ps 18:15). In the psalm as a whole, the image connects David's personal escape with both the exodus and God's original creation, when "a wind from God swept over the face of the waters" (Gen 1:2 NRSV). The psalmist also connects God's breath with creation: "By the word of the LORD the heavens were made, and all their host by the breath of his mouth" (Ps 33:6 NRSV).

In contrast to God, *idols are breathless and uninspired. The human attraction to idol worship, stemming from a trust in one's self-sufficiency, conflicts with the biblical insistence on dependence upon God for our very breath: " 'Woe to him who says to a piece of wood, "Awake!" . . . There is no breath at all inside it.' " (Hab 2:19 NASB; cf. Ps 135:17; Is 44:9-20; Jer 10:14). Appropriately, faithless and wicked human acts are judged by the breath of God: "With the breath of his lips he will slay the wicked" (Is 11:4 NASB). In the NT this breath of judgment is, in turn, transformed into the "sharp sword" that comes out of Christ's mouth in Revelation 19:15.

Ezekiel's famous prophecy derives much of its power from the evocative image of breath: "Again He said to me, 'Prophesy over these bones, and say to them, "O dry bones, hear the word of the LORD." Thus says the Lord GOD to these bones, "Behold, I will cause breath to enter you that you may come to life." ' " (Ezek 37:4-5 NASB). Ezekiel's prophecy of reinspiration parallels creation. God recreates life by giving breath to creatures whose reliance on the flesh has failed them. Just as God revivifies the remains of his people, the resurrected Jesus imparts the Holy Spirit to his disciples by breathing on them (Jn 20:22).

Breath is life; its absence is *death. Life is as hard to hold as your breath. Life fades as quickly as a mist or your breath on a cold morning (Jas 4:14). Some of the most profound biblical meditations on human limitations draw on the image of breath: "Surely every man at his best is a mere breath" (Ps 39:5 NASB). The word translated as "vanity" over two dozen times in Ecclesiastes and signifying purposelessness, emptiness and evanescence is yet another Hebrew word for breath (hebel). In these cases the constraints of human life are not due to disobedience or to ignorance of God: the image of breath conveys the mere fact of the limits of human life.

Breath evokes God's original connection to all creation; corporate and individual salvation, judgment, and the restoration of the faithful; and the ambivalence about worldly success and failure that marks the life of God's faithful people.

See also HOLY SPIRIT; MOUTH; WIND.

BIBLIOGRAPHY. H. W. Wolf, *Anthropology of the Old Testament* (Philadelphia: Fortress, 1974).

BRICKS

The most commonly used building material of ancient biblical times, bricks were usually made of mud or *clay mixed with sand and chopped *straw. This mixture was baked either in the sun or (especially for more decorative or important buildings) in pottery kilns. Kiln-burnt bricks were durable but much less abundant and were virtually unknown in Palestine until the Roman period. The cheaper and easier sun-dried bricks abounded throughout the ancient world.

Sun-dried bricks appear hard and permanent but crumble easily with rain or temperature change. Isaiah sends a warning from God to the Israelites who arrogantly boast that although "the bricks have fallen down," they will rebuild with *stone (Is 9:10; NIV). Stone is long-lasting; the bricks here picture quickly crumbling construction, possibly even of the heathen

*altars that God's disobedient people set up throughout their land to imitate the altars of the nations surrounding them. According to Isaiah such idol worshipers provoke God to his very face, "offering sacrifices in gardens/ and burning incense on altars of bricks" (Is 65:3). Such altars were made according to human rather than divine plans. They would not last, not only because the bricks would crumble but ultimately because the Lord pronounced judgment on Israel for her sinful *idolatry (see, for example, the entire passage of Is 9:8-21.)

Bricks often appear in contexts where people are constructing their own proud, temporal plans rather than obeying the eternal God. Therefore in Scripture bricks often carry negative connotations and associations: they show the limited, temporal creations of human beings, especially when those human beings have set themselves against the eternal God. The builders of the tower of *Babel begin by saying to each other, "Come, let's make bricks and bake them thoroughly" (Gen 11:3). Verse 4 even comments on their use of bricks rather than stone, which became less abundant as the people moved eastward. The bricks in this story are the concrete building blocks of the people's prideful plans. The bricks rising up toward the heavens help picture the people's hardened *hearts as they yearn for the heights and the power that belong only to God.

The most extensive mention of bricks comes in the story of the Israelites in *Egypt (Ex 1). Again, the people in control are asserting their own prideful will in rebellion against the Almighty God: the Egyptians cruelly force on God's chosen people "hard labor in brick and mortar," and their leader *Pharaoh refuses to heed God's command to let the people go (1:14; 5:2).

In each story God's supreme power prevails: he stops the building of the city and tower of Babel; he delivers his people from the hand of Pharaoh; later he punishes his people for their idolatry. Again and again bricks tell the story not only of hard, rebellious hearts but also of the fleeting, transitory rise to power such hearts enjoy.

See also BABEL, TOWER OF; CLAY; STONE.

BRIDE, BRIDEGROOM

Ideally both the bride and bridegroom are symbols of the joyful anticipation of becoming one, the final physical act of union. This God-ordained delight in creativity is reflected in the participants, blessed by this opportunity that brings immediate joy and future bliss. These are the young man and woman preparing for the journey of life, founding a *home and starting a *family, the building blocks of the Hebrew culture. For the young man, the choice of the bride was the key to the future of his line. For the bride the betrothal was the key to her whole life.

In most cultures the bride is the great transitional symbol for the young woman. Marriage marks the end of *virginity, youth and dependence on parents. In earlier cultures it was close to the time of her physical maturation. It came at the moment when she appeared most physically desirable. Though marriage was usually negotiated between two families, based on cultural factors rather than on the personal preferences of the adolescents involved, it would determine almost every element of the remainder of a woman's life. Not only did she leave her home and cleave to her husband, but she also became a functional part of the new family. She now assumed the role of *wife, and potentially of mother, the part for which she was considered destined. It would be largely as a result of the manner in which she functioned in the marriage that she would find her role in society and her fulfillment as a *woman. Under the law of coverture she was also now "covered" by her husband's status and actions. To remain unmarried was practically unthinkable for women in ancient times. Yet though marriage was rarely a matter of choice for young women, the Scripture presents the bride as a willing and happy young woman, filled with the joys of anticipation.

For the bridegroom, marriage marks the end of adolescent independence and the beginning of family responsibility. Hebrew law shows that it was somewhat less important that he be a virgin, though *purity was encouraged. He also might take more than one wife or concubine, as did some of the patriarchs and numerous of the kings. (The culmination of this was in the vast numbers of Solomon's wives and concubines, some of whom were probably political acquisitions.) If his brother died before producing male heirs, a man was expected to marry his brother's *widow. Apparently this custom was still alive in Jesus' day (Mk 12:19ff). Also, there are examples in which young men were offered sisters— Laban gives Jacob both Leah and Rachel, Samson's Philistine in-laws offer him his wife's sister as well.

The bridegroom was portrayed as a victor: he had wooed and won the beautiful and virtuous maiden, thereby winning greater respect in the community, greater financial resources and the potential of heirs. A man's sons were counted as part of his wealth, as we see in the book of Job. We later discover that the end of a civilization is signaled by the fact that "the voice of the bridegroom and bride shall be heard . . . no more" (Rev 18:23). This is John's solemn warning to the doomed Babylon.

The Wedding Customs of the Hebrews. The union of the man and the woman in *marriage is the mark of the new family. The family unit was particularly essential for those peoples committed to the covenant of Abraham. The choice of a bride and the establishment of a new family ensured that the tradition would continue. The wife was expected to pass on customs and family lore to children. Among the patriarchs this meant a particular search for the woman who would be the right wife and mother. The quests for Rachel and Rebekah are important indications that the family of Abraham thought alliances within the tribe and faith essential. This is also the reason that Samson's parents worry about his mar-

rying outside of his tribe, following his physical desires rather than his familial obligations (Judg 14:2). Later, when God selects *Mary to be the mother of Jesus, we again see the importance of the selection of the right mother, the model of obedience and faith.

The choice of the bride, establishing the bride price and the betrothal period all culminated in the central activity. Weddings apparently bore little relationship to the royal ceremonies that we have seen in the last two centuries. Rather, in a ceremony symbolizing the bringing of the bride into the groom's house, the elaborately dressed and richly bedecked bride (Is 61:10) was escorted to meet the groom. It is this procession, full of *music and laughter, that we see in the biblical symbolism surrounding marriage.

Because the ritual of marriage also celebrates the *sexual life of men and women, the day is usually filled with erotic references. The Hebrew groom and his friends would come out of his house to wait for the bride and her parade of family and friends, accompanied by musicians and the sound of tambourines. The expectant groom, outfitted in his finest apparel, wore a garland or a special crown, signifying his authority. We know that the bride wore a *veil, perhaps a symbol of her virginity, which shielded her identity until the ceremony was completed (Gen 29:23-25). In Matthew 25:1-13 we see the practice of the maidens waiting for the bridegroom, lighting their *lamps and joining the nocturnal procession. Jesus admonishes them to be prepared, lest they miss the *feast.

The actual ceremony may not have been any more elaborate than modern Jewish exchanges of vows. The main event was the entrance into the bedchamber, where the newlyweds would consummate their union. The celebration might last for a week or two, with much merrymaking and singing. Samson's wedding was apparently a drunken brawl—and the source of later problems. His taunts and prolonged entertainment of his Philistine in-laws led him to violence and to abandonment of his new bride. At the wedding at Cana (Jn 2:9) we see that even in more sedate circumstances, lavish indulgence in wine was expected. It was apparently the bridegroom's obligation to furnish the refreshments for the occasion.

If the *Song of Songs is any indication, Israelites found genuine pleasure in both male and female *beauty and sexuality. Westerners are sometimes astonished at the delight in the beauty of the male that we see here and in Psalm 45, which celebrates David's splendor. In the Song of Songs we have what appears to be an epithalamium, a marriage song, that celebrates the attributes of the bride and groom. Their physical beauty and explicit appeal is powerful in Near Eastern imagery, which uses all the senses, particularly the senses of sight and smell. The bride is pictured as pure, natural, and welcoming; the bridegroom as handsome and strong, eager for the consummation of the marriage.

The marriage ceremony itself is not pictured, probably because it is taken for granted that the audience knows exactly what is involved. But we do know from anthropologists that the Near Eastern ceremonies are less religious than social. The ceremonies lead up to the consummation, celebrating the hopes for a new life growing out of these two lovers. The mystery of the joining of the male and female is central to the story of the Jewish people. The selection of the mate is portrayed as a key decision for the man, worth traveling miles for or waiting as long as seven—or even fourteen years—for the right woman (see Jacob). She becomes the custodian of his seed, the key to his future. It is essential that she be a pure and worthy vessel.

Scripture chronicles a number of weddings. The most cursory accounts of the joining of lives in marriage occur in Genesis: *Adam and *Eve (Gen 2:22-24), Isaac and Rebekah (Gen 24:61-67), Jacob and Leah/Rachel (Gen 29:21-30). Psalm 45 is thought to be a song for a royal wedding procession. The poem portrays David as a victor—the very image of male beauty—and the processions of both bride and groom full of splendidly dressed folk wend their way to the entrance to the palace. In the Song of Songs the celebration of the wedding occurs in the very middle, surrounded by courtship lyrics. The book of Revelation gives us a spiritualized wedding of the *Lamb and those who believe in him. These all are moments of great *joy and *hope—the beginning of a new life for the bride and the bridegroom, a time for the family and the community to celebrate a new union.

Symbolic Brides and Grooms. The imagery of bride, groom and wedding is also a rich source of figurative discourse in the Bible. Many scholars have interpreted the rich language of the Song of Songs symbolically, assuming that although the primary meaning of the book concerns human sexual intimacy, the writer was ultimately describing the relationship between God and his people, between Christ and the *church.

The figurative meaning of the wedding experience appears most extensively and clearly in *Hosea, who sees the relationship as a parallel to that between God and Israel. God instructs the prophet to take to himself "a wife of harlotry . . . for the land commits great harlotry by forsaking the LORD." (Hos 1:2) Like Yahweh and his chosen people, the married couple should be bound together by mutual love and respect. When the bride proves neither pure nor faithful, she betrays the bridegroom and becomes a symbol of Israel's perfidious flirtation with other religions. The wife's infidelity is the symbol of the people's infidelity; the husband's pain in betrayal mirrors God's anguish at his wanton creatures. This extended imagery in Hosea, which was to prove the basis of much biblical imagery of the bride and bridegroom, was based on his own painful experience. Modern scholars suspect that his unfaithful wife Gomer was, in fact, a priestess of a fertility cult worshiping her pagan god with cult *prostitution. She thus becomes a symbol of both physical and metaphysical unfaithfulness.

Symbolic uses of wedding imagery are common in the Gospels. Jesus' first miracle was the changing of *water into *wine at the wedding in Cana—a ceremony that prefigures both the experience of love and the transformed significance of the bread and wine at the Lord's Supper. Jesus also uses the image of the bridegroom and the ceremony of the attendant *maidens in his parable of the foolish virgins. The preparations for the wedding and the loving attention to the coming of the bride become a parable for the coming of God's *kingdom on earth. When Jesus says, "I go to prepare a place for you," he reminds us of the diligent and loving bridegroom making his preparations for the shared home during the time of happy anticipation, that delicious time before the connubial bliss.

Paul was the first to make a clear use of the bride metaphor for the church. Christ is the "head," and the church eagerly accepts his headship, just as the bride places herself under the guidance and protection of her husband (2 Cor 11:2). The imagery of the prophet Hosea is now transformed and expanded; the image of his whoring wife has been purified and has now become the great symbol of the church, to be presented to God as a spotless bride.

In the magnificent culmination of this symbolic development, the book of Revelation, the splendid imagery is expanded to symbolize the eschatological community of the New *Jerusalem uniting with Christ—the eschatological Bridegroom. The great controlling image of the last section of Revelation (Rev 19:7-9) is the marriage of the *Lamb:

The bride makes herself ready, clothed in fine *linen, bright and pure;

The invitation is issued for the marriage *supper;

The magnificent processional with the triumphant hosts tramples everything in its path;

The gathering for the marriage supper involves elaborate preparations;

The new home is to be the new Jerusalem in which the glory of God furnishes *light, making lamps and oil unnecessary;

The guests arrive, none admitted except those whose names are written in the Lamb's book of life;

The refreshments will be the *water of life without price, and twelve kinds of *fruit.

The wedding ceremony is now the moment when Christ's church joins with him in the sacred mystery. The NT ends with the words the invitation to this sacred experience—the Spirit and the Bride say, "Come!"

See also FEAST, FEASTING; HUSBAND; MAN, IMAGES OF; MARRIAGE; WEDDING; WIFE; WOMAN, IMAGES OF.

BIBLIOGRAPHY. R. Batey, *New Testament Nuptial Imagery* (Leiden: E. J. Brill, 1971).

BRIDLE

The image of the bridle is used in the Bible primarily as an image of restraint and control. Job complains that the afflictions he has received from God have led to his enemies' throwing off restraint (literally, "let-

An ancient horse and bridle.

ting loose the bridle") and attacking him (Job 30:11). One of the indicators of the strength of Leviathan is that he cannot be subjected to such restraint, for "Who would approach him with a bridle?" (Job 41:13 NIV).

Exercising self-restraint, especially over the *tongue, is associated with this image in a number of places (Ps 39:1; Jas 1:26; 3:2-3). Without such self-control, a person "deceives himself and his religion is worthless" (Jas 1:26). The contrast between those able to exercise such restraint over themselves and the "horse and mule, which have no understanding but must be controlled by bit and bridle" is drawn out in Psalm 32:9.

The judgment of God on his enemies is pictured as a bridle "that leads them astray" (Is 30:28), an image applied specifically to Sennacherib being made to return to Assyria after threatening to invade Jerusalem (2 Kings 19:28; Is 37:29). Titus is instructed to "silence" (literally, "stop the mouths of") false teachers who are leading others astray (Tit 1:11).

See also HORSE; SELF-CONTROL; TONGUE.

BRIER

Briers surely would evoke negative memories for persons living close to the land. Everybody hates briers; they are an infuriating ground cover that trips, scratches and generally makes walking through them miserable. Briers don't just cause pain—they make you suffer. The scratches can make one's bare legs and ankles feel like they are on fire. In fact, briers and *suffering are practically inseparable in the Bible. Even the thought of being beaten with briers (Judg 8:7, 16) or having them shoved down on one's head (Jn 19:2) is painful.

Briers are used metaphorically to depict the devastating result of God's judgment—turning pleasant and productive *land into wasteland (cf. Is 5:6; 7:25; 32:13; Heb 6:8). The lasting image of briers as a nuance is seen in the familiar representation of an unpleasant person or circumstance as "a thorn in one's flesh" (Ezek 28:24; 2 Cor 12:7).

Being extremely hardy, briers are especially hard on the weak things. Small, delicate plants are no match for the voracious appetite of the brier. Jesus

had this in mind when he told the parable of the sower (cf. Mt 13:7; Mk 4:7; Lk 8:7). Finally, there is that ironic picture of the crown of thorns fashioned for Jesus as a way to mock him. The shameful tearing of his flesh is the outward display of inner suffering. Whether physical or metaphorical, briers and misery go hand in hand.

See also THORN.

BRIMSTONE

Brimstone is an archaic word for sulfur, which occurs naturally as a yellow mineral. In Palestine it is found at the surface around the Dead Sea where it has probably been formed from the breakdown of the sulfates in the sedimentary rocks. One of the few *minerals to *burn, sulfur produces an acrid and poisonous smoke made up of the oxides of sulfur. Because of this property, burning sulfur has been used as a fumigant and disinfectant for millennia, although it is unclear whether the Jews used it for this purpose.

Burning sulfur was the main element in the destruction of *Sodom and Gomorrah (Gen 19:24). References to this event, which is something of a pattern for divine judgment, occur subsequently in Scripture (Deut 29:23; Lk 17:29). Elsewhere burning sulfur is a frequent element in *judgment (Job 18:15; Ps 11:6; Is 30:33; 34:9; Ezek 38:22). In Revelation the image of burning sulfur occurs at a number of points (9:17-18; 14:10; 19:20; 20:10; 21:8), everywhere in the context of judgment. Although burning sulfur is plainly a tool of retribution on the enemies of God, there is the possibility that there is also a reference to the fumigation of the wicked and their works. If so, it reminds us that evil is so contagious and serious that ultimately this world will need disinfecting.

See also FIRE; MINERALS; SODOM AND GOMORRAH.

BROAD. *See* WIDE, WIDENESS.

BROKENNESS

Brokenness is most commonly employed in the Bible as an image for people overwhelmed by troubles. In the OT this is commonly expressed by saying that the heart or spirit is "broken." The image represents feelings of anguish and despair, and a loss of hope or a sense of well-being. A broken *heart or spirit can result from suffering, persecution and sorrow (Job 17:1; Ps 34:18; 69:20; 109:16; 147:3; Prov 15:18; Is 61:1; 65:14). It can also result from a recognition of the devastation of God's judgment on the sins of others (Jer 23:9; Ezek 21:6) or one's own *sin (Ps 51:17).

Many times these broken people turn to God for help. Several confessions of brokenness occur in the immediate context of petitions for, or confessions of, faith in God's rescue (Ps 34:17-18; 69:16-20; 109:16-21). This openness awakens God's compassion and moves him to bind up the brokenhearted (Is 61:1). In Psalm 147:2-3 the psalmist employs the language of healing the brokenhearted to celebrate God's saving actions toward the postexilic community in their struggle against political opposition and economic adversity.

In some contexts a broken person is one who responds to the prompting of the Holy Spirit in *repentance (Ps 51:17; Is 57:15). A brokenhearted person is the opposite of the self-made, hardhearted person. The fundamental difference between these two types of individuals is most evident in their reactions to being confronted with their own sins. The key element is that the brokenhearted person repents.

The accounts of the lives of Israel's first two kings, Saul and *David, as presented in 1 and 2 Samuel are telling in this regard. Both fail to carry out God's will. Saul violates Samuel's instructions to wait for him to sacrifice (1 Sam 13:8-10) and fails to completely destroy the Amalekite king and livestock (1 Sam 15:7-9). David commits adultery with *Bathsheba and has her honorable husband intentionally murdered in battle to cover up the *adultery (2 Sam 11:1-27). Both must be confronted by God's prophets in order to bring them to an acknowledgment of sin (1 Sam 13:11; 15:17-19; 2 Sam 12:1-12). Most modern readers, who consider David's offenses much graver than Saul's, are shocked to discover that Saul has the kingdom taken away from him (1 Sam 13:13-14; 15:26-29) while David is forgiven (2 Sam 12:13).

The explanation for this seeming injustice lies in the differing responses of the two men when confronted with their sin. In response to Samuel's accusations Saul first argues, then confesses, "I have sinned" (1 Sam 15:24, 30). This minimizing confession (the Hebrew could be translated, "I have violated a cultic regulation") and his further responses—self-excuse, blameshifting and greater concern for avoiding the consequences of one's actions than for the wrong itself (1 Sam 15:15, 20-30)—reveal a heart that is still resistant to God's verdict.

David's response to Nathan's parable exposing his sin is a remarkable contrast. He says simply, without qualification, protest or defense, "I have sinned against the LORD" (2 Sam 12:13). Unlike Saul, David is truly broken by God's verdict against him, vindicating the biblical assessment of David's character that he was a man after God's own heart (1 Sam 13:14; Acts 13:22).

At the outset of his public ministry Jesus quotes Isaiah 61:1 to explain his own mission (Lk 4:18-19). Subsequently, he displays great concern for binding up the brokenhearted in his focus on the spiritually "sick" (Mt 9:12; Mk 2:17; Lk 5:31), his frequent calls for repentance (Mt 4:17; Mk 1:15; Lk 13:3), his gentle dealings with sinful people (Lk 7:36-50; 19:1-10) and his parables of acceptance for the repentant (Lk 15:11-32; 18:9-14).

See also CONTRITE, CONTRITION; HEART; MELT, MELTING; SIN; SUFFERING; WEAK, WEAKNESS.

BRONZE

The patriarchal period of ancient Israel occurs in what modern historians have called the Bronze Age, and the time of the settlement of Canaan marks the change from the Bronze Age to the Iron Age. Bronze, a combination of copper and lead, was one of the earliest alloys to be widely used during the OT period. It was later replaced by brass (an alloy of copper and tin); therefore, most of the references to bronze (154 of the 160 occurrences) are in the OT.

Use of bronze as a figure of speech is concentrated in the OT poetry and prophets (two-thirds of the uses in these books are figurative) and the book of Revelation. When used figuratively, bronze often connotes strength, as seen in Job's questions "Do I have strength of stone? Is my flesh bronze?" (Job 6:12), or when describing Leviathan, who cannot be fettered, it is said that "iron he treats like straw and bronze like rotten wood" (Job 41:27 NIV; *see* Animals; Mythical Animals). In Jeremiah's call to service he is told that God has "made you a fortified city, an iron pillar and a bronze wall to stand against the whole land" (Jer 1:18 NIV). Hard and smooth, in judgment the ground will be made infertile: "I will break down your stubborn pride and make the sky above you like iron and the ground beneath you like bronze" (Lev 26:19 NIV; cf.. Deut 28:23; Job 37:18). Polished and shiny, bronze was used for *mirrors in the ancient world and is associated with shining and radiance. Bronze as associated with radiance is found in Revelation 1:15: "His feet were like bronze glowing in a furnace, and his voice was like the sound of rushing waters" (NIV). Ezekiel's heavenly creatures had legs that "gleamed liked burnished bronze" (Ezek 1:7), and later Ezekiel encountered a man whose "face shone liked polished bronze" (Ezek 40:3).

A very evocative use of bronze is its association with *bondage and captivity. Bronze shackles symbolize the treatment of fallen leaders by victorious adversaries. Two famous examples are *Samson: "Then the Philistines seized him, gouged out his eyes and took him down to Gaza. Binding him with bronze shackles, they set him to grinding in the prison" (Judg 16:21), and Zedekiah: "Then he put out Zedekiah's eyes, bound him with bronze shackles and took him to Babylon, where he put him in prison till the day of his death" (Jer 52:11).

Nearly half of all the references to bronze refer to its use in the *temple or tabernacle. From altars to *bowls, *cups, columns and frying pans, bronze was the metal of choice for implements and structures. This sturdy and easily worked metal was used throughout the Israelites' worship space.

Another sizable group of bronze references are to bronze in *warfare. Here bronze is used to describe booty (Josh 6:24; 22:8) and the implements of war. Goliath goes forth to fight with "a bronze helmet on his head" and wears "a coat of scale armor of bronze weighing five thousand shekels." On his legs he wears "bronze greaves," and he carries a bronze javelin on his back (1 Sam 17:5-6 NIV). *Helmets, *swords, spear tips and *shields all could be made of bronze or covered with it (*see* Armor).

See also IRON; METALS; MINERALS; STONE; WOOD.

BROOK

English-speaking readers unfamiliar with the rugged terrain and arid climate of Palestine are likely to miss the significance of brook imagery in the Scriptures. The two principal Hebrew words for brook (*nahal,* used 140 times, and *'āp̄íq* used 15 times) have been variously translated "brook," "stream," "ravine," "torrents," and "valley." In many cases these words fail to bring to the minds of English readers the phenomena crucial to the images employed by the biblical writers.

The *nahal* was a stream bed (commonly known as a wadi) in which water flows only after periods of rainfall. Otherwise it is dry. Job employs the inter-mittence of the brook as an image of the unreliability of his friends when he complains, "My brothers have dealt deceitfully like a brook. . . . When it is hot they vanish from their place" (Job 6:15-17 NKJV). When the rains did come, there were often dangerous flash-floods in the stream beds. It is to one of these that the psalmist refers when he writes, "The cords of death entangled me; the torrents of destruction overwhelmed me" (Ps 18:4 NIV). Amos, wanting to evoke the power of a rain-swollen brook without the implication that it will soon run *dry, calls for right-eousness to advance "like a never-failing stream" (Amos 5:24 NIV).

The *'āp̄íq* was the deepest water channel in a valley, gorge or ravine. In the drier parts of Palestine these brooks were not easy to find, nor did they always contain water. In Psalm 42:1 a deer's agoniz-ing search for these brooks is used to picture an unsatisfied longing for God. Likewise in Psalm 126:4 the restoration of the exilic community is compared to the replenishment of water in the brooks of the Negev by the rains.

Another image evoked by brooks is that of re-freshment. Many have found puzzling the reference to *drinking from a brook in Psalm 110:7 at the end of a series of statements about the exalted and favored status of the messianic king. Perhaps the point of this statement is that the king is favored by God in finding a brook with water in it to refresh himself from the weariness of battle.

See also DRINK; RIVER; RAIN; VALLEY; WATER.

BROTHER, BROTHERHOOD

The two great commandments, to love God and to love one another, address the divine and human categories of biblical relationship. Human loves such as *marriage and *friendship assume exclusive, inti-mate, volitional relationships; even love of neighbor implies a face-to-face act of kindness rather than a general feeling of goodwill. But brotherhood is a larger, more inclusive category that sometimes de-notes a connection of blood, sometimes a personal affection and sometimes a bond of allegiance such as that represented by a tribe, nation or spiritual com-munity. Most importantly, the terms *brother* and *brotherhood* imply an egalitarian relationship rather than an image of hierarchy, such as parent/*child,

*father/*son or patriarch/clan.

Many, if not most, of the characteristics of brother/brotherhood could also be extended to the biblical references to *sister(s). Although there is no specific use of the term *sisterhood* in the Bible, yet it is clear from the context of many passages where spiritual brotherhood is understood that the lan-guage is meant to be gender inclusive. The NRSV translates "brothers and sisters" in instances when it feels a mixed-gender group is being addressed.

A strong line should be drawn between literal and figurative references to brother or brothers. Ironi-cally, in the biblical record the dominant image asso-ciated with literal brothers is frequently one of discord, strife, deceit, even hatred and *murder. The first crime was fratricide. But when the word *brother* or *brothers* is used metaphorically, it takes on the characteristics of similarity and unity of purpose as-sociated with the term *brotherhood.*

Literal Brother(s). Human experience shows that relationships within the family are often the most difficult. This is especially true between siblings: envy, jealousy, competitiveness and rejection seem to occur with an almost "natural" frequency. Genesis sets the pattern for the rest of the Bible in its narra-tives of antipathy between brothers. *Cain's hatred for *Abel is the archetypal example. His "am I my brother's keeper?" stands as the epitome of heartless indifference. The first epistle of John glosses the story of Cain in particular and brotherly love in general by citing them as evidence, respectively, of inherent wickedness or of true faith: "For this is the message that you heard from the beginning, that we should love one another, and not be like Cain who was of the evil one and murdered his brother. And why did he murder him? Because his works were evil and his brother's righteous" (1 Jn 3:11-13 RSV; cf. 2:9; 4:20). The love of brothers, then, is a concrete image of the most fundamental message of the Bible, "that we should love one another."

Not only Cain and Abel, but Isaac and Ishmael, *Jacob and Esau, and *Joseph and his brothers all demonstrated the pattern of fraternal strife, treach-ery, rejection, revenge, even attempted murder. There is strife between brothers even in the *womb: Rebekah was told that two nations strove within her (Gen 25:22-23); and Perez and Zerah, sons of Judah by Tamar, also struggled for primacy of birth (Gen 38:29-30). Rachel was fiercely jealous of her sister Leah's childbearing (Gen 30:1-8). In the Gospels, Jesus' half- or step-brothers and sisters also exhibited contention with or indifference to his following God's plan of salvation and did not believe on him (Jn 7:3-10; Mt 13:56; Mk 6:3). The prodigal son's brother objects to the mercy shown his brother (Lk 15), and Martha complains against *Mary (Lk 10:39-40).

The rest of the Bible builds on these portraits of fraternal hatred and treachery in Genesis. Like a Renaissance revenge tragedy or Machiavellian in-trigue, some of its most chilling scenes document betrayal and violence between brothers, or brothers and sisters. For example, Abimelech kills his seventy brothers for power over Shechem (Judges 9), Amnon *rapes his sister Tamar (2 Sam 13), Adonijah tries to steal the throne from *Solomon (1 Kings 1) and Jehoram kills all his brothers when he becomes king (2 Chron 21:4; see also 2 Chron 22:8, 10). These typical narratives expand into horrifying images of civil war or last-days treachery. Judges portrays the civil war between "the children of my brother Benjamin" and the rest of Israel. Isaiah 19:2 and Ezekiel 38:21 record the horror that "every man's sword will be against his brother." In the apocalyptic "day of wrath" fraternal treachery will achieve such a level that brother will betray brother to death in order to escape *persecution (Is 9:19; Mt 10:21; Lk 21:16).

In contrast, harmony between literal brothers is a distinctively minor theme in biblical narrative. Jacob and Esau, and Joseph and his brothers are ultimately reconciled but at great emotional cost. "A brother offended is harder to win than a strong city" (Prov 18:18 NASB).

While the narratives tell the ugly reality, biblical laws and Proverbs evoke the ideal: a poor brother should be extended generosity (Deut 15:7-11) and never be humiliated (Deut 25:7); the sower of discord among brothers is an *abomination (Prov 6:19); and a brother is "born for adversity," that is, as a support, a *helper (Prov 17:17). Strife between brothers is not the norm but is unnatural and perverse. The divine plan was for intimacy between God and man and among the human family.

Figurative Brothers and Brotherhood in the Old Testament. The OT also recognizes the concept of a brotherhood based outside of blood kinship. On the simplest metaphorical level, brother (or sometimes, sister) connotes similarity: Job in his distress cries, "I am a brother of jackals and a companion of ostriches" (30:29) and "I have said . . . to the worm 'my mother and my sister' " (17:14), meaning that he identifies his condition with the cursed nature of these unclean creatures. The OT supplies several other metaphorical uses and images for brothers: equals in status or calling, a synonym for friend or beloved, and a community of believers.

Equality is an inherent feature of the language of brotherhood and sisterhood. It is not in hierarchical terms that the people of God address each other but in the assumed egalitarian relation of brothers and sisters. Thus the Bible uses fraternal language to describe a group that has the same calling or rank. "Brother" kings (1 Kings 9:13; 20:33), "brother" prophets (1 Kings 13:30), "brother" Levites and priests (2 Chron 39:34; 35:5-6), even false priests who eat bread together (1 Kings 23:9) are types of fraternities. (In Ezekiel, Jerusalem's unholy alliances with her "sister Samaria" and "sister Sodom" are viewed as a vile kind of sorority, Ezek 16:45-61; 23:11-33.) This sense of brotherly equality can be used to rhetorical advantage. David goes as far as calling his outlaw soldiers brothers (1 Sam 30:23)

and addresses the elders of his people as "my brethren, my bone and my flesh" when trying to persuade them to restore him to the throne (2 Sam 19:12).

In several cases brother is used as a synonym for beloved or friend. David calls Jonathan "brother" in his *lament over his death (2 Sam 1). And the beloved in the Song of Songs wishes at one point that her lover was also her brother (8:1). Even more frequently the lover refers to his beloved as his sister (Song 4:9-12; 5:1-2; 8:8). The usage is clearly to make the emotional attachment stronger through the figurative sense of brother or sister, meaning similarity. Both speakers imply that the relationship consists of, or desires to be, one of identicalness.

Whether singular or plural, brother/brethren is a synonym for members of a spiritual community. Hosea 2:1 succinctly states the point: "Say to your brethren, 'My people' " and Malachi 2:10 rhetorically asks, "Have we not all one Father? Has not one God created us?" The condition that makes all men brothers is the fact that there is one God who is the father and creator of all. Without a transcendent Father there can be no universal brotherhood. This idea is more pronounced in the NT where *Gentiles as well as Jews are included in the family of God.

Psalm 133 contains the most extended praise of brotherhood in the OT. "Behold, how good and how pleasant it is for brethren to dwell together in unity" (Ps 133:1). The psalmist uses two striking images of *anointing or *baptism to describe this cenobitic lifestyle. The first compares true brotherhood to the drenching of holy *oil, from head to toe, upon the high priest Aaron (Ps 133:2). Traditionally used to sanctify people and things for special roles or functions (e.g., to anoint kings, priests and prophets), oil is also a symbol of the richness of life as well as of the Holy Spirit. The psalmist also pictures brotherly unity like the *dew of Mount Herman, the highest peak in the land of Israel. The dew flows out to, and one might say anoints the other mountains of *Zion, where "the LORD commanded the blessing—eternal life" (Ps 133:3). The psalm's baptism-like imagery parallels and foreshadows the baptism of tongues of *fire that were manifested by another dwelling together in unity when the disciples were all with one accord in one place on the day of *Pentecost (Acts 2). The psalm's similes suggest that brotherly unity is an epiphanic experience, combining calling, holiness, life and power.

Brother(s) and Brotherhood in the New Testament. Jesus draws the best distinction between the biblical senses of literal and spiritual brothers: when a crowd tells him his mother and brothers desire his attention he asks, "Who are my brothers? Whoever does the will of my Father in heaven is my brother and sister and mother" (Mt 12:46-50; Mk 3:35; Lk 8:19-20). Here he authorizes fellow believers—or better, fellow doers—as the truest form of family, as persons with whom we have the most in common. In this context Jesus himself becomes the "firstborn of many brethren" (Rom 8:29) within the spiritually born family of God that takes precedence over one's natural *family.

The community of believers in the NT is alluded to more by the plural word *brethren* (which clearly includes women) than by any other figurative language, certainly more than by the "called-out ones" *(ekklēsia)*, or church. Brotherhood is based on similarity of belief and on the equality of believers. Christ underscores both points when he tells his disciples they should not desire to be called master or *teacher, "for One is your Teacher, and you are all brothers" (Mt 23:8).

In the Gospels, Jesus emphasizes two relational issues critical to brotherhood: forgiveness and factionalism. Right relationship is based on the ability to forgive, and Jesus sets the standard high: first be reconciled with your brother even before worship (Mt 5); a brother can sin against you seventy times seven and you must *forgive him from the *heart (Mt 18:21,35). Yet the gospel message of love extends beyond the family of faith. Jesus warns against brotherhood becoming cliquish: Don't greet only your brothers, for what reward is there in that? Love even your enemies (Mt 5). When you throw a *banquet, extend the invitation to strangers (Luke 14:12). The family of God should always be open to new *adoptions. Jesus emphasizes the high standard of love and the evangelical purpose of brotherhood.

In the Epistles, Paul and the other writers continue and expand the composition of NT brethren and brotherhood. First, "brethren" frequently prefaces Paul's teaching and exhortations. A common phrase is "I urge you, brethren" (Rom 11:25; 12:1; 15:30; 16:17) or, "I do not want you to be ignorant, brethren" (2 Cor 1:8). He uses the epithet rhetorically to call attention to key points (Gal 5:11,13), especially when there is some allegorical or nonliteral meaning (1 Cor 10:1; Gal 3:15; 4:28).

Second, his concern about order versus division in the church is strengthened by the images of unity and equality that brotherhood evokes. Paul stresses the word *brethren* when correcting the division and sectarianism in the Corinthian church. Having the "same mind and same judgment, perfectly joined together" describes the desired quality of similitude in brotherhood (1 Cor 1:10, 11). In other words, "be of one mind . . . love as brothers" (1 Pet 3:8). Even believing slaves and masters are viewed as "brethren" (1 Tim 6:2; also see Philemon). Yet brotherly equality is never used as an excuse not to serve one another.

Yet another defining aspect of brotherhood, its privilege and evidence, is service. The Thessalonians know all about brotherly love because they ministered to the needs not only of Paul but of all the brethren in Macedonia (1 Thess 4:9, 10). "Know this, beloved brethren, that if someone wanders from the truth and a brother turns him back, he has saved a soul from death and covered a multitude of sins" (Jas 5:20; see also Heb 3:12). The brethren keep each other in the truth and support the weak (Gal 6:1;

1 Cor 8:12). Romans 14 is all about not causing a brother to *stumble. We even ought to lay down our lives for the brethren (1 Jn 3:16). James calls attention to the needs of brothers *and* sisters (2:15).

Finally, Paul's language of brotherly love is passionate, intimate and affectionate. There is or should be an intensity about the brotherly bond. The Philippian brethren are "beloved and longed-for" (Phil 4:1); he tells the Thessalonians he is "endeavoring eagerly to see your face with great desire" (1 Thess 2:17), and he encourages the church members to "greet one another with a holy kiss" (1 Cor 16:20). It is a language of presence. In contrast, the church is instructed to honor secular authority, but to love the brotherhood (1 Pet 2:17).

In sum, the language of brotherhood means something more than simply believers. It is the most common and familiar appellation within the analogy of the family of God. For that reason, perhaps, it has become a buried metaphor that we no longer regard. But it is indeed an image for the ideal of closeness, like-mindedness and unity that should exist among fellow believers. Its implied egalitarianism is important; and most of all, it is *"good" and "pleasant."

See also ABEL; CAIN; FAMILY; FORGIVENESS; JOSEPH THE PATRIARCH; SISTER; STUMBLE, STUMBLING BLOCK.

BRUISE

In English, the term *bruise* usually refers to a contusion with no break in the skin surface, identifiable by discoloration. Sometimes the term is used metaphorically to speak of hurt feelings or spirit. Whereas in modern parlance a bruise is viewed as a minor injury and is almost a positive image (e.g., "he escaped with only a few bruises"), in the Bible the image is stark and powerful, with connotations of serious and repeated injury that is virtually a death blow. No single biblical term names the image; instead a number of words encompass the semantic idea of bruise, all of them denoting injury, pain and *wound.

Recent translations correctly tend to use graphic language that is more in keeping with the biblical sense. For example, the NIV translates "Blows [bruises] and wounds cleanse away evil, and beatings purge the inmost being" (Prov 20:30). The psalmist cries, "My wounds [bruises] fester and are loathsome because of my sinful folly" (Ps 38:5). Through Isaiah, the Lord declares to his disobedient people that over their entire body there are "wounds [bruises] and welts and open sores" (Is 1:6). The term translated "bruise" in Song of Songs 5:7 is rendered "emasculation" in Deuteronomy 23:1 and has crushing and cutting associated with it. An interesting usage is Jeremiah 13:23, where one of the most frequent terms used for bruise *(ḥᵃbûrâ)* refers to the stripes/spots on a tiger/leopard. Another term is variously translated "bruised" (Lev 22:24), "stuck" (1 Sam 26:7) and "fondled" (Ezek 23:3).

The most pregnant of usages is found in several pivotal redemptive texts. In Genesis 3:15 the serpent receives the promise that the offspring of the woman will bruise (NIV "crush") his head, and he will bruise his *heel. The action of bruising/crushing spells defeat for the kingdom of evil and death, and redemption and victory for the kingdom of righteousness and life (cf. Rom 16:20) at the cost of the sacrificial death of Jesus Christ.

In Isaiah 53:5 we hear that the *suffering servant, ultimately fulfilled in Jesus Christ, was pierced, crushed and bruised (NIV "wounded") for our forgiveness, redemption and peace. Further, the Lord is pleased to bruise (NIV "crush") him as a guilt offering, and as a result the redemptive purposes of God will be accomplished (Is 53:10).

Finally, the servant of the Lord will take "bruised reeds," an image of broken and fragile people (the term encompasses the notions of splintered, crushed and oppressed, cf. 1 Sam 12:3-4; Is 36:6; Amos 4:1) and heal and restore them to strength and fullness (Is 42:3; cf. Mt 12:20). In these bruised and oppressed people, and the action of bruising and crushing in the accomplishment of their redemption, we sense the power and pain that this image invokes.

See also HEEL; WOUND.

BUILD, BUILDING

To build is to exercise a primal urge to impose human order and control on the materials with which the world presents us. It is an implied resistance to both inertia and decay, and it answers to a deep-seated human need to produce something tangible and permanent. Something built is an achievement.

Most of the four hundred biblical references to building describe the literal process or product of building a physical phenomenon. In the Bible we read about the building of *cities, *towers, sheepfolds, *houses, roads, *fortresses, *walls and tombs. *Altars get built most frequently, with nearly fifty references. Sometimes we read about the materials used, such as *stone, *brick or *wood (Neh 3:35; Am 5:11; 1 Kings 15:22) or occasionally—in more expensive buildings—*silver, *bronze and *iron (1 Kings 7:9-12). References to building cluster in the books that describe the building and rebuilding of the *temple—Kings, Chronicles, Ezra, Nehemiah—and in the prophets (where building is either a positive image of blessing or figures somehow in oracles of judgment). The main picture that emerges from this world of busy building is simply one of human industry and purpose along the lines of the assertion of Ecclesiastes 3:3 that there is "a time to build." This picture of industriousness is tinged with a strong religious identity and a sense of reliance on God's providence, as expressed in the psalmist's declaration that "unless the LORD builds the house, those who build it labor in vain" (Ps 127:1 NRSV).

In addition to images of human building, the Bible posits a God who builds. He builds material things, first of all. In a day when the work of an architect and builder were not differentiated, God is portrayed as a master builder in his work of creation.

God is a hands-on builder: "My hand laid the foundation of the earth" (Is 48:13 RSV). The work of God in creation is described in terms of *foundations and beams being laid (Ps 102:25; 104:3); of measurements being determined, a line being stretched, bases sunk and a *cornerstone laid (Job 38:4-6); of upper chambers being built in the heavens (Amos 9:6). We also find concrete references to God's employing such devices or instruments as calipers and tape-measures, buckets and scales (Is 40:12; Jer 31:27; Job 26:10; 38:4-7).

What is celebrated in all this imagery is God's careful planning in creation and the intricacy and permanence of what he created. In the wisdom writings and psalms, God's work of building creation is related specifically to his superior knowledge or understanding (Job 38:4; Ps 136:5) and *wisdom (Prov 3:19-20). This comes to fullest expression in the vivid poetic portrait of a personalized Wisdom operating as an master craftsperson alongside God in an expert and playful way (Prov 8:27-31), a passage that presages NT pictures of the Word and Christ as active in the work of creation (Jn 1:1-5; Col 1:15-17; 2:3; cf. 1 Cor 8:6).

In addition to being the builder of the visible creation, God is variously pictured as building *Jerusalem (Ps 147:2) and the remnant of Judah (Jer 31:4, 28). Furthermore, God gives such explicit instructions about the building of the *tabernacle and the *temple that he emerges as the ultimate builder of these sacred places as well.

As we move toward more figurative images of God as builder, we find pictures of God as the one who builds the communal life of his people. Thus in prophetic visions of redemption God builds a secure environment for his people (Ps 69:35; Is 44:26; 65:21-11; Ezek 28:26). Salvation itself is God's building project (Is 26:1-2).

This becomes even more spiritualized in the NT, where frequently we hear overtones of temple building. Christians are portrayed as "God's building" (1 Cor 3:9), "rooted and built up" in Christ (Col 2:7). The church is the house of God (1 Tim 3:15) that stands on God's firm foundation (2 Tim 2:19). It is a house "built upon the foundation of the apostles and prophets, Christ Jesus himself being the cornerstone, in whom the whole structure is joined together and grows into a holy temple in the Lord; in whom you also are built into it for a dwelling place of God in the Spirit" (Eph 2:20-22 RSV). Christians individually (1 Cor 3:16-17; 6:19) and corporately (2 Cor 6:16) are the temple of God. Jesus promised to "build" his church on the rock of Peter's confession that Jesus is "the Christ, the Son of the living God" (Mt 16:16-18).

The image of building is used to picture the life choices that individuals make in following or refusing God's way. Jesus paints a memorable portrait of wise and foolish house builders (Mt 7:24-27; Lk 6:47-49; 18; cf. Jesus' parables of builders in Lk 12:13-21; 14:28-30). Individual Christians build on the foundation of Jesus Christ, and the adequacy of the material with which they build will be tested at the Last Judgment (1 Cor 3:10-15).

A further cluster of passages can be added if we are aware that the root word for *edify* and *edification* names the act of building (e.g., Rom 15:2; 1 Cor 14:5, 26; Eph 4:29). As a variant, we find passages that refer to "building up" the body (Rom 14:19; 1 Cor 8:1; 10:23; 14:3, 12; 2 Cor 10:8; 12:19; 13:10; Eph 4:12; 1 Thess 5:11).

Underlying these references to the church as a building is the understanding that "the builder of all things is God" (Heb 3:4 RSV). His ultimate feat of building is a heavenly "city which has foundations, whose builder and maker is God" (Heb 11:10 RSV), whose glory outshines everything imaginable (Rev 21:11), an inviting house with many rooms that Christ himself has prepared (Jn 14:2-3).

See also ALTAR; BABEL, TOWER OF; BRICK; CITY; CORNERSTONE; FORTRESS, STRONGHOLD; HOME, HOUSE; STONE; STRONGHOLD; TEMPLE; TOWER; WALL; WOOD.

BULL. *See* CALF; CATTLE.

BURDEN, LOAD. *See* HEAVY.

BURIAL, FUNERAL

In the biblical narrative it is customary for successive generations to be buried in the family tomb, either a natural cave or one cut from rock. Thus in the patriarchal narratives we find Sarah (Gen 23:19), Abraham (Gen 25:9), Isaac and Rebekah, Leah (Gen 49:31) and Jacob (Gen 50:13) all buried in the cave of Machpelah east of Hebron. Individual burial is sometimes necessitated by death at a distance from the family tomb, so Deborah is buried near Bethel (Gen 35:8) and Rachel on the road to Ephrath (Gen 35:19-20; *see* Bethlehem), their tombs being marked by an oak and a pillar respectively.

Besides weeping, *mourning includes rending one's garments and donning sackcloth (Gen 37:34-35), scattering dust on the head, wallowing in ashes, weeping and lamentation (2 Sam 1:11-12; 13:31; 14:20; Is 3: 24; 22:12; Jer 7: 29; Ezek 7:18; Joel 1:8; Amos 8:10; Mic 1:16; for Tyrian seafarers, Philistia and Moab, see Ezek 27:30, 32; Jer 47:5; Is 15:2-3; Jer 48:37) and the period of mourning might last for as long as seven days (Gen 50:10).

In the exceptional circumstance of Jacob and Joseph in Egypt, the bodies are prepared by embalming, and Joseph is placed in an Egyptian coffin (Gen 50:2-3, 26). The process of Egyptian mummification required removal of the viscera for separate preservation and packing the body in salt in order to remove moisture. The body was then packed with an impregnated linen and entirely wrapped in linen. In Genesis 50:3 we read of the embalming of Jacob taking forty days, and the Egyptians mourning seventy days.

Prompt burial, including that of the bodies of criminals who had been hung, is required by Mosaic law (Deut 21:22-23). Contact with the dead and also formal mourning bring ceremonial defilement. In addition to weeping, mourning includes actions such as tearing *garments and unbinding the *hair. But in Israel both priests (Lev 21:5) and people (Lev 19:27-28; Deut 14:1) are forbidden to cut their flesh, the corners of the beard and other such mutilations and changes of appearance. These and other practices, such as eating tithes in mourning or offering them to the dead (Deut 26:14) are Canaanite practices and are expressly forbidden. In Deuteronomy we find express limits for mourning, where women captured in war might mourn their parents for one month before marrying their captors (Deut 21:11-13) and Israel's leaders Aaron (Num 20:28-29; Deut 10:6) and Moses (Deut 34:5-8) are each honored with thirty days of mourning.

The account of Abner's burial in 2 Samuel 3:31-39 gives us a glimpse of practices in Israel. The bearing of the body on a bier to its place of interment was probably typical (2 Sam 3:31). Once Israel enters the land we find a preference for people to be buried in their ancestral inheritance in a family tomb (Gideon, Judg 8:32; Samson, Judg 16:31; Asahel, 2 Sam 2:32; Ahithophel, 2 Sam 17:23; Saul, 2 Sam 21:12-14). Samuel (1 Sam 25:1, cf. 28:3) and Joab (1 Kings 2:34) are each buried in their "house," but this may simply mean the family tomb. This general custom agrees with the notion that the dead rest with their ancestors (lit. "fathers"; e.g., 1 Kings 1:21; 2:10; 11:43).

In the cultural setting of the Bible it is a great misfortune not to be properly buried (1 Kings 13:22; Jer 16:6). Archeological evidence shows that tombs were usually located outside a town or city. There is some archaeological evidence for family tombs consisting of irregular rock-cut chamber (or chambers) with benches, reached by a short, sloping shaft blocked by a stone cut to fit over the entrance. But Isaiah has harsh words of condemnation for the palace treasurer Shebna, who is hewing his "grave on the height" and chiseling his "resting place in the rock" (Is 22:16). Pottery and other objects have been found in Israelite tombs, but they are not as elaborate as Canaanite provisions for the dead. However, Canaanite religion and burial practices were a threat to true worship of Yahweh in Israel. Isaiah 57:7-13 alludes to the wicked who make their tombs on the mountainsides, engage in idolatrous practices. Memorial pillars were sometimes erected in Israel as elsewhere in antiquity, honoring the names of the deceased (cf. Gen 35:20; 2 Sam 18:18; 2 Kings 23:17; cf. Is 56:5). Common people were laid to rest more simply in a tract of land outside Jerusalem (2 Kings 23:6; Jer 26:23), a practice that was no doubt paralleled at other towns.

In keeping with the ceremonious tone of Hebrew history, funerals are recorded with great detail. But unlike our modern ceremonies, they consist primarily of burying the body. The burials of kings and other rulers of Israel are recorded in Scripture, suggesting again the importance of the emerging story of the Israelite nation as the family of God. Those whose burials are described include Jacob (Gen 50); Nadab and Abihu (Lev 10:4-7); Aaron (Num 20:22-29); Moses (Deut 34); Joshua and Joseph (Josh 24); King of Ai (Josh 8:29); Gideon (Judg 8:32); Samson (Judg 16:31); Eli (1 Sam 4:14-18); Samuel (1 Sam 25:1); Saul (1 Sam 31:10-13); Asahel (2 Sam 2:32); Abner (2 Sam 3:31-39); David (1 Kings 2:10-12; 1 Chron 29:26-28); Solomon (1 Kings 11:41-43); Jeroboam and Rehoboam (1 Kings 14:19-20, 31); Asa (1 Kings 15:23-24); Ahab (1 Kings 22:37-40); Ahaziah (2 Kings 9:27-28); Jehu (2 Kings 10:34-36); Joash (2 Kings 12:19-21); Josiah (2 Kings 23:30) and Jesus (Mt 27:57-60; Mk 15:42-46; Lk 23:50-56; Jn 19:38-42).

The grave of an executed criminal, rebel or enemy was not honored with a proper burial, and in some instances (Achan, Josh 7:26; Absalom, 2 Sam 18:17; the king of Ai and the five Canaanite kings, Josh 8:29; 10:27) was only marked by a pile of stones. Cremation was not a Hebrew practice, but in extreme circumstances, such as when the bodies of Saul and his sons' are shamefully hung from the wall of Beth Shan, a corpse might be burned and the remains later buried in the ancestral tomb (1 Sam 31:12-13; cf. Amos 6:10).

Notable deaths sometimes occasioned poetic *laments. So David laments over Saul and Jonathan (2 Sam 1:17-27) and Jeremiah and others over Josiah (2 Chron 35:25). Professional mourners sometimes appear (cf. Jer 9:17-18; Amos 5:16). In Jeremiah we find the mourners' fast broken after the funeral by a meal (Jer 16:7; cf. Hos 9:4). The funeral of Judean kings is sometimes occasioned by a great bonfire in their honor (2 Chron 16:14; 21:19-20; Jer 34:5).

In the NT we find some mourning and burial scenes. A throng of mourners at Jairus's house weep and lament the death of his daughter (Mk 5:38; Mt 9:23), making a great disturbance and presumably beating their breasts in grief (as Lk 18:13; 23:48). Similarly Stephen's burial is accompanied by deep mourning (Acts 8:2). Jairus even hires pipers for the mourning of his daughter (Mt 9:23), presumably to accompany a formal dirge.

Some accounts give us glimpses of the preparation of a corpse for burial. Tabitha (Dorcas), whom Peter raised, was washed and displayed in an upstairs room (Acts 9:37). The arms and legs of Lazarus and Jesus are bound in linen bands impregnated with aromatic perfumes, and a piece of linen is wrapped around their heads (Jn 11:44; 20:6-7). Normal Jewish burial customs are reflected in the anointing of Jesus' feet or head at Bethany (Mt 14:3-9; Jn 11:2; 12:7); but when the women visit the tomb to anoint Jesus, their plans are averted (Mk 16:1; Lk 23:56).

The practice of burial in an earthen or rock tomb coincides with the imagery of going "down" to the grave (Ps 22:29; 28:1; 30:3, 9; 88:4; 115:17; 143:7) and into an abyss (Ps 88:11), a depth (Ps 63:9; 88:6) or even a prison or place of confinement (Ps 88:8). It is a realm of gloom and darkness where the light of the sun cannot penetrate (Ps 88:6; 143:3), a realm of silence (Ps 94:17; 115:17). Imagery of decay is also associated with burial, for the dead return to the dust from which they came (Ps 90:3; 104:29; cf. Gen 3:19).

See also DEATH; GRAVE; MOURN, MOURNING.

BIBLIOGRAPHY. E. Bloch-Smith and R. Hachlili, "Burials," *ABD* 1:785-94.

BURNING. *See* FIRE.

BURNING BUSH

The burning bush is a *theophany. While in one sense Exodus 3:1—4:23 is about *Moses's encounter with the divine, it is primarily concerned with God's revelation of himself (see Deut 33:16; Mk 12:26; Lk 20:37; Acts 7:30-34). Accordingly we find God sharing his personal name with Moses in Exodus 3:14. The bush itself was most likely some kind of bramble, and the fire burning the bush was in the form of the *angel of the Lord, since the phrase in verse 2, "appeared to him in a flame of fire" (NRSV), probably conveys the idea of "as a flame of fire."

That God reveals himself as a fire is an image of his *holiness. Fire is often pictured biblically as a purifying and refining instrument of God's holiness. Furthermore, Exodus 3:5 contains the command for Moses to remove his sandals (*see* Barefoot), "for the place on which you are standing is holy ground." (See also the parallel in the calling of Joshua in Josh 5:15.)

That God reveals himself as a *fire is also an image of his *glory. This particular self-revelation of God should not be seen primarily as something designed to produce *fear—though understandably it does so (Ex 3:6)—for the fire is not consuming (though it certainly could be, see Deut 4:24, 9:3, Heb 12:29). Rather the burning bush is meant to convince Moses of the majesty of God and to stand as a visible reminder in the many dark times ahead. Thus it is no accident that this act of God's self-revelation takes place at *Sinai, where God would soon reveal his holiness and glory to the entire nation of Israel.

See also BAREFOOT; FIRE; GLORY; MOSES; SINAI.

BUSH, BURNING. *See* BURNING BUSH.

BUTTER

The image of butter in the Bible is rendered problematic by uncertainty over exactly what *milk product is in view in various passages. Butter, curds and cream are all made by churning milk, and translators do not always agree as to which is in view. Recent translations reduce the ten instances of *butter* in the KJV to just one—Psalm 55:21, where it is texture not nutrition that is in view: "His speech was smoother than butter, yet war was in his heart; his words were softer than oil, yet they were drawn swords" (RSV). The process of making butter yields the proverb "Surely the churning of milk bringeth forth butter, and the wringing of the nose bringeth forth blood: so the forcing of wrath bringeth forth strife" (Prov 30:33 KJV).

See also MILK.

BUZZARD. *See* BIRDS.

C

CAIN

To readers of the Bible, Cain's impact may seem disproportionate to the space his story occupies, though his appearance as the first son of *Adam and Eve, born outside Eden, is strategically located in the biblical narrative (Gen 4:1-17). Cain reappears in at least three brief allusions in the NT, where features of his archetypal profile are evoked, and he plays a prominent role in Jewish thought (cf. 4 Macc. 18:11; Josephus *Ant.* 1.52-66).

Cain in the Old Testament. The name Cain *(qayin)*, while etymologically associated with words for "smith" or "song," stands in narrative juxtaposition with Eve's exclamation at his birth: "I have acquired *(qānîtî)* a man from Yahweh [or by Yahweh's help]" (Gen 4:1). What sort of son is this first of the firstborn of humankind that Eve has acquired? Whereas his younger brother *Abel is a migratory keeper of flocks, Cain is a settled tiller of the soil. Although the two brothers are characterized by this fundamental rivalry of the ancient world (cf. Jacob and Esau, Gen 25:23-28), their more significant rivalry is revealed in the offerings they bring to the Lord. Cain offers "some of the fruit of the soil" (Gen 4:3 NIV), but Abel offers "fat portions from some of the firstborn of his flock" (Gen 4:4). From a Levitical perspective both are acceptable gift offerings to God, but the more copious description of "fat portions" and "firstborn" of Abel's sacrifice hints at a richer offering than Cain's.

God's favoring Abel's offering and his refusal to favor Cain's entices our sympathy for Cain. But then the downcast face slips like a mask to reveal Cain's inner anger. The Lord probes the source of Cain's anger and instructs him in the two ways: "Do what is right and you will be accepted; do not do what is right, and sin, like a beast, is crouching at your door, ready to have you. Master it!" (Gen 4:7).

Cain is speechless, but his actions typify those who have chosen the second path and are consumed by anger. Divine instruction exacerbates sin, and *brother *farmer invites brother *shepherd into a field, assaults and kills him. Anger begets *murder, and the promising bond of brotherhood is ruptured as sibling rivalry degrades to fratricide. The one who sacrificed his firstborn of the *flock and offered them to the Lord is now slaughtered by a firstborn and given to the earth. When God inquires, "Where is your brother Abel?" Cain responds in shocking but memorable callousness: "I don't know. Am I my brother's keeper?"

For the first time, Abel is not silent. His *blood cries out to the Lord from the ground. The ground Cain's hands tilled to yield his offering to the Lord has now opened its mouth to drink in Abel's blood from Cain's hand, and now it yields a voice of *lament and condemnation. Cain's judgment is just. Now when he works the ground, it will no longer yield its crops for him. He will be "a restless wanderer on the earth." The once settled farmer now enacts a self-accusing mockery of his slain brother's nomadic life.

Cain is most eloquent when pleading his case in self-pity: "My punishment is more than I can bear! Today you are driving me from the land, and I will be hidden from your presence" (Gen 4:14 NIV). The echo of *Adam's recent expulsion from the good land of Eden (Gen 3:24) is too close to be missed, but the larger narrative pattern of Israel's history is also forecast. Israel, when she has sealed her choice of the path of disobedience to Yahweh's way, will be *exiled from the land of promise, scattered as a people and separated from the *temple presence of the Lord. Cain's punishment bears these same features in his restless alienation from the land and from the presence of God, and his laboring under the threat of death. His punishment is mitigated when a "mark" and a divine edict protects him from the threat of *vengeance.

Cain, the archetypal exile, lives in the land of Nod, "wandering" east of Eden. He becomes a metaphor for all those whose misdeeds have brought them under the curse of heaven. Yet the narrative betrays complexity behind these images of arid, isolated and rootless judgment. Cain fathers a son and goes about building a *city to stay his *wandering and a lineage to perpetuate his life, issuing in vengeful Lamech. But Cain's lineage is only a spur on the main line of the narrative, for Adam and Eve have a new son, Seth, who is born to replace Abel and establish a righteous line of descendants.

Cain in the New Testament. Abel heads the list of worthies in Hebrews 11. This allusion to the Cain and Abel story throws the brothers into bold contrast with Abel coming to the fore. "By faith Abel offered to God a more acceptable sacrifice than Cain's" (Heb

11:4 NRSV), and God approved him as righteous. Abel's inner faith and consequent divine approval are in focus, not the type of offering he brought to the Lord.

In 1 John 3:11-15 the author expands the Cain-killed-Abel motif to illustrate the consequences of hating rather than loving one's brother. Cain, we read, "belonged to the evil one" (1 Jn 3:12; an estimate in tune with the Jewish *Apocalypse of Abraham* 24:5, which finds Cain "led by the adversary to break the law"). He murdered his brother simply because his own actions were evil and Abel's were righteous. Likewise, the world hates believers simply because they are righteous and love one another. Anyone who hates his brother is a murderer like Cain.

In Jude 11 false teachers, who are characterized as speaking abusively and ignorantly and living by instinct like unreasoning animals, are said to have "taken the way of Cain." The story and image of Cain appear barely beneath the surface in Romans 7:11-25. Sin that lurked at Cain's door and desired to have him, now seizes the opportunity in the commandment and "killed me" (Rom 7:11). Like Cain, the "I" has been instructed in the good and knows it but does evil nonetheless, a captive slave of sin. And like Cain, who finds the sentence of wandering and the specter of death more than he can bear, the cry is uttered: "Who will rescue me from this body of death?" (Rom 7:24).

A cluster of negative images ripple out from the Cain narrative. His name remains indelibly associated with images of *anger, *murder and a waywardness unchecked by wisdom, a cursed wanderer whose sage informs all who might be tempted to leave the fertile fields of faith to scavenge for existence in the barren land east of Eden.

See also ABEL; BROTHER, BROTHERHOOD; CRIME AND PUNISHMENT; VENGEANCE; WANDERER, WANDERING.

BIBLIOGRAPHY. N. T. Wright, "Echoes of Cain in Romans 7," in *The Climax of the Covenant* (Minneapolis: Fortress, 1992) 226-30.

CALF

Cattle in general were of great importance economically in both nomadic and agricultural conditions. They were raised as a source of *milk (Is 7:21-22) as well as meat. Calves, like the adult bovids they would become, were a symbol of wealth and prosperity. Successful calvings were a mark of *blessing (Job 21:10), and large herds of cattle made one rich. When Saul defeats the armies of Agag, he disobeys God and does not destroy the fat calves and *lambs (1 Sam 15:9). Instead Saul tries to keep them for himself as spoils from the victory God gave him. His attempt to boost his wealth only succeeds in having the kingdom wrested from him and given to David (1 Sam 15:27-29).

In addition to suggesting prosperity the youthfulness of the calf suggested playful strength and boundless energy (Ps 29:6; Mal 4:2). Like other animals that required training, calves served metaphorically for unbridled human behavior that required chastening (Jer 31:18; Ps 68:30). As agricultural peoples the Israelites and their neighbors were familiar with the devotion of a cow to her calf (1 Sam 6:7) and what stresses could loose such bonds (Jer 14:5).

A calf is also a picture of *substitution, although it is not as common a sacrificial animal as is the bull. A year-old calf serves as a burnt *offering (Lev 9:3), and a calf of no specified age as a sin offering for Aaron (Lev 9:2, 8; cf. Heb 9:12, 19). In a *covenant-making rite similar to those attested among their neighbors, the Israelites passed between the parts of a slaughtered calf to ratify a covenant (Jer 34:18; cf. Gen 15:9-10). The implication here is that whoever breaks the covenant will be butchered and torn apart like the slaughtered calf.

A fatted (grain-fed, stall-kept) calf also symbolized hospitality and celebration. When guests arrived, proper etiquette dictated a meal with meat (Gen 18:7; 1 Sam 28:24). This show of proper respect for the guest also provided an opportunity to display the prosperity of the host. The indolence of the calf tied in its stall for fattening typifies those who do no work (Jer 46:21). A diet of fatted calves marks an opulent, indulgent life style (Amos 6:4). The fatted calf appears as a symbol of exuberant celebration in the parable of the *prodigal son (Lk 15:23). In the days prior to refrigeration, meat was used quickly; hence the amount of food butchered indicates the size of the celebration. A feast built around the slaughter of a "fattened calf" might well include as many as two hundred guests (*see* Hospitality).

Calves and bulls played a prominent role in the art and religious texts of Mesopotamia, Asia Minor, Phoenicia and Syria. In the biblical narrative, golden calves were worshiped under Aaron at Sinai (Ex 32) and later under Jeroboam I (1 Kings 12). In both cases the calves were identified as representations of Yahweh and linked to his power in bringing the people out of Egypt.

The calf, as the issue of the powerful bull (*see* Ox, Oxen), functions as a symbol of potential power and perhaps even symbolizes the relationship of the king to deity with overtones of divine kingship. A calf's head decorated the back of Solomon's *throne (1 Kings 10:19). Calflike feet contribute to the wonder of the composite creatures in Ezekiel's (Ezek 1:7). The second of the four living creatures surrounding the heavenly throne in the Apocalypse has the features of a calf (Rev 4:7 NASB).

In the future age the calf, as representative of defenseless domesticated creatures, will peacefully coexist with wild animals (Is 11:6). This juxtaposition of wild and tame animals living in harmony stresses the placidness of calves and their vulnerability and uses the calf as a symbol of tranquillity and peace.

See also ANIMALS; CATTLE; OX, OXEN.

CALLING, VOCATION

Calling or vocation is the action of God in summoning people to specific tasks or roles. A sense of sanction or *apologia* attaches to a calling from God: if a person is called by God to a task or position, this is regarded within the Bible as constituting a sufficient defense of a person's committing himself or herself to it. In addition to such sanction, we can note the element of compulsion: if God calls a person, it is never in doubt that a person is under obligation to obey the summons. The Puritan division of callings into the two categories of general and particular remains a valid distinction for categorizing the Bible's images of calling. The general calling is the call of God to believe in him as Lord and Savior and to follow his prescriptions for living. Particular callings are God's leading into specific tasks and roles in life.

General Calling. The first person to receive a direct call from God to live the godly life of faith and obedience was *Abraham (Gen 12:1-9). The content of the calling was specifically to "go from your country and your kindred and your father's house to the land that I will show you" (Gen 12:1), but Abraham's response was really a response of faith and obedience to all that God designed for Abraham's life of relationship to him. W. R. Forrester correctly claims that "Abraham was the first man with a definite, explicit sense of vocation. 'Faith' ever afterwards was a response to a 'call' from God" (Forrester, 23). The imagery surrounding this original vocation story in the Bible is primarily threefold. One motif is the aura of divine *authority as God's transcendent *voice comes from beyond the earthly sphere to lay a claim upon his creature. A second is the sense of creaturely obligation to obey, pictured as Abraham's breathtakingly prompt and decisive response: "So Abram went, as the LORD had told him" (Gen 12:4 RSV). A third motif is the element of faith and trust that such response requires, as Abraham commits himself to a life of following God's leading to an unidentified "land that I will show you" (Gen 12:1).

Subsequently in the OT the general call of God is extended to nation of Israel, and again it is primarily a spiritual call to faith and obedience. In fact the spiritual vocation of OT Israel was virtually synonymous with the idea of the *covenant. The specific word *calling* is not a relevant consideration here, but instead the general pattern of covenant relationship between God and Israel, based on a premise of obedience/blessing and disobedience/curse. The passages that highlight the national calling of Israel are the giving of the law at Mt. Sinai, Moses' farewell discourse in the book of Deuteronomy, where he accentuates the obligations of a people that have been called by God to live in a distinctive way, and the lament of the prophets that the nation has not lived as God has called it to live.

By the time we reach the NT, the specific word *calling* is used in passages that speak of God's summons of people to a life of faith in Christ and his regeneration of their hearts that enables them to follow that summons. We read variously about being "called into the fellowship of [God's] Son, Jesus Christ our Lord" (1 Cor 1:9), "called . . . out of darkness into [God's] marvelous light" (1 Pet 2:99), "called in the one body" of believers (Col 3:15) and "called to be saints" (1 Cor 1:2). Paul wrote to Timothy about "the eternal life to which you were called when you made the good confession" (1 Tim 6:12 RSV), and to the Thessalonians about being called "through our gospel" to be saved (2 Thess 2:13-14). Here the calling of God is the general call to salvation and sanctification that comes in the same form to all people.

Calling or vocation stories are a genre within the Gospels. Usually the designation is applied to the stories in which Jesus called the twelve disciples to follow him in a life of religious instruction and service. Although the disciples are in some sense a special case, in another sense they are representatives of the human race generally, called to follow Christ as their leader and savior. But the Gospels actually contain many "calling" stories in which Jesus confronts people with his claims as the Savior of the world and summons them to commit their lives to him.

Particular Callings. *The call to religious service.* In addition to the general calling to the life of faith and obedience to God, the Bible gives numerous pictures of God's calling of people to specific roles and tasks. Sometimes these are specifically religious ones. Thus in the OT we find some memorable "calling" scenes. One is the calling of *Moses on the occasion of the *burning bush (Ex 3—4), where God summons Moses and promises to equip him for the task of leading his people out of *bondage in Egypt. The role to which Moses is here called is partly spiritual—to be a spiritual leader—and partly political—to guide a fledgling nation in the position of an authority who makes the crucial decisions for the entire group. God also commissioned Aaron and his sons to the duties of Israelite worship (Num 18:1-7). Gideon too is called by God to a position of national leadership (Judg 6).

Equally dramatic are the calling scenes of some OT prophets. Chief among them is Isaiah, whose call is accompanied by a majestic scene of God's sitting on his heavenly throne and the prophet's sense of unworthiness to be God's messenger, followed by God's equipping him when a seraphim places a burning coal from God's altar on Isaiah's lips (Is 6:1-8). Similar calls are recorded for Jeremiah (Jer 1), Ezekiel (Ezek 1—3), and Amos (Amos 7:15). The three dominant motifs in these calling stories are (1) an overpowering vision of God's authority, (2) a sense of human unworthiness to accept the call, (3) God's overcoming any resistance and equipping the person to fulfill the demands of the calling and sometimes (4) God gives a confirming sign that will equip the person to accomplish the call.

The NT counterpart to the vivid OT calling scenes is the story of Paul's conversion on the way to

Damascus (Acts 9:1-19), where the dominant image pattern is the dazzling *light of God, the resultant temporary *blindness and helplessness of Paul and his recognition that he is encountering the heavenly Lord. While on one level this is the general call to salvation for Paul, it is more than that: God is also calling Paul to be "a chosen instrument of mine to carry my name before the Gentiles and kings and the sons of Israel" (Acts 9:15 RSV)—in other words, to be an apostle and missionary. Paul accordingly begins most of his epistles by asserting in one form or another that he was "appointed a preacher and apostle and teacher" (2 Tim 1:11 RSV).

In addition we may note the calling or vocation story as a subgenre in the Gospels. All of these stories narrate Jesus' calling of one or more of his twelve disciples. The call itself is static (to follow Jesus as a disciple), as is the response (immediate leaving of everyday duties to follow Jesus), though the circumstances in which Jesus finds various disciples is diverse. The images that dominate the scenes are the authority of the one who calls over a person's life and the instantaneous and lifechanging outcome of the call in the life of the disciples.

Beyond specific calling scenes, the dominant image of calling to religious office in the NT occurs in lists of church offices (Eph 4:11; 1 Cor 12:28), where the emphasis is on God's equipping people with the requisite "gifts" (endowments and aptitudes) to perform designated religious services within the church. Here we get an impression of the democratization of the calling to religious service, in the sense that the possibility of spiritual vocation is extended to ordinary people, not simply the giant figures whose callings were dramatic and extraordinary. What is retained, though, is the tremendous dignity that attaches to a religious calling and the sense of obligation that believers feel to respond to any call that comes from God.

Ordinary vocations. We come, finally, to ordinary vocations—ordinary tasks and roles that people fill in the world. Quite apart from specific images or pictures of God's calling people to these offices, we should note first that it is simply in accord with the Bible's picture of God's sovereign providence for the human race that the roles and tasks in which people find themselves are part of God's design for their lives. The picture that emerges from the Bible is that God has arranged society in such a way that there are farmers, housewives, hunters, soldiers, kings, chariot drivers and dye makers. Within the framework of overriding divine providence, it is a fair inference that no one else but God could have called people to their places in the world.

Specific passages confirm the general pattern. God "chose" David and "took him from the sheepfolds" to be the king of Israel (Ps 78:70-71). Political leadership as a vocation also emerges from Samuel's comment to King Saul that "the LORD anointed you king over Israel" (1 Sam 15:17).

The most extended picture of ordinary skills as a calling from God occurs in two passages that describe God's calling and equipping of the artists who worked on the *tabernacle (Ex 31:1-6; 35:30—36:2). The specific imagery of calling pervades the passages, with such terms as "called," "filled with the Spirit of God," "appointed," "inspired," "filled with ability." And the tasks to which the people were thus called and for which they were equipped are the abilities required by the specific tasks facing the artists: "craftsmanship," "cutting stones," "carving wood," "embroidery," and "ability and intelligence to know how to do any work in the construction of the sanctuary."

Two NT passages confirm that the ordinary roles and tasks of life are, indeed, callings from God. Paul answered the question of how conversion affects one's vocations in life by saying, "Let every one lead the life which the Lord has assigned to him, and in which God has called him. . . . Every one should remain in the state [KJV, calling] in which he was called" (1 Cor 7:17, 20 RSV). In other words, conversion to Christ does not require a change in one's vocation in the world. In a parallel passage John the Baptist answered the question raised by those whom he had baptized regarding what they should do about their vocations by advising them to remain in their existing vocations, with care to pursue them in a moral way (Lk 3:12-14).

Summary. God's calling of people extends to both the spiritual life of faith and sanctification—a call to enter God's *kingdom and live as upright citizens of that kingdom—and to human life in the fabric of earthly society. The imagery centers around the fact that two people are involved in the transaction—an authority figure (God) who issues the call and a subordinate figure who responds to the call. In the Bible, vocation never exists in freestanding isolation; it always presupposes a relationship between God and the creature. In keeping with the different levels on which the two stand, God's call is something that a person is obligated to obey. In fact, calling stories can also be called "response stories." It is no exaggeration that in the Bible's picture of calling we can find the Christian life in microcosm.

See also ABRAHAM; AUTHORITY, DIVINE AND ANGELIC; ISRAEL; MOSES; PROPHET, PROPHETESS; WORK, WORKER.

BIBLIOGRAPHY. W. R. Forrester, *Christian Vocation* (New York: Scribner's, 1953); P. S. Minear, "Work and Vocation in Scripture," in *Work and Vocation,* ed. J. O. Nelson (New York: Harper & Brothers, 1954), 32-81; L. Ryken, *Redeeming the Time: A Christian Approach to Work and Leisure* (Grand Rapids: Baker, 1995).

CAMEL. *See* ANIMALS.

CAPTIVE, PRISONER. *See* BONDAGE/FREEDOM; PRISON.

CATALOGS. *See* RHETORICAL PATTERNS.

CATTLE

Cattle played a central role in the economic life of biblical peoples. They served a variety of functions, including plowing (Deut 22:10; 1 Sam 11:5), *threshing (Deut 24:4), pulling carts (1 Sam 6:7), providing *milk (Deut 32:14; Is 7:22) and meat (1 Sam 28:24), and serving as *sacrifices (Lev 1:2). Cattle were considered property, and their well-being was regulated in the Mosaic law (Ex 20:10; Lev 19:19; Deut 22:10; 25:4). Ultimately God is the owner of "the cattle on a thousand hills" (Ps 50:10 NIV).

Owning large herds of cattle was a mark of wealth (Gen 13:2; Job 1:3; Eccles 2:7). The seven sleek and lean cows of *Pharaoh's dream (Gen. 41:1-4) made an apt figure for the prosperity and prostration of all Egypt. Livestock is frequently mentioned as a *blessing of God for obedience (Deut 7:14; 28:4; 30:9; Zech 2:4). In the same way, seizing the livestock of the enemy was often one of the benefits of victory in war (Deut 2:35; 3:7; 20:14; Josh 8:2; 1 Sam 23:5). Conversely, one sign of God's displeasure was the diminishment and destruction of cattle (Lev. 26:22; Deut 28:51; Jer 5:17). In one of Job's speeches he attacks the traditional view that successful herding depended on one's righteousness. He comments regarding wicked people: "Their bulls never fail to breed. Their cows calve and do not miscarry" (Job 21:10 NIV).

Closely connected with the image of cattle as signifying God's blessing is that of God's protection of the cattle. Isaiah prophesies of God's provision for cattle in the future messianic kingdom (Is 65:10). The book of Jonah ends with God rebuking *Jonah for his lack of compassion for the Ninevites, in sharp contrast to God's own concern even for the cattle dwelling there (Jon 4:11).

Biblical authors also employ various types of cattle as symbols or metaphors. In the Song of Moses the majesty of the tribes of Ephraim and Manasseh is compared to that of a firstborn bull (Deut 33:17). In Psalm 68:30 the psalmist emphasizes the power of Egypt by calling it "a herd of bulls among the calves of the nations." Perhaps the calf and cow of Isaiah 11:6-7 should be taken as metaphors for the weaker and more harmless nations of the earth, who will dwell peacefully with aggressive peoples in the messianic kingdom.

The cattle of Bashan were renowned for their quality. Hence the psalmist compares his opponents to bulls of Bashan in strength (Ps. 22:12). Ezekiel, summoning the carrion-eating *animals to a feast on the corpses of the hordes of Gog, tells them the *banquet will be like feasting on the livestock of Bashan (Ezek 39:18). Amos felicitously dubs the Samaritan gentlewomen "cows of Bashan" when rebuking their wretched excess and indolence (Amos 4:1).

The rambunctiousness of calves made an apt figure for God's people freed from oppression in the day of the Lord: "You will go out and leap like calves released from the stall" (Mal 4:2; see also Ps 29:6). Calves were also used as *sacrifices (Lev 22:26; Num 23:1). Jeremiah 34:18 reflects the use of a calf for a formal *covenant-making ceremony, in which the contracting parties walked between the halves of a slaughtered calf while swearing an oath. The notorious use of calves as idols in the wilderness (Ex 32) and by Jeroboam in the northern kingdom of Israel (1 Kings 18:28-33) may reflect the use of the bull to represent the Egyptian god Apis or the Canaanite practice of representing gods riding on bulls or calves.

Since every head of cattle was precious, eating a calf was reserved for only the most special occasions. Thus Amos points to banqueting on fattened calves as evidence of excess (6:4). In the parable of the *prodigal son, the father's decision to kill a fattened calf shows that he regarded his son's return as a matter for high celebration (Lk 15:23).

See also ANIMALS; CALF; MILK; OX, OXEN.

CAVE

Caves are natural openings and hollows in the rocks of *mountains and hills. They are especially prone to form in limestone, and since limestone is plentiful in Palestine, so are caves. Three main motifs of caves appear in the Bible: caves as *burial sites, as dwellings and as *hiding places.

The most prominent burial cave is the celebrated one at Machpelah (Gen 23; 25:9; 49:29-32; 50:13). NT examples are the tomb of Lazarus (Jn 11:38) and of Jesus (Mt 27:59-61).

References to dwelling in caves are similarly sparse but evocative. One of the most tragic verses in the Bible is Genesis 19:30, which tells us that Lot "dwelt in a cave with his two daughters" (RSV). Dwelling in a cave is here an image of primitivism and perhaps even barbarism, of life reduced from the civilized state and the material prosperity that Lot had known heretofore, and of fearful exile (Lot "was afraid to dwell in Zoar").

The purported security of caves is challenged by Jeremiah in his oracle of judgment against Edom when he asserts that God will bring it down even though its people "live in the clefts of the rock, who hold the height of the hill" (Jer 49:16 RSV). And in the awe-inspiring catalog of people persecuted for their faith in Hebrews 11, we read about believers "wandering over deserts and mountains, and in dens and caves of the earth" (Heb 11:38 RSV).

Most caves mentioned in the Bible are those used as hiding places. Usually they are places of safety and rescue, as when David hid from Saul in caves (1 Sam 22:1-2; 24; Ps 57:1). Obadiah hid a hundred prophets in two caves to escape death at the hands of Jezebel (1 Kings 18:4, 13), and Elijah likewise hid from Jezebel in a cave (1 Kings 19:9) at which God appeared to him (v. 13). In a time of oppression by the Midianites, the Israelites "made for themselves the dens which are in the mountains, and the caves and the strongholds" (Judg 6:2 RSV).

A whole tradition of desert spirituality arose, which recognized that the solitude of a cave can provide a place to hear the "gentle whisper" of God (1 Kings 19:12). But if caves can be secret hiding places, they can also become prisons, as when Joshua traps five enemy kings in a cave at Makkedah, and then makes it their tomb (Josh 10:16-27).

See also BURIAL, FUNERAL; HIDE, HIDING; ROCK; STRONGHOLD.

CEDAR. *See* LEBANON; TREE, TREES; WOOD.

CENTER. *See* MIDDLE, CENTER.

CHAFF

Chaff evokes an image of lightness, instability and worthlessness. Scripture uses many *harvest or agricultural images as figures of judgment: *pruning, pulling weeds, *threshing, picking, sorting sheep and goats, and winnowing (Mt 13:30; Lk 22:31). In winnowing, *grain is threshed in order to separate the kernel of grain from the husk and *straw. The mixture is thrown into the air with a winnowing fork or shovel. The *wind blows the light husks away, the heavier straw falls near the edge of the threshing floor, and the grain falls back to the floor to be collected. Both the light husks and the heavier straw are referred to in the words translated "chaff" in the Bible.

In Scripture chaff illustrates something that is trivial, harmless and light: "slingstones are like chaff" to leviathan (Job 41:28 NIV; cf. 13:25). Furthermore, chaff is something that is ephemeral, dead and worthless in contrast to something that is stable, flourishing and alive. The wicked are like chaff compared to the righteous, who are like a living, *fruitful tree (Ps 1:3-4). Chaff is something that is easily driven away and discarded by the wind. Again, such are the wicked (Ps 35:5; cf. Job 21:18; Is 40:24; 41:15; Jer 13:24; Dan 2:25). In Scripture the image of chaff parallels images of blown tumbleweeds (Ps 83:18; Is 7:13), fine dust (Is 29:5; 41:2), the morning *mist, the early *dew and smoke escaping through a window (Hos 13:3).

One of the terms used for chaff, *qaš*, also includes the meaning "straw" or "stubble" (cf. Ex 5:12). Metaphorically, chaff pictures something not worth keeping, to be burned up by *fire— whether God's enemies (Ex 15:7; Num 1:10) or apostate Israel (Is 5:24) or the faithful being sifted by Satan. This is the category of imagery John the Baptist uses when he speaks of Jesus with a winnowing fork in his hand to gather the wheat into the barn and to burn up the chaff (*achyron*) with fire (Mt 3:12; Lk 3:17).

See also FIRE; GRAIN; HARVEST; STRAW; THRESHING, THRESHING FLOOR; WHEAT.

CHAOS

When Paul rebukes the Corinthians for their un-

seemly style of worship, he founds his argument on God's character: "God is not a God of disorder but of peace" (1 Cor 14:33 NIV). Paul may have easily drawn such an understanding of God from the Scriptures. Wherever the images of chaos (confusion, disorder, meaninglessness and formlessness) are present in Scripture, they are uniformly understood as standing in opposition to God and his *creation purposes. Thus even an archetypal image like the *sea, which represents chaos in ancient Near Eastern mythology and world literature in general, takes on an added significance in the Bible precisely because of its tie to creation. Whereas in the Near Eastern myths there is a static, unresolvable, dualistic tension between chaos and order, in the Bible there is a dynamic, historical tension between chaos and personal Creator.

In the beginning God finds the earth to be "formless (*tohú*) and empty" (Gen 1:2); but through a series of creative acts, God imposes order upon the cosmos. The order is declared to be "good." Adam, who is made to share God's image as well as the divine impulse toward order is to "rule . . . over all the earth and over all the creatures" (Gen 1:26). This contrast in Genesis between the formlessness of the primordial cosmos (Gen 1:2) and the harmony developed within the creation order (Gen 1:3—2:25) will eventually become the starting point for nearly all subsequent images of chaos.

In several instances God is depicted as actively bringing chaos to bear on man's rebellion. Such is the case with the Tower of *Babel when its builders were confounded in their ability to communicate with one other (Gen 11:7). In his prophecy against Edom, Isaiah reveals God as the *"builder" of chaos: paradoxically, the Creator God will "stretch out the measuring line of chaos and the plumb line of destruction" (Is 34:11). Like many images of judgment, chaos is seen as a temporary reversal of the creation order, a reversal ultimately calculated to secure redemption.

Generally speaking, however, chaos seems not to be the direct result of divine intervention; rather it is intrinsically characteristic of any society, culture or institution that divorces itself from the one "who holds all things together" (Col 1:17). The connection between spiritual bankruptcy and the decay of the moral/societal order is a recurring prophetic theme, especially with Isaiah (Is 9:15; 19:12; 24:10), and is also expanded on in the first chapter of Romans. Paul is also one of several NT writers who, building on biblical and mythological tradition, employ the sea as a metaphor for chaos in the individual's psychological processes (Eph 4:14; Jas 1:8). Yet ultimately the biblical tradition decisively departs from the mythological dualism of order and chaos in that the former anticipates a new earth where "there is no longer any sea" (Rev 21:1) nor any chaos, but only a perfected, ordered realm under God.

See also CREATION; ORDER; SEA.

BIBLIOGRAPHY. B. W. Anderson, *Creation Versus*

Chaos: The Reinterpretation of Mythical Symbolism in the Bible (New York: Association Press, 1967); S. Niditch, *Chaos to Cosmos: Studies in Biblical Patterns of Creation* (Chico, CA: Scholars Press, 1985); B. Waltke, *Creation and Chaos* (Portland, OR: Western Baptist Theological Seminary, 1974).

CHARACTER TYPES

Most character types receive extended treatment in individual articles in this dictionary, and the discussion that follows is therefore mainly a taxonomy of character types arranged in a master plan. The idea of character types is rooted in the theory of *archetypes*—recurrent phenomena that keep coming up as we read literature, including the Bible. Of course archetypes occur in literature and the Bible because they are present in life itself.

The two most enduring elements in narrative works are undoubtedly *plot and character. As we read, we pay attention not to only the action as it develops but to the people who play out that action. We evaluate the reality of the characterization, noting the individuality of the portraits created by the author, but also recognizing ourselves, our friends and our enemies. This element of recognition is sometimes so pronounced that we realize we are reading the portrayal of a character type; that is, a person who for all his or her individuality also displays certain traits that are repeated again and again throughout literature.

The usefulness of being aware of character types as we read is that they help the material to assume a more familiar shape to us. Archetypes are the basic components of literature, including the Bible. Being aware of them makes the text we are reading at a given moment fall into place. Furthermore, because archetypes appear throughout the Bible, they become a leading means by which the Bible as a whole becomes a unified book to us.

An important thing to note about character types is that many of them exist in a dialectical form, meaning that we find good and bad versions of them. Thus we find the ideal *husband and the tyrannical husband, the ideal *wife and the shrewish wife, the model *child and the problem or wayward child (*see* Favored Child, Slighted Child). The benevolent *king finds a counterpart in the *tyrant, and the virtuous grandmother like Timothy's grandmother is balanced by the wicked *queen Athaliah, who sets out to kill off the entire royal family (2 Kings 11:1). The *saint is defined partly in antithesis to the *sinner.

As an extension of the importance of the dialectical principle, the general headings of *hero and *villain also pervade the world of character types. Regardless of the specific moral or social role that a character fills in the clusters that appear below, the deep-structure reality underlying the whole scheme is the impulse of a character type toward goodness or evil. The reason for not including a separate section on heroes and heroines (though *see* Hero, Heroine) is that except for character types who fall into the category of villain, the Bible holds out the possibility of virtually any type becoming heroic. We can speak of the king as hero, the mother or father as hero, the *priest as hero. Nor is the list limited to people of high social standing, as often prevails in extrabiblical literature. With moral and spiritual integrity as the determining qualification for heroism, the *servant or singer or *farmer can emerge within a given story or proverb as an exemplary and representative person.

Placing a character into his or her archetypal category does not cancel the individuality and uniqueness of the character. It only identifies the character at a general level in addition to an individual level. As members of the genus *"sibling rival," such species as *Cain and *Abel, *Jacob and *Esau, and *Joseph and his brothers all possess their own unique ways of pursuing their rivalry with a sibling. Placing individuals into the right character type can even be a way of highlighting the individuality of a character by leading us to note the specific ways a character fleshes out the type. Characters are more than types, but they are not less. While the type should not be allowed to become a substitute for the individual, we will see biblical characters more accurately if we place them into their archetypal category.

As with plot motifs, there is no single scheme by which to arrange the whole lexicon of character types. If there is a single principle underlying the following clusters of character types, it is the importance of role or function in determining categories. A secondary principle is moral experience (producing types like the proud person or the liar) and spiritual experience (resulting in types like the penitent and the sinner).

Family Roles. If we doubt that the Bible is a book about and for *families, the large number of character types based on family roles should prove the point. The basic family unit consists of the *wife and *husband. The addition of *children (*see* Daughter; Son) introduces the roles of *mother and *father, as well as *brother and *sister. More specific types fall under these categories, such as the *barren wife, the fruitful wife and the *widow. Children spawn a cluster of antithetical character types, including the *favored child and slighted child, the *elder child and *younger child, the model child and the wayward or problem child. *Sibling rivals also loom large in the Bible.

Vocational Types. In literature as in life, people's vocations determine types into which they fall. Usually these types are determined by functions that a character habitually fills based on his or her vocation. In the Bible the *servant and steward loom large, not only as a reflection of ancient social practices but also because the Bible elevates the image of servanthood to define the creature's/believer's relationship and duties toward God. Even the *slave can become a positive image in such a worldview, though more often slaves appear in the familiar role of an oppressed person. The Bible has been called a book by workers about workers for workers (*see* Work, Worker), for in it we find a host of specific vocations represented, including *shepherd, *nurse, *farmer, *hunter, *fisherman, craftsman and merchant. The scribe can be either a court or a religious figure in the Bible, and the poet similarly can be either a court poet writing as a professional or a private composer (usually of devotional poetry). The military world generates its own cluster of character types, including the warrior (*see* Battle Stories), spy (*see* Spy Stories), *watchman and messenger or courier. The royal *court also contributes a range of vocational types.

Authority Figures. A small but important category of character types consists of human authority figures (see Authority, Human). The most important of these is the *king and more infrequently the *queen. We also catch glimpses of the actual political importance of the courtier—an adviser to the king or ruler, such as Joseph, Mordecai and various advisers named in the OT historical chronicles. In a book where divine and human judgment looms large, it is not surprising that the judge is an evocative, awe-inspiring figure. And corresponding to the archetypal servant and steward is the master. Beginning with the book of *Exodus, moreover, we find references to various leaders, including generic leaders like *Moses, the elders among the traveling Israelites during the exodus and the OT judges. The reformer can also be an *ad hoc* authority figure if the reform is successful.

Religious Figures. The Bible is a religious book, and the prominence of religious character types attests this. One cluster is vocational or professional in nature. Here we find *prophet/prophetess, *priest, church elder and deacon/deaconess, singer in the temple, *disciple, missionary, sage or wise man, *pilgrim, and *teacher or rabbi. Another grouping of religious types is defined more by spiritual standing than by vocational role. Here we find the *martyr, *suffering servant, convert (*see* Conversion), penitent (*see* Repentance) and *saint.

Social Types. Social roles also account for a large cluster of character types. The lover and the beloved, for example, are recognizable types, as are the *bride and bridegroom. The *matchmaker or go-between and the *virgin are related figures. Age generates character types, chiefly at the two ends of the age spectrum: the *young person and *old person. Other character types defined in terms of social role include the *neighbor, host (*see* Hospitality), *guest, property owner (*see* Own, Owner) and *witness.

An additional set of social types consists of the unfortunates of society. The list includes the *beggar, runaway, outcast, prisoner (*see* Prison; Bondage; Slave) and *wanderer. In a more ambivalent status we find the *foreigner or sojourner (*see* Wanderer) or *exile, and the traveler (*see* Travel Story).

Functional Character Types. Another set of character types is defined by the narrative function they fill in the dynamics of a story or situation. The

*trickster and *eavesdropper are examples. So are the *underdog and the *avenger. The *substitute plays a specific role in a story, as do the deliverer (*see* Rescue), the *quester and the *sufferer. Unidealized types include the *dupe (the easily deceived person), the *giant, the churl or *refuser of festivities and the *tempter. A stock character is the attendant or confidant(e) of the hero or heroine. Spouses, of course, often fill this role; but other examples include Aaron in relation to Moses, Jonathan to David, Mordecai to Esther, Elisha to Elijah, the disciples to Jesus.

Villains. Various types of *villains make up the final category. While some characters in the stories of the Bible exist in our imaginations as villains simply because they are antagonists to good characters, most villains are defined in terms of a specific character trait or vice, social role, or function in a situation or action. The archetypal villains of the Bible include the *prostitute, *seducer/seductress, *adulterer, traitor, *rebel, *murderer, oppressor or persecutor, *tyrant, *tyrannical father/husband, *domineering mother/wife, *thief, *trickster, *robber, hypocrite or deceiver, liar, flatterer, coward, fool (*see* Folly), *drunkard, wayward child and false religious leader. Whatever specific vice a villain displays, he or she belongs ultimately to the archetype of the *sinner.

See also PLOT MOTIFS.

CHARIOT

In the nearly 150 references to chariots in the Bible, three categories of references dominate: chariots as royal vehicles, chariots as battle vehicles and the divine chariot. Chariots were used for *warfare, *hunting, parade and *travel. In warfare they were a mobile platform from which to shoot volleys of arrows to soften up enemy infantry. If the chariot came to a standstill, javelins could be used for throwing or thrusting. Chariots served as arms for flanking or pursuing. In hunting, game would be driven across the path of the chariot on suitable terrain. In Egypt the Pharaoh and royal family were conveyed in chariots in a procession to the temple on a feast day. Travel in chariots is implied in various texts (e.g., 2 Kings 5:9), but this would have been impractical and very fatiguing since there was insufficient space for a seat.

References to chariots in battle present a varied picture. "Chariots of iron" carries a technical force denoting military superiority—an insurmountable force on the plains (Josh 17:16, 18; Judg 1:19; 4:3, 13 RSV). We also read about the noise produced by chariots in battle (Judg 5:28). Overall, the references to battle chariots paint a picture of great military strength—a swarming and frightening power on the battlefield.

Yet chariots do not assure success in battle, and several famous stories of defeat are associated with chariots. Chariots become ineffective when they become mired in water or mud (Ex 14:25; Judg 4—5). Ahab's chariot becomes the site of his death when he disguises himself in a futile attempt to cheat the divine oracle (*see* Cheat the Oracle) and is struck by a stray arrow shot by an enemy soldier at random (1 Kings 22). The war chariots of Joram and Ahaziah become their funeral cars (2 Kings 9:24-26; 28). We read about the hamstringing of horses and burning of chariots as a decisive disarmament of a defeated enemy (Josh 11:6; cf. 2 Sam 8:4). When the poet

An Egyptian war chariot.

wishes to paint a picture of God's final defeat of human striving, he describes God's burning the chariots with fire (Ps 46:10).

Even in battle references, chariots are usually understood to be a royal image. Large numbers of chariot horses can be a measure of the might of a king (2 Sam 8:4; 1 Kings 4:26; 10:26-29). This same quality of being an index to a king's wealth and power can make chariots an image of royal exploitation of a nation's people, as the king takes their sons to serve his military machine (1 Sam 8:11-12). The chariot as a status symbol is implied in the aspiring Absalom's getting himself "a chariot and horses, and fifty men to run before him" (2 Sam 15:1 RSV).

Elsewhere the chariot is an image of swift movement. Jehu was legendary for his speed in the chariot; in fact, he is said to drive it "furiously" or "like a maniac" (2 Kings 9:20 NRSV), as he uses it to deliver divine justice to Joram (2 Kings 9). Sometimes the chariot is a means of quick flight (1 Kings 12:18; 18:44).

The chariot is important in biblical imagery about God the Divine *Warrior. God makes the *clouds his chariot, a metaphor based on the swift horizontal movement of both chariots and clouds (Ps 104:3). In the vision of Ezekiel the throne of God is supported by the winged living creatures and the wheels of a chariot aligned in their movement, creating a vehicle that not only flies through the sky but moves along the ground (Ezek 1:5-15). The vision of Ezekiel draws on several images: a *storm, a cherubim *throne and a cloud chariot (cf. Nahum 1:3; Ps 18:7-15). This would not have been foreign to the ancients: an Assyrian relief at Maltaya depicts a goddess on a throne supported by composite winged creatures that ride on the back of a walking *lion

(*ANEP* § 537). Ezekiel develops such a portable divine throne with biblical imagery about God. His living creatures have faces of a man, a lion, an *ox and an *eagle, reflecting the power and sovereignty of God over each of the great spheres of creation. The nails in the rims of the chariot wheels have become eyes, reinforcing the expression of divine omnipresence depicted in the four faces. The eyes, growing out of the image of the chariot wheel, come to serve as an independent metaphor of the divine omnipresence as "the eyes of Yahweh that range throughout the earth" in Zechariah 4:10 (cf. Rev 5:6).

The motif of the divine chariot appears elsewhere as well. Elijah is taken into heaven in "a chariot of fire" drawn by "horses of fire" (2 Kings 2:11-12 RSV). When God opens the eyes of Elisha's servant, he sees that the mountain around Dothan is "full of horses and chariots of fire" (2 Kings 6:17 RSV). Covering the ark of the covenant in the temple is a "golden chariot of the cherubim that spread their wings and covered the ark" (1 Chron 28:18 RSV). In Zechariah 6 four chariots, drawn by horses of varied colors, come from the presence of God to execute judgment.

The image of the chariot appears three times in the NT. Philip witnesses to an Ethiopian eunuch riding in a royal chariot (Acts 8:28-38). By implication at least three people can get into this chariot: the driver (Acts 8:38), the Ethiopian eunuch (8:28) and Philip (8:31). As a court official of Candace, queen of the Ethiopians, the chariot is again associated with royalty and its retinue. In the visions of Revelation the noise of the wings of the terrifying locusts is "like the noise of many chariots with horses rushing into battle" (Rev 9:9), and chariots appear in the catalog of evidences of the commercial might of Babylon (Rev 18:13).

See also DIVINE WARRIOR; WARFARE.

BIBLIOGRAPHY. Y. Yadin, *The Art of Warfare in Biblical Lands* (London: Weidenfield and Nicolson, 1963).

CHARMS. *See* MAGIC.

CHEAT THE ORACLE

Stories in which a human character tries unsuccessfully to escape the fulfillment of *an oracle or prophecy are familiar to ancient literature. The most famous example in Greek literature is the Oedipus story, where human characters' attempts to evade a horrible prophecy of fratricide and incest lead to its tragic fulfillment. The Bible contains more than a dozen examples of the archetype. In none of these stories does anyone successfully cheat God's oracle. Sometimes the results are tragic, but there are also comic variations in which people's inability to thwart an oracle produces a happy ending. As we might expect, plot reversal is common in these stories when characters who think they can cheat the oracle find that they cannot. The ingredients that make up a cheat-the-oracle story are four: (1) God prophesies what will happen in a person's life; (2) the person is deluded into thinking that he or she can outwit the *prophecy; (3) the person either ignores the prophecy or implements a series of actions designed to refute it; (4) God's prophecy is fulfilled.

The Tragic Thread. The *tragic thread begins with the story of the *Fall (Gen 3), where Satan instills in *Eve the vain belief that she can eat the forbidden fruit with impunity (cf. Eve's admission that "the serpent beguiled me, and I ate" [Gen 3:13 RSV]). Other tragedies fit the pattern as well. *Samson becomes so overly confident in his ability to conquer all situations with his superior strength (despite his repeated violations of his Nazirite vow) that even after his hair has been cut, "he awoke from his sleep, and said, 'I will go out as at other times, and shake myself free.' And he did not know that the LORD had left him" (Judg 16:20 RSV). No biblical character undertakes more elaborate means to circumvent God's prophetic word than King Saul, who first thinks that he can trick the prophet Samuel into thinking that he has obeyed God's command (1 Sam 15) and then thinks he can prevent *David from becoming his successor as God promises (1 Sam 15:15-18) and as Saul himself senses at a relatively early point (1 Sam 18:7-9).

OT history provides further examples. Although the oracle that Rebekah consulted predicted that "the elder shall serve the younger" (Gen 25:22), Isaac attempts to trick the oracle when he makes plans to confer his blessing on Esau rather than Jacob (Gen 27). When God announces that the Israelites who believed the majority report of the *spies will inhabit the Promised *Land, a remnant tries unsuccessfully to conduct a foray into Canaan (Num 14). Ahab chooses to disregard Micaiah's prophecy that he will be killed in battle, only to die from a stray arrow drawn "at a venture" (1 Kings 22:1-40). Jonah tries to evade God's oracle of judgment against Nineveh by refusing to pronounce it.

In the NT, when Jesus predicts that Peter will deny him three times before the rooster crows, Peter presumptuously denies it and aggressively follows Jesus into the courtyard precincts, where his very attempt to refute Jesus' prediction of denial puts him into the position in which he fulfills the prophecy.

The Comic Thread. Stories in which human characters try unsuccessfully to trick an oracle are not uniformly tragic. In Virgil's *Aeneid* the Harpy's prediction that the Trojans would be reduced to eating their tables is fulfilled when the travelers arrive in Italy and eat the barley cakes on which their meat and fruit had been served. In one of Ovid's stories, Deucalion and his wife Pyrrha, sole survivors of a universal flood, are initially horrified at the command to throw the bones of their great mother behind them; but when they decide that their mother is the earth and her bones the stones, they obey the oracle and the earth is repopulated. The Bible too has its comic versions of the cheat-the-oracle motif.

Dorothy Sayers called the *Joseph story the happiest and "most charming of all the cheat-the-oracle stories." As in the Oedipus myth the very steps Joseph's brothers take to thwart the prophetic dream of their eventually *bowing down to him lead directly to its fulfillment. But whereas the brothers had envisioned Joseph's elevation to be bondage to them, it turns out to be redemptive, as Joseph himself observes to his brothers at the end of the story: "As for you, you meant evil against me; but God meant it for good, to bring it about that many people should be kept alive" (Gen 50:20 RSV; cf. Gen 45:7-8).

With the *covenant promises that God pronounces on the patriarchs in Genesis serving as a backdrop, *Pharaoh's futile attempts to oppress the Hebrew nation emerge as attempts to defeat the oracles of God. God had promised repeatedly to "multiply" the patriarchs' descendants, and this language is deliberately echoed in Exodus 1:7-20. The narrator tells us laconically, "But the more [the Hebrews] were oppressed, the more they multiplied and the more they spread abroad" (Ex 1:12 RSV). In other words Pharaoh becomes yet another victim of the ironically doomed attempt to cheat a divine oracle that had predicted numerous descendants for the patriarchs.

The earthly life of *Jesus provides examples at both the nativity and the crucifixion and resurrection of how a futile attempt to thwart God's oracle can lead to a happy conclusion. At the nativity Herod's attempt to defeat the prophecy that from Bethlehem "shall come a ruler who will govern . . . Israel" (Mt 2:6 RSV) is thwarted by the wisemen's returning by another route and the escape of the holy family into Egypt. Jesus' subsequent life, moreover, unfolds against a background of OT messianic prophecies (reaching as far back as Gen 3:15) about a coming savior who would defeat evil and establish an eternal kingdom of peace and righteousness. *Satan's attempt to thwart this prophecy of Christ's victory is frustrated in the wilderness temptation. Furthermore, the crucifixion, which Satan and Jesus' enemies no doubt expected to put an end to their troubles with Jesus, leads directly to the fulfillment of God's plan for salvation history, inasmuch as it is through Christ's atoning sacrifice that Satan's defeat is secured. In the words of one of Paul's sermons, the very people who crucified Christ "because they did not . . . understand the utterances of the prophets . . . fulfilled these by condemning him" (Acts 13:27 RSV; cf. v. 29, which states that "they had fulfilled all that was written of him"). Moreover, thinking to kill Christ, his enemies actually made possible the resurrection that sealed Christ's conquest of sin and death.

A final category of stories with happy endings are those in which a prophecy of death or calamity is overcome by God's retracting the oracle. Thus God sent Isaiah to Hezekiah with the oracle that "you shall die, you shall not recover" (Is 38:1 RSV). But when Hezekiah repented, God added fifteen years to his life. God similarly relented in his prophecies to destroy a nation in response to the intercession of

Moses (Ex 32:9-14) and the repentance of Ninevah (Jon 3:10).

Summary. Stories of futile attempts to circumvent an oracle from God are built on a dichotomy between God and people. Above all, they tell us something about the divine-human relationship, in which God is sovereign and people are finite, rebellious, arrogant and presumptuous toward God's sovereignty. Human characters in these stories face an option and exercise a choice: to accept the divine purpose or to rebel against it. To adopt the second plan of action leads to inevitable defeat for the people who undertake it. The most obvious virtue these stories enjoin is submission to the divine will. The cheat-the-oracle stories in the Bible demonstrate the truthfulness and reliability of God's word and the folly of trying to thwart it. They celebrate God's superiority over people.

See also COMEDY; ORACLE; PROPHET, PROPHETESS; TRAGEDY.

BIBLIOGRAPHY. D. L. Sayers, "Oedipus Simplex: Freedom and Fate in Folk-Lore and Fiction," in *The Poetry Search and the Poetry of Statement* (London: Victor Gollancz, 1963) 243-61.

CHEMOSH. See GODS, GODDESSES.

CHERUBIM. See MYTHICAL ANIMALS.

CHILD, CHILDREN
Of the more than five hundred biblical references to child and children, about half are literal. Allusions to children in the poetic and prophetic books of the OT as well as in the Gospels are mostly figurative.

The age span implied in the term *child* is imprecise. It includes the preborn (Job 3:16), infants (yet uncircumcised), weaned children (Ps 131:2) or persons of any age who are thought of as heirs or progeny, such as the children of *widows, who are called to care for their parents (1 Tim 5:4). Childhood contrasts the present time with the past (Gen 8:21; Is 47:12, 15; Ps 37:25; Mk 9:21). The phrase "When I was a child" suggests a considerable time gap (Hos 11:1; 1 Cor 13:11; Gal 4:3). Youthful days are recalled as a time of vigor that is lost in later life: Job recalls a man whose "flesh is renewed like a child's; it is restored as in the days of his youth" (Job 33:25 NIV).

The Symbolism of Childhood. The symbolic meaning of the child image is best understood by dissimilarity from adulthood. Paul says, "When I was a child, I talked like a child, I thought like a child, I reasoned like a child. When I became a man, I put childish ways behind me" (1 Cor 13:11 NIV). Though the speaker suggests relief from childhood, childish ways are a blend of powerful innocence and frustrating immaturity.

In a positive light, childhood represents simplicity and *innocence. An innocent child is cherished by his or her parents (Ps 103:13; Lk 9:48). Humble in heart (Mt 18:4), a child understands things "hidden

from the wise" (Lk 10:21) and offers praise to God that silences avengers (Ps 8:2). It is in these respects that Jesus deems childlikeness as the essential quality for entering the *kingdom of heaven (Mt 18:3; 19:14; Mk 10:15; Lk 18:16). Jesus evokes an aura of innocence and ignorance when he calls his disciples "children!" (Mk 10:24). Paul's phrase "dear children" suggests both his affectionate care and their naiveté (1 Cor 4:14; Gal 4:19; 1 Jn 3:18, 4:4)

The two sides of childishness as opposed to adult ways are clearly stated by Paul: "Brothers and sisters, do not be children in your thinking; rather, be infants in evil, but in thinking be adults." (1 Cor 14:20 NRSV). Of differences between children and adults, he names the positive—an innocence toward evil—and the negative—a thoughtlessness toward life.

In one sense childish immaturity is relished as a revelation of the learning process. Children can perform simple tasks like writing (Is 10:19). They perceive basic truths like "knowing" when to leave the *womb (Hos 13:13), being known by one's actions (Prov 20:11) and seeing *idolatry as wrong (Jer 17:2). But they need defense from complexity. We recall the psalmist, who measures his words so as not to "betray your children" (Ps 73:15), or Paul, who speaks to new believers "as to my children" (2 Cor 6:13).

Yet in their immaturity children are prone to evil (Jer 4:22), learn slowly (Is 28:9; 1 Cor 13:11) and resist work (Mt 11:16) or pain (Hos 13:13). They are also quick to *rebel. For example, Job prays each day for his children in case they have *cursed God in their hearts (Job 1:5; cf. Is 1:2,4; Is 30:1). The negative signs of childhood are most frustrating when they endure into adulthood.

Children as Learners. Children are in need of knowledge. Ignorant of good and evil, among other things, they need to learn (Deut 1:39). After God delivers Israel it is said, "Remember today that your children were not the ones who saw and experienced the discipline of the LORD your God . . . who saw what he did for you in the desert until you arrived at this place" (Deut 11:2, 5 NIV). Parents are responsible to teach their children of God's justice, both his judgment and his mercy. Admonitions to "train up a child in the way he should go" are many (Deut 4:9-10; 6:7; 29:29; 30:2; 31:13; 32:46; Josh 4:6; Ps 34:11; 78:4-5; Is 38:19; 54:13; Joel 1:3; Eph 6:4).

The common teachability of children is celebrated throughout Scripture, whereas their occasional rebellion is deplored. Jesus called a child to stand among them to illustrate teachability (Mt 18:2-4). This teachable spirit was among the qualities for which Jesus praised children, welcomed them and likened the kingdom to them (Lk 9:48; 10:21; 18:16). A child's teachable attitude is a model for the Christian's life.

Learning entails discipline (Prov 22:15; 23:13; Heb 12:8). Unteachable children rebel against it (Is 30:9; Jer 5:7; Ezek 20:18, 21; Mt 10:21; Tit 1:6). By contrast, obedient action signals learning (1 Pet

1:14; 1 Jn 3:18). John sums up the attitude of a teacher/parent: "I have no greater joy than to hear that my children are walking in the truth" (3 Jn 4 NIV).

Adults who are intimidated by a task liken themselves to a child. Solomon prayed: "I am only a little child and do not know how to carry out my duties" (1 Kings 3:7 NIV). At Jeremiah's similar confession the Lord promises knowledge: "Do not say, 'I am only a child.' You must go to everyone I send you to and say whatever I command you" (Jer 1:6-7 NIV).

Children as Dependent. Children represent dependence in two ways: parents are dependent upon their children as a guarantee of future generations; hence, their moral and physical well-being in old age makes them dependent on their infants. Children, however, are dependent on their parents for nurture in their youth. The protection of children is a major theme.

Parental pride stemmed from dependence upon their children for a *name in the future (Gen 31:43; 42:36; 48:6, 11). Children carry the parents' reputation (Ex 2:2-3; 21:4; Job 5:25; 21:8; Lk 7:35. The psalmist echoed the opinion of all when he said, "Sons are a heritage from the LORD, children a reward from him" (Ps 127:3).

The childless are pitied in the Bible (Gen 15:2-3; 38; 42:36; 1 Chron 2:32; Mt 22:24-25; Mk 12:19-22; Lk 20:28-31). The result of childlessness is grim: "[Shimei's] brothers did not have many children; so their entire clan did not become as numerous as the children of Judah" (1 Chron 4:27). Childlessness is a sign of judgment (Lev 20:20, 21; 26:22). Fertility signals blessing both on and off the battlefield (Deut 7:14; 1 Chron 7:4; Job 5:25). Couples without children earnestly pray for them (Gen 20:17; Rachel, Hannah, Lk 1:7).

Children likewise depend on their parents: for protection from military conflict or other danger (Gen 21:23; 32:11; 33:14; Ex 2:2-3; 22:24; Num 32: 16-17, 24, 26), for proper provision (Gen 31:16; 47:24; Mt 15:26) and for nurture (Ruth 4:16; Ps 131:2; Is 66:13; Joel 2:16; Mt 23:37; 1 Thess 2:11; 1 Tim 5:10). Ideally, parents also provide a homeland (Josh 14:9; Jer 30:20; Acts 7:5). It is their great sense of responsibility that prompts their continued quest for the *Promised Land.

Without parents or in evil times, children are vulnerable to hunger (1 Sam 2:5; Lam 2:19); one prophet describes "the infant's tongue sticks to the roof of its mouth; the children beg for bread but no one gives it to them" (Lam 4:4 NIV). Defenseless on their own, children also face danger (1 Kings 8:12; 10:1; Job 5:4; 24:9; Is 13:18; Jer 40:7; Lam 2:11, 19; Rev 12:4-5).

Harm comes when parents are rendered helpless (Jer 47:3; 49:10; Lam 1:5, 16) or are the cause of the child's suffering by personal sin (Hos 1:2, 5:7, 9:12). Worst are scenes of intentional harm from their parent in cases of cannibalism (Deut 28:55, 57), of jealousy (2 Chron 22:11) or idol worship that demands child sacrifice (2 Kings 17:31; Is 57:5; Jer 6:11; 9:21; 18:21; Ezek 16:36; 23:37; 29). Specific stories of dependent children are especially potent. Moses, in the *ark amidst the reeds, while in danger of death as a male *baby in Egypt, is also in danger from the river. Jesus as a baby is endangered in the same way (Mt 2:8).

The children of Abraham were privileged to have a dependable *father: as his seed, they reap the benefits of the gospel (Acts 13:26, 33; Rom 9:7; Gal 3:7; 4:1). Likewise children of believing parents are blessed (1 Cor 7:14). Fathers were responsible for demonstrating and instilling proper moral direction (Gen 18:19; Deut 30:19)

The most enduring image of peace entails the safety of a child among natural danger, an image of God's care for the entire earth:

> The wolf will live with the lamb, the leopard will lie down with the goat, the calf and the lion and the yearling together; and a little child will lead them. The cow will feed with the bear, their young will lie down together, and the lion will eat straw like the ox. The infant will play near the hole of the cobra, and the young child put his hand into the viper's nest. (Is 11:6-8 NIV)

Both parent and child are cared for by God's promise that sin will not be punished to further generations: "In those days people will no longer say, 'The fathers have eaten sour grapes, and the children's teeth are set on edge'" (Jer 31:29). God promises to be dependable for future children: "All your sons will be taught by the LORD, and great will be your children's peace" (Is 54:13).

Children as Reflections of Parents. The parents' dependence upon the child stems from the fact that the child reflects their care for him or her, and indeed, their own character. Images of children reflect a parent's present situation as well as future potential.

When children are included in an assembly of the whole, they represent the totality of the man as a member of his clan. Just as childlessness resulted in smaller clans among Israel, so the image of children gathered around their father suggests present status. There are twenty-four references to this sort of blessing. Similar consequences are meted out for sin: God regrets Israel's sin before she is exiled to Babylon, saying, "Your descendants would have been like the sand, your children like its numberless grains" (Is 48:19).

Future danger for the children results from parental sin. A past generation's sin is remembered by saying: "To this day, their children and grandchildren continue to do as their fathers did" (2 Kings 17:41). Nehemiah referred to a generation of children who spoke only the language of the idols, not "the language of Judah" (Neh 13:24). These comments indicate that children are an unchangeable reflection of past actions.

Connections between parents and children in the present tense are made as well: "If a man denounces his friends for reward, the eyes of his children will fail" (Job 17:5 NIV). Passages promising even more forceful destruction for one's children because of sin are many (Ex 20:5; 34:7; Num 14:18, 33; Deut 5:9; Ps 103:17; 109:9-10, 12; Is 47:8-9; Jer 2:9; 32:18; 36:3; 38:23; Ezra 5:17; Rev 2:23). These examples are summarized by God's statement: "Because you have ignored the law of your God, I also will ignore your children" (Hos 4:6 NIV). This pattern makes the cry of the crowd at Jesus' trial all the more stark: "Let his blood be on us and on our children!" (Mt 27:25 NIV).

At the same time, benefits toward children are also a reward (Deut 23:8; Is 29:23; 59:21; 65:23; Jer 30:20; Ezek 37:25; Zech 10:7). They are a sort of leverage toward obedience: "that it may go well with you and your children after you" (Deut 4:40; 4:29; 6:2; 12:25, 28 NIV). The Proverbs are clear: the righteous are repeatedly promised blessing for their children (Prov 13:22; 14:26; 20:7; Ps 37:26). Repentance also brings blessing: "So there is hope for your future," declares the Lord. "Your children will return to their own land" (Jer 31:17; Zech 10:9 NIV). Likewise, the gospel is "for you and for your children" (Acts 2:39).

Children as Cherished. Though subject to normal human perversions, in general, the overwhelming image of children in the Bible is that they are cherished by their parents, by their nation and by God. Parents dote on their children with devotion unparalleled in other relationships. Their ardent prayers to bear children (Gen 15:2-3; 16:1-2; 20:17; 1 Sam 1:27; 2:20; 1 Sam 54:1) and their celebrations at the birth of a child (Jer 20:15; Lk 1:66) demonstrate this. Parents store up wealth for their children (Ps 17:14) and want to give them good gifts (Mt 7:11; Lk 11:13; 2 Cor 12:14). Parents become desperate if their child is near death (1 Kings 17:23; 2 Kings 4:18-30; Mk 5:39-40; Mk 7:30; Jn 4:49).

Specifically named children of the Bible are always cherished. As a baby, Jesus is adored by all who meet him: the wise men (Mt 2:8, 11), the shepherds, Anna and Simeon. Those who are the "only child" are noted with special care (Prov 4:3; Zech 12:10; Lk 9:38). Jephthah agonizes over his vow to sacrifice the thing he first sees because it is his precious only *daughter whom he sees first (Judg 11:34). In Nathan's story to David the poor man cares for his sheep as for an only daughter (2 Sam 12:3). Two women fight before Solomon over one living child after another child dies (1 Kings 3:18). Joash, the child king, is guarded in secret by his *mother's sister (2 Chron 22:11).

Except in times of idol sacrifice, Israelites as a nation cherish children (Judg 18:21; Ps 127:3; Is 7:14; 9:6; Hos 9:16; Mic 1:16; Mt 2:18; Mt 19:29). God's laws and edicts cherish children (Lev 18:21; 20:3-4; Deut 33:9; Josh 1:14; Mal 4:6). God himself defends them (Ps 72:4; Hos 11:10). Jesus stopped for children, took time with them

(Mt 18:5; 19:13; Mk 10:16; Lk 9:48; 13:34) and healed them (Mk 7:30). Love for children is one evidence of "a people prepared for the Lord" (Lk 1:17; Mal 4:6).

Hebrews claim to be Abraham's children and thereby privileged (Jn 8:39, 41). They are addressed as such occasionally (Acts 13:26). But children of Abraham are redefined after Christ's resurrection as anyone who accepts his promise (Gal 3:7). Abraham's children are God's children.

God's children are especially cherished and privileged (Jn 1:13; 11:52). John, "the disciple whom Jesus loved," captures this tone when he addresses "dear children" seven times in his first epistle (1 Jn 2:1, 12, 13, 18, 28; 3:1, 7). God has compassion on his children (Jer 31:20) and never forgets them (1 Sam 49:15). They have eternal contentment, eternal life (Lk 20:36; Gal 4:31; 1 Jn 3:2; 1 Jn 4:4; 1 Jn 5:19). The right to be God's child is extended to all (Jn 1:12; Rom 8:16, 21; 9:8; 1 Jn 5:1), to Gentile and Jew alike (Gal 4:28). Just as one's behavior signals one's family background (1 Jn 3:10), so God's children are called to behave as children of the King (Deut 14:1; Eph 5:1, 8; Phil 2:14-15; 1 Jn 3:18; 1 Jn 5:2).

These images of children add warmth and depth to the promises that God looks on us as a father looks on his children. Younger and different from adults in maturity and innocence, a child is dependent on others, in a position to learn, and reflects the present situation and future hope of his or her parents; above all, a child is cherished. As children of God we yearn for the contentment that comes naturally to children; we adjust our position to assume the stance of a child because we understand that Jesus said, "Anyone who will not receive the kingdom of God like a little child will never enter it" (Mk 10:15 NIV). Most of all, we rest like a child, content that he deals with us "as a father deals with his own children" (1 Thess 2:11 NIV).

See also BABY; BARRENNESS; BIRTH STORY; BIRTHRIGHT; ELDER CHILD, ELDER SIBLING; FAMILY; FATHER; FAVORED CHILD, SLIGHTED CHILD; MOTHER; ORPHAN; YOUNGER CHILD, YOUNGER SIBLING.

CHILDBIRTH. *See* BIRTH.

CHILDLESSNESS. *See* BARRENNESS.

CHOICE, STORIES OF

The element of choice is almost synonymous with storytelling, and it is hard to imagine a good story without the element of choice in it. After all, the most common narrative strategy is to put the protagonist into a situation that tests him or her and requires a choice. In the Bible this quality of stories and of life itself is given a moral and spiritual depth, for the universe is understood to be a battleground in which good and evil vie for mastery of people's souls.

The quality of choice as a condition of human life is inherent in the story of *paradise (Gen 2), where the very presence of a forbidden *tree places *Adam and *Eve in a position of having to choose whether to obey or disobey the prohibition. The first recorded human choice is a tragic one—eating the forbidden tree and thereby causing the fall of the human race and the universe. Pursuant to the Fall, God does not change the ground rules for human life. People still have the capacity to choose for or against God and between good and evil. *Cain chooses evil; Noah, good. Lot chooses selfishness and worldly-mindedness; *Abraham generally lives by faith and chooses to believe the promises of God. *Jacob's checkered life gradually moves from a series of poor choices to better ones. *Joseph chooses the moral life and the life of faith. From the very start of its portrayal of human life, then, the Bible concentrates on the person at the crossroads; and as we read, the godly life emerges in our imaginations as above all, a life of choice.

Some of the choices that remain in our memories from reading the Bible are *tragic ones. The nation of *Israel generally chooses poorly, beginning with the *exodus and continuing through every successive era, including that of the judges and kings, until it is finally carried off into *exile. In many cases the nation's tragic cycles are tied to leaders who choose *idolatry. Some of the characters who choose poorly are full-fledged tragic heroes, most notably *Samson and King Saul. Even in the stories of biblical characters who are mainly virtuous, we often see the contrary impulse toward a bad choice, as in Gideon's making of an idol (Judg 8:22-27) or *Moses' striking the rock in anger in a manner that leads God to judge him (Num 20:10-12). *David's domestic and political decline begins with an immoral choice to commit *adultery and to *murder.

On the other side we remember the heroes and heroines of the Bible chiefly for their courage at crucial moments of choice. We think of Abraham obeying God's command to leave his native land and later to offer his son; of Joseph refusing the solicitation to sexual sin; of Moses repeatedly taking his stand on God's instructions instead of giving in to popular opinion; of *Ruth heroically choosing to commit herself to a new life as a foreigner, out of loyalty to her mother-in-law; of *Esther agreeing to enter the king's presence with her petition; and of the prophets pronouncing God's word even at the cost of persecution. There is no more moving gallery of characters who made the great choice than the roll call of the heroes of faith in Hebrews 11, where the formula "by faith" is an equivalent for "by choice."

In the Bible the spiritual life is essentially one of choosing for God. We see this most forcefully in a famous moment when the departing leader Moses sets "life and death, blessing and curse" before the nation of Israel, accompanied by the command "therefore choose life" (Deut 30:19 RSV). In the same vein are Joshua's charge to the nation, "Choose this day whom you will serve" (Josh 24:15 RSV), and Elijah's chastising his nation on Mt. Carmel for

limping between two opinions instead of following God (1 Kings 18:21).

Some genres of the Bible presuppose an element of choice. One of these is the commandments that are constantly set before followers of God. To command something is to say, "Do this, not that," thereby implying that people must make a choice in the matter. Similarly in wisdom literature the observations and commands that make up the proverbs presuppose choice as a condition of the listener's life. This is accentuated when (as in Prov 1—9) the imagery of the two paths is present. Of similar import are some of the psalms, such as Psalm 1, which present the reader with a choice simply by painting a heightened contrast between good and evil.

In the Gospels Jesus himself, as well as his claims, become the focus of implied choice. Repeatedly the stories that comprise the Gospels portray characters either accepting or rejecting what Jesus says about himself and the spiritual life. Some people turn away from Jesus sorrowful; others eagerly embrace his message. In both instances we witness the momentous drama of the soul's choice, which is a main theme of the Bible. This is a drama in which the reader of the Bible participates, inasmuch as reading the Bible presupposes choice on the part of the reader as a condition of reading.

See also BIBLE; BLESSING; CURSE; IDOLATRY; REWARD; SIN; TRAGEDY.

CHRIST. *See* JESUS, IMAGES OF.

CHRIST HYMN

The genre known as Christ hymn is a NT form. Its dominant motif is to praise the person and work of the incarnate *Christ. As such, the genre is an outgrowth of the OT *praise psalm, its hallmark being that the object of praise has now become specifically Christ. The Christ hymn also has strong affinities with the *encomium (a poem in praise of either a quality or character type), with such motifs as the praiseworthy acts and qualities of the subject, the subject's distinguished ancestry, the superiority motif and the command to the reader to emulate. The canon of Christ hymns includes the prologue to John's Gospel (Jn 1:1-18), the hymn of the servant Christ in Philippians 2:5-11, the creed embedded in 1 Timothy 3:16 and the poem in praise of the supremacy of Christ in Colossians 1:15-20. In addition, passages in Hebrews and Revelation have the general qualities and motifs of the Christ hymn.

While the individual hymns have their distinctive themes, they also share common image patterns and motifs. Because Christ came from heaven to earth, the imagery of *heaven and *earth, *high and *low, figures prominently. The deity of Christ results in cosmic imagery, including the motif of Christ's being eternal (*see* Cosmology). Because Christ is the incarnate deity, some of the hymns play on the antithesis of human (including the vocabulary of "flesh") and divine. The theme of distinguished ancestry takes the form of a divine ancestry in the prologue to John's Gospel. The redemptive mission of Christ produces the imagery of *light coming to darkness. Allusions to the redemptive life, death and resurrection of Christ naturally appear, and also to his work in creating the world. Other motifs include fullness, *glory, arrival or "coming" and the motifs of "beginning" and *first. The overall direction toward which all these motifs press is the supremacy of Christ.

See also ENCOMIUM; SING, SINGING.

BIBLIOGRAPHY. R. P. Martin, *A Hymn of Christ* (3d ed.; Downers Grove, Ill.: InterVarsity Press, 1997); idem, "Hymns, Hymn Fragments, Songs, Spiritual Songs," *DPL* 419-23.

CHRISTUS VICTOR. *See* JESUS, IMAGES OF.

CHRONICLES, BOOKS OF

The books of Chronicles offer many opportunities for appreciating literary imagery. In their own right the books display a variety of artistic qualities, but comparisons with its main sources (1 and 2 *Samuel, 1 and 2 *Kings) offer a great advantage for those pursuing the imagery of Chronicles.

The precise date of the chronicler's writing is unknown. In general terms we may say with confidence that he wrote to the those who had returned from *exile in Babylon sometime between 520 and 400 B.C. His readers had come back to the *land of promise, but they failed to see the rich blessings for which they had hoped. The chronicler creatively composed his own version of Israel's past to encourage these postexilic Israelites to pursue the attitudes and actions that would lead to further blessings from God.

As with all biblical books that are largely composed of narrative, the message of Chronicles does not appear explicitly on the surface of the text. Instead, it is communicated through a number of subtle artistic devices. Two examples of the chronicler's literary techniques are his use of structural and thematic imagery.

Structural Imagery. The chronicler does not order his history with purely chronological interests. Instead he orders his materials so that their very structure convey his message. The most dominant use of this technique appears in the large-scale structure of Chronicles. The chronicler organizes his record in a way that speak to the needs of his readers. Consider the following outline of his books:

The Privileges and Responsibilities of God's
    People (1 Chron 1:1—9:34)
The Ideal United Monarchy (1 Chron
    9:35—2 Chron 9:31)
The Divided Monarchy of Judgment and
    Blessing (2 Chron 10:1—28:27)
The Reunited Monarchy of Hope (2 Chron
    29:1—36:23)

To grasp the significance of this structure we must remember that the history of Israel could have been recorded in countless other ways. The books of

Samuel and Kings, for instance, illustrate two ways it could have been done. Why did the chronicler choose to convey his history of Israel as he did? His four stages of Israel's history convey much more than data about the past. On the contrary, each segment of the history has symbolic significance for the chronicler and his original readers.

First, the opening genealogies and lists (1 Chron 1:1—9:34), which do not appear in Samuel or Kings, provid the chronicler's unique perspective on the identity of his readers. He traces the origins of the tribes of Israel from *Adam (1:1—9:1) and closes with lists of those who have returned from Babylon (9:1-34). By this means the chronicler establishes that the postexilic Israelites are the rightful heirs of Israel's history. Without explicitly declaring his view, he symbolically establishes the relevance of his entire historical record for the readers of his day. This history is their heritage.

Second, having established the contemporary value of his history, the chronicler arranges his record of *David and *Solomon with symbolic value as well. He presents the reigns of David and Solomon as ideals to which postexilic Israel should aspire (1 Chron 9:35—2 Chron 9:31). The record of Samuel and Kings report both the good and bad in the lives of these kings; however, the chronicler omits most of their shortcomings and adds tremendous accomplishments. In this way his history of Israel's monarchy begins with models for his readers. Once again, he does not explicitly state this point of view, but his arrangement of the material communicates this outlook.

Third, the chronicler's version of the divided monarchy (2 Chron 10:1—28:27) differs from parallels in Kings in a number of ways. To begin with, the chronicler ignores the history of the northern kingdom; from his vantage point only events in Judah are important because his readers live in Judah. Moreover he frequently arranges the reigns of Judah's kings into periods of *blessing and *judgment. Each of these periods offers his readers the opportunity to see the consequences of fidelity and infidelity in the past. These examples both encourage and warn the postexilic readers about their own lives.

Fourth, after a reunion of north and south at Hezekiah's *Passover celebration, the chronicler traces events in the reunited monarchy (2 Chron 29:1—36:23). These last reigns form a series of failures followed by hopeful acts of divine grace. The final demonstration of divine mercy is the release from exile that the postexilic readers have recently experienced (2 Chron 36:20-23). The records are arranged in this way to give the readers of Chronicles hope for their own future.

The large-scale arrangement of the chronicler's history illustrates one way in which structural imagery works in the books of Chronicles. Each portion of the history reflects more than information about their past; each section holds symbolic value for its first readers.

The chronicler also uses structural imagery on a smaller scale. This artistic technique appears so often that we must limit ourselves to just two examples. The first appears in the middle portion of the genealogies (1 Chron 2:2—9:1). While these chapters focus on the breadth of the tribes to be counted among the people of God, the tribes appear in an order that is unique in biblical records. Moreover, uneven amounts of material are given to various tribes. Figure 1 illustrates the resulting pattern.

Judah (1 Chron 2:3—4:23; *110 verses*)
  Simeon (4:24-43; *20 verses*)
  Transjordanian Tribes (5:1-26; *26 verses*)
  Reuben (5:1-10; *10 verses*)
  Gad (5:11-17; *7 verses*)
  [Brief Narrative (5:18-22; *5 verses*)]
  Half-Tribe of Manasseh (5:23; *1 verse*)
  [Brief Narrative (5:24-26; *3 verses*)]
Levi (1 Chron 6:1-81; *81 verses*)
  Issachar (7:1-5; *5 verses*)
  Benjamin (7:6-12; *7 verses*)
  Naphtali (7:13; *1 verse*)
  Manasseh (7:14-19; *6 verses*)
  Ephraim (7:20-29; *10 verses*)
  Asher (7:30-40; *11 verses*)
Benjamin (1 Chron 8:1-40; *40 verses*)

Fig. 1. Structural pattern in genealogies of 1 Chronicles 2:2—9:1

This structural pattern hardly seems accidental; the symbolic value is manifold. For instance, Judah is privileged with the first place (1 Chron 2:3—4:23). As the tribe from which David's royal line came, this first place is appropriate. The Benjamites are last, but privileged with much attention (1 Chron 8:1-40). This tribe remained faithful to the Davidic line, and much of its territory is included in the postexilic province of Judah. The importance of the Benjamites in the postexilic community is reflected in their prominence in the genealogies. At the center of the order is the tribe of Levi (1 Chron 6:1-81). Just as Moses ordered that the Levites should be central in the camp of Israel (Num 2:17), the Levites are central in these genealogies. This central position also points to the importance of the temple and its personnel in the postexilic community. In this way the chronicler's structuring of this material conveys a symbolic message to his readers. It gives them a picture of the priorities that they must follow in their own day.

Another example of structural imagery appears in the account of David's widespread support (1 Chron 11:1—12:40). The chronicler omits all the material from Samuel related to David's struggle with Saul (2 Sam 1:1—4:12). He gathers several texts together (2 Sam 5:1-3; 5:6-10; 23:8-39) and adds his own material (1 Chron 12:1-40) to create a temporal and geographical image of the support for David's kingship. The following chart illustrates the resulting A B C D C' B' A' pattern:

A) Anointing at Hebron (Establishment in Jerusalem) (1 Chron 11:1-9)
  B) Military Support at Hebron (1 Chron 11:10-47)
    C) Military Support at Ziklag (1 Chron 12:1-7)
      D) Military Support at the Desert Stronghold (1 Chron 12:8-19)
    C') More Military Support at Ziklag (1 Chron 12:20-22)
  B') More Military Support at Hebron (1 Chron 12:23-37)
A') More on the Anointing at Hebron (1 Chron 12:38-40)

As this outline suggests, the chronicler arranges this material geographically. With the exception of 1 Chronicles 11:4-9, each location is mentioned twice. This repetitive structure has the effect of echoing the theme of widespread support for David time and again. David's kingship is presented as being without significant opposition.

Beyond this, comparisons with the chronology of 2 Samuel demonstrate that the chronicler's outline also has a pattern of chronological mirroring. David's time at the strongholds (1 Sam 22:1-5; 23:14, 29) precedes his stay at Ziklag (1 Sam 27:6). His time at Ziklag precedes the anointing at Hebron (2 Sam 5:1-4). In this light we can see that the chronicler presents his account with a temporal regression followed by a temporal progression. The effect of this structural arrangement is to present David's anointing as an immediate *fait accompli*. The readers are then led through the events that precede it and back to the anointing itself. In this manner the chronicler conveys symbolically that David's anointing was unopposed then, just as his throne should be unopposed in the postexilic period.

Thematic Imagery. Another way the chronicler communicates his message is by thematic imagery. Often these themes appear in the reiteration of certain terms; sometimes they emerge in the repetition of similar scenes. Several motifs deserve special mention.

All Israel. One of the chronicler's favorite terms is "all Israel" (*kol yiśrā'ēl*). This and similar expressions appear throughout his history (1 Chron 11:10; 12:38; 14:8; 15:3, 28; 18:14; 19:17; 21:5; 28:4, 8; 2 Chron 1:2; 7:8; 9:30; 10:16; 11:3, 13; 12:1; 13:4, 15; 18:16; 24:5; 28:23; 30:1; 31:1; 35:3). They reflect his keen interest in the unity of God's people.

The chronicler's image of "all Israel" is both narrow and broad. On the one hand, he considers those who have returned from exile to be the *remnant of all Israel. The representatives of Judah, Benjamin, Ephraim, Manasseh and Levi who have returned to the land (1 Chron 9:2-34) represent the people of God (2 Chron 36:23). As such, they play a key role in the restoration of the kingdom of Israel.

On the other hand, the chronicler also broadly identifies God's people with all twelve tribes of Israel. In his view the restoration of Israel is incomplete so long as some of the tribes remain separated from the Davidic king and the Jerusalem *temple. To demonstrate his view, the chronicler includes both northern and southern tribes in his genealogies (1 Chron 2:3; 4:24; 5:1, 11, 23; 6:1; 7:1, 6, 13, 14, 20). He presents the ideal of a united kingdom under David and Solomon. He depicts the reunification of the northern and southern kingdoms in the days of Hezekiah (2 Chron 30:1-31:1).

The chronicler's imagery of "all Israel" may be summarized in this way: the returnees are the remnant of all Israel, but they have to pray and work for the restoration of the full extent of all Israel.

King and temple. The chronicler's history also reveals that he is deeply concerned with the centrality of Israel's king and temple. In his history, king and temple are frequently repeated images that are fundamental to the life of Israel.

For example, the genealogies give special attention to David's royal family (1 Chron 2:10-17; 3:1-24) along with long lists of priests and Levites (1 Chron 6:1-81). Moreover, his record of David and Solomon's ideal kingdoms depict the kings as enthusiastically devoted to the service of the temple (1 Chron 17—29; 2 Chron 2—7).

One of the most striking ways in which the chronicler brings this theme to the foreground is by repeating scenes of joy and celebration in worship. Time and again he describes the music and enthusiastic participation of Israel when the kings give proper attention to the temple (e.g., 1 Chron 16:1-42; 23:5; 25:1-31; 2 Chron 5:12-13; 7:6; 23:13, 18; 29:25-30; 34:12). These repeated scenes of joy in worship offer the chronicler's readers guidance for their lives. They can expect the joy of blessings from God as they give proper attention to the temple.

Divine blessing and judgment. The chronicler's history also repeats the imagery of blessing and judgment through divine intervention. Unlike the books of Kings, Chronicles seldom speaks of divine judgment being delayed or mollified. Instead it repeatedly connects fidelity with immediate blessing, and infidelity with immediate judgment (e.g., 1 Chron 28:9; 2 Chron 6:14; 7:11-22; 15:2; 16:7-9; 21:12-15; 24:20; 25:14-24; 28:9; 34:24-28).

The standards for divine judgment and blessing vary. At times the chronicler emphasizes obedience to the Mosaic law (1 Chron 6:49; 15:13, 15; 16:40; 22:12-13; 28:7; 29:19; 2 Chron 6:16; 7:17-18; 12:1-2; 14:4, 6; 15:12-15; 17:3-9; 19:8-10; 24:6, 9; 25:4; 30:15-16; 31:3-21; 33:8; 34:19-33; 35:6-26). At other times he repeats scenes of response to prophetic/priestly instruction (2 Chron 11:2-4; 12:5-8; 20:14-20; 21:12-19; 24:19-25; 25:7-10, 15-20; 26:17-20). Blessings come to those who upheld the purity of temple worship (2 Chron 15:1-19; 17:1-6; 24:1-16; 29:1—31:21; 34:1—35:19). Humble reliance on God instead of human strength brings good (1 Chron 5:20; 2 Chron 13:18; 14:7; 16:7-9; 20:1-30; 32:20-22). When the people of God and their kings turn to sin, immediate retri-

bution often follows in the form of illness or military defeat (1 Chron 10:1-14; 2 Chron 13:1-16; 16:12; 18:33-34; 21:15-19; 25:14-24; 26:19-20; 28:1-5; 33:1-11). Even so, when the people come under God's judgment, they can be restored to blessing by humbly seeking God through repentance and prayer (1 Chron 21:1—22:1; 2 Chron 7:13-15; 12:1-12; 33:10-13). By repeating these images of judgment and blessing, the chronicler shows his postexilic readers the ways to secure divine blessing in their day. The full restoration of Israel will come only as they live in fidelity to the Lord.

Summary. We remember historical writing such as we find in the two books of the Chronicles partly as a series of memorable characters and moments. These images include Uzzah's dying "on the spot" when he touches the ark of the covenant, David's dancing in abandon as the ark is carried into Jerusalem, David's gathering materials for the building of the temple, the extended descriptions of the temple as built by Solomon, Solomon's prayer of dedication and God's glory filling the temple at the dedication, the visit of the Queen of Sheba to see Solomon's court, the defeat of Sennacherib's army by an angel of God, Josiah's rending his clothes when the newly discovered copy of the law is read, and the destruction of Jerusalem and the temple at the time of the exile.

See also KINGS, BOOKS OF; SAMUEL, BOOKS OF.

BIBLIOGRAPHY. M. J. Selman, *1 & 2 Chronicles* (TOTC; Leicester, U.K. and Downers Grove, IL: InterVarsity Press, 1994).

CHURCH

The Bible provides a rich kaleidoscope of imagery about the church composed of around one hundred metaphors and statements. The thread on which all other jewels are hung is the idea of the church as an *ekklēsia* ("assembly," "gathering"). This word, taken from common usage where it applied to the "calling out" of citizens for a civic meeting or of soldiers for battle, is used extensively throughout the Old and New Testaments to refer to the people of God (e.g., Deut 4:10; 9:10; 31:30; Mt 16:18; 18:17; Acts 5:11; Rom 16:5; 1 Cor 1:2; Eph 1:22; 3:10; Heb 12:23).

A second background factor is the idea of the *kingdom of God. Its relation to the church has been much debated, but the two cannot be identical even though there are areas of overlap. The church is the partial fulfillment of the kingdom of God in the here and now and serves as a primary agent of the kingdom; hence it is appropriate to apply some kingdom imagery to the church itself (e.g., Col 1:13). But the thrust of the post-Pentecost portrayal of the church lies elsewhere. Some of the most important images cluster around the focal points of past continuity, present identity and future fulfillment.

Continuity with the Past. Those images which draw on the past roots of the people of God stress that the followers of Jesus Christ stand both in continuity with the people of the older covenant and as the fulfillment of that *covenant. They are now, in Christ, all that the older covenant longed to see. So Christians are a new *Israel, the spiritual *seed of Abraham (Gal 3:29, 6:16), ruled over by and belonging to God himself (1 Pet 2:9-10) and composed of all those who have faith in Christ, whatever their racial or cultural background.

Central to OT religion was the *temple. The church of Jesus Christ does not worship at a temple but has *become* the temple. God now lives both among and within his people, not in buildings but in a living community (1 Cor 3:16-17; 2 Cor 6:16-18; Eph 2:20-21). This metaphor is implicit in the frequent references to *building (e.g., Mt 16:18; 1 Cor 3:9; 2 Cor 10:8; 13:10; Jude 20). Given that the church is the place where God dwells by his Spirit, people must live in unity with each other and in holiness of life. Integral to the temple was the priesthood. Under the new covenant, all believers have become priests (1 Pet 2:9; Rev 1:6; 5:10; 20:6), once more bringing into actuality the unfulfilled design of the old covenant (Ex 19:6).

The picture in John 15:1-17 of Jesus as a *vine and his disciples as *branches who need to remain in him and derive their life from him is equally an OT image. Israel was spoken of in Isaiah 5:1-7 as a much-loved vineyard, which had only produced bad fruit and was thus destined for destruction.

Identity in the Present. The bulk of images focus on the character of the church in the present age. The primary one is that of the church as a *body. This image is initially used to stress the dependence of members on one another in the face of tendencies, such as their differing gifts or their different cultural and social backgrounds, which might cause them to pull apart from one another. The key issue is the quality of relationships and mutual responsiveness that believers have with each other (Rom 12:3-8; 1 Cor 12:12-31). Commitment to one another was essential because they "were all baptized by one Spirit into one body" (1 Cor 12:13 NIV). The nature of their fellowship life is far more profound than when people gather because they merely have a common interest or wish to pursue a common goal.

The concept of the body is also developed in other ways. It indicates that the church is a living organism, not a religious organization. As such it not only has coherence, but it should expect to grow and develop (Eph 4:1-16; Col 2:19). Bodies also have *heads from which commands are received and which enable them to function. So it is with the church. Ephesians 1:22 and 4:15 and Colossians 1:18-19 make clear that Christ is the head of the church.

A second image that is developed in a number of ways is that of the church as a *household. A more inclusive social unit than our contemporary family, it nonetheless picks up the idea of the church as a *family brought in to being by the faithfulness of God's son, Jesus (Heb 3:1-6). As in any family, relationships are maintained by members behaving appropriately to one another. So the focus here is on the correct behavior of members in the household of God (1 Tim 3:15; Gal 6:10, see also the household codes of behavior, e.g., Eph 5:22—6:9; Col 3:18—4:1; 1 Tim 3:1-13 and 5:1-20).

Further images arise naturally from the everyday world in which Jesus and his followers lived. These include the image of a *flock being cared for and guided by a *shepherd (Jn 10:1-21; see also Lk 12:32; Acts 8-29; 1 Pet 5:2-4) and of "God's field" in which the word of the gospel is planted and watered by persons but is germinated by God himself (1 Cor 3:6-9; *see* Farming).

Images that Point to the Future. The people of God look forward to the complete realization of their salvation in the future. This theme is particularly captured by the image of the church as the *bride of Christ (Jn 3:29; Mt 9:15; 25:1-13; Mk 2:19; Lk 5:34-35). Paul exploits this metaphor in two ways. He speaks both of the love Christ had for the church (Eph 5:25) and of the consequent need for the betrothed to keep herself pure for the coming of the bridegroom on their *wedding day (2 Cor 11:2). Revelation 19:7 brings the picture to a climax by foreseeing the wedding *banquet when at last, after all the suffering and necessary preparation, the bride and groom are finally united and the festivities begin.

See also BODY; BRANCH; BRIDE, BRIDEGROOM; BUILD, BUILDING; FAMILY; FLOCK; HEAD; HOUSEHOLD; ISRAEL; KINGDOM OF GOD; SEED; TEMPLE; VINE, VINEYARD; WEDDING.

BIBLIOGRAPHY. P. S. Minear, *Images of the Church in the New Testament* (London: Lutterworths, 1961).

CHURL. *See* REFUSER OF FESTIVITIES.

CIRCUMCISION

Circumcision is a symbolic act that functions as a powerful image throughout the Bible. It was the sign of the *covenant between God and *Israel (Gen 17:11; cf. Acts 7:8; Rom. 4:11) whereby he had chosen them and given them the promise "[I will] be God to you and to your descendants after you" (Gen 17:7 RSV; cf. Deut 7:7-9).

Circumcision as Ancient Rite. During OT times circumcision was practiced by most of the other nations near Israel, including the Egyptians, so in and of itself it was not a distinguishing mark. But the significance attached to it by Israel was unique. Among the other Semitic peoples and in Egypt, it was not generally applied to infants, and its significance is unclear. It was perhaps an initiation rite associated with puberty, a symbolic sacrificing of the reproductive powers to the gods, or even a token human sacrifice. Only in Israel did it have a clearly defined theological significance that extended beyond the individual who received it to his family and the wider community. The requirement of a ceremonial flint rather than a bronze or iron knife suggests the great antiquity of the rite itself (Josh 5:2).

Circumcision as Membership or Covenant. Before the establishment of a central sanctuary, circumcision served as the main symbol of God's covenant with Israel and as a symbol, in turn, of Israel's commitment to keep his covenant. Dire consequences attended those who failed to comply (Ex 4:24-26). It was the sine qua non of membership in the covenant community (Gen 17:14), perhaps even a test of loyalty (Gen 34). It could express a powerful recommitment (Josh 5:2-8). The Philistines alone among Israel's immediate neighbors did not practice circumcision. The automatic equation of foreskins and Philistines lies behind Saul's stipulation that David pay a bride price of one hundred foreskins (1 Sam 18:25). Because of the traditional hostility between them, "uncircumcised" came to be summary term for wicked and godless (e.g., Judg 15:18; 1 Sam 17:26; 2 Sam 1:20). Ezekiel extends the label to most of Israel's enemies in describing them as the dead nations who formerly terrorized the land (Ezek 32:17-32) but who will now be relegated to the recesses of Sheol without honor (Ezek 32:27) among the "uncircumcised."

Circumcision as Genuine Belief. Against this background it is remarkable to find the charge of "uncircumcision" leveled at Israel. "Their ears are uncircumcised so that they cannot hear!" says Jeremiah of the inhabitants of Jerusalem (Jer 6:10). He charges the whole of Israel with being "uncircumcised in heart," so that whether they practice physical circumcision or not, there is no difference between Israel and all the other nations who really are uncircumcised (Jer 9:26; cf. 4:4). They are equally wicked and godless. This awareness that outward obedience through the act of circumcision did not necessarily imply the obedience *of the heart,* and that "uncircumcision" of heart will lead to loss of the covenant blessings appears already in the Pentateuch (Deut 10:16; Lev 26:41). Stephen levels the same charge against his fellow Jews (Acts 7:51). In spite of these hints about the obsolescence of circumcision, some early believers had difficulty abandoning the outward sign.

Circumcision as Old Law. Picking up where he had interrupted Stephen, Paul develops the theme further, not only making the basic point about the redundancy of circumcision and law-keeping (Rom 2:25-29) but also warning (with caustic humor), "Watch out for the mutilation *[katatomē].* We are the [true] circumcision *[peritomē],* we who worship by the Spirit of God, who glory in Christ Jesus" (Phil 3:3). Elsewhere he dared wish that agitators for circumcision would amputate or castrate themselves (Gal 5:12). Christians, Paul believed, have been circumcised in Christ (Col 2:11), because they have been given a new heart by the Spirit; and chiefly for this reason, Paul strongly opposed those who wanted to make Gentile converts accept the literal sign of circumcision (Acts 15:1-29). "Neither circumcision nor uncircumcision means anything; what counts is a new creation!" (Gal 6:15, 5:6 NIV).

Thus time and the establishment of successive covenants radically change the symbolism of circumcision. An ancient ritual becomes the primary mark of a keeper of the covenant. And after Christ, it serves as an emblem of the unkeepable law that cannot save.

See also COVENANT; GALATIANS, LETTER TO THE.

BIBLIOGRAPHY. R. G. Hall, "Circumcision," *ABD* 1:1025-31; J. M. Sasson, "Circumcision in the Ancient Near East," *JBL* 85 (1966) 473-76.

CISTERN

Cisterns are *water reservoirs, which can include both large public water works and small home cisterns. Modern urbanites, particularly in the West, tend to overlook the importance of water conservation for the life and well-being of a community. In an era when water pours from faucets hot and cold, the significance of a cistern is easily lost. The limited *rainfall of Israel made cisterns an absolute necessity, and it is likely that in dry settled areas most homes had a cistern fed by rainwater gathered on the roof during the rainy season. Most of the cisterns that have survived were cut into the limestone in a bottle shape, plastered to help retain the water and sealed with a *stone to prevent contamination and evaporation. Freestanding containers of various materials were also employed in a manner much like the "water barrel" of the more recent past.

It is not always possible to distinguish cisterns from *pits in the OT (e.g., Ex 21:33-34). The word *bôr* is used for both cistern and pit (the related *b'r* refers only to cisterns), though never for a well, despite some English versions. These water storage structures were usually cut into rock and were common in both the city and the countryside (2 Chron 26:10). They could also serve as *hiding places (1

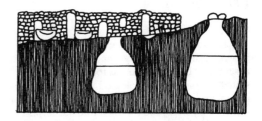

A cross-section of cisterns dug from limestone.

Sam 13:6), prominent landmarks (1 Sam 19:22), temporary *prisons (Jer 38:6) and dumping places for corpses (Jer 41:7).

Along with *house and *vineyard, having your own cistern completes the image of the secure and good life in a peaceful society (Deut 6:11 [NIV "well"]; Neh 9:25). *Drinking from a cistern may even connote ownership and thus epitomize retaining possession of one's *land (2 Kings 18:31; Is 36:16) or taking possession of someone else's land (Deut 6:11). Thus David requests water from the cistern at Bethlehem during his conquest of that city (2 Sam 23:15-16).

But *bôr* (cistern) can also mean "dungeon," so that Joseph identifies the *bôr* (dungeon) into which Potiphar threw him (Gen 40:15) with the *bôr* (cistern) into which his brothers threw him (Gen 37:24), thus signaling the parallel descents from prestige, first in his father's house, and then in Potiphar's. This association of cisterns with temporary prisons (cf. especially Jer 38:6) or "holding tanks" explains the image of the Babylonian captivity in Zechariah 9:11, where the empty cistern suggests the "lifelessness" of the captivity.

The sanctity of water rights becomes a metaphor for the sanctity of marriage. One's wife is a cistern of life (Prov 5:15), and the admonition to "drink water from your own cistern" (Prov 5:15) extends the imagery of "possession" noted above, so that one does not dispossess another of his "waters" nor cause his own to be "scattered abroad."

In Jeremiah 2:13 a cistern is contrasted with a well so as to create a negative image. Yahweh is the fountain of living water who has been abandoned for broken cisterns that hold no water at all. In this colorful passage there seems to be an implicit assumption that cistern water is inferior: cisterns are difficult to maintain, and the water was subject to becoming stale and harboring parasites.

See also RAIN; WATER; WELL.

BIBLIOGRAPHY. O. Keel, *The Symbolism of the Biblical World* (New York: Crossroad, 1978) 69-73; P. Williams, "The Fatal and Foolish Exchange; Living Waters for 'Nothing': A Study of Jeremiah 2:4-13," *Austin Seminary Bulletin,* Faculty Edition 81 (1965) 3-59.

CITIZEN. *See* LEGAL IMAGES.

CITY

The biblical image of the city is cast against the ancient Near Eastern background of the metropolis as a fortified habitation. Just as today, the city represented a profound technological and social accomplishment. Its basic identity has always been that of humanity *en masse*, and it is therefore not surprising that in the human imagination the city becomes humanity "writ large"—a representative that pictures in heightened form what is good and bad in human behavior. Another archetypal pattern to which the biblical city adheres is that it presupposes as its opposite the rural countryside, with the city participating in a grand antithesis of civilization versus nature, the communal versus the individual, culture versus the uncivilized or barbaric (*see* Country, Countryside).

The city's development required strong social ties to supplant traditional tribal identity. These ties were a combination of political and religious interests. The temple and palace were bound up together, constituting the social adhesive necessary for large-scale community life. This intertwining of religion and culture is reflected in such features as the king claiming divine sonship and approval, and the temple being the center of record keeping for commerce and the depository of tributes. In light of this it is not surprising to find the Bible using the image of the city for moral and spiritual lessons.

Lest these lessons be misapplied, it needs to be clearly stated that the city itself is not inherently evil or good, for the biblical image displays both dimensions. If cities like *Sodom, Tyre and *Babylon represent people in community against God, the OT *Jerusalem and the New Jerusalem of the Apocalypse picture the ideal of people in unity with each other and God. If the city is a place of *sexual perversion and *violence, it is also a safe refuge for congregated humanity against the dangers of nature. One of the terrors in Psalm 107 is the spectacle of people wandering "in desert wastes, finding no way to a city to dwell in," and its God-sent remedy is that God "led them by a straight way, till they reached a city to dwell in" (Ps 107:4, 7 RSV).

The Primeval City. The first explicit mention of a city is found in Genesis 4:17, where it is reported that *Cain named a city Enoch after his firstborn son (whose name may mean "to dedicate"). To this common source the author connects all civilization (cf. Gen 4:18-22). The naming of a city after oneself or one's progeny can easily be seen as an act of self-aggrandizement; however, the very act of constituting this city is the fruition of Cain's own search for security in the world. When Cain murders his brother *Abel, God pronounces a curse on him by declaring, "You shall be a fugitive and a wanderer on the earth" (Gen 4:12 RSV). Cain's desperate plea for mercy proceeds from his fear that "whoever finds me will slay me" (Gen 4:14). Thus he prevails upon God to provide him special protection (Gen 4:15). Cain's fear, seen in light of his subsequent building of a city, reflects his love for the city and the security it offers. But the city is cast under the shadow of Cain and is thus identified with the *seed of the *serpent rather than the seed of the woman (Gen 3:15).

The negative characterization of Cain and his association with urban life is the beginning of a wholly negative characterization of the city in the Bible's primeval history (Gen 1—11), which begins with the picture of a perfect *garden and then degenerates into life in a city. The early shadow cast over the city in the story of Cain combines with its wholesale condemnation in the *Babel episode to form a parenthesis around the early history of humankind. Lest this negative theme seem disrupted by the *flood, we should note that accursed Ham is connected with the continuation of city life in Genesis's next explicit mention of a city (Gen 10:12).

The intention of the builders of Babel (both the city and the tower, cf. Gen 11:4) is twofold: to reach heaven with their temple/tower and to make a name for themselves. Cain's desire for renown, repeated in the *taunt of his murderous descendant Lamech (Gen 4:23-24), reaches its climactic expression at Babel. Humankind, under the guise of religious pursuit, expresses its autonomy in technological achievement. This account is rife with divine irony. God has to descend (Gen 11:5) in order to investigate the height of human accomplishment. The solidarity of language that made this attempt plausible becomes the first casualty of divine displeasure (Gen 11:7-9, cf. 11:1). The ensuing confusion of language becomes a guard against similar future efforts. In the Babel episode we see the consummate marks of humankind's idolatrous rebellion against God. Humanity subverts God's blessed order—in this case the solidarity of human language and human skill in technological achievement—and turns it toward self-glorification. Whereas before the fall all of culture was to be given over to the glory of God, now humans turn culture into a tool of rebellion.

Early Genesis thus establishes a general worldview in which the image of the city is an anti-God state of affairs that attempts to thwart God's rule over the world. It is a place where culture subverts religion for its own purposes rather than advancing the glory of God. Genesis provides this background to an Israel living in the midst of a futile creation, a theme developed in the Exodus account of Israel's oppressive servitude to an Egyptian city-building program (Ex 1:8-14; 5:5-21). God's original intent for his image bearers was to build society for the glory of God. They were to multiply and spread out over the earth, extending the rule of God over creation as God's vice-regents (Gen 1:26-28). Because they exercised autonomy, the first man and woman were cursed and driven out of God's presence to await the fulfillment of God's promise to deliver them from that curse (Gen 3, esp. vv. 15 and 24). All efforts at city building from this point on are reassertions of that original autonomy.

In contrast to the anti-God city dwellers, those who fear God are described as *wanderers and *shepherds. Abel's case is obvious enough, but Enoch (not Cain's son) is equally an example. We read that he "walked with God" (Gen 5:22, 24). The verb form (Heb *hlq* in the hithpael) indicates a manner of life which in other contexts describes the life of a shepherd wanderer (Gen 13:17; 48:15). Enoch followed God from place to place.

Abraham and the City. Immediately following the failed urban venture of Babel comes the account of *Abraham's call and obedience (Gen 12). In response to God's call Abraham resolves to leave the security of the great city of Ur (highly developed, according to archaeological testimony) to take up the life of a wandering shepherd. As with Enoch, his security will be found in the assurance of God's presence rather than in the company of other people (Gen 15:1). This contrast between God's people and the rest of human society is further reflected in

Abraham's relationship with his nephew Lot. When they prosper to the point of needing to separate, Abraham gives Lot his choice of which portion of the land he will occupy (Gen 13:8-9). Lot chooses the well-settled Jordan valley, which includes the cities of Sodom and Gomorrah, synonyms for wickedness. Although Lot is judged by God to be the only righteous man there, his misguided desire for the security of the city is again reflected in his appeal to the angels as they lead him away. He pleads that they not take him to the mountains but let him turn aside to Zoar (which means "small," Gen 19:18-22). Within the context of the story and as evidence of the ironic attachment of Lot to a wicked and civilized lifestyle in which he lives with a bad conscience (2 Pet 2:7-8), Lot whimpers that he cannot conceive of life without at least a little "sin city" as his residence, and his subsequent experience with his daughters shows that although one can take one's children out of Sodom, one cannot take Sodom out of one's children.

Abraham, on the other hand, is content to be a wanderer in the very land that God has promised to give him as an inheritance. He refuses to pay tribute to the king of Sodom (Gen 14:17, 21-24), reserving his tithe for Melchizedek (whose name means "king of righteousness"), the king of Salem (vv. 18-20), anticipating the future of that city to become known as "Jerusalem." So resolute is Abraham to wait on God that he refuses from Ephron the Hittite the gift of a *burial site for Sarah, insisting on paying for land promised to him by God (Gen 23). The basis of this refusal is his confessed identity as "a stranger and a sojourner" among them (Gen 23:4). Lest we begin to think that the city is inimical to the life of faith, though, we need to take into the account that although Abraham wandered about "living in tents" (Heb 11:9), he nonetheless "looked forward to the city which has foundations, whose builder and maker is God" (Heb 11:10 RSV).

Thus early Israel is presented with a worldview that divides the world into two kinds of people, based on their relationship to the human city. This worldview is rightly discerned in Augustine's *City of God*, where Augustine writes, "I classify the human race into two branches: the one consists of those who live by human standard, the other of those who live according to God's will. I also call these two classes the two cities, speaking allegorically. By two cities I mean two societies of human beings, one of which is predestined to reign with God for all eternity, the other doomed to undergo eternal punishment with the Devil" (*City of God* XV.I).

For the Israelites the cities of Egypt are to be abandoned as they set out following Yahweh as sojourners toward the Promised Land. They are to understand Egyptian antipathy toward them as the classic hostility between city builders and shepherd wanderers and to see God's providential preservation of the nation through separation (Gen 46:33-34). Furthermore, because Moses describes the settlements of Canaan in terms similar to Babel (Deut 1:28; 9:1), they should look toward the conquest of those great cities as joining in this classic conflict, though even there is a vestige of approval of cities when inhabited by God's people (see Deut 6:10-13, which lends sanction to the Israelites' fearing God in "great and goodly cities" that they did not build but are allowed to possess).

Jerusalem. This worldview persists throughout the Bible, with the city of humankind consistently identified as the human-made city, with one exception. In Deuteronomy 12 Moses anticipates a point in the future when God will choose a city where his presence will be uniquely manifested. This city will not glorify the name of a human but will be the place where *God's* name will dwell. Of course, this is fulfilled in David's capture of Jebus, its dedication as *Jerusalem (2 Sam 5) and its establishment as the religious center—first in the bringing of the ark (2 Sam 6) and eventually in the building of the *temple (1 Kings 5). Up to that point God's people are to live the life of sojourners, waiting for God's city. Jerusalem will constitute the city for which they have waited. However, they are to maintain an ongoing confession of what G. von Rad called "Israel's credo": "My father was a wandering Aramean" (Deut 26:5). This perpetual outlook, even in the settled, stable Jerusalem of the monarchy, indicates that Jerusalem *per se* is not the higher reality toward which God's people are ultimately to look. However Jerusalem serves as a pattern for that ultimate city of God.

The most extensive picture of Jerusalem as the idealized city of God is set forth in the Psalms. It is a city that God builds (Ps 48:8) and protects (Ps 46:4-5). As a metonym for God it is an object of praise (Ps 87:3). Its defender is the Lord's anointed king (Ps 101:8). God's people sing a song for its peace and security (Ps 122; 51:18), knowing that it will only prosper through the Lord's favor and not through human effort (Ps 127:1). The tribute of nations will come to this city because of God's presence there (Ps 68:29). When nations come up against it, they are attacking God and will be subject to divine retribution (Ps 79:1; 137:7). In Jerusalem God's people will worship him (Ps 102:21; 116:19). Its placement in the hills signifies God's protection over the city (Ps 125:2). For those in exile, especially as they dwell in the quintessential city of the humanity, Babylon, Jerusalem's memory is a source of simultaneous sorrow and comfort (Ps 137:5). Even then it is to remain a source of confidence and hope for the future (Ps 137:6).

The City in Old Testament Prophecy. At the height of OT idealization of Jerusalem, we find the greatest contrast between God's city and the human city. But the idealistic description of Jerusalem exceeds the attendant realities. Failure to recognize this causes Israel to presume upon God's favor toward his city, not repenting of the injustice that prevents her from reflecting her heavenly antitype (Mic 3:11-12). Jeremiah corrects these misconceptions in two ways.

In declaring the inevitability of the exile, he speaks of a future city that will surpass the present. Whereas Jerusalem has been known as the place where God's *ark-*throne dwells, this future Jerusalem in its *entirety* will be the throne of God (Jer 3:16-17). God's wrath is to be poured out against the once holy city because in its pridefulness it has become like the city of humans (Jer 13:9-14).

Secondly, as Jerusalem's residents are cast into *exile, they are to maintain their perspective that the city of God has not failed, only Israel's faithful depiction of it in theocratic Jerusalem. God commands them to "seek the welfare of the city where I have sent you into exile, and pray to the LORD on its behalf; for in its welfare you will find your welfare" (Jer 29:7 RSV). They are once again relegated to the status of aliens, waiting on the eschatological hope of the New Jerusalem of which the prophets spoke. In the future, Jerusalem will once again be a glorious city, so expansive that stone *walls cannot encircle it (Zech 2:4). However this city will not be without protection, for the *glory of God will be its wall (Zech 2:5). The glory cloud associated with the name of God, which departed from Jerusalem in Ezekiel's vision of exile (Ezek 10:18-19), will return in a more expansive way, signifying God's renewed favor toward Jerusalem (Zech 1:17). But the rebuilt city of Nehemiah's day falls far short of these descriptions. This eschatological city is a pilgrim destination not only for Israelites but for the nations (Mic 4:2; cf. Is 2). It will be called "Sought Out" (Is 62:12 RSV). It will be the worship center of the world (Is 2:3).

The city is a major image of OT prophetic literature, where it is finally an ambivalent image. On one side, the city is a major image of evil (Is 14:21), climaxed in the awesome entities called *Babylon (Is 47; Jer 50) and Tyre (Ezek 27—28), which are literal geographic and political phenomena but go beyond that to be a spiritual force of evil as well. The "exultant city that dwelt secure," thinking itself supreme, is transformed under God's judgment into "a desolation," a "lair for wild beasts," so that "every one who passes by her hisses and shakes his fist" (Zeph 2:15 RSV). The city of the prophetic imagination is so godless that when one runs through the streets of Jerusalem in quest to find just one good person, the *quest is futile (Jer 5:1-5). Yet even in God's rejection of the wicked city we are led to see the city's inherent value in its good manifestation, as pictured by Jeremiah's weeping over the fall of Jerusalem.

But the prophetic city is also an image of divine blessing and of the good life. The picture of future bliss that Zechariah envisions is a street scene, not a country scene: "Old men and old women shall again sit in the streets of Jerusalem. . . . And the streets of the city shall be full of boys and girls playing" (Zech 8:4-5 RSV). The apostate city "shall be rebuilt upon its mound" (Jer 30:18). Isaiah's most extended picture of *restoration is that of a rebuilt city (Is 60—62) that is "a praise in the earth" (Is 62:7). The restored city of the apocalyptic imagination is also a world center of worship (Is 2:3; Jer 3:17).

Summary. Standing on the threshold of NT literature, the image of the city in the OT can be seen as two-fold. In the creation that God established there is one city to be built. That city will extend the glory of God throughout the earth. Humanity exercises autonomy, wresting the city from divine service and to self-glorification. From that point on the city is a symbol of that rebellion. Those who ally themselves with it align themselves against God. Those who look to God are patient wanderers, waiting in faith for him to establish his city. In the theocracy the city of Jerusalem takes on the character of the city of God. But in its failure to reflect its heavenly counterpart, it is swept away for the coming of that counterpart in its consummate form. The city itself is neither good nor bad; its identity depends on the spiritual state of its inhabitants: "By the blessing of the upright a city is exalted, but it is overthrown by the mouth of the wicked" (Prov 11:11 RSV; cf. also v. 10).

Jesus and the Apostles. The city assumes literal and symbolic importance in the Gospels. As an itinerant teacher and miracle worker, Jesus frequents the cities of Palestine, most notably Jerusalem and Samaria. Although Jesus sometimes achieves success in these cities—witnessed in the large-scale conversion of Samaritans (Jn 4:39) or the triumphal entry of Jesus into Jerusalem—the general pattern in the Gospels is to link belief with the common people of the countryside and villages and unbelief and hostility with the cities. Two common pictures that emerge from the Gospels are Jesus preaching to appreciative crowds and working miracles in the countryside, and Jesus engaging in conflict with antagonists in the city, especially Jerusalem, site of the religious establishment. Nor should we overlook that Jesus is arrested, tried and sentenced to execution in a city that he had characterized as "killing the prophets and stoning those who are sent to you." Yet even in uttering that accusation, Jesus is pictured as weeping over this wicked city, desiring to gather its "children together as a hen gathers her brood under her wings" (Mt 23:37 RSV; cf. Lk 19:41).

The world that we enter in the book of *Acts is the most modern in all the Bible by virtue of its urban identity. Most of the action occurs in the famous cities of the Greco-Roman world, not in local villages or the countryside. This prevailingly metropolitan world is, moreover, international and cosmopolitan. There is a sense in which the city is vindicated in the history of the early church—not in the sense that the city is mainly good or cordial to the gospel but in the sense that the city is where most people now live and where the influential power structures exist. Even though the cities Paul visits are mainly hostile to him and his message, it is in these very cities that small churches are planted. It is easy to see that the mission strategy of the early church was to evangelize the city. It is no exaggeration to say that in Acts the church is almost exclusively associated with the city, within which (to be sure) it is a tiny and persecuted minority.

The picture of the city as church site is reinforced by the letters to the seven churches in Revelation 2—3.

New Jerusalem. The ultimate vindication of the city comes in the apocalyptic vision of New Jerusalem, which descends from heaven (Rev 21:2), symbolic of its divine origin and its transcendence of human and earthly reality. With the appearance of this heavenly city, "the kingdom of the world has become the kingdom of our Lord and of his Christ" (Rev 11:15). Its ancient rival, Babylon, which attempts to subvert it, will ultimately be destroyed and cast down (Rev 18). This New Jerusalem will have no temple, "for its temple is the Lord God the Almighty and the Lamb" (Rev 21:22 RSV), and it will need no sun, since God's glory will be its eternal light (v. 23). Furthermore, "The kings of the earth shall bring their glory into it" (v. 24 RSV). The curse of the Fall will be removed and, along with it, the injustice and futility that characterized life in the city of man.

The Life of Faith. In summary, the image of the city in the Bible is dual, not uniform. Whether we use Augustine's designations of *city of God* and *city of man,* or M. Kline's corresponding terms of *metapolis* and *megapolis,* the distinction is one of future destiny and life in the present. Metapolis was

offered to man at the beginning in the prophetic sanctions of the Covenant of Creation, [and] is again offered as the final goal of the process of cosmic redemption. It is promised as the crowning achievement of Christ, the redeemer-king. Towards it the people of the covenant wind their historical way as pilgrims in a wilderness. . . . [But] over against the heavenly city stands the other city, mundanely present and visible to all. Although the term "city of man" used for this other city marks, in the first place, the contrast between human political government as an interim product of common grace and the city of God as a holy eschatological kingdom produced by redemptive grace, "city of man" also carries a negative religious charge insofar as it connotes the apostate character borne by this city in its development under the hand of fallen mankind. (Kline, 112)

In light of the complex that makes up the image of the city, the Christian life is to display certain characteristics. First, the Christian is a citizen of God's city through righteousness based on faith, not on the works of the law. By analogy, Paul compares these two outlooks to the "Jerusalem above" and the "present Jerusalem" (Gal 4:22-26; cf. Phil 3:20). People who attempt on their own to justify themselves before God are citizens of the latter, while those who look to Christ in faith are citizens of the former.

Second, the Christian life is marked by respect for human government as God's provisional source of order since the Fall and prior to the consummation (Mt 22:21; Rom 13:1-7; 1 Pet 2:13-17); therefore, the believer is to live like a Joseph or a Daniel in relating to the surrounding world. The ancient *Epistle of Diognetus,* a defense of Christianity, describes

Christians as those who "dwell in their own countries, but only as sojourners; they bear their share of all responsibilities as citizens, and they endure all hardships as strangers. Every foreign country is a homeland to them, and every homeland is foreign. . . . Their existence is on earth, but their citizenship is in heaven" (*Epistle to Diognetus* 5.1-9)

Third, the life of faith is to be a life of confidence in God's promise to establish his city. Hebrews speaks of the faith by which Abraham "sojourned in the land of promise, as in a foreign land, living in tents. . . . For he looked forward to the city which has foundations, whose builder and maker is God" (Heb 11:9-10 RSV). Heavenly citizenship is to be the ground of confidence in life's trials, the goal toward which life is directed.

But a significant difference distinguishes the NT believers from their OT counterparts. Of the latter we are told, "All these people were still living by faith when they died. They did not receive the things promised; they only saw them and welcomed them from a distance" (Heb 11:13 NIV). While the Christian is to continue in this alien mode until the consummation (1 Pet 1:1; 2:11), in a very profound and real sense the pilgrimage has ended because of Christ's atoning work (Eph 2:19). Through the persevering, substitutionary faithfulness of Jesus (Heb 12:2), Christians "have come to Mount Zion and to the city of the living God, the heavenly Jerusalem" (Heb 12:22 RSV). So while the geopolitical manifestation of God's city is yet future, it has been eternally established in the heavens through Jesus' work, and believers in Jesus have already taken up residence there (Jn 14:1-3) through union with him (Eph 2:6).

Therefore the church of Jesus lives in the world now as God's holy "city set on a hill" (Mt 5:14). Augustine described it thus: "The humble City is the society of holy men and good angels; the proud city is the society of wicked men and evil angels. The one City began with the love of God; the other had its beginnings in the love of self" (*City of God* 14.13).

See also BABYLON; COUNTRY, COUNTRYSIDE; JERUSALEM, NEW JERUSALEM; SODOM AND GOMORRAH.

BIBLIOGRAPHY. J. M. Boice, *Two Cities, Two Loves* (Downers Grove, IL: InterVarsity, 1996); J. Ellul, *The Meaning of the City* (Grand Rapids: Eerdmans, 1970); M. G. Kline, *Kingdom Prologue* (S. Hamilton, MA: M. G. Kline, 1991) 100-117, 165-70; J. Timmer, "The Bible and City," *Reformed Journal* (October 1973): 21-25.

CIVIL DISOBEDIENCE

Civil disobedience is not the invention of the modern age. The Bible records approximately a dozen examples of legitimate civil disobedience. Most examples occur when a government specifically commands individuals to disobey God, so that civil disobedience is at the same time religious obedience. In such cases, God commends those who suffer consequences at the hands of the government for the sake of righteousness, and he usually *rescues them.

One cluster of examples occurs when a ruler either prohibits the worship of God or commands the worship of some other god. The story of Shadrach, Meshach and Abednego (*see* Daniel) illustrates three godly men's response to the *Babylonian king Nebuchadnezzar's decree that the "peoples, nations, and languages . . . fall down and worship the golden image" that Nebuchadnezzar had erected (Dan 3:5 NRSV). Because such a command contradicts the first commandment forbidding *idolatry, these men refuse to *bow down. When confronted by the king with their disobedience, they claim to be obeying a higher authority that overrides that of the king (Dan 3:16). Although God saves them from their punishment, they acknowledge that whatever the outcome of their punishment, they *fear God more than they fear men (vv. 17-18). God's rescue of these men fully commends their action as a legitimate case of civil disobedience.

A similar case occurs when Darius, the Persian ruler, forbids prayer to any god but the king for thirty days (Dan 6). The issue behind this case is faithfulness to God, and Daniel refuses to be unfaithful despite the government's decree (Dan 6:5). He not only continues to pray three times a day as he has done before, but he makes no attempt to disguise his actions. Accordingly he is thrown into the *lions' den as punishment. Once again, however, God demonstrates to Daniel's persecutors that God's law is higher by delivering him from death in the den.

In the NT the most significant challenge to God's commandments occurrs when the Jewish leaders command the disciples "not to speak or teach at all in the name of Jesus" (Acts 4:18 NRSV). However, having the command from Christ to proclaim the gospel to all nations (Mt 28:19-20), the apostles refuse. Peter replies to their command, "We must obey God rather than men" (Acts 5:29 RSV). From then on the church is persecuted with flogging, imprisonment and death for their refusal to comply with the government's decree.

Other cases involve people who disobey government injunctions that do not directly demand that they disobey God but that do involve their tacit compliance in unrighteous practices. In the events leading up to the exodus, the Hebrew midwives help the Hebrew women to deliver their children and hide them despite *Pharaoh's decree to put all the newborn males to death (Ex 1:15-22). God commends these midwives for their fear of him, blessing them with households of their own. In similar manner Moses' mother disobeys the king's edict to destroy Hebrew males (Ex 2:1-10).

Soon after this, Moses himself participates in civil disobedience, leading the children of Israel out of Egypt against Pharaoh's will. He begins his career of civil resistance when he kills an Egyptian taskmaster who has beaten a Hebrew slave (Ex 2:11-12), his first recorded act of choosing to share ill-treatment with the people of God (Heb 11:24-25). Because God commanded him to lead the people out of Egypt, by God's direction he assaults Pharaoh and his people with a series of plagues that persuade the king to finally release the people (Ex 6—12). However, soon after he has let them go, Pharaoh pursues them with the intent to reenslave them. Moses is God's agent in the miraculous defeat of the Egyptian army by the *sea (Ex 14). Although he had ostensibly negotiated with Pharaoh for his people's release, Moses is in fact instrumental in forcing Pharaoh to release the people, an act he performs at God's command.

In another act of civil disobedience, Rahab the Canaanite hides the Hebrew spies from her city leaders (Josh 2). Rahab fears the God who has given her land to these people, and she desires to fight on the side of Yahweh (Josh 2:9-13). Thus she hides the spies who come to her and lies to the king of Jericho, saying that they have already left the city (Josh 2:5). God commends her act, claiming that her faith and obedience saved her from death at the Israelites' hands (Heb 11:31).

Some of the prophets also disobey their kings at God's command or in response to God's condemnation of their rule. King Ahab attempts several times to kill Elijah because of his message. Elijah announces a great drought on the land and is then forced to hide from Ahab's wrath (1 Kings 17). In addition, Elijah humiliates and slays the prophets of Baal, who the king supports, and then flees to Sinai (1 Kings 18). Obadiah similarly disobeys the king to obey God. When Jezebel attempts to kill all of God's prophets, Obadiah hides a hundred of them in caves and provides them with food (1 Kings 18:4). God praises him for this act, declaring that "Obadiah feared the LORD greatly" (1 Kings 18:3).

The NT also endorses stories of people protecting those who are persecuted by the government. The three wisemen worship the infant Jesus and disobey Herod's command to inform him about the newborn king (Mt 2:7-12). When the Jews and King Aretas attempt to capture and put the newly converted Paul to death, several of his disciples hide him and then helped him escape by letting him down in a basket through one of the city wall's openings (Acts 9:20-31; 2 Cor 11:32-33).

Finally, even Jesus refuses to submit to the religious authorities of his time. Although he has no complaint against the Roman civil authority, he consistently challenges the authority of the Jewish leaders. He heals a man on the Sabbath and overturns the tables of the moneychangers and vendors in the temple (Mt 12; 21). Although he commands submission to the governing authorities, Jesus demonstrates that his own authority is greater than that of the ruling priests because his authority comes from God. Thus he shows that in some cases in which God's authority conflicts with that of a government, civil disobedience is necessary.

See also BABYLON; BONDAGE/FREEDOM; EGYPT; EXODUS, SECOND EXODUS; PHARAOH; RESCUE.

CLAY

Although clay played a much more central role in ancient Near Eastern life than it does today, it is still familiar enough that Jeremiah's description of a local craftsman could easily apply to a modern studio artist (Jer 18:3-4 NASB). In addition to the many daily uses of clay vessels, artisans used clay to make molds in which to cast metal objects (1 Kings 7:46; 2 Chron 4:17). Its physical properties—pliable in one form, brittle in another—as well as its practical uses make clay a powerful biblical metaphor.

Beginning as a pliable and impressionable substance (Job 38:14; Ps 40:2), clay provides an excellent image for human beings as the work of God's creative hand (Is 64:8; Jer 18:6; Job 10:9; 33:6). The potter collecting clay (or mortar) worked it into the proper consistency by treading it, perhaps in the pit where he dug it (Nahum 3:14). The psalmist contrasts the treader's foot stuck in the clay with the secure foothold God provides after drawing him up

An Egyptian potter shapes clay on a potter's wheel.

out of the slippery *pit (Ps 40:2). The prophet warns of impending *judgment, a trampling on rulers as a potter treads his clay, suggesting a treading in preparation for God's reforming and refashioning (Is 41:25). As the master potter, God has the unquestionably sovereign right to give each of his creations a specific shape and purpose according to his will (Is 29:16; 45:9; Rom 9:21).

The fragility of dried, unfired clay offers a vivid depiction of weakness in words (Job 13:12), spirit (Ps 31:12), kingdoms (Is 30:14; Dan 2:41-42; Lam 4:2) and earthly existence in general (Job 4:19). Just as defiled vessels are to be shattered according to OT ritual laws (Lev 6:28; 11:33; 15:12), so those who dishonor God will be judged (Ps 2:9; Is 41:25; Jer 19:1-11; 22:28; 48:38; Rev 2:27). Those who serve God, however, are like earthen vessels containing valuables; they are both precious and useful to him (2 Cor 4:7; Tim 2:20; Acts 9:15). The hand of God that forms and transforms humans (Is 64:8) is echoed in the story of Jesus' applying healing clay to blind eyes (John 9:6-15).

See also BRICKS.

CLEAN AND UNCLEAN. *See* ANIMALS; CLEANSING; FOOD; PURITY.

CLEANSING

The biblical imagery of cleansing extends well beyond the approximately seventy-five appearances of the word in English translations. The context for this important biblical image is a complex portrayal of what is clean and unclean. To appreciate the image we must rid ourselves of many of our ideas of what is unclean and therefore requires cleansing, since these tend to be only hygienic. Though this is an important element of cleansing in the Bible, it is only part of the picture. In the Bible what is unclean can include *disease, dry rot in buildings, discharge from the sexual organs, corpses, certain animals, *sin and wickedness, *Gentiles, *demons or demonic possession of human beings, and even the common in contrast to the *holy. Part of the picture is ethical, but the ritualistic and physical also have their part.

At the heart of cleansing, especially in the OT, is the motif of ritual *purity and impurity. As stipulated by religious law (much of which is encapsulated in Lev 14—16 and Num 8; 19), a person or an object might be judged to be in a state of uncleanness that would prevent having any contact with the *temple or holy place. This state of impurity could be transferred, as when an unclean object (such as a corpse or menstruating woman) was touched. Ritual cleansing was the means by which the condition of impurity could be righted. While the spiritual principles underlying the need for cleansing in the Mosaic law are universal, the specific rituals that governed so much of Jewish religion were abrogated by the NT teaching concerning what it means to follow Christ. This was dramatically evidenced in Peter's vision (Acts 10) of clean and unclean *animals (in symbolic reference to the current distinction of Jew and Gentile), and in Christ's teaching about defilement coming from within a person, not from outside (Mk 7:19).

Throughout the Bible the cleansing of the body is highly regarded and practiced. No doubt this had important consequences in the prevention of disease. The attitude behind this high standard of hygiene is the biblical valuing of the bodily and physical. God is understood to be ruler over every part of human life and the created world. The human being is a psychosomatic unity, bearing God's image in this unity.

In the earliest times the distinction between clean and unclean *food did not obtain (Gen 9:3), though there is already a distinction between acceptable and unacceptable animal *sacrifices. Later, in the period of the establishment of the law, a distinction between clean and unclean animals for food is established, having the effect of making the law permeate every part of Hebrew life through ritual.

What was regarded as unclean grew even more complex as the requirements were added to in later centuries. Leviticus 11:1—17:16 portrays what is unclean and therefore requires cleansing. It is a set of instructions to the Hebrew priests in dealing with uncleanness, and it presents detailed distinctions between the clean and unclean. Its climax is the institution of the Day of *Atonement, the point of which was the cleansing of the sanctuary and the nation in God's eyes.

There were two dynamically related pairs of contrasts in the OT: between the holy and the common, and between the clean and the unclean. Both the clean and the unclean are subdivisions of the common. The common, in other words, is itself not in principle unclean, even in a fallen creation. But it can be defiled, thus requiring cleansing. There were some realities that could not be undefiled or cleansed, such as certain animals and *death. Some things, however, could be rendered holy by prescribed ritual, a process that could pertain to either persons or things. Even the high *priest was not exempt from sin, and provision was made for his cleansing (Lev 4:3-12).

The prophets in their teaching reinforced the necessity of cleansing from uncleanness, with a strong ethical emphasis, though presupposing the Levitical status quo. In later postexilic times, including the world of Jesus' life and ministry, the religious leaders extended the distinctions between clean and unclean laid down in the Mosaic law, thereby earning Jesus' condemnation for the false burden they imposed.

The OT picture of uncleanness vividly serves to convey the reality of the need for cleansing and atonement before God, with his requirement of sacrifice as the remedy. In his teaching, Jesus emphasizes moral rather than ceremonial purity, focusing on the heart of the separation between humankind and God. His teaching seizes the essence of OT teaching. His doctrine is expressed in his actions. Jesus reaches across the social divide to those who are outcasts and marginalized, touching the untouchable. The leper, the woman with a discharge of blood and even a dead body receive the touch of cleansing and of life.

The NT is triumphantly rich in its portrayal of the cleansing of human sin. Its picture of what cleanses includes the *water of life (Jn 3:5; Eph 5:26; Heb 10:22; with the literal necessity symbolizing the deeper cleansing); the *blood of Jesus (1 Jn 1:7); the word spoken by Jesus (Jn 15:3); the *sacrifice of the *Lamb of God (1 Cor 5:7); *faith in Jesus (Acts 15:9; Heb 10:22) and *forgiveness that comes after confessing sin (1 Jn 1:9). The image of water is particularly vibrant, for the water of life offered by Jesus is clean and life-giving to *drink (Jn 4:13-15; 7:37-39).

In the NT *baptism becomes a master image of cleansing. The spiritual significance of *washing with water in baptism, as practiced by John the Baptist, was in fact rooted in OT rituals of purification. Bathing was prescribed by the ceremonial law for people considered unclean (e.g., Lev 14:8, 9; Lev 15). Bathing and ceremonial washing were also associated with ordination to the priesthood (Lev 8:5, 6) and preparation to enter the Holy of Holies on the

Day of Atonement (Lev 16:3-4). Ritual purification through washing was linked symbolically with prayer for spiritual cleansing (see Ps 51:1-2, 7-10).

The Bible concludes with a proclamation that the clean (i.e., the cleansed; see Ezek 36:25-29) will enter the new creation, heaven itself. For the clean—Jew and Gentile alike, men, women and children—disease, death, the torment caused by evil spirits, the distress of broken relationships and the opposition of the natural world to humanity are gone forever. The holy, the clean and the common world are at last one, thanks to the cleansing brought about for the entire creation by the sacrifice of Christ (Rev 21: 26, 27; 22:14, 15).

See also BLOOD; DISEASE AND HEALING; FORGIVE-NESS; HOLINESS; PURITY; SACRED SPACE; SACRIFICE; WASH, WASHING.

BIBLIOGRAPHY. J. Neyrey, *Paul in Other Words: A Cultural Reading of His Letters* (Louisville: Westminster John Knox, 1990).

CLOSE. *See* SHUT, CLOSE.

CLOTHING. *See* GARMENTS.

CLOUD

Rarely do clouds appear in the Bible in a simple meteorological context, but the limited references to clouds and *weather reveal that the Hebrews were careful observers of nature. Elijah's servant knew that a cloud rising from the sea meant *rain (1 Kings 18:44) and that in contrast the high cirrus clouds from the desert were known to be rainless (Jude 12). The very first mention of clouds comes after the *flood where God establishes a new relationship with humankind through Noah, symbolized by a *rainbow in the clouds (Gen 9:12-17).

After the *exodus from Egypt, when the Israelites wander in the wilderness for forty years, their journey is marked by a pillar of cloud by day and a pillar of *fire by night (Ex 13:21, 22; 14:19, 20, 24, see later reflections in Neh 9:12, 19; Ps 78:14; 99:7; 105:39; and 1 Cor 10:1-2). Exodus 16:10 associates the cloud in the wilderness with the "*glory of the LORD." The cloud and the fire represents God's presence with them during their sojourn.

The cloud represents God's presence but also his hiddenness (see Lam 2:2). No one can see God and live, so the cloud shields people from actually seeing the form of God. It reveals God but also preserves the mystery that surrounds him.

During their wilderness wanderings, the Israelites camp for a long time at the foot of Mount *Sinai. While there, God reveals himself and his law to Moses and the people on top of the mountain. As the people look at the mountain, they hear and see "thunder and lightning, with a thick cloud over the mountain" (Ex 19:16 NIV, cf. also 24:16, 18; 34:5). Once again God's appearance is marked by cloud.

Also in the wilderness, God instructs the Israelites to build a place where they might worship him. We know this mobile sanctuary as the *tabernacle or tent of meeting. God makes his presence known there by means of a cloud that fills the most holy part of the building (Ex 33:9, 10; 40:34-38; Lev 16:2; Num 9:15-23). When the *temple later replaces the tabernacle as the place where God makes his presence known to Israel, that building too is filled with the cloud of God's glory (1 Kings 8:10-11; 2 Chron 5:13-14). Centuries later, when God turns against Israel because of its sin, he abandons his temple. Ezekiel sees this as the departure of the cloud from the Holy of Holies (Ezek 10:3-4).

A number of passages associate God's appearance as a *warrior with the cloud. Isaiah looks into the future and sees God moving in judgment against Egypt:

See, the LORD rides on a swift cloud
    and is coming to Egypt.
The idols of Egypt tremble before him,
    and the hearts of the Egyptians melt within
    them. (Is 19:1-2 NIV)

Clouds serve as God's war *chariot in the imagination of the OT poets and prophets (Ps 18:9; 68:4; 104:4; Dan 7:13; Nahum 1:3). This image of the warrior god riding a chariot into battle is an ancient one, antedating the Bible in Canaanite mythology, where Baal is given the frequent epithet "rider on the clouds."

While biblical writers associate clouds primarily with the appearance of God, they occasionally exploit other aspects of clouds to render vivid their ideas. Clouds are ephemeral, illustrating the *transience of life (Job 7:9), of safety (Job 30:15) and, in the light of God's grace, of human sin (Is 44:22). In Isaiah 18:4 God pronounces that he will quietly sneak up on Cush in judgment; he will be quiet like a "cloud of dew in the heat of harvest." Proverbs 16:5, on the other hand, likens a king's favor to "a rain cloud in spring."

The NT use of the cloud theme, however, returns to the theophanic, or more specifically Christophanic, function. At the transfiguration God spoke out of a cloud to identify Jesus as "my Son, whom I have chosen" (Lk 9:35). Jesus, like God in the OT, rides on a cloud (Acts 1:9). One of the most pervasive images of Christ's return is as one who rides his cloud chariot into battle (Mt 24:30; Mk 13:26; 14:62; Lk 21:27; Rev 1:7; cf. Dan 7:13).

See also DIVINE WARRIOR; GLORY; RAIN; WEATHER.

COLD. *See* TEMPERATURE.

COLORS

The ancient Hebrews experienced color primarily through nature; colors suggested to them elements of the physical world. Blue was the color of the sky, green the color of *grass and plants, red the color of *blood, white the color of *wool and *snow. These natural associations remain to some extent universal but have been weakened in modern society, which primarily experiences color through manufactured items of synthetic hues. The Hebrew vocabulary for color was quite limited, with only three distinct color words and essentially no words for painting, the visual arts or the concept of color and hue.

Colors are symbolic in the Bible because of their repeated use in certain contexts in ancient culture. Consider a modern example. Red and green have become associated with Christmas by repeated use in American culture. Neither color has any necessary or inherent connection with the significance or celebration of Christmas; however, for an American the holiday can be suggested by the use of these colors. Similarly the colors of the Bible are not symbols in the sense that "blue means this" or "red means that." The colors found in the Bible are symbolic because of their primary association with elements of nature and their use within the cultures of the biblical times.

The spectrum of colors is first implied in the Bible by the *rainbow God set in the sky as a sign of the *covenant he made to preserve life after the great flood (Gen 9:12-17). Colors are first named in the Bible when the Lord describes the *tabernacle and its contents to Moses. Blue, purple, and scarlet color the *linen curtains that form the tabernacle, the *garments of the high priest and the coverings for the holy altars and articles (Ex 25—28). The ephod of the high priest was woven of gold, blue, purple and scarlet yarn. Twelve colorful, precious gems, each representing a tribe of ancient Israel, were inset in the ephod (Ex 28:15-21). Colors make the place where God meets with his people visually appealing, but because of repeated use in ancient culture, they are suggestive as well.

In ancient culture the blue, purple and scarlet suggested wealth and royalty. Colored textiles were produced from natural dyes that were rare and expensive. Only wealthy and powerful *kings could afford to decorate their palaces with colored textiles (e.g., Esther 1:6; and frequent mention of royal robes as booty, e.g., Judg 5:30; Josh 7:21). In NT times Lydia could sustain an entire business dealing in purple cloth (Acts 16:14). Blue, purple and scarlet colored the tabernacle of ancient Israel, suggesting that Yahweh was the wealthy and powerful God-king, who brought an impoverished people out of *slavery in Egypt to make them a mighty nation. Because of their associations with deity and power, blue and purple were apparently also used to decorate idols in biblical times (Jer 10:9).

Blue. In ancient thought the sky was believed to separate the place of the gods from the human realm. Therefore blue, the color of the sky, could appropriately suggest the boundary between God and his people and symbolize his majesty. Like purple, blue was an expensive dye and thus connoted wealth and prestige. Blue was the dominant color of the vestments of ancient Israel's high priest (Ex 28). The high priest wore an outer garment of solid blue over the white robe of the priesthood. He was the boundary between the human and divine realms, moving in both as he ministered in the Holy of Holies.

Blue also separated the holy articles of the tabernacle from the people. When the tabernacle was dismantled and moved, solid blue cloths covered the ark of the covenant, the table of the presence, the golden lampstand and altar, and all of the tools used in the tabernacle (Num 4). Israel was a nation set apart for God, but the high priest and the most holy things were specially designated for the Lord's service. In this context blue suggests the boundary of holy separation unto the Lord. The blue coverings protected the sanctity of the holy things from the Israelites during times when the tabernacle was being dismantled and moved.

Purple. In biblical times purple dye was expensive. Therefore purple was worn only by those of high rank in royal courts (e.g., Dan 7:5, 16, 29). Because of this association the color suggests the power and wealth of royalty. A purple robe was placed on Jesus while soldiers mocked him (Jn 19:2, 5). In the tabernacle of ancient Israel the bronze altar on which the sacrificial animals were burned was covered in a solid purple cloth for travel (Num 4:13). In John's apocalyptic vision *Babylon, the great harlot, is dressed in purple, the color of political wealth and power, and in scarlet, the color of sin (Rev 17:4, 18:16). She is an image of the horror of the world's wealth and power corrupted by sin.

Scarlet. Scarlet (red), the color of blood, also colored the linen curtains of the tabernacle. One layer of the roof covering of the tabernacle was made of ram's skin dyed red (Ex 26:14). While it might be pressing the symbolism too far to say that the tabernacle, the place where God met his people, was symbolically covered with blood, the ritual slaughter of sacrificial animals in that place would only have reinforced the association of the color red with the blood of sacrifice (cf. Lev 14:4, 6, 49-52). In the book of Hebrews the cleansing efficacy of this sacrificial blood is explained as foreshadowing the blood of the ultimate and final sacrifice—Jesus Christ (Heb 9:11-28). The writer of Hebrews recalls that Moses used scarlet wool and animal blood to cleanse both the people and the tabernacle itself (Heb 9:19).

A visual contrast between scarlet and white is found in Isaiah 1:18: "Though your sins are like scarlet, they shall be as white as snow" (NIV). The contrast between scarlet and *white expresses the transition from guilt to purity worked by God's forgiveness. The biblical association of the color scarlet with sin continues in the imagery of modern literature, for instance in Nathaniel Hawthorne's *The Scarlet Letter.*

The two associations of the color scarlet—with blood and with images of sin—converge in John's Apocalypse, where Babylon, the great harlot, appears dressed in scarlet sitting on a scarlet beast covered with blasphemous names. In this scene of horror the harlot is drunk with the blood of those who bore testimony to Jesus (Rev 17:3-6).

Black. *Black is seldom used as a color in the Bible (Lev 13:31, 37; Song 1:5; 5:11; Zech 6:2, 6; Rev 6:5). It is often associated with the threatening presence of God in dark times of divine judgment upon sin and *evil. Throughout the OT, images of the coming of God in judgment are painted in hues of black. In anger God parts the heavens and comes down with dark *clouds under his feet; he is covered in darkness when he shoots his *arrows (Ps 18:9, 11). The day of the Lord, a day of judgment for sin, is described by the prophets as "a day of darkness and gloom, a day of clouds and blackness" (Zeph 1:15; Joel 2:2). The Gospels report that when Jesus died on the cross, bearing God's judgment on sin, darkness fell over the whole land (Mt 27:45; Mk 15:33; Lk 23:44). Generally, black simply describes an object's colors; but in about a quarter of its uses, it clearly accompanies God's judgment. In the Bible it is not used as an image of sin.

White. *White is used in biblical imagery as the contrasting opposite to black and darkness. It colors scenes of redemption from God's wrath and suggests the absence of darkness. It is the color of heaven's garments and symbolizes a dazzling *purity that dispels the darkness of divine wrath (Is 1:18; Dan 7:9; Mk 16:5; Rev 3:4). It is often used to describe the radiance of light in contrast to the darkness of divine wrath on evil and sin. For instance, in contrast to the image of God wrapped in darkness and descending to earth in judgment (e.g., Ps 18:7-11), Jesus is clothed in robes "as white as light" (Mt 17:2 NIV) when he is transfigured on the mount. In the book of Revelation the redeemed wear white garments (Rev 3:4; 6:11; 7:14; initiates were dressed in white linen in ancient religions), ride white horses (Rev 6:2) and have a white stone upon which is written a new name (Rev 2:17; cf. angels in white, Jn 20:12). Images of the new heaven and earth in Revelation are all white and light. There is no black or darkness in them, for the dark shadow of divine judgment will never again fall upon God's new creation, which has been made eternally pure by the blood of the Lamb.

Colors are not mentioned frequently in the Bible. However, in two instances a brilliant spectrum of color is found. One instance is of the colorful gemstones set in the ephod of the high priest (Ex 28:15-21). The other is in the visions of the heavenly city made of *jewels (Is 54:11-12; Rev 21:10, 18-21). In these images the visual beauty of color is combined with the splendor of jewels to express the opulence found in God's presence.

It is difficult to know with certainty which jewels the ancient words refer to and hence to know their colors. Nevertheless, imagine the visual delight of ruby reds, sapphire blues, emerald greens, amethyst purples, and pearly whites. The sparkling colors on the ephod of the high priest foreshadow the beauty of the heavenly city, suggesting that to be where God is, is to be in a place of unimaginable beauty, power and wealth. The heavenly city of eternal life is colored with every hue of the rainbow, the sign God first gave of his promise to preserve and not to destroy the life he had created (Gen 9:12-17).

See also BLACK; JEWELS AND PRECIOUS STONES; WHITE.

COLOSSIANS, LETTER TO THE

The purpose of Paul's letter to the Colossians is to refute the so-called Colossian heresy, a gnostic type of philosophy that taught that though Christ provided a good spiritual beginning, there was a deeper fullness available to those followers who would avail themselves of an ancient *gnōsis,* or knowledge. The *gnōsis,* said to have been corroborated by fresh revelations, instituted a system of arcane rites and legalistic asceticism. Paul answers this heresy with the brilliant assertion of the complete supremacy and adequacy of Christ.

Central to Paul's answer is the image of the cosmic Christ as given in the great Colossian *Christ hymn (Col 1:15-20). The hymn sings successively of Christ as creator, goal and sustainer of the universe, and reconciler of all things by his cross. The vision unabashedly asserts Christ's supremacy—"so that in everything he might have supremacy" (Col 1:18 NIV).

The key motif in Colossians is knowledge. Paul fights the fire of gnostic thinking with a fiery Christian *gnōsis.* Indeed, the initial mention of knowledge comes in his introductory prayer as he asks God to fill the Colossians with "the knowledge of his will through all spiritual wisdom and understanding" (Col 1:9 NIV). Significantly, the word he uses for knowledge is *epignōsis,* "full knowledge." His prayer was for a full decisive knowledge that would instill a spiritual *wisdom. The closely following Colossian hymn flames with the essential cosmic *gnōsis.* Also as Paul goes on to define the purpose of his ministry in Colossians 1:24—2:4, he describes it in terms of *gnōsis:* "to make known . . . the mystery" (Col 1:27 NIV). "My purpose is that they may be encouraged in heart and united in love, so that they may have the full riches of complete understanding, in order that they may know the mystery of God, namely, Christ, in whom are hidden all the treasures of wisdom and knowledge" (Col 2:2, 3 NIV). The reader should note that though the knowledge motif is not explicit after Colossians 2:3, it informs the remainder of the letter, because the practical wisdom for holy living (Col 3:1—4:6) rests on the *epignōsis.* In fact Paul alludes to it in the charge with which he opens this practical section, a call to focus on such knowledge: "Set your hearts on things above. . . . Set your minds on things above" (Col 3:1-2 NIV).

A parallel motif, mentioned just twice but of immense importance, is *plērōma,* "fullness" (*see* Fill, Fullness). Its first use is at the end of the Colossian hymn: "For God was pleased to have all his fullness dwell in him [Christ]" (Col 1:19 NIV). The reference to fullness here is an intentional slap at the false teachers, who apparently used the same word, *plērōma,* to denote the totality of all the thousands of divine emanations of lesser gods. The sense is that Jesus is not one of the lesser gods of the fullness. He is *the* Fullness. Colossians 2:9 puts it even more explicitly: "For in Christ all the fullness of the Deity lives in bodily form" (NIV). Fullness denotes the totality of divine power and attributes in Christ. Knowledge of this fullness is part of the *gnōsis* for which Paul prayed for the Colossians. Divine fullness establishes Christ's superiority beyond doubt. And with this, his adequacy to meet every believer's need fills his followers: "and you have been given fullness in Christ" (Col 2:10 NIV). Christ can hold all the fullness of deity, believers cannot. But believers are full of his fullness. This grand motif then informs the section on practical living.

Crucial to the understanding of Colossians is the metaphorical use of *circumcision. Normally circumcision does not refer to death but only to the cutting away of a small portion of flesh. Here in Colossians 2:11-15, however, it provides a gruesome metaphor for crucifixion. Jesus' "circumcision" on the *cross involved not the stripping away of a piece of flesh but the violent removal of his entire body in death. The Colossians who have been "given fullness in Christ" (Col 2:10) and are "in him" (Col 2:11), share spiritually in this circumcision, this death. Their sinful nature has been cut away; they have died to their former way of life.

The book of Colossians has remarkable spiritual symmetry. Its purpose is to refute gnostic thought by demonstrating the complete supremacy and adequacy of Christ. In doing this Paul fights fire with fire—the opponents' knowledge is countered by the full knowledge of Christ. The luminous Colossian hymn explodes with a brilliant revelation of the cosmic Christ (Col 1:15-20). Paul applies this understanding to the Colossians: they share in Christ's fullness (Col 2:9-10); they died in Christ's circumcision (Col 2:11-15); they must not be subject to legalism (Col 2:16-17), mysticism (Col 2:18-19) and asceticism (Col 2:20-23). They must fix their hearts and minds on the grand *gnōsis* above (Col 3:1-3). Then they will be able to put off the earthly nature (Col 3:5-11) and put on the qualities of the new nature (Col 3:12-17). They will live as they ought—as wives, husbands, children, slaves and masters (Col 3:18—4:1).

Colossians also contains conventional epistolary imagery and motifs. The gospel is something that bears *fruit and *grows (Col 1:6, 10). Christ's work of redemption is a *rescue story and a story of transfer from the *kingdom of darkness to the kingdom of God's Son (Col 1:13). God's wisdom and knowledge are *treasures (Col 2:3). Believers are both rooted and built up in Christ (Col 2:6). The lost state is a condition of being dead (Col 2:13). In the act of *redemption the condemnation that comes from the law is both canceled and nailed to the cross (Col 2:14). Sanctification consists of putting vices to death (Col 3:5). Spiritual virtues are clothes that one puts on (Col 3:9). Colossians is also memorable for its *paraenesis,* or section of exhortations, which includes lists of vices and virtues (Col 3:1—4:6). The latter includes one of two "household lists" in the NT, outlining the proper duties of spouses, parents and children, masters and servants.

See also CHRIST HYMN; EPHESIANS; FILL, FULLNESS.

BIBLIOGRAPHY. A. T. Lincoln, *Paradise Now and Not Yet* (Grand Rapids: Baker, 1991 [1981]); C. F. D. Moule, " 'Fullness' and 'Fill' in the New Testament," *SJT* 4 (1951) 79-86

COMBAT. *See* BATTLE STORIES; DIVINE WARRIOR.

COMEDY AS PLOT MOTIF

Comedy means two distinct things in literary criticism. One category is the humorous or laughable (*see* Humor). But comedy also denotes a type of story pattern. In fact it is one of four phases of the monomyth (see Plot Motifs). A full-fledged comic plot is a U-shaped story that descends into potential tragedy and then rises to a happy ending as obstacles to fulfillment are gradually overcome. Some comic plots record only the upward movement from bondage to freedom.

The progression of a comic plot is from problem to solution, from less than ideal experience to prosperity and wish fulfillment. The comic plot is the story of the happy ending par excellence. The plot consists of a series of obstacles that must be overcome en route to the happy ending. These obstacles may be blocking characters who thwart the desires of the protagonist(s), or they might be external circumstances or inner personality traits. The general movement is toward the establishment of some type of ideal society at the end, and an important feature of comic plots is the gradual assimilation of the *hero or heroine into society (in contrast to *tragic plots, where the protagonist gradually becomes isolated). The typical ending of a comic plot is a *marriage, *feast, reconciliation or *triumph over enemies. As for the blocking characters, they are either converted and assimilated into the ideal society, or they are banished from the scene of festivity.

The overall comic movement is accompanied by a host of familiar story elements and stock characters, including disguise, mistaken identity, intrigue, character transformation from bad to good, surprise, miracle, providential assistance, reversal (sometimes sudden) of misfortune, *rescue from disaster, *poetic justice, the motif of *lost and found, reversal of conventional expectations (so that, for example, the younger child is preferred over the older or the humble over the aristocratic) and sudden release. Whereas tragedy stresses what is inevitable, comedy is built around the unforeseen.

Several biblical stories are virtual case studies in comic plots. The story of *Ruth, for example, begins in tragic loss and then traces the gradual conquest of obstacles to a happy ending. The story of *Esther is similar, as a whole nation is exposed to threat before a counterplot suddenly reverses the fortunes of both the nation and the protagonists, Esther and Mordecai. The stories of *Abraham and Sarah's quest for a son, of *Joseph's eventual attainment of his prophesied destiny and of the *prodigal son of Jesus' parable also illustrate the form. The stories of Job and of Jesus in the Gospels are also U-shaped stories with happy endings, despite the preponderance of tragedy and suffering that occupy the center of the stories.

The truth is that that comedy is the dominant narrative form in the Bible. There are relatively few full-fledged tragedies in the Bible. The materials for tragedy are everywhere in the stories of sin and disobedience, but the Bible is almost completely an anthology of tragedies averted through characters' *repentance and God's *forgiveness. The comic plot is the deep structure of biblical narrative. It is the implied story of the OT prophetic books, which predict dire *judgment but almost invariably end with scenes of *restoration and festivity. It is the story of the individual's redemption from evil and punishment to salvation.

The overall plot of the Bible is a U-shaped comic plot. The action begins with a perfect world inhabited by perfect people. It descends into the misery of fallen history and ends with a new world of total happiness and the conquest of evil. The book of Revelation is the story of the happy ending par excellence, as a conquering hero defeats evil, marries a bride and lives happily ever after in a palace glittering with *jewels. Within this master plot of comedy, numerous individual U-shaped stories populate the Bible—stories of heroes like Gideon, Deborah and *David who conquer military foes, of protagonists in Jesus' parables who find a *pearl of great price or a lost *sheep, of the nation of Israel marching through the *wilderness to a promised *land, of the NT church facing *persecution and yet conquering the world.

See also BIBLE; CHARACTER TYPES; PLOT MOTIFS; TRAGEDY AS PLOT MOTIF.

COMFORT

The Bible is as confident about the possibility of real and lasting comfort in Christ as it is realistic about the sorrows of life: "Blessed are those who mourn, for they will be comforted" (Mt 5:4 NIV). The essence of comfort is that it is reciprocal: someone extends the comfort, and someone else receives it.

Although images of comfort are relatively scarce in the Bible, touching examples of comfort are numerous. Comfort is usually tendered in the context of *mourning for the dead, most often by family members. So Rebekah comforts Isaac after the death of his mother (Gen 24:67), and *David comforts Bathsheba after the death of their first son (2 Sam 12:24). *Ruth's loyalty to Naomi in her grief is a powerful expression of kinship, and the comfort that Ruth in turn receives from Boaz (Ruth 2:13) is a reward for her faithfulness. Part of the power of the parable of the good Samaritan (Lk 10:25-37) lies in the fact that relief comes from outside the normal bonds of family and community.

No comfort is also a recurrent biblical motif. Rachel in Ramah symbolizes the futility of comfort for the grief-stricken, "weeping for her children and refusing to be comforted, because her children are no more" (Jer 31:15; Mt 2:18 NIV). False comfort is a telltale sign of false prophecy (Zech 10:2). The sufferings of *exiles (Lam 1) and victims of oppression are exacerbated by the fact that "they have no comforter" (Eccles 4:1). In the day of earthly judgment the social order collapses, and not even family members are able to give condolence (Jer 16:7). Worse still, the "good things" provided by earthly comforts will prove to have been no comfort at all when compared with the comfort that only the righteous receive hereafter (Lk 16:19-31).

Misguided attempts to comfort are perhaps even worse than a lack of comfort. *Job's "comforters" are the classic example. When Job's acquaintances "heard about all the troubles that had come upon him, they set out from their homes and met together by agreement to go and sympathize with him and comfort him" (Job 2:11 NIV). Eliphaz, Bildad and Zophar begin well, sitting in commiserative silence with him for seven days and seven nights. But these would-be comforters eventually give Job more discomfort than comfort, becoming a case study in how *not* to minister to the grieving. For their false accusations, trite moralisms and doctrinal misapplications, they deserve the rebuke Job later gives them: "Miserable comforters are you all!" (Job 16:2 NIV).

The failure of earthly comforts and comforters to provide lasting succor points to a need for comfort that only God can satisfy. He is "the Father of compassion and the God of all comfort" (2 Cor 1:3 NIV; cf. Phil 2:1). Like a good shepherd, God comforts his *sheep with *rod and staff (Ps 23:4), providing guidance, protection, rescue and even correction. Divine comfort is more frequently expressed anthropomorphically. According to the psalmist the contented believer is "like a weaned child with its mother" (Ps 131:2 NIV; cf. Is 66:13), able to rest in the Lord's arms without agitation. Full *atonement for sin and full *restoration of the exiles to Zion prove Isaiah's claim that "the LORD comforts his people and will have compassion on his afflicted ones" (Is 49:13 NIV). The very cadence of the words that introduce the comfort motif in Isaiah has a soothing effect: "Comfort ye, comfort ye my people, saith your God" (Is 40:1 KJV; cf. Zech 1:13)

The comfort that the incarnate Christ offers is exemplified in his *weeping with Mary over the death of Lazarus (Jn 11:33-36) and most of all in his raising him back to life (vv. 38-44). The pathos of Christ spills over into the lives of believers, "so that we can comfort those in any trouble with the comfort we ourselves have received from God" (2 Cor 1:4-5 NIV).

Recent translations tend to render the Greek *paraklētos* as "Counselor," but the nuance of the more traditional "Comforter" should not be abandoned. By guiding Christ's disciples into all truth (Jn 15:26) and remaining with them always (Jn 14:16), the Holy Spirit sets their troubled hearts at rest (Jn 14:1, 27).

See also MOURNING; SUFFERING; WEEPING.

COMMANDMENT. *See* LAW.

CONCEAL. *See* COVER, COVERING.

CONFIDENCE

Confidence denotes trust in something or someone. It involves a high degree of certainty and faith, often in a person, to act in accordance with our expectations or hopes. We can have confidence in God and in our standing with him. We can also have confidence in others to trust them with intimate details of our lives.

Scripture shows that confidence in God will never lead to disappointment. Out of the fifty-three references in Scripture to confidence, approximately half refer to the ability to have confidence in the Lord or one's standing before him. Time and time again those who trust in the Lord see victory; believers can know that there is certainty and security in Christ. As Proverbs 3:25-26 states, "Have no fear of sudden disaster or of the ruin that overtakes the wicked, for the LORD will be your confidence and will keep your foot from being snared" (NIV). Those who trust in God will not be disappointed, but those whose confidence lies elsewhere will come to ruin (see also 2 Chron 32:7-8; Ps 71:5; Jer 17:7-8; 2 Cor 3:4-5; Eph 3:12; Phil 3:3; Heb 3:14). Likewise, confidence of our standing with God allows us to declare that we "will see the goodness of the LORD in the land of the living" (Ps 27:13). We can approach God with confidence, knowing that we will not be destroyed by his wrath because of our sin, but rather will be loved and heard because of our redemption (Heb 4:16; 10:19; 13:6; 1 Jn 3:21).

Placing confidence in the righteous is also a safe bet. Paul has confidence in the Corinthians (2 Cor 2:3; 7:4, 16), who bring him pride, encouragement and joy. Likewise, the godly *wife has her husband's full and loving confidence (Prov 31:11).

However, Scripture condemns those who place their confidence in themselves or in unrighteous persons. Jesus speaks harshly against such arrogance and tells the parable of the Pharisee and the tax collector to warn against confidence in oneself (Lk 18:9; cf. Job 6:19-20; Jer 49:31). Confidence in another person places him or her in front of God (Ezek 29:16) and in some situations may even result in misery: "Do not trust a neighbor; put no confidence in a friend. Even with her who lies in your embrace be careful of your words. For a son dishonors his father, a daughter rises up against her mother" (Mic 7:5-6). Confidence in oneself or another not only takes the place of God, but it also results in disappointment and ruin. Finite beings cannot bring fulfillment, according to Micah 7:5-6, and only God has control over life circumstances. Idols are mute and senseless, and "those who make them will be like them, and so will all who trust in them" (Ps 115:8).

The Bible also warns about whom we place in our confidence; human beings, being sinful creatures, will betray a confidence (Prov 11:13; 20:19; 25:9).

Samson's faith in Delilah led to his eventual capture by the Philistines, humiliation and death (Judg 16:15-30). Yet the Bible tells us that the upright are placed in God's confidence (Ps 25:14; Prov 3:32). The wise discern whom they may trust and are careful to be worthy of the confidence of God and others.

See also FAITH; FORTRESS; FOUNDATION; ROCK.

CONSTELLATIONS. *See* COSMOLOGY.

CONSTRUCTION. *See* BUILD, BUILDING.

CONTRITE, CONTRITION

In English Bibles the words *contrite* or *broken (in reference to the heart/spirit) occur a relatively few number of times, but the concept of *humility and acceptance of divine providence born out of trials is quite prominent. Throughout Scripture the theme is repeated that the contrite enjoy a special place in God's care. They may carry *wounds from the tragic events of their lives, but God delights in the humility born of this brokenness. "For this is what the high and lofty One says: . . . 'I live in a high and holy place, but also with him who is contrite and lowly in spirit, to revive the spirit of the lowly and to revive the heart of the contrite' " (Is 57:15 NIV; *see* High; Low).

The English Bible terminology for contrition is not clear, in part because the same Hebrew word *(dākâ)* (literally, "crush") is used to describe those who are devastated by an action, as in Job 5:4 when Eliphaz describes the plight of the fool's offspring: "His children are far from safety, crushed in court without a defender," (NIV) and an action which humbles one without disabling the person. The crushing here refers to exploitation and being rendered powerless. Such events may have happened to the contrite, but the nuance is different. The contrite have been bruised and injured, but it is their pride that has been irretrievably crushed. The crushing events of life do not automatically make one contrite. They may result either in bitterness (Ex 1:14; Ruth 1:20) or genuine contrition as with Nebuchadnezzar (Dan 4:37).

Broken/contrite must therefore be distinguished from actions that leave one devastated, immobilized, crushed, hardened or embittered. The contrite, the person broken in the right place, has been bruised or crushed in a way that results in true *humility. This person does not carry the anger, fear of punishment or lowered self-esteem that characterize the bitter person.

Adversity or a heightened awareness of sin can result in a stripping away of the natural *pride, leaving a tender and contrite heart. One passage that deeply shapes the image of contrition is Psalm 51, in which David, humbled by the prophetic denouncement of his sin with Bathsheba, declares that "The sacrifices of God are a broken spirit; a broken and contrite heart, O God, you will not despise" (Ps 51:17 NIV). In this psalm David also uses the related image of being brokenhearted.

Repentance: A Defining Characteristic. In some contexts a broken person is one who responds to the prompting of the Holy Spirit in repentance (Ps 51:17; Is 57:15). A brokenhearted person is the opposite of the self-made, hardhearted person. The fundamental difference between these two types of individuals is most evident in their reactions to being confronted with their own sins (e.g., David and Saul). The contrite person repents and is humbled.

Hearing and Responding to God's Word. The humble and contrite are able to hear God and tremble at, rather than mock, his word: "This is the one I esteem: he who is humble and contrite in spirit, and trembles at my word" (Is 66:2 NIV). The contrite and humble can be trusted with the word they hear not to distort it to their own personal ends. Paul clearly links humility and hearing God when he writes about his thorn in the flesh: "To keep me from becoming conceited because of these surpassingly great revelations, there was given me a thorn in my flesh, a messenger of Satan, to torment me" (2 Cor 12:7 NIV).

A Unique Access to God. God delights in the prayers of the humble. Those who come without dark ulterior motives or in violation of his explicit commands, but as *children to a loving parent, receive his hearing. The contrition may be the result of an affliction sent against them; nonetheless, if they are humble, God inclines his ear toward them. "When I shut up the heavens so that there is no rain, or command locusts to devour the land or send a plague among my people, if my people, who are called by my name, will humble themselves and pray and seek my face and turn from their wicked ways, then will I hear from heaven and will forgive their sin and will heal their land" (2 Chron 7:13-14 NIV). By contrast the worship of the proud wearies God: "Never again will you be haughty on my holy hill. But I will leave within you the meek and humble, who trust in the name of the LORD" (Zeph 3:11, 12 NIV).

There is no clear image for the contrite, but contrition or humility is often shown through bowing. Ahaziah's messenger to Elijah "went up and fell on his knees before Elijah. 'Man of God,' he begged, 'please have respect for my life and the lives of these fifty men, your servants!' " (2 Kings 1:13 NIV). Similarly, the man with leprosy in Mark 1:40-45 comes to Jesus on his knees, begging for healing (Cf. Mk 5:6; 10:17).

True contrition can come in variety of ways. One is an awareness of *weakness, failure or sin. Clearly David stands as an example here (Ps 51) of someone broken by sin, but so do Manasseh (2 Chron 33) and Nebuchadnezzar (Dan 4). Secondly, an encounter with God can produce contriteness. Isaiah writes that he saw the Lord "high and lifted up" (6:1), and through this he came to know his own uncleanness and the uncleanness of the people of God. "Woe is me," he exclaimed. Receiving the *cleansing of God, he was able to hear and respond to the call of God

upon his life: "Here I am; send me." His ministry follows his heightened awareness of the holiness of God and his own sin. Saul reported that on the Damascus Road: "We all fell to the ground, and I heard a voice saying to me in Aramaic, 'Saul, Saul, why do you persecute me? It is hard for you to kick against the goads' " (Acts 26:14 NIV). The proud Pharisee is led blind and defenseless into the city he was prepared to enter with power and authority. A third avenue to contrition is providential events beyond our control that defeat our myths of being in control of our lives. We sense no alternatives and feel boxed in, cornered, with nowhere to go, nowhere to turn. Job senses this as he lost all and sits in despair, but recovers after an encounter with God teaches him that "I spoke of things I did not understand, things too wonderful for me to know" (Job 42:3 NIV) and "My ears had heard of you but now my eyes have seen you" (Job 42:5 NIV). Finally, the dark night of the soul can produce contrition. At times God withdraws from his people. Contrition is birthed by the sense that one cannot control God. The psalms include a number of cases of crying out to God and experiencing his silence (Ps 22; 88; 102). Paul relates how he sought God about a problem he terms his "thorn" and found that God would not remove it because "My grace is sufficient for you, for my power is made perfect in weakness" (2 Cor 12:9 NIV).

See also BROKENNESS; HEART; HUMILITY; LOW; PRIDE.

CONVERSION

To be converted is to undergo a change of direction. This is the essential core of the imagery surrounding conversion in the Bible. While the term itself is rarely used in the Bible, stories of conversion are prominent, chiefly in the NT. OT counterparts are heathens who reject their own traditions in order to embrace the Jewish faith and God. The common denominator in all of the biblical references to conversion is that the individual recognizes his or her need for the one true God and rejects all other alternatives. Typically this action is referred to as "having faith." Biblical synonyms for conversion include *repentance, receiving *salvation and believing. The biblical imagery accompanying conversion is consistently one of dramatic change; thus those who always believed or always knew of God are not referred to as converts. The children of Israel and Jesus' disciples in his lifetime never had clear moments of conversion recorded in the Bible, although clearly the same faith was necessary.

We read about godly men and women in the OT, but we catch few glimpses of conversions. *Jacob's life was so changed by his encounter with God in his *wrestling match at the brook Jabbok (Gen 32:22-32) that it can be regarded as a conversion story. The call and obedience of *Abraham to leave his father's house and religion constituted a change of life so radical as to be a conversion—a change of direction, with a drastic new ritual of *circumcision as the accompanying sign (Gen 17). Thereafter, those who wished to become Jewish proselytes and accept the God of Abraham were also circumcised. Circumcision was thus the OT symbol for conversion to a belief in God, signifying the accompanying dramatic change in the individual's life.

Other OT examples of conversion involved not only a change in the individual's religion but a change in culture and lifestyle as well. Rahab is the first recorded proselyte. According to Hebrews, the necessary factor was that she had faith, which she demonstrated by calling the Hebrew God "God in heaven above and on earth below" (Josh 2:11 NRSV; cf. Heb 11:31). Because she acted on her confession by hiding the spies, she and her family were saved and became a part of the nation of Israel. Another OT convert was Ruth, who abandoned her own people and gods to follow her mother-in-law from her native Moab to Israel. In her statement of faith she declared, "Your people shall be my people, and your God, my God" (Ruth 1:16 NRSV). Thus Ruth too believed God and converted to the Hebrew religion.

The OT also contains stories of foreign rulers or peoples who believed God or who repented from their sins for his sake, but who are not cited as converting to Judaism. In this category are the people of Nineveh, who repented from their wickedness at Jonah's warning, and King Darius of Persia, who, convinced by Daniel's miraculous survival of the lions' den, made a law demanding that his kingdom worship "the living God," whose "dominion will be forever" (Dan 6:26). Similarly, God humbled King Nebuchadnezzar of Babylon to a confession of faith by sending a period of madness upon him for seven years (Dan 6). At the end of this time Nebuchadnezzar praised God as "the Most High . . . who lives forever" (Dan 6:34). These people repented of unbelief and sin and confessed a faith in God. If they indeed held onto that faith, then they could be considered among those believers who "hear the word of God and do it" (Luke 8:21). More ambiguous is the case of Naaman. After he was healed of leprosy under Elisha's direction, he took earth from Israel back home with him, in keeping with ancient belief that linked deities with specific regions, but he also asked pardon for bowing with his master in the house of Rimmon (2 Kings 5:17-19).

The NT contains a far more vivid picture of conversion. The chief symbol of conversion is *baptism. Such a symbol is two-fold, for it is at once the literal baptism in water that Jesus called for in the Great Commission and also the baptism in the *Holy Spirit, which is the seal of the new believer's faith and salvation (Mt 28:19; Eph 1:3). In addition to this symbol Jesus refers to conversion in symbolic illustrative language. He calls it being born again of water and the Holy Spirit (Jn 3:5), moving from *darkness to *light (Jn 3:21), drinking from the living *water that is himself and having rivers of living water flowing from the believer's own heart (Jn 7:38), and

moving from death into life (Jn 11:25). In addition he illustrates conversion with the parable of the sower, claiming that those who believe are like the good soil in which the seeds grow successfully (Lk 8:5-15). This bearing of *fruit is illustrative of those who "when they hear the word, hold it fast in an honest and good heart, and bear fruit with patient endurance" (Lk 8:15 NRSV)

The most paradigmatic conversion story in the Bible is that of Paul (Acts 9:1-22; 22:1-16)—a story so famous that to this day we speak of a "Damascus road experience" as a metaphor for sudden conversion. At its core it is a story of a person's life totally reversed—from a zeal to persecute Christians to a zeal to preach the gospel. The imagery of the conversion itself highlights its dramatic nature, with a flashing light that blinded Paul, a falling to the ground in submission, a miraculous accusing voice from heaven, temporary blindness, a speechless group of onlookers and the subsequent falling of scales from the eyes of the convert. The immediate result is boldness in proclaiming Jesus. The essential motifs stand silhouetted: a personal and overpowering encounter with Christ, submission to God, a casting off of something (picturing as losing a weight or impediment), senses heightened, vision restored, the washing of baptism to symbolize cleansing from sin, and a new lifestyle and values.

Although the most radical conversion story is that of Paul, many other examples of conversion appear in the NT. Among them are Cornelius, the first Gentile convert (Acts 10); the jailer converted by Paul and Silas (Acts 16:13); Zacchaeus, the tax-collector (Lk 19:1-10); the thief on the cross next to Jesus (Lk 23:39-43); and the many people, both Jews and Gentiles, converted at Pentecost and subsequently (Acts 2:38-41). Some of these converts believed directly because of Jesus' words and miracles, and others believed because of the apostles' words. Yet one of their common bonds was that they were often the most unlikely to have been saved. Often they were Gentiles who had never heard of the God of Israel or sinners whose actions were obvious and repulsive to those around them. As John comments, very few of the righteous Pharisees believed in Christ (Jn 7:48). Thus the essential element in each of these converts appears to have been a willingness to recognize sinfulness, to abandon all past beliefs and to believe the gospel in its entirety. Jesus reminds the Pharisees of that, commenting that clearly the chief priests did not believe all that Moses had said or else they would have believed him (Jn 5:46).

Mention must be made, finally, of NT characters who refuse conversion when it is offered to them. This is the implied state of those who reject Christ's claims in the Gospels, focused most clearly in the case of the rich young man who "went away sorrowful" (Mt 19:22 RSV; Mk 10:22) because he could not meet the demand of conversion, namely, to give up his riches. Equally memorable is the great refusal— King Agrippa, who dismisses Paul's presentation of the gospel with a statement in Acts 26:28 that is variously translated as "Almost thou persuadest me to be a Christian" (KJV) and "In a short time you think to make me a Christian!" (RSV).

Conversion is above all an initiation—an entry into something new. It also involves reversal—a casting off of the old and embracing of the new. It is a cataclysmic event in the life of the convert. Conversion focuses on the moment (even if long in preparation), and it portrays the person at a crossroads. It involves a turn of direction in a person's life and is the supreme example of the biblical motif of newness (*see* New), best expressed in the classic passage: "If anyone is in Christ, there is a new creation: everything old has passed away; see, everything has become new!" (2 Cor 5:17 NRSV).

See also BAPTISM; CLEANSING; FAITH; NEW; REPENTANCE; REVERSAL.

COPPER. *See* MINERALS.

CORINTHIANS, LETTERS TO THE

Paul's concern in 1 and 2 Corinthians is the reconciliation of division, a topic given theological expression at 2 Corinthians 5:16-21. In 1 Corinthians the fracture lines run between members of the congregations in areas such as the status of groups and individuals, litigation, *marriage, *food, *idolatry, the Lord's *Supper, and spiritual gifts. In 2 Corinthians the divisions lie between Paul himself and the members. The burden of the imagery in both letters is to counter the divisiveness endemic to this context by asserting unity and order against fragmentation.

Since in both Roman and Jewish tradition the human body could symbolically replicate the social group, it is perhaps not surprising that Paul's most explicit unifying imagery should involve the human body (1 Cor 12:12-31). This extended analogy of the community with the body (directly expressed at 1 Cor 12:28) is introduced to substantiate his claim that the many spiritual gifts come from one and the same Spirit (1 Cor 12:11). Yet since ancient Mediterranean peoples regarded some parts of the body (the *head, the *eyes, etc.) as more honorable than others (see Julius Pollux, *Onomastikon* 2.36), to use body imagery to express unity carried the risk of confirming existing status divisions in the community based on the possession of charismatic gifts. Paul's awareness of this danger emerges when he somewhat artificially seeks to overturn the accepted low status of some bodily organs (1 Cor 12:24-25).

The most persistent image that runs through both letters, however, is of *building, specifically, of house construction. The literal basis for such imagery encompasses the household as the original conversion group (1 Cor 1:16; 16:15) and the organization of the community into house churches (1 Cor 16:19). This image thus evokes the sense of integration derived from a single architectural unit and also the cohesion and exclusiveness that characterized the *family as the strongest social unit in the Mediterranean world of this period, bound together by group honor. Although the main Greek noun and verb that combine these words (*oikodomō* and *oikodomeō*) are translated in the Vulgate as *aedificatio* and *aedificare*, leading to the English "edification," we should not too readily allow such a semantic shift to obscure their original sense for Paul.

Paul launches upon this theme to strengthen his criticism of the factions that look to him or Apollos: "for we are God's fellow-workers, you are God's farm, God's building [*oikodomē*]" (1 Cor 3:9 NIV). Apollos has built upon a *foundation laid by Paul, and each will receive a reward depending on the foundation used and the manner of building (*epoikodomeō;* 1 Cor 3:10, 12, 14).

Later, Paul inserts into his two discussions of idol meat statements of the importance of the community being built up (*oikodomeō*), as opposed to being inflated with knowledge (1 Cor 8:1), or subject to everything being permitted (1 Cor 10:23). The necessity of community construction is again prominent in his desire to regulate potentially divisive charismatic phenomena so as to build up the Corinthian church, to which end Paul employs the nominal (*oikodomē;* 1 Cor 14:3, 5, 12, 26) and the verbal forms (*oikodomeō;* 1 Cor 14:4, 17). He emphasizes the priority of the spiritual gifts that involve rational discourse as opposed to glossolalia, which is nonrational; for the first builds up the community (*ekklēsia*) and the second only the individual involved (1 Cor 14:4-5). Paul summarizes his position: "Let all things be done for building up [the community]" (1 Cor 14:26 NRSV).

Paul reiterates this imagery in 2 Corinthians and explicitly connects it with the main issue in this letter by stating in two key places—at the beginning and end of the extended defense of his ministry (2 Cor 10:8; 13:10)—that he received his authority from the Lord for the purpose of building them up (*oikodomē*), not tearing them down, and furthermore that this was his whole aim (2 Cor 12:19).

A different deployment of house imagery comes in 2 Corinthians 5:1-10, for here Paul integrates it with imagery of the body in an important statement of his views on resurrection and final judgment. He contrasts our body, or earthly home (*oikia*), with God's building (*oikodomē*), the eternal dwelling (*oikia*) not made by human *hands that awaits us in heaven. Although the emphasis here is individual rather than social, the close connection Paul sees between these two visual fields suggests why he has employed both of them as the main images to promote unity in the congregation.

Paul further develops this imagery to remind his readers that they are actually the place where God's Spirit lives (*oikei*), his *temple (*naus;* 1 Cor 3:16, 17; 2 Cor 6:16). In the example from 2 Corinthians, this image is used to emphasize the exclusive nature of the community in relation to the world of unbelievers, although at a more exalted theological level than the simpler intimacy of the domestic household (*oikos*).

Related to house imagery is Paul's use of the words *"brother" (adelphos) or *"sister" (adelphē) to refer his fellow believers some forty times in 1 Corinthians and some twelve times in 2 Corinthians. Paul regarded the imagery of fictive kinship as vital to underline the cohesiveness and distinctive identity of the congregations.

In 2 Corinthians a pivotal image for expressing his position is that of the diakonos, the "humble *servant" (2 Cor 3:3, 6, 8, 9; 4:1; 5:18; 6:3-4; 8:4, 19, 20; 9:1, 12, 13; 11:8, 15, 23), which here conveys the meaning of a broker acting between heavenly patrons and human clients, but is also related to the household theme, since the original meaning of diakonos is someone who waits at table.

Yet Paul did not see himself merely as a brother or a servant, for he also asserted his authority as a *father, akin to a pater familias in the Roman social system that obtained at Corinth (Joubert). Thus he addresses his readers as those he has begotten in Christ Jesus (1 Cor 4:15), as his "beloved *children" (1 Cor 4:14; so also Timothy at 1 Cor 4:17), or simply as "children" (2 Cor 6:13) for whom he lays up an inheritance (2 Cor 12:14). A vital aspect of this metaphorical patria potestasi is that they must be obedient to him (2 Cor 2:9; 10:6), even to the extent of adhering to his direction to excommunicate a sinful member (1 Cor 5:1-5).

The most striking use of imagery in healing the breach between himself and his readers in 2 Corinthians occurs at 3:3—4:6, where the Mediterranean social reality of group *honor is again evident. To demonstrate the proof of his claim not to peddle the Word of God as others do (1 Cor 2:17), Paul proposes that the presence of God flows like *light from Christ (the image [eikōn] of God), to his gospel and then, as a result of his humble service (diakonia), onto believers, who reflect that unveiled light more brightly than Moses on Sinai.

Finally, Paul reinforces his authority by the use of imagery from *warfare (2 Cor 6:7; 10:3-5) and from *athletics (1 Cor 9:24-27). On the other hand, he also uses images that emphasize his lowliness, such as a captive dragged along in disgrace at the end of Christ's *triumphal procession (2 Cor 2:14) or an earthenware vessel (2 Cor 4:7). While visual images of this type no doubt assisted an ancient audience that was listening (rather than reading) to get the point, the apostle himself warrants the importance of one image in particular by noting that he resolved "to hold before his mind's eye [eidenai] nothing but Jesus Christ, and him crucified" (1 Cor 2:1).

See also BUILD, BUILDING; HOME, HOUSE; FAMILY; SERVANT.

BIBLIOGRAPHY. S. J. Joubert, "Managing the Household: Paul as Paterfamilias of the Christian Household Group in Corinth," in Modelling Early Christianity: Social-Scientific Studies of the New Testament in Its Context, ed. P. F. Esler (London and New York: Routledge, 1995) 213-223; B. J. Malina, The New Testament World: Insights from Cultural Anthropology (Rev. ed., Louisville, KY.: Westminster John Knox, 1993); S. Pogoloff, Logos and Sophia: The Rhetorical Situation of 1 Corinthians (SBLDS 134; Atlanta: Scholars Press, 1992); B. Witherington III, Conflict and Community in Corinth: A Socio-Rhetorical Commentary on 1 and 2 Corinthians (Grand Rapids: Eerdmans, 1995).

CORN. See GRAIN; WHEAT.

CORNERSTONE

The cornerstone is the principal *stone around which construction in antiquity was achieved. In the lexicon of biblical images of architecture, no image is more evocative than the cornerstone, the focal point of a building, the thing on which it most depends for structural integrity. Thus early in the catalog of God's acts of creation in Job 38:6, the divine voice from the *whirlwind asks regarding the world, "Who laid its cornerstone?"

Overshadowing all biblical references is the messianic use of the image. Its first appearance describes the vindication of Israel's king: "The stone which the builders rejected has become the head of the corner" (Ps 118:22 RSV). Although the original meaning of the text is uncertain, the Aramaic paraphrase of the Targum clearly understands the passage in a royal sense: "The young man which the builders abandoned is among the sons of Jesse and is worthy to be appointed to kingship and rule." The passage is taken to refer to David (cf. Tg. Ps 118:23-26).

The explicit Davidic interpretation of the Targum may help explain why Jesus used this passage in reference to the parable of the *vineyard tenants (Mk 12:1-12). Just as the wicked vineyard tenants (= the ruling priests) rejected the vineyard owner's (= God) son (= Jesus), so the "stone" (= Jesus, Israel's true king) rejected by the "builders" (= the ruling priests) would become the cornerstone (= foundation of God's restored people), which would in turn be the foundation of a new community of faith (cf. Acts 4:10-11; 1 Pet 2:4-5). The climax of all these references speaks of "Christ Jesus himself as the chief cornerstone" (Eph 2:20) of the metaphoric *temple consisting of believers.

The cornerstone image is further amplified by allusions to the "stone of stumbling" and "rock of offense" images found in Isaiah (8:14; 28:16). The combination of these Isaiah passages, along with the one cited above from Psalm 118:22 (cf. 1 Pet 2:4-10), links the early church's understanding of faith with its emerging Christology: to the one who has faith, Jesus Christ is the chosen, precious *foundation stone; but to the one who does not have faith, he is a stone of *stumbling.

See also FOUNDATION; STONE; STUMBLE, STUMBLING; TEMPLE.

BIBLIOGRAPHY. F. F. Bruce, "New Wine in Old Wine Skins: III. The Corner Stone," ExpT 84 (1972-1973) 231-35; J. D. M. Derrett, " 'The Stone That the Builders Rejected,' " in *Studia Evangelica IV*, ed. F. L. Cross (TU 102; Berlin: Akademie, 1968) 180-86.

CORROSION. See RUST.

CORRUPTION

Corruption is a decay into a state of rottenness. Although the Bible supplies images of physical corruption—the stench in Egypt after some of the *plagues; the *worm-infested manna that some people left until the sabbath (Ex 16:20); the whitewashed tombs to which Jesus compares the Pharisees, "full of the bones of the dead and of all kinds of filth" (Mt 23:27 NRSV); the diseased Herod "eaten by worms" in his entrails (Acts 12:23)—corruption is mainly a moral and spiritual quality.

The theme of corruption by sin is a major one in the Bible. Synonyms for the word *corruption* include pollution, decay, uncleanness, defilement and profaning. In the OT especially, corruption appears numerous times as a description of those who have departed from God's commandments and turned to their own sinful ways. It therefore implies a deterioration of something or someone that was once righteous or whole into something sinful or dirty. But the word is not merely limited to *sin; it is also used to describe the state of decay that results from physical *death or the physical destruction, dismantling or damaging of an object. Thus the biblical authors see the corruption of physical things and the corruption of moral beings as analogous.

From the very first sin, corruption tainted all human beings. Just before the flood, God looked down and saw that "the earth was corrupt in God's sight, and the earth was filled with violence" (Gen 6:11 NRSV). In fact the evil was so pervasive that only Noah was righteous before God, and among the rest "every inclination of the thoughts of their hearts was only evil continually" (Gen 6:5 NRSV). Unfortunately, as the psalmist observes, the flood did not change the condition of human hearts. God still "looks down on humankind to see if there are any who are wise, who seek after God," and he still sees that "they have all gone astray, they are all alike perverse; there is no one who does good, no, not one" (Ps 14:2-3 NRSV; cf. Rom 3:10-12). The key to such sin is rebellion, for people believe that there is no God, no one to hold them accountable for their deeds (Ps 14:1). Throughout the Bible the source of corruption is a desire to follow one's own inclinations in the belief that God will never punish sinners.

The chief appearance of corruption in the Bible relates to the OT depiction of Israel's continual disobedience of God's statutes. In setting up the nation of Israel, God had attempted to create a people who were his own possession, set apart from the other nations by their holiness and obedience to him. He told them, "Do not defile yourself in any of these ways, for by all of these practices the nations I am casting out before you have defiled themselves.

Thus the land became defiled; and I punished it for its iniquity, and the land vomited out its inhabitants (Lev 18:24-25 NRSV). Accordingly he gave them the law, which set out clear guidelines for what this holiness looked like. God laid out elaborate directions for the immoral acts he forbade and for the animals and diseases he considered unclean and desired the Israelites to purify from their congregation. Thus God's instructions were, "You are to distinguish between the holy and the common, and between the unclean and the clean" (Lev 10:10 NRSV). He forbade a large spectrum of acts, from touching a dead carcass or eating animals with split hooves that did not chew the cud, to not "making yourselves detestable" by having *sexual relations with animals or with anyone who was not a nonrelative, of the opposite sex and married to the individual.

In addition to these laws, God gave the Israelites several laws demanding that they not be corrupt in their attitudes toward God. They were not to swear falsely by God's name, thus "profaning the name of your God" (Lev 19:12 NRSV). God thus declared that his name was vulnerable to slander and derision if his people misused it. Part of the reason for the Babylonian captivity was God's displeasure at King Zedekiah, who falsely swore allegiance to King Nebuchadnezzar in God's name before rebelling against him (2 Chron. 36:13). In addition to this injunction, God also condemned *idolatry, calling it corrupt and evil in the sight of the Lord and worthy of provoking him to anger (Deut 4:25). However, even before Moses came down the mountain after receiving this command from God, the Israelites demonstrated their propensity to disobey it by constructing for themselves a golden calf for worship. Since they did not even obey Moses while he was alive, he predicted before his death that the Israelites would fall into corruption: "For I know that after my death you will surely act corruptly, turning aside from the way that I have commanded you. In time to come trouble will befall you, because you will do what is evil in the sight of the LORD, provoking him to anger through the work of your hands" (Deut 31:29 NRSV). Moses' prediction is the story of the OT, for all of its books retell this repeated cycle of sin, God's punishment, repentance and God's gracious forgiveness.

God found his covenant people to be corrupt in numerous ways, ranging from the degraded practices of idolatry, human sacrifice and temple *prostitution to an inability to keep the law that ought to have been the easiest to keep, the sabbath. No nation has ever been more disinclined to give themselves a rest from their labors than the Israelite people. Among other violations they were found guilty of selling merchandise on the sabbath and of not giving the land its sabbath rest (Neh 13:17; 2 Chron 36). The extent of their sin demonstrates the utter depravity sin causes in people's hearts and the alienation from God it causes. God could not describe Israel's sin adequately enough. Isaiah elaborately depicts it in his address to them, although the enumeration is incapable of covering the extent of it: "Ah, sinful nation, people laden with iniquity, offspring who do evil, children who deal corruptly, who have forsaken the LORD, who have despised the Holy One of Israel, who are utterly estranged" (Is 1:4 NRSV). Israel's sin was in fact so complete that it followed the nations' ways "and acted according to their abominations, within a very little time you were more corrupt than they in all your ways" (Ezek 16:47 NRSV). Thus the story of Israel is a story of a fall from righteousness into utter corruption.

In addition to enumerating Israel's specific sins, the Bible offers a metaphorical portrayal of her sins. Isaiah describes Israel as a rebellious child who is more headstrong than the animals. Although "the ox knows its owner, and the donkey its master's crib," Israel is more foolish than the animals, and despite God's constant entreaties, she refuses to know or understand her master's call (Is 1:3). Jeremiah has several less than flattering comparisons for the Israelites' disobedience. He calls Israel "a restive young camel interlacing her tracks," an animal in heat with unrestrained lust, desperately and nondiscriminatingly searching for a lover (Jer 2:23-24). He also describes her as a "whore with many lovers" who "took her whoredom so lightly" that "she polluted the land, committing adultery with stone and tree" (Jer 3:1-2, 9). The prophets' graphic metaphors of Israel's corruption were startling and unappealing, unsuccessfully attempting to shock Israel into repentance.

God does not merely consider corruption as affecting the individuals involved in the acts; he also describes corruption as defiling his physical creation. Repeatedly God warns the people not to defile the land they have been given by sinning. In God's description of the Canaanites' sins and punishment, he states that the land itself was defiled by their sins, being "filled from end to end with their uncleanness"; therefore, God "punished it for its iniquity, and the land vomited out its inhabitants" (Lev 18:25 NIV). Indeed all of "the earth lies polluted under its inhabitants," who have "transgressed laws, violated the statutes, broken the everlasting covenant" (Is 24:5 NRSV). Such a statement on sin's defilement of the land parallels Paul's account of creation's "bondage to decay," from which it will not be freed until Christ comes again.

Like the rest of creation, humankind's subjection to physical death and decay is a consequence of moral corruption, and the Bible even describes it as "corruption" that God saved Christ's body from experiencing (Acts 2:27). Indeed the Bible declares that the only escape from the effects of physical death is the Christlike pursuit of righteousness. Paul warns, "If you sow to your own flesh, you will reap corruption from the flesh; but if you sow to the Spirit, you will reap eternal life from the Spirit" (Gal 6:8 NRSV). Thus the direct result of moral corruption is physical corruption through death, and only redemption by Christ's blood and pursuit of righteousness by the

power of the Spirit can overcome the inevitable effects of corruption.

Although the NT in many ways echoes the OT description of corruption, it adds several new twists to God's perspective on corruption. The most obvious difference is Jesus' statement on the law. God himself had set up the elaborate system of rules that the Israelites were to follow in order to be set apart as holy to God. However Jesus told the Pharisees that they had missed the whole point of the law. In his indictment of their hypocrisy, he declared that they preferred to follow the outward form of the law, to be clean according to the law, without recognizing that the law was meant to encourage them to look at the cleanness or uncleanness of their hearts. He rebuked them, saying, "It is not what goes into the mouth that defiles a person, but it is what comes out of the mouth that defiles," for "what comes out of the mouth proceeds from the heart" (Mt 15:11, 18 NRSV). Thus Jesus made clear to the Pharisees that although the law had been from God and he had desired them to obey it, the law was meant to point them not to their need for external, physical cleanliness, but to their need for internal freedom from corruption.

Paul seconded Jesus' command, saying "I know and am persuaded by the Lord Jesus that nothing is unclean in itself; but it is unclean for anyone who thinks it is unclean" (Rom 14:14 NRSV). In Titus 1:15 he echoes this: "To the pure all things are pure, but to the corrupt and unbelieving nothing is pure. Their very minds and consciences are corrupted" (NRSV). The NT proposed in these statements that the external regulations the law imposed were intended to point the believer inward to his heart.

In addition to pointing the believer inward, the NT writers also provide a laundry list of corruptions to be avoided. When Jesus describes the truly unclean deeds, he mentions "fornication, theft, murder, adultery, avarice, wickedness, deceit, licentiousness, envy, slander, pride, folly" (Mk 7:21-22 NRSV). Paul adds to this vice list, describing people "of corrupt mind and counterfeit faith" who "also oppose the truth" (2 Tim 3:8). Among the list of sins included in the passage, he mentions those who are "lovers of themselves, lovers of money, boasters, arrogant, abusive, disobedient to their parents, ungrateful, unholy, inhuman, implacable, slanderers, profligates, brutes, haters of good, treacherous, reckless, swollen with conceit, lovers of pleasure rather than lovers of God, holding to the outward form of godliness but denying its power" (2 Tim 3:2-5 NRSV). Such a list offers one of the most complete and succinct pictures of corruption in the whole Bible, for it includes many miscellaneous sins not often considered as wrong. In essence, however, Paul is condemning the things that he encourages the Ephesians to leave behind: "put away your former way of life, your old self, corrupt and deluded by its lusts, and . . . be renewed in the spirit of your minds" by embracing a "new self," like God in "true righteousness and holiness" (Eph 4:22-

24 NRSV). Here Paul offers the only way to avoid corruption: by renewing our minds in the word of Jesus Christ.

In addition to providing many images of corruption, the Bible also offers an inkling of what the fate of the corrupt will someday be. Once Christ has established his kingdom, he will abolish all corruption and create a country for his people where no corruption will exist. Isaiah describes this kingdom as containing a highway "called the Holy Way," prophesying that "the unclean shall not travel on it, but it shall be for God's people" and "no traveler, not even fools, shall go astray" (Is 35:8 NRSV). In Revelation, John describes Christ's kingdom as New Jerusalem, which will likewise remain unpolluted, for "nothing unclean will ever enter it, nor anyone who practices abomination or falsehood" (Rev 21:27 NRSV). As for the corruption of the nations, God promises to judge it as he does the symbol of their system of sin, "the great whore who corrupted the earth with her fornication" (Rev 19:2 NRSV). Likewise God promises judgment for the corrupt themselves. He promises judgment, saying, "their place will be in the lake that burns with fire and sulfur, which is the second death" (Rev 21:8 NRSV). Thus God not only offers portraits of corruption in the Bible but also foretells the imminent demise of all who act corruptly.

See also DEATH; DECAY; PURITY; RUST; SIN; WHOLE, WHOLENESS; WORM.

COSMOGONY. *See* COSMOLOGY.

COSMOLOGY

The common theme and goal of *creation narratives and cosmological speculation in any era, ancient or modern, is a coherent articulation of the forces (divine or natural) that will account for the observable universe. In any culture this usually entails a positing of the unseen (forces or personified forces usually understood as deities) acting upon the seen (natural world) and an elaboration of the role they play from the beginning of time until the end. The goal of any creation story is to explain the events by which the gods (or God, in the case of the Hebrews) brought *order out of *chaos and to elaborate the ongoing struggle against the forces of chaos and *evil that continually attempt to subvert order and uncreate the universe.

The task of identifying and communicating the attributes and roles of such forces taxes the human vocabulary to the limit and invokes the fullest use of the imagination through appeals to symbols, metaphors and analogies based inevitably on experience of the observable world. In assessing older cosmologies the inescapable conundrum of metaphor resurfaces. Did the ancients intend their metaphors as analogies, or did they really believe them? (Modern cosmologists usually make clear that their analogies are not to be taken literally, but are merely concessions to the uninitiated and ignorant lay person.) The

simplicity, beauty and supreme literary art of the descriptions (usually couched in poetry) of the ancient authors suggest a consummate skill in the manipulation of verbal images on a par with any modern author or composition.

This mastery urges us to view these authors as peers, which they are; but in so doing we risk assuming that their view of the cosmos is, like ours, informed by empirical and quantifiable study. It is not. (A twentieth- century cosmology violates the innocence of the ancient text.) Subsequent interpreters of the ancient texts understood the metaphors in an extremely literal way, suggesting that the authors themselves may also have conceived of their images in a very concrete way. If this is so, then the images of ancient poetry, including those preserved in the OT, reflect an actual view of the cosmos—a view so different from our own that to understand it we must set aside our own assumptions about the universe.

The images of the cosmos in the OT do not attempt to present an exhaustive explication of a complete cosmology. They are instead snippets, passing allusions to a common literary background of the ancient Semitic people. Only the literature of neighboring cultures presents a more coherent and complete presentation of this shared cosmological outlook.

Order vs. Chaos. The Babylonian creation story, the *Enuma elish,* along with other accounts, tells that a primordial goddess, Tiamat, and her consort, Apsu, gave birth to monstrous gods. (The procreative activity of the gods and subsequent feuding of offspring are common themes in Mediterranean cosmologies.) After several generations Ea, the god of wisdom, killed Apsu. In response Tiamat bred monsters by her son Kingu to avenge Apsu's death. Of all the gods only Marduk, the son of Ea, dared challenge Tiamat. By the aid of magic, Marduk overcame Tiamat with his bow and *arrows. (His victory offers an etiology for the rise of *Babylon, the city whose patron god he is, to political power.) Marduk built the heavens and the earth by recycling the remains of Tiamat. He split her body like a clam, making the firmament from the top half to hold back the upper waters from flooding the earth. From the bottom half he made the mountainous foundations of the sea (cf. Job 26:10). He imprisoned the monster allies of Tiamat in the watery caverns of the underworld. He created stations in the sky for the great gods (constellations) and established the calendar by orchestrating their rising and setting—the year, the months and the days. He built gates for the sun to enter in the east and exit in the west and gave the moon elaborate orders about how to shine. (The sun shines under the firmament by day and through the starry windows by night.)

This mythological background common to all Semitic peoples forms the background tapestry upon and against which the author of Genesis weaves a monotheistic account. The many parallels in outlook between Genesis and the *Enuma elish* stem from a similar understanding of the physical shape of the universe and should present no surprise, but the salient differences are significant.

Genesis as Systematic Cosmology. Whereas the prophets delight in the verbal artistry and familiar poetic images of older mythical accounts of creation, the author of *Genesis studiously avoids any such allusions to polytheistic ideas. The outlook of the Genesis narrative with regard to the physical geometry of the universe still holds much in common with the stories of neighboring cultures, but the differences cry out for attention. The Genesis account does not attempt an exhaustive treatment but simply asserts a monotheistic Creator. Instead it goes out of its way to avoid certain terms that are essential to the telling but hazardous to its meaning. For example, the *sun, most easily referred to by the common noun šemeš, is instead called "a greater light to rule the day," and the *moon, yārēaḥ, by "the lesser light to rule the night" (Gen 1:16 RSV). The author appears to have deliberately avoided šemeš and yārēaḥ because, in addition to designating the astronomical objects, the words also commonly name the deities Sun and Moon (Deut 4:19; 17:3; 2 Kings 23:5; Job 31:26; Jer 8:2). A desire to avoid any suggestion of condoning idolatrous worship may be posited to account for the circumlocutory wording. The story does not deny that the sun and moon are God's agents to regulate the agricultural activities of humanity and the attendant feasts (Ps 104:19). It denies that sun and moon should be worshiped for this service.

The Babylonian Tiamat is present as Hebrew tᵉhôm, the *Deep, but she is not personified in the Genesis account as a deity to challenge the Creator. (Other occurrences of tᵉhôm in Scripture do clearly allude to the Deep as a mythological enemy of the Creator.)

The Babylonian Apsu corresponds conceptually to the waters above the firmament. *Firmamentum* is the Latin translation for Hebrew rāqîaʿ, a pounded brass dome over the earth, "hard as a molten mirror" (Job 37:18), which separates the waters above from the waters below and keeps them from flooding the world (Gen 1:7). The sweet *rain waters are allowed to enter through the *windows of heaven (Gen 7:11). The *stars, windows in the firmament, could be sealed up to prevent rain or light from coming through (Job 9:7; cf. Judg 5:20, where stars fight Sisera by raining and flooding Kishon). By collusion with the "springs of the Deep" (tᵉhôm), the chaos waters struggle against God's imposed order and attempt to once again flood what God has ordained as dry land. God's thundering rebuke is necessary to keep the rebellious sea in its place. The waters of the Deep flee at the Lord's rebuke. They return to their appointed boundaries, which they should not trespass, and they never again cover the earth (Ps 104:6-9).

Some elements of the story are pressed into theological service. The *seven-day cycle of creation foreordains the observance of the *sabbath (Gen 2:2; Ex 20:10). Zechariah imagines that the seven lights of the menorah are the seven *eyes of the Lord, symbolism that etymologizes the seven visible heavenly bodies that form the basis for the seven-day week (Zech 4:10). (The Hebrews borrowed the seven-day week from the Babylonians, who based it on the sun, the moon and five planetary gods.) Zechariah has kept the historic connection intact but demythologized the pagan gods into agents (or spirits, Rev 5:6) that do God's bidding, God's allies maintaining the order of creation. The symbolism of these seven moves fluidly among various categories: eyes of God, spirits, stars, angels (Rev 5:6; cf. 1:20; 3:1; in antiquity "the eyes of the king" were his spies).

The Genesis account stands distinct from other creation stories in that it has no use for an original goddess in a procreative role. The fierce monotheism of the author sanitizes the imagery with which his audience is familiar, retaining the primitive/simple view of the world (the solid firmament of the heavens and the pillars supporting the earth in a primal sea) but extirpating any traces of competition or threat from vanquished deities. There are no other deities, no lesser gods participating in the creative act either as allies or foes and certainly not as cosmic sex partners to fructify the earth. Genesis is cosmology stripped of its mythology, sterilized of its polytheistic infection.

Mythical Poetic Allusions as Cosmology. By contrast the wisdom and prophetic portions of the OT are largely poetry. And poetic imagery and characterization easily give rise to (and paradoxically, perhaps also stem from) a view that natural phenomena are actors and agents participating in a divine plan. The words and images employed in poetry boldly allude to the mythological background of the Semitic peoples. The poets persist in dealing with the conflict between good and evil in the ancient and familiar terms of the cosmic conflict between chaos and order at the beginning of time. Here too the Creator accomplishes his purpose by his word and wisdom, but he is opposed by a primeval cast of enemies. John's cosmology develops this theme of Creator as Word (Jn 1:1; cf. Prov 8:22; Wis 9:1).

The poets do struggle to imagine the cosmic birth, and they do resort to creative analogies. The original sea burst from its *womb (Job 38:8). The morning gives birth to *dew (Ps 11:3). But this does not suggest dalliance by *weather gods. On the contrary the rhetorical "has the rain a father or who has begotten the drops of dew?" underscores the profundity of human ignorance and hints at the inadequacy of older cosmologies based on *sexual imagery (Job 38:28).

The key members of this cast from the Semitic creation drama remain as players on the OT stage, sometimes with the same names (Hebrew cognates of Akkadian words). The *Sea, the *Serpent, the Apsu waters (the waters above the firmament), the zodiac constellations (*host of heaven) and the council of the gods all appear in tantalizing references to these older beliefs, reshaped by the poets and prophets in their attempt to communicate God's role in the cosmos and the eternal significance of religious and political occurrences.

The Sea. Genesis does not attempt to explain the origins of the Deep *($t^e h\hat{o}m$)*. It is simply there (Gen 1:2). Just as obviously, it is the *enemy. The restless sea constantly attempts to escape its prescribed boundaries. It wears away the land. Not content to buffet the shore with its breakers, it sends *storms (Rahab) as invasions (Jer 51:42), trespassing beyond its domain, flooding the good earth, destroying life and undoing the order of the world: "Thou dost rule the raging of the sea; when its waves rise, thou stillest them" (Ps 89:9 RSV). The rebuke of the Lord chastens the sea; it flees to its place (Ps 104:7-9). The Lord tramples the waves of the sea (Job 9:8) and sets limit for the "proud waves" (Job 38:11).

Habakkuk characterizes the rebellion of the earth in echoes of the Semitic creation story. The Lord readies his bow and puts *arrow to the string. He cleaves the earth with *rivers. The *mountains writhe at his appearance, while the waters rage and the Deep roars in defiance (Hab 3:9-10). The creation is defined in terms of controlling the waters: "God called the dry land Earth, and the waters that were gathered together he called Seas" (Gen 1:10 RSV). "He binds up the streams so that they do not trickle" (Job 28:11 RSV). "The earth is the LORD's . . . for he has founded it upon the seas, and established it upon the rivers." (Ps 24:1-2 RSV). If water is God's enemy, then it also symbolizes his people's foes: "He drew me out of many waters. He delivered me from my strong enemy" (Ps 18:16-17 RSV).

Before creation, the Deep had no shape, but was "without form and void" (Heb. *$t\bar{o}h\hat{u}$ $w\bar{a}b\bar{o}h\hat{u}$*). Where this phrase recurs in Scripture, it clearly alludes to primeval chaos (Is 40:17; Jer 4:23). But Isaiah also uses the pair in parallel with spirit evils as a mythic personification of "uncreation," as spirits called Confusion and Chaos, or Destruction and Atrophy (Is 34:11). This mythic background to the image of the sea permits great latitude in interpreting even seemingly common contexts. For example, the sea in Deuteronomy 30:13, "Who will cross over the sea?" becomes "Who will descend into the abyss?" (*abysson*, Rom 10:7, with no precedent from the LXX, which translates with the Greek word *thalassa*, "sea"). Against such a mythic background as this, Mark's rhetorical question "Who then is this that even the wind and the sea obey him?" becomes an argument for Christ's deity (Mk 4:41).

The Sea has several aliases: the Deep, the Abyss. It does not rage alone in its rebellion against God; it also has allies: Storm (Rahab) and Sea-serpent (Dragon, Leviathan). The sea is almost inseparable from the storms it brews. The poetic personifications of God's enemies blur the identities of Sea, Storm and Serpent, which are frequently paired or even substituted for each other.

Rahab ("Storm," "Arrogance," "Bluster"). In a hymn of praise to the Creator, the psalmist says, "Thou dost rule the raging of the sea; when its waves rise, thou stillest them. Thou didst crush Rahab like a carcass, thou didst scatter thy enemies with thy mighty arm" (Ps 89:9-10 RSV). "By his power he stilled the sea; by his understanding he smote Rahab" (Job 26:12 RSV). "Was it not thou that didst cut Rahab in pieces?" (Is 51:9 RSV). "God will not turn back his anger; beneath him bowed the helpers of Rahab" (Job 9:13 RSV). Who are these helpers of Rahab? The Sea as Abyss is the prison of rebellious spirits and the keeper of the dead (Job 26:5). It parallels Abaddon as keeper of shades and evil powers (cf. Ps 88:11; Rev 9:11).

Sea Serpent. The waters rage not only because of the storm, but because of the sea monster who roils the sea and stirs up the tempest (Job 41:25) and the waves (Ps 93:4; 88:7; 42:7). The sea, like the *serpent, undulates and hisses, rising up to strike the land. Leviathan "makes the deep boil like a pot" (Job 41:31 RSV). His tail thrashes the Deep (Job 41:32), creating cosmic destruction (Rev 12:4, cf. 9:10, 19). The primordial sea serpent goes by several names (Dragon, Leviathan, Tannin) and is sometimes difficult to distinguish from Rahab, with whom it appears in parallel. The defeat of the Deep and the monster in it are linked. "Was it not thou that didst cut Rahab in pieces, that didst pierce the dragon? Was it not thou that didst dry up the sea, the waters of the great deep; that didst make the depths of the sea a way for the redeemed to pass over?" (Is 51:9-10 RSV). "By his power [the Lord] stilled the sea; by his understanding he smote Rahab. By his wind [spirit] the heavens were made fair; his hand pierced the fleeing serpent" (Job 26:12-13 RSV). Much of the biblical imagery closely resembles descriptions of the sea serpent familiar from Ugaritic myth as the seven-headed serpent (ANET 138b). "Thou didst divide the sea by thy might; thou didst break the heads of the dragons on the waters. Thou didst crush the heads of Leviathan, thou didst give him as food for the creatures of the wilderness. Thou didst cleave open springs and brooks; thou didst dry up ever-flowing streams" (Ps 74:13-15 RSV). This battle took place "in the midst of the earth" (Ps 74:12).

The battle that witnessed the subduing of the serpent is in the distant past, but the war is not over. Its aftermath overflows into the present age. Occasionally the imagery applies to present enemies. Among various other mythical *animals, Egypt is a subdued sea-monster, a "Rahab who sits still" in contrast to the trashing, twisting serpent (Is 30:7; cf. Ps 87:4). "In that day . . . the LORD will punish Leviathan, the fleeing serpent, Leviathan the twisting serpent, and he will slay the dragon that is in the sea" (Is 27:1 RSV; Leviathan here may refer to Israel's, and therefore God's, enemies; the dragon is Egypt, cf. Ezek 29:3).

The Lord's allies still struggle against the spiritual evils (Eph 6:12). The forces of order and chaos still skirmish, and a final battle looms at the end of time. For this reason Scripture sometimes refers to the dragon in future battles (Gen 3:15; Rev 12:9; 20:2). These ancient images of the sea serpent as primordial enemy and personification of evil informed the ancient listeners' understanding of the imagery and the literary uses of the serpent in both Genesis 3:1 and Revelation 12:3-4. The magical powers of serpents reflected in these views also motivated the practice of serpent worship (2 Kings 18:4). Even the methods of snake charmers could also apply on a cosmic scale (Ps 58:5), so that those "who are skilled to rouse up Leviathan" tried to manipulate celestial events (Job 3:8 RSV).

Apsu. The OT refers to the Apsu waters of Semitic mythology as the "waters above the firmament" (Gen 1:6-7). "Praise him, you waters above the heavens" (Ps 148:4). Just as there are rivers in the deep, there are also streams above the firmament (4 Ezra 4:7). In addition to *storehouses for the water above the firmament (Ps 33:7), there are also storehouses for the *wind (Ps 135:7), the *snow and the *hail (Job 38:22). *Angels control these elements at God's command (Ps 148:2, 8; Rev 7:1). Later interpreters understood quite literally that when God made the winds his messengers and *fire and flame his ministers, these were angels (Ps 104:4; cf. Heb 1:7; 1 Enoch 70ff.).

Since the heavens were solid, everything that passed beneath the firmament (e.g., the sun, the clouds) must enter and exit at the eastern and western gates of heaven (Ps 19:4-6; 65:8). These are the same doors that shut out the waters above the firmament (Job 38:8). The clouds rise at the ends of the earth; the sun enters at its gate. The mountains are the doorposts, the *pillars of heaven, which support the firmament like a tent (Job 26:10). Like the sun, God enters the world below the firmament at the mountainous gateway. His named habitations are all lofty peaks: Paran in Teman, Horeb, *Sinai, Seir, *Zion (Hab 3:3). The Lord goes forth in the whirlwinds of Teman (Zech 9:14). The mountains smoke at his tread (Ps 104:32; 144:5). The pagans also believed that their gods inhabited the mountains and hills (Ezek 6:3; cf. Ps 121:1; Jer 17:2).

God's voice *thunders upon the many celestial waters where he sits enthroned above the flood (Ps 29:3, 10). He has built for himself an upper room that rests on the firmament. The light and the clouds are God's garments. When he leaves his chamber above the firmament and passes under the vault of heaven, riding his *chariot and the *wings of the wind, he carries the rain waters in his cloud garments (1 Kings 8:12; Ps 104:2-3; 18:10; 68:4; 97:2; Prov 30:4). The wicked imagine that God cannot see them when he is above the firmament (Job 22:13).

The mythological Apsu waters do occur in Hebrew poetry, but standard translations disguise them. English versions generally render the Hebrew *'ēp̄ es,* or occasionally the dual form *'op̄sāyim,* as "end," "extremity," "nothingness." In several poetic passages, however, "ends of the earth" *('ēp̄ es)* occurs in parallel correspondence to "waters of heaven" (Prov 30:4) or "the farthest seas" (Ps 65:5). Traces of the watery Apsu as God's enemy remain: "The adversaries of the LORD shall be broken to pieces . . . The LORD will judge the ends of the earth" (1 Sam 2:10).

Divine Council. The celestial counterpart to the social institution of the "elders in the gate" (Deut 21:19; Ruth 4:1-11; Ps 107:32; Prov 31:23) who serve as judges (see Ex 21:6 and 22:8, where *'elōhîm* means "judge"; cf. Ps 82:1), the divine council appears frequently in Near Eastern mythology. It is a board of advisors or counselors with whom the supreme deity consults, an "assembly of the holy ones" (Ps 98:5). "God has taken his place in the divine council; in the midst of the gods he holds judgment" (Ps 82:1 RSV). These divine beings are not the peers of God: "There is none like thee among the gods, O Lord" (Ps 86:8 RSV; cf. Ps 135:5). "For who in the skies can be compared to the LORD? Who among the heavenly beings is like the LORD, a God feared in the council of the holy ones, great and terrible above all that are round about him?" (Ps 89:6-7 RSV; cf. Ps 138:1). Although among Israel's neighbors these were clearly lesser deities, the Jews understood them as high-ranking angels. In keeping with this view the LXX often translates these "sons of God" or even "gods" as angels (Deut 32:8; Ps 8:5; 138:1 [LXX 137:1]). The NT often follows the LXX, so that "thou hast made him little less than God" (or gods, Ps 8:5) appears as "a little lower than the angels" in Hebrews 2:7.

Even though he is not loyal to God, Satan, by virtue of his rank as a (fallen) divine being, is permitted to appear at meetings of the council on a day when "the sons of God" *(b'nê 'elōhîm)* come to present themselves before the Lord (Job 1:6; 2:1). Satan's role as "accuser" requires this (Zech 3:1; Rev 12:10). The prophet Micaiah pictures another such meeting: "I saw the LORD sitting on his throne, and all the host of heaven standing beside him" (1 Kings 22:19 RSV). This council recommended, and the Lord approved, the dispatch of an angelic emissary with a lying spirit to "inspire" Ahab's prophets to give misleading advice/oracles (v. 22). The ancient tradition of worshipping these lesser deities was no longer a legitimate option for Jews. They merited no worship (Ps 73:25). Nor are Christians to worship angels (Col 2:18).

The Hosts of Heaven. The celestial conflict visible in the cosmos is waged by two opposing armies, God's army" against "the devil and his angels" (Gen 32:1-2; Mt 25:41). Both of these can be termed *hosts* in the archaic sense of "army." Most often the host of heaven designates the troops of Satan and evil spirits associated with astral worship (Acts 7:42). Occasionally *"heavenly host" may name God's angels (Lk 2:13; cf. legions of demons, Mk 5:9; but legions of angels, Mt 26:53). These alternative gods held genuine attraction, but were also a source of fear (Jer 44:17-25; *see* Idolatry). As the Israelites and Judeans struggled with their loyalty to monotheism, the worship of these lesser deities plagued their cosmic outlook. Prophetic denouncements measure how astral worship had run rampant (Amos 5:26; Zeph 1:5; Jer 19:13). Since the Hebrew poets also present these cosmic players as God's enemies, their personification is a necessary part of their character.

The Fall of Angels and the Rebel Constellations. In the Semitic creation stories the various lesser deities are tethered in position as the zodiac. Mesopotamian star-gazers thought the constellations were tethered to the earth by halters or lead-ropes (cf. "Can you bind the chains of the Pleiades, or loose the cords of Orion? Can you lead forth the Mazzaroth in their season, or can you guide the Bear with its children?" Job 38:31-32 RSV). The monsters aiding Tiamat were imprisoned in the watery caverns of the underworld. The image of these allies of evil appears in several biblical passages: "The shades below tremble, the waters and their inhabitants" (Job 26:5 RSV). Not all primeval creatures were evil. The gryphon-like cherubim and seraphim, the OT analogues to composite beings, do God's bidding (see illustrations 231-36 in Keel).

Second Temple readers of Scripture understood Isaiah's taunt against the king of Babylon to describe the fall of Lucifer as well: "How you are fallen from heaven, O Day Star, son of Dawn! . . . You said in your heart, 'I will ascend to heaven; above the stars of God . . . I will make myself like the Most High.' But you are brought down to Sheol, to the depths of the Pit" (Is 14:12-15 RSV). "The Lord will punish the host of heaven . . . they will be shut up in a prison . . . the moon will be confounded and the sun ashamed" (Is 24:21-23 RSV); that is, the sun and moon will be exposed as not being real deities (Jer 8:2 and Deut 17:3; cf. Rev 20:1-3; 12:9).

NT authors share this interpretation of Isaiah's taunt. Jude admonishes believers that even angels can fall, rebellious angels who "did not keep their own position" (Jude 6). With deliberate cosmic imagery, he characterizes those who oppose godliness as "wild waves of the sea" (i.e., allies of rebellious Sea) and "wandering stars for whom the nether gloom of darkness has been reserved for ever" (Jude 13 RSV). 2 Peter recounts that God did not spare the angels when they sinned, but cast them into *hell and committed them to *pits of nether gloom to be kept until the judgment (2 Pet 2:4; cf. Job 4:18). Paul refers to these rebel angels as "things under the earth" when he predicts that everything that has rebelled against God will eventually bow to Jesus (Phil 2:10).

Angels. Although the Genesis account is curiously silent on the role of angels at creation, other passages speak out. God created all the host of heaven by the breath of his mouth (Ps 33:6). At the founding of the world, the morning stars burst for joy and all the sons of God sang together (Job 38:7; Ps 148:3). After God determined the number of the stars and called

them all by name (Ps 147:4), he fixed the number of nations according to the number of the sons of God (angels, Deut 32:8). The spirits or angels that God created first helped with the work of creation.

He appointed angels over various realms: *fire (Rev 14:18), *water (Rev 16:5), winds (Rev 7:1), individuals (Mt 18:10; Acts 12:15), churches (Rev 1:20), countries (Dan 10:13, 20-21; 12:1) and weather phenomena such as *hail and *snow (Job 38:22). Angels take care of transporting the dead (Lk 16:22) and watch over the living (Ps 91:11). They are present at cosmic events like the Parousia (Mt 24:31).

To the degree that the NT depends on Judaism, it also participates in the elaborate Jewish naming system for angels. The various terms used to refer to these elemental spirits are sometimes positive, sometimes negative but always notoriously difficult to define. They are usually rendered according to etymology, the meaning and interpretation to be supplied by the reader from the context. They include thrones, dominions, principalities, authorities, rulers, powers, elemental spirits, princes (Dan 10:13; Lk 22:53; Rom 8:38; 1 Cor 15:24; Eph 1:21; 3:10; 6:12; Col 1:16; 2:15).

Several passages suggested angelic intermediaries to Second Temple exegetes. To these early interpreters of Scripture, when the Lord addressed elements of creation, he appeared to be speaking to his messengers. "Fire and hail, snow and frost, stormy wind fulfilling his command" (Ps 148:8 RSV) seemed to be angels, part of his host (Ps 148:2). Angels controlled the storehouses of snow (Rev 7:1; Job 38:22). Fire and lightning attended him as heralds (Ps 97:3-4; 144:6; 135:7). Angels surfaced in the interpretations of some texts where they did not appear obvious at all. In the NT angels give the law (Acts 7:53; Gal 3:19; Heb 2:2); although the OT account does not specifically mention angels, perhaps the fire or the voice was so understood (Deut 4:12). Alternatively, the *finger of God (Deut 9:10) may have been understood as a spirit of God (compare Lk 11:20 and Mt 12:28).

Heavens as Billboard. The mythological identification of stars with angels and with the host of heaven suggested to the people of the Bible that God by his word orchestrated the celestial drama, even the motions of the heavenly bodies, and that they mirrored a divine script for events of cosmic significance on earth. Bright and noticeable stars of the heavens represent noteworthy persons on earth (kings). The machinations above portend events below. Joseph's dream casts celestial bodies as surrogates for important figures in his clan (Gen 37:9). The parents are sun and moon; the twelve brothers match the twelve signs of the zodiac. Balaam, the enigmatic pagan prophet unexpectedly inspired by the spirit of Yahweh to utter oracles, reluctantly says, "A star shall come forth out of Jacob" (Num 24:17). The same logic leads the Magi to the new king (Mt 2:2), and much later the same astral symbolism illuminates

Christ as the Morning Star heralding the dawning of a new age (Rev 22:16).

New Testament Cosmology. The NT often assumes the cosmological imagery of the OT. *Thunder, the voice of God in the OT (Ps 18:13; 29), is too powerful to understand (Job 26:14). For John the thunderous voice from heaven is from God and can be interpreted, although he dutifully records that some deemed it the voice of an angel and others thought it was merely thunder (Jn 12:29). The true identity of Christ gains greater import because the spirits who reveal it in their confessions are the very beings who have secret knowledge of cosmic events (Mk 1:34; 3:11-12). They are the ones he will disarm (Col 2:15) and the powers in heaven, on earth and under the earth that will ultimately bow (Phil 2:10; cf. Mt 8:29).

Cosmic disturbances call for disruptions in the created order. The signs accompanying the crucifixion are clear indications of the cosmic conflict. The fabric of the universe threatens to unravel as God does battle with evil: the sun grows dark (Lk 23:44-45); a torn curtain exposes the sanctity of God's former house as an unmistakable token of a new order; the pillars of the earth shake (Job 9:6; Ps 75:3); even rocks cannot hold themselves together. Tombs open and release their prisoners as the enemy in the Deep admits defeat (Mt 27:51).

In Paul's doctrine of salvation the fallenness of the cosmos is symptomatic. No creature is exempt: "For the creation waits with eager longing for the revealing of the sons of God; for the creation was subjected to futility, not of its own will but by the will of him who subjected it in hope; because the creation itself will be set free from its bondage to decay and obtain the glorious liberty of the children of God. We know that the whole creation has been groaning in travail together until now" (Rom 8:19-22 RSV; cf. Hosea 4:3).

The return of the Son of Man calls for similar disturbances: "And there will be signs in sun and moon and stars, and upon the earth distress of nations in perplexity at the roaring of the sea and the waves, men fainting with fear and with foreboding of what is coming on the world; for the powers of the heavens will be shaken" (Lk 21:25-26 RSV). The language borrows the themes of the prophets (Joel 2:10, 31; Hab 3:10-15).

As the original enemy of God at creation, the old sea, parallel to Death and Hades (Rev 20:13), must pass away (Rev 21:1). At the end of days God still sits enthroned above the waters; but the crystal sea is calm, smooth as glass, subdued by the master's voice (Rev 4:6; 22:1; cf. Ps 104:7; 106:9; Mk 4:39). The cosmos will be remade without the rebellious elements.

See also ANGELS; CHAOS; CREATION; DEEP; DIVINE WARRIOR; EARTH; ENEMY; HEAVEN; MOON; MYTHICAL ANIMALS; SEA; SERPENT; SUN; SUN, MOON, STARS.

BIBLIOGRAPHY. R. Graves and R. Patai, *Hebrew Myths: The Book of Genesis* (New York: McGraw-Hill, 1963). O. Keel, *The Symbolism of the Biblical World: Ancient Near Eastern Iconography and the Book of Psalms.* Warsaw, IN: Eisenbrauns, 1997 repr.).

COSMOS. *See* COSMOLOGY; WORLD.

COUNCIL, DIVINE. *See* ASSEMBLY, DIVINE.

COUNTRY, COUNTRYSIDE

The Bible does not decisively distinguish *country* from *nation* or *land*. The image accordingly encompasses two distinct meanings. *Country* denotes "homeland"—the place where one lives—while *countryside* is the "landscape outside of towns"—the natural realm beyond the reach of the city.

Country as Homeland. The implied norm in the Bible is that people have a base, a place with which they identify and to which they belong. Moving from that place in anything other than a temporary way is seen as atypical, something worth commenting on, as when *Abraham was told to "go from your country and your kindred and your father's house to the land that I will show you" (Gen 12:1 RSV). As late as Genesis 24 Abraham still talks of the home of his relatives as "my country" (Gen 12:4).

References such as these are rooted in a universal human impulse, especially pronounced in primitive cultures, to regard one's identity as rooted in the country of one's origin. Despite *Jacob's twenty years of residence in Haran, his country remained the land of Israel, the land of his "kindred" (Gen 32:9). In the Bible, one's country is in some sense one's identity. Thus when Jonah's terrified fellow sailors want to know who the stranger is with whom they are dealing, they ask Jonah, "What is your country?" (Jon 1:8).

The story of Naaman (2 Kings 5:1-19) is a good index to what the motif of one's country means in the OT. The leading characters in the story are all associated with specific locales—Naaman with Syria, the maid with Israel, Elisha with Samaria. When Naaman is told to wash in the Jordan, he is offended, regarding the supposed superiority of the rivers of Syria with a sense of pride. After his healing, Naaman returns home with two mule loads of earth from Israel, showing how the ancient mind even linked deities with specific countries.

The dominant image of the country as a homeland that determines identity is doubtless the OT motif of the Promised Land, built around such motifs as possession, blessing, goodness and abundance. Beginning with the covenant promises to Abraham, the motif of a land that will eventually become a homeland for individuals like the patriarchs and the corporate nation of Israel reverberates through the OT. The image of the Promised Land is the goal toward which the entire Pentateuch points, as captured especially in the evocative archetype of a *land flowing with milk and honey and the anticipatory codification of laws to be implemented when the nation enters its homeland. The Promised Land is partly possessed in the books that recount the conquest of Canaan, and it remains the reference point for those who lived through the *exile and return. In keeping with the idea that land or country determines identity, the motif of the Promised Land defines Israel in terms of a covenant relationship with God, with the gaining of the land a sign of God's covenant blessing and its loss as a symbol of Israel's apostasy.

Following the pattern of many of the Bible's master images, the OT image of country becomes spiritualized in the NT. The writer of Hebrews takes up the image of "belonging place" and concludes that the true homeland of the OT believers was heaven: "For people who speak thus make it clear that they are seeking a homeland. If they had been thinking of that land from which they had gone out, they would have had opportunity to return. But as it is, they desire a better country, that is, a heavenly one" (Heb 11:14-16 RSV). In the same vein Philippians 3:20 asserts that "our commonwealth is in heaven."

The Countryside as Natural Landscape. The basic identity of the countryside is that it is the implied antithesis or complement to the town or *city. The countryside is the area outside the city or village. Several traits dominate our experience of countryside in the Bible.

One is the sheer range of specific images that comprise the composite image. Other articles in this dictionary explore variations on the theme: *forest, *garden, *grove, *mountain, *pasture, *plain, *river, *wilderness. It is also apparent that the great preponderance of action in the Bible occurs in the countryside rather than the city. The countryside is where the patriarchs and Israelites wandered, where battles were often fought, where *farming in the predominantly agrarian society of the Hebrew nation took place and where Jesus spent much of his time as an itinerant teacher and miracle worker. As this list suggests, the countryside in the Bible rarely possesses the familiar pastoral associations of an aesthetic escape from the city to natural beauty. Instead it is simply the arena for human activity, and most towns simply merged into the countryside without people feeling a sharp cleavage between them. The countryside could be either hospitable or hostile, but it was rarely an aesthetic retreat. To the biblical imagination, for example, *mountains conveyed size and power, but their beauty is not mentioned.

As with many biblical images the countryside is an ambivalent image in the Bible. On one side, it is a place of fertility, abundance and sustenance. The master image of *abundance is *harvest, as in the story of Ruth and the parables of Jesus. The same spirit of the provision of the countryside breathes through the farmer's viewpoint of the provisions of the earth in Psalm 104:10-18. When Jesus' disciples are hungry on the sabbath day, they get *food by wandering through the *grain fields (Mk 2:23). One of the few occurrences of the conventional pastoral evocativeness of the lush countryside is Psalm 23:2, with its matchless picture of green pastures and still waters. Similar images of abundant country life greet us in the pastoral interlude of Abraham and Sarah's ideal *hospitality to angelic visitors (Gen 18:1-8); in the picture of Job's prosperity (Job 1:3; 42:12) and in such agricultural parables of Jesus as those of the sower (Mt 13:1-9), the workers in the *vineyard (Mt 20:1-16) and the prosperous farmer (Lk 12:16-21).

Elsewhere, the countryside is the place of privacy or escape from the more populous town or city. It was a place of physical escape for David when fleeing from Saul (1 Sam 22—24) and for Elijah (1 Kings 17:1-7). It is also a place of psychological and spiritual retreat—the place, for example, where Isaac walks "to meditate in the field in the evening" (Gen 24:63) and where he first meets Rebekah; the place where Elijah meets God in the form of a still, small voice (1 Kings 19:9-13); the place to which Jesus retreated to pray (Mt 14:23; Mk 6:46; Lk 6:12).

An idealized country landscape has always been prominent in love stories and love poetry. The classic examples in the Bible are the idealized farm locale in which the love of Ruth and Boaz springs up and progresses and the rustic pastoral landscape that lights up the *Song of Songs. The countryside in the Song of Songs is, in fact, the one notable exception to remarks made above about the scarcity of the idealized pastoral landscape of aesthetic retreat that is so prominent in literature generally. The Song of Songs portrays ideally ardent lovers in an ideally *flowery and fruitful landscape, portrayed partly as an escape from the ordinary world. In particular, the two pastoral invitations to love (Song 2:10-15; 7:11-13) use the conventional motif of inviting the beloved to a walk in the countryside, offering the aesthetic delights of the countryside itself as the reason to accept the invitation.

But if the countryside can be a place of natural abundance, escape, spiritual retreat and romance, it is also the place of danger and death. In the story of *Joseph and his brothers (Gen 37), for example, the countryside itself conspires against the boy hero. A stranger finds the lost boy Joseph wandering in a field far from home. The landscape itself aids the brothers in their conspiracy, being replete with open *pits and wild *animals in whose blood a garment can be soaked. The countryside poses a continuous threat to the Israelites in their wilderness wanderings. Elsewhere we read about the countryside—the noncity— as the place where an enemy army waits in ambush (2 Kings 7:12), where the desert is so laden with the threat of wild animals and thirst that only God can save his people there (Is 43:19-20), where a *forest can be so dangerous that it "devoured more people that day than the sword" (2 Sam 18:8), where people wander in heart-wrenching destitution until "they reached a city to dwell in" (Ps 107:4-9). Throughout the OT the open country is associated with the threat of predators, treacherous pathways and either flood or drought.

In sum, in contrast to the pastoral idealizing that

sees the countryside as automatically superior to the city, the Bible gives no reason to believe that people in either locale are in a better or worse position before God or that one cannot live the godly life in either place. Deuteronomy 28:3 declares regarding those who obey God, "Blessed shall you be in the city, and blessed shall you be in the field" (RSV). Correspondingly for those who disobey, "Cursed shall you be in the city, and cursed shall you be in the field" (Deut 28:16 RSV; cf. Ezek 7:15 and 6:56).

See also ANIMALS; CITY; FARMING; FOREST; GARDEN; GROVE; LAND; LAND FLOWING WITH MILK AND HONEY; MOUNTAIN; PASTURE; PLAIN; RIVER; VALLEY; WILDERNESS.

COURAGE

The Bible supplies us with a rich store of images for courage. This is no surprise, since the Bible is about small people accomplishing great deeds with God's help. The images of courage are as various as the mighty deeds celebrated in the biblical canon.

The vocabulary of courage is especially rich in the OT. Biblical Hebrew employs a number of idioms for courage, only some of which can be translated into English term-for-term understandably. One common expression for courage was the word *heart*. This usage corresponds roughly to our own; the English word *courage* comes to us from the Latin word *cor* ("heart"). The "bravest warriors" (Amos 2:16 NIV) of Israel were literally "strong of heart." Loss of heart meant a loss of courage. This could be expressed in a number of ways: the heart "goes out" (Gen 42:28, author's translation), "falls" (1 Sam 17:32, author's translation), "faints" (Job 23:16), "fails" (Jer 4:9, author's translation) or "melts" (Ezek 21:7). Hebrew idioms also linked courage with the *hands and *knees. Gaining and losing courage were expressed with the phrases "strengthening/loosening the hands/knees." (2 Sam 16:21; Job 4:4; Is 13:7; Ezek 7:17).

One striking feature of biblical depictions of courage is the close link between courage and the expectation of success. With the possible exception of David's *lament for Saul and Jonathan (2 Sam 1:19-27), the biblical writers never picture courage as a grim stoicism in the face of defeat. On the contrary the frequent exhortations to "be strong and courageous" are grounded on God's promise of success (Deut 31:6; Josh 1:6-9; Judg 7:9-15; 2 Chron 32:7; Hag 2:4; Acts 27:22).

Many dramatic biblical narratives recount how individuals acted on God's promises to gain victory in *battle in the face of overwhelming human odds. In such stories as that of Jael (Judg 4:17-21), Gideon (Judg 7:1-25), Jonathan and his *armor bearer (1 Sam 14:1-14), *David against Goliath (1 Sam 17:1-54), Jehoshaphat (2 Chron 20:1-30), and Hezekiah (2 Chron 32:1-23), the people of God, despite being outnumbered, take on the *enemy with the belief that God's power is sufficient in their weakness. These narratives of bravery in battle helped to form

the self-understanding of the early church. Paul especially employed the language of courage in *warfare as a metaphor for his own ministry (2 Cor 10:1-6) and for the ministry of the church as a whole (Eph 6:10-20).

Since *weakness and *brokenness are a large part of the human condition, obedience to God can require courage in all kinds of situations. Women like Ruth (Ruth 3:1-7), Abigail (1 Sam 25:14-31) and Esther (Esther 4:10-5:2) took huge personal risks to intercede for others. The magnitude of the task involved made the building of the *temple an occasion for courage (1 Chron 22:13; 28:10); and in the building of the second temple, this was compounded by opposition and the harsh conditions of life for the returnees (Zech 8:9,13).

The early church, taking its cue from the courage of prophets who confronted kings (2 Sam 12:1-14; 1 Kings 18:16-46; 22:1-28; Is 7:1-25; Jer 36:1-32), sought and received the help of the Holy Spirit to proclaim the good news with boldness in all situations (Acts 4:29; 13:46; 18:26; Eph 6:19; Phil 1:14; 1 Thess 2:2).

Jesus himself went beyond the outer limits of human courage by daring to die, not for good people but for *sinners (Rom 5:6-8). The author of Hebrews saw in Christ's display of courage the inner dynamic that drives all people who possess biblical faith. He characterizes the Christian life as one of *"boldness," *"confidence" or "courage." (Heb 3:6; 4:16; 10:19; 10:35) Chapter 11 recounts the great *heroes of faith as examples of those who did not "throw away" their "confidence" (Heb 10:35) because they were looking to the eventual reward of their faith (Heb 11:6, 13-16). The crowning example—the "author" of believing courage—is Jesus. His endurance of the cross (Heb 12:2-3) is the model to which those who are "losing heart" should look. After encouraging the readers to consider their sufferings a sign that they have become, like Jesus, sons of God (Heb 12:5-11), he closes with an exhortation to strengthen feeble arms and weak knees (Heb 12:12). This language, clearly borrowed from Isaiah 35:3-4, is a call to regain courage.

See also BATTLE STORIES; BOLDNESS; CONFIDENCE; FAITH; HEART; HERO, HEROINE; HUNTING; TREMBLING, SHAKING, BODILY ANGUISH.

COURT. *See* ROYAL COURT.

COURTROOM. *See* LEGAL IMAGES; JUDGMENT; ROMANS, LETTER TO THE.

COVENANT

The image of covenant or agreement is the primary way in which the Bible portrays the relationship between God and his people and (to a lesser extent) to the human race in general. While many horizontal relationships are described as covenantal (including *marriage and various pacts between friends or among enemies), the Bible's imagery of covenant focuses primarily on the covenant between God and humankind.

The Covenants of Genesis. We catch the first hints of the covenant motif in Genesis 2, where God establishes what is sometimes called a "covenant of works" with *Adam and *Eve. It is a covenant that establishes the obligations of the creature toward God, as well as an outline of the consequences for disobeying. God's part of the covenant is to establish Adam and Eve in a perfect world where all their needs are met by divine provision. Adam and Eve's debt of gratitude can be paid by obeying God's injunction not to eat from the forbidden *tree upon penalty of *death (Gen 2:16-17). This language of command will be an important part of the imagery of the covenant throughout the Bible.

The second covenant that we read about is the one God makes with Noah immediately after the *flood. Here the language is much more explicitly covenantal: "Behold, I establish my covenant with you and your descendants after you, and with every living creature that is with you . . . that never again . . . shall there be a flood to destroy the earth" (Gen 9:8-11 RSV). This is a covenant with the entire creation, including nature as well as people—"a covenant between me and all flesh that is upon the earth" (Gen 9:17 RSV). The sign of this covenant is the *rainbow, "a sign of the covenant between me and the earth" (Gen 9:13).

While these are true covenants, the covenant of *redemption and grace that governs the Bible begins with *Abraham, and it is here that the main image patterns of the covenant become firmly established. Right at the outset, in the story of the call of Abraham, the most obvious rhetorical pattern is the language of command and promise: "Go from your country and your kindred and your father's house to the land that I will show you. And I will make of you a great nation, and I will bless you, and make your name great, so that you will be a blessing" (Gen 12:1-2 RSV). The command implies an obligation of obedience on the human party in the covenant. The promise is essentially one of *blessing, which extends to a range of things, including land, descendants and the presence and protection of God. As Abraham obeys, a third motif is added to command and promise in the form of reward. This motif begins with Genesis 12:7, where God *rewards Abraham for his obedience by renewing and extending the covenant. Thereafter in the book of Genesis the renewal of the covenant in the form of command, promise and reward punctuates the action.

An important aspect of the covenant in Genesis and later is that it is an agreement between unequals. God is the sovereign being who initiates the covenant, who announces its conditions to people and who rewards the human recipients of the covenant with promise and blessing. Every time we hear the contractual language of the covenant as it enters the action, we sense at once that the speaking voice is a transcendent one, coming to earth from above, and that the covenant is something *conferred*

upon the human recipient. In that sense it is a covenant of grace, as seen especially in the case of *Jacob, who receives the covenant promise at Bethel before he has done anything meritorious that might deserve his receipt of it (Gen 28:13-15). Similarly in the ritual "cutting of the covenant" between God and Abraham, Abraham sleeps; and God alone, in the form of a smoking pot and flaming torch, passes between the animal carcasses, symbolic of the fact that the covenant belongs to God alone (Gen 15:7-21). There is a sense too in which God himself is the chief blessing conferred by the covenant, as hinted at when God tells Abraham "I am your *shield, your very great reward" (Gen 15:1 NIV).

The imagery of promise and reward is noteworthy for its extravagant magnitude or *abundance. The descendants promised to Abraham are variously compared to the dust of the earth (Gen 13:16), the *stars in the heavens (Gen 15:5) and the sand on the seashore (Gen 22:17). God promises to make of Abraham "a great nation" (Gen 12:2), and from the covenant line "all the nations of the earth" shall be blessed (Gen 22:18). The same magnitude is present when the covenant promise is extended to Isaac (Gen 26:4) and Jacob (Gen 28:14).

The Exodus. Important developments occur as we see the covenant extended in the remaining four books of the Pentateuch. The primary change is that the covenant is no longer established with a series of patriarchs and their families but with an entire nation. The imagery that arises in renewals of the covenant is no longer individualistic but national, as the nation of Israel becomes "a people holy to the LORD your God," a people the Lord has chosen to be a people for his own possession, out of all the peoples that are on the face of the earth (Deut 14:2 RSV).

A new image enters when God couches his covenant in terms of the suzerainty treaties of the ancient Near East. Hittite rulers (or suzerains) laid claim to the loyalty of their vassals in formal contracts whose ingredients included (1) identification of the suzerain in terms evoking awe and fear, (2) a historical prologue in which vassals were reminded of the king's acts of benefit to them and (3) obligations of vassals to their lord, including commands, a claim to absolute loyalty (along with a renunciation of all other political loyalties) and a statement of blessings and curses that will result from obedience or disobedience to the treaty. Both the Decalogue and the book of Deuteronomy bear resemblance to this contractual treaty motif, with the implication that they are not so much law as they are covenant. God's covenant with individuals and with the human race is essentially a treaty. God the great king enters into a relationship with his servant people. It is thus a political-*legal metaphor of God's relationship with his people. This covenant is not an agreement between two equal parties. Quite the contrary, it is a relationship initiated by a lord or suzerain with his vassal. The covenant makes certain requirements and stipulates both blessings and curses for the covenant parties, depending on their faithfulness to the terms of the covenant. Thus in the Siniatic covenant of Exodus 19—20, we find God in the place of the suzerain and Israel as his vassal. Much of Exodus and Deuteronomy is commentary and exposition of the covenant initiated at *Sinai.

Another new development in the imagery of the covenant is that it is linked even more explicitly with a choice between obedience and disobedience, blessing and curse. The rhetoric is now one of a great either-or that requires a nation to choose or reject God. The classic text is Deuteronomy 11:26-32, where Moses sets before the people "a *blessing and a *curse: the blessing, if you obey the commandments of the LORD your God . . . and the curse, if you do not obey" (RSV). Near the end of his farewell discourse Moses uses the same rhetoric, putting "life and good, death and evil" before the nation (Deut 30:15-20). Deuteronomy 28—30 is an extended elaboration of the theme.

The extravagance of the imagery of blessing is still present, but it is given a larger scope that can appropriately be called national, in contrast to the more familial promises to the patriarchs. Thus Moses paints a picture of national prosperity in the Promised *Land when he outlines the results of obedience to the commands of God: God "will give the rain for your land in its season and grass in your fields for your cattle, and you shall eat and be full" (Deut 11:14-15 RSV).

The Prophets. The state of the covenant is a dominant theme in OT prophecy, where a major image pattern revolves around the faithlessness of the chosen nation and its failure to live up to its covenant obligations. Isaiah 24:5 contains this list of parallel actions: "they have transgressed the laws, violated the statutes, broken the everlasting covenant." The covenant is variously portrayed as having been "broken" (Jer 11:10; cf. Ezek 17:15-19), "abandoned" (Jer 22:9 NRSV), "transgressed" (Jer 34:18), not remembered (Amos 1:9), "corrupted" (Mal 2:8) and profaned (Mal 2:10).

Yet among the five dozen direct references to the covenant in the OT prophetic books are numerous references to God's faithfulness to his covenant. Six times God promises to establish an "everlasting covenant" with his people (Is 55:3; 61:8; Jer 32:40; 50:5; Ezek 16:20; 37:26). God holds fast to his covenant (Is 56:4) and keeps it (Dan 9:4). One could say that in many ways the OT is the story of God's continuing fidelity to his covenant in the face of his people's infidelity. One of the most powerful images of this is found in the Hosea 1—3, where the prophet takes the prostitute Gomer for a wife as a parabolic representation of God's faithfulness to his people. In this passage we find a picture of God's fidelity to a people who have broken faith and therefore have no claim on him.

The Davidic Covenant. The covenant that God establishes with *David (2 Sam 7:9-16) is carried over from the OT to the NT. In this covenant God promises a *kingdom to David's line that "shall be established

for ever." This is ultimately a messianic prophecy of what God will do for the human race in the redemptive work of Christ. Subsequently, in the prophets we are introduced to God's plan to make a "new" covenant with his people (see esp. Jer 31:31-34 and Ezek 34:25-32). This new covenant will be written directly upon the *heart, since the hearts of stone of God's people will be replaced by hearts of flesh (cf. Heb 8). Thus a living and beating heart is an essential image to the concept of new covenant.

The New Covenant. The covenant is not as pervasive and explicit in the NT as it is in the OT, though it remains an implied theological framework in which the person and work of Christ are understood as completing and fulfilling the OT covenant. Two-thirds of the NT uses of the word *covenant* appear in the epistle to the Hebrews. The dominant image patterns there identify the NT covenant as *"new" (Heb 8:8, 13; 12:24; 9:15) and "better" (Heb 7:22; 8:6). In terms of the theological argument of Hebrews, the new covenant is better because it is final, permanent and once-for-all, as well as being secured and mediated by *Christ instead of by human priests and the sacrifices they performed. The imagery surrounding the covenant in *Hebrews is thus strongly tied to sacrifice.

Other NT passages reinforce the motifs that reach their definitive expression in Hebrews. Elsewhere too, the covenant is declared to be "new" (Lk 22:20; 1 Cor 11:25; 2 Cor 3:6). As in Hebrews, the covenant is associated with *blood (Mt 26:28; Mk 14:24; Lk 22:20; 1 Cor 11:25). By implication the OT sign of the covenant, *circumcision, gives way to communion as the sign of the new covenant (1 Cor 11:25).

See also ABRAHAM; CIRCUMCISION; DAVID; ISRAEL; LAW; MOSES; SINAI.

BIBLIOGRAPHY. D. Hillers, *Covenant: The History of Biblical Idea* (Baltimore: Johns Hopkins University Press, 1969); M. G. Kline, *Treaty of the Great King* (Grand Rapids: Eerdmans, 1963).

COVER, COVERING

The fundamental idea of covering is that of concealment, either physically or metaphorically. What is covered is separated from and rendered unknown or unacceptable to potential viewers.

The biblical account offers a detailed description of the coverings made for various items and compartments associated with the *tabernacle and the *temple (Ex 37:9; 40:3, 19-21, 28, 33; Lev 16:13). The hiding of these items signified the people's inability to manipulate God. Viewing an object or person gives one the opportunity to study, evaluate, judge or control. The covering of the place of God's presence and the holy objects associated with it discouraged the people from thinking of God as easily comprehended and managed.

The image of concealment also relates to the removal of grounds for offense. In some passages God's outrage over an unjust killing is pictured as the blood of the slain lying exposed on the ground (Gen

4:10; Ezek 24:7). Job implores the earth not to cover his blood so that God will see and attend to the unjustness of his lot (Job 16:18). The parallelism of Psalm 32:1 (Rom 4:7) suggests that the idea of sins being forgiven can be pictured as hiding sins from view, so as not to take offense at them (cf. Prov 10:12; 1 Pet 4:8).

Throughout the Bible, people and objects are concealed to protect them. The psalmist likens God's protective power to the covering of a bird's *wings (Ps 91:4). In a context recounting God's displays of power over creation and in history, God's word of comfort to Israel through the prophet Isaiah portrays God's protective concern for his people as his covering them with the *shadow of his *hand (Is 51:16). Job's contention that "Death is naked before God; Destruction lies uncovered" (Job 26:6 NIV) indicates that both lie within the purview of God's awesome power.

The protective nature of coverings extends to situations in which people are in danger of violating social or cultic boundaries. Genesis 9:23 describes Shem and Japheth as walking in backwards and covering their father's nakedness. Similarly the coverings on the furnishings of the tabernacle and temple protected the people from approaching God in an unworthy manner. So also in the throne room scene in Isaiah 6:2, the cherubim are depicted as covering their faces and feet with their wings as a protection from the majestic holiness of God. God covers Moses with his hand while he passes by to shield Moses from observing his *face because "no one may see me and live" (Ex 33:20). Moses' face is radiant from the enounter, so radiant that he must cover his face with a veil to alleviate the fear of the Israelites (Ex 34:29-35). For Paul, Moses covered his face not only because the Israelites could not gaze upon his glory but because that glory was fading (2 Cor 3:17-13).

Covering also occurs to prevent shame. In Genesis 3:7 once the pre-Fall union between Adam and Eve has been disrupted, they make coverings for themselves because they are conscious of being exposed. In Hosea's portrayal of God's judgment against Israel, the Lord is depicted as a husband reclaiming his wife's *garments so that she and her unfaithfulness will be publicly exposed (Hos 2:9-10). The Mosaic law required those with infectious diseases to cover part of their faces and cry "unclean!" to prevent exposure of their disfigurement to the community. In cases of mourning, the practice of covering one's face or head (2 Sam 15:30; Esther 6:12; Jer 14:3-4) concealed temporary lapses in personal hygiene.

In many of the examples given above, covering also indicates alienation. Lamentations 3:43, 44 provides a sobering example of this connection where it portrays God as covering himself in righteous indignation and cutting off all access to himself by his people in prayer.

See also GARMENTS; HIDE, HIDING; VEIL.

CRAWL

Crawling is generally a negative image, associated with uncleanness. In the OT, things that crawl along the ground are to be detested and are often associated with *idolatry (Ezek 8:10). Under OT law all crawling animals are unclean to touch or eat (Lev 22:5) and things destined to crawl are considered *cursed. This detestation can be seen in the original curse God gives to the *serpent in the *Garden of Eden: "Cursed are you above all the livestock and all the wild animals! You will crawl on your belly and you will eat dust all the days of your life" (Gen 3:14 NIV). Similarly, Israel's *enemies are given a curse reminiscent of the serpent's fate (Mic 7:17).

Crawling is also associated with *humiliation and *shame. When Jonathan and his armor bearer go out to meet the Philistine army, the Philistines say to themselves, "Look, the Hebrews are crawling out of the holes they were hiding in" (1 Sam 14:11 NIV). They humiliate the Israelites in the use of the image, placing shame on their actions.

In the OT, crawling creatures is a catch-all term for reptiles and associated animals. In Deuteronomy 32:24 the reference is to poisonous snakes; in Micah 7:17 it refers to all snakes; in Habakkuk 1:14 it refers to all water animals except fish. In Leviticus the reference is to those small animals that can render one unclean: "If he touches any crawling thing that makes him unclean, or any person who makes him unclean, whatever the uncleanness may be" (Lev 22:5 NIV). The connection of crawling things and ritual pollution is exploited by Ezekiel when he records, "So I went in and looked, and I saw portrayed all over the walls all kinds of crawling things and detestable animals and all the idols of the house of Israel" (Ezek 8:10 NIV).

See also ANIMALS; HUMILITY; PURITY; SERPENT; SHAME.

CREAM. *See* BUTTER; MILK.

CREATION

In the Bible, *creation* refers both to the act by which God created the universe and to the product of that process. The prime text is the creation story in Genesis 1, but that account is richly embellished with a host of later references to creation. Underlying the individual image patterns is the premise that the *telos* of creation is to serve and glorify God. The *Christ hymn of Colossians 1 asserts regarding Christ that "all things were created through him and for him" (Col 1:16 RSV), while the song of the elders in Revelation 4 ascribes glory to God bcause he has "created all things, and for [his] pleasure they are and were created" (Rev 4:11 KJV).

Rule vs. Energy. One of the first patterns that draws our attention in the creation narrative is the contrast (perhaps tension) between rule and energy, order and exuberance, instantaneous creation and biological generation. On the one hand, God's act of creation is a great ordering process. The earth begins "without form and void" (Gen 1:2 RSV); God proceeds to organize this primal *chaos. This motif takes its place in an ancient context of rival creation myths that centered around the ordering of chaos. Mesopotamian, Egyptian and even Vedic Indian mythologies all talk about a chaos that is hostile to the creator god. In each case, the creator god beats back the chaos to provide order, though chaos always remains a threat. The Bible's creation story is partly similar, inasmuch as God brings order out of chaos, but the biblical account is totally free of any sense of threat or hostility in the chaos that God molds. The emphasis throughout the Bible is that God controls the forces that seek to lead to dissolution rather than wholeness in the world.

As God orders the elements, he utters commands that instantaneously produce objects. Some of his specific acts are acts of ordering, with verbs such as "made," "separated" and "placed" dominant in the process. The story itself follows a fixed pattern for each day of creation, consisting of five formulaic parts: announcement ("and God said"), command ("let there be"), report ("and it was so" or "and God made"), evaluation ("it was very good") and placement in a temporal framework. Even the division into days lends an orderly quality to the creation.

But balancing these images of order are images of fertility and energy. Here the language of God's miraculous creative word gives way to the language of biological generation as we read about "plants yielding *seed," "fruit trees bearing fruit in which is their seed," waters that "bring forth swarms of living creatures" and a command to the creation to "be fruitful and multiply and fill the waters in the seas, and let birds multiply on the earth." Here is the imagery of overflowing energy and abundance. Against the set formula for each day of creation is the sheer variety of things created and verbs used to name what God did ("created," "said," "saw," "called"). Balancing the sameness of each day of creation is the progression underlying the days of creation.

This same balance between creation as rule and energy persists throughout the Bible. On the one side we have pictures of God drawing "a circle upon the face of the waters at the boundary between light and darkness" (Job 26:10 RSV), of building the earth like a building (Job 38:4-6) and prescribing bounds, bars and doors for the ocean, saying, "Thus far shall you come, and no farther" (Job 38:10-11 RSV; cf. Prov 8:26-29). But in the other vein we find references to the sea teeming "with things innumerable" (Ps 104:25), and to a world "full of thy creatures" (Ps 104:24).

Images of Goodness and Delight. Another dominant image is the image of "the good earth." The fact that God personally brings the material world into being and and labels it "good" and "very good" stands in marked contrast to later Greek and other philosophical and theological perspectives, which view the material realm as intrinsically evil and morally suspect. But that simple observation hardly

does justice to the enthusiasm with which God views the work he has done. God's declaration is both a benediction and an expression of joy. *Good* means "It's wonderful!" *Very good* is equivalent to saying, "It's perfect!"

The joy with which God creates is a theme in the book of Job and several of the Psalms. In Job 38—41 God responds to Job's complaint against him by reminding Job of the greatness of his power and the wonder of his works, thus bringing Job back to an appropriate sense of awe. In the process, God recounts to Job the majesty of the *stars and other cosmic structures, the variety of the *weather and the delightful assortment of living creatures that inhabit the earth. One cannot read these chapters without being struck by the delight God takes in the multifaceted world that he has made and the exotic creatures he has brought into being (including the ostrich, the hippopotamus and the crocodile).

In the Psalms the emphasis is more on the joy that the creation takes in its Creator than the delight of the Creator toward his works. But in fact the former is simply an appropriate response to the latter. Thus Psalm 104 speaks of God's wonderful provision for all of his creatures and concludes with the hope that God will rejoice in his works, even as his works rejoice in him (Ps 104:31). Leviathan frolics in the ocean (Ps 104:26), while a personified *Wisdom "rejoiced in his inhabited world" as God created that world (Prov 8:30-31). Similarly, Psalm 148 summons all of creation to praise the Lord who has made it. Through such images we see how much pleasure is involved in creation. God takes pleasure in the wide variety of physical forms and behavior patterns found in creation, while the creation rejoices in the God who has made it.

Artistry and Craftsmanship. One result of believing that God created the universe is that the visible world is regarded not simply as a set of data but as someone's achievement. This accounts for the images of artistry and craftsmanship with which biblical writers portray creation. One can scarcely talk about Genesis 1, with its elaborate symmetry and ritualistic patterning, without thinking in artistic terms. God first creates three settings (light, sky and sea, dry land and vegetation) and then, in the same order, fills them with appropriate agents (light bearers, birds and sea creatures, land animals and people). The overall effect is that of an artist filling in a canvas. In Genesis 2 an anthropomorphic God plants and waters a garden, forms *Adam and animals from the ground and removes a rib from Adam's side to fashion *Eve. He creates a world that is both functional ("good for food") and aesthetically beautiful ("pleasant to the sight," Gen 2:9). It is no wonder that the psalmist views the creation as the work of God's *fingers (Ps 8:3) or that the wise man pictures the *mountains as being "shaped" by God (Prov 8:25).

But the favorite image of biblical writers in this regard is that of *building and architecture. The sheer solidity and permanence of the earth leads to the metaphor of God's laying foundations for the earth (Job 38:4; Ps 102:25; 104:5; Prov 8:29; Is 48:13). Creation is a building with a *cornerstone (Job 38:6). An atmosphere of careful planning, functional soundness and aesthetic harmony surrounds images of God's determining measurements, stretching a line, sinking bases, marking out and weighing (Job 38:5-6; Prov 8:27-29; Is 40:12).

Domestic Imagery. By an extension of such anthropomorphism, God's creation of the world is compared to ordinary domestic routines. The result is the domestication of wonder, as God is portrayed as controlling the forces of nature as effortlessly as a person performs the household routine.

For example, in his picture of God covering the earth with the ocean "as with a garment" and the waters fleeing at his rebuke (Ps 104:6-7), the psalmist pictures God as a divine parent tucking in children and scolding them. God "stretched out the heavens like a tent" (Ps 104:2), and he scatters frost as easily as a person tosses out the accumulated ashes of the day (Ps 147:16). He "shut in the sea with doors" and made "clouds its garment, and thick darkness its swaddling band" (Job 38:8-9). He also "wrapped up the waters in a garment" (Prov 30:4).

Creation *ex Nihilo*. Although the Bible does not make quite as much of the fact that God created the universe out of nothing as Christian theology has, it is nonetheless an important biblical motif. Hebrews 11:3 is the most explicit text: "By faith we understand that the world was created by the word of God, so that what is seen was made out of things which do not appear" (RSV). This picture of creation has implications for our understanding of God (he is distinguished from what he created) and the creation itself (it totally depends on God but does not emanate from him). Biblical images of creation distinguish with great care between the Creator and the creation (Rom 1:25). Indeed, the second commandment against graven images (Ex 20:4-6) reflects the language of Genesis 1 and makes it clear that God is extremely jealous that he not be confused or identified with anything within the realm of creation.

The highest scorn and most severe judgments fall on those who blur this distinction. Thus Israel is severely chastened for worshipping the Lord through the image of the golden *calf (Ex 32:1-29). The northern kingdom is eventually destroyed for repeating the same error by perpetuating the sin of Jeroboam the son of Nebat (1 Kings 12:25-33; 2 Kings 17:21-23). The woodsman who creates an *idol out of a piece of *wood in the form of a man and bows down to worship it, after having first used other portions of the log to cook his lunch and warm himself, is mercilessly satirized (Is 44:13-20). Finally, the apostle Paul declares how the wrath of God is revealed against all ungodly idolaters who have suppressed the knowledge of the truth "and exchanged the glory of the immortal God for images resembling mortal man or birds or animals or reptiles" (Rom 1:23). The biblical image of

creation as the product of a divine Creator in one sense empties nature of divinity, in contrast to the tendency of polytheism (which populates the landscape with local deities) and pantheism (which equates the visible creation with deity).

Creation as Revelation. But the same view of creation that empties nature of divinity also makes it a revelation of God and leaves it filled with pointers to God. The fact that all things find their origin in the creative work of God means that everything, in some way, bears witness to the creation and is revelatory of the Creator. According to the Bible every *rock and *tree and creature can be said to testify of God, declare his glory and show forth his handiwork (Ps 8:1; 19:1; 104; 148). We might accurately speak of the creation as divine messenger (cf. Ps 104:3-4).

The book of Proverbs strikingly develops this motif with its personification of Dame Wisdom, who describes how she was with the Lord while the earth was created and its foundations established in wisdom (Prov 8:22-31). The point is that God created the world in a way that reflects the divine wisdom, the pattern of which is discernible for those who vigorously seek after it (Prov 8:1-21). But since the source of that wisdom is God himself, wisdom must begin with an appropriate acknowledgment of and reverence for the Lord (Prov 1:7). This divine wisdom is so thoroughly imprinted on the creation that Paul declares that all those who refuse to acknowledge this testimony of God's existence and power are without excuse in the face of prospective judgment (Rom 1:18-21).

The Bible thus surrounds the creation with images of knowledge and wisdom. The voice from the *whirlwind at the end of the book of Job adduces the order and power of the creation as evidence of God's superior knowledge (Job 38:2) and power (only God can control the creatures that are enumerated). In the Psalms we find references to how God "by strength . . . established the mountains" (Ps 65:6), "in wisdom" made all creatures (Ps 104:24) and "by understanding made the heavens" (Ps 136:5). Not surprisingly, the creation itself "declares knowledge" (Ps 19:2).

Redemption as Creation. A final motif is the biblical writers' treatment of *redemption as a crowning work of God's creation. This is not surprising, since much of what is important in creation has been damaged or destroyed by the Fall. As we might expect, therefore, redemption and creation are intertwined in the Bible.

Christ's work of redemption is described as restoring those aspects of the creation that were lost or damaged as a consequence of the *Fall. The person who is regenerated in Christ is "a new creation" (2 Cor 5:17). While the Fall subjected the whole creation to futility, it waits eagerly for the time when it will be set free from its present *bondage to *decay into the freedom of the glory of the children of God (Rom 8:19-21). Creation is a spectator of human redemption, inasmuch as its own liberation is vested in the liberation of the sons of God. It is also a chorus that celebrates human redemption; for when God begins his final reign, the trees of the forest sing for joy, the sea resounds and the fields are jubilant (Ps 96:12; 98:7-8). While the original creation was marred by sin, Christ's work of redemption and restoration will bring about a new heaven and a new earth in which righteousness dwells (Rev 21:1).

See also ADAM; ANIMALS; COSMOLOGY; EARTH; EVE; GARDEN; GENESIS; PARADISE; PLANTS; SUN, MOON, STARS.

CRIME AND PUNISHMENT

The crime-and-punishment motif makes up a small library of the world's literature, and we could predict that it would loom large in a book as concerned with *evil and its consequences as the Bible. Crime-and-punishment stories follow a simple format: the antecedents, the occurrence and the consequence of a crime—what led up to it, how it was done and what followed as a result of it. The logic underlying the motif is firm and impeccable: what people sow, they reap. The literary version of this principle is called *poetic justice. It should be noted that the crime need not be a civil crime; more often it is simply a violation of God's moral law.

The Bible's first and prototypical story of crime and punishment is the story of the *Fall (Gen 3). The crime consists of *eating the *fruit that God had forbidden. Its antecedent is the subtle temptation of Eve by the *serpent (identified elsewhere in the Bible as *Satan). Most of the story is devoted to the punishment of this crime, as God arrives in the Garden as a judge and pronounces a *curse on all three principals in the drama of sin, ending with the expulsion of *Adam and *Eve from the Garden of Eden.

The story of *Cain and *Abel (Gen 4:1-16) provides the fullest manifestation of the motif. The entire story is built around the premise of a career in crime. In sequence we read about the criminal's family, vocational and religious background (Gen 4:1-4); the motive for the crime (Gen 4:4-5); the criminal's counseling history (Gen 4:6-7); the circumstances of the crime (Gen 4:8); the arrest, trial and sentencing of the criminal (Gen 4:9-12); the criminal's appeal of his sentence (Gen 4:13-14); the judge's modification of the sentence (Gen 4:15); and the serving of the sentence, as Cain becomes the first guilt-haunted *wanderer in the world (Gen 4:16).

After these first two stories of crime and punishment, we are rarely allowed to forget the motif as we read the Bible. When the wickedness of the human race becomes "great in the earth," with people's thoughts being "only evil continually" (Gen 6:5 RSV), God punishes the world with a "clean sweep" *flood. Thereafter the book of Genesis becomes a small anthology of crime-and-punishment stories— Lot and his family punished for an ill-advised move to *Sodom (whose wickedness is punished by God in cataclysmic fire and brimstone), *Abraham and

Sarah punished for their expedient act of having a child by Hagar, *Jacob punished for his self-seeking behavior toward Esau, *Esau punished for his insensitivity to the spiritual benefits represented by his *birthright, *Joseph's brothers made to pay the consequences for their crime against their brother.

The epic of the *Exodus too contains its share of stories in which people's offense is punished, usually by God's supernatural intervention into earthly affairs. *Pharaoh's hardness of *heart is punished by the ten *plagues, eventuating in his own death. The Egyptian army's pursuit of the Israelites ends in their perishing in the Red Sea. Interspersed throughout the Mosaic laws of the Pentateuch is the prescription of God's laws that must be obeyed and punishments for their violation. The people's craving for meat, accompanied by a murmuring spirit, is punished by a plague (Num 11); and Miriam's rejection of Moses' authority, by temporary leprosy (Num 12). Similarly Moses' anger, self-importance and pride in striking the rock (Num 20:1-13) are punished by his exclusion from the Promised Land; the people's impatience is punished by an attack from fiery serpents (Num 21:4-9); and the rebellion of Korah, Dathan and Abiram meets a swift end in death (Num 16). On a national scale the ignominious murmuring of the Israelites, and especially their tenfold testing of God (Num 14:22), result in a forty-year wandering in the *wilderness until the generation of the rebellious has died.

The pattern of crime and punishment in the OT historical books, beginning with *Judges, is too pervasive to permit documentation here. The general pattern, among both leaders and the nation, is to follow a cycle of apostasy, calamity (sent as a punishment from God), repentance and deliverance. While this pattern shows God's design to be ultimately redemptive, the tragic dimension of the equation is expressed particularly in the motif of crime and punishment. Within this general sweep of OT history, some individual stories of crime and punishment stand out in our memories: Achan's greed; *Samson's foolish arrogance, sensuality and weak will; Saul's disobedience; *David's committing of *adultery and *murder; Jezebel's sordid life and sordid death; the rash greed of Elisha's servant Gehazi, who is punished with leprosy; and the downfall at God's initiative of such pagan rulers as the king of Tyre, Nebuchadnezzar and Belshazzar. Overriding all is the national *exile of Israel and Judah after a heartrending history of disobeying God's covenant.

The NT is less replete with examples and images of crime and punishment than the OT, though the doctrine of eternal punishment in hell for all who reject Christ becomes fully articulated. Jesus' discourses and parables yield the most vivid images: it is better to enter into eternal life blind and without one's limbs than to have one's "whole body be thrown into hell" (Mt 5:27-30); the foolish mistake of building a house (= a life) on sand results in a great fall (Mt 7:24-27); the five unprepared virgins are permanently barred from the wedding feast (Mt 25:1-13); the wicked and slothful servant is cast "into the outer darkness" (Mt 25:15-30); the goats will be separated from the sheep to "go away into eternal punishment" at the final judgment (Mt 25:31-46); those who place everyday concerns above the messianic banquet will be permanently excluded from salvation (Lk 14:15-24); the rich man is punished in the afterlife for his lack of compassion in the present life (Lk 16:19-31).

NT narrative provides a few additional examples. Judas reaches a terrible end after his betrayal of Jesus (Mt 27:9-10; Acts 1:18-20). Ananias and Sapphira's experiment in hypocritical fraud yields them a speedy death (Acts 5:1-11). When Herod Agrippa 1 aspires to godhead, "immediately an angel of the Lord smote him; . . . and he was eaten by worms and died" (Acts 12:21-23 RSV).

The book of *Revelation too can be read in a new light if we keep the pattern of crime and punishment in the background. The crime consists of the demonic and human worlds' rejection of Christ and pursuit of evil. The main images of the crimes of the human race fall into four categories—taking the side of evil rather than Christ, battling against Christ, persecuting the followers of Christ and pursuing commercial and materialistic interests with no concern for spiritual matters (Rev 18). The punishment unfolds in interim stages—progress reports on God's punishment of an evil world—and reaches its finale in the confinement of Satan and evildoers in the lake of fire. The dominant images of punishment in Revelation are images of physical torment on either a cosmic scale (earthquakes, hail, fire, water turned to blood, darkness, locusts), an international scale (warfare and famine, Rev 6:1-8) and a personal scale (sores on people, scorching from the sun, people gnawing their tongues in anguish, Rev 16:10).

See also ADULTERY; CURSE; EVIL; EXILE; FALL FROM INNOCENCE; MURDER; PLOT MOTIFS; THIEF; TRAGEDY.

CROOKED

The comparison between crooked and *straight probably stems from the image offered by the paths of Palestine. The topography of Bible lands required that main highways follow ridges and valleys or run either along the coastal plain or desert plateau. Corvée labor over the centuries made them level and straight for use by armies and the chariots of royal messengers and processions (Is 40:3; 45:2; 49:11). In stark contrast to the highways, the byways connecting villages twisted and wandered (Judg 5:6). These little paths were intended to be traveled on foot or by donkey and negotiated the hilly terrain by means of hairpins and switchbacks, never as the crow flies. The crooked, twisting path required a much longer walk than the straight line between the journey's beginning and end. Every inhabitant of Palestine held a mental picture of such circuitous paths,

making "crooked ways" and the "way of the crooked" a vivid and common image applied to one who avoids the difficult, acts unpredictably and fails to do what is right (Ps 125:5). "The highway of the upright turns aside from evil" (Prov 16:17 RSV).

Whatever is crooked bends away from what is straight. Thus whenever the Bible speaks about crooked things, it presupposes a straight standard, a standard grounded in the character of God himself: "Good and upright is the LORD" (Ps 25:8 NIV). Since the Lord is upright, his people must be upright. God himself commends Job for being "blameless and upright, a man who fears God and shuns evil" (Job 2:3 NIV). The uprightness of the righteous is an important theme to the psalmist, who observes that God Most High "saves the upright in heart" (Ps 7:10 NIV) and concludes that "it is fitting for the upright to praise him" (Ps 33:1 NIV). Paul insists that elders in the church be upright (Tit 1:8).

The wicked are crooked rather than upright: "God made mankind upright, but men have gone in search of many schemes" (Eccles 7:29 NIV). They make their own roads crooked. Their highways lead to desolation and destruction (Is 59:7-8). Peter identifies Balaam son of Beor as the spiritual ancestor of all those who "have left the straight way and wandered off" (2 Pet 2:15 NIV; cf. Num 22:32). The difference between two moral paths is a dominant motif in the book of Proverbs. In the words that Wisdom speaks, "there is nothing twisted or crooked" (Prov 8:8 RSV). "Wisdom will save you from the ways of wicked men, from men whose words are perverse, who leave the straight paths to walk in dark ways, who delight in doing wrong and rejoice in the perverseness of evil, whose paths are crooked" (Prov 2:12-15 NIV). A "crooked mind" and a "perverse tongue" go together (Prov 17:20 RSV). It is better to follow the Lord, for "he will make your paths straight" (Prov 3:6 NIV; cf. Is 26:7).

In a time of spiritual lethargy an entire generation may decline from God's upright standard. Moses laments that the children of Israel are a "warped and crooked generation" (Deut 32:5 NIV), arguing that such corruption is poor repayment to the God who is himself "upright and just" (Deut 32:4). Peter summarizes his Pentecost message: "Save yourselves from this crooked *generation" (Acts 2:40 RSV). Paul too pleads with the early church not to repeat the error of their forebears but to live instead as "children of God without fault in a crooked and depraved generation" (Phil 2:15 NIV). The label "crooked generation" recalls Jesus' name for his enemies, "generation of vipers" (Mt 3:7; 12:34; 23:33; Lk 3:7), itself linked to the mythological descriptions of God's enemy, the twisting *serpent (Is 27:1).

Since God is upright, he sets himself against those who are crooked. David praises the Lord for the shrewdness of his dealings with the crooked (2 Sam 22:27; Ps 18:26). Even the person who steals away from the right path cannot escape divine judgment, for "he who takes crooked paths will be found out" (Prov 10:9 NIV), and all "those who turn to crooked ways the LORD will banish with the evildoers" (Ps 125:5 NIV).

The preacher of Ecclesiastes uses the idea of crookedness to display his sober view of life under the sun and his healthy respect for divine providence: "Consider what God has done: Who can straighten what he has made crooked?" (Eccles 7:13 NIV). God intends some things, at least, to be crooked. It is better to bend one's own will to such things than to try to unbend them.

God has appointed his own Son as king in order to straighten out whatever is crooked. The king makes his approach on a smooth, straight highway, not a crooked one: "Prepare the way for the Lord, make straight paths for him. Every valley shall be filled in, every mountain and hill made low. The crooked roads shall become straight" (Lk 3:4-5 NIV; cf. Is 40:3-4).

See also STRAIGHT.

CROSS

In the ancient world the word *cross* was often synonymous with crucifixion. It sometimes only consisted of an upright stake, but usually a cross beam was attached either on the top or in the middle of the stake. Crucifixion as a form of execution probably originated with the Persians. It was later appropriated by Alexander the Great, adopted by the Romans and finally abolished by Constantine. It should be noted that the reference to the condemned person hanging on a tree in Deuteronomy 21:22-23 is not a reference to execution but is a public display of God's *curse subsequent to stoning.

In the first century A.D. crucifixion was one of the strongest forms of deterrence against insurrection or political agitation in Roman provinces. Crucifixion was preceded by scourging. When the victim was affixed to the cross, he was stripped and mocked. The pain was extreme. After the victim died, the body was often left on the cross to decay and become food for scavengers.

The imagery of cross in the Synoptic Gospels expresses radical discipleship that leads to *suffering and sometimes to *martyrdom. Jesus demands that his followers be willing to deny themselves and "take up the cross" (Mt 16:24; Mk 8:34). Luke's version (9:23) emphasizes a daily commitment to this task. The expression "take up the cross" recalls the common practice of the condemned person carrying the cross beam to the place of execution. Such a demand entails that all who follow Jesus must be prepared to suffer and be crucified. Jesus' road to suffering and eventual death by means of the cross became an example of obedience and commitment to God for all who would become disciples. In this respect the call to discipleship is a call to both self-denial and suffering. In John the notion of being "lifted up," which is understood as being part of the glorification process, is associated with Jesus' crucifixion (Jn 3:14;

12:32-34). Here the cross signifies victory.

The image of cross in Paul is theological in import. Paul's interest is in the saving significance of the cross as *atonement and not in the historical reconstruction of the event. Paul interpreted Jesus' agonizing and humiliating experience on the cross as an expression of obedience (Phil 2:8), which accomplished the required *redemption. Paul's preaching of the cross, namely the crucifixion of the Messiah, does not correspond to established ideas of salvation in the Greco-Roman and Jewish religions (1 Cor 1:17-18). Rather it is seen as divine *wisdom. Not only does cross become associated with the death of Jesus, but more importantly it becomes inseparably bound to all components of Christian salvation. For Paul the cross is the revelation of God's power and wisdom. It dramatically signifies an all-encompassing reconciliation: it bridges the gap between humanity and God (Col 2:14); it breaks the barrier between Jew and Gentile (Eph 2:16); and it restores the entire cosmos (Col 1:20). Similar emphases on the effects of the cross are also described in Hebrews 12:2 and 1 Peter 2:24.

See also ATONEMENT; CRIME AND PUNISHMENT; CURSE; SUFFERING; SUFFERING SERVANT; WISDOM.

BIBLIOGRAPHY. M. Hengel, *Crucifixion in the Ancient World and the Folly of the Message of the Cross* (Philadelphia: Fortress, 1977).

CROSS BEFORE CROWN

Christianity is the religion of the agony and the ecstasy, with the former preceding the latter. Romans 8:17 sounds the keynote: Christians are "heirs of God and fellow heirs with Christ, provided we suffer with him in order that we may also be glorified with him" (RSV).

Other NT passages give us variations on the theme. 2 Timothy 2:12 sets up this causal connection: "If we suffer, we shall also reign with him" (KJV). In the verses preceding this, Paul elaborates a similar theme with the pictures of a soldier who remains single-minded in the service of his superior, an athlete "who is not crowned unless he competes according to the rules," the "hard-working farmer who ought to have the first share of the crops" and himself as someone who is "suffering and wearing fetters like a criminal" in order to "obtain the salvation which in Christ Jesus goes with eternal glory" (RSV).

Philippians 1:29 has similar import: "For it has been granted to you that for the sake of Christ you should not only believe in him but also suffer for his sake" (RSV). Elsewhere Paul pictures himself as "on the point of being sacrificed," having "fought the good fight" and "finished the race," so that "henceforth there is laid up for me the *crown of righteousness" (2 Tim 4:6-8 RSV). James writes, "Blessed is the man who endures trial, for when he has stood the test he will receive the crown of life which God has promised to those who love him" (Jas 1:12 RSV). Romans 5:2 asserts that "we rejoice in our hope of sharing the glory of God" and then immediately follows with a list of virtues that suffering produces in Christian character (Rom 5:3-5).

The first epistle of Peter is a small classic on the subject of suffering for the sake of Christ. Here too we find an implied sequence of suffering as a prerequisite or prelude to *glory. "Do not be surprised at the fiery ordeal which comes upon you to prove you," writes Peter, "but rejoice in so far as you share Christ's sufferings, that you may also rejoice and be glad when his glory is revealed" (1 Pet 4:12-13 RSV). Similarly, elders who fulfill their calling sacrificially will receive "the unfading crown of glory" at the appearing of Christ (1 Pet 5:1-4). Again, "After you have suffered a little while, the God of all grace, who has called you to his eternal glory in Christ, will himself restore, establish, and strengthen you" (1 Pet 5:10 RSV).

A more generalized version of the same rhythm appears in the OT. Job's sufferings are the prelude to his seeing God. Psalm 34:19 asserts, "Many are the afflictions of the righteous; but the LORD delivers him out of them all." Psalm 30:5 states a rhythm that the Psalms reenact many times: "Weeping may tarry for the night, but joy comes with the morning" (RSV).

See also CROSS; CROWN; GLORY; SUFFERING.

CROSSING. See JOSHUA, BOOK OF.

CROWN

Crowns typically depict some state of *honor or *blessing for those who wear them, although occasionally the opposite image is ironically presented. Perhaps the most straightforward use of this imagery concerns the crowning of an Israelite ruler (Judg 9:6; 2 Kings 11:12; 1 Chron 20:2; 2 Chron 23:11; Esther 2:17; 8:15).

Possession of a *king's crown by another connotes the usurpation of that king's power. In 2 Samuel 1:10 an Amalekite reports to David that he killed Saul. As proof he brings to David Saul's crown and armband. David responds by mourning for Saul, since he considered it unlawful to kill the Lord's anointed. Such restraint against his Israelite rival may be contrasted to 2 Samuel 12:30, where David accepts the crown of the defeated king of Rabbah, thus symbolizing the transference of power to David.

Crowns also represent God's relationship to the king. It is ultimately God who places the crown on the king's head (Ps 21:3). As such, the king's crown may be thought of as a sign of his representative rule of what is in reality God's kingdom. God's displeasure with his anointed king results in the dissolution of the God/king relationship: "You have renounced the covenant with your servant and have defiled his crown in the dust" (Ps 89:39 NIV). In a similar vein, the sage reminds us that "riches do not endure forever, and a crown is not secure for all generations" (Prov 27:24). The crown that Yahweh places on the king's head is conditional on the king's covenant loyalty.

Quite often in both the NT and OT, crowns are symbols of God's blessings on his people. At times the specific nature of that blessing is not made explicit (e.g., Prov 10:6, "Blessings crown the head of the righteous"). However in this example the blessing may involve safety from some threat, since the second half of verse 6 promises "violence" for the wicked. Other passages speak of "gray hair" (Prov 16:31) and "grandchildren" (Prov 17:6) as crowns and signs of God's favor. A "crown of splendor" is promised for those who get wisdom (Prov 4:9).

Three passages in Isaiah take this crown imagery a bit further. In Isaiah 35:10 "everlasting joy" is said to crown the head of the redeemed (see also Is 51:11). The context of this passage is the return of the *exiles to *Zion from *Babylon. Although there is some question whether or not the immediate, historical context of this passage is eschatological and heavenly, the notion of "everlasting joy" certainly signifies a perpetual, ongoing state of blessedness for God's people in light of his redemption of his people. Hence this imagery would seem to have a clear biblical-theological connection to the eternal blessedness of the Christian, in light of the more developed NT teaching of the eternal *afterlife.

Isaiah 28:5 employs crown imagery in another sense. There it is Yahweh himself who will be "a glorious crown, a beautiful wreath for the remnant of his people" after he punishes prideful Ephraim. The point of this larger pericope (Is 28) is Judah's righteous rule of its people as opposed to the northern kingdom's injustice. Yahweh himself is the crown, the kingly presence, the symbol of Judah's just rule.

An alternate image is expressed in Isaiah 62:3. Here it is Zion/Jerusalem who will be "a crown of splendor in the LORD's hand." The exiles will return from Babylon, and Jerusalem will no longer be deserted. Rather, she will be a blazing touch, a beacon of righteousness for the nations. Jerusalem is Yahweh's royal adornment. This royal city will now be the seat from which Yahweh's rule of the nations will go forth. A similar imagery is employed in Zechariah 9:16. Yahweh will appear, Israel will be delivered: "The LORD their God will save them on that day as the flock of his people. They will sparkle in his land like jewels in a crown" (NIV).

Crown imagery in the NT is used in three distinct senses. First, Paul refers to the churches at Philippi (Phil 4:1) and Thessalonica (1 Thess 2:19) as his crown. His labors in building up these communities of believers are Paul's source of hope and joy. They are, to pick up on the imagery of Isaiah 62:3, Paul's royal adornment for his work as Christ's ambassador of the gospel. Second, crowns are rewards for those who remain faithful to the gospel. Paul awaits the "crown of righteousness" that Christ, the Judge, will award him "on that day" (2 Tim 4:8). Those who love God and persevere under trial will receive the "crown of life" (Jas 1:12; Rev 2:10; 3:11 [?]). Elders who are faithful to the flock will receive "the crown of glory" when the Chief Shepherd appears (1 Pet

5:4). Christians who are conformed to the image of Christ will one day share in his royal status as coheirs with him. The benefits of Christ are imputed to the believer, but in order for the believer to benefit from Christ's work, Christ, the sinless one, became sin for us; he laid aside his crown of honor and put on a crown of *thorns (Mt 27:29; Mk 15:17; Jn 19:2, 5; cf. Phil 2:6-8; Lam 5:16). As the exalted Christ, however, he is adorned with a new crown fitting his authority and universal dominion (Rev 6:2; 14:14).

See also BLESSING; GLORY; HONOR; KING, KINGSHIP; REWARD.

CRUCIFIXION. *See* CROSS.

CRYING. *See* TEARS; WEEPING.

CRYSTAL. *See* HEAVEN; JEWELS AND PRECIOUS STONES; PERMANENCE; SEA.

CUP

For the biblical writers, what gives a cup significance is not its appearance but its contents. A cup may hold a blessing—liquid that sustains life, quenches *thirst, engenders fellowship—or it may hold a *curse—liquid that induces *drunkenness or even *death.

Literal uses of the word *cup* often carry positive associations. In Nathan's parable in 2 Samuel 11:1-4, the poor man loves his lamb so much that he lets it drink from his own cup. Jesus commends the kindness of any who will give his disciples a cup of cold *water (Mt 10:42).

Since a cup can convey love, comfort, strength and fellowship, biblical writers sometimes use cup as a symbol for all the benefits God provides, as in Psalm 23 where the psalmist proclaims, "my cup overflows" (v. 5 NIV; also Ps 16:5; Ps 116:3; 1 Cor 10:16). But in the OT, cup is most often used figuratively as a symbol of God's *judgment against sin. God is pictured punishing wicked, rebellious people by making them drunk (Is 51:17, 22; Jer 25:15-16; Ezek 23:31-34; Mk 14:36).

*Drunkenness may seem a mild picture for divine wrath compared to the horrors of *war, natural disaster and *disease that God is shown visiting on *sinners. But in a way, the cup of wrath is a particularly dark symbol of judgment. It plays against our expectations of a generous *host who offers pleasure and fellowship. Instead God is seen personally handing sinners their destruction and forcing them to drink. In Jeremiah 25:27 God tells the nations, "Drink, get drunk and vomit, and fall to rise no more."

The image of the cup of wrath carries special horror because drinking (unlike being overtaken by *battle, *earthquake or *plague) is something a person does deliberately. Drunkenness implies a humiliating progression: people begin confident of their power to handle the *wine, but it eventually masters them. In several passages that feature the cup of God's wrath, we see that sinners start out arrogant

(see Ps 75:4-5; Jer 49:12-16; Rev 18:6-8) but lose any vestige of human dignity as they drink the cup God hands them "down to its very dregs" (Ps 75:8). They stagger and fall unconscious in the streets (Is 51:17-20); they are exposed and disgraced (Hab 2:16); they go mad (Jer 51:7); they are scorned and "walked over" by their enemies (Is 51:23). Yet clearly their own choices, not God's capricious anger, have precipitated their destruction.

When we remember the predominant use of cup imagery in the OT, Jesus' repeated use of the word *cup* to signify his impending death takes on great significance. When he pleads, "Abba, Father. . . . Take this cup from me" (Mk 14:36), we realize that his anguish grows principally from the prospect of feeling the full weight of his Father's *anger against sin fall on himself. Jesus' ordeal is especially poignant because he, alone among humankind, does not deserve God's wrath, yet he chooses to surrender to crucifixion so that sinners can receive forgiveness. As the soldiers come to arrest him, humility and heroism mingle in his words: "Shall I not drink the cup the Father has given me?" (Jn 18:11).

Because Jesus drinks the cup of death, he can offer his followers the cup of the new covenant. "Drink from it, all of you," Jesus tells the disciples at the Last Supper. "This is my blood of the covenant which is poured out for many for the forgiveness of sins. I tell you, I will not drink of this fruit of the vine from now on until that day when I drink it anew with you in my Father's kingdom" (Mt 26:27-29). All who accept Jesus' sacrifice for themselves can appropriate the blessings of forgiveness, fellowship with God and other believers, and certainty of eternal life that this cup of the new covenant holds (see 1 Cor 11:25-26). But any who take Jesus' sacrifice lightly or reject it completely will find themselves drinking the cup of God's judgment (see 1 Cor 11:27-30; Rev 17:3-6; 18:6-8).

See also DRINK; DRUNKENNESS; HOSPITALITY; JUDGMENT; WATER; WINE.

CURSE

The term *curse* has a considerable range of reference in the Bible. English versions translate as "curse" the Hebrew synonyms 'ārar, qālal and 'alâ, which correspond to the Greek *kataraomai*, *katara* and *epikataratos*, and the Hebrew *ḥāram* and *ḥērem*, which correspond to the Greek *anathematizō* and *anathema*. The imagery of curse relates to three contexts in Scripture: the created order, interpersonal relations and God's *covenant relationship with Israel.

Creation Curse. Often the effect of a curse is to be cut off from one's natural community and environment. The first biblical occurrence of curse falls on the *serpent, who is not so much "cursed above all the livestock" as the NIV renders it, but more properly, "*from* all livestock," that is, from among the community of *animals. The ground too is cursed and is alienated from *Adam, who no longer can enjoy easy access to its produce (Gen 3:17). Only later, in the case of *Cain, does God issue a curse against a person, whereby he is then driven from the *land and presumably his people as well (Gen 4:11). This curse that alienates Adam and then Cain from the land prefigures the curse of *exile that will be experienced by Israel.

Interpersonal Curses. When curses against land and persons occur in the literature of the surrounding Near Eastern societies, the initiative is entirely human. Curses in the OT may also be invoked by human agents, sometimes as a retaliatory speech-act, as in the case of Joshua, who consigns the Gibeonites to slavery (Josh 9:23; cf. Gen 9:25; 27:29), or as an invocation (Judg 21:18; 1 Sam 26:19) or as an expression of self-malediction (Jer 20:14-5). Yet the biblical idea of curse is distinct from contemporary nonbiblical parallels in that the latter was essentially theurgical, or *magical, while the former was theological in focus and so arose out of broad ethical considerations. Thus the biblical writers replace the original magical background of curse with a covenantal context.

This is not to say that all cursing in the Bible is done with reference to God. There are numerous instances where *curse* is merely a synonym for *"taunt" or "slander" (e.g., Ex 21:17; 1 Kings 2:8; Ps 37:22; 62:4; Prov 26:2; 27:14), and in this regard to curse is in effect to "turn my glory into shame" (Ps 7:2). From the wicked this cursing-as-slander provokes indignation, a common theme in the poetic books.

Covenant Curses. In *Deuteronomy, *Israel swears to their willingness to keep Yahweh's *covenant with a series of solemn "Amens" (Deut 26:15-26). In Deuteronomy 27—28 Yahweh recites Israel's prospects of *blessings and curses, a recitation that bears on every sphere of existence. Should Israel depart from him in going after other *gods: "The LORD will send on you curses, confusion and rebuke in everything you put your hand to, until you are destroyed" (Deut 28:20 NIV). At stake is Israel's national identity, whether it will be as "head" (Deut 28:13) or as "tail" (Deut 28:44), whether Israel will be a recipient of the blessings of God or a recipient of his wrath. The ultimate curse of *exile would mean nothing less than the removal of that which makes Israel glorious: the divine presence.

It is arguable that the force of Deuteronomy 28—29 lies in its images of curse as constraint. As God's appropriate response to disobedience, the curse threatens to deprive covenant violators of security, freedom, health and blessings. Israel under the curse will be partially or entirely constrained from enjoying certain blessings, resulting in a debasement of their God-given identity. Within the NT we find the sense of curse as constraint and debasement in the imagery of spiritual *slavery (e.g., Jn 8:34-47; Rom 6:20; Gal 4:8; Jude 6).

The motif of God's covenant curse expressed as the "wrath of God" is experienced by Israel most prominently in its conquest by Babylon and the ensuing *exile. The exile is the reflex of the *exodus. The covenant-making God who battles for Israel at the exodus becomes "like an enemy" (Lam 2:5) when Jerusalem is destroyed for its covenant unfaithfulness. Even though Israel returns to the land, the NT finds a situation in which Israel remains in spiritual exile within the land, with the pious still yearning for the "consolation of Israel" (Lk 2:25), the "redemption of Jerusalem" (Lk 2:38). Broadly speaking, the story of *Jesus is of the messiah offering to Israel the promised return from exile and the blessings of a new covenant (Mt 5:1-12). But Israel is largely unreceptive, and Jesus pronounces curses upon the nation (e.g., Mt 11:20-24; Mk 11:12-14, 20-21; 12:1-11) and warns of a coming great national disaster (Mk 13:14-23; Lk 13:34-35; 19:42-44; 21:20-24). Jesus takes upon himself the "curse of the law" (Gal 3:13), the penalty for Israel's (and the world's) unfaithfulness, and thus provides a pathway of salvation through the coming judgment for all those who will follow him. In this way, "the blessing of Abraham" comes upon the Gentiles (Gal 3:14). Israel and the Gentiles are redeemed from the "present evil age" (Gal 1:4; 4:3-9). Ultimately, however, the NT speaks of an eschatological curse, a final *judgment, in which those who reject God's salvation perish in their separation from God.

See also ADAM; BLESSING, BLESSEDNESS; COVENANT, TREATY; EXILE.

CURTAIN. *See* VEIL.

D

DAGON. *See* GODS, GODDESSES.

DANCING

Dancing, in its essence, is always symbolic. It is laughter; being pleasant; turning in a circle; whirling, running and leaping—an agile leaping that becomes an artistic rhythmic body movement expressing feeling and thought.

In the Bible the same Hebrew words can also signify a mother's pain in labor (Mic 4:9; Is 21:3; *see* Birth), a warrior's fall when slain (Ezek 30:4), an animal's leap of terror or delight (Ps 29:6; Is 13:21) or a scoffer's disdain (Job 30:1).

Symbol of Praise. Dancing is primarily a physical and visual means of *praising, honoring and thanking God. In the Bible it is often combined with song and instrumentation. Movement joins human and inanimate sound to praise God. Dance is one way of thanking and confessing God before others. The psalmist tells us to praise God "with tambourine and dance; . . . Let everything that breathes praise the LORD!" (Ps 150:4, 6; 149:3 NRSV).

Dancing and instrumentation are related to *prophecy. Miriam the prophetess commanded the women of her time to thank God for making them victorious over their Egyptian enemies (Ex 15:20-21). The context here is a postbattle victory celebration, usually led by women meeting returning warriors. This is also the proper understanding of Isaiah 52:7, which should be translated "How beautiful are the *dancing* feet *of the women* [a feminine participle in Hebrew] who spread the good news of peace"). Dancing was used to celebrate God's victory in battle and the human *"weapons" who were used by God (Judg 11:34; 1 Sam 18:6-7; 21:11; 29:5; *see* Divine Warrior). The prophets who met Saul also danced and played instruments (1 Sam 10:5).

In the Bible dancing always symbolizes *joy, the opposite of *mourning: "You have turned my mourning into dancing; you have taken off my sackcloth and clothed me with joy" (Ps 30:11 NRSV; cf. Lam 5:15; Eccles 3:4).

When *David and the Israelites dance, sing and play instruments as the *ark of the covenant comes into Jerusalem, David's uninhibited dance to God is described as a whirling, sporting, agile leaping. On the one hand, praise of God is more important than class, status

and propriety (2 Sam 6:14-21). On the other hand, this ecstatic worship of God is not more important than obedience (2 Sam 6:5-7; 1 Chron 15:2).

As with all the arts, dancing is not limited to the pious. It was an integral part of everyday events in antiquity. The young women danced at the *vineyards while playing their hand drums (Judg 21:21; Jer 31:4, 13). The Shulammite's dance was as beautiful as two dance troops (Song 6:13). When the *prodigal son repented, the father ordered a feast and a company of dancers (Lk 15:23-25).

Since dance was part of everyday life in the ancient

A bronze figure of an Etruscan girl dancing.

world, it was part of evil activities as well. Herod's daughter danced so effectively before the guests that she won the head of John the Baptist from the reluctant Herod (Mt 14:6, 7; Mk 6:22). The Amalekites ate, drank and danced when they defeated the Philistines (1 Sam 30:16). The misled Israelites danced when they gave credit to their handmade calf for all their success instead of giving it to the living God (Ex 32:4, 19; 1 Kings 18:26).

Symbol of Freedom and Equality. A brief but profound metaphoric use of dance occurs in the NT. Jesus describes his ministry of *eating and *drinking as a call to dance: "We played the flute for you, and you did not dance" (Mt 11:17; Lk 7:32 NRSV). Dance here symbolizes joy in living, a freedom to enjoy God's material gifts and to enjoy the company of all people, sinners included (Lk 7:34). Even as Jesus was accused by the pious of being "a glutton and a drunkard, a friend of tax collectors and sinners," so too Queen Michal "despised" David in her heart for leaping and dancing "as any vulgar fellow might" (2 Sam 6:16, 20 NRSV).

Dance in the Bible symbolizes praise, freedom and equality. An apt summary of its significance is found in the personification of *wisdom, a crucial quality needed by artists (Ex 28:3; 31:3, 6; 35:10). Wisdom itself dances, makes sport, laughs. As God created the world, wisdom was God's architect, daily dancing before God's face (Prov 8:30). God created the world with a dance-like joy, and we humans are to respond with a joyful dance.

See also MUSIC.

BIBLIOGRAPHY. J. Eaton, *The Psalms Come Alive: Capturing the Voice and Art of Israel's Songs* (Downers Grove, IL: InterVarsity Press, 1986) 102-15; W. O. E. Oesterly, *The Sacred Dance: A Study in Comparative Folklore* (Cambridge, UK: Cambridge University Press, 1923).

DANGER, STORIES OF

Stories of danger have high appeal because they grip the reader's attention and emotions. The Bible appeals to this deep-seated human interest. *Hero stories especially trade in danger, in keeping with their impulse to show courageous people who encounter and overcome extraordinary circumstances. To rank as a story of danger, a story must portray a threat to the protagonist in sufficient detail to elicit the reader's experience of the danger involved. In keeping with the Bible's premise of the primacy of the spiritual realm, the danger is often moral and spiritual rather than physical.

The stories of *Genesis, the Bible's "book of beginnings," provide repeated examples of danger. When *Abraham and later Isaac find themselves in a foreign nation in the company of a wife who might appeal to the king of that region, they respond to the dangerous situation with fear and expediency (Gen 12:10-20; 20; 26:6-11). Hagar confronts danger in the *wilderness in the form of possible death (Gen 16:7-14), and Lot has reason to be fearful of what might happen to him while living in a wicked city under God's judgment (Gen 19; *see* Sodom and Gomorrah). Sometimes the danger is more imagined than actual, as when the guilt-laden *Jacob, preparing to meet *Esau, fears retaliation from his brother, who is lavishly forgiving (Gen 32—33:14). The patriarch who undergoes the most dangers is *Joseph—sold into slavery in a foreign country, subjected to sexual temptation and imprisoned on a false accusation.

The epic of the *Exodus is built from start to finish around the danger motif. The nation itself is endangered when "there arose a new king over Egypt, who did not know Joseph" (Ex 1:8 RSV; *see* Pharaoh). *Moses, the future deliverer of Israel, faces danger of extinction at his very *birth (Ex 2:1-10). Once the march through the wilderness begins, the story is a veritable catalog of dangers—of starvation and lack of water, from hostile surrounding nations, from snakes and predators, from tensions within the traveling community, from God's dramatic acts of *judgment against sinners, of dying in the wilderness. The story of the conquest narrated in Joshua replaces the dangers of traveling with those of *battle.

The book of *Judges, being a collection of *rescue stories, naturally gives us heightened images of danger. One thinks of Ehud carrying out a daring assassination in the enemy king's own chamber, Deborah leading an army against a superior enemy, the timid Gideon pulling down an altar and later carrying out a nighttime raid against the feared Midianites, *Samson entering battle as a solitary strong man instead of leading a supportive army against the Philistines. In subsequent OT history, *David's life during his years as a fugitive is a series of narrow escapes. His most troublesome danger, though, proves to be moral danger when he succumbs to the temptation of adultery and engages in a cover-up by murdering.

As one pages through the books of Kings and Chronicles, the primary impression is not the danger posed by foreign invasion but the dangers of *idolatry and other forms of sin, which elicit striking displays of divine judgment. We observe Solomon's decline into sinful idolatry and indulgence in his later years. We read haunting verdicts of a king who "did not turn from his evil way" (1 Kings 13:33), of another who "did what was evil in the sight of the LORD, and . . . provoked him to jealousy" (1 Kings 14:22), and of a king who "sold himself to do what was evil in the sight of the LORD" (1 Kings 21:20). In these historical chronicles we move in a world where a *lion kills a prophet who disobeys a command from God (1 Kings 13), the fire of God repeatedly destroys groups of fifty men in one fell swoop (2 Kings 1), a greedy prophet and proud king are struck instantaneously with leprosy (2 Kings 5:20-27; 2 Chron 26:16-21), and an evil king is smitten in his bowels with an incurable *disease (2 Chron 21:18). The prophets who bear God's unpopular word to wicked kings live a life of continuous danger, and characters of exemplary virtue, like Naboth, are likewise people at risk in an evil society (1 Kings 21). In the world of political power struggles that we read about here, the danger of beheading is always lurking in the background (2 Kings 10).

People living in *exile are also in danger. In the literature of the exile we have stories about the Jews threatened with annihilation by Haman's plot against them (Esther), Daniel's three friends thrown into a fiery furnace and Daniel cast into a lions' den (Daniel).

The same atmosphere pervades the NT. Jesus' life as portrayed in the Gospels is one of intermittent threats to his life, beginning with his birth and culminating in the religious establishment's successful plot against him in the events surrounding the crucifixion. The story of Paul and other disciples in the book of Acts is similarly one of continuous narrow escapes, punctuated by imprisonments and *martyrdoms.

The stories of danger in the Bible underscore several things about this book. One is the reminder of the dangerousness of life that is the common human lot—yet another dimension of the Bible's realism. A second is the heightened sense of watchfulness by which the Bible encourages us to live, realizing that there is danger to the soul as well as to the body. Third, although the writers of the Bible did not compose fictional accounts of danger to make their stories more gripping and entertaining, the presence of danger as a motif in biblical narrative does link the stories of the Bible with popular narrative through the centuries, and as such it provides an additional avenue toward experiencing the Bible as literature.

See also ADVENTURE STORIES; BATTLE STORIES; DEATH; ENEMY; HERO, HEROINE; JUDGMENT; LION; MURDER STORIES; RESCUE; SERPENT; WARFARE; WILDERNESS.

DANIEL, BOOK OF

Although the first half of Daniel (Dan 1—6) consists of narratives arranged in chronological order and its second half (Dan 7—12) of chronological visions, the book is unified by theme (the sovereign Lord's control over, and ultimate disposition of, human power); by its central character, Daniel himself; by structure (see Sims); and by imagery. While much of the imagery in Daniel is peculiar to the book—e.g., terrifyingly ferocious hybrid beasts (Dan 7—8; *see* Monster), mysterious *fingers writing a king's fate on his palace wall (Dan 5), the dead apotheosized from the dust to shine as *stars in the sky (Dan 12)—much of the imagery is conventional. Even images common to the Hebrew Scriptures, however, are stamped with Daniel's unique signature: "balances" represent not only even-handed justice but also God's active determiner of judgment (Dan 5:25-30; *see* Scales), as in the *Iliad* and the *Aeneid;* and while the *"horn" (qeren) is still a general symbol of power and means of domination, here it takes on an independent demonic life (Dan 7—8).

Images of divine, human and *animal forms pervade the whole, binding together the seemingly disparate genres, languages, characterizations and historical perspectives of the book. One of these categories is at times transfigured to another (Dan 4:19-27; 10:4-12), at times they are conflated (Dan 7:1-15; 8:19-26), and yet again the forms are discretely maintained (Dan 2:36-45; 6:18-23). Other image clusters appear—vegetation, heavenly bodies, *metals, physical geography, forces of nature, *garments, artifacts, *food and *drink—but observation shows all such imagery to be closely associated with one or more of the primary image groups: divine, human, animal. For instance, while *"mountain" and *"stone" stand separately as metaphors for divine presence and power (Dan 2:35, 45; 9:16, 20; 11:45), in Nebuchadnezzar's

dream a stone cut miraculously ("without hands") from a mountain destroys the statue in human form that represents human kingdoms; and the stone is then transformed into a mountain, representing God's kingdom superseding human-ruled kingdoms (Dan 2:35, 44). Later when Daniel's dream reveals the ruler of this kingdom of God to be "one like the Son of man" (Dan 7:13-14), the transmutation has come full circle: a divine form (the stone) destroys a human form (the statue, an image parallel in its feet to the "fourth beast," Dan 7:7-12) and then instead of a stone, a human form is divinely empowered to rule by the "Ancient of days" (Dan 7:13-14). Significantly, the human form representing earthly kingdoms in the narratives (Dan 2) is metamorphosed into animal forms in the *apocalyptic visions (Dan 7—8, a bestialization foreshadowed by the humiliation of Nebuchadnezzar, Dan 4:30-33). Then in angelic narrative earthly rulers once more are represented in human forms (Dan 11).

Although Nebuchadnezzar's kingdom is represented in his dream as a great *tree cut down to a stump (Dan 4:10-12, 20-23), in life his pride leads to the humiliation of sinking from human to animal form (Dan 4:33), and his restoration to sanity and erect posture (symbolized in the dream by the sprouting of the stump, Dan 4:26) results from his penitent recognition of his insignificance compared with the sovereignty of the Most High (Dan 4:34-36).

Another illustration of this interconnectedness involves imagery describing how the destruction of human kingdoms is hastened and accomplished. Once the "great image" representing the human kingdoms of history is crushed by the stone, the *"wind" drives into oblivion its debris "like the *chaff of the summer threshingfloors" (Dan 2:35 RSV). The same image of natural force (representing divine power) brings forth from the "great sea" (human populations) four beasts (Dan 7:2-3), the fourth of which was "exceeding terrible" and "seemed greater than his fellows" (Dan 7:19, 20 RSV). It is metamorphosed in the next vision into a "he-goat" whose "notable horn" is broken and multiplies into four horns "toward the four winds of heaven." The strongest "little horn" (Dan 8:9-11, 23-25), an angel explains to Daniel, after his kingdom is "divided toward the four winds of heaven" (Dan 11:4), will "magnify himself above every god" (Dan 11:36) and finally "come to his end with none to help him" (Dan 11:45 RSV). While the imagery of winds dividing and ultimately destroying the forces of *evil clearly represents God's providential control, that imagery primarily supports the impression that human rulers who ignore or oppose God's rule move ineluctably toward bestiality and defeat. Such examples as these indicate that image clusters other than those involving divine, human or bestial form are secondary and supplementary.

The pattern described runs consistently through the twelve chapters of Daniel. Divine, human and animal figures predominate, if not in number then in thematic importance, from the triumph of healthier, handsomer and wiser men resulting from a refusal to eat a diet of meat and drink not divinely prescribed (Dan 1), through the contrast between men who survive the fiery furnace and men who perish in the flames in spite of their bowing down to the idol (Dan 3), through a representation of the divine in the form of "fingers of a man's hand" writing while Daniel reminds the idolatrous Belshazzar of Nebuchadnezzar's humiliation in animal form for not recognizing the rule of God (Dan 5), through depiction of human kings as anomalous beasts and the "most High" God as a human figure on the *throne of heaven giving universal lordship to "the *Son of man" and communicating with the human prophet by a humanely considerate angel (Dan 7—8), through Daniel's vision of the divine in the form of a "man clothed in linen" who compassionately strengthens the prophet overwhelmed by visions of bestial, blasphemous kings (Dan 10), and finally to the solemn oath of the divine "man clothed in linen" that the time for judgment on the wicked who arrange temple sacrifices of abominable *animals and the time for vindication of, and everlasting life for, God's people is already determined, though not revealed (Dan 12).

The thematic importance of this dynamic interplay among three major categories of imagery is exemplified at the center of the book (Dan 6). The enemies of God and of his "holy people" are destroyed by the very beasts they had planned to employ in Daniel's destruction (Dan 6:12-13). The human figure of Daniel kneeling in *prayer before an open window facing *Jerusalem and later raised upright and unhurt from the pit "because he believed in his God" stands out sharply against the image of the men who hated and plotted against him being thrown alive (with their families) into the den and torn apart by the very beasts they placed there to devour Daniel (Dan 6:24). The invisible deity's presence has been made evident by his angel who "shut the lions' mouths" (Dan 6:22), thus showing his dominion as complete "in heaven and in earth" (Dan 6:27). Here the nondiscursive truth of the imagery is expressed discursively in the words of a pagan monarch: Yahweh rules over the divine, the human and the bestial "enduring for ever . . . even unto the end" (Dan 6:26; cf. 2:47; 3:28-29; 4:3, 17, 34-35). In addition, this message of the imagery is made explicit by the narrator (Dan 1:2), by Daniel himself (Dan 2:20-22, 37-38; 4:24-25; 5:18-21; 7:14, 18-21, 27), by the "watchers" in Nebuchadnezzar's *dream (Dan 4:17) and by angels (Dan 8:25; 11:45; 12:1-3, 7, 12-13).

Finally, for all the intricacy of the image patterns and their interrelationships, we remember the book of Daniel partly as a gallery of memorable narrative moments: four homespun young men, who excel the courtly sophisticates in their wisdom; a symbolic figure made of various *metals and *minerals; a

furnace heated seven times hotter than usual, with Daniel's three friends and a divine companion walking in it unsinged; Nebuchadnezzar's sudden insanity as he reveled in his proud achievements, followed by his eating *grass like the *ox and having his nails grow like birds' claws; a supernatural hand writing on the wall at a royal feast; Daniel's surviving a night in a lions' den.

See also APOCALYPSE, GENRE OF; APOCALYPTIC VISIONS OF THE FUTURE.

BIBLIOGRAPHY. D. N. Fewell, *Circle of Sovereignty: A Story of Stories in Daniel 1-6* (Sheffield: Almond, 1988); P. A. Porter, *Metaphors and Monsters: A Literary-Critical Study of Daniel 7 and 8* (Coneictanea Biblica, OT Series 20; Uppsala: CWK Gleerup, 1983); J. H. Sims, *A Comparative Literary Study of Daniel and Revelation: Shaping the End* (Lewiston, NY: Mellen, 1995).

DARE. *See* BET, DARE.

DARKNESS

Darkness has no existence by itself, being definable simply as an absence of light. It is a physical and spiritual reality as well as an apt symbol for some of the profoundest human experiences. With approximately two hundred references, darkness is a major actor in the biblical drama. The book of *Job, a vision of calamity and despair, is a small anthology of descriptions of darkness, with three dozen instances. Darkness stands out from virtually all other literary images, which are finally ambivalent (having both good and bad manifestations), because it is uniformly negative in its import. The best way to organize the biblical imagery of darkness is first to note what it represents in itself and then to observe what God does in regard to it.

The Cosmic Conflict. The primeval mind envisions life and even the cosmos as a conflict between *light and darkness, viewed as combatants struggling for control of the world (*see* Cosmology). The first biblical references to darkness hint at such a picture. We read that "the earth was a formless void and darkness covered the face of the deep" (Gen 1:2 NRSV). God's first creative act is to produce light and separate it from darkness, with overtones of light's conquering darkness (Gen 1:4-5). It took God to set a "boundary between light and darkness" (Job 26:10). The cosmos is kept intact only by the governing power of God, and one way in which the prophets envision a coming *apocalyptic judgment is to picture it as a return to the primeval *chaos in which the earth is "waste and void" and the heavens have "no light" (Jer 4:23; cf. Is 5:30).

Throughout the Bible, darkness is an implied contrast to light, regardless of whether the darkness is physical or symbolic. In fact, sixty verses present light and darkness as a contrasting pair, and being brought out of darkness into light is a major biblical image of redemption.

Physical Darkness. Darkness as a physical feature

of daily living accounts for a large cluster of biblical passages. At the neutral end of the spectrum, *nightly darkness simply signals the end of the working day for humans and the active time for nocturnal animals (Ps 104:20). The palpable quality of darkness in a pre-electrical era is suggested by the way in which the writer to Hebrews lists darkness in a catalog of things "that can be touched" (Heb 12:18). The connotations of this palpable nightly darkness are usually sinister. Darkness is variously associated with groping to find one's way (Job 5:14; 15:25), inability to progress down a pathway (Job 19:8), a house being broken into (Job 24:16), undesignated *"terrors" (Job 24:17; cf. Gen 15:12), a place "where evildoers may hide themselves" (Job 34:22), the wicked shooting at the innocent from ambush (Ps 11:2), "the haunts of violence" (Ps 74:20), stumbling (Prov 4:19) and gloom (Is 58:10; Joel 2:22). The cloak of darkness makes it the natural time for adulterous adventure: it is "in the twilight, in the evening, at the time of night and darkness" that the "young man without sense" commits *adultery with the wily seductress (Prov 7:7, 9 NRSV).

In short, darkness keeps some very bad company, made all the more devious by virtue of the concealment of evil activity from ordinary view. Paul provides an apt summary of this side of darkness when he commands Christians to "take no part in the unfruitful works of darkness, but instead expose them. For it is shameful even to mention what such people do secretly" (Eph 5:11-12).

Figurative Meanings. Based on its physical properties, darkness becomes a rich source of metaphor for spiritual realities. If light symbolizes understanding, darkness represents ignorance (Ps 82:5), folly (Eccles 2:13-14), a silencing of prophetic revelation (Mic 3:6), the state of the human mind unilluminated by God's revelation (2 Pet 1:19), falsehood (1 Jn 1:6) and the loss of walking in God's truth "because the darkness has brought on blindness" (1 Jn 2:11 NRSV). If light symbolizes good, darkness is the corresponding image for evil people "who forsake the paths of uprightness to walk in the ways of darkness" (Prov 2:13 NRSV; cf. Prov 4:19). In Jesus' mysterious picture of the eye as "the *lamp of the body," physical *blindness becomes a metaphor for the lost state (Mt 6:22-23; Lk 11:34-36).

On the logic of night bringing the day's activity to its cessation, darkness becomes an image for *death or the grave (Job 10:21-22; Ps 88:12). Darkness is the leading image in Job's poem cursing the day of his birth and expressing his wish for death (Job 3). The cessation that darkness brings to human activity makes it the natural associate of the *prison and dungeon (Ps 107:10, 14; Is 42:7; 49:9). Even if a literal prison is not in view, the paralysis that darkness brings to human activity makes it seem prisonlike, and eight biblical verses give us a picture of "sitting" in darkness.

Light is the generic biblical image for divine favor and human prosperity, and darkness is accordingly the absence of these (Ps 88:6). Thus Job pictures his erstwhile prosperity as a time when God's lamp shone over his head and "by his light I walked through darkness," this being the time "when I was in my prime, when the friendship of God was upon my tent" (Job 29:3-4 NRSV). Correspondingly, the fall of the wicked from prosperity is pictured as a time when "the light is dark in their tent" and when the wicked "are thrust from light into darkness" (Job 18:6, 18 NRSV). Similarly when the psalmist prays for misfortune to befall his enemies, he asks that "their way be dark and slippery" (Ps 35:6 NRSV). Amos declares the sobering message that the complacent people who speak glibly of the coming day of the Lord will find that "it is darkness, not light" (Amos 5:18, 20 NRSV).

Darkness as a Spiritual Force. The power of darkness in the NT is so vivid that it is more than a symbol, becoming nothing less than a spiritual reality. Jesus himself spoke of "the power of darkness" (Lk 22:53), and Paul spoke of how Christians do not battle against physical *enemies but against "the cosmic powers of this present darkness, against the spiritual forces of evil in the heavenly places" (Eph 6:12 NRSV). The context into which darkness is here placed is the cosmic spiritual battle between good and evil, God and *Satan. "What partnership is there between righteousness and lawlessness?" Paul asks. "Or what fellowship is there between light and darkness? What agreement does Christ have with Beliar?" (2 Cor 6:14-15 NRSV). The world itself is divided into "children of light" and children "of the night or of darkness" (1 Thess 5:5). The ultimate power of darkness was manifested with the temporary triumph of evil as Christ hung dying on the cross—a triumph of evil that took the form of a three-hour darkness that left people awestruck (Mt 27:45; Mk 15:33; Lk 23:44).

Summary. Considered in itself darkness it thus a strongly negative image in human experience. It is physically oppressive; it is the natural environment for a host of evil happenings; and it is associated with death, imprisonment and ultimate evil. Darkness is in principle associated with evil, opposed to God's purposes of order and goodness in the universe and in human society. The question then becomes what God does with regard to darkness, and whether, in fact, he is lord over it.

God's Power Over Darkness. It is important to dissociate the biblical imagery of darkness and light from any conception of dualism, as in the religion of Zoroaster. Darkness in the Bible is not equal in power to light. The occasional impression that it is equal is a result of the realism of the Bible about the power of evil in the world. However darkness exists only within God's control. God knows "the place of darkness," even though people do not (Job 38:19). He also "knows what is in the darkness" (Dan 2:22). People who think that the Lord does not see what they do in the dark are mistaken (Ezek 8:12); indeed, "there is no gloom or deep darkness where evildoers may hide themselves" (Job 34:22). The speaker in Psalm 139 admits defeat in his imaginary escape from God into darkness with the acknowledgement that "even the darkness is not dark to you [i.e., God]; the night is as bright as the day, for darkness is as light to you" (Ps 139:12 NRSV). In fact God is even pictured as the creator of darkness: "I form light and create darkness" (Is 45:7 NRSV).

God's power over darkness is evident in the fact that he uses it to achieve his purposes. He uses darkness to cover himself from human view, for example. In OT theophanies the concealing or covering quality of darkness makes it part of the means of God's appearance. When God performs the ritual of "cutting the covenant" with Abraham, for example, "when the sun had gone down and it was dark, a smoking fire pot and a flaming torch" (images of God's appearance) passes between the divided carcasses (Gen 15:17 NRSV). In other words God himself is cloaked from human view by the veil of darkness. When God appears on Mt. *Sinai, he is shrouded in awe-inspiring darkness (Ex 20:21; Deut 4:11; 5:22-23). When he appears as a *storm God, darkness is prominent in the appearance (2 Sam 22:10, 12; Ps 18:9, 11; 97:2). God is even said to "dwell in thick darkness" (1 Kings 8:12; 2 Chron 6:1), a transcendent spiritual being veiled from human view. On the premise that a mortal cannot see God and live (Ex 33:20), God's veiling of himself in darkness is an act of mercy toward the human race.

God also uses darkness to bring judgment upon evildoers. At the time of the exodus, the ninth *plague was a three-day darkness so intense that the darkness could be "felt" (Ex 10:21-23). When the Egyptians pursued the fleeing Israelites, God not only drowned the Egyptians but also used darkness to barricade them from the Israelites (Josh 24:7). In the apocalyptic vision of coming judgment, God is portrayed as sending darkness on the earth as a form of punishment (Is 13:10; 60:2; Ezek 32:7-8; Joel 2:2, 31; Amos 8:9; Zeph 1:15; Rev 16:10). When God predicts that he will "execute acts of judgment," the imagery is that of the day being dark (Ezek 30:18-19) and of his pursuing "his enemies into darkness" (Nahum 1:8). Darkness even becomes a designation for *hell itself (Mt 8:12; 22:13; 25:30; 2 Pet 2:4, 17; Jude 6, 13). In each of these passages, God is emphatically the one who sends disobedient creatures into the darkness of hell.

Deliverance From Darkness. The greatest of God's acts in regard to darkness, though, is his spiritual *rescue of people from darkness through the work of Christ. God himself "is light and in him there is no darkness at all" (1 Jn 1:5). Christ is a light that "shines in the darkness, and the darkness did not overcome it" (Jn 1:5). Whoever follows Jesus "will never walk in darkness but will have the light of life" (Jn 8:12). Jesus came "as light into the world," so that everyone who believes in him "should not remain in the darkness" (Jn 12:46). In a similar vein Paul writes that believers in Christ once "were darkness, but now in the Lord you are light" (Eph 5:8 NRSV).

Whether as a symbol or as a spiritual principle, darkness is the thing from which God in Christ delivers people. It thus figures in some of the great images of redemption that we find in the Bible. With the coming of Jesus "the people who sat in darkness have seen a great light, and for those who sat in the region and shadow of death light has dawned" (Mt 4:16 NRSV; cf. Lk 1:70). To escape the lost state requires nothing less than a divine rescue mission: Christ "has rescued us from the power of darkness and transferred us into the kingdom of his beloved Son" (Col 1:13 NRSV). Those who believe in Christ as savior are "a chosen race, a royal priesthood, a holy nation, God's own people, . . . called out of darkness into his marvelous light" (1 Pet 2:9 NRSV). For people who are God's children, "the darkness is passing away and the true light is already shining" (1 Jn 2:8 NRSV).

See also BLACK; BLINDNESS; CHAOS; LAMP; LIGHT; NIGHT.

BIBLIOGRAPHY. E. R. Achtemeier, "Jesus Christ, the Light of the World: The Biblical Understanding of Light and Darkness," *Interpretation* 17 (1962) 439-49.

DAUGHTER

Women in Scripture are nearly always identified as the daughter of their *father. Many significant daughters are only named as such: consider the daughters of Lot (Gen 19), Pharaoh (Ex 2:5; Heb 11:24), Jephthah (Judg 11:34ff), Job (Job 42:15), Herodias (Mt 14:6), Jairus (Mk 5:23) and the Syrophoenician woman (Mt 15:22). Others are named but only known for the deeds to which they had access through their father: Rebekah, whose parents' relation to Abraham brought his servant to her in search of a wife for Isaac (Gen 24); Michal, daughter of Saul, who married David (1 Sam 18:17); Rachel and Leah, daughters of the crafty Laban, who became Jacob's wives (Gen 29). We recall also those who acted as daughters: Ruth to Naomi (Ruth 4:15), Esther to Mordecai (Esther 2:7). Like a *son, a daughter is a reflection of the parents; in turn, her individual character casts a positive or negative shade on the future of their name.

A daughter depends on a parent's provision, and with few exceptions a daughter is treasured by her parents. Jephthah mourns the vow that dooms his daughter (Judg 11:35); Job's beautiful daughters are each given an *inheritance (Job 42:15); Jairus and the Syrophoenician woman frantically beseech Jesus on behalf of their daughters (Mt 15:22; Mk 5:23). Jesus suggests the treasured, privileged status of a crippled woman by calling her the "daughter of Abraham" (Lk 13:16).

Commonly parents prize and prioritize a daughter's safety. The prophets typify a daughter as "tender and delicate" (Is 47:1), "a lady of the kingdom" (Lam 2:15) and as "jealously possessed" (Jer 14:17). A *virgin daughter is considered vulnerable, and any

193

violation of her is a calamity (Lam 2:13). Along with sons, daughters are often expected to reap the benefits of their parents' righteousness (Ezek 14:20). At times a daughter's future hinges on a parent's desires or needs: Lot and the Benjamite offer their daughters to strange men; Michal becomes David's wife as a battle reward from Saul; Herodias's daughter is made to dance before Herod; Leah and Rachel wait on Laban's plans. A daughter receives an inheritance, good or bad, from her parents.

A daughter determines the honor of her parents by her action. Parents value daughters in part because their provision is reciprocated in future dependence that they have upon her. Though not responsible to carry on the family name, daughters participate in the advancement of their father's name by behaving with dignity, preserving their purity until a suitable or even advantageous marriage can be arranged. The prominent negative example is Lot's daughters, who behave shamefully in an effort to preserve the family name after they are cut off from their culture, alone with their father on the mountain (Gen 19:31). By contrast both Esther and Ruth behave as daughters to their guardians in a crisis situation, and by their prudent actions they preserve their family name. By virtue of the fact that they are not actually daughters of their guardians, they are included in the list of great heroes of a nation as her daughters. Thus the link with the idiomatic usage of *daughter* begins. Esther represents the nation of Israel in her courageous appearance before Xerxes, and Ruth is grafted into the family of Israel and is the great-grandmother of David, the great king.

These aspects of the image of a daughter help inform our understanding of the idiomatic use of the image in the prophetic writings. Often the word *daughter* is found in expressions such as "daughter of Zion" (e.g., Is 1:8; Jer 4:31; Mic 4:10; Mt 21:5), "daughter of Sidon" (Is 23:12) and "daughter of Babylon" (Jer 50:42). This Hebrew idiom reflects a double metaphor common in the culture of the ancient Near East: a capital city was personified as a woman, and the inhabitants of that city collectively as her "daughter." A pagan city was personified by a female goddess whose husband was the local patron deity; *Zion or *Jerusalem remained distinct as she whose husband was the one true God, Yahweh. During times of war when a city was overrun and its population exiled, the city was considered to be a *barren woman, rejected by her husband-deity (Is 54:1). Thus her daughters, the collective inhabitants, depended on her for identity but also shaped her future by their actions. For instance, Isaiah proclaims to "barren" Jerusalem, "Rejoice, O barren woman!" (Is 54:1) and prophesies a return of the inhabitants to that city and an unprecedented future glory for it. Because of Isaiah's use of these idioms, Jesus fulfills prophecy by addressing Jerusalem as "daughter of Zion" (Mt 21:5), and the apostle Paul quotes Isaiah 54:1 and announces in Galatians 4:26 that Jerusalem above is "free" and

that she is the "mother" of Christians.

In the historical situation of conquest and exile, the OT prophets judge or bless given cities from the view of the daughter image. Isaiah announces doom on the population of Sidon: "You will exult no more, O crushed virgin daughter of Sidon; rise, cross over to Cyprus—even there you will find no rest" (Is 23:12 NRSV). Jeremiah proclaims woes on the Egyptians: "Go up to Gilead and get balm, O Virgin Daughter of Egypt! But you multiplied remedies in vain; there is no healing for you" (Jer 46:11 NIV). The Lord says to his people through the prophet Zechariah, "Shout and be glad, O daughter of Zion. For I am coming, and I will live among you" (Zech 2:10 NIV). This follows his prophecy of the end of the exile, "Come, O Zion! Escape, you who live in the daughter of Babylon" (Zech 2:7 NIV). God's people living in exile in Babylon with the inhabitants of that city remain distinct as the citizens of Zion, she who belongs to Yahweh. These few examples demonstrate the idiomatic link between a daughter-people and a mother-city.

Perhaps the "daughters of Jerusalem" from Solomon's Song summarize the daughter image best. Heirs to the glorious promised inheritance of that city, the friends of the bride are repeatedly admonished to let their actions preserve the great blessing bestowed upon them: "I adjure you, O Daughters of Jerusalem, do not arouse or awaken love until it is ready" (Song 8:4 NRSV). The practical parental nature of this advice brings the image of a daughter to life. Whether literal or allegorical in its interpretation, this passage demonstrates the image of a daughter as one who receives great blessing and is responsible to let her actions preserve the honor of that blessing.

See also SON; VIRGIN; WOMAN, IMAGES OF.

DAVID

Mentioned a thousand times in the Bible, David is the biblical man for all seasons, the most complex and many-sided human character in Scripture. Simply to name the roles that David fills suggests why he has inspired so many images of him, both within the Bible itself and in subsequent traditions. David was variously *shepherd, fugitive, politician, *king, poet, musician, *prophet, *warrior, *friend (the Jonathan story), lover, *father, *sinner (*adulterer and *murderer), penitent and "type" of *Christ. David is unique among biblical characters by virtue of being fully known to us both from the outside (as subject of narrative writing) and from the inside (as writer of lyric poems). While many postbiblical exegetical and literary traditions take extravagant liberties with biblical data, the traditions stemming from David can all find a biblical basis. This includes the Puritan image of David the reformer—the true child of God resisting the assaults of a tyrannical king (Saul), beset by slanderers and enemies; the champion who fought against God's enemies; the king who reformed the nation and established worship on a holy foundation.

The role in which David is best known to the Western imagination is that of boy *hero and giant killer. When David kills Goliath he becomes an instant public hero, a civic liberator providing possible inspiration for fictional heroes following in his wake from Beowulf to Jack (of the beanstalk). To this day we read in the newspapers about someone's pulling off a "little David" act in sports or politics, or about a "David and Goliath" contest. The image of David the warrior, of course, expands into his adult career, as epitomized by the women's chant that "Saul has slain his thousands, and David his ten thousands" (1 Sam 18:7; 21:11 RSV). David's success in expanding the territory of Israel was unequaled in the annals of Israelite history.

David's career as a national hero was preceded by his career as an underdog. The youngest son, belittled by his older siblings (1 Sam 17:28-29), David was considered so unlikely a candidate among Jesse's sons to be anointed as the future king that he had to be summoned from tending the *sheep after the other brothers had been passed over (1 Sam 16:6-11). Subsequently he had a career as fugitive, fleeing from the wrathful Saul, living continuously on the edge. There is even a touch of David as rebel and desperado. Jesus cited David as a precedent for disobeying the levitical laws on the basis of the time David ate consecrated bread to feed his hungry men (Mt 12:3-4; Lk 6:3-4). Then there is David the political strategist. Even after he was anointed king of Judah, David had to undertake a long process of consolidating his power until he eventually became king of the entire nation (2 Sam 2—5).

The facets of David's character that render him most lifelike, however, appear less in his heroic moments than in his times of error and failure. These are the stories that are for the most part edited out of childhood Sunday school curricula, such as the affair with *Bathsheba and the taking of the national census (2 Sam 11; 24). One of the most noteworthy features of the David story is that it begins with heroic promise but becomes a story of *crime and punishment. In his career as a sinner, moreover, David becomes a classic case of one sin leading to another, as he degenerates from adulterer to murderer. Although David responds to his sin by being the ideal penitent, his subsequent life is dominated by family discord and political troubles. David the failure is the common person's David—a flawed figure in whom readers can see themselves.

In the later phases of his life David emerges as a tortured parent. He suffers greatly because of his sons, yet curiously we never see him warning them about the evils of excessive ambition and sexual indulgence. Possibly he was too concerned about losing face before them to instruct them as effectively as he could have, using his own experiences as object lessons. For anyone familiar with Shakespeare's *King Lear,* it is impossible not to read the story of David's later life without being aware of the parallels. In both

stories personal failings produce tragic results: the collapse of nations and the disintegration of families in the form of children rebelling against a father and siblings preying on each other.

NT references to David present him both as an ancestor and as a type of Christ. David freed Israel from the terror of literal bondage to Goliath and the Philistines; Christ freed all people from spiritual bondage to Satan and death. David was a prophet and king; so was Christ. God established a *covenant with David promising him an eternal kingdom (2 Sam 7:12-16) which was ultimately Christ's *kingdom. All of the Gospels identify Christ as the son of David; Matthew and Luke do so formally with complete genealogies. If it seems difficult to consider a man with David's large-scale failures as a type of Christ, one may return to the Lord's words to Samuel as he prepared to anoint Saul's successor: "For the LORD sees not as man sees; man looks on the outward appearance, but the LORD looks on the heart" (1 Sam 16:7 RSV).

The complexity of David evident in postbiblical traditions is present within the Bible itself, where various writers give complementary (but decidedly divergent) images of David. In the two books of Samuel the life of David is interpreted as a literary tragedy. Until the Bathsheba and Uriah debacle, David's career is one of heroic success. The providential theme is evident in God's anointing of David as king and in repeated references to God's giving David success; furthermore, the chronicler selects material for inclusion that idealizes David. After the Bathsheba incident, a pattern of judgment for sin dominates the action. By contrast the writers of Kings and Chronicles omit references to Bathsheba and Uriah, select for inclusion material that highlights David's religious and military achievements, and repeatedly regard David as the norm of a godly king by which to judge evil kings (e.g., 1 Kings 9:4; 11:4, 6; 15:3).

Putting these two traditions together gives us the right slant for interpreting David's life, which was indeed both heroic and *tragic. While the OT histories record David's many achievements and his occasional failures, the *Psalms reveal David's deep understanding of God's forgiveness and the joy of reconciliation with him (e.g., Ps 32). Paradoxically, therefore, the figure of David is a figure of hope for humanity: no matter how deep a person descends and regardless of how tragic the circumstances of life become, something can be made of life. The David of the Psalms, beset by trouble and guilt, is the very touchstone of spiritual trust in God. As a respected leader who gave in to sexual sin and who mismanaged child rearing, David is someone whose story is reenacted in every generation. Yet he stands as a tribute to divine grace, so that even such a person can be declared "a man after God's own heart" (1 Sam 13:14; Acts 13:22).

See also BATHSHEBA; CHRIST; CHRONICLES, BOOKS OF; HERO, HEROINE; JERUSALEM; KING; SAMUEL, BOOKS OF.

BIBLIOGRAPHY. W. Breueggemann, *David's Truth in Israel's History and Imagination* (Philadelphia: Fortress, 1985); R-J. Frontain and J. Wojcik, eds., *The David Myth in Western Literature* (West Lafayette, IN: Purdue University Press, 1980); D. M. Gunn, *The Story of King David* (JSOTSup 6; Sheffield: JSOT, 1978).

DAVIDIC COVENANT. *See* COVENANT.

DAY, DAY OF THE LORD

The Day of the Lord and related ideas occur most frequently in the prophets, the parables and sayings of Jesus, the book of Revelation, and other portions of the NT dealing with the *end times. Images and ideas associated with the Day of the Lord can also be found in the historical books of the OT and in the Psalms.

The term *Day of the Lord* is sometimes used by the prophets to refer to any specific period of time in which the God of Israel intervenes in human affairs to save and judge (Is 13:6; Ezek 13:5; Amos 5:18). In many cases the day was named after the group of human beings that was the target of God's intervention. We find references, for example, to "the day of Midian," (Is 9:4) and "the day of Egypt" (Ezek 30:9). Many times the day is named for what God was to do or what was to happen: "day of trouble" (Ezek 7:7), "day of rebuke" (Hos 1:9), "day of punishment" (Is 10:3), "day of vengeance" (Is 63:4), "day of doom," (Jer 51:2), "day of darkness" (Joel 2:2) or "day of the LORD's anger" (Zeph 2:2). Often when a prophet has already begun to describe a specific series of God's acts, he will continue his description with a reference to "that day" (e.g., Is 11:10; 15:20; 24:27; 30:23; Jer 25:33; 29:16; 30:7; 48:41; Mic 3:4; 4:7; Zech 2:11; 9:16; 14:13).

In some prophetic texts "the day of the Lord" refers to an event so cataclysmic that it ends an age of the world (e.g., Joel 2:28—3:21; Zech 14:1-21). This usage passed over into the NT, where the Day of the Lord refers to God's judging action when Christ returns at the end of the age (e.g., 1 Thess 5:2; 2 Thess 2:2; 2 Pet 3:10).

It is most commonly believed that the Day of the Lord has its roots in Israel's holy war experiences. Certainly images of *warfare predominate in those passages dealing with the Day of the Lord. Frequently there are descriptions of armies marching to the decisive battle, including their gathering (Is 5:26; Zeph 3:8; Zech 14:2; Rev 16:14; 19:19); their equipment and *weaponry (Is 22:5-7; Jer 46:3-4; Ezek 38:4-6; Joel 3:10; Rev 19:1-14); the sights, sounds and smells of the armies on the march and rushing to the attack (Is 5:28; Jer 47:3; Joel 2:4-5); and the visceral fear and anguish of those facing battle (Is 13:7-8; 21:3; Jer 30:5-6; 49:24; Ezek 7:17; 30:4, 9). Graphic images of suffering, death, destruction and dislocation usually follow (Is 3:25—4:1; 10:4; Jer 25:33; 49; 26; 51:3-4; Lam 1:3, 5; Ezek 24:20; 30:4; 39:3-4; Obad 11-12, 14; Zech 14:2).

These climactic events were given the name Day of the Lord because God's personal action was believed to be the decisive factor in the course of events. His personal involvement was signified by such phrases as "the day of [the Lord's] vengeance" (Is 34:8), "the day of [the Lord's] anger" (Is 13:13; Lam 1:12, 21-22; 2:1; Zeph 2:2-3), "the day of the Lord's sacrifice (Zeph 1:8), "the day of the wrath of the Lord" (Ezek 7:19), "the day I punish Israel" (Amos 3:14), "the day when I take from them their stronghold" (Ezek 24:25), "the day that I cleanse you" (Ezek 33:33), "the day I visit them" (Jer 27:22), "the day that I make them my jewels" (Mal 3:17) and "the day I rise up for plunder" (Zeph 3:8).

In both Testaments a variety of images for God's appearance among people is employed to express God's personal involvement in the events of the Day of the Lord. Most frequently God's appearance and action are described in terms of cosmic catastrophes, including raging *fires (Is 10:16; 38:22; Joel 2:30; Amos 1:14; Zeph 3:8; 2 Pet 3:7, 10; Rev 16:8), *whirlwinds and *storms (Is 28:2; 30:30; Jer 25:32; Ezek 38:22; Zech 9:14; Rev 16:21), shaking of the *heavens and the *earth (Is 2:10, 19; 13:13; 23:11; 24:18-20; Ezek 38:19; Hag 2:21-22; Joel 3:16; Rev 6:12-14; 16:17-20), *floods (Is 28:2; Jer 47:1-7) and the *darkening of the heavenly bodies, either by clouds or eclipses or by some unexplained phenomenon (Is 5:30; 13:10; 24:23; Ezek 32:7-8; Joel 2:15; 3:15; Amos 8:9; Zeph 1:15; Mk 13:24 par. Mt 24:29 and Lk 21:25; Acts 2:20; Rev 6:12). The poetic description of God's personal intervention on behalf of Israel in Psalm 18 is heavily indebted to this tradition of theophanic imagery.

The blowing of a *trumpet is often mentioned either as a signal of God's appearing or as a signal/alarm that God's work in judgment or salvation is about to begin (Is 27:13; Ezek 7:14; Hos 5:8; Zeph 1:16; Zech 9:14; Mt 24:31; 1 Cor 15:52; 1 Thess 4:16). The blowing of trumpets during the siege of Jericho (Josh 6:6-27) probably gives us an idea of the historical background for the trumpet image. It is probably also appropriate to read the description of God's appearing on Mt. Sinai (Ex 19:16-20) in light of its associations with the images employed to describe the Day of the Lord.

Since God's actions are irresistible, there is no escape for those against whom he acts. Several passages describe a divine process of elimination in which God employs several methods against his enemies, and every one of them is eventually destroyed by one method or other. The combinations include *fear, *pit and *snare (Is 24:18; Jer 48:43-44); *lion, bear and *snake (Amos 5:19); and *sword, pestilence and *famine (Ezek 7:15). The significance of the triad of seven-fold judgments (seals, trumpets and bowls) in Revelation 6—12 and 16 may be at least partly the inescapability of God's judgment.

The inescapability of God's actions may also be indicated by describing their overwhelming power and scope. Isaiah 2:12-21 pictures a destruction so universal that people will hide in caves. Revelation 6:14-16 adds the scene of people vainly calling the mountains to cover them in order to escape from God's wrath. Other passages describe an enemy attack so swift and so far-reaching that the victims have no time or place for flight (Is 10:3-4; 20:6; Jer 25:35; 46:6; 50:24; Amos 2:14-16; Mk 13:14-20 [Mt 24:15-22, Lk 21:20-24 par.]). Several NT authors compare the coming of the Day of the Lord to the coming of a thief in the night, indicating that God's actions will be inescapable because they will catch the unprepared by surprise (Mt 24:43-44 [Lk 12:39-40 par.]; 1 Thess 5:2; 2 Pet 3:10; Rev 16:14-15). Similarly, other parables compare the return of Jesus to a master returning to his home unexpectedly after a long journey (Mt 24:45-51 par. Lk 12:42-46).

Invariably the Day of the Lord is associated with acts of violent *judgment. It is not surprising, then, to find the biblical authors using images of great slaughter and desolation to describe the aftermath of God's action. Among the images commonly employed are those of large numbers of bodies falling on the battlefield or in the streets (Is 34:2-3; Jer 25:33; 49:26; 51:3-4; Lam 2:21; Ezek 24:21; 30:7; 39:11-16; Amos 8:3), large quantities of *blood being shed (Is 34:5-7; Jer 46:10; Ezek 32:6; Zeph 1:17), the pouring out of human blood as a winepress squeezes juice out of pressed grapes (Is 63:1-3; Lam 1:15; Joel 3:13; Rev 14:19; 19:15), the feeding of carrion *animals on masses of corpses (Ezek 32:6; 39:4; Rev 19:17-18, 21) and the desolation of buildings and lands or their occupation by wild animals (Is 23:1; 24:3-12; 34:8-17; Jer 18:16; 46:19; 50:26; Ezek 30:7; Joel 2:3; Rev 18:2).

Biblical authors also attempt to impress on their audiences the emotional impact of the Day of the Lord by describing the reactions of those who experience God's activity. For those who suffer under God's judgment, the reaction is usually described in terms of traditional ancient Near Eastern mourning practices, such as wearing sackcloth, sitting on the ground, wailing loudly and throwing dust or ashes on oneself (Is 3:18-24; 22:12; 24:7-9; Jer 25:34; 47:2; Lam 1:2; 2:10-11; Ezek 7:18; Amos 8:10; Zeph 1:8-9; Mt 8:12; 22:13; Rev 18:9-18).

Finally, the Day of the Lord will be a day in which the oppressed people of God will experience deliverance. This is often described in terms roughly opposite to those describing God's judgment, including victory in battle (Obad 17-18; Zech 9:15; Mal 4:4; 2 Thess 2:8; Rev 19:19-21); reoccupation of territory (Is 35:8-10; Obad 19-21; Zeph 3:18-20; Zech 14:10-11; Rev 21:22-27); replenishment of waterways, fields, crops and domestic animals (Is 25:6; 29:17; Hos 2:21-22; Joel 2:18-24; 3:18; Zech 9:17; 14:8; Rev 22:1-2); rebuilding of dwellings (Amos 9:14; Rev 21:2, 9-21) and rejoicing (Is 29:19; Zeph 3:14; Rev 21:4).

One of the most vexing problems for a student of the Bible is how to understand the varied images associated with the Day of the Lord. This puzzle-ment is at least partly due to the great flexibility and variety of uses to which the biblical authors put these images. For example, scholars still debate whether the description of a locust plague in the book of *Joel is figurative language for invasion by a human army or whether the battle imagery in the book is figurative language for the devastation caused by locusts. What are we to understand by the locusts from the bottomless pit in Revelation 9:1-11? The description of the battle of Aijalon in Joshua 10:1-15 seems to employ images associated with the Day of the Lord in a straightforward historical sense. Yet some of the same language is used in a highly figurative way in Psalm 18.

As the disproportionately fewer number of NT references in this article indicates, the NT writers tend to use less of the traditional imagery associated with the Day of the Lord and speak more straightforwardly about a coming universal judgment. Perhaps this is a clue that at least the images most frequently used by the prophets had become stock metaphors for God's action in judging and saving.

See also APOCALYPTIC VISIONS OF THE FUTURE; DIVINE WARRIOR; END TIMES; JUDGMENT.

BIBLIOGRAPHY. G. B. Caird, *The Language and Imagery of the Bible* (Grand Rapids: Eerdmans, 1997 [1980]); G. von Rad, "The Origin of the Concept of the Day of Yahweh," *JSS* 4 (1959) 97-108; D. Stuart, "The Sovereign's Day of Conquest," *BASOR* 221 (1976) 159-64.

DAY OF YAHWEH. *See* DAY, DAY OF THE LORD.

DEAF, DEAFNESS

Literal physical deafness is not mentioned often in the Scriptures. Most of the references to deafness are figurative. Deafness symbolizes spiritual stubbornness or willful refusal to hear and obey the word of God (Jer 5:21; Ezek 12:2) and is caused by *sin (Ps 38:13, 18). Israel is portrayed as a servant with *ears, but not hearing and obeying her Lord (Is 42:18-20; *see* Obedience). The prophetic role is pictured as calling the Israelites to hear the word of God because their sins have deafened their ears (Is 43:8). The Israelites in turn are pictured standing with their hands over their ears, refusing to hear the prophets even while judgment falls on them (Zech 7:11-14). They are deaf like the *idols they serve (Deut 4:28; Ps 115:4-8; Rev 9:20).

Sometimes spiritual deafness is pictured as being imposed by God (Deut 29:4; Is 6:9-10), which is a figurative way of saying that those who continually stop their ears to God's word are confirmed in that state. The restoration of Israel from exile is partly symbolized by the spiritually deaf hearing and obeying the word of God (Is 29:18; 35:5).

In the NT, deafness and other infirmities are at times attributed to demon possession (Mk 9:14-29) or judgments from God for sin (Jn 9:2; cf. Ex 4:11). As Jesus proclaimed the word of salvation, his healing of the deaf and people with other infirmities symbolized the defeat of sin and *disease (Mk 7:31-37), fulfilled prophecy (Is 35:5) and proof that he was the Messiah (Mt 11:5; Lk 7:22).

Deafness also symbolizes the refusal of the Jews to accept Jesus as their Messiah (Acts 28:26-27; cf. Is 6:9-10), especially the crowds who hear the parables of Jesus amidst their struggle for food and power or their misdirected messianic fervor, but without spiritual desire to know and obey God (Mt 13:14-16; Mk 4:10-12; Lk 8:10).

See also BLIND, BLINDNESS; EAR, HEARING; DISEASE AND HEALING; IDOLATRY; OBEDIENCE.

BIBLIOGRAPHY. C. D. C. Howard, "Blindness and Deafness," DJG 81-82.

DEATH

Death is the greatest of humankind's enemies, a relentless Grim Reaper that shows no respect for age or wealth. It robs parents of a precious child, leaving them to mourn their loss for the rest of their lives. It deprives wives and children of their breadwinner and protector, leaving them vulnerable in a hostile world. It takes away an aging spouse, leaving a gray-haired senior citizen without a lifelong companion and closest friend. Sometimes it arrives suddenly and unannounced; at other times it approaches slowly, as if stalking or taunting its helpless victim. Sometimes it hauls away its victims en masse; on other occasions it targets individuals. It uses a variety of methods and weapons, but only rarely does it capture its prey without inflicting pain and terror. Power, beauty and wealth can usually overcome any obstacle, but in death they meet their match. As the eighteenth-century poet Thomas Gray wrote, "The boast of heraldry, the pomp of pow'r, And all that beauty, all that wealth e'er gave, Awaits alike the inevitable hour; The paths of glory lead but to the grave" (Elegy Written in a Country Churchyard, stanza 9).

In the ancient Near Eastern world in which the Bible originated, death was called "the land of no return" and was viewed as an inescapable underworld *prison. The OT pictures the realm of death (or Sheol) as being under the earth, comparing its entrance to a deep *pit (Ps 88:4-6). Those who descend into this subterranean region are cut off from God's mighty deeds and from the worshipping community of faith (Ps 6:5; 30:9; 88:10-12; Is 38:18). With rare and only temporary exceptions (e.g., 1 Sam 28:12-15), a trip to the underworld is a one-way journey (2 Sam 12:23).

The Canaanite myths picture death as a god who greedily and continually demands human flesh to devour. One text depicts death as having "a lip to the earth, a lip to the heavens . . . and a tongue to the stars" (Gibson, 69). Death compares his appetite to that of *lions and then boasts, "If it is in very truth my desire to consume 'clay' [human flesh], then in truth by the handfuls I must eat it, whether my seven portions [a full, complete amount] are already in the bowl or whether Nahar [the river god who transports victims from the land of the living to the underworld]

has to mix the cup" (Gibson, 68-69).

The Bible does not deify death, but it does personify it as a *hungry (Is 5:14; Hab 2:5) and crafty enemy that uses snares to *trap victims (Ps 18:4-5) and sneaks through windows to grab children (Jer 9:21). Death is "the last *enemy" (1 Cor 15:28), whose fatal sting is sin (1 Cor 15:55-56; cf. Hos 13:14), an inescapable (Ps 89:48; Eccles 8:8), terrifying (Heb 2:15) and relentless (Song 8:6) foe with which no one can strike a lasting bargain (Is 28:15, 18).

Perhaps the most striking images of death are to be found in the concluding chapter of Ecclesiastes. Qoheleth, the main speaker of the book, has treated death as a major theme. Death renders everything in life meaningless. In Ecclesiastes 12:1-5 he likens the aging process to an encroaching storm. The deteriorating *body is represented by a house that, along with its inhabitants, slowly falls apart. Although this is debated, it is hard not to recognize some nearly allegorical connections between the inhabitants of the house and body parts. For instance, when the text says that the grinders cease because they are few, it is hard not to recognize an allusion to teeth. In verses 6 and 7 death is likened to the destruction of precious items. A silver cord is snapped; a golden *bowl is smashed.

Despite death's great power and hostility, it is ultimately subject to God's sovereignty. Ironically, death finds its origin in God, who decreed that death would be the ultimate penalty for disobedience to his revealed command (Gen 2:17; 3:19; see also Ps 90:3-11). When the first couple ate the forbidden fruit and rebelled against God, death accompanied sin into the world and has reigned over humankind ever since (Rom 5:12-21; 6:23; Jas 1:15). Nevertheless, death remains under God's authority. God can use it as an ally against the objects of his wrath (Ex 15:12 [where the "earth" is best understood as the underworld]; Hos 13:14 [best translated as an invitation to death to serve as God's instrument of judgment against his sinful people]) or God can deliver the objects of his favor from its powerful grasp before they descend into its depths (Ps 18:4-19; 116:3-8). In the story of Israel's covenantal relationship with God, death epitomizes the destructive consequences of a broken covenant (Deut 28:45, 48, 61) which can only be reversed by God's life-giving power (Ezek 37).

In the end God will eliminate death from his world, swallowing up the great swallower once and for all (Is 25:6-8). This conquest of death is not strictly a future event however. It began with Jesus, who conquered sin when he satisfied God's righteous requirements and died a sacrificial death for sinners (Rom 5:12-21). He then conquered death when he rose from the *grave on the third day (Rom 6:9-10), destroying in the process the power of *Satan, who uses the fear of death as a weapon against humankind (Heb 2:14-15). Jesus' resurrection guarantees the future resurrection of his people (1 Cor 15:12-28) and the fulfillment of Isaiah's vision (1 Cor 15:50-54). Death, the final enemy whose "reign" of futility and decay extends over the cosmos (Rom 8:20-21), will be destroyed. Never again will God's people experience death's sorrow and pain, for it will have no place in the new world order (Rev 21:4). With the hope of the resurrection to sustain him, the apostle Paul viewed death as a defeated foe (1 Cor 15:55-57; 2 Tim 1:10) that cannot separate God's people from his love (Rom 8:38-39) or his presence (Phil 1:21-23). Through saving faith in Jesus they have already passed from death to life (Jn 5:24-27).

Jesus' victory over death only benefits God's people (Rev 20:6). Those who have not been the objects of his saving work will someday rise from the grave, but only so they may stand before his holy *throne of judgment for final sentencing. They will then be thrown into the lake of fire, which the apostle John calls the "second death" (Rev 20:14; 21:8).

See also BURIAL, FUNERAL; CORRUPTION; COSMOLOGY; DECAY; GRAVE; JUDGMENT; MOURN, MOURNING; MURDER STORIES; PIT; RESURRECTION; SIN.

BIBLIOGRAPHY. L. R. Bailey, *Biblical Perspectives on Death* (Philadelphia: Fortress, 1979); M. C. de Boer, *The Defeat of Death: Apocalyptic Eschatology in 1 Corinthians 15 and Romans 5* (Sheffield: JSOT, 1988); O. Keel, *The Symbolism of the Biblical World* (New York: Seabury, 1978); L. I. J. Stadelmann, *The Hebrew Conception of the World* (Rome: Pontifical Biblical Institute, 1970) 165-76; N. J. Tromp, *Primitive Conceptions of Death and the Nether World in the Old Testament* (Rome: Pontifical Biblical Institute, 1969); H. W. Wolff, *Anthropology of the Old Testament* (Philadelphia: Fortress, 1974) 99-118.

DEATH AND REBIRTH. *See* REBIRTH.

DEBT, DEBTOR. *See* LEND, LENDING.

DECAY

The biblical image of decay is usually a dark one, carrying connotations of *death, *judgment, and the horror of gradually turning into nothing. Appearing by itself, the image carries little joy or hope. Only when it appears in stark contrast to images of life triumphant over death does decay no longer suggest an inevitable end.

At its most benign the image of decay conveys the notion of mortality. This is the import of God's words to *Adam, "Dust you are and to dust you will return" (Gen 3:19 NIV). Job acknowledges this as well in his question to God, "Remember that you molded me like clay. Will you now turn me to dust again?" (Job 10:9 NIV). In these instances the image of turning back into dust provides a vivid reminder of the fleeting and fragile nature of human life. The prophet Habakkuk also recognizes the fragility of life: at the very sight of God's wrath and power, the decay of his *trembling body begins within the very marrow of his *bones (Hab 3:16).

The most haunting portrait of human decay in the Bible is the detailed metaphoric account of the physiological symptoms of old age that comes near the end of the book of Ecclesiastes. Introduced to give urgency to the command to "remember your Creator in the days of your youth," the portrait comes to dominate the passage with its picture of failing sight, hearing and sprightliness in walking, as well as a loss of appetite, speech and ability to sleep (Eccles 12:1-5). After this depressing picture of physical decay, death itself is described as the final cessation (Eccles 12:6-7).

Although mortality is a universal human condition, the decay that comes with death carries a special connotation of judgment for those who defy God. The psalmist declares, "You, O God, will bring down the wicked into the pit of corruption" (Ps 55:23 NIV). Here the image is that of a grave in which the bodies of the wicked decay. Likewise the writer of Proverbs declares, "The memory of the righteous will be a blessing, but the name of the wicked will rot" (Prov 10:7 NIV). The power and essence of this image is annihilation. Death is only the beginning of God's judgment; the decay that follows ensures that every trace of the wicked will eventually come to nothing. As an image of judgment, decay renders a wicked life inconsequential; it becomes as though it had never existed.

Thus decay is an image that points toward nothingness. Speaking through the prophet Hosea, God condemns Judah for abandoning the Lord and turning to idolatry. With striking effect, God turns this same image upon himself: "I am . . . like rot to the people of Judah" (Hos 5:12 NIV). God employs an image of decay to present the most powerful illustration possible of how little regard Judah has for him.

It is the terrible prospect of coming to nothing that leads Job to lament that "man wastes away like something rotten" (Job 13:28 NIV). Death's permanence is inescapable, and Job knows it; nevertheless, he wishes out loud before God: "If only you would hide me in the grave and conceal me till your anger has passed . . . if a man dies, will he live again?" (Job 14:13, 14). Job leaves his own question unanswered, but in spite of the imminence of death and decay, he appears to entertain a fleeting hope that the answer will be yes.

It would seem that death and decay are inevitable: "No man can redeem the life of another . . . no payment is ever enough—that he should live on forever and not see decay" (Ps 49:7, 9 NIV). Nevertheless, Job's hope is not utterly vain. Taking refuge in the power of the Lord, the psalmist declares, "You will not abandon me to the grave, nor will you let your Holy One see decay" (Ps 16:10 NIV). In this passage decay is no longer the prominent theme because the image has been robbed of its finality; instead, the focus is on the power of the Lord to grant and sustain eternal life.

In the NT both Peter (Acts 2:29-33) and Paul (Acts 13:35-39) interpret this psalm messianically: the psalmist is speaking of Jesus, who did not decay upon his death but was instead resurrected by God.

Paul declares that "the one whom God raised from the dead did not see decay. Therefore . . . through Jesus the forgiveness of sins is proclaimed to you" (Acts 13:37, 38 NIV). Here the image of decay is that of a vanquished enemy; the element of judgment has been removed. Death and decay are no longer threats, since the power of God in Christ's resurrection has taken away their finality, which Job had found so dreadful. Decay returns to being simply an image of mortality—albeit a changed mortality, since it rests in the larger context of God's power to raise the dead through Christ.

See also CORRUPTION; DEATH; NEW; RESURRECTION.

DECEPTION, STORIES OF

Stories of deception, which are usually built around a character's disguise, incorporate several *plot motifs that make for good stories, including intrigue, dramatic irony, suspense, *reversal and discovery. Deception appears in the Bible in both *comic and *tragic modes.

The story of the *Fall (Gen 3) contains a latent deception motif. *Satan enters a serpent to conduct his temptation of *Eve, and his destructive intent is masked as benevolent concern for humankind. Fearful for *Abraham's life as they travel to foreign realms, Abraham and Sarah resolve to tell a half-lie about their relationship wherever it seems expedient (Gen 12:10-20; 20; cf. Gen 26:6-11). The most full-fledged deception story in Genesis is *Jacob's deception of his father by means of disguise when he steals the *birthright from his older brother *Esau (Gen 27). Tamar plays the role of a *prostitute to trick Judah into raising offspring for her (Gen 38), and Laban tricks Jacob with a substitute bride (Gen 29:21-25). When Jacob's daughter Dinah is raped by Shechem, her brothers trick the men of Shechem's tribe by getting them to be *circumcised and then killing them while they are suffering the results of their operation (Gen 34).

Later OT stories also sometimes hinge on deception and disguise. The Gibeonites dress as travelers from a distant land in order to gain a peace treaty with Israel (Josh 9). King Saul disguises himself when he consults the witch of Endor (1 Sam 28:8). Both Ahab (2 Chron 18:28-33) and Josiah (2 Chron 35:20-27) undertake futile disguises as they go into their final battles. *David's son Amnon pretends to be ill as an aid to his raping his sister Tamar (2 Sam 13:1-14). On the positive side, the crafty *lefthanded Ehud carries his homemade sword on the unexpected right side where it avoids detection, in effect providing Ehud with a disguise during his daring assassination of the Moabite king Eglon (Judg 3:15-30). Jael is equally adept at deception when she lulls Sisera into a false sense of security with acts of *hospitality (Judg 4—5).

But stories of deception can also be happy stories of divine deliverance. One thinks of Joseph's concealing his identity from his visiting brothers until the opportune time for disclosure (Gen 42—45), the Hebrew midwives' lying to *Pharaoh (Ex 1:15-21), Moses' family hiding him in a basket in the Nile and even getting paid for caring for him (Ex 2:1-10), Rahab's hiding of the *spies (Josh 2:1-14), Michal's arranging a household idol with goat's hair to aid David in his escape from Saul's executioners (1 Sam 19:11-17) and the wisemen's tricking Herod by returning home by a different route (Mt 2:12).

In the Bible, then, deception can be either good or bad. It can be God's means of deliverance and retribution on evil kings or nations. But it can with equal ease be the doomed stratagem used by an evil person in a bad cause.

See also CROOKED; ESAU; JACOB; PLOT MOTIFS; REVERSAL; SATAN.

DEEP

The imagery surrounding the word *deep* in the Bible falls into five distinct categories. The simplest use is "the literal, physical quality of being far below the surface of the ground." Thus mire can be deep (Ps 69:2), as can the root of a plant (Ps 80:9), water (Ps 69:2; Prov 20:5; Lk 5:4), a *pit (Prov 22:14; 23:27), a *hiding place (Jer 49:30) or a *well (Jn 4:11).

As is almost always the case with the imagination, metaphoric meanings are rooted in the physical properties of a thing. Based on the physical quality that something deep extends for a long distance and is hidden from view, the term becomes a metaphor to denote intensity—of *darkness (fifteen occurrences in NRSV, nine of them in the book of Job) and of *sleep (eight instances). If darkness and sleep can be deep, so can *guilt (Ezra 9:7), *evil in the human heart (Ps 36:1; 64:6) and secret plans (Is 29:15). Based on the archetypal associations of height with emotional well-being and lowness with distress or depression, the psalmist cries to God "out of the depths" (Ps 130:1), which in its original context also suggested a metaphoric sea of troubles. Again, if the quality of being deep denotes going far below the surface, it can readily become a metaphor for that which is profound, as distinct from shallow. Here we have references to "the deep things of God" (Job 11:7; Dan 2:22; 1 Cor 2:10) and the thoughts of God (Ps 92:5; Rom 11:33), as well as "sighs too deep for words" with which the Holy Spirit intercedes for believers (Rom 8:26).

The most numerous references are to "the deep" or its variants "the deeps" and "the depths." There are approximately forty of these references to the ocean or *sea. The Hebrews were not a seafaring people—the psalmist's statement in Psalm 104:25 that "yonder is the sea, great and wide" is laughably vague compared with the minutely detailed pictures of life on the land that have preceded it. The sea for the Hebrews was accordingly a fearsome and alien abode of *monsters and the site of *storms. One of the most salient features of the sea for the Hebrews was simply that it was deep (in contrast to our customary phrase about "the high seas"), with connotations of fearsome and uncontrollable power, as well as its being a mysterious realm where forces were hidden from human understanding. Some notable instances include the statement in the *creation account that "darkness covered the face of the deep" (Gen 1:2; cf. Prov 8:28), the Red Sea through which God led the Israelites and in which the Egyptians perished (Ex 15:5, 8; Ps 77:16; 106:9) and the sea into which Jonah was cast (Jon 2:3, 5)

Such references to the sea as "the deep" imply something about the *cosmology of the earliest biblical writers, though it is hard to disentangle cosmological from merely metaphoric statements. It seems clear, for example, that the ancient Hebrews viewed the ocean as being fed by fountains or springs (Gen 7:11; 8:2; Job 38:16; Prov 8:28). Also present in the Hebrew imagination is the picture of a three-tiered universe in which the earth is situated between the heaven above and "the deep" beneath (Gen 49:25; Deut 33:13; Ps 135:6). These same "deeps" are the abode of sea monsters and forces of chaos as in Psalm 74:13-14 (see Monster).

Beyond this subtext of ancient cosmology may lie overtones of other ancient myths, though this is speculative. One of the primary Hebrew words for deep, t'hôm (a flood of water), comes from the same root as Tiamat, the name of a Babylonian goddess who represents chaos. When the god Marduk sends a mighty wind down her mouth, she is destroyed, enabling Marduk to create the heavenly firmament from one half of her body, the earth from the other. Some commentators see traces of this myth in Genesis 1:1-10, which culminates in the separation of the dry land from the waters under the sky: "The earth was a formless void and darkness covered the face of the deep, while a wind from God swept over the face of the waters." (Gen 1:2 NRSV). Similarly, the OT imagery of God's conflict with the deep and its dragons may derive from Canaanite sources.

In addition to the depths of the sea, biblical writers refer to the depths of the earth. The image of "depths" is variously associated with Sheol, the *grave, the Pit, the abyss and the bottomless *pit, in each case having overtones of death (the cessation of life) and/or hell (a postmortem existence of punishment). Sometimes the depths of the earth are simply the grave (Ps 63:9; 86:13; Rom 10:7). Such references can, of course, become metaphoric for calamity, distress or depression (Ps 71:20; 88:6). Other references push the image from a neutral death to a hell-like place where demons reside and evildoers are punished (Prov 9:18; Lk 8:31). Sometimes, indeed, it is impossible to know whether a reference crosses the boundary from death to hell (e.g., Is 14:15). In a category by itself is the reference in Psalm 139:15 that the speaker's fetus was "intricately woven in the depths of the earth," an allusion to an ancient myth that all living things were produced from a cosmic womb at the center of the earth.

The appearance of "the deep" as a combined reference to sea and earth in apocalpytic visions deserves comment as a separate category. In the book of Revelation all of the dread figures of evil are pictured as arising from either the ocean or the earth (e.g., Rev 9:1-2; 13:1, 11), reminding us of the OT motif of the deep and its allies as God's enemies. The beasts and the antichrist who emerge from the deep in the end times (Dan 7:3; Rev 11:7) fight against those who hold fast to God's word. While God maintains control of the abyss in Revelation, he allows the beast and Satan to come forth from it, and their blasphemies deceive many (Rev 20:1-10; cf. 13:1-8). After the ultimate defeat of Satan and the beast, heaven and earth are recreated, but "there is no longer any sea" (Rev 21:1). At this point the only thing resembling the deep is the "lake of fire," a place of eternal torment for the beast and the damned.

From the beginning of Scripture to the end, references to "the deep" and "the depths" are images of terror with associations of danger, chaos, malevolent evil and death. "The deep" is a major negative archetype in the biblical imagination—a place or state of mind or soul that one would wish to avoid but that no one can completely avoid.

See also CHAOS; COSMOLOGY; DARKNESS; DEATH; MONSTER, MONSTERS; PIT; SEA.

BIBLIOGRAPHY. O. Keel, *The Symbolism of the Biblical World: Ancient Near Eastern Iconography and the Book of Psalms* (Warsaw, IN: Eisenbrauns, 1997 repr.).

DEFORMITY

The essential meaning of deformity is a lack of *wholeness, a flaw, a deviation from the norm. Deformity is unnatural and as such is a misfortune. Deformity is also viewed in the Bible in symbolic terms, shifting from a dominant OT image of unholiness to a NT pointer to the saving power of God in redemption.

Early in the biblical narrative God mandated that physically deformed or defective persons and animals be excluded from the most important acts of Jewish life. The physically imperfect were not allowed in the holy places as *priests or as *sacrifices. Leviticus 21 and 22 give a thorough catalog of the various imperfections that excluded a priest or a sacrificial animal from the presence of the Lord. In case the catalog of defects overlooked anything, it says that "no man who has *any* defect may come near" (Lev 21:18 NIV, emphasis added). Only the physically perfect could come, lest the sanctuary be desecrated (Lev 21:23).

With respect to people this prohibition of the flawed coming before God was most specifically for the priestly offices. However it is likely that this exclusion was extended beyond those offices into the greater society, for in the NT the lame and blind were brought to the temple gates and steps to beg from those permitted to enter (Acts 3:2). This intolerance for the physically flawed must be seen in terms of training in holiness in the history of redemption. Deformity in the OT is strongly associated with and treated similarly to ceremonial uncleanness (see Purity). This provided a powerful image that the requirements of God are moral perfection and *holiness of character.

In the OT, then, deformity serves as an image of the absence of holiness, accentuating by contrast the holiness of God. By thus divorcing deformity from any possible link to human responsibility for the flaw, the Bible suggests that holiness is not just a moral quality. The lame, the mentally disabled, the maimed and the *blind are self-evidently less than whole. God, who is holy (perfect), demands that those who come before him be holy too. To be less than whole is to be unholy.

When Jesus the Messiah came preaching and healing, he inaugurated a reversal in treatment of the flawed and deformed. We see this transition strikingly displayed in Matthew 21:12-15, where Jesus comes into the temple area, drives out all the merchants and their customers, and calls those buying and selling "robbers." Then immediately we read, "The blind and the lame came to him *at the temple,* and he healed them" (Mt 21:14, emphasis added). Here we see the morally imperfect shunned, but the physically flawed welcomed, a boldly revolutionary outlook. Jesus' miracles of healing give eloquent testimony to just what sort of Messiah he was. What mattered to God was no longer physical wholeness or perfection. Instead, wholeness and deformity were a matter of the heart, of spirit and of truth (Jn 4:19-24).

The healings Jesus performed were potent eschatological signs of the final day when all physical deformity will be eliminated (Is 35:5-6; 61:1-2; Zeph 3:19: "I will rescue the lame and gather those who have been scattered"). In the NT, however, until the day of cosmic healing and restoration arrives, there is acceptance of physical flaws. When Philip baptized the Ethiopian eunuch, a person who was shunned and unclean for his physical deformity in OT times was now welcomed and made a full brother. Paul prayed for his *thorn in the flesh to be removed, but it became clear to him that it was God's will for him to live with the difficulty.

The goal of life is wholeness. In a physically and spiritually fallen world, deformity is an inevitable part of life. The goal of redemption is to correct deformity—to present the church of Christ as "a radiant church, without stain or wrinkle or any other blemish, but holy and blameless" (Eph 5:27 NIV).

See also BLINDNESS; DEAF, DEAFNESS; DISEASE AND HEALING; HOLINESS; LEPER, LEPROSY; PURITY; WHOLE, WHOLENESS.

DEMONS

The word translated "demon" in the literature preceding and contemporary with Scripture is not always negative. An example of the neutral use remains in the Greek philosophers' label for Paul, "a proclaimer of strange divinities" (Gk *xenōn daimoniōn,* Acts 17:18), revealing a broader conception of demon in antiquity ("divine being" analogous to the "sons of God" in the OT) than that understood in today's English.

Demons as Fallen Angels. The origins of demons, like those of *Satan and the *angels, are obscured in the mythological language of texts that allude to a cosmic struggle before the *creation of the world. The titles used for them are equally vague: "first causes" (*archai,* Col 1:16), "rulers" *(archōn),* "authorities" *(exousiai),* "principalities" *(kyriotētes),* "things above, things on earth, things below" (Phil 2:10) and many others. These ancient spirits, fallen angels allied with Satan against God, remain the devil's henchmen and do his bidding just as obedient angels carry out God's orders. The cosmos (God's *ordered* world assailed by chaos) and its creatures, including humanity, serve as a battleground, disputed territory in the larger struggle between the mostly unseen forces of *light and *darkness.

The language and imagery of angels and demons exhibits many parallels. Angels come in "legions" (Mt 26:53) and so do demons (Mk 5:9). Angels have "rulers" or "princes" (Dan 12:1) as do demons (Eph 2:2). The "host of heaven" may be angels (Lk 2:13) or demonic idols of the zodiac (Acts 7:42). Angels or other heavenly beings were pictured with wings (Is 6:2), so were demons ("An [evil, idolatrous] spirit oppresses you with its wings," Hos 4:19). While the wings of demons oppress, those of the Almighty serve as an image of comfort (Ps 91:4) and healing (Mal 4:2). Angels bring messages by dreams (Mt 1:20; 2:12, 13, 19, 22; 27:19), so do evil spirits (Job 4:16; 27:20). Demons deceive through mimicry by exploiting these parallels. The devil appears as an angel of light (2 Cor 11:14). Demons promulgate seductive doctrines, too creative for the human mind (1 Tim 4:1) and fortify their deceptions with miracles (Rev 16:14, cf. Jn 10:21).

Nature as Demons in the Cosmic Struggle. The ancients in Palestine and neighboring countries found in the violence of nature tangible evidence of this cosmic battle. The *winds (Heb *rûhôt,* Gk *pneumata,* both meaning 'spirits') that brought yearly destruction and seasonal pestilence were caused by evil spirits (Thompson, 1:33). That God himself traveled in the company of *storms was further proof of their divine nature (Job 38:1; 40:6; Ezek 1:4; Zech 9:14). The *thunder accompanying nature's violence is the voice of God or his angel (Jn 12:28-29), and the *stars of heaven fight in God's earthly battles (Judg 5:20). The symbolism of Revelation reinforces the equation of angels and stars (Rev 1:20). The meteors, because of their association with seasonal *plagues and fevers, were understood from Greece to Mesopotamia as disease-bearing demons descending to earth (especially during the dog days of summer, see Homer, *Iliad* 22.30; Pliny, *Nat. Hist.* 2.107; cf. Rev. 8:10). Jesus also evokes this imagery, asserting that he has seen Satan "fall from heaven like lightning" (Lk 10:18).

The primordial waters, rebelliously surging and struggling to escape their divinely ordained boundaries (Job 38:8, 11), required the rebuke of the Lord (Ps 104:7; Heb *gāʿar* and Gk *epitimaō,* "to rebuke," are exorcistic terminology). The Gospels revisit this motif when Jesus "rebukes" the wind and the sea (Mt 8:26; Mk 4:39; Lk 8:24). The disciples' astonished response, paraphrased as "what sort of person commands the elemental spirits?" is consistent with their literary background. The OT pictures storms from the *sea as mythological monsters, enemies of the Lord to be slain by him (Job 9:13; 26:12-13; Ps 89:11; Is 51:9).

Demons as Disease. For the peoples of the Bible the prevailing understanding was that *diseases were the consequence of *sin (Jn 9:1; Acts 28:4; Rev 18:4). The cure could require turning the flesh over to Satan for destruction so that the spirit might be saved (1 Cor 5:5) or at least instructed (1 Tim 1:20). When the righteous suffered, they were being harassed by Satan or his angels (Lk 13:16; 2 Cor 12:7). By contrast the diseases of the wicked were inflicted by God's angels (1 Chron 21:16; 2 Chron 32:21; Acts 12:23). Many diseases were dealt with through exorcism, not only the familiar epilepsy but also fever (Lk 4:39), posture problems (Lk 13:16), *deafness (Lk 11:14), muteness (Mk 9:25) and *blindness (Mt 12:22). Outside of Scripture we find even more spirits of disease; demons of tetanus, hemiplegia, tuberculosis, headache, nightmares, crib death, spontaneous abortion, *homosexuality, livestock plagues, crop blight, sour milk and more.

Demons as Animals. Not only storms and illnesses were in league with the devil, but so too were particularly sinister elements of the *animal kingdom. These could be identified by their habits. Any creatures that could see at night (and so must be in league with darkness), hissed (giving off evil spirits), were poisonous (and hence allied with the anti-Creation forces) or inhabited desolate regions (where demons were known to cavort) were linked to the Prince of Darkness. Such a list includes many familiar "unclean" animals (see Animals of the Bible)—*snake (Ps 91:13), owl, raven (Zeph 2:14), bat, frog (Rev 16:13-14), jackal (Is 24:13), hyena, *lion (Ps 91:13), scorpion (Lk 10:19; Rev 9:2-11); also many mythological creatures such as basilisk, leviathan, tannin, behemoth, the Repha'im (goat-like spirits of the dead, Is 14:9; 2 Chron 11:15; Lev 17:7; Is 8:19); and the many awe-inspiring denizens of visions and mythology (see Mythical Animals of the Bible).

These animals lived in the desolate, uninhabited lands far from the cities as did the demons they represented. Demons, perhaps even in the form of animals, haunted the waterless wastelands (Is 34:11-15; Mt 12:43; Rev 18:2). Evil spirits drove the humans they plagued toward their own abode in the *wilderness (Lk 8:29). To confront the devil God's Spirit drives Jesus into the wilderness where he is "with the wild beasts" (Mk 1:12). Mark's audience, knowing the beasts of the wilderness as the Devil's allies, needed no help seeing the ominous connotations in this phrase. Ancient ruins were also haunted by their former inhabitants as ominous animals (Job 3:14; Ezek 26:20; Rev 18:2). Passersby such ruins

habitually warded off the spirits by waving the hand and whistling (Zeph 2:14; Jer 18:16; Lam 2:15; Job 27:23). Such locales where demons held sway were truly "Godforsaken."

Demons as Pagan Gods or Idols. When God established the nations, "he fixed the bounds of the peoples according to the number of the sons of God" (i.e., the divine beings, Deut 32:8 RSV), suggesting that each nation has a spirit assigned to it. The angel sent to explain Daniel's vision was opposed and detained three weeks by the prince of Persia (Dan 10:13) until Michael, the prince of Israel (Dan 12:1), came to help. These princes would seem to be the "divine beings" appointed over each nation. While Israel is ruled by God's angels, pagan nations are ruled by fallen angels that inspire and empower their *idolatry and serve as national gods. Thus the gods of the nations and their idols are demons (Rev 9:20).

Similar to viewing pagan gods as demons is viewing idols as demons. To the ancients, idols, images or even uncarved sticks and rocks were home to spirits (Jer 2:27; cf. Gen 28:18; Homer *Iliad* 22.126). They believed that a demon inspired (lived in) the idol, so they sometimes used the word *idol* in parallel or interchangeably with *demon* (Deut 32:16; Zech 13:2). "For all the gods of the people are idols, but the LORD made the heavens" (Ps 96:5). "They sacrificed their children to demons [Heb *šēdîm*, a word for demon borrowed from Akkadian], the blood of their children to the idols of Canaan" (Ps 106:37-38 RSV). "They sacrificed to demons who were not God, to gods whom they have not known," (Deut 32:17). (The LXX twice translates Heb *'elôhîm* "god[s]" with *patachra*, the Persian word for "idol," Is 8:21; 37:38). Paul asserts that meat offered to idols is really offered to the demons behind the idol (1 Cor 10:19-20). Idolatry was inspired by a spirit of harlotry (Hos 4:12, 19; 5:4).

Demons as Political, Emotional and Psychological Problems. Just as demons lay behind physical problems, evil spirits were also viewed as agents of emotional problems. Demons interfered in the international politics of Persia, Israel and Greece (Dan 10:13; 10:20; 12:1). Local political intrigue, such as the enmity between Abimelech and the rulers of Shechem, also indicated the work of an evil spirit from God (Judg 9:23). Behind the paranoid behavior of King Saul lurks "an evil spirit from the LORD" (1 Sam 16:14-23; 18:10; 19:9). The errant *oracle by the king's prophet is explained as the work of "a lying spirit" from among the host of heaven which stands before the Lord (1 Kings 22:22). Matthew's Gospel identifies jealousy with the description "evil eye," familiar to all Mediterranean peoples as a demonic designation (Mt 20:15, cf. 6:23). The terminology applied to these evils shows that behind them the ancients saw demons, the personified agents of evil in a fallen world.

See also ANGELS; COSMOLOGY; DISEASE AND HEALING; EVIL; MYTHICAL ANIMALS; PLAGUE; SATAN; SEA.

BIBLIOGRAPHY. R. C. Thompson, *The Devils and*

Evil Spirits of Babylonia (2 vols.; London: Luzac and Company, 1904).

DEN

The two dozen biblical references to dens evoke an image different from that of the *cave, which is usually a dwelling or hiding place for people. Dens are primarily lairs (homes) or hiding places of animals. They are chiefly linked in the Bible with lions (approximately a dozen references) but sometimes with undifferentiated *"animals" (Job 37:8), adders (Is 11:8) or jackals (Jer 51:37). The most famous of these animal dens is without doubt the *lions' den (probably a large cistern) into which Daniel was cast and in which his life was miraculously spared (Dan 6).

The status of the den as the abode of wild animals determines its meaning when it is associated with people. When Jesus says that the commercial interests in the temple precincts have made it "a den of robbers" (Mt 21:13; Mk 11:17; Lk 19:46 NRSV; cf. Jer 7:11), he intensifies his indictment of the sellers by implicitly portraying them as a pack of predatory animals as well as by reflecting the practice of *robbers to make their hideouts in mountains caves. When the usual association of a predatory animal's den with violence to people is neutralized, the image is part of God's redemptive or providential salvation of people, whether in history (Dan 6) or the coming millennium (Is 11:8). Reversing this pattern, God's judgment against evil nations is portrayed as transforming cities—the very epitome of human civilization—into the dens of wild animals (Is 32:14; Jer 51:37; cf. Nahum 2:11-12).

The den is thus chiefly portrayed in the Bible as a dwelling place of destruction, terror or assembled evil. It is associated with predatory animals, *night, *darkness and robbers, with overtones of fear, deception, impending doom and secrecy. Sometimes God uses such mass evil for purposes of his judgment against evil nations, but God is also capable of overriding the terrifying aspects of dens for his redemptive purposes.

See also CAVE; ROB, ROBBER.

DESCENT

The imagery of physical descent—of going down—is part of the directional imagery of the Bible that is often close to the surface as we read. But the human imagination has nearly always used directional imagery for symbolic meanings as well. In the Bible, as in classic Christian texts like Dante's *Divine Comedy* and Milton's *Paradise Lost,* much of the vertical imagery is predicated on the premise of a three-tiered universe consisting of *heaven, *earth and *hell. Descent from one of these levels to the next is always a possibility.

A leading cluster of biblical images is based on the general premise of the human imagination that up is good and down bad, that *high is desirable and *low undesirable, that to ascend is positive and to descend

negative. Such imagery underlies Jesus' parable of the wedding guest, accompanied by his advice, "When you are invited, go and sit in the lowest place, so that when your host comes he may say to you, 'Friend, go up higher' " (Lk 14:10 RSV).

Descent is sometimes associated with danger and deprivation, as when *Joseph and Jeremiah are lowered into a *pit as a place of imprisonment (Gen 37:24; Jer 38:1-13). Rescue consists of being drawn up out of a pit (Ps 40:2). *Jonah's ignominious attempt to flee from God and his prophetic mission is a successive descent—down into the depths of a ship and then down into the sea. His song from the watery depths (Jon 2) is built on images of descent, followed by ascent when he calls on God. Almost as ignominious as Jonah's descent is that of the willful Samson in Judges 14, where we read five times (Judg 14:1, 5, 7, 10, 19) that he or his father "went down" to Timnah to secure Samson's marriage to a pagan woman. Other figurative descents describe a change of fortune from blessing to deprivation, with more than two dozen references to people or nations being "brought low" or "laid low."

The ultimate human descent is the descent into Sheol, the *Pit, or the *grave, with fifty biblical references. Descent thus used refers to the thoroughly tangible picture of going down into a grave and returning to the dust (e.g., Job 7:9; Ps 22:29; Ezek 31:17). Yet the image of physical descent to the dust is never far removed from the image of descent to the underworld, however vaguely conceived. Thus following Ezekiel's prediction of the razing of Tyre, the metaphysical comes into view: "Then I will thrust you down with those who descend into the Pit, to the people of primeval ruins, with those who go down to the Pit. . . . I will bring you to a dreadful end, and you shall be no more" (Ezek 26:20-21 RSV).

Another category of images of descent in the Bible is more positive, based on the premise of a two-level universe in which God and his heavenly abode are above the earth. God's coming down to earth is thus an image of the intervention of a transcendent God into the flow of human activity on earth. Descent accompanies God's appearances to his people, whether directly or through the mediation of angels, as in *Jacob's dream (Gen 28:12; see also Dan 4:13, 23; Mt 28:2; Rev 10:1; 18:1; 20:1). In the anthropomorphic world of the OT, God's interest in what is happening on earth results in a succession of occasions when God "comes down"—to investigate rebellion (Gen 11:5; 18:21), to display his power (1 Kings 18:38; 2 Kings 1:10; 2 Chron 7:1), to *rescue his own (Ex 3:8; Ps 18:9; Is 64:1) and to execute judgment against those who deserve it (Mic 1:12).

God also descends to earth for purposes of revelation. He descends to Sinai in terrifying natural phenomena to give the Ten Commandments to Moses (Ex 19:18, 20). Here the image of descent combines the ideas of divine self-disclosure (theophany) and divine condescension. Both of these converge in the incarnation of Christ. In his discourse on himself as the bread of heaven, Jesus speaks of having come "down from heaven" seven times in just twenty-five verses. Here the imagery of descent is positive, part of a divine rescue mission to the human race that cannot save itself and that is dependent on the intrusion of the supernatural into the earthly sphere. In the eschaton God himself "will descend from heaven" and believers will rise with him (1 Thess 4:16-17), and in the ultimate climax of human history "Othe holy city, the new Jerusalem" will come "down out of heaven from God" (Rev 21:2 RSV).

The theme of ascent and descent is a favorite in John's christology. As the full realization of God's coming down into earthly affairs, Jesus relates his own person and ministry to OT images of descent, such as the stairway, or *ladder, in Jacob's dream (Gen 28:12 NIV; Jn 1:51) and the bread from heaven (Ex 16; Jn 6:31ff.). Such images attest to Jesus' identity as both revelatory agent and redeeming life-source. Yet Jesus was not only revealer and redeemer but victor as well. In his descent to the underworld (1 Pet 3:19; Eph 4:9-10), being made like sinful man in his death, he vanquishes sin and death (1 Cor 15:55). The descent of Christ is thus the definitive descent for both God and humanity.

Special note can also be made of the imagery of descent in connection with the appearance of the *Holy Spirit. At Jesus' baptism "the Holy Spirit descended upon him in bodily form like a dove" (Lk 3:22 NIV; cf. Jn 1:32-33). The image of descent is also found in the account of the coming of the Spirit on the day of *Pentecost, especially in the repeated emphasis on the pouring out of the Spirit (Acts 2:17, 18, 33). Descent is thus an image particularly associated with the empowering ministry of the Holy Spirit.

If the descent of a transcendent God can represent divine self-disclosure and spiritual empowering, in other contexts it is an image of divine judgment against sinful humanity. Thus God "came down to see the city and the tower, which the sons of men had built" at *Babel (Gen 11:5 RSV), later saying, "Come, let us go down, and there confuse their language" (Gen 11:7). Using the same word as is used in Exodus 19:20 to describe God's theophany on Sinai, Micah asserts that "disaster has come down from the LORD to the gate of Jerusalem" (Mic 1:12 NRSV). Even when God is not said to descend, the imagery of descent is associated with punishment on those who have done evil. In the NT, Jesus sees *Satan fall from heaven like lightning (Lk 10:18), echoing the vision of Isaiah 14:12-20, in which Lucifer's grand ambition of ascending into heaven results only in his falling to destruction and previewing Satan's being cast into a bottomless pit (Rev 20:1).

See also ASCENT; COSMOLOGY; DEEP; GRAVE; HELL; HIGH, HEIGHT, HIGH PLACE; LOW; PIT.

BIBLIOGRAPHY. G. C. Nicholson, *Death as Depar-* ture: *The Johannine Descent-Ascent Schema* (Chico, CA: Scholars Press, 1983); J. W. Pryor, "The Johannine Son of Man and the Descent-Ascent Motif," *JETS* 34 (1991) 341-51.

DESOLATION. *See* WASTELAND.

DESCENT (continued / DEUTERONOMY, BOOK OF)

DEUTERONOMY, BOOK OF

The image that dominates the book of Deuteronomy is the concluding scene of the death and burial of Israel's great leader *Moses on top of Mount Nebo (Deut 34). From that high vantage point on the eastern boundary of Canaan, Moses could see the Promised *Land, but he could not enter it. Moses' death outside the land of promise is a key metaphor for the inevitable limits of human life and the ultimate dependence of God's people on the judging and saving power of God. This climactic scene casts a long shadow over the rest of the book of Deuteronomy and shapes the form, structure and images of this fifth book of the OT.

Deuteronomy contains a large middle core of laws (Deut 12—28). But the rest of the book contains several other literary forms, including narratives (Deut 1—4), exhortations (Deut 6—11), liturgical material (Deut 29—31), a poetic song (Deut 32) and blessings (Deut 33). Deuteronomy describes itself as "this book of the torah" (often translated as "this book of the *law," e.g., Deut 29:21; 30:10; 31:26 NRSV). Deuteronomy's self-description as *torah* refers not so much to a legal code as to a program of catechesis, a process of education in faith from one generation to another based on a distillation of essential tradition and cast as the concluding words of Israel's leader, Moses. It is this catechetical image of an old teacher sharing his last and most important teaching with a new generation shortly before his death that defines the form of Deuteronomy. A dying Moses in effect replaces himself with a written book of instruction to guide and shape the lives of this and all new generations of God's people far beyond his lifetime (Deut 31:24-29).

The structure of Deuteronomy is defined by a series of five superscriptions or subtitles that mark the major divisions of Moses' address to this new generation:

1) "These are the words" (Deut 1:1)

2) "This is the law *[torah]*" (Deut 4:44)

3) "This is the commandment—the statutes and ordinances" (Deut 6:1)

4) "These are the words of the covenant" (Deut 29:1)

5) "This is the blessing" (Deut 33:1)

These five superscriptions join with the key chapter of Deuteronomy 5 and the account of Moses receiving the Ten Commandments to form a road map of the structure of the book. Deuteronomy 5 is a miniature version of the book as a whole. It begins with the overall theme: "Not with our ancestors did the LORD make this covenant, but with us, who are all of us here alive today" (Deut 5:3 NRSV). The reader is invited to join in a transformative journey that moves in four stages: (1) from the past story that anchors the community's identity ("I am the LORD your God, who brought you out of Egypt" [Deut 5:6]) to (2) the commandments and laws that shape and guide the present (Ten Commandments [Deut 5:7-21]) to (3) provisions for future covenant making that lead the community onward through adversity (Deut 5:22-31) to (4) God's ultimate assurance of blessing ("that you may live, and that it may go well with you" [Deut 5:32-33]). The movement of Deuteronomy 5 from past to present to future provides a map to the overall structure of the book of Deuteronomy, which moves through a similar series of stages: from the community-forming story of the past (Deut 1—4) to the community-shaping law for the present (Deut 6—28) to the community-sustaining provisions for a new covenant with future generations (Deut 29—32) to God's ultimate blessing of the community as it moves through death to life (Deut 33—34).

Apart from the Ten Commandments in Deuteronomy 5, one of the most significant texts is Deuteronomy 6:4-5: "Hear, O Israel: The LORD is our God, the LORD alone. You shall love the LORD your God with all your heart, and with all your soul, and with all your might" (NRSV). These words are a positive restatement of the first and most important commandment for Deuteronomy, "You shall have no other gods before me" (Deut 5:7 NRSV). Israel's love of God was to begin from the inner will and mind (*"heart") and flow out to animate the whole being or self ("soul") and thereby extend to every outward action of the *hands and *body ("might"). The command to love God was to be continually discussed, bound on the hand, fixed on the forehead and nailed to every doorpost. The love of God alone was to guide each person's every action, thought and movement (Deut 6:7-9). The varied laws that follow in the covenant of Horeb in Deuteronomy 6 to 28 flow out of this key imperative to "love the LORD your God."

Another notable image is the simultaneous affirmation of two *covenants that enrich and give nuance to Deuteronomy's theology. The *covenant of Horeb (Deut 6—18) emphasizes God's gracious election of Israel and the expected human responsibility for obedience to the laws and will of God. But this covenant of Horeb ends ultimately in *curse and *exile (Deut 28:45-68). Deuteronomy 29:1 presents a second covenant of Moab made "in addition to the covenant that [the LORD] made with them at Horeb." The Moab covenant emphasizes much more the judging and saving activity, not of humans but of God, in the face of the failure and limitations of human power and *obedience (Deut 29—32, cf. Deut 32:39). The two emphases—on human obedience (the Horeb covenant) and divine promise and power (the Moab covenant)—remain side by side in Deuteronomy, even as God's promise and blessing predominate and overcome the limitations of human failure and *rebellion (Deut 33—34).

Research in this century has shown a formal correspondence between the covenant forms of the book of Deuteronomy and ancient Near Eastern treaties. This discovery throws light on the basic imagery of the book of Deuteronomy. It is the treaty between a great king (God) and his servant people (Israel). Thus the book as a whole presents God in his relationship to his people with political overtones.

One text in Deuteronomy that stands out from all the others in terms of density of imagery and poetic power is the Song of Moses in Deuteronomy 32. The song is a catechetical capsule of God's history and relationship with Israel. God is portrayed in a wide array of metaphors: as the *Rock (Deut 32:4, 15, 18, 30, 31); as an *eagle caring for its young (Deut 32:11); as a *father disciplining and nurturing his children (Deut 32:6, 10, 13-14); as a *mother who gave birth to Israel (Deut 32:18); as a *divine warrior who fights against the arrogant and powerful and on behalf of the powerless (Deut 32:35-36, 40-42).

Images of nature also play a major role in the Song of Moses as they shift dramatically from soothing images of a gentle, nourishing *rain and soft *dew on the *grass (Deut 32:2) to violent images of chaotic and destructive forces unleashed by nature on a rebellious people of Israel. The *land "flowing with milk and honey" (Deut 31:20) turns into "a desert land . . . a howling *wilderness waste" (Deut 32:10). The divine eagle who gently cares for its young (Deut 32:11) becomes "the teeth of beasts" and "venom of things crawling in the dust" (Deut 32:24). God's gift of the sumptuous "fat of lambs and rams" (Deut 32:14) is turned by the people into fat sacrificed to other gods (Deut 32:37-38). A people "fat, bloated, and gorged" on the produce of the land (Deut 32:15) become people suffering "wasting hunger" and "burning consumption" (Deut 32:24). Canaan's "fine wine from the blood of grapes" (Deut 32:14) turns into "grapes of poison" and "the poison of serpents, the cruel venom of asps" (Deut 32:32-33). The cool and refreshing rain and dew that begin the poem (Deut 32:2) give way to the fiery *anger of God that "burns to the *depths of Sheol," that "devours the earth and its increase and sets on fire the foundations of the mountains" (Deut 32:22 NRSV). In each case the forces of nature turn into instruments of God's judgment against a sinful Israel.

But the Song of Moses makes one last, crucial turn in its use of nature imagery. In the end God will again turn and fight for Israel, defeating its *enemies and restoring God's people to its land. The heavens that were once witnesses against Israel (Deut 31:28) will sound the voice of praise for Israel, and God will "cleanse the land for his people" (Deut 32:43).

See also BLESSING, BLESSEDNESS; COVENANT; CURSE; EXILE; LAND FLOWING WITH MILK AND HONEY; LAW; MOSES.

DEW

Dew is moisture condensed from the warm air by the cold ground. It is important in Palestine and Syria for the prosperity of cultivated crops and natural vegetation. From April to October there is little rain, so dew is essential for the continued flourishing of vegetation. In some of the wilderness areas the heavy dews are the primary source of water for the natural vegetation, crops, vineyards and even for small animals. OT references to dew include the night and morning mists as well as the ground dew (Ex 16:13; Num 11:9; 2 Sam 17:12). To be exposed to the night air is to become covered in dew (Judg 6:37-40, Song 5:2; Dan 4:15).

At the literal level dew is part of God's creative work in nature. Along with *rain, ice, frost and the sea, the creation of dew points to the glory of the God's creative power (Job 38:28-30; Prov 3:20). It is linked with rain as something on which nature depends and whose existence in turn depends on the word of God (1 Kings 17:1).

The symbolic meanings of dew flow from its physical properties. Because dew is a source of the very water on which life depends, it symbolizes blessing, favor or prosperity. When Isaac blesses Jacob, he asks that God give him "the dew of heaven" along with "the *fatness of the earth" and "plenty of grain and wine" (Gen 27:28 RSV). In a promise of *blessing, God describes himself as "dew to Israel" (Hos 14:5). Dew is associated with the of provision of *manna in the wilderness (Ex 16:13-14; Num 11:9). The promise of blessing, whether to Esau (Gen 27:28), covenant Israel (Deut 33:13) or restored Israel at a point in the future (Zech 8:12), is pictured as dew from heaven, along with the earth's abundance of crops and new wine (Deut 33:28). In the eschaton the blessing and prosperity of restoration of the remnant of Jacob will be "like dew from the LORD" among the peoples (Mic 5:7). The favor of a king is like dew on the *grass in contrast to his rage, which is like the roar of a lion (Prov 19:12). By contrast, lack of dew was considered an evidence of curse, the reversal of blessing (2 Sam. 1:21; 1 Kings 17:1; Hag 1:10).

Because of the association of dew with *morning, the image of dew points to life, youthfulness and resurrection. Job laments that he thought he would live a long and full life, like dew lying on a branch all *night (Job 29:19). In Psalm 110:3 the poet puts dew alongside the imagery of *womb and morning as an image of how "youth will come to you" (RSV). In the day of salvation the dead in the dust of the ground will live as dew brings back life to the earth (Is 26:19).

The physical properties of dew also yield a kaleidoscope of individual symbols. The covering and refreshing quality of the dew on Mt. Hermon pictures the kindred unity of those who believe in God and join together in pilgrimage to the temple (Ps 133:3). Elsewhere the ability of dew to enclose every exposed surface is used to describe how an army will trap those it is pursuing (2 Sam 17:12). The fact that dew evaporates quickly in sunlight makes it a symbol of something that is *transient and ephemeral, simi-

lar to *chaff or smoke escaping through a window (Hos 6:4; 13:3; cf. Ex 16:13-14; Is 18:4).

Dew is a multifaceted image and symbol whose usage in the Bible is firmly rooted in the climatic conditions of a region where dew serves a vital function relatively foreign to the experiences of the Western world.

See also BLESSING; MORNING; RAIN; TRANSIENCE; WATER.

DISCERNMENT

Discernment is an act of *wisdom or detection marked by an insight into a person's character or by an event that comes through insight that goes beyond the facts given. In Scripture people can discern matters in an explicitly spiritual manner (1 Cor 2:14) or through their own cultivated powers (Job 34:4).

Discernment is always to be desired. Those without discernment are looked down upon (Deut 32:28), whereas the discerning are considered wise and knowledgeable (e.g., Prov 8:9; 14:6; 15:14; 16:21; 17:24). Discernment is often sought in political matters (Gen 41:33, 39; 2 Sam 14:17; 1 Kings 3:9) as well as in spiritual matters to guide us in holy living (Prov 28:7; Hos 14:9; 1 Cor 2:14; Phil 1:10). Even God uses discernment in examining our actions and state of *heart (Ps 139:3).

The thirst for *guidance or discernment is universal; the righteous and unrighteous alike have a perceived need for insight, but it is only truly available through God. Paganism uses magic and divination to gain insight (1 Sam 28); kings and rulers have their advisers (Gen 41:33); and moderns turn to friends, therapists and consultants. But God's children are advised to look to him (1 Kings 3:9; Ps 119:125). For example, God gives *Joseph, the wisest and most discerning man in Egypt in his time, the ability to discern the meanings of *dreams (Gen 41:1-40).

One of the clearest examples of discernment is Solomon. Rather than grabbing for riches or fame or power, *Solomon asks the Lord for a discerning heart (1 Kings 3). His request is granted, and he quickly becomes renowned throughout many countries for his great wisdom. As the epitome of a wise, discerning person, the bulk of the book of *Proverbs is assigned to him, dedicated to his son "for attaining wisdom and discipline; for understanding words of insight" (Prov 1:2 NIV). His voice echoes in the book of Ecclesiastes as the one who searches "to study and to explore by wisdom all that is done under heaven" (Eccles 1:13 NIV), looking for meaning to life. The conclusion is this: the whole duty of man is to "fear God and keep his commandments" (Eccles 12:13 NIV). In fact Solomon's wisdom was so great, he kept peace between Israel the surrounding nations, making him the only OT ruler whose reign was filled with peace and prosperity.

In contrast, Lot displayed a real lack of discernment a number of times. When he and Abram parted company to settle their flocks, Lot chose the fertile land near Sodom and Gomorrah, even though it was filled with wickedness (Gen 13). Later, when the three messengers of the Lord came to take Lot out of Sodom, he offered his daughters to the men of the town who want to rape the messengers (Gen 19:7-8); and he hesitated before leaving his home to flee (Gen 19:16). Because of these unwise actions, his wife was killed (Gen 19:26), he was forced to hide in a cave (Gen 19:30), and his daughters turned to sleeping with him in order to continue the family line (Gen 19:31-38). None of this would have occurred had he used discernment in leading his family.

See also ECCLESIASTES, BOOK OF; GUIDE, GUIDANCE; PROVERBS, BOOK OF; SOLOMON; WISDOM.

DISCIPLE, DISCIPLESHIP

Like the master-apprentice relationship, though in a religious context, the *teacher-disciple relation is a socially recognized quasi-contractual institution primarily for the purpose of learning. Although the term scarcely appears in the OT, the concept is implicit in the companies, or schools, of the *prophets. Examples include the apprenticeship from early childhood of Samuel to Eli and the service given to Elisha by Gehazi, who on occasion acted for him with delegated powers (1 Sam 2:11; 2 Kings 2:3; 2 Kings 4:29). Isaiah looked to certain assistants to take care of his writings and their transmission, and Jeremiah's secretary Baruch received a word from the Lord in the manner of his principal (Is 8:16; Jer 45). Earlier, Joshua succeeded Moses after serving a term of apprenticeship "since youth" (Num 11:28 NIV).

Discipleship in the New Testament. The Gospels refer to John the Baptist as having disciples, some of whom transferred to Jesus when he began his ministry (Jn 1:35ff). Discipleship becomes a prominent theme in the life and teaching of Jesus. In Acts, Luke routinely uses the term *mathētēs* for believers, but it is nowhere used in the Epistles, where words like brothers, church, believers and saints are preferred.

Although the *Twelve are named collectively and individually in the Gospels, the designation "disciple" was applied more widely. Luke mentions that the audience for the Sermon on the Plain was "a great crowd of his disciples" and large numbers of others (6:17). He gives 120 as the number of the believers in Jerusalem prior to *Pentecost (Acts 1:15), and in Luke 8:2 he also mentions the women within the company of traveling disciples.

To be a disciple was not merely to be a frequent listener to the teaching of Jesus, but to be "with him" as he moved about in itinerant ministry (Mk 3:14). An imperative invitation from Jesus to join his disciples seems to have been typical (e.g., the peremptory "follow me" to Levi [Mk 2:14]), but there are also instances of volunteering (Lk 9:57). John reports Jesus' assurance that he will not reject those who come to him (6:37). John, who has a distinctive emphasis on belief as the mark of the disciple, seems to allow that it was possible, at least temporarily, to

be a "secret" disciple (12:42; 19:38). Jesus called his disciples from a range of social and occupational backgrounds.

Commonly, the disciples would have been a highly visible group behind Jesus, not unlike *sheep following a shepherd. The disciples controlled access to the master and had responsibility for logistics (Mk 10:13; 6:37). They provided some of the money the group needed for themselves and to give to the poor (Lk 8:3). Submitted to Jesus' discipline, they aimed through obedience to resemble him, as indeed he invited them to do: "Everyone who is fully trained will be like his teacher," Jesus once said (Lk 6:40 NIV).

Jesus' mobility seems to have been greater than that of John the Baptist and the contemporary Jewish rabbis, and with the numerous healings and other miracles that he did; to follow Jesus was to follow more than a teacher of the law. When he sent the Twelve (called "apostles") and later seventy-two disciples in pairs to communities he had not yet visited, they were his representatives and endowed with his power to heal, exorcise *demons and bring signs of the *kingdom. After Jesus' ascension, "making disciples" in the power of the Holy Spirit among all the peoples of the earth was the "Great Commission" entrusted to the disciples (Mt 28:19-20).

Disciples play a functional part in many of the incidents narrated in the Gospels, and they provide the occasion for much of the teaching. Integral to the gospel plot is the betrayal by Judas, one of the Twelve. In the metaplot of salvation-history, the disciples are to the church and the kingdom of God what the patriarchs were to Israel (Mt 19:28). A common motif is the disciples' slowness to understand that Jesus would have to suffer and rise from death in order to complete the pattern of his *obedience to the Father.

The Meaning of Discipleship. The NT concept of discipleship begins with the literal pictures of the Twelve as presented in the Gospels. The main meanings of the image include following Christ, loyalty to Christ and his work on earth, self-denial, aptness both to learn from Christ and to teach what has been learned, authority as Christ's spokespersons, and power to perform signs and wonders. An important image of the disciple is given in John 9. A man *blind since birth is healed by Jesus (Jn 9:1-12), and the Pharisees investigate the miracle. The man who was healed becomes exasperated at the persistent questioning and asks, "Why do you want to hear it again? Do you want to become his disciples?" (Jn 9:27 NIV). The Pharisees become angry and describe themselves by declaring, "We are disciples of Moses!" (v. 28). Here a disciple is one who aligns with a particular teacher who acts as a spokesperson for God: "We know that God spoke to Moses"(v. 29).

From literal beginnings discipleship acquires metaphorical authority for all believers in Christ. The connotations of relatedness, trust and obligation endure through successive generations. The image is radical, for a changed life is fundamentally assumed; and it is dynamic, for progress and development are of the essence. According to the NT, whether or not one becomes a disciple of Jesus will be of huge importance for every individual at the judgment.

Although the call to discipleship is for "all peoples," relatively few respond because Jesus demands priority above all social bonds, including those of kin. Discipleship is expressed in an obedience that is righteous and loving, even of enemies, to the point of one's own death. It thus supplies a new paradigm for the old one of legal righteousness. The term is polysemic and generative, and it takes the serving disciple into the Way that crosses from here and now to the glory of the kingdom: "Whoever serves me must follow me; and where I am, my servant also will be" (Jn 12:26 NIV).

See also JESUS; TEACHER, TEACHING; TWELVE.

BIBLIOGRAPHY. J. D. G. Dunn, *Jesus' Call to Discipleship* (Cambridge, UK: Cambridge University Press, 1992); R. P. Meye, *Jesus and the Twelve: Discipleship and Revelation in Mark's Gospel* (Grand Rapids: Eerdmans, 1968); M. J. Wilkins, *Following the Master: Discipleship in the Steps of Jesus* (Grand Rapids: Zondervan, 1991).

DISEASE AND HEALING

The Bible writers present a largely prescientific view of illness and see external forces as playing a significant part in the causation of disease. Sometimes the agent of disease is explicitly said to be *evil in origin, though permitted by God. The *sufferings of Job are explained in this way (Job 2:1-8). Another example is the apostle Paul, who describes his "*thorn in the flesh" as "a messenger of Satan" (2 Cor 12:7 NIV). Although the Lord's response in this case is to encourage Paul in his *weakness to rely on God's power, such enemy activity is elsewhere opposed, and healing is seen as one of the means of demonstrating the arrival of the kingdom of God (e.g., Lk 13:10-16, cf. Lk 11:20).

Illness is one of the key enemies over which Jesus takes authority in the first few chapters of Mark's Gospel (e.g., Mk 1:32-34, 40-42; 2:1-12). Good health and healing are seen as marks of the blessing of God, and illness as an indication of his disfavor (Deut 7:15; 1 Sam 5:9; Ps 38:3; 41:1-4). God should therefore be consulted when someone becomes ill. King Asa, who sought help "only from the physicians" (2 Chron 16:12 NIV), is implicitly criticized for this. In several of the Psalms (e.g., Ps 32; 38; 41; 107) a number of symptoms are set out and then clearly related to the guilt of the suffering individual. God is actively involved in sending illness as a means of discipline or judgment (e.g., 2 Sam 12:15; Job 5:17-18; Ps 32:3-5; 38; Hab 3:3-5; Acts 12:21-23). This theme is picked up by Paul in his teaching on the Lord's Supper (1 Cor 11:27-32 NIV), where he says that the sin of eating and drinking "without recognizing the body of the Lord" leads to judgment and explains "why many among you are weak and sick."

Another example of this is the case of Miriam in Numbers 12. When she and Aaron speak out against their brother Moses, God's response is to afflict her with *leprosy. Then following Moses' intercession on her behalf, her punishment is commuted to a seven-day period of isolation outside the camp. The link between suffering illness and becoming an outcast is made explicit in Jeremiah 30:17. Related to this are the instructions for the recognition of infectious skin diseases set out in Leviticus 13. On making such a diagnosis the priest is to declare the sufferer "ceremonially unclean" (Lev 13:3) and place him in isolation. The terrible consequences of disobeying God are spelled out in Deuteronomy 28 and include a number of *curses associated with illness. On the other hand, God's promise to those of his people who obey his law is that "I will not bring on you any of the diseases I brought on the Egyptians, for I am the LORD who heals you" (Ex 15:26 NIV). The link between sin/forgiveness and illness/healing is further implied by the psalmist's description of the Lord as the one "who forgives all your sins and heals all your diseases" (Ps 103:3). This theme is reiterated by Isaiah: "No one living in Zion will say, 'I am ill'; and the sins of those who dwell there will be forgiven" (Is 33:24 NIV).

In the Gospels the link between sin and illness is suggested by the account of the healing of the paralytic in Mark 2:1-12 (par. Mt 9:1-8 and Lk 5:17-26). Rather than attend immediately to the physical problem of the man brought to him, Jesus begins by assuring him that his sins are forgiven. This link is made explicit by Jesus in John 5:14 and by James in his epistle: "Is any one of you sick? He should call the elders of the church to *pray over him and anoint him with oil in the name of the Lord. And the prayer offered in *faith will make the sick person well; the Lord will raise him up. If he has sinned he will be

A crippled man (probably from polio) sacrifices to Ishtar, a goddess of healing.

forgiven. Therefore confess your sins to each other and pray for each other so that you may be healed. The prayer of a righteous man is powerful and effective" (Jas 5:14-16 NIV). On the other hand, as John 9:2-3 shows, it is a mistake to assume that there is always a connection between disease and a specific sin in the life of the individual sufferer.

The book of Isaiah begins with an oracle that uses

the imagery of "*wounds and *bruises and open sores" (Is 1:6) to describe the effect of God's judgment on the nation of Israel. Other prophets use similar language. Jeremiah often uses pictures of disease and healing to describe the destruction and subsequent *restoration of Jerusalem (e.g., Jer 10:19; 14:17; 15:18; 30:12-17; 33:1-9; see also Mic 1:9). False prophets who proclaim an optimistic future are said to "dress the wound of my people as though it were not serious" (Jer 6:14 NIV; see also Lam 2:13-14). The prophet Nahum uses similar terms to describe the fate of the Assyrian capital, Nineveh (Nahum 3:18-19). Along the same lines the prophet Hosea uses pictures of sickness and sores to illustrate the effects of invading forces on the territories of Ephraim and Judah (Hos 5:8-15). Here again restoration is seen in terms of healing: "Come, let us return to the LORD. He has torn us to pieces but he will heal us; he has injured us but he will bind up our wounds" (Hos 6:1 NIV).

Miracles of healing are seen particularly in the ministry of *Jesus. Even when the apostle Peter himself seems to be the agent of healing, he makes it very clear to Aeneas that "Jesus Christ heals you" (Acts 9:34). Matthew makes a point of stressing that Jesus healed "every disease and sickness among the people. News about him spread all over Syria, and people brought to him all who were ill with various diseases, those suffering severe pain, the demon-possessed, those having seizures, and the paralyzed, and he healed them" (Mt 4:23-24 NIV). This stress on Jesus healing "every" disease comes again in Matthew 9:35 and is part of the commission given to the twelve (Mt 10:1). The Gospels record Jesus quoting what must have been two well-known proverbs in connection with medicine: "Physician, heal yourself!" (Lk 4:23) and "It is not the healthy who need a doctor, but the sick" (Mt 9:12 and parallels). Isaiah's prophecy claims that the wounds of the *Suffering Servant result in healing for his people (Is 53:5). Peter picks this up in his first epistle: "He himself bore our sins in his body on the tree, so that we might die to sins and live for righteousness; by his wounds you have been healed" (1 Pet 2:24 NIV). Although many have taken this to mean physical healing, the context suggests that the spiritual healing of a restored relationship with God is what Peter has in mind here.

In describing the healing miracles of Jesus, Luke, a doctor, emphasized the power of God (e.g., "the power of the Lord was present for him to heal the sick" [Lk 5:17] and "the people all tried to touch him, because power was coming from him and healing them all" [Lk 6:19]). Similarly in Acts Peter describes "how God anointed Jesus of Nazareth with the Holy Spirit and power, and how he went around doing good and healing all who were under the power of the devil, because God was with him" (Acts 10:38 NIV). For Luke also the healings Jesus brings about are enacted parables of what it means to be under the rule of the kingdom of God (Lk 10:9).

The healing properties of the balm of Gilead (Gen 37:25; Jer 43:11) were well known. In Jeremiah its unavailability symbolizes the dire situation facing the nation of Israel: "Why then is there no healing for the wound of my people?" (Jer 8:11; cf. Jer 51:8 NIV). Ezekiel's vision of the new temple includes the picture of a mighty river along whose banks grow fruit trees. "Their leaves will not wither, nor will their fruit fail. Every month they will bear, because the water from the sanctuary flows to them. The fruit will serve for food and their leaves for healing" (Ezek 47:12 NIV). This imagery is picked up in Revelation where "on each side of the river stood the tree of life, bearing twelve crops of fruit, yielding its fruit every month. And the *leaves of the tree are for the healing of the nations" (Rev 22:2 NIV). The healing effects of the sun are underlined by the promise of Malachi's prophecy: "But for you who revere my name, the sun of righteousness will rise with healing in its wings" (Mal 4:2 NIV).

The Pastoral Epistles apply the concept of health and wholeness to the teaching that takes place within the Christian community. False teaching within the body of Christ has the effects of gangrene, something which both spreads easily and is immensely destructive. Against this, Paul wants church members to be "sound in the faith" (Tit 1:13; 2:2), which will happen as they are taught and encouraged to hold onto "sound doctrine" (1 Tim 1:10; 6:3; 2 Tim 1:13; 4:3; Tit 1:9; 2:2, 8).

See also AFFLICTION; BRUISE, BRUISING; DEFORMITY; DEMONS; EVIL; JESUS; KINGDOM OF GOD; SUFFERING; WEAK, WEAKNESS; WOUND.

DISGUISE. *See* DECEPTION, STORIES OF.

DISOBEDIENCE. *See* CIVIL DISOVEDIENCE; LAW, REBEL, REBELLION; SIN.

DIVIDING WALL. *See* EPHESIANS, LETTER TO THE; WALL.

DIVINATION. *See* MAGIC; ORACLE.

DIVINE COUNCIL. *See* ASSEMBLY, DIVINE.

DIVINE COURT. *See* ASSEMBLY, DIVINE.

DIVINE SHEPHERD. *See* SHEEP, SHEPHERD.

DIVINE WARRIOR

As the Israelites celebrated their deliverance from the Egyptian army on the far side of the sea, they envisioned God as a great warrior who fought on their behalf: "The LORD is a warrior; the LORD is his name" (Ex 15:3 NIV). At the other end of the canon, the church expectantly awaits the return of Jesus also in martial imagery: "Out of his mouth comes a sharp sword with which to strike down the nations" (Rev 19:15 NIV). Indeed, throughout the Bible God appears as a powerful soldier who asserts his power against the evil of the world.

Israel and the entire ancient Near East knew almost constant *warfare. Armies were always on the move, either in the interest of expanding imperial territories or defending against foreign encroachment. A warrior was a powerful person, either dangerous or comforting depending on whether he was attacking or defending. The biblical writers recognized God's sovereignty over their history, and as they witnessed victory or defeat in warfare, they envisioned God's presence in martial categories.

God as Israel's Commander-in-Chief. God promised to protect Israel against their *enemies as long as Israel remained loyal to him (Deut 28:7). When the need arose he revealed himself in the guise of a warrior. One of the most dramatic appearances of the divine warrior took place on the eve of the battle of Jericho. Near the city, Joshua encountered a figure with a drawn *sword (Josh 5:13-15). Upon inquiry, the soldier identified himself as "commander of the army of the LORD." Joshua's response, similar to Moses' response to the *burning bush, leaves no doubt that the soldier is none other than God himself. God gives instructions to Joshua concerning the siege of Jericho (6:2-5), prefaced by the statement "I have given Jericho into your hands" (v. 2). The strategy results in the destruction of the imposing walls of the city without the army touching them, clearly demonstrating the divine origin of this victory.

Throughout the OT, God repeatedly fought against Israel's flesh-and-blood enemies. Sometimes he used no apparent means to accomplish the victory, as in the case of Jericho; at other times he used nature itself (Josh 10:9-15). Still another method included the armies of Israel (2 Sam 5:22-25).

Throughout the OT, Yahweh is invoked by his epithet $S^e\underline{b}\bar{a}'\hat{o}t$. This epithet, though debated, is most naturally translated "armies," or more traditionally, "hosts." We are not surprised to find its occurrence in passages associated with the divine warrior theme. For instance, when *David confronts Goliath in battle, he exclaims, "I come against you in the name of the LORD Almighty, the God of the armies of Israel" (1 Sam 17:45 NIV). The Lord's armies are both human and angelic.

The primary symbol of God's presence with the army was the *ark of the covenant. Normally located in the most holy place of the sanctuary, the ark was removed in order to accompany the army during times of war. The account of the defeat of Jericho focuses on the ark of the covenant. The parade that circles the city walls centers on the ark, which symbolizes God's presence and power, the ultimate cause of the collapse of the city. The ark also led the Israelites as they marched in the *wilderness toward the Promised Land. The battle call that began each day of march indicates quite clearly that the procession of Israel toward Canaan was the march of an army:

Rise up, O LORD!
May your enemies be scattered;
may your foes flee before you.
(Num 10:35 NIV)

The story of the defeat of the Israelite army at the hands of the Philistines, with the consequent capture of the ark demonstrates that the ark is not a magical talisman but a powerful symbol of God's power that cannot be manipulated apart from the will of God (1

A mesopotamian warrior god shoots his lightning arrow.

Sam 4:1-11). The following episode makes it clear that God is able to win the battle if he so chooses: the Philistines cart the ark back to their home country and God responds by afflicting the Israelites with disease and trouble (1 Sam 5:1—7:1).

The Divine Warrior For and Against Israel. When God appears as the divine warrior in the OT, he most often comes to save his people from their enemies. This happens from the time of the crossing of the Red Sea until late in the history of Israel.

The divine warrior theme is closely connected to the idea of *covenant in the OT. God reveals himself as *king through covenant-treaty and then promises to protect his subject people from danger threatened by their enemies. We can see this in the blessings that flow if the law of the covenant is obeyed. In Deuteronomy 28:7 God the king promises that if Israel obeys him, "The LORD will grant that the enemies who rise up against you will be defeated before you. They will come at you from one direction but flee from you in seven" (NIV). He does this many times in the history of Israel, appearing in a variety of forms and using different means to win the battle.

God often uses forces of nature, his own creation, as his weapons. At the crossing of the Red Sea when Israel is saved and Egypt judged, God uses the *winds to push back the waters of the Sea to allow Israel safe access to the other side and then collapses the waters to kill the Egyptians (Ex 14 and 15). Later when Joshua fights against a coalition of southern Canaanite kings, God uses large *hailstones to kill the enemy and causes the *sun to stop in the sky so there would be more daylight in which to finish the battle (Josh 10:1-15).

On other occasions God uses his heavenly army to fight Israel's enemies. Perhaps there is a hint of this during David's wars with the Philistines when God instructs David to wait until he hears the sound of marching in the balsam trees before he attacks. The sound of marching indicates that "the LORD has gone in front of you" (2 Sam 5:22-25 NIV). A vivid picture of God's heavenly army is presented in 2 Kings 6:6-23, when the Arameans move against the city of Dothan where the prophet Elisha and his followers are located. The defenseless city and its inhabitants are easy prey to the foreign army, and one of Elisha's servants trembles with fear. To calm him, Elisha prays that God would show him the reality of the situation. In response the servant sees the Aramean army surrounded by the "horses and chariots of fire" (2 Kings 6:17) of the divine army.

But perhaps most frequently, God uses his people to win the battle, though the people he has chosen are hardly experienced soldiers or large armies. The two most notable instances of this are Gideon and David. God chooses Gideon to rid the land of the foreign intruder (Judges 6–8). As he sets out to gather his army, God warns Gideon that he has too many soldiers in his army. He then instructs his human war leader to pare the army down from an original thirty-two thousand to a small force of three hundred, which he then uses to defeat Midian's superior force.

On an individual level we observe the same principle at work in the hand-to-hand combat of David and Goliath. Goliath is a mercenary, an experienced soldier fully armed with formidable weapons. David, on the other hand, is visiting from tending his father's flock, without armor and armed with a simple slingshot (1 Sam 17). In this story we observe not only the principle that large numbers are unnecessary in the battles of the divine warrior, but also that superior weaponry is unneeded. David expresses his trust in the ability of God the divine warrior to win the battle in his challenge to Goliath:

You come against me with sword and spear and javelin, but I come against you in the name of the LORD Almighty, the God of the armies of Israel, whom you have defied. This day the LORD will hand you over to me, and I'll strike you down and cut off your head. Today I will give the carcasses of the Philistine army to the birds of the air and the beasts of the earth, and the whole world will know that there is a God in Israel. All those gathered here will know that it is not by sword or spear that the LORD saves; for the battle is the LORD's, and he will give all of you into our hands. (1 Sam 17:45-47 NIV)

The significance of the divine warrior motif in these stories is that God is the one who wins victories for Israel. They defeat the enemy, not because of their own strength or superior intelligence but because God has fought for them. As God himself expressed to Gideon, "You have too many men for me to deliver Midian into their hands." Why are there too many men? The Lord feared that Israel "may boast against me that her own strength has delivered her" (Judg 7:2 NIV).

Since it is God who delivers as divine warrior, the only proper response to victory is a *psalm of praise.

For instance, Psalm 98 was sung immediately following victory. Other striking examples of songs sung after victory may be found in Exodus 15, Judges 5 and Psalm 24.

But God also fights against Israel. The divine warrior theme plays an important role in Israel's defeats as well as its victories. In his covenant with Israel, God not only promises his military help when his people trust and obey him but also indicates that he will abandon them and even fight against them if they are rebellious. As the blessing of divine military victory flows from obedience to the law, so defeat will follow disobedience:

The LORD will cause you to be defeated before your enemies. You will come at them from one direction but flee from them in seven, and you will become a thing of horror to all the kingdoms on earth. Your carcasses will be food for all the birds of the air and the beasts of the earth, and there will be no one to frighten them away. (Deut 28:25-26 NIV)

Immediately following the great victory over the powerful city of Jericho, Israel under Joshua experiences a devastating defeat from the tiny city of Ai, whose name means "ruin" (Josh 7). The defeat is attributable to the disobedience of one member of the covenant community, Achan, with the result that God does not appear as divine warrior on their behalf. Israel "violated the covenant" (Josh 7:11), so God "would not be with [them] anymore" (Josh 7:12).

Most striking, though, is the destruction of *Jerusalem at the time of the Babylonian attack that led to the *exile. The book of Lamentations records the lament that follows the devastation of that city and its *temple. The faithful demonstrate the proper perspective on the matter. It was not the Babylonians who caused the horrible destruction, but rather:

The LORD is like an enemy;
  he has swallowed up Israel.
He has swallowed up all her palaces
  and destroyed her strongholds.
He has multiplied mourning and lamentation
  for the Daughter of Judah. (Lam 2:5 NIV)

Throughout Lamentations, God is pictured as a warrior who fights against and not for his chosen people.

The Divine Warrior As Future Deliverer of Israel. Though to many the exile seemed like the end to Israel's relationship to God, in reality it was just a new beginning. In 539 B.C., through an edict from the Persian overlord Cyrus, a small remnant returned to the land and eventually rebuilt the temple. Nonetheless, Israel was just a shadow of its previous greatness and continued to live under foreign domination.

God gave the prophets of the time a vision of a changed future. It would be a future in which God's people would no longer be dragged underfoot. This vision was inaugurated by the divine warrior theme. God would appear and fight on behalf of his people in order to free them from their enemies. Examples may be found in the late exilic and postexilic prophets Daniel and Zechariah:

In my vision at night I looked, and there before me was one like a son of man, coming with the clouds of heaven. He approached the Ancient of Days and was led into his presence. He was given authority, glory and sovereign power; all peoples, nations and men of every language worshiped him. His dominion is an everlasting dominion that will not pass away, and his kingdom is one that will never be destroyed. (Dan 7:13-14 NIV)

A day of the LORD is coming when your plunder will be divided among you. . . . Then the LORD will go out and fight against those nations, as he fights in the day of battle . . . Then the LORD my God will come, and all the holy ones with him. (Zech 14:1, 3, 5 NIV)

It is on this note that the OT ends, looking forward to a reappearance of the divine warrior.

Jesus the Divine Warrior. Jesus' ministry opens in the Judean wilderness. John the Baptist announces his coming with words reminiscent of the late prophets of the OT:

But after me will come one who is more powerful than I, whose sandals I am not fit to carry. He will baptize you with the Holy Spirit and with fire. His winnowing fork is in his hand, and he will clear his threshing floor, gathering his wheat into the barn and burning up the chaff with unquenchable fire. (Mt 3:11-12)

Though not using specifically martial imagery, John's words anticipate a combative Messiah. Thus when Jesus begins his ministry by *healing, performing exorcisms and preaching the good news, John is confused to the point of even questioning Jesus' identity (Mt 11:1-19).

Jesus responds to John's questions, brought by John's disciples, by his actions of healing, exorcisms and preaching. As subsequent events and the book of Revelation demonstrate, Jesus intended thereby to show his continuity with the divine warrior theme, though the object of his warfare has shifted from the flesh-and-blood enemies of God's people to the spiritual powers that empower evil in the world.

Thus Paul could later look back on the death, *resurrection and *ascension of Jesus Christ in the light of divine warrior imagery. For instance, in Colossians 2:13-15 he culminates his argument with divine warrior language: "And having disarmed the powers and authorities, he made a public spectacle of them, triumphing over them by the cross" (Col 2:15 NIV). In Ephesians 4:8 he cites an OT divine warrior hymn (Ps 68) and so casts the ascension as a triumphal parade: "When he ascended on high, he led captives in his train and gave gifts to men. (NIV) Thus the divine warrior theme is pressed into service in the NT to describe Jesus' victory over Satan on the *cross.

Though Satan was defeated, the NT also understands that for a time he is still able to cause great distress. The period of time between the cross and Christ's return is the time between the battle that secured the ultimate victory and the final defeat and cessation of hostility. In the meantime the battle continues, and the church is called upon to wage war against God's enemies just as Israel was God's army in the OT. The difference is that the church's weapons are spiritual, not physical:

Finally, be strong in the Lord and in his mighty power. Put on the full armor of God so that you can take your stand against the devil's schemes. For our struggle is not against flesh and blood, but against the rulers, against the authorities, against the powers of this dark world and against the spiritual forces of evil in the heavenly realms. (Eph 6:10-12 NIV; cf. 6:10-20)

The Divine Warrior's Final Battle. Though Jesus defeated Satan on the cross, the NT informs us that the Jesus, the divine warrior, will appear again in the future to finalize the victory and to rid the cosmos of Satan and all evil. According to the *apocalyptic writings of the NT, the church is in the same situation as the Israelites at the end of the OT period: waiting for a decisive intervention of the divine warrior.

Jesus himself taught that he would return as a warrior. In the so-called Little Apocalypse of Mark 13, he warns of the future violent end to history when he will return on the "clouds." This reference to the vehicular cloud evokes memories of Yahweh as the one who rode clouds into battle on behalf of his people (Ps 68:4; Dan 7:13; Nahum 1:3).

However it is the book of *Revelation that is replete with references to the coming battles of Jesus the divine warrior. Revelation 19:11-17 is made up of a pastiche of passages from Deuteronomy, Psalms and Isaiah that describe Yahweh as the divine warrior. In this passage Jesus appears on a war horse with drawn sword. He is dressed "in a robe dipped in blood" (Rev 19:13). The armies of heaven march behind him. He then engages in victorious warfare against "the beast and the kings of the earth and their armies" (Rev. 19:19).

Thus from Genesis to Revelation we encounter the image of God as a warrior. The object of his warfare changes throughout redemptive history. In the OT, God fights against flesh and blood enemies. In the NT, Jesus directs the church in a battle against the spiritual forces of evil while it also anticipates the climactic war that takes place at the end of history.

See also ARMOR; ARROW, ARROW OF GOD; BATTLE STORIES; ENEMIES; WEAPONS, HUMAN AND DIVINE.

BIBLIOGRAPHY. V. Eller, *War and Peace from Genesis to Revelation* (Scottdale, PA: Herald Press, 1981); M. C. Lind, *Yahweh is a Warrior* (Scottdale, PA: Herald, 1980); T. Longman III and D. G. Reid, *God is a Warrior* (Grand Rapids: Zondervan, 1995); G. von Rad, *Holy War in Ancient Israel* (Grand Rapids: Eerdmans, 1991 [1958]).

DOGS

Although the phrase "a dog's life" epitomizes a life of ease devoid of anxiety in contemporary Western society, a "dog's life" in a biblical context shocks the reader with visions of squalor, dismal poverty and the life of a pariah at the bottom of the social scale.

Dogs are repeatedly depicted in terms of their disgusting and inadequate diet. Typically they devour what is left over after humans are finished eating, and

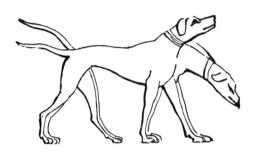

A pair of prized Egyptian hunting dogs.

that is usually described as mere crumbs (Mt 15:26, 27; Mk 7:27, 28). One certainly does not give them quality fare (Mt 7:6). Consequently dogs are never satisfied and are constantly on the lookout for nourishment. Since what they manage to scavenge is inadequate, they may consume what is repulsive (Prov 26:11; 2 Pet 2:22) or what is not fit for human consumption (Ex 22:31).

Of all the domesticated animals there is a particular revulsion for the dog, who alone is willing to eat humans corpses, a fact that is reprehensible to every human and exploited uniquely by the book of Kings as a *curse that comes upon wicked dynasts (1 Kings 14:11; 16:4; 21:23, 24; 2 Kings 9:10, 36). A threatened psalmist mingles all these elements when he describes his enemies as those "howling like dogs and prowling about the city. They roam about for food, and growl if they do not get their fill" (Ps 59:14-15 NRSV). The metaphor applies appropriately to Israel's greedy leaders: "They are dogs with mighty appetites; they never have enough" (Is 56:10 NIV).

It is not surprising that dogs are more than once juxtaposed with *swine in the Bible (Is 66:3; Mt 7:6; 2 Pet 2:22) for both are ritually unclean animals whose repulsive behavior even for animals strikes humans as foolish or even bizarre.

After making the point that human existence is "full of evil" (Eccles 9:3), Qoheleth, the main speaker in the book, does state that it is better to be alive than dead, though only barely: "even a live dog is better off than a dead lion!" (Eccles 9:4 NIV).

To identify oneself as a dog is therefore to draw attention to one's miserable condition as an inconsequential creature ("a dead dog" 1 Sam 24:14; 2 Sam 9:8 NRSV) or to the miserable treatment that one is receiving (1 Sam 17:43; 2 Sam 3:8; 2 Kings 8:13). To refer to another human as a dog is to insult the

other as among the lowest in the social scale (2 Sam 16:9). Jesus seems to intentionally echo Jewish sentiments toward Gentiles when he rebuffs the entreaty of the Syro-Phoenecian woman with the words, "it is not right to take the children's bread and toss it to their dogs" (Mk 7:27 NIV). But accepting the designation—and the priority of Jews and then Gentiles—she responds in faith, "Yes, Lord, . . . but even the dogs under the table eat the children's crumbs" (Mk 7:28 NIV). Paul, on the other hand, spares no imagery when he warns the Philippians against the Judaizers who are attempting to rob them of full membership in the people of God: "Watch out for the dogs!" (Phil 3:2).

See also ANIMALS.

DOMINEERING MOTHER, WIFE

Shrewish wives have been a staple of comic literature through the centuries. The Bible has its version of the same archetype in the form of *mothers and *wives who dominate either their *children or *husbands, though in the Bible it is cause for *tragedy rather than laughter.

The book of Genesis provides the earliest examples (as it does for most patterns of family relationships). The motif emerges in latent form when *Abraham, for the first time in the narrative, "hearkened to the voice of Sarai" (Gen 16:2 RSV) rather than God when Sarah proposed having a child by her maid. Sarah's domination in the situation proceeds when, in response to Hagar's taunting, Sarah not only "dealt harshly" with Hagar but also pressured her husband to the point that he responded, "Behold, your maid is in your power; do to her as you please" (Gen 16:6). A generation later Rebekah tries to outwit her decrepit husband and pushes her compliant son *Jacob into a plot to deceive his father in the celebrated case of the stolen blessing (Gen 27). Later still Potiphar's wife, skillful in perpetrating treachery against the virtuous young servant *Joseph, uses racial rhetoric to inflame her husband to imprison Joseph, contrary to anything he would have done if left to his own designs (Gen 39:6-20).

Later OT history provides further examples. Delilah, though never technically identified as a wife, plays the role of the domineering female by contriving to rob *Samson of his strength and deliver him into the power of her compatriots (Judg 16). Solomon provides the most extravagant example of all: his one thousand wives and concubines "turned away his heart after other gods" (1 Kings 11:4). The wicked Jezebel dominates her husband Ahab by inclining him toward pagan religious practices (1 Kings 16:29-33) and by grabbing the initiative in seizing Naboth's vineyard for her pouting husband (1 Kings 21). The narrator, in fact, describes Ahab as someone who "sold himself to do what was evil in the sight of the LORD" and as someone "whom Jezebel his wife incited" (1 Kings 21:25; cf. Rev 2:20-23, which apparently seizes upon Jezebel as an OT epitome of apostasy).

The shrewish wife makes an appearance in the book of Proverbs. "A wife's quarreling," claims one of the proverbs, "is a continual dripping of rain" (Prov 19:13 RSV). Again, "It is better to live in a corner of the housetop than in a house shared with a contentious woman" (Prov 21:9; 25:24 RSV). Finally, "A continual dripping on a rainy day and a contentious woman are alike; to restrain her is to restrain the wind or to grasp oil in his right hand" (Prov 27:15-16 RSV). While the picture of *Job's wife is not completely clear, there may be a touch of the shrew in her: she gives her husband some very bad advice in encouraging him to "curse God, and die," to which Job replies, "You speak as one of the foolish women would speak" (Job 2:9-10 RSV).

The only NT example of the archetype is Herodias. She hoodwinks her husband into granting her whatever she wishes when her daughter dances before him, an intrigue that eventuates in the beheading of John the Baptist (Mk 6:14-29).

See also MAN, IMAGES OF; MOTHER; TYRANNICAL HUSBAND, FATHER; WIFE; WOMAN, IMAGES OF.

DONKEY, ASS

We must take care not to read our own attitudes toward the donkey into the biblical materials. In Christian tradition the ass is a symbol of absurdity (cf. the motif of the ass musician) and obstinacy, as well as the mount of the demon of sloth; and the red donkey becomes a figure of Satan. But respected rabbis rode asses. Furthermore, Ugaritic sources depict deities on the backs of donkeys, Islamic tradition calls several heroes "donkey-riders" and the early Christian tale *Vita Sanctae Pelagiae Meretricis* presents as the apex of beauty and sensuality a woman riding on a donkey. Clearly attitudes have differed from place to place and time to time. Not all have consistently thought the donkey "perverse" (Plato) or "the meanest of animals" (Minucius Felix).

In the Bible the donkey is a beast of burden (Gen 42:26) and a plower of fields (Is 30:24). But its main function is as a vehicle for rich and poor alike (cf. the popular story of Balaam's ass in Numbers 22). Despite its widespread use by all, the donkey and the mule were also evidently a staple of ancient Near Eastern royal ceremony. In 1 Kings 1:33-44 *Solomon rides David's mule to Gihon to be anointed king (cf. 2 Sam 13:19; 19:26). Riding on a donkey for ceremonial entry into a city is already an act of kingship in the royal archives of Mari; and in the old Sumerian text "Gilgamesh and Agga," the sons of kings ride donkeys. It has been urged that because Genesis predicts kingly descendants for Abraham's offspring, the frequent reference to the donkeys of the patriarchs may be a royal motif.

The royal associations of the donkey are behind Zechariah 9:9, a prophecy of Jerusalem's king riding on an ass. Matthew 21:5 and John 12:15 cite this prophecy as having been fulfilled in Jesus' entry into Jerusalem. That Jesus rides not a war *horse but the donkey of Zechariah 9:9 makes him (like Moses, who also rode an ass [Ex 4:20]) "meek." His chosen beast does not show him to be a poor or common man but a *king, albeit one who does not conquer. Clearly he is innocent of the charge of rebelling against Caesar. A man on a donkey is not looking for war. One is reminded of the Eastern iconographic tradition in which Christ rides his donkey sidesaddle—the traditional posture of a woman, not a *warrior.

Zechariah 9:9 is not the only OT text about donkeys connected with Jesus' triumphal entry. Not only does the prophecy that the disciples will find a colt (Mk 11:2 and parallels) remind one of 1 Samuel 10:1-9 (Samuel's prophecy of the finding of lost asses), but the seemingly superfluous mention that this colt will be "tied" probably alludes to Genesis 49:11 ("binding his foal to the vine and his ass's colt to the choice vine" RSV). This line was given a messianic interpretation in Judaism (cf. Gen 49:10 LXX; rabbinic sources naturally associate Gen 49:11 and Zech 9:9).

See also ANIMALS; HORSE.

DOOR

Doors and doorways are places of transition. We move through them to the outside or into another room to greet new people; we close doors and find quiet and solitude. The door is an important symbol for the biblical writers. The doorway, *gate, portal or entryway is often associated with entrance into areas of great spiritual significance. The various courts in the *temple area were marked by walls and portals, and the Holy of Holies in the temple was sealed off for all but one day of the year (*see* Sacred Space). Then the high *priest, after appropriate ceremonies, would enter to represent the people before God.

The biblical writers use this almost primal association of doors and religious boundaries, but more often the imagery of door is connected quite closely to its literal work of *opening and closing (*see* Shut, Close) and of *hiding and revealing. The door is one of the most significant parts of a house, and at times biblical writers use it as a synecdoche for an entire house (*see* Home, House). In the well-ordered, God-fearing Hebrew home, doors were to bear words testifying to God's truth (Deut 6:9). This figurative language speaks of a house oriented around God's law.

The Closed Door Hides. The closed door literally keeps those outside from seeing and hearing what is going on inside (1 King 14:6). The closed door hides the activities of the *prostitute, but the open door where she sits seeking to entice men is mysteriously inviting (Prov 9:14). Job implies that to violate a shut door by *eavesdropping or loitering would be an action worthy of divine punishment. In his own defense he claims that he has not "lurked at my neighbor's door" (Job 31:9 NIV). Jesus uses this image, with a hyperbolic edge, when he calls for people not to pray like the hypocrites who make showy public prayers, "But when you pray, go into your room, close the door and pray to your Father, who is unseen. Then your Father, who sees what is done in secret, will reward you" (Mt 6:6 NIV). Privacy would be a scarce commodity in first-century Palestine. Many of the houses would only have had one interior door, and that was for a storage closet.

The Closed Door Excludes. Just as the drawn curtain and closed door of the temple excluded unauthorized persons from the sacred spaces, so doors in everyday life exclude one. After the brutal rape of Tamar by Amnon, he ordered her put out and the door bolted behind her (2 Sam 13:17, 18). The brutality of the rape is reprehensible, but for Tamar this act of exclusion is utterly devastating.

The image of the closed door that will not yield to knocking is used by Jesus. A time will come when those who have rejected him will be excluded from the festivities by a closed door that will not be opened (Mt 25:10; Lk 13:25; Rev. 3:7).

The Door as Spiritual Entryway. Jesus refers to himself as "the door" (Jn 10:9). In the context this certainly refers to being a door for the *sheep and hence the gate or entryway to salvation. When the risen Christ stands at the door and knocks—"Here I am! I stand at the door and knock. If anyone hears my voice and opens the door, I will come in and eat with him, and he with me" (Rev 3:20 NIV)—the door symbolizes the need for a decision and the potential exclusion of Christ.

The door imagery is also used to give a word of comfort to beleaguered Christians when Christ declares, "I know your deeds. See, I have placed before you an open door that no one can shut. I know that you have little strength, yet you have kept my word and have not denied my name" (Rev 3:8 NIV). Paul used the metaphor of God's opening the "door of faith" (Acts 14:27) as showing the exclusive way of faith as the portal through which people enter the *kingdom of God.

The Door as Opportunities for the Gospel. Paul uses door imagery three times to figuratively describe opportunities provided for the spread of the gospel. This imagery contains the idea that the open door makes possible that which a closed door would not. These references hearken back to Hosea 2:15, which speaks in salvific terms of a "door of hope" that the Lord will provide. Paul writes that "a great door for effective work has opened to me" (1 Cor 16:9 NIV). When he visited Troas, Paul found that "the Lord had opened a door for me"; later he prayed that "God may open a door for our message" (Col 4:3). In all of these references door speaks figuratively about an opportunity to spread the gospel.

Key Events at Doors. We can note, finally, some famous moments in the Bible in which the crucial event happens at a door. The list includes the monster *sin either couching (RSV) or crouching (NIV) or lurking (NRSV) at the door of *Cain's heart (Gen 4:7), the closed door of the *ark that signals safety for Noah and his family (Gen 6:16; 7:16), the door of Lot's house that foils the would-be rapists (Gen 19:10), the blood-signed doorposts of the Israelites on the evening of the

*Passover (Ex 12:22-23), the locked doors of Eglon's chamber that enable Ehud to make his getaway after the assassination (Judg 3:23-25), the "ancient doors" that are commanded to be lifted up so the King of glory may come in (Ps 24:7, 9) and the door of every individual's soul at which Jesus stands and knocks, ready to enter and sup (Rev 3:20).

See also GATE; OPEN, OPENING; SHUT, CLOSE.

DOVE

The dove is above all a *bird for *sacrifice, as was true already in the time of Abraham (Gen 15:9). According to Leviticus 1:14, if one's offering is a burnt offering of birds, then they will be turtledoves or young pigeons. The unpleasant ritual, which involves the priest wringing the neck, draining the blood and tearing off the wings, is recounted in Leviticus 1:15-17. Elsewhere we read that doves and pigeons are the offerings of the poor, those who cannot afford a sacrifice from a *flock (Lev 5:7; 14:21-22). But these are perhaps not the poorest of the poor, for there are those who cannot even afford to offer birds (Lev 5:11). In addition to being burnt offerings, pigeons and doves can be sin offerings (Lev 5:7-10; 12:6 [for purification after childbirth; cf. Lk 2:22-24]; 14:22, 30 [for the cleansing of leprosy]; 15:14 [for cleansing from a bodily emission]). When Jesus overturns the seats of those who sell pigeons in the *temple, he is disrupting the activities of suppliers of sacrifices for the temple (Mt 21:12 par.).

When the rains that have flooded the earth cease, Noah, after an unsuccessful experiment with a raven (black and unclean, cf. Deut 14:11-20), three times sends forth a dove (*yônâ*). The first time it returns to a waiting Noah (*Nōaḥ*) because it finds no "resting place" (*mānôaḥ*). So he puts forth his hand and, seemingly with affection, takes the bird into the ark. The second time it returns with a freshly plucked olive leaf—a sign of renewed fertility and so of dry ground—and consoles Noah. The third time the dove does not return, for it has found another place to nest. Although Noah's dove is seemingly nowhere mentioned or even alluded to in the Bible outside of Genesis 8, the image of a dove with an olive branch in its break has appropriately become a sign of peace: the storm is over.

The voice of the dove is mentioned in Isaiah 38:14: "I moan like a dove" (RSV; cf. Is 9:11, "we moan and moan like doves"; Ezek 7:16; Nahum 2:7). Because that voice can sound sad to us, human lamentation is likened to it (e.g., the "mourning dove").

The dove appears in a number of metaphors and similes. Ephraim "is like a dove, silly and without sense, calling to Egypt, going to Assyria" (Hos 7:11 RSV). This is an unusual comparison in that here no good quality is in view. But the same notion may lie behind Matthew 10:16, where the disciples are to be wise as *serpents (cf. Gen 3:1) and "innocent" as doves. Because doves are harmless and not particularly bright animals, this may mean that the disciples should emulate the dove's ignorance, at least when it comes to evil (cf. Rom 16:19).

In Hosea 11:11 Israel's speedy return from exile is likened to the swift flight of doves (cf. Is 60:8, implying the domestication of pigeons). Israel may also be implicitly likened to a dove in Psalm 68:13, but the meaning of the Hebrew is disputed. The thought of swift flight further appears in Psalm 55:6: "O that I had wings like a dove!" In Psalm 74:19 the righteous psalmist prays that "the soul of thy dove" not be delivered "to the wild beasts." Here the dove is a victim (cf. its sacrificial role).

The dove's ability to hide and nest in hidden, out-of-the-way places is the basis for comparisons in Song of Songs 2:14 (a plea for a lover to leave home); Jeremiah 48:28 (mocking advice to Moab to find a refuge from God's wrath); and Ezekiel 7:16 (of Jerusalemites fleeing judgment). Because of the dove's softness, beauty of feathers and eyes, and affection for and faithfulness to its mate, Song of Songs several times likens the lover to a dove (e.g., Song 1:15; 2:14; 4:1; 5:2, 12; 6:9).

Because of our tendency to think of the other world as above our heads, winged animals generally symbolize spiritual things throughout world mythology. So it is not surprising that the most striking appearance of dove imagery in the Bible belongs to the baptismal narratives, where the *Spirit of God *descends from heaven "like a dove" (Mt 3:16 par.). Whether the expression qualifies Spirit, so that we are to envisage the Spirit as having the form of a dove, or whether the words are adverbial and refer instead to the manner of the Spirit's descent is unclear. But one should probably think of Genesis 1:2, where the Spirit of God, water and the image of a bird recur (*merahepet* = 'move' or 'hover' is avian imagery, cf. Deut 32:11). The Talmud (*b. Hag.* 15a) likens the brooding of the Spirit over the waters at creation to the fluttering of a dove, and 4Q521, a Dead Sea Scroll fragment, gives Genesis 1:2 an eschatological reapplication: the Spirit will hover over the saints in the latter days. So the dove at the baptism seemingly means that Jesus brings a new creation.

See also BIRDS; EAGLE; HOLY SPIRIT.

DOWNPAYMENT, EARNEST. *See* LEGAL IMAGES.

DRAGON. See MONSTERS.

DRAMA. *See* THEATER.

DRAWING NEAR. *See* NEAR, DRAWING NEAR.

DREAMS, VISIONS

Dreams and their uses and images are an integral part of the oldest stories both within the Bible and without. The ancients recognized both dreams and visions but frequently used the terms interchangeably. Scripture mentions night visions (Dan 2:19; 7:2, 7, 13; Micah 3:6; Acts 18:9) and visions of the night

(Gen 46:2; Job 4:13; 20:8; 33:15; Is 29:7). Just as with visions, so also the text often specifies that dreams happen at night (Gen 20:3; 31:24; 40:5; 41:11; 1 Kings 3:5). In poetic passages especially, dreams occur parallel to visions (Job 33:15; Is 29:7; Dan 7:1-2). Given this usage it would be unwise to attempt any distinction, other than the obvious, that visions are usually daytime events while dreams seem confined to the night. God breaks into the human experience through both dreams and visions.

Dreams as the Voice of God in the Night. The frequency and significance of dreams mentioned in Scripture stems from their import as divine revelation to a particular individual. All dreams in antiquity were not necessarily considered divine, but with few exceptions (see below) ordinary dreams and nightmares play little or no part in the plot of most biblical narratives. The text repeatedly mentions dreams as one of the common means of "inquiring of the Lord" (a technical term for seeking an oracle), raising the possibility that dream seeking is the method of inquiry when no method is specified, especially when the word of the Lord comes by *night (1 Sam 3, esp. v. 15; 2 Sam 7:4, 17).

At times divine messages receive indirect mention (i.e., cryptic to us as foreigners) when the context or situation imply the medium of a dream. The "word of the Lord" need not be overtly labeled a dream to be one. The text sometimes mentions such revelatory encounters without using the word *dream*. Perhaps many more "inquirings of God" actually refer to dreams even without directly mentioning them. The word of the Lord comes at night to Nathan (2 Sam 7:4, 17 par. 1 Chron 17:3, 15) and to Gideon (Judges 6:25; 7:9). Isaiah says, "My soul yearns for you in the night, my spirit within me earnestly seeks you" (Is 26:9 NRSV). Hosea observes that prophets in particular stumble by night (Hos 4:4). Micah describes the absence of revelation as a night without a vision (Micah 3:6). When the word of the Lord came to Zechariah, he relates, "In the night I saw . . . (Zech 1:8 NRSV). Night is the expected time to hear the voice of God or witness his revelation. Even so the OT also sets the precedent for even daytime visions accompanied by deep sleep (Gen 15:12), and the NT follows (Acts 10:10; 22:17).

Dreams as Transparent or Obscure. In some dreams the narrative is streamlined or God speaks directly (Gen 31:24); others are symbolic, yet still obvious. *Joseph's brothers need no interpreter to understand the standard symbolism in his dreams (Gen 37:8). Even his doting father wearies of their transparent meanings. The dream of Gideon's enemy needs no explanation (Judg 7:13). Other dreams couch their truth in metaphor so obscure that a skilled wise man (such as Joseph or Daniel) is required to render them intelligible. *Pharaoh's cows do require explanation (Gen 41), and so do the baker's and the butler's dreams (Gen 40:5-19). (Pharaoh's dream is given twice to mark it as sure; Peter's vision [Acts 10:16] occurs three times to mark its significance, but he doesn't understand it until later [v. 17].) Nebuchadnezzar's dream ups the ante, requiring not only interpretation but recall as well (Dan 2). Some dream revelations are so difficult for humanity to understand that to do so is like trying to read a sealed *scroll (Is 29:11). In his allusion to Isaiah's metaphor, John observes that humanity is unworthy to open the scroll (Rev 5:1-2), implying that if revelatory dreams are obscure, it is because God has no people worth talking to.

Dreams as Oracles (Answers Sought from God). The very common OT phrase "inquired of the Lord" indicates consultation of the divine *oracle, often by dreams. In most ancient societies, people sought out divine oracles by sleeping in sacred precincts that would inspire a dream, so called incubation dreams. The pharaohs record that they slept in temples seeking dreams, as did the royalty at Ugarit. The Assyrian monarch, as chief of the oracle priests, received dreams at night in the temple. Greek suppliants learned how to be cured through dreams given in the temple of Asclepius.

The Bible mentions that pagan deities communicated in this way (Is 65:4), but some of the OT heroes seem to have contacted God in a similar fashion. Jacob, because of a dream, anoints his stone pillow and gives it the name Beth-El, "sanctuary" or "god-house" (Gen 28). Samuel, when the word of the Lord and visions had become infrequent, slept not in his own quarters as did his mentor Eli, but in the sanctuary instead (1 Sam 3:1-3), probably seeking his initial oracular dream (1 Sam 3:7). The vividness of the voice in his dream vision (1 Sam 3:15) seems to have awakened Samuel, disrupted the oracle and astonished him; but it did not astonish the experienced Eli. (The career of Samuel as God's mouthpiece is bracketed by the voice incident of 1 Sam 3:1, which establishes him as prophet [1 Sam 3:20], and the Endor incident of 1 Sam 28:14, marking his final oracular insight into the future. In each case once for his predecessor and once for his replacement, the oracle forebodes ominous consequences.) Solomon slept at the great high place in Gibeon for his dream from God (1 Kings 3:4, 5). When this expected channel is shut down, Saul complains that God no longer answers him by dreams (1 Sam 28:15).

Like the technique of incubation dreams in the OT, in the NT visions come to those who pray: Zechariah (Lk 1:10-11), Jesus at the Transfiguration (Lk 9:29), Cornelius (Acts 10:2-3), Peter (Acts 10:9-10; 11:5), Paul (Acts 9:11-12; 22:17; 23:11).

God uses dreams to reveal his message; however, some forms of oracular inquiry are off limits. Necromancy (consulting the spirits of the departed) is strictly prohibited as an abomination (Lev 19:31; 20:6; Deut 18:11), yet the lure of predictions from the dead kept the practice alive. Passages in Isaiah refer to incubation dreams in tombs to obtain revelations from nether-world deities and spirits (Is 8:19-20; 28:15-22; 65:4). In the ancient world the belief was prevalent that spirits of the departed could impart their dim understanding of the future to those in this world through dreams. As in other cases (see Oracles) it is not the oracular technique that is unacceptable, but service to any spirit other than God (Ex 20:5).

Dreams as Oracles. Dreams, then, are clearly a large subset of oracles. Just as oracles from God can come through pagan prophets (Balaam), so too the dreams of the enemy can be omens from God (Judg 7:13-15). God does not hesitate to send dreams to non-Israelites (Gen 20:3; Mt 27:19). In response to Jacob's financial concerns, God sends a dream to Jacob in order to inform him that his attempts at animal husbandry had nothing to do with the amazing increase of the flocks for which he had contracted with Laban as his wages (Gen 31:10-12). This God-given insight to Jacob, the supplanter (his Hebrew name means "Heel" or "Crook"), parallels the figure of wily Odysseus and his divine gift of craftiness.

Dreams as Spirits or Angels: Angels as Dreams. Underlying the use of dreams as revelation is the tacit belief that spirits bring the dream. Such a view is nearly universal in cultures which value dreams. The OT states both that the Lord and the angel of the Lord appears or speaks in dreams: "God said in a dream" (Gen 20:6), "God came in a dream by night and said" (Gen 31:24), but also "the angel of God said in a dream" (Gen 31:11). Angels debate and explain Daniel's vision (Dan 8:13-16). The Hebrew and Greek words translated "angel" mean "messenger." *Angels naturally accompany the dream messages they carry. Based on such OT precedents all the angel appearances that Matthew narrates occur "during a dream" (Mt 1:20, 24; 2:12, 13, 19, 22). In fact, visions and angels coincided so often that the appearance of an angel suggests to Peter an "unreal" state of mind (Acts 12:9). An angel brings John's apocalyptic vision (Rev 1:1).

As a dark parallel to God's use of dreams, God's enemies also manipulate humanity's thoughts. The people of antiquity reasoned that if angels were the messengers that brought God's message in dream form, bad angels, messengers of *Satan, could bring bad dreams. For Job, as for his contemporaries in Mesopotamia and Greece, the dream "amid visions of the night" is carried by a "spirit," an "indiscernible form" and a "voice" that "glides past the face," producing "chills," uttering "a stealthy word" that "the ear receives as a whisper" (Job 4:12-16). Outside of Scripture the phrase "terrors of the night" designates nightmares, and it appears in a list of spiritual evils in Psalm 91:5. The amulets and incantations (see Magic) written by contemporary exorcists focused on preventing nightmares by adjuring demons not to return. Sexual dreams were viewed as demonic *rape (cf. Tobit 6:14). Texts such as Psalm 91 and 121 provide comfort and allay such very real fears by assuring God's sleepless protection.

Dreams as Deception from Evil Sources. Some dreams are not merely benign. Some scare and terrify (Job 7:14). When a prophet misinterpreted his vision, it came from a lying spirit (1 Kings 22:22-23) or was faked (Jer 23:16, 27, 32). "The teraphim utter nonsense, the diviners see lies, the dreamers tell false dreams" (Zech 10:2 NRSV). Against this background, dreaming indicates self-delusion (Jude 8).

Dreams as Unreal, Nothing or Ephemeral. While God may speak through dreams, not all dreams are from God. Many are simply an annoying distraction. The people of the Bible did not insist on shoehorning all dreams into a supernatural category. Their metaphors equating dreams with phantoms and nothing betray such an understanding. Joseph's brothers mock "the dreamer" and attempt to short circuit his dreams, suspecting they are the product of Joseph's ego (Gen 37:19-20). Israel's enemies are not to be feared; they are like dreams (Is 29:7). The restoration of Zion made the people feel like "those who dream" (Ps 126:1). After envying the prosperity of the wicked, the psalmist comes to see that their transitory success ending in sudden ruin makes them as insubstantial "as a dream when one awakes" and "as fantasies" (Ps 73:20). Sirach disparages dreams: Divinations and omens and dreams are folly; and like a woman in travail, the mind has fancies (Sir 24:5).

Dreams as the Human Condition. There are hints in the Bible of dreams much more like those of today. Isaiah's metaphor, "As when the hungry dream of eating and awake unsatisfied" alludes to recurrent nightmares or Sisyphean dreams (Is 29:8). In the apocrypha, Sirach mentions one "troubled by the visions of his mind like one who has escaped from the battle front" (posttraumatic stress disorder, Sir 40:6). In his pragmatism the Preacher expresses his frustration with dreams as unreliable and difficult to interpret: "A dream comes with much business" (Eccles 5:3 RSV). His observation that "when dreams increase, empty words grow many" (Eccles 5:7 RSV) also suggests a surfeit of dream interpretations. For Job, who has become the Almighty's target, even sleep provides no comfort because "then thou dost scare me with dreams and terrify me with visions" (Job 7:14 RSV). Yet even these most human of dreams could provide counsel (Ps 16:7).

Dreams as Spiritual Health. The observation that "the word of the LORD was rare in those days; there was no frequent vision" comments on the moral decay of Israel (1 Sam 3:1 RSV). Sin in the camp prevents the dream oracle from functioning (1 Sam 14:37-38). The loss of oracles and dreams signifies abandonment by God (Mic 3:6-7). The country's spiritual ruin becomes real ruin as "her prophets obtain no vision from the LORD" (Lam 2:9 RSV). The Lord promises to replace Ezekiel's proverb, "Every vision comes to nought," with the "fulfillment of every vision" (Ezek 12:22, 23 RSV). The prophecy that dreams and visions will return assumes as a prerequisite the purifying of the nation and a pouring out of God's spirit (Joel 2:28; Acts 2:17).

See also ANGEL; APOCALYPSE, GENRE OF; CHEAT THE ORACLE; DANIEL, BOOK OF; JOSEPH THE PATRIARCH; ORACLE; PROPHECY, GENRE OF; PROPHET, PROPHETESS.

DRINK, DRINKING

Drinking is employed figuratively in a variety of ways in Scripture to indicate partaking in or even experiencing something. In this sense the oppressed spirit may be said to drink poison (Job 6:4), the brokenhearted may drink *tears (Ps 80:5), *lovers may drink of love (Prov 7:18; Song 5:1) or the *land may drink *rain (Deut 11:11; Heb 6:7).

The symbolism of drinking the *wine in the Lord's *Supper is that of partaking in the benefits of his death for us (Mt 26:27; Jn 6:53-56; 1 Cor 10:16; 11:25-29). Similarly, drinking together, like *eating together, demonstrates a common bond, in that all share in the same activity. The fact that at the Last Supper all drink from the same *cup indicates a fellowship both with the Lord and with other Christians. This, Paul tells us, is naturally incompatible with *idolatry of any kind (1 Cor 10:21). Similarly, because all Christians are indwelt by the same *Holy Spirit, they share a common spiritual experience and can be said to all drink of the one Spirit (1 Cor 12:13).

On occasion drinking describes an appetite for what is wrong. Individuals are said to drink *evil (Job 15:16), or scorn (Job 34:7) or *violence (Prov 4:17; 26:6). Having metaphorically drunk the *blood of the saints, the wicked are condemned to drink water turned to blood in the last days, an echo of the plague suffered by the Egyptians (Rev 16:6).

To drink from a *cup handed to you by the Lord means accepting your lot, a metaphor frequently used in prophetic writings to describe the bitter end of the wicked. The cup, described as containing divine *judgment and wrath, is one from which they have no choice but to drink (Job 21:20; Ps 75:8; Is 51:22; Jer 25:15-26; 49:12; Ezek 23:32-34; Obad 1:16; Hab 2:15-16; Rev 14:8, 10). Jesus used a similar image to indicate his willingness to accept his Father's purpose for him, which included the suffering of the *cross (Mt 26:42; Jn 18:11). It is apparent that his disciples did not really understand what he meant when they told him that they too could drink of the same cup, although in so doing they unwittingly predicted their own martyrdom (Mt 20:22-23; Mk 10:38-39).

Drinking can equally be a satisfying and refreshing exercise (Ps 110:7). God's people are pictured as being suckled by a *nursing *mother (Is 60:16; 66:11). Experiencing the blessings of the kingdom is like drinking new wine, for which the Jews were reluctant to abandon the old ways (Lk 5:39). It was in this respect that Jesus appealed to the spiritually thirsty to come to him and drink (Jn 4:9-14; 7:37-39; Rev 21:6).

Isolated references to drinking include David's refusal to drink the *water for which his men had risked their lives, in that it would be like drinking their blood (1 Chron 11:17-19). The pagan seer Balaam likened the unstoppable progress of the Israelites to a lion or lioness, taking its prey and drinking the blood of its victims (Num 23:24). Unhelpful alliances between God's people and either Egypt or

Assyria are described as drinking from either the Nile or the Euphrates rivers (Jer 2:18). The would-be adulterer is cryptically advised to drink water from his own *cistern (Prov 5:15)!

See also CUP; DRUNKENNESS; EATING; MILK; NURSE; THIRST; WATER; WINE.

DROUGHT. *See* DRY.

DRUNKARD

Judging from the vividness of the Bible's pictures of the drunkard, this character type elicited special moral *disgust from the writers of the Bible. The denunciations of the drunkard in the Bible (Prov 23:20, 31) already establish the moral essence of the drunkard as a type to be avoided. Drunkenness is a distinguishing sign of a wayward son (Deut 21:20; Lk 15:11-13).

The classic portrait of the drunkard occurs in Proverbs 23:29-35. Here the drunkard suffers from a range of psychological aberrations, including woe, sorrow, strife, complaining and hallucinations. Physical signs include unexplained wounds, red eyes, unbalanced walking and incoherent conversation. Other biblical portraits fill out the picture: drunkards reel and stagger (Ps 107:27; Is 24:20; 29:9; Hab 2:15), tread in their *vomit (Is 19:14), exhibit signs of madness (Jer 51:7), lose their clothing and appear *naked to public view (Hab 2:15), and are so devoid of judgment as to sell a girl for *wine to drink (Joel 3:3).

The portrait assumes more specific form when we turn to narrative examples of the drunkard. The drunken Noah lies naked in his tent (Gen 9:20). The drunken Lot commits incest with his daughters (Gen 19:30-38). Nabal and Ahasuerus lose their judgment while drunk (1 Sam 25:36; Esther 1:10-12). Several kings are recorded in the OT as being assassinated while drunk (1 Kings 16:9; 1 Kings 20:16). It is no surprise that kings are warned to steer clear of intoxicating drink because of its bad effects on a person's judgment (Prov 31:4-5).

Because drunkenness produces such vivid physical results, the drunkard emerges as one of the most repulsive character types in the Bible. The experience of the drunkard is epitomized by the statement that although wine "sparkles in the cup and goes down smoothly," at last "it bites like a serpent, and stings like an adder" (Prov 23:31-32 NIV).

See also DRUNKENNESS; WINE.

DRUNKENNESS

The OT is full of references to drunkenness, both as a literal physical phenomenon and as a graphic metaphorical symbol portraying a wide variety of emotional, spiritual and moral states. The stark images evoked by the biblical authors are often so dramatic that to comment on them would seem superfluous, even detrimental. However, to gain an overall view we will consider drunkenness first from a literal, then from a figurative perspective.

The OT prophets inveigh vehemently against the moral decadence of the judges who pervert the course of justice in eighth-century B.C. Judah: "Woe to those who are heroes at drinking *wine and champions at mixing drinks, who acquit the guilty for a bribe, but deny justice to the innocent" (Is 5:22, 23 NIV). Similarly, Amos castigates the rulers of Israel who "drink wine by the bowlful" (Amos 6:6). Qoheleth praises those rulers who drink "for strength and not for drunkenness" in contrast to those who "feast in the morning" (Eccles 10:16-17). The absolute disgust and moral repugnance of Yahweh's prophets rings through Isaiah's condemnation of the dissolute temple personnel: "Priests and prophets stagger from beer, and they are befuddled with wine; they stagger when seeing visions, they stumble when rendering decisions. All the tables are covered with vomit" (Is 28:7, 8 NIV). Nevertheless, in spite of the prophetic abhorrence of this sordid squalor, there is something inherently very humorous about the marvelous description of the drunkard by the writer of Proverbs. Wine, in the end, "bites like a snake, and poisons like a viper." The drunkard's eyes "will see strange sights," and his mind will "imagine confusing things" (Prov 23:29-35 NIV).

Human wickedness is not slow in exploiting the lowered guard induced by drunkenness. Lot's daughters got themselves pregnant by their father under the strong influence of alcohol (Gen 19:33, 35). Both Amnon (2 Sam 13:28) and King Elah of Israel (1 Kings 16:9) were assassinated while in a drunken stupor. David tried to cover up his adultery with Bathsheba by getting Uriah drunk (2 Sam 11:13). Noah exposed himself while drunk (Gen 9:21), leading to the cursing of Canaan. Habakkuk pronounced woes on those who deliberately get their neighbors drunk "so that they can gaze on their naked bodies" (Hab 2:15).

The metaphorical usages of the image of drunkenness are varied. The storm-tossed sailors, mounting up to the heavens and crashing down to the depths, reel and stagger like drunken men (Ps 107:27). The apostle Paul uses the picture of nighttime drunkenness as a foil for the alert self-controlled behavior of the Christian who walks in the light of day (1 Thess 5:7, 8).

Those under the influence of strong emotional or spiritual experiences are likened to those who are intoxicated: Hannah, in deep emotional trauma, was mistaken for a drunken woman (1 Sam 1:13); Jeremiah was "like a drunken man, like a man overcome by wine, because of the Lord and his holy words" (Jer 23:9 NIV); and the disciples at *Pentecost, speaking in tongues under the influence of the baptism of the Spirit, invited the mocking response "they have had too much wine" (Acts 2:13 NIV).

But by far the largest number of references to drunkenness occur in the Prophets as a metaphor of God's *judgment. Babylon, Edom, Moab and Egypt are all caused to drink of the cup of Yahweh's judgment and to reel and stagger under the wine of God's wrath (Jer 25:15). Sometimes they are God's historical judgments against these political nation-states for their acts of cruelty and defiance; other times the nations stand as types of the world as a whole, about to suffer God's eschatological fury at the end of the age. There are images of eternal drunken stupor (Jer 51:57), madness (Jer 51:7), defiant laughter (Jer 51:39), dizziness (Is 19:14), staggering (Jer 25:15)—an awesome picture of human confusion and helplessness brought upon themselves by their God-defying arrogance.

See also DRUNKARD; WINE.

DRY, DROUGHT

Drought is an image of *suffering in the Bible, but even more dominant than that is the constant motif of the threat of drought. Drought was a dangerous reality of the ancient Near East, one that could precipitate *famine. Abraham, Isaac and Jacob were all forced to relocate because of drought-related famine (Gen 12; 26; 41). In Egypt, *Joseph rose to prominence because of his able management of the country's food supply under drought conditions (Gen 41). Elijah ministered to a widow in Zarephath who expected to die from a drought-induced famine (1 Kings 17:7-24). *Jonah experienced a micro-drought as he grew faint under a blazing sun and hot east wind (Jon 4:8). Nearly all of the major biblical images of drought occur in the OT.

The background against which biblical references must be understood is the aridity of the land of the Bible, with the image of a "*dry and *thirsty land" epitomizing the situation (Ezek 19:13 NIV; see also KJV rendering of Ps 63:1). In particular it was the drying up that came from the heat of summer that constituted an annual worry, as "heat and drought snatch away the melted snow" (Job 24:19). In such a world, drought is always the implied opposite of *water and *rain. Only a tree "planted by water, that sends out its roots by the stream," does "not fear when heat comes" and is not anxious "in the year of drought" (Jer 17:8 NIV).

Drought is above all an image of natural terror. Jeremiah equates "a land of drought" with such parallel terrors as *wilderness, *pit, *darkness and "a land where no one travels and no one lives" (Jer 2:6 NIV). When the prophetic imagination pictures a coming judgment, it produces images of a *river that becomes "parched and dry" (Is 19:5), the drying up of pools (Is 42:18) and the transformation of a fertile nation into "a wilderness, a dry land, a desert" (Is 50:12). Conversely, restoration and blessing are pictured in terms of parched ground being turned into pools of water (Is 41:18) and the pouring out of "water on the thirsty land, and streams on the dry ground" (Is 44:3).

In the OT drought is linked to the motif of *covenant *blessing and *curse. God brought Israel out of Egypt into a *land flowing with milk and honey. This was his covenant gift to his people; however, their continual enjoyment of this *paradise was partially contingent on the nation's covenant loyalty. Deuteronomy 28:22 warns the covenant

breakers of Moses' day that among other things, "the LORD will strike you . . . with scorching heat and drought." If Israel rebelled against Yahweh, he would discipline them by drying up the milk and honey. The experience of a drought, then, was meant to be more than physical and financial. For the reflective Israelite it was evidence of God's displeasure and a call to repentance (cf. Joel 1—2). Drought was not just a curse; it was a sign of Yahweh's grace in that it drove the sensitive Israelite back to God.

The covenant curse of a literal drought was transformed by the psalmists and prophets into an image to describe the emotional pangs suffered under God's wrath or discipline. They described their emotional turmoil in terms of the physical strains of hunger and thirst experienced in a drought. Drought reduces the visual floral evidence of God's favor to the tiresome emptiness of a barren *wasteland. Likewise, God's discipline removes the spiritual and emotional signals of his favor (peace, fulfillment, happiness) from one's spiritual landscape. David says, "O God, you are my God, earnestly I seek you; my soul thirsts for you, my body longs for you, in a dry and weary land where there is no water" (Ps 63:1 NIV). Joel observes, "Even the wild animals pant for you; the streams of water have dried up and fire has devoured the open pastures" (Joel 1:20 NIV). In the same way the reversal of drought is an image depicting God's blessing: "For I will pour water on the thirsty land, and streams on the dry ground; I will pour out my Spirit on your offspring, and my blessing on your descendants" (Is 44:3 NIV).

The imagery of drought is scarce in the NT. The parable of the seeds briefly picks up on the image in Luke 8:6: "Some fell on rock, and when it came up, the plants withered because they had no moisture" (NIV). James employs the image when he describes the transience of a wealthy life: "For the sun rises with scorching heat and withers the plant; its blossom falls and its beauty is destroyed. In the same way, the rich man will fade away even while he goes about his business" (Jas 1:11 NIV).

See also CURSE; FAMINE; HUNGER; LAND FLOWING WITH MILK AND HONEY; RAIN; THIRST; WASTELAND; WATER.

DUNG

Surprisingly, references to dung can be found many times in the OT but only once in a key NT passage (Phil 3:8). "Dung" is the KJV preferred translation for several Hebrew and Greek terms. Other translations prefer to use "refuse," "rubbish," "waste," "filth," "offal," "dirt," "rubble" or "garbage." More explicit words for accurately rendering the biblical terms, such as "excrement," "feces" or "manure," have rarely been chosen by translators. Yet the strength of the image in the dung metaphor is preserved by not watering down its meaning from biblical times.

Dung is first associated with the *sacrificial rites of Israel. Since dung was an unclean substance, God mandated that it needed to be burned *outside the encampment and later, outside the gates of Jerusalem (Ex 29:14; Lev 16:27; Neh 3:13, 14). Dung was also used as fertilizer (Lk 13:8). However the metaphorical power of dung's coarse connotations is found in the various contexts of judgment pronouncements in the OT prophetic and historical books.

For example, in 1 Kings 14:10 dung is a metaphor applied to the ruling family of Jeroboam, where God says he "will utterly consume the house of Jeroboam, as a man burns up dung until it is all gone" (RSV). The corpse of Jezebel is to be scattered like excrement in a field, "so that no one can say, 'This is Jezebel' " (2 Kings 9:37 RSV). In Ezra 6:11 King Darius warns that anyone who interferes with the restoration of Israel's temple is to have his home turned into an outhouse—destroyed—"made a dunghill" (RSV).

Besides the judgment of dung being pronounced on Israel's *enemies (Ps 83:10; Is 25:10), the majority of dung judgments are assessed against Israel, the very people of God. Graphic examples of these judgments are found in the Prophets (e.g., Jer 9:22; 16:4), but the most extreme metaphor for God's displeasure with his people relates prophetic judgment to spreading excrement across the faces of *apostate Israel (Mal 2:3): "Behold, I will corrupt your seed, and spread dung upon your faces, [even] the dung of your solemn feasts" (KJV). Such strong language expresses God's right as Creator of all things—even dung—to use any creature or created substance as a means of expressing his divine will.

NT metaphorical use of dung is limited to Philippians 3:8, where Paul is comparing the *glory of his past natural life as a prominent Hebrew to his present servant role as Christ's apostle. "I count all things but loss . . . and do count them but dung [Gk *skybalon*], that I might win Christ" (KJV) forcefully expresses Paul's extreme attitude toward his past human attainments. The glories of gaining and serving Christ make Paul's religious prestige seem like mere excrement!

Several other coarse English colloquialisms would more closely suggest the negative inflections of *skybalon*. The coarseness and repulsiveness of the dung metaphor vividly expresses many spiritually unsavory judgments on human sin and wrong priorities.

See also DISGUST, REVULSION.

DUNGEON. *See* CISTERN; PITS.

DUPE

The archetypal *character type of the dupe is a person easily tricked and taken advantage of. The dupe is usually a comic type—the butt of a well-deserved joke—but occasionally in the Bible there is a tragic undertow.

*Eve is the original dupe in the Bible, too easily swayed by the temptation of the serpent when she should have remained obedient to the command from God (Gen 3:1-6). Her's is a sin of gullibility (Gen 3:13; 2 Cor 11:3; 1 Tim 2:14), the root trait of the dupe. Perhaps the innocent *Abel is naively trusting of his murderous brother when he agrees to "go out to the field" as though it were an invitation to a pleasurable stroll (Gen 4:8 RSV). Also in Genesis, Egyptian kings are readily deceived by Abraham and Isaac about the identity of their wives (Gen 12:10-20; 20; 26:6-11). *Esau is the proverbial "sitting duck" when Jacob bargains for the *birthright with the smell of stew in the air (Gen 25:29-34), and Isaac appears in the same role in the story of the stolen blessing, even though Isaac makes an attempt to penetrate Jacob's disguise (Gen 27). Other dupes in Genesis include *Jacob in the incident of the substitute bride (Gen 29:21-25) and in his sons' deception of him regarding the fate of *Joseph, Judah as he is tricked by Tamar (Gen 38) and the men of Shechem when they allow themselves to be circumcised as a prelude to their own slaughter (Gen 34).

Subsequent OT history also produces its gallery of dupes. *Pharaoh believes women to pose no threat to him, yet he is repeatedly outwitted by women. Even his own daughter plays a role in his being tricked into paying Moses' mother for taking care of her own son (Ex 1—2). Joshua is taken in by the neighboring Gibeonites, who pose as travelers from a distant land in order to gain a peace treaty (Josh 9). The hapless Eglon is so thoroughly tricked by Ehud's promise of a "secret message from God" for him that he rises ceremoniously to receive a dagger thrust into his fat belly (Judg 3:15-23). Sisera is beguiled into taking a nap in Jael's tent, only to find himself impaled through his temples (Judg 4:17-22; 5:24-27). *Samson has a fatal weakness for succumbing to the tears of a devious Philistine woman (Judg 14:16-18; 16:18-21). *David is tricked by Nathan's parable into pronouncing a verdict against himself (2 Sam 12:1-15). Herod is duped by the wisemen when they return home by an alternate route (Mt 2:12).

Stories of hiding (*see* Hide) often turn on an authority figure who is tricked. Thus Rahab deceives the king's squadron by hiding the spies on the roof of her house (Josh 2:1-7), and Rachel fools Laban by concealing the household gods in the camel's saddle (Gen 31:33-35). In a similar incident Michal arranges a household idol with goat's hair to deceive Saul's executioners as David escapes (1 Sam 19:11-17).

If there is a lesson to be learned from the relative prominence of the dupe in the Bible, in addition to constituting material, it is the need for watchfulness. The price of allowing oneself to be deceived or tricked can be the thwarting of one's plans and even the loss of one's life. Furthermore, God reduces evil characters to the status of dupe as part of his judgment against them.

See also CHARACTER TYPES; DECEPTION, STORIES OF; TRICKSTER.

DUSK. *See* TWILIGHT.

DUST. *See* MORTALITY.

E

EAGLE

The eagle, a large, solitary *bird of prey, is known for its keen eyesight, power and sharp beak and talons. With a wingspan up to seven and a half feet, it hunts high in the air and swoops down on its prey at great speed. Eagles mate for life and care for their young in nests, called aeries, high in trees or rocky ledges. This provides protection for the eaglets, which remain helpless for a long period, up to 100 days. Palestine is home to four varieties of eagles, of which the most common is the short-toed eagle.

Israelites were forbidden from eating birds of prey such as vultures, hawks and eagles "because they are detestable" (Lev 11:13). Yet many of the some thirty references in Scripture depict the eagle, not as detestable, but as an image of *strength and deliverance.

The eagle portrays speed and power in biblical images (2 Sam 1:23; Is 40:31; Jer 4:13). Along with three other creatures of strength—the *lion, the *ox and humans—it appears as one face of the four mighty cherubim who attend the *throne of God (Ezek 1:10-14; Rev 4:7).

The eagle symbolizes the speed and power of both God's deliverance and God's destruction. Speaking of how he delivered Israel from Egypt, the Lord says, "You yourselves have seen what I did to Egypt, and how I carried you on eagles' wings and brought you to myself" (Ex 19:4 NIV). Similar images of God's protection as an eagle, swift and powerful, are found in Deuteronomy 32:11 and Revelation 12:14. Isaiah 40:31 is the famous passage relating the renewing strength God gives to his followers: "But those who hope in the LORD will renew their strength. They will soar on wings like eagles; they will run and not grow weary, they will walk and not be faint" (NIV).

The eagles' hunting skill and sudden attack on their prey lend themselves to images of sure and sudden disaster in depictions of God's judgment. In the OT prophets the mighty nations of Assyria and *Babylon are portrayed as eagles bringing disaster on God's people because they have broken covenant with him (Lam 4:19; Ezek 17:3, 7; Hos 8:1). Jeremiah depicts divine judgment against Moab and Edom as an eagle swooping down with wings outspread (Jer 48:40; 49:22). In a scene of final judgment in Revelation, the gliding eagle appears in midair to announce the woes of the imminent disaster that the Lord is sending on the inhabitants of earth (Rev 8:13).

See also BIRDS.

EAR, HEARING

In the Bible the ear is synonymous with the *heart and *mind as an organ of cognition (Prov 2:2; Is 6:9-10), and true hearing involves listening and understanding (Job 34:16). The ear is personified as hearing and understanding (Job 13:1), seeking knowledge (Prov 18:15) and testing words (Job 12:11). To "incline" the ear is to be favorably disposed to what is heard (Jer 34:14; Ps 31:2). To have *"deaf," *"heavy" or "uncircumcised" (*see* Circumcision) ears is to reject what is heard (Jer 6:10; Acts 7:51). "Itching" ears are only favorably disposed to what is already found agreeable (2 Tim 4:3).

*Idols are deaf (Deut 4:28; Rev 9:20), but God is personified as having ears (1 Sam 8:21) and hearing his people (2 Sam 22:7). *Prayers and petitions to God begin with a request to God to "incline your ear" (Ps 17:6). God hears his people groaning in bondage (Ex 3:7), facing their enemies in battle (Is 37:17), crying out in barrenness (Gen 30:6) and complaining when unjustly treated (Jas 5:4). God hears the prayers of the righteous (Ps 17:1; 1 Pet 3:12) and those asking according to his will (1 Jn 5:14). Thus God always heard the prayers of Jesus (Jn 11:41-42; Heb 5:7). God also hears the arrogance of humanity (2 Kings 19:28) and its plotting (Num 12:2). His ears are hard of hearing or deaf to the prayers of *sinners and those refusing to hear him (Is 59:1-2; Jn 9:31).

Unlike ancient religions that sought revelation through the *eye and through visions, biblical people primarily sought revelation through the ear and hearing. Hearing symbolizes the proper response to God in the Bible. God opens the ears to hear his word (Job 36:10; Is 50:4-5), gives the ears of the *prophets his revelation (Is 22:14; 50:4-5) and exhorts his people either directly or through prophets to "hear" his revelation (Deut 5:1; Jer 2:4; Rev 2:7). To faithfully hear God's voice requires personal apprehension, acceptance and *obedience (Mt 7:24, 26; Lk 11:28; Jas 1:22-25). Lack of hearing is the decisive spiritual failure and rebellion against God (Is 48:8; Heb 3:7-8).

Jesus is God's incarnate Word, and thus God commands us to listen to Jesus in *faith and obedience (Mt 17:5). The parable of the sower demonstrates that the efficacy of Jesus' proclamation of the *kingdom depends on faithful hearing. Thus Jesus' stress upon "Let anyone with ears listen!" (Mt 13:9 NRSV). To hear the words of God is to be a *child of God (Jn 8:47) and a *sheep hearing the voice of the Shepherd (Jn 10:3, 16, 27). Not to do so is to be spiritually hard of hearing (Mt 13:14-16) and to remain unforgiven (Jn 12:47-49). Hearing is blessing and life, and not hearing is judgment (Job 36:10-12; John 5:24).

See also BLIND, BLINDNESS; DEAF, DEAFNESS; EYE, SIGHT.

EARNEST MONEY. *See* LEGAL IMAGES.

EARTH

"Who has held the dust of the earth in a basket, or weighed the mountains on the scales and the hills in a balance? . . . He sits enthroned above the circle of the earth, and its people are like grasshoppers" (Is 40:12, 22 NIV). " 'Heaven is my throne and the earth is my footstool. Where is the house you will build for me? Where will my resting place be? Has not my hand made all these things, and so they came into being?' declares the LORD" (Is 66:1-2 NIV). Isaiah's imagery of earth as God's footstool and of God's weighing the dust of the earth conveys the greatness of God, who transcends his creation. Unlike the fertility gods of the pagan religions and manmade idols, he is beyond everything that he has made.

The Psalms use imagery to praise God not only as Creator but also as Sustainer of the earth. This is the theme of Psalm 104. He created the heavens and "set the earth on its *foundations; it can never be moved" (Ps 104:5). He provides water, food and shelter for the great variety of the earth's creatures and marks off the seasons (Ps 104:10-23). God is active in sustaining and regulating his creation: "When you send your Spirit, they are created [i.e., the creatures], and you renew the face of the earth" (Ps 104:30). However, when he judges, "He looks at the earth, and it trembles" (Ps 104:32; see also Ps 147).

Humanity's relationship to the earth is crucial to understanding the earth imagery in the Bible. "The LORD God formed man [*'ādām*] from the dust of the ground [*'ªdāmâ*]" (Gen 2:7 NIV). The future of humankind and the earth are profoundly bound together. After *Adam and Eve's act of rebellion in Eden, God passed judgment: "Cursed is the ground because of you: through painful toil you will eat of it all the days of your life. It will produce thorns and thistles for you, and you will eat the plants of the field. By the sweat of your brow you will eat your food until you return to the ground" (Gen 3:17-19).

Human actions defile and corrupt the earth: "The earth is defiled by its people; they have disobeyed the laws, violated the statutes and broken the everlasting covenant. Therefore a curse consumes the earth; its people must bear their guilt" (Is 24:5, 6 NIV).

Hosea, Jeremiah and Amos employ the image of the earth *mourning as a result of people's evil deeds (Hos 4:1-3; Jer 12:4; 23:10; Amos 1:2). Hosea laments that there is "no faithfulness, no love, no acknowledgment of God in the land" (Hos 4:1 NIV). As a consequence the "land mourns [dries up], and all who live in it waste away: the beasts of the field and the birds of the air and the fish of the sea are dying" (Hos 4:3 NIV).

The earth as we know it is spoiled and awaits renewal. Several biblical writers use the image of *garments as an image of *transience in their prophecies about the earth's future (Ps 102:25-26; Is 51:6). The writer of Hebrews quotes Psalm 102,

> In the beginning, O Lord, you laid the foundations of the earth,
> and the heavens are the works of your hands.
> They will perish, but you remain;
> they will all wear out like a garment.
> You will roll them up like a robe;
> like a garment they will be changed.
> But you remain the same,
> and your years will never end.
> (Heb 1:10-12 NIV)

There will be "new heavens and a new earth" (Is 65:17, 2; 2 Pet 3:13; Rev 21:1). Isaiah gives us a wonderful picture of the renewed earth "full of the knowledge of God as the waters cover the sea" (Is 11:9 NIV). "Instead of the thornbush will grow the pine tree, and instead of briers the myrtle will grow" (Is 55:13 NIV). Symbols of *death and the *curse are replaced by those of life.

Psalm 96 describes the earth rejoicing before God who comes to judge and renew it. Fields and forests are personified as singing in the presence of God. "Sing to the LORD a new song; sing to the LORD, all the earth. . . . Let the heavens rejoice, let the earth be glad; let the sea resound, and all that is in it; let the fields be jubilant, and everything in them. Then all the trees of the forest will sing for joy; they will sing before the LORD, for he comes, he comes to judge the earth'" (Ps 96:1, 11-13 NIV; see also 98:7-9).

See also CORRUPTION; COSMOLOGY; CREATION; DEATH; DECAY; HEAVEN; LAND; TRANSIENCE.

EARTHQUAKE

The eastern Mediterranean area is prone to earthquakes. These events, which have caused devastation and loss of life throughout history, are caused by episodic movement of the earth's crust along a complex network of faults as the African and Arabian tectonic plates progressively collide with the Eurasian plate. In the Palestine area the main earthquake zones are along the line of the Jordan valley where the Arabian tectonic plate is sliding northwards against the African plate on which Palestine occurs. This is a simpler form of the situation in coastal California. Other earthquake zones are along the Jezreel Valley and southern Turkey. A significant feature of Scripture is its refusal to invoke a mythological explanation of earthquakes.

Some references to earthquakes appear to be bald statements of historic fact and seem to have little, if any, symbolic value (Amos 1:1, cf. Zech 14:5; Acts 16:26). Most references, however, particularly in the poetic parts of the Bible, accord a high degree of symbolism to earthquakes. Earthquakes in Scripture are often seen as manifestations of the direct action of God's power. The example that is probably alluded to most is the earthquake at the giving of the law at *Sinai (Ex 19:18). In their poetic reviews of the *Exodus, later writers seem to have emphasized this element (Ps 68:8; 77:18; 114:4-7) and broadened its scope to cover the whole exodus event. Matthew's linkage of the earthquake at Jesus' crucifixion with the rending of the temple *veil (Mt 27:54) is thus far more than a statement of physical cause and effect: it is profoundly symbolic. The *covenant inaugurated at Sinai is now ended. In Revelation at least some of the earthquake imagery relates back to *Sinai (Bauckham).

Although earthquake imagery is everywhere associated with God acting, the precise emphasis varies. A number of references invoke the imagery of God marching out to do battle (Judg 5:4; Ps 68:7-8; Joel 2:10-11; Mic 1:4; see Divine Warrior). Other references associate earthquakes with a *theophany, a manifestation of God to the world (Ps 97:4-5; 99:1; Is 64:2-3). If there is any symbolism to do with the earthquake at Christ's resurrection associated with the rolling back of the stone (Mt 28:2) it may lie in this area. Many other references refer to the shaking of the earth (often accompanied by *wind and *fire) when God judges the nations or the wicked (Is 13:13; 24:18-20; 29:6; Jer 10:10, Ezek 26:18; 38:19-20; Joel 3:16; Nahum 1:5-6). In this context the reference in 1 Kings 19:11 may be a symbolic way of suggesting that this was not a time of God's *judgment.

From this association of earthquakes with God's revealing himself comes the substantial presence of this imagery in apocalyptic literature. Thus Hebrews, drawing on Haggai 2:6, looks forward to the final shaking of the heavens and the earth (Heb 12:26-27). Revelation, also drawing on the many references in Scripture, includes a number of references to earthquakes (Rev 8:5; 11:13, 19; 16:18-20). The fact that the area of the seven churches in western Turkey is prone to earthquakes (Laodicea, Sardis and Philadelphia suffered in the great earthquake in A.D. 17 and Laodicea was badly damaged in A.D. 60) must have heightened the imagery to the original hearers.

Earthquakes reminded men and women then as well as now that the only fixed ground is God himself. Not even the earth is ultimately stable. They also point to the fact that one day God will shake down all human kingdoms with the appearing of Christ in Glory (Zech 14:4-5).

See also COSMOLOGY; THEOPHANY.

BIBLIOGRAPHY. R. J. Bauckham, "The Eschatological Earthquake in the Apocalypse of John," *NovT* 19 (1977) 224-33.

EAST

The Semitic cultures of the ancient Near East tended literally to orient themselves (i.e., to face) east (Heb *qedem* "forward," "east"). Ancient maps, even through the Middle Ages, typically placed the east, not the north, at the top. The Israelite tabernacle and Solomon's *temple are both expressly erected to face east. This orientation pervades much biblical literature to affirm the east as the source from which blessing and respite come (Gen 2:8; Rev 7:2-3), perhaps echoing the westward movement of the *sun from the east. The direction one faces points to origin and not destination, a fact confirmed by the words for past and future, cognate with the terms for east and west. The past is "the days in front/before" (*qedem;* 2 Kings 19:25; Ps 44:2) and the future is "the after-part (*'aḥ*ᵃ*rît*) of days" (Gen 49:1; Num 24:14). The imagery is of one heading into the unknown future backwards (west) by facing the past (east). In the same way spatial orientation toward the east, such as the east gate of the temple, has come to imply and endorse in certain narratives movement away from the east.

Movement toward the east in Genesis, consequently, consistently appears in the context of rebellion and sin. *Adam and Eve are expelled in an eastward direction from Eden (Gen 3:24), a direction in which the murderer *Cain also moves (Gen 4:16) as well as a humanity that refuses to obey God and erects the tower of *Babel (Gen 11:2-4). The momentum of catastrophe is finally reversed by *Abraham's movement away from the east toward the west, even as he forbids his family to return east (Gen 24:5-8). Catastrophe continues to strike those who, like Lot, prefer to move eastward (Gen 13:11-13). Years of swindling, deception and strife accompany Jacob's return to the east (Gen 29:1); it is Abraham's offspring who receive a lesser inheritance who move eastward (Gen 25:6).

The same pattern emerges outside Genesis. The first of the twelve tribes to disappear in history are precisely those (Reuben, Gad and half of Manasseh) who provoke Moses' anger in preferring to stay east of the Jordan and not inherit the promised land on the western side (Num 32:19; Judg 18:7). When God's *glory eventually departs from Israel, boding calamity for Jerusalem, it is toward the east that he moves (Ezek 10:18-19 11:22-23); restoration means God reverses this movement in Ezekiel 43:2-5. The Babylonian exile is a tragic return to the east, essentially starting over and undoing all that had been achieved from the time when Abraham first left the territory of Babylonia long before.

Apart from this *cosmic significance, a geographical dimension applicable only to Israel and her immediate neighbors emerges from the presence of the desert to the east. The arid eastern wastes produced a scorching sirocco *wind (from Arabic *šarqî* "east wind") that destroyed human endeavors (Ezek 27:26; Ps 48:7), blighted vegetation (Ezek 17:10; 19:12) and dried up water sources (Ex 14:21;

Hos 13:15; *see* Dry, Drought). This hot east wind became a metaphor for anything that was totally worthless (Job 15:2-3 NASB). If pursuing the wind is pointless (Eccles 6:9), the pursuit of the east wind in particular is the height of absurdity (Hos 12:1). Those who live in the east, characteristically portrayed as nomads with tents and camels (Jer 49:28-29; Ezek 25:4), behave like the east wind when they invade and destroy the settled area of Israel (Judg 6:3, 33; 7:12).

See also NORTH; SOUTH; SUN; WEST.

EATING

With seven hundred references to the act of eating (not counting references to *drinking and *food), we can say with confidence that eating is a master image of the Bible. No biblical image combines the literal and the figurative, the physical and spiritual, more inextricably than does the imagery of eating. In the OT ceremonial laws, rules governing eating are at once physical reality (a health measure) and covenant sign. The references to eating serve as a reminder of the physical identity of people in the world, but they are equally a reminder of the spiritual realities of biblical faith. Both literally and figuratively, eating communicates the paradigm of a providential creator and a dependent humanity. It also demonstrates the news of God's most gracious acts.

Literal Eating. Eating in the Bible is a continual reminder of elemental human existence in the world. Ancient literature generally was preoccupied with eating (in Homer approximately one line in thirty concerns the preparation or consumption of food). We read that "Esau ate and drank, and rose and went his way" (Gen 25:34 RSV). This is simply the way it is for humans living in the world. King Saul, having "eaten nothing all day and all night," reluctantly ate meat and bread before leaving the house of the *witch at Endor (1 Sam 1:20-25). "Our fathers ate the *manna in the wilderness," Jesus said in his discourse on the *bread of heaven (Jn 6:31 RSV). This, then, is one image of eating in the Bible—an image of the sustenance of physical life. At this level eating is variously an image of human durability (to eat is to perpetuate life) and of vulnerability (it is an act that people need to perform continuously and that is not assured), and it is an index to God's provision for his creatures.

Eating in the Bible is a prime evidence of God's providence, sometimes the result of miraculous provision. God reminds the Israelites that during their wilderness wanderings they have been totally dependent upon him and "have not eaten bread" so that they "may know that I am the LORD your God" (Deut 29:6). God commands the ravens to feed Elijah in the morning and evening at the brook Cherith (1 Kings 17:4-6), and the widow at Zarephath, after passing a test by providing her last food for a *meal for Elijah, is rewarded with an inexhaustible food supply until the drought ends (1 Kings 17:8-16). In the NT several of Jesus' most famous miracles involve supply-ing food for hungry masses.

As an image of elemental human sustenance, eating can have negative overtones as well. In a fallen world, finding food to eat can be a burden. Part of the original *curse of the Fall was that "in the sweat of your face you shall eat bread" (Gen 3:19 RSV). The sheer repetitiveness and monotony of having to eat has a burdensome side to it: "All the toil of man is for his mouth, yet his appetite is not satisfied" (Eccles 6:7 RSV).

Literal eating, however, can be more lavish than simply eating food to sustain life. The *banquet is the supreme example—not just eating, but luxurious eating, with overtones of festivity and sociability. It is also part of the high value placed on *hospitality in the Bible and in ancient cultures more generally. The picture of Abraham nonchalantly standing by his angelic visitors as they eat his hastily prepared but lavish meal epitomizes this dimension of eating in the Bible (Gen 18:1-8). Even when a meal was relatively modest, the social meaning of shared eating is that of mutual fellowship and trust. And even modest eating can be an occasion of enjoyment as the writer of Ecclesiastes repeatedly suggests (Eccles 2:24-25; 5:18; 9:7).

Physical eating, even while retaining its literal qualities, takes on a symbolic or moral meaning as well. It is sometimes an implicit moral test in the Bible. The primal sin was an act of eating from the forbidden *tree in the middle of the Garden. Jesus reversed the pattern by abstaining when Satan *tempted him with food. Abstinence is sometimes a moral virtue, as in not eating the forbidden foods of the Mosaic code (where refraining from eating is sometimes nothing less than a sign of covenant obedience) or in Nazirites' abstaining from certain foods. We think also of *Daniel and his young friends, who refuse to eat the rich food of the Babylonian king, and of NT commands to abstain from food offered to idols. *Fasting, so important in the Bible, is likewise a form of abstinence. Even when eating is not forbidden, its abuse in the form of excess or gluttony is viewed as a moral issue: the wise man warns his son against it (Prov 23:1-3, 20-21; 28:7), and Paul denounces those whose "god is the belly" (Phil 3:19) and who are "lazy gluttons" (Tit 1:12).

Excessive eating can thus be a sin, but even what we might consider to be ordinary eating can be an index to a sinful attitude. Eating is one of the pictures Jesus used to portray how indifference to the call of God in the ordinary circumstances of life can lead one to miss the kingdom of God: of people in any era of history it can be said that, as in the days of Noah and Lot, "they ate, they drank" and went about the business of life to the exclusion of God (Lk 17:27-28). In the time of Amos, eating "lambs from the flock and calves from the midst of the stall" became a picture of the indifference of the wealthy to the "ruin of Joseph" (Amos 6:4-6 RSV).

Eating, in short, signals larger issues. Above all it points to a lifestyle. How and what one eats in the

Bible identifies one as godly or ungodly, moral or immoral. Jesus' propensity to eat with a broad range of people, including "sinners" (Lk 15:2), signaled such things as an affirmation of earthly life as good in principle, the wide scope of his salvation and the joyousness of that salvation. The book of Ecclesiastes repeatedly offers eating and drinking in contented enjoyment as a feature of the God-centered life (Eccles 2:24-25; 3:13; 5:18; 8:15; 9:7). The other general lesson that emerges from the Bible's references to physical eating is simply its importance. Life depends on it, and one's moral and spiritual standing is revealed by it.

Eating as Metaphor. When we turn to metaphoric uses of eating, we find a wide range of life's activities pictured as eating. Judgment and destruction are a leading cluster. A conquering army is a metaphoric *sword that devours flesh (Deut 32:42; cf. 2 Sam 18:8). Eating becomes symbolic of divine judgment when the *fire of God "devoured" offending persons (Lev 10:2) and when God is said to have "swallowed up" his enemies in anger (Ps 21:9). James warns wealthy and self-indulgent people that the *rust of gold and silver "will eat your flesh like fire" (Jas 5:3). From time immemorial *death or the *grave has been a personified eater that devours its prey (Prov 1:12).

Assimilating religious knowledge and growing spiritually from it are likewise compared to a process of eating and digestion. Paul fed immature Christians with *"milk" because they were not ready to digest solid food (1 Cor 3:1-2), and Hebrews 5:11-14 repeats the image. Similarly Peter enjoins his audience to "long for the pure spiritual milk, that by it you may grow up to salvation" (1 Pet 2:2 RSV). God's true *shepherds feed the people with knowledge and understanding (Jer 3:15). Conversely, the absence of hearing the words of the Lord is a *famine on the land (Amos 8:11). Assimilating *folly or falsehood is likewise pictured as assimilating food into the body (Prov 15:14).

Elsewhere indulgence of the *sexual appetite is pictured in terms of eating. The loose woman seduces her naive victim with the invitation to "take our fill of love till morning" (Prov 7:18). The *adulteress "eats, and wipes her mouth" (Prov 30:20). The positive counterpart occurs in the *Song of Songs, where the delights of mutual love are pictured as eating and being satisfied (Song 2:3-5; 4:11-16).

In its ultimate metaphoric reaches, to eat is to participate in God's salvation in Christ. The parables in which Jesus pictures a messianic banquet illustrate this, as does the picture in Revelation 19:9 of the marriage *supper of the Lamb. Christ himself stands as a self-invited guest knocking at the door of the human soul, waiting to be asked to "come in to him and eat with him, and he with me" (Rev 3:20 RSV). Jesus is the bread of life that people must eat to gain eternal life (Jn 6:25-40). Most graphic of all is the Lord's Supper, in which believers eat the bread as symbolic of sharing in Christ's bodily death (1 Cor 11:23-29).

Summary. Eating is at once a physical and spiritual reality in the Bible. At a physical level it is a continuous evidence of God's daily provision for people and animals as well as an image of creaturely dependence on the Creator (Ps 104:27-30). The same two meanings—divine provision and human neediness—apply at a spiritual level. In view of this we might well conclude that the imagery of eating in the Bible evokes a picture of the world as a cosmic table of provision, and eating as the prerequisite for physical and spiritual life. The goal of human life is eating—to be numbered among those whom Christ allows to "eat and drink at my table in my kingdom" (Lk 22:30).

See also APPETITE; BANQUET; BREAD; DRINKING; FAMINE; FOOD; FRUIT; HOSPITALITY; MANNA; MEAL; MILK; PURITY; SUPPER.

EAVESDROPPER

Eavesdropping in the form of people overhearing a conversation is both a fact of life and an archetypal motif in literature. Whereas the dominant image is the negative one of a meddling eavesdropper, the Bible at least partly redeems the image.

The negative image is present, to be sure. Sarah overhears God promise *Abraham that she will bear a son in the spring and laughs in unbelief and bitterness. She is rebuked by God and lies about having laughed (Gen 18:9-15). Rebekah overhears her husband Isaac dispatch *Esau to hunt for game as a preview to his conferring the father's parting blessing on Esau as the firstborn son (Gen 27). She uses her knowledge to mastermind an elaborate intrigue in which *Jacob deceives his elderly father and steals the blessing. All four principals end up losers in this drama of intrigue that started with eavesdropping. Also in the tragic mode is Peter's denial of Jesus, in which Jesus is forced to overhear the betrayal.

But beyond these negative instances, overhearing a conversation can be redemptive for someone. Gideon's confidence is bolstered when he enters the Midianite camp by night and overhears a Midianite recount his dream in which a cake of barley bread rolls into camp and smashes a tent, confirming the certainty of Gideon's success in battle (Judg 7:9-14). Mordecai is able to save the king's life when he catches wind of a plot to kill the king (Esther 2:21-23). In similar fashion Paul's nephew hears about an intended plot against Paul's life, thereby setting in motion a counterplot to protect Paul (Acts 23:12-35). Moses' sister Miriam in effect eavesdrops on Pharaoh's daughter as she discovers the infant Moses floating on the Nile River (Ex 2:4-8). People who overhear David's confident words regarding Goliath pass them on to Saul, opening the way for David's exploit (1 Sam 17:31). Naaman apparently overhears the wish of his wife's maid that he visit Elijah in Israel (2 Kings 5:1-4), thus preparing the way for his miraculous healing.

See also EAR, HEARING.

ECCLESIASTES, BOOK OF

The dominant organizing motif in the book of Ecclesiastes is the *quest, as the protagonist of the work searches to find meaning and satisfaction in life. Transitions between units of the book keep the quest motif constantly in our consciousness as we read: "again I saw," "then I saw," "so I turned to consider," "I turned my mind to know and to search out and to seek." At the end of the book the writer tells us that he has reached the goal of his quest: "The end of the matter; all has been heard" (Eccles 12:13 RSV).

While pursuing his quest the narrator retrospectively recalls a series of dead ends that he pursued. The informing metaphor of the book, though never mentioned explicitly, is the labyrinth or maze, with its series of pathways that entice the quester to follow one dead end after another. Corresponding to the quest motif is the imagery of seeing, *searching and *finding. In a single specimen passage (Eccles 7:26-29) we read, "I found" (four times), "to find the sum," "have sought repeatedly," "have not found," "I have not found."

The key phrase in the book, occurring more than thirty times in twelve chapters, is "under the sun" (or its variant "under heaven"). Central to any interpretation of the book, this phrase implies life lived by purely earthly and human values without recourse to a supernatural level of reality. There is an implied alternative to life under the *sun, expressed most explicitly in the assertion that "God is in heaven, and you upon earth" (Eccles 5:2 RSV). The upper level in this metaphoric two-level universe (see Cosmology) keeps revealing itself in passages where God is conspicuously mentioned (e.g., Eccles 2:24-26 and 5:18-20). In contrast to the ceaseless striving evident in the human world, "whatever God does endures for ever" (Eccles 14:13 RSV), so that we are enjoined to "consider the work of God" (Eccles 7:13 RSV).

Equally recurrent (31 times) is the image translated "vanity" in some English versions but meaning "vapor" or "breath" in the original. As a quality of life under the sun, this image connotes emptiness, insubstantiality, elusiveness and brevity. A related image is the spectacle of "striving after wind" (e.g., Eccles 2:17).

To make the picture of life under the sun palpable to our imaginations, the writer repeatedly roots us in the world of elemental nature. We move rather continuously in a world of sun and *wind, *sheep and *vineyards, *sowing and *harvesting, *cloud and *water. Human activity has this same elemental quality, as we hear about being born and dying, toil and sleep, war and peace, worshiping and looking after one's possessions. Within this cycle of elemental human activity, special attention is given to the triad of *eating, *drinking and toiling. This imagery appears in both the despairing "under the sun" passages and in the positive, God-centered passages (e.g., Eccles 2:24-25). The anti-escapist implication is important: the God-centered life does not substitute another world for this one, but it brings a transcendent system of values into the earthly sphere.

The image of *appetite, though mentioned only a few times, is another informing metaphor for the book. In particular it is the voice of unsatisfied desire: "The *eye is not satisfied with seeing" (1:8), "his eyes are never satisfied" (4:8), "yet his appetite is not satisfied" (6:7).

Part of the modernity of this book lies in the space it gives to acquisitiveness, conceived chiefly in urban terms, as we find repeated references to acquiring, *building, commerce, money, goods, possessions and even investment (Eccles 11:1-2). Contributing equally to the modern spirit of Ecclesiastes is the motif of *pleasure and enjoyment. Sometimes this motif takes the form of searching for an elusive enjoyment. But enjoyment is also commended in the positive passages (e.g., Eccles 9:8) and is even declared the gift of God (Eccles 1:25). The ultimate tragedy for the preacher is not being able to enjoy life's good things (Eccles 6:2, 3, 6). The mere light of the sun is said to be "pleasant for the eyes" (Eccles 11:7), and a major message of Ecclesiastes is that one does not have to look far to find enjoyment.

Overall, we should note the dynamic nature of the imagery of Ecclesiastes. Things are constantly in flux as we move through the book. The cycles of life are prominent. People are very busy ordering their affairs and searching for satisfaction. The survey of social classes and activities is very thorough despite the brevity of the book. One of the great appeals of Ecclesiastes is the way it touches all the bases of life. Perhaps the breathtaking energy that prevails in the world of the book partly explains the power of the passage near the end that describes the physiological symptoms of *old age, ending in *death (Eccles 12:1-7).

See also FIND, FOUND; GOOD LIFE, THE; QUEST; SOLOMON; TRANSIENCE; WISDOM.

EDEN. *See* GARDEN.

EGYPT

From the very beginning of the biblical narrative, Egypt is presented as an imposing place of abundance and power. Although the relationship between the people of God and Egypt is sometimes ambiguous, more often than not, contact with that ancient empire and imitation of its ways are evaluated as negative and self-destructive.

Soon after his call, *Abram travels to Egypt to escape famine. Although he is blessed materially during his sojourn there, nevertheless Abram deceives *Pharaoh out of fear for his life and is forced to leave Egypt in disgrace (Gen 12:10-20). Because of its rich fertility the land of Egypt is associated with Eden, yet at the same time it is connected with *Sodom and Gomorrah (Gen 13:10). Here again, it symbolizes a *tempting place in which there might be both material gain and personal demise.

The story of *Joseph reflects this ambiguity in a more subtle manner. Joseph is sold by his brothers into servitude in Egypt, and he begins his stay there in charge of Potiphar's house. Temptation appears in the form of attempted sexual seduction, but Joseph maintains loyalty to his master and to his God. He is unjustly thrown into *prison, yet with divine help he interprets Pharaoh's *dreams, is released from prison and is elevated to the position of vizier (Gen 39—41). Egypt is once more a place of refuge from *famine, and Jacob's sons and their families are sovereignly placed in a bountiful region for sustenance and self-preservation (Gen 42—47). Ironically, however, Joseph's economic policies help create the absolute authority (Gen 47:20-26) that another Pharaoh, who does not remember him, will utilize to so cruelly mistreat the people of God (Ex 1—5).

After the Exodus, Egypt becomes a negative symbol in two ways. On the one hand, Egypt represents *bondage and oppression. Israel's servitude is mentioned on a number of occasions in the legal corpus as a reminder not to forget that experience of abuse. God's people are not to treat the alien and the unfortunate in their midst as their taskmasters in Egypt had treated them. Israel is to be a different kind of place: one of *refuge, grace and social concern (e.g., Ex 23:9; Lev 19:34; Deut 5:12-15; 15:12-15; 16:9-12; 24:17-22). Years later, in a biting social critique, Amos will rhetorically call to Egypt to bear witness to the oppression within Israel: the injustice of the people of God has led them to become like their ancient victimizers (Amos 3:1-2, 9-10; 8:8). In the NT, *Jerusalem is figuratively equated with Egypt (and Sodom; cf. Gen 13:10) because of its violence toward the Messiah and the two witnesses (Rev 11:8).

With the foundation of the monarchy, Egypt becomes a symbol in another sense as well. Egypt embodies the political and military temptation to turn to idolatrous superpowers instead of to Yahweh in times of acute national crisis. Several prophetic texts denounce this lack of faith. For Isaiah, Egypt's shade cannot provide protection, but only shame and defeat (Is 30:1-5; cf. 20:1-6; 31:1-7); Ezekiel likens Israel and Judah to two promiscuous *sisters, who go whoring after various empires, one of which is Egypt (Ezek 23); Hosea mocks Israel as a senseless *bird that flits from one nation to another in search of aid (Hos 7:11-12). The envoy of Assyria ridicules the ineffective help of the Egyptians as a splintered reed that pierces and wounds the hand that grabs it (2 Kings 18:19-25; cf. Is 36:4-10). Jeremiah decries the flight to Egypt after the destruction of Jerusalem by those who do not trust in Yahweh's protection and provision, and he decrees judgment on those who move there (Jer 42—43).

Lastly, the defeat of Rahab the sea-*monster (an echo of the Near Eastern tale of the struggle between Baal and Yam) is occasionally a metaphor for Yahweh's victory over Egypt (Is 30:7; Ezek 29:3-5; Ps 74:13-14, 87:10 [Heb 11]; see Divine Warrior). Yet in the future this very same Rahab will one day recognize Yahweh as Lord (Ps 87:4 [Heb 5]). This eschatological hope finds an echo in Isaiah 19:18-25.

See also BONDAGE AND FREEDOM; EXODUS, SECOND EXODUS; JOSEPH THE PATRIARCH; MOSES; PHARAOH.

BIBLIOGRAPHY. N. Frye, *The Great Code: The Bible and Literature* (Boston: Routledge and Kegan Paul, 1983).

ELDER CHILD, ELDER SIBLING

The position of the eldest *child conjures up images of *blessing, favoritism and a double *inheritance—all the benefits of primogeniture (Deut 21:17). Indeed, the firstborn child in biblical times is given a privileged status in the family. Isaac intends to give Esau the *birthright blessing despite God's words to the contrary (Gen 27:1-4). Leah, not Rachel, is given first in marriage (Gen 29:26). The greatest disaster that God can work upon Egypt is the destruction of the eldest child in each household (Ex 12:29-30). God claims the firstborn for himself but accepts the tribe of Levi in exchange (Ex 13:11-16; Num 3:12-13; Num 8:16-18).

Yet not unexpectedly in the economy of God's work, these expectations for the eldest child are frequently reversed (*see* Younger Child). The first genealogy in Genesis 5 recounts the lineage, not from father to eldest son, but from father to chosen son (e.g., Seth, not *Cain). The birthright is given to Isaac, not Ishmael (Gen 17:18-19); to *Jacob, not *Esau (Gen 27:28-29); to Judah, not Reuben (Gen 49:3-4). *Joseph is displeased when Jacob crosses his hands and gives the greater blessing to Ephraim, the younger son, rather than to Manasseh, the older (Gen 49:17-18). Quite apart from considerations of birthright, the OT rings the changes on the motif of the younger who achieves precedence over an older sibling: Rachel is preferred before her older sister Leah; Joseph is the son of destiny rather than his older brothers; *David is chosen king even though he is the youngest son in the family; *Abel receives God's favor rather than Cain; Saul's daughter Michal is preferred to her older sister Merab; *Moses overshadows his older brother Aaron. The heroic deliverer Gideon too is youngest in his family (Judg 6:15).

In the parable of the prodigal son, Jesus switches attention at the end to the peevish elder brother who refuses to rejoice at his younger sibling's return. In a pointed rejoinder to the Pharisees, who instigated the spate of parables in Luke 15 with their criticisms of Jesus' sinful dinner partners, Jesus casts his critics in the role of the carping elder brother.

On the other hand, eldest children are not unmitigated disasters. Although one line of characters represent the disappointment of failed expectations, another group consistently points to the true elder son, Christ, the firstborn among many children (Rom 8:29; Col 1:15; Heb 1:6). God names the entire nation of *Israel as his firstborn (Ex 4:22). Similarly, Samson and Samuel bring redemption to their people, albeit imperfectly, foreshadowing Jesus, who not only rejoices with the Father when the prodigal son returns but goes himself into the pigpen to rescue his younger siblings.

See also BROTHER; FIRST; SISTER; YOUNGER CHILD, YOUNGER SIBLING.

BIBLIOGRAPHY. F. E. Greenspahn, *When Brothers Dwell Together: The Preeminence of Younger Siblings in the Hebrew Bible* (Oxford: Oxford University Press, 1994).

ENAMELED IMAGERY. *See* HARD, HARDEN, HARDNESS; HEAVEN; JEWELS AND PRECIOUS STONES; PERMANENCE

ENCOMIUM

The encomium is a lyric piece, whether in poetry or prose, that is written in praise of either an abstract quality or a general character type. Originating in ancient cultures and practiced with zest during the English Renaissance, the form is actually universal. Its practitioners have followed a set of five main formulas with almost technical precision. The motifs are these: (1) introduction to the subject of *praise, sometimes including a definition of the subject; (2) the distinguished ancestry of the subject, or "praise by what kind he came of"; (3) a catalog of the praiseworthy acts and qualities of the subject; (4) the indispensable or superior nature of the subject, sometimes accompanied by comparison to lesser subjects and/or a listing of the rewards that accompany the object of praise; (5) a conclusion urging the reader to emulate the subject.

The canon of biblical encomia includes several psalms that praise the godly person (Ps 1; 15; 112; 128) and Psalm 119 praising God's *law. Two passages in Proverbs employ the standard motifs to praise *wisdom (Prov 3:13-20; 8), and the book as a whole ends with a famous acrostic encomium that celebrates the ideal wife (Prov 31:10-31). In the NT the *Christ hymn belongs to the genre of the encomium. The *Beatitudes paint a composite portrait of the ideal follower of Christ, accompanied by a catalog of the rewards that such a person will receive. In addition, two famous prose encomia take moral or spiritual qualities for their subject—love in 1 Corinthians 13 and faith in Hebrews 11. The song of the *suffering servant in Isaiah 52:13—53:12 is a parody of the conventional encomium, inasmuch as it partly reverses the usual motifs and in effect praises the subject for qualities that the world at large would consider ignomious—grounds not for praise but for rejection.

See also CHRIST HYMN; PRAISE PSALMS.

ENCOUNTER, DIVINE-HUMAN

The divine-human encounter, familiar to ancient epic and mythological literature, is one of the most recurrent "type scenes" in the Bible, whose central message revolves around the meeting of *God and people in either reconciliation or *judgment. While occasionally these encounters are initiated by the human party (on the premise, "Draw near to God and he will draw near to you" [Jas 4:8 RSV]), the

customary pattern is that God initiates the encounter. An aura of the *holy or numinous permeates the resulting encounter. The key ingredient in these encounters is the intrusion of a word or appearance from a supernatural realm into the earthly sphere. Sometimes an *angel is God's agent in the encounter; on other occasions the divine appearance is apparently direct. In either case a tremendous sense of authority accompanies the one who appears from the transcendent realm. Permeated with a sense of momentousness that is overpowering, the human thus encountered responds with either conversation or action or both.

The most direct and vivid encounters appear in the earliest books of the Bible, where face-to-face dialogues are common. The pattern begins in Genesis 3, where God appears as a parent and judge, ferreting out the truth from his reluctant children, pronouncing judgment and promising redemption (Gen 3:8-23). Subsequently God appears to *Cain to reason with him and pronounce judgment on him (Gen 4:6-15) and to Noah in the events surrounding the *flood (Gen 6—9). Beginning with the call of Abraham (Gen 12:1-9), God's encounters with the patriarchs *Abraham, Isaac and *Jacob (but not *Joseph) punctuate the action of Genesis (Gen 13:14-17; 15:1-16; 17:1-22; 18; 22; 26:24-25; 28:10-22; 32; 35). These encounters are mainly restatements of the covenant, and although usually cast as conversations, they actually carry the force of a divine oracle.

A similar pattern pervades the epic of the *Exodus. Here too the series begins with the call of the *hero (*Moses) in the story of the *burning bush (Ex 3:1—4:17). When Moses plays the role of reluctant prophet of God's messages of judgment, God appears to him as instructor and coach (Ex 6:1-13; 7:8, 14, 19; 8:1-5). After the march of the nation has begun, God repeatedly speaks to Moses (usually in crisis situations) to instruct him in the next move, and sometimes in either vindication of Moses (Num 12; 16) or in judgment of him (Num 20:10-13). The most dramatic divine-human encounters of the exodus occur with the giving of the *law at Mt. *Sinai (Ex 19:9-25; 33:1-34:35). The motif of the divine-human encounter receives its most explicit form when we read that "the LORD used to speak to Moses face to face, as a man speaks to his friend" (Ex 33:11 RSV). Equally important as a summary of the essence of such encounters is the detail that Moses' face shone after his encounters with God, requiring Moses to wear a *veil, which he took off when he "went in before the LORD to speak with him" (Ex 34:29-35). Moses' life ends with an encounter with God on Mt. Pisgah (Deut 34).

The life of Moses' successor, Joshua, is likewise permeated with divine-human encounters with the formula "the LORD said to Joshua" appearing a dozen times. In these encounters, God appears chiefly as instructor in how to conduct the affairs of the nation in their conquest of the Promised Land. The pattern continues into the book of *Judges, where highlights include God's call and equipping of Gideon (Judg 6:11—7:14) and the appearance of angel to announce the birth of *Samson (Judg 13). The books of Samuel contain similar encounters, beginning with God's calling the youthful Samuel (1 Sam 3) and continuing with the life of *David, where Nathan serves as the agent of God's encounter (2 Sam 7; 12:1-15). God's encounters with the kings of Israel and Judah come through his spokesmen, the prophets.

God's encounters with his *prophets are a staple of prophetic literature. The formula that "the word of LORD came" to a prophet (or variants such as, "Thus says the LORD") is so numerous as to make specific reference superfluous. Of special note, though, are scenes of prophets' *calling (Is 6:1-8; Jer 1; Ezek 1-3; Amos 7:15; Jon 1:1-2; 3:1-4). The story of Elijah is not only punctuated by the motif of God's commanding his prophet to undertake specific tasks, but also enlivened by the wilderness scene in which God appears to Elijah as he sits under a broom tree and provides him with food and water. This is followed by a full-fledged encounter scene in which God appears to Elijah in a cave in the form of a still small voice (1 Kings 19:4-18). The latter episode underscores a common motif in which God strengthens his prophets by his encounters with them.

No divine-human encounter is more dramatic and vivid than the voice from the *whirlwind that provides the climax to the book of Job (38-41:6). In a barrage of rhetorical questions, God turns the tables on Job (who has tried to bring God to trial) and asks Job a series of questions that demonstrate God's superior knowledge and power. While seeming to focus on God's transcendence, the two speeches also paradoxically show God's immanence—his closeness to his creation and the wonder of his providential management of nature. In keeping with the two-person nature of divine-human encounters, Job responds with humility, contrition, repentance and worship (Job 40:3-5; 42:1-6).

In the NT the incarnation of Jesus is itself a prolonged divine encounter with the human race, as John intimates in the *christological hymn with which he begins his Gospel (Jn 1:1-18). Beyond this general pattern we can note that the encounter story is a prominent subgenre of the Gospels. The stories in which Jesus confronts Zacchaeus (Lk 19:1-10) and the Samaritan woman at the *well (Jn 4:1-42) can perhaps be taken as prototypes of a numerous class of encounter stories in the Gospels. Of special note also is the story of the *conversion of Paul (Acts 9:1-9).

What is the meaning of the biblical motif of the divine-human encounter? Above all, it is the paradigm of the Bible's view of reality, the heart of which is that God communicates to people and enters their lives providentially and redemptively as well as in judgment. People are not left as orphans in the universe. They are instead the recipients of a divine word and of divine provision for their earthly and eternal needs. In addition to the specific narrative archetype of the divine-human encounter, the Bible itself possesses the quality of an encounter. Its claim upon its readers to respond is coercive in a way that ordinary literature is not. The Bible presupposes response as a condition of reading it.

See also BURNING BUSH; MOSES; PROPHET, PROPHETESS; WHIRLWIND.

END TIMES

The imagery of end times refers to a specific category of *apocalyptic images of the future. For purposes of this article the designation "end times" excludes other related topics, including *afterlife, *heaven, *hell, millennium (whose position relative to the end of history is never completely clarified in the Bible) and *second coming. While "end" here refers primarily to the end of human history, we need to note that NT eschatology makes this timeline more explicit than does OT prophecy, which contains visions of something terminal that may be closer to the writer's time than the end of human history.

The Bible's images of the end are built around a cluster of time images. One of these is the image of "latter days" (Jer 23:20; 30:24; Ezek 38:16; Jas 3:5) or "last day(s)" (Jn 6:39-40, 44, 54; 11:24; 12:48; 2 Tim 3:1; Jas 5:3; 2 Pet 3:3). Another motif is "the end" (Dan 8:17; 9:26; 10:14; 11:35, 40; 12:4, 9, 13; Mt 10:22; 13:39-40, 49; 24:3, 6, 13-14; 28:20; etc.). Yet another image is a coming *Day of the Lord (two dozen references). While the details of sequence are not always clear in these references, they establish an important aspect of the Bible's view of history, namely, that it is moving in linear fashion to an appointed consummation.

Jesus' Imagery of the End. Jesus' Olivet Discourse in Matthew 24—25 (cf. Mk 13; Lk 21) can serve as a blueprint to the Bible's images of the end. Underlying the images and events is a discernible timeline, indicated by the word pattern of "then" and "immediately after" (RSV). The discourse itself is occasioned by the disciples' question, "What will be the sign of your coming and of the close of the age?" (Mt 24:3). Jesus proceeds to outline a discernible sequence in which some of the phases may overlap. It begins with the appearance of false christs and an era of *warfare, *earthquakes and *famines, all of which are "but the beginning" of the sequence (Mt 24:5-8). "Then" will come a time of tribulation for Christians, accompanied by false *prophets who will mislead many and by the worldwide proclamation of the gospel, "and then the end will come" (Mt 24:9-14). "Then" will come a time of "great tribulation" and the appearance of false christs and false prophets who work signs and wonders (Mt. 24:21-28). "Immediately after" the tribulation there will be cataclysmic destruction of natural forces as the sun is darkened, the *moon fails to give its light and the *stars fall from heaven (Mt 24:29). "Then" the sign of the *Son of man will appear in heaven, and Christ will send his *angels to gather the elect from the earth (Mt 24:30-31). This is followed in Jesus' discourse by a series of parables that have as their common point a final judgment of all people (Mt 24:32—25:30), climaxed by the judgment scene that is prefaced by the statement, "When the Son of man comes in his glory . . . then he will sit on his glorious throne" (Mt 25:31-46 RSV).

Here, then, is an important repository of biblical images of the end. It is a nightmare vision of cosmic collapse, an equally violent disruption among people and nations, persecution for believers and spiritual deceitfulness and power by evil forces. The only positive note for Christians is the possibility of heroic endurance ("he who endures to the end will be saved" [Mt 24:13; Mk 13:13 RSV]) and the certainty that at the very end Christ will appear as divine rescuer.

The Book of Revelation. The book of *Revelation follows the same events as Jesus' outlines in the Olivet Discourse, elaborated in fuller detail and presented in a cyclic manner in which we retread the same territory, though with increasing intensification as we move through the book. Even if we interpret the book of Revelation as portraying recurrent patterns of fallen history, it seems incontrovertible that the book also portrays in symbolic manner what will happen at the end of human history.

One prominent image pattern is cataclysmic natural upheaval and decay. Two complementary motifs drive the point home—sudden cataclysm and what we might informally call "the slow burn." On the cataclysmic side we encounter a continuous pattern of earthquakes, the sun becoming black and the moon like blood, the stars falling from the sky, mountains and islands being removed from their place, hail falling, and the earth and sky fleeing away. Balancing this are pictures of a gradual process of environmental distress: *famine, pestilence, a third of the *earth and *trees burnt up, all green *grass burnt up, a third of sea creatures dying, a third of the *rivers made bitter and people scorched by *fire and heat.

Disaster in nature has as its counterpart disaster among people and nations. *Warfare is one image of social disintegration, as in the increasingly sinister sequence of four *horse visions (Rev 6:1-8) or the destructive forces that are unloosed at the river Euphrates (Rev 9:13-19). More prevalent than war is the image of *persecution of believers by forces of evil (Rev 6:11; 11:7-10; 12:17; 13:5-18) and images of *torture (e.g., Rev 9:1-11). A related image pattern is the human toll that all this natural disaster takes on people in the form of pain and *suffering (Rev 16:8-11, 21).

While such events as cataclysmic upheaval in nature and violence among people might be a picture of the earthly and human sphere left to its own disintegration, the book of Revelation views these developments on earth as part of a process of divine *judgment against a wicked human race. At this point the imagery of the two spheres—the heavenly and the earthly—becomes important. The book of Revelation presupposes a two-tiered universe (or three-tiered, if we add hell) in which reality is divided between an unseen heavenly realm and the earth. The general pattern of Revelation is to shuttle back and forth between these and for events to be visited upon earth from a heavenly source, as though they are being stage-managed by a higher power (e.g., Rev 7:3; 8:7-12; 9:13-15; 16:1-21). Indeed, the tumultuous events at the end of history are explicitly presented as the outworking of the wrath of God (Rev 14:9-11; 15:1), and the events can therefore be interpreted as images of divine punishment against sinners.

This, in turn, ties into the motif of angelic and *demonic actors in the final events of history. On one side we find an abundance of references in Revelation to angelic agents who are very busy carrying out God's revelation and judgment and protecting the followers of the *Lamb. On the other side are demonic figures—a dragon who is identified with *Satan, beasts from the *sea and from the earth, and "demonic spirits" (Rev 16:14). The main image pattern associated with both types of supernatural creatures is supernatural power over people. There is a major contrast between the revelation or unveiling in which the angels consistently engage and the elaborate powers of deception associated with the forces of demonic evil.

According to the visions of Revelation, the end times will be characterized by a great spiritual struggle between good and evil. This *battle will involve masses of both people and supernatural creatures. Thus we read variously about a war in heaven (Rev 12:7-12); the dragon's war against the offspring of the woman, the church (Rev 12:17); the beast from the sea making war on the saints (Rev 13:7); the assembling of the kings of the earth at Armageddon (Rev 16:16); the *armies of earth arrayed against Christ (Rev 19:19); and a final gathering of the nations as they "marched up over the broad earth and surrounded the camp of the saints and the beloved city" (Rev 20:7-9).

While all of these motifs characterize the end times generally, at the *very* end of history stands a final judgment, a time of transition in which evildoers descend to hell and believers enter an eternity of bliss in *heaven. In Jesus' Olivet Discourse this judgment is pictured in a series of parables and in the awe-inspiring judgment scene in which God divides the *sheep from the *goats. Other images of final judgment occur at memorable junctures in the book of Revelation—in the vision of the winepress of God's wrath (Rev 14:17-20), in the doom of *Babylon (Rev 14:18), in the casting of the two demonic beasts into the lake of fire (Rev 19:20), in the scene of the great white throne (Rev 20:11-14).

Other New Testament Images. Other NT images fill out the general picture provided by the Olivet Discourse and the book of Revelation. While some eschatological passages depict a gradual process of disintegration, a complementary motif stresses the unexpected suddenness with which events at the very end will happen. Thus Jesus speaks of the Son's coming suddenly (Mk 13:36) and of the final day coming "upon you suddenly like a snare" (Lk 21:34 RSV), while Paul speaks of "sudden destruction" (1 Thess 5:3). The most frequent NT image is that of a *thief that comes unexpectedly in the night (Mt 24:43; Lk 12:39; 1 Thess 5:2, 4; 2 Pet 3:10; Rev 3:3; 16:15).

Scattered NT passages also fill out the picture of the spread of evil in the final days of human history. One of the most haunting images is that of "the mystery of lawlessness" and "the lawless one" that will appear (2 Thess 2:7-9). Earlier in that same passage Paul speaks of "the man of lawlessness" as "the son of perdition, who opposes and exalts himself against every so-called god or object of worship" (2 Thess 2:3-4 RSV). The picture that emerges is of a total collapse of moral standards as society preys upon itself and creates a totally secular entity. John gives us a similar image in the figure of the *antichrist(s) (1 Jn 2:18, 22; 2 Jn 1:7), associated like the lawless one with spiritual deception of people.

Life in the end times receives composite treatment in two epistolary passages. One is 1 Thessalonians 5, where believers are commanded to live differently from their surrounding culture, which is characterized by the imagery of *darkness and debauchery. The other is 2 Peter 3, a small classic on how to live in the last days. Here the degenerate cultural situation is described as a time of scoffing about the return of Christ and of people "following their own passions" (2 Pet 3:3).

A final striking image of the end is the picture Peter paints of the final conflagration. Nothing in Revelation is quite as decisive as this picture of the very end of earthly existence: "The heavens will pass away with a loud noise, and the elements will be dissolved with fire, and the earth and the works that are upon it will be burned up. . . . The heavens will be kindled and dissolved, and the elements will melt with fire!" (2 Pet 3:10, 12 RSV).

Old Testament Premonitions. With the NT imagery to guide us, it is obvious that OT prophetic visions use the same image patterns. What is not always clear is whether the OT visions predict *the* end or simply an end to an empire or historical era. Two prophetic books may be taken as exemplary of visions of the final end.

The second half of *Daniel is an *apocalyptic vision of the future in which images of the end figure prominently. Couched in the strange imagery of beasts and *horns, the general pattern resembles NT images of the end. One motif is that of empires vying for power, conquering and succeeding each other, exerting themselves against God. Images of calamity, divine wrath and military destruction are pervasive: "they shall fall by sword and flame, by captivity and plunder" (Dan 11:33 RSV); "there shall be a time of trouble, such as never has been since there was a nation till that time" (Dan 12:1 RSV).

The prophecy of Zephaniah covers similar territory. It is a nightmarish vision of God's sweeping away everything from the earth (Zeph 1:2). The slaughter of judgment that God has prepared is ironically pictured as a grand "sacrifice" to which God has "consecrated his guests" (Zeph 1:7). We read further that "a day of wrath is that day, a day of distress and anguish, a day of ruin and devastation, a day of darkness and gloom, a day of clouds and thick darkness" (Zeph 1:15 RSV). Imagery of torture and mutilation is present in the picture of people's blood "poured out like dust, and their flesh like dung" (Zeph 1:17). God will make "sudden end" of all the inhabitants of the earth (Zeph 1:18). Productive land will be transformed into a desert (Zeph 2:13-15); battlements will be "in ruins" and streets "laid waste" (Zeph 3:6).

Summary. While the Bible's apocalyptic images of the future mingle pessimism and hope, the hope belongs to events that either transcend or follow the end of earthly history. The end times themselves portray the proverbial doomsday. For unbelievers there is no hope at all. For believers the only hope is that of heroic endurance to the end and intervening rescue by Christ to a heavenly reward.

Two main principles underlie the Bible's images of the end. One is their cosmic scope. Prophecies of the end times are not stories of individuals but of natural forces and nations, both political and spiritual. Events at the end are happening on a huge scale, creating an impression of a stampede of masses toward a terrible destruction. The second pattern is that the images of the end are predominantly images of terror—a terror made all the more forceful by their power or hugeness (e.g., earthquakes, floods, invading armies, demonic forces) and the suddenness with which they inflict destruction on the earth. The major lessons that these visions of the end teach are the predictable spread of evil, the certainty of God's wrath and judgment against evil, the need for endurance (Rev 13:10) and a stance of preparedness for what is coming (Mt 24:25).

See also AFTERLIFE; ANTICHRIST; APOCALYPTIC VISIONS OF THE FUTURE; COSMOLOGY; DAY, DAY OF THE LORD; DIVINE WARRIOR; JUDGMENT; KINGDOM OF GOD; MILLENNIUM; REVELATION, BOOK OF.

BIBLIOGRAPHY. R. J. Bauckham, *The Theology of the Book of Revelation* (Cambridge: Cambridge University Press, 1993); K. E. Brower and M. W. Elliott, eds., *'The Reader Must Understand': Eschatology in Bible and Theology* (Leicester: Apollos, 1997); G. B. Caird, *The Language and Imagery of the Bible* (Grand Rapids: Eerdmans, 1997 [1980]); J. B. Green, *How to Read Prophecy* (Downers Grove, IL: InterVarsity Press, 1984).

ENDANGERED ANCESTRESS

The close proximity in *Genesis of three episodes that center on the abduction or possible abduction of a Hebrew patriarch's wife has given rise to the image of the "endangered ancestress." These incidents, recorded in Genesis 12:10-20; 20:1-18 and 26:1-11, follow a very distinctive plot. The patriarch and his wife move to a new location. Fearful that the men of this region will kill him in order to have his wife, the patriarch persuades her to pretend that she is his sister. On the first two occasions, involving *Abraham and Sarah, the plan backfires. The patriarch's wife is taken first by the Pharaoh of Egypt and then by Abimelech, the king of Gerar. Both times God intervenes, restoring Sarah to Abraham. On the third occasion, concerning Isaac and Rebekah, the ruse is uncovered by the foreign ruler before any abduction occurs.

Although these incidents are frequently viewed as placing the ancestress in jeopardy, it is the continuation of the line or "seed" through whom God's blessing will be mediated to the nations of the earth that is really endangered. Significantly, in the second episode, which comes immediately prior to the birth of Isaac, the narrator emphasizes that Abimelech did not touch Sarah (Gen 20:4-7). The reader is left in no doubt that Abraham is the father of Isaac.

Some commentators have viewed the wife/sister incidents as praising the sagacity of the patriarchs. On the contrary, these incidents reveal a failure to trust God for protection. In spite of the ingenuity of Abraham's plan, he fails to protect his wife Sarah. Only God's intervention resolves the complication created by the ruse. Although Pharaoh and Abimelech are not exonerated for taking the patriarch's wife in the first two incidents, it is noteworthy that on the third occasion, Abimelech highlights the potential danger of the patriarch's deception: "What is this you have done to us? One of the people might well have slept with your wife, and you would have brought guilt upon us" (Gen 26:10 NRSV). In light of these factors the incidents were clearly never intended to applaud the deceptive behavior of the patriarchs.

See also WOMAN, IMAGES OF.

ENEMY

The world of the Bible is populated with a wide variety of enemies. If a first-time reader of the Bible were to begin with the thought that a "religious" book would be filled with sublime spirituality, remote from the realities of human existence, they would surely be surprised. If we were to extract the "enemies" from all of the Bible's narratives, prophecies, psalms, proverbs, Gospels and letters, the text would be riddled with gaps and the story would be reduced to nonsense. Enemies are a problem for which God provides the solution.

Because much of the Bible is the story of *Israel, most of the enemies we encounter are enemies of Israel. Israel's enemies are primarily the "nations," ethnic and national groupings who appear under various names but in general blend into one category of those who are not Israel, the *Gentiles. They are *idolatrous and opposed to Israel and Israel's God.

Even where the enemies are personal, such as the ones we often encounter in the book of Psalms, they are reminiscent of Israel's national enemies. In sketching the profile of enemies in the Bible, we can effectively speak of both national and personal enemies together. The more dramatic distinction lies between human enemies and spiritual enemies, and the latter being more fully developed in the NT.

Enemy Behavior. How does Israel view its enemy? The enemy is hateful (Deut 30:7), full of insults (Ps 55:12), *curses (Num 23:11; 24:10), taunts (Deut 32:27) and slanders (Satan, 1 Tim 5:14). He gloats when he *triumphs (Lam 2:17; Mic 7:8) and is full of braggadocio (Ex 15:9; Ps 13:4).

The enemy inflicts *suffering and distress on Israel (Deut 28:53, 55, 57). He encircles *Jerusalem and lays siege (1 Kings 8:37; Lk 19:43), destroys and tramples down the Lord's sanctuary (Ps 74:3; Is 63:18), plunders Jerusalem's treasure (Lam 1:10) and penetrates the most holy place of the *temple to create the "abomination of desolation" (e.g., Dan 9:27). Then, having overcome Jerusalem, he boldly cries out, "Aha! The ancient heights have become our possession" (Ezek 36:2 NIV).

The approach of a great enemy is a fearsome thing, even when viewed from the ramparts of a *walled city. In Isaiah 10:28-34 the approach of an enemy (probably Assyrian) army is measured by an itinerary that draws ever closer to Jerusalem—day by day, encampment by encampment, fear upon terror, they finally arrive at Jerusalem's gates. Enemies overrun the land (Amos 3:11), disturbing the normal course of daily life, business and travel, so that even the main roadways are abandoned (Judg 5:6-7; Zech 8:10). An enemy can be in an uproar (Ps 74:23) and seem like "waves" that "rage like great waters" (Jer 51:55 NIV). The enemy *pursues (Ps 143:3; Hos 8:3) and overtakes (Ps 7:5). He has the power to crush (Ps 143:3), defeat (1 Kings 8:33), oppress (Num 10:9; Ps 42:9) and persecute (Deut 30:7). Daniel has a vision depicting enemy empires as fearsome hybrid *monsters arising from the *sea and bringing awful suffering upon the people of God (Dan 7:1-8, 19-25). A victorious enemy extracts a price by demanding tribute (Ps 89:22) or enslaving Israel and taking her into *exile.

Enemies abound in the psalms. Frequently they are personal rather than national enemies, but the imagery is not greatly different. The enemy is full of hate (Ps 25:19; 69:4), hurls insults (Ps 55:12), *persecutes (Ps 9:13), conspires and imagines evil (Ps 41:5, 7), seeks *revenge (Ps 44:16), pursues and overtakes (Ps 7:5), surrounds (Ps 17:9) and attacks (Ps 27:2), threatens to take one's life (Ps 64:1), and brings on social shame (Ps 31:11; 69:19) or the darkness of despair (Ps 143:3). In the case of the psalms of *David, the line between national and personal enemies can be thin indeed, for Israel's enemies are easily imaged as David's own enemies (e.g., Ps 18). It is as if there is a common stock of "enemy" imagery that is rooted in the world of tribal, ethnic and national hostility but is equally applicable to enemies "within the walls."

The NT places its emphasis on spiritual enemies, though these have their precedent in the *monsters of the OT. These are the "cosmic" enemies that are imaged in the mythological symbolism of Israel's neighbors. The names are varied: Leviathan, Rahab and the dragon, or sea monster (see Cosmology; Monsters). In the NT the chief spiritual enemy is *Satan, or the devil, who prowls like a roaring *lion, "looking for someone to devour" (1 Pet 5:8 NIV). In Jesus' parable of the wheat and the weeds (Mt 13:24-30), it is the enemy (the devil, Mt 13:39) who sows weeds among the wheat of the kingdom of God. Ephesians speaks of the "evil one" who shoots fiery darts at believers, and the nefarious "rulers," "authorities," and "cosmic powers of this present darkness" (NRSV) mount a formidable opposition that must be resisted by the armor and weaponry of God (Eph 6:10-17). In Romans 6—8 we encounter a trilateral alliance of spiritual powers: sin, flesh and death, with an unwilling accomplice—the law (see Romans). And in 1 Corinthians, death is the "final enemy": "the sting of death is sin and the power of sin is the law" (1 Cor 15:56 NRSV). But in Revelation we see the cosmic enemies of the OT resurfacing in the "great dragon" (Rev 12) and the "beast coming out of the sea" (Rev 13). These evoke potent and satanic forces of evil that oppose God's purposes in history.

The Divine Enemy. Since he is the deliverer and defender of Israel, we expect to find Yahweh described as an enemy to Israel's enemies (Ex 23:22). But he can also be an enemy to Israel's disobedient king Saul (1 Sam 28:16). Even more striking is the turnabout image of Yahweh as Israel's enemy (Is 63:10). This is the consequence of Israel's breaking covenant with Yahweh. *Blessing is exchanged for *curse; deliverance is exchanged for wrath; triumph is exchanged for defeat. Israel, despite its status as the people God has chosen to dwell amongst, is not inviolable (Jer 7:4-15). God arms himself, strings his bow (Lam 2:4) and strikes Jerusalem "as an enemy would" (Jer 30:14). Jerusalem laments in anguish, "The Lord is like an enemy; he has swallowed up Israel" (Lam 2:4-5 NIV).

In these moments Israel's enemies become the armies and weapons of God, who allows Israel's enemies to defeat, rule over or take disobedient Israel into exile (Lev 26:16-44). God "delivers over" or "abandons" Israel to her enemies (1 Kings 8:46; Neh 9:27, 28). Deuteronomy 28:25 evokes a memorable scene of Israel's defeat at the hand of enemies: "You will come at them from one direction but flee from them in seven (NIV).

On the personal level, Job thinks God considers him an enemy (Job 13:24; 33:10) and is assailing him as an army would: "His anger burns against me; he counts me among his enemies. His troops advance in force; they build a siege ramp against me and encamp around my tent" (Job 19:12).

Paul develops this motif by speaking of humans apart from Christ as indeed enemies of God. But here the emphasis is on the enmity of the human heart as contrasted with the love that God extends toward his human enemies. The Colossian believers are reminded that they were formerly alienated from God and enemies in their minds because of their evil behavior (Col 1:21). And the wonder of the gospel is that while we were still God's enemies, he *reconciled us to himself through the death of his Son (Rom 5:10).

God's Defeat of Enemies. The main plot line of the biblical story is God's defeat of evil and the establishment of a new *creation. The final enemy and embodiment of evil is Satan, a rebel against the divine order, and one who must be defeated. With him no peaceful reconciliation is possible. The historical enemies of Israel are those who align themselves against God's purposes and against God's design in choosing Israel as his own people. Wittingly or unwittingly, they are accomplices with the ultimate enemy, and this spiritual reality is expressed in the OT by speaking of the nations' *gods. Israel's warfare against the nations is a serious matter in the course of redemptive history, and the conquest of the nations of Canaan has its basis not only in the divine promise of a land to *Abraham and his descendants, but also in the spiritual reality that the sin of these nations eventually will have "reached its full measure" (Gen 15:16). The nations that inhabit the Promised Land do not simply happen to be in the wrong place at the wrong time as Israel enters. The biblical story assumes that the day of judgment has arrived for these nations. In this sense they are Yahweh's enemies first and Israel's enemies second. But their immediate role is always determined by the sovereign will of God. The nations of Canaan, as well as the great empires of the biblical world (Assyria, Babylon, Egypt), may readily be used by God as a means of disciplining and bringing judgment upon Israel.

The imagery employed to speak of God's defeat of these enemies is varied, though much of it is stock imagery. The emphasis alternates between God the *divine warrior defeating the enemy and Israel defeating the enemy, with the underlying premise being that no true victory on the battlefield comes without God's help. God promises to go with Israel and fight for Israel in order to give them victory (Deut 20:4). God puts the enemy to flight, making them turn their backs and run (Ex 23:27), scattering them (Num 10:35) and sending Israel in pursuit. With God as their commander, five Israelite warriors will chase a hundred, and a hundred will chase ten thousand (Lev 26:7-8). When Israel is in a desperate plight, God saves or redeems her from the hand of the enemy (Ps 106:10) and rescues her from powerful enemies (Num 10:9; Judg 8:34; 2 Sam 22:18; Ps 18:17). God promises to drive out the Canaanites before Israel (Deut 32:21; 33:27), to thrust them out of the land (Deut 6:19). Israel will in turn be given the plunder of the nations (Deut 30:7), the land of her enemies will be hers. A recurring image associated with the acquired inheritance of the land is God's giving Israel *"rest" from her enemies (Deut 12:10; 25:19; Josh 23:1).

Frequently we read of God delivering enemies into Israel's hand (Deut 23:14), of his handing them over for execution (Josh 21:44; Judg 3:28; 1 Sam 26:8; cf. Judg 16:23-24). God is imaged as crushing the head of his enemies (Ps 68:21) or trampling them (Ps 60:12; 108:13). Solomon's enemies will "lick the dust" (Ps 72:9) and God reduces enemies to fine dust. They are as ephemeral as blown chaff (Is 29:5), and like the beauty of the field that passes with the season, Israel's enemies will vanish like smoke (Ps 37:20). The boastful mouth of the enemy will be silenced (Ps 143:12). Even more colorfully, Yahweh's *sword devours the flesh of his enemies and his *arrows are drunk on their blood (Deut 32:42). In the *exodus, God causes the sea to engulf Israel's enemies (Ps 78:53). Endless ruin overtakes God's enemies, and their cities are uprooted (Ps 9:6).

Some images speak of judgment, of avenging the blood of God's servants or taking *vengeance on his enemies (Deut 32:43), of repaying the enemy all they deserve (Is 66:6). Enemies cast shame upon God's people, and God in turn shames them by exalting his own people (Mic 7:10) and causing enemies to cower before Israel (Deut 33:29). God blesses and honors his people, exalting them in public view, by preparing a table for them in the presence of their enemies (Ps 23:5).

The crowning point of these OT cameos of divine triumph is God's subduing David's enemies (1 Chron 17:10): he places enemies *under the feet of the Davidic king as his royal footstool (Ps 110:1) and extends the king's *scepter so that he rules in the midst of his enemies (Ps 110:2). In the NT we repeatedly find the image of Psalm 110:1 used to speak of Christ's victory over his enemies. Christ's enemies are a footstool for his feet, or placed "under his feet" (Ps 8:7). These are spiritual enemies (Acts 2:35; Eph 1:19-22; Heb 1:3, 13; 1 Pet 3:22), though when Jesus recites the psalm in the Gospels, he seems to have in mind his earthly accusers (Mt 22:44; Mk 12:36; Lk 20:43). In 1 Corinthians we see that Christ must reign until he has put all enemies under his feet (1 Cor 15:25), the "last enemy" being *death (1 Cor 15:26; cf. 15:54-57). And Hebrews speaks of the ascended Christ waiting for his enemies to be made his footstool (Heb 10:13).

Other NT images of triumphing over the enemy include Jesus giving the *Seventy disciples his authority to overcome all the power of the enemy (Lk 10:19). The author of Hebrews recalls the language of the OT as he speaks of a raging *fire that will consume the enemies of God (Heb 10:27). In Revelation, fire comes from the mouths of the two witnesses and consumes their enemies (Rev 11:5), and later they *ascend to heaven with their enemies looking on (Rev 11:12).

Shamed By the Enemy. In a cultural milieu where social standing is measured on a scale of *honor and *shame, a person's or a nation's enemies are an ever potential source of shame. When Moses descends from *Sinai, he sees that Aaron has lost control of the people and Israel has become a laughingstock to their enemies because Israel is running wild (Ex 32:25). The psalmist speaks of being scorned, disgraced and shamed by enemies (Ps 69:19). And when *Jerusalem falls, enemies laugh at her destruction (Lam 1:7). Of Jerusalem it is said:

All your enemies open their mouths
    wide against you;
they scoff and gnash their teeth
    and say, "We have swallowed her up.
This is the day we have waited for;
    we have lived to see it. (Lam 2:16 NIV)

The depth of defeat is imaged in shame as God allows Israel's enemies to gloat over her (Lam 2:17), makes Israel serve her enemies under an iron yoke (Deut 28:48; Jer 15:14; 17:4) and delivers Israel's grain as food for her enemies (Is 62:8).

The ultimate shaming of a righteous Israelite comes to focus on Jesus crucified on a Roman cross. He is executed by Israel's ruling enemy, Rome. Stripped naked, suffering the most humiliating of public executions, he is shamed by the taunts of his passing enemies, most of whom are his fellow Israelites (Mt 27:37-44; Mk 14:27-32; Lk 23:35-39; cf. Ps 22:6-8).

Entreaties to God Regarding Enemies. The biblical text echoes with entreaties to God to do something about the enemy. The psalms in particular provide many examples where an individual or the community beseeches God: "Give us aid against the enemy" (Ps 60:11 NIV; Ps 108:12); "Protect my life from the threat of the enemy" (Ps 64:1 NIV). And in Lamentations, Jerusalem cries out, "Look, O LORD, on my affliction, for the enemy has triumphed" (Lam 1:9 NIV). Sometimes an appeal is made to God's own honor: "How long will the enemy mock you, O God?" (Ps 74:10, 18 NIV). The afflicted do not hesitate to suggest how God might deal with the enemy: "Let death take my enemies by surprise" (Ps 55:15); "Strike all my enemies on the jaw; break the teeth of the wicked" (Ps 3:7); and "May [God's] enemies be scattered" (Ps 68:1).

These cries of *lament are the hinge on which numerous biblical stories turn from oppression to freedom, from conflict to victory. The Israelites in Egypt "groaned in their slavery and cried out" to God, and God "heard their groaning and remembered his covenant" with their ancestors (Ex 2:23-24 NIV). In the psalms this "cry" and "groaning" is frequently focused on the enemy, such as the anguished rhetorical lament, "How long will my enemy triumph over me?" (Ps 13:2 NIV). This cry finds its echo in Paul's anguished lament, perhaps expressing the plight of Israel under the law: "Who will rescue me from this body of death? (Rom 7:24 NRSV). The resolution of this cry is expressed in the psalms of thanksgiving, where we find expressions like, "you lifted me out of the depths and did not let my enemies gloat over me" (Ps 30:1 NIV; cf., e.g., Ps 18). This basic pattern of movement from lament in the face of enemies to praise for divine victory over enemies offers a way of viewing the biblical story in its entirety. Israel, beset and oppressed by enemies, cries out for a deliverer; God triumphs over the enemies and delivers Israel, bringing vindication and abundant blessings. This pattern comes to full expression in the plight of Israel's *exile and the hope of a *return and *restoration of Israel.

The pattern may be observed in Jesus, who recapitulates the story of Israel. Jesus is beset by his enemies, who nail him to a cross. There he cries out with the voice of Israel, "My God, my God, why have you forsaken me?" These words come from Psalm 22 (Ps 22:1 NIV; Mt 27:46; Mk 15:34), where the righteous one is encircled by enemies who are imaged as strong bulls, roaring lions and dogs. God triumphantly raises Jesus—the representative and true Israelite—from the dead and places his enemies under his feet.

Unlikely or Turnabout Enemies. Sometimes *family and *friends turn out to be enemies. The Lord says of Israel, "Lately my people have risen up like an enemy" (Mic 2:8 NIV). Jesus startlingly declares that he has come "not . . . to bring peace, but a sword," to turn family members against each other so that "a man's enemies will be the members of his own household" (Mt 10:36 NIV; cf. Mic 7:6). Paul says to the Galatians, "Have I now become your enemy by telling you the truth?" (Gal 4:16 NIV), and he warns the Philippians of the "many" who now live as enemies of the *cross of Christ (Phil 3:18). The ultimate irony is that Israel, in its response to the gospel and the ingathering of the Gentiles, is "an enemy on your [Gentiles'] account; but loved on account of the patriarchs" (Rom 11:28 NIV). And James reminds his readers of the dividing line between a friend and an enemy of God: "Anyone who chooses to become a friend of the world becomes an enemy of God" (Jas 4:4 NIV).

A Transformed Response to Enemies. In the OT the response to the enemy overwhelmingly takes on the imagery of hate, conflict and warfare. There are exceptions, of course, such as the peaceable Abraham who seeks to resolve conflicts and only goes to war in order to rescue Lot's family and others who have been taken captive by marauding armies. But the exodus, conquest and establishment of the Davidic kingdom exercise a formative power on our overall perception of enemies in the OT. Enemies evoke fear or valor, defense or flight, curses and dire oracles. A counterpoint to this prevailing flow of imagery is found in Proverbs 25:21-22 (NIV): "If your enemy is hungry, give him food to eat; if he is thirsty, give him water to drink. In doing this, you will heap burning coals on his head, and the LORD will reward you." Jesus, speaking in a social climate where hatred of the enemy (Rome) is aligned with righteousness and zeal for Israel's God, makes a hallmark of his teaching—love of the enemy—all the

more striking: "You have heard that it was said, 'Love your neighbor and hate your enemy.' But I tell you: Love your enemies and pray for those who persecute you" (Mt 5:43-44 NIV), or as Luke has it, "Love your enemies, do good to those who hate you" (Lk 6:27 NIV; cf. Lk 6:35). Nowhere is this more brilliantly enacted than in the scene of Jesus' crucifixion, when he prays, "Father, forgive them, for they do not know what they are doing" (Lk 23:34 NIV).

Paul echoes Jesus' teaching of love for the enemy by quoting from Proverbs 25:21-22 (see above) and rounding it off with the instruction, "Do not be overcome by evil, but overcome evil with good" (Rom 12:20 NIV). Paul himself is not without enemies, and he carries out an ongoing struggle with those who oppose his gospel and mission. Some of his words regarding his enemies—his wish that the Judaizers would "emasculate themselves" (Gal 5:12) or his warning to the Philippians to "watch out for those dogs" (Phil 3:2)—would seem to betray his instruction to love the enemy. But those who would judge Paul must first take into account his burning love for Israel and the Gentiles, his use of rhetorical conventions that allowed for this vivid language, and his passion and zeal for God's truth. Paul's enemies are "enemies of the cross" (Phil 3:18), and as such they evoke some of the OT imagery of divine enemies. But within Paul's scheme of enemies, the ultimate enemy is Satan, and with him are aligned the various principalities and powers, and the alliance of sin, flesh and death. These are the enemies that will be trampled (Rom 16:20) and placed under the feet of Christ (1 Cor 15:24-28). So confident is Paul of the triumph of Christ, that he engages the ancient rhetoric of taunting the final enemy, death: "Death has been swallowed up in victory. Where, O Death is your victory? Where, O Death, is your sting?" (1 Cor 15:54-55; cf. Is 25:8; Hos 13:14).

See also BABYLON; BATTLE STORIES; COSMOLOGY; DIVINE WARRIOR; EGYPT; EXILE; GENTILE; MONSTERS; PERSECUTION; SATAN; TRIUMPH; UNDER THE FEET; VENGEANCE, REVENGE.

ENLIGHTENMENT, STORIES OF. *See* EPIPHANY, STORIES OF.

ENTHRONEMENT. *See* KING, KINGSHIP; TRIUMPH.

ENTRYWAY. *See* DOOR.

EPHESIANS, LETTER TO THE

The opening chapter of Ephesians unfolds the rich dimensions of God's grace in Christ in sonorous tones that evoke a liturgical setting. This characteristic and the probability that Ephesians was written as a circular letter to be read by several churches may account for the lack of personal address so characteristic of Pauline letters. Ephesians employs a wealth of imagery, and much of it belonging to either the cosmic, heavenly dimension or the horizontal, earthly dimension. But overarching the entire letter is a prevailing theme of unity, the reconciliation of all things in Christ.

The Cosmic Dimension. Ephesians takes the big view of God's redeeming action in Jesus Christ. The letter enlists imagery that reaches for the broadest categories of time and space. The humble, struggling Christian communities of Asia Minor are revealed as engaged in a redemptive drama that is both staggering in its cosmic dimensions and compelling in its call for participation.

The majesty of Christ is chiefly portrayed in imagery of heavenly kingship. God has raised Christ from the dead and seated him at his right hand "in the heavenlies" (Eph 1:20). The image of Christ's being seated at the "right hand," the place of kingly power and privilege, echoes Psalm 110:1, which speaks of a royal figure who will be seated at God's right hand and whose enemies God will make into the *king's royal footstool. It is an image of royal exaltation that assumes a sovereign's triumph over hostile powers. Ephesians carries forward this kingly and militaristic image by speaking of God's placing "all things under his feet" (Eph 1:22), and though the image of a footstool and "things under his feet" are nearly synonymous, a different OT text is now being employed. It is Psalm 8:6, where humankind is regaled as crowned with "*glory and *honor," its dominion over God's creation symbolized by "all things" placed *"under their feet." Christ is the fulfillment of Israel's national kingship and *Adam's creational rule, he is the sovereign over a new *creation that has been secured by God's mighty redemptive power. But the "things" placed in submission under Christ's feet are not earthly animals but wayward spiritual beings enumerated as "rule and authority and power and dominion and every name named" (Eph 1:21). Christ is imaged as the triumphant, cosmic warrior-king and heavenly "Adam." As the climax of the biblical drama in which Israel has failed in its role of a new Adam amidst the errant nations, with Israel's king bearing the crown of the Adamic ideal, Christ now fulfills Israel's redemptive role and is given universal reign. He is the one Lord over all things, the cosmic reconciler.

The stature of Christ as Lord of the cosmos is staggering in its immensity. "All things" in heaven and earth are "headed up," or "summed up" in him (*anakephalaioō*, Eph 1:10). More pointedly, God has given Christ as "head over all things *for* the church" (Eph 1:22), God's new redemptive society—a bold claim for the Christian communities precariously planted in a few urban seedbeds of the northeastern Mediterranean world. The Greek grammar of Ephesians 1:22 is ambiguous in itself, but probably complements the preceding image of headship: The church is the *"fullness" of Christ, the concentrated expression of Christ's sovereign rule, who in turn is the one "who fills all in all," or, to paraphrase, he "fills the cosmos with his sovereign rule." These images of heavenly enthronement and cosmic "fill-

ing" strike a fine balance between Christ's immanence and transcendence. The cosmic Lord and reconciler of all things is also Lord over the church.

The picture of the enthroned Christ "in the heavenlies" is a clue that we have stepped into a drama in which the height of conflict and triumph are in the past. The vanquished opponents, the cosmic powers and dominions, are now "under his feet." The events of Christ's *cross, death (Eph 1:20; 2:16) and *resurrection (Eph 1:20; 2:6) have faded into the background, and the focus has shifted to the drama of exaltation and enthronement. Ephesians 4:8-10 pans the preceding scenes of the drama through imagery borrowed from Psalm 68:18: Christ is depicted as a mighty warrior who "ascended on high," took "captivity captive" and gave gifts to people (with the image of "receiving gifts from people" in Ps 68:18 now turned on its head). In Psalm 68 the warrior is God, who drives his armed chariotry from Sinai and gallantly ascends the temple mount of Zion, his royal palace. That picture is now tipped on end, transposed onto a vertical plane of earth and heaven, with Christ triumphantly ascending to the heavenly temple "mount." The picture is further interpreted: "When it says, 'He ascended,' what does it mean but that he had also descended into the lower parts of the earth? He who descended is the same one who ascended far above all the heavens, so that he might fill all things" (Eph 4:9-10 NRSV). Here the "lower parts of the earth" is not an allusion to "hell" (as in 1 Pet 3:19); the phrase "of the earth" simply unpacks what is meant by "lower parts" ("lower parts, that is, the earth"). A two-storied universe is envisioned, with Christ descending to earth in his incarnation and then ascending "far above the heavens" to take his heavenly throne. The point of this brief sketch is that the ascended Christ has given gifts to outfit and enable the church, "the body of Christ" (Eph 4:12), to be built up and prosper. He has distributed his booty; in his triumph he divides "the spoil with the strong" (Is 53:12).

The "heavenly realms," or "heavenlies," is a distinctive image of Ephesians, though it is consistent with Jewish cosmology of the period. It represents both the upper reaches of the cosmos as well as the realm of spiritual beings and divine transcendence. As part of the cosmos the "heavenlies" share in both the present evil age and in the age to come. Thus we read of "principalities and powers" in the heavenlies (Eph 3:10; 6:12) controlled by "the ruler of the power of the air" (Eph 2:2), as well as believers who were once "dead" and followers of the ruler of this world (Eph 2:1-2) but are now "seated in the heavenlies" with Christ (Eph 2:6). The throne of God and Christ should probably be envisioned as situated in the highest reaches of heaven. The Ephesian believers, though their feet are firmly planted on the soil of western Asia Minor, are already "raised up" and occupying a transcendent position with Christ who is "over" all things and "far above the heavens" (Eph 4:10). It is a powerful image, perhaps shaped on the anvil of liturgical vision and imagination, in which worshipers share in the heavenly voices of praise and partake of the heavenly blessings (Eph 1:3). It is a parallel and spiritual world. We are invited to imagine a heavenly realm that is hierarchical and bears its own mysteries, including "families" of created beings (probably angels both good and evil) somehow analogous to those on earth (Eph 3:15). But it is also a fearsome realm, still inhabited by malignant pockets of the defeated forces of evil, cosmic powers "of this present darkness," "spiritual forces of evil" who assail the church (Eph 6:12).

The Earthly Dimension. Ephesians 2:11-22 views this great story along more horizontal lines, speaking of the human condition before and after Christ's work, with an emphasis on the reconciling work of Christ as it culminates in a new human community made up of formerly disparate peoples. The entire passage may be viewed as a narrative that utilizes vivid images drawn from the story of Israel.

The recipients of this letter are seen from the perspective of one who stands within historic Israel and speaks to people who realize that they have been overwhelmingly blessed by their inclusion in the newly constituted people of God. Viewed through Israelite eyes, the human family is divided in two: Israel and the Gentiles, the chosen people of God and the wayward nations, the true humanity and the beastly empires of Daniel's vision (Dan 7). The status of "Israelite," determined by birth, was sealed by *circumcision, a ritual cutting off of male genital flesh.

There follows a series of exclusionary images. The Gentile audience was formerly scorned as "uncircumcision" (*akrobystia*) by those who proudly called themselves "the circumcision" (*peritomē*, Eph 2:11). They were "*without* Christ;" that is, they were outside of the chosen people in whom the Messiah, the true king and deliverer of Israel, was rooted. They were "*separated* from the commonwealth of Israel," like impoverished outsiders who gazed longingly across the border at the privileged people in their fair land. They were "*aliens* to the covenants of promise" (*see* Foreigner), having no access to the series of historic divine transactions that promised the blessings of a true humanity, a justly ordered society, a restored creation and the abiding and glorious presence of the one God. They were "*without* hope and *without* God (*atheioi*) in the world," a people separated from the Creator and covenant God, listless vagabonds upon the earth with no future worth living for. Viewed from the ramparts of Zion, they were "far off" (Eph 2:13), over the horizon. These images form a picture of irrevocable *ex*clusion, of particularized privilege, of clearly marked insiders and outsiders.

This division climaxes in the central image of a "dividing wall" (*mesotoichon*) that symbolizes the "hostility" between these two partitions of humanity (Eph 2:14), an enmity sharpened by "the law with its commandments and ordinances" (Eph 2:15). We

may visualize the Herodian *temple and the *wall that divided the Court of the Gentiles from the inner courts of Israel. In the microcosm of the temple, this wall represented the Jewish vision of the world and its nations, where the law served as an "impenetrable fence and iron wall" separating Israel from the nations (*Letter of Aristeas* 139).

But the unexpected has taken place. As if in a military assault, Christ, the Messiah of Israel, has "broken down" (*see* Tear Down) the dividing wall, he has "put to death" the hostility, by abolishing the "law with its commandmendments and ordinances" (Eph 2:14-16). The goal of "making peace" and "reconciling" the two groups has been achieved through Christ's death. This event is briefly alluded to by images of "the blood of Christ" (Eph 2:13) and "his flesh" (Eph 2:14); the divisive "circumcision in flesh by human hands" (Eph 2:11) has been overcome by Christ's own fleshly mutilation (cf. the "circumcision of Christ," Col 2:11). With this victory achieved, Christ "came" and "proclaimed peace" to those "far off" (Gentiles, cf. Deut 20:10) and to those "near" (Israel, cf. Is 57:19). As in the OT, images of divine triumph merge into images of creation: the triumph of Christ over "hostility" leads to the creation of "one new man" (Eph 2:15), "one body" (Eph 2:16), "one new humanity in place of the two" (Eph 2:15 NRSV). Jew and Gentile are joined in the body of Christ, the New Adam, to become, as it were, a "third race" fitted for life in the new creation. The cosmic reconciliation has its counterpart in the reconciliation of Jew and Gentile into one.

But then the metaphor shifts: The Gentiles are "no longer strangers and aliens" but "fellow citizens with the saints and members of the household of God" (Eph 2:19). And the household of God is a temple. The mythic stories of the ancient Near-Eastern gods, who struggled and triumphed over the forces of chaos, followed a progressive pattern of conflict, victory, exaltation, housebuilding and celebration. This archetypal story pattern may be broadly observed in Ephesians, with significant elements appearing in this passage. Christ has triumphed over the barrier of hostility between Jew and Gentile (in addition to the hostility between God and humanity) and now proceeds to build his house, his temple. The foundation consists of "apostles and prophets" of the early church, with Christ himself as the *"cornerstone" (Eph 2:20). This structure grows organically into a "holy temple" (Eph 2:21) built of redeemed humanity, "a dwelling place for God" (Eph 2:22, cf. the "fullness" indwelling the "body" in Eph 1:23). The central symbol of God's dwelling within the "body" of Israel, the Jerusalem temple, is figuratively assaulted, torn down and replaced by this new temple built of sanctified "building blocks" of Jews and Gentiles. The image of "access" (*prosagōgē*, Eph 2:18; 3:12) to God also fits within this temple imagery, for the term is used in the Greek translation of the OT for approaching God in the sanctuary with sacrifices (e.g., LXX Lev 1:3; 3:3; 4:14), and in Greek

239

literature it is used of the right of an audience with a king. Paul speaks of "bending his knees" as he approaches the divine throne with his petitions (Eph 3:14).

Images of the Church. A good deal of the imagery of Ephesians may be categorized as images of the *church. We have observed the images of "one new man" (Eph 2:15-16) and the related images of "household" and "holy temple" (Eph 2:19-22). And the image of the church as Christ's "body" has been introduced (Eph 1:23). The relationship between this body imagery, which is further developed in Ephesians 4—5, and the Adamic imagery is frequently overlooked. The archetypal pattern of "old Adam" and "new Adam," old humanity and new humanity, is ever shaping this language. Thus when the readers are instructed to "put off" (apothesthai) the "old man" (palaion anthrōpon), corrupt and deluded by its lusts (Eph 4:22 NRSV), and to "put on" the "new man" (kainon anthrōpon), distinguished by righteousness and holiness (Eph 4:24), a corporate image of an old and new humanity is being invoked. Believers are part of a new Adamic community that is "created in the likeness of God" (Eph 4:24). By contrast, the character of the old humanity is itemized in a list of degrading vices that are to be given up—or risk loss of the inheritance of the kingdom of God (Eph 4:25-32; 5:3-5).

The image of a corporate "body of Christ" (Eph 1:23; 2:16; 3:6; 4:4, 12, 16, [25]; 5:23, 30) is closely related to this Adamic imagery, for in the Pauline thought-world Christ is the new Adam, the true imprint of the divine image. The body of Christ is an organic, growing entity, whose head is Christ (Eph 4:15). Paul even speaks as a personal trainer who leads the body of Christ in a body-building program (Eph 4:16, 29; 5:29). From the "head" the whole body is "joined and knit together by every ligament with which it is equipped, as each part is working properly," and Christ "promotes the body's growth in building itself up in love" (Eph 4:16 NRSV).

The image of Christ as *"head" (Eph 1:22; 4:15; 5:23) in Ephesians poses a problem of interpretation. If we are to understand it as a "head" attached to a "body," this "body" metaphor should certainly be distinguished from 1 Corinthians 12, where members constitute various parts of the body of Christ, including the head (1 Cor 12:21) and parts of the head (*ear, *eye, *nose; 1 Cor 12:16-17). The image of Christ as "head" in Ephesians should not be understood as part of the image of the "body of Christ" but as a separate christological (rather than ecclesiological) image indicating the sovereignty of Christ. Otherwise we would have to imagine a headless body, since Christ serves as "head of all things" in Ephesians 1:22-23.

The relationship between Christ and the church is developed in a metaphor of the church as the *bride of Christ (cf. 2 Cor 11:2). Christ's love for the church transcends human examples of a husband's love for his wife: Christ "gave himself up for her"—an allu-

sion to the cross (Eph 5:25). This was to sanctify the church for himself as a bride. The imagery of *cleansing her through "the washing of water by the word" evokes the Christian rite of *baptism, and secondarily the prenuptial bath of Jewish marital custom. The *washing, and indeed the entire metaphor of a bride, undoubtedly owes something to Ezekiel 16:8-12, where Jerusalem is depicted as an abandoned newborn girl who is saved and nurtured by God, and in her nubility bathed in water and taken by God as his wife. In the marriage ceremony of Ephesians 5:17, the church is presented to Christ in splendor as a clear-skinned *maiden, "without a spot or wrinkle or anything of the kind—yes, so she may be holy and without blemish" (NRSV).

The church as the "household" of God (Eph 2:20) is an image rooted in the social reality of the early Christian communities, which commonly met in household settings. In Ephesians 5:21—6:9 the conventional form of a "household code," well known in the ancient world, is adapted to Christian use as instructions are given for the proper behavior of *husbands and *wives, parents and *children, *slaves and masters in family households newly constituted under the Lordship of Christ.

In a memorable display of imagery, the people of God are exhorted as the army of Christ to be prepared for spiritual warfare. The enemy is not palpable "flesh and blood" but a formidable array of elusive but hostile spiritual powers: the "devil," or the "evil one," the "rulers" and "authorities," the "cosmic powers of this present darkness" and the "spiritual forces of evil in the heavenly realms." Against such enemies conventional weaponry is useless; they must take up the "whole *armor of God" (Is 59:17-18; cf. Wis 5:17-20): the belt of truth, the breastplate of righteousness, shoes for proclaiming the gospel of peace, the *shield of faith to extinguish flaming arrows, the helmet of salvation and, finally, the defensive weapon of the "*sword of the Spirit, which is the word of God" (Eph 6:14-17). The church, like Israel when it entered the land, still has its battles to fight. Its spiritual enemies—though decisively defeated at the battle of the cross—continue to attack and resist the people of God.

Mystery. Ephesians lets its readers in on a cosmic secret, a "mystery" (mystērion, Eph 1:9; 3:3, 4, 9; 5:32; 6:19), a chapter of God's eschatological plan that was laid "before the foundation of the world" (Eph 1:4), that was formerly concealed and now has been revealed in Christ. This mystery has been made known to Paul by a revelation (Eph 3:3)—though it has also been revealed to other apostles and prophets by the Spirit (Eph 3:5)—and the opening two chapters of Ephesians have unfolded Paul's understanding of the mystery (Eph 3:4). The essential outline of the mystery is that Gentiles are now fellow heirs, members of the same body, sharers in the promise with believing Israelites who have followed Jesus Christ (Eph 3:6). But the mystery includes a "vertical" dimension, the union of Christ with his church, a "great mystery" (Eph 5:32). The mystery has not been revealed to the cosmic powers (cf. 1 Cor 2:6-8), but the curtain is now being lifted and the mystery disclosed to them. The "rulers and authorities" are spectators as the wisdom of the Creator God's cosmic drama is now being acted out in the story of the church (Eph 3:9-10).

Power. Imagery of power is abundant in Ephesians, perhaps as an explicit response to the religious environment of Ephesus and other cities of Asia Minor where sorcery and evil spirits were a common and ominous feature of popular religion. This spiritual climate may have elicited the multiple names of the dark forces enumerated in Ephesians: "powers" (Eph 1:21), "rulers" (Eph 1:21; 6:12), "authorities" (Eph 1:21; 3:10; 6:12), "dominions" (Eph 1:21), "cosmic powers" (Eph 6:12) and the "ruler of the power of the air" (Eph 2:2). These names evoke a cosmos inhabited by a multitiered and malignant hierarchy of evil power. Formerly these names would have struck terror in the hearts of many recipients of this letter. But Ephesians begins with a joyous affirmation of the power of God in Christ to perform his will, work redemption and secure his blessings for his people in the face of any and every opposition that can be named. In Ephesians 1:19 the theme of power is explicitly emphasized: "the immeasurable greatness of his power . . . the working of his great power."

The greatest display of God's power was when he raised Christ from the dead and exalted him to his right hand in the heavenly realms, leading captivity captive (Eph 4:8), subjecting all powers to his sovereign control (Eph 1:20-22). Later we read that God's power is displayed in God's grace working in Paul (Eph 3:7), and that God's power can strengthen believers by the Spirit (Eph 3:16) and accomplish "far more than all we can ask or imagine" (Eph 3:20 NRSV). Finally, in facing their spritual enemies, believers are to "be strong in the Lord and in the strength of his power" (Eph 6:10). The same divine power that enabled Christ to triumph over his enemies is active within the church, and that power will allow it to "stand" firm in the face of spiritual assault. Images of divine power emerge in God's "raising up" those who were "dead" in their sins and seating them in the heavenlies with Christ (Eph 2:5-6), in Christ's breaking down the dividing wall, abolishing the law, putting to death the hostility between Jew and Gentile (Eph 2:14-16) and in his building a new temple (Eph 2:20-21). And it is the "armor of God," the weaponry of the powerful *divine warrior, that is employed by the church in its battle against the spiritual powers (Eph 6:10-17).

Other Imagery. A variety of other images may be briefly reviewed. Believers must no longer be immature "children," who are "tossed to and fro by waves and blown about by every wind of doctrine" or trickery or craftiness (Eph 4:14). The picture is of a boat at sea in the hands of inexperienced sailors. Incapable of holding their course, they are subject to whatever forces of wind and wave beat upon them or carry them along (cf. Heb 13:9; Jas 1:6; Jude 12, 13). An opposite, positive image, one of stability, is that of being "rooted and grounded in love" (Eph 3:17).

In Ephesians, Paul is memorably imaged as a prisoner "in the Lord" (Eph 4:1), or a prisoner "for Jesus Christ" (Eph 3:1; *see* Prison). Even more strikingly, he is an "ambassador in chains" (Eph 6:20). As an official representative of his heavenly Lord, Paul has not been granted diplomatic immunity. The calling card of his diplomatic mission is inscribed with a logo of suffering. So even now Caesar's instruments of power are the means by which this ambassador of the heavenly Lord boldly delivers the good news of the mystery of reconciliation.

The imagery of *family is a constant in Paul's letters. In the first half of Ephesians we repeatedly find imagery that evokes a picture of a *father with extravagant and immeasurable "riches" (Eph 1:7, 18; 2:7; 3:8, 16) who lavishes them on his *adopted children (Eph 1:5), his heirs (Eph 3:6) who will one day receive his *inheritance (Eph 1:14, 18; cf. 5:5).

The vivid image of a *sleeper awakened, rising from the dead, and greeted by the morning light of Christ, the dawn of a new creation, is memorably set out in verse structure (Eph 5:14), perhaps as a line from an early Christian baptismal hymn. The brilliant light of Christ is an image that finds company in the repeated theme of *"glory" in the doxological language of chapter one (Eph 1:6, 12, 14, 17, 18) and in the prayer language of chapter three (Eph 3:13, 16, 21). The prayer that the "eyes of your heart be enlightened" (Eph 1:18), while odd to modern Western ears, speaks of the illumination of the *heart as the perceptive seat of practical reason and wisdom, not of the emotions. And it is fitting that the people of God are "children of *light" and not *"darkness" (Eph 5:8), their works the "fruit of light" (Eph 5:9) rather than the "unfruitful works of darkness" (Eph 5:11), which are performed in the shadows but will be exposed by the light (Eph 5:12-13).

In Ephesians it is as if a narrative world of triumph and reconciliation embracing heaven and earth is constructed and then filled in with various images that furnish, populate and dramatize the action within this new world. A new creation is emerging, and its outline may be seen in the church, whose unity is celebrated in a litany of oneness in Ephesians 4:4-6: "one body . . . one Spirit . . . one hope . . . one Lord, one faith, one baptism, one God and Father of all, who is above all and through all and in all" (NRSV).

See also ARMOR; COSMOLOGY; ENEMY; EXALTATION, ENTHRONEMENT; HEAVEN; TRIUMPH.

BIBLIOGRAPHY. G. B. Caird, *Paul's Letters from Prison* (NC1B; Oxford: Oxford University Press, 1976); A. T. Lincoln, *Ephesians* (WBC; Dallas: Word, 1990); idem, *Paradise Now and Not Yet* (SNTSMS 43; Cambridge: Cambridge University Press, 1981).

EPHOD. *See* ORACLE.

EPIPHANY, STORIES OF

One of the most common narrative patterns is the archetypal movement from ignorance to insight. The literary term for this climactic moment of insight or *revelation, *epiphany,* was popularized by twentieth-century fiction writer James Joyce. The stories of the Bible are replete with moments of epiphany in which characters have a sudden experience of realization. While it is a rare story in which characters do not discover something significant, the term *epiphany* is best reserved for stories in which the whole action moves toward a climactic moment of insight into the nature of people or reality or (more often) the nature of God.

Such, for example, is the experience of *Abraham and Isaac on Mt. Moriah, where suddenly (as in a dream) the two catch sight of a ram caught in a thicket (Gen 22:14), thus making good Abraham's earlier claim that "God will provide himself the lamb for a burnt offering" (Gen 22:8 RSV) and leading Abraham to name the place "The LORD will provide" (Gen 22:15). The moment of epiphany is tragic when the deceived Isaac and then the duped Esau discover the trickery that has been visited on them by *Jacob in the story of the stolen blessing (Gen 27:32-35). When Jacob receives the covenant blessing in his dream at Bethel, he awakens from sleep and says, "Surely the LORD is in this place; and I did not know it. . . . How awesome is this place! This is none other than the house of God, and this is the gate of heaven" (Gen 28:16-17 RSV). In the same way, as Jacob wrestles with the *angel of God, he gradually comes to perceive the supernatural identity of his opponent, finally concluding, "I have seen God face to face" (Gen 32:26-30). On the eve of Jacob's escape from Laban, God appears to him in a dream and reveals that it was divine providence, not Jacob's ridiculous attempts at animal husbandry, that produced so many striped and spotted sheep and goats (Gen 31:11-13).

The list of characters who recognize God's presence in the midst of extraordinary experiences keeps expanding. Hagar sees God's omniscience and calls God "a God of seeing" (Gen 16:7-14). The Egyptians are made to understand the truthfulness of God's oracles when the tenth plague kills their firstborn (Ex 12:29-36). Rahab claims that her compatriots understood God's omnipotence when they heard of the Red Sea deliverance (Josh 2:11). Elisha's servant is dismayed by the siege of Dothan until God opens his eyes to see that "the mountain was full of horses and chariots of fire round about Elisha" (2 Kings 6:15-17). Divine handwriting on a wall brings Belshazzar to awareness of his own impending fall (Dan 5). As the psalmist contemplates the possibility of escaping from God's presence, he is led to realize that God will be present even if he escapes through space (Ps 139:7-10) or into darkness (vv. 11-12).

*Quest stories often move toward moments of epiphany in which the quester's goal is realized at last. The whole book of *Job, in which the protagonist is in quest for an explanation of the nature of his suffering, moves toward the climactic revelation of God's superior knowledge and power in the voice from the whirlwind (Job 38—41). After searching for meaning and satisfaction in all the wrong places, the narrator in *Ecclesiastes reaches "the end of the matter" in which "all has been heard," and the insight is summarized in the command, "Fear God, and keep his commandments; for this is the whole duty of man" (Eccles 12:13 RSV). Elijah's quest to bring his nation to repentance reaches a temporary climax on Mt. Carmel, where the whole nation is witness to the fact that Jehovah is the only true God (1 Kings 18). The psalmist's quest to find a solution to his problem of envying the prosperous wicked is realized in a sudden moment of epiphany that comes to him as he worships God (Ps 73:16-17).

While most stories of epiphany center on insights that characters realize about the character or work of God, the dynamics of recognition can also occur on a more human level. Thus Joseph's brothers experience a moment of recognition when *Joseph reveals his identity to them in Egypt (Gen 45:1-15), and recognition is forced on a heretofore unsuspecting Boaz in a vivid midnight encounter with a woman (Ruth 3:8-12). An obtuse Eli is led to see how thoroughly he had misjudged the behavior of Hannah (1 Sam 1:12-17). The *trickster Jacob, who had deviously exploited family members' appetites (Gen 25:29-34; 27), receives his comeuppance in similar manner when he awakes the morning after his wedding to find Leah rather than Rebekah beside him (Gen 29:25).

Characters can also come to insight about their own sinfulness; examples include Elijah on the occasion of his *call to be a prophet (Is 6:5), Peter during his denial of Jesus (Mt 26:74-75; Mk 14:72; Lk 22:60-62) and Judas Iscariot when he realizes what he has done in betraying Jesus (Mt 27:3-5).

The NT is a veritable anthology of epiphany stories, as characters repeatedly reach insight into the divine identity of *Jesus and the way in which he is the agent of salvation in their lives. In a sense the epiphany story is the natural medium for narrating the life of the incarnate Christ. The first characters to recognize him as the Messiah are Zechariah (Lk 1:67-80), Simeon (Lk 2:25-35) and Anna (Lk 2:36-38). At the other end of Jesus' life stands the centurion who exclaims on the death of Jesus, "Truly this was the Son of God!" (Mt 27:54 RSV; cf. Lk 23:47). Between are a host of people who recognize that Jesus is their Savior, including the Samaritan woman and her fellow townspeople (Jn 4:1-42), Peter when he is rescued from drowning (Mt 14:33), the three disciples who witness the transfiguration (Mt 17:1-13; Mk 9:2-13; Lk 9:28-36), Zacchaeus (Lk 19:1-10), the disciples who witness Jesus' first miracle (Jn 3:11), John the Baptist on the occasion of Jesus' baptism (Jn 1:29-34), the man born blind who received sight (Jn 9:35-38) and the penitent thief who requests salvation from Jesus on the cross (Mt 26:74-

75; Mk 72; Lk 23:39-43). The miracles of Jesus are usually accompanied by the insights the onlookers achieve into the divine power of Jesus. The postresurrection appearances by Jesus to his followers are also stories of revelation and recognition.

Similar stories of recognition occur in the book of *Acts as a series of people come to believe in Christ as their Savior. Such are the stories of those who are converted on Pentecost (Acts 2:37-42); the lame man who was healed (Acts 3:8-10); Simon the sorcerer (Acts 8:12-13); the Ethiopian eunuch (Acts 8:34-38); Paul, from whose eyes scales fell off (Acts 9:1-19) and many other converts.

The purpose of the Bible is to move its readers to epiphany—insight into their own condition, into the nature of reality, and above all, into the possibility of redemption through God's provision. Stories of epiphany enhance this general orientation of the Bible.

See also QUEST; REVELATION/RECOGNITION STORIES.

EPISTLE

The structure and imagery of the NT epistles are governed by the conventions of letter writing. They are innovations constructed on Greek and Roman models, which had three main parts: introduction (sender, addressee, greeting); text or body; and conclusion (final wishes or greetings). With this structure as the core, the NT epistles show important additions. The cursory "Greetings!" *(chairein)* of the Graeco-Roman letter becomes the theologically charged "Grace *[charis]* to you and peace from God" (RSV) in NT epistles. Their conclusions include not only final good wishes but also solemn benedictions. More important are two totally new units—a *thanksgiving* (a liturgically formulated statement of thanks and/or *prayer for the spiritual welfare of the recipients and/or a commendation of their spiritual virtues and *blessings) and a *paraenesis* (a list of moral exhortations, including both positive and negative commands, as well as such motifs as proverbial wisdom, lists of virtues and vices, and extended exhortations on a single moral topic). The *paraenesis* typically comes after the doctrinal middle section of an epistle. More generally, we know that letters are consciously composed with paragraphs as the basic unit of composition, so that the ability to "think paragraph" is one of our greatest assets when reading an epistle. Epistolary conventions and stereotyped language and formulas are thus one image pattern found in all of the NT epistles.

Another set of images follows from the implied relationship between sender and recipient. An epistle presupposes two parties, an author and an intended audience; and the picture of both is important as we read the NT epistles. Paul, especially, places himself into his letters as a real-life person. He talks about his *authority as an apostle, about his spiritual autobiography, about his *travels, about his doctrinal convictions. Similarly, we pick up a picture of the

audience as we wind our way through an epistle. The audience is usually corporate (a church or body of Christians in a given locale) but is sometimes a private person. In both cases we pick up clues about the audience's identity and situation. Context, in other words, supplies imagery and motifs for an epistle. The *Corinthian church, for example, was an unruly, immature and divided church. The recipients of the letter to the *Hebrews were dispersed Jews, possibly in Rome, who were in danger of relapsing into Judaism. The relationship between author and recipient is not that between two equals; the apostolic author writes as an authority figure, the source not only of advice that the recipient is expected to follow but also of rebuke.

The NT epistles are occasional letters (called forth by specific occasions or situations), and this too supplies imagery, motifs and content for the epistles. Only rarely (most notably in the epistle to the *Romans) do we find systematic treatises on a theological topic. The general format is to take up questions or points of controversy that are known to exist in the life of the church or individual who is addressed. It is a fair inference that the recipient(s) of a letter already knew the author's views on the central issues of the Christian faith. The author takes these for granted and directs his remarks instead to more specific questions, doubts, errors or problems. What emerges, therefore, is an ever-expanding picture of the early church in various regions of the Graeco-Roman world.

In this regard we can note that the *city is a major image in the epistles. Most of the epistles are addressed to churches or individuals living in metropolitan areas (in contrast to the more agrarian atmosphere of the Gospels). The *church is another major image; in fact, we rarely lose sight of the local church as we read the epistles. While the city in which a church or group of Christians resides is large, by comparison the church emerges as a small, beleaguered entity, almost overwhelmed by the broader social and cultural context. A strong sense of antithesis is assumed to exist between the two, or where it is absent, the audience is admonished not to live by the standards of the surrounding culture. Other social units, such as the *family/household, men and women as separate genders, and masters and *servants are also important in the epistles. Images of worship and church offices (including the minister or pastor) are a major cluster, and references to the OT *law are numerous. We can note also that the epistles contain many specific place names and individual persons' names, reinforcing the point that individuals in their real-life situations matter in the Christian life—that God's *kingdom on earth, in fact, consists of specifics and that the Christian faith does not whisk people away to an etherealized "spiritual" world.

Another real-life aspect of the epistles is the impression they give of being written in relative haste and in response to an occasion instead of being composed like an essay in someone's study. One result is the degree to which they depend on oral effects. The author's voice is a speaking voice. Paul's style is frequently oratorical and even homiletic (sermonic) in its effect and *rhetorical strategies, and we infer that he dictated his letters. Virtually all of the NT epistles were "open letters" read orally and publicly in churches, hence direct addresses to the audience are common.

Stylistically, despite all the informality noted above, the epistles display a full range of poetic and rhetorical effects. For all their theological and moral content, they appeal to the imagination with concrete images and metaphors. The language is frequently vivid. Embedded in the prose we find *proverbs and aphoristic sayings, liturgical formulas, creedal affirmations and hymns (see Christ Hymn). The rhetorical techniques are numerous: antithesis, parallelism, apostrophe (addresses to someone absent as though present), rhetorical question, paradox, question-and-answer construction, exclamation, repetition (including word patterns) and satire.

See also APOCALYPSE, GENRE OF; GOSPEL GENRE.

BIBLIOGRAPHY. D. E. Aune, *The New Testament in Its Literary Environment* (Philadelphia: Westminster, 1987) 158-225; W. G. Doty, *Letters in Primitive Christianity* (Philadelphia: Fortress, 1973); S. K. Stowers, *Letter Writing in Greco-Roman Antiquity* (Philadelphia: Westminster, 1986).

EPITHALAMIA. *See* SONG OF SONGS; WEDDING.

ESAU

The most obvious thing that we might associate with Esau is that he belongs, along with his brother *Jacob, to a group of pairs of biblical siblings whom we naturally remember together—*Cain and *Abel, Rachel and Leah, *Mary and Martha, the *prodigal son and elder brother. The characters in each pair are foils to each other and *sibling rivals.

Esau is mentioned by name more than eighty times in the Bible, and he is a more major actor in Genesis than we tend to realize, being named sixty times in the book. A number of important archetypes converge in Esau: he is the wild man, the *dupe (dimwitted victim), the *villain (a would-be murderer), the problem child, the *elder child supplanted by the younger, the progenitor of a nation and the profane person who is insensitive to spiritual values. The images linked with him include his hairy skin and ruddy complexion, a proverbial "mess of pottage," the field, the *hunting of game, a cry of protest when he discovers a lifechanging *deception and an embrace of a guilty *brother in a famous reconciliation scene.

The image of Esau as wild man begins with his *birth story, which stresses the laughable aspects of the two brothers' births. Esau, the firstborn, "came forth red, all his body like a hairy mantle" (Gen 25:25 RSV), earning him the name equivalent to "hairy"

and the nickname "red" (Gen 25:29). In contrast to the "homebody" Jacob, Esau "was a skillful hunter, a man of the field," whom his father preferred "because he ate of his game" (Gen 25:27-28 RSV). The story of the exchanged *birthright (Gen 25:29-34) stresses Esau's uncouth manners, and a literal translation of his statement to Jacob is "let me gulp some of that red stuff" (Gen 25:30). The staccato succession of five verbs at the end of the story (Gen 25:34) likewise draws attention to Esau's unpolished callousness. This uncomplimentary portrayal of Esau, progenitor of Israel's rival nation Edom, prompted Gunkel to comment wryly, "These are neighborly kindnesses." In keeping with his identity as a hunter rather than a *shepherd or *farmer, Esau "dwelt in the hill country" (Gen 36:8).

Corresponding to Esau's unrefined callousness is his moral and spiritual insensitivity. In the story of the exchanged birthright, Esau is a slave to his *appetite, unable to delay immediate gratification for the sake of future benefit. The narrator highlights this with his parting shot: "Thus Esau despised his birthright" (Gen 25:34 RSV). Esau is a classic case of someone who *misprizes something valuable. The writer of Hebrews cites Esau as an example of someone who was "immoral or irreligious ["profane" KJV, "godless" NIV] . . . who sold his birthright for a single meal" (Heb 12:16 RSV). To add to the picture of Esau as villain, he plots the *murder of his brother when Jacob cheats him out of their father's blessing (Gen 27:41-42). Moreover, as a problem child Esau's marriages to pagan women make life "bitter" and "weary" for his parents (Gen 26:34-35; 27:46). There is no indication in the biblical text that Esau is responsive to God, as the flawed Jacob certainly is. Romans 9:10-13 links Esau's forfeiture of the covenant promise to God's election of Jacob, in the process quoting Malachi 1:3 to say that God hated Esau.

Most of the references to Esau in the Bible are to his role as progenitor of the nation of Edom, for whom his name is often used as a personification. Esau is associated with Edom by wordplay, with the word for "red" sounding in Hebrew somewhat like Edom and the word for "hairy" sounding something like Seir, land of the Edomites. The *oracle that Rebekah received during her troublesome pregnancy predicted that "two nations are in your womb" (Gen 25:23), confirming Esau's role as the father of a nation. The genealogy in Genesis 36 states baldly, "Esau is Edom" (Gen 25:8). The after-history of Esau's antagonism against Jacob includes the fact that although David subjugated Edom (2 Sam 8:11-14; 1 Chron 18:13), it later revolted and actually defeated Judah during the reign of Ahaz (2 Chron 28:17).

If the images associated with Esau are mainly negative, they are not wholly so. Esau elicits our feelings of pity by default when he is the victim of deceit. While the tone of the story of the exchanged birthright is disparaging throughout, the same cannot be said of the story of the stolen *blessing. Any reader's heart aches for Esau when, upon his discovery of what Jacob has done to him, he cries out "with an exceedingly great and bitter cry" and pleads with his father, "Have you but one blessing, my father?" (Gen 27:34-38 RSV). We are also moved by the pathos of Esau's regret over his self-failing when we read that "when he desired to inherit the blessing, he was rejected, for he found no chance to repent, though he sought it with tears" (Heb 12:17 RSV).

More positively, Esau wins our admiration by being lavishly *forgiving when he and Jacob meet after Jacob's twenty-year exile (Gen 33:1-11). Whereas the guilt-haunted Jacob goes to meet his brother extravagantly over-prepared and formal, "bowing himself to the ground seven times," Esau is spontaneously good-willed, running to meet Jacob, embracing him, falling on his *neck and *kissing him (Gen 33:3-4).

This, then, is Esau—a character almost as many-sided as his brother Jacob. Whatever human sympathy might flow to Esau as the victim of deceit and as an example of a forgiving spirit on one occasion is overwhelmed by the negative side of his character. On a human plane Esau is the dimwitted outdoorsman, a slave to his stomach, a dupe ready to be exploited, unable to dispense with instant gratification for the sake of eventual *reward. On a spiritual plane he is the archetypal "profane" person (Heb 12:16 KJV)—the person of misplaced values with an inadequate regard for spiritual realities. To this day we have a proverb about selling one's birthright for a mess of pottage.

See also BIRTHRIGHT; BROTHER; DUPE; ELDER CHILD, ELDER SIBLING; JACOB; MISPRIZING; SIBLING RIVALRY.

ESCAPE, STORIES OF

With well over a hundred references to escaping and a similar number of references to *"fleeing," the Bible portrays a world in which people live in an awareness of the need to escape from a range of dangerous situations, both physical and spiritual. The motifs of escape and *rescue are closely related and sometimes overlap, but while rescue is deliverance with the aid of an outside agent, escape simply refers to the release experienced by the person or nation who escapes. Noah and his family stage the first escape in the Bible when they circumvent the death-bringing power of the flood.

Sometimes the people who escape are guilt-haunted people who are forced to flee the consequences of their own unwise choices. Lot escapes natural cataclysm when the angels lead him from *Sodom after he has made a worldly minded choice to move there (Gen 19). *Jacob escapes from his brother, *Esau, after cheating him, thereby bringing a death threat on himself. *Moses is in a similar situation when he has to escape from Egypt after killing a taskmaster. *Jonah escapes death at sea when God sends a huge fish to rescue him after his rebellious behavior.

More often, though, people who escape do so in acts of heroism—the two spies escaping from Jericho after being hidden by Rahab, Ehud escaping from the palace of Eglon after a clever assassination, *David escaping from the paranoid Saul. It is often either the clever or the strong who escape. *Samson is in the latter category when he carries off the gates of Gaza by night (Judg 16:1-3). On other occasions it is the lone survivor from disaster who escapes to bring the message of calamity (Job 1:13-19).

Individual escapes, though, seem small and isolated compared with the great escape of the OT—the *exodus of the Israelites from Egypt. Here is a story with all the suspense and danger of escape stories at their best—a build-up of tension and hostility, nighttime preparations for the escape (accompanied by awe-inspiring religious ceremony), waiting for the word that will commence the escape, a quick getaway when the Egyptians discover the death-bringing plague, and miraculous rescue as the nation makes its decisive break with Egypt on the far side of the sea.

The NT stories of escape are just as dramatic, and they typically involve the escape of either Christ or his followers from their persecutors. Joseph and Mary escape Herod's plot to kill Jesus. Jesus escapes from his enemies as they stand ready to stone him (Jn 10:31-39), Peter escapes from prison (Acts 12:6-11), Paul escapes from a conspiracy to kill him (Acts 23:12-35) and from death by drowning (Acts 27:27-44). In the apocalyptic vision of terror narrated in Revelation 12:1-6, Christ escapes Satan's plot by ascending into heaven, and the church similarly escapes the designs of Satan by fleeing into the wilderness.

While the escape motif is the special domain of narrative, it is not absent from the lyric poetry and wisdom literature of the Bible. The psalmist praises a God to whom "belongs escape from death" (Ps 68:20 RSV) and pictures his own believing community as having "escaped like a bird from the snare of the fowlers" (Ps 124:7 RSV). The proverbs of the OT are an implied strategy for escaping from the traps that ensnare the human race when it is morally and spiritually careless. For example, "an evil man is ensnared by the transgression of his lips, but the righteous escapes from trouble" (Prov 12:13 RSV); and "he who pleases God escapes" the ensnaring woman, "but the sinner is taken by her" (Eccles 7:26 RSV).

The individual escape stories of the Bible seem to gesture toward the Great Escape—*redemption from sin. Thus we read in the NT about how to "escape from the snare of the devil" (2 Tim 2:26), and about the impossibility of escaping if we neglect "such a great salvation" (Heb 2:3; see also Heb 12:25). The writer of 2 Peter also talks about how to "escape from the corruption that is in the world" (2 Pet 1:4) and about those who have "escaped the defilements of the world through the knowledge of our Lord and Savior Jesus Christ" (2 Pet 2:20).

See also BONDAGE AND FREEDOM; EXODUS, SECOND EXODUS; FLIGHT, CHASE AND FLIGHT; PRISON; RESCUE.

ESTHER, BOOK OF

The book of Esther is one of the most carefully crafted stories in the Bible. It is replete with the ingredients that audiences through the centuries have most valued in stories: heightened conflict between good and evil, a beautiful and courageous *heroine, lurid scenes of *banqueting and carousing, a palace with a harem, romantic *love in the specific form of the Cinderella motif (an orphan girl from an enslaved nation who marries the king), a *villain who makes the reader's blood boil, helpless victims who are *rescued just in time, intrigue, suspense, *reversal, decisive moral choice, climax, *battle, and *poetic justice. By means of all this richness of story material, the book tells a story of the providence of God, who (though not named in the story) controls events for his purposes of judgment and salvation.

Structure and Unity. The plot of the book is the usual U-shaped plot of *comedy in which events descend into potential *tragedy but rise suddenly to a happy ending. A series of obstacles are overcome, including the extreme villainy of the nation's enemy, Haman, and the obtuseness of a despotic king, Ahasuerus. The resulting rescue story consists of three phases. The first two chapters, narrating the king's rejection of Vashti and marrying of Esther, are the background to the conflict between Haman and the Jews. Chapters 3 to 7 narrate, step by step, how Haman plots against Mordecai and the Jews and how the Jews develop a counterplot. The final three chapters narrate the aftermath of the struggle—the deliverance of the Jews. The basic rhythm of the story is thus a build-up of tension, followed by its release. In the words of the story itself, the action is a movement "from sorrow into gladness and from mourning into a holiday" (Esther 9:22 RSV).

The cast of characters also supplies unity to the story. At the center is the titular heroine, whose Babylonian name ("Star") hints at her resplendence and courage. Esther's characterization is unified by two motifs—an identity crisis (as she tries initially to live in two worlds) and transformation through *ordeal. Mordecai, a courtier by profession, is the conventional attendant on the protagonist—a character necessary for the action but subordinate to the heroine in the design of the story. The portrait of Ahasuerus is a *satiric one in which the king is held up to ridicule every time he enters the action. Queen Vashti is mainly a foil to the king, a moral norm that heightens the king's status as a playboy and dunce. And Haman is the demonic villain, the person of uncontrollable *pride and thirst for revenge (see Vengeance, Revenge). It is no wonder that it became a convention for Jewish audiences to boo and hiss and rattle noisemakers whenever Haman's name was mentioned during oral readings of the story.

Image Patterns. The *court provides a leading cluster of images in the story, in contrast to the pastoral world of the book of *Ruth (the other major heroine story in the OT). The story opens with an extended scene of courtly splendor, banqueting and carousing, as though the action had been scripted for a modern movie. Courtly protocol is a constant presence in the story, especially as it relates to people interacting with the king. We also catch a glimpse of protocol as it prevails in the harem of an Oriental court. The language of royal decrees figures prominently as well, with implications of despotic power reinforced by numerous images of monarchy (*throne, *scepter, *crown, palace *garden, signet *ring, etc.).

As an extension of the courtly motif, the imagery of *feasting pervades the story. The action begins with an extended scene of lavish banqueting and entertainment, though of a somewhat coarse moral tone. As a foil to this scene we have the fasting of Esther and her compatriots at their moment of greatest crisis (Esther 4:16). But this quickly gives way to the ostensibly festive banquets that Esther puts on for the king and Haman. Finally, when the Jews are allowed to defend themselves, they respond throughout the realm with "gladness and joy" and "a feast and a holiday" (Esther 8:17). And after the victory is secured, we also have heightened pictures of feasting (Esther 9:19, 22).

Nation and politics are another key ingredient. Ahasuerus is portrayed as head of an entire nation, with an efficient national postal system at his disposal (Esther 1:22). On the other side it is not simply a family but the entire Jewish nation that is threatened by the king's decree plotted by Haman. The hostility between Mordecai and Haman seems to have a national origin as well. The rescue is likewise national in scope, as is the celebration. In fact, the whole story serves as an explanation of the Jewish *festival of Purim.

Clothing (see Garments) is important in the story. Mordecai dons the conventional garb of *mourning by rending his clothes and putting on sackcloth and *ashes (Esther 4:1). Esther puts on royal robes before entering the king's presence (Esther 5:1). Mordecai is clothed in royal robes when he is honored for having uncovered a plot against the king's life (Esther 6), and when Esther's case is approved by the king, Mordecai goes out from the king's presence "in royal robes of blue and white, with . . . a mantle of fine linen and purple" (Esther 8:15 RSV). Haman's face is covered as he is led away disgraced after the king misconstrues Haman's desperate plea to Esther upon her couch in a farcical reenactment of the jealous *husband motif (Esther 7:8).

Feminine perspective is important in the story as well. From start to finish we are aware that this is the story of a heroine. The moral virtue of Vashti functions as a rebuke to the sensual and drunken behavior of her husband at his stag party. Virtually the entire second chapter is devoted to feminine experiences in a harem, with an emphasis on physical beauty as the leading criterion by which the king's consort will be chosen. In her interactions with her uncle Mordecai and her husband the king, Esther behaves with the modesty and submissiveness that would have characterized women in the ancient world in their interactions with men. The essence of femininity is heightened, moreover, through the foil of the coarseness and obtuseness of most male behavior in the story. By the end of the story Esther, not the king, is the character who calls the shots for a nation, reinforcing the status of the book as a story about a heroine.

Finally, running counter to the imagery of feasting and feminine refinement and courtly splendor, we find an undertow of images of battle, cruelty and torture. People who enter the king's presence without his holding out the golden scepter are killed (Esther 4:11, 16). The edict against the Jews stipulates that the Persians "destroy," "slay" and "annihilate all Jews, young and old, women and children, in one day" (Esther 3:13 RSV). But the most vivid image by far is the seventy-five-foot-high gallows that Haman constructs for Mordecai and on which he himself is hanged. Subsequently we are led to picture the bodies of Haman and his sons dangling from gallows and the Jews smiting "all their enemies with the sword, slaughtering, and destroying them" (Esther 9:5 RSV).

The book of Esther presents us with a kaleidoscope of vivid and contradictory images. For heightened action the story is perhaps unsurpassed within the pages of the Bible.

See also BEAUTY; QUEEN; RUTH, BOOK OF; WOMAN, IMAGES OF.

EVE

Mentioned by name only four times, Eve is nonetheless a major biblical character and archetype. She is a person of multiple roles, and her characterization is ambivalent—both good and bad—as is true of all but a handful of characters whose stories are narrated in the Bible. She is the prototypical *woman of the human race, matching *Adam's status as the prototypical man. The images most strongly associated with her are *wife and *husband, rib, *serpent, forbidden *fruit, *eating, and the *curse of pain in childbearing.

Made from Adam's rib, Eve is flesh of Adam's flesh (Gen 2:23). Eve shares equally with Adam the quality of being made in God's image (Gen 1:27), just as the two together receive the command to have dominion over the earth (Gen 2:26-28).

Eve is also the first mother, leading Adam to give her the name *Eve* with the explanation that she is "the mother of all living" (Gen 3:20 RSV). The second time she is named in Scripture confirms this prophetic name given to her by Adam: "Now Adam knew Eve his wife, and she conceived and bore *Cain, saying, 'I have gotten a man with the help of the LORD' " (Gen 4:1 RSV). Adam's comment about Eve's status as the mother of all living looks backward as well as forward by echoing God's command to

Adam and Eve jointly to "be fruitful and multiply, and fill the earth" (Gen 1:28 RSV).

Again, Eve is the first *wife. She and Adam are the first couple, the prototypical husband and wife. When God first brought Eve to Adam, the writer of the account describes it in terms of the original institution of marriage (Gen 2:24), in words that Jesus quoted in his teaching on marriage (Mt 19:4-6; Mk 10:7-9). As Adam's wife, Eve is the archetypal companion and helper. In the quaint archaism from the KJV, she is Adam's "helpmeet," that is, "a helper fit for him" (Gen 2:20 RSV).

Even in the judgment scene immediately after the *Fall, Eve's characterization is positive. Whereas Adam tries to evade responsibility by blaming both God and Eve (Gen 3:12), Eve courageously and straightforwardly admits what has happened (Gen 3:13). And while pronouncing a curse on Eve in the form of pain in childbearing and being ruled by her husband (Gen 3:16), God at the same time declares Eve as the one through whose seed the Savior will arise to crush the serpent (Gen 3:15).

So much for the positive side of Eve. The negative side centers in Eve's status as the first human to fall. Having said that, we must insist that the tradition of Eve as a temptress, and the broader tradition of misogyny that sees her as a troublesome helpmeet and crooked rib, is wholly a product of postbiblical traditions. In the Genesis account of the Fall, Eve does not tempt Adam; she eats first and "she also gave some to her husband, and he ate" (Gen 3:6 RSV). There is no story of temptation here, although God says to Adam in the judgment scene, "you have listened to the voice of your wife" (Gen 3:17 RSV).

This is not to say that Eve escapes stigma for her role in the Fall. Paul draws attention to Eve as someone deceived by the serpent's cunning (2 Cor 11:3), but the focus is not on Eve's inherent sinfulness. Still, Eve does here fit the conventional role of a warning against sin—not as the one who seduces Adam into sin but as the one seduced into sin by Satan. In 1 Timothy 2:14 Eve's being deceived and sinning first is offered as a reason (buttressed by the fact that she was created second) for her subordinate role in marriage, but here too there is no trace of the archetype that has been so powerful in the postbiblical tradition of Eve as a seducer to sin. We also need to note that the fall of the human race is traced back to Adam, not to Eve (Rom 5:12-14).

A final picture of Eve that stays in the imagination is the pathos of her actions in the Fall and its aftermath. As we read the story of Satan's temptation of Eve in the Garden, we wince at her false reasoning about why it would be desirable to eat the forbidden fruit (Gen 3:1-6). Eve is here the victim of temptation, not the tempter. We relive the disillusionment that comes with the first couple's self-consciousness and shame and their awareness of their alienation from God (Gen 3:7-8). Once Eve has admitted her *guilt in the judgment scene (Gen 3:13), she is silent and chastened, bearing the harsh prophecies of God that she will follow her husband, serve him and bear her children in pain. She wordlessly follows Adam out of the Garden. The fallen Eve then joins Adam in their harsh life outside of Eden, disillusioned as she sees her firstborn become a murderer of his brother and an exile from human society (Gen 4:1-16).

See also ADAM; DECEPTION, STORIES OF; FRUIT, FRUITFULNESS; GARDEN; GUILT; INNOCENCE, FALL FROM; SERPENT; TEMPTATION, TEMPTER; WIFE; WOMAN, IMAGES OF.

EVENING. *See* NIGHT; TWILIGHT.

EVIL

The Bible tells the story of evil—its origin, its battle against good and its ultimate defeat at the hands of an eternally good God. Being so integral to the story from start to finish, evil emerges consistently in a large pattern of biblical images. In general, Scripture communicates the nature and activity of evil through images of (1) *light and *dark, (2) direction, (3) the *hunt, (4) agriculture, (5) the *body and (6) ordinary domestic life. Diverse as they are, these images all picture evil as the undesirable perversion of good.

Evil and Good: Darkness and Light. Evil in Scripture consistently appears next to and opposed to good. In Genesis 2:9 the first mention of the *tree of the knowledge of good and evil exposes that great divide. On the one hand is the source of all goodness, an eternally good God who created all things "very good" (Gen 1:31 NIV); on the other hand is anybody or anything opposed to God's perfect nature and activity. *Adam and Eve internalized that great divide for the human race when they disobeyed God and then came to know good and evil (Gen 3:22). The whole story of human beings in relation to their Creator continues to develop in the context of this opposition between good and evil, with people loving evil rather than good, for example (Ps 52:3), or calling good evil and evil good (Is 5:20). The prophets call God's people to hate evil and love good (Amos 5:15), and Hebrews 5:14 describes the "mature" as those who have "trained themselves to distinguish good from evil" (NIV).

Clearly then the Bible most often distinguishes evil, not in isolation but rather in relation to good—that is, to God. God sets his face against evil and evildoers (Ps 34:16; Jer 23:30). God's goodness is primary; evil opposes his goodness: that opposition best expresses the nature of evil.

The Bible portrays this opposition of evil to good through images of *darkness and *light. From the very beginning when God spoke the light into being, saw that the light was good and separated the light from the darkness, the light became associated with good, with God himself. Darkness, by contrast, works as the opposite of light and goodness, most often picturing a world of evil, alienated from God. Job 34:22 speaks of evildoers futilely attempting to hide from God in dark places and deep shadows. Into

the darkness of this world came the light of Jesus Christ, but people "loved darkness instead of light because their deeds were evil" (Jn 1:4-5; 3:19-20). "The people walking in darkness" are the sinful people who will see the "great light" of the promised Christ (Is 9:2).

The shining of light in the darkness gives a picture not just of original creation, not just of Christ's coming, but also of each individual's redemption from the evil of sin and death: "You were once darkness," Paul writes to the Ephesians, "but now you are light in the Lord" (Eph 5:8 NIV).

Images of Direction. Scripture also portrays this opposition of evil to good through images of direction. Good is the divinely intended *pathway or direction toward God and light and life; evil leads off in the opposite direction toward darkness and death. David, in his final song, rejoices that he has "kept the ways of the LORD" and "not done evil by turning from my God" (2 Sam 22:22 NIV).

This directional, even geographical, picture of evil builds steadily throughout the Old Testament. The prophets, as well as David and Solomon, often speak of "turning from" evil (Ps 18:21; 34:14; 37:27; Prov 13:19; Jer 18:11; 25:5; Ezra 33:11). Human beings are pictured as on a journey, choosing a direction in which to travel: either an "evil path" (Job 22:15; Ps 119:101; Prov 28:10), or the "highway of the upright," which "avoids evil" (Prov 16:17 NIV).

The NT develops this pattern of directional imagery less consistently, partly perhaps because Jesus Christ arrives and says of himself, "I am the way" (Jn 14:6). In the perfectly righteous Son of God, the picture of the path toward God and away from evil comes to life. Through his shed blood he made "a new and living way" to draw near to God (Heb 10:19-22). When Paul speaks of those who "reject the truth and follow evil," we understand that he means those who reject Jesus Christ and turn away from him who is the only way to God (Rom 2:8). When Paul tells Timothy to "flee the evil desires of youth, and pursue righteousness," we understand that he is directing this young man to turn his heart away from the world and toward Christ (2 Tim 2:22).

Images of the Hunt. Paul's advice to Timothy both continues the directional imagery and introduces another pattern of images: evil imaged as a *hunt. Both actions and agents of evil appear as aggressive pursuers of human souls to "ensnare" them (Prov 5:22). Evil desires *"trap" the unfaithful, and sinful talk "traps" an evil man (Prov 11:6; 12:13). Often we see an evil person's trap springing backward and capturing the very one who set it: the one who "leads the upright along an evil path will fall into his own trap," according to Proverbs 28:10 (NIV). In the subsequent chapter, "an evil man is snared by his own sin" (29:6). When *David prays for evil to "recoil" on his *enemies, we see a similar ironic picture of this evil turning back from the hunted to attack the hunter (Ps 54:5). When God warns *Cain about his need to master the evil in his heart, he metaphorically pictures evil as a monster "crouching" at Cain's *door, ready to destroy him (Gen 4:7).

The hunt most often ends with death: it seems appropriate that in the end evil (personified) "will slay the wicked" (Ps 34:21 NIV). The whole context of pursuit (*see* Flight), capture and death suggests not only a hunt but a broader battle as well—a *war, even. Scripture's imagery establishes evil as the great adversary that threatens death and that must itself be "swallowed up" by God in the end (Is 25:8). The Bible often shows this adversary focused in the person of *Satan, the "evil one," the ultimate enemy of God (Mt 6:13; 13:19; 1 Jn 2:13-14). Often, however, evil is itself spoken of as the great adversary, simply that which in any form opposes, hunts down and tries to kill the good.

Agricultural Images. Not only on the larger scale of chase and battle but also in the smaller world of agriculture (*see* Farming), Scripture paints pictures of evil and the destruction and death it brings. The many and various layers of biblical pictures effectively communicate the pervasive influence of evil in all the layers of this fallen world. In the world of agriculture, evil most often shows itself in the form of ugly, unwanted or hurtful growth, such as *thorns (2 Sam 23:6-7), *grass (Ps 92:7), stubble (Mal 4:1) and weeds (Mt 13:37-43). Each of these four references speaks specifically of the people who have given themselves to evil. The pictures not only expose the evil of these "evildoers" but also show the ends to which such people will finally come: the thorns (evil people) will be "cast aside" and "burned up." Evildoers, though they spring up and flourish like grass, will be "forever destroyed"; the stubble, representing the arrogant and evil, will be set on *fire in the *day of judgment with not a root or branch left. Finally, in Matthew's account, Jesus even explains the imagery himself, calling the weeds "sons of the evil one"—*sown by the devil, destined to be pulled up and thrown into the fire by God's angels. Again the good is present by contrast: Matthew's "good *seed," for example, represents the "sons of the kingdom," planted by Jesus Christ, the *"son of Man," and destined to "shine like the sun" with God forever.

Agricultural images also use the rules of nature to reveal moral laws regarding good and evil. Job's friend Eliphaz, although he does not correctly apply the principle to Job, rightly understands that those who plow evil will reap it in the end (Job 4:8): evil will bring destruction and death. The prophet Hosea accuses God's people of having planted wickedness; therefore, they are reaping evil and eating the fruit of deception (Hos 10:13). By contrast he exhorts them to "sow for yourselves righteousness" and "reap the fruit of unfailing love" (Hos 10:12). Scripture presents evil not as random acts, disconnected from causes or consequences; rather, evil grows from opposition to God and brings about evil results: "A man reaps what he sows" (Gal 6:7-8). The well-known teaching concerning the love of money as "a

*root of all kinds of evil" adds to this agricultural pattern, which shows the inevitable progression of evil: from seed to root to plant to fruit.

Images of the Body. In a few instances Scripture refers to evil as an entity independent of any doer. Job laments that "when he hoped for good, evil came" (Job 30:26). Modern usages and discussions of evil tend to treat it much more as a separate, abstract entity, however. Job might be said to speak in this way because he does not understand the heavenly actors he cannot hear or see (*see* Blind; Deaf). In the overwhelming majority of biblical references, evil is connected to an agent, human or other. Since in most cases the agent is human, it is not surprising to find a whole series of images that portray evil in connection with various parts of the human body.

The *mouth, for example, often finds its place in pictures of evil: the wicked man has trouble and evil "under his tongue" (Ps 10:7); his mouth both "gushes evil" and "gulps down evil" (Prov 15:28; 19:28); his pursed *lips show him "bent on evil" (Prov 16:30). The lips especially are pictured as either feeding, *spitting out or concealing the contents of an evil heart.

The *heart is central in Proverbs and in all of Scripture, evil ultimately takes over that symbolic innermost part of the human body and from there gushes forth either blatant evil or deceptively words and deeds. What of "fervent lips with an evil heart"? They are "like a coating of glaze over earthenware," Proverbs 26:23 (NIV) claims, with a characteristically homey and unmistakably clear simile. Consistently, throughout both the OT and NT, the heart is pictured as the place where good or evil resides and rules a person. Jesus explained that no *food going into a person's *stomach could corrupt a person; rather, all the evils coming out of the heart make a person unclean (Mt 15:16-20; Mk 7:17-23).

*Eyes picture the presence or absence of evil in a person as well. Isaiah refers to evil people as those with "an eye for evil" (Is 29:20). The righteous one, by contrast, "shuts his eyes against contemplating evil" (Is 33:15). Most of the images of eyes in relation to evil, however, ask us to imagine the eyes of God, who in his holiness and omniscience sees all good and evil utterly clearly. The historical books of the OT in particular include over forty references to those who "did evil in the eyes of the Lord." According to Habakkuk, God's eyes are "too pure to look on evil" (Hab 1:13). The eye imagery offers one of the best imaginative understandings of evil: that which offends the eyes of our holy God. God does look on evil, as he teaches Habakkuk, but with the ultimate purpose of redemption for the repentant and wrath for the unrepentant. Like the wise king in Proverbs 20:8, God will "winnow out all evil with his eyes." Without the eyes of God looking on, evil would not be evil. When God declares that he will fix his eyes on the unrepentant "for evil and not for good," he clearly means not that any evil will emanate from himself but that because of his own holy self, evildo-ers must end in wrath and judgment: total separation from God will be the inevitable final stage of their evil (Amos 9:4).

*Hands provide pictures of evil in action as well (Job 8:20; Ps 71:4; 125:3; Is 56:2; Jer 23:14; Mic 7:3). The hand of God is never associated with evil, but all these pictures of evil hands take on their full significance in contrast to the hand of God, which throughout Scripture pictures his righteous and lov-ing connection to his creation. From the mouth to the heart to the eyes to the hands to the feet (Prov 4:27; 6:18), the Bible offers a fleshed-out portrait of evil, a vivid series of pictures that human readers cannot fail to understand.

Images of Ordinary Domestic Life. The final category of images might be titled "All the Rest"; however, the concrete, everyday quality they all share might well entitle them to a unique grouping, one dealing with issues of ordinary domestic life. These images seem especially close to home; they effectively communicate the ways in which evil winds itself into all the ordinary threads of life.

OT passages at times picture evil as a *guest who comes to stay, or "dwell in your tent" (Job 11:14). David condemns his enemies, "for evil finds lodging among them." In fact, according to Proverbs 17:13, evil will never leave the house of one who returns evil for good: evil is a guest who wants to settle down forever. This picture points not only to the undesir-able nature of the guest but also to the wrong and the responsibility of the one who would entertain such a guest.

Evil shows itself through a number of other bib-lical pictures from daily life: dirtiness and cleanliness (Prov 20:30; Jer 4:14; see Purity); *birth (Job 15:35; Ps 7:14; Is 59:4); purging, *drinking, and *eating (Deut 13; 17; 22; Job 15:16; 20:12; Prov 19:28). Finally, numerous references to repaying evil for good use the common example of paying back a loan to picture the contrariness of evil: good comes first, and then evil perverts it and tries to replace it, "paying back evil for good" (Ps 35:12; 38:20; 109:15; Prov 17:13; Rom 12:17; 1 Pet 3:9).

All the scriptural images of evil in one way or another point us back to the good. For in the dark-ness the light shines; a direction is wrong because it turns from the right way; the hunted one runs from the hunter who traps to kill, into the arms of one who frees and gives life; weeds and thorns are defined in terms of the desirable plants from which they differ and which they can harm; the human body acting out evil in all its different parts is the perversion of Eden and readies us to see the Savior who came to us in the flesh. In all these images the Bible tells the whole story of evil and good, pointing continually toward the one good God who is the story's beginning and end.

See also ANTICHRIST; BODY; CRIME AND PUNISH-MENT; DARKNESS; DEMONS; EAR, HEARING; EYE, SIGHT; FARMING; HANDS; HARVEST; HEART; HUNTING; LIPS; MOUTH; SATAN; SIN; SOW, SOWING, SOWER; TEMPTA-TION, TEMPTER; TRAP, TRAPPING.

EXALTATION, ENTHRONEMENT. *See* ASCENSION; HIGH, HEIGHT, HIGH PLACE; EPHESIANS.

EXCREMENT. *See* DUNG.

EXECUTION. See CRIME AND PUNISHMENT; CROSS; STONING.

EXILE

Exile is both a *plot motif and a *character type. The essential ingredient in both cases is a person who has been banished from a native place and is now living or *wandering in foreign parts. While we ordinarily link the state of exile with judgment against someone for wrongdoing, in the Bible this is by no means always the case. In fact all true believers are pictured as being exiles from their true homeland.

An exile story is preceded by a scene of banish-ment and a subsequent journey, and the Bible con-tains some memorable examples. The prototype is the expulsion from the *Garden (Gen 3:24), which in a single moment made the entire human race an exile from its original home. It is impossible to overstate the importance of this banishment, which not only awakens the wellsprings of human regret and nostalgia but is also the starting point of every subsequent human story—the backdrop to all that is recorded in the Bible.

Other scenes of banishment follow the original one. *Cain is banished "from the presence of the LORD" (Gen 4:16 RSV) as the sentence for having murdered his brother, *Jacob is forced to flee for his life after having cheated his brother (Gen 27:41—28:5), and *Joseph is sold into slavery in a foreign land (Gen 37:25-28). *Moses flees to Midian to avoid Pharaoh's death threat (Ex 2:15). Similarly, *David repeatedly flees from Saul, and later in life he is temporarily banished from the throne by Absa-lom's rebellion. In the story of *Jesus' nativity, the *flight into Egypt is a banishment (Mt 2:13-15). In virtually all of the older literature, life at *court was a precarious existence, dependent on the whims of the ruler. The Bible accordingly records instances of people banished from court, including Adonijah (1 Kings 2:26-27), Shimei (1 Kings 2:36-38) and Haman (Esther 7:5-10). To see banishment "writ large," we can turn to the OT prophetic books with their vivid pictures of what it will be like for the nation to be conquered and carried away into captivity.

While banishment is the moment in which a person becomes an exile, being an exile is the condi-tion of life that follows. Exile encompasses a social role involving fringe status and a psychological state that includes as its salient features a sense of loss or deprivation and a longing to *return to (or arrive at) a homeland. Whenever an exile is experiencing pun-ishment for a crime, moreover, the state of exile is accompanied by feelings of *guilt and perhaps remorse (as in the book of *Lamentations). Even more important for Israelite culture would be the sense of *shame that attaches to such an exile. Above all, the exile is a displaced person. Moses sounds the authentic note when he calls his first son Gershom, "for he said, 'I have been a sojourner in a foreign land' " (Ex 2:22 RSV).

Exile in the OT is mainly national. The nation that arises from the patriarchs and their sons in Egypt is the first victim of national exile in the OT. The journeying of the nation in the *wilderness during the exodus is very much the story of exiles passing through alien territory, always longing for a promised *land. On an even larger scale are the exiles of Israel and Judah later in Jewish history. The imagery of exile is mainly contained in the prophets' visions of coming exile, but we catch the flavor of what it was like for a nation to live in exile in the narratives of Daniel and Esther. What emerges is the picture of a minority group with few rights, always threatened with the imposition of pagan practices from the surrounding culture, always vulnerable to the superior power of the surrounding political structure, always longing to get back to the homeland.

Individuals as well as nations go into exile. Such is the idyllic story of *Ruth. Although the English poet John Keats pictured her as "sick for home . . . amid the alien corn," the focus of the biblical story is instead on the way in which Ruth found acceptance in a foreign culture and religion. It is the happiest story of exile on record.

For the emotions that accompany exile we can turn to several psalms. Psalms that recall the banishment of the nation by conquering forces include Psalms 74 and 137. The spiritual longing that accompanied exile for a person whose religion centered around pilgrimages to worship God in the temple in Jerusalem is captured in Psalms 42—43, the song of the disquieted soul.

The imagery of exile reaches its metaphoric climax in Hebrews 11, which portrays people of faith as "strangers and exiles on the earth" seeking "a better country, that is, a heavenly one" (Heb 11:13, 16 RSV). At the physical level, the state of being an exile retains its negative qualities in this passage, as we read about people living in tents rather than houses, sharing ill-treatment with the people of God, suffering for Christ, being tortured and wandering over the desolate parts of the earth. Yet the chapter implies that the state of exile is the inevitable lot of all who follow Christ, who was himself an archetypal exile—a person who in his life had nowhere to lay his head (Mt 8:20) and who in his death "suffered outside the gate in order to sanctify the people through his own blood" (Heb 13:12 RSV).

See also BONDAGE AND FREEDOM; EXODUS, SECOND EXODUS; GARDEN; LAND; RETURN; WANDERER, WANDERING; WILDERNESS.

EXODUS, BOOK OF

The book of Exodus is the story of Israel's birth. It tells of her lengthy period of enslavement in *Egypt and of the Lord's deliverance for the purpose of making her a "kingdom of priests and a holy nation" (Ex 19:6 NIV). More specifically, the narrative moves from slavery in Egypt to deliverance under *Moses (Ex 1—15); describes the journey to Mt. *Sinai, also called Horeb (Ex 16—19), where the law is given (Ex 20—24); and gives detailed instructions for building the *tabernacle (Ex 25—40). These final chapters also include the famous story of the "golden calf" and its consequences (Ex 32—34).

Unifying Motifs. The book of Exodus tells the story of Israel' s birth by means of various intertwining motifs. What may perhaps give some unity to this variety is the theme of *God's presence with his people*. This overarching theme can be broken down into smaller themes. One is continuity with past promises. Israel's presence in Egypt is not an accident. God is with his people as they enter Egypt (Gen 46:3). The fact that Exodus 1:1 is virtually a verbatim repetition of Genesis 46:8 (see also Gen 46:26) highlights the intention of the author to set Israel's stay in Egypt in the context of God's promises to the patriarchs (cf. also Gen 15:13-16). In delivering the Israelites, particularly in light of their pattern of *rebellion (see below), God demonstrates his faithfulness to the past. Israel's birth is an inexorable product of God's design, reaching back beyond the book of Exodus.

A second motif is *deliverance from *slavery*. While the Israelites are in Egypt, God hears their cry and is determined to deliver them (Ex 3:7-10). He is ready to bring them across the *sea despite apparent failure (Ex 14:10-14). The dominant motif used to describe God's role in this deliverance is that of *divine warrior. Despite the fact that Israel was "armed for battle" (Ex 13:18), the battle to deliver the Israelites is God's battle: "The LORD will fight for you" (Ex 14:14). The angel of God leads the Israelites to the sea and stands as a buffer between them and the Egyptian army at night (Ex 14:15-20). After crossing the sea, the Israelites recount in song the glorious deeds of their warrior God: "The LORD is a warrior; the LORD is his name" (Ex 15:3 NIV).

A third theme centers on *the *tabernacle*. Exodus 25—40 (excluding Ex 32—34) present in detail instructions for the erection of the tabernacle. It is here that the Lord's abiding presence with his people is seen: "So the cloud of the LORD was over the tabernacle by day, and fire was in the cloud by night, in the sight of all the house of Israel during all their travels" (Ex 40:38 NIV). The simple fact of the mobility of the tabernacle further highlights its function as God's abiding dwelling place with his people. Moreover, it is God's *holy presence with his people that is the issue. The specificity of the instructions for its construction demonstrates the holiness of this dwelling for Israel's holy God.

Fourth, *the *law* is a master image in the book of Exodus. The giving of the law (19—24) is a written record of God's provision for his people. The reception of the law on Mt. Sinai is the central focus of the

Israelite emigration from Egypt. The law is not a burden; rather, it is God's declaration of the people's proper response to his presence to insure that it would remain. It is because the Israelites were to become God's "kingdom of priests" and "holy nation" that they received special instructions indicating their responsibility in this relationship (Ex 19:5-6).

Another prominent theme that appears in Exodus is *Israel's grumbling and disobedience.* Throughout the book there is an undercurrent of Israel's disbelief in God's deliverance despite the wonder of what they had seen. A hint of this is seen even in Moses' reluctance to receive God's call to deliver the Israelites (Ex 3—4; especially 4:13). The first reaction of the Israelites to God's deliverance is complaint (Ex 5:1-21), which is followed once again by Moses' reluctance concerning the task before him (Ex 6:12). When the time comes to cross the sea, Israel doubts God at the first sign of trouble, which results in Moses' strong rebuke of their lack of faith (Ex 14:10-14). No sooner have they crossed the sea than they begin grumbling in earnest. First the *water is bitter, but the Lord makes it sweet (Ex 5:22-27). Then they have no *food, so God gives them bread and meat (Ex 16). However, having received the miraculous provision of food, they immediately begin to complain again about lack of adequate water, which the Lord again provides (Ex 17:1-7). The grumbling of the Israelites surfaces in outright rebellion in Exodus 32, when in Moses' prolonged absence on the mountain, the Israelites erect an *idol, thus breaking the first two commandments. The theme of grumbling and disobedience serves to contrast the behavior of the Israelites with God's patient and persistent presence with his people

Creation is another theme throughout the book. The language of Exodus 1:7 ("The Israelites were fruitful and multiplied greatly and became exceedingly numerous, so that the land was filled with them") reminds one of Genesis 1:28 ("be fruitful and increase in number; fill the earth"). While in Egypt the Israelites fulfill the mandate of creation to increase. It is precisely this numerical expansion that alarms the "new king" (Ex 1:8) and motivates him to attempt various ways to curtail their growth. Pharaoh's sin is not so much in enslaving the Israelites as in attempting to reverse the creation mandate.

In this respect the significance of both the *plagues and the crossing of the sea comes into sharper focus. The plagues are in effect a reversal of God's created order. They are the punishment and eventual destruction of the *enemies of God by unleashing the chaotic forces of creation: *water is affected (first plague); *darkness returns where there had once been light (ninth plague; esp. 10:21); *animals and other creatures suffer (e.g., fifth plague); even humans die (tenth plague). In the end the Egyptians are destroyed by water as the waters that God had once tamed at creation are unleashed. The Israelites, however, are immune from this crea-

tion reversal. They are, in fact, "created" by being brought through the parted waters (as were the waters in Gen 1:6-10) and are formed into a holy nation.

To carry the creation imagery further, some have argued that the *tabernacle itself is an earthly representation of Edenic glory, where God's presence dwells in its fullness as it once had in the *Garden. In this sense the tabernacle is another act of creation where once again God and his people dwell together.

The *anti-epic or antiheroic motif* is also important. Traditional epics praise the writer's nation; this epic reserves its praise for God. Epic leaders are normally figures overflowing with confidence; *Moses is a reluctant leader. Instead of telling a story in which a human warrior leads his nation to victory through superhuman feats on the battlefield, this epic attributes the mighty acts of deliverance to God. The traditional motif of armed conflict is replaced by moral and spiritual warfare. The disparity between divine virtue and human *weakness is accentuated by the way the Israelites put God to an ignominious test ten times (God's verdict in Num 14:22, confirmed by ten events in which the nation murmurs or rebels against God's providence). The anti-epic theme of Exodus reaches its climax in the Moses' song shortly before his death (Deut 32).

Master Images. Along with the motifs noted above, the book of Exodus is unified partly around master images, some of them recurrent archetypes and type scenes. Overarching everything else is the image of the *journey (which is even named in the book's title) as this *travel story traces the physical movement of the fledgling nation from Egypt across the *wilderness. Traveling communities naturally experience conflict—with their environment, with deprivation, with neighboring nations, with God, with leaders—as well as tension among the travelers themselves. Other archetypes cluster around the journey that is at the heart of this book: *initiation, ordeal, *testing, *quest for a promised land, *rescue.

The story qualities of the book are also important. The epic of the exodus is an *adventure story par excellence. The nation's life is a continuous narrow escape. Human nature is heightened (as it always is in stories of travel and war). Miraculous events happen regularly. Danger and suspense prevail. Variety of adventure takes the form of juxtaposed differences in type of threat, length with which an event is narrated, scene of action, harshness or mildness of the action and type of story material (e.g., external action interspersed with speeches or lawgiving).

The action also possesses its own type scene—a combination of ingredients that keeps recurring. The sequence—crisis (an implied test of the people), complaint, call to God, divine rescue, revelation/rebuke by God—is repeated many times (e.g., Ex 14:10-18, 30-31; 15:22-26; 16:1-7, 31-35; 17:1-7). In the later stages (including examples in the book of *Numbers), the revelation increasingly involves judgment or punishment as there is a progressive falling out between the nation and God.

Specific images also recur, including *fire, *water, *earth, *rock, *mountain, *eating, *manna, desert, meat, craving and *arm (especially the arm of God). Elemental nature is important in the story, both in the ten plagues and in the story of wilderness survival. We also remember evocative individual pictures, such as the individual plagues, the parted sea, the *land flowing with milk and honey that is the goal of the quest, the dancing around the golden calf, Moses dashing the tablets of the law to the ground in a moment of horror, the shining face of Moses after he meets with God, sudden death as God's punishment, water flowing from a rock.

See also ARM; BONDAGE AND FREEDOM; CREATION; DEUTERONOMY, BOOK OF; DIVINE WARRIOR; EGYPT; EXILE; LAW; MANNA; MOSES; MOUNTAIN; NUMBERS, BOOK OF; PHARAOH; PLAGUES; SEA; SINAI; SLAVERY; TABERNACLE; THEOPHANY; WARFARE; WILDERNESS.

BIBLIOGRAPHY. R. B. Dillard and T. Longman III, *An Introduction to the Old Testament* (Grand Rapids: Zondervan, 1994); J. I. Durham, *Exodus* (WBC 3; Waco, TX.: Word, 1987); D. A. Gowan, *Theology in Exodus* (Louisville: Westminster John Knox, 1994); M. G. Kline, *Images of the Spirit* (Grand Rapids: Baker, 1980).

EXODUS, SECOND EXODUS

The motif of the exodus (as distinct from the book of Exodus) is one of the unifying images of the Bible. The literal exodus of Israel from Egypt is narrated in the last four books of the Pentateuch and thereafter becomes the single richest source of allusion for OT writers. It sums up the story of OT redemption. In the NT this literal deliverance is metaphorically and spiritually fulfilled in the *atonement of Christ. The main meaning of the image is enshrined in the common metaphoric use that the term has attained in Western society: the exodus was a journey of deliverance from *bondage to freedom and fulfillment (a promised *land).

Moses sounds the keynote for the OT importance of the exodus in his farewell discourse to Israel:

Ask now about the former days, long before your time, from the day God created man on the earth; ask from one end of the heavens to the other. Has anything so great as this ever happened, or has anything like it ever been heard of? Has any other people heard the voice of God speaking out of fire, as you have, and lived? Has any god ever tried to take for himself one nation out of another nation, by testings, by miraculous signs and wonders, by war, by a mighty hand and an outstretched arm, or by great and awesome deeds, like all the things the LORD your God did for you in Egypt before your very eyes? You were shown these things so that you might know that the LORD is God; besides him there is no other. (Deut 4:32-35 NIV)

In Moses' own words, the Exodus is an amazing series of events that provide a key for interpreting the Pentateuch. More pointedly, God's deliverance in the exodus occasioned the beginning of *writing* Scripture. Though Genesis deals with history prior to the exodus, the first five books of the Bible find their origin in the events surrounding the exodus.

No other OT motif is as crucial to understand. No other event is so basic to the fabric of both Testaments. Our concepts of deliverance and atonement, of God dwelling with his people, of God taking a people for himself and so forth have their roots in this complex of events. And precisely because it so permeates the Bible, the interpretation of the exodus and its motific usage are a challenge.

What Constitutes the Exodus? In order to consider its symbolic usage, three related questions must be answered: (1) What is the historical endpoint to the complex of events?—in crossing the Red Sea? in coming to Sinai? in completing the tabernacle? at the time of the first failure to go up into Canaan? at the end of the forty years of wandering? in crossing the Jordan into the promised land? in the essential success of the conquest during the generation of Joshua? in the final completion of the conquest generations later? (2) Once the boundaries of the exodus event are settled, what are the prominent subplots within the larger story that will be used symbolically? (3) What do the various motifs signify?

On the basis of Joshua 4:19-24, Psalm 114 and the Pentateuch's conclusion, which ends at the point that Israel is ready to enter the Promised Land, the bounds of the exodus event can fairly be seen as encompassing everything from the bondage in Egypt up to the preparations to cross the Jordan after forty years of wilderness wandering. It is, of course, still legitimate to distinguish a desert (wilderness) motif as a subplot within the larger complex; but the deliverance and wandering are so tied together that they can best be treated together. The conquest motif can be seen as something different, though obviously it is a continuation of the exodus.

Motific Language. Having settled what will be used as the limits of the exodus event, identifying which subplots are prominent and used as motifs is still a challenge. The following subplots and images seem to be used as motifs in the Bible with reference to the exodus: *tabernacle, *altar, desert, *wilderness, wandering, *forty years, *mountain of God, dark *cloud, pillar of *fire/*cloud, *divine warrior, *arm/*hand of the Lord, leading, *shepherding, carrying, highway in the wilderness, oppression, deliverance from oppression, dividing waters, *plagues, *judgments, miracles, mighty deeds, *Passover, firstborn spared, *banquet (Ex 24), the *rock in the wilderness, water from the rock, *manna, riding on *eagles' wings, *theophany, mediator, voice of God, *covenant, and images related to *law and lawgiving.

Moreover the language in the historical sections of the Pentateuch describing the exodus, and the motific language used by later writers to reflect on the exodus events, may also vary widely. For example, Isaiah often speaks of a highway in the wilderness, but the historical accounts do not use the language of "highway." Certain other motifs are so connected to the exodus that one wonders whether every occurrence of such motifs is an exodus reflection. For example, do all uses of the divine warrior motif indicate the exodus motif?

One of the signal images that points to the exodus is the hand and arm of the Lord. In fact, the tandem phrase "his mighty hand and outstretched arm" becomes almost a formulaic shorthand in the OT for the power of God displayed in the exodus. While this phrase usually makes literal reference to the exodus itself, various prophetic and poetic books use the image of hand and arm to evoke a sense of the power of the exodus in new situations requiring deliverance (e.g., Is 52:10).

Metaphoric Meanings. The central meaning of the exodus is deliverance or salvation. For this reason the exodus became the ground or rationale for Israel's *obedience, identity and belief. Concerning obedience, the exodus is the basis on which God calls Israel to enter into covenant relationship with him (Ex 20:2; Deut 5:6); and it is also the basis on which Israel is to treat aliens, slaves and others with deference (Deut 15:12-18). Concerning identity, the exodus is that moment in which God forged Israel as his people (Ex 19:5), a kingdom of *priests (Ex 19:6) and a nation independent of the dominion and rule of other nations. Concerning belief, the exodus is the evidence for trusting in the power, lordship, righteousness and love of God. He is able to deliver by means of great power (Deut 4:32-35), he acts for the oppressed (Deut 10:12-22), and he acts out of love (Deut 7:7-8). The exodus motif was used by prophets and poetic writers to transfer the significance of the original exodus to new situations requiring deliverance, obedience, identity or belief. For example, Isaiah uses exodus imagery to evoke in his listeners faith and hope that God will lead a second exodus and bring the Israelites out from exile with the same wondrous deeds and power he displayed in the exodus from Egypt (Is 40:1-11).

The Exodus Motif. The first motific use of the exodus is found in Joshua 4:19-24, where the parting of the Red Sea is explicitly likened to the parting of the *Jordan. This passage provides a clear biblical example for motific and typological work.

The broad strokes of the use and development of the exodus motif in the OT might go something like this: The entry into and conquest of the Promised Land in Joshua is the exodus experience of the next generation. The book of *Judges is structured around cycles of oppression and deliverance for Israel by the hand of the Lord as they cried out for help. The books of *Samuel-*Kings can be seen as a movement from the impermanence of the exodus wanderings to a stable situation with *king and *temple and then the ultimate reversion back to an oppressive situation. The prophets transform the original exodus into a new exodus. In the same way that God delivered Israel from Egypt in the past, he will deliver Israel in the future from bondage in the *exile.

The NT borrows the exodus motif in a number of instances: John the Baptist's ministry is summarized in the words of Isaiah 40:3-4 as the one "preparing the way in the wilderness." Jesus is the new Moses, who spent forty days in the wilderness without eating and who gives a sermon on the mountain to bring new light to the law. Indeed, when Jesus speaks of his resurrection, he speaks of leading an exodus (Lk 9:31). 1 Corinthians 10:1-5 says that Christ is the rock that was there in the wilderness of the exodus. Hebrews links Moses and Jesus (Heb 3:1-18), the Israelite and the Christian (Heb 4:1-3), the tabernacle and the heavenly temple (Heb 9:1-10), and the high priest and Jesus (Heb 6:20). Moreover, Hebrews 12:18-24 suggests a move from Mt. Sinai to Mt. Zion (similar to what the prophet Isaiah is doing with his transformation of the exodus motif and his focus on Zion). Finally, the book of Revelation has numerous examples of the use of the exodus motif (e.g., the plagues, a woman delivered on eagle's wings to the desert [Rev 12:14]).

A specific example, Psalm 144, will clarify how biblical writers use the exodus symbolism. At first blush there seems to be nothing referring explicitly to the exodus. However, in the psalm, God is called Rock, and the divine warrior is clearly invoked (Ps 144:5-7); there is oppression from foreigners against which the psalmist cries out; and there are mighty waters from which he must be rescued. The final outcome is peace in the land for family and livestock.

Development in the Motif. With the progress of the history of redemption, there is also development in the meaning of the exodus motif. The exodus story is repeated several times—in the crossing of the Jordan, in the repeated deliverance from oppression during the period of the judges, in the restoration from exile, in the first coming of Christ and in his final coming.

Hope is imparted through the transferal of the power and emotion associated with the exodus to other similar situations in the history of Israel from which God's people needed deliverance. As great as the deliverance of Israel in the exodus was, Christ's salvation is greater (Heb 2:1-4). One can hear echoes of Deuteronomy 4:32-35 (quoted at the beginning of this article) in the following description of the salvation of which the exodus is the forerunner:

> For if the message spoken by angels was binding, and every violation and disobedience received its just punishment, how shall we escape if we ignore such a great salvation? This salvation, which was first announced by the Lord, was confirmed to us by those who heard him. God also testified to it by signs, wonders and various miracles, and gifts of the Holy Spirit distributed according to his will. (Heb 2:2-4 NIV)

See also ARM; BONDAGE AND FREEDOM; CREATION; DIVINE WARRIOR; EGYPT; EXILE; EXODUS, BOOK OF; MANNA; MOSES; MOUNTAIN; PHARAOH; PLAGUES; SEA;

SINAI; SLAVERY; TABERNACLE; WARFARE; WILDERNESS.

BIBLIOGRAPHY. D. Daube, *The Exodus Pattern in the Bible* (London: Faber & Faber, 1963); T. Longman III and D. G. Reid, *God Is a Warrior* (Grand Rapids: Zondervan, 1995); R. E. Nixon, *Exodus in the New Testament* (London: Tyndale, 1963); S. Talmon, "The Desert Motif in the Bible and in Qumran Literature," in *Literary Studies in the Hebrew Bible*, ed. S. Talmon (Leiden: E. J. Brill, 1993) 216-54.

EXORCISM. *See* DEMONS; MAGIC.

EXPIATION. *See* ATONEMENT.

EXPRESSIONS, FACIAL. *See* FACE, FACIAL EXPRESSIONS.

EXPULSION. *See* EXILE; FALL FROM INNOCENCE.

EYE, SIGHT

The Bible makes frequent references to the literal organ of sight (e.g., Gen 3:6; 30:41). The eyes were regarded as a source of *beauty (1 Sam 16:12; Song 1:15; 4:1, 9; 5:12; 6:5; 7:4), and the cruel punishment of putting out an enemy's eyes bears witness to the disabling effects of *blindness (e.g., Judg 16:21; 2 Kings 25:7; Jer 39:7). However sight belongs to the common stock of spiritual imagery, perhaps because of its obvious connection to *light. Spiritual sight or insight is a widespread metaphor throughout the Bible. Seeing is sometimes connected with hearing as a metaphor for spiritual perception or knowledge (e.g., Prov 20:12; 22:12; Is 6:10). In the Bible, however, sight is accorded less theological significance than hearing.

The notion of the "evil eye" that is common throughout most religious traditions is notably absent from the Bible (though Gal 3:1 may be a veiled reference). Belief in the "evil eye" was criticized by preachers in the early church.

A God Who Sees. One cluster of images revolves around the anthropomorphic portrayal of God, to whom human body parts are figuratively attributed. God is frequently described as one who sees (e.g., Ps 33:18). In the creation narratives God is described frequently as looking at his *creation (Gen 1:4, 10). His seeing is followed by moral appreciation—"it was good." By extension God sees all that takes place on earth. He is omniscient (Job 28:10; Ps 139:16; Prov 15:13; Heb 4:13). Ezekiel expands this sense of God's capacity for seeing in his description of visions of God with living creatures around him, all covered with eyes (Ezek 1:18; 10:12).

Sometimes God is petitioned to see (Ps 17:2; 2 Chron 6:20). He sees the evil perpetrated by people (Jer 16:17), though we are sometimes told that he cannot look upon evil (Hab 1:13). Indeed, God can refuse to see—with the connotation that help will not be forthcoming (e.g., Is 1:15-16). Inevitably God's seeing sometimes results in acts of judgment (Job 34:21; Ps 66:7; 94:9; Prov 15:3; 2 Kings 4:34-35; Amos 9:4, 8).

God's seeing leads to protection of those whom he loves. "The eye of the LORD is on those who fear him" (Ps 33:18 NRSV; cf. Deut 11:12; 1 Kings 8:29, 52; 9:3; 2 Chron 6:20, 40; 16:9; Ps 34:15; Ezra 5:5; Neh 1:6; 1 Pet 3:12). What God looks for is truth (Jer 5:3) and the opportunity to benefit people (Jer 24:6). By contrast, *idols are frequently described as being blind (Ps 115:5; 135:16).

Human Insight and Knowledge. Sight is frequently used as a symbol of human understanding (e.g., Gen 3:5; Jer 5:21). Usually there is an element of opinion or exercise of judgment (Prov 3:7; Jer 7:11). Sight is often applied to spiritual insight (Ps 119:18, 37), which may occur through the study of the law (Ps 19:8) or be the direct gift of God through his Spirit (Eph 1:17-18). Such understanding may become darkened or be blinded (Mt 13:13; Lk 24:16; 2 Cor 4:4). The immediate result of the *Fall, as described in Genesis, is that *Adam and Eve receive a measure of spiritual and moral insight—their eyes are opened and innocence is lost (Gen 3:5-7). In Ecclesiastes 2:12-14 the wise person is contrasted to the fool using the image of eyesight.

People can become blind due to their refusal to respond to God's word. This was to be the outcome of Isaiah's ministry (Is 6:10). God permits the people to persist in their insensitivity (cf. Deut 29:4; Jer 5:21). Jesus quotes this passage from Isaiah in the parable of the sower to explain the case of those who fail to respond to his message (Mk 4:12). Likewise Acts 28:26-27 quotes the same passage to comment upon the lack of response to the Christian message on the part of the Jews. Paul does likewise in Romans 11:8.

The desire to see God is vouchsafed only to the "pure in *heart" (Mt 5:8). People look to God for guidance (Ps 25:15; 32:8; 123:1; 145:15). Indeed, they need God to give them sight (Gen 21:19). Care needs to be taken over what is seen (Job 31:1; Ps 101:3, 6; Prov 4:25), for the eye can be damaged or obscured (Mt 7:3-5) and can become the channel of spiritual evil (Eccles 4:8; Mt 5:29; 6:22-23). On these occasions radical treatment is called for, and Jesus advocates tearing the eye out (Mt 5:29; 18:9).

Prophets are sometimes described as "seers" (e.g., 2 Sam 24:11; Is 29:10). They are especially gifted with spiritual insight from God. The story of Elisha and the armies of Yahweh is instructive. In the first instance, Elisha is unable to perceive that God's angelic forces are to be engaged in the forthcoming conflict. In due course, however, his eyes are opened (2 Kings 6:17, 20). In *apocalyptic writings such as Daniel, Ezekiel and Revelation, "the heavens were opened" to disclose visions of deity (e.g., Zech 1:18; *see* Dreams, Visions). It is principally in apocalyptic visions that God is "seen." Usually this occurs in the form of messianic incarnations (e.g., Dan 10:5-6), and the context is generally eschatological (Is 33:17; Ezek 38:23; cf. Rev 1:7).

One of the most prominent expectations of the Messiah is that he should bring "recovery of sight to the *blind" (Lk 4:18), a function amply fulfilled in the ministry of Jesus in various miracles. Mark relates the healing of the blind man at Bethsaida where there is gradual recovery of sight (Mk 8:22-26), and Matthew recounts the healing of two blind men (Mt 9:27-31), a healing clearly related to the exercise of faith (v. 29). One of the most famous healings of a blind man is that of Bartimaeus, a story common to all of the Synoptic Gospels (Mt 20:29-34; Mk 10:46-52; Lk 18:35-43). Once again the exercise of faith is connected with the healing (Mk 10:52). Matthew adds other instances (Mt 15:30; 21:14). Jesus discusses the effect of his own public ministry in terms of Isaiah 6:10 in Mark 4:10-12. The relationship between faith and sight is more explicitly explored in John (e.g., 4:48; 14:8, 11; 20:8, 29). The centerpiece of this theme is the healing of the man born blind (9:1-41), where physical sight and spiritual illumination are both concerned. John sums up the results of Jesus' public ministry by quoting once again from Isaiah 6:10 (Jn 12:40).

Idioms. The principle of *lex talionis,* intended to limit excessive revenge, was expressed in terms of "an eye for an eye" (Ex 21:23-25; Lev 24:20; Deut 19:21). Direct confrontation was "face to face," literally "eye to eye" (Num 14:14), and actions done "before their eyes" (Gen 42:24; cf. Jer 32:12). When a person's judgment is described, especially in the OT, it is "in the eyes of" that person (e.g., 2 Kings 10:5; 1 Chron 13:4; cf. Mt 21:42; Mk 12:11). Stubbornness is "doing what is right in one's own eyes" (e.g., Judg 17:6; 21:25; Ps 36:2; Prov 3:7; 10:10; 12:15; 16:2; 21:2; 30:12f; Is 5:21). Instead it is best to do what is right "in the eyes of the LORD" (e.g., 1 Kings 15:5, 11; 2 Kings 14:3). To look around is to "lift up the eyes" (e.g., Gen 13:10, 14; 18:2; 22:4, 13; 24:63-64), and "to fix one's eyes upon" is to turn one's attention to someone or something (Gen 44:21; Ps 119:6, 15; Ezek 20:24; Lk 4:20). Things can happen "in the twinkling of an eye" (1 Cor 15:52).

The pupil or "apple" of the eye is very precious, and this expression is used to describe a person who is very dear to God (Ps 17:8; Zech 2:8). It can imply the quality of God's protective care (Deut 32:10). A teacher's instruction may be similarly described (Prov 7:2).

The Eyes as Expressing Feelings. The eyes are held to express a wide range of emotions, both positive and negative. They can express physical and emotional well-being (1 Sam 14:27; Ps 38:10), enlightenment (Ps 19:8), delight (Ezek 24:16), humility (Ps 123:2), sympathy or pity (Deut 7:16; 19:13, 21; 25:12; Ezek 16:5) or generosity (Prov 22:9; Mt 6:22). They can also express a lack of physical and emotional well-being (Deut 28:65; Job 17:7; Ps 69:3; Lam 5:17), a loss of understanding (Job 17:7), grief (Ps 6:7; 31:9; 88:9; 119:136; Jer 9:1; Lam 1:6; 2:11; 3:48-49), arrogance (2 Kings 9:22; Ps 18:27;

Prov 6:17; 21:4; 30:13; Is 5:15; 37:23), a lack of sympathy (Prov 28:27; Mt 13:15), greed (1 Sam 2:29, 32), stinginess (Prov 23:6; Mt 7:22), envy (Mt 20:15), mockery (Ps 35:19; Prov 30:17), cunning and deceit (Ps 35:19; Prov 6:13; 10:10; 16:13, 30), hatred (Job 16:9), lust (Ps 73:7; Prov 17:24; 27:20; Eccles 2:10; 4:8; Ezek 6:9; Mt 5:29; 2 Pet 2:14; 1 Jn 2:16) and flirtation (Is 3:16).

See also BLIND, BLINDNESS; DISEASE, HEALING; EAR, HEARING; HEART; LIGHT; SIN.

EYE OF THE NEEDLE
In Matthew 19:24 (cf. Mk 10:25; Lk 18:25) we find the statement of Jesus: "it is easier for a camel to go through the eye of a needle than for a rich man to enter the kingdom of God" (NIV). There is no historical evidence to suggest that "eye of the needle" refers to a narrow gateway for pedestrians. It is an example of hyperbole, familiar in rabbinic teachings, and signifying something both very unusual and very difficult. The Talmud speaks of an elephant passing through the eye of a needle to evoke an impossible situation, and a camel is portrayed as dancing in a very small measure.

EZEKIEL, BOOK OF
The opening vision of the book of Ezekiel sets the tone for all that follows with its busy, bustling activity. The vision of the glory of God is not static and temple-bound, as in Isaiah 6, but is filled with motion, and even more remarkably, it is located in Babylonia by the Kebar river (Ezek 1:3). The vision begins by describing the approach of a windstorm (*rûaḥ s̆eʿārâ,* Ezek 1:4), an "immense cloud with flashing lightning and surrounded by brilliant light" (NIV). This mighty wind recalls not only *creation, where the spirit (*rûaḥ*) of God was hovering over the waters (Gen 1:2), but also the *flood, where God sent a wind (*rûaḥ*) to dry up the floodwaters (Gen 8:1). The connection with these two pivotal events of protohistory is underlined as the chapter unfolds by reference to an awesome "expanse" (*rāqîaʿ,* Ezek 1:25) over the cherubim, like that of Genesis 1:6-8. God's radiance is compared to a *rainbow in the clouds on a rainy day (Ezek 1:28), which evokes Genesis 9:13-16. These references set the tone of the book as an account of creation-uncreation-recreation, similar to that of the early chapters of Genesis.

The message of *judgment that predominates in the early chapters of Ezekiel culminates in the departure of God's *glory from the *temple. This leads to the *exile, a situation of chaos analogous to the flood. Yet from the outset the rainbow's assurance of hope strikes an optimistic note in the midst of the gathering gloom. Ultimately that hope finds expression in the vision of *restoration that centers around the return of God's glory to fill the restored temple.

Images of movement predominate in the description of God's glory. The windstorm itself is in motion, while the living creatures it contains not only have legs but *wings as well (Ezek 1:6-7). Torches are moving back and forth between the creatures (Ezek 1:13), while alongside the creatures are "wheels within wheels" (Ezek 1:16). All of these move together and stop together under the control of the spirit (*rûaḥ*, Ezek 1:20). This mobility prepares the reader for the departure of God's glory from the temple in Ezekiel 10, in response to the abominations described in chapter 8—a slow, halting departure in an easterly direction, toward the exiles in Babylon. At the same time, however, God's mobility also permits the hope that his glory will return in the same way that it went. The certainty of that hope is communicated in the vision of God's glory returning to the new temple from the *east, the direction in which it had earlier departed (Ezek 43:2). Prior to that return the people themselves will be prepared by the coming of God's spirit *(rûaḥ)*, bringing life to the dry *bones (Ezek 37:1-14), just as in creation God breathed life into the first man. That life is immediately expressed in movement as the resurrected army comes to life and stands upon its feet (Ezek 37:10).

The conversion of static imagery to an active picture can also be seen within the restored temple, where the *"sea" of the old temple—a vast pool meeting the requirements for cleansing purposes—has been transformed into a *river flowing outward from the temple, expanding as it goes and bringing life to everything it touches (Ezek 47:2-12). Likewise, at the pilgrim *festivals the worshippers are not simply to present themselves before the Lord but to pass in front of him in a great two-way stream, from north to south and from south to north (Ezek 46:9).

In expressing his message of judgment, Ezekiel uses a wide variety of vivid imagery. He employs the language of unfaithfulness: *Jerusalem is like an adopted *daughter that has rebelled (Ezek 16); Jerusalem and Samaria are like two *sisters united in their addiction to *prostitution (Ezek 23). He speaks of uselessness: Jerusalem is like a charred *vine (Ezek 15); her prophets are like a whitewashed *wall that is on the point of collapse (Ezek 13:10-16); her rulers are impotent in the face of impending disaster (Ezek 7:27); her princes are like trapped *lions (Ezek 19). He addresses the inevitability of judgment: Jerusalem is the meat in a cooking pot, to be cooked until burned to a crisp (Ezek 24); the time has now come for disaster to fall (Ezek 7:2), a judgment that begins in symbolic manner with the temple (Ezek 9:1-11). He acts out in graphic form the siege of Jerusalem and the fate of her inhabitants, besieging a clay model (Ezek 4:2), eating defiled *food (Ezek 4:9-13), cutting off his *hair and dividing it into thirds: one-third to be burned in the city, one-third to be struck with the sword outside the city and one-third scattered to the wind, with only a few hairs preserved (Ezek 5:1-4). Judgment will fall not only upon Israel and Judah but also upon the surrounding nations: the great ship Tyre will sink without trace along with its proud king (Ezek 27-28); the mighty river monster (crocodile?) Egypt, will be hooked like a fish (Ezek 29:3-4).

Alongside the images of judgment are equally vivid words of hope. God will replace the former bad *shepherds with a new good shepherd, a new David (Ezek 34:23). God will protect the weak sheep from the strong (Ezek 34:17-22). God will perform heart surgery on his people, removing their old *heart of *stone and replacing it with a new heart of flesh (Ezek 11:19). The renewed people will be restored to a renewed *land, a new *garden of Eden (Ezek 36:35), where they can once more be fruitful and multiply (Ezek 36:11).

The central thrust of all of these images is the sovereign activity of God. The message to the unfaithful people of Judah and Jerusalem is this: the great *King of all the earth is coming for judgment—who then will escape? But the message to the faithful remnant is also a message of God's sovereignty: God himself will act to restore his people and recreate his land—who then can prevent it? God will act, and will act decisively, in judgment and blessing for the sake of the glory due his name (Ezek 36:32, 38).

See also CREATION; EXILE; GARDEN; GLORY; JERUSALEM; JUDGMENT; LAND; TEMPLE.

EZRA, BOOK OF

A primary image pattern in the book of Ezra stems from the situation that it describes: return from *exile and rebuilding the *temple provide the basic framework of the book. From start to finish, the book of Ezra breathes the spirit of a new beginning, after exile, in the original promised land. This imagery of *rebirth extends to two primary areas—the rebuilt temple (in contrast to *Nehemiah, where the city dominates) and the reinstitution of worship practices. These images are supplemented in chapters 9 and 10 by the imagery of *repentance and *reform.

Within the framework of a return to something previously lost, the main image pattern of the book centers around a binary opposition between clean and unclean (*see* Purity). According to Leviticus 10:10, a primary duty of Israel's priests was "to distinguish [literally, 'separate'] between the holy and the common, and between the unclean and the clean" (NRSV; see also Ezek 44:23). *"Holy" refers to anything set apart and specially devoted to God. The "common" in the life of Israel is what is ordinary, normal and not specially consecrated to God. "Clean" conveys the idea of purity; it is the proper state of both the holy and the common in Israelite life. "Unclean" refers to what is impure or contaminated, contrary to holiness. By definition, what was holy also had to be clean, whereas the common could be either clean or unclean. This way of looking at the world provides important background for understanding the book of Ezra and in particular its use of the motif of "separation from the unclean."

Whereas the prophet *Ezekiel had condemned the preexilic priests for failing to follow Leviticus 10:10 (Ezek 22:26), Ezra is presented as the faithful priest—note his descent from the "chief priest

Aaron" (Ezra 7:1-5)—who *does* instruct the people on how to keep the clean and unclean separate. This interest in priestly concerns is not surprising. Not only does the book of Ezra narrate the reconstruction of the temple, but it is also interested in other aspects of temple life: the accessories (Ezra 1:6-11; 5:14-15; 6:5; 7:19; 8:25-30, 33-34), the personnel (Ezra 2:36-63, 70; 3:8-12; 6:18, 20; 7:7, 12-13, 24; 8:15-20, 24; 9:1; 10:18-24), the *feasts and *sacrifices (Ezra 3:1-6; 6:3, 9-10, 17, 22; 7:17; 8:35; 10:19). The story is not only *about* the temple, but it is also written from a temple-centered perspective. The world of the temple, with its emphasis on holiness and ritual purity, is the ideological point of reference from which the narrative world is interpreted.

In Ezra, holy people and holy things are distinguished from the ordinary. On the spatial level, the site of the temple is especially sacred (*see* Sacred Space). It is the place where sacrifices were made to God (Ezra 3:1-6). It is the "house of the LORD" (Ezra 1:3), set apart by a special dedication festival (Ezra 5:13-18). Furthermore, people and things that belonged in the temple were deemed to be holy. Thus, the *priests and Levites were set apart as a special subset of the nation. In their capacity as celebrants of the *Passover festival, the priests and Levites were "clean" because they "had purified themselves" (Ezra 6:19; literally, "made themselves clean"). At another time Ezra tells a group of priests who are charged with guarding temples vessels: "You are holy to the LORD, and the vessels are holy" (Ezra 8:28). Put simply, the temple is the realm devoted exclusively to the Lord.

Even more important is the separation of the clean from the unclean. If the priests and Levites were "holy," especially set apart to God, the whole of the nation was to be "clean" and separated from people who were deemed unclean. Throughout the narrative, the group referred to as "the neighboring people" (literally, "the peoples of the lands," Ezra 3:3; 6:1, 2, 11), "the people of the land" (Ezra 4:4; 10:2, 11) or "the nations of the land" (Ezra 6:21) are defined as unclean. "Pollution" (*ṭum'âh*, literally, "uncleanness") attaches to them (Ezra 6:21) primarily because they practice *"abominations" like the Canaanites who inhabited the land before them in pre-exilic times (Ezra 9:1, 11).

In the theology of the book, clean and unclean cannot be mixed but must be kept separate (Ezra 6:21). If the two are mixed, the clean is corrupted and becomes unclean. This explains the great interest in the issue of intermarriage. Ezra is appalled to learn that many Jews, including priests and Levites, had not separated themselves from the surrounding nations but had taken foreign women for their wives. Clean and unclean were no longer separate: "the *holy seed* has mixed itself with the peoples of the land"

(Ezra 9:1-3 NRSV, emphasis added). The boundary between clean and unclean had been violated; the holiness, the separateness, of the Jews was being destroyed.

The appropriate response to the threat of mixture or contamination of the clean by the unclean is active separation. Ezra demands that the community end the practice of mixed *marriages. He also requires that Jewish husbands dissolve existing marriages by "separating themselves" from their foreign wives (Ezra 10:11) and "sending them away with their children" (Ezra 10:19). Anyone who refused to comply was "banned [literally, "separated"] from the congregation of the exiles" (Ezra 10:8).

The concern for the purity of the "holy seed" also explains the strong interest in genealogies (Ezra 2:1-63; 8:1-14). Lines of descent play a crucial role in defining the holy people. Any Jew who could not prove his lineage was defined as "not belonging to Israel" (Ezra 2:59). Particularly problematical was the case of those who claimed to be priests but could not find their names in the appropriate genealogical lists. Until they could prove their lineage by an alternate method, they were deemed to be "unclean" and prohibited from eating from "the most holy food" (Ezra 2:62-63). This is another form of separation of clean (or holy) from the unclean. The boundary between the holy and the unclean was to be maintained at all costs. The obviously unclean (foreign wives and their children) had to be excluded from the community, but also those who were not unambiguously "clean" (that is, of Israelite descent) were separated in some way from the realm of the holy.

This binary opposition between the clean and the unclean explains why even non-Jews who claimed to worship the Lord were excluded from the reconstruction of the temple. The leaders of the surrounding people saw no boundary between themselves and the Jews. They focused on what united them to the Jews: "Let us build with you, for we worship your God as you do" (Ezra 4:2). But the response of the Jewish leaders was based on a radical sense of unbridgeable separateness between the two peoples. Even an apparently mutual devotion to the Lord cannot overcome this division. The Jewish leaders responded, "You shall have no part with us [literally, "it is not to you and to us"] in building a house to our God; but we alone will build to the LORD" (Ezra 4:3 NRSV). In the ideology of the book, the concept of "you *and* us," the togetherness of Jew and Gentile, is inconceivable. From the Jewish vantage point, it can only be "we *alone*" building a temple for "*our* God."

See also CLEANSING; EXILE; HOLINESS; JERUSALEM; PRIEST; PURITY; REPENTANCE; RETURN; SACRED SPACE; TEMPLE.

F

FACE, FACIAL EXPRESSIONS

The face is an ever-changing billboard signaling our own attitudes and reactions. In turn, we read the faces of others. The face contains most of the clues we seek as to the mental state of another person. Much of what we know about others we learn from their faces before they even speak. It offers no surprise then, that in the Bible the face is often described as indicating emotions and attitudes.

Face as Self. One's face is one's true self. To honor the face is to honor the person (Lev 19:32). The king's question "Why is your face sad?" means "Why are you sad?" (Neh 2:2). The face is so much one's self that the word for face functions almost as a reflexive pronoun; for example, Job's leanness testifies to his face (Job 16:8). With childlike simplicity we instinctively attempt to hide our whole selves by covering only our face (Ex 3:6). Since the face is the essence of the person, abuse is directed at the face (Mk 14:65; cf. Deut 25:9).

Literature employs the symbolism of the face to expose nature and character. Just as the face of *Moses showed that he had been with God (Ex 34:29), so also the company of the divine transfigures the appearance of Jesus (Mt 17:2). The true character of the martyr Stephen flashes on his visage—a combination of innocence, power and grace that Luke describes as the "face of an angel" (Acts 6:15). A "face like lightning" along with other attributes suggests that the man in Daniel's vision is no mortal (Dan 10:6; cf. Lk 24:4). John's vision of one like the son of man describes him with a "face like the sun" (Rev 1:16). The creatures that surround the throne of God and worship him portray elements of creation. The third animal represents humanity and so has the "face of a man" (Rev 4:7; cf. Ex 25:20; Is 6:2; Ezek 1:10; 10:14).

Face as Presence. The Hebrew expression "to (his) face" means simply "before," or "in front of," and appears in many NT citations of the OT (e.g., Mt 11:10; Mk 1:2). To "see the face" is to gain acceptance to one's presence (Gen 32:20; Esther 1:14; Acts 20:25). The face of Moses, because he had been in the presence (before the face) of God, shone (Ex 34:29; 2 Cor 3:7). The devout live as if in the presence of God, obeying his command "Seek my face" (Ps 27:8). The believer's current understanding of God is as "in a *mirror dimly, but then face to

face" (1 Cor 13:12 RSV; cf. 2 Cor 10:1; 1 Thess 2:17; 3:10; 2 Jn 12; 3 Jn 14).

Face as Intent. Simply because the front is not the *back, a face implies direction and intent. Intent extends to resolve and purpose (Num 24:1; Prov 17:24). To set one's face toward or against evokes resolve and determination (Lev 17:10; 20:3; 2 Kings 12:17; Lk 9:51,53). "I have set my face against this city for evil and not for good" (Jer 21:10 RSV; cf. 44:11). Even inanimate objects may be said to face one direction or another. Paul's ship "could not face the wind" (Acts 27:15).

Face as False or Deceitful. The face so transparently manifests one's attitude and mood that the best way to disguise feelings is to alter one's visage, to be a hypocrite (Grk *hypokritēs,* "a play-actor," Mt 6:16). The difficulty of maintaining such a ruse prompts the accused to request an audience with their accusers "face to face" (Acts 25:16). Disguising the face is an attempt to hide the truth from others or to hide from the truth oneself (Job 24:15).

A changed visage, however, need not reflect dishonesty. A washed face, like washed hands, represents a fresh start (Gen 43:31; Mt 6:17) and a wiping away or hiding of a former state.

Face as Light and Dark. The metaphor of *light emerging on the face is common. Faces beam. Faces glow. Understanding dawns on the face. Faces break out in a grin. Smiles flash across the face. The bloom of youth appears there too. A shining human face stems from healthy skin, cared for with oil (Ps 104:15), in contrast to the starving whose "visage is blacker than soot" (Lam 4:8 RSV).

The ultimate blessing is to have the Lord's face shine upon you (Num 6:25; Pss 31:16; 67:1). "Restore us, O God; let thy face shine that we may be saved" (Ps 80:3, 7 RSV). This shining face of God is linked to teaching his statutes and keeping the law (Ps 119:135). Outside the canon we find in 4 Ezra a statement of sharp contrasts: "The faces of those who practiced self-control shall shine more than the stars, but our faces shall be blacker than darkness" (4 Ezra 7:55).

Face as Hidden or Covered. A hidden face not only denies what it refuses to see but refuses to admit that it is present: "You shall cover your face, that you may not see the land; for I have made you a sign for the house of Israel" (Ezek 12:6 RSV).

"Hide thy face from my sins, and blot out all my iniquities" (Ps 51:9 RSV), the psalmist prays. The second of the two parallel units raises the ante by asking that God not only deny the sins' existence but actually wipe them out. While God may anthropomorphically hide his face, humans do so literally. To our own detriment we have found God's chosen one repulsive and deplorable and so have hidden our faces from him (Is 53:3). To see the face of God is linked to worship (Rev 22:3-4), hinting that when God hides his face, he not only withdraws his presence and benevolent guardianship but also shuns the human offerings of worship and prayer. To hide the face is to break off communication (Deut 31:17-18; 32:20), often implying revulsion and abhorrence. A hidden face ignores requests for help (Ps 13:1; 69:17) and refuses to answer (Ps 102:2). The poets equate this lack of divine oversight with the absence of God's spirit (Ezek 39:29), even comparing it to *death and the *pit (Ps 143:7).

Among humans, to look another in the face is to ask for equal standing, recognition between peers (2 Chron 25:17). As a gesture of *humility, to *bow the face is to hide it in symbolic self-denial and deference or respect (Josh 5:14; 1 Chron 21:21). At the sound of the "still small voice" of God, Elijah wrapped his face in his mantle (1 Kings 19:13). In the new covenant, worshipers will be able to stand before God with unveiled face (2 Cor 3:18), and in the remade world they will see the face of God (Rev 22:4). In the great day of wrath, people will scramble to hide from the face of the one seated on the throne (Rev 6:16).

Mouth. The constituent elements of the face each communicates on its own. The *mouth can both disarm with a smile and antagonize with a threat. Job's smile encouraged his associates when they had no confidence of their own, and they appreciated the light of his countenance (Job 29:24). The psalmist laments that his enemies gape at him or make mouths at him (Ps 22:7).

Nose. Perhaps because the spirit of the body (the *breath) comes and goes through the *nose, it is an indicator of one's spirit, especially *anger. The nose is heated in anger, reminiscent of the snorting of a *horse. The imagery of human anger in turn expresses divine anger and "hot displeasure" (Deut 9:19). "Turn thy fierce wrath" (Ex 32:12) is literally "the burning anger of thy nostrils." In contrast, patience and being "slow to anger" is literally to be "long of nose" (Ex 34:6), perhaps meaning slow to heat up, as in Priscilla's metaphor of the captain in *The Courtship of Miles Standish:* "He's a little chimney and heated hot in a moment." Haughtiness shows clearly in the image of a raised nose (Ps 10:4).

Eyes. As perhaps the most expressive single element of the face, contact with the *eyes is essential to nonverbal communication. The eye, as a window to the soul, serves as an gauge of the wholeness, the spiritual and physical well-being of the individual. Even today, but more so in the past, the windy and dusty environment of the Middle East afflicts the eye

with many *diseases. The eye also serves as an indicator for various other systemic diseases, reflecting one's health and spiritual condition all in one, for "the light of the body is the eye" (Mt 6:22; cf. Prov 30:13; Lam 5:17).

Unaware that the eye only sensed reflected light, the ancients held that the eyes emitted a power that illumined objects. Thus darkness was not merely the absence of light, but the forces of darkness overpowering and swallowing up the human ability to see. In such a worldview the eyes actively emitted messages, expressing an attitude with every observation.

Nowhere is this view of the magical power inherent in the observer's eye more evident than in the almost universal ancient belief in the power of the evil eye. Some people, it was thought, could bring about calamity by casting a spell with an "evil eye." The expression of jealous sentiments or even compliments were viewed as harboring vengeful spirits that would subsequently destroy what had been admired. In accordance with this outlook, the phrase "evil eye" in Scripture is usually rendered conceptually as "jealousy." The literal phrase "Is thine eye evil because I am good?" (Mt 20:15 AV) becomes "Do you begrudge my generosity?" (RSV).

But the eye betrays the inner spirit and may be selfish and hoarding (Prov 22:6) or bountiful and generous (Prov 22:9). Eyes can be sharpened like weapons (Job 16:9) and narrowed to a threatening squint (Ps 35:19; Prov 6:13; 10:10; Job 15:12). The eyes communicate the whole range of human emotions: suspicion (1 Sam 18:9), haughtiness (Ps 101:5; Prov 6:17), arrogance (Is 2:11; 5:15; Ps 101:5; 18:28), humility (Job 22:29), pity (Deut 7:16).

The power of the eye is not exercised only for evil. The poet testifies to the power of a look: "You have ravished my heart with a glance of your eyes" (Song 4:9 RSV). The eyes attract attention for their beauty (Song 1:5; 4:1; 5:12) or occasionally for their lack of beauty (Leah, Gen 29:17). Artificial enhancements such as eye makeup attempt to take advantage of the beauty and power of the eyes (2 Kings 9:30; Jer 4:30; Ezra 23:40). The eyes are deep pools into which we stare to fathomed the depth of the other's character by long contemplation (Song 7:4). Yet even a lover's stare can be uncomfortable (Song 6:5).

Face as Emotions. The face displays the whole range of human feelings. It grows pale in crisis: "Jacob shall no more be ashamed, nor more shall his face grow pale" (Is 29:22 RSV); "Why has every face turned pale?" (Jer 30:6 RSV; cf. Joel 2:6; Nahum 2:11). Faces flushed with *pain and agony are "faces aflame" (Is 13:8). The *fire of the Lord, like a flame, will produce scorched faces (Ezra 21:3). Faces also grow "red with weeping" (Job 16:16). *Tears are an unmistakable sign of sorrow that the Lord will wipe away from all faces (Is 25:8).

"A glad heart makes a cheerful countenance" (Prov 15:13 RSV), but in the counterintuitive logic of Ecclesiastes, "by sadness of countenance the heart is made glad" (Eccles 7:3 RSV). Life is bittersweet and sadness makes the laughter more poignant. A fallen countenance indicates displeasure (Gen 4:5-6), but Eli can see on Hannah's face that she is no longer sad (1 Sam 1:18). Ezekiel reproaches those who because of their abominations have faces covered with horror and *shame (Ezek 7:18). Other prophets describe the face similarly: "Dishonor has covered our face, for aliens have come into the holy places of the LORD's house" (Jer 51:51 RSV); "Shame has covered my face" (Ps 69:8 RSV); "Fill their [unbeliever's] faces with shame" (Ps 83:16 RSV).

See also ANGER; FOREHEAD; GESTURES; EYES, SIGHT; FEAR; GLORY; HAPPINESS; LIPS; MOUTH; NOSE; SHAME; TONGUE.

FACIAL EXPRESSIONS. *See* FACE, FACIAL EXPRESSIONS.

FADE, FADING
The Bible uses the word *fade* primarily to denote the *transience of human life and the futility of sin. Nearly always the imagery of *grass or *plants and their short lives is used to remind people of their short stay on earth. The word *fade* thus has a two-pronged focus: it emphasizes that all humans will die and that only God is eternal, and it also emphasizes that the wicked will be judged and destroyed by God, but the righteous will ultimately be rewarded.

At a literal level, fading is a specific image within the more general category of transience and *mutability. It denotes a gradual diminishment of either *light, sight or vitality in plant life, usually as a way of emphasizing the transience and sorrow of life. Job, for example, comments that "as the cloud fades and vanishes, so those who go down to Sheol do not come up" (Job 7:9 NRSV), and the psalmist compares people to grass: "In the morning it flourishes and is renewed; in the evening it fades and withers" (Ps 90:6 NRSV). This transience brings pain and suffering to human beings. Job mourns, "My eye has grown dim from grief, and all my members are like a shadow" (Job 17:7). Likewise the psalmist laments how his *eyes "grow dim with waiting" for his God and through the sorrow that inevitably accompanies life (Ps 69:3; 88:9). For Paul the enduring splendor of the new covenant is far superior to that of the old covenant; the glory of the old is illustrated by the fading glory of Moses' face, which he hid behind a *veil after being in the presence of God (2 Cor 3:7-11). In contrast to such human and earthly fading, God is eternal and never changes: "The grass withers, the flower fades, when the breath of the LORD blows on it; surely the people are grass. . . . But the word of our God will stand forever" (Is 40:7-8 NRSV).

More specifically, the image of fading is used to denote the punishment that will come to the wicked (*see* Crime and Punishment). Job declares of them, "They are exalted a little while, and then they are gone; they wither and fade like the mallow; they are cut off like the heads of grain" (Job 24:24). The psalmist echoes this, declaring that the wicked "will soon fade like the grass, and wither like the green herb" (Ps 37:2 NRSV; cf. Isaiah's picture of people dwindling as punishment for their guilt [Is 24:6]). In keeping with the Bible's view of humankind as universally sinful, such fading is ascribed to the entire human race: "We all fade like a leaf, and our iniquities, like the wind, take us away" (Is 64:6 NRSV).

However, the Bible speaks of a method of escaping this inevitable process. The key lies in redemption by the imperishable and precious blood of Christ, which enables people to be "born anew, not of perishable but of imperishable seed, through the living and enduring word of God" (1 Pet 1:23 NRSV). If this happens, resurrection also becomes possible, so that "what is sown is perishable, what is raised is imperishable" (1 Cor 15:42 NRSV).

In addition to eternal life, God also promises eternal reward to those who are faithful in life. Jesus commanded his disciples, "Do not store up for yourselves treasures on earth, where moth and rust consume and where thieves break in and steal, but store up for yourselves treasures in heaven" (Mt 6:19 NRSV), for this treasure will be "an inheritance that is imperishable, undefiled, and unfading" (1 Pet 1:4 NRSV). Even the trials that made the eyes of Job and the psalmist dim can bring forth benefit in heaven, for such trials are meant to test "the genuineness of your faith—being more precious than gold that, though perishable, is tested by fire—may result in praise and glory and honor when Jesus Christ is revealed" and in a "crown of glory that never fades away" (1 Pet 1:7; 5:4 NRSV). Thus the Christian has hope in Christ that he or she may escape the fading caused by death and sin.

See also CORRUPTION; DECAY; GLORY; RUST; VEIL.

FAITH
Images of faith are rare in the Bible. This is partly because faith is an instrument. Although it is nothing in itself, saving faith appropriates Jesus Christ and everything he has to offer (Jn 11:25-26; 14:1; Acts 16:31; 1 Jn 3:23). Faith is the means *by which* a person is justified (Rom 3:28; Gal 2:16; 3:8, 24) and the action *through which* a person receives the righteousness of Christ (Rom 3:22; Phil 3:9). Believers are also sanctified (Acts 15:9; 26:18) and adopted by faith (Gal 3:26). A second reason that biblical images of faith are rare is that faith is a uniquely human possibility. Nothing in the natural world, where most biblical imagery originates, can serve as a suitable analogy for faith.

The Bible may be short on images of faith, but it is long on examples of trusting and believing. Faith is a way of life for the righteous, who "live by faith" (Hab 2:4; Rom 1:17; 2 Cor 5:7; Gal 2:20; 3:11). *Abraham is the quintessential person of faith (Gal 3:9). Because he trusted in God's word, which entailed (from the broadest perspective) the *covenant (Gen 17), the gospel (Gal 3:8), heaven (Heb 11:10), the child of promise (Heb 11:11) and the resurrection (Heb 11:19), "it was credited to him as righteousness" (Gen 15:6 NIV; cf. Rom 4:3-12). Again and again the psalmist asserts that he trusts "in the LORD" (e.g., Ps 31:6; 55:23) rather than in his *horse and *chariot (Ps 20:7; cf. Is 31:1), his bow (Ps 44:6), his bank account (Ps 49:6; cf. Jer 48:7), himself (Ps 49:13) or his political leaders (Ps 118:9).

The writer of Hebrews 11 offers a complete catalogue of the heroes and heroines of faith, but even he runs out of time to list them all (Heb 11:32). The lives of these men and women show that faith is an unshakable belief that God will do everything he has promised to do even before there is visible evidence to that effect. In short, "faith is being sure of what we hope for and certain of what we do not see" (Heb 11:1 NIV; cf. Heb 11:13; 1 Pet 1:8). For John and Thomas, seeing was believing (Jn 20:8, 27-28), but for every believer since the ascension of Jesus Christ, *not* seeing is believing (Jn 20:29): "We live by faith, not by sight" (2 Cor 5:7 NIV).

The lives of the faithful show what faith can do. In the OT faith enables the believer to offer better sacrifices as *Abel did (Heb 11:4), to build an *ark as Noah did (Heb 11:7), to follow God on life's journey as Abraham did (Heb 11:8), to endure suffering for the sake of Christ as Moses did (Heb 11:26), to cross through the deep waters as the children of Israel did (Heb 11:29) and so on. In the NT faith can even enable a disciple to walk on water (Mt 14:22-36). Indeed "everything is possible for him who believes" (Mk 9:23 NIV). More than anything else, faith produces good works (Phil 2:17; 1 Thess 1:3; Jas 2:14-26).

Are *any* of the heroes and heroines of the Bible without faith? No, because faith in God is the defining virtue of the Christian (Jn 6:29). The epistle to the Hebrews asserts that "without faith it is impossible to please God, because anyone who comes to him must believe that he exists and that he rewards those who earnestly seek him" (Heb 11:6 NIV). Even a forgotten figure like Ebed-melech is saved on the basis of his trust in the Lord (Jer 38:7-13; 39:15-18).

Faith is frequently measured in quantitative terms. Jesus commends the centurion for his "great faith" (Lk 7:9; cf. Mt 15:28). He chides his disciples, by contrast, for having little (Mt 6:30; 8:26; 14:31) or none (Mk 4:40). Jesus wonders if he will find any faith at all when he returns (Luke 18:8). Though the faith of some may be weak (e.g., Rom 14:1), there is always room for it to grow (Lk 17:5; 2 Cor 10:15; 2 Thess 1:3).

Even in small doses, genuine faith is potent stuff. This is not due to the power of the faith itself but to the power of the God in whom faith is placed. Jesus tells his disciples that if they have faith the size of a *mustard seed they will be able to move mountains—or at least mulberry trees (Lk 17:6). Indeed "nothing will be impossible" for a disciple with mustard-seed-sized faith (Mt 17:20), though the mustard is the smallest of all *seeds (Mk 4:31).

What is faith like? It is like an open door into a relationship with God (Acts 14:27). It is like a *shield that protects God's soldiers when they are under spiritual attack (Eph 6:16; cf. 1 Thess 5:8; 1 Pet 1:5). Faith can be defended (1 Tim 6:12), grasped firmly (1 Tim 1:19; Heb 4:14), held in trust (Jude 3) and—best of all—shared (Philem 1:6). Perhaps faith is even like a sailing vessel, since it is susceptible to shipwreck (1 Tim 1:19). But the true believer keeps the faith (2 Tim 4:7).

"And what more shall I say? I do not have time to tell about Gideon, Barak, Samson, Jephthah, David, Samuel and the prophets . . ." (Heb 11:32 NIV).

See also ABRAHAM; MUSTARD SEED.

FALL FROM INNOCENCE

The motif of a "fall" in the sense of sudden decline from an ideal state is a major archetype of literature. The genre is *tragedy, with its change of fortune from prosperity to calamity. Strictly defined, falling from innocence is a decline from moral innocence to a state of sinfulness. But in more general terms the motif of *innocence can be construed as ignorance or lack of knowledge (*Joseph's initiation into the adult world of *sibling hatred, sexual temptation and injustice), youthful naiveté (the succumbing to sexual temptation by the "simple young man without sense" in Prov 7:6-27) or a state of prosperity not yet informed by suffering or loss (the story of Job's loss).

The phrase *fall from innocence* does not occur as such in Scripture, but the idea helps to shape the contours of the total biblical narrative. Human history begins in innocence and then descends into tragedy, eventually to rise to a happy ending for those who accept God's offer of salvation. Within this overall U-shaped plot, a series of "falls" constitute a powerful witness to the awful depths of moral failure compared to the purity of God manifested in created beings, both angelic and human. Within the Bible we find two decisive falls, both key moments of creaturely history, and a myriad of recurrent falls to which the human race is subject as a result of the two primal falls.

The Fall of Satan. One of the two is the prehistoric fall of *Satan and the disobedient *angels. The Bible gives only hints of this fall (with most people's more detailed picture probably coming from Milton's elaboration of it in *Paradise Lost*). The imagery of Isaiah's taunt against the king of *Babylon (Is 14:12-21) gestures toward a more-than-earthly act of rebellion against God. The oracle of judgment against the king of Tyre in Ezekiel 28:11-19 is even more readily interpreted as a veiled narrative of Satan's fall in heaven. In both visions the fall is a punishment for Satan's titanic ambition and pride that prompt him to aspire beyond his creaturely limitations.

The NT contains cursory passages that hint at a fall (or a series of falls) for Satan and his legions. Christ speaks of Satan's falling from heaven (Lk 10:18) and being "cast out" (Jn 12:31); Romans

16:20 speaks of Satan's being crushed. Jude 6 describes the angels who "did not keep their own position" and were punished by being kept "in eternal chains in the nether gloom until the judgment of the great day" (RSV). 2 Peter 2:4 has a similar account of God's not sparing "the angels when they sinned" but casting them "into nether gloom" until the judgment (RSV). Revelation 12:7-12 narrates an epic war in heaven, ending with the dragon and his angels being "thrown down to the earth." Unlike the fall of Adam and Eve, where the act of disobedience itself constitutes a fall, the fall of the *demons is the punishment meted out by a wrathful God subsequent to the sinful action.

The Fall of Adam and Eve. The second decisive, once-for-all Fall is that of *Adam and *Eve in Paradise (*see* Garden). The picture of innocence that was lost is painted in Genesis 2. Several motifs converge in the actual story of the Fall (Gen 3). One is the temptation of the woman by Satan, who entices Eve to eat of the forbidden *tree. The actual Fall consists of disobedience—doing what God has forbidden the human pair to do upon penalty of death. Like the fall of Satan, this human Fall includes an aspiration to exceed the bounds God has established for his creatures (Gen 3:5). The Fall is immediate upon eating the forbidden tree, as Adam and Eve at once know that they are *naked (Gen 3:7) and fear the sound of God *walking in the garden (Gen 3:8). The impulse to cover themselves and to hide from God embodies the essential change that has occurred, encompassing shame, self-consciousness, the experience of loss and the awareness of separation from God. As in the story of Satan's fall, the loss of innocence is accompanied by divine *judgment as God pronounces a *curse on Adam and Eve and expels them from the garden of innocence.

NT commentary on Genesis 3 elaborates its essential features. It is viewed as the original and prototypical Fall, the cause of all subsequent falls (Rom 5:12-21; 1 Cor 15:21-22). Although Genesis 3 puts the emphasis on the willful disobedience of Adam and Eve, the NT commentary evokes a complementary picture of the pathos of Eve as a victim of Satan's seduction (1 Cor 11:3; 1 Tim 2:14).

Subsequent Human Falls. Because the human race fell with Adam and Eve, no subsequent human fall is a fall from absolute innocence but is instead only relative, a regression from an already corrupted state. Pursuant to the Fall of Adam and Eve, the rest of primeval history (Gen 4—11) is a series of consequent falls. Key events include *Cain's murder of *Abel (followed by banishment), the degeneration of the human race to the point that God destroys the world with a flood and the wicked ambition represented by the Tower of *Babel (ending in banishment in the form of dispersal). This downward spiral of the human race is traced in hammer-like progression and vivid imagery in Romans 1 as well.

In subsequent history the most prominent category of falls is that of leaders and kings, and within

that category most of the examples illustrate the motif that "pride goes before destruction, and a haughty spirit before a fall" (Prov 16:18). One thinks of *Moses, *Samson, Saul, *David, *Solomon (whose besetting sins were sensuality, luxury and paganism as well as pride), Nebuchadnezzar, Haman and Belshazzar. To these can be added the ignominious prophet Jonah, who falls from being God's respected prophet, and the arrogant wealthy people of Psalm 73, who despite their invulnerability are set "in slippery places" so that they will "fall to ruin" and be "destroyed in a moment" (Ps 73:18-19). All of these make notable errors of judgment and commit acts of disobedience, for which God judges them. In a word they fall from a state of favor and/or prosperity.

But if the literary imagination has gravitated toward rulers as the most prone to great falls, it has certainly not limited itself to the grand and mighty. Within the Bible any lapse into sin by a nation or individual is viewed as a fall. Even predominantly good characters undergo falls in the Bible, including such heroes as Abraham, Jacob, Gideon, Elijah and the disciples of Jesus. The OT history of the nation of Israel is a continuous cycle of fall, repentance and restoration. NT churches too undergo falls. The church at Ephesus is warned that it has "fallen" from its first love (Rev 2:4-5), and Paul marvels that the Galatian Christians are so quickly "turning to a different gospel" (Gal 1:6 RSV). The possibility of falling is a continuous danger for all who live in a fallen world, where anyone, at any time, can fall into "the snare of the devil" (1 Tim 3:7 RSV) or "fall into temptation, into a snare, into many senseless and hurtful desires that plunge men into ruin and destruction" (1 Tim 6:9 RSV). In a precarious world such as this, the constant injunction is, "Let any one who thinks that he stands take heed lest he fall" (1 Cor 10:12 RSV).

This sense of the precariousness of life in a fallen world—the readiness with which people can make a wrong choice and slide into misfortune—is reinforced by the parables of Jesus. Here we find a veritable gallery of ordinary people who fall from actual or potential grace either in this life or in the life to come: a slothful servant who receives some of his master's property but loses his master's favor through timidity; invitees to a banquet who are rejected by the giver of the banquet when they refuse the invitation; a self-righteous Pharisee who leaves a prayer session condemned; a rich man who ignored the plight of a beggar at his gate and whose fortune is reversed in the afterlife; an enterprising farmer whose complacent plans for retirement are dashed on the eve of the completion of his building project. These are not falls from innocence, but they are falls from prosperity and favor through wrong choices.

Although the fall from innocence is a narrative pattern, it lurks in the background of some nonnarrative genres as well. The *lament psalms typically hint at a fall that the person in crisis has undergone.

One of them recalls, "I said in my prosperity, 'I shall never be moved,'" only to find that God hid his face and he "was dismayed" (Ps 30:6-7 RSV). The speaker in Psalm 73 recalls a narrowly averted fall with the memory of how "my feet had almost stumbled, my steps had well nigh slipped" (Ps 73:2 RSV). In the Proverbs too, giving in to folly is repeatedly portrayed as eventuating in a fall. The steps of the loose woman, for example, "follow the path to Sheol" (Prov 5:5 RSV), and calamity comes upon the wicked suddenly (Prov 6:15). Similarly, "the wicked are overthrown" (Prov 12:7) and "cast down to ruin" (Prov 21:12), "poverty and disgrace come to him who ignores instruction" (Prov 13:18), and "a fool's mouth is his ruin" (Prov 18:7). Again, "a man's folly brings his way to ruin" (Prov 19:3), and "the wicked are overthrown by calamity"; whereas "a righteous man falls seven times, and rises again" (Prov 24:16). The general outlook that emerges from wisdom literature is that life is a series of *traps and pitfalls just waiting to bring a person down, with the *path of wisdom the only sure antidote.

Biblical history reflects the moral tension between God and sinful human beings, the universal conflict that generates a drama of opportunity, choice and consequence. Time and again, moreover, the wrong choice is made. Loss follows loss, creating a downward spiral that, apart from divine intervention, leaves all people without peace and without hope.

See also ADAM; APOSTASY; CORRUPTION; EVE; GARDEN; REBELLION; SIN; TEMPTATION, TEMPTER; TRAGEDY.

FALL OF ADAM AND EVE. *See* FALL FROM INNOCENCE.

FALL OF ANGELS. *See* COSMOLOGY; FALL FROM INNOCENCE.

FALLING AWAY. *See* APOSTASY.

FAMILY

The Bible begins with the biological family as the central social context of human life and as a chief means of God's communication with human beings. This social view of the family becomes extended into a spiritual and heavenly reality, with the community of God's people as a metaphoric family.

Stories About Families. Before exploring specific images of the family in the Bible, we would do well to note the genre or plot motif of family stories. This genre dominates the domestic epic of *Genesis, where the sphere of action is not the nation but the family, and where the crucial events do not occur in the court and on the battlefield (as other ancient epics would have it) but around the *home. Beginning with the birth of Cain (Gen 4:1), the history narrated in Genesis is a succession of family narratives, as we read about the families of *Adam and *Eve, Noah, *Abraham, Lot, Isaac, and *Jacob. The idyll of *Ruth is cut from the same cloth: it is a domestic

history, focused on the family and family relationships.

With the exodus and the monarchy the focus becomes more public, but even here the stories about national leaders seldom lose sight of the domestic lives of people. Moses is not only leader but also brother, husband and father in the epic of the exodus. The judges are not known to us as domestic figures; but David, filling roles of *son, *brother, *husband and *father, is a family man. *Job's family history envelopes the story of his personal suffering; and the book of *Proverbs is, from one point of view, a book of parental instruction for children.

By comparison, the NT gives us fewer stories about families. But it does give us glimpses of families in miracles involving children, as well as in the domestic scene of Jesus' visits in the home of Mary, Martha and Lazarus. Family scenes are more plentiful in the book of Acts, where scenes of preaching, conversion and baptism sometimes include the family unit.

The Family as the Primal Human Unit. The physical family first appears in Scripture as God's provision for human companionship and generation. The first family, Adam and Eve, are the prototypical *husband and *wife, joined in marriage to "one flesh" (Gen 2:24). The perfection of that abbreviated family becomes contrasted to the predominantly negative story of a family at odds with itself when Adam and Eve begin to produce children (Gen 4).

More than any other book of the Bible, Genesis is the book of families, and several key motifs can be noted, each of which is woven into the rest of the Bible. Already in Genesis 5 we encounter the genre of the genealogy. Implicit in this ancient preoccupation is an important biblical and human image of the family—that of the generation or procreation of the human race. The family perpetuates the human race and provides continuity. The fact that genealogies are based on names suggests a further dimension of this *generation: the way in which the family extends a person's physical life beyond his or her individual life span. The family is also an image of fertility as imaged by the OT (especially the patriarchal) motif of children and lineage as *"seed."

A second family motif in Genesis is the repeated picture of the family as the main social context within which people live their daily lives. Although individuals and families have dealings with the outside world, they are largely self-contained entities in the ancient world. We most naturally think of characters like Abraham and Sarah, Isaac and Rebekah, Jacob and Esau, and Joseph and his brothers in a family context. The family is thus an image of life at its primal social level, appropriate to the book of beginnings. The patriarchal families, moreover, represent the origin of the nation of *Israel.

Thirdly, one cannot read the book of Genesis without a depressing awareness of what a deeply flawed institution the family is in a fallen world. The family stories of Genesis are stories of squabbling spouses, *sibling rivals and deceitful children who have a tendency to thwart their parents' dreams for them. The book of Genesis is a virtual casebook of dysfunctional families.

Yet a final image of the family in Genesis provides a message of hope. The family is the unit through which God perpetuates his *covenant. The first example is the story of Noah's family, as God calls Noah and his whole family into the ark to be preserved from the flood. Here, as often in Scripture, *family* means a whole clan or household, rather than the nuclear families common in many parts of the twentieth-century world. In OT times people lived primarily in patriarchal groups that grew as sons brought wives and children into the clan. Noah's family included his wife and his sons and their wives (Gen 6:18). God poured his saving grace on the whole family unit and established with them "a covenant for all generations to come" (Gen 9:12 NIV).

From the beginning, then, Scripture establishes the family as the social unit into which God put human beings and the channel through which he deals with them. The family is an inherently ambivalent image of disappointment and struggle on the one hand, and of hope and blessing on the other. The family in Genesis is at once an image of security and *protection, and of conflict and victimization.

The Family as Covenant Unit. The covenants of God with the patriarchs are stories of *blessings to families and descendants, *generation after generation. The channel is long. God promises Abraham that his offspring will be as numerous as the dust of the earth and that from the generations of his offspring will come great nations and kings (Gen 13:16; 17:5-6). Choosing to work in this large way, through generations of families, God carries out this work through the smallest details of conception and *birth (Gen 17:21). Each divinely-ordered detail joins the larger flow of events that God shapes into human history, which moves along from one generation to the next. In the second of the Ten Commandments, God explains his dealings with people in these same generational terms, "punishing the children for the sin of the fathers to the third and fourth generation of those who hate me, but showing love to a thousand generations of those who love me and keep my commandments" (Ex 20:5-6 NIV).

God worked through Abraham's family as he promised: through the generations to King David and through more generations to Jesus Christ. In Jesus the channel narrowed to one brilliant point and then burst forward into a wide stream. Psalm 22 pictures the huge throng of people "from all the ends of the earth" who will finally worship God: "All the families of the nations will bow down before him" (Ps 22:27 NIV). This picture of all the families of the nations worshiping the Christ is the glorious end toward which all the generations are moving.

In the meantime, in any particular generation somewhere between the beginning and the end, God consistently channels his grace and justice through family units, however large or small. For the first *Passover in Egypt, for example, God told the Israelites to sacrifice one *lamb for each family (Ex 12:3). Each household in Egypt was judged or passed over, according to the presence or absence of sacrificial blood on the door frame of the house. God sent his grace or judgment, family by family, as he visited Egypt that night.

When Rahab, the prostitute from Jericho, put her trust in Israel's God and hid the other spies, she saved not only her own life but also "her father and mother and brothers and all who belonged to her" (Josh 6:23 NIV). The Israelites later destroyed the city of Jericho but spared Rahab with her family. By contrast, we read in the very next chapter of Achan, who stole plunder for himself from Jericho. In a frightening example of God's response to unconfessed sin, the other Israelites stoned him and all his family. Thus justice came to Achan's whole family, whereas grace came to Rahab's whole family.

In the NT as well we see God reaching into whole family units. Cornelius received a heavenly command to send for Peter, who would bring a message through which Cornelius and all his household would be saved (Acts 11:14). When Lydia opened her heart to Paul's preaching in Philippi, she "and the members of her household" were baptized (Acts 16:15). In Philippi as well, the jailer of Paul and Silas came to believe in God, "he and his whole family" (Acts 16:33), whereupon the whole household was immediately baptized.

Here then is a second biblical image of the family—not just a biological and social unit but the one through which God perpetuates his blessings and judgments. God does not limit himself to this channel, however. In fact, the biblical meaning of *family* comes to exceed its physical and social identity. Next to the physical family emerges a spiritual one.

The Human Family Redeemed. The Bible also gives us pictures of the family as a combined physical and spiritual institution in its ideal form. One dominant image is that of reconciliation and harmony. Malachi 4:6 provides the most evocative image: the Messiah "will turn the hearts of the fathers to their children, and the hearts of the children to their fathers" (NIV). Here is the antithesis of the images of family discord and fragmentation that seem to be the norm in the OT narratives.

A second image is that of order. The family structure is not random but ordered. The "household codes" of duties in the NT (Eph 5:22—6:4; Col 3:18-21) delineate the interdependent and complementary roles and obligations, with the husband/father as the head who loves his wife and children, the wife who submits to the headship of the husband/father and respects him, children who obey parental authority, and parents who train their children in the fear of God without exasperating them. To this can be added the detail from the requirements for eldership that an elder must be someone "whose children believe and are not open to the charge of being wild and disobedient" (Tit 1:6 NIV).

A third image of the redeemed family is that of care and compassion for family members. Jesus castigated the Pharisees for not contributing to the support of their parents (Mt 15:4-6). Paul prescribed that children or grandchildren "put their religion into practice by caring for their own family and so repaying their parents and grandparents, for this is pleasing to God," adding that "if anyone does not provide for his relatives, and especially for his immediate family, he has denied the faith and is worse than an unbeliever" (1 Tim 5:4, 8 NIV).

The Family as Metaphor for Spiritual Reality. The Jewish people took to heart God's covenant with Abraham. They knew that they were in his family as it was continuing through the generations and that through this family all peoples of the earth would be blessed. When the blessing came in the form of Jesus, one of his first messages to God's people was that they must look through the earthly family to see the heavenly one. "If you were Abraham's children," Jesus told the Jews, "then you would do the things Abraham did" (Jn 8:39 NIV). In this passage Jesus points the Jews to the God who must be their Father, and to himself, the one who can show the way to that Father (Jn 8:42). He points to the one everlasting family—a spiritual family, the family of God.

To those who won't "see through" the physical to the spiritual, Jesus' message seems jolting. When his mother and brothers waited to see him, he asked, "Who is my mother, and who are my brothers?" His question implied the existence of a family far more lasting than the physical one. Pointing out his disciples as his family, Jesus explained: "Whoever does the will of my Father in heaven is my brother and sister and mother" (Mt 12:48-49 NIV).

The heavenly family is eternal, whereas the earthly one is temporary, a distinction that Jesus made clear. In fact, he predicted that he himself would turn "a man against his father, a daughter against her mother" (Mt 10:35) in households where conflict arises between those who belong to the eternal Father and those who do not. Primary commitment must go to the heavenly Father. Jesus continued, "Anyone who loves his father or mother more than me is not worthy of me; anyone who loves his son or daughter more than me is not worthy of me" (Mt 10:37 NIV).

The coming of Jesus makes the call much more concrete, but in effect this call to love God and be part of his family is the same call that came to Abraham, the father who loved God more than he loved his son Isaac. God made Abraham to be the physical father of many nations and at the same time the spiritual father of those who have faith like his in the heavenly father (Gal 3:7). The spiritual family of Abraham emerges more distinctly with the coming of Christ, who came from Abraham's line, but who came to extend that line into all the world.

The writer of Hebrews develops Christ's picture of his brotherhood with all believers, who belong to "the same family" with the one who "had to be made like his brothers in every way" in order to make perfect atonement for their sin (Heb 2:11,17). The "family of believers" (Gal 6:10), or the "family of God" (1 Pet 4:17), becomes a familiar picture in NT teaching. As Christ's followers developed into the early Christian church, they saw themselves, Jew and Gentile, as "members of God's household"—the extended family of God—through Christ's reconciling death on the cross (Eph 2:19).

The Church as Metaphoric Family. Once we are alerted to the analogy between the family and the *church, it becomes evident that the metaphor is worked out in detail. First, a family has a father. Each extended family or household had a patriarch, the oldest living male. Abraham, for example, was the father of Israel. A father was called the *"head" of a family or a clan (e.g., 1 Chron 8 and 9). This head of the clan was the biological source for the family, and the one who took responsibility for the family and had authority over it. In the NT as well, the man is called the "head" (1 Cor 11:3; Eph 5:23). In each of these NT passages, however, the social phenomenon of a family head is linked to a spiritual reality—the headship of Christ over the church.

Again, although the church is sometimes pictured as a *bride (Rev 21:2), the more common image is that of *children of a heavenly father. *God is first called "Father" in Deuteronomy 1:31, as Moses recalls for the Israelites how God carried them in the desert "as a father carries his son." Isaiah develops the image: "But you are our Father," he tells God, even though his physical fathers among the Israelites have repudiated him (Is 63:16). When the child foretold in Isaiah 9 is called "Everlasting Father," the way is clear for Christ to come and show God the Father to us in his own flesh. God appears as Father on almost every page of the NT. Jesus taught his disciples to pray first, "Our Father" (Mt 6:9). God is pictured in Scripture as both father and mother. "As a mother comforts her child," he tells his people, "so will I comfort you" (Is 66:13 NIV). The concept of God as parent communicates not only headship but loving care and comfort as well, as seen in Deuteronomy 1 and Isaiah 63, where the father carries and stays by his child. God says of his chosen people, "When Israel was a child, I loved him" (Hos 11:1 NIV).

To be a child of God is to know this kind of support, not just from above but from fellow believers as well. Paul tells the Galatians to "do good to all people, especially to those who belong to the family of believers" (Gal 6:10 NIV). "God sets the lonely in families" (Ps 68:6 NIV)—not just in the care and comfort of human families but ultimately in the fellowship of the people of God. God's family will be known, Jesus taught, by his followers' love for one another (Jn 3:35).

Being part of God's family means also to originate from him and to take his name. The tribes of Israel were named according to the fathers who began each biological line. Abraham's physical offspring came from his physical seed and are called his children. But Paul explains in Galatians that the true seed to which Abraham's family leads us is Jesus Christ (Gal 3:15-19): "If you belong to Christ, then you are Abraham's seed" (Gal 3:29 NIV). Believers receive Abraham's family name and enter his line on their own through faith in Christ.

Paul speaks in Ephesians 3:14-15 of the Father God, "from whom his whole family in heaven and on earth derives its name" (NIV). The Greek word for family here is *patria,* implying clearly the father or patriarch as the originator of the family. For God's family, the one and only originator is the heavenly Father who takes as his children all who accept his Son and who thereby take his name, his identity, his reputation. Ephesians 3:15 may also be translated "from whom every family in heaven and on earth derives its name." God is the eternal Father, the ultimate origin of any family of any kind that could ever exist.

In view of the foregoing, when the writers of the epistles refer to their fellow believers as "brothers" and "sisters" in the Lord more than a hundred times, they are not simply using a decorative or emotionally compelling image. The physical family is not a concrete picture of an abstract idea; rather, it is one step toward an even greater reality. These writers are addressing fellow members of an eternally real spiritual family, whose origin is the ultimate reality, God. The family members are unified by the seed and blood of Christ. When the writer of Hebrews says, "Keep on loving each other as brothers" (Heb 13:1), he does not mean that Christians resemble brothers; he means that they participate in the true family of God and so must act accordingly.

To see Christians as members of God's family is to see many other related pictures in Scripture. For example, Jesus told Nicodemus that he must be "born again" (Jn 3:3), and the NT continues this way of describing our entrance into a new spiritual family (1 Pet 1:23; 1 Jn 3:9). Images of food relate as well, for people ordinarily take their sustenance within the household unit. So when Paul tells the Corinthians that they are ready only for *milk, not solid food, he is speaking as a parent to infants of matters pertaining to the family (1 Cor 3:1-2). As "infants in Christ" the Corinthians are not spiritually mature and ready to take more complex instruction.

*Adoption appears as another strand wound in with pictures of the family of God. Paul tells the Ephesian believers that God has "adopted" them "as sons through Jesus Christ" (Eph 1:5). Before this adoption a person is like an alien or slave, but an adopted child has been taken into the family of God (Gal 4:1-7). The family as an economic unit emerges in the picture of God's children as "heirs of God and co-heirs with Christ" (Rom 8:17 NIV). As Scripture progresses, questions of the Israelites' *inheriting the Promised Land become less important than questions of the true children of Abraham inheriting

eternal life and the kingdom of God (e.g., Mk 10:17; Lk 10:25; Col 1:12; Heb 9:15).

Summary. The Bible is a story about God's family from beginning to end. God made families in the first place partly as a biological and social basis for the human race and partly as the channel of his grace and judgment. God is also making for himself a family of sons and daughters who will serve him and praise him and reign with him in his kingdom forever (Rev 22:3-5).

See also BROTHER, BROTHERHOOD; CHILD, CHILDREN; DAUGHTER; ELDER CHILD, ELDER SIBLING; FATHER, FATHERHOOD; FAVORED CHILD, SLIGHTED CHILD; HOME, HOUSE; HOMECOMING, STORIES OF; HUSBAND; MOTHER, MOTHERHOOD; SIBLING RIVALRY; SISTER; SON; WIFE; YOUNGER CHILD, YOUNGER SIBLING.

FAMINE

Most biblical references to famine are to literal famine. Periodically, throughout the Middle East, agricultural communities were victims of climatic variations that resulted in poor *harvests and therefore in severe shortages of *food for both people and animals (Gen 41:29-31; 2 Kings 4:38; Acts 11:28). Because of the unpredictability of these famines, the risk was a continuing reason for trusting God for his provision (Ps 33:18-19; 37:19). Part of God's ultimate *blessing for Israel would be a *land untroubled by famine (Ezek 34:29; 36:29-30).

Frequently famine conditions were local and contributed to the movement of those afflicted from country to country in their search for food (Gen 12:10; 41:57; Ruth 1:1; 2 Kings 8:1). This was the immediate reason for Israel's stay in Egypt, which culminated in their enslavement and the subsequent *exodus (Gen 47:1-6). Famine could also prevail as the result of foreign invasion, or more particularly, siege (2 Kings 25:1-3; Jer 32:24; 52:6; Ezek 5:12, 16-17)); and the severe shortages of food could lead to people taking desperate measures (2 Kings 6:24-29; Neh 5:1-3). Famines are also predicted as part of the chaotic conditions relating to the end-time tribulation (Mk 13:8; Rev 6:8; 18:8).

Although some biblical periods of famine carry no moral or spiritual implications, it was regarded as one of a number of divinely ordained scourges that God uses to punish both his people and others for their sins (Deut 32:24; 2 Sam 21:1; 1 Kings 17:1; Ps 105:16; Is 14:30; 51:19; Jer 11:22; 14:11-18; 24:10; 42:13-17). For Israel it is a *curse particularly associated with breaking God's *covenant (Deut 28). The conditions for relief are consequently tied in with the willingness of the people to repent and to seek the Lord (1 Kings 8:32-40; 2 Chron 20:8-9). In Job's case, Eliphaz argued this principle in reverse, implying that Job's *sufferings were the result of his unconfessed sins. Job had only to put matters right and he would enjoy God's blessing once again (Job 5:20, 22). In certain circumstances, however, God's judgment was irreversible (Ezek 14:12-14).

Figurative references to famine are few, although there are many relating to *hunger and to *thirst. Amos predicted "a famine of hearing the words of the LORD" (Amos 8:11-14 NIV) when part of God's judgment on his people would be the withdrawal of his word through his prophets. People would be eager to hear the message, but it would be too late. Those particularly affected would be young people, possibly because while their elders had heard God's word and had rejected it, the next generation had never had that opportunity.

Famine also plays its part in the background to Jesus' parable of the *prodigal son. It was when he had foolishly spent his inheritance that famine struck the land where he was living, reducing him to the meanest conditions. At this point he came to his senses and began on the long road back to his father (Lk 15:14-20). While it would be wrong to invest every detail of the parable with spiritual significance, Jesus is certainly implying here that it is only as we come to an awareness of our spiritual need that we will we be prepared to consider repentance.

Because of its extreme nature, famine, along with trouble, hardship, *persecution, *nakedness, danger and *sword, is regarded as one of the worst troubles that this world can throw at us. As such it stands in sharp relief to the constant love of Christ from which nothing can separate Christian believers (Rom 8:35).

See also ABUNDANCE; CURSE; DRY, DROUGHT; FARMING; FOOD; HARVEST; LAND OF MILK AND HONEY.

FAR

At its most basic, the term *far* is a spatial image denoting relative distance. Something far is remote or distant. The hundred or so biblical usages that fall into this category are largely neutral in association, simply identifying the location of something. The image becomes symbolic when a person's remaining at a distance from something is a sign of *fear (Mt 26:58; Lk 23:49) or awe, either before God himself (Ex 20:18), before an act of *judgment (Rev 18:10, 15) or before mystery (Eccles 7:24, Jer 23:23). In addition to being a spatial image, the motif can refer to time, either past (Is 45:21) or future (Dan 8:26).

It is when we move from the spatial level to metaphoric and spiritual uses that the biblical imagery of being "far" assumes its true profundity. At a metaphoric level, being far from something is used in the Bible to symbolize a sense of separation or loss, as when the psalmist appeals to God not to be far away (Ps 10:1; 22:19) or complains that his friends are far off (Ps 38:11). Isaiah complains that righteousness and truth are "far from us" (Is 59:11 RSV; cf. 59:14). In contrast, God assures Israel that "I bring near my deliverance, it is not far off" (Is 46:13, cf. Deut 30:11-14).

In the context of God's *covenant with Israel, distance takes on a spiritual significance. *Israel, *Jerusalem and specifically the *temple, are "the place . . . which the LORD your God chooses, to set his name there" (Deut 14:24 RSV). The Gentile nations live "at a distance" or "far off" (Deut 29:22; Jer 9:26; Acts 2:39; 22:21), in contrast to Israel who has been brought *near (e.g., Ex 19:4).

This notion of physical/spiritual distance from God is then developed in several ways. Being far from God is a symbol of *rebellion: "This people draw near with their mouth and honor me with their lips, while their hearts are far from me" (Is 29:13 RSV, cf. Mk 7:6). They are physically located in the place of worship, but their hearts are still far off. We meet the same sense that rebellion means going "far away" in Isaiah 57:9 and Ezekiel 23:40, and of course in the evocative "far country" to which the rebellious younger son travels in the parable of the lost son (Lk 15:13). To be far off can also signal being removed from God's blessing (Lk 16:23).

But the reversal of being far from God becomes one of the Bible's most endearing images of redemption, as God promises to "save you from afar" (Jer 30:10). Here the image of *return comes into play, as in the picture of the prodigal who resolves to return to his father, who sees him "while he is yet a distance" and runs to him (Lk 15:20). God promises to address those who are far off (Is 33:13) and show his glory "to the coastlands afar off" (Is 66:19) and to draw the distant Gentiles to himself (1 Kings 8:41; Zech 6:15). This is what excited Paul as he wrote to the Gentile Ephesians: "But now in Christ Jesus you who once were far off have been brought near in the blood of Christ" (Eph 2:13 RSV).

See also NEAR, DRAWING NEAR; SACRED SPACE.

FAREWELL DISCOURSE

A farewell discourse in the Bible is an address given by a prophetic leader to his followers at or close to the occasion of his death, exhorting them regarding their conduct in the future and prophesying what that future will involve. The genre was described by E. Stauffer in an appendix to his *New Testament Theology* (1955 [1941]), who identified the most noteworthy characteristics as (1) a summoning of followers, (2) an announcement of the approaching departure of the patriarch or prophet, (3) a theological review of history, (4) exhortations to remain faithful, (5) revelations about the future, (6) warnings against false *teachers, (7) predictions of woes and controversies, (8) words of comfort and promise, (9) *prayers and *blessings for those left behind, (10) appointment of a successor or successors, and (11) worship or prayer. In addition to these we could note that in many farewell discourses the speaker asserts his own integrity and puts himself forward as an example to his followers. Nowhere do all these elements appear, but many texts have several of them.

The initial paradigmatic farewell discourse in the OT is *Jacob's farewell in Genesis 48—49. Jacob summons *Joseph and makes him promise to bury him with his fathers. He worships, reviews the history of God's dealing with his family, blesses his progeny, prophesies regarding his descendants, predicts conflicts and gives instructions about their future.

Much of Jacob's discourse is echoed in *Moses' farewell blessing in Deuteronomy 31—33, especially the blessing of the tribes in chapter 33. But there is also a summoning of Israel, Moses' prediction of his imminent death, the commissioning of Joshua, a historical review of the *covenant faithfulness of God (esp. in the song in chap. 32), exhortations to remain faithful and predictions of failure and disaster.

Joshua' s farewell in Joshua 23—24 also begins with a summoning of Israel and a statement of his approaching death, but it develops more the hortatory aspect, with historical review as a means of reinforcing the exhortation. Here too are some implied predictions, particularly about how the survivors of the previous occupants of the land will become "snares and traps for you" (Josh 23:13).

1 Samuel 12 is Samuel's farewell address, in which he asserts his integrity, reviews history, exhorts the people to remain faithful and predicts punishment if they do not. However, Samuel does not predict his death, which does not occur until some time later. Other OT examples are Joshua's farewell to Israel (Josh 22—24) and David's last words to his people (1 Chron 28—29).

In the NT the pattern is preserved, though somewhat modified. In particular, the principal danger is no longer from pagans and their false gods living in the same land but from heretics living in the same church and their false teachings. So the warnings are now directed specifically against false doctrine. Such warnings are the most consistent feature of NT farewell addresses.

Perhaps the best example is Paul's farewell to the Ephesian elders (Acts 20:17-38). Paul summons the elders to Miletus, declares his integrity, predicts his and their future ordeals and the fact that he will not see them again, exhorts them to keep watch over themselves and the flock, warns them against false teachers who will come, and prays with them.

Other farewell discourses are evident in some of the epistles. 2 Timothy clearly bears the marks of a farewell discourse. We can note the expectation of an imminent departure (2 Tim 4:6), assertions of integrity (2 Tim 1:3-12), exhortations to remain faithful (2 Tim 1:13-14; 3:14-17), warnings against false teachers (2 Tim 2:16-18; 3:6-9), predictions of tribulations and testing for the church (2 Tim 3:1-9), and even some historical review (2 Tim 1:5; 2:8-13; 3:10-11). *2 Peter also has these characteristics.

Of course the central figure of the NT is Jesus, and some discourses of Jesus have the character of a farewell address. In John 13—17 Jesus predicts his departure and prepares his disciples for the future. In addition to the usual elements, such as the awareness of imminent death (Jn 13:1), revelations about the future (Jn 14:29), warnings about future testing (Jn 15:20-21), exhortations to keep the master's words (Jn 14:21-23), promises of comfort (Jn 14:1) and prayer and blessing (Jn 17), there is a foot washing (Jn 13) and a command to love one another (Jn 13:34).

In the Synoptics, Jesus' comments immediately prior to his ascension bear a few of these characteristics but probably ought not to be regarded as farewell discourses. However, the Olivet Discourse (Mt 24—25; Mk 13; Lk 19) appears to be a farewell address. The focus on the predictions of disaster, warnings against false teachers, exhortations not to be deceived but to be alert and predictions of the future of God's people show it to be of this genre.

Note can be made, finally, of a genre of farewell stories that may omit the formal farewell discourse but have the same flavor and emotional effect. Moments of parting fill our memories from the pages of the Bible: Rebekah's parting from her family amid their wishes for her (Gen 24:59-61), Jacob and his mother weeping at his parting (Gen 28:2-5), Moses' father-in-law leaving him after a visit in the wilderness (Ex 18:27), Elijah's departure from Elisha (2 Kings 2:1-12). Even the benedictions in the NT Epistles have the quality of a farewell.

See also BLESSING; HOMECOMING, STORIES OF; JOURNEY.

BIBLIOGRAPHY. E. Stauffer, *New Testament Theology* (London: SCM Press, 1955).

FARMING

From the beginning of the Bible nearly to its end, we move in a predominantly rural and agrarian world of field and *vineyard, *cattle and *herds, *sowing and reaping. Although *cities existed in the world of the Bible, the majority of the people were directly dependent on the land for their livelihood.

Even a king like Saul and a prophet like Elisha are summoned to their calling while plowing in the field, the latter with a whopping twelve yoke of oxen (1 Sam 11:5; 1 Kings 19:19). When a king covets something, it turns out to be a neighbor's vineyard (1 Kings 21:1-16). When *drought strikes, the king responds by going in search of water and *grass for his *horses and mules (1 Kings 18:5). When Samuel tries to dissuade the Israelites from taking a king, his warning is slanted toward a nation of farmers: "He will take the best of your fields and vineyards and olive orchards and give them to his servants. He will take the tenth of your grain and of your vineyards and give it to his officers and to his servants. He will take . . . the best of your cattle and . . . the tenth of your flocks" (1 Sam 8:14-17 RSV). When a foreign invader wants to entice a farming culture to surrender, his threat is posed in agrarian terms: "Make your peace with me and come out to me; then every one of you will eat of his own vine, and every one of his own fig tree . . . until I come and take you away to a land like your own land, a land of grain and wine, a land of bread and vineyards, a land of olive trees and honey" (2 Kings 18:31-32 RSV). The romance of farming is evident in the story of *Ruth and the pastoral love lyrics of the *Song of Songs. In the NT, Jesus' parables are saturated with references to farming—*workers in a vineyard, lost *sheep, a rich farmer who rebuilds his *barns, *seeds growing secretly, sowing and reaping, *wheat and weeds.

While it might be true that people living in ancient Palestine would inevitably turn to farming for their livelihood, we can also link the prominence of farming in the Bible to broader theological themes of *land and promise. God's covenant with Abraham and his descendants included the promise of a land, and as the nation of Israel headed toward settlement

Egyptian farmers plowing and sowing seed.

in Canaan, a *"land of milk and honey," the blessings God promised took on a strongly agrarian content. It seems plausible to conclude that the prominent OT interest in farming occurs against a backdrop of the covenant promises of God.

The prominence of farming in the ancient world is also attested by military practices. To deliver a death blow to an enemy, a conqueror would sometimes raze a city and then *sow salt on it (Judg 9:45; Jer 48:9 NIV). This was an action designed to bring agricultural death to a region, inasmuch as saline soil is lifeless and unproductive (Ps 107:34).

On a broad definition of farming as livelihood from plants and animals, the biblical references encompass both nomadic and settled types of farming, with shepherding the dominant activity of the former and cultivation of crops of the latter. Four main types of farming can be discerned in the Bible: grain farming, growing vineyards, cultivating olive orchards and raising livestock. Habakkuk 3:17 hints at the range of farming activities with its mention of fig tree, vines, olives, fields, flocks and herds. The prophet Amos, who identifies himself as a herdsman and dresser of sycamore trees, likewise covers the territory, with references to sheep, cows, summer *fruit, vineyard, *grapes, *gardens and sowing seed.

A few facts about agriculture in ancient Palestine will help to explain references in the Bible. Farmers did not live on the plots of land that they tended; instead they resided by night in villages and towns, going out to their fields as the season required. A degree of tension existed between nomadic shepherding and more sedentary agriculture (see especially the story of *Cain and *Abel, Gen 4:2-5). Cultivated fields and orchards were often located near sources of water, and even summer dew was helpful to plants in the arid climate of Palestine. Crops fell into two main categories—*grains (with

barley and wheat the most common) and food crops (including vegetables, fruits, grapes and olives). The main obstacles with which farmers contended were drought, weeds, invasions of *locusts and other pests, inhospitable terrain or rocky soil, and invading armies during harvest time (Judg 6:2-4). In a climate where summer is a six-month drought, crops depended on "early *rains" during late November and December, and "latter rains" that brought crops to fruition in March and April.

A good index to the feelings awakened by farming in the OT is the alluring pictures of the Promised Land and the poets' pictures of the *good life in the psalms. The most evocative picture of the land to which the descendants of Jacob were headed when they left Egypt was its designation as "a good and broad land, a land flowing with milk and honey" (Ex 3:8, 17 RSV). Whereas in literature generally, farming is viewed as the antithesis of the city, in the OT it is contrasted with the *wilderness. Thus Moses follows up his reminder of the wilderness wanderings with the comment that "God is bringing you into a good land, . . . a land of wheat and barley, of vines and fig trees and pomegranates, a land of olive trees and honey" (Deut 8:1-9 RSV). Similarly, the proof of the land's desirability that the twelve spies brought back was agricultural proof—a gigantic cluster of grapes, along with pomegranates and figs (Num 13:23). The psalms are obviously the product of a nation of farmers and are replete with pictures of *weather, land and livestock that only a farmer knows (Ps 65:9-13; 104:13-16; 107:37-38; 144:12-14). So are some of the OT proverbs, which take their place in the ancient literature of farming known as the "eclogue" (Prov 24:30-31; 27:23-27; 28:19).

The Mosaic laws confirm the agrarian status of Hebrew society. The system of religious *festivals was largely built around *harvest times—the *Passover at the beginning of barley harvest in early spring, the Feast of Weeks at the end of the wheat harvest in late spring and the Feast of Tabernacles at the end of the fall harvest of grain and fruits. Moses' list of blessings for obedience to God and curses for disobedience is a largely agricultural vision (Deut 28—29). Incidental laws likewise presuppose a farming milieu, with stipulations about returning a neighbor's stray *ox or *sheep (Deut 11:1-2, 4), about the sowing of grain (Deut 11:9-10) and its reaping (Deut 24:19-21; 25:4), about not coveting a neighbor's ox or *donkey (Ex 20:17). The requirement that land lie fallow during the year of Jubilee was an early system for land conservation as well as a sacrifice (Lev 25:8-12). It would not be misleading to say that in the OT farming is a chief arena within which people make their moral and spiritual choices.

The cycle of life for farmers is set by the vegetative *seasons. The key points are sowing or planting, cultivation (including watering and *pruning) and harvest or reaping, and the Bible is filled with references to all three. Although we rightly think of the early Hebrews as partly nomadic, it is significant that from the beginning the calendar was based on a farming cycle (with emphasis on harvest). A helpful way to grasp biblical images of farming is to relate them to the natural cycle of the farmer's year, and it should be noted in advance that figurative uses of the phases of farming are closely linked with the physical cycle.

Plowing and Planting. It is crucial in farming to prepare the soil properly. Anyone who fails to do this cannot expect a harvest (Prov 20:4). The chief means of soil preparation is plowing (also called "tilling" in the English Bible). Plowing or tilling is so central to the agricultural process that sometimes a biblical farmer is called simply a tiller ("worker" in the original Hebrew) of the soil; examples include *Adam (Gen 2:15), *Cain (Gen 4:2) and Noah (Gen 9:20). Plowing and harvest are paired as together constituting the essentials of farming (Gen 45:6) and as a time of visible industry when one might be tempted to work on the sabbath but is forbidden to do so (Ex 34:21).

Plowing is a rich source of metaphor in the Bible. We read about plowing iniquity (Job 4:8; Hos 10:13) and about oppressors who plow upon the back of a victim and make long furrows (Ps 129:3). When Samson's bride divulges his secret to her compatriots, Samson speaks of them as having "plowed with my heifer" (Judg 14:18). Other usages include references to breaking up of fallow ground for overcoming *hardness of *heart (Jer 4:3) and, in Jesus' well-known parable, fixing one's gaze on the plowing to be done for single-minded dedication to the work of the kingdom (Lk 9:62).

The imagery of plowing is important in OT eschatological visions. The time will come when Israel will no longer have to go out to war in defense of her land but will be able to turn "*swords into plowshares" (Is 2:4; Joel 3:10; Mic 4:3). Elsewhere the future is pictured as a time when there will be no need to work the fields, either because others will look after this (Is 61:57) or because such will be the richness of God's blessing that the harvest will overtake and precede the planting (Amos 9:13)! The connotations become negative in the oracles of judgment. God's judgment against Judah is pictured as the doom of perpetual plowing without harvest (Hos 10:11). There are also references to *Zion being "plowed as a field," equated in parallelism with Jerusalem becoming "a heap of ruins" (Mic 3:12; Jer 26:18).

Planting and sowing belong with plowing as the activities that initiate the agricultural process. Along with plowing, they are an image of hope and industry. A survey of the well over a hundred biblical references is a virtual catalog of farming practices, as we hear about the sowing of grain fields and the planting of gardens, *trees, vineyards, and olive groves. This is part of the Bible's picture of the good life. The psalmist pictures God's blessing in terms of people's sowing fields, planting vineyards and getting a fruitful yield (Ps 107:37). In Isaiah's golden-age vision of Israel restored, the people "shall plant vineyards and eat their fruit" (Is 65:21; cf. Jer 29:5; Amos 9:14).

Figurative uses abound (see Sow, Sowing, Sower). Emotional experience is in view in the comment about sowing in tears and reaping in joy (Ps 126:5), and moral experience in references to sowing iniquity (Prov 22:8; Job 4:8; Gal 6:7-9). The righteous are said to be planted in the house of God (Ps 92:12-13; Jer 17:8). Children are like olive shoots around the table (Ps 128:3). Israel is repeatedly pictured as a vineyard planted by God (Ps 80:8-11; Is 5:1-4; Jer 2:21).

Tending the Crops. Not much could be done in ancient Palestine to nurture the crops that had been planted. The grain fields, vineyards and orchards awaited the rains that would enable them to grow. James gives us the picture of the farmer who "waits for the precious fruit of the earth, being patient over it until it receives the early and the late rain" as an example of patience (Jas 5:7 RSV).

The biblical writers spring a surprise on us by treating God as a cosmic gardener who tends the trees and crops and who waters and nurtures the plants and animals of the earth (Ps 104:10-18; cf. Lev 26:3-4; Is 27:3). The water that God sends is drenching or light as soil conditions require (Ps 65:9-10). In the eschaton the showers will be abundant, as will be the harvest that comes from them (Joel 2:23-26; Mal 3:10). In some passages Israel herself is pictured as God's flourishing grain and blossoming vine (Hos 14:7; cf. Is 37:30-31).

Pruning is the other main task of cultivation, and again the most evocative examples are ascribed to God. Sometimes God's pruning is a picture of judgment against evil (Is 18:5-6). But in Jesus' parable of the vine and vine dresser, pruning is a picture of good farming practices—an image of nurturing for the benefit of the vineyard and the increase of its harvest (Jn 15:1-6). Addressing the urban dwellers at Rome, Paul uses some of the finer points of olive tree cultivation in developing an analogy of how God saves the Jews and Gentiles (Rom 11:17-24).

Harvest. The rhythm of farming is the cycle of "seedtime and harvest" (Gen 8:22). Plowing and planting represent hope; harvest represents fruition and reward. The one is a picture of risk, the other of security. The main biblical images of harvest are the ingathering of grain or fruit, *threshing, the *winepress and the *storehouse. References to harvesting are virtually all positive (but see Hos 6:11, for an exception), and reaping is a uniformly positive image. But such specific images of harvesting as threshing, winnowing and treading are images of *judgment.

As is true of other phases of the farming process, the literal images of harvest provide a rich repository of symbolism for biblical writers. The most important of these are the use of harvest to picture God's final judgment against evil (Joel 3:13; Mt 13:30; Rev 14:17-20) and the ingathering of persons in salvation (Mt 9:37-38; Mk 4:29; Lk 10:2; Jn 4:35; Rev 14:14-16).

See also ANIMALS; BARN; CALF; CATTLE; DONKEY, ASS; DRY, DROUGHT; FAMINE; FLOCK; FRUIT, FRUITFUL-NESS; GARDEN; GLEAN; GOAT; GRAFTING; GRAIN; GRAPES; HARVEST; HERDS; LAND; LAND FLOWING WITH MILK AND HONEY; NATURE; OX, OXEN; PASTURE; PLANTS; PRUNING; SEED; SHEEP, SHEPHERD; STORE-HOUSE; THRESHING, THRESHING FLOOR; VINE, VINE-YARD; WHEAT; WINEPRESS.

BIBLIOGRAPHY. O. Borowski, "Agriculture," *ABD* 1:95-98; J. A. Thompson, *Handbook of Life in Bible Times* (Downers Grove, IL: InterVarsity Press, 1986).

FASTING

In modern society fasting is seen primarily as a means of protest or threat of self-destruction to put the pressure on higher authorities in order to attain the benefits or claims of the people involved. In other words, it is political in its character. Mahatma Gandhi of India during his fight against British rule, Young Sam Kim of Korea in his protest against the military dictatorship and the comedian Dick Gregory in his struggle against the violation of the civil rights of Native Americans exemplify this.

In the biblical context, however, fasting carries a different meaning. It is not a way of asserting one's will but a means of opening oneself to the work of God, expressing profound grief over *sin and point-ing to one's ultimate dependence on God for all forms of sustenance. Fasting is the act of abstaining from *food for spiritual reasons and primarily con-notes an openness to divinity and a posture of *hu-mility. It involves *prayer, *grief, penance, seeking *guidance and piety. But fasting was widely abused, so it can also carry the imagery of hypocrisy and religious display (Is 58; Mt 6).

One of the most familiar examples of fasting in the Bible is *Jesus' fasting for forty days in the *wilderness in order to prepare for his ministry (Mt 4:2). This is obviously the antitype of *Moses' fasting for forty days on Mount Sinai in order to receive the law and guidance in the wilderness (Ex 34:28; Deut 9:9). Jehoshaphat proclaims a fast throughout all Judah to seek the Lord when the sons of Moab and Ammon come to make war against him (2 Chron 20:3). While the church of Antioch fasts and prays (Acts 13:3-4), they are commanded by the Holy Spirit to send Paul and Barnabas as missionaries. Fasting and prayer are frequently associated with people seeking and preparing themselves for divine communications. Through fasting, they can devote themselves to communion with God.

Fasting bears the imagery of grief. When Saul and Jonathan are killed on the battlefield, the inhabitants of Jabesh-gilead bury their bones and fast seven days (1 Sam 31:13). *David mourns and weeps and fasts when he hears of the deaths of Saul, Jonathan and Abner (2 Sam 1:12; 3:36). Nehemiah fasts at the news of the fall of Jerusalem (Neh 1:4). When Haman issues the edict to kill the people of Mordecai, the Jews fast, weep and wail for their destiny (Esther

4:3). Fasting is associated with sincere grief and mourning, particularly with the death of the beloved, a sudden calamity and threat of death. It is an expres-sion of deep sorrow and anger.

Fasting carries the imagery of penitence (*see* Re-pentance). For example, Ahab, the king of Israel, fasts at Elijah's threat to destroy his household for having taken Naboth's vineyard (1 Kings 21:27). He tears his clothes, puts on sackcloth and goes about de-spondently. Ahab humbles himself before the Lord and seeks his mercy. The Lord sees this and with-draws the evil he had proclaimed against him (v. 29). Israel as a corporate group fasts on the occa-sion of repentance. Particularly on the Day of Atonement, the people of Israel are commanded to fast in repentance (Lev 16:29, 31; 23:27, 29, 32). At the time of Nehemiah the people of Israel as-semble in sackcloth with dirt on them and fast. They confess their sins and the iniquities of their fathers (Neh 9:1-3; 1 Sam 7:6; 2 Sam 12:16). Fasting is practiced during the course of repentance of sins as a symbol of humility and as a means of seeking the mercy of the Lord.

Fasting is used as a means of piety. The psalmist confesses that he humbled his soul with fasting (Ps 35:13) and that when he wept in his soul with fasting, he was publicly insulted (Ps 69:10). In the NT, Anna, a prophetess and a widow to the age of eighty-four, never leaves the temple, serving night and day with fasting and prayer (Lk 2:37). The disciples of John the Baptist and the Pharisees fast regularly. Particu-larly, the Pharisees are reported to fast twice a week (Lk 18:12; see extrabiblical sources *Didache;* 8:1; *Psalms of Solomon* 3:8). Fasting is conducted for the sake of personal piety and spiritual discipline.

The imagery of piety goes together with fasting; however, fasting also bears the opposite imagery, that of hypocrisy. Isaiah 58:3-6 shows that the fasting of the Israelites as a religious devotion does not match their behavior toward their neighbors. They do evil in the sight of the Lord even during the period of fasting. They only fast to display their godliness to men and gain their admiration. They do not do it for the glory of God. Therefore the Lord proclaims that he will not accept them (Jer 14:2). The same phe-nomenon can be observed in the NT. The Pharisees disfigure their faces in order that their fasting may be seen by men and are exposed for their hypocrisy by Jesus, who advises them to anoint their heads and wash their faces so that their piety and devotion might be directed only to God (Mt 6:16-17). Fasting itself is not condemned, but if it is conducted as a means of seeking self-glory, it is an image of hypoc-risy.

Generally, fasting does not carry positive and bright imagery. The Hebrew expression for fasting, "afflicting the soul," fits well with the imagery of disfiguring the *face, *weeping, lying on the ground, putting *ashes on the head and putting on sackcloth.

See also ASHES; FOOD; GRIEF; MOURNING; PRAYER; WEEPING.

BIBLIOGRAPHY. S. Lowy, "The motivation of Fasting in Talmudic Literature" *JJS* 9 (1958) 19-38; E. Wetermarck, "The Principle of Fasting," *Folklore* 18 (1907) 391-422.

FAT, FATNESS

In a fat-phobic society it is hard to imagine fat and fatness as conveying anything other than sloth, laziness, *disgust and even loathing. Yet when we turn to Scripture, we find fat and fatness used repeatedly to represent *prosperity, *blessing, *abundance and bounty.

Fat and fatness appear almost exclusively in the OT, with the exceptions of the fatted *calf of Luke 15 (where it is clearly a symbol of lavish generosity) and Romans 11:17 (where in the KJV Paul speaks of our grafting into the olive tree to partake of "the root and fatness"). Within the OT, images of fat and fatness can be carefully nuanced in several different ways. For our purposes, however, it will do to break these down into two general categories: as images of God-given or of ill-gotten prosperity.

First, fat and fatness are repeatedly used as a straightforward image of God's blessing. In Genesis 27:28 Isaac blesses Jacob, saying, "May God give you of the dew of heaven, and of the fatness of the earth, and plenty of grain and wine" (NRSV). In verse 39 Esau is told that his home will be "away from the fatness of the earth." We find this use of fat and fatness in several passages (Job 36:16; Ps 36:8; 63:5; 65:11; 92:15; Is 30:23; Jer 31:14; and others). In some of these passages, modern translations avoid the literal use of fat and fatness, substituting other images of prosperity, but the KJV reads "fat" or "fatness" in them all.

We should be aware that often fat and fatness denote the best part of a gift or *sacrifice. In Genesis 4:4 Abel's sacrifice is described as the "fat portions" (NRSV). In Genesis 45:18 Pharaoh gives Israel Goshen, where they can live off of "the fat of the land." In the OT cult, described thoroughly in Leviticus, "All fat is the LORD's" (Lev 3:16 NRSV) precisely because it represents the best part of the sacrifice.

Another way to understand how fat and fatness are images of blessing is to examine how they are contrasted to leanness, especially in Psalm 106:15 where the psalmist, speaking of Israel's sin in the wilderness, says, "And he gave them their request, but sent leanness into their soul" (KJV; see also Num 13:20; Is 10:16; 17:4; 24:16). Two other places where fat is used to indicate blessing are Genesis 41, where Pharaoh describes his dream of the lean and fat *cows (see Joseph's interpretation, vv. 25-32), and the occurrences of fat and fatness in Proverbs (Prov 11:25; 13:4; 15:30; 28:25).

However, fat and fatness do not get only favorable press. Both Deuteronomy 31:20 and 32:15 seem to link Israel's growing fat on the Lord's blessings to their turning away. Nehemiah 9:25, part of Ezra's confession, also gives this impression. This prepares us for the second general usage of fat and fatness, that of ill-gotten prosperity.

The supreme image of this kind of fatness is Eglon, who is introduced to us in Judges 3:17. No doubt his fatness has been gained by exploiting the Israelites (among others). Eglon's name is based on the root word for "calf," and the incipient symbolism of the story includes the image of Eglon as the fat calf being readied for slaughter. The Bible's condemnation of abusive fatness is not limited to foreign powers preying on Israel, however. In fact, the great majority of negative uses of the image involve the leaders and people of Israel (1 Sam 15:22; Job 15:27; Ps 17:10; 73:7; 119:70; Is 1:11; 6:10; 34:6; Jer 5:28; Ezra 34:3ff; 39:19; 44:15).

Fat and fatness, then, can be used either to show God's blessings showered in abundance upon the earth, or the misuse of these same blessings by the complacent, greedy and wicked.

See also ABUNDANCE; BLESSING; EATING; FAMINE; PROSPERITY.

FATHER, FATHERHOOD

To trace the image of the father through the Bible is to see the general outlines of biblical theology in microcosm. The major chapters in the story are (1) fatherhood as an ideal created for good by God himself, (2) the failure of reality in a fallen world to match the ideal and (3) God as the perfect father who alone can redeem the failure. With nearly a thousand uses of the explicit vocabulary of fatherhood in English translations, the image of the father is a major biblical archetype. Yet we should note at the outset that we find no extended teaching about being a human father or well-developed pictures of a father's relationship to his *children. Furthermore, we do not find many good fathers in the Bible; in fact, it is difficult to think of a human father who functions well over the course of his lifetime.

The absence of fully developed pictures of fatherhood does not mean that the Bible fails to give us a memorable gallery of fathers. Men we remember at least partly as fathers include *Adam, Noah, *Abraham, Lot, *Jacob, Isaac, Manoah, Eli, *David, *Solomon, *Job and Joseph the father of Jesus. In addition, unnamed fathers are important in the Psalms and Proverbs.

The Ideal Father. For the ideal father we are largely left with the commands that the Bible gives to fathers. We do not actually have pictures of fathers who live up to those commands very thoroughly. To begin, we can infer from the emphasis in OT on the fathers as clan leaders through whom genealogies are traced and about whom most biographies are written that fathers are the heads of their families. We find dozens of references to "father's house" as a way of designating the parental home or place of origin. While religious instruction is a joint responsibility of both parents, in the Bible it is more the domain of fathers than of *mothers (Prov 1:8; 4:1; 6:20; 13:1; 15:5; 27:10). The psalmist writes of how "our fathers

273

have told us" of God's past deeds (Ps 44:1; 78:3) in fulfillment of Moses' command in his *farewell discourse to "remember the days of old . . . ask your father, and he will show you" (Deut 32:7 RSV). Fathers simply held a position of authority in ancient cultures that is quite foreign to most modern ones.

We are also given a sense of the dignity and worth that biblical cultures attach to a father's role. Psalm 127:4-5 is the key passage, with its comparison of a father's children to *arrows and its declaration that "happy is the man who has his quiver full of them," and its picture of the strength and *honor that come to a father of sons "when he speaks with his enemies in the gate" (RSV). The ideal for a father is to have a wife "like a fruitful vine" within his house, to have children "like olive shoots" around the table and to see one's "children's children" (Ps 128:3-4, 6 RSV).

A good father takes responsibility for the spiritual welfare of his family. Job offers sacrifices on behalf of his children (Job 1:5); Joshua and his household serve the Lord (Josh 24:15). Both Deuteronomy 6:4-9 and Proverbs (e.g., 1:8: "Listen, my son, to your father's instruction") portray fathers as teachers. Nor does a good father neglect the physical welfare of his children. The good fathers we encounter in the Gospels look to Jesus for their children's needs, especially physical ones (Mt 17:14-18; Lk 8:40-56; Jn 4:43-54). It would be unthinkable for such a father to give his children stones or snakes (Mt 7:9-11).

The apostle Paul may have been a bachelor, but he seems to have understood what sonship and fatherhood are all about. He invariably opens his letters with a blessing "from God our Father" (e.g., 1 Cor 1:3; Eph 1:2). He also serves as a father to Timothy (1 Tim 1:2) and Titus (Titus 1:4), his *"sons" in the Christian faith (cf. 1 Thess 2:11).

Fatherly Failures. Adam was the father of the human race. The legacy he left his children is original sin (Rom 5:12-14). One result of that unhappy inheritance is that most biblical fathers are failures. David is a premier illustration of an inattentive father who refuses to protect his *daughter Tamar, to discipline his son Amnon or to be completely reconciled to his other son, Absalom (2 Sam 13). David is preceded by Eli (1 Sam 3:10-14), whose sons scandalize both the Israelites and God himself.

Some fathers love not wisely, but too well. Abraham favors Isaac over Ishmael (Gen 21). Isaac in turn dotes on *Esau rather than *Jacob (Gen 25:28). When Isaac becomes the stooge in Jacob's gambit to steal the *birthright (Gen 27:1-40), he gets as much as he deserved. Jacob repeats the sin of his father by loving Joseph more than all his other sons (Gen 37:3-4). His favoritism brings envy, hatred, treachery and bereavement to the family. Eli loves his sons more than he loves God (1 Sam 2:29), and their deaths are a reproach to him for his sin (v. 34; cf. 4:11). David rules over a family broken by incest and fratricide (2 Sam 13). If only he had disciplined Absalom as strenuously as he later grieved for him!

Other fathers fail to protect their children from secular influences. Although Lot takes his daughters out of Sodom, he does so too late to keep the impulse toward sexual perversion from them (Gen 19:31-36). Achan traffics in stolen foreign merchandise, and his sins are visited upon his children (cf. Ex 20:5), with the whole family dying because of his spiritual neglect (Josh 7).

The NT exhortation to fathers not to "provoke your children to anger, but bring them up in the discipline and instruction of the Lord" (Eph 6:4 RSV; cf. Col 3:21) hints at the spectacle of the tyrannical father (see Tyrannical Husband, Father). Perhaps the clearest biblical example of the exasperating father is King Saul, whose volatile temper frightens both his children and their best friends (1 Sam 19-20).

We also find the inept, bumbling father of popular literature in the Bible. Sometimes we find moments in which fathers seem to be incapable of any better response than passive anger while events transpire that are contrary to their will. Examples include Abraham's dismay at sending Hagar away with Ishmael, whom he had sired in a bad decision (Gen 21:8-11), Jacob's disapproval of events surrounding the *rape of Dinah and the revenge that his sons exact for it (Gen 34:5-7, 30) and David's *anger regarding his son's rape of his daughter Tamar (2 Sam 13:21). Other bumbling fathers are easily deceived by their children: Lot (Gen 19:30-38), Isaac (Gen 27) and Jacob (Gen 37:31-35). David mismanages his grief over the death of his son Absalom (2 Sam 18:33-19:8); Noah becomes a shameful spectacle to his sons as he lies naked in his tent in a drunken stupor (Gen 9:20-25); Jephthah makes a rash vow that dooms his daughter to perpetual *virginity (Judg 11); Samson's father allows Samson to order him around as though he were the child rather than the parent (Judg 14).

Against this backdrop of the failure of fathers stands the image of God the Father, who exemplifies all those characteristics that the flesh-and-blood fathers lack: patience, kindness, firmness, attention. In fact, our very disgust with the failures of fathers stems from our intuitive understanding of what a true father should be, so that the negative character type inevitably brings with it, as a shadow entity, the positive.

God as the Perfect Father. The litany of paternal failure serves as a reminder that only one father is good: *God the Father. However the patriarchs may have felt about their fathers, they each came to understand that the God of their fathers could be trusted. He is the "one Father" over all his children (Mal 2:10; Mt 23:9; 1 Cor 8:6; Eph 4:6). God is a loving Father who has compassion on all his children (Ps 103:13). He created them (Deut 32:6); he carries them in his *arms (Deut 1:31); he provides what they need (Mt 6:25-34); he gives them good gifts (Mt 7:7-11; Lk 11:11-13); he offers them true *bread (Jn 6:32); he "disciplines those he loves, as a father the son he delights in" (Prov 3:12 NIV). God has a father's love for *orphans (Deut 10:18; Ps 68:5; Jas 1:27) and little ones (Mt 18:10-14).

Jesus calls God "Father," especially in the Gospel of John. Because he is the only begotten Son of God (Jn 3:16), some aspects of his divine sonship are unique. Jesus is the only Son who is one with the Father (Jn 10:30, 38; 14:10-11), has inner knowledge of the Father (Mt 11:27; Jn 5:20, 10:15; Lk 10:21-22), has seen the Father (Jn 6:46), shares the Father's glory (Jn 17:1ff.) and so forth. Yet Jesus also shows us what kind of a heavenly Father we have. He teaches us to go to our Father for everything we need (Mt 6:9-13; Lk 11:2-4). There is no need to be reticent, for we are to call him *Abba* (Mk 14:36; cf. Rom 8:15, Gal 4:6). There is no need to be timid, for he has a big house with plenty of rooms to spare (Jn 14:6; cf. Jer 3:19). There is no need to be fearful, for God will run to us, throw his arms around us and kiss us when we return from our prodigal wanderings (Lk 15:20). "How great is the love the Father has lavished on us, that we should be called children of God!" (1 Jn 3:1 NIV).

The relationship between God the Father and God the Son is the perfect pattern for father-son relationships. The Father takes justifiable pride in the Son's activities (Ps 2:7). He loves the Son and is well-pleased with him (Mt. 4:17). For his part the Son submits to the will of the Father in all things (Mk 14:36; Lk 22:42; Jn 14:31). One of their favorite father and son activities is planning and accomplishing redemption (Jn 6:44; 12:50; 14:6, 21). To be a good father is to be like God the Father: "You, therefore, must be perfect, as your heavenly Father is perfect" (Mt 5:48; cf. Lk 6:36). Successful fathering is obedient sonship. Like Isaiah (Is 63:16; 64:8), good fathers call God "Father."

Summary. The images of fathers that emerge from the biographies of the patriarchs in Genesis can serve as a summary of how the Bible portrays fathers. The patriarchs are obviously progenitors of a line of descendants. As such they are agents of blessing, not only in the blessing they pronounce on their sons but as fathers of the faithful in salvation history. These fathers are heads of their clans and overseers of the economic fortunes of their families. When negotiations with outside parties are required, the proverbial "buck" stops with the father. At their best these fathers are spiritual paragons—building altars, obeying messages from God, insuring that their sons marry well, even showing a willingness to sacrifice a promised son in an act of supreme obedience to God.

But Genesis also gives us an anatomy of how fathers fail. The practice of dishonesty and expediency in a father (Gen 12:10-20; 20) is imitated by his son (Gen 26:6-11). Fathers stand ineffectually wringing their hands or boiling with anger as they watch the wreckage of their children's lives or the wrangling of their wives. Fathers display favoritism toward children with tragic results. Overshadowing everything is the image of a heavenly Father who deals with his human children as human fathers

were created to do.

In short, fathers in the Bible are a paradigm of the human condition. Their behavior ranges from the very good to the very bad. Yet God does not give up on them, and by divine grace they even manage to make a mark for good in the world and in their families.

See also CHILD, CHILDREN; DAUGHTER; GOD; MOTHER, MOTHERHOOD; SON; TYRANNICAL FATHER, HUSBAND.

FAVORED CHILD, SLIGHTED CHILD

Among the archetypes of the family are the familiar favored child and slighted child, both of them evidence of a dysfunctional family. Although it produces the syndrome of *sibling rivalry, favoritism is really a failure of parenting, inasmuch as the favor and slight are defined in terms of how children are viewed and treated by parents.

The *younger child who is preferred over the *elder child is so common in the OT as to be an archetype. Nor is it necessarily a sign of a dysfunctional family: when God favors a child, divine sovereignty and moral justice lie behind the favoring and slighting. Thus God favors *Abel over *Cain, Isaac over Ishmael, *Jacob over *Esau (Mal 1:2-3; Rom 9:13), *Joseph over his brothers, *Moses over Aaron, *David over his brothers.

The archetypal slighted child, though, is a pathetic figure, whether or not the child is morally deserving of the slight. Cain, disfavored by a heavenly Father, is a figure of tragic rebellion, tapping our wellsprings of regret. Esau, crying out when he discovers that Jacob has supplanted him in the story of the stolen blessing, is equally heart-rending. Pathos surrounds the understated story of Leah, the substitute bride who wins a husband before her sister Rachel but loses the contest for Jacob's favor.

See also CHILD, CHILDREN; ELDER CHILD, ELDER SIBLING; SIBLING RIVALRY; YOUNGER CHILD, YOUNGER SIBLING.

FEAR

Fear in the sense of terror is a formidable part of the Bible's picture of life in a fallen world. While the Bible offers no psychology of fear, we can categorize the images of fear by the things that cause fear, the physical results of fear and biblical characters caught in moments of terror.

The origin of fear in the Bible can be traced to *Adam after the *Fall, when he responds to God by saying, "I heard the sound of you in the garden, and I was afraid" (Gen 3:10 NRSV). It is no exaggeration to say that after that terrifying moment in the *Garden, the human race has lived with the constant possibility and even threat of being afraid.

Causes of Fear. Although there is a desirable reverential fear of God, the Bible also portrays *God's actions* as being causes of terror, especially—but not only—for those who do not trust in God. At the burning bush Moses "hid his face, for he was afraid to look at God" (Ex 3:6 RSV). Job confesses regarding God that "I am terrified at his presence; when I consider, I am in dread of him" (Job 23:15 RSV). God accosts Judah with the questions "Do you not fear me?" and "Do you not tremble before me?" (Jer 5:22 RSV). Isaiah pictures evil people fleeing from "the terror of the LORD" three times in a single chapter (Is 2:10, 19, 21).

In the NT Jesus tells people to fear him who "has power to cast into hell" (Lk 12:4). Fear falls on those who hear about God's judgment against Ananias and Sapphira (Acts 5:5), and the writer to Hebrews assures us that "it is a fearful thing to fall into the hands of the living God" (Heb 10:31 RSV). In the Gospels people were afraid of Jesus because of his miracles (Mk 5:33; 10:32; 11:8; Lk 5:26), as were the disciples at the transfiguration by the presence of Moses and Elijah (Mk 9:6) and upon hearing the voice of God (Mt 17:6). At the empty tomb the women were afraid when Jesus' body was gone (Mt 28:8; Mk 16:8).

A second cluster of images centers on the *threatening forces of nature*. In a prayer of imprecation the psalmist asks God to "terrify them with thy hurricane!" (Ps 83:15 RSV). Psalm 46, even though it asserts the believer's freedom from fear, is nonetheless a catalog of natural disasters that would ordinarily instill fear, including *earthquake and perhaps tidal waves (Ps 46:2-3). Psalm 91, a catalog of dangers, contains vivid pictures of "the terror of the night," "the arrow that flies by day," "pestilence that stalks in darkness" and "the destruction that wastes at noonday" (possibly sunstroke or heat exhaustion; Ps 91:5-6 RSV). Job interprets his illness as "the terrors of God" arrayed against him (Job 6:4; cf. 7:14). Predators were equally a cause for fear (Job 39:19-20; 41:14; *see* Animals), and Israel's *wanderings in the *wilderness were a continuous narrow escape because of the presence of poisonous snakes and scorpions, as well as the absence of food and water, so that Moses speaks of "that great and terrible wilderness" (Deut 1:19; 8:15; cf. Is 21:1).

A third cause of fear in the Bible is *death and calamity*. Saul is "terrified" by the *witch's prediction of his death (1 Sam 28:21). The psalmist describes "the terrors of death" that come upon him and the accompanying "horror" that "overwhelms" him (Ps 55:4-5). Another psalmist attests, "Afflicted and close to death from my youth up, I suffer thy terrors" (Ps 88:15 RSV). Job speaks of being "in terror of calamity from God" (Job 31:23). When Jeremiah is released from imprisonment at the hands of Pashhur the priest, he says, "The LORD does not call your name Pashhur, but Terror on every side. For thus says the LORD: Behold, I will make you a terror to yourself and to all your friends. They shall fall by the sword of their enemies while you look on" (Jer 20:3-4 RSV; cf. 20:10).

People also fear the *actions of other people*. Haman is "in terror before the king and the queen" when his plot against the Jews is divulged (Esther 7:6). The slander and intrigue of David's *enemies against him constitute for him "terror on every side" (Ps 31:13). Paul's timidity to preach in Corinth is portrayed by him as coming "in weakness and in much fear and trembling" (1 Cor 2:3), and Paul recalls his entry into Macedonia in terms of "fighting without and fear within" (2 Cor 7:5). On a similarly psychological note, the psalmist dreads his own "reproach" or "disgrace" (Ps 119:39 NIV).

Numerous references to fear center on the *experience of warfare or the fear of a rival nation*. Part of the explanation is the ancient practice of invading *armies terrorizing their enemies in an attempt to demoralize them (2 Chron 32:18; Is 7:6; Hab 1:9). In a variation on that theme, God's deliverance of Israel becomes an occasion for fear to strike the nations who hear of the deliverance (Ex 15:11, 16; 23:27; 34:10; Deut 4:34; 26:8; 34:12). Beyond terror as a weapon, it is simply something that accompanies war: Isaiah describes the impending invasion by Assyria as "sheer terror" (Is 28:19); Jeremiah describes people's looking for peace and finding terror (Jer 8:15; 14:19).

A final category of images of fear is to be found in the *eschatological images of the end*. The book of Revelation is an ever-expanding vision of horror, but other visions of the end are also a repository of terror. In a moment of wry humor, Amos pictures the *Day of the Lord as being like a man who "fled from a *lion, and a bear met him" (Amos 5:19 RSV). In his Olivet Discourse Jesus gave us memorable images of wars and rumors of wars, famines and earthquakes (Mt 24:5-7; Mk 13:6-8). Elsewhere Jesus predicted a time of coming catastrophe so terrible that people will ask the mountains to fall on them and the hills to cover them (Lk 23:30; cf. Rev 6:12-17). Equally memorable are the images of cataclysmic upheaval in nature and persecution that pervade the book of Revelation.

To sum up, biblical images of fear cluster around the character and works of God, the forces of *nature, death and calamity, people and their actions, warfare, and the end of history. It is important to note that in regard to all of these causes of fear, the Bible repeatedly holds out the possibility (sometimes phrased as a command) that those who trust in God are exempt from being afraid.

Physical Results of Fear. The human manifestations of fear include melting, trembling, paralysis and fainting. The human faculty with which fear is linked is the *heart (Deut 20:3; 28:67; 2 Sam 17:10; Ps 27:3; Is 7:4; 35:4).

Fear experienced metaphorically as a process of *melting is applied to the nations who hear of Israel's deliverance at the Red Sea (Ex 15:15), Israelites who are fearful of serving in the army (Deut 20:8), the inhabitants of Jericho who hear of Israel's success (Josh 2:9, 11, 24), the fearful spies (Josh 14:8), the hypothetical warriors in Hushai's counsel not to attack David (2 Sam 17:10), the Babylonians in Isaiah's vision of their doom (13:7), Israel on the eve of invasion (Ezek 21:7) and the Egyptians (Is 19:1).

*Trembling is a physical manifestation of fear (Ex 15:15; 19:16; Deut 2:25; 1 Sam 28:5; Job 4:14; Ps 55:5; Is 64:2; Ezek 26:16; 32:10; Dan 5:19; Hab 3:7; Mk 5:33; 16:8; 1 Cor 2:3; Jas 2:19). To this can be added Ezekiel's vivid metaphor of national leaders being "palsied by terror" (Ezek 7:27 RSV). The trembling of the fearful is metaphorically compared to the pangs of a woman in labor (Is 13:8; 21:3; Jer 30:6; 48:41).

At the opposite end of the spectrum from trembling are paralysis, immobility and fainting. When the leaders of neighboring nations hear of the Red Sea deliverance, Moses predicts, "terror and dread" will cause them to be "as still as a stone" (Ex 15:16). When the drunken Nabal sobers up and learns that he has been rude to David the previous day, "his heart died within him, and he became as a stone" (1 Sam 25:37). Fainting also occurs as an expression of fear (Deut 20:3; Job 23:16; Jer 51:46; Ezek 21:7; Lk 21:27).

Biblical Characters Who Fear. Finally, biblical images of fear include a gallery of characters caught in memorable moments of fear. Indeed, we encounter more than two hundred occasions when a biblical character is said to "fear" or be "afraid" (or in a variant told not to fear or be afraid, usually with the implication that the person thus addressed *is* afraid). The most memorable examples include Adam immediately after the Fall (Gen 3:10); Sarah when the divine visitor catches her eavesdropping (Gen 18:15); Lot and his daughters, fearful of staying in Zoar (Gen 19:30); Jacob after the dream of the ladder (Gen 28:17); Moses after killing an Egyptian (Ex 2:14) and at the burning bush (Ex 3:6); Aaron and the Israelites when Moses' face shone (Ex 34:30); Gideon destroying an altar to Baal by night (Judg 6:27); the youthful Samuel after receiving the vision regarding Eli's sons (1 Sam 3:15); David when captured by Achish (1 Sam 21:12) and when the ark of God was moved (2 Sam 6:9); Elijah when Jezebel vowed to kill him (1 Kings 19:3); the sailors when God punished Jonah's flight with a storm (Jon 1:5); the disciples when caught in a storm on the lake (Mt 8:26; Mk 4:40) and when Jesus walks on the water (Mt 14:27; Mk 6:50); the women at the open tomb (Mt 28:10; Mk 16:8); the shepherds at the nativity when the angel appeared (Lk 2:9-10), and the disciples at the transfiguration (Lk 9:34).

See also FEAR OF GOD; MELT, MELTING; TERROR, STORIES OF; TREMBLING, SHAKING, BODILY ANGUISH.

BIBLIOGRAPHY. E. W. Conrad, *Fear Not Warrior: A Study of 'al tîrā' Pericopes in the Hebrew Scriptures* (Chico, CA: Scholars Press, 1985).

FEAR OF GOD

The fear of God is distinct from the terror of him that is also a biblical motif (*see* Fear). Encompassing and building on attitudes of awe and reverence, it is the proper and elemental response of a person to *God. This religious fear of God is a major biblical image

for the believer's faith. In fact, there are well over a hundred references to the fear of God in the positive sense of faith and obedience. To "fear" God or be "God-fearing" is a stock biblical image for being a follower of God, sometimes in implied contrast to those who do not fear him. The very frequency of the references signals that the fear of God is central to biblical faith, and the relative absence of this ancient way of thinking in our culture should give us pause. It is important to note, however, that the preponderance of references occur in the OT, perhaps implying that a permanent change (though not an abrogation) occurred with the incarnation of Christ, who calls his disciples friends rather than servants (Jn 15:15).

What images should we associate with this mysterious "fear of God"? The actions most frequently associated with fear of God are serving God (Deut 6:13; 10:20; 1 Sam 12:24) and *obedience to his commandments (Deut 31:13; 1 Sam 12:14). The fear of God is linked to *wisdom (Ps 111:10; Prov 9:10; 15:33) and is part of the *covenant between God and his people (Ps 25:14; 103:17-18). To fear God is to be in awe and *reverence of him (Ps 33:8; Mal 2:5 RSV) and to trust him (Ps 40:3; 115:11). Fearing God means hating and avoiding evil (Prov 8:13; 16:6). It is not too much to say that fearing God is virtually synonymous with having saving *faith in him. Deuteronomy 10:12-13 is an apt summary of what is encompassed in the fear of God: "And now, O Israel, what does the LORD your God ask of you but to fear the LORD your God, to walk in all his ways, to love him, to serve the LORD your God with all your heart and with all your soul, and to observe the LORD's commands and decrees" (NIV).

The fear of God is a fundamental quality of those who have an experiential knowledge of who he is. The experience of the sailors in the book of *Jonah provides a good illustration of this and of the difference between *terror of God and saving fear of him. When Jonah tells the sailors that it is the Lord "who made the sea and land" who has sent the storm upon them, they are terrified (Jon 1:9-10). But once the storm has abated, they "greatly feared the LORD" (Jon 1:16) in the sense of being filled with awe and reverence, making sacrifices and vows to him. The significance of the latter response is that it is born out of some knowledge, however small, of who God is (see Prov 2:5, which equates "the fear of the LORD" with "the knowledge of God"). It also hints at something that the biblical passages imply—that the fear of God stems especially from an experience of his transcendence and divine power.

The fear of God produces practical results, as it does with the awe-filled sailors who offer sacrifices. When God gives the law to Israel through Moses, the command to fear the Lord occurs repeatedly, often coupled with the command to obey God's decrees (cf. Deut 5:29; 6:24; 10:20). Thus the fear of the Lord appears as a contrast to sinful deeds (Lev 19:14; 25:17, 36, 43) and has the force of a moral imperative.

Several biblical characters are explicitly said to exemplify the fear of God, sometimes confirming its relationship to obedience. After *Abraham has obeyed God's command by showing his willingness to sacrifice his son Isaac, an angel of the Lord declares to him, "Now I know that you fear God, because you have not withheld from me your son" (Gen 22:12 NIV). *Joseph, a man of integrity, attempts to allay his brothers' fears with the comment, "I fear God" (Gen 42:18). God himself twice describes Job as "blameless and upright, a man who fears God and shuns evil" (Job 1:8; 2-3 NIV). Lest we begin to think that the fear of God is an OT image only, Paul makes the evocative statement that "we know what it is to fear the Lord" (2 Cor 5:11 NIV).

The Bible also gives us pictures of people who do not fear God. By the time Moses has brought seven different plagues upon Egypt, *Pharaoh knows God well enough to fear him properly, but he does not do so. Though Pharaoh appears to repent, Moses replies, "I know that you . . . still do not fear the LORD God" (Ex 9:30). Even after Pharaoh allows Israel to flee Egypt, his disobedience in giving pursuit indicates that he does not fear God. As a consequence, God destroys Pharaoh's army, just as he promises to bring judgment upon all those who do not fear him (Mal 3:5), while preserving those who do (Mal 3:16-17). The horrifying picture of sinful humanity painted in Romans 3:10-18 winds its way to the climactic statement, "There is no fear of God before their eyes" (NIV).

For those who do fear God the resulting benefits are many: God will bring blessing upon them (Ps 115:13) and will confide in them (Ps 25:14). They will avoid evil (Prov 16:6), and God will have *mercy upon them (Lk 1:50). Moreover, those who fear God will gain life (Prov 19:23), knowledge (Prov 1:7) and wisdom (Prov 9:10). The wisdom that begins with the fear of God is closely related to knowledge and obedience (Ps 111:10). The fear of God is a fundamental quality of people who know and obey God.

In the NT the fear of God is a significant component of the gospel. In the face of worldly threats, Jesus instructs his disciples to fear God (Lk 12:5). For the Gentiles who are outside of God's covenant with Israel, the fear of God marks the beginning of the way to salvation through Christ, as we learn when Peter visits Cornelius' house and declares that God "accepts men from every nation who fear him and do what is right" (Acts 10:35 NIV). Regarding the early church we read, "Encouraged by the Holy Spirit, it grew in numbers, living in the fear of the Lord" (Acts 9:31 NIV).

See also FEAR; GOD; HOLINESS; REVERENCE; TERROR, STORIES OF.

FEAST, FEASTING

Feasts in the Bible are images of *joyful voices, festive *music and *dancing, and abundant *food. They are not simply parties, but celebrations of God's goodness toward his people. Feasts provide occasions of fellow-

ship with one another and with the Lord to remember and to celebrate what wonderful things God has done. The Hebrews had numerous harvest periods spread throughout the year. This resulted in many feasts, all celebrations of the faithfulness of God's provision and the land's fertility (hence the appeal of the fertility god Baal and other Canaanite religions).

What Feasts Celebrate. The beginning of certain relationships in the Bible was formally marked with a festive meal. For instance, when Isaac made a peace treaty with Abimelech, king of the Philistines, he prepared a feast, after which the men swore their *oath to each other (Gen 26:26-30). *Weddings in biblical times were celebrated with a feast that often lasted several days (Gen 29:22; Judg 14:10-17; Jn 2:1-11). It is therefore especially fitting that when God formally established his relationship with his people in the *covenant given to Moses on Mount *Sinai, he established feasts to commemorate and to celebrate this blessed relationship.

Six feasts and one fast (Yom Kippur) commanded by the Mosaic covenant were celebrated annually to commemorate God's continual goodness toward his people (Ex 23:14-17; Lev 23; Num 9:1-14; Deut 16:1-17). In the springtime the Feast of *Passover occurs one day before the seven-day Feast of Unleavened Bread. Together these two feasts commemorate the night in Egypt when the *angel of death passed over those who had marked their homes with lamb's blood. The Feast of Unleavened Bread begins the very next day to commemorate the resulting hasty departure from Egypt that began the *exodus.

The Feasts of Firstfruits and of Weeks are celebrations of the *harvest, reminding God's people of the goodness of the land into which he had finally brought them. The autumn feasts begin with the Feast of Trumpets, also called Rosh Hashanah, which marks the beginning of the civil new year. The Feast of Tabernacles (or Booths), also called Succoth, commemorated God's sustenance during the difficult and threatening journey from Egypt to the *"land flowing with milk and honey."

After the *exile, the celebration of another feast was added to the Jewish calendar, the Feast of Purim. This feast commemorates the deliverance of God's people from genocide in fifth-century Persia, demonstrating that his covenant promise to protect his people extended even outside the ancient borders of the Promised Land. The OT book of Esther describes the story of this deliverance and establishes the annual celebration of this feast.

A final feast was added to the Jewish calendar in the second century B.C. after Judas Maccabees reclaimed the *temple in Jerusalem from the defilement of the Seleucid king Antiochus Epiphanes. Hanukkah, or the Feast of (re-)Dedication (Jn 10:22) celebrates this improbable victory and the rededication of the temple to the Lord.

The feasts of the Bible celebrate God's faithfulness to his people in preserving and protecting them and in bringing them into close fellowship with himself and with each other. However, God was also faithful to his promise of *judgment when his people disobeyed the covenant. In those times when God's people turned away from him to idolatry, the feasts became painful remembrances of the broken covenant. From its beginning the northern kingdom of Israel was prone to *idolatry after building substitute temples to keep the people from celebrating the feasts in Jerusalem in the southern kingdom. But the feasts celebrated at these idolatrous shrines were not acceptable to God. The prophet Amos brought God's indictment against them: "I hate, I despise your religious feasts; I cannot stand your assemblies" (Amos 5:21 NIV). In the wake of Jerusalem's later destruction, the author of Lamentations expresses the desolation of the once-blessed land: "The roads to Zion mourn, for no one comes to her appointed feasts" (Lam 1:4 NIV). When the people's fellowship with God is broken by their disobedience to his word, there can be no joyful feast. A fast of repentance for sin is the only remedy.

How Feasts Were Celebrated. Each of these feasts was celebrated by refraining from the usual work of the day, by assembling together in fellowship and by eating a festive meal of meat, *grain (i.e., *bread) and *wine that had been ritually offered to God. These special sacrificial offerings renewed fellowship between a holy God and his sinful people, expressing the covenant relationship between them. Because of God's goodness, these days were to be celebrated with great joy by everyone living in the land, including men and women, boys and girls, servants, widows, orphans, and even foreigners.

When David made Jerusalem the capital city of God's nation and his son Solomon constructed the temple there, Jerusalem became "the city of our festivals" (Is 33:20) because God's presence was there in a special way (Deut 12). This central location for the feasts highlighted God's desire to dwell with his people in joyful assembly. Three times a year the men of God's people were to come to Jerusalem with offerings for the Lord in celebration of the Feast of Unleavened Bread, the Feast of Weeks and the Feast of Tabernacles (Deut 16:16).

*Solomon dedicated the temple in Jerusalem, appropriately on the Feast of Tabernacles, with a magnificent fourteen-day feast, offering tens of thousands of animals in festal sacrifice for a vast assembly of people (1 Kings 8:62-66; 2 Chron 7:1-10). The Feast of Tabernacles annually had reminded the people how God had dwelt with them in the desert in a lowly tent. Now he would dwell among them in a splendid temple in the capital city of their nation. Solomon's festive crescendo looked back on how God had indeed been with his wayward people through their exodus journey, how he had brought them into the land, established them as a nation and given them a king, and how he now would dwell among them in a magnificent temple. The descendants of Abraham had become a sovereign nation, just as the Lord had promised so long ago! The people left the feast with hearts overflowing with praise for all that God had done.

New Testament. The apostle John tells that Jesus went up to Jerusalem to celebrate the Feast of Tabernacles at the temple. In Jesus, God came in the flesh to celebrate with his people. On the last and greatest day of the Feast of Tabernacles, God incarnate stood in his temple calling out to his thirsty people to come to him and *drink (Jn 7:37). How ironic that his unrecognized voice was a disturbing presence in the festivities that had for so long been celebrated to welcome his presence!

The *Lord's Supper focuses the elements of the Feast of Unleavened Bread in the person and work of Jesus Christ. The bread and wine first offered by Jesus to his disciples at Passover is the sign of the beginning of a new covenant established in his death (Mt 26:17-30; Mk 14:12-26; Lk 22:1-23). This solemn but festive meal instituted by Jesus is to be repeated by the assembly of the Christian church in remembrance of him (1 Cor 11:23-26). The significance of Passover, the greatest of the Jewish feasts, is redefined in the death of Jesus, who is himself the final and ultimate Passover lamb, whose body and blood provide the bread and wine for the sacramental meal that unites God to his people in Christ (1 Cor 5:8). Therefore, the Christian sacrament of Holy Communion is a symbolic feast that commemorates and celebrates God's love for his people in establishing a new covenant with them in Christ who saves them from sin and death.

The kingdom of God proclaimed by Jesus is described in the parables as a great feast to which people from around the world and throughout the epochs of history will come (Mt 8:11; 22:1-14; Lk 14:15-24). It is a joyful celebration of God's faithfulness to his promises that extends from the first to the last moment of history. Moreover, the image of the kingdom of God as a great feast is portrayed as a marriage *banquet, expressing the joy of the most intimate fellowship between the Son of God and his *bride, believers from all ages of time (Mt 22:1-14; Rev 19:9).

Feast as a Sign of Future Blessing. When God's people returned from the judgment of *exile and began rebuilding the temple in Jerusalem, the feasts were renewed as a sign that the Lord was still in covenant relationship with his chastised people (Ezra 3:1-6). About this same time the prophet Zechariah foresaw a day when people of all nations would perpetually celebrate the Feast of Tabernacles, signifying God's dwelling with them, and would come to Jerusalem to worship the King of the earth, the Lord Almighty (Zech 14:16-19).

The imagery of the biblical feast is an image of the joyful celebration of the love of God for his people, which came to ultimate fruition in the death and resurrection of Jesus Christ. On Mount *Zion of Jerusalem, the central location of all biblical feasts, the Lord Almighty has prepared, as Isaiah predicted:

a feast of rich food for all peoples,

a banquet of aged wine—
    the best of meats and the finest of wines.
On this mountain he will destroy
    the shroud that enfolds all peoples,
the sheet that covers all nations;
    he will swallow up death forever.
The Sovereign LORD will wipe away the tears
    from all faces;
he will remove the disgrace of his
    people from all the earth.

                      The LORD has spoken.
                      (Is 25:6-8 NIV)

The imagery of biblical feasting still points to the future, when the Lord God will resurrect all his people from every age to live with him in eternal joy. Every feast celebrated to the Lord is but a foretaste of that glorious day.

See also BANQUET; BREAD; DANCING; DRINKING; EATING; FESTIVAL; FOOD; JOY; MUSIC; REFUSER OF FESTIVITIES; SALVATION; WEDDING; WINE.

FEET

Though feet are sometimes associated with objects such as chests and tables (e.g., Ex 25:12), the Bible refers mainly to the feet of human beings and animals. "From head to foot" is a way to describe the whole of a person (2 Sam 14:25; Is 1:6). There are also occasional anthropomorphic references to the feet of God, such as his promise to glorify the place of his feet (Is 60:13; Ezek 43:7; Zech 14:4).

One of the basic aspects of hospitality in Bible times was the *washing of a guest's feet (Gen 18:4; 19:2; 24:32; Judg 19:21; 1 Sam 25:41). A reference in Moses' blessing to Asher of the extravagance of bathing the feet in *oil (Deut 33:24) indicates the prospect of considerable wealth. To wash the feet is associated with going home and being unlikely to go out again that day (2 Sam 11:8). Thus the beloved complains that she cannot come to the door since she has washed her feet (Song 5:3). Jesus serves his disciples by washing their feet, the act of a menial *servant (Jn 13:2-11). This service, which has on previous occasions been performed for him (Lk 7:44; Jn 11:2; 12:3) establishes a pattern for his disciples (Jn 13:14-16; 1 Tim 5:10).

Ritual washing of the *hands and feet occurs frequently (e.g., Ex 30:19). Although it sounds rather gruesome, God's people can look forward to bathing their feet in the *blood of wicked (Ps 58:10; 68:23).

Feet also figure in situations in which someone has authority over a person or place. People have rights over land touched by their feet (Deut 2:5; 11:24; Josh 1:3; Ps 122:2) and lose rights over land their feet no longer walk on (2 Chron 33:8). Related to this is the idea that vanquished *enemies are *under the feet of their conquerors (Josh 10:24, 1 Kings 5:3; Ps 8:6; 45:5; 110:1; Is 49:23; 60:14; Mal 4:3). The NT stresses the authority of Christ over all things in this way (Mt 22:44; 1 Cor 15:25ff.; Eph 1:22; Heb 2:8) and the eventual victory of

Christian believers over Satan and his followers (Rom 16:20; Rev 3:9).

To fall at someone's feet voluntarily is a mark of reverence (1 Sam 25:24; 2 Sam 22:39f.; Esther 8:3; Acts 10:25), and many of those who meet Jesus fall at his feet (e.g., Mk 5:22; Rev 1:17). In Revelation the angel guiding John refuses to allow him to fall at his feet and directs him to worship God instead (Rev 19:10; 22:8). Sitting at someone's feet is an act of submission and teachability (Lk 8:35; 10:39). Seizing the feet of another is an act of supplication (2 Kings 4:27; Mt 28:9); a particular example may be the uncovering of Boaz's feet by Ruth in order to indicate her desire that he become her kinsman-redeemer (Ruth 3:4-8).

To be able to negotiate rough terrain like a nimble-footed deer is an image applied to the life a righteous person (2 Sam 22:34; Hab 3:19). Obedience to God guarantees that one's feet will not slip (Ps 17:5), for God is said to guard the feet of his saints (1 Sam 2:9). This is related to the desire for feet to be on level ground (Ps 26:12; Prov 4:26; Heb 12:13) in a spacious place (Ps 31:8) on firm ground (Ps 40:2) and guided by the *lamp of God's Word (Ps 119:105). The Bible records several prayers that feet will not stray (Ps 44:18; 119:101; Prov 6:18) or rush to sin (Prov 1:16; Is 59:7; Jer 14:10). A feature of the Messiah's ministry is that he will guide feet into the way of peace (Lk 1:79).

On the other hand, sin is characterized by feet that slip or *stumble (Job 12:5; Ps 37:31; 56:13; 66:9; 73:2; 116:8; 121:3). Along similar lines, feet may be caught in a snare or a net, or put in shackles (Ps 25:15; 57:6; 105:18; Jer 18:22; Lam 1:13). One such *trap is flattery (Prov 29:5), and the psalmist prays to be delivered from those who would trip him up (Ps 140:4).

Going barefoot is interpreted in a number of ways: either reverence at the presence of God (Ex 3:5), a result of judgment (Is 20:2) or a sign of *mourning (Ezek 24:27, 23).

Feet are not normally considered particularly attractive and may be thought of as inferior (1 Cor 12:15, 21). But they become beautiful when they belong to someone who uses them to carry the good news of God's salvation (Is 52:7; Nahum 1:15; Eph 6:15; *see* Dancing). Should the message be rejected in any particular place, the bearers of the gospel are to shake the dust off their feet (Mt 10:14) as a sign of protest (Acts 13:51) and refuse to have anything at all to do with the place.

See also BAREFOOT; HEEL; SHOE, SANDLE; STUMBLE, STUMBLING BLOCK; TOE; UNDER THE FEET.

FENCE, FENCED PLACE

The idea of a fence or fenced place is translated various ways in English versions of the Bible, including "fence," "fortified city," "fortifications," "wall" and "hedge." Virtually all of the references to the imagery of fence in English translations are to "fenced cities," that is, fortified *cities (*see* Wall). In distinction from walls of fortification, fences and hedges were less elaborate partitions used in domestic areas like homes or farms. Fences usually consisted of a stone wall, while hedges were composed of shrubbery, often *thorny plants (Mic 7:4). Jesus' famous aphorism about going "out to the highways and hedges" (Lk 14:23 RSV) evokes the picture of hedges as out-of-the-way places where one would have to actively search for people.

Because fences were usually rather slight constructions, the psalmist's imagination gravitates toward the fence as an image of something easily destroyed. In protesting people who oppress him in a time of weakness, he asks how long his tormentors will shatter him "like a leaning wall, a tottering fence" (Ps 62:3 RSV). In a similarly negative usage, the prophet Nahum scornfully compares Nineveh's princes to "clouds of locusts settling on the fences in a day of cold—when the sun rises, they fly away; no one knows where they are" (Nahum 3:17 RSV).

Mainly, though, the fence or hedge is an image of *protection and safety against thieves or predators. Satan pictures God's protection of Job with the image of God's having put a hedge around him (Job 1:10). Judah's predicted exile is pictured as a *vineyard whose hedge God will remove (Is 5:5; cf. Ps 80:12). In one of his parables Jesus pictures the preparations that a good owner would undertake when planting a vineyard, including setting a hedge around it, digging a *pit for a wine press and building a *tower to protect it (Mt 21:33; Mk 12:1). Hedges might also become places of *hiding (Jer 49:3).

In metaphoric uses, the image of God's fencing a person in can have negative connotations of confinement. Thus Job pictures God as fencing him with oppression (Job 3:23) and as walling up his way so that he cannot pass (Job 19:8), and in Hosea 2:6 God predicts that he will fence in the path of Gomer.

See also PROTECTION; WALL.

FESTIVAL

In the Bible a festival is a periodic religious celebration, sometimes at a special place and therefore involving a journey. Festivals call for a cessation to ordinary workaday activities and replacing them with communal activities that are special to the religious occasion.

Israelite festivals were crucial to a sense of national unity. There were frequent public festivals, including the weekly sabbath, the monthly new moon festival and three main annual festivals—*Passover and Unleavened Bread (celebrating the exodus), *Pentecost or Weeks (celebrating the end of the barley harvest) and Tabernacles or Booths (celebrating the final harvest ingathering). By NT times two others had been added: Purim (celebrating the victory of Esther and Mordecai over Haman's genocide plot, Esther 9) and Lights or Hanukkah (commemorating Judas Maccabeus's cleansing of the Temple in 164 B.C., referred to in Jn 10:22). It is evident from these examples that festivals celebrated two types of occa-

sions—faith events in salvation history (such as Passover) and nature events in the yearly cycle (such as Pentecost). The Feast of Booths combined the two, celebrating both harvest and the memory of Israel's wilderness wanderings.

The images associated with festivals in the Bible cluster around six motifs: breaking the routine, lavish abundance (especially of food), ceremony or ritual, sacrifice, community, holiday spirit and a religious focus on God. A good summary of what the OT festivals were like appears in Leviticus 23 and Numbers 28—29, and the generalizations that follow are amply illustrated from these chapters alone.

Hebrew Festivals as God Intended Them. That the festivals would be a *break from the routine* was assured by the stipulation that on a festival day "you shall have a holy convocation; you shall do no laborious work" (repeatedly in Lev 23 and Num 28—29 RSV). Some of the festivals required the Israelites to change their locale in order to participate in the festival. The pilgrimage to Jerusalem became an established part of Hebrew religious life and was a complete break from ordinary life at home. At the Feast of Booths the people camped out for seven days in booths made from tree branches and leaves.

*Feasting—at once a break from the routine and an example of *abundance*—dominates our impression of OT festivals. Although meat was relatively scarce in Hebrew society, it was conspicuously present at several of the festivals, where the requirement of animal sacrifices insured a large-scale banquet of meat. *Wine, an image connoting both richness or abundance and celebration, was likewise in full evidence at the festivals. So prominent is the image of feasting that most of the festivals are actually called feasts in the OT. The sheer quantity of ingredients for the sacrifices of the festivals itself constitutes an image of fullness.

Hebrew festivals were also filled with *ceremony* or *ritual*. All of the festivals involved doing prescribed activities. At *Pentecost, for example, a sheaf of *grain and two loaves of *bread were waved before the Lord (Lev 23:15-17). At the Feast of Trumpets a memorial would be proclaimed with blasts of trumpets (Lev 23:24). At the Feast of Booths people would "hold a holy convocation and present an offering by fire to the LORD" (Lev 23:36). Everywhere we turn in the accounts of OT festivals, we find ceremonies. No doubt this was a large part of the appeal of the festivals, as it is with our holiday rituals.

Sacrifice or *offering* was another constant motif in Hebrew festivals. Most of the festivals were accompanied by either animal *sacrifice or a harvest *offering. Every sacrifice or offering was specifically prescribed, such as "two lambs a year old without blemish, and one young bull, and two rams" (Lev 23:18), or "three tenths of an ephah of fine flour for a cereal offering, mixed with oil" (Num 28:12). The meaning behind such sacrifices was that of giving up something to God; the benefit was in the element of sacrifice, not in something that God himself needed (as was the case with pagan gods).

Images of *community* pervade the OT festivals, which were the opposite from solitary events. For one thing, every member of the religious community would have celebrated the same festival at the same time. It seems plausible to believe that the festivals with their sacrifices resembled potluck meals, with some of the food reserved for the priests and the remainder available for others. In some of the prescriptions we specifically find the injunction to include the entire community, as when Moses told the people that "you shall rejoice in your feast, you and your son and your daughter, your manservant and your maidservant, the Levite, the sojourner, the fatherless, and the widow who are within your towns" (Deut 16:14 RSV). We can infer that the pilgrimages to Jerusalem involved group caravans and the mingling of children from friends' families, resulting in the type of situation where Jesus' parents naturally assumed that their son was with "kinsfolk and acquaintances" (Lk 2:44).

A *holiday spirit* also pervaded OT festivals. Along with all the solemnity, the Israelites were commanded to "rejoice before the LORD your God," to "rejoice in your feast" (Deut 16:11, 13 RSV) and to "rejoice, you and your households, in all that you undertake" relating to the sacrifices (Deut 12:7 RSV). In the book of Esther we read regarding the Feast of Purim that "the Jews of the villages, who live in the open towns," commemorate the day "as a day for gladness and feasting and holiday-making, and a day on which they send choice portions to one another" (Esther 9:19 RSV). Isaiah describes "the night when a holy feast is kept" in terms of "gladness of heart, as when one sets out to the sound of the flute to go to the mountain of the LORD" (Is 30:29 RSV). The Psalms give us pictures of shouting at the worship that transpired at the *temple. In short, festivals were accompanied by high-spiritedness and a letting go of usual inhibitions.

Finally, for all their social functions, OT festivals were also *religious festivals,* kept first of all to God. The phrase "to the LORD" runs like a refrain through the prescriptions for the feasts. The gatherings were "a holy convocation." In a word, the festivals were worship experiences in which the believer encountered God and received a blessing from him. We need not, of course, drive a wedge between the social and spiritual dimensions of the festivals. If the smell of roasting meat was "a pleasing odor to the LORD" (Num 28:8), it also promised a barbecue meal. If *animals and *grain were sacrifices to God, they also provided the materials for a community meal.

Perversions and Warnings. From the prophetic books come pictures of the perversion of festivals. One is neglect. Malachi, for example, pictures people as offering blind, lame or sick animals in sacrifice instead of unblemished ones (Mal 1:8-14). Isaiah describes Israel's sin of not calling upon God, of being weary of him and of not bringing offerings and sacrifices (Is 43:22-24).

The more customary abuse was apparently nominal observance—going through the motions like a tiresome requirement, instead of making the festivals an expression of the grateful heart. Malachi pictures people performing sacrifices while saying to themselves, "What a weariness this is" (Mal 1:13 RSV). In a similar vein Amos portrays merchants as waiting impatiently for the end of the new moon and sabbath so they can begin their sale of grain (Amos 8:5).

In light of these perversions God is pictured by the prophets as despising people's offerings and festivals (Is 1:13-15; Amos 5:21-23). Elsewhere, God promises to bring an end to sham sacrifices and observance of festivals (Hos 2:11; Amos 8:10).

Festival Imagery in the New Testament. The NT presents both continuity and innovation in regard to religious festivals. On the one hand, Jesus and his disciples are described as participating in statutory Jewish festivals. But there is an element of fulfillment and abrogation as well as observance of OT festivals. Jesus turns the ceremonial *water into *wine at the *wedding at Cana to symbolize his transformation of OT rituals (Jn 2:1-11). While attending the Feast of Tabernacles, Jesus proclaims himself as the fulfillment of OT prophecy (Jn 7:37-39). The atoning events of Passion Week are set against a background of the Passover, again suggesting Christ's fulfillment of what the sacrificial system foreshadowed.

From Pentecost onward the apostolic writers lose interest in OT festivals because they have lost their significance. The death and resurrection of Christ have achieved what the rituals could not. At a stroke, the need for such symbolism has been erased, as the book of Hebrews elaborates at length. Joining in public festivals is now a matter of personal choice, and Christians are not to judge each other's decisions since the OT festivals were "only a shadow of what is to come," with the substance belonging to Christ (Col 2:16-17). Festal imagery remains a source of metaphor for spiritual reality, of course: Christians "have come to Mount Zion and to the city of the living God, the heavenly Jerusalem, and to innumerable angels in festal gathering" (Heb 12:22 RSV).

The other new development in the NT is the institution of the Lord's Supper, which was at first a shared meal, but which did not have the extravagance of a feast. When Paul, writing about the Lord's *Supper, enjoins the Corinthians to "celebrate the festival" (1 Cor 5:8), the terminology brings to mind the OT Passover. But the accompanying statement that "Christ, our paschal lamb, has been sacrificed" (v. 7) also signals that the OT sacrifices have been replaced by something new.

See also FARMING; FEAST; HARVEST; OFFERING; PASSOVER; PENTECOST; REFUSER OF FESTIVITIES; SACRIFICE; SEASONS; TEMPLE; TIME.

FESTIVITIES, REFUSING. *See* REFUSER OF FESTIVITIES.

FIFTY

The figure fifty carries with it a number of connotations. When applied to age, fifty conveys the sense of a full measure of years. It does not mark the end of life, but rather the age at which a person takes a rest from labor. For example, it is only men ranging from thirty to fifty years old who are to serve in Israel's tent of meeting (Num 4:3, 23, 30). When the Lord instructs Moses to set apart the tribe of Levi specifically for priestly duties, he stipulates that fifty years will be the retirement age for Levites, though they may continue to assist with their former duties (Num 8:25, 26). This association of fifty years with the fullness of age may shed some light on the meaning of the Jews' retort to Jesus, "You are not yet fifty years old, . . . and you have seen Abraham!" (Jn 8:57 NIV). If fifty is the age at which one gains the maturity and respect due an elder, then the Jews' comment attacks the reliability of Jesus' claim based on his relative youth. Thus, the age of fifty conveys a sense of completion and the wisdom of long experience.

But fifty is more than just a landmark in an individual's life; the number fifty also carries great significance in Israel's calendar. God instructs Moses that the timing of the Feast of Weeks is to be fifty days after the *sabbath on which the firstfruits of the harvest is first given as a wave offering—that is, the day after *seven sabbaths (or forty-nine days) have elapsed (Lev 23:15, 16). On that fiftieth day Israelites must make another wave offering of firstfruits, a sin offering, and they must observe the day as a sabbath (Lev 23:17-21). Since the forty-ninth day is also a sabbath, the fiftieth day stands out as a special second sabbath. (Later this day is called *Pentecost, the Greek term for fifty.) The imagery of fifty, consequently, contains a sense of special sabbath rest.

The association of fifty with liberty as well as rest emerges in God's establishment of the Year of Jubilee. Every seventh year is to be a sabbath year, in which the land lies fallow (Lev 25:4); but after seven sabbath years have passed, Israel is to observe the fiftieth year as a second sabbath year—a Year of Jubilee (Lev 25:11-12). In this year, on the Day of Atonement, a *trumpet blast signals the return to its original owner of any land sold and the *freedom of any Israelites in the land who have been sold as servants (Lev 25:28, 40). Ideally, a Jubilee year would occur at least once in the lifetime of every Israelite. Thus the greatest significance of fifty as a recurring image is its associations with sabbath rest and liberty.

The theme of liberation also appears in the context of Israel's exile in Babylon. In Ezekiel, Israel's return from exile is to happen in accordance with the year of Jubilee. Although God has given Israel to his servant Babylon as a gift, it is only a temporary one that must be returned in the "year of freedom" (Ezek 46:16, 17). Israel can look forward with hope to the approaching fiftieth year of exile as the end of domination by Babylon. Just as the land and individual Israelites are God's possessions, so also the entire nation belongs solely to God, who will take it back at the Jubilee. Here fifty as an image of liberation finds powerful new meaning to an exiled Israel, remembering past glory and hoping for restoration by God.

See also FIRST; FIVE; FORTY; FOUR; HUNDRED; ONE; PENTECOST; SEVEN; SEVENTY; THREE, THIRD; TWELVE; TWO.

FIG, FIG TREE

Well known in antiquity for its sweet taste and protective shade, the fig tree appears in the biblical record first in the prototypical tragedy of the Fall of humanity (Gen 3). In this archetypal *fall from innocence, one consequence of the original pair's succumbing to temptation is their attempt to cover their *nakedness before God with fig leaves.

The fig tree was one of the most important domesticated plants in the biblical era and was widely cultivated throughout Palestine. It grows best in moderately dry areas that have little or no rain during the period of fruit maturation. The tree was cultivated for its delicious fruit and appreciated for its dark green and deeply lobed *leaves, which produced a welcome shade (Mic 4:4; Zech 3:10; Jn 1:48).

These features of fruitfulness and shade make the fig tree a ready symbol for God in *covenant relation to his people, as is the *vine, with which it is often linked. Thus God is portrayed as having seen in Israel prospects of productivity as one "seeing the early fruit on the fig tree" (Hos 9:10 NIV), which, appearing in late spring, gives promise of later fruitfulness. As covenant beneficiary, Israel could enjoy the God-given prosperity and security experienced in the Solomonic ideal: "each man under his own vine and fig tree" (1 Kings 4:25 NIV).

Failure to keep covenantal standards to be fruitful could mean the loss of safety and God's judgment, a theme often repeated in prophetic pronouncements. Jesus utilized the motif of the fig tree in similar fashion, warning of the danger of spiritual fruitlessness (Lk 13:6-9), a condition which if uncorrected would spell disaster (Mt 21:19-21). Jesus uses a barren but leafy fig tree to illustrate how Israel, typified in its leadership, had a showy religion that was of no value and was worthy of judgment because it bore no fruit in their lives (Mk 11:12-21).

At its most basic level the fig tree is viewed as a wonderful part of settled life. It symbolized the good life, and to live under one's fig tree stood for a life of settledness (fig trees took several years of difficult labor to establish), *joy, *peace and *prosperity. In his taunt, the king of Assyria uses the fig tree as part of his picture of the life he claimed that he wanted to extend to Israel: "Do not listen to Hezekiah. This is what the king of Assyria says: Make peace with me and come out to me. Then every one of you will eat from his own vine and fig tree and drink water from his own cistern" (Is 36:16 NIV).

The fig tree is part of the eschaton because it is a

good thing worthy of the new order and represents the pleasures of food and settled domestic life. Fig trees are portrayed as part of this new age by Micah and Zechariah, since they symbolize how the best of the present age will continue when God's reign is fully established: " 'In that day each of you will invite his neighbor to sit under his vine and fig tree,' declares the LORD Almighty" (Zech 3:10 NIV; also Mic 4:4).

See also FRUIT; LEAF; TREE, TREES; VINE, VINEYARD.

FILL, FULLNESS

At its most positive, the biblical image of fullness is a supreme image of *abundance—the maximum satiety that we can imagine for something. In this positive sense, fullness connotes an ideal or a goal toward which the human spirit aspires and for which it longs. It implies not lacking and not falling short of a standard. But negative qualities can also be full, turning the ideal into a vision of *terror and divine *judgment.

Fullness as Abundance. At the level of human life cycle, the ideal is to die "old and full of years" (Gen 25:8; Gen 35:29; Job 42:17 NIV), with one's life expectancy having been completed. The same quality appears in nature, where for example in Pharaoh's dream, the years of plenty are pictured as *seven heads of grain that are healthy and "full" (Gen 41:7). On a family level the parent is happy whose "quiver is full" of arrows, that is, children (Ps 127:5). In an agrarian society abundance is having barns "filled with every kind of provision" (Ps 144:13 NIV). In a drought-prone land the ideal is to have "streams . . . filled with water to provide the people with grain" (Ps 65:9 NIV). All of these positive meanings of fullness converge in the book of *Ruth, where the image of fullness counteracts the motif of emptiness at the levels of the individual, the family, society and nature (Rauber).

The physical quality of being full or complete can also have an ethical dimension, expressing the virtue of honesty. God required that people should use "a full and just weight" and "a full and just measure" (Deut 25:15 RSV). God wants "the full tithes" brought "into the storehouse" (Mal 3:10 RSV). People who have stolen must make restitution in full (Lev 6:5).

Spiritual Fullness. Fullness also assumes a spiritual quality in Scripture. It characterizes the actions and character of God. Thus God's *glory fills the earth (Ps 72:19; Jer 23:24; Is 6:3; Ezek 43:5). So does his love (Ps 119:64). God is "full of compassion" (Ps 116:5 NIV) and "full of . . . mercy" (Jas 5:11 NIV).

Divine fullness is repeatedly associated with Jesus, where the added motif of fulfillment is a frequent part of the picture. Christ "came from the Father, full of grace and truth" (Jn 1:14 NIV). Through Jesus, the Father showed the human race "the full extent of his love" (Jn 13:1 NIV). Jesus came that people "may have life . . . to the full" (Jn. 10:10 NIV). Paul draws

on the theme of God's glory that fills the earth (Ps 72:19; Is 6:3; Jer 23:24; Ezek 43:5) and is particularly pleased to dwell in Zion (Ps 132:13, 14) when he speaks of Christ as the locus where "God was pleased to have all his fullness dwell" (Col 1:19 NIV) and "the whole fullness of Deity dwells bodily" (Col 2:9 NRSV). In the scheme of salvation history, moreover, Christ came "when the fullness of time was come" (Gal 4:4, KJV).

Fullness is also a prominent motif in the work of the *Holy Spirit, as reported in the NT. In the events surrounding the nativity, John the Baptist, Elizabeth and Zechariah were "filled" with the Holy Spirit (Luke 1:15, 41, 67). In the book of Acts, individuals or groups are said to be either "filled" or "full" of the Holy Spirit no fewer than eight times. Ephesians 5:18-20 exhorts believers to "be filled with the Spirit." In all these passages the image implies being empowered by the Holy Spirit to an extraordinary degree and receiving that power from a source beyond oneself.

The ideal of being spiritually complete applies also to believers both individually and corporately. At a corporate level the kingdom of God will be complete when "the full number of the Gentiles has come in" (Rom 11:25 NIV). In a similar vein, Jesus could claim, "I have not lost one of those you gave me" (Jn 18:9 NIV), again expressing an ideal of the body of the redeemed being full, lacking nothing. As Christ's body, the church is "the fullness of him who fills everything in every way" (Eph 1:23 NIV).

To be spiritually full and complete is also an individual goal. To be "filled to the measure of all the fullness of God" (Eph 3:19 NIV), to "have been given fullness in Christ" (Col 2:10 NIV), to have God "fill you with the knowledge of his will through all spiritual wisdom and understanding" (Col 1:9 NIV), to "put on the full *armor of God" (Eph 6:11 NIV), to "be complete, equipped for every good work" (2 Tim 3:17 RSV)—this is the NT ideal for the Christian.

The motif of fullness in the double sense of abundance and completeness is prominent in millennial visions of the coming kingdom. In that day "the earth will be full of the knowledge of the LORD" (Is 11:9; Hab 2:14 NIV). It will be a time when "the threshing floors will be filled with grain" and when "you will have plenty to eat, until you are full" (Joel 2:24, 26 NIV). Furthermore, "The city streets will be filled with boys and girls playing" (Zech 8:5 NIV).

At its most positive, then, the biblical image of fullness is an ever-expanding vision of what the human spirit most longs for. A survey of passages listed in a concordance will reveal that fullness is variously associated with health, satiety, maturity, blessing, wealth, justice, light, wisdom, silver and gold, time, value, and restitution.

Fullness as a Negative Image. If good things can be full, so can *evil and *judgment. By the time we reach Genesis 6:11, the earth is said to have been "corrupt in God's sight and full of *violence," so that God's "heart was filled with pain" (Gen 6:6 NIV). Subsequently, the sin of the Amorites of Canaan will become so evil that it will reach a point of "full measure" (Gen 15:16) where God's judgment will be executed upon them by Israel's conquest. But in an ironic twist, Paul can speak of the Jews who are "filling up the measure of their sins" so that God's wrath is overtaking them (1 Thess 2:16 RSV).

A violent society is "full of blood" (Is 2:16), "full of bloodshed and . . . full of violence" (Ezek 7:23 NIV). A morally corrupt society is pictured as being "unclean with the pollutions of the peoples of the lands, with their *abominations which have filled it from end to end with their uncleanness" (Ezra 9:11 RSV). In this vein, prophetic visions of the future sometimes become a surrealistic vision of terror in which houses are "full of howling creatures" (Is 13:21 RSV; see Animals), waters "are full of *blood" (Is 15:9 RSV) and "all tables are full of *vomit" (Is 28:8 RSV).

A society filled with evil becomes the object of God's complete judgment. Here we find a cluster of passages that speak of God's "full wrath" (Ps 78:38 NIV), of a prophet's being "full of the wrath of the LORD" (Jer 6:11 NIV) and of the "full strength" of the cup of God's wrath (Rev 14:10 NIV).

As with the positive images of fullness, a survey of passages listed in a concordance will reveal an ever-expanding vision of how terrible evil can be when it is full. In the Bible we can find the quality of fullness ascribed to shame, misery, deceit, bribes, boasting, evil, guilt, vengeance, hypocrisy, darkness, bloody hands, poisonous tongues and adulterous eyes. Fullness is likewise ascribed to a city with idols and a land full of adulterers, bloodshed, violence and injustice.

See also ABUNDANCE.

BIBLIOGRAPHY. D. H. Rauber, "Literary Values in the Book of Ruth," JBL 89 (1970) 27-37.

FILLING. See FILL, FULLNESS; HOLY SPIRIT.

FILTH. See DUNG.

FIND, FOUND

With well over five hundred occurrences of the vocabulary of finding, it is no exaggeration to say that the Bible is a book in which people are continuously finding something or being found. Many of the references are to everyday circumstances of finding something that has been hidden or lost (see Lost and Found), but symbolic meanings also converge in the imagery of finding.

Finding often relates to righteousness and *sin, for example. In all parts of the Bible, God speaks of looking for righteousness and instead finding sin in his people. Such a theme begins with *Sodom and Gomorrah (Gen 18) and ends in Revelation. In Exodus and Numbers, God leaves specific instructions for what must be done to those "found" in a

crime. In 1 Kings 21:21 Ahab expresses such a meaning when he is caught in a sin by Elijah, and he asks mockingly, "Have you found me, O my enemy?" (NRSV). Throughout the psalms the psalmist hopes for such justice, begging God to find out the sin of the wicked and to punish it. In Jeremiah, Micah and the other prophets, God finds sin in his nation of Israel; and in Daniel 5:27 God finds similar unrighteousness in Babylon, declaring that Babylon has been "weighed on the scales and found wanting."

In the NT, God's measuring of his people shifts slightly from finding sin to not finding righteous deeds. Jesus warns the people of the necessity of being found bearing fruit, representing his message in a parable in which the master returns to find what his slave has performed while he was absent (Mt 21:19; 24:46). The apostles warn their churches that they must be found pursuing God and without unrighteousness (2 Cor 5:3; 2 Pet 3:14; Rev 2:2; 3:4). The climax of God's searching of people's souls occurs in Revelation, where God judges the nations, rejecting any whose names are not found in the book of life (Rev 20:15). To the very end of the Bible, therefore, God emphasizes the sin that he finds in humanity.

As a contrast to the unrighteousness found in humanity, God emphasizes the righteousness that can be found in himself and in those who are following him. The Philistines found no fault in David (1 Sam 29:3, 6), and in contrast to the evil of Babylon, the Babylonian and Persian kings typically can find no wrong in Daniel (1:19; 5:11). When the Israelites disobey God, he ironically demands of his people, "What wrong did your ancestors find in me?" (Jer 2:5). The biblical statements about Jesus' righteousness are the strongest statements of a comprehensive *search being made of him and no sin being discovered (Mal 2:6). In the Gospels, Pilate and the Pharisees could find no guilt in Jesus (Lk 23:4; Jn 19:4). Finally, in Revelation, when no one was righteous enough was found to open the scroll, only Jesus was holy enough to perform the job (Rev 5:4-5).

The imagery of finding is also used in contexts that discuss human *quests to find meaning and satisfaction in life. Here seeking connotes a strenuous search in which something is long sought. When such a thing is found, it is often rare or precious. In many passages God repeats his invitation that those who seek him will find him (Deut 4:29; Mt 7:7-8; Lk 11:9). However, God also expresses his grace, maintaining that he was found by those who did not seek him (Is 65:1; Rom 10:20). Yet due to the disobedience of his people, God also expresses that such grace can be rescinded, declaring that Israel would be unable to find him due to her great disobedience (Amos and Hosea). In fact, few find the narrow road that leads to righteousness and knowing God (Mt 7:14).

To those who desire to find God, he promises many blessings. He promises that his people will "find rest for [their] souls" in him (Jer 6:16; Mt

11:29). God also provides refuge for his people, and what is found in God is so precious that it cannot be found anywhere else (Ps 61:4; 69:20). The wisdom found in God is equally precious: such wisdom, "who can find?" (Prov 20:6; cf. Prov 31:6, on the rarity and value of a virtuous wife). In his parables comparing the kingdom of heaven to finding treasure in a field or a *pearl of great value (Mt 13:34, 36), Jesus demonstrates that knowing God is precious. But Jesus also emphasizes that God must be sought directly, for a mere seeking of the benefits of knowing him will never be fruitful. Paradoxically, he who finds his life will lose it, but he who loses his life for Christ's sake will find it (Mt 16:25).

See also GUILT; LOST AND FOUND; QUEST; SEARCH, SEARCHING; SIN.

FINGER

Finger(s) appears thirty-one times in the Bible. A finger can often be an image that brings with it *mercy/grace or *judgment. The nuances associated with this word are remarkable. A partial list of its various uses follows: denoting power or authority (Gen 41:42; Ex 8:19; 1 Kings 12:10; 2 Chron 10:10; Esther 3:10; Mk 7:33; Lk 11:20; 15:22); assigning blame (Is 58:9; 59:3); communicating or writing (Ex 31:18; Deut 9:10; Prov 6:13; Dan 5:5); work [of] (Ex 8:19; Ps 8:3; 144:1; Prov 31:19; Is 2:8; Mt 23:4; Lk 11:20, 46); bringing mercy/aid (Mt 23:4; Mk 7:33; Lk 11:46; 16:24); associated with sexuality (Song 5:5); unit of measure (Jer 52:21); touching as source of belief (Jn 20:25, 27).

The biblical image of the finger carries with it the general notion of power and influence. More specifically, fingers often represent the source of deliberate action; as such, the activity of the fingers reflects the character of their owner. The phrase "the finger of God" is often used in Scripture to indicate God's authority (Ex 31:18; Deut 9:10), his signature or trademark (Ex 8:19), his work (Ps 8:3) or his power (Ex 8:19).

Both the *arm and *hand are more common biblical images of power; however, because of its relative size, the image of a single finger can represent the smallest increment of power or influence. One example is the young men's advice to Rehoboam that he should boast, "My little finger is thicker than my father's waist" (1 Kings 12:10; 1 Chron 10:10) when comparing the power he would wield over Israel with that of Solomon. Likewise, when God commands Satan concerning Job, he forbids him to lay even a finger upon Job himself (Job 1:12). In the NT, Jesus condemns the Pharisees for burdening people with their interpretations of the law, and then refusing to lift a finger toward helping them with that burden (Mt 23:4).

More frequently, fingers function as an image of activity, whether human or divine. When fingers portray human activity, they can be the source of either good or evil: the one who seeks wisdom is instructed to take wise teachings and "bind them on

your fingers" (Prov 7:3). It is the Lord himself who prepares the psalmist's fingers for battle (Ps 144:1). In these instances the fingers receive direction toward righteous action. But human fingers can also produce evil. The motif of fingers working evil is most prevalent in Isaiah. Here it is fingers that produce idols (Is 2:8; 17:8); the pointed finger, connoting accusation and malice, yields a "yoke of oppression" (Is 58:9). Consequently, the fingers as agents of wickedness become stained with guilt (Is 59:3).

Nevertheless, the image of fingers can also convey divine power in action, whether the activity be for *creation, revelation or judgment. In the work of creation the Lord makes the heavens and fashions the moon and stars with his fingers (Ps 8:3). Here the picture is that of God the artisan, forming his work with dexterity and precision, or as H. W. Wolff expresses it, "the artistic filigree-work in the delicate web of the constellations" (Wolff, 68). As a revelatory image it is the "finger of God" that writes the Ten Commandments on tablets of stone for Moses (Ex 29:12; Deut 9:10). Moreover, in the NT it is the "finger of God" by which Jesus drives out demons, thus proclaiming the arrival of the kingdom of God (Lk 11:20). When God sends the plague of gnats upon Egypt, it is his finger that Pharaoh's magicians understand to be the agent of judgment (Ex 8:19). In Daniel bodiless fingers actually appear before Belshazzar and record God's judgment of him on the wall (Dan 5:5). In each case, finger imagery conveys the power and immediacy of God's action.

The image of the finger also turns up in the joint activity of the *sacrifice, where God meets his people. In God's instructions to Moses regarding sin offerings, finger imagery plays a key role. For regular sin offerings as well as on the Day of Atonement, God's instructions for the priest include dipping a finger into the *blood of the sacrifice and sprinkling it either on the altar (Lev 4:6ff) or, on the Day of Atonement, on the cover of the ark of testimony (Lev 16:14, 19). Here there is a double image: human fingers do as God commands—a picture of *obedience; but at the same time the priest, acting on behalf of the sinner(s), appears before God with blood-stained fingers—a picture of guilty sinners cast before the judgment and mercy of God.

See also ARM; FOOT; HAND; TOE.

BIBLIOGRAPHY. H. W. Wolff, *Anthropology of the Old Testament* (Philadelphia: Fortress, 1974).

FIRE

Fire, which (the apocryphal) Ecclesiasticus 39:26 groups with *water, *iron, *salt, flour, *milk, *honey, *wine, *oil and clothing as a basic necessity, is the servant of human beings. It cooks their *food (Ex 12:8; Is 44:15-16; Jn 21:9), makes them warm (Is 44:15; Jn 18:18) and gives them *light to see (Is 50:11; Mt 25:1-13). It can be part of a manufacturing process (Gen 11:3) and can refine *metals (Is 1:25; Mal 3:2-3). It also burns refuse (Lev 8:17). Because starting a fire is work (cf. 2 Macc 10:3), it is prohibited on the *sabbath (Ex 35:3).

But fire, which can terrify as well as benefit, is also an instrument of *warfare. Throughout the Bible many battles end with the victors (sometimes at God's command) burning down the city of the losers (e.g., Josh 6:24; 8:8; 11:11; Judg 1:8; 1 Kings 9:16; cf. Mt 22:7). This is why war itself or its fury can be likened to, or spoken of, as fire (Num 21:28; Is 10:16; Zech 12:6).

Fire can be the instrument of execution for criminals (Gen 38:24; Lev 20:14; 21:9; Josh 7:15; cremation is otherwise not practiced in the Bible; see Crime and Punishment). So it is in Daniel 3, where rescue from fire is a miracle (cf. Heb 11:34). Shadrach, Meshach and Abednego, although thrown into Nebuchadnezzar's fiery furnace, survive the *ordeal without harm. The event causes the pagan king to bless the Hebrews' God and to promote the three youths.

Unlike Greek mythology, the Bible has nothing to say about the origin of fire. But this very silence compels readers to presume fire to be one of the gifts of creation. Already *Abel brings fat portions of his firstlings to sacrifice (Gen 4:4), implying a burnt offering. (Incidentally, although Genesis 4:4-5 does not inform us how *Cain and Abel recognize that God has regard for the sacrifice of Able but not of Cain, commentators have long speculated that, as in other OT stories, divine fire burns up one offering but not the other.)

Religious Uses. Beyond the common secular uses, people also used fire for religious purposes. In Numbers 31:22-23, for instance, fire is an instrument of ceremonial purification. More importantly, *sacrifices—not just "burnt offerings"—are typically burned (cf. Lev 2:2, etc.). Perhaps we should find here a symbol: the fire represents God's desire to destroy sin and to purify his people (cf. Is 6:6-7). Moreover, the smoke from fire rises, which is an appropriate indication of the symbolic movement of sacrifice: the offerer on earth is seeking to communicate with God in heaven (cf. incense and prayer ascending to heaven, Rev 8:4; Phil 4:18).

The practice of burning offerings is not confined to Israel. The OT refers, for example, to the sacrificial burning of children by pagans and apostate Jews (e.g. Lev 18:21; Deut 18:10; 2 Kings 16:3; 17:17; 21:6; 23:10; Jer 7:31; 32:35). Several of these refer to the cult of Molech and use the phrase "make their sons and daughters pass through the fire" (RSV). Reference is also made to "strange" or "unholy" fire, which seems to involve fire taken from elsewhere than the official *altar. According to Leviticus 6:8-13 the fire on the altar of burnt offering should be ever-burning: the priests must not allow it to go out. It is a sign of God's continual presence.

Theophany of Fire. In Genesis 15:17 the presence of God appears as a smoking fire pot and a flaming torch, and in Exodus 3:2 God makes himself known to Moses "in a flame of fire out of the midst of a bush" (RSV; see Burning Bush). This association of God with fire runs throughout the Bible. God descends upon Mount *Sinai "in fire" in Exodus 19:18. (That there is thunder encourages one to think of the lightning; but that there is smoke and a mountain moves one to envisage a volcano; cf. 2 Sam 22:8-9.) When Ezekiel tries to describe the indescribable—that is, the form on the divine *throne—he says, "Upward from what had the appearance of his loins I saw as it were gleaming *bronze, like the appearance of fire enclosed round about; and downward from what had the appearance of his loins I saw as it were the appearance of fire, and there was brightness round about him" (Ezek 1:27 RSV). In Revelation 4:5 lightning flashes from God's throne.

Often the imagery of God's appearance is clearly that of a *thunderstorm, and the fire that is mentioned must be akin to *lightning. In Psalm 18:14 (a battle theophany), lightning flashes are God's *arrows (cf. Ps 144:6). Psalm 29:7 says that "the voice of the LORD flashes forth flames of fire. The voice of the LORD shakes the wilderness" (RSV). In Ezekiel 1:4 the prophet sees "a storm wind" come "out of the north, and a great cloud, with brightness round about it, and fire flashing forth continually" (RSV).

That God should appear as fire is appropriate for many reasons. Just as all physical life depends on the fire that is the *sun (cf. Rev 16:8), so does all spiritual life depend on God. Just as fire both purifies and destroys, so does God *purify the righteous and destroy the wicked ("for our God is a consuming fire," Heb 12:29 RSV). Just as fire lights up the *blackness of night, so does God overcome the dark powers of evil. Just as fire is mysterious and immaterial, so too is God enigmatic and incorporeal. And just as fire is always flickering and changing its shape and cannot be held for examination, so is God always the indefinable who is beyond our grasp. (It is striking that in 1 Kings 19:12, in the revelation on Horeb [= Sinai] to Elijah, God is not in the fire as he is for Moses on Sinai, but in the silence. Here God, against expectation, dissociates himself from a traditional constituent of the theophany. He need bind himself to no natural element.)

If God himself appears as fire, so do the things around him. His throne is "fiery flames," its wheels "burning fire" (Dan 7:9). His angelic servants are "flames of fire" (Heb 1:7, quoting LXX Ps 104:4; and Lk 10:18, the devil as lightning or a meteor). Between the cherubim are fire and coals of fire (Ezek 10:2, 6-7). Before God's throne is a "sea of glass mingled with fire" (Rev 15:2; cf. 1 Kings 7:23; 2 Chron 4:2), and from before God issues a "stream of fire" (Dan 7:10). The "seven spirits of God" are "torches of fire" (Rev 4:5). Heavenly chariots are made of fire (2 Kings 2:11; 6:17). Even the eyes of the glorified Jesus and other heavenly creatures are like flames of fire (Dan 10:6; Rev 1:14; 2:18). In Acts 2:3-4 the Holy Spirit too is associated with fire ("tongues as of fire"; cf. Is 5:24).

Fire from God. During the exodus God makes a *pillar of fire to lead his people in the wilderness.

The pillar is the outward sign of God's guiding presence (Ex 12:21; Num 14:14); the same presence covers the tabernacle (Num 9:15-16).

But it is much more typical for supernatural fires to be destructive. Fire falls from heaven and consumes *Sodom and Gomorrah (Gen 19:24), Nadab and Abihu (who conduct improper ritual, Lev 10:1-2), murmuring Israelites (Num 11:1), soldiers of Ahaziah (2 Kings 1:10; cf. Lk 9:54), Job's flocks (Job 1:16), and Gog and Magog (Rev 20:9; cf. Ezek 38:22; 39:6). Sometimes the image is of something like lightning (e.g., Ex 9:24; Num 11:1); other times one thinks rather of a volcanic eruption (e.g., Sodom and Gomorrah).

Fire also occasionally falls not to consume the wicked but to consume a sacrifice, a circumstance that shows God's reality and approval (Lev 9:24; Judg 6:21; 1 Kings 18:24: "the God who answers by fire, he is God" [RSV]; 1 Chron 21:26; 2 Chron 7:1; Lk 9:54: "do you want us to bid fire to come down from heaven?" RSV). In Revelation 13:13 making fire fall from heaven is a "great sign," yet something that the eschatological false prophet can nevertheless do.

God's Wrath and Eschatological Fire. In what seems to us to be bold anthropomorphism, God's *anger burns like a fire (Hos 8:5). It is hot, and he pours it out like fire (Nahum 1:6; cf. Lam 2:4). Isaiah 66:15 (God comes in fire to "render his anger in fury") and Jeremiah 15:14 (God says, "in my anger a fire is kindled which shall burn for ever"; cf. 17:4) are typical. Prophecies of destruction by fire are often simply figurative ways of saying that God's judgment is sure or thorough (e.g., Ps 97:3; Is 33:12; Joel 2:3; Mic 1:4). For Ezekiel "the fire of my wrath" is a fixed expression (Ezek 21:31; 22:21, 31; 38:19).

The images of God's fiery wrath vary from text to text. In several texts the image is of God as a mythical, fire-breathing *monster (cf. Job 41:19-21; Rev 9:17; 11:5). Thus in Psalm 18:8 smoke comes from his *nostrils, devouring fire from his *mouth (cf. 2 Sam 22:9); and Isaiah 30:33 likens the Lord's breath to a stream of *brimstone (cf. 65:5). But in Jeremiah 21:14 one sees a forest fire; in Lamentations 1:13, lightning ("from on high he sent fire"); in Malachi 3:2, a furnace ("a refiner's fire"); and in Isaiah 30:33, a carefully stacked pile of *wood.

The association of fire with wrath and the fact that God sometimes destroys the wicked by raining fire make it natural that eschatological judgment be depicted as fire. 2 Thessalonians 1:7 says that the Lord Jesus will be revealed "from heaven with his mighty angels in flaming fire" (RSV). Revelation's accounts of the latter days are filled with fire—falling from heaven (8:7, 8; 13:13; 16:8), coming from the mouths of humans and beasts (9:17-18; 11:5), punishing the wicked (14:10; 17:16; 18:8). Furthermore, although the prophecy in Zephaniah 3:8 ("in the fire of my jealous wrath all the earth shall be consumed" RSV) is probably figurative (cf. Deut 32:22; Amos 7:4), the one in 2 Peter 3:7, according

to which the world is now "stored up for fire," [RSV] should be taken literally.

Most commonly the object of eschatological fire is not the world as such but the people in it, especially the wicked (cf. Heb 10:27). There are a variety of pictures. Fire will burn up dross to refine metal (Mal 3:2); it will burn like an oven (Mal 4:1); it will burn up unfruitful trees (Mt 3:10), unfruitful branches (Jn 15:6, though this may be only parabolic, since the Fourth Gospel and the Johannine epistles do not mention eschatological fire otherwise), tares (Mt 13:40) and *chaff (Mt 3:12). It will even burn up flesh (Jas 5:3).

Fire belongs not only to the moment of the final judgment but also to the world of eternity; it is the fearful antithesis of the kingdom of God. Already Isaiah 66:24 speaks of a fire that will not be quenched. In the NT this is assumed to be the everlasting and tormenting fire of *hell (Mt 5:22; 13:42; 18:8-9). Revelation 20:10, 14-15 envisages a frightful "lake of fire" into which the devil and his false prophet, death and hades, and all evildoers are cast at the end. Hell is nonetheless also said to be, paradoxically, dark (Mt 8:12; 2 Pet 2:17; Jude 13).

The expectation of eschatological fire may provide the background for some NT texts that are otherwise obscure. When John the Baptist, in a prophecy of the last judgment, warns of a baptism of fire, the image is of a *river or stream of fire (cf. Dan 7:10); so we should perhaps imagine an eschatological stream of fire by which the wicked are consumed and the righteous refined (cf. Zech 13:9). The obscure Mark 9:49, according to which "everyone will be salted with fire" (RSV), could presuppose the same idea. (Salt preserves, while fire destroys; eschatological fire does both.) In 1 Corinthians 3:10-15 the judgment day is a fire that tests all: it burns up the dross and refines that which is truly valuable.

In Isaiah 4:5, however, eschatological fire is not destructive. In the latter days there will be over Mount Zion a cloud by day "and smoke and the shining of a flaming fire by night" (RSV). This prophecy recalls the pillar of fire of the exodus (cf. Ex 58:8). As in 2 Kings 6:17 (the fiery hosts that protect Elisha) and Zechariah 2:5 ("I will be to her [Jerusalem] a *wall of fire round about" RSV), here God protects his people with fire.

Fire Metaphors. The Bible is full of metaphorical uses of fire. The *tongue is a fire insofar as it is a small thing that can have large and destructive consequences (Jas 3:5-6; cf. Prov 16:27). God's word is fire in that it destroys (Jer 5:14; 23:39). To *melt as wax before fire is to suffer swift and total eradication (Ps 68:2; 97:5). Being tested by God is like being purified by fire (Is 43:2; Jer 6:29; 1 Pet 4:12). Jealousy is like fire in that it devours (Deut 4:24 [of God]). So too are *sexual lust (Prov 6:27; Hos 7:6-7; 1 Cor 7:9) and anger (Eccles 28:10-11). To be plucked like a brand out of the fire (Amos 4:11; Zech

3:2) is to be *rescued from great danger.

See also ALTAR; BRIMSTONE; BURNING BUSH; HELL; JUDGMENT; LAMP; LIGHT; LIGHTNING; SACRIFICE; WOOD.

FIREWOOD. *See* WOOD.

FIRMAMENT. *See* COSMOLOGY.

FIRST

First indicates the one coming or ranking at the beginning of a series; the first precedes all others in time (the earliest), order (in contrast to second) or importance. Fundamentally, it corresponds to the ordinal number *one, as in the first river (Gen 2:11) or the first month (Gen 8:5). Harvests had "firstfruits"—the initial evidence of the bounty at hand—and then the remainder of the crop. As to children, the Bible often designates the firstborn (e.g., Gen 35:23; 36:15; 38:6). Literally, of course, that refers to the first *child born to parents— whether the child is male (Gen 27:19) or female (Gen 19:31). In this biological sense Jesus was Mary's first *son (Lk 2:7).

Being first connotes the beginning of something—hence the significant references to the first month or day (e.g., Gen 8:13; Ex 40:2), or the first year of a reign (e.g., 2 Chron 20:3; 36:22; Dan 1:21; 7:1). As a condition of uncorrupted beginning, this first state is sometimes presented as a norm of superior spirituality (Jer 7:12). Returning to it is either a restoration of God's favor and *blessing (Is 1:26; Jer 33:7, 11) or a spiritual revival (Rev 2:4-5).

Firstfruits. In the OT the Hebrew words translated "firstfruits" refer either to the portion of the crop that is the first to be ripe (Neh 10:35; Num 13:20; Ezek 44:30) or to the part that is best (Num 15:20; 2 Chron 31:5). God institutes a principle (and a *festival) in which the firstfruits of the crop (e.g., Ex 23:16, 19; Lev 23:10, 17, 20) and the first shearing of the fleece of *sheep (Deut 18:4) are offered in *sacrifice to him. When *Nehemiah's contemporaries determine to return to the Lord's ways, they reinstitute the practice of bringing firstfruits to the Lord to support the *priests who serve in his house (Neh 10:35-37; 12:44). The sage believes it is a part of *wisdom for all God's people to honor him with the firstfruits of their substance (Prov 3:9). First and best might both account for God's considering Israel to be the firstfruits of his *harvest (Jer 2:3).

Paul utilizes the metaphor of firstfruit *(aparchē)* to speak of the relationship between the resurrection of Christ to the resurrection of the dead (1 Cor 15:20, 23). Christ's resurrection is the "firstfruit of those who have fallen asleep" (1 Cor 15:20), and like the firstfruits of the harvest, it is a taste and a guarantee of the full harvest of resurrection yet to come. Likewise the Holy Spirit is called "firstfruit" in Romans 8:23 (cf. Holy Spirit as "downpayment" in 2 Cor 1:22; 5:5; Eph 1:14), a foretaste of the heavenly divinely bestowed life of the age to come. And when Paul speaks of his first converts in a region, he calls them the "firstfruits" (Rom 16:5; 1 Cor 16:15), in that they are the firstfruits of God's eschatological harvest from among the nations.

Firstborn. Firstborn sons have special importance since they insure the existence of the *family into the next *generation. Just as the firstfruits of the harvest belong to the Lord, so he insists that the firstborn of every *womb—animal and human—also belong to him (Ex 13:2, 12; 22:29; 34:19; Num 3:13). In so doing God claims the future of the nation for himself. He institutes a procedure of *redemption so the Israelites can regain possession of their firstborn (Ex 13:13, 15) though the *sacrifice of firstborn of clean animals (viz., cows, sheep, or goats) to the Lord (Num 18:15, 17). Later God selects the Levites for himself instead of the firstborn among Israel (Num 3:41, 45; 8:18).

Being born first establishes a child in a special place of prominence. The firstborn receives a double portion of the father's inheritance (Deut 21:17). The importance of identifying the firstborn emerges in the incident recorded in Genesis 38:28, where to avert mistake, the midwife ties a scarlet thread around the hand of the twin that emerged first from the womb.

Firstborn assumes a symbolic value due to the pervasive emphasis and importance given to the first one. One of Job's friends, Bildad, opines about Job's condition, "death's firstborn devours his limbs" (Job 18:13 NIV); that is, Job has encountered the strongest that death could throw up against him. Here we see that *firstborn* moves beyond the literal "one who was born first in time" to the concept of first in importance. Thus in the OT we read about nations and rulers who are "first" (Num 24:20; Esther 1:14; Dan 6:2). Of special importance is the case of David, of whom God says, "I will also appoint him my firstborn, the most exalted of the kings of the earth" (Ps 89:27 NIV). Literally, David was neither the first king of Israel nor the first son born to his parents. Firstborn here speaks of preeminence; God appointed David to the *position* of firstborn.

This idea best explains the title firstborn applied to Jesus in Colossians 1:15, 18. Jesus occupies the position of preeminence in *creation and in *resurrection, the restoration of God's created order (cf. 1 Cor 15:20, 23; Heb 1:6; Rev 1:5). Christ is the first and the last (Rev 1:17; 2:8; 22:13). Likewise, though Christians are conformed to the image of Christ, he occupies the exalted position of firstborn among all his siblings (Rom 8:29). At the same time, just as Israel was God's special nation, so the NT authors identify Christians as the firstborn (Heb 12:23) and God's firstfruits (Jas 1:18; Rev 14:4).

Although the associations of being first are thus overwhelmingly positive signposts of preeminence or precedence, the Bible characteristically throws in a surprising reversal of assumptions about first being best. The OT story of the *younger sibling supplanting the firstborn is so common as to become an archetype. Thus Isaac is given precedence over Ishmael, *Jacob over *Esau, *Joseph over his ten older brothers, Ephraim over Manasseh (Gen 48:13-14), *David over his brothers, Rachel over Leah. To this motif we can add Jesus' paradoxical rhetoric in which the first are said to be last and the last, first (Mk 9:35; Lk 13:30; cf. Lk 22:26).

See also ADOPTION; FRUIT, FRUITFULNESS; HARVEST; RESURRECTION; SON.

BIBLIOGRAPHY. G. M. Burge, "First Fruits, Down Payment," *DPL* 300-301; P. T. O'Brien, "Firstborn," *DPL* 301-3.

FIRSTBORN. *See* BIRTHRIGHT; FIRST; SON.

FIRSTFRUITS. *See* FIRST; FRUIT, FRUITFULNESS.

FISH, FISHER, FISHING

Fish are a distinct branch of the created order, created on the fifth day by God along with winged creatures with which they are frequently associated (Gen 1:20-23). Paul regarded them as a different type of flesh (1 Cor 15:39). Since they are part of creation, humans are expected to exercise dominion over them (Gen 1:26, 28; Ps 8:8). There is little classification of fish other than the division into clean and unclean (Lev 11:9-12). Human beings are warned not to worship them (Deut 4:18 cf. Ex 20:4).

Like all of creation, fish suffer at the exercise of divine *judgment (Is 19:8; 50:2; Hos 4:3; Zeph 1:3). They were destroyed in the pollution of the Nile and in the first *plague of Egypt (Ex 7:17, 21; cf. Ps 105:29), and they can equally expect to suffer on the *Day of the Lord (Ezek 38:20). By contrast, they feature in great abundance even in the Dead Sea in

Fishers work their nets from a boat.

Ezekiel's ideal future (Ezek 47:10).

Fishing and Sea Images. The image of fishing is occasionally used to describe the judgment of God on individuals and peoples (e.g., Eccles 9:12; Amos 4:2; Hab 1:15-17; Ezek 26:5, 14; 29:3-7). Jeremiah 16:16 likens the gathering of the nation for blessing and judgment to the activity of a fisherman (cf. Ezek 32:3).

The Galilean setting of *Jesus' ministry creates

rich metaphorical connotations. Jesus calls at least seven fishermen (notorious for their roughness) to be amongst his disciples (Mt 4:18-22; Mk 1:16-20; Lk 5:1-11). From the outset their calling is linked to their commissioning to be "fishers for people" (Mt 4:19). The imagery appears to have less of the connotation of possible judgment, which it has in the OT. The disciples are engaged in the messianic harvest begun by Jesus. Indeed, Luke's account suggests a messianic abundance of fish to be caught (Lk 5:6-10). This is captured once more in the feedings of the five thousand (Mt 14:13-21; Mk 6:30-44; Lk 9:10-17; Jn 6:1-14) and the four thousand (Mt 15:32-39; Mk 8:1-10). Consciously reflecting the miraculous provision of *food for Israel in the *wilderness, Jesus is also depicted as feeding his people. Such provision is observable in Matthew 17:24-27, where a fish becomes the provider of temple tax for Jesus and his disciples.

In Matthew 13:47-50 the kingdom of God is likened figuratively to a dragnet in which all kinds of fish are swept up together. In John 21:9-13 when the risen Lord eats fish with his disciples (cf. Lk 24:42), the symbolic link with the messianic feeding of the multitudes and the recommissioning of, in this case, Peter is reestablished. No symbolic significance for the number of 153 fish in John 21:11 has achieved widespread support.

Images of Judgment. An important aspect of biblical attitudes toward fish is the deep-seated fear of the sea, doubtless occasioned by its inaccessibility throughout much of Israel's history. At the beginning of time the earth was a formless and chaotic void to which God brought order in his act of *creation (Gen 1:1). The sea harbored fearful monsters such as Leviathan (Job 41), an image that reappears in the picture of the Beast from the Sea in Revelation 13:1-10 (*see* Monsters). In this sense there must be some relationship to the fearsome reality of the dragon in Revelation 12.

The image of the great fish in *Jonah must not be confused with images of dragons of the deep. In his desire to escape the call of God, the prophet set out to *sea, the very symbol of *chaos and danger. In his case the big fish became a source of salvation, preserving him from the inevitable death by drowning (Jon 2:1-10; 4:9-11). However historical this incident may be, the fish must be understood symbolically as representing God's grace of deliverance and *salvation. More allegorical readings, which identify the fish as representing the Babylonian *exile, are rather fanciful.

Early Church. Despite the fact that neither Paul nor any other NT writer uses this imagery, the early church in the first centuries was not slow to make full use of fish and fishing in its art and literature. Generally this is linked to the image of the church as a *boat, the place of safety and salvation (cf. Noah). The fish is one of the symbols of Peter and is sometimes used also as a symbol of *baptism. The Greek capitals ICHTHUS ("fish"), it is frequently pointed out, can be made to represent in Greek "Jesus Christ, God's Son, Savior."

See also ANIMALS; BIRDS; BOAT; HUNTING; MONSTERS; SEA.

FISHING. *See* FISH, FISHER, FISHING.

FIVE

The number five is a small round number used throughout the Bible. It is the number of *fingers on one *hand and therefore can stand for a handful, possessing a completeness within itself. One thinks at once of the five books of the Pentateuch and the five-discourse arrangement of material in the Gospel of *Matthew.

At times five is used to represent a small sum, numerically insignificant within a larger scheme but paradoxically possessing high value nonetheless. When Abraham pleads with God for the city of Sodom (Gen 18:22-33), he begins by asking God to spare Sodom if *fifty righteous people are found there. When God accepts, he pleads for five fewer, suggesting that the loss of five is insignificant in its consequence. He does this twice before boldly asking for ten fewer. In the NT, Paul stresses the superior value of a mere "five intelligible words" over "ten thousand words in a tongue" (1 Cor 14:19 NIV).

At other times the number five indicates just recompense or bounteous reward. *Thieves must repay five times the value of oxen they steal (Ex 22:1). The Israelites are to reclaim their firstborn with a payment of five shekels each (Num 3:47). Benjamin was honored by Joseph with five times more food than his brothers (Gen 43:34) and five sets of clothes (Gen 45:22).

Most commonly five is represented as half of the basic number ten. Throughout the measurements for the *tabernacle and the *temple, parallel units of five are used. Ten curtains covered the tabernacle in two groups of five (Ex 26:3). Each wing of the cherubim in the temple was five cubits long, totaling ten cubits (1 Kings 6:24). In the parable of the ten virgins, Jesus divides them in half between five wise and five foolish (Mt 25:2).

The number five thus variously represents a small but significant number within a larger mass, abundance on a small scale or (when used in pairs) a pointer to the completeness and totality of ten.

See also FIRST; FORTY; FOUR; HUNDRED; ONE; PENTECOST; SEVEN; SEVENTY; THREE, THIRD; TWELVE; TWO.

FLAG. *See* BANNER.

FLAME. *See* FIRE.

FLEE, FLIGHT

While the Bible paints many pictures of routine actions in a daily setting, it also captures people in moments of crisis, as the motif of flight attests. Well over two hundred references to people's fleeing from

something convey a sense of the vulnerability of people living in the world of the Bible and of the dangers that frequently beset them.

Not surprisingly, approximately half of the references to flight occur in the *battle stories of the OT historical books. In fact, the motif of flight and chase is endemic to battle itself, inasmuch as the whole point of joining battle is to dislodge an opponent from the territory it is occupying. A related (though small) category of references is *apocalyptic, with people portrayed as fleeing to the *mountains (for example) to escape the judgment of God. On a positive side, the besieged woman of Revelation 12 (representing Israel and the church) flees from the dragon into the *wilderness and is spared. Of a similar nature is the flight of Lot and his family from *Sodom just before its conflagration.

Beyond the military and eschatological references, the Bible's memorable stories of flight portray characters fleeing for their lives from powerful figures who wish to destroy them. Thus *Jacob flees for his life from *Esau and later from Laban, *David flees from a paranoid Saul and later from a usurping son Absalom, and Elijah flees from Jezebel after she declares war on the prophets of God. The fledgling nation of Israel flees from Egypt, and centuries later the holy family flees *to* *Egypt to escape Herod's plans for genocide. *Moses flees for his life after slaying an Egyptian taskmaster. In an ignominious and futile venture, Jonah attempts to flee from the presence of God, a feat that Psalm 139:7-12 had long since declared to be an ironic impossibility.

See also BATTLE STORIES; FEAR; FLIGHT, CHASE AND FLIGHT; HIDE, HIDING; RUNAWAY; TREMBLING, SHAKING, BODILY ANGUISH; WANDERER, WANDERING.

FLESH. *See* BODY.

FLIGHT, CHASE AND FLIGHT

The *flight* (or *chase and flight*) motif predominates both divisions of the biblical canon and is expressed in a variety of terms. Essentially, the motif portrays the nature and character of relationships individuals have with the Lord God, with each other and to the realities of sin, righteousness and judgment. Additionally, this motif functions to structure the sequence of action in a number of biblical narratives.

The presence of the flight motif in narrative sections often structures the story, moving the action from conflict toward resolution. The structural components of this motif are not static in order or in appearance; rather, the fluid nature of the pattern enriches a close reading of the text. The first element of the pattern includes a situation of conflict between individuals or the Lord beginning the action. The inflaming situation could be jealousy (Gen 27), barrenness (Gen 16:1-5) or a change of attitude (Gen 31:2). Second, a departure or a chase results. The intensity of an interpersonal conflict will put one to flight, driving an individual away (Gen 16:6), or it may result in a chase (Gen 31:23). Third, a divine or a human intervention occurs. The purpose of intervention varies and its location in the story line is fluid. It appears after the chase begins to protect the pursued (Gen 31:24), and it emerges before the chase begins to encourage the pursuer in the pursuit (Judg 20:18, 23). Ultimately, the intervention serves God's intention to rescue or to discipline (Judg 9:56-57).

Finally, the outcome is detailed. A conflict, a chase and an intervention create a tension in need of resolution. In some accounts the outcome includes an escape (Judg 9:5), the capture of the hunted individual (Judg 8:28) or a reunion between parties in conflict (Gen 33:1-20). Other narratives, such as those of Saul and David, move from a temporary solution or lull in the action to a continuation of the conflict and the chase. The structure of this motif creates a number of tensions regarding the chase and facilitates characterization and the exposure of the motive.

The OT gives us stories of individuals who flee from the Lord (*Adam and *Eve, Gen 3:8-9; *Cain, Gen 4:12-16; *Jonah, Jon 1:3) and of those who flee to him as a refuge in order to enjoy the security of a divine haven (David, 2 Sam 22:3; Jer 16:19; Ps 59:17; 142:5).

Relationships between biblical characters often degenerate into a conflict resulting in a flight or a chase. A historical investigation of the OT canon reveals the flight, chase and flight motif structures and develops these relationships (Sarai and Hagar; *Esau and *Jacob; Jacob and Laban; *Joseph and Potiphar's wife; Joseph and his brothers; *Moses and Pharaoh; Abimelech and Jephthah; Israel and the tribe of Benjamin; Saul and *David; Absalom and David). Sadly, the motif reveals the heartache of dysfunctional relationships between members of the covenant community.

We also see the motif developed in the stories of the relationship between God, Israel and the nations. The *Joshua conquest narratives illustrate the structure and the theology of the flight motif. The conquest of the Promised Land is undertaken on the basis of covenant *blessings and *curses related to chase and flight (Lev 26:7, 17, 36; Deut 28:7, 25). Each conquest episode in Joshua 2—11 pictures Israel either chasing or being chased on the basis of their covenant loyalty. The hymns of Hannah (1 Sam 2) and David (2 Sam 22—23), and the prayer of Solomon (1 Kings 8) celebrate God's covenant loyalty in matters of flight and chase. The *divine warrior will chase his *enemies and bring them to judgment. Although some may attempt to elude the pursuit of the Lord, the prophets predict the Lord's inescapable chase in eschatological contexts (Rev 9:6). The joy of this eschatological setting is the flight of sorrow and sighing (Is 35:10), and the related gladness of security (Is 51:11).

The NT exhorts God's people to flee unrighteousness (1 Cor 6:18; 10:14; 1 Tim 6:11) and to pursue righteousness and all its attendants (Rom 12:13; 14:19; 1 Cor 14:1; 1 Thess 5:15; 1 Pet 3:11). The nature of this flight and chase reveals one's character and motives.

See also BATTLE STORIES; ENEMIES; FEAR; FLEE, FLIGHT; HIDE, HIDING; RUNNING.

FLIGHT. *See* FLEE, FLIGHT; FLIGHT, CHASE AND FLIGHT.

FLINT. *See* MINERALS.

FLOCK

In the biblical world, a flock is almost always a group of *sheep, though occasionally a group of *goats is involved. When the specific image of flock is used (as distinct from sheep), the image incorporates what might be called the group dynamics of the sheep as a community of animals. The exception is the use of the term *flock* to indicate abundant numbers (Ps 107:41; Ezek 36:37-38) or to refer generically to livestock as a possession, as in the nearly fifty references to "flocks and herds," a stock epithet for sheep and cattle, respectively.

The importance of the image of the flock (almost two hundred biblical references) should not be surprising in view of the pastoral setting of Israel's history. At its most general, flocks are an image of *abundance, *prosperity and the *blessing of God. The growth of the flocks and *herds of Abraham and Lot that required them to separate is an index to the fact that "Abram was very rich" (Gen 13:2 RSV). Jacob's "large flocks" (Gen 30:43) are an evidence of his economic success as well as the favor of God (Gen 31:12). In fact, the size of a family's flocks was a quick way to assess its financial rating (Gen 24:35; 29:2). In Deuteronomy, with its characteristic blessing/curse motif, a flock's size is explicitly related to Israel's obedience or disobedience to God (Deut 28:4, 18). At the most elementary level, then, flocks of sheep represent earthly abundance and security, often viewed as the covenant blessing of God as a reward for obedience (e.g., Deut 8:13; 15:14; 2 Chron 32:29).

As a visible picture of abundance and the good life, a flock of sheep produces strong connotations of well-being and even aesthetic beauty to a *farmer's eyes. These feelings lie behind the references to flocks in the collection of pastoral love lyrics known as the *Song of Songs. Here flocks refer to the wealth or value that the lover possesses in his beloved or to the beauty that he sees in her. Thus we find references to the woman's hair as "a flock of goats, moving down the slopes of Gilead," an image of value, and her teeth as "a flock of short ewes that have come up from the washing," a reference to wetness and *whiteness (Song 4:1-2; 6:5-6 RSV).

The group qualities of a flock of sheep emerge, not in the literal pictures of shepherding that we find in the Bible, but in the metaphoric passages describing the care of God for his people. These metaphors are rooted in the characteristics of actual flocks. Most of the references are positive. The "oneness" of the flock, belonging to one shepherd, is an image of security and community (Jn 10:16). Similarly, God as shepherd gathers his flock together (Is 60:7; Jer 23:3), keeps it as a possession (Jer 31:10), seeks it out (Ezek 34:12), protects it (Ezek 34:22), encloses it in a sheepfold (Mic 2:12) and feeds it (Ps 79:13; Is 40:11; Mic 5:4). Perhaps the OT visions of the covenant people as God's flock can be regarded as finding their fulfillment in NT references to the church as a flock (Acts 20:28; 1 Pet 5:2).

On the negative side, in bad times God's people, like sheep, are scattered (Jer 10:21; 23:2) and doomed to slaughter (Zech 11:4, 7). If there is the proverbial "strength in numbers" as sheep are congregated into a flock, the flock can also be an image of vulnerability. Thus we find references to the disciples as a "little flock" that needs to be commanded to "fear not" (Lk 12:32) and to attacks from a *wolf as the *hireling abandons the flock (Jn 10:12; cf. Acts 20:29).

In summary, the image of the flock is both a physical reality and spiritual symbol. In the agrarian world of the Bible, flocks of sheep are part of the daily routine for a nation of farmers. This picture of the good life is given spiritual significance by being linked to God's blessing for obedience and to the sacrificial system in which people were commanded to give from their flocks to God (e.g., Lev 1:2; 5:6; 27:32). As a fully developed metaphor, the flock is an apt picture of the combined people of God under his care.

See also ABUNDANCE; FARMING; GOAT; HERD; HIRELING; LAMB; PASTURE; SHEEP, SHEPHERD.

FLOOD

Nothing captures the destructive, death-dealing potential of *water like the image of a flood—whether it be a flood that rises slowly and inexorably to drown the land, or a flood that thunders unexpectedly down a mountain gully, sweeping away everything in its path. Scripture uses both kinds of imagery, sometimes describing flooding like that of the Nile in *Egypt (see Jer 46:7-9), at other times suggesting the kind of flash floods experienced in Palestine when *storms in the mountains sent water gushing down the dry wadis (see Job 27:19-20). Although we know flooding can be beneficial, the Bible almost never uses flooding as a positive image. Isaiah 66:12, where God promises that wealth will come to his people "like a flooding stream" (NIV), is a rare exception.

Noah's flood (Gen 6—8) with its cataclysmic, universal impact gives dramatic expression to the major themes that will be carried by flood imagery throughout the Bible. This first and most far-reaching of floods demonstrates God's sheer power: as he had created a world teeming with life, he could as easily destroy it. God declares, "I am going to bring floodwaters on the earth to destroy all life under the heavens, every creature that has the breath of life in it. Everything on earth will perish" (Gen 6:17 NIV). The first flood also expresses God's hatred of *sin. God's *heart is filled with *pain (Gen 6:6) when he

sees how humans have corrupted the good world he has created. In his righteousness God determines to wipe out evil. So he says to Noah, "I am going to put an end to all people, for the earth is filled with violence because of them" (Gen 6:13 NIV).

Beyond demonstrating God's power and his hatred of evil, Noah's flood also embodies God's determination to bring new life out of the chaos wrought by human sin. God will find a way to rescue those who trust in him, carrying them through disaster and giving them a fresh start. Thus God shuts Noah and his family and the *animals in the *ark, and they float on the flood until the waters recede. Then God tells them, "Come out of the ark.... Bring out every living creature that is with you . . . so they can multiply on the earth and be fruitful" (Gen 8:16-17 NIV).

After the description of the great flood in Genesis 6—8, flood imagery is concentrated in the poetic books of the OT—especially Job, Psalms and several of the prophets. Sometimes flood imagery is used principally to testify to God's awesome power, as when the book of Joshua describes how God stopped the flow of the Jordan "at flood stage" (Josh 3:15) to allow his chosen people to enter the Promised Land. Joshua explains to the people, "The LORD your God . . . did this so that all the peoples of the earth might know that the hand of the LORD is powerful and so that you might always fear the LORD your God" (Josh 4:23-24 NIV).

More commonly flood imagery is used to picture God's determination to punish sin. Whereas judgment came in the form of a literal flood in Noah's time, later references often use flood figuratively to represent any retribution God brings either on his own people (for example, Jerusalem, referred to poetically as Ephraim, in Isaiah 28:1-2) or on their enemies (for example, Assyria in Isaiah 30:27-31). Like the worldwide deluge of Genesis, flood images often suggest that God works on a large scale, bringing nation against nation to accomplish his purposes. Jeremiah pictures God's use of Pharaoh's armies this way: "See how the waters are rising . . . they will overflow the land and everything in it, the towns and those who live in them. The people will cry out . . . at the noise of enemy chariots . . . The LORD is about to destroy the Philistines" (Jer 47:2-4 NIV).

Sometimes flood images are used figuratively to represent deep, seemingly overwhelming troubles, which are not necessarily punishment from God but which provide an opportunity for God to rescue his people. The kinds of troubles represented by flood imagery include *death ("the cords of death entangled me; the torrents of destruction overwhelmed me" [Ps 18:4 NIV]); loneliness ("Your terrors . . . surround me like a flood. . . . You have taken my companions and loved ones from me" [Ps 88:16-18 NIV]); public derision ("Those who sit at the gate mock me . . . deliver me from those who hate me, from the deep waters" [Ps 69:12-14 NIV]); and *war ("when men attacked us . . . the torrent would have

293

swept over us, the raging waters would have swept us away" [Ps 124:2-5 NIV]). In every kind of trouble, God can be counted on to save those who put their trust in him. Thus David exults in Psalm 18: "He reached down from on high and took hold of me; he drew me out of deep waters" (Ps 18:16).

The dual themes of God's punishing and saving power are expressed by Isaiah when he prophesies that God will "come like a pent-up flood" to "repay wrath to his enemies," but the Redeemer will come to save those who repent of their sins (Is 59:18-20 NIV). These dual themes continue to be embodied in NT uses of flood imagery. Writers look back on Noah's flood as foreshadowing the judgment that will come on people who persist in their sinfulness, but the picture of Noah also reinforces God's promise to save and protect those who put their trust in Christ as Savior (see Mt 24:37-41; 1 Pet 3:18-2; 2 Pet 2:4-10).

The parable of the wise and foolish builders in Luke 6:46-49 uses flood imagery as a forceful reminder that a spiritual house cannot stand unless it is built on Jesus and his words. Those who do will be like the wise man who built his house on the *rock: "When a flood came, the torrent struck that house but could not shake it" (Lk 6:48 NIV). However, those who fail to listen to Jesus and obey will be like the foolish builder with no foundation: "The moment the torrent struck that house, it collapsed and its destruction was complete" (Lk 6:49 NIV). As in Noah's day, so in Jesus' day and ours: the disastrous consequences of sin can utterly destroy, but God's saving power will provide refuge.

See also ARK; CHAOS; COSMOLOGY; DEATH; JUDGMENT; RESCUE; RIVER; SIN; WATER.

FLOWERS

The flowers, blooms and blossoms referred to in Scripture, as well as their equivalent actions—to flourish, to bloom, to blossom—illustrate several prominent biblical themes such as *pride, *beauty, *love, *restoration and *transience. Flower imagery in descriptions of the *tabernacle and of Solomon's *temple and in the *Song of Songs largely develop the themes of beauty and love, whereas those referring to pride, transience and restoration are typically found in the Psalms and the Prophets.

Two Hebrew words comprise most of the references usually translated generically as "flower," "bloom," "blossom" and their verb formations. Their root or extended meanings convey a sense of the vivid character and emotional associations that biblical writers attached to them. *Peraḥ* suggests an image of breaking forth, budding, sprouting, even bursting. *Ṣîṣ* has evokes a shining, sparkling or gleaming. The first associates flowers with a spectacular, spontaneous growth and the second with a glorious, radiant, shimmering beauty.

The most frequently mentioned specific flowers are traditionally translated "lily" and "rose" (Heb *šûšan* and *ḥᵃḇaṣeleṭ* respectively). Students of Pales-

tinian botany tell us that neither of these is probably the correct translation, however. The lily familiar to most readers, the white or "Easter" lily *(Lilium candidum)*, grows in remote regions of Israel but does not fit the description attributed to it in the biblical text as growing in valleys, among brambles or in pasture land. The common rose is not native to this region either. Many commentators now assume, for example, that the phrase "lilies of the field" means any of the showy, attractive flowers that burst forth in glorious profusion in the springtime on the plains, *pastures and hills of the Carmel and Sharon regions, which are proverbial for their fertility and beauty. These flowers include ranunculus, anemone, cyclamen, tulip, hyacinth, narcissus, crocus, iris and orchid. Any reference to lilies or roses in the following discussion could therefore just as easily be substituted with one of these species or could be understood to be making a generic reference to flowers.

In the accounts of the furnishing of the Mosaic tabernacle (Ex 25:31-34; 37:17-20; Num 8:4) and the Solomonic temple (1 Kings 6:18, 29, 32, 35; 7:19, 22, 24, 26, 49; also 2 Chron 4:5, 21), flowers, particularly almond blossoms and lilies, figure prominently, justifying the later psalmic reference to the "beauty of holiness." The lampstands of the tabernacle, and later of the temple, were designed as almond *trees and their "bowls" (i.e., cups holding the *oil and wick) as almond blossoms. Additional almond blossoms decorated the "stems" of the lampstand, suggesting a graceful art-deco-like style. (For another view of the lampstands as representing an edenic *"tree of life," see Myers). We should also recall *Aaron's rod that sprouted almond blossoms and even ripe almonds. It was placed in the *ark of the covenant under the mercy seat. On the gold and cedar walls of Solomon's temple were engraved cherubim, palm trees and both open flowers and closed buds; and on the doors of olive and cypress were more open flowers. More spectacular, the bronze pillars were adorned with lilies and pomegranates four cubits (approximately six feet!) in size; and the sea of bronze, whose brim was shaped like a lily blossom, was further ornamented with two rows of lily buds around it. Some temple music also evoked floral settings; several psalms are labeled to be sung to the tune "Lilies" (see headings to Psalms 45, 69 and 80 NIV).

Given that, as Hebrews 8:5 tells us, these things were built after a pattern in heaven, we are justified in viewing their function as more than superficial or merely ornamental. Without attaching any particular symbolic or allegorical meaning to the use of flowers in the tabernacle/temple design, we may affirm an organic principle that the flower ornament contributes to the sanctity of the whole and that beauty, rightly appreciated, is a reflection of the divine and a prompt to godliness. Jesus takes just such an interpretation of flowers in the only NT reference to their beauty, the famous "Consider the lilies of the field, how they grow; they neither toil nor spin; yet . . .

Solomon in all his glory was not arrayed like one of these" (Mt 6:28-29 RSV; Lk 12:27). The beauty of one single flower in a meadow is more gorgeous than all the riches of *Solomon, Jesus declares, and the flower did not have to worry about getting riches to clothe itself. The flower's beauty teaches much about the *glory that God gives (grace) and much about the vanity of human effort to duplicate it.

Flowers are also the language of *love, as florists tell us; and the *Song of Songs, a love poem set in a *garden, supports this truism. The sensuous quality of flowers—their *colors, shapes and scents, their delicacy of touch—are analogous to the delightful sexuality of physical love and provide the famous similes in the poem: "I am a rose of Sharon, a lily of the valleys" (Song 2:1 NIV). Because the female speaker is the pursuer and the male the pursued, the poem has lent itself to an allegorical interpretation of the church seeking its bridegroom, Christ. Lilies and pomegranate blooms are the dominant flowers, and the spring setting assures that the flowers are at their zenith of brilliance: the flowers appear, spring has come; winter is past, the vine blossoms are fragrant (Song 2:12, 13).

Flower imagery describes or is associated with both the male and female lovers: she "is a lily among thorns" (Song 2:2 NIV); "his lips are like lilies, dripping with myrrh" (Song 5:13 NIV); her breasts are like two fawns feeding among the lilies (Song 4:5); he is in a garden, feeding among the lilies, gathering lilies (Song 6:2, 3); her waist is a heap of *wheat surrounded by lilies (Song 7:2). This garden is a locus of lovemaking, for "there," says the Shulamite girl, "I will give you my love" (Song 7:12 NIV). If Alter is right, that the poem's references to flowers, spices, *fruits and fauna have erotic associations, then the Song of Songs is surely one of the tenderest of such poems. It does not stoop to crude analogies of mechanics or animalism or the language of domination, but provides instead parallels to an idyllic, pastoral garden; a cultivated, sensuous, beautiful place; by definition not wild, but tended to with love and care.

While flowers inherently convey images of beauty and love, they also by their nature suggest fragility, transience and sudden decay after a brief moment of splendor. Individual blossoms or flowers last but a few days on the stem. Dislodged by a puff of wind or the shaking of an insect, their papery petals litter the ground and soon fester. Such is the metaphor used in the Psalms, the Prophets, and the NT for the life of a person who "flourishes" like the flower or like the *grass one day, but the next day is gone. The tone is not elegiac or regretful, as one might expect to find in pagan literature on the brevity of human life, however. The usual contexts are judgment on the proud and wicked, whose deeds will not survive for a very long time, and God's power in comparison to the paltry deeds of the wicked. Conversely, since the flowering of a plant is in some sense at its prime or its most glorious moment, when all the juice and

sap are rising in the springtime, the righteous are also compared to a flowering or flourishing of a plant.

The typical image of human transience occurs in Psalm 103: "*As for* man, his days *are* like grass; as a flower of the field, so he flourishes. For the wind passes over it, and it is gone" (Ps 103:15 NKJV; see also Ps 90:6; Hos 13:15). He is here today and gone tomorrow, as in Job's account of human life: "He comes forth like a flower and fades away; He flees like a shadow" (Job 14:2 NKJV). Human frailty naturally contrasts with God's *permanence, and human *weakness with the eternal Word: "All flesh *is* as grass, And its loveliness is like the flower of the field. . . . The grass withers, the flower fades, . . . But the word of our God stands forever" (Is 40:6, 8 NKJV; see also 1 Pet 1:24, 25).

In the Prophets, particularly Isaiah, flower imagery is used not merely to point out human *mortality but also to illustrate the judgment of the proud or ungodly. Flowers do not simply fade or wither, but are trampled under foot, turned to dust or cut off with *pruning hooks: "Woe to the crown of pride, to the drunkards of Ephraim, Whose glorious beauty is a fading flower Which *is* at the head of the verdant valleys, . . . Behold, the Lord, . . . like a tempest of hail, . . . Like a mighty flood of waters, . . . will bring *them* down to the earth . . . [and they] will be trampled under foot (Is 28:1-4 NKJV; see also Is 5:24; 18:5). Nahum sees God's power to rebuke his enemies in his ability to *dry up seas and rivers and to make the many flowers of Carmel and Lebanon wilt (Nahum 1:4). So too the proud Nebuchadnezzar is pictured as "flourishing" in his palace prior to his dream of a tree whose "height was great" and whose magnificence was evident "to the ends of the earth" until the command was given to chop it down (Dan 4:4, 11, 14). And James 1:10-11 also views the rich man passing away like the flower of the field under the burning heat of the *sun, its beauty perishing.

Yet the prophets not only pronounce judgment but also promise *restoration, and flower imagery figures in this as well. Isaiah's famous "The desert shall rejoice and blossom as the rose; It shall blossom abundantly and rejoice" (Is 35:1, 2 NKJV; see also Is 27:6) is one example of God's restoring ability to turn a *wasteland into a *garden. Hosea also illustrates the theme: "I will be like the dew to Israel; He shall grow like the lily, And lengthen his roots like Lebanon" (Hos 14:5). The Psalms also sing of the righteous, not the wicked, flourishing like grass or the flower (Ps 72:7, 17; 92:12-14). Proverbs too reminds us that the righteous will "flourish," that is, break forth and sprout like foliage (Prov 13:28; 14:11). Thus the flower is not always a symbol of pride, but it can also represent a blessing of favor. In this positive vein, the bud or sprout observed growing from the stump of a dead tree is an image of hope: "For there is hope for a tree, If it is cut down, that it will sprout again, And that its tender shoots will not cease. Though its root may grow old in the earth,

And its stump may die in the ground, *Yet* at the scent of water it will bud" (Job 14:7-9 NKJV).

As it does in most cultures, the language of flowers in the Bible serves a number of proverbial or traditional functions: as symbols for love, the brevity of life and the glory of the holy and eternal. Although our knowledge of specific biblical flowers or blossoms and their meanings is somewhat limited, yet we sense that the biblical writers shared this Wordsworthian sentiment: "The meanest flower that blows can give / Thoughts that do often lie too deep for tears."

See also BEAUTY; COLORS; GARDEN; GLORY; GRASS; LOVE; PLANTS; SEASONS; SEX; TEMPLE; TRANSIENCE; TREE OF LIFE; TREES; WASTELAND.

BIBLIOGRAPHY. R. Alter, *The Art of Biblical Poetry* (New York: Basic Books, 1985) chap. 8; C. Meyers, "Lampstand," *ABD* 4:141-43; M. Zohary, *Plants of the Bible* (New York: Cambridge University Press, 1982).

FLYING. *See* BIRDS; WING.

FOLLOWER. *See* LEADERSHIP.

FOLLY

Folly is the opposite of wisdom in the Bible, and the fool is the opposite of the wise person. While the culture of our own day gives no vivid conception of what constitutes folly, to the ancient mindset folly was a living reality, not only having a definite meaning but also conveying palpable images. The classic text is the book of *Proverbs, buttressed by several verses in *Ecclesiastes. More than anything else, folly is half of a binary image in which its great opposite is *wisdom.

Fools and Folly as Negative Images. The book of Proverbs gives us a composite portrait of the archetypal fool. Fools are *angry, arrogant and self-centered. Their tempers are quick to flare up (Prov 14:17, 29; 29:11). They seem to enjoy quarrels and fights (Prov 20:3). They trust their own fund of knowledge and refuse to take advice from anyone else (Prov 12:15; 28:26). Fools are "wise in their own eyes" (Prov 26:5); they even reject the guidance of their parents as beneath them (Prov 15:5). Fools also find it impossible to control their emotions and their actions (Prov 12:23); they lack control in many areas of their lives, but especially in their ability to control their *tongues (Prov 10:14; 17:28; 18:13).

Other images accrue to the fool and his folly. Proverbs 14:24 tells us that "folly is the garland of the fools" (RSV). The fool is also blind. The wise person "has eyes in his head"—that is, is clear thinking and can easily navigate the obstacles of life. In contrast, the fool lives blindly, walking into all kinds of problems and difficulties (Eccles 2:12-17; Jer 5:21). The most persistent image pattern associated with folly is that it is inevitably self-destructive: it "misleads" the fool (Prov 14:8), it is itself "the punishment of fools" (Prov 16:22), it "tears down" a house (Prov 14:1), it "leads to ruin" (Prov 19:3),

and it is so powerful that even "a little folly outweighs wisdom and honor" (Eccles 10:1 RSV).

But perhaps the most developed image of folly and the fool in the Bible is found in Proverbs 9, where folly is likened to a loose woman who is calling for men to join her for a meal. She tempts them with "stolen water" and "bread eaten in secret" (with probable sexual overtones), but once she gets these "simple men" in her house, she kills them (Prov 9:13-18; *see* Seductress). This picture of Dame Folly is contrasted in the chapter with Lady Wisdom (Prov 9:1-6).

The Bible uses a number of telling and at times humorous images to portray the actions of the fool. The talk of fools is like whips on their own backs (Prov 14:3). One might as well cut off one's foot as send a message via a fool (Prov 26:6). Fools naturally revert to their folly like a *dog returns and consumes his own *vomit (Prov 26:11). Indeed, the fool is so closely tied to his folly that you could put him in a mortar and pound him with a pestle but still not get the folly out of him (Prov 27:22).

Another cluster of images shows the tendency of folly to make itself obvious. Thus "the mind of a fool broadcasts folly" (Prov 12:23 NRSV), "the fool displays folly" (Prov 13:16 NRSV), "the simple are adorned with folly" (Prov 14:18 NRSV), and "the foolish woman is loud" (Prov 9:13 NRSV). Other images show how thoroughly folly permeates a fool's life: a fool is "immersed in folly" (Prov 17:12 NRSV) and "folly is bound up in the heart of a boy" until "discipline drives it far away" (Prov 22:15 NRSV). Folly can actually become an insatiable appetite on which "the mouths of fools feed" (Prov 15:14) or something that fools uncontrollably "pour out" (Prov 15:2).

Jesus likens the fool, who is the one who does not listen to his wise teachings, to a person who builds a house, not on the rock but on the sand (Mt 7:24-27). In a later parable Jesus describes those who do not live in the light of his return as foolish virgin bridesmaids who do not bring enough oil for their lamps to await the coming of the bridegroom (Mt 25:1-13). Similarly, in Jesus' parable about the smug farmer who trusts in his own wealth (Lk 12:13-21), God pronounces the worldly minded farmer a "fool."

This ever-expanding vision of folly has its deep structure of causes. The theological root cause is that "the fool says in his heart, 'There is no God'" (Ps 14:1 RSV), confirming by negative example that "the fear of the LORD is the beginning of knowledge" (Prov 1:7 RSV; *see* Fear of God). Secondary causes of the fool's self-destructive behavior are lack of discipline (Prov 5:23) and an unwarranted confidence in his or her own wisdom (Prov 3:7; 16:2; 30:12).

Wise Fools. While the Bible does not highlight the archetypal wise fool of literary tradition, the NT does include the motif. The key passage is 1 Corinthians 1:18-31, where Paul introduces the theme that God "chose what is foolish in the world to shame the wise," with the gospel itself representing "God's foolishness" that is "wiser than human wisdom" (NRSV).

See also DUPE; ECCLESIASTES, BOOK OF; FEAR OF GOD; PROVERBS, BOOK OF; TEACHER, TEACHING; WISDOM.

FOOD

Food fills the Bible from beginning to end, just as it fills a human life day after day. In the OT food offers pictures of God's providence, the pleasurableness of his *creation and the proper ordering of life. Food in the NT offers all these pictures but takes them to more complex levels of symbolism, which come together most fully in the person of Jesus Christ, the food from heaven.

Food as Provision. Food shows the abundant providence of God. People in Scripture do not find food as a random good but receive it as a gift from God's hand. In the Garden of Eden *Adam and Eve first receive from God "every seed-bearing plant on the face of the whole earth and every tree that has fruit with seed in it" and were told, "They will be yours for food" (Gen 1:29 NIV). God's provision extends further than just to human beings: "And to all the beasts of the earth and all the birds of the air and all the creatures that move on the ground— everything that has the breath of life in it—I give every green plant for food" (Gen 1:30 NIV). The bounty and extent of God's provision shows clearly in the recurring "all" and "every" of this Genesis narrative: no living creature anywhere, anytime, is overlooked in God's plan to meet one of life's most fundamental needs.

The psalms many times praise God for such full provision for the needs of all living things. Psalm 104, for example, celebrates the God who "makes grass grow for the cattle, and plants for man to cultivate— bringing forth food from the earth" (Ps 104:14 NIV). The psalmist looks out over this earth full of creatures, from coneys to lions to humans, claiming: "These all look to you to give them their food at the proper time. . . . When you open your hand, they are satisfied with good things" (Ps 104:27-28 NIV). The original giving of food in Eden grows into a continuing picture of God's hand outstretched to provide food.

Moses, addressing the Israelites about to enter the Promised Land, reminds them of how God has provided *manna as food in the wilderness: "He humbled you, causing you to hunger and then feeding you with manna . . . to teach you that man does not live on bread alone but on every word that comes from the mouth of the LORD" (Deut 8:3 NIV). God's physical providence is to turn them in humble submission and attentiveness to the all-provident God.

When the prophet Elijah tells King Ahab that God will stop the rain for several years thus bringing about severe *famine in Israel, he is showing an idolatrous people, this time through the withdrawal of food, that they need the one God who controls and provides all things (1 Kings 17:1). Elijah himself is given provision: water from a brook and *bread and meat brought by ravens morning and evening. Through the food, God reveals himself to his obedient servant who indeed lives according to every word that comes to him from the mouth of the Lord. And when the brook dries up, God in his providence takes Elijah to a starving widow who first receives unending stores of flour and oil, who later receives the gift of restored life for her son, and who finally believes in "the word of the LORD" from Elijah's mouth (1 Kings 17:7-24). God's provision of food for this widow of Zarephath is the first step in turning her to himself.

Food as Pleasurable. God not only provides, and provides abundantly for his creatures, but he also provides an immense variety of pleasurable flavors, textures, colors, shapes and smells, all of which indicate the joy and delight of the Creator with his creation. From the abundance of seed-bearing *plants and fruit-bearing *trees in Eden, to the broader diet including all living things allowed by God after the *flood (Gen 9:3), the foodstuffs mentioned in the biblical texts grow in number and variety. Not just fruit, but *figs (Deut 8:8), apples (Prov 25:11), pomegranates (Joel 1:12), *grapes (Mt 7:16) and melons (Num 11:5) appear. Grapes provided fresh fruit (Num 6:3), dried raisins (1 Sam 25:18), sweet juice (Is 49:26), *wine (Prov 3:10) and vinegar (Ruth 2:14). For his first miracle Jesus chooses to change water to wine at a *wedding celebration in Cana of Galilee, facilitating the enjoyment and indeed showing the source of the pleasurable fruit of the earth (Jn 2:1-11).

The land promised to God's people is described over and over again in Scripture as a *land flowing with milk and honey (e.g., Ex 3:8). God desires to give his people not just basic food but much pleasurable food—even *honey, a highly-valued delicacy. Herbs and spices, such as *salt, are given by God to increase the flavor of foods. "Is tasteless food eaten without salt," Job asks, "or is there flavor in the white of an egg?" (Job 6:6 NIV). As Job compares the unhelpful advice of his friends to bland, unseasoned food, his comparison assumes the basic good of taste and flavor, gifts from a delightfully creative God, small signs of his pleasure in his creation.

Food as a Symbol of Order. Through food God signals not random provision or pleasure but rather a certain intended order to life. In Eden he chooses to use a fruit tree as a symbol of the knowledge of good and evil; and the act of eating that fruit constitutes Adam and Eve's disobedience (Gen 2:17). Food marks the proper limits. The most basic, concrete stuff of life pictures the most basic level of *obedience or disobedience. And the fact that God designed humans to take that stuff into their bodies so that it becomes part of them offers a perfect picture of opening themselves up to good or evil, taking in either one or the other so that it becomes part of them.

After Adam and Eve eat the fruit, part of God's resulting curse involves the whole process of cultivating and eating food. The original, perfect order of that process is disrupted along with everything else in the Fall. Now the ground is cursed, producing *thorns and thistles. It yields food, not freely as before but only through painful human toil and *sweat (Gen 3:17-19). After the flood, God looks with pleasure and mercy on righteous Noah, promising never again to *curse the ground in response to human sin, but promising rather to continue the process of seedtime and harvest, cold and heat, summer and winter, all in their proper order, "as long as the earth endures" (Gen 8:22 NIV). The *seasonal cycles that produce food today, even with the thorns and thistles and toil remaining from the original curse, continue as signs of God's ordered providence for his people. Clearly the order is not perfect or identical to that of Eden: after the flood God declares a "fear and dread" on the part of animals and birds and fish toward humans, who can now eat "everything that lives and moves," not just vegetation (Gen 9:2-3 NIV). God's providence allows this change in the boundaries of his provision, which continue, but without the original harmony of Eden. Signs of both grace and sin evidence themselves in all of life, even in the ordering of the food we eat.

When sin entered the human race through the eating of that fruit in Eden, sacrifices of food to God became part of the necessary order. In a sense the sacrificial food in the OT stands between human beings and God, whereas before the Fall they were in direct communion. The food on the *altar represents not only separation but also restored communion, through the humility and repentance of the sacrificer, and ultimately through the perfect atoning sacrifice of Jesus Christ. *Leviticus records a series of complex laws regarding which foods were clean or unclean to sacrifice or eat. In the first five chapters of Leviticus, five different kinds of sacrifices (burnt, grain, fellowship, sin and guilt offerings) involve bulls, rams, birds, grain, oil, salt, *goats, *lambs—all with carefully prescribed procedures and orders; for example, only an animal that has a split hoof and chews the cud is "clean" and can be eaten. Through this intricately ordered system of food, God shows his people the life-and-death significance of purity and defilement—not just physically but more important, spiritually—in relation to their God. So Daniel, when he refuses to disobey God's laws concerning the food he should and should not eat, is staking his life not just on physical purity but on the purity of his obedient heart (Dan 1).

Scripture's notice of amounts of food distributed also gives a sense of a divinely intended order. The Israelites in the wilderness are given manna daily, and they are to gather only enough for each day, no more. When they greedily try to gather extra, it rots overnight and develops maggots. Only on the sixth day can they gather double, and the extra does not rot, but stays fresh for the day of rest (Ex 16:16-26). God intends the daily provision of just enough food to depict his sufficient daily care for his people. He means the special distribution before the sabbath to indicate the special holiness of that day.

In the Bible God creates a well-ordered earth, able to produce enough food for the creatures living on it. His providence is sufficient for all, and he clearly grieves over and cares for those who receive too little when the balance and order of food distribution is disturbed. Scripture often pictures God's hand as reaching specifically to the poor and the hungry. "He upholds the cause of the oppressed," the psalmist writes, "and gives food to the hungry" (Ps 146:7 NIV). "He has filled the hungry with good things but has sent the rich away empty," Mary sings in Luke 1:53 (NIV). Hoarding or consuming excess is consistently condemned. The wise Solomon advises eating "just enough" honey; "too much of it, and you will vomit" (Prov 25:16 NIV).

Spiritual Food. Especially in the OT, physical food clearly pictures providence, pleasure and God's intended order. But another level of imagery exists in relation to food: a metaphorical level. For example, Isaiah calls, "Come, all you who are thirsty, come to the waters; and you who have no money, come, buy and eat" (55:1 NIV). Isaiah goes on to develop his food metaphor until he declares at the end of verse 2: "Your soul will delight in the richest of fare." We understand that Isaiah refers to food for the soul, spiritual food.

Jesus begins to explain the distinction between physical food and spiritual food when he tells his disciples not to worry about what they would eat or what they would wear. "Life is more than food, and the body more than clothes," he told them (Lk 12:23 NIV). In this passage Jesus does not denigrate the value of physical food, but he affirms God's providence over that area of life and challenges his followers to seek a whole different realm, his kingdom (12:31).

With his own words and actions, Jesus illustrates how to go about seeking the kingdom (Lk 12:22-34). Once, when his disciples urge him to eat something, Jesus tells them he has food to eat that they know nothing about (Jn 4:32). He uses Isaiah's metaphor, referring to that "richest of fare" in which the soul delights. When his disciples do not catch on, Jesus explains, "My food is to do the will of him who sent me and to finish his work" (Jn 4:34 NIV). Seeking God and his kingdom becomes his food in that it draws him, fills him and nourishes him.

Jesus not only talks about spiritual food, he *becomes* spiritual food for his followers, a living metaphor to take in and live. After miraculously feeding a crowd of five thousand from one little boy's lunch, Jesus cautions his disciples: "Do not work for food that spoils, but for food that endures to eternal life, which the Son of Man will give you" (Jn 6:27 NIV). His disciples are impressed by the miracle of the physical food, which they connect with the OT miracle of manna in the wilderness. But as they converse, Jesus turns their eyes from the actual bread to the God who sends that bread from heaven and who has sent that bread most fully in the form of his son.

The passage climaxes in that great declaration, "I am the bread of life. He who comes to me will never go hungry, and he who believes in me will never be thirsty" (6:35 NIV). Jesus is manna from heaven, bread, the food that will satisfy the souls and give eternal life. He is the word proceeding from the mouth of God by which men and women live (see Deut 8:3; Is 55). Jeremiah writes, "When your words came, I ate them; they were my joy and my heart's delight, for I bear your name, O LORD Almighty" (Jer 15:16 NIV). When Christ, who in the beginning was the Word, comes to his followers, he comes as the food that gives life (Jn 1:1).

John 6 continues in a long discourse on Jesus as food. Jesus makes the metaphor utterly graphic, insisting that unless believers eat his flesh and drink his blood, they have no life in us: "For my flesh is real food and my blood is real drink" (Jn 6:55 NIV). What shall we do with such a living metaphor? Those who hear it call it a "hard teaching" (Jn 7:60 NIV). For one thing, apart from the shocking prospect of eating another person, any Jew would know the divinely established ceremonial laws forbidding the eating of the *blood of any animal. Each animal had to be completely drained, because "the blood is the life, and you must not eat the life with the meat" (Deut 12:23 NIV). When Jesus reverses this law in himself, he means that through his blood shed for his own, they can take his life, the life of God, into themselves.

The blood smeared on the doorframes of the Israelites in Egypt saved them from death. In memory of that exodus, God's people celebrate the *Passover every year, with the sacrifice of lambs and the feast of unleavened bread (Ex 12). When the Israelites receive God's law at Mt. Sinai, the blood of the sacrificed animals is sprinkled on the people, to represent "the blood of the covenant" of God with his people (Ex 24:8). From the biblical perspective all that bread and all that blood are signs of the flesh and blood of Jesus Christ, who comes and delivers his people from eternal wrath, by offering himself as the perfect sacrificial lamb for sins.

At the first Lord's Supper Jesus celebrates the traditional Passover meal with his disciples and reveals to them the full meaning of that feast. Offering the bread, he says, "This is my body" (Mt 26:26). He then offers the cup and tells them, "This is my blood of the covenant, which is poured out for many for the forgiveness of sins" (Mt 26:28 NIV). In truly eating that feast—that is, in personally accepting the sacrifice of Jesus—a person takes into himself the death and life of God's Son. When a person eats food, that food goes into him and becomes a part of his own living body. So Paul writes to the believers in Corinth: "We always carry around in our body the death of Jesus, so that the life of Jesus may also be revealed in our body" (2 Cor 4:10 NIV).

Jesus as the believer's food offers the perfect culmination of all the references of food in the Bible.

For from the beginning, the only living food was Christ. Paul writes of Moses and the Israelites: "They all ate the same spiritual food and drank the same spiritual drink; for they drank from the spiritual rock that accompanied them, and that rock was Christ" (1 Cor 10:3-4). In his providence God planned from before the foundations of the earth to send the bread of life, to give abundant life, to offer a way to restore the order of Eden, where human beings know full communion with God.

The NT develops other food imagery to show spiritual truth metaphorically. Jesus is not only our bread but living water, welling up like a spring inside his disciples, to eternal life (Jn 4:14). Individual foods emerge as metaphors: *milk, for example, pictures the first basic instruction for "infants in Christ" and "solid food" becomes the more advanced teaching for the more mature believers (1 Cor 3:1-2; Heb 5:12-13). Jesus used salt to give a picture of his followers and their effect on this earth (Mt 5:13).

But Jesus himself is the center to which one must come when looking at the food imagery in Scripture. Those who have eaten his flesh and drunk his blood will find themselves at that final feast, the wedding supper of the Lamb (Rev 19:7-9). That celebration will be the last supper on the other side of Jesus' death. There he will not be the Lamb ready to shed his blood, but the Lamb risen and glorified and ready to embrace his bride, the church he purified through his own death. "Blessed are those who are invited to the wedding supper of the Lamb!" (Rev 19:9 NIV).

See also ABUNDANCE; ANIMALS; APPETITE; BANQUET; BREAD; DRINKING; EATING; FAT, FATNESS; FIG, FIG TREE; FISH, FISHER, FISHING; FRUIT, FRUITFULNESS; GARDEN; GRAIN; HONEY; HUNTING; LAND FLOWING WITH MILK AND HONEY; MANNA; MEAL; MILK; STEW; STOMACH; SUPPER; TABLE; THIRST; TREE, TREES; WHEAT; WINE.

FOOL. See FOLLY; SLUGGARD.

FOOTSTOOL. See UNDER THE FEET.

FOREHEAD

The two dozen references to foreheads in the Bible fall into three main clusters. The most numerous are references to the forehead as a place where one wears an identifying mark, either literal or figurative. At the institution of the Passover, Moses told the people that the perpetual remembrance of God's deliverance of them would be as a reminder and emblem "on your forehead" (Ex 13:9 16 NRSV). In his *farewell discourse, Moses commanded that his words should be fixed "as an emblem on your forehead" (Deut 6:8; 11:18 NRSV). The engraved gold signet bearing the motto "holy to the Lord" was worn by Aaron on his forehead as God's designated high priest (Ex 28:36-38). In apocalyptic visions, people's foreheads receive marks of identity, either good (sometimes for purposes of protection) or bad (Ezek 9:4; Rev 7:3; 9:4; 13:16; 14:1, 9; 17:5; 20:4; 22:4). Jeremiah 3:3

uses the image of "the forehead of a whore" to picture someone who refuses to be ashamed.

Second, the hardness of a forehead made it a symbol of stubbornness and *rebelliousness (Is 48:4; Ezek 3:7). The positive side of the image is that it can also picture the courage and persistence of a good person in standing up to evil (Ezek 3:8-9).

Third, the condition of a person's forehead was crucial to a priest's determination of whether or not a person had leprosy (Lev 13:41-43; see also 2 Chron 26:19-20).

The most famous forehead in the Bible is Goliath's. As David ran toward the heavily armored giant, the stone from his sling sank into Goliath's forehead, "and he fell face down on the ground" (1 Sam 17:49 NRSV).

See also FACE, FACIAL EXPRESSIONS; HEAD.

FOREIGNER

The image of the foreigner, stranger, sojourner or alien is a major biblical archetype. Its meaning is fluid, shifting from the literal status of the OT patriarchs and the nation of Israel to the NT emphasis on Christians as people whose citizenship is in heaven rather than on earth. The idea of a foreigner is definable partly by its opposite—the citizen or native-born. The foreigner lives in a double awareness: a sense of an identity that has been lost or forfeited, and an awareness of being homeless or strange in his or her current environment.

In the Bible the image of the foreigner is always that of the alien who lives in a country not of his or her own origin, either as a *guest or as a permanent resident. It is not used of other nations, for whom the most common term is *Gentiles. The foreigner is thus in the peculiar position of having divided customs, loyalties and laws, and of being uprooted from his or her homeland. The sense of estrangement is central to the concept of the foreigner as the image develops throughout the Bible.

The Old Testament: Literal Foreigners. According to the biblical history, being an exile in the world is first of all a universal human condition. *Adam and *Eve's eviction from the *garden of Eden begins the displacement for the entire race, a displacement highlighted by *Cain's banishment from society to be a *wanderer (Gen 3:23; 4:12). This displacement is further universalized at the Tower of *Babel when the division into separate languages begins the process of differentiating nations and ethnic groups (Gen 11:1-9). The condition of *exile is first of all a *curse.

But it becomes more than that in patriarchal history, where it plays a central role. From the moment that *Abraham obeyed God's call to "go from your country and your kindred and your father's house to the land that I will show you" (Gen 12:1 RSV), the father of the faithful became an alien. His descendants, Isaac, Jacob and Joseph, followed the same path. Here the state of being a sojourner is not a curse but a condition of the *covenant, an act of

*obedience to a God who promises great things to those who follow him. On a human level, though, being a foreigner implies a sense of rootlessness and longing for rest. We catch the tones of this weariness in the account of the birth of Joseph's first son: "He called his name Gershom; for he said, 'I have been a sojourner in a foreign land' " (Ex 2:22 RSV).

As we move from Genesis to Exodus, the scope broadens from the stories of individual aliens in the covenant line to the whole nation of Israel. It begins innocently enough with the shift of *Jacob's residence from a famine-ridden land to the fertile region of Goshen in Egypt. Initially it appears to be a benevolent exile; in fact, when Jacob arrives in Egypt he speaks of the "evil" of his life of "sojourning" and "the life of my fathers in the days of their sojourning" (Gen 47:9 RSV). When we read further that *Joseph "settled his father and his brothers, and gave them a possession in the land of Egypt, in the best of the land" (Gen 47:11 RSV), it almost seems that Jacob has attained a homeland. But when "there arose a new king over Egypt, who did not know Joseph" (Ex 1:8 RSV), the curse of being a stranger in a strange land reasserts itself, and *Egypt becomes an evocative "house of bondage" (Ex 20:2) for the entire nation of Israel.

In patriarchal and early Israelite history, the image of the foreigner is ambivalent. On the one hand, it is an image of vulnerability. The history of the patriarchs and Israelites is a continuous narrow escape. Typical events include having one's wife taken into a foreign king's harem, fearing for one's life, experiencing run-ins with locals over the use of a well, paying an exorbitant price for a burial plot, having to send off to the homeland for a wife for one's son, being an easy victim of treachery and injustice when the boss's wife uses racist language to make a false charge of rape stick, being subject to slavery and genocide. Foreigners expect little, and often their expectations are realized. We catch the hint of the foreigner's low status in *Ruth's surprised question after Boaz has expressed compassion for her: "Why have I found favor in your eyes . . . when I am a foreigner?" (Ruth 2:10 RSV). Both Joseph and Jacob express a desire that their bones be carried back to their homeland (Gen 50:12-13, 24).

Vulnerability and lack of secure status are only half of the equation, however. The other half is that the sojourner is repeatedly pictured in the OT as the special recipient of God's favor, protection and benevolent concern. We find this in OT civil laws. Specimen entries in the Mosaic law include these: "You shall not wrong a stranger or oppress him, for you were strangers in the land of Egypt" (Ex 22:21 RSV; cf. Ex 23:9); "You shall not strip your vineyard bare, neither shall you gather the fallen grapes of your vineyard; you shall leave them for the poor and for the sojourner" (Lev 19:9-10 RSV); "The stranger who sojourns with you shall be to you as the native among you, and you shall love him as yourself; for you were strangers in the land of Egypt" (Lev 19:34

RSV). The same motif appears in the Psalms (e.g., Ps 39:12; 146:9) and in the prophets (e.g., Zech 7:9-10; Mal 3:5). On some occasions God enables an Israelite foreigner to contribute significantly to the welfare of another country; the list includes Joseph, Daniel, Nehemiah and Esther. Thus if the life of the exile is a continuous narrow escape in the Pentateuch, it is also a continuous drama of God's providential grace and provision.

Once the Israelites are given the *land of Canaan after the conquest led by Joshua, the image of foreigners shifts from the Jews to those Gentiles who live with them. Although in some cases these arrangements were made by trickery, as with the Gibeonites in Joshua 9, in other instances foreigners chose to be associated with, or even integrated into, the life of Israel. Notable examples include Rahab and Ruth, both of whom become ancestresses of Christ (Mt 1:5). God commands that his people extend the same care to foreigners that he does. Having their own homeland requires now a generosity toward those who find themselves displaced and alienated. The foreigner, along with the *widow and the *orphan, is both particularly vulnerable and particularly blessed as he or she comes under the special care of God. The two-sided nature of foreignness is thus maintained.

Being a foreigner receives another twist during the time of the prophets. As these spokespersons increasingly denounce the sins of Israel and Judah, the concept of (although not the term for) foreigner moves from the alien who lives in the land to the Gentile nations that surround the land. While acknowledging the evil of both Jews and Gentiles, the prophets also announce a time when all nations will share in God's blessings (Ezek 47:22). This inclusion of the Gentiles is already foreshadowed in the repentance of Ninevah (Jon 3:10), the worship of God by Nebuchadnezzar (Dan 4:34-35) and the generosity of Cyrus, who is called "my shepherd" (Is 44:28 RSV).

The image of the foreigner or exile assumes a totally new meaning with the *exile. Here the exile is an image of God's judgment and assumes strongly negative overtones. The heart longing of the exiled Jews was to return to the homeland, an event that a remnant finally achieved.

The New Testament: Spiritual Pilgrims. In the NT the image of the sojourner comes to focus on the people of God as pilgrims and strangers in the world. On the one hand, the notion of foreigners as defined by national, ethnic or racial origins is dismissed. Jesus includes among his followers a Syro-Phoenician woman (Mk 7:24-30), a Roman centurion (Mt 8:5-13) and a promiscuous Samaritan (Jn 4:1-42). Following Jesus' resurrection and ascension, Paul announces that the mystery that has been hidden from all the ages is that the church of God will be composed of both Jews and Gentiles without distinction (Eph 3:1-6).

With the old notion of foreigner eradicated, however, the image continues, though in a metaphoric rather than national sense. Now all believers in Christ are considered pilgrims and aliens, people who live their lives as strangers on this earth while they journey toward their true home in heaven. This image of Christians as foreigners retains some of the ambivalence that it has in the OT. To be a foreigner is to feel the effects of sin; without sin there would be no displacement, no vulnerability, no homesickness. On the other hand, to be a foreigner also means to experience the exquisite protection of God, and so to understand just how much one needs that protection.

The example of Jesus exemplifies the sojourner's life in the new dispensation. Jesus himself encapsulated his *wanderer status with the aphoristic observation that "foxes have holes, and birds of the air have nests; but the Son of man has nowhere to lay his head" (Mt 8:20 RSV). The broader spiritual context of Jesus' incarnate life is that Jesus "comes" (Jn 3:19; 12:46-47; 18:37) or is "sent" (Jn 3:17; 10:36; 17:18, 21, 25) as the unrecognized (Jn 1:10) stranger into this world for a time (Jn 9:5, 39; 11:27; 13:1; 16:28; 17:11, 13). He claims that his "kingdom is not of this world" (Jn 18:36; cf. 8:23; 17:13-16). As followers of Jesus and strangers in the *world, his disciples will have "trouble" (Jn 16:33; cf. 16:20) and be hated (Jn 15:18, 19).

The apostle Paul epitomizes the NT foreigner. Outcast from his prestigious position among the Pharisees and wandering from city to city as itinerant tent maker and preacher, he poignantly states, "To the present hour we hunger and thirst, we are ill-clad and buffeted and homeless" (1 Cor 4:11 RSV). Other believers, such as Priscilla and Aquila, likewise experienced the disconcerting effects of being evicted and living as foreigners (Acts 18:2). The apostle Peter generalizes the notion of being a foreigner to all believers when he beseeches believers "as aliens and exiles to abstain from the passions of the flesh that wage war against your soul" (1 Pet 2:11 RSV). He also enjoins "the exiles of the Dispersion" (1 Pet 1:1, RSV) to "live your lives as strangers here in reverent fear" (1 Pet 1:17 NIV).

The climactic NT transformation of the foreigner into a spiritual symbol of the Christian life is the book of Hebrews, especially the encomium in praise of faith (Heb 11). Here we read that "by faith [Abraham] sojourned in the land of promise, as in a foreign land" (Heb 11:9 RSV). His heirs of faith "acknowledged that they were strangers and exiles on the earth" (Heb 11:13 RSV). All of them "make it clear that they are seeking a homeland. If they had been thinking of that land from which they had gone out, they would have had opportunity to return. But as it is, they desire a better country, that is, a heavenly one" (Heb 11:14-16 RSV). It is small wonder that this image of the pilgrim stranger, the believing foreigner in a hostile world protected by the constant care of God, has remained one of the most powerful images of the Christian life, because it is true to the facts of the Christian life on earth and hope of heaven. We can, of course, find OT premonitions of the pilgrim spirit, as in the psalmist's comment, "I am a sojourner [NIV stranger] on earth; hide not thy commandments from me!" (Ps 119:19 RSV).

See also EXILE; FAR; GENTILE; GUEST; HOSPITALITY; HOME, HOUSE; HOMECOMING, STORIES OF; LAND; WANDERER, WANDERING.

FOREST

At its simplest level, the forest is that which is other than towns and cultivated fields. As such, it represents uncultivated nature that needs to be cleared for use (Josh 17:15, 18). On the other hand, the planting and nurturing of forests can itself be a form of cultivation (Is 29:17; 32:15; 44:14; Eccles 2:6). In fact, Psalm 104:16 pictures God as cosmic planter and waterer of forests.

As a wooded area separate from towns and cultivated fields, the forest is the abode of wild *animals, especially nocturnal predators. We thus find references to "every wild animal of the forest" (Ps 50:10 NRSV), the "boar from the forest" that ravages a cultivated field without walls (Ps 80:13), "animals of the forest" that "come creeping out" while people sleep at night (Ps 104:20), "wild animals in the forest" (Is 56:9), "a *lion in the forest" (Jer 12:8; cf. Amos 3:4; Mic 5:8) and a forest in which wild animals devour people (Hos 14:5). Here the forest is an image of *terror. The forest *fire is another image of terror (Ps 83:14; Is 9:18; Jer 21:14; Ezek 20:46; Jas 3:5). In the same category is the forest damaged by a thunder *storm (Ps 29:9; Is 7:2).

On the positive side, the forest is a source of lumber, hence the references to the felling of trees in a forest (Deut 19:5; 2 Kings 19:23; Is 10:34; Jer 10:3; Zech 11:2). Nehemiah successfully requested timber from "the king's forest" (Neh 2:8), suggesting the value that forests held in the ancient Near East. As a source of lumber, the forests of *Lebanon are in a class by themselves—a recognized standard of excellence (Ezek 31:3), the source of choice lumber when Solomon pursued his lavish building projects (1 Kings 7:2; 10:17, 21; 2 Chron 9:16, 20). The cedars of Lebanon are legendary in the Bible, with nearly two dozen references.

As an image of *nature and of growing things, the forest is also a symbol of prosperity, and it retains that meaning even in prophecies of impending destruction of a nation. We read, for example, about how God will destroy "the glory of his forest and his fruitful land" (Is 10:18 NRSV) and about how "the forest will disappear completely, and the city will be utterly laid low" (Is 32:19 NRSV). Although these references to the forest appear in oracles of *judgment, the forest itself retains its identity as a standard of value and *prosperity. The forest also appears in oracles predicting restoration, and in particular forests are enjoined to break into celebration at God's acts of redemption (1 Chron 16:33; Ps 96:12; Is 44:23), technically an example of "pathetic [sympa-

thetic] fallacy" (picturing facets of nature as identifying with human emotions).

Forest imagery in the Bible participates in the incipient symbolism that characterizes the Bible at every turn. Many of the literal references noted above carry religious and moral meanings beyond the literal. The growth of the forest or its being buffeted in a windstorm are the direct result of divine activity. The forest readily becomes a picture of God's judgment (Is 10:17-19; Hos 2:12) or restoration (Is 29:17; 32:15; Mic 7:14).

See also ANIMALS; LEBANON; PLANTS; TREE, TREES; WASTELAND; WILDERNESS; WOOD.

FORGIVENESS

The approximately 125 direct references to forgiveness in the Bible are mainly straightforward in nature and do not themselves point to the imagery surrounding forgiveness. The key to understanding the imagery of forgiveness is that it views sin as *something that needs to be eradicated or removed.* Complementing this motif is one that focuses on *disrupted relationships between people that need to be restored.* In both cases the imagery of forgiveness revolves around solving a problem through either the removal of something or reconciliation with someone.

Almost all of the biblical pictures of forgiveness are pictures of divine forgiveness. But on the human plane, we have *Joseph's forgiveness of his villainous brothers, *Esau's forgiveness of *Jacob and *Jesus' command that people forgive their fellow humans "seventy times seven" times (Mt 18:22; Lk 17:4), buttressed by a parable involving the canceling of debts (Mt 18:23-35). The imagery of an equation appears in Jesus' statements about God's forgiving people as they forgive others (Mt 6:12, 14-15). The parable of the *prodigal son and the forgiving father is a picture of human forgiveness but also a metaphor of God's forgiveness (Lk 15:11-32).

Forgiveness as Removing Sin. Most of the biblical images of forgiveness involve getting rid of *sin in one form or another. Some of the imagery is spatial, as sin is removed (Ps 103:12; Zech 3:9), cast into the *depths of the sea (Mic 7:19), "swept away . . . like a cloud and . . . like mist" (Is 44:22 RSV), cast *behind God's back (Is 38:17), "set aside" (Col 2:14) or "put away" (Heb 9:26). In a variation, sin is *covered (Ps 32:1; Rom 4:7), so as to be put out of sight, or blotted out (Ps 51:9; Jer 18:23). If we begin with the premise that sin is an inner defilement, forgiveness can be pictured as a process of *washing (Ps 51:7; Is 4:4; Acts 22:16), *cleansing (Lev 16:30; Num 8:21; Ps 51:2; Is 4:4; Jer 33:8; Ezek 36:33; Zech 13:1; 1 Jn 1:7, 9), receiving "a clean *heart" (Ps 51:10) or being "purified with blood" (Heb 9:22). *Color symbolism seizes upon red as the color of sin, and forgiveness is accordingly the purging of the scarlet substance so as to leave behind an object as *white as *snow and *wool (Is 1:18).

Sin is also viewed as a debt or penalty, with the result that forgiveness becomes a paying or pardoning of the debt (Mt 6:12; Is 40:2) and a canceling of "the bond which stood against us with its legal demands" (Col 2:14 RSV). In a similar vein are various examples of God's *not* doing something in regard to sin—not counting it (2 Cor 5:19), not *remembering it (Jer 31:34; Heb 8:12), not reckoning it (Rom 4:8). Forgiveness is also a matter of God's hiding his face from someone's sin (Ps 51:9; see Jer 16:17 for the opposite picture).

A similar cluster of images focuses on freeing from *bondage and healing from disease. If sin is a burden that a person carries, forgiveness is Christ's bearing "our sins in his body on the tree" (1 Pet 2:24), or God's "nailing it to the cross" (Col 2:14). Forgiveness is also a setting free from bondage (Acts 13:38-39; Rom 6:7, 18; Gal 1:4; Rev 1:5). A strong connection was made by people in biblical times between human sinfulness and physical ailment. Accordingly, we find passages that view forgiveness as a process that simultaneously rids the body of *disease (Ps 32:1-5; 103:3; Is 53:5; Mt 9:2, 5; Mk 2:5, 9; Lk 5:20, 23; 1 Pet 2:24).

Forgiveness as Reconciled Relationship. The second major motif focuses on the restored relationship between God and the sinner that occurs with forgiveness. The classic picture is the father's welcome of the returning prodigal (Lk 15:11-32). Romans 5:10-11 paints a similar picture of reconciliaiation accompanied by *joy (cf. 2 Cor 5:19; Col 1:22), while other passages use the image of "making *peace by the blood of his cross" (Col 1:20 RSV; cf. Eph 2:15). Forgiveness is the reconciliation of people "who once were estranged and hostile in mind" with God (Col 1:21 RSV). From the Gospels we have pictures of Jesus having *table fellowship with tax collectors and *sinners.

The specific attributes of God that are most often pictured with declarations of his forgiveness are *mercy, grace and steadfast love. In fact, a stock formula that appears verbatim seven times in the Bible is that God is "merciful and gracious, slow to anger and abounding in steadfast love" (Ex 34:6; Neh 9:17; Ps 86:15; 103:8; 145:8; Joel 2:13; Jon 4:2; modified in 2 Chron 30:9; Neh 9:31; Ps 111:4; 112:4). The imagery surrounding God's forgiveness is characterized by magnitude and lavishness. It is "abounding," not half hearted. God does not simply remove human sin—he removes it "as far as the east is from the west" (Ps 103:12), thereby evidencing love as large "as the heavens are high above the earth" (Ps 103:11). In Jesus' picture of the father who forgives his prodigal son, the father does not simply accept the son—he runs to embrace him and throws an elaborate party (*see* Banquet). Balancing the imagery of magnitude is that of tenderness: the song of Zechariah speaks of the forgiveness of sins "through the tender mercy of our God" (Lk 1:77-78), and Psalm 103 balances the imagery of vast space with a picture of God pitying people "as a father pities his children" (Ps 103:13).

On the human side of this transaction, forgiveness is pictured as based on a person's taking the initiative in asking for it. The person who eventually experiences forgiveness begins as a penitent—a person sorry for sin who asks God to forgive. Penitential psalms, like Psalms 32 and 51, picture the range of human feelings and attitudes that make up the penitent. To receive God's forgiveness, one must ask for it (2 Chron 33:12-13). The psalmist declares that God is "good and forgiving" to all who call on him (Ps 86:5). The imagery of forgiveness as a process that the penitent undertakes is also evident in the path to forgiveness that Leviticus 6:1-7 outlines and that the OT system of sacrifices pictures in more general terms.

An important additional motif is the "before and after" nature of the experience of forgiveness. Forgiveness is a change of status from *guilt to declared innocence (cf. Ex 34:7, with its image of God's clearing the guilty; Ps 32:5; Jer 33:8). There is a psychological dimension to this "before and after" experience, with anxiety and psychosomatic symptoms preceding the act of being forgiven, and relief and joy following it. Psalm 32:1-2 sounds the keynote when it pronounces the forgiven person as "blessed." The human response to God's forgiveness is also love of God—a love that Jesus claimed was proportionate to the magnitude of the forgiveness that the penitent has received (Lk 7:36-50).

Summary. The overriding aura that surrounds the Bible's imagery of forgiveness is threefold, revolving around the driving need that the human heart feels for forgiveness, the decisiveness of the act by which God discards sin and the lavishness of God's mercy in forgiveness.

See also ALTAR; ATONEMENT; BONDAGE AND FREEDOM; CLEANSING; COVER, COVERING; GUILTY; MERCY; OFFERING; PEACE; PRODIGAL SON; REPENTANCE; SACRIFICE; SIN; SINNER; SNOW; WHITE; WOOL.

FORSAKE, FORSAKEN

Images of forsaken people, especially *women, appear throughout the Bible. While God has always been a God of *mercy who never forsakes those in need, abandoned people nevertheless existed and were abused in biblical times.

In the Bible the word *forsake* and its synonym *abandon* were used in two ways: in one meaning, *forsake* was a verb that meant to forget or discontinue performing a specific action; in the other meaning, *forsake* conveyed the abandonment of individuals who had no one else to care for their distresses. Both uses are important in the Bible, and when God speaks of Israel, he links the two uses. Because women were far more helpless than men, requiring legal, financial and physical protection from men, the individuals most often abandoned or forsaken in the Bible are women. Such abandonment was a disgrace as well as an inconvenience, and it typified such outcast individuals as *widows, *orphans and *foreigners.

In the OT history of Israel, the imagery of forsaking and being forsaken revolves around the *covenant that God establishes with his people. On the one hand, God establishes his own character as a faithful God who would never forsake his people. Moses gives Israel numerous promises from God that "because the LORD your God is a merciful God, he will neither abandon you not destroy you"; therefore, they could face their adversaries fearlessly, backed by a God who "will not fail you or forsake you" (Deut 4:31; 31:6 RSV). However, God also warns Israel that if his people forget him, he will forsake them to their enemies as punishment for their sin (Deut 28:20). Unfortunately, this is exactly what they do: God himself predicts that Israel will abandon the God who made them; and beginning in *Judges, the Bible recounts how the people "abandoned [God] and worshiped other gods" (Deut 31:17; 1 Sam 12:10; 1 Kings 8:57; 19:10). God abandons Israel to one *enemy nation after another; yet despite their punishment, they can never fully repent from their *sin.

In Isaiah God addresses the captive nation of Israel as though she were a distressed woman, his cast-off *wife. Promising her an end to her abandonment and an apocalyptic future of security and provision, he calls Israel to "forget the shame of your youth, and the disgrace of your widowhood" (Is 54:4 RSV). Instead, he reassures her with the security of a permanent *home and *husband, proclaiming, "Your Maker is your husband, the LORD of hosts is his name . . . . For the LORD has called you like a wife forsaken and grieved in spirit, like a wife of youth when she is cast off, says your God. For a brief moment I forsook you, but with great compassion I will gather you . . . . O afflicted one, storm-tossed and not comforted, behold I will set your stones in antimony, and lay your foundations with sapphires" (Is 54:5-7, 11 RSV). Such a declaration encompasses all that the forsaken woman most lacks: a husband who loves her, cares for her physical needs, *protects her from harm and showers her with wealth and assurances of permanency. God explicitly pledges his upcoming faithfulness to her, saying, "You shall no longer be termed Forsaken, and your land shall no more be termed Desolate; but you shall be called My delight is in her, and your land Married" (Is 62:4 RSV). Israel is indeed God's redeemed *bride, a colorful picture of God's swift erasure of the lonely woman's abandonment and disgrace.

Throughout the Bible, God expresses a special compassion and care for individuals who are abandoned and in need. The psalmist expresses God's enduring faithfulness to those who love him: "I have been young, and now I am old; yet I have not seen the righteous forsaken" (Ps 37:25 RSV). He expresses that God is more faithful than any other on earth, for even "if my father and mother forsake me, the LORD will take me up" (Ps 27:10). He calls himself the "father of orphans and protector of widows," and with his own hand he "executes justice for the orphan and the widow" and "loves the strangers, providing them with food and clothing" (Ps 68:5; Deut 10:18). God demanded that Israel to do the same, commanding, "You shall not abuse any widow or orphan," and reminding his people to care for the strangers in their land (Ex 22:22; Deut 10:19). Furthermore, God set up a specific system for their provision in Israel by allowing them to *glean any leftover food from the grain fields, olive trees and grapevines (Deut 14:29; 24:19-21). When Israel disobeys him, their treatment of orphans and widows is one of the charges God brings against them (Is 1:23; Ezek 22:7). Thus, God understood the plight of the most forsaken in society and compassionately endeavored to care for them.

Forsaken women are an archetype in the Bible. Some of them are rescued from their plight by God: Hagar (Gen 16:7-14; 21:8-19), Leah (Gen 28:30), Tamar (Gen 38), *Ruth and Naomi, and the widows in dire straits miraculously rescued by Elijah and Elisha (1 Kings 17:8-15; 2 Kings 4). In keeping with the realism of the Bible, not all forsaken women fare as well. One thinks of Jephthah's daughter (Judg 11:29-40), of the Levite's concubine left outside the door to be abused (Judg 19) and of Tamar, abandoned after her *rape by Amnon (2 Sam 13:1-19).

The imagery of forsaking also clusters around God's commands, some of which warn against forgetting or forsaking a duty. Above all, God's people are repeatedly enjoined not to forsake or neglect obeying him. The book of Proverbs is a repository of warnings not to forsake good behavior. The teacher commands his pupils not to forsake his teaching or their parents' teaching (Prov 4:2; 6:20). He commends the attainment of wisdom, promising, "Do not forsake her, and she will keep you; love her, and she will guard you" (Prov 4:6 RSV). One of the virtues praised in Proverbs is never to forsake a friend (27:10). Not forsaking virtue thus supplements the larger biblical motif of not forsaking the needy.

While the motif of forsaking is predominantly a negative image, naming a state that should be avoided, there are a few instances where it assumes the positive meaning of abandoning something bad. Thus we read about forsaking wrath (Ps 37:8), transgressions (Prov 28:13) and idols (Ezek 20:8). The classic passage is Isaiah 55:7: "Let the wicked forsake their way, and the unrighteous their thoughts; let them return to the LORD, that he may have mercy on them, and to our God, for he will abundantly pardon" (NRSV).

We might say that in the Bible the ultimate consolation is to know that one is not forsaken by God (approximately ten references). The ultimate ignominy is to forsake God or his ways (nearly twenty references). The ultimate horror is to be forsaken by God (2 Chron 29:6; Ps 22:1; Mt 27:46).

See also FOREIGNER; ORPHAN; WANDERER, WANDERING; WIDOW.

FORTRESS, STRONGHOLD

OT battle stories have as one of their staples fortresses—thick-walled cities, often on high mountains, meant to be impenetrable and intimidating to enemies. Yet of the approximately thirty-five references to fortresses in English Bibles, most are metaphoric pictures of God and his acts of salvation.

The first mention of a fortress comes in the story of David's capturing *Zion, or *Jerusalem, from the Jebusites (2 Sam 5:6-7). David made this *city his capital: a great, prosperous, central fortress in Israel. David knew many fortresses first-hand, so when he calls the Lord his fortress, he is clearly picturing strong *walls and high defenses—a secure place where no evil can enter (2 Sam 22:2; Ps 18:2).

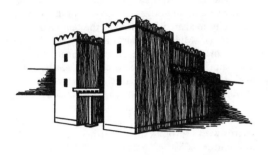

Artist's rendering of a fortresslike temple discovered at Sichem. Its walls were fifteen feet thick.

God often protected David physically, but when David and other OT writers call God their fortress, they primarily picture God as the unshakable strength of their souls, the source of hope and salvation that no *enemy—physical or spiritual—can ever threaten. David calls God "the strength of his people, a fortress of salvation" (Ps 28:8 NIV). Psalm 62 is a song about finding rest for the soul: "He alone is my rock and my salvation; he is my fortress, I will never be shaken" (Ps 62:2 NIV). In this psalm David uses the metaphor of a besieged fortress to picture himself, with "leaning walls and tottering fence"; his enemies "fully intend to topple him" (Ps 62:3-4). He may be referring to assaults on his kingship in his later years. And yet he looks to the God of his salvation as a refuge and a fortress in which he can place all his trust.

Often *rock and fortress are used together to refer to God (2 Sam 22:2; Ps 18:2; 31:3; 71:3). Fortified cities were built, if possible, high on a cliff or *mountain, with the rock providing an unshakable foundation and impenetrable defense. Isaiah accuses the Israelites of forgetting God their Savior: "You have not remembered the Rock, your fortress" (Is 17:10 NIV). Without their Rock, he tells them, they will fall to the enemy, both physically and spiritually, and the fortress of Jerusalem will be abandoned (Is 32:14). In a similar vein Nahum compares the fortress of godless Nineveh to fig trees that will spill their ripe fruit into the hands of the enemies who shake them; its gates will be wide open to its enemies (Nahum 3:12-13). By contrast, "he who fears the

Lord has a secure fortress" (Prov 14:26 NIV).

Images of fortresses in Scripture turn our eyes from earthly cities, which fall and decay, to a heavenly city, Mount Zion, the New Jerusalem described in Revelation 21. That city has a "great, high wall," thick and shining with gold and precious stones. Its gates will never be shut, and "nothing impure will ever enter it" (Rev 21:12, 17-21, 25-27). The enemy will finally be conquered, and God will rule there forever. Scripture pictures this God as the only fortress in which we can surely rest our souls as we look for the eternal city.

See also CITY; JERUSALEM; MOUNTAIN; REFUGE; ROCK; WALL; ZION.

FORTY

The period of forty days or years is an important one in Scripture and in Jewish tradition. As the church fathers observed, it is most often associated with hardship, *affliction and punishment (cf. Augustine, *De Con. Ev.* 2.4.8-9; *see* Crime and Punishment). The flood of *judgment in Noah's day lasts forty days (Gen 7:4). So does the *fasting of Moses (Ex 24:18; Deut 9:9) and Elijah (1 Kings 19:8). The generation in the *wilderness wanders for forty years (Ex 16:35; Ps 95:10). Israel is in the hand of the Philistines for forty years (Judg 13:1). Forty days is the length of time Ezekiel lies on his side to symbolize the punishment of Judah (Ezek 4:6). *Jonah prophesies that Nineveh will be destroyed in forty days—a prophecy which proves to be contingent because the forty days become a period of repentance that nullifies the forecast (Jon 3:4).

Forty is usually just a round number or estimation, not a precise reckoning. The ancients, who had neither wristwatches nor appointment books and did not live with technology's demand for exact numbers, did not in general share our preoccupation with numerical or chronological precision. There is only one absolute date in the entire rabbinic corpus—the Messiah will come 4231 years after creation (*b. 'Aboda Zara* 9b). The NT, like Plato, supplies only relative dates: things are placed successively, not on a time line. To judge from ancient Jewish epitaphs, people often did not even accurately know their own age: the excessive number of tombstones with ages ending in zero or five show that often just a round estimate was made. The lack of numerical exactness explains why in the Bible *three, *seven, and forty appear with inordinate frequency: three is a few, seven a few more, and forty a lot more. These numbers are approximations. Matthew can even use "three days and three nights" for the time Jesus is in the tomb, from Friday evening until Sunday morning (12:40). In accord with this sort of imprecision, forty days means a relatively long time (e.g., 1 Sam 17:16; Acts 1:3); as does forty years (Judg 3:11; Acts 4:22; 7:23). There are, however, occasional instances in which forty seems to be a precise reckoning (e.g., forty stripes, Deut 25:3; cf. 2 Cor 11:24).

In Matthew 4:2 Jesus' experience of "forty days

and forty nights" recapitulates Israel's forty years in the wilderness. Like Israel he is *tempted by hunger (Ex 16:1-8), tempted to put God to the test (Ex 17:1-3) and tempted to *idolatry (Ex 32). Furthermore, in his answers to *Satan, Jesus quotes from Deuteronomy 6:13, 16 and 8:3—texts about Israel's wilderness experience. Most commentators, beginning with Irenaeus, also find a deliberate allusion to the lengthy fasts of Moses and Elijah: these too last "forty days and forty nights."

See also FASTING; FIRST; FIVE; FOUR; HUNDRED; ONE; SEVEN; SEVENTY; THREE, THIRD; TWELVE; TWO; WILDERNESS.

FOUND. *See* FIND, FOUND.

FOUNDATION

The Hebrew verb *yāsad* ("establish," "found," "fix"), with its various derivatives and NT equivalents, refers to the founding or establishing of *cities and *buildings, especially *temples, according to prescribed plans. The plans, known by revelation and tradition, included consequences that made them apt illustrations for the security of godliness or the perils of wickedness. As one might expect, the bases of structures such as *altars and the foundation *stones of buildings or city *walls are primarily in view (Acts 16:26; Rev 21:14; Is 54:11-12). Similarly, the author of Hebrews alludes to foundational doctrines as the basis of spiritual maturity (Heb 6:1, *themelios*) and the male seed as the basis of a covenantal household (Heb 11:11, *katabolē*); and Paul speaks of an initial group of converts as a foundation of ministry (Rom 15:20; 1 Cor 3:10-16). Biblical buildings and cities were only as substantial as their foundations, which were symbolically related to the behavior of the people. Thus houses and walls might be impressively painted, yet without deep foundations they were flimsy and insecure. In catastrophic judgments the "exposure of foundations" meant complete destruction (Deut 32:22; Ps 18:15; Ezek 13:14; Lk 6:49).

Literal usage in the Bible focused on the construction of temples and cities (e.g., 1 Kings 16:24). Solomon's temple was built on large blocks of high quality stone (1 Kings 5:17; 6:37; 7:10). The foundation of the postexilic temple was celebrated as an assurance of the enduring love of the Lord for Israel (Ezra 3:6-12; 1 Chron 16:34; Zech 4:9; 8:9) as well as a prophetic exhortation to consider the ethical implications of the occasion (Hag 2:15-19). The sacral significance of the founding of a temple or city was mentioned negatively with Jericho, where because of child sacrifice a curse was pronounced by Joshua that was fulfilled in Ahab's reign (1 Kings 16:34).

The figurative meaning is an architectural metaphor that pictures God as the Creator of the *earth (*see* Cosmology) and the builder of his promised city and family/nation. The literal and figurative nuances are mediated by passages that refer to the Lord as the ultimate builder of *Zion and its temple in which his

people are to find *refuge (Is 14:32; 44:28). Metaphorically, the primary builder is divine rather than human; the blueprint is God's plan or decree; and the "structure" is personalized as creation, the household of God or individuals. The heavens and the earth belong to the Lord because he founded them and sovereignly governs everything in them according to his eternal plan (Ps 24:2; 78:69; 89:11[12]; 102:26; 104:5; Prov 3: 19; Is 48:13; 51:13, 16). History unfolded the divine purposes of creation so that truths were progressively revealed that have been hidden since the foundation (creation) of the world (Ps 78:2; Mt 13:35).

In the ancient Near East, temples of the sovereign deities were thought of as microcosms of the world. The deity mediated life through the temple in the "center" (*see* Middle, Center) of the city, which was in turn the "center" of the earth. The image was of the temple and city as the navel (*omphalos*) of the world. In truth, this was Yahweh's right by creation through his temple in Zion (Ps 48; Ezek 5:5). Life and security were to be found in his word and city; thus the people of God had a secure hope based on his trustworthy promises. Though they may have had to live in tents like Abraham, by faith they were to look "forward to the city with foundations [in antithesis to ungodly alternatives], whose architect and builder is God" (Heb 11:10 NIV; Rev 21:14, 19). This kind of faith in God's word was as secure as founding one's house (life) on bedrock (Lk 6:46-49), and it evidenced the Father's election of believers in Christ from the foundation (creation) of the world (Mt 25:34; Eph 1:4; 2 Tim 2:19; Heb 4:31). The notions of plans, policies or resolutions as the basis of events and relationships applied as well to human rulers who formed enclaves against the Lord and his anointed ruler (Ps 2:2; 31:13) and who determined policies for their people (1 Chron 9:22; Esther 1:8; 8—9).

Peter and Paul give the architectural metaphor its most complete expression. 1 Peter 2:6 quotes Isaiah 28:16, which was a message of judgment to the proud *drunkards of Ephraim (Is 28:1) and the scoffers of Jerusalem (Is 28:14), who boasted about their respective covenants with false gods as refuges from the Assyrian scourge. God laid a precious, tested *cornerstone in Zion, the place of his presence, as a sure foundation for faithful believers (cf. Ps 48:8). That stone, said Peter, was now Christ (NT references agree with the LXX's messianic addition "in him"), the unique son of the only living God (Mt 16:18), who was crucified by men but chosen by the Father and precious to him and believers (cf. Jn 17:5, 24; 1 Pet 1:19-20; Rev 13:8). Believers, Peter adds, are living stones that are building a spiritual house (the new temple), offering acceptable sacrifices based on historically validated faith and hope. The corner/foundation stone (*themelios*) functionally determined the basis and orientation of the building, so that God's blueprint for creation and redemption rested on the accomplishments of Christ. Peter added a quotation from Psalm 118:22 to affirm that God's foundation stone that unbelievers had rejected had become the capstone of completion that vindicated believers and condemned unbelievers according to the decree of God (also quoting Is 8:14). In short, Jesus is both foundation of God's holy city and fulfiller of its blueprint by securing believers according to the divine plan.

In Romans 9:32-33 Paul conflated Isaiah 8:14 and 28:16 to underscore Israel's lack of faith. Ephesians 2:20-21 welcomed all believers to God's household that is being built on Christ as cornerstone and the apostles and prophets as foundation stones (also Mt 16:18). The personalized temple is being built on and in Christ to become indwelt by the Holy Spirit.

In summary, God's plan for creation is the basis or foundation of the heavens and the earth, the nation, Zion and its temple, which are fulfilled in Christ, who is completing the plan through chosen believers. The new creation and holy city in Revelation 21 confirm the security of faith, hope and love in the household of God (1 Tim 6:17-19). All alternatives to these truths are "houses built of clay on foundations of dust" (Job 4:19).

See also BUILD, BUILDING; CITY; CORNERSTONE; COSMOLOGY; ROCK; STONE; TEMPLE; ZION.

FOUNTAIN

A *fountain* is a stream of *water; it is specifically a source of water. As such it is very similar to two other English words, *well* and *spring*, both treated separately in the dictionary. Indeed, most English translations are somewhat arbitrary in their translation of a number of Hebrew and Greek words into one of these three English equivalents.

The word *fountain*, like well and especially spring, is associated with the general biblical image of water as life. Since the fountain more precisely indicates the source or origin of water, its figurative use often means source of life. As such, it is not at all surprising that Psalm 36:9 refers to God as the "fountain of life" (NIV). The context of the psalm is God's sustaining his creatures through *food and *drink and also through his protection.

*Zion's reputation as the location of the *temple, the symbol of God's presence with his people, surely explains the reference in Psalm 87:7 where the psalmist happily exclaims, "All my fountains are in Zion." That is, Zion, the place where the faithful meet their God, is the source of their life.

In the book of Proverbs wisdom and its derivatives are associated with the "fountain of life." Proverbs 13:14 specifies the "teaching of the wise" as a fountain of life, and Proverbs 18:4 has an interesting twist on this theme when it describes not the fountain of life but the "fountain of wisdom" as a "bubbling book." Elsewhere phenomena associated with wisdom, for instance the "mouth of the righteous" (Prov 10:11 NIV) and "understanding" (Prov 16:22 NIV), are called a "fountain of life." That wisdom is

connected with the source of life is not at all surprising in light of the close connection between God and wisdom in that book. Indeed, Proverbs 14:27 makes this clear when it brings together the "fear of the LORD" (called the "beginning of knowledge" in Prov 1:7) with the "fountain of life" (NIV).

Though the most frequent use of the fountain image is found in its connection with God, other associations are also made. It is, for instance, an important image for a woman. Here again the fountain image is similar and is often used hand in hand with well and spring imagery. In Proverbs 5:18, the reader is encouraged to allow his wife to be a fountain of blessing. The context is obviously *sexual, and the allusion is to the woman's vagina, a well-watered place, which also is the source of human life (see also Song 4:12, where a different Hebrew word is used).

Sometimes the image simply implies an abundance of water and fits in with that general image's function as a metaphor for life or cleansing. For instance, see Joel 3:18 in the context of an eschatological salvation oracle that envisions God's people as the recipients of fertility and *blessing, whereas in the next verse God's enemies live in desolation. Zechariah 13:1 also begins an eschatological salvation oracle describing a fountain that will be opened and that will cleanse David and the inhabitants of Jerusalem.

Jeremiah uses the dual image of spring and fountain when he describes the depth of his grief at the sight of the suffering of his people. In Jeremiah 9:1 he rhetorically expresses his wish that his head become a "spring of water" and his eyes "a fountain of tears" (NIV).

See also BROOK; RIVER; SPRING OF WATER; WATER; WELL.

FOUR

Grouping objects or phrases in fours is a Hebrew literary technique used to picture universality. Just as naming the extreme points of *east, *west, *north and *south suggests everything else between, so biblical sets of four elements or poetic lines serve as an image indicating universal participation or including aspects not specifically mentioned.

Isaiah 58 offers an elaborate example. Verses 6 to 8 give four generalized aspects of justice (as God's fast), four specific acts of compassion and (borrowing Exodus imagery) four consequent blessings. Verses 9 and 10 together cite four blessings and four actions chiastically (i.e., the first two and last two lines promise, and the middle four lines command). Because they occur in fours, the specific examples imply all others.

Some of the completeness associated with four has a spatial or geographic basis. The four directions, for example, yield four *winds (ten references) and four corners of the earth (Rev 7:1). Rectangular courts or buildings have four sides (Ezek 42:20) and four corners (Ezek 46:21).

The number four occurs so often in apocalyptic

visions like Daniel, Ezekiel and Revelation that they constitute a category by themselves. We read variously about four beasts, four heads, four kings, four living creatures, four angels, four horns. In some passages the main meaning seems to be completeness or supremacy. Ezekiel's visions begin with four living beings, whose four faces reveal creation's superiorities—humankind, *lion (wild beasts), *ox (domestic animals) and *eagle (birds of the air). Representing universal worship, they support the crystal expanse under God's throne. Four somewhat similar living creatures appear in Revelation to portray universal observation (full all around with eyes) and adoration (not ceasing to praise) (Rev 4:6-8). Beyond the meaning of completeness, the prevalence of four in apocalyptic visions may convey a mystic aura for supernatural events and settings.

Another concentration of the imagery of four occurs in the descriptions of the OT *tabernacle (Ex 25—39), where again the associations may combine completeness and mystical aura. We thus read about four rings of gold, four cups, four pillars, four horns, four bronze rings and four rows of precious stones (see Jewels and Precious Stones).

The number four appears in what has come to be called a "number parallelism" in Amos 1—2 and Proverbs 30. Amos gives the reader a series of judgment speeches against various nations and begins by noting "for three sins . . . even for four." He then goes on and explicitly describes only one or two offenses. However, the intended effect of the parallelism is to impress the reader that there are many other unspecified sins at issue here. The nations have "gone over the top" and thus deserve their judgment.

Another prominent four is the refrain in Revelation of every "tribe, tongue, people and nation" gathered as God's people. A foursome is named with various patterns in Revelation 5:9; 7:9; 10:11; 11:9; 13:7; 14:6 and 17:15—each time to underscore acceptance or rebellion, the universal possibility of God's salvation or judgment upon those resisting God's comprehensive grace.

See also FASTING; FIRST; FIVE; FORTY; HUNDRED; ONE; SEVEN; SEVENTY; THREE, THIRD; TWELVE; TWO.

FOX. See ANIMALS.

FREEDOM. See BONDAGE AND FREEDOM.

FRIENDSHIP

A number of features of biblical friendship are conventional if compared to ancient cultures in general. In the classical tradition, for example, conventions prescribed that friends (1) are equals and are similar in class, interests and character, (2) share *meals and spend time together and (3) follow virtue. While not explicitly stated, these motifs are present in biblical pictures of friendship as well. One of the psalmists, for example, speaks of "my bosom friend in whom I trusted, who ate of my bread" (Ps 41:9 RSV), and another psalmist addresses his friend as "you, my equal, my companion, my familiar friend. We used to hold sweet converse together; within God's house we walked in fellowship" (Ps 55:13-14 RSV).

In both classical and biblical traditions, a friend was a support and a counselor. For example, "a friend loves at all times" (Prov 17:17 RSV); that is, even in bad times. Again, "faithful are the wounds [criticisms] of a friend" (Prov 27:6 RSV); and "the pleasantness of one's friend springs from his earnest counsel" (Prov 27:9 NIV). But as in classical culture, biblical writers also think in terms of the category of false friends who give bad counsel or betray, such as Job's "comforters" or Judas, whom Jesus calls "friend" (Mt 26:50; see also 2 Sam 13:3; Ps 41:9; 55:12-14; Jer 38:22; Lam 1:2; Mic 7:5). The disciples in their abandonment of Jesus and Peter in his denial likewise enact the familiar category of friends who prove faithless in the time of crisis.

The classical tradition held a special place for friendship between males, and we catch hints of this exaltation of male friendship in the Bible too. In his elegy for Jonathan, *David asserts that his friendship with Jonathan meant more to him than his relations with any of the women in his life: "Your love to me was wonderful, passing the love of women" (2 Sam 1:26 RSV). Similarly, the most famous NT example of friendship, that between *Jesus and his disciples, involves a masculine group. Even so supreme a precept as one's willingness to die for a friend, extolled in various classical sources referring to Damon and Pythias or Pylades and Orestes, is paralleled by Christ's teaching, "Greater love has no man than this, that a man lay down his life for his friends" (Jn 15:13 RSV; see also 2 Sam 16:16-17 and 1 Chron 27:33).

Friendship with God. What, then, is distinctive about the biblical image of friendship? Aristotle thought there could be no friendship between a god and a man, any more than a man could be a friend to his slave or his tools, because they were too dissimilar in nature. But the Bible radically rejects secular thought on this point. Few things could be more unnatural and incomprehensible to the pagan imagination than the willingness of the God who created the universe out of nothing to become a friend of mortals whose lives are a mere breath. The whole plan of salvation is an act of friendship whereby God took on human likeness so that people might take on his likeness, transforming *enemies into friends (Phil 2:5-8; Heb 2:17; 1 Jn 3:2). The high point of this motif is Jesus' statement to his disciples, "No longer do I call you servants . . . but I have called you friends" (Jn 15:15 RSV).

Friendship with God goes beyond simply the personal *loyalty implied by any friendship; it includes faith and obedience as well. The psalmist states forthrightly that "the friendship of the LORD is for those who fear him" (Ps 25:14 RSV). In three scripture references Abraham is identified as the friend of God (2 Chron 20:7; Is 41:8; Jas 2:23). The last of these links God's friendship toward Abraham with

Abraham's *faith and actions of *obedience; indeed, Abraham is a byword for obedient faith. In the very conversation in which Jesus announced to his disciples that he considered them his friends, he added, "You are my friends if you do what I command you" (Jn 15:14). Friendship with God is thus not a friendship between equals, and the loyalty God expects has an exclusive quality that does not characterize human friendships. On the issue of allegiance, James wrote, "Do you not know that friendship with the world is enmity with God? Therefore whoever wishes to be a friend of the world makes himself an enemy of God" (Jas 4:4 RSV).

In other ways the friendship of God has the qualities of human friendship. Friendship implies favor toward one's friend, and the friendship of God entails just such favor, as witnessed by Job's statement late in his time of suffering that God's earlier favor toward him was the era when "the friendship of God was upon my tent" (Job 29:4 RSV). Friendship implies the sharing of information about oneself. Psalm 25:14 links the friendship of God with the fact that God makes his covenant known to his friends.

The Imagery of Friendship. The Bible uses two consistent images in its representation of friendship. The first is *the knitting of souls*. Deuteronomy provides the earliest mention of this category of a "friend who is as your own soul" (Deut 13:6 RSV), a companion of one's inmost thoughts and feelings, resulting in an intense emotional attachment. It is well illustrated by Jonathan and David's friendship: "The soul of Jonathan was knit to the soul of David, and Jonathan loved him as his own soul" (1 Sam 18:1 RSV; cf. 20:17). Characteristic expressions of this union of hearts are an affectionate embrace or *kiss, *weeping, gift-giving and *vows of loyalty. After the slaying of Goliath, Jonathan made a covenant with David, and the gestures of friendship were Jonathan's giving David the gifts of his robe, *armor and *weapons (1 Sam 18:3-4). David and Jonathan also pledged to protect each other's families after either one's death (1 Sam 20:11-16), a promise David subsequently kept by giving sanctuary to Jonathan's son Mephibosheth (2 Sam 9). Later, when Saul's wrath required David to flee, there was a moving departure scene between the soul-mates: "They kissed one another, and wept with one another," departing in peace because they had sworn in the name of the Lord that God would bind them and their descendants forever (1 Sam 20:41-42).

Examples of this kind of friendship in the NT are chiefly identified by use of the word *philia,* the Greek term for friendship, and its cognates. Characteristics similar to the friendship of Jonathan and David's are evident in such friendship. Jesus wept for the death of Lazarus, whom he called "our friend Lazarus" (Jn 11:11). In the same account, the Greek word for friend is used to describe Jesus' love for his friend Lazarus (Jn 11:3, 35-36). Jesus and John "the disciple whom Jesus loved" (Jn 20:2) embraced freely (Jn

13:23), and Jesus made a covenant with him to look after his mother after his death (Jn 19:26-27). One sign of the "soul-knit" relationship between believers in the NT is the greeting with a "holy kiss" (Rom 16:16; 1 Cor 16:20; 2 Cor 13:12; 1Thess 5:26; 1Pet 5:14). Given such familiarity, "friend" naturally became another name for believers or brothers in the Lord: "The friends greet you. Greet the friends, every one of them" (3 Jn 15 RSV). The privileges and roles of a biblical soul mate, then, involve intimacy, loyalty and a strong emotional attachment.

The second image that the Bible uses to represent friendship is *the face-to-face encounter,* an "interface." This is literally the image used for Moses' relationship to God: in the tabernacle God spoke to Moses "*face to face, as a man speaks to his friend" (Ex. 33:11; see also Num. 12:8). The face-to-face image implies a conversation, a sharing of confidences and consequently a meeting of minds, goals and direction. In three scripture verses Abraham is identified as "the friend of God" (2 Chron 20:7; Is 41:8; Jas 2:23). Behind the epithet may lie the event of Abraham's hosting of three angelic visitors, one of whom was God (Gen 18). Following the meal, after the two angels had proceeded to Sodom to warn Lot, God takes Abraham into his confidence, asking himself, "Shall I hide from Abraham what I am about to do?" (Gen 18:20). God and Abraham then engage in a dialogue based on the intimacy of friends, with the imagery of Abraham's drawing near to God (Gen 18:23; *see* Near, Drawing Near) and the give-and-take dialogue in which Abraham and God deliberate over the fate of Sodom. A form of friendship is implied, surely, by the NT image of the believer's one day seeing God "face to face" (1 Cor 13:12).

One of the benefits of face-to-face encounters between friends is the heightened insight and stimulation that such encounters produce. A proverb that highlights this mutual sense of well-being is the famous one in Proverbs 27:17: "Iron sharpens iron, and one friend sharpens another" (KJV). This is similar to the statement of English Renaissance essayist Francis Bacon that conversation makes a "ready" person—ready for the world, ready for practical action.

Summary. Friendship entails responsibilities and benefits. The proverb that "a friend loves at all times" (Prov 17:17) expresses both an obligation and a benefit. In a similar vein is the proverb that "there are friends who pretend to be friends, but there is a friend who sticks closer than a brother" (Prov 18:24 RSV). In the Bible friendship is a mutual improvement activity, honing one for godly use. Biblical friendship is a face-to-face encounter, signifying proximity, intimate revelation and honesty. It is also a bonding of affections and trust, knitting one's very soul to another. In its ultimate reaches, it is union with God.

See also ENEMY; FAMILY; LOYALTY; NEAR, DRAWING NEAR.

FRUIT, FRUITFULNESS

Not counting three dozen occurrences of *fruitful,* the word *fruit* appears more than two hundred times in English translations. Three main meanings are discernible: (1) fruit in the modern sense of a specific food group, linked especially with fruit *trees (Gen 1:11; Neh 9:25; Ps 148:9; Eccles 2:5; Is 17:6); (2) the edible product of any tree or *plant (Gen 3:2-6; Ex 10:15); (3) by metaphoric extension, the result of an action, including offspring as the result of sexual relations.

References to fruit in the Bible portray it as either good or bad. According to a famous statement made by Jesus in the Sermon on the Mount, "Every sound tree bears good fruit, but the bad tree bears evil fruit" (Mt 7:17-19 RSV; Lk 6:43; see also Mt 3:10; Lk 3:9). This dualism is present already in the *Garden of Eden. While satisfying the human appetite through eating of the fruit of the garden is good in itself, the fruit of the forbidden tree is invested with the potential to bring *death into the universe. The primal sin consists of *Eve's eating the fruit of the forbidden tree and giving some to her husband, who also eats (Gen 3:6). However we understand this fruit, the outcome of tasting it is *shame (Gen 3:7 cf. 2:25), *pain, *suffering and ultimately death (Gen 3:16-19). Here, surely, is the archetypal bad fruit of human experience.

If the forbidden fruit has overtones of the supernatural, so does the fruit that appears in the celestial paradise at the end of the Bible. Flowing through the middle of the new Jerusalem is "the river of the water of life," and on either side of the river is "the tree of life with its twelve kinds of fruit, yielding its fruit each month" (Rev 22:1-2 RSV; cf. Ezek 47:12; *see* Tree of Life). Its fruits serve for the healing of the nations, symbolic of abundant life and a reversal of the Fall of Genesis 3. Here, surely, is the archetypal good fruit of human experience.

Fruit as an Image of Abundance. Abundant fruit is symbolic of the richness and creativity of God. The world as created by God was prolific in its fruitfulness: "fruit trees bearing fruit in which is their seed" (Gen 1:11-12) and "every tree with seed in its fruit" (Gen 1:29). Jeremiah links three of the most evocative OT images of richness when he lists "wine and summer fruits and oil" (Jer 40:10, 12).

As an image of *abundance and divine *blessing, fruit is conspicuously present in descriptions of the superiority of the Promised *Land, which is repeatedly portrayed as abundantly fruitful (Ex 3:8; Num 12:27; Deut 8:8). When the twelve spies return, the proof of the land's desirability is "fruit of the land" (Num 13:26). The fruitfulness of the land is linked to covenant obedience. An obedient Israel could expect God to preserve the fruitfulness of the land: "the land will yield its fruit, and you will eat your fill" (Lev 25:19 RSV). *Prosperity was expected (1 Kings 4:25). Even in time of war, fruit trees were not to be destroyed (Deut 20:19-20). When Nehemiah recalls the superiority of the Promised Land, the picture includes "vineyards, olive orchards and fruit trees in abundance" (Neh 9:25). Disobedience, however, leads to God's judgment upon the land of Israel (Jer 4:26), as upon the land of other nations (e.g., Is 10:18; Jer 48:33).

By extension, both *children (Gen 30:2; Deut 7:13; Mic 6:7; Ps 21:11; Is 13:18; Lk 1:42) and offspring of animals (Deut 28:4, 11; 30:9) are described as fruit. Human fertility is both the promise (Gen 17:6; 28:3; 48:4) and the command of God (Gen 1:22, 28; 8:17; 9:1, 7). In this sense a *wife can be described as a "fruitful vine" (Ps 128:3). Children are "the fruit of the *womb" and as such "a heritage from the LORD" (Ps 127:3).

A summary of fruit as a supreme image of earthly abundance is found in Moses' picture of how "the LORD your God will make you abundantly prosperous in all the work of your hand, in the fruit of your body, and in the fruit of your cattle, and in the fruit of your ground" (Deut 30:9 RSV; cf. 28:11).

First Fruits. Fruit also figures prominently in the OT ceremonial laws. Fruit trees were regarded as unclean for the first three years. The crop of the fourth year was described as the first fruits and belonged to the Lord (*see* First). From the fifth year on the fruit could be eaten.

Because everything belongs ultimately to God, the first ripening of the *harvest was ritually offered to him (e.g., Is 28:4; Jer 24:2; Mic 7:1). This extended to children (Ex 13:2-16) and *animals (Num 3:12-16). The metaphor is used to describe Israel (Jer 2:3). To consume the first fruits as any other crop would be to profane it, for it was regarded as sacred (Lev 19:23-25; cf. Deut 20:6; 28:30; Jer 31:5; Neh 10:35-36).

The *resurrection of Jesus is described by Paul as "the first fruits of those who have fallen asleep" (1 Cor 15:20, 23 RSV), clearly with an eye both to his chronological priority and to the expected messianic abundance. By extension, the *Holy Spirit is described as the first fruits (Rom 8:23). We might compare this with Paul's description of the Spirit as a "guarantee" (2 Cor 1:22; Eph 1:13-14) of a greater amount to follow.

Metaphoric Extensions. The consequences of an action are frequently described as its fruit (Jer 17:10). Creation is the fruit of God's work (Ps 104:13). In later Judaism, especially, the righteous person was described as bearing good fruit (Prov 31:31; Is 3:10), while the unrighteous person would bear bad fruit (Prov 1:31; Jer 6:19; 21:14; Hos 10:13; Mic 7:13). The tongue is capable of bearing both good and *evil fruit (Prov 12:14; 18:20). Heresy leads to unfruitfulness (Jude 12). Conversely, prayer and worship are described metaphorically as the fruit of the *lips (e.g., Prov 12:14; 13:2; 18:20; Is 57:18; Heb 13:15).

Bearing fruit is an archetype for righteous living in OT wisdom literature. Psalm 1:3 sounds the keynote, describing the godly person as "a tree planted by streams of water, that yields its fruit in its season" (RSV; cf. Jer 17:7-8). In the NT, Matthew, especially, draws upon such imagery from the wisdom tradition. John the Baptist urges the fruit of repentance and warns that unfruitful trees will be cut down and burnt (Mt 3:8-10). Jesus himself confirms this judgment and points out that false prophets can be identified in the same way as trees are identified, by their fruit (Mt 7:15-20; cf. 12:33). Seed that has been sown on good ground is extremely fruitful (Mt 13:23). Ultimately the kingdom belongs to those who produce its fruit (Mt 21:43). James draws upon the same wisdom tradition (Jas 3:17).

Paul uses the metaphor of a fruitful harvest to describe the outcome of his own ministry (Rom 1:13). For Paul continuance in life promises further fruitful labor (Phil 1:22). The gospel, like righteousness, bears fruit (Col 1:6, 10). In terms of behavior Paul echoes the language of the wisdom writings, writing of the "fruit of the *light" and the "unfruitful works of *darkness" (Eph 5:8ff). In Hebrews discipline "yields the peaceful fruit of righteousness to those who have been trained by it" (Heb 12:11 RSV).

Literal fruitfulness is, of course, dependent on an adequate sources of water. Thus *water becomes a potent metaphor for the Spirit (Ezek 47:1-12; Jn 7:37-39).

In Galatians 5:22-23 Paul employs the image of the "fruit of the Spirit" to describe the workings of God's Spirit in contrast to the "works of the flesh" (Gal 5:17-21). Here Paul draws an intended contrast between the naturally growing fruit of God's Spirit and the sin that is the outcome of humanity's actions independent of God.

*Thorns and thistles enter the scene following the spoiling of the Garden of Eden through sin (Gen 3:17-19). They represent the encroachment of untamed nature. They can be the result of idleness (Prov 24:30-31) or the judgment on a city (Is 34:13). In either case, creation is out of control. The nature miracles of Jesus give some idea of what might have been had sin not intervened (e.g., Mk 4:35-41; 6:30-44; Jn 2:1-11; cf. Heb 2:8-9). Metaphorically speaking, unfruitfulness strangles spiritual life and vigor (e.g. Mk 4:7,18-19). Isaiah describes Israel as unable to bear the fruit expected of her (Is 5:2, 4). The unfruitful *fig tree, representing Israel, is cursed by Jesus (Mk 11:12-14, 20-25; Mt 21:18-22). The unwholesome consequences of idolatry and injustice are referred to a "wormwood," a notoriously bitter and poisonous fruit (Deut 29:18; Amos 5:7; 6:12), which can spread throughout the whole community of Israel.

See also ABUNDANCE; FIG, FIG TREE; FIRST; FOOD; GARDEN; GRAPES; HARVEST; TREE, TREES; TREE OF LIFE; VINE, VINEYARD.

FUGITIVE. *See* RUNAWAY.

FULLNESS. *See* FILL, FULLNESS.

FUNERAL. *See* BURIAL, FUNERAL.

FURNACE. *See* REFINING.

G

GABRIEL. *See* ANNUNCIATION.

GALATIANS, LETTER TO THE

Galatians is a lively letter of rebuke and correction in which the readers are addressed in direct and arresting language. In its sustained interaction with the ideas and motives of his opponents, who threaten to lead the Galatians astray from the true gospel, Paul's letter burns with the heat of conflict and sparks an array of colorful imagery.

Bondage and Rescue. Galatians begins with the remembrance that Christ in his death has "set us free from the present evil age" (Gal 1:4 NRSV). The motif of *bondage, imprisonment or enslavement to a power or situation beyond human deliverance is one that recurs throughout the letter. It describes the human plight of bondage outside of Christ, a condition to which the Galatians risk returning. As for the Jews, who are under the law, "the Scripture" has "consigned," "hemmed in," or "imprisoned" *(synkleiō)* all things under the power of *sin (Gal 3:22). Before faith arrived, Israel was "held in custody" *(ephrouroumetha)* and "locked up," or "consigned" *(synkleiō),* under the law (Gal 3:23; 4:4-5). This situation is also pictured as "enslavement" *(dedoulōmenoi)* to taskmasters known as the "elements," or preferably, "elemental spirits of the world" *(stoicheia tou kosmou,* Gal 4:3, 8-9). These spirits are otherwise depicted in an image reflecting the Galatians' pagan past when they were subject to "beings by nature not gods," which Paul can also call "weak and beggarly elements" (Gal 4:8-9). The picture of enslavement is completed with the image of "works" associated with life under the *law, the keeping of laws and regulations regarding *circumcision, *food, *days, months and years (Gal 2:16; 3:2, 5, 10; 6:4; cf. 4:10).

Into this bleak world of enslavement a mighty deliverer was subversively and quietly "sent," "born of a woman, born under the law, in order to redeem those who were under the law" (Gal 4:4-5 NRSV). The image of redemption recalls Israel's release from slavery in Egypt. Christ, like a new Moses (and born like Moses, within Israel under bondage), has brought about a new exodus. Why, asks Paul, would these Gentiles, "formerly enslaved" *(edoulousate)* and now "set free from the present evil age," submit again to this "yoke of slavery" (Gal 5:1)? It is as if

*Israel were to return to *Egypt, a band of slaves return to their cruel master.

Family and Household. Paul's letters consistently evoke the picture of believers as a *family, and this aspect is well developed in Galatians. We must first envision a large, prosperous household in the ancient Mediterranean world, with numerous family members of extended relationships, household slaves and even ancestors whose memories can be evoked. The household Paul addresses is the "household of faith" (Gal 6:10) whose members are his "brothers and sisters" *(adelphoi,* literally, "brothers," carries this inclusive sense: Gal 1:11; 3:15; 4:12, 28, 31; et al.), whom Paul, as elder brother, can address as "little children" (Gal 4:19). They have all been adopted (Gal 4:5) into this household as "children" *(hyioi,* literally "sons," Gal 4:5-7) of God, and by his Spirit they are enabled to call God their "Abba, Father" (Gal 4:6). As children they are now heirs. This family status is new-found and a quantum leap forward, for formerly they were slaves—both Jews and Greeks—in bondage to the present age. Now within their new family the old human distinctions are broken down; there is neither "Jew nor Greek," "slave nor free," "male and female," but all are one in Christ (Gal 3:28). This image of a household merges into the ideal of a new humanity, for it is "a new creation" that erases and supplants a human community fractured along the line drawn between "circumcision" and "uncircumcision" (Gal 6:15). Christ is Lord (Gal 1:3) of this household, and Paul regards himself as a "servant of Christ." The Galatians can observe and judge for themselves whether Paul has lately turned his back on his master to please someone else (Gal 1:10).

Paul again employs the picture of a household as he gives the Galatians a lesson in genealogy and traces the ancestry of this new family *not* through the lineage of the "slave woman" Hagar but through the "free woman" Sarah (Gal 4:22-26), for "she is our mother" (Gal 4:26). Those who preach a "different gospel" are of a different lineage of Abraham—through Hagar and not through Sarah. As descendants of Abraham (Gal 3:7), "Abraham's offspring, heirs according to the promise" (Gal 3:29 NRSV), the Galatians are descendants of the "free woman," a household characterized by freedom. The same "false brothers" *(pseudadelphoi)* who in Jerusalem "slipped in to spy on the freedom we have in Christ Jesus, so that they might enslave us" (Gal 2:4 NRSV) are now active in Galatia. Paul did not submit to them in Jerusalem, and the Galatians should now look out for the same sinister infiltration of their household. Like their free ancestor, the Galatians are to "drive out the slave and her child" from their household, "for the child of the slave will not share the inheritance with the child of the free woman" (Gal 4:30 NRSV). This inheritance is nothing less than the kingdom of God (Gal 5:21).

The "right hand of fellowship" (Gal 2:9) is a sign of familial bonds that run deeper than differences within the family. But there are also images of estrangement from the family: "deserting" the one who called them (Gal 1:6), "alienating" themselves from Christ (Gal 5:4), or "falling away" from the grace of their divine patron (Gal 5:4). True family members will restore with a spirit of gentleness those who are caught in sin (Gal 6:1).

Again we find household imagery in the story of Israel under the law. Israel was like an heir who was still a minor. Though "lord of all the property" (Gal 4:1), Israel was no different than a slave. Until the "the appointed end of guardianship [prothesmia] set by the father" is reached, an heir is "under guardians and trustees" (Gal 4:2). The law was a "disciplinarian" (paidagōgos, Gal 3:24-25), a household servant entrusted with the supervision of the child's education and discipline. In the heat of Paul's conflict with the judaizers, this metaphor of minority status is more virulently portrayed as slavery under the "elemental spirits," or "basic principles [stoicheia]" that are "of this world" (Gal 4:3, see above; for the range of interpretations, see DPL, 229-33).

Covenant. The OT imagery associated with the divine *covenant plays an important role in Galatians. The covenant that God made with *Abraham and his offspring (Gen 15) was ratified by God and was not annulled by the law that came four hundred thirty years later (Gal 3:17). The inheritance of the original covenant was based on promises, not on law (Gal 3:18). Paul reinforces the security of the original covenant by taking an illustration from daily life (Gal 3:15), that of a human covenant (or possibly a "last will and testament," though the same term, diathēkē, is used in both Gal 3:15 and 17): once ratified, it cannot be altered or annulled. Paul calculates that this image will subvert the Judaizers' arguments and deployment of imagery, which probably presented Abraham as the first proselyte, who was given the commandment of circumcision (Gen 17:10) and in fact was obedient to the commands, decrees and laws of God (Gen 26:5). Paul demonstrates that the law was "added" later because of Israel's "transgressions" (Gal 3:19), but it did not override the previous covenant established on divine promises (Gal 3:21). In fact, Paul argues, the law was inferior in that it involved a mediator, *Moses, who stood in for the twelve tribes of Israel. But God is one (Gal 3:20), and he originally made a covenant di-

rectly with Abraham, the single progenitor of the one people of God constituted by faith (and not law) and the one "seed," Jesus Christ (see Wright).

If the law was added on account of transgressions, the result was that transgressions did in fact amass in Israel, as the national history recounts in detail. When Paul speaks of the *curse that falls on "everyone who does not observe and obey all the things written in the book of the law," he is recalling the covenant curses that would fall upon Israel if they were to break the covenant (Deut 27:26; 28:58-68). These curses did indeed fall upon Israel and culminated in the nation's *exile from the land of promise and blessing. The shadow of this curse still hung over Israel. Even though Israel had physically returned to the land, the time of renewal had not arrived. Paul finds the solution to this covenant dilemma in Jesus Christ, who as representative of Israel has taken upon himself the "curse of the law" and exhausted it in his death on the Roman cross, the accursed hanging "on a tree" (Gal 3:13; cf. Deut 21:23). With this obstacle of the law removed once and for all, the blessings promised to Abraham's true descendants flow freely, overpouring the banks of believing Israel and spilling out upon the Gentiles (Gal 3:14). The central image of Christ's death in Galatians is set firmly within the imagery field of the covenant.

Jerusalem and Sinai. Geographical images are overlaid with allegory in Galatians. Paul begins with Jerusalem as the symbolic center of Israel's history and now the widely regarded hub of the early Christian movement with its acknowledged leaders, James, Cephas and John (Gal 2:9). Paul retains the traditional Jewish imagery of "going up" (Gal 1:17, 18; 2:1) to *Jerusalem, but he also subverts the favored symbol of Jerusalem as the exalted *center of the world (cf. Is 2:2-3). His apostleship and gospel did not originate with Jerusalem's commission, authority or instruction but was received directly from God through Jesus Christ (Gal 1:1). It is a revelation (Gal 1:11-12, 16) from heaven. Paul is at pains to show that Jerusalem and its leaders exercise no centripetal force on him (Gal 1:18; 2:1-2), and he will not grant its leaders absolute authority or status as "pillars" (styloi, Gal 2:9) of the new *temple, the church.

This subversion of Jerusalem's place on the new map of the world is deepened by Paul's opposition to the work of the judaizers at Galatia. Set against the glossary of Scripture's imagery of Jerusalem, we see Paul invoking images reminiscent of prophetic denunciation. These judaizers are missionaries of a "different gospel" who claim to derive their warrant from Jerusalem. The sacred mount of Jerusalem finds its correspondence with "Mount Sinai in Arabia" (cf. Gal 1:17). This *mountain, revered in holy memory for its awesome revelation of God, the giving of the law and the disclosure of the sacred sanctuary with its functions, has now fallen under the shadow of a new and grander revelation.

Jerusalem, the fair-skinned "daughter *Zion" (Is 1:8), has taken on the tragic and weathered likeness of "Hagar, from Mount *Sinai, bearing children for slavery" (Gal 4:24). This image is akin to Isaiah's likening Zion, its walls evacuated by the exile, to an abandoned *wife (Is 49:14) or a bereaved and barren *mother (Is 49:20-21). The present Jerusalem, representing Torah-based religion, is still in exile with her children, born "according to the flesh."

Cutting and Crucifying the Flesh. Were Christian readers not so familiar with the text of Galatians, they might be repulsed by Paul's use of imagery associated with bodily markings and mutilation. *Circumcision is the central image, and as a verb or noun it appears thirteen times. Circumcision was the bodily marking that indicated membership in the covenant community for every male Israelite, and it was a practice that set Israel off from most of its Gentile neighbors. The Greek term for circumcision is *peritomē*, literally a "cutting around," in this case a ritual cutting off of the foreskin of the penis. It was a bloody and painful operation, and this dimension of the image should not be lost as we consider how it would have registered on the minds of the Gentile adult males who would have read or heard this letter. Circumcision was not practiced in the Hhellenistic Gentile world, where it was regarded as barbaric and perverse. But for Israel it was a holy rite filled with special meaning.

The judaizers had persuasively overridden Gentile revulsion and aversion to pain by promising eternal gain. But Paul subverts their arguments by exploiting the physical reality of the symbol and invoking some counter-imagery. The strength of his imagery is a testimony to the force of his rejection of this "fleshly" rite, an attitude that would have been unthinkable for the pre-Christian Paul. With earthy forthrightness he wishes that those who pressure the Galatians to be circumcised would go the whole way and castrate themselves (Gal 5:12). If the judaizers wish to promote fleshly mutilation, Paul can play their game: he has "the marks *[stigmata]* of Jesus branded" on his body (Gal 6:17 NRSV), the true bodily markings of a disciple of Christ. This image may carry reference to the actual physical scars left by his apostolic hardships and persecutions (e.g., 2 Cor 11:23-29), authentic signs of his allegiance to his crucified Lord. For Paul sees the bloody cross and fleshly mutilation of Christ as the bloody post on which the gate to the new creation pivots. By union with Christ, "the world has been crucified to me, and I to the world. For neither circumcision nor uncircumcision is anything; but a new creation is everything" (Gal 6:14-15 NRSV).

Those who preach circumcision are ashamed of the cross, the central symbol of fleshly mutilation, and wish to escape Jewish persecution for proclaiming the cross of Christ as the exclusive ground for entry into the people of God (see Col 2:11-12, where identification with Christ's death is partaking in the "circumcision of Christ"; cf. Eph 2:11, 13). The echo of a story of *David (1 Sam 18:25-27) may be faintly overheard in the judaizers' boast in the Galatians' "flesh," their collection of Gentile foreskins (Gal 6:12-13). Paul remembers with fondness the Galatians' former and honorable willingness to tear out their own eyes and give them to Paul for the sake of the gospel (Gal 4:13-15). Now, like beasts, they are shamefully reduced to "biting and devouring" one another (Gal 5:15).

Other Images. Paul's letters frequently evoke the routine tasks of life in field and town. The Galatians are a community that must bear one another's burdens, the troubles and hardships of others (Gal 6:2). But this is not to the exclusion of carrying their own load, bearing their own portion of work and minding their own business when it comes to testing the quality of labor (Gal 6:4-5). Paul is concerned that his own *work not be wasted (Gal 4:11); as one who has labored hard, he does not want to rebuild what he formerly tore down (Gal 2:18). Field and hearth are evoked in images of *sowing (to the flesh or Spirit) and reaping a *harvest (of corruption or eternal life; Gal 6:8-9), the *fruit of the Spirit (Gal 5:22) and the little *leaven that leavens the whole batch of dough (Gal 5:9).

God can be described as "the one who calls you" (Gal 5:8). When he called the Galatians (Gal 1:6), it was a call to freedom (Gal 5:13), and although the Galatians responded in faith to what they heard (Gal 3:2, 5), they seem now to be deserting the one who called them and reverting to bondage. God has also called Paul (Gal 1:15), a calling modeled after the call of the *prophets (Is 49:1, 5). Believers respond by calling back to God through the Spirit, who from their hearts trains their tongues to call out "Abba, Father" (Gal 4:6). This theme of speech, both human and divine, is extended as Paul "speaks," yet wishes to be present and change his "tone" (Gal 4:20), as Scripture speaks (Gal 4:30) and the promises of God are spoken (Gal 3:16).

Viewing his ministry among the Gentiles as a foot *race, Paul sought assurance from the Jerusalem church that he "was not running or had not run in vain" (Gal 2:2). The Galatians too are running a race: "You were running well," says Paul. But suddenly there has been an interference in their progress: Who "cut in on you?" (NIV), or "cut you off?" (Gal 5:7). Alternatively the whole course of the Christian life may be viewed as a walk, a Jewish image commonly used for living in accordance with the law. For Paul it is no longer law that guides but the Spirit. Thus he instructs the Galatians to "walk in the Spirit" (Gal 5:16), to be "guided" by the Spirit (Gal 5:18) and to "keep in step with" *(stoicheō)* the Spirit (Gal 5:25).

Paul is aware of a divine timetable that transcends human reckoning. There is the date "set by the father" (Gal 4:2), the arrival of "the fullness of time" (Gal 4:4) and the arrival of the "proper time" in which he will "reap a harvest" (Gal 6:9). But the observance of holy times prescribed by the law—days, months, seasons, years (Gal 4:10)—are part of the old calendar ruled by the "basic elements." They are to be abandoned in light of the arrival of the fullness of time.

Paul quite naturally invokes images of conception, birth and lineage. He speaks of the concrete Hebrew image of "seed" (vs. the "seeds," Gal 3:16 etc.) in speaking of the offspring of Abraham to whom the promise was given. This imagery evokes a world in which the bearing of offspring is not a matter of personal pleasure and indulgence but a means by which humans join in the process of divine promise and fulfillment. Conception and birth are opportunities for human participation in God's grace as the *barren woman who has known no *birth pangs rejoices to find herself pregnant and the *mother of more children than one who has a husband (Gal 4:27; citing Is 54:1). Or Paul can liken his relationship to the Galatians to a mother undergoing the pangs of childbirth again, "until Christ is formed in you" (4:19). It is as if the Galatians have reverted to a prenatal condition.

Paul's reference to his former zeal for the traditions of his ancestors (Gal 1:15) summons scenes of violence against the early Christian communities (Gal 1:13, 23). But zeal is also a positive impulse, and for pious Jews it called forth a distinguished cast of characters in Israel's story, including Phineas (Num 25:6-13), Elijah (1 Kings 17:1—2 Kings 2:15) and the more recent Maccabbean heroes. Paul may be evoking memories of the prophet Elijah when he speaks of his having gone away into Arabia (Sinai?; cf. Gal 4:25) and afterwards returning to Damascus (Gal 1:17; cf. 1 Kings 19:8, 15). Zeal is valued by the judaizers, but it is misplaced zeal (Gal 4:17-18). In contrast, the whole of Paul's letter exudes a dynamic zeal for the gospel and for the Galatians' participation in the true gospel.

See also ABRAHAM; BONDAGE AND FREEDOM; CIRCUMCISION; COVENANT; JERUSALEM; LAW; ROMANS, LETTER TO THE; SINAI; ZION.

BIBLIOGRAPHY. N. T. Wright, "The Seed and the Mediator: Galatians 3:15-20" in *The Climax of the Covenant* (Minneapolis: Fortress, 1992) 157-74.

GALL

"That is a bitter pill to swallow" is a near equivalent to the metaphorical usage of the word *gall* in the Bible. It denotes a bitter, hard experience of life. Proverbs 3:4 warns that the *adulteress may entice with charms as sweet as honey and yet will lead her victim to a bitter end (*see* Seductress). The psalmist uses gall as a way of describing how it feels when there is no one around to comfort you in times of trouble (Ps 69:20-21). The author of Lamentations uses the word to describe the intense *shame, despair and bitterness the destruction of Jerusalem and the collapse of Judah has brought about (Lam 3). Yet it must be pointed out that one of the Bible's most beautiful descriptions of hope in the midst of despair was penned in this very context: "Because of the LORD's great love we are not consumed, for his compassions never fail. They are new every morning; great is your faithfulness (Lam 3:22-23 NIV).

Gall is also used to denote in a very graphic way the yellowish-brown secretion of the liver (Job 16:13). It is the label given the stupefying concoction offered our Lord as he was being crucified to help him deal with the pain (Mt 27:34). It is significant that Jesus refused and chose instead to experience the full bitterness of the situation, which included not only physical pain and shame, but unfathomable mental and spiritual anguish.

See also SWEET.

GARDEN

Throughout the Bible, the garden as a well-*watered space set apart for the intense cultivation of *plants is an image of both *nature and *sacred space. At a literal, physical level the garden is a place of life richly nourished, well attended to and appointed for the enjoyment of its human owners or residents. As such, it is a touchstone of such motifs as provision, *beauty, *abundance and the satisfaction of human need. Next to heaven, it is the preeminent image of human longing.

Associated as it is with life at its fullest, one should not be surprised to find that the garden is one of the framing images of the total Bible story. In Genesis 2 *Adam is provided the Garden of Eden as a perfect abode and workplace. In Revelation 21 the New *Jerusalem is described as the ideal joining of garden and *city. The city of God descended from *heaven has a *river of life issuing from beneath God's *throne, much as a *fountain arose in the midst of Eden's garden. The river is lined with trees whose *fruit is for *food and whose *leaves are for the healing of the nations.

It is useful to notice at the outset the categories of gardens in the Bible. A basic distinction exists between *the* garden—the garden of God in Eden—and *gardens*—places that share the qualities of the original Paradise but lack its unique status. The garden in the *Song of Songs is almost as distinctly a world of its own as the Garden of Eden and is obviously the archetypal garden of love that has reverberated throughout human history, especially in literature. At a more otherworldly level, we find the image of the heavenly paradise. Finally, there are the two gardens of Jesus' passion and resurrection—the Garden of Gethsemane and the garden of Jesus' tomb.

The Garden of God. The human race has always pictured perfection as an enclosed garden, lush with vegetation and suffused with tranquillity. As we unpack the meanings of the paradisal image, it is important to be aware that this is the Bible's picture of how God intended human life to be lived. The Garden of Eden is more than a place; it is also a way of life and a state of soul. Because God himself planted the Garden of Eden (Gen 2:8), there is something prescriptive as well as descriptive in the image of the original garden of perfection and its successors.

The term *paradise* derives from the Persian word for a walled garden. Although the word is not used for the garden of Genesis 2 (which is instead called "the Garden of Eden" and "the garden of God"), it is nonetheless the Bible's version of Paradise. While Genesis 2 does not ascribe a wall to this perfect place, the impression is clearly one of secluded protection, an impression reinforced after the expulsion when a flaming *sword bars reentry, implying a *gate of entry into the garden. The terms used for *plants and *animals in Genesis 2 are different those used in Genesis 1; they refer to plants and animals cultivated and controlled by people in contrast to the cosmic scope of the preceding chapter. The enclosed nature of the perfect garden itself captures an essential quality of it—its difference from ordinary life. The very simplicity of life in the garden is part of its difference from the complexities of civilization, as signaled partly by the unashamed *nakedness of Adam and Eve in the garden. The enclosure is a fixed barrier between original perfection—an ideal past—and fallen experience. It may also imply the limits and finitude of human life even in its original perfection.

Other motifs may also be discerned in the paradisal garden of Genesis 2. One is provision. The image is perennial and universal, but it no doubt had added resonance for an agrarian society living in an arid region. Because gardens are watered, they are places of abundant vegetation. Such a garden is, moreover, a picture of the *perpetual* *abundance and nourishment of nature, along the lines of the tree of Psalm 1 that never withers. It goes without saying that this green world is also a place of natural beauty. Paradise combines the utilitarian need of being "good for food" with the aesthetic ideal of being "pleasant to the sight" (Gen 2:9). The ideal is timeless, making Paradise (in the words of C. S. Lewis) a region in the mind that does exist and should be visited often.

If the Garden of Eden is an image of divine provision, it is paradoxically also a place of human labor. Gardens, after all, require cultivation. Genesis 2 tells us that God took the newly created Adam and "put him in the garden of Eden to till it and keep it" (Gen 2:15 NRSV). In addition to its status as an image of nature and relaxation, therefore, the garden is also an image of human industry, work and striving. The garden is a place prepared for humankind, but also a place requiring ongoing human upkeep. The presence of the tree of life suggests that the garden comprehends the very principles of abundant life and growth, and in this setting the natural corollary of idealized growth is idealized work. Adam's labor is fulfilling of both himself and his environment. Implied here is the norm of perfect activity in time. So are introduced two pervasive themes of the biblical record: God is ever providing a place as well as promising new and more perfect places, even as humankind is enjoined to collaborate in obedience to the unfolding divine purpose. Eden, Canaan, Heaven: the sequence lists the gifts of a loving *providence, contingent, as the Deuteronomic tradition puts it so well, on acceptance and obedience.

Harmony is a major meaning of the image of Paradise. Adam and Eve are pictured as living in harmony with nature, including both plants and animals. They also live in harmony with each other. But overshadowing this harmony on the natural and human planes is the open communion of Adam and Eve with God. The garden may be enclosed, but it also opens upward to God, who visits the garden that he has planted, "walking in the garden in the cool of the day" (Gen 3:8 RSV). When Adam and Eve are expelled (see Exile) from the garden, they lose more than a place—they also lose a spiritual status based on unfettered communion with God.

Two further motifs can be noted in connection with the Garden of Eden. In contrast to the earthly paradises of the classical tradition, this garden is not a place of inviolable retirement, but a place of continuous moral *testing, as indicated by the presence of a forbidden tree in the middle of the garden. Related to this is the motif of the garden as a place of radical choice. In fact, we associate the original garden with the most decisive choice in the history of the world. Dominating our impression as we read Genesis 2 is our awareness that Paradise has been lost.

Ordinary Gardens. The motifs of Paradise are retained in subsequent gardens mentioned in the Bible. These lesser gardens are still ideals, though they lack the uniqueness of the original garden. The garden of God remains the touchstone of abundant natural growth and therefore of human prosperity. When Lot lifted up his eyes toward the plain of the Jordan, he saw it was "well watered everywhere like the garden of the LORD" (Gen 13:10 RSV). In a vision of *Zion restored, Isaiah envisions a desert transformed "like the garden of the LORD" (Is 51:3 RSV; cf. Ezek 31:9; 36:35).

But even when no explicit reference is made to the Garden of Eden, biblical references to gardens retain its essential physical identity of being well-watered, green and fruitful. These gardens are not only images of nature but also implied pictures of *farming. Along with their being watered, the thing that is most often noted about the gardens mentioned in the Bible is that they are planted. They do not happen naturally. A stock picture of industry and reward for labor in the prophetic visions of future restoration is that of planting gardens and eating what they produce (Jer 29:5, 28; Amos 9:14). The garden's status as a blessing from God is underscored by the motif of the destroyed garden in oracles of judgment (Joel 2:3; Amos 4:9).

Whereas the Garden of Eden was planted by God, the gardens of the ordinary world are images of human status and achievement as well as images of nature. They are associated especially with the courtly life. When the kingly narrator of Ecclesiastes catalogs his material accomplishments, the list includes the statement "I made myself gardens and parks, and planted in them all kinds of fruit trees" (Eccles 2:5 RSV). We might note in passing that the Bible makes no sharp distinction among the terms *garden, orchard, *grove and park. In the ancient world kings and other people of rank had the prerogative of the finest gardens, a practice evident in the royal bower and garden of the Song of Songs.

The Garden of Love. A leading branch of the literature of paradise is the garden of love, and the Bible does not disappoint us in the matter. The Garden of Eden already hints at the motif, inasmuch as Adam and Eve are the prototypical *husband and *wife, with God instituting *marriage and *sexual union as part of their garden existence (Gen 2:24-25).

The Song of Songs is the world's most famous garden of love. Here the paradisal motifs become transformed into romantic realities. The beauty of the surroundings is an extension of the *beauty of the beloved, and the sensory pleasures of the place mirror the pleasure the couple finds in their mutual love. The abundance and provision of the garden are metaphoric of the richness and value the two lovers find in each other. The enclosed nature of the garden of love captures the seclusion, privacy, intimacy and security that the lovers feel in their love, as well as hinting at the way in which the lovers are a world complete to themselves. The walled garden also becomes a symbol of the bride's chastity (Song 4:12). The harmony that the couple finds with their environment reflects the harmony of their relationship with each other.

The Celestial Paradise. The Bible also makes paradise a *heavenly reality. Three NT passages associate the term *paradise* with a heavenly experience (Lk 23:43; 2 Cor 12:4; Rev 2:7), though without giving details of the place. The primary text is the vision of the New Jerusalem, which is a walled city to be sure, but one that possess paradisal features of a river with a tree of life on either side, yielding fruit for the nations (Rev 22:1-2). Although the original paradise had been largely a secluded world, inhabited by just two people, the heavenly paradise is more populated and more open. The walls are graced by twelve resplendent jewel-gates that are perpetually open (Rev 21:25). Apparently a redeemed earth will be in perpetual commerce with the garden-city, for the traffic through the gates will involve "the glory and the honor of the nations" (Rev 21:26). In these pictures of the open enclosure, we see affirmed the sacred space that is whole and integral yet in eternal transaction. The celestial paradise, and to a lesser degree the original paradise, are built around a paradox: they are closed and yet open.

The Gardens of Jesus' Life. The two gardens most strong associated with Jesus are so different in physical properties and connotation that we scarcely think of them as gardens in the sense of the paradisal garden, yet the Gospels treat them as gardens. The Garden of Gethsemane is a place of ultimate anguish, of suffering and betrayal, of arrest and violence. Given the conventions of a garden, it is almost an antigarden—a surrealistic inversion of expected qualities of a garden. Yet it also shares something important with the original Paradise: it is a sacred

space within which a radical decision is made that reverses the course of human history.

The garden of the resurrection is even more of a synthesis, and the *resurrection story itself takes on added meanings if we allow some of the garden motifs to flow into the experiences that transpired on resurrection morning. There can be no doubt that the site of the resurrection was a garden: John 19:41 tells us that the place of the tomb (near the site of the crucifixion) was a garden, and Mary Magdalene mistakes the risen Jesus for the gardener (Jn 20:15). It is fitting that a garden provide the context for the Easter miracle, inasmuch as gardens have been identified throughout history with the heightening of life and growth. The first garden accommodated the first *Adam; the Easter garden accommodated the second Adam. As Paul exclaims, "If, because of the one man's trespass, death reigned through that one, much more surely will those who receive the abundance of grace . . . reign in life through the one man, Jesus Christ" (Rom 5:17 RSV). The resurrection offers a new horizon for humankind, with a world defined not by death but by life, with the prospect of growth into the fullness of the stature of Christ. All of this is enhanced if we allow the conventional meanings of the garden—abundant provision, human longing satisfied, harmony achieved, love triumphant—to flow into this one.

Summary. What then does the image of the garden mean in the Bible? It is an image of the ideal that heightens whatever activity occurs within it. It signals nature at its best, romantic love at its best, human well-being at its best, spiritual reality at its best. The garden of bliss is a moral and spiritual norm against which fallen experience is judged and toward which the human spirit aspires.

See also ABUNDANCE; ADAM; ANIMALS; BEAUTY; EVE; FOUNTAIN; FRUIT; GROVE; HEAVEN; JERUSALEM; LOVE STORY; NATURE; PLANTS; SACRED SPACE; SEX; SONG OF SOLOMON; SPRING OF WATER; TREE, TREES; TREE OF LIFE; WATER; ZION.

BIBLIOGRAPHY. P. Morris and D. Sawyer, *A Walk in the Garden: Biblical, Iconographical and Literary Images of Eden* (Sheffield: JSOT, 1992).

GARMENTS

The imagery of garments and clothing is of the major importance in the Bible. Its significance can be physical, economic, social, moral or spiritual. The imagery of investing and divesting a person of clothing is usually symbolic of larger issues. The function of clothing, moreover, is multiple: clothing can protect, conceal, display or represent a person's current state and can be symbolic of moral and spiritual qualities. The fact that garments wear out is also important.

God, as well as people, is portrayed as wearing garments. Garments can occur in everyday settings or religious settings. Clothing ranges from the endearing reference to how Samuel's mother "used to make for him a little robe and take it to him each year" as he was growing up (1 Sam 2:19 RSV) to the resplendent *wedding garments of a royal wedding (Ps 45:13-14), and from the coarse sackcloth worn in mourning to the otherworldly dazzling clothes of *angels and the transfigured Christ. Literal and figurative meanings are intertwined in virtually every category of usages. It is no exaggeration to say that one can trace the whole outline of biblical theology and salvation history through the motif of clothing.

Economic Importance. References to clothing should resolve any doubt that the biblical world was largely a subsistence economy. Garments are obviously scarce and therefore valuable. A man who takes a second wife shall not diminish the clothing of the first wife (Ex 21:10). If an Israelite takes a neighbor's garment in pledge, he is to return it before sundown because "it may be your neighbor's only clothing to use as cover" (Ex 22:26-27 NRSV; 24:13). In his vow Jacob links "bread to eat and clothing to wear" as the staples of life (Gen 28:20; cf. 1 Tim 6:8, which enjoins Christians to be content if they have food and clothing). An ultimate image of destitution is to "lie all night naked, without clothing, and have no covering in the cold" or to "go about naked, without clothing"(Job 24:7, 10 NRSV). Because garments are so valuable in a subsistence economy, their wearing out (Ps 102:26; Is 51:6 8; Heb 1:11) or being eaten by moths (Job 13:28; Prov 25:20; Is 50:9; 51:8) becomes an image of *terror.

In keeping with clothing as a valued item, we note also its prominence in the taking of plunder by a conqueror (Ex 3:22; 12:35; Josh 22:8; Judg 8:26; 1 Sam 27:9; 2 Kings 7:8; 2 Chron 20:25). When Samson needs thirty garments to pay off a wager that he has lost, he undertakes a plundering expedition to exact the agreements from victims (Judg 14:19). With the wealthy, clothing becomes an image of *abundance (1 Kings 10:5; 2 Chron 9:4; Zech 14:14). Of similar import is the prevalence of clothing as a formal gift (Gen 24:53; Judg 17:10; 1 Kings 10:25; 2 Kings 5:5, 23, 26; 2 Chron 9:24). Rich clothing is both a sign and source of commercial power for the nation producing it (Ezek 27:24).

As an image of basic human need, clothing can, by a logical extension, become an image of God's provision. Clothing (along with food) is one of two areas of human life regarding which Jesus prohibits worry in his discourse against anxiety (Mt 6:25-30; Lk12:23-28). During the forty years of wilderness wanderings, God's provision for the Israelites is seen partly in the fact that their clothes do not wear out (Deut 8:4; 29:5; Neh 9:21). One of God's first acts of provision for humankind after the fall is to make "garments of skins for the man and for his wife" and clothe them (Gen 3:21). By a further extension, lavish adornment of clothes can become a sign of God's special blessing on a nation (Ezek 16:13; cf. Is 23:18, where fine clothing is an image of abundant provision "for those who live in the presence of the LORD").

The Clothing of God and Nature. Nature is part of the clothing of God in the Bible, as God is "wrapped in light as with a garment" (Ps 104:2 NRSV). Clothing is also combined with conceptual imagery (words naming qualities) to render the attributes of God vivid. Thus God is "clothed with honor and majesty" (Ps 104:1). He also puts on "garments of vengeance for clothing" (Is 59:17; cf. Is 63:2-3), and he is "splendidly robed, marching in his great might" (Is 63:1).

To the poetic imagination, various forces of nature are like clothing. Thus the *clouds are the garment for the sea (Job 38:9); the *sea, in turn, covers the *deep "as with a garment" (Ps 104:6 NRSV); and God clothes the *heavens with *blackness (Is 50:3). God is said to clothe the *grass of the field (Mt 6:30; Lk 12:28). God's omnipotence over the forces of nature is pictured as his wrapping up the waters in a garment (Prov 30:4). The *transience of nature is also pictured by garment imagery: the forces of nature "will all wear out like a garment," and God will "change them like clothing" (Ps 102:26 NRSV; see also Is 50:9; 51:6, 8; Heb 1:12). The impenetrable skin of Leviathan is like an outer garment that no human can strip off (Job 41:13).

Garments of Festivity. A notable garment motif is that of festal garments. Here fine and white clothing symbolizes celebration. Employing ancient images of festivity, the writer of Ecclesiastes commands that life be lived with zest: "Let your garments always be white; do not let oil be lacking on your head" (Eccles 9:8 RSV). In one of Isaiah's oracles of coming salvation, he commands *Zion to "put on your beautiful garments" (Is 52:1).

Every society has its rituals of "dressing up" for special occasions, and we catch glimpses of it in the Bible as well. On the momentous night of Ruth's betrothal, she washes, anoints herself and puts on her best clothes as her preparation for springing a surprise on Boaz on the *threshing floor (Ruth 3:3). The attractive clothing of the beloved is an archetypal image of romantic *love (Song 4:11), where the adornment of *jewelry is an extension of clothing (Song 1:10-11; 4:9). The supreme occasion of dressing up is the *wedding (Ps 45:13-14; cf. reference in Jesus' parable to the importance of appropriate wedding garments [Mt 22:11-12]).

Images of Mourning and Desolation. Whereas festive garments are a *comic motif, linked with celebration and a happy ending, their *tragic counterpart is garments associated with *mourning or desolation. We thus read about prison clothes (2 Kings 25:29; Jer 52:33), *widow's garments (Gen 38:14, 19), "captive's garb" (Deut 21:13) and "*mourning garments" (2 Sam 14:2). Clothing oneself in sackcloth is a ritual of repentance or dismay (Gen 37:34; Esther 4:1; Ps 69:11; Is 37:1). Lepers wore torn clothing to advertise their diseased state to the public (Lev 13:45).

Another major motif is the tearing of clothes as a ritual gesture of grief or as an act of uncontrollable rage. Indeed, one of the best indices to the emotionalism of the ancient Hebrews is the frequency with which we read about people tearing their garments in a display of strong feeling. To cite just three specimens, Reuben tears his clothes when he returns to the pit and finds *Joseph missing (Gen 37:29), Ezra rends his garments when he learns about the Israelites' intermarriage (Ezra 9:3), and King Hezekiah tears his clothes when he receives the threatening letter from the Assyrian king (Is 37:1). If we trace the three dozen explicit references to people's tearing their clothing, we find four main categories of crisis—grief or mourning over the loss of something or someone, sorrow for sin in an act of *repentance, *fear or alarm and *anger or frustration.

Putting On and Taking Off Clothes. The actions of putting clothing on and putting it off constitute another major motif. The specific meaning of investing a person with a garment depends on what kind of clothing is in view. When a priest puts off his ordinary garments and puts on *linen garments to perform his religious functions, the action signifies consecration of the priest for spiritual duties (Ex 29:1-9; 40:12-15; Lev 6:11; 16:1-4). To remove the priestly garment means a cessation of sacred duties and a return to the ordinary routine (Lev 16:23-23; Ezek 44:19). In a prophetic oracle of judgment, the putting off of garments carries the meaning of exposure and shaming (Is 47:2). When Esther puts on her royal robes before standing in the court of the king's palace, it betokens her assertion of the rights of the queen (Esther 5:1; cf. Acts 12:21). Repeated references to putting on sackcloth picture a person's assuming the rituals of either mourning or repentance.

The most extreme form of divesting clothing is expressed by the strongly negative action of stripping, implying subjection to a being or army with superior power. The act of humbling is implied in the picture of counselors and priests being led away stripped (Job 12:17, 19; cf. Job 19:9). When kings are stripped of their robes, it is a way of saying that they have been conquered (Is 45:1). Stripping corpses on a battlefield is a part of taking booty (1 Sam 31:8; 2 Sam 23:10; 1 Chron 10:8). Aaron's garments are stripped from him and put on his son at his death (Num 20:26-28).

By an easy progression the literal investing and divesting of garments becomes overtly metaphoric of spiritual states. Thus we read about the need to "cast off the works of darkness" (Rom 13:12 RSV) and "put off the old nature" (Col 3:9; see also Eph 4:22). Contrariwise, when Job sums up his life he claims, "I put on righteousness, and it clothed me; my justice was like a robe and a turban" (Job 29:14 RSV). In Isaiah's apocalyptic vision Jerusalem is enjoined to "put on your beautiful garments" (Is 52:1), and God is said to "put on righteousness" (Is 59:17). Paul instructs believers to "put on the new nature" (Col 3:10). And in the future life believers will "put on imperishability" (1 Cor 15:53).

The Morality of Clothing. Several different moral themes converge in the Bible's references to clothing. As an antidote to the feminine tendency toward extravagant clothing, two NT epistles warn against placing unwarranted value on external apparel and commend modesty in clothing (1 Tim 2:9; 1 Pet 3:3). James warns against preferential treatment of people who can afford "fine clothing" as contrasted with the economically disadvantaged who dress poorly (Jas 2:2-3). Paul counts it as one of his moral virtues that he "coveted no one's silver or gold or clothing" (Acts 20:33 NRSV).

Elsewhere the clothing of the destitute becomes a touchstone of moral compassion—an image of *mercy. In Jesus' account of the final judgment, clothing the *naked is placed in the same category as caring for the sick, visiting the prisoner and welcoming the stranger as acts that provide entry into heaven (Mt 25:36-43; cf. Ezek 18:7, 16). In Job's great oath of innocence, one of the acts that he implicitly ascribes to himself is that he did not allow anyone in his purview to "perish for lack of clothing, or a poor person without covering" (Job 31:19 NRSV). When Dorcas dies, the tribute to her acts of mercy is the clothing that widows had received from her hand (Acts 9:39). Similar concern that the poor be clothed is evidenced in the Mosaic law (Deut 24:12, 17), reflecting God's identical concern (Deut 10:18). Conversely, to divest the poor of their clothing is portrayed as a heinous sin (Job 22:6; Amos 2:8).

Clothing of Deceit. Garment imagery is not uniformly positive in the Bible. If its covering quality makes it an image of warmth and protection, that same quality can make it an image of deceitful concealment. Here we have images of false prophets who come in *sheep's clothing but inwardly are ravenous *wolves (Mt 7:15) or of *Jacob donning the clothing of *Esau to trick his blind father and steal the blessing (Gen 27:15, 27). The crafty left-hander Ehud hides his homemade spear under his clothing on the unexpected right side, thereby escaping detection (Judg 3:16). David's wife Michal tricks her father's soldiers by covering goats' hair with David's clothes (1 Sam 19:13), while Saul puts on clothing of disguise in an effort to escape detection when he visits the witch of Endor (1 Sam 28:8). Most deceitful of all are the men of Gibeon, who secure a treaty with the Israelites under false pretenses when they assumed worn-out clothes and pretend to come from a distant country (Judg 9:5, 13).

The Old Testament Ceremonial Law. Clothing is prominent in the Mosaic laws as well, where it assumes ritual significance. The priest's investing and divesting himself of his special garment has already been noted. The largest cluster of references (30) is to the washing of clothes as a hygienic precaution or a symbol of purification. A prohibition of wearing garments made of more than one type of cloth signifies sanctification or purity (Lev 19:19; Deut 22:11). Cross dressing between men and women is disallowed (Deut 22:3, 5).

Transcendent Clothing. Dazzling garments are

a leading feature of the portrayal of transcendent or heavenly beings. Here we find a mingling of the familiar and the unfamiliar, or the raising of something commonplace to a realm beyond the earthly. The most famous instance is Jesus' transfiguration, when "his clothes became dazzling white" (Mt 17:2; Mk 9:3; Lk 9:29). In similar manner, the "Ancient One" on the throne in Daniel's apocalyptic vision wears clothing that was "white as snow" (Dan 7:9). Angels too are portrayed as wearing "dazzling clothes" (Lk 24:4; Acts 10:30) or "clothing white as snow" (Mt 28:3). The priestly garments of OT worship are only slightly less otherworldly than those of supernatural beings (Ex 28). And the redeemed saints in heaven are garbed in resplendent white robes (Rev 3:4-5; 4:4; 7:9, 13; 15:6; 19:14).

Christ and Clothing. Many of the foregoing motifs converge in the life of Christ. His birth as a naked infant, followed by his being wrapped in the swaddling cloths that were used in that time, signifies his humanity. The compassion and miraculous power of Jesus are encapsulated (as with the click of a camera) in the moment when a woman stricken with a blood ailment for years is immediately healed when she touches the hem of Jesus' garment (Mt 9:18-2; Mk 5:25-34; Lk 8:42-48; cf. Mk 6:56). Clothing imagery pervades the *passion of Christ, as Jesus is stripped of his clothing and invested with a royal robe in a public mocking (Mt 27:28-31; Mk 15:17-20; Jn 19:2-3), has his clothing divided among the soldiers (Mt 27:35; Mk 15:24; Lk 23:34; Jn 19:24) and is wrapped in a burial cloth. In his glorification in heaven Jesus appears again in transcendent clothing (Rev 1:13).

Salvation History. It is also possible to trace the main outlines of salvation history by means of garment imagery. Clothing is first present in the Bible by its absence, as the nakedness of Adam and Eve is an index to their pristine innocence and freedom (Gen 2:25). After the Fall, clothing becomes a symbol of the need for human shame to be covered. The *fig *leaves with which Adam and Eve attempt to conceal their shame are a pathetically ineffectual effort to deal with human guilt (Gen 3:7). Only God can provide adequate clothing for the human race after the Fall (Gen 3:21).

After early Genesis, clothing becomes an image for both sinfulness and redemption. On the side of sin, for example, we read about the arrogant wicked whose "violence covers them like a garment" (Ps 73:6 NRSV) and about faithless men "covering [their] garment with violence" (Mal 2:16 RSV). Jeremiah pictures a priestly class "so defiled with blood that none could touch their garments" as they wandered through the street (Lam 4:14 RSV). Ezekiel uses garment imagery to picture Israel's apostasy: "You took some of your garments, and made for yourself colorful shrines, and on them played the whore" (Ezek 16:16 NRSV).

But on the other side we find salvation pictured as a garment: "I will greatly rejoice in the LORD, my whole being shall exult in my God; for he has clothed me with the garments of salvation, he has covered me with the robe of righteousness" (Is 61:10 RSV) and a "mantle of praise" (Is 61:3). Ezekiel pictures God's love for Israel in the imagery of a betrothal ritual involving clothing: "I spread my skirt over you, and covered your nakedness: yea, I plighted my troth to you and entered into a covenant with you, says the Lord GOD, and you became mine" (Ezek 16:8 RSV). In Christ's letter to the church at Laodicea, he pictures salvation as "white robes to clothe you" (Rev 3:18 RSV).

The classic garment passage used to portray God's forgiveness of sin is the one involving the priest Joshua (Zech 3:1-5). Dressed in "filthy clothes" as he stands before the angel of the Lord, accused by Satan, Joshua hears the angel command onlookers to remove his filthy clothes and put "festal apparel" on him. Here, in symbolic action, is the story of salvation. In fact, the angel explains that the action is "an omen of things to come," which will be accomplished by "my servant the Branch," that is, the Messiah (Zech 3:8). This redemption reaches its consummation in heaven, where believers, as Christ's bride, have "washed their robes and made them white in the blood of the Lamb" (Rev 7:14 RSV). The church herself is like "a bride adorned for her husband" (Rev 21:2 RSV).

Summary: Clothing in the Story of Joseph. Many of the biblical motifs of clothing converge in the story of Joseph (Gen 37—45), in which garment imagery appears at every transition point in the action. As the favored son of Jacob, Joseph is invested with a special garment that symbolizes his exalted status with his father (Gen 37:3). When Joseph's brothers strip him of the robe, the action signals Joseph's fall from favor and entrance into a life of suffering (Gen 37:23). Reuben tears his garment in a gesture of anguish when he returns to find the pit empty (Gen 37:29), and the brothers use the garment to deceive their father into believing that Joseph is dead (Gen 37:31-33). The garment that Joseph leaves in the hands of his temptress testifies to his moral integrity (Gen 39:12), though Potiphar's wife cleverly uses the garment to carry out her deception (Gen 39:12-18). In keeping with the social practice of virtually every culture to make clothing match an occasion, we are given the random bit of realistic detail that Joseph shaves and changes his clothes before leaving prison to appear before Pharaoh (Gen 41:14). And Joseph's rise from the status of prisoner to the second most powerful ruler in the realm is accompanied by the king's arraying Joseph "in garments of fine linen" (Gen 41:42). In the scene of festivity that accompanies Joseph's disclosure of his identity to his brothers, he gives as a gift to each brother "a set of garments," giving "five sets of garments" to Benjamin (Gen 45:22).

See also ARMOR; CLOTH; COVER, COVERING; LINEN; MOURN, MOURNING; NAKED, NAKEDNESS; SILK; WOOL.

GATE

Most of the nearly 350 references to gates in the Bible involve *city gates. Passages describing the layout of the *tabernacle and *temple (including Ezekiel's vision of a restored temple) are likewise replete with references to various gates, some of which bear specific names. In all instances the image of the gate is that of an entryway into something. Because entryways are public places, there is also an emphasis on communal activities that occur at gates.

Protective Gates. For ancient Israelites the most important element of defense against external forces was the fortified *wall encircling a city. The city gate, however, constituted a breach in the wall, and hence was the most vulnerable point of the defense. The elaborate gateways that have been revealed by excavation were both massive and ingenious. The gate of a city was closed each night (Josh 2:5) to protect the inhabitants. If the presence of a city gate represented safety and security, the ultimate horror was to live in a city "that has no gates or bars" (Jer 49:31) or a city "without walls, and having no bars or gates" (Ezek 38:11).

Since most OT cities were less than twenty acres in size, one or two city gates were sufficient. The gates were situated to provide access to roads, water sources and so forth, but care was also taken to make them defensible. Apparently it was customary to make the approach ramp up to the gate from the right so that attackers, most of whom would carry their shields on their left arms, would be exposed to fire from the city walls. Not only were the gates strong and visually impressive, but they were probably made more beautiful by the *bronze sheeting that covered the doors. Thus we find references to breaking "in pieces the doors of bronze" (Is 45:2) and shattering "the doors of bronze" (Ps 107:16). The purpose of the bronze was to make the doors somewhat fire resistant, since fire was an obvious offensive weapon for breaching the gates: "When the troops were about to capture the tower and were forcing the door of the courtyard, they ordered that fire be brought and the doors burned" (2 Macc 14:41 RSV).

Since gateways protected cities not only from military attack but also from the intrusion of unwanted strangers, their use was regulated. The position of gatekeeper is an OT fixture, with the majority of references occurring in connection with the temple. The position of gatekeeper implies the act of guarding against illegitimate entry, whether into a city (2 Kings 10), a king's court (2 Kings 11:4-9) or the temple (2 Kings 12:9; 2 Chron 23:19).

The connotations of a gate of defense are ambivalent. On the one hand, it is an image of safety, with the closed gate representing safety for residents by night or for a city under attack. Thus we find references to the strength of "those who turn back the battle at the gate" (Is 28:6), to the victorious gathering for celebration at the city gate (Judg 5:11), to God's strengthening "the bars of your gates" (Ps 147:13). But gates were the vulnerable part of a city

wall, hence an image of precarious safety and insecurity. They were the focal point of attack (Ezek 21:15, 22). If the gate fell (was "possessed"), the city itself was considered to have fallen (Gen 22:17; 24:60). One could even be trampled in the press of people going through a gateway (2 Kings 7:20; Job 5:4).

Social and Legal Aspects. Because city gates were public passageways, they took on the nature of a "public square" where legal and civil events occurred. Even farmers slept in the towns at night, so the gateway was the most frequented place in town. It was where one met with others (2 Sam 15:2) and gossiped (Ps 69:12; cf. the prayer for the virtuous wife that her works might "praise her in the city gates" [Prov 31:31]). The city gate was also the appropriate place to make public announcements and demonstrations. In Proverbs the personified figure of *Wisdom cries out "at the busiest corner . . . at the entrance of the city gates" (Prov 1:21 NRSV; see also 8:3). Markets were located near the city gate as well (2 Kings 7:1), and gates were sometimes named for special commodities—the Sheep Gate (Neh 3:1), the Fish Gate (Neh 3:3), the Horse Gate (Neh 3:28).

Of special note is the phrase "sitting in the gate" in the OT. Immediately inside many city gates was an area where officials met and deliberated. To "sit in the gate" (or its variant "sit in the seat") implied one's prominence in the community. Thus it is an index to the extent of Lot's assimilation into the wicked city of Sodom that the angelic visitors find him "sitting in the gateway" (Gen 19:1). Even kings sometimes positioned themselves "in the gate" (2 Sam 18:24; 19:8). It is part of the honor of the virtuous wife of Proverbs 31 that "her husband is known in the city gates, taking his seat among the elders of the land" (Prov 31:23). To sit in the gate was to have a voice in setting policy; thus in the list of three progressive actions listed in Psalm 1:1, the climactic identification with evil is to "sit in the seat of scoffers."

*Legal activity was common in the gate area. Already in the Mosaic law the city gate was designated as the place of legal tribunal (e.g., Deut 21:19; 22:15; 25:7). Contending with one's enemies in the gate (Ps 127:5) implies legal negotiations. When Boaz insists on carrying out his desire to marry Ruth with complete adherence to established rules, he negotiates with his rival at the town gate (Ruth 4:1). The pattern was established even before the Israelites settled in cities, with Moses judging the people "in the gate of the camp" during their wilderness wanderings (Ex 32:26). Sometimes punishment or justice was meted out at the city gate (Deut 17:5; 21:21). At Joshua's command, the King of Ai was hanged and his body was thrown down "at the entrance of the gate of the city" (Josh 8:29; see also 2 Kings 10:8-9).

Because so much commercial and civil business was transacted at the city gate, it became a prime image for prophetic denunciations of a corrupt society. Thus we find references to "the afflicted at the gate" (Prov 22:22), about setting "a trap for the arbiter in the gate" (Is 29:21) and about dishonest people who "hate the one who reproves in the gate, and abhor the one who speaks the truth" (Amos 5:10 NRSV). Jeremiah's picture of desecrating the sabbath is one of people's bringing in burdens "by the gates of Jerusalem" (Jer 17:21, 24, 27). The antidote is to "hate evil and love good, and establish justice in the gate" (Amos 5:15 NRSV).

Figurative Uses. While the majority of biblical references are to literal gates, they also assume figurative qualities. Sometimes they are a synecdoche for an entire city: "Her gates shall lament and mourn; ravaged, she shall sit upon the ground" (Is 3:26 NRSV); "Wail, O gate; cry, O city" (Is 14:31 NRSV); "The LORD loves the gates of Zion more than all the dwellings of Jacob" (Ps 87:2 NRSV). The psalmist apostrophizes the gates of the temple, commanding them to open to allow entry to God: "Lift up your heads, O gates! and be lifted up, O ancient doors! that the King of glory may come in" (Ps 24:7 NRSV).

Since the primary function of a gate was to provide entry, gates can symbolize entrance into any realm. Thus we read about the gate of heaven (Gen 28:17), gates of *death (Job 38:17; Ps 9:13; 107:18), gates of righteousness (Ps 118:19), gates of Sheol (Is 38:10), the gateways of the *morning and *evening (Ps 65:8). The gates of Hades, representing the power of evil forces, will attack the church but cannot overcome it (Mt 16:18). Jesus used the imagery of a gate for entrance either into life or into destruction (Mt 7:13-14). In this picture the "narrow gate" and the hard road restricts those who gain life to a minority. By contrast, the wide gate that leads to destruction is easily entered.

Jesus elaborates the image of the gate (*"door" in some older translations) in his Good Shepherd Discourse (Jn 10:1-17). The good shepherd "enters by the gate" and leads his sheep out through the gate of the sheepfold, an image of safety. In an extension of the metaphor, Jesus calls himself the gate: "I am the gate. Whoever enters by me will be saved" (Jn 10:9 NRSV).

There is, finally, an apocalyptic image of particular power. The purpose of a gate in a fallen world is to be closed for purposes of protection by night and during attack. However, in the coming day of Israel's glory, the protection of gates will be unnecessary, because the threat of evil will have been removed: "Your gates shall always be open; day and night they shall not be shut" (Is 60:11 NRSV). Again, the gates of the New Jerusalem "will never be shut by day— and there will be no night there" (Rev 21:25 NRSV).

See also CITY; DOOR; WALL.

GEHENNA. *See* HELL; VALLEY.

GENEALOGY. *See* GENERATIONS; TIME.

GENERATION(S)
The image of generation covers several distinct phe-

nomena in the Bible—some positive, some negative. On the positive side, the motif of the continuity of the human race and the covenant community throughout history is instinctual in human experience. This motif reaches it apex in the psalms, where we read about future generations who will serve God (Ps 22:30), about telling God's glorious deeds to the next generation (Ps 48:13) or generations to come (Ps 71:18) or to the coming generation (Ps 78:4, 6; Ps 102:18), about recounting God's praise "from generation to generation" (79:13 NRSV) and about lauding God's works from "one generation . . . to another" (Ps 145:4 NRSV). Equally evocative is the motif of God's acts standing to "all generations" (a dozen times in the Psalms). The motif of the continuity of the human race spawns the motif of "generation to generation," while God's judgments against those who hate him is formulated in the motif "to the third and fourth generation" (Ex 20:5; Deut 6:9).

Elsewhere, a generation designates an era defined in terms of the life span of a group. Sometimes the connotation is neutral (Mt 24:34; Acts 13:36), but in the overwhelming majority of cases the term *generation* is preceded by a pejorative adjective, turning the designation into an assessment of an entire culture. Thus we read about a "*crooked generation," a "perverse" or "faithless" generation, an *"evil" or "wicked" generation and an *"adulterous" generation. In short, the motif of generation signals a thoroughgoing doctrine of the fallenness of human society.

The righteous are commended when they remain faithful in the midst of a sinful generation. Noah was found righteous in his generation (Gen 7:1). David's mighty acts are comprehended in the simple epitaph to which every Christian should aspire: he "served the purpose of God in his own generation" (Acts 13:36 NRSV). Paul exhorts the godly to play it straight, living "blameless and innocent, . . . without blemish in the midst of a crooked and perverse generation, in which you shine like stars in the world" (Phil 2:15 NRSV).

The difficulty of living such a life heightens the importance of commending the works of the Lord from one generation to the next (Ps 145:4). The introduction of "another generation . . . who did not know the LORD or the work that he had done for Israel" (Judg 2:10) sounds an ominous note at the beginning of Judges. The only antidote for this calamity is to "tell to the coming generation the glorious deeds of the LORD" (Ps 78:4 NRSV). The recitation of these deeds is done with an optimistic and forward-looking faith, for it is done for the sake of "children yet unborn" so that they might "tell them to their children" (Ps 78:6; cf. 102:18). A desire to preserve faith within the family in this way motivates the psalmist to pray for longevity: "So even to old age and gray hairs, O God, do not forsake me, until I proclaim your might to all the generations to come" (Ps 71:18 NRSV).

The word *generation* is often used in a formula that expresses the eternity of God's rule: "His kingdom endures from generation to generation" (Dan 4:34 NRSV; cf. Lam 5:19). Not only his being but also his purposes (Ps 33:11), faithfulness (Ps 89:1), *hospitality (Ps 90:1), renown (Ps 135:13) and dominion (Ps 145:13) will endure "through all generations."

As God hints already in his *covenants with Noah and *Abraham (Gen 9:12, 17:9), covenant blessing will be poured out upon "a thousand generations" of those who love him and keep his commands (Deut 7:9). This perpetual and exuberant outpouring of divine favor stands in marked contrast to his "punishing children for the iniquity of parents, to the third and the fourth generation of those who reject me" (Ex 20:5 NRSV). Even the figure one thousand does not function as a terminus for divine blessing, since God "remember[s] his covenant forever" (1 Chron 16:15). No wonder the formula used to express God's eternity is also used to express the eternity of the adoration of his people: "From generation to generation we will recount your praise" (Ps 79:13).

See also CHILD, CHILDREN; SEED.

GENESIS, BOOK OF

The title of the book tells us what it is about. Genesis is the "book of beginnings"—the definitive source of how the universe, human history and salvation history began. Much of the content of the book stems from this orientation—the genealogies, the preoccupation with "the generations" of various families and the occasional etiologies (stories of how people or places got their names). Genesis is preeminently the story of *first things—the first couple, the first *son, the first *garden, the first *sin, the first *rainbow, the first fratricide, the first *wanderer, the first multilingual community and so on.

The general outline of the book is a two-fold division: eleven chapters are devoted to primeval history (the origin of the world) and twenty-nine chapters to patriarchal history (the origin of the nation of Israel). While to modern readers the entire book has the aura of ancient literature, the primeval history is farther removed from ordinary history, more elemental, less specific, than the patriarchal history is. Primeval history is concerned with universal patterns of creation and fall, sin, judgment and restoration; whereas patriarchal history focuses on specific family histories.

Some of the unifying patterns in the book are thematic. God's sovereignty permeates the book from start to finish. God is a transcendent deity in the story of creation, the sovereign judge in the stories of the *Fall and the *flood, the authority figure in the stories of the patriarchs, beginning with his call of Abraham. Another unifying theme is the conflict between human waywardness and God's goodness. Repeatedly God chooses humanly unpromising material with which to work. A related tension is that between divine *judgment and divine *mercy.

The divine-human relationship is a preoccupation in the book of Genesis. The dominant motif by which this relationship is pictured is that of *covenant—an agreement (sometimes replete with contract imagery) that God makes with either the human race or individuals. There is actually a series of covenants in Genesis: a covenant of works with *Adam, a covenant of grace with Noah and a covenant of faith with *Abraham and the subsequent patriarchs. The motif of the covenant is accompanied by subordinate image patterns of promise, fulfillment, obligation (the requirement of *obedience), *reward and punishment (for disobedience; *see* Crime and Punishment).

Genesis also has a narrative unity. One aspect of it is the cast of characters. God is the protagonist of the overall story—the one who creates the universe, establishes the terms of its existence and oversees its unfolding as sustainer, guide and judge. But human characters are important too, and from a human perspective Genesis is a collection of *hero stories. Despite the wealth of secondary and minor characters, the main outline is the story of a handful of strong, fully developed characters: *Adam and *Eve, Noah, *Abraham and Sarah, *Cain and *Abel, Isaac and Rebekah, *Jacob, and *Joseph. These are primarily domestic stories—stories dealing primarily with families instead of nations.

Genesis is a book of archetypes. The original act of *creation is an archetype of new beginnings, accompanied by image patterns of fertility and abundance. The *Garden of Eden (Gen 2) is the archetypal earthly paradise, a place of pastoral bliss, provision and human innocence. The story of the Fall (Gen 3) is built around the archetypes of *temptation, *crime and punishment, *fall from innocence and *initiation. The story of the *flood (Gen 6—9) is a story of crime and punishment, cataclysmic destruction of the world and *rescue. Later stories reenact this basic repertoire of archetypal plot motifs.

In addition, the story of patriarchal history is governed by the *quest motif, with an accompanying emphasis on *journeying (the book of Genesis is an anthology of *travel stories, beginning with Noah's sea voyage). The life of Abraham is the first chapter of an epic quest, as God calls him to leave his native *land and journey to the land that God will show him. Added to this quest for land is the quest to achieve fulfillment of God's promise of a son and descendants. The later patriarchs continue these two quests, which are placed within the framework of the covenant, so that the patriarchs are not only in quest to find a homeland and perpetuate a line of descendants but also to please and obey God.

The book is also rich in archetypal character types, as we find a veritable gallery of universal characters: *heroes and heroines, guilty children, *fathers and *mothers, *husbands and *wives, *villains, *tricksters, *wanderers, *sibling rivals, sexual perverts, foreign *kings (authority figures), *brides and leaders of clans. Vocational types also abound: shepherds (or simply keepers of herds), tillers of the soil, *builders, homemakers, *hunters, *servants, butlers, bakers, rulers and courtiers (including interpreters of dreams).

A leading cluster of images is the *family. Already in primeval history, but in more accentuated fashion in patriarchal history, we move in a world of family relations. Because of the covenant motif, a strong sense of family destiny pervades Genesis, with the whole clan, generation after generation, preoccupied with producing descendants who will become a nation. The genealogies of Genesis are themselves a major image in the book. The fertile *womb (the raising up of *seed) is a major positive image; *barrenness is a human curse that women (especially) are willing to do almost anything to avoid. In keeping with the domestic emphasis of the book, the image of the *tent is pervasive as a scene of action. The families of Genesis are hardly idealized; in fact, the image of the dysfunctional family pervades the book. We read about the ultimate family dysfunction—fratricide—and about secondary dysfunction—hatred, jealousy, deceit of family members. Yet the picture is not totally negative: sibling reconciliation and family reunion figure prominently in two of the family histories.

The world of Genesis is a predominantly pastoral world in the broad sense of a world of nature, *farming and *shepherding. Only a few episodes are set in a city or court (where it turns out that people are very concerned with agrarian matters). For the most part we move in a world of desert and countryside. Dreams mainly consist of natural imagery. We are rarely allowed to lose awareness of the importance of sheep, goats and camels. The need for *water is a major motif, and it is almost synonymous with life and prosperity, just as its absence is a guarantee of want and even death. The related image of the *well figures prominently, both as a source of life-sustaining water for people and herds and as the social center of the community.

The life cycle contributes another nexus of images. *Birth stories are a prominent subgenre in Genesis. There are also memorable *death and *burial scenes. Continuity of *generations is important, where the father's blessing of his sons on his death bed is a ritual of major significance. The image of the *birthright assumes greater than normal importance in a story in which covenant lineage and blessings accompany the birthright.

A final image cluster focuses on worship of God. The building of *altars is a major sign of being a worshiper of the true God. The imagery of sacrifice is less pervasive than it became later in Hebrew history, but it is present as early as the story of Cain and Abel and their respective offerings (Gen 4:1-7). *Circumcision is the covenant sign. *Dreams sometimes carry a sacred message from God, and the *naming of children and places signals larger spiritual issues. Most pervasive of all are the divine-human

dialogues that permeate the book, and they are so direct that we hear little about humans praying to God, only of God's initiating conversations with mortals.

A final quality of Genesis that comes under the rubric of imagery is its thoroughgoing realism. Two aspects of it are especially worthy of note. One is evident in the selectivity of material: the writers include imperfect behavior as well as the good qualities of characters. There is almost more shadow than light in these hero stories, as the authors paint their heroes "warts and all." A second aspect is the elevation of the commonplace to a level of chief importance. Genesis is not primarily the story of international history but of family history. Except for the epoch-making events of primeval history, most of the events recorded in Genesis would not make the newspaper today, but would circulate within a family.

See also ABEL; ABRAHAM; ADAM; BABEL, TOWER OF; CAIN; COSMOLOGY; COVENANT; CREATION; EGYPT; ENDANGERED ANCESTRESS; ESAU; EVE; FLOOD; GARDEN; JACOB; JOSEPH THE PATRIARCH; SIBLING RIVALRY; SODOM AND GOMORRAH.

GENTILE

"Gentiles" is the general English rendering of the Hebrew terms *gôyim* and *'ammîm* and the Greek term *ethnē* when these terms are interpreted to refer to non-Israelites or non-Jews.

This is the most basic social, ethnic distinction that can be made—"not us" (like the Japanese term for foreigners, *gai jin*). In Pauline letters the word *akrobystia*, "foreskins" or "uncircumcision," is used to describe the Gentiles (Rom 2:26-27; 3:30; Gal 2:7; Eph 2:11; Col 3:11; cf. Acts 11:3). This term was created by the Jews in contrast to *peritomē*, *"circumcision." In the OT circumcision was the covenant sign for the people of God (Gen 17:11). As such, circumcision symbolized consecration to God (cf. Gen 17:1), and it naturally became a mark of *Israel's distinctiveness. On the contrary, uncircumcision represented the Gentiles, those outside the *covenant with God. Because the Gentiles were not dedicated and sanctified to God (Ezek 23:30), uncircumcision became a symbol for stubbornness and unbelief (Lev 26:41; Deut 10:16; 30:6; Jer 6:10; 9:25ff). The Gentiles as uncircumcision were indeed the people of *rebellion and disobedience, and they were thus viewed with contempt (Judg 14:3; 15:18; 1 Sam 14:6; 17:26, 36; 2 Sam 1:20; 1 Chron 10:4). In Christ, however, there is no distinction between circumcision and uncircumcision (1 Cor 7:19, Gal 5:6; 6:15; Col 3:11).

In Romans 11:17-24 the Gentiles are identified with the wild olive tree in contrast to the good olive tree. The olive tree was one of the most extensively cultivated fruit trees in the Mediterranean region and an important source of revenue (1 Sam 8:14; 2 Kings 5:26). Israel is pictured as an olive tree in the OT: "The LORD called you a thriving olive tree with fruit beautiful in form" (Jer 11:16 NIV; see also Hos 14:6). It signifies their spiritual blessing, prosperity and beauty (cf. Ps 52:8; 128:3). For Paul, in contrast, the wild olive tree, which by nature bears small and worthless fruit, is emblematic of the unfruitfulness of the Gentiles. The Gentile Christians, however, are now engrafted into the cultivated olive tree, the (believing) Jews.

The Gentiles are also regarded by Jews as *dogs and are so called in the incident of the Syrophoenician woman (Mt 15:26; Mk 7:27). When saying "Do not give dogs what is sacred" (Mt 7:6 NIV), Jesus quite possibly has the Gentiles in view. Moreover, it is written in the Jewish literature that "as the sacred food was intended . . . not for the dogs, the Torah was intended to be given . . . not to the Gentiles" (Babylonian Talmud Hagigah 13a). In the Bible the dog appears as an utterly unclean animal. A filthy scavenger, the dog wanders about the fields and streets of the cities, disposing of refuse and even dead bodies (1 Kings 14:11; 16:4; 21:19, 23; 22:38; 2 Kings 9:10, 36; Ps 59:6, 14; Lk 16:21). The animal thus symbolizes uncleanness (Prov 26:11; cf. 2 Pet 2:22; Rev 22:15), not affection and loyalty as in contemporary Western society. For the Jews the Gentiles are like dogs in their way of life: they live without the Torah, especially without its purity laws (1 Cor 9:21). Interestingly enough, however, in Philippians 3:2 Paul contemptuously calls Judaizing intruders "dogs."

While there are "righteous Gentiles" who, though they do not have the law, paradoxically show by their actions that it is written on their hearts (Rom 2:14), the term *Gentile* would remind a Jew of his greatest enemies. The "table of nations" in Genesis 10 provides a "map" of the Gentile world—an introduction to the antagonists in this story. From them certain paradigmatic Gentile enemies will emerge: *Egypt and Amalek of the Exodus story; the Hittites, Girgashites, Amorites, Canaanites, Perizzites, Hivites and Jebusites of the Conquest story (Deut 7:1; Josh 3:10; 24:11); the Assyrians and *Babylonians of the Exile story (see Christensen, 4:1037-39). Furthermore, the Gentile rulers are characterized as "lording it over them" (Mt 20:25; Mk 10:42; Lk 22:25); Jesus is "handed over" to the Gentiles and they do their awful work on him (Mt 20:19; Mk 10:33; Lk 18:32; Acts 4:27); Jerusalem will be "trampled" by the Gentiles until the "times of the Gentiles is fulfilled" (Lk 21:24). Paul can tick off the situation for Gentiles: "Separate from Christ, excluded from citizenship in Israel and foreigners to the covenants of the promise, without hope and without God in the world . . . far away" (Eph 2:12-13 NIV), their thinking is futile (Eph 4:17). Gentiles (and governors and kings) are the focus of the disciples' (or a select person's, Acts 9:15) "witness," and they cannot be expected to receive it gladly (Mt 10:18). In fact, Gentile hostility is aligned with Israel's hostility toward Jesus.

Yet a dramatic reversal of fortune enters as the gospel is spread throughout the world, and now in Christ God is even the God of the Gentiles (Rom 3:29), whom he calls "my people" (Rom 9:24-25). The former black sheep of the human family are now the envy of Israel, the chosen *son (Rom 11:11). Gentiles have become obedient servants (Rom 15:18) and share in the Jews' spiritual blessings (Rom 15:27). The Gentiles now join the congregation of praise as full members of the chorus (Rom 15:9-11), full citizens and members of God's household. As aliens from the "commonwealth of Israel," "strangers to the covenants of promise" and those who were "far off," they have now been made participants— even building stones—in a new *temple of God (Eph 2:11-22 RSV). In Acts we find that God has poured out his favor and Spirit "even upon the Gentiles" (Acts 10:45; 11:1, 18), a gift which many of them receive gladly (Acts 13:48), though the precise terms of their inclusion in the people of God is a matter of dispute (Acts 15:5-20).

See also BABYLON; CIRCUMCISION; COVENANT; DOG; EGYPT; FOREIGNER; ISRAEL.

BIBLIOGRAPHY. D. Block, "Nations," *ISBE* 3:492-96; D. Christensen, "Nations," *ABD* 4:1037-48.

GENTLENESS

"Gentle" or "gentleness" appears over twenty times in English translations of the Bible. In Proverbs we find two striking images of gentleness in its disarming power: "A gentle tongue can break a bone" (Prov 25:15 NIV) and "a gentle answer turns away wrath" (Prov 15:1 NIV).

The imagery of power and wrath that is so frequently associated with God is penultimate to his ultimate image as one who is gentle and merciful. For Elijah it is not the fierce *wind or the fearsome *earthquake or the blazing *fire of Sinai that bears the word of God but the "gentle whisper" (1 Kings 19:12 NIV). Gentleness is an image of God's ultimate subversive power that undercuts the power structures of this world. This is seen when Jesus, adopting imagery evocative of personified Wisdom in the apocryphal book of Sirach 51:23-26, describes himself as "gentle and humble in heart," his "yoke is easy" and his "burden is light" (Mt 11:29). James, in much the same vein, speaks of *wisdom "from above" as "gentle" as well as "peacable," "willing to yield, full of mercy and good fruits" (Jas 3:17 NRSV). Within the Bible we find gentleness associated with love and kindness (Acts 27:13; 1 Thess 2:7; 1 Tim 3:3; Phil 4:5; Col 3:12), meekness (Jer 11:19; Zech 9:9; 2 Cor 10:1) and *humility (Eph 4:2; 1 Pet 3:4).

Paul, the formerly zealous persecutor of the church, recognizes that gentleness does not come naturally for many. He explicitly lists gentleness as a fruit of the Spirit (Gal 5:23), a virtue that is planted and flourishes where God dwells by his Spirit. It is to be "put on" with other Christian virtues such as compassion, lowliness and patience (Col 3:12). Gentleness is Paul's preferred means of dealing with the church at Corinth: "What do you wish? Shall I come to you with a rod, or with love in a spirit of Gentleness?" (1 Cor 4:21). In speaking of his ministry among the Thessalonians, Paul's gentleness takes on maternal imagery: "like a nurse taking care of her children" (1 Thess 2:7). If gentleness is a *fruit of the *Spirit, it is certainly a quality to be sought in church leaders (1 Tim 3:3; 2 Tim 2:25; cf. Heb 5:2). Even sinners are to be restored to the community with gentleness (Gal 6:1). The picture of believers, individually and corporately, is of a gentle people who follow in the footsteps of their gentle Lord and master. Clearly this is not a gentleness that is naive or spineless but a gentleness that lives with principled firmness like the innocence of doves lives with the shrewdness of snakes (Mt 10:16).

See also HARD, HARDEN, HARDNESS; HUMILITY; MERCY.

GESTURES

The narration of gestures that accompany certain actions or emotions summons a vivid picture of act and actor. For participants of a given culture, the mere mention of the gesture is sufficient to communicate both a state of mind and attitude or even supply an unnamed emotion. The Bible contains many such allusions, now veiled by time and cultural distance.

Worship. The most numerous category is gestures associated with *worship and *prayer. Prayer in many ancient societies, and particularly in Israel, was practiced with raised and open *hands (1 Tim 2:8). Prayer and open hands occur as poetic parallels (Ps 141:2; Is 1:15). The mention of raised hands by itself also serves to indicate prayer, as when Moses "stretched out his hands to the LORD" (Ex 9:29, 33 RSV). The palm up gesture was probably one of several ritual motions integral to prayer (Job 11:13). Solomon "arose from before the altar of the LORD, where he had knelt with his hands outstretched to heaven" (1 Kings 8:54 RSV) as did Ezra (Ezra 9:5). Jeremiah envisions the people's prayer for help as "the daughter of Zion gasping for breath, stretching out her hands" (Jer 4:31 RSV; Lam 1:17). Perhaps when they were raised, the upturned palms metaphorically wafted the prayer upward: "Let my prayer be counted as incense before thee, and the lifting of my hands as an evening sacrifice" (Ps 141:2 RSV). Perhaps in popular conception the spirit, soul or heart ascended with the prayer. The imagery of Lamentations is even more direct, "Let us lift up our hearts with our palms to heaven" (Lam 3:41). The psalmist identifies the acceptable worshiper as one "who has clean hands . . . and who does not lift up his soul to what is false" (Ps 24:4 RSV). The act of raising the hands also reminded the suppliant that the prayer would go unheeded if the hands were "full of blood" (Is 1:15) or if there were "violence in my hands" (Job 16:17). The open palms also indicate a request of God: "Lift your hands to him for the lives of your children" (Lam 2:19 RSV); "I will lift up my hands and call on thy name" (Ps 63:4 RSV).

Raised hands were variously directed at different times in history: "Hear the voice of my supplication . . . as I lift up my hands toward thy most holy sanctuary" (Ps 28:2 RSV; cf. 1 Kings 8:38). Solomon knelt in the temple with his hands outstretched toward heaven (1 Kings 8:54, cf. Ps 5:7). Daniel prayed at a window open toward Jerusalem (Dan 6:10).

Scripture also mentions other positions and actions in association with prayer and worship. A long litany of descriptive terms refers to gestures of homage and loyalty: bending over, falling on the face (1 Sam 24:8, 14; 1 Kings 1:31), stooping (Ps 22:30; 1 Kings 19:18; 2 Chron 29:28; Is 45:23), *bowing the head (Is 58:5; Micah 6:6), bowing down (Dan 3:4), bowing the head between the knees (1 Kings 18:42; 2 Kings 4:34), standing and serving (Dan 3:3, 12; Mt 6:5; Mk 11:25), kneeling (Dan 6:11). The mere act of bending over implied loyalty and the service of worship. Naaman, the healed Syrian, was troubled by the implications of his obligatory bowing in the temple of the god Rimmon and asked in advance to be forgiven (2 Kings 5:18).

Deference and Obeisance. The proper attitudes for prayer and worship borrow heavily from the postures of obeisance. The service of deity and royalty share much terminology: "They bowed low and fell prostrate before the LORD and the king" (1 Chron 29:20 NIV). Those who approach the kings must bow (Gen 23:7; 2 Sam 9:6) and stoop (Esther 3:2), bow to the ground (2 Sam 14:33) or even fall (Gen 50:18).

As is widely attested in the ancient world, to beg a request of a superior one would grab his *feet (2 Kings 4:27). The Syrophoenician woman probably grabbed Jesus' feet (Mk 7:25). After the resurrection the disciples take hold of Jesus by the feet and worship him (Mt 28:9). Although it is not always stated, such actions often included *kissing the feet. The woman who was a sinner expressed her adoration by kissing Jesus' feet repeatedly (Lk 7:45). The vivid imagery of the phrase "lick the dust" may also refer to the practice of kissing the feet in subservience (Ps 72:9-11; Is 49:23; cf. Ps 44:25).

Greeting the Deity. Adoration of deities also found expression in kisses. The OT describes the faithful as those who have not bowed the knee to Baal and whose *mouths have not kissed him (1 Kings 19:18). Hosea speaks of those who kiss *calves (Hos 13:2). The kiss was part of Hebrew worship too: "Serve the LORD with fear, with trembling kiss his feet" (Ps 2:11 RSV, or even the older reading "kiss the Son" if the emendation to "kiss his feet" is unwarranted). Job denies that any of his actions can be construed as expressions of loyalty to pagan gods or being "false to the God above." Among other false deeds he mentions if "my mouth has kissed my hand; this also would be an iniquity" (Job 31:27-28 RSV). Perhaps this gesture symbolizes the "lifting up the soul" (Ps 24:2).

Greeting (Kiss). The *kiss in Scripture is an almost universal greeting (Rom 16:16; 1 Cor 16:20; 2 Cor 13:12; 1 Thess 5:26; 1 Pet 5:14) or farewell (Ruth 1:14; 1 Kings 19:20; Acts 20:37). Joseph kisses his father goodby even after he has died (Gen 50:1). In poetry the kiss parallels meeting (Ps 85:10) and is a sign of friendship or goodwill (Prov 24:26). Friends kiss at meeting and parting (1 Sam 20:41). Family members kiss each other, especially long lost family members (Gen 29:13; 33:4; 45:15; 48:10; Lk 15:20). Subordinates kiss masters. Kings kiss those beneath them (2 Sam 19:39).

Some kisses, those of peers, are to the face, some even on the lips between close friends (Prov 24:26). The common habit of kissing did not dilute the ardor of the lover's kiss (Songs 1:2), nor the suggestive kiss of an impudent woman (Prov 7:13). A kiss to superiors may be given to the feet as the recurring phrase "he bowed and kissed" intimates (Ex 18:7; note also 1 Kings 2:19 where the MT has "he bowed," but the LXX reads "he kissed her"). The difference between obeisance (probably bowing to kiss the feet) and a kiss on the face was not lost on Absalom who "stole away the hearts of the men of Israel" by treating them more as peers than servants (2 Sam 15:6).

The kiss, while expressing subservience, also marked one's approach as open and vulnerable. As a parallel in our society, an open hand extended in greeting underscores that the approaching person is unarmed. The kiss used as greeting extends the intimacy of the *family, assuring the greeted of the goodwill and protection of the offerer. A greeting psychologically disarms the other person. For those who would violate the rigid code of these interpersonal dynamics, the greeting gesture offers great potential for abuse. Such abuse was apparently not uncommon: "Profuse are the kisses of an enemy" (Prov 27:6 RSV). The dangers of feigned friendship occasionally became immediate realities. Joab treacherously eviscerates Amasa while greeting him (2 Sam 20:9-10). Judas revisits this traitorous plot, hoping his unobtrusive gesture, now a coded signal, will pass unnoticed. Jesus calls his disciples' attention to the perfidy, but does not thwart the plan (Mt 26:47; Lk 22:48). An obligatory social gesture such as a greeting can also function as a more subtle weapon. When withheld, it becomes a snub and a provocation. Jesus' prodding, "You gave me no kiss," acknowledges a social slight, perhaps an intended sign of disrespect (Lk 7:45).

Joy and Happiness. Many of the characteristic gestures and expressions associated with happiness hold elements in common even across disparate cultures, probably because they relate directly to physiological changes that are themselves universal. These include a "shining face" (Job 29:24), "light of the face" (Ps 89:15), likening the smile of the king to life-sustaining sunshine (Prov 16:15), the smiling face of God (Num 6:25; Is 60:1-5), the use of the noun *light* (Heb *'ôr*) and the verb *shine* (Heb *nāhar*) to mean "smile" (Is 60:5; Jer 31:12; Ps 34:5) and similarly for Hebrew *ṣāhal* and *ṣhr* "to shine" (Ps 104:15).

The *eyes in particular convey joy (1 Sam 14:27, 29; Ezra 9:8). The zest of life is stored in the eyes (Ps 13:3; 38:10). Living by God's commands "enlightens the eyes" (Ps 19:9). "The poor man and oppressor . . . the LORD gives light to the eyes of both" (Prov 29:13 RSV).

The joyful hold their head high (Ps 110:7). City *gates joyfully fling themselves open as if tossing the head in triumph (Ps 24:7, 9). A joyful worshiper throws the *head (*horn) high like a wild ox. "My horn is exalted in the LORD" (1 Sam 2:1 NKJV). The psalmist names God "the lifter of my head" (Ps 3:3 RSV). Clapping, the most portable and easily mastered of all musical instruments, accompanies shouts of celebration (Ps 47:1; Nahum 3:19).

Sadness and Mourning. In contrast to joy, an emotional burden bows *down the head (Gen 4:5) and puts one's *horn in the dust (Job 16:15). The one who laments is "bowed down and in mourning" (Ps 35:14 RSV). The required gesture of mourners is "sitting in the dust" (Is 47:1) or even to rolling in dust (Micah 1:10). The mourners say, "Our soul is bowed down to the dust; our body cleaves to the ground" (Ps 44:25 RSV). A mourning "soul cleaves to the dust" (Ps 119:25 RSV) perhaps sharing in the dusty destiny of the departed as symbolic participation in the nether world (Job 40:13; Ps 7:5).

Along with activities such as wailing, the mourner also dishevels the hair, wears torn clothes and tosses dust or *ashes into the air to settle on the head (2 Sam 1:2; Neh 9:1; Esther 4:1; Job 2:12; Is 58:5; Jer 6:26; Rev 18:19). Mourners in antiquity also engaged in self-mutilation. The prophets of Baal demonstrated their zeal by gashing themselves (1 Kings 18:28). This behavior may be linked to mourning the seasonal death of Baal as seen in the lack of rain (1 Kings 18:1). The worshipers bringing offerings to the temple of the Lord had shaved their *beards, torn their clothes (see Garments) and gashed their bodies (Jer 41:4). The word for mourning in NT Greek stems from the word for "to cut oneself" *(koptomai)*, hinting at the historic connection between the two actions, whether or not NT mourners still inflicted wounds on themselves (e.g., Lk 8:52).

Shame and Remorse. Self-mutilation may survive symbolically in a milder form in the *beating of the *breast (Lk 23:48). The sinful man cast down his eyes and beat his breast as signs of remorse (Lk 18:13). A similar gesture, probably a token form of self-flagellation, expresses Jeremiah's remorse and shame: "I smote upon my thigh" (Jer 31:19 RSV; cf. Ezek 21:12). The grieving "eat the bread of mourners" and "cover the lips" (Ezek 24:16-17). In response to shame, the nations "cover the mouth" and "lick the dust like a serpent" (Micah 7:16).

Anger and Aggravation. *Anger sometimes found expression in a clap of the hands. In frustration and anger at Balaam's failure to curse Israel, Balak struck his hands together (Num 24:10). Job observes that God sends the east wind against the wicked. "It claps its hands at him, and hisses at him from its place" (Job 27:23 RSV). Ezekiel's hand clap portends of doom: "Clap your hands, let the sword come down twice, thrice" (Ezek 21:14 RSV).

Additional gestures were used to express pent-up anger venting itself in physical reaction. The Jews became so frustrated at Paul's presentation of the gospel that the only way of they could think to register their protest was to cry out, wave their garments and throw dust into the air (Acts 22:23). The Lord "will shake his fist at the mount of the daughter of Zion" (Is 10:32 RSV). Shaking the head and the fist naturally accompany a diatribe (Job 16:4). Poets summon images of the wicked as aggressive carnivores: "they gnashed their teeth at me" (Ps 35:16 NIV).

Exaggerated *facial gestures accompany verbal taunts: "They make mouths at me; they wag their heads" (Ps 22:7 RSV). A beleaguered psalmist cries out, "I am an object of scorn to my accusers; when they see me, they wag their heads" (Ps 109:25 RSV, cf. Pss 22:7; 105:25). All who pass a ruined city clap their hands, hiss and wag their heads (Lam 2:15). Such gestures may also serve to ward off the evils that lurk in such desolate places (Zeph 2:14-15; Jer 19:8).

As an expression of disdain one might shake the dust from one's feet (Acts 13:51) or clothes (Acts 18:6), as if to suggest that even your dirt is bad company. Alternatively, the gesture may suggest a desire for complete disassociation in view of impending judgment (Mt 10:14).

A person who squints and purses the *lips betrays a scheming mind: "He who winks his eyes plans perverse things, he who compresses his lips brings evil to pass" (Prov 16:30 RSV). The wicked winks (narrows) his eyes (Prov 6:12).

Public addresses in the NT generally begin by mentioning that the speaker motioned for silence with the hand to quiet the crowd (Acts 12:17; 13:16; 19:33; 21:40; perhaps 26:1). The captors of the stolen Levite impose silence on him with the words, "Keep quiet, put your hand upon your mouth" (Judg 18:19 RSV).

See also BOWING; BREAST; FACE, FACIAL EXPRESSIONS; FEET; GARMENTS; HAND; KISS; KNEE; LIPS; MOURN, MOURNING; NOSE, NOSTRILS; PRAYER; WORSHIP.

GETHSEMANE. *See* GARDEN.

GIANT

The sway that giants have held over the human imagination is in excess of the number of their appearances in the Bible, where a great deal of mystery surrounds the references. We might note at the outset, then, that one of their associations is that of mystery—something beyond our ability to fully comprehend.

Four Hebrew words are translated as "giant" in various English translations. *Nephilim (n$^e\bar{p}$ilîm)* are mysterious preflood beings (Gen 6:4), rendered un-

forgettable in the evocative statement that "there were giants in the land" (KJV). *Anakim ($^{ca}n\bar{a}q\hat{i}m$)* were tall pre-Israelite inhabitants of Canaan (Deut 2:10-11, 21; 9:2), who in the report of the *spies are said to be descendants of the Nephilim (Num 13:33). *Rephaim (r$^e\bar{p}\bar{a}$'îm)* were likewise pre-Israelite inhabitants of Canaan (Deut 2:11; 3:11-13), not necessarily of gigantic proportions. And finally, *gibbor (gibbôr)* is a term used to designate a military hero or strong man, though it is uncertain whether they were gigantic in height and weight. With the possible exception of the Nephilim, who remain shrouded in mystery, all of the biblical giants are oversized humans whose superior size made them feared on the battlefield. The military province of the biblical giant is attested by the way references to them cluster in *battle contexts (2 Sam 21:16-22; 1 Chron 20:4-8).

In reading the passages describing the *giantesque inhabitants of Canaan, it is relevant to note that the Hebrews were a race of modest physical proportions. The majority report of the spies who returned from Canaan confirms this: the inhabitants were "men of great stature," said the spies, while "we seemed to ourselves like grasshoppers, and so we seemed to them" (Num 13:32-33 RSV).

The image of giants becomes more evocative when we move from classes to individuals. Nimrod, "the first on earth to be a mighty man" and "a mighty hunter before the LORD" (Gen 10:8-9 RSV), may have been a giant. Because of the link between the Rephaim and the land of Bashan, the powerful OT figure of Og, king of Bashan, may belong to the rank of giants. His *bed—made of iron and more than thirteen feet long and six feet wide—was of gigantic proportions (Deut 3:11). Even if this indicates royal magnificence rather than necessity, Og's mystique as a giant figure is fueled by the picture. The most celebrated giant of the Bible is the Philistine Goliath, the very epitome of more-than-ordinary size and strength (1 Sam 17). In Ezekiel 32:27-32, the catalog of powerful warriors fallen into Sheol includes ones that in the original Hebrew go by the name that is sometimes translated "giant."

Giants are a negative image in the Bible. They may have superior physical strength in battle, but they are pagans with whom God is displeased. These giants instill fear in God's people, but the interesting thing is that (except for Nimrod) God always instructs his people to destroy them, which they do. It is hardly too much to say that in the Bible giants are towering physical specimens on the verge of being toppled. These figures also have overtones of being grotesque freaks, as in the reference to the giant of Gath who was "a man of great stature, who had six fingers on each hand, and six toes on each foot, twenty-four in number" (2 Sam 21:20 RSV). The fate of this monster can stand as a summary of what giants in the Bible do and what God does to them in return: "When he taunted Israel, Jonathan . . . slew him" (v. 21).

See also GIANTESQUE MOTIF; MONSTER, MONSTERS

GIANTESQUE MOTIF

In addition to stories involving *giants, we find examples of the unexpectedly or extraordinarily large in the Bible. These texts are examples either of something miraculous or of the fictional preposterous. The "giantesque" is a prominent motif in the Bible.

One example is the story of *Samson. Since Samson is not identified as a giant, presumably he was of robust but ordinary physique. His exploits, though, are superhuman: killing a *lion barehanded, catching and torching three hundred foxes, killing a thousand warriors with the jawbone of an ass, carrying off city *gates, snapping ropes with which he was tied.

The story of *Jonah likewise specializes in the unexpectedly large. The narrative is either a fictional and embellished exaggeration of actual happenings or (in keeping with Jesus' implied view of the story in the NT) a true story in which God intervened miraculously. In either case, the story deals in bigger-than-life events. The first is God's sending his timorous prophet alone to preach a sermon of *judgment to the dread nation of Assyria, known for its terrorism. Equally huge is the "great fish" that God appointed to swallow Jonah (Jon 1:17), followed by Jonah's staying in the fish's belly a humanly impossible three days and three nights. When Jonah finally arrives in Nineveh, the writer amplifies the magnitude of the *city (making it a moral monstrosity as well as a physical reality) by referring to the entire city-state area (hence the information that the city was "three days' journey in breadth" [Jon 3:3]). Never in the history of the world has an eight-word sermon (Jon 3:4) resulted in such a mass conversion as the city of Nineveh experienced—a repentance so overwhelming that even the *animals were covered with sackcloth and made to *fast (Jon 3:7-8). Balancing the miraculously large *fish, God produces a shade plant overnight (Jon 4:6). Jonah even pouts on a huge scale (Jon 4:1-4, 8-9).

The master of the giantesque was Jesus. His most characteristic rhetorical effect—more frequent even than his fondness for paradox—was the preposterous exaggeration, often used in the service of *satire. Among Jesus' humorous vignettes based on overstatement are the spectacle of a camel passing through the eye of needle, someone taking elaborate precautions to strain out a gnat and then proceeding to swallow a camel, and a person with a beam of *wood protruding from his eye solicitously trying to remove a speck from his neighbor's eye. Elsewhere we are asked to consider the possibility that one's right *hand does not know what the left is doing, the advice of plucking out just one *eye or one arm as the sole cause of sin, the sight of *mountains tumbling into the sea because a person has adequate faith to perform the feat, and the miraculous growth of a mustard plant that becomes a gigantic *tree whose branches reach into heaven. G. K. Chesterton claimed in *Orthodoxy* that the diction used *about* Christ has been serious, but the diction used *by* Christ "is quite curiously gigantesque; it is full of camels leaping through needles and mountains hurled into the sea." E. Trueblood, who explicates the pattern in full detail, compares Jesus' overstatements to "our conventional Texas story, which no one believes literally, but which everyone remembers."

Another source of the giantesque is the visionary literature of the Bible, where fantasy is a frequent genre. Here we enter a world where a river overflows an entire nation (Is 8:5-8), where a ram's *horn grows to the sky and knocks *stars to the ground (Dan 8:9-10), where a treetop can reach into the *clouds and serve as a shade for "all great nations" (Ezek 31:3, 6) and where a *locust can be amplified into a being as terrifying as a warrior (Rev 9:7-11). To which we might add the "mighty angel" who sets his "right foot on the sea, and his left foot on the land" (Rev 10:1-3), a "great red dragon" whose tail sweeps down a third of the stars of heaven (Rev 12:3-4), and a serpent whose mouth pours forth "water like a river," capable of sweeping a woman away with the flood (Rev 12:15). In short, much of what happens in the *apocalyptic writings of the Bible exists on a cosmic scale, at a magnitude known only in our imaginations, not in the empirical world in which we live.

Giantesque imagery also appears in passages that portray God. God's steadfast love is as great "as the heavens are high above the earth" (Ps 103:11). His faithfulness extends "to the clouds," his righteousness is "like the *mountains," and his judgments are "like the great *deep" (Ps 36:5-6). His power and righteousness "reach the high heavens" (Ps 71:18-19). God is so huge that he can gather "the waters of the sea as in a bottle" and "put the deeps in *storehouses" (Ps 33:6-7).

The *tour de force* in the Bible's giantesque passages is the portraits in Job 40—41 of Behemoth and Leviathan. The real-life phenomena on which the portraits are based are apparently a hippopotamus and a crocodile respectively, but by the time the time the imagination has worked its amplifying magic on them, they are clearly bigger-than-life specimens.

See also GIANT; MONSTER, MONSTERS.

BIBLIOGRAPHY. E. Trueblood, *The Humor of Christ* (New York: Harper & Row, 1964).

GLASS. See HEAVEN; PERMANENCE; SEA.

GLEAN

Although the word *gleaning* may conjure up a romantic image of cloud-filled skies, tall sheaves of *grain and joyous peasant girls, the actual biblical custom was rooted in the practical necessity of caring for the poor. The Mosaic *law stipulated that owners allow needy persons to gather the grain that remained after the reapers had made a single sweep of their fields (Lev 19:9-10; Lev 23:22; Deut 24:19-21).

While the romantic notion may be sentimentalized, the powerful pastoral image is not inappropriate to the biblical idea of gleaning. The simple injunctions in Leviticus and Deuteronomy are fleshed out in the example of *Ruth, who, coming to Bethlehem with her mother-in-law Naomi, takes on the multiple roles of alien, maiden, provider and redeemer as she gleans in the fields of Boaz.

Although the fields suggest a pastoral setting appropriate for the great grandparents of King David, this is also the time of the judges, a period marked by disobedience to God and violence in the land, when there is a real danger that a woman may be molested as she gleans in the fields of Israel (Ruth 2:22). Yet Ruth proves her own words that "your people shall be my people, and your God my God" (Ruth 1:16 RSV) as she undertakes to provide for herself and Naomi according to the law. Similarly, Boaz shows himself to be a godly man as he not only allows gleaning in his field but shows generosity to the *foreigner in the land (2:8-16). Thus the centrality of gleaning, a word used no less than eleven times in the second chapter of this book, reinforces the covenantal relationship into which Ruth and Boaz enter.

The literal image of gleaning also provides a haunting picture of judgment and misery. In Jeremiah 6:9 gleaning depicts God's complete *judgment of the nation. *Grapes are used for this image because unlike grain, one can more completely strip the *vines. In Joshua 24:6 and Micah 7:1, gleaning symbolizes the misery of *poverty; and in Job, we find the cruel irony of the righteous gleaning in the wicked person's vineyard (Job 24:6).

See also FARMING; GRAIN; GRAPES; HARVEST; VINE, VINEYARD.

GLORY

With references in English Bibles ranging from 275 (NIV) to 350 (RSV), glory is one of the master images that helps to tell the story of the Bible. A survey of the references yields a tour of the some of the Bible's great moments—from the giving of the law (Ex 24:12-18), to the *wilderness wanderings of Israel (Num 14:10, 21, 22; 16:19, 42; 20:6), to the worship of God in the *tabernacle (Lev 9:6, 23) and *temple (1 Kings 8:11; 2 Chron 5:14), to the call and prophetic vision of the prophets Isaiah (Is 6) and Ezekiel (Ezek 1), to the birth (Lk 2:9) and transfiguration of Jesus (Lk 9:31; 2 Pet 1:7), to the final, apocalyptic scene of the holy city *Jerusalem descending in the clouds (Rev 21:23-34).

Glory includes splendor, *beauty, magnificence, radiance and rapture. In the Bible it is primarily a quality ascribed to God and places of his presence, including places of *worship and *heaven. The glory of God is an image of his greatness and transcendence, and it is associated with the huge aspects of earthly experience—with the *sun and *moon, for example (Ps 19:1) instead of a field, or with a powerful *thunderstorm (Ps 29:3, 9) instead of a gentle rain. To encounter the glory of God is always awe inspiring and numinous.

Because glory appears as a stock evaluative term to ascribe greatness to God, it may appear to be more of an abstraction than a concrete image. A good starting point, therefore, is the Shekinah of God that appeared in visible form in both the tabernacle and the temple. When the tabernacle was dedicated, a *cloud of glory covered the tent and the glory of God filled it, subsequently appearing as a cloud by day and a pillar of fire by night in the wilderness wanderings of Israel (Ex 40:34-38). A similar event accompanied the dedication of the temple (2 Chron 7:1-3), where the glory of God had a palpable identity. We can catch glimpses of this in references in the Psalms to the presence of God in the temple: "The LORD is in his holy temple" (Ps 11:4 RSV); "O LORD, I love the habitation of thy house, and the place where thy glory dwells" (Ps 26:8 RSV); "So I have looked upon thee in the sanctuary, beholding thy power and glory" (Ps 63:2 RSV).

Glory is an image of divine transcendence as it makes itself visible to people. It combines awe and *terror, and it simultaneously invites approach and distance. When Moses encounters the glory of God on Mt. *Sinai, the visible manifestation is a cloud that covers the *mountain and brilliance "like a devouring *fire" (Ex 24:16-17). When Moses requests to see God's glory, it is so intense that God has to shield him from the full effect (Ex 33:18-23). In Psalm 29, the song of the thunderstorm, "the God of glory" is said to thunder upon the waters (v. 3), filling human observers with such wonder and terror that they cry, "Glory!" (v. 9). God brandishes glory as a soldier wields a sword. Both sacred and dangerous, glory inspires awe, fear and respect on the part of the beholders. When Isaiah and Ezekiel individually encounter the glory of God in a vision, their response is to feel small and unworthy (Is 6:5; Ezek 1:28). The glory of God is in some sense communicable by those who have seen it, for Moses' face shone whenever he spoke to God (Ex 34:29-35).

The fifty references to the glory of God in the psalms are epitomized by Psalm 24:7-10, a litany that celebrates the presence of God as he is encountered in worship. This passage repeatedly invites the "King of Glory," the great and mighty Lord of hosts, to "come in" and join the congregation. Here glory is a friend, not a foe. At the same time, this king of glory is grand—"strong and mighty," "mighty in battle." And it is not just *any* door that he is invited to enter, but the "ancient doors" of the temple.

Glory is a prominent image in the eschatological images of the OT, as the prophets foresee a new day—a time in which "the glory of the LORD shall be revealed and all flesh shall see it together" (Is 40:5 RSV). The nations will flood into Jerusalem because "the LORD will arise upon" the city and "his glory will be seen" there (Is 60:2). All will come to Jerusalem to "drink deeply with delight from the abundance of her glory" (Is 66:11). The eschatological revelation of glory enacts a series of unparalleled transformations—a transformation of human relationships, society at large, the human heart and even the whole world. To those in need of hope, the promised theophany inspires the stamina to face difficult circumstances and to believe once again.

The NT boldly identifies Jesus as glory, and in doing so it weaves together nearly all the strands of glory. Glory pervades the divine genealogy that John provides for Jesus at the beginning of his Gospel: "We have beheld his glory, glory as of the only Son from the Father" (Jn 1:14 RSV). At the birth of Jesus "the glory of the Lord shone around" the shepherds (Lk 2:9) and the *angelic host proclaimed, "Glory to God in the highest" (Lk 1:14). Although the specific word *glory* does not appear in the accounts of the transfiguration of Jesus, it is a supreme instance of Christ's visible glory. His *resurrection is an example of glory (Lk 24:26; Rom 6:4; 1 Pet 1:21), as is his *ascension (1 Tim 3:16). Paul calls Jesus "the Lord of glory" (1 Cor 2:8) and speaks of "the glory of God in the face of Christ" (2 Cor 4:6). To experience the glory of God in Christ has mystical overtones in many passages where the word appears, and it is always an encounter with God's transcendence. When the dying Stephen gazes into heaven, he sees "the glory of God, and Jesus standing at the right hand of God" (Acts 7:55 RSV).

The NT eschatological visions share with the OT ones an emphasis on the motif of future glory. Christ himself will come "in his glory, and all the angels with him" (Mt 25:31; cf. Mk 8:38; 13:26). The emphasis in NT eschatological passages, however, is on the way in which believers will share the glory of Christ. Peter speaks of being "a partaker in the glory that is to be revealed" (1 Pet 5:1) and of believers who have suffered being restored by God "who has called you to his eternal glory in Christ" (1 Pet 5:10). The affliction of life, writes Paul, "is preparing for us an eternal weight (*see* Heavy) of glory beyond all comparison, because we look not to the things that are seen but to the things that are unseen" (2 Cor 4:17-18 RSV). "Christ in you" is "the hope of glory" (Col 1:27), and when Christ appears "you also will appear with him in glory" (Col 3:4).

The foregoing references are only the tip of the iceberg. Glory is one of the great positive images of the Bible, the language of the mystic and of the believing heart that has glimpsed the greatness of God. It is paradoxically a divine quality that is remote from human finitude and yet is held out to believers as something they will share.

See also BEAUTY; CLOUD; FIRE; GOD; HEAVY; HOLINESS; LIGHT; SINAI; TABERNACLE; TEMPLE; ZION.

GO UP. *See* ASCENT.

GOAT

The primary mention of goats in Scripture relates to their part in the OT sacrificial system. Bulls, rams, goats, *lambs, *doves and pigeons were all used,

some of them interchangeably, to burn in sacrifice to God for the purpose of *atonement and *worship. Goats, however, played a distinct symbolic role in the ceremonies required by God for the annual Day of Atonement. In those ceremonies, and in several other scriptural passages, goats primarily give us a picture of *sin, its consequences and the need for atonement and forgiveness.

Once a year, God instructed the Israelites, atonement had to be made for all the sins of all the people, who would then be clean before the Lord (Lev 16:29-34). On the tenth day of the seventh month, the high priest was to take with him into the most holy place a young bull for a sin offering for himself and his household, two male goats for a sin offering for the people, and two rams for burnt offerings. The two goats constituted the most unique and symbolic element of the Day of Atonement: the priest cast lots to select one goat "for the LORD" and the other "for the *scapegoat" (Lev 16:8). The first goat was slaughtered, its blood taken into the most holy place and its body taken outside the camp and burned. The NT book of Hebrews symbolizes the costly death of Christ, who also "suffered outside the city gate" to take away our sins (Heb 13:12 NIV). But when Jesus offered himself as the perfect sin offering—one sacrifice for sins, for all time—he finished the sacrifice and sat down at the right hand of God (Heb 10:12).

The high priest presented the other goat alive before the Lord, laying his hands on the goat's head and confessing over it all the Israelites' sins, putting them on the goat's head, and then sending the goat away into the desert (Lev 16:20-22). That scapegoat (literally, "goat of removal"), carrying all the sins of the people far away, becomes a symbol of Christ as well, who took our sins on himself in order to remove them from us "as far as the east is from the west" (Ps 103:12). The picture of substitutionary atonement in these lowly goats is a beautiful and holy one, not to be forgotten, even though a more consistent pattern of scriptural imagery connects Christ's death with the sacrifice of the lamb offered for the *guilt offering and for the *Passover sacrifice.

Other scriptural mentions of goats attribute more of a natural wildness to them than to lambs. They are more often pictured, for example, on the high mountains or leaping about or pushing to the head of the *flock (Job 39:1; Ps 104:18; Is 13:21; Jer 50:8). In Daniel's prophetic vision a great goat, representing a powerful empire, charges across the whole earth without touching the ground and attacks a huge *horned ram (a rival empire), knocking him down and trampling on him (8:5-8).

Probably the best known biblical picture of goats comes in Jesus' parable of the sheep and the goats (Mt 25:31-46). The shepherd (*see* Sheep, Shepherd) represents the Son of Man finally separating the righteous (the sheep) from the cursed (the goats). The point of the parable is the inevitable coming judgment, according to the heart and life of each individual person. Jesus' listeners would have recognized the picture of a large flock made up of hundreds, often thousands of various cattle all mixing and grazing together. The process of separating out one kind from another, for purposes of tallying, breeding and sacrificing, occurred regularly.

Ezekiel as well used this process as a picture of judgment: distinguishing "between one sheep and another, and between rams and goats" symbolized for him the judgment of God on Israel for their ungodly treatment of the poor and needy (34:17-24). Ezekiel and Jesus both talk about love for the rest of the flock, specifically about the sharing of water and food with the weak and lowly, the ones with whom the shepherd identifies.

In Ezekiel's picture, however, there are good and bad sheep and rams and goats. In the NT picture the sheep are saved and the goats are lost. In Jesus' parable of final judgment, God is no longer judging the nation of Israel; rather, he is calling out of all the nations one peculiar people who are his own (Mt 25:32). Ezekiel prophesied about this Shepherd and his sheep (Ezek 34:23-31). His flock will be finally distinguished as one kind, his own sheep, the ones who truly followed him. The goats come to represent all the others who mixed with the flock but who were not known by the shepherd as his own.

Goats, then, are most often associated in Scripture with sin in one way or another. (To this day we stigmatize an athlete whose lapse contributed to the defeat of his or her team as the "goat" of the loss). In the sacrificial system, goats carried sin; and in Jesus' parable, they are the ones whose sin has not been forgiven. The biblical pictures of goats illustrate the human need for the forgiveness of sin.

Lest we think that goats are irredeemably bad animals in the Bible, we find a minor motif that grows out of the fact that goats' hair is used in making valuable *cloth (as cashmere is made from goats' hair today). The curtains of the tabernacle were made from goats' hair (Ex 25:4; 26:7; 35:6, 23, 26; 36:14; cf. Num 31:20). In addition, we note that the enraptured lover in the Song of Songs intended a compliment when he compared his beloved's *hair to that of "a flock of goats, moving down the slopes of Gilead" (Song 4:1; 6:5 NRSV). While this could evoke a sketchy visual picture of cascading hair, or hair flowing in the wind, it is more likely a value image in which the beloved's hair is compared to its most valuable counterpart in nature.

See also ANIMALS; FLOCK; HORN; LAMB; SCAPEGOAT; SHEEP, SHEPHERD.

GOD

Most investigations of the view of God in the Bible focus on something other than images of God. Many focus on the names of God (e.g., *Yahweh, Elohim, Adonai*), the attributes of God or the work/roles of God (creator, judge, redeemer). When images come into play, they tend to be those that seem to come closest to being titles for God, such as *King, Lord and *Father, or those that are widely known, such as

*shepherd and potter. Though it is right and proper to explore the person and work of God in each of these ways, it is primarily through images that God opens up to us and reveals something of his divine nature, purposes, character and activities.

Types of Imagery for God. There are various kinds of images of God in the Bible. Indeed, all the different types of figurative language seem to be represented there. For example, we find *circumlocution*—a roundabout way of referring to someone or something—as in "the Majesty on High" (Heb 1:3 NRSV) or "the Mighty One of Jacob (Gen 49:24), and *metonym*—using the part for the whole—such as "the name" of God (Jer 27:12-15). But in the Bible the comparative forms of figurative language—*simile, metaphor, analogy, parable*—are most often used for God. This is understandable, since through this imagery we proceed from the known to the lesser known or unknown, making it an excellent way to talk about God. Our daily speech and our formal exchanges are full of such language, as is the Bible with its contents ranging from everyday discourse to theological reflection. Comparative language, then, is the way God mostly communicates to us. The full range of comparative language—similes, metaphors, analogies and parables—is found in biblical depictions of God, and in places it reaches toward, but does not quite cross, the borders of allegory.

Some of the comparisons are of a conventional kind and have a familiar ring. An example would be God as king (e.g., Ex 15:18). Psalms and Proverbs, echoing as they do the corporate worship of Israel and commonsense reflection on everyday life, tend to contain more stock metaphors than other forms of literature. Other metaphors are novel and surprising, sometimes even shocking. Here we could place God as singer (e.g., Zeph 3:17) and as a drunken soldier (Ps 78:65). The Prophets and the Gospels contain many such comparisons, as do singular books like Job and novel forms like the Epistles. And there are always comparisons that are on a line between these two. Here, perhaps, we could place God as father, since it moves from being a more formal description of God as the creator, preserver, savior and guide of the nation (e.g., Jer 3:4, 19) to an intimate address of God as "my father" by the individual believer (e.g., Rom 8:15). Another example might be God as the vinegrower and Israel as the *vine, for this is subject to various permutations (e.g., from Is 15 to Jn 15). Sometimes, as in the Prophets and the Epistles, comparisons are mixed with one another to provide variations on a theme or, as the Psalms and Job have done intensively, to add freshness to what is being said.

One of the difficulties in deciding whether a statement contains an image of God is deciding whether a living or dead metaphor is involved. This is not the same as talking about conventional and novel comparisons, for even stock images, both in corporate worship and in everyday communication, can have vitality for those who hear and use them.

Dead metaphors are those whose original point of comparison has been so subsumed in the use of the word that it no longer registers in people's imaginations. In this case, a word now has a literal rather than figurative sense. A good example would be speaking of people as the "offspring" of God, as Paul does on the Areopagus (Acts 17:28), for this no longer has any biological connotations and means only that God is the ultimate source of all creatures.

Sacred and Religious Images. Given the religious nature of the images of God, many would expect to find sacred places, people and objects being a fertile source of language about God. If this were the case, it would position God in the religious rather than profane sphere of life. God is obviously associated with such places as the *temple, such figures as the *priests, and such objects as *sacrifices. One of the regular epithets for God is the "Holy One" (Josh 24:19), though this increasingly develops a moral rather than a cultic meaning (Is 6:3). God is also described as taking the place of the temple in the heavenly city (Rev 21:22), and God's Son is described as the *Lamb sacrificed for the sins of the world (Rev 5:6). On the whole, however, the realm of the sacred is not a major source of figurative language for God.

The reason for this is not hard to seek. God is the God of the whole world and everything in it. God cannot be confined to the sacred dimension of life. God created everything, indwells everything and transforms everything. And in some degree everything reflects something of God, images God in the fuller sense in the case of human beings (Gen 1:26) or reveals some aspect of God in the case of the material world (Ps 8:1-9). This means that everything and anything can become a vehicle for comprehending God.

Family and Relationships. Many references to God stem from the circle of the immediate and extended family. In the OT, references to God as *father, occurring first in Deuteronomy, are not numerous (Deut 32:6). They occur mostly in the Prophets and the Psalms, with a more poetic flavor in the latter. References are mostly metaphorical and relate particularly to God's being the creator and provider, and later the *rescuer and *guide (Is 64:8), sometimes with a special concern for the powerless (Ps 68:5). In the mouth of the king in Psalms, but on the lips of Jesus in the Gospels, this address gains a new intimacy (Mt 18:10). God is also husband of the people (Is 54:5), a description that denotes uniqueness of the bond established through the covenant. In Hosea, for example, God refuses to abandon Israel in spite of their adulterous liaisons with foreign gods, and he makes extreme effort to woo them back again (Hos 2:4—3:5). Here God is the deeply wounded, betrayed lover who remains totally committed to the original bond.

With respect to the wider family, God is described as *redeemer (Is 41:14), a term that has strong overtones of the kinsman fulfilling an obligation to members of the family who require their benevolent assistance (cf. Ruth 4:1-12). Though God is never called *mother or *wife—understandable in view of Israel's temptation to follow after the fertility gods of the surrounding nations—various comparisons with the work of a mother or wife do appear in the biblical writings. So God is likened to one who is pregnant (Is 6:3-4), gives *birth (Is 42:14), acts as midwife (Ps 22:9-10), *nurses (Is 49:15), is a homemaker (Ps 123:2). All gender-related language in the Bible is metaphorical, so there are no sexual connotations involved in references to parents or spouse. Among other relationships taken up into images of God, one that does not occur often but is still prominent is that of God as *friend (Ex 33:11; Is 41:8; Jas 2:23). This speaks of the frankness and honesty of God in communicating with certain people and suggests the role of a benefactor with a protégé rather than a relationship of equals.

Civic and Military Life. The most common image for God from political life is that of *king. This image appeared even before Israel had a monarchy (Ex 15:18). It is used, especially in the prophets and the psalms (Is 41:21; Ps 44:4), to express God's national and universal, political and cosmic preeminence and sovereignty. The psalmist's addressing of God sometimes as "my king" indicates that it was not purely a general ascription (Ps 5:2).

God is also frequently referred to as lawgiver (Deut 5:1-22) and as judge (Gen 18:25). These are civic roles. The first plays a special role in the OT, and the second a major role throughout the whole Bible. The first identifies God as the one who provides basic instruction for the people in their moral, religious and civic obligations, the second on God as the one who will ensure that these are not transgressed or that people are not wrongly oppressed through their abuse. There are other references to God as advocate (Is 1:18), drawn from the language of local courts (see Legal Images). Here it is God's impartiality and integrity, especially toward the needy, that is chiefly in view (Deut 10:17b-18a).

Since *war, as someone has said, is merely politics by another name, pictures of God as *divine warrior (Ex 15:3) overlap with these civic metaphors. All aspects of military endeavor—from consulting about, preparing for, declaring of, fighting in, and finally to winning a war—are given figurative meanings. In the later books of the Bible the imagery is used particularly of God's intervention to bring in the eschatological age. A variant on this imagery is God as the Mighty One (Deut 32:4), or as the *enemy (Lam 2:4). In some of the ancient poetic sections of the Bible, God is occasionally represented as the divine rider of the skies (Deut 33:26) or of the *clouds (Ps 68:5). This also reflects a military setting. (This is certainly so with the description of Christ as the divine rider in Revelation 19, with its various references to the implements of war.) Many other references to different facets of the experience of battle are applied to God's struggle for the chosen people's allegiance and holiness in the face of all the forces that seek to subvert these.

Work and Technology. Besides being spoken of generally as Maker (Job 4:17; 32:22; 35:10; Prov 14:31; 17:5; 22:2; Is 17:7), a wide range of human occupations and current technologies are called into use to describe various facets of God's work. The most common are *shepherd (Ps 23:1), potter (Is 64:8), *builder (Ps 102:25) and *farmer (Ps 80:8; Hos 10:11). Sometimes particular forms of these are in view, as in comparisons between God as crop farmer, winegrower and orchardist. Other images based on work include God as metalworker (Is 1:24-26) and tentmaker (Ex 25:9). Some images are drawn from work associated particularly with the home: God as knitter (Ps 139:13-16), weaver (Job 10:10-12), clothes maker (e.g., Gen 3:21; Is 45:5), gardener (e.g., Gen 2:8) and housecleaner (e.g., Is 14:23). These are among the earliest images of God to appear in the Bible. Secondary images within these general ones also occur. With respect to farming, God appears as the one who prepares the soil, *sows or plants the seed, tends, waters and *prunes, then reaps, *harvests, binds or *threshes, and places crops in a *storehouse.

All aspects of God's work can be referred to by such images—creation, providence, compassionate care, bringing of justice, redemption, community-building, sanctification, future transformation—not just the more menial tasks in which God is engaged. Since technology was involved in all of these, it is clear that in these comparisons there is no discrimination against work based on human inventions in favor of that which is more in touch with the created order or life in the home. Even the farmer uses technology, for example the plough; and simple technology was not absent from the home. On the other hand, some types of work taken up figuratively into descriptions of God, for example metalworking, were at the leading edge of ancient technology (it was metalworkers who developed the first factories in Israel). Industrial imagery, therefore, is not foreign to the OT.

Communication and Help. One of the most common appellations of God in the Bible is instructor or *teacher (Ex 4:15). This divine role has application to leaders among the people, to individual believers and to the people as a whole. So integral is this to God that the conjunction of *Wisdom (Prov 8) and the Word (Jn 1:1-18) with God is extremely close. Included within the role of the teacher is that of mentor: God is the one who not only tells but also shows people what to do so that they can imitate the divine example (Deut 10:18-19). God is presented as a role model as well as teacher. Other images portray God as composer (Deut 31:19) and as singer (e.g., Zeph 3:17).

God is once entitled healer (Ex 15:26) but many times described as one engaged in healing activities (e.g., Is 20:36; *see* Disease and Healing). Uppermost here is God's capacity to save people from disease or make them whole from sickness, though the latter is often closely associated with the *forgiveness of sins (e.g., Ps 103:3). Here we should also place references to God as helper (Ps 10:14), especially of the powerless, and protector (e.g., Ps 116:6) of the poor, humble, bereaved, innocent, *weak and needy, as well as those often unjustly treated, such as *women, *workers, *foreigners, *slaves, *orphans and the persecuted. God is also portrayed as the *comforter (e.g., Is 40:1ff) and as the savior (Ps 25:5) of both individuals and the people.

Nature. *Nature is a surprisingly fertile field for images of God. In view of the fact that the God of the Bible is intensely personal and that human beings are the high point of creation, one might have expected otherwise. That this is not the case underlines again how God is the source, the sustainer and the ultimate goal of everything, and that even subhuman forms of life can reflect something of God. Each, as Paul says, has its particular "beauty," or "glory" (1 Cor 15:40-41).

In this category we have some of the most common images of God in the Bible. For example, God is *light (Ps 27:1), *fire (Deut 4:24; 9:3) and *rock (Ps 18:2, 31, 46). (The latter is usually combined with *fortress, thus containing elements of a military metaphor.) These speak respectively of the incomparable glory, the passionate justice and the monumental strength of God. There are other, more occasional images, including God as Lord of *Banners (Ex 17:15 NIV), a sign of victory over the enemy.

In many places similes or metaphors compare God to an *animal. They include the *lion (Hos 11:10), leopard (Hos 13:7) and *eagle (Deut 32:11-12). God is also likened to a bear who has lost her cubs (Hos 13:8) and to a hen hiding her chicks under her *wings (Ps 17:8-9). There seems to be no discrimination against any particular species or animal. Even though Satan can be compared to a lion (1 Pet 5:8) so also, as just mentioned, can God and Christ (Rev 5:5). They are lion-like in different ways, or to different ends. All this is possible because the creatures God has made reflect, in one way or another, aspects of the God who made them.

Interpreting Images of God. The presence of this wide range of imagery in the Bible has been subject to differing evaluations. For some this concrete language is an embarrassment; others welcome it. There are two issues here: First, are there any signs of a progression from more to less concrete, from figurative to more abstract, language for God in the Bible? Second, how satisfactory is this language for properly understanding or communicating God?

The first question raises the wider issue of the role of anthropomorphic language in the Bible. In retrospect, this debate was actually too anthropocentric in character, for it should have been broadened to include what we might term *cosmomorphic* language for God; that is, reference to nonhuman, whether animal or material, as well as human forms for divine realities. Anthropomorphic language is strongly present in the earliest parts of the Bible, where we have reference to God *walking in the Garden of Eden (Gen 3:8), closing the door of the Ark (Gen 7:16), *smelling the aroma of Noah's sacrifice (Gen 8:21) and *descending to have a closer look at the tower of *Babel (Gen 11:5). God is also described in many places as having *arms (Num 11:23), *hands (Ps 111:7), a *mouth (Deut 8:3), a *voice (Deut 30:20), *eyes (Deut 11:12), *ears (Ps 5:1) and, more generally, a *face (Ps 114:7). Likewise, God is portrayed as experiencing a wide range of human emotions, such as regret (Gen 6:6), *anger (Ex 15:7), jealousy (Ex 20:5) and loathing (Lev 20:23).

But in all this, God's sovereignty and transcendence are never in doubt. God is everywhere not only larger than human life but unmarked by human failings and unbound by human limitations. This language has a different atmosphere from descriptions of the Greek Olympian gods, who for all their larger-than-life character, have many recognizable human failings and limitations. This is true even of the early chapters of the OT, where the degree of anthropomorphism is only relative, as well as of the nonnarrative books of the Bible, from the early to the late prophets and throughout the psalms. An interesting test case of the compatibility of anthropomorphic language with an emphasis on the transcendence of God is the second part of Isaiah (40—66), which contains the most exalted and sublime statements about the incomparability of God in the entire Bible.

In all these writings God is clearly God and not human (Hos 11:9), and God's thoughts and ways surpass human understanding (Is 55:8-9). The wisdom writings highlight this powerfully; for example, the book of Job, especially its closing chapters (Job 38—42), and Ecclesiastes, especially certain statements within it (Eccles 4:1-3). What makes these works particularly interesting is that the tradition from which they stem drew heavily on observations of the natural and human world for its understanding of God's ways. In the NT the picture is no different. *Jesus consistently and innovatively speaks of God and the *kingdom of God in language drawn from everyday life, using a wide range of similes, metaphors and parables. Though this may be less marked in Paul, it is certainly present in his letters. And at the end of the NT the book of Revelation is as full of anthropomorphic language as it is of the incomparability and omnipotence of God.

So we cannot say that there is a development from more to less concrete language for God in the Bible. In every period we find anthropomorphic, and within that, figurative language in plentiful supply. Some metaphors run like a thread through the whole Bible as different writers play variations on a theme with them. Good examples of this are portrayals of God as father, judge, shepherd, builder, potter, teacher and light. As this list of images suggests, it is not only those that stem from the most personal dimensions of life that keep recurring in the Bible, but also those from all areas of life and levels of existence. There are two basic reasons for this. One

is that imagination is basic to all understanding and communication. We cannot think or talk without it. It is, echoing the title of a recent book, metaphors that we live by. Even abstract language simply replaces one kind of figurative language for another, one that is generally less dynamic in character and less accessible to the majority of people. (In relation to God—one thinks here of Tillich's description of God as "the Ground of Being"—such language often draws in part on the imagery of *depth [Ps 139:7] rather than *height [Dan 4:17], imagery the Bible also uses in a more concrete way.) Another reason, as already noted, is God's ability to turn anything that exists to linguistic effect precisely because of its divine source and its being a reflection of divine realities. Because God has set up the creation in a way that provides correspondence of some kind between human and divine realities and has established language as the vehicle through which this primarily takes place, images of God are basically reliable. The basis for this lies in the Bible's insistence that there is a close identification, indeed intrinsic coherence, between what God says and what God does (Gen 1:1; Jn 1:1).

This raises the issue of how far this language can take us into comprehending God. Even if it is unavoidable and appropriate, how reliable is it? It could be said that since figurative language is at the heart of the way we talk about everything, this is all that we have; therefore, we have to be content with it. If images of God are more basic than concepts of God—even though concepts of God are not alien to the Bible and in any case flow out of its images—then they are the foundation on which all other thinking about God takes place. Not only is there no other route to divine truth, but this is the best route to divine truth. We can go further than this. It is, after all, God who has spoken to us in this way. Interesting in this regard is the way passages presented as springing directly from God's mouth invariably contain a high level of figurative language (e.g., Ex 3; Jer 14). Whether God spoke these directly or they are prophetic recastings of messages is not really the point, for in either case there is a felt consistency between such language and God. Given the Bible's view of its God-breathed character—however this took place—images of God are trustworthy because, whether directly or indirectly, they flow out of the imagination of God!

Keeping a close correlation between images and what they convey therefore becomes important. For example, we should appreciate that when the glory of God is pictured as light (Ps 27:1), this is the best way of conceiving that glory. The image is indispensable to the idea. Though we can have the idea without the image and at times gain something in the process, overall we lose more than we can ever gain if we dispense with it, especially the vividness, vitality and vibrancy of what is being communicated. That is a crucial part of what is being communicated, not just an adjunct to it.

This is even more the case in connection with what are termed "root" metaphors. These are metaphors that are so intrinsic to what they are communicating that they are literally indispensable. While it is not always easy to distinguish a root metaphor from others that are significant or secondary, it has been argued, for example, that the image of God as father is one of these. To dispense with it, or to use the language of "parent," is not enough. Certainly it needs to be buttressed by feminine imagery for God, as the Bible itself does, and there is probably more room for this now than during the biblical period. But if we let it go, then we let go something intrinsic to our understanding of, and relationship with, God. This is not the case, however, with the description of God as king. Other terms might well be able to capture the essence of this, for example God as governor. While king pictures someone more exalted, it also depicts a more unapproachable and hierarchical figure. In other words, God is king-like in some ways but not in others. The image of God as governor has different advantages and limitations.

So, then, we should not set up an opposition between the concreteness of figurative language and the spirituality of God. This is a tendency among those who argue that it is only by the so-called *via negativa,* through using words that tell us what God is not, that we can attain the deepest understanding of God. The Bible certainly has room for such language. Dramatic examples of it occur in the description of God at the opening of Isaiah 40 and in the addressing of God by Paul at the close of Romans 11. In these passages God is variously portrayed as incomparable, immortal, inexhaustible, unsearchable and inexplicable. It is important to note that the way God is mostly talked about in these passages is still at root figurative: it is simply figurative in a negative rather than a positive way. It rightly keeps before us the difference between God and everything else and prevents us from taking positive comparisons too literally. But it is not the preferred language for God in the Bible. Instead, as we have seen, there is constant use of the *via positiva,* language that starts from human realities but goes beyond these in exploring divine realities.

See also ARROW, ARROW OF GOD; CREATION; DIVINE WARRIOR; FATHER; FIRE; FORTRESS; GLORY; GOD AND PEOPLE IN COMPARISON; GODS, GODDESSES; HOST, GOD AS; GOODNESS; KING, KINGSHIP; LIGHT; MOTHER; REDEEM, REDEEMER; ROCK; SHEEP, SHEPHERD; TEACHER, TEACHING; WAITING ON GOD; WEAPONS, HUMAN AND DIVINE; WORK, WORKER; WORSHIP.

BIBLIOGRAPHY. R. Banks, *God the Worker* (Valley Forge, PA: Judson, 1994); E. Barbotion, *The Humanity of God* (Maryknoll, NY: Orbis, 1976); O. Keel, *The Symbolism of the Biblical World* (Winona Lake, IN: Eisenbrauns, 1997 [1978]); G. A. F. Knight, *A Christian Theology of the Old Testament* (London: SCM Press, 1959).

GOD AND PEOPLE IN COMPARISON

Psalm 8 is a classic statement of comparison between God and people. In verse 4 the psalmist's question to God, "What are human beings?" (RSV) was generated by his contemplation of the three realities of the inanimate creation, humanness and the divine. The reason the psalmist could even pose this question is that humans are image-bearers of God (Gen 1:26-27) and are self-aware. Because of the *imago Dei* ("image of God"), the following comparisons can be discerned in Scripture.

At the heart of the *imago Dei* is personality. God and humans can communicate intelligently together (Ps 8; Is 6:8-13). Both can receive information (Gen 1:28-30; Heb 1:1-2), conceive thoughts (Gen 2:19; 2:23) and process information (Is 1:18-20). Although God's knowledge is limitless in accuracy and content (Rom 11:33-34; Mt 11:21-24), human knowledge is incomplete (1 Cor 2:9; 13:12) at its best and twisted at its worst (Eph 4:17-18). The affective dimension of God (Gen 6:6; Mt 25:21; 2 Cor 7:6) is always perfectly balanced and not dependent on anyone outside the triune Godhead for its completion (Hos 11:8-9; Acts 17:25; Jn 17:24-26). God is the lover who never stops loving (Jer 31:3; Hos 11:1-9). Although humans can express noble emotions (Ps 13:5-6; Mk 12:20:30; 2 Cor 1:24—2:4; 2 Jn 4), their love often diminishes (Rev 2:4), is prostituted by loving the evil (2 Tim 3:2, 4) and rejoices in the wrong thing (Ps 13:4; Mic 3:2; 1 Cor 13:6). They also give themselves to "degrading passions" (Rom 1:26). God's choices are always wise and right (Gen 18:25; Is 10:13; Rom 16:27), whereas human choices are often perverse (Rom 1:32).

Although there are some overlaps in the following, comparisons are also seen in such areas as character (Is 54:5; Hos 3:1-3; Jer 5:7, 8; 1 Pet 1:14, 15), metaphors/similes (Jn 1:19; Is.1:6, 7; Lk 3:22; Mt 10:16), familial relationships (Jer 5:7, 8; 31:32; Eph 5:28; Rev 21:2) and occupational images (Ps 23; Zech 11:17; Mt 13:55; Jn 10:11; 1 Cor 3:5-17; Heb 11:10; 1 Pet 5:2). Although time- and space-bound image-bearers (Ps 90:9-10; 139:7-9) do share some finite continuities with the eternal (Ps 90:2), unlimited (Ps 139:7-9), nondependent (Acts 17:25) God, they will always be dependent creatures (Gen 1:27; Ps 100:3) in need of other humans (Gen 2:18), divine information (Mt 4:4; 1 Cor 2:6-9) and God himself (Jn 15:5, 11; 17:3; Ps 16:5-11; 1 Cor 6:17).

See also GOD; GOODNESS.

GODS, GODDESSES

The Lord, who brought Israel out of *Egypt with a strong *arm and who cared for her like a compassionate mother, faced competitors for his affection. The prevalence of gods in the world of the Bible is suggested in God's words to Jeremiah that apostate Israel has "as many gods as you have towns" (NIV) and as many *idolatrous altars as Jerusalem has streets (Jer 11:13). The real enemy of true knowledge of God is not atheism ("The fool says in his heart, 'There is no God,' " Ps 14:1 NIV; Ps 53:1). The real enemy is rival gods, and the defining challenge is "Choose for yourselves this day whom you will serve" (Josh 24:15 NIV). In the language of the Bible, Yahweh is the God of gods, "For the LORD your God is God of gods and LORD of lords, the great God, mighty and awesome, who shows no partiality and accepts no bribes" (Deut 10:17 NIV; cf. Ps 82:1; Ex 15:11; Ps 96:4). Paul acknowledges that "indeed there are many 'gods' and many 'lords' " (1 Cor 8:5).

The biblical assessment shows no interest in granting a sympathetic hearing to foreign gods or the nuances of their theologies. These gods are false and worthless. Their existence, if it extends beyond the idols that are made by human hands, is *demonic. Idols are unable to do anything more than what their makers can empower them to do. They cannot move from place to place, let alone provide anything good for their makers. The foolishness of idol worship, however, does not even compare with the tragedy of the children of Abraham prostituting themselves to false gods who only bring them harm, while the true God offers a relationship of love and joy.

The worship of false gods arouses intense emotion from God. The pouring out of drink offerings to other gods provokes God to *anger (2 Kings 22:17; Jer 7:18). God displays a "how dare they" attitude at the amazing impertinence of his people in committing *abominable acts, in worshiping false gods and then assuming the protection of the true God when they are in his house (Jer 7:9-11). When *Moses exhorts the Israelites not to worship other gods, he reminds them that their God is a jealous God who will be angry with them if they sin in this way (Deut 6:15; 32:16).

Unlike and Inferior to Yahweh. God is a spirit and not "like gold or silver or stone—an image made by man's design and skill" (Acts 17:29). Other gods can lay no claim to the creator role (Jer 10:11). Where other gods fail to protect their people, Yahweh comes through. This is sharply illustrated in the story of Elijah's contest with the prophets of Baal (1 Kings 19:18) and when the Lord protects Jerusalem in response to Hezekiah's prayer (2 Chron 32). A recurring theme is that these gods of the nations "are not gods at all" (Jer 2:11 NIV; 5:7; 16:20; Is 37:19; 2 Kings 19:18).

When Daniel, and not the king's wise men, succeeds in interpreting the king's dream, Nebuchadnezzar exclaims, "Surely your God is the God of gods" (Dan 2:47 NIV). Nebuchadnezzar later proclaims that only the God of Shadrach, Meshach and Abednego can save people from being burned up in the furnace (Dan 3:29). God is described as "above all gods" (Ps 95:3; 97:9; 135:5; 136:2; 1 Chron 16:25-26; 2 Chron 2:5), and he alone is to be feared (Ps 96:4; 1 Chron 16:25). When the Philistines put the captured *ark of Yahweh in a temple of Dagon, Dagon is found fallen on his face before the ark of the Lord. The Philistines put him upright again. The

following day he has fallen prostrate again, with his head and hands broken off (1 Sam 5:1-5). The clear implication is that Dagon has been shown to be a lesser power, if not fraudulent. In language that is foreign to the modern sense of precision, the OT writers are willing to speak of Yahweh as "God of gods and LORD of lords" (Deut 10:17). There are a number of *taunts in which the writers vividly capture the limitations of the idols which were so widely worshiped: "But their idols are silver and gold, made by the hands of men. They have mouths, but cannot speak, eyes, but they cannot see; they have ears, but cannot hear, noses, but they cannot smell; they have hands, but cannot feel, feet, but they cannot walk; nor can they utter a sound with their throats" (Ps 115:4-7 NIV; cf. Ps 115:2-8; 135:15-18; Is 14:12-21; Jer 10:1-6).

One of the most graphic indictments of idolatry are the depictions of how idols are made. And undergirding this is the implied question, Where did it derive its power? Nebuchadnezzar has an image constructed, and he then commands people to worship it (Dan 3). The story carries with it a mocking, *satirical tone. The Israelites in Jeremiah's day are "worshiping what their hands have made" (Jer 1:16), which the prophet judges as absurd. Isaiah captures the irony of worshiping what one's hand have made: "A man too poor to present such an offering selects wood that will not rot. He looks for a skilled craftsman to set up an idol that will not topple" (Is 40:20 NIV; see Wood). In explaining why the gods of the surrounding nations had not saved them from Assyria, Hezekiah says they are "not gods but only wood and stone, fashioned by human hands" (Is 37:19).

Distant Gods. The gods are seen as distant by those who worship them. When Nebuchadnezzar asks his wise men to tell him his dream and interpret it, they reply that only the gods can do such a thing, "and they do not live among men" (Dan 2:11 NIV), they are unavailable to help the wise. Thus the pagans view their gods as powerful but unavailable to help them. The nearness and responsiveness of the true God is immediately contrasted when he reveals the dream and its interpretation to Daniel. In the contest between Baal and Yahweh on Mount Carmel, Baal does not answer to his priests' entreaties, and Elijah taunts the false prophets: "Shout louder! . . . Surely he is a god! Perhaps he is deep in thought, or busy, or traveling. Maybe he is sleeping and must be awakened" (1 Kings 18:27 NIV). Earlier Moses had asked rhetorically, "What other nation is so great as to have their gods near them the way the LORD our God is near us whenever we pray to him?" (Deut 4:7 NIV).

False Lovers and Saviors. In Hosea, Gomer's *adultery with other men is a symbol of the Israelites' false worship of idols (Hos 3:1). When the half-tribe of Manasseh is unfaithful to God, they are described as "having prostituted themselves to the gods of the peoples of the land" (1 Chron 5:25;

337

see Prostitute, Prostitution).

In times of trouble the Israelites turn to God for help, pointing out the inability of their own so-called gods (Jer 2:28). When God punishes his people for their idolatry, the idols will not be able to save them from God's punishment. (Jer 11:12).

Gods Doomed for Destruction. The idols were military targets for ancient Israel, and the biblical record speaks of them as ripe for destruction. When the Israelites enter the Promised Land, they are

A naked fertility goddess on a Canaanite cultic object.

commanded to destroy everything there connected with idol worship (Deut 7:5-6). King Asa destroys the false gods that have been constructed in Judah (2 Chron 14:2-6). After a defeated Philistine army leaves its gods behind, David orders them burned (1 Chron 14:12). On the final Day of the Lord, Yahweh will destroy "all the gods of the land" (Zeph 2:11; cf. Nahum 1:14). At that time all the nations will worship the true God (Zeph 2:11). Their destruction is also prophesied in Jeremiah 10:11. In Psalm 82 we find an imaginary scene from the divine assembly. Yahweh presides over the great assembly of gods and indicts them for their failure to defend the weak and the needy against the unjust. God's judgment is that these "sons of god" is the "you will die like mere men; you will fall like every other ruler" (Ps 82:6 NIV).

Gods of Counterfeit and Seductive Faith. Jeroboam, in setting up new temples in the Northern Kingdom, makes an idol in the shape of two *golden *calves (perhaps associated with Baal worship) and tells the people, "It is too much for you to go up to Jerusalem. Here are your gods, O Israel, who brought you up out of Egypt" (1 Kings 12:28 NIV). God tells Jeroboam, "You have done more evil than all who lived before you" (1 Kings 14:9). In a syncretism that marks the religious life of the ancient world, when the Assyrians relocate Gentiles into Israel, they worship both Yahweh and pagan gods (2 Kings 17:27-40).

Territorial Gods. In the ancient world, gods are linked to territory (*see* Land) and place in a manner that easily escapes the modern reader. Against this

backdrop is the seemingly outrageous claim of Israel that their God is the God of the entire world. In fact, the distribution of the gods according to nations with their territories is attributed to Yahweh's original sovereign will. He installed the "sons of god" as heavenly guardians for the peoples of the earth, with Israel as his own people: "When the Most High apportioned the nations, when he divided humankind, he fixed the boundaries of the peoples according to the number of the gods [or sons of god]; the LORD's portion was his people, Jacob his allotted share" (Deut 32:8-9 NRSV).

The Lord is angered by the notion that his territory is limited to the hills, and a man of God declares, "This is what the LORD says: 'Because the Arameans think the LORD is a god of the hills and not a god of the valleys, I will deliver this vast army into your hands, and you will know that I am the LORD' " (1 Kings 20:28 NIV). The story of Naaman illustrates the point. Naaman wants to worship Yahweh but finds it inconceivable to do so without standing on Israelite soil even in his native Syria: "let me, your servant, be given as much earth as a pair of mules can carry, for your servant will never again make burnt offerings and sacrifices to any other god but the LORD" (2 Kings 5:17 NIV). Mountains also are seen as the place where gods dwell or reign, and this notion is not foreign to Hebrew thought. The psalmist asks, "Why gaze in envy, O rugged mountains, at the mountain where God chooses to reign, where the LORD himself will dwell forever" (Ps 68:16 NIV). In the end "the mountain of the LORD's temple will be established as chief among the mountains, it will be raised above the hills, and all nations will stream to it" (Is 2:2 NIV).

Gods of Shame and Punishment. Because the Israelites served foreign Gods, their punishment consists in being made to "serve foreigners in a land not [their] own" (Jer 5:19 NIV). The psalmist warns that "all who worship images are put to shame" (Ps 97:7 NIV). Baal is referred to as "that shameful god Baal" (Jer 11:13 NIV). Following other gods is listed among the ways that the Israelites broke the *covenant God had made with them (Jer 11:10, 2 Chron 7:19). Therefore he will bring disaster on them, especially in the form of the exile (Jer 16:10-11; 1 Kings 11:33). God urges his people not to "follow other gods to your own harm" (Jer 7:6 NIV).

Ensnaring Gods. A theme of the conquest of Canaan is that the worship of idols in the Promised Land must not be allowed to continue. They must be destroyed so that Israel will not become ensnared (Deut 7:16; *see* Trap). Anyone who is found continuing these practices is to be stoned to death on the testimony of two or three witnesses, for the land must be purged of evil and pollution (Deut 17:2-3). All the objects of idol worship are to be completely destroyed. The Israelites are not even to take the *silver and *gold from an idol, for then it would ensnare them (Deut 7:25). The Israelites are not to intermarry with pagan peoples for this will also ensnare them in idolatry (Deut 7:3-4). Nor are the Israelites even to inquire as to how the surrounding nations worship their gods, for this too will ensnare them (Deut 12:29-31). These gods are slave masters and otherwise destructive to those who worship and follow them. This motif is picked up in Galatians, where Paul says that the Galatians, before they knew God, were slaves to "those who by nature are not gods" (Gal 4:8).

Gods of the Old Testament World. The above discussion has been organized around broad biblical motifs associated with the pagan gods/goddesses and their worship. But the deities of the nations had distinct characteristics, much of which we learn about from historical ancient Near Eastern sources outside the Bible. The Bible does not mention very many foreign gods by name, but some gods and goddesses play a particularly memorable role within the stories of the Bible. The following profiles of a few significant deities will highlight the nature of these gods and their appearance on the pages of the OT.

Ashtoreth was a female deity, a mother goddess, widely worshiped throughout Palestine. She was known for her powers of fertility, love and warfare. Some of the precision of Hebrew terminology is lost in translation and so current English translations use *Ashtoreth* to refer both to the goddess and her cult object, the Asherah pole (e.g., Ex 34:13). In Canaanite mythology she is frequently portrayed as the consort of Baal. During the period of the judges the Israelites turned to worship "Baal and the Ashtoreths" (Judg 2:13; 10:6), and the worship of Ashtoreth was a severe problem in Israel during the days of Samuel (1 Sam 7:3-4; 12:10). Her prominence in Israelite culture, where her worship made severe inroads, can be seen in *Solomon building a temple for her (1 Kings 11:5; 2 Kings 23:13). She is referred to as the "Queen of Heaven" (Jer 7:18; 44:17).

Baal is the most frequently appearing foreign deity in the Bible. The word *ba'al* means "master," "lord" or "husband," and the term frequently appears in the Bible in numerous place names such as Bamoth Baal, Baal Meon, Baal Peor, Kiriath Baal. As a proper name its reference is somewhat complex. In general Baal is a *storm and fertility god, and a prominent Baal is the West Semitic god known otherwise as Hadad. But the reference to Baal seems to be fluid, and a number of local Canaanite deities were called Baal. Baal-Berith, or "Lord of the Covenant," was a Canaanite Baal deity worshiped at Shechem (Judg 8:33; 9:4) and was probably the same as El-berith, "God of the covenant" (Judg 9:46). Baal-Zebub was a god who was believed to cause and cure disease. Ahaziah is denounced for having consulted Baal-Zebub and not Yahweh after his injury: "Is it because there is no God in Israel that you are going off to consult Baal-Zebub, the god of Ekron?" (2 Kings 1:6 NIV).

Because of the established nature of this deity in the preexisting cultures of Palestine and his associa-

tion with fertility, Baal worship was a constant lure to the Israelites. Could Yahweh, the God of Sinai and of the wilderness, produce crops and assure a fruitful life in the land of Canaan? We observe in the pages of the OT a running conflict between Yahweh and Baal worship, a conflict epitomized in the story of Elijah versus the prophets of Baal on Mount Carmel (1 Kings 18:16-46). The question posed is, Which deity will provide the rain to break the drought and famine in the land? Is Yahweh equal to the challenge or will the vaunted powers of Baal, the storm and fertility god, be displayed and win the contest? The story offers a classic power encounter between two deities and their followers, with Yahweh emerging victorious. Many examples of imagery, particularly storm imagery (*thunder, *lightning, riding the *clouds) used to describe Yahweh in the OT is imagery that has its counterpart in Baal mythology (as discovered in the Ugaritic texts of northern Syria). The implicit claim in attributing these varied images to Yahweh is that Yahweh is greater than Baal and that no powerful deed attributed to Baal is beyond the ken of Yahweh. It is in effect a war of myths, a theological apologetic against Canaanite paganism. Thus Psalm 29, with its storm and thunder imagery, may be an instance in which Canaanite praise of Baal is appropriated and radically refocused on Yahweh.

Chemosh was the god of Moab. Very little is known about this god from extrabiblical sources, but he may have been a god of war. Chemosh plays a part in a war narrative in 2 Kings 3. At a point when the battle with Israel has turned against him, the king of Moab offers his own son to Chemosh: "Then he took his firstborn son, who was to succeed him as king, and offered him as a sacrifice on the city wall. The fury against Israel was great; they withdrew and returned to their own land" (2 Kings 3:27 NIV; Jer 48:7, 13, 46). Solomon built a high place for Chemosh (1 Kings 11:7) which Josiah later destroyed (2 Kings 23:13).

Dagon was the principal deity of the Philistines. He was originally (third millennium B.C.) a patron deity of middle Mesopotamia, where he was regarded as the divine ruler of the land. Later he was also worshiped in Syria and then Palestine. Dagon was regarded as the father of Baal, and during *Samson's time he was worshiped at Gaza (Judg 16:21-23). During the days of Samuel he was worshiped at Beth-Shan (1 Sam 5:2-7). In the memorable story of the Philistines capturing the ark of the covenant, they take it to the temple of Dagon. On two successive mornings the statue of Dagon is found fallen on its face in front of the ark of the Lord. Thus Dagon acknowledges the lordship of Yahweh. When Saul is slain on Mt. Gilboa, his head is hung by the Philistines in the temple of Dagon (1 Chron 10:10) as a gory emblem of the victory of their god.

Marduk was the patron god of Babylon and regarded in Mesopotamian cosmology as the supreme ruler. His role is well defined in the famous

Enuma Elish epic, which justifies the rise of Marduk to be leader of the Babylonian pantheon. His name appears only once in the Bible. Jeremiah prophecies that when judgment comes on Babylon, even Marduk will be terrified: "Announce and proclaim among the nations, lift up a banner and proclaim it; keep nothing back, but say, 'Babylon will be captured; Bel will be put to shame, Marduk filled with terror. Her images will be put to shame and her idols filled with terror' " (Jer 50:2 NIV). Bel in Akkadian, like Baal in Canaanite, is an honorific title meaning "lord." As such it did not refer to any single deity, but it eventually came to refer to Marduk, who could be called Bel Marduk or simply Bel. In Jeremiah 51:44 Yahweh promises to "punish Bel in Babylon and make him spew out what he has swallowed" (NIV). Babylon will soon give up its Judean captives. Isaiah engages in satire as he depicts the religious processions in Babylon, in which the images of the Bel, and Nebo his son, are paraded on the backs of beasts:

> Bel bows down, Nebo stoops low;
> their idols are borne by beasts of burden.
> The images that are carried about are
> burdensome,
> a burden for the weary. (Is 46:1 NIV)

Molech was the Canaanite deity to whom Israel, in times of *apostasy, sacrificed *children. The identity of Molech has been the subject of extensive investigation, with some suggesting that Molech was a god of the underworld who had origins in Punic religion. Molech appears approximately fifteen times in the OT, and is a striking image of what the Bible finds utterly abominable in idolatry. Israel is explicitly commanded not to give any children to be sacrificed to Molech (Lev 18:21; 20:3-5). The penalty for this behavior is to be "cut off" from Israel. No contempt is spared for Molech, who is called "the detestable god of the Ammonites" (1 Kings 11:5, 7; 2 Kings 23:13). And in Josiah's reform at Jerusalem, the places in the Valley of Ben Hinnom where Israel had sacrificed their sons and daughters to Molech are desecrated (2 Kings 23:10; cf. Jer 32:35). It is this grisly image of a god who devours sons and daughters, the dearest things in life, that is most memorable.

Gods of the New Testament World. We encounter only a few names of gods in the NT. While a knowledge of the many gods that form the background of Greco-Roman religion is helpful for study of the NT (e.g., the goddess Aphrodite), the following are the principal deities that are actually mentioned in the NT.

Artemis (or *Diana*) was worshiped in Greece as the daughter of Zeus and twin sister of Apollo. Her temple at Ephesus, a center for Paul's missionary activity in the Aegean world, was one of the seven wonders of the world. Local myth claimed that her image had fallen from the sky (Acts 19:35). The worship of Artemis at Ephesus was associated with mystery rites and the practice of *magic, or sorcery.

In the book of Acts the silversmiths at Ephesus, who made votive wares, rioted when Paul's preaching and success at gathering followers of Jesus threatened their livelihoods (Acts 19:23—20:1). And in the book of Ephesians, where the victory of Christ over the principalities and powers is underscored, we may have a pointed response to the malignant powers that inhabited the world of Ephesian magic.

Hermes, or *Mercury,* was Zeus's (see below) attendant and spokesperson and was believed to be the guide of the living and the dead, a patron of those who traveled the roads, and a god of abundance and prosperity. In Acts 14 Paul and Barnabas are at Lystra and Paul heals a crippled man. When the crowd sees what Paul has done, and seized with wonder, they cry out, "the gods have come down to us in human form!" (Acts 14:11 NIV). The observers identify Paul as Hermes and Barnabas as Zeus, and proceed to prepare to worship them. Because Paul was "the chief speaker" in the incident, he perhaps seemed to fill the role of Hermes, the spokesperson for Zeus.

The Unknown God with an altar dedicated to it in Athens (Acts 17:23) becomes the basis for Paul's famous Areopagus speech. The ancient writers Pausanias and Philostratus speak of altars to unknown deities set up in Athens. And Diogenes Laertius tells of one occasion in which "anonymous" altars were built in order to avert a pestilence that threatened Athens on one occasion. In a world of many gods with varied spheres of influence, an altar to an "Unknown God" was a prudent thing and a tacit admission that the world of the gods was beyond human comprehension.

Zeus was the supreme god of the Greeks and a god of weather. In Lystra (see Hermes above) after a miraculous healing, Paul is identified as Hermes and Barnabas as Zeus (Acts 14:12). It is not clear why Barnabas was so identified except that there was a local temple to Zeus, and Zeus and Hermes were imaged as wanderers. So when a miraculous healing was effected by one of two visitors to their city, the identification may have seemed strikingly apparent.

See also GENTILE; GOD; IDOL, IDOLATRY; SATIRE; TAUNT; WOOD; WORSHIP.

BIBLIOGRAPHY. W. F. Albright, *Yahweh and the Gods of Canaan: An Historical Analysis of Two Conflicting Faiths* (Garden City, NY: Doubleday, 1968); F. M. Cross, *Canaanite Myth and Hebrew Epic: Essays in the History of the Religion of Israel* (Cambridge, MA: Harvard University Press, 1973); E. Ferguson, *Backgrounds of Early Christianity* (2d ed.; Grand Rapids: Eerdmans, 1993); R. MacMullen, *Paganism in the Roman Empire* (New Haven, CT: Yale University Press, 1981); M. S. Smith, *The Early History of God: Yahweh and the Other Deities in Ancient Israel* (San Francisco: Harper & Row, 1987).

GOLD

The large number of references to gold in the Bible (425) springs a paradox on us: valued because of its rarity and difficulty to attain, gold is yet one of the most frequently mentioned physical phenomena in the Bible. The primary quality of gold in these references is its value. A secondary quality that is often assumed is its *permanence and durability. A recognized standard of value, gold is associated especially with the *tabernacle and *temple, with the court and, by extension, with the affluent class more generally.

Clearly associated with riches and power (Is 60:17), the possession of gold is one of the distinguishing marks of the wealth of Abraham (Gen 13:2) and the royal authority of Joseph (Gen 41:42), Xerxes (Esther 4:11) and Mordecai (Esther 8:15). Royal *crowns are usually made of gold (2 Sam 12:30; 1 Chron 20:2; Esther 8:15; Ps 21:3; Zech 6:11; Rev 4:4; 9:7; 14:14). Gold was one of the three gifts presented to the infant Jesus by the wisemen (Mt 2:11) in their quest to find the "king of the Jews." King *Solomon's greatness is underlined by the fact that he "made silver and gold as common in Jerusalem as stones" (2 Chron 1:15 NIV). The relative merits of *silver and gold emerge from the levy imposed on Judah by Neco, king of Egypt: a hundred talents of silver and a talent of gold (2 Chron 36:3).

The superior value and permanence of gold make it a frequent reference point in comparisons that we find in the Bible. In Nebuchadnezzar's vision, the head of the statue (representing his own Babylonian empire) is "made of pure gold" (Dan 2:32), a sign of its superiority to the lower parts of the statue made of lesser metals. In the following chapter the huge image of himself that Nebuchadnezzar forces his subjects to worship is made of gold (Dan 3:1), as pagan images often were. In describing the consequences of the fall of Jerusalem, Lamentations focuses on gold to highlight the former *glory of the city and its citizens: "once worth their weight in gold," they are now "considered as pots of clay" (Lam 4:2 NIV).

Whenever a biblical poet wants to signal superiority, gold is the image of choice. In the Song of Songs the beloved uses the imagery of gold three times in one description of her lover: referring to his *head, his *arms and his *feet (Song 5:11, 14, 15). In Job the value of wisdom is indicated by the fact that "it cannot be bought with the finest gold" (Job 28:15, cf. vv. 16, 19). Along similar lines, the psalmist identifies God's laws as being "more precious than gold, than much pure gold" (Ps 19:10; cf. Ps 119:72, 127). In Proverbs wisdom is described as a better investment even than gold (Prov 3:14; 8:10; 16:16). The value of gold is so great in the biblical imagination that it can even represent God, as in the statement of Eliphaz the Temanite to Job that if he repents, then "the Almighty will be your gold" (Job 22:25 NIV).

Gold became such a touchstone of value that in NT times some apparently thought that the gold that overlaid Herod's temple was more significant than the temple itself, an idea that Jesus condemns in no uncertain terms: "Woe to you, blind guides! You say, 'If anyone swears by the temple, it means nothing; but if anyone swears by the gold of the temple, he is bound by his oath.' You blind fools! Which is greater: the gold, or the temple that makes the gold sacred?" (Mt 23:16-17 NIV).

Because gold is rare and therefore precious, it was used in biblical times for the manufacture of articles viewed as particularly special, notably furniture and other artifacts for the tabernacle (Ex 25—26; 28; 30—31) and the temple (1 Kings 6—7). We find a similar correlation between gold and "noble purposes" in 2 Timothy 2:20.

The Bible also records the misuse of gold. In warning the people of Israel against making *idols, God tells Moses to specify the error of using gold or silver in this way (Ex 20:23). Under Aaron's leadership they do so, though not for the last time in their history (Ex 32:2-4; Judg 8:24; Ps 115:4; Acts 17:29). Such idols were either solid gold or carved from *wood and then covered with gold (Is 40:19; Hab 2:19). But gold has no right to such honor; as God points out through Haggai, the world's silver and gold ultimately belong to him (Hag 2:8).

One aspect of the value of gold is its relative indestructibility. It is therefore seen as a source of security, which is one of the reasons why, from the perspective of *faith, it is so dangerous to be rich. Job states that it would be wrong to "put my trust in gold" or say "to pure gold, 'You are my security' " (Job 31:24 NIV). Similarly, God's warning through Ezekiel to the Israelites is that "they will throw their silver into the streets, and their gold will be an unclean thing. Their silver and gold will not be able to save them in the day of the LORD's wrath. They will not satisfy their hunger or fill their stomachs with it, for it has made them stumble into sin" (Ezek 7:19 NIV).

The ideas of immense worth and indestructibility combine in the description of *heaven as a city of "pure gold" (Rev 21:18, 21). Paul urges the *Corinthians to build carefully in their spiritual work, using gold (among other things) rather than combustible materials such as *wood, hay or *straw (1 Cor 3:12). Several Bible characters refer to themselves being tested and coming forth as gold (Job 23:10; Zech 13:9; Mal 3:3). Peter refers to faith being even more valuable than gold because even though it survives the refining process, it will perish in the end (1 Pet 1:7, 18; cf. Jas 5:3). The process of testing the purity of gold by melting it in a furnace is seen as a metaphor for the way the human heart is tested by God (Prov 17:3). Proverbs 27:21 uses the same illustration of the testing effect of the praise that people receive.

See also BRONZE; IRON; JEWELS AND PRECIOUS STONES; METALS; PERMANENCE; PROSPERITY; SILVER; TABERNACLE; TEMPLE; WOOD.

GOLDEN AGE. *See* MILLENNIUM; NEW.

GOLIATH. See BATTLE STORIES; DAVID.

GOMORRAH. *See* SODOM AND GOMORRAH.

GOOD LIFE, THE

Two contexts will contribute to our understanding of the Bible's images of the good life. One is to recognize how prominent the motif of the good life is to literature in general and indeed to the very idea of civilization. The human race longs for the good life and attempts to create it in real life. As an extension of that attempt, or as compensation when the attempt fails, the human imagination pictures the good life in literature and art. Most literature gives us an implied picture of an ideal. Sometimes it awakens in us an awareness: "This is better than real life." On other occasions literature portrays a world of disorder and *bondage. But even here the effect is to make us realize: "There must be something better." The history of literature is partly a record of the human race's quest for the good life.

The Bible adheres to this general principle, but in addition its images of the good life will be highlighted if we are aware of how closely aligned the Bible's pictures of the good life are to several related topics. These include *blessing, *goodness and *pleasure.

Narrative Vignettes. One source of pictures of the good life in the Bible comes from the narratives, which are dotted with specific moments, characters and settings that picture an ideal. Paradise is the original and prototypical good life. Its specific ingredients include a protected and beautiful environment, harmony with *nature and God, moral innocence, and the satisfaction of all human *appetites, including the urge for human companionship, *sexual gratification, *food, *leisure and meaningful *work. It is a picture of God, people and nature in perfect interrelation.

Abraham and Sarah's entertainment of three heavenly visitors (Gen 18:1-15) is a vintage picture of the good life as the ancient world envisioned it. It is a pastoral image, with its conventional agrarian prosperity and its rural setting far removed from the scene of urban degeneracy that unfolds in the very next chapter (the destruction of Sodom and Gomorrah). The generosity of ideally hospitable *hosts, attested by the lavish meal that Abraham and Sarah manage to produce in impromptu fashion, adds a specifically human and moral dimension to the picture. To this we can add that the spectacle of a visit by heavenly *guests (one of whom is God) further idealizes the situation, doubly and triply so when the human couple is rewarded with a divine promise of the birth of a son the next spring.

Subsequent events in the life of Abraham and Sarah can also be construed as snapshots of the good life, and in each case the picture gestures toward the value system that prevails in the Bible. To a culture that values children as highly as the Israelites did, any * birth story ranks as a manifestation of the good life. But when the child that is born is a son who has been promised for twenty-five years to a couple too old to produce children naturally, the effect is heightened (Gen 21:1-7). A three-day journey that has as its goal a father's sacrifice on an altar of his only son, a son

of covenant promise, would not ordinarily be a candidate for an image of the good life. But when the event is a supreme display of *faith in God, rewarded by the sparing of the son's life through the mediacy of a substitutionary atonement that points forward in Scripture to the ultimate substitutionary sacrifice, even such a story contributes to the "good life" motif.

In fact, any divine-human encounter that eventuates in God's blessing of someone is a picture of the good life as the Bible conceives it. Even when *Jacob is running for his life as a guilt-haunted sojourner, the vision of a ladder (see Jacob's Ladder) with angels descending and ascending is an experience that can only be called good (Gen 28:10-22). So too the ordeal of Jacob's *wrestling with an angel of God, for all its terror, is the turning point of Jacob's life and as such is a picture of the good life (Gen 32:22-32). It is followed by a scene of human reconciliation in which long-estranged brothers are harmoniously reunited (Gen 33:1-11), another picture of the good life.

The book of *Ruth is an especially clear example of how a story constitutes a picture of the good life. Ruth is the story of a heroine who herself embodies the qualities of a good life—virtue, loyalty, hard work, modesty, humility, gentleness, godliness and courage. She is rewarded with a home, marriage and a child. The broader social and natural world in which Ruth's story unfolds is likewise a picture of the good life as conceived in pastoral and agrarian terms. Its keynotes include harmony with nature and its cycles, *abundance, *harvest and provision. The world of the story is an ordered world in which Boaz carries out the legal obligations of marriage with meticulous attention, and his generosity to the gleaning of the sojourner Ruth shows his fulfillment of covenant obligations toward the disadvantaged.

The stories of the Bible are replete with images of the good life. To catalog them all would be the subject for an extensive book. What is important is the principle of the matter and the need to be alert to the frequency with which biblical narrative encapsulates its moral and spiritual truths by giving us narrative pictures of the good life. If we organize these pictures into "master images," the composite picture would include the Bible's famous *birth scenes, scenes of *worship and *pilgrimage, scenes of romantic and married love, scenes of the harmonious or *reunited *family, religious *festivals and *sabbath observance, military conquests, harvests, secure dwelling on one's *land or in one's house, and scenes of *repentance and *forgiveness. The narrative frame of the book of *Job (Job 1:1-5; 42:10-17), with its pictures of Job's domestic life, material prosperity and divine favor, provides a good summary of the narrative portrayal of the good life in the Bible.

The Poetry of Praise. A second major repository of images of the good life in the Bible is the poetry of praise. Some of this falls into the genre of the *encomium—a poem or prose piece that praises a general character type or an abstract quality. Other poems fall into a more general category of praise. The principle is simple: whatever a person praises is an implied picture of what is desirable.

A survey of the Bible's encomia is a good starting point. Psalm 1 is an encomium praising the godly person. What emerges is a composite portrait of a character and lifestyle that includes as salient features abstaining from "the wicked way," delight in the law of God, a vitality and productiveness comparable to those of a *tree planted by streams of *water, and an assurance of standing approved by God in the judgment. In a similar vein, Psalm 15 asks the question of who can worship God acceptably. The answer is an idealized portrait of a person whose goodness is seen in such virtues as honesty, good will toward others, aversion to evil and generosity with possessions.

Psalms 112 and 128 are companion meditations on the person who is blessed by God. According to Psalm 112 the good life consists of producing successful descendants, possessing wealth and riches, having a righteousness that endures forever, inner security that does not panic in adversity, and stability that outlasts persecution and looks in triumph on one's enemies. Psalm 128 paints a picture of the good life that includes the enjoyment of the rewards of one's labor, happiness, a fruitful wife, a family of children around the table, natural prosperity during one's lifetime and grandchildren.

Other encomia provide additional images of the good life. Proverbs 31:10-31 is a heightened picture of all that a husband might desire in a wife and all that a wife might aspire to be. 1 Corinthians 13 is a portrait of the good that love produces, while Hebrews 11 is a companion piece that praises the good life that ensues from the quality of faith in people's lives.

Individual *praise psalms can also be repositories of images of the good life. Psalm 16 is a small classic on the subject of the contented soul. As the litany of contentment unfolds, we find an ever-expanding list of things that add up to a good life: God as one's chosen portion and *cup, faith in God's *providence, gratitude that one's literal and figurative surveying lines have fallen in pleasant places, a goodly heritage, instruction from God, a rejoicing soul and secure *body, and the presence of God in one's life and *afterlife.

Similarly, the "songs of *ascent" sung or recited en route to *Jerusalem on pilgrimages (Ps 120—134) provide a many-sided picture of what OT believers found satisfying as they took stock of their lives at spiritually reflective times. We read about resting secure in the sufficiency of God's protection, the ecstasy of worship, faith in God, awareness of God's providential acts of *rescue and physical provision, the blessings of family, a secure nation and community, and fellowship among believers. Here is the good life as the biblical imagination conceives it.

Wisdom Literature and Beatitudes. Wisdom literature is an additional repository of images of the good life. In fact, the entire book of *Proverbs presents variations on that theme. The ever-expanding picture of the good life built up by the individual proverbs includes as its keynotes obedience to God's rules for living, *wisdom and discretion in making moral choices, self-control and discipline, moderation, honest dealing, generosity, industry and diligence, cheerfulness, and a lifestyle governed by wisdom and understanding.

The book of *Ecclesiastes too gives us pictures of the good life. These appear as the positive foil to the melancholy list of dead ends that the speaker chased in his futile attempts to achieve the good life by purely human means and by living only with earthly values in view. In the interspersed God-centered passages (Eccles 2:24-26; 3:10-13; 5:18-20; 9:7-10; 12:13-14) we catch glimpses of what the good life looks like. It is a life of joy in one's work and in such commonplace activities as *eating and *drinking and even beholding the sun (Eccles 11:7). It is a life of zest in which one performs whatever his or her hand finds to do, a life of festivity and enjoyment of life with one's spouse, and a life characterized by fear of God and obedience to his commandments.

*Beatitudes are like proverbs in their brief and fragmentary format. They too give us in piecemeal fashion the ingredients of the good life as biblical writers picture it. The premise underlying the beatitude as a genre is that blessing is the goal of life and that the good life consists of living in such a way as to secure the blessing of God and people. Over a hundred beatitudes scattered throughout the Bible can thus be viewed as "notes" toward the good life. Together they yield a composite picture of the moral behavior and values that lead to God's blessing in a person's or a family's life.

Summary. The Bible is a book that calls its readers to a higher and better life than people gravitate to by inclination. One way it does this is with frequent pictures of the good life. These pictures sum up the biblical worldview and value structure. They also appeal to something at the core of human longing. When we encounter these images of the good life, we feel ourselves to be in touch with life as God intended it. Entering into the spirit of these images is a homecoming—a return to the *Garden of Eden and a foretaste of the ultimate good life in heaven.

See also ABUNDANCE; AFTERLIFE; CHILD, CHILDREN; FAT, FATNESS; FEAST, FEASTING; FIG, FIG TREE; FOOD; GARDEN; HOME, HOUSE; HOSPITALITY; HOST, GOD AS; PEACE; PROSPERITY; PROVIDENCE; TREE OF LIFE; VINE, VINEYARD; WORSHIP; ZION.

GOODNESS

Goodness is a mysterious term that communicates a sense of delight and fathomless depth—a glad mystery. A review of the words *goodness* or *good* as found in the Bible quickly reveals the reason for this: goodness in the Bible is God himself. The Father, the Son and the Holy Spirit *are* good, *do* good and *create* good. God's people are not good in themselves but become capable of doing good through the empowerment of God's Spirit and the presence of God in their lives through Jesus Christ. What then is goodness? How does the beauty of the Bible's imagery uncover for us the richness of the words *good* and *goodness* that appear more than six hundred times in the Bible?

The Goodness of God. Goodness is in accordance with *God's nature. As it is in the nature of water to be wet or fire to be hot, it is the nature of God to be good. This characteristic is not changeable or diminishing, nor does it have a beginning or an end. When Moses requests to see the glory of God, God replies, "I will make all my goodness pass before you." But "you cannot see my face; for man shall not see me and live" (Ex 33:19-20 RSV). God's goodness is here an image of mystery, transcending human comprehension. During the same encounter, God passes before Moses and proclaims, "The LORD, the LORD, a God merciful and gracious, slow to anger, and abounding in love and faithfulness, keeping steadfast love for thousands, forgiving iniquity and transgression and sin, but who will by no means clear the guilty" (Ex 34:6-7 RSV). All of these qualities—mercy, grace, love, faithfulness, forgiveness and righteousness—are what it means for the Lord to be good.

This sense of the goodness of God encompassing many things is echoed in the Psalms. The goodness of the Lord can be seen "in the land of the living" (Ps 27:13), implying that human life in this world is the arena within which God's goodness is accessible to us. In Psalm 31, a psalm of thanksgiving for deliverance, the poet exclaims, "O how abundant is thy goodness, which thou hast laid up for those who fear thee" (Ps 31:19 RSV), and the catalog of evidences includes God's righteousness, steadfast love, compassion, faithfulness, grace and generosity. Psalm 145, a praise psalm, likewise extols God's "abundant goodness," linking it with such moral and spiritual attributes as greatness, majesty, righteousness, mercy, steadfast love, compassion and providence. God is good in his very being: Jesus asserts that "no one is good but God alone" (Lk 18:19 RSV), and the psalmist writes, "Thou art my Lord; I have no good apart from thee" (Ps 16:2 RSV).

Not only *is* God good; he *does* good. The psalmist links the two when he writes, "Thou art good and doest good" (Ps 119:68 RSV). In the OT, God "promised good to Israel" (Num 10:29) and kept his promise. Although Joseph's brothers "meant evil against" him, "God meant it for good, to bring it about that many people should be kept alive" (Gen 50:20 RSV). At the dedication of the temple, the people "went to their homes joyful and glad of heart for all the goodness that the LORD had shown to David his servant and to Israel his people" (1 Kings 8:66 RSV). In Psalm 23, a psalm that catalogs God's acts of provision, the poem rises to a confident prediction that God's "goodness and mercy shall follow me all the days of my life" (Ps 23:6). In the

NT, God is similarly portrayed as the God who *does* good. Jesus "went about doing good" (Acts 10:38). Paul expressed the confidence that "in everything God works for good with those who love him" (Rom 8:28 RSV).

The Good Creation. There is probably no more famous biblical passage built around the theme of what is good than the six declarations in the *creation story (Gen 1) that "God saw that it was good," culminating in a seventh statement that "God saw everything that he had made, and behold, it was very good" (Gen 1:31 RSV). Here is another cluster of biblical images of the good—the creation that God called into being and that continues to bless the human race. God's creation, including people, who are created in his image, is an extension of his own goodness; no wonder it is good in principle. Paul's asserts that "everything created by God is good" (1 Tim 4:4 RSV).

Because of the link between God and his creation, human life in this world is viewed in the Bible as good in principle. Two passages in the book of Jeremiah can be taken as a summary. The redeemed "shall come and sing aloud on the height of Zion, and they shall be radiant over the goodness of the LORD" (Jer 31:12 RSV), and the picture of God's goodness that follows includes *grain, *wine, *oil, *flocks and *herds, life so full that it is "like a watered *garden," and people rejoicing in *dance (Jer 31:12-13). People thus blessed "shall be satisfied with my goodness, says the LORD" (Jer 31:14). Here the goodness of God extends to the good things of this life—images of human satisfaction as well as God's inherent goodness of character.

A similar catalog of images of the good construed as the blessings of God on his creatures occurs two chapters later: "There shall be heard again the voice of mirth and the voice of gladness, the voice of the bridegroom and the voice of the *bride, the voices of those who sing, as they bring their offerings to the house of the LORD. Give thanks to the LORD of hosts, for the LORD is good, for his steadfast love endures for ever!" (Jer 33:10-11). This is indeed the proverbial good life, with God and people in harmony and people rejoicing in both God and the human blessings that he bestows. The goodness of God is not isolated from life but is the basis for what is good in it.

The Fruit of the Spirit. People, made in God's image and restored to that image by redemption, are also capable of good. Their actions, like God's in a perfect sense, are declared to be "good." The "good deeds" of Hezekiah were so noteworthy that they were committed to a written record (2 Chron 32:32). The writer of Proverbs declares that "a good man obtains favor from the LORD" (Prov 12:2) and is filled with the fruit of his deeds (14:14). Joseph of Arimathea was "a good and righteous man" (Lk 23:50), and Barnabas was "a good man, full of the Holy Spirit and of faith" (Acts 11:24). Here then is another category of goodness in the Bible—characters who display the godlike qualities that the Bible portrays as comprising the ultimate good.

Goodness is one of the celebrated *fruits of the Spirit that characterize those who belong to Christ (Gal 5:22-24). We noted earlier that God is the source of all goodness; hence, "he who does good is of God" (3 Jn 11). Human goodness is not self-generated: "No one does good, not even one" (Rom 3:12), Paul writes; and again, "nothing good dwells in me" (Rom 7:18). Yet Paul can enjoin those who have the Spirit to "do good to all men" (Gal 6:10), just as Jesus commanded his followers to "do good to your enemies" (Lk 6:35). Jesus also taught that "a good tree bears good fruit" (Mt 7:17).

The Cosmic Conflict. An important aspect of goodness in the Bible is that it is set over against its opposite. The backdrop is the biblical assumption of a great spiritual conflict between good and evil. Virtually every story in the Bible gives us a variation on the theme. The conflict begins in Paradise, with its tree of the knowledge of good and evil (Gen 2:9, 17). After eating from the forbidden tree, Adam and Eve know good and evil (Gen 3:22). Thereafter good and evil are intertwined—the lot of those living in a fallen world.

A prime responsibility for those living in such a world is to discern good from *evil (2 Sam 14:17; 1 Kings 3:9; Heb 5:14). Another is to do good rather than evil, to actively choose good over evil (Ps 34:14; 37:27; Prov 14:22; Is 7:15, 16; Amos 5:14, 15; Rom 12:9; 1 Pet 3:11). Goodness is something that must be actively sought (Prov 11:27). Another variation on the theme is that the human race is assumed to fall into two categories: the good and the evil (Prov 15:3; Eccles 9:2; Mt 5:45; 12:35; Jn 5:29), just as actions are assumed to be either good or evil (Eccles 12:14; 2 Cor 5:10). The resolution of the cosmic conflict of the ages will occur in the eschaton, and although the words *good* and *goodness* do not appear in English versions of the book of Revelation, a major meaning of the book is the final and conclusive triumph of good over evil.

Images of the Good. The image of goodness, along with the stock adjective *good*, is the most frequently used biblical term to denote what is positive in human experience. Something of its richness will emerge if we simply note the range of things that various biblical writers declare to be good. In one category we find obviously moral and spiritual phenomena. We are invited to "taste and see that the LORD is good" (Ps 34:8 RSV). Giving thanks to God is good (Ps 54:6; 92:1), and being near to God is good (Ps 73:28). So are the hand of God upon a person (Neh 2:18), God's statutes and commandments (Neh 9:13), the promise of God (1 Kings 8:56), the godly life (2 Chron 6:27), and doing justice, loving kindness and walking humbly with God (Mic 6:8).

But the list of good things keeps expanding into less obviously "spiritual" areas of life. A *pasture can be good, for example (1 Chron 4:40; Ezek

34:14). So can the work of *building a *wall (Neh 2:18) and finding a *wife (Prov 18:22). Believers' dwelling in unity is good (Ps 133:1). So are a word in season (Prov 15:23); *eating, *drinking and finding enjoyment in *work (Eccles 5:18); *wisdom (Eccles 7:11) and a conscience free from guilt (Acts 23:1; 1 Tim 1:5). The fruit of a tree can be good (Mt 7:17), as can the gifts parents give to their children (Mt 7:11) and the precepts of a wise person (Prov 4:2). Even affliction can be good (Ps 119:71).

Summary. The references to goodness in the Bible tell us that God is good and that through his life in us we grow in goodness and in our likeness to him. Meditating on the goodness of the Lord engenders a sense of true virtue that speaks to the best that is in each believer. As creatures made in the image of God, we can aspire to goodness, surrounded by a world and society that includes much that is good.

See also BEAUTY; CREATION; EVIL; GOD; GOOD LIFE, THE; PEACE; WISDOM.

GOSPEL GENRE

As literary documents, the Gospels are encyclopedic forms that bring together a range of different genres. These include biography, historical narrative, *hero story, journal, *parable, drama, dialogue, sermon or oration, saying or *proverb, *satire, poetry, *tragedy and *comedy. In addition we find a collection of narrative subtypes that make the Gospels distinctive: annunciation and nativity stories, calling or vocation stories, witness stories, encounter stories, conflict or controversy stories, pronouncements stories (in which an event is linked with a memorable saying by Jesus), miracle stories and passion stories (dealing with the trial, death and resurrection of Jesus). Despite this variety, unifying motifs and image patterns can be found in the Gospels.

The Centrality of Jesus. The point of focus in the Gospels—the center where all the rays meet and from which they issue—is Jesus. The Gospels exist to paint a portrait of Jesus and to give a record of his life and teaching. Specifically, three types of material can be discerned: (1) Jesus' *teaching and preaching, (2) Jesus' actions and (3) people's responses. In the third category two main motifs are the growing faith of the disciples and the growing hostility of the religious establishment. In addition, Jesus' dialogues and debates are a hybrid of all three of the central motifs: they are a form of teaching, they have the force of narrative action, and they involve the responses of people to Jesus and he to them.

The story of the Samaritan woman at the *well (Jn 4:1-42) illustrates the overall dynamics. In this encounter story Jesus uses dialogue to teach about himself and to initiate action in the woman's life, and the story itself embodies the woman's response to Jesus in the form of coming to faith. The story of the woman caught in *adultery (Jn 8:1-11) is similar: Jesus' dialogue with the onlookers and the woman has the force of an action; the altercation with the religious leaders is built around the responses of the primary actors in the drama; and the effect of the conflict is that Jesus teaches something important about sin, judgment and forgiveness.

The four Gospels, which are complementary rather than contradictory accounts, give their own interpretive slants on the life of Jesus. To *Matthew, for example, Jesus is the royal Messiah who fulfills OT prophecy. *Mark accentuates the humanity and suffering of Jesus. *Luke highlights Jesus' humanitarian compassion for the outcasts of his society. *John's Gospel presents a poetic Jesus, who teaches by means of great symbols. As for alleged contradictions among the four accounts, we should remember that as a traveling teacher and miracle worker Jesus would have reenacted similar events and discourses on different occasions. We might also compare the diverse accounts of identical events to the sports replay on television, where we get the same event from different angles, at different speeds, with varied verbal commentary and interpretation superimposed.

Narrative as the Primary Form. Above all, the Gospels tell a story. Narrative is the organizing framework within which the sayings and discourses are arranged. As stories, the Gospels are episodic rather than unified around a progressive action. They are cycles of material rather than single narratives, with the variety further intensified by the mixed-genre format noted above.

The virtue of the episodic plot is that it captures the nature of Jesus' life. The apparent randomness of incidents effectively portrays Jesus in his manifold roles. This same randomness also conveys a general sense of the life Jesus lived, and it creates in our imaginations the qualities of the world in which Jesus lived and acted. During his public years Jesus traveled, preached, led a group of disciples, performed miracles, engaged in dialogue with people, defended his actions and beliefs in open debate, and was finally put on trial and crucified. Given the many-sided nature of his life, the mixture and arrangement of ingredients that we find in the Gospels capture the reality of Jesus' life. An inner consistency emerges as we read, and we come to expect that something different will happen every few minutes as we read, as we do in reading an adventure story.

Individual narrative units are best approached with ordinary tools of narrative analysis. The primary questions to ask are the familiar ones of setting, characterization and plot: Where? Who? What happens? The basic rhythm is that of problem moving toward solution or conflict moving toward resolution or encounter moving toward disclosure and response.

Structure. The Gospels follow a loosely chronological structure as they recount the life of Jesus, mainly during his three years of public life. They begin either with Jesus' birth or his initiation into his public ministry and end with his trial, crucifixion and resurrection. Within that general pattern we have no way of knowing exactly how strictly chronological the accounts are, though it seems obvious that the writers rearranged chronology to fit other organizational schemes. Matthew, for example, organizes his material into alternating sections of narrative and discourse, so that the miracles and parables (for example) are mainly collected into separate sections, regardless of when they actually happened.

The kaleidoscopic structure of the Gospels is accentuated by the writers' preference for the brief unit as the basic building block of their books, though this is less true of John. The one- or two-paragraph report of an event or dialogue is the staple. Instead of looking for plots in the ordinary sense, therefore, we need to think in terms of a mosaic or collage of units, looking for connections among collected units rather than continuous narrative flow.

The Cast of Characters. We can visualize the Gospels as concentric rings of characters. At the center is *Jesus. Next to him in importance is a small group of disciples. Almost as prominent are the scribes and Pharisees (the religious establishment), a continuous presence in the Gospels. Beyond them is the crowd of ordinary people, sometimes a nameless mass, at other times represented by a particular named person. The overall effect is to show Jesus silhouetted against a world of hostility and occasional loyalty, betrayal, hypocrisy, formalized religion, envy, human need and suffering.

The crowds are typically caught between the claims of Jesus and the religious establishment. In this middle position crowds as well as individuals are often poised at a moment of choice. Jesus is shown trying to persuade them, either by word or miracle or disparagement of his antagonists. Given this implied struggle for the minds of the onlookers, we can see why Jesus and the Pharisees so often initiated conflict with each other.

Because the Gospels contain so much dialogue and encounter, individual units are often dramas in miniature. We can profitably imagine such scenes as dramas being played on a stage or as scenes photographed by a television crew. We find distant or overview shots, close-ups, shifts from one speaker to another, shots of the crowd and so forth.

Setting. Geography plays an important role in the *travel stories that make up the Gospels. We move in a world of place names that reinforce the identity of Jesus as a traveler and that keep the action rooted in the real world. Place often figures prominently in the individual episodes, in which miniature dramas are often placed in a specific setting. Sometimes geography is used for structural or symbolic purposes; Jerusalem (for example) becomes the locus of rejection of Jesus, while the towns and countryside are more accepting of Jesus' claims.

As we read the Gospels, we also enter the special world that they create in our imaginations and that becomes familiar to us the more we read them. That world is an elemental world of hills, *water, lake, evening, *morning, *boats, waves, *thirst, *house and *eating. We are frequently in the world of *nature. A certain solid realism emerges, as does a very human Jesus firmly situated in everyday earthly life.

Style. The most notable stylistic trait of the Gospels is the economy of words and details. The writers' preference for the brief unit is even more pronounced than in the OT. Episodes are relatively self-contained. The style is spare and unembellished, except in the extended discourses of Jesus. Drama and dialogue are the preferred means of telling the story about Jesus. The spirit that breathes through this blend is the momentousness of what is recorded. Though the characters are ordinary people and the settings everyday, the events are momentous, worldchanging, epochmaking.

Summary. The Gospels are a mixture of the familiar and unfamiliar. They combine simplicity and difficulty. The surface details are straightforward, but their significance requires interpretation and sometimes remains elusive. The overall message of the Gospels is easily grasped, but we never get to the end of their meaning. The hero of the story is in some ways like other heroes, but his claims (such as the ability to forgive sin and his own divine identity) and his miraculous powers are unique.

See also JESUS; JOHN, GOSPEL OF; LUKE, GOSPEL OF; MARK, GOSPEL OF; MATTHEW, GOSPEL OF.

BIBLIOGRAPHY. R. A. Burridge, *Four Gospels, One Jesus?* (Grand Rapids: Eerdmans, 1994).

GRAFTING

The agricultural image of grafting occurs once in the Scriptures, although it builds on other images repeated in the both the Testaments. In Romans 11:17-24 the image of grafting is borrowed from the care of olive trees to describe the relationship of Israel to the gospel and the position of the *Gentile believers. The grafting image depends directly on the OT picture of Israel as God's olive tree (see Hos 14:5-7 for one example of many passages). It also recalls Christ's own metaphor of the *vine and *branches recorded in John 15. In Romans, Paul synthesizes and extends the metaphor of Israel as God's olive tree to illustrate how the Gentile believers as "wild olive shoots" are grafted into the olive tree to replace those branches that have been "broken off."

Grafting was a sound agricultural practice that enabled new growth to rise from old stock. Usually a branch from a cultivated tree would be grafted onto a wild tree in order to produce orderly fruit. The tree would be made profitable by the new branches. The image in Romans, however, is of the reverse action. The wild branches are grafted into the established tree. The benefits, then, are enjoyed by the branches. Symbolically, the new branches—the Gentile believers—enjoy a new intimacy with the established roots of God's interaction with the human race. From those same roots they will profit from enrichment and growth.

Finally, Paul reminds his readers that the graft is a position of grace, not of nature. It is "contrary to nature"; it is supernatural. Because of its supernatural

characteristics the engrafted branches should feel no spiritual pride, only gratitude. At the same time, hope is established for the supernatural reinstatement of the discarded natural branches into God's olive tree.

See also FARMING; GENTILE; PRUNING; TREE, TREES.

GRAIN

Because it is such a common yet vital part of life, grain is a rich and varied biblical image that can carry connotations of blessing, provision, judgment or sacrifice. That grain is a familiar yet evocative image is evident by its role in the *sacrificial *worship of Israel. As part of the ordination of the Aaronic priesthood, God instructs Moses to burn a grain offering on the *altar each day for seven days (Ex 29:37-41 NIV). Grain also plays a prominent sacrificial role in the life of every Israelite: it is a portion of the firstfruits *offering at the start of *harvest, to be waved before the Lord in thanksgiving for the season's crops (Lev 23:10, 11).

Grain is an image of *blessing in the form of a bountiful harvest. When the aged Isaac blesses *Jacob, he offers his son "the earth's richness," all of which he sums up as "an abundance of grain and new wine" (Gen 27:28 NIV). Likewise, in his final blessing of the tribes of Israel, Moses describes the land of Canaan as "a land of grain and new wine" (Deut 33:28 NIV). In thanksgiving for a plentiful harvest, the psalmist uses the image of a *valley "mantled with grain" to describe God's rich blessing (Ps 65:13 NIV).

In these instances grain is a metaphor for the myriad of blessings that God produces from the earth. But in a context of *hunger and want, the image becomes even more powerful. When blessings are few and need is great, grain also functions as an image of God's specific provision. In speaking of Israel's *forty years of wandering in the desert, the psalmist refers to the life-sustaining *manna God provided as "the grain of heaven" (Ps 78:24 NIV).

Perhaps the most vivid examples of grain as an image of divine provision occur in the OT account of *Joseph, a major theme of which is God's providence and provision for the family of Jacob. The image of grain appears repeatedly throughout the narrative, sometimes as a subtle testimony to divine provision and sometimes as a simple allegory. For example, grain functions allegorically in a number of prophetic *dreams that are pivotal to the story. When Joseph dreams that his brothers' sheaves bow before his own (Gen 37:7, 8), it is clear that each sheaf of grain represents the person who bound it. This is certainly his brothers' understanding of the image. Similarly, when Pharaoh dreams of seven thin heads of grain swallowing seven robust heads (Gen 41:5-7), Joseph equates each image with an event—seven years of plenty followed by seven years of *famine (Gen 41:26, 27).

But grain as an image of provision occurs more subtly in the narrative. A dream of grain provides the means for Joseph's liberation from prison and rise to authority, as well as a warning of the impending famine (Gen 41:27, 40); the storing and distribution of grain becomes the focus of Joseph's energies (Gen 41:49, 56); the purchase of grain provides the occasion for Joseph to meet his brothers in Egypt and is the means by which Joseph becomes his brothers' master, as his own dream had foretold (Gen 42:6). Moreover, it is with grain that Joseph saves his family from the famine, ultimately bringing them to live in the lushness of Goshen. Joseph himself confirms that all that has happened is part of God's plan to save people from the famine (Gen 50:20). Thus the image of grain establishes divine provision as a major theme of the narrative. Through Joseph God provides not only for Egypt and for Jacob's family but also for the future nation of Israel, which will grow and thrive in Egypt, as God promises to Jacob (Gen 46:3).

Just as the presence of grain suggests God's bounty and provision, so also can its absence suggest the replacement of God's blessing with *judgment. In his declaration of God's judgment upon an idolatrous Israel, the prophet Hosea likens the nation's worship of idols to a stalk of grain without a head; it is a fruitless harvest, producing nothing (Hos 8:7). Similarly, the reaping of grain is a familiar biblical image of judgment. Job sees death as the inevitable judgment upon evil men, who "are cut off like heads of grain" (Job 24:24 NIV). When God promises to bring defeat and exile on Israel as judgment for rebellion, the prophet Isaiah compares the coming destruction to a reaper gathering grain. While most will perish, a few *gleanings will remain—a remnant who will repent and return to God (Is 17:5-7).

In the NT the image of grain carries still different connotations. In Jesus' parable of the sower, the focus shifts from impending harvest to the growth of the *seed that is sown. In the good soil the kernels grow and produce a crop (Mk 4:8). Here, as with the parable of the growing seed (Mk 4:26-29), the growing of grain illustrates the vast potential of the emerging kingdom of God. Meanwhile, the attendant image of grain being cut at the coming harvest/judgment lurks in the background, lending urgency to the present concern for a growing crop.

In John's gospel Jesus uses the image of grain to explain the purpose and meaning of his approaching death: "Unless a kernel of wheat falls to the ground and dies, it remains only a single seed. But if it dies, it produces many seeds" (Jn 12:24 NIV). Here Jesus employs the image of grain to describe the paradox of life emerging from death. As with the planting of wheat, Jesus' death is necessary in order to bring about new and abundant life. While the element of judgment may be absent, the image in this context is multifaceted. Grain dying in order to produce anew conveys not only the notion of purposeful sacrifice but also the sense of God's bountiful blessing and faithful provision for those whom he loves.

See also BREAD; FARMING; FOOD; GLEAN; HARVEST; THRESH, THRESHING FLOOR; WHEAT; WINE.

GRANARY. *See* BARN.

GRAPES

The grape, a major crop in biblical times, was grown in *vineyards for wine production; consequently, a land abounding in vineyards was symbolic of *abundance and *prosperity. Most of the biblical references to grapes elicit a picture of successful agriculture, the most vivid image being the gigantic cluster of grapes that the twelve spies brought back from the Promised Land as evidence of its fertility (Num 13:23).

On one side, then, we find grapes as an image of abundance and *pleasure. When the kinsmen of Gaal decided to hold a festival, they "went out into the field and gathered the grapes from their vineyards, trod them, and celebrated" (Judg 9:27 NRSV). The point is heightened by the example of self-denial in the Nazirites, who do not "drink any grape juice or eat grapes, fresh or dried" (Num 6:3 NRSV). The mere prospect of grapes is pleasant to the eyes: the invitation of the lover in *Song of Songs to his beloved includes the statement "let us go out early to the vineyards, and see whether . . . the grape blossoms have opened" (Song 7:12 NRSV). In the coming golden age, according to Amos, there will be such an abundance that "the treader of grapes" will overtake the sower (Amos 9:13).

In the Bible the success or failure of crops is often linked to people's obedience or disobedience, as rewarded by God's blessing or punished by his judgment. Grapes participate in this pattern. The failure of a grape crop to reach maturity signals disaster in the land. Accordingly, oracles of judgment in the OT sometimes include the prediction that disobedient people will be deprived of the pleasure and sustenance of grapes (Deut 28:39; Is 18:5; Mic 6:15), and the premature demise of the wicked person is pictured as a vineyard shaking off its unripe grape (Job 15:33). In a variation of this image, God pictures a wayward Judah as a vineyard that he planted to produce good grapes but that has instead yielded wild grapes (Is 5:2, 4; cf. Mt 7:16; Lk 6:44). In several prophetic passages the image of "sour grapes" that set one's teeth on edge is used to picture sin and its unpleasant effects (Jer 31:29-30; Ezek 18:2).

A final image is that of treading grapes in a *winepress as part of a grape harvest. It appears in *apocalyptic visions of the coming age as an image of divine blessing (cf. Amos 9:13, with its picture of a grape harvest so abundant that people will still be harvesting when it is time to sow the next year's crops, and so luscious that the very hills seem to drip with wine), but also as an image of divine *judgment (Is 63:3; Lam 1:15; Joel 3:13). The ultimate example of the latter motif is the scene of Revelation 14:18, where the angel swings his sharp sickle, harvests the grapes from the earth's vine and throws them into the winepress of God's wrath.

See also VINE, VINEYARD; WINE; WINEPRESS.

GRASS

Many grasses have grown in Palestine, but the Bible seemingly does not distinguish one from another or even differentiate grass from grass-like herbs. The fifty references to grass in the Bible fall mainly into three categories: grass as an agricultural staple for the *pasturing of livestock, the loss of grass as an act of divine *judgment, and grass as a symbol of human *transience, mutability and mortality.

According to the Bible, ever since the sixth day of creation grass has been the divinely-provided food of *oxen (Num 22:4; Job 40:15; Ps 106:20; Dan 4:25), *cattle (Deut 11:15; Ps 104:14; Jer 50:11), *horses (1 Kings 18:5), mules (1 Kings 18:5) and wild asses (Job 6:5; see Donkey, Ass). Grass is thus one of the *blessings of the created order. In a rural economy based extensively on grazing, grass is an image of fertility; its presence insures *abundance (Ps 147:8). Given the frailty of grass, its thriving presence is also a sign of God's *providential care. In Jesus' discourse against anxiety he adduces God's care over the grass as part of a "how much more" argument: "If God so clothes the grass of the field, which today is alive and tomorrow is thrown into the oven, will he not much more clothe you?" (Mt 6:30 RSV; Lk 12:28). The point is that God can be expected to provide all the more for those created in his image.

This positive image of grass as sustenance for animals and the object of God's beneficent providence is numerically the smallest category in the Bible. God's judgment is often pictured as the taking away of grass. Moses prophesies that disobedience to the covenant will move God to make the land of promise a burnt-out waste, a place where no grass can sprout (Deut 29:23; see Wasteland). Jeremiah 14:5 offers an instance of this coming to pass: the hind, because of God's judgment upon Judah, forsakes her newborn calf because there is no grass. Similarly, Amos 7:2 holds forth for Israel the prospect of judgment in the form of *locusts who devour the grass of the land. In Isaiah 15:6 an oracle against Moab foresees a desolation of waters and the withering of grass. The threat eventually becomes an eschatological motif on a worldwide scale. In Revelation 8:7, after the opening of the seventh *seal, the first angel blows a *trumpet and a third of all *green grass is burnt up.

The largest category of references to grass in the Bible is based on the dramatic changes of fortune that grass undergoes in a *dry climate. Grass in shallow soil, subject to the vagaries of drought and *rain, is a changeable phenomenon, quickly green when it has moisture and just as quickly brown when it lacks water. In such a climate even the morning *dew can renew grass (Ps 90:5). Another factor is the grass that grows on housetops. Seeds inevitably sprout on the roofs of mud houses, but soon after appearing with the rain they wither, for their *roots are shallow, and they cannot endure the *sun and *winds (2 Kings 19:26; Ps 129:6; Is 37:27). Although the ability of grass to flourish quickly usually implies its imminent destruction, sometimes the quick growth is a positive image of *prosperity (Is 66:14).

Mainly, though, references to grass use climatic conditions as a metaphor for human frailty and *transience. In Palestine the rainy season (October through April) is followed by a long dry season. Little grass endures the dry heat, so the green grass that soon dries up becomes a fitting symbol of all that is short-lived. The most obvious quality of grass in a dry climate is that it withers (Ps 102:4, 11; 129:6) and fades (Ps 37:2). For the psalmist the oppression of the wicked is made easier to bear by the thought that they are like grass; that is, they will soon fade and wither (Ps 37:2). More often than not, however, Scripture employs the theme as a warning for the righteous. We are to face our mortality and the swiftness with which our lives pass. All flesh is like grass (Is 40:6-8; quoted in 1 Pet 1:24-25). As Psalm 90:5-6 has it, to be human is to be like grass and like a dream that quickly disappears. Elsewhere the psalmist acknowledges that he is like an evening shadow that withers away like grass (Ps 102:11). We flourish only momentarily (Ps 103:15); then like the grass, we die (Is 51:12). To live as though it were otherwise would be folly (cf. Jas 1:10, where the rich are warned that they, like the *flowers of the grass, will fade away in the midst of their pursuits).

A minor motif draws upon blades of grass as an image of large numbers. Like the sands of the seashore, blades of grass are too numerous to count. Thus in Job 5:25 a large number of descendants is compared to "the grass of the earth," and in the coming age the offspring of Jacob "shall spring up like grass amid waters" (Is 44:4).

See also CATTLE; DRY, DROUGHT; GREEN; OX, OXEN; PASTURE; PLANTS; RAIN; SHEEP, SHEPHERD; TRANSIENCE; WASTELAND.

GRAVE

The grave conjures up many kinds of images, most of them negative. In its most concrete expression the grave is simply a tomb or place of *burial (Gen 35:20; Mk 16:3). Often, however, imagery of the grave as the abode of the dead is evoked. Sheol (Heb) and Hades (Gk) represent the lowest place imaginable in contrast to the highest heavens (Is 7:11; Mt 11:23). The grave does not simply represent a termination of life but points beyond it to a place where two irreconcilable destinies coexist (Lk 16:22, 26).

The grave is the epitome of *darkness (Job 17:13; 18:18; Lam 3:6). Spatially, its abode is the farthest recess from light, a prison detaining one from life and activity in the upper world. It is described as "the *pit," and its entrance as going down "into the dust" (Job 17:14, 16). The grave is ritually unclean (Num 19:16) and is a place where such detestable nighttime activities as necromancy take place (1 Sam 28:8; Is 45:18-19; 65:4) .

Loneliness and solitude (Ps 31:17-18; Is 47:5) represent the chief epithets on the gravestone. It is a place where one's only companions are *worms (Job 17:12, 14), consuming the last vestiges of the flesh that represents the experience of pleasures in the life above. In this sense, experience in the grave is the very antithesis of the enjoyment of life. It is the absence of companionship, the love between man and woman, the sounds of joy and laughter, sampling the fruits of one's labor or participation in worship (Ps 88:10-12; Is 38:18).

By way of contrast the grave also presents a positive image. The social outcast Job looks to the grave for consolation (Job 3:11-19), for there the strife of the upper world ceases. In an even greater sense the grave represents ultimate paradise for the miserable Lazarus (Lk 16:22, 25). This parable highlights the antithetical nature of the experience of the grave for its occupants with respect to their experience in life and their ultimately separate destinies.

Epithets are intimately connected with the grave. The manner in which a person goes to the grave acts as a stamp of finality on the traits that characterized the person's life. Negatively, a person could go down to the grave in sorrow (Gen 44:29), as being dumbfounded (Ps 31:17), as violently slain (1 Kings 2:9) or as alive (Ps 55:15). Positively, the ideal epithet was to retire from this life in peace (1 Kings 2:6), where the absence of strife at death symbolizes harmony both in this life and in life beyond the grave (see Afterlife).

Familial associations are symbolized by the grave. A common metaphor for going to the grave is the phrase "he slept with his fathers" (of David, 1 Kings 2:10) or "he was gathered unto his people" (of Abraham, Gen 25:17). The grave is both a temporary generational gap and the ultimate gathering place of the *family.

In Semitic imagery the grave was the entrance to the underworld, just as the *womb represented an entrance to life *from* the underworld (Ps 139:15). For those who never enter into life, the womb is a tomb, as both Job and Jeremiah observe in lamenting the day of their respective births (Job 3:10-16; Jer 20:17).

The grave is not only represented by spatial imagery, but it is often personified as death itself. Here the negative aspects of the grave as Sheol are prominent. Death and the grave are personified as a tyrannical monarch over the kingdom of the dead (Hos 13:14). The grave is also personified as a powerful *trap with cords that entangle its victim (2 Sam 22:6; Ps 18:5) or as a secure *prison with bars to retain its prisoners (Job 17:16). It allows no escape or return to enjoyment of life in the upper world (Job 14:12). For the wicked dead the grave represents a place of punishment and eternal torment (Mt 10:28; see Crime and Punishment) and of separation from all sources of help or rescue (Lk 16:24).

The grave and death are also personified as having insatiable *appetites (Is 5:14; Hab 2:5; Prov 27:20; 30:15-16). Here the grave as Sheol is associated with *swallowing (Prov 1:12; Ps 141:7), which is also represented by the god *Mot* (= death) in Canaanite mythology. In an interesting play on this metaphor, the Lord reverses the curse of the grave by "swallow[ing] up death for ever" (Is 25:8 RSV; cf. 1 Cor

15:54-57). Here the grave is transformed into a profoundly positive symbol in which those who "die in Christ" are not in Hades but rather are united with Christ (Lk 23:43; 2 Cor 5:8; Phil 1:23). For the righteous, then, the grave becomes a symbol of ultimate hope. This was true even for the miserable Job (cf. Job 19:25-26).

See also BURIAL, FUNERAL; DARKNESS; DEATH; PIT.

BIBLIOGRAPHY. D. J. A. Clines, *Job 1-20* (WBC; Dallas: Word Books, 1989); O. Keel, *The Symbolism of the Biblical World* (Winona Lake, IN: Eisenbrauns, 1997 (1978).

GREAT HIGH PRIEST. *See* PRIEST.

GREEN

Green is the *color of vegetative life. It is an ideal image, denoting the condition toward which the natural world tends in its positive condition. It connotes security, sustenance and *beauty. More than any other color, it represents *nature in its ideal form. The reference in Psalm 23:2 to "green *pastures" and "still waters" (RSV) is one of the most evocative pictures in all of poetry. Throughout the Bible green is a positive norm, and its absence is viewed as death bringing. Correspondingly, green is a sign of God's favor and provision, and its deprivation, of his judgment and disfavor.

The equation of green with life and abundance first appears at the very climax of the *creation, where God gives the animals he has created "every green plant for food" (Gen 1:30 RSV). As a second *Adam after the flood, Noah receives the same provision except that God gives Noah "every moving thing" as well as the green plants for food (Gen 9:3). Thereafter the greenness of the vegetative world is the biblical standard for nature's abundance. In Joel's prophecy the fact that "the pastures of the *wilderness are green" is made parallel to the picture of "the tree [that] bears its fruit" and "the fig tree and vine [that] give their full yield" (Joel 2:22 RSV). Cut from the same cloth is Jeremiah's picture of a *tree planted by water whose "leaves remain green," so that "it does not cease to bear fruit" (Jer 17:8 RSV).

The greenness of nature is an aesthetic delight as well as a functional prerequisite to life. In the "green pastures" and "still waters" of Ps 23:2 we picture the sheer delight to the eyes represented by a lush pastoral landscape (the *sheep, we might note, are not actually eating and drinking but resting at midday). Or the associations might be the *softness of green grass as a place to sit, as in the account of how Jesus "commanded them all to sit down by companies upon the green grass" (Mk 6:39 RSV) before feeding them, in a story that echoes Psalm 23 with its scene of Jesus as a shepherd (Mk 6:34) teaching at lakeside (water). In the Song of Songs the fact that "our couch is green" (Song 1:16) is part of the aesthetic beauty of the lovers' bower.

If green denotes life and God's favor toward people and nature, its absence is evidence of *death and God's *judgment or disfavor. We accordingly find a cluster of death images in which nature is described as not being green: "his branch will not be green" (Job 15:32 RSV); "the grass is withered, the new growth fails, the verdure is no more" (Is 15:6 RSV); "dry up the green tree" (Ezek 17:24); "devour every green tree" (Ezek 20:46). The apocalyptic version of this image is the vision of the first trumpet in Revelation, where one of the natural disasters is that "all green grass was burnt up" (Rev 8:7 RSV).

As we move from these literal, physical references to green vegetation, we find three symbolic uses in Scripture. First, if greenness is so strongly linked in our minds with nature's life and food, it is inevitable that the human imagination would turn it into a symbol of prosperity. Thus we have the psalmist's picture of the righteous being "like a green olive tree the house of God" (Ps 52:8 RSV) and fruitful in old age, "ever full of sap and green" (Ps 92:14 RSV). In the same vein is the wise man's claim that "the righteous will flourish like a green leaf" (Prov 11:28 RSV) and Jeremiah's picturing Judah in its prosperity as "a green olive tree, fair with goodly fruit" (Jer 11:16 RSV).

Secondly, in a country prone to drought, for biblical writers greenness symbolizes imminent decline or death. Green vegetation can dry up suddenly. The KJV has a famous saying in Job about the wicked person's being "green before the sun" (Job 8:16); that is, on the verge of being scorched. When the psalmist wishes to picture the imminent fall of the wicked, he predicts that the wicked will "wither like the green herb" (Ps 37:2).

Finally, because of the association of greenness with life, it was connected in ancient times with fertility religions. The OT uses the stereotyped expression "under every green tree" eleven times (Deut 12:2; 1 Kings 14:23; 2 Kings 16:4; 17:10; 2 Chron 28:4; Is 57:5; Jer 2:20; 3:6, 13; 17:2; Ezek 6:13) in reference to outdoor pagan religious rites. Unfaithful Israelites set up pagan shrines and practiced sacred prostitution among *groves of trees.

See also COLORS; DRY, DROUGHT; GARDEN; GRASS; LEAF; NATURE; PASTURE; PLANTS; TREE, TREES; WASTE-LAND; WILDERNESS.

GRIEF

The Bible gives us memorable images of grief, from *Job sitting in ashes to the *Suffering Servant of Isaiah, rejected even as he bears the grief of others. The English word *grief* translates several Hebrew and Greek words and today refers primarily to mental suffering. But in scriptural usage it encompasses both physical and emotional *pain, in keeping with the Hebrew idea of the human being's essential unity. Grief may come in response to sorrow over personal (Ps 51:1-4) or corporate (Lam 3:51) sin or as a reaction to individual (Ps 35:14) or group (Job 30:25) suffering. It has both dramatic internal and external expressions. Vivid biblical pictures of men and women overtaken by

grief reveal its nature and poignancy.

In grief Job rends his mantle and shaves his head on hearing that all his sons and daughters are dead (Job 1:20). He sits down among the *ashes, his body afflicted with sores. His friends find him almost unrecognizable, and in sympathy they also rend their mantles and sprinkle dust on their heads (2:12). David reveals his grief in words and action. He tells how it takes over his life: "My eyes grow weak with sorrow, my soul and my body with grief" (Ps 31:9 NIV). He acts out his grief by tearing his garments and lying on the ground when he hears that Absalom has struck down all his sons (2 Sam 13:31). His cry "my son, my son," as he mourns the *death of Absalom, portrays grief unforgettably (2 Sam 18:33).

The epitome of grief, however, is God's Suffering Servant. Despised and rejected, he bears the griefs of others and thereby heals them (Is 53:3-5). The word *grief* here literally means "sickness," but it refers to sickness of the mind and soul as well as the body. Christ, the fulfillment of the Suffering Servant, suffers both physical and mental grief and heals *diseases of both body and soul.

Along with Job and David, many characters throughout the Bible demonstrate grief by means of the violent gesture of tearing their *garments, showing outwardly what they feel inwardly. The destructive action reveals the sudden and sharp emotion that overshadows all ordinary concerns, such as care for appearance and possessions. Wearing torn clothes suggests that one's life, too, is irrevocably changed, and for the worse. It also indicates the desire to share another's grief as Hushai's torn robe shows his sympathy with his king (2 Sam 15:32).

Sudden loss, or the fear of it, provokes the expression of violent grief. In *Joseph's story, Reuben and then Jacob rend their clothes, believing Joseph dead (Gen 37:29, 34). All the brothers repeat the gesture when they fear for Benjamin, whose sack holds Joseph's silver cup (Gen 44:13). Jephthah tears his clothes in grief for his daughter (Judg 11:35). Tamar, raped and dismissed by her brother Amnon, tears her "ornamented robe" (2 Sam 13:19 NIV).

It is grief for assaults on God's honor or his nation's welfare that causes some to tear their clothes. Such are Joshua and Caleb (Num 14:6); Hezekiah's men who report Sennacherib's threat (2 Kings 18:37); Hezekiah (2 Kings 19:1); Josiah (2 Kings 22:11); Mordecai (Esther 4:1) and Ezra (Ezra 9:3). Likewise, Barnabas and Paul tear their clothes in grief when the crowds at Lystra acclaim them as the gods (Acts 14:14).

God notes Josiah's action as harmonious with his heart: "Because your heart was responsive and you have humbled yourself . . . and tore your robes and wept in my presence, I have heard you" (2 Kings 22:19 NIV). Otherwise, wearing torn clothes means mere compliance with a custom. Thus the prophet Joel instructs Israel: "Rend your heart and not your garments" (Joel 2:13 NIV).

Among prominent causes of grief are children disobedient to God's laws. A foolish son is a grief to his mother and father (Prov 17:25). Esau's Hittite wives were a source of grief to Isaac and Rebekah (Gen 26:35). God spares the wicked sons of Eli only to grieve his heart (1 Sam 2:33). David knew the grief of rebellious children (2 Sam 13:21; 15:30). God too is grieved by his rebellious children of Israel (Ps 78:40). Paul reminds God's children by faith in Christ not to "grieve the Holy Spirit" (Eph 4:30).

Eventually grief will give way to *joy, its opposite. Christ tells his disciples at the Last Supper, "Your grief will turn to joy," and "No one will take away your joy" (John 16:20, 22 NIV). Peter speaks of believers rejoicing in hope even while they suffer grief in all kinds of trials (1 Pet 1:6). Grief is wiped out in heaven; joy is the order of eternity (Rev 21:4).

See also ASHES; DEATH; DISEASE AND HEALING; FATHER; MOTHER; MOURNING; PAIN; PASSION OF CHRIST; SUFFERING; SUFFERING SERVANT.

GROAN, GROANING. *See* SIGH, SIGHING.

GROVE

In the OT we find the oak favored for its shade and thus as a place for deliberation (1 Kings 13:14) or to bury the dead (Gen 35:8; 1 Chron 10:12). Oaks are also associated with idolatry. The KJV translates the Hebrew *ăšērâ* as "groves" or "high places" (e.g., Ex 34:13; Deut 16:21; 2 Kings 17:16). But the Hebrew term is probably referring to an image or cult-pole of the Canaanite goddess Asherah, consort of El, and is more correctly rendered directly into English as *Asherah* and *Asherim* (pl.). However, the notion of a sacred grove is found in the Bible, for Hosea speaks of Israel sacrificing "under oak, poplar, and terebinth because their shade is good" (Hos 4:13 RSV; cf. Deut 16:21). Abraham is camped at the "oaks of Mamre" (Gen 18:1); the Israelites camp at an oasis with a grove of seventy palm trees and twelve *springs of water (Ex 15:27); and Deborah holds court under the "Palm of Deborah between Ramah and Bethel" (Judg 4:5). The grove evokes a place of cool shade in an arid land, a natural place to encamp, to worship and to congregate and carry out the business of society.

See also GARDEN; TREE, TREES.

GROW, GROWTH

The image of growth is applied to the nation of Israel, to individuals and to rulers. Although it is a prominent image in Scripture, it does not enjoy the preeminent role that it currently has in Western culture. In the Scriptures persons grow in knowledge and virtues, but metaphors related to discipline, shaping, molding and submitting are more prominent.

Through the prophet Isaiah the Lord said of the people of Israel: "They are the shoot I have planted" (Is 60:21 NIV). Despite this, Israel was not faithful to God; and this too is described with allusions to growth: "I had planted you like a choice vine of

sound and reliable stock. How then did you turn against me into a corrupt, wild vine?" (Jer 2:21 NIV). Even then, they could return. Through Hosea this is what the Lord said when Israel returned seeking forgiveness: "I will be like the dew to Israel; he will blossom like a lily. Like a cedar of Lebanon he will send down his roots; his young shoots will grow. His splendor will be like an olive tree, his fragrance like a cedar of Lebanon. Men will dwell again in his shade. He will flourish like the corn. He will blossom like a vine" (Hos 14:5-7 NIV).

The godly person is sometimes portrayed as one who is "like a tree planted by streams of water, which yields its fruit in season and whose leaf does not wither" (Ps 1:3). The picture is of a *tree that is *fruitful because it has strong *roots and is well *watered. The same ideas are found in Psalm 92:12-15 and Jeremiah 17:7ff. The illustration used in these passages is that there is strength and fruitfulness in the spiritual realm only by trusting God, delighting in the law of the Lord and living rightly.

These images show God's sovereignty and power to revive, but at the same time they show human responsibility to respond positively to God. Another strand of OT teaching is that God controls the growing and fading of the power of rulers. The prophet Isaiah said that God "brings princes to naught and reduces the rulers of this world to nothing. No sooner are they planted, no sooner are they sown, no sooner do they take root in the ground, than he blows on them and they wither, and a whirlwind sweeps them away like chaff" (Is 40:23, 24 NIV).

In the NT the picture of growth is used in various ways. In the Sermon on the Mount, Jesus refers to the fact that God creates beautiful plants: "See how the lilies of the field grow" (Mt 6:28 NIV). Jesus told his disciples not to worry but to seek first God's kingdom and righteousness (Mt 6:31-34). God clothes the short-lived plants so very well and will not have any less care for those who follow him.

Among the parables of the kingdom are several about *seeds and growth. In the parable of the *sower, the seed refers to "the message about the kingdom" (Mt 13:19 NIV) or the word of God (Lk 8:11). Jesus' explanation is about whether or not it grows, and if so, how well. For example, early growth may not survive or can be choked "by life's worries, riches and pleasures" (Lk 8:14 NIV).

Jesus told another parable (Mt 13:24-30, 36-43) in which the enemy sowed weeds among the *wheat. Both weeds and wheat were allowed to grow. The point here is that in the life of the kingdom, God is active and so is the devil. Ultimately there will be judgment, but in the meantime all genuine spiritual growth is accompanied by opposition. Other relevant parables are the growth of seed (Mk 4:26-29) and the *mustard seed (Mt 13:31ff and parallels).

Paul used the image of growth to describe his preaching work (1 Cor 3:5-9). The principle was that Paul "planted the seed, Apollos watered it, but God made it grow" (1 Cor 3:6 NIV). Another image in Paul's letters is the analogy of new birth and growth (e.g., 2 Cor 5:17; Gal 6:15). Peter also used this image when he wrote, "Like newborn babies, crave pure spiritual milk, so that by it you may grow up in your salvation" (1 Pet 2:2 NIV).

See also FARMING; FRUIT, FRUITFULNESS; MUSTARD SEED; PLANTS; SEED; SOW, SOWING, SOWER; WATER.

GRUMBLING. *See* EXODUS, BOOK OF.

GUARD

The imagery of the guard was important in the ancient world, and the Bible reflects this with well over 150 (NIV, 180) references to guard(s). Guards served to *protect rulers, their possessions and their edicts. They were employed throughout the ancient Near East by Egyptian pharaohs (Gen 37:6), Babylonian kings (Dan 2:14) and Israelite rulers (2 Kings 11:4-6). Guards also watched over prisoners (Jer 32:2). In the NT there was a guard assigned to watch Jesus' grave (Mt 27:65), and Herod Antipas had bodyguards (Mk 6:27). *Angels served as God's guards to protect the entrance to the Garden of Eden (Gen 3:24) and to watch over the Israelites in the wilderness (Ex 23:20). Most importantly, God serves as a guard to protect his people (Ps 25:20; 86:2; 91:11; 97:10; Prov 2:8).

In essence a guard symbolizes protection and *watchfulness. His entire occupation requires him to encompass and shield his charge from harm or to restrain prisoners from escape. The Philippian jailer was going to take his own life when he awoke after an earthquake and assumed his prisoners had escaped (Acts 16:27). A guard is also a picture of power. This power is located in the authority that is over the guard. Jehu, king of Judah, ordered his guards to kill all the worshippers of Baal, and it was done (2 Kings 10:25).

These images of protection, watchfulness and power evoke feelings of deep security for the believer who, like Paul, trusts God for *protection. "I know whom I have believed, and am convinced that he is able to guard what I have entrusted to him for that day" (2 Tim 1:12 NIV).

A guard also inherently suggests opposition. Without an *enemy there would be no need for guards. Human guards serve as the physical backdrop for the spiritual opposition of *Satan to God and his kingdom. Christians thus need to guard themselves from Satan's attack (Eph 6:10-18 ; 1 Pet 5:8).

Metaphoric uses of the image sometimes suggest a quasi-psychological picture of self-discipline. The psalmist, for example, prays, "Set a guard over my mouth, O LORD; keep watch over the door of my lips" (Ps 141:3 NIV). In Proverbs we read variously about how understanding will guard the wise person (Prov 2:11) and about the need to guard understanding (Prov 4:13; cf. 7:2), one's heart (Prov 4:23), lips (Prov 13:3), mouth (Prov 21:23) and soul

(Prov 22:5). Equally metaphoric is the picture of how "righteousness guards the man of integrity" (Prov 13:6 NIV).

See also BONDAGE AND FREEDOM; PRISON; PROTECTION; WATCH, WATCHMAN.

GUARDIAN. *See* AUTHORITY, HUMAN; GALATIANS.

GUEST

The image of guest is informed by two different guest types that are familiar to the social milieu of the biblical world. One of these is the unexpected guest, who is the recipient of the lavish *hospitality rituals of the ancient world (along with occasional surprises). The other is the invited guest, called to witness events and be in relationship with the host.

Unexpected Guests. The partly nomadic culture of the early OT narratives makes unexpected guests common. Messengers from God come as guests (Gen 12:16; 18:1-8; 19:3, 24; 20:7, 18; 2 Sam 3:20; Judg 13:2-7). In their travels, Abraham and Sarah are unanticipated guests of *Pharaoh and then Abimelech, thus Sarah is pursued as a mate by both (Gen 12:11-20; 20:1-18). Abraham's servant seeks to be Rebekah's guest when she demonstrates the sign of God's chosen mate for Isaac (Gen 24:12-27). The Queen of Sheba invites herself to Solomon's court (1 Kings 10:1-13), as does Ruth to Boaz's field and *threshing floor (Ruth 3:7-14). In travel, David visits the house of Nahor and Abigail and the house of priests (1 Sam 21:1-10; 25:4-12). The scheming Gibeonites, neighbors to Judah, disguise themselves as wandering travelers with elaborate props of moldy *bread and tattered *garments, attempting to gain a treaty of peace with the mighty nation (Josh 9:3-15). The prophet Elisha is welcomed to the guest room of a Shunamite woman and her husband whenever he passes by (2 Kings 4:8-10).

Being a guest is sometimes treacherous in the OT: Lot's male guests are sought for sexual pleasure by the men of his city (Gen 19:1-13); the Levite who is a guest at a Benjamite home finds his concubine raped and dead in the morning (Judg 19:1-28); Jael's guest, the fleeing villain Sisera, receives a place to rest but also a stake driven through his temples while he sleeps (Judg 4:17-21).

The *adulteress extends repeated invitations in Proverbs (Prov 2:16-19; 5:3-5; 7:6-27). A solo youth walking home at dusk is prey for her, and the teacher pleads, "Do not let your heart turn to her ways or stray into her paths" (Prov 7:26 NIV). Two personified women—*Wisdom and *Folly—prepare elaborate *banquets for their invited guests. Those who entertain the invitation of Folly do not know "that her guests are in the depths of the grave" (Prov 9:18 NIV).

A standard of guest etiquette exists for both unexpected and invited guests. Both are responsible not to insult the host by ingratitude (Prov 23:1-3, 6-8) or by refusing the provisions offered (Lk 10:7-8;

1 Cor 10:27). They must refrain from dominating the host's household by ordering *servants, making demands or taking anything not offered, including a particular place at the *table (Prov 25:6-7; Lk 14:7-11). They must also be properly attired (Mt 22:11-14).

They can expect to be cared for—be fed, have their *feet washed, be given a place to *rest, be protected. *Banquets in honor of guests are common (Gen 18:1-8; Esther 1:5, 9; 2:18; 5:4-12; 1 Kings 10:4-5; Ps 23:5; Rev 9:9, 17), and guest bedrooms are found in both the OT and NT (2 Kings 4:8-10; Mk 14:14; Philem 22).

Invited Guests. Formally invited guests expect to witness and celebrate an event. Haman and King Xerxes spring to mind as those for whom Esther's dinner series is planned. *Joseph's brothers nervously await the elaborate dinner that he orders for them when they return with Benjamin. Daniel declines invitation to the banquets of Babylonian kings. The psalmist celebrates the banquet prepared before him by God (Ps 23:5).

Celebrants of a sacrifice serve as God's invited guests to witness his redemption and justice. They are consecrated (1 Sam 16:5); that is, they are cleansed and prepared for *worship (Ex 40:9-15). Those who execute God's judgment are consecrated in a similar way (Is 13:3). These roles come together when the Lord promises to consecrate guests for a "sacrifice" on the day of Judah's judgment (Zeph 1:7).

Guests also serve as witnesses to other events. Absalom and Adonijah each invite guests to witness their attempted accession to the throne (2 Sam 15:7-12; 1 Kings 1:5-10; cf. 1 Sam 16:13). Perhaps the guests of the *bridegroom are called to witness, as well as to celebrate (Mt 9:15; 22:2, 10; see Wedding). The disciples are invited to witness the last *supper, which involves celebration and prophecy, a promise and a *sacrifice (Lk 14:12-31). At times it is implied that the guests witness an *oath, such as Zacchaeus's promise to repay (Lk 19:8) and Herod's oath to Herodias's daughter (Mt 14:7-9).

Humanity is God's invited guest in the cosmos (Gen 1:26-30; Heb 11:13). The psalmist writes, "I am your passing guest, an alien, like all my forebears" (Ps 39:12 NRSV). While the phrase "passing guest" may suggest the "unexpected guest" idea, it connotes the speakers feelings rather than God's wishes. The rest of the Bible portrays God actively seeking individual humans as his guests. We understand the guest relationship as invited: first, because humans were created by God; second, because Israel so rarely seeks God of her own volition; and third, because God is never a stranger to the activity of any human.

God hosts his chosen people in the *wilderness (Gen 15:13-21; Deut 26:5-8) and the *Promised Land (Gen 15:7; Deut 26:9); the *exiles return as God's guests to Jerusalem (Is 55:1-3). Though many know of his invitation, they chose to act as passing guests, having needs met but not abiding in relationship with God. The psalmist, seemingly intimate with God, questions man's ability to be in the presence of God's holiness, asking, "LORD, who may dwell in your sanctuary? Who may live on your holy hill?" (Ps 15:1 NIV; cf. Lk 14:15; 16:9; Mt 8:11).

*Jesus, "the image of the invisible God," answers this question, expanding the guest image. He invites people to be his guests and serves them lavishly (Lk 12:37; 22:27) and humbly (Jn 13:1-17), ultimately giving his life to save his guests (Mk 10:45), as oriental hospitality requires in extreme cases. Though in human form, he extends the same invitation as God has done for Israel. But his invitation is responsive (Mt 12:28; Jn 1:10-14); if people wish to be the guests of God, they must also invite Jesus to be theirs. Jesus radically alters their ideas of a guest, because as Messiah, he is not the type of guest they were expecting.

According to custom, the host by offering and the guest by accepting give tacit approval of one another (2 Jn 10-11). The Pharisees condemn Jesus for being "the guest of a sinner" (Lk 19:7) because they teach that even to enter the home of an unclean person makes one unclean, or at least vitiates the consecration procedure (Jn 18:28). Thus Peter is not easily convinced to invite Cornelius's messengers as guests into his home, and later to be himself the guest of Cornelius (Acts 10:13-16, 28). Yet Jesus intends to be the guest of sinners (Mt 9:9-13). He invites himself to dinner with Zacchaeus and encounters Pharisees while the guest of people whom they would never acknowledge (Lk 19:2-7). This recalls his story of the wedding banquet to whom all types of people are invited when the originally invited guests decline (Mt 22:2-14; Lk 14:16-24). He is the guest of *sinners, and in unmistakable imagery, he promises communion with God only if an invitation be extended to him (Rev 3:20; Jn 14:6).

Jesus invites guests from all nations to the banquet of communion with God (Is 25:6-8; 55:1-5; Rev 19:9). It is this great wedding banquet of the kingdom of heaven, the ultimate guest/host affair, that partially concludes John's dramatic vision and the story of the Bible as a whole (Rev 22:17).

See also BANQUET; FOREIGNER; HOSPITALITY; HOST, GOD AS.

GUIDE, GUIDANCE

The richness and variety of this motif are evident in the number of words used in Scripture to express the concept. At least twelve different terms (nine Hebrew and three Greek) are employed. Although the concept can be used in a more down-to-earth way, such as in guiding a cart (2 Sam 6:3) or a detachment of soldiers (Jn 18:3), its most frequent usage is filled with religious and providential significance.

The most dramatic biblical image of guidance is found early in the OT, where the *theophanic presence of Yahweh guides the fledgling nation of Israel via a *pillar of *cloud by day and a pillar of *fire by night (Ex 13:21). This truth was still rehearsed much later in Israel's history (Neh 9:12, 19; Ps 78:14), and Yahweh himself promised to give such guidance, even in difficult circumstances (Is 42:16). Other texts develop the theme of guidance in different ways but never depart from the basic truth of the presence of God as foundational to all guidance (Ps 23:3).

Another notable picture of guidance is of Yahweh as *shepherd (Ps 23; 78:52; Is 40:11; 49:10). An integral part of the biblical notion of guidance, this picture culminates in Revelation 7:17, where the *Lamb leads martyred saints "to *springs of living water" (NIV).

In addition to his direct involvement in guiding his people, Yahweh also has human agents and divinely appointed means to assist his people. Godly parents (Prov 4:11), *prophets (1 Sam 12:23; Lk 1:79) and other advisers (Prov 11:14) serve as God's "tour guides" through life. The Word of God is itself closely linked to guidance for the believer, and it is described as "a *lamp to my feet and a light for my path" (Ps 119:105; cf. Prov. 11:22). In a similar way the Holy Spirit guides the apostles (and by extension believers generally) "into all truth" (Jn 16:13). The prerequisites for guidance include *humility (Ps 25:9), integrity (Prov 11:3), *discernment (1:5) and *wisdom (Prov 16:23).

The theme of guidance is also seen from a negative angle when God censures false prophets, phony leaders and pagan techniques of seeking guidance. For example, the leaders of wayward Israel are guilty of *misguiding* God's people (Is 3:12; 9:16), a theme echoed in the NT when Jesus calls the Pharisees "*blind guides" (Mt 15:14; 23:16). In addition, failure to offer guidance to widows and aged parents is deemed reprehensible (Job 31:18; Is 51:18). Pagan practices such as divination (2 Kings 16:15), consulting mediums (1 Chron 10:13) and inquiring of *idols (Hab 2:19) are summarily condemned.

The actual images by which God literally or metaphorically guides people are vivid and varied. He guides them by his unfailing love and his strength (Ex 15:13), with light and truth (Ps 43:3), with his counsel (Ps 73:24) and with his hand (Ps 139:10). God led Abraham's servant to the right wife for Isaac by an answered prayer (Gen 24:10-27) and Paul into Macedonia by a *dream of a man saying, "Come over to Macedonia and help us" (Acts 16:9). He gave Gideon direction by means of a "fleece test" (Judg 6:36-40). We can find examples in the Bible of a range of ways in which God provides this guidance—through his revealed Word (with its moral guidance), the example and teachings of Jesus, the indwelling presence of the *Holy Spirit, the influence of godly models (including spouses and parents), and the exhortations of spiritual leaders or advisers.

To be thus guided or led by God is most naturally pictured by biblical writers as movement along a path or way. The range of things *into which* God guides people are varied: a land, right or safe paths (Ps 23:3), "what is right" (Ps 25:9), truth (Ps 25:5), "the way everlasting" (Ps 139:24) and God's "holy mountain"

for worship in the temple (Ps 43:3). Saints of all ages rejoice that "this God is our God forever and ever; he will be our guide even to the end" (Ps 48:14 NIV).

See also DISCERNMENT; DREAMS, VISIONS; HOLY SPIRIT; LAMP; LAW; ORACLE; PATH; PROPHET, PROPHETESS; SHEEP, SHEPHERD; WISDOM.

GUILT

Guilt, a concept found more frequently in the OT than the NT, is difficult to define precisely given the various nuances it takes on in the Bible. Throughout Scripture there is little distinction made between guilt, *sin and punishment (Gen 4:13; Is 6:7; 22:9; Jer 30:14-15; *see* Crime and Punishment). For the biblical writers guilt is not primarily an inward feeling but rather a state that arises because of a violation of divine law—that is, sin, either of commission or omission—against God or one's neighbor (Num 5:5-6).

Types of Guilt. The concept of guilt progressively develops throughout the Bible. In the early OT there is a strong sense of corporate responsibility (Ex 20:5-6). Individuals may bring guilt upon entire groups. In Leviticus 4:3, for example, the priest's sins "bring guilt upon the people." Individuals may bring guilt upon the rest of the members of the community (Gen 26:10; Deut 24:4). Later, Jeremiah warns that his killing will result in a corporate guilt (Jer 26:15).

In like fashion, guilt by association is also a possibility. The Israelites are instructed to rebuke their neighbors to avoid guilt (Lev 19:17). A man's family, even if ignorant of his sin, bears his guilt, and they and his animals are liable for punishment (Josh 7). And Eli is judged as guilty for not restraining his son's sins (1 Sam 3:13-14).

The OT also describes a type of unintentional guilt as seen in king of Gerar's question to Abraham: "How have I wronged you that you have brought such great guilt upon me and my kingdom?" (Gen 20:9) Instructions are even given (to Moses) as to what should be done if people sin unintentionally (Lev 4; see also Lev 22:15; Deut 19; 22:8).

The prophets present a different understanding of sin and guilt. In them the idea of personal responsibility clearly emerges with an emphasis on motive and inner spirit (Is 1; 57:15; 58:1-12; Mic 6:8). The notion of individual guilt and sin is heightened among the prophets (Ezra 33:12-20; Jer 31:29-30).

Although the concept of guilt is less frequent in the NT, in Jesus' teaching it takes on deeper and even more personal implications. The inner (*heart) motive of the guilty party (Mt 5:21-22) is emphasized, and degrees of guilt are seen in light of individual motive and knowledge (Lk 11:29-32; 12:47-48). Guilt is connected to forgiveness of sin as a debt owed to God (Mt 6:12; 18:21-35).

Guilt has serious consequences. The NT writers speak of it as "deserving of punishment" (Mt 26:66; 1 Cor 11:27; Jas 2:10). Paul's understanding of guilt universalizes and further internalizes the debt to God which results from sin: all are guilty before

God (Rom 1:18—3:20).

Images of Guilt. Because of the importance of community in the Bible, guilt is seen as both collective (Ex 20:5-6; Is 65:7) and individual (Deut 24:16; Ezra 18:2-4). Because of its varied manifestations, a number of provocative images are present. Guilt as stain is a popular image. Saul's house is described as "blood-stained" because of killing the Gibeonites (2 Sam 21:1). Joab, who kills during peacetime, is described by David as having his belt and sandals stained with blood (1 Kings 2:5-6). Isaiah equates guilt with blood-stained *hands (Is 59:3; see also Is 1:15-17) and speaks of scarlet and red crimson as representative of the sins of God's people (Is 1:18). The stain of guilt is so powerful that it cannot be washed away with soda and soap (Jer 2:22).

Guilt connected with images of the human body is also common. The promiscuous *adultery of a *prostitute is one such symbol. In Jeremiah 20:20-25 God compares the sin of worshiping the Baals with such widespread adultery. Elsewhere, under the Levitical code, touching the bodies of the "ceremonially unclean" brings about guilt (Lev 5:2).

Disgrace and shame also come about as a result of sinning against God (Jer 3:25). The day of the Lord brings judgment to the guilty: "their faces will be covered with shame" (Ezra 7:18). This image is also present in Daniel's prayer where he confesses that the Israelites' guilt covers them "with shame" (Dan 9:7-8).

Guilt is also described by the psalmist as something that existentially overwhelms the *sinner (Ps 40:12; 65:3), perhaps most clearly viewed through the image of a "burden too heavy to bear" (Ps 38:4).

Remedies for Guilt. The notion of guilt's connection to punishment is found from early in the Bible (Gen 4:11-15) and throughout the OT and NT. Because guilt requires some sort of punishment (Deut 19:11-13, 21), to avoid this consequence action must be taken to remove the guilt. In the OT, elaborate sin (Lev 4:11—5:13) and guilt (Lev 5:14-

6:7) offerings are present for expiation, and restitution is prescribed in relevant cases (Lev 6:1-7). Those who sin defiantly and neglect the required *atonement for sin are "cut off" and remain in their guilt (Num 15:31).

Beyond the OT system of sacrifices and rituals designed for purification lie a number of compelling images which address human guilt. The *washing away of sins is a prominent biblical symbol. James commands believers to "wash your hands" as a requirement for entering God's presence (Jas 4:8-10; cf. Ex 30:17-21). Salvation is described as a washing experience (Jn 13:8; 2 Cor 6:11; Tit 3:5). Also the popular NT image of water symbolizes *baptism, and baptism in turn symbolizes a salvation where guilt is removed (Acts 2:38; 22:16).

Guilt is also removed by the burning away of dross. The *day of the Lord will be like a "refiner's fire" purifying his people (Mal 3:2; cf. Zech 13:9). Such a purifying fire is also at work in cleansing guilt in Is 4:4. *Cleansing is also in mind in the prophet Isaiah's commissioning by God. A live coal touches his mouth and his "guilt is taken away and [his] sin atoned for" (Is 6:6; cf. Lev 16:12).

The *covering up of guilt is also a recurring image. Blessed is the one "whose sins are covered" (Ps 32:1). The Lord himself covers the sins of his people (Ps 85:2). Job, in a somewhat cryptic passage, speaks of God covering his sins by sealing his offenses "up in a bag" (Job 14:16-17).

Finally, *blood which earlier corresponded with the stain of guilt can also serve to atone for sin. Sprinkling with blood can both cleanse and consecrate (Lev 14:6-7; 16:18-19; cf. 1 Pet 1:2). In fact, it is faith in the blood of Jesus Christ that is the ultimate remedy for human guilt, bringing full and final atonement to those who believe (Rom 3:23-25).

See also ATONEMENT; BLOOD; CLEANSING; COVER, COVERING; CRIME AND PUNISHMENT; PURITY; SIN; SINNER; WASH, WASHING.

H

HABAKKUK, BOOK OF

Habakkuk's prophecy deals with the prophet's uncertainties regarding divine holiness and justice in light of a world that is permeated by godlessness and injustice. The tone of the book is philosophical/theological, as evidenced by its subject matter.

Beneath the surface of the prophecies lies an unexpressed narrative of Habakkuk's personal spiritual *quest. Trapped in a sinful society, his faith wavers so that he confronts God about his inactivity in the face of the prevailing corruption. A complication arises, for God's answer only acerbates his soul further. How could God use as an instrument of *judgment a nation more wicked than his own? A point of crisis has come for which only the divine answer can be sufficient. God reveals to his troubled prophet the standards of his *justice and tells Habakkuk of the Chaldeans' coming judgment in the light of the operation of divine government. Driven to prayer, Habakkuk is allowed to see God's justice in action in the past liberation of Israel from its oppression and his victorious leading of them to the land of promise. Habakkuk is convinced; his spiritual quest is concluded. He will trust God come what may.

The structure of the book reflects this quest in a dialogue format. A rehearsal of Habakkuk's questions and God's answers achieves cohesion in the first two chapters. The questions are cast in the familiar *lament form. The second of God's answers is composed as a series of woe oracles. Clear opening formulae and stitch words are also in evidence, as well as inclusio (Hab1:12—2:1) being bracketed with the idea of reproof, and Habakkuk 2:4-20, with enclosing statements that contrast the unrighteous Chaldean with the righteous who live by faith.

Two primary sources of imagery are used to embody the prophet's vision—*nature and *warfare. In both spheres the predominant mood is one of terror, as foreign *armies invade and conquer, as God makes people like *fish of the *sea (Hab 1:13-17), as God shakes the nations and scatters the *mountains (Hab 3:6), as mountains writhe and waters rage (Hab 3:10). It is no wonder that the prophet's body *trembles and quivers (Hab 3:16), for the prophecy is largely one of *judgment and woe.

Habakkuk's literary artistry is seen especially in his free use of simile and metaphor. Thus the Chaldean is pictured as a man who gives his neighbor a drink in seeming *hospitality. The metaphor quickly gives way to allegory. The apparently innocent *cup contains a draught of wrath, for it is designed to get its partaker drunk. However, *drunkenness alone is not the motive of the untrustworthy friend. Having got his neighbor drunk, he denudes him. The Chaldeans' cavalry is portrayed as advancing on *horses swifter than leopards and fiercer than evening *wolves. Like vultures bent for prey or as a mighty dust cloud gathering sand, they come seeking spoil and taking vast numbers of prisoners (Hab1:8-9). Although the captive people are like fish caught in a net (Hab 1:14-15), their eventual vindication is represented as a case in which a creditor calls in his debt (Hab 2:7-8).

In another simile God's glory is compared to the rising *sun, and in his actions in delivering his people at the exodus he is described as a *Divine Warrior subduing his foes. This latter figure appears in the midst of a pericope (Hab 3:3-15) containing two ancient poems: a theophanic narrative (Hab 3:3-7) and victory psalm commemorating Israel's *exodus and journey toward the Promised Land (Hab 3:8-15).

These poems bear the marks of genuine epic themes and style throughout. The central focus is on a *hero, who is God himself. Likewise, epic elements can be seen in the stylistic employment of literary features common to epic genre: static epithets, set parallel terms, and the use of vocabulary and themes common to the commemoration of the exodus event.

Habakkuk's use of these poems is a stroke of literary genius. Not only do they provide the climactic source for Habakkuk's spiritual quest, but they also allow the necessary conclusion both to that quest and to the problem of the believer's attitude toward life's seeming inequities. Through it all, people who are called to a life of faith and faithfulness must abandon themselves to their *Redeemer in absolute trust (cf. Hab 2:4, 14). This yields the most famous picture in the book—the speaker's decision to trust God:

> Though the *fig tree do not blossom, nor *fruit be on the *vines, the produce of the olive fail and the fields yield no *food, the *flock be cut off from the fold and there be no *herd in the stalls, yet I will rejoice in the LORD, I will joy in the God of my salvation. (Hab 3:17-18 RSV).

Even in these circumstances God "makes my feet like hinds' feet, he makes me tread upon my high places" (Hab 3:19 RSV).

See also PROPHECY, GENRE OF.

HADES. *See* HELL.

HAGGAI, BOOK OF

Haggai, whose ministry lasted only a few short weeks in 520 B.C., speaks during a critical juncture of Israel's restoration. Although the people have begun the process of resuming their lives in Jerusalem following the *exile, the *temple of the Lord still lies in ruins. This fact becomes the burden of Haggai's prophetic work.

The book of Haggai is written in third person prose. Stylistically, this separates Haggai from most of the other prophetic books. Attempts have been made to identify a poetic original that lay behind the present prose, but such reconstructions are unconvincing. That is not to say, however, that Haggai is devoid of literary technique. Many literary devices are found throughout the text, giving it a unique style somewhere between simple narrative and poetry.

The structure of Haggai may be readily discernible, because four oracles comprise the book. Each oracle begins with the date of the prophecy, followed by a form of the divine messenger formula ("Thus says the LORD of hosts"; cf. Hag 1:2; 2:1, 11, 20). The first oracle (Hag 1:1-11) sets forth God's reproach of his people for not rebuilding his temple. Following this oracle the reader is provided with the faithful response of the people to this message (vv. 12-15). The second oracle (Hag 2:1-9) addresses the complaints of certain members of the community who feel the new temple pales in comparison to the temple "in its former glory" (Hag 2:3 NASB). The third oracle (Hag 2:10-19) explains that the uncleanness of the people has resulted in their lack of blessing. "I smote you . . . yet you did not come back to me," the Lord chastises (Hag 2:17 NASB). The last oracle (Hag 2:20-23) assures the election and exaltation of the Davidic line through Zerubbabel. A keen observer will note that the four oracles are set in a parallel pattern, where one and three tend toward indictment, and two and four assure *hope and the *blessings of God.

Cohesion among these oracles is maintained through the use of four major literary techniques. First, Haggai has a special affinity for *rhetorical questions*. All but the final oracle contain at least one rhetorical question. The images called to mind are striking (Hag 1:4, 9; 2:3, 12-13, 19). Second, the repetition of *key phrases* throughout the text bring a singularity to the prophecies. "Consider your ways!" Haggai twice writes (Hag 1:5, 7 NASB), and again, "Consider from this day onward" (Hag 2:15, 18 NASB). Likewise, the Lord twice states that he is "going to shake the heavens and the earth" (Hag 2:6, 21 NASB), calling to mind the imagery of an eschatological *earthquake familiar to apocalyptic imagery

(cf. Rev 6:12; Heb 12:26). Third, despite the prose style of Haggai, there is the use of *parallelism*. Haggai utilizes antithetical parallelism (i.e., the juxtaposition of opposites) as a means to intensify his message. For example, in chapter 1: "You have sown much but harvest little" (Hag 1:6; see also Hag 1:4, 9-10). Fourth, *allusions* to other texts and quotations abound as well. Haggai 1:6 has striking connection with Deuteronomy 28:38-40, and 2:17 with verse 22 of Deuteronomy 28. Indeed, the whole context of blessings and cursings undergird the tone of these oracles. The command to Zerubbabel and to Joshua, the high priest, to "take courage" echoes the same command given in Joshua 1:9 before the entry of Joshua and the children of Israel into the Promised Land. Also, twice the Lord tells the restored remnant, "I am with you." These words call the reader back to the covenantal promises of God made during the time of the Patriarchs and Moses (see Gen 46:3; Ex 3:12; etc.) and are magnified through the promise of Immanuel, "God with us," found in Isaiah's prophecy (Is 7:14).

Imagery used in the book of Haggai is subtle but overwhelming. The stark contrast between the "paneled houses" (Hag 1:4) of the Israelites and the desolation of the house of the Lord would contain no mystery to the hearers of the oracle. They would be challenged to action. The agrarian (or economic) motif that appears at two critical points in the text is similarly worth note. God's own judgment on the people is symbolized in the weak *harvest (Hag 1:6, 10-11; 2:16). His blessing, by parallel, is in the abundant harvest (Hag 2:19). The place of the *temple is especially crucial to the text, and the questions over its glory yield to a powerful figure of God's *glory and sovereignty: "Does it not seem to you like nothing in comparison [with Solomon's temple]?" the Lord asks (Hag 2:3 NASB). If so, the point has been missed. "The silver is Mine, and the gold is Mine," says the Lord. "The latter glory of this house will be greater than the former" (Hag 2:8-9 NASB). Why? Not because of gold or external embellishments, but because the Lord himself will inhabit it in his *fullness (cf. Hag 2:5). From this foundation Israel can be assured of having the Davidic line restored, "a signet *ring" for God himself, because "I have chosen you, declares the LORD of Hosts" (Hag 2:23 NASB).

Finally, the name *Haggai* itself deserves comment. As is the case with the other postexilic prophets (i.e., Zechariah and Malachi), the prophet's given name has a complementary, almost indicative, relationship to his call and ministry. The name *Haggai* means "festal" and derives from the Hebrew root (*ḥag*, "feast, festival") closely associated with the pilgrimage *feasts of *Passover, *Pentecost and Tabernacles. Although one cannot state definitively the occasion suggested by the prophet's name, it does find purpose in the message that the prophet is charged to give concerning the rebuilding of the temple. Since the pilgrimage feasts all centered around the temple, without it these feasts could not possibly be kept. Thus the message of Haggai to rebuild the temple is an implicit call back to the *feasts ordained by God through the Mosaic covenant. When the people completed their work on the temple, the high holy feasts could once again be enjoyed and the covenant fulfilled (see Ezra 6:13-22).

See also PROPHECY, GENRE OF.

HAIL

Hail occasionally accompanies *thunderstorms in Syria and Palestine. When it does, it is destructive to crops, *vineyards and olive plantations. Biblical imagery regularly associates thunder, bolts of *lightning, sleet and *snow with hail (Ps 78:47-48; 148:8); and like them, hail is described in terms of divine weaponry.

Like lightning strikes or floods, when such "natural" disasters caused human fatalities, ancient cultures fitted the events into a framework of personal vengeance or punishment administered by the power behind the *storm. As such, hail inevitably evoked fear and images of devastation for people of biblical times. Ignorant of the meteorological forces that produce hail, the ancients postulated heavenly *storehouses stocked with water, snow and ice (Job 38:22). These *weapons stockpiles were reserved for the day of battle and war (Job 38:23). For the Hebrew poet, God as *Divine Warrior brandishes these weapons so that "out of the brightness of his presence clouds advanced, with hailstones and bolts of lightening" (Ps 18:12 NIV).

In a few instances biblical references to hail are part of a wider declaration of God's power. The query, "Have you seen the storehouses of the hail?" implies that God's control over nature, which humanity cannot even understand, is sufficient answer to Job's complaint (Job 38:22). The psalmist calls attention to God, who "hurls down his hail like pebbles" (Ps 147:17 NIV), and to "lightning and hail, snow and clouds, stormy winds that do his bidding" (Ps 148:8 NIV).

Since God wields his weapons in judgment, hail frequently appears in the context of God's power expressed in judgment. Haggai places hail in parallel with blight and mildew as fulfillment's of the Deuteronomic *curses (Hag 2:17; cf. Deut 28:22). Punishment rains down as hail on Pharaoh (Ex 9:13-35), on God's apostate people (Ps 78:47; Hag 2:17) and on the enemies of Israel (Josh 10:11). On the basis of such past precedents, hail became an archetypal expression of God's future judgment (Is 28:17; 30:30; 32:19; Ezek 13:11, 13). The descriptions of huge hailstones killing people (Rev 16:21, note the second exodus context; cf. Josh 10:11), accompanied by *fire, *blood and burning *brimstone (Ezek 38:22; Rev. 8:7), extend the image of hail into the eschatological realm of apocalyptic judgment.

See also DIVINE WARRIOR; LIGHTNING; RAIN; SNOW; STORM; THUNDER; WEATHER.

HAIR

Surrounded by rituals and symbolic overtones, hair has always been important and controversial in societies, and the Bible runs true to course on the matter. With nearly a hundred references, human hair ranks as an important biblical image, and the range of the references renders it complex as well. In addition, some of the specific images are among the memorable details and scenes of the Bible.

At the most mundane level, hair signals a person's health or lack of it. Leviticus 13—14 is a melancholy litany, finally repulsive to read, of how hair could signal *disease or uncleanness in Hebrew life, with the priests serving as the community's health inspectors in the matter. Equally negative are the ancient customs of tearing out one's hair as a sign of *grief or devastation (Ezra 9:3; Ezek 23:34; Jer 7:29) or of pulling out someone else's hair in personal combat (Neh 13:25). Excessive growth of a man's hair has overtones of the barbaric, as in *Esau's hairiness (Gen 25:25) and Nebuchadnezzar's state during his derangement, when "his hair grew as long as eagles' feathers, and his nails were like birds' claws" (Dan 4:33 RSV).

Mainly, though, hair is a positive image in the Bible; and moderately long hair is an aesthetic norm, as is dark hair. A mark of Absalom's handsomeness was his profuse crop of hair—so profuse that cutting it was an annual festival, with scales on hand to assist gloating and to lend charisma to his celebrity status in the neighborhood (2 Sam 14:25-26). To the love-struck male in the *Song of Songs, the beloved's hair and its bewitching movements are "like a flock of goats, moving down the slopes of Gilead" (Song 4:1; 6:5 RSV), primarily a comparison of value rather than a visual correspondence. The maiden, for her part, admires her man's "wavy" locks, "black as a raven" (Song 5:11 RSV).

Based on the premise that a full head of hair is the norm of health, vigor and *beauty, we find a motif of the ignominy of being without hair. In the day of judgment, says Isaiah, God will become a divine hair cutter: "In that day the LORD will shave with a razor . . . the head and the hair of the feet, and it will sweep away the beard also" (Is 7:20 RSV). In a surrealistic touch Micah evokes the image "bald as an eagle" as the children of Judah go into exile (Mic 1:16; *see* Baldness). Similarly, Jeremiah's vision of a desolate people includes the picture of every head shaved (Jer 48:37). Isaiah predicts a time for the women of Judah when "instead of well-set hair, baldness, . . . instead of beauty, shame" (Is 3:24 RSV). And the naughty neighborhood boys taunt the prophet Elisha with the shout, "Go up, you baldhead!" (2 Kings 2:23 RSV).

The length of person's hair has often signaled larger issues, and we catch hints of this in the Bible as well. The OT prohibition of "rounding off the hair on your temples" (Lev 19:27) was designed to set Israel apart from the practices of surrounding pagan nations (Jer 9:26; 25:23). Ezekiel's prescription for priests in the new era is that they will neither "shave their heads or let their locks grow long; they shall only trim the hair of their heads" (Ezek 44:20 RSV). By the time we reach the NT, Paul considers long hair to be the norm for women but degrading for men (1 Cor 11:14-15). Excessive attention to hair, such as fancy braiding of it, can signal a worldly minded preoccupation with externalities (1 Tim 2:9; 1 Pet 3:3).

Sometimes the treatment of hair is a direct part of a religious practice. Total shaving of one's hair was thus part of a ritual of purification (Lev 14:8-9; Num 6:18-19). Nazirites were prohibited from cutting their hair at all while they were under their vow (Num 6:5, 18), symbolic of being set apart to holiness—a sign of ascetic renunciation, not of physical attractiveness.

Anointing hair with *oil was a ritual, though not a religious one. It was instead a ritual of beauty (Ruth 3:3), festivity (Eccles 9:8) or *hospitality (Ps 23:5).

At the far end of the continuum we find references that are overtly symbolic. *White or gray hair as a sign of old age is an archetype in the Bible (Deut 32:25; Ps 71:18; Is 46:4), where such maturity is a sign of *honor and beauty (Prov 20:29). On the other hand, the elderly are especially pitiable and vulnerable figures, so that grief befalling someone with gray hairs is especially intense (Gen 42:38; 44:29, 31). Because it represents a small feature of one's body, either the single hair or the combined hairs of one's head appear in declarations about the extent to which God will protect or spare a person (1 Sam 14:45; 2 Sam 14:11; Lk 21:18; Acts 27:34). The individual hair's smallness is also the frame of reference in the proverb about choice warriors who could "sling a stone at a hair, and not miss" (Judg 20:16 RSV). Working the other way, the large numbers of a person's hairs makes them a norm for something large or numerous, such as calamities that have overtaken a person (Ps 40:12), one's enemies (Ps 69:4) and the magnitude of God's providential knowledge and care of a person (Mt 10:30; Lk 12:7). Finally, white hair as a sign of ancientness is raised to a transcendent plane in pictures of God's having white and fiery hair (Dan 7:9; Rev 1:14).

We also recall a few memorable pictures from the Bible involving hair. One is the scene of the long-haired *Samson lying with his head in Delilah's lap, first to have the seven locks of his head woven into a web and then to have them cut off (Judg 16:15-21). In the same story the growing locks of Samson after his shaving are symbolic of revival of soul and body (Judg 16:22). The Gospels give us the picture of Mary's anointing the feet of Jesus and wiping them with her hair in an extravagant gesture of devotion (Lk 7:38, 44; Jn 11:2-3).

What, then, is the significance of hair in the Bible? Simply its importance as a literal, physical phenomenon, as something whose treatment gestured toward larger moral and spiritual issues, and as a symbol.

See also BALDNESS; BEAUTY; HEAD; HONOR; SAMSON.

HAMMER

The Hebrews used two words for hammer. The blunt-nosed forge hammer (*paṭṭîš*) was used by metal smiths (Is 41:7). It was also used to break rocks (Jer 23:29). The *maqqebet*, also a blunt-nosed instrument, could also be used to forge metal (Is 44:12) or to drive pegs (Judg 4:21; Jer 10:4). It was also used to cut stone and may have existed in a sharp-nosed version. More probably, the stone-cutting *maqqebet* was also a blunt-nosed instrument used with a chisel (cf. 1 Kings 6:7 NIV).

The hammer, perhaps the most ancient of tools, is used only to effect change. God's judgment, intended to produce change, is his hammer. The hammer-like prophetic word resists any change itself while it reshapes people and events into a new, predetermined form (Jer 23:29). Jeremiah's characterization of Judah as the *rock to be broken by this hammer develops the imagery of a hard, stubborn, brittle rather than malleable people who refuse to submit (Jer 5:3; Ezek 3:7-9; 36:26). Babylon also is a hammer in its role as God's instrument for *judgment (Jer 50:23), but ironically, it is one that can itself be broken. Centuries later in a twist on this image, the Maccabees (derived from *maqqebet*) were the hammers God used to smash the oppressors of the Jews.

The positive results God obtains by use of the hammer stand in contrast to those of human artisans. As the chief tool of the smith, the hammer played a key role in the creation of all the images of gods made with human hands (Is 41:7; 44:12; cf. Jer 10:4). God's people mold and fashion their own malleable gods, but the immutable God molds and fashions his own people. The changes humans might make to places of worship were also unacceptable, hence the prohibition against using "profaning" iron tools on the *altar (Ex 20:25; Deut 27:6; cf. 1 Kings 6:7).

Feminist interpretations have found sexual symbolism in Jael's murder of Sisera (Judg 4:21), with the tent-peg as a phallic symbol (Bal, 227-228). This interpretation is perhaps overdrawn, but it is correct to see the hammer in that narrative as a man's tool (cf. the "workman's hammer" of Judg 5:26), enhancing the theme of gender reversal in the Deborah story. (Perhaps heightening such imagery and sexual symbolism, the Hebrew word for hammer, *maqqebet*, means "piercer," while the related word for female, *neqēbâ*, means "pierced," although it is difficult to prove that the original listeners made such connections.)

See also WEAPONS, DIVINE AND HUMAN.

BIBLIOGRAPHY. M. Bal, *Death and Dissymmetry: The Politics of Coherence in the Book of Judges* (Chicago: University of Chicago Press, 1988) 227-28.

HAND

The term *hand* evokes images of both power and

grace, *blessing and *curse. The literal referent is the body part at the end of the *arm (Gen 3:22; Mt 5:30; Mk 3:1), although occasionally hand can refer to the entire arm (2 Kings 5:18) or to parts of the hand, such as the *fingers or wrist. To wear *rings or bracelets "on the hand" means to wear them on the fingers (Gen 41:42; Jer 22:24; Lk 15:22) or wrist (Ezek 23:42).

Literal Use of Hand. The word *hand* occurs approximately 1,800 times in the English Bible. One third of the occurrences refer to the physical entity. The hand enables a person to do tasks (Judg 5:26; Lk 6:1), to hold tools and *weapons (Num 35:18; Lk 9:52) and to take and possess objects (Ezek 39:9; Rev 7:9). What a person makes or crafts is often called "the work of the hands" (Deut 28:12; 31:29; Ps 90:17; Lam 4:2 NIV).

The hands are used in various symbolic acts. To clasp or shake hands is to consummate an agreement (Is 2:6). Celebration (Ps 47:1) or derision (Job 27:23) is expressed by clapping the hands. To put a hand over the *mouth indicates silence (Job 21:5) and upon the head, grief (2 Sam 13:19). *Washing the hands is for cleansing (Mt 15:2) but also announces innocence (Mt 27:24). To *kiss one's own hands is to express pride (Job 31:27), and to lift "holy hands" is an act of *worship (1 Tim 2:8).

Figurative Use of Hand. Approximately two-thirds of the occurrences of hand in the Bible are used in a figurative or metaphorical way. Five primary ideas seem to be associated with this image.

Power and strength. Moses warns God's people not to assume that the power of their hands will be the reason for their prosperity (Deut 8:17). In the pivotal redemptive event of the exodus, God informs Moses that only a "mighty hand" will compel Pharaoh to liberate the Israelites (Ex 3:19-20; 6:1; 7:4-5; 13:9, 14, 16; Deut 9:26). God's "outstretched hand" will fight against his people in judgment (Jer 21:5), but it will also be the agency of redemption and restoration (Ezek 20:33-34). To be engraved on the hands of God was to be at the center of his power and control of history (Is 49:16). Zechariah sings of Messiah's power (hand) to save his people from their enemies (Lk 1:71, 74), and John points to the keeping power of the "hand" of Christ (Jn 3:35; 13:3).

In a particularly poignant text the psalmist celebrates the joy of sins forgiven and then testifies to the consequences of God's hand "heavy upon me" (Ps 32:4 NIV). Images of power in both judgment and grace are evoked. While the consequences of unconfessed sin are painful, the faithful presence of God was something to celebrate.

Several idioms using hand also relate to strength or power. To "strengthen the hands" of someone was to enable someone who needed help (Is 35:3; Jer 23:14). To "slack one's hand" was to give up and not to show the power and strength possible (Josh 1:6). Isaiah describes the Assyrians as "drained of power" (literally, "small of hand," 2 Kings 19:26; Is 37:27).

In a related image of power, agency is often implied. God speaks "by the hand of" the prophets (1 Sam 28:15; Ezek 38:17; cf. Jer 37:2), and a person can be commissioned or ordered "by the hand of" a superior (1 Kings 2:25; Jer 39:11).

Authority, control or possession. The "hand" of Israel grew steadily stronger against Jabin (Judg 4:24). And in a military image the hand on the *neck indicated victory and authority over one's enemies (Gen 49:8). Christians are assured that no one is able to pluck them out of God's hand (Jn 10:29).

The idiom "given into the hand of" is used to speak of exercising *authority. All of creation is "given into the hand of" humankind to rule (Gen 9:6, cf. 1:26-28). The nation of Israel was given "into the hands of Moses and Aaron" (Num 33:1). Joshua declares that the Lord has delivered "into the hand of" the Israelites all the land of Canaan (Josh 2:24; cf. 6:2; 8:1; Judg 3:28). To "open the hand" (Deut 15:8, 11) or "shut the hand" (Deut 15:7) expresses action of giving or withholding blessing. God "opens his hand" to satisfy the desires of his creation (Ps 145:16).

Right hand. In these occurrences different terms for hand are used that emphasize the right side (Heb. *yāmîn*, Gr. *dexios*). Two domains of imagery emerge. The first is one of prominence or favored position. Aaron and his sons were to be sprinkled with *blood on their right *ear, thumb and big toe (Ex 29:19-20; cf. Lev 8:23-26; 14:14-28). To be seated at the *right hand is to occupy a position of recognition and prestige. Solomon's mother was given a throne at the right hand of the king (1 Kings 2:19). The messianic king is ordered to be seated at the right hand of the Lord, a position of conquest and rule (Ps 110:1; cf. Mt 22:44). Jesus announced his destiny to be seated at the right hand of God (Mk 14:62; Lk 22:69). Finally, to have extended the right hand was an indication of specification and favor (Gal 2:9; Rev 1:17). On several occasions both right and left hand are combined to indicate such a favored position (cf. Prov 3:16; Mt 20:21).

The second domain of "right hand" portrays an image of intense power and strength. Most frequently it is used by the psalmists of the Lord as a God who rescues and sustains by means of his mighty "right hand" (Ps 17:7; 18:35; 21:8; 118:15b-16; 138:7; cf. Ex 15:6, 12). It is recorded of Jael that "her hand reached for the tent peg, her *right hand* for the workman's *hammer" (Judg 5:26, emphasis added). The conquering Jesus is portrayed as holding the seven stars in his "right hand" (Rev 1:16; cf. 1:20; 2:1). The accuser stands at the right hand (Ps 109:6), as does a friend to protect (Ps 16:8).

A *left-handed person was sometimes described as "restricted/bound in his right hand" (e.g., Ehud, cf. Judg 3:15; 20:16; note the play on words with Benjamin, "son of my right hand"). The symbolic significance of the right and left hands are evidenced in Joseph's attempt to change his father's deliberate crossing of his hands in the blessing of Ephraim and Manasseh (Gen 48:13-18). At the judgment the rejected *goats are sent to the left (Mt 25:31). And Qoheleth states that the heart of the fool inclines to the left (Eccles 10:2).

Consecration and designation. The idiom *"lay hands on" occurs frequently in Scripture. Hands were laid on people for designation of both blessing (Gen 48:13-17; Mt 19:13) and judgment (Lev 24:14). The laying on of hands signified commissioning for a special task or office. By such a symbolic act Joshua was commissioned to don the mantle of Moses' leadership (Num 27:18), Saul and Barnabas were appointed as kingdom emissaries (Acts 13:1-3), and leaders in the church were recognized (1 Tim 4:14; 5:22).

Hands were laid upon animals in the various *sacrifices for *atonement and other cultic functions (e.g., Ex 29:10, 15; Lev 1:4; 3:2, 8, 13; 16:21). Whether the laying on of hands is an act of transfer is unclear. Leviticus 16:21-22 explicitly describes transfer, and it appears to be the image carried forward by the NT (1 Pet 2:24; Heb 13:11-12). The act seems to be primarily one of designation.

A related idiom is to "fill the hand." Throughout Exodus 29:9-35 (cf. Ex 16:32), Moses is told to "fill the hand" of Aaron and his sons. While the actual point of the idiom is unclear, it indicated a designation, or perhaps empowerment, of these people to their priestly tasks.

Side, coast or border. The bank of a *river is designated by the term *hand* (e.g., Nile, Ex 2:5; Jordan, Num 13:29). To be "at the hand" of someone is to be at that person's side (1 Sam 19:3). The side projections or sockets in the frame of the tabernacle are "hands" (Ex 26:17, 19), and in 1 Kings 7:32 the axles of a chariot are called "hands," presumably referring to a side mount of the wheel. In Ezekiel 21:19 "hand" refers to a signpost on the road for the king of Babylon, indicating a direction either to the right or left side in the fork of the road.

Summary. While the hand is a body part at the end of the arm, it is much more than this in biblical imagery. Whether in performing tasks, expressing power and authority, or designating purpose and function, the hand is a pervasive picture reflecting the wishes and will of the entire person.

See also ARM; FINGER; FOOT; GESTURES; HANDS, LAYING ON; HANDS, WASHING OF; LEFT, LEFT-HANDED; LEG; RIGHT, RIGHT-HANDED.

HAND OVER. *See* BETRAY, BETRAYAL.

HANDS, LAYING ON OF

While the touch of the human *hand conveys differing intentions and evokes a gamut of feelings, the gentle, firm gesture that is the laying on of hands intends the sense of imparted power. The *right hand in the Bible is a symbol of strength and authority, especially of God's saving and ruling his people (e.g., Ex 15:6; Ps 17:7; Eph 1:20). This ceremony represents God's commission, blessing and equipping for service (e.g., Num 27:18-23; Gen 48:1-20; Deut 34:9).

Jesus blesses the *children with his touch (Mk 10:16), and often his healing is conveyed by such contact (Mt 8:3; 9:20; Lk 4:40). The apostles impose hands in healing (Acts 28:8), commissioning (Acts 13:3) and, on exceptional occasions, upon the reception of the *Spirit (e.g., Acts 8:17; cf. Deut 34:9).

Expectation of *blessing accompanies the ceremony. The congregation sees it as effective as well as symbolic, as the Spirit conveying that which is agreed upon by persons of faith. So Timothy's gifts are recognized by prophetic insight (1 Tim 1:18) and confirmed by the laying on of hands by Paul and the elders (1 Tim 4:14). Further gifts of power seem to be bestowed through the ceremony itself (2 Tim 1:6, "the gift of God, which is in you through the laying on of my hands" NIV).

The early church considers this practice to be among subjects of instruction so accepted that they do not need to be repeatedly established, mentioning it along with "repentance . . . faith in God, instructions about baptism . . . the resurrection of the dead, and eternal judgment" (Heb 6:1-3 NIV).

See also BLESSING; HAND; HOLY SPIRIT; RIGHT HAND.

HANDS, WASHING OF

The *hands are the essence of the individual. Hands communicate our attitudes and perform our deeds. They speak more eloquently than our words, since the actions of the hands come from the *heart. Through hands come blessing and healing, or bloodshed and deeds of wickedness. The condition of the hands portrays the condition of their owner. It is no wonder that the Bible speaks of *blood being on the hands (Gen 4:11; 2 Sam 4:11; Ezek 23:37, 45). The Hebrews also speak of *evil, treason or *guilt as being "in the hand" (1 Sam 14:10; 26:18).

If dirty hands represent past mistakes, *clean hands represent contrition and a fresh start. The temple ritual prescribed the washing of hands (Ex 30:17-21). Those who ministered were to wash their hands as a "perpetual ordinance" so that they might not die as they approached the *altar. The act of hand washing also appears elsewhere in biblical literature as a symbol of *innocence and *purity of *heart. The elders of a town washed their hands as a symbol of their innocence in the death of a man found near their town (Deut 21:6). But the Hebrews had no monopoly on such obvious symbolism. Pilate can hardly be accused of bowing to Jewish custom when he too washed his hands before the crowd to demonstrate his innocence in Jesus' death (Mt 27:24).

Clean hands protest innocence not only with regard to murder and death but to any offense. Hebrew poets describe heartfelt professions of innocence and purity as having "clean hands" (Job 17:9; 22:30; Ps 24:4; 26:6). The exhortation of James parallels the two ideas: "Wash your hands, you sinners, and purify your hearts, you double-minded" (Jas 4:8 NIV).

In a continuing search for *holiness, the requirements of the priestly class frequently became generalized for the laity. The Pharisees adopted as their own the hand-washing stipulations of the priests, and they accused Jesus' disciples of "eating with unclean hands" (Mk 7:1-8; Lk 11:38). Their offense at the disciples' failure to abide by the more stringent standards provides Jesus the opportunity to teach that hand washing is symbolic. A person is not spiritually contaminated by unclean hands but rather by unclean handiwork.

In some cases a ritualized *washing seems an inadequate gesture of remorse and contrition. Jesus strikingly captures the idea of hands as agents of sin in his admonition (with hyperbole, we hope!), "And if your right hand causes you to sin, cut it off and throw it away; it is better that you lose one of your members than that your whole body go into hell" (Mt 5:30 NRSV). Rabbinic evidence plausibly points to the "sin of the right hand" being masturbation. (In Matthew it follows a discussion of lust with amputation similarly suggested as the solution.) The extreme remedy emphasizes that outward conformity to the law or upright behavior is like clean hands, a symbolic gesture that cannot cleanse the mind if it longs for evil. Again, the work of the hands betrays an unclean heart.

Both the OT and NT record that human concerns of ritual purity, symbolic purity of heart and even simple daily needs of cleanliness converge to make the plainly visible hands a powerful symbol of the condition of our invisible heart before God.

See also CLEANSING; GUILT; HEART; INNOCENCE, INNOCENT; PURITY; SIN; WASH, WASHING.

HANGING

Hanging (by a noose) was rarely a means of execution until Roman times. The two clear instances of death by hanging recorded in the Bible are suicides: Ahithophel (2 Sam 17:23) and Judas (Mt 27:5). The reference in Esther to a gallows and hanging (2:23; 5:14; 6:4; 9:13-14; 9:25) is to be taken as impaling on a sharp upright stake—a favored method of execution by Assyrians and Persians (Ezra 6:11). The exact method of hanging mentioned in the execution of Pharaoh's baker is not known, but the hanging very probably refers to his body being publicly displayed after the execution (cf. 1 Sam 31:12).

Previously killed bodies were hung up on trees or stakes (usually by their hands, Lam 5:12). Such hangings were to expose the body to public scorn; they were symbols of the person's total disgrace and rejection by God. They were to be limited to one day (Deut 21:23). Examples include Joshua stringing up five Amorite kings (Josh 10:26) and the Philistines' triumphant display of Saul and Jonathan (2 Sam 21:12).

Paul uses this imagery to illustrate the atoning purpose of Christ's death: "Christ redeemed us from the curse of the law by becoming a curse for us, as it is written: 'Cursed is everyone who is hung on a tree' " (Gal 3:13 NIV; the cross is called a tree also in Acts

5:30; 10:39). Christ's cry of anguish (Mt 27:46) indicated a real, if temporary, rejection by God the Father. His death was also a dramatic rejection by the jeering crowds (Lk 23:35). No one could be brought lower than being publicly hung. Would God subject his Son to such ignominy? The NT writers draw out the irony: the God of love stooped as low as anyone could to redeem humankind.

See also CRIME AND PUNISHMENT; CROSS; CURSE.

HAPPINESS

The tired farmer has finished his long day in the *vineyards. The sun is going down. He sits down under one of the many *fig trees surrounding his humble house. His wife, who spent the day in the field alongside her husband, sits down beside him. Looking into the valley below at the fruitful *vines, they reflect that this has been a good year. The crop is thriving. They gave *birth to their third *child. The king, a faithful servant of Yahweh, has finally secured the borders and guaranteed the *peace and safety of his people. This is the OT image of happiness.

Such an idyllic image, however, was probably realized only briefly: "During Solomon's lifetime Judah and Israel, from Dan to Beersheba, lived in safety, each man under his own vine and fig tree" (1 Kings 4:25 NIV). The prophet Micah looked forward to the day when "every man will sit under own vine and under his own fig tree, and no one will make them afraid" (Mic 4:4 NIV). The references to trees harks back to Eden, where Adam and Eve were free to seek rest and shade under the *trees of the *Garden (Gen 2). The God-fearing man was promised: "Your wife will be like a fruitful vine within your house; your sons will be like olive shoots around your table" (Ps 128:3 NIV; cf. Ps 113:9). OT depictions of bliss include military security, agricultural *abundance, ownership of *land, fertility and the leisure of rest in the shade.

This image of happiness is given shape by the *covenant made with Abraham (cf. Gen 12, 15, 17). The covenant *blessings of the Law (e.g., Deut 28) are simply the outworking of these promises. Thus under the old covenant, happiness was a sign of God's covenant favor and the proof that God keeps his promises.

For Israel under the monarchy, happiness was directly connected to the covenant faithfulness of the king. When the king kept the covenant, the people were blessed. Under the wise rule of Solomon, "The people of Judah and Israel were as numerous as the sand on the seashore; they ate, they drank and they were happy" (1 Kings 4:20 NIV). Even the Queen of Sheba declared, "How happy your men must be! How happy your officials, who continually stand before you and hear your wisdom!" (1 Kings 10:8 NIV). It is striking that not once after the death of Solomon do the books of Kings record anyone's being happy.

The NT both maintains and transforms the OT

image of happiness. The new covenant believer is still happy under the shade of a vine. But now the vine is Jesus himself (Jn 15:1). And his kingdom, now manifest as the church, gives the shade of happiness to all who seek its *protection (Mk 4:30-32). The old covenant image was primarily in terms of circumstantial well-being. The new covenant image of happiness is centered on the person Jesus Christ: "Rejoice in the Lord always. I will say it again: Rejoice!" (Phil 4:4 NIV).

In the NT happiness has a moral dimension. One is to use it not just for self-indulgence but as an occasion of thanksgiving: "Is anyone happy? Let him sing songs of *praise" (Jas 5:13 NIV). There is also an emphasis in the NT on the happiness that will be present at the final restoration. Not only will there be no more tears in heaven, but the sadness and alienation that marked the old order will be replaced, for the former things have passed away (Rev 21:4 RSV).

See also BLESSING; CHILD, CHILDREN; FIG, FIG TREE; GOOD LIFE, THE; LAND; PRAISE PSALMS; PROSPERITY; VINE, VINEYARD; WORSHIP.

HARD, HARDEN, HARDNESS

The quality of being hard rather than *soft, stiff instead of pliable, is hardly mentioned at all in the Bible as a physical property. Instead it is a psychological, moral and spiritual quality that covers a range of attitudes, including refusal to listen, inability to understand, irrationality and rebellious disobedience. The part of the body that most often gets metaphorically hardened is the *heart; the image of being "stiff-necked" is a variant. A survey of instances of hardening will reveal the nuances of the image.

The most famous instance of hardening of heart is Pharaoh and the Egyptians. Sometimes God is said to harden the hearts of the Egyptians (ten references); on other occasions Pharaoh does the hardening (nine references). In either case, the image names the act of an evil person's strengthening of resolve to counter an action that God desires. When God hardens a human heart, as in the statement that "it was the LORD's doing to harden their hearts so that they would come against Israel in battle, in order that they might be utterly destroyed" (Josh 11:20 RSV), the image names the instrumentality by which God achieves his purpose through the actions of evil people (see also Rom 9:7).

Other instances paint a picture of rebellion against God's providence. Psalm 95:8 exhorts the Israelites, "Harden not your hearts, as at Meribah" (RSV). The narrative of the event (Ex 17:1-7) shows it to be an occasion when the Israelites complained against Moses because of their lack of water, and a later reference to the event lists it as one of ten times that Israel put God to the test (Num 14:22). From this we can infer an incipient rebelliousness in the image of humans hardening their hearts. This is confirmed when the writer of Hebrews twice links the Israelites' hardening of their hearts in the *testing in the wilderness with *"rebellion" (Heb 3:8, 15).

Elsewhere, hardening of heart is a refusal to listen to God's invitation, as when Hebrews 4:7 contrasts hardening one's heart with hearing the voice of God. Ezekiel 3:7 links "a hard *forehead" and "a stubborn heart," in a context of how "the house of Israel will not listen" to the prophet. In other usages this refusal to respond extends itself into a refusal to obey God's law for living. Thus Isaiah 63:17 links hardness of heart with straying from God's ways and not fearing God. Similarly, Jesus states that Moses had allowed a certificate of divorce "because of your hardness of heart," even though it was contrary to God's intention (Mk 10:5). Hardening of heart in these passages is a determined refusal to obey the known commands of God.

A final cluster of usages treats hardness of heart as a spiritual *blindness, an ignorance, even an irrational distortion in one's mental processes. Jesus is grieved at his adversaries' "hardness of heart" when they object to his healing the man with the withered hand on the sabbath (Mk 3:5), with the implication that they simply do not understand his redemptive work in the world. When Jesus walks on the sea, the writer comments that the disciples "did not understand," that "their hearts were hardened" (Mk 6:52; see also Mk 8:17). Jesus equated blinded eyes with a hardened heart (Jn 12:40). Other passages speak of a hardened mind (2 Cor 3:14) and darkened understanding and ignorance "due to their hardness of heart" (Eph 4:8).

In all instances, the motif of hardness is implicitly contrasted with its opposite. Softness or pliability toward God means to be enlightened by God's truth, obedient to God's commands and compliant with God's will.

See also BLIND, BLINDNESS; CLAY; FOREHEAD; HEART; REBELLION; SOFT.

HARP

Genesis 4:21 reports that harps go back to a certain Jubal, "father of all who play the harp and flute" (NIV). Throughout the Bible harps are mentioned mostly in the contexts of either celebration or mourning, with the former being more common. Other uses of harps are hinted at. For example, in Psalm 49:4 a harp accompanies the psalmist's expounding of a riddle, and it was David's skill at the harp that soothed Saul when an "evil spirit from God" came upon him (1 Sam 16:16, 23, 18).

The playing of a harp appears to have been part of the official trappings of Israelite cultic life. Certain individuals were assigned to carry out this duty in the context of the worship service (e.g., 1 Chron 15:16, 21; 16:5; 25:3, 6). This cultic setting is likely the proper context in which to view the repeated references to harps in the Psalms. Likewise, the playing of harps also seems to have accompanied the prophetic function (1 Sam 10:5; 2 Kings 3:15). Harps are, therefore, instruments that accompany both worship and divine speech. This imagery is drawn out most fully in the psalms and the prophetic literature.

The psalms are full of passages that enjoin the faithful to *praise the Lord with the harp (among other instruments). Song and *musical accompaniment are proper expressions of love and devotion toward God. The cause for praise may be the *ark's return to Jerusalem (2 Sam 6:5), victory in *battle (2 Chron 20:28) or the dedication of the *wall of Jerusalem (Neh 12:27). More commonly, the psalmist enjoins worshippers to praise the Lord with the harp for more general reasons: for deliverance from harm (Ps 43:4; 57:8; 81:2; 98:5), for being who God is (Ps 33:2; 92:3; 150:3), for his faithfulness (Ps 71:22). In Psalm 137:2 the devastation of the Babylonian captivity brings such mourning that singing ceases: "There on the poplars we hung our harps" (NIV). In Revelation 5:8-9 the twenty-four elders sing a "new song" of praise to the *Lamb, accompanied by harps. In Revelation 14:2 the new song is on the lips of the 144,000, a symbolic number describing the church, which is described as "those who had been victorious over the beast and his image and over the number of his name" (Rev 15:2 NIV).

Harps are not only connected with the praise of God, however. They also accompany the prophetic word of *judgment against the nations: Moab (Is 16:11), Tyre (Is 23:16; Ezek 26:13). In fact, music on the harp accompanies the destruction of obstinate nations (Is 30:32). Singing with the harp is sometimes symbolic of the godless joy of the wicked. Such singing, however, will cease when Yahweh devastates the earth (Is 24:8). This imagery is employed one last time in Revelation 18:22 with respect to the destruction of *Babylon, the symbol of world opposition to God. In Daniel the playing of harps accompanies the worship of idols (Dan 3:5, 7, 10, 15). Shadrach, Meshach and Abednego refuse to worship, which leads to the famous fiery furnace episode. Of course, although Israel's proper worship of God includes the playing of harps, the playing of harps does not guarantee such proper worship: complacency in Israel's worship is condemned (Amos 6:5; Is 5:12; 14:11).

The most vivid picture that most people have of biblical harps is of the *golden harps in the heavenly visions of Revelation (Rev 5:8; 14:2; 15:2). It is not so much the sound of the harps that is important here as their golden quality. They belong to a pattern of enameled imagery that combines *hardness of texture and brilliance of *light, to suggest a realm that transcends the *"soft," vegetative, cyclic world of earthly existence.

See also MUSIC; TRUMPET.

BIBLIOGRAPHY. O. Keel, *The Symbolism of the Biblical World* (Winona Lake, IN: Eisenbrauns, 1997 [1972]) 346-52; V. H. Matthews and I. H. Jones, "Music and Musical Instruments," *ABD* 4:930-39.

HARVEST

To understand the approximately one hundred references in the Bible to reaping and harvest, we need to be aware of the predominantly agrarian world of the Bible from Genesis through the life of Christ. Until we reach the urban world of the missionary efforts of Paul and the early church, we move in a largely rural world of *farming, with its attendant sowing and harvesting. In that world, harvest is both an event of great annual importance and the preeminent image of *abundance (Ezek 36:30) and *reward for labor (Prov 20:4). In the OT, moreover, harvest is bound up with the central ethical and religious life of the believing community.

Real Harvests and Moral Implications. We can begin by noting the part harvesting plays in the natural rhythm and annual calendar in biblical times. More than two dozen references in the Bible pair *sowing and reaping, seedtime and harvest. The harvest of various crops was so prominent in the agrarian world of the OT that specific harvests were used as dating devices: "in the days of the wheat harvest" (Gen 30:14); "at the beginning of the barley harvest" (Ruth 1:22; 2 Sam 21:9); "when the grape harvest is ended" (Is 24:13). The system of Hebrew religious feasts also largely revolved around an agricultural timetable in which harvest was prominent. The three main *festivals of OT religion were scheduled to coincide with the three harvest seasons—the *Passover with the barley harvest, the Feast of Pentecost (or Feast of Weeks) seven weeks later during the *wheat harvest and the Feast of Booths (also known as "the feast of ingathering" [Ex 23:16]) at the end of the year during the fruit harvest. To this must be added the Feast of First Fruits in which farmers brought a sheaf of the first fruits of a harvest to the priest (Lev 23:9-14). In all of this we can glimpse the overriding importance of harvest to biblical people.

The ethical significance of harvest in biblical times emerges when we consider the stipulations of the Mosaic code. Both Leviticus and Deuteronomy contain commands prohibiting farmers from harvesting their fields to the very edges and from *gleaning their fields thoroughly (Lev 19:9; 23:22; Deut 24:19). Instead they were to leave part of the crops for the poor and the sojourner (*see* Foreigner). Harvest was thus an indicator of the Hebrews' obedience to the moral obligations of their *covenant with God. In the OT prophets' oracles of *judgment against Israel and Judah for their moral and spiritual waywardness, the imagery of failed harvests is a sign of God's judgment against the failure of people to live up to their covenant obligations (Is 16:9; 17:11; 18:5; 32:10; Jer 8:20; 12:13).

In view of the foregoing we can catch something of the range of feelings that harvest elicited from people in biblical times. The very designation "first fruits" expresses the excitement of the first ripening of a crop, the promise and foretaste of the full harvest, an excitement heightened by the religious rituals surrounding the event. Harvest was accompanied by feelings of generosity awakened by the sight of the poor of a community being provided for as they gleaned in the fields owned by others. Harvest was a time of *joy—joy as exultant as soldiers' dividing plunder (Is 9:3), joy accompanied by *shouts (Ps 126:5). Although harvest was never a prominent part of the covenant blessings that God promised to his people, there are hints that it was so interpreted: "Isaac sowed seed in that land, and in the same year reaped a hundredfold. The LORD blessed him" (Gen 26:12 RSV). When David prays for the blessing of God on his nation, his requests include the petition, "May our barns be filled, with produce of every kind" (Ps 144:13 NRSV). In Psalm 1:3 the blessed person of the covenant is compared to a productive tree that yields its harvest of *fruit.

The Bible implicitly ascribes harvests to God rather than to the natural process per se or to fertility gods. The story of *Joseph's sojourn in Egypt hints at this. The focus of Genesis 41—45 is on the seven years of plentiful harvests followed by seven years of failed harvests in Egypt. These were presaged by the dreams of Pharaoh and Joseph's interpretation of them (Gen 41:7-11; 15-32). What emerges is that the God of Israel is in charge of harvests, not the fertility gods of Egypt or Canaan: "God has revealed to Pharaoh what he is about to do" (Gen 41:25 RSV).

All these motifs converge in the book of *Ruth, a pastoral idyll that is a harvest scene par excellence, no doubt explaining why the book has been traditionally read in Hebrew circles during the Feast of Weeks, a harvest festival. The picture of Boaz's plentiful harvest is an implicit sign of God's covenant blessing on Boaz for his religious obedience and moral integrity. Boaz's generosity to Ruth as she gleans in his field is a case study in obeying the command to leave part of the harvest for the poor and the sojourner. The progress of the harvest—Ruth arrives in Bethlehem at the beginning of the barley harvest (Ruth 1:22) and is betrothed to Boaz at the end of the barley and wheat harvests (Ruth 2:22)—becomes a metaphor for the progress of the romance going on between Ruth and Boaz. The *"seed" that the marriage produces is itself a kind of harvest of the couple's love. Throughout the story the harvest is a joyous occasion, the reward for labor and obedience to the law of God.

While a successful harvest was a supreme image of abundance and blessing, failed harvests are an image of *terror in the Bible. Indeed, so many references fall into this category that harvest finally emerges from the pages of the Bible as a precarious thing. Any number of things can destroy a harvest: *rain during harvest time (1 Sam 12:17), marauding *enemies (Judg 6:4-5; Jer 5:17), *fire (Job 31:12) or *drought (Amos 4:7). In an agrarian milieu the primal fear is a failed harvest (Is 32:10).

Because harvest is of central importance, it becomes a focus for teaching values. In fact, harvest time reveals the character of those who live in an agrarian society, as seen especially in its proverbs. Industrious people reap a good harvest, while

*"sluggards" do not (Prov 20:4). Those who sleep through a harvest fail to capitalize on a good opportunity (Prov 10:5). The industrious ant is praised as a model because "it prepares its food in summer, and gathers its sustenance in harvest," a rebuke to the lazy person addicted to sleep (Prov 6:8-9 NRSV). Harvest is also a source of metaphor and simile: "Like the cold of snow in the time of harvest [a reference to the harvester's desire for cool weather during harvest] are faithful messengers to those who send them" (Prov 25:13 NRSV). "Like snow in summer or rain in harvest, so honor is not fitting for a fool" (Prov 26:1 NRSV).

Symbolic Harvests. Inevitably a people for whom harvests were central to living would turn to them as a source of symbols. In the Bible the imagery of reaping what one has sowed is applied to a range of life situations (Job 4:8; 13:26; Prov 22:8; Hos 8:7; Hag 1:6; Jn 4:37; Rom 1:13; 1 Cor 9:11; 2 Cor 9:6, 10; Gal 6:7, 8, 9). Elsewhere the metaphors are vigorous as we read about a symbolic sowing of righteousness and reaping of steadfast love (Hos 10:12), a plowing of wickedness and reaping of injustice (Hos 10:13), a coming apocalyptic age in which "the one who plows shall overtake the one who reaps" (Amos 9:13 NRSV), when a "harvest of righteousness . . . comes through Jesus Christ" (Phil 1:11 NRSV) and "a harvest of righteousness is sown in peace for those who make peace" (Jas 3:18 NRSV). In both Testaments particular actions associated with the time of harvest are images of divine judgment against evil, for example, the sickle and *winepress (Joel 3:13), the separation and burning of the weeds (Mt 13:30), the chaff burned or blown by the wind (Ps 1:4; 35:5; Mt 3:12) and the vintage harvest, an event closely associated with the treading of grapes in the *winepress, an image evoking the blood of judgment (Rev 14:17-20). It is important to note, however, that the image of harvest itself is seldom a negative image of judgment (Hos 6:11). The reaping of the grain crop in Mark 4:29 is a positive image of gathering people into the kingdom. Likewise the picture of the son of man reaping with a sharp sickle in Revelation 14:14-16 is probably a positive image of the (wheat) harvest of the redeemed, the harvest signaled by the "first fruits" of the "redeemed" in Revelation 14:1-5, but this is followed immediately by the vintage harvest, an image of judgment (Bauckham, 94-98).

Jesus, a master of harvest metaphors, sees harvest time in two ways—as a time of opportunity in the here and now and as a time of final judgment. The idea of harvest as opportunity is presented in Matthew 9:37-38 and its parallels in Luke 10:2 and John 4:35, where Jesus sees sinners in need of salvation as a field of *grain needing to be harvested. The situation calls for mobilization of workers, for everyone knows that a ripened harvest can be lost without timely attention.

Harvests figure prominently in Jesus' parables. The abundant harvests in the parable of the sower (or the parable of the soils) represent people who hear the word and understand it (Mt 13:8, 23). In the parable of the wheat and weeds, the grain must be allowed to grow up with a poisonous weed known as darnel until the harvest, symbolic of how Christians must live in the world with unbelievers until the final judgment (Mt 13:24-30, 36-43). The farmer who repeatedly returns to the labor depot to recruit more workers to harvest his vines is a picture of God's *kingdom in which reward is based on grace rather than on merit (Mt 20:1-16). The rich farmer preoccupied with building bigger barns to store his harvest is an example of self-defeating worldly-mindedness (Lk 12:13-21).

Summary. At a physical level, harvest is perhaps the preeminent image in Scripture of abundance and its accompanying emotions. Its failure is the ultimate terror for a farming society. If we trace the principles that underlie the physical and metaphoric harvests of the Bible, they include at least the following: (1) the joy of reaping the riches of responsible investment of time and effort; (2) the fulfillment of the creation's intended purpose, which is to be fruitful; (3) an occasion on which to capitalize for God's glory, including the evangelization of a lost world; (4) God's blessing on those who follow him and judgment against the disobedient; (5) an occasion that simultaneously rewards a person for labor and tests a person's moral and spiritual status; (6) the consummation of a process that must be worked out over time, like the full program of God's kingdom—"first the stalk, then the head, then the full grain in the head" (Mk 4:28 NRSV).

Salvation history is itself like a slow movement toward a climactic harvest. God and those who work for him sow the field of the world. God tends his growing crop as it moves inexorably toward a final harvest. When the crop is ripe, God harvests it, separating the fruit and grain from the refuse and *chaff.

See also ABUNDANCE; BLESSING; CHAFF; CURSE; FARMING; FAT, FATNESS; FRUIT, FRUITFULNESS; GLEAN; GRAIN; GRAPES; JOY; JUDGMENT; SOW, SOWING, SOWER; THRESHING, THRESHING FLOOR; VINE, VINEYARD; WINEPRESS.

BIBLIOGRAPHY. R. J. Bauckham, *The Theology of the Book of Revelation* (Cambridge: Cambridge University Press, 1993); O. Borowski, *Agriculture in Iron Age Israel* (Winona Lake, IN: Eisenbrauns, 1987).

HEAD

As the uppermost and most prominent feature of the human body, the very center of life, the head serves as the image for many important theological statements in the Bible. The term *head* appears over four hundred times in Scripture, often with a great deal of symbolic value attached to it.

Literal Usage. Biblical writers conceived of the head as the seat of life; consequently, they used the term to refer to the life of the individual. In contexts of *warfare and conflict, cutting off the head is a powerful symbol of victory, because it represents the

death of the opponent. Perhaps the most significant of these references is found in Genesis 3:15, in the context of God's curse on those who rebelled against his authority in the Garden. In reference to the serpent, God announces that the woman's offspring will "crush your head," thus representing its destruction. Later, David confidently proclaims to Goliath, "I will strike you down and cut off your head!" (1 Sam 17:46). After Saul impaled himself and died, the Philistines took his head and hung it in the temple of their god, Dagon (1 Chron 10:9-10). In both of these instances the severed head represents the decisive defeat of the enemy. Simlarly, the execution of John the Baptist because of his opposition to the moral evil of the unlawful union between Herod Antipas and Herodias was carried out with the executioner decapitating John and bringing his head to the perpetrator on a platter (Mk 6:24-28). John's head represents not only his death but a cessation of his hostility toward the couple.

Because of the vulnerability of the head, the psalmist rejoices in his God "who shields my head in the day of battle" (Ps 140:7 NIV). In spiritual struggle God protects his people with "a helmet of salvation" (Is 59:17; 1 Thess 5:8). Paul presents this helmet as essential to the believer's successful resistance of the attacks of the hostile principalities and powers (Eph 6:17; *see* Armor).

As the part of the body that represents the whole person, there are many symbolic and ritual actions described in the Bible that are focused on the head. When a priest or a king is consecrated to his specific service, his head is *anointed with *oil. In obedience to God's command (Exod 29:7) Moses poured some of the anointing oil on Aaron's head to dedicate him as a priest (Lev 8:12). Similarly, Samuel took a flask of oil and poured it on Saul's head when anointing him as king over Israel (1 Sam 10:1).

*Mourning and *grief are expressed through shaving the head, covering the head, or placing dirt or *ashes on the head. Job shaved his head after he was struck by an unbelievable set of calamities (Job 1:20). Tamar put ashes on her head to convey her sense of shame and despair after being *raped by Amnon (2 Sam 13:19). In response to Absalom's conspiracy, David both covered his head (2 Sam 15:30) and later put dirt on his head (2 Sam 15:32) as he wept over the grievous situation.

The head is also the focal point for receiving *blessing. The proverb thus speaks of blessings that "crown the head of the righteous" (Prov 10:6 NIV). At the end of his life Jacob uttered blessings over the two sons of Joseph: "Israel reached out his right hand and put it on Ephraim's head . . . [and] he put his left hand on Manasseh's head" (Gen 48:14 NIV).

Conversely, the head is also the place for confirming or conferring *guilt. The law instructs all those who hear a blasphemer to lay their hands on his head before he is stoned (Lev 24:14). Repeatedly throughout the OT the guilt of people's *sins is said to come to rest on their own heads. In announcing the impending judgment of the day of the Lord, Obadiah warns, "Your deeds will return upon your own head" (Obad 15 NIV). For Joab's murder of two Israelite commanders, Solomon exclaimed, "May the guilt of their blood rest on the head of Joab and his descendants forever" (1 Kings 2:33 NIV). In the various *atonement rituals one's own guilt before God could be transferred and placed upon a sacrificial animal. Either the person bringing the offering or the priest would lay their hands on the head of the animal prior to the *sacrifice (Lev 1:4; 3:2, 8, 13; 8:14, 18, 20, 22). In the Day of Atonement ritual the priest "is to lay both hands on the head of the live goat and confess over it all the wickedness and rebellion of the Israelite—all their sin—and put them on the goat's head" (Lev 16:21 NIV).

Symbolic Uses of Head. Perhaps stimulated by reflecting on the function of the physical head in relationship to the *body, many ancient and biblical writers used the term *head* as a symbol for leadership and ruling *authority. When the Ammonites made war on Israel, the elders of Gilead appealed to Jephthah to be their commander. They told him, "we are turning to you now; come with us to fight the Ammonites, and you will be our head over all who live in Gilead" (Judg 11:8 NIV). Jephthah agreed, "and the people made him head and commander over them" (Judg 11:11 NIV). Head can stand not only for the person in authority but also for the seat of authority as in Isaiah 7:8: For the head of Aram is Damascus, and the head of Damascus is only Rezin" (NIV). Some notion of authority or leadership appears to be present in 1 Corinthians 11 when Paul speaks of God in his relationship to Christ, Christ in his relationship to humanity and man in relationship to woman (1 Cor 11:3). The symbolism of the head is also applied to Jesus to express his ruling authority over the evil principalities and powers (Col 2:10).

As an image of the relationship of Christ and the church, Paul adopts the symbolism of head in connection to the body (Col 1:18; 2:19; Eph 4:15; 5:23). He appears to rely on a widespread and common conception—illustrated especially in the medical writers, Plato and Philo—that there is a twofold sense of leadership and source of provision denoted by the head when it is used in association with the body. Thus when Paul speaks of Christ as the head, he implies that he not only provides leadership to the church but that he nourishes the body by supplying whatever it needs for its ongoing growth and development (see esp. Col 2:19; Eph 5:23).

The image of the head is also applied to the role of the man with respect to his wife (Eph 5:23). Since Christ in relationship to the church is the model held out for the man to emulate, the twofold pattern of leadership and source of provision would apply to the interpretation of this text. As head, the husband is called to provide leadership in the *marriage based on the self-sacrificial loving example of Jesus, who has the best interests of his bride as the goal (Eph 5:25-28). The image also suggests that the husband is called to provide for his wife in the way Christ provides for the church, nourishing and cherishing her (Eph 5:29).

See also ANOINTING; ARMOR; AUTHORITY; BODY; HAIR; HANDS, LAYING ON OF; MARRIAGE.

BIBLIOGRAPHY. C. E. Arnold, "Jesus Christ: 'Head' of the Church" in *Jesus of Nazareth: Lord and Christ. Essays on the Historical Jesus and New Testament Christology*, ed. M. M. B. Turner and J. B. Green (Grand Rapids: Eerdmans, 1994) 346-66; J. A. Fitzmyer, "Another Look at *KEPHALĒ* in 1 Corinthians 11:3," *NTS* 35 (1989) 503-11.

HEALING. *See* DISEASE AND HEALING.

HEARING. *See* DEAF; EAR, HEARING.

HEART

In antiquity very little was known about the heart, whose rhythmic beating coincided with all the functions of life and whose cessation meant death. The references in the Bible to the heart as a physical organ are few and by no means specific (e.g., 2 Kings 9:24), but the word *heart* is often used of such things as personality and the intellect, memory, emotions, desires and will.

Personality. The heart is used metaphorically to describe the intangibles that constitute what it means to be human. In this sense it is the antonym of the "flesh" or *body. We see this in the psalmist's confession, "My flesh and my heart may fail, but God is the strength of my heart and my portion forever" (Ps 73:26 NIV).

To use a modern idiom, the heart is often used in the Bible to describe "what makes us tick," that is, human personality. In other words, the heart is used to describe those dynamic forces that make us unique individuals. As such, the heart can be imbued with moral qualities. For instance, the poet in Psalm 131:1 claims that his "heart is not proud" (cf. 2 Chron 32:26). Hearts can also be "evil" (1 Sam 17:28) or "deluded" (Is 44:20; cf. Jer 17:9).

In this regard we also find complex metaphors concerning the heart among the writers of the Bible. A heart not yet bound to God may be referred to as an "uncircumcised heart" (Deut 10:16; Jer 9:26; Rom 2:29; *see* Circumcision). On the other hand, hearts can be transformed from self-serving to God-fearing. Ezekiel describes the process as transforming hearts of *stone into hearts of flesh (Ezek 11:19). In another place, the prophet refers to this transformation as the reception of a "new heart" (Ezek 18:31).

It is because the heart stands for human personality that God looks there rather than at our actions to see whether we are faithful or not. We are called upon to seek God with all our heart (Deut 4:29; 6:5), so that is where he looks to see if we are his people (1 Sam 16:7).

Our personality is a function of many different aspects of our being, including our thinking, remembering, feeling, desiring and willing. It is therefore not surprising that the Hebrew word for heart, *lēb,* is used as an image of these as well.

Intellect and Memory. We associate thought and memory with the brain today, but in the idiom of the Bible, thinking is a function of the heart. The psalmist thought about his present difficult situation in the light of his past. As he "remembered [his] songs in the night," he says, "My heart mused and my spirit inquired" (Ps 77:6 NIV). As a prelude to the *flood, the book of Genesis tells us that God noted "how great man's wickedness on the earth had become, and that every inclination of the thoughts of his heart was only evil all the time" (Gen 6:5 NIV).

When the Bible reports internal dialogue, whether silent *prayer to God or simply thought, it uses the idiom "in the heart." For instance, Hannah prayed to God "in her heart" (1 Sam 1:13); and throughout the book of Ecclesiastes, the Teacher's mental processes are reported as something he said "in his heart" (e.g. Eccles 2:1, 15). As Mary witnessed all the wonderful things that happened at the time of the birth of her child, Jesus, she is said to have "pondered them in her heart" (Lk 2:19).

Emotions. According to biblical usage, the heart is the source from which the emotions flow. Aaron's heart flows with *joy when he sees Moses (Ex 4:14). Leviticus 19:17 warns God's people not to hate their brother in their heart. Fear is expressed as a loss of heart (Deut 1:28), indicating that courage is also a heartfelt emotion (Ps 27:3). These and many other emotions—for instance, despair (Deut 28:65), sadness (Neh 2:2), trust (Ps 28:7) and *anger (Ps 39:3)—are said to come from one's heart.

The heart is the seat of desire as well. Ill-fated Shechem, son of Hamor the Canaanite, has his "heart set on Dinah" the daughter of Jacob (Gen 34:3, 8). Abner asks David if he can set things in motion for the king so David can "rule over all that your heart desires" (2 Sam 3:9). The psalmist tells his hearers to turn to God so he can give them the "desires" of their heart (Ps 37:4).

Will. The heart not only thinks and feels, remembers and desires, but it also chooses a course of action. Jesus himself taught that "out of the heart come evil thoughts, *murder, *adultery, *sexual immorality, *theft, false testimony, slander" (Mt 15:19 NIV). The obstinacy of the human heart is also an act of will (Deut 2:20), and here we may mention the many references in the book of Exodus to the "hard heart" of *Pharaoh (e.g., Ex 4:14, 21; 7:3; 8:15). This is a heart that refuses to choose in accordance with God's will, which leads ultimately to the Egyptian king's destruction.

On the positive side, the Bible talks of a heart that prompts a person to give a gift to the Lord (Ex 25:2). It speaks of the "integrity" of a person's heart (1 Kings 9:4) and of a "discerning" heart (1 Kings 3:9).

God's Heart. Perhaps the most striking use of heart in the Bible is in reference to *God (Gen 6:6; 8:21). The usage is similar to that applied to human-

kind and should be a reminder that we are created in the image of God (Gen 1:26-27). God, after all, is a personal being who thinks, feels, desires and chooses.

One of the most intriguing passages in this connection is found in Hosea 11. The prophet quotes God as saying that, while he will indeed punish Israel for their rebellion, he will not completely destroy them. The decision to refrain from their utter destruction was not easy; it was the result of God's inner turmoil:

My heart is changed within me;
    all my compassion is aroused.
I will not carry out my fierce anger,
    nor devastate Ephraim again. (Hos 11:8-9 NIV)

In the verse that follows, God justifies his change of mind on the basis of his divinity. Humankind, when angered, is naturally inclined toward a course of destruction of those who offend. But God is divine, not human, so his grace wins out.

See also BODY; HARD, HARDEN, HARDNESS; MIND; STONE.

BIBLIOGRAPHY H. W. Wolff, *Anthropology of the Old Testament* (Philadelphia: Fortress, 1974).

HEAT. *See* TEMPERATURE; WEATHER; REFINING.

HEATHEN

In the KJV the word *heathen* appears 143 times in the OT, where it is a translation of the Hebrew *gôyîm,* a plural noun that once meant "nations" in general but came to mean specifically "nations other than Israel." Despite a sometimes comic connotation in the twentieth century, the Hebrew term in its narrow sense and its early seventeenth-century English translation are serious words indicating a distinction between God's people and the other peoples. One of the most basic divisions in Hebrew thought (as in many other cultures) was that of "us" and "them." *Heathen* has the particular connotation of those who are different and religiously offensive.

In the OT the heathen appear almost always in relation to Israel. There are two primary images evoked by heathen. One is the means by which Israel's God punishes his people for their sins, which they have often committed in imitation of the heathen. The other is a means by which God shows his righteous power, as in Psalm 110:6: "He shall judge among the heathen, he shall fill the places with the dead bodies; he shall wound the heads over many countries" (KJV).

The religion of the heathen is *idolatry, always a temptation to the Israelites, who did not "destroy the nations" in the Promised Land as the Lord had commanded, but "were mingled among the heathen, and learned their works" and "served their idols: which were a snare unto them" (Ps 106:34-36 KJV).

Of those kings singled out for practicing "the abominations of the heathen," Manasseh of Judah is the one to whom the most detailed imagery is devoted: he reconstructed "the high places" destroyed by Hezekiah, constructed "*altars for Baal," and placed "a graven image" of the goddess Asherah in the Jerusalem temple. In the temple courts he "built altars for all the host of heaven," which he worshipped. Furthermore, Manasseh gave a son of his as a burnt offering to Molech, practiced *magic, and "dealt with familiar spirits and wizards" (2 Kings 21:2-7).

Among the images associated with the heathen are the especially notable ones of *prostitution and pollution in the allegory of Aholah and Aholibah, two sisters representing Samaria and Jerusalem, respectively. God promises to punish Aholibah because she has "gone a whoring after the heathen" and is "polluted with their idols" (Ezek 23:30 KJV). Indeed, when the Babylonians captured Jerusalem, the heathen possessed God's *"inheritance" and "defiled" his "holy temple" (Ps 79:1; see Purity).

Another frequent image is that of dispersion. God scattered Israel "among the heathen," where the chosen people "profaned" the "holy name." But Ezekiel's prophecy is that God, for his name's sake, will gather them "from among the heathen," return them to their own country, purify them, change their hearts and make them prosper in the sight of the heathen left in the land (Ezek 36:19-36).

Those heathen, however, remained a source of contamination. After the rebuilding of the *temple, the Jews who had returned from exile observed the *Passover, along with "all such as had separated themselves unto them from the filthiness of the heathen of the land" (Ezra 6:21 KJV).

Yet in contrast to the usually hostile OT view of all nations but Israel, there are injunctions like that in Exodus 22:21: "Thou shalt neither vex a stranger, nor oppress him: for ye were strangers in the land of Egypt" (KJV). Individual foreigners, like Ruth (a proselyte), were to be treated kindly; and at least some of the Israelites believed that even among the heathen "a pure offering" would be made for the God of Israel (Mal 1:11) and that he would bring "the sons of the stranger, that join themselves to the LORD" to the "holy mountain," where God's temple was to be "an house of prayer for all people" (Is 56:6-7).

Certainly that idea of the acceptance of *foreigners who seek Israel's God was a driving force in the spread of the gospel beyond the people of Israel. In the NT *heathen* is used only seven times in the KJV, where it is twice a translation of the Greek adjective *ethnikos(-oi)* and otherwise a translation of the related plural noun *ethne*, as when Paul, citing Genesis 12:3, 18:18 or 22:18, writes: "And the scripture, foreseeing that God would justify the heathen through faith, preached before the gospel unto Abraham, saying, In thee shall all nations be blessed" (Gal 3:8 KJV). In effect, by following the Great Commission the early Christians were working to eliminate the heathen, as heathen, by converting them into God's people.

In John's Revelation the final word on the hea-

then is given. Those that remain in *rebellion, symbolized by *Babylon (14:8), will experience a complete judgment; but heaven will be populated with many from heathen nations who follow Jesus. The *Lamb is worshiped by those from "every tribe and tongue and people and nation" (Rev 5:9 NKJV).

See also BABYLON; EGYPT; FOREIGNER; GENTILE; IDOLATRY; ISRAEL; PURITY.

HEAVEN

Heaven is the eternal and transcendent world that is the abode of *God, the *angels and glorified believers (*see* Saints). The imagery and motifs by which it is portrayed are numerous. NT pictures are more detailed than OT ones, which mainly picture heaven in generic terms as the transcendent "other" world where God lives.

Heaven as Dwelling Place. The most frequent association with heaven is that it is the place where God dwells. The epithet "God of heaven" is recurrent in the OT (e.g., Gen 24:7; 2 Chron 36:23; Neh 2:4). In Isaiah's vision of heaven the train of God fills the space (Is 6:1). In the parallel passage in Ezekiel the vision of what the prophet sees "above the firmament" is likewise dominated by the figure of God (Ezek 1:26-28). Throughout the heavenly visions of Revelation the presence of God and Christ is a constant reference point for what happens in heaven. Heaven is nothing less than the "holy and glorious habitation" of God (Is 63:15 RSV; cf. Deut 26:15). At the top of the *ladder joining heaven and earth in Jacob's vision stands God (Gen 28:13). When the dying Stephen gazes into heaven, he sees God and Christ (Acts 7:55-56).

God is the central inhabitant of heaven, but not its only resident. The angels live there as well, as more than a dozen verses tell us and as Jacob's vision with its imagery of *angels ascending and descending the ladder (Gen 28:12) makes clear. The company of the redeemed also lives in heaven: at the end of Elijah's earthly life, God took him up to heaven by a *whirlwind (2 Kings 2:1), and the book of Revelation repeatedly portrays glorified saints as inhabiting heaven. A preponderance of the Bible's pictures of heaven show it to be a crowded place. Crowd scenes along the lines of Micaiah's sight of God "sitting on his throne, with all the host of heaven standing beside him on his right hand and on his left" (1 Kings 22:19 RSV; 2 Chron 18:18) are common.

Spatial Imagery. In the Bible heaven is emphatically a definite locale. To enter it is to enter a definite space. Jesus called it "a place" (Jn 14:2-3). If we ask where this heavenly place is, the answer overwhelmingly is that it is above the earth. Vertical imagery dominates in the placing of it. Heaven is thus a place from which God looks down to the earth (Ps 14:2; 80:14; 102:19), as well as the place from which Christ came down (Jn 6:33, 38, 41, 42; see Descent). Correspondingly, heaven is the place to which people look up from earth (Deut 30:12; 2 Kings 2:1; Lk 18:13), and it is the place to which Christ *ascended after his earthly life (Acts 1:2, 10, 11, 16). The point of this vertical imagery is obvious: heaven is both remote from earthly reality and a higher, superior mode of existence.

The sheer separateness of heaven from earth is suggested by some passages. When the writer of Ecclesiastes lays down the principle that "God is in heaven, and you upon earth" (Eccles 5:2 RSV), the point is that heaven is a different level of reality than earth is. The parable of the rich man and Lazarus speaks of "a great chasm" fixed between heaven and hell, that "none may cross from there to us" (Lk 16:26 RSV), reinforcing the sense of heaven as having its own space.

Specific types of place fill out the spatial pictures of heaven. The nearly a dozen references to God's *throne in heaven lend a royal quality to it, indicative both of the splendor of the place and the authority of the God who rules the universe from heaven. Heaven is a stately *house with many rooms, specifically prepared by Christ for his followers (Jn 14:1-3), leading us to view it as a place where people live. Sometimes heaven has the features of a celestial *temple (Is 6:1; Rev 3:12; 11:19; 15:5), in keeping with the *worship that occurs there. More than anything else, though, heaven is a *city (Rev 20—22) replete with *walls, *gates and *streets, an emblem of believers in community unified in the worship of God. Surprisingly, this city also possesses the features of an earthly paradise (Rev 2:7; 22:1-2; see Garden).

Enameled Imagery. Poets have always depended on enameled imagery when portraying heaven. Such images combine *hardness of texture and brilliance of *light, to suggest a realm of superior *permanence, value and splendor when compared with the cyclic, vegetative world in which we live. *Jewel imagery is the most prevalent type of enameled imagery. Ezekiel's vision of a heavenly level of reality is replete with such imagery—flashing *fire and *lightning, burnished *bronze that sparkles, gleaming chrysolite, and sapphire (Ezek 1). To this we can add the memorable pictures in Revelation of a sea of glass, like crystal, the appearance of God in splendor like that of jasper and carnelian, golden *crowns, gates of *pearl, a city of pure *gold.

In addition to jeweled imagery, physical *light and its equivalent, *glory, are recurrent in biblical images of heaven. In the heaven portrayed in Revelation, the light of the *sun and *moon are no longer needed, "for the glory of God is its light, and its lamp is the Lamb," and by the light of heaven "shall the nations walk" (Rev 21:23-24 RSV; cf. 22:5).

Additional Image Patterns. The remoteness of heaven is sometimes pictured by a veiling technique. It is the lot of humans that they can see the heavenly realm only "dimly" (1 Cor 13:12 RSV) or "through a glass, darkly" (KJV; see Mirror). When Jesus ascended into heaven in the presence of his disciples, "a *cloud took him out of their sight" (Acts 1:9). To receive a vision of heaven requires a *door to be opened: "After this I looked, and lo, in heaven an open door!" (Rev 4:1 RSV; cf. Rev 15:5; 19:11). To enter heaven is to have the *veil removed and to be allowed to see "face to face" (1 Cor 13:12).

The purity of existence in heaven and the spiritual perfection of those who are "enrolled in heaven" (Heb 12:23) are expressed by imagery of *washed robes (Rev 7:14), *white *garments (Rev 3:5, 18; 4:4; 6:11; 7:9, 13), clothing of "fine *linen, bright and pure" (Rev 19:8) and chaste people who are "spotless" (Rev 14:4-5).

A pattern of symbolism is also woven into the pictures of what the redeemed receive when they enter heaven. Daniel pictures them as shining "like the stars for ever and ever" (Dan 12:3 RSV), symbolic of permanence and glory. The book of Revelation also creates a symbolic reality (images used to symbolize reality) with its pictures of the redeemed receiving such things as the morning star (Rev 2:28), a white *stone with a secret name written on it (Rev 2:17) and *water from a fountain of life (Rev 21:6). Similarly, those who enter heaven will become *pillars in the temple of God (Rev 3:12). It seems plausible to interpret these images as symbols of spiritual realities. So too with the abundance of images of dimensions, design and decoration in the account of the New *Jerusalem (Rev 21:9-27), which creates a symbolic opulence that contrasts with the stark simplicity of the opening verses of the Bible.

The Imagery of Mystery and Strangeness. While not a major motif in biblical images of heaven, beings that have never existed in human experience are included in the visions of Ezekiel and Revelation. Examples from Ezekiel's vision include living creatures with four faces, four wings and with soles like those of a *calf's foot (Ezek 1:6-7; see Mythical Animals). These creatures move about in a riot of motion, and something that looks like torches of fire moves among them (Ezek 1:13). In addition, there is a celestial *chariot replete with gleaming wheels which have rims full of *eyes (Ezek 1:15-18). To mystify us still further we read that "the spirit of the living creatures was in the wheels" (Ezek 1:21). The book of Revelation, with its pictures of creatures with six wings "full of eyes in front and behind" (Rev 4:6-8), likewise contains the motif of strangeness. The effect of all this is to reinforce the difference between heaven and earth and to underscore the sense of mystery surrounding heaven. At the far reaches the motif of incomprensibility enters: "No eye has seen, nor ear heard, nor the heart of man conceived what God has prepared for those who love him" (1 Cor 2:9 RSV).

Heavenly Ritual. Compared to the relatively plentiful descriptions of heaven as a place, the Bible gives little information about the activity that transpires there. Activity in heaven consists almost entirely of *worship (e.g., Rev 4; 5; 7:9-12). Revelation 14:4 adds the picture of the redeemed following the Lamb wherever he goes. Although the motif is not elaborated, we also read that God will "dwell" with his people and "be with them" (Rev 21:3).

The Transformation of Fallen Earthly Reality.
A major motif in the biblical imagery of heaven is the transformation of earthly experience into a different mode. Half of the equation is the negation or canceling out of fallen earthly experience. There will be no more *hunger or *thirst, no more scorching heat (Rev 7:16). God will be wipe *tears away (Rev 7:17; 21:4), and *death, *mourning and *pain will vanish, "for the former things have passed away" (Rev 21:4 RSV). As part of this exclusion of *evil, heaven is a protected place: "Nothing unclean shall enter it, nor any one who practices abomination or falsehood" (Rev 21:27 RSV). The sheer freedom from fallen experience is pictured by city gates that "shall never be shut by day—and there shall be no night there" (Rev 21:25 RSV).

The other half of the equation is the creation of earthly categories into something *"new." The main example is the new heaven and new earth that fills the last two chapters of the Bible, as well as the image of New *Jerusalem, with its suggestion of earthly reality raised to a higher level of perfection. The rhetoric of comparison is sometimes used to assert the superiority of heaven to *earth. The writer of Hebrews claims that people of faith "desire a better country, that is, a heavenly one" (Heb 11:16 RSV), and Paul declares that "the sufferings of this present time are not worth comparing with the glory that is to be revealed to us" (Rom 8:18 RSV).

Human Responses. The two dominant human responses to new life in heaven are *joy and satisfaction. The joy of heaven's inhabitants is pictured by the intermittent scenes of praise in the book of Revelation, along with the white robed conquerors waving *palm branches (Rev 7:9) and guests at a *wedding *supper (Rev 19:1-9). This is buttressed by the imagery of some of Jesus' parables, where attaining heaven is compared to attending a *banquet (Lk 14:15-24) or entering into the joy of one's master (Mt 25:21, 23). There is also the evocative picture of Hebrews 12:22, which pictures believers as having come to "the city of the living God, the heavenly Jerusalem, and to innumerable angels in festal gathering" (RSV). Images of satisfaction emerge from the pictures in Revelation of saints being guided by a divine *Shepherd to *springs of living water (Rev 7:17) and having access to "the *tree of life with its twelve kinds of fruit, yielding its fruit each month" (Rev 22:2 RSV).

From the perspective of life in this world, heaven is the object of human longing and the goal of human existence. The book of Hebrews employs the imagery of *quest to express this reality: "These all died in faith, not having received what was promised. . . . For people who speak thus make it clear that they are seeking a homeland" (Heb 11:13-14 RSV). In addition to being the goal of a quest, heaven is the reward for earthly toil, as in Paul's picture of himself as having "finished the race" and looking forward to "the crown of righteousness" (2 Tim 4:7-8). So too in Peter's vision of "the chief Shepherd" conferring "the unfading crown of glory" on those who have

served faithfully (1 Pet 5:4). Heaven is also portrayed as a rest after labor: those who die in the Lord "rest from their labors, for their deeds follow them" (Rev 14:13 RSV). Similarly, "there remains a sabbath rest for the people of God," which believers "strive to enter" (Heb 4:9-11 RSV).

Summary. The imagery used to portray heaven is a mingling of the familiar and the unfamiliar, the earthly and the more-than-earthly. Heaven is a place, but not exactly like earthly places. It contains recognizable features, but the motifs of strangeness and transcendence keep alive our awareness that earthly images do not exist in the ordinary manner in heaven. Some of the images, in fact, strike us as obviously symbolic, including the enameled imagery that suggests a place of superior permanence and value without inclining us to believe that heaven has literal streets of gold or gates of pearl.

See also AFTERLIFE; ANGEL; APOCALYPSE, GENRE OF; CITY; COSMOLOGY; CROWN; GARDEN; GLORY; HEAVENLY ARMIES/HOSTS; HELL; JERUSALEM; KINGDOM OF GOD; REVELATION, BOOK OF; SACRED SPACE; TREE OF LIFE; WORSHIP.

HEAVENLIES. *See* EPHESIANS, LETTER TO THE; HEAVEN.

HEAVENLY ARMIES/HOST

The "heavenly hosts" made famous by English translations of the Bible have two distinct meanings: one is a reference to the *stars; the other to God's celestial armies, presumably of angels. Sometimes the two references seem to merge. In fact, the two meanings of the Hebrew phrase for "host of heaven" ($ṣ^eḇā'$ $haśśāmayim$), namely, "celestial bodies" and "angelic beings," reflect a probable association between angels and stars and planets in the Hebrew imagination. The heavenly hosts of stars, moreover, sometimes have associations of *idolatry, since surrounding pagan nations were given to astrology and worship of the heavenly bodies.

The Celestial Bodies. The most frequently observable heavenly host is the stars. By virtue of their infinite number, their brilliant light, their strength and their identity with a specific ruler, the stars are termed "hosts" in Scripture and are named under the created domain of Yahweh (Neh 9:6; Ps 33:6; Is 40:25-26; 45:12). Created in a group (Gen 1:16), they stand, along with sand, as an image of a vast number from God's covenant with Abraham onward (Gen 15:5; 22:17, 26:4; Neh 9:23).

As a host collectively, the central quality of the stars is vastness, but they serve several other purposes that frame our understanding of "heavenly hosts." According to Deborah's song of victory they fight as a host at the will of God (Judg 5:20). They also offer praise to God (Ps 148:3; Job 9:7; 38:7) as well as testifying to God's sovereign power. The latter motif is well summarized in Isaiah 40:26 (RSV):

Lift up your eyes on high and see:
who created these?

He who brings out their host by number,
 calling them all by name;
by the greatness of his might,
 and because he is strong in power
not one is missing.

Because of such associations of transcendence it is not surprising that the celestial bodies as a "heavenly host" became the object of pagan worship. The nation of Israel was not immune to the appeal of such paganism. Israel and Judah joined pagan nations in worshiping the "starry host," and for their adoration of the created order and perverse concept of the divine, they were judged by Yahweh (Deut 4:19; 2 Kings 17:16; 23:4-5; Jer 8:2).

God's Armies. While the worship of pagan deities as a heavenly host is forbidden in the Bible, there is a sense in which the biblical imagination, inspired by God himself, gives us a related image of God's heavenly "armies." This image of a heavenly host hinges upon the image of God as a *king whose courts are filled with followers and who commands a great army in accomplishing his will (see Divine Warrior). This image is common to the portions of Scripture that involve images of *battle: the OT history and poetry, and the prophets of both the OT and NT. This heavenly host is a vast number of *angelic beings, mighty and noble, who relate to Yahweh as knights related to feudal kings: in homage, in service and in battle. They are a vast army, loyal to the purposes and desires of God.

Mighty Nobles. The psalmist and John the seer attribute these hosts with might and nobility. John pictures their vast number, "thousands upon thousands, and ten thousands upon ten thousands" (Rev 5:11 NIV), and their noble appearance, "riding on white horses and dressed in fine linen, white and clean" (Rev 19:14 NIV). He also describes them as an army following the one whose name is "the Word of God" (Rev 19:13 NIV). John uses the language of noble warriors to describe his vision. The splendor of such an army brings glory to him who leads them. The psalmist addresses the heavenly hosts as "you mighty ones who do his bidding, who obey his word" (Ps 103:20 NIV); he also addresses them directly as angels and as "heavenly hosts" in the same passage (Ps 103:19, 21). The heavenly hosts are thus majestic representations of the glory of God.

Homage and Service. One function of these hosts is to worship and honor God. Like the medieval practice of homage in which the kneeling vassal's hands are enclosed by his lord's, so the hosts in heaven present themselves to the Almighty in worship. It is as the angels are assembled before God that *Satan approaches him about Job (Job 1—2). Nehemiah praises God by recounting that "the host of heaven worships you" (Neh 9:6). Isaiah sees the angels, who eternally remind each other of the glory of God, saying "Holy, Holy, Holy, is the LORD of hosts; the whole earth is full of his glory" (Is 6:3 RSV); John's revelation also includes a glimpse of a great gathering of angels who praise God constantly

with similar words (Rev 7:11). By their submissive presence and incessant worship the heavenly hosts contribute to the *glory that surrounds the *throne of God.

From their stance of humility before God, these mighty nobles are commissioned by him to deliver messages to humanity. One of the two worshiping seraphim touches Isaiah with the burning coal, delivering the forgiveness of God; only after this encounter does God himself speak to Isaiah (Is 6:1-8). Joshua encounters a member of the heavenly host who identifies himself as the "commander of the army of the LORD" (Josh 5:14); John records a vision of angels who guard the corners of the earth and one who holds his *seal (Rev 7:1-2). These and others serve the purposes of God by delivering his messages. The psalmist addresses them as "servants who do his will" (Ps 103:21 NIV). The incarnation is announced to the shepherds by the only earthly appearance of the host as a group when they join Gabriel to continue their worship and deliver God's message of hope to humanity (Lk 2:13-14).

Warriors. Beyond messages, the heavenly hosts deliver the *judgment of God by fighting as a mighty army. In one scene God asks for a volunteer from the hosts, and a single spirit steps forward to accept the task (1 King 22:19-23). The idea of the heavenly host, or the hosts of God, is metaphorically applied to certain human armies as well. Israel, emerging from Egypt, is commanded to arrange herself "according to [her] hosts" (Ex 6:26 NASB); God calls them his own as they proceed successfully, and his will is accomplished (Ex 7:4; 12:51; Num 33:1). Isaiah describes how the Lord creates a host from the troops of an idolatrous nation to judge Israel (Is 13). Heavenly hosts battle for the Lord, and he also employs the might of human armies to serve his ends.

In summary, all of the hosts of heaven were created by God to serve him. Those described as surrounding his throne serve him as worshippers, messengers and soldiers.

See also ANGEL; ARMY, ARMIES; COSMOLOGY; DIVINE WARRIOR; STARS.

HEAVY

The literal use of the word *heavy* (having physical mass) occurs only twice in the Bible. In 1 Samuel 4:18 Eli is said to be heavy, and in 2 Samuel 14:2 Absalom's hair is heavy. The rest of the 376 instances of the root *kbd* in the Hebrew Bible, as well as the very few instances of Greek *boreō* or *phortizō* in the NT, are richly figurative with a wide range of usage.

Negative Connotations. The dominant usage of *heavy* is negative in connotation and may be divided into three subgroups (see Harris et al.). The first has to do with insensitivity or dullness of the human body. The term is used for the *hardening of Pharaoh's *heart in Exodus. The term is also used of *eyes (Gen 48:10), *ears (Is 6:10), *tongue (Ex 4:10) and *hands (Ex 17:12). These ponderous attributes are sometimes related to an infirmity but more often are symptomatic of a spiritual problem. The NT uses the Greek *boreō* in this bodily sense for the heavy eyes of the disciples as they slept while Jesus prayed on the night he was betrayed.

A second subgroup with negative implications relates to severity and is found in terms of work, slavery, warfare, plague or famine. In many of these situations the hand of the Lord is described as heavy (1 Sam 5:6, 11; Ps 32:4). In other situations the one with the heavy and oppressive hand is human. Often the severity is in terms of a *yoke (1 Kings 12:4). This makes Jesus' declaration that his yoke is easy (Mt 11:30) all the more significant, because it is for those loaded down *(phortizō)* under a heavy burden (Mt 11:28).

The third negative subgroup concerns magnitude of size or numbers. It is used when describing the greatness of *sin or when a tremendous army is arrayed against God's people. The sin of *Sodom and Gomorrah is very heavy. Edom comes out to confront Israel with a "heavy" people (Num 20:20).

Positive Connotations. But in a very different area of OT usage, the root *kbd* is used in a more positive way. In Genesis 13:2 we are told that Abraham is very "heavy." Here the context is his material possessions: he is a substantial or noteworthy man. In other places the persons for whom the root *kbd* is used are variously described as *honorable, impressive, full of dignity, *heroic or, most significantly, glorious.

The most important use of *kbd* is the "heaviness" of God. It is most commonly translated as his *"glory." The LXX translates these instances with *doxa*. God's name is glorious (Ps 66:2; 79:9). God is the king of glory (Ps 24:7-10). It is in this connection that *kbd* takes on its most substantial meaning. When the glory of the Lord is revealed, his presence is made known. He manifests his presence through radiance, *fire or *cloud. When the glory of the Lord passes before Moses, or takes up residence in the most holy place in the *tabernacle and *temple, or vacates the temple in Ezekiel's vision (Ezek 11), the very *foundations of the earth *tremble under the weight of glory.

Although the NT uses *boreō* and *phortizō* only a few times, it uses *doxa* some 170 times. Jesus speaks of his own glory, of the glory of his Father, of the glory of his followers. In all instances the reader must allow the positive understandings of the OT *kbd* to inform the reading. The *doxa* of the NT carries the same sense of great importance and splendor coupled with a manifestation of the presence of God. "For this slight momentary affliction is preparing for us an eternal weight of glory beyond all comparison" (2 Cor 4:17 RSV).

One of the most dramatic examples of the "weight of glory" is in the account of Christ's first miraculous sign (Jn 2:1-11). Jesus created a prodigious amount of wine—20 to 180 gallons for a wedding party that clearly needed only a modest amount. In this way, we are told, Jesus revealed his

doxa, and his disciples therefore put their faith in him. For the disciples the enormous amount of splendid wine revealed the "weight" of the person in their midst.

See also GLORY; HARD, HARDEN, HARDNESS; HONOR.

BIBLIOGRAPHY. R. L. Harris, G. L. Archer and B. K. Waltke, *Theological Wordbook of the Old Testament* (Chicago: Moody Bible Institute, 1980) 426-27.

HEBREWS, LETTER TO THE

Virtually all the images in Hebrews are associated with its extensive comparison and contrast of the OT cult with the redemptive work of Christ, which supersedes it. The overall argument of Hebrews is developed with a series of pictures drawn from the world of OT worship and the portrayal of their superior NT counterparts. Both simple and elaborate metaphors are used throughout Hebrews to clarify the argumentation and to illustrate the points made. This comparison and contrast is part of the eschatological development of OT images under the influence of Jewish *apocalyptic and early Christian tradition. Specific contrasts, each with too many instances to allow for reference here, include the divine versus the *angelic, the OT prefiguration versus the NT fulfillment in Christ, earthly versus divine *priesthood, the temporary versus the permanent, old *covenant versus new covenant and the *earthly versus the *heavenly.

Images of Christ. A central image in Hebrews is Christ as the *Son of God (Heb 1:2, 5, 8; 4:14), as begotten by God (Heb 1:5). This Son is a "chip off the old block," being "the reflection of God's glory and the exact imprint of God's very being" (Heb 1:3 NRSV). As Son of God, Christ is the heir of all things (Heb 1:2; *see* Inheritance). *Moses was over God's *house as a servant, but Christ is over God's house, the church, as a Son (Heb 3:1-6). As Son of God, Christ "sat down at the right hand of the Majesty on high," symbolizing that he can exercise the power of God as a vicegerent (Heb 1:3; cf. 1:13; 8:1; 10:12; 12:2). He is also portrayed as a *king anointed by God, having a *throne and *scepter (Heb 1:8-9), his power symbolized by his *enemies' being made a "footstool" for his *feet as he sits on his throne (Heb 1:13; 10:13).

Perhaps the dominant image in Hebrews is Christ as high *priest (Heb 2:17; 3:1; 4:14-15). In fact, the entire picture of Christ as high priest may be viewed as an extensive metaphor for his redemptive work. Unlike the high priest of the Aaronic priesthood, Christ is sinless because of his obedience as a Son of God, and he does not need to offer sacrifices for his own sin. Also unlike the Aaronic high priest, Christ is a high priest after the order of *Melchizedek. This is to say that Christ and his priesthood are eternal (Heb 4:14—5:10; 6:19-20; 7:1-28). With Christ as an eternal high priest in the presence of God, the Christian has an anchor of the soul, a source of stability and confidence about salvation, confidence as a *ship has in the anchor that moors it (Heb 6:19-20).

Unlike the priesthood of Aaron, which served God in an earthly *tabernacle, Christ serves as high priest in the heavenly sanctuary. This heavenly sanctuary is pictured as providing the model for the OT tent of meeting or tabernacle (Heb 8:1-5; 9:1-14, 23-28). Christ is pictured as the high priest entering behind the curtain into the Holy of Holies in the heavenly tabernacle, into the presence of God once for all to fulfill his priestly duties on the Day of Atonement (Heb 6:19-20).

Images of Atonement. Images of *atonement account for another cluster. The high priest of the Aaronic priesthood atoned for the sin of himself and the people once a year on the Day of Atonement with the *blood of a bull and a goat. Christ's work of atonement is depicted as a complex of two images: as Christ entering the heavenly sanctuary and offering himself as an atoning sacrifice on the *altar of God, and also as entering the Holy of Holies with his own blood to effect atonement for the people (Heb 2:17; 9:6-14, 23-28; 10:1-10). Unlike the Aaronic priesthood, which sprinkled the people with blood each year, Christ as priest sprinkles his people only once for the cleansing of their sins (Heb 10:19-25). Whereas the Aaronic priesthood offered sacrifices for sin daily, Christ offered himself as a sin offering only once (Heb 10:11-18). As the bulls and goats who supplied the blood for the Day of Atonement were burned outside the camp, Christ as the atoning sacrifice died outside the city gate (Heb 13:11-13). By offering himself, a perfect sacrifice rather than one which had to be offered each year, Christ effects a new covenant. As people's wills only take effect when they die, and as the original covenant on Mount *Sinai was effected by the sacrifice of calves and goats, so the new covenant is effected by the death and blood of the perfect sacrifice, Jesus Christ (Heb 9:15-22; cf. 8:6-13).

Images of Salvation and Apostasy. Another image pattern focuses on the process or state of salvation. The preconversion state of humanity is portrayed as a person's being "held in slavery by the fear of death" (Heb 2:15 NRSV). To come to salvation is depicted with the image of *drinking, as to have "been enlightened, to have tasted the heavenly gift, and have shared in the Holy Spirit, and have tasted the goodness of the word of God and the powers of the age to come" (Heb 6:4-5 NRSV). God's laws are put in the minds and *hearts of Christians and written there as well (Heb 8:10; 10:16). As Son of God and heir of all things, Christ can make Christians heirs of salvation (Heb 1:14) as they become *children of God (Heb 12:5-11). Through faith and patience Christians inherit the promises (Heb 6:12) and the promised eternal inheritance (Heb 9:15). Through faith Noah was an heir of righteousness, and *Abraham, Isaac and *Jacob were heirs of the promise (Heb 11:7-9).

Several metaphors depict the Christian life after salvation. Using a *building metaphor, initial instruction about the gospel and the Christian faith is laying a foundation for the Christian life (Heb 6:1-2). A mixed metaphor from education and physical development and nutrition describes growth in knowledge of the Christian life. The new Christian is an infant in need of the *milk of basic Christian instruction, and the mature Christian is an adult who can eat the solid food of more advanced instruction (Heb 5:12-14). Another metaphor is the people of God as strangers (see Foreigner) or *pilgrims on the earth seeking a homeland, a heavenly country where God is portrayed as a builder preparing a *city for his people (Heb 11:10, 13-16). There is also a metaphor of God as a parent who disciplines his children with discipline that yields the "peaceful fruit of righteousness to those who have been trained by it" (Heb 12:5-11 NRSV). Christians are *athletes engaged in training (Heb 5:14; 12:11). They struggle against sin in which all encumbrances must be removed, as if in a marathon in which all extra weight must be shed. All of chapter 11 is a presentation of the faithful of the past as a crowd assembled at an arena to watch Christians run this marathon of spiritual perseverance (Heb 12:1-4).

Backsliding or *apostasy in the Christian faith is described with a variety of images. The image of the *wilderness generation and its hardness of heart in rebellion against God and its ultimate failure to enter God's rest in Canaan portrays a Christian whose heart is evil and unbelieving and who turns away from God in disobedience and never enters God's *rest in heaven (Heb 3:7—4:13). Apostasy is to "have once been enlightened, to have tasted the heavenly gift, and have shared in the Holy Spirit, and have tasted the goodness of the word of God and the powers of the age to come, and then have fallen away" (Heb 6:4-6 NRSV). Apostasy is also powerfully depicted as "crucifying again the Son of God and holding him up to contempt" (Heb 6:6 NRSV), and as having "spurned the Son of God, profaned the blood of the covenant by which they were sanctified, and outraged the Spirit of grace" (Heb 10:29 NRSV). For the apostate there is no longer a sacrifice for sin (Heb 10:26). An apostate is portrayed with the agricultural metaphor of ground that drinks up rain and produces a crop of *thorns and thistles and is only good to be burned (Heb 6:7-8).

*Creation imagery also occurs in Hebrews. God built creation as the work of his hands (Heb 1:10; 3:4). The earth and heavens are like *garments that wear out and are rolled up and changed (Heb 1:10-12). Within creation, human beings are a little lower than the angels, crowned with *glory and *honor, with all things subjected under their feet (Heb 2:7-8).

Other Images. Miscellaneous images include the atoning work of Christ as "tasting death" (Heb 2:9); Christ as the "forerunner" (Heb 6:20), the "pioneer of salvation" (Heb 2:10) and the "pioneer and perfecter" of faith (Heb 12:2); God as a "consuming fire" (Heb 12:29); and Abraham's descendants "as many as the stars of heaven and as the innumerable grains of sand by the seashore" (Heb 11:12 NRSV). Finally, the ability of the word of God to judge the soul is vividly described as "living and active, sharper than any two-edged sword, piercing until it divides soul from spirit, joints from marrow; it is able to judge the thoughts and intentions of the heart. And before him no creature is hidden, but all are naked and laid bare to the eyes of the one to whom we must render an account" (Heb 4:12-13 RSV).

The foregoing catalog of images in Hebrews is far from exhaustive. Hebrews is continuously imagistic; the writer is as much a poet as a theologian. A specimen passage that illustrates the vigor of his imagination is this picture of what it means to believe in Christ as savior:

> You have come to Mount Zion and to the city of the living God, the heavenly Jerusalem, and to innumerable angels in festal gathering, and to the assembly of the firstborn who are enrolled in heaven, and to God the judge of all, and to the spirits of the righteous made perfect, and to Jesus, the mediator of a new covenant, and to the sprinkled blood that speaks a better word than the blood of Abel. (Heb 12:22-24 NRSV)

See also ANGEL; APOSTASY; ATONEMENT; BLOOD; COVENANT; HEAVEN; MELCHIZEDEK; MOSES; PILGRIM, PILGRIMAGE; PRIEST; REST; SACRIFICE; SON OF GOD; TABERNACLE.

BIBLIOGRAPHY. W. J. Moulton, "The Relay Race," *ExpTim* 33 (1921-1922) 73-74; V. C. Pfitzner, *Paul and the Agon Motif* (NovTSup 16; Leiden: Brill, 1967); W. G. Johnsson, "The Pilgrimage Motif in the Book of Hebrews," *JBL* 97 (1978) 239-51; D. Kidner, "Sacrifice: Metaphors and Meaning," *TynB* 33 (1982) 119-36; E. Käsemann, *The Wandering People of God: An Investigation of the Letter to the Hebrews* (Minneapolis: Augsburg, 1984).

HEDGE. See FENCE, FENCED PLACE.

HEEL

People who walk incessantly and who engage in physical combat are more conscious of the importance of the heel than others, as the ten biblical references to heel show. Here we find literal pictures of a *snake biting a horse's heels and sending its rider sprawling (Gen 49:17), of pursuing someone's heels (Gen 49:19), of people marching at a leader's heels (Deut 33:3; Judg 5:15), of a *trap seizing a person by the heel (Job 18:9) and of *terror chasing a person by the heels (Job 18:11). The general tenor of these images (with exceptions) is to link the heel with potential disaster, thus painting a picture of vulnerable humanity.

The most famous literal heel in the Bible is the heel of *Esau that *Jacob's hand gripped as Esau came out of Rebekah's womb (Gen 25:26). The incident was so noteworthy (and perhaps laughable) in the family that it gave Jacob his name as (translated

variously) "one who grabs by the heel" or "who struggles" or "who supplants." Figurative meanings are intertwined with the literal picture in this passage, since to grab by the heel in the ancient Near Eastern usage meant "to deceive." Jacob proves himself a heel-grasper by swindling his brother out of his inheritance and tricking his father into giving him the blessing intended for Esau (cf. Hos 12:3; *see* Trickster; Deception, Stories of).

The heel appears in figurative statements about opposition from an *enemy. In John 13:18 Jesus applies Psalm 41:9 to Judas. The psalmist speaks of a "bosom friend's" betrayal, shamefully "lifting the heel" against him, perhaps an image of turning and walking out in a time of need or of shamefully crushing under the foot. An important text is Genesis 3:15, where part of God's curse on the serpent is: "I will put enmity between you and the woman, and between your offspring and hers; he will strike your head, and you will strike his heel" (NRSV). This is the promise of redemption, with Christ, the seed of the woman, delivering a more destructive blow to Satan than he will bring against Christ.

See also FEET.

HEIGHT. *See* HIGH, HEIGHT, HIGH PLACE.

HEIR. *See* INHERITANCE; LEGAL IMAGES.

HELL

The best known biblical image for hell derives from a deep, narrow gorge southeast of Jerusalem called *gê ben hinnōm*, "the Valley of Ben Hinnom," in which idolatrous Israelites offered up child sacrifices to the gods Molech and Baal (2 Chron 28:3; 33:6; Jer 7:31-32; 19:2-6 NIV). Josiah defiled the *valley to make it unacceptable as a holy site (2 Kings 23:10), after which it was used as a garbage dump by the inhabitants of Jerusalem. As a result, the Valley of Ben Hinnom became known as the dump heap, the place of destruction by *fire in Jewish tradition. The Greek word *gehenna*, "hell," commonly used in the NT for the place of final punishment, is derived from the Hebrew name for this valley.

This valley was also regarded as an appropriate image of hell due to its association with the place to deposit the bodies of those slain in *battle by God's *judgment. Jeremiah prophesied that the valley would be used as a mass *grave for the corpses of the people of Judah killed by an invading army (Jer 7:30-34; 7:30-34). The prior association of the place with cultic abominations, the exposure of the bodies to carrion-eating *birds and *animals and the unceremonious nature of the burial indicate that the dead lie under God's *curse. Many of the prophets had visions of a decisive battle between God and his *enemies in the vicinity of Jerusalem (Is 66:14-16; Ezek 38-39; Joel 3:12-13; Zech 14:12-15). Ezekiel describes a valley in which the scavenged remains of the enemy soldiers (Ezek 38:4) will be buried in order to remove the defilement of dead bodies lying out in the open (Ezek 38:11-12). Isaiah mentions an unnamed place near Jerusalem in which the bodies of God's enemies lay under God's continuing curse: "Their *worm will not die, nor will their fire be quenched, and they will be loathsome to all mankind" (Is 66:24 NIV). Jesus' depiction of hell in Mark 9:47-48 brings together these prophetic images.

Were this all the Bible had to say about hell, it would be horrible enough. The sight of mutilated corpses, human bones, maggots, flies, animals and birds ripping strips of flesh off dead bodies as well as the smell of rotting and burning flesh convey a sense of horror and revulsion to which those who have viewed the aftermath of modern atrocities and warfare can fully attest (see Disgust, Revulsion).

But an additional aspect, that of *fire and burning, is also associated with hell, and this field of imagery also has roots in the OT. As Isaiah 66:24 suggests, the Valley of Ben Hinnom would be a place of burning long after the practice of child sacrifice had ceased. Throughout the Scriptures the execution of judgment is frequently portrayed with images of burning. In the sacrificial system the burning of the animal produced an aroma "pleasing to the LORD" (Lev 3:5; 4:31). The destruction by fire of *Sodom and Gomorrah (Gen 19) and Jericho (Josh 6) may be patterned after the symbol of a burning sacrifice. The point of burning seems to be that it destroys something offensive to God's holiness and that the smoke acts as a sign that the offensive thing is in fact being destroyed.

Other kinds of judgment can also be described as burning. In Deuteronomy 29:23, 24 the land of Israel will become a "burning waste" as a consequence of covenant breaking. This same kind of language is used to describe the *exile. In Zechariah 3:2, for example, Joshua the high priest is called "a burning stick snatched from the fire" in reference to his returning from exile. Throughout the prophetic books God's judgment on both the wicked nations and Israel's disobedience is referred to in these terms (Is 1:25; 7:4; Zeph 1:18; 3:8; Zech 13:8, 9). God's anger is often described as "burning against" an individual or nation (Ex 4:14; Num 11:1-3; 12:9; Josh 7:1). In Malachi 3:2 and 4:1 the Day of the Lord is likened to a "refiner's fire" and a "furnace."

This theme continues throughout the NT. Evangelism is described as "snatching others from the fire" (Jude 23). Jesus speaks of the "fire of hell" (Mt 5:22; 18:9) and the "fiery furnace" (Mt 13:42). Revelation describes the place of final punishment as a "lake of fire" (20:14-15). By using the symbol of judgment by fire, the biblical writers communicate to their readers that the judgment is catastrophic and that it satisfies the requirements of God's holiness (cf. Heb 12:29).

Burning is not only an image of the satisfaction of God's holiness, but also of the *suffering of those undergoing judgment. Revelation 14:10 warns that worshipers of the "beast" will be "tormented with burning sulfur" (see Brimstone). Here we have the image of bodies capable of feeling pain being subjected to the agony of being burned. This is in keeping with the general view of the NT that hell is punishment experienced as suffering in body and soul (Mt 10:28; Rom 2:8-9; Jude 7). In the parable of the rich man and Lazarus, Jesus describes the dead rich man as suffering in agony in a fiery place (Lk 16:23-25). So great are the torments of hell that its inhabitants will be engaged in "weeping and gnashing of teeth" (Mt 13:42, 50; 22:13). The impression left by these descriptions of unbearable heat, the noxious odor of burning and the sound of weeping has inspired many a harrowing sermon and such awful scenes in literature as the desert of burning sand and fiery rain in Canto 14 of Dante's *Inferno*.

In the NT the torment is described as continuous and eternal (Mt 3:12; 25:41; 2 Thess 1:9; Jude 7) and conveyed most vividly by Jesus' quotation from Isaiah 66:24, "Their worm does not die, and the fire is not quenched" (Mk 9:48). In Revelation 14:11 the idea of eternal punishment is pictured by a column of smoke rising from hell forever. John adds that the suffering continues without respite: "There is no rest day and night for those who worship the beast and his image" (NIV). Contrast this with the continuous blessedness of the righteous, who are serving God "day and night" in his temple in Revelation 7:15.

Hell is also pictured by the image of *darkness. A place of "blackest darkness" is reserved for the habitually wicked (2 Pet 2:17; Jude 13). Jesus talks of those who will be thrown "outside, into the darkness" (Mt 8:12 NIV). This image appears to indicate consignment to *chaos, being shut out of God's favorable presence and his good creation, since creation began with God calling light out of darkness (Gen 1:1-3; see also 2 Thess 1:9; 1 Jn 1:5).

The images of darkness and fire appear contradictory, but they should be regarded as symbols pointing to a reality more horrific than either symbol can convey by itself. In fact, biblical images of hell leave many details to the imagination, perhaps because no picture is capable of doing justice to the reality.

Because no other biblical figure speaks more often of hell than Jesus, it is no surprise that he speaks most forcefully about the need to avoid hell. Jesus uses the images of gouging out one's *eye and cutting off one's *arm or *foot as symbols of the drastic measures one is justified in taking to escape the horrors of hell (Mt 5:29-30; 18:7-9; Mk 9:42-48).

See also AFTERLIFE; CHAFF; BRIMSTONE; CRIME AND PUNISHMENT; DARKNESS; FIRE; HEAVEN; JUDGMENT; PAIN; PIT; SODOM AND GOMORRAH; TERROR, STORIES OF; TORMENT; VALLEY; WEEPING; WORM.

BIBLIOGRAPHY. K. E. Brower and M. W. Elliott, *"The Reader Must Understand": Eschatology in Bible and Theology* (Leicester: Apollos, 1997).

HELMET. *See* ARMOR.

HELP, HELPER

More than 200 occurrences of the words *helper* and *help* confirm a pillar of biblical doctrine—that people are not self-sufficient but require help from beyond themselves. The ultimate helper is God. Moses names one of his sons Eliezer, saying, "My father's God was my helper" (Ex 18:4 NIV). One of Isaiah's servant songs asserts that "the Sovereign LORD helps me" (Is 50:7, 9 NIV). In his farewell blessing to his nation, Moses repeats the insight: "Who is like you, a people saved by the LORD? He is your shield and helper, and your glorious sword" (Deut 33:29 NIV). Moses accompanies the assertion with a cluster of metaphors that paint a majestic Near Eastern image of deity, filled with anthropomorphic imagery (Deut 33:26-27). This passage also illustrates how the vocabulary of helping in the OT often carries an implied martial meaning.

Psalms of *rescue and *protection are a particularly rich source of poetry that praises God as helper. In Psalm 121, a pilgrim "song of ascents," the traveler begins by lifting his eyes to the hills, contemplating the dangers of the journey that lies before him, and is led to ask, "Where does my help come from?" (Ps 121:1 NIV). His reply is, "My help comes from the LORD, the Maker of heaven and earth" (Ps 121:2 NIV). The rest of the poem is a meditation on the ways in which God helps the traveler, and it includes the evocative epithet of God as "keeper" (Ps 121:5 RSV).

Other psalms echo the motif of God as helper. God is "helper of the fatherless" (Ps 10:14) and the soldier's helper (Ps 27:9) who allows the *warrior to "look in triumph" on his enemies (Ps 118:7). Sometimes the image of help is joined with related images to intensify the effect. Thus God is a "help and deliverer" (Ps 70:5). In Psalm 115 the declaration that God is their "help and *shield" is said of three different groups (Ps 115:9-11). Psalm 46 is a small classic on the subject, with God being called "an ever-present help in trouble" (Ps 46:1) who can be trusted to lend military help to his own city "at break of day" or "right early" (Ps 46:5 RSV).

The book of Hebrews, which was probably written for Jewish believers, appropriates the OT image from Psalm 118:6-7 to encourage the church. "So we say with confidence," the author writes, "The Lord is my helper; I will not be afraid. What can man do to me?" (Heb 13:6 NIV). Jewish believers were well versed in OT imagery. They would have sung this psalm to praise God for past deliverances. They understood that joy and victory belonged to them. The *Holy Spirit too is a helper—one who "helps us in our weakness" (Rom 8:26 NIV).

God is not the only helper in the Bible. People also fill that role. Isaiah paints a utopian picture of a society in which "each helps the other and says to his brother, 'Be strong!' " (Is 41:6 NIV). Paul and Barnabas were aided by John, who "was with them as their helper" (Acts 13:5 NIV), and later Paul sent two "helpers" to Macedonia (Acts 19:22). God gave Aaron as a helper to Moses, and Elisha to Elijah. The most famous human "helper" in the Bible is *Eve, who was created expressly to be a "helper suitable" for *Adam (Gen 2:18, 20 NIV).

The Bible's imagery of helping is far removed from any stigma of being servile or ignominious. On the contrary, to be a helper is an honorable role—an opportunity to fulfill a need. The gifts of the Spirit include serving (Rom 12:7) and "those able to help others" (1 Cor 12:28). Two dozen references to helping and helpers in the Epistles give an ever-expanding picture of how eagerly the early Christians helped each other and the cause of the church.

See also EVE; HOLY SPIRIT; PROTECTION; RESCUE.

HERALD. See AUTHORITY, HUMAN.

HERMES. *See* GODS, GODDESSES.

HERO/HEROINE

A hero or heroine cannot simply be equated with the protagonist of a story; he or she might be a secondary character rather than the leading character. Furthermore, not all protagonists are heroic. Heroes and heroines possess at least five traits: (1) they are representative figures for the culture producing them; (2) their experiences and struggles are ones with which a culture identifies and therefore experiences as something shared; (3) they embody values or virtues that a culture wishes to affirm; (4) although they need not be wholly idealized, they are mainly exemplary figures to whom a culture looks up as being worthy of emulation; (5) they capture the popular imagination. The corresponding functions that heroes perform in a culture are primarily two— they function as an inspiration and they codify a culture's values and beliefs.

A hero or heroine is a construct created by the imagination from real-life materials. Life itself furnishes the data from which the human race creates its heroes, but a hero never exists in its pure form in real life. A literary hero is a distillation from available material, and the process of distillation involves selectivity and highlighting. Creating heroes and heroines is one of the most important things a society does, partly because it is a chief means by which a society transmits its values and its moral identity.

The main literary genre devoted to the heroic impulse is the *hero story,* and the Bible is an anthology of such stories. An image of a hero can also emerge from such genres as lyric poetry, proverbs and prophecy. Furthermore, although *heroic qualities* might be the basis for defining a hero, the most recurrent categorization of the heroes of the Bible (as in literature generally) is by *role,* with a character's virtues often closely linked to that role. The framework for biblical heroes and heroines that follows is a broad-stroke overview that uses familiar images of the hero and heroine for its basic terminology.

Aristocratic Heroes. The ancient world was enamored of the power and authority represented by rulers. The chief literary media for expressing this image of hero were the *court chronicle,* listing the major public (and occasionally private) events in the lives of *kings and *queens, and the *epic,* which praised a nation partly by elevating the ruling class. We can see this pattern in the OT (though it is barely discernible in the NT). *David is the towering figure—the king most frequently adduced as a standard by which to measure kingly achievement in his successors—but the court chronicles more generally attest the ancient conviction that kings and rulers were the most important figures in society and imply awe for the *authority they represented. In the older way of thinking, a nation's whole destiny was tied to the ruler as representative, a conviction reinforced in the OT by the assumption that a king was the one through whom the *covenant would be honored or dishonored, with resultant national *blessing or misfortune. Of course a king can be a villain as well as a hero, and a notable feature of OT court chronicles is how many of the rulers were villainous rather than heroic.

Kings and queens are frequent candidates for literary treatment because they are the power figures with authority to rule a group. That principle can make other figures on the social scene candidates for heroism as well, and these are especially prominent in the OT. One category is the clan leader, especially the patriarch. The evocative triad of *Abraham, Isaac and *Jacob are the heroes of Genesis. (Luther called them "next to Christ and John the Baptist, . . . the most outstanding heroes this world has ever produced.") The sons of Jacob, themselves progenitors of the subsequent tribes of Israel, are only a step behind. *Moses and Joshua are the heroic leaders of the *exodus and conquest. The book of *Judges elevates the figure of the judge to heroic status. To be genuinely heroic, however, all of these biblical figures need to possess certain moral and spiritual qualities. These include good judgment, decisive leadership, adherence to the true religion coupled with avoidance of idolatry, godliness and obedience to God's covenant commands. But the core around which those qualities are ranged is the role of leader.

In addition to elevating rulers to heroic status, the ancient world championed the figure of the warrior as hero (*see* Battle Stories; Warfare). While this is less of a preoccupation in the OT than in parallel ancient literature, it is a major OT image of the hero. Except for the patriarchs, OT rulers were also warriors and generals; and some of these martial heroes are known to us more for their battlefield exploits than for their acts of government. While the literature of warfare is largely a masculine world, women such as Deborah and Jael (Judg 4—5) occasionally join the ranks. Heroic qualities that characterize the warrior include courage, physical strength and dexterity, and superior military strategy. We should also note that it is an axiom in martial literature that the decisive events of history occur on the battlefield. The writers of OT

military history accept as equally axiomatic that human qualities rarely bring victory by themselves but only through the assistance of God. In some of the OT victories, God is actually the champion warrior (*see* Divine Warrior).

Religious Roles. People can also achieve the status of heroes by virtue of their religious roles. In some cases these roles place people into an elite social category comparable to the political aristocrats of a society; in other cases the heroism arises from God's having singled out a person for a heroic role. The Bible gives us four main categories of elevated religious roles. The first group to be the acknowledged religious elite of their society was the OT *priestly caste, whose main function was to represent the people to God, especially through the sacrificial system. Later in OT history *prophets became the most visible class of religious heroes, known chiefly for their courage in bringing God's word of judgment to apostate people and nations. The NT church elevated the figure of the missionary to a status comparable to the OT prophet. The essence of the heroic missionary is evangelistic fervor combined with indefatigable energy in traveling with the gospel. A second NT group of religious figures is the disciples, who in the Gospels are often obtuse and unbelieving but are nonetheless elevated by virtue of their special call from Jesus, their status as the definitive first followers and companions of Jesus, and their subsequent role in proclaiming (and in some cases writing down) the gospel concerning Jesus.

The Common Person as Hero. Despite the ancient (even perhaps universal) impulse to honor the powerful figures in a society, people at the lower end of the social spectrum can achieve heroic status as well. The pastoral image of the *shepherd, for example, has been idealized throughout literary history. *Abel stands at the head of the biblical pastoral tradition, and the patriarchs are quasi-shepherd figures. But David remains in our imaginations as a heroic shepherd figure, especially in the celebration of the typical events in the shepherd's ideal day in Psalm 23. Wisdom literature, despite its courtly milieu, finds a place of honor for the shepherd (Prov 27:23-27). And Jesus provides the apotheosis of the shepherd-hero in his picture of the good shepherd (Jn 10:1-18).

By extension, the Bible finds a place for the *farmer—the "tiller of the soil"—as a figure worthy of honor and emulation (*see* Farming). *Adam and *Eve, placed by God "in the garden of Eden to till it and keep it" (Gen 2:15 RSV), are the first example. Beginning with the settlement of Canaan, biblical writing reflects an agrarian milieu, with the farming family as one of its heroes. Even a king like Saul plows in his field (1 Sam 11:5), and the prophet Elisha is called from plowing in the field with "twelve yoke of oxen" (1 Kings 19:19). In the parables of Jesus the industrious farmer is implicitly honored as a worthy figure.

Ancient literature finds a small place of praise for the faithful servant, but in general the role does not excite heroic visions. The Bible, however, elevates the role of the *servant, especially as a metaphor of the believer's relationship to God. But even at a human level we find heroic servants in the Bible, including Abraham's servant who conducts the courtship by proxy of Rebekah and Isaac (Gen 24), Naaman's servant girl who is instrumental in his healing from leprosy (2 Kings 5:1-14) and the faithful servants of Jesus' parables and sayings.

*Child heroes have always held a special place in people's hearts and imaginations, and the Bible occasionally satisfies our liking for such figures. The prime example is David, homespun giant slayer who performs his feat with a sling and a stone. In the same category is the boy Samuel, singled out by God to carry a prophetic message to his master, Eli the priest. Josiah was a mere eight years old when he assumed his godly reign as king of Judah (2 Kings 22:1-2). The virgin *Mary rises to heroic status in her acceptance of her role in the annunciation story (Lk 1:26-56). We also catch glimpses of youthful heroism in characters whose stories are not fully told, such as Miriam when her baby brother *Moses was entrusted to the Nile River, and Jesus as a boy of twelve years confounding the rabbis in the temple (Lk 2:46-47).

Reversals of Heroic Conventions. The Bible delights in reversing human conventions, exalting the *younger over the *elder or declaring that strength lies in *weakness. This subversive impulse underlies some of the images of heroes as well (see Antihero). The Bible idealizes the *martyr, for example, because martyrs represent the highest degree of loyalty to God. The prototype is righteous Abel, murdered by his brother precisely because his deeds were righteous (1 Jn 3:12). Thereafter "the blood of innocent Abel" becomes the fountainhead from which flows "the righteous blood shed on earth" (Mt 23:35; cf. Lk 11:50-51). The roll call of the heroes of faith in Hebrews 11:35-40 includes a moving tribute to martyrs, who are highlighted in the book of Revelation as well (Rev 6:9-11).

Closely related to the martyr is the *suffering servant—the figure who undergoes unmerited suffering that is redemptive in the life of others. Examples include *Joseph (who undergoes calamity that rescues his family and the world from famine), Moses (the persecuted leader who intercedes with God for his nation) and Jeremiah (the weeping prophet who is despised for his courage in declaring God's word of judgment). The first epistle of Peter is a small treatise on the honor of suffering for the sake of Christ. The archetype reaches its zenith in the four servant songs of Isaiah and in the atoning life and death of Christ.

Intellectual Heroism. In the world's literature heroes have mainly been characterized by physical accomplishment. An alternative is the hero or heroine known chiefly by mental ability. The ancient equivalent of the modern detective seems to have been the interpreter of dreams. Two biblical charac-

ters who rise to heroic status through their ability to interpret *dreams are Joseph and *Daniel. The most prevalent intellectual hero of the Bible is the *wise man—the person with superior insight into living. The wise man is often a rabbi or *teacher, another heroic figure in the Bible.

Of course teachers require learners, and the Bible elevates those who learn and who value knowledge and instruction, as in the book of Proverbs and the example of Jesus' disciples. If the wise man/teacher is the protagonist of the book of Proverbs, the actual hero of wisdom literature is the person who heeds and practices the advice of the wise man—the wise person, in other words. "Who is like the wise man?" asks the writer of Ecclesiastes rhetorically (Eccles 8:1). Again, "Wisdom is better than weapons of war" (Eccles 9:18 RSV). Solomon's fame is based as much on his wisdom as his material prosperity (1 Kings 10:1-9).

We also find examples of the contemplative as hero—in the psalms that praise the act of meditation; in the pictures of Jesus alone on the mountain or in the wilderness; in Mary the mother of Jesus, who pondered Jesus' sayings in her heart; in Mary the sister of Martha, as she sat at the feet of Jesus.

Another heroic quality greatly prized in ancient cultures was eloquence, and we can accordingly speak of the articulate hero. When the youthful David is recommended to Saul, his qualifications are not only that he is a "brave man and a warrior" but also that he "speaks well" (1 Sam 16:18 NIV). Moses fears that his lack of eloquence disqualifies him as a candidate for leadership (Ex 4:10), so God gives him Aaron as a spokesman, thereby confirming that the quality of being articulate was necessary for a heroic leader. One of the most apparent gifts of the prophets in the OT and Paul in the NT was their oratorical ability, and Jesus was likewise an expert in public speaking and witty repartee in dialogue and debate.

Lovers as Heroes. Heroism is usually defined by action, but occasionally a literary tradition makes *feeling* the norm by which heroism is achieved. The largest category is love literature (see Love Story), and the lover as hero has had a significant place in the history of literature. The supreme example in the Bible is the couple in the *Song of Songs, who are paragons of attractiveness, titans of romantic emotion and masters of the poetic rhetoric of romance. The narrative counterpart of these lyric lovers include Adam and Eve, Jacob and Rachel, Boaz and Ruth, and Joseph and Mary, all of whom are implicitly idealized in their roles as lovers.

As a sidelight, we should note in passing that although the Bible ultimately espouses a moral and spiritual conception of heroism, it does not completely omit the universal human tendency to elevate people who are physically attractive in appearance. While it is true that feminine beauty can be deceitful and vain (Prov 31:30) and that God looks on the heart instead of on the appearance as people do (1 Sam 16:7), we nonetheless find examples of heroic characters whose credentials include impressive appearance. Sarah strikes people as "very beautiful" (Gen 12:14), Rebekah "was very fair to look upon" (Gen 24:16) and Rachel "was beautiful and lovely" (Gen 29:17). Abigail was "of good understanding and beautiful" (1 Sam 25:3), and Esther was taken into the royal harem as a candidate to become queen because she met the preliminary requirement of being "beautiful" (Esther 2:2-3).

So too with some of the male heroes of the Bible. Joseph "was handsome and good-looking" (Gen 39:6). On the very occasion that Samuel mistakenly thinks that God has chosen Jesse's son Eliab as the future king because he is impressive of stature and is told not to look on external appearance, we nonetheless read regarding David, the young son of choice, that "he was ruddy, and had beautiful eyes, and was handsome" (1 Sam 16:12 NRSV).

Domestic Heroes. *Wives and *mothers also rise to heroic status in the Bible. The virtuous wife of Proverbs 31:10-31 is a composite of all that a domestic heroine might aspire to be, and we should note in this regard that physical attractiveness is regarded as suspect (v. 30). For narrative fleshing out of the portrait of the ideal wife and mother, we have the stories of Mary the mother of Jesus, and Hannah, the mother of Samuel. David had ample reason to marry Abigail as soon as possible after her churlish husband died, for she was obviously a consort worthy of any man (1 Sam 25).

Exemplary Character as Heroic. In addition to the social roles covered above, the Bible offers us many models of persons who are heroic and worthy of emulation simply because of their individual character traits, which are usually made apparent in actions in a narrative (as compared with a writer's ascribing a quality to a character). The Bible participates in one of the most universal of all literary impulses—to embody representative and exemplary human experience in the form of characters placed in concrete situations and undertaking actions that display a sense of what is right and wrong, valuable and worthless. Every story in the Bible is in some sense an "example story," along the lines of the statement in 1 Corinthians 10:11 that the historical records of the Bible "were written down for our instruction." Biblical narrative, like narrative generally, pursues two complementary ways of instructing us: it gives us positive models of behavior to emulate and negative examples to avoid. The positive examples are images of heroism.

Sometimes we find an extended portrait of heroism, as in Ruth's loyalty, Elijah's faithfulness to his prophetic calling and resourcefulness in survival, and Daniel's courage, integrity and devotion to God. But the Bible's specialty is the brief vignette in which characters are illuminated as it were from the side by flashes of kindness, moral or physical strength, devotion, perseverance, faith, wisdom, and many other heroic traits.

The Bible exhibits a thoroughgoing realism in showing such heroism intermingled with the failings that are common to humanity. (There are only a handful of wholly idealized characters in the Bible.) But the failings of heroes and heroines serve as a foil to these same characters' heroic traits and acts, and they send the message to the reader that people do not need to be perfect to be heroic.

The composite hero that emerges from the pages of the Bible is the saint—the person characterized chiefly by faith in God and obedience to God's commands. The archetypal gestures of this hero or heroine are submission to God, *prayer, piety, reliance on God, *repentance, *humility and *faith. This figure is at odds at many turns with the conventional hero of literature, whose typical gestures include pride, self-reliance, acquisition of power, material prosperity, sexual gratification and self-assertion. While such saintly heroism is within any believer's reach, biblical narrative tends to elevate heroes and heroines who display them with extraordinary courage and boldness in hostile or difficult circumstances. The heroes and heroines whose stories are recorded tend to be the Josephs and Elijahs and Pauls, or the *Ruths and *Esthers of the world.

Hero Stories. While the labels "hero" and "heroine" denote a character type, that designation does not do justice to the genre of hero stories. Such stories are built around a representative and exemplary protagonist who in some sense embodies the experiences and ideals of the culture producing him or her. The essential rule for interpreting a hero story is to go through the action as the observant traveling companion of the hero or heroine. Related plot motifs that almost always figure in a hero story are the *test motif and the *ordeal, since these provide the occasion for the hero to assert and live up to his or her identity. In addition, if we arrange hero stories into a composite story, several distinct type scenes emerge, including the hero's birth (*see* Birth Story), *initiation, *calling, and encounter with the divine (*see* Divine-Human Encounter). Many hero stories also end with an account of the hero's death.

Jesus as Hero. It will have been obvious from the foregoing discussion that *Jesus encompasses virtually all of the heroic images that the Bible gives us. The pattern of his life even follows the familiar cycle of events that hero stories often give us, including a miraculous birth, a calling to a special life, an initiation into that life, achievement and a notable death. In the case of Jesus we can add the further phases of resurrection and ascension into heaven. Specific images of the hero also cluster in Jesus' life, including leader, priest, prophet, shepherd, martyr, suffering servant, wise man, teacher and orator/debater/poet. In his moral and spiritual life too, Jesus is the supreme examplar of moral virtue, obedience to the Father, self-sacrifice and prayer.

Summary. The Bible gives us a gallery of memorable heroes and heroines. It encompasses virtually every heroic image that exists. Two passages can be taken as a summary of the whole. While the announced focus of Hebrews 11 is the heroism of faith, as the roll call unfolds, we catch glimpses of many of the heroic themes of the Bible. The life of Christ too sums up the biblical ideal of heroism.

See also ABRAHAM; ANTIHERO; CHARACTER TYPES; DAVID; ESTHER, BOOK OF; INITIATION; JESUS; JOSEPH; KING; MARY THE MOTHER OF JESUS; MOSES; ORDEAL, STORIES OF; PRIEST; PROPHET, PROPHETESS; QUEEN; RUTH, BOOK OF; SHEEP, SHEPHERD; TEST, TESTING.

HIDE, HIDING

The essential idea of hiding is concealment, and a figur-ative extension to include the modern idea of a "cover-up" seems so natural that it may be treated as part of the literal meaning. *Hide* and its inflected forms appear well over two hundred times in the OT (KJV), translating fourteen different Hebrew roots, six of which are translated "hide" only once and two of which account for over half the occurrences. Though not perfectly synonymous, most of the words have considerable semantic overlap. Of the thirty-five appearances in the NT, twenty-eight translate *kryptō* and its derivatives and four more *(para)kalyptō*, whose more common opposite *apokalyptō* ("reveal") suggests something of the larger semantic field to which *hide* belongs: secret, mystery, disguise, dissembling, *veil, *darkness, *searching, *burial and (most basic of all) *cover. Thus occasionally the image of hiding is present even without the word itself.

Protection. In biblical narratives many people hide, or are hidden, to escape *enemies: the infant *Moses, the spies in Jericho, Jotham (Judg 9:5), Israelites (1 Sam 13:6; Jer 16:16), *David many times, Elijah and other prophets (1 Kings 17:3; 18:4, 13; 22:25; Jer 36:26), Joash, Moabites (Is 16:3), Jesus (Jn 8:59). Hiding also occurs to avoid confrontation or publicity (Lk 1:24, the pregnant Elizabeth; Jn 7:10; 12:36; 19:38, Joseph of Arimathea) or to express a feeling of unworthiness (1 Sam 10:22; 1 Chron 21:20; Job 29:8, 10; Dan 10:7; cf. Is 6:2). Moses hid his face when he saw the *burning bush (Ex 3:6)—a detail echoed first in God's shielding him from the *"glory" (Ex 33:22) and then in Moses' own veiling to protect the people (Ex 34:35). People hide possessions in the hope of saving them (Judg 6:11; 2 Kings 7:8; Mt 25:18). Sometimes the attempt to hide is futile (Gen 3:8, Adam and Eve; Deut 7:20; Josh 10:16; Mk 7:24; Lk 8:47, the healed woman in the crowd). Sometimes the attempt is courageously forgone (Is 50:6; Jn 18:20).

Many of these stories readily invite moralistic commentary, and their lessons are embodied in numerous imagined scenes of hiding—proverbial or eschatological. To hide from impending evil is a mark of wisdom (Ps 55:12; Prov 27:12; 28:28) or poverty (Job 24:4). Already for the writer of Job, Adam's hiding had become proverbial for *guilt (Job 31:33 KJV) and the wicked would be hidden only in the dust; that is, the *grave (Job 40:13). Evil, if hidden to be savored, proves unbearable (Job 20:12). Nowhere can *sinners escape divine wrath (Job 34:22;

Amos 9:3), though they seek refuge in *caves and crags and cry to the *mountains, "Fall on us, and hide us" (Rev 6:16 NIV; cf. Lk 23:30; Is 2:19; Hos 10:8). The righteous, however, may hide "for a little moment, until the indignation be overpast" (Is 26:20 KJV; cf. Zeph 2:3), and Job in his desperation sees even Sheol as such a *refuge (Job 14:13). Images abound of hiding as divine *protection. God's people are "hidden ones" (Ps 83:3) dwelling in God's "secret place" (Ps 91:1), hidden with God's hand or quiver (Is 49:2) or *wings or tent or presence (Ps 17:8; 27:5; 31:20). "Thou art my hiding place" (Ps 32:7; 119:114 KJV). The *dove "hiding in the clefts of the rock" (Song 2:14 JB), an image from nature, has been interpreted allegorically; the phrase is familiar in hymnody.

Hiding to Keep Others from Knowing. Hiding is essential to an act such as ambush (2 Kings 7:12) or setting a *trap (Prov 1:17); both ideas are also used figuratively (e.g., Job 18:10; Ps 10:8-9; 56:6; 9:15; 35:78; 140:5; 142:3; Jer 18:22). Withholding information is the prerogative of someone with higher status—the king (1 Sam 20:2-3) or God (Gen 18:17; 2 Kings 4:27)—though some interpret Job 3:23 and 10:13 as accusatory; but to conceal things *from* such figures is difficult (Gen 47:18; Josh 7:19; 2 Sam 14:18; Acts 26:26; 1 Sam 3:17; Ps 10:11; Is 29:15). In Luke 19:42 it is in part Jerusalem's own imperceptiveness that hides what it should know; for God has "not spoken in secret" (Is 45:19; cf. 48:16), and God's commands are "not hidden" (Deut 30:11; cf. Ps 119:19). Words themselves may operate to obscure (Job 42:3). But some things are not to be hidden but taught (Job 15:18; 27:11) or proclaimed (Ps 40:10; 78:4), as the similitudes of a candle and a city on a hill teach (Mt 5:14-15). Indeed, that "there is nothing . . . hid, that shall not be known" (Mt 10:26 KJV) is not threat but promise.

Achan in Joshua 7 tries unsuccessfully to hide two things, his loot and his guilt. Others try to hide hatred (Prov 10:18) or shameful things (2 Cor 4:2) or, like Adam, hide themselves to avoid detection (cf. Job 24:15). But such hiding is futile (Ps 44:21; 69:5; 90:8; Prov 28:13; Jer 16:17; 23:24; 49:10; Hos 5:3; Rom 2:16; 1 Cor 4:5). Moreover, the devout want nothing hidden, no "secret faults" (Ps 19:12; cf. 139:23-24), and they indeed find it a comfort to be fully known (Ps 38:9; 139:12, 15; Is 40:27-31). Not only evil works but also good cannot be hidden (Eccles 12:14; 1 Tim 5:25); those who follow the instruction to conceal their good deeds will be rewarded openly (Mt 6).

A subsidiary meaning of hiding is to *store up and thus keep safe; hence the figures of "hiding words in one's heart" (Ps 119:11; cf. Prov 2:1; Lk 2:19) and of cultivating the inner, "hidden" self (1 Pet 3:4; cf. Ps 51:6). Buried *treasure may be brought forth by human industry (Deut 33:19; Job 28:11); its figurative equivalent, *wisdom, is harder to find (Job 28:21), though not impossible (Prov 2:4-5). A treasure stored in heaven is the promised "hidden *manna" (Rev 2:17). With more sinister meaning, hidden from human knowledge is the store of future events (Job 3:10; 15:20), and to say that "sin is hid" in this sense (Hos 13:12) indicates that eventually retribution will come.

Hiding to Avoid Knowing. A common idiom, to "hide one's face" (or eyes), means to refuse to notice something and thus avoid responding to it. Such behavior is condemned when people thereby evade responsibility (Lev 20:4; Prov 28:27; Ezek 22:26; cf. Is 53:3; 58:7; Deut 22:1-3), but not when the ignorance is unintentional (Lev 4:13f; 5:3-4).

This idiom is used frequently of God, with four interrelated emphases: (1) a general sense of divine aloofness (e.g., Job 13:24; Ps 104:29; 143:7; cf. Job 23:9), perhaps temporary (Is 8:17); (2) God's particular refusal to countenance sinners (Deut 31:17-18; 32:20; Is 1:15; 59:2; 64:7; Jer 33:5; Mic 3:4; cf. Hos 13:14), again perhaps temporary (Is 54:8; 57:17-21; Ezek 39:23-29); (3) a petitioner's cry for succor (Ps 13:1; 27:9; 44:24; 69:17; 88:14; 102:2; Lam 3:56 ["ear"]; cf. Ps 22:1), often reflecting more the speaker's *feeling* of forsakenness than an actuality; and (4) with "not," rejoicing in God's response (Ps 22:24).

Related to the first of these, note *Cain's expression of a sense of having lost God's favor: "From thy face shall I be hid" (Gen 4:14 KJV). Such a sense may be illusory, as suggested in Cowper's familiar lines: "Behind a frowning providence / He hides a smiling face." Yet a fifth emphasis takes quite the opposite direction, when it is one's sins, not oneself, that God is asked not to see (Ps 51:9). Or, in a different idiom, the sins themselves are "hidden"—that is, forgiven (Is 65:16; cf. Jas 5:20; Mic 7:19; Ps 32:1; 85:2).

Mystery. The hiding of God's face does not wholly explain Isaiah 45:15: "Verily thou art a God that hidest thyself, O God of Israel, the Savior" (KJV). For hiding has yet another sense, which springs from the very nature of deity. God's judgments are "unsearchable" (Rom 11:33), and "the skies are the hiding-place of his Majesty" (Hab 3:4 NEB; cf. Ps 18:11; 1 Tim 6:16). God is hidden from human knowledge except by revelation (*apokalypsis,* Mt 11:27; cf. Ps 81:7; Judg 13:18) to those able to receive it. God's "marvelous work" is hidden from "the understanding of [the] prudent" (Is 29:14 KJV), a statement quoted by Jesus (Mt 11:25) and by Paul (1 Cor 1:19), who continues at length to discourse of "the hidden wisdom" (1 Cor 2:7; cf. vv. 9, 10) now being revealed. Earlier, Isaiah spoke of new revelation in his time from the treasury of "hidden things" (Is 48:6), and Deuteronomy 29:29 distinguished between what had been revealed and what was still secret. Now a yet fuller revelation of "the mystery . . . hid from ages" is announced by Paul "to the saints" (Col 1:26) and to "all" (Eph 3:9); though it remains hidden to the "lost," whose minds are "blinded" (2 Cor 4:3-4; cf. Eph 4:18)—as it had been even, at times, to the disciples (Lk 9:45; 18:34; 24:25). But some things remain secret (Acts

1:7; cf. Job 24:1).

In this doctrine three themes converge: divine ineffability, God's willed and incremental self-revelation, and human failure, through sin, to understand. But if revelation depends on spiritual discernment, from the viewpoint of human wisdom, revelation may seem instead a hiding (1 Cor 1:17-24). In a sense the Incarnation itself is a disguise (Jn 1:10), though one designed for faith to penetrate. And "all the treasures of wisdom and knowledge" are said to be hidden in Christ (Col 2:3), not in "traditions of man-made teaching" (Col 2:8, NEB)—nor yet hidden in the Gnostic sense, as for a coterie.

Similarly, when Jesus spoke in *parables things that had been "kept secret" (Mt 13:35), he simultaneously revealed to those with spiritual ears and concealed from the perverse. (Compare the paradoxically mysterious "revelation" in *dreams and *apocalypses.) This principle underlying the genre is also a theme in some parables. Images of God's kingdom emphasize the preciousness and power of the invisible and unregarded: a hidden treasure worth all one's wealth (Mt 13:44), a pinch of yeast "hid" in a bushel of flour (*see* Leaven), able to enliven the whole (Mt 13:33), a seed growing secretly ("he knows not how," Mk 4:27 RSV).

Insofar as *burial is hiding, this image speaks also of death and resurrection (cf. Jn 12:24) and thus of baptism (Rom 6:4-5) and the life of the believer. "Your life is hid with Christ in God" (Col 3:3 KJV): present here are several senses of hiding—treasuring, protecting, awaiting fuller revelation.

See also APOCALYPSE, GENRE OF; COVER, COVERING; GRAVE; PARABLE; PROTECTION; SEARCH, SEARCHING; STORING UP; TREASURE; VEIL.

BIBLIOGRAPHY. S. E. Balentine, *The Hidden God: The Hiding of the Face of God in the Old Testament* (Oxford and New York: Oxford University Press, 1983); M. Bockmuehl, *Revelation and Mystery in Ancient Judaism and Pauline Christianity* (Tübingen: J. C. B. Mohr, 1990); R. E. Brown, *The Background of the Term "Mystery" in the New Testament* (Philadelphia: Fortress, 1968); R. F. Capon, *The Parables of the Kingdom* (Grand Rapids: Zondervan, 1985).

HIGH, HEIGHT, HIGH PLACE

Height is one of the major "value" images of the Bible. It names a quality rather than a quantity to be measured. For premodern people height was like *light and *darkness—an image that elicited awe, like the idea of space in an expanding universe for contemporary people. Height also has a theological value and has thus always been inextricably present in religious thought and language. Even in nonreligious contexts height retains an evocative power. We speak of high culture, high art, highways, the higher life, higher animals and the higher processes of the brain. The Bible itself is replete with references to high priests as well as to "high places," which, though usually higher in altitude, have greater significance than their measurable height. The image of height is thus an essential element in verbalizing our response of *worship, admiration or reverence, whether to the Most High God or to qualities of the created world and people that we supremely value.

Height as an Image of Transcendence and Deity. The most ultimate meaning conferred on height in the Bible is as an image of transcendence (the otherworldly) and the divine. Implicit in this imagery is an implied vertical hierarchy in which God and the unseen spiritual world that he inhabits are qualitatively "above" earthly experience. We should not ignore the physical basis of such imagery: the "heavens are high above the earth," as the psalmist puts it (Ps 103:11), and the human imagination has always pictured *heaven as being "up." God is therefore named as being "high" in the Bible. This is encapsulated in the epithet "Most High," which occurs well over fifty times (NRSV). God is "high and lofty" (Is 6:1; 57:7, 15), the one who is "high above all nations" (Ps 113:4), and he dwells "in the high and holy place" (Is 57:15). Of similar import are two dozen evocative references to God as being "on high."

By extension the imagery of height is associated with the spiritual experiences and worship of humans. Again we should not understate the importance of the physical basis of such imagery. *Mountains and hills are literally the places where earth touches heaven, and they are also the point from which vision is possible. Numerous religious experiences in the Bible occur on mountains or hills (e.g., *Abraham's encounter with God on Mt. Moriah, Moses' encounters with God on Mount *Sinai, the placing of the *temple on Mount *Zion, Jesus' transfiguration). In fact, one could trace a great deal of salvation history by following the motif of high places through the Bible.

The use of the actual term translated "high place(s)" in the Bible is complex. It essentially refers to an eminence, natural or artificial, where worship by sacrifice or offerings was made. When Canaan was invaded by the Israelites returning from Egypt, cultic sites had been established in numerous high places and were associated with immoral practices. They had features such as standing *stones, *prostitution and other fertility rites, images, and Asherah poles. These negative associations did not devalue the essential concept of using some high places for proper worship any more than the use of *altars in pagan worship made altars themselves inappropriate. Examples of true worship occurring on high places include the sacrifices offered by Samuel (1 Sam 9:12-14); the band of prophets coming down "from the high place" with musical instruments (1 Sam 10:5 RSV; cf. 10:13); Solomon's offering a thousand burnt offerings on Gibeon, "the principal high place" (1 Kings 3:4 NRSV; cf. 2 Chron 1:3); and references to worship on high places under the rule of good kings (e.g., 1 Kings 15:11-14; 22:43).

The archetypal positive high place is *Sinai, where

the law was given by God in awesome circumstances. The "mount" or hill of the Sermon on the Mount (Mt 5—7) symbolically links Christ's message with Sinai as a new law proclaimed by Jesus, a law fulfilling and making perfect and achievable the old. A whole section of the Psalms (120—134) bears the heading of "songs of ascent," meaning that these psalms were sung or recited on pilgrimages to worship God in the temple in *Jerusalem. The opening line of Psalm 121 ("I lift up my eyes to the hills") embodies the pervasive biblical tendency to use the imagery of physical height to express spiritual transcendence.

Although worship on high places is thus not always bad, the seventy biblical references to high places overwhelmingly refer, not to true worship or even necessarily to elevation of site, but rather to pagan shrines used for the worship of idols. The archetypal negative high place, significantly a manmade one, is *Babel, where humankind sought to control heaven. A constant OT theme is the need for God's people to avoid the pagan high places, which were rivals to the true place of worship, which was eventually associated with Jerusalem. In the power struggle between the northern and southern kingdoms, Jeroboam built "houses on the high places" as an alternative focus to Jerusalem (1 Kings 12:31 RSV), making Israel sin because of the lack of ritual purity and the assimilation of pagan elements in such sites.

The battle for the right kind of high place was indicative of the moral and religious struggles of the people, leading to either God's blessing or judgment in history (Deut 27—28). This is why the Bible takes the destruction of unworthy high places so seriously. Gideon is a hero for destroying the altar and *grove of Baal, a heavily symbolic act that roused God's people to purity (Judg 6). A similar symbolic victory is achieved by Elijah on Mount Carmel (1 Kings 18).

Height as an Image of Power and Exaltation. High places also have overtones of dominance, control and lordship, as demonstrated by Babel or by the temptation of Christ upon "a very high mountain" (Mt 4:8, 9). Canaanite seals portray Baal astride mountains, and some texts describe him as "rider of the clouds." The Bible speaks of the true and only God as riding or walking in the heights (Amos 4:13; Mic 1:3). *Battles in the biblical region often took place on hills or mountain slopes. To possess the heights, therefore, gave supremacy (Num 21:28; 2 Sam 1:19, 25). In fact, the association of power with height may further explain the use of elevated sites as shrines.

The imagery of height is implicit in the rich biblical symbolism of exaltation, ascending and being lifted up. The Bible often speaks of God being responsible for exalting people (e.g., Num 24:7; Deut 28:1, 43). Jesus himself went through various stages of exaltation. Rather grimly, he was lifted up on the cross, an act compared by Jesus to the lifting up of the saving effigy of the snake in the wilderness (Jn 3:14, 15). Then his body was raised up from the dead at his resurrection. Finally, Christ went up into the sky in his ascension, sitting down "at the right hand of the Majesty on high" (Heb 1:3 RSV). When Christ returns, we are told, those of his people who are alive then will be lifted up to meet him in the sky, following those raised and lifted up from the dead (1 Thess 4:13-18).

Metaphoric Uses. Height also appears in the Bible as a metaphor. The NT, for example, contains an evocative image pattern built around the phrase "from above." To enter the *kingdom of God one must be "born from above" (Jn 3:7). According to the testimony of John the Baptist, Christ is "the one who comes from above" and is therefore "above all" (Jn 3:31; cf. Jn 8:23). According to James every perfect gift "is from above, coming down from the Father of lights" (Jas 1:17 RSV), and divinely conferred wisdom is "from above" (Jas 3:15, 17).

The greatness of God's loving kindness is as high as the heavens (Ps 103:11). God's ways as compared with human ways are like the height of heaven in comparison to earth's highest mountains (Is 55:9). The immensity of height cannot separate us from God's love (Rom 8:39). The bearer of the good news is beautifully compared with the lights of a town set high on a hill—lights that cannot be blocked from view because of their altitude (Mt 5:14).

See also ALTAR; ASCENSION; ASCENT; COSMOLOGY; DEEP; DESCENT; HEAVEN; MOUNTAIN; NARROW, NARROWNESS; SINAI; WIDE, WIDENESS; ZION.

HIGH PLACE. *See* HIGH, HEIGHT, HIGH PLACE; MOUNTAIN.

HIGH PRIEST. *See* PRIEST.

HIGHWAY. *See* EXODUS, NEW EXODUS; PATH.

HILL. *See* MOUNTAIN.

HIP. *See* THIGH.

HIRELING

A hireling was a *wage earner or day laborer hired (usually on a temporary basis) to perform manual or skilled labor for a specific occasion. The exact nature of the work or service performed varied widely. Day laborers might be hired for general labor (1 Sam 2:5), agricultural work (Lk 15:17, 19), horticultural tasks (Mt 20:1, 7) or even work on a fishing boat (Mk 1:20). Skilled laborers included goldsmiths (Is 46:6), masons and carpenters (2 Chron 24:12), and mercenary soldiers (Judg 9:4). In the Bible the image of the hireling embodies three main meanings: deprivation, transience and self-service.

The lot of a hireling is above all a picture of deprivation and harshness. We can catch the flavor of what it meant to be a hireling by the way in which Deuteronomy 24:14 links the hired worker with the poor, the needy and the alien, and Malachi 3:5 with the widow, the fatherless and the alien. The three

references to hired workers in the parable of the *prodigal son (Lk 15:15, 17, 19) gain their point from our awareness that hired servants were the lowest of three categories of servants—bondsmen (slaves with good family standing), *servants (subordinates of the slaves) and hired servants (hired for the occasion). Because hirelings were prone to exploitation, specific laws were instituted to guarantee their rights (Lev 19:13; Deut 24:14-15). Despite these measures it is clear from the prophets that hirelings were exploited and that this exploitation was one of the reasons that Israel suffered God's judgment (Mal 3:5; Jer 22:13). The image of the hireling as a spectacle of misery is underscored in Job's memorable simile: "Has not man a hard service upon earth, and are not his days like the days of a hireling? Like a slave who longs for the shadow, and like a hireling who looks for his wages, so I am allotted months of emptiness, and nights of misery are apportioned to me" (Job 7:1-3 RSV).

Hirelings also symbolize transience. They lived a hand-to-mouth existence on a subsistence wage. The NIV three times links the hired worker with the "temporary resident" (Ex 12:45; Lev 25:6, 40). When Isaiah wishes to stipulate the brevity of the time before God's judgment will fall upon a nation, he uses the phrase "like the years of a hireling" (Is 16:14; 21:16). Hirelings, being assured of work only as long as a task required them, had no job security. Once the task was completed, they were on their way. The only thing that holds the hireling is the prospect of payment at the end of the day (Job 7:2). This picture of hired servants as day laborers who receive their payment at the end of a day led Jesus to use them in his parable of the workers in the *vineyard (Mt 20:1-16), where it is important to the logic of the parable that people who have worked differing lengths of time receive the same payment.

In negative usages the biblical hireling becomes a symbol of self-service. Hirelings would not work beyond the end of a contract because they had no vested interest in the result of their labor. This is precisely the point in the most ignominious reference to a hireling—the hireling in Jesus' good shepherd discourse who abandons the *sheep when a wolf comes (Jn 10:12-13). The hireling runs because the sheep are not his and he cares only for himself.

See also SHEEP, SHEPHERD; WAGES; WORK, WORKER

HISTORY

Several distinct types of history can be found in the Bible. On the human plane are personal histories or biographies, family histories and national histories (which can be the history of Israel, God's chosen nation, as well as of various pagan nations). The Bible also tells the story of actions in which God is a direct actor or protagonist. As part of his master history, God oversees human histories. This combined history of the Bible, often called "salvation history," is the metahistory of the Bible.

The Bible's picture of history is strongly linear,

moving toward a goal of consummation to be followed by eternity. In all spheres history is given a strongly providential cast, with the outcome of human actions regarded as either produced or influenced by God's activity. Biblical history is also viewed through a moral lens in which people's success or failure is attributed to whether they do good or evil. The primary form in which this history is embodied is narrative, but we also infer history from such genres as law, lyrics, epistles and prophetic utterances. Significant shifts occur as we move from the OT to the NT.

Genre Features. It is safe to say that the ancient world did not regard historical writing in the same way that we view it in the modern era, where history is a largely scientific record of verifiable events, governed by evidence and proof. As modern historical methods emerged in the nineteenth century, modes of criticism sprang up that were suspicious of the biblical text for not conforming to this new genre and for the alleged scientific unreliability of its narrative. Understanding the forms of history in the Bible itself can help to correct some of the misleading claims.

The Bible itself never refers to any of its genres as history. Yet this should not obscure the extent to which the Bible consciously deals with historical events from start to finish. Sometimes the genres advertise their preoccupation with history, as with "chronicles" or genealogies. Certainly there is implicit evidence in the OT of a vocation of court chronicler; and we find references to underlying historical sources, such as the "Book of the Annals of the Kings of Israel," the "Book of the Wars of the Lord" (Num 21:14) or the "Book of Jashar" (Josh 10:13; 2 Sam 1:18). Even narrative sections of the Bible that do not have the feel of official history are rooted in space-time history and deal with events that are recorded as having really happened. The history narrated in these parts of the Bible is virtually never universal or comprehensive. It deals instead with only a short segment of time and is limited to a small group of people. Yet paradoxically this carefully limited history claims to be a complete and sufficient revelation of God's purposes.

Even nonnarrative parts of the Bible that may seem not to be history turn out to be ineluctably historical. The law, for example, is set in the ongoing drama of the flight from Egypt, the search for the *Promised Land and the setting up of a worshiping community. The whole focus of the law is the giving of the covenant on Mt. *Sinai, subsuming the earlier covenants with the patriarchs; and this covenant-giving is an actual event with its own drama of divine manifestation and human failure and dereliction. Furthermore, the way in which the law is given in a historical context and by means of historical narrative suggests that it can be properly understood only within Israel's history, which in turn is evaluated by the standard of the law.

The conquest of the Promised Land and sub-

sequent settlement, *exile and restoration likewise tell the history of a nation. This history is told not only by political writers like Ezra and Nehemiah but also through the prophets, who give us a picture of spiritual and moral history. We cannot understand the decline and fall of Judah and Israel as they were led into exile without the perspective of the prophets Isaiah and Jeremiah. On the other hand, the prophetic witness of Elijah and Elisha is found only in the books of Kings, not in separate books of prophecies; and this history is rightly titled "the former prophets" in the Hebrew Bible because it renders a prophetic interpretation of the history of Israel. The Psalms also include historical accounts that reinforce motifs found in more detail in the narrative sections of the OT.

The prominence of biography—stories about individuals—in the Bible is noteworthy and is itself an important image of biblical history. In the Hellenistic world biographical writing was regarded as a species of history. Biblical history highlights this biographical principle; we tend to remember even the court chronicles partly as a gallery of memorable individuals. The individuals whose lives are thus recorded range from the aristocratic to the common; consequently, both sides of the scholarly debate about whether biblical history is aristocratic or commonplace can find support for their views.

On one side is the view of scholars like Hermann Gunkel and Erich Auerbach that biblical narrative eschews the aristocratic and inclines instead to a democratic view that ordinary people make history. The focus of biblical biography is often on the domestic life of characters, even when they are national leaders. In the folk history of the Bible, many a passage reads like a page from a personal or family diary: "So Isaac departed from there, and encamped in the valley of Gerar and dwelt there. And Isaac dug again the wells of water which had been dug in the days of Abraham his father" (Gen 26:17-18 RSV). It is hardly a matter of national importance that Abraham and Lot had a family quarrel about how to manage their flocks together; that Rebekah's nurse was buried under an oak below Bethel; that Joseph shaved and changed his clothes before going to see Pharaoh; that David, as the family's "gofer boy," took ten loaves to his brothers on front line duty and was put down by his oldest brother when he arrived; or that Benaiah slew a lion in a pit on a day when snow had fallen. Gunkel writes *(The Legends of Genesis)* that "the material of Genesis . . . contains no accounts of great political events, but treats rather the history of a family." The material consists of "anecdotes of country life, stories of springs, of watering-troughs, and such as are told in the bed-chamber." Throughout biblical narrative we find stories that we can envision being circulated within families or among neighbors rather than being recorded in national records. Human greatness of itself is scorned in these private histories. In the NT every major character is either a middle-class person or a member of more impoverished classes, producing a world that Auerbach describes as entirely real, average and ordinary.

At the same time, however, a principle of selectivity is at work in the OT that regards the leaders of a clan or nation as the ones who are most important in the history of a nation. While Abraham is the leader of a family rather than a nation, and a domestic rather than political hero, he is nonetheless important enough in his world to enter into relations with Pharaoh and other leaders. Although the patriarchs are clan leaders, they are also progenitors of a nation, so that in later years people looked back on their biographies as being part of national history. The books of Samuel, Kings and Chronicles bear all the traits of court history, focusing on national leaders and events. Some of the OT prophets are motley figures from obscure backgrounds, but others are from the elite of the court and priesthood. Furthermore, the prophets' recorded exploits tend toward interaction with kings and courtiers.

Although the Bible eschews myth, focusing instead on events in space-time history, it contains within it a genre that parallels ancient myths by being a story of what God does. The *creation story gives us this form of history in its pure form, ascribing all acts in the narrative directly to God as sole actor. However, at any point in the Bible we can find ascriptions of events to the direct activity of God. Partly because of this interpenetration of the divine into the flow of human history, the history of what happens to people and nations is always placed into a broader framework of interpretive significance.

As with modern, secular views of history, biblical history has a cause-effect sequencing. But the causal interpretation of history in the Bible is moral and spiritual rather than strictly political, military or economic. In biblical history no event, no matter how private, commonplace or domestic, is a purely human event. Even the birth of a baby or a shower of rain can be attributed to the *providence of God, and the death of a baby or the failure of a crop can be an expression of God's judgment. History in the Bible is neither fated nor arbitrary. People determine the course of human history and are never the playthings of the gods. The story of Noah's *flood is a judgment on human sinfulness, not the sleep-starved gods' solution to human noise and ruckus (as a Babylonian flood story has it!).

Biblical history was not written in a vacuum but within an awareness of the types of oral and written records that surrounding cultures were producing. The result is combined congruity and incongruity with the surrounding cultures. Sometimes OT writers borrow mythic language and motifs from surrounding pagan cultures, subverting them by ascribing to Yahweh what pagan religions attributed to their gods. Mythic stories of the gods give way to divine and human events in the actual world, and the actions are once-only historical events, not subject to the timeless recurrence of myth. But in other ways biblical history resembles that of nonbiblical cultures.

The OT records the wars and accomplishments of kings in a way that partly parallels the court histories of surrounding nations. Luke begins his Gospel by outlining a historical method that would have seemed familiar to Greek and Roman historians of his day (Lk 1:1-4). Historians used sources both for data and as models, and we should not overlook in this regard the indebtedness of NT writers to OT historians. Thus Luke tells the birth narrative of Jesus in a style and manner that evokes the ethos of the OT, such as the story of the birth of Samuel.

Because history is viewed in the Bible as under God's control, it is confessional—a commemoration and praise of what God has done and an expression of faith in this God who acts. The acts of God are a revelation of his character, an act of "making known" to his people (Ps 103:7). The recital of history expresses a theology of who God is, with emphasis on *judgment and *redemption (Ps 78; 105; 106). The works of God are accordingly not to be forgotten (Ps 78:7) but instead are to be passed on from one generation to another (Ps 78:5-6; 145:4) as a statement of faith. Calling to mind the acts of God is an exercise of private meditation (Ps 77:11-12) as well as of public of worship.

The Old Testament. Within the parameters noted above, four images dominate OT history. One is the *covenant—the agreement that God makes with the human race (Adam and Noah), with the patriarchs, with the nation of Israel (which is both a political and spiritual kingdom) and with David (2 Sam 7:12-16). In the OT the *history of the covenant* is partly a history of promise and fulfillment and at other times of provisional promise that remains unfulfilled because of human disobedience. Covenant history is a narrative of faithfulness and *apostasy, with an accompanying *blessing and *curse of God on individuals and on the nation of Israel. Because of the back-and-forth movement between these two poles, the history of God's covenant dealings is partly a history of *rescue or deliverance of repentant people. We see this pattern of history in microcosm in the book of *Judges, with its repeated cycle of Israel's doing "what was evil in the sight of the LORD," followed by God's subjecting Israel to surrounding nations, followed by national repentance, in response to which God raises up a deliverer who leads the nation out of servitude.

No sharp distinction can be made between this history of the covenant and the *national or political history of Israel* in the OT. This is a story of national destiny, as God delivers the nation from Egypt with a miraculous *exodus and leads it to a *Promised Land. The leading images in this history are victory, wandering, defeat, conquest, settlement, *exile and *restoration. Interspersed with these are the patterns of obedience/blessing, apostasy/judgment and repentance/restoration noted above. National destiny is seen in terms of victory or defeat over enemies. Rebellion, faithfulness and repentance are key motifs of human behavior; whereas mercy, goodness and anger characterize God's actions. If there is a hero, it is God himself (e.g., Ps 145), since the behavior of the nation is more often than not a story of ignominy.

Overlapping the histories of the covenant and the nation is *prophetic history.* This history deals with the same material as the OT narratives, though it fills in some of the gaps with more details than the historical chronicles provide. The prophets speak out of specific historical situations, with a sense of history being made even as they speak. The motifs resemble what we find in biblical narratives, with a focus on past and current apostasy, coming judgment and a promised restoration. God's continuing purposes are emphasized, frequently centered around *Jerusalem. The Mosaic covenant is linked with the Davidic covenant, as in Jeremiah 33:23-36. A very full rehearsal occurs in Ezekiel 20. However, Ezekiel several times moves away from the straightforwardly historical to an allegorical account (e.g., Ezek 16 and 23, where images of prostitution are extremely dramatic). The distinctively new thread in the prophetic books is apocalyptic history, depicting a future time of judgment and redemption. Some of this history is messianic, fulfilled in the incarnation of Christ; some of it predicts future events that stand between Christ's life and the final judgment, which it foreshadows; and some of it leaps all the way forward to the very end of history.

A final image of history in the OT that should not be overlooked in these grandiose movements is the biographical strand, built around the premise of ordinary people with ordinary destinies who matter to God. Some of these *private histories* draw upon larger motifs, as individuals, like the nation, find themselves surrounded by enemies, in need of God's mercy and rescued by God. Sometimes stories of personal testimony of salvation are individual reenactments of national and covenant history. But we also find distinctive motifs, such as individual sin, sickness, defeat, depression and deliverance along the lines of the psalmist's statement that "this poor man cried, and the LORD heard him" (Ps 34:6 RSV).

If we are looking for a synthesis of types of OT history, the book of *Ruth will suffice. It is the biography of an individual but also the history of a family. Although the brief genealogy that concludes the book links the offspring of Ruth and Boaz with "Jesse, the father of David," the story was originally preserved and circulated among family members and neighbors, not at court. This genealogy is a both a patriotic national reference and a messianic reference, making this history of an obscure woman and her family a chapter in salvation history.

The New Testament. NT history presupposes OT patterns and builds on them. Continuity is obvious. Matthew begins his gospel with a genealogy that traces Jesus' lineage back through Hebrew history. When we look at Stephen's defense (Acts 7:1-53) or Paul's sermon at Antioch (Acts 13:16-41), we find the familiar OT figures and historical motifs of covenant and Israelite destiny, God's providence and human rebellion. As might be expected, NT refer-

ences to OT history are especially heavy where the audience is perceived as Jewish. The epistle of Hebrews, with its theological argument dealing with historical precedents to the new Christian faith and its famous list of exempla of faith (Heb 11), is one example among many.

Where the audience is Gentile, more use is made of creation as the sign of God's covenant (Acts 14:15-17; 17:22-31) and of personal testimony (Acts 22:3-21; 26:4-23; Gal 1:13—2:15)—yet both features are typical of the OT as well (as in the Psalms). Even Gentile audiences view the salvation events of their own time through the lens of Israelite history, however. The OT remains the foundational history for the early church as well as for the writers of the Gospels. Similarly, the history of the latter times that we find in NT *apocalyptic writing is cut from the same cloth as OT prophecy of the end times. As we move from OT history to NT history, we find that story shapes story, with NT authors finding the history of Israel (including its prophetic history) to be a fitting schema for telling the new story.

Along with continuity we find innovation as the NT creates its unique history. The most obvious new element is that OT history is viewed as a foreshadowing, and NT history as its fulfillment. The story of God's salvation history is now strongly christological: "In many and various ways God spoke of old to our fathers by the prophets; but in these last days he has spoken to us by a Son" (Heb 1:1-2 RSV). We might speak of NT history as incarnational, focusing on what *Jesus did and taught while he lived on earth. OT motifs of *battle and conquest give way to patterns of Christ's *death and *resurrection. The theological patterns that make up the history of individual believers in the NT are repeatedly rooted in the life of Christ for their historical grounding (1 Cor 15:3-8; Phil 2:5-11; Heb 5:7-9; 13:12).

The second major innovation is that the history of Israel has become a spiritual rather than a political and national entity. The new Israel encompasses Gentile believers rather than the physical descendants of Abraham (Rom 9:6-9), and these Gentile believers obtain the salvation that "Israel failed to obtain" (Rom 11:7). Accordingly, NT history is not the history of a nation but the history of the Christian church. The book of Acts is the central text, but the epistles are likewise set in specific historical situations, as is the book of *Revelation. Like OT covenant history the history of the early church is theologically oriented; but its theology is rooted in the Gospels, not in the patriarchal and national past. It is the history of a kingdom, to be sure; but it is specifically Christ's spiritual and eternal kingdom, not a temporal kingdom in a promised land. Yet it is important to note that this new history is still patterned in terms of covenant mercy, salvation and obedience, working itself out in the spiritual destiny of believer's personal and church lives.

Furthermore, the history of the NT is even more specifically salvific than that in the OT. Whereas OT history ranges over all spheres of life, NT history primarily shows Christ's acts of salvation and the responses of people as they choose or reject Christ. The NT is preeminently the history of the individual soul's choice. These individual stories are more theologically paradigmatic of conversion and redemption, more readily recognizable as the story of Everyman or Everywoman than the OT biographies. Such personal histories are rendered universal by being grounded in Christ's historical death and resurrection, which are viewed as events in which the believer shares (Rom 6:4-5; Col 2:12). We find here a merging of the historical and transhistorical in which individual history merges into universal history.

Summary. Biblical faith differs from many religions by being firmly rooted in history. Biblical history includes numerous interrelated threads, including the personal, the familial, the national and the spiritual. Within the overall linear movement of history from the beginning of the earth to its end, there is also a strongly cyclic pattern involving constant movements from sin to salvation, from apostasy to judgment to restoration, from desolation to deliverance. The Bible certainly takes history seriously. Yet according to the Bible, it is possible to overvalue history. For history, after all, will have an end. At every moment of earthly history, moreover, there is a level of reality that transcends history and that is more real than temporal history (2 Jn 2:17).

See also ACTS OF THE APOSTLES; CHRONICLES, BOOKS OF; GENESIS, BOOK OF; GOSPEL GENRE; JUDGES, BOOK OF; KINGS, BOOKS OF; PROVIDENCE.

HOLINESS

The modern experience of the holiness of God, and consequently the modern understanding of holiness, have been dulled by the tendency to flatten human existence and experience to things rationally discerned. Understanding holiness as it is imaged in Scripture requires that we be open to the rawness of the human experience of God's holiness. Biblical descriptions of holiness tend to be dynamic and emotive.

The Holiness of God. As a fundamental characteristic of God, holiness finds clear expression in the words of the seraphim in Isaiah 6:3: "Holy, holy, holy is the LORD of hosts" (NRSV). The thrice repeated *holy,* a Hebrew idiom for the superlative, conveys the Israelite understanding of Yahweh as the most holy God. This holiness is described and experienced in a number of ways.

The holiness of God, experienced as sheer force, is manifested on those occasions when the deity appears in a *theophany. In texts such as Exodus 3 and 19—20 the presence of God is experienced in *fire, *earthquake, *thunder and *lightning, a loud *trumpet blast, *smoke, dense *clouds, and deep *darkness. Nahum 1 describes the appearance of a holy God with great force:

The mountains quake before him,

and the hills melt;
the earth heaves before him,
  the world and all who live in it.
    (Nahum 1:5 NRSV)

Such manifestations of the holy God present serious risks to those nearby, so precautions must be taken to ensure that the danger posed by God's holy presence is mitigated. At the *burning bush God commands Moses to remove his sandals, "for the place on which you are standing is holy ground" (Ex 3:5 NRSV; cf. 19:10-25). But even with such provisions the theophany of Yahweh is so overwhelming that the Israelites respond with *fear and *trembling (Ex 20:18-19).

Such references to the peril posed by the holiness of God do not necessarily imply any moral judgment on offending parties apart from their inherent profaneness. This is illustrated by the brief narrative about Uzzah's contact with the *ark of the covenant (2 Sam 6:6-8). Stretching out his hand to steady the ark as it teetered on a cart, Uzzah was struck dead. The threat posed by the holiness of the ark, derived from the holiness of Yahweh, may be compared to our modern experience of the nonmoral danger posed by imprudent contact with an electrical current.

Just as the ark of the covenant is holy because of its association with God, so too it is possible for places and days to be holy. Thus Mt. *Sinai and later Mt. *Zion were considered holy because of the presence of Yahweh. Similarly, the Holy of Holies in the *temple, where God was thought to dwell, was so fraught with danger that only the high *priest could enter it and then only once a year. Finally, the *sabbath is holy because of a special association with God (Gen 2:3; Ex 20:8-11).

When we turn to the actions of God in the Bible, they are, of course, the actions of the holy God. A convenient way to characterize them is provided by Exodus 34:6-7, the self-proclamation of God's name and nature:

The LORD, the LORD, a God merciful and gracious, slow to anger, and abounding in steadfast love and faithfulness, keeping steadfast love for the thousandth generation, forgiving iniquity and transgression and sin, yet by no means clearing the guilty, but visiting the iniquity of the parents upon the children and the children's children to the third and fourth generation. (NIV)

In these verses we see a symmetry between God's commitment to *justice and God's *mercy. There is a tendency to see these as contradictory, but the biblical writers hold these actions together as characteristic of the holy God.

Divine holiness allows God the freedom to act in unexpected ways. Thus in Hosea 11:9, after an agonizing reflection on Israel's unfaithfulness (Heb 11:1-8), God determines not to execute justice on Israel, as one might expect, but rather mercy: "for I am God and no mortal, the Holy One in your midst, and I will not come in wrath." Here the holiness of

God becomes the basis for God's freedom to act in gracious ways when one might expect only judgment.

The holiness of God, then, is manifested in a number of ways: in phenomena that we would tend to see as disruptions in nature, in deadly power and in both justice and mercy.

Holiness in the Human Sphere. The experience of God's holiness calls for a human response. It has been suggested that this human response to God's holiness is to be manifested in cleanness, understood in the OT in three different ways: (1) in priestly literature as ritual *cleanness; (2) in the prophets as the cleanness of social justice; (3) in the wisdom tradition as the cleanness of individual morality.

The concern for ritual, social and individual cleanness is united in Isaiah 6:5, where in response to his vision of the holy, divine King, Isaiah exclaims that he is doomed, "for I am a man of unclean lips, and I live among a people of unclean lips; yet my eyes have seen the King, the LORD of hosts" (NRSV). In this cultic setting in the temple, the reference may be simply to ritual uncleanness or may move into the moral and social spheres as a description of the ethical uncleanness of Isaiah and the people of Judah. Isaiah is preserved only by the cleansing act of a seraph touching his lips with a live coal from the *altar. Elsewhere in Isaiah, Judah's failure to exemplify the holiness of God becomes the basis for the divine *judgment of Judah, which the prophet describes. Similarly, in the NT Ananias and Sapphira die as a result of an affront to the holiness of God by their deceit (Acts 5). In this and other contexts the judgment of sin flows from the holiness of God.

The preparation for admission to the presence of God is also found in those texts that scholars designate "entrance liturgies" (e.g., Ps 15; 24). Here the prerequisite for entrance to the temple precincts is to have "clean hands and pure hearts" (Ps 24:4 NRSV). The overlap between the ritual and moral content of such prerequisites is clear.

Priests and prophets were held with special regard in Israel because of their unique contact with God. This contact with the divine gave them special status in the community but also presented special dangers. For example, the public attitude toward prophets was usually ambivalent, in part at least because of the abnormal behavior they sometimes exhibited. This abnormal behavior was attributed to their special contact with God.

It is also possible for communities to be holy. Thus Israel is called to be a holy people (Ex 19:6; Lev 19:2), meaning on the one hand that they are to be different and distinct from other peoples on the basis of their relationship with Yahweh. But there is an added ethical dimension here: there is to be a moral difference in Israel. As a holy people Israel is to reflect the moral holiness of Yahweh its God. Similarly, members of Paul's churches are called "the saints." They are to be holy in character, and their behavior is to reflect their inspiration by the Holy Spirit. Thus Paul's paraenesis has a dual focus: as part of the holy people, Christians are to be holy; this holiness is to reveal itself in abstention from immoral behavior and the manifestation of the gifts of the Spirit.

From Old Testament to New Testament. In the OT, the holy is untouchable by humans. Moses was told to remove his shoes because the ground was holy. The people at Sinai were forbidden to touch the mountain. Moses' face was veiled from human view. The Holy of Holies in the temple was carefully protected from contact by the worshipers, and the high priest performed elaborate rituals before being allowed to enter God's presence.

One cannot help but be struck by the contrast in the NT. With the incarnation of Christ the holy has become touchable. John records that his "hands have touched" the eternal deity (1 Jn 1:1). The masses pressed upon Jesus, and a woman was healed when she touched his garment. The resurrected Jesus invited doubting Thomas to touch his wound prints. At the crucifixion the veil of the temple was rent, making the holy place accessible. Believers now "have confidence to enter the Most Holy Place by the blood of Jesus, by a new and living way opened for us through the curtain, that is, his body" (Heb 10:19 NIV).

Summary. The Bible uses a rich set of images in an effort to capture in some approximation the overwhelming experience of God's holiness. But beyond the pyrotechnics we see divine holiness expressed in the dual concern for justice and mercy. Human response to an encounter with the holy God may take several forms, but ultimately it leads to a transformation of those who enter into the presence of God.

See also CLEANSING; FEAR OF GOD; GLORY; GOD; HOLY SPIRIT; JUDGMENT; JUSTICE; MERCY; PRIEST; PURITY; SACRED SPACE; TEMPLE; THEOPHANY; TOUCHABLE, UNTOUCHABLE.

BIBLIOGRAPHY. J. G. Gammie, *Holiness in Israel: Overtures to Biblical Theology* (Minneapolis: Fortress, 1989); R. Otto, *The Idea of the Holy* (London: Oxford, 1958).

HOLY OF HOLIES. *See* SACRED SPACE; TABERNACLE.

HOLY MOUNTAIN. *See* MOUNTAIN; ZION.

HOLY SPIRIT

The Holy Spirit, the third member of the godhead, fulfills an ongoing but invisible role of connection and communication between people and God. Awareness of the Spirit's presence differs in expression between the OT and NT, but reliance upon it as a signal of the presence of God is constant. Biblical images of the Spirit emphasize the senses, things known best by experiencing them: the force of *wind, the intimacy of *breathing, the instincts of a *dove, the energy of *fire, strong *comfort and the fragrant balm of *oil.

Wind and Breath. The movement created by a breath or wind captures a primary function of the Holy Spirit. In the Hebrew text of the OT the word *rûaḥ* serves to mean either "wind," "breath" or "spirit" and is the normal word for "spirit," including the Spirit of God. Hence the very use of the word sets up resonances between Spirit and wind, and between Spirit and breath. Although in the Greek of the NT *pneuma* more rarely means "wind," the verbal form, *pneō*, means "to blow," and the resonances remain. The common image, which all three meanings share, is that of invisible forces or life energies whose sources cannot readily be observed but whose effects are transparent and sometimes even violent. Here we need to be reminded that wind in the region of Palestine is not always refreshing, cool or gentle. Hot winds from the desert may bring crops to ruin, and underline the fragility and vulnerability of the human sphere to forces which persons cannot control or manipulate. Humans do not create the wind, but it can uproot trees, trace patterns in a field of corn or drive ships.

Like the wind, the creative power of the Holy Spirit is beyond all human ability or comprehension. Wind underlines the fragility and vulnerability of the human sphere to forces that persons cannot control or manipulate. Jesus uses the mystery of the wind's movement to describe the Holy Spirit's creative work in the process of being born again. He seems to use the wordplay or double imagery for Nicodemus: "The wind *[pneuma]* blows *[pnei]* where it wills . . . but you do not know from where it comes . . . so is everyone who has been born of the Spirit *[ek tou pneumatos]*" (Jn 3:8). The issue for Nicodemus is that to be reborn by the agency of the Holy Spirit involves forces and transformations far beyond human capacities or human understanding alone (Jn 3:3-13). It seems appropriate, then, for the coming of the Holy Spirit at *Pentecost to be signaled by a sound "as of a rushing mighty wind" (Acts 2:2 KJV). Like wind, the Spirit comes with a force that cannot be easily resisted by human means, a blowing movement that shapes the hearts of the disciples into courageous forms.

Genesis 1:2 speaks of the *rûaḥ* from God blowing over the face of the waters. Although some translate this as "a wind from God" (NRSV), it is more likely a reference to the Spirit of God. The psalmists also acknowledge the creative power of God's spirit: "When you send your spirit, they are created, and you renew the face of the earth (Ps 104:30 NIV; cf. Ps 33:5). In Genesis 1 the Spirit, "hovering over the waters," brings order and differentiation of roles out of *chaos (*light and *darkness, *land and *sea, *day and *night).

While the historians of the OT record the occurrences of the Holy Spirit's work, the poets and prophets describe his creative power. Echoing God's breathing life into *Adam, Ezekiel gives us the vivid image of the Holy Spirit blowing on the dead and their coming to life (Ezek 37:1-14). In his vision Ezekiel sees a valley of dry *bones grow tendons, flesh and skin at the command of God and then rise to their feet, alive at his breath (Ezek 37:9, 10). Israel will no longer be a mere assortment of "dry bones" (Ezek 37:1, 13). God explains Israel's only hope: "I will put my spirit in you and you will live . . . then you will know that I the LORD have spoken and that I have done it" (Ezek 37:14 NIV). In Zechariah, God gives another reminder: the force of change comes "not by might nor by power, but by my Spirit" (Zech 4:6 NIV).

This accords with a major theme in Paul, the capacity of the Holy Spirit not only to transform but to bring life out of nothing. After ascribing metaphorical *resurrection to the God who "gives life to the dead and calls into existence the things that do not exist" (Rom 4:17, of Abraham's faith relating to the "slaying" of Isaac), Paul explicitly ascribes to the Spirit the power of resurrection (Rom 8:11). The Spirit stands in contrast to human capability alone. Dead people cannot raise themselves. Indeed the physical body will be exchanged for a "spiritual body" (1 Cor 15:44), a mode of existence animated, empowered and characterized by the unhindered operation of the Holy Spirit as agent of new creation and transformation, in this case a transformation into the image of Christ (1 Cor 15:49). In both initial and ongoing ways, "the Spirit gives life" (2 Cor 3:6 RSV), a work associated with strength and power. The Spirit's transformative work can also be described as the "washing of regeneration and renewal in the Holy Spirit" (Tit 3:5-7 RSV).

Images of Personal Relationship. After Jesus ascends to heaven, the Holy Spirit abides within believers, according to Jesus' request that the Father provide a Paraclete for the disciples (Jn 14:26; 16:7 KJV). This Paraclete is one who comes alongside the believer to "guide into all truth" (Jn 16:13 KJV) and to "[help] us in our weakness" (Gk *synantilambanetai*, Rom 8:26 RSV). The Spirit comforts believers by "[testifying] with our spirit that we are God's children" (Rom 8:16). And he is our perfect advocate before a holy God; he intercedes or speaks for us with "groans that words cannot express . . . in accordance with God's will" (Rom 8:26, 27 NIV). The Holy Spirit's role as "Advocate" or "Paraclete" (Gk *paraklētos*) of the believer combines the work of a friend who also frankly tells you what is wrong (it can mean prosecuting counsel, defending counsel or friend), but only so that, once it is exposed, it can be put right. There is nothing enigmatic about the image of a Paraclete. It is part of the Paraclete's comfort and encouragement to dispel illusion but to love us still.

In this context of personal relationship, we find the possibility of wounding the Spirit. In Isaiah 63 the very passage that speaks of the Spirit caring for Israel like cattle in a valley, protecting them from hostile powers like cattle raiders and robbers (Is 63:14), also declares, "they [Israel] grieved his Holy Spirit" (Is 63:10). Ephesians 4:30 likewise urges,

"Do not grieve the Holy Spirit of God" (NIV). These scenes heighten the image of the Holy Spirit as an intimate tutor and caretaker whose heavy investment in our well-being should be honored by obedience.

In ascribing personhood to the Spirit the NT writers open the way for later trinitarian theology. Jürgen Moltmann, the most creative writer on this subject, writes convincingly that the mutuality of oneness and differentiation within the Holy Trinity provides the model for what it is to be truly a "person" for humans: working together in social commonality without absorbing the other's identity into oneself and one's interests. But supplementary language is needed to stress that the Spirit is "supra-personal," not "subpersonal." Some of the church fathers spoke of an "interpenetration" (perichoresis) between the Spirit, Christ and the Father.

Dove. The mystery and motion of wind and breath links us with images of the Holy Spirit as a *bird. The Spirit first appears in Scripture "hovering over the waters," just as a bird might (Gen 1:2 NIV). The initial appearance of the Holy Spirit in Mark's Gospel is at the baptism of Jesus when the Gospel writers agree that the Spirit descended "like a dove" (Mk 1:10; Mt 3:16, 17; Lk 3:22; Jn 1:32, 33). The image of a *dove has little to do with "peace," as it is sometimes mistakenly interpreted. The one whom the Spirit rests will quickly be driven into the *wilderness where he will encounter temptation (Mk 1:12), and he will soon be cast into ministry that is fraught with conflict and controversy. The soft descent of a dove does evoke the movement of the Spirit from heaven "above" to earth "below." The bird imagery may also be meant to echo the Genesis creation narrative and suggest the beginning of a new creation in Israel's Messiah. Others find in the dove a recall of the messenger of good news in the story of the dove returning to Noah with a fresh olive leaf in its mouth (Gen 8:11).

Anointing Oil. Whether for buildings or appointed people, the *oil of *anointing symbolizes the presence of the Holy Spirit throughout Scripture. Things anointed with oil are set apart as holy unto God. Thus God instructs *Moses to create a special anointing oil as the house of Aaron is chosen to serve God in the *tabernacle (Ex 30:25). Precious spices are mixed with olive oil and used to anoint places where the Spirit of God would dwell; everything in the tabernacle is anointed (Ex 40:9), as well as the heads and garments of Aaron and his sons (Ex 29:7, 21; Lev 21:10). Men not individually appointed are specifically prohibited from anointing (Ex 30:32).

According to the psalmist, being anointed with oil signals the presence and favor of God (Ps 23:5; 89:20); the chosen of God are anointed with "the oil of joy" (Ps 45:7). Isaiah explains, "The Spirit of the Sovereign LORD is upon me because the LORD has anointed me to preach good news to the poor . . . to bestow on them a crown of beauty instead of ashes, the oil of gladness instead of mourning" (Is 61:1-3 NIV). Ezekiel describes how rejecting or spurning the Spirit is like using anointing oil for something other than his *worship (Ezek 16:18; 23:41). According to Zechariah's vision, those who stand in the presence of God's *throne are anointed with oil (Zech 4:12). The Holy Spirit abides in vessels dedicated to him, and anointing oil is a symbol of that dedication and identification with him. Paul links anointing and sealing with the gift of the Spirit: "He anointed us, set his seal of ownership on us, and put his Spirit in our hearts as a deposit, guaranteeing what is to come" (2 Cor 1:21-22 NIV).

Pouring Out and Filling. The Spirit of God is not a projection of human religious consciousness. The Bible consistently stresses the Spirit's "otherness" or transcendence. Paul stresses this in 1 Corinthians 2:12: "we have received not the spirit of the world, but the Spirit that is from God" (Gk, to ek tou theou: "the out-of-God One"). Hence biblical writers use what many call "dynamistic" imagery. Ezekiel says "the Spirit fell upon me" (Ezek 11:5). Through Isaiah, Ezekiel and Joel, God promises to "pour out my spirit on your offspring" (Is 44:3), "on the house of Israel" (Ezek 39:27-29) and finally "on all flesh" (Joel 2:28, 29; Acts 2:17). At Pentecost, we read, "all of them were filled with the Spirit" (Acts 2:4). For Paul the Spirit is a "first installment" of more to come (2 Cor 1:22).

First Fruit and Down Payment. Paul uses the metaphors of "first fruit" and "down payment" for the gift of the Holy Spirit. The *first *fruit (aparchē) of the *harvest is literally the first fruit of the crop that comes to ripeness. It is a foretaste of good things to come. In Israel's cultic practice the first fruit was the portion of the harvest or the *flock that was to be dedicated to Yahweh (Deut 16:2; 18:4; Num 18:8-12; Neh 10:35-37; 12:44). But Paul reverses the relationship of giver and recipient. God gives the Spirit to his people as a first fruit of the whole of *salvation that still awaits them (Rom 8:23). The emphasis is on the qualitative: believers can have confidence in the goodness of their salvation because the Spirit represents a portion of what is to come. Indeed, their experience of future *adoption will be just like the Spirit they now possess, but even more so.

The Holy Spirit is also the arrabōn, a first installment, deposit, pledge or a down payment. In a marketplace transaction it represents the portion of the purchase price paid in advance, a payment that guarantees future payment of the whole. In 2 Corinthians 1:22 Paul speaks of the Spirit as the down payment, or "guarantee" (RSV), that God's promises will be true. This guarantee is also a *"seal" (sphragis, sphragizomai), implying God's mark of ownership. In 2 Corinthians 5:5 Paul candidly describes the eschatological tension Christians face as they examine their own mortality ("the earthly tent" that will be "destroyed") while looking forward to their redemption ("a building from God, a house not made with hands, eternal in the heavens," 2 Cor 5:1 RSV). Believers groan with anxiety as they long for this *redemption, and God gives the Spirit as the guarantee of their future resurrection life. Likewise in Ephesians 1:14 the Spirit is God's down payment on the believer's future, an interim gift, a prelude and foretaste of the inheritance that is to come.

Gift, Giver and Fruit Bearer. The Spirit is the enabling power of God who is given as a gift (Acts 1:4; 2:38; 10:45) to the church and multiplies gifts within the church. Although the NT never uses the term "gifts of the Spirit," Paul's association of "gift" language with the Spirit's activity makes this a legitimate image. We need not deliberate over the precise nature of the gifts of the Spirit in order to capture the gist of this image. An abundance of "gracious gifts" *(charismata)* and "things of the Spirit" *(pneumatika)* are associated with the Spirit's activity (Rom 12:6-8; 1 Cor 12:8-10, 27-30; Eph 4:11): miracles, prophecies, "tongues," deeds of service and gifts of ministry, to name but a few. The Spirit is a liberal provider for the church, building it up and enabling it to carry out its life and mission.

Individuals also benefit from the giving and enabling power of the Spirit. Paul, who uses the term "first fruits" for the Spirit, fittingly speaks of the "fruit of the Spirit" in human lives. Those who live by the Spirit are not characterized by the "deeds of the flesh" but by the "fruit of the Spirit" (Gal 5:16-26): "love, joy, peace, patience, kindness, goodness, faithfulness, gentleness and self-control" (Gal 5:22-23 NIV). The Holy Spirit is a personal and regenerative force that bears in human lives the new fruit of the age to come.

Flame and Fire. John the Baptist announces that the one to come after him will baptize Israel with the "Holy Spirit and fire" (Mt 3:11; Lk 3:16). The expression is probably a hendiadys, meaning a deluge of "Spirit-and-fire," and it finds precedent in Jewish texts which allude to the judgment that will accompany the recreative activity of the Messiah (see Turner, 344). *Fire is an appropriate image for a Messiah who would not be entirely gentle but would testify to the coming *judgment of God on an unrepentant Israel and would himself undergo a frightful deluge of judgment at the cross.

With the rushing wind that sweeps through the house at Pentecost, we read of "tongues of fire that separated and came to rest on each" (Acts 2:3 NIV). After this, each is "filled with the Holy Spirit" and speaks with "other tongues" (Acts 2:4). Both wind and fire are common features of theophanies in the Bible (e.g., wind, 2 Sam 22:11, 16; fire, Ex 19:18), and the Jewish writer Philo imagines the voice of God as taking the form of flames when the law is given (Philo *Decal.* 46). Like the image of wind, the tongues of fire suggest a divine power invading the gathered community in Jerusalem. The image of the Spirit as fire is also evoked in a setting where spiritual gifts are being exercised in the midst of the worshiping community at Thessalonica. Paul, in addressing the "testing" of prophecy, instructs the Thessalonians that they must not "quench" the Spirit (1 Thess

5:19). The true activity of the Spirit is subject to discernment, but where it is truly present it should not be snuffed out like a lamp light or a fire.

It is fundamental that each piece of imagery about the Spirit should be allowed to interact with others. Thus, while the creativity of the Spirit may invite attention to novelty, the Holy Spirit's role as the Spirit of truth (Jn 14:17) means that the Spirit's action will remain coherent and self-consistent from age to age and from place to place.

See also ANOINTING; BREATH; DOVE; FIRE; FIRST; FRUIT, FRUITFULNESS; GOD; OIL; WIND.

BIBLIOGRAPHY. G. D. Fee, *God's Empowering Presence: The Holy Spirit in the Letters of Paul* (Peabody, MA: Hendrickson, 1994); J. Moltmann, *The Spirit of Life* (London: SCM, 1992); M. M. B. Turner, "Holy Spirit," *DJG* 341-51.

HOME, HOUSE

"Home Sweet Home" has become a sentimental cliché, but it still expresses that longing, even when the reality is not so sweet. The Anglican Alternative Service Book (1980) contains a well-loved prayer that begins "Father of all, we give you thanks and praise, that when we were still far off you met us in your Son and brought us home."

If some kind of *house* is necessary for human physical survival, a *home* is necessary for human fulfillment—emotionally, mentally and spiritually. This convenient modern distinction between *house* (implying "nothing but a building") and *home* (implying "where and with whom I belong") was not always made by preliterate societies. So *house* and *home* are frequently used interchangeably in the Bible. In fact the English "home/house" translates a rich variety of words in both Hebrew and Greek.

Old Testament. *Tent.* The word used, for example, in Judges 19:9, 2 Samuel 20:1 and 2 Kings 13:5 means "tent" in English, which spotlights the origin of the Hebrew people. They were a nomadic, *wandering people, and their homes were portable. The story of humankind as told in the OT is full of people being made homeless or wandering in deserts. *Adam and *Eve were banished from the best home imaginable (Gen 3:23-24). *Cain became a fugitive after killing his brother (Gen 4:14). The race's founding father, *Abraham, traveled from (modern) Iraq to Egypt and back to Canaan and may never have lived in a house ("My father was a wandering Aramean," Deut 26:5 NIV; but cf. his residence in Gerar, Gen 20:1), and the only land he owned was a family burial plot at Machpelah (Gen 23). The chosen people were exiled in Egypt, and the forty years of desert wandering under Moses vividly portrays a people whose home is (perforce) the desert; able to survive in tents, yet all the while yearning for their real home, the *Promised Land.

To complete the story the Israelites were to be uprooted again, after a few centuries of settled life in their homeland. The exiles in Babylon longed for home ("By the rivers of Babylon we sat and wept when we remembered Zion. . . . How can we sing the songs of the LORD while in a foreign land?" Ps 137:1, 4 NIV). Not only their home but also their God seemed far away.

So the Hebrew house was originally a tent, and the Hebrew way of life was unsettled, longing for a home. This longing was naturally focused on God ("make the Most High your dwelling" Ps 91:9 NIV).

Resting place. The *dove, venturing from the ark, could find "no resting place for the sole of her foot" (Gen 8:9 NKJV). The word is used in Numbers 10:33 of a place where the Israelites could rest on their journey. In Ruth 3:1 it is a home, a place where she would be provided for. The image is of relief from struggle, taking a deep breath and relaxing in security.

Place to lie down. Linked with the above is a word used of the animal world in Isaiah 65:10 and Proverbs 24:15, where people are seen as part of the animal kingdom in need of a lair (*see* Den).

Place to return to. The word implying "brought back" is used of home in Ruth 1:21 (and 1 Sam 18:2; 2 Sam 14:13; Job 39:12). The same word in Isaiah 30:15 is translated "in returning and rest shall ye be saved" in the KJV. The NIV favors "repentance." The idea throughout is of the satisfaction of returning home after being away.

Home/House. The usual words for home/house appear, as we might expect, hundreds of times in the OT. The meaning is often house (i.e., the building) as in Exodus 9:19-20, where the need is to get the cattle indoors because of the forthcoming plague of hail. Leviticus 18:9 uses *home* in the sense of family dwelling. The general idea of "home" and "at home" appears frequently (e.g., Gen 43:26; Deut 24:5; 2 Kings 14:10). *House,* meaning "household," appears first in Genesis 18:19 and often thereafter. It usually means the whole of the domestic staff as well as the family. It is used to mean "dynasty," as in the "house of David" (e.g. 1 Kings 12:19).

Eternal home. Ecclesiastes 12:5 sees death as our "eternal home." The emphasis is on finality: once you get there, you will never come back. For the image of death as the passage to a welcome home, we have to await the NT.

God's house. "I rejoiced with those who said to me, 'Let us go to the house of the LORD' " (Ps 122:1 NIV). The Jerusalem *temple was a place of pilgrimage because it was where God had chosen to be (Deut 12:4-5; 1 Kings 8:29; 2 Kings 23:27). Not that Israel's God was a mere localized spirit: "The heavens, even the highest heaven cannot contain you. How much less this temple I have built!" says Solomon (1 Kings 8:27 NIV). But that lofty view was difficult to maintain in the midst of the Canaanites and Philistines who worshiped other gods. Had God not been specially present in the tabernacle and the ark of the covenant? In Exodus God commands to Moses, "Then have them make a sanctuary for me, and I will dwell among them" (Ex 25:8 NIV). And

later symbolism of God's presence with the ark of the covenant is evident: "Let us bring the ark of the LORD's covenant from Shiloh, so that it [or 'he'] may go with us and save us from the hand of our enemies" (1 Sam 4:3 NIV; 1 Sam 4:1-7:1; 2 Sam 6). Isaiah, however, echoes Solomon: "Heaven is my throne, and earth is my footstool. Where is the house you will build for me?" (Is 66:1 NIV). God was at home both on earth and in heaven. The OT thus foreshadows the Incarnation.

Other references. The word *house* can mean circumstances or living conditions as in Exodus 13:3 and Deuteronomy 5:6 ("the house of bondage" KJV; "land of slavery" NIV). Another unusual use refers to one's character or reputation (e.g., "her house leads down to death" [Prov 2:18]).

New Testament. There is no sharp break between the OT and NT use of home/house in the everyday sense; however, the Christian church began to use the image to apply to itself, and the revelation of eternal life was seen as the final and ideal home.

My place. The word used in John 1:11; 16:32; 19:27; 20:10 and Acts 21:6 suggests "one's own (place)," where one has a right to be expected. In John 1:11 Jesus, the "Word made flesh," has a right to be at home with his own people but is rejected. Titus 2:5 uses another word which implies *remaining* at home.

Household. Family extends to "home" and *"household" (Mt 8:6; 10:25; Lk 10:5; 15:16; Acts 16:31-34; 1 Cor 11:34; 14:35). Hospitality is enjoined in 1 Timothy 3:2, and there is a good example of it in Acts 16:15.

Body. The human *body is our home. This is the context of the parable of the evil spirit (Mt 12:44; Lk 11:25). Paul extends the metaphor in 2 Corinthians 5:1-10. Our body is our "earthly *tent" but while we are "at home in the body" (2 Cor 5:6), we are away from the Lord. If we are preoccupied with selfish concerns, we leave no room for God in our lives. Paul extends this picture in describing the spiritual builder in 1 Corinthians 3:10-15. The Christian's body is a house for God to live in (Jn 14:23; 1 Cor 3:16-17; 6:19-20; Eph 3:17). So Christians, in the plural, form the household of God, God's family on earth.

The church, the household of God. The church is both God's home on earth (Mk 13:34-35) and our home as members of his household (Eph 2:19; 1 Tim 3:15; 2 Tim 2:20-21; Heb 3:6, 10-21). We are a spiritual house, built with living *stones (1 Pet 4:17). The private house was literally the house of God in being a place of worship in the early church (see Acts 2:46).

The world. The idea of household management extends to stewardship and economy (from the Greek word *oikos,* "house") and then further to "stewardship of the world," and then it becomes a word for "the *world" itself. It is used in this sense, for example, in Matthew 24:14 (and Lk 2:1, 4:5; Acts 17:6; Rom 10:18; Heb 1:6; Rev 16:14).

Heaven. Jesus gives us a heart-warming glimpse of the life to come in God's house (Jn 14:1-4). The house is full of rooms prepared for us to live in. This holds out a positive view of life after death that far outshines the "long home" of Ecclesiastes 12:5. In the Father's house are summed up all the longings of the human race for a secure and settled future. The "hopes and fears of all the years" are embraced in the ultimate ideal home, a picture mirrored by J. R. R. Tolkien in his description of Rivendell in *The Lord of the Rings*.

Jesus at home. Jesus was born in Bethlehem, but his childhood home was Nazareth (Mt 2:23). He seems to have lived for a time in Capernaum (Mk 2:1). He was obviously very much "at home" with Martha, Mary and Lazarus in Bethany (Jn 11).

In a wider sense, Jesus saw the world as his home ("his own people," Jn 1:11), but he was never settled. "The foxes have holes and the birds of the air have nests but the Son of Man has no place to lay his head" (Mt 8:20 NIV). This was true of his way of life but also reflects his yearning to be in his true home at the Father's *right hand (Heb 12:2). Jesus called his followers to leave their homes (Lk 18:29-30). Paul warns us that it is possible to be too much at home in the everyday world (2 Cor 5:6), and the writer to the Hebrews reminds us that "here we do not have an enduring *city" (Heb 13:14 NIV). Jesus was totally "at home" wherever he was. His disciples find that a difficult act to follow!

Conclusion. Against a background of nomadic life, the biblical images of home and house tend to emphasize security and appropriateness. It is interesting that in secular thought, at least from Plato on, home has been seen as that which is private and distinct from public or political. The home was the domain of the female and the children rather than the male. It was denigrated, seen as unimportant, not the focus of life as it should be. A "stay-at-home" is a weakling; a "homebird," an unadventurous person; the kitchen sink and the hot stove, targets of feminist anger.

To these negative views of home we have to add the influence of modern transport and general mobility, which is creating a rootless society. Many people live out of suitcases in hotel rooms and do not know where home is. Mix in wars, which have made millions homeless, and we have a cocktail of homelessness and rootlessness that threatens to shatter society altogether.

It is not surprising that fundamentalist nationalism is on the increase. Ethnic groups demand a return to their roots, a defense of their land. Human beings need home, somewhere they know that they belong. To destroy the concept of home is to destroy humanity itself.

See also DEN; FOREIGNER; HEAVEN; HOMECOMING, STORIES OF; HOSPITALITY; HOST, GOD AS; HOUSEHOLD; PROMISED LAND; TABERNACLE; TEMPLE; TENT; WANDERER, WANDERING.

BIBLIOGRAPHY. M. Lurker, "Haus" and "Fels," in *Worterbuch Biblischer Bilder Und Symbole* (Munchen, 1973); J. H. Elliott, *A Home for the Homeless: A Sociological Exegesis of 1 Peter, Its Situation and Strategy* (Philadelphia: Fortress, 1981); K. A. Rabuzzi, "Home," *Encyclopaedia of Religion*. New York: MacMillan, 1987).

HOMECOMING, STORIES OF

American novelist Thomas Wolfe wrote a novel that proclaimed *You Can't Go Home Again*, but the stories of the human race are nonetheless replete with homecoming stories of people who *did* go home again. Storytellers and audiences love stories of homecoming for their emotional potential. Homecoming stories are far from uniform, for depending on the situation, a homecoming can evoke anticipation, joy, fear, sorrow, nostalgia or rejection.

The Bible does not contain an abundance of homecomings (being essentially a book about sojourning), but the ones that are present are memorable. The archetype behind all homecomings is the story of Genesis 2—3. Ever since the human race was expelled from a perfect *garden—its original state— it has lived in a state of restless *exile and has longed to return to its original home. Individual and collective homecomings are simply variations on the original text.

The first homecoming recorded in the Bible is the return of Noah and his family to dry land after the flood. The second is *Jacob's return to the land of his youth after a twenty-year sojourn in Haran. The motif of homecoming is present by its suppression in the story of the family reunion between *Joseph and his family, which occurs not in the homeland but in Egypt, though the human dynamics in this story of a family reunion are those of a homecoming story. The alien setting leads Joseph to extract a deathbed oath that his bones will be returned to Palestine. Other stories of individual homecomings in the OT include the return of *Moses to Egypt after sixty years in Midian, a bitter Naomi's return to Bethlehem (Ruth 1:19-22) and Gomer's return to *Hosea.

More prominent are the OT stories of national homecoming. After Israel's long exile in Egypt, the entry of the nation into the *Promised Land is a homecoming of sorts, even though the patriarchs had never actually owned the land of Palestine. Secondly, the return of a remnant after the Babylonian exile is experienced strongly as a homecoming. Also, in a metaphoric sense, the cycle of Israel's *apostasy followed by return to God and right worship is like a series of spiritual homecomings.

The most explicit homecoming story in the NT focuses on *Jesus' homecoming to his home town of Nazareth. It is portrayed as a disappointing experience, for people who know him refuse to accept him as more than the son of the local carpenter and of Mary (Mt 13:54-58; Mk 6:1-6; Lk 4:16-30). The experience even produced one of Jesus' classic aphorisms—"A prophet is not without honor except in his own country and in his own house" (Mt 13:57

RSV). In a more generic sense the experience of the incarnate Christ in coming to the human race was a kind of homecoming that produced two responses. The *Christ hymn that opens John's Gospel provides an exposition on this. The very world that Christ created "knew him not" (Jn 1:11). In his incarnation Christ "came to his own home, and his own people received him not" (Jn 1:11). But there were also those "who received him, who believed in his name" (Jn 1:12).

The most famous homecoming story in the Bible is without doubt the story of the *prodigal son's return to his home and father after a journey of rebellion, rejection of parental values, dissolute behavior and destitution (Lk 15:11-32). The actual homecoming is richly visualized: the father catches sight of his son "while he [is] yet at a distance" (NIV) and runs to meet him; he embraces him and kisses him (Lk 15:20). The celebration too is narrated in relative detail (Lk 15:22-24). This is how a homecoming ought to be orchestrated, we tell ourselves. And through it all we have the emotions proper to a homecoming, from the prodigal's sense of having returned a failure to the father's relief and joy that his son is back to the older brother's resentment at the attention that has been lavished on an unworthy upstart brother who has returned.

The believer's translation to *heaven is also viewed as a homecoming in a famous eschatological vignette. Jesus portrayed heaven as a stately "house with many rooms," which he described as a place that he will prepare for his followers, promising to take them to himself (Jn 14:1-4).

See also EXILE; HEAVEN; HOME, HOUSE; PRODIGAL SON; RETURN; REUNION, RECONCILIATION.

HOMOSEXUALITY

The Bible rarely speaks about homosexual behavior. Accounts of intended homosexual rape in Sodom (Gen 19) and Gibeah (Judg 19) use no images, but they tell the stories with harsh and disturbing narratives that prove to be quite evocative for the rest of the canon. From Genesis, *Sodom becomes an image for gross immorality in 2 Peter 2:6-8 and Jude 7; but in such contexts as Isaiah 1 and Ezekiel 16, the Sodom symbol refers rather to all injustices, including *adultery and neglect of the poor. Certainly, in terms of imagery the Bible does not have the category "homosexuality," but rather "homosexual behavior" or "homosexual acts." In fact, homosexuality as an "identity" is arguably a modern construction.

Leviticus 18:22 proscribes the act of a male lying with another male, classifying it as an "abomination" or "detestable thing." The Hebrew word comes from the root "to abhor," and the image emphasizes both ritually and ethically God's call to reject such behaviors. Leviticus 18 also includes commands against incest, adultery, sacrificing children to Molech and intercourse with animals as similar examples of "defilement" of God's land and people. The chapter's concluding warning entails imagery of the land spewing out those who have made it unclean with their *abominations.

Under the overarching figure of "bloodguiltiness" (that persons are responsible for their own death), Leviticus 20 commands the death penalty for various sexual immoralities, including the "abomination" of males lying together. The images of defilement, land spewing out uncleanness and bloodguiltiness are particularly strong in this section of Leviticus that modern scholars have named the "Holiness Code" (Lev 17—26).

Similarly, when Paul uses the image of not inheriting the *kingdom of God to describe ten kinds of "unrighteous" people (1 Cor 6:9-10), he includes *malakoi* (the "soft" or passive participants in homosexual acts) and *arsenokoitai* (the active instigators— a graphic term for "those who perform male coitus") as well as thieves, drunkards and the covetous. Likewise, 1 Timothy 1:9-10 adds *arsenokoitai* to liars and perjurers in listing more than a dozen "rebellious" types for whom the law is made. This image insists that everyone needs the law (for we all rebel against God) and drives us to the gospel announced in 1 Timothy 1:9-11.

The most important imagery for homosexual acts is the language in Romans 1 of "exchanging" God's purposes and of God letting go. Some dishonored God by substituting idols for God; therefore, God "gave them up" to their own lusts (Rom 1:18-25). Others God "gave up" to their depravities, such as envy, gossip and arrogance. Romans 1:26-27 declare that God gave over to their degrading passions both women and men who "exchanged" natural functions for unnatural. These three image sets are examples of warning, for Romans 2:1 insists that everyone is without excuse since all practice such rebellion against God.

While references to homosexual acts are quite limited in Scripture, they become a powerful image for those who in their blindness have given up God's good gift of healthy sexuality and have exchanged it for something degrading and unnatural. Homosexual acts become a symbol in Scripture for violating a basic principle of holiness: mixing that which the Lord declared should be separate.

See also ABOMINATION; MAN, IMAGES OF; PURITY; SEX; WOMAN, IMAGES OF.

HONEY

In biblical times honey was known for its sweetness (Judg 14:14; Ps 19:10; 119:103; Prov 24:13; Ezek 3:3; Rev 10:9-10) and its medicinal qualities (Prov 16:24). It was considered a delicacy and was sometimes presented as a valued gift (Gen 43:11; 1 Kings 14:3; 2 Chron 31:5; Ezek 16:13, 19; 27:17). For these reasons honey often indicated or symbolized *abundance and *prosperity (Deut 32:13; Job 20:17; Ps 81:16; Jer 41:8). At least twenty times (e.g., Ex 3:8, 17; 13:15) the OT calls the Promised Land of Palestine a *"land flowing with milk and honey" (NIV), a description that appears to be a stock expression for a land abounding in *pasture land and flowering *plants. It is possible that the syrup of the date *palm, rather than the honey of wild bees, is in view here (see KB^3, 213 and Borowski, 127). If so, then honey suggests agricultural abundance (Deut 8:8; 2 Kings 18:32).

Isaiah ironically reverses this symbolism when he prophesies that the sign-child Immanuel will soon eat curds and honey (Is 7:15). Initially one might think the prophet is encouraging Ahaz and his court by foretelling a time of prosperity and divine blessing, but he quickly makes it clear this is not the case. Foreign nations will invade the land and devastate its crops, forcing Immanuel and other survivors to subsist off the land (Is 7:22). In this harsh setting honey becomes a symbol of deprivation and judgment. When Immanuel eats the wild honey he finds in the fields, he will be reminded of the consequences of rebellion against God and of the importance of obedience. (Is 7:5 might be paraphrased, "Curds and honey he will eat, so that he might learn to reject what is wrong and to choose what is right.") Honey is also associated with deprivation in Matthew 3:4 (see also Mk 1:6), which identifies John the Baptist's diet as consisting of locusts and wild honey. Like Elijah of old, John is an example of self-denial to a society desperately in need of repentance and spiritual renewal.

Biblical authors sometimes use the image of eating honey to refer to pleasurable experiences. The wise father of Proverbs encourages his son to temper his enjoyment of life (symbolized by eating honey) with *wisdom (Prov 24:13-14), and warns that pleasure ("honey") must be pursued in moderation (Prov 25:16, 27; 27:7). In the love song attributed to Solomon, eating honey symbolizes *sexual pleasure (Song 4:11; 5:1; cf. Prov 5:3). When *Samson finds honey in the lion's carcass on the eve of his wedding (Judg 14:8-9), he may be viewing it as an omen of the sexual pleasure that will soon be his. Perhaps he considers it an aphrodisiac that will invigorate him for the marriage chamber. (On the physically invigorating powers of honey, see 1 Sam 14:26, 29; 2 Sam 17:29.) Prophetic spokesmen for God compare their reception of divine revelation to eating honey (Ezek 3:3; Rev 10:9-10; cf. Ps 119:103).

See also LAND FLOWING WITH MILK AND HONEY; SWEET.

BIBLIOGRAPHY. O. Borowski, *Agriculture in Iron Age Israel* (Winona Lake, IN: Eisenbrauns, 1987); S. D. Waterhouse, "A Land Flowing with Milk and Honey," *AUSS* 1 (1963) 152-66.

HONOR

Honor is a biblical term for respect, esteem, high regard and reward. It appears nearly 150 times in the English Bibles. Honor can be seen as an image for respect paid to superiors: God (2 Sam 2:30; 1 Tim 1:17), Christ (Jn 5:23), the emperor (1 Pet 2:17), church officers (Phil 2:25, 29), the elderly (1 Tim 5:1-3) or parents (Ex 20:12; Eph 6:2). Honor can also be something bestowed as a reward for virtuous behavior: for honoring God (1 Sam 2:30) or serving Christ (Jn 12:26); for manifesting wisdom (Prov 3:16), graciousness (Prov 11:16), discipline (Prov 13:18), humility (Prov 15:33), peaceableness (Prov 20:3), righteousness and mercy (Prov 21:21). Biblical images of honor also include examples of persons whose achievements bring honor to them: Joseph (Gen 41:41-43), Phinehas (Num 25:7-13), Joshua (Num 27:18-20), Solomon (1 Kings 3:13), Abishai (1 Chron 11:20-21), Daniel (Dan 2:48), Mordecai (Esther 8:15) and the apostles (Mt 19:27-29).

To honor someone or something is to acknowledge and show respect for the authority or worthiness of the object of one's honor. To show honor entails an affective side (a feeling of respect or reverence) and a set of outward manifestations, such as gestures (*bowing before or being attentive) or actions (conferring titles or privileges). All these ways of showing honor elevate the person or thing that is honored. In addition to the primary meaning, honor is used in the Bible to name something possessed by certain people or things as an innate quality.

Honor, moreover, is viewed from both external and internal perspectives. Outwardly, honor encompasses rank, wealth or public respect. Inwardly, it means nobility and integrity of mind and character. In the OT these meanings occasionally merge, for often when God blesses Israel, he expects the two kinds of honor to go hand in hand. Indeed, when the nations or individuals disappoint God with a dishonorable character, God often deprives them of their public tokens of esteem. However, the NT authors draw a sharp distinction between the two forms of honor, declaring that because the world is corrupt, those whom it honors are usually corrupt themselves. Therefore the NT suggests that the proper honor to seek is honor of character, which will reap public dishonor on earth but public acclaim in heaven.

OT Images of Honor. An important OT theme is that all humans are endowed with an innate honor by virtue of their creation in the image of God. While we might infer this from the creation story, it is stated overtly in Psalm 8:5, which claims that God has made people "a little lower than God, and crowned them with glory and honor" (NRSV). Hebrews 2:7 quotes this passage with approval.

For women in biblical times, honor is essentially bound up in the bearing of children. *Barrenness is the height of disgrace, even greater than a woman's personal physical unattractiveness (which was also an important factor in a woman's acclaim). Leah believes this so sincerely that she hopes that Jacob will honor her after she bears six sons for him; her sister is so convinced of it that she tells Jacob she will die if she cannot bear a child (Gen 30:20). Hannah, the mother of Samuel, is loved by her husband but still finds life to be painful as a barren woman. For such women, having children means the respect, dignity and security equivalent to financial success for men.

For biblical men, honor is more complicated. Sometimes honor means a wisdom and intelligence worthy of acclaim by others, a characteristic men such as *Solomon possesses. Honor is sometimes a function of political or social position, often earned by the possession of *wisdom or character: *Joseph, Mordecai and *Daniel all act as important leaders in the courts of foreign kings by virtue of their trustworthiness and good advice. A third kind of honor is the honor possessed by those with wealth, glory and fame, such as Solomon and Nebuchadnezzar. Such honor is also the most superficial and fleeting.

Moral Foundations. The book of Proverbs suggests the connection between behavior and the receiving or conferring of honor. Examples include statements like these: "Whoever pursues righteousness and kindness will find life and honor" (Prov 21:21 NRSV); "The reward for humility and fear of the LORD is riches and honor and life" (Prov 22:4 NRSV); "It is not good to eat much honey, or to seek honor on top of honor" (Prov 25:27 NRSV); "Like snow in summer or rain in harvest, so honor is not fitting for a fool" (Prov 26:1 NRSV); "It is like binding a stone in a sling to give honor to a fool" (Prov 26:8 NRSV); "A person's pride will bring humiliation, but one who is lowly in spirit will obtain honor" (Prov 29:23 NRSV).

Divine Justice as a Foundation. Throughout the Bible God demonstrates his desire that people conform to his system of honoring, both by revering God and by aspiring to his value system themselves. This theme occurs again and again in the OT as God tries to show his people that blessings come from him and that the only way to receive them is paradoxically to humble themselves and honor God. God declares this very succinctly in his condemnation of Eli: "Those who honor me I will honor, and those who despise me shall be treated with contempt" (1 Sam 2:30 NRSV). This is a repeated lesson of the OT, though God's people are slow to learn it.

One of the clearest examples of this can be seen in the parallel stories of Saul and *David. Saul is eager to obtain honor for himself and uninterested in paying respect to God. When Samuel tells him to destroy all of the spoil and people of Amalek, Saul keeps the king and some of the best spoils for himself. When confronted by his sin Saul shows a characteristic unconcern for God's honor and a preoccupation with his own public image. He says to Samuel, "I have sinned; yet honor me now before the elders of my people and before Israel, and return with me so that I may worship the LORD your God" (1 Sam 15:30). For his disregard of God and overriding desire to build himself up before his public, God revokes Saul's *crown, giving it to a man who had God's own system of honor.

David, by contrast, is so zealous to honor God that when the ark is returning to Jerusalem during his rule, he strips down to a scanty garment before all the people and dances "with all his might before the LORD." His wife Michal, disgusted with this public display, ridicules David, sneering, "How the king of Israel has honored himself today . . . [behaving] as any vulgar fellow." To her derision David replies that his dancing was for the Lord. God's treatment of both people involved demonstrates his opinion on the issue: whereas Michal bears the disgrace of never bearing children, David is given the honor of having an everlasting kingdom (2 Sam 6:14-23 NRSV). God promises that he will "raise up your offspring after you, one of your own sons, and . . . I will establish his throne forever" (1 Chron 17:11-12 NRSV). God is pleased by David's *humility and praise of him.

Nevertheless, even those to whom God had given the worldly honors of power, fame and riches must learn the boundaries of his goodness. Again and again God teaches the rulers of both Israel and other nations that their honor on earth must be accompanied by humility, since God has given the honor in the first place. Thus the OT is a testimony to the fact that ultimately God alone is the possessor of honor and worthy of being honored. When God ends the disgrace of Hannah's barrenness, giving her a much-longed-for son, she voices this important biblical doctrine: "[God] raises up the poor from the dust; he lifts the needy from the ash heap, to make them sit with princes and inherit a seat of honor. For the pillars of the earth are the LORD's" (1 Sam 2:8 NRSV). Echoing this theme the psalmist confidently declares, "On God rests my deliverance and honor," because God himself is "full of honor and majesty" (Ps 62:7; 111:3). Psalm 50:23 ties all these verses together: those who have honor must thank God for it, for "those who bring thanksgiving as their sacrifice honor me" (NRSV).

The Command to Honor. In addition to using the word *honor* as a noun, the Bible also uses it as a verb. The Bible is filled with injunctions to honor various things. Above all, of course, the believer is commanded to honor God with obedience and love. However, the Bible deems many other parties to be worthy of honor. Among these are the elders of the NT church, anyone in a position of authority over an individual (such as a slave's master) and the state of marriage (1 Tim 5:17; 6:1; Heb 13:4).

The most repeated command of all of these is to honor one's father and mother. This command is first given to Israel by Moses, and Jesus reiterates it, declaring the evil hypocrisy of the Pharisees who use their laws to keep people from doing so (Ex 20:12; Mt 15:4). In fact, the command is so important to God that any Israelite who curses or strikes a parent is to be put to death (Ex 21:7). Parents and other authority figures are types, in individuals' lives, of God's ultimate authority; therefore, God holds it to be extremely important that his people offer them respect by obedience and outward manifestations of esteem.

New Testament Developments. In contrast to God's often immediate punishment of pride with dishonor in the OT, the NT sets up the antagonism between the honor of good character and the honor of prestige. God especially condemns the Pharisees, who, like OT figures such as Balaam and Saul, loved the approbation of men more than the praise of God (Mt 23:6). Unlike these figures the Pharisee's pride will not be rewarded with shame until Christ comes again (Lk 14:7-10). Thus the NT declares that the only way to earn eternal "praise and glory and honor" is to cultivate a genuine and thriving faith, so that "by patiently doing good" (1 Pet 1:7) we will receive eternal life (Rom 2:7). Such eternal glory can only be gained at the expense of honor on earth, for Christ guaranteed his disciples that the one who loves him will be despised by the world (Jn 15:19). Therefore, dishonor by man and honor by God are an inevitable pair.

In ancient societies, honor is tied up with hierarchical social and political structures. The NT is more democratic than this, viewing honor as something of which all people are potentially worthy. Paul in addressing the church at Corinth is mindful of their struggle for honor according to the conventions of Greco-Roman society. Paul eschews the honor of worldly wisdom and power for the *"folly" and *"weakness" of the cross (1 Cor 1:18—2:5). For God has chosen the foolish and weak things of the world "to shame" the wise and strong (1 Cor 1:27). The quest for honor has led the Corinthians to lawsuits among believers. But Paul sets a different standard for honor in which struggles for honor through lawsuits are shameful (1 Cor 6:5) and being cheated or wronged is honorable. Within the body of Christ, as opposed to the civic body of Corinth, the less honorable members are treated with special honor, for God "has given greater honor to the parts that lacked it" (1 Cor 12:22-24).

Sometimes the word love is used as a synonym for honor. Paul tells the Romans to "love one another with mutual affection; outdo one another in showing honor" (Rom 12:10). The highest example of such honor is the example of Christ: in washing the disciples' feet he pays them the honor of service, of subjecting his own priorities to their interests. Such honoring of others is tied up with humility, which, as stated above, is the method of obtaining true honor—both honorable character and honorable distinctions in eternity.

Summary. Honor is a biblical image for the esteem and high regard due to God, to all human beings and, in a special sense, to human beings like parents, the elderly and those in authority. In addition to didactic passages that explain and enjoin legitimate honor, biblical images of honor include examples of persons whose characterizations represent them as having achieved honor.

See also GLORY; SHAME.

BIBLIOGRAPHY. B. Malina, The New Testament World: Insights from Cultural Anthropology (Atlanta: John Knox, 1981); H. Moxnes, "Honor, Shame, and the Outside World in Paul's Letter to the Romans" in The Social World of Formative Christianity and Judaism, ed. J. Neusner et al. (Philadelphia: Fortress, 1988) 207-18.

HOPE

Although the word hope appears more than 150 times in English translations, the imagery surrounding it is less plentiful. Even as an abstraction, however, hope has some of the vigor of an image when it appears in the evocative triad of faith, hope and love (1 Cor 13:13) and as the climactic item in a catalog of the virtues produced by suffering (Rom 5:4-5). The essential quality of hope is that it is oriented to something in the future that one expects but does not yet possess (Rom 8:24-25).

The abstraction begins to assume some of the concreteness of an image when we observe the prepositions with which hope is linked in the Bible. We read that people hope in God or Christ (a dozen references), God's steadfast love (Ps 33:18; 147:11), God's word (Ps 119:81, 114, 147; 130:5) and the promise of God (Acts 26:6). Biblical writers set their hope on God (Jer 14:22; 1 Tim 5:5), Christ (Eph 1:12) and "the grace that Jesus Christ will bring you when he is revealed" (1 Pet 1:13 NRSV). They hope for God's salvation (Ps 119:166) and a future *restoration from *exile (Jer 31:17). We also read about the hope of God (Jer 17:13), the *resurrection of the dead (Acts 23:6), sharing the *glory of God (Rom 5:2), glory (Col 1:27), *salvation (1 Thess 5:8) and eternal life (Tit 1:2).

We can note additionally the qualities that are associated with hope. Hope is variously something for which one waits eagerly (Gal 5:5) or patiently (Is 8:17), something that is unshaken (2 Cor 1:7) and steadfast (1 Thess 1:3). Hope is something that is "set" on its object (1 Tim 4:10; 5:5; 6:17) and that is itself "set before" the believer as an encouragement (Heb 6:18). The coordinates of hope are joy (Rom 5:2), faith (Heb 11:1), perseverance (Rom 5:3-5) and endurance (1 Thess 1:3).

We come, finally, to the indisputable images for hope in the Bible. Hope is a *door (Hos 2:15), "an anchor for the soul, firm and secure" (Heb 6:19 NIV) and a helmet (1 Thess 5:8; see Armor). Hope is "stored up for you in heaven" (Col 1:5 RSV). It is something inside a believer (1 Pet 3:15 RSV) and something into which one is born (1 Pet 1:3). Those who hope for the messianic age are "prisoners of hope" (Zech 9:12 RSV). There is a sense too in which many of the Bible's *apocalyptic visions of the future are images of hope for the believer—something tangible toward which believers look as an eventual reality and around which they orient their present lives.

See also AFTERLIFE; APOCALYPTIC VISIONS OF THE FUTURE; FAITH; HEAVEN; PEACE; PERSEVERANCE; PROMISED LAND; RESTORATION; RESURRECTION; SALVATION.

HOREB. See SINAI.

HORN

The literal image of horn is of the animal horn as an effective defensive *weapon. The Bible does not distinguish between horns and antlers, so horn refers to pointed bony structures on the heads of male *sheep, *goats, deer, *cattle, *oxen and so forth. They give the animal a regal look and provide such an impressive defense mechanism that their imagery was widely employed to represent power. The metaphorical value of the horn comes primarily from the fact that the size and condition of an animal's horns are indicative of its power, status and health.

Animal horns were used for a variety of purposes, including the carrying of oil, but no metaphorical development of this function occurs in the Bible. When used as a (quasi-)musical instrument, a horn is, with few exceptions, called a *"trumpet."

In general, *horn* represents power or status in a social context. In Deuteronomy 33:17 Moses compares the tribes of Joseph to "a firstborn bull, [whose] horns are the horns of a wild ox" because Ephraim and Manasseh were large and powerful. Therefore, "lifting up the horn" of someone means bestowing power, joy, health and prestige (Ps 92:10; 1 Sam 2:1). Conversely, "cutting off the horn" is the removal of one's power or influence (Ps 75:10; Jer 48:25). Since God is the source of strength to those who trust in him, David declares, "The LORD is . . . the horn of my salvation, my stronghold" (Ps 18:2 NIV par. 2 Sam 22:3). In Revelation 5:6 the lamb has seven horns—his kingly power is perfect.

By metonymy, horn came to symbolize those who had power: political or military. In Mesopotamian art, horns indicate deity and deified kings from Naram-Sin on. Thus in Daniel 7—8 the horns represent successions of kings or multiple branches of military power. The book of Revelation also picks up this kind of imagery: both the dragon and the first beast in Revelation 12—13 have ten horns, which Revelation 17:12 explains as ten kings. In Zechariah 1:18-21 the metaphor is taken both ways: the horns represent both the foreign powers themselves (Zech 1:18) and the condition of their strength and influence (Zech 1:21).

Since horn is a symbol of power, particularly kingly power, it is not unnatural that it represent God's anointed one (Messiah). Psalm 148:14 and Ezekiel 29:21 possibly use "horn" as a metonym for the expected Messiah.

Horns also became a symbol for radiance. In Habakkuk 3:4 the Lord's splendor is like the *light: "rays flash from his hand" (NIV, lit. "horns are from his hand," cf. KJV). Psalm 132:17 parallels "horn" and "lamp"—"I will make a horn sprout for David; I have prepared a lamp for my anointed" (RSV). Thus the Hebrew verb *qāran*, which may have originally been a verbal form of *qeren*, the word for horn (cf. Ps 69:31 [69:32 in Heb]), in Exodus 34:29-30 means "to shine." (This is the source of the medieval idea that Moses had horns.)

The sacrificial *altar, similar to other ancient Near Eastern altars, had four horns, which were projections on the four corners of the top (Ex 27:2), on which blood was smeared. The altar of incense also had four horns. The horns of an altar, whatever their original purpose, probably came to symbolize the power of that altar. Just as the cutting off of Moab's horns was a destruction of Moab's power, so the cutting off of the horns of the altars at Bethel symbolized the destruction of their religious or cultic power (Amos 3:14). Also, something gave Adonijah the idea that the horns of the altar were a surety against being killed (1 Kings 1:50-53). Probably Adonijah knew that Solomon would hesitate to have him dispatched if it would mean an implicit challenge to the power of God.

See also ALTAR; ANIMALS; MYTHICAL ANIMALS; TRUMPET.

BIBLIOGRAPHY. M. L. Suring, *The Horn-Motif in the Hebrew Bible and Related Ancient Near Eastern Literature and Iconography* (Berrien Springs, MI: Andrews University Press, 1982).

HORROR, STORIES OF. *See* TERROR, STORIES OF.

HORSE

In the Bible the horse most often appears in the context of battle. Horses were used to pull war chariots. Later, as better saddles and riding gear were developed, cavalry units appeared in some Near Eastern armies (Yadin, 4-5.) Because it was essential for success in battle, the horse became a symbol of military might and national security (Ps 20:7; Is 30:16). Kings accumulated horses for their chariot corps. The Phoenician king Azitawaddu even attributed his large stable of horses to the kindness of Baal and the gods (Pritchard, 499-500.)

Contrary to the typical ancient Near Eastern mindset, Israel's God had a low opinion of horses and chariots. Israelite kings were not to accumulate horses (Deut 17:16), nor were Israel's armies to fear horses and *chariots (Deut 20:1). Because of their great strength and speed (Jer 12:5), charging horses were a terrifying sight (Hab 1:8) and could cause an enemy to panic (Jer 8:16). But, like men, they are made of "flesh" (Is 31:3) and are no match for the Lord, whose supernatural enabling is the true key to success in battle (Ps 20:7; 33:17-20; 76:5-7; 147:10-11; Prov 21:31; Is 31:3; Hos 14:3).

Throughout Israel's history the Lord demonstrated his superiority to horses and chariots. At the Red Sea he annihilated Pharaoh's horses and chariots (Ex 14:9, 23; 15:1, 19-21; Deut 11:4; Is 43:17). At the waters of Merom he defeated the Canaanite coalition with its hordes of horses and chariots and then commanded Joshua to burn the chariots and hamstring the horses (Josh 11:4-11; cf. 2 Sam 8:4). At Taanach he defeated Sisera's charging horses and iron chariots by causing the Kishon River to flash flood (Judg 4:15; 5:4-5, 19-22).

OT prophets envisioned future battles when the

Lord would destroy the horses of his enemies (Jer 50:37; 51:21; Mic 5:10; Hag 2:22; Zech 10:5; 12:4; 14:15). As scavengers devour their carcasses, the Lord's glory and superiority will be apparent to all (Ezek 39:17-21; cf. Rev 19:18). When the Lord establishes his kingdom of peace, warhorses will disappear from the streets of Jerusalem (Zech 9:10).

The OT sometimes depicts the Lord, in his role of *divine warrior, as possessing horses and chariots (Hab 3:8, 15). He has horses and chariots of *fire

An Assyrian war horse

which protect his people (2 Kings 6:17) and he can make his foes run in panic at the sound of imaginary horses and chariots (2 Kings 7:6). In the case of Elijah the prophet's word was likened to horse and chariots because of its effectiveness (2 Kings 2:11-12).

Horses sometimes appear in visionary literature. In the first of his eight night visions, Zechariah saw a man riding a red horse with red, brown and white horses behind him (Zech 1:8). Though some have attempted to find symbolism in the colors, it is more likely that the colors of the horses are mentioned simply to lend vividness and realism to the description. Horses of four different colors also appear in Zechariah's eighth night vision (Zech 6:1-8). Here the variations in color correspond to the four points of the compass and distinguish the four distinct units of the divine army. In a vision of eschatological judgment, the apostle John saw four horsemen riding different colored horses (Rev 6:1-8) The white horse symbolizes the outbreak of a war of conquest; the red horse, bloodshed; the black horse, famine; and the pale horse, death. In a later vision the Lord Jesus and his heavenly armies appear on white horses as they ride forth from heaven to destroy God's enemies (Rev 19:11, 14, 19, 21).

Horses are well known for certain characteristics, such as aggressiveness and stubbornness. The wisdom and prophetic literature of the OT sometimes alludes to these characteristics for poetic purposes. For example, the people of Judah sinned with all the vigor of a horse charging into battle (Jer 8:6). They chased false gods like a stallion looking for a mare in heat (Jer 5:8) and pursued foreign alliances like a mare looking for a well-endowed stud horse (Ezek 23:20). Sinners and fools are often like stubborn horses that need to be whipped before they will cooperate (Ps 32:9; Prov 26:3).

See also ANIMALS; CHARIOT; WARFARE.

BIBLIOGRAPHY. M. A. Littauer and J. H. Crouwel, *Wheeled Vehicles and Ridden Animals in the Ancient Near East* (Leiden: E. J. Brill, 1979); J. Pritchard, *Ancient Near Eastern Texts Relating to the Old Testament* (3rd ed.; Princeton: Princeton University Press, 1969); Y. Yadin, *The Art of Warfare in Biblical Lands* (London: Weidenfeld and Nicolson, 1963).

HOSEA, BOOK OF

The prophecy of Hosea revolves around the theme of faithfulness and unfaithfulness. The reader is immediately introduced to Israel's lack of faith toward its *covenant with God by Hosea's own symbolic portrayal of that relationship via his marriage to unfaithful Gomer. As Gomer proved to be untrue to her husband, so had Israel, forsaking her divine husband *(ba'al)* for another god (*Ba'al*, Hos 2:16-17). As Gomer had gone into *prostitution, thereby alienating herself from Hosea, so faithless Israel stood in danger of being cut off from God. Even the children born during Hosea's marriage symbolized God's reproof of Israel: *Jezreel,* reflecting both the place name of royal infidelity to God's commission (2 Kings 9:7—10:28) and Israel's coming exile, "God will scatter" (Hos 1:4-5); *Lo-Ruhamah,* "no compassion" (Hos 1:6); and *Lo-Ammi,* "not my people" (Hos 1:9-11). And as Hosea sought out Gomer, so Israel's hope lay solely in God's redeeming love for his wayward people (Hos 3:1-5).

Structurally, the marriage theme of the first three chapters is presented in a neat chiastic pattern: *marriage and reunion (Hos 1:2-9; 3:1-5), covenant renewal (Hos 1:10—2:1; 2:14-23), Israel's *judgment (Hos 2:2-4, 9-13), and a centerpiece emphasizing condemnation for promiscuity (Hos 2:5-8). Before the final subscription (Hos 14:9), one encounters a collection of judgment oracles (Hos 4—8), each built around an imperative heading: "hear!" (Hos 4:1), "sound the *trumpet!" (Hos 5:8), "put the trumpet to your lips!" (Hos 8:1) and a double set of oracles that, though intended to warn of judgment, give instructions designed to convince Israel to mend its ways: "do not rejoice" (in spiritual infidelity, Hos 9:1) but rather "return" (to the Lord, Hos 14:1).

Israel's spiritual condition is described by no fewer than fifteen words for sin as well as by prominent themes: prostitution (Hos 1—3; 4:14-15, 18; 5:3-4; 6:10; 7:4; 8:9; 9:1), the covenant (Hos 2:18; 4:2; 6:7; 8:1-14; 9:11; 10:3; 13:16) and idolatry (Hos 4:10, 17; 8:4-6, 13-14; 9:10, 15; 10:5; 11:1; 12:11). Israel stands in need of *repentance (Hos 2:14; 3:5; 5:6; 6:6-7; 7:8-10; 14:4-6) and genuine righteousness (Hos 10:12; 12:6; 14:9) if the spiritual condition symbolized by the three children is to be reversed (Hos 2:23).

Although Hosea sometimes presents God's case against Israel in a manner approaching the language of the law court (Hos 4:1-4, 15; 5:1, 5, 7; 8:1, 12-13), like Amos and Micah the prophet draws on common examples from the natural and agrarian worlds to illustrate his message. He speaks of *earth and sky (Hos 2:21-23), *sun (Hos 6:3), *snow (Hos 9:8), and winter and spring *rains (Hos 6:3-4); of wild (Hos 2:12, 14, 18; 4:3; 5:14; 7:11-12; 8:9; 11:10, 11; 13:7-8) and domesticated creatures (Hos 2:11; 4:16; 5:6; 10:11); of plowed fields (Hos 12:11; cf. 10:12), *sowing and planting (Hos 2:23; 8:7; 10:12, 13), *harvest (Hos 6:11) and *threshing (Hos 2:6, 8-9, 11; 9:1-2); and of products of the field (Hos 2:9), *vine and *tree (Hos 2:12, 15; 9:2, 10; 10:1; 12:1), as well as blighted trees (Hos 9:16) and wild and forbidding plants (Hos 2:6, 12; 9:6; 10:4, 8). All of this is woven into a vivid prophetic tapestry through colorful literary figures. Particularly striking similes (Hos 2:3; 4:16; 5:10, 12, 13; 8:9; 9:10; 10:4, 7, 10, 11; 13:3) and metaphors (Hos 9:8; 10:11) are often brought together in contextual concatenations.

Particularly picturesque are the clusters in the judgment oracles of Hosea 5 to 7. Here Judah's leadership is denounced as being like those who treacherously move boundary stones (Hos 5:10), and its priests are depicted as being no better than murderous marauders (Hos 6:9). Spiritually, Israel's love for God is pictured as being as fleeting as a morning cloud and early *dew (Hos 6:4), while its political agenda is uncontrollable as a wild *donkey in heat (Hos 7:9-10) or a senseless *dove, always flitting back and forth between various world powers rather than relying on God himself. Israel has shown itself to be as untrustworthy as a faulty bow that causes an archer to miss the mark (Hos 7:6). Sadly, like a man whose *hair has gradually grayed or an unturned pancake that is near to burning (Hos 7:7-9), God's people seem unaware of their mortal danger. Therefore God will send his judgment to consume them as surely as a hungry moth or advancing rot (Hos 5:12) or a *hunter bringing down *birds with his net (Hos 7:12).

A poignant instance of Hosea's artistry is seen in his masterful employment of literary motifs to illustrate Israel's spiritual condition. God is presented as a faithful husband to Israel, his unfaithful wife (Hos 2:2, 16, 19-20; 3:1-5; 9:1) and mother of his Israelite children (Hos 2:2, 5; 4:5), and as a father to a wayward son (Hos 11:1-3). God is also Israel's *redeemer who brought his children out of Egypt (Hos 11:4; 12:9; 13:4), cared for them in the *wilderness (Hos 13:5) and, having settled them in the *land of promise, blessed them with abundant produce such as *grain, *wine and *oil (Hos 2:8). Rather than responding gratefully to him, Israel had turned away from him (Hos 7:14), with the result that God must take away these signs of his goodness (Hos 2:9). The Assyrian east *wind that Israel coveted so greatly (Hos 12:1) will prove to be an invading wind sent by

God (Hos 13:15) to yield a harvest of judgment (Hos 6:11).

Through it all, however, Israel may take hope. To be sure, God must discipline his people sorely, but the Divine Healer will bind up their *wounds (Hos 6:1). Using the familiar third day motif (Hos 6:2), Hosea assures his readers that God will revive them and restore the grain, wine and oil that symbolize his blessings on a faithful nation (Hos 2:20; 14:7).

See also COVENANT; PROPHECY, GENRE OF; PROPHET, PROPHETESS; PROSTITUTE, PROSTITUTION.

HOSPITALITY

Biblical pictures of hospitality exist within a context of ancient attitudes toward the duty of hospitality. For the Greeks hospitality was a sign of being civilized, and its religious importance is suggested by the fact that the chief deity, Zeus, was god of hospitality. For the Egyptians, being hospitable helped to secure a favorable existence in the future life, and the Romans made entertaining strangers a sacred duty. In biblical culture too, extending hospitality was not a courtesy but an obligation. Lot's offer of his daughters as sexual gratifiers in deference to his visitors (Gen 19:4-8) shows the extreme value that people in such a milieu placed on hospitality (cf. also Judg 19:22-26).

Facing Danger at the Boundaries. Social context helps to explain these attitudes toward hospitality. *Travel in the ancient Mediterranean world was fraught with physical danger and social tension. Inns were few and far between, and travelers were dependent on locals for life-sustaining *water and *food as well as for shelter and safety from attack. Since Palestine was inhabited by a variety of groups whose political boundaries and alliances were in flux and whose values and beliefs often clashed, people sensed the social tension and threat to the cohesion of their communities that the arrival of strangers posed. These needs and tensions were addressed in a fairly standardized code of hospitality practices.

The Hospitality Code. Hospitality customs provided ways whereby strangers could be welcomed and made guests and might depart as friends instead of as strangers or enemies. For this process to run smoothly people had to carry out their roles as host, stranger/guest or servant. There were four phases in hospitality: initial invitation, screening, provision and protection, and departure.

Outsiders were suspect and had to be approached cautiously, but for a community not to approach them with a ready invitation would be dishonorable and could result in violence. During the nomadic period strangers approaching an encampment might be intercepted before reaching it (Gen 18:2), thus it became customary for travelers approaching a town or city to wait in an open place, such as the *well or the city *gate for a preliminary invitation to be extended (Gen 19:1-2; 24:23-25, 31-33; Ex 2:20; 1 Kings 17:10; 2 Kings 4:8-10; Job 31:32; Acts 16:13-

15). The failure of a community to approach the strangers and issue an invitation before nightfall to dine and lodge in an established household was a serious breach of honor signifying an insult toward the strangers and an indication of the locals' bad character (Judg 19:15, 18; cf. v. 20, where the custom is properly enacted).

Strangers had to be assessed in some way to discern their intentions (Josh 2:2-3; Gen 19:4-5; 42:7). In various biblical contexts we observe instances of this. In the NT a traveling teacher, might be asked to speak (Acts 13:15). A letter of recommendation might be presented but was not always accepted (Rom 16:3-16; 1 Thess 5:12-13; 2 and 3 John). The stranger would either be asked to leave (cf. Mk 5:17, where the Gerasenes ask Jesus to leave) or would be advanced to the next step and received as a guest.

The host assumed the responsibilities of providing food, water and lodging for the guests and their animals (Gen 24:23-25; 26:30; 33:1-33, 54; 43:16, 24). The host usually was a male head of household but might be a woman of means. Examples include the widow who hosted Elijah (1 Kings 17:10); the wealthy woman who set up a room for Elisha (2 Kings 4:8-10); the NT women who provided for Jesus (Lk 8: 2-3); Jesus' friends Mary and Martha, who took him into their home (Lk 10:38; Jn 12:1-3); and the women of the early church who hosted church meetings and, like Lydia, provided for traveling missionaries (Acts 16:13-15).

The provision and protection extended in hospitality were well defined and elaborate. Acceptance of strangers as guests was signified by washing the guests' feet (Gen 18:4; 19:2; 24:32; neglected in Lk 7:36-50) and by providing a meal. The meal, prepared and served by women and household servants, might be lavish and could include entertainment (music, dancing) and discussion of Torah. In order not to insult the guests and dishonor the host, the meal must be the best the host could provide, as with the choice *calf, curds and *milk that Abraham provided for three angelic visitors. Additional honor would be signified by inviting a (male) guest to speak or *anointing his head with *oil and by giving him an honored place at the host's table. It was also the duty of the host to provide protection from harm (Gen 23:7-9; Josh 2:1-6; 2 Kings 6:22-23; cf. Gen 19, where Lot is unable to fulfill this duty). The reference in Psalm 23:5 to a table prepared in the presence of enemies may refer to the desert code of hospitality in which the fugitive from blood vengeance could find safety within a tent for the space of one day and two nights. Significantly, this psalm ends with the poet contrasting such temporary hospitality to God's house, in which he can dwell (literally "return to") forever.

Departure was the final phase in the cycle of hospitality. Customarily guests could expect to stay in one household for no more than two nights (cf. *Didache* 11.5). It would be rude and dishonorable for a guest to prolong the stay unless the host clearly extended the invitation (the extended stay in Judg 19:1-9 is extraordinary). The goal at this final phase of hospitality was to have the guest depart in peace without having disrupted the social harmony of the household or the community—as when Isaac sends Abimelech and his advisers off after a feast celebrating a peace treaty (Gen 26:26-31). A generous host would send guests off well fed and supplied for the journey (*Didache* 11.6, 12 suggests sending missionaries off with food, but not money; cf. Rom 15:24).

Extraordinary Hospitality as Israel's Mandate. When we turn from the mechanics of hospitality to its broader meanings, several distinct themes emerge. One is the OT mandate from God that his chosen nation protect the rites of hospitality as part of its moral and spiritual covenant with him.

While all the peoples of the ancient Near East practiced hospitality toward strangers, the Israelites understood their participation in these practices in the light of their unique history as the people of God. Their traditional ancestor Abraham was a "sojourner" (*see* Foreigner), and stories of the traveling patriarchs and the Hebrews who were resident aliens in Egypt and wandering strangers in the wilderness are archetypal and prototypical: "For the LORD your God . . . executes justice for the orphan and the widow, and . . . loves the strangers, providing them food and clothing. You shall also love the stranger, for you were strangers in the land of Egypt" (Deut 10:17, 19 NRSV; cf. Deut 26; 5-9; Ex 22:21; Lev 19:33-34). Israelite hospitality went beyond the merely customary and took its impetus from something other than fear of the stranger. It arose from the heart of a people whose identity and home rested in the God who had made them no longer strangers: "You shall not oppress a resident alien; you know the heart of an alien, for you were aliens in the land of Egypt" (Ex 23:9 NRSV). Proper treatment of the stranger, then, was a just and grateful act in response to God's loving provision (Deut 24:17-19) and revealed the character of God's people.

Within such an ethos, breaches of hospitality were punished and the practice of hospitality rewarded. In the former category are the Ammonites and Moabites (Deut 23:3-4), the Benjamites (Judg 19:15, 18) and the churlish Nabal (1 Sam 25:1-13; 36-38). The rewards that come to those who extend ideal hospitality are even more noteworthy. Abraham and Sarah, who "entertained angels unawares" (Heb 13:2 RSV), were rewarded for their pastoral hospitality with the promise that their son would be born within the year (Gen 18:1-15). Abigail won herself a husband with her generous hospitality to David (1 Sam 25:14-35, 39-42). The widow at Zarephath who gave Elijah her last food was rewarded with a jar of meal and cruse of oil that did not fail until the famine was over (1 Kings 17:8-16). The Shunammite woman who made a cozy guest room for Elisha (replete with bed, table, chair and lamp) was rewarded with a son (2 Kings 4:1-17). Hebrews 11:31

attributes Rahab's being spared when Jericho fell to her having "given friendly welcome to the spies" (RSV).

In a category by itself is the ironic list of hospitable acts that Jael performed for the hapless Sisera (Judg 5:25-26 RSV):

He asked water and she gave him milk,
  she brought him curds in a lordly bowl.
She put her hand to the tent peg
  and her right hand to the workmen's mallet;
she struck Sisera a blow,
  she crushed his head,
  she shattered and pierced his temple.

God's provision for Israel in the OT takes on some of the qualities of human hospitality (*see* Host, God as). God hosted the people of Israel in the wilderness, providing water, food and protection (Ex 15:24-25, 27; 17:1-7; 23:20-23). He screened them prior to their entry into Canaan (Num 14:21-24; Deut 1:34-35; Heb 3:18-19; 4:6). He invited them into a *Promised Land prepared for them—a place full of food, a place of which God says, "The land is mine; with me you are but aliens and tenants" (Lev 25:23; see also Deut 26:9). The application is even broader in Psalm 104, where the psalmist sees the cosmos as God's *garden in which all living creatures receive provision. God's hospitality is actually festive, as he makes available "wine to gladden the human heart, oil to make the face shine, and bread to strengthen the human heart" (Ps 104:15 NRSV). In a similar vein, in Proverbs 9 Wisdom, a personified attribute of God, builds a house and extends an invitation to the *good life, pictured as a lavish banquet (Prov 9:1-6). In contrast, Folly, an unworthy and wily hostess, can only offer stolen water and "food eaten in secret" (Prov 9:14-18).

The Church as House of Hospitality. The NT likewise abounds in references to hospitality. The record of Jesus' life as an itinerant teacher and miracle worker is a virtual chronicle of hospitality received (Mt 26:6; Mk 1:29; 7:24; 14:3; Lk 7:36; 14:1, 12; Jn 12:1-2). The most famous pictures of that hospitality are Mary and Martha's entertainment of Jesus (Lk 10:38-42) and the occasion when Jesus invited himself to the house of Zacchaeus (Lk 19:1-10). In his Olivet Discourse, Jesus made hospitality to himself and to his missionary "brothers" the key to entering the kingdom of heaven in his statement, "For I was hungry and you gave me food, I was thirsty and you gave me something to drink, I was a stranger and you welcomed me" (Mt 25:35 NRSV). When Jesus dispatched his followers, he sent them out on the assumption that they would depend on hospitality as they traveled (Mt 10:9-14; Mk 6:7-10; Lk 9:1-4). Failure on the part of villagers to provide such hospitality was said by Jesus to seal their doom (Mt 10:14-15; Mk 6:11; Lk 9:5).

Similar pictures of hospitality pervade NT glimpses of life in the early church (Acts 2:46). Hospitality was key to the missionary endeavor of the early church, as evidenced by the way the ministries

of Peter (Acts 10:6, 18, 32, 48) and Paul (Acts 16:15; 18:7; 21:4, 8, 16; 28:7) relied on a supply of hospitable contacts as they traveled on their missionary ventures. Corresponding to these pictures of hospitality are NT injunctions to practice it: "Extend hospitality to strangers" (Rom 12:13 NRSV); "Do not neglect to show hospitality to strangers, for by doing that some have entertained angels without knowing it" (Heb 13:2 NRSV); "Be hospitable to one another without complaining" (1 Pet 4:9 NRSV). The qualifications for a bishop included the showing of hospitality (1 Tim 3:2; Tit 1:8). The same qualification applied to widows who wished to be "put on the list" of Christian workers (1 Tim 5:10).

The Kingdom: Ultimate Hospitality. The *kingdom of God and heaven are figured as places and times where God will fulfill the desire and promise of unspoiled ultimate hospitality—unending feasting in God's vast abode, heaven. The criterion for entering heaven is acceptance of the offer of salvation in Christ. In a surprising reversal early in the book of Revelation, the individual who accepts Christ is pictured as the host, with Christ as the self-invited guest who says, "Behold, I stand at the door and knock; if any one hears my voice and opens the door, I will come in to him and eat with him, and he with me" (Rev 3:20 RSV). Later, those who enter heaven are pictured as guests at a marriage supper of the Lamb (Rev 19:7-9). The Apocalypse ends with a final invitation: "The Spirit and the bride say, 'Come.' And let everyone who hears say, 'Come.' And let everyone who is thirsty come. Let anyone who wishes take the water of life as a gift" (Rev 22:17 NRSV).

See also DRINKING; EATING; FOREIGNER; GUEST; HOST, GOD AS; SUPPER; WANDERER, WANDERING.

BIBLIOGRAPHY. S. C. Barton, "Hospitality," *DLNTD* 501-7; L. Casson, *Travel in the Ancient World* (London: Allen & Unwin, 1974); J. Koenig, *New Testament Hospitality: Partnership with Strangers as Promise and Mission* (Philadelphia: Fortress, 1985).

HOST, GOD AS

The Bible's picture of *God as a host is rooted in the actions of human hosts: as a divine host, God performs the same activities as human hosts do. The context for the biblical image of God as host is the extreme value that the ancient world placed on the obligations of hosts to their guests. The ancient Greeks made *hospitality a mark of civilization itself, the Romans made it a sacred obligation, and the Hebrews evolved an elaborate code of hospitality in response to the conditions of nomadic life, where travel required a different type of accommodation from a stationary inn. Human hosts offered their guests protection, lodging and food. The actions of God that are described by the metaphor of the host follow the same pattern, with references to the provision of food being most numerous. The discussion that follows limits its focus to passages where God *extends beneficence* to his creatures, often *issuing an* *invitation* or command to accept the provision in such a way as to suggest the actions of a host.

Physical Provision. God's extension of food to his creatures begins with the creation of the world. The climax of Genesis 1 is God's statement that to all animals of the earth he has "given every *green *plant for food" (Gen 1:30 RSV). Later OT references picture God as a host who provides for *animals (Ps 104:27-28; Job 38:39-41). But of course it is the human creature that is usually pictured as the recipient of God's provision of food.

Such provision begins in the *garden. Genesis 2 is governed by the motif of God's wonderful provision for the human race, and the content of that provision is partly what a host provides—a secure and attractive place in which to live and rest, food and companionship. The first words that God speaks to Adam are "You may freely eat [or, more strongly, you shall eat] of every tree of the garden" (Gen 2:16 RSV).

The metaphor of God as host is not overtly stated in the story of the *exodus, but it is evoked as we read. With the nation of Israel utterly dependent on God for its survival in the wilderness, God provides both protection and food. Notable instances are *manna and *water from the rock (Ex 17:1-7), as well quail (Ex 16). Although the writer of Exodus does not use the image of God as host, the retrospective reflection of the psalmist comes closer to doing so: Psalm 78:19 pictures God as spreading a *table in the wilderness, and Psalm 105:39-41 is even more specific in its references to hosting:

He spread a cloud for a covering,
    and fire to give light by night.
They asked, and he brought quails,
    and gave them bread from heaven in
        abundance.
He opened the rock, and water gushed forth;
    it flowed through the desert like a river. (RSV)
This experience of special provision in the wilderness, however, was preparatory for life in the Promised Land, which typically carries the description *land flowing with milk and honey (twenty times). Hardly limited to the abundance of *cattle, *goats and bees, this phrase pictures the whole experience of living in the Promised Land as eating a rich *banquet from God's own table (Deut 6:3).

The climax of OT references to God as host is without doubt Psalm 23. This poem begins by comparing God's provision to that of a shepherd for his *sheep, but already here the provisions thus metaphorically portrayed remind one of what a human host provides for a guest. In the last two verses of the psalm, moreover, the imagery becomes that of the host-guest relationship, with references to preparing a table, anointing a head for purposes of refreshment, providing an overflowing *cup and dwelling in a house.

In the NT Jesus is a literal host on several recorded occasions. He turned water into wine to keep festivities going at a *wedding party (Jn 2:1-10).

Twice he miraculously fed thousands of people (Mt 14:15-21; 15:32-38), and he taught that he himself was the bread of life, the true manna sent from heaven (Jn 6:30-51). After his resurrection he served bread to disciples from Emmaus (Lk 24:30) and prepared a breakfast of bread and fish for Peter and the other disciples (Jn 21:9-14).

Sacred Meals. Among the five offerings of the sacrificial system, the peace offering is unique in that the priest would burn a portion of it on the *altar "as food" for the Lord (Lev 3:11, 16). The name of this particular offering is related to the Hebrew word for peace and well-being. These offerings were made in response to a vow or voluntarily, as well as in response to answered prayer (Lev 7:11, 16). At the heart of the ritual was a meal of celebration to be shared together by those who brought the sacrifice, the priests and the Lord. This communion prefigures the fellowship that Christians enjoy with Christ, who gives them his "flesh" and "blood" to consume (Jn 6:53-58).

The fulfillment of this prefiguring sacrifice is the Lord's *Supper, instituted by Jesus. Here, surely, is the supreme instance of God as a host who provides the materials for a meal and invites people to participate. At the Last Supper itself (Mt 26:26-29) Jesus served his disciples *bread and *wine, using the host's language of invitation: "Take, eat . . . drink of it." The same terminology is picked up in the instructions for the Lord's Supper in 1 Corinthians 11:23-26. A leading motif that enters the picture at this point is the obligation of human guests to accept the divine host's invitation.

The Banquet of Salvation. The most numerous cluster of references to God as host are metaphoric ones in which the language of physical food and drink is used to portray spiritual salvation. The motif reaches back to the OT. Isaiah portrays God as inviting people to help themselves free of charge to water, wine, milk and bread (Is 55:1-2) and as making "for all peoples a feast of fat things, a feast of wine" (Is 25:6 RSV). Equally evocative are the millennial pictures of the mountains dripping with *wine and the hills flowing with milk (Joel 3:18; Amos 9:13). The composite picture evokes a sense of abundance, satisfaction and joyful celebration all made possible by the lavish generosity of God.

The metaphoric feast of salvation to which God invites reaches its high point in parables and sayings of Jesus. One thinks at once of the parable of the banquet that God insists must be well attended (Lk 14:15-24)—a parable occasioned by someone's glib statement, "Blessed is he who shall eat bread in the kingdom of God" (Lk 14:15). Twice we read about people who will "sit at table in the kingdom of heaven/God" (Mt 8:11; Lk 13:29), to which can be added Jesus' statement about "those who have continued with me in my trials" being allowed to "eat and drink at my table in my kingdom" (Lk 22:18-30). In the parable of the *prodigal son, the forgiving father throws a lavish banquet to which he invites the neighborhood (Lk 15:22-24).

Jesus tells the Samaritan woman at the well that he can provide water that brings eternal life (Jn 4:13-14) and invites the thirsty to come and drink from him (Jn 7:37-39). In washing the disciples' feet Jesus performs a host's function (Jn 13:1-17). In an eschatological saying Jesus compares the coming day to a *marriage feast, picturing the reward of "those servants whom the master finds awake" as having the master "gird himself and have them sit at table, and he will come and serve them" (Lk 12:36-37 RSV).

As some of these passages show, it is impossible to separate the eschatological references from references to salvation. The heavenly banquet begins on earth at the moment of belief in Christ as savior, and it is consummated in a coming heavenly kingdom. The book of Revelation brings the eschatological references to their culmination, with its pictures of a celestial "marriage supper of the Lamb," to which the redeemed are invited (Rev 19:9), and an invitation to anyone who is thirsty to "take the water of life without price" (Rev 22:17).

Summary. Throughout the Bible, God is clearly the one who provides food for all life. Beyond this comprehensive care for creation, God issues an invitation to enjoy the benefits of redemption that are often poetically depicted in terms of abundant food or a banquet. Actual food is a tangible blessing and is sometimes provided by miracles that reveal a facet of God's nature, but words for food also stand as metaphors of the good life God grants to his own people. The fellowship and rich provision lost in Eden is fully restored only in the New *Jerusalem, but the present experience of God's goodness sustains his people who live according to the promise of a happy future.

See also BANQUET; DRINKING; EATING; FOREIGNER; GARDEN; GOD; GUEST; HOSPITALITY; LAND FLOWING WITH MILK AND HONEY; MANNA; SUPPER; WANDERER, WANDERING; WEDDING.

HOSTS OF HEAVEN. *See* HEAVENLY ARMIES/HOST.

HOUR

The Bible's use of the term *hour* might best be summarized by the colloquial phrase "time's up!" As the bell sounds for the boxer at the end of his round or the team at the end of their match, so it sounds for Jesus at the time of his crucifixion or the world at the time of his return. It serves as a reminder that God is not only involved in events but orders their timing. Even those things that may appear arbitrary in fact follow a schedule laid down by a timeless God.

The use of the hour image is most striking in John's Gospel. Here Jesus makes it plain from the very outset that his life and work is ordered by the Father's chronology, not his own. Thus he cautions his mother at the wedding feast in Cana that "my hour has not yet come" (Jn 2:4 NRSV). As time goes by, he prepares his disciples for the fate that awaits

him. Once in Jerusalem, where his confrontation with the religious leaders is inevitable, he declares that the "hour has come for the Son of Man to be glorified" (Jn 12:23 NRSV). From this point onward the chain of events unfolds that ends in his death and resurrection. The repeated use of "hour" heightens the anticipation of this "grand finale."

Other NT writers, reflecting on the death and resurrection of Christ, use *hour* to describe a new era inaugurated by him. This is the final hour, or phase, of God's plan, ushered in by his son. It is an hour of opportunity: "The hour has come for you to wake up from your slumber" (Rom 13:11 NIV). However, it is also an hour of urgency, for God's clock ticks on toward the end of all things: "Dear children, this is the last hour, as you have heard that the antichrist is coming" (1 Jn 2:18 NIV). In many instances the reminder of the hour is used as a moral goad to make the most of the time remaining.

As he reflects from his exile on the island of Patmos, John sees another hour on its way. This is the "hour of trial that is going to come upon the whole world"(Rev 3:10 NIV), the "hour of judgment" (Rev 14:7 NIV). As the description of the Apocalypse is revealed to John, it becomes apparent that God has deliberately restrained his powers of judgment for this very hour. Just as Jesus awaited his hour to act, so too God will wait. John describes the "four angels who had been kept ready for this very day and hour" (Rev 9:15 NIV). God not only obliges us to follow his timing but does so himself. He acts in judgment *at the appointed hour,* not a moment before or after.

The image is a very potent one today, particularly in a Western context with its obsession with time and punctuality. Events are not random, but rather they follow a schedule preordained by God. In a world that has deluded itself that it will live forever, this image carries the Bible's reminder that one day our time will be up.

See also DAY, DAY OF THE LORD; SEASONS; TIME.

HOUSE. *See* HOME, HOUSE.

HOUSEHOLD. *See* FAMILY; GALATIANS, LETTER TO THE; HOME, HOUSE; TIMOTHY AND TITUS, LETTERS TO.

HOUSETOP

The key to understanding biblical references to the housetop is to know that the architecture of houses included flat roofs as a salient feature and that regular household activities occurred there. The Mosaic law even stipulated that house builders must build a railing for the roof to prevent injury from falls (Deut 22:8). Some of the activity that occurred on housetops (such as drying fruit or clothes) was routine, some was private and some was intended to be in public view.

Some of the typical housetop activities were religious. Josiah pulled down pagan altars that Ahaz had placed on a rooftop (2 Kings 23:12). Jeremiah denounced the apostate practice of using housetops to burn incense and offer drink offerings (Jer 19:13; 32:29). On the positive side we find the picture of Peter going "up on the housetop to pray" and receiving the vision of ceremonially unclean animals descending from heaven (Acts 10:9 RSV). In the time of Nehemiah, worshipers celebrated the Feast of Booths by making booths on their housetops (Neh 8:16).

Housetops also provided a place for relatively private experience to transpire. Thus we read about people going to the housetop to *sleep (1 Sam 9:25) and about a depressed person's lying awake "like a lonely bird on the housetop" (Ps 102:7). The house-top as a place of solitary seclusion emerges from the proverb that "it is better to live in a corner of the housetop than in a house shared with a contentious woman" (Prov 21:9; cf. 25:24). Rahab managed to hide the two spies by placing stalks of flax over them on the rooftop (Josh 2:6-7).

Paradoxically, the housetop, by being open to public view, is also a place for public actions in the Bible. Public *mourning occurs there (Is 15:3; Jer 48:38). So does the public festival at which Samson pulls down the temple of Dagon (Judg 16:27). That the housetop is a place of proclamation is evident in Jesus' injunction to his disciples to "proclaim upon the housetops" what he has taught them in secret (Mt 10:27; cf. Lk 12:3). When Absalom supplants David as king and wishes to assert his authority, he has a tent placed on his housetop and proceeds to have intercourse with David's concubines "in the sight of all Israel" (2 Sam 16:22).

Memorable housetop scenes remain with anyone who has read the Bible: *David pacing on his house-top late in the afternoon on a spring day and seeing the attractive *Bathsheba bathing (2 Sam 11:2) and the paralytic's friends opening the roof to let down the stricken man for Jesus' healing (Mk 2:4; Lk 5:19).

Finally, there are figurative references to house-tops. The shallowness of the root system of *grass that grew on some rooftops made grass on the housetops an image of human transience and vulner-ability (2 Kings 19:26; Ps 129:6). And as a way of stressing the urgency of leaving behind earthly con-cerns when the prophesied catastrophe strikes Judea, Jesus' command is not to go down from the house-top to get possessions out of one's house (Mt 24:17; Mk 13:15; Lk 17:31).

See also HOME, HOUSE.

HUMILITY

The terminology for humility appears nearly a hun-dred times in the Bible, referencing multiple mean-ings. Humility reflects godly character (Ps 45:4)—even Jesus was humble (Mt 11:29). It is also associated with *wisdom (Prov 11:2; Jas 3:13) and meekness (Job 8:7; Zeph 3:12). Paradoxically, the humble deserve *honor (Prov 15:33; 18:12) and the humbled will be exalted (Mt 23:12; also Lk 14:11).

The humble are known for their *fear of the Lord (Prov 22:4) and their righteousness (Num 12:3;

Zeph 2:3; Acts 20:19; Phil 2:3), but false humility comes from the ungodly, who have no place in heaven (Col 2:18, 23). Believers are commanded to assume humility before everyone (Phil 2:3; Titus 3:2) and especially to humble themselves before God (Ex 10:3; Prov 6:3; Mt 18:4; Jas 4:10). They are even to be clothed with humility (Col 3:12; 1 Pet 5:5). Often humility comes in the form of *testing or discipline (Deut 8:2; 1 Kings 11:39).

Humility is always the proper posture before God and others; by contrast, *humiliation* is never seen as a virtue in Scripture. On the contrary, it is often a punishment brought on by God (Mal 2:9; Lk 13:17) or one's own doing (Prov 25:7; Lk 14:9). Humiliat-ing others is a sin (1 Cor 11:22).

See also FEAR OF THE LORD; PRIDE.

HUMOR

The Bible is predominantly a serious rather than a funny book. Yet it would distort the Bible to suppress the humor that is present. Arranged on a continuum that ranges from the least intellectual (slapstick com-edy) to the most intellectual (irony and wordplay), we can say that the humor of the Bible tends toward the subtle. The best way to organize our thinking on the matter is to categorize types of humor in the Bible.

Situation Comedy. Situation comedy consists of embarrassing, inopportune or simply humorous situ-ations. The humor arises from the plot, even though certain personality types account for some humorous situations.

The highly unexpected event in which one or more persons are caught off guard is an important subtype. When *Jacob arrives in Haran and meets the pretty Rachel at the well, his masculine adrenaline starts to pump. He who had earlier been called "a quiet man, dwelling in tents" (Gen 25:27 RSV) suddenly emerges as a weightlifting wonder, single-handedly moving the stone at the well that ordinarily could be moved only with the combined strength of the neighborhood shepherds (Gen 29:2-10). It was an emotionally taxing experience for Jacob, who promptly lost his head, "kissed Rachel, and wept aloud" (Gen 29:11 RSV). The excited Rachel promptly ran and told her father (Gen 29:12). The scene is ready for television filming.

Consider too the following unexpected events that leave the man speechless when confronted un-expectedly with a woman lying next to him: Jacob: "and in the morning, behold, it was Leah" (Gen 29:25); Boaz: "at midnight the man was startled, and turned over, and behold, a woman lay at his feet!" (Ruth 3:8). In the latter incident Boaz falls back on the stock question, "Who are you?" only to have the woman respond not only with an answer to the question but with a command to Boaz to hurry up and propose to her (Ruth 3:9)!

People whose frustration reaches a breaking point can likewise make a humorous spectacle of them-selves. One of the funny incidents in the life of Paul was the occasion when the Jews became so angry and frustrated at Paul's speech that the only way they could adequately express their pent-up rage was to wave their garments and throw dust into the air (Acts 22:23).

Another branch of situation comedy is the humorous comeuppance of a villain (the humorous side of poetic justice), especially the sudden turning of the tables on an unsuspecting villain. The career of Haman in the story of *Esther is a classic case. More subtle is the case of Eglon, the "fat calf" (a literal translation of his name) who has oppressed the people of God through exploitation. He is the victim of an elaborate and deadly practical joke by the clever left-hander Ehud, who stage manages the original case of the disappearing sword (Judg 3:15-30). There is even the scatological humor of the king's attendants standing around in consternation, hesitant to open the chamber door because they think the king is going to the toilet, while in fact the dung is seeping out of his pierced intestine. To catch of the humor of it all, we need to remember that this story belongs (as does much of the OT) to a category of writing that we know as slave writing, which often possesses a mocking tone at the expense of an oppressive nation.

The Bible contains two examples of characters who "mouthed off" while inebriated and then have to face the repercussions in a startled moment of discovery the next morning. One is Gaal, who the morning after a wine festival at which he had asked, "Who is Abimelech, . . . that we should serve him?" (Judg 9:28) went to the city gate to have a view of the surrounding hills. He was terrified at the sight of Abimelech's warriors moving down the mountains, to which Zebul (who had informed Abimelech of Gaal's insulting words) first humored Gaal by claiming that he merely saw "the shadow of the mountains as if they were men" (Judg 9:36) and then asked with equal humor, "Where is your mouth now, you who said, 'Who is Abimelech, that we should serve him?'" (Judg 9:38). Another loudmouth is Nabal, who was rude to David's men when they requested provisions. His wife Abigail intervened to placate David, thus saving him from David's revenge. "And in the morning, when the wine had gone out of Nabal, his wife told him these things, and his heart died within him, and he became as a stone" (1 Sam 25:36-37).

Ineptitude can also be a source of situation comedy. The pool party described in 2 Samuel 2:12-16 is an example. When twelve young men on each side are invited to "arise and play," each one "caught his opponent by the head, and thrust his sword in his opponent's side; so they fell down together" (RSV). It would appear to be a classic case of excellent offense neutralized by deficient defense.

Humor Arising from Character. Some comic literature locates humor in character rather than plot. The picaro (likable rogue), for example, is a comic type. Picaros have a knack for getting themselves into difficult situations, but their resilience and good-heartedness wins our sympathetic laughter rather

than our loathing. The *trickster is a common variation on the theme.

*Jacob and Laban are the classic instances of the trickster in the Bible, and when the pair gets together during Jacob's twenty-year sojourn in Haran, the sparks fly as both try to outwit the other. Here are two tricksters who richly deserve each other. Laban begins his grand enterprise of taking advantage of a wealthy relative already when Abraham's servant arrives to claim Rebekah. Upon meeting Rebekah at the well, Abraham's servant lavishes jewelry on her (Gen 24:22), after which she runs home with the news and the tangible evidence of wealth glittering in everyone's view. When Laban saw the ring and the bracelets on his sister's arms, he was suddenly hospitable to Abraham's servant, saying, "Come in, O blessed of the LORD; why do you stand outside?" (Gen 24:30-31). Years later when Jacob, the heir in the same family, arrives, Laban remembers the financial rating of the family: "When Laban heard the tidings of Jacob his sister's son, he ran to meet him, and embraced him and kissed him, and brought him to his house . . . and Laban said to him, 'Surely you are my bone and my flesh!' " (Gen 29:13-14 RSV).

This is only the beginning of tricks. It is followed by the incident of the substitute bride, with Jacob ending up serving Laban fourteen years rather than seven for Rebekah. There is also the battle over Jacob's wages (Gen 30:31-36) that includes Jacob's laughable attempts at animal husbandry (the placing of striped rods before the healthy sheep and goats during the act of mating). The seesaw battle of wits becomes a humorous mockery of materialism.

Another picaro and trickster is *Samson. While we rightly remember him mainly as the archetypal strong man, Samson also has a comic career. He enjoys playing tricks on people, telling riddles that people cannot answer, "getting even" (the foxes used to torch the Philistines' grain fields), escaping from apparently certain captivity (walking off with city gates or allowing himself to be bound with ropes and then snapping them in a feat of strength) and telling lies (the deceitful replies to Delilah when she asks the secret of his strength).

In the Gospels, Peter is a partly comic type. An impetuous person, Peter has a particular knack for saying foolish things. Today we would identify him as someone who "puts his foot in his mouth." Perhaps because of his temperament, Jesus gave him the humorous nickname "Rocky."

Satiric Humor. Satire is the exposure of human vice or folly through either rebuke or ridicule. A great deal of OT satire is at the expense of a foreign oppressor and has the mocking tone of slave literature. Exodus 1—2 contains major examples. The more *Pharaoh tries to stamp out the Hebrews, the more they multiply (Ex 1:12). Pharaoh obviously thinks women are beneath his bother (Ex 1:16), yet the story repeatedly shows women outwitting him. When he commands the midwives to kill the Hebrew males at birth, they reply satirically that they are foiled in the attempt "because the Hebrew women are not like the Egyptian women; for they are vigorous and are delivered before the midwife comes to them" (Ex 1:19 RSV). In the story of Moses' rescue, Pharaoh's own daughter contributes to the welfare of the future deliverer of a rival nation, while Moses' mother gets paid for taking care of her own son.

Equally mocking is the list of hospitable acts that Jael performed for Sisera as he fled from Deborah's army (Judg 4—5). First she covered him with a rug (Judg 4:18). When he was cozy, he said, "Pray give me a little water to drink; for I am thirsty" (Judg 4:19). A little *water*? A captain deserves better: "He asked water and she gave him milk, she brought him curds in a lordly bowl" (Judg 5:25). One already catches the mocking and sarcastic overtones. Jael's next act of hospitality was to "put her hand to the tent peg and her right hand to the workmen's mallet," crushing Sisera's head (Judg 5:26). To complete the mockery, the poet multiplies the terms for Jael's actions ("struck," "crushed," "shattered," "pierced") and for its effects (Sisera "sank, he fell, he lay still at her feet; at her feet he sank, he fell; where he sank, there he fell dead," Judg 5:27). This in turn is followed by the mocking picture of Sisera's mother gazing through the lattice as she waits for her warrior son's return, as well as the fantasy that runs through the minds of the "wisest ladies" of the Canaanite court about the warriors' delay being caused by their "finding and dividing the spoil" (Judg 5:28-29).

OT taunt songs likewise belong to the category of satiric humor. Isaiah 44:12-20, for example, heaps up scorn on the pagan who fashions an idol from wood that he has also used for fuel and then bows down to the idol, saying, "Deliver me, for thou art my god!" Even funnier is Elijah's taunting of the prophets of Baal on Mt. Carmel: either Baal "is musing, or he has gone aside [to relieve himself], or he is on a journey, or perhaps he is asleep and must be awakened" (1 Kings 18:27).

Some of the satiric barbs in Proverbs also make us laugh. An example is the excuses of the lazy person when the alarm wakes him in the morning: "There is a lion outside! I shall be slain in the streets!" (Prov 22:13 RSV). An exaggerated version of the slothful person yields the picture of the sluggard who "buries his hand in the dish, and will not even bring it back to his mouth" (Prov 19:24 RSV). The portrait of the nagging spouse is likewise humorous: "a wife's quarreling is a continual dripping of rain" (Prov 19:13 RSV; cf. 27:15). On the subject of social pests, "he who meddles in a quarrel not his own is like one who takes a passing dog by the ears" (Prov 26:17 RSV), while "he who blesses his neighbor with a loud voice, rising early in the morning, will be counted as cursing" (Prov 27:14 RSV). Similarly, "Like a madman who throws firebrands . . . is the man who deceives his neighbor and says, 'I am only joking!' " (Prov 26:18-19 RSV).

Ecclesiastes 10 also has a few humorous sketches: the shortsighted person who does not consider the consequences of actions (Eccl 10:8-9), the dunce (Eccl 10:10), the person who puts on a good show but overlooks the obvious (Eccl 10:11) and the fool who is worn out by his own *folly (Eccl 10:15).

Humorous Sarcasm. The Bible also has examples of sarcasm. We have already noted Elijah's sarcasm at the expense of Baal's prophets on Mt. Carmel. The book of Job contains several examples, beginning simply with the designation of Job's acquaintances as "friends" and "comforters" when they mainly attack Job and render his life miserable by their presence. With this as a context Job gets off some delicious one-liners. At one point he calls his friends windbags: "Shall windy words have an end?" (Job 16:2). On another occasion he responds to a long speech by Zophar with the sarcastic comment "No doubt you are the people, and wisdom will die with you" (Job 12:2). The voice from the *whirlwind also resorts to some sarcasm. As God asks Job eighty scientific questions that are obviously beyond Job's comprehension, he interrupts the biology test to assert to Job, "Surely you know!" (Job 38:5); and again, "You know, for . . . the number of your days is great!" (Job 38:21).

Exasperation sometimes drives people to sarcasm. Achish, king of Gath, is an example: observing David play the madman, Achish said to his servants, "Lo, you see the man is mad; why then have you brought him to me? Do I lack madmen, that you have brought this fellow to play the madman in my presence?" (1 Sam 21:10-15).

Jesus could be sarcastic too: on one occasion he observed that he had to make his way to Jerusalem, "for it cannot be that a prophet should perish away from Jerusalem" (Lk 13:33). On another occasion, when Jews stood with stones in their hands ready to throw at him, Jesus said, "I have shown you many good works from the Father; for which of these do you stone me?" (Jn 10:32).

Irony. Irony is another source of humor in the Bible. Verbal irony involves saying one thing while meaning its opposite. It is based on incongruity, and in its humorous reaches it often involves pretending an obvious impossibility to be possible or asserting something that is obviously contrary to the facts.

When Jacob runs away secretively from Laban with his family and herds after years of hostility between the two, Laban finally catches up with the group, hoping for some type of retaliation. He says with mock hurt, "Why did you flee secretly, and cheat me, and did not tell me, so that I might have sent you away with mirth and songs, with tambourine and lyre?" (Gen 31:27 RSV). Laban is a master of the straight-faced deceiver: in the incident of the substitute bride, when Jacob awakes the next morning to find Leah in bed, Laban suddenly becomes the helpful travel guide, explaining native customs to a foreigner: "It is not so done in our country, to give the younger before the first-born" (Gen 29:26 RSV). The information is obviously true, but a little belated.

When Moses confronts Aaron with his offense in

carving the golden calf "with a graving tool" (Ex 32:4), Aaron's explanation of how it all happened is a small classic: the people gave him their jewelry, he "threw it into the fire and there came out this calf" (Ex 32:24). There is also the case of King Saul, assuring Samuel that he had destroyed the Amalekites while the lambs and oxen that had been spared form a musical backdrop: "And Saul said to [Samuel], 'Blessed be you to the LORD; I have performed the commandment of the LORD.' And Samuel said, 'What then is this bleating of the sheep in my ears, and the lowing of the oxen which I hear?' " (1 Sam 15:13-14 RSV). When Abraham has to buy a cave to bury Sarah, he bargains with the Hittites in a session governed by straight-faced deceit. Despite all the statements about giving the land free of charge, Abraham ends up paying an exorbitant fee for the cave (Gen 23:8-15).

Treating an obvious impossibility as a possibility is a form of verbal irony. It occurs on a grand scale when the voice from the whirlwind asks Job a series of questions about Leviathan—whether Job can reel him in with a fishhook or put a rope in his nose, or whether the beast will "speak to you soft words" and "make a covenant with you," or whether Job will "play with him as with a bird" or "put him on leash for your maidens" (Job 41:1-5).

Dramatic irony is created when the audience's superior information is in contrast to that of one or more characters in a story, and this too can result in humor. In the story of Ehud's assassination of Eglon (Judg 3:15-25), the writer in effect exchanges a grim wink with the reader at the expense of the doomed victim. We know, as Eglon does not, that Ehud, a left-hander, is carrying a homemade weapon on the unexpected right side, where it escapes detection. Ehud's words, like his sword, are double-edged, with his mention of a "secret message" for the king. The king is so impressed by the solemnity of the moment that he rises from his seat to receive the "secret message from God," which turns out to be a sword in his fat belly. Other "gruesome wink" stories in the OT include the story of Dinah (Gen 34), Judah and Tamar (Gen 38), and the Amalekite king Agag, who comes cheerfully before Samuel, thinking that if he has survived thus far he will be released, only to find that Samuel has other intentions: "Samuel hewed Agag in pieces before the LORD in Gilgal" (1 Sam 15:32-33 RSV).

Obtuseness can be a form of humor to the on-looker who "knows better." In the story of Peter's *rescue from *prison and his subsequent inability to get into a prayer meeting (Acts 12:12-17), the maid Rhoda, recognizing Peter's voice at the gate, runs to the group instead of letting Peter in. The rest of the group is equally obtuse, concluding that it cannot be Peter but must be "his angel!" As the resurrected Jesus begins to converse with the two men of Emmaus, one of them asks, "Are you the only visitor to Jerusalem who does not know the things that have happened there in these days?" (Lk 24:18 RSV). The masterpiece of obtuseness is the responses of the Pharisees to Jesus' healing of the man born blind (Jn 9), as they try vainly to deny the healing of the blind man in the face of overwhelming proof.

What's in a Name? Some of the humor in the Bible revolves around the *names of characters. We should remember that in the biblical world names were viewed as defining a person and were something that a person either lived up to or had to live down. The birth story of Jacob and Esau stresses the laughable aspects of the event (Gen 25:24-26), and the names of the brothers, based on events at their births, are approximately equivalent to "Hairy" and "Grabby." The name Isaac, meaning "he laughs," is based on the occasion when Abraham laughed in God's face when God predicted the birth of a son in Abraham's old age (Gen 17:17-19). The churl Nabal was as unfortunate in his name as in his personality and premature death: in Hebrew the word *Nabal* sounds like the word for "fool," so when Abigail meets David, hoping to placate him after her husband's insult, she says, "Let not my lord regard this ill-natured fellow, Nabal; for as his name is, so is he; Nabal is his name, and folly is with him" (1 Sam 25:25 RSV).

The crowning instance is the nickname that Jesus gave to Peter. When Jesus pinned the name "Rocky" on Peter at Caesarea Philippi, Peter was anything but a stable personality, which is what the image of the rock betokens. In fact, no sooner did Peter receive the nickname than Jesus had to rebuke him with the comment, "Get behind me, Satan!" (Mt 16:23). At the time the name was given, it was an ironic and humorous incongruity, as when we call a tall man "Shorty" or an overweight one "Slim." But the irony proved redemptive and prophetic, for Peter turned out to be a rock, and what started as a joke ended as a fact.

Jesus as Humorist. If there is a single person within the pages of the Bible that we can consider to be a humorist, it is without doubt Jesus. There is a subtle, playful quality to his mind that is unmistakable and that emerges most clearly if we take time to distill his humorous sayings from the seriousness that also pervades his words. Jesus was a master of wordplay, irony and satire, often with an element of humor intermixed.

The most characteristic form of Jesus' humor was the preposterous exaggeration (*see* Giantesque Motif), handled most convincingly in E. Trueblood's small classic *The Humor of Christ*. The recorded speeches and conversations of Jesus give us many humorous vignettes: people cleaning the outside of a cup but not the inside before drinking, straining out a gnat and swallowing a camel, the outdoor and ruggedly dressed John the Baptist as a weakling and fancy dresser, lighting a lamp and then putting it under a basket or bed, going to an all-night party without sufficient oil for the small hand-held lamps of Jesus' day, trying to remove a speck out of someone's eye with a log in their own eye, hiring a band to play while putting their money into the offering plate.

Summary. Either to underemphasize its humor or overemphasize it distorts the Bible. Although the Bible is a predominantly serious book, one of its points of humanity is its humor. The humor of the Bible is not of the rollicking type but the subtle and intellectual type for which the term *wit* is often an accurate designation.

See also COMEDY AS PLOT MOTIF; SATIRE; TRICK-STER.

BIBLIOGRAPHY. E. Trueblood, *The Humor of Christ* (New York: Harper & Row, 1964); G. Webster, *Laughter in the Bible* (St. Louis: Bethany Press, 1950).

HUNDRED

In the Bible as elsewhere, the figure of a hundred suggests a quantity of substantial size. This is particularly so when applied to age: Abraham is one hundred years old when Sarah bears Isaac (Gen 17:17). The fact that he is exactly one hundred underscores the magnitude of the miracle and, correspondingly, the magnitude of God's faithfulness in his promise to Abraham. Similarly, Isaiah describes the vast blessing of life in the new heaven and new earth in terms of great age, such that "he who dies at a hundred will be thought a mere youth" (Is 65:20 NIV).

Since a hundred equals ten tens, the figure also conveys an image of a round, complete number. Consequently, units of Israel's soldiers appear repeatedly in groups of either hundreds or *thousands (i.e., ten hundreds, e.g., 2 Sam 18:4). Likewise, when Jacob buys land from the sons of Hamor at Shechem, the sum is one hundred pieces of silver (Gen 33:19). While Jezebel is killing of the prophets of the Lord, Obadiah hides a hundred of them in two caves, bringing them food and water (1 Kings 18:4).

In the NT the figure of one hundred vividly conveys the sense of a complete number. In Jesus' parable of the lost *sheep (Mt 18:12-14; Lk 15:4-7), when one sheep out of a hundred wanders off, the number of those remaining seems lacking and incomplete by comparison. Only when the man has found his hundredth sheep is he satisfied. To grasp the power of a hundred as an image of completeness, one need only consider hypothetical variations on the parable. If Jesus had told a story of a man with ninety-nine sheep who loses one and is left with ninety-eight, the sense of completeness in the numbers would be substantially less, as would the *rhetorical power of the parable.

Because it conveys the notion of a large, complete number, a hundred is also a significant biblical image describing factors of return. For example, the first season that Isaac plants crops in Gerar, the Lord blesses him with a hundredfold yield (Gen 26:12). Here the image is that of complete *blessing, according to God's promise to Abraham. When God promises the land of Canaan to Israel, he commands their obedience, for which he promises to reward them with astounding victories against their more numer-

ous enemies—first at a ratio of one to twenty, then at a ratio of one to one hundred (Lev 26:8).

In the NT this imagery is echoed by Jesus in his parable of the sower (Mt 13:3-8; Mk 4:3-8; Lk 8:5-8). The one who receives the seed of the word of God and keeps it will produce a hundredfold crop (Lk 8:15). More explicitly, Jesus promises a hundredfold return for those who deny themselves the comforts of this world for his sake. Then, to this already monumental promise of reward, Jesus adds a still greater promise—eternal life (Mt 19:29; Mk 10:29-30). As the crown of his promise, the blessing of eternal life towers above even the magnificent blessing of a hundredfold return for one's sacrifice. In these instances the image of hundred as a factor of return speaks of the vast and complete blessing that God can produce in and for his people.

See also FIVE; FORTY; ONE; SEVEN; SEVENTY; THOUSAND; THREE, THIRD; TWELVE; TWO.

HUNGER

Hunger and its close associate *famine were powerful images to the ancient Near Eastern mind. In Palestine *harvest was dependent on adequate and timely *rainfall. Consequently, the specter of hunger stalks Abraham (Gen 12:10), Isaac (26:1), Joseph (41:27, 54), the people of Israel both in Egypt and in Sinai, David (2 Sam 21:1), Elijah (1 Kings 18:2), Elisha (2 Kings 4:38; 8:1) and many others. The attraction of Canaanite fertility gods arises from the desire to control this uncertainty (e.g., 1 Kings 18:23-39). The search for food plays an important part in the unfolding history of Israel. Most significantly, Israel experiences physical hunger in the *wilderness (e.g., Ex 16:3). Hunger is therefore a potent image for the Hebrew poets (e.g., Ps 107:5, 9, 36; cf. Neh 9:15).

In the NT, provision of food for the hungry is incumbent upon Jesus' followers (Mt 25:31-46), a command taken seriously by the early church (e.g., Acts 6:1-6; 2 Cor 8-9).

Hunger as a Metaphor. Hunger can result from disobedience to God (e.g., 1 Kings 17:1; 18:17-18; Hag 1:6, 9-11; 2:16-17). Deuteronomy, however, makes it clear that the satisfaction of physical hunger is insufficient for the well-being of the Israelites: "One does not live by *bread alone, but by every word that comes from the mouth of the LORD" (Deut 8:3 NRSV). Certainly, Deuteronomy threatens Israel with physical hunger if they stray from the path of obedience (Deut 278:48; 32:24). Jeremiah 14 expresses this insight in poetic terms, and Amos reiterates this warning (Amos 4:4-6). He develops the image by envisioning a worse predicament—that of a famine of God's word (Amos 8:11-12). However, he also prophesies a future time of superabundant blessing (Amos 9:13). Isaiah also extends the image from physical suffering of the desert journey home (Is 41:17-20) to forthcoming spiritual salvation as well (Is 44:3).

In the temptation in the wilderness (Mt 4:1-11),

Jesus symbolically reenacts the experience of Israel in the wilderness. Jesus is guided in his responses to Satan precisely by the reflection on Israel's wilderness experience (Deut 6—8; cf. Mt 4:4, 7, 10). Whereas Israel's experience was mixed, Jesus triumphs over the hardship and the *testing.

Jewish expectation was that God would relieve the hunger of the poor (cf. Lk 1:53; *see* Poverty) and, true to his messianic task, Jesus feeds the hungry (Mk 6:30-44; 8:1-10). In his teaching, however, Jesus focuses on spiritual hunger and, metaphorically, on thirsting for righteousness before God (Mt. 5:6), though even here the physical element is not completely spiritualized (cf. Lk 6:21). For Paul, hunger demonstrates that he is still awaiting the consummation of salvation. It even authenticates his ministry (2 Cor 11:21; cf. 1 Cor 4:11).

John presents a thoroughgoing development of the metaphor of hunger. With clear reference to the experience of Israel in the wilderness, Jesus not only provides food for the crowd (Jn 6:1-14), but describes himself as the Bread of Life meeting spiritual as well as physical needs (Jn 6:31-58). Revelation repeats earlier warning (Rev 6:8) but looks forward to the time when hunger will be no more (Rev 7:16; 21:4).

See also BANQUET; BREAD; FAMINE; FASTING; FEAST, FEASTING; FOOD; SUPPER; THIRST.

HUNTING

Hunting, one of the oldest activities known to humankind, is one of the fundamental archetypes of human culture and of animal behavior. The peaceful edenic coexistence of humans with animals is replaced after the flood by "fear and dread" as animals are sanctioned as human food (Gen 9:2-3). Among the Bible's vivid images of hunting and hunters are a few men (in the biblical world it is foremost a male activity) who are so skilled at hunting that their very names evoke the hunt. But hunting also provides images of pursuing one's *enemies or being pursued by them. And even *God is imaged as the divine hunter who tracks down his enemies.

Hunting sets human cunning and invention against the acute senses and varied speed, power and ferocity of a wild *animal. Although most meat in biblical times was derived from domesticated animals, Israel and other ancient cultures were heirs to thousands of years of hunting practice and a varied arsenal of of *weapons, entrapments and strategies for hunting wild game. Hunters used ingeniously constructed snares and *traps to catch *birds and some land animals. Nets could catch birds and small animals, while larger animals could be driven into specially constructed cul de sacs and then killed. Deep pits, or cisterns, camouflaged and lightly covered, entrapped large animals which were then killed by weapons. A hunter could stealthily creep up on his prey and then close the remaining distance with a deadly javelin or arrow, though these weapons were more likely to be used by warriors and royalty. Hunt-

ing *dogs were also used and prized in Egypt, Syria, Assyria and Palestine. Without the advantage of modern firearms, the hunter of the ancient world relied not only on well-fitted weapons but on finely honed skills and a deep familiarity with the habits of his prey.

Nimrod and Esau are the most unforgettable hunters in the Bible. Nimrod was "a mighty hunter before the LORD," and his reputation was memorialized in the proverbial saying "Like Nimrod, a mighty hunter before the LORD" (Gen 10:9). Esau is perhaps the most memorable of hunters. This ruddy complexioned son of Isaac cuts a manly figure as "a skillful hunter, a man of the open country" (Gen 25:27), one adept with "quiver and bow" (Gen 27:3). He is to bring his father some savory game from the hunt and then receive the patriarchal *blessing. But while he is hunting, the plot reverses, and Rebekah and Jacob's trickery turn Esau into a tragic figure who is cheated by a scheme of camouflage and bait befitting his own skills as a cunning hunter.

Hunting was closely akin to warring, and the accomplished hunter and skilled warrior were frequently one and the same. We find Benaiah, one of David's "mighty men," David's elite corp (2 Sam 23:20 par. 1 Chron 11:22), in a memorable cameo of bravery, danger and cold: "he went down into a pit on a snowy day and killed a lion." On a day when most men stayed close to the hearth, Benaiah found a lion trapped in a snowy pit, and added luster to

A hunter prepares to shoot his prey.

heroism by entering the earth's icy maw to take on this most dangerous of beasts. Even the young David presents his credentials to Saul as one who has rescued his father's sheep from the paws of the bear and lion (1 Sam 17:34-37). To be a great hunter, literally a "champion of game," was a claim associated with royal status. Gilgamesh, the ancient Sumerian king of Uruk, is depicted as a great hunter in the *Epic of Gilgamesh,* and the palace art of Assyria often depicts Assyrian kings in hunting scenes. The reality was, however, that royal hunts were often highly ritualized and choreographed events that supported a mythology of the king as a fearless hunter.

The Bible sometimes adopts a prey's-eye-view of the hunter. Those who in a moment of weakness have given their unlimited pledge to their neighbor or bound themselves to another are to make every effort to flee for their lives: "Free youself, like a gazelle from the hand of the hunter, like a bird from the snare of the fowler" (Prov 6:5 NIV). The image of an animal stalked by a hunter is found in the language of Israel's lament. "Those who were my enemies without cause hunted me like a bird" (Lam 3:52). Frequently the psalmists speak of personal adversaries capturing them by hidden pitfalls, snares and nets (Ps 31:4; 35:7-8; 64:5; 140:5; 142:3; cf. Ps 9:15). Here the imagery of the hunter and the hunted is negatively conceived as the righteous are unwittingly caught in the trap devised by their wicked predators.

God is sometimes depicted as a hunter who always gets his prey. In a rhetorical question aimed at Job, God asks, "Do you hunt the prey for the lioness and satisfy the hunger of the lions?" (Job 38:39 NIV). God does. The psalmist calls on God to let "disaster hunt down men of violence" (Ps 140:11). The image of God the hunter can take a chilling turn as Israel becomes the frightened prey, left with no recourse but to hide in the hills. In Amos we find an image of Yahweh's coming judgment on Israel: "Though they hide themselves on the top of Carmel, there I will hunt them down and seize them" (Amos 9:3 NIV). And in Jeremiah God says, "I will send for many hunters, and they will hunt them down on every mountain and hill and from the crevices of the rocks" (Jer 16:16 NIV). On the day of the Lord all of the enemies of Yahweh will flee his wrath "like a hunted gazelle," fleet footed and darting this way and that, desperately trying to escape its inevitable doom (Is 13:14 NIV). The image of the divine hunter is used of ancient Near Eastern gods such as Ningirsu, the god of Lagash, who holds his enemies in a hunting net. Within this broader context we can place texts such as Ezekiel 17:20, where God says, "I will spread my net over him [Zedekiah], and he shall be caught in my snare" (NRSV; cf. Ezek 12:13; 19:8; 32:3). The cunning and deadly accuracy of God the hunter is a fitting image of divine power, royalty and sovereign control over the affairs of this world.

See also ANIMALS; BIRDS; FISH, FISHER; FISHING; TRAP, TRAPPING; WEAPONS, HUMAN AND DIVINE.

BIBLIOGRAPHY. O. Keel, *The Symbolism of the Biblical World* (Winona Lake, IN: Eisenbrauns, 1997 [1978]) 89-95.

HUSBAND

By definition a husband is someone whose identity is relational to a *wife. *Adam is the prototypical husband of the human race. His sons in the Bible are numerous, and those we remember significantly as husbands include *Abraham, Isaac, *Jacob *Moses, Boaz, *David, *Solomon, Ahab and Joseph the husband of Mary. Among these, Boaz and Joseph stand out as ideals. We might note in passing how few men in the Bible are delineated in their husbandly role in any degree of detail.

Boaz emerges in the book of *Ruth as a full-fledged picture of all that a husband should be. A godly employer (Ruth 2:4) and a prosperous *farmer, he is *gentle and generous to his future betrothed long before he knows that he is a candidate to marry her. He values Ruth for her godliness and because she is "a woman of worth" (Ruth 3:10-11 RSV). He acts decisively and honorably to claim Ruth once she has indicated her interest in marrying him. Boaz is a kinsman- redeemer who provides for the material needs of Ruth and her mother-in-law, and he is a sire to Ruth's child.

A similar image of Joseph the husband of Mary emerges. When his unmarried fiancé becomes pregnant, he, "being a just man and unwilling to put her to shame, resolved to divorce her quietly" (Mt 1:19 RSV). Subsequently we catch glimpses of Joseph as Mary's companion in the travels of life, in worship, in child rearing.

The Role Defined. The role of the husband is defined in the creation story. At a physical level Adam provides the substance for his wife, who is in some sense his alter ego (as the very word *woman* hints, a similar relation can be observed in the Hebrew words for man, *'îš*, and woman, *'iššâ*). Husband and wife thus share the same human identity before God. They are also "one flesh" (Gen 2:24), denoting sexual union (2 Cor 6:16) and intimacy. Here then is a major part of what it means to be a husband: it means to be incomplete in oneself and to require union with a wife to find solace for what would otherwise be an unquenchable longing for a mate (Gen 2:18-13). Companionship—two forming one—is thus a major aspect of being a husband. While we have virtually no extended pictures of how husbands and wives relate to each other in the Bible, we nevertheless infer a picture of husband and wife accompanying each other through the joys and sorrows of life as well as the tasks of work and parenting and the exercise of the religious life.

As Genesis 2 implies, an important role of a husband is that of *lover and *sexual partner* to his wife. The ideal lover of the Bible is the male protagonist in the *Song of Songs—ideally ardent in his devotion and praise of his beloved, ideally attractive to her and other women, sexually confident, physically strong and a veritable poet in his wooing of his beloved. The narrative portrayals of husbands as lovers tone down the voltage, as we are mainly told that these men "knew" (KJV, RSV, NRSV) their wives, an evocative euphemism that suggests the mystery and levels of intimacy that sexual union between spouses implies. 1 Corinthians 7:1-7 elevates the sexual role of a husband to a connubial duty. The love of a husband for his wife is viewed in Ephesians 5:1-33 as a natural inclination (Eph 5:28-29), a moral command (Eph 5:33) and an analogy to the love of Christ for his church. Using the imagery of water flowing from a fountain, Proverbs 5:15-19 pictures the urge for sexual satisfaction as a natural appetite that seeks its fulfillment and enjoins the husband to "be infatuated always" with the "the wife of your youth."

Another role of husband is that of *provider*. This is not an explicit command but the implied picture that emerges from biblical stories about families. Husbands oversee the means of livelihood (in the biblical world almost always some form of agriculture) and wives oversee the household. Perhaps this division of duties can be traced back to the curse in Genesis 3, where Eve's role is that of mother (Gen 3:16) and Adam's is that of farmer and breadwinner (Gen 3:17-19).

An additional husbandly role is *head of the family*. This image reaches definitive form only in the NT, where the husband is explicitly said to be "the head of the wife," to whom wives must "be subject in everything" (Eph 5:23-24; see also 1 Cor 11:3; 14:34; Col 3:18; 1 Pet 3:1-6; cf. 1 Tim 2:11-14). It seems safe to infer that throughout the OT the headship of the husband is taken for granted. Even in stories that feature heroines (Ruth, Esther) the husbands are the authority figures with whom primary power resides within the world of the story.

A further dimension of a husband's relationship to his wife is the religious sphere, where there is both an equality and a hierarchy. While in Christ "there is neither . . . male nor female" (Gal 3:28), and although husband and wife are "joint heirs of the grace of life" (1 Tim 3:7), other signs point to a degree of headship in the husband's role. Although God sometimes appears to the wife in the OT (Judg 13:2-7), in the overwhelming number of cases he appears to the husband. In discussing worship practices, Paul differentiates between men and women, underscoring that "the head of a woman is her husband" (1 Cor 11:3) and elsewhere directing women to "keep silence in the churches" and "ask their husbands at home" if they have questions (1 Cor 14:34-35). Although the historical and social circumstances that evoke Paul's instructions are debated, the image remains.

Husbandly Virtues and Vices. A picture also emerges of the moral virtues that make up the ideal husband. Chief of these is an ardent love of one's wife. The *Song of Songs pictures this ardency as an overflowing romantic passion, while several passages in the NT epistles portray it more as a conscious moral commitment (Eph 5:25, 28-29, 33; Col 3:18). Exclusive devotion of husband to wife is pictured as a relinquishing of the parent-son relationship as primary in deference to a cleaving to one's wife (Gen 2:24; Mt 19:5; Mk 10:7). Sexual faithfulness is a virtue enjoined of husbands (Prov 5:15-23) as is lifelong faithfulness to the covenant of marriage (Mal 2:13-16). Nurturing one's wife is another husbandly virtue (Eph 5:29), with gentleness an accompanying trait (Col 3:19). Husbands are also enjoined to "live considerately with [their] wives, bestowing honor on the woman as the weaker sex" (1 Pet 3:7 RSV). Similar language is used in the command that a husband "take a wife for himself in holiness and honor" (1 Thess 4:4).

If this is the ideal, the husbandly vices are the reverse of these qualities. The golden mean is moderation between the extremes of being either a tyrant or a wimp. One abuse is to be overbearing (*see* Tyrannical Father, Husband). But the opposite abuse is also possible, with Ahab, the infantile king ruled by his wife Jezebel, as the key exhibit. Even husbands whom we regard as predominantly good husbands, like Abraham and Jacob, appear in a bad light at moments when they abdicate their role as accountable head of the family, charged with maintaining family harmony (Gen 16:1-6; 29:31—30:24). Again, if sexual faithfulness to one's wife is the prescribed virtue, conducting an extramarital affair is an ignominy for a husband, as in the case of David with Bathsheba. The churlish Nabal is simply a foolish husband whose lapses require the deft diplomacy of his impressive wife Abigail (1 Sam 25).

God as Husband. The most important husbandly image in the Bible is not human but divine, as God is portrayed as the husband of his redeemed, who metaphorically constitute his bride and wife. "Your Maker is your husband," Isaiah says regarding God (Is 54:5 RSV; see also Jer 31:32). Several strands make up the motif of God as husband.

One is the image of *God as lover*. It begins with God's act of betrothal, as God declares regarding Israel, "You were at the age for love; and I spread my skirt over you . . . yea, I plighted troth to you and entered into a covenant with you, says the Lord GOD, and you became mine" (Ezek 16:8). As divine lover God promises to love his people freely (Hos 14:4). Israel's early relationship to God is pictured in parallel terms as displaying the love of a bride (Jer 2:2).

A second image is that of *God as jilted husband*, the victim of a wife's adulterous unfaithfulness. The book of Hosea is the extended text on the subject, as Israel is portrayed as a faithless wife whom God reclaims. In graphic language Hosea portrays faithless Israel as a wife, decked with her rings and jewelry, going after her lovers (Hos 2:13). Throughout the OT prophetic books, in fact, idolatry is pictured as *adultery (Ex 34:15-16; Lev 17:7; Jer 3:6). The betrayal is so great that God declares regarding Israel, "she is not my wife, and I am not her husband" (Hos 2:2 RSV). He even writes a bill of divorce (Is 50:1).

God as husband reaches a third dimension when God is portrayed as the long-suffering and *faithful husband who restores a faithless wife*. Again the book of Hosea is the major text, as God's relationship to Israel is imaged in the marital history of Hosea and Gomer. Despite a momentary impulse to abandon his idolatrous wife, God calls her "like a wife forsaken and grieved in spirit, like a wife of youth when she is cast off," as God reclaims her "with great compassion" (Is 54:6-7). Similar language of romantic passion appears in the book of Hosea, where God's compassion for a wayward wife "grows warm and tender" (Hos 11:8) and heals his spouse's "faithlessness" (Hos 14:4).

In the NT the metaphor of the divine husband takes a specifically Christocentric form. In Ephesians 5:21-32 Paul elaborates the analogy between a human husband and Christ. Both are the head of a wife. Human husbands are commanded to love, serve, nourish and cherish their wives, just as Christ does his church. In the book of Revelation too, Christ is the husband of the church, his bride (Rev 19:7-9; 21:2)

See also FAMILY; FATHER, FATHERHOOD; MAN, IMAGES OF; LOVE STORY; MARRIAGE; MOTHER, MOTHERHOOD; SEX; TYRANNICAL FATHER, HUSBAND; WIFE; WOMAN, IMAGES OF.

HYDROMANCY. *See* ORACLE.

HYMN. *See* CHRIST HYMN; MUSIC.

HYPOCRITE

The word *hypocrite* is based on the Greek theatrical words that mean "actor" or "to play a part." The essential identity of hypocrites, therefore, is that they pretend to be something they are not. Psalm 26:4 calls them "false men" and "dissemblers" (RSV), but in the Gospels the implications are more specific: hypocrites pretend to be paragons of religious piety while lacking spiritual virtue in their inner souls. They honor God with their *lips, but their *heart is far from him (Mk 7:6).

The *Pharisees are the prototypical hypocrites of the Bible. A composite portrait is easy to assemble from Jesus' denunciations of them. They are ostentatious when they give alms with the intent that people will praise them (Mt 6:2). They pray in the synagogues and street corners so people will take note (Mt 6:5). When they fast, they disfigure their faces (Mt 6:16). They tithe their garden produce but neglect "the weightier matters of the law, justice and mercy and faith" (Mt 23:23). In Jesus' caricature of them, they clean the outside of a drinking cup but ignore the filth inside it (Mt 23:25). They are self-righteous (Mt 23:29-30), they teach people false religious beliefs (Mt 23:16-22), and they prevent people from entering the kingdom of heaven (Mt 23:13-15). They try to trap Jesus by pretending to be perplexed about issues (Mt 22:15-22). We are not surprised that they have a special place in hell (Mt 24:51). Jesus' climactic exposure of hypocrites is to picture them as "whitewashed tombs, which outwardly appear beautiful, but within are full of dead men's bones and all uncleanness" (Mt 23:27 RSV).

See also PHARISEE.

I

IDLENESS. *See* SLUGGARD.

IDOL, IDOLATRY

With an outlook that is commonplace in our time but was radical in its own, the prophets and poets of the OT consistently denounced idols as mere sticks and stones, the handiwork of humans. On such occasions their rhetoric verges on the genre of prebattle *taunt (Is 57:13; cf. 1 Kings 18:27). They repeatedly point to the irony of an idol maker worshiping his own creation (Is 44:19; Hos 13:2; Hab 2:18). Idols stand motionless, mute and dumb, like scarecrows in a cucumber patch (Jer 10:5). Isaiah mockingly commiserates with the poor weary beasts forced to transport the worthless cargo of idols (Is 46:1) as they traveled to and from ceremonies. The idols themselves decay and come to ruin (Ezek 6:6). They have human features that do not function, making them subhuman rather than superhuman (Ps 115:4-8). The NT picks up the OT refrain (Acts 17:29; Rom 1:18-32).

Idols as Deceit. Because idols are no-account gods, only the deceived (1 Cor 6:9; Eph 5:5-6) worship them; and when they do, they worship the Deceiver (Rev 12:9). False gods make people false (2 Kings 17:15). Those who engage in idolatry "suppress the truth" (Rom 1:18-25). Idolaters are grouped with liars (Rev 21:8); idol worship is lies that lead people astray (Amos 2:4). Yet the paradoxical nature of idols persists, and a simple piece of *metal, *wood or *stone becomes a genuine spiritual evil. In nearly the same breath, Paul says that the idol is "nothing" (1 Cor 8:4) and that it is empowered by a demon (1 Cor 10:20).

Idols as Spirit Habitations. Of course, idol craftsmen and worshipers alike understood that they had made the idol. We know from both Egyptian and Mesopotamian records that an idol's inauguration required an elaborate, magical nocturnal ceremony that "opened" its eyes, "washed" its mouth and endowed it with "life." These rituals rendered the artwork suitable for the presence of the god. Opposing these very beliefs, Jeremiah repeats his accusation against the goldsmith's image: "There is no breath in them" (Jer 10:14 RSV; 51:17). Once it had become inspired, the idol was treated royally, dressed in kingly robes, carried in procession, offered the choicest foods. The temple staff served as its courtiers

in a spiritual kingship. (Hebrew, like many ancient languages, uses the same word for both temple and palace.)

Idols as Personifications. Treating the idol as a person no doubt made the abstractions of deity and spirit easier to deal with. Monotheistic prophets and idol worshipers alike personified the idols, albeit for different purposes. The idols will reveal their nondivine status when "all gods bow down before him" (Ps 97:7 RSV). Similarly, when the Lord comes, "the idols of Egypt will tremble at his presence" (Is 19:1 RSV). The naming of rocks (e.g. Bethel, Ebenezer; see "Idols as Witness" below) verges on personification.

Idols and Pagan Gods as Demons. Idols and pagan gods are parallel ideas (Lev 19:4; Deut 32:21; Is 45:20) and are even equated (Ps 96:5). "All the gods of the people are idols" (1 Chron 16:26 RSV). The author of Deuteronomy lumps foreign gods, idols and demons all together (Deut 32:17). The LXX translators understood the Hebrew ʾlōhāyw (Is 8:21, either "his gods" or "his God") to refer to pagan gods and so rendered it by *ta patachra* (a Persian word for idol borrowed through Aramaic into Greek, so also in Is 37:38). Sometimes the context suggests that the term *idol* means "god": "My idol did them" (Is 48:5 RSV); "to carry the good news to their idols" (1 Chron 10:9 RSV). The Philistine "cursed me by his idols" (LXX Ps 151:6; cf.1 Sam 17:43, which reads "by his gods"). The "sacred tokens of the idols of Jamnia" (2 Mac 12:40) means amulets naming pagan gods.

Because the Jews understood pagan gods to be *demons, idols and demons are commonly paired (e.g., Zech 13:2). So too are demons and idol worship (Rev 9:20). In some cases the word *idol* appears to refer to demons. The Greek term *eidōlon*, in addition to the standard meanings—"image," "idol," "false god"—retains the classical meaning "phantom (of the dead)" and the demons that empower and inhabit the idol. Although poorly documented in Koine lexica, several passages point to the overlap of meaning. Hosea says an (evil) spirit of harlotry (idolatry) has led the people astray (Hos 4:12; 5:4) and oppresses them (Hos 4:19). An early Christian writer of pseudepigrapha, placing in Solomon's mouth the words "I became a laughingstock to the idols and demons," gives the idols not only personality but a "spirited," vengeful attitude (*Testament of Solomon* 26:7). Paul sees demons lurking behind idols (1 Cor 10:20; cf. Ps 97:7 with Phil 2:10).

Idols as Symbols of Power. On the one hand, the idol is not really the deity but only a handle to use in dealing with the spirit, the real power behind the idol. On the other hand, it becomes so identified with the god that the two are hard to separate. The genius of the symbol is that it gives humans a way to manipulate their gods. The presence of a god can be demanded in war, for oracles, at home, on a journey. Idols represent the presence of the god at state functions. (The religious and political are not clearly demarcated in antiquity.) They are dressed up for festivals, even carried to other cities for meetings (Is 46:1; Ps 68:24-25). Portable gods filled the need for divine accompaniment (Job 12:6). With similar hopes, the Israelites take the *ark of the covenant into battle, attempting to force God to join in the battle on their side. At the arrival of the ark the Philistines exclaim in dismay, "A god has come into the camp. Woe to us!" (1 Sam 4:5).

One cannot miss the symbolism of submission intended by the charade between the idol of Dagan and the ark of the Lord (1 Sam 5:3-5). (Akkadian omen texts fret about idols that have fallen down and what dire consequences such events portend.) The (dis)pleasure or the health and well-being of the god is reflected in the national fortunes, with or without an idol. Sometimes merely owning an idol gives power. Micah's Levite is enlisted to join the migration of the Danites because he has an idol usable for divination (Judg 18:18). Rachel's thievery of Laban's idols might have been for their power or for their significance with respect to inheritance and blessing or both (Gen 31:19-35). Idols were frequently one of the spoils of war (Hos 10:5). At times Mesopotamian gods are said to be "in exile" (captured). The ark, even without an image of God, still represents his presence and blessing, so the Philistines cart it off as trophy of war (2 Sam 5:21). A curse to its captors, its mere presence blesses Obed-edom's house upon its return (2 Sam 6:11).

Idol as Witness. Just as Paul says "God is my witness" (e.g., Rom 1:9; Phil 1:8), so also idols that stand for the presence of gods function as witnesses to oaths that sealed treaties, covenants and religious vows. Many of the circles of stones uncovered by archaeology are probably to be understood as divine assemblies of witnesses. The prophets berate the idolaters since their "witnesses neither see nor know" (Is 44:8-9 RSV). In addition to the prophetic calls against witnessing idols, the narrative portions of the OT contain vestiges of such an outlook. Jacob and Laban erect a stone heap with a name meaning "witness" (Gen 31:44-52). Isaiah predicts an *altar and a *pillar to the Lord in Egypt as a "sign and witness" (Is 19:19-20). An altar, not for sacrifice but for a witness of proper worship, stands at the tribal border (Josh 22:26-27, 34). The religious compo-

nent of other stone witnesses is less clear. Perhaps large stones, permanent elements of the landscape, played the role of a mute audience to historic events, serving as a fixed, tangible anchor to unwritten history (1 Sam 6:18). The concept of stones as testifying witnesses lives again in Jesus' words, "If these were silent, the very stones would cry out" (Lk 19:40 RSV).

Idolatry as Actions. The *gestures of idolatry employ unmistakable acts of submission and worship. *Bowing, the proper attitude for *prayer (1 Kings 18:42; 2 Chron 29:29), is also performed before idols (2 Kings 5:18; Is 44:15). (The Hebrew ideas of "bowing down," "serving" and "worshiping" are nearly interchangeable and are forbidden of idols [Ex 20:5]). On other occasions worship is described by the phrase "lift the eyes" both of idols (Ezek 18:6,12,15; 33:25; Ps 121) and also of God (Ps 123:1). Some gestures of worship are confined to idolatry because they require an image. Such actions include kissing Baal or a calf (1 Kings 19:18; Hos 13:2) or kissing one's hand (Job 31:27). The latter is perhaps to be construed as presenting one's soul to the deity (Ps 24:4) and may be connected to artistic depictions of worshipers with a hand to the mouth or with an outstretched hand. In a radical departure from their neighbors' practice, the Israelites' symbol for God was the absence of an image above the cherubim on the ark of the covenant.

Idolatry as Sin and Abomination. The Bible reserves some of its strongest language for idolatry: abhor, detest, provoke, rebellion (1 Sam 15:23), stubbornness (Hos 4:16), disobedience, brutishness

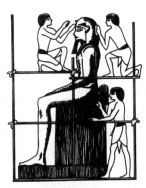

Egyptian artisans make a statute of Thutmose III. The scene informs our understanding of idols that are "the work of human hands" (Ps 115:4 NRSV).

(*see* Abomination). The prophets characterize idolatry as a pigheaded, willful disobedience of God's law and even of natural laws—the kind of disobedience that would not occur to dumb animals, implying that idol worshiping humans are baser than the brutes (Jer 8:7). Even so, the Bible and Jewish tradition record that some of the heroes of the past (or members of their entourage) succumbed to syncretistic thinking and to the seductive power of idolatry:

Jacob (Gen 28:22; 31:19-35); Gideon (Judg 8:26-27); Micah (17:5; 18:14-20); David (19:13).

Idolatry as Political Prostitution. In the shifting tide of politics, political marriages were vulnerable (1 Sam 18:26; 25:44; 2 Sam 3:14). As the experience with Solomon's wives shows, political alliances cemented by marriage stemmed from and lead to foreign politico-religious entanglements and so may also be characterized as lewd and idolatrous. Because of compromising political involvement, Judah is a wanton wench (Ezek 16), Samaria a slut (Ezek 16:46), Babylon a bimbo (Rev 17).

Idolatry as Religious Unfaithfulness. The most common and well-developed metaphor refers to idolatry as sexual impurity. But the metaphor reflects a link to, perhaps even an origin in, an idolatry built on many forms of sexual excess. Just as sexual purity was a religious mandate under the prophets (Ezek 22:7-11), idolatry made the opposite claim. Fertility cults encouraged instead the flaunting of human sexuality as a means of insuring the fecundity of the earth through sympathetic magic. Historically, idols represented nature gods, fertility gods and goddesses (Baals and Asherahs) and had long associations with fertility cults and their practices—practices believed necessary to ensure successful grain and livestock production. The rites prescribed ritualized *prostitution, both female (Gen 38:21; Deut 32:18; Hos 4:14) and male (Deut 32:18-19; 1 Kings 14:24; 15:21; Rev 22:15), incestuous relations (Ezek 22:9-11; cf. 1 Cor 5:1, 11) and the sharing of one woman by several generations of men (Jer 5:7-8; 13:27; Amos 2:7). The stone idol or wooden pillar with its phallic symbolism seems to have been viewed as the mystical sire of resulting offspring or even of the people (Jer 2:27).

In such a religious climate the prophets found in the image of an unfaithful wife an obvious analogue for a nation abandoning its own deity for that of another people. Brazen and wayward, she breaks covenant and troth (Ezek 16, esp. 16:8), defiles herself with idols (Ezek 23:7, 37), commits adultery with stone and wood (Jer 3:9). The prophets even dared to characterize the nation as a religious nymphomaniac (Jer 5:7-8; Ezek 16:32). In this context God is a "jealous God" (Ex 20:5) and refuses to share his praise with idols (Is 42:8).

Idolatry and sexual immorality continue hand in hand in the NT, where idolatry appears in lists of sins that include several labels for illicit acts (Acts 15:20; 1 Cor 6:9; cf. 1 Pet 4:3; Rev 22:15). Luke vividly conveys Paul's revulsion at Athens, a city which, in its desire not to offend any god, became "full of idols" (Acts 17:16).

Idolatry as Desires Even Without Idols. While idolatry is clearly a code name for violation of purity laws, especially (but not only) sexual ones, it eventually comes to designate lawless living in general (Col 3:5; 1 Pet 4:3). The association with lawlessness derives from its origins in the express violation of sexual social mores to insure the fecundity of the earth. Yet zeal or pious disdain for idolatry must not breed lawless retaliation, so Paul cautions that even the justified abhorrence of idols doesn't justify lawless acts against the idol's temple (Rom 2:22). Since an idol is an object of adoration, "one who is covetous" becomes "an idolater" (Eph 5:5; 1 Cor 5:10) and any earthly desires, "sexual immorality, impurity, lust, evil desires and greed," become idolatry (Col 3:5). A similar list of "works of the flesh" includes idolatry (Gal 5:19-21). Ultimately, any violation of God's law is idolatry, and idols may serve as an image and label for all that is anti-Christian (1 Jn 5:21).

See also APOSTASY; DEMONS; GOD; GODS, GODDESSES; HIGH PLACE; PILLAR; STONE; WOOD; WORSHIP.

IGNORANCE REMOVED BY INSIGHT. *See* EPIPHANY, STORIES OF.

IMAGE OF GOD. *See* ADAM.

IMMORTALITY

Images of immortality are an intensified version of images of *permanence. Immortality is the ultimate type of permanence. Since nothing earthly and tangible is immortal, there is an implicit recognition that images cannot do justice to the quality of being immortal. In place of concrete images, therefore, we find writers employing the *via negativa*, in which immortality is expressed in negative terms—"immortal" (not mortal), "imperishable," "not wither," "unfading." In addition, we find conceptual terms that name the quality of immortality rather than giving pictures of it: "eternal" (approximately 75 occurrences, NRSV), "everlasting" (nearly 60), "forever" (350).

When writers do resort to concrete imagery to picture immortality, the main technique is "enameled" imagery—imagery that combines *hardness of texture and brilliance of *light, suggesting a realm that is exempt from the cyclic changes and *decay of the earthly, vegetative world. *Jewel imagery is the most customary type of enameled imagery. Ezekiel 28:13-14 is a typical example, picturing a transcendent realm in terms of precious stones and "stones of fire." The book of Revelation likewise gives us glimpses of an immortal realm pictured by "a sea of glass mixed with fire" (Rev 15:2), "golden bowls" (Rev 15:7), a holy city possessing "the glory of God and a radiance like a very rare jewel, like jasper, clear as crystal" (Rev 21:11 NRSV). The image of a *golden *crown is another evocative NT image for immortality (2 Tim 4:8; Jas 1:12; 1 Pet 5:4).

The reality of an eternal realm is pervasive in the Bible—a main pillar of biblical faith. Yet the imagery for such an important belief is somewhat minimal, suggesting the inability of earthly imagery to capture its reality.

See also PERMANENCE

INCENSE

The high priest enters the dimly lit tabernacle with

trepidation. In one hand is a censer, hot with glowing coals from the *altar. In the other are two handfuls of incense. As he moves behind the curtain into the Holy of Holies, he puts the incense on the coals, producing a fragrant *cloud over the *ark of the covenant, the footstool of Yahweh. Thus the place of the Presence is shrouded in aromatic smoke, and the priest is hindered from seeing the forbidden throne of God.

An Element of Worship. Incense is a physical reminder of an eternal reality. It penetrates our imagination in settings of worship throughout Scripture. From the revelations to both Isaiah and John, we understand that incense signals the everlasting worship of Yahweh. In his vision Isaiah "saw the LORD seated on a throne, high and exalted, and the train of his robe filled the temple. . . . And the temple was filled with smoke" (Is 6:1, 4 NIV). Part of John's record describes twenty-four elders: "Each one had a harp and they were holding golden bowls full of incense, which are the prayers of the saints" (Rev 5:8 NIV). John's explanation echoes the psalmist, who first poses the simile: "May my prayer be set before you like incense" (Ps 141:2 NIV). The poet-prophets of Scripture consistently include incense in describing the true worship of God.

The poetic prominence of incense suggests its historical significance; indeed, incense surpasses *sacrifice as a common practice in Hebrew worship. To mirror the eternal reality of Yahweh's throne, the historical law includes detailed instructions for the temporary *tabernacles and *temples of Israel. It required the priests to "place the gold altar of incense in front of the ark of the Testimony and put the curtain at the entrance to the tabernacle" (Ex 40:5 NIV). The only incense permitted was specifically formulated for and limited to this particular use (Ex 30:34-38). The high priest was to burn the incense each morning and evening "so incense will burn regularly before the LORD for the generations to come" (Ex 30:7-8 NIV). As the smoke of the incense ascended from the altar, it served as a miniature replica of the *glory-cloud of God on Mount Sinai. Thus as Aaron stood in God's house with the miniature glory-cloud, he would be reminded of his fellowship meal with God on the smoky mountain (Ex 24) and of the terror that glory-cloud evoked.

As he obediently observed the Day of Atonement during what Luke termed "the time of incense," Zachariah, father of John the Baptist, linked the worlds of the OT and NT as Gabriel announced the prophetic work of his coming son (Luke 1:10); a prayer of centuries was being answered. The magi were also unwitting links as they presented incense as a gift to the newborn Jesus (Mt 2:11). They fulfilled prophecies that anticipated nations thronging to the Messiah "bearing gold and incense and proclaiming the praise of the LORD" (Is 60:6). And we wait still for the day when "in every place incense will be brought to [his] name" (Mal 1:11 NIV).

This string of scenes captures the general place of incense in worship. But God's indignant words to *idolaters through the prophets suggest its significance more specifically. From the tragic wider scope of references to incense, we see that it signals reverence, a pledge of allegiance and, finally, a desire to please a deity and curry favor.

To Declare Allegiance and Seek Favor. The function of incense is highlighted by its abuse in Israel's habit of idolatry. One offers incense in reverence to a being to whom all one's allegiance is pledged because one depends on that being for sustenance and survival and because one wants to garner the favor of that being. The psalmist's *prayers are like incense for this reason; he hopes to please Yahweh and gain continued protection by his fragrant declaration of allegiance. In this context the prophets provide a veritable catalogue of Israel's sinful use of incense.

The prophets summarize the misplaced allegiance, explaining that Israel burns incense "to vanity" rather than to the Lord (Jer 18:15), to Baal (Jer 7:9; 11:13, 17), to "the queen of heaven" and other gods (Jer 44), to graven images (Hos 11:2) and even to the tools of work that provide food (Hab 1:16). Israel disregards God's commands for worship. They burn incense in his temple but dedicate it to other gods or burn it elsewhere: in their own homes (Jer 19:13), on a hilltop in the shade of trees (Hos 4:13; see Grove) or in rooms prepared for worship of another. They transgress specific commands for use, employing what is intended only for the Lord in the worship of other gods (Ezek 23:41; Hos 2:13). The Prophets match the Law in specific detail of how thoroughly Israel disregarded the commands of God. Jeremiah articulates their crucial mistake as a failure to trust that God is their provider.

Like a tithe, incense indicates one's reverent allegiance and dependence upon God. In all of its sensory vividness, it is indeed an appropriate model for prayer.

See also ALTAR; ASCENT; IDOL, IDOLATRY; SMELL, SCENT; SMOKE; WORSHIP.

INCREASE, STORIES OF

While the total number of increase stories is not large, they appeal to something deep-seated in human longings. These accounts draw our imaginations to contemplate the mystery and wonder of God's workings and of his willingness to be generous to people.

A leading OT example of the motif is *Job, who lost all of his family and all of his livestock, only to find his fortunes restored, giving him "twice as much as he had before. . . . And the LORD blessed the latter days of Job more than his beginning" (Job 42:10, 12 RSV). In fact, a comparison of the number of Job's livestock at the end of the story with the number at the beginning shows that the number doubled. This is a story of virtue rewarded and prosperity not only restored but magnified. Out of sorrow and tragedy God chose to bring increase and blessing.

Four further OT stories of increase have the

common touch. The widow of Zarephath shared her last meal and oil with Elijah and was rewarded by having the meal and oil miraculously replenished until God sent rain on the earth (1 Kings 17:8-16). The widow of one of the sons of the prophets appealed to Elisha when her creditors threatened to make her two children slaves. Elisha instructed her to borrow vessels from all her neighbors, and God miraculously filled all of them with oil (2 Kings 4:1-7). Another story of increase involving Elisha is the miraculous feeding of a hundred men from someone's offering of first fruits (2 Kings 4:42-44). These are stories of God's compassion and provision extended to the needy who are devoid of resources. The cryptic story of Jabez is so brief as to tease us into wanting more information: "Jabez called on the God of Israel, saying, 'Oh that thou wouldst bless me and enlarge my border. . . .' And God granted what he asked" (1 Chron 4:10 RSV). This seems to be a story of God's generosity to the heart that longs for more.

There is also a communal story of increase at work in the OT. If one traces the word *increase* through the book of Genesis, one finds numerous promises that God will increase the numbers of the patriarchs' descendants (e.g., Gen 16:10; 17:2; 26:24), a promise repeated in Deuteronomy (e.g., Deut 6:3; 7:13; 8:1) as the Israelites contemplate entering the Promised Land. OT history confirms that this story of increase actually occurred, an early instance being the humorous story told in Exodus 1 of how the more the Egyptians persecuted the Israelites, the more they increased (Ex 1:7, 8, 12). Similarly, prophetic visions of a restored Israel include the motif of the people increasing in number (e.g., Jer 23:3; Ezek 36:11; 37:26). A NT counterpart is the statement in Acts 12:24 that "the word of God grew and multiplied."

We can even find hints of the motif of increase in the OT proverbs. The path of the righteous, for example, "is like the light of dawn, which shines brighter and brighter until full day" (Prov 4:18 RSV). While "wealth hastily gotten will dwindle," the person "who gathers little by little will increase it" (Prov 13:11 RSV). When the wicked perish, "the righteous increase" (Prov 28:28).

The best-known NT stories of increase are several of Jesus' parables and miracles. Parables that employ the motif include those of the *sower and the *seed, with its spectacular result of a hundredfold *harvest (Mt 13:3-8); the grain of *mustard seed that grows into a gigantic tree in which birds nest (Mt 13:31-32; Mk 4:30-32; Lk 13:18-19); the leaven, in which a small quantity of yeast is sufficient to *leaven as much as thirty-six quarts of dough (Mt 13:33-35; Lk 13:20-21); and the talents, in which two stewards double their master's money through aggressive investment (Mt 25:14-17). Jesus closes the parable of the talents with these words: "For to every one who has will more be given, and he will have abundance" (Mt 25:29 RSV). The parables of the kingdom are essentially stories of increase.

Some of Jesus' miracles follow the same pattern. On one occasion Jesus increased five small barley loaves and two fish into food for five thousand people, with twelve baskets of food left over (Jn 6:5-13). On another occasion seven loaves and a few small fish were multiplied to feed four thousand, with seven basketfuls left over (Mk 8:1-9). These stories remind us of the great generosity of Jesus and of his divine power over nature. Andrew's question about the five loaves and two fish at the feeding of the five thousand, "What are they among so many?" (Jn 6:9) is answered by the story itself: with God there is more than enough.

The increase motif is also present in the NT epistles, where the story of sanctification is a story of growth and increase. "Grow up to salvation," we read (1 Pet 2:2 RSV), and "Grow in the grace and knowledge of our Lord and Savior Jesus Christ" (2 Pet 3:18 RSV). Again, "We are to grow up in every way into him who is the head, into Christ" (Eph 4:15 RSV). The sanctified life is one of "increasing in the knowledge of God" (Col 1:10 RSV). The writer of Romans adduces Abraham as someone who "grew strong in his faith" as he waited twenty-five years for the birth of his promised son (Rom 4:20). To this can be added the famous passage in Romans 5:3-5 that catalogs the virtues produced by suffering—a story of ever-expanding Christian character in which one virtue produces the next. A parallel passage in 2 Peter 1:5-8 lists the virtues with which a believer is expected to add to faith, with the final product being that a person will "abound." In short, the life of faith is a grand story of increase in which grace increases thanksgiving (2 Cor 4:15), in which God provides the resources for the harvest of righteousness to increase (2 Cor 9:10) and in which faith and love increase (Phil 4:17; 1 Thess 3:12; 2 Thess 1:3).

See also LEAVEN, LEAVENING; MUSTARD SEED; NUMBERS; SEED; SOW, SOWING, SOWER.

INCUBATION DREAMS. *See* ORACLE.

INFANT. *See* BABY.

INHERITANCE

Receiving an inheritance from one's *father is a socio-legal practice well attested throughout the history and variety of cultures of the Bible. An inheritance was the gift of a good father to his *children (Prov 13:22). A major purpose of OT inheritance legislation was to provide for real property to be passed on in the family line (Num 27:1-11; Deut 21:15-17).

Most OT references to inheritance are to the *land of Canaan as the inheritance that God promised to his people (Deut 12:9, 10; 31:7; Ps 105:9-11). This was God's pledge to care for his people and provide them security. An even richer use of the imagery is found in texts that speak of *Israel as God's inheritance (Deut 32:9) or God as Israel's inheritance (Jer 10:16). God belongs to Israel and

Israel belongs to God.

The image receives greater spiritual definition in NT texts that identify the inheritance of God's people as the *kingdom of God (1 Cor 6:9, 10), eternal life (Mk 10:17), salvation (Heb 1:14) and the new *heavens and the new *earth (Rev. 21:7). It is a *"blessing" (1 Pet 3:9) whose certainty rests on the promise of God who gives it (Gal 3:18; 4:13). It is "imperishable" (1 Cor 15:50).

The power of the inheritance imagery is seen in the breadth of use in which NT writers employ it. In Colossians 1:12-13 the imagery of being "rescued from the dominion of darkness," "brought into the kingdom of the Son he loves" and gaining a "share in the inheritance of the saints in the kingdom of light" echoes the experience of Israel in its exodus and inheritance of the land. In Romans and Galatians it is used to convince God's people of their freedom from pursuing righteousness through works of obedience to the law (Gal 3:29; 4:1, 7). The promise character of the inheritance is strong in these texts, and it is a call to rest by *faith in that promise of God (Gal 3:18; Rom 4:13). In a context like Rom 8:17, this liberation from the pursuit of righteousness producing works is a liberation for joyful service.

This theme of joyful service is more clear in another set of texts, where the inheritance of eternal life has clear implications for the ethical character of the believer's present style of living. That is, the certainty and joy of the inheritance is used to motivate to righteousness (Tit 3:7; Gal 5:21; Eph 5:5), particularly brotherly love (1 Pet 3:9) and care for the needy who are fellow heirs of the kingdom (Jas 2:5).

In other texts the imagery of the overwhelming richness of the inheritance is used to encourage those who are suffering and have given up much for the sake of that inheritance (Mt 19:29, Rev 1:7). In this way it is used to move Christians to focus their vision on their rich and glorious future (Eph 1:18) when they will be transformed (1 Cor 15:50). That matchless inheritance encourages the believer to endurance and faithfulness (Heb 1:14; 6:12).

The close relationship of the Christian's inheritance to God himself is the basis of the use of the imagery to elicit praise from God's children as they look at the present experience of their inheritance and look forward to the future fullness of God's gift (Eph 1:14; 1 Pet 1:4). The appropriate response is the praise of his glory!

This wide range of use of inheritance by NT authors demonstrates the power of the imagery. It liberates, assures, motivates to righteousness, encourages and elicits praise.

See also BIRTHRIGHT; BLESSING; FATHER; GENERATION(S); KINGDOM OF GOD; LAND; PROMISED LAND.

INITIATION

The word *initiation* does not occur in the Bible. But there are a number of rites and acts that conform with the definitions of initiation by ethnologists and historians of religion, who distinguish between collective initiation and individual initiation. Initiation is also a plot motif in the Bible.

Initiatory Rites. The rites described by M. Eliade as age-group initiations include the practice of *circumcision, which in the OT serves as both an ethnic and a religious sign of belonging to the people of Israel (Ex 12:48; cf. Acts 10:45; Gal 2:9). Commanded by God (Gen 17:9-14), first performed on Abraham and his family (Gen 17:24-27), and enforced by the law (Lev 12:2), circumcision was to be practiced by the heads of families on all home-born males, as well as on *foreigners and *slaves in Israel (Gen 17:12-13). The ethnic and spiritual significance derives from the promises given to Abraham in Genesis 17:6-7: "I will make you very fruitful; I will make nations of you, and kings will come from you. I will establish my covenant as an everlasting covenant between me and you and your descendants after you for the generations to come, to be your God and the God of your descendants after you" (NIV).

In contrast to widespread customs in other cultures where children were usually circumcised at puberty, circumcision in the OT was practiced on the eighth day of a boy's life, with only a few exceptions: Abraham was ninety, Ishmael thirteen (Gen 17:25). And later, after the rite had been neglected during the *wilderness wanderings, Joshua circumcised an entire generation of male Israelites (Josh 5:1-7). As a sign of belonging to the community of the covenant, circumcision was so important that Ezekiel even speaks of a separation between the circumcised and the uncircumcised after death (Ezek 31:18). Circumcision also means a special responsibility of the people toward God (Jer 9:25-26).

Metaphorically, the initiation rite of circumcision can signify *purity, *holiness and the love of God. It implies the purity of a believer's speech, as when Moses bemoans his "uncircumcised lips" (Ex 6:12) that will not convince Pharaoh. It can also mean a readiness to obey God—or its absence can mean the opposite—as when Jeremiah talks of the "uncircumcised ear" of the people (Jer 6:10). In the NT, Paul takes up an OT metaphor when he talks of "circumcision of the heart" (Rom 2:29; cf. Deut 10:16, 30:6) to distinguish a mere outward religiosity from a truly believing heart that loves God. In his quarrel with Jewish Christians who want to make circumcision a prerequisite of the Christian faith (Acts 15:24; Gal 6:12), Paul, although having been circumcised himself (Phil 3:5), insists on circumcision being vain without faith (Rom 3:30) and obedience (Rom 2:25). He declares it as not necessary for Christians (Gal 2:3-5) and as having been abolished by the gospel (Eph 2:11; Col 3:11), and he warns that its observation as a Christian initiation rite subjects the believer to the old covenant of works (Gal 5:3ff.). The Christian church is the new Israel, as Paul tells the Philippians: "We are the true circumcision, who worship God in the spirit" (Phil 3:3 RSV).

In the NT, *baptism takes the place of circumcision as an initiation rite: "In him you were also circumcised, in the putting off of the sinful nature, not with a circumcision done by the hands of men but with the circumcision done by Christ, having been buried with him in baptism and raised with him through your faith in the power of God, who raised him from the dead" (Col 2:11-12 NIV; cf. Rom 6:4). This meaning of baptism coincides with the death-rebirth significance of other initiation rites described by modern ethnology.

The origin of Christian baptism may be the baptism performed by John the Baptist, who makes it an expression of repentance. That Jesus himself undergoes this rite at the beginning of his ministry (Mt 3:13-17) is an act of submission to God's will and of identification with his people. Although Jesus himself did not baptize, the early church adopted baptism as a sign of initiation into repentance and faith. At the same time it implied entrance into the fellowship of believers: "Those who accepted his message were baptized, and about three thousand were added to their number that day" (Acts 2:41 NIV). Thus baptism also has a community-building function, since among the believers there is "one Lord, one faith, one baptism" (Eph 4:5).

An additional figurative meaning is introduced by John the Baptist, who speaks of Jesus as he "which baptizeth with the Holy Ghost" (Jn 1:33 KJV). Jesus himself insists on baptism being a *spiritual* birth and an act of initiation when he tells Nicodemus, "no one can enter the kingdom of God unless he is born of water and the Spirit" (Jn 3:5 NIV). He then promises this baptism to the disciples (Acts 1:5), and it is also experienced by the Gentiles (Acts 11:15-16).

Vocational Initiation. What ethnology describes as vocational initiation—that is, the introduction of an individual into the role of shaman, counselor and healer—is structurally equivalent to, but also markedly different from, the calling and appointing of prophets in the OT. A number of prophets undergo a rite that makes them fit for their job. Isaiah, who feels he is a man of unclean lips, is touched by an angel with a live coal and thus cleansed of his iniquity and sin and prepared for proclaiming the truth of God (Is 6:6-10). Similarly, Jeremiah's mouth is touched by God, which makes him fit for uttering God's warnings in the face of the people (Jer 1:9); and Ezekiel is made to eat a scroll containing lamentations (Ezek 2:9-3:2). A distinctive rite is missing in the calling of Moses (Ex 3) and later of Samuel (1 Samuel 3) as prophets, but their appointment is as clearly an instance of vocational initiation as the anointing of Israel's kings such as Saul (1 Sam 9) and David (1 Sam 16), who are invested with royal authority through an official act.

In the NT, the appointment of the seven "men . . . who are known to be full of the Spirit and wisdom," (Acts 6:3 NIV) who are to oversee the distribution of food in the early church, may be seen as a similar vocational initiation. They are placed before the apostles, who pray and lay their hands on them (Acts 6:1-6). This ceremony has been considered the original institution of the office of deacon.

Initiation as Plot Motif. If initiation is understood in a more general sense as "the action of beginning, entering upon, or 'starting' something" (OED), it can be viewed as an archetypal biblical plot motif, since a large number of stories represent such an introduction to a new way of life, even without rites and formal ceremonies. The first initiates in the Bible are Adam and Eve, who are initiated into the conditions of human life in God's created world (Gen 2) and later into the conditions of life in a fallen world (Gen 3).

One action in which this motif is commonly realized is the *journey. The three stages of initiation that ethnologists have isolated—exit from the previous state, transition and entrance into the new state—can be found in such journeys as that of Abraham, who left Chaldea and traveled west to Canaan (Gen. 12). The youthful Jacob and Joseph both undertake journeys of initiation into adulthood. The pattern is reenacted in the eastward journey of the people of Israel from Egypt through the wilderness to Canaan, and it can also be found in Ruth's moving from Moab to Bethlehem with her mother-in-law Naomi (an initiation into a new faith and a new ethnic community).

Initiation stories do not always entail a journey, however. Gideon's initiation into judgeship is by way of an encounter with an angel and a pair of supernatural signs (Judg 6:1-24). The boy *David is initiated into the world of military heroism by means of his single combat with Goliath (1 Sam 17). The boy Samuel is initiated into a prophet's life through dreams in the night (1 Sam 3:1-14). In the kingly life of David as narrated in 2 Samuel, David's life prospers until the debacle with Bathsheba and Uriah (2 Sam 12), which proves to be David's initiation into a life of the retributive consequences of sin. God's allowing Satan to bring calamity onto Job brings about Job's initiation into a life of suffering and deprivation. The events of *Pentecost are the disciples' initiation into the age of the Holy Spirit. In view of the placing of Jesus' baptism and wilderness temptation early in the Gospels, these events might plausibly be interpreted as Jesus' initiation into his redemptive ministry.

Initiatory processes can be described in terms of their positive or negative outcome. In Christ's parable of the *prodigal son (Lk 15:11-32), there is a negative initiation (through his riotous living the young man is exposed to poverty, moral destitution and despair) and a positive one (the reception by his father reintroduces him to social acceptability and sonship). Negative initiations include the initiations of *Adam and *Eve into *sin and its consequences (Gen 3), of *Cain and *Abel into violence and *murder (Gen 4), of the tower-builders in *Babel into linguistic confusion (Gen 11) and of Judas into the satanic plan to betray Jesus (Jn 12:27). Some initiation stories show blessings or curses in disguise:

*Joseph's betrayal by his brothers leads to slavery in a foreign country, but its further consequence is the rescue of the starving people of Israel in Egypt, which is in turn an initiation into slavery.

The NT contains numerous positive initiations. Jesus' healings bring sufferers into a new healthful existence. Sometimes, as in the story of the lame man whose friends carried him to Jesus (Mk 2:1-11), this coincides with an initiation into a new life of righteousness before God. The latter is, of course, the central meaning of such *conversion experiences as that of the woman caught in *adultery (Jn 8:3-11), of Zacchaeus (Lk 19:1-10) and of Paul (Acts 9). Even when conversion is a process of gradually growing faith, it can be seen as an initiation. Thus J. Augustine has shown how in the Gospel of Mark the disciples undergo a series of "initiatory steps" and how the story of the Gospel itself has an initiatory function, "as it initiates the reader beyond the disciples' own understanding through the way the narrative unfolds" (Augustine, 394, 396). In addition to the NT conversion stories, the teachings and parables of Jesus speak of *entering* the kingdom of God, and statements in the epistles speak about the *new* life in Christ (*see* New).

See also BAPTISM; CIRCUMCISION; CONVERSION; JOURNEY; ORDEAL, STORIES OF.

BIBLIOGRAPHY. M. Eliade, *Birth and Rebirth: The Religious Meanings of Initiation in Human Culture* (New York: Harper, 1964); J. H. Augustine, "Mark," in *A Complete Literary Guide to the Bible*, ed. L. Ryken and T. Longman III (Grand Rapids: Zondervan, 1993) 387-97.

INJURY. *See* WOUND.

INN

In contemporary life the inn is one of our most positive and common images of *traveling—the public lodging for a night's rent, the place where a weary traveler can find *food, comfort and a *bed. The Bible is nearly devoid of this image, largely because the ancient code of *hospitality was so strong a force that private citizens lodged travelers in their homes. Thus in Job's great oath of innocence he asserts that "the sojourner has not lodged in the street; I have opened my doors to the wayfarer" (Job 31:32 RSV). We can, however, trace an evolution from the private lodging of travelers in the OT to the rise of inns by the time we reach the NT.

In the OT we catch only occasional glimpses of travelers spending the night in public inns. The two spies who came to Jericho intended to lodge overnight at the prostitute Rahab's house, which must have been an inn as well as a brothel. Rahab's inn of ill repute fits into an extrabibilical tradition that regards both inns and innkeepers with suspicion. In the Song of Songs the lover's invitation to his beloved to take a romantic trip into the countryside includes the inviting prospect of staying overnight in a village inn: "Let us go forth into the fields, and lodge in the

villages" (Song 7:11 RSV). And Jeremiah's dream of escaping an evil society includes the wish "O that I had in the desert a wayfarers' lodging place" (Jer 9:2 RSV), with the prophet perhaps picturing himself as setting up such a place on the route of a trading caravan, where inns were sometimes located.

There are hints of change in the NT. On an occasion when Jesus' teaching of the crowds continued until sundown, the disciples urged Jesus to "send the crowd away, to go into the villages and country round about, to lodge and get provisions" (Lk 9:12), evoking our more familiar picture of actively finding and paying for a night's food and lodging. In the parable of the good Samaritan too we have the picture of the inn as a neutral place (as opposed to a private home) where food and lodging are paid for (Lk 10:29-35).

But the best known inn in the Bible may not actually have been an inn. When Luke tells us that the newborn infant Jesus was placed in manger "because there was no room in the inn" (Lk 2:7 NIV), the term used is *katalyma*, which may refer to the small guest quarters of a private residence. In this case the infant is placed in a makeshift crib in the part of the home where the animals were sheltered. But this meaning is not certain, and a specific inn at Bethlehem may be indicated. Whether we are to visualize the familiy turned out of an inn or a guest room, the irony of the Messiah being born in such poor circumstances is striking. And the manger and its setting take on some of the qualities of an inn—a place of retirement for the night, a place of protection from the elements, a scene of domestic activity.

See also GUEST; HOME, HOUSE; HOSPITALITY.

INNER, INSIDE, WITHIN

The vocabulary of being inside or within someone or something appears slightly fewer than three hundred times in English translations of the Bible. Some of the usages are merely terms designating physical or spatial location, but even these references tend to accrue symbolic overtones such as *holiness or the spiritual/psychological as distinguished from the physical/external.

One cluster of references focuses on the physical *body, especially of *animals used in OT sacrifices. The chief repository of these references is *Leviticus. Another minor series uses interior imagery to identify a center of power or influence. Thus to appear before a king ordinarily entails finding one's way to the "inner court" of the palace (Esth 4:11; 5:1 NIV).

The biggest cluster by far refers to the *sacred space that surrounds *worship at the *tabernacle and *temple. The temple references include not only the accounts in the books of Kings and Chronicles but also extensive occurrences in Ezekiel's vision of restored temple worship. To these can be added an evocative reference in Hebrews to Christ's having entered "the inner sanctuary behind the curtain" (Heb 6:19 NIV).

In worship imagery inner space denotes sacred space—a holy place set apart for special activities and protected from ordinary people and life. The implied contrast of many of these spatial references is between inside and outside, the inner and the *outer, with the former in each case representing higher value and sanctity. Perhaps no other feature of tabernacle and temple architecture so obviously symbolizes spiritual status as this spatial pattern.

Another set of spatial references uses the imagery of being inside something as meaning secret or *hidden, though short of implications of holiness. Eglon's servants hesitate to check on their king because they assume that he is "relieving himself in the inner room of his house," that is, his toilet (Judg 3:24). In times of *battle, kings and generals in danger try to hide in inner rooms (1 Kings 20:30; 22:25), while on a positive note a future king might be secretly anointed in a secret inner chamber (2 Kings 9:2). Similar positive connotations occur in Jesus' command to avoid ostentatious *prayer in public places and instead to "go into your room and shut the door and pray to your Father who is in secret; and your Father who sees in secret will reward you" (Mt 6:6 RSV).

A significant further use of the imagery of inner and inside denotes the inner psychological and spiritual core of a person, usually in implied differentiation from (and even contrast to) the external person and behavior that is open to public view. Given the lyrical genre in which the psalms are written, we expect the motif to appear, and it does—not with the vocabulary of "inner" (which appears only once in the NIV) but in conjunction with the preposition within. Here we find references to a person's *heart melting within him (Ps 22:14) or growing hot within her (Ps 39:3), and to God's law being "within my heart" (Ps 40:8). Psalms 42—43 (a single poem) ring the changes on the speaker's soul being cast down "within" him (Ps 42:5, 6, 11; 43:5). Elsewhere we find a range of emotions that are said to be "within" the speaker—anguish (Ps 55:4), anxiety (Ps 94:19), a wounded heart (Ps 109:22), quietness of soul (Ps 131:2), a fainting spirit (Ps 142:3-4). Especially noteworthy is Psalm 103, a psalm of praise in which the speaker addresses his inner being to praise God: "all my inmost being, praise his holy name (Ps 103:1).

The classic lyric passage is Psalm 51, expressing David's feelings of contrition upon being confronted with his sin. Whereas most *lament psalms protest the behavior of external *enemies, the foe in this case is inner and spiritual—*sin and *guilt. The whole orientation of the psalm is accordingly inward. The premise of the psalm is that God desires "truth in the inward being" (Ps 51:5 RSV). In keeping with this interior emphasis, the psalmist prays the God will cleanse him from spiritual pollution, teach him wisdom "in the inmost place" (Ps 51:6 NIV), create in him a pure heart (Ps 51:10) and "renew a steadfast spirit within me" (Ps 51:10 NIV). Even the motif of sacrifice is spiritualized and internalized in this mildly

revolutionary psalm: "You do not take pleasure in burnt offerings. The sacrifices of God are a broken spirit" (Ps 51:16-17 NIV).

Beyond the psalms, too, the locational image of being inside is used to portray interior spiritual experience metaphorically. In his epistle, Peter commends the adornment of the "inner self, the unfading beauty of a gentle and quiet spirit, which is of great worth in God's sight" (1 Pet 3:4 NIV) as opposed to extravagant physical adornment. Jesus denounced the Pharisees for keeping up pious external appearances while they are "like whitewashed tombs," actually full of uncleanness within (Mt 23:27 NIV; cf. Mt 23:25-26; Lk 11:39-41). The principle of the matter was stated by Jesus in this form: "Whatever goes into a person from outside cannot defile. . . . It is what comes out of a person that defiles. . . . All these evil things come from within, and they defile a person." (Mk 7:18-23 NRSV).

Within this image pattern the inner person is the essential spiritual core of a person. Such a conception underlies Paul's comment that "though outwardly we are wasting away, yet inwardly we are being renewed day by day" (2 Cor 4:16 NIV). And again, "I pray that out of his glorious riches he may strengthen you with power through his Spirit in your inner being, so that Christ may dwell in your hearts through faith" (Eph 3:16-17 NIV).

An additional motif makes the individual believer reside in God or Christ. The key text is Colossians 3:3: "Your life is now hidden with Christ in God" (NIV). Fitting into this pattern are the approximately one hundred occurrences each of the phrases "in the Lord" and "in Christ."

While the biblical imagery of something's being on the inside rather than the outside begins as a simple indication of physical location, it ends by pointing to something deeply spiritual. In fact it is at the core of biblical religion, as expressed by Samuel on the occasion of the anointing of the boy David as king: "the LORD does not see as mortals see; they look on the outward appearance, but the LORD looks on the heart" (1 Sam 16:7 NRSV)

See also HEART; HIDE, HIDING; OUTER, OUTSIDE; SACRED SPACE.

INNER PARTS, BOWELS

"I am the one who examines kidneys and hearts." So reads a literal translation of Revelation 2:23. The NIV rightly translates this verse as "I am he who searches hearts and minds." A comparison of the two translations reveals the shift in the metaphors for emotions that has taken place since the time Jesus spoke these words.

Exactly where in the body one locates the focal point of emotion is somewhat arbitrary. For modern speakers of English it is the *heart. Our language is full of colorful expressions that employ and play with this idiom. For the biblical writers and their secular contemporaries, the so-called seat of emotions was the bowels, the inner parts or the *belly. In fact, the biblical terms that refer to the inner parts are often translated *"heart" in modern versions (cf. Jer 31:20, Philem 1:20).

It is easy to surmise why intense feelings were expressed by the image of the "inner parts." The image was probably born out of the physiological experience that often accompanies intense emotion. When one feels appalled by a terrible crime, for example, real nausea may accompany the emotion. Hence, we express our feelings by saying, "That makes me sick." It is understood that whether or not physical discomfort is truly experienced, the speaker is expressing emotional *disgust.

The terms in the original languages that refer to the inner parts do not in and of themselves designate whether the feeling being expressed is positive or negative. For example, the Hebrew term used for the beloved's erotic passion in Song of Songs 5:4 is the same term found in Jeremiah 4:19 to voice his distress. In other words, the sort of emotion expressed by a reference to the inner parts is to be discerned by the context rather than by an appeal to the original languages.

Biblical writers lacked modern terminology for abdominal parts. References specifically to the bowels or intestines are few and calamitous. An OT ritual trial of a wife accused of infidelity by her husband includes the *curse for a guilty wife: "Now may this water that brings the curse enter your bowels and make your womb discharge, your uterus drop!" (Num 5:22 NRSV).

Combat and suicide produce a cluster of references as well. When the crafty left-hander Ehud plunges his homemade sword into Eglon's fat belly, the victim's intestine is pierced and the dung seeps out, perhaps explaining why the king's attendants assumed that he was going to the toilet after Ehud made his getaway (Judge 3:22-25). When Joab strikes Amasa with his sword, the victim's entrails pour out on the ground (2 Sam 20:10). Judas Iscariot, perhaps in an inept suicidal hanging, is described thus: "he burst open in the middle and all his bowels gushed out" (Acts 1:18 NRSV).

Disease accounts for further references. The curse pronounced by Elijah on King Jehoram includes the melancholy prediction that the king "will have a severe sickness with a disease of your bowels, until your bowels come out, day after day, because of the disease" (2 Chron 21:15 NRSV). Two years later the king's "bowels came out because of the disease, and he died in great agony" (2 Chron 21:19). The NT counterpart is the arrogant Herod, who accepts the acclaim of the crowd that he is a god and is immediately smitten by God and "eaten by worms and died" (Acts 12:23 NRSV).

See also BELLY; DISGUST, REVULSION; HEART; STOMACH.

INNOCENCE, INNOCENT

To be innocent is to be free from *guilt, blameless, *clean or righteous. The quest for innocence is the central theme of the Scriptures. Such innocence was the original state of the human race, and the Bible records the quest of the soul to regain a state of righteousness before God. To be guiltless, blameless, pure, holy and innocent remains the deepest cry of the human soul.

Even though the specific word *innocence* does not appear in the text, the first picture—and perhaps the most enduring image—of innocence in the Bible is that of *Adam and *Eve as unfallen humans in a perfect *garden (Gen 2). The aura of the story of life in Paradise is that of new beginnings, freshness, an unsmirched quality. The premise of the story is that Adam and Eve have not yet disobeyed and are therefore sinless. Specifically they are "innocent" of the experiential knowledge of evil, as attested by their not having eaten of the *tree of the knowledge of good and evil (Gen 2:16). The image that symbolizes this innocence is that they "were both naked, and were not ashamed" (Gen 2:25 RSV).

While innocence in an absolute sense is not possible for fallen humans, it is possible in a relative sense, and the Bible accordingly speaks of innocent people in the sense of their being righteous or not deserving of some calamity that has befallen them. *Martyrs, for example, are innocent—that is, undeserving of their murder—as in Jesus' comment about "all the righteous blood shed on earth, from the blood of innocent Abel to the blood of Zechariah the son of Barachiah" (Mt 23:35 RSV). In the book of Job, which revolves around the spectacle of the suffering of someone who has done nothing to deserve it, we find numerous references to good people as "innocent" or "blameless" (Job 1:1, 8, 22; 4:7; 17:8; 22:19, 30; 27:17). The psalms make a similar equation of morally righteous people with innocence (Ps 15:5; 19:13; 94:21), as does the book of Proverbs. Here, then, is a major image of innocence in the Bible—paragons of virtue whose righteous behavior exempts them from deserving the misfortunes that befall them in an oppressive world (see also Dan 6:22). The passages that employ this motif usually pit the innocents against oppressive antagonists in such a way as to evoke the picture of the archetypal innocent victim.

The innocence of virtuous people is connected in the Bible with the *heart and the *hands—the heart because innocence is an inner quality and the hands because the washing of hands is an archetype of being clean. Abimelech protests that his sin of ignorance was undertaken "in the integrity of my heart and the innocence of my hands" (Gen 20:5). The speaker in Psalm 73:13 protests, "All in vain have I kept my heart clean and washed my hands in innocence" (RSV; cf. Ps 26:6). Job 22:30 pictures God as delivering "the innocent man" through the cleanness of his hands. Pilate washed his hands in a false innocence when he delivered Jesus to the Jews (Mt 27:24). The innocence for which David longs in Psalm 51:10 is pictured in the imagery of a clean heart.

Occasionally innocence in the Bible is the ignorance of people who do something wrong in unawareness rather than in conscious sin. Thus Abimelech responds to the dream that God sent him: "Lord, wilt thou slay an innocent people?" (Gen 20:4 RSV), meaning that he had taken Sarah into his harem in ignorance of the fact that she was a married woman. In a variation on that theme the NT twice pairs wisdom and innocence, with innocence having connotations of being exempt or ignorant of deviousness or evil: Jesus instructed his disciples to "be wise as serpents and innocent as doves" (Mt 10:16 RSV), and Paul wanted the Christians at Rome "to be wise about what is good, and innocent about what is evil" (Rom 16:19 NIV).

The most numerous category of references to innocence in the Bible centers on the shedding of "innocent *blood." There are nearly two dozen instances of the idiom, which refers to the *murder of people who did not deserve this fate. The innocence in view is of course not absolute, yet the choice of the terminology of innocence highlights the heinous nature of murder.

The supreme example of innocence in the Bible is, of course, *Jesus. When the centurion at the crucifixion "saw what had taken place, he praised God, and said, 'Certainly this man was innocent!'" (Lk 23:47 RSV). The testimony of Scripture is that Jesus "committed no sin" (1 Pet 2:22) and that he was "without sin" (Heb 4:15). Pilate found "no basis for a charge against this man" (Lk 23:4 NIV), finally declaring that "this man has done nothing wrong" (Lk 23:41 NIV). Jesus himself asked at one point, "Which of you convicts me of sin?" (Jn 8:46).

The innocent Jesus remains the model that his followers aspire to emulate. Paul prays that the Philippian Christians "may be pure and blameless for the day of Christ, filled with the fruits of righteousness that comes through Jesus Christ" (Phil 1:10-11 NIV). He is confident regarding the Corinthian Christians that Christ "will sustain you to the end, guiltless in the day of our Lord Jesus Christ" (1 Cor 1:8 RSV). To the Thessalonians, Paul expresses the prayer that God "may establish your hearts unblamable in holiness" (1 Thess 3:13 RSV). He enjoins the Philippians to "be blameless and innocent, children of God without blemish" (Phil 2:15 RSV). The possibility of being "blameless" or "without spot" in Christ is repeatedly held out as a possibility (Eph 1:24; 5:27; Col 1:22; 2 Pet 3:14; Jude 24).

See also CLEANSING; GUILT; HEART; FALL FROM INNOCENCE; MARTYR; PURITY; SIN; SINNER; SNOW; WHITE; WOOL.

INNOCENCE, FALL FROM. *See* FALL FROM INNOCENCE.

INSIDE. *See* INNER, INSIDE, WITHIN.

INSTRUCTION. *See* TEACHER, TEACHING.

IRON

The history of smelting technology informs the im-

ages of *metals in Scripture. While the text offers only a glimpse at ritual vestiges of the shift from stone to copper and *bronze tools (Ex 4:25; Josh 5:2; cf. Gen 4:22), the transition from bronze to iron provides the backdrop for the Israelite struggle for independence from oppressive neighbors cunningly maintaining a monopoly on iron forging technology through treaties with clans of smiths (Judg 4:17; cf. Gen 4:22).

A durable iron *weapon held its edge while instantly blunting or even breaking a bronze sword. The superiority of iron weapons repeatedly placed the Israelites at a distinct military disadvantage. Even their agricultural tools required costly Philistine maintenance (1 Sam 13:20-21). When Israel first entered the land, they were dependent upon the Canaanites for iron working (1 Sam 13:19-22). For reasons both economic and mystical, the Philistine-controlled craftsmen carefully guarded their trade secrets so that "not a blacksmith could be found in the whole land of Israel, because the Philistines had said, 'Otherwise the Hebrews will make swords or spears!'" (1 Sam 13:19 NIV). The song of Deborah describes the tribes as unarmed peasants (Judg 5:7-8). A paucity of weapons clearly hampers Saul's attempts at autonomy (1 Sam 13:22). The military successes of David rest in part on increased availability of iron tools (2 Sam 12:31). The obscure foreign origins of *barzel*, the Hebrew word for iron, suggest that the term was borrowed along with the technology.

Iron occurs symbolically with several connotations. First, as the hardest metal known at that time, it carried an aura of the highest level of technological innovation. Even though the production of iron eventually spread quite widely, several requirements retarded this spread: access to jealously guarded secrets, sources of ore, a knowledge base and a significant level of skill. The smiths carefully shielded their secrets from all outside their clan. The mystery and magic surrounding smelting, and especially the higher temperatures and quality controls necessary for iron production, made smiths the wizards and high priests of technology and an essential element in any plans for independence or military expansion.

The mystical associations of iron continued in later Judaism, which held the names of Jacob's wives to have magical curative properties for binding evil spirits because their initial letters spelled out the word for iron (*brzl*—Bilhah, Rachel, Zilpah, Leah). Job cites the hiding of iron in the earth as an example of divine, inscrutable wisdom (Job 28:2). Playing on the mystique of iron, Jeremiah mentions that the "sin of Judah" is written with an iron stylus (Jer 17:1), suggesting that the very hardness of his writing tool (he compares it to a diamond stylus) also implies a permanence of what is written (cf. Job 19:24).

The terror of the iron chariots (Josh 17:6; 17:18; Judg 1:9; 4:3; 4:13) comes in part from their actual effectiveness and in part from incorporating the symbolic technological advantage of invincible components, an advantage denied Israel for a time. The mystery of iron working, the irony that a flat iron hammer should pound out a sharp edge, provides the setting for the proverb "As iron sharpens iron, a friend sharpens a friend" (Prov 27:17 NLB), where accountability to a peer and tough-minded interaction produce a razor sharp mind and keenness of character.

Second, iron symbolizes great power and persistence. Behemoth owes his strength to "limbs like bars of iron" (Job 40:18), and Leviathan's mythical strength "counts iron as straw" (Job 41:27). To be put in irons makes escape impossible (Ps 107:10). The "iron pillar" (Jer 1:18) symbolizes unconquerable strength while the "necks of iron" represent an unrepentant persistence that will not be broken (Is 48:4). The scepter or rod of iron represents an harsh or unyielding reign (Ps 2:9; Rev 2:27; 12:5; 19:15). In a similar vein an unrelenting drought is symbolized as a bronze sky and an iron earth (Lev 26:19; Deut 28:23).

Finally, in Nebuchadnezzar's dream the relative value of metals plays an important role in Daniel's description of the four world empires (Dan 2:41). While iron is the least-valued metal in this ranking, it is superior in strength, hinting at a government lacking in religious values or cultural achievement, but ruling with an unbending will. Similarly, in Daniel's vision the "teeth of iron" are unbreakable and represent unrelenting cruelty (Dan 7:19). The prophet Amos alludes to the unmerciful savagery of war as "threshing sledges of iron" (Amos 1:3).

See also BRONZE; CHARIOT; METALS; SWORD; WEAPONS.

IRONY. See HUMOR; RHETORICAL PATTERNS.

ISAIAH, BOOK OF

The book of Isaiah is literarily and thematically creative and complex: *remnant, *blindness, *justice, *holiness, and cosmic *mountain are but a few of the many disparate motifs and images in Isaiah. However, two primary motifs—the *Holy One of Israel (the King) and *Zion (his intended royal habitation)—permeate the book and bring order to its complexity. The Holy One of Israel desires to dwell in Zion (Is 7:14); but in order to do so, he must first purify not only her (Is 1:24-26) but the surrounding nations (Is 13—23) and even the entirety of the created order (Is 24:1-6). The process of purification, embracing *cleansing and healing, structures both halves of the book in ever-expanding concentric circles. In the first half of the book, judgment spreads from Zion (Is 1—12) to the surrounding nations (Is 13—23) until finally all of *creation is involved (Is 24—27). Then the process is repeated, this time describing restoration rather than *judgment, which expands outward from Zion (Is 40—59) to the nations (Is 60—64) and ultimately embraces the entire *heavens and *earth (Is 65—66).

Holy One of Israel and Zion. Holiness is the primary attribute of God as king (Is 6:1-3; 63:15) and the chief pillar of God's heavenly throne (Is 43:15). Except for Lord (Yahweh) and God, the "Holy One of Israel" is the most common name by which Isaiah portrays God (30 times)—an appellation all the more striking because the title rarely occurs in the OT outside of Isaiah. The appellation "Holy One of Israel" becomes the motif to which all other images of God refer: the Holy One of Israel is the Creator of the universe (Is 17:7; 41:20; 43:15; 45:11) as well as Israel's *redeemer (Is 41:14; 43:14; 47:4; 48:17; 49:7; 54:5), her *lawgiver (Is 5:24), her *light (Is 10:17), her *help (Is 31:1) and her *joy (Is 12:6; 29:19; 41:16).

Complementing the pervasive use of the "Holy One of Israel" to represent God, Zion is the prevailing metaphor employed in Isaiah to represent God's people. Central to the Zion motif is the image of Zion as a *mountain and/or a *city. The multitude of other miscellaneous images portraying Israel—new *bride/wife (Is 62:5), harlot (Is 1:21), *barren woman (Is 54:1), *garden (Is 51:3), *vineyard (Is 5:1-7) and wayward child (1:2) to mention only some—are simply alternate pictures of Zion; they are subimages of the Zion image. Two of the three key elements of the Abrahamic promise are expressed in the Zion image: place (*land) and people (*seed). The third element, relationship with God, is expressed in the purification theme. God wants to dwell with his people (Is 7:14), so he will purify them. While other prophets and psalmists use the Zion motif, it is Isaiah who brings it into fully three-dimensional complexity.

The book of Isaiah uses abundant and diverse imagery to portray Yahweh and Israel, but the foundational motifs to which all others refer are Yahweh as the Holy One of Israel and Israel as Zion. The Holy One of Israel and Zion are the twin poles around which the prophecy orbits. The drama of the prophecy swirls around God's desire and intention to dwell in the midst of his people and their absolute inability to have him among them. The tension created by the unholy state of Zion structures the collection of prophecies and is the "plot line" along which the "story" advances.

The Theme of Purification. By purifying her, the Holy One of Israel will bring Zion from death to life. For Isaiah, purification involves a painful cleansing and healing process. Including healing as part of the purification process (Is 1:5-6 and 1:24-26) is unusual. This peculiar picture of purification, healing included with the cleansing, captures what elsewhere may be thought of as redemption; indeed, Isaiah links purification with redemption (Is 1:24-26 and 1:27).

Images of *cleansing and *healing abound (Is 1:5-6; 6:10; 19:22; 53:5). Cleansing most often takes the form of judgment, and healing the form of salvation. While the cleansing and healing images exist side by side, it is the first half of Isaiah that is laden with cleansing judgment imagery and the latter half with healing salvation imagery. The cleansing aspect of purification involves purging evil (and therefore people) from Israel, perhaps best captured by the prophecies reducing Israel to a righteous *remnant (Is 6:11-13). Healing, on the other hand, is visualized by images of *restoration, a new *exodus and an abundant population inhabiting a new heaven and new earth.

Zion is the epicenter from which purification rumbles through the surrounding nations and to the entire created universe. Chapters 1—39 present the necessity for and means by which judgment will be accomplished in Zion, the surrounding nations and the entire created sphere. In chapters 40—66 the dominant theme is salvation for Zion, the nations and the created order. The cleansing and healing processes begin in Zion, the center of Isaiah's universe, and move out to the entire created realm and universe. The account of cleansing Zion and her surroundings, followed by the subsequent healing of these same entities, structures the book of Isaiah.

The Necessity for Purification and Its Process. The necessity for and manner of the purification of Zion is laid out in the first five chapters and introduces Isaiah's prophetic commissioning (Is 6:1-13), where Isaiah first encounters the Holy One of Israel. Cherubim are flying around him, proclaiming the holiness of the one reigning on his exalted, heavenly throne. Confronted with this vision and proclamation of Yahweh's holiness, Isaiah despairs on account of his own impurity. The account of Isaiah's purification symbolizes the necessity for cleansing and healing and foreshadows the purification process that will be at the heart of the relationship between the Holy One of Israel and Zion.

Lack of purity is primarily a result of not knowing God (Is 1:2-3). *Blindness is used as the major image for ignorance of God (Is 6:9-10; 26:11; 29:9, 18; 35:5; 42:7, 16, 18-19; 43:8; 56:10). Zion's blindness is demonstrated in three ways: injustice (i.e., ill treatment of widows, orphans and poor [Is 1:17, 21]), foreign alliances (Is 31:1) and *idolatry (Is 1:29-30). Unjust treatment of fellow Israelites reveals a lack of knowledge of God's grace (Is 1:3, 16-17). Turning to foreign nations for military defense and to idols for providential care reveals a lack of faith that God can defend and provide.

The lawsuit (*see* Legal Images) prosecuted in chapters 40—48 not only argues that if Zion (Israel) knew her God, she would not have behaved as she did, but it also argues for the power of God to cleanse and purify her as he said he must. Purification means the removal of unrighteousness and injustice through cleansing judgment. It also embraces the healing restoration of these attributes by means of salvation.

Justice and righteousness are a primary poetic word pair in the first half of the book (Is 1:21, 27; 32:1). In the second half salvation is paired with righteousness (Is 45:8; 51:1-8), indicating a movement from the cleansing of judgment to the healing of salvation. While judgment and blessing/salvation

are interspersed throughout the text, the general thematic focus moves from the necessity of purifying judgment to the inevitability of judgment to judgment proper and finally beyond judgment to healing. The same Holy One of Israel that judged will be the one who heals (Is 6:10; 19:22; 53:5; 57:18), bringing the purification process to its completion. A holy, purified, priestly nation will return to inhabit Zion (Is 52:11-12), bringing offerings and holy things for worship in a new heaven and earth (Is 66:20-21).

Isaiah's Creativity with the Zion Motif. *Zion, the mountain, the city and site of the *temple, signifies several things: the place of God's rule (Is 24:21-23), *refuge (Is 14:32), *peace (Is 2:2-5), *justice (Is 1:21; 33:5) and *judgment (Is 24:21-23); the source from which word and law issue (Is 2:1-4) and the holy dwelling whose *foundation is God (Is 28:16; 33:6). She is a city that is alternately sinned against and sinful like Sodom. Zion plays other roles: the empty buildings awaiting the return of her people, the messenger to other empty cities (Is 40:9) and the recipient of the message. God is concerned for her ramparts and walls, her foundation. The new city will have *walls called "Salvation" and *gates named "Praise" (Is 60:18). Yahweh will be her foundation (Is 33:6), sun and moon (Is 60:19). Her defense and her destruction are his alone to dictate.

These diverse movements in imagery are not random; they mirror the shift in the prophecy from the Holy One of Israel's cleansing of Zion to his healing of her. In this process Zion is transformed from ruins to a gleaming city (Is 61:4), from desert to *garden (Is 35:1-2), from empty to bursting (Is 54:1), from silent to bustling, from languishing/sad to bountiful/joyous. As mountain of God, Zion replaces Sinai (Is 2:3; 4:5-6) and becomes the highest of the mountains (Is 2:2-3). Zion is judged and becomes empty, her gates languish and *mourn, and then with the promise of inhabitants, she becomes hopeful that she might become the one no longer deserted, a mother of many. Similarly, she is portrayed as the harlot, bereft of husband and children, who becomes the wife of the Holy One of Israel with many children (Is 1:21; 54:1). Zion has unruly children (Is 1:2-4), who are *orphaned and then restored (Is 60:4) by the Holy One of Israel. While Zion is portrayed as impure city and wife being made pure, the Holy One of Israel is the light that becomes a consuming fire (Is 10:16) and then the bright light of salvation (Is 60:1).

Other Motifs. The cleansing and healing process of Zion and its environs that structures the book is complemented by diverse foundational images and motifs: the *divine warrior, the *exodus motif, the royal motif, the creation motif, the remnant motif, the image of the *arm/hand of the Lord, the *covenant lawsuit, the *servant of the Lord. So, for example, the Holy One of Israel is the divine warrior (Is 63:1-6), who by the might of his arm will discipline Zion (Is 5:25) and then lead her in a new, greater exodus (Is 40:10-11) into the new heaven and earth he will create. He prosecutes his covenant lawsuit (Is 1 and Is 41—48) and will use his servant (Is 42:1-9; 49:1-11; 50:4-11; 52:13—53:12) to both accomplish his task and rule the new order.

Isaiah is creative with motifs and images found elsewhere in the Bible, for example, the *arm of the Lord, the new exodus and the new creation. The arm of the Lord image is used in the rest of Scripture almost exclusively as a stock motif to signify God's saving power as exhibited in the exodus from Egypt. While Isaiah employs it similarly (Is 63:12), the arm of the Lord in Isaiah additionally becomes the power to rule (Is 40:10), the symbolic gesture in covenant making (Is 62:8) and the hope of the nations for bringing justice (Is 51:5; 52:10—53:1).

Using the language of the exodus from Egypt (*wilderness, way through the desert, *cloud by day, going before and behind), Isaiah transforms the faith grounded in that first *exodus into hope for a second exodus from exile in Babylon.

Except for the book of Genesis, Isaiah is virtually the only other book of the OT to employ the Hebrew word for "create" (Gen 1:1) to address God's creative role. Isaiah actually speaks of creation more often (and more diversely) than Genesis. God creates Zion as the new Sinai (Is 4:5), Jacob as his people (Is 43:1), salvation for his people (Is 45:8), new things (Is 48:7), *darkness/disaster (Is 45:7), praise on the lips of the mourner (Is 57:19), Jerusalem as a delight (Is 65:18) and a new heaven and earth (Is 65:17).

Purification is Permanent. The Holy One of Israel's purifying process from Zion to the surrounding nations to all of creation moves the prophecy forward in two cycles—cleansing and healing. The nations will come to Zion and be included (foreshadowed in Is 2:1-4 and repeatedly referenced in Is 40—66). The drama will conclude on a new stage—a new heaven and a new earth; the old heaven and earth having witnessed to covenant violation, now give way to a new created order. The witnesses at the beginning of the prophecy give way to new witnesses at the end, the redeemed who have returned. And it is the all-pervasive purification motif that alone explains the strange ending to Isaiah:

As the new heavens and the new earth that I make will endure before me," declares the LORD, "so will your name and descendants endure. From one New Moon to another and from one Sabbath to another, all mankind will come and bow down before me," says the LORD. "And they will go out and look upon the dead bodies of those who rebelled against me; their worm will not die, nor will their fire be quenched, and they will be loathsome to all mankind. (Is 66:22-24 NIV)

No longer will there be impurity in Zion. Cleansing will never again be necessary. Once for all, the Holy One of Israel will have removed all that is wicked from the midst of Zion. For those redeemed witnesses who will stand on the walls of the new Zion and look out, the gruesome scene outside the walls will give hope that only light remains in God's dwelling place; darkness and wickedness will be forever beyond Zion's borders.

See also BLIND, BLINDNESS; CREATION; DIVINE WARRIOR; EXILE; EXODUS, SECOND EXODUS; HOLINESS; JERUSALEM; JUSTICE; MOUNTAIN; PURITY; REMNANT; RESTORE, RESTORATION; SINAI; SUFFERING SERVANT; ZION.

ISLAND

The Hebrew word *'iyyîm* can refer to islands proper or to coastlands, lands accessible by sea. Only a few islands bear any significance in the OT: Cyprus, whose inhabitants are the Kittim, Rhodes and Crete, known as Caphtor (Javan, Elisah and Tarshish are also named). Although Solomon and then Jehoshaphat engaged in some seafaring expeditions (cf. 1 Kings 9:26-28; 22:48), the Israelites were not a seafaring people and their first port city, Joppa, did not come into their possession until the time of the Maccabbees. Apart from Noah's *ark, the story of *Jonah contains the only seafaring episode in the OT. For Israel, knowledge of the islands and coastlands of the Mediterranean was based on hearsay, the best source being the Phoenecians, their seafaring neighbors.

In both Isaiah's and Ezekiel's oracles against the Phoenecian city Tyre, the collapse of the great sea trading city evokes a response from the islands and coastlands of the Mediterranean (Ezek 26:18; cf. Is 23:2, 6). But most of the OT's references to islands occur in Isaiah, where they form an element of the prophet's universal vision. The islands are an image of the far-flung and little-known nations across the Mediterranean world. God will reach out his hand to the dispersed remnant of his people, scattered among the nations and even the isles, and gather them (Is 11:11). In the midst of destruction a note of hope is sounded as voices of praise to God are heard coming from the islands of the sea (Is 24:15). In Isaiah 40—66 the islands play various roles, including chorus, *witness and *pilgrim. They are weighed like dust in God's scales (Is 40:15), they are silenced (Is 41:1; cf. 23:2), they tremble with *fear before the Lord (Is 41:5), they will put their hope in the *law of the Lord (Is 42:4), they are instructed to sing a "new song" (Is 42:10), to proclaim their praise to the Lord (Is 42:12) and to listen to the testimony of the *Servant of the Lord (Is 49:1). Though the islands will not escape the wrath of the *divine warrior (Is 59:18), they wait in hope for God to exercise his saving power (Is 51:5), and finally they will bring their tribute to *Jerusalem (Is 60:9). Even the most distant islands will be included in God's redemptive work as messengers are sent to proclaim God's *glory to islands that have not heard or seen (Is 66:19). For Isaiah the islands are images of the ends of the earth, borders of the known world that nevertheless fall under the sovereignty of Yahweh.

In the NT the islands appear primarily in Acts, where Cyprus (Acts 11:19-20; 13:4; 15:39) is a mission field and the islands of Crete, Cauda and

Malta play their roles in the account of Paul's voyage and shipwreck on the way to Rome (Acts 27:1—28:11). In this story, Malta is an island of deliverance from the deadly sea as well as a venue for the gospel of new life. The entire episode stands in suggestive counterpoint to the ending of the first volume, Luke's Gospel: the passion and resurrection of Jesus is echoed in Paul's near death and deliverance. But this time the good news is proclaimed not in Jerusalem but on a remote island and then in Rome. In Titus 1:5 we learn of a successful planting of churches in Crete. In the mission of the early church Isaiah's vision of Yahweh's heralds to the islands (Is 66:19) is enacted, and the islands become images of spiritual awakening, fertile soil for the planting of the gospel. In only one case is an island associated with hardship, John's exile on the island of Patmos, but even this becomes the venue for an unsurpassed vision of God's saving work that includes representatives of every tribe, language, people and nation (Rev 5:9).

See also GENTILE; JONAH THE PROPHET; SEA; SHIP, SHIPWRECK.

ISRAEL

The name *Israel* is used in the Bible with a number of referents. Traditionally associated with the ancestor *Jacob, whose name was changed to Israel after a nocturnal wrestling match with a mysterious figure (perhaps God) in Genesis 32, the name was subsequently applied to various collective entities in the Bible: the descendants of Jacob as a group; the *twelve tribes of the Israelite confederacy of premonarchic times; the united kingdom under the rule of David and Solomon; the northern kingdom after the division of united Israel; the southern kingdom of Judah, especially after the fall of Samaria to the Assyrians; the remnant of Israelites who survived the Babylonian exile; the ethnoreligious community who saw themselves as God's chosen people; and the early Christian community. This variety of referents allows the name Israel to be associated with the broader image of the people of God. A number of ancillary terms, such as *covenant and *circumcision, could be used to evoke the image of Israel as the people of God.

In the OT two streams of tradition shaped the image of Israel. One is the stream of promise, which began with the narratives of *Abraham and Sarah and proceeded through the other ancestral narratives of Genesis, finding its culmination in the divine promises made to *David in 2 Samuel 7. The other is the stream of deliverance and *covenant articulated in the book of Exodus. As a community Israel was always to remember that its identity was to be shaped by its memory of slavery in Egypt and deliverance by the Lord. Living under the promise, with the memory of its past slavery and deliverance and the challenge of covenant, Israel was called to become a faithful community.

This image of Israel as the people of God comes to expression in the book of *Deuteronomy. Here

the grand streams of tradition are woven together into a characterization of Israel's identity. Several aspects are important. First, Israel is to demonstrate unswerving, exclusive loyalty to Yahweh. Flowing out of the first commandment (Deut 5:5-7), this loyalty is expounded throughout Deuteronomy 1—11, where we find the repeated command and warning to maintain undivided loyalty to Yahweh. Second, Israel is to remember that they had been chosen by God for a special relationship: "For you are a people holy to the LORD your God; the LORD your God has chosen you out of all the peoples on earth to be his people, his treasured possession" (Deut 7:6 NRSV; cf. Deut 14:2). Their relationship with Yahweh was not based on any merit of their own. This is made abundantly clear in Deut 9:4-6. Third, as a people who had been delivered from slavery, Israel is to remember its past. This memory was to shape Israel's life as a community both in its social relationships and in its observance of the proper worship of Yahweh: "Remember that you were a slave in the land of Egypt, and the LORD your God brought you out from there with a mighty hand and an outstretched arm; therefore the LORD your God commanded you to keep the sabbath day" (Deut 5:15 NRSV; cf. Deut 15:15; 16:12; 24:18, 22). Fourth, Israel is not to replicate the social stratification and oppression of Egypt but rather to establish itself as a true community in which fraternity was to be the hallmark. Many of the regulations of Deuteronomy 12—26 reflect this vision of Israel as a fraternal community. The call to manifest justice and righteousness within the communal life of Israel is to be taken seriously. This concern for justice is shown in the frequent reminders that Israel is not to take advantage of those who are weakest in their society, specifically the widow, orphan and resident alien (Deut 10:17-18; 24:17; 27:19). In broad strokes these are some of the characteristics associated with the image of Israel as the people of God.

The contours of this image of Israel and its vocation provided the basis for much of the prophetic critique of Israel. The specific accusations of individual prophets vary, but they cluster around the issues of failure to exhibit undivided loyalty to Yahweh and failure to establish justice within the community.

New Testament. In the NT the early Christian community came to identify itself with Israel as the people of God. Occasionally this was done through a direct application of the name Israel to the early Christian church. In Galatians 6:16, after a vigorous polemic against those who would require Gentile Christians to be circumcised, Paul said, "As for those who will follow this rule [i.e., the gospel]—peace be upon them, and mercy, and upon the Israel of God" (NRSV). Here the expression "Israel of God" is taken to be a reference to the early Christian community, which accepted the gospel as preached by Paul.

More often the NT alludes to this image by using words that would immediately evoke the image of

Israel as the people of God but without explicitly calling the church Israel. A prime example of this is 1 Peter 2:9: "But you are a chosen race, a royal priesthood, a holy nation, God's own people, in order that you may proclaim the mighty acts of him who called you out of darkness into his marvelous light" (NRSV). Here we find a coalescence of terms derived from the larger image of Israel as God's chosen people (cf. Ex 19:5-6), but which here are reapplied to the early Christian community. Each of the terms has its antecedent in the OT, where it was used to refer to Israel. What we see is a broadening of the image of Israel to include those who were not Jews genealogically. This broadening is obvious in the case of the expression "chosen race," which in the context of 1 Peter's exhortation to the Christian community could not refer to racial identity on a biological level but rather to membership in the redefined Israel.

A similar reapplication and redefinition takes place with the term *circumcision*. In the controversy over inclusion in the people of God and the basis of that inclusion, Paul frequently uses circumcision as a term to refer to those who were now part of the people of God. In Philippians 3 Paul redefines circumcision so that it remains a sign of membership in the people of God but is no longer evidenced in a physical attribute. Thus he would say to the Philippians: "Beware of the dogs, beware of the evil workers, beware of those who mutilate the flesh! For it is we who are the circumcision, who worship in the Spirit of God and boast in Christ Jesus and have no confidence in the flesh" (Phil 3:2-3; Rom 2:26-29). Paul argues that circumcision may well be a characteristic of the people of God, but he redefines circumcision to mean a spiritual rather than a physical attribute:

> So, if those who are uncircumcised keep the requirements of the law, will not their uncircumcision be regarded as circumcision? Then those who are physically uncircumcised but keep the law will condemn you that have the written code and circumcision but break the law. For a person is not a Jew who is one outwardly, nor is true circumcision something external and physical. Rather, a person is a Jew who is one inwardly, and real circumcision is a matter of the heart—it is spiritual and not literal. Such a person receives praise not from others but from God. (Rom 2:26-29 NIV)

In Ephesians this emphasis on a new definition of circumcision is developed so that those who were uncircumcised have now been incorporated into Israel, that is, into the church (Eph 2:10-13).

Covenant also became an important term that could be used to evoke the image of the people of God. The words of Jesus during the Last Supper, "This is my blood of the covenant, which is poured out for many" (Mk 14:24 NIV; cf. Mt 26:28; Lk 22:20; 1 Cor 11:25), provided the early church with a fundamental means of understanding the significance of Jesus' passion. Furthermore, based on the words of Jeremiah 31:31-34, in which the prophet spoke of a "new covenant" that God would establish, NT writers frequently refer to the relationship established with God through Jesus as the new covenant (2 Cor 3:6; Heb 8:8; 8:13; 9:15; 12:24). The implicit contrast between the "old covenant" and the "new covenant" provides some NT writers with another means of evoking the image of the church as a newly constituted and redefined Israel. If we remember that the covenant established at Mt. *Sinai (Ex 19—24) provided Israel with its identity as the people of God, then the NT references to a new covenant also would have had the ability to evoke the image of the people of God as a way of understanding the identity of the church.

This application of the image of Israel to the early Christian community may have been natural when the early church was largely Jewish in composition, but with the expansion of the Gentile mission and the decline of the Jewish-Christian community, the identification of the church with Israel became more difficult and required theological creativity. An extended discussion of this relationship is undertaken by Paul in Romans 9—11. There Paul argues that the revelation of divine grace through Jesus Christ had not resulted in God's abandonment of Israel, but rather in an enlargement of Israel to include those who had been *grafted onto the olive tree. Paul's understanding of Israel transcended the traditional definition to become an image of the faithful human community without regard to the former divisions between Jews and Gentiles.

Summary. The Bible uses the image of Israel as God's chosen people to speak of those who have been called by God into a special relationship. In the OT there was strong emphasis placed on the ethnoreligious community established through the gracious acts of Yahweh in the exodus from Egypt and the conclusion of a covenant at Mt. Sinai. In the NT the church adopted the language and images associated with Israel to assist the development of its self-understanding. This stressed the continuity with its Jewish heritage, while at the same time acknowledging the novelty of God's grace in Jesus Christ. Israel became a defining image for the self-definition of the Christian community.

See also ABRAHAM; CIRCUMCISION; CHURCH; COVENANT; EXODUS, SECOND EXODUS; EXILE; GENTILES; LAW; PROMISED LAND; RESTORE, RESTORATION; SEED; TEMPLE.

BIBLIOGRAPHY. P. S. Minear, *Images of the Church in the New Testament* (Philadelphia: Westminster, 1960).

J

JACKAL. *See* ANIMALS.

JACOB

The stature of Jacob in the Bible is attested by the fact that his name appears 350 times. Nearly half of the references occur in Genesis. Overall, the name *Jacob* can refer to a number of entities: the patriarch and ancestor Jacob; the united nation of *Israel under David and Solomon; Israel, the northern kingdom that broke away from the Davidic dynasty after the death of Solomon; Judah, the southern Israelite kingdom that remained under the rule of the Davidic dynasty; or Israel in a broader, ethnoreligious sense.

The Genesis narrative divides the story of Jacob into two phases—the cycle of stories in which Jacob is the protagonist (Gen 26—36) and the *Joseph narratives (Gen 37—50), in which Jacob plays a supporting role. The first of these cycles forms a U-shaped *comic plot in which events descend into potential tragedy but rise to a happy ending. The turning point in this movement is Jacob's submission to God in the famous *wrestling scene at the brook Jabbok, which is the closest the OT comes to a *conversion story. The shape of Jacob's life during this era falls into a three-part structure, based on a pattern of withdrawal and return: childhood in the parental home, a twenty-year exile in Haran and a *return to the land of origin. At the beginning of each of these phases, we find a divine appearance that foreshadows the ensuing phase of the hero's life: an oracle to Rebekah that predicts Jacob's conquest of his brother (Gen 25:23), the vision at Bethel in which Jacob receives the covenant *blessing (Gen 28:11-17) and the wrestling at the Jabbok in which Jacob receives his covenant name and a new identity (Gen 32:22-31). The underlying contrast that organizes the plot is human unworthiness contrasted with divine grace. The unifying action is the hero's long struggle to become a godly person—a type of *quest.

The main role that Jacob fills in salvation history is that of patriarch. Jacob appears thirty times in the Bible as a member of the evocative triad of Abraham, Isaac and Jacob—the esteemed patriarchs of the nation of Israel. Already as we read his story in Genesis, we are aware that we are reading the story of a patriarch, partly because even before his birth we hear the oracle that God gives to Rebekah announcing that Jacob is the character of destiny. The patri-archal status of Jacob is heightened by our awareness that the nation itself is named after Jacob's new name, Israel, reinforced by more than 150 references to him later in the Bible that link him with the nation. Within the Genesis story itself the role in which we most often see Jacob is that of father of a clan.

The story of Jacob in Genesis is also a richly human story. His story is the single richest repository of *humor in the Bible. Much of the humor stems from the fact that Jacob is an archetypal *trickster. When he gets together with his uncle Laban, who belongs to the same type, the sparks fly in a battle of wits.

Furthermore, Jacob is an aggressive and colorful character who generates conflict wherever he goes. This is well captured by the focus of the Genesis story on Jacob's name. In the ancient world, *names captured people's identity and was something had either to live up to or live down. Jacob received his name, which can be loosely translated "Grabby" (literally, "he grabs the heel"), in the comic birth scene that stresses the laughable qualities of both brothers' first appearance into the world (Gen 25:24-26). When *Esau learns of how Jacob has stolen his blessing, he asks, "Is he not rightly named Jacob? For he has supplanted me these two times" (Gen 27:36 RSV). The hero's name also becomes the focus of the wrestling scene when the angel asks, "What is your name?" and then gives him a new name ("he who strives with God") that redirects but does not obliterate Jacob's essential identity as the one who strives and overcomes. Like Homer's Odysseus, Jacob basically lives up to his identity throughout his story, though he becomes a much mellower figure after his conversion at the Jabbok.

The image of Jacob that emerges from the Genesis account revolves additionally around the archetypes to which he adheres at various stages of the action. The motif of *sibling rivalry explains much of the early action. This rivalry is heightened by the way Jacob and Esau are foils to each other—the one "a quiet man, dwelling in tents," the other "a man of the field" (Gen 25:27). Then too, Jacob belongs to the biblical archetype of the *younger child who supplants the elder. Subsequently, Jacob becomes the guilt-haunted *wanderer, the lover, the victim of comic comeuppance (in the substitute bride incident), the successful entrepreneur (he surely ranks among the most industrious workers within the pages of the Bible) and the worshiper. In his encounter with his brother Esau, he is a guilt-stricken penitent. Beginning with the Joseph story, Jacob recedes into a somewhat shadowy background figure—the deceived authority figure in the family who is more pathetic than strong.

The images that we naturally associate with Jacob are relatively numerous. He is repeatedly associated with his family: references to his roles as husband and father are most numerous; and after that, references to his roles as son, brother and nephew predominate. The image pattern of *stones unifies the story of Jacob (Gen 28:12, 18, 22; 29:10; 31:45-52; 35:14). Other images that highlight his life include *flocks and herds, *tent, *well, *food, *travel, *ladder, pottage, goat skins, a river, and a *garment dipped in blood used to deceive him.

Although Jacob's identity later in the Bible is almost exclusively that of the progenitor of a nation and a shorthand way of referring to that nation, there are two notable exceptions. In Romans 9:13 God's love of Jacob and hatred of Esau is used to illustrate and confirm the doctrine of divine election. And Jacob emerges as a hero of faith in the famous roll call in Hebrews 11 (vv. 9, 21).

See also ESAU; DECEPTION, STORIES OF; JACOB'S LADDER; SIBLING RIVALRY; TRICKSTER; YOUNGER CHILD, YOUNGER SIBLING.

JACOB'S LADDER

Beloved by children and painters, extravagantly allegorized throughout the history of biblical interpretation (Jeffrey) and an inspiration to hymn writers, the evocative image of Jacob's ladder is mentioned only once in the Bible. Fleeing to Haran after decisively alienating his brother *Esau, *Jacob spent a night sleeping on a stone for a pillow. As he slept, Jacob "dreamed that there was a ladder set up on the earth, and the top of it reached to heaven; and behold, the angels of God were ascending and descending on it! And behold, the LORD stood above it" (Gen 28:12-13 RSV). From the top of the ladder God conferred the *covenant *blessing on Jacob (vv. 13-15).

The story itself implies the main motifs that we are intended to see in the picture. God's position at the top of the ladder from which he pronounces the covenant blessing is an image of divine transcendence and *authority. But the fact that the ladder joins God and Jacob, the divine and the human, along with the ceaseless movement of *angels up and down the ladder, makes Jacob's ladder at the same time an image of God's immanence—of his closeness to his human creatures, as Jacob's response upon awaking suggests: "Surely the LORD is in this place; and I did not know it" (Gen 28:16 RSV). Furthermore, the two-way movement suggests the two ways in which humans interact with God—by receiving what God sends to earth and by aspiring upward toward God in heaven.

It is no wonder that the image of the ladder has been interpreted in visionary and mystical ways. The ladder appeared to Jacob in a *dream. In the dream, moreover, earthly reality opened up into a vision of God and *heaven. Jacob's ladder is an image of the *holy or numinous, as the narrative hints when it tells us that Jacob "was afraid, and said, 'How awesome is this place! This is none other than the house of God, and this is the gate of heaven'" (Gen 28:17 RSV). In the NT, Jesus echoes Jacob's dream when he tells Philip and Nathanael that they "will see heaven opened, and the angels of God ascending and descending upon the Son of man" (Jn 1:51 RSV).

See also ASCENT; DESCENT; JACOB.

BIBLIOGRAPHY. D. L. Jeffrey, "Jacob's Ladder," *DBTEL* 388-90.

JAMES, LETTER OF

The images in the book of James cluster around key themes, including the *tongue, *faith and works, the rich and poor, the unregenerate self and *salvation, and the Christian life and *hope.

The Tongue. The most elaborate and interactive images in James are related to the theme of the *tongue. The tongue's evil inclination and the powerful consequences of its use are portrayed with personification and a variety of metaphors. The tongue is a braggart *boasting of great exploits (Jas 3:5). It is also a small *fire that can create a great forest fire—a fire that receives its evil powers from gehenna, or *hell, and can destroy the fabric of life (Jas 3:5-6). It is a world of unrighteousness or iniquity within the body that stains the entire body, an evil sphere of influence that destroys moral *purity (Jas 3:6). It is a "restless evil, full of deadly poison," constantly looking for ways to harm others (Jas 3:8 NRSV).

The need to control the tongue and the intimate connection of the tongue to the whole body are depicted with vivid images. To control the tongue is to control the body as a bit and *bridle in a *horse's mouth control its body (Jas 1:26; 3:2-3) or as a pilot's use of a rudder steers a large *ship (Jas 3:4). To be perfect and religious is to be able to bridle the tongue (Jas 1:26; 3:2). The difficulty, if not the impossibility, of controlling the tongue is illustrated by contrasting the animal world, which has been tamed by humankind, to humankind, which cannot tame its own tongue (Jas 3:7-8).

Images from nature highlight the inconsistency of the tongue in producing both blessing and cursing, a violation of its created purpose of producing blessing only (Jas 3:10). A spring does not issue both fresh and brackish water, and salt water cannot yield fresh (Jas 3:11-12). Plants in nature produce their own kind of fruit. Fig trees cannot produce olives or *grapevines produce *figs (Jas 3:12). Perversely, though, people use the same tongue to utter *cursing and *blessing.

Faith and Works. In his famous discussion of the relationship between *faith and works, James employs a number of images for faith without works.

Such faith is dead, just as the body without the spirit is dead (Jas 2:17, 26). It is also *barren (Jas 2:20). To demonstrate the futility of faith without works, James pictures the poor, whose needs for *food and *clothes are glibly dismissed with the words "Go in peace; keep warm and eat your fill" (Jas 2:14-17). James also uses an ancient metaphor of the *mirror as self-improvement, based on moral examples reflected to us for imitation. To simply hear the word and not do it is to be like those looking in a mirror (moral example) who quickly forget what they saw when they walk away from it (do not imitate). Perseverance in the perfect law of liberty (moral example) is required in order to be hearers who do not forget but act (Jas 1:23-25).

Rich and Poor. Many images in James cluster around the theme of the rich (*see* Wealth) and the poor (*see* Poverty). The rich should not boast, because they are short-lived mortals who disappear like a *flower in the field that blooms one day and is withered the next by the scorching heat (Jas 1:9-11). The *transitory nature of riches is depicted as something that rots and as moth-eaten clothes (Jas 5:2) and as the *rusting of gold and silver (Jas 5:3; *see* Corruption; Decay). This rusting wealth laid up by the rich in spite of the needs of the poor tells against the rich in judgment, as portrayed in the image of the rust eating their flesh (Jas 5:3) and of the rich having *fattened their hearts for the day of slaughter like livestock (Jas 5:5). God's awareness of the plight of the poor is depicted by the image of a court in which the church is warned not to favor the verdict of the rich by giving them a seat of *honor in the proceedings (Jas 2:1-11; *see* Legal Images), and by the image of the unjustly withheld wages of the poor who *harvested the crops of the rich crying out to the ears of God (Jas 5:4). To remain unstained or morally pure is partially defined as caring for the *widows and *orphans, two of ancient society's poorest groups (Jas 1:27).

Other Images. Many images are used to characterize the human plight, God's work in salvation, the Christian hope and the Christian life. There is no place for boasting in this life because it is so short and fragile, like a *flower scorched by the sun and withered (Jas 1:9-11) or a *mist that appears for a little while and disappears (Jas 4:14). Personal desires are personified as fishermen who tempt, lure and entice *fish, and as a *mother who gives *birth to sin, which in turn gives birth to death (Jas 1:14-15). Cravings are at war within a person (Jas 4:1).

Salvation is birth by the word of truth so that we can become firstfruits of God's creatures (Jas 1:18). It is also pictured as ridding ourselves of the rank growth of wickedness as we would strip off dirty *garments in order to welcome the implanted word that has the power to save our souls (Jas 1:21). A personified mercy triumphs over judgment (Jas 2:13). The Christian hope is to be justified by faith and become a friend of God like *Abraham (Jas 2:23), blessed with every perfect gift from the Father

of lights—the God who controls the heavenly worlds and keeps the universe regulated (Jas 1:17). It is also to be rich in faith and heirs of the kingdom (Jas 2:5). While awaiting the Judge who is standing at the doors (Jas 5:9), Christians are to be patient like a farmer awaiting *rain (Jas 5:7).

The Christian life is expressed in such images as becoming a *servant or slave of God (Jas 1:1), resisting temptation and receiving a *crown of life (Jas 1:12), bridling the tongue (Jas 1:26; 3:2-5), remaining pure and undefiled before God through care for the poor and oppressed, being unstained by the world (Jas 1:27), possessing a gentleness born of *wisdom (Jas 3:13), having a harvest of righteousness sown in peace (Jas 3:18), resisting the devil who *flees (Jas 4:7), drawing near to God and God in turn drawing near, cleansing the hands and purifying the heart (Jas 4:8), and being humble before God, described as laughter turned to mourning and joy to dejection (Jas 4:9-10).

The *law is paradoxically a "law of liberty" (Jas 1:25; 2:12). It is also a "royal law" because is comes from Christ the king (Jas 2:8). Christians are the twelve tribes of the Dispersion (Jas 1:1), wandering in the hostile world outside their true homeland, a place where it is possible to wander from the truth (Jas 5:19-20). The Christian who doubts is like the wave of the *sea moved at the mercy of the wind, double-minded, unstable (Jas 1:6, 8; 4:8), having cravings at war within (Jas 4:1) and being a friend with the world, which is enmity with God (Jas 4:4).

The epistle of James, though written in prose, is so laden with images and metaphors that it ranks as poetic prose. The moral core around which these images exist is the need for faith to express itself in works. The author is interested in the practical outworkings of faith, and he accordingly gives us a series of pictures of what faith looks like—in the confronting of trial, in regard to speech and obedience to God's law, in response to gradations in people's social standing and to people in economic need, in the exercise of patience and *prayer for the sick (*see* Disease and Healing).

See also FAITH; POVERTY; TONGUE; WEALTH.

BIBLIOGRAPHY. D. Y. Hadidian, "Palestinian Pictures in the Epistle of James," *ExpT* 63 (1952) 227-28; L. T. Johnson, "The Mirror of Remembrance (James 1:22- 25)," *CBQ* 50 (1988) 632-45; A. B. Spencer, "The Function of the Miserific and Beautific Images in the Letter of James," *Evangelical Journal* 7 (1989) 3-14.

JEREMIAH, BOOK OF

The first edition of Jeremiah's prophecies was reduced to ashes by king Jehoiakim (Jer 36:1-6). Perhaps this explains why the organization of the book of Jeremiah is difficult to understand. The divergences between the Septuagint (the Greek OT) and the traditional Hebrew text in length and arrangement of the book suggest that there was some fluidity in these areas.

The structure of the book is loosely historical, although some of the material is arranged thematically, perhaps by Jeremiah's scribe, Baruch (Jer 36:27-32; 45:1-5). The book is perhaps best described as an historical anthology. In addition to prophecy and historical narrative, the finished work includes a legal brief (Jer 2:1-3:5), a sermon (Jeremiah's famous "Temple Sermon," Jer 7:1-15; 26:1-6), a letter from home (Jer 29:1-23) and a series of soliloquies (Jeremiah's heart-rending "Confessions," Jer 15:10-18; 17:9-18; 18:18-23; 20:7-18).

The broad emphases of Jeremiah's prophecy are easily discernible. They appear already in the prophet's call, which uses figurative language to describe his commission to proclaim both *judgment and *salvation to Judah and the nations. Jeremiah's call came as early as 627 B.C., although his ministry was centered around the desperate situation that existed just before, during and immediately following the collapse of Judah and Jerusalem in 587/6 B.C.

Jeremiah's call employs words that picture the nations as edifices or *plants that were to be established or destroyed: "See, today I appoint you over nations and kingdoms to uproot and tear down, to destroy and overthrow, to build and to plant" (Jer 1:10 NIV; see Build, Building; Tear Down). This predominantly negative imagery recurs like a refrain throughout the book, describing the *judgment of Judah and other nations as well as Judah's ultimate *restoration (e.g., Jer 12:14-17; 18:7-10; 24:6; 31:28; 42:10; 45:4).

Two visions immediately follow the call narrative. The first involves a wordplay on an observed almond branch (sqd), signifying God's watching (sqd) over his word to bring it to pass (Jer 1:11-12). In the second vision, Jeremiah was shown "a boiling pot, tilting away from the *north," representing the coming divine judgment against Judah for her sin (Jer 1:13-14 NIV).

In the book of Jeremiah, God's central charge against the people of Judah was that they had broken their *covenant with him and had turned instead to other *gods (Jer 11:1-10; 22:8-9). Judah had been established in a special relationship with God, like a *bride (Jer 2:2). She is described as the *firstfruits of God's *harvest (Jer 2:3), his *vineyard (Jer 12:10), his *flock (Jer 13:17) and his firstborn *son (Jer 31:9, 20). However, she had forsaken the spring of living *water and had dug out her own *cisterns that could not hold water (Jer 2:13).

Jeremiah presented the family of the Rechabites (Jer 35:1-19) and their faithful adherence to the prohibitions imposed by their forefather as a visual example of the *obedience that God desired but had not found in Judah. Instead, Judah had given her allegiance to idols, and these are the subject of many of Jeremiah's oracles. He charged that *idolatry had proliferated until it was widespread (Jer 11:13) and acceptable even within and around the holy *temple (Jer 7:30-31; 19:5-6; 32:33-35). He accused entire families of idolatrous practices (Jer 7:17-19) as well

as every level of officialdom (Jer 2:26-28). These idols are compared to a "scarecrow in the melon patch" (Jer 10:5 NIV). They are worthless and fraudulent—no comparison to the Lord Almighty who created all things (Jer 10:1-16). Jeremiah likened Judah's unfaithfulness to God to that of an *adulterous woman (Jer 3:20; 5:7) or a *prostitute (Jer 2:20; 3:1-3; 4:30; 13:26-27), whose appetite for foreign gods is compared to the desire of a she-camel or wild *donkey in heat who sniffs the *wind in her lust (Jer 2:23-24).

In addition to idolatry, the nation's abandonment of God's law manifested itself in social decay and immorality (Jer 5:1-9; 7:5-8), including unspeakable acts of violence in the valley of slaughter (Jer 7:30-32). Jeremiah accused the false prophets of abetting this spiritual decline (Jer 14:14-16; 23:9-40). The prophets prophesied "peace, peace, when there was no peace" (Jer 6:14; 8:11). Jeremiah urged the people of Judah to turn away from their faithlessness by describing in fearsome imagery the judgment God must otherwise bring on the nation. That judgment would be like a scorching, scattering desert wind (Jer 4:11; 13:24), like eating bitter *food and *drinking poisoned water (Jer 8:14; 9:15; 23:15), like the violence and *shame of *rape (Jer 13:22) or the *pain of childbirth (Jer 4:31; 13:21; see Birth), like a furious *storm (Jer 23:19) or the very disintegration of all order into the precreation *chaos (Jer 4:23-26).

But Jeremiah did not limit his exhortation to repentance to words. His first trip to the *potter graphically illustrated that just as the potter can alter his intentions for the vessel he is forming on the wheel, so God can revise his plans for a nation on the basis of their actions (Jer 18:1-2). If Judah would repent, judgment could still be averted.

But because the people of Judah had *eyes but could not see and *ears but could not hear (Jer 5:21), they rejected Jeremiah's visual and vocal message. The nation did not repent of its wickedness. Unlike the storks, *doves, swifts or thrushes, who know their appointed migratory times and routes (see Birds), Judah is described as being as directionless as a *horse in battle (Jer 8:4-7). The prophecy of Jeremiah therefore turns to a pronouncement of impending judgment. Thus, Jeremiah's second trip to the potter was for a visual depiction of God's verdict against the nation. Judah would be smashed just as the potter's jar was smashed (Jer 19:1-13). Judah had been planted in the land like a choice vine of sound and reliable stock but had become a corrupt, wild *vine that had to be uprooted (Jer 2:21).

Jeremiah also symbolized and represented the coming judgment of which he spoke in his own person and actions. He buried a *linen belt until it became rotten and useless to demonstrate that Judah had become rotten (see Decay) and was no longer able to be used by God to bring himself *honor (Jer 13:1-11). Jeremiah remained unmarried and childless and was prohibited from entering a house where there was mourning or rejoicing in order to demonstrate that the offspring of Judah would perish and that there would soon be neither mourning for the dead nor rejoicing with newlyweds in the land (Jer 16:1-9). The inevitability of the nation's judgment was further signified by God's denying to Jeremiah his intercessory role as a prophet (Jer 7:16; 11:14; 14:11-12). Jeremiah's arrest, beatings (Jer 20:1-2) and imprisonment in the king's dungeon (see Prison) and his later near-death in the cistern (Jer 37—38) point toward the coming captivity and near extinction of the nation of Judah at the hands of the *Babylonians (Jer 39). Toward the end of his ministry, when the exile had already begun, Jeremiah encouraged the people of Judah to submit to Nebuchadnezzar by placing on his own neck a yoke of straps and crossbars (Jer 27). Even the emotions of Jeremiah, which have earned him the moniker "the *weeping prophet," not only manifest his melancholy but also demonstrate God's own sorrow over having to so severely judge his chosen people (e.g., Jer 4:19; 13:15-17).

The positive side of Jeremiah's message, corresponding to the "building" and "planting" of his prophetic call, involves the motif of a *remnant (e.g., Jer 3:14; 23:3; 30:10-11; 50:20) that would be delivered from captivity and returned to the land of promise (Jer 3:18; 16:14-15; 29:10-14; 30:17—31:40; 50:19). After seventy years of captivity (Jer 25:12), a righteous Branch would come to rule on David's throne (Jer 23:3, 5-6; 33:14-26). The proclamation of this future *restoration centers in the portion of the book of Jeremiah known as the Book of Consolation (Jer 30:1-33:26). Jeremiah communicated this positive message of restoration visually by buying a field in the besieged land of Judah in order to demonstrate that "houses, fields and vineyards will again be bought in this land" (Jer 32:15 NIV). Indeed, Jeremiah's own deliverance from prison (Jer 40) pointed toward the future deliverance of the people he represented from their Babylonian captivity.

The images in which Jeremiah's twin messages of judgment and restoration find their fullest expression are the images of the *cup of the *wine of God's wrath and the new *covenant. Jeremiah was commanded to take from God's hand the cup filled with the wine of his wrath and make the nations to whom God sent him drink it (Jer 25:15). This cup represents God's judgment and was to be taken to "all the kingdoms on the face of the earth" (Jer 25:26 NIV). At the top of the list were Jerusalem and the towns of Judah (Jer 25:18). Judah would be handed over to the army of Nebuchadnezzar, described as a *lion coming out of his lair (Jer 4:7), whose unstoppable advance would be "like the roaring sea" (Jer 6:23 NIV), or "like the clouds, his chariots like a whirlwind, and his horses swifter than *eagles" (Jer 4:13 NIV). His soldiers are all mighty warriors, whose quivers carry as much certainty of death as an open *grave (Jer 5:16). A "tester of *metals" would assay Judah, the ore (Jer 6:27). The Gentile nations too

would experience God's judgment, and this forms the substance of Jeremiah's "oracles against the nations" (Jer 46—51). However, the universal and final character of the prophesied judgment forces one to look for its ultimate fulfillment at a later time.

The situation is similar with the image of the new covenant (Jer 31:31-34). Jeremiah described this new covenant with God as involving an intimate personal relationship, the forgiveness of sins and a disposition toward God that would no longer be characterized by intransigent and rebellious hearts upon which sin is permanently "engraved with an iron tool, inscribed with a flint point" (Jer 17:1 NIV), but rather by receptive hearts on which the law of God is written. This new covenant, like the cup of the wine of God's wrath, would also be extended to the Gentile nations (Jer 3:17).

The book of Jeremiah ends, however, on a negative note. There was turmoil within the tiny community that remained in the land of Judah, and despite Jeremiah's protests, they eventually fled to Egypt (Jer 40—44). The realization of this prophesied new covenant, therefore, was also to be experienced in a later day.

The NT authors find the ultimate fulfillment of Jeremiah's images of the cup of the wine of God's wrath and the new covenant in the person and work of Jesus Christ (cf. Mt 26:27-28). Jesus drank from the cup of God's wrath to experience the full judgment of God against the sin of humankind (Mt 26:39; Jn 18:11). In so doing, he opened the way for the redemption of a remnant into an everlasting, new covenant with God, whose laws are written on their *hearts (Heb 8:6-13).

See also BABYLON; BUILD, BUILDING; COVENANT; HEART; JERUSALEM; JUDGMENT; PROPHECY, GENRE OF; REMNANT; RESTORATION; TEAR DOWN.

JERUSALEM

The imagery of Jerusalem plays a profound role throughout both Testaments and has been central to the religious consciousness of believers in every age. As the plan of redemption unfolded in the Bible, Jerusalem became a leading symbol of Israel's belief that God ruled over the earth and that he had established *David and his sons as his human viceregents. As such, Jerusalem became the image of Israel's grand imperial hopes.

Many interpreters trace the biblical origins of Jerusalem to the ancient Canaanite site of Salem, the city of the priestly king *Melchizedek (Gen 14:18). This identification is not altogether certain. We know, however, that the site was called Jebus before David conquered it (2 Sam 5:6-10; 1 Chron 11:4-9). Jerusalem is also identified as Mt. Moriah, the place where *Abraham offered Isaac as a sacrifice (Gen 22:1-2; 2 Chron 3:1).

The central theological significance of Jerusalem first became apparent when David conquered the Jebusite city and established it as the capital of Israel (2 Sam 5:6-10 par. 1 Chron 11:4-9). David's decision to secure Israel's throne in Jerusalem established Jerusalem as the permanent home of Israel's human monarchs.

Nevertheless, Jerusalem became more than the nation's human monarchical center. One of David's earliest royal acts was to bring the *ark of the covenant, the very footstool of God (1 Chron 28:2), to reside in Jerusalem (2 Sam 6:17). By doing so, David also established Jerusalem as the seat of divine kingship (Ps 78:68; 132:13-18).

The establishment of divine and human kingship in Jerusalem was furthered by the construction of Solomon's *temple (2 Chron 3:1-17). *Solomon brought the nation of Israel to its economic zenith (2 Chron 9:1-28). With the nation secure on all sides, Solomon built a permanent temple palace for God (1 Kings 6:1-38). Thus during Solomon's reign, Jerusalem reached its high point in the OT period.

Jerusalem was so prominent in the imagination of the Israelites that it came to serve as a synecdoche for the nation as a whole (Is 2:2; Amos 2:5; Mic 4:1). God's administration of *blessings and *curses on Jerusalem was perceived as salvation and judgment on the entire nation.

On the one hand, the prophets warned that Yahweh would withdraw his presence from Jerusalem as a result of Israel's enduring *apostasy. The Babylonians defeated Jerusalem in 586 B.C. and took the people of Judah into *exile. The destruction of Jerusalem symbolized the rejection of Israel. The blessings that once dwelt in the city were gone. "I will reject Jerusalem, the city I chose, and this temple, about which I said 'There shall my Name be'" (2 Kings 23:27 NIV).

On the other hand, Israel's hopes for restoration from exile were expressed by the image of a *restored Jerusalem. When Israel returned from exile in 539/8 B.C., rebuilding the temple and city was among the top priorities of those who returned from exile (2 Chron 36:23; Neh 2:5,18; 6:15-16). Restoration of the nation was inconceivable without the reestablishment of Jerusalem as the seat of divine and Davidic kingship.

The restoration of Jerusalem after the exile provides an essential background for understanding the centrality of the city in the NT. Jesus proclaimed that the work of Christ constituted the restoration of the people of God from captivity (Lk 4:18-19). As such, Jesus' work was closely connected with Jerusalem because he inaugurated the *kingdom of God, the worldwide imperial destiny of God's people. This empire could be realized, however, only in association with Jerusalem as the place of divine and Davidic kingship.

As a result, Jesus performed many activities in the vicinity of Jerusalem. For instance, his triumphal entry (Lk 19:38) symbolized the victorious return of Davidic kingship to Jerusalem. Christ's death, *resurrection and *ascension, and the giving of the Spirit took place in the vicinity of Jerusalem and were closely associated with Christ's exaltation to the

*throne of his father David (Acts 2:29-36). Besides this, Jesus devoted himself to the work of his Father in the temple (Lk 2:49). He also cleansed the temple as the place of prayer out of zeal for the palace of Israel's Divine King (Mt 21:12-16; Mk 11:15-18; Lk 19:45-46; Jn 2:13-16).

The positive role Jerusalem serves in NT kingdom imagery finds a counterbalance in the motif of judgment against Jerusalem. Jerusalem was the setting for the ultimate rejection of Christ. God's chosen son of David was refused his rightful place as king of Israel. For this reason, as the prophets warned preexilic Jerusalem of the impending judgment as a consequence of their infidelity, Jesus prophesied that Jerusalem would once again be destroyed (Lk 21:1-24). Using the same imagery that the prophets employed to describe Jerusalem's fall in 586 B.C., Jesus described the immanent destruction of Jerusalem, which occurred in A.D. 70 (Mt 24:15-25).

Despite the destruction of Jerusalem, the city's importance had not come to an end. The author of Hebrews forbids Christians to give allegiance to the old city of Jerusalem but insists that they look to the new city by the same name (Heb 10:39; 12:22). As he put it, "For here we do not have an enduring city, but we are looking for the city that is to come" (Heb 13:14 NIV). The NT connects Christian eschatological hopes to the New Jerusalem, a *heavenly city that will far transcend the glory of its earthly counterpart (Gal 4:26; Heb 12:22). As the earthly Jerusalem came to symbolize Israel's imperial destiny, the New Jerusalem signifies the full realization of that kingdom vision.

Finally, the apostle John portrayed the wonder of the new *heavens and new *earth by drawing attention to the royal city at its center (Rev 21:22-24). In the New Jerusalem the people of God will enjoy unhindered worship and fellowship under the great Davidic king, Jesus Christ (Rev 21:3-4). The new city will be without a temple, for "the Lord God Almighty and the Lamb are its temple" (Rev 21:22 NIV). As a result of the Divine King's presence, the glory of God will provide light for the city and the nations, and kings "will bring their splendor into it" (Rev 21:24 NIV). The New Jerusalem symbolizes the culmination of Jerusalem imagery throughout the Bible. It is the full realization of the imperial destiny of the people of God. The New Jerusalem represents the time when the reign of God will be fully actualized on earth through the vice-regency of the great Son of David.

See also CITY; DAVID; KING, KINGSHIP; RESTORE, RESTORATION; TEMPLE; THRONE; ZION.

JERUSALEM AND SINAI. *See* GALATIANS, LETTER TO THE

JESUS, IMAGES OF

It is no surprise that a teacher whose instruction abounded with images, who called himself the gate for the *sheep pen (Jn 10:7) and the *bread of life

(Jn 6:35), who carried out a colorful ministry of preaching and miracles should leave us with multiple images of his life and ministry.

Throughout history a number of images of Jesus have been coined that highlight an aspect of his ministry to the exclusion of others, but some, like magician or revolutionary leader, seem to distort the Jesus of the canonical Gospels. Other images—such as mystic, moral leader, social reformer, motivational speaker, entrepreneur or salesman—are drawn from or applied to his ministry in ways that narrow and distort his person. Others—such as lunatic, fraud, deceiver, opportunist, cult leader—are intentionally derogatory and without foundation in the Gospels and historical investigation.

Here we will explore the a wide variety of images offered by the Gospels and the rest of the NT within the setting of the canonical Scriptures as a whole. No single master image of Jesus will suffice to integrate the kaleidoscope of images offered in the biblical literature. Nor would it be desirable, for these multifaceted images find strength in their variety and the light they shed on each other. These images, some originating with Jesus himself and others crafted by the early church from the stuff of life and the story of Israel, have proven their worth as a powerful means of comprehending the ministry and person of Jesus.

Images of Humanity. The NT presents Jesus as truly human. From his incarnation to his tireless healing and serving of common people, his life is marked with a profound connection to humanity. Perhaps nothing so reminds us of this fact than the perspectives on Jesus as seen through the eyes of his detractors, whether in Galilee, Jerusalem or hometown Nazareth. Jesus is seen as a blasphemer (Mt 9:3; Mk 2:7; Lk 5:21), a deceiver of Israel (Mt 27:63), as demon-possessed (Jn 7:20) or an agent of Beelzebub's kingdom (Mt 12:24; Mk 3:22). He is also declared mad (Jn 10:20), an evildoer (Jn 18:30) and a perverter of the nation of Israel (Lk 23:2). People accuse him of bearing false witness (Jn 8:13) and of trying to persuade people not to pay taxes (Lk 23:2). For the apparent sin of socializing with sinners he is called a glutton and a drunkard (Lk 7:34). Finally, his own hometown dismisses him as only a carpenter's son (Mt 13:54-57).

Against this backdrop the NT presents Jesus as the one "Who, being in very nature God, did not consider equality with God something to be grasped, but made himself nothing, taking the very nature of a servant, being made in human likeness" (Phil 2:6-7 NIV). We find him born into poor, if not desperate, circumstances with a cruel king seeking his life. As a young child he lives a refugee existence and then grows up the son of an artisan in a small village of Galilee. Though close by the acclaimed city of Sepphoris (which was being rebuilt in Hellenistic style during his years at Nazareth), the Gospel story does not register this fact. It portrays his hometown as ordinary ("Nazareth! Can anything good come from

there?" Jn 1:46 NIV) and far from the center of Israel's religious and political power, Jerusalem. He shares the lot of many in Israel and among humanity, fully experiencing the joys, the hardships and everyday routines of life. A variety of NT images form a picture of Jesus' identification with humankind.

Being found in human form (Phil 2:8). Jesus' birth is one of the primary images of his humanity: "But when the time had fully come, God sent his Son, born of a woman, born under law" (Gal 4:4 NIV). The Gospels' birth accounts, on the one hand, bear all the marks of a birth in a Jewish family of common means yet strained circumstances. Though the birth stories are punctuated with extraordinary signs—angels, songs, prophecies, extraordinary visitors and palace intrigue—these events do not lift Jesus out of the circumstances of Jewish life and the ordinary nature of his childhood and family. The effect is to underscore the estimation of the writer of Hebrews: "We do not have a high priest who is unable to sympathize with our weaknesses" (Heb 4:15 NIV).

With loud cries and tears (Heb 5:7). Jesus' humanity is clearly imaged in his emotional states. Jesus' ministry offers a full range of human emotions and physiological states: He experiences hunger in the wilderness (Mt 4:2; 21:18), is angered by stubborn hearts (Mk 3:5), feels deep compassion for the harassed and helpless crowd (Mt 9:36; 14:14; Heb 4:15), is moved to tears at Lazarus's death (Jn 11:35; cf. Heb 5:7), becomes indignant when children are rebuked (Mk 10:14), is joyful in the Spirit (Lk 10:21; cf. 15:11; 16:24; 17:13), loves his friends and disciples (Jn 11:3; 20:2), marvels at the faith of the centurion (Mt 8:10), sighs deeply when tested by the Pharisees (Mk 8:12) and, weary from his journey, thirsts for water (Jn 4:6; cf. Jn 19:28).

The prospect of the cross only intensifies the imagery of Jesus' emotions: he is distressed under the prospect of the "baptism" he must undergo (Lk 12:50); he is overwhelmed with sorrow, even to the point of depression, in Gethsemane (Mt 26:37-38; Mk 14:33-34); agonizing to the point that "his sweat was like drops of blood falling to the ground" (Lk 22:44 NIV; cf. Heb 5:7); and in addition to suffering extreme physical pain on the cross (Mt 16:21; 17:12; Mk 8:31; Heb 2:9-10, 18; 5:8; 1 Pet 2:21), he feels forsaken by God (Mk 15:34). This catalog exhibits the range of Jesus' emotions presented in the Gospels and the presence of these emotions presents a vivid image of his full humanity.

Increased in wisdom and stature (Lk 2:52). The words written of the young Samuel, that he "continued to grow in stature and in favor with the Lord and with men" (1 Sam 2:26 NIV) are echoed in Luke's words that Jesus "grew in wisdom and stature, and in favor with God and men" (Lk 2:52). We find Jesus in the temple at age twelve, amazing the teachers of the law with his insight and then returning home with his parents and living in obedience to them. An essential mark of human life is multifaceted development, and the Bible, while not dwelling on this theme, gives every impression that Jesus' development is human.

Shepherd of the sheep. Jesus claims this image for himself when he declares, "I am the good shepherd" (Jn 10:14 NIV). Peter speaks of "when the Chief Shepherd appears" (1 Pet 5:4 NIV), and in Revelation we hear that "the Lamb at the center of the throne," a prominent christological image in the apocalypse, "will be their shepherd" (Rev 7:17 NIV). The image of the shepherd arises from the everyday agrarian life of Palestine and has two complimentary connotations in the OT: it is used for individuals who guide and protect people (Ps 78:72; Is 40:11); and more commonly, it is a metaphor for leaders such as kings or prophets (2 Sam 5:2; 7:7; 1 Kings 22:17). This is often expressed negatively ("people without a shepherd") when the absence of leadership causes hardship (Ezek 34:2; Zech 10:2; 11:17). The image of Jesus as shepherd builds on this OT trajectory of the image by conveying his care that climaxes in his death: "the good shepherd lays down his life for the sheep" (Jn 10:11 NIV). Even closer to the OT tradition is Jesus' response to the gathered crowds: "he had compassion on them, because they were harassed and helpless, like sheep without a shepherd" (Mt 9:36 NIV; cf. 1 Pet 2:25). But the shepherd image is not entirely one of protection and comfort; it includes an element of judgment and discernment: the Son of Man in his glory will separate humanity "as a shepherd separates the sheep from the goats" (Mt 25:32 NIV).

Bridegroom and bride. Jesus refers to himself as a *bridegroom when observers compare him and his disciples with John the Baptist: "How can the guests of the bridegroom mourn while he is with them? The time will come when the bridegroom will be taken from them; then they will fast" (Mt 9:15 NIV). The image of Jesus as a bridegroom may be implied in the parable of the ten *virgins who await the arrival of the bridegroom (Mt 25:1-13). It is certainly an image used by Paul when he speaks of Christ's love for the church and his desire that the church be presented to him "radiant . . . without stain or wrinkle or any other blemish, but holy and blameless" (Eph 5:27 NIV). This image of the most intimate bond of commitment and loving relationship is fully developed in Revelation, where John portrays "the wedding of the Lamb" to the bride, the church, who has made herself ready in "fine linen, bright and clean" (Rev 19:7 NIV; see Rev 21:2, 9; 22:17).

Abused one. Jesus identifies with humanity by fully experiencing its *pain and *suffering. The images of abuse found in the OT have a haunting terror. The violence and violation are so complete that they seem to loom much larger than the space allotted to them. A graphic picture of abuse can be found in the story of the Levite's concubine where a gang "raped her and abused her throughout the night" (Judg 19:25 NIV). Biblical literature is not afraid to present us with images of abuse, and no one receives it more forcibly than Jesus. The picture of the suffering servant in Isaiah 53 was seen by early Christians as forecasting the abuse suffered by Jesus: "He was despised and rejected by men, a man of sorrows, and familiar with suffering. . . . We considered him stricken by God, smitten by him, and afflicted. But he was pierced for our transgressions, he was crushed for our iniquities . . . and by his wounds we are healed" (Is 53:3-5 NIV).

In the Gospel passion narratives, Jesus is beaten, abandoned and has no one to speak for him; he is taunted and mocked and finally subjected to the shame of being stripped naked and publicly executed. He stands as one who experiences the dark and tragic side of abuse without assuming a "victim" mentality. He faithfully and unflinchingly suffers, but he understands the violation and, consequently, models the hope that there is a God who cares deeply about the suffering, the injustice and the pain. He is one who empathizes with our sufferings (Heb 2:17-18).

Refugee, stranger and scorned one. Jesus spends his first months as a refugee as his parents flee with him to *Egypt (Mt 2:13-15). As an adult he suffers rejection in his hometown (Lk 4:29) and the scorn of righteous society. He experiences the stigma of a stranger even before the full rejection of his crucifixion. He lives as a *wanderer (Mt 8:20), he speaks the language of the common person and works with his father in a simple trade that combined the functions of logger, carpenter and craftsman (Mk 6:3), and he very likely suffered the ignominy of being labeled an illegitimate child (Jn 8:41).

Friend of sinners. Jesus is a true friend. In the Gospels he takes part wholeheartedly in friendship, spending time with people, eating, talking, attending and hosting parties (Mt 26:17-30). He is known as "a friend of tax collectors and sinners" (Mt 11:19; Lk 7:34 NIV), a reputation that wins him the scorn of those who maintain the boundaries of purity. Filled with grief, he weeps over the death of a friend (Jn 11:35). And he declares himself to be the friend of his followers: "You are my friends. . . . I have called you friends, for everything that I learned from my Father I have made known to you." (Jn 15:14-15 NIV).

Dinner guest and host. A recurring image of Jesus in the Gospels is his table fellowship with tax collectors and *sinners. We find Jesus having dinner at Levi's (Matthew's) house with "many tax collectors and sinners" eating with him and his disciples (Mk 2:15; Mt 9:10; Lk 5:29). Jesus quotes his critics as saying of him, "Here is a glutton and a drunkard, a friend of tax collectors and 'sinners' " (Mt 11:19 ; Lk 7:34). On another occasion we find him at a Pharisees house where he is visited by a woman of questionable reputation (Lk 7:36-50; 19:1-10). The Pharisees, who are scandalized by his breaking down the boundaries of purity erected by their traditions, condemn him with the words, "This man welcomes sinners and eats with them" (Lk 15:1-2 NIV). Luke casts Jesus' meal scenes in the style of a Hellenistic symposium, a banquet in which the principal entertainment is the discussion of philosophical issues. And we must recall the feeding of the five thousand (Mt 14:13-21; Mk 6:32-44; Lk 9:10-17; Jn 6:1-15) and four thousand (Mt 15:32-39; Mk 8:1-10), where Jesus is host to the common people of Galilee. All of these meal scenes are living pictures of the kingdom's divine offer of forgiveness and wide welcome to sinners, a glimpse of the day when "Many will come from the east and the west, and will take their places at the feast with Abraham, Isaac and Jacob in the kingdom of Heaven" (Mt 8:11 NIV; Lk 13:29; cf. Is 25:6-8). At his last supper, Jesus plays the host to his disciples and declares that he "will not drink of this fruit of the vine from now on until that day when I drink it anew with you in my Father's kingdom" (Mt 26:29 NIV; Mk 14:25; Lk 22:18).

Controversialist. One of the most prevalent images of Jesus in the Gospels is Jesus as controversialist. Wherever he goes, controversy seems to follow. The scribes and the Pharisees are his most frequent opponents in controversy, challenging his words and actions and eventually trying to catch him in a misstep in order to bring him down. Jesus displays a wisdom and cunning that foils his foes and delights the common people who observe from the sidelines. He speaks with authority and subtly takes command of the situation, never departing from an encounter without leaving a provocative saying, an intellectual timebomb that lodges in the mind. The topics of controversy are ones that are central to Israel: the true keeping of the *Sabbath (Mk 2:23-28), the validity of *divorce (Mk 10:2-9), the true nature of purity (Mk 7:1-8), the essence of the *law (Mk 12:28-34), the authority to *forgive sins (Mk 2:1-12), the necessity of *fasting (Mk 2:18-22), whether or not to pay taxes to Caesar (Mk 12:13-17), the nature of the *resurrection (Mk 12:18-27) and the future of Israel (Mk 12:1-12). These are issues that drive to the heart of what it means to be true Israel, and the scribes and Pharisees, who are usually at the center of these controversies, are ones who care deeply about these issues. But Jesus' conflict with these religious leaders as well as with the Sadducees and priests runs parallel with his conflict with demons and *Satan, and the plot line of both of these conflicts runs on a trajectory through the deliberations of the Sanhedrin, of Pilate and Jesus' death on a cross. Jesus the controversialist is vindicated in his resurrection and, in the temporally distant horizon beyond the Gospels, in the destruction of Jerusalem in A.D. 70 (e.g., Lk 19:43; 21:20).

Head of family. When Jesus is told that his mother and brothers are standing outside waiting for him, Jesus turns to the assembled group and says, "Who are my mother and brothers?" Looking at the group he declares "Here are my mother and my brothers!" (Mk 3:34 NIV). Jesus creates a surrogate *family, a fictive kinship around himself. When Jesus calls a disciple and says, "Let the dead bury their own dead" (Lk 9:60 NIV), it is a call to leave behind old family relationships and join the new family of Jesus' followers.

This is a fitting prelude to the NT image of *adoption. With family membership as the primary source of social, religious, economic and political security and fulfillment, to move from one family system to another was an event of life-changing importance. Adoption is used in the NT as an effective image of God's blessing on his people (Rom 8:23; 9:4), with important echoes of Israel's story as Yahweh's adopted nation. It is by adoption that believers join the family of God, and this occasion of happy celebration is captured in the liturgical language of Ephesians 1:5. Believers are adopted by virtue of their union with Christ, the Son of God.

This image of family is replayed in Romans as Paul speaks of Christ as the "firstborn among many brothers" (Rom 8:29 NIV). In Hebrews we read that "Jesus is not ashamed to call them brothers" (Heb 2:11 NIV), and the author of Hebrews has Jesus adopt the voice of Psalm 22:22, "I will declare your name to my brothers." Just as Moses was faithful as a servant in all God's house, "Christ is faithful as a son over God's house. And we are his house" (Heb 3:5-6 NIV). Clearly the images of familial relationship were significant for the first audiences of these letters, for they met in households and considered themselves as an alternative family under a new head of household.

Israel. Jesus is several times imaged as *Israel. Hosea's description of the *exodus is applied to Jesus' return to Palestine with Mary and Joseph: "out of Egypt I have called my son" (Hos 11:1; Mt 2:15 NIV). In submitting himself to the *baptism of John, a symbolic call and enactment of national repentance and preparation for the restorative work of God, Jesus identifies with Israel in its plight of spiritual *exile. Jesus' *temptation in the *wilderness (Mt 4:1-11; Lk 4:1-13) is recounted as a parallel of Israel's wilderness experience. As suffering servant and the one who representatively undergoes the death of exile and the restoration of resurrection, Jesus identifies himself with the nation Israel.

Images of Deliverance and Salvation. With images reminiscent of the *exodus, Jesus sets his people free from multiple facets of *bondage. Some of these images of deliverance implicitly equate Jesus with Israel. Other images associate Jesus with *Moses or with God. Although images from Israel's salvation history lie behind the master image of Jesus as deliverer, his actions to deliver Israel and the Gentiles transcend what we might have anticipated from the OT.

Savior. In contemporary Christian parlance the term *savior* is nearly synonymous with Jesus. It may come as a surprise then that, strictly speaking, the term *savior* (Gk *sōtēr*) appears only twenty-four times in the NT, with eight instances referring to God and sixteen referring to Jesus Christ. In the Gospels, Jesus is referred to as savior only once, and that in anticipation of his birth (Lk 2:11). In the Pauline letters *savior* refers to Jesus (rather than God) in six out of twelve instances, and all but two (Eph 5:23; Phil

3:20) of these occur in the Pastoral letters. But these statistics do not reveal the entire pattern, for we find the words *salvation* (*sōtēria*) and *save* (*sōzō*) used many more times in the NT, and frequently with Jesus as the subject. The image of Jesus as savior is well established by the NT, bringing many texts into its orbit.

In Jewish texts that speak of a Messiah or messianic figure, the term *savior* is not used. But the general image of salvation is present, for a messianic figure is to serve as God's agent in delivering Israel from its plight of sin, oppression, disease and every sort of brokenness, a condition of spiritual exile from the full blessings of the age to come. The images of savior and salvation primarily evoke the saving action of Yahweh, the God of Israel. This image is encoded in the Hebrew name Jesus, *Yēśûaʿ* (shortened to *Yēśû*), meaning "Yahweh saves," or "May Yahweh save" (cf. Mt 1:21).

Luke is the Gospel writer who best highlights the profile of Jesus as a savior. Jesus arrives on the stage of Israel's drama at an hour when the nation has long been groaning under spiritual exile and bondage to foreign rule. The angel declares to the shepherds that "a savior" is born (Lk 2:11) in the city of David, but the unspoken fact is that a "savior" is already enthroned in Rome—Caesar Augustus, whose monuments declare him "savior of the world." Against this backdrop the anticipation of a savior within Israel seems fraught with danger, as the pious figures we meet in Luke's Gospel invoke OT promises of deliverance. Zechariah speaks of a "mighty savior" and of being "saved from our enemies" (Lk 1:69, 71 NRSV). Simeon, who has been looking for the "consolation of Israel," thanks God that he has lived to see God's "salvation" (Lk 2:30) in the face of the infant Jesus. And the aged Anna rejoices over the child in the presence of all who are "looking for the redemption of Jerusalem" (Lk 2:38 NRSV). John the Baptist also speaks of a great judgment and renewal within Israel associated with the coming of the Lord. Luke summarizes John's activity with the biblical image of preparing a highway for the *divine warrior so that "all flesh shall see the salvation of God" (Lk 3:6 NRSV; cf. Is 40:5 LXX). We are not led to expect a savior who will bring "spiritual" salvation.

The surprise is that Luke's Gospel defines this savior in a way that reshapes Israel's expectation of salvation as well as our own. Jesus the Savior delivers Israel from the deepest dimensions of its plight, its spiritual state of sinfulness and bondage to Satan. But this salvation turns out to be a broadly encompassing salvation aimed at whole persons and communities. Salvation is a comprehensive image that embraces a number of benefits brought about through God's saving action in Jesus. Modern English translations correctly bring out the sense (with the word *heal*) but mask the recurring use of Greek words for "save" (*sōzō*) or "salvation" (*sōtēria*). When Jesus proclaims, "Your faith has saved you," whether from sins (Lk 7:50), from a hemorrhage (Lk 8:48), from *lep-

rosy (Lk 17:19) or from blindness (Lk 18:42), it is in the sense of "Your faith has made you whole" (Gk *sesōken*, "has saved," is used in each case). The Gerasene man, delivered from a "legion" of demons and now "clothed and in his right mind," has been "saved" (*esōthē*, Lk 8:35-36 NRSV). Jairus is not to fear but "only believe," and his daughter "will be saved" from death (Lk 8:50). By identifying these key events as acts as salvation, the work of the Savior, Luke invites us to view all of the other healings and deliverances as salvation. The Savior is at work in Israel, opening the eyes of the *blind, unstopping the ears of the *deaf, causing the lame to leap and proclaiming liberty to the captives (Is 35:5-10; Is 61:1-2). These are all concrete images of Israel's end-time salvation, and they are "this day fulfilled in your hearing" (Lk 4:21).

These images of salvation are instances of people experiencing the power of the *kingdom of God in Jesus' presence (cf. Lk 18:18, 24, 26). The Savior brings an outward change with a corresponding inner transformation. We find this epitomized in the story of Zacchaeus. Jesus tells the despised and ostracized tax collector, Zacchaeus, "I must stay at your *house* today" (Lk 19:5). At his house Zacchaeus repents, and Jesus the guest declares, "today salvation has come to this *house* (Lk 19:9). Salvation is present with Jesus the Savior. Zacchaeus voluntarily vows to give half of his possessions to the poor and give restitution to those he has defrauded (Lk 19:8). A man and his household experience the Savior, and the effects are felt in his hometown Jericho. The Son of Man has come for this, "to seek out and to save the lost" (Lk 19:10 NRSV). But at the hour of his greatest act of salvation, the joyful voices that celebrated his birth as Savior are replaced by the threefold jeer of those he came to save: "He saved others, let him save himself if he is the Messiah of God, his chosen one" (Lk 23:35 NRSV; cf. Lk 23:37, 39).

The Savior's death on a Roman cross is God's paradoxical means of salvation (Lk 9:24), his taking upon himself the woes of Israel and of the world. But this rejected and crucified Savior is raised and exalted to God's *right hand, and proclaimed by the apostles as the "Leader and Savior" who gives "repentance to Israel and the forgiveness of sins" (Acts 5:31 NRSV). The image of Jesus the Savior is so closely joined with God the Savior that in Titus the two are joined in the image of "our great God and Savior Jesus Christ" (Tit 2:13 NRSV). In the cross and resurrection of Jesus the biblical story of salvation has reached its climax. The return of this Savior in glory is the "blessed hope" of the church (Tit 2:13; cf. Phil 3:20). This will be the moment of the Savior's restoration of all things, the full blossom of Israel's multifaceted hope of salvation.

Leader and pathbreaker. Deliverance in ancient Israel is almost always associated with a leader whom God raises up for the task. Moses, the various judges and later figures like Esther and Ezra, all illustrate how God mediates his deliverance through a leader.

Jesus' leadership is implicitly acknowledged by the numerous times the Gospel writers describe Jesus as having followers (i.e., Mt 4:20) who receive instruction from him and participate in his mission (Lk 10:3). Both Mark and Luke develop the motif of Jesus setting his face toward Jerusalem and moving along the "way," the highway of salvation spoken of in Isaiah 40:3-5. On this highway the Lord returns to Zion, leading his disciples as a renewed Israel in a second exodus. This is the highway John the Baptist prepares in the wilderness for the "Coming One" (Mk 1:2-3, 7).

In Acts 3:15; 5:31 and Hebrews 2:10; 12:2, the Greek term *archēgos* encapsulates the image of a "captain," a "pioneer leader," or more fully, "one who goes first, leading the way" (but rendered "author" and "prince" in the NIV). Attributed to Jesus, this image may recall the exodus, with Jesus, the eschatological leader of the people of God, forging a path of life and salvation, overcoming death and every hostile cosmic power, and going ahead to prepare a place for us.

Lord. The title Lord is so commonly used of Jesus in the NT that the distinctive features of this image, like those on a well worn coin, are not easily recognized. Occasionally this image of sovereign authority is put in bold relief. In Philippians 2:9-11 the obedient servant who has suffered death on the cross is "highly exalted" and given the throne name "that is above every name, that at the name of Jesus every knee should bow . . . and every tongue confess that Jesus Christ is Lord" (RSV). That name is "Lord." A potent image of lordship in the NT is mined from Psalm 110:1, where the heavenly Lord says to David's "lord," his royal descendant, "Sit at my right hand, till I make your enemies a footstool" (RSV). The image of Jesus seated "at the right hand" of God with enemies "under his feet" speaks of his cosmic lordship (1 Cor 15:24-26; Eph 1:20-22; Col 3:1; Heb 1:3; cf. Heb 8:1; 10:12; 12:2).

Divine warrior. Jesus' ministry begins with a strength and an assurance born of solitude and the spiritual battle fought in the Judean wilderness. Luke describes his readiness for ministry as having "the power of the Spirit" (Lk 4:14), enabling Jesus to wage battle (Lk 4:18). John the Baptist highlights the warrior aspect of Jesus' ministry: "But after me will come one who is more powerful than I, whose sandals I am not fit to carry. He will baptize you with the Holy Spirit and with fire. His winnowing fork is in his hand, and he will clear his threshing floor, gathering his wheat into the barn and burning up the chaff with unquenchable fire" (Mt 3:11-12 NIV). As the Gospel narratives unfold, particularly in Mark and Luke, we find Jesus entering into combat with demons, driving them out in a style evocative of Joshua and his warriors driving the Canaanites from the Promised Land. Jesus' conflict with the Pharisees and Jewish authorities is cast in much the same style, with the result that they conspire to kill him. In his stilling of the raging sea, Jesus demonstrates the power of the divine warrior over the forces of *chaos, symbolized by the monster *Sea in the OT (Job 26:11-12; Ps 65:7; 74:13; 89:9-10; Is 51:9-10; Hab 3:8, 15).

Christus Victor. The Christus Victor motif offers an alternative perspective on the work of Christ, viewing the cross and resurrection from the standpoint of conflict and victory over Satan, sin and death rather than ceremonial sacrifice for sins. It is a perspective that sees the plight of Israel and humankind as bondage to a power rather than laboring under guilt (though these are not ultimately exclusive perspectives). The cross and resurrection form the climax of the paradoxical battle that engages spiritual and human forces within Israel, with the cross, the harsh symbol of coercive Roman power, transformed into the symbol of Christ's victory. In the words of Paul, "having stripped off the powers and authorities, he made a public spectacle of them, and led them in triumphal procession on the cross" (Col 2:15). In his resurrection from the dead he has vanquished the ancient enemy:

"Death has been swallowed up in victory."

"Where, O death, is your victory?
Where, O Death, is your sting?"
(1 Cor 15:54-55 NIV; cf. Hos 13:14)

Since Jesus has triumphed over his enemies, "God has highly exalted him" (Phil 2:9) as cosmic Lord. He is pictured both as presently subduing his *enemies (1 Cor 15:24-26) and as reigning in triumph over his enemies, who are now "under his feet (Eph 1:19-22; cf. Ps 110:1). And he will come again in visible power and glory to vanquish the last embodiment of evil (2 Thess 2:1-12) and establish his kingdom (1 Cor 15:25-28).

Liberator of slaves. The biblical archetype of *bondage and liberation is Israel's enslavement in and exodus from Egypt. Ironically, in the biblical story deliverance entails leaving one slave master and serving another; Israel was rescued from Egypt to serve the Lord. This formative story shapes the most significant biblical stories and images of liberation. One vivid picture of bondage and liberation is found in Galatians 4:3-7. Galatians begins on the note that Christ in his death has "set us free from the present evil age" (Gal 1:4 NRSV). The bondage is described in terms of the plight of the Jews, who are "imprisoned" under sin (Gal 3:22), "locked up" under the law (Gal 3:23; 4:4-5), "enslaved" to the "elemental spirits of the world" (Gal 4:3, 8-9 NRSV). Into this bleak world of enslavement God sends a mighty deliverer, Jesus, who is "born of a woman, born under the law, in order to redeem those who were under the law" (Gal 4:4-5 NRSV). The image of redemption recalls Israel's release from slavery in Egypt. Christ, like a new Moses (and born like Moses, within Israel under bondage), has brought about a new exodus.

Similarly, in Romans 5—8 Paul sketches a drama

of bondage and liberation. A trilateral power alliance of sin, flesh and death—plus an unwilling accomplice, the law—stand opposed to the reign of God. Sin and death work together, with sin exercising its reign in death (Rom 5:21) and enslaving humankind (Rom 5:6, 14) through its ready foothold in fallen, Adamic flesh (Rom 6:12; cf. 8:6-7). Sin is a hard taskmaster who pays his wages in death (Rom 6:23). The helpless victims cry out in lament, calling for a powerful deliverer (Rom 7:24-25), and that deliverer is Jesus Christ (Rom 7:25), who enters the territory of sin "in the likeness of sinful flesh" (Rom 8:3 NRSV). Christ condemns sin (Rom 8:2-3) and brings about a dramatic rescue of those held in thrall to "the law of sin and of death" (Rom 8:2 NRSV). Like Israel in the exodus (Ex 4:22; Hos 11:1), Christ's redeemed people become the "sons of God" (Rom 8:14-17). Their deliverance is of cosmic significance, for death has extended its reign not only over the human family but over the entire created order, subjecting it to futility and decay (Rom 8:20-21). Groaning in pain (Rom 8:22), the creation awaits its coming deliverance.

Suffering servant, suffering righteous one. The writers of the NT readily identify Jesus with Isaiah's servant of the Lord, particularly as he is described in Isaiah 52:13—53:12. The heavenly voice at the baptism of Jesus echoes Isaiah 42:1—"Here is my servant, whom I uphold, my chosen, in whom my soul delights" (NRSV)—in the words, "This is my Son, the Beloved, with whom I am well pleased" (Mt 3:17 NRSV). But suffering and servanthood are joined in an important saying of Jesus in which he speaks of his ministry and alludes to his coming death: "For the Son of Man came not to be served but to serve, and to give his life a ransom for many" (Mk 10:45 NRSV). The imagery of service and giving one's life for the many seem to allude to the description of the suffering servant's death "for the many" in Isaiah 53:10-12. In Luke 22:37 Jesus speaks of the necessity of his fulfilling the text, "he was numbered with the transgressors" (Is 53:12). At the last supper, Jesus speaks of the cup, "my blood of the covenant, which is poured out for many" (Mk 14:24 NRSV). While this saying evokes the "blood of the covenant" sprinkled on the people at Sinai (Ex 24:8), the image of being "poured out" and the allusion "for many" recall the Servant's death in Isaiah 53:12.

Earlier in Isaiah (Is 42:1-6; 49:3), the servant is Israel itself. In Isaiah 52:13—53:12 the servant is one who represents Israel, who undergoes suffering on behalf of Israel, in order to save Israel from its plight of exile. The broader OT motif of Israel's redemptive suffering is here brought into its sharpest focus. And so when Jesus "fulfills" the role of the suffering servant, he is in fact taking on the role of the righteous sufferer within Israel and undergoing suffering and death on Israel's behalf. The true force of the image of the suffering servant is realized when we observe that beneath his unseemly outward appearance, the Isaianic servant is a suffering king, the

representative of his people. He startles nations and their kings (Is 52:15), he will be "exalted and lifted up" (Is 52:13), and in his eventual triumph he will "divide the spoil with the strong" (Is 53:12 NRSV).

Sacrifice. The death of Jesus is readily interpreted in terms of the OT sacrificial system. Paul speaks of God setting forth Jesus as a *hilastērion*, a Greek term variously translated as "propitiation," "expiation," "mercy seat" or simply "sacrifice of atonement" (Rom 3:25; cf. 1 Jn 2:2; 4:10). The image is of God setting forth Jesus in his death as the equivalent of the sacrifice on the annual Day of Atonement, a sacrifice made on behalf of the sins of the nation Israel. Likewise, in Romans 8:3 Jesus is sent "in the likeness of sinful man to be a sin offering" (NIV). Jesus' "blood" is also a sacrificial image, as may be seen in Paul's speech to the Ephesians where he sketches the picture of "the church of God, which he bought with his own blood" (Acts 20:28 NIV; cf. Rom 5:9; 1 Cor 11:25; Eph 1:7; 2:13; Col 1:20) and in Peter's image of "the precious blood of Christ, a lamb without blemish or defect" (1 Pet 1:19 NIV).

In Hebrews, Jesus is closely identified with the *priest (see below). Because he is without sin, he does not need to *sacrifice for himself but for the people. And the sacrifice he offers is not of bulls or goats but of himself, his own body and blood (Heb 9:12, 14, 26; 10:10). This sacrifice, unlike the repeated offerings in the OT, is offered once and for all (Heb 9:26; 10:10, 12). This imagery in Hebrews is the culmination of the NT's tendency to focus the central images of OT sacrifice on Jesus and his work. In addition to high priest and lamb of sacrifice, the metaphor of *altar is also used for his cross (Heb 13:10-12). In Hebrews the *cross of Christ is the altar on which Jesus' blood is offered, and he is the high priest who offers the sacrifice. All of the biblical images of altars of the one, true God converge on this altar. Jesus becomes the memorial of the new covenant, the place of sacrifice.

John the Baptist called attention to Jesus by proclaiming, "Look, the Lamb of God, who takes away the sin of the world!" (Jn 1:29 NIV). The image of Christ as a Passover lamb is employed by Paul (1 Cor 5:7), but in Revelation the image of Christ as a lamb achieves prominence. Jesus is the lamb that was slain (Rev 5:6, 12; 13:8). The blood of the lamb cleanses the saints (Rev 7:14) and is the means of their conquest (Rev 12:11).

Images of Care, Provision and Nourishment. A number of images may be grouped together as depicting Jesus providing for people's needs, whether in narrative actions or metaphors of his identity. His very nature is associated with blessing and providing, a fact that is richly imaged in his miraculous provision of food in his feeding of the four thousand and the five thousand, in his raising of Lazarus, and in his healing of the lepers, the lame, the deaf and the blind. The Gospels provide us with a veritable collage of Jesus as the miraculous provider.

His own description of himself as physician (Mt 9:12; Lk 4:23) points out the centrality of his healings to his whole ministry. Many of the images of provision and nourishment are quite basic, even primal, as Jesus describes himself with images appealing to our most basic needs: food, water, light, life, etc.

Kind master. The yoke can be a metaphor of slavery and the harshness of enforced subjection to a slavemaster (Gen 27:40; Lev 26:13; 1 Kings 12:4; Is 47:6). Ironically, despite his challenging call to discipleship, Jesus assures his followers that his "yoke is easy" and his "burden is light" (Mt 11:28-30). Jesus is comparing his discipleship to that of the Pharisees who, by their "traditions of men," lay heavy burdens upon men and women. In the apocryphal book known as Wisdom of Sirach, Wisdom bids listeners to "draw near to me" (Sir 51:23), and Sirach invites them to "put your neck under her yoke, and let your souls receive instruction" (Sir 51:26 NRSV). Jesus, speaking as divine wisdom, offers his "easy," or "kind," yoke. His eschatological interpretation of the law is a welcome relief to those who have toiled under the demands of Pharisaism. He is the master, but his way promises rest and peace.

Bread. The image of *bread draws on the most basic component of meals in first-century Palestine. Just as it would be unimaginable to sustain life apart from bread, so too it is impossible to live a satisfying life apart from the spiritual sustenance provided by Jesus. Jesus feeds the crowds with bread and fish, and then the next day proclaims, "I am the bread of life. He who comes to me will never go hungry" (Jn 6:35 NIV). Not only that, but he—in contrast with the manna in the wilderness—is "the bread that comes down from heaven, which a man may eat and not die. I am the living bread that came down from heaven. If anyone eats of this bread, he will live forever. This bread is my flesh, which I will give for the life of the world." (Jn 6:50-51 NIV).

In Mark's Gospel, after the feeding of five thousand and then four thousand, the disciples are with Jesus in a boat, crossing the Sea of Galilee. Jesus, detecting their concern that they have forgotten to bring bread, "except for one loaf they had with them in the boat" (Mk 8:14 NIV), tells them to beware of the yeast of the Pharisees and Herod. Puzzled, the disciples wonder if he is speaking of their having forgotten to bring bread. Jesus reminds them of the two feedings and the remaining baskets of bread. He asks, "Do you still not understand?" (Mk 8:21 NIV). Mark is leaving his readers to puzzle this out with the disciples. The "one loaf" in the boat, it seems, is Jesus himself.

At the last supper, Jesus gives thanks for the bread and says "this is my body which is given for you" (Lk 22:19 NRSV; cf. Mt 26:26; Mk 14:22). Jesus in the totality of his person and mission is the bread of life, the staple food of spiritual life.

Water. In John 4 Jesus meets the woman of Samaria at Jacob's well. The conversation moves from physical thirst and drink to Jesus' claim that those who drink the water he offers will "never thirst." It "will become in him a spring of water welling up to eternal life" (Jn 4:13-14 NIV). In John 7 Jesus appears at the temple during the Feast of Tabernacles, which commemorated Israel's wilderness experience (Num 20:2-13) and included a reenactment of the miraculous provision of water at Meribah. Here Jesus announces that if anyone is truly thirsty, he should come to him and drink (Jn 7:37-38) and receive the Holy Spirit. In both instances the symbolism of water is closely associated with the person of Jesus and the eschatological blessings offered in his person.

Vine and wine. As the "true vine" (Jn 15:1) Jesus serves not only as a source of spiritual strength and solace but also as the channel for obtaining the Spirit's presence and power. The vine is an image evoking divine blessing but also Israel, the people of God (e.g., Ps 80:8, 14; Jer 2:21; 6:9; 8:13). Jesus claims to be the *vine—the whole vine and not just the stalk—and inasmuch as his disciples remain in him as part of the vine plant, they are part of the faithful vineyard. There is a sense here that Jesus the vine sustains the disciples who remain "in him." Jesus neither explicitly calls himself nor is he referred to as *"wine," but the kingdom of God is likened to "new wine"—the first and most potent drippings of the grape—that demands new wineskins (Mt 9:17; Mk 2:22; Lk 5:37-39), and at the wedding at Cana he changes water into wine, the best wine (Jn 2:1-11), and so symbolizes the blessing of the dawning eschatological age. Finally, at the last supper, the cup of wine is "my blood of the covenant poured out for many" (Mk 14:24 NIV; cf. Mt 26:28; Lk 22:20), a sacrificial image (cf. Ex 24:3-8; Is 53:12).

Source. The image of Christ as source is perhaps most fully captured in Paul's use of "head" to describe Christ's relationship to the church as the source of its vitality (Eph 5:23; Col 1:18). Although the metaphor also speaks of his *authority and rule, the notion of source is evident in Colossians 2:19 and Ephesians 4:15-16. In Colossians the person who pursues visionary experiences ("the worship of/with angels," Col 2:18) "has lost connection with the Head [Christ], from whom the whole body, supported and held together by its ligaments and sinews, grows as God causes it to grow" (Col 2:19 NIV). This particular use of the image reflects the ancient physiological notion that the head is the source from which power flows, by route of the ligaments, to the other organs of the body. Christ the head is the source of nourishment for the church, his body.

Light. Jesus describes himself as the "light of the world" (Jn 8:12; 9:5; cf. Jn 12:35-36, 46), the "true light" (Jn 1:9). In an age when light is easily available at the flip of a switch and when its nature and speed can be studied and measured, we easily overlook the fact that for the ancients light was something imbued with mystery and power. Darkness subdues and restricts, but light revitalizes and frees by scattering the darkness, illuminating the world, arousing those who *sleep and allowing humans to carry out their lives. Matthew tells us that Jesus begins his ministry in Galilee in order to fulfill what was said by the prophet Isaiah, "The people living in darkness have seen a great light; on those living in the land of the shadow of death a light has dawned" (Mt 4:14-16 NIV). In Revelation 22:16 Jesus is also described as the "bright Morning Star," the *star that signals the dawn just as Jesus signals a new age (cf. 2 Pet 1:19). This image carries overtones of the "star of Jacob" (Num 24:17) and the "sun of righteousness" (Mal 4:2), both images of the coming deliverance of Israel.

Life. In John's Gospel, Jesus presents himself as the giver of life, the eternal life that only comes from God. The link between life and the word that proceeds from God is struck in Deuteronomy 32:46-47, where Moses warns Israel that the words of God are "no trifle for you" but "your life" (RSV). Jesus, the one sent from God and the very Word of God, claims to be life (Jn 11:25; 14:6), the very source of life (Jn 10:10). This is an astounding claim, but it is fitting that the one who "was in the beginning with God" and was present and active in the creation of all things (Jn 1:2-3) should be the source of eternal and divine life. The gift of life offered by the Tree of Life in the Garden of Eden is now offered in the person of the Word incarnate. By believing in Jesus, humans partake of the eternal life he offers (Jn 3:16). Or, more vividly, by eating the flesh and drinking the blood of Christ, they gain eternal life and will be raised on the last day (Jn 6:54). The One who is "the resurrection and the life" offers a gift that reverses the flow of life toward death: "Those who believe in me, even though they die, will live" (Jn 11:25 NRSV).

Images of Transcendence. Several NT images of Jesus either explicitly claim or allude to his divinity. Of course, it should be kept in mind that the important episodes in the Gospels narratives provide glimpses of the transcendent nature of Christ, three of which are key moments in all three Synoptic Gospels: the voice from heaven at his baptism (Mt 3:13-17; Mk 1:9-11; Lk 3:21, 22), the transfiguration and a second voice from heaven (Mt 17:1-9; Mk 9:2-8; Lk 9:28-36), and the events surrounding his death and resurrection (e.g., Mk 15:38-39; 16:1-8).

Alpha and omega. In the book of Revelation the image of Jesus as the first and last letter of the Greek alphabet, "Alpha and Omega," is set in parallel with "the first and the last, the beginning and the end" and is used of both God and Christ (Rev 1:8, 17; 21:6; 22:13). The image springs from Isaiah, where God says, "I am the first and I am the last; besides me there is no god" (Is 44:6 NRSV) and "I am he; I am the first, and I am the last" (Is 48:12 NRSV). It is an image of God as the sovereign Creator of all things and the One who brings all things to their fulfillment, the Lord of the first creation and the Lord of the new creation. In Greek thinking, "the beginning and the end" indicated the eternity of the highest god, and that idea is reflected in the biblical image. The image in Revelation closely identifies Jesus with God, the One who is prior and active in creation as well as the One who brings creation to its goal. Nothing lies outside his sovereign vision, plan and power. Those who worship him with John the Seer are reassured, "Do not be afraid; I am the first and the last" (Rev 1:17 NRSV).

Wisdom and Word of God. Jesus associates himself with divine wisdom in several passages in the Synoptic Gospels, and the theme is developed in the Fourth Gospel and epistles. The imagery is based on the Jewish tradition of speaking of God's wisdom personified, beginning with Proverbs 8, where Lady Wisdom calls out and speaks of herself as the one who was created by God at the beginning of his work (Prov 8:22), as his master worker, present at God's side at the creation of the world (Prov 8:30-31). This motif passes through later Jewish wisdom literature, particularly the Wisdom of Solomon and the Book of Sirach, before it finds its way into the NT. These apocryphal books develop the motif with the imagery of Wisdom present at God's side, active in creation and taking up residence in Israel (closely associated with the law given at Sinai).

When Jesus declares that "something greater than Solomon is here" (Mt 12:42; Lk 11:31), he is claiming to possess wisdom greater than Solomon's. But the image of Jesus as a wise man is transcended when he says "wisdom is vindicated by her deeds," in apparent reference to himself (Mt 11:16-19; Lk 7:31-35). When Jesus identifies himself, along with the prophets and "apostles," as one of Wisdom's envoys sent to Israel and met with hostile reception (Lk 11:49-51; Mt 23:34-36; cf. Prov 9:3-6; Wis 7:27), he is closely identifying himself with the very Wisdom of God. A similar image of Wisdom is evoked in Jesus' lament over Jerusalem (Mt 23:37-39; Lk 13:34-35). And in Jesus' beckoning to the weary and heavy laden to come and take his yoke upon them (Mt 11:25-30), the imagery of Wisdom lies close to the surface. The widely known book of Sirach closes with Wisdom beckoning the "uneducated" to "draw near to me . . . acquire wisdom. . . . Put your neck under her yoke and let your souls receive instruction" (Sir 51:23-27). Jesus, in comparison with the burdens of the law codified in the "traditions of men," offers a yoke that is "easy" and a burden that is "light." Heavenly wisdom is imaged as coming from above in Jesus' thanksgiving to God: "All things have been delivered to me by my Father; and no one knows the Son except the Father, and no one knows the Father except the Son and any one to whom the Son chooses to reveal him" (Mt 11:27; Lk 10:22 RSV). In Wisdom 2:13-16 the wise man "professes to have knowledge of God and calls himself a child of the Lord . . . and boasts that God is his father." The context suggests an identification with divine Wisdom, entrusted with the secret things of God and the task of revealing them (Prov 8:14-36; Wis 2:13, 16; 4:10-15).

In the prologue of the Gospel of John, Jesus is identified as the Word, the *logos,* that was "with God

... was God ... was in the beginning with God" and was active in creation (Jn 1:1-3). For those attuned to the imagery of Wisdom, the evocation could not be more forthright, and the well-known scene of Wisdom choosing Israel from among all of the nations as her dwelling place is replayed as "the Word became flesh and dwelt among us" (Jn 1:14). In Sirach 24, Wisdom, who "came forth from the mouth of the Most High" and sought a resting place among the nations, is commanded, "Make your dwelling in Jacob, and in Israel receive your inheritance" (Sir 24:3, 8 NRSV). Wisdom obeys and takes up her dwelling in the "holy tent" and is "established in Zion" (Sir 24:10-12). But Jesus, the Wisdom of God incarnate, is not known or recognized by "the world" or by "his own people" (Jn 1:10-11).

Jesus as Wisdom appears again in Paul, in an image spawned by Israel's wisdom tradition. When Paul writes that Christ is "the image of the invisible God, the firstborn over all creation" (Col 1:15), he is clothing Christ with the imagery of a preexistent Adam and of Wisdom. In Sirach 24:3-4 Wisdom is said to have "come forth from the mouth of the Most High" and "dwelt in the highest heavens" (NRSV), and in Wisdom of Solomon 7:25 Wisdom is the "pure emanation of the glory of the Almighty . . . a reflection of eternal light, a spotless mirror of the working of God, and an image of his goodness" (NRSV). This imagery is picked up even more eloquently in Hebrews 1:2-3, where Christ is the one "through whom he also created the worlds. He is the reflection of God's glory and the exact imprint of God's very being, and he sustains all things by his powerful word" (NRSV). The motif of Wisdom and its associated imagery was employed by Israel's sages and poets to search out the nature of the inner life of God and his powerful and eternal word. In the NT the story and imagery of wisdom is discovered as a garment ready made for the figure of Jesus.

Temple presence. In John we read that "the Word became flesh and made his dwelling among us. We have seen his glory, the glory of the One and Only, who came from the Father, full of grace and truth" (Jn 1:14). The image is that of the preexistent Wisdom and Word "tabernacling," or "tenting," among humankind, like the Shekinah glory that took up residence in the tabernacle at the center of Israel's encampment in the wilderness. The tabernacle and the temple symbolize God's presence in the midst of his people, in the midst of the "body" of corporate Israel. So within the NT we find the image of "God in Christ" expressed in ways analogous to the temple in Israel. Jesus mediates healing and forgiveness, two divine acts associated with the temple, and he is the new locus of the divine presence. This is sharply imaged in the Fourth Gospel in the scene (in the temple) where Jesus says, "Destroy this temple, and I will raise it again in three days," and the explanation is given that "the temple he had spoken of was his body" (Jn 2:19, 21 NIV; cf. Mk 14:58; 15:29). Jesus as temple is an image of the chosen place of God's

presence, a metaphor for what we call the incarnation.

Paul, recalling God's being pleased to have his glory dwell in the temple (Deut 12:5; Ps 68:16; Ezek 43:5), says of Jesus, "God was pleased to have all his fullness dwell in him" (Col 1:19 NIV). The metaphor of Jesus as temple is further developed in the NT to include the people of God. They are incorporated into him as a new temple, "built on the foundation of the apostles and prophets, with Christ Jesus himself as the chief cornerstone. In him the whole building is joined together and rises to become a holy temple in the Lord" (Eph 2:20 NIV). Associated with this is the image of Jesus as a "living stone," a building stone of the new temple. It was "rejected by men but chosen by God and precious to him" (1 Pet 2:4-8; cf. Is 28:16; Ps 118:2).

Son of God. The biblical image of Jesus as Son of God is frequently obscured by later doctrinal formulations of the Trinity. As true as the church's understanding may be, when we view Son of God as an image, new facets appear. It is first of all an image that grows out of the soil of Israel's story. At the exodus, God names Israel as his "son." Moses is instructed to say to Pharaoh, "Israel is my firstborn son. . . . Let my son go that he may worship me" (Ex 4:22-23 NRSV). This very image of Israel is echoed in Hosea 11:1: "When Israel was a child, I loved him, and out of Egypt I called my son" (NRSV). But within the broader body of Israel, the Davidic king, the representative of the people, is singled out for a special status of sonship. In 2 Samuel 7:14 God says of David's descendant that "I will be a father to him, and he shall be a son to me" (NRSV). And in Psalm 2:7 God declares of Israel's king, "You are my son; today I have begotten you" (NRSV). Within the OT this filial relationship of Israel and of king to God speaks of the unique place of intimacy Israel enjoys among the nations. Yet it is a relationship that is marred by sin and fractured by exile as Israel (and her king), like the Prodigal Son, goes into a distant country.

The imagery of Jesus as Son is best viewed against this backdrop. Jesus is the son born from the womb of Israel and the Davidic line, both of which carry the legacy of divine sonship. Paul evokes this rich, storied background when he writes, "But when the fullness of time had come, God sent his Son, born of a woman, born under the law, in order to redeem those who were under the law" (Gal 4:4-5 NRSV; cf. Rom 1:3-4).

Jesus' identity as divine son is confirmed at Jesus's baptism by the voice from heaven announcing, "This is my Son, the Beloved, with whom I am well pleased" (Mt 3:17; Mk 1:11; Lk 3:22; cf. Gen 22:2; Ps 2:7; Is 42:1). In the ensuing ordeal of Satanic temptation in the wilderness, Jesus is three times tempted as "Son of God," and in each case the temptation is evocative of Israel's own temptations in the wilderness. Jesus' sonship is on one level a successful replay of Israel's sonship. But whereas the sonship of Israel and of her kings was fraught with tension and disobedience, Jesus lives up to the full stature of the image of an obedient and faithful Son on intimate terms with the Father. Exceeding Israel's sonship, Jesus possesses a unique sonship outlined in the words: "All things have been delivered to me by my Father; and no one knows the Son except the Father, and no one knows the Father except the Son and any one to whom the Son chooses to reveal him" (Mt 11:27; Lk 10:22 RSV). This relationship is also evoked in Jesus' characteristic form of address to God, "Abba, Father" (Mk 14:36), a relationship that those who follow him may share (Mt 6:9; Lk 11:2; cf. Rom 8:14; Gal 4:6). The image of Jesus as Son is most eloquently set out in the Gospel of John in texts such as John 3:16: "For God so loved the world that he gave his one and only Son, that whoever believes in him shall not perish but have eternal life" (Jn 3:16 NIV).

Son of Man. This image, frequently used by Jesus to refer to himself, draws on the vision of Daniel 7 which features "one like a son of man." This background must be fully understood in order to correct the misconception that the image of "Son of Man" simply points out Jesus' human nature in contrast with his divine nature. Son of Man is not a counterweight to Son of God, as if each points to a different "side" of Christ's nature—the human and the divine. Both images are more complex than that. From the description of Daniel 7, the Son of Man is most obviously "heavenly" in his appearance, but as Daniel grasps for words, he points out this figure's remarkable trait of looking "like someone of the genus humankind."

Set within the broader context of Daniel 7, the "one like a son of man" is a corporate or representative figure. In contrast with the four composite and monstrous beasts ("unclean" by the standards of Israel's law) that represent the evil empires of this earth, the "one like a son of man" represents a truly human kingdom, Israel (cf. Dan 7:14 and 7:18), "the saints of the Most High." This truly Adamic people and kingdom is presently suffering oppression (Dan 7:7-8 and 7:19-25) under earth's ravaging beasts. The transcendent—even divine—qualities of the "one like a son of man" are imaged as he rides the chariot cloud of the divine warrior (e.g., Ps 68:4; 104:3-4). His royal stature is established as he is presented before the throne of the Ancient of Days and given "dominion and glory and kingdom, that all peoples, nations, and languages should serve him; his dominion is an everlasting dominion, which shall not pass away, and his kingdom one that shall not be destroyed" (Dan 7:14 RSV).

Clearly, then, when Jesus speaks of himself as the "Son of Man," he is evoking an image that bears with it a story of conflict and kingship. It is no accident that Jesus' own Gospel story is one of conflict with Satan and a proclamation of the presence and future fullness of the kingdom of God. The three Gospel contexts in which Jesus identifies himself by the image Son of Man—as one who seeks Israel's deliverance (e.g., Lk 19:10), who suffers Israel's exilic death and vindication (e.g., Mk 8:31; 10:45), and who is exalted and granted universal sovereignty (e.g., Mk 14:26)—all find their roots in Daniel's vision of "one like a son of man." It is a messianic image uniquely projected onto the Gospel story and focused on the figure of Jesus.

Heavenly Adam. If the image of Son of Man evokes something of the figure of Adam among the beasts, Jesus as the "image of God" prompts us to recall the biblical figure of the primal man (Gen 1:27). When we read that Christ is "the image of the invisible God, the firstborn over all creation" (Col 1:15), the biblically familiar mind returns to the story of Adam's creation. But a tension surfaces, for the text continues, "in him all things were created . . . through him and for him" (Col 1:16). Christ as the image of God is presented as a preexistent being, one logically prior to the earthly Adam and yet bearing the "image of God." The force of this seems to be that Christ bears the "human face" of God from which the earthly Adam takes his resemblance. A parallel expression may be found in Philippians 2:6, where Christ is said to be "in the form of God" and yet, unlike the earthly Adam, "did not count equality with God a thing to be grasped" (RSV; perhaps echoing Gen 3:5: "you will be like God"). The notion of Christ as the image of God also occurs in 2 Corinthians 4:4 where Paul speaks of "the light of the gospel of the glory of Christ, who is the image of God" (NRSV). Here Christ as the image of God takes on the luminescent quality of glory and recalls the picture of Adam in Psalm 8:5: "crowned with glory and honor." For Paul, the glory of Christ, the image of God, is the prototype of redeemed human glory and honor.

Finally, in 1 Corinthians 15:42-49 Paul speaks of Christ as the "last," or "second man . . . from heaven" in explicit contrast with the "first man, Adam." The first Adam "became a living being"; the second Adam, by his resurrection, "became a life-giving spirit." The first was earthly, "of the dust"; the second is "from heaven." Here the focus is not on protology but eschatology: "Just as we have borne the image of the man of dust, we will also bear the image of the man of heaven" (1 Cor 15:49 NRSV). Christ as the image of God is the prototype of humanity both originally in the first creation and eschatologically in the new creation.

Images of Vocation. *Christ, Messiah, King.* The word *christ* is so thoroughly associated with Jesus that it has virtually become a surname for Jesus of Nazareth. To discuss it as an image is something akin to archaeological recovery. But an image it is, and retrieving its luster offers insights into the Bible's portrayal of Jesus.

Behind the English word *christ* lies the Greek word *christos*, and (in the biblical tradition) behind that lies the Hebrew word *māšîaḥ*, translated into English as "messiah." Both the Greek and Hebrew terms refer to an anointed person who is set apart for a special task, such as a priest or a king. It is the image of an anointed king that interests us here. Oddly enough, the term *māšîah*, "anointed one," is only occasionally used in the OT as a one-word image of Israel's king (Ps 18:50; 132:10-17), and it is not used by the prophets as an image of the future king of the line of David (2 Sam 7:8-16). Even within early Judaism, where we do find it in texts, it is not very frequently used of the coming ruler of Israel. Nevertheless, the association of anointing with kingship is well established, and within the NT *māšîah* is obviously the Hebrew term standing behind the recurring Greek term *christos*. The link between Christ as "anointed one" and the Davidic king of the OT is underscored in Acts 4:25-26. There the apostles cite Psalm 2:2—"The kings of the earth set themselves in array and the rulers were gathered together, against the Lord and against his Anointed" (RSV)—as a prophecy of Herod, Pilate, the Gentiles and "the peoples of Israel" who set themselves against God's "holy servant Jesus," whom God "did anoint" (Acts 4:27).

The Gospels pose the question of whether Jesus is the anointed king of Israel, and though the image of this anointed one is transformed in the telling of the story of Jesus, the answer is clearly affirmative. Jesus, "the Christ," is the one who will bring Israel's hope to a climax. His anointing is a divine one, bestowed by God as the Spirit descends on him at his baptism. Jesus identifies himself as the one anointed by the Spirit "to preach good news to the poor" (Lk 4:18 NIV; cf. Is 61:1). He is the anointed king of Israel who by unexpected means will free Israel from its plight of bondage and will reconstitute those who follow him as the new people of God.

But the divine anointing by the Spirit is not the only episode of anointing in the Gospels. We find a picture of anointing in the Gospel story of a woman anointing Jesus with costly perfume (Mk 14:3-8; cf. Lk 7:37-38; Jn 11:2; 12:1-7). This literal anointing is paradoxically significant. The ointment is scandalously expensive. A woman is an unlikely candidate for anointing the Christ. Jesus interprets the act as an anointing of his body for burial. And he foretells that the woman's act will be told in memory of her wherever the gospel is preached. All of this must be set within the broader compass of Mark's "gospel of Jesus Christ" (Mk 1:1), in which Mark presents the death of Christ on the cross as the climactic moment in which a representative Gentile experiences an epiphany: Jesus is the "Son of God," or in Jewish terms, Israel's Messiah (Mk 15:39). Jesus' death is paradoxically his victory and exaltation as king, and the woman's act of anointing him is a part of this enthronement scene.

The hallmark of Jesus' proclamation, the message and enactment of the kingdom of God, is a natural accompaniment to his status as "anointed one." As the anointed king he has the authority to describe the nature of the kingdom, to dispense the blessings of the kingdom and accept people into the kingdom. The image of Christ as king is vividly portrayed in the Fourth Gospel's scene of Jesus before Pilate: "Jesus said, 'My kingdom is not of this world . . . my kingdom is from another place' . . . 'You are a king then!' said Pilate. Jesus answered, 'You are right in saying I am a king.' " (Jn 18:36-37 NIV).

In Paul's letters we encounter a fundamental aspect of the image "Christ," the corporate dimension of kingship. Like kings in general, Christ as king is the representative of his people. His accomplishment of salvation is on behalf of his people. When Paul speaks repeatedly of believers being "in Christ" and participating in the blessings of salvation, the image of a people having a corporate "share" in their "anointed one," their king, is being evoked (cf. 2 Sam 19:40-43; 20:1). By faith and baptism "into Christ" (Rom 6:11), Christians have entered into a solidarity with the anointed one so that what is true of Christ is true of his people.

In the book of Revelation we find other images of messiahship associated with the Davidic lineage: Jesus is the "Lion of the tribe of Judah, the Root of David" (Rev 5:5 NIV; cf. Gen 49:9; Is 11:10), the "Root and Offspring of David" (Rev 22:16 NIV) and the "bright Morning Star" (Rev 22:16; cf. Num 24:17-19). The image of the sword coming from Christ's mouth (Rev 1:16; 2:12, 16; 19:21) and of his judging with righteousness (Rev 19:1) are drawn from the messianic text of Isaiah 11:4. And recalling Psalm 2, where the "nations" and "kings of the earth" conspire and set themselves in opposition to "the Lord and his Anointed One" (Ps 2:2 NIV) and will be subdued, Revelation repeatedly alludes to "the nations" and "the kings of the earth" as the political powers that Christ will subdue (Rev 1:5; 6:15; 17:2, 18; 18:3, 9; 19:19; 21:24).

Destroyer and builder. Jesus is the master builder of a new *temple, but the building of that temple entails the demolition of another. The Messiah of Israel was to be a temple builder in the line of David. The messianic prophecy of 2 Samuel 7:12-14 speaks of one of the line of David whose reign God will establish and who will "build a house for my name" (cf. Zech 6:12-14). Solomon, of course, fulfills this assignment in the short term, but the expectation is extended toward the future heir of the eternal throne of David. At Jesus' trial witnesses are brought forth who say: "I will destroy this man-made temple and in three days will build another, not made by man" (Mk 14:58 NIV) Their witness is "false," or perhaps contradictory, but they seem to be presenting a garbled version of something Jesus did say, perhaps in a riddle form (which is further verified in John 2:18-22). Jesus' prediction of the coming destruction of the Jerusalem temple (Mk 13:2; Lk 19:41-44; 21:20-24) fits this pattern of demolition, and the manner in which he ties that event to his own appeal to Israel and its rejection (e.g., Lk 19:41-44) binds him closely to this coming destruction. Paul further develops the motif in Ephesians 2:14 in the image of

Christ tearing down the dividing wall between Jew and Gentile (probably a reference to the wall that separated the temple court of the Gentiles from the inner courts accessible only by Israel) in preparation for the building of a new temple for the Lord of which Christ is the cornerstone (Eph 2:19-22).

This temple-building motif is likewise rooted in the Gospels, where Jesus is alluded to as "building another" temple in three days. But more fundamentally, the image of Jesus as master builder is found in the saying of Matthew 16:18: "on this rock *I will build* my church, and the gates of Hades will not overcome it" (NIV). The temple imagery becomes more apparent against the background of Jewish cosmology, rooted in the symbolic glossary of ancient Near Eastern mythology, in which the temple was built upon a "cosmic" rock, a rock that served as a lid over the netherworld (the "gates of Hades") and in rabbinic speculation was even regarded as the site of the original paradise. When Jesus speaks of building his "church" on the "rock," he is alluding to the new rock, or foundation, of his messiahship. On this rock the new messianic community will be built and form a new "temple." He fulfills the role of the messianic temple builder, but in an unexpected manner. And as Paul will extend the imagery, this temple consists of both Jews and Gentiles who are laid on a foundation of "apostles and prophets" (Eph 2:20), or as Peter puts it, they are "living stones . . . built into a spiritual house" (1 Pet 2:4 NRSV).

Priest. In the letter to the Hebrews, Jesus is imaged as one who was "made like his brothers in every way, in order that he might become a merciful and faithful high priest in service to God, and that he might make atonement for the sins of the people" (Heb 2:17 NIV). As a great high priest (Heb 4:14) he is able to "sympathize with our weaknesses" and was "tempted in every way, just as we are" (Heb 4:15 NIV). But the focus is not on the priesthood of Aaron, whose priesthood is temporally restricted and only a "shadow" (Heb 8:5; 10:1) of the priesthood of Christ. The exemplar and lineage of Christ's priesthood is the mysterious figure of Melchizedek, who was "without father, without mother, without genealogy, having neither beginning of days nor end of life, but resembling the Son of God, he remains a priest forever" (Heb 7:3 NRSV; cf. Gen 14; Ps 110:4). Melchizedek's priesthood was based on his character and founded on the eternal will of God. Christ, like Melchizedek, is a priest "continually" (Heb 7:23) and ministers under a "better covenant" (Heb 7:22). Since he is of Davidic and not Aaronic descent, Jesus answers the description of Psalm 110:4: "You are a priest forever, according to the order of Melchizedek" (NRSV).

Whereas the Aaronic priest of the old covenant presented a sacrifice on the Day of Atonement on behalf of Israel (Heb 9:7), Jesus "as a high priest of the good things that have come," has "through the greater and perfect tent . . . entered once for all into the Holy Place, not with the blood of goats and calves, but with his own blood, thus obtaining eternal redemption" (Heb 9:11-12 NRSV). The thrust of the image of Jesus as high priest is that his ministry is absolutely effective and yet—despite the transcendent aura of its perfection, eternity and heavenly greatness—far more intimate than the Aaronic priesthood. Jesus is a priest who not only shares our humanity but offers his own blood for our atonement. The picture is much the same as 1 John 2:1-2: "But if anyone does sin, we have an advocate with the Father, Jesus Christ the righteous; and he is the atoning sacrifice for our sins, and not for ours only but also for the sins of the whole world" (NRSV).

Prophet. The crowds who follow Jesus perceive him to be a prophet (Mt 26:28; Mk 14:65; Lk 22:69; Jn 6:17). Jesus begins his ministry under the mentorship of John the Baptist, a well-known prophetic figure. Jesus becomes well known as a prophet who is mighty in word and in deed. He is, by all appearances, a prophet focused on the restoration of Israel. Even on the Emmaus Road we overhear the disciples referring to Jesus as "a prophet, powerful in word and deed before God and all the people" (Lk 24:19).

As a prophet mighty in word, Jesus proclaims with authority the arrival of the kingdom of God. Repeatedly the Gospels record him saying, "Truly I say to you," going beyond the prophetic formula, "Thus says the Lord." At Nazareth, Jesus places himself among the prophets by reading from Isaiah 61, identifying himself as the anointed servant of the Lord and responding to his hometown's rejection of him with the proverb, "No prophet is welcome in his own country" (Lk 4:24). Like a prophet, he speaks oracles of judgment against Israel: "Woe to you, Korazin! Woe to you, Bethsaida! If the miracles that were performed in you had been performed in Tyre and Sidon, they would have repented long ago in sackcloth and ashes" (Mt 11:21 NIV). But also like a prophet he speaks words of comfort: "Blessed are the poor in spirit, for theirs is the kingdom of heaven" (Mt 5:3 NIV). Finally, like a prophet, Jesus speaks in parables and performs parabolic actions, such as in the temple.

As a prophet mighty in deed, Jesus, raises the son of the widow of Nain (Lk 7:11-16), much like Elijah's raising of the son of the widow of Zarephath (1 Kings 17:17-23). Even greater than Elisha, who fed one hundred men with twenty loaves of barley bread and had some left over (2 Kings 4:42-44), Jesus feeds five thousand and then four thousand. After a feeding miracle, the people conclude that Jesus is a prophet (Jn 6:17). The disciples also regard Jesus as a prophet, and when they are snubbed by a Samaritan village, they see themselves as followers of a prophet in a bid to "call fire down from heaven to destroy them" (Lk 9:52-55; a reprise of Elijah's calling down fire on the messengers from the king of Samaria, 1 Kings 1).

Sage, wise man. The sage, or wise man, is a revered figure in the biblical and Jewish tradition. It is easy to see Jesus in the role of a sage, a figure in the tradition of wise men such as Solomon. Like a wise man, he speaks in riddle-like sayings, aphorisms and parables that subvert the accepted wisdom of the day, and parables that speak of the wise and the foolish (Mt 7:24-27; 24:45-51; 25:1-13). He is skilled in the use of rhetorical devices such as paradox, hyperbole, contrast, irony and emphasis, all designed to take hold in the mind and germinate. Like a wise man, his sayings demonstrate a wide-ranging knowledge of the world of nature—seeds, plants, flowers, trees, birds and other animals are the stuff of his speech (cf. Solomon, 1 Kings 4:33). Like an extraordinary wise man, he claims that "one greater than Solomon is here" (Mt 12:42; Lk 11:31), and indeed Jesus makes the implicit claim to be the very wisdom of God (see above). The role of a wise man should not be set apart from that of a prophet, for within Israel prophecy and wisdom had long converged in figures such as Daniel (and later, Ben Sirach).

Teacher. The disciples of John readily identify Jesus as a "Rabbi," a teacher (Jn 1:38), and he is readily called a teacher by others who meet him (e.g., Mt 8:19; 9:11; 12:38; 17:24; 19:16; 22:16; 22:24, 36). As a teacher he exhibits clarity, power and authority while displaying remarkable insight into his students and inquirers. Unlike the rabbis, he is not bound to a fixed location but teaches in the *temple (e.g., Mt 21:23; 26:55; Jn 7:14; 8:2, 20), in towns and *villages (Mt 9:35; 11:1; Mk 6:6; Lk 13:22), synagogues (Mt 4:23; 9:35; 13:54; Mk 1:21; 6:2; Lk 4:15-16, 31-33; 6:6; 13:10), *homes (Mk 2:1-2), from an anchored boat (Mk 4:1; Lk 5:3) and along the roadways (Mk 10:32-34). Jesus teaches crowds (Mk 2:13; 3:7-8; 6:34; 10:1), though his disciples ("pupils") are the special focus of his teaching (Mt 10; Mk 4:10; 8:27-32; Jn 13—17).

Jesus is a master of the spoken word and the art of rhetoric, shaping parables, aphorisms, and even longer discourses in a way that holds the attention of his disciples and the crowds. He is a penetrating and clever controversialist, silencing his opponents with wisdom and imploding their arguments. Questions, events and miracles are all occasions for teaching, and meal times become symbolic events of God's offer of forgiveness to outsiders.

Itinerant. One of the most prominent images in the Gospels is that of Jesus the itinerant teacher. Matthew twice ties healing, teaching and travel together as a summary of Jesus ministry (Mt 4:23; Mt 9:35): "Jesus went through all the towns and villages, teaching in their synagogues, preaching the good news of the kingdom and healing every disease and sickness" (Mt 9:35 NIV). Jesus' career as traveling teacher and miracle worker forms a memorable backdrop which readers familiar with the Gospels bring to any story about his ministry. From his home base in Capernaum, Jesus travels "throughout Galilee, preaching in their synagogues and driving out demons" (Mk 1:39 NIV). His trips as far north as Ceasarea Philippi and into the region of Tyre and Sidon takes him into the borderlands of Israel's

classically defined territory. He crosses to the east side of the Sea of Galilee and moves south along its perimeter. His final journey to Jerusalem is begun, as Luke records, when "Jesus resolutely set out for Jerusalem" (Lk 9:51 NIV), and his entrance into Jerusalem is the culmination of his enactment of Yahweh's return to Zion. Finally, he journeys along the Via Dolorosa, the way to his execution at Golgotha (Mt 27:31-33; Mk 15:20-22; Lk 23:26-33; Jn 19:16,17). Even after his resurrection he surprisingly appears on the road from Jerusalem to Emmaus, walking with his disciples (Lk 24:13-35), along the shore of Galilee (Jn 21) and on a mountain in Galilee (Mt 28:16-7). Finally, from the vicinity of Bethany, he ascends on his journey to heaven (Lk 24:50-51; Acts 1:9-11).

Healer. In the healing miracles the images of Jesus as the Great Physician of the body and soul is clearly established. These healings are so diverse and so immediately complete in their healing/restoration that they establish Jesus' messianic identity. When answering John's query about whether he was the Messiah, Jesus replied, echoing the words of Isaiah 35, "Go back and report to John what you hear and see: The blind receive sight, the lame walk, those who have leprosy are cured, the deaf hear, the dead are raised, and the good news is preached to the poor." (Mt 11:4, 5 NIV). The powerful works of Jesus include exorcisms (Mt 10:8; Mk 6:13; Lk 13:32), restoring sight (Mt 9:27-31; Mk 8:22-36) healing lepers (Lk 5:12-16), healing the lame (Jn 5:1-15), curing fevers (Mk 1:29-31; Jn 4:43-53), restoring a severed ear (Lk 22:51), stopping a hemorrhage (Mk 5:24-34), revitalizing a withered hand (Mk 3:1-6) and resurrections (Mk 5:35-43; Lk 7:11-17; Jn 11:1-44).

Contemplative. In the four Gospels, Jesus engages in numerous acts of devotion (solitude, fasting, prayer, meditation, Scripture reading, submission, worship). Some are done in private, others with his disciples and still others are carried out in public settings. Although these acts are often part of the background of the narrative, the Gospels present Jesus as a person whose spiritual life draws on his communion with the Father. The Gospel accounts quietly highlight what Jesus did in his "time off" and imply that his ministry flowed out of this joyful and disciplined life of the spirit. In his use of Scripture we observe a person of meditation and study. And in his prayer life (Lk 11:1), his solitude (Lk 5:16) and his fasting (Lk 4:2, 14), we encounter one whose life is lived in communion with his Father.

Summary. The sweep of OT motifs and imagery fulfilled in Jesus is memorably summarized in the words of F. F. Bruce:

> In Jesus the promise is confirmed, the covenant is vindicated, salvation is brought near, sacred history has reached its climax, the perfect sacrifice has been offered and accepted, the great priest over the household of God has taken his seat at God's right hand, the Prophet like Moses has

been raised up, the Son of David reigns, the kingdom of God has been inaugurated, the Son of Man has received dominion from the Ancient of Days, the Servant of the Lord, having been smitten to death for his people's transgression and borne the sin of many, has accomplished the divine purpose, has seen light after the travail of his soul and is now exalted and extolled and made very high. (Bruce, 21)

BIBLIOGRAPHY. R. J. Bauckham, *The Theology of the Book of Revelation* (Cambridge: Cambridge University Press, 1993); F. F. Bruce, *The New Testament Development of Old Testament Themes* (Grand Rapids: Eerdmans, 1968); R. A. Burridge, *Four Gospels, One Jesus? A Symbolic Reading* (Grand Rapids: Eerdmans, 1994); T. Longman III and D. G. Reid, *God Is a Warrior* (Grand Rapids: Zondervan, 1995); M. Magdalene, *Jesus: Man of Prayer* (Downers Grove, IL: InterVarsity Press, 1987); D. Mohline and J. Mohline, *Emotional Wholeness: Connecting with the Emotions of Jesus* (Shippensburg, PA: Treasure House, 1997); B. Witherington III, *Jesus the Sage* (Minneapolis: Fortress, 1994); C. J. H. Wright, *Knowing Jesus Through the Old Testament* (Downers Grove, IL: InterVarsity Press, 1992).

JEWELS AND PRECIOUS STONES

Jewels in the Bible fall into four main motifs. They are images of adornment and *beauty, of *wealth and power, of the numinous or *holy, and of the *permanence of the transcendent *heavenly realm. In all usages, jewels are a recognized standard of value.

It needs to be said at the outset that it is difficult to know with certainty to which specific jewels the ancient words refer (for a discussion and a chart of the various English words used to translate the references to jewels see "Jewels and Precious Stones," *IBD*, 781-89). Misguided attempts have been made to associate the qualities of a specific gem to a corresponding tribe of ancient Israel. Others, apparently with the idea of birthstones in mind, have attempted to associate the twelve precious stones in the ephod and in the foundations of New *Jerusalem with the *twelve signs of the zodiac. Though such attempts are futile, they are, fortunately, unnecessary for understanding the imagery of jewels. The individual jewels have no specific symbolism. Collectively they are the beautiful prize of wealth and power. Their presence in biblical imagery suggests that God's wealth and power are unmatched.

Jewelry as Adornment. In all societies jewels have been a form of adornment, especially for *women. When Abraham's servant wants to make a good impression on the person he hopes to win as Isaac's bride, he lavishes jewels upon her as gifts (Gen 24:22, 53). Part of the attactiveness of the woman in the *Song of Songs is that her "cheeks are comely with ornaments," her "neck with strings of jewels" (Song 1:10-11 RSV).

When the natural human impulse to beautify by means of jewelry becomes excessive, it is an index to materialistic and misguided values, and as such it is the object of God's judgment. Thus Isaiah 3:18-23 is a catalog of jewels and finery that God will take away in his judgment against a spiritually bankrupt nation preoccupied with false values. The prosperous, arrogant people of Psalm 73 likewise wear *pride as a necklace (Ps 73:6) and stand on the verge of a sudden fall (Ps 73:18-20).

The writer of Proverbs turns the adornment of jewels to metaphoric use as a way of portraying the value of *wisdom and understanding. Wisdom and discretion, for example, are "adornment for your neck" (Prov 3:22 RSV). A parent's teachings "are a fair garland for your head, and pendants for your neck" (Prov 1:9 RSV). The rewards of wisdom are similarly pictured: "She will place on your head a fair garland; she will bestow on you a beautiful crown" (Prov 4:9 RSV). Moreover, "the lips of knowledge are a precious jewel" (Prov 20:15 RSV).

Wealth and Power. Because a leading means of accumulating and saving wealth in the ancient world was to invest in jewelry, the adornment provided by jewels merges into its function as a preserver of wealth—an early version of putting money into a bank. Thus when the Israelites despoil the Egyptians after the final plague, they take "jewelry of silver and of gold" from their neighbors (Ex 11:2). Jewelry, in fact, was a leading object of plunder taken in war (2 Chron 20:25), being the most portable type of *wealth available to people before the use of coins (2 Chron 21:3). By a further extension, jewelry is a sign not only of wealth but of *authority, as when a golden chain is put around Joseph's neck when he assumes the position of a ruler in Egypt (Gen 41:42).

Jewels are thus synonymous in the Bible with wealth and power, especially of kings. Only the wealthiest could afford the luxury of gemstones. In ancient times personal power and wealth were the privilege of kings and high officials of the royal courts. Wealth (often gained through the spoils of war) and political power were mutually suggestive in the ancient world. Therefore jewels, along with *gold and *silver, were not just expensive decorations but were visual reminders of the power that had enabled a *king or *queen to acquire such wealth.

Along with literal pictures of royal wealth and power, the motif of royal jewelry is turned to metaphoric and spiritual use in the Bible. For example, Jesus pictures the kingdom of heaven as "a merchant in search of fine pearls, who, on finding one pearl of great value, went and sold all that he had and bought it" (Mt 13:45-46 RSV). The literal wealth represented by jewels here becomes metaphoric of the value of God's spiritual kingdom. A companion parable pictures the kingdom as a *treasure hidden in a field, which leads the discoverer of it to sell all that he has and buy the field (Mt 13:44). These two statements about the kingdom of heaven, both expressed in images of treasure, are reciprocal, showing the mutual worth that the kingdom of heaven has for both God and his redeemed people.

Elsewhere God is pictured as a jeweled king with a resplendent *royal court. Jewels are used to portray God as a king of unimaginable power and wealth. The image in Revelation 21 of the heavenly city, the New *Jerusalem, suggests that its king has unlimited resources. This huge city, covering about 1,400 square miles, is constructed of pure gold and precious jewels. The crown jewels of the wealthiest and most powerful kings of earth pale in comparison to this dazzling image of God's eternal city. The twelve *foundations of the city are each a different precious stone, each engraved with the name of one of the twelve apostles. Imagine the splendor of blue sapphire, green emerald, yellow topaz and purple amethyst! Gigantic single *pearls form the gates of the city, leading to streets of gold. Each pearl is engraved with the name of one of the tribes of ancient Israel. The beauty and magnificence of this place overwhelms the senses and reflects the glory of the Creator-King's infinite power and wealth.

The inscriptions of the names of God's people on the jewels of the ephod, and later on the jewels of the heavenly New Jerusalem, suggest that his people are precious and costly to the Lord God. Earthly kings acquired worldly wealth with their power, but in his war against sin and evil, the power of the divine King gained a spoil of greater value, the redeemed souls of men and women. To display the worth of his redeemed people and the great power it took to acquire them, their names were inscribed on the beautiful jewels that adorned the high *priest as he poured out the blood of sacrifice.

Images of the Holy. A further cluster of images of precious stones evokes a sense of the holy, especially the *holiness of *worship. The key passages are Exodus 28:17-20 and 29:10-13, which contain a list of jewels on the high priest's breastplate. The effect is a dazzling profusion of beauty, splendor and value, symbolic of the holiness of worship. The high priest stood at the boundary between the divine and human realms (see Sacred Space; Temple), moving in both as he ministered in the Holy of Holies, and the ephod inset with twelve precious stones engraved with the twelve tribes of Israel hinted at his more-then-human status.

Ezekiel 28:12-14 also uses the imagery of precious stones to portray the holy. Here we find a list of jewels that evoke a sense of the Edenic *glory of the king of Tyre before his corruption, as he walked "on the holy mountain of God; in the mist of the stones of fire" (RSV). Of similar texture is the vision in Ezekiel 1 of a divine throne with wheels, a vision that contains a heavy admixture of jeweled imagery.

Enameled Imagery. Throughout the centuries poets have used imagery that combines *hardness of texture and a more-than-earthly brilliance of *light to suggest a realm of transcendent permanence and value that surpasses the cyclic vegetative world of earthly existence. This too is a repository of biblical imagery of jewels and precious stones.

The motif begins already in the OT in Isaiah's vision of a restored Jerusalem in a coming golden age. He paints a picture of a jewel-bedecked city fashioned from precious stones (Is 54:11-12). This comes to fruition in the visions of heaven in the book of Revelation, where we read about a sea of glass like crystal, about the appearance of God in splendor like that of jasper and carnelian, about golden crowns, gates of pearl and a city of pure gold. The grand climax of the Bible's enameled imagery is the vision of the New Jerusalem, described by means a profusion of images of precious stones (Rev 21:9-21).

Summary. In the visions of Revelation we can perhaps see a convergence of most of the jewel motifs of the Bible. The jeweled magnificence of the city of eternal life is the setting of the consummation of the promises God has made throughout redemptive history. The power of God, promised in the OT, is now fulfilled in the person and work of Jesus Christ, the slain Lamb-King who sits on the *throne of the jeweled city. In the jewels on the ephod of the high priest and in the dazzling jewels of the eternal city, we can see the that wealthiest and most powerful God-King lives forever with his people.

See also BEAUTY; GLORY; GOLD; HEAVEN; HOLINESS; KING; PERMANENCE; QUEEN; SILVER; TREASURE; WEALTH; WOMAN, IMAGES OF.

BIBLIOGRAPHY. "Jewels and Precious Stones," in *The Illustrated Bible Dictionary* (Downers Grove, IL: InterVarsity Press, 1980) 781-89.

JOB, BOOK OF

The book of Job, largely poetic in form, is one of the most image-laden books in the Bible. It also contains some memorable individual pictures and images that remain in the memory: *Satan the accuser staging the archetypal bet with God in a heavenly court; the four-stage, hammerlike announcement by messengers to Job about the collapse of his domestic world; Job sitting on an *ash heap and his awe-struck acquaintances looking on in silence for seven days; Job's eloquent statement about knowing that his *Redeemer lives and his great oath of *innocence; and above all, the majestic traversing of nature in the speeches from the whirlwind, climaxed by the portraits of Behemoth and Leviathan (see Mythical Animals).

For all its detailed imagery and plethora of ideas about *suffering and God, the book has a firm architectonic design. The encompassing narrative has a beginning (the prologue set in heaven), a middle (a debate and God's resolution of it) and an end (the restoration of Job's fortunes). The narrative middle, in turn, reenacts some familiar archetypes. One is the *test, as God allows Satan to subject Job to suffering as a way of testing whether his devotion to God is genuinely disinterested. Job initially passes the test with patient endurance; but once the cycles of speeches begin to unfold, he loses his temper with God, as he himself acknowledges at the end when he repents of what he had earlier said (Job 40:3-5; 42:1-6).

A second pattern is plot conflict—between Job and his "friends," between rival conceptions of Job's suffering, and between Job and God (whom Job repeatedly accuses of injustice and even sadism). Even more prominent is the *quest motif, as Job undertakes a quest to understand the meaning of innocent suffering and the character of God. It is possible to trace the back-and-forth progress of Job toward understanding through the three cycles of speeches, with the voice of submission and faith in God's goodness stronger in each cycle. Early in the book Job unwittingly sets up the quest motif with his request, "Teach me, and I will be silent; make me understand . . ." (Job 6:24 RSV). At the end Job understands and submits, his journey of faith complete and his intellectual quest satisfied.

We should also note the role of irony as a unifying framework for the book. Two patterns predominate. One is the irony of orthodoxy represented by Job's counselors. They express orthodox religious belief (God is just, he punishes evildoers, human suffering is therefore punitive, Job should repent), often in the form of conventional wisdom sayings for which biblical parallels can be adduced. The irony of all this orthodoxy is that it does not apply to Job's situation, as Job protests throughout and as God confirms at the end (Job 42:7-8). Job's accusations hurled against God represent the irony of a rebellious spirit. We know from the prologue that Job's accusations are untrue (God is not attacking Job, is not unfair, has permitted but is not the cause of Job's suffering, does not regard Job as his enemy).

The image patterns in Job are so numerous that it is possible only to sketch some broad outlines. The largest single source of imagery in Job is nature. From start to finish, the speakers resort most typically to the forces of nature for the language of images by which to express their sentiments. About this nature imagery, moreover, we can discern two main traits. One is that the imagery tends to be negative, with such images as darkness, tempest imagery, deprivation of various types (*thirst, *drought, *famine) and destructiveness (broken *branches, unripe *fruit shaken off, an *eagle swooping on prey) predominating. Almost any page will illustrate the tendency. The general pattern is that of "uncreation," with the processes of God's creation of the world reversed—light turning to darkness, order in nature giving way to chaos. Corresponding to the destructiveness of nature is the huge scale on which it operates. It is the big forces of nature, corresponding to the superior power of God and the helplessness of people, that mainly come before our gaze as we read, climaxed in the pictures of nature projected by the voice from the *whirlwind. For the most part as we read the book of Job, we have little cause to look upon nature as a friend to people; it is mainly an image of terror.

The imagery associated with people is similarly terrible. Given Job's physical affliction, it is no surprise that the imagery of the human body is prominent. But the picture of the body that emerges is almost entirely negative. Disease imagery is conspicuous: flesh "clothed with worms and dirt" (Job 7:5), hardened *skin with sores breaking out afresh (Job 7:5), writhing in pain (Job 15:20), bones cleaving to skin (Job 19:20). Equally prevalent is the imagery of bodily torture, made up of a vocabulary of crushing, cutting off, seizing by the neck, dashing to pieces, slashing open kidneys, tormenting. Human isolation is the natural result of such a physical state, and we get pictures of friends and family members regarding the suffering Job as an alien, repulsive to behold (Job 19:13-19) and a laughingstock (Job 12:4). In sum, the imagery of Job embodies the spectacle of human suffering.

Another cluster of motifs centers on *warfare. Because Job believes that God is to blame for his suffering, the imagery of single combat emerges in some of the early speeches. Job pictures God as a divine shooter of poisoned *arrows, and the terrors of God are "arrayed" against him (Job 6:4). In Job's erroneous vision, God counts him as an *enemy (Job 13:24), sets him as a target for his archers (Job 16:12-13) and runs upon him "like a warrior" (16:14; see Divine Warrior). Again, God's troops come upon Job to cast up siegeworks against him and encamp around him (Job 19:12). A pattern of divestiture accompanies God's combative actions as he leads counselors and priests away stripped (Job 12:17, 19), loosens the belt of kings and the strong (Job 12:18, 21), takes away discernment from elders (Job 12:20), and strips Job of glory and takes the *crown from his head (Job 19:9).

As Job protests all of this, he envisions himself as wanting to bring a lawsuit against God (see Legal Imagery). Thus we have the judicial imagery of Job's coming to trial with God (Job 10:32), arguing his case with God (Job 13:3; 23:4), defending his ways to God (Job 13:15), eventually being vindicated (Job 13:18) and acquitted by God as his judge (Job 23:7). A whole chapter is devoted to Job's great oath of innocence (Job 31). When God answers Job from the whirlwind, the lead-in to his speeches draws upon the same courtroom imagery with such terms as "question," "contend," "argues," "put . . . in the wrong." However, there is reversal inasmuch as now it is God who brings Job to trial, after Job's futile attempts to do the same with God.

As we might expect in a work where the main action is a debate, the imagery of words and speaking is important, with nearly eighty references. This motif is especially important in the narrative links between speeches, where speakers are at pains to challenge the words of the previous speaker. The debate format is reinforced by approximately thirty instances of the verb *answered*.

Serving as a foil to the surrealistic images of suffering and uncreation are the opening and closing pictures of Job's prosperity. Here we have a concise picture of *the good life as the OT imagination pictures it: a blameless conscience, a harmonious and attractive *family, *feasting, successful *farming ventures, extensive *herds, scrupulous attention to re- ligious exercises and a long life ("and Job died, an old man, and full of days" [Job 42:17 RSV]).

The interaction between God and Job in the last five chapters is so noteworthy as to deserve comment by itself. God's poetic utterance from the whirlwind draws chiefly upon nature. God's questions directed toward Job are rhetorical counterquestions—ques- tions whose answer is obvious and whose intention is to reverse the roles of God and Job from earlier phases of the book, where Job had questioned God. On the surface, God's eighty scientific questions seem to be a *non sequitur,* inasmuch as they do not directly address the question of human suffering and the justice of God in it. But indirectly the speeches do provide answers to those questions. The underlying motif in the barrage of nature imagery is God's providential management of the world. The glory of God's *provi- dence over creation thus has the force of an *a fortiori* (how much more) statement: if God is this completely in control of even the relatively insignificant aspects of nature—aspects about which Job knows almost noth- ing—he can surely be trusted to care for humans. And in a related way, if Job cannot answer even the relatively insignificant questions God asks him about the ordi- nary creatures of nature, how can he expect to answer the ultimate philosophical questions?

As for the specifics of the speeches from the whirlwind, we can note the following features: they focus on the mysterious features of *nature, beyond human understanding; and they illustrate the huge and powerful forces of nature, beyond human strength or control. Moreover the speeches thus dramatize God's superior knowledge and power. A thoroughgoing paradox underlies the speeches: on the surface they prove God's transcendence (his superiority to the human and natural worlds), but they simultaneously demonstrate his immanence (his closeness to his creation and presence in it).

The human response to this revelation, as cap- tured in Job's replies to the voice from the whirlwind, falls into five main motifs. One is submission and resignation as Job puts an end to his debate with God and submits to God's superior wisdom and power. A second is the humbling motif, the natural effect of listening to God's speeches, as Job acknowledges that God can do all things and that he himself is "of small account" (Job 40:2-3). The silencing of Job is a third motif, as Job lays his hand on his mouth and resolves to speak no further (Job 40:3-4). The repentance motif also enters, as Job confesses that he had "ut- tered what [he] did not understand" (Job 42:3) and repents "in dust and ashes" (Job 42:6). Finally, Job actually attains the goal of all human existence—the beatific vision: "I had heard of thee by the hearing of the ear, but now my eye sees thee" (Job 42:5 RSV).

See also INNOCENCE, INNOCENT; PAIN; SATAN; SUF- FERING; TEST, TESTING; WEALTH; WHIRLWIND.

JOEL, BOOK OF

The occasion of Joel's prophecy was a plague of

*locusts that devastated the land of Judah. The prophet saw the plague as evidence of God's *judg- ment, and a dominant theme of his book is the coming *Day of the Lord as a time of impending judgment against an evil nation. That day is declared to be imminent (Joel 1:15; 2:1; 3:14), and it is "great and very terrible; who can endure it?" (Joel 2:11 RSV). Accordingly, God's people are called to repent in the hope that a merciful God will turn judgment into blessing (Joel 2:12-14).

Several prophetic genres support the basic mes- sage. As expected, oracles of judgment are placed at strategic points (Joel 2:1-11; 3:1-3). Instructional oracles warning of the need for repentance occur seven times, stated as a *lament with its call to *mourning together with a motive for doing so (Joel 1:5-7, 8-10, 11-12, 13-18, 19-20; 2:12-14, 15-17). As in other OT prophecies, however, promises of restoration balance the message of doom. In Joel we catch visions of an eschatological future, ranged on a time scheme in which key phrases are "afterward" (Joel 2:28), "in those days and at that time" (Joel 3:1) and "in that day" (Joel 3:18). The judgment of the nations, at times noted with apocalyptic fervor (Joel 3:1, 15), is blended with promises of salvation for God's people in a new age of the Spirit (Joel 2:28-29), of *peace (Joel 3:9-17) and of *prosperity (Joel 3:18-21). In keeping with the motif of judg- ment, we find judicial imagery, with God pictured as entering into litigation with foreign nations (Joel 3:1-18). God acts as a prosecuting attorney who presents his charges and enters into cross-examina- tion of the defendants, and also as a judge who delivers his decision (*see* Legal Images).

Several dominant image patterns convey the theme of *judgment. One is the imagery of *blighted nature.* As we read the book, we enter a world of destroying locusts (Joel 1:4), devastated vegetation (Joel 1:7) and failed *harvests (Joel 1:10-12, 16-20). A second motif is *invasion,* as the locusts become a metaphoric army (Joel 1:6), in appearance and move- ment like *horses (Joel 2:4) and in noise like the rumbling of *chariots (Joel 2:5), charging like sol- diers who scale a *wall (Joel 2:7) and entering houses like a *thief (Joel 2:9). A third image pattern is the *cataclysmic disintegration of the universe* (Joel 2:2-3, 10, 30-31; 3:15). People who live through this judg- ment are a case study in human anxiety: *drunkards weep (Joel 1:5), people "lament like a virgin girded with sackcloth" (Joel 1:8), priests mourn and lament (Joel 1:8, 13), farmers wail and are confounded (Joel 1:11), the elders "cry to the LORD" (Joel 1:14), people's "faces grow pale" (Joel 2:6). The focus of all this denunciation is the *degenerate religious life of the nation,* as priests and ministers are singled out by class (Joel 1:9, 13) and as religious practices are named (Joel 1:14, 16; 2:15-16), though the entire nation is called to account for what has happened (Joel 2:1).

Yet Joel differs from most OT prophetic books by balancing judgment equally with restoration and renewal, with the pivot coming in the middle of the book (Joel 2:18). The book accordingly has some of the Bible's most famous images of God's restoration of his people, and again several motifs are discernible. One is the *renewal of the natural forces* that were cursed in the first half of the book. In the place of the blighting of *nature and crops, we enter a world in which God sends *grain, *wine and *oil to satisfy his people (Joel 2:19), in which the *pastures are *green and the *tree bears its *fruit (Joel 2:22), in which *rain waters the earth (Joel 2:23) and in which harvests are abundant (Joel 2:24), in which the mountains drip sweet *wine, the hills flow with *milk, and the streams run with water (Joel 3:18). Invasion is likewise reversed as *God drives out the foreign army* (Joel 2:20) and requites the surrounding nations for their torment of Judah (Joel 3:1-8), and as he declares Jerusalem holy so that "strangers shall never again pass through it" (Joel 3:17). The earlier imagery of human desolation is balanced by *human satisfaction with God's provision* (Joel 2:26-27), and God's previous pouring out of judgment becomes a *pouring out of his spirit on all flesh* so that sons and daughters prophesy and old and young men dream *dreams and have visions (Joel 2:28-29).

What finally unifies the book of Joel is its heightened contrasts. The future is both terrifying—the coming "day of the LORD" will be "a day of darkness and gloom" (Joel 2:1-2)—and so exhilarating that one can hardly wait for it (Joel 3:28-29). God transforms the fruitful landscape into a desert (Joel 1:20; 2:3) and the desert into a fruitful landscape (Joel 2:22-25). God first uses locusts to destroy Judah's crops (Joel 1:4) and then restores "the years which the swarming locust has eaten, the hopper, the destroyer, and the cutter" (Joel 2:25). God is both a *divine warrior with a destructive army (Joel 2:11; 3:11) and a God of pity (Joel 2:18) who is a *refuge to his people (Joel 3:16). God invades nations with locusts and armies but at the same time "dwells" in Zion (Joel 3:17, 21). Zion itself is both warned of invasion (Joel 2:1) and assured of *protection (Joel 3:16). God both allows foreign nations to invade his chosen nation and judges them for carrying Judah into exile. There is no more paradoxical book in the Bible than Joel. Pervading this kaleidoscope of contrast is the tremendous energy of the imagery from start to finish, with everything heightened to a white heat of intensity.

See also ARMY, ARMIES; DAY, DAY OF THE LORD; JUDGMENT; LOCUST.

JOHN, GOSPEL OF

The author himself provides a key to the design of his book when he tells us near the end, "Now Jesus did many other signs in the presence of the disciples, which are not written in this book; but these are written that you may believe that Jesus is the Christ, the Son of God, and that believing you may have life in his name" (Jn 20:30 RSV). John was overwhelmed by the vastness of Christ, not only as God himself but

in the significance of his acts on earth. In fact, the author states hyperbolically in the last verse of the Gospel that if all that Jesus did would be recorded "the world itself could not contain the books that would be written" (Jn 21:25 RSV).

John imposes a strict and orderly framework on his narrative especially through the use of symbolism. Realizing the ability of images and symbols to unify vast tracts of experience and truth, John resorts to them so incessantly that he gives us a poetic Gospel. But whereas the book of *Revelation (which has numerous similarities to the Gospel of John) employs apocalyptic, otherworldly imagery, John uses the symbolic quality of this-worldly events in his Gospel, in the process evoking the ordinary world of first-century Palestine.

John's Gospel is perhaps the most consciously literary of the four Gospels. In particular, we may note John's preference for the relatively embellished narrative unit (in contrast to the more fragmentary and cursory style of the Synoptics), his tendency to give extended discourses by Jesus, and his reliance on great images and symbols.

Like the other Gospels, the Gospel of John follows in loose fashion the chronology of Jesus' public career. A distinctive feature of John's story is the self-conscious shaping by Jesus of his own career as highlighted by interspersed references to the *"hour" of Jesus; that is, the climax of his life in his death and resurrection (Jn 2:4; 4:21; 5:28; 7:30; 8:20; 12:23; 17:1; 31:1). Underlying the plot is a progressive intensification of conflict between Jesus and his antagonists. A general outline for the flow of the narrative is the prologue (Jn 1), followed by the book of signs (Jn 2—12) and the book of the passion (Jn 13—21). A continuous narrative thread runs through each of the two "books."

John also gives his story of Jesus' life a unifying plot: the conflict between belief and unbelief. Keeping Jesus always in the center of the action, John presents a series of responses by people who come into contact with Jesus. These responses indicate either belief or unbelief. G. W. Knight has written that John's Gospel pictures Jesus "silhouetted against a world of formalized religion, hypocrisy, envy, evil and suffering" (Knight, 169). The narrative staple of plot conflict merges with the poet's impulse to embody truth in image in several great contrasting patterns, including *light and *darkness, life and death, and acceptance versus rejection of Jesus' claims.

The most obvious pattern of John's Gospel (comparable to Matthew's interspersing of narrative and discourse) is that of combining an event involving Jesus with a discourse that interprets the meaning of the event. Thus Jesus' request for a drink from the Samaritan woman is followed by his statements about the *water of life (Jn 4), the healing on the sabbath is linked to Christ's words about his divine authority (Jn 5), the feeding of the five thousand is followed by the discourse on the *bread of life (Jn 6), and the raising of Lazarus is accompanied by Jesus' claims about being the *resurrection and the life (Jn 11). A variation consists of linking a discourse with two surrounding events. For example, the discourse on Christ as the light of the world (Jn 8) is flanked by references to the Feast of Tabernacles with its huge torches (Jn 7) and giving sight to the *blind man (Jn 9), and the discourse on the bread of heaven is placed between references to the Passover and the feeding of the five thousand (Jn 6). Alternately, a single event is linked to two discourses, as when the healing of the blind man (Jn 9) illustrates Jesus' preceding discourse about the light of the world (Jn 8) and the man's expulsion from the synagogue leads immediately to Jesus' comments about good and bad shepherds (Jn 10; see Sheep, Shepherd). The pattern that pervades all of the variations is simply the linking of event with discourse, along with the prominence of master images (*water, *light, *bread, resurrection) in the configuration. We see highlighted here the twofold way in which all of the Gospels portray their protagonist—by his deeds and his words.

John's Gospel is also known for its motif of the misunderstood statement. These dramas in miniature unfold in three stages: Jesus makes a pronouncement, a bystander expresses a misunderstanding of the utterance, and Jesus proceeds to explain the meaning of his original statement. This pattern, which occurs nine times (Jn 3:3-8; 4:10-15; 4:31-38; 6:47-58; 7:33-36; 8:21-30; 8:31-47; 8:56-58; 11:11-15; and with modification, in 2:17-22), usually revolves around a figurative statement by Jesus that a bystander interprets literally.

John's Gospel also employs number patterns in a manner similar to the emphasis on seven in the book of Revelation. Patterns of *three are prominent: three Passovers, three other feasts attended by Jesus, three witnesses by John the Baptist to Jesus' messiahship, Jesus condemned three times, three utterances from the cross, three denials by Peter, a three-stage restoration of Peter.

The imagery of *seven is likewise pervasive. The central part of the narrative is structured around seven great miracles or "signs" that Jesus performs—turning water into wine (Jn 2:1-11), healing the official's son (Jn 4:46-54), curing the paralytic (Jn 5:1-18), feeding the five thousand (Jn 6:5-13), walking on water (Jn 6:16-21), healing the blind man (Jn 9:1-17) and raising Lazarus (Jn 11:1-44). Equally important are seven great "I am" utterances by Jesus, each followed by a metaphoric description of Jesus' person and work: the bread of life (Jn 6:35); the light of the world (Jn 8:12); the *door of the sheep (Jn 10:7); the good shepherd (Jn 10:11); the resurrection and the life (Jn 11:25); the way, the truth, and the life (Jn 14:6); and the true *vine (Jn 15:1). The book also unfolds as a sevenfold witness to Christ—the witness of the Father (Jn 5:37; 8:18), the Son (Jn 8:14; 18:37), Christ's works (Jn 5:36; 10:25), Scrip-

ture (Jn 5:39-46), John the Baptist (Jn 1:7; 5:35), the disciples (Jn 15:27; 19:35) and the Spirit (Jn 15:26; 16:14).

The imagery of *witness belongs to a pattern of juridical or courtroom language, with the implication that Jesus and his claims are on trial throughout the Gospel (see Legal Images). But those who hear the evidence are also on trial, with their eternal destiny at stake. Building his account around "signs," John builds a case that demands a verdict.

John's Gospel is sometimes referred to as the "cosmic" Gospel. Whereas Matthew concentrates on Jesus as the hope of the Jews and Luke as the friend of the underprivileged, John presents a Christ of the cosmos, portrayed in universal archetypes like water, bread and light. The opening prologue already sounds the keynote. Whereas Matthew begins with a human genealogy, John begins with a divine genealogy. Echoing and parodying a centuries-old Greek hymn to Zeus, John identifies the incarnate Messiah as the divine Logos—a Word of wisdom and revelation. John thus combines pagan and Christian thought for a Hellenistic audience. Having created the universe itself, this Word enlightens every person (Jn 1:2, 9). And the images associated with him in this Christ hymn are equally cosmic—light, life, power to bring people to spiritual birth, grace. Even the crucifixion of Christ takes on cosmic overtones through the imagery of the Son of Man being "lifted up" (Jn 3:14; 8:28; 12:32, 34) and "glorified" (Jn 7:39; 12:23; 13:31; 17:1-5), as if his death on the cross is the first step in his ascension to his heavenly throne.

According to M. Tenney, the main truths of this Gospel are transmitted by fewer than two dozen images. Some are pastoral (sheep, shepherd, vine, *grain of wheat); some name universal staples of sustenance (bread, water) or common actions (*eating, *drinking, *sleeping, *birth); some are social (*bridegroom, thief, bond-*servant); some denote elemental good and evil (light, darkness); some are titles (*Father, *Son of God, *Son of Man). These images and metaphors variously highlight the indispensability of Jesus, the nature of the spiritual life for those who follow Christ and the cosmic conflict between good and evil. Above all, the imagery of John is universal.

See also BREAD; DARKNESS; GOSPEL GENRE; LIGHT; VINE, VINEYARD; WATER; WITNESS.

BIBLIOGRAPHY. G. W. Knight, "The Pioneer of Life: An Essay on the Gospels," in The Christian Renaissance (London: Methuen, 1962) 145-72; M. C. Tenney, "The Imagery of John," BibSac 121 (1964) 3-21.

JOHN, LETTERS OF

John's purpose is to strengthen the faith of genuine believers and expose the true colors of adversaries. In fulfilling this purpose, he deals with three central themes around which cluster arresting and striking images, some of which are also found in the Fourth

Gospel: (1) witness to Jesus' incarnation, (2) sharp contrast based on God's holy character, and (3) the certainty of true faith. In the process John addresses his readers in endearing terms.

Witness. John employs vivid *witness *(martyreō)* imagery (1 Jn 1:1-3; 4:14), which is of critical importance in establishing the reality of Jesus' earthly life, something that those who had seceded from the community denied (Jn 2:19, 22-23). He affirms his own personal testimony to and direct knowledge of Jesus' life and ministry by appealing to the key senses of hearing (*see* Ear, Hearing), seeing (*see* Eye, Sight) and *touching. Moreover, he uses the perfect tense for the first two verbs of 1 John 1:1 to show not only the past reality of Jesus' earthly life but also its present impact. For further literary effect he employs two different Greek verbs for seeing *(horaō; theaomai)*. He supports the witness theme by use of the images of *water and *blood (Jn 5:6). Most interpreters believe "water" is a picture of Jesus' baptism and "blood" speaks of his crucifixion. When combined with the testimony of the Spirit (Jn 5:8), such expressions refute the arguments of opponents that would deny or downplay these historical realities. John's use of witness imagery in this context (Jn 5:7-12) would probably have called to the minds of John's readers the world of jurisprudence and the necessity for at least two witnesses to establish various claims (*see* Legal Images).

Contrasts Based on God's Character. A number of ideas are expressed in sharply contrasting ways based on the truth of God's *holy character. The images John employs reflect this, as seen most notably in 1 John 1:5: "God is light; in him there is no darkness at all" (NIV). The images *light and *darkness are packed with rich connotations (cf. Jn 1:1-18). Light underscores, among other things, God's glorious character, unsurpassed moral perfection, utter separateness from creation and absolute truthfulness and righteousness. It also bespeaks God's self-revelation and finds its highest expression in his Son through whom truth is disclosed to the human race. By its very nature light exposes the true nature of something, usually leading to judgment. In any event, the entrance of light triggers irreconcilable division and irresolvable conflict. Darkness conveys its opposite: moral evil, unrighteousness, falsehood, error, willful ignorance, deceitfulness and self-deception. By introducing these metaphors John intends to demonstrate the impossibility of neutrality. This notion can be traced both in the immediate context (1 Jn 1:5—2:11) and throughout the remainder of John's letters under related images.

For example, John uses the metaphor of *walking, an image for one's manner of life, to expose the sheer inconsistency of a claim to fellowship with God with a life of sin (1 Jn 1:6-7). He does this by contrasting the phrase "walking in the darkness" (1 Jn 1:6) with "walking in the light" (1 Jn 1:7). To walk in the light is to conduct oneself in keeping with God's character and revealed truth; to walk in darkness is to live in the realm of its opposite. In parallel fashion John exposes the sheer inconsistency of a claim to be in the light with hatred toward a fellow believer (1 Jn 2:9-11).

In order to convey the idea of continuance in a certain state, sphere or person, John frequently resorts to another related image—abiding. Thus in 1 John 2:10 we read "The one who loves his brother abides in the light" (NASB). In another place he urges, "Let that abide in you which you heard from the beginning. If what you heard from the beginning abides in you, you also will abide in the Son and in the Father" (1 Jn 2:24 NASB).

Another example is the contrast between love of the world and love for the Father (1 Jn 2:15-17). The image of *world *(kosmos)* occurs frequently in John's letters and usually refers to the evil system that lies under the complete domination of *Satan and holds the great majority of people under its sway (1 Jn 5:19) and that stands in hostile opposition to God and Christians (1 Jn 3:13).

Closely associated with world imagery is John's exhortation to avoid *idols (1 Jn 5:21). Reference to idols would call to mind OT disloyalty to God. It summarizes John's concern that his readers remain true to God and not abandon their faith by accepting the false teaching that circulated so widely. It is in this sense that we should perhaps understand the "sin unto death" (1 Jn 5:16-17).

John resorts to a number of descriptive images and phrases to affirm that the human race is divided into two diametrically opposite camps. Those who belong to God are called "*children of God" (1 Jn 3:1,10; 5:2). In other places they are characterized as "born of God" (1 Jn 3:9) or simply "of God" (1 Jn 3:10; 5:19). Those who are opposed to God are called "children of the devil" (1 Jn 3:10) or "of the devil" (1 Jn 3:8). They are also labeled "false prophets" (1 Jn 4:1) and "deceivers" (2 John 7). Moreover, the advent of many "antichrists" is a sure sign that the "last hour" (2:18), a period when opposition to Christ and his followers reaches its high point, has arrived. Moreover, the image *hour suggests a period of short duration. Throughout 1 John the dividing line between these opposing groups centers around their concept of Christ, the practice of righteousness and the display of Christian love.

The Certainty of True Faith. Finally, the certainty of true Christian faith is set forth. Authentic faith has distinctive characteristics, including love for God and fellow Christians (1 Jn 3:14; 4:20), belief in Jesus (1 Jn 4:2) and indwelling by the Spirit (1 Jn 3:24; 4:13).

First, the author regularly employs family imagery to convey the message that a true believer loves both God (the believer's Father) and fellow Christian (the believer's sibling). A key verse is 1 John 5:1: "Everyone who loves the father loves his child as well" (NIV). The frequently used term *brother *(adelphos)* effectively communicates this idea and is intended by the author to include both genders. In fact, both

457

"lady" and "sister" convey the same notion in 2 John (2 Jn 1, 13 respectively) and serve as metaphors for two local church assemblies. According to John, the way one relates to a family member is a reliable measuring stick of authentic faith. In fact, one who hates a brother is labeled a *"murderer" who is devoid of eternal life (1 Jn 3:15)!

Another mark of authentic faith is belief in the Son (1 Jn 5:1, 13), who is depicted as "the word of life" (1 Jn 1), "the life" (1 Jn 1:2) or "the eternal life" (1 Jn 1:2b). Those who deny Jesus are called liars (1 Jn 2:22).

Third, John tells us that true believers are indwelt by the Spirit (1 Jn 3:24; 4:13). Two images are used to convey his ministry: the *anointing (rich in OT connotations), enables believers to know truth (1 Jn 2:20, NIV); the *seed (1 Jn 3:9) enables them to overcome sin and ensures, as the Father's offspring, their likeness to him (1 Jn 3:1-2).

Referring to himself as "the elder" in 2 and 3 John, an image which bespeaks not only physical age but also spiritual maturity and oversight, John frequently addresses his readers in endearing ways. For instance, they are his "little children" (using both *tekna* as in 1 Jn 2:1 and *paidia* in 1 Jn 2:18), "children" (*tekna* in 3 Jn 4) and "beloved" (1 Jn 2:7; 3 Jn 1, 5). In 2 John 1 he calls his readers "the chosen lady and her children" (NIV).

See also CHILD, CHILDREN; DARKNESS; EAR, HEARING; EYE, SIGHT; JOHN, GOSPEL OF; LIGHT; WITNESS; WORLD.

BIBLIOGRAPHY. G. Burge, *The Letters of John* (Grand Rapids: Zondervan, 1996); I. H. Marshall, *The Epistles of John* (Grand Rapids: Eerdmans, 1978); R. Schnackenburg, *The Johannine Epistles* (New York: Crossroad, 1992); J. Stott, *The Epistles of John* (Leicester, UK: Inter-Varsity, 1983).

JONAH, BOOK OF

The plot of the story of Jonah falls into a neat four-phase sequence as delineated by the chapter divisions: Jonah's *flight, Jonah's *rescue, Jonah's sermon and Jonah's rejection of God's grace. As even that outline suggests, the book is a *satire—the exposure of human vice through ridicule. In fact, the book is a handbook on how *not* to be a prophet. The object of satiric attack is the kind of nationalistic zeal that tried to make God the exclusive property of Israel, refusing to accept the universality of God's grace (i.e., its transcendence of national bounds). The satiric norm—the standard by which Jonah's ethnocentrism is judged—is God's character and the breadth of his grace. In this story Jonah is a great nationalist, but God is a great internationalist. The satiric tone is light and mocking as Jonah is held up to scorn by being rendered ridiculous—a pouting prophet foolish enough to undertake an anti-quest to run away from God.

The characterization of the two main characters—Jonah and God—forms a unifying motif in the story. The titular character looms like an evil spirit over the entire book. He is a surly and bigoted character whose prophetic office serves as a foil for his ignominious behavior. Only in chapter 2, Jonah's poem that celebrates God's deliverance, do we find respite from Jonah's bad behavior and attitudes. And his high point of insight into God's character there only serves to expose his ill temper later when God extends his grace beyond Jonah to Nineveh. The characteristic of God that is highlighted in the story is his grace and forgiveness, which explains why in the Jewish liturgical calendar the book of Jonah is read at the climactic point of Yom Kippur, the Day of Atonement.

The physical environment in which the action transpires shows remarkable range, considering the brevity of the book (48 verses). Much of the action occurs in elemental *nature: *sea, *water, tempest, fish, countryside, hillside, parching wind. Balancing that environment is the image of the metropolis—a city-state so large that it takes three days to traverse it and boasting a population of "more than a hundred and twenty thousand persons . . . and also much cattle" (Jon 4:11 RSV). The cast of characters is equally expansive, reaching out from Jonah as the solitary protagonist to his antagonist God, from thence to a small crew of sailors and beyond them to the world capital of Assyria (a dread city for which the mere epithet "that great city" [Jon 1:2] would have been sufficient to unleash a flood of revulsion from the original audience).

The *giantesque motif figures prominently in the story, as things happen on a more-than-usual scale of magnitude. The nature of Jonah's task, for example, is giantesque—to go as a lone prophet to preach a message of repentance to an entire world-class city, the capital of a nation known for its terrorism. The "great fish" is giantesque—big enough to swallow a man and contain him for three days. The response to Jonah's eight-word sermon is nothing less than wholesale reform. The national *repentance is lavish, extending even to the animals (Jon 3:7-8). The magnitude of God's grace is immense, sparing an entire city with a population 120,000. Even the patience of God with Jonah is large, though it fails to produce beneficial results in the surly prophet's life.

The two most famous images in the story are miraculous. One is the great fish appointed by God to be the agent of Jonah's rescue from watery death. In effect the fish becomes an actor in the story, thus rendering it a favorite with children. The other miraculous image is the plant that God caused to grow to maturity overnight to provide shade for Jonah and to teach him a lesson about the legitimacy of his grace extended to Nineveh. Two additional examples of God's controlling nature in order to teach Jonah a lesson are the worm that attacked the plant and the sultry east wind that made conditions miserable for Jonah as he sat on the hillside, hoping for a cataclysmic destruction of a city that he detested.

Additional image patterns embellish the story and

its meanings. Chapter 1 is structured as a sequence of increasing confinement and finally suffocation, from the boat's deck to its "inner part," where Jonah progresses from waking to sleeping, then being cast into water and ending up in the belly of a fish. Here is a process of attempted escape and the paralysis that it brings; it may even be a picture of a suicide impulse or death wish. The hymn of deliverance from the fish's belly (Jon 2:2-9) is constructed around the imagery of increasing confinement, followed by release of both spirit (Jonah's sudden vow to praise God) and body (his expulsion from the fish onto dry land). The poem reenacts the *death-*rebirth archetype.

The *journey motif is obviously important in the story, including an initial anti-quest as Jonah attempts to run away from God (in ironic and doomed defiance of the principle stated in Ps 139:7-12 that it is impossible to flee from the presence of the Lord). In chapter 3 the action draws heavily on biblical images of *repentance (fasting, sackcloth, ashes, public proclamation of repentance). In the closing chapter Jonah's behavior fits the pattern of the archetypal *refuser of festivities. Irony pervades the story.

See also FISH, FISHER; FLEE, FLIGHT; GIANTESQUE MOTIF; JOURNEY; RESCUE; SATIRE; SEA.

BIBLIOGRAPHY. E. M. Good, *Irony in the Old Testament* (Philadelphia: Westminster, 1965) 39-55.

JONAH THE PROPHET

If one were to come upon an entry for Jonah in *Who's Who in the Ancient Near East,* the article might include the following data: "Jonah: son of Amittai, from Gath-hepher, professional prophet, spent three days in the belly of a fish and lived to tell the tale. Greatest career achievement: brought about the repentance of Nineveh (a.k.a. Sin City), capital of Assyria." The bare facts are interesting enough to account for Jonah's being the most familiar of the minor prophets. In fact, the legendary, mythic quality ensured by the presence of the *fish makes Jonah even more memorable than most of the major prophets (Daniel and his lion-taming prayer being perhaps the only exception). Jonah also seizes our imagination by reenacting the archetypal attempt to run away from God (*see* Flee, Flight). Equally important, Christ's references to Jonah authenticate his existence and his significance for Christians.

Jonah's instant success with the people of Nineveh suggests that he was a powerful evangelist. However, a study of Jonah's actions and personal motivations reveal Jonah to be a prophet of rebellious spirit and mistaken priorities, as suggested in God's own summary at the end of the story (Jon 4:10-11). God told Jonah to "arise" and "go to Nineveh" (Jon 1:2 RSV). The text tells us that Jonah "rose" (Jon 1:3), but the ironic twist is that Jonah fled in exactly the opposite direction from what God had commanded, to Tarshish. Why? Because he could not conquer his own personal desire for vengeance (Jon 4:2). His prayer of submission in the fish's belly (Jon 2) reveals only a temporary remorse for his disobedience and probably no real change of heart toward Nineveh. When his proclamation of judgment to Nineveh results in total and sincere repentance, he asks God to kill him, preferring not to witness God's compassion on Nineveh and apparently choosing to ignore God's compassion to him when he was in the fish (thus missing entirely the beautiful symmetry of God's mercy).

Jonah's belligerence persists to the end. His final object lesson involves a shade plant to which he becomes very attached, until it withers in the hot sun. Again Jonah pleads for death. God has the final word in the book, however: "You pity the plant. . . . And should not I pity Nineveh, that great city, in which there are more than a hundred and twenty thousand persons . . . and also much cattle?" (Jon 4:10-11). Jonah's problem is that he is a great nationalist, while God is a great internationalist. Because of Jonah's rebellion and spiritual myopia, the entire book of Jonah becomes an emblem of God's sovereignty and his mercy toward repentant sinners, thus explaining why the book is read in the Jewish liturgical calendar on the Day of Atonement, celebrating God's forgiveness.

While the OT narrative and the reference to Jonah in 1 Kings 14:25 consider Jonah literally as a historical person, NT references broaden the focus to include Jonah's figurative importance. As for the historicity of Jonah, Jesus compares his own physical lodging in the grave to Jonah's parallel three-day residence in the belly of the fish (Mt 12:39-40), and he pictures the people of Nineveh who were converted in response to Jonah's preaching as standing in the final judgment (Lk 11:32). But beyond confirming the historicity of Jonah as a person, the NT treats Jonah as a type of Christ. Matthew and Luke record Christ's references to "the sign of Jonah" prefiguring his own death, burial and resurrection (Mt 12:39-41; 16:4; Lk 11:29-32).

The OT narrative, however, treats Jonah primarily as an antiprophet who undertakes an anti-quest (*see* Quest) to escape from God's presence (an ironic impossibility—witness Ps 139:7-12) and to avoid his prophetic mission. Although God uses Jonah in spite of himself, he is a small-minded, ill-tempered ethnocentrist who thoroughly disapproves of the universal *mercy of God. He is the object of *satiric ridicule in the OT book that bears his name.

See also JONAH, BOOK OF; PROPHET, PROPHETESS.

JORDAN RIVER

No river figures more prominently in the Bible than the Jordan, which is mentioned more than seventy-five times. The physical facts are that the river rises in the Lebanese mountains, flows into Lake Tiberias (Sea of Galilee) and then travels down to the Dead Sea one hundred kilometers to the south. Sinuous and often shallow, its appearance can be unprepossessing, yet it constitutes a natural barrier between the arid desert areas to the east and the fertile country toward the Mediterranean in the west.

The main meaning of the Jordan River in the Bible is double: it is a boundary, and it is in the middle of a fertile *valley. The latter dominates the first appearance of the Jordan in the Bible in the story of Lot's separation from Abraham: "Lot lifted up his eyes, and saw that the Jordan valley was well watered everywhere. . . . So Lot chose for himself all the Jordan valley" (Gen 13:10-11 RSV).

But the preponderance of references treats the Jordan as a boundary, as evidenced by clusters of passages that speak of "beyond Jordan," "on this side of the Jordan," "on the other side of Jordan" and "over Jordan." Because it is a boundary of the *Promised Land, a leading biblical motif associated with Jordan is that of crossing. Joshua 3—4 describes how, after forty years in the desert, Israel, led by Joshua, made a decisive crossing at Adam where the Jabbok enters the Jordan from the east, and how miraculously the water "piled up in a heap," as had the Red Sea at the exodus. Both events were signs to the nations of God's power (Josh 4:23-24; see also the lyric elaboration of this event in Ps 114:3, 5). Jordan thus became associated in the Hebrew imagination with a glorious entry into the Promised Land (e.g., Deut 3:17, 4:22). In later OT history the river often figures in battle narratives, again because of its status as a boundary between nations.

An additional importance of the Jordan River is simply that some major events happened there throughout biblical history. Elijah was miraculously fed by ravens at the brook Cherith, east of the Jordan (1 Kings 17:2-7). Elijah was translated into heaven shortly after he and Elisha crossed the Jordan on dry ground (2 Kings 2:7-12). The Syrian king Naaman was healed of his leprosy by dipping seven times in the Jordan (2 Kings 5:8-14). In the NT John the Baptist used the Jordan for baptism (Mk 1:5), and there he also baptized Jesus (Mk 5:9). In Jesus' ministry he sometimes made use of the river to baptize people (Jn 3:22).

Despite its descent to the lowest of all river levels, the Jordan is not a symbol of death in the Bible. Songs like "Guide me O my great Redeemer" and "Swing Low" that make this association draw on the analogy of the Promised Land with heaven, and possibly draw on the classical tradition, where the rivers Styx and Lethe mark a transition between life and death.

See also PROMISED LAND; RIVER; WILDERNESS.

JOSEPH THE PATRIARCH

The story of Joseph (Gen 37—50) has long caught the imagination of those who have read it, in large part because it embraces so many archetypal plots. On the one hand, it is the classic story of a young man's growth to maturity in which, despite setbacks, he realizes all the potential of his youth. Thus Joseph's early dreams of greatness are fulfilled not only when his brothers bow down to him, but also in his assumption of power as the right hand man of Potiphar, of the *prison keeper and finally of the *Pharaoh. The difficulties he encounters, meanwhile, show how Joseph copes with many conventional obstacles: *sibling rivalry, greed, slavery, sexual harassment, imprisonment, neglect, alienation from home and even success itself.

On the other hand, such a gently ascending plot in no way completely captures the complexity of this rich narrative. It is also the story par excellence of a disturbed family; it explores with psychological realism a house torn apart by the quarrels of mothers, a father's preferential treatment of a *younger son, that son's recognition of his own unique role and the jealous rage of the older brothers. In its presentation of Joseph as a dreamer and interpreter, the narrative unfolds the image of the prophet who is despised in his home, only to be extolled in distant lands. Furthermore, the lengthy conclusion in which Joseph tests his brothers provides both a counterpart to their earlier treatment of him and a tale of revenge turned to redemption.

The literary pattern of the Joseph story is tightly structured in a series of repetitive sequences. There are three sets of *dreams, each of which comes in a series of two: Joseph dreams of his supremacy over his family; the butler and the baker dream of their imminent fortunes; Pharaoh dreams of *abundance and *famine. These dreams are closely associated with Joseph's imprisonments in the *pit, into *slavery and in *prison, and with his rise from favored/outcast son to second-in-command of Potiphar's house, of the prison and finally of all Egypt.

Joseph also completes the literary structure of Genesis. As Abraham and Sarah, the progenitors of the Israelite race, recapitulate Adam and Eve, the forebears of the human race, so Joseph recapitulates the life of Noah. As righteous men, they save first the human race and then the Israelites from the certain destruction of flood or famine. Similarly, the story of Joseph summarizes many of the important themes that run throughout Genesis: *felix culpa* (the "fortunate fall" in which evil is turned to a better good), the image of the successful younger brother and the portrayal of Egypt as a land of both threat and promise. Furthermore, it begins the struggle between the houses of Judah (the one who will rule) and Joseph (the one who receives the double-blessing), which is continued in the rivalry between Judah and Israel.

Despite its strong literary and theological patterns, the Bible itself does not make use of the Joseph story as a paradigmatic narrative. When the story is referred to, the emphasis is on God's providential protection of Joseph and the nation (e.g., Ps 105:17). In Stephen's easy telling of the story, one is given the impression that the story was widely known and used as a picture of God's providential care (Acts 7: 9-14). Yet Joseph's life has often been seen reflected in the story of *Daniel, another interpreter of dreams who was unfairly treated, and in Jesus, who though despised by his "brothers" and sold for silver, ultimately accomplished redemption for the ones who despitefully used him.

Joseph himself is a *hero par excellence—the person of integrity and superior ability, the person who rises to preeminence in every situation in which he finds himself, every mother's dream son or son-in-law. Yet for all his success, he is also a *suffering servant—the person who undergoes unmerited suffering that proves redemptive in the lives of others. He is a case study in resilience and is generous in his forgiveness. Above all, he is a person of destiny, whose end is evident almost in his beginning, heralded by prophetic dreams of supremacy.

See also EGYPT; GENESIS, BOOK OF; JACOB; SIBLING RIVALRY; YOUNGER CHILD, YOUNGER SIBLING.

BIBLIOGRAPHY. R. Alter, *The Art of Biblical Narrative* (New York: Basic Books, 1981) 157-76; M. Steinberg, *The Poetics of Biblical Narrative* (Bloomington, IN: Indiana University Press, 1987).

JOSHUA, BOOK OF

The book of Joshua portrays key events in early Israel's life by means of vivid images. These include the actions of crossing the *Jordan River (Josh 1—5), conquering the *land (Josh 6—12), allocating the tribal territories (Josh 13—21) and learning how to *worship God as a united people (Josh 22—24). Some of the portrayals, such as God's fighting on Israel's behalf, are developed in other biblical books. The images of this book are so strong and so vivid that they are often those best remembered from childhood stories of the Bible. Their effectiveness as a means of communicating the ways of God's working with his people is enhanced by the use of three techniques: (1) the repetition of key words and phrases throughout the book, (2) the vivid and dramatic description of the images in the text and (3) the memorials of *rock piles, *altars and place names in the land.

An example of the repetition of a key word occurs at the beginning of the book. In chapters 1 to 5 the theme of crossing is emphasized by the repetition of the verbal root 'br ("to cross") thirty-one times in this section. Various groups cross through the camp of Israel (Josh 1:11; 3:2), while others cross in front of the people (Josh 3:6) or in front of Yahweh (Josh 4:13). However, this is all by way of background to the dramatic crossing of the Jordan River, where the verb 'br occurs most frequently (Josh 1:2; 2:23; 3:1, 4, 11, 14, 16, 17; 4:1, 3, 5, 7, 8, 10, 11, 12, 13, 22, 23 twice; 5:1). In fact, this is an example of what Martin Buber described as a *Leitwort* or "leading word" in the OT—a verbal root that is repeated in a variety of forms and contexts in order to stress an important thematic unity in the passage in which it appears. So Israel, its leaders, the Transjordanian tribes, the spies, the priests, the *ark and the twelve representatives cross the Jordan River.

At the center of this crossing is the dramatic picture of the waters of the Jordan miraculously stopping their flow. They back up behind a stone dam at Adam when the feet of the priests who bear the ark (symbolizing God's presence) enter the riverbed. This pictorial image intensifies the imagery of the crossing. The verbal description of the miracle at Joshua 3:14-16 is central to the account of the crossing in chapters 3 to 4. The overall event, as well as specific vocabulary (e.g., "heap" in Josh 3:16), remind the reader of Rahab's confession of the earlier miracle of crossing the Red Sea (Josh 2:9-10) and the account of that crossing in Exodus 14—15. Nor does the account itself ignore the imagery. It insists on passing the memory of the story to future generations by means of its own image, the erection of a pile of *twelve stones moved from the riverbed to Gilgal, where Joshua explains how the miracle is to be told (4:1-8, 19-24).

This central image is itself an example of other impressions that appear throughout the book. For the generation of Joshua, there is the *circumcision with flint knives and the new food eaten at the first *Passover in the Promised Land (5:2-12). For Joshua himself, there is his confrontation with the commander of the Lord's army (5:14) as a prelude to all the battles that he would soon face. For Rahab, the scarlet cord that preserves the lives of the spies, enabling them to escape from Jericho (2:18, 21), and that also rescues the lives of her family in the conquest of the city (6:17, 22-25). This cord unites the first section of the book with the second, the part that details the conquest of the land (Josh 6—12). However, it is not alone in tying the book together. The same verb that described how Israel crossed the Jordan River describes how they cross through their enemies, first Jericho (Josh 6:7, 8) and then the nations that join in coalition to oppose them (Josh 10:29-34).

The chapters describing Israel's *warfare provide some of the most vivid images in the whole Bible. Who can forget the march around Jericho seven days and seven times on the final day, followed by the blast of *trumpets, the *shout of the people and the miraculous collapse of Jericho's *walls (Josh 6:15-16, 20)? Or again, consider the victory against Ai, where in the midst of the battle (and structurally in the midst of the narrative of chap. 8), with the forces of Ai assured of a second victory and in hot pursuit of the Israelites, Joshua holds aloft his spear to glisten in the sun and signal the ambush to come out of hiding and turn the tables for an Israelite victory (8:18). Just as memorable is the picture of the participation of God, the *divine warrior, in Israel's battle against the southern coalition by raining down *hailstones and by the dramatic "standing" of the *sun in response to Joshua's prayer. The narrator celebrates this image through inserting a poem in the midst of the battle account (Josh 10:11-14).

*Side by side with these pictures of miraculous victory are gruesome images of judgment and destruction: the extermination of the army and citizens of Jericho (Josh 6:21), Ai (Josh 8:22-25) and the towns of the southern and northern coalitions (Josh 10:28-41; 11:12-20); the destruction of part of the first Israelite assault force against Ai (Josh 7:4-5); the stoning and burning of Achan and his family for Achan's theft of items devoted to God (Josh 7:24-26); the entrapment, execution and hanging up of the corpses of the five kings at Makkedah (Josh 10:16-27).

The third section, chapters 13 to 21, which describes the allotment of the tribes, can be viewed from the perspective of studying one of the largest images in the Bible, the entire land of *Israel. Here, in detail, are provided the towns and cities, as well as the boundaries and notable landmarks, that comprise the land given by God to Israel in *covenant. Scattered throughout are notes that provide vivid pictures of notable events in the acquisition of this land, whether the springs in the southern desert that Acsah requests from her father (Josh 15:16-19) or the forested hill country that the tribes of Ephraim and Manasseh clear for their dwelling (Josh 17:14-18).

The last section, chapters 22 to 24, considers the proper worship of God through the use of three powerful images: an altar, a farewell speech and a covenant. The altar forms the basis of the dispute between the tribes west of the Jordan and those who built the altar in their land east of that river. No altar was to be used for sacrifices outside the Promised Land. East of the Jordan River was outside, although the tribes of Reuben, Gad and half of Manasseh lived there. Their act of building an altar brought Israel to the brink of civil war until these two and a half tribes were able to reassure their companions west of the Jordan River that the altar was not to be used for sacrifice. Instead, it was an image or picture to remind them and their descendants of their share in the God of Israel.

Chapter 23 is Joshua's *farewell speech. Like Jacob (Gen 49) and Moses (Deuteronomy), the image is one of the tribes of Israel gathered to hear the final words of their leader. The words call them to faithfulness to God and to completion of the task of occupying the land promised to them and their descendants. Chapter 24 describes the covenant that Joshua makes between God and Israel. Like the altar built to recall the covenant in Joshua 8:30-35, a physical image of the covenant is set up again to remind the people of their promises: a stone is erected in the sanctuary of the Lord at Shechem.

The announcements of the deaths and burials of Joshua and Eleazar the high priest bring the book to a close with one final image: the return of the bones of Joseph from Egypt to their burial at Shechem with Jacob, the father of Joseph and of all Israel (Josh 24:29-33). This image draws to a close the great story of the people of God from their days in Egypt to the first generation of their possession of the Promised Land. It also prepares for the generations of the Judges who would repeatedly call the people back to the faith that they had known in Joshua's day.

See also ALTAR; BATTLE STORIES; COVENANT; EXODUS, SECOND EXODUS; JORDAN RIVER; PROMISED LAND; WARFARE.

BIBLIOGRAPHY. R. S. Hess, *Joshua* (TOTC; Downers Grove, IL: InterVarsity Press, 1996).

JOURNEY

Biblical images of journeys and portraits of sojourners illustrate the life of faith, trust and dependence that has been an abiding feature of the people of God. This biblical motif captures important aspects of Israel's earliest origins and disposition toward the world and serves as a basic paradigm for Christian existence. Several motifs make up the archetypal journey. Its essence is physical movement through space, with accompanying change of one's physical status. To journey is to be uprooted, either temporarily or for a prolonged period. A person on a journey is characterized by a certain detachment from earthly goods and comforts. The journey is an image of transition, with the traveler either headed toward a fixed place (the archetypal *quest story) or in flight away from it (sometimes in guilt, sometimes as a victim, as when Joseph's brothers sell him into slavery and send him on a journey to Egypt). In either case, a journey presupposes both a place that is left and a destination.

While the image of the journey is a predominantly positive one, it is not inherently so. People can journey away from God as well as toward him, and as a punishment for wrongdoing as well as under the blessing of God. Even Satan journeys "to and fro on the earth, and . . . up and down on it" (Job 1:7; 2:2 NRSV). Stories of guilt-haunted travelers include the youthful Jacob, who undertakes a journey of flight away from his parental home, and Moses, who does much the same after killing an Egyptian. The *wandering of the Israelites in the *wilderness for forty years is a punishment for their murmuring, a preview of the ignominious *exile into which both Judah and Israel later go for similar apostasy. Jonah attempts an ironic impossibility—fleeing from the presence of the Lord (Jon 1:3). In Jesus' parable of the *prodigal son, the journey into a far country is a journey of *rebellion, debauchery and abandonment of restraint—a journey into sin and its consequences.

The Journeys of the Patriarchs. After the downward spiral of world history recorded in Genesis 1—11, the biblical narrative begins to focus on the story of *Abraham. His story begins with a call to journey from the familiar to the unknown on the basis of God's promise, "Go from your country and your kindred and your father's house to the land that I will show you" (Gen 12:1 RSV). Abraham's threefold call to go out from country, kindred and household represents a radical break from all that previously defined his way of life. His life thereafter is characterized by his sojourning and his status as a resident alien dwelling amid a people with whom he shares neither citizenship nor abiding possession (Gen 12:10; 17:8; 23:4; Ex 6:4). Much of Abraham's life is epitomized by the simple statement that "Abram journeyed on" (Gen 12:9 RSV). As the archetype and embodiment of the people he will father (Gen 12:2), Abraham's sojourning sets a pattern for the life of faith. A sojourner for his entire life, Abraham did not come into possession of a permanent parcel of land until his death (Gen 25:7-10). His focus was not on the land but on God's call and promise—and a life of faith and trust lived before his God.

Such sojourning is a trait of all the patriarchs. Isaac also receives a promise of the land and a command not to depart from it, yet his presence in the land is also that of a sojourner, characterized by lack of permanent ties and living on the periphery of society: "Reside in this land as an alien, and I will be with you, and will bless you; for to you and to your descendants I will give all these lands, and I will fulfill the oath that I swore to your father Abraham" (Gen 26:3 NRSV). Jacob's life follows a similar pattern. Even though much of Jacob's journey is beyond the land of promise and is presented in a less than flattering light, we still find him encountering God. God's presence overtakes him on his journey—both inside and beyond the land of promise (Gen 28:13-15; 31:3; 35:1-4, 9-15), just as God had promised: "Know that I am with you and will keep you wherever you go, and will bring you back to this land; for I will not leave you until I have done what I have promised you" (Gen 28:15 NRSV). Near the end of his life Jacob reflects, "The years of my earthly sojourn are one hundred thirty; few and hard have been the years of my life. They do not compare with the years of the life of my ancestors during their long sojourn" (Gen 47:9 NRSV). Not only were the patriarchs sojourners their entire lives, but the compass of their life experience is imaged as a journey, carried out in obedience, faith and trust.

Israel's Journeys. The journeys of the patriarchs function as precursors for the journey of the nation of Israel. Israel's sojourn in Egypt has already been foreseen (Gen 15:13-14). And now Moses, in preparation for his role as Israel's deliverer, becomes a sojourner in Midian for forty years. There he fathers a son, Gershom, whose name means "a sojourner there," for Moses exclaims, "I have been a sojourner in a foreign land" (Ex 2:22 NASB).

After the exodus, Israel journeys for an entire generation in the wilderness (Ex 15:22—19:1; Num 10:11—14:45; 20). Both the journey and its wilderness location represent a locus of testing and trial, where Israel learns to trust and depend upon God. Because God accompanies Israel on its journey (Ex 33:14), there is a noted lack of attachment to permanent religious sites or structures. Mt. *Sinai is the place where Israel initially encounters God and receives the *law, but the nation does not construct a permanent sanctuary or remain there. Rather, the two main symbols of God's presence, the *tabernacle and the *ark of the covenant, are fashioned to be taken along on Israel's journey, where God leads and

accompanies them as he did the patriarchs (cf. Ex 40:36, 38).

Even after coming into the *Promised Land, Israel is enjoined to identify with the formative journeys of its past. At the offering of firstfruits Israel is to recall, "A wandering Aramean was my ancestor; he went down into Egypt and lived there as an alien" (Deut 26:5 NRSV; cf. Lev 25:23). Like Abraham, Isaac and Jacob, Israel may never ultimately do away with the tension between its identity before God as a sojourner and its promise to inherit the land. Because of Israel's past, they are also reminded to care for the sojourners who dwell in their midst: "You shall not oppress a resident alien; you know the heart of an alien, for you were aliens in the land of Egypt" (Ex 23:9 NRSV; cf. Ex 22:21; Lev 19:33-34; Deut 24:14). Those who sojourned with Israel thus enjoyed nearly the same rights, such as the right to the sabbatical fruits (Lev 25:6), the right to the tithe for the needy (Deut 14:29) and the right to sanctuary (Num 35:15; Josh 20:9).

Israel's later history reflects such self-characterization as sojourners as well. In the Psalms we find petitions offered that evoke Israel's earlier wanderings: "Hear my prayer, O LORD, and give ear to my cry; do not hold your peace at my tears. For I am your passing guest, an alien, like all my forebears" (Ps 39:12 NRSV). Again, "I live as an alien in the land; do not hide your commandments from me" (Ps 119:19 NRSV; cf. Ps 119:54; 1 Chron 29:15). The status of the patriarchs and aliens of the land is appropriated by the petitioner to reflect an attitude of reliance and dependence before God. In Isaiah, God prepares the way for a second journey of deliverance, this time from Babylon to Israel (cf. Is 35:8; 40:3; 43:19; 57:14; 62:10); and Israel's exile in Babylon is compared to its sojourn in Egypt (Is 52:4-5). Israel's unfaithfulness causes the prophet Jeremiah to want to return as a sojourner to the wilderness and causes God to act like an alien who merely sojourns with Israel (Jer 9:2; 14:8).

Journeying in the Gospels and Acts. In the Gospels and Acts the image of journeying is explored and expanded in continuity with the OT. Jesus lives the life of an itinerant preacher who has left family and possessions and who journeys from place to place, living in dependence upon God and calling others to follow him: "Foxes have holes, and birds of the air have nests," Jesus told an impulsive follower, "but the Son of man has nowhere to lay his head" (Mt 8:20 RSV). Each of the Gospels captures a different perspective on Jesus' journeys. In *Matthew, Jesus recapitulates Israel's sojourn in Egypt (Mt 2:13-15) and identifies himself with the stranger in the land (Mt 25:37-40). For *Mark, Jesus' journeys generate the thematic structure of the Gospel, particularly the final journey to Jerusalem (Mk 1:2, 3; 8:27; 9:33, 34; 10:32, 52). It is not merely a temporal or spatial journey, however. For Jesus it is movement toward his appointed goal of death on the cross; for the disciples it is a movement toward understanding who Jesus is and the meaning of his life and death—that is, his "way." The final journey of Jesus is the *via dolorosa* to the cross itself.

*Luke and *Acts develop the theme of journeying most extensively. Jesus is portrayed as the pioneer of the Christian way, whose entire life's journey typifies and is instructive for the Christian life in this world. Jesus speaks of his own death as a journey or *"exodus" (Lk 9:31). The final journey to Jerusalem is greatly expanded (Lk 9:51—19:44), serving as a context for instruction and for the gathering of a sojourning community. The undertaking of this journey is marked by a radical break with everything: "Whoever does not carry the cross and follow me cannot be my disciple. . . . So therefore, none of you can become my disciple if you do not give up all your possessions" (Lk 14:27, 33 NRSV). In Acts the journey motif is underscored in Stephen's speech, which repeatedly emphasizes the sojourning nature of God's people in the past and suggests the superiority of the traveling tabernacle over the temple (Acts 7). The early church is often simply designated "the Way" (Acts 9:2; 19:9, 23; 22:4; 24:14, 22), and Paul's journeys in Acts are a literal enactment of the motif.

In *John's Gospel the Word undertakes a cosmic journey from the Father's presence to earth. The Word becomes flesh, fulfills his Father's mission (Jn 1—18) and returns to God (Jn 18—21). Here is the mystery of the journey of the incarnation. Indeed, Christ's presence in the world is literally translated as "tabernacling among us" (Jn 1:14), similar to the tent of meeting in the OT. Christ is a sojourner in the world, as are his followers, who "do not belong to the world, just as I do not belong to the world" (Jn 17:16 NRSV; cf. vv.14-15).

Journeying in the Epistles. In addition to his many journeys recorded in Acts, Paul's epistles also evince a sojourning theology, especially concerning the Christian's posture toward the world. In writing to the Corinthians, Paul refers to human bodies as an "earthly tent" (2 Cor 5:1-4) and counsels Christians to guard against entanglement in earthly affairs (1 Cor 7:29-31). Similarly, Paul reminds the Philippians that their "citizenship is in heaven" (Phil 3:20-21).

*Hebrews recounts the significance of the journeys of Abraham and his progeny for the life of faith: "By faith Abraham obeyed when he was called to go out to a place which he was to receive as an inheritance; and he went out, not knowing where he was to go. By faith he sojourned in the land of promise, as in a foreign land, living in tents with Isaac and Jacob, heirs with him of the same promise" (Heb 11:8-9 RSV). Even though they sojourned in the Promised Land, it was never the center of their faith, for they all "died in faith, not having received what was promised," acknowledging "that they were strangers and exiles on the earth"; though in the land, they were yet "seeking a homeland" desiring "a better country that is, a heavenly one" (vv. 13-16). Hebrews broadens the sphere of the journey from

the land of promise to the whole of this earthly life as a time of sojourning while awaiting our true inheritance in heaven: "For here we have no lasting city, but we seek the city which is to come" (Heb 13:14 RSV).

This attitude of dislocation from the world is reflected in James, 1 Peter and 1 John as well. The epistle of James is addressed "to the twelve tribes in the Diaspora" (Jas 1:1), borrowing from the Jewish Diaspora to characterize the alien nature of the Christian community in the world. First Peter is addressed to "the elect aliens of the Dispersion" (1 Pet 1:1), whose earthly life is called "the time of your exile" (1 Pet 1:17; cf. 2:11). Similarly, 1 John exhorts the community not to "love the world or the things in the world" (1 Jn 2:15) and is permeated by the worldly estrangement of the sojourner, a distinguishing characteristic of God's people.

Withdrawal and Return. A circular pattern of withdrawal and return is common in literature and is likewise present in many journeys recounted in the Bible. Jacob leaves his parental home and returns after a twenty-year exile. His descendants leave Canaan for Egypt but eventually return. The tribes of Judah are carried into exile, but a remnant returns. The prodigal leaves home and returns repentant. The master in Jesus' parable of the talents goes on a long journey but eventually returns. Christ came from heaven to earth and reascended to heaven. The history of the human race is likewise a U-shaped metaphoric journey, descending from the perfection of Paradise into fallen history, but reascending (for the redeemed) into a heavenly paradise at the end. In all these stories is an inner momentum toward wholeness, completion and closure.

Summary. Biblical journeys from Abraham to the NT begin with a call from God and are oriented toward a heavenly promise. Between promise and fulfillment lies a life journey marked by trial, uncertainty and dislocation from the world. Though its path spans a variety of times, contexts and peoples, this journey with its attendant imagery exemplifies the life of faith lived in dependence on God by those who live in the tension between promise and fulfillment.

See also ABRAHAM; EXILE; FLEE, FLIGHT; FOREIGNER; HOMECOMING, STORIES OF; PATH; PILGRIM; PRODIGAL SON; QUEST; TRAVEL STORY; WANDERER, WANDERING; WILDERNESS.

BIBLIOGRAPHY. F. R. Vandevelder, *The Biblical Journey of Faith: The Road of the Sojourner* (Philadelphia: Fortress, 1988).

JOY

C. S. Lewis called joy an "unsatisfied desire which is itself more desirable than any other satisfaction." He labels it "joy" and says that it "must be sharply distinguished both from happiness and from pleasure" (Lewis, 17-18). Lewis found joy because he found God as its source.

With nearly four hundred instances of the specific

vocabulary of joy and rejoicing, joy is a major motif in the Bible. While there is joy in human life in the earthly realm, such as joy at a victory (Ps 20:5) or a harvest (Is 9:3), its overwhelming context is spiritual. The emphasis is encapsulated in famous verses expressing the sentiment that "the joy of the Lord is your strength" (Neh 8:10 NIV) and petitioning God to "restore to me the joy of your salvation" (Ps 51:12 NIV). Joy and rejoicing are a special preoccupation in the psalms (approximately 80 references) and the Gospels (approximately 40 references).

Joy is a by-product of life with God. Joy is not found by seeking it as an end in itself. It must be given by God (Job 8:21; Ps 4:7; 36:8). Therefore, it is received by faith with the gift of salvation (1 Sam 2:1; Ps 5:11; 13:5; 20:5; 21:1, 6; 33:21; 35:9; 40:16; Is 12:1; 25:9; Hab 3:18; Lk 1:47; 2:10). In the OT, joy comes with God's presence (1 Chron 16:27; Job 22:21-26; Ps 9:2; 16:5-11). In the NT that presence is identified as the Holy Spirit (Acts 13:52; Rom 15:13; Gal 5:22; Eph 5:18, 19; 1 Thess 1:6).

Joy is something that fills a person (Ps 4:7; 16:11), and is frequently associated with the heart (Ps 4:7; 19:8). "A cheerful look brings joy to the heart" (Prov 15:30). The heart can leap (Ps 28:7) or "throb and swell with joy" (Is 60:5). Tongues are filled with "songs of joy" (Ps 126:2), and a joyful heart brings forth song (Is 65:14). This energetic welling up of emotion frequently manifests itself in *shouting and *singing (approximately two dozen references for each), so that the psalms resound with a chorus of shouts and songs of joy.

Even creation joins its voice in joy. "Tabor and Hermon sing for joy at your name" (Ps 89:12); "all the trees of the forest will sing for joy" (Ps 96:12); the mountains are called on to "sing togther for joy" (Ps 98:6); and as God restores Israel, the heavens are called upon to sing and shout for joy (Is 44:23; 49:13)

Joy can sometimes be like the pleasure or pride one takes in a fine thing, a splendid sight, a stirring symbol. So in the eyes of a righteous Israelite, Mt. Zion is "beautiful in its loftiness, the joy of all the earth" (Ps 48:2; cf. Ps 137:6; Lam 2:15).

On the individual level the penitent sinner, having experienced the judgment of God, petitions God, "let me hear joy and gladness; let the bones you have crushed rejoice" (Ps 51:8). Joy can be the voice of recovery from a wayward path of guilt. The transition from mourning to joy is like turning "wailing into dancing," like changing out of sackcloth into garments of joy (Ps 30:11); the transformation is readily apparent to those who watch. And for the righteous there is the assurance that "those who sow in tears will reap with songs of joy" (Ps 126:3). God delights in showing his favor to those who love righteousness, distinguishing them above their peers by anointing them with a precious cosmetic, "the oil of joy" (Ps 45:7).

But close by the celebration of the psalms lies the sober voice of wisdom that intones the proverb:

"Even in laughter the heart may ache, and joy may turn to grief" (Prov 14:13). Or again we read that a righteous or wise son brings joy to a father's heart (Prov 15:20; 23:4; 27:11) but there is no joy for the father of a fool (Prov 17:21)

Tragically, under national judgment Israel declares that "joy is gone from our hearts" (Lam 5:15). It is "withered away" like the vine, the fig and the pomegranate on the trees (Joel 1:12). The judgment of God brings an end to the "sounds of joy and gladness," and the "voice of bride and bridegroom" are heard in Jerusalem no more (Jer 7:34; 16:9; 25:10). But the day will come when they will be heard once again (Jer 33:11). "Everlasting joy will crown their heads" as a ransomed Israel returns to Zion, and "gladness and joy" will overtake them (Is 35:10; 51:11; cf. 61:7).

It is fitting then that joy surrounds the birth of the Messiah. Even the unborn Baptist leaps for joy in Elizabeth's womb (Lk 1:44), and the angels proclaim "good news of great joy" (Lk 2:10). There is an ephemeral joy that gladly receives the word of the kingdom and then withers, a condition that lacks root (Mt 13:20; Mk 4:16; Lk 8:13), but an authentic joy accompanies the announcement of the kingdom. Jesus himself breaks out in ecstatic joy in praise of the Father who has revealed things to "little children" (Lk 10:21). It is the joy of the shepherd who finds his lost sheep (Lk 15:6) or of the woman who finds her lost coin (Lk 15:9).

This eschatological aspect of joy can be seen as Jesus invokes a heavenly scene of *angels rejoicing at the repentance of even one sinner (Lk 15:10). On the return of the seventy from a mission of victory over demonic powers, Jesus shifts the attention of these disciples from their rejoicing over vanquished spirits to rejoicing that their "names are written in heaven" (Lk 10:20). That joy will not be fully realized until the Great Day (Mt 5:21; Jude 24). In the meantime the Christian is "joyful in hope" (Rom 12:12).

For Paul and other NT writers there is a paradox to joy, for it prevails in the midst of afflictions. On this side of heaven, Christians can live joyfully in a fallen world, during the most intense persecution and through the worst *affliction. A vignette of this joy in suffering is offered as Paul and Silas are in a Philippian jail, praying and singing hymns at midnight (Acts 16:25). Followers of Christ have the powerful and guiding image of the Savior who endured the cross for the "joy set before him" (Heb 12:2).

In summary, joy is experienced through God's means of grace in the midst of life. Knowledge of God's Word produces joy (Ps 19:8; 119:16, 111, 162, 165; Jer 15:16), *worship evokes it (Ps 42:4; 43:4; 46:4; 71:23; 100:1; Lk 24:52; Jas 5:13), obedience discovers it (Ps 32:11; 64:10; 68:3; 69:32; 87:15; 97:11; 119:1; Prov 10:28; 13:9; 29:6) and work fosters it (Deut 12:18; Ezra 6:22; Eccles 2:24, 25).

The Bible describes the "deep power of joy" by demonstrating it to be more powerful, more constant and more enduring than adverse circumstances (Jn 16:20-32; Acts 16:25, 34; Rom 14:17; 2 Cor 6:10; 7:4; 8:2; 12:10; Phil 4:4). In fact the Bible urges Christians to be joyful when suffering *persecution for the faith, (Lk 6:22, 23) because in it they identify with their Savior (1 Pet 4:13). Every *trial is an opportunity for joy, because it furthers the Christian's *sanctification (Jas 1:2; 1 Pet 1:8). The Bible not only exhorts people of faith to find joy in *suffering, it says that God will give joy at the end of difficulty as a foretaste of the final *redemption (Ps 30:5, 11, 12; 51:8; 53:6; 85:6; 126:5, 6; Is 35:1, 2, 10). Joy is the believer's strength in the midst of affliction (Neh 8:10-12; Ps 28:7).

At the end of his autobiography, C. S. Lewis captures the essence of joy both as a by-product of earthly life with Christ and as a foretaste of the Christian's eternal life with the Savior: "It was valuable only as a pointer to something other and outer. . . . When we are lost in the woods the sight of a signpost is a great matter. He who first sees it cries, 'Look!' the whole party gathers round and stares. But when we have found the road and are passing signposts every few miles, we shall not stop and stare. They will encourage us and we shall be grateful to the authority that set them up. But we shall not stop and stare, or not much; not on this road, though their pillars are of silver and their lettering of gold. 'We would be at Jerusalem' " (Lewis, 238).

See also AFFLICTION; HAPPINESS; PLEASURE; SING, SINGING; WORSHIP.

BIBLIOGRAPHY. C. S. Lewis, *Surprised by Joy* (New York: Harcourt, Brace & World, 1955); W. G. Morrice, *Joy in the New Testament* (Grand Rapids: Eerdmans, 1985).

JUBILEE. *See* FARMING; FIFTY.

JUDE, LETTER OF
Though it is only twenty-five verses in length, the letter of Jude overflows with striking imagery. Most of it is aimed at adversaries who are infiltrating the believing community. Jude, believed by many to be the brother of Jesus, spares no word or image in warning his readers of the danger of these outsiders and speaking of the judgment that will certainly befall them.

A number of images suggest the community as a household to be preserved in its integrity. The opponents are "intruders" who have stolen into the community (Jude 4), which like a *household must build itself up (Jude 20), resist divisions (Jude 19) and preserve its members from destruction (Jude 22). Like a body, it must *guard against defilement or blemish (Jude 23-24), stand and not fall (Jude 24). While the insiders must stay within the boundaries of their household, the intruders transgress boundaries. They reject authority and are like the *angels who abandoned their assigned position and "left their

proper dwelling" (Jude 6 NRSV).

Images of speech hover around the theme of conflict. The opponents are "grumblers" and "malcontents" (Jude 16 NRSV), evoking memories of Israel in the *wilderness (Jude 11; cf. Ex 16—17). Their blasphemy "against the holy ones" (Jude 8) is speech that overreaches its bounds by intruding on prerogatives of heaven. It is contrasted with the words of Michael the archangel, a figure of exalted authority, who even in conflict with the devil assumed no prerogatives but said, "The Lord rebuke you!" (Jude 9). By contrast, these adversaries slander what they do not understand (Jude 10), their "mouths speak boastful [swollen] words" (Jude 16). And when their *tongues are not so engaged, they inflate language by flattering others (literally, "admiring the face") in pursuit of their own advantage (Jude 16).

A variety of sensual images is attached to the adversaries. Like irrational, wild *animals they follow their natural instincts and are destroyed by them (Jude 10). They are like the notorious inhabitants of *Sodom and Gomorrah, who indulged in sexual immorality (Jude 4, 7) and pursued unnatural lusts (Jude 7, 18). These intruders shamelessly eat at the community's sacred love *feasts, feeding themselves with abandon (Jude 12). They are "natural creatures" *(physikos),* devoid of the Spirit of God (Jude 19). These images of sensuality are associated with those of defilement or pollution: the adversaries "defile the flesh" (Jude 8), are "blemishes" (*spilas;* possibly *spilos,* "hidden reefs") on the love feasts (Jude 12), and the bodies of community members who have fallen prey to the adversaries have defiled even the tunics that cloak them (Jude 23).

Jude's most powerful indictment of his opponents is found in a cluster of concrete images evoking the skies, hills and shores of Palestine in a style reminiscent of Jesus. The adversaries are "waterless clouds carried along by the winds" (Jude 12 NRSV). Like low-hung *clouds scudding across the sky and inspiring hope of much needed rain but not delivering, they are all posture and promise and no performance. Or like late autumn fruit *trees that have borne no *fruit (despite the farmer's time and effort, cf. Lk 13:6-9) and have now been uprooted in preparation for their removal as timber or firewood (cf. Mt 3:10; Lk 3:9), they are "twice dead," fruitless and pitched on their side, though their leaves may still be green with promise. Or the opponents are like "wild waves of the sea, casting up the foam of their shame" (Jude 13 NRSV). This picture of powerful tumult is tinged with the ancient mythic symbolism of the *sea as a dark, demonic god of chaos (cf. Mk 4:35-41). The boiling white caps or discolored foam cast upon the shore is the ephemeral flimflam of the errorists' shame.

The demonic dimension is more forcefully suggested in the image of "wandering stars destined for the deepest darkness" (Jude 13). Breaking from the ancient perceived behavior of *stars following their paths in fixed formations, these stars *wander the canopy of the heavens and are fated for the gloomiest darkness. The image of stars in this context evokes celestial, angelic beings and parallels Jude's reference to the vagrant angels who are kept in deepest darkness awaiting judgment (Jude 6).

Vivid images of judgment sear the text of Jude. Divine judgment is executed in two parallel realms: the heavens, or spiritual realm, and the earthly, or natural realm. Angels who abandoned their assigned positions are now imprisoned "in eternal chains in deepest darkness" awaiting the great day of judgment (Jude 6 NRSV). Michael calls on the Lord to "rebuke" (*epitimaō*, a powerful word of effective and shattering judgment) the devil. Sodom and Gomorrah, their appetites sated on sexual immorality and unnatural lust, underwent "a punishment of eternal *fire" (Jude 7 NRSV). And believers are to save their fellows who have gone astray "by snatching them out of the fire" (Jude 23 NRSV); for even Israel, saved out of Egypt, experienced the subsequent destruction of those who did not believe (Jude 5). While the image of courtroom conviction is briefly invoked (Jude 15), it is preceded and overshadowed by the Book of Enoch's refurbished and thundering biblical imagery of the coming *divine warrior with his heavenly army: "See, the Lord is coming with ten thousands of his holy ones to execute judgment on all" (Jude 14-15 NRSV).

Finally, the false teachers are compared in thumbnail profile to a triad of wayward rogues from the OT: the way of *Cain, the error of Balaam and the rebellion of Korah (Jude 11). These names and their brief tags evoke archetypal stories of sin and its dire consequences, further unfurled in scrolls of Jewish tradition familiar to Jude's readers.

See also PETER, SECOND LETTER OF.

JUDGE. *See* JUDGMENT.

JUDGES, BOOK OF

Although Judges is replete with images, there is a central motif that organizes the entire book—the cycle. The book of *Joshua narrates Israel's history of the conquest in a linear fashion under the *leadership and faithfulness of the man Joshua. In contrast, Judges begins with a distinctly different picture. There is no leader who replaces Joshua subsequent to his death, no one man or woman to unite the people in a single-minded *quest. As a result of the loss of visionary leadership, the history of the nation of Israel degenerates into a cycle of disobedience and punishment (*see* Crime and Punishment).

This cycle proceeds as follows: (1) The Israelites commit evil in the eyes of the Lord (Judg 2:11; 3:7, 12; 4:1; 6:1; 10:6; 13:1); (2) God punishes Israel by using alien nations to oppress Israel (Judg 2:14; 3:8; 4:2; 10:9); (3) The Israelites *repent and cry to the Lord for deliverance from their enemies (Judg 3:9, 15; 6:6-7; 10:10); (4) The Lord raises up a leader to deliver his people from oppression (Judg 2:16; 3:9, 15; 10:1, 12); (5) A time of *peace is followed by the death of the judge and the return to *apostasy (Judg 3:10-11; 8:28-32; 10:2-5; 12:9-15). Contrary to some interpretations of the book, we should note that this cycle includes good as well as bad, that it is the same paradigm that exists throughout the Bible (including *Genesis, the *exodus wanderings and the historical chronicles) and human experience generally, and that it should therefore not lead us to cast everything that happens in the book of Judges in a negative light.

Within the macro pattern noted above we find a sequence of extraordinary individual acts of deliverance, and the book is, in addition to a melancholy history of a nation in decline, a collection of hero stories in which God raises up charismatic and courageous leaders to rescue a repentant nation. The book of Judges strikes the balance that Milton does in the vision of future history narrated in the last two books of Paradise Lost, where Michael tells Adam at the outset of the vision that he must expect to hear "good with bad, . . . supernal grace contending with sinfulness of men." The book of Judges presents a similar mingling.

Heroes and Heroines. The title of the book at once suggests its main image, though not in the manner commonly supposed. Only one of the judges (Deborah) is recorded as filling the function of judge (Judg 4:5). A better translation would be "warrior-ruler." The "judges" were essentially ad hoc military deliverers whom God raised up in times of military crisis to deliver the nation of Israel. The judges were, moreover, charismatic figures, not self-appointed or elected leaders. They were people whom "the LORD raised up" (Judg 2:16, 18; 3:9, 15 RSV). Seven times we read that "the Spirit of the LORD" came upon or possessed various judges. The essential role of these leaders was to deliver (nearly two dozen references), and the book itself is a small anthology of *rescue stories. The pattern is outlined early in the book: "Then the LORD raised up judges, who saved them out of the power of those who plundered them" (Judg 2:16 RSV). The high point of the rescue motif is the famous patriotic song of victory known as the Song of Deborah (Judge 5), which lingers lovingly over the details of the conquest.

At one level these stories of deliverance are success stories. After Ehud's assassination of Eglon and the subsequent military victory, "the land had rest for eighty years" (Judg 3:30 RSV). By any political standard this is a remarkable success. Other formulaic codas give similar verdicts: "the land had rest for forty years" (Judg 3:11; 5:31; 8:28 RSV); "the land had rest for eighty years" (Judg 3:30 RSV); "he had judged Israel twenty years" (Judg 16:31 RSV). Elsewhere we read about enemies "subdued" (Judg 3:30; 4:23; 8:28; 11:33) and about the nation of Israel "delivered" (half a dozen references). The fact that some of the judges themselves displayed character flaws or that during the era of the judges the nation of Israel slid into moral decline does not negate the genuine achievements of people, just as it does not do so elsewhere in the Bible. The heroic judges did what David is praised for doing, namely, serving God in his generation (Acts 13:36).

Human Giftedness. At the level of heroic accomplishment the book of Judges rings the changes on the theme of human giftedness. Of course God is the one who confers the gifts, but the agency by which he accomplishes deliverance is overwhelmingly human. What the judges have in common is that God raised them up and that they are resourceful in leading a nation. They are skillful in the techniques that are required of them, and the narrative often records their strategies in sufficient detail to enable us to see that those strategies are important.

Beyond the common thread of shared giftedness, the judges share a rich diversity. The book of Judges is built around surprises, as God's hand falls where it will—on women, on a southpaw, on the youngest of a clan, on a Nazirite whose life was accompanied by miracles. The individual judges use varied strategies, do different deeds, have different strengths and flaws. As the book of Judges celebrates human giftedness, it displays a remarkable democracy of spirit in the process. Even treachery is not bad under all circumstances. What we find here is the potential value of every person—for good as well as for evil.

The experience of Gideon can be taken as an illustration of the motifs noted above. In the first half of his story he is a case study in the inferiority complex. He is timid, slow to accept God's call and believe God's promise to equip him, and reluctant to accept leadership. Throughout the first half of the story we are led to expect that any deliverance will have to be achieved by God rather than a human. But the "making" of a hero during the first half of the story is replaced by the demonstration of heroic qualities in the second half. God drops out of the list of named characters, and the focus is placed on Gideon's sheer mastery of every situation with which he is confronted. When the nation wishes to confer *kingship on Gideon, he responds in wholly admirable fashion with the sentiment, "I will not rule over you; . . . the LORD will rule over you" (Judg 8:23 RSV). It is true that Gideon stumbles when he makes an idol that leads the nation into idolatry (Judg 8:27), but the narrator refuses to exploit the failure, giving it only a single verse. Virtually all of the space in the story is devoted to God's fashioning and using of a human hero.

Images of Violence. The world of Judges is a predominantly military world (see Army, Armies; Battle Stories). The exploits that are narrated are mainly military ones, broadly defined to include individual acts of prowess such as Jael's impromptu assassination of Sisera using household tools, Ehud's assassination of Eglon using a home-made sword and *Samson's solitary forays using such unconventional weapons as a jaw bone and foxes with their tails on fire. An atmosphere of *violence emerges from the imagery of mutilated flesh, broken *bones, crushed *heads, gouged eyes, pierced entrails, dismembered

bodies and similar atrocities. Worst of all is the gang *rape of the Levite's concubine, ending in her death (Judg 19:22-30). Whatever heroism exists in the world of Judges is colored in any reader's imagination by the sordidness of the circumstances in which the heroism occurs. The grotesqueries of the book are introduced early: "Adonibezek fled; but they pursued him, and caught him, and cut off his thumbs and his great toes. And Adonibezek said, 'Seventy kings with their thumbs and their great toes cut off used to pick up scraps under my table; as I have done, so God has requited me'" (Judg 1:6-7 RSV).

Pictures of Apostasy. The positive theme of the book of Judges is balanced by the negative theme of national *apostasy and failings in the lives of some of the judges themselves. The motif of *blindness is one of the image patterns by which the recurring cycle of self-destruction is presented. The cycle of disobedience and punishment (see Crime and Punishment) is brought on by chosen blindness to the Deuteronomic law. Throughout the book of Judges, the people do evil in the sight of the Lord (Judg 2:11; 3:7, 12; 4:1; 6:1; 10:6; 13:1). In other words, they do what is right in their own eyes (Judg 17:6).

The blindness of the leaders does not happen at once but only gradually throughout the narrative. Beginning with Gideon, each judge appears on the scene just a little more blind and oblivious than the preceding judge. Gideon leads Israel into idolatry; Jephthah sacrifices his daughter; Samson sacrifices himself; the Levite sacrifices his wife, which becomes the catalyst for Israel to nearly destroy the entire tribe of Benjamin. The characterization of the judges becomes a literary image to portray people who lose sight of God by doing what is right in their own eyes.

Gideon in some ways inaugurates the cycle. His narrative commences with an anonymous *prophet openly retelling the story of the *exodus (Judg 6:7-10). Gideon misses the recital as he hides in a wine press, *threshing wheat. Gideon is slow to recognize the *angel of the Lord who appears, insisting on his famous fleece test "to see whether God will deliver Israel by my hand" (Judg 6:36 NRSV). Similar slowness to see is repeated in the refusal of Manoah, the father of Samson, to see the Lord. Manoah, like Gideon, carries on an entire conversation with the Lord without recognizing with whom he is talking (Judg 13:16). Even here, though, the theme is not wholly negative: the characters do, in fact, come to perceive God, and they act accordingly. Gideon may miss the recital of the exodus, but it is precisely he who is granted the vision of God, as the angel of the Lord appears to him and singles him out for leadership.

Many images find their fulfillment in *Samson, who ends up blind and grinding grain around and around the prison mill. Samson is a man of vision, but his vision is skewed because he desires to appropriate everything he sees ("I saw a Philistine woman at Timnah. Get her for me, because she pleases me," Judg 14:2-3 NRSV). And in the end, he is destroyed by his own desires, his own sight—that is the irony of Samson. His punishment is telling—the Philistines gouge his eyes out. He becomes an incarnate image of Israel, a flesh and blood metaphor of a people who lose sight of God.

The final image that expresses the loss of the vision of God occurs in Judges 19 with the Levite and the concubine. On their way to the hill country of Ephraim, they stop in Gibeah and stay with an old man. A strangely familiar scene (cf. Gen 19) is repeated: the men of the city gather around the host's house and ask to "have intercourse" with the visitor, the Levite (Judg 19:22 NRSV). Again, the imagery is most telling. In Genesis God delivers Lot and his family from this tragic ordeal by striking the men with blindness. But not so in Judges. In Genesis the wicked men are aliens from Sodom and Gomorrah. In Judges the wicked men are Israelites from the tribe of Benjamin. Because the people have chosen to do right in their own eyes, God has disappeared from their sight; because they have repeatedly done evil in God's eyes, they do what is right in their own eyes.

After the rape of the Levite's concubine, the Levite dismembers her body into twelve pieces. Then he sends one piece of her body to each tribe of Israel to muster them for battle against Benjamin—one of their own. The image of the dismembered wife is symbolic of the self-mutilation that Israel will do with its own people and tribe. Because they have lost a vision of Yahweh, they have turned upon themselves and set about dismembering themselves.

The image of the *house is another informing metaphor for the book. By the time we reach the conclusion of Judges, the Israelites live in a land where a woman is not safe in her own home. In one of the most pitiful images of the Bible, the concubine collapses at the doorway of the house where her husband is staying, and her hand falls upon the threshold. This image evokes great pity but also condemns the true criminal. Ironically, grasping the threshold is an attempt to enter the supposed safety of the house. As is usual with the imagery in Judges, grasping the threshold of the door communicates two meanings. The concubine's hand also points to the man who did this heinous crime. The Levite, a man of the law, lost sight of right and wrong and sacrificed his wife to a ravenous mob. The narrative of Judges begins with two powerful and successful women: Achsah (Judg 1:13-15) and Deborah (Judg 4—5) but ends with the Levite sacrificing his wife. This is a strange, macabre act on the part of the Levite, but it summarizes and epitomizes how imagery in the book of Judges reverses normalcy and morality.

One need only contrast the action of the Levite with the action of Saul in 1 Samuel—Saul dismembered a yoke of oxen to muster the tribes in order to battle the Philistines (1 Sam 11:5-8). Even the stubborn King Saul did not stoop as low as the Levite. But in a strange twist of fate, the two images of dismemberment connect the failed king from Benjamin with the moral failure of the whole tribe of Benjamin. As is so typical with the use of imagery in Judges, the dismemberment condemns the Levite, the tribe of Benjamin and the future king from Benjamin. This is another instance where images interconnect and weave themes throughout the Bible.

More importantly, Judges ends the way it began. Even the narrative itself becomes an image. Israel at the end of Judges is stuck in the same cycle of disobedience and punishment. "In those days there was no king in Israel; all the people did what was right in their own eyes" (Judg 17:6 NRSV; 21:25). After three hundred years of exhausting endeavors on the part of Israel and her judges, there is still no visionary leader who can unite the people in a unified vision as *Moses and Joshua did.

Thus the people, living in a pluralistic society, turn to their own ways and in turn lose a vision of God. The book of Judges describes what happens to a society that loses sight of God and finds meaning solely within the individual. The image of the cycle in the end collapses tragically into a downward spiral. The narrative of Judges becomes an image of decline through its use of plot, characterization and imagery. All the other major images in Judges underscore the reason and result of a leaderless society that loses its sight of God.

Summary. The ambivalence at the heart of the book of Judges is well encapsulated in its most famous judge—Samson. Part of his story adheres to the pattern of literary *tragedy, as the writer chooses for inclusion events that reveal the flaws of the protagonist. The flaws are multiple, as we see in brief compass an ever-expanding vision of how strong people go wrong through recklessness, weak will, self-indulgence, sensualtiy, over-confidence, self-reliance, appetite, religious complacency, bad company, misplaced trust and broken vows. In view of his giftedness, Samson is a case study in how to squander God's gifts.

But the story of personal ignominy is only half the picture. The literary tragedy is also a hero story. There are ways in which Samson uses his God-given strength very well indeed in delivering his nation from their enemies. For all his human weakness, we read repeatedly that "the Spirit of the LORD" came upon Samson. We read twice that Samson judged Israel for twenty years (Judg 15:20; 16:31); obviously he did much in addition to pursuing liaisons with Philistine women. Furthermore, after falling from God's favor, Samson returns to it, as symbolized by the growth of his *hair and God's answering his final prayer for a return of strength. In case we were in any doubt that the story of Samson is a story of success as well as failure, we find Samson included in the roll call of heroes of faith in Hebrews 11 (Heb 11:32, which also names the judges Gideon, Barak and Jephthah).

See also APOSTASY; BLIND, BLINDNESS; BONDAGE AND FREEDOM; JOSHUA, BOOK OF; JUDGMENT; RESCUE; SAMSON; SAMUEL, BOOKS OF.

JUDGMENT

Judgment in the Bible is both human and divine. A judgment is an effort to correctly discern wrong from right, eventuating in a decision that is synthesized from observed experience and the precedence of the law. A judge makes the decision, determining the just reward of a person's action.

Human Judges as Peacemakers. The primary function of human judges in the Bible is to serve as agents of civil order, bringing peace to human conflict within a community. *Moses preserved order in the wilderness by serving as the first judge of Israel and appointing others to judge between conflicting accounts of daily life during the exodus (Ex 18:2-24; Deut 1:16). Under Mosaic law a judge supervised each town (Deut 16:18), sending more difficult cases to a higher court (Deut 17:8-9). By discerning rightly, these human judges preserved a climate of cooperation in the wilderness.

Because of the word used in English translations, the "judges" of the book of *Judges belong to the legal profession in the popular imagination. Yet the essential identity of these judges is that of deliverers: "The LORD raised up judges, who saved [the nation] from the hands of . . . raiders" (Judg 2:16 NIV). Deborah is the only leader in the book who held a court to which the Israelites come "to have their disputes decided" (Judg 4:5). The role of judge is rather filled by priests and prophets in premonarchical society (1 Sam 7:15—8:1). Subsequently, kings were called to judge, as we know from the historical chronicles: Nathan poses a civil case for David to judge (2 Sam 12:1-6), and Solomon has to render a verdict in the conflict of the two women over an infant (1 Kings 3:16-28). Proverbs 20:8 states that "when a king sits on his throne to judge, he winnows out all evil with his eyes" (NIV). Absalom "stole the hearts of the men of Israel" by offering to provide *justice for them, saying, "If only I were appointed judge in the land! Then everyone who has a complaint or case could come to me and I would see that he gets justice" (2 Sam 15:4-6 NIV).

An ideal human judge imitates God's righteousness (Lk 12:57; Jn 7:24) but does not attempt to usurp God's role as the final judge (Deut 1:17). He shows mature discernment in moral questions with humility, keeping God's perfect law in mind (Lk 12:57; Jn 7:24; Rom 15:14; 1 Cor 2:15; 6:1-6; 10:15; 2 Cor 13:5; Phil 1:9ff; Col 1:9; 1 Jn 4:1). Scripture lends grandeur and finality to images of judgment because God is held as the ultimate authority, the ultimate justice. As the psalmist declares, "The law of the LORD is perfect, reviving the soul. The statutes of the LORD are trustworthy, making wise the simple" (Ps 19:7). The biblical imagery of judgment rests on the assumption that God's judgments are wholly righteous and that though they are mysterious, they are the standard by which all other justice is known.

The Problem of the Unjust Judge. "Judges with evil motives" shape another set of stories and images of the human judge. Humans tend to favor their own version of wisdom; the phrase "and every man did what was right in his own eyes" summarizes an era of corruption and decline in Israel (Judg 21:25). Resistance to moral judgment assumes that the judge does not deserve his position of authority, being as error-prone as any other person. Before Israel was formed, Lot's attempted moral authority was scorned by his fellow Sodom dwellers; when he resisted their lustful intentions toward his male guests, they said: "Get out of our way. . . . This fellow came here as an alien, and now he wants to play the judge! We'll treat you worse than them" (Gen 19:9 NIV). Their scorn assumed the common difficulty of judges with corrupt motives.

Though God appoints many judges, not all judges follow his patterns of justice. A catalog of scenes paints a picture of favoritism and partiality as the common sin of judges. Favoritism defines the perversion of justice in the law (Lev 19:15). God commends those who avoid bribery and declare true innocence (1 King 8:32), whereas he despises those who take bribes (Mic 3:11; 7:3). Judges are repeatedly instructed to avoid the temptation of bribery (2 Chron 19:7) and instead to show mercy (Lk 18:6). Behind the scriptural command not to judge another person poorly (Mt 7:1; Lk 6:41-42; Jn 8:7; Rom 2:1; 14:4; Jas 4:1), we can sense the perennial tendency of human judges to abuse their authority.

The Human Judge as Literary Type. In the Bible, as in literature generally, the character type of the judge is ambivalent. At best a judge is an authority figure who represents civil order, without which a society will collapse. Thus we have pictures of Moses (Ex 18:13) and Deborah (Judg 4:5) sitting to administer judgment in civil cases (see also Deut 17:9; Ezra 7:25). Part of the comfort afforded by a just judge is that the rights of the poor and disadvantaged are defended (Prov 31:9).

But the human judge is a figure of terror as well as comfort. Because the judge oversees the punishment of offenders (Deut 25:2), a guilty person might well fear to come before a judge (Mt 5:25). The ultimate negative image is the false judge (Jer 5:28; Mic 7:3). One also catches hints of indifferent judges who need to be roused even to hear a case (Lk 18:2-6); this situation is implied by the psalms of lament in which speakers address God as a judge who needs to be roused to action.

Stories of Judgment. Judgment can also produce a narrative genre known as stories of judgment. The story of *Adam and *Eve's disobedience (Gen 3) is such, as God enters the Garden in the role of judge ferreting the truth out of disobedient children and then pronouncing judgment on the guilty parties. The story of *Cain's fratricide (Gen 4:1-16) is governed from start to finish by the dynamics of judgment, as we read in sequence about the criminal's family, vocational and religious background; his motive for crime; and his counseling history. We read about the arrest, trial, sentencing, appeal, modification of the sentence and serving the sentence. Other stories in Genesis that fit the genre of stories of judgment include the story of the *flood and the Tower of *Babel. Individual episodes in the lives of the patriarchs also contain scenes of judgment, as when Abraham and Isaac's deception of Egyptian kings comes to light or when Abraham has to cope with the fallout of an ill-advised decision to have a son by Hagar.

The epic of the Exodus is an anthology of judgment stories, beginning with the plagues that God visits upon Pharaoh for his stubbornness. When the traveling Israelites murmur or rebel, their actions result in scenes of judgment, as they are punished by death or temporary disease or attacks from fiery serpents or the earth opening up and swallowing people. The climactic judgment scene is narrated in Numbers 15, after the spies bring a defeatist recommendation, when God sentences the nation to forty years of wandering in the wilderness. The subsequent history of the nation of Israel is based on a rhythm of *apostasy, judgment, *repentance and deliverance. The OT prophetic books are stories of national judgment as well, sometimes buttressed by courtroom imagery as God calls a wayward people to account.

Within this national scope, individuals too are brought to account in memorable scenes of judgment—characters like Nadab and Abihu (Lev 10:1-8), Miriam (Num 12), Korah, Dathan and Abiram (Num 16), Uzziah (2 Sam 6:6-7; 1 Chron 13:6-10), Achan, Samson, Saul, and David and Bathsheba. Pagan kings are also brought to judgment (e.g., Nebuchadnezzar, Belshazzar). NT counterparts include the judgments rendered against Ananias and Sapphira (Acts 5:1-11) and Herod Agrippa (Acts 12:21-23).

Physical Ailments and Death. In addition to the archetypal judge and stories of judgment, the Bible elaborates the motif of judgment with a cluster of specific image patterns. In contrast to the long life promised to the righteous, Scripture images the wicked's judgment with a wide variety of ill health. *Leprosy strikes Miriam when she scorns Moses (Num 12:4-9) and Uzziah when he offers a faulty sacrifice (2 Chron 26:16-21). Jereboam chooses a personal idol and is judged by having his hand wither (1 Kings 12:25—13:6). *Barrenness is a judgment suffered by both Abimelech's household (Gen 20:17-18) and Michal, David's wife (2 Sam 6:23).

*Death as judgment comes with similar speed. A prophet lies and is then killed by a *lion (1 King 13:7-32). Uzziah touches the ark (1 Chron 13:6-14), and Josiah alters war orders (1 Chron 35:20-24); both are judged by death. A man of bloodshed is judged according to his sin (Ps 5). Whole groups are judged by death: fifty thousand for improper sacrifice (1 Sam 6:19) and another group for marrying foreign women in disobedience to the command of God (Num 25:1-10). More prominent examples include *David and *Bathsheba, whose first son dies in God's judgment of his parent's adultery (2 Sam 12:15-23); Ananias and Sapphira, whose deceit downs them both (Acts 5:1-11); and of course, Adam and Eve, who are judged with death for their disobedience in eating of the Tree of the Knowledge of Good and Evil (Gen 3). Even death is a temporary judgment, for every person will stand before God on the day of final judgment. And, as in the case of Adam and Eve, death can be seen as a judgment of mercy on a larger scale, a judgment that prevents heightened misery.

Political Ruin. The writer of Proverbs observes that "when a man's ways are pleasing to the LORD, he makes even his enemies live at peace with him" (Prov 16:7 NIV). Unlike the success of those who are blessed by God, those judged as evil encounter a wide array of frustrated attempts at self-determination. Efforts most often fail in judgment for disobeyed commands: Israel ignores Joshua's command against plundering and so loses a battle that should have easily been won (Josh 7); Micah decides to have his own idols and priests, and thus finds himself suddenly attacked (Judg 17-18); Assyrian and other captivities occur as God judges Israel's disobedience (2 Kings 17:1-23). Reuben, Jacob's oldest son, is told that he "will no longer excel" after his infidelity with his father's concubine (Gen 36:16-22; 49:4). Moses is prevented from leading the people into Canaan because of his disobedience (Num 20:9-13, 27:12-14). The reigns of both Saul (1 Sam 13:11-14) and Jereboam are cut short by their disregard for the commands of God (1 King 14:1-20). Political ruin often comes as judgment from God.

Natural Disaster. Perhaps the most astounding images of judgment are so-called natural disasters, the elements of the earth rising to overwhelm the wicked: *floods, *famines, *earthquakes, *fire, *plagues and infestations. Again, the occurrence of such disaster does not necessitate that it happens as judgment. But Scripture details numerous occasions where the explicit cause behind natural disasters is the judgment of God. Beginning with the worldwide flood of Genesis 6—9 (cf. 2 Pet 2:5), we find other images of destruction of the wicked by a flood (Job 20:28; 22:16; Nahum 1:8). A flood's irresistible force (Dan 2:26; Hos 5:10) and sudden overwhelming nature (Mt 24:38) make it a potent image of judgment.

The second prominent catalogue of natural disaster is the series brought by God to Egypt just before the exodus (Ex 5—10). The air, the water, the ground—-there is no escape from the judgment of God. At other times the Israelites are struck with plagues of human sickness, once for greed (Num 11:33-35) and another time for grumbling (Num 16:42-46). They also are judged with a serpent-infested camp (Num 21:4-9).

*Fire is another image of judgment. Inescapable and sudden like floods or plagues, fire consumes in judgment. We remember God's blessing on Elijah's sacrifice when the water-logged *altar was consumed by fire (1 Kings 18:38); but fire burned the priests, not the sacrifice, in other cases of improperly offered sacrifice (Lev 10:1-6; Num 16:35). "Fire from the Lord" burned the outskirts of the Israelite camp when the people complained about their hardships (Num 11:1-3; Ps 78:21-22); a "devouring fire" was known as judgment from the Lord for defiance of his authority (Deut 9:3; Josh 7:15; 2 Kings 1:10-12; Ezek 20:47-48). From Daniel's story we know that fire was a prominent human judgment (Dan 3). And fire is a primary metaphor for the prophets who announce God's impending judgment (Is 31:9; Jer 43:12; Lam 4:11; Amos 1:7; Mic 1:7; Zech 9:4). The final judgment of God will entail a fire that consumes the earth (Rev 16:8; 2 Pet 3:10) as well as a place of fire to which the unrepentant will go (Mt 3:12; 25:41; Rev 20:14-15).

The end of time is marked by an accumulation of natural disasters prompted by God's judgment of the earth. John the seer writes, "Therefore in one day her plagues will overtake her: death, mourning and famine. She will be consumed by fire, for mighty is the Lord God who judges her" (Rev 18:8 NIV). The history, prophecy and poetry of the Bible supply unavoidable pictures of judgment that inform our emotions when we encounter those same pictures in our experience. But the necessary context for this catalogue of observed judgments is the Bible's persistent affirmation of God as the perfect judge.

God as Perfect Judge. Even more dominant than human judgment in the Bible is the overriding motif of divine judgment. The biblical testimony is that the execution of God's judgment issues forth in praise and adoration by both humankind and the created order (Jer 51:48; Rev 19:1-2). So devastating are the effects of evil on both the human and natural worlds that in the current era the whole creation groans "as in the pains of childbirth" (Rom 8:22). Conversely, when God comes to set things right, the heavens, the sea and its inhabitants, the fields and their inhabitants, and the trees of the forest are pictured as rejoicing in celebration of God's eschatological judgment: "They will sing before the LORD . . . for he comes to judge the earth" (Ps 96:11-13 NIV; Ps 98:8).

God the Patient Judge. God's judgments are depicted as springing from his judicial wrath. Some of the vivid images used to describe the intensity of God's wrath may leave one with the false impression that the judgment of God is an uncontrolled emotional outburst. Rather, the testimony of Scripture is of God's mercy and grace striving with people until "at the right time" (Gal 4:4). God acts against evil. There is a holy timeliness and proportionality to God's judgment (Gen 18:16-33; Is 65:1-7).

The biblical authors depict God as patiently forbearing with humankind while the race continues to degenerate despite his constant pleas and warnings (Rom 2:5). When God made his covenant promise to Abraham regarding Canaan, he forewarned Abraham that the land would not be given to his descendants for four hundred years. God stated a reason for this delay: "for the sin of the Amorites has not yet reached its full measure" (Gen 15:16 NIV). The *exile provides another picture of God's forbearance. Israel's expulsion from the land with its attendant horrors was simply the forewarned consequence of covenant disobedience (Lev 26:14-39; Deut 28:15-68; Ezek 14:21-23). It was delayed over and over again (2 Kings 17:13-14; 2 Chron 36:15-16) until, as the chronicler puts it, "there was no remedy."

Judgment as God's Courtroom Scene. God's forbearance also results in the amassing of enough evidence to make the condemnation of evil and vindication of the right both inescapable and unassailable. God's intermediate and final judgments are depicted in terms of a courtroom scene. The OT *prophets regard themselves as God's prosecutors in a *covenant lawsuit against God's people (Jer 2:4-9; Hos 4; Mic 6:1-6; cf. Mt 21:33-46). In Isaiah 1:2 the heavens and earth are summoned as witnesses, harking back to Deuteronomy where these same natural elements bore witness to God's covenant with his people (Deut 4:26; 30:19; 31:28-29; 32:1). Now they bear testimony to the rightness of the impending judgment that Isaiah announces.

In the case of the final judgment, God assumes the role of both prosecutor and judge of the wicked. The books bearing witness to the resolute *rebellion of the unrepentant are opened. They collapse under the weight of the damnation they have been laying up for themselves (Ps 1:5; 5:5). Their lack of any legitimate defense results in their being cast into the lake of fire (Rev 20:11-15).

The activities and outcome of the courtroom scene differ for believers. God is still judge. Satan is now cast as the prosecutor. His accusations are answered and silenced and Satan himself is rebuked by the defense that Jesus offers on behalf of his own (Zech 3:1-5; 1 Jn 2:1; Rev 12:10-12). The righteous also fall, but in praise and adoration under the weighty realization that they are in the presence of the Judge of the Universe (Rev 4:10-11; 19:4).

Judgment as an Incremental Process. Scripture portrays God's judgments throughout history as proleptic pictures of the final judgment. God's judgment is depicted as coming in stages on a divine installment plan. In one sense the impenitent are judged already (Jn 3:18), yet God's present partial judgments on societies and individuals are meant to function as a merciful warning to them to renounce evil and submit to God (Amos 4:6-13; Rom 1:18-25; 2:1-4. See also Ezekiel's repeated refrain, "then you/they will know that I am the LORD" [Ezek 5:8-13; 6:8-10; 16:59-63]). The number of installments is limited. The Scriptures speak of the day of final payment as the "coming wrath" (Lk 3:7; 1 Thess 1:10). For the unrepentant this day of judgment is a day of fear and ghastly horror.

The Comings and Goings of God's Judgment. Judgment is often depicted as a casting away from God's presence. God is holy, and as such he cannot tolerate sin in his presence. Because the entire Garden of Eden functioned as God's sanctuary on earth, it was necessary for Adam and Eve to be expelled from it when they sinned (Gen 3:23-24). Later on, when the *tabernacle and *temple served as symbols of God's dwelling in the midst of a sinful people, regulations were established to maintain the holiness of God's dwelling place. Although the priesthood was established to secure an avenue of approach, this was done in the framework of protecting the *purity of God's dwelling place (Lev 1—10). The impure were cast outside the camp in judgment (Lev 13—14). When the Israelites refused to heed the repeated prophetic warnings regarding their religious presumption, their punishment was expulsion from the Promised Land where God had covenanted to live with his people (Jer 7:15).

In the NT period this judgment is temporarily served by the practice of excommunication from the corporate body of believers (1 Cor 5:1-5). In these cases, the expulsion includes an element of grace, meant to bring about repentance in the offending party. This gracious offer of a "second chance" is not to be presumed upon, for the day is coming when it will be offered no more.

Judgment as the Great Exposé. The popularity and success of exposé in all forms of the media may be due in part to the ability of the reader/listener to anonymously sit in judgment against the exposed. Few things can rival the protracted examination of another's sins to quiet one's own conscience and sense of depravity. In the final exposé, the shroud of anonymity will be stripped as each individual stands naked before the Judge of the Universe (Mt 12:36-37; 1 Cor 4:5; Heb 4:12-13).

The Bible portrays the human race as responding to the coming exposé in two contrary ways. The imminent final judgment is pictured in 1 Peter as the "day of visitation" (1 Pet 2:12 NKJV). God keeps himself distant from the unrepentant until the time is right for judgment (Is 13:5; 26:21; 30:27-33; 64:1; Mic 1:3). At his coming the wicked seek to hide in fear (Is 2:19-21; 26:20; Hos 10:8; Rev 6:15-17). This is in contrast to the righteous, who are pictured as awaiting God's day of judgment with great anticipation (Rom 8:23-25; 1 Cor 1:7; Phil 3:20-21; 2 Tim 4:8; Rev 6:9,10) and even quickening its arrival with prayer (Rev 22:20).

Judgment as Separation. The result will be the unveiling of the great divide. Two groups will emerge, testifying to the bipolar character of all of human history (Ezek 20:33-37; Mt 13:24-30, 47-50). Augustine aptly typified the drama played out in human history as the "city of God" versus the "city of man."

The partial separations that intermediate judgments bring about are meant to serve as a warning to the impenitent. In the flood narrative God separates the righteous (Noah and his family) before executing his judgment (Gen 6—7). During the course of the ten plagues in Egypt, this differentiation emerges before God executes the plague of the

flies (Ex 8:22-23). The separation reaches its climax in the tenth plague, where those who obediently prepare as Moses commanded them are spared the loss of a son (Ex 11—12).

Separation between the wicked and the righteous also occurs within the nation of Israel. When twelve representatives from the various tribes are sent to scout out the Promised Land, only Caleb and Joshua return confident that the Lord will prove faithful and hand Canaan over to the Israelites. When the tribes follow the advice of the ten and rebel against Moses and the Lord, the entire generation is denied entry into the land, except for the righteous Caleb and Joshua (Num 14:30).

Judgment as separation also appears in imagery related to the *harvest, a context that further enhances the notion of final and complete separation (Mt 13:36-43; Joel 3:12-13; Rev 14:14-20). Jesus is portrayed with a winnowing fork, "to gather the wheat into his barn, but he will burn up the *chaff with unquenchable fire" (Lk 3:17 NIV). In Revelation 14:14-20 two harvests, *grain and *grapes, are depicted. In both cases God's covenant people are forever separated from their enemies. The two groups are never again to be together, due to an inseparable chasm between them (Lk 16:26).

Paradoxical as it may seem, each group receives what it wanted. The wicked are shut out of God's presence for good (Rev 21:27; 22:15), while the righteous are welcomed into God's presence forever (Rev 21:3-4; 22:14). As C. S. Lewis rendered memorable in his fictional vision of hell entitled *The Great Divorce*, the final judgment is the moment at which God says to unrepentant sinners, "Your will be done." And as seventeenth-century Anglican Jeremy Taylor mused, God threatens to do terrible things to people who refuse to be happy.

The Picture of Judgment Calling for Preparation. The biblical picture is that of judgment spurring believers on to righteous living. This preparedness is not simply a matter of intellectual knowledge but of believing response to God's grace. As an act of grace God warns Noah of coming judgment and reveals a plan of salvation: the construction of the ark. Noah prepares for the judgment by obedience (Gen 6:13-22), literally building his own salvation. Similarly, prior to the destruction of the firstborn in Egypt, the Lord graciously reveals to Moses the provisions for the Passover. In language reminiscent of that describing Noah's obedience, the Israelites are said to have prepared themselves according to the Lord's instructions and are spared (Ex 12:1-28).

This emphasis on spiritual preparedness is continued in the NT. Matthew's infancy narrative is unique in recording the visit of the Magi and the ensuing conversation between Herod and the Jewish leaders regarding the place of the Messiah's birth (Mt 2:1-6). This episode at the first appearance of Jesus serves as an introduction to the failure of the Jewish leaders to prepare for the coming of God. Ironically, the religious leaders direct the Magi (who come from the lands of Israel's historic enemies) to Christ, because they know exactly where Christ is to be born (they even quote from Micah 5:2), yet they do not go with them to honor the Messiah. Their failure is clearly not lack of knowledge but unbelief.

In 1 Thessalonians 5:1-9, a passage that draws themes and images from Jesus' *apocalyptic discourse, Paul applies the need for preparation to the church. He urges his readers to prepare for the appearance of Christ. In light of the suddenness and inescapability of judgment, it is necessary for the church to be self-controlled and to exercise faith, love and hope. The exercise of these virtues is what it means to be *watchful. Those who are outside, by continuing to practice evil, will be caught unawares by Christ's return.

The Shocking Element of Judgment. The process of separating the saved from the damned will yield some surprises. The testimony of Scripture is that many will be shocked when they are barred from entering into glory. Their presumption gives way to astonishment and disbelief when the Lord dismisses them with the cutting words, "I never knew you. Away from me, you evildoers" (Mt 7:23 NIV).

To emphasize this somber truth, several of Christ's kingdom parables present a group or individual who was initially in a place of special privilege being excluded at the end (Mt 25:1-13; 14-30; Lk 19:11-27). Christ's emphasis on the sifting at the final judgment was meant to warn both his original Jewish audience and Christians reading the Gospels against becoming complacent about their relationship with God.

The extent to which *many* are surprised at God's final verdict serves as a ghastly testimony to the degree of Satan's success in passing off as truth what in reality is counterfeit. In the parable of the ten *virgins (Mt 25:1-13), the familiar tone ("Lord! Lord!" NKJV) used by the foolish virgins when they request entry into the wedding banquet indicates that they fully expect to be let in. Instead, the *bridegroom (symbolizing Jesus at his second coming) rebuffs them: "I tell you the truth, I don't know you" (Mt 25:12 NIV).

Judgment as God's Warfare and as a Cup of Wrath. Scripture graphically portrays God acting in violent judgment as a bloodstained warrior (Deut 32: 40-42; Is 13:4; 34:5, 6; 63:1-6; *see* Divine Warrior). The day of God's vengeance effects utter desolation (Is 34:1-4; 59:15-20; 65:17-25).

One of the most poignant images is that of being forced to drink a *cup of wine so potent that it causes madness and death. In the poetic and prophetic books this image is descriptive of both Israel and her enemies' experience (Job 21:20; Ps 75:8; Is 51:17, 21-23; Jer 25:15-29; Ezek 23:31-34; Obad 15, 16). The Gospels witness the climax of God's judgment when Christ freely drinks this cup of wrath (Mt 26:42) in order to satisfy God's judgment against our sins. By taking this judgment on himself, Christ then

offers a new cup of wine symbolizing the new covenant (Lk 22:20; 1 Cor 11:25-26).

When Christ comes again in judgment, the wine of God's fury is transposed from an image to the awesome reality awaiting those who refused his call. What Christ experienced at Calvary for believers in drinking this cup is reserved at the final judgment for nonbelievers (Rev 14:9-10).

Summary. Judgment in the Bible is built around a series of dichotomies. It is both human and divine, for example. Human judges are either very good (agents of civil order and justice) or very bad (selfish and partial perpetrators of moral collapse within a society). God's judgment is good news to the oppressed, who are finally saved, and bad news to evildoers, who are finally punished.

See also APOCALYPTIC VISIONS OF THE FUTURE; APOSTASY; COVENANT; CUP; CURSE; DAY, DAY OF THE LORD; DIVINE WARRIOR; END TIMES; EXILE; HELL; JUDGES, BOOK OF; JUSTICE; LEGAL IMAGES; SIN.

JUSTICE

The words *just, justice* and *justly* appear nearly a hundred times in the Bible, overwhelmingly in the OT and only a handful of times in the NT. Justice fits with the concept of law, and thus God's justice is revealed heavily in the OT. But in the NT, we are justified by God's *mercy.

Justice is one of the most outstanding attributes of God in Scripture. Time and again God is depicted as the herald of justice, especially in the Prophets (Is 28:6; 51:4-5; 61:8; Jer 9:24; 21:12; Ezek 34:16). All of God's ways are just: "He is the Rock, his works are perfect, and all his ways are just. A faithful God who does no wrong, upright and just is he" (Deut 32:4 NIV; see also Neh 9:13, 33; Is 58:2; Jn 5:30; 2 Thess 1:6). The righteous are called to mirror God's justice, for the Lord loves the just (Ps 37:28; cf. Gen 18:19; Deut 27:19; Jer 22:3). The image is so closely tied to God's character that "evil men do not understand justice, but those who seek the LORD understand it fully" (Prov 28:5 NIV).

Justice is often considered a synonym for fairness, but often God's justice equals not what is fair but what is right (2 Chron 12:6; Neh 9:33; Jer 22:15; 23:5; 33:15; Ezek 18:5). A living example is seen in Job's plight. We know from Scripture that God is always just (Deut 32:4), yet fairness is not given to Job—he suffers at God's will, despite his righteousness. There is nothing Job has done to deserve such punishment, yet he is afflicted with great pain and loss.

Yet while God's justice is often associated with punishment or wrath, mercy plays a large role in it. Isaiah prophesies that "Zion will be redeemed with justice" (Is 1:27 NIV) and "my [God's] justice will become a light to the nations. My righteousness draws near speedily, my salvation is on the way, and my arm will bring justice to the nations" (Is 51:4-5 NIV; see also Jer 30:11; Ezek 33:13-20; 34:16). Here, justice is associated with redemption and salvation, bringing deliverance to the captives and freedom to the oppressed. God's justice is never cold, for God is love. Instead it brings joy (Prov 21:15). The Psalms, in particular, sometimes express ecstatic joy that God is coming as judge (Ps 67:4; 96:13; 98:9).

The Servant figure in Isaiah is an excellent, living example of justice. Isaiah writes,

Here is my servant, whom I uphold,
  my chosen one in whom I delight;
I will put my Spirit on him
  and he will bring justice to the nations.
He will not shout or cry out,
  or raise his voice in the streets.
A bruised reed he will not break,
  and a smoldering wick he will not snuff out.
In faithfulness he will bring forth justice;
  he will not falter or be discouraged

till he establishes justice on earth.
  In his law the islands will put their hope.
    (Is 42:1-4 NIV)

This description of justice and the one who will administer justice is compelling. The reader is drawn to the strength and mercy of the Servant and longs to see the day of his coming. Justice here is personal, filled with mercy and love and deliverance; it is associated with what is right and good and holy. Integrity and truthfulness and faithfulness are implicit in the passage, revealing the nature of God's justice.

See also JUDGMENT; MERCY.

JUSTIFICATION. *See* ROMANS, LETTER TO THE; SALVATION.

K

KEYS

Keys as actual physical objects appear only rarely in Scripture, yet metaphorically they form an important connecting motif that runs between the OT and NT. As a motif, keys have long been recognized as symbols of power and authority, yet the image has more subtle overtones as well. Keys symbolize power because they are given to those who are judged trustworthy, and a key (even in ancient times) is a relatively small thing compared to that which it opens. Thus it suggests something of power, mystery and exclusivity.

In the OT keys belong to the steward of the house, the trusted servant, the one that the master has chosen to care for the household affairs. In Isaiah the prophet foresees a day when the false steward will be removed and a true steward will be entrusted with the care of Jerusalem. The image used by Isaiah is striking, for he says, "I will place on his shoulder the key to the house of David" (Is 22:22 NIV). Evidence suggests that the long and heavy keys of those days were customarily carried on one's shoulder. In addition to the obvious suggestion of authority given to the new steward, the passage also suggests that the keys are images of trust and responsibility. For the one who gives the keys, they are symbols of trust and belief in the character of the steward. For the one who receives the keys, they are symbols of responsibility.

The Gospel records include two significant uses of the key image that build on the OT suggestions. In Luke 11:52 the lawyers are accused of not fulfilling their offices of trust and responsibility. Jesus says that they took away "the key of knowledge" (NRSV), so that they not only refused to enter into knowledge themselves, but they actually prevented others from entering as well. The key controls access. The lawyers should have used their offices to gain knowledge and to unlock that knowledge for others; they were stewards of the truth. Because they did not fulfill their duties, however, it is implied that the key has been taken away.

The most famous of the key images in the Scriptures is the account of Jesus' empowering of Peter with the keys to the *kingdom (Mt 16:13-20). This passage once again builds on the twin themes of trust and authority. Peter's confession of Christ's identity forms the immediate circumstance for Jesus' grant-

ing of the keys to him. Because Peter understands who Jesus is, at least in part, he is to be trusted. Like the key of knowledge, Peter is to use the keys to *bind and to *loose. Peter, however, is responsible not only for the earthly actions of the kingdom but for the heavenly as well, since the keys in this passage seem to connect the earthly and the heavenly in one operation.

In the Revelation the image of the keys reappears. Here again the emphasis is on power and authority but also on trust and responsibility. The words of Isaiah concerning the true steward are quoted by the vision of Christ in Revelation 3:7: "And to the angel of the church in Philadelphia write: These are the words of the holy one, the true one, who has the key of David, who opens and no one will shut, who shuts and no one opens" (NRSV). The passage from Isaiah has been transformed from a future possibility to a present reality; Christ has become the steward that can be trusted. Yet the author of the Revelation carefully identifies the keys to which the Christ is referring. These are apparently not the same metaphorical keys given to Peter in the Gospels. Whereas Peter's keys were identified as the keys of the kingdom, the glorified Christ carries "the keys of Death and of Hades" (Rev 1:18 NRSV). Later in the Revelation, keys are used to open the bottomless pit to release the judgment of God.

If keys are read as part of an image pattern extending through both Testaments, it might be suggested that the responsibility of opening the kingdom of heaven has been given to the church. Human beings have been entrusted with the authority to set people free with the knowledge of the gospel. The final power of judgment, however, still rests in the hands of the glorified Christ, who will come with final power and authority.

See also AUTHORITY; DOOR; GATE; KINGDOM OF GOD.

KING, KINGSHIP

There is scarcely a grander or more widespread image used in the Bible than king. Impressive in physical appearance, honored and respected by his people, the king was the dispenser of protection, justice and mercy and a symbol of power and authority. In the Bible two royal images are found—God as king and humans as kings. It is important in the Bible's theology that the latter reflects the former and that ultimately, the two merge into one.

The Hebrew-Aramaic word for king *(melek)* is one of the most commonly used words in the OT, occurring almost 2,700 times. The same is true in the NT; the Greek word for king *(basileus)* occurs more than 125 times. When the verbal and other noun forms of these and related words are added (i.e., to reign, kingdom, etc.), we find an important biblical motif woven throughout the entire fabric of the Bible's message.

Human Kingship. By far the most common reference in the Bible is to human kings and kingdoms. The first citation is found in Genesis 14:1, referring to four Mesopotamian kings who did battle against kings near the Dead Sea, and the final citation is in Revelation 21:24, referring to the kings of the earth who will honor the heavenly Jerusalem by bringing their splendor into it. Between these we see human kings of all varieties: *Solomon in all his glory (and yet self-destructing in the end); *David, Hezekiah and Josiah as models of faith and righteousness; Jeroboam, Ahab, Manasseh and dozens of others as embodiments of wickedness in Israel and Judah; even foreign kings and emperors, most of whom are symbols of evil.

The trappings surrounding kings were the most rich and ostentatious of any group in society. Solomon's palace took almost twice as long to build as did the temple, and his wealth and fame were astonishing. His court consumed astounding amounts of foodstuffs each day; he had thousands of *horses (1 Kings 4:22-28 [MT 5:2-8]); he maintained a vast fleet of trading ships (1 Kings 9:26-28); and his wisdom, wealth and fame spread far and wide (1 Kings 10).

The king was anointed into his office. We are told specifically about the anointing of Saul, David, Solomon and Jehu (see especially the account of Jehu's anointing [2 Kings 9:1-13]). His personal symbols of royalty included royal robes (1 Kings 22:10, 30; 1 Chron 15:27), a *scepter (Gen 49:10), an ornate *throne (1 Kings 10:18-20), a *crown (2 Sam 1:10; 2 Kings 11:12), unparalleled wealth (1 Kings 10:14-29; 2 Chron 32:27-30), a personal army of troops (2 Sam 23:8-39) and burial in the royal tombs in Samaria (2 Kings 13:13) or Jerusalem (2 Kings 9:28; 2 Chron 32:33).

As rich as the pictures are of the Israelite and Judahite kings in the Bible, however, larger empires such as the Assyrian, Babylonian, Persian, Hellenistic and Roman empires exceeded those of Solomon and other kings in their wealth and luxury. Throughout the ancient Near East the king's power, wealth and stature were a symbol of the nation's.

The monarchy in Israel was supposed to contrast with that of the surrounding nations. Although it arrived relatively late on the scene in Israel's history in comparison with the offices of priest, judge or prophet, kingship nevertheless had early roots in God's promises to Abraham. Among the many blessings he was promised was that kings were to come from his line (Gen 17:6, 16; 35:11). This promise is placed into sharper focus in Jacob's blessing on his twelve sons, where royal authority is promised to Judah (Gen 49:8-12). Here Judah is to receive the obeisance of his brothers (not Joseph, as earlier is the case [Gen 37:5-11]), and the scepter, the ruling staff, belongs exclusively to Judah.

This promise comes to fruition in the establishment of the Davidic monarchy (since David was from the tribe of Judah) and in God's promise to David that his will be an everlasting dynasty (2 Sam 7:11-16). In Chronicles the eternal aspect of this kingdom is repeatedly found (e.g., 1 Chron 17:12, 14, 17, 23-24, 27; 2 Chron 9:8; 13:5, 8; 21:7), as well as the important assertion that the earthly kingdom represented by the Davidic line is to be identified with God's kingdom: 2 Chronicles 13:8 mentions "the kingdom of the LORD in the hand of the sons of David" (RSV) and 1 Chronicles 28:5 and 29:23 mention Solomon sitting on "the throne the kingdom of the LORD" (cf. 2 Chron 9:8). Israel itself was to be a "kingdom of priests" (Ex 19:6), an idea applied in the NT by Peter and John to the entire body of believers (1 Pet 2:9; Rev 1:6; 5:10).

The Israelite king was to meet several strict criteria, according to Deuteronomy 17:14-20: (1) he was to be chosen by God; (2) he was not to be a foreigner; (3) he must not accumulate horses (i.e., build up and trust in military might); (4) he must not accumulate many *wives, lest his heart be turned aside; (5) he must not accumulate *wealth for himself; (6) he must write a copy of the law for himself; and (7) he must read it and obey it.

The king, then, was not a law unto himself but rather was subject to God's law. His major function was to be an example of a humble servant of Yahweh leading the people in keeping the law. Concerning national security (a major concern in Israel and in all surrounding nations), it was Yahweh himself who was to be Israel's *Divine Warrior. Thus when Israel asked for a king like the nations to lead them in fighting their battles (1 Sam 8:5, 20), this represented a deposing of Yahweh as Israel's warrior. The same issue is at stake in the Israelites' request of Gideon to rule over them because he—and not Yahweh—had supposedly defeated the Midianites, at least in the Israelites' minds (Judg 8:22-23).

Kings were accountable to Yahweh, and the prophets were his representatives to confront them when they sinned. Over and over again prophets such as Nathan, Gad, Elijah, Elisha, Micaiah, Isaiah, Jeremiah, Amos and others confronted the kings. This contrasts dramatically with ancient Near Eastern conceptions of kingship where, for example in Egypt, the kings (pharaohs) were considered to be gods themselves. The norm in the ancient Near East—and often in Israel and Judah—was that prophets were beholden to the kings and told them what they wanted to hear (see Ahab and the 450 prophets of Baal in 1 Kings 18 and later his 400 advisory prophets in 1 Kings 22).

The special relationship of the Davidic king to Yahweh in the OT is represented well in the royal psalms (e.g., Ps 2; 18; 20; 21; 45; 72; 89; 101; 110; 132; 144). In Psalm 2, for example, the king is God's anointed one (Ps 2:2) and his own adopted son (Ps 2:7; cf. 2 Sam 7:14). The king is to be loyal to Yahweh, to establish justice and righteousness and to help the needy (Ps 72; 101). His abode is at *Zion, Yahweh's holy hill (Ps 2; 132). Yahweh gives him victory over his enemies (Ps 2; 20; 21; 110; 144).

Non-Israelite kings in the OT are almost uniformly presented in a negative light as adversaries to God's people and obstructions to God's plan. Whether they were the great Egyptian pharaohs, petty Canaanite "kinglets" (i.e., kings of small city-states) or Assyrian or Babylonian warrior-kings, they were consumed with their own power and importance and thus were opposed to Yahweh. Among the notable exceptions are several Persian kings. For example, Cyrus was Yahweh's instrument to redeem his people from exile (Ezra 1:1-4), and God called him "my shepherd" and "anointed one" (Is 44:28; 45:1). Darius was kind to Daniel (Dan 6) and Ahasuerus (Xerxes I) dealt well with Esther and Mordecai.

In the NT also, human kings are usually seen as setting themselves against Yahweh and his anointed one: Pharaoh, the Herods, Aretas and the Roman emperors are all presented thus. Such kings are known as "kings of the earth" (e.g., Mt 17:25; Rev 1:5; 6:15), "the kings of the Gentiles" (Lk 22:25) or "kings of the whole world" (Rev 16:14). Only David and Melchizedek receive a positive treatment in the NT: David, because of the promises to him about his perpetual dynasty, which Jesus Christ fulfilled completely (cf. Mt 1:1); and Melchizedek, the king of Salem (Gen 14), because of his priestly position (cf. Heb 7).

Divine Kingship. *God as King.* One of the most important ways in which the Bible speaks of God in both OT and NT is that he rules as king. We first encounter this in the song of Moses and Miriam, which affirms that "The LORD will reign for ever and ever" (Ex 15:18 RSV). This idea of God's eternal reign as king in the future is repeated numerous times (e.g., Ps 10:16; 29:10; 66:7; 146:10; Jer 10:10; Mic 4:7; 1 Tim 1:17). It is also affirmed as extending into time immemorial in the past (e.g., Ps 74:12; 93:2).

Yahweh's kingship is over his own people, including the Israelite king (e.g., Num 23:21; 1 Sam 12:12; Ps 44:4 [MT 5]; 74:12; 145:1; 44:6; Is 33:22; Ezek 20:33). However the biblical vision of Yahweh's kingship extends to the nations as well. He is sovereign over them, and they will worship him in the end (e.g., Ex 15:18; Ps 22:28; 47:2 [3], 7 [8], 8 [9]; 93:1; 96:10; Mic 4:7; par. 1 Chron 16:31; 2 Chron 20:6; Ps 97:1; 99:1; 146:10; Jer 10:7, 10; 46:18; 48:15; 51:57; Zech 14:16, 17; Mal 1:14). Beyond this, God's sovereignty extends to the elements of nature and to the gods worshiped among the nations (see esp. the kingship of Yahweh psalms: 47; 93; 96—99;

145). It is here that Yahweh as Creator-King is prominent as well.

God's rule is in the heavens, but his throne in OT times was depicted as being the ark of the covenant (1 Sam 4:4; Ps 99:1). Isaiah saw a glorious vision of the Lord sitting on his throne, high and exalted, surrounded by worshipping seraphs (Is 6:1-5). To him is due the worship of the nations (Zech 14:16, 17).

Jesus as King. The NT speaks often of Jesus as king as well. This has its roots in the OT Davidic kingship (Jesus was the son of David [Mt 1:1; Rom 1:3]) and in the OT messianic idea. The English word *messiah* comes from the Hebrew *māšîaḥ*, which mean "anointed one." These terms were taken into Greek as *messias* or translated as *christos.* Jesus the *Christ is thus the anointed king par excellence from the line of David, and numerous messianic prophecies in the OT look ahead to him. Jesus was the Son of God ontologically, as the second person of the Trinity (see Jn 1:1-18) and also as the son of David, since any Davidic king was God's "son" (2 Sam 7:14; Ps 2:7). It is in the person of Jesus Christ, then, that the images of human and divine kingship are finally and uniquely merged.

In the Gospels Jesus is called "Son of David," "King of the Jews" or "King of Israel" primarily by his opponents during his trial before Pilate (Mt 27; Mk 15; Lk 23; Jn 18—19). He did acknowledge his kingship openly in response to the high priest, however, in glorious language: "I am [the Christ], and you will see the Son of Man sitting at the right hand of the Mighty One and coming on the clouds of heaven" (Mk 14:62 NIV).

The culmination of Jesus Christ's kingship is found in Revelation. Here he is the "King of kings and Lord of lords" (Rev 19:16; cf. also 17:14); that is, occupying the same place that Yahweh occupies in the OT passages that speak about his kingship. The Lord God himself is the "King of the nations" (Rev 15:3 NRSV) or the "ages" (NIV). Indeed, most of the book of Revelation is devoted to declaring God's victory over the powers of evil.

The OT offices of prophet, priest, judge and king all coalesce in the NT in the person of Jesus Christ, who is the exalted king over all and to whom every knee will bow (Phil 2:9-11).

See also AUTHORITY, HUMAN; CHRIST; CHRONICLES, BOOKS OF; COURT, ROYAL; CROWN; DAVID; JERUSALEM; KINGDOM OF GOD; KINGS, BOOKS OF; SCEPTER; SOLOMON; THRONE; ZION.

BIBLIOGRAPHY. D. M. Howard Jr., "The Case for Kingship in Deuteronomy and the Former Prophets," *WTJ* 52 (1990) 101-15; B. Klappert, "King, Kingdom," *NIDNTT* 2:372-90; G. V. Smith, "The Concept of God/the Gods as King in the Ancient Near East and the Bible," *Trinity Journal* 3 (1982) 18-38.

KINGDOM OF GOD/KINGDOM OF HEAVEN

The kingdom of God is a governing motif of the NT,

with the term itself appearing well over a hundred times. It is particularly prominent in the Synoptic Gospels, where it serves as a leading image of Jesus' mission. Although the phrase "kingdom of God" does not appear in the OT, the theme of the *kingship, or kingly rule, of God runs in the same vein and is a favored motif of poets and prophets.

Kingship of God in the Old Testament. The psalmist declares, "The LORD has established his throne in the heavens, and his kingdom rules over all" (Ps 103:19 NRSV). And the faithful in Israel "shall speak of the glory of your kingdom, and tell of your power . . . your kingdom is an everlasting kingdom, and your dominion endures throughout all generations" (Ps 145:11-13 NRSV; cf. Ps 22:28; Dan 2:44; 4:3; 4:34; 7:27). The so-called enthronement psalms (Ps 45; 93; 96; 97; 98; 99) provide a fertile and verdant field of imagery for understanding Jesus' message of the kingdom of God. The repeated declaration that "the Lord is king" is imaginatively greeted with a joy and singing that envelopes the entire created order, with human praise and music making joined with the roar of the *sea, the clapping of the *floods, and the singing of the hills and the *trees of the forest. The *earth and all within it rejoices, for God's kingdom extends over the entire created order. These psalms celebrate the fact that God is king but also anticipate that he will "become king" in the sense of manifesting his transcendent kingship in the concrete world of people, nations and nature.

God is praised for having manifested his kingship in epochal events of Israel's history, the archetype being the *exodus and the crossing of the sea. The Song of Moses (Ex 15:1-18) recalls the mighty act of God's deliverance of his people. Israel's Lord demonstrates that he is "a warrior" (and by implication greater than the gods of Egypt, the superpower of that day; see Divine Warrior) and "will reign forever and ever" (Ex 15:3, 18). God is king over all the *creation (1 Chron 29:11), but a particular expression of his kingship is found in his relationship to his chosen people Israel (Ex 19:6; 1 Chron 28:5). *Zion and *temple are important symbols of this kingship of God, for they speak of his dwelling in the center of Israel's *sacred space and are conceived as the point where *heaven and *earth meet.

God's kingship or kingdom is the prevailing pattern in the fabric of Israel's identity. When Israel goes into *exile and Ezekiel sees the *glory of God departing from the temple (Ezek 10:18-19), it symbolizes the withdrawal of God's kingship from Israel. Israel under the judgment of exile longs for God to "be king" again, to renew his people and bring to full expression the visions of renewal unfurled in the prophets. Isaiah's visions of renewal are intimately tied to the reassertion of God's kingship in Israel and on Zion. Israel's future will include a day in which "the mountain of the LORD's house shall be established as the highest of the mountains, and shall be raised above the hills; all the nations shall stream to

it (Is 2:2 NRSV). Like many similar visions, this one speaks, without even uttering the term *kingdom of God*, of the reign of God coming to full flower in Israel. In Isaiah 52:7-10 the return from exile is imaged as a day in which a fleet-footed messenger will carry good news across the mountains of Judah, announcing *salvation to Zion: "Your God reigns!" The victorious Lord, who has "bared his holy arm before the eyes of all the nations" returns to Zion (cf. Is 59:15-21; 60:1-3; Ezek 43:1-7; Zech 2:4-12; 8:2-3). The establishment of God's kingship in Israel is a near synonym for salvation. It is the good news that Israel longs to hear.

Jesus and the Kingdom of God. When *Jesus proclaims the kingdom of God, he evokes this complex backdrop of Israel's story and symbols. In Luke we find pious Israelites longing for the kingdom under the parallel images of the "consolation of Israel" (Lk 2:25) and the "redemption of Jerusalem" (Lk 2:38). The coming climax of Israel's hope is signaled and the expectation aroused that Israel's judgment will be ended, her sins will be forgiven, her enemies will be subdued, and a renewed people will be gathered with the divine and kingly presence returned to the sacred center of Zion. Kingdom of God is an emblem intricately interwoven with Israel's story and future hope.

Matthew's favored term, "kingdom of heaven" (literally, "heavens"), is synonymous with "kingdom of God." It is a characteristic Jewish substitution of "heaven" for the sake of avoiding the divine name. It is the kingdom of the One who is in heaven; it is not a "heavenly" and "spiritual" kingdom in contrast with an "earthly" and "physical" kingdom.

Although the kingdom of God is not a political term in the usual sense, from the Jewish perspective—where religion and politics are not neatly divided—it bears political implications. If God is king, then Caesar is not (cf. Acts 17:7), nor is his client-king Herod. Jesus points out that the kingdom "is not coming with things that can be observed; nor will they say, 'Look here it is!' or 'There it is!' " (Lk 17:20 NRSV). Instead, he says, "the kingdom of God is *entos hymin*" (Lk 17:21), that is "in your midst" or "within your grasp" (*not* "within you," as if to say "in your heart"). The kingdom is mysteriously and even quietly present in the ministry of Jesus, that is, in comparison with a revolutionary uprising or the arrival of the heavenly army. Again, when Jesus says that his kingdom is "not of this world" the contrast is with a militant, revolutionary uprising in which Jesus' followers "would be fighting to keep me from being handed over to the Jews" (Jn 18:36). When Paul writes that the kingdom "is not food and drink but righteousness and peace and joy in the Holy Spirit" (Rom 14:17 NRSV), he is reminding the "strong" and the "weak" at Rome that the life of a community under the kingdom of God is not constituted on exclusionary *food laws or ascetic practices but on the formative values of righteousness, peace and joy in the Holy Spirit.

Jesus declares the kingdom to have arrived. We thus read here and there in the Gospels about the kingdom as something that has *come near* (Mt 3:2; 4:17; 10:7; Mk 1:15; Lk 10:9, 11) and that has *come to you* (Mt 12:28; Lk 11:20). This kingdom is something that is accordingly *proclaimed* to prospective citizens (nine references). Since it is a kingdom of which one becomes a citizen not by natural birth but by new birth, it is something that needs to be *entered* (16 references). Four times it is pictured as something that is *inherited* (1 Cor 6:9, 10; 15:50; Gal 5:21). The kingdom of heaven is a *secret* that is revealed (Mt 13:11; Mk 4:11; Lk 8:10), and it is heralded as *good news* (six references), just as the victory and accession of a king would be heralded (cf. Is 52:7-8). Once a person has entered the kingdom, it is something that they "possess," as in the repeated declarations in the Beatitudes of Jesus (Mt 5:2-12; Lk 6:20-26) that the kingdom is *yours* or *theirs*.

How, then, does one enter the kingdom of heaven? Whereas the theological theme of the Bible is that the kingdom is something that is conferred by God's grace through the agency of human faith, the actual imagery surrounding entry into the kingdom has an ethical slant. The *Beatitudes of Jesus, for example, paint a family portrait of those who inhabit the blessed realm of the kingdom of God: the poor of spirit, the *mourners, the meek, the merciful, the pure in *heart, the peacemakers and those who endure *persecution. To enter the heavenly kingdom, one's righteousness must be sincere (Mt 5:20). Instead of speaking the well-worn platitudes of religious devotion, one must *do* the will of the Father in heaven (Mt 7:21). It is not the proud and sophisticated but the childlike, those who recognize their dependence on the Father, who qualify for entering the kingdom (Mt 18:3-4; 19:14; Mk 10:14-15; Lk 18:16-17). Conversely, when two passages in the epistles inform us regarding who is excluded from the kingdom, it is not unbelief that is cited but the immoral behavior that manifests unbelief (1 Cor 6:9-10; Gal 5:21). We are not, of course, to understand that people can earn their way into the kingdom of God. The divine initiative in bringing people into the kingdom is vividly captured in the Johannine metaphor of "being born from above" (Jn 3:3; cf. Jn 3:5).

The general picture that emerges is that entry into the kingdom of God requires conscious decision. Rich people can scarcely enter it at all (Mt 19:23-24; Mk 10:23-24; Lk 18:24-25). It is open only to people who *repent (Mt 21:28-32) and who produce the *fruits of the kingdom (Mt 21:43). To enter the kingdom one must abandon other allegiances in single-minded devotion to the kingdom (Lk 9:59-62). People enter the kingdom "through many persecutions" (Acts 14:22), which implies opposition to the kingdom and a willingness to pay the price of suffering for the immeasurably higher value of the kingdom.

Jesus himself is the one who most regularly and boldly pictures the kingdom in images, often as signaled by the formula "the kingdom is like," and several clusters of images and metaphors emerge. One cluster emphasizes the *largeness and expansiveness of the kingdom that emerges from a *small beginning, as though both individually and corporately this kingdom is the most dynamic thing we can imagine. Here we find images of the kingdom as *seed that is *sown and yields a *harvest (Mt 13:18-23, 24-30; Mk 4:26-29), as a tiny *mustard seed that grows fantastically into a gigantic *tree (Mt 13:31-32; Mk 4:30-32; Lk 13:18-19), as a small amount of yeast that *leavens a lump of dough (Mt 13:33; Lk 13:20-21), and as a drag net that captures an abundance of fish (Mt 13:47-48), though some must be thrown out.

Another cluster of images captures the festive and *abundant nature of the kingdom, especially in its eschatological manifestation. Here we find multiple parables built on the image of the kingdom as a great *feast, whether a *wedding feast (Mt 22:1-14; 25:1-13), a worldwide feast attended by Israel's ancestors and people from east and west (Mt 8:11-12; Lk 13:28-29), or a lavish *banquet to which many are invited (Lk 14:15-24). In the feeding of the five thousand and four thousand the feasting image of the kingdom is symbolized (Mk 6:39-44; 8:1-9). Eating *bread (Lk 14:15) and drinking *wine (Mk 14:25; Lk 22:18) are images of the kingdom of God (cf. Is 25:6). It is not a time for *fasting (Mk 2:18-20), a practice associated with Israel's *exile and longing for *redemption. John the Baptist came "eating no bread and drinking no wine" (Lk 7:33-34), but Jesus "has come eating and drinking," and those who do not perceive the presence of the kingdom call Jesus "a glutton and a drunkard, a friend of tax collectors and 'sinners' " (Mt 11:19 NIV; Lk 7:34).

Other images express the way in which the kingdom of God includes some and excludes others. For example, there are keys to the kingdom that open and close it (Mt 16:19). The motif of *judgment reappears in parables comparing the kingdom to a king's settling accounts with his servants (Mt 18:23-35) and a master who assesses the behavior of stewards to whom he has entrusted his wealth (Mt 25:14-30).

Other qualities of the kingdom are captured in single metaphors. To show that God's kingdom is based on divine grace rather than human merit, Jesus pictures it as the practice of the owner of a vineyard to pay all workers equally, regardless of gradations in the quantity of effort they have exerted (Mt 20:1-16). The extreme value of the kingdom is captured in images of its being a *treasure discovered hidden in a field (Mt 13:44) or a *pearl of great value (Mt 13:45-46).

The "coming" kingdom of God, like the establishment of human kingdoms, implies the displacement of other kingdoms. It comes with the violence of conflict and *triumph over an *enemy. The conflict is vividly imaged in the parable of the strong man: "How can one enter a strong man's house and plunder his property, without first tying up the strong man? Then indeed the house can be plundered" (Mt 12:29 NRSV; cf. Lk 11:21-22). Jesus in his exorcisms of evil spirits is engaged in a conflict with the prince of *demons, *Satan. This conflict and Jesus' victory is a clear sign of the kingdom: "If it is by the Spirit of God that I cast out demons, then the kingdom of God has come to you" (Mt 12:28 NRSV; Lk 11:20). Jesus' enigmatic statement that "from the days of John the Baptist until now the kingdom of heaven has suffered violence, and the violent take it by force" (Mt 11:12 NRSV; Lk 16:16) suggests an assault and intensity on the front lines as the kingdom makes its incursion into the dominion of this age. There is more of a hint of God on the march, Jesus as the *divine warrior wresting Israel from the hands of the enemy. The climax of the conflict occurs at the cross, where Satan and the authorities claim their victory over Jesus. But in fact this is the paradoxical victory of the kingdom. There, accompanied by the *darkness and quaking of the Day of the Lord, Jesus takes upon himself the *violence and *death that was due Israel and the world. It is a victory validated by his resurrection from the dead, the intrusion of the new creation in the old.

The kingdom of God is a metaphor that evokes the grand theme of the restoration of Israel. Thus in Acts 1:6 the disciples ask their resurrected Lord, "is this the time when you will restore the kingdom to Israel?" But Israel is restored in an unexpected manner. Ethnic Israel for the most part rejects the kingdom and undergoes severe judgment (e.g., Lk 13:33-34; 21:20-14), while the Gentiles enter the kingdom and form a new people of God that is neither "Jew nor Greek" (Gal 3:28). By the end of Acts we find Paul, a prisoner in Rome, proclaiming the kingdom of God. While most Jews reject this "salvation of God," many Gentiles accept it and enter the kingdom (Acts 28:17-30). The seed of the kingdom of God is rooted and growing under the unwitting guardianship of the great Roman Empire where Caesar is king. Here is an anticipation of the time when "the kingdom of the world has become the kingdom of our Lord and of his Christ" (Rev 11:15 NIV).

See also JESUS, IMAGES OF; DIVINE WARRIOR; GOD; KING, KINGSHIP; MUSTARD SEED; THRONE; TRIUMPH.

KINGS, BOOKS OF

These books, originally one, follow closely on 2 *Samuel and take the history of Israel from David's death to the *exile. The genre of Kings is unmistakably history, therefore, but written from a theological perspective that is very different from modern secular history. This "prophetic history" shows the word of the Lord through the *prophets being fulfilled in events often generations later. It has a pronounced judgmental element. Every ruler in the northern kingdom "did evil in the eyes of the LORD," and only

seven kings in Judah were approved as having done "what was right in the eyes of the LORD" (five of those with reservations). The basis of judgment was the Deuteronomic *covenant law, which the king was to copy, read and follow (Deut 17:18). This commitment, intended to distinguish Israel from all other nations, was not honored, hence the threat of ultimate disaster spoken by Ahijah (1 Kings 14:15) that hangs over the rest of the book. The prophetic word provided an interpretive theme.

The author is not an innovator but a faithful representative of the prophetic understanding of history. God is the primary actor. The focus is outside the domain and the life span of any single human being, be he king or prophet. Surrounding nations were included in its scope. Israel's history impinged on world history when Egypt, Assyria and Babylon invaded, asserting their authority over Samaria and Jerusalem. Prophetic history embraced the destiny of the great powers (e.g., 2 Kings 24:1-3), as well as of Judah and Israel (2 Kings 23:27).

Chronology is important to the author. He seeks to date the building of the temple (1 Kings 6:1) and, using accepted formulas, he records the accession, death and length of reign of each king, though keeping the two kingdoms parallel creates a complicated pattern. Overlap between Israel and the world powers enables comparative chronology to anchor events in parallel with world history. The reigns of the world conquerors, Sennacherib (2 Kings 19:32-34) and Nebuchadnezzar (24:13-15) are both well documented outside the Bible.

So far as the structure of Kings is concerned, chronology is basic: the order of events dictates the contents. But within that general framework there is little in the way of pattern. At the beginning the kingdom is united under the aged *David and under *Solomon, but division soon takes place. By the end of the book both kingdoms have been removed. Yet the decline is not unbroken. There are examples of *repentance (1 Kings 21:27-29), especially in Judah under Hezekiah (2 Kings 18—20) and Josiah (2 Kings 22—23), but in no way does repentance bring the narrative to a climax. Short episodes are often placed side by side; summaries of reigns, with notes on sources of further information, follow one another. The kings of the two kingdoms are synchronized so as to present one people of God, despite division. The outworking of God's promise to David reiterated in 1 Kings 2:4 had been put in jeopardy, so the book ends with a great hiatus, except for the slightest glimmer of hope (2 Kings 25:27-30). The author was exercising faith in writing the book.

The structure reveals that the author has priorities. David is his ideal king against whose devotion other kings were judged: "[Solomon's] heart was not fully devoted to the LORD his God, as the heart of David his father had been" (1 Kings 11:4 NIV). Other kings, by contrast, had role models such as Jeroboam ben Nebat, "walking . . . in the sin he had committed and had caused Israel to commit" (1 Kings 16:19

NIV). Kings in the latter category had comparatively little space devoted to them unless they featured in a prophet's ministry. Even Omri, founder of a dynasty, a diplomat who put the northern kingdom on the international map, was dismissed in six verses (1 Kings 16:23-28). The idolatrous worship he promoted held the seeds of Israel's disintegration. Individuals who are prominent in the book are those who fulfilled the prophetic ideal or were themselves prophets: Elijah, Elisha, Jehu, Hezekiah, Isaiah, Josiah.

Collections of episodes in the lives of prophets have a distinctive character. Elijah appears suddenly without introduction (1 Kings 17:1) and takes center stage, opposing the king and demonstrating decisively that Israel's God was indeed God. It was he who directed the course of history (1 Kings 19:15-18) and rebuked kings through his prophets (1 Kings 20:42; 21:20-22; 2 Kings 1:16).

The Elisha narratives are episodic, swift moving, often unconnected, except that they continued to show to rulers and peasants alike that God revealed his purpose to his prophets. Indeed, this great block of fourteen chapters in the middle of Kings, nearly a third of the whole, serves as a reassuring proof that the God of their fathers was the living God who vindicated the right and brought retribution on the oppressors. Here is the source of hope in the book: the God who gave the law continued to uphold it, not only in justice but also in mercy, answering prayer and responding to faith.

The fact that the author quotes many sources when summarizing reigns complicates the task of analyzing his style of writing. Much of the book's colorful phraseology is in dialogue, presumably quoted from a source, though the fact that he includes it suggests that he appreciated its force. "As numerous as the sand on the seashore" (1 Kings 4:20) harks back to Abraham (Gen 22:17); "each man under his own *vine and *fig tree" (1 Kings 4:25) spoke of peace in Assyria as well as Israel (2 Kings 18:21); "a *lamp for David and his descendants for ever" (2 Kings 8:19) is a recurring metaphor (1 Kings 11:36; 15:4; cf. 2 Sam 21:17). These few examples suggest that the author was content to make use of prophetic turns of phrase, laying stress on the Lord's word rather than his own.

In the account of Solomon's reign the author may seem to make rather too much of Solomon's *wisdom, especially in view of his disclosures in chapter 11. There could be a strong element of irony here and in the repetition of such things as basins, shovels and sprinkling bowls of *gold or burnished *bronze among the furnishings of the *temple (1 Kings 7:40, 45, 50). These are detailed again among the booty taken by the Babylonians into exile (2 Kings 25:14). There certainly is implied criticism in the contrast between "He had spent seven years building it [the temple]" (1 Kings 6:38 NIV) and what follows: "It took Solomon thirteen years, however, to complete the construction of his palace" (1 Kings 7:1 NIV).

There is a terse humor close to irony in many accounts in Kings, such as Elijah's taunting of the so-called god Baal (1 Kings 18:27) and the contrast between Elijah's "I am the only one left" and the Lord's "seven thousand in Israel—all whose knees have not bowed down to Baal" (1 Kings 19:14-18). In the siege of Samaria Elisha's promise of abundant food was met with a classic statement of unbelief: "Look, even if the LORD should open the flood-gates of the heavens, could this happen?" What the king's officer reckoned impossible, despised outcasts rejoiced to announce as done (2 Kings 7:1-11 NIV). An example of dramatic irony occurs when Jehu kills Joram on the very site of Naboth's vineyard and throws his body where Naboth's blood had been spilt (2 Kings 9:24-26).

The author never doubts the power of the Lord to control *history. Like a farmer with his bull, the Lord will lead the great Sennacherib just where he wants him to go (2 Kings 19:28). Though much diminished, Judah has a future, which the zeal of the Lord Almighty will accomplish (19:29-31). Worse was to follow under the Babylonians, but faith would not accept that exile was the end.

See also CHRONICLES, BOOKS OF; HISTORY; JERUSALEM; KING, KINGSHIP; SAMUEL, BOOKS OF; SOLOMON; TEMPLE.

KINSMAN REDEEMER. See LEGAL IMAGES.

KISS

Every kiss is an outward expression of some presumed kind of intimacy. Biblical examples illustrate the wide variety of the nature of that shared intimacy and the degree of mutual commitment involved. Aside from Judas's treacherous kiss, the vast majority of references to kissing are in the OT, and most of these occur in a family context. Kissing as an erotic activity was known and enjoyed in this era, but the image of kissing is primarily between males in the context of a *family.

By far the most common biblical examples of kissing involve the warm emotional embracing of relatives or close friends. These are variously indications of intimacy restored (e.g., Joseph and his brothers, Gen 45:15), the intimacy of reconciliation (Jacob and Esau, Gen 33:4; the prodigal son, Lk 15:20) or intimacy disrupted (Naomi and her daughters-in-law, Ruth 1:9; Paul and the Ephesian elders, Acts 20:37). They also record, in somewhat ritual fashion, occasions of reconciliation, farewell and so forth. All are heavily charged with emotion, as is the extravagant kiss of homage and adoration of the forgiven woman in Luke 7:38. The more formal and conventional "holy kiss" of the early church (Rom 16:16; 1 Cor 16:20; 2 Cor 13:12; 1 Thess 5:26; 1 Pet 5:14) indicates the believers' shared intimacy in the grace of Christ.

The passion of the seductive kiss of illicit lovemaking is well illustrated by the footloose and wayward wife of Proverbs 7:13, who gives hints of the secret pleasures in store for her simpleton victim when she has lured him between the sheets. Appropriate romantic kissing is celebrated in the Song of Songs: "Let him kiss me with the kisses of his mouth" (Song 1:2 NIV).

Of course kissing may represent nothing more than the cynical promises of political campaigning. Absalom's kiss (2 Sam 15:5-60), which stole the hearts of the people of Israel, has its modern counterpart in today's electioneering. Such feigned intimacy may or may not deliver the goods. Judas's kiss (Lk 22:47), like Joab's sham overture that hoodwinked the unwary Amasa (2 Sam 20:10), was the ultimate in treachery, violating all propriety and social convention.

The illicit intimacy with foreign gods is well expressed by Hosea's outraged astonishment, "Men kiss calves!" (Hos 13:2 RSV). Job also recognized the possibility of secret enticement to worship the astral deities with a kiss of homage (Job 31:26-27). Finally, the metaphorical use of this figure of intimacy (e.g., "righteousness and peace kiss each other," Ps 85:10 NIV) is an indication of how varied are the images of intimacy associated with the idea of kissing.

See also FAMILY; IDOLATRY; MOUTH; SEX; SONG OF SONGS.

KNEE, KNEEL

In the thirty-five appearances of the image in Scripture, knees are most often used to signify the state of one person before another, either in submission, *blessing or *fear.

Submission or *humility is perhaps the most common image. When one places oneself in subjection to another, one kneels to the ground, lowering oneself, and at times may even fall to one's knees, desperate. Ahaziah's messenger to Elijah "went up and fell on his knees before Elijah. 'Man of God,' he begged, 'please have respect for my life and the lives

of these fifty men, your servants!' " (2 Kings 1:13 NIV). Similarly, the man with leprosy in Mark 1:40-45 came to Jesus on his knees, *begging for healing (cf. Mk 5:6; 10:17).

Often kneeling in submission and humility is seen in worshiping God or idols. In Elijah's time only seven thousand people in all of Israel did not kneel down to *idols such as Baal (1 Kings 19:18). Yet "at the name of Jesus every knee should bow, in heaven and on earth and under the earth, and every tongue confess that Jesus Christ is Lord" (Phil 2:10-11 NIV). Only God deserves worship, and on the day of the Lord every knee will be compelled to bend before God, even those who had worshiped Baal and other idols.

People fall on their knees in intense *prayer. Ezra tells of his plea to God: "Then, at the evening sacrifice, I rose from my self-abasement . . . and fell on my knees with my hands spread out to the LORD my God and prayed" (Ezra 9:5-6 NIV). When Darius decrees that only he should be worshiped, Daniel goes into his room and kneels before the Lord in prayer three times a day (Dan 6:10).

Knees are also significant in blessing and nurture. Job 3:12 and Isaiah 66:12 both depict being held and loved as when on a mother's knee. In the patriarchal period a father would place his children on his knee when blessing them (Gen 48:12).

Finally, failing or *trembling knees describe fear or *weakness. In cases of fear, all references in Scripture are associated with an act or will of God or the person of Jesus (cf. Ezek 7:17; 21:7; Dan 5:6; 10:10; Nahum 2:10; Lk 5:8). The Bible speaks of knees failing and people falling to the ground because of human weakness and exhaustion, but we also see weak knees being strengthened by God (Job 4:4; Ps 20:8; 109:24; Is 35:3; Heb 12:12).

See also BEG, BEGGING; BOWING; FEAR; HUMILITY; PRAYER.

L

LABOR. *See* BIRTH; WORK, WORKER.

LABORER. *See* HIRELING.

LADDER. *See* JACOB'S LADDER.

LAIR. *See* DEN.

LAMB

A lamb is simply a young and therefore small *sheep. Many of the nearly two hundred biblical references to lambs are therefore synonymous with those for the broader category. Lambs, like sheep generally, are a source of *wool (Prov 27:26). They are part of the herds that figure so prominently in the agrarian world of the Bible. Within the genus *sheep,* however, the species *lamb* has two distinguishing associations.

Lambs are associated with *gentleness, *innocence and dependence. Thus God as shepherd (*see* Sheep, Shepherd) gathers lambs in his arms because they are helpless (Is 40:11). In Nathan's parable of *David's greed, it is the lamb that stands for helpless innocence. In the coming millennium it is the lamb that will feed and lie

A lamb.

down with the *wolf (Is 65:25; 11:6). When a prophet wishes to paint a picture of heightened helplessness and innocence, he chooses the lamb that is led to the slaughter (Jer 51:40). The *Suffering Servant too is like a lamb led to the slaughter without uttering a sound (Is 53:7). When Jesus paints a

picture of the vulnerability of his disciples, he describes himself as sending them out as lambs into the midst of wolves (Lk 10:3).

Even more numerous are passages that associate the lamb with *sacrifice. Lambs are specifically mentioned in connection with sacrifices more than eighty times in Exodus, Leviticus and Numbers. This sacrificial motif reaches its fulfillment in Christ, who is called "the Lamb of God" (Jn 1:29, 36 NRSV) and the "paschal lamb" (1 Cor 5:7 NRSV) whose blood is "like that of a lamb without defect or blemish" (1 Pet 1:19 NRSV). The grand climax is the book of Revelation, where "the Lamb" as an epithet for Christ appears twenty-eight times.

See also GOAT; FLOCK; PASSOVER; SACRIFICE; SHEEP, SHEPHERD.

LAMENT PSALMS

Lament psalms, comprising approximately one-third of the book of *Psalms, are the most numerous category of psalms. They are also called "complaints" by the psalmists themselves. These poems contain the poet's strategy for mastering a crisis, and they can be either private (e.g., Ps 3; 4; 13; 22; 31; 39; 57; 69; 71; 77; 139) or communal (e.g., Ps 12; 44; 74; 79; 80; 94) in focus. Lament psalms are occasional poems, arising from a specific occasion in the life of the poet or his community. Common occasions for lament psalms are mockery or slander by personal *enemies, *warfare, *disease, *drought or the burden of *sin and *guilt.

Lament psalms are a fixed form consisting of five elements, which can occur in any order and can occur more than once within the same poem. Lament psalms ordinarily begin with an *invocation,* or introductory cry, to God (an element that can be repeated in the psalm as well), often accompanied by exalted epithets for God and sometimes already containing an element of petition. The *lament,* or complaint, is a definition of the crisis, the stimulus behind the entire poem, the thing to which the poet is responding. In the *petition,* or supplication, the poet outlines what he is asking God to do to remedy the distressing situation. Most lament psalms also contain a *statement of confidence in God.* A *vow to praise God* is the fifth element in a typical lament psalm. It is obvious that the lament psalm thus contains a *reversal and even a recantation: the poet begins by asserting that his situation is hopeless, and he ends with confidence. The unifying element of such a poem is the crisis to which the poet is responding.

In addition to the five elements of the form, typical poetic strategies also emerge. For example, there is a strong element of protest in many lament psalms, with the poet in effect chastising God for not having corrected a terrible injustice and sometimes charging God with being asleep (see Sleeping God Motif). In addition to the protest element, a persuasive format is evident, as the poet attempts to convince God (and at the same time his readers) that something needs to be done at once. Lament poets nearly always paint a heightened and hyperbolic portrait of the villains who need to be thwarted in their malicious actions and punished for their misdeeds.

The sense of outrage, however, is combined with statements of faith in a God who superintends human affairs and is a friend of the oppressed. Lament psalms are based on the principle of *poetic justice, and they presuppose at least two premises—that there is a right and a wrong, and that God can be trusted to vindicate the cause of the righteous. Usually the speaker makes a third assumption as well—that he belongs to the godly side. Without these premises a lament psalm is impossible.

See also LAMENTATIONS, BOOK OF; PSALMS, BOOK OF

LAMENTATIONS, BOOK OF

The despair and dismay experienced by the nation of Judah at her defeat by the Babylonians in 586 B.C. are expressed in the book of Lamentations. The book is composed of a collection of *laments and contains all of the elements that characterize that genre. Several times the Lord is called upon to look on the distress of *Zion and come to her aid (Lam 1:9-10, 11, 20; 2:18-20; 3:55-59; 5:1, 20-21).

Besides invocations and pleas for help, another attribute of laments is a complaint concerning *enemies. Judah too complains about her treatment at the hands of the nations (Lam 1:2-3, 5, 10; 3:52-54, 60-63; 4:18-20) but recognizes that all of this is from the Lord (Lam 1:5, 12-15, 17; 2:1-8, 17, 22; 3:1-18, 43-45; 4:11). Nevertheless, Judah calls down curses on those nations that participate in her demise (Lam 1:21-22; 3:59-66), Edom in particular (Lam 4:21-22). Laments also usually include the confession of sin. In Lamentations Zion acknowledges her own guilt before the Lord (Lam 1:8-9, 18, 20; 3:40-42; 4:12-13; 5:7, 16).

In the midst of all this negativity, laments regularly demonstrate a confidence in God's eventual response. The book of Lamentations expresses this unshakable confidence in the Lord in a pivotal passage that occupies a prominent central position in the book (Lam 3:21-33). Finally, laments usually end with a hymn or blessing to God, and this appears as well in Lamentations (Lam 5:19).

To intensify the effect of the laments, Lamentations employs organizational techniques as well as stark and vivid imagery. Chapter 1, an alphabetic

acrostic poem of twenty-two verses, alternates between third person references to Zion as mourning (Lam 1:1-11, 17) and examples of Zion herself mourning in the first person (Lam 1:11-16, 18-22). The *city is metaphorically described as a *queen who has become a *slave (Lam 1:1), abandoned and betrayed by her former lovers (Lam 1:2). She looks for comforting but finds none (Lam 1:9, 16-17, 21). Therefore, her mourning is bitter (Lam 1:16), and even her roads and gateways join in (Lam 1:4).

Chapter 2 is another alphabetic acrostic poem. The author recounts the ferocity of the Lord's judgment in strong metaphorical terms: "hurled down" (2:1 NIV), "swallowed up" (2:2 NIV), "cut off" (2:3 NIV), "poured out his wrath" (2:4 NIV). Judah's devastation is mourned (Lam 2:11-19) and Zion calls upon the Lord to take note of the destruction he has wrought (Lam 2:20-22). In a reversal of Israel's *divine warrior theology, the book presents God as an enemy of Israel (Lam 2:4), who has "swallowed up Israel" (Lam 2:5 NIV).

Chapter 3 is also an acrostic poem but distinguishes itself by assigning three verses to every letter of the alphabet, for a total of sixty-six verses. This highlights its pivotal position as the center of the book and draws attention to the fact that here, in a protracted individual lament perhaps to be understood as spoken by Zion herself, one finds a beacon of hope amid the darkness all around. *Hope in the Lord is encouraged (Lam 3:21, 25) in a section bracketed by testimonies to his love and compassion (Lam 3:22-23, 32).

Chapter 4 reverts back to the twenty-two-verse acrostic pattern and resumes the lamentation over Zion by reflecting on the contrast between her former and present condition: "The precious sons of Zion, once worth their weight in gold, are now considered as pots of clay" (Lam 4:2 NIV). Nevertheless, this section ends with a glimmer of hope. Confidence is expressed that Zion's punishment will end (Lam 4:22), while those who rejoice over her downfall are promised judgment of their own (Lam 4:23).

Chapter 5 is not an acrostic, but even here the twenty-two verses suggest a relation to the twenty-two letters of the Hebrew alphabet. That the orderly acrostic pattern is not present here perhaps hints at the disorderly, chaotic conditions present in Zion. This chapter concludes the author's lament and is characterized by calls upon the Lord for a deliverance (Lam 5:1, 19-21) that the author is aware must proceed from his grace (Lam 5:22).

The book of Lamentations is rightly named: its informing metaphor is weeping and lamentation occasioned by the fall of a nation.

See also JERUSALEM; LAMENT PSALMS; MOURN, MOURNING; ZION.

LAMP, LAMPSTAND

Lamps were used in Palestine from at least the seventeenth century B.C. Biblical writers mention them in homey contexts, giving the impression that they are a fixture of domestic life. The wealthy woman who equipped Elisha's guest room provided it with a bed, table, chair and lamp (2 Kings 4:10). In Proverbs 31 a lamp symbolized the efficient domestic management of the righteous woman whose "lamp does not go out at night" (Prov 31:18 NIV).

The majority of the references to lamps are to their religious or symbolic use. Lamps are most frequently mentioned in relation to the *tabernacle and *temple (Ex 25:31-40; 27:20; 1 Kings 7:49; 1 Chron 28:15). The connection between lamps and the central sanctuary is very strong. Perhaps all but two of the literal references to lamps (2 Kings 8:19; Dan 5:5) are to lamps in the central sanctuary. The golden lampstand in the tabernacle, with its vertical shaft, its three branches on each side and its cups "shaped like almond flowers with buds and blossoms" (Ex 25:34 NIV) gives the impression of a stylized tree (Ex 25:31-40; see Meyers). It is very likely that this lamp symbolized the *tree of life in the garden of Eden, which is otherwise evoked in features of the tabernacle and in the inner courts of Solomon's temple (see Adam).

Figurative Uses. Lamps and light are positive images in Scripture. When used to convey a negative message, it is generally through negation ("the lamp of the wicked is snuffed out" [Prov 13:9 NIV]) or being used to accomplish something undesired by the readers ("I will search Jerusalem with lamps and punish those who are complacent" [Zeph 1:12 NIV]).

Associated with worship. The lamp in the shrine at Shiloh is called "the lamp of God" in 1 Samuel 3:3; this suggests that its light symbolized God's presence. The lamp for the tabernacle was to be trimmed night and morning to give constant light (Ex 30:7-8). The material and deliberate style of these lamps

The seven-branched lampstand of Herod's temple.

(sevenfold gold lamps) no doubt were intended to symbolize God's perfection, splendor and holiness.

Guidance. The guidance of parents is a lamp for children (Prov 6:23), but regarding those who fail to respect father or mother, "[their] lamp will go out in utter darkness" (Prov 20:20 NRSV). In Proverbs

20:27 the image of a lamp carried from room to room may refer to the conscience: "The human spirit is the lamp of the LORD, searching every innermost part" (NRSV). The Word of God is extolled in Psalm 119 as "a lamp to my feet" (Ps 119:105). The lamp gives enough light to see one step ahead, indicating the traveler's constant need of God's Word. Peter wrote similarly of the prophetic message, "You will do well to pay attention to it, as to a light shining in a dark place" (2 Pet 1:19 NIV). Keeping the lamp lit or keeping the home fires burning are metaphors for responsibility or diligence (cf. the lamps of the wise and foolish virgins in Mt 25:1-13).

Blessing/Presence of God. A different lamp metaphor occurs in connection with God's oath that the *Davidic dynasty would endure (2 Sam 7:16). Solomon's son and grandson failed to keep the covenant. "Nevertheless for David's sake the LORD his God gave him a lamp in *Jerusalem, setting up his son after him" (1 Kings 15:4 NIV). Similarly, "I have prepared a lamp for my anointed one [David]" (Ps 132:17 NRSV). Since David's men had referred to him as the lamp of Israel, the psalmist must expect another king with David's charisma. The Lord was the source of that charisma, "Indeed, you are my lamp, O LORD, the LORD lightens my darkness" (2 Sam 22:29 NRSV), and he was to come in the person of Jesus (Jn 8:12). At the end of the Bible, when the new Jerusalem is seen coming down from heaven, lamps are no longer needed because "its lamp is the Lamb" (Rev 21:23 NRSV) and "the Lord God will be their light" (Rev 22:5 NRSV). The lamps in the opening chapter of Revelation symbolize the divine presence with the seven churches. Christ's warning that the lamp could be withdrawn connotes God's removing his active presence from them (Rev 1—3).

Witness/Proclamation. When Jesus astonished the disciples by telling them they were the light of the world, his emphasis was on allowing their lamps to shine (Mt 5:15). Of John the Baptist he said, "He was a burning and shining lamp" (Jn 5:35 NRSV). John was fearless in his exposure of wrongdoing and was noted for pointing others to Jesus, who called his followers to be equally faithful and courageous. The enigmatic saying of Jesus, "The eye is the lamp of the body" (Mt 6:22), suggests that just as a defective eye distorts an image, so divided loyalties will distort God's truth, causing it to appear as darkness—a terrifying warning. The lamps can also symbolize the good works of the righteous, whose light shines into the surrounding spiritual darkness and prompts others to glorify God (Mt 5:15-16).

When the temple was being rebuilt after the exile, Zechariah saw a vision of a bowl holding seven small lamps, each with seven wicks in a miniature candelabra (Zech 4:2). Two olive trees fed the lamps by pouring oil out of themselves: a vivid picture of the two leaders at that time, Joshua and Zerubbabel. Through them God equips his people to complete the rebuilding, despite shortages. The key message is

"Not by might, nor by power, but by my spirit, says the LORD of hosts" (Zech 4:6 NRSV).

Illumination. Zephaniah depicted the Lord searching every corner of Jerusalem with lamps to expose the complacent (Zeph 1:12). Jesus tells of a woman with a lamp searching for a lost coin to show how persevering is God's search for the lost (Lk 15:8).

Life. "The light is dark in their tent and the lamp above them is put out" (Job 18:6 NRSV). The extinguished lamp signifies the declining vitality of those who do evil; though they are still alive, their light has become darkness, the symbol of death. The lamp, by contrast, is the symbol of life, prosperity and blessing that Job had once experienced and longed to have restored (Job 29:2-3).

Domestic life. For Jeremiah the warm glow of the lamp was a symbol of the homes God was about to destroy because of his people's disobedience (Jer 25:10). Even the righteous can find themselves in darkness, yet remain within God's total purpose (cf. Mk 15:33).

See also FIRE; LIGHT; OIL; TABERNACLE; TREE OF LIFE.

BIBLIOGRAPHY. C. Meyers, *The Tabernacle Menorah* (Missoula, MT: Scholars Press, 1976).

LAND

The image of land in the Bible involves several words such as the Hebrew *'ereṣ* (usually "land" but frequently "earth") or *'ᵃdāmâ* (usually "ground" or "land") in the OT and *gē* in the NT. References generally fall into two categories. One is references to a specific geographical area. This is most commonly associated with certain groups of people or nation-states (e.g., Mt 4:15), although the *Promised Land is conceived as such because of God's promise to Abraham. The second category is references to the earth itself, either as a global entity (Gen 1:1) or as the soil or ground (Gen 1:10). In both instances one cannot exaggerate how important the image of land was to the OT mind and heart, not only in reference to the Promised Land that was eventually attained but also in the apocalyptic visions of the coming age. Next to God himself, the longing for land seems to dominate all others.

What does land mean in the Bible? First of all, it is part of creation. As such, it is one of the arenas within which people's relationship to God is lived out. In fact, man is called *'ādām* because he was formed out of *'ᵃdāmâ* (Gen 2:7). The land was where humankind's obedience to God was to be measured, both in *Adam's broader mandate to fill the earth and subdue it (Gen 1:26, 28) and in his narrower responsibility to tend the Edenic paradise where God had placed him (Gen 2:15). This latter responsibility was not limited to cultivation of the land but also included protection of it. Adam failed in this regard, allowing the serpent access to this holy ground. The result of Adam's representative act was a cosmic fall, symptomized by the infestation of the

ground with thorns and thistles (Gen 3:17-19). The ground's accursedness reflects the general alienation of people from the world due to sin. One image of land in the Bible, then, is the physical place in which humanity lives, to which it has a bodily link. Good in principle, land is cursed as a result of humanity's sin, and people are alienated from it as well as being joined to it.

A second motif is land as the object of *covenant promise—one of the preeminent images of longing in the Bible. This motif begins already with the story of *Abraham, with whom God's covenant, including the promise of land (Gen 12:1), was made. Thereafter the promise of land is a virtual obsession with the patriarchs, whose status as sojourners always presupposes an eventual land as the place where they can finally settle. The same can be said of the story of the exodus, with approximately four hundred references to land in the final four books of the Pentateuch. The land of anticipation becomes an image of *abundance (*see* Land Flowing with Milk and Honey) and also represents a hoped-for *rest from *wandering. The elaborate laws governing the use of the land after the Israelites have possessed it also show land to be an important arena of spiritual of testing to see whether the Israelites will live up to their covenant obligations.

Once the Israelites conquer the land of Canaan and settle in it, other meanings accrue to the image. One is fulfillment: what was long promised and anticipated is now a reality. A second meaning is that of possession, with God giving the nation "this good land to possess" (Deut 9:6 RSV). After all the wandering, moreover, land becomes an image of settledness and rest: "The LORD your God is providing you a place of rest, and will give you this land" (Josh 1:13 RSV). This land, in other words, is a homeland. Another motif is stewardship: God is the one who gives the land (Deut 5:31 speaks of "the land which I give them to possess"), and in dividing the land among the tribes and families, the nation is simply assigning it to people who will manage it as stewards.

The dominant image of land during the next phase of OT history, the *exile and events leading up to it, is *judgment. Not only is the nation physically separated from its land when it is carried into exile, but in the prophetic denunciations of current ills and predictions of coming judgment as well, the land figures prominently as the sphere of God's punishment on a wayward people. Image clusters include pollution, blighting and drought, and we can detect an analogy in this fall from grace to the original expulsion from the Garden of Eden. In Israelite history the land acts as a barometer of the nation's relationship with God, bearing blessings for obedience and curses for disobedience.

Finally, the "golden age" prophecies of a coming restoration never lose sight of the sway that land held over the Hebrew imagination. In the restoration God "will set them in their own land" (Is 14:1 RSV), "will bring them back to their own land" (Jer 16:15

RSV), will cause Israel to "dwell in their own land" (Ezek 28:25 RSV), "will plant them upon their land" (Amos 9:15 RSV) and so forth.

To a large extent the OT preoccupation with land as the locus of longing and covenant blessing is replaced in the NT by Christ and his the kingdom of God. The symbol of land is universalized when Paul speaks of the promise to Abraham and his descendants that they would "inherit the world" (Rom 4:13). And the pattern of exodus followed by possession of the land is echoed in Christ having "delivered us from the dominion of darkness" and "qualified us to share in the inheritance of the saints of the light" (Col 1:12-13). Not that the image of land entirely loses its appeal: the promise to the meek is still that "they shall inherit the earth" (Mt 5:5), and pilgrims still seek a "homeland" (Heb 11:14). Yet as a biblical image, land remains largely an OT image which is in the NT is invested with new meanings and points forward to the eschatological renewal of the heaven and earth.

See also EARTH; GARDEN; LAND FLOWING WITH MILK AND HONEY; PROMISED LAND.

BIBLIOGRAPHY. W. Brueggemann, *The Land: Place as Gift, Promise and Challenge in Biblical Faith* (Philadelphia: Westminster, 1977); W. D. Davies, *Gospel and the Land* (Berkeley: University of California Press, 1974); C. J. H. Wright, *God's People in God's Land: Family, Land, and Property in the Old Testament* (Grand Rapids: Eerdmans, 1990).

LAND FLOWING WITH MILK & HONEY

"A land flowing with milk and honey," a phrase that encapsulates the abundant goodness of the Promised Land, first appears in God's conversation with Moses from the *burning bush in Exodus 3:8. It subsequently occurs fourteen times in the Pentateuch, once in Joshua and several times in Jeremiah and Ezekiel within contexts alluding to Israel's history.

A few passages, such as Deuteronomy 8:7-9 and 11:10-12, give detailed descriptions of the land's suitability for agriculture. According to these descriptions, the land destined for settlement boasts abundant *water, *wheat, barley, *vines, *fig trees, pomegranates, olive *oil and *honey. The phrase "land of milk and honey" uses two important agricultural products as a summary statement about the lush conditions of the land. The twelve men who spied out the land exclaimed, "We went into the land to which you sent us, and it does flow with milk and honey!" (Num 13:27 NIV).

Why did milk and honey become the favored pair of items for the evocative epithet, when other options existed? Since the Bible does not itself explicate the epithet, we are left to surmise. Next to *bread, milk was the most important staple in the diet of the Hebrews. A land that produced an abundance of milk had to be rich in pasturage, so by extension a picture of successful farming enters one's imagination.

Honey, valued for its *sweetness rather than as a necessity of life, was rare enough to rank as a luxury. As images of desirability and abundance, therefore, these two images combine to form a picture of total satisfaction. The image of "flowing" suggests a rich fullness that surpasses all need and sets up a contrast with the arid wilderness. Perhaps they are even an example of Hebrew merism (naming opposites to cover everything between as well), suggesting the whole spectrum of food, from the necessary to the luxurious.

See also ABUNDANCE; HONEY; LAND; MILK; PROMISED LAND.

LAND OF ISRAEL. *See* LAND.

LANDSCAPE. *See* COUNTRY, COUNTRYSIDE.

LARGE, LARGENESS

Largeness in Scripture primarily pictures the nature and activity of God. It manifests itself literally on a physical level and metaphorically on a spiritual plane. Applied to humans, largeness usually portrays wrongful attempts to usurp something that properly belongs to God.

Physical Largeness. At a purely physical level, nature provides most of the images of largeness in the Bible. A *hundredfold *harvest, for example, is gigantic—a harvest *par excellence* (Gen 26:12; Mt 13:8, 23). The fish that swallows and preserves *Jonah is impressively large. So are Behemoth and Leviathan, sea *monsters so huge that only God can control them (Job 40:15—41:34). To the Hebrew imagination the mysterious and terrifying sea is "vast and spacious" (Ps 104:25). On both occasions when Jesus guides his disciples in their attempts to *fish, he shows himself to be the God in charge of all the bounty of nature by the miraculously large number of fish that the disciples find in their nets (Lk 5:6; Jn 21:6).

The human imagination tends to view largeness as a positive image. The Bible often shares this bias, picturing largeness as an image of God's bounty. Moses describes the Promised Land stretching before the Israelites as being full of "large, flourishing cities," overflowing with provisions and food—all of it given into their hands by God (Deut 6:10-12). A stock way of commending a place in the OT is to declare it large or spacious (Ex 3:8; Judg 18:10; 2 Sam 22:20). There are eight positive references to God's enlarging a person's or nation's territory (*see* Increase, Stories of). Especially memorable is the cursory account of how Jabez cried to God, "Oh, that you would bless me and enlarge my territory! . . . And God granted his request" (1 Chron 4:10 NIV). In all of these instances, a large land expresses God's bountiful provision for people.

A similar picture emerges from the OT motif of large *stones. At first we might notice the pattern only to appreciate the Bible's graphic detail. But many of these large stones connect to God in some way. Moses commanded the Israelites to set up large stones on Mt. Ebal (on the other side of the Jordan), on which to write the words of God's law (Deut 27:2). The large expanse of stone would offer a visual reminder of God's greatness and of the monumental importance of his law, the expression of himself to them. Later God told Isaiah to write his message on a "large scroll"—large so that God's words and the importance of them would be clear (Is 8:1). We read of large stones being used as a platform, or *altar, for sacrifices to God (1 Sam 14:33), and large stones were required to build the *temple of God (1 Kings 5:17; 7:10). In fact, David describes the many fine and varied materials he has assembled for the temple with the stipulation, "all of these in large quantities." He explains, "The task is great, because this palatial structure is not for man but for the Lord God" (1 Chron 29:1). The largeness of the task and of the temple reflects the largeness of God himself.

The Largeness of God. Not surprisingly, the Bible associates images of largeness with *God. Images of vast space, for example, are present in the psalmist's claim that God's love is "as *high as the heavens are above the earth" and that he removes people's sins "as far as the east is from the west" (Ps 103:11-12 RSV). God's faithfulness "reaches to the skies" (Ps 36:5; 57:10). His "righteousness is like the mighty *mountains" and his justice "like the great *deep" (Ps 36:6 RSV). Compared to God, "the nations are like a drop from a bucket" (Is 40:15 RSV), and God can hold the waters of the earth in the hollow of his *hand (Is 40:12). Imagery like this sends a simple but majestic message: God is big.

On the negative side, largeness sometimes pictures the power and judgment of God *against* people or nations. God rained huge *hailstones on the Amorites (Josh 10:11), showing his great power over nature and over his enemies. His *cup of anger, which Israel and Judah both must drink because of their sin, is "large and deep" (Ezra 23:32). The sword picturing God's judgment in Revelation 6:4 is large. God's judgment against Babylon is pictured by an angel who "picked up a boulder the size of a large millstone and threw it into the sea" (Rev 18:21 NIV). These large images of judgment portray not only God's power but also the magnitude of sin; in fact, Babylon's sin is so large that it is "piled up to heaven" (Rev 18:5). Of similar import is Jesus' claim that someone who causes God's children to sin should "be thrown into the sea with a millstone tied around his neck" (Lk 17:2 NIV), an image of huge punishment for a huge sin.

The Largeness of the Kingdom. The large catch of fish to which Jesus directed the disciples represented the bounty of nature under divine control, but when Jesus proceeded to tell Peter about fishing for men, the image expanded into a picture of the bounty of God's kingdom, which will be large and full of people (Lk 5:10). Jesus, whose most distinctive rhetorical trademark was the *giantesque exaggeration, pictured his kingdom as a tiny *mustard seed

which, when it grows, becomes "the largest of all garden plants, with such big branches that the birds of the air can perch in its shade" (Mk 4:31-32 NIV). People who leave everything to pursue the kingdom are headed for a big reward: they "will receive a hundred times as much [as they relinquished] and will inherit eternal life" (Mt 19:29 NIV). Peter learned more of the largeness of the kingdom when in a vision he saw heaven opened and a "large sheet" being let down to earth, filled with animals both clean and unclean, which he was called to eat (Acts 10:11-13). In heaven, God's kingdom will be "a great multitude that no one could count, from every nation, tribe, people, and language" (Rev 7:9 NIV).

Largeness belongs to God and his kingdom; whenever humans take God's largeness for themselves, there is danger. Even as Moses described the bountiful *Promised Land, he added a warning for the people to be careful not to forget the Lord in the midst of all their plenty (Deut 6:10). Moses predicted that when the people's herds and flocks and stores of gold and silver grew large, their hearts would become proud and turn from God (Deut 8:13). Large material *wealth is often mentioned as a lure that pulls the heart away from God (cf. the parable of the rich farmer of Lk 12:13-21). Kings were not to accumulate large amounts of silver and gold or large numbers of wives, so that their hearts would not be led astray (Deut 17:17), a prediction confirmed in the life of Solomon (1 Kings 11:3-4). According to biblical texts, the largeness that should properly fill the human heart is the largeness of God and his kingdom.

See also ABUNDANCE; BABEL, TOWER OF; COSMOLOGY; DEEP; GIANT; GIANTESQUE MOTIF; HIGH, HEIGHT, HIGH PLACE; INCREASE, STORIES OF; MONSTER, MONSTERS; MOUNTAIN; MUSTARD SEED; SMALL; STOREHOUSE; WEALTH; WIDE, WIDENESS.

LAST SUPPER. *See* SUPPER.

LAUGHTER. *See* HUMOR.

LAW

The law expresses God's expectations for the moral and spiritual conduct of Israel, the guidelines God has given to Israel to enable them to live life as he created it to be lived. The most important word for law in the OT is *tôrâ* (usually translated "law"). The precise meaning of *tôrâ* is still the subject of scholarly debate, but there is general agreement that it bears the connotations of guidance, teaching and instruction. At times *tôrâ* refers to the injunctions regulating Israel's moral, religious and civil life (Ex 24:12). At other times the term designates the entire Pentateuch (Ezra 7:2; Mt 22:40; Lk 16:16). Several other terms serve as functional equivalents of *tôrâ* in the OT. "Laws" refers to the many individual regulations. The expression "the words of the LORD" (Jer 36:8 RSV) and "words of the covenant" (Ex 34:28; 2 Kings 23:3) serve in a similar way. By the NT period the whole OT could be referred to as "the Law" (Jn

10:34; 12:34; Gal 4:21-23).

Psalm 119 is the *locus classicus* of biblical images for the law, and it can serve as a good entré into the subject. The first thing to note is the range of specific words by the which the law is called: testimonies, precepts, statutes, commandments, ordinances, ways, word. What all these terms have in common is their assumption that God gives the law in such a form that people can order their lives by it. Around these central terms the psalm weaves a tapestry of specific images. Obeying God's law is like *walking down a *path (Ps 119:1, 35, 128) and is something on which to fix one's eyes (Ps 119:6, 15). It *guards a person's life (Ps 119:9). The law is associated with delight (Ps 119:14, 24, 47, 70, etc.) and meditation (Ps 119:15, 23, 97). The law is a counselor (Ps 119:24), a song (Ps 119:54), the object of love (Ps 119:97, 127, 159) and a *lamp by which a person can see to walk (Ps 119:105). Overall, the emphasis falls on four motifs: the law (1) comes from God, (2) is intended for human benefit, (3) is a reliable guide to living and (4) illuminates one's mind or understanding.

The Books of Moses: The Law as Covenant. The law of the OT is often called "the law of Moses" (e.g., Josh 8:32; Lk 2:22) because the Bible consistently designates Moses as the one through whom God originally gave his law. For this reason the conception of law in the Mosaic period constitutes the enduring imagery of law throughout the Scriptures. Above all, the Pentateuch presents the law of God as a codification of God's *covenant with Israel. It is not an abstract moral code or a mere collection of general ethical or social principles. Instead Moses presents the law as an aspect of the covenantal relationship between God as the supreme suzerain and Israel as his vassal nation.

The covenantal nature of the OT law is evident in a variety of ways. The Ten Commandments resemble literary patterns that often appear in international treaty-covenants (also called suzerainty treaties) between ancient Near Eastern emperors and their vassal nations. Much like these treaties, the Ten Commandments contain stipulations and sanctions (Ex 20:1-18), but they are preceded by a preamble identifying the one who gives the law (Ex 20:1) and an historical prologue announcing the benevolence of the lawgiver toward the vassal (Ex 20:2; see also Ex 19:3-6). Similarly, the entire book of Deuteronomy roughly corresponds to this pattern: Preamble (Deut 1:1-4), Historical Prologue (Deut 1:5-4:43), Stipulations (Deut 4:44—36:19), Sanctions (Deut 27:1—30:20) and Succession Regulations (Deut 31:1—34:12). Moreover, the collection of laws in Exodus 21:1—23:33 is actually called "the book of the Covenant" (Ex 24:7). The imagery of God's law in Scripture is thus part of a larger conceptual framework that explains further features of it.

First, just as ancient treaties formalized a preexisting relationship, the giving of law presumes that mutual love and loyalty have been established between Israel and her divine suzerain. The Ten Commandments come to Israel *after* God redeems her from Egypt (Ex 20:1-17). In the covenantal framework the law is never intended to be a way of earning good standing before God. It is a response to God's grace, not a prerequisite to it. The proper motivation for obedience to the law is to show loyal love for God (Deut 6:1-25; Mt 22:37-40), not to earn the love of God.

Second, the law is designed to bring benefits to God's vassals. Just as ancient emperors promised to care for their people, God demonstrates his benevolence by giving his law. Rather than a burden or curse, God gives the law for Israel's well-being. Obedience to the law will bring prosperity (Deut 8:1; Josh 1:7) and make Israel the envy of all nations (Deut 4:8).

Third, the stipulations and sanctions of the law also test the loyalties of Israel to her divine suzerain. Blessings are promised to those who prove their love for God by obedience to the law (Deut 11:13). Flagrant violations of the law reveal hearts of rebellion and eventually bring severe covenant curses on the nation (Deut 27:14-26).

Throughout the Scriptures this basic covenantal framework shapes the imagery of law. The law never stands on its own; it always functions as an aspect of God's covenant with his people. Although the covenant itself has a positive meaning, the sinfulness of the human heart leads to a dominant theme of the inability of the human race to keep the covenant, giving the law a negative cast. Moses himself, after rehearsing the law before his death, gives a decidedly negative verdict on how the law will fare with God's covenant people: "I know how rebellious and stubborn you are; behold, while I am yet alive with you, today you have been rebellious against the LORD; how much more after my death! . . . For I know that after my death you will surely act corruptly, and turn aside from the way which I have commanded you" (Deut 31:27, 29 RSV).

The Psalms: Celebration of the Law. If the books of Moses give us the actual law, the psalms give us a glimpse of how the OT believer felt about God's law. The dominant motif is celebration and gratitude. The psalmists apparently feel nothing of the NT sentiment of the law as a burden. Psalm 1 strikes the keynote right at the outset: the portrait of the blessed person includes the detail that "his delight is in the law of the LORD, and on his law he meditates day and night" (Ps 1:2 RSV).

In the psalms the law is considered so precious that it is treasured in the heart (Ps 37:31; 40:8). It is to be taught to future generations for their protection and well-being (Ps 78:5-8). The one who learns God's law is considered blessed (Ps 94:12). Psalm 19, which praises God's two books of revelation (nature and the law), turns on the picture in verse 6 of the sun's spanning the entire world, so that "there is nothing hid from its heat." C. S. Lewis comments in *Reflections on the Psalms* that in this picture the sun "pierces everywhere with its strong, clean ardor.

Then at once . . . [the poet] is talking of something else, which hardly seems to him something else because it is so like the all-piercing, all-detecting sunshine. The Law is 'undefiled,' the Law gives light, it is clean and everlasting, it is 'sweet.' No one can improve on this and nothing can more fully admit us to the old Jewish feeling about the Law; luminous, severe, disinfectant, exultant." These conceptions of the law depict the positive outlook on the law as God's benevolent covenant gift to Israel.

The psalms also contain a number of compelling metaphors and similes for the law. Meditating on the law is like a *tree drawing moisture from streams of *water (Ps 1:3). The law is so good that it is more precious than finest *gold (Ps 19:10) and *sweeter than *honey (Ps 19:10). In Psalm 119, the most extended celebration of the law in the whole Bible, the law is compared to honey (Ps 119:103) and *silver and *gold (Ps 119:72). The poet acknowledges the benefit to the young (Ps 119:9) and finds obedience a delight (Ps 119:34-35). The law becomes the psalmist's comfort in the midst of suffering (Ps 119:50-52). God's law is also a touchstone of wisdom and knowledge (Ps 119:97-104).

Law in the Prophets. The dominant image of the law in the OT prophets is that of squandered opportunity. Repeatedly the prophets appeal to the original covenantal relationship, with the law as the human obligation and response to God's favor, as something the nation has disregarded. Failure to live up to the duties required by the law is the constant regret within the prophetic books, and the law emerges as the prosecutor in a covenant lawsuit of God against his people (*see* Legal Images). The prophets themselves are covenant emissaries who bear messages of *judgment in reaction to Israel's response to the law.

The prophetic message is often negative, pointing to violations of the law and their consequences. At times specific aspects of the law are addressed (Is 44:6-20). At other times the people of God are accused of neglecting the law in general terms (Jer 11:1-13). In all events, the prophets warn God's people that their violations of the law are bringing covenant *curses (Hos 5:1-15). Unfortunately, Israel and Judah refused to heed the prophetic warnings and eventually suffered the curse of defeat and *exile from the land.

Despite the severity of the curse of exile, the prophets also bring a positive message of hope regarding the law. The covenant under Moses had established that God's people would not be forsaken to exile forever (Lev 26:40-45; Deut 4:29-31; 30:1-10). The prophets remind the nation of God's promise that repentance will eventually lead to restoration and tremendous blessings in their land (Amos 5:1-15; Is 40:1-11). The prophetic assurance of *restoration forms an important element of the imagery of law. After the exile, God promises to renew his people to the ideal of the law written "upon their hearts" (Jer 31:33) as something that everyone will obey

(Mic 4:2; Is 51:4). As a result, the future of the people of God is pictured as a time of wondrous covenant blessings, culminating in victory over enemies (Is 49:23-26; 60:12) and the eventual renovation of all *creation (Is 65:17-25). The law of God holds a central place in the eschatological hopes of OT prophecy. The future age of restoration will be a time of inward renewal resulting in delight in the law. It will be a revival of attitudes toward the law established earlier in Moses' original covenant and celebrated in the Psalms (Jer 31:31-34).

Law in the New Testament: Ambivalent Images. Jesus saw himself standing in Israel's prophetic tradition (Mt 24:37; Lk 20:9-15; Mt 13:57; Lk 16:31). As a result, he and his apostles affirm the covenantal imagery of God's law by proclaiming the twofold prophetic message of blessing and judgment. Jesus and his apostles lived in a time when many in Israel professed loyalty to the law of God. Yet much of this loyalty was divorced from the law's OT covenantal imagery. By a perverse twist the law became viewed as a means of gaining right standing with God (Gal 3:1-5). *Circumcision came to be the central symbol of commitment to the law as a means of justification before God (Gal 6:12). Jesus points out, however, that this affirmation of the law is hypocritical and legalistic (Mt 23:1-4, 13).

In response to this situation Jesus and his apostles taught the inability of the law to effect salvation. In this sense the image of the law in the NT is negative. Judgment awaits those who attempt to earn covenant blessings through the law because perfect conformity is impossible (Rom 3:19-20; Jas 2:8-11). Without forgiveness and restoration through faith in Christ, the law can only bring further curses (Rom 2:5-6). It is in this sense that the apostle Paul insists that those who attempt to earn salvation through the law "will be judged by the law" (Rom 2:12).

But Jesus also teaches a positive attitude toward the law. He affirms that he did not come to annul the law of Moses (Mt 5:17-20). He even insists that his followers must conform to the law even more than his legalistic opponents (Mt 5:20; 23:3). Throughout his ministry Jesus interprets the law in ways that demonstrate its benevolent character (Mt 12:1-14). He illustrates in his life and teaching how the law is to be obeyed from the heart by those who have been redeemed to covenant blessing by belief in the gospel (Mk 12:28-34).

The image of the law in Paul's writings is much the same. On one side, "the law is holy, and the commandment is holy and just and good" (Rom 7:12 RSV). Nevertheless, those who attempt to earn salvation by the law are bound to "the law of sin and death" (Rom 8:2 RSV). The law brings people into judgment and is powerless to save; in that sense it is an image of impotence and bondage (Rom 7). In fact, Paul says, the law causes sin to increase (Rom 5:20) and brings the knowledge of sin and produces death (Rom 7:7, 13). One of the great gifts of life in Christ is that it sets the sinner free from the condemnation of the law (Rom 8:1-4). The best that can be said for the law is that it was a benevolent "custodian" (Gal 3:24-25 RSV) or "schoolmaster" (KJV) or "tutor" (NASB) to lead people to Christ, whose forgiveness alone can save a person. While the image of the custodian or tutor might include the positive associations of instruction, surviving sketches of Roman tutors who accompanied school boys throughout the course of the day usually show them with a rod in hand, implying a type of oppression. This association is reinforced by an accompanying military image of the law as a guard that holds people as "prisoners" (Gal 3:22-23 NIV). Here is the ambivalence of the NT attitude toward the law: the law cannot save and as such delivers Israel into the bondage of condemnation, but it nonetheless serves a crucial purpose in bringing people to faith in Christ as their only release to freedom.

It is perhaps too simplistic to delineate three different types of OT law: the ceremonial, the civil and the moral. In truth those distinctions are not made in the OT. More helpful distinctions might be made between criminal, civil, family, cultic and charitable laws. It is safe to say that the cultic laws, those having to do with the rituals of the tabernacle and temple, are regarded in the NT as premonitions, or types, of the saving work of Jesus Christ. The NT views the covenantal system with its law as superseded by a new covenant in which elements of the old covenant law, such as those found in the Ten Commandments, are appropriated but subsumed under the "law of Christ" (Gal 6:2), which is "faith expressing itself through love" (Gal 5:6). Paul in particular makes it clear that all laws that erect barriers of Jewish ethnic exclusivity—exemplified in male circumcision, Jewish food laws and Jewish Sabbath laws—have lost their normative value under the new covenant. Nevertheless, as a record of the divine will for Israel the law provides numerous instructive moral and spiritual paradigms for members of the new covenant.

Summary. The law is a major motif of the Bible, where it is both positive and negative. Bearing the imprint of God's moral character, the law is God's blueprint for how God intends human life to be lived. At this level the law is "holy and just and good" (Rom 7:12 RSV). But because the human race cannot meet the covenant obligations of the law, it ultimately brings bondage, from which Christ's atonement alone can free a person.

See also COVENANT; DEUTERONOMY, BOOK OF; EXODUS, BOOK OF; GENESIS, BOOK OF; LEVITICUS, BOOK OF; MOSES; NUMBERS, BOOK OF; OBEDIENCE.

BIBLIOGRAPHY. C. J. H. Wright, *An Eye for an Eye* (Downers Grove, IL: InterVarsity Press, 1983).

LAWMAKING. *See* LEGAL IMAGES.

LAWSUIT. *See* LEGAL IMAGES; JUDGMENT.

LAZINESS. *See* SLUGGARD.

LEAD

Lead is a soft, silvery-white or grayish *metal commonly used in antiquity. Although not an attractive metal like *silver or *gold, it was used because it is very malleable, ductile, dense and resistant to corrosion and because it is part of useful alloys. The references to lead in the Bible are figurative.

First, lead is used to picture the sinking of the Egyptian army: "But you blew with your breath, and the sea covered them. They sank like lead in the mighty waters" (Ex 15:10 NIV). In a memorable passage Job yearns that his words might be recorded permanently. To that end he wishes that his words might be "inscribed with an iron tool on lead, or engraved in rock forever" (Job 19:24). Here lead's low melting point (327.5 C) and its malleable nature comes into play. It may be that Job is asking that his words be inscribed by an iron tool in *rock and those letters filled with lead. This corrosion-free metal, coupled with rock, would lead to a permanent record of his words.

Lead is mentioned in lists with other metals, always near the end: "gold, silver, bronze, iron, tin, lead" (Num 31:22), implying its relatively low value. This is also seen when Ezekiel describes it as simply a byproduct of refining silver: "Son of man, the house of Israel has become dross to me; all of them are the copper, tin, iron and lead left inside a furnace. They are but the dross of silver" (Ezek 22:18 NIV).

Finally, the melting of lead and other metals is likened to God's judgment: "As men gather silver, copper, iron, lead and tin into a furnace to melt it with a fiery blast, so will I gather you in my anger and my wrath and put you inside the city and melt you" (Ezek 22:20 NIV).

See also BRONZE; GOLD; IRON; METALS; SILVER; STONE; WOOD.

LEADERSHIP

The Bible is a book built on human experience, and the experiences of leading and following form part of the fabric of our existence. The Bible does not sketch out a theory of leadership, but as is so often the case, it comments on leadership more by showing examples of leadership (both good and bad) than by direct comment. In this article, analytic categories have been used to help classify the numerous cases of leadership. Many of these leaders served in some way in all of the categories (e.g., priest, king), but they are mentioned in their primary sphere of leadership.

The Quintessential Leader. Perhaps no other person in the Bible so graphically embodies the role and character of the leader as Moses. He serves as *prophet, bringing the word of the Lord to Israel and to *Pharaoh (Ex 3—11); as *priest, officiating over the first *Passover and the consecration of the firstborn (Ex 12; 13) and confirming the covenant between Israel and God (Ex 24); as judge and wise man, hearing the various complaints of Israel (e.g., the daughters of Zelophehad, Num 27:1-4); and as political leader for the nation of Israel, leading Israel out of Egypt (Ex 12:31—15:21), commanding military campaigns (e.g., the Amalekites at Rephidim, Ex 17:8-16) and directing espionage (e.g., the exploration of Canaan, Num. 13:1-3; *see* Spy Stories).

When examined according to the leadership of Moses, the characters of Aaron and Miriam present a marked contrast. Even though Aaron has essentially seen and experienced all of the works of God that Moses has seen, beginning with the preliminary negotiations with Pharaoh (Ex 5), he does not have the moral fortitude that a leader of Moses' caliber possesses. Aaron quickly caves into the people's demand for an idol; in fact, he facilitates their request by fashioning the golden calf himself (Ex 32:4). He also quickly shifts blame off of himself and onto the people, effectively denying the responsibility a leader has for his followers (Ex 32:22). Aaron and Miriam speak maliciously of Moses, their own immediate leader, and try to assert equal rights of leadership, claiming that God has spoken through them just as much as he has through Moses (Num 12:1-2).

Political Leadership. The most easily identified leaders in society are the various political heads of state that bear titles like prince, king, judge, emperor, Pharaoh, ruler and Caesar. The rule of these various leaders is never secure, and the Bible is filled with political intrigue as distraught family members, court officials, ethnic splinter groups, religious zealots and political rivals attempt (and often succeeded at) toppling the ruler. The king serves as a symbol for power and authority. Yet the biblical writers delight in showing how fleeting the power and life of a king actually is: the king can fall to a randomly shot arrow (2 Chron 18:33); the king can be assassinated (1 Kings 16:16); a king may be felled by mental illness (Dan 4:33); and a king may be deposed by a foreign power (2 Kings 25:7). The absolute power of the king and, at the same time, its fragile nature, is reflected in the proverb: "The king's heart is in the hand of the LORD; he directs it like a watercourse wherever he pleases" (Prov 21:1).

The image of God as *king is very prominent in the Bible (*see* Royal Court), as in Psalm 84:3, "O LORD Almighty, my King and my God" (NIV), and in Jeremiah 10:10, "eternal king" (NIV; cf. Ps 48:1; Dan 4:37; 1 Tim 6:15; Rev 15:3). The language and imagery of kings and *courts is used frequently in connection with God. Examples include God's royal courts (Ps 100:4), his *throne (Ps 47:8) and his *scepter (Ps 45:6).

In the wilderness we find Moses becoming weary as he sits judging all the cases brought to him (Ex 18:13-27). On Jethro's counsel he sets up a system of deputies to judge routine cases, with the more difficult cases being handled by himself. This system of judges is institutionalized in Deuteronomy which provides for the appointment of "judges and officials for each of your tribes in every town the LORD your God is giving you, and they shall judge the people fairly" (Deut 16:18 NIV). Under the monarchy, judges are employed to carry out both judicial and administrative duties. Under David, "Kenaniah and his sons were assigned duties away from the temple, as officials and judges over Israel" (1 Chron 26:29 NIV). Judges play an important role in Jehoshaphat's attempt to have the nation ruled by the law, and to this end he "appointed some of the Levites, priests and heads of Israelite families to administer the law of the LORD and to settle disputes" (2 Chron 19:8 NIV), and he charges them to "serve faithfully and wholeheartedly in the fear of the LORD" (2 Chron 19:9 NIV).

One of the more colorful sets of leaders to emerge in Israel are the "judges." The term *judge* here is really a misnomer and *governor,* or *leader,* seems more fitting. They arise during the time of the disorganization, discord and military defeat which follows Joshua's death. When the people "cried out to the LORD, he raised up for them a deliverer" (Judg 3:9 NIV). These charismatic leaders, who display no pedigree and at times lack what would seem to be the prerequisite experience, arise and serve as "deliverers" (Judg 3:9), and most seem to judge over Israel (*see* Samson).

While political and national leadership in the biblical world is largely masculine and patriarchal, we can actually find examples of a small number of women who fill virtually every leadership role that men fill. We read about *queens as well as the customary kings; the list includes Jezebel, Athaliah and Sheba. Deborah, termed a prophetess, is the only leader in the book of Judges who actually judges (Judg 4:4-5), and she also fills the role of military leader of an army (Judg 4—5). We also read of the prophetesses Huldah (2 Kings 22:14) and Noadiah (Neh. 6:14), and the wise person and teacher, the so-called Lady Wisdom, appears repeatedly in Proverbs 1—9.

Leadership in the Tribal/Social Realm. The sense of governmental control and influence was far different in ancient Israel than what we experience today. In the OT we find law enforcement carried out at the local level by the elders of the clan, and social pressure is far more powerful in day-to-day life than governmental decrees. For instance, when a man fails to provide for his dead brother's wife by marrying her, the elders summon him, and if he still refuses, "his brother's widow shall go up to him in the presence of the elders, take off one of his sandals, spit in his face and say, 'This is what is done to the man who will not build up his brother's family line' " (Deut 25:9 NIV). In the shame-based culture of Israel such a man's lineage is known as "The Family of the Unsandaled" (Deut 25:10). The leadership in the clan moves beyond the disciplinary, but this is the level where authority resides for the typical Israelite. It is here where the eyewitness (Deut 19:15), the wise person (Prov 9:9), the elders of the *gate (Deut 21:19), the teacher and Levite (2 Chron 17:7-9) exercise considerable sway.

Leadership in the Family. The family plays a central role in the very drama of redemption seen in the Bible. The parents, or more typically the elder figures within an extended family, are held up as figures of benevolent care who are generally well intentioned. Thus Jesus can say, "Which of you fathers, if your son asks for a fish, will give him a snake instead? Or if he asks for an egg, will give him a scorpion? If you then, though you are evil, know how to give good gifts to your children, how much more will your Father in heaven give the Holy Spirit to those who ask him!" (Lk 11:11-13 NIV). Within extended and somewhat complex family and household relationships, the parental figures must exercise wisdom and diplomacy.

Typically the parent is not portrayed as a benevolent dictator, but as a wise guide. For example, when *Abraham and his nephew's herdsmen dispute over limited water and grazing land, Abraham suggests that they separate. And Abraham defers to his nephew when it came to choosing their respective territories (Gen 13). Abraham, as with other patriarchs, should be seen as a princeling, or clan leader. The positive leadership of the parent is portrayed as consisting of loving (1 Chron 17:13), correcting (Prov 29:15), disciplining (Heb 12:7), instructing (Prov 1:8), providing (Mt 7:11), praying (1 Sam 1:27) and nurturing in the faith (Eph 6:4).

The marriage relationship, too, possesses a well-defined pattern of leadership in the Bible. The headship of the husband and submission of the wife are the implied pattern throughout the OT, and it is visibly imprinted—though subsumed and modified under the new order of Christ's headship—in the so-called household codes of Ephesians 5:22—6:9, Colossians 3:18-25 and 1 Peter 2:13—3:7 (cf. 1 Cor 11:3; 14:34-35). Within the structure of the headship of the husband and father, though, wives and mothers are family leaders, too. While religious instruction is more often a fatherly image (Ps 44:1; 78:3; Prov 4:1; 13:1; 15:5; 27:10), we also find mothers instructing (Prov 1:8; 6:20). The portrait of the industrious wife and mother that concludes the book of Proverbs (Prov 31:10-31) clearly shows her to be the leader in household management. And the story of Abigail shows a woman who, when her husband fails to function as a wise leader of the family, ably and honorably steps in to compensate for her husband's abdication (1 Sam 25).

The Integrity of Leaders. Throughout the biblical portrait gallery of leaders we find an implied or forthright judgment of their character. It is God in particular who keenly examines the integrity of a leader. Sometimes the judgment is implied, but at times it is explicit, as when David implores God to judge him according to his integrity (Ps 7:8) or when the psalmist remarks that David shepherded Israel with integrity of *heart (Ps 78:72). God exhorts King Solomon to maintain his integrity and promises him that if he would walk before him in integrity of heart, his throne over Israel will be established and preserved (1 Kings 9:4-5). A direct correlation exists between the integrity of a leader and the safety of his

tenure. The leader with integrity is guarded by righteousness, but his wickedness will result in his overthrow (Prov 13:6). And the entire history of Israel, from Joshua through 2 Kings is aptly named the "Former Prophets," in part for its prophetic evaluation of this series of leaders from Joshua through Jehoiachin.

The Leader Under Moral Law. Leadership connotes a heavy responsibility for the affairs of others, for the affairs of those who follow. The leader's place of power bears an exacting weight of moral law, placed there to bring righteousness to the mundane manifestations of leadership. Proverbs brims with admonishments for the leader, reinforcing the natural dictates of conscience and giving instruction on issues such as being faithful to justice (Prov 16:10) and assuring protection for the innocent (Prov 18:5), while executing justice against those who oppress the poor (Prov 14:31) and orphans (Prov 23:10).

Breaking moral law, even if those who err are only followers, can bring judgment upon a leader. This reflects the concept that a leader is inextricably bound to his followers, those whom he leads, not unlike the head is permanently attached to the trunk of the body. We see in the story of Achan how the actions of one man brings judgment upon Israel, even reaching the place of Joshua's position as leader (Judg 7).

The Courage of Conviction. Throughout the Bible we find leaders who honorably and tenaciously maintain their convictions in the face of opposition from peers, followers and enemies. The righteous leader is aided in this struggle by two endorsements, the inner prompting of natural law, providing a strengthening of resolve, and the confirmation of God's will. The prophet Ezekiel is an example of a leader maintaining his convictions in the face of public disapprobation. Ezekiel's life becomes a living parable for the people of Israel as he shaves his head (Ezek 5:1), cooks his food over excrement (Ezek 4:12-15), lies down for hundreds of days (Ezek 4:4-8) and does not *mourn for his beloved wife (Ezek 24:15-24). In the NT we find Paul refusing to cave in to pressure when "certain men from James" arrive in Antioch and influence even Peter to separate himself from Gentile believers. Paul openly confronts Peter for his hypocrisy and will not back down from the principle that justification entails the inclusion of Jews and Gentiles in one new humanity without the barriers imposed by Mosaic law (Gal 2:11-21).

Religious Leadership. When viewed from a social perspective, the pyramid of religious organization in ancient Israel is remarkably flat. Though there is a clear sense of hierarchy in the Pentateuch, the structure of high priest, priests, Levites and people is relatively simple, and it somewhat mirrors the concentric degrees of holiness represented architecturally in the sanctuary (see Sacred Space). We do not find layers of religious bureaucracy or officially numerous purveyors of religion. The formal religious leadership can be divided into three groups: those with inherited offices (priests and Levites), those with positions that are confirmed as a result of their giftedness (prophets, overseers, elders, spiritual leaders) and those that come through the agency of others (Nazirite, Samuel dedicated in the temple, Jephthah's daughter).

In Jeremiah 18:18 three categories of religious leaders are mentioned: priest, prophets and wise men. In terms of imagery, the leadership of these groups is best seen in some exemplary leaders.

Priest. The teaching of the law is a prime responsibility of the priests. They included Ezra, who "read [taught] from the Book of the Law of God" (Neh 8), ushering in a time of repentance on the part of the Israelites (Neh 9). A thought-provoking example of a priest is Phineas, the grandson of Aaron. The righteous zeal of Phineas, who drives a spear through the embraced bodies of an Israelite and a Midianite woman, is called an "atonement" and results in God halting a plague (Num 25:6-13).

We find the Priests and Levites teaching "throughout Judah, taking with them the Book of the Law of the LORD; they went around to all the towns of Judah and taught the people" (2 Chron 17:8, 9 NIV). The priests guide the people of Israel in a disparate array of practical functions, such as ritual *sacrifice (Lev 1—7), *atonement (Lev 16:29-34) and *cleansing from diseases (Lev 13). The priests also lead the people in the various *feasts that are celebrated before the Lord: the Feast of Weeks, Trumpets and Tabernacles (Lev 23).

The formal religious establishment, however, comes in for much criticism in the OT. The priests abandon their calling, set up idols (Jer 2:8), lead people astray (Ezek 7:26), seek after money (Jer 6:13; Mic 3:11) and become corrupt (Jer 18:18). This prophetic criticism continues in the NT, where we find Jesus not only declaiming woes against the Pharisees and teachers of the law (Mt 23:1-36) but telling a parable against the priests (Mt 21:33-46). Paul seems to have Jewish leadership in mind when he speaks of those who "killed the Lord Jesus and the prophets and also drove us out . . . they always heap up their sins to the limit. The wrath of God has come upon them at last" (1 Thess 2:14-16 NIV).

Prophet. The OT is replete with the character of the *prophet. The prophet acts as a liaison between God and people, bringing *judgment (Ezek 13), encouragement (Mic 4:1-5), exhortation (Mal 2:1-9) and visions of Israel's future restoration (Is 40—66). The prophet is to speak God's word, and this is done with integrity by minor prophets like Huldah (2 Kings 22:14) and major prophets like Jeremiah, whose words are so offensive that the king burns them (Jer 36). In the case of the prophetess Deborah, her leadership is vigorous enough to extend to the actual political leadership of Israel (Judg 4).

One of the clearest NT examples of the prophet is John the Baptist. John is a leadership prophet who calls Israel to a great act of repentance, a rebirth as a nation, by descending to the Jordan and recrossing the classic boundary of Israel in a reenactment of

their ancestors' entrance into the land of promise. John's eye is on a coming renewal, or deliverance, of Israel from her bondage—and the judgment of those who would not repent. At the center of John's vision is the "Coming One," Jesus (Mt 3:1-12; Mk 1:1-8; Lk 3:1-18). Another John, the author of Revelation, unfurls his apocalyptic vision in which the kings and empires of the earth meet their demise before the Lord of heaven and his Lamb.

Wise man. The wise man is often a counselor in government or state affairs. The OT archetype of the wise man is *Solomon. At the beginning of his reign the young king offers a sacrifice at Gibeon, and Yahweh promises to fulfill one request. Solomon asks not for power or riches but for a discerning heart, the ability to judge wisely. The story of the two contending women (1 Kings 3:16-28) provides a cameo of Solomon's wisdom, as does the visit by the Queen of Sheba, who personally tests his wisdom and then declares, "How happy your officials, who continually stand before you and hear your wisdom!" (1 Kings 10:8 NIV). Another memorable image of a wise man is Ahithophel. Both David and Solomon agreed that "the advice Ahithophel gave was like that of one who inquires of God" (2 Sam 16:23 NIV).

Negative examples of the wise man also appear in Scripture. The Pharisees and Sadducees are supposed to supply wisdom and counsel for the people, both in matters of religion and temple but also in matters of daily life. However, they are quick to demonstrate that theirs is a wisdom that runs against the grain of the *kingdom of God as they are emboldened to challenge Jesus himself for his words and behavior. These wise men grouse concerning Jesus' eating with tax collectors and sinners (Mt 9:11), they conspire to test him (Mt 16:1), and they plot to take his life (Jn 11:45-53).

The ultimate wise man is Jesus himself. He speaks in parables and aphorisms as a wise man, and he compares himself to Solomon, saying "one greater than Solomon is here" (Mt 12:42 NIV; Lk 11:31). He regards himself as an envoy of wisdom (Mt 23:34-36; Lk 11:49-51) and wisdom's revealer who beckons to Israel to follow (Mt 11:25-27; Lk 10:21-22), and he implies that those who respond to him are "wisdom's children" (Mt 11:16-19; Lk 7:31-35).

Military Leadership. In the OT, leaders of warfare are sometimes generals or commanders but frequently the king himself. Saul and David are outstanding examples of warrior kings, but we also find heads of state such as Sennacherib personally leading an army (2 Kings 19—20). The ideals of king and warrior were closely associated in the ancient Near East. There is also a close association between warfare and everyday life. We may observe this in the scene of the young shepherd boy David bringing food to his brothers stationed at the front lines (1 Sam 17). In the armies that were composed largely of untrained conscripts, it was possible for warriors to rise to formal leadership roles. During the days of Saul we find the Israelite army structure beginning to take shape, and it apparently includes both tribal leadership and people who have come up through the warrior ranks. In the English translations we find the captain, a leader of thousands, hundreds or fifties (Ex 18:25; 1 Sam 8:12). After Saul, Israelite armies are divided into companies headed by "captains of thousands" (1 Sam 17:18). Later we find that David's army is led by "The Thirty," those mighty men who had proven themselves as warriors during David's years as a brigand general.

The NT supplies at least one memorable image of a military leader. The centurion who entreats Jesus to heal his sick servant tells Jesus that he need not come to his house. All Jesus must do is "say the word, and my servant will be healed" (Mt 8:8). His explanation offers a glimpse of military leadership: "I myself am a man under authority, with soldiers under me. I tell this one, 'Go,' and he goes, and that one, 'Come,' and he comes. I say to my servant, 'Do this,' and he does it" (Mt 8:9 NIV). Jesus is astonished at the faith exhibited in this man, and then he commands, "Go! It will be done just as you believed it would" (Mt 8:13 NIV).

Representational Leadership. There is a strong sense in Scripture that certain leaders represent a nation, and the focus is generally upon Israel. This representation can be for ill; in Leviticus, for example, if a priest sins, he can bring judgment on the entire nation: "If the anointed priest sins, bringing guilt on the people, he must bring to the Lord a bull without defect as a sin offering for the sin he has committed" (Lev 4:3 NIV). In a positive way we see Moses interceding on behalf of the nation with the effect of staying God's hand of judgment (Ex 32). Perhaps this representation is seen most graphically in Jeremiah, who delivers a message to the nation that a judgment is coming that cannot be stayed even by the intercession of righteous ones. To drive home his point Jeremiah declares, "The LORD said to me: 'even if Moses and Samuel were to stand before me, my heart would not go out to this people. Send them away from my presence! Let them go!' " (Jer 15:1 NIV).

In a variety of ways, leadership is offered as people stand and represent Israel, but the most striking image of representational leadership is found in the tradition of kingship in Israel. In 2 Samuel 19:40-43, after the defeat of Absalom, the men of Israel dispute with the men of Judah over who has the greater claim on king David. The men of Israel argue, "We have ten shares in the king; and besides, we have a greater claim on David than you have" (2 Sam 19:43 NIV). Immediately following, Sheba son of Bicri, initiates his rebellion with the shout, "We have no share in David, no part in Jesse's son! Every man to his tent, O Israel!" (2 Sam 20:1). This notion of representational, or incorporative, leadership is found in the NT where Christ (the Son of David) and his people are closely bound. Those who are "baptized into him" (Rom 6:11) experience the reality of his representative death for his people. What is true of Christ is true of his people.

The Bible abounds with images and metaphors of both leaders and followers. In the list below, these are divided into categories of leader and follower.

Images and Metaphors of Leaders. Various traits, qualities and manifestations of leaders are articulated throughout the NT. The apostles are literally "sent ones," or "messengers" (cf. 1 Tim 2:7; 2 Tim 1:11), a *witness to God and the gospel (Lk 24:48; Acts 1:8). In the interest of maintaining humility and preserving that honor for Jesus himself, they should not take on the title of "Rabbi" (Mt 23:8). They should regard themselves as *servants (Jn 13:16; Acts 4:29) who, following the example of Jesus, "wash one another's feet" (Jn 13:14). In the same vein, Peter exhorts elders in the church not to lord it over the church (1 Pet 5:1-3) but to serve willingly and not for personal gain. Leadership also entails collegiality, and Paul calls Titus a partner and fellow worker (2 Cor 8:23) and so demonstrates his humility even while being the archetypal leader within the early church.

Jesus tells a parable of a shrewd manager [oikonomos], or steward, in a wealthy household who, called to give an accounting of his management, shrewdly deals with his situation (Lk 16:1-12). This image carries over from Jesus' setting into the world of Christian leadership, where a leader can take the role of an administrator (kybernēsis, 1 Cor 12:28). Other workaday images evoke agricultural settings, with the leader as a hardworking *farmer who "should be the first to receive a share of the crops" (2 Tim 2:6 NIV), or a *shepherd, exhorted to care for and feed the *sheep (Jn 21:15-16; Acts 20:28-29). Or the building trade comes into play as Paul likens himself to an expert builder laying a *foundation with others building upon it (1 Cor 3:10), or Timothy as a "workman who does not need to be ashamed (2 Tim 2:15). From another perspective the leaders of the church—apostles and prophets, with Jesus as the "chief *cornerstone"—form the foundation of God's new temple. (Eph 2:20). The Bible in general lifts up those who are "used" by God. It is honorable to be a leader who is a chosen instrument, or vessel, such as Paul (Acts 9:15), to be an article of *gold or *silver in God's household, "an instrument for noble purposes, made holy, useful to the Master and prepared to do any good work" (2 Tim 2:20-21).

Paul can evoke the dynamism of the sports arena in the image of the leader as an *athlete, dedicated to competition for the sake of God (2 Tim 2:5), or a disciplined *runner in a *race (1 Cor 9:24-27). These competitors are reaching out for the victor's *crown. But Paul just as often portrays the apostolic leader in paradoxically negative images: a fool for the sake of Christ (1 Cor 4:10), or one regarded by the world as scum or refuse (1 Cor 4:13).

What images are employed to portray the desirable qualities of leaders? The great leader Joshua, who meditates on Scripture (Josh 1:8), presents a model for all. Those who follow in his train are devoted to study of the law (Ezra 7:10), flee impurity (Is 52:11), are not filled with *fear (Jer 1:7) and do not trade in falsehood (Mal 2:6). The prophecy against the house of Eli is concluded with God's promise of a future leader, "a faithful priest, who will do according to what is in my heart and mind" (1 Sam 2:35 NIV).

Jesus shows uncommon "street smarts" as he sends out the Twelve "as sheep among wolves" and expects them to be "as shrewd as *snakes and as innocent as *doves (Mt 10:16). From the human world we have the image of a leader who does not "lord it over" others (Mt 20:25) but is humble (Mt 23:8-10), one who is faithful in small matters (Lk 12:42-44) and yet possesses spiritual power (Lk 24:49). A leader is not merely a "hired hand" (Jn 10:2-15) but a true servant (Jn 13:13-16), one who recognizes that it is ultimately God who is at work (1 Cor 3:5-9) and so seeks to be proven faithful (1 Cor 4:1-13). In this context, worldly boasting in one's own accomplishments is out of place (1 Cor 9:16-23). Paul, the apostle, led by God in the triumphal procession in Christ, spreads the "fragrance of the knowledge of Christ," which to those who are being saved is the fragrance of life and to those who are perishing the fragrance of death (2 Cor 2:15-17; see Smell, Scent). For leaders in Christ's church, integrity is essential (2 Cor 4:2): they flee immorality (1 Tim 6:11), do not act from impure motives (1 Thess 2:3) and avoid presenting *stumbling blocks for others (2 Cor 6:3). The truth of the gospel is a trust that is passed on, and so leaders must keep to sound teaching (2 Tim 1:13), maintain a singleness of focus (2 Tim 2:1-23) and faithfully exercise their gifts (1 Pet 4:10).

Images and Metaphors of Followers. As a picture needs a frame, or as a frame needs a picture, the character of the leader is nothing without that of the follower. Two sorts of followers are presented to us: those who are followers of human leaders, and those who are followers of God.

An example, in the good sense, of a follower of a human leader is Joshua, the assistant of Moses. Where Moses goes, there goes Joshua, even ascending the mountain of the Lord (Ex 24:13). Joshua is so diligent and faithful to Moses that he waits on the mountainside for him, staying forty days and forty nights until Moses returns with the tablets (Ex 32:15-17). Joshua remains faithful to Moses through the long years in the wilderness. Even though Israel does not trust God and rejects Moses' leadership, Joshua remains steadfast, even at the risk of his life (Num 14:6-10). Joshua's faithfulness is rewarded, and he is raised up and given authority after the death of Moses (Deut 34:9). But even after Joshua has assumed the command and leadership of Israel, he continues to be portrayed as a humble follower of the heavenly Lord, one who readily submits to the commander of the Lord's army (Josh 5:13-15).

The Bible is full of followers of God, but no single figure illustrates this as much as Jesus. Like the *suffering servant of Isaiah 53, Jesus is oppressed for the sake of his people but does not open his mouth in protest (Is 53:7), he is resolved to do God's will even though he suffers God's blows on behalf of his people (Is 53:4, 10). His life is a declaration of what it means to follow God regardless of the bitter consequences (Mt 26:39) of a shameful death.

Followers of God are chosen (Deut 10:15). They can be likened to good soldiers of Christ (2 Tim 2:3), willing to endure hardship. They are slaves of Christ (1 Cor 7:22-23), bought with a price and ready to do his command (Jn 15:13-15). Some are deacons, such as Stephen, called to serve the church (Acts 6). Or they are workers called on to bring in the *harvest at the moment when the grain has ripened (Mt 9:37-38). As disciples of Jesus they are also his *friends (Lk 12:4), agents of Christ's love (Mt 10:42) and known by their love for one another (Jn 13:35). Paul speaks of the Philippians as partners in the gospel (Phil 1:5), and one of them is his loyal yokefellow (Phil 4:3). Frequently in Paul we find the imagery of God's household (e.g., Eph 2:19-20). They may be likened to newborn babies (1 Pet 2:2) or to obedient, beloved *children (1 Pet 1:14; 1 Cor 4:14)—God's children (Lk 20:36). All are *saints (Eph 1:1), a royal priesthood belonging to God (1 Pet 2:9) and citizens of heaven (Phil 3:20). As witnesses to the gospel some of these followers are faithful even unto death (Rev 7:14), ever obedient to God and holding onto the testimony of Jesus Christ (Rev 12:17).

In more indirect metaphors, followers of God—the people of God—are pictured as a *flock (Ps 77:20; Acts 20:28-29) or as sheep (Jn 10:1-16; Mt 10:16). God's people are like a *bride or a bridegroom, lavishly adorned with the garments of salvation (Is 61:10), or even the guests of the bridegroom—Jesus Christ (Mt 9:15). They are the *salt of the earth (Mt 5:13) or the good *seed sown in the world and growing alongside weeds (Mt 13:38). NT writers employ the imagery of real estate and architecture by speaking of a building or a field belonging to God (1 Cor 3:9-11) or "living stones" in a new *temple (1 Pet 2:5; cf. Eph 2:20-22). Finally, God's people are like a *crown (1 Thess 2:19) or a treasured possession of God (Deut 14:2).

See also DAVID; GOD; JESUS, IMAGES OF; KING, KINGSHIP; MOSES; PRIEST; PROPHET; QUEEN; SOLOMON; THRONE.

LEAF

There is a curious dualism to the Bible's use of leaf as an image. It speaks both of health and decay, of abundance and inadequacy. Not surprisingly, there are many parallels to the use of the image of *fruit.

A variety of leaves were put to practical use in ancient Near East. For example, box tree leaves were used for tanning; black berry leaves were chewed for bleeding gums or applied to burns; fig leaves were woven into baskets; olive leaves provided an astringent; and sycamore and walnut leaves were used to dress wounds (see Jacob and Jacob).

On those *trees where fruit is expected, leaves, no matter how abundant, are insufficient. Thus one of the few *curses to come from the lips of Jesus is reserved for the barren *fig tree. Looking for fruit and finding only leaves, Jesus curses the tree, saying, "May no one ever eat fruit from you again" (Mk 11:14 NIV). The following day his words come frighteningly true (Mk 11:21).

On other occasions it is not only the absence of fruit but the presence of dropping and shriveled leaves that bespeaks God's anger against his people. Thus Isaiah warns the people that they will be "like an oak with fading leaves" (Is 1:30 NIV). Jeremiah describes the day when the trees of Judah will reflect the fate of its people: "I will take away their harvest. . . . There will be no grapes on the vine. There will be no figs on the tree, and their leaves will wither" (Jer 8:13 NIV). The leaves, useless for food, are doubly useless when they shrivel and die. The image of these shriveled leaves evokes powerfully the desolation of those who fall under God's judgment.

It is precisely this sort of picture that makes Ezekiel's use of the leaf image all the more striking. In his description of the temple's restoration and the Lord's return to fill it, he describes the river flowing from the renewed sanctuary. Along its banks are trees whose fruit is for food and whose leaves are "for healing" (Ezek 47:12). Here is the abundance of God's blessing, when even the hitherto limited but essential medicinal value becomes a source of true healing. So important is this picture of the trees on the holy river bank that it is repeated in John's description of the *New Jerusalem. This time the leaves of the trees are for "the healing of the nations" (Rev 22:2 NRSV).

There are other occasions, however, when lush foliage speaks of God's blessing in a more ordinary context. Thus the righteous person of Psalm 1 is "like a tree planted by streams of water . . . whose leaf does not wither" (Ps 1:3 NIV). The one who trusts in the Lord is likened by Jeremiah to a tree whose "leaves are always green" (Jer 17:8). On a tree where we would not expect to find fruit, it is the leaves that speak of life and health and God's blessing. Like the organic picture of the vine, this is a description of the vital relationship between man and God.

See also BRANCH; FIG, FIG TREE; ROOT; TREE, TREES; TREE OF LIFE.

BIBLIOGRAPHY. I. Jacob and W. Jacob, "Flora," *ABD* 2:803-17.

LEANNESS. *See* FAT.

LEAST. *See* SMALL.

LEAVEN, LEAVENING

Used since prehistoric times, leaven includes various agents, the most common of which is yeast, causing dough or batter to rise through the process of fermentation. Yeast, a fungus that ferments carbohy-

drates in various substances, is also responsible for the fermentation in making beer, wine and spirits. Yeast occurs widely on plants and in the soil.

Leavened *bread was the normal fare for the ancient Israelites (Hos 7:4). Several texts speak of omitting the leaven for various religious purposes. Directions concerning the *Passover rite, for example, insist that leavened bread could not be eaten for seven full days (Ex 12:15). In fact, leaven could not be stored within the Israelites' houses (Ex 12:19), or even exist within the entire territory of the nation (Ex 13:7; Deut 16:4). The rite assured that later generations of Israelites would not forget God's deliverance in their swift exodus from Egypt (Ex 12:34, 39). Later instructions about sacrifices outlawed combining many of the sacrifices with leaven (e.g., Ex 34:25; Lev 2:11; 6:17). On the other hand, the peace offering employed leavened bread (Lev 7:13), and the *offering of the first fruits of the *grain harvest consisted of two loaves *baked with leaven (Lev 23:17). This was an occasion for rejoicing in God's provision.

The physical phenomenon of infiltration, as the yeast fungus multiplies throughout its medium, provides the basis for a symbolic use of leaven or yeast. The effect can be either positive or negative. One of Jesus' parables about the growth of the kingdom depended on the understanding of the hidden yet pervasive effect that yeast has on a large quantity of flour (Mt 13:33; Lk 13:20-21). This is a positive image: the kingdom message will gradually permeate the world. But most uses of the image seem to regard the idea of infiltration as negative, and this may lie behind the commands to remove leaven from bread during the sacrifices. Worship of the true God could not be combined with other gods or religions. Unleavened bread symbolized this requirement of *purity of worship.

Similarly, Jesus saw the theology of some of his Jewish contemporaries as potentially destructive to his disciples. So, for example, he warned his followers in various places to beware of the leaven of the *Pharisees, Sadducees or Herod (Mt 16:6, 11; Mk 8:15). Though the disciples were confused, Matthew makes it clear that Jesus was speaking of the *teaching* of the Pharisees and Sadducees (Mt 16:12), also identified as *hypocrisy (Lk 12:1). Likewise, Paul uses the idea of leaven's ability to permeate a batch of flour to warn the Corinthians about the potentially destructive effect of condoned *sin within their church body (1 Cor 5:6; cf. Gal 5:9). Expelling the sin from their body was akin to removing leaven, similar to what the Israelites did to prepare for the Passover. They needed to be a "new batch" of flour without yeast—which, in fact, they really were (1 Cor 5:7): "bread without yeast, the bread of sincerity and truth" (1 Cor 5:8 NIV).

See also BAKING; BREAD; SIN.

LEBANON

A northern border to Israel, an abundant, fertile

standard of earthly glory, Lebanon is the source of fine *wood for Israel and a paradise in the Hebrew imagination. Yet it is home to *idol worship and so is judged by God and dominated by God's greater glory.

Lebanon is a region made up of two *mountain chains, the coast fringing Mount Lebanon range and the lesser easterly Anti-Lebanon range, separated by the Bekaa Valley. The biblical references are probably only to Mount Lebanon itself. Here elevated heights, which reach up to ten thousand feet, give Lebanon majesty and glory (Is 35:2; 60:13) and the reputation as being the "utmost heights" (2 King 19:23 NIV). The elevation is responsible for a heavy rainfall, which falls on the heights in winter as *snow. In places, the snow lasts all year (Jer 18:14). The high precipitation and the slow melting snows, coupled with porous aquifers (Ezek 31:3-4, 7), ensure year-round fertility (Ps 104:16).

Temple-Worthy Materials. The cedars of Lebanon represent the finest of earthly materials. Solomon studied the lightness and strength of cedars (1 Kings 4:33), bargained with Hiram, who ruled the area, and created a conscript labor force thirty thousand strong to log the Lebanon cedars for the *temple in Jerusalem (1 Kings 5). Using cedar, these men, working one month out of three, built a magnificent palace out of the forests of Lebanon. The famous cedar also provided the main supports of the temple. In Song of Songs the bridegroom's carriage is made of wood from Lebanon (Song 3:9), and in Ezekiel a fine *ship is built whose mast is a cedar of Lebanon (Ezek 27:5).

In several figurative uses, the once-mighty Assyrian empire is likened to "a cedar in Lebanon, with beautiful branches overshadowing the forest; it towered on high, its top above the thick foliage" (Ezek 31:3 NIV). In a riddle to an aggressive king, Jehoash compares the king to a thistle in Lebanon and himself to the great cedar to emphasize his superiority (2 Kings 14:9). In a story about *trees, the cedar is superior to all the rest (Judg 9:15).

Every aspect of Lebanon echoes the supreme beauty and earthly glory of the cedars; its *wine (Hos 14:7), flowing *waters (Song 4:15) and *animal life (Song 4:8) are celebrated. Abundant fertility is constant (Song 4:15; Jer 18:14). Its ravishing beauty heightens the eroticism of the *Song of Songs. The *bride comes from Lebanon with its fragrance clinging to her garments (Song 4:8). She likens her groom to Lebanon itself: "choice as its cedars" (Song 5:15 NIV). The psalmist lets the entire region serve as a metaphor for abundance: "Let its fruit flourish like Lebanon" (Ps 72:16 NIV).

Lebanon is a common midrashic figure for the *temple. According to one rabbinic interpretation, it is based on a play on words involving the root *Ibn*—the temple "makes white" the sins of Israel. The use of this metaphor is well-attested in the Bible and Jewish literature of the second temple period. As the cedars of Lebanon adorned the temple, in some sense

Lebanon could stand for the *glory of the temple (Is 60:13). This identification is made explicit in Ezekiel's parable of two *eagles and a *vine (Ezek 17:3, 12), and it may also be directly in view in Jeremiah 22:23, a declaration of woe upon King Jehoiakim of Judah as the "inhabitant of Lebanon, nested among the cedars" (NRSV).

An Echo of Eden. Lebanon plays a unique role in the soul of the Israelites. In extra-biblical references Lebanon is called the home of gods (see Shehadeh), and with its superabundant fertility, Lebanon seems to echo Eden (Ps 104:16; Ezek 31:9, 16). As the way to the *Garden of Eden was barred as a result of the fall (Gen 3:24), so there is something vaguely out of bounds about Lebanon, despite its allure. It is clearly placed beyond the lands given to the Israelites (Josh 1:4); it remains unconquered, and its riches are tapped by pagan proxies (1 Kings 5:1-12). Its created beauty is repeatedly exceeded by the Lord's glory (Ps 29:5-6; Is 10:33-34; Nahum 1:4); all of its riches combined remain inadequate as a sacrificial offering (Is 40:16). God's *glory dominates even Lebanon, the most glorious of earthly creation.

As the height of created *beauty, Lebanon serves as an image of eventual redemption. One day the *wilderness will be given "the glory of Lebanon" (Is 29:17; 35:2; Is 60:13). As Lebanon echoes Eden, it reminds us that God mercifully restores lost beauty: "In a very short time, will not Lebanon be turned into a fertile field and the fertile field seem like a forest?" (Is 29:17 NIV).

Pride That Is Judged. From its prominent stance Lebanon is a chief metaphor of *judgment. Conquest of Lebanon's finest cedars is a standard boast, a statement of *pride that is judged by God (2 Kings 19:23; Is 14:8; 37:24). Being "nestled in cedar buildings" is a metaphor for security based on human accomplishment (Jer 22:23 NIV). The prophets predict a day of humbling for the proud whom Isaiah calls "the cedars of Lebanon, tall and lofty" (Is 2:13). In judgment, "Lebanon is ashamed and withers" (Is 33:9; Nahum 1:4) and is "clothed with gloom" (Ezek 31:15). Jeremiah prophesies a scene of destruction for the palace of the king of Judah: "Though you are like Gilead to me, like the summit of Lebanon . . . I will send destroyers against you, each man with his weapons, and they will cut up your fine cedar beams and throw them into the fire" (Jer 22:6-7 NIV). Because her beauty breeds pride, the last image of Lebanon is one of judgment: "Open your doors, O Lebanon, so that fire may devour your cedars!" (Zech 11:1 NIV).

See also GARDEN; MOUNTAIN; TEMPLE; TREE, TREES.

BIBLIOGRAPHY. L. Shehadeh, "Lebanon in Ancient Texts" in *Quest for Understanding: Arabic and Islamic Studies in Memory of Malcolm H. Kerr,* ed. S. Seikaly, R. Baalbaki and P. Dodd (Beirut: American University of Beirut Press, 1990) 3-13.

LEFT, LEFT-HANDED

The left side and left-handedness play a distinctively

negative role in many languages. The word *sinister* derives from the Latin term that means "on the left side." Left and right, though, can be merely neutral descriptions. In the Bible we find both neutral and negative uses.

When used for directions, left pointed to the *north because it was on one's left side when facing *east (Gen 14:15; Josh 19:27). Abraham gave Lot the choice of directions to pursue—*right or left hand—with no suggestion that either was preferable (Gen 13:9). Most uses suggest no value or preference to either; they simply identify the one in question (e.g., Lev 14:15, 26; Judg 3:21; 16:29; 1 Chron 6: 39, 44; 12:2; Neh 8:4; Job 23:9; Dan 12:7; Mk 10:37; Lk 23:33). One should go *straight and not veer either to right or left (Deut 5:32). "Long life is in her right hand; in her left hand are riches and honor" (Prov 3:16 NIV; cf. Songs 2:6; 8:3). Paul uses *weapons of righteousness to defend his ministry in both his right and left hands (2 Cor 6:7).

But a few uses suggest a distinctly negative value for the left side. When Jacob stretched out his hands to bless Ephraim and Manasseh, he deliberately crossed his arms, putting his left hand on Manasseh the *firstborn (Gen 48:13-14). Joseph objected since the right hand of blessing ought to have been placed on the oldest. In a clear instance, wisdom inclines to the right side and foolishness (*see* Folly) to the left (Eccles 10:2). It is arguable as well that Jesus' reference to the outcome of the king's judgment of the sheep and goats shows the negative value of the left: the goats consigned to eternal fire are on his left hand (Mt 25:33, 41-46). One might conclude that Jesus shows preference for the right as the hand that naturally gives alms when he tells the disciples, "Do not let your left hand know what your right hand is doing" (Mt 6:3 NIV), though this is probably another instance where the two are interchangeable.

There are, finally, references that attribute military significance to left-handedness. Among the troops of Benjamin is a group of seven hundred "crack" soldiers who are specifically said to be "left-handed; every one could sling a stone at a hair, and not miss" (Judg 20:16 NRSV). In later Israelite history we read about ambidextrous bowmen who "could shoot arrows and sling stones with either the right or the left hand" (1 Chron 12:2 NRSV). Left-handedness is also a crucial aspect of Ehud's cleverness in assassinating Eglon (Judg 3:15-23). Commentators do not agree on whether Ehud's left-handedness is a handicap that he overcomes or evidence that he belonged to a specially trained caste of warriors or simply a neutral genetic inheritance. What is indisputable is that Ehud's left-handedness means that he carries his homemade sword on the unexpected right side, thereby escaping detection in his daring assassination.

See also NORTH; RIGHT, RIGHT HAND.

LEG

The leg appears as an image of human strength in several Bible passages. The psalmist points out that God takes delight in those who fear and trust him rather than placing their faith in physical *strength, a feature which is illustrated by the strength of a horse or the legs of a human (Ps 147:10). The strength of "a mighty angel" is indicated by his having legs "like fiery *pillars" (Rev 10:1 NIV). On the other hand, times of particular stress are indicated by an individual's legs giving way (Dan 5:6) or shaking (Hab 3:16).

The legs of the beloved's lover are said to be "pillars of marble" (Song 5:15 NIV), in response to which he declares that her "graceful legs are like jewels" (Song 7:1 NIV). To "smite hip and thigh" is a particularly vigorous form of attack (Judg 15:8), while to smite one's own thigh is a mark of sorrow and repentance (Jer 31:19 NRSV; Ezek 21:12). The custom of making an oath by placing the hand under another's thigh is referred to in Genesis 24:2 and 47:29. A proverb in the mouth of a fool is likened to the legs of a lame man, which may appear to be strong but just hang limp (Prov 26:7).

At a meal, the upper leg of an animal was considered one of the more choice parts of meat (Ezek 24:4) and to be given such a portion was a mark of honor, for example bestowed on Saul by Samuel (1 Sam 9:24). The leg is often singled out for special mention in the preparation of sacrifices (e.g. Ex 12:9; Lev 1:9).

See also ARM; FINGER; FOOT; HAND.

LEGAL IMAGES

Legal metaphors abound in the Bible. Indeed, the broad outline of the biblical narrative could be summarized as an extended judicial proceeding, going from the *sin and punishment (*see* Crime and Punishment) of Genesis to the final sifting of the Last Judgment. Given the importance of the Sinaitic *law and the Mosaic code, the rules of conduct for individuals and the ceremonial law, it is not surprising that metaphors drawn from the law and legal procedures recur. But there are dangers in too simplistic an approach to these matters.

As with all metaphors, figures of speech drawn from the law and legal procedures communicate in proportion as their nonmetaphoric content is understood. In the case of biblical metaphors this presents a difficulty, since a number of different and very diverse legal systems as well as many centuries of development are involved. The cultural history and presuppositions of Anglo-American or any other legal tradition should not be imposed on such material. A further problem is to know when, or whether, a passage or word that speaks through metaphor is reality or is reality simply expressed and transposed down for our understanding.

Arranging material spread over so many centuries and traditions is difficult in a short article. One distinction lies between OT and NT. Another, based on modern notions, would be to separate concepts from civil and from criminal law. Another, within civil law, would separate metaphors from the law of persons and those from other sources, often commercial law. (It is intriguing that many biblical legal metaphors are drawn from the law of persons, that is, the law that deals with the relationship between individuals. This underlines the personal nature of a relationship with God.) The most useful broad distinction for our purposes, however, is between metaphors drawn from substantive law (i.e., the actual concepts of law that are enforced, where necessary, through legal mechanisms) and those from procedural law, including legislation and court processes.

Substantive Law. In the NT most of the metaphors drawn from substantive law and legal concepts are found in the Epistles, notably those of Paul, who was, of course, a lawyer well trained by the Jewish standards of his day. That said, we should note in passing that, as J. D. M. Derrett in particular demonstrates, a good many of the parables of Jesus are well grounded in contemporary Jewish law.

Given the destination of most of the Epistles, it makes sense to look to Roman law to provide a content for many of the legal metaphors found in them. This is further justified when one finds that Roman law is in some instances the only legal system with the concept (e.g., *adoption), or provides a fuller content for the concept being pressed into service to communicate truth (cf. citizens: aliens).

OT metaphors largely draw on Jewish law or on the common legal traditions and notions of their time. Not many metaphors found in the OT depend on legal content, but those that do are illuminating. Outstanding, but limited to the OT, is that of the kinsman-redeemer-avenger, which, as its name implies, depends upon kinship. Other concepts, such as slavery, appear in both Testaments.

Kinsman-Redeemer-Avenger. The kinsman-redeemer-avenger is not known in other legal systems as a person formally designated and with particular legal rights and duties. The kinsman-redeemer was a near blood-relative and always male. This near-kinsman (or one of them, if many) had a duty to protect his weaker relatives. He had to *redeem property belonging to relatives when they had to sell land or goods (Lev 25:23-25) and even their persons when they had sold themselves into *slavery (Lev 25:47-55). For example, Jeremiah bought land belonging to his cousin at Anathoth because he was the kinsman-redeemer (Jer 32). In the case of *Ruth, it was important that the nearer relative give up his right/duty in favor of Boaz (Ruth 4:6). The kinsman-redeemer was also duty bound to come to the defense or aid of a relative in either a legal or an actual struggle. This adds meaning to Job's foresight of the Redeemer on his side (Job 19:25) and underlies the Lord taking up the role in defense of his people when he saw no one else coming to their aid (Is 59:15b-20). That God would act as such a redeemer proved his family connection with those he was to save.

The duty of the kinsman also extended to the levirate, the begetting and raising of children with the wife of a deceased brother so as to carry on his name (cf. the case of Tamar, Gen 38; see also Deut 25:6; Ruth 2:20; 4:1-6). This particular duty was still known in NT times, underlying the question put to Jesus by the Sadducees about whose wife would a woman be, having successively married seven brothers under the levirate law (Mt 22:23-33; Mk 12:18-27; Lk 20:27-38).

The near-relative might also act as an avenger, the avenger of blood being guiltless when executing the killer of a relative, provided the killer had not lawfully sought refuge in one of the six designated cities (Num 35:9-34; Deut 19:1-13). Finally, it was the duty of the kinsman to take the side of his relative in a court action. God, or the Savior, is often so depicted (e.g., Ex 4:22-23 [sonship]; Job 19:25-27; Is 59:12-20; 63:1-5).

All these concepts of a duty to aid and rescue reflect, through their metaphoric application, the relationship of God and Christ with a believer. However, the notion is not clearly presented in the NT, save in the function of Redeemer.

Citizens: Aliens. In biblical times one's presence in a territory did not necessarily mean that one could make use of its civil courts to enforce one's rights. Sometimes one could be subject to those courts, but only as a defendant. Criminal law and its courts usually applied to all who breached it (though note the case of Jesus, below).

The application of civil law to an individual was not territorial but was based on citizenship (*see* Foreigner). The usual form was that one carried the law of one's nationality (province or allied state) like a snail carries its shell. Whether or not one's "personal" law was in effect, or one's rights protected, depended on the laws of the state or the province one happened to be in. In the Roman Empire, of course, a Roman citizen had a special position, even when in a place where Roman law was not nominally the ruling law. These concepts are powerful metaphors of the relationship of a Christian to the ways of this world and of a non-Christian to the realm of God.

In NT times both Paul, the Roman citizen (Eph 2:19; 3:20; Phil 2:12, 19; 3:20; 4:18; Gal 5:1; Phil 4:3), and Peter, the non-Roman Jew (1 Pet 1:1), use metaphors based on citizenship or the status of the alien or of the peregrine (the non-Roman citizen who moved through the empire). Citizenship was the basis on which Pontius Pilate tried to send the case of Jesus to Herod Agrippa, since Jesus, a non-Roman, came from the territory in which Agrippa was the civil power (Lk 23:6-7). Peter, the alien (stranger) speaks from that experience (1 Pet 1:1). On his journeys Paul made good use of his claim to Roman citizenship (Acts 16:16-40; 22; 25-39), and he obviously therefore knew the importance of having a "special" citizenship. He was able to appeal to Caesar (Acts 25:11) with the consequences we all know. He presents the non-Christian as not being part of God's community (Eph 2: 12, 19; 4:18; Col 1: 21), while the Christian is an alien in this world

(Phil 3:20; Eph 2:19; cf. 1 Pet 2: 9-21). As a resident alien, however, one does owe a duty to the community one resides in to respect its laws and customs as far as possible. In the OT, resident aliens were subject to Jewish religious requirements, though they could also benefit from concessions to them as the Jews had been strangers in Egypt (e.g., Ex 12:19; 48-9; 22:21; 23:9; Lev 19:34; 24:22; Num 9:14; 15:13-16; Deut 24:14-15, 17).

Slavery. *Slavery was known in OT times, although it is not particularly used as a metaphor by the prophets. Most of the time, of course, the Jews were in no condition to develop a full law of slavery, and in any event the Torah restricted the concept. Slaves held by Jews were to be well treated. Slaves who were Jews were not to be treated as slaves but rather as hired workers (Lev 25:39-43) and were liberated at the seven-year jubilee unless they requested otherwise (Lev 25:47-53; Deut 15:12-7). Aliens were more severely treated and could be disposed of in a will (Lev 25:44-6). A Jew, slave to an alien, could acquire funds and buy his own freedom (Lev 25:47-50). Alternatively, his kinsman-redeemer could redeem him (Lev 25:48-9, cf. above).

Slavery was common in NT times, being known in Greek and other contemporary law, but was most fully developed in Roman law, a fundamental division in the law of persons being that "all men are either free or slaves," as an introductory law text from the second century A.D. puts it (Gaius *Institutes* 1.9). The concomitant notion—the freedman—only existed as a developed legal concept under Roman law. Jewish and Greek slavery was mild by comparison. Under Roman law a slave was owned as a chattel. While the owner might permit a slave to transact business, profits and losses went to the owner unless he decreed otherwise as an act of grace. Injuries to the slave were injuries to the owner. If the slave did an injury to someone else, the owner was liable; or he might surrender the slave to the injured person either for punishment or, by way of formal transfer of ownership, as compensation. Children of slaves belonged to the owner of the mother even if the father were free (or even the slave owner). In short, the subjection of the slave to the owner was total, the slave having no separate legal existence except in one or two minor aspects that we might today equate with laws for the protection of animals from undue cruelty. That said, an owner could kill a slave at will. Although some owners were kind and generous, they were not required to be. A "slave of Christ" and similar expressions indicate a commitment weakened in its impact by our ignorant sentimentalism.

Entry into slavery was accomplished by birth to a slave mother, by surrender as a captive in war or by self-sale. These last two modes provide substance to such texts as John 8:34, 1 Corinthians 7:23, Galatians 5:1 and especially Romans 6:16-22. Indeed, the last citation accurately reflects the Roman principle that in Roman law someone behaving as if he were a slave would find himself deemed to be one, and would not be allowed to argue or prove otherwise.

The major distinction between a slave and any other piece of property was that the slave might, by the expressed will of the owner, be freed. Under Roman law this made the person a "freedman," not a "free man." A free man or woman was born free, although he or she could become a slave. If freed, the former slave became a "freedman," a separate status in law. A relationship continued to exist between the former master and the former slave, now a freedman, and this is only found in Roman law. The freedman was bound to respect and aid his patron, and each was bound to look after the other if he (or she) fell into want or illness (a primitive form of social security). 1 Corinthians 7:22 therefore is explicable in Roman terms, not that of the Jewish law that Jesus refers to in John 8:35. Under other legal systems freeing a slave meant that one was free of obligations to him. Under Roman law the former master and former slave had continuing mutual obligations of assistance.

Fatherhood, Family Authority. Under all legal systems relevant to biblical studies, within a family it was normal for there to be a head of the household (Roman = *pater familias*). This individual, normally male, had extensive powers in relation to his family and to those owing allegiance to him, such as slaves, employees and those resident within the household (cf. aliens, above). His authority could have many effects, and persons became subject to it in various ways, *birth or *adoption being the route for children.

Adoption: Children. Adoption is the formal legal process by which someone leaves one family and enters another, becoming subject thereby to the authority of the head of the new family. Although many arrangements are now called adoption, true adoption only occurs when the legal relationships involved are properly dealt with. Adoption is referred to five times in the Pauline epistles (Rom 8:15, 23; 9:4; Eph 1:5; Gal 4:5) and, because all the addressees would have known Roman law, is likely to have a Roman referent in all cases. The concept was unknown in Jewish law. It was used in Babylonian law as the temporary basis of an apprenticeship, ending when the skills had been learned from the father/apprentice-master. It was used in Greek law for inheritance purposes only, adoption being a deathbed arrangement. Since Christians are spoken of as the adopted sons of God, and God has not died, a Greek referent is ruled out.

In Roman law adoption was bringing into a filial relationship someone outside the family, making them subject to the authority, care and responsibility of the *pater familias,* the father of the family. The father's relationship to his children was equivalent to that of the master over his slaves, described above. A Roman child, whether adopted or natural, was always under the authority of the father until the father died or chose formally to grant the child its freedom. Until that freedom was granted, the duties, responsibilities, errors and legal advantages of the child were those of the father in much the same way as a slave was the responsibility of its owner (see above). The fatherhood of God in the NT therefore has overtones that are not relevant in the OT. Although the OT father did have considerable authority, his power was not as complete as that of Roman fathers, to whom Paul refers particularly in writing to centers governed by Roman law.

Heirs, Heirship and Inheritance, Guardianship. The proper operation of the rules of *inheritance, whatever they be, are fundamental to most early legal systems. Family lines must be preserved and property transmitted from generation to generation. Adoption in its Greek and Roman forms was an artificial way in which this could be assured, but even there natural relationships were usually the basis of inheritance (except among the Roman emperors!). Heirship and inheritance were regulated by the rules of testate or intestate succession operating on statuses defined by the law of persons.

Irrespective of how the status as heir is attained, the heir is the person who inherits or who will inherit in due course. Often in biblical times the heir is spoken of as having a stewardship over the property to be inherited (the inheritance), especially if the person owning (the "father") delegates authority to the heir to act on his behalf. *Inheritance* is therefore a concept of property, whereas *heir* is a concept of succession, the designation being a matter of the law of persons, that is, of personal status.

In the OT the giving of the *land as an inheritance to the people is celebrated by many authors (e.g., Gen 15:7; Deut 4:21; 20:16; 1 Kings 8:36; Is 60:21; Jer 3:16). The Lord is spoken of as the inheritance of the *priests and Levites (Num 18:20; Deut 18:1-2). Sometimes the figure is inverted, as when the Lord is asked to take the people as his inheritance (Ex 34:9; Ps 28:9; 33:12; 1 Kings 8:51, 53).

In the NT, attention is turned to one's status as heir rather than to its property implications, depicting the Christian being made the heir of God, jointheir with Christ (Rom 8:17). In Galatians 3:23—4:11 Paul makes use of the status of the minor heir and the appointment of a guardian (the law) whose authority lasts until the heir attains majority. Elsewhere Paul tackles the problem produced by a strict application of the metaphors of heirship, showing that the status as heir belongs to those who are the descendants of Abraham through faith, not through the flesh alone (Rom 4:13-16; 9:6-8). In these ways the status of the Christian and the expectations attached are underlined. The situation of the "heir of God" is remarkable.

Wills. A common way in which a person becomes an heir is through a will, by which the testator arranges how matters are to be after his death. The Greek term *diathēkē,* however, goes beyond testamentary wills to all arrangements and is therefore properly used as when Jesus speaks of the "new testament" in his blood (Mt 26:28; Mk 14:24; Lk 22:20). The more strict analogy of the testamentary will is found in passages such as Hebrews 9:16-18 and Galatians 3:15, where the formalities of the law round out the figure of speech.

In biblical times a will might be written, or it might be declared orally before witnesses. Paul's comment that no person alters the terms of a will duly established (Gal 3:15) therefore perfectly transposes the legal form, and he goes on to use the law of inheritance to show that the promise to Abraham took precedence over the merely mechanical concept of physical succession (Gal 3:16-25).

Purchase, Sale, Redemption. Metaphors drawn from the world of commerce are to be found here and there in the Bible. Many of these are procedures. The concept of sale, for example, is frequently connected with other notions, such as self-sale into slavery; and, of course, the idea of redemption (buying back) depends upon concepts of sale.

The concept of redemption (buying back) is intrinsic to many of the biblical metaphors that draw on legal notions. As we have seen above, the duty and right of the kinsman-redeemer was to come to the aid of his near-relatives, in whatever way they needed. In the NT the Redeemer buys the Christian back from slavery to the devil or to sin (Rom 7:14, 25). Thereafter the Christian is seen either as freed into freedman status vis-à-vis his patron, God, or remaining as the slave of Christ (see above). An alternative view is that the payment made by Christ is not a formal redemption of a chattel but rather is in satisfaction of punishment that would otherwise be imposed on one guilty of breaking the law (see below).

Price. In sale or redemption the price is a fundamental part of the transaction. That the life of the Son of God was the price of salvation for Christians places an inestimably high value on the individual.

Earnest. Earnest *(arrabōn)* guarantees the later performance of a transaction or obligation or merely proves its existence. Various legal systems had slightly different concepts. We do not know with certainty to which Paul refers in 2 Corinthians 1:22 and 5:5 and in Ephesians 1:14. Jewish, Greek and Roman law contain variants of the notion, ranging from the evidencing of a transaction, to the guarantee of the future performance of an obligation through requiring the returnable deposit of some valuable item, to part payment of a price.

Seals. Linked with the notion of earnest is that of the *seal, a concept that appears throughout the Bible. A seal can have many functions in law, usually as a matter of evidence. A seal may show that something closed has not been opened or that it is inviolate and its contents hidden until the seal is broken. Darius seals the lions' den (Dan 6:17); Jesus' tomb was sealed (Mt 27:66); the bottomless pit will be sealed (Rev 20:3). Revelation 4 tells of the opening of the Book of Seven Seals, the seal there having many aspects. Although John is told to seal one prophecy (Rev 10:4), Revelation itself was not to be sealed

(Rev 22:10; cf. Dan 12:4; Is 8:16).

Legal documents were sealed both for authenticity and to indicate finality (e.g., Neh 9:38; Jer 32:10-11, 14). Haman and later Mordecai had their authority proved by possession of the king's signet *ring (Esther 3:10; 8:8, 10). Jesus speaks of himself as authenticated and validated by God (Jn 6:27). The Corinthian believers were a seal, a proof of the authenticity of Paul's' ministry (1 Cor 9:2).

A seal might additionally indicate ownership, as in the case of Christians (2 Cor 1:22; Rev 7:2-8; 9:4) and those bearing the mark of the beast (Rev 13:16-17; 14:9; 19:20). *Circumcision was a seal of Abraham's faith (Rom 4:11), both establishing its existence in fact and acting as proof for others.

Title deeds. Title deeds, usually referring to known landmarks, are important in biblical societies. In Jeremiah 32, as noted above, the prophet buys a field from his cousin and buries evidence of the transaction. The parable thereby uses a very formal legal procedure to indicate that the captivity to come will not last forever (Jer 32:8-15).

Lawmaking, Lawgiving. The power to make law for a territory or for a people and to enforce it is fundamental to law itself. The presentation of God as the Lawgiver can be thought of as a metaphor. However, as C. S. Lewis points out in *The Pilgrim's Regress,* there are times to question which way around a figure of speech works. Our lawgiving may be an analogy of the greater, not the greater of the lesser instance.

The giving of the law at Sinai may be seen as a typical instance of the imposition of a treaty upon a subject people, making them vassals of the superior. It can also be construed as a unilateral *covenant, binding on the subservient party, and with its provisions subject to conditions suspensive and resolutary. However, as is clear from earlier judgments (e.g., Sodom and Gomorrah and Gen 26:5), the law did not come into being at its revelation to Moses. Sinai was a restatement, not an innovation.

Compliance with the requirements of the (broader) law as elaborated by the priests and lawyers was thought, by NT times, to assure one of the favor of God and, for those who thought in these terms, of salvation.

Trial. At a trial, facts are ascertained and judgment given. These procedures of law courts are peculiarly adapted to transmitting meaning in a theology that speaks of transgression and *guilt; of accusation, trial and condemnation; of redemption and of judgment. These show clearly in both Testaments.

Prosecutor. In biblical times in the Middle East there was no necessary division of function between prosecutor and judge. A lawgiver or upholder might function in both capacities. Early in the biblical narrative transgression and punishment are seen in the story of *Garden of Eden. There the Lawgiver himself acts. No formal process, accusation, proof or hearing is involved (Gen 3). At the other end of the

Bible, the Last Judgment settles matters finally within the current space-time continuum. Though the books of record are inspected (Rev 20:12), procedures are summary and there is no indictment, plea or defense. Between Genesis and Revelation the mechanisms of the court are frequently drawn in to transmit meaning. Genesis contains many examples of summary judgment, without any separation of the functions of accusation, prosecution, proof and judgment. The *flood (Gen 6—7) is one such instance, *Sodom and Gomorrah (Gen 18—19:27) another. In the latter example, there is an attempt by Abraham at a plea in mitigation of sentence (Gen 18:23-33), which is granted, but its basis not found proved.

A clear NT example of the judge as prosecutor is the situation where the Sanhedrin having interrogated Jesus on the basis of inadequate witness statements, the high priest manages to get Christ to utter words that themselves could be construed as blasphemous (Mt 26:63-6; Mk 14:61-3; Lk 22:66-71).

Any person could competently bring an accusation before a judge, and the delation of an offender was a recognized civil duty. One obvious source of prosecutors was the witnesses to a civil or religious crime. Abuse was deterred by making an unjustified accuser liable to the penalty for the offense of which he accused another. In Zechariah 3, Joshua the high priest stands before the angel of the Lord with *Satan beside him and ready to accuse him. In that instance, however, the would-be accuser is summarily dismissed; and Joshua is invested with clean *garments, the meaning of the whole scene being then explained to the prophet.

Defender: the advocate. It was competent for someone to aid a party in a court action. This was the role of the kinsman-redeemer mentioned above. It is also the role of the Paraclete of the NT, the *Holy Spirit (Jn 14:16, 26). The Roman prototype was qualified both forensically and oratorically.

Witnesses. When there is a trial, evidence is required to prove the facts upon which the case depends. This is usually given by *witnesses, although documents are also evidence (see title deeds, above).

In modern times witnesses have two manifestations: in the investigation into crime, and during the proof required for a civil or criminal action. In both instances the role of the witness is passive—to respond to questions and give information. In biblical times the role of witness was much more active, the witness being expected to be persuasive and hortatory, impassioned delivery adding force to whatever facts are testified to. A witness was expected to stick to his story, to magnify it and to seek to diminish evidence pointing to other conclusions. It is a mark of the faithfulness of early witnesses to the truth of the Christian faith that the Greek word for witness is *martyr*—a word we now use often in ignorance of its basic meaning.

Many witnesses are spoken of in the Bible, including the witness of the Spirit and of believers (Jn

15:26-7). Witnesses to the truth of Christianity may be seen as participating in the long legal process in which we are all engaged and which will eventually come to a climax in the Last Judgment.

Judgment. *Judgment is the formal decision of a matter, often involving a disposition of matters for the future. As we have seen above, summary judgments are spoken of in the Bible. These are but foreshadowing of the Last Judgment. Inherent in such matters are questions of guilt and punishment, which may also involve inquiry and prosecution. These do not seem to be used as legal metaphors but are discussed elsewhere in this volume.

It is quesstionable whether the Last Judgment is to be entirely seen as a metaphor. It will be the ultimate evaluation of each individual and a determination as to the destination of each. Different passages indicate slightly different procedures, but it is clear that God will act as judge on the basis of law he has laid down. For the Christian the Redeemer is at hand, and the Advocate will have done his work well.

Although many view judgment as something dreadful (and it may be), it is important to remember that a favorable judgment is given in many criminal cases and that in almost all civil cases one party is absolved from blame.

Criminal Punishment: Redemption. Breach of the law may have civil or criminal consequences. Where what is involved is a criminal offense for which punishment rather than civil enforcement is the penalty, other metaphors are thereby drawn into play. The substitution of someone other than the offender to incur the actual penalty was known in biblical times, although it was by no means common. Nonetheless it is that concept, and that of expiation of guilt, which underlies many of the phrases in which Christ's death on the *cross is spoken of (*see* Atonement).

Summary. There are many legal metaphors in the Bible. One should be careful not to carelessly incorporate modern notions into them. When they are explored, their colors and textures add greatly to our grasp of biblical teaching. In the case of the traditional Pauline material, Roman law often provides deep meaning.

See also ADOPTION; CRIME AND PUNISHMENT; INHERITANCE; JUDGMENT; LAW; REDEEM, REDEEMER; SEAL; SLAVE, SLAVERY; WITNESS.

BIBLIOGRAPHY. H. Danby, *The Mishnah* (Oxford: Oxford University Press, 1933); J. D. M. Derrett, *Studies in the New Testament* (5 vols.; Leiden: E. J. Brill, 1977-1989); idem, *Law in the New Testament* (London: Darton, Longman & Todd, 1970); G. Horowitz, *The Spirit of Jewish Law* (New York: Central Book, 1963); F. Lyall, *Slaves, Citizens, Sons: Legal Metaphors in the Epistles* (Grand Rapids: Zondervan, 1984); D. M. McDowell, *The Law in Classical Athens* (Ithaca, N.Y.: Cornell University Press, 1978); A. A. Trites, *The New Testament Concept of Witness* (Cambridge: Cambridge University Press, 1977).

LEISURE

Leisure is more inclusive than *play. A minimal definition is that it is time free from work and necessity. But it is also definable by certain activities (including play, cultural pursuits, recreation and social activities), and in its ultimate reaches it is a quality of life.

Thus defined, the original image of leisure in the Bible is God's rest on the seventh day of creation: God "rested on the seventh day from all his work which he had done" (Gen 2:2 RSV). Even though God proceeded to bless this day of rest from work (Gen 2:3), at its origin it had not yet become linked with worship (God did not need a day off to worship) but only with cessation from work. There is a hint of aesthetic contemplation and delight in this original image of leisure, inasmuch as we read that "God saw everything that he had made, and behold, it was very good" (Gen 1:31 RSV). To this we can add the imagery of refreshment: "on the seventh day he rested, and was refreshed" (Ex 31:17 RSV).

Sabbath rest is thus the original image of leisure. It eventually became associated with a prescribed day of worship in the weekly cycle, a day that the Israelites were commanded to keep holy, to protect from the inroads of work and to devote to rest (Ex 20:8-11). By extension, the annual *festivals of the OT calendar were also days devoted to religious exercises and communal festivity on which the Israelites were commanded to "do no laborious work" (Num 28:18, 25, 26). These religious festivals are an additional important image of leisure in the Bible. The Feast of Purim is described in the book of Esther as "a day for gladness and feasting and holiday-making, and a day on which they send choice portions [of food] to one another" (Esther 9:19 RSV). The remnant that returned from exile celebrated the Feast of Booths with "very great rejoicing" as they "kept the feast seven days" (Neh 8:17-18), camping out with families and neighbors. Even the OT pilgrimages to the temple had a leisure dimension to them (like our familiar camp or retreat experiences), combining cessation from work, travel, socializing and worship of God.

Leisure in romance and courtship is one of the themes of the *Song of Songs. The main activity of the lovers in that book is to spend pleasurable leisure time together, usually in a beautiful natural environment, in a world seemingly immune from the time pressures of life in the workaday world.

The psalms also contain a latent leisure motif. Psalm 23 is a pastoral, metaphoric account of God's provisions for his creatures. One of these is leisure—lying down in green pastures and walking beside still waters. This is a retreat experience, an oasis in the world of work and duty. In another psalm we are commanded to "be still," literally, "cease striving" (Ps 46:10). The nature psalms implicitly call us to the aesthetic and religious contemplation of *nature, and one of them explicitly links nature with leisure (Ps 104:15, 26).

The life of Jesus affords additional images of leisure. One of Jesus' most characteristic activities was attending dinners as an invited *guest. On one of these occasions Jesus turned water into *wine to keep a *wedding party going (Jn 2:1-11). The Gospels contain episodes in which Jesus not only retreated to private *prayer and meditation (Mk 6:45-47; Lk 6:12; 9:28) but also commanded his disciples to retreat from the crowds "to a lonely place, and rest a while" (Mk 6:30-32). Jesus' discourse against anxiety, especially his aphorism that enjoins people to "consider the lilies of the field" (Mt 6:25-34), is in part an endorsement of leisure as a curb to the acquisitive urge and an antidote to excessive preoccupation with the physical necessities of life. An OT example of someone who "went out to meditate in the field in the evening" is Isaac (Gen 24:63 RSV).

Another side of the Bible's pictures of leisure is its perversion in a fallen world. Paul gives us a brief catalog of degraded leisure pursuits ("works of the flesh"), mentioning immorality, impurity, licentiousness, drunkenness and carousing (Eph 5:19-21). Self-indulgent complacency emerges from Jesus' parable of the foolish farmer whose hedonistic self-reliance is captured by his inner dialogue: "Soul, you have ample goods laid up for many years; take your ease, eat, drink, be merry" (Lk 12:19 RSV). The most extended picture of misguided leisure—leisure doomed by an attempt to get more satisfaction out of it than it can by itself offer—is the quest of the narrator in *Ecclesiastes (Eccles 2:1-11). The prophet Amos used *music to symbolize a society whose leisure has degenerated into idleness, luxury, shallow entertainment, drinking and the pursuit of physical attractiveness (Amos 6:4-6).

This, then, is the biblical image of leisure: a letting go of the acquisitive urge; a rest from labor; a giving of oneself to festivity, worship and contemplation. Its proper conduct requires vigilance to protect it from its potential abuses, but in principle the main meaning of leisure in the Bible is that it is good, something that God practices and commands.

See also BANQUET; FEAST, FEASTING; FESTIVAL; NATURE PSALMS; PLAY; REST; SABBATH; WORK, WORKER; WORSHIP.

LEND, LENDING

Lending and borrowing are terms Scripture writers use to paint portraits of *blessing and *cursing. The fundamental meaning of lending is the extension of provision and generosity to someone in need; that of borrowing is dependence and neediness. Proverbs 19:17 highlights this meaning: "He who is kind to the poor lends to the LORD, and he will reward him for what he has done" (NIV).

The element of generosity inherent in lending is insured within the Bible by a consistently negative attitude toward lending money for interest (Ex 22:25; Lev 25:37; Ezek 18:8). The essential generosity conveyed by lending in the Bible is captured by the command to "be openhanded and freely lend" (Deut 15:8 NIV; see also Neh 5:8-10). In the NT lending becomes an even more lavish image of generosity, as in Jesus' commands to "give to the one who asks you, and do not turn away from the one who wants to borrow from you" (Mt 5:42 NIV) and to lend "without expecting to get anything back" (Lk 6:35 NIV). In view of this ethical undertow to lending as an act of generosity, it is not surprising that the portrait of godly people in the OT includes the detail that "they are always generous and lend freely; their children will be blessed" (Ps 37:26 NIV).

As a logical extension of the fact that "the rich rule over the poor, and the borrower is servant to the lender" (Prov 22:7 NIV), the mere ability to lend is an image of *prosperity and power. In fact, it becomes an index to covenant blessing and obedience: "For the LORD your God will bless you as he has promised, and you will lend to many nations but will borrow from none. You will rule over many nations but none will rule over you" (Deut 15:6 NIV). Again, "The LORD will open the heavens, the storehouse of his bounty, to send rain on your land in season and to bless all the work of your hands. You will lend to many nations but will borrow from none. The LORD will make you the head, not the tail. If you pay attention to the commands of the LORD your God that I give you this day and carefully follow them, you will always be at the top, never at the bottom." (Deut 28:12-13 NIV).

The ability to lend to others came from the Lord's abundant material blessings to Israel; ability to lend signified God's favor on individuals and the nation as a whole. Conversely, if Israel did not follow God, "The alien who lives among you will rise above you higher and higher, but you will sink lower and lower. He will lend to you, but you will not lend to him. He will be the head, but you will be the tail" (Deut 28:43-44 NIV). The absence of God's favor manifested itself in the need to borrow (Neh 5:4).

The manner in which people lend is one of the characteristics that defines them as righteous or unrighteous. Because the Lord is a compassionate God, specific laws are given to govern the process of lending in order to protect borrowers and to show how God calls his people to imitate the compassion and *mercy he has shown them (Ex 22:25; Lev 25:36-37; Deut 23:19-20; 24:10-17). Scripture extols the righteous for generosity and graciousness in lending (Ps 37:26; 112:5; Prov 19:17). Ezekiel differentiates a righteous father and his evil son by the manner in which they lend. The righteous father does not lend at excessive interest, but the evil son "lends at usury and takes excessive interest" (Ezek 18:13 NIV).

The Bible says little about borrowing, but the low status of the borrower is implicit in the statements about lending. While Israelites are free to lend to foreigners, they are commanded not to borrow from the surrounding nations. Balancing the promise that if Israel obeys she will "lend to many nations but will borrow from none" (Deut 18:12) is the fact that among the curses is the threat that an alien "will lend to you, but you will not lend to him" (Deut 28:44), thus making Israel the "servant to the lender" (Prov 22:7 NIV).

Ancient Near Eastern culture was not a society in which loans for commercial or business purposes would have occurred. Borrowers were men and women in desperate situations unable to provide food, clothing or shelter for themselves. The ostensibly small detail of the recorded cry of the man whose iron axhead fell into the water speaks volumes: "Oh, my lord, . . . it was borrowed!" (2 Kings 6:5 NIV). The status of borrower to lender is parallel to that of debtor to creditor or buyer to seller (Is 24:2). Lest we paint the borrower in wholly pitiable terms, however, we have a reminder that borrowers can be scoundrels too: "The wicked borrow and do not repay" (Ps 37:21 NIV).

See also ABUNDANCE; POVERTY; PROSPERITY; WEALTH.

LEOPARD. *See* ANIMALS.

LEPER, LEPROSY

The biblical word traditionally translated "leprosy" does not (at least usually) refer to what we call leprosy (Hansen's disease) but rather covers a variety of *skin *diseases, including the different forms of psoriasis and vitiligo (both of which make the skin white, cf. 2 Kings 5:27). The leprosy in Leviticus that contaminates clothing or a house is mold or mildew (Lev 13:47-59; 14:33-57).

These diseases are associated with uncleanness and entail segregation from others (cf. Num 5:2; 2 Kings 15:5; 2 Chron 26:16-21). But that segregation is not complete isolation; for although Leviticus 13:46 might mean that lepers should live by themselves, in both Testaments lepers have dealings with other people (cf. 2 Kings 7:3; Mk 14:3). One nowhere reads of leper colonies. On the contrary, lepers advertise their presence by wearing ragged clothing, looking unkempt and crying, "Unclean, unclean" (Lev 13:45).

The legislation on leprosy, which makes unpleasant reading, appears in Leviticus 13—14. It is addressed to priests and is intended to give them the expertise to diagnose when a skin eruption is truly leprous. It also instructs what rituals should be performed upon remission. There is nothing said about hygiene or treatment.

Lepers are the living dead. In Numbers 12:12 the flesh of the leper is "as of one dead," and in Job 18:13 Job's skin "is consumed, the firstborn of death consumes his limbs" (RSV). When the unnamed king of Israel is asked to heal a leper, he responds with, "Am I God, to kill and to make alive, that this man sends words to me to cure a man of his leprosy?" (2 Kings 5:7 RSV).

Leprosy can be a divine punishment, as in Numbers 12:9-16 (Miriam; cf. Deut 24.8-9), 2 Kings 5:27 (Gehazi) and 2 Chronicles 26:20 (King Uzziah; cf. Lev 14:34). But God in his *mercy also heals lepers. Instances include Numbers 12 (Miriam's seven-day

leprosy), 2 Kings 5:1-14 (Elisha heals Naaman), Mark 1:40-45 (Jesus heals an unnamed leper) and Luke 17:11-19 (Jesus heals ten Samaritan lepers).

Because of the dreadful effects of leprosy and the isolation it brings, many see it as a picture of sin. But that is not a primary connotation in Scripture. It far more symbolizes the tragic element of life and human vulnerability.

When Elisha declares, "Let him [Naaman] come now to me, that he may know that there is a prophet in Israel" (2 Kings 5:8), the implication is that only a prophet can heal leprosy. This is consistent with the circumstance that it is Moses, Elisha and Jesus who heal lepers in the Bible. It also helps explain Matthew 11:5 and Luke 7:22, where Jesus refers to his ability to heal lepers as a sign that he is "the coming one" (although Mt 10:8 also gives the authority to heal lepers to the disciples).

The beggar in Jesus' parable of the rich man and Lazarus (Lk 16:19-31) is said to have "sores" that the dogs lick. Although the text is silent on the matter, tradition has specified his disease as leprosy. This explains the designation of medieval leper houses as "Lazaries," the depiction of Lazarus of Bethany as a leper (for he has often been conflated with the figure in Luke's parable) and the use of "Lazarushian" as an adjective for leprous conditions (as in Kipling's words about Gunga Din having "Lazarushian leather").

See also DISEASE AND HEALING; SKIN.

LEPROSY. *See* LEPER, LEPROSY.

LETTER. *See* EPISTLE.

LEVIATHAN. *See* MONSTERS; MYTHICAL ANIMALS.

LEVITICUS, BOOK OF

The book of Leviticus embodies a symbolic universe of tangible imagery hardly paralleled in the rest of Scripture. It enshrines the old pattern of approaching God that typified the coming age of faith in Christ. Its distinctive assemblage of figures combines to present the sensitive reader with a lavish picture of what a relationship with the living God is like.

In Romans 10:5 Paul contrasts Leviticus and its precepts with what he calls the "righteousness that is by faith." With Christ's coming, a person's relationship to God is no longer found in relation to the symbolic order of Leviticus. Yet the *law presents us with symbols that are still applicable and enlightening today. The book of *Hebrews calls the Levitical order a "shadow of the good things to come" (Heb 10:1). Hebrews uses the laws and rituals in Leviticus to shed light on the significance of Christ's work. It invites us to approach the law with a view to finding images and symbols that enhance our appreciation of the way to God, his character, salvation and eternal things.

Paul cites Deuteronomy 25:4, "Do not muzzle

an ox when it is treading out the grain," and claims that God is not really concerned with *oxen in this commandment (1 Cor 9:9). It was really written for people. In the same way, in Leviticus God commands the Israelites not to eat any unclean *animal. In Acts 10:9-29 God shows Peter these beasts and tells him to kill and eat them. Peter eventually understands this to mean that he should accept Gentiles into the church. Thus many of the commands in Leviticus may be understood within their full canonical context as images applicable to people and their relationship to God, not only to animals or seed. (Deut 22:10 commands that an ox and an ass should not be *yoked together, and Paul in 2 Cor 6:14 seems to read this as an image concerning *marriage.)

One of the most significant images in Leviticus is that of *holiness. The command "Be holy as I am holy" is found sandwiched within a passage on unclean animals that are detestable to eat (Lev 11:44). Everything that is not holy is considered common (Lev 10:10). Common things divide into two categories, the clean and the unclean. *Cleanness in Leviticus is connected with the concept of *wholeness or completeness. Some things are by nature unclean: an animal that the Israelites would have perceived as an odd assortment of incongruous parts is considered unclean. Thus an animal that lives in the water but does not have fins and scales is not "normal" and therefore unfit for human ingestion. But persons or objects that are not categorically unclean, but are clean, can be made unclean, and they will remain unclean until they are made clean again through the means prescribed by the law. Clean things are "pure." All unclean animals in some way do not fit within normal categories and thus are unclean. Mixtures are an abomination. (This can be taken as an image that shows how the mixing of Israelite seed with Gentile seed should be shunned.)

Clean things can become holy when they are sanctified. A clean person or thing can be made either holy or unclean through contact with a sacred or polluted object. However the holy and the unclean must never come into contact with each other (e.g., if an unclean person eats holy food, he will be cut off). In the same way, anyone with a physical defect could not minister at the altar. As "cleanness" means "normal" or "pure," so "holiness" means "set apart, special." Certain objects and persons are "sanctified" or made holy in order to be fit to draw close to God's localized presence in the Tent of Meeting. A holy people are people who attend to propriety and order, preparing themselves to meet the transcendent God. Holiness is ultimately imaged in *God as the absolute Other who will not dwell among an imperfect people in a disorderly world. Only through sacrifice can God's attitude toward unclean people be changed so that he will make them holy.

A second powerful and graphic image (that comprises the first seventeen chapters of Leviticus) is the image of *sacrifice. Sacrifices of animals are required in Leviticus in order to make an unclean person or thing clean, or to make a clean person or thing holy. Israelite sacrifice is concerned with restoring the relationship between the people and God. In the Pentateuch we find the *Sinai *covenant creating a fellowship characterized by life, order and harmony. Outside this covenant is the realm of death and disorder. Sin, *disease or anything else that disturbs this order is a potential threat to the well-being of all Israel. Sacrifice restores order to the community.

One image associated with sacrifice is the worshiper confessing sin and laying his hands upon the head of the sacrificial victim. Thus the worshiper identifies himself with the doomed animal and offers it as a *ransom for his sins. Another image is the sprinkling of *blood on objects that are being made sacred. The life of the creature is the blood. Therefore eating flesh with the blood in it is regarded as taking from the life-giving God what is properly his. (Animals are expected to conform to the Sinai covenant. Animals must enjoy a *sabbath rest. The *birds of prey are detestable because they eat carrion and flesh from which the blood has not been drained properly.) The blood of the ordination ram is smeared on Aaron and his sons, thus making them holy and able to minister before the holy God on Israel's behalf.

Each bloody sacrifice provides a different image of *sin. The burnt offering portrays the person as guilty sinner, ransomed by the death of an unblemished animal. The sin offering depicts sin as that which makes the world dirty and which the blood of the animal must cleanse. The reparation offering pictures sin as a debt that a person incurs against God, paid through the offered animal.

Another sacrificial image is found in Leviticus 14:6, which recounts the rituals prescribed for the leper. This description is somewhat parallel to the manner by which Israel was made holy during the Passover event, when hyssop was used to sprinkle blood over the leper. Thus all Israel can be seen as leprous and in need of cleansing through the shedding of blood to become clean—and holy. The Day of *Atonement is the annual event on which the sin and uncleanness of all Israel are to be atoned for (Lev 16). Aaron offers two goats. The first is slaughtered at the altar. Aaron then lays his hands on the head of the other and confesses all the sins of Israel over it. The goat is then driven into the *wilderness. Thus both goats effectively cease to exist. The first disintegrates and dissolves into nothingness at the *altar, and the second disappears into the *chaos (symbolized by wilderness) outside the community of faith. One drew too near and the other too far away from God.

Just as there is no forgiveness of sins without the shedding of blood, so also in Leviticus there is no sacrifice without fire. *Fire is another powerful image in Leviticus. All sacrifices are consumed by fire. The fire at the altar is a perpetual fire, maintained vigilantly throughout each night (Lev 6:12-13). This fire has its source with God—since God originally lit it with fire from his presence (Lev 9:24). This fire consumed the first offerings made by Aaron and his sons in the midst of great joy; soon thereafter it also consumed Aaron's sons since they offered illegal fire (Lev 10:1-2). The fire offered by the priests reflects the divine conflagration. This fiery God "cooks" the sacrifices with his own flame—and savors the aroma.

The image of the fire of *judgment that consumes sinners or their ransom echoes throughout the Bible. Jesus' messianic ministry is distinguished by his baptism with the Spirit and unquenchable fire (Lk 3:16-17). Jesus cries, "I have come to bring fire on the earth, and how I wish it were already kindled!" (Lk 12:49 NIV). The eternal flame of Leviticus, which set ablaze the original altar fire and which perpetually consumed animal sacrifices, is an image of that eschatological judgment which will consume the world, cleansing it from all uncleanness and purifying and sanctifying God's dwelling place, his people.

See also ABOMINATION; ATONEMENT; BLOOD; CLEANSING; FIRE; GUILT; HOLINESS; PURITY; SACRED SPACE; SACRIFICE; SIN.

BIBLIOGRAPHY. D. Davies, "An Interpretation of Sacrifice in Leviticus," *ZAW* 89 (1977) 387-99; M. Douglas, *Purity and Danger: An Analysis of the Concepts of Pollution and Taboo* (London: Roultedge & Kegan Paul, 1966); G. J. Wenham, *The Book of Leviticus* (NICOT; Grand Rapids: Eerdmans, 1979).

LIBERTY. *See* BONDAGE AND FREEDOM.

LIGHT

The Bible is enveloped by the imagery of light, both literally and figuratively. At the beginning of the biblical narrative, physical light springs forth as the first created thing (Gen 1:3-4). At the end of the story the light of God obliterates all traces of *darkness: "And night shall be no more; they need no light of lamp or sun, for the Lord God will be their light" (Rev 22:5 RSV). Between these two beacons the imagery of light makes nearly two hundred appearances, with light emerging as one of the Bible's major and most complex symbols.

Physical Light. Light in the Bible is first of all physical, the very basis of life on the earth. This primacy of light to life itself is signaled in the Bible by the fact that God's creation of light is the first recorded event: "And God said, 'Let there be light'; and there was light. And God saw that the light was good" (Gen 1:3-4 RSV). Here is the wonder of existence springing from nonexistence, breathtaking in its suddenness and illuminating power. The apostle Paul conveys this sense of wonder over the primal creation of physical light when he links it to the life-transforming experience of conversion: "For it is God who said, 'Let light shine out of darkness,' who has shone in our hearts to give the light of the knowledge of the glory of God in the face of Christ" (2 Cor 4:6 RSV).

The first thing that biblical writers note about physical light is thus that God made it. In contrast to the pagan impulse to deify the heavenly bodies for their light-giving properties, the writers of the Bible consistently separate light from its Creator, making it an index to the divine instead of deity itself. The greatest example is Psalm 148, where the *sun, *moon and *stars are commanded to praise the Lord. And why are they thus commanded? "For [God] commanded and they were created" (Ps 148:5 RSV).

The Conflict Between Light and Darkness. Primitive thinking begins by dividing reality into a dichotomy between light and darkness, viewed as combatants in a perpetual battle for dominance. When light dawns, *chaos is again averted. We catch the strains of this primitive outlook in the Bible's *creation story, where "God separated the light from the darkness" (Gen 1:4). It is impossible to understand the biblical imagery of light without seeing it as the great antithesis and conqueror of darkness.

With the conflict between light and darkness as a context, light has the properties of rulership over the universe, with an accompanying sense of awe such as a subject might feel toward a benevolent king. We find this motif of rulership in the creation account when on the fourth day of creation God "made the two great lights, the greater light to rule the day, and the lesser light to rule the night" (Gen 1:16 RSV). As an image of order, light is the ally of people and their civilized enterprises, protecting them as they battle the forces of chaos and danger.

To the primitive mind, moreover, light is shrouded in mystery, and it retains this quality in the Bible. The voice from the whirlwind in the book of Job includes in its catalog of questions about the mystery of the origin of natural forces the query, "Where is the way to the dwelling of light?" (Job 38:19 RSV). And again, "What is the way to the place where the light is distributed?" (Job 38:24 RSV).

Along with reverence before the mystery of light, biblical writers express a terror about its absence. We catch this strain, for example, in Job's picture of deposed rulers who "grope in the dark without light" (Job 12:25 RSV) or in Isaiah's apocalyptic vision of light "darkened by its clouds" (Is 5:30) or in Jesus' metaphoric vision of good eyesight's producing a "whole body" full of light and its opposite producing a "whole body" full of darkness (Mt 6:22-23). Related are Jesus' memorable pictures of the futility of lighting a *lamp and putting it under a basket (Mt 5:15) and of the need to work "while it is day; night comes, when no one can work" (Jn 9:4 RSV).

Physical Light in the Biblical Story. Physical light retains its life-giving and protective qualities throughout the Bible, and the people who inhabit the biblical world, along with the writers who tell their story, are filled with a sense of reverential dependence on physical light. In such a world, light denotes safety. While the Egyptians were enshrouded in darkness, "all the people of Israel had light where they dwelt" (Ex 10:23 RSV). On the Israelites' subsequent march through the wilderness, God led the traveling community "by night in a pillar of fire to give them light, that they might travel" (Ex 13:21 RSV).

In the elemental world of the Bible, people live in close correspondence to the daily cycle of sunrise and nightfall. The light of dawn signals the beginning of momentous human activity. Thus it is in the early morning that Abraham sets out on his quest to sacrifice his son Isaac (Gen 22:3), that David sets out with his army (1 Sam 29:10-11), that God protects his holy city (Ps 46:5, dawn being the customary time to attack a city) and that Jesus rose from the grave. The light of dawn is also universally a time when the catastrophes of the preceding night are revealed—when the negligent Levite discovers his abused concubine dead at the doorstep (Judg 19:26-27) and the survivors of the Assyrian army find 185,000 dead bodies in their camp (1 Kings 19:35).

The book of Job is a case study in the imagery of light versus darkness. Job's early speech of despair in which he laments that he was born (Job 3) is a curse on light, which is associated with life, and a plea for darkness, which is associated with nonbeing or death. Job's deficient pictures of the *afterlife are similarly pictured as the extinguishing of light, as in the description of death as "the land of gloom and chaos; where light is as darkness" (Job 10:22 RSV). The ruin of the wicked is portrayed by Bildad in terms of light being put out and of the light being "dark in his tent" (Job 18:5-6 RSV).

Not surprisingly, the poets of the Bible give us the most rapturous pictures of the life-giving and illuminating properties of physical light. The nature poetry of the Bible and the psalms of praise are the greatest repository: God has "prepared the light and the sun" (Ps 74:16 KJV); God covers himself "with light as with a garment" (Ps 104:2 RSV); God's omnipresence is so powerful that "darkness is as light with thee" (Ps 139:12 RSV). The ultimate praise of light comes from the pen of an author who is mistakenly considered by some to be a nihilist: "Light is sweet, and it is pleasant for the eyes to behold the sun" (Eccles 11:7 RSV).

If the birth of light energized the Bible's stories of origin, the extinguishing of light is one of the notable archetypes in the Bible's *apocalyptic visions of the end. In the OT visions we read that "the stars of the heavens . . . will not give their light; the sun will be dark at its rising" (Is 13:10 RSV) and that the heavens will have no light (Jer 4:23). The NT concurs: "The sun will be darkened, and the moon will not give its light, and the stars will fall from heaven" (Mt 24:29 RSV); "The light of a lamp shall shine in thee no more" (Rev 18:23 RSV).

Physical Light and the Sacred. A final cluster of images of physical light focuses on worship and spiritual encounters with God. It would not be inappropriate to think in terms of "holy light" in these contexts, for although light is physical rather than symbolic, it expresses the mystery of divine presence. Lamps were prominent, for example, in the worship prescribed for the *tabernacle: "You shall make the

seven lamps for [the golden lampstand]; and the lamps shall be set up so as to give light upon the space in front of it" (Ex 25:37 RSV); "Command the people of Israel to bring you pure oil from beaten olives for the lamp, that a light may be kept burning continually" (Lev 24:2 RSV). The worship at the temple likewise featured lighted lamps (1 Kings 7:49; 2 Chron 4:20). Both the tabernacle and the *temple, moreover, faced eastward to allow the sunrise to filter into them.

Most notable among the lights of the temple was the Shekinah, the *glory of God. This was not ordinary physical light, but it was visible in the form of a luminous *cloud that filled holy space. When Solomon dedicated the temple, it "was filled with a cloud, so that the priests could not stand to minister because of the cloud; for the glory of the LORD filled the house of God" (2 Chron 5:13-14 RSV). This is similar to the glorious cloud that settled on Mount Sinai when Moses ascended to receive the law from God (Ex 24:15-18), after which "the skin of [Moses'] face shone because he had been talking with God" (Ex 34:29 RSV).

In the NT the ritual light of tabernacle and temple worship is replaced by the appearance of extraordinary light on people who encounter the supernatural directly. At the nativity of Jesus, light accompanies the appearance of the angels to the shepherds (Lk 2:9), and a star lights the way of the Magi to the house where they find Jesus (Mt 2:9-10). At the conversion of Paul a light from heaven flashes about him (Acts 9:3). When an angel rescues Peter from prison, a light shines in the cell (Acts 12:7).

The Primacy of Physical Light in the Bible. Although references to physical light in the Bible are outnumbered by symbolic references, it would be wrong to minimize the importance of the physical imagery of light that has just been traced. As we travel through the world of the Bible, we move in a world where physical light is a primary stage prop.

Furthermore, the symbolic associations of light to which we now turn would never have arisen if light did not possess the physical properties that characterize it: light is insubstantial but real; it emanates from a source; it illuminates darkness and allows people to see; it is a source of life. The writer of Colossians is able to speak of "the inheritance of the saints in light" and of how God "has delivered us from the dominion of darkness" (Col 1:12-13 RSV) only because of our experience of the physical properties of light and darkness.

Light as Symbol of Goodness and Blessing. At its most general level of symbolism, light represents goodness and holiness as opposed to evil. Evildoers are people "who rebel against the light . . . and do not stay in its paths" (Job 24:13 RSV). "Every one who does evil," Jesus explained, "hates the light, and does not come to the light, lest his deeds should be exposed" (Jn 3:20 RSV). When applied politically light becomes a symbol for the goodness that flows from a ruler who rules justly over his people: "He dawns on them like the morning light, like the sun shining forth upon a cloudless morning" (2 Sam 23:4 RSV).

In the NT the sanctified life is repeatedly associated with light. In the famous passage on holy living that concludes the epistle to the Romans, believers are commanded to "cast off the works of darkness and put on the armor of light" (Rom 13:12 RSV). Equally evocative is the picture in Ephesians 5:8-9: "Once you were darkness, but now you are light in the Lord; walk as children of light (for the fruit of light is found in all that is good and true)" (RSV). The calling of Christians is to "shine as lights in the world" (Phil 2:15 RSV).

Light is also a symbol of God's favor and the joy this favor brings. When the Jews were rescued from Haman's planned genocide, they "had light and gladness and joy and honor" (Esther 8:16 RSV). The psalmist does not hesitate to limit the gift of this light to those who live in fellowship with God: "Light dawns for the righteous, and joy for the upright in heart" (Ps 97:11 RSV; 112:4). Similarly, the book of Proverbs asserts that "the path of the righteous is like the light of dawn, which shines brighter and brighter until full day" (Prov 4:18 RSV). When Job pictures his former prosperity, God's favor assumes the qualities of light: "His lamp shone upon my head, and by his light I walked through darkness" (Job 29:3 RSV).

In other contexts light is associated with life, and darkness with death. In the book of Job, to be redeemed from going down to the grave is parallel to one's life seeing the light (Job 33:28), and to be brought back from the Pit is to "see the light of life" (Job 33:30 RSV). When the psalmist imagines the rich person's going "to the generation of his fathers," it calls to mind the picture that he "will never more see the light" (Ps 49:19 RSV).

Light as Symbol of Truth. A further cluster of images links light with truth and understanding as opposed to error and ignorance, and to the illumination that comes from embracing the truth. For example, "The unfolding of thy words gives light; it imparts understanding to the simple" (Ps 119:130 RSV). An OT pilgrim equates truth and light when praying that God will "send out thy light and thy truth" to "bring me to thy holy hill" (Ps 43:3 RSV). Daniel is commended as a person in whom are found "light and understanding and excellent wisdom" (Dan 5:14 RSV).

Because truth is represented in the Bible as being a revelation from God, that revelation itself is pictured as light: "Thy word is a lamp to my feet and a light to my path" (Ps 119:105 RSV). God's law can be characterized as "enlightening the eyes" (Ps 19:8 RSV). As with the law, so with the prophets: Peter describes "the prophetic word" as "a lamp shining in a dark place" (2 Pet 1:19 RSV).

A related cluster of images associates light with revelation of something that had been secret or hidden. In the hymn to wisdom in Job 28, one of the powers attributed to human ingenuity is the ability to bring to light the "thing that is hid" (Job 28:11 RSV). In the NT this bringing to light is applied to God's judgment of the individual heart. The Lord "will bring to light the things now hidden in darkness and will disclose the purposes of the heart. Then every man will receive his commendation from God" (1 Cor 4:5 RSV). The same motif appears in the OT: "He will bring forth your vindication as the light, and your right as the noonday" (Ps 37:6 RSV).

God as Light. Light also symbolizes God. In the OT we find the evocative image of "the light of [God's] countenance" (Ps 4:6; cf. Num 25-26). Isaiah's vision of the final triumph of goodness includes the assertion that "the LORD will be your everlasting light" (Is 60:19, 20). The most succinct statement is found in 1 John 1:5: "God is light and in him is no darkness at all" (RSV). James speaks of God as "the Father of lights" (Jas 1:17). Elsewhere God is simply associated with light as an image of divine glory: he covers himself "with light as with a garment" (Ps 104:2); "his brightness was like the light" (Hab 3:4); "the light dwells with him" (Dan 2:22). Ezekiel's vision of the divine chariot (Ezek 1) is a riot of brightness, flashing fire, shining jewels and gleaming metals.

By extension, God who is light inhabits a heaven bathed in light. Here light becomes the preeminent symbol for transcendence, dear to the mystics' and poets' expressions through the ages. The classic passage is 1 Timothy 6:16, which speaks of God as the one "who alone has immortality and dwells in unapproachable light" (RSV). Colossians 1:12 speaks of the believer's being qualified "to share in the inheritance of the saints in light" (RSV).

As a symbol for God, light takes the more specific form of representing the Messiah. Isaiah's prophecy predicted, "The people who walked in darkness have seen a great light; those who dwelt in a land of deep darkness, on them has light shined" (Is 9:2 RSV). Jesus applied this prophecy to himself (Mt 4:15-16). The song of Simeon calls Christ "a light for revelation to the Gentiles, and for glory to thy people Israel" (Lk 2:32 RSV). John's great prologue in praise of the incarnate Word repeatedly applies the mystical language of light to Christ (Jn 1:4, 5, 7, 8, 9). Christ declared himself to be "the light of the world" (Jn 8:12). Elsewhere he claimed, "I have come as light into the world, that whoever believes in me may not remain in darkness" (Jn 12:46 RSV).

The Community of Light. If God and his Son are light, light becomes a natural symbol for salvation and the new life. "The LORD is my light and my salvation," the psalmist testifies (Ps 27:1 RSV). The person "who does what is true comes to the light, that it may be clearly seen that his deeds have been wrought in God" (Jn 3:21 RSV). In Christ's great discourse on himself as the light of the world, those who follow Christ are defined as people who "will not walk in darkness, but will have the light of life" (Jn 8:12 RSV). According to 1 Peter 2:9, believers are those who have been called "out of darkness into his marvelous light" (RSV). An early liturgical formula, accompanied by its lead-in, is a fitting summary of this motif: "When anything is exposed by the light it becomes visible, for anything that becomes visible is light. Therefore it is said, 'Awake, O sleeper, and arise from the dead, and Christ shall give you light'" (Eph 5:13-14 RSV). The implied message is clear: if God is light, to come to God is to come to the light and to receive life. We might note also the echo of Christ's resurrection in the picture of the sleeper's arising from the dead.

Those who have been delivered "from the dominion of darkness" and transferred "to the kingdom of his beloved Son" (Col 1:13 RSV) are thus strongly associated with light as the thing that defines their very essence. Jesus called John the Baptist "a burning and shining lamp" in whose light people rejoiced (Jn 5:35). After painting a composite portrait of the ideal disciple in his beatitudes, Jesus added, "You are the light of the world. . . . Let your light so shine before men, that they may see your good works and give glory to your Father who is in heaven" (Mt 5:14, 16 RSV).

It is not inaccurate, therefore, to view the church as portrayed in the NT Epistles as the possessor and giver of light. Paul writes to the Thessalonian church, "For you are all sons of light and sons of the day" (1 Thess 5:5 RSV). As prototypical convert, Paul was sent by God to the Gentiles "to open their eyes, that they may turn from darkness to light" (Acts 26:18 RSV). This light is not only part of the church's evangelistic proclamation but also characterizes life within the church: "If we walk in the light, as he is in the light, we have fellowship with one another, and the blood of Jesus his Son cleanses us from all sin" (1 Jn 1:7 RSV).

Light in the Coming Age. The final pictures of light that we find in the Bible appear in the eschatological visions of the new age in the book of Revelation. The New Jerusalem comes down from heaven "having the glory of God, its radiance like a most rare jewel" (Rev 21:11). The city, moreover, "has no need of sun or moon to shine upon it, for the glory of God is its light, and its lamp is the Lamb" (Rev 21:23 RSV; cf. Is 60:19). To climax the motif, we read that "night shall be no more; they need no light of lamp or sun, for the Lord God will be their light" (Rev 22:5 RSV). This echoes Zechariah's similar vision of a coming time when "there shall be continuous day" and that "at evening time there shall be light" (Zech 14:7 RSV).

Summary. In all of the Bible's references to light, light is not self-generated. It comes (usually unbidden) from outside the earthly and human sphere and transforms that sphere with a transcendent splendor. As a symbol light thus pictures the simultaneous transcendence and immanence of God: it is from above, but it permeates everyday life.

A survey of light imagery in the Bible illustrates the implied thesis of this dictionary—that the main outline of biblical belief and the feelings it generates can be traced by following the Bible's master images. Light in its varied meanings is at the heart of such central biblical themes as creation, providence, judgment, redemption and sanctification. It embodies much of the theological teaching of the Bible about God, which explains why light has been prominent in the history of theology (Pelikan). In its literal, physical manifestations, moreover, light contributes significantly to the elemental quality of the biblical world, keeping spiritual reality rooted in the lives that people actually live.

The text within the Bible itself that comes closest to summarizing the range of meanings of light is 2 Corinthians 4:6: "For it is the God who said, 'Let light shine out of darkness,' who has shone in our hearts to give the light of the knowledge of the glory of God in the face of Christ" (RSV). Here is the link between creation and the new creation, between OT and NT, between the physical reality and the spiritual symbol.

See also DARKNESS; FIRE; GLORY; LAMP, LAMPSTAND; MOON; STARS; SUN.

BIBLIOGRAPHY. E. R. Achtemeier, "Jesus Christ, the Light of the World: The Biblical Understanding of Light and Darkness," *Interpretation* 17 (1963) 439-49; J. Pelikan, *The Light of the World: A Basic Image in Early Christian Thought* (New York: Harper, 1962).

LIGHTNING

A few natural elements such as *wind and *fire, perhaps because their essence is discernible yet intangible, transparent and difficult to control, occur repeatedly in literature as metaphors for the divine or the spiritual. They often do surrogate duty for the image of the invisible God. Fire represents God's presence (Gen 15:17; Ex 13:21; 14:24; Mt 3:11; Acts 2:3), his deliberate action (1 Kings 18:24, 38) or his judgment (Gen 19:24; Job 36:31-33; Sir 43:13; Mt 13:20; 18:9; Lk 9:54). The association of fire and God is so close that Scripture takes pains to distinguish them (1 Kings 19:12). After all, God is light (1 Jn 1:5; Rev 21:23) and the Father of lights (Jas 1:16). What manifestation of light could be more awesome and frightening than that most potent, uncontrollable and blinding fire—lightning? Lightning is fire on a supernatural scale with a supernatural purpose.

Lightning as God's Power and Mystery. Lightning represents one of our great primordial fears. Its grandeur and awe reduce us to frightened children, acutely aware of our powerlessness and insignificance. To observe the activity of lightning, especially in antiquity (in the absence of our current naturalistic explanations), was to witness the direct involvement and response of the Creator to creation—a creator in control of nature that seems at the same time paradoxically out of control. Lightning symbolizes at once both the untamable power and unapproachable presence of God. Biblical authors return again and again to the theme of God's control over nature as the most obvious and easily understood measure of his power (Ps 65:8; 89:9-10; 107:25-29; Acts 2:2). In the NT the obedience of nature serves as tacit testimony to Christ's deity (Mt 21:20; Mk 4:41; Col 1:17). In several biblical accounts lightning is the divine tool of choice because it is swift, precise, unambiguous and has the added advantage of putting a rebellious humanity in a respectful frame of mind (Job 36:29-33). For Job there was no hope of knowing how God "causes the lightning of his cloud to shine" (Job 37:15 RSV).

Scripture uses lightning as proof of God's terrifying presence. It frightens believer and infidel alike. Mount *Sinai flashes and smolders as evidence of God's occupancy (Ex 19:16—20:18). As proof that God attends his chosen people in battle, lightning routs his enemies (Ps 77:18; 97:4, cf. 144:6; 2 Sam 22:13-15, cf. Ps 18:14).

Lightning as Divine Weapon. Just as the Canaanite Baal and Akkadian Adad were depicted holding a lightning bolt as their emblematic *weapon, the poets of the OT employed verbal images of the conquering Lord armed with lightning. Lightning appears as the spear of God (Hab 3:11) but more commonly as the *arrow of God (Ps 7:13; 18:14; 77:18; 144:6), just as the *storm flood is the work of his bow (Gen 9:13). Even human weapons, with their flashing blades conjuring up images of lightning, intimidated the foe (Ezek 21:10, 15, 28). Lightning is again the divine weapon in the contest on Mount Carmel. Baal and his prophets were ceded every advantage (1 Kings 18:23-25). As the Canaanite storm god who wields the thunderbolt, Baal should have been in his element answering his worshipers by lightning. His failure made clear to the spectators that the God of Elijah overpowered Baal at his own game (*see* Divine Warrior).

Lightning as God's Finger. Lightning covers God's hand, suggesting that it is his *fingers (Job 36:32). The finger as opposed to the whole hand suggest a deftness and precision. It is an accurate weapon in his hands (v. 32). Elsewhere God's fingers are his supernatural agents (Ex 8:19; 31:18; Deut 9:10) or even the work of God's spirit (Lk 11:20). The law in the OT was delivered through God's fingers, but in the NT the law is delivered by angels (Acts 7:53; Gal 3:19; Deut 33:2 LXX). God's fingers are responsible for his creative acts (Ps 8:3). Lightning is also his creation (Jer 10:13:16; 51:16-19). Man's fingers, in contrast, create mere idols (Is 8:2).

Lightning as God's Agents and Angels. God's tools and weapons are often difficult to distinguish from his agents. His means easily merge with his messengers, personified and pictured as attendants, spiritual beings doing his bidding. So in the ancient mind lightning was evidence of divine activity mediated by angels. The cosmological imagery of the psalms equates the wind and fire with angels (Ps 104:4; Heb 1:7; further elaborated in the meteorological sections of 1 Enoch). The LXX understood the "furies of God's wrath" and the heat of his nostrils manifested in storms to be angels (Job 40:11).

A flaming appearance marks celestial armies, whether fiery chariots or angels on horseback, with lightning (2 Kings 6:17; 4 Macc 4:10). Angels are clothed in lightning (Mt 28:3), underscoring both the residual brightness from the presence of God (Mt 18:10; Dan 10:6, cf. Moses, Ex 34:29) and their other-worldly connection. The lightning aura surrounding the creatures in Ezekiel's vision indicates both their power over the created order and their access to God's throne (Ezek 1:13). Lightning not only marks the activity of God's loyal messengers but also traces the downward trajectory of the fallen angel (Lk 10:18).

Lightning as Swift and Omnipresent. God dispatches lightning "to the corners of the earth" (Job 37:3 RSV). There is nowhere to hide from it. Lightning, which appears in the east at the same instant it appears in the west, suggests the omnipresence of God and serves as proof of the worldwide appearance of the returning Christ (Mt 24:27; Lk 17:24).

See also ARROW, ARROW OF GOD; DIVINE WARRIOR; FIRE; STORM; THUNDER; WEAPONS, HUMAN AND DIVINE.

LILY. *See* FLOWERS.

LINEN

The word *linen* appears about one hundred times throughout the Bible, approximately 80 percent of the time in the OT. Linen is cloth made of woven flax, noted mainly for its strength, coolness and luster. It is a commodity of beauty and utility. Linen and wool were the two textiles native to Palestine and would have been worn by common persons as well as the wealthy. Nearly all references to linen in the Bible connect it directly with persons or nations of wealth and power, with priests and with God himself. For each of these three main types of usage, there are clear and consistent OT and NT counterparts.

The association of linen with earthly honor and power becomes apparent in the many OT references linking it to kings and prosperous nations. The Egyptian Pharaoh and the Persian Ahasuerus clothe Joseph and Mordecai, respectively, in fine linen to honor them for great service to the crown (Gen 41:42; Esther 8:15). The virtuous woman of Proverbs 31 wears and sells fine linen. Ezekiel records God's lament that he wrapped Jerusalem with fine linen and silk (Ezek 16:10-13) and that the prosperous city of Tyre's sail of "fine embroidered linen from Egypt . . . became [her] distinguishing mark" (Ezek 27:7). In the NT, the rich but damned Dives wears fine linen, as does the nation *Babylon (Luke 16:19; Rev 18:12, 16). Thus linen in the Bible is a "power fabric," an unequivocal sign of earthly success to persons and nations of the ancient world.

The OT contains nearly thirty references to linen as part of the priest's required garments, from turban to breeches (Ex 28—29; Lev 16). The NT counterpart to this is presented consistently—even emphatically—in all four Gospels: the linen cloths used by Joseph of Arimathea to wrap Christ's body for burial. Hebrews 7 and 8 establish the doctrinal framework for this identification of Christ as humanity's perfect and permanent high priest.

Finally, OT usages connecting linen to God himself begin with numerous references to the *tabernacle, God's temporary dwelling place among his wandering people (Ex 25:8). All of the linen gathered for the tabernacle (and later for Solomon's temple) was "fine linen" or "fine twisted linen." While linen adorns God's dwelling on earth, it also clothes the citizens of heaven, God's eternal dwelling. We see this in apocalyptic usages in Ezekiel 10:1-7, Daniel ("And I heard the man dressed in linen, who was above the waters of the river, as he raised his right hand and his left toward heaven, and swore by Him who lives forever;" Dan 12:7 NKJV), and Revelation ("And to her it was granted to clothe herself in fine linen, bright and clean; for the fine linen is the righteous acts of the saints;" Rev 19:14 NKJV; cf. Rev 15:6; 19:8 [note the recurrent phrase "bright and clean," which is probably for purity in an investiture ceremony]).

In conclusion, linen in the Bible speaks of status. To humans, linen symbolizes power, wealth, honor and success. To God, linen reflects his holiness, purchased for humans by Christ and to be worn by the church when she weds Christ, to dwell for eternity in his glory.

See also GARMENTS; WOOL.

LION

The Israelites based their opinion of the lion on their encounters with it as pastoralists (Amos 5:19). They knew the lion as a ruthless, almost unstoppable killer, taking from the *flock at will. It frequently worked from ambush, but even when not actively hunting, its roar, audible for miles, spread its fear abroad. A significant portion of the references to lion in Scripture concerns its voice (Job 4:10; Ps 22:13; 104:21; Prov 19:12; 28:15; Jer 2:15,30; Ezek 22:25; Hos 11:10; Zech 3:3; 11:3; Rev 10:3). "The lion has roared; who will not fear?" (Amos 3:8 NRSV). No doubt many more people had heard a lion than had seen one, and this enhanced the mythology surrounding lions. The Bible uses nearly a dozen words to designate lions of various ages and gender, but not all of these terms are securely defined. Hebrew šāḥaṣ clearly means lion in most instances, but some have pointed out that the word is confined to poetry and occasionally seems to refer to a more *mythical creature than a flesh and blood lion (in passages like Job 28:8; Ps 91:13). In support of this idea, Akkadian literature refers to a snake as "earth-lion." Ancient art work depicts many composite creatures with clear lion features paralleling mentions of such wonderous *animals in scripture (Ezek 1:10; 10:14; Dan 7:4; Rev 4:7; 13:2). The lion is sometimes paired with

mythical creatures such as dragons (Sir 25:16) just as it is paired with real animals. It seems to exist in a twilight between real and supernatural.

Mortal lions were frightful enough. God employed them as agents in punishment (1 Kings 13:26; 20:25; 2 Kings 17:25). The mention of their teeth, paw or mouth summoned all the fears they provoked (Joel 1:6; 1 Sam 17:37; Ps 58:6). The mouth of the lion is a predicament from which escape seems hopeless (Dan 6:22; 2 Tim 4:17; cf. Ps 22:21; Heb 11:33). To Hebrew poets, the wicked acted like lions. "Like a lion they will tear me apart; they will drag me away, with no one to rescue" (Ps 7:2 NRSV; cf. Ps 10:9; 17:12; 22:13, 21; 35:17; 57:4; 58:6; Is 5:29; Jer 4:7; 5:6; 50:17). The devil also preys on humanity as a roaring lion (1 Pet 5:8, cf. 2 Tim 4:17). Scripture compares God himself in his destructive wrath with a lion: "I, even I, will rend and go away; I will carry off, and none shall rescue" (Hos 5:14 RSV; cf. Hos 13:7; Is 31:4; 38:13; Jer 25:38; Lam 3:10-11).

Lion in the OT evokes ferocity, destructive power and irresistible strength. It is described as a bold and valiant warrior (Prov 28:1; 30:30). As in some other tribal societies, killing a lion epitomized the brave (Judg 14:5; 1 Sam 17:34; 1 Chron 11:22; 1 Macc 3:4), those stronger than lions (2 Sam 1:23), the truly lion-hearted (2 Sam 17:10). David's shock troops had faces like lions (1 Chron 12:8).

The royalty of surrounding cultures employed the lion as a symbol as did the Israelites. Ramses II and Ashurnasipal II kept live lions. The prophets likened enemy kings to predatory lions (Jer 50:17; Ezek 32:2). The lions flanking Solomon's throne serve as graphic reminders of the king's absolute power (1 Kings 10:19-20): "The dread wrath of the king is like the growling of a lion" (Prov 20:2 RSV). Solomon's temple, as God's palace, also shared lion decorations (1 Kings 7:29), as did Ezekiel's envisioned temple (Ezek 41:19). Such decorative lions may recall the image of the tribe of Judah as a lion in Jacob's blessing (Gen 49:9), as do the lions who represent members of the royal house of Judah in Ezekiel 19:2-9. Israel triumphant over her enemies fits the image of a lion: "It does not lie down till it has devoured the prey, and drinks the blood of the slain" (Num 23:24 RSV; cf. Mic 5:8). When history has reversed the nation's fortunes, the prophet caricatures his enslaved people as a snared lion led off to Babylon (Ezek 19:8-9).

The various facets of the lion's existence, as *hunter and hunted, as bold and strong or stealthy and ruthless, as all powerful or savage, permit it to represent a nation in its prime or in decline, both the wicked and the righteous, both the Almighty and evil. Scripture also presents the lion as a paradoxical image. The lion is the epitome of proud self-sufficiency (Job 28:8) and yet cries to God to be fed (Job 38:39; Ps 104:21). The lion is the quintessential carnivore, but the messianic kingdom will differ so much from the familiar world that it's lions will be vegetarian and lie down with the *lamb (Is 11:6). This kingdom will be ruled by a lion-like lamb.

When Genesis 49:9 ("Judah is a lion's whelp; from the prey, my son, you have gone up" RSV) came to be understood in later Judaism as a key messianic prophecy (cf. 1QSb 5:29; 4 Ezra 12:31-33), the image was still of the royal Messiah as military conqueror. The Apocalypse expresses this perplexing combination of *Suffering Servant and military Messiah by melding the conquering Lion of the tribe of Judah with Lamb that was slain (Rev 5:5-6). The juxtaposition of the two images of lion and lamb does not cancel the former but suggests the idea of conquest, not by destructive power but by obedience and sacrifice.

See also ANIMALS; MYTHICAL ANIMALS.

LIPS

Such a small but active part of human anatomy claims much mention and many pictures throughout Scripture, most of them relating to the quality of the *heart that produces the words lips speak.

The Bible often pictures a person's lips as constituting a separate, rational, moral agent. Hebrew literature in particular is full of synecdoche, that figure of speech in which a part assumes the qualities of a whole. If a person is untruthful, he is said to have "lying lips" (Ps 31:18; 120:2; Prov 10:18 NIV). So also appear lips that flatter, deceive, detest wickedness, promote instruction, know what is fitting, promote instruction and so forth (see especially Psalms and Proverbs). Truthful lips are even said to "endure forever," just as does a human soul (Prov 12:19).

Sometimes the lips become such independent agents that the person who owns them is at odds with them. Eliphaz tells Job that his lips testify against him (Job 15:6). The psalmist speaks of fulfilling the vows his lips promised when he was in trouble, as if an acquaintance made a promise for him and now he must keep it (Ps 66:14). "He who guards his lips guards his life" (Prov 13:3 NIV). Here the lips might be a valuable or even dangerous prisoner to be kept under guard. The lips of a fool—that is, lips not kept under guard—will "bring him strife," becoming his own enemy (Prov 18:6). In the most extreme and almost unimaginable picture, "a fool is consumed by his own lips" (Eccles 10:12 NIV).

Lips are often pictured as openings through which words come out. Job describes himself as so "full of words" that he is like a new wineskin ready to burst with bottled-up *wine; he must open his lips and let the words out to find relief (Job 32:18-20). David asks God to open his lips to praise him, for he has confessed the sin that clogged that opening (Ps 51:15). He rejoices in praising God, in not "sealing his lips" (Ps 40:9).

Yet at another point David asks God to "set a guard over my mouth" and "keep watch over the door of my lips" (Ps 141:3 NIV). The opening of the lips often appears as a door that can be opened or closed and out of which words proceed directly from the heart, the room to which the door leads. The door is only the outer visible facade; what is inside is what counts. The Lord says of the Israelites that they honor him with their lips, but their hearts are far from him (Is 29:13). When Isaiah's lips are touched by the live coal, we see an external picture of an interior cleansing: "See, this has touched your lips; your guilt is taken away and your sin atoned for" (Is 6:7 NIV).

When the heart is evil, the words that come from the lips can be deadly weapons; the picture of the guard at the door fits perfectly. The lips can "spew out" *swords (Ps 59:7); they can threaten the poison of vipers (Ps 140:3); they can work like a snare, clamping down on the unsuspecting soul (Prov 18:7).

In a somewhat more sedate pattern of images, lips also appear as surfaces on which words and qualities stick or rest. "The law of the LORD is to be on your lips," God tells Moses (Ex 13:9 NIV). "Is there any wickedness on my lips?" Job asks, almost inviting us to inspect his lips to see if any traces of wickedness can be spotted (Job 6:30 NIV). Such imagery makes words and the speaking of words even more palpable, solidly significant and lasting. Proverbs uses this picture several times, contrasting the discerning man who has wisdom "on his lips" with the foolish man who has no knowledge to be found "on his lips" (Prov 10:13; 14:7).

In an almost backwards image, Proverbs pictures lips as producing food. Instead of taking in food, as in the process of eating, lips bring forth words as *"fruit," in the process of talking. A person is spiritually nourished by this process of bringing forth a *"harvest" of fruit in words, just as he is physically nourished by taking in real fruit (Prov 12:14; 13:2; 18:20). "The lips of the righteous nourish many," as well as themselves (Prov 10:21), in contrast to the words of a fool, which attack and destroy himself and others. An adulteress's lips may seem to bring forth good food as they "drip *honey," but in the end they offer only "bitter gall" (Prov 5:3-4). Other portions of Scripture also describe words as fruit, making "the fruit of lips" into a sacrifice of praise offered up to God (e.g., Hos 14:2; Heb 13:15).

Images of lips in *Song of Songs, by contrast, simply celebrate the beauty of the lover and the beloved to each other. He describes her lips as a "scarlet ribbon," and says they "drop sweetness as the honeycomb" (Song 4:3, 11 NIV). He has found her words (and surely her kisses) truly sweet, unlike those of the adulteress in Proverbs. The lover's lips are like lilies to the beloved, "dripping with myrrh" (Song 5:13 NIV). Sight, taste, touch and smell all come alive in these sensuous images of young love.

Scripture presents a great variety of lips—from lovers', to children's (Ps 8:2), to all sorts of women's and men's, to God's (Is 11:4). All the lips in Scripture appear in the context of a righteous God who loves true words and hates false ones, and who evaluates what comes from the lips according to what is in the heart.

See also HEART; MOUTH.

LISTS. *See* RHETORICAL PATTERNS.

LITTLE. *See* SMALL.

LOAF. *See* BAKING; BREAD.

LOATH. *See* ABHOR, LOATH.

LOCUST

While locusts in the Bible are mainly a negative image, they are not wholly so. To our surprise, locusts were a ceremonially clean insect that OT Jews were allowed to eat (Lev 11:20-23). This image of locusts as an image of sustenance is rendered memorable in the picture of John the Baptist's eating of locusts and wild *honey (Mk 1:6), an image of the ascetic piety of a wilderness experience. Mainly, though, locusts in the Bible are an image of *terror and the destruction of crops, usually with the added connotation of their being an agent of God's judgment against a rebellious nation.

Underlying all this imagery are the literal facts of how locusts behaved. Locusts were voracious at all three stages of their development—a larval stage in which wingless locusts hop like fleas, a pupal stage in which the wings are encased in a sack and the locusts walk like ordinary insects, and the adult stage in which they fly. Adult locusts swarm in the air like clouds and cover the landscape where they alight, leaving it denuded.

The first destructive swarm of locusts that we read about in the Bible is the plague of locusts that falls on Egypt "to devour everything growing in the fields," establishing the locust as an agent of terrible divine judgment (Ex 10:1-20 NIV). Thus the inclusion of locust *plagues among the *curses for covenant disobedience warns the people of God not to be like the Egyptians (Deut 28:38, 42; cf. Amos

A locust.

4:9-10). It was for deliverance from such plagues that Solomon dedicated the temple (2 Chron 6:28-31).

The sheer numbers of locusts in a swarm (Judg 6:5; 7:12; Jer 46:23; 51:14), the physical resemblance of their heads to *horses' heads (Job 39:20; Jer 51:27; Rev 9:7), their unbroken advance (Prov 30:27), their ability to "strip the land" (Nahum 3:15-17) and their thunderous approach (Rev 9:9)

make a plague of locusts a suitable metaphor for an invading *army.

The prophecy of *Joel was occasioned by an invasion of locusts (Joel 2:1-11, 25), which in Joel's prophetic imagination became an emblem of divine judgment against an apostate nation. Joel describes the invasion with minute and technical accuracy, referring, for example, to "the cutting locust," "the swarming locust," "the hopping locust" and "the destroying locust" (Joel 1:4 RSV) in reference to the stages of the locusts' development. Joel compares the sight and sound of a plague of locusts to "a powerful army drawn up for battle" (Joel 2:5 RSV). The locusts approach like a black cloud or a spreading dawn (Joel 2:2). On closer inspection they look and sound like galloping cavalry (Joel 2:4), advancing like trained soldiers who march in line, not swerving from their course (Joel 2:7). Their beating wings and chomping mouths crackle like a great *fire (Joel 2:5), and like a fire they devour everything in their path (Joel 2:3; cf. 1:4).

The *tour de force* of locust passages in the Bible is the apocalyptic locusts of Revelation 9:7-11. Beginning with a literal locust as the core of the description, the author's imagination then transforms the insect into a fantastic and terrifying image of judgment. The locusts looked like "horses prepared for battle" because they came as a force and with destructive intent. The crowns of gold on their heads are the glistering effect of sun on their exoskeletons, and their "faces resembled human faces" by conveying malice and threat. The *hair like women's hair might be a fanciful account of their antennae. The lions' teeth signal the destructive gnawing ability of locusts as they chew *grain, and the iron breastplates again refer to their exoskeletons. Keeping the imagery of military attack alive, the author compares the combined sound of the locusts' wings to the thundering of horses and *chariots rushing into battle; and to heighten the destructive effect, he gives the locusts "tails and stings like scorpions."

See also JOEL, BOOK OF; PLAGUE.

LOOSE, LOOSEN

The imagery of loosening in the Bible refers to freeing or unbinding something. It pictures the removing of restraint. This can be either good, as when a prisoner is loosed from his bonds, or sinister, as when God looses his punishment on a wicked world. Except in references to such everyday occurrences as loosening a belt or *garment, the imagery of loosening something is associated with a person (usually God) who possesses superior power and authority, loosening being a display of that sovereignty.

For example, God is portrayed as using his power to loosen various elements of nature. Thus in the book of Job God looses the *thunder, looses "the cords of Orion" and looses "the bonds of the swift ass" (Job 37:3; 38:31; 39:5 NRSV). Here the imagery of loosing metaphorically pictures the empowering of nature to produce its natural effects, with

God as the implied sovereign who orchestrates the spectacle. God has similar power to control or undo people: he "looses the sash of kings" and "the belt of the strong" (Job 12:18, 21 NRSV), and he loosed Job's bowstring to humble him (Job 30:11). This cluster of images is paradoxical, inasmuch as they do not picture people being freed from *bondage but rather being divested of their strength or power. God is again the one who loosens, implying his sovereignty.

In addition, the Bible declares that God loosens has wrath on those who sin. In Leviticus, God threatens to "let loose wild animals against" Israel if she disobeys him (Lev 26:22). Throughout the Bible, God declares is intention to "let loose" on the wicked "his fierce anger, wrath, indignation and distress, a company of destroying angels" (Ps 78:49 NRSV), to "let loose on them sword, famine, and pestilence" (Jer 29:17), and to "loose . . . my deadly arrows of famine, arrows for destruction, which I will let loose to destroy you" (Ezek 5:16 NRSV). The motif of God's "letting loose" is here an image of terror and judgment—a letting go of restraint from a torrent of punishment.

But loosing can also be an image of liberation from bondage (see Bondage and Freedom). God declares his authority to free from bondage those whom he chooses. The psalmist praises God because he has "loosed my bonds" (Ps 116:16). In Isaiah, God declares exultantly that he will soon free Israel from her oppressors, so that someday the "captive daughter of Zion" will be able to loose the bonds from her neck (Is 52:2). But in return God asks Israel to be as generous as he has been, to "loose the bonds of injustice" and "let the oppressed go free" (Is 58:6).

Finally, after Peter confesses that Jesus is the Messiah, Jesus gives him authority over loosening things. He tells Peter, "I will give you the *keys of the kingdom of heaven, and whatever you bind on earth will be bound in heaven, and whatever you loose on earth will be loosed in heaven" (Mt 16:19 NRSV). Jesus clarifies the meaning of this verse in his later command to Peter and the church to confront members with their sins (Mt 18:15-20). Thus, God gave authority to the apostles to bind and loosen, or to condone or prohibit, practices that might be sinful.

Miscellaneous uses of the word *loose* occur in several contexts. Proverbs warns men to avoid the loose woman, or adulteress, who is a stumbling block to men (Prov 2:16). In such a context, *loose* comes to mean "morally unrestrained." In other contexts it is simply used for untying or freeing something in everyday terms. For example, God commands Isaiah to "loose the sackcloth" from his loins and walk around barefoot and naked for three years as an illustration of Egypt's future captivity.

See also BONDAGE AND FREEDOM; KEY.

LORD. *See* GOD; JESUS, IMAGES OF.

LORD'S SUPPER. *See* SUPPER.

LOST AND FOUND

The motif of finding falls into two categories in the Bible—the major motif of finding something (presumably for the first time) after a process of searching, and a much smaller category of references to finding or regaining something that was lost. In literature generally, the motif of lost and found is a favorite plot line of the folk tale imagination (with the finding of a lost family member popular in comic literature). While the specific terminology is relatively scarce, the pattern of lost and found is the overarching plot of the Bible. In *Adam the human race lost possession of *Garden of Eden, perfection, untarnished communion with God, *innocence and immortal bliss. In Christ, the second Adam, it can find or regain all those qualities again.

Apart from a myriad of references throughout both Testaments to physical objects, a number of significant lost-and-found motifs thread their way through the biblical record. The most obvious motif is the pastoral imagery of *sheep. In the OT the psalmist speaks of himself as having strayed like "a lost sheep" (Ps 119:176 KJV), and the prophet Jeremiah speaks of the Israelites as being lost, their "shepherds" (spiritual leaders) having led them astray (Jer 50:6). Though the OT speaks of lost sheep and of searching for sheep, it is not until the NT that much is made of sheep being found. In Matthew, Jesus announces that he came to seek "the lost sheep of the house of Israel" and commands his disciples to minister to the "lost sheep" of Israel (Mt 10:6 RSV). Jesus' references here are the high point of pastoral imagery in the biblical literature.

The *locus classicus*, however, is the three parables of Jesus recorded in Luke 15. Told to silence the Pharisees, who murmured when they saw that Jesus "receives sinners and eats with them" (RSV), the parables revolve around a lost sheep that is rescued, a woman's lost coin that is found, and a lost son who returns. In the parable of the *prodigal son (the climactic parable of the three), when the son returns from his dissolute wanderings, the father says, "this my son was dead, and is alive again; he was lost, and is found" (Lk 15:24 RSV). Metaphorically associating death with being lost and new life with being found, Jesus climaxes the figurative uses of lost and found by equating them with spiritual death and life. To be lost is to be spiritually separated from God, and to be found is to be rightly related to God in Christ. This usage has dominated our thinking about lost and found in the Bible.

Other important lost and found references include numerous citations of lost or found grace (Gen 6:8; Ex 33:16), favor (Gen 18:3; Num 11:11, 15) and wisdom (Job 32:13; Dan 5:11, 14). The references to grace and favor suggest that the Lord initiates the finding, giving kindness and compassion where they are not deserved. The references to wisdom and to God's word imply that people must actively search if they hope to find the desired object.

When Scripture refers to anything more than misplaced objects, the lost-and-found motif carries with it profound spiritual meaning. People are lost in sin and in need of being found or redeemed. Under the metaphors of lost sheep, lost coin and lost son, the Bible speaks of being lost as the critical problem in both Testaments alike. The problem is rectified by one's being found or brought back into right relationship with God in Christ, as many passages in the NT attest.

See also FIND, FOUND; INNOCENCE, FALL FROM.

LOVE STORY

A number of couples in the Bible remain in our imaginations as lovers: *Adam and *Eve, *Abraham and Sarah, Isaac and Rebekah, *Jacob and Rachel, *Solomon and his Shulammite bride, *Esther and the king, *Ruth and Boaz, *Mary and Joseph. Only two of these are in any sense full-fledged love stories, but we catch bits and snatches of romance in what we know about the other couples.

The book of *Ruth is the love story in the Bible that covers the gamut, a feat all the more remarkable when we recall its brevity. Although the following list of ingredients of a love story is not based on the story of Ruth, that story does contain all of the conventions. To begin, what we call a love story is essentially a story of courtship and its culmination in *marriage. The cast of characters in such a story is relatively fixed: an idealized and eligible couple in which both principals are worthy of each other, a group of background observers to the romance (including friends, acquaintances, townspeople and family members), a confidant, a matchmaker and a rival.

The list of typical events is equally conventional. Key moments include a memorable first meeting and first date (or its equivalent), asking others about the "eligible other," a report of the first date to a confidant, meetings (and perhaps secret rendezvous) in special places, goodby scenes, the bestowing of favors, flirtatious behavior and—as a high point—betrothal. An idealized country setting (or a park for city dwellers) is almost a requirement. The courtship includes wooing the beloved (and perhaps her mother or father) and obstacles that need to be overcome (sometimes including social factors that make it unlikely that the couple will fall in love or attain marriage). Often others (including the readers) know before the couple does that they are right for each other, lending a sense of destiny to the romance and marriage.

While the story of Ruth is a love story strongly tinged with domestic concerns, the Song of Songs dispenses with any family concerns and gives us courtship in its pure form—as nothing less than a way of life. The principals in this lyric drama are ideally ardent lovers, pursuing courtship in an ideally flowery and fruitful pastoral landscape (despite the courtly milieu that is always breaking through the rustic facade). Here we find the literature of compli-

ment, as the lovers never tire of telling the beloved how beautiful he or she is.

The *Song of Songs is the Bible's lone example of the poetry of love that makes up so large a share of the literature of love generally. Such poetry includes as its staples the impulse toward hyperbole, the search for superlatives, the metaphoric comparison of love and the beloved to the best things in nature, and the use of epithets (pet names) for the beloved. At the level of sentiment, we find vows of eternal constancy and the desire to be possessed by the beloved.

See also RUTH, BOOK OF; SONG OF SOLOMON.

LOW

The human imagination has gravitated naturally to directional imagery of high and low, up and down, as expressing qualities in human life that really exist and are important in defining persons and values. Being or becoming low is a biblical image that denotes rank or condition—a spatial metaphor defining one's position by means of comparison. Together, the extremes of *high and low define the hierarchy according to which someone may be ranked. When pondering the significance of humanity in comparison with the vastness of creation, the psalmist declares, "You made him a little lower than the heavenly beings" (Ps 8:5 NIV). Here the image of being lower describes in spatial terms the proper place of humanity in the hierarchy of God's creation. The dominion and power over the earth given to humans ranks just below that of heavenly beings. Using a simple image of physical position to illustrate the hierarchy of creation, the psalmist is thus able to describe the great wonder and immense responsibility of being a human creature of God.

Lowness also functions as an image to indicate social class. In Acts we read how the magician Simon exerted himself with such charisma that in Samaria "all the people, both high and low, gave him their attention" (Acts 8:10 NIV). The psalmist makes a similar distinction between classes of people, addressing "both low and high, rich and poor alike" (Ps 49:2 NIV). Here it is material wealth in particular that is the criterion for rank, as the two phrases are equivalents in which the middle two words are paired (high and rich), as are the first and last words (low and poor). For those who are low, there is likely to be little respect from the wealthy and powerful. Consequently, the psalmist is both "lowly and despised" (Ps 119:141 NIV). At the bottom of the social hierarchy is the slave, who exists solely as a commodity to be bought and sold. It is this rank with which Noah curses Japheth, using the superlative form: "The lowest of slaves [literally "a slave of slaves"] will he be to his brothers" (Gen 9:25 NIV).

Just as those of low social class are under the power and authority of those who are higher, so also *bowing, the physical lowering of oneself before another, is an image that conveys subservience and obedience. When Balaam meets the angel of the Lord standing in the road, he bows low with his face to the ground in a gesture of reverence and submission (Num 22:31). Likewise, when Joseph's brothers are brought before him on their second journey to Egypt, they all bow "low to pay him honor" (Gen 43:28). In both instances the lowering of one person before another is a physical image of an unseen relationship. The person who bows is surrendering to the authority of one who is both literally and figuratively higher.

Beyond simply paying honor and acknowledging authority, bowing can also function as an image of submission. Thus becoming physically low before God is an image of worship itself. When David finishes his prayer at the installation of Solomon as king, he commands the assembly, "Praise the LORD your God," to which they respond by bowing low and falling prostrate (1 Chron 29:20). Another intriguing example is Abraham's encounter outside Sodom with the three men, one of whom is God. When Abraham first sees the visitors coming, he rushes out to meet them, bowing low (Gen 18:2). Here the physical image is not merely one of respect, but of worship. The Hebrew term that is translated "bowed low" in this passage describes the physical position of *worship (cf. Gen 22:5; Ex 34:14; Ps 96:9). Thus Abraham physically lowers himself because he recognizes that God is present before him.

Whether before God or some lesser authority, bowing low is a self-humbling act that acknowledges the superiority and authority of another. But for those who will not humble themselves, the Bible is replete with images of God's humbling the high, the powerful and the proud. Here the act of *descent—becoming low—is an image of forced humility under God's overwhelming power. Isaiah declares that God "humbles those who dwell on high, he lays the lofty city low" (Is 26:5 NIV). This passage conveys an image of humbling that includes destruction, in which the city is literally made low (i.e., leveled). Likewise, Jeremiah announces that the warriors of Egypt will "be laid low" by the hand of God and turned to flight (Jer 46:15). Isaiah also promises that "the eyes of the arrogant man will be humbled, and the pride of men brought low" (Is 2:11 NIV). In this instance it is not merely physical power but sinful pride that is subject to humiliation. In each case, God exercises his dominion by bringing humility on those who would otherwise exalt themselves. There is no one who is outside God's dominion: Job muses on the universally humbling effect of death in a double image in which "man dies and is laid low" (Job 14:10 NIV) both figuratively and literally.

The biblical image of being or becoming low can thus reflect ontological or social position, a relationship of submission, an attitude of worship or the dominion of God over human power and pride. The primary feature of the image is humility, whether voluntary or forced. In general, the Bible reverses the usual meaning of the archetype by making lowness predominantly positive. Even the Bible's attitude toward the sanctity of the commonplace and the domestic is part of the pattern.

See also ASCENT; DESCENT; HIGH, HEIGHT, HIGH PLACE; HUMILITY; LYING PROSTRATE; SLAVE, SLAVERY.

LOYALTY

Loyalty is a relational term. While one can be *faithful* to an ideal, duty or vow, one is *loyal* to a person. Loyalty denotes enduring commitment to a person over a long period of time, often with the implication of the commitment persisting in the face of obstacles that threaten such endurance. A loyal *friend sticks by, proves reliable even in adverse circumstances and is faithful in his or her dealings. In the Bible loyalty points beyond human relationships to the relationship of God with his people, a relationship based on *covenant and expressive of permanent love from which no believer can ever be separated (Rom 8:35-39). Biblical images of loyalty thus fall into two categories—human and divine.

On a human level loyalty is a prime virtue without which human relationships become undependable and the fabric of society loses its stability. When Abimelech wishes to reach accord with *Abraham, he appeals to the ideal of mutual loyalty as the basis for their agreement (Gen 21:24). Abraham's servant, in quest to find a wife for Isaac, makes a similar appeal for loyal dealing with Rebekah's family (Gen 24:49), as does *Jacob in his request to *Joseph that he be buried in Canaan rather than Egypt (Gen 47:29). In all of these instances loyalty is regarded as the ultimate court of appeal for people to act with integrity in personal dealings (see also 2 Sam 2:5; 3:8; 10:2; 1 Kings 2:7; 1 Chron 19:2).

Loyalty is associated especially with friendship. The friendship of *David and Jonathan (1 Sam 20) is the classic example in the Bible. The book of Proverbs has sayings about a friend who sticks closer than a brother (Prov 18:24), who keeps secrets (Prov 11:13), who criticizes in the best interest of a person (Prov 27:6). A summary of the ideal is the proverb that "what is desirable in a person is loyalty" (Prov 19:22 NRSV). In his epistles Paul addresses his "loyal companion," or "yokefellow" (Phil 4:3), and his "loyal child in the faith" (1 Tim 1:2; Tit 1:4). Judas is the ultimate perversion of the ideal, the disloyal friend par excellence (Mk 14:44-45; Lk 22:47-48).

Ruth is a byword for loyalty, and her relationship to her mother-in-law can be seen as combining friendship and family ties. Her loyalty is expressed in unforgettable rhetoric: "Entreat me not to leave you or to return from following you; for where you go I will go" (Ruth 1:16 RSV). When Boaz first expresses his interest in Ruth, it is Ruth's reputation for loyalty that he mentions: "All that you have done for your mother-in-law since the death of your husband has been fully told me" (Ruth 2:11 RSV).

Overshadowing these images of human loyalty are references that link loyalty to God's covenant relationship with his people. On one side is the loyalty of God, who is "the faithful God who maintains covenant loyalty with those who love him and keep his commandments" (Deut 7:9 NRSV; cf. 7:12). The response that God desires is people who reciprocate by being loyal to him (Deut 18:13; Dan 11:32), based on the premise that "with the loyal you [God] show yourself loyal" (Ps 18:25 NRSV). The ultimate disgrace for a covenant people is to be disloyal (Hos 4:1).

See also COVENANT; FAMILY; FRIENDSHIP.

LUKE, GOSPEL OF

Modern readers tend to perceive the Gospel accounts as diffuse and episodic. This perception may result from the habit of reading discrete excerpts, often for devotional purposes. Reading a Gospel from beginning to end to experience the impact of the whole, however, presents a more unified impression and suggests a number of recurrent motifs and patterns. Read at one sitting, the Gospel of Luke appears more cohesive than it otherwise might seem.

The plot of Luke is structured as a *quest. Though its composition is episodic, the plot is organized in the main as a teleological journey toward completion of a goal. Christ has come to do his Father's will: to die and rise again (Lk 24:45-47; cf. Acts 1:1-8). This sense of purpose is most evident in the long middle section (Lk 9:51—19:27) that does not appear in any other Gospel. It begins with Jesus "resolutely" setting out for Jerusalem for his appointed death, burial and resurrection. Along the way he variously heals the multitudes (e.g., Lk 5:12-13, 18-26; 9:37-42) and teaches his disciples (e.g., Lk 9:1-6; 17:1-10; 21:20-36). Seen in the narrative context of Christ's purposeful move toward Calvary, all these events and teachings must be understood as *kērygmata*—proclamations of the Messiah's salvific mission.

Permeating the whole of Luke's Gospel is a sense of fulfillment, begun with Christ's first sermon at Nazareth (Lk 4:16-21) and continuing until the climactic crucifixion at Calvary. Even the frame of the Gospel suggests a quest. In its announcement of an orderly account of events certifying truth, Luke's prologue (Lk 1:1-4) promises *telos* and fulfillment. Likewise the concluding events of the meeting on the road to Emmaus and the appearance at Bethany point to the completion or fulfillment of a divine plan (Lk 24:27, 44-47), this phase of the plan now concluded in his resurrection. It may well be that the Anglo-Saxon author of the poem "The Dream of the Rood" had Luke in mind when he pictured Christ eagerly mounting and even embracing the cross as a knight entering battle, for the cross was the anticipated climax of his life.

Within the events of Christ's quest for the cross, a rhythm that alternates between crowds and individuals predominates. Often after a scene of Christ in a crowd, Luke focuses on Christ alone, or on Christ with one individual or the disciples. A poignant example is Peter's confession of Jesus as the Messiah, which follows in the narrative immediately after the feeding of the five thousand (Lk 9:10-22). The next event recorded is the transfiguration, followed by the crowd pressing again as Christ heals the boy with an evil spirit (Lk 9:28-45). While these events happened days apart, Luke compresses them in an alternating rhythm of crowd then individual that shows Christ's interest in the individuals he meets. The Zacchaeus story (Lk 19:1-10), which Luke alone records, is another scene in which the crowd is counterpointed against an individual. A profound irony underlies this incident as the individual sinner Zacchaeus is converted and the self-righteous crowd remains unchanged. Even the events of the passion narrative alternate between crowd and individual. Judas betrays Christ (Lk 22:1-6); Christ celebrates the Last Supper (Lk 22:7-38); they retreat to the Mount of Olives, where Christ prays alone (Lk 22:39-46); when he returns to his disciples, he is arrested (Lk 22:47-52); the scene reverts to the courtyard where Peter becomes the focus as he betrays the Lord and weeps bitterly (Lk 22:54-62).

Even within the crowd scenes themselves, the focus often narrows to Christ and an individual, like a zoom shot in film. Notice the zoom from the "large crowd" to the widow of Nain's son as he raises him from the dead and amazes the crowd (Lk 7:11-17). The same pattern is repeated in the raising of Jairus's daughter (Lk 8:40-55). Contained within this story is the incident of the woman "subject to bleeding for twelve years" (Lk 8:43). With the crowd almost crushing him, Jesus focuses his attention on the woman, trembling in fear, and heals her. The same pattern is apparent in the widow's offering (Lk 21:1-4), the rich functioning as foils to highlight her sacrifice of all she had.

When we turn from plot to images, the picture that emerges is of a bimodal, almost paradoxical, world. Images vary from everyday scenes to educated, even aristocratic settings. The most obvious recurrent image is the commonplace one of the road and *walking. Christ travels the roads of Palestine, stopping to teach or heal. The primary transition between incidents in Luke is Christ walking. "Then he went down to Capernaum" (Lk 4:31); "he entered Capernaum" (Lk 7:1); "one Sabbath Jesus was going" (Lk 6:1); "Jesus resolutely set out for Jerusalem" (Lk 9:51); "One Sabbath, when Jesus went to eat in the house of a prominent Pharisee" (Lk 14:1); "Jesus entered Jericho" (Lk 19:1). Each of these narrative transitions introduces a destination at which a significant event or teaching highlights Jesus' ministry among the common people. Luke's Gospel gives the impression of a series of microcosmic *teloi* within the larger macrocosm of Christ's purpose as redeemer.

A counterpart to the central image of walking is the upper class image of *banqueting. In one scene Christ is at dinner "in the house of a prominent Pharisee" and admonishes the guests to choose their seats humbly. He goes on to rebuke the *Pharisees in the parable of the great *supper, the irony of which could not have been lost on those present (Lk 14:1-24). At the home of Martha and Mary, Christ teaches that Mary had "chosen what is better" in learning from him, as opposed to Martha, who was consumed with the social obligation of feeding her guest (Lk 10:38-42). The image of banqueting reaches its climactic portrayal in the last Passover supper, in which Christ transforms the meal into a symbol of his death and second coming (Lk 22:7-22). The disciples must have remembered this meal in their postresurrection dinners with the Lord (e.g., Lk 24:30).

Even in the world of the parables that Luke alone records, the bimodal images of a commonplace world and upper class banqueting predominate. On the one hand are parables set in an agricultural world, and on the other hand are those set in a more aristocratic situation. Lukan parables in which the world is largely agrarian include the parables of the rich fool (Lk 12:16-21), the barren *fig tree (Lk 13:6-9) and the lost *sheep (Lk 15:3-7). Those that present a more aristocratic world, however, are the most memorable. Most striking is the *prodigal son (Lk 15:11-32). Here we have a son who is forced into an agrarian existence, yet his wealthy father is rich in *mercy, welcoming him back into the family. In the *same world is the story of the rich man and Lazarus, teaching that riches do not guarantee eternal bliss (Lk 16:19-31). The parables spoken to the Pharisees (Lk 14) move appropriately in a cosmopolitan world that the auditors would recognize instantly.

Omnipresent throughout the heterogeneous world of the Gospel and unifying it into a cohesive narrative is Christ himself. Providing a frame to the depiction of Christ in Luke's Gospel is the sublime account of his nativity (see Birth Story) at the beginning and his post-resurrection appearances and *ascension at the end. Of the synoptic accounts, Luke's is the most complete and elevated in its narrative of the incarnation. Luke begins with God becoming man and ends with the God-man ascending to heaven. Within this frame is a picture that emphasizes the humanity of the Messiah. Of the four Evangelists, Luke alone does not recount the miracle of walking on the water, yet five of fourteen incidents that Luke alone reports are miracle healings (Lk 7:11; 11:14; 17:11-19; 13:10-17; 14:1-6). Luke's is the Christ who turns from teaching the disciples to healing the poor or disenfranchised who are near at hand.

Luke's Gospel surpasses the others in the attention it accords to the fringe figures of society, including the outcasts, the poor, the *sinners and women. Luke repeatedly shows Jesus as the friend of sinners and outcasts. Twice in Luke's Gospel, but nowhere in the other three, we find a record of the Pharisees and scribes accusing Jesus of receiving and eating with sinners (Lk 5:29-32; 15:1-2). Luke specializes in parables that deal with finding what was *lost—a lost sheep, lost coin and lost son (Lk 15:3-32). The Jesus of Luke's Gospel defends the cause of the poor,

most notably in the parable of the rich man and Lazarus (Lk 16:19-31) and the teaching about inviting the poor, maimed, lame and blind to a banquet instead of one's rich neighbors (Lk 14:12-24). There is a revolutionary undertone as well as a cosmopolitan spirit to Luke's Gospel. Highlights include the parable of the good Samaritan (Lk 10:25-37); Simeon's song (Lk 2:31-32), with its focus on "all peoples" and "the Gentiles"; and the Great Commission that comes near the end, with its focus on bringing the gospel to "all nations" (Lk 24:47).

Luke's Christ elevates *women above their position in the Jewish economy to a position of respect and privilege. Witness the women who traveled with him and supported him in his ministry—Joanna, Susanna, Mary Magdalene (Lk 8:1-3). Women are the last to leave the cross (Lk 23:55) and the first at the tomb (Lk 24:1). In the tenderest of stories the resurrected Christ appears first to a woman (Lk 24:5-8). With a few beautiful strokes of his pen, Luke portrays a Christ who understands the lot of women and elevates them to their rightful place.

Luke's Gospel simply overflows with Christ. Christ presses his claims on everyone he meets, variously showing compassion on the disenfranchised poor or confronting the comfortable rich. Frequently surrounded by begging multitudes, he focuses attention on a single individual. Luke's Christ moves deliberately toward Calvary to do what only he could do, along the way ministering to Jews and Gentiles alike. With the earliest Christian writers we must see Luke as a consummate artist who writes an orderly and evocative account of the greatest story ever told.

See also GOSPEL GENRE; JESUS, IMAGES OF; JOHN, GOSPEL OF; MARK, GOSPEL OF; MATTHEW, GOSPEL OF; QUEST.

LUST. See ADULTERY; APPETITE; IDOL, IDOLATRY

LYING DOWN

The image of lying down is used extensively in the OT to represent conditions both of *blessing—"He makes me lie down in green pastures" (Ps 23:2 NRSV)—and of judgment—"Let us lie down in our shame, and let our dishonor cover us" (Jer 3:25 NRSV).

The blessings of lying down follow the keeping of the commandments (Lev 26:3, 6), the keeping of sound *wisdom and discretion (Prov 3:21, 24), and the direct *protection of the Lord (Ps 3:5; 4:8). Lying down while under *judgment is a symbol of *prostration, *humiliation and *death. In Ezekiel 4:4-9 the prophet is told to lie on his side daily to represent the siege on *Jerusalem for the sins of the "house of Israel." In Lamentations 2:21 and Ezekiel 32:26-32 the dead lie in the open, unburied.

In Leviticus 26:6 those who rest in God's blessings are also promised to be untroubled by wild *animals. Those who lie down in God's blessings are sometimes referred to as *sheep, with the Lord as their shepherd who makes them *rest (Ps 32:2; Ezek 34:14-15). Under these circumstances human shepherds will also find places for their *flocks to graze and lie down (Is 65:10; Jer 33:10). In the future *kingdom, animals which are natural enemies will lie down together (Is 11:6-7).

Under circumstances of judgment, however, cities and other human habitations are abandoned to the animals who will rest therein. In *Babylon, "wild beasts of the desert will lie there, and their houses will be full of howling creatures" (Is 13:21 NKJV). When "the cities of Aroer are forsaken; they will be for flocks which lie down" (Is 17:2 NKJV). Zephaniah prophesied of Nineveh, "How has she become a desolation, a place for beasts to lie down" (Zeph 2:13-15 NKJV). In times of blessing, people rest like the animals; in times of judgment only the animals are able to rest.

See also LYING PROSTRATE; REST.

LYING PROSTRATE

Lying prostrate may be variously represented in the Bible as "falling on one's face," "bowing down with one's face to the earth," "prostrating oneself," "doing reverence" or "doing obeisance." Some of the many references to mere *"bowing" may also indicate someone lying prostrate. The prohibition of bowing to *idols, for example, applied to the Israelites' prostration before Baal of Peor (Num 25:2), Cornelius's prostration before Peter (Acts 10:25-26) and John's prostration before the angel (Rev 19:10; 22:8-9). Such prostrations are only forbidden, however, when they indicate acts of improper worship.

Lying prostrate was commonly an act of respect to authority figures: to kings (1 Sam 24:8; 25:23; 2 Sam 9:6; Esther 8:3), to prophets (1 Kings 18:7; Dan 2:46), to an authoritative relative (Gen 48:12; Ex 18:7; Ruth 2:10), to masters (Mt 18:26, 29), to a military leader (2 Sam 18:21) and to a friend (1 Sam 20:41). Such respect was, of course, deemed especially appropriate in *worship to God. Abraham, Job, Joshua, Ezekiel and the Israelites at Solomon's temple dedication were among the OT figures who prostrated themselves in worship (Gen 17:3; Job 1:20; Josh 5:14; 2 Chron 7:3; Ezek 1:28). In the NT those possessed by *demons are said to fall down before Jesus (Mk 3:11; Lk 8:28).

Lying prostrate was also a frequent expression of *fear. Balaam fell down afraid when he saw the Angel of the Lord (Num 22:31) as did Daniel during one of his visions (Dan 8:17). Fear and awe of God's power and glory often resulted in worshipers prostrating themselves (Lev 9:23-24; Judg 13:20; 1 Kings 18:39; Rev 1:17).

Other reasons people prostrated themselves were to confess sin and ask forgiveness (Gen 50:18; 1 Chron 21:16-17; Lk 5:8); to offer petitions, especially to Jesus for healing (Mk 5:22; 7:25; Lk 5:12; Jn 11:32) and to give thanks (Lk 17:15-16). Not every act of prostration was sincere: Abraham laughed while prostrate (Gen 17:17); Absalom bowed himself to David while plotting against him (2 Sam 14:33). Once Naaman determined to worship the Lord, he asked Elisha to be excused if, in fulfilling his duties, he should seem to bow to his nation's god. Elisha granted this request (2 Kings 5:17-19).

See also BOWING; FEAR.

LYRIC

The term *poem* is almost synonymous with *lyric*. A lyric is a short poem, sometimes sung or accompanied by music, expressing the thoughts or feelings of a speaker who speaks in the first person ("I" or "we"). The subjective or personal element is especially regarded as the authentic note of lyric. Lyric poets speak directly instead of projecting feelings onto other characters. A lyric is in effect an utterance that is overheard, although the speaker may speak for a group or for the reader as well. A good lyric is like a good public prayer—both personal and communal, expressing what both an individual and a believing community want said.

Emotion is often regarded as the differentia of lyric, and it is true that feeling is the dominant content of lyric poetry. But the other possibility—thought, meditation or reflection as the subject of lyric—is proportionally more common in the Psalter than in lyric poetry generally. With both affective and reflective lyrics, we should not expect to find a story line. Lyric poets are much more interested in creating a mood than in presenting an action.

Lyrics are heightened speech used to express intensified feeling or insight. Because of this they often contain abrupt shifts, and they usually lack smooth transitions. Both meditative and emotional lyrics are likely to represent the poet's response to a stimulus, and there is frequently an implied situation underlying a lyric poem.

Lyrics are also brief. They should accordingly be viewed as self-contained units, not as chapters in a book. Because lyrics express a feeling at its greatest intensity, or a thought at its greatest insight and conviction, they do not express the whole truth on a topic or experience. Lyrics capture a moment and do not represent a systematic or reasoned philosophy of the subject. To this we should add that lyric is often hyperbolic, with the result that it often expresses emotional truth, not literal truth. Because lyrics are brief, unity of impact is at a premium. To read lyrics as a collection of individual verses detracts from that effect. A helpful framework for grasping the unity of a lyric is to think of it as a theme and variation on the subject.

Lyrics are normally constructed on a three-part structure. They begin with *a statement of the controlling theme or motif*. This unifying element might be a feeling, an idea or a situation to which the poet is responding. It can be established with an invocation, a reference to a situation, an address to the audience, the statement of an idea or the expression of a feeling or exclamation. The *body* of a lyric develops the controlling theme or motif. There are four means by which lyric poets develop their theme: repetition, contrast, catalog and association (branching out from one subject to a related one). Finally, lyric poems do not simply end; they are rounded off with a *note of resolution or finality.* In the Psalms this note of resolution is often a brief prayer or wish that brings the poem to a note of closure.

See also PSALMS, BOOK OF.

M

MADNESS

The modern psychological understanding of madness simply did not exist in biblical times. There are, however, examples of irrational and insane behavior. Those suffering such affliction were universally feared and shunned because it was assumed that they had had some contact with deity or the demonic (cf. 1 Sam 21:12-15). Indeed, madness was thought to be the outcome of divine punishment (Deut 28:28; Zech 12:4). God sent an evil spirit to torment Saul (1 Sam 16:14-16; cf. 1 Kings 22:19-23) resulting in depressive and murderous behavior (1 Sam 18:10-11), which could sometimes be assuaged by *music (1 Sam 16:23), though not always (1 Sam 18:10). Saul also exhibited evidence of other psychoses, including hysteria (e.g., 1 Sam 19:24) and paranoia (e.g., 1 Sam 20:30-34). The Bible clearly links his madness to his disobedience.

In Daniel 4 Nebuchadnezzar exhibits symptoms of depressive or psychotic delusion when his pride becomes overweening (vv. 32-33). His symptoms involve self-neglect, delusion and bestial behavior. It is not the psychology but the theology that interests biblical writers however. Both Saul and Nebuchadnezzar are in rebellion against God. Their behavior reflects their foolishness. Indeed, *folly is the outcome of a certain kind of madness—the refusal to live according to God's revealed wisdom and in obedience to him, which gives rise to the metaphorical understanding of madness discussed below.

In the NT Jesus frequently delivers from demons those who exhibit apparently psychotic behavior. The violence of the Gadarene demonic (Mk 5:1-20) subsides to the point where he is "in his right mind" (v. 15). Occasionally dumbness and blindness are associated with the demonic (Mt 9:32; 12:22) and may be hysterical in origin.

Each of the above examples creates the impression of chaos and disorder. This relates to the refusal to allow God his proper place of respect and control or to the direct opposition of demonic forces. Thus, metaphorically, wisdom literature uses the image of madness to describe a life lived unwisely. Ecclesiastes, for example, describes intellectual boasting as madness (Eccles 1;17; 2:12; 7:25; 9:3; 10:13). Saul is, once again, a prototype of foolish behavior because he closed his mind to God. Nabal is a fool because his behavior is heedlessly aggressive (1 Sam 25:25).

This madnnes that is folly is the faulty evaluation of God's existence and purposes (Ps 14:1; Is 32:5-6; 1 Cor 1:25, 27). Sometimes it is simply silliness (e.g., Prov 10:14; 14:15; 18:13). But frequently it derives from the inability to correctly perceive issues (e.g., Lk 11:40) or the tendency to make unworthy moral choices (e.g., Prov 9:13-18; Lk 12:20) or to engage in scoffing (Prov 1:22; 14:6). Such is madness (Lk 6:11; cf. 2 Pet 2:16).

See also DEMONS; FOLLY.

MAGIC

In the world of the Bible, filled with exorcists and magicians, mystery religions and cults inspired by evil spirits, where curses were effective against enemies and protection from evil spirits was a necessary worry of the righteous, magic was everywhere. Western preoccupation with empirical science has recently relieved much of humanity from such worries with the result that translations of the Bible have hidden much of the magic of antiquity from the modern reader.

The text of Scripture contains a handful of scattered references alongside a few incidents of confrontation between magicians and heroes of the faith: Joseph versus *Pharaoh's magicians (Gen 41:8, 24); Moses versus Pharaoh's magicians (Ex 7:11; 8:7; 9:11); Daniel versus the Chaldeans (Dan 1:20; 2:2; 4:7; 5:11); Peter versus Simon Magus (Acts 8:9); and Barnabas and Saul versus Elymas Bar-Jesus (Acts 13:8). In truth, for the inhabitants of the biblical world most confrontations between good and evil were simply the visible manifestations of a larger spiritual reality, which was the domain of magic. The few other references (apart from the contests mentioned above) only hint at how widespread was this magic outlook.

Most discussions of magic devote the initial chapter to the notoriously difficult task of defining magic, but with limited success. Sociologists usually object to cultural biases and external impositions of value-laden terms in such definitions, while theologians focus on the distinctions between worship of the Creator and manipulation of creation for selfish ends. One often encounters the summary statement that a religious leader has a congregation, a magician a clientele.

For purposes of biblical interpretation, the field

of magic is much larger than what has been traditionally called magic in English. Much of the popular understanding of religion through the ages has bordered on magic. Just as the word *hocus-pocus* has degenerated from a popular misunderstanding of the mystery of *hoc est corpus meum* ("This is my body"), so too the human propensity to postulate causes and personify the inanimate has led to repeated subversion of the mystical facet of religion. Magic in antiquity encompassed many aspects, including protection against evil spirits and other magic (spells, curses, broken oaths, jealousy), understanding and manipulating the hierarchies of angels and demons, exorcism, curing the spiritual causes of disease, controlling nature (weather, crops, host of heaven) as well as divination and oracles. But ultimately, magic may be defined as the work of magicians.

The Hebrew Bible uses a bewildering array of words to refer to individuals who performed magic or who mediated the supernatural. Although the titles are common, the narrative rarely provides details of ritual or praxis. Veiled references to obscure ceremonies remain difficult to explain (e.g., Ezek 13:19; 21:21) and are often enlightened only by cultural parallels. The wonders performed by prophetic figures in the OT foreshadow the miracles of Jesus in the Gospels. The "man of God" knows the future (Judg 13:6) and is equated with the "angel/messenger of Yahweh" (Judg 13:16). All that he says comes true (1 Sam 9:6). He sees far-away events (2 Kings 5:26). He also brings down *fire from heaven (1 Kings 18:38). He can multiply *food—bread (2 Kings 4:42-44) and *oil (2 Kings 4:1-6)—and can manipulate *rain and drought (2 Kings 8:7) and make God *thunder from heaven (1 Sam 7:10; 12:18). The man of God can heal (2 Kings 5:3; 8:7) but also afflict (2 Kings 5:27). God sends him ministers in the wilderness (1 Kings 17:4; cf. Mk 1:12).

The Hebrew terms for magicians and other mediators of the supernatural are as follows:

'aśśāpîm: "exorcists," primarily dream interpreters (Heb, Dan 1:20; 2:2; Aram, Dan 2:10, 27; 4:4; 5:7, 11, 15).

gāzᵉrîn: "diviners" (from a word meaning "to cut, decide" [Dan 2:27; 4:7; 5:7, 11]).

ḥōbēr ḥāber: "spell caster" (literally, "one who ties magic knots" [Deut 18:11; Ps 58:6; Is 47:9, 12]).

ḥōzeh: "seer," one who sees visions (Is 30:10; Mic 3:7; Amos 7:12), sometimes designating an official attached to the king (2 Sam 24:11; 1 Chron 25:5) who at the same time performs temple service with singers and Levites (2 Chron 5:12).

ḥᵃkāmîm: usually translated "wise," which hides the fact that it occasionally designates a special class of learned, shrewd men who appear with astrologers, magicians and diviners (Gen 41:8; Ex 7:11; Is 19:11; 44:25; Jer 50:35; 51:57; Esther 1:13; 6:13). They are also mentioned among the elite leadership of society along with experts in charms (Is 3:3). This term reflects a semantic development similar to English *wizard* (also derived from *wise* with specific magical connotations). Solomon's great wisdom earned him a reputation as the greatest of wizards and exorcists (1 Kings 4:29-34; Josephus).

ḥartummîm: "magician," probably of Egyptian origin meaning "dream interpreter" (Gen 41:8, 24; Ex 7:11, 22; 8:3, 14-15; 9:11; Dan 1:20).

ḥarāšîm: used only in Isaiah 3:3 to designate magic arts or pharmacopoeia, herbal medicine being the realm of the magician/physician. Both magic and medicine were obscure "sciences" practiced by curious investigating wise persons and charlatans. (Doctor is often not a positive word in antiquity!)

kōhēn: "priest," interprets or receives the oracle from the ephod, here a divining tool (1 Sam 2:28; 14:18; 23:9-12; 30:7). Note also the role of Levites as diviners (Judg 17:8—18:31; Deut 33:8). Levites also control the power of cursing (Deut 27:9-26; cf. Job 31:30; Ps 41:7).

kaśdîm: "Chaldeans," i.e., Babylonian dream interpreters (Dan 2:2, 4).

mekaśśēpîm/keśśāpîm: "sorcerers" (herbalists?). They are condemned as an abomination (Deut 18:10), introduced by Jezebel (2 Kings 9:22), called false prophets (Jer 27:9), are to be cut off (Mic 5:11) and are present in foreign courts (Ex 7:11; Dan 1:20, etc.).

mᵉlaḥᵃšîm: "enchanters," literally "whisperers" (Ps 58:6 and in Ugaritic charms, and *lāḥaś* in Ps 41:7; Is 3:3) and the "amulets" of Isaiah 3:20 (cf. 2 Macc 12:40; Mt 23:5).

mᵉnaḥēś: "omen diviners," prohibited in Deuteronomy 18:10 but practiced in Genesis 30:27 and 1 Kings 20:33; "omens" in Num 23:23; 24:1 (RSV).

meᶜōnēn: "soothsayer," who supplants true prophecy (Deut 18:14) and gives false predictions (Jer 27:9). Jacob is rejected as "full of soothsayers," to be cut off (Mic 5:12). Also the diviner's oak (Judg 9:37). (A related Arabic verb means "to whisper in the leaves," cf. Homeric oracles from Zeus's whispering oak.)

nābîʾ: "prophet," has power to heal (2 Kings 5), to resurrect (1 Kings 17:17; by touch [2 Kings 4:29-37] or even after death [2 Kings 13:21]). His clothing possessed power (mantle of Elijah [2 Kings 2:14; cf. Lk 8:44]).

qōsēm: "diviners" by casting lots (Deut 18:10; Ezek 21:26; Num 23:23) or using the *'ōb,* a "divining pit" from which spirits of the dead are conjured to answer questions about the future (1 Sam 28:8).

rōʾeh: "seer." Saul contacts Samuel to find his father's lost donkeys (1 Sam 9:9); Hanni contacts the Seer (2 Chron 16:7-10). The Seer perhaps overlaps in function with the *nābîʾ* (1 Sam 9:9).

Many of the terms for magicians are borrowed from foreign cultures (Egypt, Mesopotamia, Anatolia), and even the Hebrew ones occur in neighboring cultures to designate magico-religious functionaries. The Israelites were obviously impressed with the abilities of conjurers who used other *gods. These foreign cultures, in turn, often held Jewish magicians in awe.

The prevalence of magicians in the Jewish world points to a parallel ubiquity of magical evils. These evils and their associated magic remedies divide into two classes. Some magic was intended to do harm to one's enemies, to get even or gain advantage. This type was clearly forbidden in Scripture as well as in surrounding nations. Another type of magic was meant simply to protect a vulnerable soul against the evils loose in the world: bad dreams, unintentionally broken oaths, disease, the evil eye, miscarriage, burglary. Such evils were consequences of sin visited by unclean spirits on morally lapsed humans. Since all have sinned, all had reason to fear. Job was tormented by Satan even without cause.

Words as Magic: Curses. The author of Proverbs reassures the righteous that the "curse that is causeless does not alight" (Prov 26:2). God's word does not return without accomplishing its purpose, and humans are not to utter idle words (Is 55:11; Mt 12:36). Balaam discovers that he cannot *curse, charm or incant against Israel (Num 23:7, 23; but see 24:9). Simon Magus, himself a respected magician, fears Peter's curse (Acts 8:24)

Much of the imagery of Psalms, wherein the wicked open their mouth against the righteous and their words and whispering intend harm, probably refers to magical attempts to hex God's people. The Lord detests people who "hunt down souls" by magic rituals (Ezek 13:18-20). Psalm 109 is a long prayer that the wicked may wear their own curses as a garment. Job protests that he is innocent before his haters, saying, "I have not sinned by asking for his life with a curse" (Job 31:30).

By contrast, a broken oath left one exposed to the curses that had sealed the oath (Deut 29:21). A curse devours the earth because of guilt (Is 24:6; cf. Jer 23:10). Irrational or self-destructive behavior was blamed on bewitching by enemies. Paul uses such a metaphor of the Galatians' inexplicable reversion from faith to law (Gal 3:1). Evil spirits could themselves mislead (1 Tim 4:1).

Central to practice of magic is the idea that symbols harness the power of what they represent. Words are symbols and more. They have power in and of themselves. For John the Word is God (Jn 1:1). God's word created the heavens (Ps 33:6; 148:5-8) and sustains creation (Heb 1:3). Just as God's rebuke creates (Ps 18:15) and restores order to creation (Ps 104:7; Job 26:11), so too Jesus' rebuke heals (Mt 17:18 par. Lk 9:42; Lk 4:35, 39, 41). God rebukes the sea; so does Jesus (Mk 4:39; cf. Ps 106:9). Jesus commends the faith of the centurion who asks, "Only say the word, and my servant will be healed" (Mt 8:8 RSV; Lk 7:7). Matthew's terse description of Jesus' method of exorcism simply says, "He cast out the spirits with a word" (Mt 8:16 RSV). The ineffable name of God uttered by one pure and holy had power to recoil attackers. When Jesus says, "I am," his arresters fall to the ground (Jn 18:4). The name of Jesus spread quickly even among Jewish exorcists as a deity by whom to adjure evil spirits (Acts 19:13).

For later exorcists the recorded Aramaic utterances of Jesus became magic formulas (Mk 5:41; 7:34).

Phylacteries. Our comfortable distinctions between magic and religion fade in the realm of phylacteries (Mt 23:5). For Jews at the time of Christ, the wearing of Scripture was mandated (Deut 6:8-9; 11:18-21). Scriptures secured to the door posts protected or secured a blessing for the house in a manner similar to the blood of the *Passover lamb (Deut 6:9). The text of the Aaronic blessing (Num 6:24-26) has been found written on a silver roll from the period of just before the exile. No doubt it was worn as an amulet. The sin for which many fell in battle was not the wearing of amulets but that those amulets contained the names of foreign gods (2 Macc 12:40).

Magic as Spirits. Angels and demons represent parallel hierarchies of spiritual armies either aiding or opposing God's wonder worker. God dispatches *armies (Gen 32:2; 2 Sam 5:24), fiery *chariots (2 Kings 6:17) and legions of *angels (Mt 26:53; *see* Divine Warrior). But the devil also has his legions (Mk 5:9). The *stars are angels (Rev 1:20), and the host of heaven can either be God's army (Lk 2:13) or the demonic zodiac of idolatrous worship (Jer 19:13; Amos 5:26; Acts 7:42). The officers of these angelic armies fight against each other as they carry out their missions (Dan 10:1, 13, 20)

For the Magi (from the Persian word for astrological priest and dream interpreter, whence the Gk *magikos* and, ultimately, English *magic*) and their Jewish contemporaries, events in the heavens (i.e., cosmic events) presaged momentous changes on earth that led them to seek the Christ (Mt 2; cf. Rev 6:12-14). Falling stars or *lightning symbolized falling members of the heavenly host, whether Satan himself (Lk 10:18), Wormwood (Rev 8:10) or the nameless fallen angel who releases the scorpion demons from the bottomless pit (Rev 9:1). But the revelatory voice from heaven, whether God's or an angel's, sounded like mere *thunder to the ignorant (Jn 12:29; cf. 1 Sam 7:10; 12:18; 2 Sam 22:14).

The typical magician established a relationship with a spirit that granted the practitioner superhuman powers in exchange for co-opting his rational faculties on occasion. High-ranking demons were believed to be able to order lower-ranking disease demons away. Such thinking lies behind the accusation that Jesus "has a demon" (Lk 7:33; Jn 10:20, cf. Mt 11:18) or "has Beelzebul" (Mk 3:22, not "is possessed by" as RSV) and especially that "he casts out demons by the prince of demons" (Lk 11:15). Jesus replies that his authority comes not from tapping into a demonic hierarchy but from God, and therefore the kingdom has come. Jesus mentions Pharisee exorcists (Mt 12:27), and Jewish literature records that they healed patients by using *spittle (cf. Jn 9:6) and that magic was believed responsible for blighted crops and withered orchards (Mt 21:19). The Pharisees' confusion regarding Jesus is understandable.

In the realm of magic the spirit that possess a body

is said to be "clothed in the flesh." This phrase does not apply only to evil spirits, for "the spirit of Yahweh clothed Gideon" (Judg 6:34; RSV translates "took possession"). Paul uses the same metaphor, urging believers to "be clothed in the Lord Jesus Christ" (Rom 13:14; cf. Gal 3:27).

Demonic Diseases. Because many physical ailments were the consequences of *sin (1 Cor 11:30; Jas 5:16; cf. the popular attitude expressed in Jn 9:2), *forgiveness of sins was a prerequisite to healing (Mt 9:2-6). Sin opened one up to punishment and suffering, which might be administered by God's angels (Rev 7:2) or, alternatively, by an angel of *Satan (2 Cor 12:7, cf. Job).

It is difficult (and perhaps not desirable) to show that all *disease in the Bible had spiritual causes, but it certainly is true that evil or unclean spirits and sickness go hand in hand in the biblical world (Mt 4:24; 8:16; Mk 1:34; 6:13, 56; Acts 5:16; 8:7; 19:12). The techniques and terminology used of healing the sick are those of the exorcist. An epileptic is exorcised (Mt 17:15-18). Some who are *deaf (Mk 7:32; 9:35) and *blind are healed through exorcism (Mt 12:22). Those afflicted with muteness (whose Heb designation means "bound," presumably tongue-tied by superhuman forces) are released from demons (Mt 9:32; cf. Lk 11:14, which specifies that the demon itself was dumb). A woman is stooped because she has been "bound by Satan" (Lk 13:16). Paul's thorn in the flesh is the work of a messenger *(angelos)* of Satan (2 Cor 12:7).

Luke, the physician, narrates that Jesus rebuked a fever, suggesting an unclean spirit as the minister of the illness (Lk 4:39; fever demons appear in Akkadian magic literature and also in Jewish texts at Qumran contemporary with the Gospels, 4Q560). Using exorcist terminology, the wind and the sea are likewise "rebuked" and "muzzled" (Mk 4:39; cf. Ps 104:7; Zech 3:2). These events as narrated represent the divine as mastering and subduing evil, healing creation, undoing the Fall and reordering the chaos of Satan and his unclean spirits. Assuming the audience's familiarity with the OT magicians and wonder workers, they portray the victorious Christ as the ultimate "man of God."

Miracles as Magic? Theologians may debate how to harmonize Western empirical views of disease vectors with the spiritual causes of Scripture and to what extent disease is the result of sin or natural agents. The imagery of the Gospels, however, makes it clear that Jesus' contemporaries perceived him as a wonder-working exorcist. Jesus repeats the miracles of Elijah. His clothing can heal. He controls the *weather. He multiplies food. Like Moses, he has power over the sea, and his disciples will have Mosaic power over serpents (Ex 4:3; 7:12; Num 21:9; Lk ; Jn 3:14; 5:46). Moses survived an encounter with God in the wilderness, but Jesus faced the devil, the ultimate magician's contest. Offered a pact with the devil, Jesus declines and comes out on top. Jesus' wisdom and power over the natural world exceed

that of the renowned son of David, Solomon. The Evangelists deliberately accentuated the events in Jesus' life that show him to be greater than Elijah, more powerful than Moses (Matthew's theme, cf. Jn 5:46), even greater than Solomon (Mt 12:42; Lk 11:31).

After exorcising the dumb, Jesus is accused of being in league with Beelzebul (Lk 11:15—note the labels applied to Jesus that are elsewhere used of other magicians: "son of the devil" [Acts 13:10] and "Samaritan" [Jn 8:48; cf. Acts 8:9]), a charge he counters by observing that other exorcists are not so accused or that John the Baptizer, a righteous prophet, was similarly slandered (Mt 11:18).

Magic as Evil. Although the methods and rituals of magic are not described, the OT condemns specific practices, especially those involving the worship of spirits (Deut 18). The NT condemns magicians because, unlike Jesus and his disciples, they are in league with the devil or spirits (Acts 8:9; 13:6; 19:14) and are clearly doing the devil's bidding (Acts 13:10). The expensive books of magic destroyed at Ephesus probably contained formulas for harming opponents, seducing women, spiritual telekinesis and so forth (Acts 19:19).

Magic as Ambiguous. Some practices of the early church continue OT magic precedents. Like Elijah's mantle and Jesus' robe, Peter's shadow (Acts 5:15) and Paul's handkerchief or apron transmit healing (Acts 19:12). It is significant that Jesus forces the woman to address not his robe but his person as healer (Mk 5:25-34). Since medicine and magic were not well distinguished and neither was empirically based, the early church struggled with its attitudes toward "helpful" magic; that is, the use of herbs and potions to promote health. Even today Christians debate what forms of medical intervention trespass in the realm of spiritual wholeness and health. Judging from the number of amulets found with Christian symbols on them, certain magical practices continued to appeal to the general populace for centuries.

Charms. Certain passages of Scripture directly support a magical outlook. The songs of David, especially those composed to alleviate Saul's intermittent suffering at the hand of an evil spirit from the Lord (1 Sam 16:14; 18:10: 19:9), are an example. Documents from Qumran show that Psalm 91 was widely believed to be one of these psalms and to have curative and exorcistic powers. Rabbinic literature calls Psalm 91 "A Song for the Stricken" (by evil spirits), under the belief that the evils mention therein were demonic. Other such "Songs Against Evil Spirits" were also composed (4Q510-511). The NT corroborates such a view of Psalm 91 in that each time the psalm is quoted or alluded to, it is in the context of opposing the devil ("He will give his angels charge over you" [Lk 4:10]; "You will tread on snakes and scorpions" [Lk 10:19]; "A thousand shall fall at your side and ten thousand at your right hand" [corresponding to the demon Legion of Mk 5:9]).

*Snakes lay squarely in the domain of magic. They had been the devil in the *Garden, and they continued to represent demons on the devil's errands. Their unblinking eyes were peep holes into hell. No creature was more malevolent or more efficient at dispensing divine retribution (Acts 28:4). To tread on *serpents was to dominate the evil one (Ps 91:13; Mk 16:18; Lk 10:19). The one who charmed a serpent had power over the evil side of nature. Some serpents, deaf adders, thwarted the whispered incantations of the charmer by turning a deaf ear (Ps 58:4; cf. Jer 8:17; Eccles 10:11). Similar techniques applied to cosmic manipulations: "Let those curse it who curse the day, who are skilled to rouse up Leviathan" (Job 3:8 RSV).

Metaphors from Magic. In addition to the broad categories of a magical worldview above, many allusions to a magical outlook or ritual are scattered as metaphors throughout Scripture. The invisible yet irresistible influence that women exert on men has been integral to magic probably since the beginning. One wonders if the prophet intends his reference to the charms of the harlot as a metaphor (Nahum 3:4). Many similar English adjectives acquire a special meaning when used of women: fascinating (Lat, "spell-binding"), enchanting, charming, bewitching.

Some magical phrases almost escape detection. Around the whole Mediterranean world, the evil eye portended an act of jealous malice carried out by a vindictive demon whose attention had been called to someone's good fortune by expressing aloud some careless admiration or an envious remark. In the Gospels the phrase refers to a jealous spirit. The AV renders Matthew 20:15 literally, "Is thine eye evil because I am good?"

Revelation, shrouding political eventualities in metaphor and spiritual imagery, draws heavily on magical symbolism. The bowls of *plagues are familiar to John's readers from magic rituals in which evils are dissolved and poured out (Rev 15:7; 16:1-21). Nighttime *monsters and worries, like scorpions, frogs and foul and hateful birds (owls), already correspond to demons in popular mythology. John does not create these images but avails himself of the standard literary stock at hand (Rev 18:2; *see* Mythical Animals).

Magic as Barrier. As one of many examples, behind Naaman's request for two mule loads of Israelite soil on which to worship the God of Israel lies his belief that Elijah's God, like his own national god Rimmon, is territorial and can only be properly served on his own ground (2 Kings 5:17). Any reluctance on our part to admit these contrasts obscures the message of the text. More than the obvious differences in language, time and geography, the modern failure to see spiritual causes behind "natural" occurrences separates us from the people of antiquity and makes the imagery and meaning of their literature and language inaccessible to us.

See also COSMOLOGY; CURSE; DEMONS; DISEASE AND HEALING; EVIL; MONSTER, MONSTERS; PROPHET,
PROPHETESS; SATAN; VOW, OATH.

BIBLIOGRAPHY. P. S. Alexander, "Incantations and Books of Magic" in *The History of the Jewish People in the Age of Jesus Christ (175 B.C. - A.D. 135)*, rev. and ed. G. Vermes, F. Millar and M. Goodman (3 vols.; Edinburgh: T & T Clark, 1986) 3:342-79; J. M. Hull, *Hellenistic Magic and the Synoptic Tradition* (Naperville, IL: Allenson, 1974); A. Jeffers, *Magic and Divination in Ancient Palestine and Syria* (Leiden: E. J. Brill, 1996); M. Smith, *Jesus Exorcist* (WUNT 2/54; Tübingen: J. C. B. Mohr, 1993).

MAID, MAIDEN

The Hebrew and Greek terms translated "maid" or "maiden" are used in a variety of ways in the Bible. They may refer to a young woman of marriageable age (1 Kings 1:2-4; Esther 2:3), a *virgin (Gen 24:16; Deut 22:23), a young married woman (Ruth 4:12) or a female *servant or *slave (Gen 16:1; Ex 23:12; Ps 123:2). The image is unified by three features: vulnerable status, strong service and unusual faith.

Vulnerable Status. Youth, gender and virginity contribute to the vulnerable status of the maiden. In the ancient cultures their low status as youth is doubled by their female status; the moderate respect afforded women with age or children is not yet given. The fragile treasure of virginity is easily and irreparably lost; women are ruined if it is lost improperly. Dinah and Tamar, who are raped, and Ruth and Tamar, who are widowed early, must each endure the shame of a culture. In the Bible our imagination is introduced to Hagar, assigned to conceive a child with Abraham by Sarah, or to Zilpah and Bilhah who served Leah and Rachel by bearing children for them (Gen 16:3-5; Gen 30:4; 9-10). We think of Mary the mother of Jesus, a young virgin promised but not yet cared for by Joseph, and of the great scorn she faced when she became pregnant before her marriage.

Strong Service. Maids are dependable servants to people and to God throughout the Bible. We usually meet them as young women and do not encounter them again. Servant girls fulfill many roles: informant to Jonathan in the Absalom intrigue (2 Sam 17:17), Peter's courtyard questioner during Jesus' trial (Mt 26:69). A more prominent figure, the young Miriam guards her brother Moses's basket and negotiates nursing privileges for her mother when he is discovered by Pharaoh's daughter (Ex 2:4). Her image is echoed in the servant girl who tells Naaman to seek the prophet Elisha to be healed of his leprosy (2 Kings 5:2-4) and in Rhoda, who leaves Peter knocking at the door as she breathlessly announces his arrival (Acts 12:13-16).

Jesus uses the image of the loyal maid in his parable of the wise and foolish virgins. Demonstrating their faithful service, the wise virgins are fully prepared with extra oil as they await the bridegroom (Mt 25:1-12). Mary the mother of Jesus offers the most profound service as she answers Gabriel's stunning announcement by saying, "Behold, I am the handmaid of the Lord; let it be to me according to your word" (Lk 1:27 RSV). The strong service offered by the maids heightens the irony of their vulnerable status.

Unusual Faith. The unusual faith of biblical maids allows them to bear their vulnerable status and motivates their service. Hagar sets the standard: pregnant by Abraham and miserable under Sarah, she flees to the desert and is met by the angel of the Lord who promises numerous descendants from the child she will bear. She agrees to return to Sarah with trusting words: "You are the God who sees me" (Gen 16:13 NIV). Her simple words of faith reverberate in another maid's response to difficulty. In her unusual pregnancy Jesus' mother, Mary, is faced with certain scandal and future pain that Simeon later describes as a "sword [that] will pierce through your own soul" (Lk 2:35 NIV). Yet her song of praise, the Magnificat, reveals only humble joy in serving God (Lk 1:46-55). In their vulnerability maidens often have no earthly defense, no human recourse against harm; literally, God is their only advocate. The purity of their resulting faith teaches us the beauty of trusting fully in God.

As always, the faith of maids is justified. God cares for these dependent yet dependable women: he rescues Hagar in the wilderness, commands treatment for Zilpah and Bilhah's sons equal to Leah and Rachel's, and provides John for Mary when she loses Jesus. In the formal Hebrew law, God requires that a female servant taken by the master of the house receive the status of wife (Gen 21:15-21; Gen 49; Deut 21:10-14). In the lives of maidens who trust him, God shows himself faithful.

See also SERVANT; SLAVE, SLAVERY; VIRGIN, VIRGINITY; WOMEN, IMAGES OF.

MAIMED, HALT AND BLIND

We owe to the King James Version the triad of "maimed, halt [or lame], and blind" (Lk 14:13, 21). Together these three represent a category of unfortunates, namely, the physically deformed. People who are grouped together thus were often regarded as unqualified for certain religious ceremonies. Indeed, to have any of these defects was to be disqualified from the priesthood (cf. Lev 21:16-24, esp. v. 18). Sacrificial animals with similar defects were also to be excluded (cf. Lev 22:17-25, esp. v. 22; Deut 15:21).

Of course the ancient mind saw symbolic overtones in most physical phenomena. In the Dead Sea Scrolls some of the passages that exclude the maimed, halt and blind are applied more broadly: people with physical defects cannot participate in the final eschatological battle against evil (1QM 7:4) and cannot attend the messianic banquet (lQSa 2:3-7). This kind of interpretation is not limited to Qumran, however. According to 2 Samuel 5:8, David declared that "the blind and the lame shall not enter the house," but in the Targum the text is paraphrased: "The *sinners* and the *guilty* shall not enter the house."

It is this image of the lame and the blind as in some sense morally inferior and culturally excluded that Jesus encounters in his ministry. Evidently guided by the eschatological promises of Isaiah (cf. Is 35:5-6; 61:1-2) and other prophets (cf. Jer 31:8; Mic 4:6-7; Zeph 3:19: "I will save the lame and gather the outcast"), Jesus frequently found healing the lame and the blind (cf. Mt 11:5 par. Lk 7:22; Mt 15:30-31; John 5:3). On one occasion the lame and blind come to Jesus in the temple to be healed, with the result that Jesus is hailed as "son of David" (Mt 21:14-15). This vignette may be intended as a corrective to the Aramaic interpretation of 2 Samuel 5:8 cited above.

The parable of the great banquet (Lk 14:15-24) is perhaps the most poignant example of Jesus' challenge to the assumption that the lame and blind lack God's favor. In contrast to popular expectation, physically disabled persons, along with social outcasts and the poor, are invited in to enjoy the eschatological banquet. Jesus made the point that being lame and blind is no indication of God's disapproval or rejection.

See also ARM; BLIND, BLINDNESS; DISEASE AND HEALING; EYE, SIGHT; LEG.

MALACHI, BOOK OF

Malachi is generally recognized as the last of the OT "writing prophets." He was a later contemporary of the prophets *Haggai and *Zechariah, who addressed postexilic Judah between 520 and 518 B.C. Malachi's ministry likely dates to near 500 B.C.

Given his references to "the nations" (Mal 1:11, 14), it is possible that the victory of the Greeks over the Persians at the Battle of Marathon in 490 B.C. prompted Malachi's message. Postexilic Jerusalem was expecting the fulfillment of Haggai's prophecy about God's "overthrow of the nations," and that event may have been interpreted as the harbinger of divine judgment upon the kingdoms of the earth (cf. Hag 2:21-22 NRSV).

The literary format of Malachi is unique among the OT prophetic books. The prophet's entire message is cast in a rhetorical style known as "diatribe" or "disputation speech." The disputation speeches of Malachi are framed in a manner similar to the argumentation characterizing a formal debate, here pitting prophet against audience. Specifically, the disputation is characterized by a three-part outline, including the declaration of a truth claim by the prophet (e.g., "I have loved you," Mal 1:2), a (hypothetical?) audience rebuttal (e.g., "How have you loved us?" Mal 1:2) and a rejoinder by the prophet asserting the original premise through the presentation of supporting evidence (e.g., "Yet I have loved Jacob but I have hated Esau; I have made his hill country a desolation," Mal 1:2-3 NRSV). This literary format is an adaptation of the judicial-speech or trial-speech pattern common to OT prophetic literature (see Westermann, 169-76). Typically, the "legal-procedure" speeches in prophetic literature accuse, indict and announce judgment. All three elements may be found in Malachi.

The message of Malachi is couched in a hortatory style denoted by terse sentences and direct speech. In fact, forty-seven of the book's fifty-five verses are first-person addresses by God through his prophet Malachi. Structurally, the book consists of six oracles or disputations within an envelope composed of the superscription (Mal 1:1) and a postscript (Mal 4:4-6). Each of the disputations contrasts God's *faithfulness* with Israel's *faithlessness*. The basic message of Malachi's six disputations has been aptly summarized by J. A. Fischer: (1) God loves Jacob (Mal 1:2-5); (2) the God of Israel desires honest worship (Mal 1:6-2:9); (3) God is the father of all Israelites, and he expects loyalty and faithfulness (Mal 2:10-16); (4) God wants honesty and justice, not words, because he is truth and righteousness (Mal 2:17-3:5); (5) God is faithful to his word and desires genuine worship (Mal 3:6-12); (6) the repetition of God's desire for honesty is blended with threat of judgment (Mal 3:13-4:3). The postscript (Mal 4:4-6), though its originality is debated by biblical commentators, reminds postexilic Jerusalem of the legacy of genuine faith and true worship exemplified in the lives of Moses and Elijah.

The book's relationship to *Haggai and *Zechariah should not be overlooked. The messages of these three postexilic prophets originate in the same general time period and focus on a common theme: the *temple of God. Haggai encourages the Jewish community in Jerusalem to rebuild Solomon's temple destroyed by the Babylonians in 587 B.C. and reinstitute sacrificial ritual (Hag 1:9). Zechariah complements Haggai's challenge by summoning the people to repentance so that their worship in the new temple might be appropriate and acceptable to God (Zech 1:3; 8:14-17). Malachi completes the triad by calling for the reformation of temple worship corrupted by spiritual apathy and abuses permitted by a lax priesthood (Mal 1:7, 12; 2:8).

The book of Malachi abounds in rhetorical features and literary devices. A sampling includes:
□ anacoenosis, or an appeal to others sharing a common experience ("If then I am a father, where is the honor due me?" Mal 1:6 NRSV)
□ *encomium, or praise of an abstract quality or virtuous character trait (e.g., the description of the "ideal" priest in Mal 2:4-9)
□ the foil, or emphatic contrast (e.g., "the LORD" vs. "a foreign god" in Mal 2:11)
□ hyperbole, or conscious exaggeration for effect ("it will leave them neither root nor branch," Mal 4:1 NRSV)
□ metaphor, or direct comparison ("they will be ashes under the soles of your feet," Mal 4:3 NRSV)
□ paronomasia, or word-play (e.g., the prophet's name "Malachi" [Heb. *mal'āki*] in Mal 1:1, meaning "my messenger," and the reference to "my messenger" or *mal'āki* in Mal 3:1)

□ satire or ridicule ("Try presenting that to your governor," Mal 1:8 NRSV)
□ simile, or indirect comparison ("the day is coming, burning like an oven," Mal 4:1 NRSV)

The prophet Malachi makes use of a variety of images and symbols as he assures postexilic Judah of God's covenant love, indicts sins of hypocritical worship and social injustice, calls his audience to repentance and concludes with a mixed message: threatening divine *judgment and promising *restoration. Among the more prominent literary images and symbols employed in the disputations are:
□ the sibling rivalry of *Jacob and *Esau (Mal 1:2-3), recalling the patriarchal narratives recounting the odyssey of these twin brothers (Gen 25—36)
□ the father-son motif (Mal 1:6), appealing to the fifth commandment ("honor your father and mother," Ex 20:12)
□ the *honor-*shame motif embedded in ancient culture (Mal 1:8-9); here the prophet "shames" his audience by observing that the animal sacrifices the people offer to God in worship obviously violate protocol for similar gifts presented to the local governor
□ the stark contrast established between "unblemished" offerings and "polluted" offerings (Mal 1:13-14), harking back to the Mosaic stipulations for sacrificial offerings (Deut 15:21)
□ the tender (and rare in the OT) image of God as Father (Mal 2:10), probably in the sense of Creator of humanity (Deut 32:6), and God as the father of Israel figuratively—Israel as his "firstborn son" (Ex 4:22)
□ the "messenger" and "the messenger of the covenant" (Mal 3:1), both alluding to the divine *assembly, the heavenly court where God and the angelic beings reside. The prophets or messengers of God are thought to receive their commission and message from this setting.
□ the "refiner's fire" and the "fuller's soap" (3:2), both powerful images depicting the purifying effects of divine judgment. The image of the fuller's soap applied for the cleansing of sin in the postexilic Hebrew community is unique to Malachi in the OT. The figure of the refiner's *fire is more common (cf. Is 1:25; 48:10; Jer 6:29; 9:7; Dan 11:35; 12:10; Zech 13:9). The passage in Malachi advances the sober reminder that "the *day of LORD" is for both the righteous and the wicked. This day of judgment will see the wicked consumed by fire (Mal 4:1, where the image of fire is associated with the intense heat produced by the baker's oven) and the righteous purified by fire (Mal 3:3).
□ the symbolic "book of remembrance" (Mal 3:16). This heavenly register of the righteous and their deeds may have its earthly counterpart in the Persian "book of records" (Esther 6:1). The idea of a "heavenly book of life" is attested elsewhere in the OT (cf. Ex 32:32-33; Ps 69:28; Dan 12:1). These heavenly books become symbols of divine judgment in Daniel 7:10; 10:21 and 12:4. No doubt these references

provide the OT background for the books opened at the great white throne judgment in Revelation 20:11-15.

□ the celestial figure of "the sun of righteousness" rising "with healing in its wings" (Mal 4:2), the most well-known example of imagery in Malachi. The *sun is a symbol for God in Psalm 84:11, but "the sun of righteousness" is probably an adaptation of the winged sun-disc icon of Persian art (cf. Baldwin, 250). In ancient Mesopotamia the winged sun-disc icon represented the guardianship of the deity for the king. Malachi applies the solar epithet to God as the deity who will truly provide blessing and protection for those people overshadowed by his *"wings."

□ the pastoral image of "leaping calves from the stall" (Mal 4:2). God's restoration of his people in the Day of Lord is fittingly likened to the joyful playfulness of animals romping in the meadows in springtime (cf. Zechariah's picture of the kingdom of God, streets "full of boys and girls playing," Zech 8:5).

See also HAGGAI, BOOK OF; ZECHARIAH, BOOK OF.

BIBLIOGRAPHY. E. Achtemeier, *Nahum-Malachi* (IntC; Atlanta: John Knox, 1986); J. G. Baldwin, *Haggai, Zechariah, Malachi* (TOTC; Downers Grove, IL: InterVarsity Press, 1972); J. A. Fischer, "Notes on the Literary Form and Message of Malachi," *CBQ* 34 (1972) 315-20; A. E. Hill, *Malachi* (AB 25D; New York: Doubleday, 1998); C. Westermann, *Basic Forms of Prophetic Speech* (Louisville: Westminster John Knox, 1991).

MAN, IMAGES OF

The Bible is replete with images of man, of both wicked and righteous models of masculinity. Throughout the Bible, *God is portrayed as male, as are Christ and the *angels. Among the male roles most often depicted in the Bible are the warrior, wise *teacher/preacher, *king, *father, *son, *husband and lover. In addition to these roles, pictures of specifically male *folly occur, as well as the perfect model for righteousness in the form of Jesus Christ (*see* Jesus, Images of). Christ's identity as a man intimately related to the historical fact of the incarnation, Jesus of Nazareth. Consequently, Christ's maleness inescapably presents a model for men to emulate, though his call to follow him is extended equally to males and females.

Prominence of Men in the Biblical World. Considered sheerly in terms of power and precedence and not in terms of inherent worth or spiritual potential, the world of the Bible is in many ways a man's world. There are more stories of men than of women in the Bible. Men tend to fill *leadership roles in the biblical world. The main characters in the Bible tend to be men, making masculinity more diverse than the more specifically defined female roles. Beginning with the *creation of *Adam, men are usually portrayed as the leader of the two sexes, and therefore male characters in the Bible are often more well developed, as well as more harshly criticized.

Males are the subject of census in *Israel (Num 1:2), partly because a census is designed to assess military *strength. Firstborn males are highly prized, being said to be "the LORD's" (Ex 13:12 RSV). From the Levitical rules for *vows (Lev 27:1-8) we learn that men are more highly valued (fifty shekels) than women (thirty shekels) of the same age (twenty to sixty-two years). In OT religion, males receive the *covenant sign of *circumcision, with no counterpart prescribed for women. Males are commanded to go on a minimum of *three pilgrimages per year to *Jerusalem, with no corresponding requirement for women (Deut 16:16).

Lest this relative concentration of male images of power and importance seem to privilege them unduly in our thinking, we must remember that men are given no moral or spiritual advantage over women. In fact, because of their greater power, both physically and socially, men commit the greater wrongs. Furthermore, men are physically vulnerable in ways that women are not. Male *deaths in battle litter the text of the OT (*see* Battle Stories), and the motif of killing all males is a common one (e.g., Deut 20:13; 1 Sam 25:22, 34; 1 Kings 11:15-16; 14:10; 16:11; 21:21; 2 Kings 9:8; Mt 2:16).

In the Beginning. Whatever emerges in the Bible as distinctive to man as compared with *woman, the Bible as a canonical whole maintains the spiritual equality of man and woman before God (e.g., Gal 3:28). They jointly share the things that make up essential humanity, as we first see in the account of creation. Man and woman together receive the creation mandate to be fruitful and multiply and have dominion over creation (Gen 1:27-28). Man and woman share the image of God (Gen 2:27). Together they meet each other's need for companionship, with woman having been created so man would have a human companion and thus be complete (Gen 2:18-25). The very pairing of man and woman in the assertion "male and female he created them" (Gen 1:27 RSV) implies that together the two sexes make up humanity. The great manifestation of this essential unity is *marriage (Gen 2:23-24).

If unity thus exists from the earliest pages of the Bible, so does differentiation. Woman holds a dependent position in the creation story, having been created for the man as a "helper as his partner" (Gen 2:18-22 NRSV); man, by contrast, is endowed with a "free-standing" role, having been formed first for God alone (Gen 2:7), though God soon states that "it is not good that the man should be alone" (Gen 2:18 NRSV). The NT interprets this order of creation as endowing the male of the species with a role of *headship (1 Cor 11:3, 8-9; 1 Tim 2:12-13). The story of the Fall reinforces an early distinction between man and woman by assigning the first act of *eating the forbidden *fruit to Eve (Gen 3:6; cf. 2 Cor 11:3; 1 Tim 2:14). The *curse that God pronounces on Adam and *Eve after the Fall also contains an implied contrast: woman will *suffer *pain in childbearing (Gen 3:16), while man must struggle for livelihood against the soil (Gen 3:17-19), evoking a picture of the man as the one who as "breadwinner" provides for *family needs. Finally, God holds the man primarily accountable for the first *sin, first asking Adam to explain himself (Gen 3:11-12), just as the NT views sin as having been passed down from Adam rather than Eve (Rom 5:12-21).

Family Roles. Pursuant to the Bible's story of creation and fall, a dominant image of men comes from the domestic role of being head of a family. Throughout the OT, men are known to us most readily as clan leaders, with the patriarchs standing as the most obvious examples. To be leader of a clan entails a variety of other roles, including husband, father and *owner of a family's property. Throughout the OT, family lines are traced through the husband rather than the wife. Property is inherited by sons rather than *daughters. The nature of a man's domestic role can be summed up by the idea of headship, which is implied in the entire OT social structure as found in the *law and narratives but becomes explicit in the NT (1 Cor 11:3; 14:33-34; Eph 5:22—6:9; cf. Col 3:18-22), where such household authority extends to wife, *children and *slaves.

The Bible is filled with examples of human fathers and their relationships with their sons. Among the most touching portraits of fatherhood in the Bible is that of *Abraham, who waited years for a son and then, upon receiving him, willingly obeyed God and offered to *sacrifice the son he loved so much. *David likewise showed great love for his sons, *weeping when *Absalom died even though this occurred while Absalom was leading a *rebellion against him.

Examples of bad fathers also abound in the Bible. David, although a godly man and loving father, did not discipline his sons enough and reaped the consequences when one son *raped his half-sister and another led a rebellion against him. Eli behaved similarly, overindulging his sons and placing them before God so that eventually they became so dissipated that God took their lives and Eli's on the same day. *Jacob likewise had his faults in fatherhood, unwisely and unfairly playing favorites with his sons and suffering the consequences in the form of great family discord.

The NT tells believers that how fathers treat their children is a sign of their ability to lead: although fathers are not to provoke their children to *anger, they are also to keep their children under control with all dignity, for if they are unable to handle their own household, they cannot take on responsibilities of leadership in the household of the church (Eph 6:4; 1 Tim 3:1-7). Human fatherhood is thus a role that demands leadership and godliness.

Another important role for men is that of the husband. Paul ascribes a twofold obligation to husbands: they must be head of their wife, and they must love their wife (Eph 5:23-30; Col 3:19). Ungodly husbands in the Bible fail in one or both of these obligations—not loving their wives or not being the leader in the household—and sometimes even godly men do not perform their role of husband adequately.

One of the greatest failures along these lines is Ahab, who marries Jezebel, a Canaanite, and allows her to bring Baal *worship into Israel (1 Kings 16:31-33). Ahab also allows his wife to destroy the *prophets of God, and while he sits pouting because he cannot have Naboth's *vineyard, Jezebel sets about to kill the innocent Naboth to obtain it for him (1 Kings 18:4; 21). Although no godly men in Scripture even approach Ahab's weak and sinful abdication to his wife (and no one had quite such an evil wife), men often have difficulty being godly husbands, especially when they have households with more than one wife. The story of Abraham, Sarah and Hagar is fraught with domestic tension. And the narrative casts Abraham in a poor light as one who abdicates his responsibility and fails to deal with the dispute between his wife and her *maidservant. The story of Jacob, Leah and Rachel portrays the patriarch as a less than effective husband, showing favoritism for one wife over the other and producing a great deal more tension in a family that was already emotionally charged due to the fact that the two wives were *sisters. Foils to these failures are the stories of Boaz and of Joseph the husband of *Mary.

In addition to examples of godly husbands, the NT gives an ideal portrait of marriage under the lordship of Christ. Ephesians declares that "the husband is the head of the wife as Christ is the head of the church" (Eph 5:23 RSV). The marriage relationship is now set in a new context under Christ, with both husband and wife called upon to enact their marital roles on the model of Christ's relationship to the church. Women are directed to submit to their husbands and men are commanded to love their wives "as Christ loved the church and gave himself up for her" (Eph 5:25 RSV). Such love is to take the form of self-sacrifice, a service so complete that men ought to "love their wives as their own bodies. . . . For no man ever hates his own flesh, but nourishes and cherishes it" (Eph 5:28). Here is an image of marriage that runs against the grain of contemporary Greco-Roman and Jewish marriage ideals.

Other family roles that are uniquely masculine include son and brother. The ancient world placed a particular value on the ideal of worthy sons, and we catch hints of this in selected proverbs (Prov 10:1; 17:25; 23;15), as well as in the general orientation of the book of *Proverbs toward the speaker's son rather than his daughter. The oldest son (*see* Elder Child, Elder Sibling) held a position of privilege in ancient family patterns. The tenth *plague in *Egypt demonstrates the powerful importance of the firstborn male in ancient culture, inasmuch as the killing of the firstborn male in every household was the only plague great enough to persuade *Pharaoh to release the Israelites from Egypt.

Property Owners. In the ancient world, property was considered part of home and family, and here too men possess the power. In the Bible it is chiefly men who inherit money and possessions from their fathers, though daughters might receive an *inheritance if there are no sons (Num 27:1-11). Though men bear the benefit of the gender through which the inheritance was passed, they also suffer because of the jealousies between inheriting sons. The firstborn son holds the place of *honor, taking precedence over his brothers and inheriting a double share of his father's belongings. This position is coveted by all men, and several biblical stories reflect a concern to identify the firstborn and maintain his position. Jacob and *Esau are one example of the struggle over the firstborn privilege: their parents are careful to time even which twin was born first, and Jacob displays his wiliness in tricking his brother out of his inheritance. The tension is so great between the two brothers that their fraternal conflict foreshadows the warfare that would prevail between the two nations descended from them, Israel and Edom.

Occupational Roles and Public Positions. Unlike the biblical woman, the man in the Bible is not defined as completely by his role in family relationships. Because of the curse placed upon man at the fall, man holds a dual responsibility to be both a figure in his family and to be engaged in work that takes him into the field, that interfaces with the marketplace or that establishes him in the public square. In the culture of the Bible, occupations are often diverse and usually exclusively male. Among the most common in the OT are *shepherd, farmer and merchant, but we also encounter a number of kings and warriors. In the NT these occupations expand to more urban jobs, such as *fisherman, tent maker, tax collector and scribe. Whatever the occupation, the man is encouraged to diligence and excellence, yet admonished to be content in whatever capacity God has placed him, even if it is a position of subservience (Eph 6:5-10).

In addition to their occupations, men often play an important role in their communities, such as being an elder who stands at the *gates to discuss and judge local affairs (Ruth 4:1; Prov 31:23). The man who stands at the gates is the epitome of *wisdom and public success. Thus men's roles in the community are normally of a more public nature than those of the woman, and most examples of the "leader" in the Bible are men.

Warriors and Kings. Ancient cultures were essentially warrior cultures, which in turn were pretty solidly a man's world. The OT presupposes such a world. The warrior is characterized chiefly by physical strength and agility, *courage and tactical skill. The roll call of such figures in the OT includes Joshua and the judges Othniel (Judg 3:7-11), Ehud, Jephthah, Gideon and *Samson. David, one of the most heroic men in the Bible, is likewise a warrior. All of these warriors are specifically called by God to defend and conquer for Israel, and all are called to rely upon God's strength and not on their own. What emerges

is the image of the godly warrior, captured in the evocative phrase from the story of Saul about "men of valor whose hearts God had touched" (1 Sam 10:26 RSV).

The image of male as warrior is often associated with the image of the king. Sometimes kingship is the reward for military conquest, and kings lead their *armies into battle. Kingship plays a central role in the life of Israel, for the king is the visible representation of the power, military solidity and law for the nation. As with other masculine roles, it would be wrong to dissociate social role from spiritual considerations. Among the characteristics of good kings are obedience to God, solidity and leadership in foreign affairs, military prowess, rejection of *idolatry, and refraining from over-taxation or greedy conquest. David and *Solomon are the wisest and best of the kings: David possesses a heart for God and military leadership, and Solomon possesses wisdom and skill in foreign relations. Most OT kings are idolatrous and *evil, reinforcing the general pattern that men (like women) are neither good nor bad in themselves. They simply possess the potential to be either good or evil.

Men as Lovers. Another role of men in the Bible is that of lover. Although Isaac's marriage is arranged for him, he loves his wife, who is a comfort to him after his *mother dies (Gen 24:67). When he goes to live in Abimelech's *land and lies about Rebekah's being his sister, Abimelech detects that she is in fact his wife, having seen Isaac caressing Rebekah (Gen 26:8). His son Jacob is the classic lover among the patriarchs, falling in love with his beautiful cousin Rachel at first sight. Subsequently he works for *seven years to gain her hand in marriage, and these seven years "seemed to him but a few days because of the love he had for her" (Gen 29:20). Solomon in the *Song of Songs is also a great lover, referring to his beloved as "a lily among the thorns" and never ceasing to describe how beautiful his beloved is in all aspects of her person. Although the examples of men like these are few in the Bible, they demonstrate the Bible's recognition of the importance of the role and the strength of romantic passion that men feel for women.

In keeping with the emphasis of the Bible that God's gifts are neither automatically good nor bad but instead depend on a person's moral and spiritual use of them, we also find examples of men whose romantic and sexual passion leads them into sin. One of man's greatest weaknesses as seen by the author of Proverbs is the tendency to be led astray by lustful desire for women. Proverbs is full of admonitions to the young man to avoid the lure of the loose woman and the adulteress and instead to take delight in the wife of his *youth. However, even the best of men in the Bible can display weakness engendered by sexual passion. David is the prime example of a man who falls because of his lust for a woman. His son Amnon has a similar weakness, leading him to rape his half-sister Tamar. King Solomon is no better:

although he never commits *adultery like his father, he marries many foreign women against the command of the Lord and allows them to turn his *heart away from God. Samson is another example of a man made foolish by a woman, for his desire for Delilah leads him to entrust the secret of his strength to his *enemies, the *Philistines. In the NT, Herod is persuaded by the pleasing dancing of Herodias's daughter to foolishly promise her whatever she asks, upon which she asks for the head of John the Baptist (Mt 14:1-12).

Wicked Men. Like biblical women, men can be either very good or very bad. If men figure prominently among biblical *heroes and *saints, they are also lavishly represented in the categories of *villain and *sinner. While men are morally no worse than women, men have a propensity toward certain male vices. Even though the generic human term *man* applies equally to both sexes, exhortations against certain bad practices call men readily to mind.

Proverbs, for example, contains admonitions to avoid bad company, violence, heavy drink and laziness. Many examples of such "worthless men" or fools occur in the Bible. Among them are the wicked men of *Sodom and Gomorrah, who ask that the angels visiting Lot be brought out so they might have sexual contact with them. Similarly, the men who abuse the concubine of the Levite to death are termed "base fellows" (Judg 19:22), as are the men of David's army who greedily tried to deny a share of the booty to the soldiers who stayed with the baggage (1 Sam 30:22). Nabal is memorable as one who is "surly and mean in his dealings" in contrast with his wife Abigail, who "was an intelligent and beautiful woman" (1 Sam 25:3 NIV). Another temptation to which men are especially susceptible is too great a trust in their riches or power. King Uzziah is an example of this: he gains great military power and fame, and allows this to make him proud (2 Chron 26:18; see Pride). Thus the Bible details the sins to which men are especially susceptible as greed, *thirst for power, lust and a tendency toward laziness or dissipation.

Religious Roles. While women occasionally fill the same religious roles as men in the Bible, those roles belong overwhelmingly to men. The OT priestly class is masculine—the sons of Aaron (see Priest). The role of *prophet is likewise mainly a masculine one (cf. Lk 2:36; Acts 2:17; 21:8-9), and even more so is that of scribe. Jesus' twelve *disciples are men, though we encounter women who are close followers of Jesus (e.g., Lk 8:1-3; 23:49). And in the book of Acts and the Epistles the leading missionary figures are men, though we also find intriguing references to women engaged in missionary work (e.g., Priscilla: Acts 18:2, 18-19, 26; Rom 16:3, 19; 2 Tim 4:19). In both OT and NT the position known as elder belongs to men. Although both men and women are deacons (on women deacons, see Rom 16:1), the general impression conveyed by NT qualifications for church office is a movement in which men exercise leadership (1 Cor 11:3-16; 14:33-36; 1 Tim 3:1-13; Titus 1:5-9), while women concentrate on what might loosely be called ministries of compassion (1 Tim 5:9-14). Accounts of preaching in the NT likewise reveal a masculine slate.

See also FATHER, FATHERHOOD; HEAD; HUSBAND; KING, KINGSHIP; SON; TYRANNICAL FATHER, HUSBAND; WOMAN, IMAGES OF.

MANAGER. *See* AUTHORITY, HUMAN; LEADERSHIP.

MANNA

The word *manna* awakens sensuous images, a heaven-sent food whose literal and symbolic references enrich the Bible from Exodus to Psalms, from John to Revelation. Bible writers refer to manna in narration, exposition, argumentation and poetry and use it to recall, inspire, persuade and exhort.

Bible writers describe manna's sense appeal: its appearance—"a fine flake-like thing, fine as the frost on the ground" (Ex 16:14 NASB), but when the sun grew hot, it would melt (Ex 16:21), and "it was like coriander seed, white" (Ex 16:31); its taste—"like wafers with honey" (Ex 16:31) and like "cakes baked with oil" (Num 11:8); its odor, when hoarded "it bred worms and became foul" (Ex 16:20); its touch—"The people would go about and gather it and grind it . . . or beat it . . . and boil it . . . and make cakes with it." (Num 11:8); and its abundance—"He rained down manna upon them to eat . . . He sent them food in abundance" (Ps 78:24-25). There is a mysterious and unexplained quality about it, for when the Israelites first saw it they asked, "What is it?" (Ex 16:15), and this question (Heb *mān hû'*) became its name.

Manna—the name invites all to taste and *touch and *smell and see that the Lord is good, his gifts delicious, nutritious, abundant and free, unearned and undeserved. But one sense is missing—hearing. Or is it? The only sound associated with manna is negative, Israel's complaints: "Who will give us meat to eat? We remember the fish . . . . There is nothing at all to look at except this manna" (Num 11:4-6 NASB). Jesus himself spoke of manna by contrast: "This is the bread which came down out of heaven; not as the fathers ate, and died, he who eats this bread shall live forever" (Jn 6:58 NASB).

Manna imagery spreads throughout Scripture, sensuous multiple references to God's ability—and willingness—to provide for his children (even complaining ones) in their wilderness experiences. Jesus stresses that he himself is the ultimate manna, the true manna sent from heaven, capable of sustaining both life on this earth and life eternal.

See also BREAD; FOOD; HUNGER.

MANURE. *See* DUNG.

MARBLE. *See* MINERALS.

MARDUK. *See* GODS, GODDESSES.

MARK, GOSPEL OF

The Gospel of Mark is a biography of Jesus written according to the conventions of ancient Greco-Roman *bioi*, or biographies. By contrast with modern biographies, these lives of great men (particularly those of philosophers or writers rather than generals or politicians) were shaped over a skeleton chronology running from their birth, or entrance on the stage of public history, to their death, interrupted here and there by topical excursions. Within the restraints and freedoms of this ancient genre, Mark's Gospel renders a faithful and compelling portrait of Jesus that is grounded in history and imbued with literary patterns and imagery.

The Gospel of Mark is a biography charged with energy. It begins with a brief heading. An overture is sounded from OT texts; John the Baptist is introduced; and then Jesus, full grown and come of age, arrives at the Jordan River for his inauguration into ministry. It is as if Jesus bounds onto the stage of public history, and for three chapters his movements afford no leisure of extended conversation or discourse. Mark's use of the Greek "historic present" tense lends a sense of urgency to the story. The first eight chapters of Mark's story of Jesus move to the tempo of a verbal metronome: "*immediately* [*euthys*, 42 times in Mk] he was in the synagogue" (Mk 1:23); "*again* [*palin*, 28 times in Mk] he entered the synagogue" (Mk 3:1); "immediately he *began* [*archō*, 27 times in Mk]" (Mk 4:1). Jesus is a man of action, and where he is things happen. Not until the first passion prediction of Mark 8:27-30 does the tempo slow down. Finally, as Jesus enters Jerusalem and the passion narrative begins, time is measured more closely than ever—down to the momentous hours of his crucifixion.

Abrupt transitions and contrasting scenes laid end-to-end (parataxis) invite the listening ear to hear and the inquiring mind to see and to fill the synapses. This characteristic contributes to a transcendent enigma that inhabits Jesus' sayings, actions and self-disclosures and encompasses the Gospel itself, with its motif of secrecy (e.g., Mk 1:26, 34; 7:36; 8:30; 9:9) and its elusive and puzzling ending of *flight, *terror, amazement and silence (Mk 16:8). The effect is that the very Jesus who meets the disciples and crowds, compellingly attractive and yet elusive of their grasp, now beckons readers with equal winsomeness and puzzling invitation to explore who he is through this Gospel.

Patterns of *three emerge from the topography of this Gospel. Most notable are the three voices declaring the divine sonship of Jesus, first heralded in the Gospel's heading: "The beginning of the good news of Jesus Christ, the Son of God" (Mk 1:1 NRSV). This sonship is declared at three epiphanic points in Jesus' life, events staged at the beginning, middle and end of the Gospel: the voice from heaven at his baptism ("You are my Son, the Beloved, with you I am well pleased," Mk 1:11 NRSV), the voice from the cloud at his transfiguration ("This is my Son, the Beloved," Mk 9:7 NRSV) and the voice of the Roman centurion at Jesus' death ("Truly this man was the Son of God!" Mk 15:39 RSV). Equally significant are the three passion predictions of Mark 8:31; 9:31; and 10:33-34, emanating from the center of the Gospel and preparing readers for Jesus' ascent toward the heat of conflict in Judea and Jerusalem. The triadic pattern also emerges in the three boat scenes (Mk 4:35-41; 6:45-52; 8:14-21); the three instructions to "keep awake and watch" (Mk 13:33-37), answered by three sleepings in Gethsemane at the hour of crisis (Mk 14:37, 40, 41); the three denials by Peter (Mk 14:66-72); the three questions by Pilate to the crowd (Mk 15:9, 12, 14) and the three-step descent of the third, sixth and ninth hours from crucifixion to death (Mk 15:25, 33, 34).

Structurally, Mark's Gospel highlights a feature of biblical narrative generally—the preference for brief literary units. The result is a kaleidoscope of passages in which the subject keeps changing and is never in focus for very long. This means that the unity to be found is that of a mosaic or collage of individual passages that together produce a pattern.

Like his contemporary biographers, Mark can group stories and sayings of Jesus thematically, weaving carpets of discourse or presenting poignant sayings in anecdotal settings: the conflict stories of chapters 2 and 3, the parables in chapter 4 and the eschatological discourse of chapter 13. What first resembles a patchwork quilt, on closer inspection reveals a carefully ordered pattern, most notably a "sandwiching," or "ring" composition, in the general pattern of A-B-A (Mk 3:20-35; 5:21-43; 6:6-30; 11:12-20; 14:1-11; 14:54-72). These patterns hold meanings that invite inquiry. A more complex variation may be observed in the five conflict stories of Mark 2:1—3:6 that are topically patterned:

A	B	C	B′	A′
2:1-12	2:13-17	2:18-22	2:23-28	3:1-6
(healing)	(eating)	(fasting)	(eating)	(healing)

The central conflict (C) over fasting (Why do Jesus' disciples not fast while the disciples of Pharisees and the Baptist do?) elicits a foreshadowing of Jesus' death, but this is "ringed" by miracles of physical restoration and Torah-forbidden dining, both distinctive features of Jesus' ministry as he symbolizes the presence of the blessings of the age to come. This subtle literary pattern discloses a broader horizon of Mark's message: the dawning of a new world is viewed through the enigma of the cross. For those vested in the old order, the enacted symbols of eschatological resurrection and feasting kindle resistance and hostility, and the series of stories is sealed with a conspiracy to kill Jesus (Mk 3:6).

In addition to the more easily recognized Gospel motifs of *kingdom, gospel (good news) and *forgiveness, numerous leitmotifs are stitched into Mark's Gospel. Particularly notable are those that profile the epochal conflict between Jesus and the demonic, the disciples and the Jewish authorities. Here, as well as in his interpretation of the law, we see one aspect of Jesus' power and authority. The image of "casting out," or "driving out" (*ekballō*, 16 times in Mk), is used particularly of Jesus driving out demons and echoes Israel's driving out the Canaanites from the land. The demons are also "rebuked" (*epitimaō*, 10 times in Mk). More than simply a scolding, this is a Greek rendering of a Hebrew word (*gā'ar*) that in the OT frequently indicates Yahweh's powerful word of command (e.g., Ps 18:15), an explosive blast from his mouth that overthrows enemies. Jesus can also direct this rebuke at the raging *storm (Mk 4:39; cf. Nahum 1:4) and toward his recalcitrant disciples.

"Tempting," or "testing" (*peirazō*), is directed by *Satan, *demons, authorities and even the disciples against Jesus. And repeatedly we are reminded that Jesus (like John the Baptist, Mk 1:14), and even his disciples (Mk 13:9, 11, 12), live under the shadow of being "handed over" (*paradidōmi*) to hostile hands and even death. The Isaianic image of the "way of the Lord," a highway of divine deliverance of Israel from exile, first announced in the prologue (Mk 1:2-3), conveys the narrative forward as Jesus and his disciples travel along the "way" (*hodos*, particularly concentrated in Mk 8:22—11:1) that eventually leads to Jerusalem and the final conflict. Finally, Jesus frequently strikes fear in the hearts of the disciples and others, both friends and foes (Mk 4:41; 5:15, 33, 36; 6:50; 9:32; 10:32; 11:18). This aura of dreadful transcendence invites the readers' response as the Gospel closes—not with celebration but with the first witnesses of the empty tomb fleeing in terror (Mk 16:8).

Mark's Gospel, though unquestionably rooted and invested in the historical life of Jesus, spins a narrative world of events, characters and settings full of human interest and vivid detail. While many of these details are shared with the other Synoptic Gospels, it is worth noting what might otherwise be passed over.

Mark presents us with an abundance of dining scenes and images. To the outrage of the *Pharisees, Jesus dines with sinners at Levi's house and reinterprets purity laws pertaining to food. He defends his disciples' plucking and eating grain on the *Sabbath, and he refuses to fast. He is host to the feeding of five and then four thousand, and "loaves" and *"leaven" form an intriguing point of subsequent puzzlement and mystery. Toward the end of the Gospel Jesus hosts a final meal with his disciples where he anticipates a future meal "in the kingdom of God" (Mk 14:25). These images of eating are related in one facet or another to the arrival of the kingdom of God and the eschatological *feast in the presence of God.

An example of Mark's narrative art can be observed in the feeding of the five thousand in Galilee. There the people are described as "sheep without a shepherd," an image signifying the absence of a recognized Israelite *king worthy of the title. Mark is careful to tell us that the people are seated for their feeding on the "green grass," and that once fed, they are "filled." In a play on words perhaps carried over from the oral stage of telling this Gospel, the image of *sheep content under the care of their good messianic shepherd is underscored by the Greek assonance between "grass," *chortō* (Mk 6:39), and the people being "filled," *echortasthēsan* (Mk 6:42). Contrary to appearances, a shepherd-king is present in Israel. In typical Markan fashion we are invited to contrast the immediately preceding episode, a story of king Herod Antipas. There the ungodly ruler of Galilee hosts a festive birthday banquet, glibly offers up to half his kingdom to his dancing daughter and serves up the grisly head of an unpalatable prophet on a platter (Mk 6:17-29)!

In contrast with the courtesans and the leaders of Galilee who attend Herod's court, aside from his final days in Jerusalem, Jesus is found in rural, rustic and rudimentary settings and in the company of the little people. We find him in the wilderness, on a mountain, along the seashore or crossing the sea, in towns and villages (or avoiding them), and walking through a grain field. When he is in a building, it is typically a home and sometimes a synagogue, but always with ordinary people—even outcasts, unfortunates and rough-hewn figures—who enjoy his company, flock to him, receive his touch, are chosen as disciples and are deeply affected by his words and deeds. This image of Jesus as prophet and sage among rustics possessing faces and feelings and authentic speech would be viewed as extraordinary were it not so familiar. As Erich Auerbach has pointed out, no classical Greek or Roman writer ever shed the conceit of his top-down perspective and lent the art of vivid description and direct discourse to such individuals and settings.

The least of people play a leading role in a most striking feature of Mark's Gospel. A motif is constructed of positive and negative images of perception and comprehension: *ears that hear or do not hear, *eyes that see or do not see and *hearts that absorb with understanding or are hardened with resistance. It is an Isaianic note that again sets the tone for this Markan motif: Israel "may indeed look, but not perceive, and may indeed listen, but not understand" (Mk 4:12 RSV; cf. Is 6:9-10). While first providing a rationale for the parables of Mark 4 (outsiders hear but do not understand; insiders receive interpretation and insight), it is skillfully woven into the warp and woof of the subsequent narrative. We find the narrator's voice and the words of Jesus providing an interpretive context for this motif, but its power is delivered in living images of people who we expect to see and hear and understand but do not. These are set in contrast with the blind who see (Mk 8:22-26; 10:46-52), the deaf who hear (Mk 7:32-37; 9:25) and the seemingly hardhearted (e.g., Mk 2:13-15; 15:39) who comprehend. The Pharisees have hard hearts (Mk 3:5), and the disciples, epitomizing the condition of Israel as ever seeing and ever hearing (Mk 4:12), have deaf ears, blind eyes and hard hearts (Mk 8:17-21). This repeated refrain of imagery, set in tension with the mystery of Jesus' person, deeds and message of the kingdom, rises up to enfold the Gospel, with its final scene of an empty tomb and terror (Mk 16:8), and it poses to readers the question put to the disciples: "Do you still not perceive or understand?" (Mk 8:17).

See also GOSPEL GENRE; JESUS, IMAGES OF; JOHN, GOSPEL OF; LUKE, GOSPEL OF; MATTHEW, GOSPEL OF.

BIBLIOGRAPHY. R. A. Guelich, "Mark, Gospel of," *DJG* 512-25; W. H. Kelber, *Mark's Story of Jesus* (Philadelphia: Fortress, 1979); J. D. Kingsbury, *Conflict in Mark: Jesus, Authorities, Disciples* (Minneapolis: Fortress, 1989); D. Rhoads and D. Michie, *Mark As Story: An Introduction to the Narrative of a Gospel* (Philadelphia: Fortress, 1982).

MARKETPLACE

A distinctly public arena, a marketplace is the site of material abundance, a barometer of political and spiritual affairs and a place to seek security.

A Place of Material Goods. By implication, biblical texts show us the myriad goods of the marketplace. *Cloth and *food are available in abundance: "beautiful garments, embroidered fabric, multicolored rugs" (Ezek 27:24); linen cloth and sashes (Prov 31:24); a linen belt for Jeremiah (Jer 13:1); *bread, *wheat (Amos 8:5); *grain (Neh 10:31); *wine, *grapes, *figs, *fish (Neh 13:15-16); *doves (John 2:16); meat (1 Cor 10:25) and food for crowds listening to Jesus (Jn 6:5-7; 4:8, 32). Though merchants were traveling, not local salesmen, their luxuries—spices, precious stones and gold—were also occasionally available (Ezek 27:22).

A Political and Spiritual Barometer. Merchants also contributed to the political climate of the marketplace by setting the scales and weights by a sometimes suspicious standard (Gen 23:16; 2 Kings 7:1, 8). The charged political arena of the marketplace stemmed from the convergence of many different cultures. Open markets and trade signaled hospitality and goodwill between rulers (Gen 34:10, 21; 1 Kings 20:34).

Authority of a democratic sort was asserted in the marketplace. Mobs formed quickly in the people-filled area. When they cast a demon from a slave girl, Paul and Silas were dragged to the market "to face the authorities" (Acts 16:19).

The market was a barometer of spiritual as well as political affairs. Observance of the sabbath in the marketplace indicated renewed commitment to God (Neh 10:31), and frustrated wicked men (Amos 8:5). By contrast, disregard for God's provision was signaled by busy sabbath commerce, which continually troubled the righteous (Neh 13:15-19). Also, oppression and fraud in the marketplace were metaphors for public iniquity (Ps 55:11).

A Place to Seek Security. Above all, the market is a place to seek security, so we find people there. All types meet: teachers of the law who love to make an entrance in "flowing robes" and be greeted with respect (Mt 23:7; Mk 12:38; Lk 11:43, 20:46); dishonest merchants who cheat by "skimping the measure, boosting the price and cheating the dishonest scales" (Amos 8:5); children sitting and playing (Mt 11:16-17; Lk 7:32); loose women (Prov 7:12); day laborers looking for a job or standing around "doing nothing" (Mt 20:3); bad characters, ne'er-do-wells ready for excitement (Acts 17:5); people in storefronts with homes behind them (Zeph 1:11). People share in common the need to care for themselves.

Perhaps the most poignant marketplace images are those where a servant of God comes to the market seeking people. *Wisdom, who was with God at creation, calls out to the people in the public square, telling them where true security is found (Prov 7:12). Jesus encounters crowds of the desperate sick in the marketplace, and all who touch him are healed (Mk 6:56). He condemns the temple dove sellers: "How dare you turn my Father's house into a market!" (John 2:16 NIV). Burdened with the gospel, Paul spends his days in a tentmaker's shop, reasoning "in the marketplace day by day with those who happened to be there" (Acts 17:17 NIV). Amid people seeking to secure material needs, God's servants assert his constant promise of provision for those who trust him.

In these marketplace scenes, as with Jesus and the woman at the well, we can imagine discussions about earthly needs, about security and about the chance to become a child of God, the Great Provider. God's words through Isaiah echo in the clamorous market: "Come, all you who are thirsty, come to the waters; and you who have no money, come, buy and eat! Come, buy wine and milk without money and without cost. Why spend money on what is not bread, and your labor on what does not satisfy? Listen, listen to me, and eat what is good, and your soul will delight in the richest of fare. Give ear and come to me; hear me, that your soul may live" (Is 55:1-3 NIV).

See also WORK, WORKER.

MARRIAGE

In the Bible marriage is the primal human bond of society, the foundation of social life. Prior to a society there must be families, and before a family there exists a marriage. A marriage is a bond between two people, male and female. When we think of images of marriage in the Bible, we think first of all of famous couples—*Adam and *Eve, *Abraham and Sarah, Isaac and Rebekah, *Jacob and Rachel, *Ruth and Boaz, *Solomon and his Shulammite bride, *Esther and the king, *Mary and Joseph.

From the Bible's images of such couples, along with passages of explicit teaching about marriage, we receive an ever-expanding picture of what marriage is, including as its basic components divine institution, companionship, romantic relationship, cove-

537

nant, sexual union, joint livelihood, parenting and a shared religious life. In addition, marriage is a leading biblical metaphor for the relationship between God and the believer.

Whatever the specific motif, the foundation on which all additional images of marriage are placed is the basic principle that in marriage two become one (Mt 19:5; Mk 10:7-8). The imagery of joining accordingly plays a central role.

Instituted by God. The general framework into which the Bible places marriage is its institution by God. We might say that marriage was God's idea for the human race. In the creation story it is God himself who decides that "it is not good that the man should be alone; I will make him a helper fit for him" (Gen 2:18 RSV). It is God who brings Eve to Adam after creating her (Gen 2:22), in effect pronouncing the first marriage union in history. In the NT, too, *husband and *wife are said to be "joined together" by God (Mt 19:6; Mk 10:9). Jesus sanctioned marriage by his attendance at the marriage of Cana in Galilee (Jn 2:1-11).

Companionship. A keynote in the original institution of marriage is that it is formed as a companionate relationship between man and woman. Adam is incomplete in himself, lacking a suitable mate until Eve is created to complete him and fulfill his capacity for human companionship (Gen 2:18-22). This companionship is exclusive: it involves a leaving of the parental bond as primary and a cleaving instead to the spouse (Gen 2:24).

The longing simply to be with one's beloved is a leading motif in *Song of Songs, where marriage is pictured as the satisfaction of this longing. In the narrative parts of the Bible we are given pictures of husband and wife as companions in daily life.

Romance and Sex. The companionship between lovers, both before and after marriage, is more than friendship—it is a romantic passion. The Bible's great repository of images of romantic longing leading to marriage is the Song of Songs. The sentiments expressed in this epithalamion (wedding song) are far more rapturous and refined than either ordinary *friendship or specifically sexual relationship. The romantic relationship expresses itself in well-defined rituals of courtship and wooing (see Love Story), and it is highly verbal and poetic.

The natural consummation of romantic love is *sexual union, which encompasses spouses at physical and emotional levels and has spiritual implications as well. The archaic biblical euphemism that husband and wife "knew" each other captures the mystery and depth of sexual union in marriage. The marriage relationship is the most intimate of all human relationships. The man and the woman become "one flesh" (Gen 2:24), which denotes sexual union (1 Cor 6:16). It is relationship between one man and one woman; no rivals are tolerated. We can also note the obvious: marriage as prescribed by God is heterosexual, involving a man and a woman (Gen 2:18-24).

1 Corinthians 7:1-7 places the sexual union of married love into the category of a duty that spouses are obliged to extend to each other, showing its importance in the marriage relationship. Proverbs 5:15-19 uses the imagery of a fountain of water to picture the satisfaction of sexual appetite, and the ideal is that a husband be infatuated always with the love of the wife of his youth, who is pictured as "a lovely hind, a graceful doe" (RSV).

Covenant. The motif of a permanent bond is another dimension of marriage in the Bible. The ideal is that marriage is for life. Such permanence does not force something foreign onto romantic passion but is an ideal to which romantic love itself propels people when they are in love. The moment of epiphany toward which the Song of Songs moves is a plea for permanence in love (Song 8:6-7). This image of a permanent bond is stated by Jesus as a command: "What therefore God has joined together, let not man put asunder" (Mt 19:6 RSV; Mk 10:9).

Sometimes the Bible pictures this permanent bond in the imagery of a covenant. Malachi pictures God as "witness to the covenant between you and the wife of your youth, . . . your companion by covenant" (Mal 2:14 RSV; cf. Ezek 16:8).

Domestic Images. A further image of marriage that emerges from the narrative parts of the Bible is the joint struggle for livelihood that is necessary for marriage to survive. One of the givens of the world is that spouses together provide for the physical needs of life and family. Both husband and wife contribute to the provision of the family's physical needs (the encomium in praise of the ideal wife in Prov 31:10-31 catalogs the wife's domestic provisions).

In addition to livelihood, marriage encompasses the family responsibility of the parenting of children. Husband and wife are assumed to be the primary people who provide for the physical needs of children and nurture them morally and spiritually. A picture of joint responsibility for instruction emerges from the book of Proverbs, where we read, for example, "My son, keep your father's commandment, and forsake not your mother's teaching" (Prov 6:20 RSV; see also Prov 1:8). Of similar import is the fifth commandment in the Decalogue, which enjoins children to "honor your father and your mother" (Ex 20:12; Eph 6:2).

The structure of authority within the family is portrayed in the Bible as hierarchical, with the husband/father the accountable head of the family. We might infer this from the way the OT focuses on the heads of clans. The image of marriage as hierarchical reaches its explicit formulation in several "household codes" in the NT epistles (Eph 5:22-24; Col 3:18; 1 Pet 2:1-6).

Metaphoric Uses. Throughout the Bible, God's relationship to his people is pictured as a marriage. In this metaphor God is the husband and his people are his wife. It is not that God is male or that there are no female images of God in the Bible (see Ps 131; Prov 8—9; Is 66:13). In Israelite society the man was the head of the household, so within the marriage metaphor, it is understandable that God is cast in the role of the husband.

As noted above, Malachi speaks of marriage as a covenant (Mal 2:14), a relationship that is built on mutual love but finds expression in a legal form. Israel's relationship with God in the OT is also covenantal, as witnessed in the books of Exodus (Ex 19—24) and Deuteronomy. When Israel breaks its covenant with God, it is likened to the breaking of the marriage bond. Hosea may be the first to use this marriage metaphor when he describes the alienation between Israel and God as a break in their marriage vows. Not only does God command the prophet to marry "an adulterous wife" (Hos 1:2 NIV), but he says:

Rebuke your mother, rebuke her,
  for she is not my wife,
  and I am not her husband.
Let her remove the adulterous look from her face
  and the unfaithfulness from between her
    breasts. (Hos 2:2 NIV)

The prophet Ezekiel develops the metaphor of marriage as spiritual symbol to its greatest extent. He dedicates two long chapters to recounting the perversity of Israel's relationship to God using sexual terms. We will pass over Ezekiel 16 and illustrate the prophet's argument with Ezekiel 23. Ezekiel describes two sisters and identifies the first, Oholah, with Samaria and the second, Oholibah, with Jerusalem. These sisters became *prostitutes in Egypt, where "their breasts were fondled and their virgin bosoms caressed" (Ezek 23:3 NIV).

God then complains that Oholah lusted after Assyrian soldiers even when he was still married to her (Ezek 23:5-8). As a result, he simply gave her to them, and they humiliated her and then killed her (Ezek 23:9-10). Oholibah did not learn a lesson from her sister's fate. She found herself attracted to the Babylonians. Her rejection of the marriage bed was intense, since "she lusted after her lovers whose genitals were like those of donkeys and whose emission was like that of horses" (Ezek 23:20 NIV). In the end God will judge Oholibah, his unfaithful wife, as he did Oholah.

Other prophets also exploit the resemblance of Israel's unfaithfulness to a broken marriage covenant. In Jeremiah, God remembers when his relationship with Israel was good, using these terms:

I remember the devotion of your youth,
  how as a bride you loved me
and followed me through the desert,
  through a land not sown. (Jer 2:1 NIV)

But in the present, Israel commits spiritual *adultery. *Idolatry is adultery, as Jeremiah 3:6 makes clear: "Have you seen what faithless Israel has done? She has gone up on every high hill and under every spreading tree and has committed adultery there" (NIV).

Isaiah too makes the literary connection between idolatry and adultery. God has divorced his wife Israel because of her adultery (Is 50:1). However, Isaiah also speaks of Israel's future salvation as a restoration of the marriage relationship:

The LORD will call you back
  as if you were a wife deserted and distressed in
    spirit—
a wife who married young,
  only to be rejected. . . .
For a brief moment I abandoned you,
  but with deep compassion I will bring you back.
  (Is 54:6-7 NIV; see the whole of Is 54)

The prophets exploit the marriage metaphor most dramatically, but its contours can be discerned elsewhere in the OT as well. In the Pentateuch we hear of Yahweh's jealousy, an emotion that is only proper to an exclusive relationship like marriage (Ex 19:3-6; 20:2-6; 34:14). Also, Israel's rebellion is described as adultery and prostitution (Ex 34:15-16; Lev 17:7).

The *Song of Songs celebrates intimacy between a man and a woman. Within the context of the canon, the relationship can only be understood as that of a married couple. We could justifiably treat the Song of Songs as an extension of the marriage metaphor that occurs in many places in the Bible.

The use of the marriage relationship as a metaphor of the relationship between God and his people continues in the NT. Most notably, Paul in the book of Ephesians instructs Christians that their connection with Christ is like a marriage (Eph 5:21-33). Accordingly, wives should submit to their husbands as the church submits to Christ, and husbands should love their wives with the sacrificial love that Christ has for the church.

The book of Revelation describes the end of history, when God will once and for all destroy all evil. His faithful people will be united with him forever in glory. Not surprisingly, considering the development of the marriage metaphor up to this point in the Bible, this final union between God and his people is described as a marriage:

Hallelujah!
  For our Lord God Almighty reigns.
Let us rejoice and be glad
  and give him glory!
For the wedding of the Lamb has come,
  and his bride has made herself ready.
Fine linen, bright and clean,
  was given her to wear. (Rev 19:6-8 NIV)

See also ADULTERY; FAMILY; HUSBAND; LOVE STORY; SEX; SONG OF SONGS; WEDDING; WIFE.

BIBLIOGRAPHY. N. Stienstra, *YHWH Is the Husband of His People* (Kampen, Netherlands: Pharos, 1993).

MARTYR

The English word *martyr* is derived from the Greek *martys*, which carries the sense of "witness." In the Christian tradition, those who are martyrs have died in witness to Christ. But the image of a martyr also takes in a broader scope of those who die for a noble cause (e.g., for their country), choosing death rather than renouncing their principles or commitments. The image of *martyr* is more prominent in church history than in the Bible. It is in the centuries since the formation of the Christian church that the veneration of the martyrs and the hagiographic accounts of their lives have arisen. Nevertheless, the image of the martyr can be found in the Bible, and the broader background of Jewish martyrdom is crucial for fully understanding the imagery of the death of Jesus.

In the OT writings we find occasional glimpses of the martyr image in other contexts. *Abel is the first martyr, slain by an evil brother simply because his own deeds were righteous (Gen 4:3-8; 1 Jn 3:12), an example that prompts John to comment, "Do not be surprised, my brothers, if the world hates you" (1 Jn 3:13 RSV). Like other martyrs, Abel's influence lives on: as a model of faith, "he being dead yet speaketh" (Heb 11:4 KJV).

In the story of Saul's sons and grandsons in 1 Samuel 21 we see innocent victims who are slain because of Saul's failure to abide by an ancient agreement with the Gibeonites. They are guilty of no duplicity except through the family tie, and yet only their deaths can set the people free. The most touching OT picture of a martyrdom-like event, however, is in the book of Judges. Jephthah's daughter must carry out her father's wish because of her father's oath to God. Her life is given as forfeit for the people's victory over the Ammonites. The inspiring image of her sacrifice was kept alive by subsequent generations (Judg 11:40).

The NT is more reticent than the later church to dwell on martyrdom, perhaps for fear of detracting from the martyr par excellence: "Jesus Christ, who is the faithful witness [martyr]" (Rev 1:5; 3:15 NIV). In the crucified Messiah we see martyrdom in its purest form—the innocent slain for the guilty, and the hero for those who reject him. Isaiah's description of the *suffering servant employs language rich with the imagery of the innocent martyr: "he was crushed for our iniquities; the punishment that brought us peace was upon him" (Is 53:5-6 NIV).

The theme of Jesus' willing and noble death must be read, in part, as a noble martyr's death. The intertestamental period provides the precedent for righteous martyrs affecting the welfare of the nation Israel. The Maccabees' own self-understanding of their sacrifice is evoked in the words of a martyr: "I, like my brothers, give up life body and life for the laws of our ancestors. . . . and through me and my brothers to bring to an end the wrath of the Almighty that has justly fallen on our whole nation" (2 Macc 7:38 NRSV). In 4 Maccabees the deaths of the martyrs are understood to have redemptive value for the nation: "The tyrant was punished, and the homeland purified—they [the martyrs] having become, as it were, a ransom for the sin of our nation. And through the blood of those devout ones and their death as an atoning sacrifice, divine Providence preserved Israel that previously had been mistreated" (4 Macc 17:21-22 NRSV). Jesus' death stands squarely

within the context of the story of Israel, and in the resolution of Israel's plight the NT sees the redemption of the world. The precedent of Maccabean martyrdom and the value placed upon it (*ransom, propitiation, dealing with divine wrath) is an important backdrop against which to view the death of Jesus, even if Isaiah 53 is more to the fore.

The Bible has no aphorism about martyrs that can match Tertullian's "the blood of the martyrs is the seed of the church." But Jesus, proclaiming the coming judgment upon unbelieving Israel, invokes the memory of a whole line of martyrs: "Upon you will come all the righteous blood that has been shed on earth, from the blood of righteous Abel to the blood of Zechariah" (Mt 23:35 RSV).

In the NT, Stephen stands out as the first Christian martyr, one who exemplifies the meaning of Jesus' instruction of taking up the cross in following him (Mk 8:34; Lk 9:23). Martyrs are also highlighted in the book of Revelation, where their sacrificial witness receives special honor. When the dragon is defeated, we are told that his downfall is brought about by the saints: "by the blood of the Lamb and by the word of their testimony; they did not love their lives so much as to shrink from death" (Rev 12:11 NIV). Here the description of the "blood of the martyrs as the seed of the church" was born.

See also CROSS; PASSION OF CHRIST; SUFFERING SERVANT.

MARY THE MOTHER OF JESUS

Layer upon layer of imagery has overlaid the sparse NT facts about the historical Mary. In the Roman Catholic world her influence is all-pervasive. Mary has become an object of veneration, revered for her spotless *virginity and perfection. As such, she has inspired some of the finest artistic achievements in the Western world.

Mary's history has been shaped by different emphases in theology and devotion. The façade of Notre Dame Cathedral in Paris provides a synthesis of the ways Mary has been perceived. Above St. Anne's doorway, seated on the throne of wisdom, she is a type of the church and, as virgin mother, presents her son. In a church dominated by asceticism in the first century, Mary epitomized the virtues of the celibate life and the ideal to which all Christians should aspire. Over the north doorway Mary is depicted as Queen of Heaven. As perpetual virgin, her body and soul are triumphantly assumed into heaven, where she is crowned. The proof text used to support her assumption is the ambiguous reference in Revelation 12:1: "A great and wondrous sign appeared in heaven: a woman clothed with the sun, with the moon under her feet and a crown of twelve stars on her head" (NIV). From heaven Mary acts as protector and powerful intercessor. Above the central doorway Christ sits in judgment, while on his left Mary and John pray at the foot of the cross. Thus Mary intercedes as spiritual mother. She is viewed as a co-redemptrix who collaborates intimately with Christian redemption. Some feminist theologians have taken up this emphasis on Mary as coredemptrix, so that Mary becomes a liberating, redemptive symbol for women.

The elaborate extrabiblical traditions surrounding Mary stand as foils to the biblical portrayal. Given the scarcity of biblical data, it is strange that Mary has been idealized in so many different ways. The historical evidence about the real Mary who lived in the first century is sparse, although she is the biblical woman most often mentioned by name. Her date of birth and the nature of her death are unknown. Her parentage and background are obscure.

Mary makes few appearances in the Gospels, being most visible in the accounts of *Matthew and *Luke. From these sources we know that Mary was a Galilean Jew. At the time of the annunciation, she was betrothed to Joseph. According to Luke's narrative, the *angel Gabriel was sent to her in Nazareth with the news that she would become pregnant and give birth to a son (Lk 1:26-38). After Mary's visit to her cousin Elizabeth in the hill country of Judea and the birth of Christ in *Bethlehem (Lk 1:39-56; 2:1-20), she is mentioned on only a few occasions: at the presentation in the *temple, at the discovery of Jesus in the temple with the teachers of the law, at the *wedding in Cana and at the cross (Lk 2:21-40, 41-52; Jn 2:1-11; 19:26-27). Sometimes she is accompanied by Jesus' *brothers (Mt 12:46-50; Mk 3:31-35; Lk 8:21).

Mary's first role is that of the betrothed *virgin, singled out for momentous *blessing but also social ostracism. The trauma of her pregnancy is such that Joseph even considers divorcing her (Mt 1:19). But there are *joy and blessing as well. When Mary and Elizabeth meet, Elizabeth prophetically greets Mary as "blessed among women, . . . the mother of my Lord," blessed for believing "that what the Lord has said . . . will be accomplished" (Lk 1:42-43, 45 NIV).

Mary responds with an intense song of *praise to God (Lk 1:46-55). Her song is reminiscent of Hannah's *prayer (1 Sam 2:1-10) and of the imagery of some of the *psalms (for example, Ps 113), showing her acquaintance with the Hebrew Scriptures. As a self-portrait the Magnificat gives us a picture of Mary as blessed by God, of *humble standing, someone who fears God. She is also a poet. She identifies herself with the *"hungry" of the world and those who have longed for fulfillment of the ancient promises to *Israel. This then is one image of Mary—the betrothed who became a virgin mother, the young Hebrew woman of exemplary piety.

At the *nativity (Lk 2:4-7) Mary is the archetypal young mother who gives birth and wraps her newborn in swaddling clothes. She is also an outcast, deprived of a suitable place for childbirth and having to settle for a barn and manger. As an extension of her role as mother, she is shown briefly as the mother of a son who became a celebrity in his society. At the wedding at Cana in Galilee, where Jesus performed his first miracle, Mary seems to sense her son's divine power (Jn 2:3-5). Mary, the contemplative of her son's words, appears already at the adoration of the Magi, where we read that "Mary, treasured up all these things and pondered them in her heart" (Lk 2:19 NIV), as she did also when Jesus explained his staying behind in the temple (Lk 2:51).

Another role of Mary is the sorrower—the mother forced to *witness the *pain of her son's *suffering and execution. Already at Jesus' presentation in the temple, Simeon prophesied to her, "And a sword will pierce your own soul too" (Lk 2:35 NIV). This is a terrifying image that Luke never fully explains. Was Simeon speaking of the deep anguish Mary would suffer as she watched what happened to her child?

At an early age Jesus caused his mother and father anxiety when he disappeared for three days, eventually to be rediscovered in the temple in *Jerusalem. Mary may have witnessed his violent rejection in Nazareth (Lk 4:14-30). She must have known that some of Jesus' family thought that he was out of his mind (Mk 3:21). She was present as Jesus was *tortured and taunted on the cross (Jn 19:25-27). Her story is full of poignancy and pain.

The images we most readily associate with Mary cover the range of her life: an angel who appears before her at the annunciation, her moment of submission captured in her statement "May it be to me as you have said" (Lk 1:38 NIV), her virginity, her fiancé and husband Joseph, birth in a barn and her laying her firstborn in a manger, a furtive *flight into *Egypt on a *donkey, and grief at the cross.

The tradition that isolates Mary as a unique person elevated far beyond ordinary humanity, and even humanity itself, misses the point. According to the NT accounts, Mary is not removed from ordinary women. She is not the Queen of Heaven or the token female in the Trinity or a goddess. She is neither a matriarchal nor a fertility symbol. She has no titles or special sway in heaven. She is an ordinary woman who responded in *faith to a unique calling.

In fact, it is her ordinariness that makes her so extraordinary. We are to remember her as "blessed among women," representing qualities that, except for her bearing the Savior of the world, are open to any person. In her role as Everywoman, Mary fills an ever-expanding list of roles—humble *servant of God, idealized virgin, the mother of exemplary maternal devotion to her child, *disciple of Christ, sharer in Christ's suffering.

See also BIRTH STORY; JESUS, IMAGES OF; NATIVITY OF CHRIST; VIRGIN, VIRGINITY.

MASTER BUILDER. *See* AUTHORITY, HUMAN.

MATCHMAKER, GO-BETWEEN

The archetypal matchmaker is someone who arranges or fosters a romantic relationship. A successful matchmaker stage-manages a relationship that ends in *marriage.

The original matchmaker in the Bible is *God.

Believing that "it is not good that the man should be alone" (Gen 2:18 RSV), and because in naming the *animals it became apparent that "for the man there was not found a helper fit for him" (Gen 2:20 RSV), God fashioned a *woman from the rib of *Adam. He then "brought her to the man" (Gen 2:22 RSV), who eagerly embraced her as being "at last . . . bone of my bones and flesh of my flesh" (Gen 2:23 RSV). This was the original and prototypical matchmaking, and it was accordingly accompanied by God's instituting of marriage itself (Gen 2:24; accepted as the original institution of marriage in Mt 19:5; Mk 10:7-8; Eph 5:31).

The biblical character who most resembles the conventional matchmakers of *love stories and life is Naomi, who masterminds the romance of Ruth and Boaz (see Ruth, Book of). Her career as a matchmaker begins when Ruth returns after her first day's *gleaning in the field of Boaz and informs her *mother-in-law that she has gleaned in the field of Boaz. Naomi nearly goes into orbit, seeing at once the implications for Ruth's future: "Blessed be he by the LORD!" (Ruth 2:20 RSV). Her advice to Ruth that "it is well, my daughter, that you go out with his maidens" (Ruth 2:22 RSV) is dripping with irony. Naomi prefaces her most daring strategy as a matchmaker—sending Ruth to the threshing floor for a nighttime proposal to Boaz—with the question "My daughter, should I not seek a home for you?" (Ruth 3:1 RSV), confirming her intention to find Ruth a *husband. Naomi is personally rewarded for her efforts, taking her newborn grandson into her bosom and becoming his *nurse (Ruth 4:16).

Lesser matchmakers also appear in the Bible. *Samson's parents are virtually coerced by their unruly and strong-willed son to arrange his marriage to the woman of Timnah (Judg 14:2-3, 5, 10). The protective (and domineering?) *brothers of the female protagonist in the *Song of Songs think to oversee their *sister's finding of a husband (Song 8:8-9), but she in effect retorts that she has done just fine by herself (Song 8:10). There is also an enigmatic passage in the story of *Esther that hints that Hegai, the king's eunuch in charge of the harem, gave her advice that promoted her favor with the *king (Esther 2:15). *David's *adulterous affair with *Bathsheba uses the services of informants and messengers (2 Sam 11:3-4).

There may be a spiritualized version of the motif of matchmaking in the story of Jesus and the woman at the *well (Jn 4:1-42). An OT archetype is the story of the meeting of the future betrothed at a well (see Meeting at the Well). Some scholars believe that this is an implied backdrop to the story of Jesus and the Samaritan woman. By means of a carefully crafted persuasive dialogue, Jesus successfully completes his quest to bring the woman to *salvation. We might say, then, that Jesus is the matchmaker between the woman and God.

The conclusion to be drawn from this motif in the Bible is twofold. First, it strengthens the link between biblical narrative and literature generally. The Bible includes conventional characters like the matchmaker. Second, it reinforces the realism of the Bible, for it is a common experience of life that romances eventuating in marriage receive the help of interested third parties.

See also LOVE STORY; MARRIAGE; MEETING AT THE WELL.

MATTHEW, GOSPEL OF

Each of the four Gospels highlights or foregrounds things that distinguish it from the others. Matthew's Gospel is written for the Jews, stressing Jesus as King and as the fulfillment of OT prophecy. It has apocalyptic and ecclesiastical interests as well. The arrangement of material bears the imprint of an orderly mind and a penchant for tidy organization and grouping, traits in keeping with the tradition that the author was Matthew the tax collector and bookkeeper.

The most important feature of the book's structure is its arrangement on a principle of alternating sections of narrative and discourse, with the two loosely related in each unit, as follows: narrative of Jesus' early years (Mt 1—4) and his inaugural demands for those who wish to live in the *kingdom of God (the Sermon on the Mount in Mt 5—7); the miracles of Jesus as he *travels about (Mt 8—9) and the discourse about how his disciples are to conduct themselves on their travels (Mt 10); Jesus' conflicts with the Jews (Mt 11—12) and his *parables about entering the kingdom (Mt 13); experiences with the disciples as the core of the new community (Mt 14—17) and a discourse about the duties of discipleship within the new community (Mt 18); events surrounding Jesus' final journey to Jerusalem (Mt 19—23) and eschatological instruction (the Olivet Discourse in Mt 24—25); the events of *Passion Week, ending with the *resurrection (Mt 26—28).

While it is speculative to ascribe the five-part arrangement of discourses to a conscious imitation of the five books of the Pentateuch (though this would fit the Jewish orientation of the Gospel), the convenience of the scheme (perhaps an aid to the memory of new converts being instructed) is unmistakable. One can count off the five discourses on the fingers of one's hand, each one answering a question. The question of how citizens of the kingdom are supposed to live is answered by the Sermon on the Mount (Mt 5—7). The question of how disciples are to conduct their travels is answered by the missionary discourse on *servanthood (Mt 10). Those wanting to know what parables Jesus told about entering the kingdom will find some of them collected into a single chapter (Mt 13). The question of how disciples should live with each other finds an answer in the discourse about *humility and *forgiveness (Mt 18). The question of how it will all end receives its answer in the Olivet Discourse on the end of the age (Mt 24—25). The tidiness of the arrangement is highlighted by the way each of these sections ends with the formula "when Jesus had finished these sayings" (see Mt 7:28; 11:1; 13:53; 19:1; 26:1).

Other patterns are also evident. We find a conscious balancing of beginning and end, for example. Christ's coming to earth at the start is balanced at the end by his imminent departure to heaven. Incarnation is balanced by resurrection, birth by death. The action starts in Bethlehem and ends in Jerusalem. The light of the *nativity (Mt 2:2) is balanced by the darkness of the crucifixion (Mt 27:45). Jesus is worshiped at the nativity and mocked at the crucifixion. Between these bookends we find the story of Jesus' life and ministry.

The interlinking of narrative and teaching also characterizes Matthew's portrait of Jesus, which presents a multitude of obvious connections between Jesus' words and his deeds. If Jesus indirectly exhorts others to be meek (Mt 5:5), he himself is such (Mt 11:29; cf. Mt 21:5). If he enjoins *mercy (Mt 5:7), he himself is merciful (Mt 9:27; 15:22; 20:30). If he congratulates those oppressed for God's cause (Mt 5:10), he himself *suffers and dies innocently (Mt 27:23). Jesus further demands faithfulness to the *law of Moses (Mt 5:17-20) and faithfully keeps that law during his ministry (Mt 8:4; 12:1-8, 9-14; 15:1-20). He recommends self-denial in the face of evil (Mt 5:39) and does not resist the evils done to him (Mt 26:67; 27:30). He calls for private *prayer (Mt 6:6) and subsequently withdraws to a *mountain to pray alone (Mt 14:23). Jesus, moreover, advises his followers to use certain words in prayer ("your will be done," Mt 6:10; "do not bring us to the time of trial," Mt 6:13) and he uses those words in Gethsemane (Mt 26:41-42). He rejects the service of mammon (Mt 6:19), and he lives without concern for money (Mt 8:20). He commands believers to carry crosses (Mt 16:24), and he does so himself, both figuratively and literally.

Matthew writes self-consciously to Jews, hoping to convince them that Jesus is the promised Messiah and that OT prophecies are fulfilled in his life. There are accordingly many OT allusions and echoes in his account. In Matthew 1—5, for instance, the text again and again directs the informed reader to the foundational story in *Exodus and so teaches that Jesus is a new lawgiver whose advent inaugurates a new *exodus. Herod's order to exterminate the male infants of Bethlehem (Mt 2:16-18) is like *Pharaoh's order to do away with every male Hebrew child (Ex 1). The quotation of Hosea 11:1 in Matthew 2:15 evokes thought of the exodus, for in its original context "out of Egypt I called my son" (NIV) refers to Israel. Jesus, like Israel, is exiled to Egypt and then returns to the land of origin. Matthew 2:19-21 borrows the language of Exodus 4:19-20 so that just as *Moses, after being told to go back to Egypt because all those seeking his life have died, takes his wife and children and returns to the land of his birth, so too with Jesus: Joseph, after being told to go back to Israel because all those seeking the life of his son have died, takes his wife and child and returns to the land of his son's birth.

John the Baptist's ministry is the fulfillment of Isaiah 40:3 (LXX; see Mt 3:3), and in the OT the prophecy is comfort for the exiles in Babylon: a new exodus and return to the land lie ahead. When Jesus passes through the waters of *baptism and then goes into the desert to suffer *temptation, one again recalls the exodus (cf. esp. Deut 8:2-3). Jesus, whose *forty-day fast reminds one of Moses' forty-day fast (Ex 24:18), is like Israel tempted by *hunger (Ex 16:2-8), tempted to put God to the test (Ex 17:1-4; cf. Deut 6:16) and tempted to *idolatry (Ex 32). On each occasion he quotes from Deuteronomy—from Deuteronomy 8:3, in Matthew 4:4; from Deuteronomy 6:16, in Matthew 4:7; and from Deuteronomy 6:13, in Matthew 4:10. After all this Jesus goes up on a mountain, where he discusses the *Sinai commandments (Mt 5:17-48) and delivers his own.

Other motifs reinforce the Jewish orientation of Matthew's Gospel. The Jews made much of lineage, and Matthew begins with a human genealogy for Jesus (cf. John's divine genealogy at the beginning of his Gospel). In keeping with the Hebrew respect for prophecy, Matthew lavishes attention on Jesus' role as teacher. The Hebrews were people of the Book, and Matthew goes out of his way to assert that Jesus fulfilled and brought to consummation what had been written in the OT. The Jews were familiar with apocalyptic visions of the end, and Matthew includes the Olivet Discourse on the last things.

The Jewish imagination was exhilarated by the idea of *kingship, and Matthew obliges with an emphasis on Jesus as king and ruler of a spiritual kingdom. The theme of Jesus as king unites much of Matthew's theology. The "kingdom of God" is "his" (= Jesus') kingdom (Mt 13:41). Jesus bears royal titles, including "Son of David" (Mt 1:1-18, 20; 9:27, etc.) and "Messiah" (Mt 16:13-20; cf. 2 Sam 7). As the Son of man who sits on his throne, he will judge and rule (Mt 19:28; 25:31, 34, 40). Jesus enters Jerusalem as its king (Mt 21:5) and is crucified as "King of the Jews" (Mt 27:11, 29, 37, 42). In line with his royal status throughout the Gospel, Jesus is repeatedly portrayed as sitting, that is, taking the position of authority and rest (Mt 5:1; 13:2; 15:29; 21:7; 24:3; 25:31).

In view of this emphasis on Jesus as king, the motif of Jesus as *suffering servant at the end of the book assumes increased force. After the Last *Supper, when Jesus refuses to exercise his kingly authority (cf. Mt 26:53), he no longer positions himself as the one in authority. Instead others sit—disciples (Mt 26:36), Peter (Mt 26:58, 69), guards (and evidently the high priest; Mt 26:58, 62), Pilate (Mt 27:19), the soldiers at the cross (Mt 27:36). Jesus now stands (Mt 27:11), falls to the ground (Mt 26:39) and hangs from a *cross (Mt 27:35). His posture during the passion reflects his temporary renunciation of authority and the lack of all comfort. The king has become the suffering servant of Isaiah (cf. Mt 8:17; 12:18-21).

Geography is a unifying factor in Matthew's Gospel, and an incipient symbolism is at work in some of the places. Galilee is where Jesus begins his ministry (Mt 4:12-25) and where Jesus commissions his disciples to continue his mission (Mt 28:16-20). Within Galilee, Capernaum and Nazareth are symbols of the rejection of divine grace (Mt 11:23-24; 13:54-58). Jerusalem is the place of ultimate rejection—crucifixion—and the place of mortal enemies like Herod, Pilate and the chief priests and elders of the people.

Matthew's Gospel is partly unified by conflict and contrasts. The Sermon on the Mount ends with the famous contrasts between narrow and wide gates, true and false prophets, and the wise and foolish builders (Mt 7:13-27). All the long parables recorded by Matthew involve conflict or contrast. The light on the Mount of Transfiguration (Mt 17:1-2) is contrasted to the darkness that set in as Jesus hung on the cross on the hill of crucifixion (Mt 27:45). More generally, Jesus participates in the whole gamut of human possibilities: he is humiliated and exalted, surrounded by saints and ringed by sinners, clothed with light and wrapped in a mantle of darkness, is born and dies.

Finally, Matthew is fond of grouping his material by numerical schemes. Patterns of *three can be found in Matthew 1:1-17; 4:1-11; 6:1-18; 7:7; 8:1-15 (three miracles of healing); Matthew 8:23—9:8 (three miracles of power); Matthew 9:14-17; 10:26, 28, 31; 10:37-38; 13:1-32 (three parables of sowing); Matthew 18:6, 10, 14; 21:18—22:14 (three parables of warning); Matthew 22:15-40 (three questions by adversaries); Matthew 26:39-44; 26:69-75; 27:11-17). A *sevenfold arrangement can be found in Matthew 6:9-13 (seven clauses in Matthew's version of the Lord's Prayer); Matthew 12:45; Matthew 13 (seven parables); Matthew 15:34; 15:37; 18:22; 22:25; Matthew 23 (seven woes).

See also JESUS, IMAGES OF; JOHN, GOSPEL OF; LUKE, GOSPEL OF; MARK, GOSPEL OF.

MEAL

People in the ancient Near East customarily ate two meals each day, a light midday lunch and the main meal in the evening after work. Breakfast was a light snack, not usually considered a meal proper. A meal was never simply a time to ingest food and quench thirst; at meals people displayed kinship and *friendship. Meals themselves—the foods served, the manner in which that was done and by whom—carried socially significant, coded communication. The more formal the meal, the more loaded with messages. The messages had to do with *honor, social rank in the family and community, belonging and *purity, or *holiness. Social status and role were acted out in differentiated tasks and expectations around meals, and the maintenance of balance and harmony at meals was crucial to the sense of overall well-being. Among God's chosen people, meals became ways of experiencing and enjoying God's presence and provision.

Recognizing References and Allusions to

Meals. Biblical references to meals are sometimes indirect. Passages in which invitations are given to enter or lodge in a house almost always imply an invitation to a meal as well (e.g., Lk 19:1-10). Mention of any of the following also usually indicates a meal: *food, breaking of *bread, *drink, *cup, *eating "before the Lord," *sitting, *reclining, *table, *anointing with *oil and foot *washing or hand washing. In addition, several types of special meals occur: ceremonial meals, ritual meals, festive banquets like wedding *banquets, farewell meals and, in the NT, Greek symposium-style meals. Meals differed according to occasion (everyday or festive), time, place (temple or home, wilderness or kosher space), persons present (family or associates, guests present or not).

Social and Religious Boundaries and Meals. The meal became a place where Jews "drew the line" between insiders and outsiders in their families, communities and ethnic group. Gentiles and strangers either were excluded or had to undergo special ritual cleansing in order to participate in even ordinary meals. There were strict limitations on food, its preparation and its consumption, distinguishing between the ritually clean and the unclean. Concern for holiness, which gave rise to the kosher (*kashrut*) laws of later Judaism, reflect the Jewish conviction that God is present at meals. To eat defiled food or to eat with an "unclean" person would be inappropriate and dishonoring to God.

Sacredness and Meals. Special covenant meals held to seal and dramatize the ratification of a covenant were sacred, and God's presence was assumed. Feasts were important to Israel's worship and to the cultural rhythm of the year. These included ritual meals held to signify and remember events of God's protection and intervention in the past (as in the *Passover meal, Deut 16:1-8), and to accompany offerings and gifts celebrating God's present provision for the people. These meals are said to be held "before the LORD" or "in the presence of the LORD," and the people are encouraged to "rejoice before the LORD" (Deut 12:12, 17-18; 14:26; 16:11, 15; Lev 23:40).

God's presence was expected, awaited and enjoyed at everyday meals in devout Jewish households; all meals were sacred because God had provided them. There were no strictly secular meals: "In Judaism table fellowship means fellowship before God" (Jeremias, 115).

When Jesus gives thanks before breaking bread (e.g., Lk 9:10-17), he performs (and transforms) the blessing that was an integral part of every proper meal. The meal was a joyful time, and joyfulness and cheer could be symbolized in a meal (Prov 15:15). God's provision and care become tangible in the meal. Just as Yahweh demonstrated his love and care by feeding the people in the wilderness, so Jesus feeds the multitudes (Lk 9:10-17 par.) at miraculous meals. *Abundant provision becomes a picture of God's *kingdom, of salvation, and of God's love (Is 25:6).

Royal Meals: Power and Honor. Special meals were held to celebrate a king's coronation (1 Chron 29:22) and to celebrate victories after battle (see Is 55:1-5 and 61:6 for figurative uses). The downside of a victory meal is the defeat that it demonstrates for the conquered (see the grotesque, symbolic victory feast in Ezek 39: 17, 20). Verbs evoking meals or eating ("consume," "eat up," "devour") can be used to describe slander, defeat and judgment, as in the Apocalypse: "Come, gather together for the great supper of God, so that you may eat the flesh of kings, generals, and mighty men, of horses and their riders, and the flesh of all people, free and slave, small and great" (Rev 19:17-18 NIV; cf. Ps 27:2; Is 51:3, 17-23; 56:9-12; Jer 12: 9; Lk 22:30).

Meals and Eschatological Intimacy with God. In Revelation the picture of a meal for people of all nations, celebrating God's final victory and judgment, recalls Isaiah's vision: "On this mountain the LORD Almighty will prepare a feast of rich food for all peoples, a banquet of aged wine—the best of meats and the finest of wines. On this mountain he will destroy the shroud that enfolds all peoples, the sheet that covers all nations; he will swallow up death forever" (Is 25:6-7 NIV). The eschatological meal announces the wideness of God's mercy and universal scope of God's salvation (Mt 8:11; Lk 13:29; Is 61:3) and ultimate blessing (Mt 26:9; Mk 14:25; Lk 22:18; Rev 3:20; 19:9; 22:17). Rich feasting and universal fellowship is the very opposite of the pale and silent shroud of death.

Church Meals: Remembering and Previewing. Meals were central to the life of the early church. Luke summarizes the earliest days of the church: "They broke bread in their homes and ate together with glad and sincere hearts, praising God and enjoying the favor of all the people" (Acts 2:46, 47 NIV). Ordinary hospitality became a crucial way of supporting and sustaining missionaries and introducing newcomers to Jesus and the Way. Such meals challenged believers to cross and forsake traditional boundaries between gender, rank, religion and ethnicity. Meals became a way of demonstrating and celebrating their new kinship in Jesus' family. The *Lord's Supper and agape (love) meals were central expressions of their life together, and anything that marred the fellowship of the meal was to be avoided (Cor 10—11; Jude 12; 1). These meals were foretastes of the sweet fellowship with Jesus and one another to which the church looked forward when the kingdom would come in its fullness.

See also BANQUET; DRINKING; EATING; FEAST, FEASTING; FOOD; HUNGER; SUPPER; THIRST.

BIBLIOGRAPHY. M. Douglas, "Deciphering a Meal" in *Implicit Meanings* (London: Routledge & Kegan Paul, 1966); J. Jeremias, *New Testament Theology* (New York: Scribners, 1971); J. H. Neyrey, "Ceremonies in Luke-Acts: The Case of Meals and Table-Fellowship" in *The Social World of Luke-Acts: Models for Interpretation,* ed. J. H. Neyrey (Peabody, MA: Hendrickson, 1991) 361-87.

MEASURING, MEASUREMENT. *See* SCALES.

MEEKNESS

The key to understanding the virtue of meekness is that it is not a quality of *weakness but rather of strength. Meekness is not cowardice, timidity or lack of confidence. In classical Greek the word from which we derive *meekness* was used to describe tame animals, soothing medicine and a gentle breeze. The word also implies self-control. Aristotle describes it as the mean between excessive anger and excessive passivity, so that meekness can be regarded as strength under control.

The background for understanding the biblical virtues of meekness and gentleness is the disparagement of these virtues in the classical world and the humanistic philosophies that have stemmed from classicism. Most of the world's literature has exalted the conquering *hero who refuses to submit and who exerts his or her interests against anyone who might challenge those interests. Most cultures have reserved their rewards for people who compete successfully through strength of will and superior power. In such a context Jesus' portrait of the ideal *disciple as someone who is meek, accompanied by the promised reward that such a person will *inherit the *earth (Mt 5:5; cf. Ps 37:11), is a flat contradiction of conventional wisdom.

Meekness and gentleness appear in the Bible among lists of virtues, and two corresponding motifs are associated with them: they are commanded behavior, and *rewards are promised to people who display these virtues. Thus the psalmist can claim that God "will hear the desire of the meek" and "will strengthen their heart" (Ps 10:17 NRSV). The meek "shall possess the land, and delight themselves in abundant prosperity" (Ps 37:11 NRSV). The day will come when "the meek shall obtain fresh joy in the LORD" (Is 29:19 NRSV). Gentleness is one of the evocative nine fruits of the Spirit against which there is no condemnation of the law (Eph 5:23), and it is one of the virtues that Paul begs the Ephesians to display as they "live a life worthy of the calling" to which they have been called (Eph 4:1-2). Meekness is a virtue that NT Christians are commanded to "put on" (Col 3:12) and "aim at" (1 Tim 6:11), and Christians are repeatedly exhorted to "be" meek or gentle (Tit 3:2; 1 Pet 2:18; cf. 1 Thess 2:7; Jas 3:13, 17). Gentleness is a prerequisite for holding church office (1 Tim 3:3), and "a quiet and gentle spirit" among wives is "in God's sight . . . very precious" (1 Pet 3:4).

Yet another motif is that meekness or gentleness is commanded as the spirit in which believers are called to perform certain duties. The list of such duties includes restoring wayward Christians (Gal 6:1), correcting opponents (2 Tim 2:25), receiving the implanted word (Jas 1:21) and making a defense of the gospel (1 Pet 3:15). In many of the passages that enjoin meekness or gentleness as a virtue, it is easy to get the impression that this virtue is displayed especially in speech, a premise made explicit in the proverb that "a gentle tongue is a tree of life" (Prov 15:4 NRSV).

The two biblical characters with whom we most readily associate meekness are *Moses and Jesus. We read regarding Moses that he "was very meek, more than all men that were on the face of the earth" (Num 12:3 RSV). If we examine the life of Moses, we find good evidence that meekness is not weakness but strength under control. There is no more heroic and forceful character in the OT than Moses. He is fearless in exercising leadership against unbearable intransigence among his followers. He stands up to *Pharaoh. He defends his right to lead when his authority is challenged. He is the most visible and powerful figure in the traveling nation of Israel. Yet he does all of this in the strength of God, and he himself makes no presumption to be self-reliant, nor does he use his position as leader for self-aggrandizement. The major exception is when he strikes the rock instead of obeying God's command to speak to it, accompanied by a self importance about being the one to bring forth water ("Listen, you rebels, shall we bring water for you out of this rock?" Num 20:10 NRSV). The incongruity of Moses' behavior on this occasion with the general tenor of his life operates as a foil to highlight the prevailing quality of meekness in Moses' demeanor.

*Jesus is the supreme example of meekness and gentleness. "When he was abused," writes Peter, "he did not return abuse; when he suffered, he did not threaten; but he entrusted himself to the one who judges justly" (1 Pet 2:23 NRSV). Defiant toward the religious establishment in defending the helpless and diseased, as well as opposing evil, Jesus is self-effacing in regard to his own interests. From the cross he prays that his heavenly Father would forgive those who crucify him (Lk 23:34). No wonder he characterizes himself as being "gentle and lowly in heart" (Mt 11:29 RSV). And it is no wonder, either, that when we search our own longings we find such a person to be the one to whom we would most naturally go to "find rest for [our] souls" (Mt 11:29).

Although meekness and gentleness are robustly positive virtues, not a display of passive timidity, we can nonetheless bring them into focus if we list the behaviors they are *not*. Meekness and gentleness are the opposite of harshness, a grasping spirit, vengefulness, self-aggrandizement and lack of *self-control.

See also HUMILITY; WEAK, WEAKNESS.

MELCHIZEDEK

Melchizedek is one of the mystery figures in the Bible, a character whose evocative splendor is all out of proportion to the brevity of space devoted to him. His story is told in a mere three verses (Gen 14:18-20). After *Abraham defeats the *kings who carried his nephew, Lot, into captivity, he is met by Mel-

chizedek, who blesses him, in response to which Abraham offers him "a tenth of everything" (Gen 14:20 RSV). Who is this shadowy figure who elicits such respect from Abraham and seems to come out of nowhere to play his role on the stage of biblical history?

He is first of all an *authority figure. The associations are both royal (he is "king of Salem") and *priestly ("he was priest of God Most High"). As a person with authority he pronounces *blessing; in fact, in just two verses he is *three times said to extend a blessing (twice on Abraham, once on *God). He speaks of God as Creator and deliverer, and he is himself an agent of *peace, being associated with Salem (meaning "peace") and not having participated in the conflict in which Abraham has been a combatant. Melchizedek is also a host, bringing out "bread and wine" to Abraham, a picture that can scarcely avoid bringing associations of Communion into the consciousness of a Christian reader of the text, with an accompanying mystery about how this could be present so early in the Bible.

In the original text Melchizedek gains additional meaning by being a foil to the king of *Sodom, who also interacts with Abraham after his military conquest (Gen 14:21-24). Whereas Abraham accepts Melchizedek's *hospitality, he refuses to accept the offered gift of the king of Sodom. Melchizedek speaks in well-turned and gracious poetry, while the king of Sodom speaks in short, ineloquent and uncouth terms, essentially "Give me people. You take goods." And Abraham's wordless but eloquent response to Melchizedek contrasts with his relatively verbose and revealing disclosure of his perception of the character of the king of Sodom, with its implied accusation that the king of Sodom would later brag, "I have made Abram rich." The king of Sodom is dismissed from the scene with no regrets, while Melchizedek is a person who invites us.

This then is the original appearance of Melchizedek. It is an evocative story of mystery and authority, but we would scarcely make much of the figure if it were not for expansions on the picture later in the Bible. In a *psalm with messianic overtones, God is pictured as swearing incontrovertibly, "You are a priest for ever after the order of Melchizedek" (Ps 110:4 RSV). This would simply enhance the sense of mystery surrounding Melchizedek if it were not for further elaboration in the NT book of *Hebrews.

Hebrews 7 rings the changes on the theme of the superiority of Melchizedek and Christ as *priests to the Aaronic priesthood. Melchizedek has now become a Christ-figure. He is eternal, being "without father or mother or genealogy" and having "neither beginning of days nor end of life" (Heb 7:3 RSV). "Resembling the Son of God he continues a priest for ever" (Heb 7:3 RSV). The fact that Abraham gave him a tithe of the spoils is adduced as evidence of "how great he is" (Heb 7:4). Like Melchizedek, Christ was from a nonpriestly (non-Levitical) family, implying the superiority of his priesthood. Although the point is implied rather than stated, Melchizedek is like Christ in being a king as well as a priest. Virtually everything that the writer of Hebrews 7 says about Melchizedek adds to our impression of him as a mysterious and awe-inspiring figure.

This, then, is Melchizedek. His role in the history of doctrine is disproportionate to the little we know about him. What we *are* told arouses mystery instead of explaining matters. This enigmatic figure has captured the imagination of biblical audiences through the ages as the patron of Abraham and a precursor of Christ.

See also ABRAHAM; PRIEST.

MELT

The image of melting dominated the prescientific understanding of the world. Most of the elements of the natural world, through forces understood only by God himself, could be transformed into liquid. Humanity had learned (using techniques largely regarded as magic secrets) to manipulate and liquefy some elements and return them to their original form or to a different more useful form (Job 28:1-11). Note the awe in Job's description, not at the ingenuity of humanity but at the Creator who had hidden miraculous provision and fecundity in the earth (which we now blithely and thoughtlessly label "natural processes"). In particular, note his overly simple words for the ores in contrast to the technical names for the *metals resulting from the smelting processes: "Iron is taken from dust, and a stone he melts (into) copper" (Job 28:2). But not only *stone melted. Wax, because of its low melting point, was familiar to everyone and is a favorite simile. The earth itself, created at God's word, stood on "smelted pillars" (1 Sam 2:8) and also melted at his command (Nahum 1:4-6; cf. Ps 147:18).

Melting is destruction (Ezek 24:11) more final than the *flood (2 Pet 3:4-7). The ultimate fate of the created order is that even heaven "shall be dissolved, and the elements shall melt with fervent heat" (2 Pet 3:12 AV). This creation will be reforged. That the elements in the world consistently retain their familiar form at all is due to the sustaining power of God against the destructive forces of *chaos and evil ("in him all things hold together" Col 1:17 RSV).

Melting describes any weakening in the characteristic properties of a substance. The weakening of the ropes on *Samson's hands is the spirit of the ropes' creator at work melting them (Judg 15:14). If things made from the earth, plants and metals and other parts of creation, could melt, so also could human beings. Even today we say in English that people "fall apart" and "dissolve into tears." The weak knees and limp limbs serve as additional proof that the body of the individual is melting into its component parts. The water—one of the essential compositional elements of the body, along with earth, blood and spirit—is leaking out (1 Jn 5:6). (The heat of the sun, capable of melting wax, also

melts people until they leak water.) So the psalmist speaks of sorrow melting away the soul (Ps 119:28; cf. Job 30:16). Other poets observe that "everyone wails and melts in tears" (Is 15:3 NRSV). This melting of the soul often coincides with the loss of courage (Heb *rûaḥ,* "spirit").

The image of melting is most commonly used in the Bible to describe the effects of fear. In the expression "the heart melted," the *heart refers to the core of a person's inner being. The weakening of human resolve is the melting of a hard *heart. The result of this breakdown is often terror: "our hearts melted and no courage remained in any man." (Josh 2:11 NASB; cf. Josh 5:1; 7:5; 14:8; 2 Sam 17:10; Ps 107:26; Is 13:7; 19:1; Ezek 2:17; Nahum 2:10). "I am poured out like water . . . my heart is like wax, it is melted within my breast" (Ps 22:14 RSV) aptly describes the wasting away typical of profound physical and psychological distress.

In other passages melting signifies God's power to dismantle in judgment: "The Lord, the LORD Almighty, he who touches the earth and it melts." (Amos 9:5 NIV). The "mountains melt beneath him . . . like wax before the fire" (Micah 1:4 NIV; cf. Ps 94:5). *Mountains functioned as places and symbols of religious and political power in the ancient Near East (Is 2:14; 11:8; 30:29; 65:11, 25; Ezek 18:6; 22:9; 38:20). The image thus evokes the powerlessness of human institutions, even other gods (Is 65:7; Jer 3:23), before the God of Israel (Nahum 1:5; Ezek 35:12).

Melting is also used for the destruction of God's enemies. Psalm 58:8 compares the fate of the wicked to that of a snail "melting away as it moves along" (NIV). "As wax melts before the fire, may the wicked perish before God" (Ps 68:2 NIV)—a not so subtle request that God would "uncreate" the wicked.

The image of wax melting was familiar from the *blessing and *cursing rituals that sealed ancient treaties. A wax figurine was burned while uttering threats of similar consequences visited on anyone breaking the treaty. Fire could melt the body into its constituent elements. God had promise to melt down his people in a furnace of wrath like "silver and bronze and iron and lead and tin" and recast them (Ezek 22:20).

See also FIRE; METALS; TREMBLING, SHAKING, BODILY ANGUISH.

MERCY

The virtues are important in the Bible, but a difficulty exists in the English vocabulary for them. In the original Hebrew and Greek, virtues that receive distinct names in English Bibles often merge in ways that are virtually indistinguishable. Mercy is thus closely related to compassion in the Bible. We can profitably think of mercy as compassion in action. The Greek word from which *compassion* is derived means literally "from the bowels," denoting the visceral reaction to someone or something. Mercy, therefore, is both feeling compassion and acting upon it. Our best biblical picture of it is the figure of the good Samaritan in Jesus' parable. We read regarding the Samaritan that he "had compassion" and then acted decisively as benefactor to the wounded *traveler on the roadside, an action that identifies the Samaritan as having "showed mercy" on the wounded man—and as one who has crossed a gaping abyss of animosity between Samaritans and Jews (Lk 10:33, 37 RSV).

The Hebrew and Greek words that lie behind the vocabulary of *mercy* and *merciful* in the Bible suggest something of the difficulty we have in determining biblical references. The Hebrew *ḥesed* is often translated as "mercy," but it is also translated as "lovingkindness" and "goodness." Regardless of the Hebrew and Greek backdrop, if we look at the passages where mercy (approximately 150 occurrences in English translations) and compassion (50 references) occur in the Bible, the common definition is accurate: mercy is aid rendered to someone who is miserable or needy, especially someone who is either in debt or without claim to favorable treatment.

The most important fact about mercy in the Bible is that it is almost wholly the domain of God. There are, to be sure, references to human displays of mercy. We find mercy attributed to *Joseph's treatment of his brother's who appear before him in Egypt (Gen 43:14). One of Jesus' famous beatitudes makes the showing of mercy a hallmark of kingdom behavior, accompanied by the promise that those who are merciful will be rewarded by obtaining God's mercy (Mt 5:7). In Luke's sermon on the plain, this becomes a command to behave in such a way as to imitate God himself: "Be merciful, even as your Father is merciful" (Lk 6:36). The general thrust of Jesus' parable of the unmerciful servant is to summon people to show mercy to their fellow humans, as God has had mercy on them (Mt 18:38). But these references to humans showing mercy are statistically insignificant compared to the chorus of biblical passages that ascribe merciful behavior to God.

Mercy is one of God's most evocative attributes, and merciful behavior is among the actions of God in which biblical writers most obviously rejoice. While God's mercy encompasses all of God's benevolent acts toward his creatures, if we trace the references to God's mercy, two areas dominate—God's acts of *providence by which he sustains his vulnerable creatures, and his *forgiveness of sins. This is a way of saying that God's provision for the physical needs of people is a merciful act, as is his provision for their spiritual welfare. The latter motif is well summarized in a theological formula that appears approximately a dozen times in the Bible—that God is "merciful and gracious, slow to anger, and abounding in steadfast love and faithfulness" (e.g., Ex 34:6; Ps 86:15; 103:8 RSV). Again, God can be described as being "rich in mercy, out of the great love with which he loved us, even when we were dead through our trespasses," making us "alive together with Christ" (Eph 2:4-5 RSV). This side of God's charac-

ter is captured in the epithet "Father of mercies" (1 Cor 1:3).

In Jesus we find the mercy of God embodied and displayed in action. This divine mercy is found in the several instances where, faced with crowds or particular human needs, Jesus "had compassion for them, because they were harassed and helpless, like sheep without a shepherd" (Mt 9:36). Here the term for compassion is *splagchnizomai*, "to be moved in one's bowels." We might say, "his heart went out to the people," or "they broke his heart." In several instances we find needy people crying out to Jesus, "have mercy on me" (Mt 15:22; 17:15; 20:30-31; Mk 10:47; Lk 17:13; 18:38-39). We can then view each story of exorcism, healing and forgiveness by Jesus as a cameo of divine mercy. God's mercy is extended to the afflicted, the needy, the poor and the sinners of Israel. In the figure of Jesus the primary facets of God's mercy—forgiveness, deliverance, restoration—are given concrete shape. The *restoration promised by the prophets is at hand and moving in a quiet and mysterious way among the "little people" of Israel.

James closely reflects the ethos of mercy in the Gospel. Once again we find concrete images of mercy: caring for the fatherless (Jas 1:27), helping the *widow (Jas 1:27), respecting the poor (Jas 2:1-8), feeding the *hungry and clothing the *naked (Jas 2:1-16). Under God "mercy triumphs over judgment" (Jas 2:13 RSV).

Among Paul's several images of mercy we find an emphasis on God's freedom in dispensing mercy to whom he wills: "It depends not on human will or exercise, but upon God's mercy. . . . He has mercy upon whomever he wills" (Rom 9:16 RSV). Men and women are receptacles of this divine mercy: while some are "vessels of wrath made for destruction," others are "vessels of mercy, which he has prepared beforehand for glory" (Rom 9:22-23 RSV).

In Hebrews, Christ is the "merciful and faithful high priest" who became "like his brothers in every way" (Heb 2:17), the mediator of the divine mercy that flows from the "*throne of grace" in time of need (Heb 4:16). And in 1 Peter 1:3 we read of a "great mercy" that brings new birth through the power of resurrection. Formerly the Gentiles "had not received mercy," but now they "have received mercy" (1 Pet 2:10; cf. Hosea 1:6, 9; 2:1, 23) and so, like Israel, they have been newly constituted as "a chosen race, a royal priesthood, a holy nation, God's own people (1 Pet 2:9 RSV).

See also DISEASE AND HEALING; FORGIVENESS; SALVATION.

MERCY SEAT. *See* ATONEMENT.

METAMORPHOSIS. *See* TRANSFORMATION.

MICAH, BOOK OF

The dominant theme of Micah's prophecies is rebuke and *restoration. The book is structured around the thrice occurring admonition to hear/listen (Mic 1:1; 3:6; 6:1), with each major section being organized along similar, though not identical, lines: warning, *oracle of *judgment and *salvation oracle.

Chapters 1—2 and 6—7 show the clearest systematizing of the pattern: the double warning of Micah 1:2-7 (court setting) and Micah 1:8-16 (lament), followed by a woe oracle (Mic 2:1-5) and succeeding oracles of judgment (of disputation, Mic 2:6-11) and salvation (Mic 2:12-13) being paralleled by the double warning of Micah 6:1-8 and 6:9-16, followed by a woe oracle (of lament, Mic 7:1-7) and succeeding oracles of judgment (Mic 7:8-13) and salvation (prayer, Mic 7:14-17; hymn, Mic 7:18-20). The central portion is less standardized. Although the section opens with the usual double warning (Mic 3:1-4, 5-7) and is followed by oracles of judgment (disputation, Mic 3:8-12) and salvation (Mic 4:1-5), thereafter there is a recurring intertwining of messages of judgment and deliverance (Mic 4:6-13; 5:1-5a; 5:5b-9; 5:10-15) built around the *remnant theme (Mic 5:8).

Micah's use of language is predominantly what Northrop Frye terms *demotic* (the language of everyday speech). His is the tongue of the common man, his imagery that of everyday life. He speaks of *birth and *death (Mic 4:9-10; 5:2-3; cf. 3:2-3), of *horses and *chariots (Mic 5:10), and *cities and countries (Mic 7:12), of *temple worship together with its *idolatry, *witchcraft and *prostitution (Mic 1:7, 8; 5:12-14; 6:6-7) and of the destruction and captivity of *warfare (Mic 1:9-16; 3:12; 4:10-13, 15; 6:16; 7:8-13). Especially to be noted is the injustice of society (Mic 2:6-11; 3:1-3; 6:9-12; 7:4-6) and its leadership at every level (Mic 2:1-2, 6, 9-11; 7:3). In all of this may be noted the added touch of pathos in the prophet's own agony of heart: "Because of this I will weep and wail; I will go about barefoot and naked. I will howl like a jackal and moan like an owl" (Mic 1:8 NIV). The sentiment is clear: injustice must be overcome with justice, mercy and a humble walk with God.

Underlying the whole of Micah's prophecies is a pastoral tone. His allusions are alive with the sights and sounds of the natural and agrarian worlds. He calls attention to *mountains (Mic 1:3-4; 3:12; 6:1-2; 7:12) and *valleys (Mic 1:4, 6); to sunset and *darkness (Mic 3:6); to *earth, *sea and rushing *water (Mic 1:4; 7:12, 13, 19); to showers and *dew on the *grass (Mic 5:7); to fields and *houses (Mic 2:2; 3:12); to plowshares and *pruning hooks (Mic 4:3); to the planting of olives and *grapes (Mic 1:6; 6:15), the gathering of summer *fruit, and the *gleaning of *vineyards (Mic 7:1), and sheaves gathered on the *threshing floor (Mic 4:12-13); to *briars and *thorn hedges (Mic 7:4); and to such creatures as the jackal and the owl (Mic 1:8; see Animals). Micah's language and subject matter are often presented in a rich kaleidoscope of literary features. Among the many that may be noted are simile (Mic

1:8; 2:8, 12; 3:12; 4:10; 5:7, 8; 7:1), metaphor (Mic 2:13; 3:2-3; 5:3, 4; 7:8, 9), anthropomorphism and anthropopassionism (Mic 6:18-19), apostrophe (Mic 4:11; 6:3-5; 7:8, 10, 15-17), diatribe (Mic 3:11), hypocatastasis (Mic 4:8) and rhetorical question (Mic 2:7; 4:9; 6:7, 8, 10-11; 7:18a). One such feature, best appreciated in the Hebrew text, is the combination of assonance and alliteration in Micah 1:10-16. For example, "In Beth Ophrah [house of dust] roll in the dust" (Mic 1:10 NIV).

Several key themes run through the book. Especially important are those of the mountains as scenes and witnesses of God's activities (Mic 1:4; 3:12; 4:1-2; 6:1-2; 7:12), the remnant (Mic 4:6; 5:8), and the restoration of God's people (Mic 4:1, 6-7; 5:10; 7:7-15; cf. 2:12-13). Above all, God is seen to be Israel's king who, though he may have to chastise and correct his people, will yet restore and rule over them in power, and in an era of great peace and prosperity (Mic 2:13; 4:1-5, 6-8; 5:2-4; 7:11-12, 18-20).

Also to be emphasized is Micah's free use of well-known motifs such as the call/answer motif (Mic 3:4), the hidden face (Mic 3:4, 7) and the *vine and the fig tree (Mic 4:4). Particularly crucial is that of the *shepherd (cf. Mic 5:5-6). The motif of God as *shepherd to Israel his *flock serves as a prominent feature of the salvation oracles. It is the Good Shepherd who will gather the chastised, scattered *sheep and bring them to safe *pasture and fold (Mic 2:12-13; 4:68). Accordingly, the prophet has confident hope (Mic 7:7) that though he must pronounce Israel's present judgment, he can also declare God's forgiveness (Mic 7:18-19) and abundant provision (Mic 7:14) in accordance with the age-old provisions of the Abrahamic *covenant (Mic 7:20). Rebuke thus becomes the channel of restoration and ultimate blessings.

See also PROPHECY, GENRE OF; RESTORE, RESTORATION.

MIDDAY. *See* NOON.

MIDDLE, CENTER

The Christian medieval tradition is very aware of the middle position. In iconography and painting, the middle, besides size, serves to define the hierarchy of importance. Therefore the saint, Christ or God is always depicted in the center of the picture. In the Bible too some vividly visual scenes come to mind that illustrate the biblical usage of "middle."

The Middle as Defining Honor. The apostles James and John came to Jesus directly after he had predicted his death for the second time to request to sit at his *right and *left in his *glory (Mk 10:35-37). Their demand shows that they were interested in their own glory; that is, to be in the center of attention, rather than being sensitive to what the Lord had just entrusted to them. The Lord taught his disciples not to seek their own glory; and to illustrate that, he took a little child and had him stand in the midst of the disciples, telling them that whoever wanted to be first had to be the very last and the servant of all (Mk 9:33-36).

Revelation 5 shows Jesus as the *Lamb, standing in the center of the *throne, encircled by the four living creatures and the elders (Rev 5:6), who themselves are encircled, and thus in the center of "many angels, numbering thousands upon thousands, and ten thousand times ten thousand" (Rev 5:11 NIV). Here Christ alone is given all *worship and glory.

The Communal Concept of the Middle. The Hebrew word *tāwek,* meaning "bisection," and thus by implication "center," "middle," is mostly translated as "among" in the English versions. This word choice already highlights the concept of fellowship and communion, rather than that of supremacy and priority. Thus God says in Exodus 25:8: "Then have them make a sanctuary for me, and I will dwell among them." Though it is evident that a sanctuary serves as a place of worship and that God alone is worthy of worship, God's main goal is fellowship with his people. Naturally, this fellowship is only possible where God is the sole focus.

This communal concept of middle or center is coherent in both Testaments. Thus Jesus promises that "where two or three come together in my name, there am I with them" (Mt 18:20 NIV; "in the midst of them" KJV); and the risen Lord "came and stood among the disciples ("stood in the midst" KJV) and said, 'Peace be with you!' " (Jn 20:19 NIV). John describes as the central feature of the New Jerusalem that "now the dwelling of God is with men, and he will live with them. They will be his people, and God himself will be with them and be their God" (Rev 21:3 NIV). Earlier in Revelation, Christ is pictured as in the middle of the seven lampstands (Rev 1:13), symbolic of his honored presence in the Christian church.

Christ himself is shown in the middle, as the focal point of attention, when he was crucified "and with him two others—one on each side and Jesus in the middle" (Jn 19:18 NIV). This scene provides a striking image of Jesus as God incarnate, who committed no sin (1 Pet 2:22), taking sin upon himself as "he was numbered among the transgressors" (Is 53:12).

People at the Crossroads. A final image of being in the middle is the situation of a person or nation standing at the crossroads of decision between two alternatives. A memorable instance is Elijah's challenge to his nation on Mt. Carmel: "How long will you waver between two opinions? If the LORD is God, follow him; but if Baal is God, follow him." (1 Kings 18:21 NIV). Here, standing in the middle is an ignominious paralysis of spiritual will. Both Moses and Joshua, in their farewell discourses to their nation, picture the people as standing between two courses of action. Moses phrases the great choice as one between obedience and disobedience to the covenant, and between life and death, *blessing and *curse (Deut 30:15-20). In a similar vein Joshua challenges Israel to "choose for yourselves this day

whom you will serve" (Josh 24:15 NIV).

See also LEFT, LEFT HAND; OUTER, OUTSIDE; RIGHT, RIGHT HAND.

MIDNIGHT

Midnight comes late in the *night, even the *middle of night, as the word suggests. It is the time when under normal circumstances people *sleep. This is the word's common and ordinary use, to designate a time of *rest and quiet. Yet the Bible is silent about this meaning of the word *midnight.* In the Bible the events said to occur at midnight give us a new perspective on midnight as a time of devotion and a time of unexpected things.

A Time of Devotion. Midnight encompasses images of tranquil, constant devotion. The psalmist shows his zeal for *God and his *law by rising at midnight to offer his praise (Ps 119:62). In fact, in all the watches of the night he chooses to "remember [God]" (Ps 63:6; 119:148). By rising from his rest (presumably to return later), the psalmist demonstrates a steady devotion.

By contrast, Jesus describes a man without devotion to his neighbor. When the neighbor comes seeking bread to feed a guest at midnight, the man is unwilling to disturb his sleeping household to assist him (Lk 11:5-8).

Midnight is a time when only urgent desires are pursued. Paul, preparing to leave the city of Troas, speaks to the church there until midnight, devoted to their growth as Christians (Acts 20:7). Those things most important to us are accomplished even in the middle of the night.

A Time of Unexpected Events. Our image of midnight is shaped by the sudden events that happen then. God intrudes on the sleep of the *Egyptians when the tenth *plague strikes at midnight (Ex 11:4; 12:29). It is a time of unexpected attack. In the middle of the night *Samson tears down the *gates of Gaza while its people plan to kill him at dawn; his unexpected action spoils their plan (Judg 2:3).

Boaz discovers Ruth at his feet "in the middle of the night" (Ruth 3:8 NIV; *see* Ruth, Book of). In *Solomon's famous demonstration of *wisdom with two mothers who claim the same child, the true mother complains that her live baby was replaced with a dead child "in the middle of the night" (1 Kings 3:20 NIV). Elihu, Job's young friend, comments on God's equal view of all persons by noting that everyone dies without warning "in an instant, in the middle of the night" (Job 34:20 NIV). As Paul and Silas praise God in the Philippian jail, an *earthquake occurs at midnight that *opens all the *doors (Acts 16:25); the jailer is met with another surprise when he discovers that the prisoners have not fled, and he "and his house" are *baptized that night. In another tense moment, aboard a ship bound for Rome, Paul's guards spot land around midnight, having been lost in a storm (Acts 27:27). Such incidents surround the midnight hour with a tone of suspense and expectation that only those who are awake then might actually feel.

Midnight is also the time of the unexpected arrival of the *bridegroom in the parable of the ten virgins (Mt 25:1-13). Of the ten, five virgins have brought enough *oil to keep their *lamps burning into the late night; the other five have not and are found unprepared. The parable's purpose is to warn the followers of Jesus that his coming may be a time when they do not expect him, so they need to be constantly prepared. Indeed, in Jesus' *teaching about his return in Mark 13, he warns that he could come at any time, even midnight (Mk 13:35). He concludes his teaching with the command that his followers should "watch!"

In sum, midnight represents the depths of the night, a time of sleep, peace and quiet. Devotion is demonstrated when one awakens voluntarily at midnight, while events that disturb the night are generally unexpected. When a midnight event is anticipated, such as Christ's return, believers are called to be constantly prepared.

See also NIGHT.

MILK

The Israelites were primarily agriculturalists and *shepherds; therefore, milk was a common enough drink. However, its color, texture, use and origin all lent to milk's use as an image in the Bible.

In the first place, whole milk has a sensuous quality. Its texture is thicker than water and wine; its taste lingers on the palette. It is a pleasant taste experience, and it symbolizes blessing and luxury. This sense is evoked in the name frequently given to the land of Palestine, the *"land of milk and honey" (e.g., Ex 3:8, 17; 13:5; Lev 20:24; Num 13:27; 14:8; Deut 6:3; 11:9; Josh 5:6; Jer 11:5; Ezek 20:6). The Israelites looked at the *Promised Land as a land of great abundance and fertility. The prophet Joel looked forward to a restoration of the blessing of Israel in similar terms when he says that "the hills will flow with milk" (Joel 3:18 NIV). Job looks back on his life of wealth and good relationship with God as a time when his "path was drenched with cream and the rock poured out streams of olive oil" (Job 29:6 NIV). The sensuous quality of milk is highlighted in the *Song of Songs where deep kissing is anticipated by the remark that wine and milk are found under the woman's tongue (Song 4:11; 5:1).

Milk's luxurious and sensuous quality also stands behind its occasional mention in contexts of hospitality. Abraham rolls out the red carpet for his three special visitors, and the banquet includes milk as well as other luxury items (Gen 18:8). Deception plays a role in another scene of hospitality. After his defeat at the hands of the Israelites, Sisera, the Canaanite commander, fled and sought refuge in the tent of a woman named Jael (Judg 4). Sisera was thirsty, and in the words of the poem reflecting on the event, "He asked for water, and she gave him milk" (Judg 5:25 NIV). She showed Sisera hospitality, perhaps lulling him as much by the soporific effects of the drink as

by the kind treatment. But when he went to sleep, she killed him by driving a tent peg into his head.

Milk is striking in its *whiteness, and a few biblical passages pick up on this aspect of the drink. As Jacob looked into the future, he concluded his blessing of Judah by saying, "His eyes are darker than wine, and his teeth whiter than milk" (Gen 49:12). As the author of Lamentations recalls the past, he observes that Judah's princes were "brighter than snow and whiter than milk," but that now, after the destruction of Jerusalem, "they are blacker than soot" (Lam 4:7, 8).

Milk, of course, comes from the breasts of female mammals; thus, it can also strike the note of kinship. This may be behind the mysterious law that informs the Israelites, "do not cook a young goat in its mother's milk" (Ex 23:19; 34:26).

In a unique use of milk as an image, Job describes his creation in the following way: "Did you not pour me out like milk and curdle me like cheese, clothe me with skin and flesh and knit me together with bones and sinews?" (Job 10:10-11 NIV).

Finally, in the NT milk is a metaphor for spiritual nourishment. Peter appeals to the strong appetite of newborn babies for milk. Believers should put away malice, deceit and other vices that stunt spiritual growth, and "crave pure spiritual milk, so that by it you may grow up in your salvation" (1 Pet 2:2 NIV). But for other writers who are trying to awaken their audiences from spiritual stupor, milk is contrasted with a diet of solid food; and milk comes to represent the inferior diet of the spiritually immature. Paul gave the Corinthians "milk, not solid food," for they were not yet ready for solid food (1 Cor 3:2); and the audience of Hebrews is still in need of milk, though they should be feeding on solid food (Heb 5:12-13). Milk is an early growth formula that goes down easily; but with growth comes teeth, and further growth requires solid food.

See also DRINKING; LAND FLOWING WITH MILK AND HONEY; THIRST.

MILK AND HONEY. *See* LAND FLOWING WITH MILK AND HONEY.

MILLENNIUM

In the discussion that follows, the term *millennium* is used in its loose, popularized meaning rather than as the technical eschatological one-thousand-year phenomenon mentioned in Revelation 20:4. *Millennium* here refers to the golden-age visions of OT prophecy. No attempt is made, moreover, to tie these visions of an ideal world to a specific eschatological interpretation. Some of the prophecies of a future golden age focus on the restoration of the Jews to Palestine after the exile, others on the coming of the Messiah, and still others on the end times in a conclusive sense. But regardless of what the referent is, the image patterns and motifs are the same.

Most OT prophecies end with a vision of a golden age, and these are the main repository of millennial visions. In a prophecy like *Isaiah, however, we find interspersed visions of a coming golden age (in fact, as early as Isaiah 2 we find a millennial vision).

The Time. OT millennial visions are set in a temporal framework, as the prophets make it clear that the golden age they envision lies in the future. The millennium exists in the future tense. "It shall come to pass in the latter days," Isaiah says as he leads into his first vision of a coming golden age (Is 2:2 RSV). "In that day" is a common formula, and the dominant tense of the verbs is future.

The Land. We should not overlook the obvious: the physical setting in which the millennium will occur is a prominent motif. One motif is the *land, the physical *earth. The final verses of the book of Amos sound the keynote, as God promises,

"I will plant them upon their land,
and they shall never again be plucked up
out of the land which I have given them,"
says the LORD your God. (Amos 9:15 RSV)

Again, God's people "shall possess the land for ever" (Is 60:21 RSV), as God promises to "restore the fortunes of the land as at first" (Jer 33:11 RSV; see also Ezek 28:25).

The dominant image of the land is pastoral, with the natural landscape figuring prominently. In fact, nature will be a second Paradise: "this land that was desolate has become like the garden of Eden" (Ezek 36:35 RSV). The desert "shall blossom abundantly" (Is 35:2 RSV) and become "a fruitful field" (Is 32:15 RSV). A specifically pastoral note enters with the picture of "a pasture of flocks" (Is 32:14 RSV). The staple of pastoral literature is the verdant *pasture: "the pastures of the wilderness are green; the tree bears its fruit" (Joel 2:22 RSV). Because the millennium represents a rebirth after destruction, this natural landscape has some of the qualities of a new creation. We read that "waters shall break forth in the wilderness, and streams in the desert" (Is 35:6 RSV).

Not only is the millennial vision pastoral, but it is specifically an agrarian vision of cultivated land that produces crops. "The land that was desolate shall be tilled," we read (Ezek 36:34 RSV). In this golden age, farmers experience reward for their toil: "they shall plant vineyards and drink their wine, and they shall make gardens and eat their fruit" (Amos 9:14 RSV; see also Is 65:21-22; Ezek 28:26). The people of the new age "shall be radiant over the goodness of the LORD, over the grain, the wine, and the oil, and . . . their life shall be like a watered garden" (Jer 31:12 RSV; see also Joel 2:18).

The vision, moreover, is a vision of abundance. Everywhere we catch the note of overflowing energy and abundance: "the threshing floors shall be full of grain, the vats shall overflow with wine and oil" (Joel 2:24 RSV). Amos 9:13 is the most famous passage celebrating the millennial richness: "Behold, the days are coming . . . when the plowman shall overtake the reaper and the treader of grapes him who sows the seed; the mountains shall drip sweet wine,

and all the hills shall flow with it" (RSV; see also Joel 3:18). The millennial vision is the Bible's story of earthly *prosperity par excellence—a story in which God promises to "extend prosperity . . . like a river, and the wealth of the nations like an overflowing stream" (Is 66:12 RSV). God promises to "provide for them prosperous plantations so that they shall no more be consumed with hunger in the land" (Ezek 34:29 RSV).

The City. Although the *garden and the *city have been perennial opposites in the pastoral tradition, in the millennial vision of the Bible they complement each other and harmoniously coexist. In fact, sometimes they appear in the very same verse: "This land that was desolate has become like the garden of Eden; and the waste and desolate and ruined cities are now inhabited and fortified" (Ezek 36:35 RSV). The same verse in Amos that describes the planting of vineyards and gardens also tells us that "they shall rebuild the ruined cities and inhabit them" (Amos 9:14 RSV). Civilization and nature together make up the millennial vision: "they shall build houses and inhabit them; they shall plant vineyards and eat their fruit" (Is 65:21 RSV).

The city is finally as prominent in the millennium as is the pastoral countryside. The most prominent city is *Zion, or *Jerusalem, the holy city of the biblical imagination: "Look upon Zion, the city of our appointed feasts!" (Is 33:20 RSV). The Jerusalem of the millennium is "a praise in the earth" (Is 62:7 RSV). Some of the most famous millennial pictures are street scenes: "Old men and old women shall again sit in the streets of Jerusalem. . . . And the streets of the city shall be full of boys and girls playing in its streets" (Zech 8:4-5 RSV; see also Jer 30:18-19).

In keeping with the blending of the pastoral and the civilized, one of the most prominent features of the millennial Zion is the presence of a glorious *river (in fact, water imagery is prominent in the millennial vision generally [Is 41:18; 43:19]). This river seems to encompass more than physical satisfaction, but it is imagined as life-giving, gushing water first of all. The most extended picture is Ezekiel's vision of a river flowing from the *temple (Ezek 47). That this river is at least partly symbolic is suggested by a passage that states that "there the LORD in majesty will be for us a place of broad rivers and streams" (Is 33:21 RSV).

The People and Their Way of Life. Who will inhabit this coming glorious place of pastoral beauty and tranquillity and urban civilization? This is never spelled out specifically, but it seems taken for granted that the citizens of God's *kingdom are the redeemed of the Lord. A typical identification of the citizenry of the millennial kingdom is that found in Ezekiel 28:25: "Thus says the Lord GOD: When I gather the house of Israel from the peoples among whom they are scattered, . . . then they shall dwell in their own land which I gave to my servant Jacob" (RSV). The imagery of Israel remains dominant in millennial visions, though when viewed through the lens of NT developments one might plausibly conclude that the company of the redeemed includes Gentiles as well as Jews.

Because God is the one who inaugurates the millennium through an act of divine restoration, we often think of the millennium as a state in which the redeemed simply move in and take their ease. The contrary is actually the case: the millennium is a beehive of human activity, filled with visible industry on every hand. Some of this work is agrarian, as people plant and *harvest crops (Is 65:21-22; Ezek 28:26). Amos even paints a hyperbolic picture of such eagerness by *farmers, and such natural abundance from *nature, that the "the plowman shall overtake the reaper and the treader of grapes him who sows the seed" (Amos 9:13 RSV). A leading feature of work in the millennium is that it is productive—people who work receive the fruits of their labor (Is 62:8-9; 65:21-22; Jer 31:5).

In addition to farming, architectural *building is everywhere evident. In fact, the millennium emerges as one of the vastest building projects on record. We read of people building houses and inhabiting them (Is 65:21; Ezek 28:26). Building highways is also part of the picture (Is 40:3; 57:14; 62:10). Mainly, though, it is the cities that will be rebuilt: (Is 61:4; Amos 9:14). Sometimes foreigners are described as doing the building (Is 60:10), and sometimes even God is the one who says, "I will raise up the booth of David that is fallen and repair its breaches, and raise up its ruins, and rebuild it as in the days of old" (Amos 9:11 RSV).

A further part of the "beehive" effect of ceaseless human activity in the millennium is the influx of foreign traffic into the area, apparently in a continuous bearing of tribute. "The abundance of the sea shall be turned to you," writes Isaiah, "the wealth of the nations shall come to you" (Is 60:5 RSV), and he proceeds to paint a picture of throngs of animals and people entering the place (Is 60:6-14). In fact, the traffic is so continuous that the city's "gates shall be open continually; day and night they shall not be shut; that men may bring to you the wealth of the nations" (Is 60:11 RSV).

People will live triumphantly in the millennium. We get a strong sense of struggle being past, as people now reap the reward of victory. This is conveyed through political and military imagery of conquest. We read, for example, that "aliens shall stand and feed your flocks, foreigners shall be your plowmen and vinedressers" (Is 61:5 RSV). A key symbol of triumph in the ancient world was the ritual of leading the kings of conquered nations as trophies in a triumphal procession, and we find this image in Isaiah's millennial vision (Is 60:11). Nations that previously oppressed God's people "shall come bending low" (Is 60:14 RSV). Along with this display of power we find pictures of the wealth with which a conquering nation enriched itself: "Instead of bronze I will bring gold, and instead of iron I will bring silver" (Is 60:17 RSV).

The Peaceable Kingdom. Another leading motif in OT millennial visions is the *peaceableness of the life—its freedom from the terrors of ordinary life. American Quaker artist Edward Hicks captured the spirit of the millennium in his famous painting *Peaceable Kingdom*. One level at which this tranquillity exists is natural:

The wolf shall dwell with the lamb,
    and the leopard shall lie down with the kid. . . .
The cow and the bear shall feed; . . .
    the weaned child shall put his hand on the
        adder's den.
They shall not hurt or destroy
    in all my holy mountain. (Is 11:6-9 RSV;
        see also Is 35:9; 65:25)

In fact, God will make "a covenant of peace and banish wild beasts from the land" (Ezek 34:25 RSV).

This condition extends also to people and nations as universal peace reigns. In contrast to a world in which oppression from hostile nations threatens human security, in the millennium people will live "securely in their land with none to make them afraid" (Ezek 39:26 RSV), even able to "dwell securely in the wilderness and sleep in the woods" (Ezek 34:25 RSV). The people "will abide in a peaceful habitation, in secure dwellings and in quiet resting places" (Is 32:18 RSV).

The single most famous image of this peacefulness pictures it as a transformation of *war into peace: "they shall beat their swords into plowshares, and their spears into pruning hooks" (Is 2:4 RSV; cf. Joel 3:10). In fact, God will "abolish the bow, the sword, and war from the land" (Hos 2:18 RSV; see also Is 60:18).

An apt summary of the kinds of security that prevail in the millennium is this: "They shall no more be a prey to the nations, nor shall the beasts of the land devour them; they shall dwell securely, and none shall make them afraid" (Ezek 34:28 RSV).

The Satisfied Kingdom. Biblical visions of the millennium go beyond description of the external situation and give us a picture of the inner state of the people as well. The result is a beatific vision—a picture of how the inhabitants of the land *experience* their blessed state. Above all, they are *satisfied*. God promises that in the coming age "my people shall be satisfied with my goodness" (Jer 31:14 RSV; see also Jer 50:19). Not only will God send "grain, wine, and oil," but his people "will be satisfied" (Joel 2:19 RSV). Again, "you shall eat in plenty and be satisfied, and praise the name of the LORD your God" (Joel 2:26 RSV). God promises to "satisfy your desire with good things" (Is 58:11 RSV). The voice of satisfied *appetite runs strong in the millennial visions of the Bible: here people "come to the waters, . . . buy wine and milk without money and . . . eat what is good" (Is 55:1-2 RSV).

It is no wonder that the OT millennial visions are filled with the vocabulary of *joy, often expressed as a promise from God: "Then you shall see and be radiant, your heart shall thrill and rejoice" (Is 60:5 RSV). The people will say, "I will greatly rejoice in the LORD, my soul shall exult in my God" (Is 61:10 RSV). "Be glad," comes the prophetic voice, "and rejoice for ever in that which I create; for behold, I create Jerusalem a rejoicing, and her people a joy" (Is 65:18 RSV). Even "the desert shall rejoice and blossom" (Is 35:1 RSV).

The King of the Kingdom. The millennium is a divine monarchy ruled over by God and his Messiah. God "will become king over all the earth" (Zech 14:9 RSV), and "a king will reign in righteousness" (Is 32:1 RSV; see also Is 2:4). The Messiah will be established on the throne of David to rule an eternal kingdom (Is 9:6-7; 11:1-5). The people "will see the king in his beauty" (RSV) and will submit to him as their ruler (Is 33:17-22). The Lord "is exalted" in the kingdom (Is 33:5). He is so central that "the sun shall be no more your light by day, . . . but the LORD will be your everlasting light (Is 60:19-20 RSV).

*Worship naturally figures prominently in such a divine monarchy. We are asked to picture a realm in which "all the nations" flock to "the mountain of the LORD," saying, "Let us go up to the mountain of the LORD, . . . that he may teach us his ways and that we may walk in his paths" (Is 2:2-3 RSV). The people of the blessed kingdom "shall be called the priests of the LORD," and people will speak of them "as the ministers of our God" (Is 61:6 RSV). The prophets envision a time when "the earth will be filled with the knowledge of the glory of the LORD, as the waters cover the sea" (Hab 2:14 RSV; see also Is 11:9). Ezekiel actually devotes the last eight chapters of his prophecy to a portrayal of temple worship in the coming age.

The religious aura that envelops life in the millennial kingdom is a thoroughly moral and sacred one. The "people shall all be righteous" (Is 60:21 RSV). God himself "will fill Zion with justice and righteousness" (Is 33:5 RSV), and he "will cause righteousness and praise to spring forth before all the nations" (Is 61:11 RSV). Sanctity so infuses the realm that "on that day there shall be inscribed on the bells of the horses, 'Holy to the LORD.' And . . . every pot in Jerusalem and Judah shall be sacred to the LORD of hosts, so that all who sacrifice may come and take of them and boil the flesh of the sacrifice in them" (Zech 14:20-21 RSV).

Conclusion. The millennial visions of the OT prophetic books paint a picture of a utopia ("good place"). Regardless of how literally or figuratively one interprets the details, and independent of a specific eschatological interpretation, the imagery that fires the millennial imagination is simultaneously pastoral and urban. It is a vision of the fulfillment of human longing at every possible level. And it is a picture of moral and spiritual perfection.

See also ABUNDANCE; APOCALYPTIC VISIONS OF THE FUTURE; CITY; END TIMES; GARDEN; GOOD LIFE, THE; KINGDOM OF GOD; LAND; PEACE; TEMPLE; ZION.

MIND

Today we associate the mind with the brain. The brain and the head provide us with a number of stock images of the mind and its functions. So it comes as a surprise to many modern people that in the imagery of the Bible there is no awareness of the brain as the center of consciousness, thought or will. The processes of the "mind" are frequently associated with an organ that for us evokes the emotions, that is, the heart. English translations of the Bible vary in the extent to which they preserve the word "heart" rather than substitute a word or image associated with the mind.

In the Bible *heart* encompasses more than what we mean by *mind* (for which there is no word in biblical Hebrew). The heart is the center of the being, where the will, affections, thoughts, purposes and imagination reside. Human emotions are more frequently associated with the lower organs. In general the Bible places the psychological focus one step lower in the anatomy than do most popular modern idioms. Similarly, in the Greek NT, "mind" *(nous)* usually is used in reference to the cognitive, rational and purposive aspects of a person as well as the less concrete aspects such as heart, soul, opinion and understanding or reflection. The overlap between "mind" and "heart" is evident in Philippians 4:7: "the peace of God . . . will guard your hearts and your minds in Christ Jesus" (NIV). Or in 2 Corinthians 3:14-15 Paul can speak of the Israelites, whose "minds are made dull" because "a veil covers their hearts" (2 Cor 3:14-15; for OT examples, cf. 1 Sam 2:35; Job 10:13; 38:36).

The Bible is concerned with the right attitude of heart. The human heart, made dysfunctional by sin, must be "broken" or "crushed" (Ps 51:17), images many moderns would associate with a ruptured romance or spurned love. But for the psalmist it is symbolic of a person's humility and penitence, and is synonymous with "a broken spirit." A *"hard" or *"stony" heart does not submit to the will of God (Ezek 11:19). A *"fat" or "uncircumcised" heart fails to respond to God's will (Is 6:10; Ezek 44:7).

God knows the heart of each one and is not deceived by outward appearance (1 Sam 16:7). The godly rightly pray that God would search and know their heart (Ps 139:23) and make it *clean (Ps 51:10). The wicked, those who have willfully transgressed God's ways, need a "new heart" (Ezek 18:31), with God's law "written on the heart" (Jer 31:33). From these images it is clear that something akin to what we would call the "mind" is in view, though it includes human affections and aspirations. The heart as the spring of all desires must be guarded (Prov 4:23).

The rational capacity of the heart is evident in a number of texts. "The discerning heart seeks knowledge" (Prov 15:14 NIV) and "the wise man's heart guides his mouth" (Prov 16:23 NIV). The wise patriarchs instruct Job and utter sayings out of their heart (Job 8:10). It is the aim of the teacher to win pupils' hearts to the right ways (Prov 23:26). Jesus says it is the pure in heart who shall "see God" (Mt 5:8), and Paul writes that it is through Christ's dwelling in the heart by faith that the saints can comprehend the love of God (Eph 3:17). H. W. Wolff concludes that the heart in Hebrew "describes the seat and function of the reason. It includes everything that we ascribe to the head and the brain—power of perception, reason, understanding, insight, consciousness, memory, knowledge, reflection, judgment, sense of direction, discernment" (Wolff, 51).

Whatever else we may understand to be implied by the biblical understanding that humans are created in the "image of God" (Gen 1:26-27), the Bible presumes that the mind is part of this image. The unique attribute of this mind is its ability to know God. The distinction between the human mind and the animal mind is a basic premise that needs little elaboration. But the contrast is vividly imaged in Daniel when King Nebuchadnezzar, the leader of the great "superpower" of the day, is reduced to beastly behavior: his "mind" is "changed from that of a man" and he is "given the mind of an animal" (Dan 4:15-16 NIV; cf. the four beastly empires and the kingdom of the "one like a son of man" in Dan 7). At the same time there is a distinction between the human mind and the mind of God. Despite the vast capability of the human mind "to search out wisdom and the scheme of things" (Eccles 7:25 NIV), the depths of God's mind remains unsearchable by any human: "For my thoughts are not your thoughts, neither are your ways my ways, declares the LORD. 'As the heavens are higher than the earth, so are my ways higher than your ways and my thoughts than your thoughts' " (Is 55:8-9 RSV). In contrast with God, whose mind does not change (Num 23:19; 1 Sam 15:29), the human mind can be fickle (1 Sam 15:29) and "go limping with two different opinions" (1 Kings 18:21 RSV). Even when faced with the revelation of God's mighty power and will, the human mind can be overshadowed with doubts (Lk 24:38), dulled (2 Cor 3:14) or "blinded" by the "god of this age" (2 Cor 4:4). The Gospel of Mark provides vivid narrative images of the disciples, who follow Jesus daily, failing to perceive the full meaning of who Jesus is and what he is seeking to accomplish.

The human mind is subject to troubling thoughts (Gen 41:8) and confusion, a condition that sometimes results from divine judgment (Deut 28:28, 65). But a mind that steadfastly trusts in God will experience "perfect peace" (Is 26:3). From Paul's perspective it is as if the mind that is resistant to the "knowledge of God" is subjected to a spiritual disease. Finally, God, "gives over" such minds to the full effects of a "depraved" or "worthless" mind (Rom 1:28) that engages in beastly behavior (Rom 1:26-32). Even those who strive to keep God's ways find themselves engaged in a struggle. Paul sees this as the plight of Israel under the law (Rom 7:23), and the only solution is found in Jesus Christ, the true "image of God (2 Cor 4:4; Col 1:15), who through

the Spirit brings deliverance from the "fleshly" mind of "death" and creates a mind of "life and peace" (Rom 8:6). This is a transformation that Paul can call the "renewing of the mind" (Rom 12:2), or having "the mind of Christ" (1 Cor 2:16). Those who have experienced this transformation can be called on to be "perfectly united in mind and thought" (1 Cor 1:10 NIV; Phil 2:2).

See also HEAD; HEART.

BIBLIOGRAPHY. H. W. Wolff, *Anthropology of the Old Testament* (Philadelphia: Fortress, 1974).

MINERALS

The term *mineral* is used here in the broadest sense for anything nonliving found in the ground. Given the preoccupation of most societies past and present with the finding, mining and accumulation of mineral wealth, there is surprisingly little in the Bible on such matters, and most references are only in passing. There are two chief reasons for this. The first is the obvious point that Scripture places the emphasis on the spiritual rather than the material. The more subtle point is that ancient Israel possessed only limited mineral wealth, and its people developed only minor mining and metallurgical skills. The only metallic minerals found within its borders are, as stated in Deuteronomy 8:9, copper and iron; and nonmetallic wealth other than stone is very limited.

This limitation is surely significant: Israel was not so overflowing with wealth that its people could ever be independent of God. In fact, the main ore deposits are at the northern and southern margins of the Promised Land, and the metallurgical poverty reflected in 1 Sam-uel 13:19 may indicate the failure to take and hold on to the land. As with agricultural fertility, the mineral riches of Israel were not given unconditionally but had to be won. They were also inadequate to support any temptation for Israel to be an industrial power. By the same token, their paucity tempted no one to invade for minerals.

Although the level of mineral use in biblical times may appear to be low by modern standards, there may well have been a higher level of sophistication than we assume. Recent work on the Herodian Palace in Jericho has shown the existence of a range of pigments based on lead, mercury, copper and clay minerals. A similar complexity used in cosmetics would be probable.

As with the precious stones, biblical language does not always follow scientific classification; mineral identities are sometimes obscure. Minerals for which there are only brief references and no obvious symbolism—alabaster (Mt 26:7; Mk 14:3; Lk 7:37), lead (Ex 15:10; Job 19:24; Ezek 22:18ff.), tin (Num 31:22) and porphyry (Esther 1:6)—are omitted. The conventional division of minerals into nonmetallic and metallic is followed here.

Nonmetallic Minerals. Many of the nonmetallic minerals that are important today were either unknown or were of little use in the preindustrial world of Scripture. The chief nonmetallic mineral wealth won from the ground was *rock and *stone, with lesser contributions by flint, sulfur and so forth.

Stone. That *stone played a number of roles in the lives of people in biblical times is reflected in the complex and overlapping imagery. The Palestinian farmer eked out a livelihood in spite of the stony ground (e.g., Mk 4:5-6), for bedrock lies just below the surface of most of the Near East and all too frequently pokes through. More positively, stone was the most lasting of all building materials.

Negatively, the immutability of stone is evoked in references to spiritual *hardness (Jer 5:3; Ezek 11:19; 36:26). In an image perhaps strengthened by the *farmer's daily battle against it, stone forms the antithesis of living things. It is sterile and lifeless (Jer 2:27; Hab 2:19; Mt 3:9; 2 Cor 3:3; cf. 1 Pet 2:4), dumb (Hab 2:11; Lk 19:40), immobile and senseless (1 Sam 25:37; Acts 17:29) and inedible (Lk 4:3). The density of stone is referred to in Exodus 15:5, Nehemiah 9:11 and Proverbs 27:3.

Positively, stone is strong and seems, at least from the vantage point of a human life span, unaffected by time. This makes it suitable to bear God's words (Ex 24:12), to make boundary markers (Josh 15:6) or to form commemorations of covenants or events (Gen 31:45-54; Ex 24:4; 1 Sam 6:18; 7:12). The strength of stone is alluded to in many passages (e.g., Job 6:12; 38:30; 41:24; Lam 3:9; Ezek 3:9; Mt 7:24). It may be that something of the values of *permanence and security of rock are transmitted to stone.

In addition to these uses, stone is also used to refer to the Messiah. The imagery is derived, in the main, from three separate OT passages that center on the use of stone in *building. In Psalm 118:22 a stone cast aside by builders as useless is later found suitable of the glorious role as capstone (probably here keystone); the reference is to God's reversal of the world's verdict on Israel. The second passage is Isaiah 8:14, which centers on the paradox that while a stone (or a rock) may be vital to construction, it is also capable of causing a fatal fall (an underrated hazard to those of us who dwell in a world of electric lights); God is both savior and judge. The third verse (Is 28:16) refers to the laying of a precious and tested cornerstone—an allusion to the trustworthy, rocklike nature of God's deliverer. That these three verses were seen by the early church as referring to the Messiah is shown by the citation of the second and third references in Romans 9:33 and all three together in 1 Peter 2:6-8. The early nature of this interpretation can be seen in Acts 4:11, and its origin is doubtless to be found with Jesus himself (Mt 21:42 par.). Here and also in Matthew 3:9 the significance is heightened by similarity between the Hebrew word for stone (*'eben*) and that for son (*bēn*).

A further buttress of the messianic stone imagery may have been provided by the vision of Daniel 2. Here a divinely hewn rock fragment destroys the kingdoms of this world (Dan 2:34-35). Although the word used is translated as "rock" in most English versions, the two words are to some extent interchangeable (see Is 8:14).

Rock. The distinction between stone and *rock is far from clear in the English language. It is even less well demarcated in Hebrew, and there is some overlap (cf. Is 8:14). Nevertheless, the main imagery that has to do with rock is very different from stone. Here the fundamental concept hinges on a desert geomorphology alien to many modern Western readers, the unvegetated, bare rock outcrop or mountain mass rising up steeply from a flat plain. Here, in contrast to the open desert areas of *Sinai and the Negev, a rock outcrop would provide crevasses to hide in (Ex 33:22; 1 Sam 24:2), shade from the sun (Is 32:2), a defensible position (Ps 27:5) and a potential source of water from *springs. Seemingly based on this comes the idea that God is Israel's rock, a changeless and permanent *refuge and protector (1 Sam 2:2; 22:2-3, 32, 47) and numerous verses in the Psalms (e.g., Ps 19:14; 18:46; 62:1-2, 7). A basic passage in this imagery is Genesis 49:24, although equally significant are the many references in the Song of Moses (Deut 32:1-43). This emphasis on rock as a place of security is heightened by recurrent expressions, such as "rock of refuge," particularly in the Psalms (e.g., Ps 31:2; 62:7; 71:3). The concept of God as rock is so apposite that Rock is actually used as a name of God (2 Sam 23:3; Hab 1:12). In this context Paul's statement that the spiritual rock that accompanied the Israelites in the exodus was Christ (1 Cor 10:4) is a bold statement of his divinity.

Like stone, however, rock is naturally inhospitable to life, a feature implicit in the parable of the *sower (Mt 13:5, 20 par.). This property also underlies the water-from-rock incidents (Ex 17:1-7; Num 20:2-11; cf. Is 48:21), where it is shown that God can supply his people's needs in the hardest of places. Similarly, Isaiah 51:1 invokes the deadness of rock: out of inanimate material, God has made himself a people.

The NT usage is subtly changed, reflecting a different language, culture and geomorphology. The concept of God as Rock seems absent (apart from 1 Cor 10:4), and the imagery of rock (*petros*) is largely restricted to the idea of a firm foundation for building (Mt 7:24; 16:18).

Flint and marble. The limestone of Palestine and the adjacent areas commonly contains hard layers of flint, a pure accumulation of silica. The use of the chipped edges of flint as a surgical cutting tool is referred to in Scripture (Ex 4:25; Josh 5:2). However, it is the hardness of flint that is the basis of its use as an image in Isaiah 5:28 and Jeremiah 17:1. This characteristic is negatively referred to in Zechariah 7:12 in the context of a refusal to repent. A more positive use, referring to a resolute determination to carry out a divinely appointed task in the face of opposition, occurs in Ezekiel 3:9 and in Isaiah 50:7 (a verse probably alluded to in Lk 9:51).

Although scientifically marble is metamorphosed limestone, the writers of Scripture (and most builders since) use the term to simply refer to any hard and strong rock that can be given a polish suitable for architectural or ornamental use. The limited occurrences (1 Chron 29:2; Esther 1:6; Song 5:15; Rev 18:12) are all in the context of richness and splendor.

Salt and sulfur. The main sources of *salt for ancient Israel were the natural deposits along the Dead Sea (the Salt Sea, Deut 3:17; Josh 18:19). These are impure mixtures of various evaporated minerals out of which the more soluble halite (NaCl) is easily lost if exposed to moisture, thus allowing salt to lose its saltiness (Mt 5:13). Salt is a unique mineral in that on the one hand it is edible, flavor imparting and indeed essential for life; yet on the other hand it is also a disinfectant (cf. Ezek 16:4) and in large quantities a poison. Almost all the symbolic references in the OT seem to be based on the sterilizing and preserving qualities of salt rather than its ability to impart flavor. The idea of preservation, and hence permanence, almost certainly underlies the references to a "covenant of salt" (NIV) in Numbers 18:19 and 2 Chronicles 13:5 (cf. Lev 2:13). The reference in 2 Kings 2:20-21 may be based on the covenant symbolism of salt more than on its sterilizing ability.

Salt as a symbol of sterility or barrenness, often as a result of a curse due to a covenantal breach, can be found in several passages (Deut 29:23; Judg 9:45; Ps 107:33-34; Jer 17:6; 48:9; Zeph 2:9). Some of this imagery looks back to the destruction of *Sodom and Gomorrah in Genesis 19. Here there is an interesting comparison. On the one hand there is Lot's unnamed wife, who bears children (although with long-term negative results, Gen 19:37-38) but who becomes the very epitome of sterility and barrenness: a pillar of salt (Gen 19:26; cf. Lk. 17.32) on the other hand there is Abraham's wife Sarah, who is initially infertile but who ultimately becomes a "mother of nations" (Gen 17:16).

Most of the NT references to salt are probably best understood as references to its preservative and disinfecting ability rather than to merely adding flavor (Mt 5:13; Mk. 9:50; Lk 14:34; Col 4:6). This makes more sense of the cryptic Mark 9:49.

*Brimstone (or sulfur) occurs as a yellow mineral. In the Palestine area it occurs most commonly along around the Dead Sea. A flammable mineral, it produces an acrid and poisonous smoke, which does, however, have a use as a fumigant.

Metallic Minerals. *Gold, *silver, copper, bronze and *iron are the main metals alluded to in the Bible, although there are mentions of lead and tin. In interpreting the symbolism of the metals it should be borne in mind that there were then (as there are now) important technological and economic limits on metal use. There may be no symbolism at all attached to use of bronze for the major metalwork of the Solomonic temple; after all, what else could have been used?

Two features found in parallel cultures are significant by their absence in Scripture: there is no astrological significance to the metals, and there is no

magical power attributed either to the metals or to those that work them.

Gold. Then, as now, gold was the most precious of metals, reflecting its scarcity, malleability and resistance to tarnishing. It is often associated with God and is symbolic of his holiness, majesty and unchangeable nature (cf. the numerous references to gold in the making of the tabernacle in Ex 25—30; Mt 23:16-17). The nearer to God, the more refined the gold ("pure gold," Ex 25:17, 24 NIV) had to be.

On a human level, gold is associated with the idea of kingship, particularly kingly power, dignity and splendor (Gen 41:42; Esther 4:11; 5:2; 8:4). In Israel its use in this context typified Solomon's reign (1 Kings 10:16-22).

At times gold seems to have been used as a suitable offering in worship to God (Is 60:9; Hag 2:8), sometimes associated with incense (Is 60:6, cf. Mt 2:11). It is even a guilt offering (1 Sam 6:4; cf. 1 Pet 1:18). But the nature of gold made it inevitable that it would be also associated at times with false religion (Ex 32; 1 Kings 12:28; Ps 115:4; Jer 51:7; Dan 3:1-18; Rev 18:12, 16). It is certainly a snare and a temptation (Deut 7:25). A minor use is as an indicator of prosperity and well-being.

Silver. Although often occurring in the Bible with gold, silver never seems to be associated with the divine. This may be due to the tendency of silver to tarnish. Furthermore, the fact that silver is associated with commerce (it is the chief currency metal in Scripture) rules it out for representing anything that is holy.

Where lists are given, silver is subordinate in rank to gold—indicative of its lesser value and power (i.e., Dan 2:31-45). Silver is associated with gold in two main contexts: first as the gifts for "the dedication of the altar" (Num 7:11-86 NIV) and as acceptable offerings (Is 60:9), but second as linked with the making of idols (e.g., Ps 115:4; 135:15; Is 2:20; 30:22).

The necessity of refining silver ore gives rise to two images. In Jeremiah 6:29-30 lead is added to silver ore in the furnace to act as a flux to remove impurities. The image speaks of God's attempt to purify Israel by removing the impurities of the wicked under the Babylonian onslaught. In Ezekiel 22:20-22 Jerusalem is likened to a silver smelting furnace as an image of God's wrath.

Copper and bronze. Copper (along with iron) is a metal indigenous to the Promised Land (Deut 8:9). It is not always clear whether copper or bronze (a natural or artificial alloy with 2-16% of tin) is meant, although the context helps make it plain. Copper is soft and can be beaten; bronze is hard and can be cast to make sharp tools. Copper is a low value currency metal in the NT.

Bronze has two main symbolic meanings. Where used of "passive" objects, such as fetters, flesh, gates, bones, walls and towers (2 Kings 25:7; Job 6:12; 40:18; 41:27; Is 45:2; Jer 1:18; 15:20), it symbolizes hardness, strength and invulnerability. The mysterious bronze *pillars outside Solomon's temple (1 Kings 7:15-22) may have symbolized God's protecting power. In some cases the symbolism is primarily of impenetrability (as in Lev 26:19; Deut 28:23; Is 45:2). The association of iron with the bronze strengthens the symbolism. Where bronze is used of "active" objects, such as weapons, claws and hooves, the symbolism is of hardness and sharpness (Job 20:24; Dan 7:19; Mic 4:13). Here too iron occurs to heighten the imagery and to indicate a lethal combination of sharpness and strength. Bronze can therefore be used to symbolize both strong protection and devastating attack.

Bronze (and iron) can symbolize evildoers and enemies of God (Jer 6:28). The sense here appears to be that the wicked are hardened against God. In terms of value, bronze is plainly inferior in worth to gold (Is 60:17; Dan 2:31-45); and in this context it is a sign of things deteriorating.

Iron. Along with copper, iron is the only metal indigenous to the Promised Land (Deut 8:9). The high temperatures required to smelt iron put it at, and sometimes beyond, the limits of Israelite technology (1 Sam 13:19). Symbolically iron is a industrial and military metal only; and although valuable (2 Kings 6:1-7), it never occurs in the context of worship. In a similar manner to bronze, iron symbolizes might and even brutality (Ps 107:10, 16; Dan 2:40; 7:7, 19; cf. Rev 2:27). The temperatures reached in the iron smelting furnaces were the highest known in biblical times and are used to indicate the unpleasantness of life in Egypt (Deut 4:20; 1 Kings 8:51; Jer 11:4).

See also BRIMSTONE; BRONZE; CORNERSTONE; FOUNDATION; GOLD; IRON; LEAD; ROCK; RUST; SALT; SILVER; STONE.

BIBLIOGRAPHY. K. H. Singer, *Die metalle Gold, Silber, Bronze, Kupfer und Eisen im Alten Testament und ihre Symbolik* (Würzburg: Echtar, 1980).

MINISTER, MINISTRY

The English word *ministry* reflects several related ideas that are expressed by distinct terms in the original languages of the Bible, but these ideas point uniformly to the broad definition of ministry as service, the investment of self for another's advancement, whether in relation to God or other human beings. Prominent NT metaphors for ministry including working as a *body with many parts (Rom 12:5-8), constructing a *building (1 Cor 3:10-15) and planting and nurturing crops (1 Cor 3:5-9; *see* Farming), but the single most consistent image of ministry in the Bible is the *priest. Through a powerful progression of situations, characters and instructions in Scripture centered on the priest, ministry is defined as an investment of self for another's advancement that requires vision and daily devotion.

An Investment of Self. Priests devote their entire beings to the worship of God. All followers of Yahweh are called to "love the LORD your God with all your heart and with all your soul and with all your strength" (Deut 6:5 NIV); ministry is defined, in fact, by this type of love for God that encompasses every part of a person's being. So a catalog of selfhood emerges as the biblical writers consider what parts of a person should be dedicated to God. According to those who ministered to God, an investment of self includes valued possessions like cattle (Ex 10:26); energy; the focused devotion of time, as demonstrated by Joshua's house (Josh 24:15-16), Manasseh (2 Chron 33:16), Hezekiah (2 Chron 31:2) and the priests in general (Ex 28:35, 43; 29:30; 30:20; Num 18:2; 1 Kings 8:11); verbal praise (Ps 135:2); and musical skills (1 Chron 6:32). Self-investment includes all gifts and abilities; *prophesying, serving, *teaching, helping those in need, encouraging, governing and showing *mercy are a few (Rom 12:6-8).

Ministry is as varied as are personalities, but it is focused on glorifying God (1 Cor 12:5). Peter summarizes the Bible's consistent image of ministry as self-investment: "Each one should use whatever gift he has received to serve others, faithfully administering God's grace in its various forms" (1 Pet 4:10 NIV). By virtue of being created by God, each person is given a ministry, a way to minister to him.

Priests are highly honored by being given the opportunity to minister to God. The biblical writers speak in unison: self-sacrifice in *worship of God is the highest honor a person can enjoy. Aaron and his descendants, the Levites, first pictured self-investment by devoting their whole lives to worship God in his *tabernacle (Deut 10:8; 18:5, 7; 1 Chron 23:13); their position as priests is repeatedly counted an honor and privilege (Num 16:9; 2 Chron 29:11; Ezek 40:46; 44:15-16, 27; Heb 8:6). Special *garments (Ezek 42:14), housing (Ezek 45:4) and work areas (Ezek 46:24) were reserved for them.

Ministering before God is a sign of his favor. God honors Phineas with a lasting priesthood for his family because of his zeal for the honor of God (Num 25:11-14). God specifically chooses Samuel over Eli's sons for the position (1 Sam 2:35-3:1) and eliminates from the priesthood families who dishonor him (Neh 13:29). The psalmist agrees that only "he whose walk is blameless will minister to [God]" (Ps 101:6 NIV), and Jeremiah recalls that God's favor rests on obedient priests (Jer 33:22). Those who truly minister to God by investing themselves are highly honored.

The writer of Hebrews builds on the OT history by explaining that Jesus is the "high priest whom we confess" (Heb 3:1 NIV); he is the most valuable minister because he uses perfect abilities in a perfect way (Heb 7:26), and his ministry is superior to that of the OT priests (Heb 8:6). Jesus himself conveys the self-sacrificial nature of ministry by contrasting the tyrannical practices of the great rulers of the world with the conduct required of his followers. He concludes with his own life as an example: "The Son of Man did not come to be served, but to serve, and to give His life a ransom for many" (Mt 20:28 NKJV; see Mt 20:24-28; Lk 22:25-27).

The apostle Paul wishes to spend his life in the same way, honored to be given the same "ministry of reconciliation" that Christ had (2 Cor 5:18-19). He repeatedly employs imagery of the priesthood in commending this desire to others: wishing to pour himself out like a drink offering (Phil 2:17), naming his missionary activity a "priestly duty" and the Gentile converts as "sacrifices" (Rom 15:16-17), calling the church to "present [their] bodies as living sacrifices" (Rom 12:1). He also highlights the honor of self-investment, explaining that it is a choice made in freedom as Christ did; followers of God are invited to participate in this highest honor, to imitate Jesus the great high priest and use their freedom to invest themselves in the worship of God (Gal 5:13). The image of ministry begins, then, with self-investment.

Ministry to God. The self-investment of ministry is motivated by desire to advance another person's interest, in relation both to God and to other people. There are two images of ministry to God described in Scripture. He ordained that the ceremony, *sacrifices and *prayers of the law be performed to advance the glory of his name; the priests who ministered these things were forefathers to the wider priesthood of those who minister by the second means. As demonstrated by Jesus, through the Holy Spirit's strength, all believers minister to God by demonstrating love to other people, sharing the good news of reconciliation to God in words and action. By both the law and the Holy Spirit's power in human action, God is glorified and his purposes on earth are advanced (2 Cor 3:7).

People also are honored by each action; both observance of the law and the "ministry of the Word of God," the gospel, allow people to relate with God. All actions of mercy toward others minister to God by aiding his purpose of redemption; thus Jesus explained that love toward "the least of these" would be counted as love toward God (Mt 25:40, 45). Peter encourages use of individual gifts "so that in all things God may be praised through Jesus Christ" (1 Pet 4:11 NIV). An exuberant desire to bring praise to God is part of the image of true ministry.

Ministry of the Word of God. OT images of ministry focus primarily on ministering to God; the NT writers aim for that goal but describe ministry to people as one "of the word of God." *Minister* connotes one who brings something good, something needed: sacrifices brought to God in the OT are replaced by the gospel of Jesus brought to other people as the primary ministry in the NT. Paul uses the phrase "a minister of Christ on your behalf" to describe a fellow believer (Col 1:7 NKJV) and encourages Timothy to be a good "minister of Christ Jesus" by standing diligently against false teaching (1 Tim 4:6 NIV).

Ministry as Cooperation. True ministry finds no room for pride. The ministry of Christ to others invites metaphors of design in which the crucial paradox of human effort versus the work of the Holy Spirit is captured. Ministry to people is dependent on God, a truth illustrated by imagery from *farming and architecture. Paul tells the churches, "You are God's field, God's building" (1 Cor 3:9 NIV). He explains that human ministers are assigned different tasks according to their gifts, parallel to agricultural planting and watering, but concludes that "neither he who plants nor he who waters is anything, but only God, who makes things grow" (1 Cor 3:7 NIV). Similarly, as an architect rather than the builders has primary responsibility for the completion of a building, so God "who began a good work in you will carry it to completion" (Phil 1:6 NIV). Ministry to people is dependent on the work of God first and foremost; human ministers cooperate to accomplish his designs.

Ministry as Witness. Nevertheless, God chooses to use human ministers to represent him. Jesus named his followers "my witnesses" (Acts 1:8), echoing Isaiah's words from God to his people who ministered to him (Is 43:10, 12; 44:8).

Ministry involves the quality of work and worship offered to God. Giving a warning to anyone who aspires to be a builder without Jesus as the foundation, Paul explains that ministry is a sacrifice to God whose worth will be tested. If one offers anything beside one's best—"wood, hay or straw" instead of "gold, silver [or] costly stones"—one will be judged (1 Cor 3:12-13 NIV). So we return to the image of ministry to people as a sacrifice to God, performed by priests whose lives are dedicated to advancing the purposes and interests of God.

Motivated by Vision. The image of a minister in Scripture includes the quality of envisioning the final goal or purpose for a project and being wholeheartedly committed to that single goal. Ministering before the Lord is a sign of *vision*. Priests preserved this vision; when it falters under distracted priests, Hezekiah reinstitutes ministry to the Lord in the temple as a sign of contrition and renewed vision for bringing God honor (2 Chron 31:2).

Jesus' awareness of the chief end of his efforts prompts his obedience (Jn 17); earlier he anticipates that the world will know about him through the ministry of his followers to one another (Jn 13:35). He warns that a minister must choose to serve a single vision: "no one can serve two masters" (Mt 6:24 NIV).

Paul joins his metaphors of ministry to a sense of the long-term purpose of our lives, bringing glory to God by loving one another; he explains that various people minister "to prepare God's people for works of service, so that the body of Christ may be built up" (Eph 4:12 NIV). Different kinds of service are all motivated by a vision of honoring the same Lord (1 Cor 12:5).

A Daily Choice. Along with a sense of vision, there is a quality of repetition to good ministry. Consider Samuel's many years of service to Eli in the temple. Consider the long hours David played his harp, ministering peace to the troubled Saul (1 Sam 16:23; 18:10; 19:9). As king, David assigned Asaph and his associates "to minister [in the tabernacle] regularly, according to each day's requirements" (1 Chron 16:37 NIV). A psalmist indicates the continuous nature of temple ministry by addressing those "who minister by night" (Ps 134:1 NIV). The writer of Hebrews remembers the priests' offering sacrifices "day after day" (Heb 7:27). And John records that a great multitude in white robes stand before God's throne and "serve him day and night in his temple" (Rev 7:15 NIV). To those who would imitate his ministry Jesus instructed, "If anyone would come after me, he must deny himself and take up his cross daily and follow me" (Lk 9:23 NIV). Images of ministry consistently connote repetition and long-term daily devotion.

A Royal Priesthood. Because of the prominent record of their function, priests form the backbone of the Bible's image of ministry, with other metaphors contributing. Priesthood requires investing oneself for the advancement of others, sustaining daily devotion with a vision of honoring God. A priest's position is a high honor, indicating worthiness to minister to a holy God. Jesus is a perfect priest, superior to the order of Aaron (Heb 7:11-12, 24). All believers have been given gifts for ministry and are thus called to join the "royal priesthood . . . that you may declare the praises of him who called you out of darkness into his wonderful light" (1 Pet 2:9 NIV). By ministering to other people, believers advance the glory of God on earth.

See also BUILD, BUILDING; FARMING; PRAYER; PRIEST; TABERNACLE; TEACHER, TEACHING; TEMPLE; WORK, WORKER.

MIRROR

Though rarely referred to in the Bible, the term *mirror* is significant for interpretation. Mirror as a metaphor is provocatively used in three NT passages (1 Cor 13:12; 2 Cor 3:18; Jas 1:23).

The mirrors of antiquity were flat disks cast from bronze (Job 37:18; Ex 38:8) and then polished to be as reflective as possible. In 1 Corinthians 13:12 Paul contrasts the earthly and heavenly knowledge of God: "Now we see but a poor reflection [Gk *ainigma* "riddle," "intimation"] as in a mirror; then we shall see face to face" (NIV). Since mirrors of Paul's day did not yield the bright, clear images that silvered glass does, many have plausibly interpreted the words to refer to the inferior quality of the image. Alternatively, this enigmatic metaphor expresses not the inferior qualities of a mirror but rather that what appears in the mirror is only an indirect reflection of the viewed object, which is perplexing and requires interpretation. Paul asserts that the Christian can only see and understand God through secondary means. In the heavenly state intermediary means, such as human expressions of love (1 Cor 13) or Scripture itself (Jas 1:25), will not be necessary, for we shall see God "face to face." Paul further enhances

the mirror metaphor by comparing partial and full knowledge. God already fully knows the Christian, but Christians do not know God in full. One day all believers accepted into the heavenly kingdom will have their knowledge completed. Until that day, mirror reflections of reality are an imperfect means of understanding the riddle (Gk. *ainigma*) of life.

Although the word *mirror* does not appear in 2 Corinthians 3:18, by using the Greek verb *katoptrizō*, "to look at something as in a mirror," Paul takes the mirror metaphor one step further into the Christian spiritual life. Here the *veiling of *Moses' *glory after receiving the *law (Ex 34:33) is contrasted to the unveiling of the Christian's heart and mind to reflect the liberating work of Jesus Christ. With an unveiled mind the Christian is able to be more like Christ and so reflect the glory of God to others. In effect, Christians have the freedom and the privilege to be mirror metaphors for the virtues of Jesus Christ. We are not only imitators of those who imitate Christ (1 Cor 4:16; 11:1; 1 Thess 1:6; Heb 6:12), but direct reflectors of Christ. Those who peer into us must see Jesus.

Finally, in James 1:23-25 the writer compares the oblivious hearer of God's message to one who glances at a mirror and then instantly forgets the personal image, neglecting to tidy up or to improve oneself. The law, like a mirror, shows us our true selves. But what benefit is that if we fail to act on what we learn? In context, the Word of God is also part of the mirror metaphor. "But the man who looks intently into the perfect law that gives freedom," (Jas 1:25 NIV) presents the Scriptures as an efficacious mirror for blessing—if, that is, the Christian does not forget what he has read or seen or heard.

See also EYE, SIGHT; VEIL.

MISPRIZING, MISVALUING

To misprize something is to fail to value it correctly. Such misvaluing can occur in two ways—undervaluing (not sufficiently prizing something valuable) or overvaluing (prizing the wrong thing, or valuing something too highly). In a book as devoted to the question of values as the Bible is, it is not surprising that misprizing is a major motif.

The biblical prototype of a misprizer is *Esau, who sold his *birthright for the proverbial "mess of pottage." After recounting this appalling spectacle of indifference to spiritual values, the narrator offers as his parting shot "Thus Esau despised his birthright" (Gen 25:34 KJV, RSV, NIV), or "Thus did Esau misprize his birthright" (Anchor Bible). Hebrews 12:16 interprets Esau's act as showing him to be "profane" (KJV), "irreligious" (RSV) or "godless" (NIV), and the act itself to be irrevocable, even though Esau sought to repent with *tears (Heb 12:17).

Already before Esau's experiment in misprizing, we read about Lot's lifting up his eyes to the well-watered valley of the Jordan River and choosing its material *prosperity to the peril of his soul (Gen 13), and of his wife's inability to leave behind her materialistic lifestyle and being turned into a pillar of salt as a warning to the subsequent human race (Gen 19:26; Lk 17:32).

As these examples from Genesis suggest, much of the misprizing in the Bible consists of choosing the immediate tangible benefits of physical prosperity over spiritual values and *obedience to God. Thus Achan chose to take the spoils of *battle over obeying a divine injunction not take anything (Josh 7), and Saul complied with the people's desire to take the best of the *flocks of the defeated Amalekites (1 Sam 15). *Solomon's career follows a more general arc of devotion to affluence at the cost of devotion to God. When the psalmist recalls a crisis of *faith in which his "feet had almost stumbled" (Ps 73:2 RSV), the entire crisis turns on his being overly impressed by the apparent prosperity of the *wicked, while his recovery of faith is based on a recognition of the superior value of the spiritual life (Ps 73:23-28). In the NT Judas betrayed Jesus for thirty pieces of *silver, while Ananias and Sapphira paid the same price—a hasty death—for their choice of money over honesty (Acts 5:1-11).

Misprizing is ultimately a mistake of allegiances—exalting something over another thing that deserves a higher allegiance. The melancholy OT history of dabbling in pagan *idolatry (a history told partly by the narrative of Israel's and Judah's *kings) is a spiritually charged story of misplaced allegiance to pagan *gods and a devaluing of the true God. Jesus rebuked the domestically preoccupied Martha for being "anxious and troubled about many things" and commended Mary, who sat at his feet, for having "chosen the good portion" (Lk 10:41-42 RSV). The missionary Demas deserted Paul because he was "in love with this present world" (2 Tim 4:10 RSV).

In the value-laden world of the Bible, the constant injunction is to choose one set of values over another—to "set your minds on things that are above, not on things that are on earth" (Col 3:3 RSV). Even self-preservation can become an avenue to misprizing, as when Peter denied knowing Jesus in the interest of his own safety. Misprizing hinges on the question of what a person *treasures supremely; in the words of Jesus, "where your treasure is, there will your heart be also" (Mt 6:21 RSV).

The urgency of valuing rightly, along with the disastrous results of valuing wrongly, is a prominent motif in Jesus' *parables. In the parable of the great *banquet, people who reject the master's invitation in favor of everyday pursuits find themselves excluded from the messianic table (Lk 14:15-24). The wealthy *farmer who trusts in the abundance of his possessions is denounced by Jesus for having laid up "treasure for himself" and not being "rich toward God" (Lk 12:21). The industrious *workers in the *vineyard, not realizing that the new *kingdom is based on grace rather than merit, overvalue the role of their work in the eyes of their master (Mt 20:1-16).

In a similar way, the self-righteous *Pharisee who prays as a way of rehearsing his own virtues has a mistaken estimate of his own worth before God, in contrast to the publican who realizes his spiritual bankruptcy before God (Lk 18:9-14). Similarly, the *priest and Levite who pass by a severely wounded man wrongly value their own safety (or, in some interpretations, their chance to serve a stint in the *temple) over neighborly compassion (Lk 10:30-37).

The canon of biblical stories dealing with misprizing expands when we add the idea of misjudgment. The Bible gives us a memorable gallery of people who misjudge the character of God, the nature of the *world in which they live and their own ability to control the events of their lives. All the protagonists in stories built around the motif of futile attempts to *cheat the oracle miscalculated the sovereign power of God and their inability to thwart God's power to achieve his predicted purposes. The enterprising farmer of Jesus' parable (Lk 12:13-21) illustrates exactly how misjudgment can dominate a person's life. The farmer's preoccupation with earthly possessions misjudges what is truly valuable in life, violating Jesus' lead-in proverb that "a man's life does not consist in the abundance of his possessions" (Lk 12:15 RSV) and his follow-up comment about the need to be "rich toward God." The farmer further misjudges the duration of earthly life: he thinks that he has "many years" to take his ease and enjoy his retirement, whereas God requires his soul "this night." Finally, the farmer misjudges the purpose of life, which he thought was self-indulgent ease but which within the logic of the parable is to prepare one's soul for eternity.

The antidote to misprizing is to value supremely the spiritual and heavenly. This is the import of Jesus' command "Do not lay up for yourselves treasures on earth, . . . but lay up for yourselves treasures in heaven" (Mt 6:19-20 RSV). To value rightly is to value the *kingdom of God above all other values. The value of that kingdom is compared by Jesus to a treasure discovered in a field that is worth all a person's possessions (Mt 13:44), and to a *pearl of great price for which a merchant is willing to give all that he owns as the purchase price (Mt 13:45).

At its core, misprizing consists of choosing the wrong treasure. Jesus rendered it unforgettable in aphoristic rhetorical questions: "What is a man profited, if he shall gain the whole world, and lose his own soul? or what shall a man give in exchange for his soul?" (Mt 16:26 KJV; cf. Lk 9:25).

See also ABUNDANCE; GOLD; IDOLATRY; PEARL; PROSPERITY; SILVER; STOREHOUSE; STORING UP; TREASURE.

MIST

Biblical references to mist or vapor number fewer than a dozen, and even here the words in the original are sometimes inconclusive. Mist occurs rarely at sea level in Palestine (though regularly on the mountains), perhaps accounting for the sparsity of reference.

At a literal level, the RSV says that in paradise (*see* Garden) a "mist went up from the earth and watered the whole face of the ground" (Gen 2:6), but more recent translations reflect the interpretation that perennial underground streams are in view. In the book of *Job, Elihu's preview of the voice from the whirlwind cites the mist that *God distills in *rain as an example of God's transcendent and mysterious power over *nature (Job 36:27). Similarly, Jeremiah twice ascribes to God the act of making "the mist rise from the ends of the earth" (Jer 10:13 RSV; 51:16).

To the poetic imagination, mist or vapor is above all an emblem of transitoriness and insubstantiality, based on its tendency to dissipate quickly in the heat of the morning *sun. Isaiah thus speaks of God's sweeping away "transgressions like a cloud, and . . . sins like mist" (Is 44:22 RSV). Although English translations do not sufficiently acknowledge it, the word translated as "vanity" more than thirty times in the book of *Ecclesiastes could more appropriately be translated "mist" or "vapor." In the book of *Proverbs the fleetingness and emptiness of ill-gotten gain are compared to a mist that dissipates: "The getting of treasures by a lying tongue is a fleeting vapor" (Prov 21:6 RSV). The ephemeral quality of life itself is pictured by James as "a mist that appears for a little time and then vanishes" (Jas 4:14 RSV). Israel's unfaithfulness is pictured by Hosea as "a morning cloud" and as "the dew that goes early away" (Hos 6:4 RSV). Later Hosea uses the same imagery to describe God's impending *judgment against Ephraim: "They shall be like the morning mist or like the dew that goes early away" (Hos 13:3 RSV). In all these instances—*sins that are *forgiven, wrongly made fortunes, life, the withdrawing of love from God, prosperity on the verge of being lost— mist betokens something that disappears.

Twice it is the dimming quality of mist that is in view. Thus the blinding of Paul by the midday sun at his conversion is pictured as mist and *darkness falling on him (Acts 13:11), and one of the prophetic signs that Peter mentions in his *Pentecost sermon is the "vapor of smoke" and the sun's being "turned into darkness" (Acts 2:19-20 RSV).

A final reference is Peter's angry denunciation of false *prophets as "waterless springs and mists driven by a storm" (2 Pet 2:17 RSV). In context, mist here represents not so much transience as emptiness and worthlessness.

See also DEW; PERMANENCE; RAIN; TRANSIENCE.

MISVALUING. *See* MISPRIZING, MISVALUING.

MOLECH. *See* GODS, GODDESSES.

MONOMYTH. *See* PLOT MOTIFS.

MONSTERS

The Bible opens up a whole new world to its readers;

one with which it often finds itself unfamiliar. The biblical world is populated by spiritual beings—*angels, cherubim, *demons and monsters. Because our own world is so different from the ancient one, we will have trouble appreciating the horror that these images aroused in those who heard about them. The ancient Near Eastern cultural background to the imagery of the Bible is particularly evident in its references to monsters.

In the OT three terms are found for monsters that symbolize the threat to the divine order of the world: Leviathan *(liwyātān),* Rahab *(rahab)* and dragon or sea monster *(tannîn).* Rahab (boisterous one) is not found in any text outside the Bible; the biblical parallels suggest it is another name for Leviathan. Leviathan is described as the coiling and twisting serpent (Is 27:1), as is Rahab (Job 26:12-13); Rahab is also parallel to dragon (Is 51:9), a term also used for Leviathan in Isaiah 27:1. This imagery is significant for understanding biblical language about creation, God's wars against the nations, and the ultimate conflict that will lead to a new created order.

The Threat of the Sea Monster. In the ancient Near East a monster is a common symbol to represent a watery chaos that threatens life in the world. The chaos monster is variously depicted as a composite creature (half *lion and half *eagle), as a serpent or as a seven-headed monster. In a cylinder seal from Mari in the Akkadian Period (2350-2150 B.C.), a *god (possibly El) is seated on a mountain in the midst of the sources of the two oceans. Two goddesses embodying vegetation rise out of the two rivers that originate at the foot of the mountain, while another god (possibly Baal-Hadad, god of the *storm) combats the unruly waters with his spear. In a Syrian cylinder seal (18th-17th centuries B.C.) the *tree of life, depicting the world, is attacked by a chaos serpent, which is killed by Baal-Hadad as he strides over the *mountains brandishing a mace. In a Hittite limestone relief the coiled fiery serpent, whose body depicts the breaking of the mighty waves, is attacked by the god of storm and fertility with the help of the celestial rain gods. In a gray stone cylinder seal from the Akkadian period, two gods attack a seven-headed dragon; three of the seven heads are limp, one is being attacked, and three other heads hiss dangerously. The flames rising from the dragon's back indicate that he simultaneously symbolizes searing heat and destructive masses of water. In Egypt the monstrous serpent Apophis is the embodiment of the dark sea, the evening clouds and the morning haze. A papyrus of the twenty-first dynasty (1085-950 B.C.) portrays the sun god Re at the point of leaving the sky; a serpent stylized as wild waves pits himself against Re but is rendered harmless by Seth, the helper of Re. Helpful jackal and cobra demons draw the ship of the sun across the sluggish floods of the netherworld. In the ancient Near East the empirical world points beyond its superficial reality to spheres of divine intensive life and bottomless devastating lostness. The symbolism of the chaos threat indicates that there was no ultimate basis for security in the present sphere of existence.

The ancient Near Eastern depictions of creation provide a background for its iconography and language. The Egyptian view is known only from fragments in the alien setting of texts of the dead or from hymns and similar texts. There are numerous and varied Egyptian conceptions of creation from the primal sea, the Nun, which was unbounded, unmoved and full of potential fertility without being creative. Four pairs of gods, whose names vary, embody the world before creation: unboundedness, lightlessness, timelessness and nothingness. All take part in creating from the sea, beginning with a first piece of firm land, the "primal hill." In another version a god flew over the water in the form of a bird and laid the primal egg upon it. Very little is said about the creation of humans, other than that they arose out of the creators' tears.

The Akkadian creation epic Enūma elish ("When on High"), consisting of almost 900 lines on seven tablets, introduces us to the battle with chaos in creation. It first reports the creation of the gods by the primal couple Apsû (primeval sweet-water ocean) and Tiâmat (salt water ocean), whose waters mingled in an immense undefined mass. The uproar among the younger gods robbed aged Apsû of his repose, and he decides to destroy them; but he encounters the opposition of Tiâmat. Apsû is killed, and Tiâmat then seeks to take vengeance for her consort. Marduk enters into combat with Tiâmat and out of her slain body creates the cosmos, the heavens and the earth. As the reward for his victory, he is made lord over the gods and the cosmos. In this version of creation the primeval waters are a dangerous and threatening force.

A variation of the battle with the sea is found in the Ugaritic Baal myth (c. 15th century B.C.). The reconstruction of the epic is uncertain due to the fragmentary state of the tablets, but it seems to consist of six tablets that follow the cycle of Baal according to the annual seasons, beginning in the fall. If this is correct, Baal, the god of the storm and fertility, loses his rule to Yam (sea), the god of the winter storms. Baal enters into battle with Yam, gains the victory and builds a palace for his rule, providing for the spring rains. Baal then succumbs to Mot (death), the season of summer heat and *harvest. Finally Baal escapes the realm of the netherworld and again ascends his throne at the time of the new year. The new year is a microcosmic reflection of the first day of *creation and may be regarded as a repetition of the conquering of the primordial chaos.

Myth and ritual in the ancient Near East in similar ways portray the threat of chaos to the ordered fertility of creation. It is possible that elements of the Baal myth have influenced the Babylonian epic of creation, which is a composite of various influences. Various similarities exist between Baal's battle with the sea and the battle of Marduk with Tiâmat: both incorporate elements of the storm, and the name

Marduk seems to have the meaning "son of the storm." In the Syrian (Ugaritic) texts there is no mention of the splitting of the sea or the creating of heaven and earth out of it as in the Mesopotamian epic. The sea is considered a continuous danger in present times, as it was when the world was created; the enemy is presently an entity on earth. It is this distinct language and imagery of the Ugaritic texts that is found in the Bible to describe God's providence in creation.

The Conquest of the Sea Monster. The language of a battle against the chaos monster is used in certain biblical texts to portray the sovereignty of God in his created order. In contrast to other ancient Near Eastern texts, the Hebrew speaks emphatically of the absolute rule of Yahweh in his overcoming the threatening waters. Psalm 74 is a *lament for the destruction of the temple. The confession within this lament (Ps 74:12-17) is based on the assurance that the God who defeated the hostile waters can overcome the present *enemies. The confession explicitly links the defeat of the sea and Leviathan to the creation of the world. Similarly, in Psalm 89:9-13 the defeat of the sea and Rahab at the time of creation are presented as the ground of confidence in Yahweh to deliver from the present distress. The majestic power of God in his creative work is extolled in Job 26:5-14. The passage concludes with a reference to God's triumph over the waters of the sea, over Rahab the twisting serpent (Job 26:12-13). Job complains that God watches him relentlessly, giving him no respite, as if he were the sea or the dragon (Job 7:12), the powerful forces that God must always keep under his control (cf. Job 38:8-11, where God sets the immutable boundaries of the sea at its birth). It is probable that this same thought is found in Psalm 44:18-19 (reading dragon [tannín] instead of jackals [tanním], a change that must also be made in Ezek 29:3 and 32:2). Both the language and the imagery suggest that God crushes the wicked as the dragon. Job trembles before the power of the Creator as he contemplates challenging the justice of God (Job 9:5-14); God is the one who tramples on the high places of the sea (v. 8), who subdues the helpers of Rahab. Finally there is the reference in Job 3:8 to those who are skilled in rousing Leviathan. Here Job wishes that those with power over darkness would blot out the day of his birth; darkness is associated with the raging waters of the sea. The battle against the sea monster is prominent in Job, an image particularly appropriate to a book that confronts the problem of evil within the created order, while affirming the absolute control of God over creation. Even the forces of the dragon cannot threaten God's rule, but the ways of his order are incomprehensible.

The language used in the imagery of the crushing of the dragon is specifically Canaanite, as seen in the Baal myth. In addition to Baal's battle against the Sea and judge River (cf. Ps 93:3; Nahum 1:4; Hab 3:8, 9), there is reference to Baal destroying Litan the coiling serpent, the Tyrant with the seven heads

(KTU 1.5 i 1). The description would indicate that the Ugaritic *ltn* is a variant of the Hebrew *lwytn* as the name of the sea monster, cognate of the noun *liwyah* (wreath), with the meaning "twisting one." The heads of Leviathan in Psalm 74:13 are reminiscent of the seven heads of the Ugaritic monster. In Ugaritic the coiling serpent is also described as the dragon *(tnn)* of seven heads (KTU 1.3 iii 40-42). Other helping deities are associated with the dragon, who may be identified with the sea god Yam (KTU 1.83). These are to be conquered by the power of the sun (KTU 1.6 vi 50-52). Job speaks of the helpers of Rahab (Job 9:13) and of the hostility of Leviathan against the power of the sun (Job 3:8). The conflict against the light in the Ugaritic passage occurs at the end of the cycle, which would correspond to the beginning of the new year, corresponding also to the period immediately before creation. In the lament against his birth, Job longs for the precreation *darkness. This mythical imagery in the Bible serves both as a vivid portrayal of the power of God over creation and as a polemic against the false concepts of surrounding religions.

In the creation account of Genesis 1 the mythical language is removed entirely. Attempts to make this account dependent on *Enuma elish* must be judged a failure. Even the Hebrew word *t'hôm*, translated "deep" (Gen 1:2), is not to be derived from the Akkadian *Tiâmat*. Though the two words are derived from a common Semitic root, they are different in both spelling and gender, indicating that they are two different words. The parallels of the division of the waters and the fixing of the cosmic orders may indicate something of a polemic against the old myths, but they are unremarkable in terms of the differences; the focus in Genesis 1 is on the vegetation, sea creatures and other animals, all of which are unmentioned in *Enuma elish*. In the creation of the animals we encounter the *tannîn* as sea creatures totally subject, as are all of the other creatures of the waters above and below (Gen 1:26; cf. Ps104:25-26). The use of this term may echo the well-known battle against the waters, but the imagery has been removed entirely. Yahweh's control of the cosmic waters is simply a job of work; there is no hint of the cosmic conflict.

The Control of the Sea Monster. In Job the response of God (Job 38:1—41:34) concludes with a description of creation that is beyond human control but possesses a beauty all can recognize. The wonders of the inanimate world (Job 38:2-38) are followed by descriptions of the *lion (Job 38:39-41), the mountain *goat (Job 39:1-4), the wild ass (Job 39:5-8), the wild *ox (Job 39:9-12), the ostrich (Job 39:13-18), the wild *horse (Job 39:19-25), the hawk and the *eagle (Job 39:26-30). The second speech concludes with a description of Behemoth (Job 40:15-24) and Leviathan (Job 41:1-34), creatures not merely intended for human use, but positively dangerous and repulsive to them. God, however, rejoices in these creatures

as worthy expressions of his creative power.

The interpretation of the monster creatures of the second speech vacillates between the mythical and the real. A mythical interpretation is suggested not only by the name Leviathan but also by various descriptions that seem to be at variance with a crocodile, such as the inability to capture it (Job 41:1-8) and its ability to breath out *fire and smoke (Job 41:18-21). In Job 41:25 the gods *('elîm)*, a description of the mighty waves as helpers of the sea god *Yam*, are afraid of him. The mythical interpretation would be in harmony with the references in Job that make reference to the monster of the unruly waters (Job 7:12; 26:12-13). Behemoth is a great oxlike creature that can scarcely be captured (Job 40:24) and may be the calf mentioned in the Ugaritic texts in connection with Leviathan, the twisting serpent and the waters (KTU 1.3 iii 43-44; 1.6 vi 51-53). Against this it must be remembered that the divine speeches are completely concerned with describing the glories of the natural world. Leviathan in Job 41:5 is further described in the vocabulary of Psalm 104:26, where he is one of the creatures of the sea. The two creatures must be actual animals, described in somewhat hyperbolic terms, which may actually allude to the conquest of the waters, as elsewhere in Job, as a means of demonstrating both the dangers within creation and the absolute divine control over them.

The Historicization of the Sea Monster. It is most logical that the imagery of the defeat of the waters of the chaos monster at creation (Ps 74:12-17; 89:5-12) and the control of them within creation should be extended to other enemies of God and his people in creation. This is true especially in relation to Egypt and the birth of the nation. It is most clear in Isaiah 51:9-11, with its declaration of hope for the exiles. God's victory over chaos at creation and the exodus both provide hope for a deliverance from the Babylonians. God is declared to have hewed Rahab in pieces, to have pierced the dragon *(tannîn)* and to further have dried up the sea, the waters of the great deep *(t'hôm)*. The language of creation describes the exodus: Rahab is both the creation waters and Egypt, and by implication of the promise, Babylon is also Rahab. The wording of this passage is particularly close to Psalm 89:9-10, and it is possible it is actually dependent on the psalm.

Egypt is specifically called Rahab in Isaiah 30:7, where her help is denounced as "the silenced Rahab." The same inference is to be made for Psalm 87:4, where Rahab is mentioned alongside Babylon, Philistia, Tyre and Ethiopia as the ones who belong to Zion, probably in the sense of an eschatological vision; Egypt is the balance to the great power of Babylon. Ezekiel 29:3-5 and 32:2-8 both describe Egypt in terms of the dragon. This is not simply a crocodile but the creature of the seas (Ezek 32:2) as in Isaiah 51:9, where the term is parallel with Rahab. The fact that the dragon made the streams (Ezek 29:3) is explicable in that the monster personified the great primeval deep that feeds the streams. The dragon is given to the wild beasts for food, as in Psalm 74:14. The monster is given features of the crocodile, such as scales (Ezek 29:4), but this does not reduce it to a mere creature of the Nile. In Psalm 77:17-21 we again have a reference to the victory over the sea at the exodus as a ground for hope in the present. Though the terms for the monster do not appear here, it is expressly stated that God's conflict at the exodus was with the waters.

This close identification of *pharaoh with the dragon brings additional significance to the conflict of *Moses with pharaoh in the introduction to the plagues. There the staff of Moses turns into a serpent called a *tannín* (Ex 7:9-10); this immediately evokes images of creation as a perspective from which to understand what is happening. Both the purpose and the outcome of the battle are indicated, particularly in the reference to the *tannín* of Moses swallowing up those of the Egyptians (Ex 7:12).

The historicization of the sea monster is extended to nations other than Egypt. Jeremiah describes the Babylonian king as a *tannín* who has swallowed Israel (Jer 51:34); the imagery is continued in Jeremiah 51:36, where God will dry up her sea. There is also a reference to Babylon in Habakkuk 3:8-14, where the political conflict alluded to in verses 12-14 is described in terms of God's conflict with the waters. In Isaiah 17:12-14 the chaotic sea is a designation for Assyria. In Psalm 46:2-3 the divine conflict with the nations attacking Zion is represented as a historicization of the conflict with the waters.

The Sea Monster in Apocalyptic. The use of the dragon imagery to depict God's power over the waters at creation and over the nations within creation has its extension in God's eventual defeat of the nations and his restoration of creation. In apocalyptic the historical and mythological elements are combined in a new tension and take on a new life. Isaiah 27:1 is a very important text indicating the transition of the sea imagery into apocalyptic. Isaiah 24—27 has generally been recognized as universal in scope concerning the renovation of the earth and proto-apocalyptic in its literary character. The language of Isaiah 27:1 bears a strong resemblance to that of the Ugaritic Baal myth, which calls attention to the original power of God over creation. However, the defeat of the monster now represents the conquest of the nations opposing God. Yahweh will rule from Mount *Zion (Is 24:23), and all the nations will participate in the great eschatological *banquet (Is 25:6-8).

In the OT, apocalyptic use of the sea imagery finds its most developed application in Daniel 7. The whole vision of the exaltation of one like a son of man over the dragon is a composite of many influences, among which is the motif of the battle against the waters. The great beasts representing the nations emerge from the waters, and each in turn meets its demise, including the last indescribable beast. This imagery is taken up again and developed further in Revelation 12:1-17. This sign is a further composite of many features, but it has been pointed out that Isaiah 26:16—27:1 forms an impressive parallel to the central thought. The great dragon, who now specifically represents the devil in his opposition to God (Rev 12:9), is soundly defeated by the child of the woman, though his persecutions continue for a little while. However, the ultimate defeat of the dragon is sure (Rev 20:7-10), and there will be a new heavens and a new earth in which there is no more sea (Rev 21:1). The apocalyptic vision could conclude on no more fitting a note than to affirm that the ancient opposition to God's rule over his creation is utterly removed in the new creation.

Other Apocalyptic Monsters. Other monsters also appear in biblical apocalyptic. The beast that arises from the sea (Rev 13:1-10) and the one that arises from the earth (Rev 13:11-18) are terrifying creatures unlike any known in the real world. The red horse (Rev 6:3) and yellowish green horse (Rev 6:7) are in the same category. The *locusts of Revelation 9:1-11 are apparently real locusts transformed into monstrous creatures by the apocalyptic imagination, and the same can be said of the horses arrayed at the Euphrates (Rev 9:17-19) and the "foul spirits like frogs" that issue from the dragon's mouth (Rev 16:13-14).

See also ANIMALS; BIRDS; COSMOLOGY; DEEP; DEMONS; DIVINE WARRIOR; MYTHICAL ANIMALS; RIVER; SEA.

BIBLIOGRAPHY. J. Day, *God's Conflict with the Dragon and the Sea* (Cambridge: Cambridge University Press, 1985); A. Heidel, *The Babylonian Genesis* (Chicago: University of Chicago Press, 1942); T. Jacobsen, "The Battle Between Marduk and Tiamat," *JAOS* 88 (1968) 104-8; O. Keel, *The Symbolism of the Biblical World: Ancient Near Eastern Iconography and the Book of Psalms* (New York: Crossroad, 1985) 47-56; C. Kloos, *Yhwh's Combat with the Sea: A Canaanite Tradition in the Religion of Ancient Israel* (Leiden: E. J. Brill, 1986) 70-85; W. L. Lambert, "A New Look at the Babylonian Background of Genesis," *JTS* XVI n.s. (1965) 287-300; J. C. de Moor, *An Anthology of Religious Texts from Ugarit* (Leiden: E. J. Brill, 1987) 11, 41, 69, 99, 181-2.

MONTH. *See* MOON; TIME.

MOON

Although references to the moon and *stars are identical in frequency in the Bible (nearly seventy references), the associations are distinct. When the moon is mentioned alone (and not as part of the familiar triad of *"sun, moon and stars"), the main purpose is to demarcate a time in the monthly cycle. This is not surprising when we consider that the Hebrew calendar was a lunar calendar. The OT is replete with references to "new moon" as the occasion for monthly *festivals. Part of the Hebrew ceremonial system was to set aside the first *day of the month for a religious festival (see the command in Ps 81:3 to "blow the trumpet at the new moon, at the full moon, on our festal day" [NRSV]).

In more general ways too, the moon is used to lend a regular rhythm to earthly existence. It is the "lesser light" that *God created along with the sun to "rule over the day and over the night, and to separate the light from the darkness" (Gen 1:16-18 NRSV; cf. Ps 136:9; Jer 31:35). According to the psalmist, God "made the moon to mark off the seasons" (Ps 104:19 NRSV).

Because of its predictable regularity, the moon becomes an image of longevity and even eternity: the psalmist prays that the king might live "as long as the moon, throughout all generations" (Ps 72:5 NRSV; cf. Ps 72:7), and regarding the eternal lineage that God promises to David we read, "It shall be established forever like the moon, an enduring witness in the skies" (Ps 89:37 NRSV).

*Worship of the moon prevailed in pagan cultures surrounding OT Israel. The Israelites were specifically prohibited from doing so (Deut 4:19; 17:3; 2 Kings 23:5), and in Job's great oath of innocence he denies that he has engaged in the iniquity of worshiping "the moon moving in splendor" (Job 31:26 NRSV). The moon is here an image of abominable paganism, a temptation to be avoided by anyone pure in heart toward God.

The moon is a ready instance of God's creativity and providence. Looking up at the nighttime sky, the psalmist is led to contemplate the moon as the work of God's *fingers and as something that God "set in place" (Ps 8:3 NIV). Along with the sun, the moon belongs to God, who established it (Ps 74:16). On the basis of its *creation by God, the poet apostrophizes the moon and commands it to praise its Creator (Ps 148:3). In the ongoing providence of nature, God "gives the sun for light by day and the fixed order of the moon . . . by night" (Jer 31:35 NRSV).

A major archetype occurs in *apocalyptic visions of the future, where the moon is one of the cosmic actors in the drama of the earth's final disintegration. Usually it is pictured as not giving its customary *light (Is 13:10; Ezek 32:7; Joel 2:10; 3:15; Mt 24:29; Mk 13:24), but other motifs include its *color becoming red like *blood (Joel 2:31; Acts 2:20; Rev 6:12), a third of the moon being struck with *darkness (Rev 8:12) and unspecified "signs" appearing in the moon (Lk 21:25). In Isaiah's oracle of *judgment God is pictured as punishing the host of *heaven, and "the moon will be abashed, and the sun ashamed" (Is 24:23 NRSV). On a more positive note, the resplendent *woman who represents Israel has "the moon under her feet" (Rev 12:1 NRSV), and the heavenly *city "has no need of sun or moon to shine on it, for the glory God is its light, and its lamp is the Lamb" (Rev 21:23 NRSV; cf. Is 60:19-20). In the coming day of redemption, moreover, "the light of the moon will be like the light of the sun" (Is 30:26 NRSV).

There are, finally, miscellaneous references to the moon that show something of the power it held over the ancient imagination. Because of its association with the cycle of the day, the moon is said to have stopped when God prolonged the day of battle for Joshua (Josh 10:12-13), a motif that reappears in Habakkuk's vision of God as a divine *warrior whose theophanic appearance includes the spectacle of the moon standing "still in its exalted place" (Hab 3:11 NRSV). The light of the moon makes it a recognized standard of brightness in the lover's picture of his beloved as looking forth "fair as the moon, bright as the sun" (Song 6:10 NRSV). Correspondingly, the failing eyesight of the elderly is characterized partly by the moon's being darkened (Eccles 12:2). Associations of the moon (usually the full moon) with mental aberrations may lie behind the psalmist's declaration that under God's protection the moon will not strike the pilgrim by night (Ps 121:6; cf. Mt 17:15, where the afflicted boy is said to be "moonstruck" or "lunatic").

See also FESTIVAL; STARS; SUN; SUN, MOON, STARS.

MORNING

Morning is preeminently an image of new beginnings in human experience. It signals the end of night and the start of a new *day. Night means cessation of labor; dawn signals its beginning. Dawn is the time when the pulse of life reasserts itself. The Bible refers to dawn and morning well over two hundred times, and the largest category of references is to morning as the time when active people get going and purposeful action is initiated. If morning is the time for routine action, in the Bible it is also the most customary time for special events to occur, especially events laden with spiritual significance. In both cases, morning is God's special time, and it represents human opportunity to achieve something purposeful.

At a purely physical level the biblical imagination was adept at capturing the rapturous quality of dawn. The beginning of the day, for example, is metaphorically personified as a mythical creature (worshiped in other cultures as a deity) with *wings (Ps 139:9), who can be awakened by *music (Ps 57:8) and whose most distinctive features are his gargantuan eyelids and stunning gaze (Job 3:9; 41:18; Song 6:10). This personification presents an ambiguity, for although the morning brings light and dispels darkness, the dawn is also the begetter of the rebel morning star, associated with the underworld (Is 14:12-15). God's daily commissioning of the personified morning is a task whose moral consequences are similar to the taming of a rebellious sea and the surveillance of the Abyss and the *gates of *death (Job 38:8-17). The dawn characteristically "rises" in Hebrew writing, perhaps an echo of its underworld connections, attested elsewhere in the ancient Near East. Typically male in Hebrew, the personified dawn once appears as female in a reference to the "*womb of the morning" (Ps 110:3 NRSV), whose progeny is the rejuvenating *dew. The rapturous quality of sunrise is best captured in Psalm 19:5, where it is compared to a *bridegroom leaving his room and a strong man running a race.

Biblical references to morning are rooted in methods of calculating daily time. The Hebrews regarded a day as the unit of time lasting from evening to evening (Ex 12:18; Lev 23:32; Neh 13:19; etc.), and the most common OT word for morning *(bōqer)* means "to split" or "to break." By contrast, in NT times the day was divided into two twelve-hour segments between sunrise (regarded as beginning at six o'clock, with noon being the "sixth hour" [Lk 23:44 RSV]) and sunset (Jn 11:9). In both time schemes, morning or daybreak has the same status of dividing the time of darkness from the time of daylight, as in the reference to waiting all night "until the light of the morning" (Judg 16:2 NRSV) or to God as the One who "turns blackness into dawn" (Amos 5:8 NIV).

The dialectical contrast between *light and *darkness, *day and *night, pervades biblical depictions of the morning, for both evening and morning are boundaries that separate night from day, the one marking the subsidence of light and respectable human activity, the other presaging their renewal. As boundaries, morning and evening serve simultaneously as closure and inauguration. As closure, morning signifies the end of night and its sometimes disreputable or shameful activities, such as illicit *sex: a concubine is sexually assaulted "all through the night until the morning" (Judg 19:25 NRSV), and an adulteress suggests that a couple should "take our fill of love until morning" (Prov 7:18 NRSV).

In addition to serving as a concluding boundary for the deeds of darkness, morning brings sacred activities to a close. God finishes his daily creative work each morning in Genesis 1. The consumption of certain sacred foods reflects this pattern, for *manna must be entirely eaten before the following morning (except on the *sabbath), lest it become inedible (Ex 16:19-24). Uneaten portions of peace offerings must not remain until the following morning but are to be burned (Ex 12:10; 34:25; Lev 7:15; Num 9:12; Deut 16:4).

As an inaugural boundary, morning is the appropriate time when human beings begin a journey (Gen 21:14; 24:54; 26:31), and if one postpones departure until later in the day, the delay can result in tragedy (Judg 19:5-26). *Armies initiate *battle in the morning (Josh 8:10; Judg 9:33; 20:19; 1 Sam 11:11; 2 Chron 20:20; hence the comment in Ps 46:5 that God will protect his holy city "when the morning dawns" [NRSV]). It is in the morning that oaths are exchanged (Gen 26:31) and seed sown (Eccles 11:6).

The incipient symbolism of the Bible is evident in the way in which every part of the day (morning, *noon, evening, night) assumes ethical and spiritual significance at many points. Thus references to beginning an action at dawn or in the morning sometimes take on symbolic overtones: Abraham's rising "early in the morning" on his journey to sacrifice Isaac signals his prompt and decisive obedience to God's command (Gen 22:3); the *sun rises on Jacob as he begins a new life after wrestling with God and receiving a new name (Gen 32:31); God's *glory appears in the form of manna in the morning (Ex 16:67); Moses appears before God on Mt. *Sinai in the morning (Ex 34:2). Morning as an archetype of new beginnings appears in the reference to the morning stars' singing together at creation (Job 38:7).

Morning held a religious significance for biblical characters. It was a time of *prayer (Ps 5:3; 88:13; Mk 1:35), *worship (1 Sam 1:19) and *sacrifices (Lev 6:12; 2 Kings 3:20; 16:15; Job 1:5; etc.). Morning was a time of awareness of God's perpetual, reliable goodness: God's steadfast love and mercy "are new every morning; great is your faithfulness" (Lam 3:23 NRSV), and "every morning he shows forth his justice, each dawn he does not fail" (Zeph 3:5). In a similar vein, it is in the morning that God satisfies his people with his steadfast love (Ps 90:14) and that worshipers declare God's steadfast love (Ps 92:2). Believers wait for God to be their arm every morning (Is 33:2). Jacob anointed a stone early in the morning after receiving the dream of the ladder and the accompanying covenant *blessing (Gen 28:18). It is hardly too much to say that morning is God's special time for humans to encounter him and acknowledge that he is indispensable to life.

Because daylight dispels the cloak of darkness, morning takes on associations as a time of revelation. That revelation is by no means always positive. A foreboding or unclear *dream from the preceding night can be troubling at break of day (Gen 20:8; 40:6; 41:8). The illumination that comes with morning may bring to light crushed hopes, tragedy and disaster: Jacob discovers only on the morning after that he has married the wrong woman (Gen 29:25), and Nabal dies in the morning from the shock of the news his wife presents as the day begins (1 Sam 25:37). The death of loved ones or companions greets individuals when they arise: a mother finds her infant son dead in the morning (1 Kings 3:21), just as a man discovers his dead concubine (Judg 19:27). Because God's judgment sometimes occurs at night while humans sleep, it is the morning light that reveals to Abraham a destroyed Sodom (Gen 19:27) or to the Assyrians the 185,000 corpses slain by an angel (2 Kings 19:35). Similarly, humans who carry out God's judgment at night have the results of their work unveiled at dawn: in the morning people were dismayed upon seeing Baal's altar destroyed by Gideon (Judg 6:28).

As part of the motif of morning as the time of divine revelation, morning becomes the most appropriate time for justice to be meted out: "Every morning he [the Lord] renders his judgment" (Zeph 3:5 NRSV). This is the time of day when Moses confronts Pharaoh with punitive plagues (Ex 7:15; 8:20; 9:13). It is "in the morning" that God discloses the guilt of Korah, Dathan and Abiram (Num 16:5).

God sends his prophet to a disobedient David in the morning, informing him of the types of punishment he can expect (2 Sam 24:11, 15). The process of discovering Achan as the guilty party at Jericho occurs in the morning (Josh 7:14, 16). God destroys *Sodom and Gomorrah at dawn (Gen 19:15, 23, 27), and at dawn the Red Sea returns to normal depth, overwhelming the Egyptian pursuers (Ex 14:27). In keeping with the pattern of inevitable *judgment at daybreak, people are advised not to party and get drunk in the morning (Is 5:11; Eccles 10:16; cf. Acts 2:15) but to "execute justice in the morning" (Jer 21:12 NRSV).

The revelations of the morning can also be good. Gideon discovered God's answer to his "fleece test" in the morning (Judg 6:38), and King Darius found Daniel safe in the lions' den "at break of day" (Dan 6:19 NRSV). The servant of Elisha got up early in the morning at Dothan and saw the mountain full of horses and chariots of fire (2 Kings 6:15-17). Jesus' empty tomb was discovered in the morning (Mt 28:1; Mk 16:2; Lk 24:1, 22; Jn 20:1).

Because God's acts are especially evident at morning, morning is a time and symbol of *hope for the righteous. Those who have reason to expect vindication long for the morning as the time of God's action in their behalf: "LORD, in the morning you hear my voice; in the morning I plead my case to you" (Ps 5:3 NRSV). When a favorable verdict in God's court exonerates the afflicted at dawn, and when judgment justifiably comes upon the wicked at this time, the morning becomes a time of rejoicing and grateful praise to God: "Weeping may linger for the night, but joy comes with the morning" (Ps 30:5 NRSV; cf. Ps 59:16). Elsewhere the soul of the psalmist "waits for the Lord more than those who watch for the morning" (Ps 130:6 NRSV). In Isaiah's vision of redemption, the light of the redeemed will "break forth like the dawn," and "healing shall spring up quickly" (Is 58:8 NRSV).

The supreme instance of the morning as an image of hope is the equation of Christ with "the morning *star" (Rev 2:28 NRSV) and "the bright morning star" (Rev 22:16 NRSV). Although technically the morning star is Venus, which appears just before daybreak, it merges in the human imagination with the sun itself. Most memorable of all is the reference in 2 Peter 1:19, which exhorts believers to pay attention to the prophetic word "until the day dawns and the morning star rises in your hearts" (NRSV), a probable reference to the return of Christ (inasmuch as the designation "day of the Lord" refers elsewhere to that return [2 Pet 3:12; cf. Rom 13:12; 1 Thess 5:2).

Summary. One cannot survey the passages dealing with morning without sensing what a crucial time morning is in the Bible. It is a time for human and divine initiative. More than any other time of the day, it is the time for both the undertaking of routine activities and the occurrence of decisive or special events. Morning is at once a literal and symbolic image of new beginnings, of revelation, and of either judgment or hope.

See also DARKNESS; DAY; DEW; HOPE; HOUR; JUDGMENT; LIGHT; NIGHT; NOON; SUN.

MORNING STAR. *See* STARS.

MORTALITY

Mortality is perhaps the greatest given of human life in the world: the one thing that we know about all people is that they are destined to die. The imagery of mortality, in turn, represents people's awareness of their mortal condition.

Mortality in the Old Testament. In the curse God places on the first man, the Lord God says, "You are dust, and to dust you shall return" (Gen 3:19 RSV). Thus begins the biblical story of human mortality, the result of disobedience of God. The image of our physical return to the substance from which humans and the *animals come is important in the OT, as when the Preacher says that "man has no advantage over the beasts; for all is vanity. All go to one place; all are from the dust, and all turn to dust again" (Eccles 3:19-20 RSV). Again, "Man cannot abide in his pomp, he is like the beasts that perish" (Ps 49:12 RSV).

Righteous persons in the OT typically live long lives on earth, dying "in ripe old age, as a shock of grain comes up to the threshing floor in its season" (Job 5:26 RSV). Nevertheless, even for them, with the exceptions of Enoch and Elijah, death is "the way of all the earth," as Joshua and David each remark (Josh 23:14 RSV; 1 Kings 2:2). Just as there is "a time to be born," there is "a time to die" (Eccles 3:2). The flesh of the wise and the foolish alike will perish, and the self-assured resemble sheep with death as their shepherd: "Straight to the grave they descend, and their form shall waste away; Sheol shall be their home" (Ps 49:14 RSV). In an equally vivid picture we read that people's "graves are their homes for ever, . . . though they named lands their own" (Ps 49:11 RSV). Psalm 90:3 pictures the universal human fate in terms of people's being "turned . . . back to the dust" as the eternal God says, "Turn back, O children of men!" (RSV).

Sheol, a vaguely envisioned place for the souls of the dead in the *afterlife, is "the house appointed for all living" (Job 30:23 RSV) and a devourer that "has enlarged its appetite and opened its mouth beyond measure" (Is 5:14 RSV). It is apparently where the dead passively join their ancestors, where they are "gathered" to their "people" (Gen 25:8) or "sleep" with their "fathers" (Deut 31:16). Dead bodies, sources of contamination (Num 19:11), remain buried, as in the cave at Machpelah, where Jacob wishes to be *buried with Abraham, Sarah, Isaac, Rebekah and Leah (Gen 49:29-32), or as in the ancestral sepulchers in Jerusalem (Neh 2:3).

OT images of mortality are gloomy in spirit—a statement of defeat for human aspiration. Even though the *glory of a rich person's house may increase, "when he dies he will carry nothing away; his glory will not go down after him" (Ps 49:17 RSV). Even if a person "counts himself happy" and "does well for himself," his inevitable fate is to "go to the generation of his fathers, who will never more see the light" (Ps 49:18-19 RSV). Part of the defeat involved in mortality is that after a person's death "there is no enduring remembrance" of the person, "seeing that in the days to come all will have been long forgotten" (Eccles 2:16 RSV). Being divested is part of the picture: "As he came from his mother's womb he shall go again, naked as he came, and shall take nothing . . . away in his hand" (Eccles 5:15 RSV). As for the destination of the dead in the OT, it is a shadowy nonexistence—a "land of gloom and deep darkness . . . and chaos" (Job 10:21-22 RSV) where "the wicked cease from troubling" and "the prisoners . . . hear not the voice of the taskmaster" (Job 3:17-18 RSV).

The most haunting biblical portrait of human mortality is probably the metaphoric description of physiological symptoms of aging that appears in the last chapter of Ecclesiastes (Eccles 12:1-7). Here mortality takes the palpable form of weakening *eyesight, *trembling *hands and *arms, stooped shoulders; loss of hearing, *appetite, *sleep and speech; feebleness and danger in *walking; and loss of desire for life. By itself this is a portrait of old age rather than mortality, but it is only a prelude to the dissolution of physical life, pictured as the irremediable breaking of household objects (cord snapped, golden bowl broken, pitcher shattered), accompanied by mourners who "go about the streets" as the deceased "goes to his eternal home" and "the dust returns to the earth as it was" (RSV).

Even in the OT, however, there are several images that could be interpreted as showing the defeat of mortality. Psalm 49 is one of the most extended repositories of images of mortality in the Bible, but in the midst of the litany of *decay the poet asserts that "God will ransom my soul from the power of Sheol, for he will receive me" (Ps 49:15 RSV). The speaker in Psalm 73 declares that "afterward thou [God] wilt receive me to glory" (Ps 73:24) and that God is his great desire not only "upon earth" but also "for ever" (Ps 73:25-26). Similarly, the picture of death near the end of Ecclesiastes makes a distinction between the physical decay of the body ("the dust returns to the earth as it was") and the release of "the spirit," which "returns to God who gave it" (Eccles 12:7).

Although the great image of the dry *bones in Ezekiel 37:1-14 presents a kind of immortality, it is actually a collective triumph of "the whole house of Israel" (Ezek 37:11) over national mortality, a triumph in which the *"graves" (Ezek 37:12) are metaphorical rather than literal. The return from the dead of the widow of Zarephath's son (1 Kings 17:8-24) and the similar event with the Shunammite's son (2 Kings 4:18-37) are examples of individual, but only temporary, defeats of mortality. It is probably with Enoch, who "walked with God" and then "was not, for God took him," that we have the first OT example of the immortality of a particular human being (Gen 5:24 RSV). Another such example, with more vivid imagery, appears in 2 Kings 2:11, when "a chariot of fire and horses of fire" part Elijah from Elisha and the older prophet ascends "by a whirlwind into heaven" (RSV). Yet the cases of Enoch and Elijah are special. The most noteworthy image of general individual immortality, or at least perpetual existence, appears in the words of the angel to Daniel about the troubled time to come: "And many of those who sleep in the dust of the earth shall awake, some to everlasting life, and some to shame and everlasting contempt" (Dan 12:2 RSV). We also have Job's great vision of a blessed hope: "I know that . . . after my skin has been thus destroyed, then from my flesh I shall see God" (Job 19:25-26 RSV).

Mortality in the New Testament. In the NT such miracles of Jesus as the raising from death of the widow of Nain's son (Lk 7:11-17) and of Lazarus of Bethany (Jn 11:1-44) point to the supreme image of mortality—Jesus' own death on the *cross—and the supreme image of triumph over mortality—the *resurrection.

The Gospels describe Jesus as having given up his "spirit" (Mt 27:50; Jn 19:30) or "breathed his last" (Mk 15:37), or having committed his "spirit" to his Father and then having "breathed his last" (Lk 23:46). The images are similar, because the Greek verb *exepneusen,* translated in the RSV as "breathed his last," is closely related to the noun *pneuma,* which may be translated *"breath" or "spirit." The underlying idea, regardless of the particular Gospel, is not of some powerful trance but of death in its common, profound human sense.

That Jesus was mortal was a consequence of his humanity, but his death was purposeful in a way that most human deaths do not immediately seem to be. John 10:11 gives us the image of Jesus as "the good shepherd" who "lays down his life for the sheep" (RSV; *see* Sheep, Shepherd), while Matthew 20:28 shows Jesus as the servant who will "give his life as a ransom for many" (RSV). In 2 Timothy 1:10 Jesus is the Savior who "abolished death and brought life and immortality to light through the gospel" (RSV).

Nevertheless, the earliest Christians were soon faced with the problem of the mortality of their own flesh, and Paul writes in 1 Thessalonians 4:13-17 of how "those who are asleep," "the dead in Christ," will "meet the Lord in the air" (RSV) as he descends, as will those still living on earth at the time of the second coming. In 1 Corinthians 15 Paul combines the image of death as sleep with agricultural imagery, describing the resurrected Christ as "the first fruits of those who have fallen asleep" (1 Cor 15:20 RSV); he proclaims that "as in Adam all die, so also in Christ shall all be made alive" (1 Cor 15:22 RSV) and that "the last enemy to be destroyed is death" (1 Cor 15:26 RSV). Paul eventually returns to agriculture, a familiar subject even for first-century urban

Christians, and uses the image of "a bare kernel, perhaps of wheat or of some other grain" (1 Cor 15:37 RSV), which must be planted, as the perishable fleshly body must be buried before the resurrection, when a "spiritual body" (1 Cor 15:44) will be raised never to perish.

Revelation's images of mortality and the Christian triumph over it are apocalyptic. "Death" rides "a pale horse," followed by "Hades," and they devastate one-fourth of the earth (Rev 6:8); but eventually they relinquish "the dead in them" and are both cast into "the second death, the lake of fire," where those whose names are not in "the book of life" must also go (Rev 20:13-15 RSV). For the saved, the curse of mortality that began with the first sin has passed: "a new heaven and a new earth" will come, the "new Jerusalem" will descend from heaven, God will live with humans, and "he will wipe away every tear from their eyes, and death shall be no more" (Rev 21:1-4 RSV).

See also AFTERLIFE; BURIAL, FUNERAL; DEATH; DECAY; GRAVE; IMMORTALITY; PERMANENCE; RESURRECTION; TRANSIENCE; TREE OF LIFE; WORM.

MORTAR. *See* BRICKS.

MOSES

The dominant image of Moses in the Bible is that of lawgiver. Beginning with Exodus 20 and continuing throughout the rest of the Pentateuch, Moses regularly receives the law *from God and hands it on to Israel. (With the exception of Ezek 40—48, all legislation in the Hebrew Bible comes through Moses.) Moses himself, however, does not actually promulgate laws; he only reports what God reveals to him. So when we read of "the law of Moses" (Lk 2:22; 1 Cor 9:9), the meaning is not "the law given by Moses" but "the law given through Moses."

Next to being a lawgiver, Moses is above all else a deliverer or savior (*see* Rescue). The dramatic story of the *exodus is the story of God, through Moses, freeing Israel from *bondage and bringing them through the *wilderness to the *Promised Land. When God calls Moses in Exodus 3—4, it is for the express purpose of liberating the people (cf. 1 Sam 12:6-11). It is Moses who says to *Pharaoh, "Let my people go," who (with Aaron) is the instrument for the *plagues and who directs the actual exodus. It is no surprise that when the book of Judges tells the story of Gideon, another deliverer from foreign bondage, it makes him resemble Moses (cf. Judg 6:1-24).

While moderns do not usually think of Moses as a prophet, it is otherwise in the Bible. Moses has the Spirit of God (Num 11:17), receives a divine calling and divine *revelation (Exodus 2—3) and speaks God's word. According to Hosea 12:13, "by a prophet the LORD brought Israel up from Egypt" (RSV; cf. Ecclus 46:1; Wisd 11:1). Deuteronomy 18:15 and 18 seemingly prophesy a series of *prophets like Moses—a prophecy fulfilled in various ways

in Elijah (see esp. 1 Kings 17—19 and 2 Kings 1—2 and the lengthy list of parallels in *Pesiqta Rabbati* 4:2), in Jeremiah (compare Jer 1 with Moses' call in Ex 3) and in Jesus (cf. Acts 3:17-26). Deuteronomy 34:10 says that "there has not arisen a prophet since in Israel like Moses, whom the LORD knew face to face" (RSV; a reference to Ex 33:12ff.). Numbers 12:6-8 differentiates Moses from all other prophets by boldly asserting that God does not speak to Moses in a dream or vision but "mouth to mouth, clearly, and not in dark speech; and he beholds the form of the LORD" (RSV). The intimacy and perhaps even affection implicit in these words about God's special relationship with Moses comes to a climax at the end of the Pentateuch, where God himself buries Moses (Deut 34:6).

Moses is also remembered as: (1) a great leader—his "office" is passed on to Joshua (Num 27:12-23), and David and Josiah are made out to resemble him (see Allison); (2) an intercessor for Israel (e.g., Ex 32:11-13, 30-33 [where Moses offers his own life for his people]; Jer 15:1; Ps 99:6; 106:23—Is Moses' status as intercessor the reason why Psalm 90, which contains an intercessory *prayer for Israel, is attributed to him?); and (3) a great miracle worker (recall the ten plagues, the *manna and the water from the rock).

Despite his achievements, Moses is not presented as a conventional hero. He does not sit on a throne or plot strategy for war. He is unsure of himself and is not eloquent (Ex 3:13-4:17). He leaves no important sons and has no mausoleum. He does not act on his own devices but only at the instigation of God. (Perhaps this last fact is why he is praised as "meek," Num 12:3). In Exodus 2:14-15 Moses strikes down an unsuspecting victim, hides his act and flees into the night. Here he seems cowardly. Furthermore, because of disobedience he does not enter the *land (Num 20:10-13). So being a "man of God" (e.g., Deut 33:1; Josh 14:6) and a faithful "servant of God" (e.g., Ex 14:31; Num 12:7-8) does not eliminate sin. Moses is what God makes of him, despite himself.

The NT makes frequent reference to Moses. The most striking instances are those that compare the OT leader to Jesus Christ. As great as Moses was, Jesus is vastly superior as a lawgiver (Mt 5—7), a prophet (Acts 3:17-26), a leader and a savior (John 1:17; 2 Cor 3:12-18; Heb 3:1-5).

See also ARK; BURNING BUSH; EGYPT; EXODUS; LAW; MANNA; PLAGUE; RESCUE; SINAI; TABERNACLE; WILDERNESS.

BIBLIOGRAPHY. D. C. Allison Jr., *The New Moses: A Matthean Typology* (Philadelphia: Fortress, 1994); D. J. Silver, *Images of Moses* (New York: Basic Books, 1982).

MOTHER, MOTHERHOOD

Motherhood was considered the chief blessing for *women all through Scripture. From the first events following the creation of *Eve, the admonition to be fruitful and multiply, along with the designation of

Eve as the "mother of all living," woman's ability to conceive and bear was considered her most powerful quality. After the Fall, when Eve hears God's solemn prediction that she will bear children in pain (*see* Birth), Eve discovers the price of this creativity. The sweet-sour experience of motherhood became woman's primary role in OT culture.

Only in a rare prophecy for a tormented people does Scripture proclaim, "Sing, O barren one, who did not bear" (Is 54:1 RSV). The greatest *curse that a woman could know was to have a *barren *womb. God was seen to have a significant role in the conception of the *child. The psalmist exclaims that God has known David "from the womb." And a wayward or sinful woman might be punished by having God "close her womb." *Beauty was cherished, but fecundity was valued more over time. In fact, even Paul notes that women are saved by childbearing (Gal 4:26)—a statement interpreted in various ways over the years.

For a woman the greatest *blessing of all was the birth of a *son. Through him she became significant; for he was the inheritor of the tradition, the fulfillment of the *covenant. The *firstborn was the inheritor of the father's blessing and the major portion of his wealth. He was also dedicated to God (Ex 13:14-15). The great dream for Israel became the birth of the Messiah, the child who would prove to be the savior and king. It is in fulfillment of this promise that the angel Gabriel announced the news to the *virgin *Mary; and it is in understanding of this tradition that she humbled herself in submission to God's will. The greatest of the *birth stories is the beautiful story told in Luke that details the steps from the Annunciation to Epiphany. The Incarnation, the Word made flesh to dwell among us, must rank as the greatest of all miracles.

In the NT we see evidence that the gestation period was clearly understood, even with indications of the months in the process. When John leapt in the womb at the visit of the pregnant Mary, we even see evidence of response to God's presence among the unborn—a powerful comment on the humanity of the fetus. The birth itself was apparently handled by female relatives and neighbors (Ruth; 1 Sam 4:20), sometimes by midwives (Gen 35:17; 38:28; Ex 1:15-21). This female ceremony was undoubtedly a source of strength and community for women. A birthing stool was apparently used among the Hebrew women—two stones on which they sat or knelt. The newborn child was bathed and then rubbed with salt and wrapped in swathes of cloth (Ezek 16:4; Lk 2:7). Shortly afterward, the women of the neighborhood or the parents would name the child (Ruth 4:17).

The religious rituals for the child moved away from the female community to embrace the men as well. For boys the eighth day would be the day of *circumcision (Lk 1:59). According to the law, the woman was sequestered for a time after giving birth. The new mother would be considered unclean for seven days after the birth of a boy, fourteen after the

birth of a girl (Lev 12:1-5). She remained in the house for thirty-three or sixty-six days, until the time of her purification offering in the sanctuary (Lev 12:6-8; Lk 2:22-24).

Such laws, apparently designed by God to protect women at their most vulnerable time, contrast with the more malevolent practices of the Israelites' neighbors. For example, some of the Canaanite religions required the sacrifice of their firstborn sons to their fertility gods. The Israelites loved and protected their firstborn sons, who were dedicated to serve God through their lives. Their God cherished human life. So did the good mothers.

The Scripture does have evidence of cruel mothers and grandmothers as well as benevolent and nurturing ones (*see* Domineering Mother, Wife). We read about mothers eating their children (2 Kings 6:28-29; Lam 2:20; 4:10) and killing them (2 Kings 11:1; 2 Chron 22:10). But generally, even the most devious of women were inclined to work for the betterment of their children's lives. We may believe Rebekah to be wrong in her betrayal of her husband and her son *Esau, but she was seeking to enhance the fortunes of her favorite son, *Jacob. Scripture does not have images of child sacrifice by mothers that we see in the Greek tale of Medea. The slaughter of the innocents was instead the work of evil men—Pharaoh or Herod. When the Egyptian children died, the Israelites were given the means for protecting their children.

The role of motherhood is defined in terms of a mother's relationship to her child, and some of the Bible's pictures of mothers accordingly focus on their protection of the rights or privileges of their children. Rebekah advances the cause of Jacob. Moses' mother nurses him in secret. Bathsheba requests that Solomon accede to the throne (1 Kings 2:19). Other mothers raise their children with special care: Hannah the mother of Samuel (1 Sam 1:21-28), Mary the mother of Jesus, Elizabeth the mother of John the Baptist and the mother of Timothy (2 Tim 1:5; 3:15). Paul remembers Rufus's mother as a mother to him also (Rom 16:13), and in reminiscence he writes to the Thessalonians, "But we were gentle among you, like a mother caring for her little children" (1 Thess 2:7 NIV).

Two mothers among the OT matriarchs became powerful symbols for Paul. He saw Sarai and Hagar as the two traditions of worship, the dual paths toward salvation. Hagar, who was the slave, bore her son into slavery—the tradition of the law, or Mt. Sinai (where her descendants worshiped); whereas Sarai bore her son of the "promise" to be free, in the tradition of Jerusalem (1 Tim 2:15). This then becomes the paradigm for the traditions of works (or law) as opposed to faith (or promise/freedom; *see* Galatians, Letter to the).

In spite of the implication in Genesis 1 that God's image contains both male and female, the OT contains very little mothering imagery for God. It was perhaps to avoid confusion with the fertility cults that the Israelites were reluctant to characterize God as Mother. Also the creation as told in Genesis is not a physical process, as in most fertility religions. Although the scribes appear to have avoided any confusion with the mother goddess who tempted the Hebrews, we do find some residual mother imagery. Isaiah 50 pictures God as a mother figure; we also see it in Psalms 131:2.

Generally, however, the major features of "mother" are differentiated from those of "father." She is gentle, while he is strong; she is merciful, while he is just; she is the follower, while he is the leader. In marriage she is the one chosen, the one supported, the one who bears the children and stays at home. Hers is the passive, immanent role; his the active, transcendent one. He is the one who makes the choices, faces the outside as trader, *wanderer, *warrior, *priest or *king.

While Christ is unambiguous in speaking of God as Father, he also uses beautiful motherly imagery, for example in picturing God weeping over Jerusalem (Matt 32:37). We see in the life of Christ the importance of the mother's role. From the Annunciation to Pentecost, *Mary was focused on her child. She nursed him in *Bethlehem, fled with him to *Egypt, took him to the temple for his religious training and watched as he grew independent of her. The fact that they were still close as late as the miracle at Cana suggests that she was by then a widow, relying on him as her oldest son. She accepted his rebuff, followed him on his travels, seeking to protect him even then. When he announced that the mother or brother was not flesh and blood but a part of the family of faith, she appears to have accepted this new relationship, continuing as his disciple until she stood at the foot of the cross. Testimony to her transformed relationship, from flesh and blood to spiritual follower, is in her presence in the upper room, where she waited for the Holy Spirit with his other disciples.

In the image of Mary we see the NT emphasis on mothers as nurturers in the faith—a pattern apparent from the mother of John the Baptist to the mother of Timothy. This is a significant change from the OT mothers' limitation to childhood and flesh. Timothy's mother appears to have acted as a mother in the faith.

Revelation 12 expands the mother image to suggest that God has served as Hagar, protecting her child in the wilderness. The image of God as a mother to Israel and the faith, preserved over the centuries, is a beautiful suggestion that our God serves as both mother and father to us. Like the mothers of Hebrew history, God loves his creatures from the womb, watches over them as infants, nurtures them in their youth and mourns for them in their journeys. But his son also taught us that he can transcend the earthly role of mothers by redeeming us and giving us life everlasting.

In summary, the Bible's images and meanings of motherhood will come into focus if we simply recall the varied stories of the Bible's most famous mothers:

Eve, Sarah, Rebekah, Rachel and Leah, the mother of Samson, Ruth, Hannah, Elizabeth and Mary.

See also BARRENNESS; BIRTH; BIRTH STORY; CHILD, CHILDREN; DOMINEERING MOTHER, WIFE; EVE; FATHER, FATHERHOOD; MARY THE MOTHER OF JESUS; NURSE; WOMAN, IMAGES OF; WOMB.

MOUNTAIN

Mountains and hills proliferate in biblical landscapes, numbering approximately five hundred references. No clear distinction can be made between mountains and hills in biblical imagery. Together they represent an elevated terrain or region. A well-known rhetorical feature of biblical parallelism is that the need for similar terms in successive lines led to stock doublets that are regularly paired. "Mountains and hills" constitutes such a stock formula, being paired in parallel form forty times.

Biblical meanings of the mountain are paradoxical and even contradictory. Mountains are sometimes a symbol of *refuge and security and sometimes a threatening place of military slaughter. At times inaccessible, barren and uninhabited, mountains are nonetheless places where God's people will dwell in abundance. As sites of religious experience, mountaintops are places of pagan *worship that God denounces and of true worship that he commands. The mountains and hills of the Bible are both physical phenomena and spiritual symbols.

Mountains as Physical Places. Although mountains and hills are a prime source of symbol and metaphor in the Bible, they are also an important physical phenomenon of the world of the Bible. Mountains and hills have always been significant natural barriers that readily become geographic and political boundaries (Josh 15:8-16). Extreme conditions make them barren and often sparsely populated. Their unchanging appearance makes them a measure of permanence and solidity. Their natural features (steep slopes, rock outcroppings, sheer cliffs) make them strategic *fortress sites (Judg 6:2). Their many nooks and crannies make them places of hiding and refuge to which to *flee.

These physical qualities of mountains give them connotations of being wild, distant and alien to civilization. There are nearly a hundred biblical references to "hill country" (NRSV), implying a region sparsely populated, beyond the pale of what might be considered civilized. People flee to the hills when their city is destroyed (Gen 14:10; 19:17), and Lot lives in semibarbarous fashion in a *cave in the hills after eschewing a civilized existence (Gen 19:30). Mountains are where persecuted Christians wander in the skins of sheep and goats (Heb 11:37-38) and where Jephthah's unfortunate daughter bewails her virginity for two months (Judg 11:37-39). The descendants of the uncouth *Esau, the Edomites, settled, appropriately, in the hill country (Gen 36:8-9).

Other typical actions reinforce the alien quality of mountains in the Bible. Here is where fugitives hide (1 Sam 26:1), where routed *armies seek escape (1

Sam 14:22), where soldiers pursue their *enemies (Lam 4:19), where armies gather (1 Sam 17:3) and set ambushes (Judg 9:25). In short, hills and mountains are not inviting places. People hunt there (1 Sam 26:20), but the only agricultural activities undertaken in the hills are the planting of *vineyards (Jer 31:5) and the pasturing of *sheep (Mt 18:12) or *cattle (Ps 50:10), not the growing of crops that require tilling of the ground. For the pilgrim traveling to *Jerusalem, hills represent dangers that require God's protection (Ps 121:1-3).

On a more positive note, the elevation of hills and mountains makes them natural places for vision (Deut 34:1-4; Rev 21:10) and proclamation (Is 40:9; 52:7; Mt 5:1). Covenant making, lawgiving and *covenant renewal occur at mountains that, due to their permanence, stand as memorials to the covenant (Ex 19—20; Deut 9—10). They are also the place from which announcements are made—cursing and blessing from Ebal and Gerizim (Deut 27-28), for example, or the word of God from Zion (Is 2:3; Mic 4:2).

The Mountains of the Poets. In addition to their remoteness and ruggedness, hills and mountains are large and impressive. Their inaccessibility makes them unknown and gives them an aura of mystery. Their visible immensity makes them the benchmark for enormity. These are the qualities that impress biblical poets. In Moses' farewell blessing on Israel, he speaks at one point of "ancient mountains" and "everlasting hills" (Deut 33:15 RSV). The most striking images of the destructiveness of nature in Psalms are the shaking of mountains in *earthquakes (Ps 46:2-3) or volcanic eruptions (Ps 104:32) and forest *fires on the mountains (Ps 83:14).

As recognized standards of immensity, mountains appear in descriptions of God's divine power. When God appears (in either imagined or theophanic form) in his anger, "the foundations . . . of the mountains trembled and quaked" (Ps 18:7 NRSV). When he comes down, he touches "the mountains so that they smoke" (Ps 144:5 NRSV), and "the mountains *melt like wax before the LORD" (Ps 97:5). Mountains are the standard of ancient existence against which God's everlasting existence is measured (Ps 90:2). God's righteousness is likened to "mighty mountains " (Ps 36:6 NRSV), as is his protection of his people (Ps 125:2). He is "more majestic than the everlasting mountains" (Ps 76:4 NRSV). And God's creation even of the mountains attests his strength (Ps 65:6). In Jesus' teaching the largeness of mountains becomes a measure of what people can do through faith, as they cast mountains into the sea (Mt 17:20; 21:21).

Hills and mountains are also personified in Scripture, usually in passages of celebration. They rejoice (Ps 98:8), leap (Ps 114:4, 6), sing (Is 44:23) and praise God's name (Ps 89:12). They also "gird themselves with joy" (Ps 65:12 NRSV). Ezekiel pictures God as addressing the mountains (Ezek 6:3), which in Micah 6:1-2 are summoned to hear a covenant lawsuit.

Mountains as Sacred Sites. Almost from the beginning of the Bible, mountains are sites of transcendent spiritual experiences, encounters with God or appearances by God. Ezekiel 28:13-15 places the *Garden of Eden on a mountain. *Abraham shows his willingness to sacrifice Isaac and then encounters God on a mountain (Gen 22:1-14). God appears to Moses and speaks from the *burning bush on "Horeb, the mountain of God" (Ex 3:1-2 NRSV), and he encounters Elijah on the same site (1 Kings 19:8-18). Most impressive of all is the experience of the Israelites at Mt. *Sinai (Ex 19), which *Moses ascends in a *cloud to meet God.

A similar picture emerges from the NT, where Jesus is associated with mountains. Jesus resorted to mountains to be alone (Jn 6:15), to *pray (Mt 14:23; Lk 6:12) and to teach his listeners (Mt 5:1; Mk 3:13). It was on a mountain that Jesus refuted Satan's temptation (Mt 4:8; Lk 4:5). He was also transfigured on a mountain (Mt 17:1-8; Mk 9:2-8; Lk 9:28-36), and he ascended into heaven from the Mount of Olives (Acts 1:10-12).

The sacred mountain achieves its clearest expression in the OT motif of the mountain of God, or the holy mountain. Two separate mountains are part of the image—first Mt. Sinai or Horeb and later Mt. *Zion, on which the *temple stood in Jerusalem. The mountain of God possesses all the other mountain attributes and adds some special nuances. God's mountain is a holy place (Ex 19:23; Is 11:9) on which God dwells and reigns (Ps 43:3; Is 24:23). It is a particularly threatening place (Ex 19:23) that becomes a welcoming place for the righteous (Is 2:2-4). God speaks of planting his people on his holy mountain (Ex 15:17). The metaphor suggests a change in the mountain habitat from barrenness to fruitfulness, from isolation to activity center.

Originally the mountain of God was Sinai, but through time and the movement of Israel into the *Promised Land, Zion displaces Sinai as God's dwelling place on earth. The movement of the mountain of God from Sinai to Zion tracks with the progress of redemption (prophesied by Isaiah [Is 2:1-3; 4:5] and explicitly stated in Heb 12:18-24). The threatening mountain of holiness becomes a welcoming mountain (still holy) where God's people find refuge, peace and joy.

As the new mountain of God, Zion will be similar and dissimilar to Sinai. Both are holy places, both are associated with God's appearing and dwelling, both are places from which the law comes (Ex 19—20; Is 2:1-5), and both are covered by cloud and fire (Ex 19; Is 4:5). But precisely in these apparent similarities a critical transformation is made. Zion is a holy mountain to which people will stream rather than from which they will be fenced away (Is 2 vs. Ex 19). The nations desire the law of God. The cloud and fire on Zion are not the threats of holy, theophanic presence but the comforting images of the presence of God that guided Israel in the exodus. No longer barren, no longer uninhabited, no longer somber,

Zion is the first of many mountains to be transformed. Unimpressive in appearance and virtually indistinguishable from the hills and ridges all around it, Zion will become the chief of mountains (Ps 68:16; Is 2:1-5).

Apocalyptic Mountains. If Psalms is one main locus of mountain imagery, the visionary books are the other. In a sense all the motifs converge here. Given the way the physical elements become actors in *apocalyptic visions, it is no surprise that the mountains figure prominently in the prophetic books (Is 5:25; Jer 4:24; Ezek 38:20; Rev 6:14; 8:8; 16:20). Being poetic in style, these visions naturally take mountains and hills as sources for figurative language (Is 5:1; 10:23; 40:4; 41:15; Jer 51:25; Mic 1:4). And in visions of God's transformation of the world, mountains are participants in God's judgment against an evil world (Is 17:13; Ezek 32:5-6; 33:28; Hag 1:11) and the locus of his blessing on a renewed world (Is 11:9; 25:6; 30:29; 42:11; Jer 31:5; Ezek 20:40; Joel 3:18; Amos 9:13; Zech 8:3).

Summary. Mountains and hills are a master image of the Bible, through which one can trace the whole course of biblical history and doctrine in microcosm. They are literal landscapes in which a broad spectrum of human activity occurs. As symbols they declare the nature of God. As the place where humans encounter the divine, they epitomize how God and people relate to each other, both in history and in the eschaton.

See also FORTRESS, STRONGHOLD; REFUGE, RETREAT, SAFE PLACE; SINAI; TEMPLE; WILDERNESS; ZION.

MOURN, MOURNING

Mourning is a poignant image in the Bible used to evoke the deep anguish that is experienced when God judges or appears to be silent. *Grief at the *death of a loved one or at affliction was expressed in the Bible in different ways: by the rending of *garments, wearing sackcloth, placing dust or *ash on the head, *fasting, *beating the *breast, and wailing (Gen 37:34; 2 Sam 3:31, Neh 9:1; 2 Sam 1:11; Luke 23:27, 48). Many of these outward expressions of grief are woven into the imagery of the prophets. Joel calls the nation to broken-hearted *repentance rather than an outward show of contrition by commanding them to "rend your heart and not your garments. Return to the LORD your God" (Joel 2:13 NIV). Jeremiah *laments over the judgment, sacking and massacre of Jerusalem by using auditory imagery: "Call for the wailing women to come; send for the most skillful of them. Let them come quickly and wail over us till our eyes overflow with tears and water streams from our eyelids. The sound of wailing is heard from Zion" (Jer 9:17-19 NIV).

The profundity of grief is emphasized by likening Israel's sorrow to that of a young woman grieving for her betrothed or parents for their only son. The prophet Joel, describing the great and terrible day of God's judgment, urges the nation to "mourn like a virgin in sackcloth grieving for the betrothed of her

youth" (Joel 1:8 NIV). Amos gives a harrowing description of Israel's *judgment: "I will make the sun go down at noon and darken the earth in broad daylight. I will turn your religious feasts into mourning and your singing into weeping. I will make all of you wear sackcloth and shave your heads. I will make that time like mourning for an only son and the end of it like a bitter day" (Amos 8:9-10 NIV; see also Jer 6:26). Zechariah predicts the deep sorrow at the death of Christ by using the image of mourning for

Mourners depicted in an Egyptian tomb painting from 1345-1200 B.C.

an only child: "They will look on me, the one they have pierced, and will mourn for him as one mourns for an only child, and grieve bitterly for him as one grieves for a firstborn son" (Zech.12:10 NIV).

Lamentations conveys the horror of the destruction of Jerusalem by personifying the city as being in mourning: "Like a widow is she. . . . Bitterly she weeps at night, tears are upon her cheeks" (Lam 1:1-2 NIV). The roads too mourn because the *worship of God has ceased and no pilgrims are traveling to the festivals: "All her gateways are desolate, her priests groan" (Lam 1:4 NIV).

So terrible is God's judgment that the whole creation joins in the lament. Hosea, Jeremiah and Amos use the image of the land mourning (Hos 4:1-3; Jer 12:4; 3:10; Amos 1:2). Hosea creates the impression of total environmental desolation as the "land mourns [dries up], and all who live in it waste away: the beasts of the field and the birds of the air and the fish of the sea are dying" (Hos 4:3 NIV). This is a heavy consequence of there being "no faithfulness, no love, no acknowledgment of God in the land" (Hos 4:1 NIV). Jeremiah prophecies that before the Lord's fierce *anger "the earth will mourn and the heavens above grow dark" (Jer 4:28 NIV). The darkened heavens speak of judgment and mourning. Some of those who watched the crucifixion would have been vividly reminded of these prophecies, as "from the sixth hour until the ninth hour darkness came over all the land" (Mt 27:45 NIV).

In addition to these pictures of overwhelming sorrow and mourning, the Bible includes some wonderful descriptions of mourning being turned to *joy (Ps 126; Is 57:14-21; 61; Jer 31). Jesus read one of these passages from Isaiah, promising comfort and consolation to those who mourn over their sin, as he inaugurated his ministry: "The Spirit of the Sovereign LORD is on me, because the LORD has anointed me to preach good news to the poor. He has sent me to bind up the broken-hearted, to proclaim freedom for the captives and release for the prisoners, to proclaim the year of the LORD's favor and the day of vengeance of our God, to comfort all who mourn, and to provide for those who grieve in Zion—to bestow on them a crown of beauty instead of ashes, the oil of gladness instead of mourning, and a garment of praise instead of a spirit of despair" (Is 61:1-3 NIV; Lk 4:16-21). Mourning is forever consecrated by one of Jesus' famous beatitudes: "Blessed are those who mourn, for they will be comforted" (Mt 5:4 NIV).

See also ASHES; BURIAL, FUNERAL; DARKNESS; DEATH; GARMENTS; GRAVE; GRIEF; JUDGMENT; LAMENT PSALMS; TEARS, VALE OF TEARS; WEEPING.

MOUTH

Mouth is a major biblical image, occurring over three hundred times. It refers literally to physical openings. *Wells (Gen 29:2-3), sacks (Gen 42:27), *caves (Josh 10:18) and baskets (Zech 5:8) all have mouths of this sort. Similarly, the human mouth is an opening in the physical body. Much more often, however, the mouth is viewed metaphorically as an opening into the inner person, a window through which the soul may be viewed. Just as the content of a vessel can be known by peering in it through its mouth, so the human *heart is revealed by a person's mouth.

At the physical level the mouth is a metonym for a person's speech. When God designates Aaron as Moses' spokesperson, he states, "You shall speak to him and put the words in his mouth; and I will be with your mouth and with his mouth . . . he shall serve as mouth for you" (Ex 4:14-15 NRSV). In the calling of Isaiah to the prophetic office of speaking God's word, Isaiah's hesitancy because he is "a man of unclean lips" (Is 6:5) is canceled when a seraph touches Isaiah's mouth with a live coal from the altar (Is 6:6-7). In the psalms of lament the mouth is repeatedly the villain, representing such verbal sins as dishonesty (Ps 5:9; 144:8) and arrogance (Ps 17:10; 73:9—the preferred image for slander is *lips and *tongue). Correspondingly, silence or the withholding of speech is pictured as a closed mouth (Ps 39:9; Is 52:15).

But the mouth is more than the agent of external speech. Passages such as Joshua 1:8 connect the mouth with *thought* and knowledge: "This book of the law shall not depart out of your mouth; you shall meditate on it day and night" (NRSV; cf. Deut 30:14). In the background of such references lies the practice in an oral culture of remembering a text by reciting it.

The mouth frequently reveals *moral character.*

During Isaiah's prophetic call, a cherub touches a burning coal to Isaiah's mouth and says, "Your sin is blotted out" (NRSV), with the cleansing of the mouth symbolizing inner purification (Is 6:7). Jesus stresses that "it is not what goes into the mouth that defiles a person, but it is what comes out of the mouth that defiles" (Mt 15:11 NRSV).

Hebrew poetry often uses the words *mouth* and *heart* as synonymous parallels, because "out of the abundance of the heart the mouth speaks" (Mt 12:34 NRSV). David thus prays, "Let the words of my mouth and the meditation of my heart be acceptable to you, O LORD" (Ps 19:14). Paul, by the same device, parallels confession and saving faith in Romans 10:10: "one believes with the heart and so is justified, and one confesses with the mouth and so is saved" (NRSV).

Interior *emotions* are also revealed by the mouth. God "put a new song in my mouth," says David, indicating the joy of deliverance (Ps 40:3; 63:5). In all such usages the mouth is an opening into one's cognitive, moral or emotional state.

In oral societies, where spoken commitments are binding, oaths and testimony must be handled cautiously. A criminal can be convicted only "on the evidence [mouth] of two or three witnesses" (Deut 19:15), and one must "never be rash with your mouth" (NRSV) when making a vow in the temple (Eccles 5:2). The social damage of false testimony makes the "wicked and deceitful mouth" a favorite target of invective in the Psalms (e.g., Ps 35:21; 109:2). The false mouth, furthermore, misrepresents one's inner being, leading Jeremiah to complain that the Judeans have God "near in their mouths yet far from their hearts" (Jer 12:2 NRSV; see Is 29:13). Rather than using false testimony to harm, the just will speak out in defense of the oppressed. "Speak out [open your mouth]," Lemuel says, "for the rights of all the destitute" (Prov 31:8-9 NRSV), while Paul urges that "no evil talk come out of your mouths, but only what is useful for building up" (Eph 4:29 NRSV).

Because the mouth reveals one's inner being, the wise person exercises discretion in speech. "Those who guard their mouths preserve their lives," whereas "the mouths of fools are their ruin" (Prov 13:3; 18:7 NRSV). An aspect of this discretion involves social position, for custom dictated that one could not speak to a superior. Job remembers the days when princes "laid their hands on their mouths" in honor of his position, a gesture he himself feels compelled to make in the presence of God (Job 29:9; 40:4). The prophets describe Israel's restoration as a time when "kings will shut their mouths" in the face of God's power (Is 52:15; Mic 7:16). Paul borrows this imagery to describe the lawbreaker's humble position: "that every mouth may be silenced, and the whole world may be held accountable to God" (Rom 3:19 NRSV). By disclosing the inner person, the mouth reveals wisdom, folly and status.

See also LIPS; TONGUE.

MUCH FROM LITTLE. See INCREASE, STORIES OF.

MULE. See ANIMALS; DONKEY, ASS.

MURDER STORIES

Murder stories are sordid, awe-inspiring and fearful. They are also sometimes graphic. While biblical accounts occasionally re-create the means by which a murder is committed, *that* a murder occurred is much more important to biblical writers than *how* it occurred.

The first murder story in the Bible (Gen 4:1-16) is perhaps prototypical. The motive for the murder is envy. The design for murder is an innocent invitation to the victim to "go out to the field" (Gen 4:8 RSV). Because the focus of the story is the moral monstrosity of murder and the sanctity of life, we are given no information about the means of murder. The murderer assumes that the field itself is sufficient to conceal the body, as *Cain attempts to evade God's question about where *Abel's corpse resides. The *judgment of God in this story is its climax, as we are led (and this is common in murder stories) to feel a certain revulsion against the act. An aura of the sanctity of life hovers over the entire story. No other act carries such a strong sense of wrongness as does murder. Cain's descendant Lamech is as hardened as his progenitor, boasting of his murder in revenge for a wounding (Gen 4:23-24).

The story of Ehud's assassination of Eglon (Judg 3:15-30) is more graphic in its details than the story of Cain and Abel. The account focuses on the cleverness of the hero—a southpaw who carries his weapon on the unexpected right side (in effect a disguise) and manages to be alone with his unsuspecting victim. Ehud's words are double-edged like his *sword—deceitfully couched in terms of a secret message from God. The assassin is clever at stabbing his obese victim, clever at concealing his weapon, clever in making his getaway (locking the doors of the king's roof chamber, leading the king's attendants to assume that he is going to the toilet). Told in the mocking tone of slave literature, this murder story is filled with graphic details, including the fatness of the victim's belly, the king's fat closing over the blade, and the piercing of the king's intestine so that dung seeps out.

The preferred weapon for murder in the OT is the spear, and the belly is the destination of choice. Abner pierces Asahel with a spear that went through the belly and "came out at his back" (2 Sam 2:23 RSV), and Joab does the same to Amasa, whose bowels spill to the ground (2 Sam 20:10). A homemade version of a spear will work fine as need arises: Jael follows up her ideal hospitality to Sisera by driving a tent peg through his skull as he sleeps (Judg 4:21; 5:25-27). The murder of Absalom has a ritual feel to it: after Joab thrusts three darts into his heart as he dangles from an oak tree, ten of Joab's armorbearers surround Absalom and strike him (2 Sam

18:9-15). Stoning is the means of Naboth's martyrdom (1 Kings 21:1-16). Sometimes physical abuse rather than a weapon is the means of murder, as when the Levite's concubine is raped throughout the night and dies in the morning (Judg 19:22-26).

The victim's lack of suspicion is a typical feature in murder stories. Ish-bosheth is the classic case, murdered while taking his noonday nap in his bedroom (2 Sam 3:5-7). Uriah thinks he is simply following military orders when he goes to frontline duty and certain death (2 Sam 11:15). Assassinations are usually committed by people within the court, rendering the lack of suspicion on the part of the victim all the more surprising. Menahem assassinates Shallum to gain his throne (2 Kings 15:14). Similar motives prompt the sons of Sennacherib king of Assyria, who is assassinated while worshiping in the house of his god (2 Kings 19:36-37). Joash's servants murder him as he lies wounded on his bed (2 Chron 24:25).

The imagery of OT murder stories thus combines the violent with the domestic or commonplace. It is true that bodies are mutilated with *weapons, but the victims are usually at ease in their home environment when the horror is visited on them.

Although the killing of Jesus was technically an execution carried out by judicial bodies and designated executioners rather than a murder perpetrated by intrigue in a moment of secrecy, it has overtones of the archetypal murder story. It is a story of horrible mutilation and torture. It is done (like political assassinations) out of motives of personal envy, not because Jesus had broken a law. Significantly, Stephen in his speech at his own martyrdom claims that the Jews "betrayed and murdered" the "Righteous One" (Acts 7:52 RSV).

See also ABEL; CAIN; CRIME AND PUNISHMENT; DEATH; MARTYR.

MUSIC

Although the prohibition against images (Deut 20:4) prevented Israel from developing an impressive tradition of visual art like the Greeks, music played a central part in its life. Every facet of its life and every stage of its history were marked by music. Music was present when people greeted each other and said farewell (Gen 31:27; Lk 15:25), when they *married and were *buried (Jer 7:34; 48:36), when they went off to *war and were welcomed back from it (Judg 30:34; Is 30:32). From the least to the greatest, biblical people sang and played instruments (1 Sam 16:18; Job 30:31). At the everyday level we find romantic songs, working songs and drinking songs (Song 1:9-17; 2:15; Is 21:11-12; 22:13; Ezek 33:32). Major events in the life of the people, such as the *exodus from Egypt, conquering the Canaanites, recapturing the *ark, dedicating the *temple, crowning the *king and returning from *exile, were celebrated in music and song.

Indeed, the Israelites excelled in music, perhaps more than any of their contemporaries, and nowhere more so than in their corporate *worship. From the beginning, music and song were at the heart of temple worship (2 Sam 6:5, 14; 1 Kings 10:12; 1 Chron

An Assyrian band makes music with tambourine, lyres and cymbals.

15:15-16), a tradition that continued when the second temple was built (2 Chron 29:25; 35:15; Neh 7:1; 12:27-43). The scale on which this took place was impressive (1 Chron 15:19-21; 16:4-6, 39-42; 23:5-8; 2 Chron 5:12-13; Ezra 3:10-11). There were string, wind and percussion instruments. The number of personnel required by this extravaganza and the overwhelming atmosphere of joy and festivity are beautifully captured in several passages (e.g., Ps 68:24-27; 149; 150). All this is seen as a natural or fitting response to what God has done for his people, whether corporately (Ps 147:1) or individually (Ps 13:6; 27:5-6; 71:20-23). This role of music and song was continued in the early church (Acts 16:25; 1 Cor 14:14-15, 26; Eph 4:19; Col 3:16).

The Music of Creation and Nature. The music of creation becomes a biblical motif only in indirect or occasional ways. The repeated terms, patterns and refrains of the opening chapter of Genesis suggest at least a poetic and probably a musical dimension to the whole story of the creation (Gen 1:1—2:4). There is also a reference in Job to the morning *stars' singing together, along with angelic shouts for joy at the creation of the world (Job 38:7). Here singing becomes an image of celebration (cf. the connection between music and creation when Aslan sings creation into existence in C. S. Lewis's *The Magician's Nephew*). The psalmist sings a "new song" celebrating the redemptive work of God in which, "all the trees of the wood sing for joy" (Ps 96:12 RSV).

This language reappears in apocalyptic visions of God's future work of salvation, when "the mountains and the hills before you shall break forth into singing" (Is 55:12 RSV), probably suggesting that the creation too is the recipient of salvation. The creation's groans of travail and longing (Rom 8:23) will be turned into joyful and exuberant melodies as grasslands, hills and *valleys come alive in song (Ps 65:12-13). In Psalm 98 not only are the people of the earth enjoined to "break forth into joyous song"

when God comes to judge the world (Ps 98:4 RSV), but so are the sea, the floods and the hills (Ps 98:7-8).

The Song of the Soul. In other passages it is the individual believer who is encouraged to receive and give voice to God in song at points of need and grace. Sometimes this is meant literally (Ps 27:6; 71:22-23). In these references music is preeminently an image of *praise, associated with joy. In fact, over a hundred references in the Psalms command the use of music for praising God, and 91 out of 107 references to music in the Psalms specify God as the audience of music (including numerous references to singing "to the LORD"). It is small wonder, then, that the refusal of music becomes the most poignant way to express the Israelites' devastation as they are marched off into exile in Babylon: "On the willows there we hung up our lyres. . . . How shall we sing the LORD's song in a foreign land?" (Ps 137:2, 4 RSV). This refusal to sing at the *taunt of their tormentors to "sing us one of the songs of Zion" (Ps 137:3 RSV) shows that the equation of music and praise images a spontaneous and irrepressible upwelling of emotion, not something to be summoned by external manipulation.

In addition to expressing praise and joy, music is associated with such varied moods as consolation, thanksgiving and deliverance. When all is dark the psalmist finds that the Lord's song is with him as a kind of soothing nighttime lullaby to pacify him (Ps 42:8). Similarly, God himself is said to be the believer's song (Ex 15:2; Ps 118:14; Is 12:2). Singing is also the expression of thanks (Ps 26:7; 28:7) and acknowledgment of deliverance (Ps 51:14).

The evocative image of singing a "new song" appears nine times in the Bible (Ps 33:3; 40:3; 96:1; 98:1; 144:9; 149:1; Is 42:10; Rev 5:9; 14:3). An implied contrast to "old" songs, it is an image of the transformed life of faith, the dynamic, ever-changing

A Syrian lyre, a harplike stringed instrument.

nature of a life lived in fellowship with God, and the perpetual renewal of God's mercy in the life of a believer.

Although virtually all biblical references to music are positive, there is also a motif of music as a symbol of the human soul in disease. Amos denounces a culture for whom the music of religious ritual has become a substitute for the exercise of justice and righteousness (Amos 5:23-24). Amos also paints a picture of a decadent society whose music is part of an indulgent lifestyle that ignores social oppression (Amos 6:4-6). Isaiah paints a similar picture of indulgence as a substitute for the fear of the Lord (Is 5:11-12). The foil to these pictures of music as an index to decadence is the vibrancy of the pictures (found especially in the Psalms) of music as the expression of heartfelt devotion to God.

The Music of God. Sometimes God or his Spirit is said to be the source of the skills that produce music and song, so that music assumes the quality of a gift and inspiration (Ex 31:3, 6; 35:25; 36:1; 1 Chron 15:22; 25:7; 2 Chron 34:12; Ps 33:3). David describes himself as the God-anointed singer of Israel's songs (2 Sam 23:1). But the Bible also speaks more directly of God as a composer of songs and of the divine wisdom they contain (1 Kings 4:29, 32). In Psalm 40:3 David claims that it is God who "put a new song in my mouth" (RSV). Alongside the image of God as lawgiver, therefore, we should place the image of God as musical composer (Deut 31:19). He is also a performer: his heart "moans for Moab like a flute" (Jer 48:36 RSV), and he exults over Zion "with loud singing" (Zeph 3:17 RSV).

Summary. The book of Revelation can serve as a summary of what music means to the biblical imagination. Trumpets serve a ritualistic purpose of announcing the advent of times of judgment and redemption. References to harps lend an otherworldly atmosphere to the picture of heavenly realms (Rev 5:8; 14:2; 15:2). Most pervasive of all is the singing of the saints in heaven over their redemption and glory (Rev 5:12-13; 7:12; 11:17; 14:3; 15:3).

See also HARP; PRAISE PSALMS; TRUMPET; WORSHIP.

MUSICAL INSTRUMENTS. *See* HARP; MUSIC; TRUMPET.

MUSTARD SEED

From references in the Gospels and rabbinical writings, the mustard seed was proverbial for its smallness. Indeed, Jesus describes it as "the smallest seed you plant in the ground" (cf. Mk 4:31 NIV). Depending on the precise variety of seed, it produces a *plant that would normally reach between two and six feet in height.

In the teachings of Jesus the mustard seed is mentioned in two different contexts. First, in exhorting his disciples to exercise greater faith, Jesus uses hyperbole to say that if they would have "faith as a grain of mustard seed," they would be able to move a *mountain (Mt 17:20) or command a *tree to plant itself in the *sea (Lk 17:6).

Second, Jesus compares the *kingdom of God/heaven to a mustard seed that a man *sows in his garden (Mk 4:31-32). Two features of this illustration are striking. First, Jesus' listeners would have

been shocked by the idea of comparing the kingdom of God/heaven with a mustard seed. To them it must surely have seemed blasphemous to associated God's reign with the tiniest of *seeds. Second, Jesus focuses on the growth of the mustard seed. In spite of its minute size, it grows to become "the largest of garden plants" (Mk 4:32 NIV), big enough for the birds to perch in its branches. For Jesus it is the growth of the tiny seed into a large plant that resembles the kingdom of God/heaven. Whereas his listeners probably expected God's kingdom to be inaugurated in a dramatic, earth-shattering manner, Jesus emphasizes that from the smallest of beginnings it will slowly grow to reach its full size. This picture of gradual growth is also reflected in the closely associated parable of the *leaven (Mt 13:33; Lk 13:20-21).

See also PLANTS; SEED; SOW, SOWING, SOWER; TREE, TREES.

MUTABILITY. *See* MORTALITY; TRANSCIENCE.

MYSTERY. *See* EPHESIANS, LETTER TO THE.

MYTHICAL ANIMALS

The term *mythical animal* is more easily defined in our time than in that of the Bible. Unlike in antiquity, when travelers returned from other lands with believable stories of unbelievable beasts, today very few areas of the world where monsters could be hiding remain unexplored. The presence of monkeys and peacocks at Solomon's court (1 Kings 10:22) demonstrates a curiosity about the exotic. Other ancient texts tell of a *manticore*, a Persian word referring to a beastly monster that probably originated around a man-eating tiger. The legend of the phoenix rising from the ashes probably stems from literary embellishments of actual accounts of the flamingo nesting in caustic soda lakes. In each of these cases an inability to completely and accurately describe the natural history of foreign, rare or inaccessible animals required that the imagination supply the details. Nocturnal animals or those in the sea were especially unobservable. The carcasses of whales, sharks or even more outlandish creatures washing up on the beach served as fodder for fantastic speculation about the denizens of the deep.

A great deal of myth continues to surround some animals. Today's natural history books still devote space to demythologizing many of their subjects: snakes cannot hypnotize; goatsuckers (birds) don't drink milk from goats; lemmings don't commit mass suicide. Some myths will always accompany animals, perhaps as a result of our propensity to anthropomorphize or otherwise misinterpret their behavior. Even so, ancient literature may describe creatures that people knew could not be found on earth. Their mythical beasts, like ours, existed in a spiritual realm and symbolized spiritual truths, much as the wings of an *angel express their ability to move between heaven and earth, or the halo on a saint signifies a divine aura and marks them as more than merely human.

The art of the ancient world exhibits a variety of composite creatures with grotesque heads, lions' bodies, eagle's legs, and the talons and tail of a snake or scorpion. Even if such monstrosities did not spring from the artist's bad dreams, they no doubt enlivened the nightmares of those who saw them. The combination of lion and adder together symbolizes the evil powers that the one who trusts in God will dominate (Ps 91:13). Luke's allusion to this passage rephrases the evil symbols as serpents and scorpions (Lk 10:19). Even animals people had seen were believed to possess supernatural abilities, to be agents of, or in league with, God or the devil. Certain animals embodied evil. In fact, the identity of the animal itself is not as important as its embodiment of brute power, sinister activity or association with darkness (Ezra 32:2).

Mythical Animals as God's Enemies. The dragon and Leviathan, as primordial *Chaos, represent the original *enemy of God. In the Babylonian creation story, the *Enuma elish,* the chief god, Marduk, battles the monstrous Tiâmat, the Deep/Abyss (Heb *tᵉhôm*), and her eleven monster allies whose

A cherub engraved in ivory.

carcasses, upon their defeat, become the twelve signs of the zodiac. In contrast, the Deep *(tᵉhôm)* is not personified in Genesis 1:2, nor does it serve any etiological function in the *cosmology of Genesis. Elsewhere in the Hebrew Scriptures "the deeps" do appear in poetry parallel to the dragons (Ps 148:7), and they do teem with sea monsters (*tannînim,* Gen 1:21). The Bible assumes its readers' familiarity with a story in which God slays the primordial monster: "Was it not thou that didst cut Rahab ['Raging Storm'] in pieces, that didst pierce the dragon?" (Is 51:9 RSV). Evil, portrayed as the monster from the abyss, must be slain: "In that day the LORD with his hard and great and strong sword will punish Leviathan the fleeing serpent, Leviathan the twisting serpent, and he will slay the dragon that is in the sea" (Is 27:1 RSV). The ultimate end of the dragon/sea monster is defeat (Rev 20:2, 10). The bitter waters

of the sea where he has hidden will be no more (Rev 21:1).

Since the outcome of the cosmic battle is assured, God's enemies on earth may be likened to the dragon. Nebuchadnezzar has consumed Jerusalem with his monstrous appetite (Jer 51:34). Pharaoh, surrounded by the Nile delta, is "the great dragon that lies in the midst of his streams," thrashing futilely against God (Ezek 29:3 RSV; cf. Is 30:7). The roiling sea was evidence of the struggles of the sea serpent. Job complains that he is confined as if he were a sea monster (Job 7:12). God will deal with his enemies just as he broke the heads of the dragon and will work his salvation in the earth by defeating the anti-Creation forces of Chaos (Ps 74:12-13). Although puny man is helpless, God can reach Leviathan, the dragon, the ally of Chaos, even in his deep hiding place (Ps 74:14, cf. Ezek 29:3; 32:2).

The fantastic beasts of eschatological visions may represent political "dominions" (Dan 7:6). In the intertestamental period dragons symbolized spiritual evils (evil spirits) that incite political unrest (cf. additions to Esther 11:5-6). This use anticipates the dragon in *Revelation, where the ancient serpent is the embodiment of evil, the enemy of God and foe of his angels (Rev 12:7, 9). The evil spirits that emanate from the dragon foment war (Rev 16:13) and deceive the nations (Rev 20:3).

Mythical Animals as Heavenly Servants. The "fiery serpents" for which the Israelites feared the desert (Num 21:6-8; Deut 8:15) become further embellished as "flying serpents" (Is 14:29; 30:6). The serpents, designated by the same Hebrew word as seraphim, are distinquishable from them only by context (Is 6:2, 6). This pairing suggests that the image of a seraph may have had more in common with our idea of dragon than of angel.

The cherubim enjoy a similar angelic iconographic likeness in recent art, but representations in ancient artwork show the gods riding on gryphon-like animals or seated on thrones borne by such creatures. The repeated descriptions of the mercy seat as overshadowed by cherubim (Ex 25:18-20) or references to God riding on or enthroned above the cherubim leave little doubt that the Hebrews shared a similar conception (Ps 18:10; 80:1; 99:1; Is 37:16). The vivid, terrifying composite creatures described by Ezekiel (1:5-28; 9:3; 10:1-20; 11:20) are cherubim (Ezek 10:20). Just as cherubim guard the *Garden of Eden (Gen 3:24), God appoints as guardian of the king of Tyre a cherub who later drives the king from power for abuse of trade and violence (Ezek 28:14, 16). The living creatures (beasts) of apocalyptic literature may represent either cherubim or seraphim (Rev 4—6).

Mythical Animals as Evil Spirits. The winds that roiled the sea evinced the dual role of the sea monster as both natural and spiritual force. Several other creatures shared such a dual role. The beasts lurked in desolate ruins because of their alliance with evil, resulting in the obvious association of "demon, foul spirit and unclean bird" (Rev 18:2). Many of the animals that haunted ruins were thought to be manifestations of evil spirits. Owls, silent in flight, nocturnal and yet all-seeing, seemed particularly otherworldly. The lilith that haunts ruins is in some translations rendered as "owl," in others as a demonic "night hag" (Is 34:14 RSV). Hebrew has borrowed the word *lîlît* from the Akkadian *lilîtu,* "demon." Paradoxically, both translations may be correct, each reflecting different aspects of the same mythical embodiment in the creature we call the owl. Similarly, the *'ōhîm* of Isaiah 13:21 are rendered "doleful creatures" (AV) or "howling creatures" (RSV), but that word is recognized to mean owl, probably a borrowing of Akkadian *ahû* "ominous thing" or "owl," which the Mesopotamians believed to be a manifestation of a demon. Satyrs, evil spirits depicted with goatlike features (Is 13:21; 34:14) danced among the haunted ruins. Scripture also mentions the worship of idols carved in their shape (2 Chron 11:15; Lev 17:7).

As often occurs in preindustrialized societies, animals that call at night are known by their cry. A myth arises around a creature even if the people cannot identify which animal makes the cry. Many of these creatures have onomatopoetic names; that is, they are called by an imitation of the sound they make. Such a scenario may explain the apparent confusion or overlap of names. In addition to the examples above, animals or spirits that howled at night and cavorted in ruins include "jackals" or "goblins" (*tannîm,* Mic 1:8), the hyena (*'iyyîm,* Jer 50:39), the hedgehog or owl (*qippōd,* Is 14:23; 34:11; Zeph 2:14; *qippôz,* Is 34:15). The epithet "lair or haunt of jackals" pronounces a curse of desolation on a city (Is 13:22; 34:13; Jer 9:11; 20:22; 49:33; 51:37; Lam 5:18; Mal 1:3) but may also serve as a reference to the desert (Ps 44:19).

Mythical Animals as Translation Problems. Several words seem to apply to more than one creature—first to a "real" animal and second to a mythical one. *Leviathan* seems to be clearly a crocodile in Job 41 and perhaps when referring to Pharaoh, who "ruled" the Nile crocodiles. But elsewhere Leviathan clearly refers to a sea monster of mythical proportions. *Seraph* shares a similar ambiguity, referring to a heavenly creature, a flying serpent or a genuine biting snake (see above). The Hebrew words for sea serpent *(tannîn)* and jackals *(tannîm)* are probably not related, but are nevertheless confused in two difficult contexts (Lam 4:3; Neh 2:13). In addition, *tannîn* may designate a merely mortal serpent (Ex 7:9-10, 12). Other uses seem to play on the mythological or spiritual dimension (Deut 32:33; Ps 91:13,

cf. Lk 10:19) as do words for snake in general. In antiquity serpents seemed to have eternal life because of their supernatural ability to regenerate by shedding their skin (*see* Serpent).

Mythical Animals as Mistranslations. Several mythical animals that appear in older translations are no longer supported by current scholarship. For example, the translators of the KJV, apparently unaware of the existence of a wild ox (the aurochs or *Bos primigenius,* now extinct) around the Mediterranean, rendered the Hebrew *re'ēm* as "unicorn." For this they relied on the LXX *monokerōs* (single-horned) even though the Bible describes it as a clean (edible) animal with horns (Deut 33:17). The aurochs, a truly powerful (Num 23:22; 24:8) and untamable beast (Job 33:9-10), had existed in Palestine from prehistoric times and had acquired a reputation of mythic proportions. It had two horns that it tossed in triumph, offering Hebrew poets a vivid image of power (Deut 33:17; 1 Sam 2:1; Ps 92:10) and boundless energy (cf. Ps 29:6, where "calf" translates the Heb *ben r*'ē*mîm,* "young one of the wild ox").

Basilisk, an archaic designation for snakes, has a mythological aura. Words once rendered as basilisk under the influence of the LXX are now translated adder (Is 59:5; Ps 91:13). The cockatrice, a common symbol in heraldry, was believed to be the product of a rooster's egg being incubated by a snake and resulting in a dragonlike hatchling (Is 59:5). Older versions used cockatrice for several related Hebrew words designating serpents (Prov 23:32; Is 11:8; 14:29). Its listing with the flying serpents no doubt enhanced its mythic reputation (Is 14:29). Because of the snake's desert habitat, the prophet Isaiah uses it as a label for desert peoples, suggesting desolation, uselessness and a connection with the dark side of creation (Is 30:6).

Job 40:15-24 clearly describes the hippopotamus. The translators of the AV, unaware at that early date of the existence of the hippo, resorted to transliteration of the Hebrew name Behemoth (itself borrowed from Egyptian). In so doing they unwittingly created a mythical animal that survives to the present. Its counterpart is Leviathan (cf. Job 41, where it means crocodile, not the sea monster). The author of Job uses the two to represent but a few of the many secrets that reveal the profundity of God's knowledge, suggesting to the pious the depths of human ignorance and thus their unworthiness to question the Creator.

See also ANIMALS; COSMOLOGY; MONSTER, MONSTERS.

N

NAHUM, BOOK OF

Nahum is a neglected literary master. His use of Hebrew poetic technique, metaphor and simile in particular, is the equal of his more widely acclaimed prophetic colleagues Isaiah and Micah; but his overall message, the violent destruction of the Assyrian city of Nineveh, is not attractive or immediately relevant to modern audiences. This is a pity, since Nahum's view of God is as important today as it has ever been.

Nahum's short prophecy begins with a hymnic description of the appearance of God as a *divine warrior who has come to rescue his people while he destroys their enemy (Nahum 1:2-8). The divine warrior image is found in many places in both Testaments. Here it is accompanied by the description of God as one who rides the *clouds into battle (Nahum 1:3), dries up the chaotic waters of the *sea (Nahum 1:4) and throws the whole natural world into convulsions (Nahum 1:5). God is a warrior who cannot be conquered, a message specifically directed to the oppressive city of Nineveh but relevant for all those who try to resist God through the ages.

Nahum employs his poetic gift to ridicule God's *enemies. He taunts them by calling them *lions without lairs, unable to satisfy their cravings for prey (Nahum 2:11-13). The use of this image for Nineveh is intentional, since we have Assyrian records in which they themselves refer to their power and ruthlessness as lionlike. Isaiah, a century earlier, used the lion image in reference to Assyria in order to evoke *fear in his Israelite audience (Is 5:26-30).

In a structurally parallel passage (Nahum 3:4-7), Nahum likens Nineveh to a witch—not just any witch but one that has particular skill in love potions. She is a harlot-sorceress (see Prostitute), who for years has seduced the nations into her alliance and then exploited them. This *witch will now be humiliated in public. In addition, Nineveh is said to be like the *locust, an insect that descends on a fertile area and picks it dry (Nahum 3:14-17).

This enemy, Nineveh, has had a stranglehold on the world, and on God's people in particular. Nahum invokes the image of the yoke to describe the oppression God's people have suffered at the hand of Nineveh (Nahum 1:13). As a result, God was going to judge and destroy them. This *judgment is described as a burning up of stubble (Nahum 1:10) or the eating of a ripe *fig (Nahum 3:12). They would drink the *cup of judgment, a cup that would make them get drunk and pass out (Nahum 3:11).

Nahum speaks a powerful message by means of captivating images. Though the thrust of the book is hostile toward God's enemies, it signals grace and compassion toward his people. In other words, the book of Nahum is not ultimately dark but indeed causes us to look to the *mountains where we see "the feet of one who brings good news, who proclaims peace" (Nahum 1:15 NIV).

See also DIVINE WARRIOR; PROPHECY, GENRE OF.

BIBLIOGRAPHY. T. Longman III, "Nahum" in *The Minor Prophets*, ed. T. E. McComiskey (Grand Rapids: Baker, 1993) 765-830.

NAKED, NAKEDNESS

The biblical images evoked by the word *naked* are many and varied. They include, among other things, original *innocence, defenselessness and vulnerability; exposure and helplessness; humiliation and *shame; *guilt and *judgment; and *sexual impropriety and exploitation. Each of these various nuances needs to be carefully identified in each scriptural context, although there may, of course, be some degrees of overlap.

The most positive image of nakedness in the Bible is also the first, where we read regarding *Adam and *Eve in the *Garden that "the man and his wife were both naked, and they felt no shame" (Gen 2:25 NIV). This is a strongly positive image, connoting such prelapsarian qualities as innocence, freedom, openness, paradisal simplicity and sexual intimacy in *marriage. This striking verse at once signals implied contrasts between the original state of the human race and its later state, between paradisal simplicity and civilized complexity, between transparency and concealment, between a childlike lack of self-consciousness and adult shame over one's private body parts.

A clear case of the metaphorical usage of *nakedness* as vulnerability is found in Genesis 42:9, where Joseph accuses his brothers of coming to Egypt to spy out "the nakedness of the land" (NRSV). Similar exposure to unwanted intrusion is illustrated by Hebrews 4:13 where all things are "naked" (NRSV) before the eyes of the all-seeing God.

Nakedness as an indication of deprivation is another example in which vulnerability and unprotectedness are in view (e.g., the parable of the sheep and the goats, where "naked" is translated by the NIV as "needing clothes"). Gross exploitation of the poor is illustrated in Job 22:6, where both literal and metaphorical aspects are probably meant: "You demanded security from your brothers for no reason; you stripped men of their clothing, leaving them naked" (NIV). Deliberately stripping off the *garments as an act of humiliation is found in 2 Samuel 10:4, where Hanun, king of the Ammonites, sends away the envoys of David with their buttocks exposed. Prisoners of war were ritually stripped and led away naked and *barefoot (see Is 20:2-4). Contrary to all artistic representations, it is almost certain that Jesus was stripped naked when crucified as a criminal by the Romans.

Nakedness as humiliation leads us to consider the complex issue of shame, guilt and punishment. This sends us back to the primal couple in the Garden of Eden where, before the Fall, Adam and Eve were "both naked, and they felt no shame" (Gen 2:25 NIV). But as soon as human rebellion and self-assertiveness reared their ugly heads, shame, guilt and self-consciousness took over. Pathetic attempts at self-concealment (Gen 3:7) are replaced by God's own provision of covering (Gen 3:21). Henceforth nakedness was unnatural. Clothing is God's covering, his divine gracious response to human rebellion. Being unclothed thus becomes a metaphor for being exposed to the judgment of God. This can be seen in a very literal way in the case of the punishment for prostitution, where the skirt was lifted over the harlot's face (see Jer 13:26).

Illicit sexuality and nakedness are linked together a number of times in the Bible (although it must be made quite clear that in Genesis 3, the sense of shame in nakedness after the Fall has nothing to do with sexual relations). Ezekiel 16:36 speaks of exposing "your nakedness in your promiscuity with your lovers" (NIV). Forbidden sexual unions are spoken of as "uncovering the nakedness" of some person; for example, Habakkuk 2:15 mentions drunken orgies, where deliberate intoxication is induced as a prelude to lustful leering on nakedness.

The NT is very explicit in indicating that metaphorical nakedness is an undesirable state and that redemption means being clothed with the garments of God's salvation. Revelation 3:18 speaks of the shame of nakedness being covered with white garments bought from the risen Lord. The apostle Paul, in speaking of the eschatological hope of the *resurrection of the body, longs not to be found naked but rather to be covered with the heavenly dwelling which God himself provides (2 Cor 5:1-5).

Job said, "Naked I came from my mother's womb, and naked I will depart" (Job 1:21 NIV). There is no more poignant description than this of humanity's pathetic vulnerability and need for covering, both for this life and for the life to come.

See also BODY; GUILT; INNOCENCE, INNOCENT; SEX; SHAME.

NAME

The word *name* and its inflected forms occur nearly eleven hundred times in the KJV, almost always translating Hebrew *šēm* (also rendered "fame," "renown," "report") or Greek *onoma*. Just under half of these occurrences refer to the name of God or God's Son.

Personal and Place Names. Often *name* is merely literal, a mechanism for summoning someone (Esther 2:14), casting lots (Num 17:2-5), appointing for tasks (Num 1:5-15; 4:32; 1 Chron 16:41; 23:6, 14; Ezra 10:16), establishing legal identity (Gen 48:6; Ezra 2:61-62) and so on. About one-fifth of the occurrences of *name* simply identify persons or places ("the name of the first [river] is Pishon," Gen 2:11; "a city called Nazareth," Mt 2:23; "and his mother's name was . . . ," a common formula in 2 Kings and 2 Chronicles when introducing kings; "a man of Cyrene, Simon by name," Mt 27:32). Here its only larger significance is to show the importance of personal identity and preservation in cultural memory, an idea also attested by the inclusion in the canon of many long lists of names—indeed, Scripture mentions by name more than three thousand persons. To "greet the friends by name" (3 Jn 14) is a token of a letter writer's regard, and a name alone may arouse emotional response (Song 1:3; Jer 33:9). High value was placed on having one's name live on, in descendants (Gen 48:16; Num 27:4; Deut 25:6-7; Ruth 4:10; 1 Sam 24:21; 2 Sam 14:7; 18:18; Jer 11:19)—as it did literally for Jacob/Israel and his sons, especially Judah—and also in a reputation for achievements and piety (Sir 44:8-9, 14; cf. Ps 41:5; Eccles 6:4; Is 56:5). But "the name of the wicked will rot" (Prov 10:7 NIV; cf. Job 18:17; Ps 34:16; Zeph 1:4)—a common image is of being blotted out—or, if remembered, will have no *honor (Gen 11:4, 8 [builders of Babel]; Deut 25:10; Ps 49:11-12; Is 65:15). Also threatened thus with oblivion are whole nations (Ps 83:4; Is 14:22) and false gods (Deut 12:3).

Immortality via memory in the OT differs from that prized by Homeric heroes, for Scripture adds a divine dimension. God knows *Moses by name (Ex 33:17; 3:4); the good shepherd calls "his own sheep by name" (Jn 10:3 NIV; cf. 2 Tim 2:19). For Bezaleel (Ex 31:2), *David (1 Sam 16:3), Isaiah (Is 49:1), the apostles (Lk 6:13) and even Cyrus (Is 45:3-4), calling by name means divine selection for a task. The names of the twelve tribes are to be borne on the high priest's garments "for a memorial before the Lord continually" (Ex 28:29; cf. Ex 28:9-12, 21). The NT adapts this image to the eschatological realm, setting tribes and apostles together (Rev 21:12, 14; cf. Phil 4:3); closely related is the idea of "your names . . . written in heaven" (Lk 10:20; cf. Ex 32:33; Heb 12:23; Rev 13:8; 17:8).

Individual names in the Bible have etymological meanings, as they do today, but such associations might be ignored in choosing a name (Lk 1:59-61 attests to the weight given to family tradition). Still, in an age that tended to identify words and realities—when nominalistic philosophy had yet to develop (but see Acts 18:15)—any parallel between name and personality would be considered more than fortuitous. Names in Hebrew society had to be either lived up to or lived down. The phenomenon of self-fulfilling prophecy stemming from one's name might also have been a factor.

Many OT texts display interest in etymology. Explanations are given for more than forty place names (often with a flavor of folk etymology); many, like *Babel, Bethel, Mizpah, Peniel, Gilgal and Ebenezer, commemorate events in patriarchal or later history (Gen 11:9; 22:14; 28:19; 31:49; 32:30; 35:15; Ex 17:15; Josh 5:9; 1 Sam 7:12). Micah 1:10-15 is a tour de force of ironic wordplay on toponymic etymology. In some thirty instances in Genesis and Exodus and a dozen elsewhere, parents choose or construct a name that fits the circumstances of a child's birth, either personal (Ben-oni, "son of suffering," promptly changed to Benjamin, Gen 35:18; Samuel, "heard by God," 1 Sam 1:20 [cf. Ishmael, Gen 16:11]) or, rarely, social (Ichabod, "no glory," 1 Sam 4:21), or a name that expresses their hopes or their piety or both (Noah, "relief," Gen 5:29; *Joseph, "may God add," Gen 30:24; and note the many theophoric names beginning or ending with Υ[ah] or El). Some children, such as Ishmael and Isaac, receive a name by divine command, usually one with prophetic meaning (Solomon, Jesus, John) or even direct prophetic purpose (Isaiah's children, Is 7:3; 8:3, 18; Hosea's, Hos 1:4, 6, 9). The name *Jacob (ya'ᵃqōḇ, "let God protect") was given punningly to a child who at birth seized his elder twin's 'āqēḇ, "heel," and was later interpreted, by further wordplay, to explain his tendency to 'āqaḇ, "supplant" (Gen 25:26; 27:36). When Jacob's name was extended to his posterity, these associations were not forgotten (Jer 9:4; Hos 12:3). Abigail's similar joke about her husband's name, Nabal, meaning "worthless" or "good-for-nothing" (1 Sam 25:25), has been taken unsmilingly by generations of commentators.

Ideally, however, a name captures the essence of the person. The Creator, of course, has such discernment (Ps 147:4; Is 40:26). In Genesis 2:19 Adam has it concerning the animals and, with it, authority over them. Both discernment and authority are often implied in the changing of names. Formal renamings register a change in personality and signal a new phase of one's life. Abram, Sarai and Oshea have their names replaced (Gen 17:5, 15; Num 13:16 [Joshua]); Naomi in her sorrow thinks that she should (Ruth 1:20). Jacob, Gideon and Solomon are given supplementary names, Israel, Jerubbaal, Jedidiah—nicknames, in the old sense. So also, in the NT, are James and John (Boanerges), Simon (Cephas/Peter), the Cypriot Joseph (Barnabas) and Thomas/Didymus (Aramaic and Greek for "twin"; his true name was Judas, according to patristic tradition).

Peter and Thomas illustrate the doubling of names for practical reasons in a multilingual culture; other examples include Tabitha/Dorcas, synonyms ("gazelle"), and Saul/Paul, alike in sound, not meaning. Some NT names are Hellenized equivalents of traditional Hebrew names—James for Jacob, Jesus for Joshua. But John Mark (among others) had two names, Semitic and Roman, that were quite unlike. OT parallels (Joseph, Gen 41:45; late kings, 2 Kings 23:34; 24:17; Daniel and his associates, Dan 1:7) reflect instead imposition by foreign authority. Daniel's new name, Belteshazzar, contains the name of the god Bel (Dan 4:8). In NT times surnames were also becoming common, based on such facts as the person's home (Judas Iscariot, Mary Magdalene, Joseph of Arimathea), occupation (Simon the Tanner), politics (Simon Zelotes) or family (Simon Barjona); or the patronymic alone might be given (Bartimaeus, Barabbas).

Symbolic names and renaming abound in poetry and prophecy. The names of those traditionally pitted against God in myth (Leviathan, Rahab, the Deep, the Dragon; see Mythical Animals) or history (*Egypt, *Babylon) are used metonymically in celebrations of God's triumphs (Ps 74:13-14; 89:10; Is 27:1; 51:9-10; Rev 11:7-8; 20:2-3) or warnings to God's people. *Jerusalem may become *"Sodom" (Rev 11:8; cf. Ezek 16:46-56) or suffer a worse fate (Mt 11:23-24). Babylon is a code name for Rome, or for what Rome, in turn, stands for (Rev 17:5, 9; cf. Is 21:9; 1 Pet 5:13). Ezekiel rebukes Jerusalem and Samaria in a parable of two women whose behavior belies their symbolic names (Ezek 23). Sometimes a new epithet is condemnatory (Jer 6:30; 20:3; cf. Prov 21:24), but more often it points to redemption: the *City of Righteousness (Is 1:26; cf. Jer 33:16), *Trees of Righteousness (Is 61:3), Hephzibah and Beulah (Is 62:2, 4; cf. Is 62:12), Restorer (Is 58:12), Priests and Ministers (Is 61:6), The Lord Is There (Ezek 48:35; cf. Is 60:14, 18), City of Truth (Zech 8:3), My People, and Pitied (Hos 2:1—reversing the pessimism of Hos 1:6, 9; cf. Hos 1:10; 2:23; Rom 9:25-26; 1 Pet 2:9-10). In the Apocalypse renaming is for individuals—a new, secret name written on a white stone (Rev 2:17).

Divine Names. Three kinds of expressions are used to refer to *God: the personal name Yahweh; nouns with the generic meaning "god"—Hebrew 'ēl and its longer forms and Greek theos, often with a definite article—which in Israelite monotheism were sufficient identification for the one true God; and various terms pointing to particular attributes or roles. Compound names like El Shaddai and Yahweh Sabaoth combine the third type with the first or second. A wealth of imagery attaches to these names and the interplay among them.

The name Yahweh (appearing in texts as only the four consonants, yhwh, the Tetragrammaton) and its short form Yah occur over 6,800 times in the OT—more than any other word. The short form is common in the liturgical formula of praise, halᵉlû-yāh. The verb hāyâ, "I am" (Ex 3:14), apparently cognate, has in special cases (e.g., Deut 31:23; 32:39; Is 48:12; Hos 1:9) the force of the Name itself. "Yahweh" is God's self-revelation (Ex 3:15; 6:3), yet the debates over its meaning—ideas of absolute being, numinousness, creation and benevolent presence are all suggested—hint that God is revealed as One who cannot be fully comprehended in a word. The Name is all of God that Moses can experience (Ex 33:18-20). In both theophanies the context indicates that God's actions are as revelatory as the cryptic Name. Jacob's divine antagonist is recognized despite withholding the Name (Gen 32:29-30; cf. Judg 13:18), and it is by acts of judgment or mercy that people "know that I am Yahweh," in Ezekiel's oft-repeated phrase (e.g., Ezek 6:13; 37:13 JB).

In other cultures *ʾēl* is the name of a particular god, but in the OT the word rarely occurs as a name except in compounds. Its commonest form in Scripture is *ʾelōhîm*—not in the strictest sense a name. Occasionally in Scripture this and *theos* refer to pagan gods and exalted mortals (e.g., Ex 7:1; Judg 11:24; Jn 10:35; Acts 7:40; 1 Cor 8:5).

The attributive names are best grouped according to meaning. Lord and King explicitly indicate authority; *baʿal*, "master," fell into disuse because heathen gods were so named (compare, e.g., 1 Chron 8:33 with 2 Sam 2:10; Hos 2:17). Also suggesting supremacy are Highest (Gen 14:18-22; Num 24:16; Lk 1:35; 6:35); Sabaoth (*ṣ̌ebāʾôt*), "of hosts [armies]" (always compounded with Yahweh, and never found before the monarchic period); and Shaddai (*šadday;* Gen 17:1); the latter two are transliterations from Hebrew. From the LXX on, Shaddai in the OT has traditionally been rendered as "Almighty" (in the NT, cf. Rev. 4:8; 19:6). Distinct from this are the Mighty One (Is 1:24; 60:16) and the Power (Mt 26:64), where a common noun is absolutized as a name.

Other names use metaphors of relationship. One group is the familial: *Father (Jer 3:4, 19; Mt 5:45; cf. Aramaic *abba*, Rom 8:15), *Husband (Is 54:5; Hos 2:16) and Redeemer (Is 63:16). Closely related to these is the designation "God of [ancestors]," as in Genesis 31:5, Exodus 3:6 and Psalm 46:7, 11. Other names indicating relationship—sometimes used in parallel with the above—are *Rock (Deut 32:15; Ps 19:14 JB), *Shepherd (Gen 49:24), Savior (Is 43:3; 49:26; Lk 1:47) and Maker (Is 43:15; 45:9).

Yet another group consists of names that highlight particular attributes: God as seeing (Gen 16:13), living (1 Sam 17:26; 1 Tim 4:10), eternal (Gen 21:33; cf. Is 44:6; Rev 1:8, Alpha and Omega; Dan 7:9, Ancient of Days), true and faithful (Is 65:16, cf. Rev 19:11), awesome (Gen 31:42) and unapproachably holy (Is 57:15; Hos 11:9; cf. Is 6:3). Some expressions that remain adjectival in Scripture are in rabbinic or Christian tradition treated as names (cf. Ex 34:6, 14; Ps 7:9; 103:8). A common literary device (e.g., Num 24:16; Ps 91:1-2; Is 44:6; 49:26; Rev 1:8; cf. 1 Tim 1:17) is the cumulation of several names; and some appear among the messianic names in Isaiah 9:6.

In a special category because of its trinitarian reference is the name *(Holy) Spirit (Mt 28:19; Mk 1:8, 10; Jn 7:39; cf. Jn 4:24; Joel 2:28), with related designations (Jn 14:26: paraclete; and 15:26: Spirit of truth). Finally, some interpret the personification of *Wisdom (e.g., Prov 8) as a divine name.

In the NT the name *Jesus, meaning "Yahweh saves" (cf. Mt 1:21), is an ordinary name commemorating one of Israel's heroes, Joshua, but also approximates one of the divine titles—a connection made explicit when Jesus is called Savior (e.g., Lk 2:11; Jn 4:42; Tit 3:6 [cf. Tit 3:4]). Other divine names appropriated by or for him refer to particular roles (*Redeemer, *King, *Shepherd, *Bridegroom) or to a clearer identity with Godhead (Tit 2:13). To "confess that Jesus Christ is Lord" (Phil 2:11; cf. Mt 22:43; Rom 10:9; 1 Cor 12:3) is to accord him the "name . . . above every name" (Phil 2:9)—Yahweh—answering to his own claim "I am" (Jn 8:24, 28, 58; 18:6). The divine titles Living One (Rev 1:18 NEB) and Alpha and Omega (Rev 22:13; cf. Heb 13:8) have become his. So have the title Son of God (Mt 14:33; Lk 1:35; Jn 5:20, 25; Rom 1:4; Heb 1:2, 5)—but with a new meaning (cf. 2 Sam 7:14; Job 1:6; Dan 3:25, 28)—and more abstract titles like Holy One, Power, Wisdom, Righteousness, Amen (Acts 3:14; 1 Cor 1:24, 30; Rev 3:14).

Emerging in the NT as a name is the Word (*logos:* Jn 1:1; Rev 19:12-13). Also appropriated to Jesus are names from OT prophecy—the Anointed (*māšîah, christos),* Son of Man, Son of David, Dawn (Lk 1:78 NRSV [LXX rendering of Branch, Jer 23:5; Zech 3:8]), Emmanuel (Mt 1:23 from Is 7:14; cf. Ps 46:11), Servant (Mt 12:18)—and from OT typology: *Lamb, *Passover (1 Cor 5:7), *Adam (1 Cor 15:45; cf. Rom 5:14), *Rock (1 Cor 10:4), *Lion and *Root (Rev 5:5). Underlying much of this naming is the suggestion of uncovering previously unperceived meanings.

Idioms and Figurative Expressions. *Name* can stand by metonymy for the person bearing the name (Num 1:2; Acts 1:15; 4:10; Rev 3:4) and vice versa (Ex 32:33; Dan 12:1). God's "glorious" name (1 Chron 29:13; Ps 72:19) is to be blessed, praised, exalted, magnified, glorified, rejoiced and exulted in, thanked, hallowed, feared, loved, remembered, proclaimed, declared, waited on, walked in, desired and sought. For many of these verbs—those denoting verbal acts that necessarily include the name—*God* is virtually the object. The common expression "call on [God's] name" means literally to call on God by name. The name is, from the human point of view, the means by which God is approached and known, to the degree that God *is* known. It is also the means by which inner devotion receives outward expression (cf. 2 Tim 2:19, "names the name"), thus combining spiritual and material realms.

Name sometimes means reputation, bad (Deut 22:14; Lk 6:22) or good (Prov 22:1; Rev 3:1), sometimes fame and *honor (e.g., Deut 26:19;

2 Sam 8:13; 2 Chron 26:15; Zeph 3:20; Mk 6:14), even rank (2 Sam 23:18, 22; Heb 1:4). God gives Abraham and David "great" names (Gen 12:2; 2 Sam 7:9; cf. 1 Kings 1:47 [Solomon]). Greatest of all is God's name, in Israel (Ps 76:1) and worldwide (Deut 28:10; 1 Kings 8:42-43; Ps 8:1; 48:10; 148:13; Is 60:9; Mal 1:11), inspiring respect and even worship (1 Kings 8:41-42; but cf. Josh 9:9).

What Yahweh's fame rests on is faithfulness in keeping covenant (Ps 138:2) and power demonstrated on behalf of the nation (2 Sam 7:23; Neh 9:10; Jer 16:21; cf. Josh 7:9; Is 59:19; 64:2) and the downtrodden (Ps 74:21). The idea of acting "for thy [my, his] name's sake" often, along with the concept of maintaining personal integrity, means acting to uphold this reputation, whether by guiding (Ps 23:3; 31:3), pardoning (Ps 25:11; 79:9), sparing (1 Sam 12:22; Is 48:9; Jer 14:7, 21; Ezek 20:44) or delivering (Ps 106:8; 109:21; 143:11). Once Israel's behavior and consequent exile have undermined that reputation, Yahweh will act "for the sake of my holy name, which you have profaned among the nations" (Ezek 36:22 JB; cf. Ezek 36:19-24; also Ps 74:10, 18; Is 52:5-6; Ezek 20:9, 14, 22; 39:7, 25; Rom 2:24; 1 Tim 6:1).

Profaning the Name is more, however, than just besmirching Yahweh's reputation. The Name itself is a sacred object, to be revered (Deut 28:58; Ps 111:9; Mal 2:5; cf. Mt 6:9, "hallowed"). Its legitimate use in vows (Deut 6:13; 1 Sam 20:42; 1 Kings 2:24; Is 65:16; Jer 12:16; cf. Jer 44:26; Heb 6:16) implies such reverence. Concerning the abuse of God's name, however, Hebrew has words ranging semantically from emptiness (*šāw* "in vain") through deceit (*šeqer:* Lev 19:12; Zech 5:4) and uncleanness (*tāmē*, "defile," Ezek 43:7-8; *ḥālal*, "pollute," e.g., Lev 19:12; Is 48:11) to violent attack (*nāqab* "puncture, blaspheme": Lev 24:11, 16; cf. Acts 26:11; Jas 2:7; Rev 13:6; 16:9). The third and fourth emphasize the result, offense against what is sacred, often indirectly through false worship (Lev 20:3; 22:2; Ezek 20:39; Mal 1:12) or injustice (Jer 34:16; Amos 2:7). The other three emphasize the offender's attitude—frivolous, exploitative or antagonistic—in verbal acts involving the Name. So serious were such offenses that eventually a custom developed of avoiding even inadvertent misuse by not saying "Yahweh"—omitting it (Lev 24:11, 16); or substituting euphemisms like "another place" (Esther 4:14); "Heaven" (Dan 4:23; Mt 21:25; Lk 15:18); in early postbiblical Judaism, "the Presence" (*š^ekînâ);* or, when reading aloud, *Adonai* (hence the LXX Gk *kyrios* for Heb *yhwh* and the translation "LORD" in many English versions).

The phrase "in [someone's] name" can indicate status (Mt 10:41-42; Mk 9:41), impersonation (Mt 24:5), responsibility (Esther 2:22; Eph 5:20) or purpose (Ps 118:26; Mt 18:20). Usually, however, it claims delegated authority. Apart from acts of ministry (Deut 18:5; Mt 18:5; cf. Heb 6:10) and battle (1 Sam 17:45; 2 Chron 14:11; Ps 20:5, 7; 118:10-12; cf. Ps 44:5) and generally serving as a person's rep-

resentative (Jn 5:43; Rom 1:5; Col 3:17), the phrase is mostly associated with speech acts: formal communications from a king or leader (1 Sam 25:5; 1 Kings 21:8; Esther 3:12; 8:8) and, in God's or Jesus' name, blessing and cursing (Deut 10:8; 2 Sam 6:18; 2 Kings 2:24; Ps 129:8; cf. Is 66:5, where the claim to authority is spurious), judging (1 Cor 5:4 NRSV), proclaiming (Lk 24:47), speaking and prophesying (Ex 5:23; 1 Kings 22:16; 1 Chron 21:19; Ezra 5:1; Jer 20:9; Dan 9:6; Acts 5:28; 9:29; Jas 5:10)—sometimes falsely (Deut 18:20; Jer 27:15; 29:9)—appealing (1 Cor 1:10 [*dià*]) and commanding (2 Thess 3:6). The authority behind the command is what expels *demons (Mk 16:17; Lk 10:17; Acts 16:18), perhaps even when the name is falsely used (Mt 7:22-23) and thus profaned, but the experience of the seven sons of Sceva argues against viewing the name itself as having magic power at the user's disposal (Acts 19:13-16).

Indeed, to "know" God's name means to be in harmonious relationship with God's character and purposes (cf. Ps 91:14, where the parallel is "love me" [NRSV]), not to possess a tool of power. In the performance of miracles generally (Mk 9:39; Jn 10:25; Acts 3:6; 4:30; Jas 5:14) and in prayer (Jn 14—16), "in [Jesus'] name" is more invocation than command and involves faith (Acts 3:16). Forgiveness also is "through his name" (Acts 10:43; 1 Jn 2:12), along with life and salvation (Jn 20:31; 1 Cor 6:11; Acts 4:12), though here—as also in Acts 4:10—*name* seems a simple metonymy for Jesus himself. Similarly, following *believe* the phrases "in his name" and "in him" seem interchangeable (e.g., Jn 3:18).

Another speech act using the divine names is that involved in *baptism (Mt 28:19; Acts 2:38; 8:16; 10:48; 19:5). The imagery here is complex. It includes, besides authority, the ideas of a new identity, of a dependent relationship and of another's name as a protective covering. The latter is evident in Isaiah 4:1 in a social setting and throughout the OT in three major figures of divine-human relationship. The first is the Name, given concrete syllabic form, as both a sign and a guarantee of Yahweh's fixed character of faithfulness. "The name of Yahweh is a strong tower" (Prov 18:10), to defend, save, help, protect (Ps 20:1; 54:1; 124:8; Jn 17:11-12 NRSV); it is worthy of trust (Ps 33:21; Is 50:10; Zeph 3:12; Mt 12:21). The second is expressed in phrases like "to put his name there" (Deut 12:21), and its core meaning is divine presence. During the wanderings it refers to the guiding angel (Ex 23:21; cf. Ex 33:14) and the tabernacle (Deut 12:5; cf. Ex 20:24). Later it refers to the ark of the covenant (1 Chron 13:6) and, preeminently, the temple (e.g., 1 Kings 9:3; Ps 74:7) and Jerusalem (e.g., Is 18:7; Jer 25:29). The third applies the same imagery to God's people: Israel (Num 6:27; 2 Chron 7:14; Is 43:7; Jer 14:9; cf. Jer 15:16); prophetically, the nations (Amos 9:12; cf. Is 56:6; Zeph 2:9; Zech 14:9; Eph 3:15); and, finally, those named for Christ (Acts 11:26).

In John's apocalyptic vision all people will finally

be marked with God's name (Rev 3:12; 14:1; 22:4) or its opposite (Rev 13:17). To bear Christ's name, then, is to share his authority, protection and identity; this entails responsibility (2 Tim 2:19; 3 Jn 7; Rev 2:3) and risk (Mt 19:29), even of dishonor (Acts 5:41; 1 Pet 4:14; cf. Mt 5:11) and persecution (Mt 24:9; Lk 21:12, 17; Jn 15:21; Acts 9:16; 21:13), and introduces a quite different meaning for the phrase "for my name's sake." To acknowledge Christ's name, not deny it (Rev 2:13; 3:8), guarantees the preservation of one's own name (Rev 3:5; cf. Lk 12:8-9).

See also CHRIST; GOD.

BIBLIOGRAPHY. J. Barr, "The Symbolism of Names in the Old Testament," *BJRL* 52 (1969) 11-29; W. Eich-rodt, *Theology of the Old Testament* (2 vols.; London: SCM Press, 1961-1967); F. Hahn, *The Titles of Jesus in Christology* (London: Lutterworth, 1969); T. N. D. Mettinger, *In Search of God* (Philadelphia: Fortress, 1988); K. H. Miskotte, *When the Gods Are Silent* (London: Collins, 1967); J. A. Motyer, *The Revelation of the Divine Name* (London: Tyndale, 1959); O. Odelain and R. Séguineau, *Dictionary of Proper Names and Places in the Bible* (Garden City, NY: Doubleday, 1981); Y. T. Radday, "Humour in Names" in *On Humour and the Comic in the Hebrew Bible,* ed. Y. T. Radday and A. Brenner (Sheffield: Almond, 1990) 59-97; V. Taylor, *The Names of Jesus* (London: Macmillan, 1953); J.-J. von Allmen, ed., *Vocabulary of the Bible* (London: Lutterworth, 1958).

NARROW, NARROWNESS

Like its antithesis, *wide, narrow is an ambivalent image in the Bible. In conventional thinking narrow is negative and wide is positive, and the Bible partly agrees with this assessment. Joshua invites the tribe of Joseph to expand its allotted boundary because it is a numerous tribe that has received a hill country "too narrow" for it (Josh 17:15 NRSV). Isaiah offers as an image of discomfort a bed too short to stretch oneself on and its "covering too narrow to wrap oneself in it" (Is 28:20 NRSV).

But Jesus reverses the image in his famous aphorism that commands his followers to "enter through the narrow gate," contrasting it to the wide road that leads to destruction (Mt 7:13-14; Lk 13:24). Here narrowness is a double reference: it implies the comparative difficulty with which one lives a godly life of discipline and submission to God, and it denotes the relatively small number to whom such a life appeals compared to the easy life of self-indulgence.

See also DEEP; HIGH, HEIGHT, HIGH PLACE; LOW; WIDE.

NATIONS. See GENTILE; HEATHEN.

NATIVITY OF CHRIST

"Immanuel . . . God with us" (Mt 1:23 NIV) is the motif that permeates the accounts of Christ's nativity: *God becomes a common man; the transcendent

becomes immanent. The most beautiful story ever told is highlighted by the wonder of the incarnation, the union of the divine and the human. The exalted and the humble are juxtaposed in the nativity. *Angels in all their *glory greet common people—*shepherds, a carpenter and his fiancée—in the midst of their daily activities.

Common people take part in the nativity— *Mary, Joseph, the shepherds, Simeon and Anna. Three of the six dreams recorded in *Matthew's Gospel are given to Joseph, a humble carpenter. In *Luke's account, Mary meets Gabriel. After her initial surprise and questions about the miraculous conception and her lowly status, Mary humbly submits to her role, acknowledging herself as a *servant of the Lord (Lk 1:38). Also humble are the shepherds who are chosen to hear the first announcement of the *birth of the Messiah and are the first to proclaim his birth to their countrymen (Lk 2:8-20). Even *Bethlehem is lowly, the least significant of Judean towns; yet it is chosen as the birthplace of the Messiah, as prophesied by the *prophet to the common folk of rural Judah, Isaiah's contemporary Micah (Mic 5:2).

At the same time, the nativity juxtaposes the exalted to the humble. Mary sings an exalted hymn of praise, the Magnificat, focusing on God's humbling the powerful and raising the *weak by choosing her as the vessel to bear the Christ (Lk 1:46-55). In this respect Mary's song echoes Hannah's song (1 Sam 2:1-10); Hannah also thanked God for a son and spoke of the lowly being raised. The only *Gentiles in the nativity story are the wealthy Magi from the *east (Mt 2:1-12). They travel a great distance at their own expense and at great peril to give their gifts to the *King. A *star unlike any other guides them, pausing at *Jerusalem to wait for them and then leading them to Bethlehem. A *virgin conceives, a star guides, and angels appear to the principals in the story—all events that unite the divine and the human (*see* Encounter, Divine-Human). The nativity occurs in a context of miracles and *dreams revealed to everyday people.

Within this context of the divine-human cooperation at Christ's unique nativity are type scenes and sequences of action that remind the reader of other scriptural events. The pastoral scene of shepherds receiving the proclamation from the angels that the Messiah is born is similar in some respects to God's calling *David from tending his *sheep to rule over Israel (2 Sam 7:8). The shepherd is found worthy of God's trust. At the other extreme is the scene at the palace when Herod realizes that the Magi have not returned to bring him word of Messiah's location; he orders all boys "two years old and under" (Mt 2:16 NIV) to be killed. *Jeremiah's prophecy (Jer 31:15) links the Hebrew sorrow of this event with the parallel scene in *Moses' life when *Pharaoh ordered all newborn boys thrown "into the river" (Ex 1:22). In *Egypt and in Jerusalem, the wicked king is thwarted. Unique to the nativity account, however, is the scene in the stable (or cave, as some scholars have it). No other biblical story parallels the remarkable birth of the "Wonderful Counselor, Mighty God, Everlasting Father, Prince of Peace" (Is 9:6 NIV) in such humble circumstances. This is a unique story, and the child at the center of the events surrounding his nativity has no parallel in Scripture.

When we turn to the archetypes of the nativity, archetypal imagery of *light and *darkness predominates. Isaiah prophesies that "the people walking in darkness have seen a great light" (Is 9:2 NIV); without the Messiah, God's chosen people live without *hope, unable to see spiritually. Even more elemental than Isaiah's prophecy to the chosen people is the light and dark imagery in John's encomium to the *logos* who came for all people. John writes that the *logos* (Christ)—the Creator—was the "life" and the "light" (Jn 1:4) of all people. Of course not all people acknowledge that they are in darkness and that Jesus is the light (Jn 1:5). John associates the light of the *logos* with the light of Christ at the nativity, for he writes of the incarnation in "the Word became flesh and lived for a while among us," so that "we have seen his glory" (Jn 1:14 NIV). The Evangelist also associates John the Baptist with light imagery, writing that John was a witness to "that light" (Jn 1:7), Christ, who came into the world to give "light to every man" (Jn 1:9 NIV). Light is one of the key motifs of the stairstep parallelism in John's picture of the *logos*—Word, life, light.

In Luke's Gospel too we have reference to light and dark imagery. The angels who appear to the shepherds shine the "glory of the Lord" (Lk 2:9) around—an experience no less intense than the *shekinah* *glory that visited the Israelites of old. In his hymn of wonder, the Te Deum, Zechariah speaks of the Messiah as "the rising sun" who shines on "those living in darkness and in the shadow of death" (Lk 1:78-79 NIV), guiding them to peace. Zechariah echoes Isaiah's prophecy and explicitly links Isaiah's light with the Christ child. Extending Christ's salvific work to all people, Simeon sings in the Nunc Dimittis of the Messiah as a "light for revelation to the Gentiles and for glory to [his] people Israel" (Lk 2:32 NIV). God's primal decree is light (Gen 1:3), but from his nativity to his future reign in glory, Christ is the apotheosis of the imagery of light in the Scriptures, as the light imagery at the transfiguration (Mt 17:2) and in John's Apocalypse (Rev 1:12-16; 22:16) attest.

Perhaps we can appreciate the intensity of the nativity more fully when we see the close juxtaposition of the exalted with the humble, light with dark, palace with stable, divine with human throughout the scriptural accounts of Christ's birth. While many motifs in the nativity look backward to the OT and forward to the remainder of the NT, the story has no parallel. Neither does its protagonist.

See also BETHLEHEM; BIRTH STORY; MARY THE MOTHER OF JESUS; VIRGIN.

NATURE

We do not think of the Bible as a "nature book," yet the case for it can surely be made. The world of the Bible, for all the human activity that transpires within it, is a predominantly natural, outdoor world. From start to finish, as Bible readers we move in a world of sky and sea, rain and wind, mountain and field. Except for plot motifs and character types, no subject in this dictionary contains more articles that can be cross-referenced to it. The main biblical archetypes of nature (not counting secondary ones) include *animals, *birds, *cloud, *countryside, *drought, *fish, *flowers, *fruit, *garden, *grain, *grass, *harvest, *moon, *mountain, *pasture, *plain, *plants, *rain, *river, *sea, *sheep, *snow, *stars, *storm, *sun, *tree, *water, *weather, *wheat and *wilderness.

The Artistry and Romance of Nature. Nature is a source of artistic beauty, and the images that biblical writers associate with it often draw on the artist's world. The creation story shows nature to be the product of God's creative activity, much as a painter fills in a canvas with scenery and figures. In the creation story itself, the commendation that various aspects of nature are "good" is an implied comment on their beauty as a focus of artistic contemplation and delight, first for God, then for people. For the psalmist the heavens are the work of God's molding *fingers (Ps 19:3 RSV), and personified Wisdom pictures the mountains has having been "shaped" (Prov 8:25). Other biblical writers use architectural metaphors to describe the artistry of nature: the *earth has *foundations (Job 38:4; Ps 102:25; 104:5; Prov 8:29; Is 48:13) and a *cornerstone (Job 38:6), and the making of it was planned and executed by God, using such builder's tools as measurements, lines, markings and *scales (Job 38:5-6; Prov 8:27-29; Is 40:12).

The function of artistic beauty is to give pleasure, and images of delight are accordingly linked to nature in the Bible. The trees of paradise were "pleasant to the sight" (Gen 2:9 RSV). The matchless green pastures and still waters of Psalm 23:2-3 are supreme examples of the beauty of nature. In Psalm 19 the poet invests the commonplace with wonder as he surrounds the rising of the sun with all the excitement and delight of a *wedding and a *race (Ps 19:5). While the view of nature in Psalm 104 is mainly utilitarian, the poet incorporates pleasure images with references to the singing of the birds (Ps 104:12), "wine to gladden the heart of man" and "oil to make his face shine" (Ps 104:15 RSV). That same psalm claims that God made the sea partly as a playground in which Leviathan might "sport" (Ps 104:26 RSV; NIV "frolic"; *see* Mythical Animals). According to the voice from the whirlwind in Job 38:7, God's creation caused the morning stars to sing together and the sons of God to shout for joy.

The beauty of nature is also part of Jesus' point in his picture of "the lilies of the field," which surpass even the splendor of Solomon's clothing (Mt 6:28-

29). Equally important, Jesus' command to "consider" the lilies of the field is in part a call to aesthetic contemplation of the beauty of nature.

The largest concentration of images of the beauty of nature comes in the *Song of Songs. Love poetry the world over is filled with the beauties of nature, apparently on the premise that our sentiment for nature can be transformed into romantic sentiment. The pastoral world of the Song is a world replete with images of vineyards in bloom, flowers, pastures, springtime burgeoning of vegetation, productive fig trees and lush gardens—all that is naturally delightful, with idealized lovers placed in an ideally flowery and fruitful landscape.

Utilitarian Images. C. S. Lewis describes the Hebrew delight in nature as "both utilitarian and poetic." In the Bible the functional view of nature dominates over the purely aesthetic view. Thus the writers of the OT reveal that they belonged to a nation of farmers: people "approached Nature with a gardener's and a farmer's interest." The clearest example is Psalm 104, where nature is emphatically *good* for something (useful, in other words). The poet is interested in what the various forces of nature contribute to creation's ongoing existence—water for animals, trees for birds, grass for cattle, plants for human beings to cultivate, and so forth.

A similar view is implied in the pastoral story of *Ruth, where the purpose of a harvest is to provide food for the community. The trees of Paradise were not only "pleasant to the sight" but also "good for food" (Gen 2:9 RSV). In an agrarian society in which nearly everyone is dependent on land and nature, the luxury of contemplating nature in a disinterested way is not an option. Except for the royal bower of the Song of Songs, even the gardens in the Bible are not places for strolling but sites of farming—places where people "make gardens and eat their fruit" (Amos 9:14 RSV; cf. Jer 29:5).

Two specific images of nature flow from this. One is a pervasive concern with crops and harvests. The other is a preoccupation with weather rather than landscape (Ps 65:9-13; 104:10-18, where God as cosmic gardener and caretaker waters his creation). Lewis believes that the psalmists give us "the very feel of weather—weather almost as a vegetable might be supposed to enjoy it."

Nature also functions as moral teacher. Jesus commands us to contemplate the lilies of the field, not simply for their implied beauty but to learn a practical lesson about the uselessness of worry over one's physical needs for food and clothing (Mt 6:28-31). The OT wise man commands the sluggard to "go to the ant" to learn a lesson about self-motivated industriousness (Prov 6:6-8).

The Sublime. Nature's beauty has been appreciated within two main traditions through the centuries. The more common of these categories has often been called "the picturesque." The Bible's images of nature tend toward the other tradition, known as "the sublime." The biblical imagination gravitates toward the huge and terrifying images of nature. Thus we find a song of the *thunderstorm (Ps 29) but not of the sunset. The theophanies of God in the Psalms (Ps 18:7-15; 77:16-18; 97:2-5) give us images of a reeling earth, *trembling mountains, thick *darkness, *hailstones, thunder and *lightning. The set piece of sublime nature description in the Bible encompasses twin descriptions of Behemoth (probably a hippopotamus) and Leviathan (a glorified or mythical crocodile) that the voice from the whirlwind uses to silence and humble Job (Job 40:15-41).

Images of nature in the Bible are more often fearful than comforting. Nature in the Bible, for example, is prone to the extremes of drought and flood. When the psalmist needs images of terror in the midst of which believers trust in God, his imagination turns to images of tidal waves and *earthquakes (Ps 46:2-3). There are more references to expansive mountains and sky in the Psalms than to flowers and gardens. The same bias is evident in the catalog of nature with which God challenges Job (Job 38—39).

The sublime in nature readily becomes an image of mystery. Again, the prime example is the questions with which God silences Job. The effect of the questions that God asks in Job 38—39 is to awaken a twofold sense of human limitation—a lack of human knowledge about how the creatures of nature do what they do, and a sense of physical smallness and weakness compared with the mysterious power that many creatures possess. Even the origin of nature is a mystery to the human mind (Job 38:4-7).

Innocence Versus Experience. Some of the image patterns of nature in the Bible fall into complementary contrasts, and one of the these is *innocent nature versus fallen nature. The ideological framework behind this pattern is the premise of existence before the Fall and after it.

The original creation (Gen 1) and the Garden of Eden are the Bible's supreme images of the innocence of nature. Here is nature in its nonviolent and nurturing form, God's provision for the human race (see Adam). Innocent nature reappears in the "golden age" prophecies of a restored people who will experience the replacement of the wilderness with a garden (Is 51:3) and will "plant gardens and eat their produce" (Jer 29:5). Reversing the violence of fallen nature, "the wolf shall dwell with the lamb" and "the cow and the bear shall feed" together (Is 11:6-9 RSV). In the millennium, "instead of the thorn shall come up the cypress; instead of the brier shall come up the myrtle" (Is 55:13 RSV). Nature is thus a master image of innocence and redemption. Even in its fallen state, nature offers a setting for restorative contemplation; the winsome example in the Bible is the picture of Isaac going "out to meditate in the field in the evening," which becomes the occasion for his first meeting with his wife Rebekah (Gen 24:63 RSV).

But nature fell with the human race in the Garden. The most famous images to signal the change in nature's status are the "thorns and thistles" that now curse the ground (Gen 3:18 RSV). Predatory animals are another of the Bible's images of fallen nature: the wilderness through which the Israelites passed was a "great and terrible wilderness" populated by "fiery serpents and scorpions" and characterized by "thirsty ground where there was no water" (Deut 8:15 RSV). In Paul's evocative personification, "the whole creation has been groaning in labor pains" ever since the Fall (Rom 8:22 NRSV).

Part of the fallenness of nature is its tendency to decay. If nature is mighty in the Bible, it is also fragile. The most common archetype that biblical writers use to make the point is "the grass of the field," which seems always to be on the verge of death in the Bible's pictures of it (e.g., Ps 90:5-6; Mt 6:30). It is in the nature of the earth that it will "change" (Ps 46:2, probably a picture of land erosion), and Paul can speak of the creation being subjected to "subjected to futility" and in "bondage to decay" (Rom 8:20-21).

Another aspect of the fallenness of nature its destructive power. The positive twist on this is that it demonstrates the power and glory of God (Ps 29). But the negative side is that people are vulnerable in the face of nature's fury. A vivid image of this potential is the *flood that sweeps people away (Ps 69:2; 15; 88:17; 124:4). Correspondingly, one of the strong images of God's redemptive activity in people's lives is his rescue of people from floods (Ps 18:16; 69:14; 144:7). The prophetic vision of a time when predators will no longer "hurt or destroy" (Is 11:9) awakens our awareness of how often animals in a fallen world represent terror.

Order Versus Energy. Another complementary dichotomy that the Bible makes much of consists of the related qualities of order, design and control on the one hand and energy, abundance, excess and even chaos on the other. Nature as a mighty order—even a hierarchy of being—is evident in Psalm 148, where the poet marches down the scale of nature from "the heavens" to "the earth" to "all peoples." The notion of control underlies the picture of how God "shut in the sea with doors" and "prescribed bounds for it," saying, "Thus far shall you come, and no farther" (Job 38:8, 10-11 RSV). The daily circuit of the sun in Psalm 19:6 is another memorable image of the regularity and design of nature. The interdependent organism portrayed in Psalm 104:10-18, for all its multifarious splendor, reveals nature's order and control. The daily cycle and the other biblical *"seasons" are based on the predictable natural rhythm of "seedtime and harvest, cold and heat, summer and winter, day and night" (Gen 8:22 RSV).

But on the other side we find a certain superfluous abundance and energy in nature that always threaten to overwhelm the design that is equally a part of nature. The sheer multiplicity of natural activity that God is said to oversee in Job 38—39 creates an image of overflowing natural energy. The teeming waters of the creation account (Gen 1:20-21) are another

example. Nothing stands still in the pictures of nature in the Bible: water flows, vapors ascend, lightning flashes, the sea roars. When God waters the earth, he does so "abundantly" (Ps 65:10; 104:16). God doesn't simply have snow and hail at his disposal—he has "storehouses" of them (Job 38:22). To the biblical imagination, pastures can be so lush that they make "the wilderness drip" (Ps 65:12 RSV), a *grape harvest so abundant that the mountains and hills drip and flow with wine (Amos 9:13), and a harvest so lavish that harvesters get in the way of people who want to plant the next year's crop (Amos 9:13).

Mythical Images of Nature. The primal imagination tends to portray nature in mythical form, with the qualities of a personified deity. The Bible borders on such images, though they result from poetic license rather than literal belief. Nature speaks with the *"voice" of God in Psalm 19:1-4. God is poetically rendered as a storm God (Ps 18:7-15; 29; 77:16-18). Psalm 139:15, describing the mysterious growth of a fetus in a mother's womb, draws on the myth of surrounding cultures that all living things were generated in the center of the earth. In Psalm 104 nature's service to God is portrayed figuratively as God's covering himself with light, using the clouds as his *chariot and the winds as his messengers (Ps 104:2-4); the effect is to infuse nature itself with a sense of divine life and purpose. Later in Psalm 104 the marvelous picture of God's provision for all of nature by means of nature has the effect of making nature a single, all-embracing organism—a kind of mythical being.

Elsewhere, the personification of nature produces similar effects. The hills and valleys "clothe themselves with crops," and "they shout and sing together for joy" (Ps 65:12-13 RSV). The "floods clap their hands," and the "hills sing for joy together" (Ps 98:8 RSV). In the coming millennium the mountains and hills "shall break forth into singing, and all the trees of the field shall clap their hands" (Is 55:12 RSV; see Music).

Nature as God's Agent. The Bible's images of nature show a strongly theocentric bias. We rarely lose sight of the fact that nature is God's work, both in its origin and in its sustenance. The psalms of praise, for example, are variations on the creation story (Gen 1), emphasizing that God made the world. While the nineteenth-century Romantic tradition of nature was indifferent to how nature got here, accounting for the origin of nature is a virtual obsession with the writers of the Bible. A praise psalm seems almost incomplete if it lacks mention of the fact that "by the word of the LORD the heavens were made" (Ps 33:6 RSV) or that God "made heaven and earth, the sea, and all that is in them" (Ps 146:6 RSV).

The ongoing survival of the creation is likewise a leading arena of God's *providence in the Bible. As Psalm 147 paints a picture of the ongoing activity everywhere in nature, everything is pictured as something that God does. The climactic utterance regarding the individual creatures in Psalm 104 is that "these all look to thee, to give them their food in due season" (Ps 104:27). When God opens his hand, creatures "are filled with good things," and when God hides his face, "they die" (Ps 104:28-29; cf. Ps 145:15-16). The Bible, in short, pictures nature as a thoroughgoing dependent.

An important corollary is that the Bible pictures people as fellow dependents with nature. In the Bible people are part of nature. In the scale of nature that we traverse in Psalm 148, people are right there with the mountains and hills and snow. The formula used in Psalm 36:6 expresses it in a nutshell: "You save humans and animals alike, O LORD" (NRSV). Thus the gusto of biblical poets embraces aspects of nature that are indifferent to people or even actively hostile to them (like storms and lightning).

God's control over the forces of nature is a further image of nature's service to God. The floods "lift up their roaring," but "mightier than the thunders of many waters, mightier than the waves of the sea, the LORD on high is mighty!" (Ps 93:3-4 RSV). In several of his memorable miracles, Jesus calmed the sea of Galilee. In the song of the thunderstorm (Ps 29), a parody of Canaanite poetry based on the myth of Baal, God sits enthroned *over* the flood (Ps 29:10). God rules the raging of the sea (Ps 89:9) and "turns the rock into a pool of water" (Ps 114:8 RSV). God "turns rivers into a desert" and "a fruitful land into a salty waste" (Ps 107:33-34 RSV). In short, the Bible pictures nature as subservient to God.

Nature is also an agent of God's *covenant *blessings and *judgments. We should not overlook the fact that God makes a covenant with nature itself. After the flood, God establishes his covenant not only with Noah but also "with every living creature" (Gen 9:8-17 RSV), and in the coming millennium God will make "a covenant . . . with the beasts of the field, the birds of the air, and the creeping things of the ground" (Hos 2:18 RSV).

Throughout the OT the fecundity of nature is understood to be God's blessing for the people's covenant obedience and drought to be a judgment for disobedience. Moses sets up the ground rules before the nation enters the *Promised Land: if the people keep God's commandments, he "will give the rain for your land in its season" and "grass in your fields for your cattle," whereas if the people disobey, God will "shut up the heavens, so that there be no rain, and the land yield no fruit" (Deut 11:14-15, 17 RSV). One of the most pervasive image patterns in the prophetic oracles of judgment is God's use of natural disaster to punish a wayward people (see Amos 4:6-10 for a succinct picture). Even in narrative passages the withholding of rain can be God's chosen means of judging a nation (1 Kings 17:1) and a downpour of rain the means of military defeat (Judg 5:4, 20-21).

Nature is also pictured as a revelation of God to people. Paul's statement that "ever since the creation of the world his . . . eternal power and deity" have "been clearly perceived in the things that have been made" (Rom 1:20 RSV) sounds the keynote. The most memorable image used to praise nature as a revelation is the psalmist's picture of the heavenly bodies as "speech" uttered by a "voice" and as "words" that go out "through all the earth" and "to the end of the world" (Ps 19:1-4 RSV).

Above all, nature is the agency of God's providence in the world—in the double sense of providing for the needs of creation and guiding the history of nations and individuals. The psalms of praise regularly cite provision through nature as a chief activity of God. Psalm 147:8-9, for example, offers as evidence of God's benevolent provision for his people the fact that he "prepares rain for the earth, he makes grass grow upon the hills. He gives to the beasts their food" (RSV). When a king prays for God's provision on his nation, his request is for full storehouses of grain, as well as sheep and cattle that bear many young (Ps 144:13-14). When Jesus wants an image to picture God's universal provision for the human race, it is an image from nature: God "makes his sun rise on the evil and on the good, and sends rain on the just and on the unjust" (Mt 5:45 RSV).

Summary. Nature is many things in the Bible, and it unleashes the imagination of biblical writers. It is both artistic and useful, both picturesque and sublime. Nature can be both innocent and fallen, both an orderly, controlled design and an overflowing energy and abundance. Nature serves God—in providence, in the sending of blessing and judgment, in revealing God's nature.

See also ANIMALS; BIRDS; CLOUD; COUNTRY, COUNTRYSIDE; CREATION; DRY, DROUGHT; FISH, FISHER; FLOWERS; FRUIT, FRUITFULNESS; GARDEN; GRAIN; GRASS; HARVEST; LAND FLOWING WITH MILK AND HONEY; MOON; MOUNTAIN; MYTHICAL ANIMALS; NATURE PSALMS; PASTURE; PLAIN; PLANTS; RAIN; RIVER; SEA; SHEEP, SHEPHERD; SNOW; STARS; STORM; SUN; TREE, TREES; WATER; WEATHER; WHEAT; WILDERNESS.

BIBLIOGRAPHY. C. S. Lewis, "Nature," in *Reflections on the Psalms* (New York: Harcourt Brace & World, 1958) chap. 8.

NATURE PSALMS

Although nature imagery makes its way into dozens of psalms, the Psalter contains five poems that adhere to the specific genre of the nature psalm: Psalms 8, 19, 29, 104 and 148. These poems come from an agrarian society where everyone lived close to the soil. The nature psalms, accordingly, evince a farmer's utilitarian view of nature (preoccupation with what nature provides), as well as a more universal artistic delight in the beauty of nature. In addition, the nature psalms are firmly rooted in the doctrine that God created nature and is the source of its providence. Because the psalmists view themselves as codependents with all other aspects of creation, their gusto extends not only to features of nature that are indifferent to human concerns but even to natural forces like *hail and *lightning that are hostile to people. Also, although the nature psalmists' doctrine of creation prevents them from equating nature with the divine (in effect emptying nature of deity), they regard nature as filled with signposts and revelations of God.

While the nature psalm, unlike the *lament and the *praise psalm, is far from a fixed form, it is possible to generalize about the motifs and strategies that these poets typically employ in their nature poetry. They paint minute word pictures of nature. They always deflect the ultimate praise from nature to God. The nature psalms seem to have unleashed the imaginative wellsprings of the poets, and the imagery and figurative language are especially rich. A typical effect is that these poems awaken our elemental sense of nature and also our sense of the glory of nature and of the commonplace. The nature poets of the Psalter are especially impressed by the large and terrifying forces of nature, with the result that much of the poetry embodies the spirit of what has traditionally been called the sublime.

See also NATURE; PRAISE PSALMS; PSALMS, BOOK OF.

NEAR, DRAWING NEAR

Recent English translations use the term *near* between 250 and 300 times. In the Bible the quality of being near is variously spatial, temporal and spiritual, and it is predominantly positive in meaning.

As a spatial image, being near to something implies close connection to something within easy reach. Ordinarily this carries the positive connotation of being close to one's destination or to safety. But if the object of nearness is dangerous to well-being, the motif of things "not coming near" becomes a positive image (Is 54:14; Ps 91:7, 10). As the opposite of far, the term *near* figures in a common biblical merism of "far and near," implying that everything between is also covered.

Nearness can also picture temporal proximity—of judgment (Hos 9:7), of salvation (Is 56:1; Rom 13:11), of the kingdom of God (Mk 1:15) or of the second coming (Rev 22:12).

The most evocative uses of the image of nearness are metaphoric and spiritual. Because the covenant with Israel located the presence of God in a particular place, to "draw near" took on a symbolic significance involving not just physical but also spiritual approach. The OT presents a paradoxical picture in this regard: *Israel is invited to draw near to God's presence (Deut 4:11; 15:20; Ps 65:4) but at the same time must keep a distance (Ex 24:2; Num 2:2), so by far the most distinctive use in the OT relates to the *priests and Levites who alone are allowed to "draw near" to God as they perform the sacrifices (Lev 21:17; Num 4:19; 18:4; Ezek 40:46; 45:4; cf. Heb 10:1).

Alongside this restriction, however, we find an awareness that God can "come near" to us, quite apart from the Jerusalem cult (Ps 18:6-9; 69:18; Lam 3:57); and of course, especially in the NT we find the thought that we can "draw near" to God in prayer in any place (Heb 10:22). And in Ephesians there is

a contrast between those who were "once far off," the Gentiles, now drawing near, as was Israel's privilege, "through the blood of Christ" (Eph 2:13 NRSV). In another sense, God is already "near" to all human beings, as Paul points out in Acts 17:27-28. Much of the mystery of the divine-human relationship is captured in the evocative aphorism of James 4:8, "Draw near to God and he will draw near to you" (RSV).

See also FAR.

NECK

In Scripture the neck is sometimes associated with *beauty or *prosperity, although in itself it is usually less prominent than the *jewelry that adorns it (Gen 41:42; Judg 5:30; Prov 1:9). However, in Song of Songs 4:4 and 7:4 the lover praises his beloved's neck itself, rather than the jewelry she wears, making her the focus of his love. In the cultures of the ancient Near East, neck ornaments were worn as a sign of authority, status or beauty by high officials (Gen 41:42; Dan 5:7, 16, 29), by women (Is 3:18; Ezek 16:11) and even by camels (Judg 8:21). The author of the prologue of Proverbs appears to employ this custom as a metaphor for accepting parental instruction as a source of honor and blessing (Prov 1:9; 3:3, 22; 6:21).

Binding something such as love, faithfulness or teaching around the neck depicts keeping it near one's heart and in one's thoughts (Prov 3:3; 6:20-21). The image here is reminiscent of Deuteronomy 6:8: "Tie [God's commandments] as symbols on your hands and bind them on your foreheads" (NIV). One who follows this instruction will be guided by those things bound around one's neck (Prov 6:22).

On the other hand, being bound or seized by the neck depicts capture and subjection to others (Job 30:18; Jer 29:26). The image of a *yoke upon one's neck is often used to depict forced service to one's *enemies (Gen 27:40; Deut 28:48; Jer 27:8). Similarly, Joshua tells his army commanders to "put your feet on the necks of these [defeated] kings" (Josh 10:24 NIV; cf. Gen 49:8), declaring domination over their enemies and making them degraded and humiliated.

*Death can also be associated with the neck. Animals brought to be *sacrificed are killed by breaking the neck (Ex 13:13; 34:20; Lev 5:8; Deut 21:4, 6), and Eli falls backward off his chair and dies by breaking his neck. In addition, Jesus states that if anyone causes "a little one" to sin, "it would be better for him to have a large millstone hung around his neck and to be drowned in the depths of the sea" (Mt 18:6 NIV). Paul's companions "risked their own necks" for his sake (Rom 16:4), proving their love for him even to death.

The outward posture of the neck is often used in the Bible to indicate the inward orientation of one's heart. The metaphor of being "stiff-necked" is used frequently to describe Israel's resistance to God's lordship over the nation (Ex 32:9; 33:5; Neh 9:29; Jer 7:41; Acts 7:51). Isaiah employs the image of "walking along with outstretched necks" to portray the self-centered arrogance and defiant unconcern for injustice of the women of Jerusalem (Is 3:16; cf. Ps 75:5).

Neck is also employed in Scripture as part of the metaphor of a *yoke being placed upon the neck. This metaphor evokes the image of an *ox strapped with a yoke for the purpose of guiding its movement and therefore represents someone being brought under another's control. It is used in Deuteronomy 28:48 to symbolize Israel's cruel subjugation to foreign powers as a punishment for covenantal disobedience (Deut 28:48). The later prophets borrowed the metaphor to describe the domination of the northern and southern kingdoms by the Assyrians and Babylonians respectively (Is 10:27; 14:25; 52:2; Jer 27:2, 8, 11, 12; 28:1-14; Hos 10:11). It passed into later Judaism as a way to describe the Jews' submission to the Mosaic *law. At the Jerusalem council, when Peter mentioned "putting on the necks of the disciples a yoke that neither we nor our fathers have been able to bear" (Acts 15:10 NIV), he was referring to attempts to make Gentile converts submit to the law, even though Israel had been unable to keep it.

See also HEAD; JEWELRY; PRIDE; YOKE.

NEEDLE. *See* EYE OF THE NEEDLE.

NEHEMIAH, BOOK OF

The controlling image of the book of Nehemiah is that of starting over. This new start takes several forms: rebuilding the *walls of *Jerusalem (and defending the building project against hostile surrounding people), renewing the *covenant, reinstituting life in Jerusalem and reinstituting *temple *worship. The excitement of starting life again as God's people in the old homeland is one of the most attractive features of the book. The orderliness of the account is also one of its salient features, evident partly in the writer's penchant for lists of names—of those who worked on the walls, of those who returned from *exile, of those who signed the covenant, of those who lived in Jerusalem, of the priests and Levites, of the two great companies who gave thanks and went in procession at the dedication of the city walls. The book of Nehemiah emerges finally in our imaginations as a master image of order as well as *renewal.

Modern Western readers might be surprised by Nehemiah's strong reaction to Hanani's report that the walls of Jerusalem were in ruins and that its *gates had been destroyed by fire (Neh 1:3). On hearing this news, Nehemiah "mourned for days, fasting and praying" to the Lord (Neh 1:4 NRSV). The strength of this reaction is even more surprising since Hanani's news was old news. After all, the Babylonian king Nebuchadnezzar had destroyed Jerusalem about a century earlier. Nehemiah is not learning about some

new devastation that had recently befallen the city. What evokes Nehemiah's response is not the horror of destruction but something *inert:* the image of walls and gates lying in a state of disrepair. Clearly, Nehemiah reacts to some connotative meaning of Hanani's report, some emotive or associational dimension of the image of a wall in ruins.

Why is Nehemiah's reaction so strong? The first part of Hanani's report provides the clue: the people living back in Judah were "in great trouble and *shame" (Neh 1:3). The ruined condition of the city walls brought "trouble" or "distress" upon the people. More than that, however, it caused them shame. The image of a ruined city, or at least of ruined walls and gates, evoked feelings of humiliation. Nehemiah's charge to the inhabitants of Judah after he returned and inspected the ruined walls and gate confirms that this is the central issue: "Come, let us rebuild the wall of Jerusalem, so that we may no longer suffer disgrace" (Neh 2:17 NRSV).

Undoubtedly, the ruined walls meant that the Jews were defenseless against attack, but this is not the major problem, at least not at the level of the narrative. The crucial issue is shame. Even as the Jews rebuilt the wall, their enemies stood by mocking them (Neh 2:19; 4:1-5 [MT 3:33-37]). This prompted Nehemiah to ask the Lord to "turn their taunt back on their own heads" (4:4 [MT 3:36]). Nehemiah's apparent goal was to rebuild a wall, but that project was the vehicle for a deeper purpose: to transfer the Jews' sense of shame and humiliation on to their enemies. Rebuilding the wall achieves that ultimate goal. When this happened, Nehemiah stated that "all the nations around us were afraid and fell greatly in their own esteem" (Neh 6:15, 16). Although the Hebrew here is difficult, the point seems clear enough: Nehemiah's prayer had been answered, and now the enemies, rather than the Jews, were experiencing shame and loss of standing.

This association between dilapidation and shame begs explanation. In the ancient world, *city building was the pinnacle of a society's success, an activity that defined it as ordered, civilized and cultured. On the other hand, desolate regions without structures or with ruined structures were understood to be chaotic, disordered, uncivilized—even monstrous and ugly. Cities and buildings represented creation, life, order and beauty. Structures in disrepair and decay were associated with chaos and death. To build or rebuild a structure carried powerful emotive associations. It was more than a mere engineering activity; it was a movement from chaos to order, from death to life. This connotation can be seen in Sanballat's mockery of the Jews as they rebuilt the city wall: "Will they *revive* the stones out of the heaps of rubbish?" (Neh 4:2 NRSV). By using the *piel* stem of the verb $h\bar{a}y\hat{a}$ ("to give life, revive"), the rebuilding project is interpreted as a "life-giving" act. Magnificent buildings were the evidence of prosperity and life, dilapidation was a symptom of failure and death. Such successes and failures occurred before the watching eyes of the surrounding nations. Nations that built magnificent structures were held in high esteem by other nations. They were either honored or envied. States whose structures were destroyed or fell into disrepair were held in low esteem by others and so became objects of ridicule.

Although this ideology undergirds the book of Nehemiah, it is found elsewhere in the OT. Song writers acclaimed Jerusalem for the perfection of its beauty (Ps 48:2; 50:2; Ezek 16:14), and its city walls were a source of national pride: "Walk about Zion, go all around it, count its towers, consider well its ramparts; go through its citadels" (Ps 48:12, 13 NRSV). Kings boasted of their great construction projects (Eccles 2:4-6). Conversely, a city in ruins was a matter of national disgrace (Lam 2). When Jerusalem's walls "lay in ruins" and its gates "had sunk into the ground" (Lam 2:8), this gave Judah's enemies the excuse to "hiss and wag their heads," mocking Jerusalem with a cruel parody of the psalmist's words of praise: "Is this the city that was called the perfection of beauty, the joy of all the earth?" (Lam 2:15, 16 NRSV). The book of Nehemiah is the counterpoint to *Lamentations. It is more than a story about a mere reconstruction project. Rebuilt walls and gates are surprisingly evocative images. They speak of deeper realities: the restoration of order and life and the sweeping away of national shame.

See also EZRA, BOOK OF; EXILE; GATE; JERUSALEM; RESTORE, RESTORATION; WALL.

NEIGHBOR

"Love your neighbor as yourself," interpreted as not hurting others and doing good where we can, is a popular Western philosophy. Awareness of the "global village" has extended the idea of neighborliness to caring for deprived people anywhere in the world. That, however, falls short of what the biblical authors intended to convey by the term *neighbor*.

The command to love your neighbor is first enunciated in Leviticus 19:18, where it sums up detailed laws regulating social conduct. It is repeated eight times in the NT and is unique among ancient law codes. It is much more than a commonsense provision for social relationships. While such social niceties as not moving your neighbor's boundary stone (Deut 19:14) are common to many law codes, only the Israelites had both an explicit and implicit obligation to discriminate positively in favor of their neighbors. The stress is on caring for them as for yourself, with mutual trust and respect: "Do not plot harm against a neighbor, who lives trustfully near you" (Prov 3:29 NIV).

So there is a deep sensitivity expressed in the law on taking security for a loan. When the deal is struck, "do not go into [your neighbor's] house to get what he is offering as a pledge" (Deut 24:10). That would be to invade his privacy needlessly and to increase his embarrassment or sense of failure in asking for a loan.

Furthermore, one is to think positively toward the neighbor. "He who despises his neighbor sins" (Prov 14:21 NIV); and as for those who slander neighbors privately, God will put them to *shame (Ps 101:5). Paul gives this NT reinforcement: "Each of us should please his neighbor for his good" (Rom 15:2 NIV), the practical outworking of considering "others better than yourselves" (Phil 2:3).

In OT times the definition of neighbor was limited in practice, though not in principle, to fellow Israelites and "strangers" who willingly chose to live among them. In NT times this restriction was further narrowed: "Love your neighbor and hate your enemy" (Mt 5:43). Neighbor became no more than someone who is liked. But this reduces people to the status of an object that one chooses to love, ignore, despise, hate or perhaps even manipulate.

To counter this, Jesus tells the story of the Good Samaritan in response to a lawyer's question "Who is my neighbor?" (Lk 10:25-37). He reinstates the OT emphasis on positive responsibility, which began with the implied response to Cain's rhetorical question "Am I my brother's keeper?" (Gen 4:9). The neighbor is not a person in need but a person in relationship to another (Lk 10:36)—in other words, me in the mirror—every fellow human made in God's image and looking back at me with identical needs, feelings, hopes, desires and rights.

However much people have tried to avoid the implications, the Biblical writers use the term *neighbor* to convey the Creator's intention that human relations are to be marked by mutually supportive fellowship, not by self-interest punctuated with charitable acts.

See also ENEMY; FAMILY; HOSPITALITY.

NET. *See* FISH, FISHER, FISHING; HUNTING; TRAP.

NEW

The word *new* is a "value term" in the Bible—a word whose evocative splendor exceeds the number of references. The Bible is framed by resounding affirmations about the "new" as it is rooted in the very nature of God. Genesis opens with the account of *creation, in which all things appear newly minted by the divine word. *Revelation presents the story's close, which is also a new beginning. God the Father, in the only statement attributed directly to him in that apocalyptic chorus of many mysterious voices, proclaims, "Behold, I make all things new" (Rev 21:5 RSV). The key to understanding the image of newness in the Bible is an awareness that God is the God of new beginnings, who is continuously "doing a new thing" (Is 43:19 RSV). These new actions occur in five arenas—the original creation, providential history, advent, regeneration and apocalypse.

Genesis, the book of beginnings, opens with the aura of newness everywhere. Nothing else in the Bible quite rivals these opening pages for the sense that things are being done for the first time. The initial phrase, "In the beginning," sets the tone as the divine artist fills in the canvas of creation. In the ensuing pages we are aware as we read that we are dealing with first things—the first human couple, the first human home, the first sin, the first results of sin.

Once the creation is complete, God's new actions occur in the arena of providential history, including the world of *nature. Indeed, it is within biblical religion that history is truly allowed to be a story that goes somewhere. Neither history nor nature on this understanding is cyclical, a pointless eternal recurrence. The writer of Ecclesiastes may insist in one of his "under the sun" passages that there is no new thing (Eccles 1:9), as proved by the endless cycles of the natural elements and the tedious repetitions of human life (Eccles 1:4-11), but Isaiah represents the majority viewpoint when he portrays nature as being a perpetual fountain of new growth: "The rain and the snow come down from heaven, and return not thither but water the earth, making it bring forth and sprout, giving seed to the sower and bread to the eater" (Is 55:10 RSV). *Rain, in other words, does not simply return to its source but produces something new. In the providential view of history that the Bible repeatedly affirms, God's *mercies "are new every morning" (Lam 3:23 RSV), helping to explain the nine references to the "new song" that the life of faith constantly requires as God's providential acts unfold.

The advent that marks the beginning of the "new covenant" is the third locus of biblical references to God's new actions. While it is not always easy to determine whether the "golden age" prophecies of the OT refer to the coming of Christ or the end of the ages, it seems clear that some of them are messianic prophecies built around the motif of God's new action in Christ. In one of Isaiah's servant songs, God is quoted as saying, "Behold, the former things have come to pass, and new things I how declare" (Is 42:9 RSV). Again, "From this time forth I make you hear new things, hidden things which you have not known. They are created now, not long ago" (Is 48:6-7 RSV). This new thing is not simply the displacement of the old; it is something that perfects and completes the old. The traditional term for this is *typology*. The book of Hebrews rings the changes on this theme, declaring Christ to be "the mediator of a new covenant" (Heb 9:15 RSV), whose *atonement confers "a new and living way" of access to God (Heb 10:20 RSV).

The imagery of the "new" is used most often in connection with the regeneration of the individual. Regeneration is for the believer nothing less than a new creation: "If any one is in Christ, he is a new creation; the old has passed away, behold, the new has come" (2 Cor 5:17 RSV). Newness here indicates that a clean break is provided, with the past forgiven and transcended. This *transformation into something new is the essential spiritual reality: "For neither circumcision counts for anything, nor uncircumcision, but a new creation" (Gal 6:15 RSV; cf. Eph 4:24; Col 3:10).

Although it is in the NT that the motif of newness reverberates most intensely, OT prophecy anticipates

it. Ezekiel pictures a time when God will "put a new spirit within them" (Ezek 11:19 RSV), elsewhere quoting God's words, "A new heart I will give you, and a new spirit I will put within you" (Ezek 36:26 RSV). Such regeneration is not only an event of future history; at one point God commands Israel to "get yourselves a new heart and a new spirit" (Ezek 18:31 RSV).

The most comprehensive transformation of the old into the new occurs in the *apocalyptic visions of the Bible. Here the "new" is cosmic, though individuals will also be renewed at the consummation of history. The final and total transformation of all things is captured most vividly in the image of the "new heavens and new earth" that God will create (Is 65:17; 66:22; Rev 21:1). In this transformation believers will receive a new *name (Is 62:2; Rev 2:17). We read similarly of a "new Jerusalem" (Rev 3:12; 21:2). New songs break forth before the heavenly throne (Rev 5:9; 14:3). And if early Genesis is the archetype of new beginnings, the same aura is re-created in the last two chapters of the Bible, whose imagery returns us to the creation story with its motif of new creation and a paradisal *garden.

In summary, the God of the Bible is the God of new beginnings. He is the One who is perpetually "doing a new thing" (Is 43:19) and who makes "all things new" (Rev 21:5). His drama of renewal stretches from creation to apocalypse, with his providential and redemptive history joining the two. God, moreover, always extends an invitation to the human race to join the drama of renewal—to become a new creation and sing a new song. History and eternity are a perpetual waiting for God's new and fuller appearance.

See also APOCALYPTIC VISIONS OF THE FUTURE; CREATION; EARTH; HEAVEN; MUSIC; NATURE; OLD, OLD AGE; RESTORE, RESTORATION; TRANSFORMATION.

NEW COVENANT. *See* COVENANT.

NEW EXODUS. *See* EXODUS, SECOND EXODUS.

NIGHT

If we count both singular and plural references, the Bible contains more than three hundred references to night. Nearly a hundred verses pair *day and night to denote the entire twenty-four-hour period of a day, or perhaps the totality of time over repeated days. Another large category of references equates night with *darkness in contexts where it is the associations of darkness that are the crucial meaning. Beyond these uses, nighttime represents a discernible range of meanings in the Bible.

As the complement of daytime, night is part of a grand order that God created to organize humans and nature. This motif of day and night dividing time between them is prominent in the creation story, as well as in the repeated formula "there was evening and there was morning, the . . . day" (Gen 1: 5-31 NRSV). As created by God, day and night are his (Ps

74:16), but they exist for the benefit of the creation. Psalm 104:19-23 pictures the alternation of day and night as the organizing principle for people and animals, part of the daily rhythm by which we live. Day and night are not opposites in this scheme, like light and darkness; they are instead part of a harmonious cycle.

As an extension of this rhythm, night can become a symbol of cessation from *work, just as daylight is associated with active work. For example, in Jesus' parable the workers in the vineyard are "day laborers" who work by the day and are paid at nightfall (Mt 20:1-16), an association rendered famous in English poetry by John Milton's sonnet on his blindness ("When I consider how my light is spent . . ."). A famous aphorism by Jesus renders the image memorable: "We must work the works of him who sent me while it is day; night is coming when no one can work" (Jn 9:4 NRSV).

In keeping with night as half of a daily cycle that contributes time to human existence, many biblical references to night are simply references to when an event occurred. Some of these events are routine, such as sleeping, extending *hospitality to travelers or engaging in *sexual activity (Gen 19:34-35; 30:16). But equally numerous are references to supernatural activity by night. Revelatory appearances from God to people at night are a biblical archetype (e.g., Jacob, Samuel, Nathan, Solomon, Daniel and Paul). Night is also associated with *dreams that have momentous significance for people (a dozen references). *Angelic visits happen by night (Lk 2:8-14; Acts 5:19; 12:7; 27:23), and Jesus walked on the sea by night (Mt 14:25).

Another cluster makes night the time for spiritual devotions by people. Jesus sometimes spent nights in *prayer (Mt 14:23; Lk 6:12). In the Psalms we read about people who receive instruction by night (Ps 16:7), sing in the night (Ps 42:8), meditate by night (Ps 63:6; 119:148), commune with their heart in the night (Ps 77:6) and remember God's name in the night (Ps 119:55).

Conversely, if night is the time when a person is freed from distracting activity, it can become the occasion for troubling thoughts and emotional turmoil. The *sleepless night is itself a biblical archetype. The psalmist several times pictures night as a time of uncontrollable *weeping (Ps 6:6; 30:5; 42:3; 77:2). Other psalms make night the time of mental aberrations (e.g., the moon that strikes by night in Ps 121:6) and of unidentified *terror (Ps 91:5). Job paints a heart-rending picture of "nights of misery" that are so burdensome that when he lies down he finds that "the night is long, and I am full of tossing until dawn" (Job 7:3-4 NRSV).

From time immemorial, night has been associated with secrecy and danger. Many nighttime events recorded in the Bible have this quality. The hasty departure from Egypt at the time of the exodus was a phantasmagoria of surrealistic hurry and departure. *Jacob wrestled with an angelic opponent by night

in a terrifying struggle. Night is the time of escape for threatened people: the holy family fleeing into Egypt, Peter escaping from prison, Paul escaping from Damascus. The events of Jesus' arrest and trial were clouded by the darkness and furtiveness of night. The undifferentiated "terror of the night" of which the psalmist speaks (Ps 91:5) takes on an eschatological and ultimate intensity in Paul's evocative picture of the *day of the Lord coming "like a *thief in the night" (1 Thess 5:2 NRSV).

A further cluster of images is military. Daybreak was the customary time for attack (Josh 6:15; Ps 46:5); therefore, the secrecy of night made night a time for deployment in preparation for *battle the next day (Josh 8:3; 10:9; Judg 9:34). To attack by night was a daring and risky venture, depending in large part on surprise for its success. This is how Gideon conducted his attack on the Midianites (Judg 7:19-23). It was also by night that the angel of the Lord killed eighty-five thousand Assyrian soldiers (2 Kings 19:35; Is 37:36).

One of the most evocative biblical references to night is in a category by itself. On the night of Judas's betrayal of Jesus, upon receiving the bread of the *Passover from Jesus' hand, the text says, "he immediately went out. And it was night" (Jn 13:30 NRSV). Here literal and spiritual levels of the image combine to produce a wrenching picture of the evil soul abandoning itself to the ultimate deed of darkness.

See also DARKNESS; DAY, DAY OF THE LORD; DREAMS, VISIONS; SLEEP; STARS; TERROR, STORIES OF.

NINEVEH

As befits its origins with Nimrod, "the first on earth to be a mighty man" (Gen 10:8-11), Nineveh became the capital of the mighty empire of Assyria and was renowned as "that great city" (cf. Jon 1:2 NRSV). The context of that evocative epithet is that Assyria was known for its terrorist atrocities in warfare.

There is a pronounced play on this image of "greatness" in the book of *Jonah. The emphasis in the early scenes is on physical size and renown: Nineveh is a fabulous city, a den of iniquity three days' walk across (Jon 1:2; 3:2-3). As the story progresses, however, Nineveh's greatness is seen to lie rather in its people, who evoke God's compassion (Jon 4:11) and who respond with spectacular conversion, "from the greatest to the least" (Jon 3:3, 5). It is this reputation for repentance that endures in the Bible (Mt 12:41).

The books of *Nahum and *Zephaniah also know of Nineveh's greatness, which now, however, speaks of pride before a fall. Nineveh is the object of divine wrath, consumed as easily as fire eats up thorns or dry stubble (Nahum 1:10). Once a woman of substance, like Thebes (Nahum 3:8-10), she now suffers the indignity of *nakedness and *exile (Nahum 3:7), her seductive powers as *prostitute now reaping the whirlwind of *shame and disgrace that accompany exposure (Nahum 3:4-7). Once a *den of *lions, a safe haven where prey could be enjoyed by all who lived there, she has now attracted the attention of the divine *hunter who cannot be resisted (Nahum 2:11-13), and she has become a ruin inhabited by other, less terrifying wild beasts (Zeph 2:14-15). Once given security, like Thebes, by the water that lies in the vicinity, Nineveh is now both submerged under the floods of *judgment (Nahum 2:6) and yet also a pool with broken *walls that cannot contain escaping water (refugees escaping the onslaught, Nahum 2:8). Her *fortresses are like *fig trees whose *fruit is ripe; but ripeness is an image not of abundant blessing but of imminent judgment akin to the coming of the *locust (Nahum 3:12, 15), which makes the city not a site of fertility but a place of desolation, a dry waste like a desert (Zeph 2:13). Her people are themselves as numerous as a swarm of locusts; but now, experiencing divine wrath rather than divine compassion, they are ephemeral, vanishing suddenly when warmed by the sun (Nahum 3:15-17). They are like a *flock with no *shepherds to lead or to protect them (3:18). The imagery is similar in many respects to that which we find in respect to other fallen cities in the Bible (e.g., Babylon, Is 47; Jerusalem, Lam 1—5).

Jesus himself refers to the repentance of the Ninevites in Matthew 12:38-42 (par. Lk 11:29-32). The Ninevites repented when Jonah preached to them of a coming judgment, whereas his own generation ignored his warnings.

See also CITY; JONAH, BOOK OF; JONAH THE PROPHET; NAHUM; ZEPHANIAH, BOOK OF.

NO ABIDING PLACE. *See* PLACE, NO ABIDING.

NOAH'S FLOOD. *See* FLOOD.

NOON

Noon marks the height of the *day, when the *sun is at its highest point in the sky. At noon, *morning turns to afternoon; a time of beginnings changes to endings as the sun descends to the horizon. Since at noon the sun is at its most prominent point of the day, its *light is at its strongest. It is in association with the more pervasive image of light that noon finds its value as an image.

It is not the case that every reference to noontime has symbolic overtones. "Noon" often simply marks a time or defines the latter boundary of the morning, as when the Baal prophets are said to call on their *god from morning until noon (1 Kings 18:26). It also marks the approximate time of the midday *meal, as in Genesis 43:16, where *Joseph is said to eat with his brothers. In this sense it can mark a welcome respite from the demands of the day.

Its use as an image occurs in both positive and negative contexts. In Psalm 37:6, for instance, the psalmist urges his listeners to commit their life to God; for if they do, then he will "make your right-

eousness shine like the dawn, the justice of your cause like the noonday sun" (NIV). That is, as the noonday sun's light illumines the earth, so the godly person's virtues will be clear and obvious to all.

While *darkness is associated with evil, God and his people are bathed in the clear light of day. Thus, according to Isaiah, if the Israelites turn from oppression to justice, then "your light will rise in the darkness, and your night will become like the noonday" (Is 58:10 NIV).

Therefore, when Israel follows God, they live in the light of the noonday sun, but when they turn away from God, light becomes darkness. Eliphaz utilizes this image when he disputes Job. According to Eliphaz, God catches the crafty so that "darkness comes upon them in the daytime; at noon they grope as in the night" (Job 5:14 NIV). The prophet Amos speaks of a coming day of judgment when God will "make the sun go down at noon and darken the earth in broad daylight" (Amos 8:9 NIV).

See also DARKNESS; LIGHT; MIDNIGHT; MORNING; NIGHT; SUN.

NORTH

In Mediterranean latitudes the northern circumpolar *stars never set but remain forever in the sky, unlike those stars that rise nightly only to set in the *west. These far northern stars, picturesquely designated "the imperishable stars" in ancient Egyptian because they never set, became a picture of immortality and eternity in the ancient Near East.

It is therefore appropriate for the north to be the biblical locus for the eternal God's sacred *mountain, which goes by more than one name (Mt. Zaphon, "north;" Mt. *Zion). It is a celestial locale, not to be confused with any earthly place, for God "stretches out the north over empty space" (Job 26:7 NASB). From here God administers the cosmos, summoning the starry hosts "to heaven . . . above the stars of God . . . on the mount of assembly in the recesses of the north" (Is 14:13 NASB). The physical location of *Jerusalem, where God's terrestrial house was built by Solomon, was irrelevant to its metaphysical significance as a counterpart to the northern celestial abode: "His holy mountain, beautiful in elevation, the joy of the whole earth, Mt. Zion in the far north, the city of the great King" (Ps 48:1-2 NASB).

Although God's *glory therefore naturally emanates from the north (Job 37:22), he may also vent his anger from this direction if he is dissatisfied with humanity's behavior. It is from the north that the turbulent whirlwind comes, revealing God and his message of doom to Ezekiel (Ezek 1:4), an image undergirded by Levantine meteorological conditions where the north wind brings *rain and cold (Prov 25:23; Job 37:9; *see* Weather). "Destruction from the north" becomes a leitmotif of the prophets, particularly Jeremiah (Jer 1:13-15; 4:6; 6:1; 10:22; 25:9), underscoring that invading armies are God's disciplinary tools. This image is reinforced by the geographical reality that invaders (apart from Egypt to the south) typically came from the north, Israel being in a corridor hemmed in by the sea on the west and the desert to the east. But the metaphysical dimension emphasizing God's dwelling in the north must be seen as primary, since the leitmotif is applied to Gentile nations, often where the geographical reality does not apply (Jer 14:31; 46:20, 24; 47:2; 50:3, 9, 41-43; 51:48; Ezek 26:7).

The divinely orchestrated destruction from the north that comes upon a wicked humanity spins off an independent motif of the northern destroyer who goes too far, compelling God to "remove the northern army far from you" (Joel 2:20). Although God may use the forces of the north to discipline, these forces exhibit a self-destructive hubris that requires that they often be destroyed in turn: God will "stretch out His hand against the north / And destroy Assyria" (Zeph 2:12 NASB; cf. Ezek 39:2-4; Is 10:5-16). The motif attains its most evocative significance in the *apocalyptic figures of Gog, who comes from the north (Ezek 38:6, 15; 39:2), and the despicable king of the north in Daniel 11:21-45. The wise will leave northern climes before the area is judged (Zech 2:6).

The ominous imagery associated with the north may be a reflex of the ancient orientation assumed in the Bible where one faces east, and north is consequently to one's *left (Gen 14:15; Josh 19:27; Ezek 16:46). Throughout Semitic and Mediterranean cultures, the left side is the direction that characteristically portends catastrophe and calamity.

See also EAST; LEFT, LEFT-HANDED; SOUTH; WEST; ZION.

NOSE, NOSTRILS

Most often when the nose is referred to, it is not the focus of biblical imagery; instead a *ring or hook is the operative feature. For instance, a nose ring is a piece of adornment (Gen 24:22; Is 3:21; Ezek 16:12; *see* Jewelry). However, biblical imagery of a hook in the nose symbolizes mastery or forced leading. Prophets have used this image to warn nations of God's wrath and of their coming doom (2 Kings 19:28; 2 Chron 33:11). In Job 40:24—41:2, God asks if Job is able to trap and tame the Behemoth or Leviathan (*see* Mythical Animals) by piercing their noses.

The nose itself is the focus in four passages. Psalm 115:6 states that *idols have noses but cannot *smell, meaning they have no life or power as God does. Proverbs 30:33 uses the image to show that stirring up anger produces strife. Ezekiel 8:17 states that the Israelites are "putting the branch to their nose," which has an uncertain meaning but may connote that in seeking to injure others, they only injure themselves. In Ezekiel 23:25 God tells Israel that her enemies will come and cut off their noses and *ears, mutilating the prisoners.

Nostrils, a related image, has four uses in Scripture. Life is associated with nostrils: "The LORD God . . . breathed into [Adam's] nostrils the breath of life,

and man became a living being" (Gen 2:7 NIV; see also Gen 7:22; Job 27:3; Is 2:22). Every living thing has the breath of life in its nostrils, but only man has the breath of God in his nostrils.

The power of God is displayed with blasts from his nostrils as he parts the Red Sea and delivers David from his enemies (Ex 15:8; 2 Sam 22:16; Ps 18:5; *see* Divine Warrior); and fierceness/wrath is shown as smoke rises from both God's and Leviathan's nostrils (2 Sam 22:9; Ps 18:8; Job 41:20).

Repulsion and despising are symbolized by nostrils as well (*see* Disgust, Revulsion). In Numbers 11:20 Israel will get sick of the meat God gives them—it will "come out of your nostrils" (NIV; see also 2 Sam 10:6; 16:21; 1 Chron 19:6).

See also BREATH; SMELL, SCENT.

NOSTRILS. *See* NOSE, NOSTRILS.

NUDITY. *See* NAKED, NAKEDNESS.

NUMBERS, BOOK OF

The book of Numbers derives its name from the census lists of the number of people in each of the *twelve tribes of *Israel in Numbers 1 and 26. The Hebrew title for the book, "In the Wilderness," comes from the first verse of the book and accurately describes its setting. Numbers is the story of the people of Israel in the *wilderness as they *travel from the slavery of *Egypt toward the freedom of Canaan under the leadership of *Moses.

The book of Numbers involves an important generational transition in the story of early Israel's journey as the people of God. The transition from the old rebellious generation of the wilderness to the new generation of hope and promise on the edge of the *Promised Land forms the primary structure and theme for the book of Numbers. This structure is marked by the two census lists of the twelve tribes in Numbers 1 and 26, which divide the book into two parts.

Structure and Content. The first census list in Numbers 1 introduces the first part of the book, chapters 1—25. This first part of Numbers begins with the organization of the people of God into a highly structured holy-*war camp on the march in the wilderness (Num 1—10), contributing to the pervasive biblical imagery of God as a *divine warrior and his people as an *army. The *tabernacle, or tent of meeting—the sign of God's holy and powerful presence—stands in the midst of the camp.

An atmosphere of Israel's complete obedience to God's commands dominates Numbers 1—10, but there are some ominous undertones and reminders of danger and *death under the otherwise calm surface of Israel's compliance (Num 3:4, 10; 4:15, 18, 20; 5:2; 6:6-7; 8:19; 9:6-11).

When the preparations are completed and the march begins, the people suddenly and unexpectedly erupt into *rebellion (Num 11—12). The series of wilderness rebellions builds to a climax in the *spy story in Numbers 13—14. The members of the first generation in Numbers are condemned to die because of their refusal to enter the Promised Land and accept the gift God had striven so long to give them.

Many of the remaining chapters through chapter 25 recount further rebellions, plagues and deaths of this old rebellious generation (Num 16; 17; 20; 21; 25). Some glimmers of hope shine through along the way. God proclaims regulations for a future time when a new generation of Israelites would properly enter the Promised Land (Num 15). God gives some preliminary military victories to Israel over the king of Arad, as well as over Sihon and Og (Num 21). A final crescendo of hope and promise is sounded in the Balaam oracles (Num 22—24), which look forward to a more distant future generation. The first generation's story ends with the final rebellion of the people and the death of the remaining members of the first generation (Num 25).

The second census list in Numbers 26 introduces the second part of the book, chapters 26—36. This second census is nearly identical in form to the first census list in Numbers 1. However, those who were numbered in Numbers 26 did not include any members of the old generation who had been numbered in the census in Numbers 1. The only two exceptions were two faithful spies named Joshua and Caleb; they were members of the old generation, but they alone had acted with faith in God in the spy story in Numbers 13—14 (Num 26:63-65; cf. Num 14:5-10, 28-34).

This second part of Numbers, marked by the second census, becomes the sign of an emerging new generation of God's people who look forward in hope to entering the land of Canaan. Following the census in Numbers 26, the second part is bracketed by an inclusio in chapters 27 and 36. Both of these chapters relate a legal dispute involving the daughters of a man named Zelophehad and the issue of inheriting land once the daughters arrive in Canaan. The legal issue involving land *inheritance from one generation to the next is resolved in both cases, and the successful resolution sets a positive and hopeful tone for the entire second part of Numbers. In contrast to the deaths of a whole generation of Israelites in a series of rebellions and *judgments in the first part of Numbers, the second part does not record the death of any Israelite. The Israelites are victorious in their first military engagement with the Midianite people (Num 31). Potential crises do not turn into rebellions but are successfully negotiated and resolved (Num 27:1-11; 31:14-15; 32:1-42). Numerous laws are given that look forward to future residence in the Promised Land (Num 27; 34—36). The second half of Numbers, therefore, is uniformly hopeful and positive in tone.

Images. In spite of Israel's rebellions, a major theme of Numbers is that God's ultimate will for Israel is one of blessing and not curse. This theme is reinforced in two images. Numbers 6:22-27 sets forth the image of the priest who is to bless Israel repeatedly with the still often-used Aaronic benediction ("The LORD bless you and keep you; the LORD make his face to shine upon you, and be gracious to you; the LORD lift up his countenance upon you, and give you peace," Num 6:24-26 NRSV). The second image involves Numbers 22—24 and the tale of the professional foreign prophet Balaam and his talking *donkey. Balaam is hired by a foreign king to curse Israel, but God turns Balaam's words into words not of *curse but of lavish *blessing upon Israel and its future *king.

A number of images in Numbers play a role in the stories of the old wilderness generation and its many rebellions against God and God's leaders. The story of the bronze serpent in Numbers 21:4-9 plays upon common ancient Near Eastern associations with the snake or *serpent as a symbol of evil power and chaos from the underworld as well as a symbol of fertility, healing and life. In Numbers 21 God sends poisonous snakes as a judgment against Israel's rebellion. At the same time, God instructs Moses to erect a bronze serpent upon a pole so that "everyone who is bitten shall look at it and live" (Num 21:9 NRSV). This image of Moses lifting up the serpent in the wilderness is used by the NT text of John 3:14-15 as a precursor of Jesus who was "lifted up" on the cross, signifying both his death and his resurrection/ascension.

Other images in Numbers include the budding almond rod of Aaron (*see* Aaron's Rod) that demonstrated God's election of Aaron and the Levites as priests over the competing claims of other lay leaders among the tribes of Israel (Num 17). Images of the miraculous *manna from heaven, meat from quail and *water from the rock appear first in the book of Exodus, where they were all portrayed as God's positive response to Israel's legitimate requests for *food and water in a barren wilderness (Ex 16—17). In Numbers the manna, quail and water from the rock all become negative occasions for rebellions by Israel and Israel's leaders, including even Moses and Aaron (Num 11: 20). In the end even the leaders of Israel—Moses, Aaron and Miriam—must join the old generation of rebellious Israelites in dying outside the land of Canaan (Num 20). Thus Aaron passes on his priestly office to his son Eleazar (Num 20:22-29), and Moses lays his *hand on the head of his assistant Joshua to pass on the mantle of leadership to a new generation, who will cross over the Jordan River into Canaan (Num 27:12-23). As the old generation dies, God prepares a new generation to journey on. The book of Numbers concludes with this portrait of a new generation of Israelites poised to enter the Promised Land, chastened by the failures of the past and encouraged by the promises of hope for the future.

See also AARON'S ROD; DIVINE WARRIOR; MANNA; MOSES; PROMISED LAND; TABERNACLE; WILDERNESS.

BIBLIOGRAPHY. D. T. Olson, *The Death of the Old and the Birth of the New: The Framework of the Book of Numbers and the Pentateuch* (Chico, CA: Scholars

Press, 1985); idem, "Numbers" in *Harper's Bible Commentary,* ed. J. L. Mays (San Francisco: Harper & Row, 1988) 182-208.

NUMBERS IN THE BIBLE

Numbers play a prominent and varied role in the Bible. They appear throughout both Testaments, even though no part of the Bible has a purely scientific or mathematical purpose. The Bible's main functions are historical, theological and literary, perhaps explaining in part why when numbers occur, they are always written out in words rather than represented by symbols, which was a distinct possibility in ancient Semitic writing systems.

Numbers are not only prevalent in the Bible, but their use is varied. The history of biblical interpretation demonstrates four potential uses of numbers: conventional, rhetorical, symbolic and hidden (Davis; although the fourth category is doubtful, it is included because it has traditionally been on the agenda of discussion in biblical writings).

Conventional. Counting and numeration have been around as far back as we have records of humankind. Indeed, we have evidence of counting in the ancient Near East well before writing came into existence around 3000 B.C. As a matter of fact, the argument has been well made that writing down words and concepts, and ultimately literature itself, flowed from the practice of keeping written records of numbers of animals being transported for sale. Thus it is of no surprise that most numbers in the Bible are used in a strictly conventional way to count objects, people or anything else that comes in a quantity.

It is not unusual, even when discrete and finite groups are being counted, for the biblical author to simply give a round number for the total. A good example of the use of round numbers may be seen in the census list in Numbers 1. The number of people in each tribe of Israel is given here to the nearest hundred.

Rhetorical. Numbers may be used for literary purposes in the Bible. In these cases the numbers themselves have no symbolic meaning, but neither are they cited for conventional purposes. Two examples can be observed in the use of graded numbers and also the use of numbers in the structure of a text.

The literary convention of graded numbers, also known as X/X+1 parallelism, is illustrated by Proverbs 30:29-31 (NIV):

> There are three things that are stately in their
>   stride,
>   four that move with stately bearing:
> a lion, mighty among beasts,
>   who retreats before nothing;
> a strutting rooster, a he-goat,
>   and a king with his army around him.

This proverb begins with a parallelism that moves from a list of *three to *four things that are stately. In this case the writer then moves on to state the four things he has in mind. The move from three to four

intensifies the thought of the line.

Other examples indicate that the move from the lower to the higher number is not for the purpose of arriving at the "right" number, but to intensify the thought. Illustrative are the lists of oracles against foreign nations in Amos 1:6-2:16. For example, Amos 2:1-3 begins: "For three sins of Moab, even for four, I will not turn back my wrath" (NIV). It is interesting that the oracle then goes on to name only one sin. The graded parallelism, though, gives the impression that if needed, the prophet could illustrate with many other examples.

A second class of biblical texts that exemplify a rhetorical use of numbers are those that bear on the structure of a passage or even a book. Psalm 119 is a well-known example. By means of an acrostic, the psalm is broken up into twenty-two clearly delineated stanzas. This parallels the number of letters in the Hebrew language and imparts the impression that the poet has moved from A to Z in covering his topic. It also gives the poem an atmosphere of order.

A somewhat debated, though striking example of the use of number in the structuring of a book is the book of Revelation. The symbolic number *seven (see below) is used throughout the book, and recent studies have persuasively argued that the book may be divided into seven cycles of texts recapitulating the events surrounding the second coming of Jesus Christ.

Symbolic. Few doubt that in certain contexts in the Bible numbers take on symbolic overtones. The practice of using numbers in this way was not an innovation of the Hebrews and may be found in literature of the ancient Near East before the first writing of Scripture.

Hyperbole is occasionally employed to indicate vastness of number. For example, Daniel 7:10 describes the "thousands upon thousands" indeed the "ten thousand time ten thousand" that stood before God on his throne and attended him.

But beyond this more general use of numbers, we observe that certain numbers acquired specific symbolic meaning in biblical tradition. It is not that the number has symbolic meaning every time it appears, but through literary and cultural convention symbolic use is possible in some and without doubt in other passages. We will not go into detail about specific numbers in this article. Rather the reader is referred to individual articles on specific numbers: *one, *two, *three, *four, *five, *seven, *twelve, *forty, *fifty, *seventy, *hundred and *thousand.

While certain contexts are clear in their intention to use a number symbolically, others are debated. Perhaps the most notorious example is Revelation 20:3 and 5, which speak of the thousand-year reign of Christ. Is this number being used in a conventional sense, in which case it would be a literal thousand-year period, or is it symbolic, indicating an extremely long period of time (*see* Millennium)? This is at the root of the classic millenarian debate.

There is no magic formula to solve such questions, but certain important principles can guide one's exegetical conclusion. Perhaps the most important of these is to take into account the genre of literature of the passage. Poetry and apocalyptic use many different types of image. If a text is highly figurative in general, and if other numbers are used figuratively in the text, then that would predispose the reader to treat a number as symbolic if it is a number that is known to be symbolic elsewhere.

Hidden. Throughout the history of interpretation there have been fringe groups that have sought a "mathematical key" of some sort to unlock a secret or mystical message of the Bible. In a recent example, one self-proclaimed Bible scholar decreed that thirteen was the number of "supercompletion" and then read numbers that in some way contained the number thirteen in order to arrive at a formula for the end of the world. The Bible contains no secret or hidden uses of numbers. They are imposed from outside the text and fail to sustain support from more than a few devoted followers and usually only for a brief length of time.

See also FIFTY; FIVE; FORTY; FOUR; HUNDRED; ONE; SEVEN; SEVENTY; THOUSAND; THREE; TWELVE; TWO.

BIBLIOGRAPHY. J. J. Davis, *Biblical Numerology* (Grand Rapids: Baker, 1968).

NURSE

The nurse of biblical times does not carry the connotation of medicine or of aiding recovery from illness so much as the maternal connotation of suckling an infant *child or caring for a growing child.

The essence of nursing lay in nourishment and nurture. These twin aspects are seen in *Moses' *mother (Ex 2:7) and in *Ruth, where the reference shows that nursing was not necessarily done by the mother (Ruth 4:16). Consequently, strong attachments were formed between a child and its nurse, who on occasion retained a significant place in the family long after the child had grown into adulthood.

The caring and carrying motif was not seen as exclusively feminine. Moses complained to God of the burden of carrying the children of Israel through the wilderness "as a nurse carries an infant" (Num 11:12 NIV). Isaiah, forecasting the *restoration of Israel, prophesied that *queens would be their "nursing mother" and kings, correspondingly, would serve as their guardians or foster *fathers. Paul, alluding to Deuteronomy 1:31, speaks of God nursing the children of Israel through the wilderness (Acts 13:18).

Paul characterizes his own ministry to the Thessalonians as that of a wet nurse or mother (1 Thess 2:7). He does so to emphasize the gentleness of his approach in contrast to the popular wisdom of his day as seen, for example, in the writings of the Dio Chrysostom (A.D. 40-120), which argued that robust and vigorous methods of instruction were necessary to instruct the masses and that gentleness was the technique of a flatterer.

The image of the nurse is consistently that of gentleness, of nourishment and nurture, and of caring for and carrying a small child.

See also BABY; MILK; MOTHER.

O

OAK. *See* TREE, TREES; WOOD.

OATH. *See* VOW, OATH.

OBADIAH

The subject of Obadiah's *prophecy is the judgment of Edom. Like the canonical prophets surrounding it, Obadiah deals with the judgment of a foreign nation (Obad 1-14). Like *Joel and *Amos before it, Obadiah features God's acts of *judgment and *redemption in the coming *Day of the Lord (Obad 15-21).

These two broad divisions of the book show evidence of further structural unity. The first six verses are nearly verbatim from Jeremiah 49 (cf. Obad 1-4, 5-6 with Jer 49:14-16, 9-10) and form a distinct literary unit dealing with the despoiling of Edom's pride. The appearance of the name Yahweh (LORD) in Obadiah 1 and 4 serves to mark a clear inclusion, while Obadiah 5-6 share their own internal structure. After a hinge verse (Obad 7) predicting that Edom will be forsaken by its friends just as it had forsaken its brother Jacob, Obadiah 8-14 form a quasi-court-scene *(rîb)* oracle. Edom's sentence is declared (Obad 8-9), and the serious charges against the nation for which it has been judged guilty are detailed (Obad 10-14). The phrase "in/on the/that day" forms a stitching device throughout the entire section; the repetition producing a chorus-like effect that is almost antiphonal. The final section (Obad 15-21) comprises a kingdom oracle in which the judgment of Edom becomes typical of the future universal judgment of all nations, while God's own people experience deliverance and blessing. The name Yahweh once again bookends the section (Obad 15, 21).

The unifying motif of Obadiah is that of brotherhood, a theme that stitches together both major sections of this short prophecy. Edom's hostile actions against Jerusalem (Obad 10-11) were particularly reprehensible because that nation was descended from *Esau, Jacob's brother. Thus Edom is repeatedly called Esau (Obad 6, 8, 9, 18, 21) and reminded of its brotherly relation to *Jerusalem/*Jacob (Obad 10, 12, 17, 18). The heinous nature of its crime is underscored by declaring that Edom will be despised by the nations (Obad 2), much as Esau despised his birthright (Gen 25:34).

Just as Esau was to find his blessing through Jacob (Gen 25:23; 27:27-40), so Edom's final blessing can come only in relation to the deliverance that will come from Mount *Zion (Obad 21).

The deliverance from Mount Zion takes it place as an important part of the *mountain imagery of the book. The seemingly impenetrable mountains/heights of Edom/Esau served as an emblem of the nation's pride (Obad 3, 8). In a touch of dramatic irony, however, people from the lowlands will overcome and occupy them (Obad 19). Attention shifts to Mount Zion, which forms an important literary foil to Edom's mountainous heights. For deliverance comes to Mount Zion (Obad 17), from where deliverers will proceed to the mountains of Esau (Obad 21).

Other literary figures and imagery enhance the prophet's message. Edom's proud stronghold is likened to an *eagle's nest (Obad 4). Edom's passivity at Jerusalem's misfortune makes it like one of the invaders themselves (Obad 11). The nation's defeat will not be like looters or robbers who leave a little behind, but will be total (Obad 5-6). The final victory of Jacob/Israel over Esau/Edom is compared to a fire that easily consumes the stubble (Obad 18). Several important sub-themes provide further enrichment to the book, such as the folly of pride, the principle of *lex talionis* in judgment (Obad 16) and the restoration of the remnant of Israel together with Yahweh's universal dominion in the Day of the Lord. Indeed, Edom's hope for future blessing lay in the understanding and playing out of these crucial themes.

See also ESAU; MOUNTAIN.

OBEDIENCE

Obedience as a biblical motif emerges primarily from the many examples of individuals whose relationships with God are characterized by faithful obedience. Through repeated examples of obedient responses to God's commands, the biblical narrative paints a picture of the fundamental role that obedience plays in a proper relationship with God. The story of Noah is a simple but powerful instance. In the sparsest terms God announces his intent to send a flood and instructs Noah to build an *ark. The record of Noah's response is even more brief, as if only his obedience were of importance: "Noah did everything just as God commanded him" (Gen 6:22 NIV). The significance of Noah's obedience is borne out in the passages that follow in which God delivers Noah and his family, blesses them and makes a covenant with them never again to *flood the earth (Gen 9:1, 12).

In the OT the archetypal example of obedience to God is *Abraham, the father of the nation of Israel. When God first calls Abram out of Haran to Canaan, it is Abram's obedient response that makes it possible for God to begin fulfilling his promise to bless him and to make his descendants into a nation (Gen 12:1-4). Moreover, when God commands him to go out and sacrifice his son Isaac as a burnt offering (Gen 22:2), Abraham's obedience is so unwavering that he is ready to destroy the only living evidence of God's promise to him, since it is through Isaac that a nation is to descend from him (Gen 21:12). God responds to Abraham's obedience by reiterating his promise of great *blessing, taking an *oath upon himself (Gen 22:16-18). Thus Abraham sets the standard of obedience for Israel, his descendants.

It is Abraham's high degree of obedience that God requires of his people and nothing less. When Saul, under God's direction, defeats the Amalekites, he allows the soldiers to return with some of the livestock as plunder to be sacrificed to God in spite of God's command that everything should be destroyed (1 Sam 15:3). Because Saul fails to obey fully, God rebukes him through Samuel: "To obey is better than sacrifice, and to heed is better than the fat of rams" (1 Sam 15:22 NIV). The biblical motif of obedience conveys nothing short of total surrender to the will of God.

But God's demand for obedience is not purely arbitrary; rather, obedience is a means by which God brings blessing. When God confirms to Isaac the promise of land and innumerable descendants, he cites the obedience of Abraham as the immediate reason for such immense blessing (Gen 26:4, 5). Likewise, when God speaks to *Moses from Mount Sinai, he declares that if they will obey fully, Israel will be his "treasured possession . . . a kingdom of priests and a holy nation" (Ex 19:5, 6). Here obedience is associated with blessing such that each comprises one half of the relationship between Israel and God: it is Israel's part to obey and God's part to bless.

But the biblical image of obedience is not merely a means for gaining blessing. Just as one stands in proper relation to God by being obedient to him, so also one becomes obedient to God out of love for him. This relationship between love and obedience appears in the Shema, the heart of Israel's law. Immediately following Moses' reiteration of the Ten Commandments, he admonishes the people to keep God's commands and to teach their children to do so as well. In the very center of this message is the command "Love the LORD your God with all your heart and with all your soul and with all your strength (Deut 6:5 NIV). It is not just for blessing but out of love that Israel is to obey God.

It is this aspect of obedience that gains further prominence in the NT, surrounding the person of Jesus Christ. For Jesus, who is both the model and object of obedience, to obey God is sustenance itself (Jn 4:34). Such obedience is borne out of a love for God so complete that it defines his every action. Thus Jesus is always ready to submit his will to God's, even when faced with the bitter cup of death in Gethsemane (Mt 26:39; Mk 14:36; Lk 22:42). The apostle Paul contrasts the trespass, or disobedience, of the first Adam with the obedience of the "one man," Jesus Christ (Rom 5:12-17). And in the Philippian *Christ hymn we read that Christ was "obedient to the point of death—even death on a cross" (Phil 2:8 NRSV). The image is a remarkable one: the Son of God, who unlike mortals was not subject to the rule of death, obediently accepts death, even on a cross.

Jesus teaches his disciples of the link between love and obedience, telling them, "If you love me, you will obey what I command" (Jn 14:15 NIV). Likewise, Jesus declares the foundation of the Law and Prophets to be summed up in two commands: to love God (the Shema), and to "love your neighbor as yourself" (Lev 19:18; Mt 22:37-39). The one who loves God will also obey God, and the result will be blessing from God. Thus the motif of obedience is a key to the Bible's portrayal of God's desired relationship with his people.

See also ABRAHAM; FAITH; LAW.

ODOR. *See* SMELL, SCENT.

OFFERING

"No one shall appear before me empty-handed," the Lord says twice during the theophany at Mt. Sinai (Ex 23:15; 34:20 NIV). Offerings were a integral part of Israelite *worship, and from *Cain and *Abel down to Revelation, the image of the offering permeates the Bible. What changes over time is the idea of what constitutes a fitting offering and, more importantly, who makes a worthy offering. In the earlier books of the OT the offering is made by humans to God, and it is material. It is, most importantly, a blood *sacrifice. In the oracles of the prophets, however, and especially after the destruction of the *temple, the physical offering becomes immaterial. The offering the Lord requires is not any material thing but "a broken and contrite heart" (Psalm 51:17). In the NT there is a further development. The offering required of humans retains a double form—both material and spiritual. But the idea of the human's offering to God is eclipsed by the image of God's offering of himself in the person of Jesus, who is identified with the *lamb offered in the earlier sacrifices.

Worship and offering are inextricably linked in the OT. The Pentateuch (particularly Lev 1—7) describes several different sorts of offerings: the "burnt offering" that was the centerpiece of temple worship, the "sin offering" that restored a person or place that had become unclean, the "guilt offering" that made restitution for an unwittingly committed misdeed, the "thank offering" that offered the Lord gratitude. Each offering is intended in a different way to commemorate or restore the relationship between the Lord and his people. It is always the people who make the sacrifice, whether to please or propitiate the Lord, and what they sacrifice is very important. The law specifies the characteristics of an acceptable offering in great detail, though the primary requirement is always that the lamb or *grain or bread offered be of the very highest quality. The primary image associated with the act of offering itself is that some object is brought to a specific place and then relinquished or sacrificed. Such offerings are also often linked with an *altar.

In the Prophets the sacrifices that the law requires are put in perspective. They matter less than the inward sacrifice of righteous behavior. In Isaiah the Lord says that bringing offerings is futile and instead commands, "Cease to do evil, learn to do good" (Is 1:16-17). A similar oracle appears in Amos 5:21-22. Several passages in the Psalms declare that the Lord prefers an inward offering and that he has no need of any offering: "If I were hungry, I would not tell you, for the world and all that is in it is mine. . . . Offer to God a sacrifice of thanksgiving" (Ps 50:12, 14 NRSV).

Like the prophets, Jesus emphasizes that God requires an interior offering and that without a change of heart and behavior, any material offering is meaningless. There is a more important development in the image of offering in the NT, however: the most important offering is not just received by God; he himself makes it through the person of Jesus Christ. The NT does not reject the idea that humans must make offerings, but the focus is never on the worshipers' sacrifice. The important offering, the offering of Jesus, has been made and received, and it need not be repeated. The letter to the Hebrews is largely an expression of the idea that Christ's sacrifice has taken the place of earlier offerings and sacrifices: "He entered once for all into the Holy Place, not with the blood of goats and calves, but with his own blood, thus obtaining eternal redemption" (Heb 9:12 NRSV). Jesus takes the place of both the lamb sacrificed and the high priest who presented it at the altar. The same image of Jesus taking the place of all other offerings is presented symbolically in Revelation: the Lamb is enthroned, and there is no temple—no place of offering—in the New Jerusalem (Rev 21:22).

See also ALTAR; GUILT; SACRIFICE; WORSHIP.

OFFSPRING. *See* GENERATION(S); SEED.

OIL

Oil is mentioned nearly two hundred times in the Bible. These references cluster at two ends of a continuum: some of the uses of oil were everyday and common, while others were special and even sacred.

Oils in biblical times were obtained from a variety of sources—animal, vegetable and mineral. Deuteronomy 32:13 and Job 29:6 refer poetically to oil flowing from *rocks, an image of fertility or *prosperity. In some Jewish traditions the *tree of life in Eden was considered to be an olive tree, a sign of the importance of oil in daily living. Oil was seen as a staple and characteristic product of the *Promised Land (2 Kings 18:32; Jer 40:10). It served a plethora of purposes: a constituent of *food (1 Kings 17:12), a cosmetic (Eccles 9:7-8), a fuel for *lamps (Ex 25:6), a medicine (Is 1:6). It was also a key export (1 Kings 5:25). Oils further had a role in *sacrifices and in *anointing performed as part of investiture.

The olive was the most significant source of oil. Using poles, people dislodged olives from the tree (Is 17:6) and then reduced them to pulp. When the pulp was placed in wicker baskets, the highest and lightest grade of oil would run out, constituting the "beaten oil" that is referred to several times in the Bible (e.g., Ex 27:20; 29:40; Lev 24:2; Num 28:5; 1 Kings 5:25). After the lightest oil had been extracted, a lower-grade oil was obtained by exerting further pressure on the pulp and heating it.

Oil in Everyday Life. Along with other staples, such as grain and wine, oil was seen as an essence of life and a tangible sign of God's *blessing and favor, which could be lost by disobedience (Deut 11:13-17). It was used as food and in baking and cooking. The taste of *manna was compared to that of cakes baked with oil (Num 11:8).

Some of the anointing associated with oil was also ordinary. In a climate where dry skin was a problem, especially for travelers, anointing with oil was a refreshment (Ps 23:5, which at a literal level, however, refers to healing oil applied to an injured *sheep in the sheepfold at the end of a day). Elsewhere anointing with oil seems to be an image of high-spirited indulgence on a festive occasion (Ps 104:5; Eccles 9:8). We also catch glimpses of anointing with oil as an *honor conferred on a guest arriving for a feast (Lk 7:46).

Another common use of oil was as a healing *ointment. Psalm 23:5 puts this into a pastoral context, with its picture of a shepherd's anointing scratches or bruises of a sheep. For humans too, oil was valued for its healing properties. The oil softened *wounds, and in James 5:14 it is linked with God's active hand in healing as a response to people's prayer.

A final mundane use of oil was as a fuel for lamps. In Jesus' day the use of small, hand-held lamps was common. In view of the lamps' small capacity, carrying a supply of fuel was essential, a situation that formed the basis for one of Jesus' haunting parables (Mt 25:3-8).

Special Uses of Oil. At the other end of the spectrum, oil in the Bible is associated with the most solemn and awesome experiences of OT religious and civil life. Oil was used as part of the ritual anointing to set apart a *prophet (Is 61:1), a *priest (Lev 8:30) or a *king (1 Sam 10:1). The anointing oil is referred to as "oil of gladness," in keeping with the joyousness of the occasion.

A rich theme of anointing runs through the OT in the figure of the promised deliverer, who is twice called "the Anointed One," or Messiah (Dan 9:25-26 NIV). The anointing is figurative, invested by the *Holy Spirit (Ps 2:2; Is 61:1). In the NT the symbolism of anointing is richly associated with Jesus the Messiah (Heb 1:9) and includes the anointing by Mary (Jn 12) as well as the anointing of his corpse after his crucifixion (Jn 19:39-40).

Another context where oil is prominent is OT *worship, where it assumes sacral significance. Oil was part of the continual burnt offering and was mixed with various food offerings. It also figured prominently in ritual purification. To catch the flavor of oil as part of OT religious ritual, one can sample the one hundred references to oil in the last four books of the Pentateuch.

Even the sensory properties of anointing oil convey a sense of its richness. Such oil was above all fragrant. While olive oil was used as a base for various perfumed lotions, Exodus 30:22-33 speaks of finest spices, referring to special anointing oil made from rare and expensive scented spices. Most of these came from far-off places like India. Persia, India and Arabia were renowned for the export of aromatic perfumes. The oil of myrrh (Ex 30:23) was esteemed for its sweet perfume (Ps 45:8; Prov 7:17). Cinnamon and balsam were other ingredients of the fragrant anointing oil.

Oil as a Symbol. Such a regular feature of ancient culture and life naturally became a rich symbol. Possession of oil is a sign of prosperity and abundance, as well as of God's good provision (Job 29:6; Joel 2:24). The olive tree in Judges 9:9 boasts that by its fatness "gods and men are honored" (RSV). The seductive words of an enemy are compared to the *softness of oil (Ps 55:21). The enticing speech of the sexually promiscuous is considered to be smoother than oil (Prov 5:3).

God's favor is compared to the refreshment of anointing oil on the head (Ps 23:5; 45:7; 92:10), and a similar comparison is used to describe the ideal unity of fellow pilgrims (Ps 133:1-2). The love given by the woman in the Song of Songs, sweetened by the fragrance of her perfume, is praised, the fragrance imaging her love (Song 4:10). A good name is said to be better than good oil (Eccles 7:1, where there is a wordplay on "name" *[šēm]* and "oil" *[šemen];* cf. Song 1:3).

See also ANOINTING; DISEASE AND HEALING; LAMP, LAMPSTAND; OINTMENT.

OINTMENT

In the Bible the various words associated with perfume can be translated either "ointment" or "perfume." Ointment was a semiviscous liquid or salve that protected one's skin in a harsh climate while imparting a pleasant smell. Its sources were either animals or plants. A Red Sea mollusk was the origin of one perfume used in Palestine. The various plants used to produce perfumes and ointments were brought to Palestine mostly from other lands and included assorted spices, barks, woods, flower petals, seeds, roots, fruits and the resins of certain trees (Gen 37:25; Is 60:6; Jer 6:20). Ointments might also be simple olive *oil or the more expensive myrrh or balsam.

Some ointments were extremely rare in the ancient world and costly to obtain and possess. The sage regards ointment as precious (Eccles 7:1). Ointments might be included in the treasury of a king (2 Kings 20:13; Song 3:6-7). The prophet describes the complacent and wealthy of Israel as those who can afford the finest lotions (Amos 6:6). No wonder Jesus' disciples complained at the woman's "waste" of her expensive ointment when she poured it out on Jesus' head. It could have been sold and used more practically to meet the needs of the poor (Mt 26:9; Mk 14:4). In fact, the nard (an ointment probably from Nepal) in Mary's alabaster flask was worth three hundred denarii, nearly a year's wages (Jn 12:5; 11:2; cf. Mk 14:5). Ointment (or oil) is listed among the products that the merchants of the world trade and value (Rev 18:13).

The Bible exhibits several uses of ointment or perfume. The mention of ointment in the apocryphal book of Judith illustrates a common use: after bathing, a woman anointed herself (or her face) with precious ointment, fixed her hair and put on a splendid gown (Jdt 10:3; 16:8; cf. Ruth 3:3; 2 Sam 12:20). Ointment was used as a simple fragrance or cosmetic (Song 1:3; 3:6; 7:13; Mt 6:17). Embalming procedures used ointments, including masking the smell of the dead (2 Chron 16:14; *see* Burial). After Jesus' hasty execution and burial on Friday, the women spent the next day or so preparing spices and perfumes, expecting to finish their work early on Sunday (Lk 23:56).

*Anointing assumed an important religious significance in Israel. A specially-prepared spiced oil was considered holy anointing oil and was used for the ceremonial anointing of the "tent of meeting" (Ex 30:23-27; Num 7:1) and priests (Ex 29:7; 30:30-33; 40:15). Other objects and people were also anointed (e.g., Ex 25:6; 28:41; 29:21, 36; 40:10; Is 45:1). Anointing on the head set a person apart for God's special use (Ex 29:7; Lev 8:12; Num 3:3; Ps 105:15). In the early church Paul believed that all Christians experience God's anointing (2 Cor 1:21-22; cf. 1 Jn 2:27); that is, all believers are set apart for God's special purposes.

Anointing with oil solemnized the appointment of Israel's kings (Judg 9:15; 1 Sam 10:1; 15:1; 2 Sam 2:4; 1 Kings 1:39; 2 Kings 9:3, 6). The anointing of the king was predicated on God's selection of him to that role: he is the Lord's anointed (1 Sam 15:17; 16:6). At David's anointing with oil, God's Spirit came to rest on him (1 Sam 16:13). The concept of "the Lord's anointed" laid the groundwork for an expanded concept of "the anointed one," that is, the

Messiah (Heb) or Christ (Gk). In some texts the interchange between the literal Davidic dynasty and the coming "Lord's anointed" is clear (e.g., Ps 2:2; 45:6-7 [Heb 1:9]; 84:9; 89:20, cf. vv. 27-29). Jesus applies the text of Isaiah 61:1 to himself when he claims to be the coming one whom God has anointed (Lk 4:18). Thus the early church came to describe Jesus as "the anointed one" (Acts 4:27): anointed not with oil but with the Holy Spirit and power (Acts 10:38).

Luke records an incident of a woman of the city who was a sinner. Her understanding of Jesus' forgiveness of her sins led her to a dramatic display of love (Lk 7:37-46). In full view of the other guests and host, she kissed Jesus' feet and anointed them with perfume. Later commenting on her actions, Jesus contrasted his host's failure to provide Jesus with the customary ointment on his head with this woman's anointing of his feet. With the symbolic act of anointing, she showed her love for Jesus.

Oil was appointed as an accompaniment to prayer for healing in the early church (Jas 5:14). Oil had some medicinal value in the ancient world (cf. Is 1:6), but the use in James is more likely ceremonial or symbolic of invoking God's power to heal. This symbolic use of oil connected with healing occurs in several incidents in the Gospels (e.g., Mk 6:13). Jesus also mixed saliva with dirt to produce a kind of salve or ointment that he smeared on a man's blind eyes to effect healing (Jn 9:6, 11). The ointment that the risen Jesus suggests to the spiritually blind Laodecians has a special poignancy, since that city was in a region renown for its eye salve (Rev 3:18). The symbolic use of anointing in the NT clearly points to the presence and power of the Holy Spirit as Acts 10:38 makes explicit.

See also ANOINTING; OIL.

OLD, OLD AGE

Old age is seen in the Bible first of all as a time of human frailty. This frailty begins with the *curse of Genesis 3 in which human beings are destined to the dust from which they were created. The outworking of this curse is seen especially in Genesis 5 with the constant repetition "and he died." The frailty of the last phase of human existence is seen in the diminishing of physical abilities: sight (Gen 27:1; 48:10; 1 Sam 4:12-18; Eccles 12:2-3; *see* Eye, Sight); taste (2 Sam 19:31-39); hearing (2 Sam 19:31-39; *see* Ear, Hearing); reproduction (Gen 18:11; Lk 1:36); circulation (1 Sam 28:14); *sleep (Eccles 12:4); strength (Ps 71:9); speech (Eccles 12:4). The body changes in appearance: weight gain (1 Sam 4:12-18); gray *hair (Gen 42:38; Prov 20:29; Eccles 12:5); stooping posture (Eccles 12:3); absent *teeth (Eccles 12:3). There are psychological changes as well, such as *fear (Ps 71:9-10; Eccles 12:5) and lack of desire (Eccles 12:5).

Old age is communicated through powerful images. By far the most vivid is that found in Ecclesiastes 12:1-9, where the physiological symptoms of old age

are portrayed in the vivid metaphors of the blossoming almond tree (gray hair), the grinders ceasing (absent teeth), *windows growing dim (poor eyesight), the *doors on the street being shut (loss of hearing) and the grasshopper dragging itself along (loss of sprightliness in walking). So also death is depicted with domestic images from everyday life, each one describing the moment of death as an irrevocable household crisis: a broken golden bowl, a shattered pitcher at the spring, a broken wheel at the well. Several biblical characters are exceptions to these transformations and become powerful images: Sarah, who is beautiful in her old age (Gen 12:11, 14); *Moses and Caleb, who remain strong in old age (Deut 34:7; Josh 14:11). But these are exceptions, and the biblical norm is that one's later years are marked by decline.

This image of frailty is the root of the sense of vulnerability that accompanies old age in the Bible. This is communicated powerfully through the figure of Isaac, whose frailty in old age leaves him vulnerable to deception at the hand of his wife and son Jacob (Gen 27). Such vulnerability is reflected in the transformed value of the elderly in the society at large. There is a considerable drop in the votive value of a human being once the age of sixty is attained (Lev 27:1-8). Levites over fifty are no longer allowed to work directly in the tent of meeting (Num 8:25-26). This vulnerability is reflected in the precariousness of one's hold on power in old age (2 Sam 15, 20; 1 Kings 1) and of one's ability to control his own destiny (Jn 21:18). It is also seen in the frustration of the final years on earth (Ps 90, esp. v. 9), of the possibility of ending life in sorrow (Gen 42:38; 44:31) and in the potential for foolishness (1 Kings 11:4; Eccles 4:13; 1 Tim 4:7). Because of such vulnerability the Bible condemns any preying on the elderly and encourages care of these legitimate members of the community (Prov 19:26; 30:17; Mk 7:5-13; Acts 6:1; 1 Tim 5:13-16; Jas 1:27).

Such frailty, however, is not the only image connected with old age in the Bible. In Daniel 7:9, 13 *God is called the "Ancient of Days," a figure who possesses great power and authority. So also with human beings, old age is a sign of authority. This authority is attested in the *honor expected for the elderly (Lev 19:32; Deut 28:50; Prov 16:31; 20:29; 23:22; 1 Tim 5:1; Philem 9). This authority is linked to the wisdom that should accompany greater age and experience (1 Kings 12:6-20; Job 12:12; 15:10; Ps 37:25; 119:100) and is expressed through leadership in the community, especially in the role of dispensing justice and teaching and acting as representative for the people (Lev 4:13-15; Num 11:16-17; 16:25; Deut 21:2, 19; 22:15ff. 25:7ff. 27:1; Josh 20:4; Ruth 4; Acts 14:23; 15:2; Tit 1:5; James 5:14; 1 Pet 5:1-5).

Old age is sometimes seen as a sign of God's *blessing (Gen 15:15; 24:1; 25:7-8; 35:29; Judg 8:32; 1 Sam 25:6; 1 Chron 29:28; Job 42:17; Ps 91:16; 92:14), whereas an early death is seen as evidence of the *curse of God (1 Sam 2:31-32; Is 65:20). Death is inevitable, but the greatest curses are premature death (Is 38:10, 12; Job 36:13-14; Prov 10:27) or sorrowful death (Gen 42:38; 44:29, 31; 1 Kings 2:9) as opposed to peaceful death (1 Kings 2:6). The patriarchal figures of Abraham and Isaac become images of the blessing of old age as they die "old and full of years" (Gen 25:8; 35:29).

Old age is also depicted as a time of transition in which blessing, name, inheritance and responsibility are passed on to a new generation (Gen 27:1; 1 Chron 23:1; Ps 71:18; Titus 2:3-5). This transition is accentuated through the contrast between old and young characters and is especially noticeable in the farewell discourse narratives in the OT, where blessing is passed on to the next generation (Gen 27:27-29; 48:15-16; 49:1-28). This contrast is used by Luke in the dedication of Jesus, as the older generation, represented by Simeon and Anna, are used as images of the hope of past ages finding their climax in the messianic baby. This final image explains the possibility of old age being both a negative and positive image in the Bible; for while such a transition can be a source of honor in passing on one's heritage, it also signifies one's own passing on. Thus it is in this transfer from generation to generation that we see both the frailty and the potential of old age.

See also DEATH; HONOR; YOUNG, YOUTH.

BIBLIOGRAPHY. J. G. Harris, *Biblical Perspectives on Aging: God and the Elderly* (Philadelphia: Fortress, 1987); R. P. Knierim, "Age and Aging in the Old Testament" in *Ministry with the Aging*, ed. W. M. Clements (San Francisco: Harper & Row, 1981) 21-36; J. Laporte, "The Elderly in the Life and Thought of the Early Church" in *Ministry with the Aging*, ed. W. M. Clements (San Francisco: Harper & Row, 1981) 37-55; S. Sapp, *Full of Years: Aging and the Elderly in the Bible and Today* (Nashville: Abingdon, 1987); F. Staff, *The Bible Speaks on Aging* (Nashville: Broadman, 1981).

OLIVE, OLIVE TREE. *See* GRAFTING, TREE, TREES; WOOD.

ONE

A majority of the more than two thousand uses of "one" in the Bible refer simply to the singular rather than plural of something—one man, one woman, one hand. No deeper meaning should be construed in these instances. Three uses, though, move beyond the mere singular to suggest something more profound—oneness as a quality of God, as a symbol of unity and as an expression of the unique value of individual persons.

The Divine One. "Hear, O Israel: The LORD our God, the LORD is one" (Deut 6:4 NIV). This is the beginning of the central Jewish creed, and it is quoted by Jesus when he is asked for the most important commandment (Mk 12:29). What does the word *one* imply?

First, *God is the only God. Other gods have no rights whatsoever. They must not be worshiped (Ex 20:1-6). God has created heaven and earth. Whereas other peoples considered sun and moon as deities, Genesis 1:16 makes it clear that they are nothing but lights. God's reign is unrestricted by time and place (Deut 10:14; Ps 90:2). In OT times Near Eastern religions believed that gods had limited spheres of activity (2 Kings 5:17), so that uniqueness of God was an unheard-of claim. In 1 Corinthians 8:4 Paul denies that other gods exist at all.

Second, there is only one God for all people. His reign is not restricted to the Jews (2 Chron 20:6). Even if they do not know it yet, the nations are ruled by him (Ps 32:28). In the same way, salvation through Christ is effective for everyone (Rom 3:29-30).

Third, there are no gradations in deity. It is impossible to become God or to be God up to a certain degree. Consequently the Jews wanted to stone Jesus for blasphemy when he claimed to be one with the *Father (Jn 10:30-31). This statement implies that everything was created and lives through Christ (1 Cor 8:6). The identification of the man Jesus with God is indeed the only way to maintain both the unity of God and justification through Christ. Two gods are impossible, and a mere human being is unable to bring salvation. The man Jesus is the ultimate revelation of God's eternal nature. The resurrection confirms that Jesus' words and deeds are in unison with God's will. The glory that belongs to the only God (1 Tim 1:17) is given to Jesus (Phil 2:9-11).

The Human One. Another dimension of oneness becomes apparent in the unity of the *church. It is founded on the unity of Christ with the Father (Jn 17:21-23). The participation in Christ's sacrifice enables believers to be one *body (1 Cor 10:16-17). God's protection is necessary for this (Jn 17:11). Being united with Christ encourages love, tenderness, compassion, like-mindedness and humility—in short, the same attitude that Jesus had (Phil 2:1-11). Paul speaks of one body with many parts working together and caring for each other (1 Cor 12). Thus being "one in heart and mind" (Acts 4:32 NIV) proves to the world that the unity between Jesus and the Father is real (Jn 17:23). The ultimate reason and purpose of human brotherhood and sisterhood (Mt 23:8-10) is the glory of God.

The quality of being "one" also expresses the uniqueness of human beings. The worth of a single person in the eyes of God is expressed by the parables of the lost sheep and the lost coin (Lk 15:1-10). Here God's preference for the unimportant, the sick, the sinner is stressed even more than in the OT. Tempting "one of these little ones who believe in me" (Mt 18:6 NIV) will have dreadful consequences.

See also FIFTY; FIVE; FORTY; FOUR; HUNDRED; SEVEN; SEVENTY; THOUSAND; THREE; TWELVE; TWO.

OPEN, OPENING

The action of opening something, or something

being opened, is ubiquitous in the Bible. To open is an archetypal act mentioned well over two hundred times. While the most evocative instances are metaphoric and spiritual, we should not overlook the prominence of literal, physical acts of people opening something or having something opened before them. *Ears, *eyes and *mouths are repeatedly opened in the Bible. So are *doors, *gates and *windows. Many times *wombs are said to open upon the birth of a child. Sometimes arms—and even the *heart—are said to open.

The heavens open up at different points throughout the Bible, offering periodic glimpses into the kingdom of God. The heavens opened for Ezekiel to show him visions of God's sovereign plan for his people (Ezek 1:1). Jesus saw the *heavens torn open at his baptism to reveal the Father and the Spirit at one with the Son (Mt 3:16; Mk 1:10-11; Lk 3:21). Sometimes these rendings of the heavens come in visions, as with Ezekiel, Jacob (Gen 28:12-13) and Peter (Acts 10:11). Sometimes they seem quite literal, as with Jesus and Stephen (Acts 7:56). In either case, they are visible only to the one granted eyes to see.

Jesus told Nathanael that he would see "heaven open, and the angels of God ascending and descending on the Son of Man" (Jn 1:51 NIV), suggesting that he himself is the *ladder (as in Jacob's vision) that would finally open up heaven to earth and earth to heaven. Indeed, when the new Jerusalem comes down out of heaven from God, as John prophesies in his vision, Jesus the *Lamb of God will dwell there, himself the light for all to see, in this final and complete opening of heaven to earth (Rev 21:1-3).

Often the heavens open not to be seen but to let something in or out. God sends *chariots of fire from heaven for Elijah (2 Kings 2:11). Sometimes heaven appears as a great *storehouse that opens and sends down supplies—of manna or rain, for example (Deut 28:12). At the right times God's storehouse opens to send down judgments of earthquake, storm or hail (Job 38:22-23; Josh 10:11). God even opens an arsenal against the Babylonians (Jer 50:25). Floodgates in the heavens open up to let forth not only floods (Gen 7:11; 8:2) but *blessing (Mal 3:10) and judgment (Is 24:18). Sometimes we see heaven's opening as a door (Ps 78:23). In Revelation the door of heaven opens for John to go up "in the Spirit" and receive his vision of the end times (Rev 4:2 NIV).

God is the opener of all kinds of doors in Scripture. *Prison doors open at his command (Acts 5:19; 16:26-27). God says he will open doors and gates before Cyrus, using this metaphor to say he will allow him opportunity to be victorious in battle (Is 45:1). NT preachers speak of doors being opened by God for work to proceed and their message to enter in (1 Cor 16:9; 2 Cor 2:12; Col 4:3). When Jesus teaches his followers "Knock and the door will be opened to you" (Mt 7:7; Lk 11:9), he means that God will open the door, opening himself and all of his kingdom to those who humbly ask. "Open for me the gates of righteousness," the psalmist prays; "I will enter and give thanks to the LORD" (Ps 118:19 NIV).

In Revelation 3:20 the picture turns around: it is Jesus who stands knocking, and the person who hears his voice opens the door. The Bible calls the earth and its creatures to open themselves to God, who opens his heavens to them. They must receive his salvation, just as the earth opens itself to the rain from heaven (Is 45:8). Fundamentally, however, God is always the final opener. When Lydia believed in Christ, "the Lord opened her heart to respond" (Acts 16:14 NIV). In fact, death and destruction and all human hearts and minds "lie open" to the sovereign God (Prov 15:11; Ps 38:9; Lk 24:45).

This opening and closing between heaven and earth is often communicated in terms of parts of the human anatomy that open and close: eyes, ears, mouths and hands. God's eyes are open to all the ways of people (Jer 32:19). Many prayers ask God to come to their aid in these terms: "Give ear, O LORD, and hear; open your eyes, O LORD and see" (e.g., Is 37:17 NIV). Food and blessings we receive come from God's open hand (Ps 104:28; 145:16). And it is God who both calls people to open their eyes and ears and who, paradoxically, himself does the opening (Is 42:18; 35:5; 50:5).

"What he opens, no one can shut; and what he shuts, no one can open" (Rev 3:7 NIV). God opens what he wills (wombs (Gen 29:31; 30:22); rocks that gush water (Ps 105:41); a whole sea (Ps 74:13); the very earth itself (Num 26:10; Ps 106:17). But God's most marvelous opening is of himself to us through Christ, pictured well by the tearing open of the curtain separating the Most Holy Place from the rest of the *temple. This tearing open was as great as any rending of the heavens, for Christ's death brought "a new and living way opened for us through the curtain, that is, his body," leading us into the very presence of God (Heb 10:19-20 NIV).

See also DOOR; EAR, HEARING; EYE, SIGHT; GATE; SHUT, CLOSE; WOMB.

OPPRESSION

The experience of oppression pervades the entire Bible, although it can be of several kinds and come from different quarters. It is often associated with physical and spiritual burdens, the *violence of *war or unjust social and political systems.

When the people of God endure oppression at the hand of other nations, it is borne in either cruel servitude or war. The harsh oppression that profoundly marked the theology of the OT was the *slavery suffered in *Egypt. The Israelites were afflicted by ruthless taskmasters and threatened with infanticide; any hint of *rebellion brought more irrational demands from the *pharaoh (Ex 1—2, 5). This oppression at the dawn of the nation's history also produced another key element that becomes a recurring pattern throughout the Bible: the people of God, when desperate under oppression, cry out to him for mercy and deliverance. In Egypt the

Israelites called out to the Lord, who remembered the *covenant (Ex 2:23-25; 3:7-9; Deut 26:6-8).

In the book of *Judges Israel goes through several cycles of oppression as judgment for sin (e.g., Judg 2:18; 4:3; 10:8). Once again the people of God cry out for help (e.g., Judg 3:9,15; 6:6-7; 10:10,12). The fear and impoverishment of the oppressed is vividly pictured in the account of Gideon (Judg 6). Because of the marauding Midianites the Israelites could not tend their ravaged land, and they hid in caves; consequently, the angel of the Lord found Gideon threshing in a winepress. But Judges also demonstrates that oppression can refer to invasion and armed conflict. Oppression as attack by a foreign power is presented as a covenant *curse (Deut 28:25-37). The historical and prophetic books present a series of wars as *judgments, culminating in the destruction of *Jerusalem (e.g., 2 Kings 13:22; Amos 6:14; Jer 50:33). The agony and horror of that devastation is powerfully expressed in *Lamentations. The human loss and the demolition of the holy city and temple leave the author stunned and weeping.

The violence of oppression, however, is not only administered against God's people by other nations. The biblical text denounces the systemic oppression of the leadership of Israel against those who cannot defend themselves and who have no power—the poor, the widow, the orphan and the alien. Amos decries the "cows of Bashan"—those pampered, wealthy women who demand drink even as they exploit the needy (Amos 4:1; cf. 6:4-6). Micah describes the rulers of Judah as wild beasts who rip and eat the flesh of the people (Mic 3:1-3). Ecclesiastes says that the oppressed have no one to dry their tears and that for some it would have been better never to have been born (Eccles 4:1-3).

The pity and anger evoked by the imagery of passages like these can be contrasted with that of others that look forward to the character of the future reign of God's *anointed one. Whereas the kings and officials of Israel take advantage of the weak for their own ends (Is 10:1-4; Jer 22:15-17; Ezek 18:5-18; Amos 2:7, 5:11-12), the ideal monarch defends the afflicted and judges the oppressor (Ps 72). The Messiah will rule with justice and in *peace and *gentleness (Is 11; 42; 61). There will be no more oppression, whether of war, slavery or internal injustice. In this concern for the oppressed, he mirrors the heart of the Lord (Ps 9:9 [Heb 10]; 10:17-18; 103:6).

In the NT several of these themes reappear. Perhaps the *persecution suffered by the early church can be considered as parallel to the oppression from external sources. Apostles and other believers are subject to trials, incarceration, beatings and stoning (e.g., Acts 4; 7—8; 12; 21—28; 2 Cor 4; Phil 1). At the same time, the congregations were not exempt from victimizing the helpless in their own midst and favoring the prominent (Jas 2:1-13; 5:1-6).

The Gospels and the Epistles reveal still another dimension of oppression, the *demonic. Satan holds people under his power, afflicting some with *disease and keeping many in spiritual darkness (e.g., Lk 13:10-17; Acts 10:38; 26:17-18). However, as the one anointed by the Spirit of God, Jesus announces that his reign brings freedom from every kind of *bondage (Lk 4:18-21). In him the oppression of all humanity finds its ultimate solution.

In sum, the primary imagery of oppression is that of bondage, rights taken away, property confiscated, life threatened and resultant discouragement and fear. Oppression always has a human agent who imposes it. This archetypal oppressor might be a nation (such as the Egyptians, Philistines, Assyrians, Babylonians or Romans), but even in these instances the nation is usually represented by its bullying ruler. The gallery of oppressors from the pages of the Bible include Pharaoh, Ben-hadad, Sennacherib, Nebuchadnezzar and Herod. The archetypal oppressor might also be a class within society, such as the wealthy people in the prophecy of Amos who oppress the poor, the Pharisees of the Gospels or the Jews of the book of Acts.

See also BABYLON; BONDAGE AND FREEDOM; EGYPT; PERSECUTION; VIOLENCE, STORIES OF; WARFARE.

ORACLE

The occurrence of oracles and their many and varied associations often pass unrecognized in translation. The Hebrew phrase *šā'albᵉ* and the verb *dāraš* both translated "to inquire of," function as technical terms for consulting the deity. Both expressions can have either pagan deity or monotheistic God as object, that is, as the power behind the spirit that provides answers and predictions. In addition to narratives about obtaining oracles, these phrases are extremely common, pointing to the importance of this activity and implying a large repertoire of methods and rituals.

Oracle as Answers from God. The Scriptures allude to many methods of ancient divination. Although relatively little is known about their actual practice, among them we find the following:

Astrology (Deut 4:19; 2 Kings 17:16; 21:3-5; 23:4-5, 11-12; Jer 7:17-18; 8:2; 19:13; 44:16-19; Ezek 8:16). The *sun and *moon (Josh 10:12-13) or *stars act as Israel's allies in battle (Judges 5:20), the worship of the star god Kaiwan is condemned (Amos 5:26), and Isaiah speaks of those who "study the heavens . . . gaze at the stars, and at each new moon predict what shall befall you (Is 47:13 NRSV).

Heptoscopy, the reading of the livers of sacrificial sheep (Ezek 21:21), is neither endorsed nor prohibited in Leviticus as a form of diviniation (Lev 3:4; 9:10).

Hydromancy. Wells and springs were regarded as oracular sites in the ancient world. Springs that bubbled up were quite naturally regarded as places to consult chthonic spirits. Some place names testify to such traditions. *ʿEn mišpāt* (Gen 14:7) and the investiture ceremony at Serpent's Rock near *ʿēn rōgēl* ("diviner's spring," 1 Kings 1:9; cf. the ancient association of oracles with snakes, an example being the "Pythonic spirit," translated "spirit of divination," in Acts 16:16). Joseph used his cup for divining (Gen 44:5, 15). Rivers too have long been viewed as mythological judges.

Fleece reading appears with Gideon, but it has parallels outside Israel (Judg 6:37-40, cf. Aeneas sleeping on a fleece in the cave of divination).

Rhabdomancy, the divining by trees, wooden rods and arrows, receives mention as "inquiring of wood" (Hos 4:12; cf. Jer 2:27). Similar ideas inform the story of Aaron's magical budding rod (Num 17:7) and the magical effects of Jacob's sticks on breeding animals (Gen 30:31-39; revealed in a dream, Gen 31:10). Neb-uchadnezzar calls upon his diviner to perform an arrow ritual (Ezek 21:21); Elisha communicates future events to Joash by interpreting the actions of arrows (2 Kings 13:15). Arrows carry a coded message for David from Jonathan (1 Sam 20:20-38). Many trees hold associations with judging and giving oracles (oak of the teacher, Gen 12:6-8; diviner's oak, Judg 9:37; Deborah's palm, Judg 4:5); the angel of the Lord sat under the oak at Ophrah and prophetically motivated Gideon (Judg 6:11).

Teraphim, sometimes translated "idols" and sometimes "sculpted stones," were thought to answer questions put to them (Ezek 21:21; Zech 10:2); and the Asherah, representing the tree, was probably also used for divination (1 Kings 14:23). Teraphim are sometimes condemned (1 Sam 15:23; 2 Kings 23:24), but at other times are legitimated or tolerated (in David's house, 1 Sam 19:22-17; in Jacob's possession, Gen 31; in Micah, Judg 17:5) or are ambiguous (Hos 3:4).

Dreams were an especially common medium of divine communication. All around the Mediterranean, Assyrian kings, Egyptian pharaohs, Greek heroes and presumably everyday citizens sought out guidance from dreams. In the NT Matthew records use of dreams as warnings to Joseph, the Magi and Pilate's wife (Mt 1:20; 2:12; 2:13, 19, 22; 27:19). Acts tells of visions to Paul (Acts 16:9), Peter (Acts 10:10) and Ananias (Acts 9:10). Scripture records many dreams as messages from God. When this expected channel is shut down, Saul complains that God no longer answers him by dreams (1 Sam 28:15). Even a pagan's dream is a message from God (Judg 7:13).

Incubation dreams. In most ancient societies people sought out divine oracles as dreams by sleeping in sanctuaries. Pagan deities communicated in this way (Is 65:4) but so too did God. Because of a dream, Jacob gives the name Beth El, "sanctuary," to the dream spot (Gen 28). Samuel, when the word of the Lord and visions becomes infrequent, sleeps in the sanctuary instead of his own quarters (1 Sam 3:1-3). Solomon sleeps at the great high place in Gibeon for his dream from God (1 Kings 3:4, 5).

Necromancy, the consulting of the spirits of the departed, was strictly prohibited as an *abomination (Lev 19:31; 20:6; Deut 18:11), yet the lure of predictions from the dead kept the practice alive. Passages in Isaiah (Is 8:19-20; 28:15-22; 65:4) refer to incubation dreams in tombs to obtain revelations from netherworld deities and spirits. Isaiah 9:24 describes the wispy voice from dead spirits in the pit. In spite of the ban, a desperate Saul resorts to a medium, getting one more answer from Samuel (1 Sam 28).

The ark of the covenant was a symbol of God's presence with Israel, and in some instances it is associated with "inquiring of the Lord" (Judg 20:27; 1 Sam 14:18; 1 Chron 21:30).

Urim and Thumim are associated with the high priest and the giving of guidance (Deut 33:8, 10; 1 Sam 14:41; called "oracle" in Sirach 45:10), but their actual nature and use are difficult to determine. It has been speculated that the urim and thummim were flat objects with a "yes" and "no" side. As in a coin toss, the side(s) that landed "up" determined the answer to a query (1 Sam 14:18; cf. Prov 16:33).

The ephod eludes our firm determination. It is sometimes a divinely sanctioned garment worn by priests (Ex 28; cf. 1 Sam 2:18, 28; 22:18) and in other cases it appears as an idol consulted (Judg 8:27; 17:5; 18:14-20; 1 Sam 23:9 [cf. 14:18]; 30:7; Hos 3:4).

Oracles as Pagan or Proper Methods of Divination? The modern reader may recoil from the idea that worshipers of the God of Israel performed rituals that differed little from their pagan neighbors. Yet many of the methods used in common with neighboring cultures were acceptable. Oracular inquiry allowed for divine guidance and input: "The lot is cast into the lap, but the outcome thereof is the LORD's" (Prov 16:33). When condemnation of divination occurs in the OT, it usually takes issue with the god or spirit reached by the method, not with the method itself. Dreams from God are approved; dreams from tomb spirits are not. The oracle of the God of Israel is legitimate; that of Baal-zeboul is not (2 Kings 1:1-16). Wearing phylacteries into battle is not wrong, but they must not contain the names of pagan gods (2 Mac 12:40). So too "the sin of divination" probably means consulting other gods (1 Sam 15:23; 2 Kings 17:17).

Divination as Power. The ability to envision or manipulate the future gave the oracle great influence. *Joseph manipulated his brothers' fears about the reputation of Egyptian diviners (Gen 44:15). Ahithophel's fame for wise counsel was "as if one consulted the oracle of God" (2 Sam 16:23). Daniel's promotion to political power stemmed from his ability to interpret dreams about the future. Diviners receive mention as leaders of the people (Is 3:2, 3). The dying words of patriarchs, far seeing, laden with wisdom and couched in poetic verse, functioned as oracles (2 Sam 23:1; Deut 31:1; 33:1; Gen 49:1).

Oracles as politics and lies. The Israelites did not consider it strange that Balaam, a pagan oracle, should attempt to meddle in their future. The Lord's ability to usurp Balaam's mouth and thwart Balak's intentions served as evidence of the Lord's supreme power (Num 23:5). Israelite prophets also rendered oracles regarding foreign nations that altered the course of their neighbors' history and consequently their own. At home in the royal court, Ahithophel's good counsel to Absalom needed to be countered with bad advice (2 Sam 17:14). Bad oracles could be the result of a lying spirit sent by the Lord (1 Kings 22:22-23). Fake oracles were also a possibility (Jer 23:16).

Oracles as self-fulfilling prophecy. Elijah's revelation that Hazael will replace Ben-hadad as ruler of Syria appears to function both as prophecy and as a planted suggestion (1 Kings 19:15; 2 Kings 8:12-15). Other prophecies were brought to pass by people consciously fulfilling prophetic utterances as a form of obedience to God, as when Jehu commands his men to do "in accordance with the word [oracle] of the LORD" (2 Kings 9:25 NIV).

Oracles as self-interpreting parables. While the bulk of oracles are rendered in poetry, Balaam's oracles are labeled *parables, *proverbs or figures (Num 23:7). Nathan elicits self-condemnation from David with a parable (2 Sam 12:1-6). Jotham vividly portrays the political folly of Shechem with a parable about the trees choosing a king (Judges 9:8-15). Many other prophets participated as actors in dramatizations of future events (e.g., 1 Kings 20:35-37; Ezek 5:1-4).

Oracles as God's Word. Finally, God's word as the Law (Acts 7:38; Rom 5:2; Heb 5:12; Wisdom 16:11), or as (written) prophecy (2 Macc 2:4), or even the utterances of the early Christian prophet, are called oracles (1 Pet 4:11).

See also CHEAT THE ORACLE; DREAMS, VISIONS; MAGIC; PROPHET, PROPHETESS.

BIBLIOGRAPHY. A. Jeffers, *Magic and Divination in Ancient Palestine* (Leiden: E. J. Brill, 1996).

ORDEAL, STORIES OF

If defined broadly as a difficult or trying experience that tests the resourcefulness, character and perseverance of a protagonist, the ordeal story is almost synonymous with storytelling itself. The chief ingredients of a story of ordeal are (a) a protagonist with whom the reader undergoes the struggle, (b) a situation, event or person that resists the protagonist, (c) an encounter between the protagonist and the obstacle and (d) outcome in the form of either defeat or *triumph. The main function of this article is to suggest something of the diversity of ordeal stories in the Bible.

That diversity extends first of all to the characters who confront an ordeal. Most ordeal stories in the Bible trace the fortunes of a solitary protagonist—*David confronting Goliath in single combat, for example, or Elijah bringing God's word to an evil *king, or Jesus engaged in conflict with his detractors. A second possibility is to show a family confronting an ordeal, such as the family of *Abraham or *Jacob coping with *drought, or the family of Elimelech coping with loss in a foreign country. The NT counterparts to OT stories of family ordeals are ordeals encountered by the disciples of Christ or teams of missionaries. Third, in the Bible a nation is frequently the entity that undergoes an ordeal, as in stories of the wandering nation of Israel during the *exodus or *battle stories involving a nation. The NT parallel is ordeals involving the *church. Even more amplification occurs when Scripture treats the corporate human race as the entity that faces an ordeal—the ordeal of God's *judgment against human sin, for example, or its own impulse toward evil rather than good.

Even more diversity emerges when we consider the nature of the ordeals that characters and groups undergo. *Nature is a constant source of ordeals in the Bible, which after all is set in a geographic locale that is generally inhospitable to life. Thus we read continually about individuals, families and nations confronting drought, *floods, predators and excessive heat. In a book where most people *travel incessantly, the terrain becomes a source of ordeal, with its *rocks, its treacherous pathways, its hidden *dangers, its scorching desert conditions. It is hardly an exaggeration to say that any time the characters of the Bible step outside, they face the possibility of an ordeal.

Battle stories reveal a second source of external ordeal, as soldiers or nations have to overcome threats to their lives. In stories of single combat the ordeal consists of physical struggle with one's rival. *War stories in the Bible more often provide a wide-scale view of battlefield action, with the conflict spread over entire *armies. While the chief elements of an ordeal on the battlefield are the threats of *death, injury or capture, war stories in the Bible often reach out to show the effect on a whole society, where lack of food or threat of capture infiltrates life beyond the battlefront.

Other people are another category of external ordeal that a protagonist might encounter. There is, in fact, a large group of Bible stories that portray protagonists confronting hostile people in personal conflict. Such are the slanderers and their intrigue that trouble the psalmist in the lament psalms, the hostile King Saul, with whom David has to deal over an extended time, and brothers who try to thwart the destiny of Joseph. One quickly gets the impression when reading the Bible that living in one's family and society is itself a continual ordeal, testing one's patience and ability to survive. Leaders like *Moses, Saul and David are particularly susceptible to ordeals.

But an ordeal need not directly involve another person. It might be a task or situation. Finding adequate grazing land was an ordeal for Abraham (Gen 13). For Moses, leading a nation was a long-term ordeal. Securing the bride of his choice was a fourteen-year ordeal for Jacob (Gen 29:15-28). Overcoming childlessness was an ordeal for Abraham and Sarah, for Rachel (Gen 30:1-8), for Hannah (1

Sam). Coping with adversity and loss was an ordeal for Naomi (Ruth 1). Waiting patiently for love to mature and the wedding day to arrive was an ordeal for the bride in the Song of Songs. Being prevented from worshiping God in the temple as he lived in exile was an ordeal for the speaker in Psalms 42—43. Facing the terror of the *cross became Jesus' dark night of the soul in Gethsemane.

A further category of ordeals is personality or character traits within oneself. Characters can be their own worst enemies. Abraham's tendency to take things into his own hands and do what seems immediately expedient makes his life difficult on several occasions. Jacob's inherent competitiveness keeps getting him into trouble. The same is true of Samson's indulgent self-will and sensuality. The problems of David's later life stem from his impulsiveness with Bathsheba and Uriah. Solomon's pagan marriages turn his heart from God in his later years. Peter's unthinking rashness leads him to deny Christ. In short, the events that become ordeals for a person can be aspects of his or her own personality or character.

In a book where place figures prominently and place is often as much spiritual as physical, it is impossible to think about ordeals without thinking about specific places. The battlefield is one such place. But the *wilderness is even more striking. The ordeals of the exodus find their locus in the wilderness through which the nation of Israel passes to the Promised Land. The wilderness is also the place of Jesus' *temptation by *Satan, an ordeal that deserves special note. In fact, the ordeal in the wilderness can be viewed as a rite of passage for God's Son. Jesus recapitulates the ordeal of Israel in the wilderness, defeating Satan as the new Adam, the archetypal new man and hero. In defeating the specific temptations of Satan, Jesus encompasses his entire ministry, emerging triumphant from an ordeal designed by Satan to threaten his redemptive purpose.

Stories of *journey and *quest (Abraham's quest for a son and land, Jacob's quest to become a godly person, the Israelites' quest for the Promised Land, Paul's missionary journeys) can perhaps summarize the essential principles of the ordeal story. The physical act of travel is itself a series of obstacles that must be overcome. Some of the obstacles pertain to physical safety and survival, others to interactions with traveling companions or surrounding people. Journeys are stressful situations that test the characters who undertake them, with the result that character flaws often manifest themselves. The sheer perseverance required to complete a journey or quest becomes an ordeal.

Stories of ordeal are basic to storytelling. In the Bible, as in literature and life, they constitute an essential paradigm for what the writers want to say, and for their view of life itself.

See also BATTLE STORY; DANGER, STORIES OF; DEMONS; QUEST; SATAN; TEMPTATION, TEMPTER; TRAVEL STORY; WILDERNESS.

ORDER

Modern notions of order and disorder are largely shaped by mechanical concepts derived from Newtonian physics that suggest that the universe is an orderly, albeit supremely complex, machine. Such clockwork imagery is not found in Scripture, which sees the orderliness of the universe in much more personal terms.

Order and Covenant. According to the Genesis account, when God created the earth, he distinguished between *day and *night and set the greater and lesser lights to govern them and to mark the passage of days, *seasons and years (Gen 1:14); he reaffirmed this seasonal regularity following the flood (Gen 8:22). But Scripture sees nothing mechanical about this order, rather interpreting it as reflecting a *covenantal relationship between God and his creation (Jer 33:20, 25). Similarly, God's *providential ordering is revealed in his relationship to living creatures. God establishes an interdependency among living creatures, provides their habitat and designates their water supplies and food chains (Ps 104:27-28).

God's working outside the normal pattern of order is often described as the miraculous. Such a description is permissible as long as it is understood that God is not less actively involved in the "natural" patterns that we observe around us than in the so-called "supernatural" exceptions that we term miracles.

Order and Distinctions. Although the divine orderliness of the universe is often manifested in patterns of regularity, the divine order is most frequently described in Scripture by various separations or distinctions. For example, in the creation narrative in the first chapter of Genesis, God overcomes the formlessness of the pri-meval universe with a series of boundaries: between *light and *darkness, *day and *night, *sea and dry *land (cf. Ps 104:9), the firmament and the heavens, the creatures that live in those various realms, and human beings, created in the image of God and called upon to rule over all the rest of creation (Gen 1:1-28).

Orderliness through distinction carries over into the *worship and service of Israel in the *sabbath principle that sets apart the sabbath day and year, and the year of Jubilee; in the rituals of sanctity that separate the *clean from the unclean; by *circumcision and the *law, which distinguish Israel from the other nations; and by the word of God, which distinguishes the commandments of God from the traditions of men and the worship of the true God from that of *idols.

This pattern of distinction is reinforced by various principles of separateness embedded in the law. God commands his people that different fabrics are not to be mixed in clothing, different seeds in the field or different cattle in the breeding stalls (Lev 19:19). Likewise, the Mosaic law insists that the customary clothing that is traditional for sexual differentiation is not to be exchanged between the genders and maintains the laws of consanguinity that distinguish between neighbor and kin.

Order and Wisdom. The patterns and boundaries that reflect both the physical and moral order of the universe, while always present and integral to creation, are not always easily discerned or their utility immediately grasped. Nonetheless, even before the Fall, God gave to men and women, as his image bearers, a commission (also known as the "cultural mandate") to gain insight into this order and make explicit use of it by bringing the earth into subjection (Gen 1:28) and by being good stewards of the *garden into which they were placed (Gen 2:5). While the Fall makes fulfilling the cultural mandate more difficult, the responsibility to do so continues in the form of the biblical obligation to pursue *wisdom. Thus, in the wisdom literature of Proverbs and Ecclesiastes, part of wisdom is to be able to understand the order with which God created the world (Prov 8:22-36), to distinguish things that differ and to discern the appropriate and inappropriate times for everything under heaven (Eccles 3:1-8). Those who refuse to pursue wisdom and prefer instead to live disorderly lives are labeled in the book of Proverbs as fools and *sluggards.

Order and Salvation. If orderliness is crucial for humanity's cultural task, it is even more important for God's redemptive work. For if God and his word bring order, sin disrupts it. God's solution is to reassert order, again by distinguishing between things that differ. Thus the first redemptive promise is a promise of division between the *seed of the woman and of the *serpent, which will bring about the conquest of the serpent and a restoration of the divine moral order (Gen 3:15).

This restoration is achieved through God's work of redemption in Christ. *Jesus shows himself to be the Lord of creation in commanding the waves of the *sea to be still. He restores the moral order by his death on the cross and sets the stage for the final judgment in which all things will be set right and there will be a new heaven and a new earth (Rev 21:1).

Ultimately, the notion that God is a God of order and not of confusion (1 Cor 14:33) extends beyond the physical realm to include relationships within the state and the church. It includes God giving authority to civil rulers to protect life, to restrain evil and to provide social stability so that the gospel may be preached and lived in peace (Rom 13:1-7; 1 Tim 2:1, 2). It also embraces the obligation of church leaders to be certain that all activities within the household of God are conducted "decently and in order" (1 Cor 14:40 KJV).

See also COSMOLOGY; CREATION; WISDOM..

ORDINANCE. *See* LAW.

ORIGIN, IMAGES OF

The question of origins is a universal human preoccupation. The adopted child's quest for his or her parental origin becomes relentless once the desire is awakened. The quest for knowledge of origins is a quest for identity. The Bible is fundamentally a book about origins. It purports to give a perspective on the origin of all important things: man and woman, creatures of nature, the world itself, society, family, even the evil that resides in the universe (Gen 3). The exception is God himself, the originator of everything except evil, who has no origin of his own.

Origin identifies the root or foundational character of a thing. To identify an origin is partly to understand the essence of something; hence the relevance of images of origin. If the habitable earth was originally a garden, our understanding of it is quite different from what it would be if we regarded the earth as a mere collection of matter that by evolution became the world as we know it. The implications are quite different if we view people as having been created in the image of God as compared with viewing them as having evolved from lower animals (as captured by the comment of a well-known evolutionist about humankind: "So there he stands, our vertical, hunting, weapon-toting, territorial, neotenous, brainy, Naked Ape, a primate by ancestry and a carnivore by adoption").

The nature of origin as essence is illustrated in the creation of *Eve, who is described in Scripture as derivative from *Adam and taken from his side (Gen 2:21-22). From this origin the woman derives her name (Gen 2:23), her status as a fellow bearer of God's image (Gen 1:27), her oneness with Adam in the *marriage relationship (Gen 2:23-24) and her vocation as a suitable helper (Gen 2:20) in fulfilling the cultural mandate to fill the earth and bring it under subjection (Gen 1:26-28). Additionally, the fact that woman was made from man and not man from woman is adduced as evidence by Paul that the husband is the head of the wife (1 Cor 11:3, 8).

Creation illustrates the same principle. The creation is from God, but it was made out of nothing. This means that although God is the source of the creation, he is distinct from it, and that although the created order depends on God, it does not emanate from him and is not itself divine. The OT parable of the woodsman who creates an *idol out of a piece of *wood after having first used other parts of the wood to cook his lunch and warm himself (Is 44:13-20) points to the foolishness of idolatrous thinking and practice, in which persons worship and serve the creation rather than the Creator and imagine God to be merely some extension of the created order (Rom 1:21-25). Our understanding of origin is bound up with our understanding of the essence of something.

A final thing to note about origins is that things resemble the thing from which they originate. Conversely, things cannot have origins that are unlike them: a fresh-water *spring produces fresh *water, not salt water, and a *fig tree yields figs, not olives (Jas 3:11-12).

The Origin of Humanity. Modern discussions of the "origin of man" largely center on the method by which human life originated—whether instantaneously or by some kind of process. The biblical description of the origin and creation of humans, however, is remarkably brief, considering the importance of the subject. It consists of three verses (Gen 1:26-27; 2:7), the third and most detailed of which is full of anthropomorphic language. This does not mean that the narrative is in any way untrue; it simply suggests that Scripture makes little attempt to provide answers to the kinds of questions regarding details of the origin of human life that we might like to pose from our twentieth-century scientific perspective. What Scripture does affirm is that God himself was responsible for bringing the first man into being and that he did so by utilizing preexisting "earthy" material, which Scripture labels "the dust of the ground."

This "earthiness" of humanity is one of the most important images in Scripture related to origins. Because people are taken from the dust of the ground, they are by nature from the earth, earthy, and derived from the constituent elements to which they will eventually return (Gen 3:7). The concomitant of an earthy origin is that it instills humility and discourages pride, as well as serving as a constant reminder of death as a judgment for sin. In the OT similar applications of our earthiness are found in the book of Job and the Psalms. Most of the references emphasize the brevity and fragility of life (Job 4:19; 10:9; 7:21; 34:15; Ps 30:9; 90:3). But in at least one instance our earthiness also elicits a sympathetic and gracious response from the Lord, who "knows how we are formed, he remembers that we are dust" (Ps 103:14 NIV).

In the NT the image of humanity's earthy origin is particularly emphasized in order to contrast the earthy life of the first Adam with the spiritual life of the second Adam, Christ (1 Cor 15:47-48). Paul contrasts the earthy (those who are in Adam in his earthiness and are part of the present evil age) with those in Christ (who will be transformed [1 Cor 15:51] into new, imperishable, immortal and heavenly spiritual bodies, like the spiritual body of the resurrected Christ). Viewed from this perspective, the issue of origin is critical to salvation. Everything rests on whether an individual is "in Adam" or "in Christ." All those who trace their roots through Adam are patterned after his earthiness and shall die. Those who are found in Christ shall exhibit his Spirit life and shall be made alive (1 Cor 15:21).

Balancing the image of the earthiness of human origins is the emphasis of Scripture that people were created in the image of God. In keeping with the principle that origin determines essence, the connotations here are quite different from those of being made from the dust. As creatures made in God's image, people are unique within creation. They share divine qualities, including the power of reason, creativity (when we first read about people created in the image of God, the chief thing that we know about this God is that he creates), future immortality, and

the traits that the NT calls true knowledge, righteousness and holiness (Eph 4:24; Col 3:10). As God's image bearer, humanity receives a unique status within creation itself to be viceregents, under God, over the world that God has made (Gen 1:26-28). The exalted status that Psalm 8 ascribes to humanity ("little less than God," crowned "with glory and honor," given dominion over the visible creation—Ps 8:5-6 RSV) is specifically rooted in the fact that God "made" humanity thus.

People are by origin double creatures—both earthy and possessed of divine qualities. Even the passage that describes Adam's creation from the dust of the ground hints at this duality, since Adam did not become "a living being" until God "breathed into his nostrils the breath of life" (Gen 2:7 RSV; cf. Eccles 12:7: the physical dust of the body "returns to the earth as it was," while "the spirit returns to God who gave it" [RSV]).

The Origin of the Visible Universe. The visible universe also bears the imprint of its Creator (*see* Creation). Much that the Bible ascribes to the universe is traceable back to *God as its origin. When a person makes something, for example, we can assume that the created thing has a purpose or *telos*. The created world, we can infer from Scripture, has as its purpose to express the goodness and glory of God (Ps 19:1; 148). The *beauty of creation, too, is a beauty that can be traced back to God's handiwork (Ps 19:1); in fact, God intended creation to be both beautiful and functional (Gen 2:9; *see* Nature). Again, because God is the Creator of the visible universe, it exists to serve him (Ps 104:2-4).

A created object has design and planning behind it. The created order is such a design. Its orderly rhythms reflect a God of order (Ps 19:6; 104:19-23). Further, a person who makes something assumes a responsibility to keep it up. In large and small ways, the Bible pictures the universe as something for which God provides (Ps 104:10-30).

The creation story in Genesis 1 hints at further applications. The fact that God created the universe means that it is not self-sufficient but dependent. It is not an emanation from God and is therefore separate from God and not to be viewed as itself divine. Coming from a God who is himself good, the universe is repeatedly declared to be "good" and "very good."

In the Bible, moreover, passages dealing with God's creation of the universe often have a polemical purpose behind them, with the intention of refuting rival creation stories of surrounding pagan cultures. Whereas other creation stories are really theogonies (stories of the origins of the gods), the Bible takes the eternal existence of the Creator for granted and tells of the creation of the world. In contrast to creation myths built around the motif of conflict, in which deities battle each other, the creation story in the Bible is the epitome of harmony and order. As a result, while pagan views of the world tend toward an incipient dualism, with forces of chaos always on the verge of regaining control of the universe, the Bible portrays a God who decisively and calmly governs the world (Ps 74:12-17; 104:5-9).

The Genealogy of Salvation. The theme of a division between two humanities, in accordance with their spiritual origin, is not original to the NT but finds its roots in the original promise of redemption given to Adam and Eve (Gen 3:14-15). In this passage God declares that he will make a division within humanity by putting enmity between the seed of the woman and the seed of the serpent. The Bible thus views spiritual pedigree as very important.

Even in the period prior to the flood, the Bible traces the line of Seth as a line of life and the line of *Cain as the line of death; their intermingling results in the judgment of the flood. As God's redemptive purposes unfold in biblical history, this distinction between the godly and ungodly lines of humanity becomes even more pronounced. For example, in the blessings and curses given by Noah to his children and grandchildren we find a foretaste of genealogical blessings and curses to come (Gen 9:25-27). From the subsequent table of nations arising from Noah's descendants, God determined to call one man, Abram, of the line of Shem (Noah's son whom he had blessed), out of Ur of the Chaldees, to bring him to a new location to displace the descendants of Canaan (Noah's grandson whom he had cursed).

As God makes his covenant with *Abram and his descendants, he promises him that he will make of him a great nation in order to accomplish his redemptive purposes, through which all the families of the earth will be blessed (Gen 12:1-3). The rest of the Bible is the narrative of God's fulfillment of this promise. Israel is formed as a nation, joined to God as his people through the Mosaic covenant, entrusted with the oracles of God and given the promise of a future Messiah. It is because of Israel's privileged position and special stewardship that Jesus can declare to the Samaritan woman that "salvation is from the Jews" (Jn 4:22).

This also meant that access to the covenant promises of God in the OT was attained primarily through national origin. To be a non-Israelite was a substantial, if not absolute, disqualifier. Highly notable exceptions include Ruth the Moabite and Rahab the prostitute from Jericho, both of whom not only became incorporated into the nation of Israel but were also grafted into the genealogy of Christ (Mt 1:5). Two other important foreigners who experienced blessing through contact with Israel include the widow in Zarephath, whose son was healed by Elijah (1 Kings 17:8-24), and Naaman the Syrian, who was cured of his leprosy through Elisha (2 Kings 5:1-15). Jesus specifically appeals to these as examples of judgment on unbelieving Israel and as testimonies to God's intention to extend the blessings of the kingdom to the Gentiles (Lk 4:24-27).

Even these few examples make it clear that God's spiritual genealogy is something other than salvation by insemination, though it is no less real than physical genealogy. All who are true Israelites trace their lineage to Abraham in a spiritual rather than physical sense. Paul explains that the true children of Abraham are those who exhibit Abraham's faith in the promises of God (Rom 2:28-29; 9:6-8; Gal 3:7). It is by being in the seed of Abraham (in Christ) that the blessing of Abraham extends to the Gentiles (Gal 3:13-16). In this sense origin is integrally connected with salvation.

God is the origin of spiritual life, which bears the imprint of his moral character. A dead soul cannot produce a living one: "And you he [God] made alive, when you were dead through the trespasses and sins" (Eph 2:1 RSV). Jesus explained to Nicodemus that what "is born of the flesh is flesh, and that which is born of the Spirit is spirit" (Jn 3:6 RSV). As for the divine mystery of the origin of this life, "The wind blows where it wills, and you hear the sound of it, but you do not know whence it comes or whither it goes; so it is with every one who is born of the Spirit" (Jn 3:8 RSV). "It is the God who said, 'Let light shine out of darkness,' who has shone in our hearts to give the light of the knowledge of the glory of God in the face of Christ" (2 Cor 4:6 RSV).

The Humble Origins of Spiritual Greatness. In Scripture, groups of certain ethnic or geographical origins are sometimes viewed with a jaundiced eye, and this prejudice is often used to make a significant theological point. For example, in the parable in Ezekiel 16 God portrays Israel as a child abandoned in a field to die of exposure. God rescued her, nurtured her, married her and blessed her, only to see her prostitute herself to other gods. God begins this parable by reminding Israel of her humble origins—that her father was an Amorite and her mother a Hittite (Ezek 16:3). This evil pedigree forms a dark backdrop against which the light of God's grace to Israel can be seen more clearly and her wicked rejection of grace contrasted more starkly. The point is that Israel had no reason to take pride in herself and every reason to be grateful to God—but did not.

A different point is made from Jesus' own humble origins. Jesus was raised in Nazareth, which apparently had an unfavorable reputation (Jn 1:46). Likewise, the Galilean region in which Nazareth was located found held little prospect as a source of spiritual benefit (Jn 7:52). This particular detail was not accidental and seems to have two purposes. First, it reinforces how the Lord Jesus humbled himself and took on the form of a servant in order to accomplish his work of redemption on the cross (Phil 2:6-8). Second, it witnesses to God's intention, revealed in his prophetic word, to first reveal his gospel to those of humble origins. It was God's purpose that the people walking in darkness should see a great light (Is 9:1-2).

The apostle Paul makes the same point when he reminds us that not many believers are people of status by human standards, but that God has chosen the foolish to shame the wise and the weak to shame the strong, so that those who belong to God should boast in him and not themselves (1 Cor 1:26-31). The Bible gives us a virtual roll call of spiritual "attainers" who come from unpromising origins: *Mary the mother of Jesus (Lk 1:48), Amos (Amos 7:14), Rahab the harlot, who makes it into Jesus' genealogy (Mt 1:5), *David the shepherd boy, who has to be fetched from the sheep pasture to be anointed king of Israel (1 Sam 16:10-13). As the One who originates spiritual life, God regards the lowly (Ps 138:6), looks after the humble and contrite in spirit (Is 66:2), and gives grace to the humble (Jas 4:6; 1 Pet 5:5).

Summary. Both our human need for and our hope of salvation relate to our origin. As a consequence of sin in our natural state, we are earthy sons and daughters of Adam and offspring of the serpent. By grace we are lifted out of that lowly, sinful position to be joined in Christ to the promised Seed of the woman and declared to be true children of Abraham.

See also ADAM; ABRAHAM; CREATION; FIRST; JESUS; SEED.

ORPHAN

Orphans are mentioned more than forty times in the Scriptures. The Hebrew word for orphan refers to a *child bereft of a *father, whether or not the child's *mother is dead (see Job 24:9). In Israelite society, to be fatherless meant vulnerability to poverty and disenfranchisement. Virtually all the biblical occurrences of *orphan* refer to literal orphans; however, often orphans are used to depict loss, vulnerability and social disruption.

In the patriarchal environment of Israelite society, the father was the source of provision and protection. Without him both wife and children assumed a precarious position. This is why the plight of the *widow and orphan so often occur in tandem in the Scriptures.

The biblical use of orphan emphasizes the great need for advocacy. God himself protects the orphan (Deut 10:18; Ps 10:14, 17, 18; 68:5; Prov 23:10-11). God's care and concern is expressed primarily through his laws and commandments. The Israelites were to represent God's compassion and justice in their treatment of the orphans (Deut 14:28, 29; 16:11, 14; 24:17-22; 26:12-15). The prophetic record, however, reveals that Israel failed in this role and was judged for her failure (Is 1:23; Jer 7:6; Ezek 22:7). Malachi connects the Israelites' *oppression of the orphans with a lack of fear of God (Mal 3:5). Prophetic calls for Israel's *repentance and renewal included demands of proper concern for the orphans (Is 1:17; Jer 7:6; 22:3; Zech 7:10).

When Jesus promises his disciples, "I will not leave you as orphans; I will come to you" (Jn 14:18 NIV), he intimates that his departure would leave the disciples in an extremely desperate state. His own resurrection and the coming of the *Holy Spirit would protect and provide for his vulnerable disciples.

Care for orphans was of such high importance

that in his description of "pure and faultless" religion, James included care for the orphans (Jas 1:27).

See also ADOPTION; CHILD, CHILDREN; FATHER; MOTHER; WIDOW.

OUTCAST

The character type known as the outcast is akin to the wanderer (*see* Wandering) and the *exile. The essential quality of the outcast is that he or she has been expelled from a home (however loosely defined) and forced to travel or reside in an alien place far away. Being an outcast can be the fate of either *saint or *sinner. In either case, the outcast is a pitiable figure, enacting a pattern that everyone tries to avoid having to experience.

*Adam and *Eve are the original outcasts of the human race (just as they are the first in a number of other motifs covered in this dictionary). Their moment of transition is the archetypal and literal expulsion from the *garden of innocence. Thereafter the entire human race has been an outcast from its true home. Adam and Eve are tragic figures responsible for their condition as outcasts; their son *Cain likewise becomes a *guilt-haunted outcast—someone who goes "away from the presence of the LORD" to dwell in the land of "wandering" (Gen 4:16 RSV; see marg.). Equally pathetic is Hagar, cast out with her son Ishmael after the birth of Isaac (Gen 21:8-21). *Jacob too is cast out of his parental home through his own immoral dealings with his brother and father. Biblical outcasts also include notable sinners like the greedy Achan, who is removed from the Israelite camp with his family to be stoned and burned (Josh 7:22-26). Projected onto a national scale, the exiled nations of Israel and Judah are outcasts.

OT health laws made the outcast a familiar figure, as sufferers of various *diseases (most notably *leprosy) or people undergoing rites of purification were required to spend time outside the camp or city (Lev 13:46; 14:8; Num 5:1-4; Num 31:19). In the Gospels we catch glimpses of the plight of lepers as outcasts from society (Mk 1:40; Lk 17:12).

The outcast is a familiar figure in the Gospels. Jesus himself is alienated from the religious establishment, unwelcome in his hometown and in Jerusalem, not having a regular place of residence where he can lay his head. Furthermore, Jesus often reached out to the outcasts of society—the Samaritan woman who came to the *well at noon to avoid interaction with others, the poverty-stricken and ill, the woman caught in *adultery, shady and despised tax collectors like Zacchaeus. Luke especially defines Jesus' ministry as a ministry to outcasts. In Jesus' eschatological parables and sayings, the outcast becomes an image for the person cast into the "outer darkness" of *hell (Mt 8:12; 22:13; 25:30). Of similar import is God's banishing unbelievers with the command "Depart from me, you cursed, into the eternal fire prepared for the devil and his angels" (Mt 25:41 RSV).

Some outcasts are innocent sufferers (*see* Suffering Servant). Such is *Joseph, cast out of his parental home and sold into slavery in a foreign country. *Moses in effect exiles himself from *Egypt when he takes the side of his own nation against the Egyptian taskmasters. Prophets like Elijah and Jeremiah are sufficiently unpopular with evil kings that they often find themselves in the role of outcast. The heroes of faith celebrated in Hebrews 11, "of whom the world was not worthy," include outcasts wandering destitute "over deserts and mountains, and in dens and caves of the earth" (Heb 11:38 RSV). Jesus in his role as the one who atones for sins is the archetypal outcast—the one who "suffered outside the gate in order to sanctify the people through his own blood" (Heb 13:12 RSV), the one who cried from the *cross to his heavenly Father, "My God, my God, why hast thou forsaken me?" (Mt 27:46 RSV; Mk 15:34).

Several additional passages offer a picture of being outcast as a spiritual state. Samuel speaks consolingly to his nation by assuring them that "the LORD will not cast away his people" (1 Sam 12:22 RSV). The psalmist prays that God will not "cast [him] off" (Ps 27:9) and not cast him away from God's presence (Ps 51:11). In the story of Rahab, being an outcast from her own city is actually an image of redemption, as she and her family are rescued from the destruction of Jericho (Josh 6:22-25).

See also EXILE; FOREIGNER; LEPER, LEPROSY; PURITY; SINNER; WALL; WANDERER, WANDERING.

OUTER, OUTSIDE

Over a hundred biblical references to someone's or something's being "outside" are neutral in association, denoting simply a position outside of a building (usually) rather than inside. But references to an "outer" area are often richly connotative and symbolic. In this cluster of references, "outer" is an implied contrast to "inner." Outer *walls, for example, denote a protective barrier that renders the city inside secure. Mainly, though, references to "outer" are architectural references. Palaces, for example, have an outer court and outer rooms, with the implication that the privileged center of power resides in a more secluded inner area. The chief references are to the *temple, where the contrast between outer and inner represent gradations of sanctity. Ordinary worshipers might enter the outer court, but only the priests have access to the more holy inner recesses.

The image of "outside the camp" occurs frequently in Leviticus and Numbers. The camp of Israel is a *sacred space that is sanctified for and by the presence of God dwelling at the center of the camp (*see* Tabernacle). In order to preserve its sanctity, certain things, people and activities are carried or occur outside the camp. Leviticus prescribes that portions of *offerings that are not sacrificed on the *altar (e.g., hide, head, innards) be taken "outside" the camp and burned in a place that is ceremonially clean place (Lev 4:12; 6:11; 8:17; 9:11). But more striking is the blasphemer who is to be taken outside the camp and stoned (Lev 24:14, 14), the man who

breaks the *sabbath ordinance who is executed outside the camp (Num 15:35-36), and those with infectious skin diseases who are to be ushered outside the camp (Num 5:3-4). Following warfare with the Midianites, those who have engaged in killing must remain outside the camp for a period of purification (Num 31:19). "Outside the camp" is associated with various bodily human functions that are judged impure by the law (Deut 23:10, 12). All of these injunctions underscore the ideal sanctity of the community of Israel, the necessity of it being a *holy corporate body, a fit dwelling for the divine presence.

When Israel enters the land and establishes homes and *cities, "outside" is sometimes an image of danger or of judgment. We read of the concubine who is sent outside the house and thereby delivered over to the sexual predations of the men of Gibeah (Judg 19:25). An accused *murderer who is discovered outside a city of refuge by his "avenger of blood" is a fair target of *vengeance (Num 35:26-27). During times of warfare and siege, those who venture outside the walls of the city will face danger and death. In Josiah's reform of worship in *Jerusalem, the city is sanctified by taking objects of *idolatrous worship outside Jerusalem and destroying them by fire (2 Kings 23:4-6). And the shamefulness of divine judgment is promised for Jehoiakim, son on Josiah, who "will have the burial of a donkey—dragged away and thrown outside the gates of Jerusalem (Jer 22:19).

Aspects of the OT pattern may be observed in Jesus' judgment's against Israel. In a great reversal, Jesus speaks of the insiders, the "subjects of the kingdom" who regard themselves as Israel, being thrown "outside" and replaced "inside" by "many who will come from the east and the west" to feast with Abraham. And while the feasting goes on inside, outside there will be "weeping and gnashing of teeth" (Mt 8:10-12 NIV; cf. Mt 22:13; 25:30). The *hypocrisy of the Pharisees is highlighted by a contrast between the "inside" and "outside": outside everything appears clean, whitewashed and righteous; inside is impurity, "dead men's bones" and wickedness (Mt 23:25-28). In Mark's Gospel, "outside" is an image for those who do not comprehend the mystery of the *kingdom of God (Mk 4:11).

In Hebrews 13:11-13 the OT image of portions of sacrifices being transported "outside the camp" is poignantly invoked to interpret the death of Christ on behalf of the people of God: "The high priest carries the blood of animals into the Most Holy Place as a sin offering, but the bodies are burned outside the camp. And so Jesus also suffered outside the city gate to make the people holy through his own blood. Let us, then, go to him outside the camp, bearing the disgrace he bore" (NIV). The divine "center" has borne the searing pain of expulsion and death "outside" in order to save and sanctify his people. They too are now encouraged to follow him in suffering, knowing that short of their arrival at the "city that is to come" (Heb 13:14) they have "no lasting city," and their pilgrim pathway is sanctified by following him who went outside the gate.

Finally, in Revelation's rebirth of OT imagery the holy city of God is contrasted with the "outside," where we find "the dogs, those who practice magic arts, the sexually immoral, the murderers, the idolaters and everyone who loves and practices falsehood" (Rev 22:15 NIV). In the biblical scheme of inside and outside, we should not be surprised at reversals (just as the last shall be first, the least exalted and the lost found), but in the end no one wants to be on the outside looking in.

See also INNER, INSIDE; WALL.

OUTWITTING, STORIES OF

The Bible has a plentiful share of stories in which clever characters outwit their opponents. While the *trickster is a character type that figures in some of these stories, the genre is much more inclusive than that label indicates. In the OT the emphasis on outwitting is partly related to the status of the Israelites as a constantly threatened and often oppressed nation, for whom stories of outwitting an *enemy would have been told and retold with relish. Often such stories are simply stories of survival in a competitive world, a pattern that begins with the biographies of the patriarchs in Genesis. In the NT the personality and life situation of Jesus help to account for the prominence of stories of outwitting. While it is usually good characters who outwit evil ones, there are a few stories in which the exploits of a clever *hero are held up to implicit rebuke.

Outwitting gets off to a shaky moral start in the book of Genesis, where some guilty characters even think they can deceive God. Such are the stories of *Adam after the Fall, when he tries to evade responsibility for eating the forbidden *fruit (Gen 3:12), and of *Cain, who tries to convince God that he does not know where his murdered brother is (Gen 4:9; cf. *Jonah, who thinks he can run away from God when he responds to God's command to "arise and go" by going in a direction opposite of that commanded). *Abraham and Isaac both try to outwit a foreign king regarding the identity of their wives, but this experiment in expediency proves embarrassing to them and signals a lack of faith in God's ability to protect (Gen 12:10-20; 20; 26:6-11). *Jacob outwits his dull-witted brother in the episodes of the exchanged *birthright (Gen 25:29-34) and the stolen *blessing (Gen 27). Laban successfully outwits Jacob in the episode of the substitute bride (Gen 29:15-30), and Jacob and Laban attempt to outwit each other in an ongoing saga about Jacob's wages in livestock, a mockery of materialism (Gen 30:25-43).

The moral tone improves when we come to events surrounding the *exodus. Here the Hebrew midwives outwit *Pharaoh (Ex 1:15-22), as does the mother of Moses (Ex 2:1-10). God outwits the Egyptians by means of the *plagues and the Red Sea destruction of the Egyptian army. Rahab helps the Israelite *spies to outwit the squadron sent for their arrest (Josh 2). Of course, stories of *battle are replete with examples of one side outwitting another, as when Israel renders the forces of Ai vulnerable with an ambush that draws the soldiers out of the city (Josh 8) and surprises the Amorites by marching all night in order to attack in the early morning (Josh 10). The crafty *left-hander Ehud's assassination of the Moabite king Eglon in his private chamber while attendants mill about outside is a classic of outwitting an enemy, and the story features the mocking tone of slave literature (Judg 3:15-30). Jael's murder of the unwitting Sisera while he slept is cut from the same cloth (Judg 4:17-22; 5:24-27). *Samson's career as a strong man is a virtual case study in how to outwit an enemy nation, though the tragedy of his life is his own weakness when confronted with the wiles of pleading pagan wives who outwit him (Judg 14—16). *David follows God's advice in conducting a surprise attack on the Philistines (1 Chron 14:8-17).

Political intrigue can also become the mainspring for stories of outwitting. Saul and David play a stealthy cat-and-mouse game as the former tries to eliminate someone his paranoid mind has deemed a political threat, contrary to all evidence. While Adonijah rallies people for a coronation, Samuel quickly anoints *Solomon king (1 Kings 1:10-53). The counterplot devised by Mordecai and *Esther thwarts the intrigue that Haman plans against the Jews.

Outwitting can even be the means of bringing a person to judgment. By means of a fictional story, Nathan beguiles David into thinking that he is judging a civil case, whereas he is actually judging his own acts of adultery and murder (2 Sam 12:1-14). Something similar is found in the psalms of lament, where evildoers are portrayed as thinking they can outwit a God who seems not to see their evil (Ps 10:3-6, 11; 64:5-6; 73:11). But in sudden *reversal, God in the end turns the tables on the perpetrators of evil, in effect outwitting their grandiose plans (Ps 2:1-6; 10:12-18; 64:7-9; 73:17-20). God can thus be the one who outwits someone.

This reaches its climax in the life of Jesus, who is without doubt the greatest genius at outwitting in the pages of the Bible. As Jesus became an increasingly prominent public figure, the religious establishment of the day undertook an elaborate program of entrapment designed to thwart him. The result is a series of debates and verbal sparrings which Jesus often won through mental and verbal quickness. Here, for example, are the stories of sabbath controversy (Mt 12:1-14; Mk 2:1-12, 23-28; 3:1-6; Lk 6:6-11; 13:10-17), the question about taxes (Mt 22:15-22; Mk 12:18-27; Lk 20:19-26), discourses about divorce and remarriage (Mt 22:23-33; Mk 12:18-27; Lk 20:27-38), the question about what is the greatest commandment (Mt 22:34-40; Mk 12:28-34), Jesus' unanswerable question to the Pharisees about what they thought of the Christ (Mt

22:41-45; Mk 12:35-37; Lk 20:41-44) and the story of the woman caught in adultery (Jn 8:1-11). It is not amiss to read the Gospels as a continuous battle of wits between Jesus and his detractors. Often Jesus wins the battle by quoting or interpreting Scripture, as in Satan's *temptation of Jesus (Mt 4:1-11; Lk 4:1-12).

The most subtle form of Jesus' outwitting someone occurs in several parables that seem not to be examples of debate but that satirically and indirectly expose someone's bad attitude or behavior. The parable of the good Samaritan, for example, deflates a self-righteous lawyer who desired "to justify himself" (Lk 10:25-37). The parables of the lost sheep, the lost coin and the lost son (Lk 15) are parables of grace that silence the murmuring Pharisees and scribes, who complained that Jesus received sinners and ate with them. The parable of the foolish farmer is a put-down of a greedy man who tried to get Jesus to judge a financial squabble with his brother (Lk 12:13-21).

In summary, while it is true that God is portrayed in the Bible as choosing the foolish things of the world to confound the wise, the complementary side of the picture is that God also uses the clever wit of people to achieve his redemptive purposes. Indeed, God himself outwits the forces of evil in the Bible's drama of redemption. Because this story of redemption is a comic story with a happy ending, we find an incipient humor in the Bible's stories of outwitting.

See also CHEAT THE ORACLE; DECEPTION, STORIES OF; HUMOR; TRICKSTER.

OVERHEARING. *See* EAVESDROPPER.

OVERSEER. *See* AUTHORITY, HUMAN.

OWL. *See* BIRDS.

OWN, OWNER

Ownership is a key theme in the Bible, and it has practical as well as spiritual significance. The main meaning is possession, with implications of individual accountability and acknowledgment of God's sovereign ownership of all things.

God the Owner. God's universal ownership is vividly reinforced in the *nature imagery of Psalm 50: "Every animal of the forest is mine, and the cattle on a thousand hills. . . . And the creatures of the field are mine. . . . for the world is mine, and all that is in it" (Ps 50:10-12 NIV). In anticipation of the splendor of the coming rebuilt temple, the Lord exclaims, "The silver is mine and the gold is mine" (Hag 2:8 NIV). The Bible finds such claims fitting in the mouth of the Lord, but in the mouth of a Pharaoh or other another earthly ruler, a claim of ownership is destined for reversal. When Pharaoh boasts, "The Nile is mine; I made it for myself," the Lord likens Pharaoh to a "great monster." The divine hunter put him in his place: "I will put hooks in your jaws" (Ezek 29:3 NIV).

God's Own. But God's ownership is particularly expressed in his relationship with *Israel. At Sinai he declares, "Although the whole earth is mine, you will be for me a kingdom of priests and a holy nation" (Ex 19:5 NIV). Within Israel, God's ownership is representatively focused on the firstborn males, who are in turn represented by the Levites: "The Levites are mine, for all the firstborn are mine. When I struck down all the firstborn in Egypt, I set apart for myself every firstborn in Israel, whether man or animal. They are to be mine. I am the LORD" (Num 3:12 NIV). In Isaiah the theme of divine ownership over Israel intones a message of comfort: "Fear not, for I have redeemed you; I have summoned you by name; you are mine" (Is 43:1 NIV). But Isaiah also speaks of Israel's resistence against God's claim on them, likening them to rebellious *children who do not possess the basic knowledge that domestic animals have of their owners: "The ox knows its owner, and the donkey its master's crib; but Israel does not know, my people do not understand" (Is 1:2-3 NRSV).

Divine ownership is sometimes evoked in images of bodily markings. The *circumcision of Israelite males may be understood as a sign that they belong to Yahweh, the God of Israel. God himself declares to Israel, "See, I have engraved you on the palms of my hands" (Is 49:16 NIV). But in contrast, the suffering Job finds no comfort in divine ownership: "you keep close watch on all my paths by putting marks on the soles of my feet" (Job 13:27 NIV). In contrast with his opponents, who demand circumcision of believers, Paul says that he carries "the marks [*stigmata*] of Jesus branded on my body" (Gal 6:17 NRSV). These marks are probably the scars of the apostolic afflictions entailed in following the crucified Christ. Or as Moffatt translates it: "I bear branded on my body the owner's stamp of Jesus."

In speaking of the Lord Jesus' ownership of new covenant believers, Paul can employ the image of the *"seal" of the Spirit: God has "anointed us by putting his seal on us, and giving us his Spirit in our hearts as a first installment" (2 Cor 1:22 NRSV). The application of a personal seal to an object signifies ownership or authenticity (1 Kings 21:8; Esther 8:8), but in this case believers are not only claimed as God's own, but as God's own they are his heirs. Sealing with the Spirit is closely associated with the metaphor of *adoption (Rom 8:23) and the *inheritance that will one day be received in full: "marked with the seal of the promised Holy Spirit; this is the pledge of our inheritance toward redemption as God's own people" (Eph 1:13-14 NRSV).

Owning the Land. The chief covenantal benefit that God grants Israel is his guarantee of her ownership of the *land of Canaan. But this ownership is more like a lease, for the land first and foremost belongs to Yahweh. Israel is reminded, "The land must not be sold permanently, because the land is mine and you are but aliens and my tenants" (Lev 25:23 NIV). God is the one who leads Israel into the land and conquers the *enemy. The land is a gift, or trust, to Israel. One prominent image of land ownership in the OT is the boundary marker. Boundary markers once set are not to be moved (Deut 19:14; Job 24:2-4; Prov 23:10-11; Hos 5:10). The extensive boundary descriptions in Joshua 13—21 function something like a survey, a plat book, of God's land, which he is allotting to his tribal tenants.

Another image of land ownership is walking on the land, pacing it off, claiming it by the footfall. *Abraham appears to do this in prospect as he moves through the length of the land, building *altars, and then ironically exiting to Egypt because there is a famine in the land (Gen 12:5-10). God promises Moses, "Every place where you set your foot will be yours: Your territory will extend from the desert to Lebanon, and from the Euphrates River to the western sea" (Deut 11:24 NIV). And to Joshua he says, "I will give you every place where you set your foot, as I promised Moses" (Josh 1:3 NIV). But the image is reversed to evoke the landless condition of Israel in exile: "Among those nations you will find no repose, no resting place for the sole of your foot" (Deut 28:65 NIV). Perhaps it is the context of acquiring land by warfare that informs the image of Psalm 60:8, where the triumphant *divine warrior declares, "on Edom I hurl my shoe" (NRSV; cf. Ps 108:9).

God does not merely dole out a large stretch of land to his people; he also divides this land among the twelve tribes, insisting that each tribe must "retain its own inheritance" instead of swapping lands between tribes (Num 36:9). But for all Israel the land is given as a trust, and the divine landlord sets down the stipulations of the law. As long as the stipulations are obeyed, Israel can claim the land as her property. But should Israel disobey the stipulations of the law, the nation will be evicted. For Israelite families the land is a tangible symbol of their personal share in the inheritance of Israel. It is a heinous sin for "the wicked" to "remove landmarks" (Job 24:2 NRSV), for their actions not only threaten an Israelite family's economic support but diminish their practical enjoyment of partaking in God's blessing of land. The covenantal ownership of land in Israel functions as a "middle term" in Israel's relationship with God, a stage upon which Israel relates to God, to fellow Israelites and to the created order. "The prohibition of theft, therefore, did not imply the 'sanctity of property' *per se*, but rather *the sanctity of the relationship between the Israelite household and Yahweh*" (Wright, 135-36).

In the OT the *family is the most significant locus of ownership. The commandment against coveting—"You shall not covet your neighbor's house, . . . wife, . . . manservant, . . . maidservant, . . . ox, . . . ass, or anything that is your neighbor's" (Ex 20:17)—is a protection against violating the integrity of a family before God. Job's imagery of property wrongfully taken achieves its poignancy in the naming of those whose purchase in the family structure is most precarious: "The wicked remove landmarks; they seize flocks and pasture them. They drive away the donkey of the orphan; they take the widow's ox for a pledge" (Job 24:2-4 NRSV).

Israel continually fails to recognize that what they own has been given to them by God and is ultimately God's. God warns them: "Do not say to yourself, 'My power and the might of my own hand have gotten me this wealth.' But remember the LORD your God, for it is he who gives you power to get wealth" (Deut 8:17-18 NRSV). Although Israel is plagued with trouble because they repeatedly forget this lesson, David remembers it and is generous with what he has before God. When he gives his own silver to build the house of the Lord, he declares to God, "But who am I, and what is my people, that we should make this freewill offering? For all things come from you, and of your own we have given you" (1 Chron 29:14 NRSV). With this we may contrast the duplicity of Ananias and Sapphira (Acts 5:1-11).

To be landless is to lack a share in the covenantal *blessings of Israel, to have a precarious purchase on the "Israelite Dream." But Jesus shakes the presumptuous scaffolding that was assembled around Israel's theology of ownership and blessing. He challenges those whose ownership (and perceived divine blessing) has become their god: "Go, sell your possessions and give to the poor, and you will have treasure in heaven" (Mt 19:21 NIV). Those who live without physical property or disregard its personal claims are promised the greatest inheritance an Israelite could ever hope for: "blessed are the poor in spirit, for theirs is the kingdom of heaven. . . . Blessed are the meek, for they shall inherit the earth" (Mt 5:5 NRSV). Speaking of himself, the truest Israelite of all, he says, "Foxes have holes, and birds of the air have nests; but the Son of Man has nowhere to lay his head" (Mt 8:20 NRSV; Lk 9:58). And Paul recognizes Christ's relinquishing of "ownership" when he writes, "though he was in the form of God, [he] did not regard equality with God as something to be exploited, but emptied himself, taking the form of a slave" (Phil 2:6 NRSV).

Responsible Ownership. Personal ownership entails personal responsibility. Nowhere are the raw and everyday realities of this more memorably expressed than in the commandment regarding an ox who gores a slave. Here is an image of the property of one damaging the property of another: If an Israelite's *ox gores a fellow Israelite's *slave, the owner of the ox must repay the owner of the slave (Ex 21:32). But even the ox is an object of the owner's special care: "You shall not muzzle an ox while it is treading out the grain" (Deut 25:4 NRSV). Under OT law the land too needs special consideration. Responsible ownership of the land means allowing its prescribed and appropriate "rest" from production. On the *sabbath year it is to lie fallow, and every seventh sabbath year, the land is to enjoy an extra year of Jubilee (Lev 25). Ownership does not allow unrelenting exploitation but a stewardship that is modeled by the heavenly owner who cares for his creation.

Sometimes possessions can be betray their owners. In the skillfully rendered story of Judah and Tamar, Judah unwittingly leaves with a prostitute his signet, cord and staff as a pledge, a sort of credit card. When his daughter-in-law Tamar is found to be pregnant "as a result of whoredom" (NRSV), it is Judah's signet, cord and staff that identify him as the father of the "prostitute's" child (Gen 38:18, 25).

The Bible provides numerous images and stories of contentment with what one already owns. In Nathan's parable condemning David's sin of *adultery and *murder, one of his chief points of the story is that the rich man does not use one of his own *sheep but rather takes the only lamb of his poor neighbor (2 Sam 12:4). Proverbs warns men to "drink water from your own cistern"; in other words, to enjoy one's own wife rather than someone else's (Prov 5:15 NRSV). One of God's chief condemnations of the wealthy is that "wealth is treacherous" because those who have much never have enough: "They gather all nations for themselves, and collect all peoples as their own" (Hab 2:5 NRSV). But God warns that such greed will never bring contentment, because all people, however wealthy, must ultimately suffer the same fate. Like every person after death, "their graves are their homes forever, . . . though they named lands their own" (Ps 49:11 NRSV). And in eternity, hoarded riches will only bring the owner hurt (Eccles 5:13). Yet this does not mean that God forbids private ownership but only that he desires that each be content and generous with their own and prefer eternal possessions over earthly ones. In fact, Micah offers an inviting image of God-given ownership in the end times, when everyone will possess what they need and "they shall all sit under their own vines and under their own fig trees, and no one shall make them afraid" of losing what they have been given (Mic 4:4 NRSV).

See also INHERITANCE; LAND; PROMISED LAND.

BIBLIOGRAPHY. C. J. H. Wright, *God's People in God's Land: Family, Land and Property in the Old Testament* (Grand Rapids: Eerdmans, 1990).

OX

The imagination of ancient Mediterranean cultures was captivated by the *strength of the ox. All forms of cultural expression from the region link the image of an ox with *pride and awe in strength. From Paleolithic cave art and Neolithic bucrania (horns of the aurochs or wild ox, now extinct, mounted in what appear to be shrines) to the bull temples of Anatolia, the mythology and art of the Levant and Mesopotamia, Greece with the Io myth and Crete with its Minotaur, cultural records pay respect to this impressive beast.

Biblical images of the ox exist in tension between the ox as a symbol of fruitful power and as a symbol of unintelligent brute strength. In Scripture the ox represents the pinnacle of created strength and ability in the then-known world, but like humans it stands subject to the supremacy of *God and would be foolish to attempt defiance against him.

Power and Fertility. The wild ox was the largest, most powerful animal hunted regularly by early humans. It became for them a symbol of brute strength and majesty (Deut 33:17). In several Near Eastern mythologies the *gods were believed to own *cattle. Homer refers to the Herds of the Sun. Ishtar releases the Bull of Heaven as vengeance against Enkidu. A bull pulls the *chariot of the Hittite storm god. These views probably provided an etiology for *thunder as pounding hooves and perhaps also the hot *winds as snorted *breath. The bull's *horns, tossed in *anger or defiance, understandably came to symbolize its power. The Bible likens a triumphant person to a victorious bull lifting up its horns (1 Sam 2:1, 10; Ps 92:10). The vanquished have had their horns cut off (Ps 75:10).

The vitality of the bull, its prodigious procreative powers and the difficulties of controlling such a large animal when governed by its natural drive all contributed to the rise of the bull as a symbol of fertility. It served as the emblem of the Canaanite god Baal, whose cult was dedicated to ensuring the fecundity of the land through crops and herds. This context of *idolatry is crucial for understanding the tension of the image in Scripture. Common experience in the ancient world led to elevation of the ox as the quintessential image of strength, but it remains a created strength whose opposition to the Creator is worthless and foolish.

Bull as Leader. While "bull" is the clear meaning of Hebrew 'abbîr ("stallion," "bull," "strong" or "dominant one") in Psalm 22:13 and 50:13, elsewhere when applied to humans it is not so obviously rendered (Ps 68:31; Is 10:13: "mighty one" NIV, "bull" RSV). When the God of Jacob is termed 'abbîr in *Genesis 49:24, English translations shun the rendering "bull" to avoid confusion with Baal's representation as a bull.

Like the Nazirite *Samson, the biblical image of an ox consistently suggests that earthly strength yielded to the will of God is glorious and majestic, but when strength becomes arrogant it is quickly and pathetically reduced. In this way the ox is a metaphor of human *leadership (Is 34:7; cf. "stags," Lam 1:6). It is grouped with the images of a *lion, an *eagle and a man in apocalyptic descriptions of four living creatures that worship God (Ezek 1:10; Rev 4:7); its physical strength complements the catalog of ability captured by the other three images. King Nebuchadnezzar, who defied God, is described in his dementia as "eat[ing] grass like cattle" (Dan 4:33 NIV): a once-powerful man humbled by the judgment of God mimics the behavior of an ox. In poetry and prophecy as well, comparison to an ox can denote degradation of human glory (Ps 106:20; Prov 7:22; Is 1:3). However, in a hyperbolic parallel, submissive oxen are compared favorably to disobedient Israel (Is 11:7; 65:25). They are held up as an example of contentedness and cooperation with their Creator.

The Domesticated Ox: Service, Strength, Wealth. Another side of biblical ox imagery highlights their value as domesticated animals. In contrast to the unruly wild ox, the tame one made civilization possible (Job 39:9-12). In addition to providing dietary staples—*milk, cheese, *butter—the ox furnished the power for extensive agriculture that otherwise would have been impossible (Prov 14:4). The humped withers of the ox, which easily accomodated a simple yoke, made it easily adaptable to pulling heavy loads without choking the beast (in contrast with the horse, which could not be used for heavy hauling until the invention of the horse collar, see Firmage, 1136-37). Because of its strength, the ox was the animal best suited for plowing. It also pulled wagons and *threshed *grain, either by treading on it or by drawing the threshing sledge over it. As the quintessential herbivore, in contrast to carnivores (Is 11:7; 65:25), it required *pasture, usually on lands not serviceable for crops (Is 7:25). Oxen became the spoils of war (Judg 6:4) and served as collateral for the poor—perhaps unjustly, since tilling the ground was their only means of support (Job 24:3). Thirty-seven mentions of oxen in the Pentateuch indicate their socioeconomic importance; also, *sacrifice of the animals was a function of their immense value. Jesus highlights their value when he poignantly equates the Pharisees' *sabbath care of their oxen with his own sabbath healing of a crippled woman and a man with dropsy (Lk 13:15; 14:5).

Oxen are the dominant image used to teach the importance of respecting and caring for the material world over which humans were given dominion (Gen 1:28; Ps 8:7). The ox's loyal service and understanding cooperation (Is 1:3; Job 6:5; Hos 10:11) were not to be repaid with poor treatment (Deut 25:4). The care of animals, reflected in their condition, was to be regarded as a sacred duty (Prov 12:10). Paul applies these ideals metaphorically in his admonition that ministers of the gospel should be well cared for in each town (1 Cor 9:9; 1 Tim 5:18). Overall, the condition of one's stock, as well as their number, indicated one's wealth and well-being (Job 1:3; 42:12; Ps 144:14; Prov 15:17). The state of the cows in Pharaoh's *dream marks years of either *abundance or want (Gen 41). Samson's accusation of the townsmen, "If you had not plowed with my heifer," suggests the communal value of good care and the violation assumed without it (Judg 14:18).

Summary. In each of its contexts, whether used to connote power and fertility or strength and usefulness, the ox as an image captures the essential state of the created order: glorious capability, finite control, created to be well treated but yielded to Another.

See also ANIMALS; HORSE.

BIBLIOGRAPHY. E. Firmage, "Zoology," *ABD* 6:1109-67; esp. 1129-30, 1136-37.

P

PAIN, PANGS

In the Bible "pain" and "pangs" translate several different words and are almost always used in a metaphorical sense, often to denote great distress, *fear or anxiety. Although a few occurrences refer to nothing more than the pain that goes with human frailty and *mortality (Job 14:22; 33:19; Ps 116:3), most occurrences have to do with emotional terrors. In some cases it is the righteous or repentant who cry out to God for relief. They are "in pain" because of their *enemies (Ps 25:16-19; 55:1-4) or because of their *sin (Is 26:16-17). Often this pain is compared to a woman's labor pains.

The most frequent image of pain is associated with prophetic warnings of future *judgment and the fear and anguish that come with it. The prophets declare that Israel's enemies will be seized with great pain (Is 13:8; 21:3; 23:5; Jer 22:23; 48:41; 49:22-24; 50:43; Ezek 30:4, 9, 16). Babylon, Edom, Egypt, Ethiopia, Lebanon, Moab and Tyre will all be terrified when the Lord brings judgment upon them. Recalling past victories, the psalmist remembers times when God frightened Israel's enemies (Ps 48:4-6). But the same image is applied to Israel as well. Because of sin, judgment will befall God's people, and when this judgment comes Israel will be as "a woman in travail" suffering birth pangs (Jer 4:31 RSV; 6:24; 13:21; 30:6; Hos 13:13). Even the prophet experiences pain and terror as he becomes aware of Israel's grim fate (Jer 4:19; 15:18).

The pain metaphor is sometimes used of the period of *suffering through which God's people must pass before the day of redemption. The exile is likened to the pain of childbirth. After the daughter of Zion has suffered, she will be redeemed by God (Mic 4:9-10). Indeed, the eschatological redemption will be such that the pains of *birth will scarcely be noticed (Is 66:7-8).

This imagery is taken up in the NT. The *resurrection of Jesus "loosed the pains of death" (Acts 2:24 KJV) and now makes possible the redemption of humankind. According to Paul, "all of creation has been groaning in pain together until now" (Rom 8:22), as it eagerly awaits redemption and the revelation of the people of God (Rom 8:18-23). Paul even likens the ongoing process of the forming of Christ in his converts as going through the pain of childbirth (Gal 4:19). Reminiscent of OT imagery,

Paul avers that the Day of the Lord will come suddenly upon the ungodly, "as birth pains come upon a woman with child" (1 Thess 5:3). But these pains will not last forever. With the advent of Christ pain itself will be banished, for in that time God "will wipe away every tear from their eyes, and death shall be no more, neither shall there be mourning nor crying nor pain any more" (Rev 21:4 RSV).

See also BIRTH; CROSS; DEATH; DISEASE AND HEALING; MORTALITY; SUFFERING; SUFFERING SERVANT; WOUND.

PALM TREE

The palm *tree has a distinctive look. It has a long, slender trunk with foliage only at the very top. It also has deep, water-seeking *roots. Because of the latter characteristic, it thrives in an oasis environment.

Certain geographical locations are associated with palm trees. The Israelites camped at Elim during their wanderings in the *wilderness, and this place was notable for its *twelve *springs and *seventy palm trees (Ex 15:27; Num 33:9), the numbers suggestively coinciding with the twelve tribes and the seventy elders of Israel. Deborah held court under the "Palm of Deborah," located between Ramah and Bethel (Judg 4:5 NIV). The famous city of Jericho, built on the site of a large oasis in the wilderness, was well known as the "City of Palms" (Deut 34:3 NIV; 2 Chron 28:15).

Thus the palm tree was associated with the oasis, a place of fertility in the midst of the wilderness. It provided food in the form of the date, and its sap could be used as a sweetener or for making wine. Given these attributes, it is not surprising that the palm frequently connoted fertility and *blessing. According to Psalm 92:12 (NIV):

The righteous will flourish like a palm tree,
   they will grow like a cedar of Lebanon;
planted in the house of the LORD,
   they will flourish in the courts of our God.

The palm's function as a symbol of fertility and life likely explains its extensive use as an image in the artwork of the *temple. Palm trees were carved on the walls of the temple, the two olive doors and elsewhere (1 Kings 6:29, 32, 35; 7:36). Continuing the theme, Ezekiel's vision of an eschatological temple describes a building that also contains many artistic representations of the palm (Ezek 40:16, 22,

26, 31, 34; 41:18, 19-20, 25-26).

The palm tree produces large *leaves, or fronds. These fronds found use in the religious ceremonies of ancient Israel. On the first day of the Feast of Tabernacles, worshipers celebrated with the *fruit of trees, leafy branches, poplars and the frond of the palm, all symbolizing the fertility of *harvest. The booths in which the Israelites were to live during the *festival were constructed of palm leaves, as well as *branches from other trees (Neh 8:15). In the NT Jesus' entry into Jerusalem took on the shape of a religious festival as the crowds waved palm branches in acclamation (Jn 12:36).

The palm tree is stately and regal in appearance. Its shape and the connotation of its fertility make it an apt image of the woman (see Woman, Images of) in the Song of Songs, about whom the man exclaims:

Your stature is like that of the palm,
and your breasts like clusters of fruit.
I said, "I will climb the palm tree;
I will take hold of its fruit." (Song 7:7-8 NIV)
Isaiah exploits the idea that the palm, whose foliage bursts into the air, is the most regal of trees by citing it in implied comparison with the reed, which droops toward the ground: "So the LORD will cut off from Israel both head and tail, both palm branch and reed in a single day" (Is 9:14 NIV). The idea is that both the top and the bottom of Israel will be judged (see also Is 19:15).

See also FRUIT, FRUITFULNESS; TREE, TREES.

PANGS. See BIRTH; PAIN, PANGS.

PARABLE

Virtually all that we might say about the imagery of the parables of Jesus can be put under two headings—*realism* and *symbolism*. The literal, surface level of these simple stories is characterized by a thoroughgoing verisimilitude (lifelikeness). Yet as the very term *parable* ("to throw alongside") implies, the literal details represent something else, which is the essential method of symbolism. In addition, the narrative qualities of the parables are a virtual case study in the "rules" of popular storytelling as we find them in folk narrative, including a reliance on archetypes.

Realism. The most obvious feature of the parables is that they portray life as we find it in the world. The situations they present are utterly routine—*sowing and *harvesting a crop, extending a *wedding invitation, *baking *bread, lighting a *lamp, *traveling to a neighboring town. The people who perform these actions are equally commonplace—*farmers, homemakers, *fathers and *sons, embezzlers, *widows with limited means, merchants. In his parables Jesus gives us an unforgettable picture of peasant and bourgeois life in first-century Palestine. In keeping with this thoroughgoing realism, we can note in passing a nearly complete absence of fantasy elements such as talking animals or haunted forests.

Realism also implies attention to concrete particulars, and the parables fit the definition at this

point as well. In the parables nearly everything is concrete and tangible, as we move in a world of *seed and *wheat and *pearls and wedding *garments. The soil conditions mentioned in the parable of the soils correspond exactly to the geography and farming practices of rural Palestine. The parables' social customs too are thoroughly rooted in the particulars of the time (see especially Bailey). In short, the parables show Jesus to possess the essential gift of a master storyteller—the power of observation.

This extends as well to the memorable gallery of characters Jesus gives us in the parables. Only one of the characters (Lazarus) is named, yet as we encounter the characters of the parables we sense that we have known them all already. They are universal types, possessing the traits that we and our acquaintances possess. Never has such immortality been thrust upon anonymity. We do not need to know the name of the woman who first loses and then finds her lost coin: she is every person. The family dynamics of the parables of the prodigal son and the two brothers whose father asks them to work in the *vineyard could be observed at any family's breakfast table. The dutiful workers who complain when workers who labored a fraction of the time receive the same *wage are all of us.

The very realism of the parables express an indirect religious meaning. Overtly religious references to religious practices are rare, yet these "secular" stories embody profound spiritual meanings. We come to realize that it is in the everyday world of sowing and eating and dealing with family members that people make the great spiritual decisions and that God's grace works.

Symbolism. For all the realism of the parables, we are aware that the stories are too simple to interest us at a purely literal level. We sense intuitively that the story of the two brothers who change their minds about whether to work in their father's vineyard embodies more than a moral about being a dutiful son and helpful family member. The etymology of the word *parable* is a tip-off that the stories' imagery possesses a symbolic or allegorical level of meaning. The word implies the technique of second meaning—a comparison between two things that are set alongside each other.

Other qualities reinforce our awareness of a second level of meaning. The religious context of the parables, coupled with what we know about the didactic or instructive purpose Jesus ascribed to them, pushes us in the direction of viewing them as being allegorical. For example, many of the parables begin with a formula along the lines of "The kingdom of heaven is like . . . ," at once signaling that the literal imagery or action represents a spiritual reality. Jesus' own interpretation of two of his parables likewise establishes them as having a continuous thread of symbolism or allegory, in which details stand for something else (Mt 13:1-30). Furthermore, some of the images already possessed traditional symbolic meanings—seed as God's word, the owner of a vineyard as God, God as father and master and judge, a feast as emblematic of salvation.

Finally, despite the realism of the parables, some of them also contain "cracks" in the realism that incline us to probe for deeper meanings. Examples include unlikely reasons to avoid attending a wedding feast, the preposterous size of a *mustard plant that reaches to the heavens like a gigantic *tree, the inexplicable hiring practices of an employer whose pay scale disregards how long *workers have labored, or the extravagant risk of selling everything one owns to purchase a single pearl.

Folktale Motifs. Along with their realism and symbolism, the parables repeatedly adhere to the rules of storytelling as we find them in folk stories through the ages. They employ simple and heightened conflicts (seed versus natural forces that hinder it; character clashes between father and son or master and employer) and contrasts or foils (good stewards contrasted to a bad one; two sons who are temperamental opposites; indifferent passersby contrasted to a compassionate Samaritan). The rule of suspense is present in such forms as seed entrusted to the earth and characters put in situations that test them. The narrative situations are kept simple and uncomplicated, as we observe such actions as planting seed, hiring and paying workers, going on a journey and returning to reward or punish stewards who have been left in charge. The "dramatic rule of two" means that only *two characters are present at a given time. The rule of repetition figures prominently, especially *threefold repetition (three stewards entrusted with wealth, three passersby, three types of soil that yield no harvest and three that yield a good harvest), often combined with the rule of end stress, in which the crucial element comes last (perhaps as a foil to what has preceded).

Popular storytellers through the ages have liked the element of surprise. So did Jesus, as he told stories with surprise endings—an enterprising farmer's plans for retirement are dashed the day after completing his preparations; help for a wounded traveler comes from the least expected source; an employer's wage scale disregards the length of a worker's time spent in labor. Whatever the foreground theme of a parable is, therefore, there is often a "deep structure" element of subversion at work by which conventional ways of viewing reality and or valuing things is called into question. The general import of this technique of subversion is to announce that the new kingdom Christ announces is based on new values, with special emphasis on divine grace as opposed to human merit.

A final folktale feature of the simple stories Jesus told is their reliance on archetypes—master images that recur throughout literature and life. We think at once of such motifs as *lost and found, *robbed and *rescued, sowing and reaping, *sibling rivalry. Often these archetypes tap deep wellsprings of human psychology. The *prodigal son, for example, represents an impulse that lies within every human psyche—the impulse away from the domestic, secure, governed and morally pure, toward the distant, the *adventurous, the *rebellious, the indulgence of forbidden appetites, the abandonment to unrestraint. The elder brother in the same parable is equally recognizable, representing a middle-aged attitude that is dutiful, grudging, self-righteous and unforgiving. All employees have certain deep-seated responses toward the figure of the employer as we find him in the parables, just as the plight of the man who is traveling from Jerusalem to Jericho over a robber-infested road (the equivalent of a modern inner-city alley) evokes universal feelings of dread and *fear of *violence.

See also GOSPEL GENRE; PRODIGAL SON.

BIBLIOGRAPHY. K. E. Bailey, *Poet and Peasant: A Literary Cultural Approach to the Parables in Luke* (Grand Rapids: Eerdmans, 1976); K. E. Bailey, *Through Peasant Eyes: More Lucan Parables* (Grand Rapids: Eerdmans, 1980); C. L. Blomberg, *Interpreting the Parables* (Downers Grove, IL: InterVarsity Press, 1990).

PARADISE. *See* GARDEN.

PARALLELISM. *See* RHETORICAL PATTERNS.

PARODY

Parody is the practice of imitating an existing literary form or specific work with inverted effect. Whereas literature in general parody usually produces *humor, in the Bible it is related to spiritual meaning.

A major instance will illustrate the strategy on a grand scale. In the background of the song of the *suffering servant in Isaiah 52:13—53:12 is the literary form known as the *encomium—a piece that praises its subject with conventional formulas. Here, though, the suffering servant is praised (as it were) for all the wrong reasons. One of the standard motifs of the encomium is to praise the subject for its distinguished ancestry, a motif that is here present by its denial, as this person is said to have no distinguished ancestry or attractiveness (Is 53:2). Traditional panegyrics praise *heroes who conquer; this protagonist is praised for suffering as an outcast and even as a criminal. Epic heroes traditionally exert themselves to win rewards for themselves; this hero's exertions are on behalf of others as he becomes an offering for the sin of his people. The servant's humility unto death contrasts with the way in which conventional warriors defend themselves on the battlefield.

A large branch of biblical literature does similar things with the motif of human heroism by elevating the *antihero. Antiheroes in the Bible display an absence of the conventional traits of the hero. They are neither eloquent nor self-reliant. They are often fearful to undertake the task required of them. They lack the abilities that would enable them to achieve their tasks with purely human endowments. They may even be deeply flawed characters whose human *weakness serves as a foil to what God accomplishes through them. This is indeed the message that the antiheroic strain in the Bible delivers: the lack of people's abilities becomes the occasion for God to empower human characters or to perform successful feats himself.

Other biblical parodies do not so much reverse and refute conventional literary motifs as correct them by substituting God for either pagan *gods or human heroes. Ancient Near Eastern kings commanded obedience from their subjects in the form of suzerainty treaties. These treaties identified the suzerain, or "great king," and included a historical prologue in which the king's previous relations and benefits to his vassals were recounted, obligations of the subjects to their king were stipulated, and curses and *blessings were stated as sanctions for *obedience to the conditions of the *covenant. The Decalogue and book of *Deuteronomy follow the form of the suzerainty treaty, but the point of reversal or inversion is that it is God, not a human king, who is declared worthy of ultimate allegiance.

Psalm 29, the song of the thunderstorm, presents a slightly different slant. In the background is a body of Canaanite poetry that takes the Baal myth as its subject. The central feature of the myth is that Baal, god of the *storm and of fertility, performs an annual battle with the god of the salt sea, symbolic of death. After defeating his foe in the Mediterranean Sea, Baal moves eastward onto the coast, where he brings life-giving rain and builds a throne for himself. The storm described in Psalm 29 follows exactly this pattern, rising in the Mediterranean and moving eastward. As in the Baal myth, God is enthroned. A look at the geographic references shows that the poem is not a native Israelite poem, instead taking its place names from the region to the north. The poem, in short, is a parody, and as such it is polemical or argumentative, claiming either that what the pagans worship as Baal is really Yahweh, or showing that all that might be claimed for Baal is surpassed by Yahweh.

The beatitudes of Jesus (Mt 5:1-12) highlight the dynamics of biblical parody. Together they paint a composite portrait of the ideal person. To paint a portrait of the hero is a leading impulse of literature, especially epic and hero stories. Literature generally presents variations on the humanistic theme of self-reliant heroes who employ their power and resourcefulness to achieve personal and earthly rewards. The portrait that Jesus paints adheres to the conventional impulse to portray heroic behavior but inverts the values and rewards that are customary in literature generally. To begin, Jesus praises self-effacing behavior that is the opposite of the self-aggrandizement that the world at large regards as ideal. He also replaces worldly achievements with spiritual ones—being poor in spirit and meek, merciful and pure in heart, for example. The peacemaker replaces the epic warrior as the ideal. To complete the inversion Jesus consistently replaces political and personal rewards with spiritual and eschatological ones.

The foregoing are large-scale examples of parody. For the technique on a small scale we can turn to the book of Amos, where the prophet repeatedly shows his mastery of parody in small ways. The *praise psalms of the Bible catalog God's acts of creation and redemption; they serve as a foil to Amos 4:6-11, which catalog God's acts of disaster on his chosen nation. Obituaries lament a person after death; Amos delivers funeral rites for a nation while it is still successful (Amos 5:1-2). Priestly exhortations encouraged people to come to places like Bethel and Gilgal to worship; Amos turns the conventional exhortation on its end with shocking effect: "Come to Bethel—and transgress; to Gilgal—and multiply transgression" (Amos 4:4 NRSV). The conventional *rescue motif is actually an antirescue: "As the shepherd rescues from the mouth of the lion two legs, or a piece of an ear, so shall the people of Israel . . . be rescued, with the corner of a couch and part of a bed" (Amos 3:12 NRSV).

*Battle motifs are another major repository of parody in the Bible. The conventional arming of the hero, a picture of the warrior's innate strength and superiority, is assigned to God in the Bible, where it becomes an index to God's sufficiency (Ps 18:32-42). Or it might take the form of a boy hero finding the warrior's *armor too cumbersome for him and his choosing a homespun sling instead (1 Sam 17:38-40). The conventional boast of the warrior in his own strength (1 Sam 17:8-10) becomes a statement of praise of God's power to deliver (1 Sam 17:45-47). The conventional battle motifs of ancient epic are prominent in the book of Revelation, but they are spiritualized, picturing spiritual battle between good and evil, and featuring a *divine warrior instead of human warriors.

These are examples only of a general thread that runs through the Bible. The Bible is not a totally unique book. It shares many literary conventions and motifs with other ancient and later literature. This being the case, however, it is also true that these common motifs are slanted in the Bible to deliver a message that *is* unique, as conventional effects are inverted within a biblical view of God and people.

See also ANTIHERO; ENCOMIUM; HUMOR.

PAROUSIA. *See* SECOND COMING; THESSALONIANS, FIRST AND SECOND LETTERS TO THE.

PASSION OF CHRIST

The passion (from the Latin *patio,* "to suffer or endure") of Christ consists of the events of what is familiarly known as Holy Week—from Jesus' entry into Jerusalem on Sunday through the second day of entombment on Saturday. Events on the second Sunday constitute the *resurrection. Jesus himself is the protagonist of the passion: it is the story of his *suffering and *death from start to finish.

Several general traits of the passion story in the four Gospels should be noted at the outset. First, from a purely human point of view, it is a story of the utmost injustice and sadness. What Jesus endured would be terrible for any mortal to endure, but infinitely more so for an *innocent person and for deity. The response of the onlookers returning from the crucifixion who beat their breasts (Lk 23:48) is the natural response of anyone who looks at the events from the perspective of the Gospel writers.

Second, the narrative is nearly devoid of explicit theological commentary on the meaning of the events that are portrayed. We might say that the narrative style is "pure narrative"—an account of what people did and said, presented relatively dispassionately and without theologizing, though from a distinct point of view. Almost all the explicit commentary on the meaning of the events is dependent on the interpretation of the events provided copiously in the NT Epistles. But this is significantly supplemented by the context provided by OT messianic prophecies and pointers represented by the OT sacrificial system. Those with eyes to see and ears to hear can detect their hues and echoes within the Gospel passion narratives.

Third, anyone who reads the four Gospel accounts of the passion in sequence will be struck by how uniform they are regarding the main lines of the accounts, including the order in which events occurred. Here, more than with any other aspect of Jesus' life and ministry, all four Gospels tell the same story.

Finally, it is therefore possible to get the "lay of the land" regarding the chronology of Passion Week. It begins with a triumphal entry into Jerusalem, followed by four days of very full confrontation and teaching by Jesus (Lk 21:37-38 paints a picture of daytime teaching in the temple and nighttime lodging on the Mount of Olives). As these days unfold, Jesus' enemies resort to plotting against him, who becomes the victim of intrigue and conspiracy. On Thursday evening Jesus commemorates the Passover and institutes the Lord's Supper with his disciples in the upper room. The remainder of that night and the next day are a phantasmagoria of *suffering, desertion, captivity, trial and sentencing, climaxed by crucifixion. It all ends with death and entombment. The motifs and imagery that are built on this foundation are stark and memorable.

Climax and Finality. One of the most obvious features of the passion story is its status as the climax and finale of the Gospel narratives of the life of Christ. One index to this is the percentage of the Gospels devoted to the passion story. The Gospels devote between 20 and 30 percent of their space to the passion story. Another index to the climactic role of the passion story is the way in all four Gospels that Jesus predicts the events of Passion Week long before they occur (Mt 16:21-23; 17:22-23; 20:17-19; Mk 8:31-33; 9:30-32; Lk 9:22, 43-45; 18:31-34; Jn 10:1-18). The effect when we read the actual passion story is that we recognize it as the fulfillment, at last, of what we have been anticipating.

The climactic nature of the passion story is reinforced by the way Jesus sets his face toward Jerusalem and heads toward it in a conscious journey, with the events of Passion Week constituting the goal of the journey and indeed of Jesus' entire redemptive life. Luke 9:51 encapsulates the motif: "When the days drew near for him to be received up, he set his face to go to Jerusalem" (RSV).

The Triumphal Entry. One of the most famous images of passion week occurs right at the outset in the form of the triumphal entry into Jerusalem (Mt 21:1-13; Mk 11:1-11; Lk 19:28-46; Jn 12:12-19). Zechariah had predicted that a "triumphant and victorious" king would enter Jerusalem "humble and riding on an ass" (Zech 9:9 RSV). The spectacle of Palm Sunday fulfills the prophecy. It is an act of ironically short-lived recognition and acknowledgment on the part of the disciples and masses that the Messiah (however misconceived by the people who shout) is now here.

The image patterns are easy to see. One is *kingship, suggested by the procession itself and made explicit when the crowds shout, "Hosanna to the Son of David!" (Mt 21:9) or variants. Another motif is *honor. A third is miracle, as Jesus predicts events surrounding the disciples' finding the colt that are subsequently fulfilled. The spirit of the triumphal entry is public, festive, celebrative and ritualistic, as the crowd shouts and spreads *garments and tree *branches on the road. Jesus himself implicitly makes a statement, accepting the messianic tribute of the crowd and aggressively invading Jerusalem, right to the very *temple.

Yet there are pathos and tragedy in the triumphal entry. By week's end the crowds will be shouting, "Crucify him! Crucify him!" In Luke's account Jesus actually weeps over the city of Jerusalem and predicts its destruction (Lk 19:41-44), ending with the haunting indictment that the people who cheered him wildly "did not know the time of your visitation" (RSV).

Jesus the Victim of Intrigue. The half-week that Jesus spends teaching resembles the previous three years, except perhaps that the confrontations with the religious establishment are more intense than ever, heading toward a final showdown. The content of Jesus' teaching is also more *apocalyptic than his earlier ethical emphasis. But in many ways it seems like a half-week of business as usual, except for its foreboding setting in Jerusalem and a sinister added ingredient.

The religious establishment had dogged Jesus throughout his three-year ministry, but now we read about organized plotting and intrigue, even plans for Jesus' execution (Mt 26:3-5; Mk 14:1-2; Lk 22:1-2; Jn 11:45-57). Jesus' antagonists now have a definite plan, rendered operational by the cooperation of the traitor Judas Iscariot (Mt 26:14-15; Mk 14:10-11; Lk 22:3-6). Jesus is accordingly cast in the role of a victim of a sinister and large-scale intrigue.

The Upper Room. Jesus spends the evening of his arrest with his disciples, and several motifs cluster around this event. The place itself is an evocative image—an upper room (Mk 14:15-16; Lk 22:12-13), with associations of privacy, intimacy and retreat. An aura of the miraculous surrounds the place, inasmuch as Jesus instructs Peter and John to ask a householder about an upper room, which they find prepared for the *Passover (Lk 22:8-13; cf. Mk 14:13-16). The fact that Jesus here celebrates the Passover meal with his disciples (Mt 26:17-29; Mk 14:12-25; Lk 22:7-28) hints at the sacrificial aspect of his coming crucifixion, while his institution of the Lord's *Supper suggests a transition to a new era.

The only major deviation among the four Gospels in the entire passion story is found in John's handling of the final evening with the disciples (Jn 14—17). John dispenses with the Passover narrative and replaces it with the incident of Jesus' washing of the disciples' feet (Jn 13:1-11) and a full-fledged *farewell discourse.

Desertion and Betrayal. A leading source of the pathos of the passion narrative is the repeated abandonment of Jesus by his erstwhile companions. The most notorious example is the betrayal of Jesus by Judas Iscariot (Mt 26:14-15; Mk 14:17-21), with the dissembling kiss in the Garden of Gethsemane its most famous image.

The other disciples' desertion is only less acute and not therefore more excusable. One manifestation is the disciples' sleeping in Gethsemane while their Master agonizes over his impending suffering (Mt 26:26-46; Mk 14:32-42; Lk 22:39-46). The disciples also *flee when Jesus is arrested (Mt 46:56; Mk 14:50-52). The group desertion is highlighted by the individual denial by Peter, which we experience twice—first in Jesus' prediction (Mt 26:30-35; Mk 14:26-31; Lk 22:31-34; Jn 13:36-38) and then in its actual occurrence (Mt 26:69-75; Mk 14:26-31; Lk 22:31-34; Jn 13:36-38).

Agony, Suffering and Torture. Dominating all other images of the passion of Christ is the physical and psychological suffering Jesus endured. The psychological agony reaches its most affecting moment not in the *torture inflicted on Jesus by the soldiers after his arrest but in the solitary loneliness of the Garden of Gethsemane earlier in the evening (Mt 26:36-41; Mk 14:32-42; Lk 22:39-46). Here we view the spectacle of Jesus in his isolation, "sorrowful and troubled," abandoned by his companions, contemplating his death for the sins of the world. Here is Jesus falling to the ground in extremity of agony, praying that the *cup pass from him without his having to endure the cross, his sweat dropping like drops of *blood from him.

Once Jesus is arrested, imagery of torture and derision punctuates the action. The arresters *spit on him (Mt 26:67; Mk 14:65) and strike or *beat him (Mt 26:67-68; Mk 14:65; 15:18-19; Lk 22:63; Jn 19:1, 3). The ultimate image of physical torture is the crown of thorns placed on Jesus' head (Mt 27:18; Mk 15:17; Jn 19:2). Physical torture is supplemented by various forms of psychological suffering in the

form of mocking (Mt 26:28; Lk 22:63-65). Specific images include the scarlet robe placed on Jesus and the reed placed in his right hand (Mt 17:29), with accompanying mock homage (Mt 27:17-30; Mk 15:18-20; Jn 19:2, 5). And a conspicuous ingredient in the events at the cross is the derision heaped on Jesus, mainly by his long-time enemies, apparently supported by random passersby (Mt 27:35-44; Mk 15:29-32; Lk 23:34-38; Jn 19:23-24).

Arrest and Trial. The centerpiece of the passion story is a flurry of activity surrounding the arrest of Jesus and a series of furtive and hastily arranged trials. Literal and metaphoric darkness envelops the action. Jesus accentuates this quality with his statement to his arresters, "But this is your hour, and the power of darkness" (Lk 22:53 RSV). Equally memorable is the evocative statement that after receiving his morsel at the Last Supper Judas Iscariot "immediately went out; and it was night" (Jn 13:30 RSV).

The arrest itself is a phantasmagoria of threatening soldiers, drawn *swords and clubs (Mk 14:43-49; Lk 47-53; Jn 18:1-12). Once Jesus is arrested, moreover, the account is rather continuously permeated by the imagery of Jesus' being led, handed over, delivered, bound, seized, having hands laid on him and such like. This is the language of captivity and helplessness. We also get the impression from the text of a frenzy of physical movement from one site to another. Perhaps without our being fully aware of what we are doing, as we read the text we intuitively imagine scenes, and as we do so an additional quality enters with the prevalence of group scenes, in contrast to the privacy and loneliness of events earlier in the evening of the arrest.

Once Jesus has been placed under guard, a quasi-judicial motif takes over as Jesus is hustled from one improvised court or hearing to another. The account is filled with accusations and verdicts against Jesus, accompanied mainly by Jesus' silence (Mt 26:63) but occasionally by an authoritative pronouncement, such as Jesus' statement to Pilate "I tell you, hereafter you will see the Son of man seated at the right hand of Power, and coming on the clouds of heaven" (Mt 26:64 RSV). Jesus appears as a defendant before the deposed high priest Annas (Jn 18:13-14, 19-24), before Caiaphas the high priest (who histrionically tears his robes at a certain point in the farcical proceedings; Mt 26:65; Mk 14:63), before the chief priests and elders (Mt 27:1-2; Lk 22:66-71), and most important, before the Roman procurator Pontius Pilate (Mt 27:11-26; Mk 15:1-15; Lk 23:1-25; Jn 18:28-19:16), who is portrayed as a cowardly weakling whose most memorable gesture is washing his hands in a futile attempt to maintain his innocence in allowing the execution of Jesus.

The Crucifixion. The supreme image the world has associated with the passion of Jesus—and indeed with the Christian faith itself—is the *cross, a synecdoche for the means by which Jesus was executed. We know from extrabiblical sources that crucifixion was the cruelest form of death available—a form of torture so terrible that the Romans passed a law that no Roman citizen could be crucified, regardless of the crime. It comes as something of a surprise, therefore, that the most noteworthy feature in the account of Jesus' crucifixion in the Gospels is its rather brief, cursory nature (Mt 27:32-35; Mk 15:21-24; Lk 23:26-34; Jn 19:17-18). The effect of this notable reticence is simply to impress on us *that* Jesus was crucified and not allow that fact to become obscured with specific pictures of human *pain. All four accounts record the actual moment of death (Mt 27:50; Mk 15:39; Lk 23:46; Jn 19:30).

Two main motifs surround the experience of Jesus on the cross. One is cosmic, consisting of natural cataclysm and supernatural signs. Specific events include *darkness for *three hours (Mt 27:45; Mk 15:33; Lk 23:44-45), the rending of the curtain of the *temple from top to bottom (Mt 27:54) and an *earthquake accompanied by *graves opened and *rocks split (Mt 27:51-53).

Complementing these cosmic images are personal, human vignettes. Most poignant are the pictures of women onlookers weeping at the cross (Mt 27:55-56; Mk 15:40-41; Lk 23:48-49; Jn 19:25-27). If the dominant response among onlookers is taunting and derision (noted earlier), we also find moments of conversion and belief in the accounts of the centurion (Mt 27:54; Mk 15:39; Lk 23:47) and the penitent *thief (Lk 23:40-43). In the centurion's words, "Certainly this man was innocent!" (Lk 23:47 RSV), the injustice and tragedy of the event are highlighted.

Entombment. Following the heightened intensity of the arrest, trial and crucifixion, the passion narratives end with quietness, sorrow and defeat in the images of Jesus' entombment. All four accounts give us particularized pictures of the wrapping of Jesus' body and laying it in a tomb (Mt 27:57-61; Mk 15:42-47; Lk 23:50-55; Jn 19:38-42). Matthew's account gives a further picture of the sealing and guarding of the tomb (Mt 27:62-66). The *burial of Jesus brings the passion story to closure with the terminal imagery of entombment, enclosure, death and a dispersal of human activity.

Old Testament Motifs in the Passion. While the Gospel accounts of the passion story are told with spare, unembellished brevity, they implicitly gesture toward a context of OT motifs. The most pervasive is the motif of the Suffering Righteous, as found in the Psalms and the stories of *Joseph, *Daniel and others. The passion accounts of the Gospels draw especially on Psalms 22, 31, 34, 35 and 69 to interpret such details in Jesus' passion as the presence of enemies who plotted against Jesus, abused him, accused him, divided his *garments, offered him a *drink and anticipated his *rescue prior to death; Jesus' betrayal by a table intimate and the withdrawal of his friends; Jesus' innocence and silence; and his experience of anguish and abandonment at death. By weaving into the tapestry of Jesus' suffering and death the words and story line of the Suffering

Righteous, early Christians were able both to overcome the apparent oxymoron of the suffering of the righteous and to understand how the Scriptures themselves anticipated such an unexpected conclusion to the life of God's Messiah.

Closely related to the motif of the Suffering Righteous in the Gospels' portrayal of Jesus' passion is his identification as the Lord's *Suffering Servant. Drawing especially from Isaiah 52:13—53:12, the Gospel accounts portray Jesus as the Servant—God's "chosen one" who will complete his mission through suffering, is innocent and silent, dies "for many," is "handed over," is "numbered with transgressors" and anticipates his vindication by God. Other motifs from the OT that surface in the Gospel passion accounts include Jesus' portrayal as a martyr-prophet and as the Passover *Lamb.

New Testament Motifs. Both in the Gospels and in the rest of the NT, the saving significance of Jesus' death is represented in myriad ways. This points to our inability to exhaust the significance of the cross of Christ, but also to the necessity of communicating the meaning of the cross in fresh ways in changing circumstances. Within the NT the importance of Jesus' passion for salvation is developed chiefly through five constellations of images, borrowed from central spheres of public life in the Mediterranean world: the battleground (*triumph over evil), interpersonal relationships (reconciliation or making *peace), the *legal system (justification), commerce (*redemption) and *worship (*sacrifice).

Each of the Gospels accords privilege to its own array of motifs. The Gospel of Matthew, for example, seems concerned especially with the motif of *blood. Judas, we are told, in betraying Jesus has betrayed "innocent blood," for which he receives "blood money," later used to purchase a "Field of Blood" (Mt 27:4, 6, 8 RSV). Jesus had already rebuked the scribes and Pharisees for their complicity with their ancestors in the rejection and murder of the righteous: "that upon you may come all the righteous blood shed on earth" (Mt 23:35 RSV). Pilate washes his hands, declaring that he is "innocent of this man's blood," while the people in Jerusalem, urged on by their leaders, accept responsibility for his death: "His blood be on us and on our children" (Mt 27:24-25 RSV). These images speak of Jesus' innocence and the culpability of his opponents. Earlier, though, Jesus had employed the motif in a way that pulls our attention away from questions of innocence and blame. By interpreting his death—the pouring out of his blood—as a *covenant sacrifice for the *forgiveness of sins (Mt 26:27-28), he gives much wider significance to the blood motif and opens the possibility of forgiveness even for those most to blame.

Mark, on the other hand, is concerned throughout his Gospel to underscore the inseparable relationship between Jesus' teaching and miracles and his passion. Jesus is the powerful herald of the good news whose teaching and miraculous deeds lead to his death. The importance of this perspective is highlighted by the motif of identity and recognition that weaves its way throughout the Gospel. Who is Jesus? Within the narrative God identifies him as Son of God (Mk 1:11; 9:7), but apart from the narrator himself (Mk 1:1), the only person ever to recognize him as God's Son is the centurion at the cross (Mk 15:39). That he does so *only* after witnessing Jesus' death shows the importance in Mark's theology for people to fully integrate the way of the cross into their understanding of Jesus and of the meaning of discipleship.

One of the hallmarks of Luke's presentation of Jesus' crucifixion is present much earlier in the narrative, in Luke 9:23. Luke recounts Jesus' call to would-be disciples not only to take up the cross but to do so *daily*. According to the narrative of Luke-Acts, then, disciples may not be likely actually to face death on account of their faith in and allegiance to Jesus as Lord, but they are likely to face opposition. This is true for Peter and John in Acts 3, Stephen in Acts 6—7, and Paul in Acts 13—28. It was first true for Jesus, whose faithfulness led to his shameful suffering and execution. Opposition, then, is not a negation of faithfulness. In Luke's perspective, conflict is not necessarily even an impediment to the spread of the good news. Because Jesus is Savior (Lk 2:11; Acts 5:30-31), his death and resurrection open new doors to a universal mission, embracing both Jew and Gentile, and throughout Acts resistance does not deter but seems actually to enhance the growth of the church (cf. Acts 14:22).

As throughout the Gospel of John, so in the passion account, the Evangelist paints Jesus with royal hues, always in control of the events leading to his own death. Judas does not identify Jesus for the posse; rather, Jesus identifies himself, and with such grandeur that those who would arrest him respond as they would at a *theophany (Jn 18:3-7). The disciples do not flee at his arrest (as in Mark and Matthew); instead Jesus negotiates their release (Jn 18:8-9). Jesus accepts the title of king given him by others but interprets his royal dominion as originating in God's domain even if it is present in this world (Jn 18:36; Jesus declares that his kingdom is not *from* this world; he does not deny that his kingdom is *of* [pertains to] this world). Even his opponents acclaim him as king, albeit in an ironic way, and he is led to crucifixion as a threat to the emperor (Jn 19:1-12, 15, 21-22). Following his death he receives a burial fit for a *king (Jn 19:39-41).

Finally, we should note that the factual passion story of the Gospels becomes the central text to which the rest of the NT alludes. It is no exaggeration to say that the Epistles and the book of Revelation are an extended commentary on the soteriological meaning of the passion story.

See also ATONEMENT; BURIAL, FUNERAL; CROSS; CROSS BEFORE CROWN; DEATH; GRAVE; LAMB; PASSOVER; RESURRECTION; SUFFERING SERVANT.

BIBLIOGRAPHY. R. E. Brown, *The Death of the Messiah—From Gethsemane to the Grave: A Commentary on the Passion Narratives* (2 vols.; ABRL; New York: Doubleday, 1994); J. T. Carroll and J. B. Green, *The Death of Jesus in the Early Church* (Peabody, MA: Hendrickson, 1995); M. D. Hooker, *Not Ashamed of the Gospel: New Testament Interpretations of the Death of Christ* (Grand Rapids: Eerdmans, 1994).

PASSOVER

The account of God's *rescue of the Israelite *slaves from *bondage in *Egypt comes to a dramatic climax in Exodus 12, when the homes of the Israelites are "passed over" as the firstborn of every Egyptian household is struck dead (see Exodus, Second Exodus). This event was so significant that God instructed the Israelites to commemorate it annually by celebrating for a full week the Feast of Unleavened Bread. On the evening preceding this *festival the Israelites were also to reenact much of what originally took place in Egypt. By focusing on the Passover the Israelites remembered the single most important redemptive event in their early history. Passover continues to be the most important festival of the Jewish year.

The account in Exodus 12 provides a vivid picture of what took place during the original Passover in Egypt. Various images are highlighted by the narrator. Three are especially helpful for understanding the ritual the people were to perform. First, on the tenth day of the month the Israelites were to select for each family a year-old male *lamb or kid without defect. Four days later they were to *sacrifice it. Second, they were to sprinkle the *blood from the sacrifice on the "sides and tops of the doorframes" of their houses (Ex 12:7, 22 NIV); this would prevent a "destructive *plague" from entering and striking dead the firstborn sons (Ex 12:13, 23 NIV). Third, they were to roast the meat and, along with *unleavened *bread, eat all of it without breaking the *bones of the animal (Ex 12:8, 46). Significantly, these activities parallel closely the account of the consecration of the Aaronic priests in Exodus 29 and Leviticus 8. Here the slaughter of a ram, the sprinkling of its blood and the eating of its meat form the main elements of a consecration ritual by which the priests are set apart as holy to God. Although there are differences of detail, the same elements are present in the Passover ritual. The sacrifice of the animal atones for the sin of the people, the blood sprinkled on the doorframes purifies those within, and the eating of the sacrificial meat sanctifies those who consume it. By participating in the Passover ritual the people consecrate themselves as a nation holy to God (cf. Ex 19:6).

The crucifixion of Jesus coincides with the celebration of Passover. The NT writers saw this as deeply significant. The Synoptic Gospels (Matthew, Mark and Luke) present the Last *Supper as a Passover *meal (Mt 26:17; Mk 14:12; Lk 22:7-8), emphasizing the importance of Jesus' words and actions. This meal is subsequently commemorated in the Lord's

Supper (1 Cor 11:23-33). Elsewhere the death of Jesus is linked to the offering of the Passover sacrifice. John's Gospel alludes to this by observing that Jesus' death resembles that of the Passover sacrifice because his bones were not broken (Jn 19:36; cf. Ex 12:46). This connection is made even more explicit by Paul: "For Christ, our Passover lamb, has been sacrificed" (1 Cor 5:7 NIV). By linking the crucifixion of Jesus to the Passover, the NT writers highlight the redemptive nature of his death. Like the original Passover sacrifice, his death atones for the sin of the people, his blood purifies and cleanses, and his body sanctifies those who eat it at the Lord's Supper.

See also CROSS; EXODUS, SECOND EXODUS; FESTIVAL; LAMB; PASSION OF CHRIST; SACRIFICE; SUPPER.

BIBLIOGRAPHY. T. D. Alexander, "The Passover Sacrifice" in *Sacrifice in the Bible*, ed. R. T. Beckwith and M. Selman (Carlisle, UK: Paternoster; Grand Rapids: Baker, 1995) 1-24; J. B. Segal, *The Hebrew Passover from the Earliest Times to A.D. 70* (London Oriental Series 12; London: Oxford University Press, 1963).

PASTURE

The pasture is above all a pastoral and rural image, evoking archetypal feelings about *beauty, *nature and agriculture. To the Western imagination pastures belong to a green world, as captured in the matchless image of *green pastures and still *waters from Psalm 23:2. In a land prone to drought, as the biblical world is, the spectacle of brown pastures is an image of terror rather than *abundance and security (Jer 23:10).

The pasturelands of Israel included rich and lush regions such as the coastal plains (1 Chron 5:16) and Galilee (Josh 21:32), as well as rather arid, desertlike areas such as the Judean *wilderness (Amos 7:14) and the Negev (Gen 27:27-31). The pastures of Israel supported domesticated animals such as *sheep and *goats (Gen 29:7), *donkeys (Jer 14:6), *cattle (1 Kings 4:23) and camels (Ezek 25:5). They were also the home of wild animals such as deer (Lam 1:6), jackals (Jer 9:10-11), *lions and bears (1 Sam 17:34). While from a modern urban perspective pasture may seem rather insignificant, appropriate allotments and quality of pasturage were essential for the prosperity of settlements in the ancient world (cf. Gen. 47:3-6; Josh 21:1-42).

It is impossible to exaggerate the importance of pastureland to a pastoral economy. Joshua 21, dealing with the division of the land of Canaan, contains fifty-three references to "pasture lands" (RSV), while a similar passage in 1 Chronicles 5 contains forty-two references. Not only was pastureland the staple for sustaining livestock, it presupposed an adequate quality of soil and supply of water. Rich pastureland is so positive in the OT that it makes a frequent appearance in the idealized prophetic visions of the coming *restoration or golden age of God's favor (Is 30:23; 65:10; Jer 50:19; Ezek 34:14; Mic 2:12; Zeph 2:6-7; 3:13).

The primary image of pasture is pastoral care and supply. The people of God are often called the sheep of God's pasture (Ps 74:1; 79:13; 95:7; 100:3; Jer 23:1; Ezek 34:31). The psalmists speak of life with God as the enjoyment of safe and fertile pastures. Pastures are places of refreshment, security and satisfaction (Ps 23:1; 37:3). The prophets use the image of pasture to express the hope of restoration. God's people will enjoy both supply and security like sheep restored to rich pasturage (Is 14:30; 49:9; Jer 23:3; 33:13; Ezek 34:13-18). Even wicked rulers are pictured as shepherds caring for sheep in their pastures (Jer 25:34-38; 49:20; 50:45). In the NT Jesus uses the image of pasture to indicate the supply of all needs for the saved (Jn 10:9). Jeremiah alters the image somewhat and describes God himself as the pasture of his people (Jer 50:7). He, not the *idols or ways of the nations, is the source of care and supply.

While the pasture is mainly an idealized pastoral image of provision and natural beauty, it is occasionally a negative image. When God invades a city in *judgment, the pasture becomes a place of desolation and ruin, useful only for pasturing *flocks and herds (Is 5:17; 32:14; Ezek 25:5). Furthermore, withered pastures themselves are sometimes indicative of God's judgment (Jer 23:10; Amos 1:2).

See also ABUNDANCE; CATTLE; FARMING; FLOCK; GRASS; GREEN; LAND; NATURE; SHEEP, SHEPHERD; VALLEY.

PATERFAMILIAS. *See* LEGAL IMAGES.

PATH

The image of the path or way is pervasive in the Bible, with the references numbering approximately eight hundred. Most of these refer to the physical track over which one *walks or the act of walking in a culture where walking was the primary mode of transportation. Beyond these references to literal roads and journeys or occasional references to the natural rhythms of life and death (as when death becomes a metaphoric "way" or journey [Josh 23:14; 1 Kings 2:2; Ps 121:7-8]), the image of the path or way embodies a profound reflection on fundamental ethical themes, the conduct of God and humanity, and the character of God's salvation.

As always, symbolic meanings grow out of the physical phenomenon. Walking on a path involves choosing to enter on the path and to pursue it in a given direction, progress toward a destination, making wise rather than foolish choices along the way, taking care for safety and not getting lost, and arriving at a goal.

The Path of Life. All these elements of walking on a path are used in recurrent biblical images of the path to designate the conduct of a person's life and the results of that conduct. In a society where walking was the primary means of transportation, walking down a path could hardly avoid being a ready illustration of everyday living. References to walking in the ways of God or his law would make up a small anthology of biblical verses (there are over a hundred references in Psalms and the book of Proverbs alone). Specimen passages include the following: "he leads me in right paths" (Ps 23:3 NRSV); "I will instruct you and teach you the way you should go" (Ps 32:8 NRSV); "to those who go the right way I will show the salvation of God" (Ps 50:23 NRSV); "you search out my path . . . and are acquainted with all my ways" (Ps 139:3 NRSV).

Since walking or journeying entails purposeful action, it is no wonder that biblical writers picture the direction and orientation of one's life as a path. To picture one's life as progress along a path, moreover, captures a sense of the dynamic nature of human existence, which never stands still and in which individual choices are not self-contained but contribute to an overall pattern. This dynamic quality is expressed memorably in the statement that "the path of the righteous is like the light of dawn, which shines brighter and brighter until full day" (Prov 4:18 NRSV). In the same vein, "For the wise the path of life leads upward" (Prov 15:24 NRSV).

Within the metaphor of life as walking down a pathway toward a destination, a particularly evocative biblical image is the *two contrasting paths or "ways." Psalm 1 is structured as a prolonged contrast between "the way of the righteous" and "the way of the wicked." Passages early in Proverbs contrast "the way of evil" and "the paths of uprightness" (Prov 2:12-15 NRSV), "the way of evildoers" and "the path of the righteous" (Prov 4:14-19 NRSV). The motif of two ways implies that the universe is such that people must choose between the two, as in Moses' *farewell discourse to Israel, in which he sets before the nation a *blessing and a *curse, life and death, with the former associated with walking in the ways of God and the latter with turning from the way that Moses commands (Deut 11:26-28; 30:15-20). This is echoed in Jeremiah 21:8, where God says, "See, I am setting before you the way of life and the way of death" (NRSV). Psalm 139 ends with a contrast between the "wicked way" and "the way everlasting" (Ps 139:24). Of similar import is Jesus' contrast near the end of the Sermon on the Mount between the broad way that leads to destruction and the narrow way that leads to life (Mt 7:13-14).

Passages that portray the two ways highlight a feature of the image of the path that is implied elsewhere—that movement along a path leads to a destination and end. They also accentuate the ease with which one can take a wrong turn, along with the dangers of doing so.

In such a moral universe the manner and moral quality of one's actions are pictured as walking down either a good path or an evil path, and there are frequent encouragements or commands to walk in one rather than the other. On the one side, "Happy are those whose way is blameless, who walk in the law of the LORD" (Ps 119:1 NRSV). From Proverbs come these encouragements to pursue the right path: "keep straight the path of your feet" (Prov 4:26);

"happy are those who keep my ways" (Prov 8:32); "in the path of righteousness there is life" (Prov 12:28 NRSV). The persistent command to OT kings is to "keep the charge of the LORD your God, walking in his ways and keeping his statutes" (1 Kings 2:3 NRSV). On the other side, we are warned not to "learn the way of the nations" (Jer 10:2 NRSV), choose the ways of the violent (Prov 3:31), "enter the path of the wicked" (Prov 4:14 NRSV) or stray into the paths of the loose woman (Prov 7:25).

Even when biblical writers are actually talking about the moral life, they do not lose sight of the physical realities of walking down a path. Thus we find references to holding fast to a path and not slipping (Ps 17:5), walking on a safe rather than dangerous path (Ps 18:32), fixing one's eyes on a path (Ps 119:15) and the difference between *crooked paths (Prov 2:15) and *straight paths (Prov 4:26).

The Way of Salvation. In addition to imaging life and its moral conduct, the path image is applied to salvation itself. In the messianic prophecies of the OT, for example, the coming salvation is pictured as the preparation of a path or way. "In the wilderness prepare the way of the LORD, make straight in the desert a highway for our God" (Is 40:3 NRSV). The "new thing" that God "is about to do" is to "make a way in the wilderness" (Is 43:19 NRSV). And again, "Prepare the way for the people; . . . build up the highway" (Is 62:10 NRSV). This echoes the imagery of the *exodus, where God led the Israelites "along the way" through the *wilderness (Ex 13:21), but the "second exodus" of salvation in Christ is of universal significance, and its path is open for any believing soul to travel.

As heirs of this OT motif, early Christians found the pathway to be a fertile symbol, representative of the final salvation that God had brought. Each of the Gospels cites Isaiah 40 in a figurative relation to the preparatory ministry of John the Baptist (Mt 3:3; Mk 1:2-3; Lk 3:4-5; Jn 1:19-25). This preparatory "way" finds its fulfillment in Christ. In the book of Acts we learn that the early Christians were known as those "who belonged to the Way" (Acts 9:2 NRSV), or simply as "the Way" (Acts 19:9, 23; 22:4; 22:14, 22).

Such terminology would be familiar to anyone acquainted with Jesus' life or with the Gospels, where the life of the disciples can aptly be summed up under the metaphor "on the road with Jesus." The image of the way lends structural unity to the Gospel of Mark, where discipleship is pictured as following Jesus on his way to the cross (Mk 1:2; 8:27; 9:33, 34; 10:32, 52). A similar picture emerges from the Gospels of Matthew (Mt 3:3; 11:10) and Luke (Lk 1:76-79; 9:52; 13:22-23). In the Gospel of John, Jesus' person is uniquely identified as the way, providing access and fellowship with the Father: "I am the way, and the truth, and the life. No one comes to the Father except through me" (Jn 14:6 NRSV). In Hebrews, Christ's role as high priest provides access to God "by the new and living way " (Heb 10:20 NRSV; cf. Heb 9:8).

See also MARK, GOSPEL OF; STREET; WALK, WALKING; WILDERNESS..

PATHBREAKER. *See* JESUS, IMAGES OF.

PATIENCE

Patience usually connotes a calm, abiding endurance, sometimes associated with *wisdom (Prov 19:11) or *humility (Eccles 7:8).

Patience is a characteristic of God we may often overlook, yet Christ's *mercy toward Paul displays his unlimited patience and mercy (1 Tim 1:16), revealing the love of God for a wicked person (Neh 9:30; Is 7:13; Rom 2:4; 2 Pet 3:15). Patience is also a characteristic of an apostle (2 Cor 6:6; 2 Tim 3:10), and the believer is commanded to live patiently with others, clothing himself or herself in patience (Col 3:12; 1 Thess 5:14; 2 Tim 4:2). Patience is accompanied by mercy, especially God's mercy (Mt 18:26; 1 Tim 1:16; 2 Pet 3:9, 15), and is a fruit of the Spirit (Gal 5:22).

Patience involves *perseverance and waiting (Neh 9:30; Job 6:11; Ps 37:7; Rom 12:12; 2 Cor 1:6; Jas 5:7) but is known for yielding *fruit (Prov 25:15; Heb 6:12); thus patience will be rewarded. During Abraham's twenty-five-year wait for a son, "he grew strong in his faith as he gave glory to God" (Rom 4:20 RSV).

*Jacob's patience required his waiting seven, then fourteen years for marriage. Afterward he continued to serve Laban another six years to earn flocks for himself. During this time he endured consuming heat and frigid cold, lack of sleep, changed wages ten times and loss from his own flocks to pay for stolen animals (Gen 31:38-41). Yet through all this his lack of complaining is notable.

God's patience with his people is an outstanding example of the virtue. Though Israel turns to idols and wickedness, God pleads with them to repent and call on his name. He tells *Solomon, "If my people who are called by my name humble themselves, and pray and seek my face, and turn from their wicked ways, then will I hear from heaven, and will forgive their sin and heal their land" (2 Chron 7:14 RSV). God waits, sending his prophets for generations, before exiling Israel and Judah to foreign lands. As Nehemiah prays, "For many years you were patient with them. By your Spirit you admonished them through your prophets" (Neh 9:30 NIV).

Almost as a foil, God's own people are markedly impatient with the very One who shows such long-suffering toward them. When they travel in the *wilderness after their deliverance by God's hand from *Egypt, grumbling and impatience mark their character. Numbers 21:4-5 (NIV) comments that "the people became impatient on the way . . . [and] spoke against God and against Moses, and said, 'Why have you brought us up out of Egypt to die in the wilderness? There is no bread! There is no water! And we

detest this miserable food!" Here is the opposite of patience: rather than thanking God for the *food they have, their freedom and his visible presence with them in the wilderness, they grumble because they are taking a long route. Here impatience is shown for what it is: selfish, whiny demanding. The self is placed above God's purposes and demands that its desires be met immediately rather than according to God's perfect plan.

See also HUMILITY; PERSEVERANCE.

PEACE

For the ancient Greeks and Romans, peace was more important in theory than in practice. They deified the concept in the *goddess Pax or Eirene. She was a youthful female, holding in her left arm a horn of plenty, a cornucopia, and in her right hand an olive branch or the wealthy infant Plutus. She was one of the Horae, a goddess with power to make things grow, personifying the *seasons.

By contrast, in the Bible peace is a key characteristic of God and a prominent concept. As in its ancient counterparts, the Bible's prominent meaning of peace is political. But the political meanings of peace are associated with emotional and physical meanings and numerous images from the military, agriculture and home. The Hebrew *šālēm* (from which comes the familiar Hebrew noun *šālôm*) literally refers to being uninjured, safe and sound, or whole. The Greek *eirēneuō* refers mainly to being in political peace.

Peace as Political Justice. When Isaac and Abimelech make a *covenant of "peace," they pledge not to harm each other physically (Gen 26:29, 31; Josh 9:15). Jesus speaks of an ambassador as someone who seeks terms of peace between warring nations (Lk 14:31-32).

If "peace" is literally political negotiations, the Bible builds onto this image the larger truth of complete reconciliation, physical and emotional, between feuding parties. In the Bible genuine peace is always just and moral. God's "covenant of peace" is made possible by obedient *priests who prevent God's wrath (Num 25:12). Peace is seeking the well-being of others and of oneself. Deborah, called a *prophet and a judge, brought political, just and moral peace to Israel for *forty years (Judg 4:1-31).

Jesus preached the "good news of peace," healing and doing good (Acts 10:36 RSV). False prophets say, "Peace, peace," when there is no peace, because they have neither *healed the people's *wounds nor ended their greediness and injustice (Jer 6:14; 8:11). The biblical peacemaker is therefore physician as well as prophet. Gideon could go to Penuel "in peace," breaking down its towers and killing all the men of the *city, because he was doing *"justice" to a city that did not give the Israelites food (Judg 8:9, 17). A wise woman brought peace to the city *Abel by convicting a political rebel (2 Sam 20:1-2, 14-22).

Thus "peacemaker" was a political position, an ambassador of peace—someone who ended wars, brought physical safety and health to people, sought people's well-being, and brought justice. Jesus is the Prince of Peace because Jesus makes Jew and *Gentile one, breaking their dividing *wall of hostility and reconciling them (Is 9:6; Eph 2:14-17).

The peacemaker/prophet/ambassador is the model for the preacher. Philo notes that "heralds establishing peace" come to suspend wars, wearing sandals so as to be "very swift-footed" with the news they carry (*Embassy to Gaius* 13). So too the NT preacher is a "herald" bringing reconciliation between God and human beings, and between people (Rom 10:15; Eph 6:15; 2 Cor 5:16-20).

The biblical prophet, like the political ambassador, stood at the crossroads of advancing armies with potential good news. John the Baptist was such a prophet who was to guide people into a way of peace (Lk 1:79). Unfortunately, not all who heard him wanted to heed his message. He was killed. So was Jesus.

Peace in Figurative Language. As noted, peace in its classical understanding was personified as the youthful female Pax. Biblically, she would be a strong, wise, swift and determined *warrior, the personified Wisdom of Proverbs (Prov 3:13-17) holding a horn of plenty to signify God's riches and an olive branch as a symbol of reconciliation.

In the Bible the political and just aspects of peace are expressed in a variety of figurative images. *"Feet" is a common synecdoche for a person running swiftly over difficult terrain to bring good news (Is 52:7; Nahum 1:15; Rom 10:15; Eph 6:15). Peace guards not only one's body but also one's inmost self, the heart (Phil 4:7). It "rules" or "judges" among many hearts (Col 3:15). Peace is also personified as a scouting patrol that advances to observe an enemy's land, or as a messenger *dove (Gen 8:8-12). If a home welcomes God's messenger, that messenger's "peace" remains there; if not, the peace returns to the messenger (Mt 10:13). Peace cannot remain where it is not welcomed.

Peace also can be imaged in more organic ways. God will give peace to a repentant *Jerusalem in the same way as a mother provides a "stream" of *milk to a *nursing child (Is 66:10-13). Peace can also be a dark, fertile soil in which the *"fruit" of righteousness grows if the sower is a peaceful or just person. *Rain may contain peace (Jas 3:17-18). Peace also is the fruit sown by the Holy Spirit or through righteous discipline (Gal 5:22; Heb 12:11). What does the fruit of peace look like? It has no spots or faults (2 Pet 3:14). Peace is a quality that can grow over time if it is well planted, well sown and well watered.

See also DOVE; ENEMY; WARFARE.

PEARL

Pearls are mentioned fewer than a dozen times in the Bible, where their status as a prized *jewel make them a touchstone of *beauty, value and *permanence. Among the literal references, mother-of-pearl is one of the precious stones that Ahasuerus displays during his seven-day extravaganza (Esther 1:6), and when Paul wants a contrast to the feminine modesty that he commends, his images of inappropriate external adornment are braided hair, *gold, pearls and costly attire (1 Tim 2:9 RSV). Of similar import is the repulsive picture of the luxurious finery of the whore of *Babylon, who "was arrayed in purple and scarlet, and bedecked with gold and jewels and pearls" (Rev 17:4 RSV; cf. Rev 18:16). As a symbol of a worldwide mercantile empire, the whore of Babylon is also portrayed as trafficking in pearls (Rev 18:12).

Because of their beauty and value, pearls become a recognized standard of excellence when biblical authors wish to make a comparison. Thus "the price of wisdom is above pearls" (Job 28:18 RSV), and the gospel itself is so precious that it should not be offered to hostile people indiscriminately: "Do not throw your pearls before swine, lest they trample them under foot and turn to attack you" (Mt 7:6 RSV). Similarly, "the kingdom of heaven is like a merchant in search of fine pearls, who, on finding one pearl of great value, went and sold all that he had and bought it" (Mt 13:45-46 RSV).

The final appearance of the image in the Bible is truly resplendent. Because the pearl combines *hardness of texture with brilliance of reflected *light, it is a staple in "enameled imagery" that poets from time immemorial have used to portray *heaven. Thus pearls are prominent in the barrage of jewel imagery in John's vision of the new *Jerusalem; in fact, each of the twelve *gates of the heavenly *city is made from a single pearl, with the dazzling effect reinforced by the street of the city, which is "pure gold, transparent as glass" (Rev 21:21 RSV).

Overall, the pearl is an ambivalent image in the Bible. Its beauty and value are positive when it is associated with God's wisdom or heavenly kingdom. But its beauty and value actually become reprehensible when people use it to make an extravagant external impression.

See also JEWELS AND PRECIOUS STONES.

PEDAGOGUE. *See* AUTHORITY, HUMAN; GALATIANS, LETTER TO THE.

PENTECOST

Pentecost is significant in both the OT and the NT. *Pentecost* is actually the Greek name for a *festival known in the OT as the Feast of Weeks (Lev 23:15; Deut 16:9). The Greek word means *"fifty" and refers to the fifty days that have elapsed since the wave offering of *Passover. The Feast of Weeks celebrated the end of the *grain harvest. Most interesting, however, is its use in Joel and Acts. Looking back to Joel's prophecy (Joel 2:8-32) and forward to the promise of the Holy Spirit in Christ's last words on earth before his *ascension (Acts 1:8), Pentecost signals the beginning of the church.

The only reference to the actual events of Pentecost is Acts 2:1-3: "And when the day of Pentecost was fully come, they were all with one accord in one place. And suddenly there came a sound from heaven as of a rushing mighty wind, and it filled all the house where they were sitting. And there appeared unto them cloven tongues like as of fire, and it sat upon each of them" (KJV). Pentecost is reminiscent of the Last *Supper; in both scenes the disciples are together in a house for what proves to be an important event. At the Last Supper the disciples witness the end of the Messiah's earthly ministry as he asks them to remember him after his death until he returns; at Pentecost the disciples witness the birth of the NT church in the coming of the Holy Spirit to indwell all believers. Thus the scene of the disciples in a room at Pentecost is a type scene, bookending the beginning of the Holy Spirit's work in the church with the conclusion of Christ's earthly ministry in the upper room before the crucifixion.

The *wind and *fire imagery of the Pentecost account reverberates richly throughout the OT and the NT. The wind at Pentecost was "rushing" and "mighty," a powerful wind that nevertheless did not extinguish the tongues of fire. Scriptural references to the power of wind (always understood to be under God's control) abound (Ex 10:13; Ps 18:42 and Is 11:15 in the OT and Mt 14:23-32 in the NT are only a few examples). More significant than wind as power is wind ("breath," the same Hebrew word) as life in the OT (Job 12:10) and as spirit in the NT (Jn 3:8). Just as the first *Adam received the breath of physical life (Gen 2:7), so the second Adam brings the breath of spiritual life. The idea of spiritual life as generated by the Holy Spirit is certainly implicit in the wind at Pentecost.

Fire, the other image of Pentecost, is often associated in the OT with the presence of God (Ex 3:2; 13:21-22; 24:17; Is 10:17) and with his holiness (Ps 97:3; Mal 3:2); likewise in the NT fire is associated with the presence of God (Heb 12:29) and the purification he can effect in human life (Rev 3:18). God's presence and holiness are implied in the Pentecostal tongues of fire. Indeed, fire is identified with Christ himself (Rev 1:14; 19:12); this association naturally underlies the Pentecost gift of the Holy Spirit, who would teach the disciples the things of Christ (Jn 16:14).

The remainder of Acts 2 adds to the images with which we associate the first Pentecost. A leading picture is the miraculous speaking in foreign tongues, which enabled people from various language groups to understand the message of the apostles. A second is the bold and incisive preaching of Peter to a Jewish audience. The effect of the sermon is equally vivid, as listeners were "cut to the heart" (Acts 2:37 RSV) and instructed by Peter to "repent, and be baptized" (Acts 2:38). The narrative concludes with three thousand souls being added to the fellowship, the breaking of bread and prayers, apostolic signs and wonders, and a utopian community formed in which everyone's needs were met.

See also FESTIVAL; FIFTY; HOLY SPIRIT.

PERFUME

Neither Giorgio nor Polo nor Ralph Lauren but myrrh, frankincense and onycha perfume the pages of Scripture, tempting readers' sense of *smell with beguiling scents. Some other specific fragrances mentioned in the Bible include stacte, mint, galbanum, cumin, spikenard, saffron, aloes, camphor, calamus and cinnamon. Combinations of such fragrances with other ingredients are what Bible writers refer to when they mention spices, *ointments, *incenses, salves, embalming materials and anointing *oils.

Bible writers from Genesis to Revelation mention fragrances for many reasons, recording aromatic details to enhance poetry, history, narrative and prophecy. Scents, individually or in mixture, appear in a range of contexts: barter ("carry down the man a present, a little balm, and a little honey, spices, and myrrh, nuts, and almonds" [Gen 43:11 KJV]), commerce ("and, behold, a company of Ishmaelites came from Gilead with their camels bearing spicery and balm and myrrh, going to carry *it* down to Egypt" [Gen 37:25 KJV]), romance (Solomon to his love in a surfeiting of scents: "spikenard and saffron; calamus and cinnamon, with all trees of frankincense; myrrh and aloes, with all the chief spices" [Song 4:14 KJV]), religious ritual (in reference to the altar of incense and anointing oil: "and Aaron shall burn thereon sweet incense every morning" [Ex 30:7 KJV], and "take thou also unto thee principal spices, of pure myrrh five hundred shekels, and of sweet cinnamon half so much, even two hundred and fifty shekels, and of sweet calamus two hundred and fifty shekels" [Ex 30:23 KJV]), in poetic comparison ("ointment and perfume rejoice the heart: so doth the sweetness of a man's friend by hearty counsel" [Prov 27:9 KJV]), *worship ("and fell down, and worshipped him: and when they had opened their treasures, they presented unto him gifts; gold, and frankincense, and myrrh" [Mt 2:11 KJV]) and *burial ("and they returned [to Jesus' tomb], and prepared spices and ointments" [Lk 23:56 KJV]).

From the first book to the last, from Jesus' birth to his death, fragrances enhance the potency of the biblical story, being associated throughout with riches. Besides their use as fragrances, some of these ingredients doubled as flavorings, cosmetics (Ruth 3:3) and medicines (Jer 8:22).

See also ANOINTING; INCENSE; OIL; OINTMENT; SMELL, SCENT.

PERMANENCE

The Bible's imagery of permanence is rooted in a two-tiered conception of the universe, as captured in kernel form in the statement of the wise man that "God is in heaven, and you upon earth" (Eccles 5:2 RSV). The essential contrast of the Bible is between the unchanging *God and his time-based, contingent creation. One nexus of biblical imagery for permanence is thus the contrast between the temporal and the eternal, which ties into a corresponding contrast between the *earthly and the *heavenly.

Conceptual Imagery. The imagery used to denote the transcendent realm is partly conceptual—words naming qualities rather than tangible images. Heading the list are the words *forever* and *evermore* (nearly 650 references). Something is said to be "steadfast" nearly two hundred times. The heavenly realm is also "eternal" (approximately 75 references). The root word *endure* appears nearly 150 times. The epithet *everlasting* is also important (five dozen references).

Writers have through the centuries also resorted to the *via negativa* in talking about heaven and deity, denying to them the qualities that characterize mortal beings. Here we find such terms as *immortal* ("not mortal"; Rom 1:23; 1 Tim 1:17; *see* Mortality), *imperishable* (1 Cor 9:25; 15:24; *see* Decay) and *unfading* (1 Pet 1:4; 5:4; *see* Fade, Fading). The godly person's permanence is pictured in the image of a tree whose leaf "does not wither" (Ps 1:3 RSV; see also Ezek 47:12). The *locus classicus* for defining the permanent heavenly realm in contrast to the earthly transient realm is Paul's description of the *resurrection body in 1 Corinthians 15:35-58.

A related motif is to heighten the eternity of God by contrasting it to something transient. For example, Psalm 103:15-18 contrasts the mutability of people, who are like *grass that withers, with the "steadfast love of the LORD," which is "from everlasting to everlasting" (RSV). Again, "the mountains may depart and the hills be removed, but my steadfast love shall not depart from you" (Is 54:10 RSV). Similarly, people and plants perish, "but the word of the Lord abides for ever" (1 Pet 1:24-25 RSV). Permanence is here pictured in terms of its contrast to *transience.

Enameled Imagery. Poets have always used enameled imagery to portray permanence, especially transcendent permanence. Enameled imagery combines *hardness of texture with brilliance of light to suggest a realm more permanent than the cyclic, vegetative world in which we live. *Jewel imagery is the most prevalent type of enameled imagery. Ezekiel's vision of a heavenly level of reality is replete with such imagery—flashing *fire and *lightning, burnished *bronze that sparkles, gleaming chrysolite and sapphire (Ezek 1). To this we can add the memorable pictures in Revelation of a sea of glass, like crystal, the appearance of God in splendor like that of jasper and carnelian, *golden *crowns, *gates of *pearl, a *city of pure gold.

Nature. *Nature too has supplied poets with images by which to portray permanence. Certain features of nature become candidates for such use simply by their stability and comparative permanence. *Mountains, for example, appeal to biblical writers as an image of permanence. To the biblical imagination the mountains are "ancient" and the hills "everlasting" (Deut 33:15). When God's righteousness is said to be "like the mountains" (Ps 36:6 RSV), this is likely a reference to its permanence as

well as its magnitude. Even the constantly repeated cycles of nature can paradoxically become an image of permanence (Eccles 1:4-7). The world or cosmos is also an image for permanence in the Bible; thus "the world stands firm, never to be moved" (1 Chron 16:30 RSV; cf. Ps 93:1; 96:10).

The Things That Endure. We may note finally a list of things that the Bible declares to be permanent. Most important is *God himself, who is "the King of ages, immortal," to whom honor and glory will be given "for ever and ever" (1 Tim 1:17 RSV). God's law, too, will last "till heaven and earth pass away" (Mt 5:18 RSV), underpinning the moral fabric of the human race. The word of the Lord "abides for ever" (1 Pet 1:25 RSV). God's "steadfast love endures for ever" (Ps 136 RSV; cf. Is 54:10). Among the Christian virtues, love is the most enduring; in fact, it "never ends" (1 Cor 13:8). God's protection of his own will last "from this time forth and for evermore" (Ps 121:8 RSV).

See also DECAY; FADE, FADING; GOD; HARD, HARDEN, HARDNESS; MORTALITY; TRANSIENCE.

PERSECUTION

Persecution is aggressive and injurious behavior carried out in a hostile, antagonistic spirit, normally by a group. Persecutors are known especially for their fiery zeal (Phil 3:6), a zeal that is described elsewhere as "not based on knowledge" (Rom 10:2 NIV). Persecution itself is a *terror, more or less inevitable in the biblical world, especially the NT.

Persecution and its attendant spirit of animosity are set against the backdrop of the Bible's dramatic portrayal of *Satan's great enmity against God and his people. It is concretely expressed in the antagonism of the wicked (described as the children of the devil, Jn 8:44) toward the righteous (the children of God, Rev 12:17). It is thus no surprise that the image of persecution is so pervasive in the Bible, for it falls upon God's people by virtue of their relationship to him (Jn 15:18-21). This sense of solidarity and union with Christ and his people is movingly described in Acts 9:4, where the risen Jesus asks Saul, persecutor of followers of the Way, "Why do you persecute *me?*" In fact, persecution serves as a sign of the authenticity of one's relationship to Jesus (Mt 5:10, 12; Phil 1:29) and one's response as a veritable litmus test to determine that authenticity (Mt 13:20-21). Disciples can count on persecution. Those who respond in faith will be counted as righteous; however, "many will turn away from the faith" (see Mt 24:9-11 NIV).

In light of the above, persecution in the Bible is primarily of a religious nature (although ethnic persecution occurs, as in Esther). In this spiritual context it assumes a number of different forms: physical (*beatings, Is 50:6; stonings, Acts 14:19), verbal (mocking, Lk 23:11; insults, Ps 69:9; slander, Rev 2:9), social (excommunication or ostracism, Jn 9:22) or mental (intimidation, Lk 13:31; threats, Acts 4:21, 29). Persecution also involves or can lead to imprisonment (Mk 6:17), banishment (Rev 1:9; *see*

Outcast), even death (2 Chron 24:21; Rev 2:10).

Because persecution is inevitable for the truly righteous (Phil 1:29; 2 Tim 3:12), the people of God are exhorted to respond positively. Negative reactions such as *fear (Phil 1:28; 1 Pet 3:14; Rev 2:10), compromise (Gal 6:12), cursing (Rom 12:14), desertion (Mt 26:56), retaliation (Rom 12:17-21) or *apostasy (Heb 10:32-39) deny potential Christian witness. Instead believers are to commit themselves to God (1 Pet 4:19), rejoice because of the great eschatological *reward awaiting them (Mt 5:12), demonstrate *patience (1 Cor 4:12) and *perseverance (Heb 10:36), and pray for those who inflict persecution upon them (Mt 5:44).

See also MARTYR; OUTCAST; PERSEVERANCE; TERROR, STORIES OF; TRIAL; VIOLENCE, STORIES OF.

PERSEVERANCE

Perseverance is rooted in *confidence (in the Lord). It is produced by *suffering (Rom 5:3; Jas 1:3) and produces character, "so that [we] may be mature and complete, not lacking anything" (Jas 1:4 NIV; also Rom 5:4). *Faith requires perseverance (Heb 12:1), because the world hates believers and works to discourage them from finishing the *race. Perseverance is the mark of an apostle (2 Cor 12:12) and anyone who does the work of God. In perseverance, *strength comes from God, and God is glorified by it (Heb 11:27). He notices Christians' perseverance (Rev 2:2, 19) and *rewards them with his compassion and *mercy (1 Tim 4:16; Heb 10:36; Jas 5:11).

Paul's perseverance is perhaps the prime biblical example: "I am compelled to preach. Woe to me if I do not preach the gospel!" he writes to the Corinthians (1 Cor 9:16 NIV). After being stoned by the Jews and left for dead in Lystra, Paul gets up and goes back into the very same city (Acts 14:19-20). In fact, Paul is so set on preaching Christ that he endures terrible hardship and *persecution:

> Five times I received from the Jews the forty lashes minus one. Three times I was beaten with rods, once I was stoned, three times I was shipwrecked, I spent a night and a day in the open sea, I have been constantly on the move. I have been in danger from rivers, in danger from bandits, in danger from my own countrymen, in danger from Gentiles; in danger in the city, in danger in the country, in danger at sea; and in danger from false brothers. I have labored and toiled and have often gone without sleep; I have known hunger and thirst and have often gone without food; I have been cold and naked. Besides everything else, I face daily the pressure of my concern for all the churches. Who is weak, and I do not feel weak? Who is led into sin, and I do not inwardly burn? (2 Cor 11:24-33 NIV)

Paul's perseverance is marked by humility and lack of concern for himself. Always on his mind is the glory of Christ and his concern for the churches. He does not care for himself but continues to faithfully serve the Lord according to the *calling he received.

But perseverance is not reserved for the apostle; in Hebrews we are called to "hold unswervingly to the hope we profess, for he who promised is faithful. . . . Let us not give up meeting together, as some are in the habit of doing, but let us encourage one another" (Heb 10:23-25 NIV). The call to persevere is for all who trust Christ as their Lord.

See also FAITH; ORDEAL, STORIES OF; PERSECUTION; STRENGTH; SUFFERING; TRIAL.

PERSPIRATION. *See* SWEAT.

PERVERSE. *See* CROOKED.

PESTILENCE. *See* PLAGUE.

PETER, FIRST LETTER OF

1 Peter presents itself as a letter addressed to Christians living in the northern parts of Asia Minor. It is less personal than Paul's letters, making no specific reference to individuals and not interacting with addressees' questions or specific matters of doctrine or practice. It is nevertheless addressed to a specific situation: believers who are facing *persecution and calumny because of their profession of Christianity. The author helps his readers deal with such *suffering and exhorts them to follow the example of Christ.

In 1911 R. Perdelwitz suggested that 1 Peter was not originally a letter but two distinct homilies, 1:3—4:11 (being later combined with 1:1-2) and 4:12—5:14. The first part was held by many scholars in the first half of the twentieth century to have originally been some sort of liturgy with *baptism at its core. But more recent scholarship has tended away from these conjectures because the letter as a whole does admit of a rational unified character without recourse to such guesswork. Although many still hold to the idea that baptism is a controlling theme of 1 Peter, the letter is now more commonly seen as a unity.

This is not to say that the author may not have used sources. It is not difficult to note how frequently 1 Peter buttresses his exhortations with liberal quotation from the OT. It also appears that he may be using some other preexistent material familiar to the church. Several scholars, starting with H. Windisch (1930), have identified hymnic material in 1 Peter, usually somehow connected with the baptismal liturgy hypothesis. M.-E. Boismard professed to find four *hymns (1:3-5; 2:22-25; 3:18-22; and 5:5-9), all of which bear resemblance to highly stylized material elsewhere in the NT. He also saw fragments of hymns at 1:20 and 4:6. Since none of these pieces bears a marked metric or strophic form, such identifications must remain hypothetical; but at least we may say that whether or not the author is using sources, these passages do exhibit literarily heightened language, especially in 1 Peter 2:21-25 and 3:18-22. Both of these passages are marked by a frequency of relative pronouns, they demonstrate some alliteration (e.g., *en tō stomati* and *en tō sōmati* in 1 Pet 2:22, 24) and they allude implicitly or explicitly to OT and traditional material. Furthermore, both may be chiastic in structure. However, all of these possible hymns are better understood as christological in character rather than as focused on baptism, which is only passingly mentioned in one text.

Peter uses a number of images, mostly drawn from the OT, to depict and illumine the situation and responsibilities of his readers. The metaphor that controls these images is *Israel, the people of God. This metaphor expresses itself in four aspects: (1) that the believers as the spiritual Israel do not belong to this world, (2) that they *do* belong in God's *house (Israel) by identification with Jesus Christ, (3) that God has graciously brought them into that state of belonging and (4) that such a situation results in a kind of *warfare.

Not Belonging. 1 Peter stresses the distance of believers from the social world around them. This is derived from the fact that as God's people they are *holy;* that is, set apart for God (1 Pet 1:15-16). They are therefore referred to as sojourners and strangers (1 Pet 1:1;1:17; 2:11; *see* Foreigner), terms borrowed from OT contexts that depict *Abraham as wandering in Canaan (Gen 23:4; cf. Heb 11:13). Recent efforts have been made to identify this alienation as a literal social situation (Elliott), but the primary emphasis in the letter appears to be the distinction and separateness of believers due to the fact that their ultimate citizenship lies elsewhere than in any political entity of this present world. In particular, 1 Peter 2:11-12 specifically links recognition of alien status to the distinctive behavior patterns that mark off the believers from the *"Gentiles" among whom they live. This distinction from Gentiles is also reflected in the author's use of *diaspora* in reference to his readers. Although older commentators often took this to indicate a Jewish readership, almost all scholars are now persuaded by such passages as 1 Peter 1:18 and 4:2-4 that at least most of the audience was originally pagan in background. Thus the Jewish image of the dispersion, a reference to the fact that God's people were scattered all over the Greco-Roman world, came to be applied to Christians, who were also exiled and scattered all over the world. This may also be why Peter seemingly refers to Rome as *"Babylon" in 1 Peter 5:13—not because Rome had at that time sacked Jerusalem, but because Rome was the political center of the empire within which the people of God were scattered.

Belonging. In contrast to the stranger/sojourner images that reflect Israel's not belonging, there is a set of images that stress belonging. These references are piled on top of each other in 1 Peter 2:5-10. The most prominent of these is the various forms of house of God imagery. Since believers as Israel is the controlling motif, the house of God refers first of all to household, the people who constitute God's family. But of course "God's house" can also refer to a place of worship, the temple. The depiction of all believers

as living *stones being constructed into a spiritual *temple of God (1 Pet 2:5) on the foundation of Christ (1 Pet 2:4, 6-8) combines these meanings into a very rich and multiplex image, which is picked up again in 1 Peter 4:17, where Christian suffering is described as a judgment that begins with the house of God.

The idea of Christians as God's family is continued in 1 Peter 2:9-10, where the contrast between the readers' former and present states is spelled out, using the language of Hosea 1 and 2. Christians can therefore call God *Father (1 Pet 1:17), but of course this entails acting like his children. Also as a family the "household rules" that prevail in general social obligations (1 Pet 2:18—3:7) have their counterpart in the church (1 Pet 5:1-5).

An extension of the "family of God" and "temple" concepts is the *priesthood. Since the Levites and especially the priesthood in the OT were specially set apart for the Lord, the new people of God are also as a whole considered a priesthood (1 Pet 2:4), even as was Israel as a whole (1 Pet 2:9, which is quoting from Is 43:20 [LXX] and Ex 19:6). This priesthood offers up spiritual *sacrifices acceptable to God (1 Pet 2:5). The reference is probably to the prayers of believers, although it may also represent their righteous behavior in the face of persecution or even, as Paul says in Romans 12, their very selves, since in this one verse they are both the stones that make up the house and the priests who serve in it.

Also in this set of "belonging" metaphors is the *flock of *sheep image. Christians are referred to as the flock of God (1 Pet 5:2), picking up the common OT metaphor (e.g., Ps 78:52; 80:1; 95:7; Is 40:11; 63:11; Jer 10:21). The correlative picture of God as *shepherd is probably operative here, and possibly also a remembrance of Jesus' words recorded in John 10:11.

Initiation. Another set of metaphors develops the process of *initiation and reception into the people of God. Christians are God's flock because they were brought back to the shepherd (1 Pet 2:25). Earlier, in 1 Peter 2:9, the author points out that the elect people belong to God because they were called out of *darkness into light.

Furthermore, this entire chapter starts off with an exhortation to yearn for God's word as new-born *babies yearn for *milk (1 Pet 2:2). This image is picking up on the fact that believers have been reborn into incorruptible hope (1 Pet 1:3) by the incorruptible *"seed" of God's word (1 Pet 1:23). Since they are reborn, they have been set apart, made holy by "sprinkling" with the *blood of Jesus (1 Pet 1:2; reflecting the blood sprinkling of Israel at Sinai), which also "purchased" them from the implicit slavery of their old traditional and futile behavior patterns (1 Pet 1:18-19; probably echoing the delivery of Israel from slavery in Egypt).

The most problematic passage in the letter, 1 Peter 3:19-22, has at its center a reference to Noah's salvation by the *flood as typological of the initiation and cleansing of the believers by baptism. Whatever this enigmatic passage means, it appears the author is using an OT physical image as a metaphor for the spiritual reality of incorporation into Christ. Just as the flood rescued Noah's family by separation from the old world, so baptism rescues believers by *"cleansing" the conscience, through identification with the death and resurrection of Jesus. Again, because the people of God are holy, this involves a separation from, or "dying to," sins in order to live for righteousness (1 Pet 2:24).

Warfare. The author wishes his readers to live as God's people in the midst of a situation inherently opposed to God. Thus suffering "for the name" of Christ is to be expected from time to time and is a good thing, pleasing to God (1 Pet 4:12-14). This means that the life of the believer is going to be one of struggle; hence, 1 Peter reflects certain *warfare images. But the *battle is cognitive and behavioral, not physical.

Thus 1 Peter 1:13, which is literally translated "gird up the loins of your mind," depicts the soldier tucking up his garment so it does not become entangled when running or handling weapons. The struggle is mental, and Christians are to get their minds ready for battle. Similarly, in 1 Peter 4:1 the readers are to "arm themselves" with the same mindset that Christ had in facing suffering. So too, when faced with persecution, Christians are not to retaliate in kind, for the battle is not physical. The behavior of believers is to be governed by the *imitatio Christi* principle. Christ's suffering without retaliation left the pattern (1 Pet 2:21). As his battle was against spiritual forces (1 Pet 3:22, and probably 3:19 as well), so the believer's warfare is waged not against people but against the "fleshly desires" that "make war against the soul" (1 Pet 2:11).

See also PERSECUTION; 2 PETER; SUFFERING.

BIBLIOGRAPHY. P. Achtemeier, "New-Born Babes and Living Stones: Literal and Figurative in 1 Peter" in *To Touch the Text: Biblical and Related Studies in Honor of Joseph H. Fitzmyer,* ed. M. P. Horgan and P. J. Kobelski (New York: Crossroad/Continuum, 1988) 207-36; M. E. Boismard, *Quatre Hymnes Baptismales dans la Première Epître de Pierre* (Paris: Editions du Cerf, 1961); J. H. Elliott, *A Home for the Homeless: A Sociological Exegesis of 1 Peter, Its Situation and Strategy* (Philadelphia: Fortress, 1981); T. W. Martin, *Metaphor and Composition in 1 Peter* (SBLDS 131; Atlanta: Scholars, 1992); C. F. D. Moule, "The Nature and Purpose of 1 Peter," *NTS* 3 (1956-57) 1-11.

PETER, SECOND LETTER OF

The primary thematic concerns of 2 Peter are the contrast between false and true *prophecy, the importance of the coming of Christ in *judgment, and the danger inherent in abandoning hope in it. The book is highly graphic in its depictions, both of the end of this world (esp. 2 Pet 3:10-13) and of the

wickedness of false prophets (2 Pet 2).

2 Peter should probably be seen as bearing the form of a testament or *farewell discourse: it contains predictions of the author's death and other imminent catastrophes, along with exhortations to faithfulness and the promise of ultimate victory. One very important feature in common with many such farewell discourses is that false prophets are considered a major threat, and the readers are warned against them vigorously.

Like *Jude (which it closely resembles, not so much in actual words as in the series of depictions used), the second chapter of 2 Peter piles up a series of negative images to reinforce the danger of false prophecy and the depravity of those who do it. Imagery of sexual license is pronounced here (2 Pet 2:6, 13-14). These are probably not literal references to actual sexual depravity but metaphors for the spiritual *adultery and seductiveness that false prophecy entails. On the other hand, the fiscal greed (2 Pet 2:3, 14-15) may be a literal depiction. Certainly financial greed is a frequent motive for false prophecy (the example of Balaam being explicit here in 2 Pet 2:15). It is not clear whether the depiction of these false prophets as slanderous toward *angels (2 Pet 2:10-12) is an indication of some strange exorcistic rites or teaching, or is simply another in the series of images taken from common tradition to depict the depravity of those who depart from the truth (cf. Jude 8-10).

The "waterless *springs" and "storm-driven *clouds" in 2 Peter 2:17 are particularly forceful imagery to dwellers in Palestine, where water is such a precious and in some places rare commodity. A person in the desert who expends his effort arriving at a spring is not just disappointed when he finds it dried up; his error could be fatal. Likewise, clouds promise *rain, but clouds hard-driven by strong wind are a false hope—they either blow over or bring rain so hard it destroys a crop. False prophecy sounds and looks promising but in fact is illusory.

2 Peter also uses boldly drawn images in positive ways. 2 Peter 1:2-4 sets forth an eight-rung "ladder" to emphasize the development of Christian character (cf. Rom 5:3-5; Gal 5:22ff.). The catalog begins with the exhortation to "add" various virtues to faith. The word used here was also used to designate wealthy patrons of drama who donated money for the costumes of an acting troupe. What we are to picture, therefore, is a lavish outfitting of ourselves with the Christian virtues. Furthermore, the exhortation to pay attention to true prophecy (2 Pet 1:19) links genuine prophecy to the second coming, comparing it to "a light shining in a dark place, until the day dawns and the morning *star rises in your hearts" (NIV), an image picked up from Isaiah 60:1 (cf. Lk 1:78-79).

2 Peter is written partly in response to the problem of a delayed parousia—people are scoffing at Christians because their expectation of Christ's return has so far not been fulfilled (2 Pet 3:3-13). As

in our own day, rationalistic or scientific skepticism mocks biblical catastrophism. In 2 Peter 3:5-6 the author refers to biblical images of *creation and the *flood, both catastrophic events, to reinforce the biblical view of history as punctuated by the massively unexpected. He thus does not think of these as only images but as actual intrusions into experiential space and time. The imagery of *water and *fire dominates the discussion of cataclysmic judgment.

Overall, we can say that the imagery of the letter paints a heightened contrast between good and evil, and between true believers and unbelievers. On one side, we have the imagery of adding the Christian virtues to one's faith; of paying attention to prophecy as to a *lamp shining in *darkness; of persons living lives of holiness and godliness; of being found by Christ spotless, blameless and at peace with him—an extended picture of all that is loveliest in the Christian life. On the other side, we read about false prophets guilty of lurid vice, about God's condemning demons to hell and subjecting wicked humanity to floods and *brimstone, about the *dog returning to its *vomit and the sow wallowing in the mire, about professing Christians' being carried away by the error of lawless people. For virtually every category of experience that is named, we find good and bad manifestations—"the word of the prophets made more certain" (2 Pet 1:19 NIV), for example, set over against "ignorant and unstable people" who "distort" the Scriptures "to their own destruction" (2 Pet 3:16 NIV).

See also FAREWELL DISCOURSE; JUDE; 1 PETER; PROPHET, PROPHETESS.

PHARAOH

Egyptians gave many titles to their rulers, including Pharaoh, which functioned similarly to the English title king. But pharaohs differed from Western conceptions of *kings because Egyptians considered their ruler to be divine (*see* Gods, Goddesses). Pharaoh was the son of the powerful sun-god, Re, and became the god Osiris after death. Scripture mentions several pharaohs, either by proper name or by title; generally the most well-known pharaoh is the "pharaoh of the exodus" (Ex 4—14).

Pharaoh's most famous role is antagonist to Yahweh's protagonist in the *exodus drama. As a god and as the king of *Egypt, Pharaoh shows disdain for the Hebrew God who dares to usurp his authority: "Who is the LORD, that I should obey him and let Israel go? I do not know the LORD and I will not let Israel go" (Ex 5:2 NIV). Throughout the exodus narrative Pharaoh's major character trait continues to be his arrogant, prideful and unyielding attitude toward Yahweh, which the biblical writer refers to as a *hard or unyielding *heart on seventeen occasions in Exodus 4—14. This characteristic was so widely known that Philistines refer to the hardness of Pharaoh's heart in 1 Samuel 6:6.

King Yahweh determines to humble his rival (Ex 10:3) and to bring *judgment on all the gods of

Egypt, including Pharaoh (Ex 12:12). Through a series of ten great and terrible plagues, King Yahweh wages war against Pharaoh and defeats him. As victor, Yahweh will reign forever and ever (Ex 15:18). Yahweh is the true God and King.

Pharaoh and Yahweh also serve as foils for each other. Pharaoh rules a *land characterized by *death for Israelites, but Yahweh is a sovereign leading his people to a land of life. Pharaoh only takes, but Yahweh gives. Pharaoh is *evil, but Yahweh is good.

Pharaoh of the exodus represents all those who oppose the one true God. Those who raise themselves up against God will be brought to nothing. Yahweh raises Pharaoh up so that the whole world may know about the true King and his power (Ex 9:16; cf. Rom 9:17). Scripture gives testimony to this principle: "It is not by strength that one prevails; those who oppose the LORD will be shattered" (1 Sam 2:9-10 NIV). "God opposes the proud but gives grace to the humble" (Jas 4:6 NIV).

Pharaohs who ruled after the exodus continue to be viewed negatively by biblical writers, primarily because of Israel's propensity to make alliances with Egypt (e.g., Is 30:1-3). Later pharaohs follow in the footsteps of their illustrious ancestor who ruled during the exodus. The pharaoh in Ezekiel's prophecies (Ezek 29—32) exhibits the same arrogance as the pharaoh of the exodus, who lived over six hundred years before.

Ezekiel records that the pharaoh of his time dared to assert that he made the Nile (Ezek 29:3). Because of his pride, God promised destruction for Pharaoh and all his army (Ezek 31:11, 18). Ezekiel sees an *apocalyptic* judgment against Pharaoh; the day of judgment equates to "the day of the LORD" (Ezek 30:3).

Similarities exist among the judgments described by Ezekiel, the ten *plagues in Exodus and John's visions of divine wrath in Revelation. For example, a judgment of *darkness is spoken of in Exodus 10, Ezekiel 32 and Revelation 9. These similarities suggest that the character of Pharaoh not only exemplifies those who flout God's authority but represents the cataclysmic and eternal destiny of those who oppose the true King.

See also EGYPT; EXODUS; PLAGUE.

PHARISEE

In all literature a worthy *hero must have apt opponents to heighten his own valor. Such is the case with Milton's *Paradise Lost,* and such is the case with the antagonists in the Gospels, the Pharisees. They are model citizens of *Israel, accepted leaders simply by virtue of their zeal for the *law. But like the original Antagonist, *pride fells them.

In the Gospels the words *pharisee* and *hypocrite* are nearly synonymous. The etymology of *hypocrite* suggests "a pretender." In Hebrew culture the Pharisees pretended to be the authoritative opinion on righteousness and the law. They are convincing: fervently loyal to God, zealous for knowledge of

Scripture, respected as the authority even by those who disagreed with them. Jesus challenges their right to their assumed position and exposes their pretense and emerges as a higher authority. The Pharisees defend their stance aggressively, ultimately collaborating in Jesus' death.

The images of a Pharisee compose the portrait of a person having zeal without knowledge of the mystery of the kingdom, occupying the "seat of Moses" in Jewish culture, outstanding by all cultural measures of righteousness but threatened by the Messiah's arrival.

Zeal Without Knowledge. As a religious group the lineage of the Pharisees may be traced to the postexilic reform efforts of Nehemiah and Ezra. Their intense loyalty to God and separatist philosophy reflected the suspicion of kingdoms that lingered after the Jews' exile. In their zealous efforts to observe the law and establish boundaries demarcating true Israelite identity, they embraced oral as well as written law, thus differing from the Sadducees on the *resurrection of the *body, among other things (Acts 23:6-9). They ardently sought knowledge of God. Both Nicodemus, who questioned Christ in the night (Jn 3:1-15), and Gamaliel, who suspended judgment on the early church (Acts 5:34-39), were Pharisees.

The Pharisaic ardor for the details of the law is best described by the words of Isaiah: "So then, the word of the LORD to them will become: Do and do, do and do, rule on rule, rule on rule; a little here, a little there—so that they will go and fall backward, be injured and snared and captured" (Is 28:13 NIV).

On the Seat of Moses. In the Gospels the Pharisees command tremendous respect. This accords with their historical refusal to be loyal to Rome; they are politically influential because they were popular leaders of the people. Though subject to intra-Jewish criticism in the Qumran and other rabbinic literature, they were credited with the role of judge in Hebrew culture, "the seat of Moses" (Mt 23:2).

But the Pharisees are foremost interested in the restoration of Israel. Their concern for keeping of the law, for the sanctity of the temple, for the purity of Israel and for the full Israelite claim on the land of Israel were fired by prophetic promise and charged with political implications. For this reason we find them to be the foremost inquisitors and dialogue partners of Jesus. They rightly perceive that they share common interests with the rabbi from Galilee. Thus they send a deputation to examine John the Baptist (Jn 1:19-28), and they constantly question Jesus. But the Gospels afford little casual conversation between Jesus and the Pharisees. Stories of conflict with Pharisees dot this pathway through a drama that will climax at the cross. Jesus accuses them of abusing their power: "devour[ing] widows' houses" (Mk 12:40), taking the best synagogue seats (Mt 23:6), expecting dutiful marketplace greetings and the title Rabbi (Mk 23:7).

Blind Guides. As ideal antagonists the Pharisees share the same body of knowledge about God as the hero, Jesus, but they are *blinded by pride to the complete perspective. Their myopic vision of the law leads eventually to a decline in popular opinion and immediately to the harsh judgment of Jesus: "You blind guides! You strain out a gnat but swallow a camel" (Mt 23:24 NIV).

Though they are considered expert exegetes in the nuance of the law, Jesus condemns them as teachers of the law for expanding its intention. While they take offense to his *sabbath healing of a man with a withered *hand (Mk 3:1-5), he refers to the written law and scorns extrapolations (Mk 2:27). He claims their traditions make void the word of God (Mk 7:13) by focusing on minute details and missing the larger purpose: "Woe to you, teachers of the law and Pharisees, you hypocrites! You give a tenth of your spices—mint, dill and cummin. But you have neglected the more important matters of the law— justice, mercy and faithfulness" (Mt 23:23 NIV). A tithe of spice outweighs *justice. Jesus decries the burdens of the law that they load on the people without offering assistance (Mt 23:4).

Whitewashed Tombs. Intent on separation from all defilement, the Pharisees have applied to their table fellowship the laws prescribed for priests and sacrifices. No wonder they are offended at Jesus' fellowship with tax collectors and *sinners. Their boast in observance of the law and their contempt for sinners finds its clearest expression in Jesus' parable of the Pharisee and the tax collector. The Pharisee esteems his own *purity in prayer: "God, I thank you that I am not like other people: thieves, rogues, adulterers, or even like this tax collector. I fast twice a week; I give a tenth of all my income" (see Lk 18:9-14 NRSV). But Jesus explains that the tax collector who begged for mercy, rather than the Pharisee, was justified by prayer.

To emphasize their insufficient efforts at purity, he calls the Pharisees "whitewashed tombs, which on the outside look beautiful, but on the inside . . . are full of the bones of the dead" (Mt 23:27 NRSV). They ignore God's words to Samuel: "The LORD does not look at the things man looks at. Man looks at the outward appearance, but the LORD looks at the heart" (1 Sam 16:7 NIV). Jesus heightens the Pharisees' accepted standard of purity by reminding them that defilement is an inner condition of the heart (Mk 7:14-23).

Jealous Avengers. Jesus infuriates the Pharisees by solving their hardest riddles, surpassing their highest standards, exceeding their discernment of law. But they are prompted to action when he asserts his right to their position as religious authority. Along with miraculously healing the impure, he claims a special relationship to God (Mt 11:27; Mk 12:36; Jn 10:14-23). He also owns the messianic role with direct appeals to their treasured law (Jn 10:33, 39; 11:47). They turn to their political and religious clout for revenge; with priestly roles and political connections, they encourage his trial and crucifixion (Jn 11:47-53; 18:3).

The proverbial blindness of the Pharisees is ironically reversed when one Pharisee, Saul of Tarsus, gains sight by being blinded on the Damascus Road. His vicious persecution of Christians demonstrates the false conviction that motivates the Pharisees. After being blinded by the might of Jesus, whom he was persecuting, his myopic view of the law is corrected and he sees clearly. And we find a few other Pharisees trusting Christ (Acts 15:5; 21:20). Paul's tone of sorrow toward those opposed to the gospel (Romans) echoes Jesus' own strange request regarding his blinded condemners: "Forgive them, for they do not know what they are doing" (Lk 23:34).

See also HYPOCRITE; JESUS; LAW; PURITY

PHILEMON, LETTER TO

The brief letter of Paul to Philemon, a letter of advocacy in which Paul mediates a solution "in Christ" for the return of Philemon's *slave Onesimus, is dominated with metaphors of social relationship. The world of these metaphors is a large household established as an alternative society. Within the Roman world, the hard facts are that Philemon is a master, Onesimus is his slave (probably of high standing), and Paul is a prisoner of the state, most likely detained in Rome. Within the social relations of that world, Onesimus is a debtor to his master Philemon, for Onesimus is absent without leave from his master's household.

How this circumstance came about we cannot be certain, but recent interpretation favors the view that Onesimus has sought out Paul with the intention of having Paul, a person respected by Philemon, mediate a dispute with his master. In negotiating the safe return of Onesimus, Paul invokes the image of an alternative world of relationships and values "in Christ."

If Paul is (by all public appearance) a prisoner of Rome, he considers himself in reality a "prisoner of Christ Jesus" (Philem 1, 9) and "in chains for the gospel" (Philem 13 NIV). Paul presents himself as engaged in a military role of some kind, for he is a "fellow soldier" with Archippus. Like the household of Caesar (Phil 4:22), which included high officials and lowly *servants in the employ of Caesar—in Rome, Corinth, Caesarea or wherever—Christ has a large household over which he is Lord, and it is represented in many cities. In speaking of his "Lord" (Philem 3, 5, 16, 20, 25), Paul implies his own relationship of *slave to this head of the household. How much more so are Timothy, Onesimus and even Philemon, who are called his brothers, and Apphia his sister! Paul employs language of *familial intimacy as he speaks of being like a *father to Onesimus, who is like a *son to him. Indeed, Onesimus is Paul's "very heart" (Philem 12). Within this household Paul has several "fellow workers" (Philemon, Mark, Aristarchus, Demas and Luke; Philem 24). Finally, as was common for slaves in large households, Paul has an executive role within the household of Christ, for he could have "commanded" Philemon, but he will

appeal to the household code of love (Philem 8-9); and Philemon, instead of Onesimus, might have been the one to serve Paul in his imprisonment (Philem 13). Paul also has a public role, for he claims to be an "ambassador" (*presbytēs* in Philem 9 could also mean "old man"; but cf. 2 Cor 5:20 NIV, "Christ's ambassadors"; Eph 6:20 NIV, "ambassador in chains").

Onesimus, a slave in the Roman social system and subject to its *laws, which might justly be invoked, has a transformed status in the household of Christ. He is to be received by Philemon as "no longer a slave but more than a slave, a beloved brother . . . both in the flesh and in the Lord" (Philem 16 NRSV). Onesimus, whose name means "useful," was formerly "useless" to Philemon, "but now he is indeed useful" both to Philemon and to Paul (Philem 11 NRSV).

Philemon, the master of a sizable household in Colossae (Col 4:9) and ostensibly the patron of the church that meets in his house (Philem 2), bears a quite different role in the household of Christ. He is a dear friend, a coworker and a *brother of Paul (Philem 20) and of Onesimus, who is no longer his slave (Philem 16). Philemon has his duties and obligations within this household (Philem 8, 14, 21-22). Paul is confident that Philemon will act voluntarily in love (Philem 8), without coercion (Philem 14), because of his allegiance to the Master of the house (Philem 8) and his proven character (Philem 5-7).

In the eyes of the Roman world, Onesimus is the debtor and Philemon is due his recompense. Thus on Onesimus's behalf Paul writes an imaginary blank voucher, payable in the currency of Rome: "If he has wronged you in any way, or owes you anything, charge that to my account. I, Paul, am writing this with my own hand: I will repay it" (Philem 18-19 NRSV). But then Paul deftly recalls the ledger of accounts kept in the household of Christ. Philemon owes Paul his "own self" (Philem 19), his entrance into the household of Christ. Philemon surely can be counted on to do the right thing in repaying his indebtedness to Paul (Philem 20-21) or, more important, "refresh my heart in Christ" (Philem 20 NRSV). Hopeful of *reconciliation, Paul banks on Philemon's indebtedness and *hospitality: "welcome him as you would welcome me . . . prepare a guest room for me" (Philem 17, 22 NRSV).

See also SLAVE, SLAVERY.

BIBLIOGRAPHY. N. R. Petersen, *Rediscovering Paul: Philemon and the Sociology of Paul's Narrative World* (Philadelphia: Fortress, 1985).

PHILIPPIANS, LETTER TO THE

Paul's letter to the Christians in Philippi belongs to the genre of the thank-you note. More specifically, it is a letter from a missionary to thank his supporters for their spiritual and financial partnership in the gospel (Phil 1:5). The features of this genre include a return address and address (Phil 1:1), a greeting (Phil 1:2), a report on the progress of the mission

(Phil 1:12-26), an acknowledgment of support received (Phil 4:10-19), and final greetings (Phil 4:21-23). These standard elements are interspersed with doctrinal teaching, personal business (Phil 2:19-30) and practical advice for the church in Philippi.

The main theme of Philippians is *suffering. Paul and the Philippians have entered into "the fellowship of sharing in [Christ's] sufferings, becoming like him in his death" (Phil 3:10 NIV). Nevertheless, the dominant mood of Philippians is *joy. Paul finds it difficult to mention anything—even his own incarceration—without rejoicing over it. He rejoices about the Philippians (Phil 1:5, 25), the preaching of Christ (Phil 1:18), the help of the Holy Spirit (Phil 1:19), the fellowship of like-minded believers (Phil 2:2) and the prospect of his own death (Phil 2:17). Paul invites the Philippians to share in all his joy (Phil 1:26; 2:18). "Rejoice in the Lord always," he says. Then he says it again: "Rejoice!" (Phil 4:4 NIV).

A literary treatment of Philippians properly begins with what the letter says *about* literature. Paul closes the hortatory portion of his correspondence by providing the theological basis for a Christian aesthetic: "Finally, brothers, whatever is true, whatever is noble, whatever is right, whatever is pure, whatever is lovely, whatever is admirable—if anything is excellent or praiseworthy—think about such things" (Phil 4:8 NIV). What literary features in Paul's letter to the Philippians are lovely or praiseworthy?

To begin with, Philippians contains a number of memorable images. The setting for the epistle is a *prison (in Ephesus, perhaps, or Rome, or even Caesarea). Since Paul is "in chains for Christ" (Phil 1:13 NIV), it makes sense for him to say that his enemies are adding pressure to his chains (not "stirring up trouble," as the NIV has it) by their envious preaching (Phil 1:15-17).

A recurring motif in Paul's thank-you note is citizenship. The concept of citizenship would have been familiar to the Philippians because their city possessed a Roman charter. In fact, as many parishioners would have remembered, the apostle had taken advantage of his own citizenship on his first visit to Philippi (Acts 16:37-38). Thus when Paul urges them to "conduct [them]selves in a manner worthy of the gospel" (Phil 1:27 NIV), he uses the common civic term *politeuesthe*. He is actually commanding the Philippians to "carry themselves like gospel-worthy citizens." Their primary citizenship *(politeuma)* is not earthly but heavenly (Phil 3:20). Rather than looking to Rome for their salvation, they are to "eagerly await a Savior from [heaven], the Lord Jesus Christ" (Phil 3:20 NIV).

The theme of citizenship is fortified by a cluster of military images that arise from Philippi's military heritage. Epaphroditus is called a "fellow soldier" (Phil 2:25). Euodia and Syntyche "contended at [Paul's] side in the cause of the gospel" (Phil 4:3 NIV). Paul exhorts all the Philippians to "stand firm in one spirit" and contend "as one man for the faith

of the gospel" (Phil 1:27 NIV). The image is of a phalanx of soldiers fighting as a unit.

It is not surprising for a letter from a missionary to his supporters to include imagery from the world of finance. Becoming a Christian involves rebalancing one's spiritual books. All the things Paul used to calculate as credits—family background, educational pedigree, denominational affiliation, personal reputation—he now puts in the debit column for the sake of Christ (Phil 3:7). Apparent spiritual advantages that usurp faith in Christ are not assets but liabilities. Similarly, the letter closes with talk of gifts, financial aid, credits, accounts and payments (Phil 4:17-18). Even the phrase "giving and receiving" (Phil 4:15) is a technical term for a fiscal partnership.

Another notable metaphor in Philippians is an *athletic one: "Forgetting what is behind and straining toward what is ahead, I press on toward the goal to win the prize for which God has called me heavenward in Christ Jesus" (Phil 3:13-14 NIV).

A number of other features of Philippians deserve comment. One is the rhetorical use of the dilemma. Will Paul choose to live for Christ or "to depart and be with Christ, which is better by far" (Phil 1:23 NIV)? He is not so much "torn in two" (NIV) as he is hard pressed from both directions. The Pauline knot is cut by the affirmation that "to me, to live is Christ and to die is gain" (Phil 1:21 NIV).

Later in the epistle Paul lapses into vocabulary that is earthy, not to say vulgar: "Watch out for those dogs, those men who do evil, those mutilators of the flesh" (Phil 3:2 NIV). Although this attack is virulent, it is not personal. The point of comparing the false teachers to *dogs is that they are unclean, like Gentile outcasts in Israel (cf. Mt 15:24-27). Paul sees that those who add human works (especially *circumcision) to the finished work of Christ are outside the orthodox camp. Still worse, they "live as enemies of the cross of Christ" (Phil 3:18 NIV). This is because everything a person might contribute to his or her salvation amounts to a pile of excrement *(skybala)* compared with the pristine "righteousness that comes from God and is by faith" (Phil 3:9 NIV).

Allusions to OT literature in Philippians are sometimes overlooked, perhaps because of their subtlety. For example, Paul bases his expectation of deliverance in Philippians 1:19 on the appearance of Job before the divine court (Job 13:16). Similarly, his warnings about "complaining or arguing" and living "without fault in a *crooked and depraved generation" echo the wanderings of the children of Israel under Moses (Phil 2:14-15 NIV; cf. Num 14:27; Deut 32:5). The claim that Christ Jesus did not grasp after equality with God (Phil 2:6) may even be an allusion to the sin of *Adam, who did make a grab for deity (Gen 3:4-6).

The most important allusion of all comes in Philippians 2:9-11. Here Paul writes against the background of Isaiah's defense of monotheism. There is only one Lord, before whom every knee will bow and by whom every tongue will swear (Is 45:21-23). The effect of Paul's allusion to Isaiah is to prove that Jesus of Nazareth must be worshiped as the Lord God of Israel. Jesus has earned the "name that is above every name": Lord.

The most beautiful and familiar passage in Philippians is Paul's paean of praise for the incarnate Christ (*see* Christ Hymn):

> Who, being in very nature God,
>   did not consider equality with God something
>   to be grasped,
> but made himself nothing,
>   taking the very nature of a servant,
>   being made in human likeness.
> And being found in appearance as a man,
>   he humbled himself
>   and became obedient to death—
>   even death on a cross!
> Therefore God exalted him to the highest place
>   and gave him the name that is above every
>   name,
> that at the name of Jesus every knee should bow,
>   in heaven and on earth and under the earth,
> and every tongue confess that Jesus Christ is
>   Lord,
>   to the glory of God the Father.
>   (Phil 2:6-11 NIV)

Readers have often wondered if these highly structured verses formed one of the first hymns of the early church. On one reading, the two stanzas of the poem (one for Christ's humiliation, one for his exaltation) neatly pivot on the astonished phrase "even death on a cross!" On another reading, the hymn is organized around three nouns (*theos, doulos* and *kyrios*) which indicate three stages of the work of Christ (God, servant and Lord). Whether this is hymnody or mere poetry cannot be determined on linguistic grounds. But it hardly matters. The real beauty of the passage does not come from its lyrics but from its living, dying, living-again Lord.

See also CHRIST HYMN; JOY; SUFFERING.

PHILISTINE

In modern-day usage *Philistine* is a term of insult that suggests an uncultured, common or ignorant person. But in OT times the label referred to a people, occupying the coastal region of southern Palestine, who were anything but uncultured and ignorant (as evidenced by archaeological discoveries and biblical texts). The Philistines figure in the patriarchal narratives, the stories concerning the occupation of Canaan and the accounts of the forming and then division of the monarchy.

In the pre-Davidic narratives the Philistines are a parade example of *Israel's *enemies. By contrast, in the few prophetic passages where they are mentioned they are simply one nation among the many who will experience God's *judgment on the grounds of their hostility toward God's people and God's ways, whether manifested by *pride (Zech 9:6), greed (Ezek 16:27), malicious hostility (Ezek 25:15) or

paganism (Is 2:6). In the premonarchic period the Philistines become especially significant as the one enemy Israel was unable to conquer, despite the successive attempts of Samson, Samuel and Saul. Saul was even defeated by the Philistines in a series of battles (1 Sam 13—14; 17; 23; 31), whereas David in being able to subdue them (2 Sam 5) fully justified his claim to be God's chosen *king. In these historical encounters with Israel, the Philistines symbolize a people group with foreign, independent identity (in fact in the majority of instances the Septuagint translation of the Hebrew term uses a word that means "foreigners" or *"Gentiles").

In the historical books the Philistines are often described as "uncircumcised" (e.g., Judg 14:2). The term can be used in a derogatory fashion (as in 1 Sam 14:16) as a way of indicating the Philistine presumption in deriding Israel and Israel's God. Furthermore in 1 Samuel 17:8-54 Goliath serves as an archetype of the Philistine people and as such is a symbol of foreign enmity toward God's people and their representative David (just as David acts as an archetype of Israel). However, the Philistines are seen in a more positive light in the account of the capturing of the *ark in 1 Samuel 4. In this instance the Philistines are representative of foreign people who understand better than Israel that God's presence is associated with the ark, even though their understanding is limited and incomplete.

Despite Philistine military *strength, their gods are shown to be impotent when confronted by Yahweh (1 Sam 5:1-5). The Philistines regard their deities as uninformed. This view is unconsciously confirmed by the Philistines themselves, who need to inform their deities about the victory of their own *army (1 Sam 31:9; 1 Chron 10:9).

The Philistines are an evocative OT image. Until David conquered them, they were a persistent military threat to Israel and a lure to pagan *worship, as epitomized in the story of Samson (Judg 13—16).

See also BATTLE STORIES; ENEMY; GENTILE; SAMSON.

PIG. *See* ANIMALS; SWINE.

PIGEON. *See* DOVE.

PILGRIM, PILGRIMAGE

Although the words *pilgrim* and *pilgrimage* are absent from most English translations of the Bible, the image is a major one, encompassing some of the deepest meanings of what it means to be a follower and worshiper of God. In the OT, images of pilgrimage center around the annual pilgrimages that individuals and families made to *festivals held the *temple in Jerusalem. In both Testaments pilgrimage becomes a metaphor for the shape of the earthly life of anyone who is headed toward a heaven beyond this world. In all instances the image implies a *journey to a sacred place, and both facets are important—

the pilgrim is always a traveler, but a fixed and glorious goal is always the final destination that motivates the journey.

Literal Pilgrimages. OT pilgrimages are rooted in the worship practices that prevailed after settlement in the Promised Land. The essential corporate worship occurred at the temple in Jerusalem. Jewish males were required to worship in Jerusalem a minimum of three times a year (Ex 23:17; Deut 16:16), and it is safe to assume that other family members did so when they could. The place to which the pilgrims went was not only the center of worship but also the political center of the nation, which explains the patriotic associations evident in some of the worship psalms. Another factor that helps to explain the nature of pilgrimages is that in OT times the *shekinah* *glory of God resided in visible form over the ark of the covenant in the holy of holies. This explains the references to God's presence in the temple (Ps 11:4; 26:8; 63:2; 132:13-14) and helps to fill out the splendor that OT pilgrims associated with the place to which they were headed.

The fullest available picture of OT pilgrimages can be gleaned from the psalms of ascent (Ps 120—134), a collection of fifteen psalms that were sung on pilgrim processions to Jerusalem and at the festivals that occurred there. These psalms are an excellent index to the values and preoccupations of godly pilgrims on religious excursions. When the psalms of ascent are read in sequence, they suggest the experience of pilgrims traveling from a distant land. The cycle begins with a yearning lament: "Woe is me, that I am an alien in Meshech, that I must live among the tents of Kedar" (Ps 120:5 NRSV). This is followed by an acknowledgment of the Lord's protection of those on pilgrimage: "He will not let your foot be moved; he who keeps you will not slumber" (Ps 121:3 NRSV). Then we have the joyful arrival at Jerusalem: "I was glad when they said to me, 'Let us go to the house of the LORD!' Our feet are standing within your gates, O Jerusalem" (Ps 122:1-2 NRSV). Psalms 123—133 include various prayers, oaths and invocations uttered by pilgrims at the festival, followed by a farewell blessing of the temple servants by the departing pilgrims to complete the cycle: "May the LORD, maker of heaven and earth, bless you from Zion" (Ps 134:3 NRSV).

Psalm 84 also captures something of the flavor of the pilgrim's experience. It begins with the pilgrim's longing to arrive at the temple, perhaps accompanied by a first glimpse of the building (Ps 84:1-2). This is followed by pictures of the physical details of the temple (Ps 84:3); an exclamation regarding the blessing that attends those who metaphorically "live" in the temple (that is, worship God in his house; Ps 84:4); recollections of the excitement and blessing of the journey, including the evocative heart cry of the pilgrim, "Happy are those . . . in whose heart are the highways to Zion" (Ps 84:5-7 NRSV); a prayer for the king (Ps 84:8-9); and concluding affirmations of the high value the pilgrim places on worshiping God

at the temple (Ps 84:10-12). One reason for the strong sense of place that pervades OT worship psalms is the institution of the pilgrimage, which always orients the traveler toward an anticipated goal, a sacred place.

Though the image of pilgrimage emerged from the historical experience of Israel's thrice-yearly pilgrimages, one senses that it also encompasses broader implications for the pilgrimage of faith and trust that characterizes God's people in all times. The biblical archetype for the pilgrim of faith is *Abraham, whose account commences with the command to depart from his country and kindred on the basis of God's promise (Gen 12:1-3). Such sojourning is also a feature of Abraham's offspring, who are "aliens in a land that is not theirs" (Gen 15:13 NRSV; cf. Gen 35:27; 47:4; Ex 6:4; Ps 105:12). Jacob describes both his own life and that of his ancestors as a "pilgrimage" (Gen 47:9 NIV).

From the beginning, then, the life of faith is viewed as a metaphoric pilgrimage—a life of traveling in quest for an eventual place of rest. Because of this feature of Israel's formative past, even after the people came into the land there was always provision in the law for the *foreigners among them: "You shall not wrong or oppress a resident alien, for you were aliens in the land of Egypt" (Ex 22:21 NRSV; cf. Ex 23:9; Lev 19:34; Deut 10:18-19).

Metaphoric Pilgrimages. Pilgrimage imagery is used in a variety of ways by the prophets, particularly Isaiah. Though often entwined with images of the *exodus, Isaiah's pilgrimage motif is unmistakable in its depiction of future salvation. Just as in the temple pilgrimage, many peoples shall say, "Come, let us go up to the mountain of the LORD" (Is 2:3; cf. Is 2:1-4; Mic 4:1-8). God will bring forth water in the desert for thirsty pilgrims (Is 41:17-20; cf. Ps 84:6), and their processions will be filled with songs of rejoicing (Is 30:29; 35:10; 51:11; Jer 31:10-14). God will make for the people a highway in the wilderness (Is 35:8; 40:3; cf. Ps 84:5) and will provide divine protection along the way (Is 52:7-12; cf. Ps 121) as he draws his people from the four corners of the earth in the final, universal pilgrimage (Is 11:11-12; 19:23-25; 43:5-6; cf. Hos 11:11; Mic 7:12-13; Zech 8:7-8). While these texts do not explicitly evoke the image of pilgrimage, the image functions as a subtext for the pattern of salvation they describe.

The image of pilgrimage is also latent in the Gospels, especially the Synoptics, all of which underscore Jesus' final pilgrimage to Jerusalem. In Mark this pilgrimage is repeatedly emphasized by reminders of Jesus' final journey (Mk 8:27; 9:33-34; 10:1, 17, 32, 46, 52), which becomes the dominant image of discipleship. This motif is elaborated in Luke (Lk 9:51-19:28) and continues in Acts, where the Christian movement is referred to as "the Way" (Acts 9:2; 19:9, 23; 22:4; 24:14, 22). In John's Gospel Jesus himself is declared to be the pilgrim's *path to the Father (Jn 14:6).

The book of *Hebrews repeatedly explores the

Christian life through images of pilgrimage, often returning to biblical heroes who also undertook a faith pilgrimage. Abraham obeyed God and "set out for a place that he was to receive as an inheritance," looking for "the city that has foundations, whose architect and builder is God" (Heb 11:8-10 NRSV). His offspring all died in faith as "strangers and foreigners on the earth" because they were "seeking a homeland," looking for a "better country, that is, a heavenly one" (Heb 11:13-16 NRSV). Many other heroes of the faith are pictured as wandering in deserts and mountains and caves, yet never receiving the promise because "God had provided something better" (Heb 11:38-40 NRSV).

In light of this heritage and pattern, Christians are exhorted to "lay aside every weight" as they journey toward their goal, which is not the earthly Zion but "the city of the living God, the heavenly Jerusalem" (Heb 12:1, 22 NRSV). In similar fashion Christ is portrayed as a forerunner; he is the "pioneer of their salvation" (Heb 2:10 NRSV), as well as the "pioneer and perfecter of our faith" (Heb 12:2 NRSV).

Peter's first epistle also takes its place in the pilgrimage literature of the Bible. The Christian communities addressed are pictured as pilgrims and aliens, sojourning in exile (1 Pet 1:17; 2:11) because of social alienation and general persecution by society. The author himself reflects this stance toward the world when he says that he writes from "Babylon" (1 Pet 5:13), again alluding to the previous history and pattern of God's pilgrim people.

Summary. Throughout the Bible the faithful who follow God are pictured as either literal or figurative pilgrims. They are people of the way, people journeying rather than settled, still looking for the spiritual place that will satisfy them.

See also ABRAHAM; ASCENT; EXODUS, SECOND EXODUS; HEAVEN; JERUSALEM; PATH; TRAVEL STORIES; ZION.

PILLAR

With over a hundred biblical references (NRSV 120), pillars were obviously a conspicuous feature in the biblical world. The overwhelming number of references are to pillars in extraordinary rather than routine settings, and their main importance in the Bible is more symbolic than architectural. Most references are to pillars at sacred sites (descriptions of the *tabernacle and *temple are replete with references to pillars) and secondarily to pillars as memorials.

Pillars in the Bible are of two kinds—those that support a building and those that are freestanding. Often the latter are large *stones set up to mark a spot. They may serve as monuments to draw the attention of passersby to a significant spot, like the pillar Jacob placed on Rachel's grave (Gen 35:20). Jacob erected the stone on which he lay at Bethel as a pillar, anointed for the sacred purpose of bearing witness to his encounter with God (Gen 28:18; cf. Gen 31:13; 35:14). This role of a standing stone in bearing witness is more explicit in other passages,

where pillars are erected as witnesses to a covenant (Gen 31:44-48; Ex 24:4; Josh 24:26-27). The pillar of salt into which Lot's wife was transformed (Gen 19:26) is a variation on this motif of the pillar as a memorial, as Jesus' famous aphorism hints (Lk 17:32).

Some of the pillars that appear in religious contexts likewise fit the pattern of freestanding, nonweight-bearing pillars. Two bronze pillars, called Jachin and Boaz, stood in front of the sanctuary building in Solomon's temple (1 Kings 7:15-22; Jer 52:21-23). The symbolic function of these huge, magnificent *gateposts was probably to indicate that the Lord had passed through them, entered the temple and dwelt there in the midst of his people.

A fragment of a miniature ivory pillar from northern Syria, perhaps similar to the pillars Jachin and Boaz of Solomon's temple.

Also, these nonweight-bearing monoliths symbolized by their sheer size and mass the grandeur and stability of God, and as worshipers stood beside them they felt small.

The essential structural role of pillars within buildings is well illustrated by the story of Samson's last exploit, in which a pagan temple collapsed when Samson dislodged the two middle pillars (Judg 16:23-30). But even in this story the pillars are more than architectural phenomena, inasmuch as Canaanite shrines typically contained one or more pillars as sacral objects. The architectural function of pillars also entered ancient *cosmological pictures. Just as large buildings required pillars to support them, so the earth and the *heavens were envisaged as supported by pillars (1 Sam 2:8; Job 9:6; 26:11).

Once we grasp the special contexts in which pillars figure in the Bible, the metaphoric uses are even more evocative. In Psalm 144:12 the poet-king prays, "May . . . our daughters [be] like corner pillars, cut for the building of a palace" (NRSV). It is an image of resplendent *beauty, attractiveness and splendor. Similarly evocative is the picture of Wisdom's house as having "seven pillars" (Prov 9:1). Here too the pillars connote beauty as well as solid dependability, with the number *seven adding an aura of perfection and completeness.

645

Two key metaphorical uses of the architectural pillar refer to the pillars that supported the temple. In Galatians 2:9 Paul refers to the three leaders of the Jerusalem church—James the Lord's brother, Peter and John—as those "who were acknowledged pillars" (NRSV). This is not just an instance of the natural use of the metaphor of pillar for someone who supports others or an institution; it is related to the early Christian understanding of the Christian community as the new temple in which God is present. Just as Christians are the stones of which the temple is built (1 Pet 2:5) and the apostles and prophets the *foundation of the building (Eph 2:20), so these three key leaders in the Jerusalem church are pillars of the temple. At a later date the use of the image is broadened and applied to the redeemed community beyond death: in Revelation 3:12 Christ promises to make every Christian who is faithful unto death a pillar in the temple of God. Since the promise continues "You will never go out of it" (NRSV), the principal thought here is of a permanent place in the structure.

In 1 Timothy 3:15 the church is described as "the pillar and bulwark [better translated 'foundation'] of the truth" (NRSV). The meaning is that the church's role is to uphold the truth of the gospel. Since earlier in the verse the church has also been called "the household of God"—the temple in which God dwells—there may also be a connection with the pillars of the temple, though the image is not precise.

The two most famous pillars in the Bible were not rooted in the ground at all. The divine presence with Israel in the wilderness took the visible form of a pillar of *cloud (by day) and of *fire (by night), going ahead of the people to lead and to light the way (Ex 13:21-22; Neh 9:19). While cloud and fire symbolize divine presence, the term *pillar* simply describes the shape of the phenomenon. Again we note the aura of the sacred that frequently surrounds biblical references to pillars.

See also COSMOLOGY; FOUNDATION; TEMPLE.

PILLAR OF CLOUD/FIRE. *See* PILLAR.

PILOT. *See* AUTHORITY, HUMAN.

PIT

Although "pit" could refer simply to a hole in the ground, generally it was a *cistern several meters deep, carved in rock to collect and store precious *water. Building a cistern involved a great deal of work (Deut 6:11). A cistern usually had a small access near the top into which groundwater flowed. Dark, damp, rocky and isolated, the pit provided a near-death experience for anyone hapless enough to fall in and be stranded inside. Despair quickly followed the realization that there was no escape.

Pit as Prison. The metaphor of pit as *prison stems from actual use. A nearly dry cistern could function as a handy prison (Zech 9:11). The Hebrew designated the dungeon as *bēt habbôr,* literally,

"house of the pit" (Ex 12:29). *Joseph (Gen 37:22) and Jeremiah (Jer 38:6) are doubtless only the most famous of many prisoners kept in dark holes (Is 24:22; Ps 107:10). Water in the pit would make the event more frightening (Ps 69:1-2). The psalmist draws a parallel between God's seeming failure to answer and the unheeded cries of one caught in a pit (Ps 28:1; cf. Lam 3:55). To be pulled from a miry pit provides a vivid picture of the salvation of the helpless (Ps 40:2). To be delivered from one's enemies is to be drawn up out of Sheol (like a bucket out of a cistern, Ps 30:1). God alone redeems from the pit (Job 33:22, 28-29; Ps 16:10; 103:4; Jon 2:6). Isaiah assures us that the stooped one will not die in the dungeon ("Pit," Is 51:14).

Pit as Trap. Pits functioned as wild *animal *traps (2 Sam 23:20; Ezek 19:3-4), even as the wicked lay traps for the just (Jer 18:22). Just as an unwary domestic animal might fall into a pit (Ex 21:33; Mt 12:11), so the morally loose (Prov 22:14; 23:27), the wicked (Prov 26:27; 28:10; Eccles 10:8) or the spiritually blind (Mt 15:14; Lk 6:39) cannot avoid a pit they cannot see. The wicked one falls into his own pit (Ps 7:15) or the trap he has laid for the righteous (Ps 35:7-8; Jer 18:20). Israel itself became trapped in a pit dug by the nations (Ezek 19:8), but in the end Israel's enemies will go down into the pit (Ps 9:15; Ezek 32:18).

Pit as Despair. As an inescapable predicament, the pit serves as metaphor for depression and despair. "Going down to the pit" (whether Heb *bôr* as in Ps 28:1; Prov 1:12; Is 38:18; Ezek 26:20; or -*šāḥaṯ,* Ps 30:9), "to Sheol" (Ps 55:15) or "to the dust" (Job 17:16) captures in a phrase the hopelessness of the dying or the abject contrition of the sinful.

Pit as Grave. Although "pit" is a common metaphor for *death, it is often used to mean *"grave." Bodies were sometimes conveniently disposed of in open graves or pits (Gen 37:20; 2 Kings 10:14; Ps 5:9; cf. 2 Kings 13:21). (Note seventy bodies in one cistern: Jer 41:7.) That the slain "go down to the stones of the Pit" reflects the Palestinian practice of burying the dead on a bed of stones (Is 14:19 NRSV). Likewise, "They have silenced my life in the pit, they have cast stones over me" (Lam 3:53) refers to a different practice of covering the corpse with stones (2 Sam 18:17).

Pit as Access to the Underworld. If the grave is the *door to the *afterlife, so is the pit. The pit appears as an entrance to the underworld throughout the oldest literature. The *Epic of Gilgamesh* records that Gilgamesh was ordered by the gods to dig a hole so that the spirit of his departed friend could issue forth from the netherworld (*Tablet* 12.78; ANET, 98). Homer narrates that Odysseus dug a trench to gain access to the spirits and consult a dead seer (*Odyssey* 11.23). (Virgil allows Aeneas to use a cave to meet underworld spirits: *Aeneid* 6.237). The belief that the spirits of the dead held wisdom and insight into the future which could be tapped by necromancy was a cultural universal around the Mediterranean. The nighttime necromantic ritual seems to have involved a pit that permitted infernal deities to ascend briefly to the upper world and offer revelations. The woman of Endor, seeking an *oracle for Saul from the departed seer Samuel, witnesses "spirits" (*'ĕlōhîm*) and "an old man coming up from the earth" (1 Sam 28:13-14; cf. Is 14:9). Saul speaks with the spirit. Apparently the sound heard on such occasions was faint, "like that of a spirit from the dust" (Is 29:4).

Although the practice of consulting the dead was viewed as an imitation of the nations and a detestable thing (Deut 18:11), it was a fact of Israelite life from before the monarchy until after the prophets. Manasseh is condemned for his sanction of it (2 Kings 21:6). Isaiah mentions the idolatrous practice of sitting inside tombs and passing the night in secret places (Is 65:4) and asks, "Should they consult the dead on behalf of the living?" (Is 8:19). To the ancient mind "breathing" caves, bubbling springs and hissing vents all bore eloquent testimony to elemental spirits living under the earth, not to mention those that escaped from graves. In spite of their apparent rule now, these abyssal, chthonic forces (*katachthonioi*, "subterranean powers") will ultimately kneel and confess the name of Jesus (Phil 2:10).

Pit as Hell. Consider the short steps required to move from the pit as grave to the pit as gateway to the underworld and then to the pit as *hell itself. Amos makes the hyperbolic suggestion that by digging deep enough one might reach Sheol (Amos 9:2). The afterlife, like the pit that represents it, is pictured as dark and deep (Ps 88:6), mucky (Ps 40:2) and disgusting (Job 9:31). Those in the pit can no longer praise God's faithfulness (Ps 30:9). The righteous will not find relief from adversity until the Lord digs a pit for the wicked (Ps 94:13).

In the literature of Qumran the phrase "sons of the Pit" identifies the devil's human accomplices (1QS 5.10; 8.12; 9.20). Eschatologically, the Pit is the source of the beast (Rev 11:7). Hell with its pits of darkness will become the final prison for Apollyon, the angel of the abyss (Rev 9:11), and the fallen angels (Lk 8:31; 2 Pet 2:4). The idea that the afterlife is reached by crossing waters (cf. River Styx) appears in Paul's rendering of Deuteronomy 30:13, "Who will cross the sea?" with "Who will descend into the abyss?" (Rom 10:7 NRSV).

The Pit. Some of the references to "the Pit" (which the NRSV capitalizes in more than two dozen verses) create an evocative image that combines several of the categories named above. While these references begin as literal references to Sheol or the grave, they gather overtones of a literal and metaphoric hell also. To "go down to the Pit" is to descend to moral and psychological depths as well as physical death. In Psalm 103:4, for example, the poet celebrates the fact that God "redeems your life from the Pit." While this may refer first of all to the preservation of physical life, the redeemed soul can testify to a range of spiritual and moral "pits" from which the Christian faith has spared him or her.

See also CISTERN; DEEP; GRAVE; HELL; LOW; PRISON.

BIBLIOGRAPHY. H. A. Hoffner Jr., "Second Millennium Antecedents to the Hebrew *'ôb,*" *JBL* 86 (1967) 385-401; A. Jeffers, *Magic and Divination in Ancient Palestine and Syria* (Leiden: E. J. Brill, 1996) 167-81; N. J. Tromp, *Primitive Conceptions of Death and the Nether World in the Old Testament* (Rome: Pontifical Biblical Institute, 1969) 66-71.

PLACE, NO ABIDING

Although a main motif in the OT is movement toward a *promised land that is to be settled, another motif to be held in tension with this deals with loss of homeland, *exile and the nomadic life. *Abraham, nomadic journeying, the Israelites' forty years in the *wilderness and the Babylonian exile are examples. The most extreme case is *Cain's punishment, to be "a fugitive and a wanderer on the earth" (Gen 4:12 NRSV; cf. Ex 18:3; Ps 69:8; Lam 4:15). One resolution of this tension comes in the concept of *pilgrimage, ritualized in the OT, particularly in the three pilgrim festivals of Deuteronomy 16:16 (Unleavened Bread, Weeks and Booths). These are celebrated in the psalms of ascent (Ps 120—134), which in turn were linked to the return from exile (Ezra 7:7-10). Another resolution involves exile as temporary punishment (e.g., Jer 32; Ezek 16:53-63; cf. Ps 137).

As we move from the OT to the NT, motifs of pilgrimage and exile become images of sojourning. The pilgrim center of a literal *Jerusalem is redefined as a heavenly *city, with this earthly life taken to be the pilgrimage. Other OT images are used to reinforce this. For example, in an early Christian formulation Stephen takes the Genesis 15:1-16 account of God's promise to Abraham and subtly shifts the emphasis away from the promise of a settled land (Acts 7:3-5, paraphrasing Gen 15:1-11) to Abraham's being an alien (Acts 7:6, quoting Gen 15:13). The Greek word Stephen uses is *paroikos* (behind which lies the Heb *gēr*), variously translated as "alien," "stranger" or "sojourner" (i.e., someone living temporarily in a land with no legal rights of citizenship). The tension between permanence and temporariness is strong. Stephen uses the same term in connection with *Moses (Acts 7:29), where he plays down the idea of a settled promised land, emphasizing that even the attempt to build a dwelling place for God was doomed to frustration (Acts 7:49-50, quoting Is 66:1-2). The *tabernacle in the wilderness becomes just as much a type of true worship (Acts 7:44-45), however temporary its abiding places.

Paul takes this image up only to deny it: "You are no longer strangers and aliens, but you are citizens with the saints" (Eph 2:19 NRSV). The *church is our abiding place. But Peter uses the image twice (1 Pet 1:17; 2:11) to speak of our being *paroikia* as *paredidē moi* (strangers, sojourners) here on earth. Perhaps he is subtly echoing Christ's words about the Son of Man having "nowhere to lay his head" (Mt 8:20; Lk 9:58 NRSV). In this context Christ's example is also referred to in Hebrews 13:12-13.

It is in the letter to the Hebrews that the image is most strongly worked out. Significantly, in comparison to the other epistles, here the sense of community is quite weak. *Dispersion, exile* and *suffering* are key words. The walk of faith is basically an individual one, a faith movement, like Abraham's, which interprets movement as pilgrimage and a concomitant suffering as growth toward perfection (Heb 2:10). The object of the pilgrimage is variously defined. In Hebrews 4 it is "rest," which is placed in the creation pattern of the sabbath (Heb 4:4). It is linked to the exodus (Heb 3), with "rest" being seen as antitype of entry into the Promised Land. Disobedience and faithlessness mean that the destination remains unreached, as does reliance on one's own works. The literal historical fact that the Israelites did reach Canaan is dissolved symbolically (Heb 3:7-11, quoting Ps 95:7-11).

The OT narrative of journey is picked up in Hebrews 11. Here it is Abraham's journey rather than the failure of the exodus (Heb 11:8-10). As in Stephen's interpretation, the land Abraham settles in is and yet is not the Promised Land (Heb 11:9). It has no city and therefore is no country (Heb 11:14-16; cf. Heb 13:14). So Abraham has to live in *tents, nomadically.

How are we to keep moving and yet enter rest? The resolution seems to lie in the affirmation of the worth of this life to be lived by faith, with privileges given as if we had already arrived at the heavenly Jerusalem (Heb 12:22-24; 13:14), yet we have more to enter into (Heb 11:40; 12:27-28).

See also FAITH; FOREIGNER; LAND; PILGRIM, PILGRIMAGE; PROMISED LAND; WANDERER, WANDERING.

BIBLIOGRAPHY. D. Lawton, *Faith, Text and History: The Bible in English* (Hemel Hempstead, UK: Harvester/Wheatsheaf, 1990) 103-4.

PLAGUE

The word *plague* is borrowed from the Greek *plēgē*, meaning "blow." Like *plague*, many of the words for disease and suffering in both Hebrew and Greek, as well as in the surrounding cultures of Mesopotamia and *Egypt, derive from the vocabulary of attack and weaponry (*see* Weapons). Hebrew has *maggē pâ* ("blow," "pestilence"), *makkâ* ("blow," "disease" [especially as punishment]) and *nega'* (stroke/ plague) while Greek uses *plēgē* ("blow," "plague"), *mastix* ("whip," "illness") and *patassō* ("to smite with disease"). Consider the similar English terminology, especially the word roots behind plague (flog), affliction, scourge (whip), blight (blow), blast, stroke (strike) and more.

Plagues as Divine Weapons and Agents. Such consistency of meaning points to an almost universal human outlook on suffering that personifies the agency of *disease and views the ultimate causes as unseen and spiritual. For all ancient Mediterranean cultures, plagues were the visible manifestations of unseen weapons wielded by the country's deity (or deities) to enforce the moral and social code. The deity, using plague as a weapon (or sometimes personified as an agent), had humanity in its sights. People served as "targets" (Job 16:12). These weapons run the gamut of the arsenal then current, including *sword (1 Chron 21:16,30), mace, net (Job 19:6), bow (Gen 9:13) and arrow (Deut 32:23-24; Job 6:4; 16:13; Ps 64:7; Hab 3:9; Zech 9:14; *see* Arrow of God). Even if the weapon went unnamed, ancient assessments often identified the responsible deity. Egyptian and Akkadian texts commonly diagnose a disease as "the hand of [the god so-and-so]," usually naming a lesser, underworld deity as minister of the plague. Not unexpectedly, in such situations the Bible employs a similar phrase, "the hand of God" (Ex 9:3, 15; 1 Sam 5:11; Job 19:21).

Plagues as Divine Punishment. The image of plague as a corrective blow from on high is common both for *Israel's *enemies (Ex 9:14; Lev 26:21; Num 11:33; Deut 28:59; 29:21; 1 Sam 4:8; 6:4) and against Israel (Num 14:37; 17:13-15; 25:8-9, 18-19; 31:16; 2 Sam 24:21, 25; 1 Chron 21:22; 2 Chron 21:14; Ps 106:29-30; Jer 21:6). Job's debaters cannot bring themselves to question their assumptions of Job's guilt as the cause of his plagues (cf. Jn 9:1). Pragmatic concerns about contagion, linked to the notion of *disease as divinely ordained ostracism, made a plague a lonely ordeal (Ps 38:11). The existence of righteous people in the population could sometimes mitigate or delay the punishment, but not always (Gen 18:23-32; Ezek 14:12). Because national leaders served both as the embodiment of the deity before the people and as the embodiment of the people before the god, the people could be plagued for the failings of the ruler (1 Chron 21:8-22; 2 Chron 21:13-14, *see* King, Kingship). The logic of a single individual as moral embodiment for the whole population appears again in "as in Adam all die" (1 Cor 15:22 KJV).

The plagues of Egypt are probably natural calamities, familiar to the Egyptians and even presented in their typical seasonal order, but on a grand scale. The ancients recognized the hand of their gods in all natural events, but cataclysms were theologically significant. The disasters served as visible attacks in a cosmic contest, "judgment on all the gods of Egypt" (Ex 12:12 NIV; Num 3:4). The escalating duel between *Moses, empowered by his recent encounter with the God of the patriarchs, and the inferior gods of the Egyptian magicians also indicted the ability of *Pharaoh, as earthly representative of his god, to maintain the cosmic order in his appointed realm. His failure to uphold the spiritual health of his country, by his own admission (Ex 9:27), inevitably resulted in plagues. Witnesses to these events concluded that "the LORD is greater than all other gods" (Ex 18:11 NIV). Not only were the Lord's plagues more potent, but they could not be countered or counterfeited by *magic (Ex 7:11, 22; 8:7; but see Ex 8:18-19; 9:11).

Plague as Personified Spiritual Evil (Pagan God or Demon). Hebrew poets, like their contemporaries, occasionally described plague as a divine attendant. In the prophet's description of the Lord's stormy approach, he personifies the agents of punishment: "Before him went pestilence and plague followed close behind" (Hab 3:5 NRSV). The triad of demonic evils (*see* Demons) that in other literature accompanies Resheph, the West Semitic plague god, appears in Scripture as *hunger, heat and pestilence (Deut 23:24) or as the pair *death and destruction (Hos 13:14). Job labels his disease or its cause the "firstborn of Death" (Job 18:13 NRSV), as if his sickness were the offspring of an underworld figure called Death, analogous to "the king of terrors" who meets the wicked in the afterlife (Job 8:14 NRSV). The psalmist personifies as enemies a long litany of feared evils but reassures the one who trusts in God that the "pestilence . . . shall not draw nigh thee" (Ps 91:6-7 KJV). The pair death and plague follow the "company of destroying angels" whose members are named "anger, wrath, indignation, and distress" (Ps 78:49-50 NRSV and Job 40:11, where the LXX renders the word *wraths* [Heb *'brwt*] as "angels").

The ambiguous "destroyer" of the firstborn (Ex 12:23) is subject to comparable personification in the NT (Heb 11:28; cf. 1 Cor 10:10). While an *angel of God "smites" Herod with *worms (Acts 12:23), an angel of *Satan plagues Paul (2 Cor 12:7).

See also ARROW, ARROW OF GOD; CRIME AND PUNISHMENT; DEATH; MAGIC; WEAPONS.

BIBLIOGRAPHY. J. K. Hoffmeier, "Egypt, Plagues in," *ABD* 2:374-78.

PLAIN

There are some remarkable images involving plains in Scripture, but most of the references are quite straightforward and refer to broad expanses of land. A few refer to smaller flat areas in or near Jerusalem (Neh 3:22; Jer 21:13).

Plains are places where people settle: "As men moved eastward, they found a plain in Shinar and settled there" (Gen 11:2 NIV). But most often they are places where people gather, travel and fight battles. The flat places on both sides of the Jordan that are designated plains were the site of many important biblical events. The plain on the east side was known as the "Plains of Moab" (Num 22:1; 26:3); and the plains on the west side, as the "Plains of Jericho" (Josh 4:13).

It is hard to imagine a more evocative image than Lot choosing the "well-watered plain" (Gen 13). Because the herdsmen of Lot and his uncle *Abraham are competing for water and grazing space (*see* Pasture), Abraham suggests that they separate. Abraham, the elder, defers to his nephew, who looks and sees the "whole plain of Jordan." As Lot saw it, the plain was supremely attractive from every material

viewpoint (Gen 13:10), but it was to become a desolate symbol of judgment. The cause of this destruction was probably an *earthquake with an accompanying release and explosion of gaseous deposits. From the biblical perspective it was God's *judgment, an event that echoes throughout the Bible (Deut 29:23; Is 1:9; Jer 49:18; Lam 4:6; Amos 4:11; Lk 17:29; 2 Pet 2:6).

In 1 Kings 20 the limited territory of pagan gods is contrasted with Yahweh's rule of all creation. After being defeated by the Israelites, Ben-Hadad's advisors tell him, "[The Israelites'] gods are gods of the hills. That is why they were too strong for us. But if we fight them on the plains, surely we will be stronger than they" (1 Kings 20:23 NIV). So to show his true territory Yahweh brings the second attack, this time staged by Ben-Hadad on the plains, to the same end.

In the writings of two prophets, Isaiah and Zechariah, the image of topographical change symbolizes the intervention of God in human affairs. In Isaiah 40:4 (cf. Luke 3:4) the prophet announces that in preparation for the Lord's coming "every valley shall be raised up, every mountain and hill made low; the rough ground shall become level, the rugged places a plain" (NIV). And in Zechariah, God's angel announces that the *"mountain" of opposition against Zerubbabel's rebuilding of the temple will be leveled: "What are you, O mighty mountain? Before Zerubbabel you will become level ground" (Zech 4:7 NIV).

See also MOUNTAIN; PASTURE; SODOM AND GOMORRAH; VALLEY; WIDE, WIDENESS.

PLANTING. *See* FARMING; SOW, SOWER.

PLANTS

Plants form a major motif throughout the Bible, where they function in both literal and metaphoric ways. In a book that always keeps us close to nature and the external world, it would be surprising if plants did not function prominently. Some of the major plants of the Bible receive their own articles in this dictionary; the discussion that follows provides a general framework for how plants in general appear in the Bible.

Images of Life. Plants are organic and alive. Thus in the Bible they often serve as images of the life force. In Psalm 1, for example, in painting a heightened contrast between life and *death, the poet chooses plant imagery for the quality of being alive: the godly person "is like a tree planted by streams of water, that yields its fruit in its season, and its leaf does not wither" (Ps 1:3 RSV). When plants are used to picture life in the Bible, they are often pictured next to a supply of *water, precious in the arid landscape of the biblical writers. "The man who trusts in the LORD" is "like a tree planted by water, that sends out its roots by the stream, and does not fear when heat comes, for its leaves remain green" (Jer 17:7-8 RSV).

Plants are associated not only with life as opposed

to death but also with *growth as opposed to stagnation. Isaiah 61:11, for example, compares the Lord's *sowing of "righteousness and praise" to the way "the earth brings forth its shoots, and . . . a garden causes what is sown in it to spring up" (RSV). The Song of Songs, the biblical paean to springtime, paints a picture of how "the flowers appear on the earth. . . . The fig tree puts forth its figs, and the vines are in blossom" (Song 2:12-13 RSV). When Hosea wants an image for growth, he speaks of plants that blossom, spread out and flourish (Hos 14:5-7).

As images of life and growth, plants also embody the quality of fruitfulness and therefore abundance. Ezekiel's picture of the productive *tree epitomizes the motif: "on both sides of the river, there will grow all kinds of trees for food. Their *leaves will not wither nor their fruit fail, but they will bear fresh *fruit every month" (Ezek 47:12 RSV). To an agrarian imagination abundance is strongly linked to plants. When Moses paints a picture of the abundance of the *Promised Land that the nation of Israel will enter, plant imagery looms large: "the LORD your God is bringing you into . . . a land of wheat and barley, of *vines and *fig trees and pomegranates, a land of olive trees" (Deut 8:7-8 RSV).

The literal properties of plants as being alive, growing and fruitful make them a chief source of metaphors and similes for human life. When the poet wishes to picture the flourishing of people, they are said to "flourish like a *flower of the field" (Ps 103:15 RSV). In the vital family the wife is "like a fruitful vine" and children are "like olive shoots" (Ps 128:3 RSV). At their best, sons are "like plants full grown" (Ps 144:12 RSV).

Images of Decay and Death. The same qualities that make plants images of life also make them images of mutability. If plants can grow, they can also decline. If they live, they also die. No source of imagery for transience is more frequently used by biblical writers than plants. Thus we find references to "the fading *flower" (Is 28:4) and withered *grass (Ps 102:4, 11; 1 Pet 1:24). James elaborates the picture into an image of *terror: "the sun rises with its scorching heat and withers the grass; its flower falls, and its beauty perishes" (Jas 1:11 RSV). If it is not drought and heat that make the grass vanish, it may be the trampling of feet (Ps 58:7).

Often, in fact, a plant's quick growth is used to highlight its equally rapid decline: people flourish "like a flower of the field; for the wind passes over it, and it is gone, and its place knows it no more" (Ps 103:15-16 RSV). Psalm 90, a meditation on human mortality, makes conspicuous use of plant imagery, as God is pictured as sweeping people away "like grass which is renewed in the morning: in the morning it flourishes and is renewed; in the evening it fades and withers" (Ps 90:5-6 RSV). Again, "All flesh is grass, and all its beauty is like the flower of the field. The grass withers, the flower fades" (Is 40:6-7 RSV).

Plants in Parables, Similes and Metaphors. In addition to appearing in parables such as the *sower (Lk 8:5), the *leaven (Mt 13:33), the weeds (Mt 13:24-30) and the *mustard seed (Mt 13:31), plants are used figuratively in similes and as metaphors. Judah grows like a plant (2 Kings 19:30); the Suffering Servant will grow up "like a young plant, and like a root out of a dry ground" (Is 53:2 RSV). Jesus warns the Pharisees that "every plant which my heavenly Father has not planted will be rooted up" (Mt 15:13 RSV). The psalmist reminds us of the transience of life—a recurring biblical theme—which is like the grass and wildflowers in the short Palestinian spring, when hot winds dry up the soil and wither the vegetation, or plants are used as fuel (Ps 37:2; 102:4, 11; 103:15; 129:6; Is 37:27; Mt 6:30; Jas 1:10-11; 1 Pet 1:24). Yet the lilies' natural beauty is comparable to the glory of Solomon (Mt 6:28; Lk 12:27), and faith as small as a mustard seed can accomplish great things (Mt 17:21).

The weeds hindering the growth of crops provided illustrations of evil, such as those weed seeds ("tares," KJV) sown among the wheat (Mt 13:24, 36) and the judgment of the renegade who "springs up like poisonous weeds ['hemlock,' KJV] in the furrows of the field" (Hos 10:4 RSV). In the dry fields there are worthless thistles and prickly plants— a *curse of *Adam (Gen 3:18). They crowd out young wheat plants just as "the cares of the world and the delight of riches choke the word" of God (Mt 13:22 RSV). Such plants are fit only for burning, as are those who commit *apostasy (Heb 6:6-8; cf. Is 33:12) and the ungodly (2 Sam 23:6-7). *Thorns "are in the way of the perverse" (Prov 22:5 RSV); "like a thorn that goes into the hand of a drunkard is a proverb in the mouth of fools" (Prov 26:9 RSV). Thorns and thistles are signs of complete destruction (Is 34:13; Hos 9:6); one expects no useful fruit from such plants (Jer 12:13; Lk 6:44). However, God reveals himself to Moses in a burning bush that is not consumed (Ex 3:2-4).

The desert yields many prickly plants, as well as wormwood (which represents bitterness of soul or corruption) and gall (a poisonous drink; Deut 29:18; Amos 5:7; Jer 9:15; 23:15; Lam 3:15, 19; cf. Rev 8:10-11). But the prophet Isaiah promises that "the desert shall rejoice and blossom like the crocus ['rose,' KJV] . . . with joy and singing" (Is 35:1-2 RSV). It is also in the wilderness that God provides *manna for the starving Israelites. *Manna* literally means "What is it?" Commentators have always asked the same question—the only clue being that it "was like coriander seed, and its appearance like that of bdellium" (Num 11:7 RSV).

In contrast, where there is water, reeds abound. Pharaoh dreams of cattle feeding on the Nile-side reed grass (Gen 41:18); tall reeds (phragmites) growing in water shake in the wind (1 Kings 14:15; Mt 11:7). But it is more likely to be the papyrus sedge *(Cyperus papyrus)* that bows down its flower head like a fasting man (Is 58:5). A bruised or damaged reed (arundo; Mt 12:20) is of no use as a walking stick, yet "my servant" would not break it and throw it away, nor would he pinch out a smoldering flax lamp wick (Is 42:14; Mt 12:20). This shows that Jesus would be gentle with people according to their abilities and condition.

Symbolic Plants. Certain plant species have particular biblical symbolism. The grapevine and the *vineyard typify the people of Israel, which is pictured as "a vine out of Egypt" (Ps 80:8 RSV). Isaiah tells a parable based on the same motif: "For the vineyard of the LORD of Hosts is the house of Israel, and the men of Judah are his pleasant planting" (Is 5:7 RSV). Jeremiah sees the enemy as grape gatherers, stripping Israel of everything (Jer 6:9). The prophet Hosea also likens Israel to "a luxuriant vine that yields its fruits" (Hos 10:1 RSV; cf. Ezek 17). A vine is symbolic of safety (1 Kings 4:25) and a source of visions (Gen 40:9). Since a golden vine decorated the front of the second temple, it was significant that Jesus should say "I am the true vine" (Jn 15:1).

Religious Uses. A final cluster of plant images centers on the ornamentation of the temple furniture. We read about engraved carving of plants on the walls (1 Kings 6:29) and doors (1 Kings 6:32, 35). The bronze pillars are ornamented with lilies and pomegranates (1 Kings 7:15-22; 2 Chron 3:15-17). The *lampstand, or candlestick *(menorah)*, has seven stems in plant form, with "the flower of a lily" (1 Kings 7:26; cf. "almond blossoms," Ex 25:34). So as Israelite worshipers gazed at various accoutrements of the most sacred place of their spiritual experience, they saw not angels and cherubim but the plants of nature.

See also BRANCH; FIG, FIG TREE; FLOWERS; GRASS; LEAF; MUSTARD SEED; NATURE; PALM TREE; ROOT; SEED; SOW, SOWING, SOWER; TREE, TREES; TREE OF LIFE; VINE, VINEYARD.

PLAY

Playing in the Bible encompasses a range of human activities, most of them involving pleasurable recreation, the arts or sports.

One cluster of images surrounds the playing of musical instruments (Gen 4:21; 1 Sam 16:16-17, 23; 1 Chron 15:16, 20; Ps 33:3; 144:9; Mt 11:17; Lk 7:32; 1 Cor 14:7). Filling a role, as in a drama, furnishes another cluster. There are two dozen references in the Prophets to "playing the whore," meaning to serve the role of *prostitute. Another connotation is that of presuming to fill a role for which one is not suited, as when the townspeople taunt Lot, an outsider, for presuming to "play the judge" before them (Gen 19:9). Elsewhere the meaning is that of someone's pretending to be something that he is not, as in the proverb "Some friends play at friendship but a true friend sticks closer than one's nearest kin" (Prov 18:24 NRSV). When David pretended to be a madman, King Achish asked sarcastically, "Do I lack madmen, that you have brought this fellow to play the madman in my presence?" (1 Sam 21:15 NRSV).

Another motif is that of sport, including *children's play. The voice from the whirlwind asks Job with obvious irony whether he will play with Leviathan "as with a bird, or . . . put it on a leash for your girls" (Job 41:5 NRSV; *see* Mythical Animals). God portrays the mountains as yielding "food for [Behemoth] where all the wild animals play" (Job 40:20 NRSV). The catalog of God's provisions in *nature in Psalm 104 includes the statement that God created Leviathan to "sport" in the sea (Ps 104:26). Recreational play can also become the spectacle of pagan orgies, as in Paul's retrospect on the golden calf incident: "the people sat down to eat and drink, and they rose up to play" (1 Cor 10:7 NRSV).

The most positive images of playing occur in *apocalyptic visions of the coming *millennium. Chief among them is Zechariah's marvelous street scene of the new Jerusalem, where old men and women will sit in the streets, which will "be full of boys and girls playing" (Zech 8:4-5 NRSV; see also Jer 30:18-19; 31:4, 13-14). In Isaiah's parallel vision of the peaceable kingdom, "the nursing child shall play over the hole of the asp" (Is 11:8 NRSV).

If we extend the motif of play to playfulness, the prime biblical example is *Jesus. Jesus' discourses and his sparring with opponents (and occasionally his friends) are marked by a whimsical and playful quality. One of the most characteristic rhetorical features of Jesus' parables and discourses is the *giantesque motif—comic exaggeration designed to secure a listener's assent and produce a smile in the process. Jesus was also fond of wordplay (as when he gave the mercurial Peter the nickname "Rocky") and irony (e.g., asking the crowds who had sought out the rugged desert dweller John the Baptist whether they had gone to see a delicate dandy [Mt 11:7-8]).

See also ATHLETICS; GIANTESQUE MOTIF; LEISURE; MUSIC.

PLEASURE

Pleasure is a person's feeling of enjoyment, delight and satisfaction. By extension, the word also applies to the things that produce this feeling in people—the so-called pleasures of life. To codify the images of pleasure in the Bible, we need only ask what categories of experience give enjoyment and satisfaction to the characters and writers of the Bible. While the whole Bible depicts pleasures, it is the poetic books that particularly identify certain experiences as pleasurable. The Bible adds complexity to the picture by distinguishing between good pleasures and bad ones, true ones and false ones. It is further useful to distinguish between the pleasures of people and the pleasures of God.

The Pleasures of People. What, then, gives pleasure to the characters (including the authors) we meet in the Bible? One large category is experiences of *beauty. The beauty of *nature, for example, is a source of pleasure, as attested especially by the five nature poems in the Psalter (Ps 8; 19; 29; 104; 148; *see* Nature Psalms). The account of *rainfall and resultant crops that closes Psalm 65 (Ps 65:9-13) is so evocative that the author seems himself to have experienced the weather and growth as plants might be assumed to enjoy them. Similarly, in Psalm 147 the poet enumerates the beauties and bounties of nature—the stars, the rain and grass, the finest of the wheat, and the seasonal changes—as a way of expressing his implied pleasure in them.

Artistic beauty also gives pleasure to the people and authors of the Bible. The aesthetic beauty of the temple leads the psalmist to exclaim, "How lovely is thy dwelling place, O Lord of hosts!" (Ps 84:1 RSV). The sound of the "harp with the psaltery" is "pleasant" (Ps 81:2 KJV). Literature too can be a source of pleasure: the writer of Ecclesiastes, giving us his philosophy of composition, claims that he sought to find "pleasing words" or words of delight (Eccles 12:10 RSV).

Family life is another of the pleasures of life for the writers of the Bible. The parent whose "quiver" is full of *children is "happy" (Ps 127:5). The "blessed" man is someone whose *wife is "like a fruitful vine within your house" and whose children are "like olive shoots around your table" (Ps 128:3-4 RSV). Grandchildren are also a source of pleasure, as suggested by the psalmist's wish "May you see your children's children" (Ps 128:6 RSV). Children who are wise are a special pleasure to their parents (Prov 10:1; 15:20; 23:24-25; 27:11; 29:3).

Romantic love and *sexual fulfillment are also sources of pleasure in the Bible. Proverbs 5:18-19 is a brief celebration of the sexual pleasures of married life, accompanied by a warning to avoid the false pleasures of *adulterous sex (Prov 5:20-23). The classic text on the pleasures of romance and sex is the *Song of Songs. Some of the pleasures it catalogs are romantic and sexual, such as being in the presence of the beloved, physical contacts such as *kisses and caresses, and the physical attractiveness of the beloved, including the woman's adornments. But the genius of love poetry like that of the Song of Songs is that it shows us an entire world transformed by love. The pleasures of romance become projected onto life beyond the lovers—most notably to nature, so that the Song of Songs can also be read as a nature poem that celebrates the pleasures of the countryside and the seasons.

The pleasures of community and sociability are also praised in the Bible. It is "good and pleasant" when believers "dwell in unity" (Ps 133:1 RSV). OT pictures of *festivals and *pilgrimages to Jerusalem give us images of the pleasures of kindred spirits participating together in communal activities. In the Gospels, similarly, we find frequent pictures of Jesus enjoying the social life of dinners and retreats with the disciples.

As already hinted, experiences of *worship are a conspicuous source of pleasure in the Bible. The speaker in Psalm 42, living in exile, recalls the pleasures of worship thus: "I went with the throng, and led them in procession to the house of God, with glad shouts and songs of thanksgiving, a multitude keep-

ing festival" (Ps 42:4 RSV). Another psalmist exclaims, "I was glad when they said to me, 'Let us go to the house of the Lord!'" (Ps 122:1 RSV). Psalm 84, the prototypical worship psalm, reviews the pleasures of worshiping God in the *temple (including the pleasures of the pilgrimage).

A leading theme of the Bible is that we do not have to look far to find pleasure. The book of Ecclesiastes is filled with catalogs of the pleasures of everyday life. We read, for example, that "it is God's gift to man that every one should eat and drink and take pleasure in all his toil" (Eccles 3:13 RSV). Again, it is "good and . . . fitting" for a person "to eat and drink and find enjoyment in all . . . toil" (Eccles 5:18 RSV). "Every man also to whom God has given wealth and possessions and power to enjoy them, and to accept his lot and find enjoyment in his toil—this is the gift of God" (Eccles 5:19 RSV). The pleasures of life are within easy reach—*eating *bread with enjoyment (Eccles 9:7), living in a festive spirit (Eccles 9:8) and enjoying "life with the wife whom you love" (Eccles 9:9 RSV). To the zestful eye of the writer of Ecclesiastes, the mere light of the sun is pleasurable: "light is sweet, and it is pleasant for the eyes to behold the sun" (Eccles 11:7 RSV). The writer is so convinced of the goodness of legitimate pleasure that for him the ultimate tragedy is someone who does not enjoy the goods of this life (Eccles 6:2, 3, 6; cf. also Eccles 12:1, where the tragedy of old age is that a person has "no pleasure" in life).

Given the premise that everyday life can be a source of pleasure, virtually any daily activity can become pleasurable, and it is so in the Bible. *Land can be pleasant (Ps 106:24), speech can be pleasant (Prov 16:21, 24; 23:8), and riches can be pleasant (Prov 24:4). Even *sleep can be counted among the pleasures of everyday life (Ps 4:8; 127:2). Things that make a person glad include "a good word" (Prov 12:25 RSV; NIV "a kind word") and *oil and *perfume (Prov 27:9). Or we can consider the comprehensive picture of the pleasures of the godly and moral life, with several encomia in the Psalter providing an index to those pleasures (Ps 1; 15; 112; 128). The pleasures of living a moral life are summed up in the proverb "Wise conduct is pleasure to a man of understanding" (Prov 10:23 RSV). Among the pleasures of a virtuous life are "a pure heart and a good conscience" (1 Tim 1:5 RSV).

What gives the characters and writers of the Bible most pleasure is God. The Psalms, where we find "the language of hedonism everywhere" (Piper 1986, 17), ring the changes on the theme of the pleasures that believers find in God and his works. Psalm 16 is a small classic on the subject, with its famous images of "the lines" that "have fallen for me in pleasant places," of "fulness of joy" found in God's presence and of the "pleasures for evermore" that are at God's "right hand" (Ps 16:6, 11 RSV). The works of God are great, "studied by all who have pleasure in them" (Ps 111:2 RSV; cf. Ps 92:4). The psalmist exults in God (Ps 9:2) and is "glad in the Lord" (Ps 32:11;

cf. Ps 40:16; 70:4). A key passage in Ecclesiastes that encourages people to enjoy the pleasures of life (Eccles 5:18-19) follows the exhortation with the paradoxical addendum "For he will not much remember the days of his life because God keeps him occupied with joy in his heart" (Eccles 5:20 RSV). Human and divine pleasure are similarly joined in the exhortation of the psalmist to "take delight in the LORD, and he will give you the desires of your heart" (Ps 37:4 RSV).

The most obvious conclusion to be drawn from these images of human pleasure in the Bible is that God wants his people to be happy, and that (to use the formula of Jeremy Taylor) he threatens to do terrible things to people who refuse to be happy. Pleasure in itself is good, as the doctrines of heaven and hell confirm. God is not a celestial Scrooge who hopes that his creatures are unhappy. He is rather the God who offers his people the use of a feasting house and a "river of . . . delights" (Ps 36:8 RSV), and the One who gives the ingredients for making human life in this world pleasurable (Eccles 2:24, with its assertion that enjoyment "is from the hand of God"). The pleasures that people find in life are actually among the pleasures of God, "who delights in the welfare of his servant" (Ps 35:27 RSV).

Underlying all of the Bible's images of human pleasures is the premise that God is their source. In the words of 1 Timothy 6:17, God "giveth us richly all things to enjoy" (KJV). In the book of Ecclesiastes, too, pleasure or enjoyment is given by God; it is not something people can attain by human effort. Enjoyment, says the Preacher, "is from the hand of God, for apart from him who can eat or who can have enjoyment?" (Eccles 2:24-25 RSV). The ability to accept one's lot and "find enjoyment in . . . toil—this is the gift of God" (Eccles 5:19 RSV).

The Bible as a whole is enveloped in striking master images of pleasure. The original image of pleasure in the Bible is paradise, the *garden that God planted specifically for people, the garden that included "every tree that is pleasant to the sight" (Gen 2:9 RSV). *Paradise* is synonymous with *pleasure,* and the Genesis account differs from its ancient parallels in stressing that the happy garden was designed by God for people. The final two chapters of the Bible return us to the pleasure motif, with their pictures of joy, the passing away of human pain and sorrow (Rev 21:4) and the satisfaction of every human need (Rev 21:6; 22:2).

The False Pleasures of Sin. The Bible springs a surprise on us, or at least a paradox, by also denigrating some pleasures as bad. The paradox of bad pleasures is highlighted in the roll call of faith of Hebrews 11, where we read that Moses chose "rather to share ill-treatment with the people of God than to enjoy the fleeting pleasures of sin" (Heb 11:25 RSV). "The pleasures of sin" must mean the immediate gratification that some morally bad actions can bring. We can further surmise that pleasures can be "false" when they are morally wrong or when they are

overvalued (perhaps to the point of *idolatry).

Although in one sense the Bible endorses the person as pleasure-seeker, Paul in 2 Timothy 3:4 delineates what can go wrong with this innate human impulse to seek pleasure when he speaks of people who are "lovers of pleasure rather than lovers of God" (RSV). Peter extends the picture when he writes of people who "count it pleasure to revel in the daytime. They are blots and blemishes, reveling in their dissipation" (2 Pet 2:13 RSV). Here is a double image of false pleasures—activities that gratify the body temporarily but that are pursued excessively to the neglect of the greater good, God, and that are immoral, displeasing to God.

The most obvious category of pleasurable sins depicted in the Bible is illicit sexual activity. A memorable narrative example is David's *adultery with Bathsheba (2 Sam 11). But the book of Proverbs gives the most detailed account of the false pleasures of illicit sex. The seductress Folly assures her victims that "stolen water is sweet, and bread eaten in secret is pleasant" (Prov 9:17 RSV). The extended temptation story in Proverbs 7:6-27 is replete with evocative imagery of sexual and sensory pleasure—kisses, a couch decked with coverings, a luxurious linen bedspread, perfume, privacy and the invitation "Come, let us take our fill of love till morning; let us delight ourselves with love" (Prov 7:18 RSV). Equally vivid is the imagery of the "smooth tongue of the adventuress" (Prov 6:24 RSV) and her sexual attractiveness, identified as a "beauty" that a man would desire in his heart and imaged by the woman's captivating eyelashes (Prov 6:25).

Additional portraits of the perversion of pleasure fill out the description of false pleasures. The proverb "He who loves pleasure will be a poor man" (Prov 21:17 RSV) refers to the person who neglects the duties of work in order to do what is more immediately pleasurable. People can actually come to enjoy immoral acts, so that (for example) they "take pleasure in falsehood" (Ps 62:4 RSV). Addiction and lack of self-control are evident in people who are "slaves to various passions and pleasures" (Tit 3:3 RSV). The most detailed account of the futility and disillusionment that attend an abandonment to pleasure occurs in Ecclesiastes 2:1-11, where the author decides to "make a test of pleasure" by pursuing discreet sensuality, the acquisition of goods, sex and entertainment. But after keeping his "heart from no pleasure," he comes up empty: "all was vanity and a striving after wind" (RSV). In this famous test the ancient teacher tried to get more out of the pleasures of life than they can give, whereas other passages in *Ecclesiastes show pleasure to be something God gives.

A final image we should note is *places* of false pleasure. Ecclesiastes 7:2-4 speaks of a "house of feasting" and a "house of mirth" (NIV "house of pleasure"). In Proverbs 9:13-18 Folly has her own "house" from which she utters her seductive invitation to eat bread "in secret." The point of the spatial metaphor is at least twofold: (1) many actions require a site where they are performed and with which they are associated, and (2) an indulgent lifestyle surrounds a person and becomes the habitual "world" in which he or she resides. True pleasures are also pictured as having their special places: the psalmist finds his pleasure at God's right hand (Ps 16:11) and in the temple (Ps 84:4).

The Pleasures of God. Complementing the pleasures of people are the pleasures of God. What pleases God? we might ask. People do, first of all. We read, for example, that "the LORD takes pleasure in those who fear him" (Ps 147:11 RSV) and that "the LORD takes pleasure in his people" (Ps 149:4 RSV). God gives "wisdom and knowledge and joy" to the person "who pleases him" (Eccles 2:26 RSV). God also takes pleasure in the actions of people who follow him. The godly person's meditation can be pleasing to God (Ps 104:34). "The words of the pure are pleasing" to God (Prov 15:26 RSV), and a person's "ways" can "please the LORD" (Prov 16:7 RSV). Conversely, some kinds of people do not give God pleasure. For example, God "has no pleasure in fools" (Eccles 5:4 RSV); he has "no pleasure" in the sacrifices of people whose heart is not worshipful (Is 1:11 NIV); he is "not a God who delights in wickedness" (Ps 5:4 RSV); and the wickedness of humanity grieves him to his heart (Gen 6:6).

Second, God takes pleasure in the true worship of him. An extensive pattern of *altar imagery might be adduced here, beginning as early as the altar that Noah builds after the flood, regarding which we read that "the LORD smelled the pleasing odor" (Gen 8:21 RSV). To picture God enjoying the *smell of the sizzling animals and birds, as that odor wafts up from the altar toward heaven, is to begin to understand his delight in Noah's righteous worship. God is really taking pleasure in Noah's heart. In the many directions given by God to Moses and the Israelites are included over thirty references to the burnt offerings that have "a pleasing odor" to the Lord (see esp. Num 28—29).

Of course the pleasing sacrifices offered on an altar need to be accompanied by a *repentant *heart. It is this that truly pleases God. Psalm 51:16-17 makes this clear with its assertion that God has "no delight in sacrifice," being instead pleased with "a broken spirit" and a "contrite heart" (RSV). Similarly, praising "the name of God with a song" and magnifying "him with thanksgiving" are said to "please the LORD more than an ox or a bull with horns and hoofs" (Ps 69:30-31 RSV). As far back as the occasion of Saul's disobedience, we encounter the principle that God does not have "as great delight in burnt offerings and sacrifices" as he does "in obeying the voice of the LORD" (1 Sam 15:22 RSV). To this might be added Jesus' comment to the Samaritan woman that the worship that God "seeks" ("is pleased by," we can infer) is worship "in spirit and truth" (Jn 4:23). Turning the motif of "pleasing sacrifice" to metaphoric use, Paul calls the gifts to him from the Philippians "a fragrant offering, a

sacrifice acceptable and pleasing to God" (Phil 4:18 RSV). On another occasion, Paul urges Christians to "offer your bodies as living sacrifices, holy and pleasing to God" (Rom 12:1 NIV). God is also pleased by people's exercise of faith: "without faith it is impossible to please him" (Heb 11:6 RSV).

God also delights in his *creation. Genesis 1 exudes the pleasure of an artist in the act of creating, and the account is punctuated by the assurance that "God saw that it was good." In other words, God took pleasure in what he had created. After cataloging the splendors of created nature, the psalmist expresses the sentiment "May the LORD rejoice in his works" (Ps 104:31).

Finally, God takes pleasure in doing good to his people. Through the prophet Jeremiah he said regarding the people whom he would restore, "I will rejoice in doing them good, and I will plant them in this land in faithfulness, with all my heart and all my soul" (Jer 32:41 RSV). Moses had similarly told the Israelites that "the LORD will again take delight in prospering you, as he took delight in your fathers, if you obey the voice of the LORD your God" (Deut 30:9-10 RSV). God "delights in the welfare of his servant" (Ps 35:27 RSV). Isaiah portrays a coming golden age of which God can say, "I will rejoice in Jerusalem, and be glad in my people" (Is 65:19 RSV). In fact, God will name his restored nation "My delight is in her," for "the Lord delights in you. . . . As the bridegroom rejoices over the bride, so shall your God rejoice over you" (Is 62:4-5 RSV).

See also BEAUTY; BLESSING, BLESSEDNESS; GARDEN; GOOD LIFE, THE; LAND FLOWING WITH MILK AND HONEY; LEISURE; NATURE; PLAY; SEX; WORSHIP.

BIBLIOGRAPHY. N. Geisler, "The Christian as Pleasure-Seeker," *Christianity Today,* September 26, 1975, 8-12; J. Piper, *Desiring God: Meditations of a Christian Hedonist* (Portland, OR: Multnomah Press, 1986); J. Piper, *The Pleasures of God: Meditations on God's Delight in Being God* (Portland, OR: Multnomah Press, 1991).

PLOT MOTIFS

The material that follows is mainly a taxonomy of plot motifs. Detailed treatment of the Bible's main plot motifs can be found in individual articles as indicated. Here the point is partly to raise consciousness about the prevalence of familiar plot motifs in the Bible, partly to enlarge one's lexicon of plot motifs and partly to provide a comprehensive framework for viewing plot motifs as a single interrelated edifice.

No single framework can cover the entire range of plot motifs. There are, however, identifiable clusters that will make the details manageable. These clusters consist of four large categories of material. Some plot motifs are archetypes, such as the *initiation and *journey. Others are narrative conventions, such as *reversal and *recognition. A third category is narrative genres, such as *battle story and *love story. Still other plot motifs, such as stories of *terror and stories of *sin, are based on subject matter rather than elements of literary form.

The Monomyth. The largest single paradigm by which to organize plot motifs is the monomyth—the composite story on which all individual stories can be plotted. This "one story" of literature is organized as a circle having four phases that correspond to the four seasons. It can be diagrammed as follows:

The two phases above and below the horizontal line yield relatively few plot motifs because they

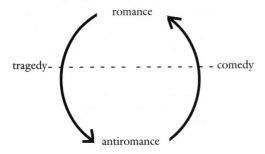

consist of static states, whereas narrative tends to focus on change and development. Plot motifs that fall into the position of romance include *prosperity stories and stories of *hospitality and *provision, as well as scenes of the *good life. In the category of antiromance we find stories of *suffering, *oppression and *bondage, and stories of sin, as well as such nightmare (*see* Dreams, Visions) categories as stories of *violence, *terror and *danger, and *murder stories.

The generic pattern of downward movement from prosperity to loss is *tragedy. Its more specific forms are the *fall from innocence, stories of *exile or banishment, the *crime and punishment motif, and stories of *misprizing.

The most numerous category of plot motifs that cluster around the monomyth are those of *comedy—the upward progress from bondage to prosperity, or from a less desirable state to a more desirable one. Here we find stories of *increase, *mercy, *reform, *reunion/reconciliation, *rebirth, *restoration, *reward, *redemption and *return. As all the preceding words with the prefix *re-* attest, the comic movement essentially reverses a negative movement with movement toward a positive goal. In addition we can note the motif of *rags-to-riches and stories of *homecoming and *outwitting.

A few plot motifs reenact the entire U-shaped pattern of the monomyth. The essential movement of the monomyth, we might note, is a constriction followed by an expansion (as some of the comic motifs noted in the previous paragraph also hint). Such is the *rescue motif; the *ordeal, *trial and *test that are successfully overcome; the *quest in which obstacles to the goal are gradually conquered; the motif of *lost and found; and the *upset victory of the *underdog.

Narrative Conventions. The next largest cluster of plot motifs stems from basic conventions of storytelling. At the heart of every story is plot conflict. The element of conflict is usually multiple, and it can exist at a number of levels—people against their environment, against other people, against society or institutions, against supernatural forces, against elements of their own character. Plot conflicts, moreover, can be physical, emotional, moral/spiritual or psychological. The structure of such conflicts is an arc of increasing struggle and tension followed by a release of tension, with resolution and closure of the conflict at the end of the story. The basic rhythm is a problem that moves toward solution—a tension that is resolved. Plots are furthermore based on a shapely pattern of beginning-middle-end. As such, they are a distillation from available materials, inasmuch as events in real life are rarely self-contained like this.

Within the linear structure of plot movement, a number of more specific motifs are recurrent. In keeping with the tendency of plot conflicts to move toward resolution of the issues that have been introduced at the outset, the motifs of *epiphany and *revelation/recognition are common. Again, the element of suspense implicit in the paradigm outlined in the previous paragraph generates such motifs as *deception, *surprise and *reversal. *Spy stories, *battle stories, *adventure stories, stories of *escape and stories of *hiding and intrigue are related phenomena. Here too we find stories of *risk, and the archetypal *bet or dare belongs to the same narrative family.

Stories hinge ultimately on the choices that characters make, and sometimes this element of choice is so prominent as to produce a category of stories of *choice. The dynamics of choice are often bound up with *test and *temptation motifs. Finally, in keeping with the principle of plots to record growth and change, the motifs of *transformation and *conversion are important.

The Journey Motif. Literal and metaphoric journeys provide a further category of plot motifs. The emphasis is on the linear progress of the action, accompanied by the growth of the characters who undertake the journey. Within this general paradigm we find *travel stories, stories of *quest and *wandering, and stories of *pilgrimage.

The Life of the Hero. Another set of motifs converges in the composite life of a *hero. The resulting pattern can be viewed as a specific manifestation of the U-shaped monomyth noted earlier. Hero stories often begin with the circumstances of the hero's special birth and infancy (*see* Annunciation; Birth Story). Heroes are usually called to a special task or destiny (*see* Calling, Vocation) and thereafter undergo an initiation. The *hero's task almost always involves an ordeal and test, and in the Bible a *divine-human encounter is often present as well. The hero's life usually ends in *triumph. If the hero's entire story is told, the last phase includes such motifs as farewell (*see* Farewell Discourse) and *burial.

Motifs of Judgment. The element of *justice also figures prominently in plot motifs. Next to the ingredient of plot conflict, no convention has been more universal as a presence in stories than *poetic justice—the practice of ending stories with virtue rewarded and vice punished. In addition, the element of judgment can be so prominent as the basic story material as to produce a genre of stories of *judgment. Stories of *revenge are rooted in the principle of judgment, as are stories of cataclysmic destruction of persons or *cities. Futile attempts to cheat God's oracle (*see* Cheat the Oracle) are also stories of judgment.

Family Stories. A final cluster of plot motifs is determined by the content of the stories, which are domestic in nature. Here we find stories built around *family relationships. Specific motifs include *marriage and *sibling rivalry as well as the genre of the *love story. Stories of family reunion and homecoming round out the cluster.

See also CHARACTER TYPES; COMEDY AS PLOT MOTIF; POETIC JUSTICE; TRAGEDY AS PLOT MOTIF.

PLOW, PLOWING. *See* FARMING.

PLUNDER. *See* TRIUMPH.

POETIC JUSTICE

Poetic justice consists of virtue rewarded and vice punished. It is one of the most common features of stories to end with poetic justice. In fact, with this device storytellers often signal their own moral allegiances or belief system. When a character is rewarded at the end of a story for his or her experiment in living, it is natural to conclude that the story offers such behavior for approval as a virtue. The opposite is true for characters or events that "lose" at the end of a story.

While a complete tabulation of biblical stories that display poetic justice is beyond the scope of this article, it is important to be aware that nearly every biblical story ends with poetic justice, not only signaling what constitutes virtue and vice in the story but also expressing a faith in divine justice as a principle of reality that will ultimately exert itself (and that often exerts itself in earthly and human life). The principle of poetic justice is succinctly stated by God in the story of *Cain: "If you do well, will you not be accepted? And if you do not do well, sin is crouching at the door" (Gen 4:7 RSV).

Poetic Justice as Narrative Convention. Poetic justice is most naturally associated with biblical narrative. Some aspects of the story of *Jacob illustrate the negative side of poetic justice. Jacob exploits his brother's eagerness for food to his own advantage (Gen 25:29-34), and he subsequently steals the *blessing from his brother by deceiving his father (Gen 27:1-40). In the episode of the substitute bride (Gen 29:15-30), a family member turns the tables on

Jacob by exploiting eagerness for Rachel and deceiving him. The *trickster is tricked, and justice for Jacob's own deception is requited.

A second example is the story of Jacob's son *Joseph and his brothers, in which poetic justice is present on multiple levels. Joseph remains virtuous during the course of his temptations and sufferings in Egypt, and he is rewarded by a meteoric rise to power in Pharaoh's court. Even though Jacob's grief over the supposed death of Joseph is in excess of his desert, he nonetheless is in some measure punished for the favoritism he showed to Joseph. Through Joseph's manipulation of his brothers, meanwhile, they are punished for the evil they did to him.

The book of *Esther also highlights elements of poetic justice, which plays itself out through the entire course of events, including the fact that those who intended to kill the Jews were themselves slaughtered. The most delicious poetic justice is reserved for the villain Haman. Guilty of overreaching hubris, Haman is forced to lead his enemy Mordecai in honor through the streets because that is the reward he himself prescribed for the person whom the king desired to honor. Then, guilty of boundless hatred for Mordecai, Haman is hanged on the very gallows that he had ordered to be built in anticipation of Mordecai's fall from favor.

*Hero stories cannot exist without poetic justice as a mainspring of the action, inasmuch as their whole thrust is to praise the central character and (as part of that impulse) to show the rewards that come to virtuous character and action. Thus Noah is rewarded for his godliness by escaping the flood. *Abraham is rewarded for his faith and obedience. *Ruth risks herself in loyalty to her mother-in-law and in committing herself to the Hebrew faith, and she is rewarded with love, marriage and family. At the end of the book of *Job, Job's fortunes are restored after he repents of his belligerence toward God, while his conceited friends are denounced by God. Gideon responds to God's call of him as military deliverer, and he proceeds to a successful military career.

Old Testament Covenant History. A broader pattern of poetic justice can be found in the story of the nation of Israel in the OT. The repeated cycle is prosperity, apostasy, subjection to an enemy nation, repentance, deliverance. Leaders such as Moses and Samuel set before the nation a great either-or in which they outline the *blessings that will come through obedience to the *covenant and the *curses that will result from disobedience (Deut 28; 1 Sam 12). Underlying this rhythm is poetic justice—reward for virtuous conduct and punishment for vicious conduct.

The same covenant context provides the backdrop to the OT prophetic books. Here punishment is predicted and predicated on the evidence that the nation has been disobedient to its covenant duties. The major theme is that God will judge disobedience. The minor theme is the call to "seek good, and not evil, that you may live; and so the LORD, the God of hosts, will be with you" (Amos 5:14 RSV), implying a principle of reward for righteous behavior.

Poetic Justice in Psalms and Proverbs. Poetic justice also underlies Psalms and Proverbs. The premise of the lament psalms (the most numerous category of psalms) is that there is a right and wrong, and that God can be trusted to vindicate the cause of the right. Psalm 73 is paradigmatic of a pattern that the psalms repeat: although the arrogant wicked flourish for the moment, God sets them "in slippery places," so that they will be "destroyed in a moment" (Ps 73:18-19 RSV), with the result that "truly God is good to the upright" (Ps 73:1 RSV) in the long run. Psalm 1 sounds the keynote right at the outset: "the LORD knows the way of the righteous, but the way of the wicked will perish" (Ps 1:6 RSV).

A similar pattern underlies many of the OT proverbs, which presuppose a causal connection between human conduct and its outcome. "Good sense wins favor," we read, "but the way of the faithless is their ruin" (Prov 13:15 RSV). Again, "A false witness will perish, but the word of a man who hears will endure" (Prov 21:28 RSV). On the one side, "Happy is he who trusts in the LORD" (Prov 16:20 RSV). On the other, "The LORD is far from the wicked" (Prov 15:29 RSV). These are randomly chosen specimens of a pattern that pervades all the proverbs of the Bible.

Poetic Justice in Salvation History. The *Bible's metanarrative itself is a story of poetic justice, based on the premise of the ultimate triumph of good and defeat of evil. Redemption is not on the basis of merit but of grace, yet the Bible pictures those who will reign with Christ as being rewarded for their faith and devotion to God. Daniel paints a picture of the final resurrection as the occasion when the dead will rise, "some to everlasting life, and some to shame and everlasting contempt. And those who are wise shall shine like the brightness of the firmament" (Dan 12:2-3 RSV). Jesus' Olivet Discourse, too, ends with a vision of those who served humanity with compassion being received into God's eternal kingdom, while those who were negligent are condemned to hell ("they will go away into eternal punishment, but the righteous into eternal life" [Mt 25:46 RSV]). The book of Revelation concludes the Bible on a note of ultimate and eternal poetic justice, with good triumphant and evil defeated.

A conception of poetic justice underlies the message of Paul, which combines personal and cosmic poetic justice. Paul characterizes humanity and consequently the world as fallen and sinful, pursuing its own perverse course (Rom 1:18-32). As a consequence there is evil and suffering in the world (Rom 5:12-21), with Paul himself as well as others in the hurch suffering from it (e.g., 2 Cor 11:23-27; 2 Tim 4:6-7). More than that, in this world there are evil forces all around (2 Thess 2:1-12). But for Paul this life on earth is only part of the story. Although there is sin and death, Paul looks to a vanquishing of evil and conquest by Christ. On one level, this involves a

personal vindication, described variously as human justification, reconciliation or sanctification. On the cosmic level, using *apocalyptic imagery, Paul speaks of a restraining force on the power of evil that is at work even now, until such a time as the full forces of evil erupt and a last battle occurs. Christ is the ultimate victor (note that Rom 8:18-22 speaks of a redemption of the created order; *see* Triumph), and at that time he hands over to God a world in which justice reigns supreme (1 Cor 15:20-28).

Summary. Poetic justice in the Bible is both a narrative convention and an expression of a moral/theological vision of human history. We should not minimize the literal appeal of poetic justice in stories. The prevalence of such narrative endings in the Bible need not point to a fictional impulse at work. The human race simply prefers to retell stories that turn out "right." Aristotle claimed that in the absence of such an ending our moral sense is not satisfied. Not every Bible story ends with poetic justice, of course, but a preference for such stories is evident.

Yet in the Bible poetic justice is more than a narrative convention. It also expresses the moral and spiritual vision of the universe that biblical faith espouses. As the literary critic John Dennis (1698) wrote, "Poetic justice would be a jest if it were not an image of the divine." The divinely created and governed laws of the universe ensure that ultimately virtue will be rewarded and vice punished. In a sense, therefore, poetic justice can be seen as an overriding theme of the entire Bible.

See also BIBLE; BLESSING, BLESSEDNESS; CRIME AND PUNISHMENT; CURSE; HERO, HEROINE; REWARD.

POOR. *See* POVERTY; RAGS TO RICHES.

POTTAGE. *See* STEW.

POTTER. *See* CLAY; GOD.

POURING OUT. *See* HOLY SPIRIT.

POVERTY

The Bible uses a variety of words for "poor" and "poverty." These terms have been the subject of etymological studies and research into possible socioeconomic and political backgrounds, as well as the focus of ethical discussions and the theologies of liberation. Both testaments offer vivid pictures of the plight and afflictions of the poor. In Scripture numerous groups suffer the pains of want and injustice: peasant farmers, wage laborers, *widows, *orphans and *foreigners.

Although descriptions of the circumstances and explicit causes of poverty are sometimes vague, many passages use verbs that graphically communicate that the poor are often victims of greed, lust for power and manipulation within the legal system. The prophets, for instance, denounce leaders and a society that "crush," "deprive," "destroy," "grind," "trample on" and "oppress" the poor (e.g., Is 3:14-15; 32:6-7; Amos 4:1; 8:4). The fundamental image of helplessness is reinforced by OT legislation designed to succor those exploited in the courts and to facilitate restitution for those forced to sell their *land and their *family members into *slavery, because of overwhelming debt (Ex 23:6-13; Lev 25; Deut 15; cf. 2 Kings 8:1-6; Neh 5). Poverty can leave a person abandoned by *neighbors, friends and family (Prov 14:20; 19:4, 7).

Several biblical texts present more extensive portraits of the conditions of poverty. Each underscores that the poor are prey to the cruelty of those in power. They often have no recourse to anyone but God. The opening chapters of *Exodus describe the groaning of the Israelites under the Egyptian yoke: forced labor and infanticide mark their existence as slaves under *Pharaoh. In Nathan's parable of rebuke to *David, he tells of a poor man whose beloved lamb is snatched away by a wealthy neighbor (2 Sam 12:1-10). Job 24 depicts the desperate lot of the poor who lack clothing, search for *food and are taken advantage of in their menial jobs. Jesus' description of the agony of the sick beggar Lazarus also emphasizes the callousness of the rich and mighty (Lk 16:19-31). Throughout the Bible, God is portrayed as One who responds to the cries of the poor, especially the needy among his people.

Jesus repeatedly demonstrates his concern for the less fortunate. In the sermon at Nazareth he declares that he has come to bring good news to the poor (Lk 4:16-21; cf. 7:18-23; Mt 25:31-46 and par.). Even though this passage also refers to spiritual realities and needs, there can be no denying that the feeding of the hungry and the healing of the sick are important elements of Jesus' ministry.

Stark realities of poverty also permeate the accounts of the early *church. Indeed, it was the poor who often responded to the gospel message (1 Cor 1:26-29). Believers share food and possessions and organize themselves to take care of the widows (Acts 2; 4; 6; 1 Tim 5); they are called to recognize the common spiritual bond between slaves and free (e.g., Gal 3:28; Eph 6:5-9) and are reminded of their obligation to help alleviate the poverty of even distant churches (Rom 15:25-27; 1 Cor 16:1-4; 2 Cor 8). James in particular portrays the critical state of the poor, who have no food, clothes or decent *wages (Jas 2:1-19; 5:1-6).

Although poverty is never a desired condition, a deeper trust in God can be generated by such circumstances. In the OT, *Ruth stands out as an example of faith; her hard work in the fields and virtuous character are rewarded with food and protection, then *marriage and a *child. Jesus offers the sacrificial generosity of a poor widow as a positive model to the disciples (Mk 12:31-44 and par.). Later Paul will set the giving of the poor Macedonian churches before the Corinthians as worthy of imitation (2 Cor 8:1-15). Jesus calls his disciples to voluntary poverty in the fulfillment of their ministry (Mk 2:23-25;

6:8-9; 10:28-31 and par.; cf. 2 Cor 4:8-10; 11:27-29; Phil 4:12-13), even as he had forgone physical comforts in carrying out his own task (Mt 8:20 and par.).

The dependence on God occasioned by material want allows for the biblical connection between poverty and piety—that is, the humble trust of the righteous. The psalms especially speak of those who are falsely accused and accosted by evildoers but who ultimately confide in divine mercy and faithfulness (e.g., Ps 34; 37; 109). This reliance on God, though, is still placed within contexts of oppression and persecution that is very real (cf. Mt 5:3-12).

Finally, it must be noted that the Bible also provides imagery of those who suffer poverty because of sloth or disobedience. The amusing image of the *sluggard (Prov 6:6-11; 10:4; 24:30-34) and the picture of excessive *feasting (Prov 23:19-21; 21:17) serve as warnings to avoid the consequences of laziness and lack of self-control. In addition, the covenant curses point to poverty as divine judgment for *sin (Deut 28:48). These curses are portrayed in the historical accounts and prophetic oracles as fulfilled in experiences of extreme want (e.g., Joel 1; Amos 4:6-10; Hag 1:5-11).

See also FOREIGNER; GLEAN; HOSPITALITY; HUNGER; ORPHAN; PROSPERITY, WAGES, WANDERER; WANDERING; WIDOW.

POWER. *See* STRONG, STRENGTH.

PRAISE PSALM

The second largest category of psalms (next to the *lament) is the psalm of praise. Usually this title is reserved for psalms that specifically praise God (e.g., Ps 8; 19; 33; 103; 104; 145-48). (Psalms praising human subjects fall into such categories as royal psalm and *encomium.) A helpful signpost to understanding the praise psalm is knowing that the English word *praise* originally meant "to set a price on" or "to appraise." From this came the idea that to praise means to commend the worth of someone or something. Praise is thus a response to the worthiness of someone or something. The psalms of praise celebrate and revere the worthiness of God.

The psalm of praise is one of the fixed forms within the Psalter, containing three motifs. Psalms of praise begin with a *formal call to praise* (e.g., Ps 33:1-3). This might consist of as many as three elements: an exhortation to sing to the Lord, to praise and to exult; the naming of the person or group to whom the exhortation is directed; and mention of the mode of praise (e.g., song, *dance, timbrel, lyre). The main section of a praise psalm is the *catalog of the praiseworthy acts and attributes of God* (e.g., Ps 33:4-19). Less frequent is the technique of painting a portrait of God (as in psalms that portray God's coming as a storm God, Ps 29). Praise psalms end on a *note of closure* with a final prayer, wish or other formula that provides a note of resolution at the end (e.g., Ps 33:20-22).

The catalog is the crucial element, and we might

note these further things about it. Because the object of praise is God, the imagery is usually sublime and exalted. God is praised both for his actions and for his character or attributes. Sometimes a praise psalm celebrates specific actions that God has performed; at other times the subject is God's habitual and universal actions. God's praiseworthy acts occur chiefly in three arenas: *nature or *creation, history, and the personal life of the believer. Common acts for which God is praised include creation, *providence (including preservation of physical life), *rescue, *salvation or *redemption, and *judgment. Sometimes the poet uses generalization; at other times, particular examples. Some praise psalms extol God for personal blessings, whereas the focus of others is communal. Because God's acts are offered as proof of his praiseworthiness, allusion to past events is a staple.

Finally, in addition to the three motifs that comprise the content of a praise psalm, we can identify certain ingredients that make up praise itself. One of these is the elevation of the object of praise. Related to this is the direction of the speaker's whole being away from himself or herself and toward God. Thus, while praise psalms are filled with the speaker's emotions, we do not look at the speaker. Instead we look *with* the speaker *at God*. Praise typically occurs in a communal setting and has a quality of testimony to it. There is a corresponding double quality to praise psalms, which look horizontally at fellow humans and vertically to God.

See also LAMENT PSALMS; NATURE PSALMS; PSALMS, BOOK OF; WORSHIP PSALMS.

PRAYER

Prayers abound in the Bible. From the time of Seth when, we are told, "men began to call on the name of the LORD" (Gen 4:26 NIV) to the culmination of history in Revelation, the people of God pray. The Bible contains nearly fifty lengthy prayers recorded in prose sections and several hundred shorter prayers or references to praying. The writers are far more interested in showing people at prayer than in telling about prayer. Consequently, the images of prayer discussed in this article are drawn from the actual practice of prayer (e.g., Dan 6:10). These prayers show that the primal images for prayer are relational. The major terms for prayer are conversational; it presupposes a mutual posture of trust and devotion; it concerns the range of life concerns; like a conversation between friends (*see* Friendship), it provides both comfort/support and challenge; and its purposes include service of others.

Prayer as Conversation. The dominant metaphor for prayer in the Bible is conversation with God. Ordinary words for speech and conversation (e.g., said, spoke, say, call, cry) describe acts of prayer as humans address the God who seeks relationship with his people. Expressive verbs for prayer (e.g., cry, beseech, seek) largely reflect the emotional state of the one praying rather than a technical vocabulary related to elaborate prayer ceremonies. In other ancient religions prayer can appear to involve a mastery of technique and esoteric knowledge. In the Hebrew Scriptures the primary image of prayer is simple *asking*, in a conversational manner. Implicit in this asking, which is neither demanding nor mere wishing, is the expectation that the asker is both humble and expectant.

The elements of speaking, waiting and listening in biblical prayer suggest a tone of conversation face to face. The person praying offers words to God and is *confident that God hears the sentiment they express (Ps 34:6; Rom 8:26-27). *Abraham's prayer for Sodom uses ordinary speech and even adopts a persuasive tone (Gen 18:23-33). *David notes the need to *wait on God in prayer (Ps 37:4; 40:1; see also Is 40:31). He describes calling out to God and receiving an answer (Ps 18:13; 30:10-11; 81:7): "When I called, you answered me; you made me bold and stouthearted" (Ps 138:3 NIV). Isaiah calls the people to repent, reminding them of the conversation to which they can return: "Whether you turn to the right or to the left, your ears will hear a voice behind you, saying, 'This is the way; walk in it' " (Is 30:21 NIV). The constant nature of the prayer dialogue is essential to the intimacy of relating to God.

Jesus models the intimate nature of prayer as conversation. He related to God as a *father, using the Aramaic *abba* (an intimate term for "father"), yet this intimacy does not diminish his sense of God's holiness. Except for his agonizing cry on the cross (Mt 27:46 par. Mk 15:34), he always addresses God as Father in prayer and teaches his *disciples to do the same (Mt 6:5-15; 7:7-11; Lk 11:2-4). Thus he makes the dialogue between God and his people a more personal conversation. He prays often (Lk 5:16) and urges his disciples to make prayer a part of their lifestyle (Lk 18:1). He instructs his disciples in prayer (Lk 9:28; 11:1) and makes prayer his first action in times of trouble. The Gospels record his praying at all important events in his life (baptism, Lk 3:21; transfiguration, Lk 9:29; selection of *twelve disciples, Lk 6:12; Gethsemane, Mt 26:36-46 par. Mk 14:32-42; Lk 22:39-46).

An exchange of confidence. Prayer is an exchange of confidence: we assume the stance of a trusting *child and pray with faith that is matched by obedience; God remembers our frailty, loves us as his children, hears and answers our prayers. Biblical praying must be set in contrast with many other schemes for influencing deity common in the ancient Near East. Biblical faith excludes any attempts to use magic or formula to control or placate God. Elijah offers a simple, straightforward prayer clearly rooted in his relationship with God, "I am your servant," while the priests of Baal vainly seek to win the favor of deity through "frantic prophesying" and bloodletting (1 Kings 18:16-38 NIV).

Our posture of trust and obedience. In many societies certain times and postures become symbols of prayer: a *bowed head, closed *eyes, folded *hands or a kneeling position. In Scripture, posture, movement and time are mentioned in relationship with prayer, but no single time, place, gesture or posture becomes a metonymy for prayer. When Hezekiah prayed for deliverance he took a threatening letter to the temple and "spread it out before the LORD" (Is 37:14 NIV). People pray while standing, kneeling, lying down, lifting their hands, sitting, bowing or pounding their chest. The physical activity symbolizes an engagement of the whole being in the act of praying. But the bodily symbol is significant only if it accurately reflects the heart's position toward God.

Prayer is deeply affected by the fact that human beings look "on the outward appearance, but the LORD looks at the heart" (1 Sam 16:7 NIV). Long prayers in public places oppose the stance that Jesus taught (Mk 12:40). Likewise, even eloquent prayers are shunned if they are spoken by the unrighteous (Prov 28:9; Is 16:12). The posture most important in prayer is a posture of rest (trust in God) and of action (obedience).

There is a deep and necessary connection between our praying and our living (Prov 15:24; Jas 5:16). *Moses and Samuel are singled out as ones who prayed effectively (Jer 15:1). Jesus modeled the posture of submitted action as he prayed in Gethsemane: "May your will be done" (Mt 26:42). Most important, his lifestyle and prayers said the same thing (Heb 5:7). Those whose prayers God honors come to him with humility and trust, as a child to a father or like a weaned child in a mother's lap (Ps 131:2), seeking love and a sense of belonging.

God's posture of mercy and grace. God positions himself to assist the upright in *heart; he answers prayer to be faithful to his own character and trusts humans with a choice of actions toward him. Often biblical characters suggest to God that he should act in a given way because his honor, glory, grace, mercy or trustworthiness demands such a response. The narrative accounts of these prayers leave the distinct impression that God is pleased when his character is appealed to but not presumed upon (Ex 32:11-14; Num 14:13-22; Deut 9:26-29; Neh 1:4-11). For example, Abraham based his prayer on God's character—"Will not the Judge of all the earth do right?" (Gen 18:25 NIV)—and Moses appeals to God's faithfulness to himself when he prays, "Why should the Egyptians say, 'It was with evil intent that he brought them out, to kill them in the mountains and to wipe them off the face of the earth'? Turn from your fierce anger; relent and do not bring disaster on your people" (Ex 32:12-13 NIV). One of Scripture's most stunning pictures of God answering prayer comes in response to this prayer: "the LORD relented" (Ex 32:14 NIV). Joshua prays with similar logic after the defeat at Ai (Josh 7:6-9); he forms his plea in the question "What then will you do for your own great name?" (NIV). Daniel and Jesus also recognize God's stance in prayer as being that of a benevolent master whose goal is to be faithful to his

own ideal (Dan 9:19; Lk 11:2).

Prayer is an exchange of confidence between God and his *covenant people: God is positioned in mercy, waiting for his people's obedience, while God's people are positioned in trust, recalling his promises. Moses and Samuel exemplify a right relationship with God: "They called on the LORD and he answered them. He spoke to them from the pillar of cloud; they kept his statutes and the decrees he gave them" (Ps 99:6-7 NIV).

The prayer life shown in the Bible does not involve technical achievement limited to a few who have learned a system of symbols and incantations, but is open to all because of God's relationship with his chosen people. The relational basis of biblical prayers is captured by Moses' great invitation to prayer: "What other nation is so great as to have their gods near them the way the LORD our God is near us whenever we pray to him?" (Deut 4:7 NIV). This accessible, inviting aspect of prayer is captured in David's statement "This poor man called, and the LORD heard him; he saved him out of all his troubles" (Ps 34:6 NIV).

Prayer across the range of life experience. God is near to us in every moment of life. Thus all realms are open to prayer. Prayers are prompted by distress (Ps 18:6), by sickness (Ps. 30:2), by a need for guidance (Ps 119:18), by repentance from sin (Ps 30:8-9), by bewilderment at God's ways (Ps 22:1) or by the hollow feeling of distance from him (Ps 33:12). The verb *seek* typically describes the action of prayer and depicts it as part of the quest after wisdom and life (Ps 119). The book of *Psalms is made up entirely of prayers, reflecting the range of emotions people experience throughout their lifetime.

Other Prominent Images for Prayer. *Intimacy with God.* Prayer is an intimate meeting with God, like resting in a mother's lap (Ps 131:2). The prophet promises that in prayer God "will quiet you with his love, . . . will rejoice over you with singing" (Zeph 3:17 NIV).

An avenue of service. Those who offer prayer in the OT and in the NT agree that one central goal of prayer should be for power to help others. Abraham, Moses, Joshua and Daniel pray on behalf of the Israelite people, as do all of the prophets. The apostles request prayer from the churches for their ministry (Rom 15:31; Col 4:3; Heb 13:18-19).

Jesus taught the disciples to use prayer as an avenue of service, not as a means of personal power. He prayed for those seen as a burden, such as children (Mt 19:13). He withdrew to pray when in need of *strength to continue ministry (Lk 5:16). His prayer of blessing and intercession in John 17 echoes the language of public prayers of the OT, furthering his image as *prophet, *priest and *king (Jn 17:1-26). The book of *Hebrews gives the picture of Jesus as high priest who "always lives to intercede for [us]" (Heb 7:25 NIV), in contrast to the image of *Satan's continual slandering of us (Rev 12:10).

Images of prayer's unique power. Uniquely, prayer

allows God's children to take part in two worlds. In Revelation the elders who minister before the Lord hold "golden bowls full of incense, which are the prayers of the saints" (Rev 5:8). Prayer is unlike most other communication, for when we pray we can expect that the One being addressed will understand our inarticulate groans and translate them into effective prayers. The picture is of a loving parent who listens to a child's confused complaint and responds to what is deeply wished but not well expressed. "We do not know what we ought to pray for, but the Spirit himself intercedes for us with groans that words cannot express" (Rom 8:26 NIV).

Though we may often feel that prayer is of little consequence, Jesus reminds us that it can do remarkable things: "If you have faith as small as a mustard seed, you can say to this mulberry tree, 'Be uprooted and planted in the sea,' and it will obey you" (Lk 17:6).

Those who prayed well. Perhaps the most indelible images of prayer in the Bible involve those who model authentic praying, such as Abraham's other-oriented prayer for Sodom (Gen 18:16-33) and his prayer for his infertile wife Sarah (Gen 15:1-4). When Israel is in *bondage in *Egypt, we are given a moving picture of God interpreting the exhausted cry of his people and acting (Ex 3:7). Moses engages in poignant dialogue with God about his fitness to lead the people (Ex 3:1—4:7). Joshua's prayer life is rich with imagery. He prays after the defeat at Ai and is told that the problem is hidden sin (Josh 7:6-15). A negative example is found in Joshua 9, when the Israelites make a foolish treaty because they "did not ask direction from the LORD" (Josh 9:14 NRSV). Joshua receives a dramatic answer to his prayer that the *sun would stand still (Josh 10:12-14). Hannah's prayer-vow for a child (1 Sam 1:10) is gripping. *Solomon's prayer for *wisdom must be considered one of the major models for prayer (1 Kings 3:5-9). Elijah and Elisha show themselves to be persons of great prayer, especially in the contest with the prophets of Baal (1 Kings 19:2-18). When surrounded by the Assyrian army, Hezekiah spreads out a threatening letter before the Lord, who is then described with majestic images (2 Kings 19:15-19). At two points Jeremiah is told to stop interceding for the people (Jer 7:16; 11:14), and his outburst of anger at God shows how true prayer is marked by honesty (Jer 20:7-18). Daniel prays three times a day and records one of the most other-oriented and God-centered prayers of Scripture (Dan 9:4-19).

Jesus' prayers are remarkable for their sheer frequency, their simplicity and their direct address of God as "Abba." Paul's prayers as recorded in his epistles show a person who is deeply thankful (Rom 1:8-9; Eph 1:3-14; 3:14-21). Hebrews gives picture of Jesus always interceding for the saints (Heb 7:25), and prayer is pictured as allowing us access to the throne of grace (Heb 4:4-16). James provides a picture of caring for the sick through prayer (Jas 5:13-18), and Revelation 4—5 vividly describes the prayer-filled heavenly worship of the *Lamb.

Prayer is shown in Scripture to be a key dimension of the divine-human relationship. It marks the people of God and is rooted in human need and divine love and sufficiency. Asking for help is the primary image for prayer in the Bible, but images of nurture, confrontation (of God by his people and of people by God), quiet communion and dialogue are very present as well.

See also BOW, BOWING; FASTING; KNEE, KNEEL; WAITING ON GOD; WORSHIP.

PRECIOUS STONES. *See* JEWELS AND PRECIOUS STONES.

PRIDE

Although the apostle Paul speaks of a healthy pride we should have in ourselves and others (2 Cor 5:12; 7:4; 8:24; Gal 6:4), the word *pride* in Scripture is more frequently used to refer to a very negative character trait that can be described as arrogant, conceited and haughty. Classical Greek and Roman cultures had a particular aversion to it, stigmatizing it as *hubris* and making virtually all their literary tragedies a variation on the theme of the self-destructive effects of pride and its offensiveness to the gods. In the Bible, likewise, such pride brings disgrace (Prov 11:2), breeds quarrels (Prov 13:10), goes before destruction (Prov 16:18) and brings humiliation (Prov 29:23).

As a character trait, pride produces a gallery of memorable characters in the pages of the Bible. We find people who ostentatiously flaunt their power and wealth. A notable instance is the Persian king Nebuchadnezzar (Dan 2—4), who erected a gold statue of himself and required his subjects to bow down to it, and who as he walked on the roof of his palace said, "Is not this great Babylon, which I have built by my mighty power as a royal residence and for the glory of my majesty?" (Dan 4:29-30 RSV). The most certain feature of pride in the Bible is that it precedes a downfall, and the story of Nebuchadnezzar runs true to form: immediately after uttering his boast, he was stricken with insanity and his kingdom was taken from him. The NT counterpart is Herod, who flaunted his royal status, prompting the people to shout, "The voice of a god, and not of man!" (Acts 12:22 RSV), whereupon an *angel of God smote him with *worms and he died (Acts 12:23).

Equally famous as an example of pride is the overweening Haman in the book of *Esther. He erupts in pride and plots revenge when his personal enemy Mordecai refuses to bow down and tremble before him. When the king desires to *honor someone, Haman says to himself, "Whom would the king delight to honor more than me?" (Esther 6:6 RSV). He accordingly proceeds to prescribe a pretentious show of *glory for himself. As elsewhere in the Bible, though, this pride goes before destruction, as Haman is forced to lavish his display of glory on his enemy

Mordecai, resulting in his own humiliation and disgrace. And eventually the proud villain is hanged on the very gallows that he had prepared for Mordecai.

Another embodiment of pride is the nation and ruler of Tyre. Ezekiel 27—28 paints an extended picture of material affluence coupled with human pride over the achievement. In an oracle of judgment against the king of Tyre, the prophet pictures his heart as being proud and him as saying, "I am a god, I sit in the seat of the gods" (Ezek 28:2 RSV). The prophetic charge is that "your heart was proud because of your beauty" (Ezek 28:17 RSV). As we come to expect, this pride comes "to a dreadful end" (Ezek 28:19 RSV). Of a similar nature is the prophetic oracle of *Isaiah in which he recounts the fall of Lucifer, an example of aspiring pride (Is 14:12-21).

Not only kings are natural candidates for pride, so are nations, often represented by their rulers, as we see repeatedly in the OT prophetic books. The king of Assyria is denounced for "his haughty pride" and "arrogant boasting" (Is 10:12 RSV), Tyre for the pride of all glory" (Is 23:9 RSV), Moab for "his pride together with the skill of his hands" (Is 25:11 RSV) and for loftiness, pride, arrogance, haughtiness of *heart and insolence (Jer 48:29-30; cf. also Zeph 2:8-11), Sodom for its "pride, surfeit of food, and prosperous ease" (Ezek 16:49 RSV), Israel for "the pride of your power" (Ezek 24:21 RSV; cf. also Amos 6:8), Judah for being "haughty in my holy mountain" (Zeph 3:11 RSV). Such references are only representative of a common motif in the OT prophecies, where proud nations are frequently actors in the divine drama of sin and judgment.

The biblical images of pride are most obviously of rulers and nations, but pride is a vice within reach of any individual with enough money or power to provide a platform for it. Isaiah paints a vivid picture of haughty women who "walk with outstretched necks, glancing wantonly with their eyes, mincing along as they go, tinkling with their feet" (Is 3:16 RSV). Similar vividness characterizes the portrait of the arrogant prosperous in Psalm 73:3-12, who (predictably) are poised on the verge of imminent ruin (Ps 73:17-20). The psalms are replete with briefer vignettes of proud people—the violent (Ps 10), the slanderer (Ps 31:18), those who sin with their *mouths (Ps 59:12), the oppressor (Ps 94:3-7), the scornful who are at ease (Ps 123:4), those with haughty *heart and *eyes (Ps 131:1). From Jesus comes the satiric portrait of the banquet guest who ostentatiously seats himself in a place of honor, only to be moved to a lower place, accompanied by the aphorism that "he who exalts himself will be humbled" (Lk 14:7-11 RSV).

As these brief pictures show, pride keeps some very bad company. It is associated with such varied vices as perverted speech (Prov 8:13), boastfulness (Jer 48:30), defiance of God (Jer 50:29), indifference to the poor and needy (Ezek 16:49), self-deceit (Obad 3), the lust of the flesh and of the eyes (1 Jn 2:16) and false trust in riches (1 Tim 6:17). Twice pride is placed in a catalog of highly charged vices (Mk 7:21-22; 2 Tim 3:2-5).

A survey of the numerous biblical passages on pride will yield the following conclusions. Pride in the Bible is not just an abstraction but instead yields a series of vivid images. It is especially linked to certain body parts: the heart, the mouth and the eyes. It is also treated as generic evil or wickedness. Material *prosperity and its accompanying power are prerequisites to pride. Morally the most common manifestation of pride is *oppression of less fortunate people. Spiritually its root sin is disregard for God or defiance of him. The leading self-delusion of proud people is their false *security in themselves and their resources. The most important thing about proud people is that God opposes them, and the most predictable thing we know about pride is that God will bring it down (see especially Is 2:12-17). Indeed, pride in the Bible seems always on the verge of being humbled. The biblical images of pride add up to such a repulsive picture that they would lead one to abhor it, yet the frequency with which it appears in the Bible suggests something of its perennial appeal to the sinful heart.

See also GLORY; HEART; HONOR; HUMILITY; OPPRESSION; PROSPERITY; REBEL, REBELLION; SIN.

PRIEST

Most references to priests in the Bible involve the priests of the Mosaic *covenant. These consisted of the Levitical priests in general—all the qualified males of the tribe of Levi—and the high priests of Aaron's family especially. In the Passover plague on Egypt, God killed all the Egyptian firstborn (*see* Elder Child, Elder Sibling) but spared the firstborn of *Israel through blood on the lintels (Ex 12). Because firstborn males among the Israelites were spared death, God had special claim on them. God claimed the entire tribe of Levi for full-life service to him as their substitute (Num 1:47-53). Thus the Levites became the priests of Israel, devoting their lives to maintaining and enforcing *worship of God, first in the *tabernacle and eventually in the *temple.

The Old Testament Priesthood. Within the tribe of Levi, Aaron and his sons were given special status as high priests (Ex 28). The high priestly family had the highest responsibility and privilege to serve in the holy place and most holy place of the tabernacle and temple. While the functions of the priests are significant, these functions must be understood as proceeding out of their identity. It is a pervasive biblical principle that nature is determinative of actions, not vice versa. The priestly identity was founded not in function but in essence.

For high priests and Levites alike, *holiness (setting apart) was the chief distinguishing characteristic. While inner moral *purity was essential, God chose to teach this lesson through the requisite physical perfection of his priests (Lev 21). But more instructive of the priestly identity were Aaron's garments and *anointing. The color and structure of his garments, revealed by God to *Moses on Mt. Sinai, corresponded closely to many elements in the likewise-revealed tabernacle design (Ex 28). Further, Aaron's anointing with *oil (Ex 40:13), which symbolized the anointing of God's Spirit, paralleled the infilling of the tabernacle with the glory-Spirit of God (Ex 40:34). Thus understood, Aaron is seen to be a minitabernacle, a shorthand version of God's dwelling place among his people (Poythress).

Functions of the high priests and Levites, seen in this light, reflect the presence and working of God among his people. When the priests received *sacrifices and *offerings, they signified God's acceptance of the one offering (Lev 1—8). When the priest ate the peace offerings with the offerers, he signified God *feasting in fellowship with them. Besides this first major aspect of the priestly functions—representing God to the people—there was a second aspect: representing the people to God. His holiness relative to the layperson allowed him access to God on behalf of the people. Although seen in many functions, such as the offering of *incense symbolizing prayer for the people (Ex 30:7-10), the most poignant example is the high priest's sprinkling *blood on the *ark on the Day of Atonement (Lev 16).

Whether a third aspect of the priest's functions or whether a consequence of the first two, we must recognize the military duty of priests. Consistent with the functions of temple priests in surrounding religions, the Israelite priest guarded the tabernacle or temple of God through threat of arms. Any who transgressed the manifested holiness of God's presence were to be slain (Num 1:53; cf. Ex 32:25-28).

While the distinction between priests and people had to be clearly maintained in order that God's utter holiness be recognized, similarities between priests and laity bring attention to the fact that all Israelites were priests in certain respects. Though they did not minister in the tabernacle or temple, they were priests in the land as a whole. For example, a rebellious city was to be offered as a burnt offering at the hand of all the laity (Deut 13:16; cf. Deut 13:10). Likewise, the Israelites were to represent God before the nations (Ex 19:6; Is 42:6). So high priest, Levite and layperson each had priestly duties in their respective venues.

God's People as Priests. Cheung has effectively argued that Israel's identity as a priestly nation has primarily to do with their redeemed status rather than their function. Being holy and redeemed people permits free access to God's service (Zech 3:7). Although *Adam had no need of redemption prior to the Fall, he rendered priestly service to God. Redeemed sinners are restored images of God, and hence priests. Adam himself, as the *imago Dei,* is the archetype for the priest (Kline). His charges to subdue the earth to *sabbath consecration to the Lord (Gen 1:28) and to defend God's holy paradise (*see* Garden) from uncleanness (Gen 2:15; cf. Gen 3:24) are priestly functions. In sum, a priest is what a human person ought to be.

But even the high priest had to atone for his own *sin before he could make *atonement for the people (Lev 16:11). And the most holy place itself had to be cleansed (Lev 16:16). The OT draws to a close with the high priest, and thus the entire nation, looking for a means of perfection (Zech 3).

In the NT the image of God's chosen nation as a nation of priests is transmuted into the image of the priesthood of believers in Christ. Through the substitutionary priestly work of Jesus, believers in him are made holy in God's presence (Heb 4:14-16; Jude 24-25). Further, they are given priestly duties in that presence (Heb 10:20-22). It is not what they do that justifies Peter's designation of the *church as a "royal priesthood" (1 Pet 2:9), but who they are as redeemed persons. As such, they serve God now in the administration of themselves as sacrifices (Rom 12:1-2), and they will wear priestly robes in eternal service in the *Lamb and God, who are the temple of the New *Jerusalem (Rev 1:6; 21:3, 22). But rather than garments sewn by human fingers, they will wear Christ himself and his perfect righteousness, which is possessed by faith (Rom 13:14; Gal 3:27).

Jesus, the Great High Priest. Perfection of the priesthood awaited Jesus. He is the perfect high priest, being the divine Son of God (Heb 7:16) who alone possesses sinless perfection, but yet being a brother to humanity through his incarnation (Heb 2:11-18). In contrast to the law-ordained, sin-tainted, perpetual and numerous sacrifices of the OT priests, Jesus was the sinless offerer of his sinless self once and for all on behalf of his people (Heb 7—10, esp., e.g., Heb 7:27; 9:12, 28; 10:10, 14). He is the high priest par excellence because he made himself the sacrifice par excellence. Not only in his offering but also in his place of service, he perfected the priesthood, for he entered into the most holy place in heaven to make atonement (Heb 9:23-24).

See also ALTAR; ATONEMENT; MELCHIZEDEK; OFFERING; PURITY; SACRIFICE; TABERNACLE; TEMPLE; WORSHIP.

BIBLIOGRAPHY. A. T. M. Cheung, "The Priest as Redeemed Man," *JETS* 29.3 (1986) 265-75; M. G. Kline, *Images of the Spirit* (S. Hamilton, MA: M. G. Kline, 1986) 35-56; V. S. Poythress, *The Shadow of Christ in the Law of Moses* (Brentwood, TN: Wolgemuth & Hyatt, 1991) 51-57.

PRIMOGENITURE. *See* BIRTHRIGHT, ELDER CHILD, ELDER SIBLING.

PRISON

As a sanction, prison is mentioned quite often in the Bible, but imprisonment was not covered in the Mosaic law, and there were no prisons, in the modern sense of long-term incarceration, in ancient Israel. Yet penal *slavery and prisons were part of the ancient Near East and were well enough known that writers could employ prison as an image effectively.

Sometimes an imprisonment was unjust (e.g., Gen 39:20; Jer 37:18); sometimes it resulted from due processes of law (e.g., 2 Kings 17:4; Ezra 7:26). Because a prisoner could be held indefinitely, release from prison is seen as God's *blessing and an answer to *prayer (Ps 68:6; 79:11; 107:10-16).

In some passages it is difficult to tell whether the reference to prison is literal or metaphorical. For example, David was not strictly in jail when he prayed, "Set me free from my prison, that I may praise your name" (Ps 142:7 NIV), but was no doubt referring to his personal circumstances at the time (compare Ps 66:11; Is 42:22; Zech 9:11). Sometimes prison serves as a ready illustration of anything or anyone that restricts an individual's freedom. Hence imprisonment imagery can refer to the wiles of an unscrupulous woman (Eccles 7:26) or to restrictive, unjust practices (Is 58:6) or merely to cutting off one's own retreat (1 Sam 23:7). It is employed by Ezekiel as part of a larger picture of Israel's king as a captured *lion (Ezek 19:9), while the apostle Paul contrasts his own confinement with the liberty of the Word of God (2 Tim 2:9): in spite of his imprisonment, the good news was still free to spread.

The apostle also uses imprisonment as a description of our fallen spiritual condition. "The whole world is a prisoner to sin," he writes (Gal 3:22 NIV). He found himself unable to free himself from the principle of *sin within his nature (Rom 7:23) and concluded that only God could do it for him. This gives particular point to Isaiah's prophecies concerning the coming One who would release captives from jail (Is 42:7; 61:1), a prediction that Jesus saw himself fulfilling: "The Spirit of the Lord is upon Me, because He anointed Me to preach the gospel to the poor. He has sent Me to proclaim release to the captives, and recovery of sight to the blind, to set free those who are downtrodden, to proclaim the favorable year of the Lord" (Lk 4:18-19 NASB). *Death, as Hades, the place where the departed gather, is seen as a prison to which Christ has the *key (Rev 1:18, 24; see Hell). This also seems to be the significance of Jesus' response to Peter's confession concerning "the gates of Hades" (Mt 16:18 NIV), although the image overlaps with that of a *city.

On other occasions, however, it is God who is pictured as a jailer from whom there is no *escape (Lam 3:7). Job is reminded of and acknowledges the futility of opposing God. "If he comes along and confines you in prison . . . who can oppose him?" (Job 11:10 NIV; see also Job 12:14; see Job, Book of). In this respect Jesus' advice about settling things quickly with your adversary before you find yourself in jail seems to be more than advice about social relationships (Mt 5:25-26; Lk 12:58-59). It underlines the need to be *reconciled to God while that is possible.

This image has a particular point when it is used to describe the *judgment of spiritual beings, including Satan (Is 24:22; 2 Pet 2:4; Jude 1:6; Rev 20:1-3, 7). Peter's tantalizing reference to the spirits Christ visited in prison (1 Pet 3:19) has attracted a wide variety of interpretations, ranging from the spirits of the departed who had never heard the gospel to the rebellious spiritual beings incarcerated before the *flood (2 Pet 2:4; Jude 1:6). Opinion is divided as to the exact significance of this verse.

See also BONDAGE AND FREEDOM; CRIME AND PUNISHMENT; DEATH; ESCAPE, STORIES OF; SIN; SLAVE, SLAVERY.

PROCESSION, TRIUMPHAL PROCESSION

Every human society has its moments of procession, but ancient cultures, rooted in ritual, seem to have specialized in them. Martial cultures have generally commemorated victories with triumphal processions, as modern cultures more customarily do to celebrate athletic or political victories.

The most prominent and regular processions mentioned in the Bible are those that occurred as part of the formal worship at the *temple in *Jerusalem. In Psalm 42:4 the speaker, living in exile, recalls a time when he led the worshipers "in procession to the house of God, with glad shouts and songs of thanksgiving, a multitude keeping festival" (RSV). Nehemiah 12:31 paints a similar picture. Elsewhere in the Psalms we read about "solemn processions . . . the processions of my God, my King, into the sanctuary—the singers in front, the minstrels last, between them maidens playing timbrels" (Ps 68:24 RSV), as well as "festal procession with branches, up to the horns of the altar" (Ps 118:27 RSV; see Ps 118:19-26 for a fuller picture, replete with images of *gates opening and people entering them).

In addition to processions as part of worship, we find OT references to political and military processions. At the Red Sea deliverance, Miriam led a procession of *dancing women (Ex 15:20), and women led David and Saul home after victory in similar fashion (1 Sam 18:6-7). First Kings 1:33-40 narrates Solomon's coronation procession, while Psalm 68:18 draws on the military practice of a *triumphant king's leading captives in procession into a *city. Isaiah gives us a picture of a coming *apocalyptic triumph in which kings will be "led in procession" as people bring "the wealth of the nations" to Zion (Is 60:11 RSV).

Jesus too is associated with a triumphal procession, though surprises are connected with it. In Zechariah's messianic prophecy of the event, we find the paradox of a "triumphant and victorious" king who is so humble as to ride on a *donkey (Zech 9:9 RSV). The fulfillment of the prophecy comes with Christ's triumphal entry from Bethany into Jerusalem (Mt 21:1-11; Mk 11:1-10; Lk 19:29-40; Jn 12:12-19). This famous moment fuses OT procession motifs, inasmuch as Jesus is hailed as a king who enters the capital city and at the same time enters the temple with a procession (Mk 11:11). Although the book of Revelation pictures no full-fledged triumphal entrance of Christ and his saints into *heaven, the motif lurks in the background of scenes in which Christ and his followers are shown conquering their enemies and entering a heaven that rings with jubilation. A similar spirit underlies the picture at the beginning of the book of Hebrews, where we read that after Christ "had made purification for sins, he sat down at the right hand of the Majesty on high" (Heb 1:3 RSV).

The climax of the triumphal procession motif in the NT is a double reference to *thriambeuō*. Translations do not agree on how to render 2 Corinthians 2:14, which is variously translated as "Thanks be to God, who in Christ always leads us in triumph" (RSV) and "Thanks be to God, who always leads us in triumphal procession in Christ" (NIV). Colossians 2:15 uses the same term in speaking of Christ's "having disarmed the powers and authorities" and making "a public spectacle of them, triumphing over them by the cross" (NIV). The frame of reference is the Roman procession in which a victorious general would enter the capital city leading his triumphant *army and/or a string of captives to be put on public display. Believers in Christ might be in either or both categories. On the one hand, they are part of Christ's victorious army (cf. Rev 19:11-13). Yet the paradox of Christians' finding their victory by being enslaved to Christ is consistent with Paul's repeated designation of his own status as a bondslave of Christ (Rom 1:1; cf. also Rom 6:16-22; 1 Cor 4:9-13; 2 Cor 6:4-10; 11:30; 12:9-10; *see* Slave, Slavery).

The paradox may go even deeper than the positive connotations of being led as a prisoner to be put on display: Christ's own triumphal procession led to his *atoning death in Jerusalem, and because followers of Christ share in his death (Gal 2:20), they are not simply paraded in triumph at the *cross (as the powers and authorities are in Col 2:15) but are perhaps led to the cross themselves as Christ was, on the understanding that this death is actually a triumph.

See also DIVINE WARRIOR; TRIUMPH.

BIBLIOGRAPHY. L. Williamson Jr., "Led in Triumph: Paul's Use of *Thriambeuō*," *Interpretation* 22 (1968) 317-32; T. Schmidt, "Jesus' Triumphal March to Crucifixion: The Sacred Way as Roman Procession," *Bible Review* 13 (1997) 30-37.

PRODIGAL SON

It is no surprise that the *parable of the prodigal *son (Lk 15:11-32) remains popular among people of all backgrounds. As a character the prodigal son evokes numerous images. He is viewed as the archetypal *rebellious teenager, so much so that many would probably define *prodigal* as "wayward" instead of "wasteful." The rebelliousness of the prodigal at the outset of the story is evocative, representing a rejection of respect for parental authority, for the domestic, for the morally correct, and an embracing of the distant, the adventurous, the indulgence of forbidden appetites, the abandonment to unrestraint, the dissolute. The prodigal's riches-to-rags progression (*see* Rags to Riches) culminates in astonishing degradation, as this Jewish youth not only works among the pigs but hungers for the pods he feeds them.

Yet as powerful as the pictures of rebellion and fall are, more powerful still are the pictures of *repentance and *restoration. The prodigal son "comes to himself," possibly revealing a penitent and humble *heart, ready to act. But repentance involves the whole person—mind, heart and will—and it is possible that he is returning to his *father with the goal of repaying his debt through work. The moving scene of his newfound resolve is eclipsed by the portrayal of his father's extravagant love, as we see the *family patriarch running to his son, refusing to hear his whole apology and restoring him to the full rights of sonship.

"The Prodigal Son" is an inadequate title for this parable. The story underlying the images above is only half the parable. Too often when we think of this parable we neglect Luke 15:25-32, the older brother's story (*see* Elder Child, Elder Sibling). Given that Jesus is telling this parable in answer to objections raised by the *Pharisees and scribes (Lk 15:1-2), whom the older brother no doubt represents, we should not neglect them. The unifying character here is the father, whose gracious love is extended to both his younger, unrighteous son and his older, self-righteous son.

See also FATHER; PARABLE; RAGS TO RICHES; REBEL, REBELLION; REPENTANCE; RESTORATION; RUNAWAY; SON.

BIBLIOGRAPHY. K. E. Bailey, *Finding the Lost: Cultural Keys to Luke 15* (St. Louis: Concordia, 1992); H. J. Nouwen, *The Return of the Prodigal Son: A Story of Homecoming* (New York: Doubleday, 1992).

PROMISED LAND

The motif of the Promised Land is a major pattern in the Pentateuch and the book of Joshua. The actual phraseology does not appear until the book of Exodus, but the motif itself arises as early as the story of God's *covenant established with the patriarchs in Genesis. Here God promises to show *Abraham a *land to which he calls him (Gen 12:1 RSV), and subsequently promises to "give this land" as Abraham journeys in *obedience to God's call (Gen 12:7; see also Gen 13:15, 17; 28:13). Once the prediction that the patriarchs will inhabit the land has been stated, later generations look back to it as something that has been promised. These references begin almost immediately in the book of Exodus, as God tells *Moses at the *burning bush, "I promise that I will bring you up out of the affliction of Egypt, to . . . a land flowing with milk and honey" (Ex 3:17 RSV; *see* Land Flowing with Milk and Honey).

The imagery of the Promised Land above all paints a picture of agricultural abundance, along with the fertile soil and provident climate required for plentiful crops. The description of Moses sounds the keynotes: "The LORD your God is bringing you into a good land, a land of brooks of water, of fountains and springs, flowing forth in valleys and hills, a land of wheat and barley, of vines and fig trees and pomegranates, a land of olive trees and honey" (Deut 8:7-8

RSV; see also Deut 11:10-12). The tangible proof of the *abundance of the land is the trophy that the twelve spies bring back from their scouting expedition—a single cluster of *grapes so lush that it needs to be carried on a pole suspended between two spies, along with pomegranates and figs (Num 13:23).

The motif that the land has been promised by God to the patriarchal line is another leading emphasis. In Exodus through Joshua, we find three dozen references to the fact that God *swore*, or vowed, to give the land to the offspring of the patriarchs. The general impression is that of a father who has earmarked a possession for a child, waiting for the appointed time to hand it over. We thus find an additional three dozen references to the fact that God will *give* the land to the nation of Israel, and another three dozen to the way in which he will *bring* the nation *into* the Promised Land.

As a land of promise the land of Canaan becomes an evocative image of longing for the Israelites as they *journey toward it. It is the goal of a forty-year quest, always beckoning and receding before the people until they actually possess it in the latter stages of the book of Joshua. After the years of *exile and *slavery in Egypt, as well as the restless journey toward the Promised Land, the Israelites naturally look upon it as a contrasting fixed point of reference. It is an image of possession and security that contrasts with nearly five centuries of Israelite history preceding its attainment. Three dozen verses refer to the Promised Land as a *possession*, or as something that the people will *possess*. The picture of the security represented by having a place of one's own after years of exile and wandering is captured in verses that speak of how the Israelites will "dwell in [their] land securely" (Lev 26:5) and "live in safety" (Deut 12:10).

This does not mean, however, that the Promised Land is a place of inviolable retirement. For one thing, as long as the land remains the object of a *quest still in progress, it is a land inhabited by natives who must be subdued (Num 32:22, 29; 33:52). The Promised Land is thus an image of conquest as well as a gift conferred by God, and the book of Joshua shows how hard the task of conquest was. Furthermore, the land that had been promised could be lost. Its possession was part of God's covenant with his people, and the covenant entailed responsibility as well as promise and blessing. In a word, the Promised Land was the Israelites' conditionally. The conditions imposed by God were that "if you walk in my statutes and observe my commandments, . . . you shall . . . dwell in your land securely," but "if you will not hearken to me, . . . but break my covenant, . . . I will scatter you among the nations" (Lev 26:3-33 RSV).

See also GARDEN; LAND; LAND FLOWING WITH MILK AND HONEY.

PROPHECY IN THE NEW TESTAMENT

The issue of prophecy in the NT raises several questions. Where are the prophets? In contrast to the OT (*see* Prophecy in the Old Testament), none of the NT authors claims to be a *prophet, with the exception of John the author of *Revelation. And though Jesus was considered a prophet by some of the Jews, Christians have given more attention to his role as Son of Man, Son of God and Savior. Second, where are the prophecies? In contrast to the literary prophets of the OT, those recognized as prophets in the NT—Jesus and John the Baptist, for example—left no written records. We have only partial information in secondhand sources about what they said. Third, what is the content of NT prophecy? The absence of a definition of prophecy leaves open a key question: What distinguishes Jesus' prophetic statements from the rest of his teachings? Though everything recorded in Isaiah is considered prophetic, not everything recorded in the Gospels should be considered prophetic. However, according to the apostle Paul, prophecy in the early church was intended to strengthen, encourage and comfort the saints, and it could result in the conviction of sinners (1 Cor 14:3, 24). That tends to broaden the possibilities of what prophecy included.

While prophecy does not cease at the end of the OT, by the time of the NT its appearance has changed. Its authority is now implicit (or supported by the statement "Truly I say to you") rather than being dependent on "Thus saith the Lord." Its language is primarily prose rather than poetry (the more common form in the OT). It focuses more on individuals than on the nation of Israel and political leaders. It summons people to come to God for salvation out of a condition of permanent rebellion rather than summoning the nation of *Israel to revival out of a condition of temporary *rebellion. In the early church it is a gift of the Holy Spirit and becomes a regular part of the *worship experience rather than being part of the public life of the nation of Israel.

At its core, however, prophecy in the OT and NT is essentially the same: it is proclamation of the divine word, first in oral form and sometimes recorded in writing. Prophets are channels for God's revelation of his perspective on right and wrong, his displeasure with sin, his pleas for people to repent, his *judgment of sinners and his promise of future salvation.

The Prophets of the New Testament. Luke and John take particular interest in references to *Jesus as prophet (Lk 4:24; 7:16, 39; 13:33; 24:19; Jn 4:19; 6:14; 7:40; Acts 3:22; 7:37). That the multitudes realized Jesus was a prophet is not surprising in light of the similarity of his preaching with that of the OT prophets: promise of the coming kingdom, call to repentance, revelation of divine truth, announcements of judgment and the authority of his teaching. But it is especially his miracles and supernatural knowledge that drew attention to his status as a prophet (cf. Elijah and Elisha). However, outside of the Gospels and Acts Jesus is not referred to as a prophet.

Other than Jesus, at least twelve individuals in the

NT are recognized as prophets. John the Baptist's announcements of impending judgment and call for repentance prompt a large following of people to conclude that he is a prophet (Mt 14:5; Mk 11:32; Lk 1:76). Jesus confirms the conclusion of the multitudes, adding that John is more than a prophet (Mt 11:9). John, the author of the Apocalypse, considers himself a prophet (Rev 1:3; 10:11; 22:7, 10, 18), though his prophecy better matches the specific genre of apocalyptic. Paul may have been considered a prophet (Acts 13:1), but he never claims to be a prophet, preferring the title *apostle*—perhaps because apostle ranked above prophet in the church. Nevertheless, portions of his letters are clearly prophetic (Rom 11:25-27; 1 Cor 15:51-52; 1 Thess 4:15-17; 2 Thess 2:1-12; 2 Tim 3:1-5).

Others in the NT who prophesy are Zechariah (Lk 1:67), Anna (Lk 2:36), Caiaphas (Jn 11:49-51); Agabus (Acts 11:27-28; 21:10-11), Judas and Silas (Acts 15:32), four virgins (Acts 21:8-9), and some (maybe all) of those named in Acts 13:1. The term *prophet* appears fourteen other times in the NT in reference to contemporary prophets, usually in the plural, suggesting that prophecy was a common part of the experience of early Christians. Paul encourages the believers to seek the gift of prophecy because it builds up the church (1 Cor 12:31; 14:5, 12). False prophecy is warned against (Mt 7:15-23; 1 Jn 4:1), and one false prophet is mentioned by name (Rev 2:20).

To understand the content of NT prophecy, we are primarily limited to Jesus, John the Baptist, Paul and the Apocalypse. Of the others who prophesy, we know only the content of Zechariah's song, what Caiaphas predicts about Jesus' death and what Agabus prophesies about the impending famine in the Roman Empire and the threat of Paul's being bound in Jerusalem. We know nothing of what the prophets proclaimed in the *worship services of the early church. Though Paul declares the purpose of prophecy to be strengthening, encouraging and comforting the saints, that does not mean that anything that builds up the saints is necessarily to be considered prophecy.

Embedded in the Gospels are many prophetic statements of Jesus, but it is impossible to isolate completely the prophetic from the rest of Jesus' teachings. No one in antiquity attempted to collect the prophecies of Jesus, nor should we. Though in many ways the Gospels are a mixture of genres, the prophetic tone of much of what Jesus said is clear.

Themes and Motifs. The inspiration for Jesus' prophetic statements is the inauguration of the *kingdom, which is mentioned over one hundred times in the Gospels (e.g., Mt 3:2; 4:17). This linked Jesus closely with the OT prophets, whose prophecies he was both fulfilling and augmenting. And events such as his transfiguration and triumphal entry fulfilled OT prophecy as well as looked forward to the consummation of the prophecies of the kingdom (Mt 17:1-13; 21:1-11). The most prominent motifs of Jesus' kingdom prophecies are as follows.

Kingdom warnings. Like the OT prophets, Jesus boldly denounces the present world order. Prophetic invective is often directed at religious institutions and leaders: John and Jesus call the Pharisees and Sadducees a "brood of vipers" (Mt 3:7 RSV; 12:34; 23:33). Jesus says the Pharisees are full of "greed and wickedness" (Lk 11:39 NIV); he calls them *"hypocrites" (Mt 15:7; Lk 12:56) and "blind guides" of the *blind (Mt 15:14); he itemizes their wicked deeds and announces woes against them (Lk 11:37-54; Mt 23:1-36). John warns the Pharisees and Sadducees, "The ax is already at the root of the *trees, and every tree that does not produce good fruit will be cut down and thrown into the *fire" (Mt 3:10 NIV; cf. Mt 12:36-37). Jesus refers to "a wicked and *adulterous generation" (Mt 12:39 NIV; Lk 11:29); he calls the temple a *"den of *robbers" (Mt 21:13 NIV).

Kingdom judgments. Contrary to the Jewish notion that all descendants of Abraham are united as God's favored people, Jesus announces that he will be the cause of divisions (Lk 12:51-53), that many Gentiles will come to the kingdom, "but the sons of the kingdom will be cast out into the outer darkness" (Mt 8:11-12 NASB), that "he who is not with me is against me" (Mt 12:30 NIV; Lk 11:23), that "many are invited, but few are chosen" (Mt 22:14 NIV), that some are blessed and some are not (Mt 5:3-12; Lk 4:25-27), that "one will be taken and the other left" (Lk 17:34-35 NIV; Mt 24:40-41), that he will separate the *sheep from the *goats (Mt 25:32-34). Jesus warns Capernaum, "It will be more bearable for Sodom on the day of judgment than for you" (Mt 11:24 NIV), and he announces that Jerusalem will be destroyed (Lk 19:43-44).

Kingdom requirements. John and Jesus offer a way out of the coming judgment and into the kingdom, if people will repent (Mt 4:17; Lk 3:3, 7; 5:32; 13:3, 5; 24:47). But radical change is required: childlike faith is necessary to enter the kingdom (Mk 10:15); the wealthy can barely get in (Mk 10:23). Synonymous with the invitation to repentance is Jesus' emphasis on *cleansing and righteousness (Mt 5:20, 48; 6:33). His cursing of the *fig tree and cleansing of the *temple are symbolic acts for God's judgment and need for cleansing (Mk 11:12-17; Jn 2:14-16). Because of a lack of repentance, Jesus pronounces woes of judgment on the cities of Chorazin, Bethsaida and Capernaum (Mt 11:2-24; Lk 10:10-15).

Kingdom conditions. In contrast to the evil in the present order, Jesus inaugurates new ways of thinking and doing things in the new society. "Yet a time is coming and has now come when the true worshipers will worship the Father in spirit and truth" (Jn 4:23 NIV). Jesus breaks with Jewish tradition and heals on the sabbath (Mt 12:9-13; Mk 2:23-28; Jn 5:2-9). In the Sermon on the Mount, Jesus establishes a new morality: "You have heard that it was said, 'Love your neighbor and hate your enemy.' But

I tell you: Love your enemies" (Mt 5:43-44 NIV). A prominent characteristic of the new order is a reversal of roles: those who are poor, who mourn, who hunger and who are persecuted are blessed (Mt 5:3-12). Those who have are given more, while those who do not have lose even what they have (Mt 13:12; 25:29; Mk 4:25). Those who are blind see, and those who see are blind (Jn 9:39-41). The lame walk, the deaf hear, and the dead are raised (Mt 11:5). Those who cling to life lose it, and those who give up life gain it (Lk 17:33; Jn 12:24-25). "If anyone wants to be first, he must be the very last, and the servant of all" (Mk 9:35 NIV; Lk 22:26-27).

Kingdom consummation. The kingdom is both present and future (Mk 1:15; 8:38); the phrase "a time is coming and has now come" underscores the already/not yet dimension of the new society (Jn 4:23; 5:24-29; 16:25-26, 32). The kingdom is near (Mt 10:7); the Son of Man will come in his kingdom (Mt 16:28). The advancement of the kingdom cannot be stopped (Mt 11:12). The events of the day of the Lord will happen unexpectedly (Mt 24:40-25:13; Lk 12:35-48). The kingdom has an otherworldly dimension: the kingdom is not of this world (Jn 18:36); sin will not be present (Jn 1:29); the kingdom is full of secrets (Mt 13:11). And the kingdom will be universal: "the kingdom of God will be taken away from you and given to a people who will produce its fruit" (Mt 21:43 NIV). It is evident that the Son of Man will usher in the age of divine victory and restoration. The salvation oracles promise rest (Mt 11:25-30), renewal (Mt 19:28), inheritance (Mt 19:29), joy (Mt 25:21), feasting (Mt 22:1-14; Lk 14:15-24) and fellowship (Lk 22:29-30).

Jesus' prophetic monologue from the last week before his crucifixion, known as the Olivet Discourse, takes on a special tone. Cataclysmic natural disasters and international wars will begin to occur (Mk 13:7-8). Terrible persecution is coming (Mk 13:9-13); the worst tribulation ever will befall the world and should be avoided if possible (Mt 24:15-28). Cosmic chaos (*see* Cosmology) will accompany the arrival of the Son of Man (Mt 24:29-31). The Son of Man will sit on the throne and judge the world, sending people to eternal punishment or to eternal life (Mt 25:31-46). These words of Jesus can be identified with the *apocalyptic genre.

Literary Devices. Though NT prophecy is largely written in prose, figures of speech typical of poetry are frequent. The figurative language heightens the impact of the prophecies and may at the same time add to the mystery of what God reveals. "His winnowing fork is in his hand . . . gathering his *wheat into the barn and burning up the chaff with unquenchable fire" (Mt 3:12 NIV; *see* Harvest; Threshing). "The kingdom of heaven has been forcefully advancing, and forceful men lay hold of it" (Mt 11:12 NIV). This generation is "like children sitting in the marketplaces and calling out to others, 'We played the flute for you, and you did not dance; we sang a dirge, and you did not mourn'" (Mt 11:16-

17). "The men of Nineveh will stand up at the judgment with this generation and condemn it. . . . The Queen of the South will rise at the judgment with this generation and condemn it" (Mt 12:41-42; Lk 11:31-32 NIV). "Woe to you, because you are like unmarked *graves, which men walk over without knowing it" (Lk 11:44 NIV). "I have come to bring fire on the earth, and how I wish it were already kindled!" (Lk 12:49 NIV).

To some of Jesus' prophetic statements he adds a parable. The parable of the wineskins (*see* Wine) illustrates the new order of the kingdom (Mk 2:21-22). A series of nine parables picture the growth and importance of the kingdom (Mt 13:1-52; Mk 4:26-29). The parable about a vineyard whose tenants kill the owner's son explains why the kingdom will be taken from the Jews and offered to another nation (Mt 21:33-43). In Jesus' Olivet Discourse he includes six parables teaching faithfulness and readiness for the arrival of the Son of Man.

Understanding Prophecy. The imagery characteristic of prophecy often confuses readers, because they become frustrated when they cannot understand prophetic passages with a quick reading. But prophecy is complex, and to understand it correctly requires a careful procedure whose principles include the following:

☐ Analyze the circumstances of the author and audience.

☐ Study the OT and extrabiblical literature for background to NT prophecy.

☐ Determine what main idea the prophecy is intended to convey.

☐ Allow for powerful patterns of speech designed more for their effect on the listeners than for giving specific information about how a prophecy will be fulfilled.

☐ Recognize that prophecy is often fulfilled in two stages—at the time of Christ's first coming and at the time of his second coming.

☐ Realize that the function of prophecy is to affect the present more than to predict the future.

NT prophecy raises many questions, but for those willing to seek appropriate answers to them, it is a fascinating and rewarding study.

See also APOCALYPSE, GENRE OF; APOCALYPTIC VISIONS OF THE FUTURE; DREAMS, VISIONS; ORACLE; PROPHECY IN THE OLD TESTAMENT; PROPHET, PROPHETESS.

PROPHECY IN THE OLD TESTAMENT

The genre of OT prophecy has been identified rightly as proclamation. Indeed, the prophets themselves often rehearse their *call to proclaim their God-given messages (e.g., Jer 1:5; 2:1). Delivered orally, their messages largely took on the form of a sermonic homily designed to make known God's intentions, with a view to admonishing or encouraging hearers to respond properly to the divine word.

Literary Genres and Forms. Prophetic messages were given in a variety of literary genres. The two most common forms are the *oracle of *judgment and the oracle of *salvation or redemption. The oracle of judgment is more frequent, and it is usually built around at least two central elements: (1) accusation, giving the reason for the Lord's judgment, and (2) the announcement proper (e.g., Amos 4:1-2). Announcements of judgment were proclaimed against foreign nations and God's *covenant people, in either case aimed at individuals, *cities or countries. At times they took on the form of a woe oracle with its customary elements of invective, criticism and threat (e.g., Hab 2:6-20).

In some instances these oracles take on a universal perspective that features end-time events often presented in apocalyptic scenes, including warfare on a cosmic scale and terrifying events in the natural world causing widespread devastation (see End Times), along with a divine intervention that terminates *evil on *earth and brings ultimate deliverance for God's people. The blending together of eschatological oracles of judgment and salvation oracles may well be designated "kingdom oracles," for the judgment serves to introduce earth's final age of peace and prosperity.

Many prophecies are instructional accounts. Typical subgenres include the covenant lawsuit, containing such elements as witnesses, charges, indictment and sentencing (Is 3:13—4:1), and the disputation, featuring declaration, discussion and refutation (Mal 1:6-14). Other instructional material may contain an exhortation or warning, with a typical call to hear what the prophet is saying, together with the motive for heeding the divine summons (Mic 3), and various wisdom sayings (e.g., Is 29:16).

Several other genres can be noted, such as satire (Amos), *lament (Ezek 19), *taunt song (Nahum 3:8-13), *vision report (Ezek 1), *prayer (Jer 14:7-9) and biographical and autobiographical accounts (e.g., Ezek 24:15-27). The prophets also utilized hymns and songs on occasion (Is 42:10-13; see Music), in at least one case being drawn from the epic cycle of the *exodus (Hab 3:3-15). The prophets made use of both dominant literary vehicles, prose and poetry, the former occurring most often in biographical or autobiographical accounts, historical notices (e.g., Jer 37—44) and vision reports, and the latter being called upon in most other genres.

Literary Figures and Motifs. Whether using strictly prose or poetry, the prophet wrote in such a heightened speech and urgency of tone and message that the result yielded a literary expressiveness that can be termed "poetic." Accordingly, one is not surprised to find the free use of many of the literary features and rich imagery common to poetry.

Especially prominent are simile and metaphor. *Hosea pictures Israel's love for God as being as fleeting as a morning *cloud or early *dew (Hos 6:4); *Obadiah likens Edom's stronghold to an *eagle's nest (Obad 4); *Habakkuk compares the Deliverer of his people to a warrior (see Divine warrior) vanquishing his foes (Hab 3:8-15); and *Nahum describes God's judgmental wrath as *fire (Nahum 1:6). *Isaiah points out that humankind (all flesh) is *grass (Is 40:6). *Zephaniah charges that Jerusalem's oppressive officials are roaring *lions (Zeph 3:3), while *Zechariah calls them foolish and worthless *shepherds (Zech 11:15, 17).

Such figures are often extended into parable and allegory. Israel is likened to a fruitless *vineyard (Is 5:1-7), while Nebuchadnezzar, a great eagle, breaks off the top shoot of a cedar tree (the king of Judah) and plants it in a city of traders (Babylon; Ezek 17:1-21). The closely allied feature hypocatastasis, which is a statement that implies a comparison, is also attested. *Amos calls the socially prominent women of the northern kingdom "cows of Bashan" (Amos 4:1), and *Micah challenges Jerusalem with a reminder that it is the watchtower of the *flock (Mic 4:8).

Several figures of speech involving substitution are also in evidence, such as metonymy, synecdoche and merism. Thus Jeremiah speaks of attacking *tongues, meaning the words that drop from them (Jer 18:18); Hosea reports that the land (i.e., God's people) has departed from the Lord (Hos 1:2). Jeremiah castigates prophets and priests as godless (i.e., the false prophets and apostate priests, Jer 23:11); Nahum foresees the besiegers' fire consuming the bars (i.e., the gates) of Nineveh (Nahum 3:13); and Amos pictures the hopeless condition of the northern kingdom before its attackers by portraying the *weakness and *thirst of its young men and women (Amos 8:13).

Kindred literary figures likewise provide picturesque imagery. Isaiah personifies the desert as glad (Is 35:1), while the *mountains and hills sing and the *trees clap their hands (Is 55:12). Micah calls upon the mountains to serve as jurors before whom the Lord will present his case against Israel (Mic 6:2). With forceful apostrophe *Joel calls on the Lord to bring down his holy forces against the *armies of the earth (Joel 3:11), while personified *Zion addresses her *enemy with advice not to gloat over her desperate condition (Mic 7:8). Anthropomorphism and anthropopathism are also in evidence. Amos reports that God's eyes are against the sinful northern kingdom (9:8), and Zechariah describes God's jealousy for Zion (8:1).

Still others may be noted. For example, the prophets (especially Malachi) often employ rhetorical question and hyperbole to underscore their point. Through Jeremiah God reminds his people of his omnipresence by asking, "Am I only a God nearby . . . and not a God far away?" (Jer 23:23 NIV). Through Isaiah he asks, "Was my arm too short to ransom you?" (Is 50:2 NIV). Utilizing ladder parallelism, Micah asks the orthodox but spiritually empty citizens of his day, "Will the LORD be pleased with thousands of rams, with ten thousand rivers of oil?" (Mic 6:7 NIV). The coming *Babylonian invaders are portrayed as advancing more swiftly than leopards (Hab 1:8).

Irony, sarcasm and satire are also found in the prophetic writings. Amos tells the Israelites, "Go to Bethel and sin; go to Gilgal and sin yet more" (Amos 4:4). In a forceful touch of situational irony, the fire intended for Daniel's three companions instead consumes those who cast them into the furnace, while the three remain unscathed within the fiery furnace (Dan 3:21-27). With biting sarcasm, Nahum predicts that Nineveh's vaunted military forces will prove to be mere weak women, and will desert during the heat of battles like grasshoppers that, having had their wings dried by the sun, fly away with the warmth of the day (Nahum 3:13, 17). In a penetrating social satire, Amos points out that although the exploiters of society have built fancy houses, they will not dwell in them (Amos 5:11-12). Jonah is reprimanded by God for having more concern for the shriveled vine that gave him protection from the *sun's heat than for the souls of the *Ninevites (Jon 4:10-11).

The prophets' artistry may also be seen in their frequent use of alliteration and assonance. Thus Joel (Joel 1:15 NIV) predicts that the coming day of the Lord will be "like destruction from the Almighty" *(kešod mišadday)*, and Nahum (Nahum 2:10) pictures Nineveh's destruction with the prediction that the vaunted city will be destroyed, despoiled and denuded *(buqâ um^{e}buqâ um^{e}bullaqâ)*. Micah portrays the judgment of his land in a similar manner (Mic 1:10-16), proclaiming that Beth Ophrah (house of dust) will roll in the dust (*'apār*, Mic 1:11), while the house of Aczib (*'akzîb*, deception) will be of deceptive and disappointing (*'akzāb*) help in the coming crisis (Mic 1:14).

The prophets also delivered their messages via symbolism, whether in actions or in words. Thus Isaiah walked naked and barefoot for three years to depict the fate of Egypt before its Assyrian conquerors (Is 20:2-4); Jeremiah warned of Jerusalem's demise by smashing a potter's jar in the Valley of Hinnom (Jer 19:1-13); and Ezekiel portrayed Babylon's siege of Jerusalem by drawing a picture on a tablet and making models of siege devices, then placing an *iron pan as a wall between himself and the city he had drawn on the tablet and turning his face toward it (Ezek 4:1-3). Apocalyptic prophecies of end-times events were frequently delivered via various symbols, especially those involving *colors (Zech 1:8), *numbers (Dan 7:24-25; 8:14; 9:24-27; 12:7-12) and *animals (Dan 2; 7; 8).

In addition to the rich kaleidoscope of literary figures, the prophets made abundant use of standard motifs and themes, such as the call/answer motif (Is 65:24; Mic 3:4; Zech 13:9), the *father and the *son (Hos 11:1-3), the *husband and the *wife (Is 50:1; Jer 3:1-10; Hos 1—3), the vine and the *fig tree (Joel 1:11, 12; Mic 4:4; Zech 3:10), and the *Day of the Lord (Joel, Amos, Obad, Zeph). Especially prominent is that of the shepherd and the sheep (Is 40:11; 63:11; Jer 23:1-4; Ezek 34; 37:24; Amos 3:12; Mic 5:4; 7:14; Nahum 3:18; Zech 10:2-3; 11:4-14;

13:7). The motif of reversal or transformation is at the very heart of prophetic vision, as the prophets repeatedly paint a picture of a great reversal that is impending or envisioned as already having happened: those currently in power will be defeated, and the weak will be exalted.

A final feature of prophetic discourse is the use of fantasy—pictures of a reality that is merely imagined and violates the norms of empirical reality. An obvious example is the presence of animals and natural forces as major actors in a prophesied drama. The setting of events is often cosmic rather than localized, as such characters as God, nations and cosmic forces perform the action. In the fantastic visions of the prophets, a *river can overflow an entire nation (Is 8:5-8), a *branch can build a temple (Zech 6:12), and a ram's *horn can grow to the sky and knock *stars to the ground (Dan 8:9-10).

The Prophet's World. To read a biblical prophecy is to enter a whole world that forms the surrounding context for the prophet's oracle. In entering these prophetic worlds, we step into a royal court with Isaiah, Jeremiah and Daniel; into a priestly world of priests and liturgy with Jeremiah, Ezekiel and Malachi; into a world of social corruption and impending upheaval with Amos, Micah and Habakkuk; and into an agrarian and pastoral world with Hosea, Joel, Amos and Micah. Above all, as readers we come to realize the full significance of Israel's spiritual condition before its sovereign, holy and covenant-keeping God.

See also APOCALYPSE, GENRE OF; APOCALYPTIC VISIONS OF THE FUTURE; DREAMS, VISIONS; ORACLE; PROPHECY IN THE NEW TESTAMENT; PROPHET, PROPHETESS.

BIBLIOGRAPHY. J. Lindblom, *Prophecy in Ancient Israel* (Philadelphia: Muhlenberg, 1962); C. Westermann, *Basic Forms of Prophetic Speech* (Philadelphia: Westminster, 1967).

PROPHET, PROPHETESS

The prophet is a strong figure in the OT. There are vast differences in the personalities and particular ministries of individual figures: Elijah, wild and somewhat isolated (1 Kings 17—19); Elisha, pastorally sensitive (2 Kings 4); Amos, possessing a strong social conscience; Deborah, the wise governor (Judg 4—5); Huldah, a noted theologian (2 Kings 22); Isaiah, the distinguished courtier; Jeremiah, the sad visionary; Ezekiel, the exiled priest, to name but a few. Nevertheless, behind these differences is a clear awareness of what it means to be a prophet. Prophets such as Elijah and Elisha cut bold figures in the narrative texts that they occupy. But even the classical "writing prophets" are not anonymous, and though we learn fewer details of their lives, their individuality is apparent in varying degrees. It is interesting that although there are many, many more male prophets than there are female, gender is never raised as an issue. The female prophets are not seen as unacceptable or inferior, rather their existence is taken for granted alongside their ability to hear from God and to speak for God.

A prophet is somebody who is close to God. He or she is expected to be able to discern what God thinks about a given situation, what his attitude is toward their behavior in the past, what he requires of them in the present and how will he act in their future. A prophet is a living example of insight, dedication, holiness and commitment (Deut 18:15-22; 2 Kings 4:9). A prophet is a person with a particular calling to see or hear what God is saying, live it out in their own lives and proclaim it to the people round about. The prophet is set apart, called and sent by God himself (Jer 1:5; 7:25; Heb 1:1).

Prophets can be described as *anointed and there is often a sense of unstoppable urgency about their messages, they feel so strongly about their message or their mission that it just cannot be held in. The prophet thus stands as a reminder that God has a will for the people, that God makes demands on the people, that God cares about what they do and perhaps most of all that God genuinely wants to communicate to them.

The persons we broadly classify as "prophets" were given various titles at various times and places in Israel's history: "seer" (rō'eh, e.g., 1 Sam 9:9, 11, 19; Amos 7:12), "prophet" (nābî', e.g., Gen 20:7; Deut 34:10; Hos 6:5), "visionary" (ḥōzeh, e.g., 2 Chron 19:2; 33:18), "Servant of the LORD" (Is 20:3; 42:19; 49:5; 50:10), "Man of God" (1 Sam 2:27; 1 Kings 13; 20:28), "Son of Man" (Ezek 2:1, 3, 6, 8, etc.). The Hebrew terms rō'eh, nābî' and ḥōzeh are sometimes used with apparent discrimination (1 Chron 29:29) and sometimes in overlapping senses. The underlying historical reality and social setting of these various titles and roles is complex and has been the subject of extensive investigation. In this article we will look at the prominent images associated with this general class of figure we call "prophet" or "prophetess."

Prophets Called. Prophets sometime record call narratives to provide evidence that they are genuine, that there really has been an encounter with God which validates the prophet's credentials. Amos describes himself as one who was minding his own business when God interrupted: "I was neither a prophet nor a prophet's son, but I was a shepherd, and I also took care of sycamore-fig trees. But the LORD took me from tending the flock and said to me, 'Go, prophesy to my people Israel'" (Amos 7:14-15 NIV).

Isaiah's call narrative is one of the most memorable, for it reminds us that some prophets are best pictured as spokespersons for the heavenly court. Isaiah's call takes place in the *temple, but it transports him to the heavenly *throne:

I saw the Lord seated on a throne, high and exalted, and the train of his robe filled the temple. Above him were seraphs, each with six wings: With two wings they covered their faces, with two they covered their feet, and with two they were flying. And they were calling to one another:

"Holy, holy, holy is the LORD Almighty; the whole earth is full of his glory."

At the sound of their voices the doorposts and thresholds shook and the temple was filled with smoke. (Is 6:1-4 NIV)

The heavenly king deliberates before his council, "Whom shall I send? And who will go for us?" Isaiah answers, "Here am I. Send me!" (Is 6:8 NIV). He is then sent on a mission to a hardened Israel; "Go . . ." (Is 6:9-13).

Jeremiah's does not record so visionary a call. A voice comes to him,

Before I formed you in the womb I knew you, . . . I appointed you as a prophet to the nations. . . . Then the LORD reached out his hand and touched my mouth and said to me, "Now, I have put my words in your mouth. See, today I appoint you over nations and kingdoms to uproot and tear down, to destroy and overthrow, to build and to plant." (Jer 1:5, 9-10 NIV; cf. Is 49:1, 5)

It is Ezekiel's encounter with the king of heaven that is most startling and even bizarre to modern readers. The description is given in imagery forged on the anvil of similitude. By the Kebar River in *Babylon, "the heavens were opened and I saw visions of God" (Ezek 1:1):

I looked, and I saw a windstorm coming out of the north—an immense cloud with flashing lightning and surrounded by brilliant light. The center of the fire looked like glowing metal, and in the fire was what looked like four living creatures. (NIV)

Here begins a language-stretching description of a vehicle borne about by *angelic creatures, by wheels within wheels, a sort of throne chariot that would capture the aspirations of later Jewish mystics who wished to ascend to the heavens, walk the heavenly plain and stand before the throne of God. The *wings of the heavenly creatures beat out a sound like "the roar of rushing waters . . . like the tumult of an army" (Ezek 1:24 NIV). Ezekiel sees someone who has "the appearance of the likeness of the glory of the LORD" (Ezek 1:28 NIV) and falls face-down before him. The sonorous voice from the throne then commissions him: "Son of man, stand up on your feet and I will speak to you. . . . Son of man, I am sending you to the Israelites, to a rebellious nation that has rebelled against me; they and their fathers have been in revolt against me to this very day" (Ezek 2:1-3 NIV).

In the NT, Paul experiences a summons from the heavenly Lord that resonates with the grandeur of these classical prophetic calls. On the Damascus Road he is intercepted by a "flashing light," a voice from heaven and a commissioning as a servant and a witness to the nations (Acts 9:1-6; 22:4-16; 26:9-18). Echoing Jeremiah's call narrative, Paul says, "God who set me apart from birth and called me by his grace, was pleased to reveal his Son in me so that I might preach him among the Gentiles" (Gal 1:15-16 NIV).

Prophets of the Spirit. The prophets are people

who experience unusual workings of God's *Spirit. Saul demonstrates dervishlike behavior that was apparently expected of prophets in his day. At Gibeah, Saul meets a procession of prophets, the Spirit comes upon him, and he prophecies. But observers wonder, "Is Saul also among the prophets?" (1 Sam 10:10-11). Later we read: "The Spirit of God came even upon him, and he walked along prophesying until he came to Naioth. He stripped off his robes and also prophesied in Samuel's presence. He lay that way all that day and night. This is why people say, 'Is Saul also among the prophets?'" (1 Sam 19:23-24 NIV). Elisha calls for a *harpist to play for him, and while he is playing, the "hand of the LORD comes upon Elisha and he prophecies (2 Kings 3:15). This image of the prophet as one who is overcome by the Spirit is variously expressed: "the power of the LORD came upon Elijah" (1 Kings 18:46); Isaiah says God placed his "strong hand upon me" (Is 8:11); and for Ezekiel "the hand of the LORD was upon him" (Ezek 1:3; 3:14). Even more dramatically, the Spirit transports Ezekiel from place to place. "The Spirit lifted me up" (Ezek 3:12 NIV), or he "took me by the hair of my head" (Ezek 8:3). More sedately, Isaiah says, "the Spirit of the Sovereign LORD is on me" (Is 61:1 NIV; cf. Lk. 4:18, 21).

Prophets of Vision. Perhaps the image most commonly associated with a prophet is that of a visionary, a seer, a dreamer of *dreams, a foreteller of the future. The foreign prophet Balaam, whose prophetic powers are taken over by Yahweh as he is employed by Balak to curse Israel, captures a facet of the prophet as seer. Introducing his *oracle, he says:

The oracle of Balaam son of Beor,
  the oracle of one whose eye sees clearly,
the oracle of one who hears the words of God,
  who sees a vision from the Almighty,
  who falls prostrate, and whose eyes are opened.
    (Num 24:3-4 NIV)

References to visions may be found in Isaiah, Ezekiel, Obadiah, Micah and Nahum, usually in introducing their entire written prophecy. But among the OT prophets it is Daniel and Zechariah who have the most striking visions, earning them the adjective *apocalyptic. These latter visions are highly symbolic. Daniel's vision of four dreadful composite beasts (*see* Monsters) arising from the *sea and "one like a son of man" coming on the clouds of heaven (Dan 7:1-14) demands the aid of an angelic interpreter (Dan 7:15-27). It is a story of four *evil and beastly empires and the vindication of the people of God, Israel, the true humanity. Along with his visionary gift, Daniel is also given the divine gift of interpreting dreams, a characteristic of Israel's wise men (Dan 2; 4). Zechariah has highly symbolic visions in the night that center around the *restoration of *Jerusalem and its temple after the *exile (Zech 1—4). In the NT, *Jesus the prophet speaks of a vision of *Satan falling "like lightning from heaven" (Lk 10:18 NIV; *see* Satan Cast Down) as the *Seventy successfully deploy their mission. This profile of the prophet as

visionary suggests an extraordinary gift and calling that sees the world and its events in a different dimension, far transcending the ordinary human experience of seeing and even dreaming. But Jeremiah would remind us that the claim of a vision is not such an elite category as some might think!

"Let the prophet who has a dream tell his dream,
  but let the one who has my word speak it faithfully.
For what has straw to do with grain?" declares the
  LORD. "Is not my word like fire," declares the LORD,
  "and like a hammer that breaks a rock in pieces?"
    (Jer 23:28-29 NIV)

Prophets of the Word. As Jeremiah would remind us, prophets are figures closely associated with the word of God. *Moses is one with whom God spoke "face to face, clearly, and not in riddles" (Num 12:8 NIV), and God promises that when he raises up a prophet like Moses, "I will put my words in his mouth" (Deut 18:15-18). The classic introduction to the words of the prophet is "Thus saith the Lord." Amos is to introduce his message with, "Now then, hear the word of the LORD" (Amos 7:16 NIV). God tells Jeremiah to "say whatever I command you," and God then reaches out this hand and touches his mouth and says, "Now I have put my words in your mouth" (Jer 1:7, 9 NIV). Later, Jeremiah says, "when your words came, I ate them; they were my joy and my heart's delight." (Jer 15:16 NIV). We read of Jeremiah and Ezekiel that "the word of the LORD came" to them (e.g., Jer 1:2, 4; Ezek 1:3). When a prophet proclaims an "oracle," or "declaration," it is a "lifting up [of the voice]" (e.g., Is 13:1; 15:1; 17:1; KJV: "burden"). With such emphasis on the word of the Lord, the prophets are among the finest wordsmiths of the Bible. They are as much poets as are the psalmists, and their use of imagery is second to none. Amos snaps us to attention with his opening prophetic words:

The LORD roars from Zion
  and thunders from Jerusalem;
the pastures of the shepherds dry up,
  and the top of Carmel withers. (Amos 1:2 NIV)

And Isaiah's panorama of the new creation enlivens our imagination:

"The wolf and the lamb will feed together,
  and the lion will eat straw like the ox,
  but dust will be the serpent's food.
They will neither harm nor destroy
  on all my holy mountain,"
              says the LORD. (Is 65:25 NIV)

Prophets of Falsehood. False prophets, both male and female, and lying prophets are found in abundance in the Bible (Jer 23:9-40; Mic 2:6-11). These are not prophets of alien or false gods, which also exist, but those who purport to speak for and on behalf of the God of Israel and yet do not speak his word or reflect his character. They stand as representatives of all those in Israel who seek to treat God as if he can be manipulated or controlled, of all those who wish to find a way of providing religious support for their own greed and immorality. We find some colorful images of these false prophets. They are those who would be happy to say, "I will prophesy for you plenty of wine and beer" (Mic 2:11 NIV). They "tell fortunes for money" (Mic 3:11), "if one feeds them, they proclaim 'peace'; if he does not, they prepare to wage war against him" (Mic 3:5 NIV). And Isaiah knows well the "prophet that teaches lies" (Is 9:15 NIV).

Prophets of Symbolic Action. The prophets are sometimes called upon to embody their message or carry out symbolic actions. Hosea's *marriage to the unfaithful Gomer illustrates God's covenant relationship with unfaithful Israel. Even his children carry symbolic names: Lo-Ruhamah, "Not Loved," and Lo-Ammi, "Not My People" (Hos 1:6, 9). Isaiah has a son named Shear-Jashub, "A Remnant Will Return" (Is 7:3), and another named Maher-Shalal-Hash-Baz, "Quick to the Plunder, Swift to the Spoil" (Is 8:1-4). Isaiah goes about Jerusalem "stripped and barefoot for three years, as a sign and portent against Egypt and Cush" (Is 20:3 NIV). Jeremiah buys a plot of *land as a sign of confidence that God will restore Israel to the land after exile (Jer 32:6-15). And Ezekiel is instructed to erect a model of Jerusalem under siege and lie down on his side behind the wall, on his left side for 390 days and then on his right side for 40 days, for the sins of the house of Israel and the house of Judah respectively. He is to cook food symbolic of the food of a city under siege (Ezek 4:1-13). On another occasion he enacts Jerusalem's departure for exile (Ezek 12:1-7). It is in this prophetic tradition that we should understand Jesus' cursing of the *fig tree and his action in the temple, symbolizing the coming destruction of the temple (Mk 11:12-21). Paul, who identifies himself as being in the prophetic tradition (see above), no doubt sees his afflictions and trials as an apostle as a physical expression of his theology of the cross (e.g., 2 Cor 4:8-9; 6:4-5; 11:23-29; 12:10). He is "persecuted for the cross of Christ" and bears on his body "the marks of Jesus" (Gal 6:12, 17 NIV), by which he may mean the scars of his punishments and afflictions for the sake of the gospel.

Prophets Rejected. True prophets stand as a challenge to the people, a reminder of their need to hear God and to obey God. Many times the challenge of the prophets is deeply resented, the people do not like to be reminded of their own failure. They want to feel that God is on their side. But the prophets make it more difficult for them to believe that they and their behavior are approved by God. The reaction is to prevent the prophets from speaking at all, or worse, to *persecute them or kill them (1 Kings 18:4, 13; Neh 9:26; Jer 11:21; Mic 2:6). Thus we find images of one hundred prophets hidden in *caves from the wicked Jezebel (1 Kings 18:4, 13) and of Jeremiah placed in a *cistern, sinking down in the mud (Jer 38:6). It is no wonder that prophets advise, "do not prophesy about these things; disgrace will not overtake us" (Mic 2:6 NIV). Prophets who will prophesy victory for a king intent on going to

war are numbered four hundred to the one Micaiah son of Imlah who will boldly speak the truth, "who never prophesies anything good" about the king "but only bad" (1 Kings 22:18 NIV). Hebrews 11:32-38 includes prophets among those "who . . . were tortured and refused to be released, . . . faced jeers and flogging, . . . were chained and put in prison . . . were stoned . . . were sawed in two . . . were put to death by the sword . . . went about in sheepskins and goatskins, destitute, persecuted and mistreated . . . wandered in deserts and mountains, and in caves and holes in the ground" (NIV).

The imagery of the rejected prophet appears at several places in the Gospels. Jesus, speaking of Israel's rejection of his followers, recalls "how their fathers treated the prophets" (Lk 6:23 NIV; Mt 5:12). He laments, "O Jerusalem, Jerusalem, you who kill the prophets and stone those sent to you" (Lk 13:24 NIV). Jesus' woes against the Pharisees unleashes a series of images of Israel's crimes against the prophets: prophets killed and then honored by tombs, prophets sent by God and then killed or persecuted, prophets who have arisen since the beginning of the world and for whose blood they will be held responsible (Lk 11:47-50). The cumulative effect is that a true prophet who visits Israel is destined to be spurned. So it is no surprise that we find stories of Jesus, who in many ways fits the mold of a prophet (Lk 24:19), rejected at Nazareth (Lk 4:24) in accord with the saying "no prophet is accepted in his own hometown" (Lk 4:24), and exclaiming, "surely no prophet can die outside Jerusalem!" (Lk 13:33 NIV).

Prophets of Kingship and Warfare. We find prophets as friends and foes of the kingly court, involved in warfare and international affairs. The prophets in Israel arise with the advent of the monarchy. It is as if a king on *Zion demands an independent voice from the heavenly court who will speak the will of the heavenly king and keep Israel's monarch faithful to his calling, or redirect him when he fails. But prophets are associated with the royal court elsewhere in the ancient Near East. They function as advisers to kings and serve in other ways, such as the foreign prophet Balaam, who is called upon by the Moabite king to curse Israel. The classical prophets Isaiah and Jeremiah have access to the royal court and audiences with the king. Isaiah in particular is a courtly figure, though he may address king Ahaz "at the end of the aqueduct of the Upper Pool, on the road to the Washerman's Field" (Is 7:3 NIV). There he calms the shaken king regarding the threatened invasion by Israel and Aram: "Be careful, keep calm and don't be afraid. Do not lose heart because of these two smoldering stubs of firewood" (Is 7:4 NIV; cf. Jer 21:10; 37:16-21).

Even more revealing is the scene of 1 Kings 22, where the kings of Israel and Judah are inquiring of the prophets whether they should attack Ramoth Gilead. Four hundred prophets advise attack. Only one, Micaiah son of Imlah, will say "only what the

LORD tells me" (1 Kings 22:14). His truth-telling gains the reward of imprisonment and a diet of bread and water—until the king returns safely! (Alas, the king dies in battle.) Earlier still, the prophets Elijah and Elisha are portrayed as figures closely associated with warfare. Elijah is swept up to heaven in a fiery *chariot, with Elisha exclaiming, "My father! My father! The chariots and horsemen of Israel!" (2 Kings 2:12 NIV). These words are uttered again by King Jehoash as Elisha is dying (2 Kings 13:14). The implication seems to be that these prophetic figures are closely associated with the *divine warrior and his heavenly army's defense of Israel. It is Elisha who repeatedly warns the king of Israel of the designs of the king of Aram, so that it is said of Elisha that he "tells the king of Israel the very words you speak in your bedroom" (2 Kings 6:12 NIV). In the face of Aramaeans surrounding the city of Dothan, Elisha is boldly confident that "those who are with us are more than those who are with them." Then the eyes of Elisha's servant are opened to see what Elisha sees: "the hills full of horses and chariots of fire all around Elisha" (2 Kings 6:17 NIV).

The classical prophets strike the image of experts in international affairs. This is fitting, of course, if they are spokespersons for the heavenly king, who is Lord not only of Israel but of the entire creation. Thus we find in the prophets numerous oracles against the nations that reflect the international climate and affairs of the day. Assyria, Babylon, Egypt, Cush, Tyre and Moab are some of the nations that occupy the prophetic sights in Isaiah and Jeremiah. Amos reads off judgments against Damascus, Gaza, Tyre, Edom, Ammon and Moab before turning his attention to the domestic sins of Judah and Israel (Amos 1—2). This role of the prophets gives them a transcendent stature as figures who occupy a high turret from which they can view the nations surrounding Israel and Judah. It is fitting that Isaiah employs the image of the prophet as a *watchman who has no developments to report at the moment, but must persist at his post:

Someone calls to me from Seir,
    "Watchman, what is left of the night?
    Watchman, what is left of the night?"
The watchman replies,
    "Morning is coming, but also the night.
    If you would ask, then ask;
    and come back yet again." (Is 21:11-12 NIV)
Later we read of the watchmen of Israel lifting up their voices, for they have spotted on the horizon the Lord returning to Zion (Is 52:8).

Prophetic Schools. The image of the prophet as a lonely figure, a "voice crying in the wilderness," is not quite accurate. Saul, for example, falls in with a procession of prophets (1 Sam 10:10). Elijah, who in scene after scene is as bold and stark figure as we might expect to find, has his disciple Elisha, who calls Elijah "My father! My father!" (2 Kings 2:12 NIV). But more striking is that both Elijah and Elisha are leading figures in a "company of the prophets" (2

Kings 2:3, 5, 7, 15, etc. NIV; "sons of the prophets" KJV) that numbers no less than fifty members (2 Kings 2:7). Isaiah speaks of binding up the testimony and sealing up the law "among my disciples" (Is 8:16). John the Baptist, a prophet in the tradition of Elijah, has his disciples (Mk 2:18; 6:29; Jn 1:35, 37; 3:22, 25), and Jesus, who presents himself as a prophet (among other roles), calls disciples to himself.

Your Sons and Daughters Will Prophesy. It is clear that God's sending of prophets to Israel is a privilege, the special provision of an extra opportunity for the people to hear what should already have been understood because of its inclusion in the law. The failure to respond to this privilege in the end leads to its removal (Mic 6:8; Ps 74:6; 1 Sam 28:6; Zech 13:3-5). The last prophet in this tradition, John the Baptist, concludes a period when prophecy appears to have died out completely. John is symbolically linked with Elijah (Mt 17:9-13). Together these two remind us of the way in which the prophets stand in the messianic tradition. There was a hope that just as the prophets of old spoke out for God and told of his intervention in human history, so in the future there would be a "prophet like Moses" who would be the precursor of the supreme intervention of God in his world, and perhaps even a prophet who could reflect God with no possibility of dilution or distortion (Deut 18:15; Mt 16:14; Jn 1:21). We might say that the entire story of the prophets, beginning with the death of Moses, is in search of another "prophet like Moses." This role is fulfilled by Jesus.

In the early church the situation appears to be slightly different. It is still important that the people should hear and heed God's word and we find again those who are specially called or gifted with prophetic skills or ministry. Acts 21:9 tells of Philip's four daughters who prophesy, and 1 Corinthians 12 and 14 speaks in some detail about the exercise of prophetic gifts. However, God has now revealed himself perfectly in Christ, and the OT vision that all would be able to hear from God and speak for God in prophetic ways (Num 11:29; Joel 2:28-32) is now assumed to have been fulfilled (Acts 2:17). Every Christian is thus potentially a prophet in a way that was not true for OT believers.

See also APOCALYPSE, GENRE OF; APOCALYPTIC VISIONS OF THE FUTURE; CHEAT THE ORACLE; DREAMS, VISIONS; END TIMES; JONAH THE PROPHET; PROPHECY IN THE NEW TESTAMENT; PROPHECY IN THE OLD TESTAMENT.

BIBLIOGRAPHY. J. Blenkinsopp, *A History of Prophecy in Israel* (Philadelphia: Fortress, 1983); K. Koch, *The Prophets* (2 vols.; Philadelphia: Fortress, 1980); J. Lindblom, *Prophecy in Ancient Israel* (Philadelphia: Fortress, 1962); R. R. Wilson, *Prophecy and Society in Ancient Israel* (Philadelphia: Fortress, 1980).

PROPITIATION. *See* ATONEMENT.

PROSECUTOR. *See* LEGAL IMAGES.

PROSPERITY

Prosperity is a close relative of *abundance, but while the latter denotes that a person possesses a superlative degree of material or spiritual blessing, regardless of whether it comes by human effort or by divine grace, prosperity is success that comes to those who have been active in achieving it. Prosperity is the state of those who "have a good reward for their toil" (Eccles 4:9 RSV). After praying that the girl who comes to the *well will be the future betrothed of Isaac, the servant of Abraham watches Rebekah intent "to learn whether the LORD had prospered his journey or not" (Gen 24:21 RSV), showing the combination of divine and human effort that results in prosperity. Of similar import is the narrator's comment that "the LORD caused all that [Joseph] did to prosper in his hands" (Gen 39:3 RSV; see 2 Sam 8:6 for a similar explanation of David's military success). The most famous statement about prosperity in the Bible—the declaration in Psalm 1:3 that the godly person prospers "in all that he does"—follows on the heels of the image of the well-watered *tree that produces its *fruit in its *season, thus defining prosperity in terms of a process that leads to fulfillment of the purpose for which a thing or person was created.

Old Testament Images of Prosperity. What does prosperity look like to the OT imagination? It is conceived first in terms of fruitful *work, resulting in sustenance of physical life. Because Israel was an agrarian nation, biblical prosperity is in large part agricultural (*see* Farming). The king's prayer in Psalm 144:12-15 is a good summary of the ideal: vigorous sons, resplendent daughters, full granaries and abundant livestock. Psalm 147:12-14 adds a nationalistic note of peace within the borders and abundant crops. Equally famous is the millennial picture of every person hosting "his neighbor under his vine and under his fig tree" (Zech 3:10 RSV); to someone living in a subsistence economy, this is modest prosperity.

A second type of prosperity highly valued in the OT is *children. We catch this note in Moses' vision of the *blessings of *obedience to the *covenant: "And the LORD will make you abound in prosperity, in the fruit of your body" (Deut 28:11 RSV; see Barrenness). The townswomen who pronounce a blessing on the newly married Ruth extend the wish "May the LORD make the woman . . . like Rachel and Leah, who together built up the house of Israel. May you prosper . . . and be renowned" (Ruth 4:11 RSV). Psalm 25:13 gives a variation on the theme of domestic prosperity with the assertion that the godly person "shall abide in prosperity, and his children shall possess the land" (Ps 25:13 RSV).

The Covenant Connection. In the OT context of the covenant, prosperity is viewed as a sign of God's approval and blessing. *Abraham and all the patriarchs were very wealthy (Gen 13:2). *David acquired great wealth, and *Solomon received even

greater wealth as a mark of his acceptance by God (1 Kings 3:13). Israel entered the *Promised Land as a special gift from God. It was very rich (Ex 3:8-9)—part of the Fertile Crescent, a lucrative trade route and much desired by other, more powerful nations. Israel, however, was to always detect the hand of God in their good fortune (Deut 8:17-20; cf. Ps 24:1). To fail to do so would lead to disaster. They were responsible for the fair and proper distribution of the prosperity God had given them (Lev 25; cf. 2 Cor 8—9; 1 Tim 6:17-19).

A righteous and obedient life ought to lead inevitably to blessing and success (Deut 29:9; cf. Josh 1:7-8). Disobedience and unrighteousness would lead to disaster and impoverishment (Deut 28:29; cf. 2 Chron 24:20; Jer 22:30). God could even transfer his proffered success to *enemies instead (e.g., Lam 1:5). So David urges Solomon to be obedient (1 Chron 22:6-16; cf. 29:23). Hezekiah is a model for all those who would seek to live prosperous lives (e.g., 2 Chron 31:21; 32:27-31). Thus prosperity becomes a mark of responsible obedience to God. Continued prosperity is seen as a reward for diligence (Prov 10:2, 27), which brings a level of security (Prov 10:15; 13:8).

The Problem of the Prosperous Wicked. But prosperity is not always accompanied by righteous behavior. The prophets both demand justice for the poor (e.g., Amos 2:6-7; Mic 3:9-12) and hold out the hope for a future time of righteousness (e.g., Is 11:6, 9; 42:1). Both Jeremiah and Habakkuk express confusion as to why the wicked so frequently prosper (e.g., Jer 12:1-2; cf. Ps 37; 73). Psalm 1 depicts the prosperity of the righteous over against the desperate plight of the wicked, but frequently there is no such certainty. The equation of righteousness with wealth and *poverty with *sin ceases to be convincing. Even with hard work the outcome is uncertain (Eccles 11:6). Often it is the wicked who prosper. Sometimes "the rich" is even synonymous with "the wicked" (e.g., Ps 10; 12). Psalm 73 recounts how the speaker came near calamity occasioned by "the prosperity of the wicked" (Ps 73:3).

The most startling image of this reversal is to be found in Job, who by the canons of received wisdom ought to have prospered. At the outset he is depicted as the epitome of the wise, righteous and consequently wealthy patriarch (Job 1:1-5). But disaster strikes and deprives him of all his prosperity (Job 1:6-22). Job reaches a milestone in his intellectual quest when he decisively dissociates prosperity and suffering from a human cause, pointing out that the wicked often prosper in this life, even receiving prominent funerals (Job 21). Job's three "comforters" apply various traditional approaches in their attempt to understand his plight but are all found wanting (Job 42:7-9). The reason for Job's temporary demise remains hidden within the inscrutable counsels of God. Prosperity cannot be viewed as a metaphor for God's approval.

New Testament Reversals. Earthly prosperity as

an extension of the spiritual life is chiefly an OT theme. Of the seven dozen uses of the vocabulary of prosperity in the RSV, only two occur in the NT. Indeed, the incarnation itself is a massive *reversal (2 Cor 8:9; Phil 2:6-8). While Jesus never criticizes prosperity per se, the beatitudes promise special blessing to the poor and woe to those who are wealthy (Lk 6:20, 24; cf. Mt 5:3). Jesus' very mission is presented in terms of redistribution of wealth and a positive evaluation of the poor (Lk 1:51-53; 4:16-19). Prosperity has ceased, then, to be a metaphor of spiritual blessing and righteousness. In fact, it can serve to insulate individuals from the more important demands of the inbreaking *kingdom of God (Lk 12:13-59). The rich young man (Mk 10:17-31) is not automatically regarded as righteous and indeed fails the test, unlike the disciples of Jesus. One's *attitude* toward prosperity is now an indicator of commitment to Christ. Zacchaeus, who has become inordinately rich as a result of usury, demonstrates his repentance by making restitution (Lk 19:1-10).

*James launches into a prophetic denunciation of the wealthy who oppress their workers (Jas 2:1-7; 4:13-16: 5:1-6; cf. Amos 4:4-6). This is not to say that poverty has become a more positive metaphor under the new covenant. It is still possible for the author of 3 John to pray for the physical as well as the spiritual well-being of Gaius (3 Jn 2). In Revelation 21 the vision of the New Jerusalem affirms prosperity and material splendor. But prosperity no longer carries a semiautomatic connotation of righteousness.

Prosperity Stories. A category of biblical stories is best termed prosperity stories. Their popularity stems from the fact that they are wish-fulfillment stories in which a reader's most cherished longings for success and security are satisfied. The story of Abraham and Sarah is a story of prosperity—a combination of material and spiritual blessings and contentment after long trial of their faith. Jacob's success with his flocks and herds while working for Laban is a story of prosperity.

The story of *Joseph is par excellence a story of success, in which the family *underdog becomes an international leader and celebrity, so wealthy and powerful that he can command the resources to relocate his entire extended family in a fertile area of Egypt. The domestic counterpart to the public success of Joseph is the story of *Ruth and Boaz, narrated in a book filled with images of natural, physical, social, moral, spiritual and family well-being.

Cultures have always looked up to leaders as models of success, and they have accordingly often defined prosperity in terms of political careers. We can place here, in addition to the life of Joseph, the careers of Joshua, David, Solomon, Mordecai and Daniel.

On a national scale the settlement of Israel in the Promised Land is an extended story of prosperity in which God's people are promised and then achieve relative material and spiritual prosperity. The single most famous image of the Promised Land as a land of prosperity is the epithet for it that reverberates through the epic of the exodus—a *"land flowing with milk and honey." The grandest prosperity story in the OT is found in the visions of the *millennium.

See also ABUNDANCE; BLESSING, BLESSEDNESS; CHILD, CHILDREN; GOLD; LAND FLOWING WITH MILK AND HONEY; POVERTY; REVERSAL; SILVER; STOREHOUSE; WORK, WORKER.

PROSTITUTE, PROSTITUTION

Literal references to named prostitutes are few in the Bible. Of three, Tamar and Rahab are treated with dignity in Israel (Gen 38:6-24; Josh 2:1-21). By contrast, Delilah fits the frequent figurative portraits and metaphors of prostitutes in both the OT and the NT.

From the most common metaphors, we understand that greed feeds the *heart of a prostitute. Whether because of genuine need or base ambition, a prostitute takes the posture of grasping, seeking satiation at all costs while also promising satiation for a price. Self-indulgence is at the heart of prostitution (*see* Self-Control).

Careless Destruction—A Prostitute's Action. A prostitute, also called a harlot, is a person who provides *sexual activity in exchange for material security. Generally a *woman, she is distinguished from an *adulterer by her lack of discrimination in partner choice. *Proverbs characterizes her as loud, defiant, brazen, undisciplined and ignorant (Prov 6:26; 9:13). She is the foil of a loyal *wife, catering her attentions to the highest bidder, pursuing self-interest with numerous men rather than faithfully supporting one man.

Delilah and the foolish woman of Proverbs illustrate in action and description the treacherous ways of a prostitute. The wise teacher of Proverbs warns against the harlot's careless attitude toward clients: "the prostitute reduces you to a loaf of bread" (Prov 6:26 NIV). For hope of payment, Delilah repeatedly betrays Samson to the Philistines (Judg 16). When Samson finally confides the truth to her deviant ear, the teacher's lament regarding another *seduction scene comes to mind:

All at once he followed her
　　like an ox going to the slaughter,
like a deer stepping into a noose
　　till an arrow pierces his liver,
like a bird darting into a snare,
　　little knowing it will cost him his life.
　　(Prov 7:22-23 NIV)

Delilah's treachery, like all prostitute actions, leads to *death; warnings against this trail to the *grave punctuate the *wisdom sayings (Prov 2:16-19; 5:3-5; 7:6-27; 9:18).

Quick Profits—A Prostitute's Goal. Delilah sets the image of the greedy, smooth-talking woman. The image is metaphorically applied to Israelites who reject God's provision to seek gain from other means.

Individuals and the Israelite nation as a whole are accused of harlotry when they seek security from mediums and spiritists (Lev 20:6), military might (Nahum 3:1-4), political alliances (Ezek 23:5-6) or commerce (Is 23:17). Because they value material gain too highly, Israelites who accept bribes and abandon God's plan of social justice are also considered harlots (Is 1:21-23). Above all these, however, *idolatry stands as the most common cause for the epithet "prostitute."

"Hear, O Israel, the LORD our God, the LORD is one" (Deut 6:4 NIV). The Israelites' monotheistic stance distinguished Judaism from the polytheism of other ancient religions; the idea of monogamy thus undergirds figurative prostitute accusations. God's *covenant with Israel is comparable to a monogamous *marriage; he provides for her, raises her to a special place of *honor and asks her to support his plan. The proper response for such provision is gratitude, love and obedience; instead Israel ignores God's provision and pursues the promises of other gods in Canaan, home of God's promise. Seven times Israel is said to prostitute itself before other gods; the strong verb position of the word aptly describes Israel's betrayal (Ex 34:15, 16; Lev 17:7; Lev 20:6; Deut 31:16; 2 Chron 21:11, 13). God says it is the "spirit of prostitution" that causes Israel to "ask counsel from wooden idols" (Hos 4:12).

From *Hosea's own painful experience with Gomer, his adulterous wife, he paints one of three OT metaphors of prostitution to describe Israel's idolatrous pursuit. Like a willful woman, Israel says, "I will go after my lovers, who give me my food and my water, my wool and my linen, my oil and my drink." Hosea explains, "She has not acknowledged that [God] was the one who gave her the grain, the new wine and oil, who lavished on her the silver and gold—which they used for Baal" (Hos 2:5, 8 NIV). Israel is like Gomer, allured by the apparent easy gain of adultery.

Gomer's action further shadows Israel's as she tastes adultery, finds it lacking for all its ease and returns to her husband. Hosea accurately anticipates Israel's action: "She will chase after her lovers but not catch them; she will look for them but not find them. Then she will say, 'I will go back to my husband as at first, for then I was better off than now' " (Hos 2:7 NIV). Like Gomer, Israel prostitutes herself for lovers/idols who promise much and do not demand as much as God. When she finds their rewards lacking, she returns to God. The image of grasping for more pleasure summarizes Israel's prostitution.

By Force or by Choice—a Prostitute's Motivation. In ancient cultures a person came to prostitution either by force or by choice. Many cultures devalued female babies, so infant girls were often left to die and then picked up by people who raised them for prostitution. Their forced condition prompted mercy. By contrast, free women prostituted themselves either in worship to a pagan god or to make a living; both realms centered on securing material

*prosperity. Though many lived anonymous, a well-known professional prostitute could become quite wealthy from the gifts of her visitors. Fertility cults that worshiped Baal advocated intercourse between worshipers and religious prostitutes—both male and female—to encourage the gods to bestow greater fertility on land, livestock and people. Before the Israelites entered the Promised Land, God cautioned them against these cults: "Be careful not to make a treaty with those who live in the land; for . . . they prostitute themselves to their gods and sacrifice to them. . . . They will lead [you] to do the same" (Ex 34:15-16 NIV). When Israel followed pagan prostitute habits, Hosea indicted the nation, saying, "You have been unfaithful to your God; you love the wages of a prostitute" (Hos 9:1 NIV). The choice for either professional or religious prostitution was self-seeking, not self-sacrificial. Judgment, not mercy, followed this choice.

The Orphan Queen's Chosen Ruin. Given the motivation of force or choice, Ezekiel's image of Israel's idolatry-prostitution holds a potent completeness: God tells of *rescuing Israel from the mud as a kicking *baby with her umbilical cord still attached, and then nurturing her and adorning her with *beauty and finery. Saved from a probable life of forced prostitution, she was blessed with the finest *food and clothes and gained fame for her beauty. Yet God explains that Israel "trusted in [her] beauty and used [her] fame to become a prostitute" who, in a repulsive twist, paid others to solicit her (see Ezek 16:3-41). Israel's idolatry is pictured as an orphan-queen's choice for professional prostitution that involved both work and worship.

Though other religions suggested spiritual, cosmic reasons for prostitution, the Bible is uniform in its description of prostitution as base and animal-like, unbefitting human dignity at any level. Israel chose to follow the cults God had warned against (Ps 106:35-39). Through Jeremiah, God notes the nation's resulting brazen and degraded state in his accusation:

> On every high hill
> and under every spreading tree,
> you lay down as a prostitute. . . .
> How can you say, 'I am not defiled;
> I have not run after the Baals?' . . .
> You are a swift she-camel
> running here and there,
> a wild donkey accustomed to the desert,
> sniffing the wind in her craving—
> in her heat who can restrain her?
> (Jer 2:20, 23-24 NIV)

God had commanded Israel, "[Do] not prostitute yourselves by going after the lusts of your own heart and eyes" (Num 15:39 NIV). In his eyes prostitution is self-indulgence, not self-sacrifice.

Devastating Judgment—a Prostitute's Future. Those who traffic in base passions with many lovers risk suffering violent abuse, punishment and even death. Ezekiel warns God's unfaithful people:

This is what the Sovereign LORD says: I will stir up your lovers against you. . . . They will deal with you in fury, they will cut off your noses and your ears. . . . They will take away your sons and daughters. . . . They will leave you naked and bare, and the shame of your prostitution will be exposed. Your lewdness and promiscuity have brought this upon you, because you lusted after the nations and defiled yourself with their idols. (Ezek 23:22, 25, 29-30 NIV)

Images of prostitution are completed by judgment. In Revelation's judgment, prostitution again assumes figurative force. *Babylon, the *city of godlessness, decadence, materialism and ruthless power, is pictured as the Great Whore "which made all nations drink the maddening wine of her adulteries" (Rev 14:8 NIV). To the terror of those who sought her, her judgment results in an endless billow of smoke (Rev 19:1-3).

Judgment for prostitution, especially of a religious nature, is finally complete and without mercy, but mercy is available for the repentant heart.

Divine Mercy—a Prostitute's Hope. Prostitution is a dark background against which God's gracious *forgiveness and restoration shine bright. All three OT allegories of prostitution end with a promise that God will take back the wayward woman, forgive her *sins and establish a new, mutually loving relationship with her (Jer 3:11-18; Ezek 16:53-63; Hos 2:14-3:5; *see* Love Story).

In the NT Gospels and Epistles this note of grace is carried forward in literal accounts of prostitution. Jesus commends the sinful woman who pours *perfume and *tears on his *feet (Lk 7:36-50), because her acute awareness of failure has opened her *heart to love and believe in him. He provokes the religious leaders, saying, "The tax collectors and the prostitutes are entering the kingdom of God ahead of you" (Mt 21:31 NIV). Paul notes that even though some of the Corinthians had been engaged in prostitution, they have now been washed, sanctified and justified through Christ (1 Cor 6:9-11). Prostitution is thus revealed as an opportunity for God's forgiving, redeeming power to be made manifest.

See also ADULTERY; APOSTASY; FOLLY; IDOL, IDOLATRY; MARRIAGE; SEDUCTION, SEDUCER, SEDUCTRESS; SEX; WOMAN, IMAGES OF.

PROSTRATE. *See* LYING PROSTRATE.

PROTECTION

The biblical imagery of protection is far more extensive than the three or four dozen uses of the word in English translations by themselves would indicate. The psalms are the largest repository of images of protection.

As a point of entry, one can notice the words that are associated with the explicit vocabulary of protection. The list of associated terms includes *guard (Neh 4:9; Ps 12:7; Jn 17:12 NRSV), spread over (Ps 5:11), deliver (Ps 59:1; 91:14) and *refuge (Ps 16:1;

Is 30:2). Each of these yields a cluster of references to protection, even though the specific vocabulary may be absent. Another important thing to know is that God is overwhelmingly the One to whom the action of protection is ascribed in the Bible.

Because protection is something that intervenes between a person and something that threatens, the imagery of *hiding becomes a leading way to picture it. We read variously of protection as a hiding in "the shadow of [God's] wings" (Ps 17:8 NRSV; 57:1), in God's "shelter in the day of trouble" (Ps 27:5 NRSV) and in the "shelter" of God's "presence" (Ps 31:20 NRSV).

Military imagery forms another cluster of references to divine protection. God, for example, confronts the psalmist's *enemies, delivering by his *sword (Ps 17:13-14). When the psalmist's enemies slander him, God shoots his *arrow and wounds them suddenly (Ps 64:7). God is a "stronghold" (Ps 27:1), as well as a "strength and . . . shield" (Ps 28:7 NRSV). He is "a rock of refuge" (Ps 31:2 NRSV), a safe shelter in which to hide (Ps 31:20). His *angel "encamps around those who fear him, and delivers them" (Ps 34:7 NRSV).

Psalms of Protection. Several psalms are built around the motif of God's protection of those who trust in him. Psalm 91 is a small classic on the topic. Here the protection of God is pictured as a shelter, a *shadow, a refuge and *fortress, a deliverance from the trap of a fowler, a parent bird protecting its young with *wings and pinions, a military *shield and a dwelling place. In addition we find heightened, hyperbolic pictures of being spared on the battlefield ("a thousand may fall at your side, ten thousand at your right hand," Ps 91:7 NRSV), experiencing immunity from epidemic illness and sunstroke, and being spared from large and small dangers in traveling. To round out the vision of protection, God speaks a vocabulary based on such words as "deliver," "protect," "be with . . . in trouble" and "rescue."

Psalm 121, the traveler's statement of trust in God's protection from the dangers of a *pilgrimage, is similar. It makes protection palpable with pictures of God's being a "help" who "will not let your foot be moved," a "keeper" who functions as a "shade at your right hand," so that "the sun shall not strike you by day, nor the moon by night." In addition, God "will keep you from all evil; he will keep your life." And the totality of God's protection is rendered memorable in the Hebrew merism (naming opposites to suggest that everything between is covered as well) that God "will keep your going out and your coming in from this time on and forevermore" (RSV).

Another strategy used in Psalms is to paint a heightened picture of *danger and *terror to serve as a foil to the confidence that comes to the person who trusts in God for protection. Psalm 46 begins with a brief catalog of natural disasters—*earthquake, tidal wave, erosion. God is then introduced as the foil to such destructiveness, being portrayed as a military conqueror who can destroy the very *weapons of warfare and as a Lord of heavenly "hosts" of *armies.

Stories of Protection. God's protection is also pictured in the form of brief narratives. Several psalms, for example, employ the motif of God's miraculous protection of his holy city against threatening armies (Ps 46:4-7; 48:4-8). We also find stories in which an unseen (or seen) God intervenes miraculously to protect an individual or nation against otherwise certain destruction. A balking donkey, for example, protects Balaam's life by refusing to walk further on the path into the drawn sword of an angel (Num 22:21-35). When Elisha and his servant are surrounded by the Syrian army at Dothan, God sends a mountain full of *horses and *chariots of *fire, buttressed by Elisha's miracle of striking the enemy with blindness and leading it to Samaria (2 Kings 6:11-23), much as the striking of the men of *Sodom and Gomorrah with blindness protects Lot and his angelic visitors from the men who are pounding on his door (Gen 19:11). God also protects the city of Samaria from the besieging Assyrian army by sending a sound like an attacking army, leading the Assyrians to abandon their camp (2 Kings 7). In a similar act of protection, the angel of God kills 185,000 soldiers of the army of Sennacherib king of Assyria by night (2 Kings 19:35-36). To this can be added the *shipwreck that Paul experiences en route to Rome, when God protects the lives everyone on board (Acts 27), followed by the episode in which God protects Paul from death when he is struck by a viper on the island of Malta (Acts 28:1-6; *see* Serpent).

Summary. The images and stories of protection in the Bible reinforce two dominant themes of Scripture: the weakness and vulnerability of people and God's sovereign power and inclination to be compassionate toward the human plight.

See also ARMOR; CITY; DIVINE WARRIOR; FORTRESS, STRONGHOLD; REFUGE, RETREAT, SAFE PLACE; WALL; WEAK, WEAKNESS.

PROVERB AS LITERARY FORM

The Bible, which is replete with concise, memorable statements known as proverbs or maxims, is one of the most aphoristic books of the world. The proverb form has identifiable characteristics or motifs, and an understanding of these can enhance one's enjoyment of proverbs and appreciation for the truth that they embody.

To begin, proverbs are memorable. Their aim is to make an insight permanent. They do this by epigrammatizing an experience, stripping it down to its essence and cutting away all that is irrelevant. To achieve such permanence the creator of a proverb tries to overcome the cliché effect of ordinary discourse with special effects of language, including imagery, metaphor and tighter than-normal-syntax. When these combine, a proverb strikes us—even on first hearing—as arresting and worthy of memory.

A second excellence of proverbs is that they are simultaneously both simple and profound. On the surface level they are easily grasped and simple to understand: "He who loves money will not be satisfied with money" (Eccles 5:10 RSV). Yet at the same time proverbs express profound principles about living, and we never get to an end of their application. The proverb about the limitations of money, for example, actually expresses a double truth—that one's appetite for money is insatiable, and that money does not satisfy permanently and at the deepest level.

Another paradox of proverbs is that they are both specific and general, both particular and universal. They often speak to a very specific area of life: "Through sloth the roof sinks in, and through indolence the house leaks" (Eccles 10:18). This proverb speaks to a universal principle of life, not simply an architectural fact of negligent building maintenance. Our metaphoric roofs leak in a myriad of life's situations. Even when a proverb speaks directly instead of metaphorically, it covers a whole category of similar events and speaks to a general tendency of life. A proverb is an insight into the repeatable situations of life, and as such it covers as many examples of the phenomenon as exist in history.

Some of the qualities noted above are true of proverbs because they are frequently expressed in poetic form. Many proverbs rely on imagery rather than abstraction: "Better is a dry morsel with quiet than a house full of feasting with strife" (Prov 17:1 RSV). Beyond this, the impulse toward comparison in the form of metaphor and simile is pervasive as one area of human experience is used to cast light on another: "The path of the righteous is like the light of dawn" (Prov 4:18 RSV).

The foregoing traits of proverbs result in tremendous compression of meaning as vast areas of human experience are bought into a single focus. The proverb is an example of the human urge for order—the impulse to master the complexity of life by bringing it under the control of an observation that explains and unifies many similar experiences. Of course the context that brings a proverb to life is not the collection of proverbs but the real-life situation to which it speaks. The truthfulness of a good proverb is its truthfulness to life. The one incontrovertible proof of a proverb is a long, hard look at life around us.

See also PROVERBS, BOOK OF.

PROVERBS, BOOK OF

The book of Proverbs is a veritable gallery of images. In fact, the OT wise men have been called the photographers of the Bible because of their reliance on observation of life. Not only do proverbs often rely on the image or metaphor as their vehicle; they are also filled with concrete pictures of actions and (even more) character types such as the fool, the sluggard and the adulterer. In addition, the writer of Proverbs had a particular knack for tying his writings together with image patterns like the path or way.

Wisdom and Folly. The two dominant images in

the book are *wisdom and *folly, and the conflict between them provides plot conflict for the book as a whole. To render these two antagonists vivid, the writer personifies them as beautiful and alluring *women (especially in Prov 1—9) who build *houses, prepare *banquets and invite the public to their side in the great conflict. The book as a whole is an ever-expanding vision of wisdom and folly, as both are given character traits, typical actions, a lifestyle and an outcome to their respective destinies.

With wisdom and folly as the presiding presences in the book, a host of character types emerge as friends of these two mighty antagonists. On the virtuous side we meet people of prudence, industry, honesty, chastity, generosity and self-control. The gallery of foolish people is larger: *sluggards, dishonest people, *drunkards, *prostitutes, *adulterers, violent people, hotheads, nagging spouses, greedy people, misers, bad neighbors, liars and simpletons. For a survey of society and social types, it is hard to match the book of Proverbs.

With this heightened contrast between wisdom and folly permeating Proverbs, a plot element of conflict also serves to unify the book as a whole. The reader, moreover, is placed in a position of having to choose between the two sides in an ongoing tug-of-war, a feeling increased by the frequency with which the content is couched as exhortations or commands.

Teacher and Learner. Wisdom literature was an instruction genre in the ancient world—the equivalent of a modern classroom lecture. We might say that wisdom is taught in the classroom of the world. The classroom milieu accounts for much of the imagery and tone of Proverbs. The authority figure is variously a *teacher, a *father or a *mother— representatives of the older generation responsible for the education of the young. The recipient of the instruction is pictured as the speaker's son. The dynamics of the educational process produce the dramatic monologues that are a staple of the first nine chapters, as well as a continuous summons to listen, accompanied by promises and blessings if the young listener will heed the instruction of his parents and teachers.

The Path or Way. The most characteristic image pattern used to portray the nature of the life of wisdom is that of the *path or way. Implicit in the image are such motifs as conscious entry into an action, habitual or long-term movement in the same direction, and arrival at a destination. The image thus pictures the conduct of a person's life and the results of that conduct. Within the imagery of the path or way we find the motif of contrasting ways of good and evil (see esp. Prov 2:12-15; 4:14-19). The resultant view of the momentousness of life's choices is summed up in the proverb "He who walks in integrity walks securely, but he who perverts his ways will be found out" (Prov 10:9 RSV). The road of right conduct is imagined as level (Prov 4:26), straight (Prov 15:21), leading upward (Prov 15:24) to life and immortality (Prov 12:28).

The book of Proverbs is particularly concerned with the destructive destination of people who choose the wrong path. For example, "There is a way which seems right to a man, but its end is the way to death" (Prov 14:12; 16:25 RSV). To give in to sexual temptation is to follow "the way to Sheol, going down to the chambers of death" (Prov 7:27 RSV). The person who "wanders from the way of understanding" (Prov 21:16 RSV) is headed for death (Prov 15:24; 16:17).

Imagery related to the path or way includes such movements as *walking, *stumbling, stepping and following, as well as to the feet as the body part that is active in the venture.

Traps and Weapons. Another cluster of images pictures the ways people can mess up their lives in terms of *traps and snares. Snares are the habitat of fools; snares avoided are the reward of the wise. Proverbs attempts to be a map of life that can help the young avoid becoming stuck. The wise man labels a wide range of foolish behavior as snares to avoid: foolish words (Prov 6:2-5), sinful talk (Prov 12:13), rash decisions (Prov 20:24) and fortunes made by lying (Prov 21:6). Snares are subtly hidden along the path to prevent progress just as these actions are. The adulterer is named a deep *pit (Prov 22:14) and a narrow *well (Prov 23:27) that "lies in wait like a robber" (Prov 23:28). To give in to sexual temptation is to be like a stag caught fast and killed by an arrow, or like a *bird that rushes into a net (Prov 7:22-23).

The way folly can destroy a person is pictured in terms of an arsenal, with wisdom as protection—a "shield to those who walk in integrity" (Prov 2:7 RSV; see also Prov 30:5). The *lips of the loose woman, by contrast, are "sharp as a two-edged sword" (Prov 5:4). A person who testifies falsely "is like a war club, or a sword, or a sharp arrow" (Prov 25:18 RSV). To deceive a neighbor is like throwing "firebrands, arrows, and death" (Prov 26:18-19 RSV). Hiring a fool is as harmful, like binding "the stone in the sling" (Prov 26:8 RSV), and hiring a passing fool or drunkard is "like an archer who wounds everybody" (Prov 26:10 RSV).

Value Terms. In a book that exists to exalt the virtues of wisdom, it is not surprising that value terms figure prominently. The most obvious pattern is that of jewels, as wisdom is variously described as "adornment for your neck" (Prov 3:22 RSV), "a fair garland for your head, and pendants for your neck" (Prov 1:9 RSV), "a beautiful crown" (Prov 4:9 RSV) and "a precious jewel" (Prov 20:15 RSV). Of similar import is the imagery of *silver (Prov 2:3; 10:20) and *gold (Prov 25:11). We also find direct assertions of the value of wisdom (Prov 8:18), as well as declarations that wisdom is better or more valuable than silver or gold (Prov 3:14; 8:10, 19; 16:16). A good wife "is far more precious than *jewels" (Prov 31:10).

A variation on the motif of the superior value of wisdom is the incipient emphasis on the practical advantages that wisdom brings to a person. If one pays close attention, following the path of wisdom emerges as a gigantic success story, made all the more attractive by contrast to the destructiveness that folly brings. This is best seen in the two encomia (praise poems; *see* Encomium) that list the rewards wisdom offers (Prov 3:13-18; 8:6-21). The book of Proverbs is a continuous call to the better as contrasted to the worse, the valuable as contrasted to the worthless.

The Professions. Because wisdom literature covers all of life, the activities portrayed in Proverbs add up to a rather comprehensive survey of the professions of life. We have occasional glimpses of people who make their living by criminal means. Elsewhere we read about *farmers and businesspeople, rulers and messengers, house builders and maids, masters and servants. The portrait of the virtuous and industrious wife that concludes the book has references to buying and selling merchandise, shipping, *planting a vineyard, cloth making and sewing, and household management.

Regardless of one's profession, the book of Proverbs is preoccupied with the virtue of industriousness and the vice of sloth. The *sluggard or lazy person is a major archetype (Prov 6:9-11; 13:4; 15:19; 19:15, 24;20:4; 24:30-31, 34; 26:14-15). Contrariwise, "in all toil there is profit" (Prov 14:23). One of the most vivid portraits in the entire book is that of the self-starting and industrious ant (Prov 6:6-8). The "hand of the diligent makes rich" (Prov 10:4 RSV) and "rules" (Prov 12:24). The plans of the diligent "lead surely to abundance" (Prov 21:5 RSV), and "the soul of the diligent is richly supplied" (Prov 13:4 RSV).

Sex and Marriage. The book of Proverbs is a repository of biblical teaching about *sex and *marriage. Faithful wedded love is held up as the ideal (Prov 5:15-19). It is contrasted to various forms of infidelity, from sexual adventure with a neighbor (Prov 6:23-35) to the brazen aggressiveness of the harlot (Prov 7), often called "the loose woman." The appeal of the wise man is to have a love affair with wisdom—to "love her," "prize her highly" and "embrace her" (Prov 4:6, 8 RSV).

*Family roles and relationships—*husband, *father, *son, *wife, *mother—are continuously present. No book in the Bible gives more prominence to *women than the book of Proverbs, and its view of women is ambivalent—they can be both very good and very bad.

Everyday Realism. Wisdom has a "here and now" emphasis. The many promises of "life" (e.g., Prov 3:16) and warnings of "death" (e.g., Prov 5:5) can be overinterpreted by those familiar with the NT use of such language. Wisdom, unlike the gospel, does not promise salvation from eternal damnation. Rather, wisdom promises successful living in God's world and relief from the pain of folly. Wisdom increases the prospect of a long life, while folly sends you down the path to an early death. In the same way, the "promises" of Proverbs should not be interpreted with the same absoluteness of the other promises of Scripture. Rather than a description of guaranteed outcomes, proverbial promises describe the quality of life typically produced by wise living.

With this emphasis on living, we naturally find references to the elemental activities that make up every person's life—*eating, *drinking, *working, *sleeping, *walking, *loving, *sexual activity, *sowing and *harvesting, laughing, speaking, listening. We read in Proverbs about taking away a *garment on a cold day (Prov 25:20), pouring vinegar on a *wound (Prov 25:20), a bad *tooth (Prov 25:19), twisting a *nose to produce blood (Prov 30:33), grabbing a passing *dog by the ears (Prov 26:17) and the trials of living with a cheerful early riser (Prov 27:14). Reinforcing this sense of people engaged in everyday life is a high incidence of references to body parts—to the *feet (fifteen references), *lips (over thirty), *hands (two dozen), *tongue (nearly twenty) and *ear (more than twenty-five). Tending in the same direction are numerous references to nature, partly because a convention of proverbs is to seek analogies between human behavior and the forces of nature. Thus we find references to *water, *wind, *night, *darkness, *light, *fountains, *mountains, *trees, *clouds and *rain.

An apt summary of the range of everyday activities over which the wise man's imagination roams can be found in the catalogs of mysteries found in Proverbs 30:18-19, 21-31.

See also DISCERNMENT; FOLLY; PROVERBS AS LITERARY FORM; SLUGGARD; WISDOM.

PROVIDENCE

The providence of God encompasses two main motifs—his *provision* for his *creation and creatures and his *control* over all events and creatures (including his *guidance of them). That provision and control exert themselves in three arenas—history, nature and the lives of individuals.

God's providential control of events in a person's life is illustrated by virtually every narrative in the Bible. Sometimes God is named as an actor in the story to signal that God is orchestrating the action; for example, regarding *Joseph's success in Egypt we read that God "caused all that he did to prosper in his hands" (Gen 39:3 RSV). This explicit reference to God as an actor is so common in biblical narrative that it becomes an understood premise that God is the one who controls events in human history. If we are looking for images (notable examples) of God's providence in the Bible—stories in which events fall into a redemptive design with a heightened and perhaps surprising intricacy—we think most naturally of the stories of *Abraham, Joseph, *Ruth and *Esther. But such a list is arbitrary, since God's providential direction of history is an axiom of all biblical narrative.

Another approach to the imagery of providence in the Bible is to look at the *praise psalms. In what areas of human life does God control events? Psalm 33 shows God's actions in creation (Ps 33:6-9), in "the counsel of the nations" (Ps 33:10-17 RSV) and in the lives of believers (Ps 33:18-22). Psalm 147 traverses similar territory: God works in *nature (Ps 147:4, 8-9, 15-18), in his compassionate dealings with the downcast (Ps 147:3, 6) and in the nation of his chosen people (Ps 147:12-20). As a third test case we can consider Psalm 103, where God's redemptive actions extend to the personal life of the speaker (Ps 103:2-5), the covenant community (Ps 103:6-18) and the cosmos (Ps 103:19-22). Some of the most vivid pictures of God's providence in the Psalter are *nature psalms in which God provides *for* nature and *through* nature (Ps 65:9-13; 104). The forces of nature serve God—the *clouds are his chariot, for example, and the *winds his messengers (Ps 104:3-4). God's intimate control over the forces of nature receives its most detailed anatomy in the message from the *whirlwind near the end of the book of Job (Job 38—39).

The realms of nature and history often merge in the providential history of the Bible, with nature becoming the means by which God controls human history. The Bible pictures God as the great dispenser of *weather—for example, keeping the storms, rainfall and sunshine in his storehouse (Ps 135:7) and sending them forth according to his plan. God can close up his storehouse of *rain and cause a famine to punish ungodliness (1 Kings 17:1). He can make ravens carry bread and meat morning and night to his servant Elijah (1 Kings 17:6). He can miraculously open up his supply of flour and oil to feed a starving widow (1 Kings 17:16). He provides not only for his people but also for all the animals and living things (Ps 147:8-9).

If these are the arenas within which God's providence works, what image patterns are associated with God as the God of providence? One is God as King. David makes the picture clear: "The LORD has established his throne in the heavens, and his kingdom rules over all" (Ps 103:19 RSV). God is "a great king over all the earth" (Ps 47:2 RSV; cf. Ps 47:7), the One who "reigns over the nations" and "sits on his holy throne" (Ps 47:8 RSV). He "sits enthroned over the flood . . . as king for ever" (Ps 29:10 RSV). Human authorities are delegated by God (Rom 13:1) and also controlled by him, so that "the king's heart is a stream of water in the hand of the LORD; he turns it wherever he will" (Prov 21:1 RSV). In addition to the power of God implicit in these pictures of his kingship is his transcendence over all earthly forces, so that "none can stay his hand or say to him, 'What doest thou?' " (Dan 4:35).

A second image pattern associated with God's providential control over earthly affairs and his intervention in them is the huge forces of nature. The God of providence is frequently depicted as the *storm God. When he comes down to *rescue someone, he does so in a riot of natural forces—*wind, *rain, *hail, *thunder, *lightning (Ps 18:10-15; 77:16-19).

But if God's providence is thus pictured in images of hugeness and power, it is expressed equally in anthropomorphic images, picturing God in human terms as having *hands, *eyes, *ears and *voice. God's hand opens to give food to creatures (Ps 104:28) and to lead a person (Ps 139:10). God's eyes "run to and fro throughout the whole earth, to show his might in behalf of those whose heart is blameless toward him" (2 Chron 16:9 RSV), and his eye "is on those who fear him" (Ps 33:18 RSV). His ears are toward the cry of the righteous (Ps 34:15), and his voice is the moving spirit in a thunderstorm (Ps 29). The point of this human imagery is to show God's closeness to his creatures and the intimacy with which he enters the flow of their lives. The God of providence is like a human companion on the journey of life.

God's providence is also pictured in geographical or spatial images in which God leads the way, shows the *path or makes a *place for his people. As a *shepherd the Lord leads his followers beside quiet waters and guides them in paths of righteousness, finally bringing them to dwell in the house of the Lord (Ps 23). He will make paths straight for people who trust in him with all their hearts (Prov 3:5-6). These familiar verses, with their comforting sense of direction and place, picture God as leader and guide all the way through life and death. Joseph grasped this aspect of God's providence when he told his brothers that God, not they, had sent him ahead to Egypt in order to preserve their family line (Gen 45:7-8). God's promise to provide a "way out" for those who are tempted makes metaphoric use of the path out of a maze (1 Cor 10:13).

There is, finally, a miscellany of memorable images from the Bible that picture God's providence. One is paradise, which is an image not only of *pleasure but also of provision. The provisions for the human race pictured in Genesis 2 include nature, food, beauty, work, moral choice, human companionship and fellowship with God. God led Israel with a pillar of cloud by day and a pillar of fire by night (Ex 13:21). He used the prayer of Abraham's servant to identify a wife for Isaac (Gen 24:10-17), a sleepless night to lead a Persian king to renew contact with Mordecai and advance the Jewish cause against Haman (Esther 6), and a dream to summon Paul into Macedonia (Acts 16:9).

All of God's leading is meant to bring people to himself. His greatest provision toward that end comes in the person of Jesus Christ, who offers the ultimate living picture of God's providence. Abraham called a certain mountain "The LORD will provide" because there God provided a *lamb for the burnt offering, sparing Isaac (Gen 22:14). Jesus, the Lamb of God, came to provide the final purification for sins (Heb 1:3). The psalmist praises God for providing redemption for his people (Ps 111:9); Jesus was the full provision of that redemption. He is the King of kings, the ruler over all, the One who leads to salvation, the culmination of the abundant providence of God. God's providence, finally, is pictured in Scripture as "glorious riches" given by God to meet all human needs, and those riches are found "in Christ Jesus" (Phil 4:19 NIV).

Within a biblical understanding, all of life is evidence of God's provision, inasmuch as all existence is dependent on God. Yet notable instances of God's special or miraculous provision make up a category of narratives within the Bible that can be viewed specifically as stories of provision. The list includes God's provision of water in the wilderness for Hagar (Gen 21:15-19), a ram as a substitute sacrifice for Abraham (Gen 22), dry land for passage through the Red Sea (Ex 14—15) and the Jordan River (Josh 3), food for Elijah (1 Kings 17:1-7; 19:4-8) and the widow at Zarephath (1 Kings 17:8-16), oil for a destitute widow to sell (2 Kings 4:1-7), a protecting army of angels for Elisha (2 Kings 6:15-17), food for the multitudes in Jesus' miracles of feeding, safety for Paul when he was shipwrecked (Acts 27) and bitten by a viper (Acts 28:1-6), and protection and sustenance for the woman (Israel and the church) miraculously spared in Revelation 12:6. The epic of the exodus is a minianthology of stories of physical provision for the traveling people of God, climaxed by God's provision of a *promised land.

Psalm 23 is perhaps the supreme biblical text on providence, and it can serve as a fitting summary of biblical images of providence. In portraying God as shepherd the poet shows him in the providential roles of provider, protector and guide. God is the active shepherd; people are the sheep totally dependent on the shepherd for their continued existence. The range of provisions keeps expanding: restoration, peacefulness, guidance and safety, freedom from fear, protection and rescue (the rod and staff), food, healing, and a perpetual or eternal dwelling place. But Psalm 23 is a poem, and its final effect is affective as well as cognitive. In picturing God's providence the poem gets us to feel the contentment that comes from resting in the sufficiency of God's providence.

See also ABUNDANCE; CREATION; DISEASE AND HEALING; DRINKING; FOOD; GUIDE, GUIDANCE; HOME, HOUSE; NATURE; PROMISED LAND; PROTECTION; RESCUE.

PRUDENCE

Prudence is a character trait that describes one's ability to exercise discretion or careful management. It connotes caution, circumspection, *wisdom and *discernment—qualities not prominent in most people.

Of the seventeen references to prudence in Scripture, fifteen are in the book of *Proverbs, given for instruction; in fact, prudence is listed as one of the purposes of Proverbs: "for acquiring a disciplined and prudent life . . . for giving prudence to the simple" (Prov 1:3-4 NIV). Time and again, prudence is associated with wisdom. Wisdom calls out, "You who are simple, gain prudence; you who are foolish, gain understanding" (Prov 8:5 NIV), and wisdom dwells with prudence (Prov 8:12). Prudent persons are wise in holding their *tongue (Prov 12:16),

thinking before they leap (Prov 14:15) and seeing danger and taking *refuge (Prov 27:12). The prudent are "crowned with knowledge" (Prov 14:18) and heed correction (Prov 15:5).

The *wife of noble character found in Proverbs 31 is an excellent example of someone who displays prudence in her daily life. She is prepared for the future, considers the needs of her *family and acts wisely rather than hastily. She is shrewd in business and gives wise and faithful instruction.

It seems that the simple are most often associated with prudence (Prov 1:4; 8:5; 19:25), perhaps because prudence tends to be meek and humble (*see* Humility). There is nothing lofty about prudence: great intelligence is not needed, and simplicity takes on a kind of splendor in this virtue. The highly educated, for their part, tend toward complicated knowledge and impressive displays of wisdom; there is no room for the simple things in complex people (cf. 1 Cor 8:2-3).

During wicked times, prudence is hardly found. In Jeremiah 49:7-8 the lack of prudent wisdom plays a part in the prophecy against Edom: "Has counsel perished from the prudent? Has their wisdom decayed? . . . I will bring disaster on Esau at the time I punish him." Because no one in Edom lives according to prudence, the Edomites' ways are wicked and hated by the Lord. In Amos 5:13, Israel has become so wicked that the prudent are driven to keep quiet; there is no place for them anymore.

See also DISCERNMENT; WISDOM.

PRUNING

The word *prune* appears in the Bible in both its literal and its metaphorical sense. In the agrarian world of the Bible, pruning was a crucial process in tending *vineyards and produce-bearing *trees. Pruning embodies a paradox of life—that *growth and productivity require deprivation and stress. If left to grow unattended, a vine or *fruit tree will produce lush foliage but little fruit. That pruning was associated with life rather than death is suggested by the stipulation in the Mosaic law that the Israelites were not to prune their vineyards every seventh year, as a part of the *sabbath rest for the *land (Lev 25:3-4).

Pruning in biblical times was done with pruning hooks (Is 2:4; 18:5). These were small, sickle-shaped knives forged at spearpoint and attached to a short handle. As a tool the pruning hook in the Bible is a physical icon symbolizing *prosperity and *peace, as suggested by three famous parallel passages that speak of beating swords into plowshares and spears into pruning hooks (Is 2:4; Joel 3:10; Mic 4:3).

The word is also used in the metaphorical sense in both the OT and the NT. In Isaiah 5:6 God refers to Israel as his vineyard which has failed to yield fruit. God therefore declares that he will remove its hedge and neither prune it nor hoe it. In such a case, pruning is seen as a caretaking action connoting concern and provision for the vineyard, and refusal to prune is an act of *judgment.

Metaphoric references to pruning reach their climax in NT usage, where it is seen as a paradoxical action demonstrating the twofold character of God's grace and judgment. Romans 11:11-24 ties up the metaphor of Israel as the vineyard in the OT and Jesus' illustration of himself as the vine in John 15 (*see* Jesus, Images of). It speaks of Jesus as the good *root of an olive *branch whose old branches (Israel) have been broken off to accommodate new *grafts, the *Gentile believers. Paul here emphasizes the duality of pruning as illustrative of the nature of God: "Note then the kindness and severity of God: severity to those who have fallen, but God's kindness to you, provided you continue in his kindness" (Rom 11:22 RSV). Thus the pruning of branches can benefit the plant as a whole while destroying the parts that do not cooperate with the rest of the body. Pruning connotes growth and peace for the whole unit of a plant (or people) rather than for individual parts that do not contribute holistically to the group.

The classic passage is Christ's "true vine" discourse in *John 15:1-11, a full-fledged development of the analogy between Christ as a vine and his disciples as branches. Drawing in minute ways on actual practices of pruning, Jesus pictures the nature of Christian growth, an important part of which is that God prunes every branch that bears fruit, "that it may bear more fruit" (Jn 15:2). Far from being an image of punishment, pruning signifies nurture, growth and fruitfulness.

See also BRANCH; FARMING; FRUIT; GROW, GROWTH; TREE, TREES; VINE, VINEYARD.

PSALMS, BOOK OF

The book of Psalms cements the importance of imagery. The book's popularity with Bible readers through the centuries stems partly from the way its images connect to our emotions and experiences. As Hebrew poetry the psalms ("songs of praise" from Hebrew), lyric poems in their genre, are marked by concise wording and frequent parallelism. A reader can expect a stated topic, a development of thoughts and emotions about the topic, and a resolution of emotions at the end. Word precision and structured phrases are methods of distillation that heighten the concentration of meaning. But the images in Psalms, hinged on metaphor and simile, put a burden of interpretation on the reader.

The Reader's Work. Images encapsule truth by placing objects side by side in comparison. In this symbolism or "putting together," from the Greek *symballein,* a lesser-known object, concept or experience is explained by its association, however small, with a more familiar one. The reader must re-create the picture of the familiar image, determine the logic of its details and then apply appropriate meaning from it to increased understanding of its partner idea. This is the process of the Greek word *metaphor,* from *meta* (over) and *pherein* (to carry): to carry over meaning from one object to another. Our emotions become involved in the carryover; we translate the emotions evoked by the familiar image to the less known. Because those emotions are often universal, the author expects this. We might say that poets do not invent metaphors but discover them. The psalmist writes in images because they enable him to capture a meaning would be unavailable in any other way. The psalmist's thought is punctuated with pictures that make the meaning clearer.

The reader's work is to unpack an image carefully so as to apply its points to a more abstract idea. He or she asks questions about the image. What relationships are suggested by this image? Consider a potter and its *clay. What does the familiar image do in relation to the other? The potter shapes and creates, hones and crafts. Why does he do this? It is the nature of his position; he is glorified by the beauty he creates in an object. How does he accomplish things? With skill, time, firing the pot in stages so as to ensure the strength of a pot. What does he not do? Take orders from the clay. The apostle Paul demonstrates application of this familiar image to an unfamiliar concept (Rom 9:21), and the psalmist does the same. Both authors expect their readers to make connections from one image to the next. The skill of inference, more than any other, is the crucial skill for reading images in Psalms.

Topics of Interest. Though the possible subject list of Psalms would be quite long, we may summarize it as we would for the Bible as a whole. By way of history, narrative, poetry and letter, the Bible defines the nature of God, the righteous and the wicked, and common human experience. The Bible as a whole also demonstrates the types of relationships that humans can have with God, now and in the future. The book of Psalms aims for these goals in a poetic form: by lining up a host of familiar pictures to hold beside any main subjects that are more difficult to understand. Relational roles, character types, landscapes and structures, professions, postures, objects and emotions—these stock the poet's arsenal of images as he explores basic topics.

Images of God in the Psalter. The psalmist expresses the difficulty of describing a *God who is unlike anything in creation: "For who in the skies above can compare with the LORD? Who is like the LORD among the heavenly beings?" (Ps 89:6 NIV). Paul describes Jesus as "the image of the invisible God" (Col 1:15 NIV), and John also describes him literarily as "the Word made flesh" (Jn 1:14). Jesus is the basis of what we comprehend about God; he is the Image, the full picture, God's self-expression (but he also uses images and is described by them). The psalmist's images glimpse individual aspects of God's nature; he catalogs facets of God's character.

Three prominent images of God are *King, warrior (*see* Divine Warrior) and *fortress. From these we observe the power of images to communicate God's character: first, by understanding details of the image and then by applying their implications to God. Other images of God in Psalms can be addressed in the same way.

Consider a king: seated on a *throne (Ps 93:2; 99:1), *crowned and robed (Ps 93:1), surrounded by nobles in waiting, sovereign over the people of his kingdom, often ruler of vast domains (Ps 47:6-7), lawgiver (93:5) and peacekeeper (Ps 74:12), judge (Ps 96:10, 13; 98:9; 99:4;), maker of *war against his *enemies (Ps 10:16) and maker of *covenants with his vassal people (Ps 25; 44; 50; 55; 74; 78; 89; 103; 105; 106; 111; 132). A king's *glory is created by his wealth, his power and the loyal praises of his subjects; in this sense the whole book of Psalms can be understood as a collection of covenant hymns from loyal subjects to their great and mighty King. The details of a king's role, appearance and ability remind us of God's authority, magnificence, strength and sovereign power. God's relationship to us is described in part by the position of a king; we owe respect and service to One whose power far exceeds our own.

Along with the image of God as king, we see him in Psalms as a warrior. Being a king requires ability as a warrior and commander of an army. The psalmist highlights God's superiority over the nations' kings by describing the physical elements as his subjects and indeed soldiers: "Fire goes before him and consumes his foes on every side. His lightning lights up the world" (Ps 97:3-4 NIV). The psalmist calls on God to do battle for him (e.g., Ps 3; 7). He finds comfort in the fact that God protects him during a battle (Ps 91), and he celebrates the victories God has won on his behalf (Ps 18; 24; 68; 98).

Psalm 18 pictures an army commander on the battlefield. The psalmist begins with the physical feats of the warrior: "He parted the heavens and came down" (Ps 18:9 NIV); this approaching warrior mounts angels rather than horses and rides on the wind rather than the ground (Ps 18:10). He camps on the battlefield, making "darkness his covering, his canopy around him" (Ps 18:11 NIV). He sends preliminary troops ahead: "Out of the brightness of his presence clouds advanced, with hailstones and bolts of lightning" (Ps 18:12). He issues preattack threats and warnings (Ps 18:13) and then attacks with "arrows and . . . great bolts of lightning" (Ps 18:14). By using nature as his weapon, this warrior exceeds all other kings in his ability to defend his people from attack. These details of a warrior's attack heighten our ability to imagine God's power to conquer what threatens us.

As king, God is sovereign over his subjects; as warrior, he rules his enemies as well. These images of God suggest relationship with those who trust him. Several other images also suggest relationships of trust between God and his people: God is a *mother who has *children (Ps 131), a shepherd with *sheep (Ps 23), a *host with *guests (Ps 23:5), a *healer with patients (Ps 6:2; 30), a judge with defendants (Ps 5:3; see Legal Imagery), a boxer with an opponent (Ps 3:7; 74:11). As we consider the details and qualities that belong to each role, these familiar pictures expand our understanding of God in rela-

tionship to us.

The psalmist's images of God extend beyond relational references to objects that express God's strength or mysterious nature. God is compared to a *shield (Ps 3:3), a *cloud rider (Ps 68:4), a shadow (Ps 91:1), a *bird (Ps 91:4) and *light (Ps 104:2). These metaphors are the work of poets who observed qualities in the created realm that reflect the Creator; they challenge us to understand God in a new way, to follow the poet's experience, matching it with our own or learning from it. We confess the personhood of God and yet find that our experience in his created realm helps us to understand him more.

For example, consider the picture of God as a fortress. Psalm 18:1-2 piles up metaphors that picture God's ability to defend the speaker from harm:

I love you, O LORD, my strength.
The LORD is my rock, my fortress and my
    deliverer;
my God is my rock, in whom I take refuge.
He is my shield and the horn of my salvation
    my stronghold. (NIV)

Fortress, like *rock, *shield and *stronghold in this psalm and shelter elsewhere, indicates that God provides protection for his people. Fortress too is a military image and thus feeds the picture of God as a warrior, but it is more defensive than much other military language associated with God. In ancient Israel, when a hostile army attacked, people in outlying areas would run quickly to the closest walled city to seek refuge, and that is the picture of the divine fortress image. Such a picture evokes feelings of comfort and confidence among those who truly follow God.

Imagery of the divine always intrigues us. Though the psalmists' images associate God with relationships and things that are common to our experience, God is fundamentally unlike any of them. Psalm 23 asserts that God is a shepherd, but he really is not a shepherd. The metaphorical statement catches our attention and requires that we meditate on the question how God is like a shepherd. Occasionally, though, the metaphor does more than intrigue; it shocks us. Psalm 78, for example, recounts the history of God's relationship with Israel; it is a relationship where Israel has been rebellious. As a result, God in his anger withdrew his presence for a period of time from his people. In Psalm 78:65-66 the poet dramatically describes God's intervention on behalf of his people:

Then the Lord awoke as from sleep,
    as a man wakes from the stupor of wine.
He beat back his enemies;
    he put them to everlasting shame. (NIV)

In these verses the psalmist likens God to a soldier who rouses himself after a night of deep *sleep induced by heavy drinking. In a word, God is a warrior with a hangover. This association intends to shock the reader into considering the relationship between the two situations: a drunken officer with his duties and a once-offended God with his covenanted people. This image uniquely captures the perspective of the one who had been waiting for rescue: the time of waiting for him seemed unusually long, as is the sleep of one who has been drunk.

Images of God in the psalms deal primarily with who he is in relationship to humanity. The things to which he is compared, the pictures drawn of him, are as varied as species. Though commonly depicted as a protector and ruler, God is also imagined by the psalmist as being mysterious and in some ways beyond description, so that every image contributes to our collective and cumulative understanding of his nature.

The Righteous and the Wicked. The psalmists do not restrict their imagination to describing God and his relationship with us. A survey of the psalms shows frequent imagery associated with the nature and behavior of both those who follow God and those who hate him.

The wicked wear *pride as their necklace; they clothe themselves in *violence (Ps 73:6). They are not in touch with divine reality; indeed their reality is an illusion, like a dream (Ps 73:20). Thus they do strange and evil things, especially against godly people. They *hunt down the righteous (Ps 10:2; 11:2), casting their nets to catch them (Ps 25:15; 31:4). They eat them like bread (Ps 14:4; 53:4). They have no regard for sacred places and enter them brazenly, like a woodcutter in the forest (Ps 74:5-7). According to their deeds, wicked people are lickened to a host of dangerous and repulsive *animals. Evil people are like *snakes (Ps 58:4), wild boars (Ps 80:13), *dogs (Ps 22:16; 59:6), bees (Ps 118:12), wild beasts (Ps 74:18), *oxen (Ps 22:21) and bulls (Ps 22:12). However, the animal most often associated with the wicked is the *lion (Ps 7:2; 10:9; 17:12; 22:13; 34; 35:16; 57:4; 58:6). In such pictures lions are dangerous, hostile and ruthless—devourers of human beings, nearly impossible to defeat.

Because of their hostility and the danger that the wicked represent, the psalmist calls on God to make them like a stillborn baby, like a snail dissolving in slime (Ps 58:8). In other words, the psalmist wanted them eradicated and shamed. Poetically, the poets of the psalms also express their confidence that God will not let the pride of the wicked go unpunished. He will blow them away like smoke and *melt them like wax that gets too close to the fire (Ps 68:2). He will put them on a path that will make them slip and fall (Ps 73:18).

Opposed to the wicked are the righteous. They are described in images conveying God's special love and care for them. They are *trees planted next to water (Ps 1:3), the sheep of God's pasture (Ps 74:1; 78:52; 79:13), a fruitful *vine (Ps 80:8) and the apple of God's eye (Ps 17:8). The righteous will blossom like a *palm tree and grow like the magnificent cedars of *Lebanon (Ps 92:12). God's blessing on them is rich because they stay near his presence and so are like an "olive tree flourishing in the house of God" (Ps 52:8 NIV). While God makes the wicked stumble

on the way (Ps 73:18), he makes the righteous as sure-footed as the deer (Ps 18:13). The righteous occasionally may begin to fall, but God will catch them before they hit the ground (Ps 73:1).

Inference is the key to unlocking an image. As fruitful vines, the righteous produce good things; they walk through difficult terrain with grace, "as the deer," and God surrounds them as a father encouraging his child to walk, ready to catch them before they are hurt in the learning process. While the tone of many images of the wicked takes on animal or savage tones, the images of the righteous sustain a tone of childlike dependence and security and beauty. We begin here to see the significant choices an author makes in choosing images to establish a tone or an attitude toward something.

Images of Experience. A survey shows that images of God and of the righteous and wicked are more numerous than any other category of image in the Psalter. Even so, these just begin to describe the incredible variety that the reader of the psalms encounters. A handful of other metaphors and similes will serve as examples of images that throw new light on things, concepts, experience, relationships and people. While simply a survey, the following section reveals the magnificent diversity of images found in the book of Psalms.

Things. The psalmists employ their poetic imagination to stimulate reflection about many tangible and intangible things, setting unexpected pictures side by side. The manna in the wilderness is the "bread of angels" (Ps 78:25), while the quantity of meat God provided to the Israelites during that period is described as so abundant that it was "like dust" or even "like the sand on the seashore" (Ps 78:27 NIV). The violence of the wicked during their attack causes blood to run "like water all around Jerusalem" (Ps 79:3 NIV). Nature is used as imagery to describe other things because it is easily recognizable, familiar.

But imagery of human-made objects is also used to describe things made by God. For instance, in Psalm 19:4-6 the psalmist describes how God pitched a *tent in the heavens for the sun, which comes bursting out in the morning with all the glory and exuberance of a bridegroom on his wedding day. Compared to God himself, however, the creation wilts. God will always remain the same, but his creation "will wear out like a garment . . . and will be discarded" (Ps 102:26 NIV).

The psalmists surround God's word with images of esteem, images that capture its qualities and effect on the reader. God's word is flawless "like silver refined in a furnace of clay, purified seven times" (Ps 12:6 NIV). It is like a *lamp that illuminates the life path of the psalmist (Ps 119:105). God's word, specifically his law, is given extended attention in Psalm 19, where it is said to surpass gold in preciousness and *honey in sweetness. The poets set images of *beauty, *purity, value and *pleasure beside the thing they most treasure.

Concepts. A concept is an abstraction, often hard for us to grasp. The poets of the book of Psalms help us by associating abstract concepts with concrete images. For instance, we may have only a vague understanding of such concepts as *forgiveness, retribution or the bonds that exist between human beings. Our understanding is heightened when we read that forgiveness is analogous on a spiritual level to a good physical washing:

Wash away all my iniquity
  and cleanse me from my sin. . . .
Cleanse me with hyssop, and I will be clean;
  wash me, and I will be whiter than snow.
    (Ps 51:2, 7 NIV)

The idea of retribution—that is, that people ultimately get what they deserve—is conveyed powerfully by the frequent image that the wicked dig a hole into which they themselves later fall (Ps 7:15; 9:15) or they get stuck in the *trap that they themselves set (Ps 9:15; 57:6).

Psalm 133 is a poem celebrating the unity in a family or community. Such intimate communion is

like precious oil poured on the head,
  running down on the beard,
  running down on Aaron's beard. . . .
It is as if the dew of Hermon
  were falling on Mount Zion. (Ps 133:2-3 NIV)

Images associated with concepts often evoke emotion: the satisfaction and relief of being clean; the frustration, surprise and anger of being suddenly caught; the soothing effect of a fragrant covering. One way to understand an image, then, is to consider the emotion that might be evoked by the scene described.

Feelings. Like concepts, experiences are often inchoate and hard to grasp. The psalmists can illuminate such experiences, whether states of mind or emotions, by drawing a comparison to something concrete and better known. The utter depression of the poet in Psalm 88 is made strikingly real by its concluding line, "The darkness is my closest friend" (Ps 88:18 NIV). The psalmist expresses the overconfidence that led to his downfall by saying his *"mountain" stood "firm" (Ps 30:7 NIV). On a more positive note, the psalmist articulates his intense desire to know God more intimately with the image of a deer that *thirsts for water (Ps 42:1; cf. 63:1).

People. We have seen how the psalmists poetically describe the wicked and the righteous as classes of people. They also recognize the similarity between humanity as a whole and the dust of the earth (Ps 90:5) or the lowly *worm (Ps 22:6), or even a phantom (Ps 39:6). A psalmist will frequently turn to imagery to describe himself in his poems. In his distress he is "poured out like water" and his heart has "turned to wax" (Ps 22:14 NIV). When irrational, he is "like a brute beast" (Ps 73:22 NIV). In his weakness the psalmist is like a "leaning *wall" or a "tottering *fence" (Ps 62:3 NIV). When he laments, he sounds like a "desert owl" (Ps 102:6 NIV).

Subgenres and Tone. The psalms' images of God, human beings and nature are widely varied. It is helpful to recall the subgenres of poetry that we most often find in Psalms: *lament psalm, *praise psalm, *nature psalm, *worship psalm and *encomium. Psalms of thanksgiving, confidence, remembrance, kingship and wisdom also occur. These subgenres are identified in part by the types of images found within them. The details of the images establish the tone of the poem. Images of water provide an excellent example: we find "still waters" to walk beside in Psalm 23 but hear cries for rescue from "the miry depths" in Psalm 69:2. Both picture water, but one has a tone of rest, the other of panic. The emotions evoked by the images in a psalm join the logic of form to help a reader identify the overall purpose of the psalm.

Mythic Borrowings and Transformations. A final significant source of imagery in Psalms is the interaction with other cultures that marked every era of Israel's history. Of special note are the creation psalms that mimic the story lines of pagan creation myth (*see* Cosmology). At the foundation of Canaanite and Mesopotamian mythology is a story of the creator god's conflict with the *sea. In the Mesopotamian myth Enuma Elish we read how Marduk confronted Tiamat (the sea), defeated her and from her body constructed the universe. In the Canaanite literature from ancient Ugarit we read of Baal battling Yam (the sea) and his cohorts, including Lotan (Leviathan). The Ugaritic text is unfortunately broken after Baal defeats Yam, but it is assumed that a creation account followed in that text.

The creation account in Genesis 1—2 is strikingly different from these stories. Due to its strict monotheism, no conflict between gods can be found in the original creation story. However, the poetic genre grants freedom to the imagination, and the psalmists make use of the creation myths of other religions to confess the superiority of God. Psalm 74:13-17 reflects on creation in this way:

It was you who split open the sea by your power;
  you broke the heads of the monster in the
    waters.
It was you who crushed the heads of Leviathan
  and gave him as food to the creatures of the
    desert.
It was you who opened up springs and streams;
  you dried up the ever flowing rivers.
The day is yours, and yours also the night;
  you established the sun and moon.
It was you who set all the boundaries of the earth;
  you made both summer and winter.

Creation here is envisioned very similarly to the Mesopotamian and especially the Canaanite accounts, in that it involved a conflict between God and the sea *monster. In a number of psalms God is described as king over the floodwaters, such as in Psalm 29, a poem long considered a reflex of Canaanite poetry.

It appears that the poets of Psalms appropriated certain vivid images from the mythology of their neighbors. This was not because they shared their theological views but indeed to debunk them. By describing Yahweh as the One who vanquished the waters of chaos, they were implicitly attacking rival religions. More broadly, the poets used water imagery not just to refer to creation but to describe the forces of chaos generally. This helps explain why the psalmist often describes his troubles with the image of being neck-deep in the waters (Ps 69:1-2) and why the Red Sea is personified and pictured as locked in conflict with Yahweh when the exodus is poetically described (Ps 77:16-20; 114). Though other images of water suggest tranquillity, this set of images demonstrates the habit of garnering imagery material from cultural associations and a wide range of experiences.

The waters are opposed to the dry land, a place of security, and nothing is more different from the sea than the *mountains. Throughout the Near East the mountains were known as the place where the gods lived. Yahweh himself accommodated his revelation to the Israelites by appearing to them first on Mount *Sinai and then instructing that his *temple be built on Mount *Zion. Psalm 48 celebrates God's presence on Zion as a sign of his protection. Psalm 46 asserts a strong confidence in God even if the mountains should fall into the heart of the sea.

Conclusion. It cannot be emphasized too strongly that this essay serves merely to skim the surface of the imagery of the book of Psalms. This dictionary's individual articles unpack many of these images in detail; here we scan the horizon line of topics on which the light of images reflects, and we grasp the crucial place of inference in reading imagery in Psalms. Like other poetry the book of Psalms consists of an array of creative language and human perception in which we recognize our own experience; but the psalms offer the unique value of being infused with God's wisdom. As such, they invite and reward the reader's long and thoughtful reflection.

See also ENCOMIUM; LAMENT PSALMS; NATURE PSALMS; PRAISE PSALMS; WORSHIP PSALMS.

PUNISHMENT. *See* CRIME AND PUNISHMENT.

PURCHASE. *See* LEGAL IMAGES.

PURITY

Purity in the Bible is primarily a concern of the cultic system, the means by which God's *holiness is established and protected. From this origin purity eventually became, especially under the influence of the classical prophets, a way of speaking about moral conduct. As the understanding of purity broadened to include moral categories of conduct, symbolic literary representations of purity seemed to emerge. The distinction between pure and impure is made by God and maintained according to his instructions. Associated with God's holiness, purity is intimately related to divine election (note the theme of becoming unclean and being cut off from the people of

God, Lev 5; 7), divine presence and divine *blessing.

Purity is achieved by effort and attention and maintained by effort and attention. For *Israel life is ever-gravitating, slipping toward impurity. Like dust and dirty dishes, uncleanness requires regular action and maintenance. Uncleanness is readily communicable, in a way that holiness is not. One can be unclean without intending to or being aware of it, as by unintentionally coming in contact with a corpse/carcass—a fundamentally unclean thing (Lev 5:2). Corpse uncleanness is a significant theme in Numbers, where a *generation is dying in the *wilderness (*see* Numbers, Book of).

The line between cultic and moral purity is not always clear, and these two kinds of purity are, in fact, closely intertwined. *Washing is the primary means of cultic purification. This is taken over as an image of moral purity in Isaiah: "Wash yourselves; make yourselves clean; remove the evil of your doings from before my eyes" (Is 1:16 NRSV; also Ps 73:13: 1 Cor 6:11; Rev 22:14-15). A similar idea carried over into Christian *baptism: "you were washed, you were sanctified" (1 Cor 6:11 NRSV; Heb 10:22). It is something of a mixed metaphor. Other familiar metaphors for purity—for example, the pristine purity of *snow and *wool—combine cultic imagery and personal piety: "though your sins are like scarlet, they shall be white as snow; though they are red like crimson, they shall become like wool" (Is 1:18 NRSV; see this imagery applied to God in Dan 7:9). By this dual concern, cultic and personal, the modern reader is reminded that communal and institutional purity was usually as much a concern for the biblical writers as personal piety, and this is classical Judaism at its best.

Whereas OT purity took on the palpable forms of cultic rituals, in the NT it is more thoroughly spiritualized. When the Pharisees challenge Jesus' casual attitude toward ritual washing of *hands, Jesus articulates the principle that "whatever goes into a person from outside cannot defile, since it enters, not the heart but the stomach. . . . It is what comes out of a person that defiles" (Mk 7:18-20 NRSV; see Mk 7:1-23 for the entire narrative). Of similar spiritual import is the assertion that "no . . . impure person . . . has any inheritance in the kingdom of Christ and of God" (Eph 5:5 NRSV).

An important biblical image of purity operates indirectly, revealing impurity through the *fire of *judgment. Purifying fire separates pure metal from dross (Num 31:23) and pure works from evil ones (1 Cor 3:13). Fire is also a symbol of God's purity and sanctifying presence. From the fearfully haunting epiphany of the smoking pot and flaming torch of Genesis 15:17 to the majestic *throne and its seven torches in Revelation 4:5, God's holiness is represented by fire. We also find fire as a symbol of the purification of the servant of God in call narratives. Isaiah's unclean *lips are purified, and he is consecrated to see God, by a live coal plucked from the *altar by a seraph (*see* Angel), all while the *temple fills with smoke (Is 6:6-8). In Ezekiel's inaugural encounter with God he paints a remarkable vision of God's presence as a gleaming amber, "something that looked like fire enclosed all around" (Ezek 1:27). This purifying fire causes Ezekiel to fall on his face, but then to be raised and filled with the Spirit. The tongues of fire that appear on the heads of those at Pentecost may have a similar symbolic meaning (Acts 2:3). Purity is revealed by fire, an apt image of its sterling essence.

*Time is frequently tied to purity and impurity. In the OT there are numerous time limits for certain uncleannesses; for example, being unclean till the evening is a frequent theme in *Leviticus: "You will make yourselves unclean by these; whoever touches their carcasses will be unclean till evening" (Lev 11:24 NIV). Corpse uncleanness requires purifica- tion rituals that take seven days: "Whoever touches the dead body of anyone will be unclean for seven days" (Num 19:11 NIV). Related to this is menstrual impurity, with its monthly uncleanness and seven-day cleansing: "When a woman has her regular flow of blood, the impurity of her monthly period will last seven days, and anyone who touches her will be unclean till evening" (Lev 15:19).

See also ALTAR; CLEANSING; HOLINESS; LEVITICUS, BOOK OF; PRIEST; SACRIFICE; SANCTIFICATION; SIN; TEMPLE.

PURPLE. *See* COLORS.

PUTTING ON, TAKING OFF. *See* GAR- MENTS.

Q

QUEEN

For the most part, queens in Scripture are the consorts of male monarchs (Neh 2:6; 2 Kings 10:13; Jer 13:18; 29:2; *see* Kings, Kingship). Though infrequently titled, the *wives of the kings of Judah and *Israel are understood to be queens (Jer 44:9). However, neither the queen of Sheba (1 Kings 10:1-13; 2 Chron 9:1-12) nor Candace of Ethiopia (Acts 8:27) is linked to a king. These solitary queens evoke images of exotic places far removed from the *land of Israel, and the queen of Sheba is praised for marveling at God's works (Is 49:12; Mt 12:42).

In general the Bible describes a queen as a *woman of elegant *beauty and privileged upbringing who either bolsters arrogance through misuse of power or strengthens virtue by commanding authority for good. Though chosen for her beauty, a queen is judged by that which she chooses to pursue (*see* Choice, Stories of).

Chosen for Her Beauty. With Queen Vashti disposed of, *Esther is chosen from among hundreds of women as the most beautiful and pleasing to the king (Esther 2:17). David first observes *Bathsheba as she bathes and so is drawn to her beauty (2 Sam 11:2-3). Ezekiel describes *Israel as an orphan nurtured to beauty so great that she "rose to be a queen" (Ezek 16:13 NIV; *see* Prostitution). A queen possesses great physical beauty.

Judged for Her Choices. After a woman's beauty has landed her on the throne, her use of power determines her reputation. Many biblical queens abuse their *authority. The archetypal *evil queen in the OT is Jezebel, who persecuted the prophets of God and ultimately met her doom by being thrown from a *window in the palace and trampled past recognition by horses (1 Kings 18:4; 2 Kings 9:33). Closely linked to her is Athaliah, her daughter, who murdered her own grandchildren after her son Ahaziah died; she then assumed the throne of Judah and was later deposed by Jehoiada the priest (2 Kings 11:1-20). Less radical abuses of power are recorded of Michal, David's first wife, who mocked his *dance before the Lord (2 Sam 6:20-23), and Maacah, Asa's mother, who was removed by her son for her *idolatrous behavior (1 Kings 15:13). An elusive reference to a female *goddess, the Queen of Heaven (Jer 7:18; 44:17), can also be placed within this category of negative images. Use of power

for personal advancement is the essential action of the evil queen (Is 47:5, 7). Revelation typifies the attitude and future *judgment of the evil queen: "In the measure that she glorified herself and lived luxuriously, in the same measure give her torment and sorrow; for she says in her heart, 'I sit as queen and am no widow, and will not see sorrow' " (Rev 18:7).

Pursuit of *wisdom, righteousness or the benefit of others typifies the righteous queen. The queen of Sheba is praised for the search for wisdom that prompts her visit to Israel (Mt 12:42; Lk 11:31). Belshazzar's queen recommends Daniel's ability and righteous actions (Dan 5:10-11). Queen Vashti is dismissed by Ahasuerus (Artaxerxes) for refusing to dance before his drunken friends, an act more of dignity than of rebellion (Esther 1:9, 11). Esther's providential ascent to the throne of Persia allows her to *rescue the Jews from almost certain annihilation at the hands of Haman (Esther 2—9). Bathsheba appeals for her son to David and is subsequently *honored by *Solomon with a chair at his *right hand (1 Kings 2:19).

Although the image of *Mary as the Queen of Heaven has been popular since the Middle Ages, the NT does not support this picture. Indeed, it makes only four references to queens: twice to the Queen of Sheba (Mt 12:42; Lk 11:31), once to Candace (Acts 8:27) and once to the harlot of Babylon (Rev 18:7). The exotic queens of the first three references represent *Gentiles coming into the *kingdom of God. The last reference picks up on the negative analogy of Jezebel, conjoining the images of ruthless queen and faithless wife to portray the empty *pride of those who oppose God.

See also BATHSHEBA; KING, KINGSHIP; WOMAN, IMAGES OF.

QUEST

A quest is an action undertaken to achieve a goal. The achieving of the goal is possible only at the expense of arduous effort and a conscious process of labor. While quest stories often involve a physical journey, people undertake intellectual and spiritual quests as well as physical ones. Even quests toward a physical goal like wealth or safety need not involve travel. Furthermore, journeys of quest nearly always involve the growth of the person undertaking the quest, resulting in a moral or spiritual quest as well as a journey through space. Usually the motif of a *search is implied by the quest.

The quest is a major plot motif of literature, and it is important in the Bible as well. In the Bible people undertake quests for a *place of residence, for fulfillment of a promise, for satisfaction in love, for *peace, wealth or *wisdom, and for *salvation.

The first full-fledged quest story in the Bible is the story of *Abraham. It begins when God calls Abraham to "go from your country . . . to the land that I will show you" (Gen 12:1 RSV). The command is accompanied by God's promise that he will make of Abraham "a great nation" (Gen 12:2), which later includes the promise of a son (Gen 15:4). The twenty-five-year ordeal that follows is fueled by the dynamics of this double quest for a land and descendants. Of course it is also a spiritual quest to obey God and exercise faith in his promises. Thus Romans 4:20-21 states that Abraham "grew strong in his faith, . . . fully convinced that God was able to do what he had promised" (RSV).

For all his journeying, Abraham never achieved the quest for the land God had promised him, and although the quest for a son was fulfilled, the promise of a multitude of descendants was not fulfilled in Abraham's life. The writer of the epistle to the Hebrews interprets this as a paradigm of the Christian quest for heaven, with Abraham belonging to the company of those who "died in faith, not having received what was promised, but having seen it and greeted it from afar" as they sought a "homeland" and "a better country, that is, a heavenly one" (Heb 11:13-16 RSV).

Subsequently the personal quest of Abraham becomes the national quest of *Israel. It begins with a journey of *exodus from Egypt. But the exodus—an immediate quest to get out of an *oppressive country—is coupled with a quest to arrive at a *promised land, as God makes clear when he calls Moses at the *burning bush: "I have come down to deliver them out of the hand of the Egyptians, and to bring them up out of that land to a good and broad land, a land flowing with milk and honey" (Ex 3:8 RSV). Through disobedience the quest becomes an antiquest—a forty-year wandering in the *wilderness—but this is only a temporary detour. God never abandons his promise nor the nation its quest to enter Canaan. The epic of the exodus is thus a full-fledged quest epic—the story of a nation's journey to establish a homeland. To it can be added the book of *Joshua, a conquest narrative built around the quest to possess the Promised Land and settle in it.

The *covenant established at Mt. *Sinai and renewed by Moses in his farewell discourse in Deuteronomy adds a spiritual dimension to the national quest of Israel. With the giving of the law the national destiny of Israel becomes that of remaining the faithful people of God. This is the ultimate quest of the nation. Through disobedience, climaxed by the exile, the nation fails to achieve its quest. Part of the pathos of the story of Israel's *apostasy is the failed quest—the sad plight of a nation that allowed itself to get sidetracked from achieving a goal set before it. But even this ignominy is not total, for a remnant undertakes a quest to rebuild Jerusalem and the temple and to reestablish a national identity in the old homeland.

Stories of individual quests fit into the broader picture of Israel's national quest. The stories of the judges are stories of individual leaders who undertook quests to *rescue the nation from oppressive foreign nations and deliver it from *bondage to idolatry and disobedience. The stories of the kings of Israel and Judah follow a similar pattern, as do the careers of the prophets.

The story of *Ruth is a self-contained quest story, as the text itself hints. When Naomi attempts to renounce her ties with her daughters-in-law, she wishes that each may "find a home" (Ruth 1:9 RSV), and later Naomi asks whether it is not appropriate that she "seek a home" for Ruth (Ruth 3:1 RSV). The seeking and finding of a home is exactly what the story recounts. For Ruth it involves both a physical journey from one country to another and a spiritual journey of allegiance and trust, as indicated by her choice of Naomi's God as her God (Ruth 1:16) and by the reference to her having taken refuge under God's wings (Ruth 2:12). It is a story of virtue rewarded, as Ruth finds a husband, a home, a son and a place among God's people (even a place in the messianic line). Like other quest stories, this one narrates the gradual conquest of obstacles that stand in the way of the attainment of the goal.

The *Song of Songs has affinities with the domestic romance of Ruth and Boaz. Underlying the collection of love lyrics is the quest for satisfaction in romantic love. The book is filled with the imagery of seeking—seeking to find the beloved, to be with him or her, to marry the beloved, to have one's romantic and sexual longings filled. Whereas the voice of unsatisfied longing permeates the book of *Ecclesiastes, the voice of satisfied desire runs strong in the Song of Songs.

*Job undertakes an intellectual quest for a solution to the problem of innocent *suffering and a spiritual quest to exercise faith in the face of his undeserved suffering. In place of the conquest of physical and human obstacles on a journey through space, the narrative substitutes an anguished debate in which Job contends with bad counselors and his own rebelliousness against God. In a nutshell it is a quest for spiritual understanding and faith. In three successive cycles of speeches, we can chart Job's gradual progress, amid fits and starts, in finding answers to his questions and doubts. The plot of this quest story is expressed in microcosm in Job's early sentiment "Teach me, and I will be silent; make me understand" (Job 6:24 RSV). Although the voice from the whirlwind does not directly address Job's questions, Job's quest for understanding and faith is achieved: he comes to trust God's design for his life. The sheer extent of God's superior power and knowledge, seen in his management of the world of nature, sends the implied message that God's control over human destinies can be trusted to be even more complete and benevolent.

The narrator of the book of Ecclesiastes likewise embarks on a quest of the mind and soul rather than a physical journey (though we can infer that the quester did his share his traveling as he chased one dead end after another). The quest of the speaker is that of the human spirit—to find meaning and satisfaction in life. He records his restless searching from the superior vantage point of someone who has achieved his goal. Sensing that life itself does not offer meaning (Eccles 1:4-11), the speaker went actively in search of it—in the pursuit of wisdom, pleasure, wealth, acquisition of goods, and work. Narrative links keep the quest motif alive: "moreover I saw," "again I saw," "I have also seen." And the imagery of achieving the goal of one's quest emerges strongly at the conclusion of the work: "The end of the matter; all has been heard" (Eccles 12:13 RSV).

Underlying the book of Proverbs is a similar quest for wisdom and understanding. The prologue to the book (Prov 1:2-6) establishes this as its purpose. The very quantity of good advice that follows implies that a person who seeks for wisdom can find it. In fact, an early passage makes the motif explicit: "My son, if you receive my words . . . if you seek [understanding] like silver . . . then you will understand the fear of the LORD and find the knowledge of God. For the LORD gives wisdom" (Prov 2:1-6 RSV).

The quest motif even enters the psalms. The *lament psalms are variations of the quest to find relief from an enemy and from the injustices of life. All of them ask for God's intervention in the situation, inasmuch as the speaker cannot find the relief for which he searches. The *pilgrim psalms remind us that the entire OT institution of pilgrimages to the temple was based on a quest—a journey to meet God at a sacred place. The penitential psalms record a sinner's quest for forgiveness. Beyond these groupings within Psalms, we find that the inner drive of the psalmists was for a fuller experience of God, as in the sentiment "For God alone my soul waits in silence; from him comes my salvation" (Ps 62:1 RSV).

The life of *Jesus also follows a quest pattern. The purpose of that life was to achieve the salvation of the human race. The very name Jesus signifies this quest: "you shall call his name Jesus, for he will save his people from their sins" (Mt 1:21 RSV). As Jesus replies to Pontius Pilate, he interprets his incarnate life in terms of a quest: "For this I was born, and for this I have come into the world, to bear witness to the truth" (Jn 18:37 RSV; cf. Jn 12:27). Jesus' final journey to Jerusalem to face trial and execution is a quest, as capsulized in Luke's statement that "he set his face to go to Jerusalem" (Lk 9:51 RSV). Many of Jesus' encounters with individuals and groups represent his quest to bring them to belief, with the conversation with the Samaritan woman at the well being the classic instance (Jn 4:1-42).

The story of the early church and its growth through missionary efforts is likewise a quest story. In its early phases it is a quest simply to get the church started in Jerusalem. But as the Christianizing of the Mediterranean world proceeds, the story can be read as a quest to evangelize the world. Within the general pattern the disciples (most notably Paul) travel extensively, always in quest to plant the kingdom and win converts.

The book of *Revelation too can be read as an epic quest that Christ undertakes to establish his rule in the world. He does so partly in combat with the forces of evil, partly in his coming to Earth to gather his church. The goal of the quest is to defeat evil and usher in the bliss of heaven.

Finally, the *Bible's overarching story of salvation history is a quest story. It begins with the tragic fall of the cosmos in Genesis 3. The goal of history is to undo the damage of sin. Not until the final pages of the Bible is that goal realized. The quests of individuals and nations make up the universal history of the world between its beginning and its end.

See also FIND, FOUND; JOURNEY; PLOT MOTIFS; SEARCH, SEARCHING.

R

RACE

Imagery of racing in Scripture involves the training, skill and awards received for *running and winning a race. In Ecclesiastes a proverb notes that it is not always the best-prepared person who wins:

The race is not to the swift
or the battle to the strong,
nor does food come to the wise
or wealth to the brilliant
or favor to the learned;
but time and chance happen to them all.
(Eccles 9:11 NIV)

The joy of a trained *athlete who welcomes the race is used to picture the *sun rising "like a champion rejoicing to run his course" (Ps 19:5 NIV).

Paul draws his imagery of a race from the Hellenistic games. Comparing life to an athletic contest was a common figure used by popular preachers of moral philosophy, so Paul is by no means coining the image. Nevertheless, it is interesting to note that Corinth was the home of the biennial Isthmian games, and that Paul would almost certainly have been present in Corinth for those games during the course of his eighteen months at Corinth (Acts 18:11). This is the background for the metaphor of 1 Corinthians 9:24-27: "Do you not know that in a race all the runner compete, but only one receives the prize? So run that you may obtain it. Every athlete exercises self-control in all things. They do it to receive a perishable wreath, but we an imperishable" (RSV). The weight of the metaphor lies on the Corinthian believers adopting the singular focus and discipline of an athlete in following Christ, something Paul exemplifies in his own life (1 Cor 9:19-23). The prize of faith is imperishable (cf. 2 Tim 2:5; 4:8; 1 Pet 1:4; 5:4), not like the celery crown that was awarded to the winner of a race at the games! The metaphor breaks down in that Christians who persevere will all receive the prize.

In Philippians 3:13-14 the focus is again on a footrace: "forgetting what lies behind and straining forward to what lies ahead, I press on toward the goal for the prize of the upward call of God in Christ Jesus" (RSV). The image of "straining forward . . . press on toward the goal" evokes the picture of the racer who looks neither to the left or to the right to check the progress of the competition or to be swayed by any diversion. The eye is on the goal post, and perhaps we are to imagine the runner leaning forward at the finish line in an added effort to be the first one to cross. In this case again, the metaphor breaks down in that all will obtain the prize. The emphasis is solely on individuals keeping their eye on the true goal of their calling. Some commentators, perhaps fancifully, see in the "upward call" an allusion to the victor's being called to the podium to receive their crown. Paul employs the image of not running a footrace in vain in Philippians 2:16 and Galatians 2:2.

In Hebrews 12:1-2 we again find the image of running a race, but now with a different emphasis: "Therefore since we are surrounded by so great a cloud of witnesses, let us lay aside every weight, and sin which clings so closely, and let us run with perseverance the race that is set before us" (RSV). Having described the great examples of faith in Hebrews 11, the author now depicts them as an amphitheater crowd of witnesses observing a later generation of faithful ones. Like athletes, they must strip off all unnecessary clothing—anything that would impede their movement and speed.

See also ATHLETICS; RUNNING; WRESTLING.

BIBLIOGRAPHY. V. C. Pfitzner, *Paul and the Agon Motif: Traditional Athletic Imagery in the Pauline Literature* (Leiden: E. J. Brill, 1967).

RAGS TO RICHES

The "rags to riches" story consists of a change of fortune from social obscurity and perhaps even *poverty to social prominence and *prosperity. Two OT stories present the clearest biblical examples. *Ruth, a *widowed *foreigner in Israelite society, from hated Moabite stock, *marries a prosperous farmer and not only becomes assimilated into Jewish society but also takes her place in the messianic line. *Esther, an *orphan member of a subjected nation living in exile, marries the Persian *king.

At times the motif of the Bible's preference of the *younger child over *elder siblings merges with the motif of rags to riches. David is so obscure that at the last moment he has to be summoned from caring for sheep to be anointed king (1 Sam 16:1-13). In the story of David and Goliath too, David enters the military world as an outsider (1 Sam 17:26) and despised youngest sibling (1 Sam 17:28-29) and leaves it a national *hero who marries the king's daughter.

The story of *Job is built around a rags-to-riches motif. First Job is stripped of his prosperity, but at the end his fortunes are restored double. The same motif is given a spiritual dimension in the OT prophetic books, where the prophet predicts a coming national destruction and disgrace but nearly always ends with a vision of national fortune lavishly *restored. The parable of the *prodigal son in the NT provides a memorable rendition of the rags-to-riches motif, possibly intended to evoke the return of a beleagured and impoverished Israel to its God.

See also POVERTY; PROSPERITY; REVERSAL; RESTORATION.

RAHAB. *See* COSMOLOGY; MONSTERS.

RAIN

Rain is one of the most positive *nature images in the Bible—even more so than in literature generally. Two factors help to explain this. One is that the world of the Bible is prone to drought and aridity (*see* Dry, Drought). The other is that the world of the OT is an agrarian world in which people are aware of their dependence on *weather.

In an agrarian world rain is first of all an image of life and *abundance, since vegetation and crops depend on it. When Moses paints a picture of the abundance of the *Promised Land, he mentions that it is "a land of hills and valleys, watered by rain from the sky" (Deut 11:11 NRSV). Prosperity is measured by God's giving "rain on the earth and . . . waters on the fields" (Job 5:10 NRSV; cf. Jas 5:18). Conversely, deprivation is portrayed as a time when there is "neither *dew nor rain" (1 Kings 17:1 NRSV; cf. Is 5:6; Jer 14:4; Amos 4:7). Rain thus becomes a key exhibit in the gallery of God's acts of provision, so that a *praise psalm, for example, includes the data that God "covers the heavens with clouds, prepares rain for the earth, makes grass grow on the hills" (Ps 147:8 NRSV; cf. Is 55:10). Paul even makes rainfall a proof for God's existence when he constructs a natural theology (Acts 14:17; cf. Mt 5:45). So vibrant are the feelings of the biblical writers for the refreshment represented by rainfall that we sometimes feel the rain almost as a plant might be imagined to experience it, as we read about "ground that drinks up the rain falling on it" (Heb 6:7). In such a world the appearance of *clouds that produce no rain is one of the ultimate disappointments (Prov 25:14; Jude 12).

In keeping with the whole tenor of the Bible to provide a supernatural or spiritual backdrop to natural phenomena, the life-giving rain is more than a simple force of nature: it is nothing less than a sign of God's blessing, usually understood as a *reward for *covenant *obedience. It is thus within the context of obedience to God's law that the Israelites receive promises of God's giving them "rains in their season," so that the "land shall yield its produce" (Lev 26:4 NRSV; see also Deut 11:14; 28:12, 24; cf. 1 Kings 8:36). In the coming renewal of the earth

too, the people will "ask rain from the LORD, . . . from the LORD who makes the storm clouds, who gives showers of rain to you, the vegetation in the field to everyone" (Zech 10:1 NRSV).

The Bible's literal references to rainfall are rooted in the actual climatic conditions of Palestine. Rain in the region is seasonal and is linked to the cycles of vegetative growth, harvest and dormancy. In brief, half the year—summer—is dry, and the other half—winter (ideally starting in October)—is rainy. A good crop requires the onset of rain to enable the *seeds to germinate and grow, and rain late in the growing cycle to bring crops to maturity. Hence the references in the Bible to early rain and later rain (Deut 11:14; Ps 84:6; Joel 2:23; Jas 5:7; the variant in Jer 5:24 is "autumn rain" and "spring rain;" cf. Job 29:23; Hos 6:3; Zech 10:1). The ideal is to have sufficient rain throughout this cycle—to have rain "in its season" (Deut 28:12; cf. Lev 26:4; Jer 5:24).

While rain and the water that it brings are generally images of desire, it makes a great deal of difference to the biblical writer's imagination how the rain falls. The most soothing of all rain images is that of the gentle shower. Here we find pictures of *mist-like rain (Job 36:27), "rain that falls on the mown grass" (Ps 72:6 NRSV) and "gentle rain" that falls on *grass (Deut 32:2). Of course after a time of drought, the sound of "rushing rain" and the phenomenon of "rain in abundance" are also welcome (1 Kings 18:41; Ps 68:9).

On the far side of the continuum, rain becomes an image of terror. Here the original carries the force of torrential rain that beats down the ground and produces floods. We read about "torrents of rain" (Job 38:25), "beating rain" (Prov 28:3), "a deluge of rain" (Ezek 13:11), "torrential rains" (Ezek 38:22) and rain that beats against a house (Mt 7:25, 27). In fact, rain is sometimes an image of oppression from which vulnerable people seek shelter, an image of the hostility of what we call "the elements" (Job 24:8; Is 4:6). The forty-day rain that produced the flood is described in Genesis in terms of the sluices of heaven being opened so the water could pour out: "The fountains of the great deep burst forth, and the windows of the heavens were opened" (Gen 7:11 NRSV).

Metaphoric references to rain follow the same contours as the literal references. Most uses are positive, but a vigorous minor thread pictures ill fortune of various types as a raining down. On the positive side, godly teaching can "drop like the rain" (Deut 32:2 NRSV), and righteousness can rain from the skies (Is 45:8). When a ruler rules justly it is like "gleaming from the rain on the grassy land" (2 Sam 23:4 NRSV). On the negative side, God rains his fierce anger upon the wicked (Job 20:23) as well as coals of *fire and sulfur on them (Ps 11:6). A "wife's quarreling is a continual dripping of rain" (Prov 19:13 NRSV)—tedious, monotonous and relentless. And "a ruler who oppresses the poor is a beating rain that leaves no food" (Prov 28:3 NRSV).

See also CLOUD; DEW; DRY, DROUGHT; HAIL; MIST; SNOW; STORM; WATER; WEATHER.

RAINBOW

A rainbow is a strikingly beautiful atmospheric phenomenon. It is an arc of *colors, displaying the spectrum, which appears occasionally at the tail end of a *rainstorm as the *sun breaks through *clouds.

The rainbow takes on potent symbolic force in the Bible, beginning with the aftermath of the *flood. After the waters recede and Noah and his family once again stand on solid ground, God reaffirms his *covenant relationship with them. The rainbow becomes "the sign of the covenant" (Gen 9:12) between God and Noah. As such, it epitomizes the new relationship that exists between human beings and their Creator.

The Hebrew word for rainbow is the same word that is used to refer to the bow as a military *weapon (*qe_et*). The idea implied in the Genesis passage seems to be that God has taken the weapon that he has used to judge his creatures and hung it in the sky. When humans see a rainbow after a *storm, they are to be reassured that "never again will the waters become a flood to destroy all life" (Gen 9:15 NIV). In this passage, then, the rainbow becomes an image of God's mercy and peace after the storm of judgment.

Interestingly, the passage itself indicates that the bow is a reminder *to God* (Gen 9:16). This is best understood as an anthropomorphism, whose actual intention is to calm human fears.

Ezekiel begins his prophecy with a description of an awesome appearance of God, surrounded by radiance "like the appearance of a rainbow in the clouds on a rainy day. . . . This was the appearance of the likeness of the glory of the LORD" (Ezek 1:28 NIV). It is likely that this alludes back to Genesis 9 and indicates that God will exercise his mercy in the context of his judgment of the people for their *sins.

The same may be said of the two occurrences of the rainbow image in the book of Revelation. In Revelation 4:3 we have a context very similar to that of the Ezekiel passage, a divine *throne theophany. John sees that "a rainbow, resembling an emerald, encircled the throne" (NIV). Interestingly—though this point is debated—the occurrence of the phenomenon in Revelation 10:1 is not associated with a divine figure, but with an *angelic one. He is described as "robed in a cloud, with a rainbow above his head; his face was like the sun, and his legs were like fiery pillars" (NIV). Here again, the allusion is to the covenant with Noah and the idea of God's grace in the midst of his judgment, which is a recurrent theme in the book of Revelation.

See also CLOUD; FLOOD; RAIN; STORM.

RAM. *See* GOAT.

RANSOM

To ransom something is to pay a price to redeem it or secure its freedom. While we remember it chiefly as an image of redemption, the image figures in a range of human activities as well. The *death of a person due to one's negligence in controlling one's *ox might require a ransom (Ex 21:30). A *woman can be ransomed (Lev 19:20), an *animal can be ransomed (Lev 27:27), individual people can be ransomed (1 Sam 14:45).

Mainly, though, ransom is an image of the redemption by which God saves people from bondage or a person from eternal death. The psalmist asserts, "God will ransom my soul from the power of Sheol, for he will receive me" (Ps 49:15 RSV; see also Hos 13:14). Isaiah speaks of "the ransomed of the LORD" (Is 35:10; 51:11), and of ransoming Israel at the cost of other nations: "I give Egypt as your ransom, Ethiopia and Seba in exchange for you. Because you are precious in my sight, and honored, and I love you, I give people in return for you, nations in exchange for your life" (Is 43:3-4 NRSV).

In the NT the act of ransoming sinful humanity is ascribed specifically to Christ (Mt 20:28; Mk 10:45; 1 Tim 2:6; 1 Pet 1:18; Rev 5:9). However, the image of ransom should not be over-interpreted. The emphasis in the image of Christ's atoning work as a ransom lies in the divine costliness and the inability of humans to rescue themselves from bondage; it does not imply a figure such as Satan who has demanded and received a ransom price.

See also ATONEMENT; REDEEM, REDEMPTION.

RAPE, SEXUAL VIOLENCE

The Old Testament often describes a society or individuals in a state of moral collapse and *rebellion against God. It is not surprising, therefore, to discover that it records some horrific incidents of sexual *violence: when people are alienated from God, depravity and violence are inevitable. Biblical stories of rape are infrequent but vivid, including the story of Dinah's rape and the resulting sexual retaliation by her brothers (Gen 34), the abuse to death of the Levite's concubine (Judg 19) and Amnon's rape of his sister Tamar (2 Sam 13:1-21). In a similar vein are pictures in the prophetic books of the ravishing of *wives and *virgins as the aftermath of a nation's being conquered (Is 13:16; Lam 5:11; Zech 14:2).

In a book as realistic as the Bible, we expect to find stories of sexual violence. What is unexpected, perhaps, is the prophets' use of savage sexual imagery. What do these images evoke? Isaiah portrays the fall of *Babylon and graphically depicts the humiliating fate of the captive *slave girl:

Go down, sit in the dust,
  Virgin Daughter of Babylon. . . .
Lift up your skirts, bare your legs,
  and wade through the streams.
Your nakedness will be exposed
  and your shame uncovered. (Is 47:1-3 NIV)

Babylon is being *judged for its war crimes. The proud, spoiled woman is ousted from her throne and sits in the dust. The lady of leisure is forced into labor, grinding flour. She is taken into *exile and is violated, her *nakedness exposed.

Jerusalem's *adultery in worshiping the false gods of the surrounding nations and breaking *covenant with Yahweh is punished equally severely. The images combined in Ezekiel's allegory seem to suggest gang rape:

> Therefore, you prostitute, hear the word of the LORD! . . . I am going to gather all your lovers, with whom you found pleasure, those you loved as well as those you hated. I will gather them against you from all around and will strip you in front of them, and they will see all your nakedness. . . . Then I will hand you over to your lovers. . . . They will strip you of your clothes and take your fine jewelry and leave you naked and bare. They will bring a mob against you, who will stone you and hack you to pieces with their swords. (Ezek 16:35-41 NIV)

Israel had adopted the sexual promiscuity of the pagan religions and practiced child *sacrifice, but its allies in these *abominations now become the means of its destruction. The language of the allegory shifts back and forth from the figure of Jerusalem the *prostitute (stripped of clothes and *jewelry, stoned and put to the sword) to the tangible destruction of the land (mounds and shrines destroyed and houses burned).

The nation (Jerusalem, Samaria, *Nineveh) as a shameless, degenerate prostitute, who is punished by being publicly abused and disgraced, is a recurrent metaphor (Jer 13:22, 26; Ezek 23; Hos 2:3, 9; Nahum 3:5-6). Jerusalem is told, "It is because of your many sins that your skirts have been torn off and your body mistreated" (Jer 13:22 NIV). Nineveh is warned, "I will lift your skirts over your face. I will show the nations your nakedness and the kingdoms your shame. I will pelt you with filth, I will treat you with contempt and make you a spectacle" (Nahum 3:5-6 NIV). The shocking images convey the prophets' abhorrence of decadence and apostasy. The picture would not be complete, however, without adding that despite Jerusalem's degradation, God promises to establish an everlasting covenant and to "make atonement . . . for all you have done" (NIV; see Ezek 16:59-63).

See also ADULTERY; PROSTITUTE; SEX; VIOLENCE, STORIES OF.

RASHNESS. *See* BRASHNESS.

REAPING. *See* HARVEST.

REBEL, REBELLION

Images of rebellion are more important than is commonly realized. English translations use the vocabulary of rebellion well over a hundred times (NRSV 126; NIV 171). The prominence of the image is explainable if we consider how thoroughly ingrained patterns of *authority were in ancient cultures. Not to respect and obey legitimate authority, whether human or divine, is to be guilty of rebellion. Within such a context the act of disobedience to God's *law is typically pictured as an act of rebellion against God. In the Bible the archetypal rebel is a figure of reproach, in contrast to the Romantic and modern glorification of the type.

The image can be traced in two complementary ways. One is to catalog the types of activity that are labeled as acts of rebellion. The Israelites rebelled against the leadership of *Moses (Num 16:41; 17:10) and against the commands of God (Num 20:24; 26:9; Deut 1:26; etc.). *Children who disobey their parents are said to be rebellious (Deut 21:18-20; Rom 1:30). In Samuel's farewell discourse to the nation, which is also an inauguration of Saul as *king, he links disobedience of God's commands with rebellion (1 Sam 12:15). In Samuel's denunciation of Saul's subsequent disobedience, he likewise calls it a *sin of rebellion (1 Sam 15:23). Subject nations rebel against their captors (2 Kings 1:1; 3:5; 18:7). Indeed, *rebels* or *rebellious* is a stock epithet to denote sin against God (Is 1:28; 30:1, 9; 58:1; Jer 5:23; 6:28; Tit 1:10).

The other way to understand the image of the rebel is to recall characters whom we remember as rebels. *Adam and *Eve are the first rebels of the human race, which itself is a corporate rebel against God. *Satan seems to have been guilty of an ill-fated rebellion against God in heaven. The gallery of famous rebels also includes *Cain; Aaron and Miriam in their rejection of the authority of Moses (Num 12); a similar rebellion by Korah, Dathan and Abiram (Num 16); King Saul; and the *prodigal son of Jesus' parable.

See also AUTHORITY; SIN.

REBIRTH

The archetypal movement from *death to rebirth has been called "the archetype of archetypes," in token of the centrality in literature and life of the pattern of *ordeal and threat moving to release and conquest. It is not primarily a literal *resurrection that is in view here (though literal resurrections represent the motif in its pure form) but a metaphoric death that leads to renewal.

The story of the *flood (Gen 6—9), for example, represents the motif on a universal level, as God destroys the entire world except for Noah's family and specimens of all animals, and then causes life to reemerge on the earth. The story of *Abraham's willingness to offer Isaac fits the pattern as well, as accentuated by the NT commentary on the event to the effect that Abraham "figuratively speaking" received his son "from the dead" (Heb 11:19 RSV). At an even more metaphoric level, *Jacob, stripped of everything except his essential self, undergoes a dark night of the soul when he *wrestles with the *angel of God and emerges from the ordeal with a new name and a new identity, entering a new era as "the sun rose upon him" (Gen 32:31 RSV). *Joseph too undergoes a series of imprisonments before his story takes an upward turn as he becomes, next to Pharaoh, the most powerful figure in Egypt.

The pattern continues in the epic of the *exodus. On a national level Israel is reborn after four hundred years of *bondage in Egypt, and later the nation dies in the *wilderness before the next generation rises to enter the *Promised Land. On an individual level Moses' parents entrust him to the Nile River in an "ark," from which he is rescued and given a new lease on life. During the ten plagues, the nation of Egypt is subjected to a series of deathlike cataclysms, somehow emerging to ordinary life after Pharaoh relents, until the final judgment against the nation is carried out. Other moments in Exodus reenact the essential movement—Miriam struck with *leprosy and then healed of it (Num 12:9-16), *Aaron's (inanimate) rod budding with blossoms, representative of life (Num 17), Moses' bronze *serpent that when looked upon heals someone who has been bitten by one of the "fiery serpents" (Num 21:4-9). The symbolism is present in latent form when the Israelites march through the Red Sea on dry land and emerge on the far side, from which they see the Egyptian army drown.

The death-rebirth pattern is intertwined throughout OT history. It is present in the ever-present rhythm of the nation's succumbing to *idolatry and *apostasy, followed by *repentance and *restoration. We see this pattern on the largest possible scale in the story of Judah's exile and restoration. Specific moments from OT history stand out as well: Hezekiah's receiving a death sentence from God and then receiving fifteen more years of life (2 Kings 20:1-11; Is 38), occasions in Elijah's life when he was kept alive in threat or famine, Naaman's dipping in the Jordan seven times and rising cured of his leprosy (2 Kings 5:8-14). *Job undergoes deprivation on virtually every level possible (physical, social, psychological, spiritual), followed by his revival and restoration to *prosperity and peace with God. Jonah descends into a watery cavern, from which he is spared; his psalm of deliverance (Jon 2) is built around the imagery of death and rebirth, *descent and suffocation followed by *ascent and *escape.

Other OT genres give their own variations on the theme. The psalms of *lament are based on a pattern of dire threat, not infrequently pictured in images of heightened danger and potential death, that finds resolution in a confidence that God will deliver. The emotional sequence in these psalms is the archetypal death and rebirth of the human spirit. Psalms of *praise, too, often praise God for delivering the speaker from deathlike conditions. Psalm 107 is a minianthology of such vignettes, as the poet narrates the plight of people in the desert, in *prison, in illness and in *storms at sea, who eventually find a city, liberation, health and a quiet haven. An ever-present pattern of Psalms is encapsulated in the statement of Psalm 30:5 that "weeping may tarry for the night, but joy comes with the morning" (RSV).

The OT *sacrificial system adheres to a death-rebirth pattern in its general orientation. The principle, never stated explicitly, is that something is given up—an animal, produce, grain—in order to secure the continued spiritual welfare of the one who offers the sacrifice. To be alienated from God is to partake of death, but to receive forgiveness is to experience new life.

OT prophetic literature, too, shows a general orientation toward a pattern of death and rebirth. The main message of the prophets is a prediction of doom and *judgment. The prophets expose the spiritual and moral death of nations, and they use cataclysmic imagery to predict a coming destruction. But the oracles of redemption use imagery of the good life to paint a picture of eventual return to God's blessing. Ezekiel's vision of the valley of dry *bones that come to life through the *breath of God epitomizes this quality of prophetic discourse (Ezek 37:1-14). The prophetic oracles of redemption are filled with rebirth imagery—people *returning to a homeland, planting, *harvesting, life springing up, *cities rebuilt. Thus although belief in a resurrection from the dead is limited to just a few OT verses (Job 19:25-27; Dan 12:2), the archetypal movement from death to rebirth underlies most of the OT, preoccupied as it is with lament giving way to praise, servitude to freedom, exile to return.

Rebirth imagery in the NT is dominated by the resurrection of Jesus from the dead, buttressed by other literal resurrections. But the more general imagery of death and rebirth also exists. Regeneration is portrayed as a being born again (Jn 3:1-8). To live the Christlike life is to be "brought from death to life" (Rom 6:13 RSV; cf. Rom 7:5-6, 10; 8:6, 10). To believe in Christ for *salvation is to be "made alive, when you were dead through the trespasses and sins" (Eph 2:1 RSV; see also Eph 2:5; Col 2:13). The hymnic fragment in Ephesians 5, perhaps part of a baptismal rite, enjoins the believer to "arise from the dead" (Eph 5:14 RSV). *Baptism itself is a death-rebirth ritual, as believers are "buried" with Christ "by baptism into death, so that as Christ was raised from the dead by the glory of the Father, we too might walk in newness of life" (Rom 6:4 RSV; see also Col 2:12; 1 Pet 3:21). Self-denial (see Self-Control) too is a kind of death to self (Jn 12:24-26).

It is obvious that the death-rebirth motif is close to the heart of biblical religion, encompassing as it does a key principle of physical, emotional and spiritual life.

See also ASCENT; BIRTH; CONVERSION; DEATH; EXODUS, SECOND EXODUS; FORGIVENESS; REFORM; REPENTANCE; RESTORE, RESTORATION; REVERSAL.

REBUKE. See DEMONS.

RECLINING

Reclining at *meals had become a custom among people in NT times. Guests would recline three to a couch in the Greco-Roman fashion, leaning on their left elbow while leaving their right hand free to dip food from the common dish. The guests on each couch reclined in such a way that each rested his head near the *breast of the one behind him. However, reclining at meals was not always the custom. In the patriarchal period diners typically ate on the floor, and in later times eating at a *table in the Egyptian fashion was the practice (although guests were reclining at Esther's *feast; Esther 7:8; see Esther, Book of).

In today's busy, urgent, work-oriented and "fast food" world, reclining in such a way may seem wasteful or lazy. Yet Jewish culture placed much importance on the evening meal. It was a time for *family and *friends to come together and fellowship with each other. Reclining was thus an integral part of the meal; it required slowing down and *resting, focusing on the relationships of those sharing the couch. Fellowship was easily established, and the meal became a time of rest rather than laziness.

Jesus reclined at meals. He is seen reclining at the table with Pharisees (Lk 7:36; 11:37), at Simon the Leper's (Mt 26:7; Mk 14:3) and at the Last Supper (Mt 26:20; Lk 22:14; Jn 13:23). He also uses the image in a parable, when the master returns home to find his servants dressed and ready for service (Lk 12:37).

See also BANQUET; EATING; MEAL; SEAT; SITTING; SUPPER; TABLE.

RECOGNITION STORIES. See REVELATION/RECOGNITION STORIES.

RECONCILIATION. See REUNION, RECONCILIATION.

RED. See COLORS.

REDEEM, REDEMPTION

In the Bible the imagery and concept of redemption are specific motifs under the broader rubric of *salvation. The specific vocabulary of redemption and its variants appears approximately 150 times in English translations, with all but 20 of the occurrences coming in the OT. At the heart of the image is the idea of paying a price to regain something that will otherwise be forfeited. Redemption thus carries double connotations: it implies deliverance and restitution but also a cost that must be paid. Distinct developments occur as we move from the OT to the NT.

Redemption in the Hebrew Law. The occasions for redemption in the biblical world were quite extensive. In the ancient world generally, the release of soldiers taken in battle might occur if a *ransom were paid. The "holiness code" of Leviticus contains numerous possibilities for redemption. A person sold into *slavery because of insolvency can be redeemed if the family's finances later improve (Lev 25:39-55); so can property or a house sold when a person needed money (Lev 25:25-34), and a similar provision ensures that *land cannot be sold in perpetuity but

always needs to be subject to possible redemption (Lev 25:23-24). A person whose *ox has gored someone to death, because the death is not a willful murder, can pay a ransom price (Ex 21:30-32) and thus circumvent the law that requires stoning the owner (Ex 21:29).

Another area of cultic redemption is the sanctifying of the firstborn (see First) males of both humans and *animals: "No one, however, may dedicate the firstborn of an animal, since the firstborn already belongs to the LORD; whether an ox or a sheep, it is the LORD's. If it is one of the unclean animals, he may buy it back at its set value, adding a fifth of the value to it. If he does not redeem it, it is to be sold at its set value" (Lev 27:26-27 NIV). The principle is that firstborn males, because they belong to God, can be recovered or restored to normal life only through the payment of a price (cf. also the ram that serves as a substitute for Isaac's life in Gen 22, and the *Passover lamb that spares the life of a Hebrew firstborn on the night of the tenth plague in Egypt).

The OT law provides three ways that forfeited property can be redeemed. First, a kinsman can buy back what has been sold (Lev 25:48-49). A favorite picture of redemption is that of Boaz exercising this role as recorded in the book of Ruth (Ruth 2:20; 3:9). Second, if prosperity has returned to the seller, he himself can buy back forfeited property or his own release from slavery (Lev 25:26-27, 49). Third, if redemption does not come through these two means, then one can wait until the Year of Jubilee when the property will be returned to its original owner (Lev 25:10, 28).

The OT construct of redemption pervades every aspect of life. All manner of things—animals and people—stand in need of redemption for a multitude of issues (e.g., being firstborn, having been dedicated to a special purpose, having been sold). *Lambs are redeemed (Ex 13:13), slaves can be redeemed (Ex 21:8), donkeys might be redeemed (Ex 34:30). A woman can be ransomed (Lev 19:20), and when Jonathan unwittingly disobeys his father's command for soldiers not to eat anything as they are routing the Philistines, the people ransom him (1 Sam 14:45).

The image of redemption involves three aspects: (1) the *"bondage" or special circumstance from which a person, object or animal needs to be freed; (2) the payment of a redemption price; (3) usually a human intermediary acting to secure the redemption. This structure can be modified by the arrival of the Year of Jubilee in which slaves are to be set free and property returned. Although it appears that this Year of Jubilee was never historically implemented, it stands as an ideal within the text of the OT.

Redemption in the OT Mosaic code is primarily moral in nature, enforced by legal procedures and sanctions. Its aim is to govern human relationships that fall into certain categories. But as is so often the case in the Bible, spiritual meanings are rooted in physical and moral ones, and the redemption of a firstborn *child understood as belonging to God already shades from moral into spiritual meanings.

The Exodus. The central OT image of spiritual redemption is the salvation accomplished by God in delivering his people out of Egypt (*see* Exodus, Second Exodus). In the OT this redemption is not spiritualized into a mere escape or deliverance. The biblical writers clearly seek to emphasize how the exodus was a redemption as understood by their culture and Mosaic law.

That law requires an intermediary to serve as redeemer. God is the redeemer of his people in the exodus. Even before the event itself, God declares, "I will free you from being slaves to them, and I will redeem you with an outstretched arm and with mighty acts of judgment" (Ex 6:6 NIV). Moses later uses the same imagery to recall the event: "But it was because the LORD loved you and kept the oath he swore to your forefathers that he brought you out with a mighty hand and redeemed you from the land of slavery, from the power of Pharaoh king of Egypt" (Deut 7:8 NIV). The same imagery lives on in later Israelite recollections of the exodus (2 Sam 7:23; 1 Chron 17:21; Mic 6:4; etc.).

God as Redeemer. As we move beyond the specific redemption represented by the exodus from *Egypt, God's redemption of his people becomes generalized into a pattern of spiritual salvation. God himself is called by the epithet "Redeemer" two dozen times. We read of God redeeming a person's soul or life from an unspecified and evocative *"pit" (Job 3:28; Ps 103:4). People invoke God to redeem them (e.g., Ps 31:5; 44:26; 69:18; 119:134). In the OT the redemption is from such varied situations as an oppressor (Ps 78:42; 119:134), "the hand of the foe" (Ps 107:2; cf. Mic 4:10), sins (Ps 130:8), "the grasp of the cruel" (Jer 15:21; cf. Jer 31:11) and death (Hos 13:14).

Two of the most memorable pictures of redemption in the OT involve the marriage relationship. The central action in the book of *Ruth is the functioning of Boaz as a kinsman-redeemer (gō'ēl) for Ruth—a near-of-kin who accepts the financial and social obligations of marrying Ruth, providing for her and raising up seed by her. In a similar manner, Hosea buys back his *adulterous wife Gomer as a symbol of God's redemption of Israel (Hos 3).

Although some scholars believe that God's deliverance of Israel in the OT implies the element of a purchase price that was a necessary part of redemption in the moral/legal code, the evidence for that conclusion seems strained. To say that God delivered his people "with an outstretched arm and with mighty acts of judgment" (Ex 6:6), though it pictures an expenditure of effort, is not in the same category of money being paid. When God redeems in the OT, the primary image is that of God's role as redeemer and its effect of deliverance, not on a price that God has paid. Of course this changes drastically in the NT.

Redemption in the New Testament. The NT image of redemption is more specifically soteriological than the OT image. The first NT reference to redemptive hope of deliverance from hostile powers (*see* Enemies) is described in language that brings to mind God's deliverance in the Exodus: "Praise be to the Lord, the God of Israel, because he has come and has redeemed his people" and brought "salvation from our enemies and from the hand of all who hate us" (Luke 1:68, 71). Redemption becomes a standard way by which NT writers refer to salvation, and it implies the payment of a price. Images of ransom and *sacrifice are an assumed part of the picture.

Although the medieval understanding of redemption was based on the premise that Christ paid a price to *Satan as a way of purchasing his own, the NT does not share such a premise. Although Christ defeats Satan in open combat (the *Christus Victor* motif; *see* Triumph), Christ does not owe or pay Satan anything. Instead Christ redeems his followers from sin, the condemnation of the *law and *death. According to the NT, "Everyone who commits sin is a slave to sin" (Jn 8:34 NIV). Sinners are "slaves to sin, which leads to death" (Rom 6:16 NIV; cf. Rom 6:23). This is the spiritual bondage from which sinners need to be redeemed, and the language of that redemption retains the OT connotations of a price that has been paid to secure the freedom of slaves. We thus read that "redemption . . . came by Christ Jesus" (Rom 3:24 NIV), who "redeemed us from the curse of the law by becoming a curse for us" (Gal 3:13 NIV). Christ came "to redeem those under law" (Gal 4:5 NIV) and "gave himself for us to redeem us from all wickedness" (Tit 2:14 NIV). One of the most vivid pictures is this one: God "has rescued us from the dominion of darkness and brought us into the kingdom of the Son he loves, in whom we have redemption, the forgiveness of sins" (Col 1:13-14 NIV).

The NT imagery of redemption stresses not only an intermediary who performs the transaction but also the price that has been paid. The keynote is that "you were bought at a price" (1 Cor 6:20; 7:23 NIV). The price of redemption is the atoning death of Christ. Thus we read that "through the redemption that came by Christ Jesus" God "presented him as a sacrifice of atonement" (Rom 3:24-25 NIV). Again, "we have redemption through his blood, the forgiveness of sins" (Eph 1:7). Jesus himself says that he has come "to give his life as a ransom for many" (Mk 10:45). The price of spiritual redemption is far greater than money, just as its result is farther reaching than OT premonitions: "For you know that it was not with perishable things such as silver or gold that you were redeemed from the empty way of life handed down to you from your forefathers, but with the precious blood of Christ, a lamb without blemish or defect" (1 Pet 1:18-19 NIV).

While NT references to redemption mainly look back to the redemption purchased on the *cross, there is also an eschatological thread in which full redemption is yet to be accomplished. When the signs of the times begin to appear, says Jesus, "stand up and lift up your heads, because your redemption is drawing near" (Lk 21:28 NIV). Paul portrays Christians as groaning inwardly "as we wait eagerly for . . . the redemption of our bodies" (Rom 8:23 NIV). The Holy Spirit is "a deposit guaranteeing our inheritance until the redemption of those who are God's possession" (Eph 1:14 NIV). The Holy Spirit has also "sealed" believers "for the day of redemption" (Eph 4:30 NIV).

See also BONDAGE AND FREEDOM; JESUS, IMAGES OF; LEGAL IMAGES; RANSOM; RESCUE; SACRIFICE; SALVATION.

REFINING

Many traditional hymns, sermons and prayers use the language of refining to interpret difficult experiences we undergo. The metaphor originates in the craft of metalworking, which comes before us very early in the Bible (Gen 4:22). Crude metals (*see* Minerals) were placed in a furnace, *workers intensified the heat with a pair of bellows, and smelting separated the dross (Ezek 22:17-22). The final stage of refining isolated pure metal from low-quality material (*see* Metals of the Bible).

Once the language of refining refers to God's Word as flawless (Ps 12:6). Mostly it is used figuratively of God's putting Israel through the heat of some *reversal or *punishment. Through this crucible their real worth is demonstrated (Prov 17:3), and the wicked are separated (2 Kings 24:14; Is 24:1). God is depicted as a worker thoroughly purging impurity among the people (Is 1:24-26; *see* Purity). Though the majority will be consumed in this *fire (Zech 13:8-9), the remainder will be purified through the *affliction (Is 48:10-11). Occasionally, God is compared to the furnace itself (Mal 3:2-3). It is the people's unfaithfulness and the subsequent divine wrath that bring about this affliction, and the latter can take various forms (Ezek 22:17-22). Elsewhere it is God's desire to preserve and enhance the people that is uppermost (Ps 66:8-12).

Though the experience of metalworking is unfamiliar to most people, we still talk about God's *"melting" our hearts, purifying or refining us. We tend to see this individualistically rather than corporately, and often stress its positive benefits rather than the element of *judgment.

See also AFFLICTION; FIRE; MELT, MELTING; MINERALS.

BIBLIOGRAPHY. R. Banks, *God the Worker: Journeys into the Mind, Heart and Imagination of God* (Valley Forge, PA: Judson, 1994).

REFORM

To reform means to reconstitute the life of an individual or nation and bring it into line with a moral or spiritual standard. In the Bible, stories of reform involve a *return to an earlier standard from which individuals or nations have drifted. Such reform is implicitly accompanied by *repentance.

The biggest grouping of reform stories in the Bible involves restoring the true *worship of God after a nation has embraced *idolatry. The prototypical reform story is that of Josiah, under whose reign the book of the *law is rediscovered and a wholesale reform of worship instituted (2 Kings 22—23). Other OT kings institute similar reforms (2 Chron 15:8-19; 29-31). When the *exiled nation of Judah returns to its native *land, *Ezra has to institute national reform regarding intermarriage with pagans (Ezra 10:1-15), and *Nehemiah oversees similar reforms of worship and *marriage (Neh 13). The prophetic counterpart of these historical annals consists of prophets' calling a nation to reform (Joel 2:12-17; Amos) or picturing God as instituting the reform of his people (Ezek 36:8-38; Zeph 3:9-13).

The Gospels contain stories of characters who accept the conditions of *salvation as taught by Jesus and subsequently reform their lives. Zacchaeus is a typical example (Lk 19:10), as is the woman who "was a *sinner" whose life is transformed by Jesus' *forgiveness (Lk 7:36-50). We leave other Gospel stories confident that characters who have encountered Jesus reform their lives, even if the text does not tell their story of reform—characters like the Samaritan woman (Jn 4:7-42) and the woman caught in *adultery whom Jesus charges, "Go, and do not sin again" (Jn 8:11 RSV).

No one in the pages of the Bible had his life more thoroughly reformed than Paul, as he sometimes notes in the autobiographical sections of his addresses or letters. The closest the OT comes to a *conversion story—the story of *Jacob's wrestling with the angel of God (Gen 32:22-32)—is the turning point in the story of an obnoxiously combative man who becomes much mellower and more sympathetic after his encounter with God (*see* Encounter, Divine-Human). At least two of Jesus' parables, too, tell of individuals who reform their lives—the younger son who comes to his senses and returns to his father's will (Lk 15:11-24; *see* Prodigal Son), and the son who conquers his surliness and reverses his initial refusal to work in his father's vineyard (Mt 21:28-31).

Although stories of reform are not as numerous in the Bible as one might expect, this relative scarcity is somewhat misleading. The entire moral and spiritual tenor of the Bible—the whole force of its incessant commands, exhortations and *wisdom sayings—is a continuous call to the reader to reform his or her life from the sinfulness that is the universal human lot. We can see this impulse in microcosm in the lists of virtues and vices embedded in some of the NT Epistles, which are nothing less than a blueprint for moral and spiritual reform.

See also CONVERSION; REBIRTH; REPENTANCE; RETURN.

REFUGE

A safe place into which to run is a universal need for all creatures, including human beings. We can all remember childhood games in which there was a place where one was "safe" and could not be touched by a pursuer or opponent. "Out there" was danger, but to reach the sanctuary or haven (even if it was only a circle drawn in the dust) meant security.

A number of Hebrew words in the OT evoke images of refuge—a place of safety from danger, relief after stress, defense from an *enemy, *protection from the heat of the sun, overall security. These images incorporate both *rocks and *fortresses on the one hand and *houses or homes on the other. A rock in the desert could be seen as a military outpost and therefore a refuge for those in *flight. The home is a refuge of a more permanent nature, one to which a wanderer can finally *return. The preponderance of biblical references to refuge declare *God to be the believer's refuge, but other major clusters of references are to the *cities of refuge and to the *altar as a sanctuary. It is also important to note that the image is largely an OT image. Of ninety-five references in the RSV to "refuge," the only NT reference is (tellingly) in the book of Hebrews (Heb 6:18-20).

We can get a feel for the range of the image of refuge by noting the leading OT words for it. *Maḥseh,* "place of refuge," is frequently used to refer to God (e.g., Ps 14:6; 71:7; 142:5). In Psalm 104:18, though, the word designates the place God has provided for animals, and in Isaiah 4:5-6 it is the canopy that God will spread over *Zion. *Mānôs,* "place of flight," is a place of safety while one *escapes from enemies (2 Sam 22:3; Ps 59:16; 142:4). The heading of Psalm 57 suggests that the Cave of Adullam, where David gathered his forces, was just such a refuge. *Miśgāb,* "high place" or "tower," was particularly dear to David in his exile (Ps 9:9; 46:7, 11; 48:3). *Mᵉ῾ōnâ,* "the arms of the Lord," comes close to suggesting eternal life, as in Deuteronomy 33:27: "The eternal God is your dwelling place, and underneath are the everlasting arms" (RSV).

Refuge from Vengeance. Prominent in the OT notion of refuge are detailed arrangements for dealing with fugitives who had accidentally caused the death of someone (Num 35:9-34; 35:6; Deut 4:41-43; 19:1-13; Josh 20:1-9; 21:13, 21, 27, 32, 28; 1 Chron 6:57, 67). Designed to prevent endless cycles of *vengeance, a network of cities of refuge enabled anyone who had unintentionally or accidentally committed a murder to be safe from retaliation by relatives of the murdered person. Something of the aura surrounding these places of refuge can be gleaned from such stipulations as that "the congregation" help to rescue an inadvertent murderer from his pursuers (Num 35:25), that enough cities of refuge be established to make the distance for reaching them a practical possibility (Deut 19:3, 8-10) and that a person fleeing from vengeance would be safe only within a city of refuge and subject to vengeance if he strayed outside it (Num 35:26-28).

What did the image of the city of refuge mean to the ordinary Israelite? It was an image at once of safety, protection from pursuit, a renewal of life that

would otherwise be doomed and a kind of salvation. The picture of the harassed fugitive finding safety is central to OT ideas of justice and salvation, and it may partly account for the popularity of the image in Psalms.

A related OT institution is the *horns of the *altar, to which a person fleeing from *blood vengeance might flee. The conditions surrounding this institution are shadowy compared with what we know about the cities of refuge, but we have narrative accounts of two people who attempted to use the horns of the altar as a place of safety from vengeance—Adonijah (1 Kings 1:50-53) and Joab, who was killed while still clinging to the altar because Solomon judged him to be *guilty rather than *innocent (1 Kings 2:28-34).

God as Refuge. For the writers of the Bible, God is the ultimate refuge. The book of Psalms is the primary text, with nearly fifty references. The writers mainly picture God as someone "in" whom the *covenant people take refuge, but sometimes the refuge is given a more specific picture. The refuge afforded by God is thus variously portrayed as a rock (Ps 18:2; 31:2; 62:7; 94:22), *wings (Ps 36:7; 57:1; 61:4; 91:4), a fortress (Ps 59:16; 71:3; 91:2) and a strong *tower (Ps 61:3). Psalm 144:2 is a good composite image: "my rock and my fortress, my stronghold and my deliverer, my shield and he in whom I take refuge" (RSV).

Eschatological References. Another leading cluster of images of safe refuge can be found in the eschatological visions of the Bible. In these visions God promises a future place of refuge for his people. People who take refuge in God will "possess the land, and . . . inherit my holy mountain" (Is 57:13 RSV). The days are coming, wrote Jeremiah, when "Judah will be saved, and Israel will dwell securely" (Jer 23:6; cf. Jer 33:16). Ezekiel paints similar pictures (Ezek 28:26; 34:28), as does Hosea (Hos 2:18). The ultimate "safe place" comes at the end of the book of Revelation, with its picture of a foursquare city with stately *walls (Rev 21:9-21), securely beyond the reach of evil (Rev 21:27; 22:15).

See also CITY; FORTRESS; GOD; PROTECTION; ROCK; SHIELD; STRONGHOLD; WALL; WING; ZION.

REFUSE. *See* DUNG.

REFUSER OF FESTIVITIES

A refuser of festivities (sometimes also called the churl) is one who, motivated by personal interests, chooses not to participate in *joyful activities of the community. In literature generally, the refuser of festivities is a comic type, the butt of laughter as he or she is excluded from the ideal society at the end of the comic plot. The Bible invests the character with a more tragic hue, inasmuch as the festivities from which the churls exclude themselves are the *salvation and eternal life that God offers. Although Christianity has often been regarded as a stern faith, by both critics and believers, the refusal of festivities is always associated with sinfully misplaced priorities, lending support to the claim of Jeremy Taylor that God promises to do terrible things to people who refuse to be happy.

While the refusal of festivities is mainly a NT motif, premonitions exist in the OT. The one indisputable example is *Jonah, who is banished to the belly of a fish while erstwhile pagan sailors experience a newfound *fear of God (Jon 1:16) and who at the end of the story pouts in *anger because he disapproves of God's *forgiveness extended to the city of *Nineveh in its wholesale *conversion, while Jonah had been hoping for an outpouring of *judgment (Jon 4:1-2). *Pharaoh refuses repeated opportunities to allow the Israelites to hold a religious *feast to the Lord, and *Job's friends virtually miss the festivity represented by Job's *restoration (Job 42:7-9). David's wife Michal is smitten with *barrenness when she rebukes David for his *dancing and celebrating with the ark of the covenant (2 Sam 6:14-23). We can also catch hints of the archetype at a national level in the prophetic pictures of Israel and Judah as refusing to listen to God or *return to him (Jer 13:10; 15:6; Hos 11:5).

The archetype becomes more decisively present in the NT, especially in the Gospels. The *Pharisees are the main refusers of festivities in the Gospels. In Matthew 11:16-19 and Luke 7:29-35 the Pharisees do not dance with the joyous nor lament with the mourners, and they accuse Jesus of gluttony, excessive drinking and bad associations. In John 9 they refuse to rejoice with the man who has been healed of *blindness. In Luke 15:1-2 they are outraged that Jesus would receive sinners and eat with them. Throughout the Gospels the Pharisees not only refuse the offer of salvation themselves but also resentfully try to obstruct others from participating in the joy of salvation. The rich young ruler leaves Jesus sorrowfully after learning that he will have to relinquish his possession to enter the *kingdom, "for he had great possessions" (Mt 19:22 RSV). This is similar to King Agrippa, who refuses Paul's call to conversion in a statement that is variously translated as "Almost thou persuadest me to be a Christian" (Acts 26:28 KJV) and "In a short time you think to make me a Christian!" (RSV).

We cannot limit the refusal of festivities only to the religious establishment, though. In the drama of the soul's choice that we find in the Gospels, people from all walks show themselves capable of the great refusal. The picture that captures it best is perhaps Jesus' *weeping over *Jerusalem, saying, "How often would I have gathered your children together as a hen gathers her brood under her wings, and you would not!" (Mt 23:37 RSV; cf. Jesus' statement in Jn 5:40 that "you refuse to come to me that you may have life" [RSV]).

We also find the refuser of festivities in Jesus' parables. The best-known example is the *elder brother of the *prodigal, who refuses to join the party thrown in honor of his reformed younger brother (Lk 15:25-32). In the parable of the *wedding feast, people preoccupied with worldly interests exclude themselves from the feast, symbolic of salvation (Lk 14:16-24; cf. a similar parable in Mt 22:1-14).

The archetypal refuser of festivities in the Bible stands as a warning not to emulate. The writer to Hebrews asks, "How shall we escape if we neglect [refuse] such a great salvation?" (Heb 2:3 RSV), adding the command "See that you do not refuse him who is speaking" (Heb 12:25 RSV).

A minor reversal of the archetype can also be noted in Scripture. There are occasions where the festivity is an immoral or ungodly one and where refusing it is a spiritual virtue. Thus Vashti refused to appear at her husband's lavish stag party (Esther 1:10-12), and *Daniel and his three friends refused the rich food of King Nebuchadnezzar (Dan 1). By faith Moses refused the plush life of the Egyptian court, "choosing rather to share ill-treatment with the people of God than to enjoy the fleeting pleasures of sin" (Heb 11:25 RSV).

See also BANQUET; CHARACTER TYPES; FESTIVAL; JOY.

REIGN OF GOD. *See* KINGDOM OF GOD/KINGDOM OF HEAVEN.

REMEMBRANCE

The biblical notion of remembrance extends far beyond nostalgic recall. It embraces a comprehensive range of human experiences, for the purpose of fully integrating faith and life and for the goal of complete *obedience to God.

Disciplined remembrance is institutionalized in biblical faith because we are called to interpret our present circumstances in light of God's known faithfulness in the past. Correspondingly, forgetfulness was seen as one of humankind's greatest spiritual maladies (hence the psalmist's call to "forget not all his benefits" [Ps 103:2 NIV]). When people had fresh experiential knowledge of God, they responded in wholehearted obedience, but forgetfulness led to *wandering from God. The book of Judges attributes the multiple problems of those days to the forgetfulness of the people: "The Israelites did evil in the eyes of the LORD; they forgot the LORD their God and served the Baals and the Asherahs" (Judg 3:7). As Kinlaw has emphasized, the Hebrew was called to walk, as it were, backwards into the future, always keeping an eye on the past through the *festivals and meditation on God's *law and acts.

From the Hebrew noun *zēker* the concept of "memorial" is drawn from the call for "remembrance." In turn, parallel nouns (like *zikkārón* and *'ozkārá*) identify memorial *offerings or memorial mementos. But whether specific cases in Scripture highlight a plea for personal remembrance (Jer 15:15), personal memorial (Mt 26:13) or examples of corporate human recall (Deut 5:15; Josh 4:4-24), biblical remembrance always focuses on people. Besides noting divine-human instances (*see* Encounter,

Divine-Human), there are evidences of interpersonal memorials, such as the one established between *Jacob and Laban (Gen 31:44-50).

The twin celebrations of *Passover (Ex 12:14) and the Lord's *Supper or Eucharist (Lk 22:19; 1 Cor 11:24-26) reflect the most prominent memorials in the OT and NT. Each recalls particular messages of deliverance and *salvation; each elicits the fullest effects of every human sense. Total sensory involvement of participants provides the compelling link between these significant historic events and the anticipation of faithful living; reverence for the past is merged with relevance in the present. Other examples of intentional recall which utilize human senses include memorials of *stones (Ex 28:12; Josh 4:4-24) and *trumpet blasts (Num 10:9, 10).

Besides instances of *prayer (Rom 1:9; Phil 1:3-4) which serve as reminders of believers' needs, tangible gifts to the poor express personal faith (Acts 10:4; Gal 2:10). Furthermore, invaluable written records were to provoke memory, such as the "scroll of remembrance" (Mal 3:16 NIV). Other written memorials include phylacteries (Ex 13:9) and the narrative account of Amalek's defeat (Ex 17:14). Jehoshaphat, son of Ahilud, personified the value of written reminders of God's work in history, serving as King David's recorder (2 Sam 8:16).

What the foregoing catalog immediately underscores is how "institutionalized" remembrance was in the experience of the biblical cultures. A host of events and tangible objects ensured that people remembered what they were called to remember.

Biblical challenges to recall God's *laws were not to be taken lightly. Israel's repeated absent-mindedness (Judg 8:34; Neh 9:16-18; Ps 78:42) always resulted in disobedience and defeat. Specifically, the Bible cautions against forgetting the guidelines of proper *worship (Num 16:36-40). Also, the celebration of Purim serves as a negative reminder of how God deals with those who scheme against Israel (Esther 9:23-28). Finally, *holiness and accompanying *guilt are linked when intentional recollection of faith in life is experienced (Num 5:11-15; 1 Kings 17:17-18).

When it comes to "remembrance," God is not satisfied with halfhearted response. The goal of complete dedication is summarized by his commands to keep the Passover observance "like a sign on your hand [behavior] and a reminder on your forehead [thoughts] that the law of the LORD is to be on your lips [communicated values]" (Ex 13:9 NIV).

Psalm 77 illustrates well the psychology and theology of remembrance in the Psalter. The psalmist begins with an expression of his struggle with his circumstances and with God (Ps 77:1-3), whom he sees as the origin of his problems (Ps 77:4-9). In the midst of his emotional turmoil, he remembers "the deeds of the LORD" (Ps 77:11), and he specifically rehearses the deliverance at the Reed *Sea (Ps 77:16-20). As a result of his remembrance his attitude changes from lament to worship (Ps 77:13-14).

Finally, we should not overlook the obvious: people forget what they do not call to remembrance (hence Samuel Johnson's observation that we need more often to be reminded than to be informed). The second epistle of Peter sounds the keynote: "Therefore I intend always to remind you of these things, though you know them and are established in the truth that you have. I think it right . . . to arouse you by way of reminder. . . . I have aroused your sincere mind by way of reminder; that you should remember the predictions of the holy prophets and the commandment of the Lord and Savior" (2 Pet 1:12-13; 3:1-2 RSV).

See also FORSAKE, FORSAKEN; LOST AND FOUND.

REMNANT

The remnant motif in the Bible is associated with a variety of images, but the starting point of the motif is with Israel, as an ethnic people, a nation and ultimately as a symbol of the people of God. These can carry either a positive connotation, such as the "righteous remnant," or a negative connotation, such as what remains following *judgment. The negative aspect of remnant is portrayed in exaggerated and colorful ways that convey the gravity of divine judgment.

Some of the most poignant examples are found in *Isaiah. Following his vision of God's throne room, the prophet is told to preach his message of doom "until cities lie waste without inhabitant . . . and the LORD removes men far away . . . and . . . a tenth remain" (Is 6:11-13 RSV). As a sign of the coming judgment and purge, Isaiah names one of his sons She'ar-jashub, meaning "a remnant will return" (Is 7:3). The male population will be so depleted, the prophet declares, that "seven women shall take hold of one man in that day, saying, 'We will eat our own bread and wear our own clothes, only let us be called by your name'" (Is 4:1 RSV). Judah will be like a hut in a cucumber field (Is 1:8) or a lonely flagpole on a hill (Is 30:17). Indeed, the devastation will be such that the nation could almost be compared to *Sodom and Gomorrah (Is 1:9).

But Isaiah's remnant idea carries with it the hope of *restoration. The judgment will act as a purge that will remove impure dross and leave behind a pure residue (Is 1:25-26; *see* Purity). Those who have faith will survive the coming *flood (Is 28:16; 30:15). A holy *seed will survive (Is 6:13). "He who is left in Zion and remains in Jerusalem will be called holy, every one who has been recorded for life in Jerusalem" (Is 4:3 RSV).

The OT remnant idea plays an important role in the NT. It helps explain why it is that not all of Israel accepted Jesus as the awaited Messiah. Jesus himself alludes to Isaiah's vision (Is 6:9-10) to explain why not all respond in faith to his word (Mk 4:10-13). Paul also appeals to OT imagery to understand Israel's unbelief: "It is not as though the word of God had failed. For not all who are descended from Israel belong to Israel" (Rom 9:6 RSV).

Paul's theology of election worked out in Romans 9—11 is in important ways based on OT ideas of remnant. Despite Israel's obstinacy, Paul is convinced that "God has not rejected his people" (Rom 11:2), and for proof he cites the example of Elijah's despair: "I alone am left, and they seek my life" (Rom 11:3 NIV, citing 1 Kings 19:10). "But what is God's reply to him?" Paul asks. " 'I have kept for myself seven thousand men who have not bowed the knee to Baal' [1 Kings 19:18]. So too at the present time there is a remnant, chosen by grace" (Rom 11:4-5 RSV).

Finally, in the apocalyptic imagery of the book of Revelation, the chosen remnant are listed as one hundred forty-four thousand, *twelve thousand faithful from each of the twelve tribes of Israel (Rev 7:2-8), but when the seer looks, this numerically defined imagery of Israel is expanded to a vision of a "great multitude that no one could count, from every nation, from all tribes and peoples and languages, standing before the throne and before the lamb" (Rev 7:9 NRSV).

See also ISRAEL; RESTORATION.

BIBLIOGRAPHY. J. C. Campbell, "God's People and the Remnant," *SJT* 3 (1950) 78-85; G. F. Hasel, *The Remnant: The History and Theology of the Remnant Idea from Genesis to Isaiah* (AUM 5; Berrien Springs, MO: Andrews University Press, 1972).

REPENTANCE

The apostle Paul notes that godly sorrow produces an earnestness, an eagerness to clear one's name, indignation, alarm, longing, concern and a readiness to see justice done (2 Cor 7:11). While Paul documents many separate images of repentance, the single most prominent biblical source of images of repentance is Psalm 51, which provides an anatomy of the *sinner's (David's) soul and emotions after the prophet Nathan confronted him with the enormity of what he had done in committing *adultery with Bathsheba and *murdering her husband (2 Sam 11—12). The psalm conveys a profound sense of both the depth of evil possible in the human *heart and the confidence of one who has experienced the effects of authentic repentance—*forgiveness and reconciliation with God. It also catalogs four facets of genuine repentance echoed by Paul: comprehension of wrong done, earnest desire for justice, desire for the presence of God, and changed action.

Wrongs Recognized. Genuine repentance begins with a clear understanding of the wrong committed. David notes his *sin as well as the person who was harmed by it and the justice of judgment against him (Ps 51:3-5); his words convey a sense of ready, willing confession backed by true knowledge. Job understands that true understanding of evil is necessary for real repentance (Job 34:31-33). Job himself ends not only by ceasing to accuse God (Job 40:4-5) but also by actively confessing that he spoke untruthfully regarding God and repenting of it (Job 42:3, 6). Several groups of people admit their wrongdoing readily, as David did: the Israelites when *Ezra reads

the *law after returning from exile (Neh 9:11), the *Ninevites after *Jonah delivers God's words (Jon 3:5-6, 8) and the crowd whose hearts are "cut to the quick" when they hear Peter on the day of *Pentecost (Acts 2:38). The repentance of the *prodigal son in Jesus' story started when he "came to his senses" (Lk 15:17 NIV). Recognition of sin is central to biblical repentance.

Cleansing Sought with Earnest Grief. Awareness of sin leads to an earnest pursuit of *cleansing. Prominent in David's prayer are urgent appeals to the character of God and requests for cleansing (Ps 51:1-2, 7-8). In addition to earnest *prayer, *tears, sackcloth, *ashes and *fasting are common expressions of this eager desire. Expressions of earnest grief are actions that can be chosen before judgment or certain consequences once judgment has been passed; several biblical stories record instances when grieving signals repentance.

Sackcloth, ashes and fasting are primary expressions of penitence. They are associated with repentance when a group of kings humble themselves before the king of Israel (1 Kings 20:31), when Hezekiah repents and asks for more life (2 Kings 19:1; Is 37:1-2), when Ahab is confronted by Elijah (1 Kings 21:27) and as part of Job's penitent posture before God (Job 16:15) as well as the psalmist's penitent pleas (Ps 69:11). Daniel prays and fasts in sackcloth to repent on behalf of his people (Dan 9:3), and the king of Nineveh leads his people "from the greatest to the least" in a similar expression of repentance (Jon 3:5-6, 8). Prophets convey God's recommendation that repentance be demonstrated in this way (Is 32:11; Jer 4:8; Joel 1:13), and Jesus himself commends it when he pronounces woe on the cities that have rejected his miracles (Mt 11:21; Lk 10:13). Dressing in sackcloth, sitting with ashes poured over one's head, forgoing the strength and satisfaction of food—these humble actions picture a pliant agreement with the accuser and an earnest desire to be forgiven.

A *soft *face and soft heart are related facets of the repentance image; Scripture commends both of these as good measures of the verity of repentance. David observes that broken contrition is a quality God desires in true repentance (Ps 51:17). The prophet Jeremiah disappointedly reports unrepentant faces that are "harder than stone" (Jer 5:3); corrupt people are likened to *bronze and *iron, and God to a tester of metals (Jer 6:27-28). Soft faces reflect soft, repentant hearts that desire God's presence, and so the prophet infers unrepentance from the faces he witnesses. David's tone confirms the necessity of this pliant quality as he is ready to be cleansed by God (Ps 51:2, 7).

New Desire for God. Earnestness is a quality commended to those who do not wish to miss experiencing the presence of God (Rev 3:19); repentance images capture this earnest desire. In his eager, pliant tone, David directly petitions for sustained audience with God: "do not cast me from your presence or take your Holy Spirit from me" (Ps 51:11 NIV). David perceives that in his guilt he has lacked "the joy of God's salvation" and "a willing spirit" (Ps 51:12 NIV).

The prophets and NT writers confirm David's hope that repentance is marked by a renewed awareness of God's closeness. Isaiah promises that "the Redeemer will come . . . to those . . . who repent of their sins" (Is 59:20 NIV), and Jeremiah reminds his audience that their forgiveness includes renewed audience with God, for they have been restored to serve God (Jer 15:19). Luke explains that the *angels rejoice over a truly repentant person (Lk 15:7) and recommends repentance so "that times of refreshing my come from the Lord" (Acts 3:19 NIV). Repentance is signaled by a new desire for and experience of the presence of God. Ultimately, the unrepentant will endure the undesired eternal separation from God that most thoroughly defines death (Ezek 18:32; Hos 11:6).

Human repentance is frequent and imperfect. NT images of human repentance underscore the action of changing one's mind or feeling deep sorrow over one's actions. While the writers of Acts and the Epistles call for and describe genuine repentance (e.g., Acts 3:19; Rom 2:4-5; 2 Cor 7:-11), the Gospels record compelling images of repentant persons, particularly in the parable of the prodigal son (Lk 15:11-24) and the story of Zacchaeus (Lk 19:8). In each narrative the penitent undergoes dramatic and immediate change, with the result that personal circumstances also change profoundly. In each case the audience, which regards the repentant person as an unlikely or impossible candidate for change, is surprised, even offended. Each of these images of repentance emphasizes the shocking nature of grace; each demonstrates that authentic repentance occurs in unlikely places and is always associated with a lavish measure of grace.

Changed Action. Changed action is the most tangible demonstration of repentance. While, like a stony face, unwillingness to glorify God signals a lack of repentance (Rev 16:9), large strides in a new direction are the most sure sign that repentance has occurred. Having requested the presence of God, David immediately describes his plan of action: to "teach transgressors your ways," leading to their repentance, and "to declare your praise" (Ps 51:13-15). He lends backbone to his earnest tone by envisioning outward change to demonstrate his inward contrition. The prophets hold changed action to be the norm for true repentance; repeated pleas to "turn from idols" dot their messages (e.g., Ezek 14:6; 18:30). NT writers Luke and John uphold this standard of changed action. In the story of the prodigal son, Luke emphasizes the new plans the son makes after his recognition of his sin (Lk 15:11-24); there is also the stunning action of Zacchaeus, who demonstrates his repentance by returning four times the amount stolen from those he had cheated as a tax collector (Lk 19:8). Simon the magician is told that

his attitude toward the Spirit's power should turn around and change completely (Acts 8:22); Luke notes Paul's praise of others who proved repentance "by their deeds" (Acts 26:20). In his messages to the seven churches of Revelation, John describes repentance as a turning back to "do the things you did at first" (Rev 2:5 NIV). Building on the steps of understanding sin, grieving separation and desiring the presence of God, changed action is the standard proof of true repentance.

Divine Repentance. The Bible demonstrates God's relational nature toward us by providing images of divine repentance. Noah's story gives us a picture of God repenting of creative action that results in evil; after seeing the evil of Noah's generation, God is sorry for and "repents" of creating humans (Gen 6:7 NKJV). Beyond this there are several OT instances of God's repenting of destructive action undertaken as punishment of evil (*see* Crime and Punishment). At the end of 2 Samuel, for example, God repents of sending a *plague on Israel in the form of an afflicting angel. After seeing the result of the plague, seventy thousand dead, God stops midcourse as the angel is on the threshing floor of Araunah the Jebusite. After begging God for *mercy, David buys the threshing floor and builds an altar. God then stands firm in his repentance and stops the plague (2 Sam 24:15-25).

Being warned by Elijah of God's coming judgment, Ahab repents, and God also changes his mind about the promised destruction (1 Kings 21:27). And in the book of Jonah, the reluctant prophet warns Nineveh of God's destructive intent. The king of Nineveh models and orders repentance, acknowledging the possibility of what does occur in the story: God will change course and repent of his action in response to Nineveh's own turning around.

Each example provides an image of God as one who stops one course of action in order to choose another. The divine changes of mind emphasize God's purity of character, *holiness and concomitant *anger over sin, and at the same time his absolute mercy and love, a love that intervenes and qualifies the terrifying hand of just punishment.

See also ASHES; FACE; FASTING; GUILT; HEART; PRAYER; PRODIGAL SON; REVERSAL; SIN; SINNER; SOFT, SOFTNESS; TEARS, VALE OF TEARS; WEEPING.

REPETITION. *See* RHETORICAL PATTERNS.

RESCUE

The Bible is filled with stories and images of rescue. It is an anthology of rescue stories, spoken and written by people who had themselves participated in a grand rescue and who want their listeners and readers to be recipients of rescue also. In fact the biblical narrative, stretching from the expulsion from the *Garden of Eden to the establishment community of the New *Jerusalem, may be viewed as a rescue story. The Bible tells a story of humankind gone astray, taking the entire *creation with it, and of God setting out to rescue his creation from its wayward and destructive course. *Abraham and his descendants, *Israel, become the particular agent of God's rescue operation. But Israel, too, goes astray much like the world at large, and a final hero emerges from Israel, *Jesus, who brings this dramatic rescue operation to its climax and conclusion. Much of the NT is an explication of the significance of the *cross and *resurrection in this grand rescue, and how a rescued people can live as those who will one day inherit and inhabit a rescued creation. But the Bible also contains numerous and smaller episodes of rescue, some of which foreshadow the grand rescue of the cross and resurrection.

Rescue is in many ways synonymous with deliverance, though the image of rescue frequently carries a sense of immediate or impending danger, of a hazardous predicament and of bold and decisive action. It speaks of courage, strength, skill and risk. Rescue easily evokes more concrete scenes than deliverance or salvation. Many Americans will never forget the television image of a man risking his life by jumping into the ice-choked Potomac River to rescue a flight attendant from the wreckage of a crashed plane. Rescues involve hapless victims who are in over their heads and cannot help themselves. They face awful consequences, often death. Rescuers take risks. They plunge into the fray.

Rescues provide the stuff of great stories. The plot motif of the rescue moves in a U-shaped pattern from the plane of everyday life to the depths of experience far from the ideal (danger, suffering, etc.) and then back to life on its former plane, but with a renewed sense of the preciousness of life. Or it can be viewed as a plot that constricts down to the climax of the rescue and then expands. Perhaps one of the best illustrations in the Bible is the condensed story in the *Christ hymn of Philippians 2:6-11. The U-shape pattern is vividly depicted here, but ironically it is traced in the story of the rescuer. For the rescuer must plunge to the depths of the human predicament in order to bring the victims to new life. Christ descends from the height of being in the form of God and equal with God (Phil 2:6) to taking on human likeness and servitude—even to the point of suffering the abysmal death on the cross (Phil 2:7-8)—and then is "highly exalted" to universal lordship (Phil 2:9-11). *Adam and *Eve had descended from a position of privilege (seeking to be "like God") to a position of servitude and bondage to *death. Christ the rescuer will bring the children of Adam and Eve to an exalted position of new humanity. As Paul elsewhere puts it, they are now "seated at the right hand of God" (Col 3:1 NIV). In this hymnic sketch of a bold rescue, the rescuer descends from an even greater height than Adam and goes to the lowest depth in order to rescue those who would otherwise be hopelessly lost.

The first great rescue story in the Bible is God's rescue of Noah, his family and the animals from the great *flood (Gen 6—9). In this story the world has become hopelessly mired in sin, and God chooses one man and his family as a sort of new Adam, whom he will rescue from a great judgment and bring safely to the other side. Noah and the animals will start the world's story on a new footing. In the NT this rescue is understood as a foreshadowing of the final rescue of God's people from a universal and final judgment (cf. 1 Pet 3:20-22; 2 Pet 3:5-7). Sadly, the descendants of the rescued Noah degenerate into godless rebellion, and the judgment at *Babel fractures the human family into many nations.

The calling of Abraham from amidst the nations and peoples is the beginning of a grand story of divine rescue that stretches from the patriarch through Israel and ends with Christ. But in the foreground we encounter numerous vignettes and stories of rescue. Abraham proves he has the right stuff when he bravely rescues Lot and others from Chedorlaomer and his coalition of kings (Gen 14). On other occasions God has to rescue Abraham from inescapable predicaments into which he delivers himself through cowardice and lack of faith in God's ability to spare his life, as when he twice lies to a ruler about his wife's identity (Gen 12:10-20; 20:1-18). God also rescues Abraham's nephew Lot from the judgment of *Sodom and Gomorrah (Gen 19; cf. 2 Pet 2:6-8), and Hagar and her son, Ishmael, from death in the desert (Gen 19).

The story of *Joseph can be read as an intricate narrative of divine rescue. Joseph is first rescued from a *cistern and the murderous intentions of his jealous brothers (Gen 37:19-30) and then rises to be the chief steward in the house of the Egyptian Potiphar (Gen 39:1-6). After escaping the *seduction of Potiphar's wife, he is put in prison to await his fate (Gen 39). But God rescues Joseph by providing the opportunity for him to use his divine gift in interpreting pharaoh's *dreams (Gen 41). Joseph then rises to be Pharaoh's chief regent in all of Egypt and is given the responsibility of preparing for the coming *famine. In the end Joseph is God's means of rescuing his entire family—the promised seed of Abraham—from a great famine that sweeps the land.

The most prominent human agent of rescue in the Pentateuch is *Moses, who was himself rescued from death as an infant (Ex 2:1-10). Moses first rescues his fellow Israelite from an Egyptian taskmaster (Ex 2:11-14), then he rescues the daughters of Reuel from hostile shepherds (Ex 2:15-19), and finally he becomes the human agent of God's rescue of Israel (cf. Acts 7:25). Israel, enslaved in Egypt, cries out to the Lord (Ex 3:7). God tells Moses, "I have heard them crying out, . . . I am concerned about their suffering. So I have come down to rescue them from the hand of the Egyptians and to bring them up out of that land into a good and spacious land, a land flowing with milk and honey" (Ex 3:8 NIV). Moses is commanded, "go . . . bring my people the Israelites out of Egypt. . . . I will be with you" (Ex 3:10, 12 NIV). The ensuing story, which includes a miraculous crossing of a body of water and a narrow escape from the clutches of Pharaoh and his troops (cf. Ex 18:10), provides the master image for many succeeding rescues in the Bible. In the *exodus a nation of nobodies, helplessly subjected to servile labor by the great superpower of the day, is rescued by the one God, constituted as one people, given an inheritance of land and privileged with the divine presence in its midst. Moses' song of deliverance (Ex 15) sounds the keynote and is a high point of the rescue motif in the Bible.

As Israel travels through the wilderness to the *Promised Land, there are several miraculous rescues that anticipate the impending entrance into the land of Canaan. Simply at the level of physical survival, the story is a minianthology of rescue stories in which God sends *food and *water to a traveling nation that faces one narrow escape after another. The episode of the fiery *serpents (Num 21:4-9) is a variation on the theme.

Other rescues of the exodus revolve around military exploits (see Battle Stories). In Numbers 10:9 God instructs that when Israel is in the land and goes into battle against an oppressing enemy, they are to "sound a blast on the trumpets. Then you will be remembered by the LORD your God and rescued from your enemies" (Num 10:9 NIV). It is as if the silver *trumpets are alarm bells that summon the great rescuer of Israel. But God does not simply rescue on demand. In Numbers 14:39-45, when Israel brashly goes up against the Amalekites and Canaanites, after recanting on their initial response to the *spy report, they are roundly defeated. The Lord does not rescue a disobedient people (Num 14:43), he instead delivers them into the hands of their *enemies. This is the first of Israel's great lessons in "no rescue." Those who presume on God will have their expectations reversed. As Amos later puts it, those who long for the *Day of the Lord (i.e., the day of God's victory) may find "that day will be darkness, not light" (Amos 5:18 NIV).

The book of Joshua is a story of a military campaign in which the occupants of the Promised Land are conquered and the *land apportioned to Israel's tribes. But one can also view the battle stories as episodes in which the Lord rescues Israel from enemies as Israel obediently enters the land and faces its inhabitants against seemingly hopeless odds. But it is in the book of Judges that the rescue motif clearly comes to the fore.

The judges are God's agents of rescue during a time of tribal rule and frequent enemy oppression in Israel. But throughout the story it is the Lord who "rescued them from the hands of all their enemies on every side" (Judg 8:34 NIV). The names of some of these judges evoke vivid scenes of Israel's cry for help and God's raising up a rescuer who delivers them from the oppressing powers of Palestine. Ehud with his concealed sword boldly dispatches the corpulent king of Moab and rescues Israel from Moabite oppression (Judg 3:12-30). Under Deborah's leadership Israel is rescued from the oppression of the Canaanite king Jabin and his commander Sisera (Judg 4—5). Under Gideon, the reluctant warrior, Israel is rescued from the hand of the Midianites (Judg 6—7). Under Jephthah, Israel is rescued from the Ammonites (Judg 10:6—12:7). And through the colorful figure of Samson, God rescues Israel from Philistine oppression (Judg 13—16). Ezra's great prayer recounting Israel's history well sums up this period: "You handed them over to their enemies, who oppressed them. But when they were oppressed they cried out to you. From heaven you heard them, and in your great compassion you gave them deliverers, who rescued them from the hand of their enemies" (Neh 9:27 NIV).

During the period of Samuel's leadership in Israel, God continues to rescue Israel from the hands of the Philistines (e.g., 1 Sam 7:8). Under Saul, the first king of Israel, the Lord rescues Israel (1 Sam 11:12-13; 14:23) while Saul's fighting men rescue Jonathan from the capricious hands of Saul (1 Sam 14:45). An ideal king is one who is capable, with God's help, of rescuing his people from enemies and other dangers. Whereas Saul ultimately fails the test, *David proves to be an exemplary king whose resume as a shepherd of Israel begins with a story of rescuing his father's sheep from the lion and the bear (1 Sam 17:35). David comes to be regarded by his loyal followers as one who "rescued us from the hand of the Philistines" (2 Sam 19:9 NIV). But David confesses that it was the Lord who "rescued me from my powerful enemy, from my foes, who were too strong for me. . . . He brought me out into a spacious place; he rescued me because he delighted in me" (2 Sam 22:18, 20; Ps 18:17, 19 NIV).

The Lord's rescue of Israel sets the tone for the various psalms that recount the mighty acts of God. Psalm 107 offers a series of four vignettes of rescue, from wandering in the wastelands, from imprisonment, from affliction brought on by *rebellion and from the terrors of the sea. In each case the subjects "cried out to the LORD" (Ps 107:6, 13, 19, 28) in their distress, and he rescued them from their plight. Psalm 91 speaks of various terrors—deadly pestilence and *plague, the terror of night and the flying arrow by day, the fearsome *lion and cobra—that might befall people. But it firmly assures that those who love the Lord will be rescued (Ps 91:14-15). In Psalm 22 the psalmist recounts the insults hurled at him by his enemies: "He trusts in the LORD, let the LORD rescue him" (Ps 22:8 NIV; cf. Mt 27:43). The psalmist's own cry to the Lord intones Israel's cry: "Rescue me from the mouth of the lions; save me from the horns of the wild oxen" (Ps 22:21 NIV; cf. Ps 35:17).

The Bible has only a few *sea stories, but the story of *Jonah is a prominent one. Jonah is first cast into the sea to quiet the *storm, where he is swallowed by a great fish. Jonah's attempted escape thus leads him into a dangerous predicament. From the belly of the fish he cries out to God in a psalm of *lament, and God rescues him. But ironically, Jonah's experience of rescue does not alter his lack of concern for

Nineveh's rescue from judgment.

The narratives of the prophets provide some of the most vivid instances of divine rescue in the OT. Elijah, for example, is miraculously rescued from starvation in a time of famine (1 Kings 17). He is God's agent for rescuing the nation of Israel from *idolatry on the occasion of the showdown with the prophets of Baal on Mount Carmel (1 Kings 18). He is rescued by divine *fire when Ahaziah sends squadrons of soldiers to seize him (2 Kings 1). Elisha too is rescued when God sends *horses and *chariots of fire that fill the hills as Elisha is surrounded by Arameans at Dothan (2 Kings 6:8-23). Rescues also happen to others who encounter the prophets, as when God rescues Naaman from *leprosy (2 Kings 5:1-14), Hezekiah from military threat (2 Kings 19) and illness (2 Kings 20), and the inhabitants of Samaria from the siege of Ben-Hadad of Aram (2 King 6:24—7:20).

The book of Daniel presents us with two memorable rescue stories in which God delivers faithful Israelites from dire danger in a foreign land. Shadrach, Meshach and Abednego refuse to worship the golden idol created by King Nebuchadnezzar and are bound and thrown into a fiery furnace. They accept the penalty, saying "the God we serve is able to save us from it, and he will rescue us from your hand, O king" (Dan 3:17 NIV). They are stunningly rescued by an angel, and when the king sees them walking among the flames unbound and unharmed, he releases them from the furnace and praises their God (Dan 3:19-30). Daniel is cast into a lion's den for refusing to compromise his allegiance and devotion to God. The king, too late in realizing that his honored servant Daniel is the victim of jealous enemies, anxiously says to Daniel, "May your God, whom you serve continually, rescue you!" (Dan 6:16 NIV). The next morning the king finds Daniel whole and well in the den, rescued by an angel who "shut the mouths of the lions" (Dan 6:22 NIV; cf. Dan 6:20). These stories of the rescue of righteous Israelites in a foreign nation demonstrate God's power to rescue his faithful ones who obey and trust the God of Israel.

The return from *exile, like the exodus from Egypt, is portrayed as an epochal rescue of Israel. A brief sampling from the prophets illustrates the variety of ways in which they use the image of rescue. Isaiah speaks of God's promise to rescue Jerusalem, shielding it from above like a bird flying overhead (Is 31:5). But God's rescue of Israel is also a matter of God's timing. His power to do so is beyond question, for he is the God of Israel's exodus: "Was my arm too short to ransom you? Do I lack the strength to rescue you? By a mere rebuke I dry up the sea, I turn rivers into a desert" (Is 50:2 NIV). Ironically, Isaiah can also speak of a future rescue of Egypt in a manner evoking Israel's rescue from Egypt: "when they cry out to the LORD because of their oppressors, he will send them a savior, and he will rescue them" (Is 19:20 NRSV).

A "no rescue" motif is also employed by the prophets. For Isaiah it depicts the plight of Israel short of God's action, for they are like a "people plundered and looted, . . . trapped in pits or hidden away in prisons. They have become plunder, with no one to rescue them" (Is 42:22 NIV). Hosea and Micah both hammer out a message of judgment on the anvil of the "no rescue" motif. Hosea depicts the Lord as a lion to Ephraim and Judah, tearing them to pieces and carrying them off "with no one to rescue them" (Hos 5:14 NIV). And Micah sees the nations treating the remnant of Jacob like a lion among the flock, mauling and mangling as it goes "and no one can rescue" (Mic 5:8 NIV).

In the NT the greatest image of rescue is the *resurrection of Jesus Christ. Arrested, tried, crucified, dead and sealed in a tomb, he is like Israel, with "no one to rescue" him. But God raises him from the dead, exalts him and enthrones him at his *right hand with his enemies *under his feet. The OT stories of divine rescue—particularly the exodus and return from exile—provide the key for understanding this great rescue. Ezekiel's vision of a valley of dry *bones coming to life (Ezek 37:1-14) is a prominent instance of the metaphor of death and resurrection applied to Israel's exile and restoration. But the pattern may be observed elsewhere in the Bible, such as in the withering, convulsing, melting and death that strikes nature and humankind when the *divine warrior marches to war (Is 24:1-13; Mic 1:3-4; Nahum 1:2-6; Hab 3:6, 8) and the rejuvenation of life and "new song" that breaks forth when he is victorious (e.g., Ps 96; 98). In his own death and resurrection, Jesus recapitulates the story of Israel's exile and full restoration. The return from exile that Israel has never fully experienced is brought to light. The rescue of Jesus from the clutches of death is the first fruits of the prophetic hope of the redemption of God's people. His rescue embraces all who follow him—both Jews and Gentiles—and in his rescue the entire created order finds its hope of rescue from death and decay (cf. Rom 8:18-23).

The book of Acts recounts episodes of rescue of early church leaders. An angel rescues the apostles from jail (Acts 5:17-26) and delivers Peter from Herod's prison (Acts 12:1-19). Paul and Silas are miraculously rescued from the prison at Philippi when an earthquake breaks open the prison doors (Acts 16:22-28). Paul is later rescued from the hands of his enemies in Jerusalem (Acts 21:27—23:35). These stories of rescue reinforce the theme that the spread of the gospel is directed by God, for whom no confinement or danger is insurmountable.

In fact the entire narrative of Luke-Acts is bracketed by the rescue motif, with the climactic rescue occurring near the center of the entire work (Lk 23—24; Acts 1). At the beginning of Luke the song of *Mary (Lk 1:46-55) and the song of Zechariah (Lk 1:67-79) sound the theme of God's rescue of Israel's righteous ones from their enemies (cf. Lk 1:74). The Gospel develops the rescue motif as it depicts Jesus rescuing many who are sick and helpless. But Luke is alone among the Gospel writers in displaying the full sweep of Jesus' *descent and *ascent: his miraculous *birth into this world, his descent to the cross and then the grave, and his subsequent resurrection and ascension to heaven. The book of Acts draws to a close with Paul, the chief herald of this story, passing through his own figurative passion and resurrection. Shipwrecked and abandoned to a stormy and malevolent *sea, Paul and his shipmates are providentially rescued on Malta (Acts 27). As if to underscore the rescue of Paul, the apostle is subsequently delivered from the deadly venom of a viper (Acts 28:1-6). In the end we find Paul strategically placed in Rome and declaring to the Gentiles the good news of God's great rescue (Acts 28:28-31)—in fulfillment of the risen Lord's promise to Paul: "I will rescue you from your own people and from the Gentiles" (Acts 27:17 NIV).

Paul employs the image of rescue as he speaks of the work of Christ as a new exodus. In Galatians 1:4 he speaks of Christ giving himself for our sins "to rescue us from the present evil age" (NIV), and in Colossians 1:13 it is God the Father who "has rescued us from the dominion of darkness and brought us into the kingdom of the Son he loves" (NIV). The "present evil age" and "dominion of darkness" evoke an oppressive regime in which men and women are held captive, in dire need of rescue. From the midst of those held in thrall to "this age," a voice cries out, "What a wretched man I am! Who will rescue me from this body of death?" (Rom 7:24 NIV). In fact, this cry appears to be Paul's taking on the voice of Israel under the *law, held in bondage because of its inability to keep the law due to the power of sin (cf. Rom 5:12—6:23). In Galatians 4:1-5 Paul sketches out the drama of divine rescue in which Israel, enslaved to the "basic principles of the world," is rescued by one sent by God and born "under the law, to redeem those under law" (Gal 4:5 NIV). But like the psalmists who speak of God's rescue as both a national and personal reality, Paul lives with the assurance that "The Lord will rescue me from every evil attack and will bring me safely to his heavenly kingdom" (2 Tim 4:18 NIV). This note is affirmed in 2 Peter: "The Lord knows how to rescue godly men from trials and to hold the unrighteous for the day of judgment, while continuing their punishment (2 Pet 2:9 NIV).

The book of Revelation provides the final glimpses of rescue in the Bible. Behind much of the cosmic battle imagery lies the assurance that Christ has rescued his followers from *Satan, *evil and *death. The premise throughout the book is that Christ "has freed us from our sins by his blood" (Rev 1:5). When the demonic dragon (see Monsters) threatens to destroy the woman (Israel) and her son (Christ), both are miraculously rescued from otherwise certain destruction (Rev 12:1-6). The interspersed pictures of the redeemed in heaven (e.g., Rev 5; 7; 14:1-5) convey a sense that they are in heaven through the rescue efforts of the divine Lamb. Just when the forces of evil seem poised for their greatest assault, the divine warrior appears (Rev 19:11-21; 20:7-10) to stay their hand.

See also BATTLE STORIES; BONDAGE AND FREEDOM; DANGER, STORIES OF; ENEMIES; EXODUS, SECOND EXODUS; RESTORE, RESTORATION; SALVATION..

RESERVOIR. *See* CISTERN.

REST

A longing for rest after exertion belongs to the universal human condition. It is, in fact, part of the rhythm of daily and weekly life. Paintings that picture the laborer returning home at the end of a working day capture feelings that even an urban dweller experiences, as does the assertion in Psalm 127:2 that God "gives to his beloved sleep" (RSV). Human rest in the Bible combines physical and spiritual meanings. For biblical writers rest is more, though not less, than utilitarian.

Rest was built into the natural rhythms of life by the Creator, who rested on the *seventh day of *creation (Gen 2:1-3). An important part of the meaning of rest is suggested by the mystery of divine rest: it draws a boundary around *work and exertion and takes a legitimate delight in celebrating what has been accomplished, without an urge to keep working. The rest of God even includes an element that is crucial for humans who rest—refreshment. Exodus 31:17 tells us that God not only rested on the seventh day but also "was refreshed" (RSV). Similar pictures of rest as a cessation of work emerge from the life of Jesus. Despite his busyness, Jesus took time for retreats from his active life (Mk 6:45-47; Lk 6:12; 9:28). He prescribed a similar pattern for his *disciples, telling them, "Come away by yourselves to a lonely place, and rest a while" (Mk 6:31 RSV).

The most obvious form of human resting in the Bible is the *sabbath—one day in seven set aside for freedom from work (Ex 20:8-11; Deut 5:12-15). It was a time of total rest within the household, with neither *servants nor *animals exerting themselves in work (Ex 23:12). We can see in this weekly rest the satisfaction of both a physical need (the reason Ex 23:12 gives for the prescribed rest is that people and animals "may be refreshed") and a spiritual requirement to set time aside for the *worship of God. Sabbath rest was buttressed by a system of *festivals that constituted an important part of Hebrew religious life.

Such rest reorients a person's values, taking attention off the workaday preoccupation with getting and spending and onto God and spiritual realities. In the Bible willingness to engage in such rest is nothing less than a *covenant sign—"a perpetual covenant" and "a sign" between God and his people (Ex 31:16-17 RSV). Yet another part of the symbolism of sabbath rest was that it pictured release from the *bondage of Israel in *Egypt (Deut 5:15). Rest is a form of freedom—from work, from human striving and acquisitiveness, from worldly preoccupations.

If willingness to rest is a sign of commitment to God, it is elsewhere viewed as a freedom from anxiety. Moses paints a picture of "the beloved of the LORD" as someone who "rests in safety" and "rests between [God's] shoulders" (Deut 33:12 NRSV). Here is a picture of what rest ultimately involves in the Bible—a relinquishing of human self-assertion and a trust in God. The psalmist enjoins us to "rest in the LORD, and wait patiently for him" (Ps 37:7 KJV). Jesus' discourse against anxiety uses a barrage of persuasive strategies urging people to cease from anxious striving as they trust in God to supply their needs (Mt 6:25-34). Rest is here a form of letting go of human control.

Taken a step further, rest as trust in God's providence becomes symbolic of *salvation itself. Isaiah quotes God as reprimanding his people for trusting in their own resources instead of accepting God's invitation: "In returning and rest you shall be saved; in quietness and in trust shall be your strength" (Is 30:15 NRSV). Jesus offers more than emotional rest when he utters the invitation "Come to me, all who labor and are heavy laden, and I will give you rest" (Mt 11:28 RSV).

The ultimate rest is *death—life's final and lasting cessation from work and action. For Job this final rest is what it is for Homer—a mere cessation, a place where "the wicked cease from troubling, and . . . the weary are at rest" (Job 3:17 RSV). This hazy OT picture of the afterlife is equally present in the formula of deceased people's *sleeping or resting with their fathers. In the NT, however, the *heavenly rest that follows life on earth is nothing less than the goal of human existence. The writer of Hebrews rings the changes on this theme, claiming that "we who have believed enter that rest" (Heb 4:3 RSV) and assuring believers that "there remains a sabbath rest for the people of God; for whoever enters God's rest also ceases from his labors as God did from his. Let us therefore strive to enter that rest" (Heb 4:9-11). And in Revelation we hear the voice from heaven saying, "Blessed are the dead who die in the Lord henceforth . . . that they may rest from their labors" (Heb 14:13 RSV).

See also BONDAGE AND FREEDOM; DEATH; LEISURE; PLAY; PROMISED LAND; SABBATH; SLEEP; SLEEPLESS NIGHT; WEAK, WEAKNESS; WORK, WORKER; WORSHIP.

RESTORATION. *See* RESTORE, RESTORATION.

RESTORE, RESTORATION

Anyone familiar with biblical religion knows how important the prefix *re-* is to the Bible and biblical theology. Biblical faith is preeminently the religion of going "back" or experiencing something "again." The imagery of restoration thus takes its place with such related motifs as redemption, *return, *reunion, reconciliation and *rebirth. Restoration denotes giving or receiving something back that was taken or *lost.

The word itself appears well over a hundred times in English translations. The first thing to note is the immense range of phenomena that are restored. A wife can be restored to her husband (Gen 20:7, 14), a son to a father (Gen 37:22), a person to an office (Gen 40:13, 21; Dan 4:34-37). People's afflicted bodies are restored to *wholeness or health (Ex 4:7; 1 Kings 20:34; 2 Kings 5:10, 14; Mk 3:5; 8:25), and even life is restored to the dead (2 Kings 8:5). *Garments are restored (Ex 22:26), stolen goods are restored (Lev 6:4-5), fortunes are restored (Deut 30:3; Ps 14:7; 53:6). *cities are restored (1 Sam 7:14; Neh 3:8), the *temple is restored (2 Chron 24:4, 12). The largest repository of explicit references to restoration is the OT Prophets, where the focus is the restoration of the nation of *Israel (Judah) after the Babylonian *exile, an event that combines political and spiritual meanings—and that carries over to the NT when the disciples ask the risen Christ on the verge of his ascension, "Lord, will you at this time restore the kingdom to Israel?" (Acts 1:6 RSV; cf. also the argument of Rom 11, which speaks of a restoration of Israel).

Sometimes the imagery of restoration has moral implications. Thus a cloak taken in pledge must be restored to the *owner before nightfall (Deut 24:13), stolen property must be restored (2 Sam 12:6), money taken by fraud is restored (Lk 19:8), a person guilty of *sin is restored by the church (Gal 6:1). Elsewhere the meaning is spiritual rather than ethical, as a person's soul is said to be restored (Ps 23:3), a person *forgiven by God is said to be restored to the *joy of salvation (Ps 51:12) and redeemed people are said to be restored (Ps 80:3, 7, 19; 85:4). Even the attainment of *heaven is viewed as a restoration: "And after you have suffered a little while, the God of all grace . . . will himself restore, establish, and strengthen you" (1 Pet 5:10 RSV).

Biblical eschatology likewise includes a restoration theme. It is most explicitly stated in a sermon by Peter, who predicts that Christ's return will be "the time of universal restoration that God announced long ago through his holy prophets" (Acts 3:21 NRSV). The whole structure of the Bible embodies this pattern, as we move from an original perfection down to the misery of fallen human history and then up to a restoration of perfection—even a paradisal perfection (Rev 22:1-2; *see* Garden). The same motif underlies the argument of Romans 8:18-25, which speaks of the human and natural worlds groaning under the burden of fallenness, waiting for an eventual redemption or restoration.

The Bible also contains stories of restoration. *Joseph is restored to a position of prominence in Egypt after having been imprisoned by Potiphar and to his *family after years of separation. *Job's fortunes are restored double after his ordeal of suffering. *David is restored to the kingship after *Absalom's temporarily successful *rebellion. The restoration of Israel prophesied by the prophets is narrated in the books of *Ezra and *Nehemiah. Peter's relationship with Jesus is restored in a manner that recapitulates his threefold denial of Jesus (Jn 21:15-17).

See also CREATION; EXILE; ISRAEL; JERUSALEM; PEACE; REBIRTH; REMNANT; RETURN; REUNION, REC-ONCILIATION; WHOLE, WHOLENESS.

RESURRECTION

The imagery of resurrection in the NT is rooted in the Gospel narratives of Jesus' resurrection, though the Epistles add imagery when the writers explore the efficacy of Christ's resurrection in the lives of believers.

The Gospel Accounts. The resurrection of Jesus from the dead is preeminently an image of new beginnings, and the image that all four Gospels include to highlight this quality is the physical dawn of the Sunday on which Jesus arose (Mt 28:1; Mk 16:2; Lk 24:1; Jn 20:1). Into this scene the writers introduce solitary or paired figures who drift or (as the news spreads) run to the tomb in the minutes of early *morning, in obvious contrast to the crowd scenes that dominate the passion story. And in another contrast to the passion story, the only cataclysmic detail in the resurrection story is Matthew's account of an *earthquake that accompanied the appearance of the *angel who rolled the *stone from the tomb's mouth (Mt 28:2).

The story of the resurrection is suffused with a quality of mystery and miracle, and this atmosphere is chiefly embodied in the numinous appearance of angels, resplendent in their transcendent *glory (Mt 28:2-4; Mk 16:5; Lk 24:4; Jn 20:12).

The supreme image of Jesus' resurrection is without doubt the stone rolled away from the entrance to the tomb (Mt 28:2; Mk 16:4; Lk 24:2; Jn 20:1). It is supplemented by the imagery of the empty tomb (Mt 28:6; Mk 16:6; Lk 24:3, 22; Jn 20:5-9).

Although the cast of characters on stage at any one time is small, the story is filled with the imagery of announcement and passing of the word. Some of it transpires between angels and *women (Mt 28:5-7; Mk 16:6; Lk 24:5-6). The women, in turn, pass the word to the *disciples (Mk 16:7, 10; Lk 24:8-10; Jn 20:18), creating an atmosphere of excited discovery and a felt need to communicate the news. In keeping with this are the related motifs of quickness and extensive motion, as characters run to and fro in a near frenzy of motion (e.g., Mt 28:8; Jn 20:2-8). This is in obvious contrast to the passion story, where we experience a progressive cessation of activity.

The motif of encounter also permeates the resurrection story. At the center of the encounters is the risen Christ, as he meets the women of his life (Mt 28:9-10; Mk 16:9, 12-14; Lk 24:36-42; Jn 20:11-29) and the two men of Emmaus (Lk 24:13-35; *see* Divine-Human Encounter). The followers of Jesus likewise encounter each other, and the sense of a small, tightly knit believing community runs strong in the narrative.

The resurrection story is marked by powerful emotions. These emotions run a notable range—dis-belief, *joy, perplexity, amazement, *fear—but they all share an intensity that is one of the leading qualities of the story (Mt 28:8; Mk 16:5, 8, 11-12; Lk 24:3, 5, 11, 32). Amid all the encounters, moreover, we find gestures of *worship and belief (Mt 18:9; Lk 24:31; Jn 20:8-9, 16, 28).

The Epistles. The imagery of Christ's resurrection extends beyond the narrative in the Gospels, as the writers of the Epistles build a theological structure around the event. The most frequently used image is supplied by the word *raised* (approximately three dozen references), accentuating two aspects of Christ's resurrection—its dynamic nature and the idea that the power came from a source beyond Christ himself. We might also see overtones of a directional symbolism, with the *grave assumed to be *"low" and the resurrection raising the dead Christ "up" from the dead. This image of raising suggests a mighty power, as Ephesians roundly describes it, "God put his power to work in Christ when he raised him from the dead and seated him at his right hand in the heavenly places" (Eph 1:20; cf. 1:19). Here we see the raising and enthronement of Christ as one fluid movement of exaltation. As a mighty act of God it evokes memories of the exodus, the biblical archetype of God's powerful saving acts.

A second leading motif is the linking of the believer's experience with Christ's resurrection, which is viewed as the model and source of the believer's future resurrection from the dead. The imagery stresses linkage or connection, with believers being "united" with Christ in his resurrection (Rom 6:5), or raised "with" Christ (Col 2:12; 3:1), or raised by the same power that raised Christ (1 Cor 6:14; 2 Cor 5:15). In a sense *baptism becomes the prime epistolary image for the believer's link with Christ, with imagery of dying with Christ and rising with him linked with the physical act of baptism.

A third cluster of verses visualizes the final resurrection of the dead at the end of history. Two main motifs are the suddenness with which the universal resurrection of all the dead will happen (1 Cor 15:51-52; 1 Thess 1:10) and the complete *transformation of individual believers as they are born into a superior state of being (1 Cor 15:35-54). Elsewhere, resurrection is imaged as an *awakening, as Daniel predicts that "many of those who sleep in the dust of the earth shall awake, some to everlasting life, and some to shame and everlasting contempt" (Dan 12:2 NRSV).

Defeating Death. The Bible records real-life resuscitations in addition to the resurrection of Jesus. OT narrative records the raising of the Shunammite woman's son through the agency of Elisha (2 Kings 4:18-37). NT narrative multiplies the examples: Jesus' raising of Jairus's daughter (Mt 9:18-26; Mk 5:22-43; Lk 8:40-56) and Lazarus (Jn 11:1-44), the raising of Eutychus through the agency of Paul (Acts 20:9-12) and Tabitha through the agency of Peter (Acts 9:36-42), and the "many bodies of the saints" that came out of the tombs after Jesus' resurrection and went into Jerusalem (Mt 27:52-53).

See also ASCENSION; BURIAL, FUNERAL; DEATH; GRAVE; MORTALITY; RESTORE, RESTORATION; REVERSAL; TRANSFORMATION.

RETURN

The approximately four hundred instances of *return* in English translations signal the importance of the return motif in the Bible. These references denote movement back either to a previous location (such as the dove returning to the ark, Gen 8:12) or to a previous condition (such as people returning to dust after death, Gen 3:10). Most of these references are neutral in association, but even at a literal level they underscore an inherent rhythm of human life—that of going out and returning to the place from which one set out. In fact, this basic rhythm of life is encapsulated in a biblical merism (the rhetorical device of naming opposites with the implication that everything between them is also included) that speaks of "going out" and "coming in" (Josh 14:11; 2 Sam 3:25; 1 Kings 19:27; Ps 121:8; Is 37:28 RSV).

The image of returning can also carry a profound spiritual meaning. To return is to *repent from *sin, thereby returning to a state of favor with God. Here we find pictures of *sinners returning to God (Ps 51:13), of God's inviting people to return to him for *redemption (Is 44:22) or for *mercy (Jer 3:12), of God's commanding his people to return from their evil ways (Jer 18:11) and of his longing that they do so (Ezek 33:11). Approximately a dozen Bible verses speak specifically of returning to God, with Isaiah 55:7 serving as a fitting epitome of the motif of return as repentance: "Let the wicked forsake his way, and the unrighteous man his thoughts; let him return to the LORD, that he may have mercy on him, and to our God, for he will abundantly pardon" (RSV). The prominence of the imagery of return to describe spiritual progress underscores an essential assumption of the Bible, where God is the starting point of all that is good; to go forward, in such a view of life, is to go back.

The imagery of returning is thus more than a physical motion. The biblical authors, notably the prophets, use the imagery of return to expound further on the nature of the turning of a human *heart. It is the return of a wayward covenant people back to their covenant Lord (Is 44:22; Jer 3:10-11, 14; 4:1; 24:7; Lam 3:40; Hos 6:1). Repentance, therefore, is a very important aspect of the image of return. The connection between repentance and returning to God is illustrated well in Hosea 14:1-2. The *return* imagery implies a wholehearted turning from reliance on one's own strengths and virtues and firm resting on the covenant character and promises of God (see also Joel 2:12-13). It is a fundamental redirection *away* from the *path of sin and self-reliance and a subsequent *return* to a place of restored fellowship and *peace. The image therefore illustrates vividly the dual nature of biblical repentance: turning away from sin and returning to God.

Stories of Return. We can note additionally a genre of return stories in the Bible. Such stories were important in the ancient world. A whole branch of classical literature dealing with the Trojan War consists of return stories, with Homer's *Odyssey* (which tells of Odysseus's ten-year journey to return to his home in Ithaca) the chief monument. Some of the Bible's stories of return are minor, others decidedly major. The first return story is that of *Jacob, who returns to the land of his parental origin after a twenty-year sojourn with Laban in Haran (Gen 31—35). Within that story the return to Bethel (Gen 35) receives special emphasis, as God renews the covenant promise he first made to Jacob when the latter was fleeing from Esau. Naomi returns to *Bethlehem after a tragic interlude in Moab (Ruth 1). The grandest of the OT stories of return is the return of a remnant of people to Palestine after the Babylonian *exile (*see* Exodus, Second Exodus).

The NT too is a repository of return stories. The magi return home by a secret route (Mt 2:12), and *Mary and Joseph return to Galilee after the flight into Egypt (Mt 2:19-23). The shepherds return to everyday life after being the first outsiders to see the baby Jesus (Lk 2:20). In an opposite mood, the witnesses of Christ's crucifixion "returned home beating their breasts" after the horrors of what they had seen (Lk 23:48 RSV). Jesus makes numerous return visits to towns during his career as an itinerant preacher and miracleworker.

The parables of Jesus also make use of the return motif. The prototype is the story of the *prodigal son, who comes to his senses and returns from a far country to his father's home, emblematic of the repentant sinner's return to God (Lk 15:11-24). The Pharisee and tax collector return home after their respective prayers at the temple—one justified, the other condemned for his self-righteousness (Lk 18:9-14). The rich man makes a futile appeal to God to send Lazarus on a return trip to earth to warn the rich man's brothers about impending judgment (Lk 16:19-31).

Yet another category of return stories is eschatological in nature, centering on what is familiarly known as Christ's "return" (even though the NT does not use that exact vocabulary). The key text is John 14:3, where Christ says, "When I go and prepare a place for you, I will come again and will take you to myself, that where I am you may be also" (RSV). This is buttressed by parables in which a master (Christ) returns after taking a long journey, calling his servants to account upon his arrival (Mt 25:14-30; Lk 12:35-40; 19:11-27).

Perhaps the motif of return is a "metanarrative" in the Bible. Although the *glory of God departed from *Zion at the exile (Ezek 10:1-22), Israel continued to hope not only that they would return to Palestine but also that God would return to Zion. This is sometimes stated explicitly (Is 52:7-10; Ezek 43:1-7; Zech 8:2-3), while at other times it is the implied story behind the establishment of the reign of God and the vanquishing of Israel's enemies (Ps 50:3-4; 96:12-13; 98:8-9; Is 4:2-6; 24:23; 25:9-10; 35:3-6, 10; 40:3-5, 9-11; 59:15-17, 19-21; 60:1-3; 62:10-11; 63:1-9; 66:12-19; Hag 2:7, 9; Zech 2:4-5, 10-12; 14:1-5, 9, 16; Mal 3:1-3). There is a sense in which Jesus' incarnation, and especially his entry into the *temple, fulfills this theme of the return of God to Zion.

See also EXODUS, SECOND EXODUS; HOMECOMING, STORIES OF; OUTCAST; PRODIGAL SON; REPENTANCE; REUNION, RECONCILIATION; RUNAWAY.

REUNION, RECONCILIATION

All of us love stories of reunion and reconciliation, partly because they are rich in emotion and partly because they appeal to a deep-seated longing to be at *one with other human beings and with God. The most famous biblical reconciliation scenes are the two family reunions that light up the book of Genesis. One is the story of *Jacob and *Esau (Gen 33:1-14), reunited after twenty years of separation. In this story Jacob is the guilt-haunted supplicant, humorously overprepared for the meeting, while Esau is generous and impulsive in his *forgiveness. Even more elaborate is the extended reunion scene when *Joseph discloses his identity to his *brothers and fêtes them in grand style (Gen 46:1—47:12).

A motif of reconciliation underlies the book of *Hosea, where the prophet obeys God's command to be reunited with his faithless wife, Gomer. In the *Song of Songs moments of separation between the two lovers are resolved in scenes of reunion. A similar motif is latent in the postresurrection appearances of *Jesus, and it becomes the dominant thread in the story of Jesus' restoration of Peter (Jn 21:15-19).

Reconciliation between persons is a pattern as well in the ethical teaching of Jesus, as Jesus outlined a protocol for being reconciled to a fellow believer (Mt 5:23-26; cf. Gal 6:1) and for forgiveness of a brother or sister who sins against oneself (Mt 18:21-22).

The motif of restoration receives a distinctly spiritual treatment in the Bible, built on the foundation of God's forgiveness of sinners. It happens on a national level in the OT, where the continuous cycle of sin-repentance-restoration is the dominant pattern in Israelite history. The prophetic books call the nation to be restored to obedience and favor with God, and they typically end with a vision of such restoration. The psalms occasionally express the wish for such restoration in the form of petitionary prayer (Ps 14:7; 53:6; 60:1; 85:1; 126:4).

Such reconciliation with God through *forgiveness is also realized on a personal level. The classic case is Psalm 51, built around the contrition of the speaker and his longing that God will "restore to me the joy of thy salvation" (Ps 51:12 RSV). The theme underlies all of the traditional "penitential psalms" (Ps 6; 32; 38; 51; 102; 130; 143). In the NT this motif becomes a full-fledged theological principle in which the key term is *reconciliation* (Rom 5:10-11;

2 Cor 5:18-20; Eph 2:16; Col 1:20, 22).

See also FORGIVENESS; PEACE; REPENTANCE; RESTORE, RESTORATION; WHOLE, WHOLENESS.

REVELATION, BOOK OF

No book of the Bible is thicker with images than the book of Revelation. In fact, one author entitled his commentary on the book *A Rebirth of Images.* Though Revelation is written in prose, its texture is poetic in its reliance on images to the nearly total exclusion of abstract or propositional discourse. Northrop Frye, the most influential archetypal critic of the twentieth century, even called the book of Revelation a "grammar" of literary archetypes—the place where we can find them in a systematic and definitive form.

The imagery of the book is in fact heavily archetypal. Its images are the universal images of the human race, the very stuff of our waking and sleeping dreams and nightmares. For all its syntactical and grammatical irregularity, the book of Revelation is the easiest biblical book to translate, because it speaks a universal language of images. As we enter the world of the book, we move in a world of life, *death, *blood, *lamb, dragon, beast (*see* Monster), *light, *darkness, *water, *sea, *sun, *war, *harvest, *white, scarlet, *bride, *throne, *jewels and *gold. Equally archetypal are the numerous references to rising and falling, high and low (or even bottomless).

The book of Revelation seems unwieldy in the sheer quantity of its details, but the organizational scheme is actually quite simple. The key to the book's structure is the *sevenfold motif that pervades it. Between the prologue (Rev 1) and epilogue (Rev 22:6-21), the book unfolds according to the following sevenfold pattern: the letters to the seven churches (Rev 2—4), the seven *seals (Rev 5:1—8:1), the seven *trumpets (Rev 8:2-11), the seven great signs (Rev 12—14), the seven *bowls of wrath (Rev 15—16), the seven events of final *judgment and consummation (Rev 17:1—22:5).

Another unifying factor is the narrative format that organizes the individual visions. For any given unit of Revelation we can ask four standard narrative questions: Where does the action occur? Who are the actors or agents? What happens? What is the result of the action?

Contrast and Balance. Contrast is a leading motif in Revelation, which confronts us with the great "either-or" of human life—the choice between goodness and evil, which are engaged in nothing less than mortal combat on a cosmic level. Within the general conflict of good versus evil we find a whole system of parallel conflicts: Christ versus *Satan, the Lamb versus the dragon, the saints versus the followers of the beast, the bride of Christ versus the whore of *Babylon, *heaven versus sinful *earth, the *city of God versus "the great city" of evil, New Jerusalem versus Babylon, the sealing of the saints versus receiving the mark of the beast.

Revelation is a book of extremes. The *cosmology moves in a huge expanse from the heights of heaven to the depths of the bottomless pit. Emotions run the gamut from the utmost desolation and lament to the highest ecstasy of celebration. God and Christ represent the absolute good; Satan and his two beasts (perhaps a demonic parody of the holy Trinity) are absolute evil.

Sometimes the dichotomies of Revelation are not so much contrasting as complementary. The most obvious example is the balance between *nature and civilization as sources of the book's imagery. One cannot miss the emphasis on nature, which for the most part is in a state of environmental disintegration. But there are probably as many city and court scenes as landscape scenes in Revelation. The imagery of elemental nature, including the forces of nature as cosmic actors in the drama of judgment, might lead us to picture the world of the book as being somewhat unpeopled, but the book is actually filled with crowd scenes.

Apocalyptic Imagery. Some of Revelation's conventions and image patterns belong to the apocalyptic genre of the book (*see* Apocalyptic Visions of the Future). The dualistic nature of the world of the book fits this pattern. Apocalyptic writing is strongly messianic, and this too underlies the book of Revelation. From start to finish the book is "the revelation of Jesus Christ" (Rev 1:1), who stands revealed in both descriptive portraits and narrative accounts of his exploits. Apocalyptic writing elevates spiritual characters like *angels and *demons to center stage, and so does the book of Revelation. *Animal symbolism and numerology (*numbers used with symbolic meaning, such as seven to denote completeness or fullness) are also prevalent. The preoccupation of apocalyptic writing with coming judgment and woes is another feature of the book.

Apocalyptic imagery is futuristic, and the entire book of Revelation assumes this as a premise. The opening verse of the book uses the formula "what must soon take place" (Rev 1:1 RSV), thereby signaling the futuristic cast of the entire book. The author himself, we should note, identifies his book as a "prophecy" (Rev 22:18), which in this case includes the implication of prediction of the future. No matter how much of Revelation strikes later readers as having been already fulfilled, much of the prophecy seems impending.

Apocalyptic imagery is also visionary. The basic premise of the genre is that it is an "unveiling" (the literal meaning of *apocalypse*) of a spiritual world that is ordinarily invisible to human sight. The world of Revelation is an "other" world in two ways: it is a world of the future that can only be imagined at this point, and it is a world that transcends the earthly order of things. In both cases the world of Revelation is beyond ordinary human access, capable of being grasped only by way of a vision that God sends to his seer John. If we are to catch a glimpse of that other world, the "door" to the other world has to be opened (Rev 4:1), or heaven itself has to be

"opened" (Rev 19:11). The repeated references to John's "looking" and "seeing" reinforce the impression that we are looking at a transcendent realm, as do references to John's "hearing" the content of his visions, as though they are beyond visualizing.

The most memorable visionary realm in the book of Revelation is of course *heaven. From time immemorial enameled imagery has been one of the chief image patterns by which prophets and poets have portrayed the heavenly realm. Such imagery combines *hardness of texture and brilliance of light to suggest a world of superior *permanence and value that transcends our vegetative, cyclic world. Thus we have images of a "sea of glass, like crystal" (Rev 4:6 RSV), a city with "radiance like a most rare jewel, like a jasper, clear as crystal" (Rev 21:11 RSV), a wall "built of jasper" in a city built of "pure gold, clear as glass" (Rev 21:18 RSV) and so forth.

The terminal imagery of the book likewise fits into its apocalyptic genre. The events portrayed are not simply futuristic but eschatological images of the *end. Underlying the surrealistic time scale of the book is a progressive intensification of judgment, from a fourth of the earth to a third to "the last, for with them the wrath of God is ended" (Rev 15:1 RSV). Earthly realities vanish: "earth and sky fled away, and no place was found for them" (Rev 20:11 RSV). The "no more" motif becomes prominent in the later phases of the book (Rev 18:22-24; 22:3-5), implying that earthly reality has been replaced by something *new.

Theatrical Imagery and Folk Literature Motifs. *Theatrical motifs and imagery pervade the book, which may show signs of influence from the conventions of classical drama. Much of the impact of the book depends on what Aristotle called spectacle—characters with physical traits ascribed to them (including attention to "costuming"), placed in specific settings, where they perform actions on the "stage" that has been created for them by the author's descriptions. The book is filled with snatches of dialogue, while on other occasions a chorus of actors sings hymns. The basic format of the book—a pageant of visions—draws on the theatrical model of a succession of scenes.

Despite its reputation for being a mystical and mysterious text, the book of Revelation partakes of a number of folk-literature motifs that make it seem more like children's stories than an esoteric guide to another world. Revelation makes limited use of animal characters, for example—the lamb, the dragon, horses of various colors, warriorlike locusts and terrifying beasts (*monsters, obviously) from the sea and earth. *Color symbolism is equally a characteristic of the popular imagination through the centuries, and we find it in Revelation—white associated with Christ, the saints in heaven and God's throne, and red in contexts of evil (warfare, the Satanic dragon and the whore of Babylon along with her beast).

The last half of the book is a spiritualized version

of familiar folktale motifs: a woman in distress who is marvelously rescued, a hero on a white horse who kills a dragon, a wicked *prostitute who is finally exposed, the marriage of the triumphant hero to his bride, the celebration of the *wedding with a *feast, and the description of a palace glittering with jewels in which the hero and his bride live happily ever after.

Symbolism. While the images of Revelation appeal to the imagination first of all at a sensory or physical level, it is important to realize as we read that these images and narrative motifs are intended as symbols of a future and/or transcendental reality. The book of Revelation uses images as symbols for characters and events that really exist or will really occur, but not in a literal manner. The four horse visions (Rev 6:1-8), for example, employ images and symbols to portray a coming era that Jesus described directly when he predicted in his Olivet Discourse that "nation will rise against nation, and kingdom against kingdom, and there will be famines and earthquakes in various places" (Mt 24:7 RSV). Another hermeneutical key to how the imagery of Revelation works is Revelation 12:1-6, which narrates the escape of a woman's child from the destructive strategies of a dragon. While we do not mistake these details for literal realities, they call realities to mind, namely, the birth of the Messiah (the child who is to rule all the nations [Rev 12:5]) from the nation of Israel (the woman in travail), the inability of Satan to destroy Christ during his earthly life and the ascension of Christ into heaven.

Symbolic imagery is present already in the letters to the seven churches. Here we read about the *sword of Jesus' *mouth (Rev 2:16), about people not having soiled their garments (Rev 3:4), about glorified believers becoming a *pillar in a temple (Rev 3:12), about Christians who have become lukewarm (Rev 3:16), about Christ standing at a *door and knocking (Rev 3:20). We do not interpret these images literally. They are physical symbols of spiritual realities. In interpreting the symbolic visions of Revelation we need not reach for esoteric meanings. The best question to ask of a given passage is, of what theological fact (e.g., redemption, judgment, good, evil) or event in salvation history (final judgment, glorification in heaven, a coming tribulation, etc.) does this passage seem to be a symbolic version? In particular, the book continuously narrates the outline of eschatological events that Jesus predicted in the Olivet Discourse (Mt 24—25).

The symbolic imagery of Revelation has an open-ended quality. The predictions of the book have been fulfilled many times in history and will be ultimately fulfilled at the end of history. To take just one example, the Babylon of Revelation was the Roman Empire for John's original audience, but it has taken many forms since then and is in fact a picture of the human race in rebellion against God, as we find it in our own culture. Revelation's visions of cosmic collapse have spoken to every generation of readers, but they have even more relevance to an age of global environmental pollution and destructive capabilities that transcend those of any previous age. The visions of Revelation are always up to date, and it is the symbolic mode of the book that makes them such.

In keeping with this symbolic mode, the imagery of the book tends to be nonpictorial. Though painters and illustrators have always tried to turn the images of Revelation into pictorial form, the imagery of Revelation resists such treatment. The book is strongly sensory and even visual (in the sense that we visualize images and symbols), but the harder we try to visualize the scenes as composite scenes, the more incomprehensible and grotesque they become. The basic rule of symbolic writing is that it does not paint pictures. It is ideographic, not pictographic. Just as the skull and crossbones on a bottle of medicine is a symbol of poison but not a picture of it, Revelation's lamb and lion are symbols of Christ but not pictures of him.

Cosmic Imagery, Surrealistic and Transformed. The book of Revelation is epiclike in the sweep of its action and settings. It encompasses all of reality, including heaven, earth and hell. Only in the letters to the seven churches are we rooted in a specific historical setting. Most other references to the earth extend to the whole earth, not a specific locale, and all nations, not a specific country. The world of Revelation is the elemental world of sun, river, ocean, mountain, stars and suchlike.

In addition to the universality implied by this cosmic imagery, we should note that cosmic forces become actors in the drama that transpires in the book of Revelation. The sun becomes black (Rev 6:12), the stars fall to the earth (Rev 6:13), a mountain, burning with fire, is thrown into the sea (Rev 8:8), and rivers become blood (Rev 16:4). The point is at least twofold: cosmic forces as actors are images of power beyond human ability to resist, and they show that events are happening at the very core of the created order.

The cosmic world of Revelation is, moreover, a surrealistic nightmare of *disease and *death and unnatural happenings. The only healthy place is heaven, but the imagery of transcendence keeps us aware that heaven is a world remote from earth in its final stages of disintegration and corruption. The imagery associated with the earth in the book of Revelation makes up a sustained surrealistic nightmare. Here we encounter such unsettling and grotesque images as water turning to blood, heavenly bodies falling from the sky, people covered with sores, gigantic locusts that attack people, the drying up of vegetation, the pollution of the environment, hailstones "heavy as a hundredweight" dropped from heaven (Rev 16:21 RSV) and vanishing islands and mountains (Rev 16:20).

The cosmos of John's vision is governed by the transformation motif, portraying a world in transition. Nothing remains static for very long. Even the cinematic structure of the book reinforces this effect, with its kaleidoscope of visions that are constantly shifting and never in focus for very long. Two main patterns of transformation dominate. The earthly sphere, subject to God's judgment, is in a process of degeneration and collapse. By contrast, the final two chapters are the Bible's second creation story, suffused with the atmosphere of God's creating "a new heaven and a new earth; for the first heaven and the first earth had passed away" (Rev 21:1 RSV). In the book of Revelation things are changing either for the worse or for the better.

Summary. A good way to make sense of the kaleidoscope of images with which Revelation bombards us is to codify them into a series of clusters under the formula "images of . . ." The main headings are the following: images of *glory, images of *heaven, images of *judgment, images of mystery, images of *redemption, images of *evil, images of *worship, images of *battle, images of earthly destruction, and images of punishment and *torture (see Crime and Punishment).

See also APOCALYPSE, GENRE OF; APOCALYPTIC VISIONS OF THE FUTURE; COSMOLOGY; END TIMES; PROPHECY, GENRE OF.

BIBLIOGRAPHY. R. J. Bauckham, *The Climax of Prophecy: Studies in the Book of Revelation* (Edinburgh: T & T Clark, 1992); idem, *The Theology of the Book of Revelation* (NTT; Cambridge: Cambridge University Press, 1993); G. B. Caird, *Commentary on the Revelation of St John the Divine* (New York: Harper & Row, 1966).

REVELATION/RECOGNITION STORIES

Recognition stories often exist apart from an element of revelation (when a character recognizes something by coincidence) but in keeping with the Bible's *providential theme, in most biblical stories of recognition a revelation occurs by God's design. Sometimes the mainspring of a story is the element of revelation by God or a person; on other occasions the main action is human recognition, with an implication that someone has revealed the thing that has been discovered.

The God Who Appears. Stories of revelation are present from the Bible's beginning. Having created Adam and placed him in Paradise (see Garden), God speaks to him to reveal the conditions of human life in the world (Gen 2). After the Fall, Adam and Eve suddenly recognize both their own *sinfulness (as symbolized by their *shame over their *nakedness) and the presence of God *walking in the garden prior to a scene of *judgment (Gen 3). Thereafter the book of Genesis is punctuated with scenes in which God appears or speaks to reveal his purposes—to Noah, to the patriarchs, to Hagar, to Pharaoh. Correspondingly, people experience a series of discoveries as the book unfolds. In particular, *Abraham and Sarah discover by steps exactly how God will fulfill the promise of a son, and *Joseph undergoes a series of experiences that on the surface cannot possibly lead to the fulfillment of his youthful dreams, while

of course they all play a part in that very fulfillment. When a person recognizes God's presence, the response is awe and *worship; highlights include Abraham's catching sight of the substitute ram (Gen 22), Hagar's recognition that God is "a God of seeing" when God appears to her in the *wilderness (Gen 16:13 RSV) and *Jacob's awaking from his *dream and concluding, "How awesome is this place! This is none other than the house of God, and this is the gate of heaven" (Gen 28:17 RSV; see Jacob's Ladder). On a human plane, points of high drama are Isaac and *Esau's trembling and crying out when they recognize that Jacob has cheated them (Gen 27:33-34) and the paralysis of Joseph's brothers when they recognize Joseph in Egypt (Gen 45:1-15).

The most customary way God reveals his presence and purpose is through appearances to human beings. We can scarcely think of the OT without remembering a host of such appearance scenes—divine appearances to *Moses in the *burning bush (Ex 3:1-6) and on Mt. *Sinai, and when God's *glory passes before Moses (Ex 33:17-23), and on numerous occasions when he instructs Moses how to proceed with the trip through the wilderness; to Gideon (Judg 7:9-15); to *Samson's parents (Judg 13); to the youthful Samuel by night (1 Sam 3); to the nation of Israel when his glory fills the *tabernacle (Ex 40:34-35) and the *temple (2 Chron 7:1-3) on the occasion of their dedications. God appears to Job in a *whirlwind (Job 38-42:6), to Elijah in a still small *voice (1 Kings 19:9-13), to Isaiah in a vision of a heavenly *throne (Is 6:1-5), to Ezekiel in a riot of whirling sensation (Ezek 1), to Nebuchadnezzar in the form of an unexpected fourth person in the fiery furnace (Dan 3:24-25), to Belshazzar in the form of a hand writing a message of *judgment on the wall (Dan 5:5-9). For the recipients of these divine revelations the experience is an encounter with the holy or numinous, even when the revelation comes in the form of *nature (Ps 19; 29; see Encounter, Divine-Human).

The human response to God's revelations is recognition. The Song of Moses pictures the nations who hear of the Red *Sea deliverance as becoming "as still as a stone" as they recognize God's power (Ex 15:16). Rahab recounts a similar recognition on the part of the people of Jericho (Josh 2:11). The newly pregnant Hannah is led by her experience to recognize God's power and *justice (1 Sam 2:1-10).

Recognizing God in Christ. The NT variations on the motif of revelation and recognition focus on the incarnate Christ. The Christ hymn that opens the Gospel of John (Jn 1:1-18) sounds the keynote when it portrays Christ as God's Word of revelation, in whom people recognize God's glory. The recognition story is one of the leading narrative genres of the Gospels; in these stories people come to recognize Christ as the promised Messiah and as Savior. Jesus is thus recognized by the wise men (Mt 2:1-12), Simeon and Anna (Lk 2:25-38), the *shepherds (Lk 2:15-20), Peter (Mt 16:13-17), John the Baptist (Jn

1:29-34), *demons (Mk 3:11), the *disciples (Jn 2:12), *women who anoint his feet (Mt 26:6-13; Mk 14:3-9; Lk 7:36-50; Jn 12:1-8), the Samaritan woman and her fellow townspeople (Jn 4:1-42), and the multitudes. The postresurrection appearances of Jesus add to the list of such stories; highlights include the appearances to Thomas (Jn 20:24-29) and the men going to Emmaus (Lk 24:13-35).

See also BURNING BUSH; ENCOUNTER, DIVINE-HUMAN; EPIPHANY, STORIES OF; GLORY.

REVENGE. *See* AVENGER; VENGEANCE/REVENGE STORIES.

REVERENCE

Even though the word *reverence* comes uneasily, if at all, to the lips of most people today, it refers to an experience that we all share. Consider the aura that surrounds the rich and powerful and their influence over people and institutions. Much of this type of reverence may be unwarranted (biblical examples of refusal to give such reverence include Esther 3:2-5; Dan 3:8-18), yet the Bible allows for some distinction of *honor to be made among people (Mt 22:15-22). Paul encourages believers to pay "respect to whom respect is due, honor to whom honor is due" (Rom 13:7 RSV). The most common gesture of reverence toward a human superior in the Bible is *bowing (Gen 23:7; 33:3; Ruth 2:10; 1 Sam 24:8; 2 Sam 14:4; 1 Kings 1:16). In surveying NT hints of what a Christian society would look like, C. S. Lewis includes among its salient features an emphasis on *obedience and outward marks of respect by subordinates toward the *authorities above them ("Social Morality," in *Mere Christianity*).

In the Bible, however, reverence is above all directed toward God, and *worship is reserved solely for the true God (cf. Ex 20:3; Deut 5:7). It is also clear from the biblical account that the reverence due God has something to do with fear, though it should not be understood as a slavish or abject fear (*see* Fear of God). Moses made this distinction clear to the people of Israel after their reaction to God's self-revelation in the *thunder, *lightning and *trumpet blast on Mt. *Sinai at the giving of the Ten Commandments. The Israelites pleaded with Moses, "Speak to us yourself and we will listen. But do not have God speak to us or we will die." Moses responded, "Do not be afraid. God has come to test you, so that the fear of God will be with you to keep you from sinning" (Ex 20:19-20 NIV).

Thus the fear of the Lord is not merely shaking in one's boots but is better understood as that curious mix of awe, fear and honor due the Almighty King and Creator of everything. This reverence/fear is, according to biblical wisdom literature, the foundation of all human knowledge (Prov 1:7).

Lewis captures the spirit of reverence in *The Lion, the Witch and the Wardrobe*, as Mr. and Mrs. Beaver explain Aslan's nature to Lucy:

"Then he isn't safe?" said Lucy.

"Safe?" said Mr. Beaver. "Don't you hear what Mrs. Beaver tells you? Who said anything about safe? 'Course he isn't safe. But he's good. He's the King, I tell you." (75-76)

See also AUTHORITY, DIVINE AND ANGELIC; BOWING; FEAR OF GOD; HONOR; KNEE, KNEEL; OBEDIENCE.

BIBLIOGRAPHY. C. S. Lewis, *The Lion, the Witch and the Wardrobe* (New York: Macmillan, 1970); idem, *Mere Christianity* (London: Collins Fontana, 1952).

REVERSAL

As far back as Aristotle, storytellers and audiences have thrilled to tales that include an element of *surprise in the form of reversal. Strictly defined, a reversal is an action that produces the opposite of the effect intended. More loosely defined, reversal encompasses any change-of-fortune story in which a sudden or decisive change is a mainspring of the plot.

The account of the Fall (Gen 3) is the first reversal story in the Bible. Thinking to become Godlike—reaching for everything—*Adam and *Eve lose it all. *Cain thinks to rid himself of a pious brother whom he envies, only to find himself condemned to the life of a restless *wanderer (Gen 4:1-16). Lot lifts his eyes to the well-watered plain of the Jordan River and chooses a land that in his mind equals material *prosperity (Gen 13), only to lose his home and his wife as that region is transformed into a *wasteland (Gen 19). *Abraham's twenty-five years of waiting for God to produce the promised son are punctuated by a series of false starts in which he undertakes actions that seem expedient but instead result in dead ends; such are the episodes involving the king of Egypt (Gen 12:10-17), the decision to have a son by Hagar (Gen 16) and Abraham's lie to Abimelech (Gen 20). On a happier note, Abraham sets out to *sacrifice his son, only to find a ram as a *substitute (Gen 22).

Reversal continues in the subsequent patriarchal narratives in Genesis. *Jacob thinks to better himself by stealing his dying father's *blessing, only to find himself an exile for twenty years in a hostile foreign locale. When Jacob returns to his parental land, he thinks that his impending meeting with his brother, *Esau, is the major problem to be solved, but instead his wrestling with God (Gen 32:22-31) proves to be the climactic event of his life. In the story of *Joseph and his brothers, the happiest of the *cheat-the-oracle stories in the Bible, everything the brothers do to prevent fulfillment of Joseph's *dreams of supremacy leads directly to their fulfillment. The moving of Jacob's family to Egypt also involves reversal, based on the "false haven" motif: thinking to settle in a place of security, Jacob's family eventually becomes an oppressed nation for four hundred years.

The epic of the *exodus also has its share of plot reversals. All of *Pharaoh's stratagems to subject the Israelites to *bondage lead to their *prosperity (Ex 1:12). Thinking that women pose no threat (Ex 1:16), Pharaoh is repeatedly *outwitted by women.

During the *plagues Pharaoh's attempts to thwart the Israelites' plans lead only to a series of plagues that eventually destroy him. Later, Balaam does all he can to pronounce a *curse on the Israelites, but when the crucial moment comes he instead pronounces a blessing (Num 22—24).

The book of Judges is a small anthology of striking reversals. The Moabite king Eglon ("fat calf") is so thoroughly duped by the crafty Ehud that when Ehud speaks deviously of having a secret message from God for him, Eglon rises solemnly, only to receive a deadly sword thrust in his fat stomach—the original case of the disappearing knife (Judg 3:21-22). The fleeing captain Sisera settles down to a cozy nap in the tent of the apparently hospitable Jael (whose name should have warned him); instead he is impaled through his skull with a tent peg (Judg 4—5). Gideon begins his story (Judg 6—8) with a severe case of inferiority complex, as virtually all the details early in the story paint a portrait of a reluctant hero. But halfway through the story our expectations are denied, as Gideon shows sheer mastery of everything that stands in his way. Thinking to perform a pious act, Jephthah condemns his daughter by his rash *vow (Judg 11). *Samson's dalliance with Delilah reaches its climax in the sudden reversal of his loss of strength (Judg 16).

The story of *Esther highlights reversal as well. Haman's story is based on the proverbial *pride that goes before a fall: overreaching himself in his pride and hatred of the Jews, he ends up overseeing the exaltation of his enemy Mordecai and dying on the gallows he had prepared for Mordecai. On a national level, the seemingly hopeless situation of the Jewish nation is reversed by a sudden victory. Reversal is more subtle in the book of *Ruth, where Boaz is surprised by an unexpected request for marriage at midnight from a widow whose age, social standing and national origin make her an unlikely consort.

The psalms of *lament present their own variation on the theme of reversal. Nearly without exception, these *quests for consolation in the face of terrible crisis include a reversal or even a recantation. After painting a picture of seemingly unconquerable threat, the poet suddenly reverses himself in a statement of confidence in God and vow to praise God. The situation that has been portrayed as hopeless turns out suddenly to be soluble after all. Other psalms can also employ the motif; for example, Psalm 73, after presenting a portrait of the arrogant wicked, reverses itself with a contrasting picture of the sudden fall of these very people. Psalms of praise sometimes celebrate God's glorious reversals that exalt the humble and topple the proud; Hannah's song (1 Sam 2:1-10) and Mary's "Magnificat" (Lk 1:46-55) are the best examples.

Psalms of *rescue are also based on the reversal motif. Psalm 107, for example, narrates the plight of four groups of unfortunates—those wandering in desert wastes, sitting in prison, suffering from illness and going down to the sea in ships. Each vignette is reversed halfway through by the intervention of God, who leads the desert wanderers to a city, liberates the prisoners, heals the ill and brings the storm-tossed sailors to a haven. *Jonah's song from the watery *deep (Jon 2) enacts the same reversal. On a spiritual and emotional level, the *guilt-haunted *sinner in Psalm 32 wastes away when he fails to declare his sin, but his plight is reversed when he resolves to confess his transgressions to the Lord.

The book of *Proverbs too is a memorable scrapbook of sudden reversals, sometimes in the form of predictions: people who get gain by violence will be trapped in their own designs (Prov 1:10-19), the *sluggard will find that his excuses for not working will bring him to sudden *poverty (Prov 6:9-11), and the person who undertakes elaborate means to avoid being brought to account for his *evil will be broken "in a moment" (Prov 6:12-15).

No genre in the Bible is more saturated with reversal than prophetic and apocalyptic literature. The oracles of *judgment are filled with visions in which current conditions are reversed, contrary to all present evidence. Above all, the nations that are currently powerful will have their prosperity snatched away from them. But in keeping with the mysteries of grace, these same books, despite all their predictions of judgment, end with a sudden reversal, not prepared for, in which the nation that has been chastised throughout the preceding visions is portrayed as being *restored to prosperity. Prophetic narrative (and not only prophetic vision) springs reversals on us—especially the book of *Daniel, where Nebuchadnezzar casts the three young men into a furnace only to find them miraculously spared, where the same king suddenly falls from power in the moment when he least expects it, where Belshazzar receives the prophecy of his imminent defeat on the very night that he throws the biggest party of his life, and where Darius needlessly spends a sleepless night after consigning Daniel to the *lions' den.

The NT has its own versions of the reversal motif. One set is the *conversion stories that abound, in which a person's whole pattern of life is reversed by his or her initiation into the *kingdom of God. Another is the motif of God's choosing people from undistinguished backgrounds, reversing the world's standards of value. The *disciples are the best examples, but the classic expression of the principle is Paul's statement that not many of Christ's followers "were powerful, not many were of noble birth; but God chose what is foolish in the world to shame the wise, God chose what is foolish in the world to shame the strong" (1 Cor 1:26-30 RSV).

The most prominent NT version of reversal occurs in the sayings and parables of Jesus. Jesus' sayings regularly reverse conventional standards or expectations, as the *first are declared to be last and the last first, as the person who loses his life is said to save it and vice versa, and as the blessed person is the one who is meek, who mourns, who suffers *persecution. A similar assault on the listener's deep structure of thought occurs with the familiar reversals that enliven Jesus' parables—the fortunes of the rich man and *beggar reversed in the afterlife, the enterprising *farmer's plans for retirement dashed the day after his building venture is completed, the religious elite passing by the wounded man while help comes from the least expected source (a despised Samaritan), and a *Pharisee going home condemned while a tax collector is justified.

The story of salvation itself is a story of reversal. Isaiah writes, "Come now, let us reason together, says the LORD: though your sins are like scarlet, they shall be as white as snow" (Is 1:18 RSV). People dead in trespasses and sins have their burial reversed (Eph 2:1, 5-6). Those who "once . . . were no people" now are God's people, and those who "once . . . had not received mercy . . . now . . . have received mercy" (1 Pet 2:10 RSV).

At least two themes emerge from the biblical motif of reversal. One is the mystery of God's providence, grace and election, as unlikely people are chosen for favor while people impressive by worldly standards are scorned. The other principle is judgment, as people who think themselves secure are actually vulnerable.

See also CHEAT THE ORACLE; PLOT MOTIFS; SURPRISE, STORIES OF; YOUNGER CHILD, YOUNGER SIBLING.

REWARD

The motif of reward is deeply rooted in the faith of the Bible, which nowhere treats the godly life as a life devoid of reward. From God's assurance to Abraham that "your reward shall be very great" (Gen 15:1 NRSV) to Christ's statement in the last chapter of the Bible that "I am coming soon; my reward is with me" (Rev 22:12 NRSV), the Bible assumes that God rewards the righteous. This is not to say that reward is based on human merit; it is based on divine grace. In fact, hovering over the Bible is the grim awareness that the *"wages" the human race has earned by sin consist of *death (Rom 6:23). This is why salvation is the serious theme of Scripture. But reward is nonetheless linked throughout the Bible to people's lifestyle and state of soul.

The Hebrew and Greek words used in the Bible for reward are rooted in the idea of payment, hire or wages. A correspondence is presupposed between work done or not done and the payment given to a person. Only once—in Jesus' parable of the workers in the vineyard who receive a payment that disregards the duration of their effort (Mt 20:1-16)—is this link severed, for the purpose of stressing that in the kingdom of God new values dominate, based on divine grace rather than human merit.

The idea of reward is richly evoked throughout Scripture as the fruit, consequence and award for goodness or righteousness in living—living that reveals faithfulness to God's commands or is based on an innate knowledge of God's goodness and nature within people who have not had the benefit of God's written Word (Rom 1:19-20; 2:6-8). The most ob-

vious division of rewards in the Bible is between earthly and heavenly rewards, physical and spiritual rewards, OT and NT conceptions of reward.

The Old Testament Vision: Earthly Rewards. A good entrée into the OT concept of reward is the portrait of the godly person in Psalm 1. The outcome of behavior that avoids various types of evil practices and roots itself in obedience to God's law is that such people "prosper" in "all that they do" (Ps 1:3 NRSV). In a similar portrait the reward that comes to those who pursue holy living is that they "shall never be moved" (Ps 15:5 NRSV). In yet another encomium the rewards for the person who fears the Lord are mighty descendants in the *land, wealth and riches, a stable life, and *honor (Ps 112). *Children too are a reward from God (Ps 127:3).

A similar outlook emerges from OT wisdom literature. "Those who sow righteousness get a true reward" (Prov 11:18 NRSV), we hear from the wise man. Again, "manual labor has its reward" (Prov 12:14 NRSV), and "those who respect the commandment will be rewarded" (Prov 13:13 NRSV). "Prosperity rewards the righteous" (Prov 13:21 NRSV), and "the reward for humility and fear of the LORD is riches and honor and life" (Prov 22:4 NRSV). The climactic sentiment in the acrostic poem praising the virtuous wife of Proverbs 31 is a wish for her reward: "Give her a share in the fruit of her hands, and let her works praise her in the city gates" (Prov 31:31).

This then is the entrenched view that pervades the OT: God will reward righteous people (those who live by his law and are marked by spiritual integrity) with the good things of this life—*family, *home, sustenance, *honor, *prosperity, success (as in Ps 18:20). This vision of the good life as God's reward appears in kernel form in the oldest confession of faith in the Bible—the Shema of Deuteronomy 11:13-21, which pronounces as a reward for obeying God's commandment the blessings of *rain, crops and *harvest (*grain, *wine, *oil, *grass, *fruit). The list of blessings for obedience in Deuteronomy 28:1-14 is similar in import.

This conception of the good life is not necessarily unspiritual, inasmuch as God is very much a part of the picture. The reward God promises Abraham is by implication God himself (Gen 15:1). The rewards of earthly prosperity, moreover, are never separated from the means by which they are attained, namely, godliness. Moses reminds his fellow Israelites that they will conquer the Promised Land not because of their righteousness but because of God's faithfulness to his covenant (Deut 9:4-5). Still, despite the stipulation of godliness as a prerequisite for reward, the OT emphasis on earthly welfare is far different from the eschatological and otherworldly emphasis of the NT.

Old Testament Stories of Reward. The motif of reward is present in narrative form as well as in the law and poetry of the OT. To begin, it is a rare biblical story that does not end with *poetic justice—with virtue rewarded and vice punished. This is simply how stories work. The underlying premise is justice, and (to use Aristotle's evocative phrase) the reader's moral sense is satisfied only if such justice prevails. Thus Abraham and Sarah's life of faith in God's covenant is rewarded with the birth of a promised son. Joseph's integrity is rewarded with his elevation to authority in Egypt. David's refusal to take Saul's life leads to similar reward. Even when the specific imagery of reward is not evoked in poetic justice, the motif is present and carries the implication of immediate and earthly reward.

In addition to the dynamics of poetic justice, some stories turn so significantly on the action of reward that we can speak of a category of "stories of reward." The story of *Ruth is one such. Boaz calls attention to the pattern when in his first meeting with Ruth he expresses the wish, "May the LORD reward you for your deeds, and may you have a full reward from the LORD, the God of Israel, under whose wings you have come for refuge!" (Ruth 2:12 NRSV). Boaz himself becomes the means by which that reward comes to Ruth when he marries her as a kinsman redeemer. The story of *Job too is a reward story, since Job's initial godliness and later reconciliation to God's providence in his life lead to his doubly restored fortunes at the end of the story. In other OT stories such paragons of courage as *Esther, *Moses and *Daniel are rewarded for their godly risk-taking. The *suffering servant of Isaiah 53 is rewarded for his sacrifice, as expressed in the imagery of military conquest—receiving a portion with the great and dividing the spoil with the strong (Is 53:12).

The New Testament Vision: Rewards in a Coming Kingdom. The motif of reward continues unabated in the NT, but it takes a different turn. The best entrée into the new vision is Jesus' famous beatitudes (Mt 5:1-12; Lk 6:20-26). In this portrait of the ideal disciple, Jesus pronounces blessing on people for the same spiritual lifestyle that the OT commends. But the focus of the rewards in the motivational section of each beatitude ("for . . .") is solidly otherworldly and even eschatological. The rewards are now such things as possessing the kingdom of heaven, receiving God's comfort and mercy, seeing God and being called children of God. And even when the imagery looks earthly (inheriting the earth) the reference probably is to a coming *millennium or new creation.

Other statements in the teaching of Jesus reinforce the imagery of spiritual and heavenly reward. Jesus encourages people to practice piety in such a way as to receive a "reward from your Father in heaven" (Mt 6:1 NRSV; see also Mt 6:6, 18). Jesus tells *parables in which the rewards that characters receive are such spiritual rewards as going home justified, or entering into the joy of one's Lord, or being carried to *Abraham's bosom. And in the Olivet Discourse (Mt 24—25), the reward that is chiefly pictured is entering into heaven and inheriting "a kingdom prepared for you from the foundation of

the world" (Mt 25:34 NRSV).

Consolation and Motivation for Endurance. In keeping with the otherworldly emphasis of NT rewards, rewards are promised less as incentives to godly living for the sake of earthly prosperity (the OT pattern) and more as motivation to endure in the faith during trying times. The prospect of an unseen heavenly reward is offered as a consolation and sustaining *hope—an encouragement not to lose heart. The book of Hebrews, addressed to people in danger of abandoning the faith in difficult times, sounds the keynote: "Do not, therefore abandon that confidence of yours; it brings a great reward" (Heb 10:35 NRSV). Again believers are encouraged to "run with perseverance the race that is set before us," looking for inspiration to Jesus, who endured the cross for the joy of eventually sitting "at the right hand of the throne of God" (Heb 12:1-3 NRSV). The seven letters to the churches in Revelation 2—3 reinforce the pattern: each ends with the promise of a heavenly reward to believers who persist in their commitment in the midst of *persecution or *apostasy.

The imagery used to portray heavenly reward in the NT stresses the transcendent permanence of the reward. From the world of athletic winners comes the image of an imperishable wreath of victory (1 Cor 9:25). The preferred image comes from monarchy, as we read about a *crown of righteousness (2 Tim 4:8), a crown of life (James 1:12) and a crown of *glory (1 Pet 5:4; Rev 2:10). In addition the book of Hebrews pictures heavenly reward by means of the imagery of *rest after labor, reserved for those who do not fall through disobedience (Heb 4:9-11).

The conditions for being rewarded are stringent. They are not simply a matter of outward behavior and observance of the letter of the law (Mt 5—7). The Bible emphasizes inner qualities, including wisdom in living (Dan 12:3), humility (Mt 10:42), faithful stewardship (Mt 25:25), generosity (Lk 6:35) and practical goodness (Rom 2:10; 1 Cor 3:8; Col 3:23-25).

See also CROWN; HEAVEN; GLORY; GOOD LIFE, THE; HONOR; INHERITANCE; POETIC JUSTICE; PROSPERITY; WAGES.

RHABDOMANCY. *See* ORACLE.

RHETORICAL PATTERNS

The adjective *rhetorical* denotes two distinct features of a discourse. It means either the persuasive strategy by which a written or oral discourse influences an audience or a set of conventional motifs or formulas that appear in a body of discourse. This article is concerned with conventional devices that appear in biblical texts. No attempt has been made to be exhaustive but only to outline some of the main features of biblical rhetoric, accompanied by sufficient examples to illustrate the devices.

Shapeliness and Completeness. The simplest of all rhetorical patterning takes the form of creating compositions that possess a sense of shapeliness and completeness. Aristotle's time-honored formula that a composition is whole and complete if it has a discernible beginning, middle and end is probably the best account that exists. The preference of biblical writers for the brief unit is obvious, but the resulting minicompositions display an artistic impulse to frame the main composition with a formal beginning and ending.

The story of Cain, for example, begins by introducing the protagonist onto the stage with an account of his birth and ends by dismissing him with a note closure ("Then Cain went away from the presence of the LORD, and dwelt in the land of Nod" [Gen 4:16 RSV]). The story of the exchanged birthright (Gen 25:29-34) begins with a brief version of "once upon a time" ("once when Jacob was boiling pottage") and ends with an account of how Esau "ate and drank, and rose and went his way," followed by the narrator's interpretive commentary on the event ("thus Esau despised his birthright," RSV). On a larger scale the story of Ruth begins by placing the family of the story into a temporal and geographic setting ("in the days when the judges ruled") and ends with a genealogy. What we see here is the impulse toward completeness and resolution—like putting a frame around a picture.

If we turn to the lyric poems of the Bible, we find the same impulse toward beginning-middle-end. Virtually every poem in the Psalter begins with a line or couplet that announces the subject of the poem: "LORD, who may dwell in your sanctuary?" (Ps 15:1 NIV). And virtually every psalm ends with a generalized, semi-detachable statement of closure that rounds out the meditation with a note of finality: "He who does these things shall never be moved" (Ps 15:5 RSV). "Blessed is the man," announces the poet as he begins a portrait of the godly person (Ps 1:1 RSV). And after assembling the portrait, the poet gives a final verdict on the two ways that have been presented in the poem: "The LORD knows the way of the righteous, but the way of the wicked will perish" (Ps 1:6).

Something similar happens in the NT Epistles. They begin in formal manner with a salutation, usually followed by a thanksgiving. Then follows the business that has occasioned the letter. The epistles do not simply end; they instead reach a note of closure with final greetings and a benediction: "The grace of the Lord Jesus Christ and the love of God and the fellowship of the Holy Spirit be with you all" (2 Cor 13:14 RSV).

Even the Bible as a whole possesses a shapeliness and wholeness. Its first two chapters portray a world from which evil is absent, as do its last two chapters. The paradisal *garden of Genesis 2 makes a reappearance in the last chapter of Revelation (Rev 22:2). The aura of the new *creation in the Bible's opening chapters is balanced by a similar aura surrounding the new *heavens and new *earth of the final chapters. The garden in which two perfect people are placed reaches a grand finale in a holy city where the host of the redeemed enjoy life forever. Between this obvious beginning and end stretch the annals of fallen human history.

Circular Structures. In its heightened form, this impulse toward shapeliness takes the form of envelope structure. Several psalms, for example, begin and end with the same line (Ps 8; 103; 106; 113; 117; 135; 147). A modification is seen in psalms that begin and end with similar imagery or vocabulary. Psalm 1, for example, begins and ends with the imagery of the *path or way. Psalm 139 opens and concludes with the imagery of God's knowing the way of the speaker.

Many OT historical narratives begin and end in similar fashion. For a traveler like *Abraham, a common pattern is to begin a story by bringing him into a region ("Abram went down to Egypt," Gen 12:10 RSV) and end by leading him out ("Abram went up from Egypt," Gen 13:1 RSV). In the chronicles of OT kings the placing is temporal rather than geographic: "Manasseh was twelve years old when he began to reign.... So Manasseh slept with his fathers, and they buried him in his house" (2 Chron 33:1, 20 RSV).

An informal name for this rhetorical pattern is "bookends." The technical Latin term is *inclusio*. Isaiah encircles a section of his prophecy with nearly identical phraseology about *darkness and distress (Is 5:30; 8:22). The woman in the Song of Songs begins and ends a meditation on her beloved by comparing him to a gazelle and young stag (Song 2:9, 17). When applied to an entire book, this impulse toward circular structuring takes the form of "ring composition," in which material is arranged in concentric "circles" around a pivot in the middle. The *Song of Songs, for example, pictures the *wedding of the couple in the middle. The book begins and ends with courtship lyrics. Between the center and the encircling bookends are songs of romantic love.

The structuring of a passage in such a way that the second half takes up parallel topics to the first half in reverse order is called *chiasm*, after the Greek word for "crossing." Even after we have conceded that many of the chiastic structures scholars have claimed for the Bible are imposed by the scholars rather than signaled by the text, it still seems conclusive that biblical writers wrote in an awareness of chiasm as a rhetorical principle. Isaiah 6:10, for example, gives us the sequence heart-ears-eyes-eyes-ears-hearts. Amos 5:4b-6a begins and ends with a command to "seek" the Lord and "live," and between this envelope we pursue the series Bethel-Gilgal-Beersheba-Gilgal-Bethel. Some of the chiastic structures are more subtle and require close reading to discover: Romans 11:33-35 follows the sequence riches-wisdom-knowledge-unsearchable judgments-inscrutable ways-mind-counselor-gift.

Theme and Variation. Few principles of composition are more recurrent than that of theme and variation. The theme of a composition is its unifying core—an idea, an image, a situation, an emotion. The variations are the specific ways the writer elaborates and develops the theme. The rhetorical principle of theme and variation imposes a double obligation on writer and reader—to find a principle that unifies the entire composition and to relate all the parts to that unifying core. A composition thus constructed adheres to a time-honored principle of "the same in the other" and "the whole in every part."

Lyric poems are the most obvious examples of compositions constructed on theme and variation. Psalm 23, for example, is constructed around the acts a shepherd performs for *sheep during the unfolding of a typical day; the variations are the specific activities that make up that composite picture. Psalm 121 is one of the "Songs of Ascent"; its core theme is God's ability to protect the traveler, and the poem accordingly constitutes a catalog of God's protective acts in the life of the *pilgrim. Psalm 104 presents variations on God's provision for *nature and through it (*see* Providence).

Most passages of expository prose likewise display obvious adherence to the principle of theme and variation. 1 Corinthians 13 rings the changes on the superiority and hence indispensability of love to the Christian life. The beatitudes of Jesus give a many-sided portrait of the ideal disciple. Jesus' discourse against anxiety (Mt 6:25-34) presents an ever-expanding picture of how futile and faithless it is for a Christian to worry about food and clothing. The Ten Commandments give specific answers to the question of how God wants his people to live.

Stories are built around the premise of a plot conflict moving to resolution. Yet even in biblical narrative the principle of theme and variation is at work. Aristotle was the first to establish as a literary principle that we must be able to see how every episode a storyteller chooses to include is relevant to the story as a whole. There is a sense, therefore, in which even narratives are constructed on a principle of theme and variation. The individual episodes in the life of *Joseph all reinforce the theme of God's providence working through the life of an exemplary character. Every detail in the story of Ruth contributes to the picture of a domestic heroine engaged in a quest for home and family.

Repetition. The importance of repetition in the Bible is universally recognized. Patterns of repetition are numerous. In biblical narrative, for example, writers often revert to a common formula or pattern as the story unfolds. Thus the book of Genesis is punctuated with the formulas "these are the generations of" and "these are the descendants of," thereby keeping alive our awareness that this is the book of beginnings. The chroniclers of the OT kings repeat formulas of the type "in the fifteenth year of Amaziah the son of Joash, king of Judah, Jeroboam the son of Joash, king of Israel, began to reign in Samaria, and he reigned forty-one years" (2 Kings 14:23 RSV). Similarly, "Jeroboam slept with his fathers, the kings of Israel, and Zechariah his son reigned in his stead" (2 Kings 14:29 RSV).

Not all repetition in Bible stories is highlighted by such formulas. The following cycle recurs in the book of Judges: the nation wanders from God's commands into idolatry; God delivers the nation into the power of a neighboring oppressive nation; the people repent and cry to God for help; God raises up a deliverer. The book of Acts has its own repeated cycle, which is arranged as a spiral of expansion as well: Christian leaders arise and preach the gospel; God performs mighty acts through them; listeners are converted and added to the church; opponents begin to persecute the Christian leaders; God intervenes to *rescue the leaders or otherwise protect the church.

Repetition is even more evident in the poetry of the Bible. The most overt example is the antiphonal Psalm 136. Some psalms employ repeated word patterns; Psalm 119 is built around such synonyms for the law as *testimonies, precepts, commandments* and *statutes*. Or a psalm might employ repeated words at the beginning of strophes (Ps 36:5, 7, 10). Alternately, the repeated vocabulary can occur at the end of units (Ps 42:5, 11 and 43:5; 46:7, 11; 49:12, 20).

Repetition also appears in prose passages. Various parts of Jesus' Sermon on the Mount, the *encomium to love in 1 Corinthians 13 and the honor roll of faith in Hebrews 11 are case studies in the use of repeated words and formulas to give force and eloquence to a prose composition. In this regard it is helpful to know that the characteristic Hebrew way to conduct an argument is not to unfold a series of logical arguments leading to a conclusion but to repeat a point so often that the audience is finally inclined to feel that the argument is valid. The book of Ecclesiastes provides numerous examples, such as the meditation on the meaningless cycles of life (Eccles 1:4-11) or the poem on "a time for everything" (Eccles 3:1-8).

Not infrequently patterns of repetition in the Bible are linked to number formulas. Psalm 29 begins with a threefold ascription of praise to God (Ps 29:1-2), and the body of the poem consists of a sevenfold catalog of actions by the "storm God," in which each clause begins with the phrase "the voice of LORD" as the subject of the action (Ps 29:3-9). The importance of threefold repetition, and of the pattern three-plus-one, is well known in both folk literature and the Bible (*see* Three, Third). Patterns of seven pervade the book of *Revelation. Wisdom writers, too, build some of their repetitions around the mnemonic device of numbers (Prov 30:15-16, 18-20, 21-31).

Binary Patterning. It is also well established that binary thinking is inherent in the human imagination and in life, and the Bible attests the truth of this (*see* Two). Many things in life simply exist as pairs. Two main categories of binary patterns exist. In dialectical rhetoric the pairs are opposites, vying for supremacy. Given the Bible's preoccupation with values, some of these opposites are recurrent and central to the meaning of the Bible—*good and *evil, *light and *darkness, *God and *Satan, *hero and *villain, before *conversion and after, life and death, health and disease, *wisdom and *folly. It is a rare passage in the Bible that does not contribute to one or more of these antithetical pairings.

But pairs can also belong to the rhetoric of complementarity. Here the two items may indeed be very different from each other, but they have been created to exist in harmony, each helping to make the other whole. Examples come readily to mind—God and people, *man and *woman, parent and *child, master and *servant, individual and community, *earth and *heaven, this life and the *afterlife, the *garden and the *city (nature and civilization), *youth and *old age. Here too it is hard to find a biblical passage that does not manifest the pattern of complementary pairs. An important theological truth to emerge from binary patterning is that whereas God created many pairs to be complementary, in a fallen world the potential always exists that these pairs will become antithetical.

Specific narratives or books of the Bible sometimes reveal even more reliance on binary patterning. In the story of Joseph, for example, we find two robes that signify favor (Joseph's robes from his father and from Pharaoh), two occasions when Joseph's antagonists use his robe to deceive an authority figure, a pair of dreams in which Joseph's family bows to him, Pharaoh's pair of dreams that Joseph interprets and two visits by Joseph's brothers to Egypt. In the Gospel of Matthew pairs of items also recur. The beatitudes balance a pronouncement of blessing with a statement of motivation, beginning with the repeated formula "for . . ." (Mt 5:3-12). In the same oration Jesus pairs such things as salt and light as metaphors of the ideal disciple (Mt 5:13-14), food and clothing as things over which people should not be anxious (Mt 6:25-31), birds and lilies as evidences of God's providential care (Mt 6:26-30), dogs and swine as animals from which to keep precious things (Mt 7:6), the narrow and broad ways (Mt 7:13-14), rock and sand as foundations for a house (Mt 7:24-27).

Balance. It is a short step from complementary pairing to the element of balance that is part of the deep structure of biblical writers' thinking and imagination. Here the essential principle is that the first item in a pair is incomplete until a second item is introduced to balance it. The most overarching example of this concerns the relationship between the OT and the NT. The OT anticipates and points forward to the NT, which fulfills it. To understand the NT fully requires knowledge of the OT promises and premonitions. Without the NT fulfillment of those promises and premonitions, the OT would be permanently incomplete and unfinished.

More localized examples of balance also exist. Once alerted to these balancing acts, when we encounter one half of some familiar biblical equations we instinctively wait for the other half—the proverbial waiting for the other shoe to drop. In the *lament psalms, for example, after the poet has painted a heightened picture of the despairing situation in which he finds himself, we learn to anticipate the good news—a statement of confidence in God and *vow to *praise him—that will balance the bad news. Once we become familiar with Paul's epistles, we intuitively prime ourselves for a pivot at which Paul moves from doctrine to application, from theology to morality. Matthew structured his Gospel on balanced sections of narrative and teaching, and John did something similar in pairing events in Jesus' life with extended discourses based on some aspect of them (e.g., the miracle of the feeding the five thousand linked with a discourse on Jesus as the bread of life). In the OT prophetic books, we come to expect that after the terrible denunciations and predictions of woe, at a late point (or interspersed throughout) the prophet will give a vision of a coming restoration to God's favor and blessing.

The most famous example of balancing in the Bible is the verse form in which biblical poets and orators spoke—parallelism. Regardless of the specific type of parallelism (synonymous, antithetic, incremental), the basic principle is that one line is balanced by the next line(s): "The LORD of hosts is with us; / the God of Jacob is our refuge;" "the LORD knows the way of the righteous, / but the way of the wicked will perish." We should not allow the simplicity of this type of balance to obscure how much of the Bible is based on it: the prophetic books and wisdom literature of the Bible, as well as the discourses of Jesus, rely on the biblical verse form of parallelism.

While biblical poetry with its parallelism is marked by the rhetoric of balance, narrative possesses it too, in ways easy to overlook. The basic rhythm of narrative is a movement in which plot conflict is balanced at the end by resolution and closure. The reader or listener experiences a corresponding catharsis (emotional purging) as tension gives way to release and equilibrium at the close. In view of the dominance of *poetic justice (good characters rewarded and evil ones punished) as the customary way to end a story, this catharsis is moral as well as emotional, as the audience is led to believe that the moral order of the universe is beneficent toward the good.

The Rhetoric of Subversion. The Bible is a supernatural revelation. As such it conveys more and different things than the unaided human reason or imagination produces. At many points the Bible challenges conventional human wisdom and ways of living. The means by which it does so is partly its rhetoric of subversion, which undermines conventional ways of thinking and valuing.

Paradox, for example, is a major biblical (especially NT) rhetorical device. The first are last and the last first (Mt 19:30; 20:16). Those who humble themselves are exalted, and those who exalt themselves are humbled (Mt 23:12; Lk 14:11; 18:14). Those who lose their life find it (Mt 10:39; 16:25). When a person is *weak, he is strong (2 Cor 12:10). Believers have nothing yet possess everything (2 Cor

6:10). What all these paradoxes have in common is that they subvert the standards by which people of the world live.

Patterns of *reversal and inversion do the same. God chooses the weak things of the world to confound the strong, and the foolish to refute the worldly-wise (1 Cor 1:18-31). The *younger child who is "unnaturally" preferred over the *elder child is so common in OT hero stories as to become the norm. Jesus told parables in which the fortunes of a rich man and beggar are reversed in the afterlife, in which help for a wounded traveler comes from the least expected source, and in which a *Pharisee goes home from temple worship condemned while a tax collector goes home justified by God.

Parody (echoing an existing piece of literature with inverted effect) is also a technique of subversion. The conventional *boast, for example, expresses the self-reliance of a warrior, while the boasts of the Bible celebrate God as the only sufficient strength. The arming of the hero is a major moment in epic literature—a celebration of the hero's human ability to conquer in his own strength—but in Psalm 18:32-35 God is the one who arms the hero. In place of the hero the Bible sometimes exalts the *antihero—the protagonist who lacks the confidence and skills of the conventional hero. The prophet Amos is a master at parody, as in the shocking inversion of the priestly exhortation to worship: "Come to Bethel, and transgress; to Gilgal, and multiply transgression" (Amos 4:4 RSV).

Rhetoric of Make-Believe. While the Bible is a very realistic book, rooted in actual, everyday events set in space-time history, there is also much about it that is fantastic. Metaphor, for example, is always a literal lie, inasmuch as it asserts something that we know to be false. "The LORD is my rock," declares the psalmist (Ps 18:2 RSV), but we know that God is not literally a *rock. God "will conceal me under the cover of his tent," writes the poet (Ps 27:5 RSV), but God does not literally put people into a *tent. The rhetoric of metaphor and simile is inherently fictional and fantastic; it plays the game of "let's pretend." Human *tongues do not literally strut through the earth (Ps 73:9); it is only the poet's imagination that makes them do so.

The Bible seems to flaunt the element of fantasy by tending toward a rhetoric of hyperbole—the exaggerated statement that conveys heightened feeling in an obviously nonliteral form (see also Giantesque Motif). "A thousand may fall at your side, ten thousand at your right hand," says the poet (Ps 91:7 RSV) in a heightened picture of battlefield deliverance. Again, "You will tread on the lion and the adder" (Ps 91:13 RSV). Similarly, the exultant confidence of David is so strong that he boasts that in God he "can crush a troop" and "leap over a wall" (Ps 18:29 RSV). The truth this hyperbolic rhetoric conveys is not literal or factual truth but emotional truth. The resulting spirit is exultant and buoyant, but it is not literal.

The *apocalyptic visions of the Bible display the element of fiction and fantasy even more overtly. In Nebuchadnezzar's vision, future political kingdoms are pictured as a human statue composed of varied metals (Dan 2:31-45). In the prophetic imagination we encounter such fantastic images as "living creatures" with "six wings, . . . full eyes all around" (Rev 4:8 RSV), two flying women with wings like those of a stork (Zech 5:9) and a beast that "was like a lion" and "had eagles' wings," which had its wings plucked off and then stood "upon two feet like a man" (Dan 7:4 RSV). The rhetoric of strangeness in apocalyptic writing expresses the supernatural and mysterious nature of the reality being portrayed.

Catalogs. Biblical writers are fond of catalogs (lists). We must remember in this regard that oral and written literature was the ancient world's method of information storage and retrieval and that oral cultures always need mnemonic (remembering) aids. Catalogs are such mnemonic devices.

Catalogs take many forms in the Bible. One is the venerable genealogy, which seems cumbersome and unexciting to modern Western readers but which remains a favorite in oral cultures to this day. The truth is that we can run into a list in virtually any part of the Bible—lists of instructions for the tabernacle and temple, lists of people who performed various activities, lists of tribes, lists of commands, lists of ingredients, lists of soldiers, lists of kings, lists of virtues and vices. We find a list of human activities for which there is a time (Eccles 3:1-8), a list of qualities that make a person blessed (Mt 5:3-12), a list of woes against the Pharisees (Mt 23), a list of human activities that will be "no more" after Babylon has been decisively defeated (Rev 21:21-24). In lyric poems we find catalogs of the attractive features of the beloved (Song of Songs), catalogs of the praiseworthy acts and qualities of God in the praise psalms, and catalogs of God's acts of protection in other psalms (Ps 91; 121). The biblical encomium (a composition in praise of an abstract quality or character type) is likewise structured as a catalog, as in 1 Corinthians 13 on the subject of love and Hebrews 11 on the subject of faith.

Rhetoric of Transcendence. In a book where an unseen spiritual world is consistently portrayed as existing alongside the visible earthly realm, it is inevitable that the writers employ a set of stock devices for portraying the transcendent realm. Biblical writers who portray heaven or spiritual beings have seven basic techniques at their disposal.

One technique is *contrast*. Heaven is "other" than what we ordinarily experience, a distinction made explicit in the familiar designation *otherworldly*. Of course the contrasts in heavenly visions build upon familiar realities in *this* world, in effect mingling the familiar and unfamiliar to evoke a picture of something different from ordinary reality. Revelation 21 makes reference to a "new heaven," a "new earth" and "new Jerusalem." We have *our* versions of *heaven, *earth and *Jerusalem, but the adjective *new* signals that the heavenly version of them is different. In the same chapter we read that "the city has no need of sun or moon to shine upon it, for the glory of God is its light" (Rev 21:23 RSV). This is obviously quite a different world from the one we inhabit.

A specific contrast is based on what past ages called enameled imagery—imagery combining brilliance of light and *hardness of texture, with *jewels topping the list. In the heavenly visions in the book of Revelation, for example, we read about a sea of glass, a river bright as crystal and a city that is "pure gold, clear as glass" (Rev 21:18 RSV). What are we to make of this imagery that appears with such consistency in visions of heaven? The best explanation is that it evokes a world of superior value, splendor and permanence than our cyclic vegetative world.

Writers who portray the transcendent also use a technique of *negation,* denying to the spiritual world the qualities of finite reality. In such "negative theology" God is portrayed in terms of what he is not— "immortal" (not mortal; Rom 1:23; 1 Tim 1:17), "beyond measure" (Ps 147:5), "unapproachable" (1 Tim 6:16). In Revelation 21:4 we read that in heaven "death shall be no more, neither shall there be mourning nor crying nor pain any more, for the former things have passed away" (RSV). In short, the transcendent can be portrayed by denying it the qualities of earth.

The way of negation has always been balanced by the way of affirmation as a means of portraying the transcendent. Using earthly images to portray God and heaven presupposes the principle of *analogy* between earth and heaven. After all, earthly language and experience are the only materials we have to portray the "other" world. This principle of analogy is evident in virtually any description of heaven that we might read. Heaven is regularly pictured as a *city with *gates and *streets, for example. In Jesus' evocative version it is a great *house with "many rooms" (Jn 14:2). Heaven has also been regularly pictured as a kingly court, replete with *thrones, *crowns and courtly attendants. Musical harmony has likewise been a prevalent image, again establishing a link between life in heaven and life on earth.

Analogy like this is metaphoric. At some level the physical image asserts something that is true of heaven. John the seer repeatedly portrays various aspects of heaven in terms of what they are "like," that is, similar to in earthly reality. It is the correspondence or embedded meaning, not the literal picture, that is important. If heaven is portrayed as a city, the physical image implies the qualities of unity and community that heaven really possesses. Jesus could compare heaven to a stately house with many rooms because there really are connections between a house and heaven—such as *refuge, *rest and living close together. Similarly with *light: certain qualities of heaven (such as the illumination that exists there) really are like light.

As we move along the continuum of imagery used to portray heaven, we move away from literal analogy toward *symbolism,* which takes greater liberties than analogy does with the physical images used. In analogy we give a degree of literal belief to the physical image, even if we entertain the possibility that it is not true of heaven in exactly the ordinary way. It seems inevitable, for example, that heaven does really possess some of the qualities of a city and house, whereas the *pearly gates and *golden streets are probably symbolic.

The great example of a book of the Bible in which the writer creates a symbolic reality is Revelation, where glorified believers are pictured as symbolically receiving such things as the morning *star (Rev 2:28), a *white *stone with a secret name written on it (Rev 2:17) and water from a fountain of life (Rev 21:6). Daniel's prophecy pictures citizens of the heavenly realm as shining "like the stars for ever and ever" (Dan 12:3 RSV), a symbol of their glory but not a literal picture of what they are. Revelation 14:4 claims that the redeemed in heaven are male virgins, doubtless a symbol for believers' purity of devotion to Christ. In one of many heavenly promises expressed in the book of Revelation, the one who enters heaven will become "a pillar in the temple of my God" (Rev 3:12 RSV), a symbolic rather than factual picture.

A fifth technique of conveying transcendence is *distancing* of the supernatural realm from earthly reality. Heaven is literally beyond our known experience. So writers describe it as physically and spiritually remote. The framework of the vision is the primary distancing device in the Bible, as writers portray heavenly reality in terms of something envisioned, not as a tangible reality that one can physically visit in this world. In the book of Revelation, John several times portrays what "seemed" to be (Rev 6:6; 13:3; 19:1, 6), implying that what he saw was at such a distance that he could not see precisely.

Writers who portray heaven also gravitate toward predictable *types of imagery.* One category, as noted above, is enameled imagery. Another category is conceptual imagery—words that name abstract qualities instead of sensations. Thus "righteousness and justice are the foundation" of God's heavenly "throne" (Ps 89:14 RSV), and "holiness befits [his] house" (Ps 93:5 RSV). God himself, the transcendent One, is repeatedly described in terms of his attributes, as well as being metaphorically called a rock and fortress.

A final technique by which to portray transcendence consists of *internalizing the effects* of heaven in either the visionary who catches sight of heaven or the actual citizens of heaven. The premise is that heaven is knowable partly by how it satisfies and delights the person or angel who resides there. The psalmist claims that he will behold God's "face in righteousness," and when he does so he "shall be satisfied with beholding thy form" (Ps 17:15 RSV). We experience the heaven of John's visions partly in terms of the beatitude of those who worship God around the heavenly throne.

Rhetoric of Genres. Many of the genres of the Bible have their own rhetorical patterns. Some common formulas of wisdom literature, for example, are the summons to listen, statements of motivation (incentives to listen and heed), series of admonitions and statements of consequences for obeying the wisdom of the teacher. Wisdom writers are also fond of using analogies to nature, as when James compares speech ("the tongue") to the rudder of a *ship and to a forest *fire (Jas 3:4-5). Sometimes wisdom teachers combine command and reward in rapid-fire sequence (Prov 3:1-12) or ask a series of rhetorical questions ending with the issue that the teacher is actually addressing (Prov 6:27-29; cf. Amos 3:3-6 for an example in prophetic literature).

Biblical prophecy too has its own rhetorical patterns. The basic form is the oracle—the statement or vision that the prophet speaks from God. Formulas such as "Thus says the Lord" or "The word of the Lord came to me, saying . . ." are common lead-ins to visions. Directly quoted speeches are a staple in these oracles. The oracles themselves fall into two main categories—oracles of judgment in which the prophet denounces vice and predicts coming calamity, and oracles of redemption in which the prophet predicts a time of restoration and salvation. The woe formula is a convention in which the prophet directly pronounces woe on people he is subjecting to satiric rebuke. Interspersed commands to reform are common, and sometimes future events are portrayed in the past tense as having already happened. Name-calling and vituperation (direct and vicious rebuke) are sometimes present: "Hear this word, you cows of Bashan," writes Amos against the wealthy women of Samaria (Amos 4:1 RSV).

To cite a third example of genre rhetoric, the NT *epistle employs a host of rhetorical features. One of these is the epistolary format itself, consisting of five items: opening (sender, addressee, greeting), thanksgiving, body, *paraenesis* (exhortations) and closing (final greetings and benediction). Specific rhetorical features keep multiplying within this format. Persuasive rhetoric takes the form of a proem (introduction to the topic and situation at hand), narration (background), proposition (the thesis to be defended), proof (including rebuttal) and epilogue. Elements of the diatribe are present: the author confronts and debates an imaginary audience, replete with direct address to imagined listeners or opponents, rhetorical questions, question-and-answer constructions, exclamations and the exposure of false reasoning or wrong conclusions. Lists of virtues and vices are a rhetorical form used by the writers of the Epistles, as is the household code that lays down rules for family living. We also find interspersed blessings, doxologies, liturgical fragments, hymns and creeds.

Wisdom literature, prophecy and epistle are specimens of the genre-specific rhetoric that prevails throughout the Bible (*see* Christ Hymn; Encomium;

Lament Psalms; Oracle; Praise Psalms; Proverb as Literary Form; Worship Psalms).

Irony. Irony falls into three categories, all of which display an element of discrepancy. Verbal irony consists of saying the opposite of what one intends. Irony of situation occurs when a situation is the opposite of what one expects or what is appropriate. Dramatic irony occurs when a reader or audience knows more than characters in a story do. The Bible contains an abundance of the latter two types.

The most pervasive irony of situation in the Bible stems from a failure of faith. Repeatedly God and we as readers have a right to expect better behavior from characters than they display. As the recipient of God's covenant blessing, for example, Jacob should have behaved in a more exemplary manner than he did until his wrestling match with the angel of God. In view of God's repeated rescue and provision for the nation of Israel, the nation of the *exodus should have risen above its continual murmuring and final decision not to enter the *Promised Land. In the Gospels, Jesus' career of teaching his disciples and performing public miracles should have produced more belief in the disciples than it did.

The other main kind of irony of situation revolves around the inversion of values noted earlier. We expect the older child to be the child of destiny, yet God chooses the younger. It is an axiom of ancient martial literature that victory goes to the warrior who has the greater strength and military equipment; yet the Bible declares that "a warrior is not delivered by his great strength. The war horse is a vain hope for victory" (Ps 33:16-17 RSV). We would expect deity to be born in more auspicious circumstances than a stable. Throughout the Bible we find continuous ironic discrepancy between expectation and reality.

Storytellers can scarcely tell a story without using dramatic irony, and because the Bible is heavily narrative, dramatic irony is pervasive in it. Repeatedly we observe characters in Bible stories who lack some of the privileged information that we possess. As we watch events unfold when Abraham lies to Pharaoh about the identity of his wife, or Jacob to his blind father about his own identity, we do so in full awareness of the information that Pharaoh and Isaac (and at another level, Abraham and Jacob) lack. Similar dramatic irony pervades the story of David, *Bathsheba and Uriah, as David ironically thinks he can keep his affair secret, as Uriah carries the instructions for his own death to his captain, as Nathan tricks David into condemning himself when David thinks he is only judging a civil case. Dramatic irony of this type is inherent in storytelling; if there is a distinctive note to it in the stories of the Bible, it is that God is a sovereign and omniscient observer of all human action, and we as readers experience the stories of the Bible in this light.

A second type of dramatic irony in the Bible is clearly rooted in a spiritual reality. The Bible repeatedly juxtaposes apparent and hidden plots. The apparent action is the foreground action—what we cannot possibly avoid seeing. In the stories of the Bible this is the earthly and human sphere of action. The apparent plots in the stories of both Joseph and Jesus, for example, have to do with human failure, suffering, injustice and victimization. The hidden plot is less evident, at least during the unfolding the action, and it concerns the ultimate purpose and outcome of the action. In the stories of Joseph and Jesus, what appears to be a series of disasters for the protagonists is really a story of providence and redemption. Because the Bible presupposes the existence of two worlds—the visible earthly world and an unseen spiritual world—this type of dramatic irony is rarely absent from the stories of the Bible.

The foregoing discussion of irony in the Bible provides only specimens of patterns that are pervasive. The Bible is a very ironic book, and awareness of ironic patterns is a major requirement for reading the Bible well.

Rhetorical Devices. We might simply note, finally, a series of common rhetorical devices that appear in the Bible. One cluster is dramatic in nature, reinforcing the degree to which the Bible employs the techniques of drama and perhaps reflecting an oral culture for much of the Bible. Direct quotation is a staple in the narrative sections. Apostrophe (direct address to someone absent as though present) is the counterpart in the poetic parts, as question-and-answer constructions are in the Epistles. Rhetorical questions presuppose a listener who will answer, as do indictments and denunciations. Of similar nature is the calling of imaginary or absent witnesses.

Devices of arrangement constitute another cluster. Parallelism of lines or groups of lines is the most frequent device of artful arrangement in the Bible. The rule of end stress means that the most important item in a series or an argument is placed last (with Jesus' parables constituting a ready source of illustrations), and oratories and epistles often end with a peroration (climactic statement, filled with eloquence). We also find stairstep arrangement, in which the last key word in one clause becomes the first key word in the next clause (Rom 5:3-5). Elsewhere a series of clauses might begin with a common phrase (1 Cor 12:8-10).

Another cluster of rhetorical devices is related to logical argumentation. The list includes the summoning of imaginary or absent witnesses to buttress the author's argument, giving the reason for a statement (known as "cause shown" [Rom 1:16]), concession, correction, exclamation for persuasive effect, exhortation, association of the author with those addressed (inclusion), indignation, mocking, interrogation, refutation and prayer.

Miscellaneous devices are likewise important. Virtually all genres have their versions of summary statements. Some books of the Bible have prologues and epilogues or postscripts. The style of the Bible tends toward aphorism (a concise, memorable saying). The authority of statements is sometimes asserted by means of such formulas as "The word of Lord came to me, saying," or "Thus says the Lord," or "Verily, verily" ("Truly, truly"). Various types of wordplay are sometimes important, but of course their effect depends on a knowledge of the original Hebrew or Greek. Oratorical and epistolary passages often heap up synonyms for the sake of emphasis.

See also CHARACTER TYPES; NUMBERS IN THE BIBLE; PLOT MOTIFS; REVERSAL.

BIBLIOGRAPHY. J. L. Bailey and L. Vander Broek, *Literary Forms in the New Testament: A Handbook* (Louisville, KY: Westminster John Knox, 1988); P. D. Duke, *Irony in the Fourth Gospel* (Atlanta: John Knox, 1985); E. M. Good, *Irony in the Old Testament* (Philadelphia: Westminster, 1965); S. Greidanus, *The Modern Preacher and the Ancient Text* (Grand Rapids: Eerdmans, 1988); G. A. Kennedy, *New Testament Interpretation Through Rhetorical Criticism* (Chapel Hill: University of North Carolina Press, 1984); N. Lund, *Chiasmus in the New Testament* (Chapel Hill: University of North Carolina, 1942).

RICHES, WEALTH. *See* PROSPERITY; RAGS TO RICHES.

RIGHT, RIGHT HAND

The predominance of right-handedness provided a ready basis for metaphors and geographic perspective in the Ancient Near East. Geographically, a natural orientation toward the Eastern *sunrise put *south on the right. In social concourse, *oaths and agreements were affirmed with the right *hand (Gen 14:22; Ezek 17:18; Dan 12:7), expressions of fellowship were sealed with a right-handed handshake (Ezra 10:19), and giving and receiving were done with the right hand (Ps 26:10; Gal 2:9).

All of this provides ready imagery whenever particular emphasis, distinct identification or full and energetic participation of a biblical protagonist is intended. Particularly instructive is the instance of the consecration of Aaron and his sons to the priesthood. In recounting this event the narrator takes great pains to prepare the reader for the climactic portion of the ceremony—the symbolic seal of ordination. The blood of the sacrificial ram for ordination is placed on the right earlobe, right thumb and big toe of the right *foot of the new priests (Lev 8:23-24). By this action each is reminded of his solemn duty to hear and obey God's Word, undertake his holy work and walk in his ways. Similar emphases may be found in the ritual for cleansing of the leper (Lev 14:14-18, 25-29).

The right hand is the preferred one in patriarchal *blessings (Gen 48:17-20); solemn oaths are made via the uplifted right hand (Is 62:8; Rev 10:5-7); and the risen Christ is portrayed as holding seven stars (the "angels" of the seven churches) in his right hand, before placing his right hand of comfort on the awe-struck, prostrate John (Rev 1:16-17).

The right hand is used particularly as a synecdoche to emphasize God's person and actions. God's right hand is said to be "filled with righteousness"

(Ps 48:10) and effective might (Ps 80:15-16; 89:13). With his right hand he delivered Israel out of Egypt (note Ex 15:6, 12, where the right-hand motif forms an important stitching device) and brought them into the *land of promise (Ps 44:1-3). God is a saving God (Ps 2:6; 98:1) who judges his foes (Hab 2:16) and delivers trusting believers from theirs (Ps 17:7). Accordingly, believers can find in God a source of omnipresent help and *strength (Ps 139:10; Is 41:10), for in him they can expect present security (Ps 10:8), *protection (Ps 121:5; 138:7), sustenance (Ps 18:35; 63:8; 73:23) and joyous victory (Ps 18:15-16) as well as the *hope of eternal *pleasures (Ps 16:11).

To be at the right side is to be identified as being in the special place of *honor (1 Kings 2:19; Ps 45:9). Thus the full participation of the risen Christ in God's honor and glory is emphasized by his being at God's right hand (Acts 2:33-34; Heb 1:3). From there he will return to *judge the world, welcoming believers to blessings on his right while assigning the wicked to the *left (Mt 25:31-46).

This last text, Matthew 25:31-46, forms part of a well-attested right hand/left hand motif emphasizing completeness or totality, often with concentration on a fixed goal. Citizens of *Nineveh "cannot tell their right hand from their left" and thus are totally spiritually ignorant (Jon 4:11 NIV), whereas godly wisdom offers long life in the right hand, riches and honor in the left (Prov 3:16). The wise person chooses the right *path (Gen 24:49; Eccles 10:2) and thus avoids such spiritual dangers as *idolatry (Deut 28:14; Josh 23:6-8) and lawlessness (Deut 17:8-12). Above all, godly individuals, and especially spiritual leaders, are to let their lives be ruled by God's Word, not deviating toward the right or toward the left, so that they may enjoy proper success (Deut 5:32; 17:18-20; Josh 1:6-9).

See also HAND; LEFT, LEFT-HANDED; SOUTH.

RIGHTEOUS REMNANT. *See* REMNANT.

RING

In the Bible rings serve as ornamentation and jewelry. Interestingly enough, all the passages mentioning rings as ornamentation occur in the book of Exodus, details delighting the reader's eye in sensuous descriptions associated with the *tabernacle. Rings are on the *ark of the covenant—"And you shall cast four gold rings for it" (Ex 25:12 NASB); the table of showbread—"And you shall make four gold rings for it and put rings on the four corners" (Ex 25:26 NASB); boards and sockets—"And you shall overlay the boards with gold and make their rings of gold" (Ex 26:29 NASB); the bronze *altar—"you shall make four bronze rings" (Ex 27:4 NASB); the altar of incense—"two gold rings for it under its molding" (Ex 30:4 NASB); the ark of acacia—"And he cast four rings of gold for it on its four feet; even two rings on one side . . . and two rings on the other side of it" (Ex 37:3 NASB); and the priestly garments—"And they bound the breastpiece by its rings to the rings

of the ephod with a blue cord" (Ex 39:21 NASB). All such visual extravagance symbolizes the beautiful, priceless character of the God who is honored by the tabernacle services, to celebrate his glory with a profusion of splendid *golden and bronze rings.

Rings used primarily as jewelry generally are mentioned either as *offerings or as symbols of authority. After Moses' impassioned speech about the tabernacle, "everyone whose heart stirred him . . . brought the LORD's contribution for the work of the tent . . . brooches and earrings and signet rings and bracelets, all articles of gold" (Ex 35:21-22 NASB). In response to a battle victory in which not one Israelite died, the jubilant people "brought as an offering to the LORD what each man found, articles of gold, armlets and bracelets, signet rings, earrings and necklaces, to make atonement for ourselves before the LORD" (Num 31:50 NASB; *see* Battle Stories).

It is when the Bible writers use rings to denote *authority, real and symbolic, that they have their greatest imagistic power. Starting life as a pampered son, undergoing a rite of passage in an Egyptian dungeon and then catapulted to power, Joseph has his new position validated by a piece of jewelry: "Then Pharaoh took off his signet ring from his hand, and put it on Joseph's hand . . . and they proclaimed before him, 'Bow the knee!' " (Gen 41:42 NASB). But a signet ring was more than just another gem; it was a finger ring bearing an engraved

A signet ring.

signature, a *seal used to officially mark documents. Thus the ownership of such a ring was synonymous with power. The Esther story parallels Joseph's: she is first a gorgeous queen, then an endangered Jew, and then she and Mordecai are restored to power: "And the king took off his signet ring which he had taken away from Haman, and gave it to Mordecai. And Esther set Mordecai over the house of Haman" (Esther 8:2 NASB).

Such power was signified by the literal giving of a ring that Jesus used it in the *prodigal son parable: "But the father said to his slaves, 'Quickly bring out the best robe . . . and put a ring on his hand . . . bring the fattened calf . . . let us eat and be merry' " (Lk 15:22-23 NASB). With these acts the father restores the prodigal to the authority of sonship, credentials joyously reinstated.

With sensuous descriptions of such tabernacle ornamentations as rings, Bible writers make vivid and hence memorable the God such trappings glorified. And with ring stories of Joseph, Mordecai and the prodigal son, other authors emphasize God's unmerited favor by associating rings with opulence, rulership and reconciliation. Such narratives become archetypes of the eternal God's providential protection of and love for his own, an omnipotent God's willingness to rescue his people from the dungeons of life's deepest problems and restore them to their heavenly heritage.

See also JEWELS AND PRECIOUS STONES; SEAL.

RING COMPOSITION. *See* RHETORICAL PATTERNS.

RISK, STORIES OF

Everyone likes stories of risk, because they provide suspenseful action. In the Bible the issues run deeper than that: the life of heroic *faith is almost synonymous with willingness to take a risk.

Noah, for example, took a risk to build a huge *ark on dry land in response to God's prediction of a *flood. For *Abraham to respond promptly to God's command to go from his native land "to the land that I will show you" (Gen 12:1 RSV) was to take a risk. Abraham's willingness to offer his son in *sacrifice (Gen 22) was in the same vein. Not all risky ventures in biblical narrative are praiseworthy: Lot took an ill-advised risk when he chose a place to live on the prospect of material *prosperity, and *Jacob's risk in pulling off the deception of his father (Gen 27) was ignominious.

Moses is a case study of someone willing to take the risk of faith. It took nerve to make numerous appearances before Pharaoh. As heroic leader, Moses repeatedly obeyed God's instructions in the face of opposition from a nation of chronic complainers. Joshua and Caleb similarly represent the voice of courageous faith when they urge the nation to enter the *Promised Land despite the apparent dangers (Num 13:30-33).

The judges too were risktakers. Ehud undertook a risky assassination with consummate resourcefulness. Deborah and Barak showed courage in leading an army against the Canaanites, as did Jael in assassinating Sisera with a tent peg and mallet. Gideon conducted a daring nighttime raid on the Midianites with a mere three hundred men. On the negative side, *Samson, for all his exploits of strength, undertook foolish risks—marrying Philistine women, posing a riddle at his wedding feast, dallying with a temptress.

Some of the most resplendent risktakers in the Bible are *women. Hannah made a spectacle of herself in praying for a child and then dared to offer her son as a child to the service of the temple. *Ruth risked herself to a new life in an alien land and in undertaking a midnight encounter with Boaz on the threshing floor. Abigail dared to intercept David as he was en route to take revenge against her churlish husband (1 Sam 25). *Esther risked herself in agreeing to petition the king on behalf of her nation.

Some of the most heroic characters from OT historical annals are known for the risks they were willing to take for God. At their forefront stands David, most notably in his readiness as a boy with a sling to go against the giant Goliath in single combat. David also took a risk in refusing to take King Saul's life, when doing so would have ensured his safety from his personal enemy. David's behavior engendered similar behavior in his followers, who risked their lives to bring him water from a well at Bethlehem during wartime (1 Chron 11:15-19). Hezekiah too risked himself for God, spreading the threatening letter from Sennacherib before the Lord in the temple instead of succumbing to his enemy's threats (2 Kings 19; Is 38).

The book of Daniel is a minianthology of risk stories. First, Daniel and his three friends dare to refuse the king's diet in deference to their own kosher diet. Then the three friends take the risk of refusing to bow down to the king's statue, despite the king's dire threats. Finally, Daniel dares to pray despite the prohibition of it.

No biblical characters are more courageous than the prophets who speak an unpopular message to evil kings. Elijah stands foremost among them in his challenges to Ahab and Jezebel, most notably when he poses the archetypal dare on Mt. Carmel, even dousing the altar thoroughly with water before calling on God to send down fire (1 Kings 18).

A similar spirit accompanies the disciples and Paul in the book of Acts. Here we find numerous accounts of bold preaching in the face of opposition and persecution, as well as journeys by dangerous means to far-flung corners of the Greek and Roman world.

In the Bible the life of faith is a life of risk. The roll call of faith in Hebrews 11 catches the spirit of it, with a catalog of risky ventures that would never have been undertaken by people concerned first for personal safety.

See also FAITH.

RIVALRY, SIBLING. *See* SIBLING RIVALRY.

RIVER

Rivers and streams have a predictable appeal to the human imagination. They attract us. As a source of water they represent life-giving qualities. Their tranquil flow makes them an image of mystery and fascination. When in Psalm 46 the poet wants a tranquil contrast to the opening imagery of cataclysmic upheaval in nature, all he has to do is assert, "There is a river whose streams make glad the city of God" (Ps 46:4 NRSV). The Christian church has evocative hymns about God's people gathering at the river and about God's perfect love being like a glorious river. The more than 150 biblical references to rivers and streams fall chiefly into six categories: a source of life, a source of *cleansing, serving as a boundary or geographic point of reference, a place of divine-human encounter, the agent of God's acts of provision/*rescue or *judgment, and a symbol.

The significance of rivers in the Bible depends much on Israel's lack of significant rivers within its territory. In contrast to the life-giving rivers that sustained Egypt and Mesopotamia (see Deut 11:10), Israel was "a land of hills and valleys, watered by rain from the sky, a land that the LORD your God looks after" (Deut 11:11-12). While countries with plentiful rivers use them as means of transportation and communication, Israel remained largely associated with the land. But though lacking perennial streams, Palestine did possess numerous wadis, or dry riverbeds, that flowed only with the runoff from the *rains—an image Job uses to describe his undependable friends: "My brothers have acted deceitfully like a wadi, like the torrents of wadis which vanish" (Job 6:15; cf. 1 Kings 17:1-7).

The association of streams with life in the Bible draws upon the arid geography of the biblical world in at least three ways. First, we are given pictures of streams flowing in the *wilderness. Thus we read about "streams of water in a dry place" (Is 32:2 RSV), "streams in the desert" (Is 35:6 RSV) and "streams on the dry ground" (Is 44:3 RSV). Second, repeatedly trees are said to grow on the banks of streams, with the implication that they do not flourish away from streams (Ps 1:4; Is 44:4; Jer 17:8; Ezek 31:4; cf. the claim in Is 32:20, "Happy will you be who sow beside every stream"). To this can be added occasional pictures of streams drying up in drought, an image of loss (Job 14:11; Ps 107:33).

Based on all these factors it is easy to glimpse what kind of river or stream the biblical people longed for: they wanted streams that were "full" (Ps 65:9), *"abundant" (Ezek 17:5, 8), "flowing" (Deut 9:21; 10:7; Ps 42:1; Song 4:15; Is 44:4; Jer 18:14), "everflowing" (Ps 74:15; Amos 5:24) and "gushing" (Prov 18:4). These qualities, in turn, are an important part of the meaning when biblical writers use rivers and streams as symbols for God and the righteous life.

In its most positive form the river figures in the Bible as part of a *garden paradise—a source of life to plants, animals and people. From the original Garden of Eden flowed a river that divided into four rivers (Gen 2:10-14). When Lot lifted up his eyes, he saw that "the Jordan valley was well watered everywhere like the garden of the LORD, like the land of Egypt" (Gen 13:10 RSV), and it represented prosperity. In Balaam's blessing on Israel we find the image of "gardens beside a river" (Num 24:6 RSV). In the psalmist's pictures of God's blessing on the earth, the image of river is prominent, with assurances that "the river of God is full of water" (Ps 65:9 RSV) and that God as cosmic gardener and caretaker causes streams to flow between the hills (Ps 104:10). In such a milieu the equation of river with prosperity is inevitable: "Thus says the LORD: '. . . I will extend prosperity . . . like a river, and the wealth of the nations like an overflowing stream' " (Is 66:12).

Symbolic uses of the river in the Bible draw chiefly on the associations of a paradisal river. We read about God's "river of . . . delights" (Ps 36:8 RSV), about "the LORD in majesty" being for his people "a place of broad rivers and streams" (Is 33:21 RSV) and about the river of heaven that flows "through the middle of the street" of the heavenly city, on either side of which is the tree of life, reminiscent of the original paradise (Rev 22:1-2 RSV). Since *Jerusalem had no river flowing through it (its water was supplied by an aqueduct [Is 7:3]), the river the psalmist pictures as flowing through Jerusalem (Ps 46:4) must be a symbol of God's presence, and a similar reading is likely for Ezekiel's vision of a river flowing from the temple (Ezek 47). Similarly, Jesus speaks of a spiritual reality when he says, "Out of the believer's heart shall flow rivers of living water," by which he meant the Holy Spirit (Jn 7:38-39 NRSV).

An important function of rivers in the Bible is to serve as boundaries and geographic points of reference. The *Jordan was the single most important river for Israel, but it lay on the periphery as Israel's eastern boundary (Num 34:12; Ezek 47:18). One does not find in the Bible the metaphor of the Jordan as the river of death to be crossed before one enters the afterlife, comparable to the River Styx in Roman mythology or the Habur River in Mesopotamia. Nevertheless, the boundary status of the Jordan, along with that of rivers in general, pervades biblical texts. The Jordan separates communities (Josh 22:11-12, 24-25; Judg 12:5-6). Rivers and wadis also define Israel's border to the north and south: "from the river of Egypt to the great river, the river Euphrates" (Gen 15:18 NRSV), the latter being The River par excellence (Ex 23:31 and elsewhere) and serving later to demarcate the boundary of the Persian province "Beyond the River" (Ezra 8:36; Neh 2:7; etc.).

Rivers can be spiritual boundaries as well as physical ones, for although God can reveal himself anywhere, rivers (like *trees and *mountains) often figure as privileged loci for divine encounters. Ezekiel and Daniel specify that they are by Babylonian watercourses when a supernatural communication comes to them (Ezek 1:1-3; 10:15-22; 43:3; Dan 10:4; 12:5-7). The Jordan River provides the context for Elijah's ascent to heaven and Elisha's confirmation as his prophetic successor (2 Kings 2:6-15). Jacob wrestles with a supernatural being all night when he crosses a river to reenter Canaan (Gen 32:22-31), and it is at the Jordan that God's voice from heaven declares Jesus to be his Son (Mk 1:9-11). Even in revelatory *dreams rivers provide the setting for divine encounters (Gen 41:1-18; Dan 8:2-6, 16). The spiritual association with living waters is significant in these contexts. Jesus speaks of the new life in Christ in terms of living water, bringing eternal life (Jn 4:10-14), and in John 7:38 (cf. Rev 7:17) Jesus promises the Holy Spirit through the living-water metaphor. Spiritual events near rivers are thus precursors of the true living water that comes from Jesus Christ.

Because of the numinous aura sometimes associated with rivers, persons who seek communication with God may do so beside a river. Paul's expectation to find a place of *prayer by a river (Acts 16:13) has earlier precedents: Ezra and his companions stop by a watercourse for several days to fast and pray for God's protection for a coming journey (Ezra 8:15-31), and the exiles lament before God "by the rivers of Babylon" (Ps 137:1 NRSV).

"Living water" is a biblical metaphor for the quality of water found in a river or stream: in contrast to stagnant, "dead" water, it moves and so is "alive." In the OT the guilt of an unsolved homicide was removed by a ritual carried out near a flowing stream (Deut 21:1-9). The Jordan, Israel's primary river, was the most potent in its vivifying capabilities: Naaman's leprosy was removed and "his flesh was restored like the flesh of a young boy" (2 Kings 5:14 NRSV) only by immersion in the Jordan, even though he had proposed alternate rivers (2 Kings 5:12). The Jordan is the source of "living" water that John the Baptist chooses to symbolically cleanse repentant Jews of their sins (Mt 3:5-11). Rivers thus have a special status as cleansers.

Rivers are finally an ambivalent image: they can be used by God to wreak havoc on his foes (Judg 5:21) or to bring salvation to his people. Thus although the Nile brings death to male Israelite infants (Ex 1:22), God's preservation of the infant Moses in a basket on the Nile (Ex 2:3-5) will ultimately result in new life for all Israelites and a bloody Nile for the Egyptians (Ex 7:15-25). In their negative manifestation, rivers may flow with blood to indicate mass death (Ezek 32:6; cf. Ex 7:15-25; Ps 78:44), and in Paul's catalog of disasters he has endured as a missionary we find the image "danger from rivers" alongside such terrors as bandits and destitution (2 Cor 11:26-27). We see the two-sided nature of rivers within *apocalyptic references to them as well. The oracles of *judgment speak of contaminated rivers (Rev 8:10-11; 16:4) and rivers that God dries up as a judgment against sinful people (Is 19:5; 42:15; 44:27; 50:2; Nahum 1:4). But the oracles of redemption give us evocative pictures of mountains and streams flowing with sweet *wine (Amos 9:13) and water (Joel 3:18).

Rivers feed into the *sea (Eccles 1:7) and partake of the sea's ominous quality: like the sea, they can epitomize undisciplined rebels who oppose the establishment of God's ordered rule. On the one hand, the Bible gives us terrifying images of swollen rivers overflowing their banks and devastating human habitation (Josh 3:15; Is 8:7-8). God is the only figure in the Bible capable of countering the hostile force of rebellious rivers, whose onslaught he repulses with divine weapons (Hab 3:8-15) that send the waters retreating in fright (Ps 114:3-5). Specifically, God splits rivers or dries them up so that they are no longer

a threat and can be crossed safely by God's people (Is 11:15-16; Zech 10:11). When Israel, Elijah and Elisha (Josh 2; 2 Kings 2) each cross the Jordan River, the miracle contains a moral dimension: it is a demonstration of the victory of God over forces of evil that attempt to hinder the movement of God's people. Any power humans have over rivers derives from God, as an expression of this moral reality: "I [God] will set his [the king's] hand on the sea and his right hand on the rivers" (Ps 89:25 NRSV; cf. 2 Kings 2:14).

Summary. Rivers and streams figure prominently in the Bible. On a physical plane, references to them keep us situated in a real world where water brings life and sustenance and its absence threatens existence. On a symbolic level, streams picture the deepest spiritual realities. The very structure of the Bible draws upon the river: the fructifying river that originates with God appropriately frames the biblical narrative from beginning (Gen 2:10-14) to end (Rev 22:1-2; cf. Ezek 47:5-12; Joel 3:18), and even human beings may be conduits of life when out of their "heart shall flow rivers of living water" (Jn 7:38 NRSV).

See also COSMOLOGY; FOUNTAIN; JORDAN RIVER; MONSTERS; SEA; SPRING OF WATER; WATER.

ROAD. *See* PATH; STREET.

ROB, ROBBER

Behind the related terms *robber* and *thief* in our English Bibles lie several words in the Greek NT and in the Hebrew OT, and significant English translations vary in their translation of these various terms. For example, in an image of ferocity, "a bear robbed of her cubs" (2 Sam 17:8 RSV; Prov 17:12; Hos 13:8), we find the verb *šākal*, "bereave" or "make childless," not the usual term for "rob," *gāzal*. English translations use the term *thief* or *robber* depending on the shades of meaning found in the original language. In English the general distinction is made between a *robber*, who uses threat or exercise of force or violence in the act of stealing, and a *thief*, who takes the property of others by stealth, cunning or sleight of hand.

In the Bible robbery in the literal sense is a despised practice, not only from the standpoint of the victim who suffers personal loss and violation but also as a flagrant infraction of the divine commandment "You shall not steal" (Ex 20:15; cf. Lev 19:13). The *curses that will befall Israel for breaking *covenant with God include robbery: "Day after day you will be oppressed and robbed, with no one to rescue you" (Deut 28:29 NIV; cf. Lev. 26:22). For this reason robbery and theft can be deployed as images of broken covenant and social ruin, as in Samaria, whose *sinful condition is unfurled as "thieves break into houses, bandits rob in the streets" (Hos 7:1 NIV).

The poor and the *weak are particularly helpless to defend themselves against robbery and need special *protection. Consequently, God's saving power is most profoundly displayed as he rescues "the poor and needy from those who rob them" (Ps 35:10). Indeed, this is divine *justice, and it is to be reflected in God's people, as they are warned to "rescue from the hand of his oppressor the one who has been robbed" (Jer 21:12 NIV; also Jer 22:3). But Israel in its unfaithfulness does not rescue victims from robbery. The parable of the good Samaritan stands in this trajectory of imagery (Lk 10:30-37). The traveler from Jerusalem to Jericho is violently attacked by brigands, stripped of all he has and left for dead. While the *priest and Levite, esteemed guardians of covenantal order, pass by turning a blind eye to their *neighbor, the despised Samaritan, ironically and extravagantly, reflects divine justice and *mercy (see comment on Hos 7:1 above).

Robbery as a socially and ethically despised "profession" becomes an effective image to unleash on those who hold it in deepest scorn. In a memorable and rhetorically effective image, Malachi depicts Israel robbing God: "Will a man rob God? Yet you rob me. But you ask, 'How do we rob you?' In tithes and offerings" (Mal 3:8 NIV).

This shocking conjunction of robbery with *worship and sanctuary recurs in Scripture. In Romans 2:22 Paul rhetorically condemns Jews: "You who abhor idols, do you rob temples?" (NIV). And the city clerk of Ephesus quiets the crowd by pointing out that Gaius and Aristarchus, Paul's traveling companions, are guilty neither of blaspheming the *goddess Artemis nor of robbing *temples (Acts 19:37). The presence in both texts of the special Greek term *hierosyleō* ("to rob a temple") reveals, however, a stock-in-trade image of a crime that was particularly heinous in the eyes of both *Gentiles and Jews. The image of robbery, rather than theft, points out the boldness of an act that violated religious sanctions and sensibilities. Paul's use of the term points out a possible Jewish motivation for robbing pagan temples, whose protection rested mainly on social regard for their sanctity. Since for the Jews idols were detestable nothings that belonged to no one in particular, their robbery and the sale of their silver or gold might be rationalized and credited to religious zeal (but cf. Deut 7:25).

Jeremiah's temple speech binds robber and sanctuary in a new image that will memorably echo in the words of Jesus: "Has this house, which bears my Name, become a den of robbers to you?" (Jer 7:11 NIV). "Is it not written: 'My house will be called a house of prayer for all nations'? 'But you have made it "a den of robbers" ' " (Mk 11:17 NIV; cf. Mt 21:13; Lk 19:46). Jeremiah proclaims that Israel, in its stealing, *murder, *adultery and *idolatry, and in its vacuous trust in the sanctity of its election and sanctuary, has turned the temple of the Lord into a robbers' *den. The image evokes *violence, plunder, plotting, squalor and hidden access in the very place intended to radiate divine holiness, mercy, beauty, worship and open invitation. For both Jeremiah and

Jesus, the divine verdict on this condition is judgment and destruction of the robbers' den, symbolically displayed in Jesus' forceful demonstration within the temple.

The Greek term (from the Septuagint) found in Jesus' condemnation of the temple is *lēstai*, frequently translated by the English "robbers." It usually refers to social bandits or brigands (in contrast to *kleptai*, "thieves"); these are peasants and others who have suffered social dislocation and injustice. Somewhat like Robin Hood and his men, they rob for a cause, resisting their oppressors and seeking to right wrongs by acts of violence. Jesus' use of Jeremiah's image of a "den of *lēstai*" is particularly prescient in light of events leading up to the Roman destruction of the Jerusalem temple in A.D. 70. Josephus tells us of revolutionary brigands, the hardcore nationalist Zealots, who violently resisted foreign influence, set up headquarters in the inner temple and remained there until their violent end.

Since Scripture overwhelmingly views robbery as a dark deed, it is startling to find *Jesus likening his own ministry to a violent "breaking and entering" and robbery of a household. In the parable of binding the strong man (Mt 12:29-30; Mk 3:27; Lk 11:21-23), Jesus likens his driving out *demons to forcefully entering a strong man's house, binding the strong man and plundering his goods (the language is more militaristic in Luke's account). The image suggests Israel as inhabited by Beelzebul, or Satan, demonized men and women as his "goods," and Jesus as "plundering" them—though in fact he is taking back what is God's own.

This picture of Jesus as brigand should not be quickly set aside, for Jesus dies a brigand's death on the cross, with two *lēstai* crucified on either side. In all likelihood these are not common criminals, or "thieves," but political revolutionaries ("bandits," NRSV; cf. Mk 15:7; Lk 23:19). Their enemy is Rome, his is Satan; their strategy is physical violence and political upheaval, his is spiritual deliverance and the mysterious invasion of the kingdom of God. Both Jesus and the bandits seek to "rob" Israel from the illegitimate grasp of a "strong man."

See also THIEF.

ROBE. *See* GARMENTS.

ROCK

In the ancient world, where explosives and powerful drills were unknown, rock—abundant and varied in shape and size—was a ready image of impervious solidity. A rock provides a solid foundation, *protection and security, but it can be a nuisance when it poses an obstacle to progress and dangerous when it falls. The Bible uses words translated "rock" in all these senses and occasionally in more specialized ways.

Much of the OT imagery has the desert as its backdrop. The sight of a rock in a barren, sunparched *wilderness lifted the spirits of the hot and weary traveler or soldier. The ministers of the righteous *king, wrote Isaiah (Is 32:2), will be like "the shadow of a great rock in a thirsty land" (NIV). The rock might contain a spring of *water (see Ex 17:6) as well as providing welcome shade from the burning *sun. The hunted, whether human or animal, could find in the rocks a *hiding place (1 Sam 13:6; Ps 104:18). Isaiah reveals a horrifying picture of people trying to hide from God among the rocks (Is 2:10, 19, 21). But ideally rock formed a sound *foundation; a rock was a *stronghold, a *fortress and a *refuge. "See, I lay a stone in Zion, a tested stone, a precious cornerstone for a sure foundation; the one who trusts will never be dismayed" (Is 28:16 NIV).

King *David knew what it was to be a fugitive in the desert, and he *worshiped God as the rock in whom he found shelter (2 Sam 22:2-4, 32; Ps 18:1-3, 31, 46). The image is repeated in Psalm 31:3; 62:1-8; and 71:3, 7. It is a short step to seeing God as redeemer, savior and deliverer (Ps 62; 95:1; 78:35). God is not only *like* a rock, however—he *is* a rock (Deut 32:30-31). The Israelites had experienced God as a safe refuge, utterly secure and dependable. As Luther was later to express it, *Ein feste Burg ist unser Gott*, "a mighty fortress is our God."

Rocks can also get in one's way. If people insist on pursuing their own way, they may find that God will get in their way as "a rock that makes them fall" (Is 8:13-14). This negative view of rocks becomes more common in the NT. Paul refers to Isaiah 8 in Romans 9:32-33. Rocks are an obstacle to agriculture as well, damaging plows or, as in the case of table rock, holding shallow soil that is easily baked in the sun and hostile to the growth of a *seed (Mt 13:5; *see* Farming). More serious still is the horror of the collapse of a building, a picture of *judgment in Luke 20:17-18. A landslide or rockfall, however, might be seen as a merciful release from the worse *pains of the judgment to come (Rev 6:15-17).

The NT uses positive images of rock just as the OT does. Simon, the leader, perhaps, of the apostles, is named Cephas, Peter, "Rock" (Mk 3:16). Peter is in some way seen as central to the foundation of the *church (Mt 16:17-19). Jesus spoke of the person who hears and acts on his words as *building on the rock, a sure foundation, whose *house will stand firm (Mt 7:24-27). Peter wrote of the church as being built on the firm granite foundation of Isaiah 28:16, built with "living stones" into a spiritual *temple, for Christ himself is the living *stone par excellence, rejected by his people indeed but chosen by God (1 Pet 2:4-8).

There remain a few unusual uses of the word *rock*. It is easy to see how God the Rock should be viewed as the *Father (Ps 28:1; 89:26; Is 51:1 NIV, "the rock from which you were cut"). It is easy too to see how *Jerusalem could be seen as a massive rock (as it literally is) and why Zechariah warned its besiegers to beware (Zech 12:3). It is less obvious that a rock could sell people (Deut 32:30), but it is God the Rock who hands over his *enemies to the slaughter. Strangest of all is the reference in 1 Corinthians 10:4

to the rock that traveled with the people of Israel in their *wanderings—a spiritual rock, says Paul, to be identified now with Christ. Paul's point of reference appears to be to a rabbinical legend.

So the word *rock* is used in Scripture with a wide variety of meanings, almost all associated with God, either as a secure foundation or stronghold or as an obstacle to evildoers. Twentieth-century city dwellers need to exercise their powers of imagination to feel the full impact of King David's relief and joy at finding a secure and shady fortress enclosing a spring of water as he was pursued by his enemies in the desert. Our view of God is enriched by the effort.

See also FORTRESS; FOUNDATION; GOD; STONE; STRONGHOLD; STUMBLE, STUMBLING BLOCK; ZION.

ROD, STAFF

Images of the rod and the staff are used somewhat interchangeably in English translations of the Bible. Six main categories may be noted: *travelers' staffs, the striped tree branches employed by *Jacob with his flocks, instruments of discipline or punishment, tools used by *shepherds, symbols of *authority and the miraculous rods of Moses and Aaron.

Staff is the customary biblical term for the walker's stick that was apparently universal in the ancient world. It is thus an icon of the traveler, symbolic of a transitory lifestyle and the vulnerability of living on the road (inasmuch as the staff was used as both a weapon and a support for the weary). When Jacob wants to identify his earlier status as a wanderer, he chooses the image of the staff: "with only my staff I crossed this Jordan" (Gen 32:10 RSV). At the first *Passover the people's readiness to be on the move is expressed in their eating the Passover meal with "loins girded, your sandals on your feet, and your staff in your hand; and you shall eat it in haste" (Ex 12:11 RSV). When Jesus wishes to picture the revolutionary nature of discipleship, he sends his disciples out devoid of customary preparations for travel—"no bag for your journey, nor two tunics, nor sandals, nor a staff" (Mt 10:10 RSV; cf. Lk 9:3)— confirming how conventional the staff is as a biblical image for traveling.

Elderly people especially need the aid of a staff in walking, and while we rightly associate such a staff with frailty, an interesting reversal occurs in the marvelous street scene of Zechariah 8:4, where the picture of old men and women sitting in the streets of Jerusalem, "each with staff in hand" (RSV), is positive in association, indicating the blessing of long life in a peaceable kingdom (*see* Old, Old Age). The staff as an icon for *pilgrimage, largely a postbiblical development, possibly has a lone biblical reference— the picture of the dying Jacob "bowing in worship over the top of his staff" as he blessed his sons (Heb 11:21 RSV), perhaps epitomizing his life as a stranger and sojourner in quest for "a better country, that is, a heavenly one" (Heb 11:16 RSV).

The fashioning of tree *branches into striped

"rods" was the province of Jacob's ridiculous attempts at an animal husbandry (Gen 30:37-4). Thinking that surrounding sheep and goats during the act of mating would influence them to produce speckled and spotted offspring, Jacob placed streaked tree branches before the mating animals. (Gen

Two types of rod.

31:10-12 records Jacob's moment of discovery that his intrigue was not the cause of his prosperity with his flocks and herds.)

Rods were also used to punish wayward *children, *slaves, fools or misbehaving adults. The RSV uses the image for discipline administered by human authorities approximately a dozen times (with nine of the references coming in the book of Proverbs) and for the oppression of a foreign nation four times (Is 9:4; 10:24; 14:29; Mic 5:1). Paul asks the Corinthians whether he should come to them "with a rod [in a mood of anger and reproof], or with love in a spirit of gentleness" (1 Cor 4:21 RSV). God's punishment, anger or rule is pictured by the rod approximately a dozen times, with the books of Isaiah and Revelation containing a preponderance of the references. Here the rod becomes an image of ultimate terror, as in references to God's breaking the rebellious kings of the earth "with a rod of iron" (Ps 2:9; cf. Rev 2:27; 19:15), as well as God's speaking of "the rod of my anger, the staff of my fury" (Is 10:5 RSV).

But the rod and staff can also be images of comfort, *protection and security. This is preeminently true of the shepherd's rod and staff. One of these was the familiar crook, used for disciplining a wandering *sheep, encircling a sheep's neck or belly to rescue it from a gully and laying across the backs of sheep for purposes of counting (the so-called rodding of the sheep) as they entered the sheepfold (Lev 27:32; Ezek 20:37). The other half of the "rod and staff" pair was a clublike *weapon used for warding off predators. The picture has been rendered forever famous by the detail in Psalm 23 that in the valley of deepest darkness, the place of treacherous gullies and lurking predators, the sheep will "fear no evil; . . . thy rod and thy staff, they comfort me" (Ps 23:4 RSV).

In the hands of a leader a rod or staff, like a king's *scepter, can also be symbolic of authority. During Israel's wilderness wanderings God told Moses at one point to "take the rod, and assemble the congregation" (Num 20:8 RSV), and Moses subsequently used the rod to strike the rock to produce water (Num 20:11; cf. Ex 17:5-6). In the book of Revelation, Christ is the One "who is to rule all the nations with a rod of iron" (Rev 12:5).

See also AARON'S ROD.

ROMANCE, ROMANTIC LOVE. *See* LOVE STORY.

ROMANS, LETTER TO THE
Paul's letter to the Romans is frequently characterized as the most theological and abstract of Paul's letters, but in fact it displays a rich variety of imagery and metaphor. The genre and rhetorical form of the letter have been widely investigated and debated. R. Jewett's identification of Romans as an "ambassadorial letter" is particularly suggestive.

Ambassadorial Letter. Jewett summarizes the scene: "An ambassador arrives in an alien court, states his credentials, and then advocates the interest of his sovereign or contituency. Similarly Paul introduces himself to the Roman churches he has not founded and then proceeds in a diplomatic fashion to provide a rationale for his forthcoming visit" (Jewett 1991, 266). Paul is addressing the various and competing house churches in Rome in an effort to unify them under the gospel and enlist their support for his coming missionary campaign to the western end of the world, Spain (Rom 15:24). The thesis, or rhetorical proposition, of the letter is stated in Romans 1:16-17: the gospel is "the power of God" for everyone who believes, an apocalyptic revelation of God's covenant faithfulness to Israel, a "righteousness of God" (NRSV) that reclaim Israel and through Israel his *creation that has gone astray. This force has been unleashed in the world through the work of Christ, and Paul the *servant of Christ Jesus is proclaiming the good news of Christ's lordship (Rom 10:9, 12-13) to the nations that they all might believe, *obey and *worship God (Rom 15:11; 16:27). From this ambassadorial perspective even the greetings of Romans 16 are not a postscript but a vital means of establishing personal ties and witnesses in Rome to the authenticity of Paul's apostolic gospel.

At various points in Romans 1:16—11:36 Paul employs the style of argumentation called "diatribe," in which a fictional interlocutor introduces objections or expresses erroneous views that Paul then answers or corrects. Or Paul simply addresses someone sitting in the front row, so to speak ("So when you, a mere man, pass judgment," Rom 2:3 NIV). This lends a dialogical air to much of the letter, evoking a lecture-hall setting in which attentive, intelligent and sometimes impertinent (Rom 9:20) listeners voice issues, and it allows Paul to project himself as a masterful speaker, thinker and polemicist. These features lend credence to the view that Romans is imbued with the characteristics of the standard "speech of exhortation" *(logos protreptikos)* used by Hellenistic philosophers to win the minds of their listeners. The dialogical nature of Romans may in fact reflect material from Paul's own tested oral argumentation, now effectively adapted to give his letter the feel of an oral address that reaches across space and time from Corinth to Rome.

As an effective rhetorician who wishes to carry his audience along with him, Paul employs a number of images and metaphors in Romans and so "sets the scene before our eyes" (Aristotle *Rhetoric* 3.10.1). Romans deals extensively with the human predicament and the saving work of God in Christ (*see* Salvation), and much of the imagery can be grouped under headings of predicament and solution. These groupings are not autonomous but complement and overlap each other in various ways.

Guilt and Justification. Paul evokes the scene of a *law court, the *judgment seat of God, where Jews and *Gentiles will one day be arraigned and judged. The imagery of the law court is particularly concentrated in Romans 1:18—3:20, where the thrust of the argument is to show that all men and women, whether Jew or Gentile, stand under condemnation. The guilt of the Gentiles before God is displayed in a mosaic of egregious vices of the Gentile world— malice, gossip, slander, hatred of God and so forth (Rom 1:29-31). But even virtuous Gentiles find their consciences acting as *witnesses, accusing or defending their very selves (Rom 2:15).

The Jews, on the other hand, are liable all the more because they possess God's *law and yet continue to *sin. A gallery of witnesses from the OT (Rom 3:10-18) bear witness to the charge that "Jews and Gentiles alike are all under sin" (Rom 3:9 NIV), "imprisoned" in disobedience (Rom 11:32 NRSV). The weight of this indictment is that "every mouth may be silenced" in the eschatological law court of God (Rom 3:19 NIV). To those who would question the *justice of the divine Judge, Paul maintains that God's judgment is based on truth (Rom 2:2), his judgments will prevail (Rom 3:4), and he alone is capable of judging the world (Rom 3:6). God is an impartial judge (Rom 3:21-22) who has demonstrated his forbearance in the past (Rom 3:25). In the end even Christians are not to judge each other, for all will stand before the judgment seat of God (Rom 14:10) and not one will escape (Rom 2:3) on the day when God judges people's secrets (Rom 2:16). God will give to each according to what they have done (Rom 2:5-6). In fact, as a counterpoint to the righteousness of God now being revealed in the gospel (Rom 1:17), the wrath of God is already being revealed from heaven (Rom 1:18) as godless and wicked men and women are being delivered over (Rom 1:24, 26, 28) as if to a three-member execution squad of sinful desire, shameful lust and depraved mind.

This would be a grim scene were it not for a remarkable fact. Prior to and in anticipation of that final day of judgment, God has already demonstrated his justice, his commitment to setting things right, in Christ, and he now "justifies" all those who trust in God's work in Christ (Rom 3:26). The divine verdict of the final judgment has already been rendered over sinners whose guilt has been exposed. But in a stunning transaction that has taken place outside the court, the guilt of sinners has been absolved as God through the *death of his faithful *Son has taken care of the dire consequences of that sin and guilt in a unique "sacrifice of atonement" (Rom 3:25 NIV). However we decide to translate the Greek word for this *atoning *sacrifice, *hilastērion*— whether "expiation" (an obliteration of sin), "propitiation" (satisfaction of wrath) or "mercy seat" (the place where God's mercy was symbolically manifested in God's sanctuary)—it covers even those sins previously committed by humankind and passed over in God's forbearance.

The force of this *justification* is not simply that a verdict is rendered and a certificate of eternal life issued to its recipients. Nor is it a legal fiction, an "as if" righteousness that does not truly describe its human subjects. Like all of God's speech, this is an *effective word* or, to use an older English term, a *rightwising* word that sets former sinners in a right (or righteous) relationship with God and anticipates a *transforming divine work in their lives. This word is spoken by the same God who brought the creation into existence by his powerful word, the one "who calls into existence the things that do not exist" (Rom 4:17 NRSV).

It is a particular expression of the powerful and transforming "righteousness of God" (Rom 3:21-22 NRSV) that Paul speaks of in his thesis statement (Rom 1:16-17). The linguistic relationship between *justify* and *righteousness* is more evident in the Greek, where they are seen to share the same root *(dik-)* and initial vocalization: *dikaioō* ("to justify") and *dikaiosynē* ("righteousness"). In Christ's work God demonstrates his justice (Rom 3:25) and justifies the ungodly (Rom 3:24, 28, 30; 4:2; 5:1, 9; 8:30; 10:10).

Bondage and Liberation. The human plight can be viewed not only in terms of human guilt but also in the dynamic imagery of *enslavement to an alien power. In this helpless state the only *hope lies in *rescue by someone mightier than the enslaving power. For Paul and other Jews the historical paradigm of *bondage was found in *Israel's enslavement in *Egypt followed by their dramatic deliverance by God and his leading them into the land of promise (*see* Promised Land). The imagery associated with this *exodus story shapes the Bible's language of subsequent events of deliverance and leaves its imprint on Romans. Isaiah memorably speaks of Israel's future return from *exile as if it were a second exodus (e.g., Is 40:3-5). First-century Jews in Palestine, however, experienced their life in the *land as a bitter irony: they had returned to the land of their ancestors, but they were under Roman domination, and their key symbols of Torah, *temple, tribe and territory fell far short of their ideal expression. Israel longed for liberation, a true exodus and restoration. When in Romans 5—7 Paul speaks of humanity in bondage, the story line and formative imagery of Israel's narrative lies just beneath the surface. How will this human plight, dramatically enacted in Israel's historical dilemma, be resolved?

Paul's analysis of the human plight, for both Jews and Gentiles, goes deeper than the historical realities of political power. He speaks of a trilateral spiritual power alliance opposed to the reign of God—sin, flesh and death—plus one unwilling but impotent accomplice, the law. It is a story of kingdoms in conflict, a battlefield and a mighty deliverer. Prior to the giving of the law to Israel, sin as a power had "entered the world," and with it came death (Rom 5:12 NIV, echoing the story of *Adam and *Eve's sin and consequent "death"). "Death reigned from the time of Adam to the time of Moses" (Rom 5:14 NIV), but with the giving of the law—as Israel's story at *Sinai amply attests (Ex 20—32)—sin multiplied (Rom 5:20; 7:8-10). Sin and death work together, with sin exercising its reign in death (Rom 5:21) and enslaving humankind (Rom 5:6, 14) through its ready foothold in fallen Adamic flesh (Rom 6:12; cf. Rom 8:6-7), where it finds ready weapons of wickedness (Rom 6:13). Sin is a hard taskmaster who pays his wages in death (Rom 6:23). The law, holy and good in itself (Rom 7:12), nevertheless is helpless before the manipulations of sin. Sin uses the law as a bridgehead (Rom 7:8) as it wages war (Rom 7:23) and takes its prisoners (Rom 7:23). Its hapless victims cry out in lament, calling for a powerful deliverer (Rom 7:24-25).

This deliverer is Jesus Christ (Rom 7:25), who enters the territory of sin "in the likeness of sinful flesh" (Rom 8:3 NRSV). But when sin and death press their claim upon this righteous One, the tables are turned. In Christ's condemnation of sin (Rom 8:2-3) there is a dramatic *reversal and rescue of those held in bondage to "the law of sin and death" (Rom 8:2 NIV). Those who attach themselves by faith to this divine deliverer, like Israel in the exodus (Ex 4:22; Hos 11:1), become the "sons of God" (Rom 8:14-17 NIV). Even Israel, in its waywardness and *hardened condition, will see the deliverer who "will come from Zion" and "turn godlessness away from Jacob" (Rom 11:26 NIV; cf. Is 59:20). The deliverance of these *children of God is of cosmic significance, for death has extended its reign not only over the human *family but over the entire created order, subjected to futility and *decay (Rom 8:20-21) and groaning in *pain (Rom 8:22) as it awaits its deliverance. The hope of creation's release lies in the revelation of the children of God, and it eagerly awaits this evidence of the defeat of death, the first light of the dawning of a new creation (Rom 8:19).

The story of Israel provides the substructure for this narrative of redemption. It is as if Paul says, "As Israel goes, so goes the world." Within Israel's story lies a finely articulated outline of the human situation, and from Israel's bosom there arises the only deliverer (Rom 1:3) who can rescue both Israel and the world.

Old Adam and New Adam. The awareness that we are not quite right, the longing to be made anew, seems etched on human consciousness. Paul's use of Adamic imagery is well developed in Romans and encompasses the contrasts of *deformity-transformation (cf. Rom 12:2) and disobedience-obedience. When Paul says that "all have sinned and fall short of the glory of God" (Rom 3:23 NIV), he is alluding to the psalmist's declaration that humans are created as persons crowned with *glory and honor (Ps 8:5), and this in turn builds upon the idea of man and woman being made in the image of God (Gen 1:28). "Since the creation of the world God's invisible qualities . . . have been clearly seen" (Rom 1:20 NIV), but the descendants of Adam have "exchanged the glory of the immortal God," who is the fitting object of worship for those who bear the image of God, for images of mortal humans and beasts (Rom 1:23 NIV; cf. Ps 106:20). In this and in their degraded behavior and animal appetites, their divine image has become badly distorted and threatens to transmogrify into the beastliness of the objects of their worship (cf. Wis 11:15-19). Humanity is not alone in this situation, for the creation in its entirety has lost its original radiant glory and been subjected to futility and decay, though not of its own will (Rom 8:20-21).

Paul explicitly develops an aspect of this Adam typology in Romans 5:12-21, where he contrasts the reign of sin and death with the reign of grace, righteousness and eternal life. "Sin entered the world through one man, and death through sin, and in this way death came to all men, because all sinned" (Rom 5:12 NIV). Adam is portrayed as a figure whose actions, as the father of all humanity, have an ongoing effect through subsequent generations. It is as if his disobedience allowed the entrance of an alien and hostile force into God's world, which all his descendants serve by their misdeeds. But if Adam's disobedience is the pattern and undoing of the many, Adam is also "a pattern of the one to come, . . . the one man, Jesus Christ" (Rom 5:14-15 NIV).

As in many a human story, new beginnings recapitulate the pattern of old beginnings—but with a difference. The story of the first Adam was a story of humans in relationship with God; the story of the second Adam is infused with divine grace and regenerative power as God uniquely embodies himself in the human story and transforms it. By the trespass of the first Adam a legacy of sin, judgment and condemnation was inherited by the many, both as a contagion and in imitation as each became his own Adam. Through the one act of righteousness the obedience of Christ, the second Adam, bestows a gift of grace—justification rather than judgment—which overflows to many (Rom 5:15). Whereas death *reigned through* the first Adam, holding his many descendants in its thrall, the many will themselves *reign in* life through the second Adam (Rom 5:17), sharing in the renewed Adamic splendor of dominion in a new creation (cf. Gen 1:28; Ps 8:6). Through the disobedience of the first Adam many were made sinners; through the obedience of the second, many will be made righteous (5:19). Behind the "one trespass" stands the disobedience of Adam in his eating from the forbidden tree; behind the "one act of righteousness" (Rom 5:18 NIV) lies the obedience of Christ in his death ("on a tree," as Paul says in Gal 3:13).

The progenitors of two humanities are contrasted, but the second is categorically different from and superior to the first in nature, action and effect. The dark and degenerative rule of death is overthrown by the radiant and generative rule of life. The malignant power of sin, accelerated by the law, is far overrun by the increase of grace through righteousness: "where sin increased, grace increased all the more" (Rom 5:20-21 NIV). Grace is neither niggling nor scheduled in its rewards.

Adam appears more covertly, but present nonetheless, beneath the argument of Romans 7:7-12. Here the picture is of sinful passions aroused by the law and bearing fruit for death. How so? "Had it not been for the law, I would not have known sin. . . . The law . . . said, 'You shall not covet.' But sin, seizing an opportunity in the commandment, produced in me all kinds of covetousness. . . . The very commandment that promised life proved to be death to me" (Rom 7:7-10 NRSV). Here speaks the voice of Israel, whose experience with the law followed precisely this pattern. But beneath the experience of Israel lies the prototypical story of Adam. Rabbinic interpretation understood the law to have existed prior to creation, and thus the commandment to Adam not to eat of the tree (Gen 2:17) was viewed as an expression of Torah. When Adam ate, the consequence was "death" and exclusion from the tree of life, the same pattern of action and consequence laid out by the law and enacted by Israel in its tragic history.

This pattern of first and second Adam, two humanities, sets Paul's gospel of redemption in a universal context that encompasses all—both Jew and Gentile—who would join by faith in service and worship to the one Lord. In joining this new humanity "our old self [Adam] is crucified with Christ" (Rom 6:6 NIV). The gospel joins people together as a new humanity in Christ. The corporate nature of this image carries over into the metaphor of the community as one body consisting of many members with complementary gifts and functions (Rom 12:4-8). By this overarching corporate imagery of a new humanity in Christ, the missionary objective of this letter is supported: "that all nations might believe and obey [God]" (Rom 16:26 NIV). Believing readers of Romans are invited to envision themselves as the corporate harbinger of a new society in a new world in which the old distinction between Jew and Gentile, Israel and the nations, is transcended.

Enmity and Reconciliation. The history of humanity is one of hostility, warfare and a longing for peace. But Paul identifies the most basic hostility as lodging in the human relationship with God. This was overcome through God's initiative at the *cross. Christ is likened to a *hero, but one who paradoxically dies not for his fatherland but for his *enemies (Rom 5:6-8): "when we were God's enemies, we were reconciled to him through the death of his Son" (Rom 5:10 NIV). Being justified, believers now have "peace with God through our Lord Jesus Christ" (Rom 5:1 NIV). The end result is the reconciliation of the world (11:15), and the diverse community shaped by the reconciling work is to "make every effort to do what leads to peace" (Rom 14:19 NIV), for God is a God of *peace (Rom 15:33; 16:20). Those outside the community are also to be engaged peacefully. Even unbelieving Israelites, who are enemies of believers as far as the gospel is concerned, are to be regarded as beloved on account of their election and their ancestors (Rom 11:28). Enemies are not to be avenged but won over with acts of *mercy (Rom 12:19-20).

Jews and Gentiles. Perhaps the most prevalent but most easily overlooked pattern in Romans is the binary contrast between Jews/Israel and Greeks/Gentiles. There are more occurrences of the Greek word *ethn_,* "Gentiles," in Romans than in any other Pauline letter (twenty-nine in Romans; ten, for example, in Galatians). A fundamental subtext of Romans is how this baseline division within humanity will be resolved in one new humanity in Christ and under one God (Rom 3:30). The culmination will be a community of doxological harmony, "one voice" glorifying the one "God and Father of our Lord Jesus Christ" (Rom 15:6 NRSV).

In Romans 1—3 Paul speaks of the "Jew" (*Ioudaios*) and then only twice uses the term in Romans 9—11 (Rom 9:24; 10:12). In contrast, Paul refers to "Israel" and "Israelite" only in Romans 9—11. "Jew" is frequently contrasted not with "Gentile" but with "Greek" (Rom 1:16; 2:9-10; 3:9; 10:12 account for all "Greek" references save one, Rom 1:14, where we find "Greeks and barbarians"). In Romans the two terms, *Israel(ite)* and *Jew,* suggest different aspects of the historic people of God. Paul's use of *Jew* generally evokes a public and forensic setting, one that is evaluative of the present identity and standing of Jews and Greeks under God. For the most part the identity of Jews was, by their distinctive ethnic and religious customs, plainly evident to the watching Roman world. But for Paul, who is a true Jew? God only knows. One may be outwardly "named" a Jew (Rom 2:17), but the true Jew is one who is a Jew on the inside, "hidden," not just outwardly identified, whose *circumcision is of the *heart rather than of the flesh alone (Rom 2:28-29).

Despite their privileges, the Jews have failings that are painfully evident. Their possession of the law, which instructs them in the very will of God (Rom

2:18), convinces them that they are "a guide for the blind, a light for those who are in the dark, an instructor of the foolish, a teacher of infants" (Rom 2:19-20 NIV). But this hubris can conceal the acquisitive sins of stealing, commiting *adultery and robbing temples (Rom 2:21-22). The seemingly indelible mark of male circumcision, the outward symbol of ethnic membership, is not enough. The outward sign is worthless without an inner correspondence in the "circumcision of the heart" (Rom 2:29 NIV).

Despite their many advantages, such as being entrusted with the *oracles of God (Rom 3:1-2), Jews join Greeks in standing guilty "under sin" (Rom 3:9), a verdict itself sealed with a chorus of scriptural oracles (Rom 3:10-18). Although the gospel comes to Jews "first" (Rom 1:16; 2:9, 10), God is not the God of the Jews alone but also of the Gentiles (Rom 3:29), for God is *one (Rom 3:30). This image of divine oneness reveals the fundamental reality coming to expression in the gospel of Jesus Christ. The one God is calling and creating one people from many. God transcends historic, temporal and ethnic distinctions between Jews and Gentiles and lays his singular claim of judgment and grace on all people. Thus Jews and also Gentiles are now "called" as people of God (Rom 9:24), for there is "no difference" in Christ (Rom 10:12 NIV). Romans displays an inexorable movement from the duality of Jew and Gentile— and the manifold plurality of Gentiles with their many *gods—to a oneness in Christ under one God. This oneness breaks down a fundamental Jewish ordering of the world.

In contrast with Jew, the term Israel or Israelite evokes the election, privilege and heritage of the historic people of God. It is the language of Paul's heart, a familial term almost, by which he displays his love and hope for his own people and laments their present waywardness. More than that, the image of Israel is of a people who enjoys the status of a uniquely advantaged minority under God: "Theirs is the adoption as sons; theirs the divine glory, the covenants, the receiving of the law, the temple worship and the promises. Theirs are the patriarchs, and from them is traced the human ancestry of Christ, who is God over all, forever praised!" (Rom 9:3-5 NIV). Here is an image calculated to puncture Gentile-Christian *pride, a pride perhaps nurtured in the sustained absence of Jewish Christians who had been expelled from Rome under the emperor Claudius and were now returning to their homes and Christian communities. Paul reminds Gentile Christians of God's promises and long-term relationship with Israel. In the extended image of the olive tree (Rom 11:16-21), Israel makes up the *root, trunk and *branches of God's cultivated olive tree, and Gentiles are only wild branches grafted in. If God prunes some Israelite branches from this tree to make room for wild branches, the Creator God can just as well graft in the pruned branches at a later time.

The inverse relationship between the failure of Israel and the fortune of the Gentiles is only temporary. While the defeat of Israel has meant riches for Gentiles (Rom 11:12), these riches have aroused Israel's envy of believing Gentiles, and this envy will eventuate in the *salvation of some Israelites as envy and desire give birth to discovery of the gift of salvation in Christ (Rom 10:19; 11:11, 14). God's fatherly rejection of Israel is only apparent, not real (Rom 11:1); it serves the larger purpose of the *reconciliation of the world (Rom 11:15).

The image of Jew and Gentile becoming one shades into an abundance of familial images. The legacy of Israel's family—*adoption, glory, temple, patriarchs and more—finds its climax in the one true Israelite, Christ, before spilling forth to those Israelites plus Gentiles who are truly the people of God in Christ. Believers are "adopted" as "sons" and "children" (Rom 8:16-17, 21) of God and address God as "Abba, Father" (Rom 8:15). *Abraham, formerly regarded as the forefather of the Jews, is "our forefather" (Rom 4:1), the "father of us all" (Rom 4:16 NIV), the "father of many nations" (Rom 4:17-18 NIV), the "heir of the world" (Rom 4:13 NIV). Thus Isaac also becomes "our father" (Rom 9:10). The "seed" of this family is transferred by promise and not flesh (Rom 9:8). Christ is the preeminent "Son" in this family (Rom 1:4), but believers as newly adopted "children" in God's family are "joint heirs with Christ" (Rom 8:17 NRSV). Paul regards fellow believers as "brothers" (Rom 1:13) and sisters (Rom 16:1)—some of whom are relatives by natural ties (Rom 16:7, 11, 21)—and encourages them in "brotherly," or familial, love (Rom 12:10 NIV). Paul can even speak of one woman as "a mother to me" (Rom 16:13 NIV), and as in a large Roman household, we meet several "fellow workers" (Rom 16:3, 9, 21 NIV). Paul fosters the intimacy of this large family in encouraging the "holy kiss" (Rom 16:16) and protects the family's integrity with a warning against "those who cause divisions" (Rom 16:17 NIV). These images are grounded in the social reality of Paul's addressing various "house" churches of Rome (Rom 16:5, and implied throughout Rom 16:3-16), communities that needed their bonds strengthened and reinforced.

Other Images. The quantity and rich variety of images that appear throughout Romans fly in the face of the common notion that this is a ponderous and abstract epistle. Paul draws on a number of areas of life to make his points.

The workaday world of the laborer is evoked in images of *wages and *work (Rom 4:4), of potter and *clay (Rom 9:20-21), of *building up (Rom 14:19; 15:1) and yet not building on someone else's *foundation (Rom 15:20). And the language of commerce is engaged to speak of carrying no outstanding debts except for love of one's *neighbor (Rom 13:8-10).

The institution of *marriage and its dissolution by death provides a metaphor (admittedly complex) for speaking of Israel's relationship to the law and subsequent discharge from its obligations (Rom 7:1-4). Those who are united with Christ in his death "die to the law" (Rom 7:4) and are like a woman now freed from her marriage bonds and able to marry another without committing adultery.

The daily rhythms of *night and *day (Rom 13:12), darkness and *light (Rom 13:12), *sleeping and waking (Rom 13:11) are employed to speak of the transition from the "night" of pagan vice to the "day" of salvation. This blends into imagery suggesting soldiers who are instructed to lay off the "works of darkness" (Rom 13:12 NRSV), to give up nights on the town invested in carousing, partying and orgies (Rom 13:13) and to put on the "armor of light" (Rom 13:12 NRSV).

In a list of denials of what can separate believers from the love of God, Paul invokes images of hardship, distress, *persecution, *famine, *nakedness, peril, *sword (Rom 8:35). These find their fount in Deuteronomy 28:53, 55, 57 and Leviticus 26:25, 33, which set out in advance the terrors that will befall unfaithful Israel (Thielman, 183). But while these *sufferings were the result of divine abandonment and defeat for Israel, they are not to be so interpreted for those who are "more than conquerors through him who loved us" (Rom 8:37 NIV). Salvation does not guarantee *escape from sufferings in this life.

Images of *eating or not eating cluster around the equally evocative images of the "strong" and the "weak" in Romans 14. The strong are able to eat all sorts of food and drink, and the *weak, who at Rome were probably vegetarians, abstain from meat and *wine (Rom 14:1-6, 14-15, 20-23). But "the kingdom of God is not a matter of eating and drinking" (Rom 14:17 NIV), and the strong ones' insistence on the freedom to eat any food should not become a *stumbling block to others. Elsewhere we hear that *appetites of any type are not to be served (Rom 16:18). And when David is cited as saying "Let their table become a snare and a trap" (Rom 11:9 NRSV), Paul probably understands it as a reference to Israel's sacrificial cult and Pharisaic cultic *purity that had trammeled Israel. Paul is convinced that "no food is unclean in itself" but is so only because one regards it as unclean (Rom 14:14 NIV). On the other hand, enemies (who epitomize uncleanness for the Jews) who *hunger or *thirst should be given food and drink as they require, with the result that burning coals will be heaped on their head (Rom 12:20). This puzzling image is taken from Proverbs 25:21-22, and while the burning shame of having one's hostility met with love comes first to mind, there is evidence that the image may originally have been derived from an Egyptian ritual signifying genuine repentance (Dunn, 751).

Images of *feet are evident in the graphic picture of *Satan being crushed under the messianic foot (Rom 16:20; cf. Gen 3:15) and the "beautiful feet" (Rom 11:15; cf. Is 52:7) of the heralds who bring the good news of salvation. The true sign of a person of God is not circumcision but *walking "in the footsteps of the faith that our father Abraham had before he was circumcised" (Rom 4:12 NIV). But footsteps are not always sure, and stumbling feet are a hazard on the spiritual *pathway. A "stumbling stone"—Christ—is laid for Israel in *Zion (Rom 9:32-33; cf. Is 8:14), and Israel's own cultic rituals are also a source of stumbling (Rom 11:9). But Israel has not "stumbled so as to fall," and "through their stumbling salvation has come to the Gentiles" (Rom 11:11 NRSV). Still, within the community of faith there is no place for stumbling stones (Rom 14:20-21), and the community must be on the watch for those who put obstacles in their way (Rom 16:17).

The imagery of foot and path finds affinity with the imagery of pursuit. Israel "pursued a law of righteousness" and failed to obtain it, for in their pursuit they stumbled over the stone laid in Zion (Rom 9:30-32 NIV). Christ, the goal (telos, Rom 10:4) of the law, became for Israel not the finish marker of their *race but a stone that caused them to stumble. In Romans 15:30 we encounter athletic imagery from another arena. Paul calls on the Romans to "wrestle together" (synagōnizomai) with him in prayer (not against God but against opponents) so that he might be "rescued from the unbelievers in Judea."

Images of the *mouth are a vehicle for portraying the desired harmony of the inner and outer person. The Mosaic reminder that the word of law is *near, "in your mouth and in your heart" (Rom 10:8 NIV; Deut 30:14), finds its gospel correspondence in confessing with the mouth and believing in the heart (Rom 10:9). Likewise the believing community is to praise God "with one mind [homothumadon] and one mouth [heni stomati]" (Rom 15:6). In contrast, the hearts of those who bring dissension and false teaching are masked with "smooth talk" (chrēstologia) and "flattery" (eulogia, Rom 16:18 NIV).

Images of unsearchable *wisdom and failed *quest reveal the paradoxes of life before God. Israel earnestly seeks but does not obtain (Rom 11:7), while the Gentiles do not seek but find (Rom 10:20). The riches and wisdom and knowledge of God are unsearchable (Rom 11:33), and it is his way to keep mysteries hidden for ages and then finally to reveal them (Rom 16:25-26). No one can know God's mind, nor does anyone serve as his counselor (Rom 11:34). It is futile and unneccessary to launch a spiritual quest to ascend to heaven to bring Christ down or to descend into the abyss to bring Christ up from the dead. In the mystery of God's ways the crucified and risen Christ is as near as the confession of the *lips and belief of the heart (Rom 10:6-9).

Paul puts several images of *hardness and disability to good work. *Pharaoh's heart is hardened (Rom 9:16-18), and he becomes an object of divine wrath and destruction. Israel was also hardened (Rom 11:7), though partially (Rom 11:25). Hardening of the heart suggests a retrenchment of mind and being before God and others, a stubborn lack of *repentance (Rom 2:5), an impenetrability at the very point where a person should be receptive and vulnerable to God and others. In the field of biblical imagery it seems to be a malignant condition that invades and impairs the organs of sight and hearing. Israel was given a "sluggish spirit, eyes that would not see and ears that would not hear" (Rom 11:8 NRSV; cf. Deut 29:4). The image of backs "forever bent" (Rom 11:10 NRSV) is graphic, though the precise meaning is opaque. Whether we should see Israel as oppressed under the burden of slavery, or laboring under a burden of grief or forever hunched over from a life of hard toil and unable to lift their gaze we cannot be sure. But it is clearly a deformed condition for creatures who have been granted the dignity of walking upright, and it suggests an inability to meet others in the eye, or to gaze into the past or future, or to fully engage in the actions of worship.

Paul can invoke priestly or cultic imagery to speak of the death of Christ as a sacrifice of atonement (Rom 3:25 NIV) or the Christian community offering themselves as a "living sacrifice" which is their "acceptable service *[latreia]*" (Rom 12:1). When he speaks of gaining "access . . . into this grace" (*prosagōgē*, Rom 5:2 NIV), the image is of Israelite and priestly access to the presence of God in the inner temple courts or holy of holies. And we read that "everyone who calls on the name of the Lord"—an image of worship—"will be saved" (Rom 10:13 NIV). But the most sustained flourish of priestly imagery comes when Paul speaks of his own mission to the Gentiles. Ultimately Paul's mission is all about worship, or service. The Gentiles, who "worshiped and served the creature rather than the Creator" (Rom 1:25 NRSV), now have Paul as their "minister of Christ Jesus" (*leitourgos*, Rom 15:16 NRSV) to direct them to the true object of their worship so that "every knee shall bow" and "every tongue shall give praise to God" (Rom 14:11 NRSV; cf. Is 45:23). He serves "the gospel of God" as a priest and fulfills his duty by making an acceptable offering of the Gentiles (Rom 15:16). He is on his way to the holy city *Jerusalem to be of service (Rom 15:25), and he is taking a contribution from the Gentiles (Rom 15:26-27) that recalls Isaiah's eschatological vision of the wealth of nations being brought to Jerusalem. The Romans are to pray that his service will be acceptable (Rom 15:31).

As we have already seen, Paul's use of *plant imagery prominently features his picture of Israel as an olive tree. But the image of the root should not be missed: "If the root is holy, so are the branches," says Paul (Rom 11:16 NIV). The life of the Gentiles in this family tree of faith is dependent on the root in Israel's ancestry which received the promises. The same point is made from an image drawn from the intersection of agriculture and hearth: "if the part of the dough offered as firstfruits is holy, then the whole batch is holy" (Rom 11:16 NIV). The image of root takes a peculiarly activist posture when it is said that "the Root of Jesse will spring up" (Rom 15:12 NIV)—presumably once cut off and now surging

forth to flourish as a full-grown tree—and will exercise its messianic rule over the nations (cf. Is 11:10).

In the end every image is enlisted in the progress of the power of the gospel (Rom 1:16-17) as it makes its way into the lost world, driving forward toward its redemptive unity in Christ. Paul's mission rides the cusp of this divine mission, and the ultimate outcome will be all nations' believing and obeying God, giving him praise and glory (Rom 16:26-27).

See also ADAM; BONDAGE AND FREEDOM; LEGAL IMAGES; REUNION/RECONCILIATION.

BIBLIOGRAPHY. D. E. Aune, "Romans as a *Logos Protreptikos*" in *The Romans Debate*, ed. K. P. Donfried (rev. and exp.; Peabody, MA: Hendrickson, 1991) 278-96; R. K. Jewett, "Following the Argument of Romans" in *The Romans Debate*, ed. K. P. Donfried (rev. and exp.; Peabody, MA: Hendrickson, 1991) 265-77; R. K. Jewett, "Romans as an Ambassadorial Letter," *Int* 36 (1982) 5-20; J. D. G. Dunn, *Romans* (2 vols.; WBC; Dallas: Word, 1988); F. Thielman, "The Story of Israel in the Theology of Romans 5—8" in *Pauline Theology*, 3: *Romans,* ed. D. M. Hay and E. E. Johnson (Minneapolis: Fortress, 1995) 169-95; N. T. Wright, "Romans and the Theology of Paul" in *Pauline Theology*, 3: *Romans,* ed. D. M. Hay and E. E. Johnson (Minneapolis: Fortress, 1995) 30-67.

ROOT

Much of the Bible presents us with an agrarian society, populated by farmers whose lives depend on their ability to grow plants (*see* Farming). It is common knowledge that a plant's growth depends on a strong root system. If the root withers from lack of *water or is torn from the ground, the plant will soon shrivel up and die (Job 8:16-19). It is not surprising then that the Bible uses the image of a well-rooted plant as a symbol of stability and growth, and the opposite image of a withered or uprooted plant as a word picture for *judgment and destruction.

In stark contrast to the wicked, who sometimes appear to be well rooted and stable (Jer 12:2) but cannot survive calamity (Job 5:3; 18:16; Mal 4:1), those who trust in the Lord are like a well-rooted tree planted by a stream (Jer 17:7-8). Even during hot weather and *drought, its *leaves remain *green and it continues to produce *fruit. In the same way the faith of the righteous sustains them through difficult times, for the God in whom they trust provides what they need and protects them from harm. NT believers are to remain rooted in the Lord Jesus (Col 2:7) and his great love (Eph 3:17-19) so that they may remain stable. When adversity comes, such well-rooted plants remain productive, unlike plants growing in *rocky soil. The latter spring up quickly but have no root system. When trouble comes, they wither (Mt 13:6, 21 par. Mk 4:6, 17 and Lk 8:6, 13).

The OT often associates the image of a root with Israel. God plants his *covenant people Israel in the *Promised Land, where they take root and grow into a large *vine (Ps 80:8-11; see also Ezek 19:10-11).

When Israel rebels against its covenant Lord, God's judgment robs the nation of its vitality and prominence, turning it into a diseased plant with *decaying and withered roots (Is 5:24; Hos 9:16). God eventually uproots his people (1 Kings 14:15), leaving them at the mercy of the hot east *wind (Ezek 17:9-10; 19:12). Nevertheless, the Lord always preserves a *remnant through judgment (2 Kings 19:30 par. Is 37:31), and he promises to someday *restore Israel's strength and influence. At that time his people will take root and become a large, flourishing *tree (Is 27:6; Hos 14:5-7).

The prophets sometimes use the image of a withered or uprooted plant to depict God's judgment on foreign nations. The powerful Amorites are seemingly as stable as a cedar or oak tree, but the Lord destroys the root system of this tall tree and bring it crashing to the ground (Amos 2:9). He threatens to destroy the Philistines' root with *famine (Is 14:30) and warns that *Pharaoh, despite being like a deeply rooted, well-watered tree, will be chopped down (Ezek 31:2-14). As the sovereign ruler of the world the Lord plants and uproots rulers as he desires (Is 40:24). The *Babylonian king Nebuchadnezzar is a prime example of this (Dan 4). As his power and jurisdiction expands, he becomes like a great tree, but then God orders that he be chopped down. Yet he also decrees that Nebuchadnezzar's tree stump and roots be preserved, so that his prominence might be restored once he has learned his lesson.

Like the OT prophets Jesus uses the symbolism of a withered or uprooted plant for judgment. In denouncing the *Pharisees he warns that every plant not planted by God will be uprooted (Mt 15:13). He curses a fruitless *fig tree, causing its roots to wither (Mk 11:12-14, 20-21). The tree represents the Jewish *generation of Jesus' day; the withering of its roots foreshadows the judgment this generation will soon experience (see also Mt 3:10; Lk 3:9).

Since a plant's root may be viewed as its very life's source, the Bible occasionally uses the image to describe the source of someone or something. According to Isaiah the ideal king of the eschaton will grow out of the "root" of Jesse, meaning that he will come from the *Davidic line (Is 11:1, 10; see also Rom 15:12; Rev 5:5; 22:16). Paul views Israel as the "root" from which the people of God spring (Rom 11:16, 18). He also warns that the love of money is the root, or source, of all kinds of *evil (1 Tim 6:10). *Idolatry and *sin in general are likened to a bitter root that poisons and defiles God's covenant community (Deut 29:18; Heb 12:15).

Finally, Isaiah uses the image of a plant shallowly rooted in dry ground to emphasize the apparent insignificance of the Lord's special *suffering servant (Is 53:2). When Israel first sees the servant, he is without majesty or attraction (Is 53:2-3), but much to their surprise, God announces the servant's vindication and eventual exaltation (Is 53:12).

See also BRANCH; LEAF; PLANTS; TREE, TREES.

ROSE. See FLOWERS.

ROTTEN. See CORRUPTION; DECAY.

ROYAL COURT

Royal courts played an important role in ancient social and political contexts, and it is not surprising to find descriptions of courts throughout biblical literature. In modern times the image of the royal court continues to be meaningful, especially in connection with human political endeavor and with the biblical portrayal of the *fearful and awesome presence of God.

The Concept of Court. The Hebrew word usually translated "court" in our English Bibles is ḥāsēr, which refers to an enclosure of some kind. While the word ḥāsēr is not widespread in Scripture, the concept or image of the court is implied in many places, particularly where we find mention of a *king and his *throne.

We would be mistaken to think of the royal court solely in terms of a room. The use of this motif in the Bible demonstrates that it also includes the idea of a retinue: the ruler, officials, *servants and *guests who would typically be in the room. This understanding of royal court as both a particular place and a group of people can be seen in the older English expression "to hold court."

Biblical Descriptions of the Royal Court. One of the strongest images we associate with a royal court is a magnificent room with splendid architecture, dominated by a throne on which a *king or *queen sits. At the rise of the monarchy in Israel, however, such grandiose embellishments were not yet present. After his coronation King Saul returned to his own house with a group of men, to carry on with his former occupation as a farmer (1 Sam 10:26; 11:4; see Farming). This description seems to bear little resemblance to our usual idea of a royal court. We also read of a "field court" (1 Sam 14:2; 22:6; 1 Kings 22:20) and a winter court (Jer 36:20-22). While these lacked the splendor of a court in a palace, the descriptions in the text show that the royal court—regardless of its appearance or location—existed for the king's purposes, whether business or pleasure.

In less than a century the royal court of Israel was transformed into a room of such magnificence that surrounding countries were awed. King *Solomon designed and directed the building of his palace, which took thirteen years to complete (1 Kings 7:1-12). Built of expensive *stone and cedar, it was furnished with valuable imported items and an immense throne made of ivory and *gold (1 Kings 10:18-25). Our initial notion of a royal court, then, is probably similar to the description of Solomon's palace court, that of a throne room fit for a king.

Upon further reflection we might picture the occupants of the throne room as well. A royal court in the ancient Near East often included magicians and astrologers (Ex 7:11; Dan 2:2; see Magic), servants and waiters (1 Kings 10:5), a *cupbearer (Neh 2:1-5) and wise men who could act as counselors (Dan 1:3-5). Other officials, such as military generals, the high *priest, district leaders and royal secretaries were also present (2 Sam 9:15-18; 20:23-26; 1 Kings 4:1-7). The recognition that all these people—servants and officials alike—were part of the royal court enhances our mental picture further, suggesting that a royal court is a place of harmonious and orderly service. The rank of these officials also indicates that the court was the place where matters of the most serious nature were discussed and dealt with. Moreover, the presence of important officials would certainly add to the grandeur of the court.

The Ruler and the Court. All aspects of the court are inseparably linked to the person for whom the court exists: the royal personage. The images associated with a king—power, majesty, regal appearance—are transferred to the royal court simply by the king's presence. Conversely, the court also enhances the king's image in that its splendor adds to his majesty. This was particularly the case if the court had been designed by the king himself; Solomon, Nebuchadnezzar and Herod were famous for the royal palaces they built. While walking on the roof of his royal palace, the Babylonian king Nebuchadnezzar remarked, "Is this not Babylon the great, which I myself have built as a royal residence by the might of my power and for the glory of my majesty?" (Dan 4:30 NASB). The physical appearance of the royal court, especially its imposing size and rich decor, could serve as propaganda to awe and intimidate foreign visitors. Once the queen of Sheba had seen the wonders of Solomon's royal court, the biblical writer notes, "there was no more spirit in her" (1 Kings 10:4-7 NASB).

By metonymy, then, the royal court is a symbol of who the king is. In this sense the royal court can convey an extremely negative picture: a brutal king, unjust and corrupt officials who take bribes, and policies that oppress the people of the *land (2 Chron 16:10; 22:2-4; Jer 22:13-19). On the other hand, the royal court can be a symbol for all that is positive about a kingdom—a just king, who with the help of wise counselors rules well and looks to the welfare of his people (2 Chron 17:3-9).

The close relationship between the king and his court can be seen in court protocol. To "enter the king's presence" was a serious matter, requiring humility (Prov 25:6-7), decorum (1 Kings 1:28, 31) and proper dress (Esther 4:2). In some nations, to enter the king's court without summons was to invite death (Esther 4:10-11, 16). The respect due the king was thus associated with his court. It is easy to see why for us the image of the royal court commands feelings of awe and respect, for it is a symbol of the king's authority.

The Function of the Royal Court. Much of the imagery associated with the royal court derives not only from its physical appearance but also from its function. One function of the royal court was its use as a place to hear appeals, try legal cases and dispense *justice. 1 Kings 7:7 describes Solomon's royal court as "the hall of judgment" (NASB). The image of such a place of *judgment evokes strong emotions, both positive and negative, in the reader. As a place of sentencing and conviction, it arouses feelings of *fear; as a place of appeal and acquittal, it assures us that justice will prevail.

Not only was the royal court a place to seek legal decisions, it was the place from which royal edicts were given. The word spoken by the king in his court was law, and the royal court can therefore be seen as the *seat of the kingdom. Here decisions affecting the entire country were made (Esther 3:8-15). This function of the royal court evokes images of authority and *wisdom: the royal counselors advising the king, the proclamation given by the king himself, and swift messengers issuing forth from the court to spread the king's law.

Another function of the royal court was its role in the process of appointment and promotion. This function was made possible by the fact that the court symbolized the king's authority and majesty. Hence a summons to court was an honor, a sign of the king's recognition (Esther 5:12). *Joseph was taken out of prison and promoted to a high position in Pharaoh's court for his wise counsel (Gen 41:39-44). It was a mark of great favor to "eat at the king's table," an honor bestowed by King David on Mephibosheth (2 Sam 9:7, 13) and the sons of Barzillai (1 Kings 2:7). It is possible that the narrator of the book of *Kings symbolically alludes to a future *hope for the exiled Jews by mentioning such an incident: 2 Kings 25:27-30 records that Jehoiachin of Judah was released from *prison by the Babylonian king, honored above other rulers in the court and allowed to eat "in the king's presence regularly all the days of his life" (NASB). The exclusivity of the royal court—and the hope that one might be honored enough to be invited there—demonstrates that the royal court can be a symbol for status and prestige.

The Divine Court. As important as scriptural references to earthly royal courts are, some of the most powerful images are evoked by descriptions of the divine court. Biblical literature portrays God as the King par excellence, sovereign ruler of the universe, and biblical descriptions of his court show that its splendor is fitting for such a king.

As throne room and temple. One of the most unusual aspects of the divine court is that it is described as both throne room and *temple. Isaiah saw God "sitting on a throne, lofty and exalted, with the train of His robe filling the temple" (Is 6:1 NASB). In the sense that the divine court serves as the seat of authority and majesty, it functions as the throne room of a palace, filled with *angelic messengers and authorities under God's rule (2 Chron 18:18; Rev 4:1-4). This corresponds to what has been mentioned above regarding the human royal court.

The picture of the divine court as a temple, however, is more complex; here the respect and honor due an earthly king are replaced by the *worship and adoration of the divine King. In his vision John sees the elders who "fall down before Him who sits on the throne, and will worship Him who lives forever," accompanied by a great crowd of people "before the throne of God" who "serve Him day and night in His temple" (Rev 4:10; 7:15 NASB). If the human royal court is an appropriate place for supplicants and envoys to show homage, how much more the divine royal court!

Temple imagery associated with the divine court also derives from the fact that Christ, who is King (*see* Jesus, Images of), acts in a priestly role on behalf of his people. We see this particularly in Hebrews, where Christ is described as "a high priest, who has taken His seat at the right hand of the throne of the Majesty in the heavens, a minister in the sanctuary" (Heb 8:1-2 NASB).

The earthly and heavenly divine court. Closely related to this idea of palace and temple is the biblical description of the divine royal court as having both an earthly and a heavenly location. The physical temple in Jerusalem can be spoken of as a royal court by virtue of the fact that God is portrayed as dwelling there as King. A certain tension arises from this description, a tension of which the biblical writers were well aware. On the one hand, the Bible portrays "the glory of the LORD" as dwelling in the tabernacle (Ex 40:34-38), and more specifically, "enthroned above the cherubim" of the *ark of the covenant (Ps 80:1 NASB; also 1 Sam 4:4). This idea of a divine dwelling place on earth is expanded in Deuteronomy 12:11, which speaks of a "place in which the LORD your God shall choose for His name to dwell" (NASB). That God's dwelling on earth is developed at length in the Zion motif, where the temple in Jerusalem (Zion) is seen as God's royal residence (Ps 48:2-3; Jer 8:19).

On the other hand, there is a definite understanding that God's royal court cannot be limited to mere earthly dimensions. When King Solomon completed the temple in *Jerusalem, he remarked, "But will God indeed dwell on the earth? Behold, heaven and the highest heaven cannot contain Thee, how much less this house which I have built!" (1 Kings 8:27-28 NASB). This thought is echoed in Isaiah 66:1, where God challenges: "Heaven is My throne, and the earth is My footstool. Where then is a house you could build for Me?" (NASB). The book of Psalms, which contains numerous references to the earthly temple as God's court, also describes the heavens as the place of God's court: "The LORD has established His throne in the heavens; And His sovereignty rules over all" (Ps 103:19 NASB; see also Ps 2:4; 11:4; 33:13-14; 115:3; 123:1).

The court as a symbol of authority. What concepts do we typically associate with these descriptions of the divine royal court? One is cosmic authority and transcendence. If the divine royal court is "in the heavens," it implies that God's lordship extends over all the universe. Another implication of this image is that when considered spatially, it shows the earth from God's perspective. God is portrayed as "looking down" on the *earth, able to perceive all that happens (Ps 33:13-14; 102:19). Unlike human kings, God has no need of counselors in his royal court (Is 40:13-14); he sees all from the heavens and acts as he wills (Is 40:21-25).

The court as a symbol of honor. Like the earthly royal court, the divine court is a symbol of honor and prestige. Christ is described as "seated at the right hand of the power of God" (Lk 22:69 NASB) and "exalted to [God's] right hand" (Acts 5:31 NASB). To be at God's right hand in his royal court is the ultimate position of majesty and power (Eph 1:20-21). This was understood in part by Jesus' *disciples who wished to sit on each side of his throne when he came into his *kingdom (Mk 10:35-40; see also Rev 3:21).

Two other concepts we might associate with the divine royal court are unapproachability and judgment. God is called "the King of kings and Lord of lords; who . . . dwells in unapproachable light; whom no man has seen or can see" (1 Tim 6:15-16 NASB). Taken with the image of God's throne as a seat of judgment (Mt 25:31-32; Rev 20:11-12), the picture of the royal court can be fearsome and terrifying. Yet the divine court can also be a very *comforting image: the writer of Hebrews tells us to "draw near with confidence to the throne of grace, that we may receive mercy and may find grace to help in time of need" (Heb 4:16 NASB).

Summary. The biblical motif of the royal court is associated with strong and often conflicting images. It can be a symbol for the transcendence of God, filled as it is with his majesty and glory. Depicted in this manner it seems unapproachable and, as the place of divine judgment, even terrifying. The awe inspired in the biblical characters by human royal courts is shared by us as we read descriptions of the divine court.

Nevertheless, given that we are citizens of God's kingdom (Phil 3:20), the biblical authors assure us that the divine court symbolizes the justice and *mercy of the King. In the final chapters of the Bible we see the hope that God's royal court will one day be in the midst of his people and open to all who serve him (Rev 21:1—22:5).

See also AUTHORITY, DIVINE AND ANGELIC; HONOR; KING, KINGSHIP; QUEEN; SCEPTER; TEMPLE; THRONE.

ROYAL PRIEST. *See* AUTHORITY, HUMAN; PRIEST.

RUBBISH. *See* DUNG.

RUDDER. *See* SHIP.

RUNAWAY

A runaway, or fugitive, is a person in flight from a threat. The person in flight may be either innocent of wrongdoing or guilty of a crime that necessitated the flight. Related motifs include *exile, *foreigner, *wanderer and *outcast, or castaway. The state of a runaway is constant restlessness and rootlessness, given the unnatural disruption represented by the person's flight, and the implied goal of such a person is to *return.

The Bible presents us with a small but vivid gallery of runaways. When life in the household of Abraham and Sarah becomes unbearable, Hagar flees into the wilderness, where she receives God's special providence (Gen 16:6-14). *Jacob is a guilt-haunted fugitive from his brother Esau's thirst for retribution, and after twenty years of conflict with Laban he runs away with his family and possessions. *Moses flees from justice after killing an Egyptian taskmaster (Ex 2:11-15). *David spends long years as a fugitive from a paranoid and jealous King Saul, and later he flees from his own court when Absalom rebels. Elijah flees from Jezebel (1 Kings 19:1-3). *Jonah undertakes a futile attempt to "flee . . . from the presence of the LORD" by going in exactly the opposite direction from what God had commanded him (Jon 1:3 RSV). The NT epistle to Philemon has as its background the escape of the slave Onesimus from his master.

The most notable runaway in the Bible is the *prodigal son of Jesus' parable (Lk 15:11-32). The foolish son's flight begins as an act of rebellion against his father. It is a journey of rebellion against parental values—away from the domestic, the secure, the governed, the morally right, and toward the distant, the exotic, the adventurous, the indulgence of forbidden appetites, the abandonment to unrestraint. The youthful runaway becomes a pitiable figure of dissolution, deprivation and poverty, betrayed by people on whom he has squandered his money. This debacle of rebellious flight from the father is reversed only when the son returns home.

See also EXILE; FOREIGNER; PRODIGAL SON; RETURN; WANDERER, WANDERING.

RUNNING

If we consider only instances of the animal or human motion of running (excluding, for example, references to running water), we find that running figures in a range of biblical usages—the running of *athletes and messengers, of warriors in *flight, of people caught up in extraordinary *joy or eagerness, of *villains bent on doing *evil. In all cases, however, running is an image of speed or haste and strenuous exertion in a momentous event.

In the case of animals, running implies speed of movement. There are prophetic warnings of *horses "swifter than eagles" (Jer 4:13 KJV) and "swifter than the leopards" (Hab 1:8 KJV), and there is a description of the running ostrich that "scorneth the horse and his rider" (Job 39:18 KJV). The speed of animals makes them a source of comparison to fast-moving people: *David says in his lament over Saul and Jonathan that "they were swifter than eagles" (2 Sam 1:23 KJV), and the historian later describes Asahel as being "as light of foot as a wild roe" (2 Sam 2:18 KJV; *see* Animals of the Bible). More generally,

the runner is a recognized standard for swiftness, so that Job can say that his "days are swifter than a runner" (Job 9:25 NRSV). Similarly, the word of God "runneth very swiftly" (Ps 147:15 KJV).

A second cluster of images links running to athletic *races. In Psalm 19:5 the athletic image suggests jubilation, as the *sun in its course through the sky "rejoiceth as a strong man to run a race" (KJV). The *Teacher replaces the jubilation of the psalmist's image with a more pessimistic image from human competition when he sees that "the race is not to the swift" (Eccles 9:11 KJV). In the NT we find the influence of Greek athletics in the readiness with which writers compare the Christian life to a race. Paul uses the metaphor in 1 Corinthians 9:24: "Know ye not that they which run in a race run all, but one receiveth the prize? So run, that ye may obtain" (KJV). Paul goes on to contrast the triumphant athlete's "corruptible crown" with the Christian's "incorruptible" one, adding, "I therefore so run, not as uncertainly" (1 Cor 9:25-26 KJV). In a similar vein the epistle of Hebrews enjoins us to "run with patience [endurance] the race that is set before us" (Heb 12:1 KJV).

Runners before a *king's *chariots were part of the glamour that attached to royalty in the ancient world. Thus when Samuel tries to dissuade the Israelites from kingship, he warns them that the royal impulse toward luxury will mean that a king "will take your sons, and appoint them for himself, for his chariots, and to be his horsemen; and some shall run before his chariots" (1 Sam 8:11 KJV). One of Absalom's first kingly gestures was to prepare "chariots and horses, and fifty men to run before him" (2 Sam 15:1 KJV; cf. 1 Kings 1:5). By extension, runners were messengers in the service of the king, as in Jeremiah's picture of a relay of runners who carry the message of the fall of Babylon (Jer 51:31; cf. 2 Sam 18:19-27).

Running as *flight from danger is another motif. Hagar runs from Sarah (Gen 16:8), and Moses accompanies the forward movement of the *ark of the covenant, symbolizing the advance of God the king and *divine warrior, with the statement "Rise up, LORD, and let thine enemies be scattered; and let them that hate thee flee before thee" (Num 10:35 KJV). As this verse suggests, retreats in biblical battles were often so disorderly as to be routs, with soldiers running as fast as they could to escape their victorious enemies, who may have been close in pursuit (see 1 Sam 14:22; 1 Chron 10:1-2; 2 Kings 25:4-5; *see* Battle Stories). As for refugees, Jesus pictures the Judeans as running "to the mountains" at the beginning of a great tribulation (Mk 13:14-16; also Mt 24:15-18 and Lk 21:20-21).

If running thus implies a more-than-ordinary desire to get away from something threatening, it can also imply eagerness to achieve something positive, sometimes accompanied by obvious *joy. Abraham ran from his tent *door to extend an invitation to three heavenly visitors (Gen 18:1-2). A miraculous infusion of energy allowed Elijah to outrun Ahab's *chariot on the trip from Mount Carmel to the gate of Jezreel as the storm clouds gathered (1 Kings 18:45-46). The name of the Lord "is a strong tower: the righteous runneth into it, and is safe" (Prov 18:10 KJV). In the coming millennium foreign nations will "run" to Israel to *worship God (Is 55:5). The climactic example is the forgiving *father in the parable of the *prodigal son, who forsakes paternal dignity as he runs to embrace his returning son (Lk 15:20). Running in such passages connotes something out of the routine, eliciting extraordinary haste. By a slight extension, running is intermixed with wonder in some memorable scenes from the Bible. The resurrection of Jesus is accompanied by a frenzy of eager running (Mt 28:7-8; Mk 16:8; Lk 11:12; Jn 20:2-4).

In contrast to running as an image of eagerness to achieve a good are passages where running implies haste and active commitment to do something evil. Elisha's *servant Gehazi runs after Naaman to claim the gift that his master had refused (2 Kings 5:20-21) and was punished for his greed and lying. The psalmist's *enemies "run and prepare themselves" to perpetrate evil without just cause (Ps 59:4 KJV). The book of Proverbs gives us pictures of people whose "feet run to evil, and make haste to shed blood" (Prov 1:16 KJV) and "feet that be swift in running to mischief" (Prov 6:18 KJV; cf. Is 59:7).

A final motif turns running to metaphoric effect in summing up the essence of godly living. The psalmist who obeys God's law claims, "I will run the way of thy commandments" (Ps 119:32 KJV). Those who wait upon God "renew their strength; . . . they shall run, and not be weary" (Is 40:31 KJV). Paul pictures the start of the Christian life as "running well" (Gal 5:7 NRSV), and he himself takes pains to make sure that has "not run in vain" (Phil 2:16 NRSV).

See also ATHLETICS; FLEE, FLIGHT; FLIGHT, CHASE AND FLIGHT; RACE; WALK, WALKING.

RUST

Rust appears twice in the NT as a potent image of the inevitable destruction and destructiveness of treasured temporal goods. It seems that the term translated "rust" has a broader connotation of the corrosion and *decay that attaches to metals of various sorts (not only iron; *see* Minerals).

Jesus himself warned his *disciples not to store up "treasures on earth, where moth and rust destroy, and where thieves break in and steal" (Mt 6:19 NIV). James makes the picture even more concrete as he speaks not simply of *treasures but of "gold and silver" that have "rotted" and "rusted": in fact, he predicts, "their rust will be a witness against you and will consume your flesh like fire" (Jas 5:2-3 NASB). This picture of the most precious metals utterly discolored, corroded through and through, shows vividly the ultimate worth of hoarded earthly riches. In these verses this *world's treasures appear not simply valueless but even harmful and malign: that very rust will consume and burn the flesh of hoarders, presumably as it witnesses against them and so consigns them to the *flames of *hell.

Conversely, the lesson Jesus would teach is to "store up for yourselves treasures in heaven, where moth and rust do not destroy" (Mt 6:20 NIV). The Son of God wants his followers to seek after the *kingdom of God and his righteousness (Mt 6:33). Such treasures are eternal, cannot be corrupted and bring to the one who has invested there the everlasting riches and *joy of heaven. For those who set their hearts on things above and not on earthly things (Col 3:1-2), Scripture promises a "city of pure gold," shining with the unending glory of God (Rev 21:18 NIV).

See also CORRUPTION; DECAY; MINERALS; STORING UP; TREASURE.

RUTH, BOOK OF

The book of Ruth is a story of *tragedy and triumph, of *death and *love. The narrative is unified by the motif of a *quest for home, as Naomi undertakes a quest to find a home for her loyal daughter-in-law Ruth (Ruth 1:9; 3:1). Within this pattern the story unfolds as the prototypical love story in the Bible. The plot builds toward the climax of the nighttime meeting between Ruth and Boaz on the *threshing floor, and each chapter contributes a phase to that action: the tragic background to the love story (Ruth 1), the courtship between Boaz and Ruth (Ruth 2), the night of betrothal (Ruth 3), the *wedding and celebration (Ruth 4). This is a U-shaped *comic plot, with events first descending into tragedy and then rising to a happy ending as obstacles are overcome.

The dominant image pattern is the tension between emptiness and *fullness. Ruth 1 is an ever-expanding vision of emptiness, moving from the natural level (*famine in the land) to the domestic level (the death of Naomi's husband and two sons) to the personal level (the widow's inner depression). Even in the opening chapter, though, there is a countermovement toward fullness, as we read about the restoration of *food to Israel (Ruth 1:6) and Ruth's refusal to relinquish her ties with her mother-in-law. References to the *harvest in Ruth 2—3 permeate the middle of the book, and the tension between emptiness and fullness is decisively resolved in the final chapter with references to the child the married couple produces and the image of Naomi laying the infant in her bosom (Ruth 4:16). This outline only hints at the detail with which the imagery of emptiness and fullness is present in the texture of the story (see Rauber).

Another cluster of images stems from the pastoral genre of the book. The story of Ruth is a pastoral idyll. The central action in Ruth 2—3 occurs in a rural world replete with references to harvesting and threshing. For the human imagination the *harvest is a master image of *abundance, and in this story references to the beginning of the barley harvest

(Ruth 1:22) and the end of the barley and *wheat harvests (Ruth 2:23) serve as a metaphor for the progress of the romance between Ruth and Boaz. References to *grain are plentiful throughout Ruth 2—3, reinforcing the pastoral world of the story and the sense of abundance that comes to dominate it.

Domestic imagery of family, offspring and lineage is likewise important in the story. The story is filled with domestic epithets that delineate family roles: husband, son, daughter-in-law, mother-in-law, next of kin. The sphere of action is the family. The quest is for home and offspring. Family relations dominate the action. The feminine focus of the story can also be noted. The protagonist is a woman, and her mother-in-law is the mainspring of much of the romantic action. The story is told from the viewpoint of women for whom domestic values are preeminent. The final human voices we hear in the story are those of the women of *Bethlehem as they pronounce their blessing on the bride (Ruth 4:14-15) and name her infant (Ruth 4:17).

Images of *loyalty are likewise important in the story. Ruth's eloquent refusal to leave her mother-in-law and her corresponding assertion of loyalty are etched in our memories as an unsurpassed expression of domestic loyalty (Ruth 1:16-17). But Naomi's persistence in finding a husband for Ruth (Ruth 3:1) is also a notable example of loyalty, for which she is rewarded at the end of the story as she gathers the infant into her bosom. Boaz's loyalty to Ruth is also an important and memorable part of the story.

The imagery of ingathering is latent throughout the story and sometimes comes to the surface. Pictures of the harvesters gathering sheaves of grain into their arms are in our consciousness as we read of the harvest and threshing. In the last chapter Naomi takes her infant grandson into her bosom. When Boaz, as yet unaware of the role he will play in the matter, commends the virtuous Ruth, he expresses the wish that "a full reward be given you by the LORD, the God of Israel, under whose wings you have come to take refuge" (Ruth 2:12 RSV). This imagery of the *wing is echoed in the next chapter when, at the memorable encounter on the threshing floor, Ruth requests that Boaz "spread your skirt over your maidservant" (Ruth 3:9 RSV). English translations miss the wordplay by not retaining the image of the wing that appeared in the previous chapter, but even so the image of ingathering is evident in Ruth's request.

The image of the sojourner or *foreigner carries an importance out of proportion to the scarcity of actual references in the book. At the outset of the story the family of Elimelech is in the position of being foreigners or sojourners in the hostile land of Moab. Ruth then courageously commits herself to accompany her mother-in-law to Bethlehem, where she is an obvious outsider in a very closed society. When Boaz discloses his admiration for Ruth's loyalty to her mother-in-law, she replies, "Why have I found favor in your eyes, that you should take notice of me, when I am a foreigner?" (Ruth 2:10). In the background is a whole chorus of passages from the Levitical law, the prophets and Psalms about God's special provision for the foreigner.

Ruth 2—3 is a study in contrast between images of *daylight/openness and *nighttime/secrecy. The first exchange between the future lovers occurs at midday and is climaxed by a shared lunch. A crowd of onlookers surrounds the couple. By contrast, the focus narrows to just the couple in Ruth 3, where the action happens at *midnight, hidden from the eyes of others (Ruth 3:14).

*Legal imagery is also important. This is most evident in the scene at the village *gate (Ruth 4:1-6), in which Boaz fulfills all legal obligations in securing his right to marry Ruth. But the language of the levirate *marriage (in which a *widow had a right to expect the next of kin to raise offspring by her) has been present throughout the story from the time that Naomi identifies Boaz as "our nearest kin" (Ruth 2:20). Then too we are never allowed to forget that Boaz is a *gō'ēl*—a kinsman-redeemer (*see* Redeem, Redemption) for the widowed Ruth.

Finally, despite all of the commonplace domesticity and privacy of the story, the imagery places the action in the mainstream of OT salvation history and even messianic history. The first hint comes in Ruth 2:11, where Boaz's description of how Ruth "left your father and mother and your native land and came to a people that you did not know before" (RSV) echoes the language used of *Abraham when God called him (Gen 12:1). Our minds also fill with the patriarchal past when the women of Bethlehem express the wish that God will make Ruth fruitful "like Rachel and Leah, who together built up the house of Israel" (Ruth 4:11 RSV). Most of all, though, we notice the genealogies at the end that link the son of Ruth and Boaz with David (Ruth 4:17-22). This is both a patriotic reference and a reference to the messianic line.

In terms of narrative art and imagery, the story of Ruth is unsurpassed in the Bible. No other story of such brevity contains such a rich literary texture.

See also FARMING; FILL, FULLNESS; FOREIGNER; HARVEST; LOVE STORY; MARRIAGE; WIDOW.

BIBLIOGRAPHY. D. F. Rauber, "Literary Values in the Bible: The Book of Ruth," *JBL* 89 (1970) 27-37; reprinted in *Literary Interpretations of Biblical Narratives,* ed. K. R. R. Gros Louis et al. (Nashville: Abingdon, 1974) 163-76.

S

SABBATH

The imagery surrounding the *seventh day of the Jewish week conveys a sense of the day's being special and sacred, but beyond that several distinct motifs emerge. The earliest references to the sabbath focus on the motif of repose or cessation from exertion. At the original sabbath, after "God finished the work" of creation, he "rested on the seventh day from all the work that he had done" (Gen 2:2 NRSV). When observance of the sabbath became one of the Ten Commandments, the example of God's *rest after six days of work remained prominent (Ex 20:8-11; Deut 5:12-15). During the *exodus, the sabbath as a day of cessation from work became institutionalized for the Hebrew nation, as the people were prohibited from gathering *manna on the seventh day (Ex 16:23-30), with the implication that the sabbath is to draw a boundary around the acquisitive urge. The motif of God's and Israel's ceasing from work on the sabbath is naturally related to being "refreshed" (Ex 31:17)—the motif of renewal as part of sabbath rest. The sabbath is also said to be "a delight" (Is 58:13). The motif of sabbath rest is turned to metaphoric use in Hebrews 4:9, which views *heaven itself as "a sabbath rest."

Second, the sabbath is linked with the motif of *remembrance and commemoration. This is particularly emphasized in the Decalogue, where sabbath observance is linked with remembering both God's resting from work during *creation (Ex 20:11) and the nation's deliverance from *bondage in Egypt (Deut 5:15). The very observance of one day in seven is something that the Israelites were commanded to "remember" to do (Ex 20:8).

Third, the sabbath is surrounded by an aura of sanctity—as something set apart from the ordinary. At its very institution God "blessed the seventh day and hallowed it" (Gen 2:3 NRSV). Thereafter this day is to be kept "holy" (Ex 20:8; 31:14; Deut 5:12), for God "blessed the sabbath day and consecrated it" (Ex 20:11 NRSV); it is the occasion of "holy convocation" (Lev 23:3 NRSV).

As an extension of the sabbath's being set apart, it is sometimes presented as a covenant sign that the nation of Israel had been set apart by God as his chosen people. Exodus 31:16-17 (NRSV) speaks of sabbathkeeping as "a perpetual covenant" and "a sign forever" between God and the people of Israel,

while Leviticus 24:8 (NRSV) speaks of sabbath observance as "a covenant forever" between God and Israel. In later prophetic books we read about keeping the sabbath as a form of holding fast God's *covenant (Is 56:6) and of the sabbath itself as a "sign" between God and Israel (Ezek 20:12, 20).

The sabbath is additionally surrounded with the motif of command and *law. Already during the exodus, Moses' prohibition of gathering manna carried the force of something that God had "commanded" (Ex 16:23). This is reinforced by the appearance of sabbath observance in the Decalogue, where it is couched as an imperative, and in later Mosaic laws (e.g., Ex 35:3; Lev 16:31; 23:3). Characteristic terms by which the motif of law is phrased include the need to "observe" the sabbath and to "keep" it (Deut 5:12, 15; Neh 13:22; Is 56:2).

Yet another motif associated with the sabbath is *worship. The first we hear about this link is in connection with special priestly *sacrifices on the seventh day (Num 28:9-10), a practice referred to later in the OT as well (Ezek 46:4, 12). In a similar vein, Isaiah speaks of coming to worship before God "from sabbath to sabbath" (Is 66:23 NRSV). In general, though, pictures of something approximating weekly Sunday worship in a Christian church do not emerge clearly until we come to the references to synagogue worship in the NT (Mk 1:21; 6:2; Lk 4:16-17, 31; 6:6; 13:10; Acts 13:14, 27; 15:21; 17:2; 18:4), where the emphasis is on reading and expounding the Scripture and debating its meaning.

Although *sabbath* refers especially to the seventh day of the week, we should note that in the OT other religious *festivals are called "sabbaths." Examples include the Day of Atonement (Lev 16:31), the Festival of Trumpets (Lev 23:24) and the Feast of Booths (Lev 23:39). Also, every seventh year is to be a sabbath to the Lord after the Israelites have entered the Promised Land (Lev 25). An extension of this is the sabbath of the *land, allowing the land to lie fallow every seven years, that Israel was commanded to observe (Lev 25:1-7).

All the foregoing OT motifs evoke a picture of the extreme importance and sanctity of the sabbath. It is not surprising, therefore, that an additional motif is the profanation of the sabbath, a particular horror to the OT prophets (Is 56:2, 6; cf. also Neh 13:17). The most common form of sabbath desecration was engaging in business on the sabbath (Neh 13:19; Amos 8:5), described with imagery of bringing merchandise through the city gates (Neh 13:19, 22; Jer 17:21, 24, 27).

When we turn to the NT, we find both continuity and modification. To begin, we can note the high number of references to events that happen on the sabbath in both the Gospels (nearly fifty references) and Acts (approximately ten references). This concentration obviously signals the importance of sabbath as a day on which decisive or controversial events happen in the lives of Jesus and the apostles. In the Gospels it is a day which fittingly frames the recreative work of God's kingdom as Jesus heals and bring wholeness to human brokenness. The idea of the sabbath as a day set apart for religious activity rather than daily work is assumed in all of these references. Yet the extreme (and potentially legalistic) forms of refraining from work that prevailed under the law are softened and set within the context of God's new redemptive work (Mt 12:1-12; Mk 2:23-28; 3:2-4; Lk 6:1-9; 13:10-17; 14:1-6; Jn 5:9-18; 9:14-16). Given this NT modification, we are left with a picture of the sabbath as a day of doing good as well as a day of worship and cessation from ordinary work.

See also SEVEN; REST; WORK, WORKER; WORSHIP.

SACKCLOTH. *See* ASHES.

SACRED SPACE

The sense of place runs strong throughout the Bible. Sacred space is a place where God is encountered in a special or direct way, by virtue of which the very place becomes *holy and set apart from ordinary space. It is a point of reference to which people return, either physically or in memory. Some sacred places are the site of once-only encounters with God, while others are places of perpetual visitation.

In keeping with the Bible's way of picturing the unseen spiritual world as reaching down into the ordinary routines of life, any place is a candidate to become sacred by virtue of a visitation from God. For *Abraham and Isaac, Mt. Moriah becomes a sacred site, not because it held any special physical property but because it is where Abraham exercised his supreme venture in faith and was rewarded by God (Gen 22). Bethel is an ordinary landscape until God appears to Jacob in a dream, whereupon *Jacob concludes, "Surely the LORD is in this place; and I did not know it. . . . How awesome is this place! This is none other than the house of God, and this is the gate of heaven" (Gen 28:16-17 RSV). God's appearance to Moses in a burning bush makes the landscape holy for Moses (Ex 3:1-6). When the nation of Israel sets up *twelve *stones of *remembrance following the crossing of the Jordan river (Josh 4), they identify the space and accompanying event as sacred. The stories of *conversion in the Gospels are replete with sites that become sacred—the well at which the Samaritan woman encounters Jesus, for example, or

the tree from which Zacchaeus is summoned by Jesus. In the Bible any site can become sacred.

Beyond these individual and localized sacred places, though, an incremental sequence of sacred places hold special meaning not simply for individuals but for the believing community through the ages. Paradise is the first sacred space that God creates for the human race (*see* Garden). It is a place planted by God himself for the first human couple, a place in which God *walks and converses with *Adam and Eve. It is also a place of prelapsarian *innocence. Throughout the Bible, Paradise (the garden *in* Eden) retains its identity of being sacred: even though the place and the spiritual state associated with it have been lost, these remain a spiritual point of reference by which to define moral and spiritual perfection for people.

The second sacred space in salvation history is Mt. *Sinai, the place where God meets face to face with *Moses and gives him the law. The sanctity of the place itself is such that before Moses ascends the *mountain the people undergo a ritual purification for three days (Ex 19:10-11). The people are prohibited upon penalty of death from even touching the border of the mountain (Ex 19:12-13). On the day of Moses' ascent the mountain is enveloped in *fire and smoke, and the "the whole mountain quaked greatly" (Ex 19:18 RSV). During Moses' stay on the mountain "the appearance of the glory of the LORD was like a devouring fire on the top of the mountain in the sight of the people of Israel" (Ex 24:17 RSV). Here truly is sacred space—a once-only experience for the people who experienced it but also a permanent image for the ages of the supernatural *glory of God.

The *tabernacle and *temple are the supreme sacred places of OT worship, the places God chooses for his "name to dwell" and which for Israel supersede and displace all the sacred spaces of Canaanite worship (Deut 12:2-5). They are not only the place of sacrifice but also the art gallery, music plaza and poetry library of the nation. Temple boundaries are strictly observed, and the space is protected from improper entry, with the holy of holies being the most sacred space of all. Hebrew worshipers make regular pilgrimages to the temple. It is a bustle of religious activity and a riot of sensations. The temple stands on a "holy hill" (Ps 43:3 RSV) and is the very place where God dwells in the form of his visible *glory (*š e kînâ;* Ps 26:8; 132:14). Even to catch sight of the temple stirs the heart (Ps 84:1-2), and it is almost beyond belief that the worshiper can say, "Our feet have been standing within your gates, O Jerusalem!" (Ps 122:2 RSV). For all of these reasons and more, the words of the prophets and finally of Jesus that God will judge *Zion and depart from this sacred space are earthshaking.

The Promised Land of OT Israelite history is sacred space for the OT Jews. In fact, the Mishnah makes explicit what is probably implied in the OT— that the degrees of sacred space in the temple, with lesser sanctity encircling the holy of holies, is a microcosm of how the Israelites regarded their own land encircled by neighboring countries (*Mishnah Kelim* 1:6-9). The Promised Land is a sacred space that one enters and leaves; there is even a hint that it is watched by angelic guardians (Josh 5:13-15). To the Hebrew imagination the land is a place of blessing that is sanctified by divine election and presence. The sanctity of the temple radiates throughout the land, which in some sense partakes of the quality of paradise.

This is strongly reinforced in some of the descriptions of the *millennium—the coming golden age that fired the imaginations of OT prophetic writers. The prophets envision a world of total peace in which people beat their *swords into plowshares and their spears into pruning hooks (Is 2:4). In this vast sacred space the Spirit will be "poured out . . . from on high," and "justice will dwell in the wilderness, and righteousness abide in the fruitful field" (Is 32:15-16 RSV). Again, "the earth will be filled with the knowledge of the glory of the LORD, as the waters cover the sea" (Hab 2:14 RSV; see also Is 11:9). In fact, the coming golden age will be so sacred that the bells of the horses will be inscribed "Holy to the LORD," and "every pot in Jerusalem and Judah shall be sacred to the LORD of hosts" (Zech 14:20-21 RSV).

Several scenes in the earthly life of Jesus constitute a composite sacred place, or a mosaic of sacred spaces. The nativity scene is such a place—a place of God's visitation of the earth and a place where the incarnate Christ is seen in palpable form and worshiped. The Mount of Olives, scene of Christ's transfiguration and ascension (among other events), is a sacred place. The upper room where Christ celebrates his final earthly *Passover is sacred because of what he inaugurates there. Most of the Bible's sacred spaces are places of transcendent beauty, but not so Gethsemane, scene of agony, and Calvary, scene of Christ's atonement for human sin and conquest of Satan. Yet they are sacred through the spiritual import of what happens there. The garden of the *resurrection is sacred to Christian memory because it is the place where death was defeated. When the promised Holy Spirit comes to the upper room where Christ's followers are gathered, this room too becomes a sacred place in Christian memory.

In addition to specific locales associated with Jesus, there is a suggestion in the NT that sacred space is in the process of being spiritualized and universalized, supplanting the OT emphasis on particular holy places like the temple. The key text is Jesus' statement to the woman at the well that the time has arrived in which no physical place is more sacred than another: "Woman, believe me, the hour is coming when neither on this mountain nor in Jerusalem will you worship the Father. . . . But the hour is coming, and now is, when the true worshipers will worship the Father in spirit and truth" (Jn 4:21, 23 RSV).

*Heaven is the climactic sacred space of the Bible.

It is preeminently the holy place that is separate from evil—from which, in fact, evil has been decisively expelled (Rev 21:27). It has all the qualities for which the human spirit longs most ardently: it is a place of bliss, of the presence of God, of human needs satisfied, of beauty, of worship. It is also permanent—exempt from decay and the possibility of being lost. While the book of Revelation is the supreme text to portray heaven, Hebrews 12:22-24 provides a brief glimpse to light the vision: "You have come to Mount Zion and to the city of the living God, the heavenly Jerusalem, and to innumerable angels in festal gathering, and to the assembly of the first-born who are enrolled in heaven, and to a judge who is God of all, and to the spirits of just men made perfect, and to Jesus, the mediator of a new covenant" (RSV).

See also BURNING BUSH; HOLINESS; PROMISED LAND; SINAI; TABERNACLE; TEMPLE; ZION.

SACRIFICE

Almost universally, the peoples of ancient cultures offered sacrifices in order to win divine favor or even to sustain their gods, as in Mesopotamia. The religion of the Hebrews was no exception, though the idea that sacrifices feed Yahweh (Lev 21:6) is an infrequent echo of other religions and is not seriously maintained (Ps 50:12-14); rather, sacrifices were gifts to honor God. *Blood, *fire and smoke are the most common images of sacrifice in the Hebrew Scriptures. Sacrifices also symbolize that we owe everything to God. Indeed, because of our *sin, we owe him our lives. The sacrifice stands in our place. The animal dies instead of us. As we will see, this image is used of Jesus' *death on the *cross.

The Patriarchal Period. In the time of the patriarchs, sacrifices were offered by individuals themselves, as *Abraham does with the ram after God tests him and then tells him not to sacrifice Isaac after all (Gen 22:13) or as *Jacob does after making his peace with Laban (Gen 31:54). In time, however, sacrifices had to be performed by the *priests and eventually only at the *temple in *Jerusalem (Deut 12:5-14), until its destruction by the Romans in A.D. 70, after which they ceased.

Temple Sacrifices: Types and Methods. Although several books of the Hebrew Scriptures deal with sacrifice, they are best explained in Leviticus 1—7. They were of two general types, animal and nonanimal. Only clean, unblemished animals could be sacrificed, specifically cattle, sheep, goats, doves and pigeons (*see* Animals). Vegetable sacrifices included *wheat, barley, olive *oil, *wine and frankincense. All sacrifices were to include *salt. All types were burned, but sometimes only a portion of the whole. Other parts of the sacrifice were to be eaten by either the priests and worshipers, the priests and their families, or only the priests.

The worshiper was to place his hands on the victim, signifying that it in some way represented him; except for national *offerings, the worshiper also slaughtered animals offered to the Lord. Provision was made for the poor, who were allowed to substitute two turtledoves or two pigeons (or for the extremely poor a specific amount of flour) in place of a *sheep, for example (Lev 5:7-13; *see* Poverty).

Specific instructions are given as to how each type was to be sacrificed. For example, the burnt offering (Lev 1), intended for *atonement or thanksgiving, had to be a bull which was to be burned completely except for the hide, which was given to the priest.

Two Assyrian men sacrifice a ram.

The blood would be sprinkled on the *altar (as was the case with all larger animals), because "the life of the flesh is in the blood; . . . as life, it is the blood that makes atonement" (Lev 17:11 NRSV).

Types of sacrifices included, besides the burnt offering, the "cereal" offering (baked or fried cakes or grain with oil and frankincense), the peace offerings (vow offering, thank offering, or free-will offering), the ordination offering, *guilt offerings and *sin offerings (to ritually *cleanse the sanctuary). That portion of the sacrifice which was to be eaten had to be consumed within one or two days as specified.

There were also daily offerings at the temple and seasonal sacrifices on behalf of the entire nation (e.g., the Feast of Firstfruits or of Unleavened Bread). Another type of sacrifice, though it did not involve slaughter, was the *scapegoat, chosen annually to receive the collective sins of the people and carry them away into the desert (Lev 16).

Abuses and Warnings. Because sacrifices could be abused, several times OT writers, especially the prophets, warn against their being performed without the proper attitude: "The sacrifice of the wicked is an abomination to the LORD" (Prov 15:8 NRSV); "the sacrifice acceptable to God is a broken spirit; a broken and contrite heart, O God, you will not despise" (Ps 51:17 NRSV); "for I desire steadfast love and not sacrifice, the knowledge of God rather than burnt offerings" (Hos 6:6 NRSV).

One of King Saul's chief mistakes occurs when, after being told to utterly destroy the Amalekites and all that they possess, he spares their king and allows the Israelites to save the best sheep and *cattle "to

sacrifice to the LORD." He is rebuked by the prophet with these words: "Has the LORD as great delight in burnt offerings and sacrifices, as in obeying the voice of the LORD? Surely, to obey is better than sacrifice, and to heed than the fat of rams" (1 Sam 15:21-22 NRSV).

In general, however, sacrifices were viewed quite positively (Ps 43:4), and in the NT Jesus shows respect for them (Lk 5:14); his famous "cleansing of the temple" was carried out to purge the profit-making activities associated with them (Jn 2:13-16).

The New Testament. Not only did the Roman destruction of the temple in A.D. 70 bring the era of sacrifice to a close; the death of Jesus, "the Lamb of God who takes away the sin of the world" (Jn 1:29 NRSV), was viewed by Christians as a sacrifice for humanity's "eternal redemption" (Heb 9:12). Jesus' sacrifice, unlike previous sacrifices, was once and for all given, there being no need for further ones (Heb 9:28; 10:1-18).

Christ served as both high priest and victim (Heb 9:11-12) in offering himself to God the Father, for "without the shedding of blood there is no forgiveness of sins" (Heb 9:22 NRSV). In so doing he fulfilled the roles of the "suffering servant" (Is 53) and of the scapegoat (Lev 16). The blood of the *Lamb and the *wood of the cross are the most pertinent images of Christ's sacrifice.

NT writings exhort Christians to live a life of sacrifice to God by their conduct—"present your bodies as a living sacrifice, holy and acceptable to God, which is your spiritual worship" (Rom 12:1 NRSV)—by their faith (Phil 2:17), by their gifts (Phil 4:18) and by offering "spiritual sacrifices acceptable to God through Jesus Christ" (1 Pet 2:5 NRSV). They are also to praise God by confessing Christ (Heb 13:15).

Not only is the individual's body "a temple of the Holy Spirit" (1 Cor 6:19), but God's people themselves constitute a priesthood (1 Pet 2:9) and in the Communion meal share in the body and blood of Christ (1 Cor 10:14-22). Christian "sacrifice" is thus both individual and corporate.

See also ALTAR; ATONEMENT; BLOOD; GUILT; LAMB; OFFERINGS; SIN; TABERNACLE; TEMPLE; WORSHIP.

SADNESS. *See* SORROW.

SAGE. *See* JESUS, IMAGES OF.

SAINTS

The character type of the saint extends far beyond the actual use of the word, which appears more often in the NT than the OT. *Saint* refers to the godly person whose spiritual and moral traits and behavior are what the Bible offers for approval and emulation. The saintly person might have roles and callings beyond the specifically spiritual side of life, but the character type itself is identified by a person's spiritual and moral qualities. The saintly person is not a self-made spiritual paragon but is instead fashioned by God's grace. Still, the Bible is full of admonitions that saints pursue conduct befitting the position they have received by grace.

To get a composite picture of the saint, we can look at NT passages that use the term, character sketches of the godly person and narrative examples of saintly characters. In keeping with the Bible's vivid consciousness of values, as we contemplate the saintly character in the Bible we are nearly always aware of the opposite character type—the *sinner.

The Epistles: Saints Defined. The NT especially goes to great lengths to describe what a saint is. Paul describes saints as "those who are sanctified in Christ Jesus, called to be saints, together with all those who in every place call on the name of our Lord Jesus Christ" (1 Cor 1:2 NRSV). Thus the saints are those who know God in Christ, and often the Bible refers to them as being the earthly representation of Christ. For instance, Ananias, the man who healed Paul of his blindness, reminded God that Paul was a persecutor of the saints (Acts 9:13). However, when Christ appeared to Paul on the road to Damascus, Christ asked Paul why he was persecuting *him* (Rom 9:4). This is in part because each saint is the bearer of the *Holy Spirit, who is the spirit of Christ sent to help them toward Christlikeness.

Ephesians provides an extensive definition of who saints are, their benefits and the expectations of their behavior. The saints were chosen "in Christ before the foundation of the world to be holy and blameless before him in love" (Eph 1:4 NRSV). The duty of the saint, then, is holiness. The passage further details how this is possible. The saint is a citizen of heaven and an *adopted child of the household of God, part of the structure built of believers that God is making into a holy *temple (Eph 2:19-21). Having heard the gospel, believed it and subsequently been marked with the Holy Spirit, the saint has been made alive with Christ, raised up with him and "seated . . . with him in the heavenly places" (Eph 2:6 NRSV). Having received with the blessings of redemption, the saint is therefore a new creature, "created in Christ Jesus for good works, which God prepared beforehand to be our way of life" (Eph 2:10 NRSV).

Other NT passages amplify the picture. The epistle to the Hebrews details the importance of faith, defined as "the assurance of things hoped for, the conviction of things not seen" (Heb 11:1 NRSV). According to Hebrews, faith is one essential component of saintliness, for "without faith it is impossible to please God, for whoever would approach him must believe that he exists and that he rewards those who seek him" (Heb 11:6 NRSV). Galatians offers a more complete list of the fruits of the Spirit, the products of an *obedient walk with God, which are "love, joy, peace, patience, kindness, goodness, faithfulness, gentleness, and self-control" (Gal 5:22-23 NRSV).

The chief virtue displayed by the biblical saint is love. The most succinct statement of the motif is 1 Corinthians 13. To the saint who is seeking reward from God, prophecy, wisdom, faith, generosity and courage are of no value unless accompanied by love (1 Cor 13:1-3). As the portrait unfolds, the picture of love becomes far broader than it is often thought to be, and in fact encompasses many of the *fruits of the Spirit, including *faith and *hope. These related virtues, though, are useless unless they flow from love. By learning to love, the saint will learn patience, kindness, humility, contentment, propriety, unselfishness, calmness, forgiveness, truthful uprightness, long-suffering, hope and endurance (1 Cor 13:4-7). The saint's walk can come only from love, for only "love never fails" (1 Cor 13:8). Thus this passage is one of the best models for saints to emulate.

Character Sketches: Saints Praised. Because the saint is a character type, character sketches in the Bible, especially in the form of the *encomium (a poem or description that praises a character type and encourages emulation) are prime sources. Psalm 1 illustrates the point. Here the godly or saintly person is contrasted to his or her opposite. As the portrait unfolds, we learn that the saint refrains from wicked behavior, bases life on God's law, is a stable and productive person who prospers in godliness, and is assured of future reward when standing in the judgment. Psalm 15 gives us a picture of the saint as ideal worshiper. That worship, though, is rooted in moral behavior that includes as typical traits a "blameless" way of life, commitment to truth and harmony with one's neighbor, honesty, and generosity. According to Psalm 112, the saint is a person who fears God and delights in his commandments, is merciful and righteous, and gives to the poor.

For a NT counterpart we can turn to the ideal disciple who emerges from Jesus' beatitudes (Mt 5:3-12). Here too the saint is characterized chiefly by spiritual qualities that run counter to worldly standards of success. Saints recognize spiritual poverty in themselves, mourn for their sins, are meek, hunger and thirst for righteousness, are merciful and pure in *heart, are peacemakers, and endure *persecution with joy. The rewards that motivate and satisfy such saints are spiritual and otherworldly: receiving a spiritual kingdom and God's comfort and *mercy, seeing God, and being called children of God.

Biblical Narrative: Saints in Action. The exhortations and sketches of saints are fleshed out in the hero stories of the Bible (*see* Hero, Heroine). Wherever an exemplary and heroic character in biblical narrative is defined by a moral or spiritual quality rather than a human role or achievement, something is added to the composite character type of the biblical saint. Of course the wholly idealized hero or heroine is a rarity in the Bible; there is no implied claim that the saints of the Bible are perfect. With that proviso in place, we can say that the hero stories of the Bible, as contrasted with those of extrabiblical literature, exalt the saint as hero above all other images of the hero. The stories of saints as we encounter them in the Bible are therefore virtually synonymous with the genre of hero stories.

The roll call includes Abel, Noah, Abraham, Sarah, Isaac, Jacob and Joseph. Subsequently we see sainthood in Moses, Joshua, Gideon, Ruth, Boaz, David, Esther, Daniel and the great prophets like Elijah, Elisha and Jeremiah. In the NT there are Mary, Joseph, John the Baptist, Anna, Simeon, the disciples, the women devoted to Jesus and the missionary Paul. The closest we come to a definitive list is Hebrews 11, which shows how varied the life situations of saintly people are. Externally, the saints of God are nearly as disparate as a cross-section of any virtuous society; spiritually they serve God above all and display moral virtues in their behavior in the world. The roll call of saints in Hebrews ends by offering Jesus as the ultimate exemplar of saintly behavior: "looking to Jesus the pioneer and perfecter" of faith (Heb 12:2 NRSV). While it would be demeaning to call God himself a saint, the behavior of the incarnate Jesus is Bible's supreme model of how saints must live. The call of saintliness is always the same—to emulate Christ in the anticipation of the reward we will receive from him.

See also FAITH; HOLINESS; MARTYR; PERSECUTION; PURITY; SANCTIFICATION.

SALE. *See* LEGAL IMAGES.

SALIVA. *See* SPIT.

SALT

Salt has literally hundreds of uses. Like other natural compounds, salt can be used negatively or positively. The Bible's writers made generous use of salt imagery, sprinkling references to its use and abuse throughout Scripture, particularly in the OT. Biblical writers are well aware of salt's properties, associating it with images of seasoning, preserving and *purifying—or with powerful images of death, desolation and *curse.

References to salt's positive qualities emphasize its seasoning, preserving and purifying properties. Job asks, "Can something tasteless be eaten without salt . . . ?" (Job 6:6 NASB). Paul admonishes the Colossians, "Let your speech always be with grace, seasoned, as it were, with salt" (Col 4:6 NASB). References to the *covenant of salt capitalize on salt's preserving qualities as symbolic of a permanent indissoluble relationship between God and his people (Lev 2:13; Num 18:19; 2 Chron 13:5). Likewise, salt is listed as a required addition to all burnt *offerings because of its preserving qualities (Ezra 6:9).

There is also a connection between salt and new beginnings or separation. Newborn *babies were rubbed with salt: "On the day you were born your cord was not cut, nor were you washed with water to make you clean, nor were you rubbed with salt or wrapped in cloths" (Ezek 16:4 NIV). To Abimelech, spreading salt on a captured *city symbolized a curse: he "razed the city and sowed it with salt" (Judg 9:45 NASB). Salt in the soil would inhibit the growth of food crops, but also it symbolized a break from the past. When Elisha treated a bad *water supply at Jericho with salt, it may have symbolized a new beginning in terms of removing the curse Joshua had leveled on it: "And he went out to the spring of water, and threw salt in it and said, 'Thus says the LORD, "I have purified these waters" ' " (2 Kings 2:21).

Jesus contrasts salt's positive and negative potential: "You are the salt of the earth; but if the salt has become tasteless, how will it be made salty again? It is good for nothing any more" (Mt 5:13). The Salt Sea (Dead Sea), the Valley of Salt and the City of Salt all connote death, desolation, despair and deserts. "All its land is *brimstone and salt, a burning waste, unsown and unproductive, and no grass grows in it" (Deut 29:23). Jeremiah associates images of bushes in deserts, stony wastes, *wildernesses and a land of salt with a person who turns away from God (Jer 17:6). Likewise, Ezekiel contrasts salt marshes and swamps with fertile freshwater sources capable of growing all kinds of *trees whose *leaves will not wither (Ezek 47:11). In Ezekiel's vision of a flourishing and vibrant Dead Sea, salt is so essential that marshes remain for its production.

See also FOOD; PURITY.

SALVATION

Biblical images for salvation describe what God has done, is doing and will do on behalf of men and women who suffer from the misery, mortality and meaninglessness of the human condition. *Salvation* refers both to an active process and to its resultant effect, both to a verb *(save)* and to a noun *(salvation)*, though it is the latter that is the special focus of this article.

Salvation History. The Bible is essentially the story of the one creature to bear God's image (human being), with *sin as the basic complication, Christ as the central character *(see* Jesus, Images of) and salvation as the unifying plot. The Bible tells of an initial condition (Paradise, *see* Garden) which is disturbed (Fall), of the consequences of this complication (sin, *death), of what is done to overcome these conflicts (the *cross) and of the resolution of the problem (*resurrection and *Pentecost)—a conclusion that improves upon the original situation. It is a mystery story, for it was not clear, before Christ, just how God could save the ungodly (Mk 4:11; Eph 1:9). The logic and scope of salvation develop as the story progresses: at the beginning it concerns God's dealings with the children of Abraham (that is, Israel), in the middle the focus turns to Jesus and his followers, and toward the end the story embraces the *Gentiles and the whole created order.

The first hint of salvation follows the account of the Fall, when God says to the serpent, "He shall bruise your head, and you shall bruise his heel" (Gen 3:15 RSV), though neither the identity of the Savior nor the means for reversing the Fall becomes clear until the NT. Nevertheless, "bruise his heel" already alludes to the cost of salvation, to the cross of salvation and to the Christ of salvation. The biblical story pictures not only the act and effect of salvation but its culmination as well, namely, the *wedding cele-bration of the *Lamb of God and his *bride, the *church (Rev 19:6-9). Between the beginning and the end of the story, the plot unfolds in the history of Israel and culminates in the *passion of Jesus Christ, when salvation is accomplished once for all, and in the life of the church, where salvation is celebrated and proclaimed. The Bible ends with Edenic imagery—the *tree of life—and with the Savior's promise to complete the saving work he has already accomplished: "Surely I am coming soon" (Rev 22:20 RSV).

The story of salvation has two main parts. The first recounts Israel's history: the saving act (*exo-dus) and the resultant effect (life in the *Promised Land). The OT recounts a story of deliverance from captivity and oppression that culminates in Israel's crossing of the Red Sea. The second part describes a new exodus—Jesus' death or "exodus" from this life (Lk 9:31) and its effect (life in the promised Spirit). The NT tells the story of how a new deliverance, a release from the *bondage of sin, was wrought by Christ's departure from this life (Rom 6:9; Eph 1:7; Col 1:20) and by the "red sea" of *blood that flowed from his cross. Christ's life, poured out on the cross, is the "power of God for salvation" (Rom 1:16 RSV).

Salvation From. The biblical language for salva-tion depicts the transition from need to fulfillment, from problem to solution—images of movement. Deuteronomy 26:5-9 briefly recounts both aspects: the salvation *from* *Egypt leading *to* life in the Prom-ised Land.

It is impossible to understand salvation apart from some notion of that from which one is saved, whether external, physical threats or internal, spiritual ones. God saves, first of all, from doom and disaster, from natural and national catastrophes alike, from *ene-mies or energies. The psalmist asks to be saved from defeat by enemy nations (Ps 44); Jesus' disciples asked to be saved from the waves that threatened to swamp their boat (Mt 8:25, *see* Water). One may be saved, second, from *disease and physical defects (Mk 5:28, 34; Jas 5:15). Many of the psalms contain "songs of deliverance" that attribute salvation to God alone (e.g., Ps 18; 30; 31; 34; 46; 91; 105; 106; 118; 136).

The biblical writers also speak about salvation from spiritual dangers: from *Satan, from the wrath of God and from sin. Jesus' exorcisms are signs that he has the power to release people from demonic possession and from the dominion of Satan (Mk 3:23-27; Lk 8:36). Equally important, however, is deliverance from the wrath of God that falls upon sinners (Rom 5:9-10) and from the day of God's judgment (Rom 2:5; 1 Thess 2:16; *see* Day of the Lord). By far the most common NT use of salvation, however, has to do with salvation from sin ("and you shall call his name Jesus, for he will save his people from their sins," Mt 1:21 RSV). To be precise, one is saved from the *penalty* of sin (Lk 7:48, 50), from

the *power* of sin (Rom 6:12-14) and from the *practice* of sin as a way of life (1 Jn 3:9-10; 5:18).

Salvation To. Whereas the verb *to save* has refer-ence to some physical or spiritual peril, the noun *salvation* pertains to the positive effects of God's saving action. In general, one is saved from bondage and brought to a state of well-being or *blessedness. Three images in particular tend to dominate the Bible's depiction of well-being.

To begin with, salvation is depicted as liberation (*see* Bondage and Freedom). The God of Israel is a Savior God because he is a God who delivers (Ex 20:2). Similarly, Jesus was sent "to set at liberty those who are oppressed" (Lk 4:18 RSV). Paul states that "for freedom Christ has set us free" (Gal 5:1 RSV) and explains that Christians have been liberated from the requirements of the *law in order to be free to love and to serve (Gal 5:13-14).

Second, the blessedness of salvation is depicted in terms of health and wholeness. *Sōtēria*—the most common NT term for salvation—carries connota-tions of health, wholeness and soundness. Mark 2:17 describes Jesus as a "physician." Jesus' ministry was to make people well. In Jesus' ministry the physical and spiritual aspects of healing miracles are linked together: when Jesus heals, there are transforming physical and spiritual effects. Jesus' healings are signs both of his saving power and of the nature of salva-tion (*see* Disease and Healing).

The third image of the well-being that defines salvation, *peace, or *shalom,* is found primarily in prophetic literature. The community of the saved is pictured by the prophets as living in a peaceful and just society in which people will live together in peace and harmony and "nation shall not lift up sword against nation" (Is 2:2-4 RSV; Mic 4:1-4; Zech 2:6-12).

Salvation In. One important image of blessed-ness is unique to the NT: union with Christ. Here one might speak of salvation *in,* for there are several images that picture salvation as a matter of being related to the Savior: "if any one is in Christ, he is a new creature" (2 Cor 5:17 RSV). Jesus is the *cornerstone and *foundation "in whom the whole structure is joined together . . . in whom you also are built into it for a dwelling place of God in the Spirit" (Eph 2:21-22 RSV; cf. Col 2:7; 1 Pet 2:4-5). Other similar images include those of *husband and *wife (Eph 5:31-32; Rev 19:7; *see* Marriage), *vine and *branches (Jn 15:1-10; Col 2:6-7) and the relationship of the *head to the *body (1 Cor 6:15, 19; Eph 1:22-23).

Not only are the saved *in* Christ, but Christ is also *in* those who are saved: "I have been crucified with Christ; it is no longer I who live, but Christ who lives in me" (Gal 2:20 RSV; cf. Jn 14:20; Eph 3:17; 1 Jn 4:16).

The Meaning of Salvation. The benefits of one's union with Christ are described in various ways. It may be helpful to group the Bible's many images into three distinct categories: new situation, new self, new steps. Salvation in the Bible is a three-dimensional phenomenon.

New situation: salvation as objective change. To be saved means, first, that one's legal status has changed, that one has acquired new rights (and responsibilities) as a result of one's union with Christ. Four leading images depict the new situation brought about by God's saving work.

The concept of *redemption* evokes imagery of the *marketplace. In the OT, redemption is a convention in which a relative sets a *family member free by buying him or her back from bondage through the payment of a *ransom (Ex 21:30). Redemption signifies a transaction where some item or person is exchanged for payment. For instance, the negligent owner of an *ox who gored a person to death could be saved from the death penalty only by the payment of a ransom "for the redemption of his life" (Ex 21:29-30 RSV).

Yahweh was understood to be Israel's *redeemer (Deut 13:5; Is 49:26). Jesus similarly appeals to imagery of redemption to explain the nature of his own ministry and death: "The Son of man also came . . . to give his life as a ransom for many" (Mk 10:45 RSV). Luke uses the term *redemption* as a general term for salvation (Lk 1:68; 2:38; 21:28; 24:21). Paul too uses the imagery of redemption (Rom 3:24; 1 Cor 1:30; Col 1:14; Gal 4:5) and declares that the price of our redemption was the blood of Christ, representing the divine life: "In him we have redemption through his blood" (Eph 1:7 RSV; cf. Heb 9:12-15; 1 Pet 1:18-19). "You were bought with a price," Paul reminds his readers (1 Cor 6:20 RSV).

Justification is an image drawn from the *law court. To be justified is to be declared *innocent by the presiding judge. "I, I am He who blots out your transgressions for my own sake, and I will not remember your sins" (Is 43:25 RSV). Here too, to be saved is to enter into a new situation, namely, the state of being acquitted that follows the legal verdict of "not guilty." Paul makes it clear that sinners are declared righteous not on the basis of their own merits or achievements (works) but rather on the basis of their standing "in Christ": "There is therefore now no condemnation to those who are in Christ Jesus" (Rom 8:1 RSV; cf. Rom 3:21-31; Gal 3:11; Eph 2:8-9). Justification, like redemption, depends on the shed blood of Christ, "who was put to death for our trespasses and raised for our justification" (Rom 4:25 RSV; cf. Rom 5:8-9). The new situation denoted by justification is that sinners who are in Christ have been formally pardoned.

To be saved is to be incorporated or *adopted* into the family of God (Ex 4:22; Hos 11:1; Gal 4:5-7). The process of adoption is linked to the work of the *Holy Spirit, whom Paul calls the "Spirit of adoption" (Rom 8:15 KJV). The company of the saved are members of God's *kingdom and God's kindred alike. One is not a child of God by nature; the image of adoption thus emphasizes the graciousness of salvation. Adoption pictures union with Christ in

terms of enjoying all the privileges that comes with one's status as a legal child of God, as "heirs of God and fellow heirs with Christ" (Rom 8:17 RSV; cf. Eph 1:13-14).

Finally, Paul depicts the new situation of the saved with an image drawn from the domain of personal relationships, *reconciliation* (*see* Reunion, Reconciliation), a picture that assumes a previous estrangement that has been overcome or healed. All people are by nature *enemies of God because of sin (Rom 5:10; Col 1:21). God is similarly alienated from human beings because of his righteous *anger (Rom 1:18). Again, it is the death of Jesus Christ that overcomes sin and averts the divine wrath: "God was in Christ reconciling the world to Himself" (2 Cor 5:19 NASB; cf. Eph 2:16). Thanks to this reconciling work, one who is in Christ enjoys restored relations with God and, like Abraham, may be called "the friend of God" (Jas 2:23 RSV).

New self: salvation as inner change. To be in Christ is, second, to undergo inward renewal. "If any one is in Christ, he is a new creation" (2 Cor 5:17). Salvation names a new subjective condition, a new self, as well as a new objective status. Perhaps the most striking image of this inner *transformation is Jesus' metaphor of *rebirth (Jn 3:3-7; cf. 1 Pet 1:23). The need for this inner renewal was perceived by the psalmist: "Create in me a pure heart, O God; and renew a right spirit within me" (Ps 51:10 KJV). The prophets also foresaw a time of national renewal and spiritual *cleansing (Ezek 36:25-28) when God would make a new *covenant by writing his law on people's hearts (Jer 31:31; Hos 6:1-3). Paul conceives of *baptism as a sign of rebirth: "We were buried therefore with him by baptism into death, so that as Christ was raised . . . we too might walk in newness of life" (Rom 6:4 RSV; cf. 2 Tim 2:11).

Jesus' resurrection is a sign that the new order has already begun. Because believers share in Christ's resurrection, Paul can refer to the "new man" (Eph 2:15 RSV). Paul calls men and women who are "in Christ" to put off their old natures "and be renewed in the spirit of your minds, and put on the new nature, created after the likeness of God in true righteousness and holiness" (Eph 4:23-24 RSV; cf. Col 3:9-10; Rom 12:1-2). "The new nature" designates a new power and a new orientation, which Paul describes as a renewal of God's image in humanity, defined by Christ. To be born anew means to join in the new humanity of the Second Adam, to be made more Christlike through the renewal of one's inner nature by the Holy Spirit (Jn 1:13; Tit 3:5).

New steps: salvation as behavioral change. The company of the saved, as a result of their union with Christ, rebirth and gift of Christ's Spirit, are expected to live differently. Not only the natures but the actions and interpersonal relations too of the saved are transformed: "If we live by the Spirit, let us also walk by the Spirit" (Gal 5:25 RSV). 1 John lays special emphasis on the moral and spiritual implications of rebirth: "No one born of God commits sin;

for God's nature abides in him, and he cannot sin because he is born of God" (1 Jn 3:9 RSV). And "he who says he abides in him ought to walk in the same way in which he walked" (1 Jn 2:6 RSV).

James teaches that salvation involves a new way of life and goes so far as to call for "works" as evidence of *faith (Jas 2:24). Salvation is received in faith but expressed in good works (2 Tim 2:21-22). Christ gave himself for the church not only to change our legal standing before God but also "that he might sanctify her, having cleansed her by the washing of water with the word . . . that she might be holy and without blemish" (Eph 5:25-27 RSV; cf. Heb 9:14). The company of the saved give evidence of their new natures by walking according to the Spirit, and in particular by the quality of their love for one another: "he who loves is born of God and knows God" (1 Jn 4:7 RSV).

The Agent of Salvation. Nothing humans do can, in and of itself, change their legal standing before God, create a new nature or radically reorient their behavior. Human beings cannot save themselves (Rom 3:24; Tit 3:5). Salvation is wrought either by God himself or by a deputy of God: "I, I am Yahweh, and besides me there is no savior" (Is 43:11). God is the ultimate source of salvation (Ps 25:5; 65:5)—the Savior (Ps 106:21) and salvation itself (Ps 118:14; Is 12:2).

In the OT, kings were expected to be saving helps (2 Sam 14:4; 2 Kings 13:5), prophets proclaimed salvation (Is 42-43), and *priests were said to be clothed with salvation (Ps 132:16; 2 Chron 6:41). The Gospels, however, apply the title Savior only to God and to Jesus (Lk 2:11; Jn 4:42). The term is used twenty-four times in the NT, sixteen times of Jesus (e.g., 2 Pet 1:1; 1 Jn 4:14) and eight times of God the Father. The name Jesus literally means "Yahweh is salvation." Mary calls her son Jesus, "for he will save his people from their sins" (Mt 1:21 RSV). He shall be called "Emmanuel, . . . God with us" (Mt 1:23 RSV)—the epitome and concrete embodiment of God's original covenant promise to dwell with his people.

Jesus' life and work demonstrates the aptness of his name (Lk 19:10; Jn 3:17). Jesus explained that he came into the world in order to save (Mk 10:45). Jesus heals (Mk 5:34) and forgives (Lk 7:47-48). He thus becomes the central character in the story of God's salvation. According to Peter's *Pentecost sermon, "There is salvation in no one else, for there is no other name under heaven given among men by which we must be saved" (Acts 4:12 RSV). Jesus is Savior because his life and work as Messiah (the Christ) fulfills the three offices of, respectively, the prophet who announces salvation (Lk 4:18-21), the priest who effects forgiveness of sins ("it is finished," Jn 19:30) and the king who rules in our hearts (Gal 2:20). Salvation, then, is being "in Christ." In Christ the saved receive a new status, a new nature and a new way of life. The believer lives in Christ and Christ lives in the believer (Jn 15:4). The original covenant

promise of God—to be their God—is thus fulfilled in a startling new way.

The Scope of Salvation. Who, or what, can be saved? The company of the saved consists of those individuals who respond to the preaching of the gospel in *repentance and *faith (Acts 2:41; 4:4). There are no limitations to the invitation to repent and believe; salvation is available to all races and classes of people (Acts 11:34-45; Gal 3:28; Tit 2:11). Yet according to Paul, salvation is not merely a rescuing of certain individuals out of a doomed world but indeed a transformation of the whole cultural and cosmic created order. What is to be saved are not only individual selves but the whole social order. "Principalities" and "powers"—forces that are either political or supernatural—are said to have been created (Col 1:16) and reconciled (Col 1:20; Eph 1:10) through Christ. Salvation here attains a cosmic reach. Indeed, the whole created order longs for an exodus event: "the creation itself will be set free from its bondage to decay and obtain the glorious liberty of the children of God" (Rom 8:21 RSV; see Rom 8:19-23, 28-29).

The Time of Salvation. Salvation is past, present and future: one who is in Christ has been saved, is being saved and will be saved. That Jesus accomplished salvation is a past fact: his death delivered us once for all from the penalty and power of sin (Jn 19:30; Rom 5:8; Tit 3:5-7; Heb 9:12). Justification, redemption and reconciliation are *faits accomplis*.

Yet salvation is also an ongoing and progressive present experience. Christians are sometimes described in the NT as "those who are being saved" (Acts 2:47; 1 Cor 1:18; 2 Cor 2:15). Those who have died with Jesus have also been raised with him and so share his life and his Spirit (Rom 6:5-14). Moreover, though salvation is a past fact, it must not be "neglected" in the present (Heb 2:3) but rather be "held fast" (1 Cor 15:2) and humbly "worked out" (Phil 2:12).

The full meaning of salvation will be known only at the last day, when the renewing process is complete (Phil 1:6). Both the OT and the NT express hope for a new *heaven, a new *earth and a new *Jerusalem (Is 65:17-25; 2 Pet 3:13). The prophets anticipate a second exodus which will bring about a greater deliverance than that from Egypt and usher in the kingdom of God (Is 51:9-11; Hos 2:16-25). The NT authors envisage a second coming of Christ (Heb 9:28; Rev 22). Salvation is a future hope that one will be spared from the divine wrath: "Let us be sober, and put on the breastplate of faith and love, and for a helmet the hope of salvation. For God has not destined us for wrath, but to obtain salvation through our Lord Jesus Christ" (1 Thess 5:8-9 RSV; cf. Rom 5:9-10). The eternal life associated with the kingdom of God is simultaneously present in Christ and future with regard to its glorious manifestation (Jn 3:16; 5:25; 11:25-26; 14:18-20; 17:24-26). The full privileges that belong to God's adopted children—the *inheritance guaranteed by one's possession of the Holy Spirit—is "kept in heaven for you" (1 Pet 1:4-5 RSV; cf. Eph 1:13-14).

The Economy of Salvation. Salvation is not a divine afterthought; on the contrary, salvation history derives from God's eternal "plan" or *oikonomia* of salvation "to unite all things" to Christ (Eph 1:10; cf. Eph 3:9; 1 Pet 1:20; Mt 25:34).

Salvation is part of the economy, first of all, of the Trinity. The plan of salvation reflects the purpose of the will of God the Father, who has sent the Son to carry it out (Eph 1:3-10). The divine righteousness has appeared in history, both in the mission of the Son, who accomplishes salvation, and in the mission of the Spirit, who applies salvation by relating believers to Christ (Jn 14-16). Salvation is thus a result of the concerted action of Father, Son and Holy Spirit: "God has sent the Spirit of his Son into our hearts, crying, 'Abba! Father!' " (Gal 4:6 RSV).

Second, salvation partakes of the economy of the gift. Salvation is not something that one can earn; it is totally unmerited— "For by grace you have been saved through faith; and this is not your own doing, it is the gift of God" (Eph 2:8 RSV). Salvation refers to the God-wrought reversal of the sinner's denial of the Creator and the created order. God's affirmation and acceptance of the sinner makes possible one's subsequent affirmation of God's *creation, covenant and Christ. "For the wages of sin is death, but the free gift of God is eternal life in Christ Jesus our Lord" (Rom 6:23 RSV).

Last, salvation belongs to the economy of eternal life. Jesus came that we might have life, abundant life (Jn 10:10). Whereas sin is life-defying, salvation is life-enhancing. Jesus is the source, condition and power of new life: "I am the resurrection and the life" (Jn 11:25 RSV). The book of Revelation brings the story of salvation to a close with the image of the tree of life, first encountered in Genesis 2, whose leaves are "for the healing of the nations" (Rev 22:2 RSV). Salvation means having a share in this paradisaical tree, planted in the presence of God, rooted in Christ and bearing the fruit of the Spirit to the glory of God.

Summary. Taken together, the biblical imagery for salvation makes up a three-dimensional description: salvation is an objectively new situation, a new self and a new way of life that is past fact, present experience and future hope, and partakes of the economy of the gift of God's own triune life—Father, Son and Spirit—to those who do not deserve it. To be among the company of the saved is to be united with him who is "the way, the truth, and the life" (Jn 14:6 KJV). It is to enjoy a new situation (the truth of our life in Christ), a new self (the life of the Spirit of Christ in us) and a new way of life (the way of righteousness defined by Christ). In the final analysis, the Bible's controlling image of salvation is neither of a process nor of a promise, but of a person: "The LORD is my light and my salvation" (Ps 27:1 RSV). "Thanks be to God for his inexpressible gift!" (2 Cor 9:15 RSV).

See also ADOPTION; ATONEMENT; BLOOD; BONDAGE AND FREEDOM; CROSS; DISEASE AND HEALING; LEGAL IMAGES; REBIRTH; REDEEM, REDEEMER; REUNION, RECONCILIATION; SACRIFICE; TRANSFORMATION; TREE OF LIFE; TRIUMPH.

BIBLIOGRAPHY. P. Fiddes, *Past Event and Present Salvation* (Louisville, KY: Westminster John Knox, 1989); D. F. Wells, *The Search for Salvation* (Downers Grove, IL: InterVarsity Press, 1978).

SAMSON
No biblical character is more paradoxical than Samson (Judg 13-16). A figure of heroic physical strength, he is also a morally and emotionally weak person whose frailty is highlighted by the *tragic pattern of the OT story. A Nazirite from birth, set apart to a holy lifestyle, Samson nonetheless specializes in liaisons with *Philistine women of questionable repute. Though a national deliverer, Samson is a lone ranger who is never seen in the company of supportive companions. Strong of body and weak of will, Samson is like the self-indulgent athlete who thrills on the field and appalls off it. In our imagination he is both prime specimen of physical strength (the biblical counterpart of Hercules) and helpless *blind man.

Some of the ambivalence surrounding Samson makes sense when we realize that the OT narrative is simultaneously a *hero story and a tragedy. We view the same events from both perspectives within the story itself. As a hero story the narrative puts Samson into a public arena and tells of national deliverance by the archetypal strong man. It is the story of a man whose *birth was miraculously foretold and whose desire for a pagan wife "was from the LORD" (Judg 14:4 RSV), a man upon whom "the Spirit of the LORD came mightily" (Judg 14:19 RSV), who judged Israel for twenty years (Judg 15:20; 16:31), whose prayer for a final victory God answered (Judg 16:28-30). He is even listed in the roll call of faith (Heb 11:32).

But when viewed as the story of a private individual, Samson's story is a tragedy that revolves around repeated violation of the Nazirite vow and the squandering of God's gifts. Public triumphs over the Philistines are, viewed from the hero's personal life, occasions of moral failure and abuse of God's gift of strength in selfish private *vengeance. At this level the story is one of weak will, self-indulgence, *appetite, the dangers of success, sensuality, overconfidence, bad company, recklessness, misplaced trust and spiritual complacency. Samson is the lonely and isolated celebrity who always seems to be looking for intimacy in self-destructive ways. He is the archetypal *trickster, with a strong admixture of the brawler.

Although cast in the form of literary tragedy, the story of Samson as told in *Judges also has a remarkably contemporary feel. It might have been written by a magazine staff writer based on material provided by a gossip columnist. The focus is as much on the sexual misconduct and marital failure of a public leader as on his political and military exploits. Yet somewhere inside this flawed man was a passion for God. God noticed and used it. So did the author of Judges, who gave Samson more space than any other judge to send the implied message "if God could use this person, he can use anyone."

See also JUDGES, BOOK OF.

SAMUEL, BOOKS OF

The books of 1 and 2 Samuel record the transition of Israel from a theocracy to a monarchy. The two books can be organized loosely around three key figures: Samuel the *prophet, Saul the failed *king, and David the great king. Each of these presents a complex of images that leave the reader with a picture of various ways to encounter and experience God.

The person of Samuel is presented to the reader in a series of events and pictures that form an image complex. Samuel is a transition figure, the prophet who judges Israel in the last days of the theocracy. From his youth he ministers close to God, usually in the midst of corrupt religious functionaries. Unlike the kings to follow, Samuel makes use of divine weaponry and brings about a miraculous deliverance (1 Sam 7). One image that is definitive for the book is that of Israel demanding a king so that it may be "like the other nations" (1 Sam 8). Samuel is distressed by this request, for to request a human king is to reject the divine King. Here we find Samuel contrasting his office of prophet with that of a king, claiming that he never exploited the people (1 Sam 12). Israel's asking for a king will be answered by God's giving them one—and refusing to listen to their lament when they later regret it. The image of the prophet in 1 and 2 Samuel demonstrates the priority of prophet over king. A king requires the prophet's anointing and is subject to their censure. A prophet speaks for God.

The image complex that is generated by the account of Saul includes the following elements. The reader is presented with a picture of the new king hiding among the baggage, trying to avoid his duty as king (1 Sam 10:22). On occasion Saul receives the *Spirit of God. This enables him to prophesy and to deliver the city of Jabesh. Another image is of the anxious Saul, watching his *army melting away, waiting in desperation for Samuel to come. Samuel is delayed in coming. After seven days, Saul takes matters into his own hands and offers a *sacrifice. For this, Samuel rebukes him and promises that his reign will come to an early end (1 Sam 13:14).

The image of Saul then becomes that of a man who can do no right. Apart from God's favor, everything he does goes wrong. The image of Saul inadvertently tearing Samuel's robe—and Samuel using the event as a sign of Saul's doom—is typical. Saul fights for Israel but fails to please God. Saul becomes insane. And his insanity leads to an attempted murder of David (and once of his own heir, Jonathan). He kills the priests of Nob. And as he consults the witch of Endor, Samuel posthumously rebukes Saul yet again.

The final image in the Saul complex is that of Saul falling on his own *sword in a desperate and faltering attempt to avoid death at the hands of his enemies. Thus, the image complex associated with Saul yields a picture of a king at odds with the living God. We find a portrait of one who puts *throne and honor before God and then spirals into a free fall of failure, jealousy, insanity, murder, foolhardiness and self-destruction.

The image complex generated by the account of David is dominated by his encounter with the giant Goliath. Here is a champion warrior whose personal victory delivers his people. Without *armor, armed only with a stone and a sling, the boy-hero brings down the monstrous challenger. This forceful image brings home the point: if God is with the king, he cannot fail.

Closely associated with this is the image of the warrior. David's reputation is ten times bloodier than Saul's (1 Sam 21:10). Warfare is to David a theater in which God's *blessings and *anointing are confirmed. However, much of David's early career is presented in conflict with Saul. Saul's jealousy over David's favor with God propels the drama of 1 Samuel to its fateful conclusion—the death of Saul and Jonathan, and David's lament over them both (2 Sam 1). It matters not to David what Saul has done to him or how irrational and unjust his behavior has been. Saul remains to the end God's anointed king, the glory of Israel. David's lament over Saul poses a striking image that illustrates the character of the great king. The surprising restraint seen in David toward Saul is echoed throughout his career. David is characterized by unexpected actions that show the inscrutable and unpredictable personality of the great king (see 2 Sam 12:18-23, 23:16-17).

David in 2 Samuel is dominated by the image of the sin with *Bathsheba and the said train of familial consequences that follow. Through episodes of deception, intrigue and finally murder, David is seen striving to gain control of the consequences of his sin. God's judgment is publicly rendered on David's family. The image of the great king fleeing from his son Absalom, climbing the Mount of Olives "weeping as he went" (2 Sam 15:13-37), shows how God deals severely with one to whom he has pledged his favor forever. David is not above the law.

After David's return to his throne, we find the poignant image of Mephibosheth, Saul's grandson. Mephibosheth has waited in longing for David's return, being unable to leave Jerusalem due to his lame condition. He has neither shaved nor washed from the day David left (2 Sam 19:24-25). Upon David's return, Mephibosheth calls him an angel of God. He refuses any inheritance, claiming that being in the presence of the king is all he needs to be content (2 Sam 19:30). Here is a moving image of loyalty, love and devotion to God's anointed king.

David's selfless zeal for God can be seen in the image of his wild *dance before God in the procession of *the ark as it is brought into Jerusalem (2 Sam

6). His wife Michal is scandalized since the king is shamefully exposing himself to the onlookers. But David defends himself on the grounds that his dance is a repudiation of his own pride. His purposeful humiliation is understood by all to be a means of bringing *glory to God. True *honor comes in humbling the self before God (2 Sam 6:22). David forms an image complex that defines the great king. The king is a deliverer, a warrior, a champion and a wise ruler. He is anointed by God and enjoys a unique relationship to him.

Another significant image complex in 1 and 2 Samuel is that of the *ark of the covenant. It signifies God's covenanted presence. When captured by the Philistines, it brings death. The image of the golden rats and boils portray the devastation brought upon those who capture the ark. The ark is holy and must be respected. Several times Israelites handled it to their own harm (1 Sam 6:19; 2 Sam 6:6-7). The image of God suddenly striking down a man who reached up to keep the ark from falling powerfully makes the point that God is dangerous, he will not be toyed with, and he is even more unpredictable than the king.

Thus 1 and 2 Samuel present a rich set of images that depict the prophet, the king and God in ways that unforgettably communicate the character and nature of Israel's relationship with God under the covenant. Jesus' title of Son of David should be understood in the light of the images of the anointed king David as seen in 1 and 2 Samuel.

See also CHRONICLES, BOOKS OF; DAVID; KING, KINGSHIP.

BIBLIOGRAPHY A. A. Anderson, *2 Samuel* (WBC 11; Dallas: Word, 1989); J. G. Baldwin, *1 & 2 Samuel* (TOTC; Downer's Grove, IL: InterVarsity Press, 1988).

SANCTIFICATION

While the word *sanctification* is used to cover a broad range of spiritual experiences, in this article it will refer to the practice of godliness in the life of a believer, and especially to the process by which a person who has been saved progresses toward the goal of becoming like God and Christ. The attainment of Christlikeness is the NT understanding of sanctification.

There is a decisive difference between OT and NT images of sanctification. In the OT, sanctification is pictured primarily in two ways—ceremonial rituals that picture *holiness and obedience to the moral *law of God. The emphasis is on external practice and conduct, though these are understood to picture an inner spiritual reality. In the NT the focus shifts from external and cultic actions to personal spiritual life, and the imagery becomes more varied.

The Life of Holiness in the Old Testament. An understanding of OT patterns of sanctification can begin with the question of why things or people need to be sanctified. The answer is that God is holy and perfect and cannot be approached by what is *sinful,

polluted or *diseased. How then do things or people become sanctified? By *washing, by abstention from polluting contacts, by ritual acts that bring *cleansing or separation from stain or pollution. The priest, for example, must wash himself, wear consecrated sacred *garments and make *sacrifice for his own sins. Also he must not touch corpses and not have *skin disease if he is to be fit to approach God in the holy place to represent a sinful people.

The gulf between God's divine nature and the human realm is bridged by the biblical concept of sanctification. The word *sanctify* comes from the Hebrew word group *qdš*, whose derivatives appear hundreds of times in the Hebrew Bible. Among their meanings are "hallow," "consecrate" and "sanctify." The central idea is setting apart from the sinful and secular for a special divine use. These ideas are integrally related to cultic practice and its central role in Israelite religion from *Moses to the final destruction of Herod's temple. The modern mind is not well equipped to process the startling and sometimes grotesque realities of this foundational idea of Judaism, which involved *animal sacrifices and the shedding and sprinkling of *blood (e.g., Lev 22:16, 32; Num 6:11; Heb 9:13). The images come from a symbolic world and culture vastly different from our own.

The primary focus of sanctification is the *tabernacle and later the *temple, along with the ceremonial rituals that occurred there. This represents the separateness of God and the physical isolation he requires for himself, his people and the accoutrements of *worship. The temple is a living, functioning symbol of God's transcendence. As *Solomon says, "I have built thee an exalted house, a place for thee to dwell in for ever" (2 Chron 6:2 RSV). Rabbinic lore teaches us that sanctity has a geographic aspect, emanating from the center of the temple and decreasing with physical distance, based on contiguity. To grasp these concepts we must imagine ourselves in the context of the grand temple structures and priestly vestments, the solemn ritual of sacrifice in its bloody cruelty, and the mass energy of large *festivals. These are the symbols by which God defines and establishes his otherness; sanctification is the means of bridging the gap.

A cluster of OT passages speak of people or *priests sanctifying themselves by a conscious action, usually as prescribed by the ceremonial law. The primary meaning is setting apart from either common use or sinful practice. The image patterns here stress washing of various kinds, not touching contaminated physical objects, avoiding spiritual contamination through intermarriage or *idolatry (pictured repeatedly in the OT as *adultery), and performing acts unique to members of the cult (e.g., *circumcision). The showbread in the temple was set apart. The *sabbath was a day set apart from other days. Purging the *Promised Land of idolatry was a sanctifying act.

If the ceremonial rituals of the Mosaic law thus

provide the leading OT motif, the second OT emphasis is living a life of obedience to God's moral law. The keynote is perhaps encapsulated in Leviticus 20:8, where God says, "Keep my statutes, and do them; I am the LORD who sanctify you" (RSV). A leading image of such a life of sanctified godliness is the *path or way. Or we might look at the portrait that emerges from several *encomia in the Psalter (Ps 1; 15; 112), where the holy person is characterized by moral conduct, inner virtue and rectitude in worship. These same psalms introduce a portrait of the wicked to show that sanctification involves separation from evil as well as positively following the paths of godliness. The book of Proverbs, too, gives an ever-expanding picture of what the sanctified life looks like, with emphasis on moral conduct.

New Testament Images. NT images for sanctification are much less cultic than the OT images. Even imagery of sanctification that is carried forward from the OT undergoes a transformation, as when the temple ceases to be a sacred site in Jerusalem and instead becomes the individual person or the fellowship of believers (1 Cor 3:16-17; 6:19; 2 Cor 6:16). The basic premise of NT sanctification is that individuals are "sanctified by faith" in Christ (Acts 26:18; cf. 1 Cor 1:2; Heb 13:12). The power for such sanctification comes from the *Holy Spirit (Rom 15:16; 2 Thess 2:13; 1 Pet 1:2). The momentousness of sanctification is expressed by the aphorism "For this is the will of God, even your sanctification" (1 Thess 4:3 KJV). The imagery by which the process of sanctification is pictured is rich and varied.

The essential pattern is twofold—an avoiding of sin and a positive practice of virtue. One cluster of images accordingly pictures the action of separating oneself from evil. Sanctification is here a matter of casting off evil practices (Rom 13:12), shunning immorality (1 Cor 6:18), putting off the old nature (Eph 4:22), putting away immoral conduct (Eph 4:25; Jas 1:21), laying aside every weight of sin (Heb 12:1). A related motif uses the language of abstaining from evil (1 Thess 4:3; 5:22; 1 Pet 2:11), renouncing it (Tit 2:12) or keeping oneself unstained by it (Jas 1:27). In more intense imagery this becomes a putting to death of sin (Col 3:12, 14) or crucifying of it (Gal 5:24). The imagery of washing, cleansing and purifying from sin is of similar import (1 Cor 6:11; 2 Cor 7:1; Eph 5:26; 1 Jn 3:3). Also present is the imagery of not being conformed to a sinful lifestyle (Rom 12:1; 1 Pet 1:14).

The positive counterpart to putting off evil is putting on the good (Rom 13:12, 14; Eph 4:24; Col 3:12, 14). The sanctified life is something one builds on the foundation provided by Christ (1 Cor 3:10-15). Again, sanctification involves supplementing faith with virtue (2 Pet 1:5). Sanctification involves producing something that was not present before—a concept implicit in pictures of sanctified conduct as fruit that is produced by a renewed nature (Gal 5:22-23; Phil 1:11). Or sanctification can be an equipping with everything good (Heb 13:21).

The imagery of process is also important, with the implication that sanctification is incremental. Sanctification thus becomes a matter of maturing into adulthood and being no longer a *child (Eph 4:13-14), of *growing up (Eph 4:15), of growing in grace (2 Pet 3:18). The imagery of overflowing abundance is also present: people "abound more and more" in godliness (Phil 1:9 RSV), "increase and abound in love" (1 Thess 3:12 RSV), become "rich in good deeds" (1 Tim 6:18 RSV) and "abound" in godliness (2 Pet 1:8 RSV). The process of sanctification can also be slow and methodical, with one virtue producing another (Rom 5:3-5), perhaps through a process of imitating what is good (3 Jn 11). Process imagery is also implied when sanctification is pictured as pressing on toward a goal (Phil 3:12, 14), as something that is not yet perfect, with the implication that the progression is toward perfection (Phil 3:12), and as a process in which God will eventually sanctify a person wholly (1 Thess 5:23).

Because sanctification is contrary to the fallen state into which people are born and become acclimated, and because it is a process, the imagery of being transformed and renewed is used (Rom 12:2; Eph 4:25). If we ask what such a transformed life actually looks like, we can do no better than to look at the passages known as paraenesis (exhortation)—commands in the form of lists of virtues to practice and vices to avoid (Rom 12:9-21; Eph 4:25-32; Phil 4:4-9; Col 3:12-17; 1 Thess 5:12-20; Heb 13:1-5).

See also BLOOD; CLEANSING; GROW, GROWTH; HOLINESS; PRIEST; PURITY; SACRED SPACE; SACRIFICE; TABERNACLE; TEMPLE; WASH, WASHING.

SANCTUARY. *See* TABERNACLE; TEMPLE.

SANDAL. *See* SHOE, SANDAL.

SARCASM, HUMOROUS. *See* HUMOR.

SATAN

The popular image of Satan as the devil dressed in red with a long tail and a pitchfork is archetypal. While the details of this portrayal of Satan are largely a figment of the popular imagination, the identification of Satan as a demonic figure and archenemy of *God does have a basis in the NT. There Satan is the devil, who stands diametrically opposed to God and human well-being. In the OT, however, the figure of Satan is more ambiguous and less clearly associated with evil.

Satanic Figures in the Old Testament. Contrary to what we might expect, Satan does not play a large role in the OT. Used in only a handful of passages, the Hebrew noun *sāṭān* is often employed to describe the character of an action or the role of the individual performing it, rather than as a proper name for the character performing an act. Thus the word *satan* is employed to describe actions of obstruction, opposition and accusation. Where it is used to refer to a celestial being, the actions of that being are usually ambiguous and open to interpretation.

To understand the OT portrayal of a celestial satanic figure, which is our primary interest in this article, we must refer to the common ancient Near Eastern image of a divine council or assembly of the gods (*see* Cosmology). The gods would meet in council to discuss important issues, to settle disputes among themselves and to determine the fate of the cosmos. Intrigue and subterfuge were characteristic of the members of the council as they jockeyed for positions of influence and settled various scores with one another. In this worldview the human world was caught up in the conflicts amongst the gods.

Within biblical literature the *divine assembly appears explicitly on a number of occasions (1 Kings 22:19-23; Job 1-2; Is 6). The council appears to have been a forum for deliberations about divine plans. The Israelites adapted the imagery of the divine assembly to their own beliefs so that Yahweh, Israel's God, was the supreme deity presiding over the council. The other members of the council, who were summoned to the presence of Yahweh, served the purposes of Yahweh and showed varying degrees of autonomy. But within Israelite texts none of the lesser beings could mount an effective challenge to Yahweh's sovereignty. The monotheistic tendencies of Israelite religion prevented such serious challenges.

The most extensive portrayal of a satanic figure in the OT is found in Job 1—2. The satanic figure of the book of Job takes a place among the "sons of God" or heavenly beings who present themselves before God as members of the divine assembly. Here the satanic figure is referred to as "the satan," with the definite article, indicating that the term is understood not as a proper name but rather as a title or office held by the individual. The role of the satan is that of an investigator, tester or prosecuting attorney who seeks to probe the character of human beings. In Job the satan describes his activity as "going to and fro on the earth." When God raises the specter of Job's blameless character and unblemished devotion to God, the satan responds with doubt about Job's integrity and the motive for his piety. Then he proposes that Job's character be tested. An affirmative response from God sets Job's trial in motion as he is afflicted with a multitude of disasters. When Job maintains his piety after the first onslaught, the satan proposes for him yet another trial, more grievous than the first. After this second trial, which leads into the series of speeches that occupy the center of Job, the satan recedes into the background for the rest of the book.

In assessing the character of the satanic figure in Job, it is important to keep in mind that it is God who draws Job to the attention of the satan (Job 1:8). Furthermore, while the satan outlines the nature of the test of Job, it is approved by God and limits for the test are set by God (Job 1:12; 2:6). The satanic figure in Job clearly works within the parameters established by God.

Is the satanic figure of Job inherently evil? While misfortune falls on Job from the activities of this figure, nevertheless there is no indication that we are dealing here with an archrival of God. Rather, the satan functions as one of the "sons of God" (Job 1:6) who present themselves to God and who receive their mandate from God. The satan in Job 1 does not present a serious challenge to God's sovereignty but works as a divine agent, testing the integrity of human beings like Job. Thus in Job the satan is an ambiguous figure who appears on the one hand to challenge God's assessment of Job's character, and yet on the other hand works within the parameters established by God.

Two other texts merit brief consideration. In Zechariah 3:1-2 the satan stands as the accuser of the high priest Joshua. This role is executed without any direct quotation of the words of the satan. Yahweh rebukes the satan, yet it is unclear whether the rebuke is a repudiation of the satan himself or of the satan's accusation against Joshua, although the latter appears more likely. Again, the character of the satan is ambiguous. In 1 Chronicles 21:1, Satan (this time without the definite article) appears as an individual who incites David to conduct a census of Israel. Of the three texts considered, this is the only one in which the term *satan*, without the definite article, is used to refer to a celestial being. This could indicate that we should understand the term as a proper name. But once again we find little indication that the satanic figure is an archrival of God.

To summarize, in the OT there is little indication that early Israel thought in terms of a personalized evil individual, Satan, who stood diametrically opposed to God as an archenemy. What we do find in the OT is an ambiguous figure, a member of the divine council, whose role appears to be that of testing and probing the character of human beings. However, it must be emphasized that this satanic figure works within the parameters established by God.

Satan in the New Testament. With the NT we find a significantly different symbolic world within which Satan functions. Building on the religious resources and thinking reflected in the apocryphal and pseudepigraphical writings of the intertestamental period, early Christianity adopted a dualism that interpreted the world as a battlefield between God and Satan. Under many guises, Satan became the epitome of evil, who would work at cross-purposes with God and humanity at every opportunity. Satan was the sworn enemy of all humanity, especially those who would claim allegiance to God. The range of names given to Satan in the NT—the devil, the tempter, the evil one, the prince of *demons, the dragon, the ancient serpent, Beelzebul, the accuser, the *enemy—is testimony to the richness of the early Christian experience and portrayal of evil. The ambiguity of the satanic figure in the OT is gone.

Two related but distinct aspects of Satan's activities are identifiable in the NT: Satan's hostility toward humanity and his animosity toward God.

Hostility toward humanity. Satan's ill will toward humanity is summed up best in 1 Peter 5:8: "Like a roaring lion your adversary the devil prowls around, looking for someone to devour" (NRSV). This statement can be elaborated by considering several of Satan's activities.

Satan is portrayed not only as the tempter who tested persons to see whether they would succumb to evil, perhaps in a way comparable to the role of the satan in Job, but also as the one who drove humans to evil. At times the dividing line between these two activities may be blurred. In the Synoptic Gospels, Jesus was led into the desert where he would not only endure but also resist temptation by the devil (Mt 4:1-11; Mk 1:12-13; Lk 4:1-13). Similarly, after Peter's confession of Jesus' identity and the subsequent passion prediction, Peter's rebuke of Jesus is condemned as another temptation of Satan (Mt 16:23; Mk 8:33). In some instances, evil actions are attributed to the agency of Satan, who has inspired, or perhaps even possessed, individuals. Thus the betrayal of Jesus by Judas Iscariot is attributed to the entry of Satan into Judas (Lk 22:3; Jn 13:27). Elsewhere, Peter's denial of Jesus is attributed to the actions of Satan (Lk 22:31), who seeks to "sift" Peter. In Acts, Ananias' deceptive scheme is attributed to Satan, who has filled his *heart (Acts 5:3).

Satan's hostility toward humans is also seen in his role as the author of misfortune, disaster and illness. In Luke 13:16 a woman who had been subject to physical afflictions for many years is said to have been bound by Satan. Paul describes his famous "thorn in the flesh" as a "messenger from Satan" (2 Cor 12:7 NRSV). Satan can also be said to hinder the actions of individuals as in 1 Thessalonians 2:18, where Paul asserts that his desire to return to Thessalonica has been thwarted by Satan.

Animosity toward God. As the opponent of God, Satan also seeks to thwart the advance of God's purposes and the Christian mission. The diametrical opposition between God and Satan is evidenced in Acts 26:17-18, where while recounting his vision of Jesus and his subsequent conversion, Paul cites Jesus as saying, "I will rescue you from your people and from the Gentiles—to whom I am sending you to open their eyes so that they may turn from darkness to light and from the power of Satan to God" (NRSV). The association of Satan with darkness and God with *light is characteristic of the broader images of *darkness and *light, *evil and good, damnation and *salvation. The important point here, however, is that this reflects the underlying antipathy between Satan and God.

The conflict between Satan and God comes to its most colorful expression in *Revelation. Here we find explicit references to the struggle between Satan and God that had broken out in heaven and was fought on the terrestrial plane. The imagery is rich: "And war broke out in heaven; Michael and his angels fought against the dragon. The dragon and

his angels fought back, but they were defeated, and there was no longer any place for them in heaven. The great dragon was thrown down, that ancient serpent, who is called the Devil and Satan, the deceiver of the whole world—he was thrown down to the earth, and his angels were thrown down with him" (Rev 12:7-9 NRSV). Here we find a rich assortment of images being employed to characterize the enemy of God. The ancient *serpent is a transparent reference to the serpent of Genesis 3 which, while not identified with Satan in the OT, came to be associated with Satan in Judaism and the writings of early Christianity. Similarly, the reference to Satan having been cast out of heaven appears to be an allusion to Isaiah 14:3-21, where the reference is directed toward the king of Babylon but here is applied to Satan. Finally, the reference to the dragon is a development of the OT references to a sea *monster (Is 27:1; 51:9), which was seen as a challenger of the dominion of God. The effect of this coalescence of imagery is to enhance the place of Satan as the archrival of God.

Summary. The biblical imagery associated with Satan shows a definite development from the OT to the NT. In the OT, Satan functions as a member of the divine council under the sovereignty of God. However, in the NT, Satan has become the devil, the archenemy of God, who mounts a significant, but ultimately futile, challenge to God's authority. Especially in the NT there is a coalescence of images and designations for Satan as the archenemy of God.

See also COSMOLOGY; DARKNESS; DEMONS; DIVINE WARRIOR; EVIL; TRIUMPH.

BIBLIOGRAPHY. P. L. Day, *An Adversary in Heaven: Satan in the Hebrew Bible* (Atlanta: Scholars, 1988).

SATAN CAST DOWN

*Satan's being cast down from *heaven is a mysterious and evocative motif that seems to cover the entire span of salvation history. The most famous account is the *war in heaven narrated in Revelation 12:7-17. "Now war arose in heaven," we read (Rev 12:7 RSV), and in the epic battle that ensues Satan and his followers are defeated by Michael and his angels. The resolution of the battle comes when "that ancient serpent, who is called the Devil and Satan, . . . was thrown down to the earth, and his angels were thrown down with him" (Rev 12:9 RSV). In context, the epic account is a flashback to Christ's conquest of Satan at Calvary (Rev 12:1-6). But other possibilities seem to converge in the account. The very presence of the story in the Apocalypse carries hints of a final defeat of Satan at the end of history. It has also been common to believe in a fall of Satan from heaven before human history began.

The latter motif rests on two OT passages, which may or may not be an adequate basis for the belief. In Isaiah's taunt against the king of Babylon, the prophet exclaims, "How art thou fallen from heaven, O Lucifer, son of the morning!" (Is 14:12 KJV). Because no mortal can be fallen from heaven, the imagination reaches out to picture Satan as the being in view. Ezekiel's oracle against Tyre elaborates the picture further, portraying a being who once resided in Eden, placed "with an anointed guardian cherub" on "the holy mountain of God" (Ezek 28:14 RSV). This being was "blameless . . . from the day you were created, till iniquity was found in you" (Ezek 28:15 RSV). Thereupon he was "cast . . . as a profane thing from the mountain of God, and the guardian cherub drove [him] out from the midst of the stones of fire" (Ezek 28:16 RSV). Again, he was "cast . . . to the ground" (Ezek 28:17).

Mystery surrounds the motif, and this mystery is intensified when we find other references to Satan's fall from heaven that make it, at least metaphorically, a repeated action. Shortly before his passion, Jesus said, "Now shall the ruler of this world be cast out" (Jn 12:31 RSV). When the *seventy returned and told Jesus that they had cast out demons, Jesus replied, "I saw Satan fall like lightning from heaven" (Lk 10:18 RSV).

See also EVIL; SATAN; TRIUMPH.

SATIRE

Satire is the exposure of human vice or folly through rebuke or ridicule. It can appear in any form or genre, including expository prose, narrative, poetry or visionary writing. It can be either a minor part of a work or the main point. It might consist of an entire book (e.g., Amos), or it can be as small as an individual *proverb. One of the conventions of satire is the freedom to exaggerate, overstate or oversimplify to make a satiric point. Overall, satire is a subversive form that questions the status quo, unsettles people's thinking, assaults the deep structure of conventional thought patterns and aims to make people uncomfortable.

Satire is made up of four identifiable elements, the chief of which is *one or more objects of attack*. An object of attack might be as specific as a single moral vice, like greed or *pride, or as general as an entire wicked society. It might be a universal quality or behavior, but it is more likely to be a historical particular, as when the OT prophets expose specific situations in specific nations or when Jesus attacks the behavior of a specific religious group of his day—the *Pharisees. The result is that satire is often topical, requiring a knowledge of the original context for its complete understanding.

The second ingredient of satire is the *satiric vehicle*—the specific form by which the satirist embodies the attack. The most common satiric vehicle is story or narrative, with characters and their actions embodying the bad behavior or attitudes that the satirist wishes to rebuke. Also common is the portrait, in which the satirist paints a word picture of a character who embodies the folly or vice that the author aims to denigrate. A single metaphor can be the vehicle of satiric attack, as when Amos calls the wealthy women of his society "cows of Bashan" (Amos 4:1 RSV) or Jesus addresses the Pharisees as

"blind guides" (Mt 23:16). Direct vituperation or denunciation is also common, with the "woe formula" heading the list: "Woe to those who are at ease in Zion" (Amos 6:1 RSV).

The third element in satire is the *satiric tone*—the author's attitude toward the subject. Two possibilities exist, known among literary scholars by two Roman satirists who became associated with the two forms. Horatian satire (named after Horace) is light, urbane and subtle. It uses a low-pressure approach in attempting to influence an audience toward a negative assessment of the thing being attacked. The book of *Jonah and some of Jesus' parables illustrate the approach. Juvenalian satire (named after Juvenal) is biting, bitter and angry, as epitomized by the book of *Amos and Jesus' oratory against the Pharisees in Matthew 23. We might say that one approach attempts to *laugh* vice or folly out of existence, and the other to *lash* it out of existence.

Finally, satire needs a *norm*—a stated or implied standard by which the criticism is being conducted. This standard of virtue or right behavior usually appears explicitly within a satiric work, though in terms of space it receives minor treatment compared to the object(s) of attack. The goal is simply to suggest, however briefly, an alternative to the scenes of foolish or wicked behavior that make up the bulk of a satiric work. Amos, for example, includes interspersed calls to right behavior and reminders that God's justice is the standard by which his nation should reform itself, and Jesus customarily accompanies his satiric parables with a proverb that names the principle that the bad behavior embodied by characters in the parable have violated. Sometimes the satiric norm is not stated explicitly but is left to the audience to infer.

It is obvious that the Bible is a thoroughly satiric book. The largest repository of satire is prophetic writing, where we encounter continuous attacks on the evils of society and individuals. The second largest category is the parables and discourses of Jesus. Satire is prominent in biblical narrative, where wholly idealized characters are a rarity and deficient or immoral human behavior is the staple. Poems can be satiric (for example, the lament psalms, with their satiric portraits of the poet's enemies), as can proverbs.

See also AMOS, BOOK OF; HYPOCRITE; JONAH, BOOK OF; PARABLES; PRIDE; PROVERB.

SAVING UP. *See* STORING UP.

SAVIOR. *See* JESUS, IMAGES OF.

SCALES

During the early development of civilization scales were used to measure weights. Virtually all commercial transactions involved the use of weights and balances. Metal pans were suspended by chords passing into the ends of a tubular beam. The plummet was situated in front of the upright support so that when the articles in the two pans were equal, the exact vertical position of the plummet would be evident. In Revelation 6:5 the scales in the hand of the third horseman, because of their commercial association, symbolize rationing and famine.

Because hand scales were open to fraudulent manipulation, the Bible contains many injunctions concerning the need for fair practices: "Use honest scales and honest weights, an honest ephah [a container for dry measure] and an honest hin [a jar for liquid measure]" (Lev 19:36 NIV).

Ancient hand-held scales.

God is often pictured in the OT as a judge holding scales. Hannah celebrates the justice of God in her prayer of thanksgiving after the birth of Samuel: "The LORD is a God who knows, and by him deeds are weighed" (1 Sam 2:3 NIV). In Proverbs 16:2 God weighs the motives of people, especially of the self-righteous. In his despair Job pleads with God for just measure: "If only my anguish could be weighed and all my misery be placed on the scales!" (Job 6:2 NIV). God is thus the supreme administrator of the scales of justice, measuring not only the motives but also the actions.

Conversely, improper use of scales is used as a symbol of total corruption within a people. Israel is castigated by the prophets for its injustice: using dishonest scales while hypocritically retaining an outward façade of devotion to God, "saying, 'When will the New Moon be over that we may sell grain, and the Sabbath be ended that we may market wheat?'— skimping the measure, boosting the price and cheating with dishonest scales" (Amos 8:5 NIV; cf. Mic 6:11). This injustice not only cheats the buyer but is an *abomination to God (Prov 11:1), who created weights and scales (Prov 16:11). In the NT, Jesus enjoins his listeners to judge others justly with an implicit reference to scales: "For in the same way you judge others, you will be judged, and with the measure you use, it will be measured to you" (Mt 7:2 NIV; cf. Mk 4:24-25; Lk 7:34-38).

Scales are also used as a symbol of God's power and exacting perfection in creation. When God made the world, he measured the waters and the heavens in his hand and "weighed the mountains on the scales and the hills in a balance" (Is 40:12 NIV). He is the master craftsman of creation, who allocates its substance and shapes its features with measured precision. But the proportions of measurement are massive and far transcend any scale imaginable for humans. Because of his great majesty and power, Israel need not fear its enemies, for in the eye of the Lord "they are regarded as dust on the scales" (Is 40:15 NIV). How ironic that the worship of God, who weighs the entire world in a balance, is traded for the worship of idols of gold measured out in a scale (Is 46:6)!

Probably the most famous use of the scale motif is in the interpretation of the writing on Belshazzar's wall (Dan 5:25-30). Because of the haughty arrogance of Belshazzar in defiling the gold vessels from God's temple and worshiping false gods, his kingdom is overthrown by Darius the Mede. God has placed Belshazzar, a great world ruler of daunting power and authority, on the scales, and he has been "found wanting." This recalls the picture of God as the just judge who ably manages the affairs of the world, and who not only measures motives and actions but evaluates and controls each person's destiny.

Thus scales invoke the motifs of justice, power and evaluation. But unlike modern symbols of "blind" justice, God sees all: "Will not the Judge of all the earth do right?" (Gen 18:25 NIV).

See also JUSTICE.

SCAPEGOAT

The scapegoat is mentioned in the Bible only once (Lev 16), as part of the ritual for the annual Day of *Atonement. The *priest was to cast lots for two *goats. One of them was then *sacrificed for a *sin offering; the other, chosen by lot as the scapegoat, was driven out of the camp alive after the priest had lain hands on it and confessed over it the sins of the Israelites (Lev 16:7-10, 20-22, 26).

The English word *scapegoat* was apparently invented by William Tyndale as an attempt to translate what literally says "for Azazel." The Hebrew term might refer to the wasteland, the inaccessible land where the animal was sent, but also to some supernatural power there, like a desert *demon. In any case, the scapegoat was certainly no sacrifice to God, for only an animal without defect could be sacrificed as an atonement (Lev 1:10). The scapegoat, however, was loaded with the sins of the people. It was supposed to carry the sins into the realm of a personified *evil force, by no means then as an offering but rather as a scorn.

The discharge of sin is not possible but by the will and in the presence of God. The whole ceremony took place at the entrance to the tent of meeting (Lev 16:7). In the presence of the Lord the scapegoat was chosen, the sin confessed and passed onto the animal. As the drawing of lots was a common means to find out God's will, even the choice of the goat was entirely his own.

The passing of the sins onto the scapegoat was a demonstrative act stressing the reality of sin almost like a physical entity. The priest was to press both his *hands on the *head of the animal, confess the sins aloud and thus "put them on the goat's head" (Lev 16:21 NIV). The man who led it into the *wilderness had to *cleanse himself before returning to the camp, to prevent "reinfection." Thus sin was considered not just a moral weakness but a dangerous threat to the community.

The goat was not killed (though in later Jewish tradition it was driven over a cliff to prevent its returning) but left to its fate. The wilderness as the sphere of *death was its rightful place. Wild beasts or maybe *demons would do as they pleased, and death would take its lawful toll. And yet even the desert was created and ruled by God. The ultimate *judgment over the animal carrying the sins of his people was his own.

The motif of a creature chosen by God carrying the sins of the people out of an inhabited place to face God's judgment reappears several times in the NT, though the image of the scapegoat is never directly applied to Jesus. Jesus is the sacrifice for our sins (Heb 10:1-18), an offering to God and not "for Azazel." Yet John the Baptist calls Jesus the "Lamb of God, who takes away the sins of the world" (Jn 1:29 NIV), and in Hebrews 13:12-13 the point is stressed that Jesus was crucified outside the *city. Again, the disposal of sin is considered as an almost physical process: sin is loaded onto Jesus; he is driven out of town and given over to God's *curse (Gal 3:13). His death is a rightful consequence of our sinning (Rom 6:23). Thus some aspects of the ultimate justification by Christ are foreshadowed in the scapegoat ritual.

See also GOAT; SACRIFICE; SIN; WILDERNESS.

SCARLET. *See* COLORS.

SCENT. *See* PERFUME; SMELL.

SCEPTER

Like *"throne" and *"crown," the scepter in the Bible is a symbol of *kingship and its accompanying authority and power. In the Egyptian writing system the scepter is the key symbol in the word "to rule," a fact that simply underscores the symbolic value of the scepter in the ancient Near East. In the OT we find scepters made of *gold and *iron. Ezekiel figuratively speaks of the "mother" of the princes of Israel as a vine whose branches were "fit for a ruler's scepter" but are so no more (Ezek 19:11, 14 NIV). The psalmist speaks of God's scepter as a "scepter of justice" (Ps 45:6), and the author of Hebrews applies that figure to Christ (Heb 1:8).

The image of the scepter can have a dynamic quality that evokes a coercive kingly power or acceptance. In the book of Esther the King Xerxes's golden scepter plays an important role. Those who approach the king without being summoned will be put to death—unless the king extends to them his golden scepter (Esther 4:11). The tension mounts as Esther boldly approaches the king on behalf of the Jews. But the king is pleased with her and extends his golden scepter (Esther 5:2; 8:4). In the psalms we see the opposite power of the scepter. The rule of the Davidic king will be extended by Yahweh's help, and the king will rule the nations "with an iron scepter" and "dash them to pieces like pottery" (Ps 2:9 NIV). Here the scepter is clearly a *weapon, and the iron seems to point to the origin of this royal symbol in the field of battle. Similarly, in Psalm 110:2 the Davidic king is assured: "The LORD will extend your mighty scepter from Zion; you will rule in the midst of your enemies" (NIV). It is interesting that only the Seer of Revelation directly applies the image of a powerful scepter (Ps 2:9) to Christ (Rev 12:5; 19:15) and his followers (Rev 2:27).

The Lord, the heavenly king, breaks the scepter of wicked rulers (Is 14:5). The OT speaks of the scepters of various nations: Babylon (Is 14:5), Persia (Esther 4:11), Moab (Jer 48:17), Damascus (Amos 1:5), Ashkelon (Amos 1:8) and Egypt (Zech 10:11). Thus it is said of the downfall of Egypt that "Egypt's scepter will pass away" (Zech 10:11). The fall of Moab is mockingly mourned, "How broken is the mighty scepter, how broken the glorious staff!" (Jer 48:17).

God's voice is his scepter by which he will even strike down Assyria (Is 30:31). Alternatively, viewed from the heavenly throne room, Judah can be called God's scepter (Ps 60:7; 108:8), the symbol and instrument of God's rule. Since Davidic kingship arises from the tribe of Judah, it is natural that the image of the scepter should be used of Judah. Jacob's patriarchal blessing over Judah promises, "The scepter will not depart from Judah, nor the ruler's staff from between his feet" (Gen 49:10 NIV). And Balaam's prophecy proclaims, "A star will come out of Jacob; a scepter will rise out of Israel" (Num 24:17 NIV), a passage viewed by Jews and Christians as a messianic prophecy.

See also CROWN; KING, KINGSHIP; THRONE.

SCRIPTURE. *See* BIBLE.

SCROLL

Until the second century A.D. most fairly lengthy documents were written on scrolls of papyrus, leather or parchment, though in Mesopotamia clay tablets were used widely. References to *book(s) in English versions of the Bible usually mean written documents in scroll form. There are three ways in which the imagery of the scroll as a particular form of written document is used in the Bible.

Ezekiel 2:8—3:2 and Revelation 5:1-5 speak of a scroll that is written "on the front/inside and the back." It was rare for a scroll to have writing on both sides. In Ezekiel the scroll, which the prophet *eats, symbolizes his message. The writing on both sides symbolizes its completeness as it comes from God.

The prophet can add nothing to it. In Revelation the same symbolism indicates the completeness of God's plan for human history.

The scroll in Revelation has *seven *seals. In the

A scroll of the torah.

ancient world legal documents had multiple seals. In Roman Asia testaments were sealed with the seals of seven *witnesses, in whose presence they were unsealed after the testator's death. Here the *Lamb that had been slain but is alive opens the seals of the scroll that promises the consummation of God's kingdom.

The most transparent and graphic use of scroll imagery is found in pictures of God's *judgment: "All the host of heaven shall rot away, and the skies roll up like a scroll" (Is 34:4 RSV); "the sky vanished like a scroll that is rolled up" (Rev 6:14 RSV).

See also BOOK; SEAL.

BIBLIOGRAPHY. B. M. Metzger, "The Making of Ancient Books" in *The Text of The New Testament* (3d ed.; Oxford: Oxford University Press, 1992) 3-35.

SEA

The sea is central to the biblical picture of the universe. Like its ancient neighbors, the Israelites believed that at creation God used a cosmic sea to create a three-tiered universe: the sea, the *heavens and the *earth (Ps 135:6; Rev 14:7). God created the cosmic sea (Ps 95:5; Jon 1:9) and gathered the waters covering the entire face of the earth into seas and established their boundaries (Gen 1:2, 9-10; Ps 104:5-9; Job 38:8-11), rooting the earth in the cosmic sea (Ps 18:15; 24:1-2). He formed the firmament to enclose the atmosphere and hold back the sea from above (Gen 1:6-8; Prov 8:27-29). The sea provides all water on the earth. Water springs forth below and drops through apertures in the firmament above as *rain and *snow, even providing water for the great *flood (Gen 7:11; 8:2). Above the heavens God's *throne floats upon the sea (Ps 29:10; Ezek 1:26). In this picture the sea is a tribute to the power of God the Creator over *chaos and may have been symbolized by the large bronze molten sea before Solomon's *Temple (1 Kings 7:23-26).

The cosmic sea, however, also symbolizes the continued threat the forces of chaos pose against God

and creation. The sea pushes against the boundaries God established for it (Job 38:8-11; Jer 5:22). The Bible adapts its neighbors' creation myths of a primeval battle between a creator god and a sea monster of chaos called Leviathan, Rahab, or the dragon or *serpent (Job 41). Unlike the myths of neighboring nations, God creates the chaos *monster and places it in the sea (Gen 1:20-21; Ps 104:24-26). The monster stirs the cosmic sea but is *wounded and subdued by God (Job 26:12; Ps 74:12-14; 89:9-10; Is 51:9) and will ultimately be vanquished in the end times (Is 27:1). As the home of the chaos monster who can be roused, the sea symbolizes the threat of the reemergence of chaos (Job 3:8). In fact, the evil world powers and the *antichrist of the last days which oppose God and his people are symbolized as beasts arising from the sea (Dan 7:3; Rev 13:1).

As Creator, God controls the sea, both producing and calming its waves (Is 51:15; Jer 31:35), and keeping it within its boundaries (Job 38:8-11; Prov 8:27-29; Jer 5:22). He can dry up the sea at will (Nahum 1:4) or unleash it to judge the world as in the flood (Gen 6—8). Thus the threat of chaos and *evil which the sea symbolizes is ultimately hollow. The parting of the Red Sea and destruction of *Pharaoh is a reenactment of the subduing of the sea and chaos monster, once more demonstrating God's ultimate authority over forces of chaos and evil (Ex 15; Is 51:9-10). This same authority is symbolized by Jesus' walking on the sea (Mk 6:45-52) and calming the sea (Mk 4:35-41). Even the beast of Revelation which arises from the sea is subdued and cast into the lake of fire (Rev 19:20).

The throne room of God contains something like a sea of glass which may refer to the cosmic sea (Rev 4:6; 15:2). The calmness of the sea symbolizes the absence of evil and chaos in heaven, for there is no "monster" of chaos able to disturb it. At the consummation, the cosmic sea is mingled with *fire, perhaps a symbol of impending judgment (Rev 15:2). After the consummation there is no longer a sea (Rev 21:1), which symbolizes no more actual or possible threat to the creation and sovereignty of God.

The sea also provides many maritime metaphors and similes. The roar of the seas is the tumult of the peoples (Ps 65:7). Both the sea and invading armies *thunder and roar (Is 17:12-14; Jer 6:23). Babylon is covered with the waves of invading armies (Jer 51:42). Those fearful of impending judgment are troubled like the sea (Jer 49:23), and the doubter is like a wave of the sea tossed by the wind (Jas 1:6). The restlessness and works of the wicked are like mud and mire tossed up by the sea (Is 57:20; Jude 13). The numerous grains of sand on the seashore are like many descendants (Gen 22:17; Heb 11:12) or sizable armies (Josh 11:4; Rev 20:8). God's forgiveness is portrayed as casting sin into the depths of the sea (Mic 7:19). It is hoped that the knowledge of God will one day *fill the earth as the waters cover the sea (Is 11:9).

See also CHAOS; COSMOLOGY; DEEP; DIVINE WAR-

RIOR; EARTH; FLOOD; HEAVEN; MONSTERS; WATER.

BIBLIOGRPAHY. J. Day, *God's Conflict with the Dragon and the Sea* (Cambridge: Cambridge University Press, 1985).

SEA MONSTER. *See* COSMOLOGY; MONSTERS.

SEA SERPENT. *See* COSMOLOGY; MONSTERS.

SEAL

The book of Job suggests the diversity of meanings for the image of seals. God's seal on the *stars symbolizes his *authority (Job 9:7); God seals his instruction to preserve it (Job 33:16). Two unusual figures compare God's control in changing things to *clay under a seal (Job 38:14), and Leviathan's strong scales form a tight seal shutting him up (Job 41:15). The latter image of securing a place occurs also in the stories of Daniel sealed in the lions' *den and Jesus sealed in the tomb (Dan 6:17; Mt 27:66)—so they cannot be removed! Satan is sealed so he no longer deceives anyone (Rev 20:3).

Seals on letters symbolize the authenticity of authority (1 Kings 21:8; Esther 3:12; 8:8-10); thus metaphorically the image connotes authenticity. Abraham's *circumcision is the seal of his righteousness (Rom 4:11); a witness sets his seal on the truth of God, and the Father on the Son (Jn 3:33; 6:27). People become seals, proving the worth of Paul's apostleship (1 Cor 9:2), and he carries the Macedonians' contribution to Jerusalem as an authenticating seal (Rom 15:28). Jeremiah acts out this symbolism by purchasing land and sealing the deed to prove God's future restoration of Israel (Jer 32:6-44).

Seal is also an image of authority itself. A king's signet seal on a document gives it the authority of the king himself; anyone illegally opening a letter sealed by the king is defying his authority. Sometimes the authority represented by a seal is given a spiritual meaning: Paul declares that God's foundation for believers is a double seal—the Lord knows those who are his, and he commands them to abstain from wickedness (2 Tim 2:19).

Because Near Eastern peoples wore engraved signet rings on their fingers (Gen 41:42; Jer 22:24) or cylinder seals on neck cords (Gen 38:18; Prov 3:3) to indicate identity or *ownership (like a coat of arms or heraldic crest), the beloved in the Song of Songs asks her lover to place her as a seal on his *arm (finger) and *heart (Song 8:6). The woman's request for permanence in love thus implies both proximity (like the seal that is always present) and the action of being claimed (as her lover stamps his beloved like an official signature on his heart).

Sealing is sometimes an image that deepens mystery. Daniel is instructed to conceal God's words by sealing the book (Dan 12:4) till the end of time (Dan 12:9); Isaiah and John are similarly instructed (Is 29:14; Rev 10:4). Later in Revelation, however, the message is no longer sealed (Rev 20:10)—thus imaging the future understanding of believers. The

image of the sealed book in Revelation underscores the worthiness of the *Lamb (Rev 5:1-2, 5, 8). When its seven seals are opened, the ensuing events reveal God's control over all nature and history (Rev 6:1-12; 8:1).

Preservation is a frequent meaning for the image of sealing (Song 4:12). Obedience to the law is preserved by the sealed *covenant in Nehemiah (Neh 9:38—10:1), and Isaiah commands God's law to be sealed among his disciples (Is 8:16). In God's treasuries God seals his promise to vindicate his people (Deut 32:33), but Job complains that God also sealed up his transgressions and glued together his iniquity (Job 14:17).

The image of God's sealing his people combines all these meanings—authenticity, ownership, mystery, worthiness, preservation (2 Cor 1:22). God's people marked by a seal are protected (Rev 7:2-8; 9:4). The *Holy Spirit's coming as promised is a seal and down payment, proof that God's people are sealed for the day of redemption (Eph 1:13-14; 4:30).

See also AUTHORITY; OWN, OWNER; RING; SCROLL.

SEARCH, SEARCHING

Life is characterized by searching. Storytellers know this better than most, and *quest* is almost synonymous with *story:* an individual who searches encounters difficulties that must be overcome and may need assistance in the process. Searching may also entail discoveries, corrections, changes in plans and growth in understanding. It is always a process rather than an instantaneous event.

The Bible shares the emphasis of life and narrative on searching. Indeed, the Bible is a book for searchers, though there are five times as many references to *finding as to searching in the Bible.

Human Searching. We can begin by noting the range of things for which people in the Bible search: people, family members, property that has been taken away, *enemies, information in historical chronicles, *food, *sheep, *pasture for livestock and *treasure. At this level the imagery of searching simply reinforces the element of human experience that forms the substratum of the Bible. Equally true to human experience is the way biblical characters' searching sometimes leads to unexpected results. Saul begins a search for his father's donkeys and ends up being anointed king (1 Sam 9—10). John's disciples seek the place Jesus is staying and find the Messiah (Jn 1:35-42). On the morning of the resurrection Jesus' followers expect to find his body in the *grave and instead find a living person. On some occasions people do not find the thing for which they search (Josh 2:22; 2 Sam 17:20; 2 Kings 2:17).

Searching takes on moral and religious overtones when people seek after qualities beyond the physical. In this category are references to searching out the commandments of God (1 Chron 28:8), searching one's spirit in the act of meditation (Ps 77:6), searching for understanding and *wisdom (Prov 2:1-5), searching the Scriptures (Jn 5:39). The book of the Bible most suffused with the act of searching is *Ecclesiastes, where the speaker undertakes the ultimate quest, to find satisfaction in life, searching in all the wrong places before coming to "the end of the matter" and concluding that the goal of life is to "fear God, and keep his commandments; for this is the whole duty of man" (Eccles 12:13 RSV).

In its most spiritual reaches, human searching is a seeking of God's *kingdom and his righteousness (Mt 6:33; 13:45-46) and of God himself (approximately forty references). Psalms is a veritable primer on searching for God. God himself invites such seeking, adding as a motivation that the person who seeks will find (Jer 29:13; Mt 7:7-8; Lk 11:9-10; cf. Deut 4:29). "Seek me and live" (Amos 5:4 RSV) is the divine invitation of the Bible.

The Searching of God. Platonic and humanistic thought has made the human search for God the basic paradigm of our existence. The Bible does not disparage human searching, but it balances it with the picture of a God who searches for people. The ultimate example is the incarnation of Christ—God reaching down to save a humanity that cannot save itself. Jesus' self-characterization to Zacchaeus expresses it aphoristically: "For the Son of man came to seek and to save the lost" (Lk 19:10 RSV). The parable of the shepherd seeking the lost sheep is the master image (Lk 15:3-7; see Sheep, Shepherd). An OT anticipation is God's prediction that he will search for his sheep (Ezek 34:11).

Another aspect of God's searching focuses on his omniscience. Thus God searches every human mind (1 Chron 28:9; Rev 2:23) and heart (1 Chron 29:17; Jer 17:10; Rom 8:27). The primary text is the opening verses of Psalm 139, where God searches out the speaker's path, heart and thoughts, with the speaker acquiescing at the end of the poem with the prayer "Search me, O God, and know my heart" (Ps 139:23).

Summary. Searching and finding are built into the very fabric of human life. In the Bible that rhythm is part of human life in the world and also part of the spiritual life. At a purely human level, we know that there is "a time to seek" (Eccles 3:6). At a divine level, people can live life in a double awareness—that God has come to seek the lost (Lk 19:10) and that the person who seeks will find (Mt 7:7-8).

See also ECCLESIASTES, BOOK OF; FIND, FOUND; QUEST.

SEASONS

Seasons are a leading image of order in the Bible. They signify regularity, predictability, cyclic succession and sometimes (when taken together) completeness or wholeness. Yet the "seasons" of the Bible are not primarily the cycle of nature during the course of a year. They are more generic in nature, signifying an appointed or appropriate time for something.

The Natural Cycle of the Year. Anyone who comes to the Bible looking for references to the four seasons will be disappointed by their scarcity. For one thing, people in the biblical world lived in just two seasons—summer and winter—with only scant awareness of brief transition seasons between these two. Spring is identified as the time "when kings go off to war" (2 Sam 11:1 NIV; 1 Chron 20:1), and it is an implied time for romance in the *Song of Songs, with its rapturous descriptions of burgeoning buds and blossoms (Song 2:11-13; 7:11-13) offered as an appropriate setting for romance.

Summer and winter are the major seasons in the world of the Bible. Summer is hot and *dry (Ps 32:4), a time of *harvest for crops (Prov 6:8; 30:25; Jer 40:10, 12; Mic 7:1). Winter is *rainy (Song 2:11; Hos 6:3), a time of inclement weather when people regard themselves as vulnerable (Mt 24:20; Mk 13:18; Acts 27:12; 2 Tim 4:21; Tit 3:12). We catch glimpses of seasonal living, especially for the privileged classes, in references to a summer palace (Judg 3:20), a winter apartment (Jer 36:22), and a winter house and summer house (Amos 3:15).

Seasons as Appointed Times. We are left then with more generic "seasons" as the customary biblical usage. To think about such seasons in the Bible is first to think about Genesis 1, which tells of God's making the *sun, *moon and *stars "as signs to mark seasons and days and years" (Gen 1:14 NIV). The lights in the sky and the seasons they pattern are regarded thereafter as "signs" of God's gracious, sovereign *ordering of all of life. Out of nothing came not randomness or *chaos but a divinely ordered progression of time, through segments called seasons, which in themselves show the pattern of life and death and life again.

The apostle Paul called rain from heaven and the crops in their seasons God's "testimony" to human beings that he exists and loves the people he created (Acts 14:17). Daniel, for one, heard the testimony, read the signs and praised God for being the wise and powerful One who "changes times and seasons" (Dan 2:21 NIV). The implication of the Bible is that every time one season changes to another we can hear God's voice promising Noah that as long as the earth endures, he will keep the rhythm of "seedtime and harvest, cold and heat, summer and winter, day and night" (Gen 8:22 NIV).

God's *providential signs require the obedience of each part of the pattern he is working out. When the psalmist writes "The moon marks off the seasons, and the sun knows when to go down" (Ps 104:19 NIV), he is celebrating the way each element of creation plays its part perfectly, as God planned. We might picture a sun and moon with wills of their own, moving about the heavens in obedience to God. "Even the stork in the sky knows her appointed seasons," Jeremiah writes (Jer 8:7 NIV), juxtaposing the life of a bird to the movement of the huge planets, and showing that on every level the created ones follow the appointment of the Creator. Jeremiah's point, however, is that one part of God's creation refuses to follow: human beings, confronted with the signs and the testimony, either fall in line and complete the pattern or turn away and break it. The passage ends with the accusation "But my people do not know the requirements of the LORD" (Jer 8:7 NIV).

The rainy season is meant to bring rain, and the season of harvest is meant to bring forth abundant crops. Such is the harmonic progression of the seasons. But harmony or disharmony in the seasons is often tied in Scripture to obedience or disobedience on the human level. This will have a familiar ring to anyone acquainted with the Renaissance concept of the Great Chain of Being, which saw a correspondence between order and disorder on the human and cosmic planes. Proverbs 20:4 makes exactly such a connection: "A sluggard does not plow in season; so at harvest time he looks but finds nothing" (NIV).

Still the connection deepens. Over and over again in the OT God tells his people that if they obey his commands, loving him and serving him, "then I will send rain on your land in its season, both autumn and spring rains, so that you may gather in your grain, new wine and oil" (Deut 11:14 NIV; also Deut 28:12; Lev 26:3-4). Jeremiah, speaking of God's people in their rebellion, charges them with lack of *fear for the Lord God, "who gives autumn and spring rains in season, who assures us of the regular weeks of harvest" (Jer 5:24 NIV). The prophet goes on to say that people's sin has kept these steady seasonal blessings away, as all parts of God's ordered world suffer the consequences of human disorder.

Yet God will bring order from all disorder in the end, in his time. When Psalm 1:3 compares the righteous person to "a tree planted by streams of water, which yields its fruit in season" (NIV), we understand that the God who first ordered the seasons of the earth can rightly order the seasons of a human life, bringing each follower of him to maturity, ripeness and productivity in his own good time. When the writer of Ecclesiastes speaks of "a season for every activity under heaven" (Eccles 3:1 NIV), we understand that the God who first ordered the seasons of the earth can rightly order the seasons of all human life, whether they be seasons of birth or death, war or peace. God divinely conducts all seasons. The one who ignores his beat will find no rain and will not flourish. The one who follows him will bring forth fruit. These are the pictures of the seasons in Scripture.

So Paul could write to Titus that "at the appointed season" God had "brought his word to light" through Paul's preaching (Tit 1:3 NIV). In the same sentence Paul specifies God as the One who promised eternal life "before the beginning of time" (Tit 1:2 NIV). He gives a glimpse here of the Creator God who first set up the seasons, who looked forward and appointed one after another, literally and figuratively, so that each season is an unfolding of a plan divinely ordered from the beginning. Seasons mean that God made earthly time and marked off parts of it according to his wisdom, so that even though we

are limited to living only one moment at a time, we can glimpse and trust the pattern of his sovereign greatness.

See also DRY, DROUGHT; FARMING; HARVEST; ORDER; RAIN; SNOW; SOW, SOWING, SOWER; WEATHER.

SEAT

In Scripture, imagery of the seat focuses on a special role or authority deserving of reverence, along the lines of God's raising the poor to "a seat of honor" (the song of Hannah, 1 Sam 2:8 NRSV). This is epitomized by the single most prominent seat in the Bible—the *mercy seat of the *ark of the covenant (approximately two dozen references).

The institution of monarchy accounts for an important cluster of seat images. *Kings sit upon a designated "seat" or *throne (1 Sam 20:25; 2 Kings 11:19; Acts 12:21). The exemplary court of Solomon that impressed the queen of Sheba so much included "the seating of his officials" at mealtime (1 Kings 10:5 NRSV; 2 Chron 9:4). Solomon's extravagant throne is called a "seat" (1 Kings 10:19; 2 Chron 9:18). The same imagery is applied to God's kingship. God takes a seat "on high" (Ps 7:7; 113:5) as a king "seated" on a heavenly throne (a dozen references in Rev). The exalted Christ is pictured as "seated on the throne of his glory" (Mt 19:28 NRSV) and as "seated at the *right hand" of God (Mt 26:64; Lk 22:69; Eph 1:20; Col 3:1; Heb 8:1; 12:2).

When a person is exalted on a special occasion, the image of the seat often denotes the *honor. Naboth is seated at the head of the assembly when he is set up for false accusation (1 Kings 21:9-12). When Haman is promoted, he is given a "seat above all the officials who were with him" (Esther 3:1 NRSV). When Job recalls his years of prosperity, he remembers taking his "seat in the square" (Job 29:7 NRSV). When the exiled king Jehoiachin is brought out of prison, he is given "a seat above the seats of the other kings who were with him in Babylon" (Jer 52:32 NRSV). Synagogues possessed "best seats" (Mt 23:6; Mk 12:39; Lk 20:46).

Elsewhere "seat" is the designated image for various functions in Hebrew society. Priests thus have a "seat at Jerusalem" (2 Chron 19:8 NRSV), and Eli the priest has a designated seat (1 Sam 1:9; 4:13, 18). The scribes and Pharisees "sit on Moses' seat" (Mt 23:2 NRSV), representing their authority as interpreters of the law. Judges sit on a "judgment seat" (Mt 17:19; Acts 25:6, 17; 26:30), and the same imagery is applied to God as judge (Rom 14:10; 1 Cor 5:10). The personified *Wisdom of Proverbs takes "a seat at the high places of the town" (Prov 9:14 NRSV). Town elders likewise have a "seat" (Prov 31:23). And Psalm 1:1 lauds the person who does not keep the company of sinners, "nor sitteth in the seat of the scornful" (KJV). In biblical idiom where a people takes their "seat" signifies not only their social standing but their character.

See also HONOR; RIGHT, RIGHT HAND; SITTING.

SEAT OF MOSES. *See* PHARISEE.

SECOND COMING

The term *second coming* is not used in the Bible, though it names an event that is important in biblical eschatology. The NT speaks instead of the *return* of Christ sometime at or near the end of human history. Both terms—"second coming" and "return"—build on the motifs of the incarnation (the "first" coming to earth) and *ascension into *heaven (from which Christ will pay a return visit to *earth).

Representations of the second coming in art have generally developed along two lines. The most popular portrays Jesus in his role at the Great *Judgment, following his return. The second has Jesus returning to earth on the *clouds, accompanied by an *army of *angels (*see* Jesus, Images of). This latter image borrows from Jesus' own rendering (cf., e.g., Mk 13:26; 14:62), itself an interpretation of Daniel's vision (Dan 7:13-14). If viewed together, these images would display in one frame the two primary emphases of NT presentations of the second coming—its certainty and suddenness on the one hand, the need for vigilant preparedness on the other.

In the NT the sudden and unexpected nature of Jesus' *return is captured in the image of the *thief who comes in the *night (Mt 24:43; Lk 12:39; 1 Thess 5:2, 4; Rev 3:3; 16:15), the master who returns after a long *journey (Mk 13:34-36; Lk 12:35-38, 42-48) and the *bridegroom who arrives in the middle of the night (Mt 25:1-13). Jesus and his first followers thus employ scenes from everyday life to depict his return.

In these examples darkness plays an obvious role. No doubt this is due both to the tendency to relate *light and *dark by analogy to God and *Satan, respectively (e.g., Acts 26:18; Col 1:13), and to the normal rhythm of life that has us active during the *day and *sleeping during the night (cf. Mk 4:27). While highlighting the abruptness of the second coming, then, these images also underscore the necessity of constant readiness, symbolized in the call to stay awake.

This dual emphasis, surprise and readiness, inspired the biblical writers sometimes to mix (or at least develop) related metaphors. For example, Jesus is coming like a thief, so his followers should keep their clothes on (Rev 16:15). Being clothed in this instance has to do with constant faithfulness in the midst of *suffering, similar to that demonstrated by Jesus in his suffering and death. Paul, on the other hand, can develop the metaphor in the other direction, insisting that Christians, who live in the light, should resist behavior characteristic of the night (e.g., drunkenness, 1 Thess 5:1-8; cf. Rom 13:11-14).

In describing the second coming of Jesus, Paul uses another cluster of images borrowed from the triumph of the *divine warrior. The *trumpet call (1 Cor 15:52; 1 Thess 4:16), for example, is reminiscent of the call to battle, just as the picture of the faithful meeting the Lord in the air (1 Thess 4:17) is drawn from the practice of coming out of the *city to welcome a returning warrior who has been successful in battle. The use of this cluster of images communicates that Jesus is God's agent of *salvation but also defines salvation, in part, as the defeat of Satan (and all that would oppose God's purpose) in cosmic warfare. The book of *Revelation, of course, continues the theme of divine warfare in relation to Jesus' return.

What is telling about Revelation's portrayal of the cosmic struggle, then, is its pervasive portrayal of Jesus as the *Lamb who defeats *evil. This suggests that the overturning of evil at the second coming will not be accomplished by force. Instead evil is overcome then, just as it is now, through faithful service that refuses worldly definitions of power and might. According to Luke, Jesus himself spoke of his return along these lines: the master who returns "will fasten his belt and have [the faithful] sit down to eat, and he will come and serve them" (Lk 12:37 NRSV). Jesus, whose earthly ministry can be characterized as "serving at the table" (Lk 24:24-27), will return to do the same.

Finally, specific images are indelibly part of our picture of the second coming. It is a cosmic event and therefore associated with nature—with images of cataclysmic destruction like the *sun being darkened, the *moon not giving its light and the *stars falling from *heaven (Mt 24:29). Because Christ will *journey from heaven to earth, his coming is associated with the heavens—with arrival on the clouds of heaven (Mt 24:30; Rev 1:7; 14:15) and *descent from heaven (1 Thess 4:15). The universal visibility of the coming is part of the picture (Rev 1:7). And everywhere the second coming is accompanied by the spectacle of people's responses of either *joy or *terror, as we read about all tribes on the earth wailing (Rev 1:7) and people hiding in *caves and among the *rocks of mountains (Lk 23:30; Rev 6:15-17).

See also APOCALYPTIC VISIONS OF THE FUTURE; DESCENT; DIVINE WARRIOR; END TIMES; JESUS, IMAGES OF; JUDGMENT; RETURN.

SECOND EXODUS. *See* EXODUS, SECOND EXODUS.

SEDUCTION

The related terms *seduction, seduce, seducer* and *seductress* provide a composite image of seduction. Seduction images in Scripture portray people being *tempted by someone or something to stray from the course they should follow. The wrong course promises *pleasures and *rewards (physical or spiritual) that are otherwise denied. Closely tied to the image of seduction is indirectness of the appeal. The one seduced is lured along a *path and incrementally turns away from where *loyalty should be placed. People may betray loyalties because of threats, by following the herd or as a simple transaction to gain money or power, but all of these are more deliberate or sudden than the path of seduction. Words used in various versions of the Bible to express the idea of seduction (*entice, beguile, lure, deceive, lead astray*) suggest both its attractive and deceptive aspects.

The Bible portrays people lured into a variety of wrong behaviors, among them the *worship of false *gods (Deut 11:16), illicit *sex (Job 31:9), theft and violence (Prov 1:10), and treason (Judg 16:5). The agents of seduction vary. The *serpent (Gen 3:1), heavenly bodies (Deut 4:19; *see* Sun, Moon and Stars), a *woman (Eccles 7:26), *family members (Deut 13:6), bad company (Prov 1:10-19), the promise of wealth (Job 36:18), false *prophets or *teachers (Ezek 13:10)—all may deceive and lead astray.

The temptation in the *Garden (Gen 3:1-6) indicates the various avenues by which temptation may penetrate the soul. The appeal may be to the senses (the forbidden *fruit is pleasing to the eye) or the *appetites (the fruit looks good for food) or the intellect (the fruit seems desirable for gaining *wisdom). But the chief force effecting this fall is the cunning argument of the serpent. Most often in Scripture it is words—persuasive, deceptive, insinuating words—that are the *weapons of a seducer. Deuteronomy warns that a relative or friend may "secretly entice you, saying, 'Let us go and worship other gods' " (Deut 13:6 NIV). Delilah, a famous temptress in the OT, nags and cajoles until *Samson divulges the secret of his strength. The adulteress of Proverbs seduces her victims with "persuasive words" (Prov 7:21 NIV; *see* Adultery) and "speech . . . smoother than oil" (Prov 5:3 NIV). Ezekiel accuses the false prophets of leading the people astray by "saying, 'Peace,' when there is no peace" (Ezek 13:10 NIV).

Like the OT prophets, the NT epistle writers warn believers against being seduced by false teachers. Through "smooth talk and flattery they [can] deceive the minds of naive people" (Rom 16:18 NIV) and take them "captive through hollow and deceptive philosophy" (Col 2:8 NIV). Peter describes false teachers thus: "They mouth empty, boastful words and, by appealing to the lustful desires of sinful human nature, they entice people who are just escaping from those who live in error" (2 Pet 2:18).

The NT often pictures people being led astray by their own sinful desires, which are personified as a seductive force that works against God's saving grace in the individual. Paul speaks of our old selves being corrupted by "deceitful desires" (Eph 4:22 NIV). James uses imagery of sexual seduction to show how our desires insidiously pull us in the wrong direction: "Each one is tempted when, by his own evil desire, he is dragged away and enticed. Then, after desire has conceived, it gives birth to sin; and sin, when it is full-grown, gives birth to death" (Jas 1:14-15 NIV).

Here James echoes a truth demonstrated all

through the Bible: succumbing to the seduction of sin ultimately leads to disaster.

See also ADULTERY; APPETITE; IDOLATRY; PATH; PLEASURE; REWARD; SEX; TEMPTATION, TEMPTER; WEALTH.

SEED
A seed is a product and a producer, a small investment with large potential value, an essential detail, a step in a continuum of reproduction. Though one, it becomes many through death. It is a treasury, an allotment, an investment whose yield depends on its environment. Having central importance in agriculture, which is common to all nations from Adam, the seed yields fertile imagery for both OT and NT principles and events. At a physical level, the image of seed is preeminently of the potential for life and generation.

Smallness—the Seed as Faith. An important aspect of the seed image is its size. Seeds are small. Their minute size is emphasized when Samson's parents are told that he cannot touch grapes, "not even the seeds" (Num 6:4). The *mustard seed, the smallest of its kind in the Near East, provides the tiny seed image in the NT (Mt 13:31-32; 17:20; Mk 4:31; Lk 17:6). Paul emphasizes size when he contrasts an adult plant to "just a seed" (1 Cor 15:37 NIV).

Value—the Seed as God's Word. A seed is valuable. A chorus of images from both OT and NT carry this nuance. Delight in the fecundity of Eden is registered by seed-bearing plants, full of sustainable promise (Gen 1:11-12, 29). Later, economic systems echo this original value placed on seeds.

Seed, in the plural sense as used both in Hebrew and Greek, was a primary means of barter in ancient cultures that depended on agriculture. Seed has economic value as both *food and future crops. During the *famine in Egypt, Joseph purchased land from desperate families, who were given seed in exchange. The seed, both planted and reserved as food, sustained them, though Pharaoh required one-fifth of it each year (Gen 47:19, 23-24). In a later famine, rising prices are recorded: "the siege lasted so long that . . . a quarter of a cab of seed pods [sold for] five shekels" (2 Kings 6:25). Seed was carefully stored for crops and could, thus gathered, be ruined by contact with *water or the disease of a carcass (Lev 11:37-38). When "shriveled beneath the clods" as in Joel, seeds are an image of financial ruin (Joel 1:17 NIV). In both OT and NT, God is described as a provider, giving "seed for the sower" (Is 55:10 NIV; 2 Cor 9:10). Seed is valued as both product and producer.

Seed is also a measure of weights and thus of value. The Pentateuch records value or size according to seed amounts: fifty shekels of silver equal a homer of barley seed (Lev 27:16); a trench is dug large enough to hold two seahs of seed (1 Kings 18:32). In both its presence and its absence, seed is an image of prosperity (Ezek 17:5; Hag 2:19).

Seed is valued according to its type. When a man's

enemy sows weeds among his *wheat, the man is asked, "Sir, didn't you sow good seed in your field?" (Mt 13:27 NIV). By its *fruit, a seed is judged on a spectrum of value.

Righteous and Wicked Seed and the Seed of Abraham. From Genesis 1 on, seeds are genetically determined, pronounced and absolute in their individual identities. In Eden each *plant bore "fruit with seed according to its kind" (Gen 1:11). It is a repeated law that a field or *vineyard not be planted with two kinds of seed (Lev 19:19; Deut 22:9). Jesus *sows good seed as opposed to the bad seed of the *evil one (Mt 13:37-41). In a metaphor of *resurrection Paul reminds us that "to each kind of seed [God] gives its own body" (1 Cor 15:38 NIV).

The seed image often denotes human lineage or heritage. The "seed" of *Eve and of the *serpent are opposed from the Fall onward (Gen 3:15). The poets and prophets describe races as the "seed of the righteous" (Prov 11:21) or "the seed of the wicked" (Is 1:4). The phrase "the seed of men" refers to a nationality (Dan 2:43 RSV mg). *Remnants from the *exile are called the "holy seed" for Judah (Is 6:13 RSV; Ezra 9:2).

One central figurative use of the seed image involves the "seed" of *David and of *Abraham. Paul refers to Jesus as the "seed of David," a well-established designation in Judaism for the awaited Messiah ("descended from David," Rom 1:3 RSV; cf. 2 Sam 7:16). This designation acknowledges Jesus' Davidic, and thus royal, descent as well as supporting his claim to be the Messiah (Jn 7:42; Acts 13:23; 2 Tim 2:8).

While "seed of David" is a specific reference, "Abraham's seed" refers to the many spiritual descendants of his unusual faith. God promises Abraham that his offspring will inherit the *Promised Land (Gen 12:7), and the Jews rightly consider themselves his seed, having descended from his son Isaac (Lk 1:55; Jn 8:33; Acts 3:25; Rom 9:7; 2 Cor 11:22). However, Paul creates a lucid argument against the law by pointing out that Abraham's descendants were heirs "through the righteousness that comes by faith," not the law (Rom 4:13 NIV). In this distinction he asserts that because Abraham was "credited righteousness" by faith and not by law (Rom 4:24), *Gentiles also descend from Abraham, heirs to God's promise and free from the law (Rom 4:13-18; Gal 3:29).

By discussing Abraham's seed Paul counters those who try to gain *salvation through observing the law (Gal 3:1-19). He argues that because the law was given 430 years after Abraham received God's promise, it is by grace and *faith that humans are credited righteousness. He makes a play on the word *seed*, suggesting that it refers to a single person, Jesus Christ: "the Seed to whom the promise referred" (Gal 3:19 NIV). Paul claims that (1) the promise to Abraham was of the Spirit (*see* Holy Spirit) and not of the law and (2) Jesus' coming brought the Spirit, thereby making Gentiles heirs "through the right-

eousness that comes by faith" (Rom 4:13). He pushes the bounds of genetic determinism past the Israelites, descended through Isaac and Jacob; he defines the seed of Abraham as all who by faith embrace the promise of the Spirit, who enables the obedience by which we are credited righteousness (Rom 4:24).

The genetic determinism of seed is fruitfully applied by metaphor to salvation. Both Peter and John describe freedom from sin as growing from a new type of seed: "For you have been born again, not of perishable seed, but of imperishable, through the living and enduring word of God" (1 Pet 1:23 NIV). "No one who is born of God will continue to sin, because God's seed remains in him; he cannot go on sinning, because he has been born of God" (1 Jn 3:9 NIV).

The Seed as God's Word or as a New Christian. Given their fragile size and potential value, seeds need nurture from their environment; they require protection, preparation and care. In prophetic scenes of safety seeds have abundant water (Num 24:7); in the Promised Land seeds "drink rain from heaven" and do not require irrigation (Deut 11:10-11). While seeds are to be sown in the morning out of caution (Eccles 11:6), God's blessing is indicated by *rain for them (Is 30:23). Praise to God from the nations is likened to seeds nurtured in a garden (Is 61:11).

Jesus' parables of the farmer and seed exemplify the seed's dependence on nurture. One farmer sows seeds on different soil; those sown among *thorns or *rocky places fail to sustain growth, while the good soil produce abundance from the seed (Mt 13:1-8). Jesus illustrates a seed's need for nurture when he explains that in the bad soil, weeds choked some seeds, while others were stolen by *thieves (Mt 13:19-23). He also likens God's word to a seed (Mt 13:23). To warn against false doctrine he tells a story of a field that is vandalized when weeds are sown among the good seeds (Mt 13:24-30); here the seeds represent Christians.

Evangelism as the Seed Process. A seed is transformed by a process called, in lay terms, *growth. Requiring time above all else, the process includes steps for both the plant and the planter: the seed dies, takes *root, sprouts and grows while the planter sows, waters, weeds, waits and reaps. The seed image metaphorically illustrates spiritual principles at all points of the growth process.

The OT images primarily involve the planter's tasks. In a direct image of watering, the ease of growth in the rain-blessed Promised Land is compared to the irrigation required in arid Egypt (Deut 11:10). The waiting required for cultivating seeds prohibits nomadic peoples from sowing seeds or planting vineyards (Jer 35:7). More figurative images pertain to sowing, a duty (Eccles 11:6) and a hardship often accompanied by *tears (Ps 126:6).

The figurative images of the NT draw multiple metaphors from the growth process. The actions of sowing and waiting represent evangelism. Knowing the value of seeds, we wait with the farmers who watch for the return of the large investment they have sown (Mt 13:3, 24; Mk 4:27); thus we learn to protect and cherish the Word and the new Christian lives that are sown as seeds on various ground. We gain a lesson in patience from the story of one farmer who sows his seeds without thought to the soil and has a drastically reduced crop (Mt 13:3-24). Jesus himself is described as the sower of good seed (Mt 13:37), that is, believers and doers of good. Sowing represents the spread of information.

Weeding and reaping follow the sowing stage. Tares that grow among wheat are eventually burned (Mt 13:39-40). Jesus also promises that his *angels will "weed out" those who practice sin, the children of the evil one (Mt 13:38, 41). Reaping metaphors seem aimed directly at eager evangelists. In a lesson on humble service, a man who sows seed sleeps and wakes to find plants sprouted, stem and stalk, all around. It is clear that while he rested, someone nurtured the seeds he had sown (Mk 4:27). Jesus thus describes the place of the Holy Spirit and of other believers in the process of conversion. He reveals the process further by explaining that those who sow the gospel message do not always reap the experience of a soul who accepts Christ's claims (Mt 25:24, 26). In familiar seed terms, Paul reiterates the process: "I planted the seed, Apollos watered it, but God made it grow" (1 Cor 3:6 NIV).

A Sacrificial Investment—the Seed as Discipleship. The image of a seed dying so as to create roots and produce other seeds is crucial among NT metaphors of *discipleship. Jesus clearly links the death of a seed and the roots and sprouts that follow with the death of a believer: "I tell you the truth, unless a kernel of wheat falls to the ground and dies, it remains only a single seed. But if it dies, it produces many seeds" (Jn 12:24 NIV). This image of seed anticipates the physical death of Jesus and of Stephen. It also encompasses a metaphorical death to self that being a disciple and a "fisher of men" requires: "Greater love has no one than this, that he lay down his life for his friends" (Jn 15:13 NIV).

Seed and Judgment. The OT images of seed often concern the crop that will result, as well as the relationships between sowing and reaping and between right living and prosperous *harvests. Because a seed's miraculous growth is a blessing of God (1 Cor 3:6; 9:10), its productivity indicates *judgment or blessing. At times the Israelites are told that their seeds will be ineffective because of their sin (Lev 26:16). Other times blessing is indicated by a seed that has abundant water (Num 24:7) or a seed that grows well (Zech 8:12). Obedience is promised a reward: to "increase your store of seed" (2 Cor 9:10).

Two principles surround the images of sowing seeds. First, sowing must be done carefully. As the parable of the farmer suggests, poor spreading of seeds indicates irresponsibility: sowing seeds by every

stream (Is 32:20), running out of seed in the *barn (Hag 2:19). Second, sowing is proportional: you reap nothing more or less than what you sow. Spiritual "seed" can be sown among people, and the sower can rightly expect a harvest (1 Cor 9:7). Although the sower may not personally gather all that he or she has sown, it will somehow be gathered (Mt 25:24, 26).

See also FARMING; GARDEN; GRAIN; GROW, GROWTH; MUSTARD SEED; PLANTS; ROOT; SOW, SOWING, SOWER.

SELF-CONTROL

Self-control is one of the few characteristics of a godly person that are not directly attributed to God's character, although it is listed in Galatians 5:23 as a *fruit of the Spirit (*see* Holy Spirit), which shows that it comes from God. Lack of self-control is the natural tendency for fallen human beings, as we see when the newly liberated nation of Israel, left to itself while Moses meets with God on Mt. Sinai, quickly turns to idol worship (*see* Idol, Idolatry) and runs wild, making itself a laughingstock to its enemies (Ex 32:25). Because of this tendency, we are continually warned against losing self-control and are called to practice self-discipline (1 Cor 7:5; 1 Thess 5:4-7; 2 Tim 3:2-4).

Self-control leads to *holiness or godliness (Acts 24:25; 1 Thess 5:6,8; 2 Tim 1:7; Tit 2:12; 2 Pet 1: 5-6) and is so crucial for Christ's followers that self-discipline is a requirement for anyone who wishes to be a leader in the church or a mentor for others (1 Tim 3:2; Tit 1:8; 2:2, 5-6; *see* Leadership). To James, practicing self- control is like breaking in an animal: "If anyone is never at fault in what he says, he is a perfect man, able to keep his whole body in check. When we put bits into the mouths of horses to make them obey us, we can turn the whole animal" (Jas 3:2-3 NIV). Paul takes this issue so seriously that he writes, "I beat my body and make it my slave so that after I have preached to others, I myself will not be disqualified for the prize" (1 Cor 9:27 NIV). Again he says,

> But among you there must not be even a hint of sexual immorality, or of any kind of impurity, or of greed, because these are improper for God's holy people. Nor should there be obscenity, foolish talk or coarse joking, which are out of place. . . . Be very careful, then, how you live—not as unwise but as wise, making the most of every opportunity, because the days are evil. Therefore do not be foolish, but understand what the Lord's will is. Do not get drunk on wine, which leads to debauchery. Instead, be filled with the Spirit. Speak to one another with psalms, hymns and spiritual songs. (Eph 5:3-20 NIV)

The contrast between self-control and lack of control is clear. Self-control is holy and pleasing to God.

*Joseph, of course, exemplifies self-control in the OT. Despite Potiphar's wife's constant attempts to *seduce him, Joseph refuses to go to bed with her.

"My master has withheld nothing from me except you, because you are his wife," Joseph tells her. "How then could I do such a wicked thing and sin against God?" (Gen 39:9). He knows the seriousness of the *sin and exercises self-control so faithfully that he even flees from her presence without his cloak (Gen 39:12).

By contrast, the young man of Proverbs 7 appears to have no concept of self-control, or of the consequences of a lack of control. As Proverbs 7:22-23 states, "*All at once* he followed her like an ox going to the slaughter, like a deer stepping into a noose till an arrow pierces his liver, like a bird darting into a snare, little knowing it will cost him his life" (NIV; *see* Trap). Self-control is lost in a moment of impulse and passion, and the cost of such lack of self-control is devastating.

See also HOLINESS; SEDUCTION, SEDUCER; SIN; TEMPTATION, TEMPTER; TONGUE.

SERAPHIM. *See* MYTHICAL ANIMALS.

SERPENT
The human psyche generally finds snakes repulsive, so that encountering one causes a shock to the system. The approximately fifty references in the Bible do nothing to soften the effect. If anything, the Bible gives us added reasons to dislike snakes.

Snakes as the Devil and His Agents. From beginning (Gen 3:1) to end (Rev 20:2) Scripture portrays the devil in the guise of a serpent. The various names for types of snakes also serve as labels for those who do the devil's bidding (Mt 3:7; 12:24; 23:33; Lk 3:7) or those whose words are poison (Ps 140:3). The plots of the wicked are like snake's eggs, inevitably hatching into greater evils (Is 59:5). That snakes haunted the same deserted ruins as *demons and other ominous beasts (scorpions, jackals, owls, ravens) enhanced their association with evil (Is 34:14-15; Mt 12:43; Mk 1:13). (The ancient association between snakes and spirits of divination appears in the *pneuma pythōna*, "Pythonic spirit," of Acts 16:16.) The expectation of power over serpents and poison symbolized for believers the waning influence of the evil one and anticipation of the age of the Christus Victor (Mk 16:18).

Snakes as Beautiful and Crafty. Yet not every biblical reference to snakes is pejorative. From a safe distance the creature's fluid grace inspired admiration (Is 27:1; Jer 46:22) or even expressions of awe (Job 26:13; Prov 30:19).

Other natural attributes of snakes lead to an alternation between positive and negative. The snake is "subtle" or "crafty" (Gen 3:1) or even "wise" (Mt 10:16). Such views probably stem from the hypnotic effect of the animal's sinuous motion. Many cultures believe that snakes hypnotize their prey, because the victim often appears mesmerized during a snake's slow but visible approach, watching until it is too late to escape.

Snakes as Danger and Punishment. In spite of their beguiling beauty, snakes posed a genuine danger. Snakes often struck from *hiding, biting without warning (Gen 49:17). This ever-present danger serves as metaphor of sudden *judgment (Is 14:29; Amos 5:19). The association of snakebite and divine judgment was not a benign literary device but a widely held belief of the general public (Acts 28:3; 1 Cor 10:9).

In an attempt to avoid being bitten, the ancient inhabitants of Palestine charmed snakes (Eccles 10:11). Some conjurors even had the audacity to take on Leviathan (Job 3:8; *see* Mythical Animals). Yet some snakes (deaf adders) proved crafty enough to thwart the murmured spells of the charmer by stopping up their ears (Ps 58:4; Jer 8:17). Such snakes are like the wicked—*evil and deceptive, dishonest from their birth. It is a measure of the serpent's *wisdom that it could not only beguile the first *woman (Gen 3:13) but also outwit the charming wizard, renowned for his wisdom. Believers must display serpentlike wisdom by anticipating and outwitting their attackers and yet remain "as harmless as doves" (Mt 10:16).

Snakes as Life. Along with the snake's paradoxical combination of wisdom and *evil, it represents not only *death but also health and life. Perhaps its ability to administer death seemed to imply authority over life. The image of the serpent in the *wilderness allowed those bitten to "look and live" (Num 21:6-9), just as looking to the Christ gives life instead of sure death (Jn 3:14-15). John invokes the image of the serpent on the *cross even though historically the Israelites had retained it as an *idol called Nehushtan, and it became a cause for *stumbling (2 Kings 18:4). The snake inherits eternal life in the Mesopotamian Gilgamesh Epic. After the hero, Gilgamesh, succeeds in his quest for the Tree of Life, he falls asleep and allows a snake to eat the plant. The snake thus acquires the ability to rejuvenate itself (by shedding its skin) rather than to die.

The ancients believed that snakes craftily acquired their poison by eating "bitter herbs" (*Iliad* 22.93-95). This understanding lies behind the dual use of several words for poison (Hebrew *rō'š* means both "bitter plant" and "venom"; Greek *ios* means both "venom" and "corrosion"). These dual meanings reflect the belief that the snake is an agent of Chaos, a member of the destructive forces that continually attempt to tear apart the fabric of *creation. Against this backdrop, Paul portrays those who would proclaim another Jesus as cunning serpents whose poison will gradually but surely corrupt pure devotion to Christ (2 Cor 11:3).

Snakes as Millennial Signpost. When the proper balance of nature has been restored, the role of the snake will change from an automatic object of dread. Instead the innocent will play without fear "over the hole of the asp," an obvious place of immense danger in this fallen age (Is 11:8 RSV). The serpent will no longer be carnivorous but will "eat" dust (Is 65:25; Mic 7:17).

See also ANIMALS; MYTHICAL ANIMALS; SATAN.

SERVANT

There are many different types of servants and service in Scripture: a personal attendant, such as Gehazi to Elisha (2 Kings 4:12); a *disciple and potential successor, such as Joshua to *Moses or Elisha to Elijah (Ex 24:13; 1 Kings 19:21); a trusted employee, such as *Abraham's servant (Gen 24:2); or those who offer service primarily for their own benefit (Josh 9:8; 2 Sam 15:34; 2 Kings 10:5). Service can be voluntary or involuntary, paid or unpaid, temporary or permanent. The difference between *slave and servant is not as clear in biblical writings as in more modern slavery situations, and not as clear in the OT as in the NT (*see* Slave, Slavery).

What all of the models have in common is the existence of a superior (whether an employer, owner or overseer) to serve and a task of service to complete. Servants are called upon to have an attitude of deference to their superiors, to seek their benefit rather than to be self-seeking and to be obedient and useful. Those served have a responsibility to care for and protect their servants. In the words of Peter's admonition, "Servants, be submissive to your masters with all respect" (1 Pet 2:18 RSV). In general a servant is of low status, though this will vary with the kind of service involved and the status of the particular master. The quality most commended in servants in the Bible is faithfulness (a dozen references), summed up by Paul's comment that "it is required in stewards, that a man be found faithful" (1 Cor 4:2 KJV).

There is thus a fairly easy transfer from the concept of human servant to that of servant of *God. Service of God is expected from all, but because of God's greatness, those who give special service and are considered worthy of the title "Servant of God" or "Servant of the Lord" are particularly revered and given high status. The title becomes appropriate for *kings (2 Kings 19:34), *prophets (1 Kings 14:18; 2 Kings 14:25; Is 20:3) the nation of *Israel (Is 41:8; Ps 136:22) and the Messiah (Is 52:13; Zech 3:8). Service of God involves *justice and righteousness (Is 32:17) as well as *worship, and the Servant of the Lord is the one who particularly portrays those characteristics. In the NT the believer is encouraged to live a life of sacrificial service to God and also to the community (Rom 12:1; Phil 2:17, 30).

But the servant concept is turned on its head because of Jesus. Jesus is Lord (Jn 13:13; Acts 10:36; 1 Cor 12:3), and to be a servant of Christ is to confess him as Lord. Yet also "the Son of man came not to be served but to serve" (Mt 20:28 RSV). This service was not just symbolic; it involved low-status tasks like washing *feet (Jn 13:1-17) and led eventually to his *death. The Master voluntarily puts himself in subjection to his own disciples, and the concept of servant leadership is born.

In the new community initiated by Jesus, leaders are to follow quite different patterns from those normally found in the world. They are not to act toward the community as *fathers, or *teachers or masters, but as servants (Mt 23:8-12). The modern church picks up this concept in theory by using words such as *deacons, ministers* or *pastors* for its leaders. The appropriation of the image of servant for believers also participates in the Bible's grand pattern of reversal of values: by worldly standards servanthood is something ignominious, but in the economics of the kingdom the epithet "servant of the Lord Jesus Christ" becomes an honorific title (Jas 1:1; cf. Col 1:7; 4:7).

See also BONDAGE AND FREEDOM; CALLING, VOCATION; LEADERSHIP; OBEDIENCE; SLAVE, SLAVERY.

SERVANT OF THE LORD. *See* SUFFERING SERVANT.

SEVEN

Of the numbers that carry symbolic meaning in biblical usage, seven is the most important. It is used to signify completeness or totality. Underlying all such use of the number seven lies the seven-day week, which, according to Genesis 1:1—2:3 and Exodus 20:11, belongs to the God-given structure of *creation. God completed his own work of creation in seven *days (Gen 2:2), and seven days constitute a complete cycle of time.

The symbolism of completeness occurs in a wide variety of uses of the number seven. For example, sprinkling the *blood of a sacrifice seven times (Lev 16:14, 19) indicates complete purification. The seven "eyes of the LORD, which range through the whole earth" (Zech 4:10 NRSV), indicate the completeness of God's sight of everything in his creation. When the prophet John sees the *Lamb, an image of Christ, "having seven horns and seven eyes, which are the seven spirits of God sent out into all the earth" (Rev 5:6 NRSV; cf. 1:4; 3:1; 4:5), the seven spirits are the fullness of the divine Spirit (*see* Holy Spirit), going out into the world as the Spirit of Christ with complete power ("seven horns") and complete knowledge and insight ("seven eyes"). The seven heads of the dragon (Rev 12:3) and the beast (Rev 13:1; 17:3, 9-11) represent the totality of Satanic opposition to God and the complete sequence of rulers opposed to God's rule. In Hebrews 1:5-14 a series of seven OT quotations provide a complete demonstration of the point at issue.

Since seven is the number of completeness, a specific series of seven can function as representative of the whole. The seven "signs" in the Gospel of John, the first two of which are numbered (Jn 2:11; 4:54) to encourage the reader to continue to count up to seven (five other events are called "signs": Jn 6:2; 6:14, 26; 9:16; 12:18; 2:18-19), are representative of the "many other signs" Jesus did (Jn 20:30). The seven parables in Matthew 13, the seven churches in Revelation 2—3, the seven characteristics of wisdom in James 3:17 and the seven disciples in John 21:2 are in each case representative of all.

The model provided by the week of six days and a *sabbath means that in a series of seven the seventh is sometimes different from the other six and climactic. The seventh of the seven signs in the Gospel of John is the *death and *resurrection of Jesus (Jn 2:18-19; cf. Jn 20:30), a climax toward which the other six signs, which are miracles of Jesus, point. In the series of seven *seal-openings (Rev 6:1—8:1) and the series of seven *trumpet-blasts (Rev 8:2—11:19), the seventh in each case is a climax set apart from the preceding six. Enoch's special importance is indicated by calling him "seventh" in descent from *Adam (Jude 14).

Sometimes the number *seventy functions like seven. Seventy years are the full human life span (Ps 90:10; Is 23:15). The table of the nations in Genesis 10 lists seventy nations, representing all the nations of the world, and the seventy disciples sent out by Jesus (Lk 10:1) may be symbolically connected with this idea.

If seven represents completeness, seventy-seven represents unrestricted and unsurpassable fullness. Thus, compared with *Cain's sevenfold *vengeance, Lamech's is seventy-sevenfold (Gen 4:24), whereas, conversely, Jesus commands *forgiveness not just seven times but seventy-seven times (Mt 18:21-22). In Luke's genealogy of Jesus he is the seventy-seventh generation of human history (Lk 3:23-38).

Sets of seven are by no means always on the literary surface but need to be detected. The book of Revelation contains seven beatitudes scattered through it (Rev 1:3; 14:13; 16:15; 19:9; 20:6; 22:7, 14). The Gospel of John contains two sets of "I am" sayings of Jesus. One set is of absolute "I am" sayings, in which the simple "I am" is a declaration of divine identity (Jn 4:26; 6:20; 8:24, 28, 58; 13:19; 18:5, 6, 8). The other is of "I am" sayings with predicates (e.g., "I am the bread of life," Jn 6:35; 8:12; 10:7, 9; 10:11, 14; 11:25; 14:6; 15:1, 5). Together they indicate the fullness of Jesus' divine identity and of his saving significance.

See also SABBATH; SEVENTY.

SEVENTY

The number and pattern of seventy occurs in some auspicious places in the biblical story. In the vocabulary of round numbers, seventy avoids the generality of one *hundred and suggests a schematic precision as a tenfold multiple of *seven. Though the significance is not always apparent or consistent, attention to seventy reveals some intriguing dimensions.

The most significant pattern of seventy begins with Genesis 10 and extends to Luke's Gospel. In the numbering of people the correlation between seventy nations and seventy heads of *Israel has long been noted. In Genesis 10 the so-called table of nations lists the seventy nations of Israel's world. Though the numeric total is not pointed out in the text, we are right to count them, for the idea of a fixed "number" of nations (according to the number of the *gods, or "sons of God") appears in Deuteronomy 32:8, and later Judaism obviously stood in a tradition of tallying the nations. This is witnessed in the notion that the Torah had been offered to the nations in seventy languages before it was given to Israel (*m. Sota* 7:5). Within the biblical narrative the one man *Abraham emerges from the midst of these seventy nations, the head of a new people of God's choosing (Gen 12). He in turn, like a new *Adam on the stage of history, becomes a family of seventy that goes down to Egypt (Gen 46:27; Ex 1:5; Deut 10:22; but cf. Acts 7:14). Thus the story of Israel's origins seems intentionally framed by two lists of seventy: the nations of Israel's world (Gen 10) and *Jacob and his descendants in *Egypt (Gen 46). Israel, though distinct in its twelvefold headship, is a microcosm of the world in this seventyfold dimension.

The seventy of Jacob become a multitude in Egypt (Deut 10:22), but they are represented by seventy elders of Israel (Ex 24:1, 9; Ezek 8:11) who are "leaders and officials among the people" (Num 11:16 NIV; cf. the seventy shepherds of Israel, possibly *angels, in *1 Enoch* 89:59-66; 90:22-25). In Exodus 24 these seventy accompany Moses and Aaron, Nadab and Abihu partway up the *mountain (Ex 24:1) to "behold God" and to *eat and *drink in his presence (Ex 24:9). The seventy are privileged above the people of Israel but much less so than *Moses and his priestly entourage. In Numbers 11 the seventy are "known as leaders and officials among the people"; they are called to approach with Moses the Tent of Meeting. When the Spirit that rests on Moses is apportioned out and rests on the seventy, they prophesy (Num 11:16, 24-25).

Within the Pentateuchal narrative the twice-repeated note of Israel's rest stop at Elim, where there were twelve springs and seventy *palm trees, offers a puzzlingly suggestive (perhaps Edenic) correlation (Ex 15:27; Num 33:9). For later Judaism the seventy elders of ancient Israel formed the basis for the seventy(-one) elders who traditionally made up the Jewish council called Sanhedrin (the Mishnah debates the number seventy versus seventy-one on the basis of Moses' being added to the seventy elders and, it seems, on the practical necessity of an odd number to avoid a tie vote in the council; *m. Sanhedrin* 1:6).

Luke's Gospel presents the unique account of Jesus' appointing seventy (some texts read seventy-two, probably reflecting a desire to have the number a sixfold multiple of twelve; see Gen 10 LXX [seventy-two nations]; Josephus *Ant.* 12.2.7 §57) *disciples who, in addition to the Twelve, are sent on a mission. The correspondence between these seventy and the seventy elders of Israel as well as the seventy nations suggests an incipient universal mission to *Gentiles initiated by Jesus. This would fit the thrust of Luke-Acts, with its clear emphasis on the gospel's moving outside the boundaries of Israel. Quite possibly we should understand the mission of the Seventy as the restored and messianic Israel initiating a universal mission that was never discharged by ethnic Israel. The Seventy's combat with *demonic powers, as well as Jesus' corresponding vision of the *fall of Satan (Lk 10:18), suggests a spiritual mission cast in a militaristic mold, with the fall of Satan corresponding with the ouster of the gods of the nations (cf. Deut 32:8; Ps 82).

If, on the one hand, this pattern of seventy among the nations and within Israel bears a plausible narrative logic, several other instances of seventy people, typically offspring of a single father, evade the pattern or stand in uncertain tension.

Jerub-Baal, or Gideon, has seventy sons (Judg 8:30). Abimelech, one of the seventy, puts himself forward as the next leader and persuades the Shechemites to come to his side. The text tells us that Abimelech murdered his seventy brothers, and it betrays a preference for the round number even though seventy minus himself leaves sixty-nine, and less one brother who escapes there are actually sixty-eight (Judg 9:1-5). In Judges 12:13-14 another judge, Abdon, has *forty sons and thirty grandsons (thus seventy "sons" in the biblical sense), who ride on seventy *donkeys.

In fact, the number of those who fall to wrath or *vengeance is frequently seventy. In each case the mark of leadership or military *strength is apparent or suggested. God strikes down seventy men of Beth Shemesh because they "looked into the ark of the LORD" (1 Sam 6:19 NIV). Seventy *thousand (in all likelihood the Hebrew word for "thousand" here designates a military division) from Dan to Beersheba are struck down as a result of David's census of fighting men (2 Sam 24:15; 1 Chron 21:14). Seventy sons of the house of Ahab in Samaria, royal princes all (2 Kings 10:1, 6), are slain by the leading men of the city at Jehu's suggestion (2 Kings 10:6-7), and seventy heads are delivered to Jehu as grisly tokens of their vote for his leadership. The Canaanite king Adoni-Bezek proclaims the scope of his sovereignty in the boast that "seventy kings with their thumbs and big toes cut off have picked up scraps under my table" as the same fate befalls him (Judg 1:7 NIV).

Quite possibly these numbers are merely a conventional round number for a large number of descendants. But from Canaanite texts we learn that the goddess Asherah, or Athirat, had seventy godsons. This echoes the defined number of "gods" already observed in Deuteronomy 32:8, and the correspondence between the divine and human realm suggests a deeper meaning. Perhaps these stories of seventy men bespeak a seventyfold dimension of Israel gone bad and under *judgment.

A sense of either loss or judgment can be associated with seventy segments of time. The Egyptians mourn Jacob's death for seventy days (Gen 50:3), a fitting offering on behalf of the nations. In contrast, we read of *Joseph's *seven days of mourning in the land of Canaan (Gen 50:10). Seventy years mark the expected boundary of a lifetime (Ps 90:10, with eighty the outer limit) or the "span of a king's life"

(Is 23:15 NIV), which is the period Tyre will be "forgotten" in judgment (Is 23:15, 17). And most memorably, seventy years of *exile and judgment will fall upon Israel, a sentence associated with Jeremiah's prophecy (Jer 25:11-12) but echoed in narrative (2 Chron 36:21) and apocalyptic (Dan 9:2; Zech 1:2; 7:5), where it is transformed into Daniel's seventy "sevens," or "weeks" (Dan 9:24). These weeks "are decreed for your people and your holy city to finish transgression, to put an end to sin, to atone for wickedness, to bring in everlasting righteousness, to seal up vision and prophecy and to anoint the most holy" (NIV). The seventyfold duration of judgment moves the story of *salvation for Israel, and thus for the nations, to its climax in the Anointed One.

See also FIFTY; FIVE; FORTY; HUNDRED; NUMBERS IN THE BIBLE; ONE; SEVEN; THOUSAND; THREE, THIRD; TWELVE; TWO.

SEX

The nations that surrounded Israel worshiped not one but many deities. To the ancient Canaanite, Mesopotamian or Egyptian man or woman, the cosmos was run by many gods as well as goddesses. Gods were not only gendered, they were active sexual beings. The great creation epic of the Babylonians, the *Enuma elish*, begins with a theogony, a recital of the generation of the gods, which leads eventually to the story of the creation of the world and human beings:

> When on high no name was given to heaven,
> Nor below was the netherworld called by name,
> Primeval Apsu, their progenitor,
> And matrix-Tiamat, who bore them all,
> Were mingling their waters, together,
> No cane brake was intertwined nor thicket
>   mattered close.
> When no gods at all had been brought forth,
> None called by names, none destinies ordained,
> Then were the gods formed within the[se two].
> Lahmu and Lahamu were brought forth,
> were called by name. (Foster, 354)

In the ancient Near Eastern worldview, the sexual activity of human beings, then, is simply an earthly reflection of what takes place in the divine realm.

The OT, however, presents a radically different theology from that of the surrounding nations. Genesis 1 and 2 announce that *God created the cosmos and the first human beings. There is only one God, and divine sexual activity does not enter into the picture of *creation. As we will see, the Bible uses sexual images to describe God; however, God is clearly neither male nor female. Sexuality is a result of creation, not a quality of the Creator. God creates both male and female "in his image" (Gen 1:27 RSV). Though God is frequently imaged as a male (king, father, warrior), it is not unusual for God to be pictured as a female (mother, Lady Wisdom). God is, nonetheless, no more a male or female than he is a *rock or a *shield (Ps 18:2).

The man and woman that God created, on the

other hand, are sexual. Indeed, immediately after the announcement that God created the male and female in his image, he blesses them and commands them to "be fruitful and increase in number" (Gen 1:28 NIV), a commission that clearly involves sexual activity. Genesis 2 retells the story of creation with a focus on this human pair. God first creates the male, *Adam. However, Adam alone is inadequate. He is lonely. God responds to Adam's loneliness by creating different *animals out of the dust of the ground and calling on Adam to name these animals. The task seems to have as its goal the discovery of a proper companion for the man, but after Adam is finished, still "no suitable helper was found" (Gen 2:20 NIV). After all, Adam is created not only from the dust of the ground as the animals are, but God also breaths life into his nostrils. Someone comparable needs to be created.

God remedies the situation by the creation of the first female, *Eve. The manner of her creation illumines the nature of sexuality. God causes Adam to fall into a deep sleep. Then he takes one of Adam's ribs, and from that rib he creates the woman. That the rib is used rather than something from the head or the foot indicates the equality between the sexes. It also indicates that the woman, like the man, can trace her origin to the combination of dust of the earth and the breath of God. Furthermore, it shows that the man and woman are a "part of each other." They were made for intimacy.

Nowhere is this intimacy more dramatically displayed than in the act of sexual intercourse. Here is a poetic reaffirmation that the man and woman really are "one flesh" (Gen 2:24). The Bible thereby explains how important sexuality is to human nature and the human experience. Accordingly, it is not at all surprising that sex, and in particular sexual intercourse, is a major topic throughout the canon.

To look at the imagery of sexuality properly, we need to explore the Bible from two perspectives: images of sexuality and sex as an image. That is, the biblical authors use the language of imagery to describe the act of sex, and they also use the language of sex to illumine other important relationships, most notably the relationship between God and his people.

Images of Sex. The Bible is not a prudish book, though interpreters through the centuries have exerted great efforts to "de-sex" the Bible (for instance, by adopting an allegorical method for interpreting the Song of Songs). But neither is the Bible pornographic or medical in its description of sexual matters. Often the biblical authors use simile and metaphor to describe the sexual organs or the sexual act.

Sexual organs. Certainly the most sexually explicit of all biblical books on the matter of sexuality is the *Song of Songs. The poet(s) of these passionate love songs often use imagery to refer to the male and female erogenous zones. Space permits only a sample. In a poem descriptive of the woman's beauty and generically identified as a song sung as a prelude to lovemaking (Pope, 55-56, 67, 142, 144), the man likens the woman's *breasts to "twin fawns of a gazelle that browse among the lilies" (Song 4:5 NIV). The image evokes the anticipation of touch. It is an image of gentleness. Later, at the end of a similar descriptive song, the man describes his beloved's body as a slender *palm tree whose clusters of fruit are her breasts. In a moment of passion he cries out, "I will climb the palm tree; I will take hold of its fruit." (Song 7:7-8 NIV). This image is more visual than the first, showing that his romantic intentions are focused on the woman's breasts.

Returning to the first descriptive song, the man's celebration of the woman's body culminates with a long section that dwells lovingly on her "garden":

You are a garden locked up, my sister, my bride;
  you are a spring enclosed, a sealed fountain.
Your plants are an orchard of pomegranates
  with choice fruits,
  with henna and nard,
  nard and saffron,
  calamus and cinnamon,
  with every kind of incense tree,
  with myrrh and aloes
  and all the finest spices.
You are a garden fountain,
  a well of flowing water
  streaming down from Lebanon.
  (Song 4:12-15 NIV)

Elsewhere in the Bible (Prov 5:15-19) as well as in other ancient Near Eastern poems, we see that the watered garden is a metaphor for the woman's vagina. We can even recognize this from the structure of the poem itself as the poet works his way down from the woman's head to the object of his most intense interest.

We will pause to consider one other text in the Song of Songs, a text that indicates that the love of the Song is not without trouble. The story is told from the woman's perspective. She hears the knock of her lover on the *door; however, she is already in *bed for the night, so she perhaps playfully tells him she does not want to rise to open the door. He responds first by trying to gain entry into the house. The NIV translates the crucial passage:

My lover thrust his hand through the latch
  opening;
  my heart began to pound for him.
I arose to open for my lover. (Song 5:4-5)

This language, however, is double entendre, and the English translations, unable to capture it, have emphasized the tame aspects of the language. A translation that emphasizes the other side of the intended meaning of the text would sound something like the following:

My lover thrust his hand through the hole,
  and my vagina was inflamed,
I arose and opened for my lover.

The Song of Songs is rich in sexual imagery. Much of it comes from the man as he describes the woman's sexual beauty and attraction, but there are examples of the woman speaking explicitly about the power of the man's beauty. In the midst of the one descriptive song of the man, the woman says,

His arms are rods of gold
set with chrysolite.
His body is like polished ivory
decorated with sapphires. (Song 5:14 NIV)

Once again the English translations are reticent and here intentionally obscure the more explicit Hebrew text. It is not his body that is like a slab of ivory, but rather his sexual organ, which is like a tusk of ivory.

The Song of Songs thus exemplifies the use of images of sex for romantic and erotic purposes. Elsewhere in the Bible we encounter images as euphemisms. The "feet," for instance, can refer to the penis or the vagina, not only in urinary contexts (1 Sam 24:3) but also in sexual scenes (Ezek 16:25). It is highly likely that the *threshing floor scene between Ruth and Boaz should be added to this list. Her uncovering of Boaz's feet (Ruth 3:4) is best understood as a sexual proposition that is temporarily declined.

Numbers 5 contains the legal procedure for suspicion of adultery. At the direction of the priest the woman drinks a potion that will have no effect if she is innocent, but will result in her "thigh" withering (Num 5:22) if she is guilty. From the earliest times this reference to the thigh was considered to be a euphemism for the vagina (Ashley, 132). See also Genesis 47:29 where it is a reference to the man's sexual organ.

Sexual intercourse. There is no verb in the Bible that means "to have sexual intercourse," rather the idea is conveyed by a series of euphemistic metaphors. The first two are used frequently enough that they may be frozen metaphors. The very common "to know" indicates that to engage in sex entails learning new things about the body and personality of one's partner (cf. Gen 4:1, 17, 25; 1 Sam 1:19). To "lie down" with someone of course hints at one of the most common positions for the sex act (Gen 19:32; 22:19; 38:26; Lev 18:22; Deut 28:30). More colorful expressions include "playing" (Gen 26:8), "plowing" (Judg 14:18) and "grinding grain" (Job 31:10).

Crude metonymy for women as sexual objects appear in Judges 5:30 (the NIV translates "girl," but the Hebrew is coarse slang; cf. Eccles 2:8, where women are referred to as "breasts").

Sex as Image. *God as husband.* God is not a sexual being (see above). As a result, he reveals himself to humanity using both male and female images. For the most part, however, God takes the role of the man in the sexual metaphor. God commands the prophet Hosea to marry "an adulterous wife" (Hos 1:2). In the second chapter Hosea speaks for God when he angrily says:

Rebuke your mother, rebuke her,
for she is not my wife,
and I am not her husband.
Let her remove the adulterous look from her face

and the unfaithfulness from between her
breasts. (Hos 2:2 NIV)

The theme continues in the third chapter when God tells Hosea, "Go, show your love to your wife again, though she is loved by another and is an *adulteress. Love her as the LORD loves the Israelites, though they turn to other gods and love the sacred raisin-cakes" (Hos 3:1 NIV). Throughout these three chapters Israel's spiritual unfaithfulness is likened to sexual unfaithfulness. The assumption is that Israel's relationship to God is like a *marriage relationship, but that they, as his wife, are sleeping with other men, that is, other gods. God demonstrates his great patience and compassion as he takes back his people who have spurned him.

Hosea is the earliest prophet to develop this analogy between sexual intimacy and the divine-human relationship at great length. The image is a natural one since the marriage relationship is the most intimate of all relationships among human beings and the sexual act is a dramatic expression of that unity. The two become one flesh as they engage in sexual relations.

The marriage relationship is also a mutually exclusive relationship. Although one can have multiple *friends, multiple *children, two parents and many business associates, one can have only one spouse. The Bible is very clear in its moral code that the sexual act can only legitimately take place within the context of the marriage relationship. Thus the image of marriage and sex, a relationship that is purely exclusive and allows no rivals, is an ideal image of the relationship between God and his people.

Consequently, when Israel flirts with and embraces false gods, the sin is rightly described as a kind of adultery. Even before Hosea, the Pentateuch, though not developing the metaphor at length, assumes that God and Israel are in a marriage-like relationship and that departures from that relationship evoke God's jealousy (Ex 19:3-6; 20:2-6; 34:14). Such lapses are described as adultery, a perverse sexual relationship (Ex 34:15-16; Lev 17:7).

Other prophets follow Hosea in condemning Israel's spiritual *apostasy by describing it as adultery: Jeremiah (Jer 2:1; 3:6), Isaiah (Is 50:1; 54) but especially Ezekiel, who devotes two long chapters (16 and 23) to charging Israel with religious unfaithfulness by means a graphic description of sexual infidelity.

Ezekiel 16 describes Israel's beginning as a birth (*see* Marriage for comments on Ezek 23). Her parentage was mixed; her father was an Amorite and her mother a Hittite. Her parents abandoned her at birth, but God came across her in the *wilderness, where he cared for her and raised her. The text then speaks of the relationship between God and Israel in unabashedly sexual terms: "Later I passed by, and when I looked at you and saw that you were old enough for love, I spread the corner of my garment over you and covered your nakedness. I gave you my solemn oath and entered into a covenant with you, declares the Sovereign LORD, and you became mine" (Ezek 16:8 NIV).

Though God gave Israel many precious presents of *garments, *jewelry and *food, she used her new prosperity to lure other lovers: "You trusted in your beauty and used your fame to become a prostitute. You lavished your favors on anyone who passed by and your beauty became his" (Ezek 16:15 NIV). Indeed, Israel was worse than a prostitute, since prostitutes at least charged for their sexual favors, while God's people actually paid to sleep with her lovers (Ezek 16:34). Because of these sins, God will punish Israel.

In most places the sexual image is used to make Israel's unfaithfulness to Yahweh graphic and repulsive. However, the image is founded on the assumption that Yahweh and Israel have an intimate sexual relationship.

For this reason the Song of Songs has long been considered a poem that celebrates God's intimate and exclusive relationship with his people. Indeed, the canonical context has been so strong that interpreters through the centuries have overlooked the obvious fact that the text is a celebration of human sexuality. The relationship between the man and the woman in the Song is highly sexual. Nowhere is their marriage explicitly asserted, but it must be assumed given the nature of sexual ethics during the biblical period. Thus the Song of Songs as a whole may be read as a song extolling not only human sexuality but also the close relationship between God and his people.

The sexual theme is continued in the NT, where it is always explicitly associated with marriage. Most notable is the book of Ephesians, where Paul associates the closeness of the marriage relationship with that which exists between Christ and the church. But mention also should be made of Revelation 19:6-8, where the final union between Christ and the church is described as the uniting of a bride and a bridegroom (Rev 19:6-8).

Lady Wisdom and Dame Folly. The book of *Proverbs, while also describing idolatry as a form of illicit sexuality, has an especially interesting development of the sexual metaphor for the relationship between God and his people. We may observe this in the personification of *wisdom and *folly as two women. The addressee of the book of Proverbs, especially notable in the first nine chapters of the book, is a young male. Life is likened to a path, and his parents are instructing him on the best way to live life. They advocate a life of wisdom and a rejection of folly. To make the point explicit, wisdom is personified as a woman:

Long life is in her right hand;
    in her left hand are riches and honor.

Her ways are pleasant ways,
    and all her paths are peace.

She is a tree of life to those who embrace her;
    those who lay hold of her will be blessed.

    (Prov 3:16-18 NIV)

With the last parallelism, the image takes a tasteful sexual turn (see also Prov 4:7-8).

The theme comes to a climax in Proverbs 8 and 9. Proverbs 8, the better known of the two, is quoted in reference to Christ in the NT at least twice (Col 1:15, cf. Mt 11:19), but our focus will be on Proverbs 9, which presents two female figures, Wisdom and Folly. In Proverbs 9 both Wisdom (Prov 9:1-6) and Dame Folly (Prov 9:13-18) are seated by their houses, overlooking the path of life. Both call to the men walking by with the same invitation: "Let all who are simple come in here!" The invitation has sexual overtones. The women want the men to come into their homes and dine with them, sharing moments of intimacy.

Who are these women? Their homes are situated on a hill (Prov 9:3, 14), where only the homes of the gods could be found. Lady Wisdom is clearly the personification of Yahweh's wisdom, which is a metonym for Yahweh himself. Dame Folly stands for all the false gods who seduce Israel into unfaithfulness against their true God. In other words, Proverbs 9 presents a fundamental religious choice to the Israelites through a sexual metaphor: With whom will they join themselves, Yahweh or the gods of the nations?

See also ADULTERY; HUSBAND; LOVE STORY; MAN, IMAGES OF; MARRIAGE; PROSTITUTE; RAPE, SEXUAL VIOLENCE; SONG OF SONGS; WIFE; WOMAN, IMAGES OF.

BIBLIOGRAPHY. T. R. Ashley, *The Book of Numbers* (NICOT; Grand Rapids: Eerdmans, 1993); B. R. Foster, *Before the Muses: An Anthology of Akkadian Literature* (Bethesda, MD: CDL Press, 1993); M. H. Pope, *The Song of Songs* (AB; Garden City, NY: Doubleday, 1977).

SEXUAL VIOLENCE. *See* RAPE, SEXUAL VIOLENCE.

SHADE. *See* SHADOW.

SHADOW

Shadows are never an image for sinister *darkness in the Bible. Rather, in the heat of Palestine, shadows are preeminently an image for *protection or *refuge, especially that which Yahweh provides.

The *wings of Yahweh provide shade to those who seek refuge in him (Ps 17:8), whether a temporary *hiding place (Ps 57:1) or a permanent dwelling (Ps 91:1). The natural basis of this image is depicted in Isaiah 34:15 (cf. Mt 23:37). But the uniqueness of the image to the psalms, with their presumed cultic setting in the *temple, has led some to suggest a connection with the wings of the cherubim. Yet the cherubim are never equated with Yahweh himself. Compare rather the ancient image of Yahweh bearing his people into the wilderness on *eagles' wings (Ex 19:4). Elsewhere one may note the protecting shadow of Yahweh's *hand, under which the "servant of the LORD" finds refuge (Is 49:2; 51:16), and the eschatological *cloud of Yahweh's *glory which will provide shade for restored *Zion (Is 4:5-6; cf. Ex 13:21).

The shadow or shade of a *tree is the customary image for the protection afforded by nations and human rulers. This image often suggests support or sustenance in addition to protection. Assyria was a "cedar in Lebanon" in which all nations once found shade (Ezek 31:3, 6; cf. Dan 4:12 for Babylon, also with the formulaic reference to birds of the air and beasts of the field). Restored Israel will be a poplar in whose shade people dwell (Hos 14:5-7), or a cedar of Lebanon providing shade for every kind of *bird (Ezek 17:23) or, finally, a mustard tree in whose *branches the birds find shade (Mk 4:32). In one of the exalted psalms celebrating divine protection, the image of a tree that protects from sunstroke is combined with a military image of an *armor bearer to produce the picture of God's being "your shade at your right hand" (Ps 121:5 NIV).

In Isaiah 32:2 the princes of restored Zion will provide protecting shade like that of a sheltering *rock in the desert. The shade of a rock, however, is never connected with Yahweh, despite the prevalence of the image of Yahweh as a rock elsewhere. In a very different setting the beloved in Song of Songs 2:3 finds her lover to be an apple tree providing shade for repose.

"Shadow" is sometimes a dead metaphor and simply signifies "protection" or "shelter" (e.g., Eccles 7:12, where "wisdom is a shelter as money is a shelter" [NIV], or the "protection" of a tent in Gen 19:8).

"Shadow of death" (e.g., Ps 23:4 KJV) is a mistranslation going back to the LXX. The Hebrew *salmāwet* is not a compound of "shadow" and "death" but is based on the root *'lm*, meaning "deep darkness." But through the LXX of Isaiah 9:2 "shadow of death" has found its way into the NT (Mt 4:16; Lk 1:79), though it remains an undeveloped image there.

On the basis of the LXX use of *episkiazō* (cf. Ex 40:35 and esp. Ps 91:4), the NT uses the image of "overshadowing" to depict not so much divine protection as a divine presence or power, such as that of the Holy Spirit at the conception of Jesus (Lk 1:35) or the cloud at the transfiguration (Mt 17:5). The popular power of such an image is seen in the effort to find healing power in the shadow of Peter (Acts 5:15).

At other times shadow can be an image of the ephemeral nature of life. Associated especially with "evening" shadows (Ps 102:11; 109:23), the ephemeral nature of life is depicted as a shadow (1 Chron 29:15; Job 8:9; Eccles 6:12). It is uncertain whether the image is based on the nonsubstantial nature of shadows (Job 17:7) or on their transitory nature (Job 14:2; Ps 144:4). See also the sense of lost opportunity suggested by evening shadows in Jeremiah 6:4. Evening shadows may, however, represent the peaceful end of the righteous (Eccles 8:13) or even a time for romantic repose (Song 2:17). The ephemeral nature

of shadows is applied in the NT to the institutions of the Mosaic *covenant (Col 2:17), which are but a shadow of the heavenly realities to come (Heb 8:5; 10:1).

Unique in the Bible is the imagery of unfaithfulness in terms of "shifting shadows" in James 1:17. Here again, however, it is not the darkness of shadows that is evil but their instability.

See also DARKNESS; PROTECTION; REFUGE, RETREAT, SAFE PLACE; SUN, MOON, STARS.

BIBLIOGRAPHY. O. Keel, *The Symbolism of the Biblical World* (New York: Crossroad, 1978) 190-92; D. W. Thomas, "*salmawet* in the Old Testament," *JSS* 7 (1962) 191-200.

SHAKING. *See* TREMBLING, SHAKING, BODILY ANGUISH.

SHAME

Shame correlates with several parallel themes such as *sin, *nakedness, reproach, humiliation and *guilt. It is, however, particularly connected with post-Fall *sexuality and humanity's broken relationship with God and others.

Shame and Relationships. After the Fall, *Adam and *Eve were ashamed to stand before God, whose test of *obedience they had violated (Gen 3:1-24). This is not surprising. But the unaccustomed sense of nakedness and shame they experience toward each other is unanticipated and clearly portrays the devastating effects of sin on the very core of our being. Shame is thus seen objectively as that moral state which exhibits the reprehensible and degrading nature of sin, and subjectively as a psychological or emotional consequence that flows from guilt and sin. The two are necessarily related. To sin and feel no shame aggravates the offense. Thus one of the strongest condemnations Paul can direct against the enemies of the cross of Christ is that they "glory in their shame" (Phil 3:19 RSV). At the same time, to continue to feel shame after sin has been forgiven would be equally inappropriate, since forgiveness removes sinful reproach through the One who endured the cross and despised its shame (Heb 12:2).

The Imposition of Shame. There is a further dimension to shame, for it is not simply something that a person brings upon himself or herself. It can also be imposed on others, and in such a case it invites retribution. For example, Tamar's *rape by Amnon is, as she declares to him before he commits it, shameful, and afterwards leaves her desolate; it also brings Absalom's *vengeance down upon his brother (2 Sam 13:13). Similarly, the humiliation of David's messengers of condolence to Hanun (who have their *beards mutilated and their buttocks exposed) results in David's waging war against the perpetrators (2 Sam 10).

Shame and Judgment. Shame and *judgment are juxtaposed so frequently that "to be put to shame" is recognized as an idiom meaning to come under God's judgment. But there is also a sense in which shame functions as a moral deterrent within the believing community. Thus when Paul cautions the Ephesians against unwholesome speech, he suggests that it is a shame to even speak in public about what evildoers perform in secret (Eph 4:12; *see* Evil). Likewise, when Paul hears of how the Corinthian believers are taking each other to court, he shames them for this disgraceful activity (1 Cor 6:5).

In sum, shame is a serious and destructive consequence of sin but happily, through the gospel, not an irremediable one. Indeed, the great image of shame is the cross, which underscores the horror of sin and the judgment of God but also offers the glory of *forgiveness and *restoration.

See also FORGIVENESS; GUILT; HONOR; NAKED, NAKEDNESS; SIN.

SHATTER. *See* TRIUMPH.

SHAVE, SHAVING

The origins of shaving and coiffure are lost in time, but social distinctions seem to have been associated with *hair quite early. A few descriptions of appearance in antiquity do occur, and as is often the case, what is normal or standard goes unmentioned while the unusual is noted. In ancient Mesopotamia a *slave was required by law to wear a haircut that identified him as a slave. A similar stipulation applied to harlots. In Egypt *priests were called "bald-headed ones," and the written sign for "mourning" consisted of three locks of hair. In both these cultures a commoner's haircut followed from his art. In Israel the average man probably cut his hair regularly; *Absalom did once a year (2 Sam 14:26). The Nazirite stands as the exception to the rule, going without shaving for the duration of his *vow. Yet even for the ordinary person, shaving marked significant events in life, and the state of one's hair served as a sign.

Hair as Symbol. Practices of shaving are rooted in how a culture views hair (with shaving being the lack or removal of hair). In Scripture luxuriant hair serves as a symbol of manliness and an (almost magical) symbol of *strength and virility (*Samson, Judg 16:17, 22; Absalom, 2 Sam 14:25-27). Within the Bible and without, many heroes have been noted for their hair. Hair, even today and certainly in times past, serves as an indication of the condition of the inner spirit (Gen 25:25-27). Revelation notes that the composite beings that come out of the pit have "hair like the hair of women" (Rev 9:8). The description offered there clearly corresponds to drawings of *demons from the period (long, disheveled hair, *lion's teeth, scorpion stings). Similarly, the symptoms of Nebuchadnezzar's illness—hair like *eagles' feathers, nails like talons (Dan 4:33)—coincide with features enumerated for demons in Mesopotamian texts. The association may be due to the lack of personal care and hygiene among the demon-possessed. Although Paul's definition may be debated, he also considered long hair unnatural (1 Cor 11:14).

Shaving as Purity or Cleanliness. By the same logic that required bare *feet (e.g., Ex 3:5; Josh 5:15) or even *nakedness for approaching the sacred, the absence of hair may have indicated that a person was hiding no impurities or uncleanness. Herodotus refers to the shaved heads of Egyptian priests as a hygienic requirement. It was also an effective method of lice control. Genesis expressly notes that *Joseph shaved before coming before Pharaoh (Gen 41:14). The law prescribed shaving as part of ritual diagnosis and cleansing of *leprosy (Lev 13:33; 14:8-9). The Levites were required to shave their entire *body (Num 8:7). The shaving required at the taking of a vow connotes not only purity but also a fresh, clean start (Acts 21:24). A Nazirite must shave if he comes in contact with impurity (Num 6:9). Contact with a woman taken in *war was forbidden until after she had shaved her head and pared her nails, as if they contained impurity (Deut 21:12). In Ezekiel's vision of a new *temple, the sons of Zadok will not shave but will trim their hair, presumably to avoid duplicating the practices of the nations (Ezek 44:20).

Shaving as Humiliation. The evidence for shaving as a form of humiliation is not clear. In the injunction not to sell or enslave the shaved foreign woman "because you have humbled her," the humbling may refer to her status as concubine rather than her temporary *baldness (Deut 21:14). Some Mesopotamian laws did punish false accusations with shaving of half the head. This is reminiscent of the treatment of David's emissaries (1 Chron 19:4). Although David and his messengers certainly considered their treatment an affront, there is evidence that the shaving was part of a ceremony to settle feuds without violence, a submission to ritualized murder rather than actual killing. If so, then David takes offense at being treated as a subordinate rather than with the peer status he was seeking. Isaiah's warning of an impending shaving of the "hair of the legs" (i.e., pubic hair), the head and the *beard may refer to a humiliating ritual of symbolic removal of "male attributes" (Is 7:20).

Shaving as Mourning. Shaving and self-mutilation on behalf of the dead are common in aboriginal societies and are usually explained by the practitioners themselves as an attempt either to propitiate the spirit of the departed or to reassure the spirit that the departed is properly mourned. Such rituals were known to the Israelites and practiced by them, although banned for the sons of Aaron (Lev 21:1, 5). Those who *mourn have "every head bald, every beard cut short and gashes on every hand" (Jer 41:5; 48:37; Is 15:2). Baldness and mourning are inseparable (Is 3:24; Ezek 7:18; 27:31; Amos 8:10). Jeremiah foresees that conditions will deteriorate so far that no one will bother to "cut himself or shave his head" on behalf of the dead (Jer 16:6 NIV).

Shaving as Nakedness and Destitution. If hair serves as a covering (1 Cor 11:15), shaving evokes nakedness. For the Hebrews the razor was a "stripper." While Job shaves to mourn his loss, the naked condition of his head also symbolizes his destitute state: "Naked came I out of my mother's womb, naked I shall return there" (Job 1:21).

Single strands of hair, each one insignificant by itself, together make up a full head of hair. A head of hair serves as a parable for a nation composed of countless, insignificant individuals. The hairs of one's head are so numerous that their true number, like the number of a nation's souls (which should remain uncounted, 2 Sam 24), is known only to God (Ps 40:12; 69:4; Mt 10:30; Lk 12:6-7). The safety of one individual is also likened to a single hair (2 Sam 14:11; Lk 21:18; Acts 27:34).

Yet in spite of their innumerablity, all the hairs of the head can be completely removed. The stark contrast of a newly naked head with its former shagginess serves as a parable for complete destruction and devastation by an *enemy (Is 7:20). Likewise, Ezekiel's audience easily recognized his dramatization of his shorn locks being flayed, burnt and scattered as a metaphor for their own future. His baldness foreshadowed their mourning (Ezek 5:1-12).

See also BALDNESS; BEARD; HAIR.

SHEEP, SHEPHERD

Sheep are the most frequently mentioned *animal in the Bible, with nearly four hundred references if we include references to *flocks. Additionally, the figure of the shepherd receives approximately one hundred references. This prominence grows out of two phenomena—the importance of sheep to the nomadic and agricultural life of the Hebrews, and the qualities of sheep and shepherds that made them particularly apt sources of metaphor for spiritual realities.

Sheep were a central part of the Israelite economy from the earliest days (Gen 4:2). *Abraham, Isaac, *Moses, *David and *Amos were all shepherds (Gen 12:16; 26:14; Ex 3:1; 2 Sam 7:8; Amos 1:1). Shepherds were not always men; shepherdesses include Rebekah (Gen 29:9) and the daughters of Jethro (Ex 2:16). Raised for both *food (*milk and meat) and *wool, sheep were a natural part of life in the arid eastern Mediterranean because they can survive with a minimum of water and *grass and can be moved to new grazing and watering areas during dry times (*see* Pasture). Sheep also figured prominently in the OT sacrificial system.

Conditions of shepherding in ancient Palestine provide the foundation for figurative references. These conditions were very different from most modern practices. Sheep were not fenced in and left to fend for themselves. Instead they were totally dependent on shepherds for protection, grazing, watering, shelter and tending to injuries. In fact, sheep would not survive long without a shepherd. Sheep are not only dependent creatures; they are also singularly unintelligent, prone to wandering and unable to find their way to a sheepfold even when it is within sight.

Sometimes other animals, such as *goats, were mixed with sheep. This situation figures prominently

in at least two biblical passages—Jacob's experiences with Laban's flocks (Gen 30—31) and Jesus' Olivet Discourse, with its picture of the final judgment as a time when God will separate sheep from goats (Mt 25:32-33).

The helplessness of sheep helps to explain the actions and qualities of a good shepherd, who in the Bible is a case study in care and compassion. It was the task of a shepherd to lead sheep from nighttime protection in a sheepfold on safe paths to places of grazing and watering. After morning grazing and watering, sheep typically lie down for several hours at midday in a *shady or cool place (Song 1:7), returning at night to the sheepfold, where the shepherd would attend to fevered or scratched sheep. To protect sheep against predators, shepherds would carry two pieces of equipment, the *"rod and staff" of Psalm 23:4, one of them a clublike weapon and the other the familiar crook used for protection, *rescue and placing across the backs of sheep to count them as they entered the sheepfold (a process known as "the rodding of the sheep"; see Lev 27:32). Psalm 23, built around a typical day in the life of a shepherd, is a virtual handbook of these shepherding practices.

Shepherds were thus providers, *guides, *protectors and constant companions of sheep. They were also figures of *authority and *leadership to the animals under their care. So close is the connection between shepherd and sheep that to this day Middle Eastern shepherds can divide flocks that have mingled at a well or during the night simply by calling their sheep, who follow their shepherd's voice. Shepherds are inseparable from their flocks, and their work is demanding, solitary and sometimes dangerous (Gen 31:38-40; 1 Sam 17:34-35). Shepherds were aided by their sons or daughters (Gen 37:12; 1 Sam 16:11) or hired help (Jn 10:12-13), again placing them in a position of authority and responsibility.

In addition to the economic context of ancient Palestine, biblical references to sheep and shepherds take their place within a huge branch of literature known as pastoral literature. In this tradition the shepherd is an idealized figure of simple virtue and spiritual leadership. The shepherd figure in the pastoral tradition is also frequently a lover (as in the Song of Song) and a poet (as in the case of David, "the sweet psalmist of Israel" [2 Sam 23:1 KJV]). In the pastoral tradition, simply to portray the shepherd's world is to evoke associations of moral innocence and exemplary leadership. We catch glimpses of this pastoral idealizing in the figure of *Abel, the "keeper of sheep" who was also an example of ideal piety (Gen 4:2-4), and the shepherds to whom the nativity was first announced (Lk 2:8).

Building upon these literal facts of sheep and shepherding, biblical writers and Jesus construct an elaborate symbolic and metaphoric framework of references. Four main strands can be distinguished.

Leaders as Shepherds. In keeping with the shepherd's role as leader and provider, biblical pastoral writings often picture civil and religious leaders as shepherds and the people as sheep. In a sense the patriarchs fit the pattern, inasmuch as they were both shepherds by vocation and the progenitors of the nation of Israel. The first decisive example is Moses, who was a shepherd before becoming leader of the Israelites (Ex 2:15—3:1), leading one of the psalmists to speak of God's leading his people "like a flock by the hand of Moses and Aaron" (Ps 77:20 RSV). Moses' successor, Joshua, was likewise designated to lead the people in order "that the congregation of the Lord may not be as sheep which have no shepherd" (Num 27:17 RSV). David is par excellence the shepherd-ruler, the one whom God "took . . . from the sheepfolds . . . to be the shepherd of Jacob his people" and who tended the Israelites "with upright heart . . . and guided them with skillful hand" (Ps 78:70-72 RSV). Although foreign kings were commonly called shepherds, even in the Bible (Is 44:28), biblical writers are reserved in using the image for their own kings. The only Israelite king who is explicitly called a shepherd is David (2 Sam 5:2), though 1 Kings 22:17 may extend the image more generally. Amos is an example of the prophet as shepherd, being a herdsman whom God took "from following the flock" and called him to prophesy to Israel (Amos 7:15 RSV; cf. Amos 1:1). Judges were also called shepherds (2 Sam 7:7).

Ecclesiastical satire—an attack on unworthy religious leaders—has been a common subgenre throughout the pastoral tradition. It is also common in the Bible, where false religious leaders are often denounced as being bad shepherds. In these denunciations it is not always possible to differentiate between civil and priestly leaders. The classic passage is Ezekiel 34, an extended passage of satiric rebuke to selfish and unreliable leaders who have not cared for the people of Israel. From Ezekiel's judgments upon these ignominious shepherds we can deduce that their role was to preserve and care for the people (not exploit them), to strengthen the weak, heal the sick, bind up the crippled and bring back the stray among them, to guide them gently and keep them together (Ezek 34:2-6). Since the unworthy shepherds care more for themselves than for their charges and have plundered them rather than searched for them, God will hold them accountable, remove them from their posts and take away their livelihood (Ezek 34:8-10). Out of this situation comes the promise of a shepherd from the line of David who will genuinely care for the people (Ezek 34:23).

Other OT prophets also use religious satire in the pastoral mode. Jeremiah attacks leaders who have mismanaged their tasks and under whom the people have lost their way (Jer 10:21; 50:6). These false shepherds themselves will be destroyed (Jer 25:34-36; cf. Zech 10:2-3; 11:15-17) and replaced by shepherds of God's choosing (Jer 3:15; 23:1-3). The culmination of this pastoral satire comes with Jesus' exposé of the hireling in his Good Shepherd dis-

course (Jn 10:1-18) and Peter's negative comments about shepherd-elders who exercise their role in greedy and domineering ways (1 Pet 5:2-3).

On the positive side, in the NT the shepherd metaphor is used to delineate how pastors and elders should fill their office. When Jesus restores Peter he uses the imagery of feeding and tending a flock to designate Peter's apostolic and pastoral task (Jn 21:15-17). Elders in the church are encouraged to watch carefully over themselves and the flock entrusted to them and are warned about those who would seek to ravage it (Acts 20:28-29). These elders are also admonished to perform their pastoral task willingly, out of a genuine desire to serve rather than for monetary reward, and to focus on being examples to the flock instead of rulers over it (1 Pet 5:3-4).

The Chosen People as God's Sheep. The word *flock* is sometimes used simply to indicate a group

A cylinder seal depicts a shepherd driving his flock of sheep.

of sheep (Ps 107:41; Ezek 36:37-38). But mostly in the OT it is used implicitly or explicitly of the people of *Israel, especially in the psalms (Ps 28:9; 68:7; 74:1; 79:13: 121:4) but also elsewhere (1 Kings 22:17; Jer 13:17; 50:6). The connection of these sheep with God is frequently implied or stated, as in references to the flock or sheep of God's *hand, *pasture or possession (Ps 95:7; 100:3; Mic 7:14). The main point is that Israel is God's possession and can look to him confidently for guidance, provision and security.

In the NT, *flock* is still used for Israel, described by Jesus as lost (Mt 15:24) as well as weakened and exhausted (Mt 9:36). Mostly, however, it refers to the remnant band of disciples he is gathering (Lk 10:3; Jn 10:1-16). On account of its smallness, Jesus talks of this as his "little" flock. Its members are commanded not to fear on that account, even with the danger of deceptive attacks from within and overt attacks from without (Mt 7:15; 10:16) and the certainty of its undergoing great tribulation in the future (Mk 14:27), because it is God who is giving it the kingdom (Lk 12:32). The image of the flock of sheep is also used of the *church (Acts 20:28-29; 1 Pet 5:2).

The metaphor of people as sheep draws in specific ways on the traits of sheep, which may be negative or positive. As sheep often do, the people are said to have gone astray, each one wandering in the direction he or she chooses (Is 53:6; 1 Pet 2:25). The passivity of sheep and their use in sacrifice make them metaphors of persecution and martyrdom (Ps 44:22; cf. Rom 8:36). In a typical flock of sheep there are domineering sheep who push the weaker sheep away from water and food, who tread the pasture down and foul the water. All of this enters Ezekiel's picture of life in the religious community gone awry (Ezek 34:17-23).

The Divine Shepherding of the Individual. In several places God is spoken of as the shepherd of an individual as well as of the people. This brings an added intimacy to the image. Thus we find God holding a rod over the sheep as they go into the sheepfold, taking note of each one as it passes to ensure that all are safely present (Ezek 20:37). Relevant too are the references to God's carrying *lambs and guiding pregnant ewes (Is 40:11) or seeking the strayed, lost, crippled and weak (Ezek 34:16), all of which speak of special divine consideration being given to those in greatest need. Psalm 23 can be read as David's personal testimony of God's provision in his life, pictured in pastoral terms. God is addressed in the most personal terms as "my shepherd" (Ps 23:1), and the catalog of provisions is both marvelously inclusive and fashioned with loving attention to the literal details of a shepherd's life.

Jesus likewise declares his pastoral concern for individuals among the flock. This is brought home forcefully in the parable of the lost sheep (Mt 18:12-24), in which the shepherd leaves the rest of the flock in order to search for a solitary lost sheep. The depth of the shepherd's concern for the individual is beautifully brought home in the descriptions of his rejoicing when he finds the sheep, his carrying it home on his shoulder and his calling together his friends and neighbors to tell them what has happened. In the parable of the good shepherd this is amplified through reference to Jesus' calling all of the sheep by name and each one of the sheep knowing his voice. He knows the individual members of the flock in the same way the Father knows him, and not only preserves their lives but gives them eternal life (Jn 10:3-5, 10, 14-15, 27-28).

God as Shepherd. One of the most endearing images in the Bible is that of *God as shepherd of his people. The first reference to this is quite early, though its meaning is not developed (Gen 49:24). While in some cases God's role as shepherd is mentioned without further explanation (Ps 79:13; 95:7; 100:3), in others God is presented as guiding (Ps 77:20; 80:1), protecting (Ps 78:52), saving (Ezek 34:22) and gathering (Jer 31:10) the people, as well as leading them out to find proper nourishment (Jer 50:19; Mic 2:12-13). Psalm 23 remains the classic text, with its picture of God as provider, guide and protector. Almost as famous is Isaiah's vision of

God's tender love for the weakest, depicted in terms of the shepherd's lifting the lambs into his arms and carrying them, as well as gently leading those who have yet to give birth (Is 40:11).

Beyond the present unfaithfulness of the people and their leaders, God looks forward to a time when the remnant of Israel, presently scattered, will be gathered again as a flock into a pen where there is safety, and out again through the gate to a place where there is ample provision (Mic 2:12-13). Through all this, God will keep careful watch over his people (Jer 31:10) and care for them (Zech 10:3). Once again the people will multiply, and God will set over them shepherds who will have their best interests at heart and look after them properly (Jer 23:4). Sometimes all this is ascribed purely to God, most notably in Ezekiel 34:11-16.

The Messiah as Shepherd and Lamb. In addition to the generalized picture of God as shepherd of his people, the Bible develops a motif that focuses specifically on the Messiah, as prophesied in the OT and fulfilled in Christ in the NT. Like David, from whom he is descended (2 Sam 5:2; 1 Chron 11:2; Ps 78:7-12), this figure is described in shepherdlike terms. Thus Ezekiel prophesies, "My servant David shall be king over them; and they shall all have one shepherd" (Ezek 37:24 RSV).

In the NT this figure is directly identified as Jesus (Mt 2:6), who parabolically speaks of himself as searching for the lost sheep and bringing it home (Lk 15:4-7) and directly identifies himself as the shepherd of the abandoned and scattered people whom he cares for and gathers (Mt 6:34; 9:36; 15:24; Lk 19:10). In his extended description of the "good shepherd" in the Fourth Gospel, we have the fullest portrait of what is involved in shepherding God's people (Jn 10:3-30). Here we have more than a parable, though less than an allegory: it is an "image field" full of rich figurative possibilities. For the first time there is reference to "other flocks" beside Israel, that is, the Gentiles. The shepherd is no longer a figure in the story but the figure around whom it all revolves. Also new is the reference to the death of the shepherd for the flock.

In a stunning turn of phrase, this death is spoken of as the death of a *lamb, the most vulnerable of the flock. Jesus is not only the sacrificial shepherd but also the sacrificed sheep, and this is why in the last book of the Bible he is described as both lamb and shepherd (Rev 7:17; cf. 14:4). Elsewhere in Revelation he is simply the lamb (Rev 5:6-14; 7:14; 14:1; 19:7). The writer to the Hebrews describes Jesus as "the great shepherd of the sheep" (Heb 13:20 RSV), and Peter attributes to Jesus the title "the Shepherd and Guardian of your souls" (1 Pet 2:25 RSV). Isaiah's vision of the suffering servant pictures him as a lamb led to the slaughter and silent before its hearers (Is 53:7; quoted in Acts 8:32).

Summary. Pastoral literature is one of the most important conventions of literature at every stage of its history. It is also important in the Bible, where the focus is less on lush landscape as an image of pleasure and escape from burdensome reality (though the references to green pastures and still waters in Ps 23:2 and the idealized landscapes of the Song of Songs gesture toward that tradition) and more on the functions performed by a shepherd on behalf of the sheep. Rooted in the sheep-shepherd relationship, the biblical imagery stresses the care and compassion of the divine shepherd and the dependence of people on God to meet all their needs.

See also FARMING; FLOCK; GOAT; LAMB; PASTURE.

BIBLIOGRAPHY. R. Banks, *God the Worker: Journeys into the Mind, Heart and Imagination of God* (Valley Forge, PA: Judson, 1994); J. Beutler and R. T. Fortna, eds., *The Shepherd Discourse of John 10 and Its Context* (New York: Cambridge University Press, 1991).

SHEOL. *See* GRAVE.

SHEPHERD. *See* SHEEP, SHEPHERD.

SHIELD

The shield was an ancient Near Eastern warrior's primary defensive *weapon. Having the right type of shield in *battle could mean the difference between life and death. Shields varied considerably in size and shape from time to time and place to place. Infantrymen without *armor preferred longer shields, while those protected by armor could afford to use a smaller shield that allowed greater mobility. Shield bearers accompanying a warrior into battle usually carried long shields. Shields took various shapes, including the circle, rectangle, triangle and figure eight. Some shields were flat, while others were convex, giving better protection against angular thrusts and arrows. Shields were made from a variety of materials, including metal, wood, leather and braided twigs. Sometimes wood and leather shields were reinforced with metal plates or inlays (see Yadin, 13-15).

Because of its importance in battle, the shield became a metaphor for *protection in both biblical and other ancient Near Eastern literature. For example, in an Assyrian oracle the goddess Ishtar assures King Esarhaddon of her protective presence: "I am your reliable shield" (*ANET*, 605). The OT frequently calls *God a shield when emphasizing his ability to protect his people. Following Abram's military victory over the kings of the East (Gen 14), the Lord appeared to him in a vision and declared, "Do not be afraid, Abram. I am your shield" (Gen 15:1 NRSV). In the conclusion to his *blessing of the tribes, Moses pictured the Lord as Israel's shield and *sword, for he had defeated their enemies (Deut 33:29). The metaphor is especially prominent in Psalms. Like a shield, the Lord protects his people from hostile enemies (Ps 3:3; 5:12; 7:10; 18:2, 30 [par. 2 Sam 22:3, 31]; Ps 28:7; 33:20; 59:11; 115:9-11; 119:114; 144:2). This shieldlike protection is evidence of his faithfulness and enables his people to

be confident, not afraid (Ps 91:4-5; *see* Fear).

Sometimes the shield metaphor appears as a royal idiom, for *kings were responsible for protecting their subjects (Ps 47:9; 84:9 [note the parallelism with "your anointed one," NIV]; 89:18 [note the parallelism with "our king"]). The author of Psalm 84 uses the image in this idiomatic sense when he declares that "the LORD God is a sun and shield" (Ps 84:11). As the just King of the world, the Lord blesses his loyal subjects. (Ancient Near Eastern kings frequently compared themselves to the *sun when speaking of their sovereignty and responsibility to protect their people. For example, Ashur-nasir-apli II of Assyria described himself as one "whose protection spreads like rays of the sun over his land" [see Grayson, 2:184]. Both Hittite kings and Egyptian *pharaohs were addressed as "the sun" because they ruled over vast kingdoms.)

In his role as a mighty warrior-king (*see* Divine Warrior), the Lord himself is depicted as carrying a shield (Ps 35:2). He shatters the shields of his foes (Ps 76:3) and destroys them with *fire (Ps 46:9 NIV—which here follows the reading of the ancient Greek version of the OT). *David pictured God giving him a shield for battle (Ps 18:35 par. 2 Sam 22:36). The image of a deity giving a king special weapons is well attested in ancient Near Eastern art and literature. For example, in an Egyptian text the god Amun says to Ramses III, "I give thee my sword as a shield for thy breast, while I remain the (magical) protection of (thy) body in every fray" (see Edgerton and Wilson, 107).

The shield metaphor is rare in the NT. Paul compares *faith to a shield, for it is able to protect Christians from *satanic attacks, likened to flaming arrows (Eph 6:16).

See also ARMOR; PROTECTION; WEAPONS, HUMAN AND DIVINE.

BIBLIOGRAPHY. W. F. Edgerton and J. A. Wilson, *Historical Records of Ramses III* (Chicago: University of Chicago Press, 1936); A. K. Grayson, *Assyrian Royal Inscriptions* (Wiesbaden: O. Harrassowitz, 1972); Y. Yadin, *The Art of Warfare in Biblical Lands* (London: Weidenfeld and Nicolson, 1963) 13-15, 48, 64-65, 83-84, 295-96.

SHIP, SHIPWRECK

Ship implies a large seagoing vessel, in contrast to a *boat, which is associated with lakes or *rivers. Biblical references to ships confirm that the Israelites were not a seafaring people. In the main they lived inland, and those who did live near the *sea lacked good harbors. The OT imagination exhibits a real fear of the sea, and most of the references to ships show a certain distance from them by describing the shipping of neighboring countries. When Solomon needed to ship *gold, he apparently had to charter Phoenician ships and sailors for the venture (1 Kings 9:26-28). In Psalm 104, after a wealth of minute word-pictures of nature on land, the poet's picture of the ships at sea is laughably vague: "Yonder is the sea, great and wide. . . . There go the ships" (Ps 104:25-26 RSV).

The NT world shows more Greek and Roman influence in its acceptance of travel by ship as a chief means of international travel, and half of the biblical references to ships appear in the NT, but even here the most vivid images are those of shipwreck. In literature generally, the ship is an image of *travel (mobility), safety and the transport of goods (usually with associations of wealth). That is the ideal, and the image of shipwreck (in the Bible as in Shakespeare) is a vivid image of *terror, insecurity and the dashing of financial dreams.

Ships in the ancient world were used to convey a variety of cargoes; they were used by messengers (Ezek 30:9); they conveyed passengers from place to place, including refugees and prisoners (Deut 28:68; Is 43:14; 60:9; Acts 27:1-2). Because of the variety and value of the goods transported, shipping symbolized *abundance and wealth (1 Kings 10:11, 22; Rev 18:11-13) and also the power and *pride that these could bring (Is 2:12-16). The initiative and profit involved in shipborne trading are used to describe the activity of the good *wife, who provides bountifully for her *family (Prov 31:14). The entire economy of a nation like Phoenicia was based on shipping, and its destruction, or the destruction of its harbors, spelled national collapse (Is 23:1-14). Equally, ships themselves could represent the threat of invasion and hostilities (Num 24:24; Dan 11:30, 40). The fact that ships could not approach the future *Jerusalem was, for Isaiah, an indication of its security (Is 33:21-23).

To the biblical landsman, ships and sailing held an element of mystery. Agur singled out "the way of a ship on the high seas" as being one of the four things he could not understand (Prov 30:18-19 RSV). Similarly, James is fascinated by the effectiveness of ships' rudders, in spite of their small size, and makes them an illustration of the power of the tongue (Jas 3:4-5). An enchanting OT picture is that of Solomon's ships that "once every three years . . . used to come bringing gold, silver, ivory, apes, and peacocks" (1 Kings 10:22 RSV; 2 Chron 9:21). It was the hazards of seafaring, however, and the risks involved, that captured the imagination of biblical authors (1 Kings 22:48; Ps 107:23-32; Jon 1:4-16; Acts 27:13-44). The apostle Paul in particular was a frequent victim (2 Cor 11:25). Storm and shipwreck provided vivid pictures of total destruction (Ps 48:7). The nation of Tyre is likened to one of its ships that goes down with all hands, together with its valuable cargo (Ezek 27:1-9, 25-36).

Only two OT stories recount full-fledged sea voyages. Noah's rescue from the *flood occurred in a ship, which is accordingly an image of preservation and reward for obedience. *Jonah's ignominious flight in a ship is an emblem of human disobedience, producing God's judgment in the form of a sea storm and the threat of shipwreck. The ship of Jonah's experience is the dominant one in the OT, where the ship is more likely to be a negative image of human vulnerability than a positive one of secure travel. The sea was to the Hebrew imagination an image of terror, a fearful and threatening world inhabited by monsters of chaos (Ps 74:13-14; Is 27:1) and so inimical to God that he set explicit boundaries to it (Job 28:8-11; Ps 104:9; Jer 5:22). Ships do not fare well in such a threatening realm. Next to the spectacle of the doomed attempt of Jonah's fellow sailors to weather the sea storm, the most vivid OT picture of sea travel occurs in Psalm 107, where we read about those "who went down to the sea in ships" and ended up reeling and staggering like drunken men "at their wits' end" (Ps 107:23-27 RSV).

Even the more positive image of shipping as representing commerce and moneymaking is largely unattractive in the Bible. Three evocative apocalyptic passages use the image of a shipping-based economy to picture humankind ordering its earthly affairs apart from God. In the OT, Isaiah 23 and Ezekiel 27 paint an extended portrait of Tyre as a commercial empire under the impending judgment of God, and the OT epithet "ships of Tarshish" becomes a symbol of human pride resulting from material prosperity. The NT counterpart is the city of Babylon in Revelation 18, a worldwide commercial success that is destroyed by God; "shipmasters and seafaring men, sailors and all whose trade is on the sea" stand far off and cry as they view the smoke of the burning city (Rev 18:17-18 RSV).

In NT times, travel throughout the Roman Empire at certain seasons of the year was frequently quicker and more efficient by ship, and because of that, sea routes became the means for the gospel to travel from place to place (Acts 13:4). Paul's missionary journeys include numerous sea voyages, and Paul himself is indelibly linked in our minds with ships. Both Homer and Virgil tell epic stories of heroes who undertake quests in ships and suffer shipwreck, and in this context the story of Paul's journey to Rome, with its accompanying shipwreck (Acts 27—28), seems very familiar. It is small wonder that Paul turns ship travel to metaphoric use in his epistles. Unstable and immature believers are "tossed back and forth by the waves, and blown here and there by every wind of teaching" (Eph 4:14 NIV), while those who reject conscience "have shipwrecked their faith" (1 Tim 1:19 NIV). By contrast, though, the author of Hebrews pictures those who have hope in God as securely riding out the storms of this life like a well-anchored ship (Heb 6:19).

See also BOAT; ISLAND; JONAH THE PROPHET; SEA; TRAVEL STORY.

SHOE, SANDAL

Wearing shoes or sandals in biblical times, as today, was primarily for protection of the *feet. Many examples of shoes, sandals and soldiers' boots have been recovered from archaeological sites in Bible lands. However, the biblical references to shoes do not focus so much on their primary physical purpose as on other factors associated with them. For example, they were relatively insignificant, inexpensive items (Gen 14:23; Is 5:27; cf. Sir 46:19). Slaves were being sold for the price of a pair of shoes in Amos's day (Amos 2:6; 8:6). John the Baptist considered himself unworthy of even carrying (Mt 3:11) or untying (Mk 1:7; Lk 3:16; Jn 1:27) Jesus' sandals, a task usually reserved for slaves (cf. 1 Sam 25:41; Jn 13:6-7).

For people who often went barefoot, lacing on sandals signified preparation for a task or journey. The instructions for eating the *Passover meal include a stipulation to eat with belt girded, sandals on and *staff in hand (Ex 12:11). Paul also used the imagery of Christians' fitting their feet "with the readiness that comes from the gospel of peace" to speak of their readiness for spiritual *warfare (Eph 6:15 NIV). Jesus told his disciples to take sandals with them when they went out to preach and heal, but little else (Mk 6:9); they were to travel light in order to be ready for anything in the ministry of the gospel. (The parallel passages in Matthew and Luke state that Jesus forbade his disciples taking sandals, but what is probably meant here is the taking of extra footwear, which would encumber them.)

Wearing sandals was a sign that someone was a free person, not a *slave (Lk 15:22). It was even a sign of *beauty (Song 7:1 [MT 7:2]). By contrast, going *barefoot was a sign of mourning (2 Sam 15:30; Ezek 24:17, 23) and a sign of respect for holy ground (Ex 3:5; Josh 5:15; Acts 7:33). It was required of captives and slaves (2 Chron 28:15; Is 20:2).

The taking off of one's sandals was involved in various legal transactions, some of which are not completely understood. The clearest example involved a widow whose brother-in-law refused to fulfill the obligations of levirate marriage; she could publicly remove her sandal and spit in his face as signs of reproach (Deut 25:9-10; cf. Ruth 4:7, 8).

See also BAREFOOT; FOOT.

SHOULDER

In the ancient Near East shoulders were used to bear objects. Clothing was draped over the shoulders, and the priest's ephod hung on his shoulders. People carried large or heavy objects such as water jars on their shoulders (Gen 24:45), and shepherds would carry *lambs draped across their shoulders behind the neck (Lk 15:5). An ox may wear a *yoke on its shoulders to do heavy work, but in cases of *slavery, the yoke is figuratively placed on human shoulders (Is 9:4). Because of this, the shoulder becomes a metaphor for labor; thus when Nebuchadnezzar drove his army in a hard campaign against Tyre, "every head was rubbed bare and every shoulder made raw" (Ezek 29:18 NIV; see also Neh 3:5).

Burden is also associated with the image. Jesus rebukes the Pharisees and the teachers of the law for imposing "heavy loads . . . on men's shoulders" without lifting a finger to help them (Mt 23:4 NIV). The law of God has become a burden, when it should

revive the soul (Ps 19:7-11). Descriptions of captivity and slavery are filled with images of burdened shoulders (Ps 81:6; Is 10:27; 14:25), implying forced submission and hard labor. The yoke, normally reserved for work animals (*see* Animals of the Bible), which captives bore on their shoulders, reveals the kind of treatment slaves were given.

Responsibility is placed on the shoulders as well. Thus when God gives instructions to mount two gemstones on the shoulders of the ephod with the names of the twelve tribes of *Israel engraved on them, he declares that "Aaron is to bear the names on his shoulders as a memorial before the LORD" (Ex 28:11-12 NIV). Aaron is to come before the Lord with the responsibility on his shoulders of caring for Israel. Likewise, Isaiah 9:6 states that "the government will be on his [the Messiah's] shoulders" (NIV), giving him both *authority and responsibility for the nations.

Other shoulder images include working shoulder to shoulder (Zeph 3:9), *rebellious Israel shoving with its shoulder (Ezek 34:21), carrying someone on the shoulders as a token of *honor (Is 49:22) and the indictment that is worn on the shoulder of the accused (Job 31:36). In Ezekiel 12 the prophet enacts the future *exile, carrying what he owns on his own shoulders and predicting the disgrace to come to "the prince in Jerusalem and the whole house of Israel" (Ezek 12:10 NIV).

See also YOKE.

SHOUT

Shouting means different things in different contexts. At a sporting event, shouting is the normal way to express *joy that one's favored team has just scored or contempt at bad officiating. In a grocery store, with soft Muzak gently persuading the customer that all is right with the world, the sound of an angry mother shouting at her defiant two-year-old is unsettling. Spilling from the open window of an apartment building, shouting takes on the uncomfortable character of an episode of *The Honeymooners*—everyone hopes the bark is worse than the bite, but one never knows. In short, all that can be said of shouting is that it is an indicator of strong emotion, and one has to search the context to identify which emotion.

The same is true regarding the Bible's use of this word. Shouting in the Bible can be a shout for joy (Ex 32:17; Judg 16:25; 2 Sam 6:15; 2 Chron 15:28; Ps 20:5; 47:1; 71:23; 81:1; 105:43; Prov 11:10; etc.), a *war cry (Josh 6:5; 1 Sam 17:52; Job 30:5; etc.), an indication of *pride or defiance (1 Sam 17:8-10; 2 Kings 7:11; *see* Rebellion) or a proclamation of something important (Gen 41:43; 1 Kings 1:34, 39; Lk 4:41; Rev 18:2).

Most frequently the shout is a shout of joy directed toward God. God is praised in this way for being Creator (Job 38:7; Ps 95:1) and providing material *blessings (Jer 31:12). But the predominant reason for people to shout in joy to the Lord is his *salvation, particularly in the context of warfare (Ps 20:6; Zeph 3:14; Zech 2:14).

See also BATTLE STORIES; JOY; TRUMPET; VOICE.

SHOWBREAD. *See* BREAD.

SHREWISH WIFE. *See* DOMINEERING MOTHER, WIFE.

SHUT, CLOSE

In the Bible, to shut or close is primarily to exercise power. Although God has the ultimate authority to shut and close things, human beings in their exercise of free will are also said to shut out the word of God from their own understanding. Thus shutting or closing is chiefly the site of a battle between divine and human wills.

At a literal level the imagery of shutting chiefly pictures the act of *protecting something inside an enclosure from an outside threat. Thus God shuts the *door of the *ark (Gen 6:16), Lot shuts the door of his *house when the men of *Sodom threaten to seize his angelic visitors (Gen 19:10), and people threatened by invasion shut themselves in their houses for protection (Is 24:10; 26:20). In addition to domestic scenes of shutting the doors of houses, the imagery appears in military situations, where people in besieged towns shut the door or *gate of a tower or city *wall (Josh 6:1; Judg 9:51). Even if there is no physical door or gate to shut, exclusion from a community is pictured by the imagery of being shut out, as Miriam is shut out of the camp during her period of *leprosy (Num 12:14-15).

The imagery of shutting is ambivalent in these contexts. While shutting brings safety to those behind the closed door or gate, the outside threat also makes the people inside *prisoners to their own house or refuge. Accordingly, for a gate to be no longer shut assumes overtones of a glorious liberation. In the millennial *kingdom, Isaiah predicts, "your gates shall always be open; day and night they shall not be shut, so that nations shall bring you their wealth" (Is 60:11 NRSV). Revelation has a similar prediction, declaring of New Jerusalem, "Its gates will never be shut by day—and there will be no night there" (Rev 21:25 NRSV).

The primary use of shutting or closing is seen in God's sovereign and ultimate authority to shut or close what he wishes. When God speaks to the church in Philadelphia, he describes himself as "the holy one, the true one, who has the key of David, who opens and no one will shut, who shuts and no one opens" (Rev 3:7 NRSV). Such ultimate authority is seen in several places throughout the Bible. God uses this power in giving power to rulers on the earth, as when he declares that he will open doors for Cyrus's conquest of the known world, so that "the gates shall not be closed" (Is 45:1 NRSV).

God's sovereignty in closing and shutting also appears in his protection of his people. When creating the world, God "shut in the sea with doors" to keep them from overwhelming the earth (Job 38:8 NRSV). He delivered Daniel from being devoured in the *lions' den by sending his angel to "shut the lions' mouths" (Dan 6:22 NRSV). In the OT, God is also viewed as protecting his people by preventing what was hurting them from closing in upon them. The psalmist begs God not to let "the Pit close its mouth over me" and to prevent his enemies from closing in on him (Ps 69:15 NRSV; 88:17). Here shutting is an image of protection or deliverance.

But the same imagery can imply *judgment, as shutting becomes withholding. God is capable of preventing childbearing, as seen when he "closed fast all the wombs of the house of Abimelech" because the already-married Sarah was living in Abimelech's house as his wife (Gen 20:18 NRSV). Similarly, God closed Hannah's womb until she was able to bear Samuel (1 Sam 1:5). He also "shut up the heavens" to prevent *rain when his people had disobeyed. He promised to do this in Deuteronomy 11:17, and he actually did so many times throughout the OT in response to Israel's unfaithfulness.

Finally, God ultimately is able to shut people in as a means of punishment for their deeds. When Korah, Dathan and Abiram *rebelled against Moses and Aaron, God caused the earth to close over their families and bring them directly to Sheol (Num 16:33). When Job was suffering and felt that God was against him, he moaned, "God has put me in the wrong, and closed his net around me" (Job 19:6 NRSV). Isaiah prophesies that in the end times God will shut up all the kings of the earth for punishment (Is 24:22). Finally, Jesus warned people to repent before God closes the doors of *heaven and it is too late for them to be saved (Mt 25:10; Lk 13:25).

The imagery of shutting is also given a human application when people are pictured as closing themselves to God. On an external, literal level, Ahaz shut up the doors of the *temple when instituting idol worship (2 Chron 28:24). Psalm 17:10 speaks of evil persons who "close their hearts to pity" (NRSV), and Proverbs warns that those who "close [their] ear to the cry of the poor" will receive no mercy themselves (Prov 21:13 NRSV). More important, God condemns his people, saying, "This people's heart has grown dull, and their ears are hard of hearing, and they have shut their eyes," thus refusing to hear and see and "understand with their heart" that God could heal them of their sins (Mt 13:15 NRSV, quoting Is 6:10).

Yet even in human stubbornness God is sovereign. Not only does he know what these people have done in secret—what they have whispered behind closed doors—but he also takes part in closing their minds to understanding him (Job 17:4; Mt 6:6; Lk 13:25). He declares in Isaiah that because people have not heeded him, he will close their eyes that they may not understand him (Is 29:10; 44:18). His sovereignty can also work in the reverse direction. In Revelation, God declares to the church in Philadelphia that because they have remained faithful, he has "set before [them] an open door, which no one is able to shut" (Rev 3:8 NRSV). This open door is an invitation into heaven. Thus even though people have the free will to ignore God, God is ultimately sovereign even in their denial of him.

See also DOOR; GATE; HOME, HOUSE; OUTER, OUTSIDE; PROTECTION; WALL.

SIBLING RIVALRY

Sibling rivalry is competition between two siblings for parental favor or *blessing and for the power and wealth that this favor entails. In OT history, where the history of tribes or even nations is often traceable back to sibling progenitors, sibling rivalry can be extended to a tribal (Judg 20—21; 1 Kings 12) or national level (Amos 1:11; Obad 10). The presence of sibling rivals in the Bible attests its common humanity, for it is a rare family in which siblings do not at certain stages compete with each other as antagonists.

*Cain and *Abel are the prototypical sibling rivals in the Bible (Gen 4:1-16). The unusual feature of their story is that the *brothers are in competition (at least as perceived by Cain, whose sacrifice God rejects while accepting Abel's) for the favor of a heavenly *Father rather than an earthly one. This story of fratricide is not only the original story of sibling rivalry but also shows its effect in the most extreme form possible—the *murder of the rival. God's judgment is resolutely set against such *sin. The story also exemplifies two important qualities of subsequent stories of sibling rivalry. One is that sibling rivalry is a manifestation of human sinfulness, such as jealousy (Gen 30:1; 37:11; Num 12), sexual misconduct (2 Sam 13) or lust for power (Judg 9:1-6). Additionally and ironically, sibling rivalry in the Bible sometimes results from God's blessing on one sibling over the other.

The most concentrated story of sibling rivalry in the Bible is that of *Jacob and *Esau, whose entire lives in the parental home seem dominated by rivalry. Opposites in temperament and ability (Gen 25:27) and each favored by one of their parents (Gen 25:28), the twins are contentious already in the *womb of their mother (Gen 25:22). To some degree they are pawns in their parents' rivalry with each other. They are rivals for the family *birthright and the father's blessing on the elder son as well as for the ongoing favor of their parents in day-to-day living. Theirs is an extended story of competition, intrigue, deception, hatred and intended murder, finally resolved by Esau's forgiving spirit in a memorable reunion and reconciliation scene (Gen 33:1-11).

*Genesis, being a book about families, is the biblical book most filled with stories of sibling rivalry. Rachel and Leah vie for the favor of their shared husband, Jacob, with childbearing being their chief weapon (Gen 23—20). Jacob's children by Leah resent Joseph and Benjamin, sons of Rachel. *Abraham's adopted son Ishmael runs afoul of Sarah's concern for the interests of her son Isaac (Gen 21:8-14; cf. also Gen 25:5-6).

The account of *Joseph and his brothers is the most extended story of sibling rivalry in Genesis. Favored by the father of the family and singled out by dream as the son of destiny, Joseph is envied and despised by his brothers. For unmitigated hatred, it is impossible to surpass this story of ten brothers ganging up on a helpless younger brother. Joseph is one of numerous younger brothers in the OT who are favored by God over the elder, resulting in tensions between them. Examples include Isaac/Ishmael, Jacob/Esau, Joseph/Reuben, Zerah/Perez, Moses/Aaron, David/Eliab and Solomon/Adonijah. The story of Joseph and his brothers also illustrates particularly well the ability of God to use sibling hatred for his redemptive purposes (Gen 45:5-8; 50:20). Thus the genre of sibling rivalry shows how God often overturns the natural order of birth to effect his divine purposes, even though at a human level we observe the spectacle of wasted opportunity for goodwill and cooperation among family members.

The biblical record of *David's life also furnishes examples of sibling rivalry. The story of David's arrival on the battlefield, where he is disparaged by his oldest brother, has sibling rivalry written all over it (1 Sam 17:24-29). David's sons, Solomon, Absalom and Adonijah, are cutthroat competitors for the throne, though it is already reserved for Solomon (1 Kings 1:5-53).

Three NT stories of sibling rivalry round out the biblical canon of the archetype. Mary and Martha become antagonists as they pursue different avenues for gaining the approval of Jesus (Lk 10:38-42). In Jesus' parable of the *prodigal son and churlish elder brother, we see a heightened contrast between adventurous youthfulness and dutiful maturity, unable to be reconciled even when encouraged by the model of a father who goes out to both brothers (Lk 15:11-32). This parable echoes the antagonism between Jacob and Esau for an inheritance, as well as OT stories in which brothers persist in hostility even though God's blessing is assured to both of them. Finally, the disciples argue like siblings, wondering who will be greatest in the kingdom (Lk 9:46-48). At root, sibling rivalry is a form of self-interest—a desire for power or privilege over someone else.

Lest we begin to think that sibling rivalry is the norm for life, the Bible provides glimpses of a foil—sibling unity. Psalm 133 asserts the loveliness of sibling unity and the blessing that accompanies it: "Behold, how good and pleasant it is when brothers dwell in unity!" (Ps 133:1). We find similar pictures in the law (Lev 18:18; Deut 15:9; 19:18) and wisdom literature (Prov 17:17; 18:19).

See also ABEL; CAIN; ELDER CHILD, ELDER SIBLING; ESAU; FAMILY; JACOB; JOSEPH THE PATRIARCH; YOUNGER CHILD, YOUNGER SIBLING.

SIGH, SIGHING

If *joy and *singing are the principal modes of

human expression in *heaven, then sighing and crying are their counterparts here on *earth. This may seem like an overly pessimistic view of things, but nothing is made more clear to us in Scripture than the fact that something tragic happened in Eden and that the appropriate human response is the sigh or groan (see Creation; Garden). The prophet Isaiah draws the comparison for us; "The ransomed of the LORD will return. They will enter Zion with singing; everlasting joy will crown their heads. Gladness and joy will overtake them, and sorrow and sighing will flee away" (Is 51:11 NIV). Paul puts it this way in the NT: "Meanwhile we groan, longing to be clothed with our heavenly dwelling" (2 Cor 5:2 NIV). Groaning is, therefore, a profound human experience.

One of the first places in Scripture the word *groan* is encountered is Exodus 2:23: "The Israelites groaned in their slavery and cried out, and their cry for help because of their slavery went up to God" (NIV). Those of us who live in a democracy resonate deeply with the Israelites, because we have tasted, and therefore appreciate, some measure of personal freedom—sometimes to a fault. Yet the Bible repeatedly makes the case for a deeper, more fundamental form of *slavery that affects each human person regardless of the form of government or current social institution that happens to be in force during their lifetime. The words of Christ bear this out. Responding to the Pharisees' arrogant claim to freedom, Jesus retorted, "I tell you the truth, everyone who sins is a slave to sin" (Jn 8:34 NIV). *Sin is the great slave master, and we are born under its tyranny. When this fact becomes clear to us, whether through revelation or tragedy, we respond with deep, soul-wrenching groans.

It is a perversion of Scripture to demand that humans *suffering the consequences of the Fall are to somehow bear up under it with a resolute grin-turned-grimace. The books of the Bible, all of which deal frankly with human suffering, know of no such stoicism. *Job was not ashamed or afraid to express his *grief to God (Job 3:24) and complained bitterly about his perception of divine indifference (Job 23:2; 24:12). The psalms, which beautifully reflect the full range of human emotion, are full of references to sighing and groaning (cf. Ps 5:1; 6:6; 12:5; 22:1; 31:10; 32:3; 38:8-9; 77:3; 79:11; 90:9; 102:5, 20). And the Gospel of Mark reports that the incarnate Lord himself, drinking deeply from his humanity, sighed on two occasions: first when he healed the deaf and mute man in the region of the Decapolis (Mk 7:34), and second as he responded to the Pharisees' cynicism near Dalmanutha (Mk 8:11-12). Our Lord experienced the frustration of being human between the Fall and the coming redemption, and his sighs reflect this.

Fortunately for us, however, our God is compassionate and responds to our groanings with kindness, and in this we have *hope even as we sigh. Returning to the book of Exodus, we read that "God heard their groaning and he remembered his covenant with Abraham, with Isaac and with Jacob" (Ex 2:24 NIV). Likewise, during the years of the judges, God repeatedly had compassion on his people as they languished under one enemy after another (Judg 2:18). Even the psalmist, who is not afraid to ask God if his *ears are stopped up (cf. Ps 22:1), is also ready to assert, " 'Because of the oppression of the weak and the groaning of the needy, I will now arise,' says the LORD. 'I will protect them from those who malign them' " (Ps 12:5 NIV).

The apostle Paul summarizes both aspects of groaning, its relevance and its resolution, at the end of Romans 8. In Romans 7 he had almost come to despair when considering the power that sin seemed to have over him, but now he exults in the hope that is ours in Christ: "We know that the whole creation has been groaning as in the pains of childbirth. . . . Not only so, but we ourselves . . . groan inwardly as we wait eagerly for our adoption as sons, the redemption of our bodies. For in this hope we were saved. But hope that is seen is no hope at all. Who hopes for what he already has? But if we hope for what we do not yet have, we wait for it patiently" (Rom 8:22-25 NIV). For Paul, groaning and hope are two sides of the same coin. If we do not groan, then hope is meaningless to us. He continues with the intriguing statement that "in the same way, the Spirit helps us in our weakness. We do not know what we ought to pray for, but the Spirit himself intercedes for us with groans that words cannot express" (Rom 8:26 NIV). Whatever it means for the Spirit of God (see Holy Spirit) to groan, it surely indicates that he standing beside us and bearing our *sorrows up to heaven. The Spirit's groaning is the ultimate sign from Christ that "surely I am with you always, to the very end of the age" (Mt 28:20 NIV).

See also BREATH; GRIEF; HOPE; SORROW; SUFFERING.

SIGHT. *See* EYE, SIGHT.

SIGNET. *See* RING; SEAL.

SILENCE

Silence communicates. It is a basic feature of human relationships, for we must often interpret the silence of others. And by its very nature silence can express a wide variety of things. Usually it is not hard to interpret—the rebellious sullenness of a child, the hush as the school principal or head teacher enters. But sometimes silence *is* hard to interpret.

It is not surprising, therefore, that silence in the Bible expresses a wide range of emotions, attitudes and states: attentiveness (Deut 27:9; Job 33:31; Acts 19:33), restraint (1 Sam 10:27; Ps 50:12; Jer 4:19), respect and awe (Job 29:21; Hab 2:20), *loyalty (Is 36:21), deep thought (Acts 15:12), acceptance of *guilt (Job 13:19; Rom 3:19), *rest after tumult or *suffering (Ps 46:10; Mk 4:39), fear of saying something wrong (Ps 39:2), even *wisdom (Job 13:5; Prov 17:28); more negatively, it can express faithlessness (Esther 4:14), *fear (Job 31:34; Acts 18:9), deep *pain (Job 2:13; Lam 2:10), rebellion (Ps 32:2; Mk 3:4), defeat or destruction (Ps 101:5; 143:12; Is 47:5), and supremely *death (Ps 31:17-18; 94:17; 115:17). Significantly, there is one Hebrew verb (used, e.g., in Ps 18:40, 101:5; Lam 3:53) that means both "to destroy" and "to keep silent."

The biblical writers also occasionally exploit the "openness" of silence—for instance, Aaron's silence in Leviticus 10:3 (grief? rebellion? submission?), the silence of *God (Ps 44:23; 83:1), the silence of *Jesus at his trial (Mk 14:61; cf. Is 53:7) or the silence in *heaven in Revelation 8:1. Also worth mentioning here are significant absences of speech where we might expect something (for instance, from Nicodemus after Jn 3:21). In all these cases, we the readers have to supply the meaning of the silence, which acts as a metaphor or parable.

See also EAR, HEARING; VOICE.

SILK

Most English translations of the Bible use the word *silk* only once—in a catalog of the worldwide mercantile goods traded by Babylon in Revelation 18:12. The RSV adds two more references (Ezek 16:10, 13). The closely related term "fine linen" appears more than five dozen times.

The associations of fine *linen and silk are clear from Ezekiel 16:13 (RSV): "Thus you were decked with gold and silver; and your raiment was of fine linen, and silk, and embroidered cloth." The *cloth in view is rare and luxurious—a "value" image. As such, it is also an image of royalty and power (e.g., Gen 41:42).

See also CLOTH; GARMENTS; LINEN.

SILVER

Mentioned nearly three hundred times in the Bible, silver is, next to *gold, the Bible's leading "value" image. Signifying both currency and *treasure, silver is a natural symbol for wealth and for what is precious. It also pictures a process of refinement that results in something pure. Often the word occurs along with *gold* to signify great wealth (more than five dozen references). References to silver can be either positive or negative, depending on the attitude with which those who deal with the silver have used it. In all cases, silver is considered beautiful and rare and as such valuable, but the Bible's distinction between true and false notions of value is relentless.

In the literal sense, silver was used in the ancient Near East both as currency and as an expensive material for making *jewelry and decorations in buildings. Beginning in Genesis, Abraham was blessed with a great deal of silver, gold and livestock; he used silvery as currency in his dealings with merchants and rulers (Gen 13:2). God commanded the Israelites to plunder their neighbors' silver and gold as they left Egypt (Ex 11:2). Thus from the very beginning of the nation of Israel, God blessed his people with wealth. Throughout the Bible, though,

silver as a symbol of wealth became a stumbling block for the Israelites, and the kings' use of silver became a fairly accurate indicator of the state of their hearts and their spiritual position before God.

Silver as an image of *temptation appears as early as the story of Joseph, when his brothers sell him to the Midianite traders for twenty pieces of silver (Gen 37:28). Later Joseph ironically shows his brothers their sin by placing a silver *cup in Benjamin's satchel and accusing them of stealing it (Gen 44:2). God understood the danger of the gold and silver with which he hoped to bless Israel and therefore warned them repeatedly against becoming ensnared by it. In his eyes the lust for wealth and the making of graven images were inextricably related (*see* Idol). As the children of Israel left Egypt, he commanded, "You shall not make gods of silver alongside me" (Ex 20:23 NRSV). When the nation entered the Promised Land, God commanded them to burn all idols, saying, "Do not covet the silver or gold that is on them and take it for yourself, because you could be ensnared by it" (Deut 7:25 NRSV). Likewise, he forbade the king to acquire for himself gold or silver in great quantity (Deut 17:17).

In the OT both good and bad uses were made of silver, and how a leader used his silver was an indication of the state of his *heart before God. The *tabernacle was constructed using silver as decoration, and later Joshua placed all the silver and gold from his conquests into the treasury of the Lord (Ex 26:19; Josh 6:19). However, during these conquests Achan committed the first sin involving spoils of war: instead of donating them to God or burning them, he stole silver and other plunder and hid them in his *tent, for which God punished him by commanding that he, his family and the plunder be stoned and then burned. Achan's sin was not an isolated event, for by the time of the judges Israel was already making molten images of silver idols (Judg 17:4). Such incidents were to mar Israel's history as long as it was a nation.

For a short period under David's reign, silver was used properly. David placed all the silver from his conquests in the temple treasury, saving it for the building of the temple under his son's reign (1 Kings 7:51). For his faithfulness and that of Solomon in building so lavish a temple, God rewarded *Solomon with riches. During Solomon's reign "the king made silver as common in Jerusalem as stones" (1 Kings 10:27 NRSV), and all his drinking vessels were of gold, "none were of silver—it was not considered as anything in the days of Solomon" (1 Kings 10:21 NRSV). However, silver was used wickedly under later kings such as Omri, who "did more evil than all who were before him" (1 Kings 16:25 NRSV), using silver to buy land to build Samaria, a city he dedicated to idolatry. Ahaz, another evil king, used the silver and gold from the house of the Lord to pay tribute to the king of Assyria, who was threatening to invade Israel because Israel had displeased God (2 Kings 16:8).

Because Israel was so disobedient in its use of wealth, God prophesied that he would take that wealth away. Ezekiel predicted that Israel would "fling their silver into the streets" because "their silver and gold cannot save them on the day of the wrath of the LORD," wrath that comes because this silver "was the stumbling block of their iniquity . . . in which they took pride" and out of which "they made their abominable images" (Ezek 7:19-20 NRSV). The Lord also criticized his people for a lack of thankfulness, saying that Israel "did not know that it was I who gave her the grain, the wine, and the oil, and who lavished upon her silver and gold that they used for Baal" (Hos 2:8 NRSV).

Examples of greed and foolishness with money also appear in the NT. Most notably, Judas agreed to betray Jesus for thirty pieces of silver—an act of which he later repented by throwing the silver on the temple floor (Mt 26:15; 27:5). Likewise, Ananias and Sapphira sold a piece of property, giving part of the money to the church with the claim that it was the full amount (Acts 5:1-11). For their sin God struck them dead before all the people as a warning. In keeping with this forbidding of greed, James warns rich believers not to keep their silver for themselves and in so doing rob their laborers, for if they hoard their wealth they will be deprived of eternal reward (Jas 5:3). Thus both OT and NT contain examples of how silver can ensnare human hearts.

The Bible also frequently uses the smelting of silver as a metaphor for the *purification of people's hearts through trial. God condemns Israel because its "silver has become dross" (Is 1:22 NRSV). As a result, God refines her "in the furnace of adversity" (Is 48:10 NRSV). Jeremiah is far less hopeful about the results of the refining process. He declares, "In vain the refining goes on, for the wicked are not removed. They are called 'rejected silver,' for the LORD has rejected them" (Jer 6:29-30 NRSV). The NT speaks in similar terms of the refining fire that will reveal the deeds of the righteous in the end times. On the foundation of Jesus Christ the builder builds with "gold, silver, precious, stones, wood, hay, straw. . . . If the work is burned up, the builder will suffer loss; the builder will be saved, but only as through fire" (1 Cor 3:12, 15 NRSV). Second Timothy 2:20-21 declares that every church contains both righteous and unrighteous believers (utensils of gold and silver and of wood and clay), but "all who cleanse themselves" of sin can become utensils of silver, "ready for every good work" (NRSV). God thus represents his people as silver that must be refined by trials to make them truly pure and righteous.

In the OT silver is also used as a symbol for all that is precious. Job declares that *wisdom is more precious than gold or silver, because gold and silver can be discovered and mined but wisdom cannot be easily found (Job 28:1, 15). The writer of Proverbs likewise says that wisdom should be sought as silver or hidden treasures, because it will bring more blessings to the person who possesses it than silver ever

could (Prov 2:4; 3:14). The psalms declare that the promises of God are precious because they are as pure as "silver refined in a furnace on the ground, purified seven times" (Ps 12:6 NRSV).

See also ABUNDANCE; GOLD; JEWELS AND PRECIOUS STONES; MINERALS; PROSPERITY; TREASURE.

SIN

The Bible is nearly as full of sin as it is of grace. Scripture records the sordid details of everything from petty embezzlement (Acts 5:1-11) to child sacrifice (Jer 7:31), from verbal abuse (2 Sam 16:5-14) to homicidal *rape (Judg 19). The staggering variety of sin in the Bible reflects the totality of human depravity, confirming the verdict that "if any one of you is without sin, let him be the first to throw a stone" (Jn 8:7 NIV).

Sin is exemplified and personified already in the opening pages of the Bible. The fall of *Adam and *Eve (Gen 3) is sin exemplified. Eating the forbidden fruit—indicative as it is of such varied sins as grasping after deity, mistrust of divine providence, disobedience of the word of God and subsequent shaming and blaming—is the paradigmatic sin. In the very next story, that of *Cain and *Abel, sin takes on palpable form as it is personified: God warns Cain, "If you do not do what is right, sin is crouching at your door" (Gen 4:7 NIV). Sin is the stalker behind the door who casts a long, dark shadow over the rest of human history. Other translations picture sin as "couching" at the door like a predatory monster that through long habitude has become domesticated (cf. Rom 7:9). The subsequent history of Genesis is replete with evidence that the stalker has no shortage of victims; these include the entire human race—of which God says that "every inclination of the thoughts of his heart was only evil all the time" (Gen 6:5 NIV)—the builders of the Tower of *Babel (Gen 11) and the sinful cities of *Sodom and Gomorrah (Gen 19). And these are only the opening chapters in the book of human sinfulness that constitutes a large part of the Bible.

The rich biblical vocabulary for sin has its origin in metaphor (as does a great deal of language). The most prominent terms in the OT all appear in Exodus 34:7: "wickedness, rebellion and sin" (NIV). *Wickedness* (Heb '*āwōn*) has its origins in the idea of bending or twisting. *Rebellion (pešaʿ)* is transgression, or breaking the law. *Sin (ḥaṭṭāʾâ)* denotes missing the mark or straying from the path. The primary NT term for sin is *hamartia*, a term that in its etymology is associated with missing the mark in archery. The more infrequent *paraptōma* suggests falling down or losing one's way (e.g., Heb 6:6). Similarly, *parabasis* ("trespass") has the obvious sense of walking away from the right path (e.g., Judas in Acts 1:25) or overstepping a proper boundary (Jas 2:9). Yet these and the other biblical terms for sin become so conventional that the metaphors behind them have vanished through long use in common discourse. What remains are synonymous and overlapping terms for sin.

What is sin like? It is often described as a form of tyranny or bondage. Sin wraps the sinner up with strong cords (Prov 5:22), and it easily entangles its victim (Heb 12:1). The reason Cain is warned not to let sin have mastery (Gen 4:7) is that sin is a *slave driver. The psalmist took the hint and prayed that sin would not rule over him (Ps 119:133). Jesus warned that "everyone who sins is a slave to sin" (Jn 8:34 NIV). Paul could vouch for the bondage of sin from his own experience as a man "sold as a slave to sin . . . a prisoner of the law of sin" (Rom 7:14, 23 NIV; cf. Rom 6). Indeed, "the whole world is a prisoner of sin" (Gal 3:22 NIV).

Sin is like falling down or turning away from a good *path. Ezekiel argues that *silver and *gold made the children of Israel "*stumble into sin" (Ezek 7:19 NIV). To sin is to go astray, turning to one's own way (Is 53:6; cf. Dan 9:11). Even though sin is a kind of *wandering, it is no accident. Both the writer of Proverbs and the prophet Isaiah observe that the feet of sinners "rush into sin" (Prov 1:16 NIV; Is 59:7; cf. Jer 8:6 NIV: "Each pursues his own course like a horse charging into battle").

Sin is costly and unsightly. It can be compared to a debt that must be paid. Sin deserves a penalty (Job 8:4) that can be laid as a charge against someone (Acts 7:60 KJV). It can also compared to an indelible stain. Sins are like scarlet; they are red as crimson (Is 1:18; see Colors).

Sin is deadly. The connection between sin and *death is emphasized in the Torah by the oft-repeated provisions for sin offerings involving *blood *sacrifice. The costliness and deadliness of sin are conjoined in Paul's memorable epigram "The *wages of sin is death" (Rom 6:23 NIV; cf. Rom 5:12). To be a sinner is to be "dead in your transgressions and sins" (Eph 2:1 NIV; cf. Col 2:13). Paul goes so far as to personify sin as a killer or an executioner: "Sin, seizing the opportunity afforded by the commandment, deceived me, and through the commandment put me to death" (Rom 7:11 NIV). Alternatively, it is the mother of all death, for "when it is full-grown, [it] gives birth to death" (Jas 1:15 NIV). A variant of the sin-as-death motif is the biblical portrayal of it as a disease of which one must be rid (Ps 32:1-5; 103:3; Is 53:5; Mt 9:2, 5; Mk 2:5, 9; Lk 5:20, 23; 1 Pet 2:24).

Although the Bible is saturated with images that portray the pervasiveness of sin, it also offers a complete remedy for sin (see Forgiveness). In order to put sin to death once and for all, Jesus Christ became sin personified on the *cross: "God made him who had no sin to be sin for us, so that in him we might become the righteousness of God" (2 Cor 5:21 NIV). Jesus put Cain's stalker to death by paying the price for sin: "Speak tenderly to Jerusalem, and proclaim to her . . . that her sin has been paid for" (Is 40:2 NIV). Again, "Blessed is the man whose sin the Lord will never count against him" (Rom 4:8; cf. Ps 32:2).

The effect of the death and *resurrection of Jesus Christ is to undo all the damage of sin. His victory gives freedom from the *bondage of sin (Jn 8:36; cf. Rom 6; 8:2). His blood is the fountain that cleanses from "sin and impurity" (Zech 13:1 NIV), that can "wash away all my iniquity" (Ps 51:2 NIV) and make my scarlet stains "as white as snow" (Is 1:18). Though sin cannot be concealed from God, it can be covered by Christ (Ps 32:1, 85:2; Is 14:17). Though "my sin is always before me," the grace of *atonement can "blot out all my iniquity" (Ps 51:3, 9 NIV; cf. Is 43:25) and "take away our sins" (1 Jn 3:5 NIV; cf. Heb 9:28). How far has God removed "our transgressions from us?" "As far as the east is from the west" (Ps 103:12 NIV).

God not only cleanses and removes sin, he also forgets it. God "remembers your sins no more" (Is 43:25 NIV; cf. Jer 31:34; Heb 8:12). Divine forgetfulness of pardoned sin is most vividly portrayed by the prophet Micah: "[God will] hurl all our iniquities into the depths of the sea" (Mic 7:19 NIV; cf. Is 38:17: "you have put all my sins behind your back" [NIV]).

The term *sinner can be used pejoratively, as when the Pharisees asked the disciples why Jesus ate "with tax collectors and 'sinners' " (Mt 9:10 NIV). On the lips of a penitent, however, it is a mark of purest piety: "God, have mercy on me, a sinner" (Lk 18:13 NIV).

Sin and its synonyms appear in many other memorable phrases in the Bible. While these phrases are not images in the strictest sense of the word, their evocative nature has transformed them into symbolic emblems: "the sin of the fathers" (e.g. Ex 20:5 NIV); "your sin will find you out" (Num 32:23 NIV); "the sins of my youth" (Job 13:26 NIV; Ps 25:7); "if your right eye causes you to sin" (Mt 5:29 NIV); "forgive us our debts" (Mt 6:12 NIV); "the unpardonable sin" (Mk 3:29 KJV); "your sins are forgiven!" (Lk 7:48 NIV); "the Lamb of God, who takes away the sin of the world" (Jn 1:29 NIV); "all have sinned and fall short of the glory of God" (Rom 3:23 NIV); "where sin increased, grace increased all the more" (Rom 5:20 NIV); "Christ died for our sins" (1 Cor 15:3 NIV); "enjoy the pleasures of sin for a season" (Heb 11:25 KJV); "if we claim to be without sin" (1 Jn 1:8 NIV); "if we confess our sins" (1 Jn 1:9 NIV). Most memorable of all, "he was pierced for our transgressions, he was crushed for our iniquities . . . and the LORD has laid on him the iniquity of us all" (Is 53:5-6 NIV).

See also ADULTERY; APOSTASY; ATONEMENT; BLOOD; BONDAGE AND FREEDOM; FALL FROM INNOCENCE; GUILT; HEART; IDOL, IDOLATRY; MURDER STORIES; PURITY; RAPE, SEXUAL VIOLENCE; REBELLION; REPENTANCE; ROB, ROBBER; SACRIFICE; SIN, STORIES OF; SINNER; STUMBLE, STUMBLING BLOCK; TEMPTATION; TEMPTER.

SIN, STORIES OF

The Bible is a book preoccupied with good and evil.

Its prevailing view of the person is that humans are flawed beings with an inherent inclination to do what is wrong much of the time. It is no surprise, therefore, that a large proportion of stories in the Bible can be classified as stories of *sin. With the *law and revealed will of God serving as a background gauge of the human heart and actions, most of these stories of sin hinge on an act of disobedience. In this sense the Bible's first story of sin, that of *Adam and *Eve's eating of the forbidden *fruit, is prototypical.

Along the lines of medieval classifications of sin (as encapsulated, for example, in Dante's *Divine Comedy*), to rehearse the best-known stories of sin in the Bible is to provide a virtual anatomy of sins. As the pages of the Bible unfold, we find stories of murder (*Cain and *Abel, Gen 4:1-16; Jezebel's murder of Naboth, 1 Kings 21), lying (the lying prophet, 1 Kings 13; Ananias and Sapphira, Acts 5:1-11), greed (Gehazi, 2 Kings 5:19-27), *adultery (*David and *Bathsheba, 2 Sam 11), cheating (*Jacob's stealing of the blessing, Gen 27), incest (Amnon and Tamar, 2 Sam 13), *rape (the Levite's concubine, Judg 19), weak *leadership (the tragedy of King Saul), squandering of God's gifts combined with breaking of a *vow to God (the tragedy of *Samson), *pride (Nebuchadnezzar, Dan 3—4), *idolatry (the golden calf, Ex 32:1-10), impatience and *anger (*Moses at the rock, Num 20:7-13) and complaining (the murmuring of the Israelites during the exodus).

This is neither to deny that the Bible also contains stories of virtue nor that the Bible shows a realism of grace as well as a realism of depravity. It is only to note that stories of sin are prominent in the Bible.

See also FALL FROM INNOCENCE; GUILT; SIN; SINNER.

SINAI

Mount Sinai, also called Horeb (Ex 17:6; 33:6), is where the *law is given to Israel through *Moses. It is known as "the mountain of God" in Exodus (Ex 3:1 NIV) and once in Numbers is called "the mountain of Yahweh" (Num 10:33). Its height and physical appearance are unimportant and so not given (and identification of the site can only be guesswork), but its location in a *wilderness where *food and *water are scarce inevitably brings to mind an image of harsh, barren rocks.

The primary meaning of Sinai has to do with its being the place of revelation where God meets Israel, the temporary junction of *heaven and *earth. Thus it is "holy ground" (Ex 3:5 NIV). When the people arrive at Sinai—the goal of the *exodus (Ex 3:12)—they must accordingly consecrate themselves through *washing and sexual abstinence, and even then they cannot come too near the mysterious *mountain (Ex 19:10-15, 21). After God (pictured as living above in the heavens) comes down to the mountain, only Moses (and in some passages Aaron also) goes up (Ex 19:20)—something that happens again and again. There in the "thick darkness" (Ex 20:21 NIV) God reveals to Moses the Ten Com-

mandments and the rest of the *law, and also—in response to Moses' request—himself (Ex 33:12-23). But the people who stand afar off only see smoke and *fire and *hear *thunder and *trumpets and experience an earthquake (Ex 19:18-19; 20:18). Like the holy of holies, into which only the high *priest can enter, Sinai is, because of God's presence, a hallowed area only a few are allowed to approach.

Though Sinai/Horeb is a constant presence in Exodus and Deuteronomy, it hardly appears again in the rest of the Bible. This is because after the revelation to Moses it plays no more significant role in sacred history. Unlike Mt. Zion, it is not closely associated with ongoing political and religious institutions; it belongs to the past.

Outside the Pentateuch, Sinai/Horeb is mentioned or alluded to in two sorts of passages—those that remember the giving of the law and attendant events (Judg 5:5; 1 Kings 8:9; 2 Chron 5:10; Neh 9:13; Ps 68:8; 106:19; Mt 4:4) and those that implicitly compare an individual with Moses. In the latter passages people do things on a mountain which are designed to remind informed hearers or readers of what Moses did on Sinai. The two most obvious examples occur in 1 Kings 19:8, 12 (Elijah, cf. Ex 33:21-23; 34:28; Deut 9:9) and Matthew 5:1—8:1 (Jesus, cf. Ex 19:3-14; 34:29; etc.; see also Jn 6:3). In the case of Jesus we see him as the new lawgiver. Just having coming out of the wilderness, where he resisted the *temptations of *Satan for *forty days and nights (parallel to the forty years of the Israelites in the wilderness), he delivers the law to his people. In Galatians, Paul develops an allegory of Sinai and the Jerusalem above, with Sinai representing the old covenant, slavery and the "present Jerusalem," in contrast with the freedom of the "Jerusalem above" (Gal 4:21-31). We also note the use of Sinai imagery in Hebrews 12:18-29, where that mountain comes to represent the old covenant while Mt. *Zion represents the new covenant that takes its place.

See also LAW; MOSES; MOUNTAIN; THEOPHANY; WILDERNESS; ZION.

BIBLIOGRAPHY. J. Levenson, *Sinai and Zion: An Entry into the Jewish Bible* (San Francisco: Harper & Row, 1987).

SINGING. *See* MUSIC.

SINNER

The opposite of the *saint is the sinner. Despite the multitude of *character types in the Bible, the basic paradigm is that characters at any given moment behave like a saint or like a sinner. The designation *sinner* seems most natural for characters (perhaps during individual episodes in their larger life story) who are known to us chiefly for their disobedience to God's commands of good conduct, and usually a flagrant offense against good characters as well.

The archetypal sinners of Christian theology and Western literature are *Adam and *Eve—prototypical because they were the first sinners. This is not to deny the possibility that they were eventually redeemed; it is only to acknowledge that they are customarily remembered for their sin. In the story of the first sin we can see the essence of what makes a sinner: disobedience to God's commands for righteousness. Famous sinners follow in the wake of Adam and Eve: Abel, Lamech, Pharaoh, a host OT kings of Israel and Judah, and such pagan tyrants as the king of Tyre and Nebuchadnezzar. From the pages of the NT we remember as sinners Herod, Judas Iscariot and those responsible for the execution of Jesus.

While it seems natural to think of these specific characters as sinners, when the Bible actually uses the word *sinner(s)* it rarely links the character type with a specific character or group. Exceptions are passages in which the people of *Sodom are identified as "great sinners against the LORD" (Gen 13:13 NRSV) and in which the designation is linked with the Amalekites (1 Sam 15:18) and the people of Zion (Is 33:14). Individually the woman who anoints Jesus is called a sinner (Lk 7:37, 39). But in nearly all the seventy times the epithet appears, it is plural and identifies a spiritual state that is understood without having to be defined. Sinners are those who are reprobate—outside of saving faith in God and opposed to the divine will.

See also SAINTS.

SISTER

In the Bible, the relationship of sister to sibling is one of the closest possible relationships. Sisters are protected by their *brothers, and the relationship of sister to siblings is often used metaphorically to portray intimacy, sometimes spiritual in nature. Sisters were "fixtures" in the large *families and closely knit families of Middle Eastern culture. This is demonstrated in the book of Job, when Job's sons invite their sisters over for a large feast (Job 1:19). At the end of the story, Job's sisters as well as his brothers visit him upon the restoration of his fortunes (Job 42:11). From such references we catch a glimpse of the importance of the relationship of sister to sibling.

Because *women were the vulnerable sex, with no way of protecting themselves in Middle Eastern culture, brothers often found it an important duty to protect their sisters from harm, especially in the case of sexual assault (*see* Rape, Sexual Violence). They took it as a personal affront if any man violated their sisters, especially if they refused to marry her afterward. In *Song of Songs, the brothers of the Shulammite take a protective interest in her sexuality, promising to reward her if she remains virtuous and to *shut her up if she is loose (Song 8:8). David's son *Absalom takes more drastic measures: when his half-brother rapes his sister Tamar, he hates Amnon so fiercely for defiling his sister that he bides his time, waiting for the right opportunity for revenge (2 Sam 13; *see* Vengeance/Revenge). Jacob's sons likewise avenge the rape of their sister (Gen 34). From such narratives emerges one of the Bible's images of sisters—vulnerable in the outside society and needing

the protection of their brothers. In response, sisters are loyal to their brothers, as in the story of Lazarus, Mary and Martha (Jn 11).

More positively, sisters can be heroic. Miriam shows herself courageous and resourceful in helping to *rescue her infant brother Moses from threatened death (Ex 2:1-10). Later she shares leadership with Moses in the Red Sea deliverance by leading the women in song and *dance (Ex 15:19-21). Jehosheba foils the attempt of Athaliah to destroy the entire royal family by hiding the son of her deceased brother King Ahaziah (2 Kings 11:1-3).

Although families may have been close in OT times, this closeness did not preclude competition and resentment within families. Sisters accordingly are sometimes *sibling rivals. The two wives of *Jacob, Leah and Rachel, were two sisters who competed for their husband's favor. Each found a specific role in which she could beat her sister: the wife whom Jacob loved was Rachel, and the wife who bore the most children was Leah. Rachel was so jealous of her sister's fertility that she told Jacob, "Give me children, or I shall die!" (Gen 30:1 NRSV). After her maid Bilhah bore two sons for her, she said triumphantly, "With mighty wrestlings I have wrestled with my sister, and have prevailed" (Gen 30:8 NRSV). In fact, the competition to bear the most children became so fierce that the sisters fell to bargaining with mandrakes for a chance to sleep with Jacob (Gen 30:15). God recognized such competition inherent to sisterly relationships and therefore included in the law a command that a man "shall not take a woman [as a wife] as a rival to her sister" (Lev 18:18 NRSV).

Even if sisters are not rivals, they might serve as foils to each other. Mary and Martha are a chief example: while the two women entertained Jesus in their household, Martha rushed frantically around the house preparing a meal for Jesus, while Mary sat quietly at Jesus' feet listening to his words (Lk 10:38-42). When Martha complained to Jesus, he answered rebukingly that her sister had "chosen the better part" (Lk 10:42). *Ruth likewise showed faithfulness in comparison to her sister-in-law (Ruth 1). While her sister chose to leave their mother-in-law and return to her own country, Ruth bravely left her home to care for her mother-in-law in her own land. In such biblical examples, two sisters often serve to highlight the honor of one at the expense of the other.

Brother-sister pairs are no less prone to disagreement. Miriam, Moses' sister, brought Aaron with her to criticize Moses for his marriage to a non-Israelite woman, saying, "Has the LORD spoken only through Moses? Has he not spoken through us also?" (Num 12:2 NRSV). For such a challenge of God's *authority, Miriam became leprous, and although she was healed when Moses prayed for her, she had to remain *outside the camp for seven days (Num 12:10-16).

Although the Mosaic law forbade *marriage between a brother and sister, there were a few cases of such marriages before God gave Moses the law (Lev 18:11). Genesis seems to imply that Cain and Abel married their sisters of necessity, since there was no one else for them to marry. *Abraham marries Sarah, his half-sister, with whom he shared a common father (Gen 20:12). Later Amram, Moses's father, married his father's sister Jochabed (Ex 6:20). Even after men ceased to marry their sisters, *sister* was an affectionate term for a husband to call his wife, and the beloved in the Song of Songs even goes so far as to wish that her lover were her brother so she could kiss him in public (Song 5:1; 8:1). Thus although marriage between brothers and sisters was forbidden, the closeness of a brother-sister relationship came to metaphorically represent the relationship of a husband and wife.

Jesus paid tribute to the high value of sisters (along with other family members) in one of his hard sayings: "Whoever comes to me and does not hate father and mother, wife and children, brothers and sisters, yes, and even life itself, cannot be my disciple" (Lk 14:26 NRSV).

Because the relationship of siblings is so strong, it comes to symbolize any close personal connection. Job despairingly feels close to all that is vile, saying "to the worm, 'My mother,' or 'My sister' " (Job 17:14). The author of Proverbs commands the wise man to "say to wisdom, 'You are my sister,' " denoting the great value of wisdom to the seeker (Prov 7:4 NRSV). To indicate the similarity of their acts, Jeremiah refers to Judah and Israel as sisters in crime, each antagonizing the other to sin more direly (Jer 3:7). Ezekiel calls Israel a part of a large family of sinners along with other evil nations: "You are the sister of your sisters. . . . Your mother was a Hittite and your father an Amorite. Your elder sister is Samaria; . . . and your younger sister . . . is Sodom with her daughters" (Ezek 16:45-46 NRSV).

Metaphoric references to sisters can also be positive. According to Jesus, "Whoever does the will of my Father in heaven is my brother and sister and mother" (Mt 12:50 NRSV). Fellow believers are also siblings: Paul and James both refer to female members of churches as their sisters (Rom 16:1; 1 Tim 5:2; Jas 2:15).

Although sisters were vulnerable within their societies and had few rights apart from the males in their lives, they are not undervalued in the Bible. Like their male counterparts, they can be either good or bad, but their value to God and their families is evident.

See also BROTHER; ELDER CHILD, ELDER SIBLING; FAMILY; SIBLING RIVALRY; WOMAN, IMAGES OF; YOUNGER CHILD, YOUNGER SIBLING.

SIT

Most of the more than three hundred references to sitting in the Bible merely denote the posture of sitting rather than *standing or *walking. But the remaining references assign special and even ritual meaning to the posture of sitting.

The most prominent among these usages is the motif of sitting in the city *gate, which carries legal and legislative overtones. The area inside the gate of ancient cities was where official business was transacted, where public announcements were made, where town officials deliberated policy and where legal or judicial transactions occurred. Within this context, to "sit in the gate" meant to be a prominent citizen of the town, probably one of the elders who determined policy for the community. Such, for example, are Lot (Gen 19:1), Job (29:7) and the husband of the virtuous wife of Proverbs 31 (Prov 31:23). Sometimes *kings sat at the gate of a city (2 Sam 18:24; 19:8). In the progressive identification with evil that is traced in three parallel clauses in Psalm 1:1, the climactic ignominy is to sit in the seat of scoffers. Kings too had gates to their court, and to "sit" at the king's gate meant to be a courtier—an adviser to the king, with privileges of access denied to ordinary citizens. Such is Mordecai (Esther 2:19, 21; 5:13; 6:10).

Another special seat is the royal *throne (1 Kings 2:19; Esther 5:1). To sit on the throne is the kingly counterpart of sitting in the gate (1 Kings 16:11; 22:10. 19; Jer 22:30). Of similar import is the motif of sitting on the *right hand (Mt 20:21; Mk 14:62; Heb 1:4). Correspondingly, a king's consort might sit beside him while others in the court presumably stood (Neh 2:6).

Quite apart from its link to special places, the posture of sitting is associated with specific dignitaries possessing authority. Judges trying a *legal case sat (Judg 4:5; Ruth 4:1-1; Jer 26:10; Dan 7:9). People sat to await an *oracle from a prophet (2 Kings 4:38; Ezek 8:1). Wise men, teachers and rabbis sat to *teach (Prov 9:14; Mt 5:1; 13:1; 24:3). Finally, there is sometimes an implied *honor in sitting while someone with lesser status stands (Gen 18:8; Lk 12:37; Jas 2:3).

A final ritual meaning of sitting is to sit in *ashes to signify *mourning (Job 2:8; Jon 3:6; Lk 10:13).

See also LYING DOWN; LYING PROSTRATE; RECLINING; SEAT; STAND, STANDING; THRONE; WALK, WALKING.

SKIN

The biblical word for skin refers to the outer covering of the *body and is differentiated from "flesh." Of the more than sixty references to skin in the Bible, nearly two-thirds appear in the book of Leviticus, with the book of Job providing the next largest number of references. Skin is predominantly an image of human frailty, vulnerability, *disease and physical *suffering. Skin is subject to disease and *decay.

The preoccupation with skin in Leviticus has to do with diseases of the skin, especially *leprosy. The image is primarily one of terror, inasmuch as the catalog of skin ailments evokes a sense of potential disease lurking in one's future, of physical discomfort as the symptoms are described and of appearing submissively before the *priests who enforce the health code for the community. The book of Job reinforces these associations with its pictures of physical suffering, as we enter a world where "skin hardens, then breaks out afresh" (Job 7:5 RSV), where "by disease [one's] skin is consumed" (Job 18:13 RSV) and where the sufferer's "bones cleave to [his] skin" (Job 19:20 RSV). Here the nadir of Job's vitality is portrayed by suggesting that his *bones are weaker than his skin. The proverb "I have escaped by the skin of my teeth" (Job 19:20 RSV) also points to his desperate condition because he is left with nothing but the skin on his *teeth, which, of course, is nothing at all. Things do not improve elsewhere, as we read about skin wasting away (Lam 3:4) or about oppressors tearing the skin off their victims and flaying it (Mic 3:2-3).

Some exceptions to the main images of skin should be noted. Skin as an image of transience is countered in Jeremiah 13:23, where we read about the Ethiopian's inability to change his skin or the leopard its spots, followed by the negative application that someone accustomed to doing *evil cannot do good. The one genuinely positive image of skin is the shining skin of *Moses when he comes down from *Sinai (Ex 34:29-34), a notable image of the holy or numinous in the Bible. Of course, all this negative thrust must be tempered by the Scriptures' unremitting sense that our bodies were created by God and are "good."

When we move from human skin to animal skins, the picture becomes more positive, beginning with God's making "garments of skins" to clothe *Adam and *Eve after pronouncing the curse following the Fall (Gen 3:21 RSV). Negatively, the *goats' skins that Rebekah placed on *Jacob's arms and neck (Gen 27:16) become an image of deception in a story of trickery. The greatest number of references to animal skins, however, have to do with the material from which the dyed cloth for the *tabernacle was made. Here skin becomes an image of richness and color.

See also BODY; BONE; DECAY; DISEASE AND HEALING; LEPER, LEPROSY.

SLAUGHTER. See ALTAR; BATTLE STORIES; SACRIFICE.

SLAVE, SLAVERY

In the Bible a slave is the economic asset, legal property and complete responsibility of his or her purchaser. While the words are sometimes used interchangeably, a lower social status generally distinguishes a slave from a *servant, but advancement is possible and very common. Though the slave is subject to perpetual *bondage, God, who created all persons with dignity, oversees slavery in Scripture. Further, from the biblical perspective every person is subject to slavery, either to *sin or to *God.

An Economic Asset. Whether gained by simple purchase or by military conquest, a slave was an economic asset in ancient societies. Slaves had market value (Gen 37:28; Ex 21:32; Ezek 27:13; Acts 16:19); they could be bought and sold (Lev 25:44-45); they could be passed on as *inheritance (Lev 25:46). Among the Israelites, only people from other nations were to be sold as slaves in a demeaning sense—notably the Canaanites, who were cursed as "the lowest of slaves" (Gen 9:24 NIV) and described (in the memorable phrasing of the KJV) as "hewers of wood and drawers of water" (Josh 9:18-27).

Those bought with money or born in the master's home had special privileges (Gen 17:12, 23, 27; Ex 12:44; Lev 22:11). One thinks of *Joseph, purchased by Potiphar, given much responsibility and yet called a slave by Potiphar's wife (Gen 39:1-19). Conquered slaves performed heavy labor (1 Kings 9:21). The Israelites in *Egypt were subdued for fear of their potential military might and made to perform the labor befitting such defeat (Ex 1:1-14). *Solomon conscripted *foreigners for his slave labor force but assigned Israelites positions on the servant level: government officials, officers, captains, soldiers and the like (1 Kings 9:21-22).

Slave purchase was common but was surveyed by the divine *justice of God. Abraham (Gen 17:23), the Preacher of Ecclesiastes (Eccles 2:7) and Hosea (Hos 3:2) purchased slaves. After seeing the Israelites' misery, God himself metaphorically purchased them by defeating the Egyptians who resisted Moses (Ex 3:7; 15:16; 2 Pet 2:1).

In times of hardship Hebrew communities were threatened by the possibility of enslavement. Elijah's prayer kept a *widow's *sons from being taken as slaves to satisfy her debt (2 Kings 4). In postexilic Judah, excessive interest charges caused many families to sell themselves as debt-slaves, though they were purchased from bondage by righteous men whenever possible (Neh 5:8). Also, while just economic gain was permitted, "slave traders" are included with "liars and perjurers" in a list of things "contrary to the sound doctrine" of the early Christian church (1 Tim 1:10 NIV). God provided laws and judgment to monitor the institution of slavery. Still more dignity accrues to the status of being a slave in NT times if we consider the "household duties" passages of Ephesians 5:21-6:9 and Colossians 3:18-4:1, where the very placement of slaves in lists with other *family members suggests that their status was that of members of the *household.

Legal Property and Responsibility. Because slaves were valuable as an economic asset, they were counted as *legal property that required care. The *doulos* word group from which slave is derived assumes a status of ownership, dependence and *obedience under a single master.

Because kidnapping fellow Israelites as slaves threatened the Hebrew community, it was punishable by *death (Deut 24:7). Though permitting some *beating, the law made direct prohibitions against beating slaves to death (Ex 21:20). The Hebrews were commanded to provide asylum for mistreated slaves (Ex 21:21; Deut 23:15). Priests, as exemplary followers of the law, were to treat purchased slaves as part of their household and *eat with them at *table (Lev 22:11). An Egyptian slave who was abandoned by his master when he became ill contrasted pagan ways with God's protective directions about slavery (1 Sam 30:13); in a similar manner, the NT centurion who sought Jesus for his sick servant mimicked the Hebrew ideal (Lk 7:2). Because of God's laws, Hebrews were known among the nations as being good masters.

*Women and *children were especially protected. Women could not be sold to foreigners (Ex 21:8) and were privy to equal rights if *adopted or given in *marriage (Ex 21:9). Children of slaves belonged to the master, so if a man slave accepted a *wife from his master, he would generally choose to become a servant for life (Ex 21:6). One example was Ziba, Saul's servant, who served Saul's sons with his entire family for life (2 Sam 9:9-10).

The slave-master relation parallels ours with God because we are called to be accountable to him (Rom 14:4; Eph 6:9; Col 4:1; 2 Tim 2:21). He also assumes responsibility for us: "As the eyes of slaves look to the hand of their master, as the eyes of a maid look to the hand of her mistress, so our eyes look to the LORD our God, till he shows us his mercy" (Ps 123:2 NIV).

Subject to Perpetual Bondage. Images of bondage link the economic significance of slavery to the image of spiritual *idolatry, paving the way for one of the Bible's richest *salvation pictures. We easily recall slaves who were mistreated: Joseph, the Hebrews under Egyptian and Babylonian empires, the Egyptian slave whose master leaves him, the postexilic Jews in Nehemiah 9:36. Harsh bondage of enforced subjection is often pictured as a burdensome *yoke of labor (Gen 27:40; Lev 26:13; 1 Kings 12:4; Is 47:6). Yet figurative use of the image yields a more vivid picture.

Both slavery and idolatry entail bondage, that is, complete subjection to a master's will. Egypt, "the house of bondage," and Babylon are metonymies for idolatry and slavery, and their *gods are metaphorical masters (Ex 20:2-4; Deut 5:6-8; Ps 137; Lam 1:1-2; Rev 11:8; 18:13). The important figurative jump is not from slavery to freedom, but from slavery to sin to slavery to God, *darkness to *light, falsehood to truth. Though the Lord's "yoke is easy" and his "burden is light" (Mt 11:30 NIV), a yoke still exists.

The Bible assumes universal service on earth; the issue is whether one's master is God or sin (Rom 6:15-23). Indeed, all of *creation suffers in bondage to decay after the Fall (Rom 8:21). Unredeemed sinners are in bondage to sin, specifically *evil powers such as elemental religious deities (Gal 4:3), gluttony (Rom 16:18) and lusts (Tit 3:3). As Peter points out: "A man is a slave to whatever has mastered him" (2 Pet 2:19 NIV; see also Jn 8:34). Judgment awaits those who falsely assume that redemption is self-mastery rather than the freedom to chose God as master (Ps 12:4).

This aspect of perpetual bondage is developed most extensively in the teachings and active examples of Jesus and of Paul. Jesus' parables affirm the slave's subservient and obligatory allegiance to a single master as an illustration of service under God (Mt 8:9; 18:21-34; 25:14-30; Lk 17:7-10). He exemplifies voluntary slavery, humbling himself as a human being, embracing death, even symbolically by *washing the apostles' *feet (Jn 13:12-17; Phil 2). He teaches that true greatness in Christian service is the humble position of the godly slave, the last as first, an antithesis to the status-conscious world (Mt 20:27; Mk 10:44). His death is the redemptive payment for the deliverance of many from the slave market of sin (Mk 10:45; Rom 3:22-24). His perfect life demonstrates that freedom is not autonomous perfection but rather a chosen relationship with God that requires obedient rejection of sin's bondage.

Paul directs the early church accordingly. Salvation is presented as a spiritual manumission involving a change of masters, expressed allegorically as freedom to be Sarah's "children of promise" who serve Christ in the Spirit with a view to total redemption in the new creation (Gal 4:21-31; Rom 6:14; 8:18-25). "Slave of Christ" is Paul's christological restatement of Moses' first command: one is not to have compromising relationships with any other masters (cf. Lev 25:55; Deut 6:4; Mt 6:24); accordingly, Christ's *douloi* represent his cause and, in the final analysis, give account only to him.

Paul's own testimony illustrates the choice between masters. He confesses slavery to sin because "what I want to do I do not do, but what I hate I do" (Rom 7:15 NIV) but chooses to be a slave to God's law (Rom 7:25). Also, echoing Jesus' example (Mk 10:44), he calls himself a slave to all people for the sake of the gospel (1 Cor 9:19) and further makes his own *body a slave "so that after I have preached to others, I myself will not be disqualified for the prize" (1 Cor 9:27 NIV). His life is a threefold example of voluntary slavery.

Paul also handled an unusual difficulty in the early church. In a culture whose slave trade was a primary business, his metaphorical relation of sin to slavery had the natural effect of making believers desire social freedom. Believers also responded to his call to serve each other by volunteering to sell themselves for others' freedom. Believing in God's providential placement of his children, Paul's representative principle concerning slavery was to remain in the state in which one was called (1 Cor 7:17-24; cf. 1 Pet 2:18). He clearly states that the primary goal of a slave was not social freedom but rather freedom to serve the supreme Lord (Rom 14:7-8; 2 Cor 5:15).

Temporary Status. A final important aspect of slavery in the Bible is that it is only temporary. Without choice to be a bondservant, a slave is not owned for life. Advancement is also possible; indeed, slaves of God are adopted as sons by God (Jn 8:35-36; Gal 4:1-9). In the scope of eternity also, slavery is a temporary condition: "it will be the same for priest as for people, for master as for servant, for mistress as for maid, for seller as for buyer, for borrower as for lender, for debtor as for creditor" (Is 24:2). Individual responsibility before God reverberates in thirteen different predictions of judgment for all persons, "slave or free" (1 Kings 14:10; 21:21; 2 Kings 9:8; 14:26; 1 Cor 12:13; Gal 3:28; Eph 6:8; Col 3:11; Philem 15-16; Rev 6:15; 13:16; 19:18).

See also BONDAGE AND FREEDOM; SIN; WORK, WORKER.

BIBLIOGRAPHY. S. S. Bartchy, "Slave, Slavery," *DLNTD* 1098-102; M. A. Dandamayev, "Slavery (Ancient Near East) (Old Testament)," *ABD* 6:58-65; M. I. Finley, *Ancient Slavery and Modern Ideology* (New York: Viking: 1980); K. Hopkins, *Conquerors and Slaves* (New York: Cambridge University Press, 1978); D. B. Martin, *Slavery as Salvation* (New Haven, CT: Yale University Press, 1990).

SLEEP

Since sleep is a nightly human need, it is not surprising that it receives frequent mention in the Bible. Sleep may be divinely-induced, as when God "caused the man [Adam] to fall into a deep sleep" (Gen 2:21 NIV). Sleep may also prompt *dreams and visions. Jacob (Gen 28:10-22), Joseph (Gen 37:5-11, 19), Ezekiel (Ezek 1:1—3:15), Daniel (Dan 7:1—8:27), Zechariah (Zech 1:7—6:8), Joseph (Mt 1:18-25), Peter (Acts 10:9-23) and John (Rev) are among the Bible's more notable dreamers and visionaries. As Pharoah's baker discovered (Gen 40:16-22), not all dreams are good dreams—some are nightmares.

Biblical sleep usually has negative connotations. Nightmares are not the only calamities that befall those who slumber. During sleep a dead *baby might be swapped for a live one (1 Kings 3:20), a tent peg might be driven through one's skull (Judg 4:21), the bridegroom might return unexpectedly (Mt 25:5) or one might fall from a window during a long sermon (Acts 20:9).

Too much snoozing may also result in poverty. "How long will you lie there, you sluggard? When will you get up from your sleep? A little sleep, a little slumber, a little folding of the hands to rest—and poverty will come on you like a bandit and scarcity like an armed man" (Prov 6:9-11 NIV; cf 19:15, 20:13). Here the rhythm of the poetic verse contrasts the slowness of sluggard's nodding off to sleep with the swiftness with which poverty will overtake him.

Given the hazards of sleep, it is little wonder that the wicked—like anxious King Nebuchadnezzar (Dan 2:1)—struggle with insomnia. Evildoers "cannot sleep till they do evil; they are robbed of slumber till they make someone fall" (Prov 4:16 NIV).

Sleep is altogether sweet for the righteous, since the Lord "grants sleep to those he loves" (Ps 127:2 NIV). The righteous may sleep peacefully because they know that "he who watches over Israel will neither slumber nor sleep" (Ps 121:4 NIV). So Jesus napped in a boat during a terrible storm (Lk 8:22-25), both receiving and trusting in his Father's watchful and unsleeping care. In its positive associations sleep is a sign of spiritual and psychic health: "I will both lie down and sleep in peace; for you alone, O Lord, make me lie down in safety" (Ps 4:8 NRSV). The wise person "will not be afraid" when lying down, and his or her "sleep will be sweet" (Prov 3:24 NIV). Sleep is also the reward of the honest laborer: "The sleep of a laborer is sweet, . . . but the abundance of a rich man permits him no sleep" (Eccles 5:12 NIV).

The Bible also uses sleep as a metaphor for the *death of the righteous. "Christ has indeed been raised from the dead, the firstfruits of those who have fallen asleep" (1 Cor 15:20). In Christ, death is nothing more than a nap from which the righteous will awaken to endless day.

See also AWAKENING; BED, BEDROOM; DREAMS, VISIONS; NIGHT; REST; SLEEPING GOD MOTIF; SLEEPLESS NIGHT.

SLEEPING GOD MOTIF

The idea of a sleeping deity seems at first to be inappropriate to the Bible. After all, Psalm 121:4 assures us that God neither slumbers nor sleeps. Of course the motif of a sleeping deity is primarily a feature of the anthropomorphism of pagan religions. It reaches its most memorable moment in the Bible when Elijah begins to taunt the 450 prophets of Baal at noon on the day of the showdown on Mt. Carmel. "Cry aloud," mocks Elijah, "for he is a god; . . . perhaps he is asleep and must be awakened" (1 Kings 18:27 RSV). Similar scorn appears in some of the prophetic taunts directed toward pagan worshipers: "Woe to him who says to a wooden thing, Awake; to a dumb stone, Arise!" (Hab 2:19 RSV).

But the Bible itself does not lack the technique of anthropomorphism: we do find poets picturing God as needing to be aroused from slumber. The primary repository of passages is the psalms of *lament, in which the speaker, distressed at God's inaction to date, gives vent to his feelings by portraying a sleeping God. "Awake, O my God," he exclaims (Ps 7:6). Again, "Rouse thyself! Why sleepest thou, O Lord? Awake!" (Ps 44:23 RSV). "Bestir thyself, and awake for my right" (Ps 35:23 RSV; see also Ps 59:4-5).

In a counterpart to the personal psalms of lament, the OT prophets plead with God in similar terms to deliver an exiled nation: "Awake, awake, put on strength, O arm of the LORD; awake, as in days of old" (Is 51:9 RSV). A statement of confidence can be expressed in the same imagery: "The LORD . . . has roused himself from his holy dwelling" (Zech 2:13 RSV).

What are we to make of such a surprising ascription of *sleeping to the God of the Bible? It fits into a thoroughgoing anthropomorphism in which God, even though he is spiritual rather than material, is metaphorically described as having body parts like an *arm and ear and in which he performs human activities such as changing his mind or *smelling the aroma of offerings. The sleeping God motif appears in the Bible in contexts of individual or national oppression. To picture God as needing to be awakened thus expresses human emotion rather than a theological fact about God.

See also SLEEP.

BIBLIOGRAPHY. B. F. Batto, "The Sleeping God: An Ancient Near Eastern Motif of Divine Sovereignty," *Biblica* 68 (1987) 153-77; T. H. McAlpine, *Sleep Human and Divine in the Old Testament* (Sheffield: JSOT, 1987).

SLEEPLESS NIGHT

In literature generally, the sleepless *night is an archetype of the *guilty conscience or the soul in turmoil. In the Bible too, people who have sleepless nights usually have good reason for their unsettled experience, and many of the sleepless nights in the Bible belong to pagan kings.

As part of the Bible's celebrated emphasis on the importance of the commonplace, a key event in the book of Esther is the sleepless night of King Ahasuerus, who asks that the royal chronicles be read and discovers that he has neglected to honor Mordecai for saving his life from plotters (Esther 6:1-3). On the night that Daniel spent in the lions' den, King Darius—who had "labored till the sun went down to rescue" Daniel—fasted, "and sleep fled from him" (Dan 6:14, 18 RSV). Kings who receive prophetic dreams do not sleep well: Nebuchadnezzar's "spirit was troubled, and his sleep left him" when he received the dream of the kingdoms (Dan 2:1 RSV), and a *Pharaoh has his sleep interrupted by two prophetic dreams (Gen 41:1-8). While all of these sleepless nights were distressing for the persons involved, they were noteworthy occasions of God's achieving his purposes. This is also true of *Jesus' night of agony in Gethsemane, a foil to the ignominious sleeping of the disciples. The boy Samuel too was awakened three times by dreams sent from God, and the prophetic message God entrusted to him was so momentous that he "lay until morning" thinking of what he had to tell Eli (1 Sam 3:15 RSV).

Elsewhere sleeplessness is the fate of people who fall into "at risk" categories. Thus "the surfeit of the rich will not let them sleep" (Eccles 5:12 RSV), and the portrait of *suffering humanity in Psalm 102 includes the detail of lying awake (Ps 102:7). The separated lover in Song of Songs has her own version of a sleepless night: "I slept, but my heart was awake" (Song 5:2 RSV). The missionary's career, too, is beset with sleepless nights (2 Cor 6:5; 11:27).

Not all sleepless nights are negative. The lover of God's law in Psalm 119 declares that "my eyes are awake before the watches of the night, that I may meditate upon thy promise" (Ps 119:148 RSV; cf. Ps 63:6). Another psalmist claims that "at night [the Lord's] song is with me" (Ps 42:8), and Job 35:10 gives us the evocative phrase about God as the One "who gives songs in the night" (RSV). David's zeal to build a temple was such that he hyperbolically refused to "give sleep to my eyes or slumber to my eyelids, until I find a place for the LORD" (Ps 132:4-5). And one of seven beatitudes in the book of Revelation pronounces, "Blessed is he who is awake" when Christ comes (Rev 16:15 RSV).

The foil to the sleeplessness of the restless has always been the peaceful sleep of the clean conscience and the honest *worker. If "the surfeit of the rich will not let him sleep," "the sleep of a laborer" is "sweet" (Eccles 5:12 RSV). The litany of contentment that makes up Psalm 16 includes the declaration that "my soul rejoices; my body also rests secure" (Ps 16:9 NRSV). Such peaceful sleep is ultimately the gift of God. The psalmist asserts, "In peace I will both lie down and sleep; for thou alone, O LORD, makest me dwell in safety" (Ps 4:8 RSV). It is "in vain," writes the poet, that a person rises up early and goes late to rest, "eating the bread of anxious toil; for [God] gives to his beloved sleep" (Ps 127:2 RSV).

See also AWAKENING; NIGHT; REST; SLEEP.

SLIGHTED CHILD. *See* FAVORED CHILD, SLIGHTED CHILD.

SLUGGARD

The character type known as the sluggard is a lazy person. In the Bible the archetype appears only in the book of Proverbs, where the idle person's behavior unleashes such a torrent of scorn from the wise man that he emerges as an important, though minor, biblical type.

To someone who values an industrious spirit and lifestyle, the sluggard is guilty on several counts. The sluggard begins the day awry by staying in *bed when he should be beginning his *work (Prov 6:9-10); he finds preposterous reasons to avoid going to work, such as the possibility of there being a *lion on the road (Prov 22:13; 26:13). As for excessive devotion to one's bed, "as a door turns on its hinges, so does a sluggard on his bed" (Prov 26:14 RSV). The sheer lack of exertion is captured by the caricature of the sluggard's burying his *hand in the dish but being too lazy even to bring the *food to his *mouth (Prov 19:24; 26:15).

The external symptoms of the sluggard all bespeak a lack of work. "The way of a sluggard is overgrown with thorns" (Prov 15:19 RSV). The wise man "passed by the field of a sluggard" (to get his day's shot of superiority?), and the lazy man's *vineyard was "all overgrown with thorns; the ground was covered with nettles, and its stone wall was broken down" (Prov 24:30-31 RSV). Among industrious sorts, such spectacles of mismanagement due to laziness always elicit a heavy dose of disapproval.

The impracticality of it all plays into the scorn the diligent direct against the sluggard. In a world where human labor is God's appointed means of provision (Gen 3:19), the sluggard is just asking for trouble. Because he "does not plow in the autumn," he "will seek at harvest and have nothing" (Prov 20:4 RSV). The sluggard will experience sudden poverty that comes like an armed man (Prov 6:11; 24:34). The "idle person will suffer hunger" (Prov 19:15 RSV), and although his soul craves, it will get nothing (Prov 13:4).

See also FOLLY; POVERTY; WORK, WORKER.

SMALL

In English *little* can sometimes carry more emotion than *small*. While to accuse someone of small-mindedness is quite insulting, it lacks the invective of an expression like "the little cunning of little minds." "Little sneak" sounds more contemptuous than "small sneak"—the latter may simply be a sneak of small stature.

In the Bible the term *small* and related concepts such as "little" and "least" similarly have many meanings and emotional colorings. This reflects a usage of belittlement, but often reversing or subverting normal perceptions. "Small" can apply to measure, such as stature, or to value. The image has many uses, often for dramatic effect, as when our Lord spoke of the tiny *mustard seed and its subsequent *growth (Mt 13:31) or pointed out the vast significance of the *widow's mite (Lk 21:2). There is ironic contrast, too, in the fact that a few loaves and some small *fish fed several thousand (Jn 6:9—a lesson in *faith, like the mustard seed); that a thousand would flee from *one person (Is 60:22; cf. also Is 29:5); and that an adolescent, *David, too young to be a soldier, slew the *giant Goliath (1 Sam 17). Similar irony is displayed when *James pictures the effect of a large *ship's small rudder, using it to illuminate unforgettably the effect of the *tongue (Jas 3:4).

Stature can play an important part in the course of events and thus become a feature of a biblical narrative. This is clearly apparent, of course, in the height of Saul and of Goliath (both of whom trusted in their virility rather than in the living God, in contrast to the relatively short David). It is there, amusingly, in the diminutive Zacchaeus, who had to climb a tree in order to see Jesus (Lk 19). In ancient times biography was not preoccupied with the image of a person, as it is now, so stature was recorded only if it was significant to the acts of a person. Thus we know that Jesus was neither very tall nor very short, as there is no record of his stature.

In very many instances the Bible uses *small* as an opposite to *great*, in reference to rank, station, the range of society and possibly height. A common phrase refers to crowds, the "small and great" (e.g., Esther 1:5; Job 3:19; Jon 3:5; Rev 11:18). Individuals are sometimes singled out by size-related terms, as in "James the less" (Mk 15:40), possibly referring to age. *Small* can refer to *children and the *young (Mt 18:6, 10, 14; Mk 9:42). *Little* can be a term of endearment, as when the apostle John speaks of the hearers of his letter as "my little children" (1 Jn 2:1, 12; *see* John, Letters of)—a gentle way of affirming his apostolic *authority. The image of smallness has powerful uses within a cluster of meanings: despised, apparently unremarkable, relatively powerless, marginalized. All these usages are ironic, as in the biblical

perspective the subject in fact has great significance, one with eternal ramifications. Thus there is the key idea of a small, faithful *remnant (Ezra 9:8; Jer 23:3; Rom 11:1-6). There are small places and little nations that need to be seen in a new perspective, such as *Bethlehem, Nazareth and the small nation of God's Old Testament people (Amos 7:2; Mt 2:6; Jn 1:46). Psalm 119:141 speaks of the pain of being put down and despised, even though one is faithful to God. The apostle Paul sees himself genuinely as less than the least of all God's people (Eph 3:8). Paul points out the symbolic significance of being small and the least—the impact of the small and despised is evidence of the gift of God's grace and his loving hand in history.

See also INCREASE, STORIES OF; LARGE, LARGENESS; LEAVEN, LEAVENING; MUSTARD SEED; ONE; REMNANT; SEED.

SMELL, SCENT

The primary sensation in the Bible is hearing (*see* Ear, Hearing). By comparison, scriptural imagery of smelling and scent is quite rare. Still, smell is not unimportant in the Bible, as a survey of related words like *stink, stench, fragrant/fragrance* and *perfume will demonstrate. Smells in the Bible, as in life, are either positive or negative.

The anthropomorphic *God of the OT is pictured as smelling the pleasing odor of a burnt *offering (nearly forty OT references; cf. Gen 8:21; Ex 29; Lev 1—3; Num 15; 28). The meaning of this positive imagery of scent is the satisfaction God experiences in the proper *worship of him and the acceptance of a *sacrifice as a propitiation for sin. We should also note that a characteristic way in which God derides *idols is by pointing out that they have no sense of smell (Deut 4:28; Ps 115:6).

Human smells in the Bible are varied. Jacob appropriates the smell of his brother to deceive his blind father (Gen 27:276). A *trumpet call metaphorically smells the impending *battle (Job 39:25). The sparing of Daniel's three friends in the *fiery furnace is so miraculous that they emerge without the smell of fire on them (Dan 3:27). In the Song of Songs the lover praises the scent of the beloved's *garments (Song 4:11) and *breath (Song 7:8), and the imagery of fragrance wafts throughout the lyrics of this epithalamion, or wedding song (Song 1:12; 2:13; 3:6; 4:10, 16; 5:13; 7:1). The *robes of the king in Psalm 45, another epithalamion, "are all fragrant with myrrh and aloes and cassia" (Ps 45:8 RSV). Two OT passages (Eccles 7:1; Song 1:3) employ wordplay in comparing a good name *(šēm)* to fragrant *anointing *oils *(šemen).*

A major positive cluster emerges from the fragrance of various aspects of OT worship. The fragrant *incense used in worship (mentioned a dozen times in the Pentateuch) was so "holy to the LORD" that anyone who duplicated it for ordinary use was to "be cut off from his people" (Ex 30:37-38 NIV). The fragrant incense of priestly offerings is also associated with temple worship (2 Chron 2:4; 13:11). The NT counterpart is the perfume with which Mary anointed Jesus' feet (Jn 11:2; 12:3-5).

By metaphoric extension, fragrance is attributed to the knowledge of Christ (2 Cor 2:14), those who follow and proclaim Christ (2 Cor 2:14-16), the sacrifice of Christ for those who believe in him (Eph 5:2) and the gifts of believers to a missionary (Phil 4:18). In Paul's extended analogy comparing the variety of gifts in the church to parts of the human body, Paul questions where the sense of smell would be if the whole body were hearing (1 Cor 12:17).

Negative smells also appear. Two of the ten *plagues were accompanied by terrible stench (Ex 7:18, 21; 8:14). The aftermath of battle includes the inevitable stench of dead corpses (Is 34:3; Joel 2:20; Amos 4:10). Human *death more generally produces stench (Jn 11:39; 2 Cor 2:16). According to a famous proverb, "dead flies make the perfumer's ointment give off an evil odor" (Eccles 10:1 RSV). Sometimes bad smells are part of God's *judgment, as when he promises that "instead of perfume there will be a stench" (Is 3:24 NRSV).

See also ALTAR; INCENSE; NOSE, NOSTRILS; PERFUME; SACRIFICE.

SNAKE. *See* SERPENT.

SNARE. *See* TRAP.

SNOW

Actual experience with snow was rare for biblical people. Snow would occasionally fall in Jerusalem, which is situated on a mountain top, but the sight of snow was for the most part a distant sight, rendered luminous by its presence on mountaintops remote from where most people actually lived, such as Zalmon or *Lebanon (Ps 68:14; Jer 18:14), and perhaps accounting for the quality of transcendence sometimes attributed to snow by biblical writers. Given the climatic context, the paucity of biblical references to actual snowfall makes sense; snow is more often used as a symbol. Still, the nearly two dozen biblical references show that snow was important to the writers' imaginations.

The rarity of contact with snow is hinted in the story of Benaiah, "a valiant man" and "a doer of great deeds" (2 Sam 23:20 RSV). One of his deeds was to kill a *lion in a pit "on a day when snow had fallen" (2 Sam 23:20 RSV; *see* Hunting), a detail that shows that snowfall was considered noteworthy. When the biblical poet says that God "gives snow like wool" and "scatters hoarfrost like ashes" (Ps 147:16 RSV), the point is partly that God can control the mysterious and awe-inspiring (because rarely experienced) forces of nature as easily as people perform routine daily tasks. In a climate where snow falls only once every several years and can cause hardship for people not prepared for it, snow is naturally linked with other large and hostile forces of nature—*fire and *hail, frost and *stormy winds (Ps 148:7). The re-

sourcefulness of the virtuous and industrious wife in Proverbs 31 is reflected in the fact that "she is not afraid of the snow for her household, for all her household are clothed in scarlet" (Prov 31:21 RSV). Mystery and power combine when the voice from the whirlwind in Job asks, "Have you entered the storehouses of the snow, . . . which I have reserved for the time of trouble?" (Job 38:22-23 RSV; cf. Job 37:6, where all God has to do to send snow is tell it to go).

Among figurative references to snow we find that it is first of all snow's *whiteness that is important. The color of *leprosy is three times compared to the whiteness of snow (Ex 4:6; Num 12:10; 2 Kings 5:27). Whiteness combines with *purity in passages that compare the *forgiveness of sins to snow (Ps 51:7; Is 1:18). The whiteness of snow and *milk is part of an idealized picture of prosperous princes (Lam 4:7). The most noteworthy image pattern of the whiteness of snow is pictures of the transcendent brightness of God himself (Dan 7:9), of Christ at his transfiguration (Mk 9:3), of the angel who appeared at the resurrection (Mt 28:3) and of Christ standing amid the *lampstands in John's vision (Rev 1:14).

Other properties of snow figure in miscellaneous ways. Snow is associated with harsh cold (Ps 147:16-17; 148:8; Prov 25:13; 31:21) and with refreshing coolness (Prov 25:13; *see* Weather). The fact that snow falls on the earth and stays there, causing crops to grow, figures in Isaiah's simile asserting that God's word does not return to him empty but accomplishes its purpose (Is 55:10-11). And the fact that snow melts quickly and then vanishes in warm temperatures is used in Job 24:19 to picture the destruction of the wicked.

For people living in climates where snow falls abundantly every winter, snow is an image of the commonplace. The opposite is true for the writers of the Bible, where snow assumes qualities of something rare, exotic, noteworthy and resplendent.

See also HAIL; LEBANON; PURITY; WEATHER; WHITE; WOOL.

SODOM AND GOMORRAH

The *sin and destruction of Sodom and Gomorrah described in Genesis 19 are a symbol throughout the Bible for those who choose to oppose the purposes of God and a paradigm of devastating divine *judgment. Though the account of these *cities of the *plain reaches its climax with the raining of burning sulfur from heaven, the reader is actually introduced to them earlier in the narrative.

Sodom and Gomorrah are first mentioned in the table of nations as part of the territory of the Canaanite clans (Gen 10:19). This subtle connection with the *curse of Noah's son Ham (Gen 9:18-27) hints at *evil and perhaps some relation with *sexual perversion. When Abram and Lot are forced to go separate ways because of the rivalry between their herdsmen, Lot chooses the well-watered plain for himself (Gen 13:10-12). These verses are full of echoes of earlier stories, all of which end in disaster. Lot sees that the plain is "like the garden of the LORD" (Gen 13:10 NIV) and, like Eve in Eden, is tempted by what is "pleasing to the eye" (Gen 3:6 NIV); the plain is also "like the land of Egypt," yet Egypt had been the scene of Abram's lack of faith and *shame (Gen 12:10-20); and Lot moves *east toward Sodom (v. 11), even as all the earth had moved "eastward" to Shinar and with hubris built the Tower of *Babel (Gen 11:1-9). In other words, the sin and judgment of Sodom and Gomorrah are part and parcel of the broader framework of humanity's *rebellion. The text moves beyond these literary subtleties to advise that these cities later will be destroyed (Gen 13:10) because of their great wickedness (Gen 10:13).

The material prosperity of the city of the "well watered" plain of the Jordan is confirmed by a portrait in Ezekiel 16:49 of the residents of Sodom as suffering from "pride, surfeit of food, and prosperous ease" and not aiding the poor and needy (RSV). It was Sodom's *prosperity that doubtless attracted Lot to it. That he lived in a place of sexual perversion with a very bad conscience is suggested by the comment in 2 Peter 2:8 that Lot was "vexed in his righteous soul day after day with their lawless deeds" (RSV).

Lot's move from "near Sodom" to the city itself (Gen 13:12; 14:12) means that the fate of Sodom and Gomorrah now becomes intricately interwoven with the life of the patriarch. Abram rescues his nephew from capture by Kedorlaomer and so saves the goods and people of Sodom (Gen 14:1-16). The interchange between Abram, *Melchizedek and the king of Sodom after the battle, however, serves to locate the account of Sodom and Lot within the history of faith and *blessing (Gen 14:17-24). Abram is blessed by Melchizedek, but he refuses to accept the offer of the king of Sodom. Thus Sodom continues to develop as a symbol of temptation away from dependence and *obedience to God. Abram demonstrates the character God desires; Lot is his foil, the contrasting picture of *weakness and carnality.

The appearance of the visitors in Genesis 18 adds another level to the imagery of Sodom and Gomorrah. On the one hand, the "outcry" against them (Gen 18:20; cf. Gen 19:13) takes the reader back to Genesis 4:10 and reinforces the earlier links with humanity's evil, and *Abraham's intercession for however few righteous might live in these cities again underscores his own just life (Gen 18:16-33; cf. Gen 12:1-3); on the other hand, his discussion with the Lord also ties the story into the promise of the *seed and the future nation (Gen 18:10-17). Lot's own descendants will be the fruit of incest and the fathers of Moab and Ammon, *enemies of Israel (Gen 19:30-38). Beyond the enduring general symbol of Sodom as opposite of what is pleasing to God, therefore, lie the realities of political conflict in the history of the nation.

The contrasting of Lot and Sodom with Abraham is highlighted by parallels in the *hospitality extended toward the divine messengers (Gen 18:1-8; 19:1-3). But the story in Genesis 19 quickly degenerates into a spiral of sin. The attempt at sexual violation by the entire male population, the offer of Lot's daughters in the messengers' stead, the mocking of his future sons-in-laws, Lot's hesitation to leave Sodom and his plea not to have to flee far away, and the fateful backward glance of his wife fill out this portrait of rejection of God's ways (Gen 19:4-26). All Abraham sees afterward is the smoke of the judgment (Gen 19:27-28).

The character and fate of Sodom and Gomorrah reappear often in the Bible. Sometimes the allusions are clear even though the names are not used. Rahab shows hospitality to strangers and protects them from a mob (Josh 2); Judges 19—21, with the cruel *rape of the Levite's concubine in Gibeah, the offer of a *virgin daughter to save the visitor and the desperate measure to preserve the seed of Benjamin, resounds with parallels to Genesis 19. It is possible, too, that the biblical phrases that describe judgment as *fire and *brimstone are anchored in that dreadful destruction on the plain.

These two cities, however, are also cited explicitly as paradigms of what is ungodly. Most often a particular sin of Genesis 19 is not mentioned; rather, Sodom and Gomorrah serve as a byword for evil. They represent what is unnatural (Deut 32:32). *Jerusalem is like them because of *oppression and hollow religiosity (Is 1:10; 3:9; Jer 23:14). Jesus says that the nation's rejection of his message and person makes his audience guiltier than Sodom and Gomorrah (Mt 10:11-15; 11:20-24). For killing its divine messengers, the city of David in the future will be called Sodom (Rev 11:8). In two passages the comparison with Sodom and Gomorrah is based on a list of sins (Ezek 16:46-56; Jude 7). Sexual perversion does not appear in the prophetic list, but in the context the *idolatrous activity of Israel and Judah is repeatedly pictured as promiscuity (Ezek 16:15-43). In Jude the sexual sin is clearly alluded to. So Sodom and Gomorrah represent self-destructive depravity, although the nature of the sin that is denounced varies from passage to passage.

Finally, the divine chastisement of Sodom and Gomorrah is a symbol of total and irrevocable judgment. In the OT this imagery can be used of other nations (Is 13:19; Jer 49:18; 50:40; Zeph 2:9) or of the people of God (Lam 4:6; Amos 4:11). In the NT, Sodom and Gomorrah are an example and metaphor of the future day of judgment. At that time people will be judged for not repenting and for rejecting God's Son and salvation (Mt 10:15; 11:23; Lk 17:28-36; 2 Pet 2:7-11).

See also BRIMSTONE; CITY; HOSPITALITY; JUDGMENT.

BIBLIOGRAPHY. R. Alter, "Sodom as Nexus: The Web of Design in Biblical Narrative" in *The Book and the Text: The Bible and Literary Theory*, ed. R. M. Schwartz (Oxford: Basil Blackwell, 1990) 146-60; L. D. Hawk, "Strange Houseguests: Rahab, Lot and the Dynamics of Deliverance" in *Reading Between Texts: Intertextuality and the Hebrew Bible*, ed. D. N. Fewell (Louisville, KY: Westminster John Knox, 1992) 89-97; R. I. Letellier, *Day in Mamre, Night in Sodom: Abraham and Lot in Genesis 18 and 19* (Leiden: E. J. Brill, 1995).

SOFT, SOFTNESS

The words *soft* and *softness* are not often found in English translations. The Hebrew and Greek words that are sometimes translated "soft" or "softness" occur more frequently. Given the relative prominence of the language of softheartedness among contemporary English-speaking Christians, it is surprising that this language appears only rarely in the Scriptures, and then with a different meaning.

Softness as Weakness. In English, "softheartedness" usually refers to a sensitivity to others, or to a quickness to respond to conviction of *sin with *repentance. The Hebrew word most frequently standing behind the "soft" of English translations appears in Job 23:16, the only biblical text to speak specifically of softheartedness: "For God made my heart *weak*, and the Almighty terrifies me" (NKJV). Based on this verse's synonymous parallelism—a common feature of Hebrew poetry—a softened *heart is a fearful heart (*see* Melt for the meaning of the related image of a melting heart). Similarly, Deuteronomy 20:8 employs the Hebrew word to describe an individual fearful of *warfare ("fainthearted," NASB).

The image of the soft heart has implications for the meaning of more common image of the *hard(ened) heart. The hard heart is the heart fortified against the natural *fear of God to resist his will: "They made their hearts as hard as flint and would not listen to the law or to the words that the LORD Almighty had sent by his Spirit through the earlier prophets" (Zech 7:12 NIV).

Another Hebrew word can be translated "make soft" in the sense of dissolving. Job 30:22 ("Thou dost lift me up to the wind and cause me to ride; and thou dost *dissolve* me in a storm," NASB) pictures Job's personal ruin. Psalm 107:26 describes the failure of human courage in the midst of a *storm at *sea: "They rose up to the heavens, they went down to the depths; their soul *melted away* in their misery" (NASB).

Softness as Gentleness. The same Hebrew word conveys the sense of *gentleness or tenderness. Its use in Deuteronomy 28:54, 56 points out the unspeakable horrors of siege, as it describes "the most gentle and sensitive man among you" (NIV) resorting to cannibalism. Speech is often described as "soft" in the sense of gentleness. In Job 41:3 the Lord asks Job concerning Leviathan (*see* Mythical Animals), "Will he make many supplications to you? Or will he speak softly to you?" In Psalm 55:21 the psalmist describes (insincerely) peaceable words as "softer than oil" (NASB). The power of gentle speech is portrayed strikingly in Proverbs 25:15,

where the "gentle tongue" (NIV) has the power to break *bones. Likewise, Proverbs 15:1 tells us, "A soft answer turns away wrath" (NKJV). The apostolic writings often enjoin Christians to engage in gentle speech and behavior (Gal 5:22; 2 Tim 2:24; Tit 3:2; Jas 3:17).

Soft as Indulgent. To highlight the rugged integrity of John the Baptist's *ministry, Jesus contrasts him with those who wear "soft garments" and live in *kings' palaces (Mt 11:8 NKJV; Lk 7:23). The same Greek word, *malakos*, is translated "homosexuals" in 1 Corinthians 6:9, describing a type of "soft" men—most likely men who submit to *homosexual advances.

See also FEAR; HARD, HARDEN, HARDNESS; HEART; MELT, MELTING.

SOJOURN, SOJOURNER. *See* FOREIGNER; WANDERER, WANDERING.

SOLAR IMAGERY. *See* SUN; SUN, MOON AND STARS.

SOLDIER. *See* ARMY, ARMIES; BATTLE STORIES.

SOLOMON

Historically, Solomon was widely recognized for his fabulous wealth. He was so wealthy that he might as well have had Midas's mythic golden touch, for everything he used on a daily basis was *golden. In his day he made *silver "as common . . . as stones" (1 Kings 10:27 NIV). The OT records further that his *wisdom "surpassed the wisdom of all the people of the east, and all the wisdom of Egypt" (1 Kings 4:30 RSV) and was such that "all the earth was seeking the presence of Solomon, to hear his wisdom that God had put in his heart" (1 Kings 10:24). Christ speaks of Solomon's wisdom and suggests (by use of parallel structure) that it went beyond mere human wisdom, that it was spiritually regenerative: he likens it to Jonah's preaching, and the queen of Sheba to the Ninevites (Lk 11:31-32).

So vast is the biblical image of Solomon's preeminence that today we are most familiar with his name as possessive adjective: Solomon's mines, Solomon's wealth, Solomon's *wives, Solomon's *temple. No other person ever receives God's carte blanche offer "Ask what you wish me to give you" (1 Kings 3:5 NASB). He is a person of unfathomable wealth and power, an image of unlimited potential.

Unfortunately, Solomon ultimately becomes an image of wasted potential and position. He inherits David's firmly established *kingdom, at peace with all surrounding *kings (1 Kings 2:12; 4:24). He inherits the task of building God's temple. But while his kingdom is secure, his heart for God is not, perhaps evinced best when he builds himself a palace four times the size of the temple (1 Kings 6:2; 7:2). When he chooses to *worship the pagan deities of his many foreign wives, God takes away the realm that Solomon could have passed on to his *children.

The image of the wasted Solomon is used most effectively in the book of *Ecclesiastes. The "Preacher" in that book is associated with Solomon. He is one who has wisdom, power and women but cannot find meaning "under the sun."

Christ puts Solomon and his wealth in divine perspective when he points out in the Sermon on the Mount that even Solomon couldn't buy the exquisite clothing of the lily of the field (Mt 6:28-29). Solomon made his earthly mark and at times used his gifts to honor God, but his spiritual choices show that he valued temporal luxury over eternal *inheritance.

Solomon's wisdom is acknowledged in Matthew 12:42. But Jesus' wisdom makes Solomon's pale by comparison.

See also ECCLESIASTES; DAVID; PROSPERITY; WISDOM.

SON

In the Bible a son is a male begotten by a *father. In a broader sense sonship denotes a range of familial, hereditary, social and theological relationships. Biblical references to sons need to be understood in context of the extreme value that ancient cultures placed on sons.

Perpetuating Life. In the ancient way of thinking, the life of a father is continued in his son. A major ingredient in a father's feeling that his life on earth has fulfilled its purpose is the presence of a son to perpetuate his lineage (Gen 15:2-4). Thus institutions such as polygamy, levirate *marriage and even *adoption were established in order to save a father's life on earth. Something of the profundity of the image of perpetuating oneself in one's son is captured by the comment that *Adam "became the father of a son in his own likeness, according to his image" (Gen 5:3 NASB).

From this understanding, a son is called a *"seed" (*zeraʿ*). In Genesis 15:2 Abraham complains that God has not given "seed" to him, and in Genesis 22:16-18 God promises Abraham after the test, "Because you have done this thing, and have not withheld your son, your only son, indeed I will greatly bless you, and I will greatly multiply your seed as the stars of the heavens, and as the sand which is on the seashore; and your seed shall possess the gate of their enemies. And in your seed all the nations of the earth shall be blessed, because you have obeyed My voice" (NASB; cf. Gen 24:7). Onan was ordered to go in to his brother's wife and perform his duty as a brother-in-law to her, to raise up seed for his brother (Gen 38:8).

Since the life of one's father passed on to his son, a son usually was called by the name of his father. "The one who is called by the name of his father" is a designation for a son generally in the Bible (Gen 48:16). From this analogy, Ruth was said to raise up the name of the deceased when she gave birth to a son through Boaz (Ruth 4:11-13), and the son was called "a restorer of life" (Ruth 4:15 NASB). In Genesis 3:15 the messianic redeemer is designated as

the seed of woman, and Isaiah 53:10 says the Messiah will see his seed after his death.

The social manifestation of this view of sons as perpetuating a family's line was *inheritance. A son was to inherit the property of his father. In particular, the first son inherits a double portion of all that his father has (Deut 21:17). For this reason the tenants in Jesus' parable attempt to kill the heir in order to take his inheritance (Mt 21:38; Mk 12:7; Lk 20:14). If the father was too old to care for his family, the first son took his father's responsibility and exercised authority over the household (Gen 24:50, 55). Thus the Israelite women called the (grand)son of Naomi born to Ruth "a sustainer of your old age" (Ruth 4:14 NASB).

Sons as an Image of Honor. In Homer's *Odyssey* nothing is valued more highly than a worthy son. Some of the same sentiment underlies biblical attitudes, and the book of Proverbs gives us a glimpse of it. Positively, "a wise son makes a father glad" (Prov 10:1 NASB; 15:20). The speaker also asserts, "My son, if your heart is wise, my own heart also will be glad" (Prov 23:15). Conversely, "a foolish son is a grief to his father, and bitterness to her who bore him" (Prov 17:25 NASB). Ways in which an unworthy son brings shame (Prov 10:5; 17:2; 19:26) have as their logical concomitant the ideal of raising a proverbial son that "maketh not ashamed."

In the Bible sons are even viewed as the symbol of the father's might or strength. Jacob calls Reuben, his firstborn, "my might and the beginning of my strength" (Gen 49:3 NASB). The expression "beginning of strength" is used on several other occasions in the Bible in reference to the firstborn (Deut 21:17; Ps 78:51; 105:36). That is, children are the strength of the father in war or in labor power, and the firstborn is the beginning of it. The sons of Jacob demonstrated their power when they destroyed Hamor and his son Shechem, who raped their sister (Gen 34). The psalmist compares the "sons of one's youth" to "arrows in the hand of a warrior" (Ps 127:4 RSV), adding, "How blessed is the man whose quiver is full of them; they shall not be ashamed, when they speak with their enemies in the gate" (Ps 127:5 NASB).

Christ as Son. There are approximately 150 NT references to Christ as "the Son," "Son of God" or "Son of Man." As a trinitarian term, *sonship* images relationship between Christ and the Father. Building on the image of human sonship noted above, it is also a designation of honor and exaltation, heightened by the epithet "only begotten." It is important, though, to distinguish at this point between human sons and the divine Son, inasmuch as *begetting* is a metaphoric term, not referring to either emanation or creation. The second person of the Trinity is a son also in his obedience to the will of the Father regarding the incarnation and *atonement.

The Son as Symbol. A striking image of sonship in the Bible is the description of *Israel as the son of God. The Lord calls Israel "my son" (Ex 4:22-23; Is 43:6; Hos 11:1). Accordingly, the Lord is called

Israel's father (Is 63:16; Jer 3:4, 19). Since Israel is the son of God, "my people who are called by my name" (Deut 28:10; 2 Chron 7:14) is the Lord's special designation for Israel. Further, the Lord, the owner of the *land (Ps 24:1; Deut 10:14), gives Israel the land of Canaan, flowing with milk and honey, as an inheritance (Deut 15:4; 19:10; 20:16; Ps 135:12; Is 19:25).

In the NT the imagery of sonship is applied to believers in Jesus, and we should note that used in this way it is not a gender term but includes both men and women. John and Paul in particular develop the concept of sonship to describe the relationship between God and the believer. The overall plan of God's salvation is "the revealing of the sons of God" (Rom 8:19 NASB). In order to fulfill the plan, God sent his Son into the world, born of *woman (Gal 4:4-5). The *Gentiles receive the adoption of sonship through his *Spirit, the spirit of adoption (Rom 8:15). The spirit of adoption causes them to cry out to God, "Abba! Father!" and the Spirit bears witness that we who are being led by the Spirit of God are sons of God (Rom 8:14). Furthermore, the sons of God will be heirs of God and fellow heirs with Christ (Rom 8:17), inheriting the *kingdom of God which is prepared from the foundation of the world (Mt 25:34; Lk 12:32; 1 Cor 6:9-10; 15:50; Gal 5:21; Eph 5:5). At that time the Lord will say, "He who overcomes shall inherit these things, and I will be his God and he will be My son" (Rev 21:6 NASB).

See also BIRTHRIGHT; CHILD, CHILDREN; DAUGHTER; INHERITANCE; FATHER; SEED.

SON OF DAVID. *See* JESUS, IMAGES OF.

SON OF GOD. *See* JESUS, IMAGES OF; SON.

SON OF MAN. *See* JESUS, IMAGES OF.

SONG. *See* MUSIC.

SONG OF SOLOMON. *See* SONG OF SONGS.

SONG OF SONGS

The most persuasive interpretation of the title Song of Songs, taken from the first two words of the Hebrew text, is that it is the best of all songs. Certainly the book's pervasive and compelling use of imagery lends credence to this claim. No other book of the Bible is so thick with simile, metaphor and other artful examples of language.

The most egregious errors in the interpretation of this book arise because of a failure or unwillingness to recognize its proper poetic quality. The imagery is too often treated as allegory in the negative sense, the characters and the images standing for persons or qualities for which there are no hints in the text itself. Or the literary allusions are turned into real people and events, as happens in the various dramatic interpretations of the Song.

But the Song is neither allegory nor drama. There is no plot or narrative, and no historical characters are involved, except by allusion (Song 3:7; 8:10-12). Rather, the Song is composed of loosely connected lyric poetry that expresses an emotion, indeed one of the most powerful of emotions: love. A prose description of love would not be as powerful. The poetic imagery expresses an emotion that transcends simple statement. It preserves a level of mystery and appeals to more than the mind—to the whole person.

Nature Imagery. Dominating everything else in the Song is the fact that it is a collection of pastoral love poetry. The conventions of pastoral, one of the most common literary conventions at every stage in the history of literature, are easy to grasp: the setting is rustic, the characters are *shepherds and shepherdesses (usually a fictional disguise), and the actions are those customarily done by shepherds and shepherdesses. Pastoral love poetry, specifically, adds wooing and courtship to the activities performed by the characters. In pastoral love poetry, *nature supplies most of the images by which the lovers express their romantic passions, including their praise of the beloved. Subtypes of pastoral love poetry include the invitation to love (an invitation to the beloved to stroll in a flowery and fruitful landscape is a metaphoric invitation to marriage and the life of mutual love [Song 2:10-15; 7:10-13]) and the emblematic blazon or *wasf* (the beloved is praised by cataloging his or her beautiful features and comparing them to objects in nature [Song 4:1-7; 5:10-16; 6:4-7; 7:1-5]).

Nature imagery permeates the Song, and here we will only mention briefly the *flowers, *fountains, *gardens, orchards, *vineyards and *animals that ornament this passionate love poetry. In the first place, many of the scenes of intimacy take place in natural settings. We read of the lovers' tryst in a forest *bedroom (Song 1:16-17). They find each other in verdant gardens (Song 6:2-3) and meet under an apple tree (Song 8:5). Such peaceful, romantic natural settings are contrasted with the hostile urban settings where the two lovers are separated from one another (Song 5:2-8).

The physical beauty of the couple is described using nature imagery. The man is like a gazelle or young stag on spice-laden *mountains (Song 8:14). The woman is like a *palm tree, her *breasts like clusters of the vine (Song 7:7-8). Perhaps most powerful is the description of the woman's body as a garden or a fountain (Song 4:12-5:1). In this *wasf* the climactic focus is on the woman's vagina, likened to a marvelous and sweet-smelling garden, a well-watered fountain. These are common ancient Near Eastern images of a woman's vagina.

The metaphors of the book consistently draw upon nature, but it is important to realize that the correspondence is not primarily based on visual similarity. The point of the comparisons is instead the *value* that the speaker finds in his or her beloved. The lovers and their love are compared to *the best things* in nature. The poetic mode of the Song is not pictorial but emotional and sensuous in nonvisual ways (including tactile and olfactory). More than anything else, images of nature portray the *quality* of the beloved, and here we can see evidence of the Hebrew fondness for structure and for how things are formed. The comparison of the woman's *teeth to sets of twin shorn *sheep fresh from washing (Song 4:2) is a typical specimen, capturing such qualities as whiteness, wetness, symmetry, completeness and flawlessness. A woman's breasts are not visually like two fawns (Song 4:5), but the imagery captures her modesty (a passerby will not get close to two fawns) and their softness to the touch.

Courtly Imagery. One of the paradoxes of pastoral poetry is that it arose only with the rise of *cities and civilization. Images of a royal *court, with all its wealth and opulence, frequently break through the fictional façade of the Song's pastoral world. The world of the Song is filled with expensive clothes, *perfumes, rich *foods, gems and erotic leisure. As early as Song 1:4, the woman addresses her lover as her king; in Song 7:5 the woman's head is said to "crown" her and her *hair is a "royal tapestry." This language has mistakenly led some to argue that the Song is a story of a royal pair, perhaps Solomon and his Egyptian queen, but the language is love poetry, where the woman is a *queen in the eyes of her lover and the man is a *king in the eyes of his beloved.

The allusion to Solomon and his luxurious carriage in Song 3:6-11 adds to the royal motif. It is unclear whether we are to imagine the woman being carried in the carriage or the man being connected with it, but the point is that the lover and the beloved are associated with this object of royal luxury and leisure.

The wealth of the court is reflected in a number of the images in the Song, including those having to do with clothes, perfumes, food, gems and architecture. The *veil, except in one instance, probably associates the woman with royalty and marriage (Song 4:1, 3; 6:7). The evidence indicates that Israelite women normally did not wear veils except during marriage ceremonies and among the wealthy and sophisticated classes. The one exception is Song 1:7-8, which is likely a reference to the fact that *prostitutes also wore veils. In this instance the woman chides the man, asking him not to make her act like a prostitute as she seeks him out. But in the many other cases where the Song mentions a veil, a royal and perhaps marriage context is evoked.

*Oils and spices are images of both court and nature. They were expensive and so the property of the rich only. Already in Song 1:2 the woman comments on the enticing fragrance of her lover, and the compliment is returned in Song 4:10. Of course, this image evokes the sense of *smell, once again reminding the reader that the emotion of love is a multifaceted sensual experience.

The beauty of both the man and the woman is compared to the beauty of precious gems. Looking at Song 5:10-16 alone, we see the man's head compared to *gold, his eyes to *jewels, his arms to rods of gold set with chrysolite. His body (the term more likely refers to his phallus) is a tusk of ivory decorated with sapphires, and so on. In a word, his physical beauty is attractive, even stunning, to behold.

Finally, the architectural images also partake of a courtly milieu. The woman's *neck, for example, is compared to David's *tower, in all likelihood to emphasize its grace and dignity (Song 4:4).

Family Imagery. Munro rightly identifies a series of metaphors in the Song which arise from the family. Interestingly, there is little marital imagery as such—no references to *husband and *wife (except perhaps when the man refers to the woman as his "bride" [Song 4:8-12; 5:1]), but there are significant references to mothers and siblings.

The mothers of the woman and the man support the relationship (Song 6:9; 8:5). The home of the former is a secure place for intimacy (Song 3:4; 8:2). Interestingly, the fathers are never mentioned in the Song; the woman's *brothers seem to take the place of her father. As opposed to her mother, the brothers are an obstacle to love's intimacy, and she struggles to be free of their influence (Song 1:5-7; 8:8-12).

At one point the woman declares her wish that her lover were her brother, so that she might be intimate with him publicly as well as privately (Song 8:1). On the other hand, the man will often endearingly refer to his beloved as "his *sister" (Song 4:9-10, 12; 5:1-2).

Summary. The world of the Song is a world of heightened emotion. Its genius is that it enables us to view the world as experienced by people intoxicated with love (cf. the references to love as being better than wine [Song 1:2; 4:10], meaning more emotionally intoxicating than wine is physically intoxicating). The imagery of the Song is pastoral, passionate, erotic, sensuous, hyperbolic, metaphoric and affective. The style aims at an association of feelings and values rather than visual correspondence, and the imagery is symbolic rather than pictorial, figurative rather than literal.

See also LOVE STORY; MAN, IMAGES OF; MARRIAGE; SEX; WOMAN, IMAGES OF.

SORCERY. *See* MAGIC.

SORROW

Every kind of human *grief, sadness and sorrow is depicted in Scripture, whether as the result of adverse circumstances, sickness, parting, personal loss, failure or *sin. In sorrow the *heart, the core of the emotions according to the Hebrews, becomes heavy and is downcast. Most of the scriptural references are to the literal sorrow of men and women (Ps 116:3; Rom 9:2), but in two respects sorrow is also attributed to God.

Human sorrow in the Bible is a response to calamity. It is the picture of Jacob protesting that his gray head will go "down to the grave in sorrow" over his allegedly dead son Joseph (Gen 42:38 NIV), or

Rachel weeping for her dead children "and refusing to be comforted" (Jer 31:15 NIV; cf. Mt 2:18), or Jesus in Gethsemane, his soul "very sorrowful, even to death" (Mt 26:38 RSV par. Mk 14:34). Specific images associated with sorrow include *eyes growing *weak (Ps 6:7; 31:9); a troublesome burden in one's heart (Ps 13:2); a state of being overcome (Ps 116:3), or overwhelmed (Mt 26:38; Mk 14:34); soul weariness (Ps 119:28); something that is added to *pain, wears a person out and robs a person of rest (Jer 45:3); physical exhaustion (Lk 22:45); and an anguish of heart (Rom 9:2).

Sorrow is also associated with *God. First, there are occasions when God is described as being sorry for something he has done. At the time of the *flood "the LORD was grieved that he had made man on earth, and his heart was filled with pain. So the LORD said, 'I will wipe mankind, whom I have created, from the face of the earth—men and animals, and creatures that move along the ground, and birds of the air—for I am grieved that I have made them' " (Gen 6:6-7 NIV). Similarly, the failure of Israel's first king, Saul, is pictured as grieving God (1 Sam 15:11, 35).

There are also times when God is pictured as being saddened because of the calamities his own *judgments have caused. So it was with the *plague he had sent as punishment for David's numbering of the people (2 Sam 24:16; 1 Chron 21:15). He similarly grieves over his devastated *land (Jer 42:10), and he is even depicted as wailing and *weeping over the destruction of Moab (Jer 48:32), even though he himself is clearly responsible for it.

References like these, if taken strictly literally, call into question factors like God's perfect foreknowledge and purposes in the *world, which would certainly not have been the intention of those who employed them, for we are told on more than one occasion that God does not change his *mind (Num 23:19; 1 Sam 15:29; Ps 110:4). Rather, they fall into a category known as anthropomorphisms, where God is described in human terms. Just as the biblical authors could speak about God's arm or his hand, they could also describe him grieving or *repenting, that is, changing his mind about what he had done.

Having said this, however, Scripture makes it clear that God does feel sorrow, and it is in this respect that we turn to the second aspect of the use of this image. The disobedient actions of people are described as making him sad. So the *sin of *Sodom and Gomorrah was so "grievous" to him that he visited those places with his judgment (Gen 18:20). The sins of his own people had a similar effect (Ps 78:40). Isaiah describes them as grieving God's *Holy Spirit by their *rebellion (Is 63:10), an image taken up in a NT context by Paul: "Do not grieve the Holy Spirit of God, with whom you were sealed for the day of redemption" (Eph 4:30 NIV). The language, though human, is applicable to the personal relationship believers have with God, who is no mere power or mind, impassive and static; and this, in turn, becomes a powerful moral incentive.

See also GRIEF; HEART; MOURN, MOURNING; PAIN; SUFFERING; TEARS.

SOUTH

It is unfortunate that no English translation distinguishes the quite different Hebrew words for "south," each designating contrasting perceptions of this direction. The term *têmān* or *yāmîn*, "right hand," "south," provides a cosmic orientation that assumes individuals anywhere on earth are facing the rising *sun, so that their *right hand points south, an orientation Israel shared with other cultures in the ancient Near East (cf. on the extreme southern tip of Saudi Arabia the modern state of Yemen, whose name means "south" or "right hand"). The beneficent and salutary connotations associated with the right hand may encourage a favorable perception of the south when this term is used: "Awake, O north wind, and come, O south wind! Blow upon my garden" (Song 4:16 NRSV).

On the other hand, the term *negeb* has to do with a localized geographic orientation specific only to the territory of ancient Israel, the extensive desert directly south of the fertile hills and lowlands of Judah. The south from this narrow point of view represents a region hostile to life; it is "a land of trouble and distress, of lioness and roaring lion, of viper and flying serpent" (Is 30:6 NRSV). The inimical aura cannot be confined but breaks out and threatens the verdant areas to the *north: "As whirlwinds in the Negeb sweep on, it comes from the desert, from a terrible land" (Is 21:1 NRSV). As predictably as cold comes from the north, so "out of the south comes the storm" (Job 37:9 NASB) and hot air: "When you see the south wind blowing, you say, 'There will be scorching heat'; and it happens" (Lk 12:55 NRSV; cf. Job 37:17).

Both the beneficent and the hostile dimensions of the south are exploited simultaneously when God is depicted as having his residence in the south (*têmān*) on a *mountain that is identified by a number of different names (Mt. *Sinai, Mt. Horeb, Mt. Paran, Mt. Seir). God administers *justice to the cosmos from this southern locale by (1) beneficently coming to the *rescue of those in need and (2) bringing destruction upon those who afflict the helpless (Deut 33:2; Judg 5:4-5; Hab 3:3-6). The imagery of the hot and violent southern *winds enhances this picture whenever God decides to "march forth in the whirlwinds of the south" (Zech 9:14 NRSV), resulting in garments that "are hot when the earth is still because of the south wind" (Job 37:17 NRSV).

*Wisdom may be yet a third aspect associated with the south. Because wisdom is a characteristic feature of the high *gods of the ancient Near East, the association of the south with wisdom may result from its association with one of the dwelling places of God. A city in Edom named Teman ("south," "right hand") was identified as a hub of wisdom and good counsel (Jer 49:7). One of Job's friends comes from here, Eliphaz the Temanite, a counselor who epitomizes the best of traditional wisdom as he *wrestles with Job's dilemma (Job 2:11; 4:1). Later rabbinic tradition suggested that any "who desires to become wise should turn to the south [when praying]" (*b. Baba Batra* 25b). It is unclear whether the *tabernacle *lamp was placed on the south side of that structure as an echo of such illumination from the south, but it is at least consonant with the notion (Ex 26:35; 40:24).

See also EAST; NORTH; RIGHT, RIGHT HAND; WEST.

SOW, SOWER, SOWING

In an agrarian economy, the sowing and planting of crops is a major event, the timing of which depends on the type of *seed, for which there is always a "time" (Eccles 3:2). In the Bible, God is viewed as the One who instructs the farmer how to do his work rightly (Is 28:29). Sometimes plowing the soil and planting went together; at other times one followed the other so that some seed fell on *paths, *rocky ground or *weed-infested soil (Mk 4:1-9).

Human Sowing. Sowing is spoken of figuratively for setting various things in motion. In both the OT and the NT it is used for engaging in a righteous or loving activity (Prov 11:18; Eccles 11:1; Hos 10:12; cf. Jas 3:18), for initiating *evil and disrupting unity (Job 4:8; Prov 6:14, 19; 16:28; 22:8) and for undertaking a spiritual task (Gal 6:8-9). Linked with *harvesting, it gives birth to proverbs about the link between energy expended and outcome expected, such as "you reap whatever you sow" (Gal 6:7 NRSV), "one sows and another reaps" (see Job 31:8; Mic 6:15; cf. Jn 4:37) or "those who sow in tears reap in joy" (see Ps 126:5; Prov 22:8). It is also a metaphor for giving, which if done sparingly will result in a small return, if done generously in a large return (2 Cor 9:7-10).

In Paul the image of sowing is connected with the passage from earthly to *heavenly life. In 1 Corinthians 15:35-38 he echoes Jesus' words about the grain of *wheat falling into the ground before it can bear *fruit (Jn 12:24). Our present existence is physical in form and perishable in kind: it exhibits *weakness and dishonor. The future form will be spiritual and immortal: it will radiate power and *glory (1 Cor 15:36-38, 42-44).

Divine Sowing. Sometimes God is pictured as metaphorically supplying the seed and therefore always capable of increasing it (2 Cor 9:9-10) or sowing it, such as when he is described helping Israel to flourish again (Jer 31:27), multiplying its inhabitants, *animals and *cities, and increasing the amount of good they do (Ezek 36:9-11), all of which brings delight to both God and the nation (Hos 2:23). It is also used to describe God's indiscriminate giving to the poor (2 Cor 9:9; *see* Poverty), as well as God's supplying and multiplying people's capacities to act righteously (2 Cor 9:10).

On other occasions *Jesus is the sower (Mt 13:37), the seed represents the message that he

preaches (Mk 4:14), and his hearers are represented by the different soils on which it lands. Jesus interprets such references allegorically to explain how the gospel often falls on hearts that are *hardened, superficially ready or encumbered with worldly concerns. This, combined with interference from *Satan, difficulties and *persecutions, or anxieties, desires and greed, prevents the Word from taking deep *root. Only when it falls into genuinely fertile and cultivated soil will it flourish, but then it does so exponentially (Mk 4:1-9, 13-20).

In other *parables Jesus explains how God's *work in the world grows at God's hands even when someone is *sleeping (Mk 4:26-29), and how the outcome of this provides a haven for people of every kind (Mk 4:30-21).

See also FARMING; FRUIT, FRUITFULNESS; HARVEST; ROOT; SEED.

BIBLIOGRAPHY. R. Banks, *God the Worker: Journeys into the Mind, Heart and Imagination of God* (Valley Forge, PA: Judson, 1994).

SPARROW. See BIRDS.

SPEW. See SPIT; VOMIT.

SPIRITUAL FOOD. See FOOD.

SPIES, SPYING

Spying, "the second oldest profession," has been a standard weapon in power games since the dawn of history. Israelite leaders from Moses onward (Num 13) regularly used spies to report on *enemy movements and targets. The handful of OT spy stories are strikingly modern and surprisingly ambivalent: spies are depicted as *heroes or *villains, depending on the side for whom they are working.

The universal dislike of foreign spies is well illustrated in the dramatic irony of Joseph's encounter with his brothers in Egypt. He accuses them of coming "to see where our land is unprotected." They, unaware of his true identity, protest, "Your servants are honest men, not spies" (Gen 42:9-11 NIV). Spying is clearly disreputable if one is being spied upon.

But if the spies are working for God's people, then the image becomes positively romantic. Joshua's spies are popular heroes who take refuge beneath the roof of Rahab, who practices the oldest profession, prostitution (Josh 2). During the Israelite massacre of Jericho, she whom the law condemns is rewarded by a commando-style *rescue (Josh 6:20-23).

Other twists in the moral maze include Esther, applauded for concealing her Jewish identity and becoming a classic agent of influence as queen of Persia (Esther 2:20). Ehud the judge became a folk hero for worming his way into King Eglon's chamber to deliver "a secret message"—deftly, with a concealed dagger (Judg 3:19-23).

The NT has little time for spy stories. Only two references are made in passing, both dismissive. Spies are sent, like secret police, to record Jesus' words in the hope of trapping him (Lk 20:20-26). And Paul refers to false teachers as agents of influence who covertly infiltrate the church to subvert its freedom in Christ by encouraging legalism (Gal 2:4).

Furthermore, the NT maintains that the spy's currency of duplicity and falsehood cannot be cashed by people of truth and righteousness who have "renounced secret and shameful ways [and] do not use deception" (2 Cor 4:2 NIV). It effectively outlaws the profession in the service of the gospel; the *weapons of Christian warfare are not those of the world (2 Cor 10:4).

See also DECEPTION, STORIES OF; SPY STORIES; WARFARE.

SPIT

The image of spit, when combined with the related images of saliva, spew and *vomit, illustrates the great flexibility of figurative language in the Bible. Of the thirty-three uses of these words, only seventeen refer to a literal spitting or vomiting; the rest are wholly figurative. And of the seventeen literal references, only three have no additional figurative value: Jonah 2:10 (though even here the whale's vomiting Jonah probably signifies disgust) and Proverbs 23:8 and 25:16. An analysis of the figurative meanings reveals quite a variety.

In ten of the literal references to spitting, it is a social insult. To spit in the face is an extreme insult or expression of contempt (e.g., Deut 25:9), complained of by Job (Job 17:6; 30:10) and supremely applied to Jesus (Mt 26:67; 27:30; etc.). In a related motif, spitting and vomiting are gestures of revulsion and rejection. The action of the *stomach in vomiting, or of the *mouth in spitting, becomes a vivid image of rejection. God will spit out the Laodiceans (Rev 3:16), and the land will spit out Israel if the people do not obey (Lev 18:28; 20:22).

Elsewhere spitting and vomiting are related to madness or *folly. David's letting saliva run down his *beard (1 Sam 21:13) was an act of resourcefulness that enabled him to escape death while a captive. In the biblical world, wallowing in vomit is a vivid image for folly (Prov 26:11) or spiritual incomprehension (Is 19:14; 28:8; Jer 48:26). In a related picture Peter portrays false *teachers as *dogs returning to their own vomit (2 Pet 2:22).

Lest we think the imagery of saliva wholly negative, though, we find a motif of its healing power (*see* Disease and Healing). In several of his miracles of healing, Jesus used saliva (Mk 7:33; 8:23; Jn 9:6), which fits with the Jewish and Hellenistic belief in the healing properties of saliva.

See also DISGUST, REVULSION; MOUTH; VOMIT

SPOILS, DIVIDING. *See* TRIUMPH.

SPOT

Spot or *taint* suggests a conspicuous tinge of something offensive, such as a blemish, stain or other

impurity, which renders the object no longer pristine or pure but rather contaminated in some way. In the Bible both literal and figurative senses are anchored in the *holiness of Yahweh, who demands from his *covenant people both ritual and moral purity (Lev 11:45).

Examples of literal imagery include Leviticus 13, where individuals with *skin "spots" were to be inspected by the *priests to determine whether they were ritually clean or unclean. In a similar vein, objects tainted with mildew were rendered "unclean" (Lev 13). The *sacrifice of an animal with any kind of defect was unacceptable to God (Ex 12:5; Deut 17:1). No Aaronic descendant with a physical blemish could serve as a priest (Lev 21:17-21).

These images are also used in a figurative sense, as for example in Jude 23, where the writer vividly captures the depraved condition of unredeemed human nature by describing it in terms of "clothing stained by corrupted flesh" (NIV). James exhorts his readers to keep themselves from being "spotted" by the world (Jas 1:27). Elsewhere he describes the *tongue as that which "stains" the whole person (Jas 3:6). Conversely, a pure *church is described as free from "spot or wrinkle" or any other blemish (Eph 5:27 NRSV). And most important, the Lord Jesus himself is described as One who "offered himself unblemished to God" (Heb 9:14 NIV) as a "lamb without blemish or defect" (1 Pet 1:19 NIV).

See also CLEANSING; HOLINESS; PURITY.

SPOUSE. *See* HUSBAND; WIFE.

SPRINGS OF WATER

Water is a precious resource in the Middle East, and much of what is available comes from natural springs or *fountains. Springs in the Bible have associations similar to those of *rivers and *water, but a spring is even more evocative, being upsurging, "living" water that becomes synonymous with the sustaining and refreshment of life. As a perpetual and continuous flow of water, a spring embodies a principle of natural provision that is abundant and irrepressible. Springs in the Bible are almost uniformly positive in association, and the number of references is approximately fifty (since *wells are frequently located at the sites of springs, some English translations have fewer references to *spring* in deference to *well*). In many of the passages cited below, God is clearly the One who has power to produce and dry up springs of water.

The imagery of springs of water is integral to Holy Land geography and climate. Because external moisture supplies are precarious, underground sources of water are especially valued. Moses could hardly have given a more favorable description of the *Promised Land than this one: "For the LORD your God is bringing you into a good land, a land with flowing streams, with springs and underground waters welling up in valleys and hills" (Deut 8:7 NRSV). Psalm 104, one of Scripture's most evocative pictures of God's natural provision, includes the picture of how

God makes "springs gush forth in the valleys" (Ps 104:10 NRSV).

The terrain of Palestine accounts for several features of the springs mentioned in the Bible. Springs frequently appear in a desert or *wilderness landscape (Gen 36:24; Ps 84:6; 107:35; Is 35:7; 41:18; 43:19). Related to this, springs are often part of a desert oasis where travelers can be sustained or even rescued (Gen 16:7; Ex 15:27; Num 33:9). In an arid land, springs of water are inevitably linked with vegetation, where it would otherwise be unlikely (Gen 49:22; Is 44:18). *Gardens are likewise associated with springs (Is 58:11; 61:11). Part of the importance of springs in the Bible is the location of wells near them (Gen 24:13, 16, 29, 42-43, 45; 26:19).

Compared with wells and *cisterns, springs have the advantage of being in constant motion. They represent not simply water but abundance of water. In the psalmist's imagination, springs are linked with torrents (Ps 74:15). In Proverbs 8:24 the essential quality of springs is that they are "abounding with water" (NRSV), and Isaiah speaks of "a spring of water, whose waters never fail" (Is 58:11 NRSV).

Based on all of this it is not hard to see why springs would be highly valued in the world of the Bible. In Joshua 15:18-19 Caleb's daughter asks him to give her possession of some springs as part of her dowry, calling the springs a blessing. In an arid land, springs can assume such importance that they become geographic points of reference (Josh 15:9; 18:15; Judg 7:1).

Some of the imagery of springs in the Bible is latent rather than obvious, and some is based on ancient cosmology. The Hebrews imagined the oceans to be fed by springs or fountains (Gen 7:11; 8:2; Job 38:16 NIV). Although the river flowing from the Garden of Eden is not called a spring, the fact that it arises from a source like a headwaters and then divides into four *rivers gives it the quality of a spring (Gen 2:10-14). This is echoed in Ezekiel's vision of a stream springing up from the temple and issuing in a tree-lined river (Ezek 47:1-2, 12).

Although most of the associations with springs are positive, there are terrors as well. Because of the scarcity of water resources, the threat of impurity of springs and wells is a major concern (Lev 11:35-36; 2 Kings 2:19-22). Stopping up springs was a military tactic designed to harm the enemy (2 Kings 3:19, 25; 2 Chron 32:3-4). God's judgments include using springs for floods (Gen 7:11; 8:2), drying up springs (Jer 51:36; Hos 13:15) and defiling and polluting springs (Rev 8:10-11; 16:4).

The symbolic meanings of springs are wide-ranging and flow from the physical properties noted above. Human corruption is portrayed as polluted, spoiled or dried-up springs (Prov 25:26; Jer 2:13; Jas 3:10-12; 2 Pet 2:17). On the positive side, "faithfulness will spring up from the ground" (Ps 85:11 NRSV). In a psalm praising *Zion and filled with patriotic devotion, the climactic praise is the statement "All my springs are in you" (Ps 87:7 NRSV). The "springs of life," metaphoric for a person's inner identity and its manifestations, flow from the heart (Prov 4:23 NRSV). A husband's *sexual appetite is like a spring of water that should remain his private domain with his spouse (Prov 5:16). The beloved's eyes "are like doves beside springs of water" (Song 5:12 NRSV). A chaste bride is an enclosed garden within which is "a spring *shut up, a fountain sealed" (Song 4:12 NKJV).

The symbolic uses of the spring of water reach their climax in pictures of salvation. According to OT apocalyptic visions, in the coming messianic age spiritual springs of water will appear in the wilderness (Is 43:19) and will guide the redeemed there (Is 49:10), and as noted above, the redeemed themselves will be "like a spring of water, whose waters never fail" (Is 58:11 NRSV). These prophecies find fulfillment in NT references to the water of salvation that becomes in people "a spring of water gushing up to eternal life" (Jn 4:14 NRSV), the "springs of the water of life" that satisfy glorified saints in heaven (Rev 7:17 NRSV) and the salvation that Christ offers to thirsty people "as a gift from the spring of the water of life" (Rev 21:6 NRSV).

See also BROOK; CISTERN; FOUNTAIN; RIVER; WATER; WELL.

SPRINKLE

Sprinkling in the Bible is a ritual act that symbolizes a spiritual reality. The overwhelming preponderance of references occurs in the books of the Pentateuch that lay out the ceremonial laws. There are two root words in the OT for "sprinkle": *nāzâ* and *zāraq*. They are synonymous in meaning, with the difference having to do with amount of material (almost always liquid) sprinkled. The former, *nāzâ*, is done with the fingers and is a relatively light distribution of *blood, *oil or *water. More copious amounts (handfuls) of those substances are distributed when *zāraq* is used. There is no such distinction made for sprinkle in the NT, where the Greek word is *rhantizō*.

In the Bible, sprinkling serves two related but separate functions in the religious life of God's people. One is to consecrate or hallow objects or people to the Lord. Whether *altars, *garments or people, that which is sprinkled is marked as something now holy to the Lord (Ex 24:3-8).

The second function was for cleansing or for expiation of *sin. After Aaron's sons were killed because they had approached the holy place unworthily, the Lord made provision for a more sanctified approach for *priests who would follow: "He shall sprinkle some of the blood on it with his finger seven times to cleanse it and to consecrate it from the uncleanness of the Israelites" (Lev 16:19 NIV; see also Ex 29:20 for purification rites for priests). The cleansing role of sprinkling was also integral to the sacrifice of the sin offering (Lev 5:9). Water was to be sprinkled for the sake of purity when someone had become defiled by touching a corpse (Num 19).

In the NT the ritualistic sprinkling of the OT ceremonial laws becomes metaphoric. The letter to

A pharaoh is purified by gods sprinkling the water of life.

the Hebrews shows how sprinkling as both consecration (a new priesthood daring to enter the most holy place) and *cleansing has its fulfillment in Jesus Christ, the ultimate priest who became the ultimate blood sacrifice:

> He entered the Most Holy Place once for all by his own blood. . . . The blood of goats and bulls and the ashes of a heifer sprinkled on those who are ceremonially unclean sanctify them so that they are outwardly clean. How much more, then, will the blood of Christ, who through the eternal Spirit offered himself unblemished to God, cleanse our consciences from acts that lead to death! (Heb 9:12-14 NIV)

Christ's atoning sacrifice represents "sprinkled blood that speaks a better word than the blood of Abel" (Heb 12:24 NIV). In metaphoric applications to believers, we read about human "hearts sprinkled clean from an evil conscience" (Heb 10:22 RSV) and about sanctified Christians as having been set apart "for obedience to Jesus Christ and sprinkling by his blood" (1 Pet 1:2 NIV).

See also CLEANSING; BLOOD; OIL; WATER.

SPY STORIES

Spy stories are a branch of *battle stories. While not numerous in the Bible, they play a crucial role in several OT events. Spy stories are stories of secrecy, intrigue and danger. *Spies themselves are a case study in vulnerability. When Joseph wishes to terrify his brothers, he charges them with being spies (Gen 42:9-16, 30-34). Genuine spies were courageous warriors required to travel over rough terrain and show considerable diplomatic skill if questioned.

Spy stories first become important in the Bible in the events surrounding the entry of the nation of Israel into Canaan. As part of a deliberate military strategy, Moses dispatches *twelve spies (one from each tribe) to check out the land (Num 13). The advice of ten of the spies that the nation not enter the Promised Land ranks as an ignominious chapter of weak faith, judged severely by God. Joshua and Caleb, on the strength of their advice to conquer the land, rank as heroic figures in their role as spies.

For the dangerous side of spying, we have the story of the two spies whom Joshua sends into Jericho (Josh 2). They are nearly discovered, escaping only by the cleverness of Rahab when she hides them under flax on the roof of her house. Subsequently, we read about spies who are dispatched to Ai (Josh 7:2) and Kadesh barnea (Josh 14:7). Spy stories are also present in the book of Judges (Judg 1:23-24; 18:2, 14, 17). In later history David also employed spies (1 Sam 26:4; 2 Sam 10:3).

Two NT references round out the canon of biblical spy stories. Although the religious establishment's attempts to entrap Jesus and bring him to trial are only once said to be the work of spies (Lk 20:20), in a sense the ongoing intrigue of the scribes and *Pharisees against Jesus is an extended spy story. Paul makes metaphoric us of the imagery of spying when he claims that the Judaizers who wish to impose Jewish rites on Christians are "false believers secretly brought in, who slipped in to spy on the freedom we have in Christ Jesus" (Gal 2:4 NRSV).

See also SPY, SPYING.

SPYING. *See* SPIES, SPYING.

STAFF. *See* ROD, STAFF.

STAIN. *See* SPOT.

STAND, STANDING

Among postures portrayed in the Bible, standing is a major image. Most of the more than six hundred references denote presence or location, as when we read about "towns that stood on mounds" (Josh 11:13 RSV), the Lord's tabernacle that "stands" in Israel (Josh 22:19), people who stand at a specific place (Judg 7:21; 9:7) and "standing grain" (Judg 15:5). But the imagery of standing also comes to connote specific qualities and attitudes, both literal and figurative.

While some of the positioning uses of the image are neutral, others imply a special quality to being present at a given place. For example, when the psalmist exclaims, "Our feet have been standing within your gates, O Jerusalem!" (Ps 122:2 RSV), we catch the notes of *worship in a sacred place; this standing entails a spiritual posture as well as a physical one. Standing becomes almost numinous when we read of prophets, priests and people "standing in the house of the LORD" (Jer 28:5 RSV). It can be an expression of *reverence, as when the *remnant that returned to Jerusalem stood before the book of *law when it was opened (Neh 8:5).

Standing is sometimes a posture for *prayer. For example, Hannah stood while praying for a child (1 Sam 1:26), and Solomon stood to utter his dedicatory prayer at the temple (1 Kings 8:22). In Jesus' parable (Lk 18:9-14) both the Pharisee and the tax collector stood to pray—the former pompously (and presumably in a conspicuous place at the temple), while the publican stood "far off" (probably in the temple's outer court).

A cluster of images associates standing with commitment to a godly purpose. Nearly a dozen exhortations in the Epistles to "stand firm" (or "stand fast") evoke an image of fixed commitment to God and the Christian faith, as opposed to abandoning one's resolve. Similar qualitative meanings accrue when people are said to be of "good standing" (1 Tim 3:13) or "high standing" (Acts 13:50; 17:12) and in the picture of believers who "stand mature" in godliness (Col 4:12 RSV).

Another cluster associates standing with *authority. A *king, for example, stands as head over a people (1 Sam 19:20), and a *prophet stands as head over those who prophesy (1 Sam 19:20). The *priests of the tribe of Levi were appointed to "stand and minister in the name of the LORD" (Deut 18:5 RSV). "Standing by" an authority is a related image of attendance upon an authority figure, whether priestly (Zech 3:5) or kingly (2 Sam 13:31). Six dozen references to standing "before" God or an earthly authority evoke a picture of formal reverence or service on the part of subjects. Thus the person "skilful in his work . . . will stand before kings" (Prov 22:29 RSV). Overtones of authority are also part of more than a dozen references to standing in awe of either God or human authority.

The image of taking a stand appears in contexts of *warfare (2 Sam 2:25; 20:11; 1 Chron 11:14), where it implies a defensive posture. The ultimate defeat is to "have no power to stand before your enemies" (Lev 26:37 RSV). The image pictures conquest when it is said of a nation that "not a man shall be able to stand against you" (Deut 7:24 RSV; cf. Deut 11:25; Josh 1:5; 1 Kings 10:4). Standing guard is a related image (Neh 7:3; 12:25).

Building on some the usages noted above, standing is also an image of permanence. Vows, for example, are said to "stand"—that is, remain in effect (Num 30:4, 7, 11). God's counsel "shall stand" (Is 46:10 RSV), and his kingdom "shall stand for ever" (Dan 2:44 RSV). A house built on a *rock stands when floods come, whereas a house built on sand collapses (Mt 7:24-27). "The house of the righteous will stand" (Prov 12:7 RSV). Conversely, destruction is pictured in terms of altars not standing (Is 27:9). Most emphatically of all, God's Word and love will stand forever (Ps 89:28; Is 40:8).

See also BOWING; LYING DOWN; SITTING.

STARS

The nearly seventy references to stars in the Bible highlight their status among the heavenly bodies. In a large number of instances, stars are mentioned with one or both of their familiar companions in the skies—the *sun and the *moon. Together these three were created by God to rule the *day and

*night (Gen 1:16-18; Ps 136:9; Jer 31:35). The stars thus help to divide day from night, as in the reference to builders of the wall in Nehemiah's time laboring and standing guard "from break of dawn until the stars came out" (Neh 4:21 NRSV).

A series of associations gather around the stars as objects of God's *creation. They signal transcendence, for example: "See the highest stars, how lofty they are!" (Job 22:12 NRSV). Stars are evidence of God's artistry: in Psalm 8:3 stars and the moon are the work of God's molding "fingers" (NRSV). There is something cheerful about stars; at creation "the morning stars sang together" (Job 38:7); Psalm 148 speaks of "shining stars" (Ps 148:3 NRSV). Stars can also be images of *glory, as in Paul's assertion that there is a specific "glory of the stars; indeed, star differs from star in glory" (1 Cor 15:41 NRSV). As physical features of the heavens, stars have from time immemorial seemed to the human imagination to be wanderers in vast space, and the Bible includes a reference to "wandering stars" (Jude 13 NRSV). The stars are part of God's providential control as well as the product of his creativity, as God "determines the number of the stars; he gives to all of them their names" (Ps 147:4 NRSV).

The stars of the sky sometimes also signify huge *numbers. Ten times in the Bible the stars are used as a standard by which to declare something (usually descendants) to be "numerous."

When we move from literal to figurative references, interesting developments emerge. God's masterminding the Israelite defeat of the Midianites, partly through the use of a rainstorm that mired the enemies' chariots in mud, is described figuratively as a battle of the stars: "The stars fought from heaven, from their courses they fought against Sisera" (Judg 5:20 NRSV). The stars as actors in God's cosmic drama are an archetype in *apocalyptic visions of the end of history, where they are described either as ceasing to give light (Is 13:10; Joel 2:10; 3:15) or as falling from heaven (Mt 24:29; Mk 13:25).

Stars also become symbols of people. In Daniel's apocalyptic vision, those who will awake to everlasting life "shall shine . . . like the stars forever and ever" (Dan 12:3 NRSV; cf. Phil 2:15). False teachers who deviate from the truth are, as noted above, "wandering stars" (Jude 13). In Revelation 1:20 the seven stars "are the angels of the seven churches" (NRSV), and the twelve stars of the woman in travail identify her as Israel (Rev 12:1). Whereas the ancient pagans worshiped the stars (see Acts 27:20 for a reference), the NT metaphorically calls Christ the *morning star (2 Pet 1:19; Rev 22:16). In addition to stars, there is *the* star of the Bible—the star that led the wise men to Jesus at his nativity (Mt 2:2, 7, 9-10).

Virtually all the biblical star motifs converge in the book of Revelation, where more than a dozen verses contain images of stars. Christ holds mysterious stars (angels of the churches, we learn later) in his hand (Rev 1:16; 2:1). Christ is himself "the bright morning star" (Rev 22:16 NRSV). To the believer who overcomes, Christ promises to give "the morning star" (Rev 2:28 NRSV), apparently symbolic of eternal life in heaven, and perhaps of Christ himself. Amid the cataclysmic events at the end of history, stars fall from the sky (Rev 6:13; 8:10; 9:1; 12:4) and refuse to give their light (Rev 8:12). A mythical star named Wormwood contaminates the waters of the earth (Rev 8:11), and Israel, portrayed as a woman, wears "a crown of twelve stars" (Rev 12:1 NRSV).

In sum, stars in the Bible are images of mystery. At a literal level they demonstrate God's awe-inspiring creativity and *providence. In symbolic uses they appear in apocalyptic visions of impending cosmic events that we can barely imagine, and they represent such transcendent beings as saints in eternal glory and the resplendent ascended Christ.

See also COSMOLOGY; MOON; NIGHT; SUN; SUN, MOON, STARS.

STATURE, BODILY. *See* BODY.

STEW

Unlikely as it may seem, one of the most familiar stories in the Bible is about stew. It would actually be more accurate to say the story is about character. But the word *stew* in the context of a discussion of the Bible reminds us immediately of the story of *Jacob and *Esau. The characters of the twin sons of Isaac and Rachel are exposed for all to see, as Esau foolishly trades his *birthright to Jacob for a bowl of stew (see Gen 25).

Now there is absolutely nothing remarkable about stew—it may be wholesome, savory and tasty, but it remains a very common and humble sort of *meal. It is this very fact that gives the story of Jacob and Esau its power. The trade gave Jacob, in essence, something for nothing; in choosing the stew, however, Esau "despised his birthright" (Gen 25:34 NRSV). The potential power, wealth and honor of his birthright were cashed in for the proverbial "mess of pottage." We all shake our heads in amazement at Esau's lack of foresight. Stew in this story becomes a touchstone for character, as Esau reveals that he is a slave to his stomach, unable to deny himself immediate gratification for the sake of future benefit, while Jacob shows himself to be an opportunist, ready to use anything that presented itself in his self-interest. We might note in passing that the original Hebrew stresses Esau's uncouth manners and speech patterns, as he tells Jacob, "Let me gulp some of that red stuff."

There is a lesser-known story in the Bible in which stew is a key ingredient as well. 2 Kings 4:38-41 gives us a rather odd little tale about Elisha converting a bad stew into a wholesome one. There are undoubtedly many reasons this story is included in the canon, but an obvious one is that it underscores Elisha's role among everyday folks. Unlike Elijah, who dealt mainly with royalty, Elisha was God's mouthpiece primarily for the common people. It is also significant that the miracle took place during a *famine (2 Kings

4:38), showing God's concern for his servants.

See also FOOD.

STEWARD. *See* AUTHORITY, HUMAN; LEADERSHIP.

STIFF-NECKED. *See* NECK.

STOMACH

The stomach is part of a cluster of biblical images centering on *food and *eating. On the physical level it is both literally and by synecdoche or metonymy associated with bodily *appetite and sustenance. As such it signals larger moral and spiritual issues of personal values, self-control, self-indulgence and the state of one's soul. Another cluster of images draws upon the stomach simply as the vulnerable midregion of the body.

Stomach imagery is first of all used in reference to bodily satisfaction. Having one's stomach filled suggests comfort and wealth, or being satisfied. In his farewell discourse, when Moses paints a picture of the *good life that awaits the Israelites in the *Promised Land, the image of the full stomach is one of the details: "when you eat and are satisfied" (Deut 6:11 NIV; cf. Job 20:22-23, where the full stomach is an image for plenty). Conversely, an empty stomach represents bodily deprivation and discomfort, sometimes as a result of God's judgment for disobedience: "Therefore, I have begun to destroy you," the Lord tells Israel. "You will eat but not be satisfied; your stomach will still be empty" (Mic 6:13-14 NIV; see also Amos 4:6). The prodigal of Jesus' parable was so hungry that "he longed to fill his stomach with the pods that the pigs were eating" (Lk 15:16 NIV). An OT proverb combines the full stomach as emblem of plenty and the empty stomach as an example of want: "The righteous eat to their hearts' content, but the stomach of the wicked goes hungry" (Prov 13:25 NIV; also Prov 18:20). A full stomach, in other words, is an image of the *good life, a *reward for godly behavior.

The importance of the full stomach is highlighted by the way the two most significant temptations in biblical history center on appeals to the stomach. *Satan uses the natural appetites of the stomach in *tempting *Eve, twisting the original and good purposes of the appetite to his own gain (Gen 3:6). Later, while Jesus is *fasting forty days in the *wilderness, Satan's first tactic is the appeal of food to the stomach: "If you are the Son of God, tell these stones to become bread" (Mt 4:3 NIV). While Adam and Eve fell to sin, Jesus triumphed over the appeal of the stomach's appetites and Satan's lie that we must satisfy our desires.

In the Bible the stomach sometimes reveals the condition of a person's soul. A popular saying of the time is quoted by Paul—"Food for the stomach and the stomach for food" (1 Cor 6:13 NIV)—revealing the depraved state of those who seek to satisfy the appetites of the sinful nature. Similarly, the "enemies of the cross of Christ" are destined for destruction because "their god is their stomach" (Phil 3:18-19 NIV). The meaning of this is debated. Perhaps it is a reference to libertines whose appetites draw them away from Christ. Or it may be a reference to Jewish Christians who promote and adhere to Jewish food laws and so misconstrue the gospel. The biblical case against the stomach is not only that it can become an obsession but also that it can never be permanently satisfied: "All man's efforts are for his mouth, yet his appetite is never satisfied" (Eccles 6:7 NIV).

Jesus turned the physical process of digestion to metaphoric use in teaching that it is one's inner soul, not one's physical stomach, that makes one clean or unclean. He said, "Don't you see that whatever enters the mouth goes into the stomach and then out of the body? But the things that come out of the mouth come from the heart, and these make a man 'unclean' " (Mt 15:17-18 NIV; cf. Mk 17:19).

A prophetic motif is for a prophet to eat a *scroll as a metaphor for assimilating a message from God (Ezek 3:3; Rev 10:9-10). The scroll John eats turns his stomach sour, symbolic of the judgmental content of the visions God entrusts to him. In a related usage, Zophar's portrait of the misery that awaits the wicked includes the account of how, "though evil is sweet in his mouth . . . his food will turn sour in his stomach" (Job 20:12, 14 NIV). In a follow-up image recounting the fate of the wealthy wicked, "God will make his stomach vomit" up his riches (Job 20:15 NIV).

The most famous stomach in the Bible is surely that of the "great fish" in which *Jonah is preserved from a watery death. Despite the positive connotations of Jonah's being preserved, the surroundings could hardly have been pleasant, and the culmination of the event is Jonah's being vomited onto dry land.

A final usage of the stomach in Scripture is violent mutilation of someone's body. Thus we read about Abner's thrusting his spear into Asahel's stomach (2 Sam 2:23), Joab's stabbing Abner in the stomach in retaliation (2 Sam 3:27) and Recab and Baanah's stabbing Ish-Bosheth in the stomach (2 Sam 4:6).

Although the Bible contains a few pictures of the full stomach as a physical condition toward which people aspire on their earthly sojourn, most of its references to the stomach do not convey a positive picture. The preponderance of images surround the stomach with intruding weapons, with sourness and vomiting, with hunger pangs and insatiable appetite, and with obsessive devotion to eating until it becomes a god.

See also APPETITE; BELLY; FOOD.

STONE

Nothing could be more lifeless than a stone. Selected and displayed in a prominent place, however, a stone can bear a message and almost become personified. Thus Joshua's stone at Shechem "heard all the words of the LORD; . . . therefore it shall be a witness against

you, if you deal falsely with your God" (Josh 24:27 NRSV). Stones appear as *witnesses in other passages as well. A *covenant is made, a sacrificial meal eaten, and stones serve as witnesses (Gen 31:44-54). Archaeologists have uncovered several circles of stones (some with *eyes or *hands on them) almost certainly representing witnesses to covenants or other religious rites.

Stone imagery primarily conveys the concept of lifelessness. When Moses received the Ten Commandments, they were written on tablets of stone, a fact that seemed to prophets of a later generation symbolic of hard, unresponsive hearts: "I will remove from your body the heart of stone and give you a heart of flesh" (Ezek 36:26 NRSV; cf. Jer 31:33). Paul took up the contrast between "the ministry of death, chiseled in letters on stone tablets," and the greater glory of the ministry of the Spirit (2 Cor 3:7-8 NRSV; *see* Holy Spirit), which transformed lives.

Stones of great density and weight are a powerfully destructive force when set in motion. A stone cut out "not by human hands" strikes the feet of Nebuchadnezzar's dream statue, shattering the *gold, *silver and other layers that represent world empires. This supernatural stone grows to fill the earth and is depicted as God's invincible *kingdom (Dan 2:34-44). The stone endures, whereas successive world kingdoms fall, never to rise again. That unchanging, enduring quality lies behind Jacob's name for God, the *Rock (KJV: "stone of Israel," Gen 49:24).

That Jesus was *tempted to turn *wilderness stones into *bread is significant. *Satan's temptation was to do something that would have immediate appeal. But God does not need to stoop to "bread and circuses" to gain a following.

Appropriately, the Lord's *temple was built of costly dressed stone (1 Kings 5:17), a building material more enduring than manufactured *brick. It was meant to stand for the truth—God is with us—and indeed the Lord said to Solomon when the temple was consecrated, "My eyes and my heart will be there for all times" (1 Kings 9:3 NRSV).

But that unique privilege carried with it the fearsome implications of God's holiness. If his people turned aside from following him as Lord, Israel would be cut off from their *land and the temple would become a heap of ruins (1 Kings 9:6-9). Isaiah was aware that this threat would soon be carried out: "The LORD of hosts, him you shall regard as holy. . . . He will become a sanctuary, a stone one strikes against" (Is 8:13-14). The same God becomes both a sanctuary and a stone to trip over, depending on the response people make to his holiness. Those who make the Most High their dwelling place will find his *angels keeping them from stumbling against this stone (Ps 91:12; cf. Mt 4:6). Moreover, God's purpose for *Jerusalem will be fulfilled, despite the intrigues of Israel's leaders (Is 28:14).

God's future purpose, revealed to Isaiah, was to

lay in *Zion "a foundation stone, a tested stone, a precious cornerstone, a sure foundation" (Is 28:16 NRSV) and to use *builders of *justice and righteousness. The *cornerstone here is part of the foundation, whereas in other contexts it could be the key top stone (Zech 4:7, 9). The NT makes use of both senses. The top stone of an arch or pediment proved that the architect's instruction had been carried out and so exactly illustrated the work of Christ, the "living stone" (1 Pet 2:4). Peter also quotes Psalm 118:22: "The stone that the builders rejected has become the very head of the corner" (1 Pet 2:7 NRSV) together with Isaiah 8:14. These references were linked by the first Christians because they point to Jesus as the Messiah foretold in the Scriptures (cf. Acts 4:11): though their Messiah had caused division and was rejected by many, this had been predicted. Jesus himself was the source of this application of Psalm 118:22, to which he added a reference to the stone of Daniel 2:34: "Everyone who falls on that stone will be broken to pieces; and it will crush anyone on whom it falls" (Lk 20:17-18). This dreadful picture of judgment from the lips of Jesus is found only in the Gospels.

Paul conflated Isaiah 28:16 and Isaiah 8:14 to explain Israel's failure to accept righteousness through faith; they had stumbled whereas Gentiles had believed (Rom 9:33). In Ephesians 2:20-21 he draws on the temple-building metaphor to construct his famous vision of the *church, made up of believers from far and wide, "built upon the foundation of the apostles and prophets, with Christ Jesus himself as the cornerstone. In him the whole structure is joined together and grows into a holy temple in the Lord" (Eph 2:20-21 NRSV).

In Nehemiah 4:2 Sanballat asks, regarding the Jewish returnees' efforts at rebuilding Jerusalem's *wall, "Can they bring the stones back to life from those heaps of rubble—burned as they are?" (NIV). This is an interesting metaphor in relation to Peter, who would add that individual believers are "like living stones" (1 Pet 2:5). Meditation on his name had perhaps convinced him that he was not the only one who would be called Peter, a stone.

Mention should be made, finally, that stones are a unifying motif in the story of Jacob as narrated in Genesis, embodying important facets of this hero's life and personality.

See also BRICKS; BUILD, BUILDING; CORNERSTONE; ROCK; STONING; STUMBLE, STUMBLING BLOCK.

STONING

Stoning was the most common method of biblical execution (Lev 24:13-16; Deut 17:2-7), and the images of it are evocative, to say the least. Stoning was a *death of surpassing brutality. Rabbinic lore describes how a man was to be thrown from a cliff and crushed on the chest with a large *stone. If still alive, the victim was then pelted with smaller stones until dead. This ghastly image is magnified by the fact that stoning was a communal sentence carried out by the common people. It was excommunication from the community in the most dire sense. Furthermore, the *weapons were the very stones of the land of Israel.

Most of the crimes for which stoning was prescribed were public offenses against the integrity of the community of faith, and this explains the communal nature of its method. Blasphemy, *idolatry, spirit divination, false *prophecy, *adultery, the disobedience of a son and child *sacrifice were all to be punished by stoning. A particularly heinous offense was *seducing others to forsake Yahweh (Deut 13); there was to be no compassion or mercy, even between *family members. Thus Achan and his family are stoned for stealing sacred spoils and "troubling" Israel (Josh 7:1-26).

The most graphic images of stoning come from the NT, with Stephen's untimely death by stoning at the hands of a mob (Acts 7:58) and the attempted stoning of Jesus by his own townspeople (Lk 4:29). The unsettling brutality of stoning expresses the seriousness with which Israel viewed the sanctity of the community and the danger for those who transgressed. Offenders were crushed by the stones of the land and by the hands of the people.

See also CRIME AND PUNISHMENT; STONE.

STOREHOUSE

The storehouse is a biblical image for abundance and security (either true or false). It was a place designated for storage of either agricultural produce or the *treasures of a kingdom or temple. In its metaphoric uses the biblical storehouse is the place where an anthropomorphic God keeps the forces of *nature (*see* Cosmology).

From the earliest days of the Bible, wealth was seen as a sign of *blessing and storehouses as evidence of accumulated wealth. Thus the storehouses of a rich man would be both extensive and full—a sign of his well-being. In a prosperous land like Egypt before the famine, full storehouses would be a reassurance to the people of their continuing security. During Egypt's prosperous years Joseph "stored up huge quantities of grain, like the sand of the sea; it was so much that he stopped keeping records because it was beyond measure" (Gen 41:49 NIV). "When famine had spread over the whole country, Joseph opened the storehouses and sold grain" (Gen 41:56 NIV).

The other kind of storehouse was a treasure house at a court or *temple. The storehouses of a powerful deity would be full of treasure, evidence of the deity's power. In the Bible we find occasional references to the storehouse of the temple (1 Chron 26:15) and to royal storehouses and storehouses in outlying districts (1 Chron 27:25).

Human storehouses can be a negative image as well as a positive one. In the ancient world when a king was toppled and his national god with him, an empty temple storehouse would bespeak the complete bankruptcy of the king and people. In a variation on that theme, God's coming judgment against

Israel is pictured as the nation's storehouse plundered of its treasures (Hos 13:15). Even a full storehouse can be a negative image of misplaced trust and values. One thinks of the rich *farmer of Jesus' parable, whose worldly-minded confidence in his large storehouses of *grain is an image of misguided reliance on wealth. His *barns become an example of a useless storehouse when his soul is required of him the day after his building project and plans for retirement are completed (Lk 12:15-21). The OT parallel is King Hezekiah, who in a mood of careless *pride in his achievement shows off his storehouses to the envoys of Babylon (2 Kings 20:13; Is 39:2), only to have them return as conquerors and carry off the treasure.

God is the One whose storehouses are mentioned most often in Scripture. Like a wealthy landowner he has full storehouses, and he dispenses their goods to those who work the land. In almost all cases the storehouse is an image associated with God's provision in nature. In a vision of God's blessing, Moses in his farewell discourse to Israel claims that God "will open the heavens, the storehouse of his bounty, to send rain on your land in season" (Deut 28:12 NIV). In the picture of nature that emerges from Job 38, God has storehouses of *snow and *hail (Job 38:22), while in the psalms an anthropomorphic God puts the *water of the *sea into storehouses (Ps 33:7) and brings wind from his storehouses (Ps 135:7). The image captures both the *abundance and the perpetual supply of God's creation.

In summary, storehouses in the Bible are usually a sign of prosperity and blessing. When a good storehouse fulfills its purpose, it has three qualities: its contents are abundant (adequate to meet needs when they arise), valuable and secure. God's storehouses possess these qualities. An empty or plundered storehouse is an image of terror, ultimately traceable to God's judgment against sin. While a storehouse can become a temptation to misplaced trust in earthly prosperity, it more often represents reward for either work or faithfulness to God. In the last book of the OT, God challenges his people to test him by bringing "the whole tithe into the storehouse, that there may be food in my house, . . . and see if I will not throw open the floodgates of heaven and pour out so much blessing that you will not have room enough for it" (Mal 3:10 NIV). Here is an image of the earth itself as God's storehouse of blessing.

See also ABUNDANCE; BARN; PROSPERITY; TREASURE; STORING UP.

STORING UP

Storing up is essentially an image of gradual accumulation. Such accumulation may be either positive or negative. Negatively, storing up is an image of futility when one stores something impermanent and unreliable (Mt 6:19), wrongly acquired (Mic 6:14), wrongly desired (Lk 12:21) or ostentatiously displayed (1 Kings 20:17). But storing up can also have

the positive overtones of proper *prudence (Prov 30:25), due *reward (Prov 15:6), value rightly ascribed (Mt 6:21) or providently saved as an *inheritance for one's *children (Ps 17:14; Prov 13:22). Storing up can also be a picture of *abundance, as when under Joseph's superintendence the Egyptians "stored up huge quantities of grain, like the sand of the sea," for use during *famine (Gen 41:49 NIV).

The motif of storing up is mainly a metaphoric image in the Bible, used for a range of meanings. Negatively, God stores up wrath or punishment for wicked people (Job 21:19; Rom 2:5). Paul connects this with the thought that God postpones judgment to allow time for *repentance. Closely connected with this is the thought of storing up *sin or *guilt before God (Hos 13:12; 1 Thess 2:16; cf. Gen 15:16). There comes a point, then, when *judgment must fall.

On the positive side, God stores up *blessings for the righteous (Ps 31:19; Eccles 2:26; 1 Tim 6:19; cf. 2 Tim 4:8; 1 Pet 1:4). Closely associated with this is the idea of *treasure in *heaven, a favorite image used by Jesus himself (Mt 6:20; 19:21; Lk 12:33). Eschatological overtones surround this motif, as in the image of "the hope that is stored up for you in heaven" (Col 1:5 NIV). We can also store up God's Word, *wisdom or knowledge in our hearts (Job 23:12; Ps 119:11; Prov 2:1; 10:14; Is 33:6). Along these lines Paul calls the gospel a "treasure in clay jars" (2 Cor 4:7 NRSV). A natural extension of this is the idea of the qualities of character (Mt 12:35) or particular thoughts (Lk 2:19) that we store up within ourselves.

See also ABUNDANCE; BARN; STOREHOUSE; TREASURE.

STORK. *See* BIRDS.

STORM

Storms provide many and varied biblical images, some times even contradictory ones. The storm is a danger and a necessity. It gives life through its *water but *death through its violence. As an uncontrollable force of *nature, it is both a tool of *judgment in the hand of God and an evil threat to God's people, an agent of chaos against God's ordered world.

Storm as Wind. The *wind as an unseen force, but with plainly evident power and effects, serves as the ideal metaphor for God as powerful yet unseen actor (Jn 3:8; 4:24). In fact, neither Hebrew *rûaḥ* nor Greek *pneuma*, both words having the meanings "wind," "spirit" and "breath," required that the speaker or hearer make a distinction among those ideas. For biblical protagonists the wind often served as evidence of the presence of God. *Adam and *Eve heard the "sound of the LORD God walking . . . in the cool [i.e., breeze; Heb *rûaḥ*] of the day" (Gen 3:8 NIV). God's aid and presence in *battle are assured by the sound of his *army in the treetops (2 Sam 5:24). The presence of God's Spirit is proven by the sound of a "mighty rushing wind" (Acts 2:2). A good wind/spirit is God's blessing (Ps 143:10).

*Breath too was a sign of the activity of God. The proof that *idols are false *gods is that, unlike God, they have no breath *(rûah)* in them (Jer 10:14) nor do they instill their spirit in humanity as the breath of life (Gen 2:7). When the breath returns to a person, so does the soul (1 Kings 17:17, 22).

Storm as Deity. The biblical writers were well aware that their neighbors worshiped storm gods. The Hittites had Teshub, the Akkadians and Aramaeans had Hadad. At Ugarit, Hadad was the principal deity under the generic term Baal. The obvious link between the fecundity of the *earth and the coming of the *rains gave rise to the worship of a storm god who every year died and was brought back from the underworld, coinciding with the blossoming of the crops (*see* Resurrection). The fear of rainless storms (Prov 25:13), *drought, crop failure, *flood and so on ensured a thriving cult around the god who strides the *sea, rides the *clouds and brings the rains. In contrast, the OT ultimately sees God's power, but not God himself, in the forces of nature (1 Kings 19:11-12).

Storm as God's Attendant. Scripture stops short of claiming that God *is* a storm but repeatedly asserts that the storm warns of God's approach (Is 29:6). He is surrounded by tempest (Ps 50:3). A tempest marks the presence of God (Heb 12:18). His way is in whirlwind and storm (Nahum 1:3; Zech 9:14). The storm is not the Lord; rather the storm attends the Lord, just as he is accompanied by servants/*angels named *lightning, flame, *famine, pestilence and the like (Hab 3:5). Even so, to the poet *thunder is God's *voice (Job 40:10), and he speaks from the whirlwind (Job 40:6).

Storm as God's Agent of Judgment. The storm accompanies God as his agent and means of punishment, a palpable expression of his *anger. "Look, the storm of the LORD! Wrath has gone forth, a whirling tempest" (Jer 23:19 NRSV). A great wind kills Job's children (Job 1:19). The storm epitomizes fears, both real and imagined (Job 27:20-23). "My brethren are treacherous as a torrent-bed" (Job 6:15 RSV). In the primitive cosmology of the Hebrews, the Lord stores up the winds in chambers or *storehouses at the corners of the world, releasing them to do his bidding (Job 37:9; Jer 10:13; cf. Rev 17:1). The spottiness of rain offered mute testimony to a divine plan (Amos 4:7).

The caprice and unpredictability of storms made their violence seem like personal animosity. The Israelites and their neighbors alike feared the sea. Jonah knows God's wrath lies behind the raging sea (Jon 1:9-12). The inhabitants of Malta thought a viper (*see* Serpent) had been sent against Paul because he had escaped the *judgment of the storm (Acts 28:4). Paul's confidence in God freed him from the fear possessing those around him (Acts 27:20-25).

As a symbol of judgment, the storm also makes a fitting metaphor for impending battle. The prophets repeatedly resort to storm imagery. Both war and storms serve God's ends (Is 28:2). Both gather ominously before they break (Jer 25:32). Both swiftly sweep away and overpower the individual (Prov 1:27; Is 5:28; Hab 3:14). Both rage until they spend themselves and disappear (Ps 57:1). Both leave carnage and destruction in their wake (Prov 10:25; 28:3). Like war and the peace that follows it, a storm stands in stark contrast to the clear skies and calm that follow (Job 37:21). As battle is likened to *harvest, so too the storm winnows the wicked (Wis 5:23) and drives them away like *chaff (Job 21:18; Ps 1:4; 83:13; Is 17:13; 40:24).

Storm as God's Enemy. To be precise, it is the mythological *Sea (the Deep, the Abyss) and its ally, the Sea Monster (the Dragon, Leviathan; *see* Mythical Animals), that are God's *enemies. The storm that comes from the sea is the product of their rebellious thrashing and raging against God and his order (Job 41:31). The water that lashes the land is an invasion from the stormy sea. It floods the land and threatens all that breathe. The flood story serves as a reminder that God alone keeps the Sea from reclaiming the dry land.

The ancient Semitic myth of a god battling the Sea was familiar to the people of the eastern Mediterranean. The Bible repeatedly alludes to that theme but consistently places the Lord in the victorious role. "The LORD sits enthroned over the flood" (Ps 29:10 NRSV). "Thou didst trample the sea with thy horses" (Hab 3:15 RSV). The Lord is "mightier than the thunders of many waters . . . than the waves of the sea" (Ps 93:3 RSV; 107:29). The violence of the sea is reinterpreted so that the sea will "roar" and "the floods clap their hands" in praise of the Lord (Ps 98:7-8 RSV). A mundane account of the Lord's provision for crossing the Red Sea in Exodus 14 appears poetically reworked as a battle between the Lord and the surging Sea in Exodus 15 (cf. Ps 114:3, 5; Is 51:9-10). The stilling of the storm by the Lord's rebuke (Ps 18:15-16; 104:6-7; 106:9) has literary links to this ancient imagery (Mt 8:26; Mk 4:39; Lk 8:24).

Storm as Evil Spirit. If a storm could be termed an evil wind, it could also be an evil spirit. Akkadian writings explain seasonal storms as *demons or winds stirred up by the *wings of demons, providing an etiology for why they occur at the same time as seasonal fevers and *plagues (also believed to be the work of demons). The Jewish understanding held that pagan gods were actually demons that had tricked Gentiles into worshiping them. Thus the force behind the storm was evil and was attempting to rage out of control and destroy God's order. This amalgam of pagan storm god and demonic tempest was kept under control by the "rebuke" of the Lord.

Storm as Flood. Storm is symbolically the Sea out of its borders. The great flood represents the ultimate storm. Not only did God allow the *Deep to escape its bounds, to which he had subjected it at *creation when he imposed order *(kosmos)* on the surface of the deep *(tehôm,* Gen 1:2, 6), but he also let water flood in from above the firmament. "All the fountains of the great deep burst forth, and the windows of heaven were opened" (Gen 7:11 RSV). The two sources of water resulted in a cataclysm.

Smaller floods also occurred. Water could appear in dry channels without hint of rain. "You shall not see wind or rain, but that stream-bed shall be filled with water" (2 Kings 3:17 RSV). The wise man who builds on the *rock does so to be safe from seasonal flash floods. "The flood," "the torrent," "the raging waters" are real dangers (Ps 124:4-5 RSV). It would be easier to build on the flat alluvial sand at the bottom of a *valley, but the sudden torrential streams after a rain would shift the sands and undermine the house's *foundations, a foolish risk (Mt 7:24-27). Such floods, damaging while they lasted, quickly disappeared; thus "the wealth of the unjust will dry up like a torrent" (Sirach 40:13).

As dangerous as such floods could be, they were also necessary for life. Such water from nowhere exemplified divine blessing, prompting the prayer "Restore our fortunes, O LORD, like the watercourses in the Negeb" (Ps 126:4 RSV).

The Psalm of the Thunderstorm. Psalm 29 combines so many of these storm motifs that it deserves special mention. This parody of Canaanite poetry based on the Baal myth describes a storm rising in the Mediterranean Sea and then moving *eastward onto the coastal region, and thence to the *mountains and on to the *wilderness. The sequence of the psalm captures the aesthetics of a storm as nature lovers often describe it, from anticipation through awe to subdued calm. The psalm's threefold ascription of praise to the God of the storm is followed by a *sevenfold narrative account of what "the voice of the LORD" does.

At a literal level the poem does an admirable job of re-creating the events of a moving thunderstorm. But the poem is also polemical, in effect stating that Yahweh is actually the One who does what the pagans ascribe to Baal. The terminology and vocabulary of the psalm place it farther north than the nation of Israel, confirming that the poem is a parody of existing Canaanite poetry. Actions that the pagans ascribe to Baal and that the psalmist ascribes to God include God's conquest of the sea and his moving to land, where he is enthroned. Instead of being a God *of* the storm, though, God sits enthroned *over* the flood, and not simply after an annual conquest of the sea but *for ever* (Ps 29:10).

Storm as Suffering. One's problems can be depicted as wind or the storm personified as enemy and agent of destruction (Job 30:22). The unjust anger of the wicked is likened to a flash flood (Ps 124:3-5). One in need of comfort or haven is "storm-tossed" (Is 54:11). One beset by doubts is like a boat bobbing on the deep, driven aimlessly by the wind (Jas 1:6).

See also COSMOLOGY; CLOUD; DIVINE WARRIOR; FLOOD; HAIL; LIGHTNING; RAIN; SEA; THUNDER; WEATHER; WIND.

STORM OF GOD. *See* COSMOLOGY; DIVINE WARRIOR; STORM.

STRAIGHT

The shortest distance between two points is a straight line. We all know this from experience, even if we never understood high-school geometry. However, using the word *straight* in this manner can lend it a very utilitarian feel. If we never take any detours, we never see any of the scenery. So we end up being a bit ambivalent about this word; is it good to be straight, or are we limiting ourselves?

This is largely a result of the cynical age we live in, which has filled many words with meanings contrary to their original connotation. For example, the image conjured up by *straight* is confusing because we use it to connote two diametrically opposed modes of behavior. On the one hand, when people refer to someone as being "straight-laced" or as "walking the straight and narrow," their meaning is often pejorative. This is simply another way of accusing someone of self-righteousness. On the other hand, if someone is characterized as being a "straight shooter" or "level-headed," they are being complimented on their integrity and honorable character. This double usage produces a kind of schizophrenic haze around the word and robs us of its power to convey the reality of a God whose existence defines the standard that gives *straight* its meaning.

The Bible consistently uses this word in a positive sense. The image of a straight *path or way appears approximately twenty times (chiefly in Psalms, Proverbs and Ecclesiastes). Those who continue on the straight path are the ones whose *walk is in accordance with God's walk, while those leaving the straight path are *rebels against God and are therefore in danger of his *judgment. Scripture's use of *straight* conveys a sense of steadfast purpose and clarity of vision provided by God himself (cf. Prov 3:6; 4:11, 25; 11:5; 15:21). The detours to be avoided are not the ones that would be beneficial for enriching one's life but are unnecessary and damaging because they ignore the standard of God's character and would have us striking out on our own (cf. Ps 107:7; Prov 2:13; 5:5).

The word *crooked* is actually a better word to describe self-righteousness. "The straight way" is synonymous with righteousness—not self-righteousness but God's righteousness.

See also CROOKED; JUSTICE; PATH.

STRANGER. *See* FOREIGNER.

STRAW

Straw appears almost exclusively in the OT, and it draws on the agrarian setting of the ancient Middle East. Literally, straw is the stalk of the *grain, which was separated from the grain at *harvest time by the winnowing process. The worthless *chaff was blown away in the *wind, but the straw, which is a bit heavier, fell near the threshing floor and was collected for *animal food or used in the making of *bricks or ceramics. Two-thirds of the references to straw in the OT are to its use as animal food (Gen 24:25, 32; Judg 19:19) or in *building materials (e.g., Ex 5, where the tormenting Egyptian taskmasters compel the Israelite slaves to gather their own straw for the making of *bricks).

In a figurative sense, straw denotes anything lacking in strength, substance and significance. Job likens human implements and *weapons to straw in contrast with the mighty creative power of God (Job 41:27, 29). Isaiah notes that the *enemies of God and his people will be destroyed like straw in a *fire (Is 5:24; 25:10). Jeremiah equates the dreams of false prophets with straw, while God's word is likened to grain (Jer 23:28). Finally, Isaiah's vision of the future foresees a time of harmony and peaceful coexistence when domestic animals will feed alongside of wild predators and "the lion will eat straw like the ox" (Is 11:7 RSV; 65:25).

A solitary use of straw in the NT uses the imagery of building. Rather than contrasting the *weakness of humanity with the power of God, Paul compares a Christian worker's effective and lasting ministry with that which is temporary. Straw denotes an inferior *foundation that will be revealed and destroyed on that *"Day" (1 Cor 3:12-13).

See also THRESHING, THRESHING FLOOR.

STREAM. *See* BROOK; RIVER.

STREET

The word *street* has a distinctly urban flavor. Even the book of Revelation's vision of the new *Jerusalem includes a street (Rev 21:21; 22:2). For this reason the Bible's images associated with *street* and related words like *square, corner* and *alley* appear to be different from those associated with more neutral terms like *path, way* and *road*. The colors and connotations of events said to take place "in the streets" have to do with masses of people and the often harsh realities of *city life. They are, of course, varied and mixed, reflecting the heterogeneous and cosmopolitan nature of any city.

A Public Place. As a setting in the Bible the street first of all symbolizes open communication and widespread exposure. It is the place immediately outside the privacy and insulation of the *home (Gen 19:2; Judg 19:20; Job 31:32; cf. Prov 22:13). To be in the street or the city square is to be instantly accessible, visually and audibly, to the masses. It is the location for public meetings (Ezra 10:9; Neh 8:1; Job 29:7), public ministries (Lk 13:26; Acts 5:15) and public occasions of *honor (Esther 6:9; cf. Mt 6:2, 5).

Wicked deeds done "in the streets" therefore constitute brazen, high-handed acts of defiance, performed for all to see. The *evil men of Jerusalem openly proclaim to Jeremiah, "We will burn incense to the Queen of Heaven . . . just as we and our fathers . . . did in the towns of Judah and in the streets of Jerusalem" (Jer 44:17 NIV). This open practice of *idolatry leads Ezekiel to portray their shamelessness allegorically: "At the head of every street you built your lofty shrines and degraded your beauty, offering your body with increasing promiscuity to anyone who passed by" (Ezek 16:25 NIV).

Counteracting this are prophetic proclamations made "in the streets," which by the same token symbolize the way God intends his words to be universally made known. Thus Jeremiah is commanded, "Proclaim all these words in the towns of Judah and in the streets of Jerusalem" (Jer 11:6 NIV). Jesus draws on this imagery as he directs the *Seventy(-two) to proclaim *judgment in the streets of towns that reject the message of the *kingdom (Lk 10:10). The broad hearing the streets offer is the reason Lady *Wisdom makes her plea in the public squares (Prov 1:20).

A Window into the City's Common Life. Second, the street as a setting in the Bible represents what is commonly true of the mood, spirit and well-being of the city. Streets typically line the entirety of a city and serve as its reference points. Descriptions of what takes place "in the streets" therefore function as generalizations about what is going on in the city as a whole.

There is a universal quality to streets, whether what is depicted in them is good or bad. This is made explicit when the prophets predict *suffering to take place "in every street": "There will be wailing in all the streets and cries of anguish in every public square" (Amos 5:16 NIV; see also Is 51:20; Jer 48:37-38; Lam 2:19; 4:1; Nahum 3:10). On the other hand, widespread *joy and *prosperity are also depicted as street scenes: "Once again, men and women of ripe old age will sit in the streets of Jerusalem. . . . The city streets will be filled with boys and girls playing there" (Zech 8:4-5 NIV; see also Ps 144:14; Jer 33:10). Want to know the people of a city? Look at the streets.

Further, searches for particular individuals within an entire population must take place in the streets: "Go up and down the streets of Jerusalem, look around and consider, search through her squares. If you can find but one person who deals honestly and seeks the truth, I will forgive this city" (Jer 5:1 NIV; see also Song 3:2; Lk 14:21). Go through the streets, and you will cover everything and everyone.

A Place of Shame and Disrepute. Finally, the street as a setting in the Bible presents soiled and tainted images. Homes are wholesome environments, streets are not. Every city dweller knows about the seedy and often sleazy side to life "on the streets."

Street people, both the despised and the pitied, therefore have an air of *shame and disrepute about them. The *adulteress of Proverbs 7 is a "streetwalker," an evil *seductress who must be out to lead simpletons astray: "now in the street, now in the squares, at every corner she lurks" (Prov 7:12 NIV). Lamentations depicts the fate of the disobedient, who have been reduced to the shame of street life because of their *sins: "Those who once ate delicacies are destitute in the streets" (Lam 4:5 NIV; see also 2:12; 4:8, 14).

Streets themselves, unlike homes, are often squalid and full of refuse. They are the place for thrown-away and worthless things (cf. Lam 4:1; Ezek 7:19). This is why the image of unburied dead bodies in the street evokes such horror and contempt—people are treated as rubbish (Is 5:25; Jer 14:16; Lam 2:21; Ezek 11:6; Rev 11:8). Streets are also places of mud and trampling (Ps 18:42; Zech 10:5). Those defeated in military conquest are its human equivalents (Is 51:23; Mic 7:10). In short, streets, like the people associated with them, are dirty and *forsaken.

These images, however, are what makes Jesus' *banquet parables so powerful (Mt 22:1-14; Lk 14:15-24). After his initial invitation is spurned, the master of the banquet commands, "Go out quickly into the streets and alleys of the town and bring in the poor, the crippled, the blind and the lame" (Lk 14:21 NIV). The gospel message is that the people of the street, the shamed and the disreputable, may now enter the kingdom.

In summary, the street scenes of the Bible embody pretty much the same range of activities and associations found in street scenes in contemporary cities.

See also CITY; PATH.

STRENGTH. *See* STRONG, STRENGTH.

STRIFE

The biblical image of strife and related synonyms calls to mind an intense conflict in interpersonal relationships (on an individual or group level), characterized by discord (1 Cor 1:10) and antagonism (Mt 10:34-36), the sources of which may range from a mere difference of opinion to rivalry (Phil 1:15) and even to violent hostility (Is 58:4; *see* Violence, Stories of). Although it usually manifests itself in verbal forms (e.g., quarreling over words, 1 Tim 6:4; or the *law, Tit 3:9), strife may degenerate to downright brawls (Is 58:4) or other forms of violence (Ps 55:9; Hab 1:3).

In the Bible strife is the inevitable result of the *sinful nature (Gal 5:20), *evil desires (Jas 4:1), *pride (Pr 13:10), selfish ambition and envy (Jas 3:14), hatred (Prov 10:12) and *anger (Prov 30:33—note the colorful metaphors). It is a vice that is characteristic of the wicked (Prov 6:14; Rom 1:29) and is hated by the Lord (Prov 6:19).

As a result, the Bible frequently warns against strife (Prov 17:14) and commands the godly to avoid it (Rom 13:13) as well as contentious and quarrelsome people (Rom 16:17). The latter are vividly likened in Proverbs to charcoal and *wood for "kindling strife" (Prov 26:21 NIV). Those who avoid strife are regarded as honorable (Prov 20:3).

Biblical examples of strife include the civil *war in Israel (Judg 20:20), the disagreement between Paul and Barnabas (Acts 15:39), the conflict between the *Pharisees and Sadducees (Acts 23:7), and the situation in the Corinthian church (1 Cor 1:10).

See also ANGER; REUNIONS, RECONCILIATION; SIBLING RIVALRY; VIOLENCE, STORIES OF.

STRIKE DOWN. *See* TRIUMPH.

STRONG, STRENGTH

Unlike an attribute such as righteousness, strength in the Bible is applied to natural as well as supernatural and human beings.

Certain objects in nature are commonly seen as strong, their symbolic potential sometimes becoming explicit in similes. Inanimate objects mentioned in Scripture as strong include the *sea (Is 43:16), *stone (Job 6:12), flint (Ezek 3:9), *iron (Dan 2:40), *sun (Rev 1:16), *thunder (Ps 29:4) and *wind (Ex 14:21; Acts 2:2). Strength in animate creation is observable in oaks (Amos 2:9; *see* Tree), the *lion (Judg 14:18; 2 Sam 1:23; Prov 30:30), the wild *ox (Job 39:11), the *horn (Deut 33:17), the *horse (Job 32:21), Behemoth (Job 40:16; *see* Mythical Animals), Leviathan (Job 41:22) and the ox (Prov 14:4), but not appreciably in ants (Prov 30:25).

In the supernatural realm *God is inherently strength (Job 26:14; Ps 24:8; 89:8; Rom 1:20). He is the mighty God (Is 10:21; Jer 32:18), Mighty One (Is 1:24; Mt 26:64), particularly through his *hand (Ex 13:9) and *arm (Jer 21:5). His strength reveals itself not only in *creation (Ps 65:6; 74:13; Is 40:26; Jer 10:12) but also in past (Ex 32:11), present (Prov 23:11) and future (Is 40:10; Zeph 3:17) deliverance of his people and *judgment of his *enemies (Jer 50:34; Nahum 1:3; Rev 18:8). By it he *guides (Ex 15:13) and preserves (1 Pet 1:5). Strength is likewise a prominent attribute of the Messiah (Ps 45:3; Is 9:6; 11:2; Mt 3:11; Heb 1:3), who also is the object of God's strength in his conception (Lk 1:35), ministry (Mic 5:4) and *resurrection (2 Cor 13:4). Moreover, relative strength extends to *angels (Ps 103:20; 2 Pet 2:11) and *Satan (Mt 12:29; Lk 10:19).

But the fullest development of strength imagery is found in its application to humankind, especially as human strength is related to God's. All human strength comes from God (1 Chron 29:12; Ps 63:35), whether it is thought of as common vital strength (Deut 8:17-18; Ps 90:10), unusual physical power (Judg 16:28) or the military might of an enemy *army (Is 28:2). How fitting that response to this gift is to love God with all one's strength (Deut 6:5; Judg 16:30; 2 Sam 6:5, 14; 2 Kings 23:25; Eccles 9:10). Persons especially endowed, notably *Samson (Judg 14—16; Heb 11:34), *David (1 Sam 17—19), Saul and Jonathan (2 Sam 1:19-27) become symbols of strength. Yet even though it is God's gift, strength is inferior to *wisdom.

Human strength may also stand in contrast to God's. That God is infinitely stronger than humans is a frequent theme in Job (Job 9:4, 19; 36:5, 22). Yet paradoxically God can allow *Jacob to prevail against his strength (Gen 32:28). Further, human strength can become perverted (Amos 6:13) and should not be trusted (1 Sam 2:9; Ps 147:10; Is 30:3; 31:1; Jer 9:23; Hos 10:13; Zech 4:6), since it will be brought low (Is 1:31; 2:12-17). That human strength must bow to God's power (Is 25:3; 1 Cor 1:26-27) is an overarching biblical theme (Gen 6:4; 11:6; Rev 19:18). The only true human strength is found in God (1 Sam 23:16; Ps 18:1; 28:7-8; 59:17; Is 40:29-31) and in *weakness (2 Cor 12:9-10). *Egypt (Ezek 30:6) and its *pharaoh (Ex 5:2), Philistia and its Goliath (1 Sam 17:8-10), Assyria (Is 10:13) with its Nimrod (Gen 10:8-12) and *Babylon (Hab 1:11; Rev 18:16) with its Nebuchadnezzar (Dan 4:30) are memorable images of misdirected might.

The theme of strength is developed along psychological lines as well as physical. Strong *faith is informed (Rom 15:1) and resolute (Rom 4:20; 1 Jn 2:14). Strength is *courage (Josh 1:6; Lk 22:43; 1 Cor 16:13; Col 1:11), *confidence (Prov 31:25), *knowledge (Acts 18:24) and convincing proclamation (Mic 3:8; Lk 24:19; Acts 7:22; 2 Cor 10:4).

Strength can characterize not only humans themselves but also elements of our experience, as we sense the strength of *sin (1 Cor 15:56), love and *death (Song 8:6). Finally, the image of strength as clothing or *armor (Ps 18:39; 93:1; Eph 6:10-11) suggests its being a personal possession and invites comparison with similar imagery (Gen 3:7, 21).

See also WEAK, WEAKNESS.

STRONGHOLD

Although the terms *stronghold* and *fortress* are somewhat interchangeable, the former is a more generic image than the latter. Both constitute places of safety from the *enemy. Rather than necessarily a *walled fortification, though, a stronghold may be any inaccessible place of *refuge, especially an elevated one. The KJV generally uses "high *tower" rather than the NIV's and other versions' "stronghold." The fifty biblical references to strongholds (NIV; sixty-two in NRSV) fall into two categories: in the narrative and prophetic books strongholds are literal places of military refuge, while in Psalms they tend to be metaphors for God.

The many literal strongholds in the Bible shed light on the metaphorical strongholds the poets celebrate. Having watched David find strongholds in *caves, deserts and hills as he flees the pursuing Saul, we grasp the vividness of his picture when he calls God "my stronghold, my refuge and my savior" (2 Sam 22:3 NIV). The stronghold is generally used in scriptural poetry to picture the safe, eternal refuge of the soul in *God. Such a picture offers security, strength and confidence: one can almost identify with that eagle God described to Job, which builds "his nest on high," "dwells on a cliff" and makes a "rocky crag" his "stronghold" (Job 39:27-28 NIV).

The stronghold saves from the enemy, and it is the salvation of God our stronghold that Scripture repeatedly celebrates. Again David speaks of his God as "the horn of my salvation, my stronghold" (Ps 18:2 NIV). "The salvation of the righteous comes from the LORD," he writes, and the next line follows naturally: "he is their stronghold in time of trouble" (Ps 37:39 NIV). We can understand the feelings evoked by the image of the stronghold when we observe the threats with which it is often paired: trouble, enemies, oppressors, pursuers. These cannot reach or destroy the one who has found refuge in God's saving presence.

That presence is often pictured in terms of a *temple or *tabernacle where God dwells. Often a temple within a *city was the city's highest point and its stronghold; in Shechem, for example, all the citizens under siege went and hid in "the stronghold of the temple" (Judg 9:46). David calls God "the stronghold of my life" and goes on to picture that stronghold in terms of "the house of the LORD, . . . the shelter of his tabernacle . . . high upon a rock" (Ps 27:2, 4-5 NIV). Elsewhere he calls God "my stronghold" and goes on to picture himself as led by God's light and truth up to "your holy mountain . . . the place where you dwell" (Ps 43:2-3). In his holy tabernacle, which signifies the presence of God the Most High, is the stronghold that saves the soul.

Ezekiel addresses the Israelites who put their trust in the literal stronghold of the Jerusalem temple: "the stronghold in which you take pride, the delight of your eyes, the object of your affection" (Ezek 24:21 NIV). God tells them through Ezekiel that he is about to desecrate his sanctuary. God's people had ceased to seek the true spiritual stronghold—God himself—of which the physical temple was only a sign.

Scripture gives pictures of those who have tried to build their own strongholds apart from the presence of God. Such strongholds are generally shown to be high places of pride that will be brought down low in the end. It is predicted that God will "bring . . . down to everlasting ruin . . . the man who did not make God his stronghold but trusted in his great wealth" (Ps 52:5, 7).

The true stronghold in Scripture is indeed a *high, lofty place. One can reach that place, however, only by bowing low before the God of *salvation. The Bible pictures his presence as the only true stronghold.

See also CITY; FORTRESS; JERUSALEM; MOUNTAIN; REFUGE, RETREAT, SAFE PLACE; ROCK; WALL; ZION.

STUMBLE, STUMBLING BLOCK

A little misstep of the feet, a sudden trip over an unseen obstacle, the awkward and suspended moment of uncertain recovery or fall, these are the common experiences of life on two legs. By the democracy of mishap, stumbling has become a well-worn image of all sorts of human foibles, from faltering speech to social blunder, and even the inadvertent discovery of something wonderful ("The weary explorers stumbled upon an ancient Mayan city").

The Bible repeatedly uses the image of stumbling, and the English language and its stock imagery of moral misstep has been shaped by it. For example, "stumbling block," the contribution of William Tyndale's English translation of the Bible (1526), is an image shaped from an expression current in his day, "to stumble at a block"; that is, to stumble over a tree stump. For many modern Westerners, tree stumps do not form the most ready image of a stumbling block. In fact, we do not have nearly as many occasions for physical stumbling as did Tyndale, much less for the inhabitants of the ancient biblical world. The rocky, rutted *paths, *streets and roads of Palestine, even at their stone-paved best, were an uncertain footing compared to our everyday concrete and asphalt walkways. Diverted eyes or darkness of night were open invitations to stumbling feet.

The Bible produces an array of vivid images of stumbling, from which we can sample a few. On the battlefield disobedient Israel will stumble "as though fleeing from the sword, even though no one is pursuing them" (Lev 26:37 NIV). *Pharaoh Neco's warriors will stumble over each other at the battle of Carchemish on the Euphrates (Jer 46:6, 12, 16). Indeed, the battlefield is the occasion for the stumbling of many an army: over corpses, on uneven ground, in weariness and in fearful *flight. On the domestic front the mischievous and malicious must be commanded not to "put a stumbling block in front of the blind" (Lev 19:14 NIV). More poignantly, in Israel's spiritually sickened condition, priests and prophets, befuddled with *wine and beer, "stumble when rendering decisions" (Is 28:7 NIV). "At midday" Israel stumbled "as if it were twilight" (Is 59:10 NIV), and even truth "stumbled in the streets" (Is 59:14 NIV). In the best of times "we all stumble in many ways" (Jas 3:2 NIV). It is then that one turns to a friend like Job, whose words "supported those who stumbled" and "strengthened faltering knees" (Job 4:4 NIV).

The Hebraic metaphor of life as a *"walk," a *"pathway" or a "way," forms the scenic backdrop for much of the Bible's imagery of stumbling. Wisdom provides the context for sharp contrasts. Those with sound judgment, who walk in the ways of *Wisdom, have great peace and will not stumble (Prov 3:23; 4:12). Those who follow the way of the wicked, who travel in deep *darkness, do not even know what makes them stumble (Prov 4:19). These are sound reminders for us, whose physical pathways have been smoothed and straightened and well lighted, but whose moral pathways are strewn with stumbling blocks.

Like wisdom, Israel's divine *law and *covenant form an illuminated pathway through life. Those who love God's law cannot be made to stumble (Ps 119:165). "The ways of the LORD are right; the

righteous walk in them, but the rebellious stumble in them" (Hos 14:9 NIV), and Isaiah speaks of the Lord making "the way of the righteous smooth" (Is 26:7 NIV). But the antithesis of Israel's single-minded worship of the One God is, in Ezekiel's language, the setting up of "idols in their hearts" and thus putting "wicked stumbling blocks before their faces" (Ezek 14:3, 4, 7 NIV; see Idol). Although avoidance of stumbling can be a sign of God's care for his faithful ("You have delivered me from death and my feet from stumbling, that I may walk before God in the light of life" [Ps 56:13 NIV]), the Lord himself may place a deadly stumbling block in the path of the righteous person who has turned to evil (Ezek 3:20).

The paradoxical image of a divine stumbling block is memorably shaped in Isaiah:

And he [the Lord Almighty] will be a sanctuary;
    but for both houses of Israel he will be
a stone that causes men to stumble
    and a rock that makes them fall.
And for the people of Jerusalem he will be
    a trap and a snare.
Many of them will stumble;
    they will fall and be broken,
    they will be snared and captured.
    (Is 8:14-15 NIV)

This passage, with its conjunction of sanctuary/*temple and stone/rock of stumbling, stands in contrast with the *restoration of Israel and *Zion's temple in Isaiah 28:16:

See, I lay a stone in Zion,
    a tested stone,
a precious cornerstone for a sure foundation;
    the one who trusts will never be dismayed.
    (NIV)

Paul, contemplating Israel's unbelief before Christ, identifies Jesus as Isaiah's stumbling stone. In light of Christ, the divine *foundation stone of a new temple, he reassembles Isaiah's words into new verse:

See, I lay in Zion a stone that causes men to
    stumble
and a rock that makes them fall,
and the one who trusts in him will never be
    put to shame. (Rom 9:33 NIV)

It is as if Israel, *running a *race in pursuit of righteousness, stumbled over the goal marker, Christ the "stumbling stone" (Rom 9:32), and kept running in pursuit of a "law of righteousness," which it has not attained. But Paul will not bury or dislodge this stumbling stone to accommodate Israel's blindness or sensibilities (cf. Rom 11:9, quoting Ps 68:23-24 LXX). The offensiveness of "Christ crucified" is a "stumbling block [skandalon] to Jews and foolishness to Gentiles" (1 Cor 1:23 NIV), a nonnegotiable symbol of the wisdom of God and an indelible hallmark of Paul's gospel. Peter's desperate attempt to divert the pathway of the Messiah from the scandal of death had proven futile and badly mistaken. Peter, the foundation rock of the messianic community, the new temple (Mt 16:18), had suddenly become a stumbling block [*skandalon*] to the Messiah (Mt 16:23).

While Paul elevates the offense of Christ, he strenuously avoids and warns against placing an unnecessary "stumbling block" in the pathway of Jews or Greeks, and certainly before a fellow believer (1 Cor 10:32; 2 Cor 6:3). At Rome the concern is eating meat and thus offending "the weak" who maintain a religiously motivated vegetarianism (Rom 14:20); at Corinth it is the exercise of knowledge and freedom by eating meat that has been offered to idols and thus causing weaker ones to stumble (1 Cor 8:9). No food is unclean, but love demands consideration for the conscience and spiritual vitality of others. Stumbling blocks not only trip, but they can "destroy your brother or sister for whom Christ died" (Rom 14:15 NIV). This concern echoes Jesus' warning against placing a stumbling block before "little ones who believe in me": "Woe to the world because of stumbling blocks! Occasions for stumbling are bound to come, but woe to the one by whom the stumbling block comes!" (Mt 18:6-7 NRSV).

See also FEET; PATH; STONE; WALK, WALKING.

STUMBLING BLOCK. *See* STUMBLE, STUMBLING BLOCK.

SUBSTITUTE, SUBSTITUTION

A substitute is someone or something who takes the place of someone or something else. The basic motif is exchange. While Christ's substitutionary *atonement is the central theological doctrine of the Christian faith, the imagery of substitution in the Bible is remarkably scarce. Because Christ fulfilled the OT sacrificial system, it is easy for a NT reader to see a substitutionary aspect in OT animal *sacrifices (which took the place of the penalty that sinful humanity would otherwise have to pay before a just God), but the portrayal of sacrifices in the OT does not stress this aspect.

We do find a full-fledged OT portrayal of substitution in the song of the *suffering servant in Isaiah 53, with its conspicuous emphasis on the way the servant was *wounded for *sinners (Is 53:4-6, 11-12), his righteousness likewise causing "many to be accounted righteous" (Is 53:11 RSV). Also, we can perhaps see a foreshadowing of Christ as substitute in the ram caught in a thicket that is sacrificed in place of Isaac (Gen 22).

The Levites are another major OT example of substitution. Behind the choice of a tribe of priests lies God's claim that "on the day that I slew all the first-born in the land of Egypt, I consecrated for my own all the first-born in Israel" (Num 3:13 RSV). The Levites represent that first-born of the whole nation: "And the LORD said to Moses, 'Behold, I have taken the Levites from among the people of Israel instead of every first-born'" (Num 3:11 RSV; see also Num 3:40-51).

Substitution is suggested in the NT principally in prepositional phrases built around what Christ has done *for* those who believe in him. In the Good Shepherd discourse, Jesus pictures how he will lay down his life "for the *sheep" (Jn 10:15). In the Epistles we likewise read that "Christ died for the ungodly" (Rom 5:6 RSV), that "Christ died for our sins" (1 Cor 15:3 RSV; cf. 1 Pet 3:18) and that Christ "has died for all; therefore all have died" (2 Cor 5:14 RSV; see also 2 Cor 5:15).

There are also miscellaneous references to substitution. In OT sacrifice, substitution of good animals for inferior ones was disallowed (Lev 27:10, 33). Jesus denounced the *Pharisees for substituting human tradition for the commandment of God (Mk 7:8). Even more ignominious is the downward spiral of the human race as it substituted ("exchanged") human and animal images for the glory of God (Rom 1:23; cf. Ps 106:20). Some substitutes are clearly illegitimate, such as false balances or weights (Prov 11:1; 20:23); this lends further honor to the substitutes that God declares suitable, most notably his own Son.

Substitution also occurs in contexts of a generous offer by someone to take the place of someone under threat. Judah offers himself for his youngest brother, Benjamin (Gen 44:33). *Moses, as intercessor on behalf of his sinful nation, is willing to have his name excised from God's book if God will accept him as a substitute for the nation (Ex 32:30 32). Paul expresses a similar wish (Rom 9:3).

See also ATONEMENT; SACRIFICE.

SUBSTITUTION. *See* SUBSTITUTE, SUBSTITUTION.

SUCKING. *See* BREAST; NURSE.

SUFFERING

Suffering in the Bible is usually understood as a distinctively human experience, and thus the imagery of God's suffering and the story of the incarnate Son offer remarkable insights into God's redemptive love.

Prior to Christ, *suffering* in the Bible typically refers to an anguished mortal who is reeling from *painful circumstances (Job 1) or a desperate, tormented soul crying out in *sorrow and *fear (Lk 16:19-31). Without question, voices of *oppression, agony and deprivation resound in unmistakable images of the emptiness of life (Eccles 1:18), the discomfort of sickness (Jer 10:19) and the frustration of unrealized hopes (Jon 4:6). These and other images help to explain why human life is "full of turmoil" (Job 14:1 NASB).

It is useful to keep in mind that suffering is of three main types. *Punitive suffering,* also called retributive suffering, is tragic suffering (*see* Tragedy)—the deserved punishment for a mistake that a person has made. *Innocent suffering* is unmerited suffering. Both can become *redemptive suffering,* either for the sufferer as he or she is refined or ennobled by it or for the benefit of others (the *suffering servant motif).

The Suffering God. Though numerous people in Scripture feel anxiety, pain and trouble, the more profound biblical message is not human suffering. God himself is not too powerful or too lofty to feel sorrow, disappointment and grief—not just after but before the incarnation. Examining only some of the images of his distress lead us to a clear sense of the true nature of the loss, trouble and pain that constitute suffering. Whereas other religions portray a deity that serenely transcends human suffering, at the heart of the Christian faith stands the mystery of a suffering God.

In Genesis, God sentences *Adam and *Eve (Gen 3:8-24) and drives them out of the Garden (Gen 3:24 NASB), stationing angelic sentinels at the gate. He expels the man and woman from the *Garden to live outside, under decrees of trouble and death. Human sorrow aside, the couple's rebellion obviously grieves God even as it arouses his anger. He is suffering. 2 Peter offers a similarly vivid image of God enduring sorrow and disappointment when certain angels rebelled and sinned against him (2 Pet 2:4). The image here is of a jailer turning away all would-be excuses and calls for leniency and isolating the transgressors.

Elsewhere in the biblical narrative God bears totally undeserved irreverence, disrespect and unbelief. Early in human history as wickedness spreads, God grieves that he ever created anyone (Gen 6:6). Such regret continues as Israel wanders for forty years in the wilderness, grieving the Spirit more than once along the way (Neh 9:20; Ps 78:10, 40; Is 63:10). Later the Hebrews continue to burden God by turning repeatedly to idolatry (Judges). Time and again in Judges, God's anger either "burned" or "was kindled" against Israel (e.g., Judg 2:14; 3:8; 4:2; 6:1; 10:7), and he either "gave" or "sold" his people into the hands of their enemies. This image of a merchant delivering goods to the Canaanites is heavily ironic: the holy and blameless Yahweh must suffer the indignity of turning over his beloved nation to its oppressors that he might maintain his covenant righteousness. There were no surprises, however; he had known long before that disappointment, pain and loss would come (Deut 31:17-18).

The image of God's *face possibly expresses God's desire to break fellowship but also perhaps hints at divine sorrow. The psalmist, exasperated at God's apparent disregard of Israel's troubles, asks,

Why dost Thou hide Thy face,
And forget our affliction and our oppression?
(Ps 44:24 NASB)

Elsewhere in Psalms the speaker is burdened by a lack of intimacy with God, asking, "Why dost Thou hide Thy face from me?" (Ps 88:14 NASB). Isaiah uses a similar image to describe God's reaction to wayward Judah. His suffering the *shame of their wickedness was clear enough: he was "hiding His face" from the chosen people (Is 8:17 NASB; 59:2). Interestingly, John writes in the Apocalypse that at the great white throne of judgment the process is reversed: "I saw . . . Him . . . from whose presence [literally "face"]

earth and heaven fled away" (Rev 20:11 NASB), probably in fear.

God continues to suffer in the NT, of course, as Jesus endures trial after trial. Two particular moments are worth noting because they capture remarkably the spirit of Yahweh's earlier experience with Israel. The first combines the same blend of long-suffering and judgment found in Isaiah. On his way to Jerusalem, Jesus encounters the Pharisees, who evoke from him a painful plea and warning divided by a powerful image: "O Jerusalem, Jerusalem! . . . How often I wanted to gather your children together, just as a hen gathers her brood under her wings, and you would not have it! Behold, your house is left to you desolate" (Lk 13:34 NASB). Mercy and grace are evident, as is the Son's immeasurable distress.

In a second key scene, Lazarus's tomb, Jesus displays a similar distress. His weeping (Jn 11:35), the well-known detail here, may show less of his suffering than his being "deeply moved in spirit," "deeply moved within" (Jn 11:33, 38 NASB). Obviously he knows his power to raise Lazarus; the pain and being "troubled" (Jn 11:33) seem to come from the disciples' assumption that Jesus could not raise Lazarus, a manifestation of unbelief in his deity. The real distress results from a failure to acknowledge him, to know him, as God (cf. Ps 46:10; Is 1:3; Jer 31:34; Hos 2:20). Herein lies a continuous thread of divine suffering throughout the biblical narrative.

Finally, Paul provides a vivid image of divine suffering in redemption. In Romans 8:18-30 the "sufferings of this present time" (NRSV) find a voice in the "groanings" of the creation and of the children of God (Rom 8:22-23). And God through his Spirit joins in the suffering lament of the creation, interceding "with sighs too deep for words" (Rom 8:26). Here we find an echo of Yahweh's solidarity with his people in Egyptian bondage: "The Israelites groaned under their slavery, and cried out. Out of the slavery their cry for help rose up to God. God heard their groaning, and God remembered his covenant with Abraham, Isaac, and Jacob. God looked upon the Israelites, and God took notice of them" (Ex 2:23-25 NRSV). Viewed from this perspective, the entire story of God's redemption of humanity through Israel, and climaxing in Jesus, is a story of God's taking the suffering of the world upon himself.

Images of Human Suffering. Biblical images of suffering by God and by mortals are many and varied. Turning to humanity, one finds that in the NT (KJV) seven different Greek words convey the ideas of suffering (Rom 8:18; 2 Cor 1:7; Col 1:24; 1 Pet 5:9), suffering long or having patience (Rom 9:22; 2 Cor 6:6; Gal 5:22; Eph 4:2; 2 Tim 4:2; Jas 5:10), suffering loss (1 Cor 3:15; Phil 3:8), suffering need (Phil 4:12), suffering *persecution (Rom 12:14; 1 Cor 4:12; 2 Cor 4:9; Rev 12:13), suffering *shame (Acts 5:41) and suffering *violence (Mt 11:12). Whether the sufferer is entrapped in circumstances, attacked by physical or spiritual powers or lacking means of sustenance, that person is portrayed as enduring these problems because they inhere in the experience of a fallen humanity whose deeds and desires are foreknown by God. The foundational message of the Bible, moreover, is that this innocent One has tolerated the trouble and burden of human depravity since Eden. The Bible, then, displays not just the plight of Hebrew slaves in Egypt or dispersed Jews in the wilderness or persecuted missionaries across Turkey and Greece. More important are the instances of God's own suffering.

Suffering is also related in the Bible to sanctification and growth in Christian character. The key passage is Romans 5:3-5, a catalog of the virtues that suffering produces. Here suffering is pictured as a story of *increase. Elsewhere the NT Epistles portray suffering as a process of refinement. Hebrews 12:10-11 portrays the discipline of suffering as something that God brings "for our good, that we may share his holiness," which will happen only "to those who have been trained by it" (RSV). Similarly, "whoever has suffered in the flesh has ceased from sin" (1 Pet 4:1 RSV).

An additional motif is suffering as a necessary prerequisite to *glory. We are "heirs of God and fellow-heirs with Christ," writes Paul, "if indeed we suffer with Him in order that we may also be glorified with Him" (Rom 8:17 NASB). Similarly, "If we suffer, we shall also reign with him" (2 Tim 2:12 KJV). Again, "For to you it has been granted for Christ's sake, not only to believe in Him, but also to suffer for His sake" (Phil 1:29 NASB). 1 Peter is a small classic on the subject of suffering for Christ's sake, and the motif of suffering as prelude to glory makes an appearance here too: "To the degree that you share the sufferings of Christ, keep on rejoicing; so that also at the revelation of His glory, you may rejoice with exultation" (1 Pet 4:13 NASB).

Stories of Suffering. We can also recognize a genre or plot motif best called stories of suffering. The *passion of Christ is the supreme story of suffering in the Bible, with key ingredients being the *taunting of enemies, the experience of false conviction, the crown of *thorns and crucifixion on a cross. In the OT, the story of *Job is the most prolonged story of suffering. The oppression of *Israel, first in Egypt and then in *exile, constitutes stories of national suffering. The prophetic version of national suffering is encapsulated in the books of Jeremiah and Lamentations. The *lament psalms tell a story of human suffering, as do four "servant songs" in the book of Isaiah (Is 42:1-4; 49:1-6; 50:4-9; 52:13—53:12). Stories of *martyrdom are also stories of ultimate suffering.

See also AFFLICTION; GRIEF; LAMENT PSALMS; PAIN; PASSION OF CHRIST; PERSECUTION; SIN; SUFFERING SERVANT; SORROW; TORMENT; VIOLENCE, STORIES OF.

SUFFERING SERVANT

Exaltation through humiliation is the central motif of the fourth servant song of Isaiah (Is 52:13—

53:12), from which we derive the label "suffering servant." The variety of images used to support this central motif makes "suffering servant" one of the richest messianic titles in both the OT and the NT. The archetype is usually construed to include anyone who suffers redemptively for the benefit of others. The first example in Scripture is *Joseph, who undergoes calamity that proves redemptive for his family and an entire world in famine (Gen 45:5-8; Gen 50:20). The lives of *Moses, the unappreciated leader who intercedes with *God on behalf of an ignoble nation, and *Jeremiah, the weeping prophet, also fit the archetype.

Though some have seen the servant of Isaiah's "servant songs" (Is 42:1-4; 49:1-6; 50:4-9; 52:13—53:12; there is some discussion as to the extent of the first three) as corporate *Israel, when we read back from the NT the servant of the fourth song should be understood as messianic. Both the NT writers and Jesus himself repeatedly refer to this servant song to substantiate messianic claims (e.g., Mt 8:17; Mk 9:12; Jn 1:29; Rom 5:19; 1 Pet 2:21-25; see also Mt 12:18-20 as it echoes Is 42:1-4).

While there are important connections among the four servant songs, the suffering servant's exaltation through humiliation is most clearly revealed in the fourth song (cf. Is 50:6, where the third song mentions suffering as part of the servant's commission). The suffering servant stands as a sign to kings and nations (Is 52:13-15). He "shall be exalted and lifted up" (Is 52:13 NRSV; interestingly enough, the Hebrew wording here is the same as in Is 6:1). He will serve as a sign, not despite his humiliation but because of it. His example thus represents the posture that truly righteous people hold before a holy God. The suffering servant will grow up "like a root out of dry ground" (Is 53:2 NRSV). While this could be taken as a *blessing—plant life emerging from arid soil—it is most likely meant to portray the opposite. The context speaks of rejection and isolation, pointing to a meager plant struggling for survival in a land of sparse vegetation.

Perhaps the dominant image associated with the suffering servant is the *lamb used as a *sin offering in OT practice (Is 53:4-9). The *wounds of the servant are graphically described, how he bears the infirmities and *diseases of human beings and their rightly deserved punishments. Here we find the roots of the doctrine of substitutionary *atonement. Upon this one lamb, curiously silent in his suffering—unlike Job, Jeremiah and others—the sins of all the *sheep are laid (see Jn 1:29). On their behalf he is cut off from the land of the living.

It is essential to recognize that God is the one who punishes the servant, as Isaiah 53:4 and 53:6 make clear. God demands a *sacrifice for sin, and it is the servant who pays it. Thus we find the servant in the seemingly paradoxical position of being humiliated by God and yet exalted for his *obedience to him. Through this obedience the suffering servant provides life, *light and righteousness for many (Is

53:10-11). The suffering servant is also a royal figure (Is 53:12). Through his obedience to the point of humiliation, he receives the spoils of victory due a king. In his place of exaltation he continues his work on behalf of the people of God through intercession for them.

As Peter writes, the suffering servant is a type and model for those who follow (1 Pet 2:21-25). The suffering servant is the supreme image of endurance and trust, demonstrating exaltation through humiliation and bearing a *cross to gain a *crown. The missionary career of Paul, frequent sufferer in his *journeys, is a paradigm of the Christian's life as a suffering servant of Christ.

See also ISAIAH, BOOK OF; JESUS, IMAGES OF; SUFFERING.

SULFUR. *See* BRIMSTONE; MINERALS.

SUMMER. *See* SEASONS.

SUN

Most of the Bible's 150 references to the sun are to the sun as the source of *light. These literal references to the physical light of the sun focus on two related motifs—the sun as an image of the common routine of life and the sun as part of a daily cycle. The cyclic nature of the sun's daily course is rendered memorable in Psalm 19:6: "Its rising is from the end of the heavens, and its circuit to the end of them" (NRSV). The sun governs the sequence of the *day, as captured in references to sunrise, *noon and twilight. It is an image of order in the Bible—a point of reference in a predictable universe. When the sun goes down, people retire and predators emerge; "when the sun rises," animals retreat and "people go out to their work" (Ps 104:20-23 NRSV).

One of the goals of the poets of the Bible is to awaken the mind from the lethargy of the familiar so that we can sense the wonder of the common rhythms of *nature. The writer of Psalm 19, for example, invests sunrise with the excitement of a *bridegroom emerging from his chamber on his *wedding day or an *athlete running a *race (Ps 19:5). In the same vein is the assertion of the writer of Ecclesiastes that "light is sweet, and it is pleasant for the eyes to see the sun" (Eccles 11:7 NRSV).

The penetrating heat and light of the Mediterranean sun (Ps 121:6; Is 49:10; Rev 7:16) and the fact that as it crosses the heavens daily it "sees" all that happens on the face of the earth may be the reason why, in ancient Near Eastern mythology, the sun *god is the god of justice, the judge of gods and humans. The Babylonian ruler Hammurabi is depicted receiving his laws from the sun god. This illuminates Psalm 19, where the description of the sun's daily movement prefaces a meditation on the law of the Lord. The link is the statement "nothing is hid from its heat" (Ps 19:6). The sun is the symbol of the all-seeing *eye of the Lord, the judge and lawgiver.

Merely as a physical phenomenon, the sun is an ambiguous image. It is the ultimate source of life and as such is a fitting metaphor for *God himself (Ps 84:11). Yet the psalms evoke vivid pictures of the terror of sunstroke and heat exhaustion, perhaps captured most vividly in the image of the sun as a malevolent foe that strikes by day (Ps 121:6; cf. Ps 91:6). One of the Dantesque pictures in the book of Revelation is the scorching heat of the sun that scorches sinners, who respond by *cursing God instead of *repenting (Rev 16:8-9).

Our life is very obviously dependent on the heat and light of the sun. Therefore we find that in the Bible the failure of the sun, and the other heavenly lights, to shine is a symbol of God's *judgment. Initially this appears in prophecies of judgment on specific nations: *Babylon (Is 13:10) or *Egypt (Ezek 32:7). It then becomes part of the imagery of the final *Day of the Lord (Joel 2:10, 31, quoted in Acts 2:20; also Mk 13:24-25; Rev 6:12). This indicates the significance of the fact that whereas Mark 15:33 says that during Jesus' crucifixion "darkness came over the whole land," Luke 23:45 adds, "while the sun's light failed" (NRSV).

The obverse of judgment for the wicked is *blessing for the righteous. Following the Day of the Lord the righteous do not need the sun anymore, because God becomes their source of life in a more direct way than before. Isaiah 24:23 says "the moon will be abashed and the sun ashamed" when the Lord of hosts reigns in *Jerusalem and manifests his *glory. Isaiah 60:19-20 takes this further. There will be no more need of sun or *moon because "the LORD will be your everlasting light, and your God will be your glory" (NRSV). In Revelation the new Jerusalem has no need of sun or moon because "the glory of God is its light, and its lamp is the Lamb" (Rev 21:23; cf. Rev 22:5).

Such use of common cultural imagery is also seen in Malachi 4:2: "But for you who revere my name the sun of righteousness shall rise, with healing in its wings" (NRSV). This draws on the imagery of the sun as a source of life. The mention of *wings probably arose from the use of the winged solar disk as a symbol in ancient Near Eastern art. The depiction in Mesopotamian art of the sun god with rays emanating from his shoulders may also be relevant. The imagery of Revelation 12:1-6 of the woman "clothed with the sun," who gives birth to a son whom a dragon tries to devour, seems to draw on a myth about the sun god which occurred in various forms in the Mediterranean world and depicted the battle between good and *evil. Whereas some Roman emperors claimed identification with the sun god, John is inspired to use the imagery, combined with imagery from the OT, to claim that *Jesus is the true Savior from evil.

See also COSMOLOGY; DAY, DAY OF THE LORD; MOON; STARS; SUN, MOON, STARS.

SUN, MOON AND STARS

Just over a dozen references to the evocative triad

"*sun, *moon and *stars" have etched the three on the minds of Bible readers through the centuries. It is as though together these three rule the sky in the imaginations of biblical writers.

Of course biblical writers steer a wide path around the pagan religious practice of worshiping the sun, moon and stars. Biblical writers know that the three owe their existence to a transcendent Creator, who created them at the same time on the fourth day of creation: "God made the two great lights, the greater light to rule the day, and the lesser light to rule the night; he made the stars also. And God set them in the firmament of the heavens to give light upon the earth, to rule over the day and over the night" (Gen 1:16-18 RSV; cf. Jer 31:35). This magnificent passage provides the clue to understanding why the three are so ineluctably joined in the Bible: together they are celestial lightgivers to the earth, and together they account for the entire daily cycle of *day and *night.

Whenever a subsequent biblical author is speaking of the heavenly bodies in a comprehensive way, the familiar triad is a likely choice. Moses warns the Israelites not to *worship what they see when they lift up their eyes to heaven and "see the sun and the moon and the stars, all the host of heaven" (Deut 4:19 RSV). The psalmist enjoins the sun, moon and "shining stars" to praise God (Ps 148:3 RSV). When the writer of Ecclesiastes wants to picture the waning of an elderly person's eyesight, it is the light of the sun, moon and stars that is "darkened" (Eccles 12:2 RSV). When Paul needs analogies to explain the difference between one's earthly body and resurrected body, he reaches to the sun, moon and stars as an illustration of the principle that the glory of one thing differs from that of another (1 Cor 15:41; we can note also the connotations of splendor that the triad holds for the biblical imagination).

On the strength of the Joseph story, the sun, moon and stars acquire symbolic associations with the patriarchs and nation of Israel. The association starts with the dream of the youthful Joseph in which the sun, moon and eleven stars bow down to him (Gen 37:9). This reappears in the vision of the woman in travail in Revelation 12:1, symbolizing the nation of Israel that produced the Messiah, and identified as Israel by being "clothed with the sun, with the moon under her feet, and on her head a crown of twelve stars" (RSV).

The most numerous category of passages that link the sun, moon and stars is *apocalyptic visions of coming cosmic collapse. Here we find pictures of the three ceasing to give their light (Is 13:10; Ezek 32:7; Joel 2:10; 3:15; Mt 24:29; Rev 8:12) or (more vaguely) of their containing "signs" that will distress and perplex people on earth (Lk 21:25).

On one level, the combination of sun, moon and stars simply impresses a person who observes the sky. They imply a certain security and predictability to people who dwell beneath them. They also enhance one's picture of the power of God over his creation.

The feelings of security drop away in apocalyptic visions of the end, but God's control over those cataclysmic events remains.

See also COSMOLOGY; MOON; STARS; SUN.

SUNSET. *See* TWILIGHT.

SUPPER

The Greek word *deipnon*, infrequently translated "supper," is usually translated "banquet," "feast" or "meal" (meaning especially the main evening meal). Accordingly, "supper" evokes the associations surrounding biblical *hospitality and *meals. Central to the meaning of the supper in NT times is the ancient practice of eating three meals during the course of a day. Breakfast was as simple as a slice of dry bread dipped in wine, and lunch was eaten wherever one happened to be. Supper was the main meal of the day. It occurred at sunset, after the work of the day was finished, and the entire household was present. It was a leisurely meal at which family members and guests conversed at length. It was a time to relax. In contrast to our own use of *supper* to connote informality as compared with the more dignified *dinner*, supper to biblical people suggested comparatively abundant food, coming at the end of the working day and thus embodying longing, satisfaction and reward for labor.

There is no Hebrew word for supper, but OT meals and hospitality practices are foundational to NT suppers. Particularly important are the Passover meal, the prophetic visions of the messianic *banquet (Is 25:6-8) and the whole cycle of offerings, *feasts and *covenant meals eaten "before" or "in the presence of" the Lord. The custom of holding farewell dinners before the departure of honored family members and friends (e.g., Gen 27:1-40) should also be kept in mind.

Modern English translations of the Bible generally restrict the use of *supper* to three major events: Last Supper, Lord's Supper and *marriage (or *wedding) supper of the *Lamb. These suppers should be seen alongside other banquets, dinners, feasts and meals in both OT and NT, and especially Jesus' lifelong practice of participating in and hosting meals where he demonstrated acceptance by welcoming *sinners and outcasts as friends. The *kingdom comes tangibly and God's shalom becomes manifest at meals with Jesus.

The Last Supper (Mt 26:17-30; Mk 14:12-26; Lk 22:7-30) is both a *Passover meal (Lk 22:11) and a farewell banquet in Jesus' honor. It is a meal among former strangers who have become friends, forming a new kind of family with Jesus as head of household. The elements of the supper (unleavened bread, cup of wine) are Passover elements (Ex 12; Deut 16) which Jesus, presiding over this remembrance of ancient deliverance, reinterprets and renames, designating himself as the sacrificial lamb for the coming ultimate deliverance. The Last Supper carries all of the ceremonial significance of the Passover as a familial and faith-community bonding event.

Paul's comments in 1 Corinthians are our primary source of information about the Lord's Supper. Paul precedes his description of it with teachings about "spiritual food" and "spiritual drink" (see 1 Cor 10:1-13), using images from the exodus-wilderness narratives (Ex 16—17) and religious meals in the ancient Near East (especially Hellenistic cultic sacred food and drink, through which the gods could thus be reached or placated). Paul sounds a clear warning against slipping into *idolatrous practices that use *food and *drink magically (1 Cor 10:14), effectively defying Jesus' lordship and deity. When Paul outlines the proper practice for the Lord's Supper (1 Cor 11:17-34), the keynote is its status as a sacred meal that uses divinely sanctioned food and drink and commemorates the atoning death of Jesus. Paul teaches that the authenticity of the supper is based on the living lordship of Jesus Christ reflected in believers' relationships within the new family of God—their life together is practiced in the supper. He scolds the Corinthians: "When you come together, it is not the Lord's Supper you eat" (1 Cor 11:20 NIV), because the people's behavior is incommensurate with the etiquette Jesus outlined and demonstrated for his disciple-friends (1 Cor 11:21-22; cf. Lk 14:7-14).

The wedding supper of John's apocalypse (Rev 19:9, 17-18) arises from and evokes the promises, grandeur and hopes of the OT messianic banquet prophecies (Is 25:6-8), royal wedding banquets and victory banquets. Victory and consummation for the church and its Lord also spell final defeat and judgment for God's enemies, pictured in the grotesque fare of the "great supper of God" (Rev 19:17-18; cf. Ezek 39:17-20). But the final word is an open, hope-filled invitation:

The Spirit and the bride say, "Come."
And let everyone who hears say, "Come."
And let everyone who is thirsty come.
Let anyone who wishes take the water of life as a gift.(Rev 22:17 NRSV)

To sum up, suppers evoke the blessing of God's presence, our belonging and friendship in Jesus' family, the joyful celebration of victory and God's deliverance, and the hopeful expectation of vindication. All these motifs flow together in the evocative KJV image of Christ standing at the *door of a person's heart, inviting himself to "come in" and "sup" with anyone who will open the door (Rev 3:20).

See also BANQUET; DRINKING; EATING; FEAST, FEASTING; FOOD; HOST, GOD AS; MEAL; PASSOVER; WINE.

SURPRISE, STORIES OF

Surprise is a common ingredient of stories. Life itself contains surprises, good and bad, but their prevalence and impact in stories are partly a literary convention. Familiarity with stories of surprise does not mitigate the effect of surprise for a reader. On the contrary, the impact is all the greater when we know that the surprise is coming. Freed from the element of novelty, we can respond to the inherent "surprisingness" of the event.

Surprises often take the form of meetings. *Adam and *Eve behave as though they are surprised to find God taking his accustomed walk in the *Garden after they have eaten the forbidden fruit (Gen 3:8). Characters who encounter God unexpectedly include Hagar (Gen 16:13), *Jacob (Gen 28:10-17; 32:22-30), *Moses (Ex 3), Gideon (Judg 6), Samson's parents (Judg 13), Elijah (1 Kings 19:9-18), Isaiah (Is 6:1-5), Ezekiel (Ezek 1), Nebuchadnezzar (Dan 3:24-24), the two men from Emmaus (Lk 24:30-32) and others to whom *Jesus appears after his resurrection. People too can surprise each other in encounters. Jacob is doubtless surprised by *Esau's generous and forgiving behavior when they are reunited (Gen 33:1-14). *Joseph's brothers are shocked by his revelation of himself in Egypt (Gen 45:1-15). *Ruth springs a surprise on Boaz in an intimate midnight encounter on the threshing floor (Ruth 3:6-13). Esther surprises Haman with her identity and counterplot, and Ahasuerus with a disclosure of Haman's plot against the Jews (Esther 8).

Another category of surprise stories focus on events that turn out contrary to expectation. Eve enthusiastically names her firstborn Cain, exclaiming, "I have gotten a man with the help of the LORD" (Gen 4:1 RSV); doubtless *Cain's parents are surprised by how tragically their hopes for their son turn out. *Abraham and Sarah might well have been surprised by the immediate consequences of their decision to have a child by Hagar (Gen 16:1-6). Isaac and Esau are surprised by their discovery of how Jacob and Rebekah have stolen the blessing (Gen 27:30-35). Moses comes down from Mt. Sinai with God's law written on two tablets only to discover that the nation has resorted to idolatry (Ex 32:15-19). The Levite is surprised to find his concubine lying dead at the door, and the nation is shocked by the news (Judg 19:27-30). Both Samson and Saul are so positively endowed by God as to be ranked among the "most likely to succeed," with the result that their tragic failures are a surprise. After the catalog of success stories in Hebrews 11 has led us to expect an unmitigated record of triumph, we are presented with surprising examples of terrible failure when judged by ordinary external standards (Heb 11:35-38).

Some of the Bible's stories of surprise involve characters who are brought to a sudden awareness of something they have done in ignorance. Tamar presents Judah with evidence of his liaison with her when she was disguised as a prostitute (Gen 38:1-30). Jacob is surprised the morning after his wedding to find that "behold, it was Leah" to whom he "went in" the night before (Gen 29:25 RSV). We can readily imagine Jephthah's response when the first person to meet him as he returns home from battle is his own daughter (Judg 11). David is surprised by the personal application of Nathan's fictional account of a sinful act, inasmuch as David thought he was simply judging a civil case (2 Sam 12). On the day after the drunken Nabal insulted David, his wife Abigail tells him what he had done, "and he became as a stone" (1 Sam 25:37). Events can be so surprising as to produce shock: when Jacob is informed that Joseph is still alive, "his heart fainted, for he did not believe them" (Gen 45:26 RSV).

Other surprises turn on God's revelations (see Revelation/Recognition Stories). Three times in Genesis, for example, an Egyptian king is surprised by the revelation of what he has done in taking a patriarch's wife into his harem (Gen 12:10-20; 20; 26:6-11). After Jacob's elaborate but ridiculous attempts at animal husbandry, he would have reason to be surprised by the dream revelation that the multiplying of his flocks and herds had a genetic cause arranged by God, and not the rigmarole of branches placed in front of the animals during their mating (Gen 30:37—31:12). God surprised Belshazzar with a prediction of his impending judgment so dramatically (a mysterious hand that writes on the wall) that the king "was greatly alarmed, and his color changed" (Dan 5:9 RSV).

Quite apart from special revelations, God's providential acts prove to be surprising in the pages of the Bible. Not only is the life of the infant Moses spared through a daring act of his parents, but his mother actually gets paid for taking care of her own child (Ex 2:1-10). The first appearance of *manna was a surprising discovery for the Israelites (Ex 16:13-15), and we might infer that subsequent acts of provision during the wilderness wanderings also had an element of surprise. God surprises Gideon by reducing his army to three hundred men (Judg 7:4-7). Everyone present is surprised by young David's conquest of Goliath with a stone from a sling (1 Sam 17). The court of Nebuchadnezzar is surprised by the robustness and skill of Daniel and his three friends after ten days of simple fare (Dan 1).

Keeping in mind that human character is one of the sources of narrative surprise, sometimes we as readers are surprised by developments in the stories of the Bible. After the reluctance of Moses and Gideon to be leaders has been clearly established, we are surprised by their sheer mastery of situations once they assume leadership. Again, both Moses and Gideon become so idealized in our imaginations that we are surprised by a character flaw that emerges in each of them (Num 20:1-13; Judg 8:22-28). Job is legendary for his patience in the prologue to the book of Job, but thereafter he surprises us with the vehemence of his accusations against God. Solomon's wisdom too was legendary, which renders his apostasy late in life a surprise to us. Elijah surprises us by experiencing a case of burnout after his greatest victory (1 Kings 19), and Hezekiah by coming to a disappointing end after the spiritual "high" in the events surrounding God's extending of his life (Is 37—39).

Still another category of surprise stories hinges on

characters who are suddenly judged by God. Lot's wife is instantaneously turned into a pillar of salt when she looks back to Sodom (Gen 19:26). We can infer that Pharaoh is surprised by the retributive power of God during the plagues and at the Red Sea destruction. Miriam is instantaneously smitten with leprosy (Num 12:9-16), as is Elisha's servant Gehazi (2 Kings 5:19-27). Nebuchadnezzar is smitten with insanity at the very apex of his earthly success (Dan 4:28-33), and Ananias and Sapphira are smitten dead for their lying (Acts 5:1-11). Though not directly judged by God, the men of Succoth and Penuel who refuse to help Gideon in his pursuit of the Midianites are no doubt surprised to see him return and make good on his threat to flail them with briers and tear down their tower (Judg 8). Samson is apparently surprised that his strength has left him after he discloses its secret to Delilah (Judg 16:20). Both Ahab (2 Chron 18:28-33) and Josiah (2 Chron 35:20-27) think a disguise will preserve their life in battle but are killed anyway.

*Battle stories include accounts of surprise as a military strategy. At the battle at Ai, Joshua uses an ambush to draw the *army of Ai out of the city and then surprises the city by entering it from behind (Josh 8:14-22). Ehud surprises his victim Eglon with a dagger thrust when Eglon expects to receive a secret message from God (Judg 3:12-30). Gideon's nighttime raid on the Midianite army uses surprise to throw the enemy into a panic (Judg 7:19-23). Judges 9 revolves around a series of surprises, including the braggadocio Gaal's shock at seeing enemies moving down the hillsides toward him and Abimelech's being crushed when a woman pushes a millstone onto him from a tower.

The OT proverbs, too, contain brief vignettes of people who are surprised by sudden judgment—as sudden as fish or birds are caught in a net as "it suddenly falls upon them" (Eccles 9:12 RSV). Poverty surprises the *sluggard by coming upon him like a *robber (Prov 24:34). Even the psalms contain brief surprise stories, as when the prosperous arrogant are set "in slippery places" and "destroyed in a moment" (Ps 73:18-19 RSV).

Jesus' parables are a minianthology of surprise stories. Despite their prevailing realism and avoidance of fantasy, many of them contain a surprising twist—a pay scale that totally disregards how much time workers have worked, a spurned father's irrational lavishness in forgiving a *prodigal son, help to a wounded traveler coming from the least expected source, implausible excuses not to attend a banquet, a servant whose debt is forgiven but who refuses to be lenient with people who owe him money. We also find stories with surprise endings, such as when a rich farmer's plans for retirement are dashed the day after he completes his work, or when sons reverse what they tell their father about working in vineyard at the breakfast table, or when a Pharisee goes home condemned while a tax collector goes home justified. Still other parables are built around surprised discoveries—finding *treasure hidden in a field, a *pearl of great price, a *wedding guest without a wedding garment.

This element of surprise suffuses Jesus' teaching as well. His Beatitudes, for example, give a surprising version of the conditions that make a person happy or blessed, as do some of the promised rewards (such as the meek inheriting the earth). Jesus' relative leniency regarding sabbath observance is a source of continual surprise to the religious establishment of the day. Other verdicts on conventional experiences are also surprising, such as the statement that a poor widow who put a minute amount of money into the temple treasury has given more than rich people who contributed ostentatiously.

The *apocalyptic visions and eschatological discourses of the Bible are yet another repository of surprise stories. Predictions of the future foretell surprising reversals of conditions that currently exist, such as when prosperous nations or groups are said to be headed for destruction. The kaleidoscopic structure of the prophetic books in effect springs one surprise on us after another. The most notable example is the book of Revelation, where one moment Jesus is *lion and a verse later a *lamb (Rev 5:5-6), or where we read about extravagant preparations for a battle that is never described (Rev 16:12-16). An added element of surprise in the eschatological parts of the Bible is the suddenness with which the final events will engulf people. In the Epistles, for example, the day of the Lord will come like a *thief (1 Thess 5:12; 2 Pet 3:10). Jesus used the same image to depict the suddenness with which his return will occur (Mt 24:43; Lk 12:39), and he told parables that reinforce how surprised some people will be when the eschaton arrives (Mt 24:36-25:1-31). To this we can add how surprised people are by the verdict that is rendered on their earthly life in Jesus' picture of the final judgment (Mt 25:31-46).

The drama of redemption itself is a story of surprises. God's choice of the unlikely person begins in Genesis and extends through the familiar preference in the OT for the younger over the older sibling (see Younger Child). Underlying the surprise of God's choices is the principle that "the LORD sees not as man sees; man looks on the outward appearance, but the LORD looks on the heart" (1 Sam 16:7 RSV). The life of Jesus participates in this pattern of surprises. As the song of the servant in Isaiah 52:13-12 predicts, the Messiah lacks external signs of impressiveness that we would expect of such an exalted figure; indeed, even to speak of the exaltation of a servant is surprising. Jesus' earthly life too is a series of surprises, as he identifies with the poor and humble and eschews an earthly kingdom. When Paul reflects on all this, he concludes that God's calling of Christians was an extended surprise and shock in its violation of worldly standards of likely candidates for salvation, as God chose "foolishness" over "wisdom" (1 Cor 1:18-31).

What are we to make of the prevalence and variety of the surprise motif in the Bible? At a purely literary level we can recognize this as one of the things that make the Bible an interesting rather than dull book to read. At another level we can sense something of the realism of life and mystery of human personality to which these surprises attest. At an even more profound level, the surprises of the Bible have something to do with divine *providence, *judgment and *redemption. Overall, the pervasive element of surprise in the Bible shows the need to live in a spirit of watchfulness about one's own behavior and attitudes.

See also REVERSAL.

SWADDLING BANDS

Swaddling bands consisted of a *cloth tied together in bandagelike strips. After an infant was born, the umbilical cord was cut and tied, then the *baby was washed, rubbed with salt and wrapped with strips of cloth (Ezek 16:4). This provided the child with warmth, protection of extremities and a sense of security.

In the OT, God is pictured as "swaddling" the sea at creation with thick *darkness (Job 38:9). Israel is described as an unswaddled *child abandoned by her *mother until God comes and cares for her (Ezek 16:1-7). The birth narrative of Jesus in Luke stresses that the baby was wrapped in "swaddling clothes" by his mother, *Mary (Lk 2:7 KJV). This wrapping and placement in a manger acted as a sign to the shepherds, who were instructed to find the baby in Bethlehem (Lk 2:12, 16).

As an image, swaddling bands convey two meanings. First, they reflect parental care and compassion. When Mary swaddled Jesus, she showed the care of a good mother (cf. Wis 7:4-5). Despite austere surroundings and the likely presence of barnyard animals, Jesus was protected and warmed in his mother's care (see Animals). Likewise, God was in no way obligated to choose Israel or to care for its daily needs. Yet his tender nurturing strengthened Israel, and from Abraham God made a great nation (Gen 15:5).

Second, for a child swaddling symbolizes total dependence. Incapable of tending to its own needs, a baby will not survive unless it receives the care of others. Israel's survival as a nation rested in God's hand (Ps 124:1-2). The humility of Jesus' incarnation is shown in his subjection and dependence on his earthly parents, though he was the Creator and Sustainer of the universe (Col 1:16-17).

See also BABY; BIRTH STORY; LINEN.

SWALLOW

In the natural world, victor and victim are defined by one simple act: the victor *eats, the victim is eaten. A leopard dramatically demonstrates her dominance when upon capturing an antelope, she drags it into her tree and leisurely dines. Most dramatic of all is when one creature unhinges its jaws, opens wide its tremendous *mouth and with a single gulp swallows the opponent whole. The Scriptures employ this powerful language to show the utter domination of one party by another.

Pharaoh and his magicians are no match for the Lord and his servants. This is dramatically shown in the encounter of the staffs that turn into serpents in Exodus 7. Aaron throws his staff to the ground, and it becomes a huge *serpent. Not to be outdone, Pharaoh's magicians do the same with their staffs. But Aaron's serpent proceeds to swallow Pharaoh's serpents (see Aaron's Rod).

The same thing happens, but on a much larger scale, when the foolish Pharaoh and his host are vanquished in the *sea. Exodus 15 records Israel's victory song: "The enemy boasted, . . . 'I will gorge myself on them' " (Ex 15:9 NIV). But "you stretched out your right hand and the earth swallowed them" (Ex 15:12 NIV).

An equally powerful display of the utter dominance of the Lord occurs when Korah and his followers rebel against Moses. Moses calls an assembly and states the need for the rebels to die in a totally new way so that there will be no mistake about who holds authority. As soon as he finishes speaking, "the ground under them split apart and the earth opened its mouth and swallowed them, with their households and all Korah's men and all their possessions" (Num 16:31-32 NIV).

The *grave, or Sheol, is personified as swallowing a person whole. This fact adds to the humiliation and fear of the grave (Prov 1:12; see Death). It is in the context of the grave, that great mouth dreaded by all, that the most awesome swallowing of all will take place, in fulfillment of Isaiah 25:7-8: "On this mountain he will destroy the shroud that enfolds all peoples, the sheet that covers all nations; he will swallow up death forever" (NIV). Paul shows that at the resurrection, "when the perishable has been clothed with the imperishable, and the mortal with immortality, then the saying that is written will come true: 'Death has been swallowed up in victory' " (1 Cor 15:54 NIV).

See also EATING; MOUTH; THROAT.

SWEAT

The word sweat occurs only twice in the NIV, yet almost everyone in the Western world, whether Christian or not, could paraphrase part of the first Bible verse in which it occurs: "By the sweat of your brow . . ." (Gen 3:19 NIV). Sometimes plain reality is the best method of Scripture memorization. "By the sweat of your brow" is such a powerful metaphor because it speaks to the double-edged nature of human labor. We feel good when we work up a sweat and accomplish something; yet all of us know the frustration of *working ourselves to the bone only to have it go for naught. The writer of the book of Ecclesiastes (Eccles 2:17-23) complains long and hard about this fact, and it resonates powerfully within our aching souls.

The other biblical occurrence of the word sweat

is also widely known: the scene of Christ in the *Garden of Gethsemane pleading with his Father to spare him the *cross if possible. It is intriguing how this image of Christ's travail corresponds to the awful prediction made by God in the original Garden (cf. Gen 3:19). These two uses of the word sweat are like bookends in the drama of the Fall of humanity. At one end we see a dejected pair of human beings told they will *suffer much futility because of their disobedience. Nothing will ever work out perfectly in this life. At the other end we see Christ suffering to the point of sweating drops of *blood as he contemplates his *journey toward the cross. All the futility of life is wrapped up in that image of drops of blood spattering the ground where Christ *weeps. His willingness to suffer the wrath of God on our behalf squeezes the last drop of sweat from the human brow. At the right hand of the Father, Christ sweats no more—and neither shall his people.

See also WORK, WORKER.

SWEET

The adjective sweet—in both literal and figurative usage—appears more frequently in the OT than in the NT. In literal usage it describes the taste experience associated with *honey or sugar; in figurative usage it generally describes a pleasant experience. In fact, the word pleasant appears in parallel constructions with sweet.

Sweet is used more often to describe a *smell (an example of synesthesia so familiar that it is almost transparent as a figure) than a taste. Sweet is usually paired with savor or *incense with reference to the smell of burnt *offerings in altar worship, from Noah through the wilderness wanderings to the *idolatrous days preceding captivity in Babylon. After Noah left the ark, he built an altar "and took of every clean beast, and of every clean fowl, and offered burnt offerings on the altar. And the LORD smelled a sweet savour; and the LORD said in his heart, I will not again curse the ground any more for man's sake" (Gen 8:20-21 KJV). Concerning Aaron's priesthood, we read, "And thou shalt burn the whole ram upon the altar: it is a burnt offering unto the LORD: it is a sweet savour, an offering made by fire unto the LORD" (Ex 29:18 KJV). "And Aaron shall burn thereon sweet incense every morning" (Ex 30:7 KJV).

Regardless of how sweet the smell of burnt offerings might be, God is always more interested in the condition of the *heart and the life: "I will bring evil upon this people, even the fruit of their thoughts, because they have not hearkened unto my words, nor to my law, but rejected it. To what purpose cometh there to me incense from Sheba, and the sweet cane from a far country? Your burnt offerings are not acceptable, nor your sacrifices sweet unto me" (Jer 6:19-20 KJV). Several passages note sweet smells' tendency to sour as a result of foolishness or sin. Note the vividness of the following simile: "Dead flies cause the ointment of the apothecary to send forth a stinking savour: so doth a little folly him that is in reputation for wisdom and honour" (Eccles 10:1 KJV). "Because the daughters of Zion are haughty," their health and their ornaments will be taken away, and "instead of sweet smell [of perfume] there shall be stink" (Is 3:16, 24 KJV).

Sweet is also used in the Bible to designate fresh or drinkable *water, much as it is today (Ex 15:25; Jas 3:11). Spices and *ointments used for burials (Mk 16:1; Jn 12:3; 2 Cor 16:4), cosmetics (Esther 2:12; Is 3:24) and consecrating *oil (Ex 30:23-5; Ps 45:8) are also described as sweet.

The clearly figurative uses of *sweet* and *sweetness* are numerous and varied, sometimes appearing in interesting combinations with the literal use of the words. The "sweetness" referred to in Jotham's charming parable in Judges 9, for example, is literal; but it appears in a discussion among a *fig tree and some other trees regarding which of them should be king of trees (Judg 9:11). In Samson's riddle the use of *sweet* and *sweetness* is not as figurative as its structural context, but its use is still interesting—"Out of the strong came forth sweetness. . . . What is sweeter than honey? and what is stronger than a lion?" (Judg 14:14, 18 KJV)—a simile within a riddle.

Not surprisingly, the poetic books—Job, Psalms, Proverbs and the Song of Songs—abound in this usage, and Paul, as shown below, repeatedly builds on old covenant *sacrifice imagery to describe the life of the Christian. David is called "the sweet psalmist of Israel," surely a positive appellation (2 Sam 23:1 KJV). Note the bitterly ironic tone in the following passages from Job. Zophar advises Job regarding the wicked and the *hypocrite, "Though wickedness be sweet in his mouth, . . . yet his meat in his bowels is turned, it is the gall of asps within him" (Job 20:12-14 KJV). Job, observing that the wicked seem to die unaccused and unpunished, says, "The clods of the valley shall be sweet unto him, and every man shall draw after him, as they are innumerable before him" (Job 21:33 KJV). In a passage especially rich in figurative language, the *womb—a synecdoche for the mother of the sinner—"shall forget him; the worm shall feed sweetly on him" (Job 24:19-20 KJV). Finally, God, speaking to Job, seems to be suggesting subtlety and mystery through his use of *sweet* in one of his several rhetorical questions that leave Job humbled: "Cants *thou* bind the sweet influences of Pleiades, or loose the bands of Orion?" (Job 38:31 KJV).

In the psalms the judgments of the Lord are praised for their metaphorical sweetness: "More to be desired are they than gold, yea, than much fine gold: sweeter also than honey and the honeycomb" (Ps 19:10 KJV). Similarly, the words of God are called sweet (Ps 119:103; 141:6). The speaker in Psalm 104:34 writes, "My meditation of [God] shall be sweet" (KJV). Human-to-human communication is also counted as pleasant in Psalm 55:14: "We took sweet counsel together, and walked into the house of God in company" (KJV). These passages certainly affirm language, thought and the

gift of communication as graces.

The wise author of Proverbs describes several experiences, actions and concepts as sweet: sleep (Prov 3:24), "the desire accomplished" (Prov 13:19 KJV), words, again compared to honey (Prov 16:24), a *friend (Prov 27:9) and, of course, knowledge and *wisdom (Prov 24:13-14). Proverbs 16:21 offers a somewhat less clear figure: "The wise in heart shall be called prudent; and the sweetness of the lips increaseth learning" (KJV). Perhaps "the sweetness of the lips" suggests asking questions politely; or it may refer to keeping *silent and listening. Irony and paradox color the following passages from Proverbs—and, interestingly, all of them use an *eating or *drinking metaphor with the word *sweet*. "The full soul loatheth an honeycomb; but to the hungry soul every bitter thing is sweet" (Prov 27:7 KJV). The speaker in the next passage is the "foolish woman" who calls "passengers who go right on their ways": "Stolen waters are sweet, and bread eaten in secret is pleasant" (Prov 9:17 KJV; *see* Seduction). Note the parallelism: sweet equals pleasant. "Bread of deceit is sweet to a man; but afterwards his mouth shall be filled with gravel" (Prov 20:17 KJV). "The morsel which thou hast eaten shalt thou vomit up, and lose thy sweet words" (Prov 23:8 KJV).

*Sleep is again called sweet in Ecclesiastes 5:12: "The sleep of a labouring man is sweet, whether he eat little or much; but the abundance of the rich will not suffer him to sleep" (KJV). *Sweet* and *pleasant* are again equated in Ecclesiastes 11:7: "Truly the light is sweet, and a pleasant thing it is for the eyes to behold the sun" (KJV).

The line between literal and figurative becomes very faint in the Song of Songs, due in part to the unabashedly sensuous nature of the work. Both the masculine and the feminine speakers use *sweet* to describe both each other and the ointments and spices that enhance their experience of each other. She compares him to other men with a simile and then uses *fruit and taste imagery to describe her experience of him: "As the apple tree among the trees of the wood, so is my beloved among the sons. I sat down under his shadows with great delight, and his fruit was sweet to my taste" (Song 2:3 KJV). He says to her, "Sweet is thy voice, and thy countenance is comely" (Song 2:14 KJV). Literal myrrh and spices appear in Proverbs 4:10 and 5:5, while Proverbs 5:13 reads, "His cheeks are as a bed of spices, as sweet flowers: his lips like lilies, dropping sweet smelling myrrh" (KJV). She says of him, "His mouth is most sweet: yea, he is altogether lovely" (Prov 5:16 KJV). And he says to her, "The roof of thy mouth [shall be] like the best wine for my beloved, that goeth down sweetly, causing the lips of those that are asleep to speak" (Prov 7:9 KJV).

Regardless of whether we see the work as a picture of God's desired relationship with his chosen people, or of Christ the bridegroom (*see* Jesus, Images of) with the church, his *bride, or simply as an inspired affirmation of the goodness of erotic love between proper partners (or all of the above), it remains the most beautiful poem in the Hebrew and Christian Bibles. If *sweet* here means "pleasant," as it does so many other places, then we have another figurative device at work in the Song as well: understatement.

Three passages from Isaiah are heavy with irony and bitterness, yet use sweetness imagery. "Woe unto them that call evil good, and good evil; that put darkness for light, and light for darkness; that put bitter for sweet, and sweet for bitter!" (Is 5:20 KJV). The city of Tyre is told, "Take an harp, go about the city, thou harlot that has been forgotten; make sweet melody, sing many songs, that thou mayest be remembered" (Is 23:16 KJV). "They shall be drunken with their own blood, as with sweet wine" (Is 49:26 KJV).

In the NT the figurative use of sweetness is found primarily in Paul's letters and in Revelation. Revelation 5:8, while not using the word *sweet,* describes the twenty-four elders falling down before the *Lamb "having every one of them harps, and gold vials full of odours, which are the prayers of the saints" (KJV). Could these odors be anything but pleasant and sweet? Revelation 10:10 seems to echo Ezekiel 3:1-3. Ezekiel reads, " 'Eat this roll [scroll], and go speak unto the house of Israel.' . . . Then did I eat it; and it was in my mouth as honey for sweetness" (KJV). Revelation reads, "It [the little book] was in my mouth sweet as honey: and as soon as I had eaten it, my belly was bitter" (KJV). Each of these is interesting in light of the passages—in Psalms, primarily—that describe words as sweet.

Paul's echoing of OT sacrifice imagery is obvious and revealing of this imagery's importance in his thinking. As Norman Friedman has observed, "A given poet's preoccupation with certain settings, situations, and characters will be seen, when viewed in the perspective of his total achievement, *to act as a symbolic key to his ultimate vision of life, just as his recurring metaphors, when systematically inspected, will do*" (31, emphasis added).

In letters to three different audiences, Paul uses very similar figures. "For we are unto God a sweet savour of Christ, in them that are saved, and in them that perish: To the one we are the savour of death unto death; and to the other the savour of life unto life" (2 Cor 2:15-16 KJV). As in some passages from the OT cited above, the same smell can be sweet or unpleasant depending on one's spiritual condition. Notice also how closely Paul identifies the Christian with the sacrifice of Christ, calling to mind his admonition to present our bodies as living sacrifices (Rom 12:1). Christ's work on the cross is addressed in Ephesians: "Be ye therefore followers of God, as dear children; And walk in love, as Christ also hath loved us, and hath given himself for us an offering and a sacrifice to God for a sweetsmelling savour" (Eph 5:1-2 KJV). Finally, "I am full, having received of Epaphroditus the things which were sent from you, an odour of a sweet smell, a sacrifice acceptable, wellpleasing to God" (Phil 4:18 KJV). Here individ-

ual acts of grace and charity are imaged as pleasing, acceptable worship, evidence of one's identification with Christ and his sacrifice.

See also HONEY; INCENSE; SACRIFICE; SMELL, SCENT.

BIBLIOGRAPHY. N. Friedman, "Imagery: From Sensation to Symbol," *Journal of Aesthetics and Art Criticism* 12 (1953) 25-37.

SWINE

The *law of Moses considers pigs "unclean" and not to be eaten by the people of Israel (Lev 11:7; Deut 14:8). While this puts them in a category containing many other creatures, in practice they were a prominent member of this category, since in many other parts of the ancient world pigs were kept as domestic animals and valued as *food. Thus eating pork is instanced as a key example of unclean, pagan practice in Isaiah 65:4 and 66:17, which attack Israelites who participate in pagan cults. Especially in view of Isaiah 66:3, which refers to the offering of pigs' blood in *sacrifice, it is likely that in these verses the eating of pork pertains to a sacrificial rite, even though the eating of pork offered in sacrifice was not common in ancient Near Eastern religion. For a biblical writer, of course, the association of pigs with *holiness, which these apostate Israelites claim to gain from their pagan rites (Is 65:5; 66:17), is heavily ironic.

In the later biblical period, Jewish abstention from pork was a notable distinctive that marked them out from *Gentiles. In the persecution under Antiochus Epiphanes, which aimed to eradicate the distinctives of Jewish religion, loyal Jews treated abstention from pork as a test of their loyalty to God's law. The Maccabean martyrs died for refusing to compromise on this point (2 Macc 6:18-20; 7:1). Part of Antiochus's desecration of the *temple consisted of offering pigs in sacrifice (1 Macc 1:47), since pigs, as unclean, were not among the animals used for sacrifice according to the law of Moses (*see* Animals of the Bible).

Although the classification of pigs as "unclean" is a technical one that does not refer to their physical dirtiness, in the ancient world pigs were generally considered dirty animals. They were often allowed to roam loose and scavenge in the streets, as *dogs did. This increased the symbolic association of uncleanness with pigs in the Jewish mind, and in a later period both *pigs* and *dogs* became derogatory terms for Gentiles. An obvious association of pigs with Gentiles appears in the NT, where when pigs appear as domestic animals it is a clear indication that the story has entered Gentile territory, as in the cases of Jesus' encounter with the demoniac Legion (Mk 5:11-14) and the *prodigal son's degradation to swineherd (Lk 15:15-16).

"Like a gold ring in a pig's snout is a beautiful woman without good sense" (Prov 11:22 NRSV). The point here is the incongruous contrast between the beautiful ornament and the animal, which is probably considered dirty and perhaps also ugly (though this would be the only evidence that pigs were thought ugly).

The association of pigs with dogs occurs both in Matthew 7:6 and in 2 Peter 2:22. The former verse should probably read as chiastic parallelism:

Do not give what is holy to dogs;

and do not throw your pearls before swine,

or they [the swine] will trample them under foot

and [the dogs will] turn and maul you. (NRSV)

Some interpreters have seen here a prohibition on preaching the gospel to Gentiles (symbolized as dogs and swine; cf. Mt 10:5), but it seems more likely that simply unreceptive hearers are in view, people who treat what is supremely valuable (like *pearls) as worthless and contemptible. Such people need not be Gentiles, but the saying may compare them with typical Gentiles, regarded by Jews as contemptuous of the holy and precious things of God's law.

In 2 Peter 2:22 two proverbs are applied to the case of Christians converted from a pagan background who return to their immoral pagan way of life. Once again the traditional association of dogs and pigs with Gentiles may be in view, as well as the more general association of these animals with dirt. The two proverbs give examples of the unpleasant habits of the two animals. The first is quoted from Proverbs 26:11; the second ("The sow is washed only to wallow in the mud," NRSV) is preserved elsewhere in the *Story of Ahiqar*. Pigs enjoy bathing in *water, but not for the sake of cleanliness, since they equally enjoy wallowing in mud. The pig in question has been to the public baths and washed itself *clean, but immediately dirties itself again. The bathing may suggest baptism as the converts' "cleansing of past sins" (2 Pet 1:9 NRSV).

See also ANIMALS; DOG; GENTILE; PURITY.

SWORD

The sword was the most important *weapon of *warfare in the ancient Near East and in the Greco-Roman world. Ranging from sixteen inches to three feet in length, with one or both sides sharpened, this implement was used for thrusting and slashing opponents in armed conflict. Most of the over four hundred occurrences of the term in the Bible are to be understood in a literal sense, but *sword* also came to acquire a set of figurative meanings.

Because it commonly occurs in narratives describing *battle, "the sword" became a symbol for warfare. "Putting a city to the sword" is another way of saying "going to war." Defeat was spoken of as "falling by the sword" (see Jer 19:7). The OT prophets pointed to a time in the future when there would no longer be war, and the sword would be absent. Hosea proclaims, "I will abolish the bow, the sword, and war from the land; and I will make you lie down in safety" (Hos 2:18 NRSV). Isaiah depicts this as a time when "they shall beat their swords into plowshares" and "nation shall not lift up sword against nation" (Is 2:4 NRSV).

Even beyond the context of warfare, the sword represents bloodshed and *strife. Nathan's prophetic announcement to David that "the sword shall never depart from your house" (2 Sam 12:10 NRSV) indicated that there would be discord and violence among family members in succeeding generations. Absalom's conspiracy against his father is one illustration of what Nathan prophesied (2 Sam 15—18).

The sword also symbolizes divine *judgment. The psalmist warns, "If one does not repent, God will whet his sword" (Ps 7:12 NRSV). Scripture even speaks of God's judgment as "the sword of the Lord." In the outpouring of God's wrath on the day of *vengeance, Isaiah says that "the sword of the LORD is bathed in blood" (Is 34:6 NIV). Jeremiah speaks of the inescapability of God's judgment: "the sword of the LORD devours from one end of the land to the other; no one shall be safe" (Jer 12:12 NRSV). Jesus is depicted as bearing a sharp, two-edged sword in his *mouth (Rev 1:16), which he will use "to strike down the nations" (Rev 19:15 NRSV) at the consummation.

The power of civic authorities to punish and execute wrongdoers is depicted by the image of the sword. In his letter to the Romans, Paul says that the governing *authority "does not bear the sword for nothing. He is God's servant, an agent of wrath to bring punishment on the wrongdoer" (Rom 13:4 NIV). The passage therefore speaks of the divinely granted role of local governments to punish those who violate public laws.

Because of the sword's capacity to inflict *wounds, it is used to symbolize anything that causes harm and injury to people. The psalmist says of his *enemies that their "tongues are sharp swords" (Ps 57:4 NIV), and the writer of Proverbs observes, "Rash words are like sword thrusts" (Prov 12:18 NRSV). A promiscuous woman wounds those allured and taken in by her: "In the end she is bitter as gall, sharp as a double-edged sword" (Prov 5:4 NIV). A false witness is like a sword because of the damage this person can do (Prov 25:18). Those who exploit the poor for their own gain are said to have *teeth that are swords (Prov 30:14).

A few passages in the Bible use this instrument of piercing to symbolize something good—the Word of God. God's Word is represented as a sword because of its ability to penetrate a human life. Isaiah prophesied that God would make the mouth of the *Servant of the Lord "like a sharp sword" (Is 49:2 NRSV). His message would have a powerful impact on humanity. In Paul's depiction of believers' ongoing struggle with the forces of *evil, he pictures the Word of God as a sword that functions as part of their protective *armor (Eph 6:17). Jesus himself had set the example of intimate acquaintance with the written Word of God which issued in appropriate application to each of the devil's three solicitations to evil (Mt 4:1-11; *see* Satan). The writer of Hebrews also likens the Word of God to a sword: "Indeed, the word of God is living and active, sharper than any two-edged sword, piercing until it divides soul from spirit, joints from marrow; it is able to judge the thoughts and intentions of the heart" (Heb 4:12 NRSV). God's Word can reach into the deepest recesses of our beings and have a transformative effect on our lives.

See also ARMOR; ARROW, ARROW OF GOD; BATTLE STORIES; WEAPONS, HUMAN AND DIVINE.

SYMBOLIC NUMBERS. *See* NUMBERS.

T

TABERNACLE

Next to the *temple, the tabernacle is the most important place of *worship in the Bible. The biblical imagery falls naturally into three categories—the original tabernacle and its furniture, subsequent OT allusions to the tabernacle, and NT portraits in John, Acts and especially Hebrews and Revelation.

The Tabernacle in Exodus. One of two primary image patterns associated with the original tabernacle is artistic and architectural. The chapters that describe the materials that went into the building of the tabernacle are an artist's delight—a riot of *color, texture and design. An aura of careful planning weaves these sensory images into a composite unity. In addition to the physical properties of the tabernacle, a motif of worship practices is interwoven, as we are never allowed to lose sight of the fact that this lavishly adorned and colorful tabernacle existed for the purpose of religious ritual and worship.

Because the physical properties of the tabernacle reflected the purpose of religious use, it is possible to see an incipient symbolism at work. A long line of modern interpreters have viewed the tabernacle as a collection of symbols about Christ—red for Jesus' *blood, blue for *heaven and so forth (*see* Colors of the Bible). The problem with such interpretations is that no matter how much they depend on earlier interpretations, all those interpretations represent nothing more than guesses and arbitrary associations. To really understand the background of the tabernacle, one must examine what the symbols meant to ancient Israelites.

Size and Shape of the Tabernacle. The tabernacle was a *tent—an ornate tent to be sure, but a tent nonetheless. It was built during the *wilderness period, when the people of God were *journeying from Egypt to the Promised Land and were all living in these easily transportable residences. Thus it is understandable that the tabernacle, God's residence on earth, would be constructed in the form of a tent.

The book of Exodus tells us that God gave instructions for the building of his own residence. God told *Moses in detail how to build the tabernacle (see the recurrent refrain "make them according to the pattern shown you on the mountain" in Ex 25:9, 40 NIV). After the instructions were given and before they were carried out, Israel turned away from God and worshiped the golden *calf (Ex 32). Moses,

though, interceded for his people, and God forgave them. The last part of the book of Exodus narrates how Israel carried out God's construction plans to the letter (compare Ex 35—38 with Ex 25—27). When the building was finished, God filled it with his cloud of *glory, symbolizing his holy presence in the midst of his people (Ex 40:34-38).

Physically, the tabernacle was tripartite: one entering the outer court could proceed directly forward to the holy place, and the most holy place (the "holy of holies") was directly behind the holy place. In the early period all Egyptian temples, modeled after wealthy homes, were tripartite and approached in this direct linear manner; some Canaanite temples (e.g., Ugarit, Shechem) were tripartite; Mesopotamian temples possessed an entirely different structure. Israelites thus would have recognized some features of the tabernacle as simply standard features of Egyptian temples. Other features of the design,

The tabernacle in the wilderness.

however, sent a clear message. The innermost shrine of almost all ancient temples contained a sacred bark on which was mounted the deity's image; Egyptian temples also sometimes boasted shrines for tutelary deities on either side of the holy of holies. The tabernacle's architecture proclaims: there is only one God, and you shall have no graven images of him.

The tabernacle was modest by ancient temple standards; compare the daily offerings of fifty-five hundred loaves of bread in Theban temples of Ramses II. The outer court was one hundred cubits long and fifty cubits wide, but the tabernacle itself thirty cubits long and ten cubits high and wide. Some other temples from this period were of comparable size, but the tabernacle was smaller than most Canaanite and much smaller than Egyptian, Mesopotamian and Hittite temples. Egyptians also used tent-shrines, however, as did some nomadic peoples, and the tabernacle apparently was larger than most of these. During Israel's travels in the wilderness the tabernacle was in the midst of a rectangular camp, just as Ramses II's royal tent was during his military campaigns.

Contents of the Tabernacle. All the dye colors and materials reported in Exodus were available in *Egypt in the period of Moses; Egypt had employed the construction techniques for up to fifteen centuries. Some materials have no symbolic significance except perhaps to testify that God is practical: the Israelites used acacia *wood (often used in Egyptian construction) because it was the only kind of wood available in the Sinai desert! It also has a high tolerance for heat. (Had later Israelites invented the story of the tabernacle, they surely would have used cedar wood, as in Baal's temple and *Solomon's temple.)

The most expensive colors and metals were used nearest the ark; materials declined in value as one moved away from the ark. In the ancient Near East this progression of value signified gradations of *holiness, hence that the deity must be approached with great reverence and awe.

The *ark of the covenant resembled the sacred barks of deities kept in the innermost shrines of ancient temples. Because artists often used cherubimlike figures on *throne pedestals, the cherubim atop the ark symbolize a throne; thus God is "enthroned" above the cherubim (1 Sam 4:4; 2 Sam 6:2; 2 Kings 19:15; Ps 80:1; 99:1; Is 37:16; cf. Num 7:89; Ezek 9:3). Other ancient Near Eastern temples (e.g., Minoan, Assyrian, Hittite) had *tables of offering, but in Israel's tabernacle the *priests rather than a deity consumed the bread (Lev 24:9). *Sacrificial altars regularly appear in ancient temples, along with standard types of sacrifices: thank offerings, *sin offerings, *atonement offerings. But most ancient peoples also had offerings to persuade deities to send rain or other favors; Yahweh promised his people to *bless them if they simply kept his *covenant. Temples with sacrificial altars needed *incense altars to cover the stench of burning flesh, as in the tabernacle. *Lampstands were also necessary in such temples so priests could see in the sanctuary, secluded as it was from the profane light of the world.

Many ancient Near Eastern temples provided the deity with a throne, footstool, lamp, table, chest and bed. The tabernacle has no chest and bed, which would imply that God has bodily needs (cf. Ps 50:8-14). Egyptian, Canaanite or Hittite priests would get the deity up in the morning and entertain it with dancing girls and so forth; but Yahweh is not a god of wood or of *stone like those *gods (Ps 135:15-18; Is 46:5-11; see Sleeping God Motif).

The Purpose of the Tabernacle. Ancient peoples understood temples as houses of gods. Thus peoples typically thought that gods provided the temple designs (Thoth in Egypt; Ningirsu in Gudea, Cylinder A); thus they showed more interest in the accounts of such architecture than we do today (e.g., Baal Epic). People also understood that an earthly temple merely reflects the glory of the deity's heavenly home (*Babylonian Esagila;* compare also excavated Baal temples with the Canaanite myth of his heavenly house). The earthly pattern had to correspond with the heavenly to make the deity comfortable on earth; the specific instructions in Exodus (Ex 25:8-9; 29:45) may imply a similar idea. Just as Canaanite, Egyptian and Mesopotamian temples often pointed to the *cosmic* reign of their deities (e.g., the blue, star-studded ceilings of Egyptian temples), Israel could worship God in his tabernacle yet acknowledge that he fills heaven and earth (1 Kings 8:27; Is 66:1-2). A temple did not imprison a deity; it merely provided a place for the worshiper to approach the deity with appropriate reverence.

Although the tabernacle was God's dwelling, God *descended* on it to meet the assembly (Ex 33:9). Thus it ultimately merely symbolized a concept represented in Moses and the Prophets: God's presence is available to his people (Ex 33:9-11). The tabernacle communicated God's holiness, his oneness and his presence among his people.

During the period of the wilderness wanderings, the tabernacle signified God's presence as divine *warrior. Numbers 2 presents a picture of the Israelite camp as it was on the march from Egypt to the *Promised Land. The tabernacle is a tent pitched in the midst of the tribes. In other words, God's tent occupies the place of the warrior-king in a battle camp. Thus it is not surprising that when the tabernacle was taken down, the ark, which was normally housed in the holy of holies, led the march, which began with the acclamation "Rise up, O LORD! May your enemies be scattered; may your foes flee before you" (Num 10:35 NIV). And when the ark comes to rest at a new encampment, the cry is "Return, O LORD, to the countless thousands of Israel" (Num 10:36 NIV).

The Tabernacle Elsewhere in the Old Testament. Some writers have argued that the tabernacle existed in the temple, but it is more likely that the *Philistines destroyed it at Shiloh (1 Sam 4:11-22; Ps 78:60; Jer 7:12-15) and only the ark remained, though the Israelites constructed another tabernacle for it before the temple (2 Sam 6:17; 1 Kings 1:39; 2:28-30). Nevertheless, Israelite worship frequently designated the tabernacle as God's dwelling place, sometimes referring figuratively to the temple (Ps 27:6; 76:2). This language made good sense in the ancient world; Canaanites similarly had spoken of the "tabernacle" of their chief god, El.

One who longed for God might thus long to be in his "tabernacle," that is, dwelling in his presence like the priests and Levites who served in the temple

(Ps 15:1; 27:5; 61:4; Levites originated many of the psalms—1 Chron 16:4-6, 41-42; 25:1-7; 2 Chron 29:30). God promised that his tabernacle would be with his people forever, for his covenant was that he would dwell with them and be their God (Ezek 37:27; cf. Ezek 43:7, 9; Ex 29:45-46).

New Testament Tabernacle Imagery. The earliest Christians occasionally mentioned the tabernacle; the word's most prominent NT occurrences are in John, Acts and especially Hebrews and Revelation.

Jesus as the Tabernacle. We have already seen how the primary function of the tabernacle is to represent God's holy presence on earth. The Gospel of John begins by announcing that the very Word of God took on human form. In the words of John 1:14, "The Word became flesh and made his dwelling among us. We have seen his glory, the glory of the One and Only, who came from the Father, full of grace and truth" (NIV). In Greek, "made his dwelling" (*skēnoō*) is a verbal form of the word for tabernacle. In this way the author of the Gospel intends us to see Jesus as the fulfillment of the tabernacle. God is indeed present among men and women!

The tabernacle in Stephen's speech in Acts 7. Non-Christian Hellenist Jews charge Stephen with two offenses: speaking against Moses or the *law, and against "this holy place," the temple (Acts 6:13-14). Many Jewish traditions preserved after the temple's destruction in A.D. 70 record the zeal many Jews had for the temple and its special holiness, so these charges were substantial. Stephen refutes the charge that he is against the law of Moses, quoting it through much of his response. He is, however, opposed to the way his accusers view the temple.

Stephen responds both that the temple is not the focus of God's revelation and that history proves that God's people reject the deliverers he sends them (Acts 7:9, 27, 35-37). He points out that God can reveal himself anywhere, including Mesopotamia, Egypt or a "holy place" on a desert *mountain (Acts 7:2, 10-17, 33). Paraphrasing Amos 5:25-27, Stephen warns that Israel had a tabernacle in the wilderness but turned it into a further occasion for *idolatry (Acts 7:40-44); he then reminds his hearers that God did not allow *David to build the temple but Solomon (Acts 7:46-47), and that God never needed an earthly temple anyway (Acts 7:48-49; Is 66:1-2). Like Jesus (Mk 12:10-11 with Ps 118:19-27; Jn 14:23), Stephen undoubtedly anticipated the new temple Jesus will build among his people (Eph 2:19-22; Rev 21:3).

The tabernacle in Hebrews. As noted above, the tabernacle of Exodus probably pointed to a heavenly tabernacle, as did many other ancient Near Eastern temples. Jewish people in the first century A.D. often paralleled the heavenly and the earthly (e.g., the heavenly Sanhedrin); naturally the rabbis and various apocalyptic writers thus envisioned a temple in heaven. Wisdom of Solomon (9:8) and Philo, building more overtly on Plato's principle of ideal proto-

types and earthly shadows, took the matter further.

Although using Platonic language like *copy* and *shadow* (Heb 8:5), the writer of Hebrews portrays a heavenly tabernacle closer to that of apocalyptic visionaries of his day. He emphasizes the reality of the heavenly tabernacle to show the secondary nature of the earthly one: now that we have access to the heavenly house of God in Christ, we need no longer resort to the earthly one. Contemporaries like Philo allegorized the tabernacle: linen represented the earth, dark red the air, the *seven-branched lampstand the seven planets, and so forth. The writer of Hebrews, however, avoids such allegorical typology and contents himself to observe that the holiest place in the tabernacle was off limits to anyone but the high priest once a year (Heb 9:6-7), and that this condition obtained up to the present age, until God revealed himself fully to his people (Heb 9:8-10; cf. Rev 11:2). But Jesus, as the high priest after the order of *Melchizedek (Heb 5—7), has inaugurated the future era of God's presence (Ps 110:1, 4). Now all believers have direct access to God's presence (Heb 4:16), the reality toward which the tabernacle in Israel's midst always pointed (see Ex 33:9-11, above).

The tabernacle in Revelation. Revelation's images of God's heavenly throne room allude back to the wilderness tabernacle. It contains an altar of incense (Rev 5:8), an altar of sacrifice (Rev 6:9), the ark (Rev 11:19; cf. Rev 15:5-8) and so forth. The "sea of glass" (Rev 4:6-7; 15:2) alludes to the *sea in Solomon's temple (1 Kings 7:23; 2 Chron 4:2, 6), which reinforced the idea that the deity in that temple reigned over all creation. In the Hebrew Bible the covenant containing stipulations and *curses (*plagues) against the disobedient was deposited in the ark; thus Revelation 11:19 may indicate further *judgments to come. Some Jewish pietists felt that the temple had been defiled, and once it was destroyed in A.D. 70, Jewish people could look only to the heavenly temple and the future rebuilding of an earthly one in the time of the *kingdom. Revelation promises that the heavenly ark, once concealed (like the earthly one, behind a curtain), will be exposed to public view (Rev 11:19).

Most important, Revelation declares that the tabernacle that long represented God's dwelling among his people will be among his people forever (Rev 21:3). Despite Ezekiel's vision of an eschatological temple (Ezek 40—46), Revelation is interested only in what that temple ultimately symbolized: God dwelling with his people (Ezek 43:7-12; cf. Ezek 11:16; 36:27; 37:14, 27-28; 39:29). In keeping with Johannine theology (Jn 14:23; 15:1-6), God and the *Lamb will be their people's temple, and they will need no other (Rev 21:22; cf. Rev 3:12).

See also ALTAR; ARK OF THE COVENANT; LAMP, LAMP-STAND; PRIEST; SACRED SPACE; SACRIFICE; TEMPLE; WORSHIP.

BIBLIOGRAPHY. A. Badawy, *A History of Egyptian Architecture: The Empire (1580-1085 B.C.)* (Berkeley:

University of California Press, 1968); U. Cassuto, *A Commentary on the Book of Exodus* (Jerusalem: Magnes, 1967); F. M. Cross Jr., "The Tabernacle: A Study from an Archaeological and Historical Approach," *BA* 10 (September 1947) 45-68; R. J. Forbes, *Studies in Ancient Technology,* 9 vols. (Leiden: Brill, 1966); M. Haran, *Temples and Temple-Service in Ancient Israel* (Oxford: Clarendon, 1978); K. A. Kitchen, "Some Egyptian Background to the Old Testament," *Tyndale Bulletin* 516 (1960) 4-18; S. Lloyd, *The Archaeology of Mesopotamia* (London: Thames and Hudson, 1978); A. Lucas, *Ancient Egyptian Materials and Industries,* rev. J. R. Harris (London: Edward Arnold, 1962); J. A. Scott, *The Pattern of the Tabernacle* (Ph.D. diss., University of Pennsylvania; Ann Arbor, MI: University Microfilms, 1978).

TABLE

Tables are central to everyday life in the Bible, serving domestic, ceremonial and business or commercial functions. The image comes to stand for fellowship with others and with God at *meals and ceremonies around tables. In the end, Jesus promises his disciples the ultimate blessing of a place at "my table in my kingdom" (Lk 22:30).

Tables for Eating. In earliest OT times a "table" was often an animal hide spread on the floor of a tent or on the ground (see Is 21:5), and possession of a wooden table and ability to entertain with plenty of *food were signs of wealth. But by NT times even common people had tables around which to *eat. Biblical references to tables are sometimes indicated by the use of certain verbs that imply the presence of a table, as in 1 Samuel 20:5, where the verb *yāšab* ("sit") is correctly translated "sit at table" ("dine with the king" NIV; "sit with the king at the meal" NRSV see also Gen 43:32-34; 2 Kings 25:29). In the NT the verb "to *recline" implies the presence of a table. At formal meals male guests would recline (leaning on the left elbow, leaving the right hand free for eating) on low couches around the outside of a U-shaped table; women and *servants served from the inside the U.

Customs and Manners. An invitation to share a meal at someone's table was a sign of *friendship (Ps 128:3; Lk 14:10), welcome and *honor, as well as required hospitality to strangers (Gen 18:1-5; Judg 13:15). The Joseph story contains a table scene demonstrating some basic features of ancient Near Eastern custom: separate tables for people of different ethnic backgrounds; people's refusal to eat with others they consider unworthy or unclean; places assigned according to rank and relationship to the host; plenty of food, with the most food going to the one of highest honor (Gen 43:31-34). To insult one's host or to share table fellowship while slandering or betraying him was a poignant picture of betrayal and the loss of friendship (Ps 41:9; Dan 11:27; Lk 22:21).

Royal Tables. To dine at the *king's table is an honor; it is to enjoy the favor, *protection, *prosperity and power of the king (2 Sam 9:7-13; 19:28; 1 Kings 2:7). Refusing the king's invitation insults him (1 Sam 20:29; Esther 1:12). To be disinvited from sitting at the king's table and reduced to "eating the crumbs" from underneath it instead is a picture of humiliation and defeat (Judg 1:7; used figuratively in Ezek 39:20 and Mt 15:21-28). The size and richness of the food and *drink on the ruler's table are signs of wealth and power and, ultimately, of God's *blessing (1 Kings 4:27; 10:5; 2 Chron 9:4; Neh 5:17).

A Full Table: Blessing or Decadence. A substantial table spread with plenty of food shows God's blessing and provision and can evidence *shalom,* God's peaceful *justice (Neh 5:17; Job 36:16; Ps 23:5; 78:19). A table spread with kosher food, surrounded by ritually pure, righteous people with whom to share it, is goodness made tangible (e.g., Ps 128). On the other hand, a king's or nation's or individual's injustice and decadence may be displayed on a too-elaborate table spread with too much rich food while the poor suffer (Is 28:8; *see* Poverty).

Ceremonial Tables. Both *tabernacle ("tent of meeting") and *temple furnishings included tables. The table of the *bread of the presence held the special ceremonial bread signifying God's presence (tabernacle: Ex 25:23-30; 31:8; 37:10-16; 39:36; 40:4, 22-23; Lev 24:6; Num 4:7; temple: 1 Kings 7:48; 1 Chron 28:16; 2 Chron 4:19; 13:11; 29:18; Heb 9:2). Solomon had ten tables made for the temple (2 Chron 4:8), according to David's instructions (1 Chron 28:16). Ezekiel describes a *wooden *"altar" or "table" in his vision of the new temple (Ezek 41:22) and mentions *twelve tables in all, eight of them for slaughtering *sacrifices (Ezek 40:39-41) and four of cut *stone for holding the tools and flesh offered to God (Ezek 40:42-43). These could be approached and used only by ritually pure *priests (Levites, Ezek 44:16). "The table of the LORD" in the OT is the table for burnt *offerings.

Malachi prophesies against people who cynically mimic heartfelt *worship by bringing improper, unclean sacrifices; he says they do not "respect the table [or altar]" (Mal 1:7, 12).

Idol Worship and True Worship. In contrast to the holy tables for tabernacle and temple worship, tables and altars used in *idol worship (Is 65:11; Jer 17:2; 1 Cor 10:21) become symbols of God's absence or disfavor, of impurity and dishonor, and of the futility of idol worship. The prophets of the false *god Baal are said to "eat at Jezebel's table" (1 Kings 18:19 NIV; this phrase probably reflects a royal stipend or support at royal expense). Paul warns that sacrifices to idols "are offered to demons, not to God" (1 Cor 10:20 NIV), contrasting the good and holy use for the Lord's Supper of the "Lord's table" with the "table of demons" (idol worship). "Lord's table" becomes code for the meal and practice of the Lord's Supper and the authentic Christian fellowship enacted there.

Table Service. Jesus conducted much of his ministry and teaching around tables (Mt 26:7; Lk 5:29-32; 7:36-50; 14:1-24) and was criticized by the *Pharisees for eating with tax collectors and *sinners, because to do so implied acceptance of persons customarily deemed unworthy of sharing a meal with good people. The notion of willingness to put aside personal gain and rank to take on women's and servants' roles of table service is central to Jesus' teaching for disciples/followers: "For who is greater, the one who is at the table or the one who serves? Is it not the one at the table? But I am among you as one who serves" (Lk 22:27 NRSV). Accordingly, "to wait on tables" literally and metaphorically described the work and office of diaconal service (Acts 6:2). A Christian church leader, in contrast to an OT king or person of wealth, shares and serves at tables with people of all sorts—not just those of equal or higher social status.

Kingdom Tables: Blessing and Judgment. Jesus' promise of the eschatological kingdom centers on a table signifying ultimate blessing and belonging, but also final judgment for the unfaithful who refuse his invitation. He says to his disciples, "You are those who have stood by me in my trial; and I confer on you, just as my father has conferred on me, a kingdom, so that you may eat and drink at my table in my kingdom, and you will sit on thrones judging the twelve tribes of Israel" (Lk 22:28-30 NRSV).

See also ALTAR; BANQUET; EATING; FOOD; GUEST; HOSPITALITY; HOST, GOD AS; MEAL; SUPPER.

TAINT. *See* SPOT.

TASTE. *See* SWEET.

TAUNT

Taunting is most often found in the OT as a collective action inflicted by a group on another group or individual. References to taunting, mocking and jeering are found most often in Psalms and the Prophets, although we also find accounts in the narratives.

Two major uses of the word are apparent. In Psalms and the Prophets, the word appears in the context of a lament: an individual or a spokesperson for Israel *laments how the nations or evildoers have taunted him and his nation (Neh 4:4; Ps 42:3, 9-10; 44:13-16; 79:4; 89:50-51; 137:1-3; Lam 3:14, 61, 63; Zeph 2:8). In the second case, taunting appears as a warning from God of future punishment, declaring that the nations will taunt Israel if the people continue to disobey (1 Kings 9:7; Jer 24:9; Ezek 5:15).

The taunt was a conventional feature of ancient *warfare, and the martial world accordingly supplies some of the most vivid biblical pictures of taunting (*see* Boast). Lamentations 1:7 gives a brief picture of a foe who "gloated over her, mocking at her downfall" (RSV). The classic passage is Goliath's taunting of the Israelite army (1 Sam 17:8-10, 44). David's reply is itself a taunt, defying Goliath in the name of the Lord and predicting victory (1 Sam 17:45-47). In later Israelite history Benhadad and Ahab exchange insults (1 Kings 20:10-11), and Sennacherib sends emissaries to taunt Hezekiah's charges (2 Kings 18:19—19:13; Is 36—37).

A second context for taunting is religious, in a manner akin to the bumper sticker "If your god is dead, try mine." Elijah taunts the priests of Baal on Mt. Carmel, jeering that perhaps Baal is musing, or on a journey or *sleeping (1 Kings 18:27). Here the religious taunt serves as a psychological weapon as well as making a theological statement. Similar religious taunts appear in Isaiah 44:9-20 and Habakkuk 2:18-20. God himself gets into the mocking mode in Psalm 2, where he is pictured as sitting in the heavens and laughing in derision at the conspiring nations.

Yet another class of taunting is personal. Elisha endures the jeering of boys until God punishes the forty-two young offenders by sending bears to kill them (2 Kings 2:23-24). Job in his suffering pictures onlookers as making sport of him (Job 30:1-15). The most ruthless taunting is that which Jesus received from his enemies during his trial and crucifixion.

Taunting even produced an ancient literary genre known as the taunt song—a formalized putdown of an opponent, usually employing conventional motifs. The religious taunt, for example, catalogs the lifeless features of a pagan idol, in contrast to the living and transcendent God (Ps 115:2-8; 135:15-18; Jer 10:1-16). A related category is prophetic passages that predict the downfall of wicked nations with an element of almost personal animosity toward the defeated (Is 14:12-21). The military counterpart exists in some of the songs of victory that do more than celebrate a victory by mocking the defeated *enemy (Ex 15:1-18; Num 21:27-30; Judg 5).

There are also miscellaneous taunts. Psalm 52:6-7 pictures the righteous person as mocking the person who trusted in riches instead of making God his refuge. Isaiah taunts the harlot (Is 23:15-16).

Finally, prophetic denunciations often contain an element of the taunt, discernible whenever the denunciation is directed toward a specific person or group. Sometimes such denunciation is identified as taunt, as in Habakkuk's prophecy against the Chaldeans: "Shall not all these take up their taunt against him, in scoffing derision of him?" (Hab 2:6 RSV). The spirit of the taunt pervades Amos's fiery denunciations ("Hear this word, you cows of Bashan. . . . Come to Bethel, and transgress" [Amos 4:1, 4 RSV]), and Isaiah's sarcastic description of the haughty daughters of Zion captures the taunting quality of much prophetic discourse: these women "walk with outstretched necks, . . . mincing along as they go, tinkling with their feet; the Lord will smite with a scab the heads of the daughters of Zion" (Is 3:16-17 RSV). Of special note is a subgenre of the doom song in which the prophet pictures the demise of a nation before it actually takes place—a kind of obituary for someone still alive (Is 14:3-21; Jer 38:22; Ezek 27—28; Amos 5:3).

While it is an innate human tendency to taunt one's enemies if their past offenses seem excessive, the picture of ancient practices that emerges from the Bible suggests something more formalized. Here taunting has become a ritual, generating its own rhetorical forms.

See also BOAST; ENEMY.

TEACHER, TEACHING

The events, activities and images that mark education in our age are missing from education in the biblical world. The classroom with professional teachers who are trained as much in pedagogy as in a content area is simply not present in the Bible. The education of ancient Israel was closer to what might be termed deliberate encultural or nonformal education. There are hints of a school at the central sanctuary and the presence of literacy indicates deliberate instruction, but the biblical images of education and teaching are generally not oriented to schooling activities. This article seeks to catalog the principal features of teachers, teaching and learning in the Bible.

God the Teacher. *God is the great teacher of the Bible. The whole course of the biblical story can be viewed as God's instruction. We find him instructing with commandments and object lessons in Eden, and the giving of the *law at *Sinai is for Israel an archetypal teaching event. Rhetorical questions imply the obvious: "Who was it that taught him knowledge?" (Is 40:14 NIV). "Can anyone teach knowledge to God?" (Job 21:22 NIV). Human teachers may have things to learn from their students, but with God, teaching flows one way.

It may seem an understatement to say that God "teaches more to us than to the beasts of the earth" (Job 35:11 NIV), but it is a logical assumption that the Creator God is involved in a broad program of instruction that includes the nonhuman world. Like a parent, God "taught Ephraim to walk" (Hos 11:3). Like a *warrior, he trains hands for *battle (2 Sam 22:35; Ps 18:34; 144:1). But for Israel, God's instruction is symbolized by his law, torah. The lessons of the divine teacher are prized among his students: "Blessed . . . is the man you teach from your law" (Ps 94:10, 12 NIV). The psalmist can confess, "Since my youth, O God, you have taught me" (Ps 71:17). His instruction, encoded in statutes, precepts and commands, and preserved in the book of the law, evokes from his pupils the highest praise: "perfect, . . . trustworthy, . . . right, . . . radiant, . . . pure, . . . sure and altogether righteous, . . . more precious than gold, . . . sweeter than honey, than honey from the comb" (Ps 19:7-10 NIV). Such a treasure is meant to be shared, and in Isaiah's vision of the "last days," the enrollment in God's school of Torah will multiply beyond bounds as the nations will stream to Zion, begging to be enrolled under the divine teacher and saying, "he will teach us his ways so that we may walk

in his paths" (Is 2:3; Mic 4:2).

In this school of divinity it is not the precocious but the humble student who is most suited for instruction in God's ways (Ps 25:9). These are the ones who submit to divine instruction with the plea, "teach me to do your will" (Ps 143:10 NIV), "teach me your way" (Ps 25:4-5; 27:11; 86:11). Eliphaz, thinking he has discovered the root of Job's dilemma, intones this theme as he counsels Job to submit himself to the divine teacher, to "accept instruction from his mouth and lay up his words in your heart" (Job 22:22).

The NT is able to look back on a completed Hebrew Bible and regard it as God's Word, God's instruction, "God-breathed" Scripture (2 Tim 3:16). The former lessons of the divine teacher are committed to the text of the Law, the Prophets and the Writings. As Paul says, "these things . . . were written down for our instruction" (1 Cor 10:11 RSV). But the NT writers are also aware of another vital and dynamic source of ongoing divine instruction, the instruction of the *Spirit. Even surpassing Israel in the *wilderness, to whom God gave his "good Spirit to instruct them" (Neh 9:20 NIV), Jesus tells his disciples that "the Holy Spirit . . . will teach you all things" (Jn 14:26; cf. Jn 6:45; 1 Jn 2:27). Paul offers a one-word image of this phenomenon, Believers are "God-taught" (*theodidaktos*) how to love one another (1 Thess 4:9).

In Proverbs divine instruction is embodied in the personified figure of *Wisdom. Wisdom calls out and beckons to men and women to heed her words: "Choose my instruction instead of silver, knowledge rather than choice gold, for wisdom is more precious than rubies, and nothing you desire can compare with her" (Prov 8:10-11 NIV). Wisdom is the emissary of God, whom the Lord "brought . . . forth as the first of his works" (Prov 8:22) and was "the craftsman at his side" (Prov 8:30) as he created the world. This wisdom that ordered the splendor of this world now turns teacher and beckons, "Listen to my instruction and be wise; do not ignore it" (Prov 8:33).

The voice of Wisdom points to God as the source of wisdom, so wisdom is to be found in the "fear of the Lord" (Job 28:20-28; Prov 1:7; 9:10). Human understanding alone, though it is God given, is not sufficient for wisdom: "Trust in the Lord with all your heart and lean not on your own understanding" (Prov 3:5 NIV). The pursuit of knowledge attempted without reference to God is at best precarious and distorted, and if persistently pursued becomes seriously misleading and damaging. However, wisdom embraces understanding, correctly understood, ("understanding is a fountain of life," Prov 16:22 NIV) and the emotional heart of a person ("guard your heart, for it is the wellspring of life," Prov 4:23 NIV). Wisdom, and with it true teaching, encompasses both mind and heart.

Jesus as Teacher. *Jesus is the supreme expression of the divine teacher, showing compassion combined with clarity, power and authority in his instruction. Unlike the rabbis, who teach in fixed locations, we find Jesus teaching in the *temple (e.g., Mt 21:23; 26:55; Jn 7:14; 8:2, 20), in towns and *villages (Mt 9:35; 11:1; Mk 6:6; Lk 13:22), in synagogues (Mt 4:23; 9:35; 13:54; Mk 1:21; 6:2; Lk 4:15-16, 31-33; 6:6; 13:10), in *homes (Mk 2:1-2, the house in Capernaum may have served as a teaching center), as he travels along the road (Mk 10:32-34), and even from an anchored boat (Mk 4:1; Lk 5:3). The image of Jesus the teacher is of one who is adaptable to any venue and is as much at home under the open sky as under the roof of a house or synagogue. While the rabbis exclusively teach their chosen circle of students, we find Jesus teaching the crowds (Mk 2:13; 3:7-8; 6:34; 10:1), though his disciples, literally "pupils" (*mathētai*), are a special focus of his teaching (Mt 10; Mk 4:10; 8:27-32; Jn 13—17). Perhaps there is no better image of a pupil of Jesus than Mary of Bethany, "who sat at the Lord's feet and listened to his teaching" (Lk 10:39 RSV; cf. Acts 22:3). In contrast with her sister Martha, who is "anxious and troubled about many things" (serving her guests!), Jesus says, "Mary has chosen the good portion, which shall not be taken away from her" (Lk 10:41).

Jesus' teaching is attuned to the needs and questions of his audience, and he effectively responds to living situations that present themselves to him. He takes seriously that the "medium is the message" and teaches in a manner that supports his gospel. He deftly employs parallelism (and perhaps rhyme in his language of Aramaic) as well as rhetorical devices such as paradox, hyperbole, riddles, contrast, irony and emphasis, all no doubt designed to take hold in the memory. In his carefully crafted *parables he shows himself capable of shaping the familiar and commonplace into poignant and provocative means of teaching. The *kingdom of God is like a *mustard seed, a fishing net, a precious *pearl or a woman searching for a *lost coin. His sharp and witty sayings, like proverbs, are searching and memorable.

Jesus' parabolic acts, such as his temple "cleansing" (Mk 11:13-17) and the cursing of the fig tree (Mk 11:12-14, 20-26) reveal the nature of his mission. He also uses the interpretation of miracles (Mk 2) as an opportunity for teaching. Jesus' teaching is powerfully shaped by his correlation of words and actions, such as his offer of forgiveness conjoined with his open table fellowship with sinners and tax collectors.

Finally, the ministry of Jesus shows that the character and quality of life of a teacher is as important as creativity and skill in using effective teaching methods. The authority of his teaching is readily recognized by those who encounter him (Mk 1:21-22), and in all four Gospels he is addressed as "teacher" (e.g., Mt 19:16; Mk 4:38; Lk 9:33; Jn 1:38).

Levites and Prophets. Among the teachers of the OT, the Levites are instructors of Israel. In addition to their assistance with *priestly duties in the temple, part of their calling is to help foster and preserve the knowledge of the law and maintain its central place in Israel. *Moses' blessing to Levi speaks of Levites's position as teachers in Israel: "He teaches your precepts to Jacob and your law to Israel. He offers incense before you and whole burnt offerings on your altar" (Deut 33:10 NIV). At times the Levites seem to serve as itinerant teachers (2 Chron 17:7-9). The image of the Levites as teachers may be observed during Josiah's reign when they are described as the ones "who instructed all Israel" (2 Chron 35:3 NIV). This role of the Levites as instructors certainly continues through the *restoration following the *exile when the Levites are described as the ones who "instructed the people in the law" (Neh 8:7 NIV). The function of the Levites as teachers is seen in two prophetic denouncements of their corruption of the office, the most biting being Micah's assessment: "Her leaders judge for a bribe. Her priests teach for a price, and her prophets tell fortunes for money. Yet they lean upon the Lord and say, 'Is not the Lord among us? No disaster will come upon us.'" (Mic 3:11 NIV). In an admonition of priests and Levites, Malachi directs the Levites to follow the example of Levi and teach the law with impartiality, teach it so as to lead people into the truth (Mal 2:1-9).

Classroom scenes may not be a dominant image of education in Scripture, but there are vignettes of classroom learning. Isaiah may be evoking a scene of rote instruction in the lines, "Do and do, do and do, rule on rule, rule on rule; a little here, a little there" (Isaiah 28:10 NIV). During the time of the monarchy an institution was in place that, in some earlier English translations, was rendered as the "schools of the prophets," but recently is translated "company of the prophets" (2 Kings 2:15; 4:1; 4:38; 5:22; 6:1; 9:1). This, in fact, bears some resemblance to the relationship between Jesus and his disciples.

Imitation. In the NT one of the key concepts in spiritual formation is imitation. This fits within the widespread Hellenistic tradition of regarding personal examples and models as an important means of moral instruction. There is a clear sense that imitation is something that naturally occurs without deliberate effort, and consequently there is the concern for the character of the teachers (Lk 6:39-40). But imitation is also something that can be deliberately fostered. The imitation of Christ is rooted in Jesus' call to his disciples to "follow me." Paul seems to imply an analogous imitation of Christ in Philippians 2:5-11, where the focus is on the self-giving and servanthood of the preexistent Christ as he becomes human, descends to death on a cross and is then exalted by God. 1 Peter 2:21 presents Christ as an example for those slaves who must endure abuse at the hands of their masters. Paul admonishes his hearers to "imitate me as I imitate Christ" (1 Cor 11:1; cf. 1 Cor 4:16; Phil 3:17; 1 Thess 1:6). In Ephesians we even find a call to "be imitators of God" (Eph 5:1). And in Hebrews godly figures of Israel's past, such as

Abraham (Heb 6:13-15), are called up as models for imitation by those who through faithfulness "are inheriting the promises" (Heb 6:12).

Sanctuary and Home. *Tabernacle worship instructs Israel that God is holy yet merciful, that he may be approached only with reverence and costly *sacrifice (e.g., Ex 29; Heb 9:20-28; 10:19-22). Clearly what is said in worship is instructive, but the layout, furnishings and symbols of the sanctuary also convey much (*see* Sacred Space). The *festivals provide one of the most deliberate forms of instruction in ancient Israel. And in the Passover ceremony the centrality of education is shown in the well-known question that marks its beginning, when the child asks, "What does this ceremony mean to you?" (Ex 12:26 NIV). The parents then explain what the Passover symbolizes. The Scripture reading, teaching, feasting and ceremonies of the Jewish festivals perform a deliberate educational dimension, usually recalling epochal moments in Israel's past.

If in the modern world the presumed locus of formal education is the school, in the world of ancient Israel the normative locus of education is the *home. In Deuteronomy 6:20-25 parents are to be prepared to answer their children's questions about the meaning of the law and its origin. And in an even more colorful passage (Deut 6:6-9), parents are instructed to speak of these commandments throughout the day: "Impress them on your children. Talk about them when you sit at home and when you walk along the road, when you lie down and when you get up" (Deut 6:7 NIV). These, of course, depict the ideal. In Jeremiah the family supporting and passing on *idolatry to the next generation is tragically and graphically described: "The children gather wood, the fathers light the fire, and the women knead the dough and make cakes of bread for the Queen of Heaven. They pour out drink offerings to other gods to provoke me to anger" (Jer 7:18 NIV).

The responsibility for passing on the faith from one generation to another is evident in the NT. Parents have a major role in this: "Fathers, do not exasperate your children; instead, bring them up in the training and instruction of the Lord" (Eph 6:4 NIV). But others in the Christian community play a role too. The commission Jesus gives to all his disciples is to go, make disciples, baptize and teach (Mt 28:19-20). Paul's instructions to Timothy are in keeping with this: "the things you have heard me say in the presence of many witnesses entrust to reliable men who will also be qualified to teach others" (2 Tim 2:2 NIV), and "continue in what you have learned . . . because you know those from whom you learned it, and how from infancy you have known the holy Scriptures" (2 Tim 3:14-15 NIV).

Varied Images of Instruction. In traditional societies such as we encounter in the Bible, a principal educational outcome desired by a teacher is that the instruction be handed on to the next generation. And so we find images of teaching as "receiving" and a "handing on," or "delivering," of sacred knowl-edge (1 Cor 11:2, 23; 15:3; 2 Thess 2:15; 3:16; Ps 79:13, 145:4). Another outcome of instruction is causing people to remember. This can be seen most classically in Moses' instruction in Deuteronomy where the people are to remember how they provoked God to *anger by their *rebellion (Deut 9:7). And they are also to remember that they possessed the *Promised Land because of God's action and not because of their merit (Deut 9:4).

In the Bible we find instruction occurring in a variety of forms and venues. Ezra, both a priest and a scribe, publicly teaches and interprets the law to the people (Ezra 7:6, 10). We catch a glimpse of instruction taking place in the *family (Deut 6:4, 7) and of the Levites carrying out an itinerant ministry of instruction (2 Chron 17:7-9). Isaiah instructs by dramatizing his message, walking *naked and *barefoot (Is 20), Jeremiah smashes a potter's vessel in the place of the potsherds (Jer 19), and Ahijah tears his coat into twelve pieces and gives ten pieces to Jeroboam (1 Kings 11:29-31). Education at the central sanctuary is observed in the nurturing of Samuel who is brought there as a young boy (1 Sam 1:24-28). And in a much different context we find Paul carrying on a mentoring relationship with Timothy (Acts 16; 2 Tim 1). In fact, the very form of the letters to Timothy and Titus is imbued with instruction set within a call to imitate Paul.

In Paul's letters we find some unique images of teaching, including the schoolmaster, or tutor, mentioned in Galatians 3:24-25 and in 1 Corinthians 4:15. The metaphor is based on the Greek and Roman pedagogue, a trusted male attendant, usually a *slave, who had the general supervision of the pupil's education and saw him safely to and from school. This is Paul's metaphor for the role of the law—a tutor that has led Israel to faith. In 2 Timothy 2 a whole series of metaphors applying to Christian ministry in general is unfurled, but in their first instance they apply to the teaching ministry of Timothy. Here we find the images of the single-minded soldier (2 Tim 2:4), the *athlete who competes according to the rules (2 Tim 2:5), the hard-working *farmer (2 Tim 2:6), the *workman who needs not be ashamed (2 Tim 2:15), the false teaching which spreads like gangrene (2 Tim 2:17) and the notion of a cleansed vessel being available for use (2 Tim 2:21). But most fundamentally, in 1 Corinthians, Paul asserts that teaching is a gift of the Holy Spirit, given by God for the formation of the church (1 Cor 12:28; Eph 4:1; 1 Tim 5:17)

See also DISCIPLE, DISCIPLESHIP; FEAR OF GOD; LAW; PARABLE; WISDOM.

TEACHING. *See* TEACHER, TEACHING.

TEAR DOWN

The imagery of tearing down is, not surprisingly, an overwhelmingly negative one. Most biblical instances of tearing down arise out of two significant and related biblical contexts: the tearing down of structures related to *idolatry and the tearing down of a city's defenses. These objects of destruction are related because they typify opposition to the one true *God. In the one case an object related to pagan *worship, carefully and often artistically constructed as the focal point of a human culture opposed to the true God, is violently dismantled. In the case of a city the tearing down of *walls and ramparts graphically and forcefully images the defeat of a society's pride and sufficiency.

Religious Reform. Stories of religious renewal, the battle against idolatry, frequently call for violent means. The Lord tells Gideon to "tear down your father's altar to Baal and cut down the Asherah pole beside it" (Judg 6:25 NIV). Jehu and his men tear down the temple of Baal in Samaria (2 Kings 10:27; cf. 2 Kings 11:18; 2 Chron 23:17). Josiah tears down the quarters of the male shrine prostitutes in the *temple of Yahweh (2 Kings 23:7) and pulls down *altars (2 Kings 23:12; 2 Chron 34:7). Metaphorically speaking, Ezekiel sees Jerusalem's destruction as if a *prostitute is handed over to her lovers: "they will tear down your mounds and destroy your lofty shrines" (Ezek 16:39 NIV). These violent acts of tearing down are memorialized in Scripture as acts of righteousness and zeal, examples of the proper response to idolatry.

Military Assault. Military strategies have frequently entailed tearing down a country's or city's defenses, or breaking down its infrastructures. Tearing down is not only a means of routing an enemy from its fortress but of bringing *shame, ruin and sometimes total desolation upon its society. *Fortress towers are particularly appropriate for tearing down. Thus Gideon swears to the men of Peniel, "When I return in triumph, I will tear down this tower" (Judg 8:9 NIV), and later he "pulled down the tower of Peniel and killed the men of the town" (Judg 8:17 NIV). In the spirit of the prophetic oracles against the nations, Ezekiel declares that the walls of Tyre will be destroyed, her towers pulled down (Ezek 26:4). Amos and Micah foresee a day when an enemy will overrun Israel, pulling down her *strongholds and plundering her fortresses (Amos 3:11; cf. 3:15; Mic 5:11). We visualize lofty structures reduced to a pile of stones, soldiers taking pleasure in their work. The psalmist recalls the unforgivable cheer of the Edomites as Babylon destroyed Jerusalem: " 'Tear it down,' they cried, 'tear it down to its foundations!' " (Ps 137:7 NIV). It is fitting then that the false prophets who proclaim "peace, peace" when there is no peace are likened to builders of a flimsy wall covered with whitewash; Yahweh will tear down that wall and lay bare its foundation (Ezek 13:14).

What is true of nations is frequently true of individuals: Since the wicked "show no regard for the works of the LORD and what his hands have done, he will tear them down and never build them up again." (Ps 28:5 NIV). Even the considered world of wisdom can employ the metaphor of tearing down, for the pathway of the wise leads through conflicts likened to battle. Subversive wisdom is like when "a wise man attacks the city of the mighty and pulls down the stronghold in which they trust" (Prov 21:22 NIV).

Not to Tear Down but to Build Up. The epitome of tearing down is the destruction of *Jerusalem, the climax of Yahweh's war against his disobedient covenant people: "The LORD determined to tear down the wall around the Daughter of Zion" (Lam 2:8 NIV). The prophet Jeremiah, as an agent of the heavenly king, is appointed "over nations and kingdoms to uproot and tear down, to destroy and overthrow, to build and to plant" (Jer 1:10 NIV). Specifically, he proclaims the coming fall of Jerusalem. But even this catastrophic judgment will pass, and divine discipline will give way to Israel's *restoration. God promises that "I will bring them back to this land. I will build them up and not tear them down" (Jer 24:6 NIV; cf. 31:28; 42:10). Paul speaks with a prophetic consciousness and a clear sense of his own role in the restoration of the people of God as he adopts Jeremiah's metaphor in speaking of the apostolic authority that "the Lord gave us for building you up rather than pulling you down" (2 Cor 10:8; cf. 13:10).

Varied Metaphors. An assortment of metaphorical uses stands in interpretive relief against the rhythms of Israel's judgment and restoration. Job translates his personal afflictions and loss of honor as God's tearing him down "on every side until I am gone" (Job 19:10 NIV). What hope is there when "what he tears down cannot be rebuilt" (Job 12:14)? Hezekiah, speaking of illness that led him to the border of death, exclaims that "like a shepherd's tent my house has been pulled down and taken from me" (Is 38:12 NIV). And the proverbial wisdom of Israel sees justice in God's ways: "The LORD tears down the proud man's house, but he keeps the widow's boundaries intact" (Prov 15:25 NIV). On the other hand, it is an abysmal shame when a *woman or a *king who bears the responsibility of building a household or a nation engages in tearing it down through self-centered *folly (Prov 14:1; Prov 29:4). And even when prudence seems to guide the prosperous farmer to reason that "I will tear down my barns and build bigger ones" (Lk 12:18), it is condemned by Jesus as foolish presumption.

Perhaps the most positive biblical perspective on tearing down is found in the long view of the Preacher, who reasons that, just as there is "a time to kill and a time to heal," there is "a time to tear down and a time to build" (Eccl 3:3). Surely this is true of God's ways with his people.

See also CITY; FORTRESS; JERUSALEM; STRONGHOLD; WALL.

TEARS

Tears are a manifestation of strong emotion, usually of *grief. In the Bible, whereas tears are uncontrollable with "weeping," when associated with "crying" they are more frequent and multicaused. Tears are shed as marks of *humility (Ps 80:5; Acts 20:19), frustration (Jer 9:1) and disappointment (Lam 1:16). While the actual Hebrew and Greek words for tears occur only thirty-six times in the OT and NT, tears are often implied. However, in texts where other verbs of *weeping are used, these are sometimes translated with a phrase that includes *tears* (more commonly in recent versions than in the KJV). The tears in Genesis 27:38 become explicit in Hebrews 12:17. Even more indirect expressions such as "dried up" (Ps 69:3) or "poured out" (1 Sam 1:15; Job 30:16; Ps 22:14; 42:4; Lam 2:11, 19) may reflect contemporary notions of the physiology of tears.

Characters in biblical narrative shed tears in a wide variety of circumstances: entreaty, whether on one's own behalf (Gen 27:38) or for the sake of others (Esther 8:3; Mk 9:34), especially in *prayer to God (1 Sam 1:10; 2 Sam 12:22; 2 Kings 20:3; Job 16:16, 20; Lam 2:18-19); *joy (Gen 43:30); grief for loved ones who have died (Rebekah for her nurse, Gen 35:8; David for Absalom, 2 Sam 18:33; Rachel for her children, Jer 31:15 and Mt 2:18; Mary for Lazarus, Jn 11:33; disciples for Jesus, Mk 16:10 and Jn 20:11; friends for Dorcas, Acts 9:39 NEB); grief for national *apostasy (Ps 119:136) or disaster (Is 16:9; Lam 1:2, 16; Lk 23:28; though Ezek 24:16 hints that tears may be insufficient); depression or spiritual longing (Ps 42:3); maltreatment (Ps 31:9; Eccles 4:1; Acts 20:19); *exile anticipated (Jer 9:18) or realized (Ps 137:1); physical *suffering interpreted as divine disfavor (Ps 6:6-7; 39:12); and remorse (Peter in Mt 26:75). Often we cannot pinpoint a single emotional source. Mixed emotions are ascribed to the elders in Ezra 3:12, and the tears of the woman who was forgiven much (Lk 7:38, 44) surely spring from joy and gratitude mingled with compunction. In many passages, commentators read tears as tokens of contrition and penitence even when these feelings are not explicitly named.

Christ weeps for his dead friend Lazarus (Jn 11:35), for a spiritually unresponsive and therefore doomed *Jerusalem (Lk 19:41) and in his own inner struggles (Heb 5:7, an allusion to Gethsemane and perhaps to other, unrecorded episodes). Beyond these specific scenes, he is identified as the "man of sorrows . . . acquainted with grief" of Isaiah 53:3 (KJV), and already in earliest Christian times some of the psalms of *lament were read as referring to him. His tears are a mark of his humanity, both part and symbol of his self-emptying.

Christ's tears of compassion for his people are foreshadowed in the OT by those of Jeremiah, both in his prophecy (Jer 9:1; 13:17; 14:17) and in the book of *Lamentations ascribed to him (Lam 2:11; 3:48-49). Paul is a follower of Christ in this respect, moved to tears by the *strength of his caring for his converts, whether in person (Acts 20:31) or in writing (2 Cor 2:4).

Tears associated with sorrow for one's *sin are, for obvious reasons, especially prominent in homiletic and devotional traditions. Peter's tears after denying his Lord, the copious outpouring by the woman who washed Jesus' feet with her tears (identified in tradition with Mary Magdalene, the weeper at the tomb) and the penitential cries found in the psalms attributed to David (e.g., where tears seem a natural expression of the "broken and . . . contrite heart" of Ps 51:17)—these are the chief texts used in making a firm link between tears and repentance. There are, however, occasions of weeping when the genuineness of the emotion is uncertain. The tears shed in Jeremiah 3:21, for example, are little more than an attempt to avert the justifiable wrath of God. Very often the context of disobedience and *idolatry in which such weeping is set throws in doubt its sincerity.

Scripture suggests that God will relieve people of their tears, unless one is guilty of an irrevocable misdeed (the case of Esau, Heb 12:16-17) or unrepentant despite distress (Mal 2:13 in the more traditional reading). It is true that David's infant *son dies (2 Sam 12:22-23), but the Lord sees Hezekiah's tears and heals him (2 Kings 20:5 par. Is 38:5). "Thou hast delivered . . . mine eyes from tears," says the psalmist (Ps 116:8 KJV), and the tears of "Rachel" will end in the exiles' return (Jer 31:16). Indeed there is assurance that "weeping may endure for a night, but joy cometh in the morning" (Ps 30:5 KJV), and that "they that sow in tears shall reap in joy" (Ps 126:5 KJV); this *hope is echoed in Luke 6:21 and John 16:20. The point is not merely that the dismay represented by tears will eventually be replaced by *joy, but that tears can be a path to joy and are therefore good. Somewhat related in exegetical tradition is Psalm 84:6, "Who passing through the valley of Baca make it a well"; despite the different metaphor (*water replacing *drought), the miracle is similar. But the word *bākā'*, treated in the KJV as a place name, is translated literally in the LXX, and the subsequent Vulgate rendering *vallis lacrymarum* gave rise to the familiar English phrase "vale of tears," which has become a metaphor for the whole of our earthly pilgrimage. Already in Isaiah the idea of an end to weeping is given an eschatological turn (Is 30:19; 35:10; 51:11; 65:19; and esp. Is 25:8: "The LORD God will wipe away tears from off all faces"). This last image is quoted twice in the book of Revelation (Rev 7:17; 21:4).

Visual images associated with tears include *eyes dimmed (Ps 38:10), a face disfigured by weeping (Gen 43:31; 2 Sam 12:20; *see* Deformity) and the image of exaggerated flow—a *fountain (Jer 9:1, 18) or *river (Ps 119:136; Lam 2:16, 18) of tears, enough to drench a *bed (Ps 6:6) or fill a *wineskin (Ps 56:8). This last image (*nō'd*, KJV "bottle") may begin as a play on *nōd* ("wandering") in the preceding hemistich, but the conceit that develops of God's preserving the tears of sufferers becomes the dominant theme of the verse, being paralleled in the succeeding clause. Beyond the purely visual are such figures as that of tears contaminating one's drink (Ps 102:9) or replacing food and drink (Ps 42:3; 80:5;

127:2, "bread of sorrows").

See also LAMENT PSALMS; MOURN, MOURNING; WEEPING.

BIBLIOGRAPHY. T. Collins, "The Physiology of Tears in the Old Testament," *CBQ* 33 (1971) 18-38, 185-97; I. Hausherr, *Penthos: The Doctrine of Compunction in the Christian East* (1944) (Cistercian Studies 53; Kalamazoo, MI: Cistercian, 1982); F. F. Hvidberg, *Weeping and Laughter in the Old Testament: A Study of Canaanite-Israelite Religion* (Leiden: Brill; Copenhagen: A. Busck, 1962); M. Ross, *The Fountain and the Furnace* (New York: Paulist, 1987).

TEETH

Teeth are primarily used as symbols of the attempted consumption of ill-gotten gain, taken by force from the powerless. But teeth also symbolize good consumption, as in the lover's consumption with his teeth of the love from the beloved in *Song of Songs, or when the Lord makes the repentant Israelites like a many-toothed threshing sledge crushing the mountains.

Teeth are an image of power, whether good or bad, and of a seemingly unconquerable state. From the mighty Leviathan, who has "fearsome teeth" (Job 41:14 NIV; *see* Mythical Animals), to the small but destructive locusts of the first woe in Revelation (9:8), which have teeth like a *lion, teeth symbolize conquering and unstoppable power. In Daniel's vision the second beast, who is introduced with the comment that "it had three ribs in its mouth between its teeth," is told to eat its fill of symbolic flesh (Dan 7:5 NIV). The fourth beast in Daniel's dream, which is "very powerful," has large iron teeth that allow it to crush and devour those it attacks (Dan 7:7). The image of destructive teeth is applied to Israel's neighbors when they attack. In Joel, when Israel is invaded and laid waste, the destruction is likened to that which comes from the teeth of a lion.

Another graphic image from Scripture is that of "gnashing of teeth." In the OT the emphasis is on enemies who grind their teeth as a taunt and as a sign of derision. The ungodly gnash their teeth at the stumbling and defenseless (Ps 35:16), including the Israelites in the time of the destruction of Jerusalem (Lam 2:16), but eventually the Lord will *rescue them. Gnashing of teeth is an expression of strong and often violent anger, rage or fury that can boil over into an all-out attack, usually physical, at any moment. The furious crowds gnash their teeth at Stephen (Acts 7:54) before dragging him out of the city and stoning him. However, the example of Stephen is an exception to the general NT pattern, where gnashing of teeth is done by those overcome with grief. In seven occurrences it is in the formulaic expression "weeping and gnashing of teeth" (e.g., Mt 8:12). Consequently, weeping and gnashing of teeth becomes a description of *hell, the place of *judgment reserved for those who do not enter the kingdom. There will be burning (Mt 13:42) and

darkness (Mt 8:12) there, and the judged will be cut to pieces (Mt 24:51). Here the OT and NT pictures merge: the wicked, who have gnashed their teeth in *anger all their lives, will continue to do so, but now at God's behest, in hell.

The breaking of teeth symbolizes defeat. The teeth of the wicked are broken; they are not allowed to use them to devour the weak/righteous who trust in God. Though they may roar and growl like lions, evil people will have their teeth broken by the Lord. For a lion to have its teeth broken was to be mortally wounded. It now "perishes for lack of prey" (Job 4:11 NIV). Here teeth are a symbol of the power of evil people to consume the defenseless and even to provide for themselves and their own. When justice comes, evil will have its teeth broken; that is, it will be defeated. One of Job's righteous acts was to break the teeth and fangs of the wicked (Job 29:17). God, in protection of the psalmist, breaks the teeth of wicked men "whose teeth are spears and arrows" (Ps 57:4 NIV), who seek to consume the defenseless (Ps 3:7; 37:12-13; 57:4; 58:6; 112:10; 124:6).

Being able to simply taste food but not digest it is a graphic image of a punishment both to Israel and to Israel's enemies. When the Israelites, sick of *manna, grumbled for meat, they were given quail. "But while the meat was still between their teeth," the Lord killed them (Num 11:33 NIV). Similarly, the Lord promises to take the forbidden food out of the mouths of Israel's enemies (Zech 9:7). Here food gotten by sinful means is tasted but will never reach the belly.

Finally, a number of the references to teeth are quite ordinary. Healthy white teeth are a symbol of beauty. In the Song of Songs the beloved's beauty is extolled with the description that her teeth are "whiter than newly shorn and washed sheep" (Song 4:2; 6:6) and that they are "evenly paired" (none is missing, Song 4:2; 6:6). The beauty of teeth is in part related to their fragile nature, heightened in ancient times with the lack of modern dental restoration. The value of teeth, and the penalty for those who are responsible for knocking out the teeth of others is addressed in the Law (Ex 21:23; Lev 24:20). Job points to the elemental nature of teeth when he describes his current state as "escaping by the skin of his teeth," which means to have only what is left of your body and nothing more (Job 19:20 NIV).

See also EATING; MOUTH.

TEMPERATURE

In a world without air conditioners, gas furnaces or aspirin, the biblical authors view temperature as an uncontrollable force affecting many areas of human existence. Also, without precise measuring instruments, their descriptions of temperature are limited to broad terms like *hot* and *cold*, which their audiences will presumably understand from personal experience. The universal experience of temperature provides the basis for a number of metaphorical uses.

Nature. Temperature words literally describe basic physical conditions. Isaiah chides the *idol maker who makes a *god from one half of a *tree and a *fire from the other half and says, "Ah, I am warm, I can feel the fire!" (Is 44:16 NRSV). Physical warmth is the only thing such a god can provide. Heat and cold are also often used as time markers because they recur in nature in regular cycles. Nehemiah orders that "the gates of Jerusalem are not to be opened until the sun is hot" (Neh 7:3 NRSV), the time of broad daylight when approaching enemies are easily spotted. The "heat of day" is the regular time for an afternoon rest, which allows Rechab and Baanah to catch Ishbosheth unawares by attacking then (2 Sam 4:5; also Gen 18:1). Genesis 8:22 seems to use temperature as a marker for broader time periods, when God promises Noah that "seed time and harvest, cold and heat, summer and winter" will never cease (NRSV).

Like all natural phenomena, temperature is created and controlled by God. This control is often cited to demonstrate that God transcends human limitations, as biblical characters cannot modify their environment. Elihu, charging Job of blasphemy, notes that God sends "cold from the scattering winds"; this being so, who is Job to speak, "whose garments are hot when the earth is still because of the south wind" (Job 37:9, 17 NRSV)? Job's inability to control temperature highlights his human frailty, which contrasts with the power of the God who rules the cold. This rule is evident in God's case against Israel's idolatry. "Does the snow of Lebanon leave the crags of Sirion?" God asks. "Do the mountain waters run dry, the cold flowing streams? But my people have forgotten me" (Jer 18:14-15 NRSV). God's reliability is compared to the constant cold of *snow-fed *springs.

Exposure and Shelter. Because temperature is under God's control and human beings are its helpless victims, exposure to the elements is a frequent metaphor for the hardships of life. Jacob complains to Laban that "by day the heat consumed me, and the cold by night," yet Laban has not appreciated his *sacrifice; rather, "you have changed my wages ten times" (Gen 31:40-41 NRSV). Jacob's protest is echoed in Jesus' parable of the laborers in the *vineyard. Those who have worked all day, representing faithful servants who have suffered for the *kingdom, are outraged when latecomers receive the same amount as "us who have borne the burden of the day and the scorching heat" (Mt 20:12 NRSV). A veteran of such *hardship, Paul lists exposure to harsh temperature among his *sufferings for the gospel: "[I went] many a sleepless night . . . cold and naked" (2 Cor 11:27 NRSV). He is certain that his willingness to undergo such hardship will silence those who question his character.

Exposure to temperature is the particular plight of the poor and oppressed, whom the righteous are responsible to assist. Job insists that of those who "have no covering in the cold," all he encountered were "warmed by the fleece of my sheep" (Job 24:7;

31:20 NRSV). Job's kindness contrasts with the indifference of James' hypothetical *hypocrite: "If a brother or sister is naked . . . and one of you says to them, 'Go in peace; keep warm and eat your fill,' . . . what is the good of that?" (Jas 2:15-16 NRSV). A friendly greeting or concerned *prayer is not enough when someone is in need, as true faith will work to relieve the suffering of the helpless.

The danger of exposure provides a vivid metaphor for divine wrath in the form of extreme heat. Moses promises that those who break the covenant will be *plagued with "fever, inflammation, with fiery heat and drought" (Deut 28:22 NRSV), things from which there is no escape. The inescapable doom of the wicked is assured when the fourth bowl of wrath is poured onto the *sun in Revelation 16:8-9, "and it was allowed to scorch them with fire; they were scorched by the fierce heat" (NRSV). On a more positive note, eschatological *blessing may take the form of protection from severe temperatures. Isaiah's purified *remnant will receive "a shade by day from the heat" (Is 4:6 NRSV), and John's multitude in *white robes "will hunger no more, and thirst no more; the sun will not strike them, nor any scorching heat" (Rev 7:16 NRSV).

Things that are pleasant or refreshing are often compared to the pleasant relief of a cool breeze or a cold *drink on a hot day. "Like the cold of snow in the time of harvest are faithful messengers to those who send them. . . . Like cold water to a thirsty soul, so is good news from a far country" (Prov 25:13, 25 NRSV). Jesus, in commissioning the Seventy, uses cold *water to represent the most basic act of *hospitality: "whoever gives even a cup of cold water to one of these little ones" (Mt 10:42 NRSV) will receive blessing, refreshment from God in return for refreshing God's servants.

Spiritual Life. Temperature is not only an external sensation. The biblical authors did not need thermometers to recognize the heat of fever or the cold clamminess of a corpse. The NT often describes inner life in terms of bodily temperature, most frequently using inner cold to represent spiritual deadness. Jesus warns that in the last days, "because of the increase of lawlessness, the love of many will grow cold," suggesting that *persecution and hardship will lead believers to stop practicing their faith (see Mt 24:9-13).

John's Gospel uses cold to stage Peter's denial of Christ. After insisting that he will never fall away and fighting to prevent Jesus' arrest, Peter follows the mob into the courtyard of the high *priest's house. While Jesus stands trial, Peter stands in the cold *darkness "warming himself" at the soldiers' fire (Jn 18:18 NRSV). The cold night seems to pervade his spirit and strip his courage, as his fiery zeal turns to three chilling denials of his Master.

Temperature as a gauge for spiritual activity also underlies Jesus' rebuke of the Laodiceans. Jesus knows the works of the Laodiceans: "You are neither cold nor hot. I wish that you were either cold or hot"

(Rev 3:15 NRSV). The Laodiceans provide neither healing nor refreshment because they are spiritually "lukewarm," lacking any inner desire to work for Christ. This lukewarmness is identified with spiritual complacency in Revelation 3:17-19.

Rage. The warm blush of *anger underlies the biblical image of "hot wrath," an indication of extreme inner activity that can erupt in violence. Images of boiling rage are often applied anthropomorphically to God, expressing his wrath over, and the impending *judgment of, sin and idolatry. Moses vividly recalls that when the Israelites worshiped the golden *calf, "I was afraid of the anger and hot displeasure with which the LORD was wrathful against you" (Deut 9:19 NASB), an inner heat that almost boiled over to their destruction (Ex 32:10). The same word *(hēmâ)* is used by the psalmist when he begs God, "Do not rebuke me in your anger, or discipline me in your wrath" (Ps 6:1; 38:1 NRSV). Such heat imagery is consonant with passages describing God's wrath as the "kindling" of a consuming "fire" (Jug 2:14; 10:7).

See also ANGER; DRY, DROUGHT; FIRE; MELT, MELTING; SNOW; WATER; WEATHER; WIND.

TEMPLE

Not surprisingly, given the temple's central role in Jewish society, the biblical imagery surrounding it is particularly rich and suggestive. The temple presents a fascinating range of symbols and, in light of the biblical prohibition against graven images, a surprising emphasis on the visible nature of revelation communicated by the dwelling of *Israel's invisible *God (e.g., Ps 48:4-8, 12-14). No doubt the songs, fragrances, *prayers and rituals surrounding a visit to the temple, the biggest structure of its kind in the ancient Near East, left an indelible impression on the senses and served as a fountainhead of religious imagery. After all, the temple was not only the worship center of Hebrew culture but also the art gallery, concert plaza and poetry library.

God's Dwelling Place. The temple in its most basic sense symbolizes the dwelling place of God. This is underscored by numerous references to the temple as the "house of God" or the "house of the LORD." Its other titles include "the sanctuary" or at times simply *Zion—as the psalmist emphasizes, "For the LORD has chosen Zion; he has desired it for his habitation" (Ps 132:13 NRSV; cf. Ps 9:11; 74:2; 76:2; Joel 3:17). In lieu of the carved deity symbolizing the presence of the *gods in pagan temples, the architecture and increasingly precious metals encountered as one neared the holy of holies emphasized God's presence. Indeed, at its dedication the manifestation of his presence proved overwhelming: "a cloud filled the house of the LORD, so that the priests could not stand to minister because of the cloud; for the glory of the LORD filled the house of the LORD" (1 Kings 8:10-11 NRSV; cf. 2 Chron 5:14; 7:1-2; Ezek 43:5; 44:4). The two massive pillars of the forecourt are also symbolic of God's

entrance into his abode (1 Kings 7:15-22; cf. 43:4).

However, the image of God's dwelling in a habitation constructed by human *hands may appear problematic, or at best paradoxical. On the one hand, the temple provided a place for worship and a tangible reminder of God's presence, *blessing and *protection; on the other hand, its presence might lead to the perspective that God may be circumscribed. Criticism of the latter perspective is evident in Isaiah

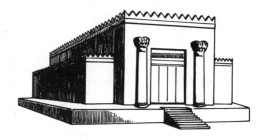

A reconstruction of Solomon's temple with the pillars Jachin and Boaz at the entrance.

66:1: "Thus says the LORD: Heaven is my throne and the earth is my footstool; what is the house that you would build for me, and what is my resting place?" (NRSV; cf. Deut 4:7; Ps 145:18; Acts 7:48; 17:24). Even at the temple's dedication, *Solomon acknowledges that God is not "contained" in it. "But will God indeed dwell on the earth? Even heaven and the highest heaven cannot contain you, much less this house that I have built!" (1 Kings 8:27 NRSV). Other passages unite both dimensions without any apparent tension: "The LORD is in his holy temple; the LORD's throne is in heaven" (Ps 11:4).

The answer to this paradox lies in the fact that the temple is an *earthly archetype of the *heavenly reality, just as *Moses constructed the *tabernacle after the heavenly pattern revealed to him on *Sinai (Ex 25:9, 40). This contrast between the heavenly and the earthly is also underscored in several passages of Hebrews: "They offer worship in a sanctuary that is a sketch and shadow of the heavenly one" (Heb 8:5 NRSV; cf. Heb 9:1, 24). Specific aspects of God's heavenly abode are duplicated in the temple. For example, God's dwelling in a veil of smoke and *darkness is replicated in the holy of holies (2 Sam 22:12; Ps 18:11; 97:2; Rev 15:8).

Symbol of Divine Victory. The temple was more than God's earthly dwelling place. It was also a potent symbol of God's victory over his *enemies. We may see this in 2 Samuel 7, the story of *David's abortive desire to *build the temple. David felt guilty that he lived in a permanent *home while God still lived in a *tent (2 Sam 7:2). He expressed his desire to built a permanent structure to the prophet approved the idea. Later, however, ~~to~~ Nathan, telling him that David ~~build a~~ temple.

~~The~~ 2 Samuel 7 centers on a play on ~~the word~~ *bayit*, which is rendered in various ~~En~~glish versions (though not the ~~NRSV which trans~~lates "house" consistently). David is secure ~~and at rest~~ in his *bayit* (house; cf. 2 Sam 7:1) but wants to build God a *bayit* (temple; cf. 2 Sam 7:5). God rejects David's plan but tells him *he* will build *for David* a *bayit* (a dynasty; cf. 2 Sam 7:11). The one who follows David in his dynasty will be the one to build the "house of God." This one of course is Solomon, whose name means "peace." The point is that the temple symbolizes victory over the enemies of God and peaceful settlement in the *land. David was the conquest completer, but he was also "a warrior" (1 Chron 28:3); so the time was not right for the temple. His son Solomon built it.

In this way the temple is a symbol of establishment and victory. As such, it falls into the pattern of ancient Near Eastern mythology (in particular the Baal Epic of ancient Ugarit), which presents a pattern of *warfare followed by the proclamation of the god as *king and the commemoration of victory through the building of a new divine residence.

The Temple and Creation. Yet God's celestial and terrestrial abodes are not always contrasted; often they are depicted as complementary. That is, the temple also represents the entire cosmos; it is a microcosm of all creation. "He built his sanctuary like the high heavens, like the earth, which he has founded forever" (Ps 78:69 NRSV). Since the temple speaks of all creation, Habakkuk declares, "The LORD is in his holy temple; let all the earth keep silence before him!" (Hab 2:20 NRSV). Similarly, Isaiah's vision of God's *glory filling the temple is accompanied by the angelic antiphony "Holy, holy, holy is the LORD of hosts; the whole earth is full of his glory" (Is 6:3 NRSV).

Both the temple and the tabernacle embody a theology of creation and God's presence within it. Consequently there are parallels between the *Genesis creation account and the accounts of the building of the tabernacle and the temple. The significance of the *light of creation and the light in the tabernacle (Ex 25:31-40; 37:17-24) is retained in the temple (2 Chron 13:11). Similar to the *seven *days of creation, the temple took seven years to complete, a fact that emphasizes God as its builder rather than Solomon or David. The objects in the temple bear creation symbolism as well. For example, the placid *waters of the bronze reservoir in the court of the *priests represent God's victory over the waters of chaos, as celebrated in Psalm 93, which connects the creation of the world, the raging chaotic waters and the *holiness of God's house. Both God's creation and his acts of creation are often imaginatively portrayed in the temple.

As a symbol of pristine creation the temple evokes the *Garden of Eden, or paradise. Ezekiel depicts the primordial *rivers (Gen 2:10-14) emerging from below the threshold of the temple (Ezek 47:1). He also suggests that the perfection of Eden is cultivated in the temple by its proximity to the *tree of life. "Their leaves will not wither nor their fruit fail, but they will bear fresh fruit every month, because the water for them flows from the sanctuary" (Ezek 47:12 NRSV). The psalmist longs for the delights of such a paradise: "Happy are those whom you choose and bring near to live in your courts. We shall be satisfied with the goodness of your house, your holy temple" (Ps 65:4 NRSV; cf. Ps 36).

Place of Communication. The temple, moreover, represents a place of communication with and about God. Its priests had access to the mind of God (Deut 33:8) and instructed the people in the *law. This instruction in Torah which emanates from temple is projected onto the age to come when the nations shall stream to *Zion (Mic 4:2), the place of *prayer for all nations (Is 56:7; Jer 7:11; Mk 11:17). It was a place to pronounce *vows and fulfill pledges. Even during the time of *exile, when the temple was in ruins, the people of Israel would direct their prayers toward the temple, knowing that God would hear (1 Kings 8:28-29; Ps 138:2; Dan 6:11; Jon 2:7). In Luke's infancy narrative the temple is the place where the pious receive *revelation concerning God's coming *salvation and where Jesus, even as a child, expounds God's Word. In Acts the early church does not abandon the temple but preaches in its precincts.

Cosmic Center. Not only did daily economic, political and religious life orbit the *Jerusalem temple, but it symbolized the center of the cosmos, the meeting place between heaven and earth, the center to which distant communities would send delegations to offer *worship. Ezekiel describes it as located in the "center of the nations" and as "the navel of the earth" (Ezek 5:5; 38:12 NRSV mg.). Hence actions that take place in its precincts take on special significance, such as Jesus' prophetic act of cleansing the temple (Mk 11:15; Lk 19:45; Jn 2:15) and the rending of the temple *veil brought about by Jesus' *death (Mt 27:51; Mk 15:38; Lk 23:45; cf. Heb 6:19; 9:3; 10:20).

The Temple and Holiness. Because the temple represented the dwelling place of God on earth, it was a symbol of *holiness. The deeper one penetrated the temple precincts, the greater the sanctity one encountered. Unlike a synagogue or church, the inside of the temple itself was not a place of public worship. The spread *wings of the cherubim on the *ark of the *covenant in the holy of holies suggest a picture of divine sanctity and protection (1 Kings 8:6-7; cf. Gen 3:24; Is 6:2-3).

Since the temple represents all creation, the *purity rules surrounding it had implications for categorizing everything, including people, in terms of clean and unclean. For example, the first gradation of holiness prevented *Gentiles from approaching the inner precincts. Ezekiel is exhorted to "mark well those who may be admitted to the temple and all those who are to be excluded from the sanctuary" (Ezek 44:5 NRSV). In Herod's temple there was a wall or marker that warned Gentiles not to proceed further under penalty of death. Paul is falsely accused of defiling the temple by bringing Gentiles past this barrier (Acts 21:28). This image is taken up in Ephesians 2:14, which maintains that Christ's death "has broken down the dividing wall" (NRSV) between Jew and Gentile.

The Temple and Community. Since sacred concepts of boundaries, holiness and God's presence undergird the identity of the people of God, the temple often symbolizes God's people. For Isaiah the restoration of the temple mount and of the people are synonymous (Is 51:16); Ezekiel's vision of the *restoration of the temple is a vision of *hope for Israel (Ezek 40:1—43:12). Numerous biblical authors employ the temple as a symbol of the rise and fall of God's people according to their moral, ethical and spiritual condition (Ps 79:1; 114:2; Jer 24; Ezek 9:6; 43:10; Dan 8:13; 11:31; Rev 11:1). Similarly, the *disciples' discussion of the temple in the Gospels sets the stage for Jesus' prophetic discourse concerning the nation of Israel (Mt 24:1; Mk 13:1; Lk 21:5). John in particular emphasizes the function of the community, Jesus' body, as the temple that bears God's presence (e.g., Jn 2:19-21; 4:21-24).

Paul as well understands the redeemed community, the *church, as the dwelling place of God: "Do you not know that you are God's temple?" (1 Cor 3:16). Accordingly, it has implications for separation from the unholy and ungodly (cf. 1 Cor 3:17; 6:19; 2 Cor 6:16; Eph 2:21). 1 Peter speaks of Christ and believers as "living stones" that are "built into a spiritual house" (1 Pet 2:4-5 NRSV). Revelation addresses the faithful as pillars of the temple (Rev 3:12) but also emphasizes that there is no longer any need for a temple because of the unmediated presence of God in the New Jerusalem (Rev 21:22), which, because it is fashioned as a cube (Rev 21:16), suggests the shape of the holy of holies.

The Temple and Justice and Peace. The temple is pictured as the embodiment of God's people's longing for *justice, *peace and *blessing. This was true while the temple was standing and was only intensified by its destruction. The temple is related to the dispensation of law and justice; in it the law was both taught and practiced. The prophets were quick to remind people of the offensiveness of temple worship if not accompanied by justice (Is 1:10-17; Hos 6:6; Amos 5:21). Accordingly, the psalmist makes a connection between the physical and ethical preparation necessary for those who would "ascend the hill of the LORD" or "stand in his holy place" (see Ps 24:3-6; cf. Ps 15): the physical ascent of the temple mount into God's presence must be matched by an ethical ascent.

This fits well with the emphasis on the temple's physical *beauty. The religion of the Bible tolerates no graven images of the deity, but it was not bereft

of artistic achievement. Psalm 84 celebrates the beauty of *Zion, which certainly would have included the temple building itself. It expresses the psalmist's longing to be in the vicinity of this marvelous building.

Moreover, the temple symbolizes peace and *rest. Because the glassy *sea of the temple is associated with God's victory over chaos in creation, the temple is associated with the *sabbath rest that accompanied the completion of the world. The temple is spoken of as his "resting place" (Ps 132:14; cf. Is 66:1), and Solomon is chosen to be its builder because he is a "man of peace" (1 Chron 22:9). The completion of the temple is symbolic of the sabbath God grants Israel from its warring past. Hence it is from its origin a place of rest (cf. Ex 20:25). In Revelation the altar of the temple is pictured as the place where the martyrs rest until the time of the end (Rev 6:9-11).

Image of Christ. Like the tabernacle before it, temple imagery is associated with *Jesus Christ in the NT. After all, the temple represented God's presence on earth, and Jesus is the fullness of that presence in bodily form. A rumor had reached the high priest that Jesus had foreseen the destruction of the temple (Mk 13:1-2) and attributed to him the claim that in *three days he would build another, but "not made with hands" (Mk 14:58; cf. Jn 2:13-22). His opponents knew what he was saying: that he would stand in place of the temple as the presence of God.

Conclusion. Given such a richness of imagery surrounding the house of God, it is little wonder that God's people have always passionately yearned for life inside its courts: "Surely goodness and mercy shall follow me all the days of my life, and I shall dwell in the house of the LORD my whole life long" (Ps 23:6 NRSV).

See also ADAM; ALTAR; JERUSALEM; LAMP, LAMPSTAND; OFFERING; PRIEST; SACRED SPACE; SACRIFICE; TABERNACLE; WORSHIP; ZION.

BIBLIOGRAPHY. D. M. Knipe, "The Temple in Image and Reality" in *Temple in Society*, ed. M. V. Fox (Winona Lake, IN: Eisenbrauns, 1988) 105–38; J. D. Levenson, *Sinai and Zion: An Entry into the Jewish Bible* (Minneapolis: Winston, 1985).

TEMPTATION. *See* TEMPTER, TEMPTATION.

TEMPTER, TEMPTATION

In a book preoccupied with good and *evil and the need for people to choose between them, it is no surprise that the temptation motif looms large. The root meaning of temptation is that it *tests* a person, with the person's response determining his or her identity. Temptation stories can thus be viewed as a particular category within the archetypal *test motif. The ingredients that converge in a full-fledged temptation story are fixed. The two principal actors are a tempter (whose chief trait is subtlety) and a victim of temptation (who is often gullible or weak-willed). The action consists of three main motifs—a process of manipulation by which the tempter allures the victim to do a forbidden or wrong thing, the process by which the victim deals with the allurement (usually first resisting but then gradually succumbing) and final closure, in which the intended victim either thwarts the tempter or assents to the forbidden action. Most temptation stories end in victory for the tempter, but this is not the only possibility.

The Wiles of the Tempter. The most famous temptation story in the Bible is the one that precedes the fall of *Adam and *Eve (Gen 3:1-6). Despite its brevity, it contains all the essential ingredients. The tempter's subtlety consists of his casting God's prohibition of the forbidden *tree in the form of an incredulous question (Gen 3:1), contradicting God's predicted punishment for disobedience of the edict (Gen 3:4) and giving the woman a reason for desiring the forbidden *fruit (Gen 3:5). In the process of Eve's gradual weakening, she amplifies the original prohibition beyond what God had said ("neither shall you touch it" [Gen 3:3 RSV]), and she produces three impeccable reasons for eating the forbidden fruit as she contemplates the possibility of doing so (Gen 3:6). Eve and Adam's succumbing to the temptation is narrated with breathtaking matter-of-factness: "She took of its fruit and ate; and she also gave some to her husband, and he ate" (Gen 3:6 RSV).

The NT counterpart of this temptation story, prototypical for the NT and a balance to the temptation of Adam and Eve, is *Satan's temptation of Jesus in the wilderness (Mk 1:12; Lk 4:1-12). Christ, the second Adam, undoes what the first Adam did, thwarting Satan and robbing him of final victory. In John Milton's formula, here is paradise regained, compensating for paradise lost. The usual ingredients are present, including a subtle tempter who can quote Scripture to his own purpose, a back-and-forth sally in which the intended victim consistently thwarts the tempter, and closure in the form of Satan's slinking off in defeat.

Other full-fledged temptation stories fill out this biblical genre. In the *Joseph story Potiphar's wife is the archetypal seductress who tempts Joseph to engage in *sexual sin; Joseph resists the temptation but loses his standing in Potiphar's household (Gen 39:6-20). Less virtuous is the naive "young man without sense" of Proverbs 7:7 (RSV), who after an elaborate invitation from an adventuresome *adulteress "at once . . . follows her, as an ox goes to the slaughter" (Prov 7:22 RSV). Another classic temptation story with sexual overtones is the story of *Samson and Delilah (Judg 16), based on a *three-plus-one pattern in which the intended victim resists the temptation three times but then tragically succumbs.

In all of these stories the tempter plays a key role. When the tempter is a woman, the resulting archetype is the temptress. The Bible gives us a memorable gallery of temptresses (though Eve is not among their ranks, that being a postbiblical tradition) in addition to those already noted. Job's wife tempts

her suffering husband to "curse God, and die" (Job 2:9). Jezebel tempts her husband to take by devious means the vineyard that he covets (1 Kings 21). Solomon's pagan wives together and by a gradual process "turned away his heart after other gods" in his latter years (1 Kings 11:4 RSV). It is small wonder that the narrator of Ecclesiastes claims to have "found more bitter than death the woman whose heart is snares and nets, and whose hands are fetters" (Eccles 7:26 RSV). In the book of Proverbs a personified Folly tempts passers by to "turn in here" and partake of her lavish *banquet of *folly (Prov 9:13-18).

Temptations Within and Without. In addition to these full-fledged temptation stories governed by an aggressive tempter who stage-manages the temptation, we can find the motif surfacing in briefer versions throughout the Bible, where the common pattern is for the victim to be tempted by circumstances and inner desires rather than an external agent of temptation. Sexual temptation is one example of such temptation in the Bible. *Bathsheba does not have to make a play for David in order to be the occasion of his sexual temptation; the beauty of her nude body is enough to set the dynamics of inner temptation in motion for the sexually aroused David (2 Sam 11). Judah (Gen 38) and Samson (Judg 14:5—16:1) are additional examples of males who are driven by their own desires when confronted with feminine attractiveness, easy prey to sexual temptation. The antidote to such behavior is faithful marriage: "Because of the temptation to immorality, each man should have his own wife and each woman her own husband" (1 Cor 7:2 RSV).

The largest category of self-tempted characters in the Bible is those who find the appeals of materialism irresistible and who accordingly succumb to greed. The motif starts when Lot is tempted to choose the material prosperity represented by the well-watered Jordan valley, at the price of spiritual compromise (Gen 13). The roll call of characters tempted by the greed for money and goods includes Achan (Josh 7), Ahab in the story of Naboth's vineyard (1 Kings 21), the rich young ruler who "went away sorrowful; for he had great possessions" when Jesus told him that the cost of being a disciple would be to sell all that he had and give it to the poor (Mt 19:22 RSV), the rich farmer of Jesus' parable who succumbed to the temptation to lay up treasure for himself instead of being "rich toward God" (Lk 12:21), Judas in his betrayal of Jesus for thirty pieces of silver, and Ananias and Sapphira (Acts 5:1-11). Given people's readiness to succumb to the temptation of materialistic greed, no wonder Paul says that "those who desire to be rich fall into temptation, into a snare, into many senseless and hurtful desires that plunge men into ruin and destruction" (1 Tim 6:9 RSV).

Ambition can also tempt the mighty who are greedy for power and leadership. King Saul is such, tempted to secure his position by remaining popular with his followers when they want to spare the best of the spoils instead of following the command of God (1 Sam 15). Absalom, impressed with his own rating in popularity polls, is tempted to rebel against his father and grab the kingship for himself (2 Sam 15:1-12). Herod Agrippa I is tempted to hubris when he dons his royal robes and accepts the acclaim of the people to be "a god, and not a man" (Acts 12:22 RSV). The temptation to a ruler's *pride reaches its apex in Ezekiel's narrative of the self-temptation and fall of the king of Tyre (Ezek 27—28), where the imagery even has overtones of Satan's original temptation and fall.

False worship also tempts people in the Bible. Temptations to idolatry are a leading leitmotif in OT history. The NT counterpart is *apostasy—falling away from the newly founded Christian faith into various forms of false doctrine and lifestyle. Thus Paul expresses fear that "the tempter had tempted you and that our labor would be in vain" (1 Thess 3:5 RSV), and the writer of Hebrews is clearly worried that his readers, formerly Jewish in their religious practices and beliefs, will "drift away" from their Christian convictions (Heb 2:1).

Sometimes something as reflexive as the urge for self-preservation can tempt a person to do something wrong. This is the story of Peter's denial of Jesus, where despite his best intentions, Peter's impulse to save himself leads him to deny his loyalty to Jesus three times.

While we rightly think of temptation as a narrative motif, it underlies some nonnarrative parts of the Bible as well. In Psalms, for example, wicked oppressors are often said to be tempted to think that God either does not see what they do or will not intervene. The "man greedy for gain curses and renounces the LORD. . . . All his thoughts are, 'There is no God' " (Ps 10:3-4 RSV). Slanderers "hold fast to their evil purpose, . . . thinking, 'Who can see us? Who can search out our crimes'?" (Ps 64:5-6 RSV). In short, they are tempted to a delusion, for it turns out that God does see them and is willing to intervene (Ps 64:7). In Psalm 73 it is "the people" who are tempted to ask regarding the arrogant wealthy, "How can God know? Is there knowledge in the Most High?" (Ps 73:11 RSV). The speaker in that psalm undergoes a great crisis of faith as he is tempted to envy the prosperity of the wicked and to decide that the godly life is not worth the sacrifices required.

A latent temptation theme also underlies some of the OT proverbs. In fact, the book of Proverbs is an ever-expanding picture of threats to the godly life. We read between the lines that the young person addressed in the book faces a more or less constant series of temptations—to cast his lot with the violent, not to heed his father's instruction, to choose folly rather than wisdom, to give in to the sexual allurement of the "loose woman," to be slothful instead of industrious, to grab ill-gotten gain, to engage in dishonest business practices, to be quick-tempered and quarrelsome, to become a winebibber. The constant thrust of OT wisdom literature is to "choose

this, not that," as even the prevalence of antithetical parallelism often shows (e.g., "A man of quick temper acts foolishly, but a man of discretion is patient" [Prov 14:17 RSV]).

The Bible's Anatomy of Temptation. From the Bible's temptation stories we can piece together the dynamics of how it works. Temptation exists in the first place because the moral and spiritual world, in the view of the biblical writers, is such that a great battle between good and evil is raging at every moment. For people living in a fallen world, life at every moment is at a transcendent crisis in which a person's allegiance is claimed by God and counterclaimed by Satan and evil. The wisdom literature motif of the two paths or two ways sums it up. The temptation stories of the Bible, moreover, send the message that the power and attraction of evil are great, not minor.

Temptation itself is a lack of self-control, a letting go, a letting down of one's guard. The person who allows "the iniquities of the wicked [to] ensnare him" and who "is caught in the toils of his sin" has one basic problem: "he dies for lack of discipline" (Prov 5:22-23 RSV). Paul's analysis of what goes wrong when married people fall into sexual sin is that Satan tempts them "through lack of self-control" (1 Cor 7:5 RSV).

In this great conflict between good and evil, human choice is assumed to exist and is in fact the universal human lot. No one is forced to succumb to temptation. People choose to do so. Stories of temptations that are successfully resisted, such as David's resistance to the suggestion that he put an end to the king who torments him, prove that people have a power of choice when confronting temptation. 1 Corinthians 10:13 makes it explicit: "God is faithful, and he will not let you be tempted beyond your strength, but with the temptation will also provide the way of escape, that you may be able to endure it" (RSV).

The stakes involved in temptation are not small but monumental. The imagery associated with succumbing to temptation is awe-inspiring in its destructiveness. Not infrequently the result of giving in is literal or figurative death. The picture in Proverbs 7:21-27 is an apt summary: to succumb to temptation is to be like an *ox going to the slaughter, a stag whose entrails are pierced by an arrow, a *bird caught in a snare and a one-way ticket "down to the chambers of death" (RSV).

Finally, despite all the external circumstances and agents that elbow their way into a person's consciousness and beckon toward evil, they do not *cause* anyone to give in to temptation; they merely provide *the occasion for* moral choice. The enemy is within, as the epistle of James makes explicit: a "person is tempted when he is lured and enticed by his own desire. Then desire when it has conceived gives birth to sin; and sin when it is full-grown brings forth death" (Jas 1:14-15 RSV). The antidote therefore is to guard one's inner heart and soul: "keep your heart with all vigilance; for from it flow the springs of life" (Prov 4:23 RSV).

See also APOSTASY; SATAN; SEDUCTION; SIN; STUMBLE, STUMBLING BLOCK; TEST, TESTING.

TEN COMMANDMENTS. See LAW.

TENT

The patriarchs and their households were nomadic and lived in tents (Gen 12:8; 26:25; 31:25; Heb 11:7), as did all the people of God during the *journey to the *Promised Land (Ex 13:20; 15:27; 19:1). This period left an indelible impression on the Israelites (Ex 32:21ff.), and the words "To your tents, O Israel" (see 2 Sam 20:1; cf. 1 Sam 4:10 NIV) became a common idiom for returning to their homes. Soldiers continued to live in tents in times of *war (2 Kings 3:9), and during *festivals the Israelites stayed in tents (Lev 23:42-43). The imagery of tent dwelling served to remind Israel of God's provision to them during the *wilderness wanderings and their continued dependence on him once settled in the Promised Land.

The Physical World and Body Compared to a Tent. Pitching a tent may depict an act of establishment. For example, although God is literally the designer of the large pavilion-style tent of the *tabernacle (Ex 25:9), most references compare God's establishing the created order to the setting up and laying out of a huge marquee (Ps 19:4-5; Is 40:22; 44:24; 45:12; 51:3); it is God who has founded creation and continues to care for it. Interestingly,

Large nomadic tents, perhaps like Abraham's.

the tense used sometimes suggests this is a continuing rather than once-for-all activity (Ps 104:2), suggesting that God is always active as the Creator.

In the OT a comparison is also drawn between the human *body and a tent. The body's well-being is like a secure tent (Ps 16:9), and its vulnerability through illness, age or *death is like a tent under siege or a tent whose cords are pulled up (Job 19:12; 4:21; Is 38:12). In the NT the impermanence of the body is compared to a tent that "I will soon put away" (2 Pet 1:13-14). This happens most fully and

eloquently in the writings of Paul, himself a tentmaker, who emphasizes the burden and longing of our earthly existence for *heavenly permanence: "we know that if the earthly tent we live in is destroyed, we have a building from God, an eternal house in heaven" (2 Cor 5:1; also 2 Cor 5:2-5). Our future form will be eternal, not something that can be easily destroyed like a vulnerable man-made tent but rather firm and sure, built by God himself. (It should be noted that nowhere here is the notion of an immortal soul in a temporary body.)

The People's Fortunes and God's Presence as a Tent. God's *restoring, extending and securing of the people are described in terms of the mending (Amos 9:11), erecting (Is 54:2-3) and enlarging (Is 33:20) of a tent. In the NT the first of these events is prophetically viewed as being fulfilled in the birth of the church (Acts 15:16-17).

The most original metaphorical use of tent language is of God's "moving about from place to place with a tent as my dwelling" (2 Sam 7:6-7), a reference to the tabernacle. Here God is described as a nomad pitching and moving his tent among and alongside the people. Some of this language persists even after the temple replaces the tabernacle (1 Chron 9:19). With its destruction a more mobile picture of God's presence with the people *returns (Ezek 37:27; Joel 3:17; Zech 2:10), as also a more intimate picture of God's dwelling in the individual *heart as though pitching his tent there (Is 57:15).

In the NT this comes to glorious expression in the picture of God's *Son "pitching his tent" among us (Jn 1:14; cf. Ex 40:34). The wonder of this is beautifully evoked in the opening words of John's first letter (1 Jn 1:1-2). Jesus has also "pitched" a true tabernacle in the heavens, of which the former was only a *shadow and copy (Heb 8:2, 5), and the day is coming when God will "stretch his tent" over all those who have suffered the great tribulation (Rev 7:15), providing *rest and security.

Although it does not occur in the NT, Paul's working with his hands while fulfilling his apostolic vocation provides the basis for the metaphor of "tentmaking" often used of nonprofessional missions today.

See also PLACE, NO ABIDING; TABERNACLE; TRANSIENCE; WANDERER, WANDERING.

BIBLIOGRAPHY. R. Hock, *The Social Context of Paul's Ministry: Tentmaking and Apostleship* (Philadelphia: Fortress, 1980); M. Seale, *The Desert Bible: Nomadic Tribal Culture and Old Testament Interpretation* (New York: St. Martin's, 1974).

TERAPHIM. See ORACLE.

TERROR, STORIES OF

While it would be a mistake to claim for the Bible the same impulse that lies behind modern horror stories, with their premise that it is fun to be frightened in one's leisure time, it is indisputable that the stories of the Bible have a large ingredient of terror. This is truer of some biblical genres than others; the stories of terror are concentrated in the historical chronicles, the prophetic and apocalyptic visions, the psalms, and the *passion of Christ. The main agents that people fear in these stories are *nature, personal and national *enemies, and *God.

To rank as a horror story, a narrative must do more than recount a *violent or terrifying event; it must be told in such a way as to make the reader feel the terror. By this criterion the story of *Cain's murder of *Abel is not a horror story, because the main event, though violent, is described in a single verse, whereas the story of the flood is a horror story because we relive (however briefly) the terror of the rising floodwaters until all human and animal life is extinct (Gen 7:17-24). Even the receding of the water (Gen 8:1-12) has a certain terror about it. While the book of Genesis is not a concentrated collection of horror stories, we do remember some stories as stories of terror—the threat to the angelic visitors to Lot's house and the subsequent destruction of *Sodom (Gen 19), the offering of Isaac (Gen 22), and *Joseph's being seized by his brothers (Gen 37:12-28).

In the epic of the *exodus we experience the ten *plagues as scenes of terror (Ex 7—12), as well as the earth's swallowing the rebels (Num 16) and the attack of the fiery serpents (Num 21:4-9). In later Jewish history the story of the concubine who is raped to the point of death is a story of terror (Judg 19). One of the ingredients of terror is a sense of inescapable calamity, and by this criterion the story of Naboth's vineyard is a story of terror (1 Kings 21).

The psalms are filled with vivid pictures of terror—sometimes recalled, sometimes averted, sometimes projected as coming in the future. The *lament psalms often paint a heightened picture of the threat that surrounds the speaker—threats that lead the speaker to claim that his "bones are shaking with terror" and that his "soul also is struck with terror" (Ps 6:2-3 NRSV). The evildoers of Psalm 10 pursue their victims like a predator and wait in ambush for them before trapping them in a net. Plotting slanderers represent "terror all around" to the speaker of Psalm 31:13 (NRSV). Nature too supplies images of terror in the psalms—as in the song of the *thunderstorm (Ps 29), the cataclysmic forces of nature in Psalm 46:2-3 or the desert and sea *storm of Psalm 107.

Even when nature is not itself the terror, poets draw from nature as a source of metaphors. Thus the sudden fall of the arrogant wicked is pictured as their being "swept away utterly by terrors" (Ps 73:19 NRSV), and military threat is portrayed as "raging waters" that destroy a nation (Ps 124:5 NRSV). A psalm of *rescue or deliverance like Psalm 91 is a catalog of terrors, with references to "the terror of the night," *arrows that fly by day, "pestilence that stalks in darkness" and "the destruction that wastes at noonday" (NRSV), military threat, and dangers of journeying such as *lions and *snakes. Finally, visions of God's future judgment of evil is pictured in images of terror: "pursue them with your tempest and terrify them with your hurricane" (Ps 83:15 NRSV).

A third major repository of stories of terror is the *prophetic and *apocalyptic books of the Bible. Here the forces of nature and the destructive power of *armies combine to produce visions of terror for all people living through the era that is predicted. A typical specimen is Jeremiah 48:44, which forecasts that "everyone who flees from the terror shall fall into the pit, and everyone who climbs out of the pit shall be caught in the trap" (NRSV). Daniel is so troubled by the terrifying beast visions he received that he records, "As for me, Daniel, my thoughts greatly terrified me, and my face turned pale" (Dan 7:28 NRSV). In NT apocalyptic, Jesus paints a picture of the coming destruction of *Jerusalem with people fleeing to the *mountains in terror, anguished pregnant women, rumors of military invasion, *famines and *earthquakes (Mt 24). The motif of eschatological terror reaches its climax in the book of Revelation, a pageant of terrifying scenes of horrifying judgments as the whole earthly order collapses.

The *passion of Christ too is an extended scene of terror. Not only do we witness the victimization of an innocent person condemned in courts of law, but we are also led through a series of terrifying scenes of bodily mutilation and pain, accompanied by severe psychological suffering. The grisly story of the beheading of John the Baptist (Mt 14:1-12; Mk 6:14-29; Lk 9:7-9) foreshadows these later scenes of terror in the passion of Jesus.

See also BATTLE STORIES; DEATH; FEAR; FLEE, FLIGHT; FLOOD; JUDGMENT; MONSTER, MONSTERS; MYTHICAL ANIMALS; NATURE; STORM; THUNDER; THEOPHANY.

TERROR. *See* FEAR.

TEST MOTIF

The test motif is almost synonymous with story itself, inasmuch as the most common way to organize a story (even when recounting a real-life event) is to portray the protagonist in a situation that tests his or her identity and ability. If a force actively pulls the protagonist to do a wrongful action, the result is a temptation story (*see* Tempter, Temptation), but this is a relatively small category of stories of testing. The Bible is a collection of test narratives, and the view of life that emerges is that life is a continuous testing, with events at every point eliciting responses from a person that at the same time define that person's character. The specific vocabulary of testing occurs more than two hundred times in English translations of the Bible.

In stories of testing, the link between action (plot) and character is very close. Action is character; character is action. When God tests *Abraham by commanding him to offer his son Isaac (Gen 22), Abraham's prompt and decisive obedience demonstrates his character, in which faith is the dominant ingredient. When on an earlier occasion Abraham and Sarah find themselves to be sojourners in a potentially hostile foreign land, their response of fear issuing in expediency is a manifestation of their flawed character at their moment of choice. When *Jacob arrives at his uncle's home for an extended stay, his ability to establish himself as an adult undergoes an extended test—a test in which Jacob's responses (competitiveness, physical stamina, perseverance, resilience) demonstrate his character.

Because character is determined by responses to tests, we remember many biblical characters especially for their heroism or ignominy in isolated moments of specific testing. *Adam and *Eve are famous chiefly for their failing the test posed by the serpent in the *Garden. We remember Abraham for passing the test of loyalty when he offered Isaac, *Joseph for resisting sexual sin, *David for giving in to sexual sin, *Daniel for praying when the lions' den loomed, *Ruth for remaining loyal to her mother-in-law and *Esther to her nation. One of the most endearing sides of Jesus' character and personality to emerge from the Gospels is the way he handled the continuous testing posed by people and circumstances during his public years.

If we recognize the centrality of the test motif to narrative itself, it becomes virtually impossible to classify the things that test a person. All of life tests us. The external world of nature and weather tests us. Specific people, as well as the entire social environment, test us. Personal relationships test our identity and loyalties, bringing out character traits in the process. It is true, of course, that the Bible tends (as does literature in general) to show characters in extraordinary or unusual situations that test them—a journey, for example, instead of a routine day at home, or a controversial encounter with a personal enemy rather than a conversation with a spouse or friend. Still, the Bible's thoroughgoing realism gives us to understand that our essential identity consists our responses to the events that make up our lives in the world.

If there is anything distinctive to the test motif in the Bible, it is the testing that transpires between God and people. In keeping with the providential assumption of the Bible that all events in a person's life are ultimately arranged by God, we find the motif of God's testing people. While this is explicitly stated only a dozen times, it is impossible to read the stories of the Bible without interpreting the events that test the human characters as from God, to determine characters' moral and spiritual standing. The reverse of this is also possible: people test God. The associations of such testing are usually negative, and they cluster around the behavior of the Israelites during the *exodus *wanderings (though see also Jesus' warning to Satan during the wilderness *temptation "not to tempt the Lord your God" [Mt 4:7 RSV]).

Several of the Bible's passages of interpretive commentary on the test motif supply a framework within which to understand it. 1 Corinthians 10:13 informs us that (1) the testings that a person undergoes are not unique but are "common to man" and (2) God will not allow a person to "be tempted beyond your strength, but with the temptation will also provide the way of escape, that you may be able to endure it" (RSV). In other words, passing the tests of life is always a possibility. 2 Corinthians 13:5 exhorts Christians, "Examine yourselves, to see whether you are holding to your faith. Test yourselves" (RSV). Here we are encouraged to become readers of our life stories, to determine our identity and take corrective action if needed.

Furthermore, testing produces growth in character (see Increase, Stories of): "Count it all joy, my brethren, when you meet various trials, for you know that the testing of your faith produces steadfastness. And let steadfastness have its full effect, that you may be perfect and complete, lacking in nothing" (Jas 1:2-4 RSV). The book of Hebrews, addressed to Christians enduring persecution, likewise stresses endurance, or "holding fast," as the virtue required to pass a test (Heb 3:6; 4:14; 10:23). Finally, the goal of life itself is linked to the test motif: "Blessed is the man who endures trial, for when he has stood the test he will receive the crown of life which God has promised to those who love him" (Jas 1:12 RSV).

Romans 5:3-5 catalogs in ladderlike sequence the specific virtues produced by suffering: "We rejoice in our sufferings, knowing that suffering produces endurance, and endurance produces character, and character produces hope, and hope does not disappoint us" (RSV). The same writer offers Abraham as an example of someone who "grew strong in his faith" as he went through the test of waiting twenty-five years for the birth of his promised son (Rom 4:20 RSV).

See also Cross Before Crown; Ordeal, Stories of; Tempter, Temptation; Trial.

THAT DAY. *See* Day, Day of the Lord.

THEATER

The only incident recorded in the Bible as taking place in a theater is the riot that Demetrius, an idol maker, provoked against Paul in Ephesus (Acts 19:29, 31). However, theater is also used figuratively in the New Testament. In 1 Corinthians 4:9 Paul says that the apostles "have been made a spectacle to the world, both to angels and to men" (NKJV). The Greek word for "spectacle" is *theatron*, the same word used for the theater in Acts 19. In Hebrews 10:33 the Greek term for Hebrew believers who "were made a spectacle" (NKJV) is *theatrizō*. In both of these passages the emphasis is on how the persecutions of believers make them a show or a theater of faith, to the world and to the angels.

Other miscellaneous theatrical effects are present in the NT as well. A Greek play, Menander's *Thais*, is the source of Paul's quoted proverb that "evil company corrupts good habits" (1 Cor 15:33 NKJV). The *"hypocrite" epithet that Jesus tossed scornfully toward his antagonists is based on the Greek word for "actor," with its meaning of pretending to be something that one is not. When Peter exhorts his audience to "add" faith to their virtue (2 Pet 1:5), he uses the word that was used of wealthy patrons who paid for the costumes and equipment of an acting troupe. What we are to picture, therefore, is extravagant endowment and equipping—an outfitting of oneself with virtue the way patrons equipped a group of actors.

We can find dramatic performers in the Bible among the OT prophets who engaged in what today we would call street theater. Ezekiel performs the upcoming siege of Jerusalem with a model of the city and by acting out the citizens' future deprivations (Ezek 4—5; 12). Hosea's marriage to Gomer, Isaiah's three years of nakedness representing the future of Egypt (Is 20:1-6) and Agabus's binding of himself to represent Paul's subjugation (Acts 21:11) are other symbolic prophetic performances. The master of such theater was Jeremiah (Jer 13:1-7; 17:19-27; 19; 27; 32:1-25; 51:59-64).

Writers of at least three books of the Bible may have composed their work with theatrical models in mind. The book of *Job is constructed out of dialogues, as dramas are, and has a dramatic prologue and epilogue. Job's friends, moreover, function as the chorus of ancient theatrical performances. The book of *Mark has been found to resemble Greek tragedy following Aristotelian norms (Bilezikian). These norms include a prologue (Mk 1:1-15), complications (Mk 1:16—8:26), a recognition scene (Peter's confession, Mk 8:27-30) and a reversal of the fortunes of the leading character followed by the denouement (Mk 8:31—16:8). The book of *Revelation likely shows the influence of Greek theater. It is filled with dramatized scenes and dialogue, characters and events placed in elaborately embellished settings, the costuming of characters, and ritualistic movement of characters, as though stage managed.

Other biblical passages have dramatic qualities. The *Song of Songs, for example, contains an abundance of dialogue, and the characters are characteristically placed in specific settings (in fact, dramatic theories and even dramatizations have been offered throughout the history of this book's interpretation). The Songs of Ascent, Psalms 120—34, were performed by Hebrew pilgrims on the way to Jerusalem to celebrate their traditional feasts. Psalm 124:1 and Psalm 129:1 have instructions for the participation of the pilgrims. Other passages suggest possible actions to accompany the recital of the songs: "I will lift up my eyes to the hills—From whence comes my help? My help comes from the LORD" (Ps 121:1-2 NKJV).

More generally, it is useful to be aware of how strongly dramatic the Bible as a whole is. Everywhere we turn in this book we find an abundance of quoted speeches, snatches of dialogue, stationing of characters in a setting and *gestures by characters. While biblical cultures did not produce theater in its pure form, the dramatic impulse permeates the Bible.

See also CHARACTER TYPES; COMEDY AS PLOT MOTIF; HYPOCRITE; TRAGEDY AS PLOT MOTIF.

BIBLIOGRAPHY. G. Bilezikian, *The Liberated Gospel: A Comparison of the Gospel of Mark and Greek Tragedy* (Grand Rapids: Baker, 1972).

THEOPHANY

Theophany is derived from two Greek words meaning "God" and "to show." A theophany, then, is a manifestation of the deity. Appearances of *God mark significant events in the life of *Israel in the Hebrew Scriptures. Over the course of time, descriptions of the deity become increasing mystical and less personal, as the Lord's omnipotence and cosmic majesty are emphasized. Other ancient peoples created statues, paintings and other representations of their *gods. Perhaps because they were forbidden to make "graven images" (Ex 20:4 KJV), the Hebrews valued even more the verbal descriptions of encounters with their God they found in their Scriptures.

The Old Testament. Genesis describes a personal, familiar relationship between humans and God in the *Garden of Eden (Gen 3:8-11). As a result of the Fall, however, humanity is estranged from its Maker. Stories of encounters with the Lord are treasured and preserved in Scripture; writers often embellish and extend the work of previous writers, especially in the prophetic books.

Sometimes in the Hebrew Scriptures, God is personified in the forces of nature: "The LORD also thundered in the heavens. . . . And he sent out his arrows, and scattered them; he flashed forth lightnings, and routed them" (Ps 18:13-14 NRSV). The Lord is also described like a Canaanite divine *warrior: "You brandished your naked bow, sated were the arrows at your command. . . . The sun raised high its hands; the moon stood still in its exalted place, at the light of your arrows speeding by, at the gleam of your flashing spear. In fury you trod the earth, in anger you trampled nations" (Hab 3:9-12 NRSV). *Fire, *lightning, *storm and *cloud often mark these descriptions, along with *fear on the part of any observing the deeds of the Almighty.

The patriarchs. The accounts of the patriarchs reveal a more personal relationship between them and their God than appears elsewhere in the OT. When the Lord first calls Abram, he *says* to Abram, "Go from your country and your kindred and your father's house to the land that I will show you" (Gen 12:1 NRSV). A little later the Lord *appears* to Abram and says, " 'To your offspring I will give this land.' So he built there an altar to the LORD, who had appeared to him" (Gen 12:7 NRSV). The patriarchs often mark the spots of their encounters with God, as Abram does here and as *Jacob does at Bethel after *dreaming of a *ladder on which "the angels of God were ascending and descending" (Gen 28:12-19 NRSV); such narratives authenticated various sanctuaries.

A famous encounter between the Lord and

Abram occurs when Abram "looked up and saw three men standing near him" (Gen 18:2 NRSV). Gradually it becomes clear that one of these three is the Lord, who makes known his intention to judge the cities of *Sodom and Gomorrah. Abram then begs that the righteous be spared the divine retribution (Gen 18:2-32).

Some scholars consider only the most dramatic encounters with God, such as *Moses and the *burning bush episode, as theophanies. An intermediate phase in this process of encounters with the deity may be seen in *Jacob's struggle with "a man" who must leave at "daybreak." Jacob clearly considers the struggle to have been with the Lord: "So Jacob called the place Peniel, saying, 'For I have seen God face to face, and yet my life is preserved' " (Gen 32:24-30 NRSV). Furthermore, as a result of this encounter Jacob's name is changed to *Israel (Gen 32:28); name changes often follow theophanies (e.g., Abram/Abraham; Sarai/Sarah; and in the NT, Cephas/Peter; Saul/Paul), an indication of some profound spiritual change or *blessing.

One of the most dramatic theophanies in the OT occurs when Moses goes up on Mount Horeb: "There the angel of the LORD appeared to him in a flame of fire out of a bush; he looked, and the bush was blazing, yet it was not consumed." When Moses turned aside to examine this strange phenomenon, "God called to him out of the bush, 'Moses, Moses!' And he said, 'Here I am' " (Ex 3:2-4 NRSV). The danger inherent in encounters with the divine is made explicit later when Moses begs God to show him his *glory. The Lord replies, " 'I will be gracious to whom I will be gracious, and will show mercy on whom I will show mercy. But,' he said, 'you cannot see my face; for no one shall see me and live' " (Ex 33:18-20 NRSV).

Job. Another memorably dramatic theophany in the OT occurs in the theodicy of *Job. Having lost his children, his possessions and great wealth, his health and his reputation, Job persists in maintaining his innocence before the Lord, whom he begs for an explanation as to why such a crisis has fallen upon a faithful worshiper of God. Eventually he is granted a divine visit (*see* Divine-Human Encounter): "Then the LORD answered Job out of the whirlwind" (Job 38:1 NRSV). However, instead of giving him an answer to his questions, God asks Job a series of questions of his own: "Where were you when I laid the foundation of the earth? Tell me, if you have understanding. . . . On what were its bases sunk, or who laid its cornerstone when the morning stars sang together and all the heavenly beings shouted for joy?" (Job 38:4-7 NRSV). Thus the Lord reassures Job of his power to sustain him by a recital of the glories of his creation. "Then Job answered the LORD: 'I know that you can do all things, and that no purpose of yours can be thwarted' " (Job 42:1-2 NRSV).

The prophets. In the OT, God is always transcendent, apart from his creation, though it may reflect his glory and power. An episode with Elijah would seem to emphasize this point. The Lord tells Elijah to stand on Mount Horeb while he passes by: "Now there was a great wind, so strong that it was splitting mountains and breaking rocks in pieces before the LORD, but the LORD was not in the wind; and after the wind an earthquake, but the LORD was not in the earthquake; and after the earthquake a fire, but the LORD was not in the fire; and after the fire a sound of sheer silence" (1 Kings 19:11-12 NRSV).

Prophets frequently encounter God in *dreams and visions, as does Daniel in Babylon. After seeing four apocalyptic beasts, he watches as "an Ancient One took his throne, his clothing was white as snow, and the hair of his head like pure wool; his throne was fiery flames, and its wheels were burning fire. . . . A thousand thousands served him" (Dan 7:9-10 NRSV).

Elsewhere in the books of the prophets, theophanies are especially associated with the calling or commissioning of the *prophet as God's messenger, indicating that human beings have a vital role to play in the divine drama. For example, Isaiah describes his own commissioning in such terms: "In the year that King Uzziah died, I saw the Lord sitting on a throne, high and lofty; and the hem of his robe filled the temple. Seraphs were in attendance above him; each had six wings" (Is 6:1-2 NRSV). As the house fills with smoke, the prophet responds with dread before such a vision but is purged of his *sin and hears "the voice of the Lord saying, 'Whom shall I send, and who will go for us?' " Isaiah answers, "Here am I; send me!" (Is 6:4-8 NRSV).

Ezekiel's call is described in similar terms, with "living creatures," cherubim, as guardians of God's throne: "And above the dome over their heads there was something like a throne, in appearance like sapphire; and seated above the likeness of a throne was something that seemed like a human form" (Ezek 1:26 NRSV). The prophet concludes that "like the bow in a cloud on a rainy day, such was the appearance of the splendor all around. This was the appearance of the likeness of the glory of the LORD" (Ezek 1:28 NRSV).

The New Testament. Some scholars use the term *theophany* only in reference to the OT because of the NT's theology of the incarnation ("the Word became flesh and lived among us, and we have seen his glory, the glory as of a father's only son, full of grace and truth," Jn 1:14 NRSV). Nevertheless, it cannot be denied in a number of important passages in the NT the writers draw on the theophanic tradition to give emphasis to a dramatic moment. This is especially true of episodes in the life of Jesus when the Gospel writers make his divinity "shine through." As John explains, "No one has ever seen God. It is God the only Son, who is close to the Father's heart, who has made him known" (Jn 1:18 NRSV).

The life of Jesus. In Luke's infancy narrative he describes the heavenly message of the *birth of the Christ to *shepherds in the fields at night, using some of the familiar terms of theophany: "Then an angel of the Lord stood before them, and the glory of the Lord shone around them, and they were terrified." Quickly the *angel reassures the shepherds and presents them with "good news of great joy for all the people: to you is born this day in the city of David a Savior, who is the Messiah, the Lord" (Lk 2:8-11 NRSV).

The next important event in the story of Jesus' life and ministry occurs at his *baptism in the Jordan *River: "suddenly the heavens were opened to him and he saw the Spirit of God descending like a dove and alighting on him. And a voice from heaven said, 'This is my Son, the Beloved, with whom I am well pleased' " (Mt 3:16-17).

One of the most dramatic theophanies in the NT is the transfiguration of Jesus, which occurs when he takes three of his disciples with him "up a high mountain, by themselves. And he was transfigured before them, and his face shone like the sun, and his clothes became dazzling white" (Mt 17:1-2 NRSV). Seeing Jesus with Moses (representing the *law) and Elijah (*prophecy), Peter wishes to build a memorial of the scene. "While he was still speaking, suddenly a bright cloud overshadowed them, and from the cloud a voice said, 'This is my Son, the Beloved; with him I am well pleased; listen to him!' " (Mt 17:4-5 NRSV). Both the dazzling *light and the *voice from heaven emphasize the primacy of Christ.

The death of Jesus is marked in special ways, and elements of theophany are used for this emphasis: "At that moment the curtain of the temple was torn in two, from top to bottom. The earth shook, and the rocks were split. The tombs also were opened." When the centurion and his soldiers see these events, they say, "Truly this man was God's Son!" (Mt 27:51-52, 54 NRSV).

The *resurrection of Jesus has long been viewed as an event of the utmost importance, certifying as it does his divinity. Again, theophanic elements are used to describe it: "And suddenly there was a great earthquake; for an angel of the Lord, descending from heaven, came and rolled back the stone and sat on it. His appearance was like lightning, and his clothing white as snow. For fear of him the guards shook and became like dead men." Reassuring the *women who mourn Jesus, the angel announces that "he has been raised, as he said" (Mt 28:2-4, 6 NRSV).

Finally, Jesus' *ascension, apparently from the Mount of Olives, is described in familiar terms: "he was lifted up, and a cloud took him out of their sight" (Acts 1:9 NRSV). What follows conforms to the pattern of heavenly messengers who explain what has happened: "suddenly two men in white robes stood by them. They said, 'Men of Galilee, why do you stand looking up toward heaven? This Jesus, who has been taken up from you into heaven, will come in the same way as you saw him go into heaven' " (Acts 1:10-11 NRSV).

Other New Testament theophanies. Outside of the Gospels the most prominent NT theophany occurs on the day of *Pentecost, when the *Holy Spirit first appears to the gathered followers of Christ: "And suddenly from heaven there came a sound like the rush of a violent wind, and it filled the entire house where they were sitting. Divided tongues, as of fire, appeared among them, and a tongue rested on each of them." Being filled with the Spirit, the disciples are miraculously able to communicate with each other in their native tongues (Acts 2:1-4 NRSV), a reversal of the Tower of *Babel story (Gen 11:1-9).

Other NT theophanies include the dramatic conversion of Paul on his journey to Damascus, when "suddenly a light from heaven flashed around him. He fell to the ground and heard a voice saying to him, 'Saul, Saul, why do you persecute me?' " (Acts 9:3-4).

Finally, John's vision in Revelation, reminiscent of those of Isaiah and Ezekiel, is of "one like the Son of Man, clothed with a long robe and with a golden sash across his chest. His head and his hair were white as white wool, white as snow; his eyes were like a flame of fire, his feet were like burnished bronze, refined as in a furnace, and his voice was like the sound of many waters" (Rev 1:13-15 NRSV). John also uses the "four living creatures" found in OT prophetic visions (Rev 4:6).

In these ways the NT writers highlighted important events in the life of Christ and of the early church, drawing readily from the tradition of theophany found in the Hebrew Scriptures.

Summary. A theophany is an appearance of God. In a religion where artistic representation of deity is forbidden, verbal descriptions increase in importance. Even such descriptions, however, must remain indirect. Our survey has shown that biblical revelation provides a rich variety of windows to the nature of God.

Nonetheless, a handful of images are used recurrently through the Bible. The two most important of these are related. God often appears in the form of fire and smoke (or cloud). Fire attracts and frightens. It purifies and destroys. Smoke, on the other hand, conceals, indicating that while our glimpse of Godhead is accurate, it is also shielded. We learn true things about God, but our knowledge is never exhaustive. Of course the most dramatic and complete "appearance of God" is Jesus Christ. He is the very Word of God, who lived among us in flesh and blood (Jn 1).

See also ANGEL; ANNUNCIATION; BURNING BUSH; DREAMS, VISIONS; EARTHQUAKE; FACE, FACIAL EXPRESSIONS; FEAR OF GOD; FIRE; GLORY; GOD; LIGHT; LIGHTNING; SINAI; SMOKE; STORM; WORSHIP.

THESSALONIANS, FIRST AND SECOND LETTERS TO THE

The imagery most memorably associated with 1 and 2 Thessalonians is apocalyptic or eschatological in nature. It can be broadly discussed under the headings of arrival (which includes images of space and movement), sights and sounds, *times and *seasons, conflict and *triumph, *persecution and hostility.

The Great Arrival. The well-known image of *parousia*, which means "presence" or "arrival," is used of the Lord Jesus Christ six times in the two letters (1 Thess 2:19; 3:13; 4:15; 5:23; 2 Thess 2:1, 8). Parousia itself does not denote a movement or "coming," but the context sets the scene for us to picture Christ's coming from a place off the *world's stage. The term could be used in Greek literature to refer to the arrival of a deity, a ruler or an *army. The Thessalonians have "turned to God from idols . . . to wait for his Son from heaven" (1 Thess 1:9-10 NRSV), an event associated with the climactic moment when he will "descend from heaven" (1 Thess 4:16 NRSV). An associated movement from "below" is implied as the dead in Christ "rise" (1 Thess 4:16). Those who are alive, who "remain" on earth, are pictured as dramatically "caught up *[harpagēsometha]* in the clouds" to "meet the Lord in the air" and "be with the Lord forever" (1 Thess 4:17 NRSV). The word translated "meet," *apantēsin*, was used of a delegation sent forth from a *city to greet a visiting dignitary and formally escort him into the city. Here a scene of "horizontal" earthly diplomacy is recast on a vertical plane. Believers are pictured as meeting the *descending Lord "from heaven." The end of the story is sketched by the words "so we will be with the Lord forever" (1 Thess 4:17 NRSV), but the direction of this mininarrative suggests that the Lord's people meet him to accompany him as he lays claim to his earthly city.

Second Thessalonians fills in the picture of what will have transpired in the earthly city prior to the arrival of the Lord (2 Thess 1:10). A certain "lawless one" will have staged his own parousia, led people astray by his mighty works, signs and lying wonders empowered by *Satan (2 Thess 2:9), and taken his seat in the *temple of *God (2 Thess 2:4). At the moment he is active though "restrained," but when that restraint is removed (2 Thess 2:6-7), he will boldly exercise his deceptive power. But it will not last. His final episode will be his annihilation at "the manifestation of his [Jesus'] parousia" (2 Thess 2:8). With ultimate consequences of this weight, no wonder that Paul asks for *prayer that "the word of the Lord may spread rapidly" (or "run swiftly," *trechē;* 2 Thess 3:1 NRSV).

Sights and Sounds. Aural imagery plays a notable role in these events, but they are prefaced by "the word of the Lord" which has "sounded forth," or loudly rung out, from Thessalonica throughout Macedonia and even into Achaia (1 Thess 1:8). This proclamation of the gospel finds its counterpart in the arresting sounds that will attend the coming of the Lord: the "cry of command," the "archangel's call" and the "sound of God's trumpet" (1 Thess 4:16 NRSV; cf. 1 Cor 15:52). All these sounds accompanying the parousia evoke a scene of *battle and the coming of God as a *divine warrior (cf. Num 10:9; Josh 6:5; Judg 6:34-35; 7:20; Joel 2:1; Zeph 1:16; Zech 9:14). The brightest of visual images is of the Lord "revealed from heaven with his mighty angels in flaming fire" (2 Thess 1:7-8 NRSV). The imagery of *fire, recalling the description in Isaiah 66:15 of the arrival of the divine warrior, reinforces the theme of *judgment that accompanies this arrival of Jesus.

Times and Seasons. "The times and the seasons" (note the assonance of *chronos* and *kairos;* 1 Thess 5:1 NRSV) of these eschatological events are fraught with uncertainty. On the one hand the season of eschatological *harvest has begun, for the Thessalonians have been divinely chosen "as the first fruits for salvation" (2 Thess 2:13 NRSV). But believers must be prepared, for "the day of the Lord will come like a thief in the night" or "like labor pains come upon a pregnant woman" (1 Thess 5:2-3 NRSV). The image of uncertainty in a *thief's coming is well understood even today. Just when people are self-assured of their "peace" and "security," the thief arrives. The arrival of labor pains can be more closely calculated through recent developments in Western medicine. But we need only imagine ourselves a few generations back to appreciate the mystery and miscalculations attending the prediction of the onset of *birth pangs.

These images of indeterminate arrival trigger a series of contrasts between *darkness/*night and *light/*day. The Jewish sectarians of the Qumran Scrolls called themselves "sons of light" and their *enemies "sons of darkness." In much the same way, Paul refers to the Thessalonian believers as "sons of light and sons of the day, . . . not of the night or of darkness" (1 Thess 5:5 RSV). The metaphor is then extended: they should keep awake and not *sleep, stay sober and not get *drunk (1 Thess 5:6-7). The images of being awake and sleeping are elastic, however, for within a few sentences they signify those who are alive or dead in Christ, both of whom will "live with him" (1 Thess 5:10).

In drawing an eschatological line between light and darkness, Paul seems to be breathing the same metaphorical air as the *War Scroll* of Qumran, where the "sons of light" will battle the "sons of darkness." But where the Qumran sectarians saw the hordes of Belial in the thronging armies of Rome and the mass of apostate Israel, Paul enjoins the Thessalonian believers to be ready for a different sort of spiritual conflict: "put on the breastplate of faith and love, and for a helmet the hope of salvation" (1 Thess 5:8 NRSV).

Conflict and Triumph. The eschatological scenarios sketched in these letters have at their heart the theme of conflict and deliverance. The imagery of the coming of the Lord with his *archangels is mined from the OT imagery of the divine warrior who arrives with his *heavenly hosts to deliver his people and execute judgment against his enemies. In the final chapter of the biblical story, the people of God are a mixed group of Jews and *Gentiles, and the subjects of judgment are now unbelieving Jews as well as Gentiles. Thus the Thessalonian believers await the "Son from heaven, . . . Jesus, who delivers us from the coming wrath" (1 Thess 1:10). On the other hand, it is the Jews, who killed Jesus and the *prophets and have persecuted followers of Jesus, who now—like the Canaanites of old (Gen 15:16; Dan 8:23)—have "filled up the measure" of their *sins (like a measuring cup topped off) so that God's wrath is at last overtaking them (1 Thess 2:15-16). But believers are "not destined for wrath but for salvation" (1 Thess 5:9). The Lord is the avenger (1 Thess 4:6), and he will bring "sudden destruction" on those who reside in darkness (1 Thess 5:3-5; see Vengeance, Revenge).

The *day of the Lord will not come without a preface of *rebellion in which the lawless one "opposes and exalts himself above every so-called god or object of worship" and *seats himself in the "temple of God," the earthly symbol of the heavenly throne room of God (2 Thess 2:4 NRSV; cf. Dan 8:13; 9:27; 11:31; 12:11). Here is an eschatological recasting of cosmic hubris, the distillation of wickedness in a figure who is a satanic parody of Jesus, tricked out with wonders, signs and powerful manifestations that deceive his deluded and perishing throngs (2 Thess 2:9-10). The arrival of the Lord Jesus will bring his sudden defeat: he will destroy the lawless one "with the breath of his mouth, annihilating him by the manifestation of his coming" (2 Thess 2:8 NRSV). The imagery of destructive *breath draws on the messianic conqueror's victory portrayed in Isaiah 11:4: "with the breath of his lips he shall kill the wicked" (NRSV). The accompanying image of annihilation by powerful "manifestation" captures the OT pictures of the destructive potential of a divine theophany in the context of judgment.

Persecution and Hostility. Apocalyptic conflict and divine victory are the culmination of a process that is already under way. Images of conflict and *hardship are woven into these letters. The Thessalonians, like the apostle, his fellow missionaries and believers residing in Judea, are under persecution. The gospel was first preached under "great opposition" (1 Thess 2:2 NRSV) at Thessalonica, and the Thessalonian believers *suffered at the hands of their compatriots (1 Thess 2:14). Their suffering is a piece of a broader fabric. They should not be "shaken by these persecutions" but continue to "stand firm" (1 Thess 3:3, 8); they were forewarned of this work of the "tempter" (1 Thess 3:4-5), who earlier is said to have "blocked" the way (1 Thess 2:18) of Paul's attempts to revisit the Thessalonians. Now they are encouraged to maintain their identity as *children of the light and of the day, to put on the *breastplate and helmet and to "build each other up" (1 Thess 5:5, 8, 11).

In the second letter we find that Paul has been boasting among other *churches of the Thessalonians' steadfastness and *faith in the face of persecution and affliction (2 Thess 1:4). The Thessalonians should pray that Paul and his fellow missionaries might be "rescued from wicked and evil people" (2 Thess 3:2 NRSV), and Paul prays that the Thessalonians themselves will be *strengthened and guarded "from the evil one" (2 Thess 3:3 NRSV).

The overall image is of a community of believers who are under fire and are best encouraged by seeing themselves as soldiers in conflict who must maintain their strength, defense and sure hope in the final outcome of the *battle. The urgent correction that the victorious "day of the Lord" is *not* "already here"—despite reputed dispatches from the front (2 Thess 2:2 NRSV)—reinforces the broader image of a sustained conflict that has not yet reached its climax.

Images of Family. Paul frequently invokes the language of *family relationships when writing to his congregations. A pervasive Pauline image is applied also to the Thessalonians: they are his *adelphoi* (literally, "brothers"), a term of spiritual sibling relationship in Christ that is well rendered "brothers and sisters" (NRSV). In this spiritual family they are beloved by God their *Father (1 Thess 1:1, 3; 3:11, 13; 2 Thess 1:1-2), who has given them eternal encouragement and hope (2 Thess 2:16). Paul himself dealt with the Thessalonians "like a father with his children, urging and encouraging . . . and pleading" that they live lives worthy of their calling (1 Thess 2:11-12 NRSV).

More poignantly, he paints an image of himself not as a demanding apostle but as one who was "gentle" (*ēpioi;* some manuscripts have the less probably reading "babes," *nēpioi*) among the Thessalonians, "like a nurse tenderly caring for her own children" (1 Thess 2:7). A wet *nurse who is more gentle with her own *children than with others may be in view, but the focus is on a *mother's special tenderness as she nurses her own, gently lisping baby talk while holding the babe to the nourishing warmth and security of her bosom. Throughout this passage Paul contrasts his manner of ministry with the privileged and strident manner that he might have adopted as an apostle (and that was evidently practiced by some). The imagery of *gentleness was used by certain itinerant Cynic philosophers, who held it as an ideal in contrast to others of their colleagues who adopted a harsh style.

Paul's paternal and maternal imagery carries over into his recollection of his abrupt departure from Thessalonica (Acts 17:1-10): "we were torn away from you" (1 Thess 2:17 NIV). The term *aporphanizō* can be used to speak of children "orphaned" or, as here, of parents losing their children. Paul, the encouraging father and tender mother, had suddenly and painfully been removed from his children. In contrast with the first letter, 2 Thessalonians notably abandons this tender parental imagery as Paul adopts a more admonitory tone.

Images of Model and Imitation. The practice of imitating human exemplars, moral and otherwise, was highly regarded in the ancient world, and Paul instinctively uses the imagery of imitating concrete expressions of embodied faith to instruct and encourage believers. The Thessalonians "became imitators [mimētai]" of Paul, their immediate exemplar of joy in persecution (1 Thess 1:6 NRSV). But Paul was shaped after the prototype of the Lord Jesus (1 Thess 1:6). In fact there are other imprints of this prototype, for in their suffering at the hands of their compatriots, the Thessalonians have become imitators of the "churches of God in Christ Jesus that are in Judea," who suffered at the hands of their fellow Jews (1 Thess 2:14 NRSV). In turn the Thessalonian believers have become "an example [typos] to all the believers in Macedonia and in Achaia" (1 Thess 1:7 NRSV).

Typos in secular Greek can refer to the procedure of casting or striking a die on *metal, the product of that casting or die, or the impression that a casting or die-cut product makes on malleable material. A signet *ring is shaped by the typos of its mold; the ring's raised signet is a typos that leaves its own typos in wax. Typos in more abstract contexts comes to mean a model, prototype, pattern, impression or version of an original document. The Thessalonians, then, have corporately become a "striking model" of the transforming power of the gospel, for the heat of persecution has not cast a character of *fear and bitterness but of "joy inspired by the Holy Spirit" (1 Thess 1:6-7 NRSV), whose re-creative work in the community should not be extinguished or quenched (1 Thess 5:19). And in 2 Thessalonians 3:7 we find that Paul's laboring *night and *day is held up as an intentionally shaped model (typos) of *discipleship that the Thessalonians should obediently imitate (mimeisthai).

Images of Labor and Idleness. The images of Paul's "labor and toil," his working "night and day" and not being a "burden" to any of the Thessalonians (1 Thess 2:9 NRSV) are contrasted with images of idleness and living on the dole at Thessalonica. This imagery of labor is not focused on Paul's work of ministry so much as his practice of supporting himself by *tentmaking. The imagery reflects the realities of Paul's trade: laboring from early in the *morning to late in the day, working by *hands with tools, leather, fabric and stitching, seated in uncomfortable postures in a dimly lit shop. The *wages were enough for life's necessities (see Hock, 26-49).

Paul employs work imagery in commending the Thessalonians for their "work of faith and labor of love" (1 Thess 1:3 NRSV), in commanding them to "respect those who labor [in the gospel] among you" (1 Thess 5:12 NRSV), in encouraging them to continue to "build each other up" (1 Thess 5:11 NIV) and in urging them not to be weary in doing what is *right (2 Thess 3:13). But more striking is the forthright instruction to "work hard with your hands" (1 Thess 4:11). The reason for this instruction becomes clear: among them are ataktoi, translated "idlers" or "those who live irresponsibly," who need to be admonished. In 2 Thessalonians these ataktoi appear again as those who are "living in idleness" (2 Thess 3:6 NRSV). Now with even greater force Paul appeals to his own example, which they are to imitate: "we were not idle [ētaktēsamen], . . . and we did not eat anyone's bread without paying for it; but with toil and labor we worked night and day, so that we might not burden any of you" (2 Thess 3:7-8 NRSV). As if this were not enough, Paul lays down the *law: "Anyone unwilling to work should not eat" (2 Thess 3:10 NRSV). With a play on words that may be rendered in English, Paul addresses those who are "not busy" (mēden ergazomenous) but are mere "busybodies" (periergazomenous) who do not work, commanding and exhorting them "in the Lord Jesus Christ to do their work quietly and to earn their own living" (2 Thess 3:12 NRSV). Like no other Pauline epistles, 1 and 2 Thessalonians establish and reinforce a work ethic.

Images of Honor and Shame. Paul speaks within a culture in which men and women are motivated by *honor and *shame. It is instructive to observe some of the images of shame and honor that Paul employs to reinforce the standards of life within the family of Christ.

The honored value of believers is evident in their having been "chosen by God" (1 Thess 1:4 NRSV), a reality made evident in their spiritual work and labor (1 Thess 1:3). They are encouraged in the *path of honor to live lives worthy of their calling (1 Thess 2:11-12). Their imitation of the apostle and the Lord has increased their honor by making them a showcase for believers in Macedonia and Achaia (1 Thess 1:6-7). Paul does not seek doxa—"glory" or "praise"—from mortals (1 Thess 2:6). The Thessalonians are the emblems of Paul's hope and joy, and they will be his "crown of boasting" at the coming of the Lord, his "glory [doxa] and joy" (1 Thess 2:19-20 NRSV). It is to their honor that they contribute to Paul's honor, and they too will share in the honor of God's "kingdom and glory [doxa]" (1 Thess 2:12 NRSV; cf. 2 Thess 2:14).

The Thessalonian Christians' public shame as they are mistreated by opponents of the community of faith is translated into honor within the community, for this shameful path to true honor is the way first forged by their Lord Jesus (1 Thess 2:14-15), who will manifest himself in radiant *glory (2 Thess 1:9). In fact their persecutions and *afflictions contribute to their honor by making them "worthy of the kingdom of God" (2 Thess 1:5 NRSV). To shun praise from mortals and to abandon tactics of flattery and greed (1 Thess 2:5-6) in favor of gentleness and *hard work are badges of honor among the true apostles and people of Christ.

The way of honor lies along the path of living to please God. Shameful ways must be left behind. Fornication is to be abandoned in favor of learning "how to control your own body [or 'how to take a wife for himself'] in holiness and honor, not with lustful passion, like the Gentiles" (1 Thess 4:3-5 NRSV). Darkness and night are associated with shamefulness, for they overcome their subjects with drunkenness and sleep (1 Thess 5:4-7). Those who labor and lead in the community are to be esteemed with honor (1 Thess 5:12-13), and the words of those who prophesy are not to be despised (1 Thess 5:20). Idleness is singled out as the most shameful behavior in the Thessalonian community (2 Thess 3:6-13). Those who do not obey Paul's instructions regarding idleness and work are not to be shunned, not as *enemies but "so that they may be ashamed" (2 Thess 3:14 NRSV).

See also APOCALYPTIC VISIONS OF THE FUTURE; DIVINE WARRIOR.

BIBLIOGRAPHY. T. Longman III and D. G. Reid, *God Is a Warrior* (Grand Rapids: Zondervan, 1995).

THIEF

In English the general distinction is made between a *robber*, who uses the threat or exercise of force or violence in the act of stealing, and a *thief*, who takes the property of others by stealth, cunning or slight of hand. The distinction is not rigid, however, for in John 10:1-10 the images of thief and robber are parallel descriptions of the one who enters the *sheep pen, and the thief is described as a violent person, one who kills and destroys the *flock.

Stealth and cunning are inclined toward the darkness of night. Job considers those "who rebel against the light, who do not know its ways or stay in its paths" (Job 24:13). These include the *adulterer, those who break into houses, and the *murderer, who "in the night steals forth like a thief" (Job 24:14). The thief is double faced: one person during the day and another at night or in private. Operating in the darkness (a darkness quite unknown to many people today who live in well illuminated urban and suburban areas), the thief hopes to evade detection, capture and exposure to punishment and public shame. A thief may be found among one's closest companion, such as Judas, the disciple of Jesus, who was entrusted with the money bag and yet was a thief who helped himself to the funds (Jn 12:6).

Thieves are unwelcome intruders who secretly bypass the conventions of their society to acquire what is not their own. Avoiding the light and public exposure of day (Jer 49:9; Obad 5), they take advantage of those who sleep. Breaking into houses (Hos 7:1), entering through windows (Joel 2:9) and avoiding the gate (Jn 10:1), they bypass the designated entrance ways into private space.

The thief is usually one who secretly disregards the values of the community and so is despised. But even here a proverbial saying allows an exception: "if he steals to satisfy his hunger when he is starving" (Prov 6:30 NIV). The prevailing overtone of *shame, of loss of *honor, is accented by Jeremiah when he speaks of Israel "as a thief disgraced when he is caught" (Jer 2:26; cf. 48:27). The theme of national shame is epitomized when Israel's rulers are "companions of thieves," loving bribes and chasing after gifts (Is 1:23). A thief unveiled is a person unfit

for participation in the community. Job captures the ancient Near Eastern attitude as he describes his mockers as the sons of those he formerly disdained, "banished from their fellow men, shouted at as if they were thieves" (Job 30:5). The theme of banishment culminates in Paul's warning that thieves, along with drunkards, slanderers and swindlers, will not inherit the kingdom of God (1 Cor 6:10).

From the victim's point of view, the thief drives home the lesson that riches and material possessions are precarious treasures. Jesus instructs his followers to lay up treasure in heaven "where no thief comes near and no moth destroys" (Lk 12:33 NIV; Mt 6:19).

In some instances the image of a thief evokes the element of *surprise, with none of the negative overtones that are assumed elsewhere in the Bible. Jesus, urging his disciples to be "ready" for the coming of the Son of Man, uses the image of a thief arriving suddenly. And Paul echoes the image in warning the Thessalonians that "the day of the Lord will come like a thief in the night" (1 Thess 5:2), though believers, who do not live in darkness, need not be taken by total surprise. In Revelation Jesus warns, "Behold, I come like a thief!" (Rev 16:15 NIV). This is obviously not an image of Jesus coming to take what is not his own. Whether it be the church at Sardis (Rev 3:3) or believers in general, the image is intended to inspire wakefulness and preparation.

See also ROB, ROBBER; SURPRISE, STORIES OF.

THIGH

Thigh as a biblical image is filled with powerful connotations. There are often undertones of *sexuality or procreation. For instance, it is shameful for a woman to expose her *legs (Is 47:2), and the *priest's undergarment must reach down to the thigh, to avoid incurring guilt and dying (Ex 28:42-43). The patriarchs took oaths requiring an individual to place his *hand under the thigh of the person to whom the *vow was made. For example, *Abraham tells his chief servant, "Put your hand under my thigh. I want you to swear by the LORD . . . that you will not get a wife for my son from the daughters of the Canaanites" (Gen 24:2-3 NIV). Placing the hand on the thigh, so close to the genitals, would create a sense that the oath was being made in the presence of one's descendants, with them as witnesses to the vow. Other interpretations suggest that the powers associated with the loins are invoked in the taking of the vow, or that the *covenant of *circumcision is connected with the covenant established by the oath.

The association of the thigh and procreation is carried further in Numbers 5:11-31, which sets forth a test for a wife suspected of *adultery. If guilty, she will be *cursed with a swelling abdomen and a thigh that wastes away. The association may also be found in Deuteronomy 33:11, in which Jacob curses all who oppose Levi: "Smite the loins of those who rise up against him" (NIV).

Perhaps the most familiar association of the thigh

comes from Jacob's struggle with the angel in Genesis 32. Defeated by the *angel, his hip dislocated, he comes into a new relationship with *God, one of dependence on the Lord. This event was so significant that "to this day the Israelites do not eat the tendon attached to the socket of the hip, because the socket of Jacob's hip was touched near the tendon" (Gen 32:32).

Because the thigh is one of the choicest pieces of meat, it figures prominently in offering regulations. The thigh is presented during the consecration and ordination of priests (Ex 29:22; Lev 8:25-26), as a fellowship offering (Lev 7:32-34) and after a Nazirite's period of separation (Num 6:20). Because the thigh contains such choice meat, it is part of the Levites' share of the offerings made to the Lord (Lev 10:14-15).

In addition, one's *sword is strapped to the thigh for quick defense or attack (Judg 3:16, 21). Also, Christ's *name is written on his thigh and robe in Revelation (Rev 19:16).

See also LEG; VOW, OATH.

THIRD. *See* THREE, THIRD.

THIRD DAY

The nearly four dozen biblical references to "the third day" highlight the importance of this motif. Some of the references seem simply to be coincidental, as when Laban catches up with the fleeing Jacob on the third day (Gen 31:22), when David comes to Ziglag on the third day (1 Sam 30:1), when Jesus and his disciples arrive at a marriage at Cana on the third day of their journeying (Jn 2:1) and when cargo is thrown overboard on the third day of a storm (Acts 27:19). Physical conditions lead Jacob's sons to take vengeance on the family of Shechem on the third day after the adult males had been *circumcised and "were sore" (Gen 34:25). In the overwhelming number of occurrences, though, the third day has either a ritual or a sacral significance.

A minor motif is court rituals involving events on the third day. Joseph imprisons his brothers for three days (Gen 42:18). Rehoboam asks for three days to consider what his political policy will be (1 Kings 12:12; 2 Chron 10:12).

The third day has a ceremonial significance as well. At Mt. *Sinai the Israelites perform ritual purifications for God's appearance on the third day (Ex 19:10-16). The meat left from *sacrifices was to be destroyed on the third day (Lev 7:17-18; 19:6-7). We also read about purification by *water on the third day (Num 19:12, 19) and about sacrifices being offered on the third day (Num 19:20). When God heals Hezekiah, the king goes up to the *temple on the third day (2 Kings 20:8), and when Esther decides to confront the king with her plea, she asks for a three-day fast from her compatriots, after which she dons her royal robes and enters the king's presence (Esther 4:16; 5:1).

The motif reaches its sacral climax in the third-day resurrection of Jesus. In fact, a dozen NT passages refer to "the third day" on which Jesus was raised, with one of the references speaking of how Jesus "was raised on the third day in accordance with the scriptures" (1 Cor 15:4 RSV). At least two "third day" moments in the OT foreshadow the rising of Jesus on the third day: it is on the symbolic third day that Abraham comes to the mountain where he and Isaac encounter God and find a substitutionary ram that saves Isaac's life (Gen 22), and Jonah is released from the belly of the fish on the third day (Jon 1:17; cf. Mt 12:40).

See also THREE, THIRD.

THIRST

Living in arid lands without modern *water systems, the people of the Bible were acutely aware of the pains and perils of being without water. In the biblical literature thirst is often frightening and life-threatening, as opposed to the modern experience of temporary discomfort. The Israelites in the *wilderness complain to Moses, "Why did you bring us up out of Egypt to make us and our children and livestock die of thirst?" (Ex 17:3 NIV).

Thirst is a mark of our humanity, and so we see even more clearly Jesus' solidarity with us when he cries, "I am thirsty" (Jn 19:28 NIV), and dies following a *drink. The absence of thirst in the eschaton speaks of a new order radically unlike the present age: "Never again will they hunger; never again will they thirst. The sun will not beat upon them, nor any scorching heat" (Rev 7:16 NIV).

OT writers recognize that *God is the One who ultimately quenches thirst. Usually he accomplishes this through natural processes: *rain, *springs, cycles of growth and *harvest (see Ps 104:10-15). But sometimes he intervenes miraculously, as when he brings water from the *rock in the *Sinai wilderness (Ex 17:4-7). Such a miracle makes clearer what is always true: God alone is the source of all resources necessary for life.

God can withhold resources if he wishes, and Moses and the prophets remind the Israelites that God will punish them with drought and thirst if they break their *covenant relationship with him (see Deut 28:47-48; Is 5:12-13; Hos 2:2-3). Sometimes physical thirst is what turns people to God. In their distress they call to him, and he meets their need (see Judg 15:18; Ps 107:5-9; Jer 14:1-7).

Not surprisingly, thirst is often used figuratively in Scripture to represent spiritual dissatisfaction or the passionate quest for God. "Blessed are those who hunger and thirst for righteousness," Jesus proclaims, "for they will be filled" (Mt 5:6 NIV). Such soul thirst, though painful, is a prerequisite for spiritual growth, for people must want God before he can give himself to them. In Psalm 42 this kind of soul thirst is expressed beautifully: "As the deer pants for streams of water, so my soul pants for you, O God. My soul thirsts for God, for the living God" (Psalm 42:1-2 NIV; see also Ps 63:1: "My soul thirsts for you . . . in a dry and weary land where there is no water" [NIV]; Ps 143:6-7).

God desires that emotional and spiritual emptiness will drive people to discover his grace. Thus he pleads in Isaiah 55:1-3, "Come, all you who are thirsty, come to the waters. . . . Come, buy wine and milk without money and without cost. . . . Give ear and come to me; hear me, that your soul may live" (NIV). The thirst is not condemned by the Lord, but people's methods for satiating this thirst are often found to be wanting. Thus Jeremiah speaks of Israel's rejecting the best water available, a fresh water spring (the Lord), in favor of the low-quality water of a broken *cistern (*idols): "My people have committed two sins: They have forsaken me, the spring of living water, and have dug their own cisterns, broken cisterns that cannot hold water" (Jer 2:13 NIV).

In the NT, particularly in John's writings, it is Jesus who can quench our soul thirst. Thus Jesus proclaims to the woman at the *well, "Whoever drinks the water I give him will never thirst. Indeed, the water I give him will become in him a spring of water welling up to eternal life" (Jn 4:14 NIV). In John's vision of heaven in Revelation 7:16-17, an elder explains, "Never again will [the inhabitants of heaven] thirst . . . for the Lamb at the center of the throne will be their shepherd; he will lead them to springs of living water" (NIV).

In spite of the NT emphasis on Jesus' quenching our spiritual thirst, the parable of the *sheep and the *goats in Matthew 25:31-46 suggests that Jesus himself (the Son of Man in the parable) experiences a kind of soul thirst. The story illustrates that Jesus' longings can be satisfied only when his followers give *food, water, clothing, companionship or comfort to the needy: "Whatever you did for one of the least of these brothers of mine, you did for me" (Mt 25:40 NIV). Thus the NT echoes the OT in its insistence that God wants to fill both people's physical needs and their spiritual thirst.

See also CISTERN; DRINKING; DRY, DROUGHT; HUNGER; SPRING OF WATER; WELL.

THORN

In two dozen books of the OT and NT, thorn imagery pokes its way into poems, stories, histories and parables. From the romantic "Like a lily among the thorns, So is my darling among the maidens" (Song 2:2 NASB) to the threatening "I will thrash your bodies with the thorns of the wilderness," (Judg 8:7), Bible writers find varied uses for such imagery, but their references to thorns are *always* negative.

Some authors use thorn imagery in comparisons: "The way of the sluggard is as a hedge of thorns, But the path of the upright is a highway" (Prov 15:19 NASB); "Instead of the thorn bush the cypress will come up" (Is 55:13 NASB); "Like a thorn which falls into the hand of a drunkard, So is a proverb in the mouth of fools" (Prov 26:9 NASB); and Jesus' "Grapes are not gathered from thorn bushes, nor figs from thistles" (Mt 7:16 NASB).

Other writers capitalize on thorns' worthlessness, using them as metaphor for that which needs to be discarded or burned: "Every one of them will be thrust away like thorns" (2 Sam 23:6 NASB); "They were extinguished as a fire of thorns" (Ps 118:12 NASB); Like tangled thorns . . . they are consumed (Nahum 1:10); and "if it yields thorns . . . it ends up being burned" (Heb 6:8 NASB).

Some passages accentuate the negative aspects of thorns by associating them with thistles (Gen 3:18), snares (Prov 22:5), nettles (Prov 24:31) and briers (Is 32:13). Other texts reference thorns when mentioning punishment or *torture: "As pricks in your eyes and as thorns in your sides" (Num 33:55 NASB); "And the soldiers wove a crown of thorns and put it on [Jesus'] head" (Jn 19:2 NASB); and finally Paul's "thorn in the flesh" (2 Cor 12:7) to symbolize his personal torment.

It is significant to note that thorns are in some cases associated with the judgment of Israel's exile. Thus in Isaiah we read that Israel, God's vineyard, will be overgrown with "briers and thorns" (Is 5:5-6) and "all the land will be briers and thorns" (Is 7:23-25 NRSV; cf. Is 32:13; Ezek 28:24; Hos 9:6; 10:8). Here perhaps is an echo of the condition that befalls Adam when he and Eve are exiled from the Garden (Gen 3:18). When Jesus in his parable speaks of some seed being sown among thorns (Mk 4:18-19 and par.), he may have in mind the continuing condition of Israel being in spiritual exile despite its return to the land.

From Genesis to Jesus, from the prophets to Paul, Bible writers sprinkle thorn imagery throughout Scripture to emphasize their messages of punishment, worthlessness and nonproductivity.

See also BRIER; PLANTS.

THOUSAND

Thousand, whether used alone or in some multiple, clearly represents a round number for a large group. In some uses it appears that *thousand* is to be taken almost literally, as in "a thousand pieces of silver" (Gen 20:16) or, more likely, in "1,775 shekels" (Ex 38:28) and in dimensions of *land (Ezek 45:1, 3, 5-6; 48:8-10; cf. Rev 21:16).

Most often *thousand* represents the largest round figure that can exist in multiples for counting. The actual number may or may not be intended as precisely literal (see, e.g., the lists of the numbers of people in the various tribes in Num 1), yet the objective is to convey actual details. The numbers of soldiers in *Israel's and its enemies' *armies, the numbers of those killed in battles, and the numbers of members of the various tribes of Israel are typically given in quantities of thousands (a significant majority of uses in the Old Testament; cf. Lk 14:31; Rev 7:1-8; 9:16; 14:1, 3). Spoils of *war occur in multiples of a thousand (e.g., 1 Chron 5:21), as do possessions (Job 1:3). In many instances "about a" before "thousand" shows that a round number is intended (e.g., Ex 12:37; 32:28; Josh 4:13). The

Evangelist counts the number of men whom Jesus fed in terms of thousands (Mt 14:21; 15:38). The early church grew in multiples of thousands (Acts 2:41; 4:4). Wealth is given as thousands of pieces of *silver or talents (4 Macc 4:17; Mt 18:24; Acts 19:19). About two thousand *pigs met their *death in the region of the Gerasenes (Mk 5:13).

Thousand also serves as a nonliteral symbol for a large quantity. *Moses appeals for the numerical growth of Israel "a thousand times" what it already is (Deut 1:11 NIV). He promises that the Lord is faithful to those who love him "to a thousand generations" (Deut 7:9 NIV; cf. Ps 105:8). *God possesses the *cattle on a thousand hills (Ps 50:10). A *day with the Lord surpasses a thousand anywhere else (Ps 84:10), and those thousand pass by quickly, they are so delightful (Ps 90:4). Prosperous *vineyards are those containing a thousand vines (Is 7:23). Paul preferred five words of *prophecy to ten thousand in a *tongue (1 Cor 14:19). God's eternality means that to him the length of a day and that of a thousand years are virtually the same— they pass by equally quickly to him (2 Pet 3:8; cf. Ps 90:4). A thousand years also constitutes the time that *Satan is bound in the abyss, which is also the length of the millennium, the time between the two *resurrections (Rev 20:2-7). Most scholars doubt that John intends to specify the length of time strictly literally.

To summarize, *thousand* means "large quantity." It can indicate some precision— presumably Mark meant to distinguish between five thousand and four thousand who feasted as the result of Jesus' miracles (Mk 8:19-20). Certainly "twenty-three thousand" deaths in 1 Corinthians 10:8 indicates some specificity. *Thousand* may indicate relatively large numbers (cf. one *king with ten thousand soldiers versus another with twenty thousand; Lk 14:31). Or *thousand* can simply be "a very big number" with no intention to specify how big.

See also HUNDRED; NUMBERS OF THE BIBLE.

THOUSAND YEARS. *See* MILLENNIUM.

THREE, THIRD

Occurring in the Bible as often as it does, the figure of three is an evocative image, rich with connotations. On the surface it is simply a tidy number; partly due to its prevalence in literature, its familiarity to the reader can make it seem a more natural quantity than *two or *four. Thus the dreams Joseph interprets for Pharaoh's cupbearer and baker are rife with quantities of three (Gen 40:10), and Jonah is stuck in the belly of a fish for three *days and three *nights (Jon 1:17).

But the significance of three as a literary motif is not purely arbitrary. Three is the minimum number necessary to establish a pattern of occurrences. A single event can be pure chance; a pair can be mere coincidence; but three consecutive occurrences of an event serve as a rhetorical signal indicating special significance. For example, only after the Lord calls to Samuel for the third time does Eli realize that it is the word of the Lord coming to the boy (1 Sam 3:8).

Because the number three conveys a sense of significance, biblical episodes that occur in sequences of three often generate a sense of expectation; once an event has occurred for the third time, something new and unexpected is likely to happen. For instance, the angel of the Lord appears in the path of Balaam's donkey but is invisible to Balaam; when the donkey turns aside, Balaam beats it. After this episode has occurred three times over, the donkey suddenly speaks to Balaam (Num 22:28). Similarly, Elijah has a sacrifice and *altar on Mt. Carmel doused with *water a full three times before the *fire of the Lord comes down to consume it (1 Kings 18:34). In the NT, Jesus prays in Gethsemane three times over and each time discovers his disciples *sleeping; only then does the mob arrive to arrest him (Mt 26:36-47; Mk 14:32-43). In each of these instances the triple occurrence of an episode generates an expectation in the reader that a new and significant turn of events is about to take place.

Thus an episode occurring in threes is a motif that points to further developments yet to unfold. But three also conveys a sense of completeness or thoroughness to the episode itself; when an event happens three times over, the reality of that event gains emphasis. When Peter denies for the third time that he knows Jesus, it conveys the sense that he has denied Jesus utterly; the denial is seemingly permanent (Mt 26:74; Mk 14:71; Lk 22:60; Jn 18:27). In Luke's Gospel, following Peter's three denials is a parallel episode in which Pilate speaks to the crowd regarding Jesus' fate. Three times Pilate tries to release Jesus, and three times the chief priests and rulers reject him; this repetition indicates the thoroughgoing nature of their rejection (Lk 23:13-25). Then, following Jesus' *resurrection, he appears to his disciples. According to John's Gospel, upon his third appearance to them, Jesus asks Peter three times if he loves him, and each time Peter confirms that he does (Jn 21:15-17). Thus Jesus restores Peter's relationship to him in a manner that emphasizes the certainty of his restoration as thoroughly as Peter's earlier denial was emphasized. The threefold occurrence of each episode underscores its reality and significance.

Whatever the specific effects, the pattern of threefold repetition is recurrent in folk literature from all cultures. Examples abound in the Bible. Jesus told parables involving three stewards, three types of soil that are inhospitable to crops and three degrees of abundance from soils that produce crops, three invitations to a banquet, and three travelers who encounter a wounded man on the road. The book of Job is structured as three symmetrical cycles of speeches. Peter sees sheets filled with animals and hears an accompanying voice three times (Acts 10:16). In the annunciation story surrounding the birth of Samson (Judg 13), we hear the announcement from the angel and the prohibitions of the Nazirite *vow three times—by the angel to Manoah's wife, in her recounting of the event to Manoah and in a return visit from the angel. The Aaronic benediction consists of three pairs of statements (Num 6:23-24).

A related motif is three plus one, in which a common element occurs four times, but with a crucial change introduced the fourth time. Delilah's *temptation of Samson (Judg 16:4-21) presents the pattern in its pure form. Other examples include the fable of Jotham (Judg 9:7-15), the ascent of Elijah into heaven (1 Kings 2) and a formula found in OT prophecy and wisdom literature, "for three transgressions . . . and for four" (Amos 1:3, 6, 9, 11, 13; 2:1, 4, 6) or "three things . . . and four" (Prov 30:18-19, 20-23, 29-31).

The figure three also establishes a sense of finality and completeness in the account of Jesus' *death and resurrection. When Jesus rises on the third *day (see Third Day), the ordeal that he had so dreaded a few *nights before in Gethsemane is finished, and his victory over *sin and death is complete; three days is enough. Paul recognizes this when he declares of Jesus, "Death no longer has mastery over him" (Rom 6:9 NIV). Three speaks of the totality and sufficiency of the work of Jesus Christ. Here as well, the figure three connotes significance, sufficiency and completeness.

See also FIFTY; FIRST; FIVE; FORTY; FOUR; HUNDRED; NUMBERS IN THE BIBLE; ONE; SEVEN; SEVENTY; THIRD DAY; THOUSAND; TWELVE; TWO.

THRESHING, THRESHING FLOOR

Threshing was an essential step in the yearly *grain *harvest. After the cereals had been cut, it was necessary to separate out the kernels before they could be ground into flour. This could be done by hand by simply beating them out of the stalks using flails (Ruth 2:17). Large quantities of grain involved using threshing floors: open, exposed areas of hard or rocky ground. There the sheaves were deposited, and the kernels were crushed out under the hooves of an *ox or a heifer (Job 39:12), which was driven round and round the area. Mosaic law decreed that these animals should not be muzzled (Deut 25:4), for even the animals were allowed to share in the harvest, a fact used by Paul in his teaching about the support of Christian workers (1 Cor 9:9; 1 Tim 5:18).

Alternative methods of threshing were using the wheels of a cart or a threshing sledge made of boards studded on the underside with either sharp stones or the equivalent in iron. These were dragged over the stalks by the animal, with someone standing on the board. Some sorts of grain were too delicate for this method and needed to be threshed by hand (Is 28:27-28). The resulting mixture of *chaff and kernels were then winnowed by tossing them into the air and letting the breeze carry the light chaff away while the heavier kernels fell straight down.

Threshing was so much part of the process of producing food that, along with the *winepress, the threshing floor summed up harvest and therefore God's provision for his people (Deut 16:13; Joel 2:24). Conversely, empty threshing floors and winepresses spelled famine (2 Kings 6:27). Being conveniently located open places, threshing floors could be used for other purposes (1 Kings 22:10), the most famous being the site of the *Jerusalem *temple (2 Sam 24:18-25; 2 Chron 3:1). Threshing floors could also be misused (Hos 9:1-2).

Egyptians winnow grain (left) and thresh with oxen (right).

In an agrarian world like the biblical world, the threshing that accompanies *harvest is a supreme image of *abundance. The annual process of threshing had something of the quality of a social ritual, and during the time of threshing the threshing floor became a site of family and community activity. Threshing was sometimes done at night to take advantage of the winds. In addition, as the grain accumulated, it became necessary to protect it from theft. These dimensions explain why it was common for threshers and even their families to sleep near the site of the threshing floor.

Threshing was used as a figure of the violence inflicted by one people on another (Is 21:10; Amos 1:3), particularly in judgment (Jer 51:33; Mic 4:11-13; Hab 3:12). John the Baptist used the process to describe messianic activity (Mt 3:12; Lk 3:17). The instruments involved in threshing could, in turn, symbolize instruments of judgment (Is 41:15). The skills required in threshing mirror the divine intelligence in the way God handles people and nations (Is 28:24-29). The worthless *chaff represented anything useless or of no account, or anything that would pass away without trace (2 Kings 13:7; Dan 2:35; Hos 13:3).

The animals, because of the liberty they enjoyed in eating part of the crop, could represent a carefree attitude (Jer 50:11; Hos 10:11). The Christian mission was also described in terms of plowing and threshing (1 Cor 9:10).

Isolated references to threshing include the description of Leviathan, probably the crocodile (Job 41:30), the wise king's dealing with the wicked (Prov

20:26) and the Lord's gathering of scattered Israelites (Is 27:12).

See also CHAFF; GRAIN; HARVEST; WINEPRESS.

THROAT

This image of throat conveys powerful messages in the Bible. The number of instances in which the Hebrew term *nepeš* should be translated "throat" and not "soul," "life," "breath" or some such term is debatable and depends on the context. But in certain cases the meaning "throat" seems clear. The throat is one of the most sensitive areas of the human *body, and any imagery using this symbol will therefore bring strong and vivid reactions from the reader or hearer.

At times the throat is said to reflect the condition of a person's *heart or soul. Psalm 5:9 states, "Their throat is an open grave; with their tongue they speak deceit" (NIV; see also Rom 3:13). Something as unclean as an open *grave so closely associated with an individual's soul would be appalling to a Jew. Not only would such persons be ritually unclean, but their very souls would be considered unclean. Jesus' words in Matthew 12:34 are given greater strength in light of this image.

A *dry throat depicts great tiredness or weariness. Psalm 69:3 and Jeremiah 2:25 depict people who have run themselves to exhaustion without stopping for rest or *water. They are intent on one thing only, and continue to run after it or call to God until that desire is satisfied. Psalm 69:3 says, "I am worn out calling for help; my throat is parched" (NIV).

Furthermore, the throat is an image of life, especially threatened life. Psalm 115:7 depicts lifeless *idols who cannot "utter a sound with their throats" (NIV), while Proverbs 23:2 and Jeremiah 4:10 speak of knives or *swords being held to one's throat, threatening one's life. The idea of life being found in the throat involves both the fact that two major arteries run along the throat and that living beings breathe and speak with the throat. Thus the throat is a symbol of vitality and life; to threaten one's throat is to threaten one's life.

See also BREATH; MOUTH.

BIBLIOGRAPHY. H. W. Wolff, *Anthropology of the Old Testament* (Philadelphia: Fortress, 1974) 10-14.

THRONE

The image of a throne is one of the most glorious and evocative in the entire Bible. It denotes authority, power, majesty and splendor. In the vast majority of cases, the Bible's references to thrones are positive, referring to the benevolent power and splendor attendant upon the human throne or—to an infinitely greater degree—the divine throne. The throne imagery conveys one of the most fundamental biblical motifs, that of God's reign as King (*see* King, Kingship). Many scholars have seen the kingdom of God as the one central, unifying motif in the Bible, and the imagery of the throne is fundamental to that motif. The term occurs about 135 times in the OT

and about 61 times in the NT.

Physical Thrones. In a small number of cases, references to thrones are to the actual physical seat on which a king sat. Several of these have to do with *Solomon's throne (1 Kings 2:19; 10:18, 18; 2 Chron 9:17, 18); one reference is to a throne that Solomon had brought out for his mother, placed next to his own (1 Kings 2:19). Solomon's throne was very impressive, inlaid with ivory and overlaid with fine gold; six steps led up to it, and its back had a rounded top. A *lion—a universal symbol in the ancient Near East of royal power and *authority—stood beside each armrest.

Numerous ancient reliefs show kings seated on their thrones (see *ANEP*), sometimes flanked by lions, as Solomon was (e.g., *ANEP*, nos. 332, 458). Solomon's throne was housed in the great Hall of Justice, which was paneled with cedar from floor to ceiling. Other scriptural references to physical thrones include Joash's (2 Chron 23:20), Ahasuerus's (Esther 5:1), the Ninevite king's (Jon 3:6) and Herod's (Acts 12:21).

Symbols of Authority and Majesty. More commonly, biblical imagery of a throne is evocative of authority, power, majesty or splendor.

Human thrones. Biblical references to human thrones most commonly refer to the kingly authority and power inherent in them. Thus reference to a king's throne or to his sitting on the throne signifies power and authority to rule. Such references include the thrones of the Egyptian *pharaoh (Gen 41:40; Ex 11:5; 12:29); Israelite or Judahite kings such as Elah (1 Kings 16:11), Ahab (2 Kings 10:3), Jehu (10:30), Joash (11:19) or Jeroboam (11:19); the Babylonian kings Nebuchadnezzar (Jer 43:10) and Belshazzar (Dan 5:20); and the Persian Ahasuerus

An ancient Persian throne and footstool.

(Esther 1:2). Human thrones are to be places of righteousness and justice (e.g., Prov 16:12; 20:8; 25:5; 29:14).

The Davidic throne. The most common reference to human thrones, however, is to the throne of *David (about 30 percent of all references to thrones). This has its basis in the great promise of what has come to be known as the Davidic covenant, in which God promised David that his descendants would rule in perpetuity on the throne in Israel. This promise was first given to David by Nathan the prophet (2 Sam 7) and is referred to many times after that: in 1-2 Kings and 1-2 Chronicles, the book of Psalms (see especially Ps 89; 132), Isaiah and Jeremiah (see Is 9:7; 16:5; Jer 13;13; 17:5; 22:4, 30; 29:16; 33:17; 21; 36:30) and the NT (Lk 1:32; Acts 2:30). This promise came to its ultimate fulfillment in Jesus, the son of David par excellence (Mt 1:1; Lk 1:32).

God's throne. By far the most common biblical reference to a throne, however, is to God's throne (close to 60 percent). God's kingship is affirmed many times in Scripture, and his throne is a visible proof of his sovereign rule. The Lord presides from his throne, surrounded variously by all the host of heaven (1 Kings 22:19; 2 Chron 18:18), a rainbow like emeralds (Rev 4:3), twenty-four other thrones (Rev 4:4), a crystal-clear sea of glass (Rev 4:6) and countless numbers of angels (Rev 5:11). His is a holy throne (Ps 47:8), glorious in its appearance (Is 63:15; Jer 14:21; 17:12; Mt 19:28; 25:31) and eternal in its duration (Ps 9:7; 45:6; 93:2; Lam 5:19; Ezek 43:7; Heb 1:8; Rev 1:8; 5:13).

It is a spectacular throne, variously described as flaming with *fire (Dan 7:9), glittering with sapphires (Ezek 1:26; 10:1), flashing and crashing with *lightning and *thunder (Rev 4:5), dazzlingly *white (Rev 20:11), from which flows a *river of living water (Rev 22:1).

Some thrones in Scripture are set up in opposition to God, such as the corrupt throne in Psalm 94:20, the royal thrones of *Babylon (Is 14:13; cf. Is 47:1) and Tyre (Ezek 28:2), and even *Satan's throne (Rev 2:13; 16:10). Yet these thrones represent no power or appeal when compared to the power and splendor of God's throne.

References to God's throne are found most often in the book of Revelation, appropriately enough, since this book describes God's final victory over Satan and the forces of evil. The royal motifs found throughout Scripture find their climax at the end of history in this image-laden book in the Bible.

See also AUTHORITY, DIVINE AND ANGELIC; KING, KINGSHIP; ROYAL COURT; SEAT.

THUNDER

Thunder is a vivid biblical image, appearing two dozen times. The meaning of the image is linked to thunder's physical properties as a force of terrifying power beyond the human, accompanied by *lightning and other aspects of *rainstorms.

The primal imagination links thunder with the presence, power and wrath of deity. In the Bible, accordingly, most references make thunder a manifestation of *God. Within this, four motifs appear.

Sometimes thunder is simply one of the forces of *nature controlled by God. Thus God "made a decree for the rain, and a way for the lightning of the thunder" (Job 28:26 RSV; see also Job 38:25). The preeminent example is Psalm 29, the song of the thunderstorm, where the metaphoric voice of God thunders as the *storm unfolds. Sometimes such divine control over thunder expands into the storm God motif, in which the focus is not so much a literal storm as a symbolic use of natural forces to picture the power of God. Thus the psalmist claims that "the crash of thy thunder was in the whirlwind; thy lightnings lighted up the world; the earth trembled and shook" (Ps 77:18 RSV).

A second cluster of images make thunder a symbol for the transcendent power of God. On the day of God's speaking from Mount *Sinai, "there were thunders and lightnings" (Ex 19:16 RSV). Job asks, "The thunder of his power who can understand?" (Job 26:14 RSV). The *voice from the *whirlwind challenges Job with the question "Can you thunder with a voice like [God's]?" (Job 40:9 RSV). In the little *creation story of Psalm 104, it is God's thunder that makes the personified *waters take to *flight (Ps 104:7). The equation of thunder with supernatural power also appears in the book of Revelation (Rev 6:1; 10:4; 14:2).

As an extension of the power of God, thunder is one of God's *weapons against his *enemies (*see* Divine Warrior). Thunder and *hail are prominent in the seventh *plague (Ex 9:13-35), for example. In the case of the plagues, Moses' ability to influence the presence of thunder by his prayers marks him as a holy person and his God as a powerful God. "I will spread out my hands in prayer to the Lord. The thunder will stop" (Ex 9:29). Hannah's song of praise claims that "the adversaries of the LORD shall be broken to pieces; against them he will thunder in heaven" (1 Sam 2:10 RSV). When God "thundered with a mighty voice . . . against the Philistines," they were thrown into confusion and defeated by the Israelites (1 Sam 7:10 RSV). Isaiah predicts that Israel's foes "will be visited by the LORD of hosts with thunder and with earthquake and great noise, with whirlwind and tempest, and the flame of a devouring fire" (Is 29:6 RSV).

Yet another category of references extends the power of God in the specific direction of divine wrath and *judgment against evildoers. For example, in the middle of Samuel's farewell discourse as Israel's prophet, God sends thunder and rain in the *harvest season so the people can see that their wickedness is great in asking for a *king (1 Sam 12:17-18). In one of the visions of Revelation, flashes of lightning and peals of thunder, accompanied by an *earthquake, usher in the final judgment (Rev 16:18).

The image of thunder in the Bible is based on a paradox: it is a force of nature that consistently images forth something beyond nature, namely, the presence, power and judgment of deity, evoking primarily awe and dread.

See also DIVINE WARRIOR; LIGHTNING; NATURE; STORM; VOICE; WEATHER.

TIAMAT. *See* COSMOLOGY; DEEP; MONSTERS; MYTHICAL ANIMALS.

TIME

With biblical references to "time" and "times" in contemporary English translations numbering anywhere from 738 (NRSV) to 887 (NIV), it is obvious that the Bible shares the Western preoccupation with time. Biblical writers, moreover, show a sophisticated and complex awareness of many different types of time. The claim can surely be argued that the Bible is even more oriented toward sacred time than it is toward *sacred space. As we unravel the strands in biblical images of time, it will become apparent that to biblical writers time encompasses much more (though not less) than the succession of events in this world.

Life Under the Sun: Natural Time. Most direct biblical references to time are neutral in association, denoting simply when something happens. Contrary to a common misconception that the Bible does not deal with cyclic time, many of these references imply an awareness of human life lived in terms of its *seasons or cyclic repetitions. We might profitably think of such time as natural time, rooted in the natural *creation.

This type of time is part of God's original creation. God's first act of creation was to create *light and separate it from darkness. Thereafter each of the days of creation concludes with variations on the formula "There was evening and there was morning, one day" (Gen 1:5, 8, 13, 19, 23, 31 RSV). Subsequently the Bible contains numerous pictures of daily life based on the cycle of *morning and *evening, *day and *night, all of them based on the premise of a twenty-four-hour day resulting from the daily course of the sun. Psalm 104 portrays the provisions God has made for the world by his creation, and the specific provision that the sun and moon confer on the world is time (Ps 104:19-23)— the orderly alternation between *darkness and *light, with corresponding actions ascribed to animals and humans. Nearly two thousand biblical references to "day" and "days" attests the extent to which the daily cycle organizes people universally.

A second cycle of life is the week of *seven days. It too is rooted in God's creation of the world, with a seventh day of rest completing six days of work (Gen 2:1-3; Ex 20:8-11). To divide human life into the week as a unit of time, so common in contemporary life (we think of many activities as occurring "once a week"), is thus of very ancient lineage, with Hebrew life built solidly around an inviolable *sabbath. As an extension of the weekly cycle we find over 250 biblical references to the month or "new *moon." As with many of the references to days and weeks, a particular concentration of references to the month occur in connection with the Mosaic religious rituals, suggesting an aura of the sacred that surrounded the most common units of time for believers in biblical times.

Third, the annual cycle was a prominent ordering device for biblical societies built around *farming. The year itself was based on an agrarian cycle of *sowing or planting, growth and *harvest. The annual religious *festivals were linked to this vegetative cycle. The 750 biblical references to the year confirm the extent to which the biblical mind thought in terms of the annual cycle as a unit of time.

A final unit of cyclic time in the Bible is the life cycle of the individual. It follows a pattern from birth to death. There is even a conventional norm for a full cycle of life—threescore years and ten (Ps 90:10). In the Bible the awareness of the human life cycle is accentuated by a strong awareness of the generations' succeeding each other, as in the genealogies and the assertion in Ecclesiastes 1:4 that "a generation goes, and a generation comes" (RSV; cf. Ps 78:5-7).

In view of the foregoing, we can see how misleading are some of the claims that the Bible does not encourage a cyclic view of time. From start to finish, the Bible measures time in terms of recurrence and repetition. This is, in fact, one of the prime biblical images for human and divine order, pattern and design. The godly life is in part a life ordered by the natural units of time, invested with sacred significance partly by being linked to religious practices and rituals. This is not to say that the biblical concept of time as cyclic partakes of pagan beliefs in a natural religion based on the dying and resurrected year. Instead we can picture the biblical concept of cyclic time as being rooted in a *covenant relationship with God, who prescribes appointed times for spiritual duties.

The Bible's distinction is not between cyclic and linear conceptions of time but between cyclic time as fallen and as redeemed. *Ecclesiastes is the classic text on the subject. The cycles of natural and human life are in themselves meaningless, leading nowhere and investing human life with a quality of utmost monotony (Eccles 1:4-11). But it is possible to see these same cycles as positive, from both a human and a divine perspective. The most famous biblical comment on time is the poem on the subject of "a time for everything" (Eccles 3:1-8). Here is a memorable portrait of life under the *sun, arranged in a cyclic pattern. The tone is positive, with the keynotes being timeliness, resignation and acceptance of time as the arena of human activity, buttressed by the assurance that God "has made everything beautiful in its time" (Eccles 3:11). Ecclesiastes also gives us a God's-eye view of time (Eccles 1:10-22). We learn here that time is God's gift to the human race (Eccles 1:10-11), that God has implanted within the human mind a capacity for transcendence of time (Eccles 1:11), that the proper human response to time is to enjoy it (Eccles 1:12-13; 22), that the limitations imposed on people by time is for the purpose of instilling reverence before God (Eccles 1:14-15) and that time is the arena within which God tests people's spiritual identity and in which they determine their eternal destiny (Eccles 1:16-21).

It is wrong to claim, therefore, that the Bible discourages us from viewing time in cyclic terms; instead it offers the possibility of investing such earthly time with a transcendent and even divine perspective and significance. It is a mark of human wisdom to "know the time" for performing a human act (Eccles 8:5) and to be among those who know the times (Esther 1:13). The writer of Psalm 90 concludes a moving portrait of the mutability of human life in a time-bound world with the prayer that God will "so teach us to number our days that we may get a heart of wisdom" (Ps 90:12 RSV). Using time well is above all a matter of "redeeming the time" (Eph 5:16 KJV) or "making the most of the time," within a context of urgency provided by the knowledge that "the days are evil."

We might note finally an important byproduct of the way the Bible continuously shows people living in the ordinary, earth-bound cycles of time. As this dictionary shows in myriad ways, biblical faith in God does not remove people from earthly life and whisk them away to some ethereal spiritual realm. Instead the great spiritual issues are resolved in the earthly flow of things. Belief in God does not raise a person above the routines of life, but it brings the transcendent into those routines with the promise of redeeming them.

Historical Time. In addition to measuring time in terms of the natural cycles, biblical writers arrange life into historical eras. This too is a way of patterning time. The genealogies are an obvious example of the impulse. The book of Genesis arranges its chronology of the early history of the human race and the covenant line in a series of ten "generations" (Gen 2:4; 5:1; 6:9; 10:1; 11:10; 11:27; 25:12; 25:19; 36:1; 37:1). Biblical narrative generally relates events to a chronological scheme. Sometimes the chronology focuses on the personal life of a person: "Abram was seventy-five years old when he departed from Haran" (Gen 12:4 RSV). In the court histories, time is marked off by the reigns of national rulers: "in the fifth year of Joram the son of Ahab, king of Israel, Jehoram . . . began to reign" (2 Kings 8:16 RSV); "in the first year of Cyrus king of Persia" (Ezra 1:1 RSV); "when Quirinius was governor of Syria" (Lk 2:2 RSV).

Here too, a main lesson is simply the seriousness with which the Bible regards human life in this world. Additionally, by so consistently rooting events in space-time history, the Bible separates itself from the mythological impulse to situate events in a fictional realm that transcends the ordinary world. The Bible deals with real people who actually lived and events that actually happened. Finally, historical time is linear, having a once-only quality that removes it from the repetitive cycles of natural time. The only qualification necessary to make here is that sometimes Israelite history shows a cyclic pattern, as in the cycles of evil, judgment and repentance that pervade the book of Judges.

Kingdom Time. If the foregoing concepts of time are shared between the Bible and human experience generally, the Bible also gives us a complex of concepts that are unique to it. A series of related conceptions of time can be subsumed under the rubric "kingdom time," meaning they are related to a transcendent reality that is either above ordinary time or reaches down from a transcendent sphere to create a story of salvation history.

Prophetic time is evident in the prophetic books. It is a sometimes bewildering mixture of references to historical time, the natural cycles of days and years, and future messianic or apocalyptic events. It is a commonplace that time is radically telescoped in some of these prophetic visions, sometimes referring to an imminent military event, sometimes predicting events in the incarnate life of Christ and sometimes portraying events that will occur before the end of history and at its consummation. The orientation of prophetic time is to *the future,* whether immediate or distant, but the future is portrayed as having urgent implications for the present.

Eschatological time is a category within prophetic time. Its distinction is that it predicts what conditions will be like at "the close of the age" (Mt 24:3 RSV), at the end of history. Such time is a mixture of mystery ("you do not know when the time will come" [Mk 13:33 RSV]) and specific time sequences (Jesus' Olivet Discourse in Mt 24—25 contains a fully developed chronology of what will happen "then" or "after" an event). Eschatological time is not simply oriented to the future but specifically to *the *end.* Occasionally this is underscored by terminal imagery of "the last day" (e.g., Jn 6:39-40; 11:24) or "last days" (2 Tim 3:1) or "the last time" (1 Pet 1:5). Even without such imagery, we receive a strong impression as we read the eschatological visions of the Bible that we are being given a preview of final things.

Third, we find a time line that might be called *the time of salvation.* It encompasses messianic history and more. Central to this conception of time is a "great divide" that parcels out universal history into eras before Christ and after Christ, and personal history into before and after conversion. To read the messianic prophecies of the OT prophets is to enter a world energized by excitement and longing for what will be at some future point. NT writers live in an awareness that the time that had been predicted has now arrived. Jesus himself claimed that "the time is fulfilled, and the kingdom of God is at hand" (Mk 1:15 RSV), while Galatians 4:4 pictures Christ's birth as occurring "when the time had fully come" (RSV). More generally, NT writers view postincarnation believers as living "in these last days" (Heb 1:2 RSV) or at "the last *hour" (1 Jn 2:18 RSV). If the orientation of the OT prophets is futuristic, the focus of the NT is *the present:* "Behold, now is the acceptable time; behold, now is the day of salvation" (2 Cor 6:2 RSV). A similar division of time into "before" and "after," or "once" and "now," characterizes the life of the individual believer. "Once you were darkness," states Ephesians 5:8, "but now you are light in the Lord" (RSV). People who were "once . . . far off" have "now . . . been brought near" to one another in Christ (Eph 2:13 RSV), and those who "were once estranged and hostile in mind" have "now" been reconciled in Christ (Col 1:21-22 RSV).

A final dimension of kingdom time is the time between Christ's *resurrection and the coming eschaton. For want of a better term, we can call this *the time of waiting*. The NT church at every era is "between the times." It both participates in the new possibilities that Christ brought into the world and waits in longing for the consummation of redemption. On the one hand, Christians live in an awareness of "the mystery hidden for ages and generations but now made manifest to his saints" (Col 1:26 RSV). But on the other side, the creation and church "groan inwardly" as they wait for their final redemption (Rom 8:23 RSV). One of the surprising things about this interval of waiting is that NT writers regard it as a short time whose end will come quickly. According to 1 Corinthians 7:29, "the appointed time has grown very short" (RSV), and in the book of Revelation we read that Christ is "coming soon" (Rev 22:20 RSV) and that Satan "knows that his time is short" (Rev 12:12 RSV).

Summary. Biblical images of time are sufficiently complex to require our best efforts to keep them all separate. A passage where they all converge is 2 Peter 3. Peter writes this eschatological passage in an awareness of living in "the last days" (2 Pet 3:3). The scoffers he refutes base their skepticism about Christ's second coming on the cyclic succession of nature that has persisted since the creation of the world (2 Pet 3:4). But Peter in turn adduces historical events that happened once for all as a precedent for Christ's second coming (2 Pet 3:5-7). Peter also paints vivid pictures of the eschatological end of time that will mark the transition from earthly history to eternity (2 Pet 3:7, 10-11). He portrays the present age as being an urgent time for repentance and salvation (2 Pet 3:9) and a time of "waiting for and hastening the coming of the day of God" (2 Pet 3:11; cf. also 2 Pet 3:14). Permeating all these references to earthly time is the conviction that God is both above time and in control of it: "with the Lord one day is as a *thousand years, and a thousand years as one day" (2 Pet 3:8 RSV).

See also CREATION; DAY; END TIMES; GENERATION(S); HOUR; MOON; SABBATH; SUN; THOUSAND; WAITING ON GOD.

TIMOTHY AND TITUS, LETTERS TO

The three letters of 1 Timothy, 2 Timothy and Titus are commonly called the Pastoral Letters. Here Paul addresses his two trusted assistants chiefly regarding matters of internal church order. The major images and motifs of each of these letters bear a close family

resemblance and may conveniently be treated together.

Paul and His Pastors. *Paul.* Paul is imaged as a "herald," "apostle" and "teacher of the Gentiles" (1 Tim 2:7; 2 Tim 1:1), as well as a spiritual father to Timothy and Titus. In 1 Timothy his former religious zealotry is portrayed in dark terms—he was a blasphemer, a persecutor and a *violent man (1 Tim 1:13), the "worst of sinners" (1 Tim 1:15). But he is now a grateful recipient of divine *mercy (1 Tim 1:16) and an "overflow" of divine grace (1 Tim 1:14). He stands in eternal obligation to his divine Savior and benefactor, and discharges his duty as a head servant in the household of God.

*Suffering for the gospel is a hallmark of Paul's apostleship (2 Tim 1:8, 12; 2:9), and 2 Timothy presents a memorable image of Paul as *prisoner: he is a "prisoner of Christ" (2 Tim 1:8), "chained like a criminal" (2 Tim 2:9; cf. 1:16). To this is added the pathos of abandonment and desertion (2 Tim 1:15; 4:10), danger and impending death. At his first court defense there was no one to support him. All had deserted him, and only the Lord was by his side (2 Tim 4:16-17). In contrast, Onesiphorus "searched and found" Paul in Rome (2 Tim 1:17), but as Paul writes, only Luke is with him (2 Tim 4:11). Paul's endangerment is vividly imaged in his *rescue "from the lion's mouth" and his confidence that the Lord will rescue him from every evil attack and save him for his heavenly *kingdom (2 Tim 4:18). This rescue does not preclude *death, a death imaged as an imminent "time of departure" or as being "poured out as a libation offering" (2 Tim 4:6).

*Athletic metaphors provide a vivid retrospect of Paul's apostolic ministry: "I have fought the good fight, I have finished the race, I have kept the faith" (2 Tim 4:7). A victor's "*crown of righteousness" is being set aside for Paul, to be given on "that day" by the Lord, the righteous judge (2 Tim 4:8). All of this lends poignancy to Paul's plea for his beloved Timothy to "come soon" (2 Tim 4:9). He is to "come before winter" (2 Tim 4:21), when the shipping lanes will close, and to bring Paul's cloak, books and parchments (2 Tim 4:13). These few material possessions, left behind in Troas, evoke a scene of unpredicted itinerary, the need for the warmth of clothing, of companionship through the coming winter and the hope of a little remaining time well spent with books and parchments. Apostolic virtue and power are no hedge against human vulnerability.

Timothy. 1 Timothy has frozen in time the image of a youthful Timothy, one who must guard against being judged by his appearance and despised for his youthfulness (1 Tim 4:12). Paul regards him as a "true son in the faith" (1 Tim 1:2, 18; cf. 2 Tim 1:2; 2:1), but Timothy must maintain his role as leader within a delicate balance of family relationships in which he is an elder *son and sibling in the household of faith (1 Tim 5:1-2). Timothy is heir to a maternal heritage of sincere Christian faith evoked in the names of his mother Eunice and grandmother Lois

(2 Tim 1:5). This spiritual foundation is imaged in a firm faith rooted in his knowing "the sacred writings that instruct in salvation" since childhood (2 Tim 3:14-15). But heritage bears responsibility, and Timothy is not only to guard the "good trust" given to him (2 Tim 1:14) but to entrust it to other faithful people (2 Tim 2:2). With his youthfulness we find a vulnerability marked by *"tears" (2 Tim 1:4), but tenderness is no exemption from serving as "a good soldier of Christ Jesus" (2 Tim 2:3) and "suffering for the gospel" (2 Tim 1:8). A good soldier knows when to *flee and when to pursue: Timothy is to "flee" youthful passions and "pursue" righteousness, faith, love and peace (2 Tim 2:22). And as a minister of the faithful and sound word of the gospel, he must *"guard" what has been entrusted to him (1 Tim 1:14).

Titus. Much like Timothy, Titus is Paul's "loyal child," but his profile is more mature. Paul left Titus behind in Crete to "put in order what remained to be done" and "appoint elders in every town" (Tit 1:5 NRSV). Titus receives from Paul various directives on church order and controversy, and is expected to provide a model of "good works, . . . integrity, gravity and sound speech" (Tit 2:7 NRSV). He is to "exhort and reprove with all authority," and let no one look down on him (Tit 2:15 NRSV). Throughout this brief letter Titus appears as a faithful lieutenant who can be trusted to receive orders and execute them without pampering.

Our Great God and Savior. In 1 Timothy, *God is imaged as dwelling in transcendent splendor. Doxological language piles honor upon praise to God: "the King of the ages, immortal, invisible, the only God . . . honor and glory forever and ever" (1 Tim 1:17 NRSV; cf. 1 Tim 6:15-16). Christ too is radiant with the brightness of heaven that suffuses the story of a mediator who moves between *heaven and *earth: "There is one God; there is also one mediator between God and humankind, Christ Jesus, himself human, who gave himself a ransom for all" (1 Tim 2:5-6 NRSV). Remarkably, in Titus 2:13 we read of "the manifestation of the glory of our great God and Savior, Jesus Christ." It is quite probable that the titles "God" and "Savior" both refer to Jesus Christ (see commentaries for detailed consideration). In this case Christ, in his manifestation, is ascribed the highest divine status.

The bright imagery of *"epiphany" is a recurring motif in these Pastoral Letters. It is underscored in the hymn of 1 Timothy 3:16, with its alternating images of his earthly (E) reception (flesh, nations, world) and heavenly (H) exaltation (spirit, angels, glory):

He was revealed in flesh, (E)
   vindicated in Spirit, (H)
   appeared to angels, (H)
proclaimed among Gentiles, (E)
believed in the world, (E)
   taken up in glory. (H)
   (author's translation)

With this sovereign now ascended to heaven, his people await the "blessed hope and the manifestation [*epiphaneia,* "epiphany"] of the glory of our great God and Savior, Jesus Christ," (Tit 2:13 NRSV; 1 Tim 6:14). In 2 Timothy, Christ's worthiness of *worship—"honor and glory" (2 Tim 4:18)—is similarly evoked in the luminescent language of his "appearing," or "epiphany," both in the past (cf. Tit 3:4) and yet in the future (2 Tim 4:8) when his heavenly kingdom will be revealed (2 Tim 4:1, 18).

The images of Savior and *salvation are characteristic of these letters in a way not found in the other Pauline letters. In Titus the theme of epiphany is associated with God's timely and mighty action in Christ Jesus as "the goodness and benevolence toward humankind of God our Savior" (Tit 3:4 NRSV). In his benevolence God embodies the key virtue of an ideal Hellenistic ruler—*philanthrōpia* (from which the English *philanthropy* is derived), a love of his subjects. Christ has come "into the world to save sinners" (1 Tim 1:15) and, like God (1 Tim 1:1; 2:3; Tit 1:3; 2:10; 3:4), he is now hailed as "Savior" (1 Tim 4:10; Tit 1:4; 3:6). The images of God and of Christ as Lord, King and Savior (*see* Jesus) stand in implied contrast with earthly "kings and all who are in high position" (1 Tim 2:2), for Caesar too would claim the titles *dominus, deus, soter* (lord, god, savior). In 2 Timothy we find that God's grace "has now been revealed through the appearing of our Savior Christ Jesus" (2 Tim 1:10). Christ's entry into the world is through the focal point of Israel's story, the "descendant of David" (2 Tim 2:8). The work of this mighty Savior (2 Tim 2:10) is contrasted with human helplessness ("not according to our works," 2 Tim 1:9).

Accompanying the epiphany of the Savior is the theme of salvation accomplished. The characteristic Pauline tension between present and future is for a moment eclipsed by the image of the risen Christ (2 Tim 2:8) having *already* "abolished" *death (cf. 1 Cor 15:26) and brought "life and immortality" to light (2 Tim 1:10). Nevertheless, the future hope is maintained as we find that those who die with Christ will also live (the resurrection of the dead has not yet occurred, 2 Tim 2:18) and reign with him (2 Tim 2:11-12) in "eternal glory" (2 Tim 2:10).

Christ's work is not limited to past and future, for even now he is active, rescuing Paul from the *lion's mouth and evil attack (2 Tim 4:17-18), proving himself faithful (2 Tim 2:13) and "guarding" the deposit that he has entrusted to Paul (the meaning is disputed, see commentaries) until "that day" (2 Tim 1:12).

The Household. In the Pastorals the image of the church as the "assembly [*ekklēsia*] of the living God" (1 Tim 3:15) takes second place to the image of the "household of God" (*oikia theou,* 1 Tim 3:15). The household is first of all a relational image, a large and extended family including various associates and household servants known affectionately as "brothers and sisters" (e.g., 2 Tim 4:19, 21). But closely related is the architectural imagery of the church as *"pillar" and "foundation of the truth" (1 Tim 3:15). This evokes a building under construction (elsewhere a *temple, cf. Eph 2:19-22), rising up from the ground, with the *foundation and weight-bearing pillars built of the most reliable and enduring material to be found: truth.

1 Timothy is particularly characterized by its sustained attention to the qualities of leaders—called overseers/elders and deacons—within the household of God. A striking correspondence is drawn between the virtues of male household *leadership (including marriage and parenting) and the qualifications for leadership in the household of God (1 Thess 3:1-12). The listing of virtues and vices is also a significant feature of Titus. Behavioral concerns are to the fore in the ordering of the household of God, whether it be elders/overseers (Tit 1:5-9), *older men and women (Tit 2:2-3), *young men and women (Tit 2:4-6), *slaves (Tit 2:9-10) or Cretans. It is as if the reinforcement of virtue and "sound teaching" in company with "order" (Tit 1:5) serves as a hedge against destructive false teachers who threaten the believing communities in Crete. The charismatic gifts of ministry (Rom 12; 1 Cor 12) have receded into the background to leave a profile of the practical virtues of character.

In 2 Timothy we find members within the church likened to household utensils of *gold and *silver or *wood and *clay; some for special, or "honorable" (timē) use and others for ordinary, or "dishonorable" use (atimē). The context of this metaphor is a comparison between those who are faithful to the truth and those who have turned from the truth. Those who cleanse themselves will become "special [timē] utensils, dedicated and useful to the owner of the house, ready for every good work" (2 Tim 2:21-22 NRSV).

As in a large household of the ancient Mediterranean world, the welfare of extended family and associates is a concern. In 1 Timothy the care for *widows, women of a most vulnerable status, comes into view (1 Tim 5:3-16), and an established household ministry of widows emerges. Widows called to this service of the household of God are *married to Christ. For them to remarry a human husband would be a capitulation to sensual desire, a "lusting away" from Christ, a violation of their first pledge (1 Tim 5:11). The profile of a widow who qualifies for support and service is that of an esteemed matron in the household of God, at least sixty years old, a "one-man woman" who has raised her children, is devoted to prayer (1 Tim 5:5), has proven her *hospitality, washed the *feet of the saints and otherwise demonstrated her capacity for good works (1 Tim 5:9-10). Young widows, by contrast, are not likely candidates for the office, for they are susceptible to "living indulgently" and thus being "dead" even as they live (1 Tim 5:6). The ideal picture of a young widow is one who remarries, bears children and responsibly manages her own family affairs (1 Tim

5:14). She will escape the trap of living in idleness and gadding about as a gossip and a busybody (1 Tim 5:13; cf. 5:15).

The household imagery continues with a distinct portrait of feminine *beauty. It is defined not by braided *hair or *gold or *pearls and expensive clothes but by modest dress and the spiritual adornment of good deeds (1 Tim 2:9-10). True beauty is inward—like a "pure heart" (Tim 1:5)—and expressed in virtues such as faith, love, holiness and modesty (1 Tim 2:15). *Women are imaged as living their lives within the bounds of their culturally defined setting: learning quietly and submissively, maintaining their silence in the worship assembly and not exercising unseemly authority over men. A rationale is found in appealing to the archetypal figures: as man is to *Adam, so woman is to *Eve. But the godly woman carries the distinction of being "saved through the childbearing" (1 Tim 2:15; see Birth), an obscure image perhaps alluding to womankind's participation in bearing the offspring (the Messiah) who will crush the head of the deceiver, the serpent (Gen 3:14-16).

The household of God is forging a new society within society at large, and in this vein 1 Timothy subverts the world's meaning of wealth through memorable imagery. "The love of money is the root of all kinds of evil" (1 Tim 6:10 NRSV). Those who desire and pursue after wealth suffer a host of unforeseen consequences: falling into *temptation, becoming ensnared by a *trap, plunging into ruin and destruction, *wandering waywardly and being pierced with *pain (1 Tim 6:9-10). The pursuit of godliness as a means of "gaining wealth" is the occasion for a play on words: "there is great gain in godliness—with contentment" (1 Tim 6:6). But this is no excuse for withholding support from the minister of the gospel! Scripture provides a memorable image of the right relationship between a worker and the fruit of labor: "Don't muzzle an ox while it is treading grain" (1 Tim 5:18; cf. Deut 25:4). *Prosperity is put in its place by means of a brief sketch of life framed by a maxim: "We brought nothing into the world; we can take nothing from it. If we have food and clothing, we will be content with these" (1 Tim 6:7-8). The wealthy should not set their hope on "the uncertainty of riches" but on God. Their cultivation of the good life should be transposed into a spiritual key: to "share," to "be rich in good works" and to "store up for themselves a treasure of a good foundation for the future, so that they may take hold of the life that really is life" (1 Tim 6:19 NRSV; see Treasure).

Household Controversies and Interlopers. Life within the household of God carries its own tensions and subversive threats from adversaries, much of it centered on words. Some are led astray by "myths and endless genealogies," "speculations," "profane myths and old wive's tales" (1 Tim 1:4; 4:7) which subvert the household's story and purpose. This is "what is falsely called knowledge" (1 Tim

6:20). Some, like mariners who have lost their course, have "shipwrecked their faith" (1 Tim 1:19), and others have "gone astray" (1 Tim 6:21). Some, like branded slaves, have seared their consciences as with a hot iron (1 Tim 4:2) and placed themselves in the service of falsehood. Two individuals have been "handed over to Satan," under whose bitter tutelage they will "learn not to blaspheme" (1 Tim 1:20). In 2 Timothy we encounter Hymenaeus and Philetus, who have "swerved from the truth" (2 Tim 2:18 NRSV) and are "overturning the faith of some" (2 Tim 2:18), and Alexander the coppersmith is named as one who did Paul "great harm" (2 Tim 4:14). Then there is the damning image of those who are condemned as "having a form of godliness but denying the power thereof" (2 Tim 3:5 KJV). Spiritual danger is all around, and the household is to be on the lookout for "deceitful spirits," the "teachings of demons" (1 Tim 4:1) and the "snare of the devil" by which he holds people "captive to do his will" (1 Tim 3:7; 2 Tim 2:26).

In 2 Timothy we encounter a mini-daytime drama based on localized events: false teachers infiltrate households and take captive "silly women, overwhelmed by their sins and swayed by all kinds of desires, who are always being instructed and can never arrive at a knowledge of the truth" (2 Tim 3:6-7 NRSV). The point of this imagery is the character of these particular women, not of their gender.

Sound and Unsound Words. The crux of conflict is words—words that compose the Word of God and Christian teaching, and words that foster controversy and error. The verbiage of those in error is colorfully denigrated. It is "wrangling over words" (*logomachein*, 2 Tim 2:14), "profane chatter" (*bebēlos kenophōnias*, 1 Tim 6:20; 2 Tim 2:16), talk that spreads "like gangrene" (2 Tim 2:17), and "stupid and senseless controversies" that "breed quarrels" (2 Tim 2:23). These "myths" and "disputes about words" (1 Tim 6:4) must be opposed by a bulwark of "sound," or "healthy," teaching (1 Tim 1:10; 2 Tim 1:13; Tit 2:1, 8), a diet of nourishing words (1 Tim 4:6), the "sure saying" (2 Tim 2:11), the "good entrustment" (2 Tim 1:14), the "faithful word" (Tit 3:8), the "word of truth" (2 Tim 2:15) that is to be "rightly divided," or "explained," a foundation of "faithful" and "sound words" (1 Tim 1:15; 4:9; 6:3; 2 Tim 2:19). The elders/overseers that Titus appoints are to have a "firm grasp of the word that is trustworthy in accordance with the teaching," able to "preach with sound doctrine and to refute those who contradict it" (Tit 1:9 NRSV). But even apart from human involvement, the "word of God is not chained" (2 Tim 2:9). It is "God-breathed" (*theopneustos*, 2 Tim 3:16), an image evoking the memory of the *breath of life that God breathed into the mouth of Adam.

These images of established and sound teaching evoke a standard of truth by which persons and communities are to be ordered and identified. "Sound words" order lives of "good works." Titus

is to be "in all respects a model of good works" (Tit 2:7 NRSV), and although God has saved his people "not because of any works of righteousness that we had done" (Tit 3:5 NRSV), he desires his people to be "zealous," "ready" and devoted to "good works" (Tit 2:14; 3:1; 3:8, 14). Even the submissiveness of *slaves in the community is highlighted as "an ornament to the doctrine of God our Savior" (Tit 2:10 NRSV). This theme of encouraging good works resonates with the image of God as an instructor in the virtues of the age to come (*see* Teacher). In Titus 2:12 we read that the grace of God has appeared, bringing salvation to all and "training us to renounce impiety and worldly passions, and in the present age to live lives that are self-controlled, upright and godly" (NRSV).

See also CHURCH; SALVATION; WOMEN, IMAGES OF.

TOE

Of the thirteen times the image is used in Scripture, the most common references to toes are found in the rituals of ordination for *priests (Lev 3:23-24) and *cleansing from infectious skin diseases (Lev 14:14-28). Here the lobe of the right *ear, the thumb on the right *hand and the big toe on the right foot (*see* Feet) are marked with *blood (and *oil, for the person who had been sick). The foot often symbolically indicates the destination or inclination of a person and at times is a symbol for the entire person himself; thus marking the toe with blood or oil symbolizes either the consecration or the cleansing of the entire person.

Another reference to toes is in Judges 1:6-7: the toes are cut off King Adoni-Bezek when he is captured after battle, in the typical treatment commonly given to *prisoners of war; this relatively small *wound would disable a warrior and force him to crawl along the ground. Ironically, this is the same punishment Adoni-Bezek had dealt to his own foes (seventy petty kings). He died in Jerusalem, probably of infection brought on by his wounds.

Toes are also mentioned in 2 Samuel 21:20 and 1 Chronicles 20:6 in reference to a Philistine soldier who had six fingers on each hand and six toes on each foot; he was killed by King David's nephew after taunting Israel. In the book of Daniel, King Nebuchadnezzar has a dream of a statue whose toes are made of *clay and *iron, symbolizing the division of a kingdom (Dan 2:41-42), often interpreted as Rome.

See also FINGER; FEET.

TOMB. *See* BURIAL, FUNERAL; GRAVE.

TONGUE

Just as the words uttered by the tongue are symbols, so too the word *tongue* occurs frequently with symbolic import. These symbolic uses fall into four main categories. (1) By metonymy, tongue stands for the language used by the tongue. Glossolalia, speaking in tongues, is a subset of this use. (2) Tongue often points to an individual utterance, particularly, but not exclusively, in the wisdom literature (Psalms, Proverbs, Isaiah and James 3:1-12) and sometimes to the utterer. (3) Sometimes tongue refers to the shape of an object. (4) Tongue can convey nonverbal messages.

Tongue as Language. Most nations are delineated along linguistic boundaries (cf. Gen 11); therefore, tongue often means speaker group (Ps 114:1; Esther 1:22; Is 2:11; and many times in Revelation). Speaking in tongues (glossolalia) can refer to human languages ("tongues of men," Acts 2:11) or to ecstatic speech ("tongues of angels," 1 Cor 12—14). Glossolalia is a sign both of prophetic inspiration by the Spirit (Acts 2:4, 18; 19:6; "speaking mysteries in the Spirit," 1 Cor 14:2 NRSV), and of direct revelation from God (1 Cor 14:6). Tongues and communication are inseparable. This is why Paul insists that "tongues" should be interpreted: their presence in the church symbolizes God's intention to speak to his people. At the same time, however, "tongues are a sign not for believers but for unbelievers" (1 Cor 14:22 NRSV). Paul has just quoted Isaiah 28:11, where "tongues" signify God's judgment against rebellious Israel. So if tongues alone are used when unbelievers are present, they will only receive a sign of their judgment and will not hear the message that could save them (1 Cor14:23-25).

Tongue as Utterance. The tongue denotes the whole person, the abundance of the *heart out of which the *mouth speaks: "A man of perverse heart does not prosper; he whose tongue is deceitful falls into trouble" (Prov 17:20 NIV; cf. Ps 39:3). In the phrase "their tongue struts through the earth" (Ps 73:9 RSV), the tongue stands for the person. The propensity to allow the tongue to misrepresent the person lies behind John's exhortation, "let us not love with words or tongue, but with actions and in truth" (1 John 3:18 NIV). Expressions of love must be made real with deeds, not merely lip service.

Because the tongue betrays one's thoughts and attitudes, it also represents a lifestyle. "Your sin prompts your mouth; you adopt the tongue of the crafty" (Job 15:5 NIV) seems to focus on a way of speaking, but "your tongue plots destruction; it is like a sharpened razor, you who practice deceit" (Ps 52:2 NIV) points to a whole lifestyle. Such people can be addressed as "you deceitful tongue!" (Ps 52:4 NIV; 120:3).

The great power of the tongue finds expression in its characterization as a weapon for harm—a *sword (Ps 57:4, 64:3), *serpent's tongue (Ps 140:3), a deadly *arrow (Jer 9:8)—or an instrument to heal (Prov 12:18; 15:4). Nor is it hyperbole to admit that "the tongue has the power of life and death" (Prov 18:21 NIV). The unruly power of the tongue is most vividly expressed in James 3, where the tongue is "a fire, a world of iniquity . . . a restless evil, full of deadly poison" (Jas 3:6-8 NIV). On the other hand, "whoever would love life and see good days must keep his tongue from evil" (1 Pet 3:10

NIV). Alongside this negative emphasis, the tongue focuses the right response of praise toward God (Ps 51:14; 126:2; Is 45:23; Acts 10:46; Rom 14:11).

Tongue as Gesture or Shape. The Hebrew word for "tongue," when used as a verb, carries with it the negative associations and is translated "to slander" (Ps 101:5; Prov 30:10). But the tongue need not speak in order to harm. Presumably a mere human gesture, sticking out the tongue is a symbol of rude dismissal toward God (Is 57:4).

And finally, the shape of the tongue produces extended meanings: tongues of *fire (Is 5:24; cf. Acts 2:3); tongues of *gold (Josh 7:21); tongue of the *sea (probably the Nile, Is 11:15). The spit of land protruding into the Dead Sea was called "the Tongue."

See also MOUTH; TEETH; VOICE.

TORMENT

Biblical images of torment and the meanings readers attach to those images vary widely. Torment, *suffering and *torture are consistently associated with *hell and the *demonic. For instance, Jesus is said to torment the demons who punish those they inhabit (Mt 8:29). The eschatological images of the book of Revelation include pictures of eternal punishment for the devil and those who have aligned themselves with the devil, including very specific images of endless burning (Rev 14:10-11; 20:10; see Fire; Satan).

Perhaps even more familiar to readers of the Bible is the fiery torment described in the Gospel narrative about Lazarus, the rich man and Abraham (Lk 16:19-31). In this story, Lazarus the leper, after having been ignored by the rich man at whose gate he begged daily, is carried by the *angels to sit at Abraham's side (*see* Abraham's Bosom). The rich man goes to hell instead and, as he suffers eternal torment, begs Abraham to allow Lazarus, whom he can see, to bring him a bit of *water to cool his burning *tongue. Abraham reminds him that he received his good things while he was on the earth, that now their relative positions are reversed and that the chasm between them cannot be crossed.

In each of these instances the image of torment originates in a response to *sin or separation from *God. Moreover, each image emphasizes the eternal nature of this punishment, which is dispensed by God. The biblical writers present the burning lake and smoking sulfur of Revelation, along with the burning tongue of Lazarus, as a permanent, unchangeable situation.

While many people assume that Paul is the NT writer who provides the most terrifying images of hell, it is actually Jesus who (appropriately) pictures the place of eternal punishment. Jesus gives us images of a place "where their *worm does not die, and the fire is not quenched" (Mk 9:48 RSV) and of being cast "into outer darkness" where "men will weep and gnash their teeth" (Mt 25:30 RSV).

On the other hand, the Bible provides many images of torment that is, at least relative to the torment mentioned above, fleeting. Sometimes the torment originates with those who reject God yet have the power to inflict suffering on God's people (e.g., Ps 73). In many other instances the torment comes from on high, either as punishment for the wicked or as chastisement of the wayward faithful (e.g., Jer 25:27-38).

Perhaps the most compelling and complex image of torment in the Bible occurs in the book of Job, where a good man is tormented because of a bargain made between God and the devil, a bargain that the good and generous Job knows nothing about. After losing his possessions, family and health in the bargain, Job disregards the counsel of those around him and refuses to *curse God. In this instance the biblical writer gives us an image of torment that suggests both inexplicability (in stark contrast to the other images mentioned here, which suggest purpose and *justice) and divine sovereignty (consistent with the previous images). God authors all torment, these images suggest, and even the righteous may suffer.

See also CRIME AND PUNISHMENT; HELL; PAIN; SUFFERING; TORTURE.

TORTURE

Torture is the infliction of *pain on someone. The people of the Bible did not live in a gentle culture, and torture was common, especially in warfare. In the OT such *violence was a part of the Israelite nation's interactions with other nations and of their treatment of their *priests and *prophets. In the NT, *suffering figured largely in the lives of Christ and his followers, who suffered for the sake of righteousness. While the means of torture in the Bible are numerous and diverse, torture is often related to *beating and *death, and is used more often for the purpose of cruelty or the infliction of pain than for the eliciting of information.

Atrocities in War and at Home. In OT times torture was often employed in times of warfare, but despite its frequency, God was not pleased with it. When the king of Babylon defeated Israel, he "slaughtered the sons of Zedekiah [the king of Israel] at Riblah before his eyes," before blinding him and binding him to be sent to Babylon (Jer 39:6-7 NRSV). According to one interpretation, even David engaged in cruelty in warfare: when he vanquished Ammon he brought out the people of the city "and set them under saws, sharp iron instruments, and iron axes and made them pass through the brickkiln" (2 Sam 12:30 NASB; compare RSV, NRSV and NIV, which indicate forced labor rather than torture). His vicious treatment of Ammon was probably a response to the nation's own cruelty in warfare. At the beginning of Saul's rule, when members of the Israelites tried to make a peaceful treaty with Ammon, the Ammonite king would agree only if his army could first gouge out the eyes of all of the Israelites to ensure that they could never attack his people (1 Sam 11:2). Later, God judges Ammon for their cruelty,

condemning them "because they ripped open the pregnant women of Gilead" in the pursuit of their own gain (Amos 1:13 NASB). Damascus was an equally bloodthirsty nation: God condemns them "because they threshed Gilead with implements of sharp iron" (Amos 1:3 NASB). Thus in Amos, God judges several nations for their unnecessary cruelty, but the practice was nevertheless widespread in ancient times.

Individuals in Israel were also known to treat each other harshly. Some Benjaminite men "wantonly raped . . . and abused" a girl "all through the night until the morning" (Judg 19:25 NRSV). Many of the prophets were mistreated and even put to death. For instance, Jeremiah was beaten several times, was put in the stocks and was thrown in jail (Jer 20:2; 37:15). He describes himself as "a gentle lamb led to the slaughter," ignorant of the plots against him (Jer 11:19 NRSV). Hebrews describes the many OT heroes who suffered *persecutions and tortures at the hands of the unrighteous: "Others experienced mockings and scourgings, yes, also chains and imprisonment. They were stoned, they were sawn in two, they were tempted, they were put to death with the sword . . . destitute, afflicted, ill-treated" (Heb 11:36-37 NASB). Many prophets were stoned, such as Zechariah and those stoned by Ahab and Jezebel; Isaiah was sawn in two, and countless other men of God were ill-treated by Israelite rulers (1 Kings 19:10; 1 Chron 24:21). Thus even in peaceful times, torture was a problem in Israel.

The Cost of Discipleship. The NT mentions torture as often as the OT does; however, its references are primarily to the sufferings of Christ and his apostles at the hands of rulers who hated the gospel. In the NT torture often takes the form of beatings. The NT, though, focuses less on the details of the torture or beatings than on the spiritual implications, such as the fact that the Christian suffers with Christ and will receive a reward for enduring persecution. The NT is not the place to look for graphic depictions of torture.

The greatest example of torture in the NT was the *passion of Christ, which combined both physical suffering and the indignity of ridicule. Before Jesus was sent to Pilate, the men who kept him "spat in His face and beat Him with their fists; and others slapped Him" and ridiculed him (Mt 26:67 NASB). In addition, these men "blindfolded Him and were asking Him, saying, 'Prophesy, who is the one who hit You?' " (Lk 22:64 NASB). After Pilate's sentence, they put a purple robe on him and a crown of thorns on his head, spitting on him and beating him on the head with a reed (Mt 27:29-30). The crucifixion (*see* Cross) itself was another painful torture, and Christ's antagonists compounded his agony by further mocking him and giving him water mixed with vinegar when he asked for a drink (Mt 27:33-44).

Christ, who suffered such great rejection and torment, told his disciples that they too must expect such treatment. Indeed the early church was not received warmly in any nation in which it sprang up, and early Christians were subjected to torture. However, the NT Epistles contain few details about these sufferings; they focus more on the importance of bearing this suffering righteously than on accounts of the ordeals. Peter explains that believers ought to suffer just as Christ suffered, because it was Christ's suffering that brought them their salvation, and "by His wounds you were healed" (1 Pet 2:24 NASB). Peter notes that Christ faced suffering with quiet acceptance: "While being reviled, He did not revile in return; while suffering, He uttered no threats, but kept entrusting Himself to Him who judges righteously" (1 Pet 2:23 NASB).

Because he suffered so righteously and so generously for them, Paul considered it an honor that he and his brothers and sisters could suffer with Christ. He says to the Philippians, "For to you it has been granted for Christ's sake, not only to believe in Him, but also to suffer for His sake" (Phil 1:29 NASB). Likewise, Peter counsels Christians not to be "surprised at the fiery ordeal among you," because not only does it come for their testing, but it is a blessing to "share the sufferings of Christ" (1 Pet 4:12-13 NASB). Similar encouragements appear throughout the NT, aimed at keeping the church strong in times of persecution.

While few details of the gory tortures suffered by believers appear in the New Testament, a few can be found in or inferred from Paul's letters to his churches. In 2 Corinthians he provides a glimpse of the trials he had experienced in his ministry as he endured "far more labors" and "far more imprisonments" than other members of the church: "beaten times without number, often in danger of death. Five times I received from the Jews thirty-nine lashes. Three times I was beaten with rods, once I was stoned" (2 Cor 11:23-25 NASB).

While most biblical descriptions of torture allude to events that have already happened, Scripture does contain a few general references to a future torture that all sinners will experience. The descriptions of hell in the Gospels offer the first glimpse of this future punishment. For example, Christ tells a story of a poor man, Lazarus, who goes to heaven while his rich neighbor is sent to Hades. In Hades, a "place of torment," the rich man is in so much agony that he begs Abraham to send Lazarus "that he may dip the tip of his finger in water and cool off my tongue; for I am in agony in this flame" (Lk 16:24, 28 NASB). Abraham refuses, stating that an unbridgeable gap separates heaven from hell. The word translated "torment" in Luke 16:28 is also used to refer to the testing of metals by flame and beating. Elsewhere Jesus describes hell as a place of outer darkness where "there shall be weeping and gnashing of teeth" (Mt 25:30 NASB).

The book of Revelation provides an eschatological vision of the torments God will inflict on the earth and its sinful inhabitants. With the blowing of the seven trumpets seven plagues fall on the earth. The first four trumpets involve the burning of a third of the earth, a destruction of a third of the sea and its life, an embitterment of a third of the springs of fresh water, and an obscuring of a third of the heavens (Rev 8:7-13). While these trials clearly affect the people of the earth adversely, the fifth trumpet brings a direct onslaught of torture upon human beings. An angel is sent to earth with the keys to the bottomless pit, which he opens, letting smoke "like the smoke of a great furnace" billow out of it to obscure the sky (Rev 9:2 NASB). Out of this smoke terrible demonic locusts come upon the earth with power like that of "the scorpions of the earth" (Rev 9:3 NASB). These locusts are permitted to touch nothing but persons lacking "the seal of God on their foreheads," and "they were not permitted to kill anyone, but to torment for five months" with stings like those of scorpions (Rev 9:4-5 NASB). The anguish of the tormented will be so great that they "will seek death and will not find it" (Rev 9:6 NASB). Finally, the sixth trumpet is blown and a third of humankind is killed by a series of plagues (Rev 9:13-21).

Because the nations do not repent after the blowing of the trumpets, God sends seven bowls, or plagues, upon the earth. The first is "loathsome and malignant sore[s]" upon the people (Rev 16:2 NASB); the second the destruction of the seas; the third the bloodying of the earth's rivers; the fourth the scorching of people with fierce heat; the fifth great darkness that makes people gnaw their tongues in pain; the sixth the drying of the Euphrates; and the seventh a great earthquake and one hundred-pound hailstones to destroy the earth (Rev 16).

Finally, because the nations still do not repent, God will judge all evildoers in the last judgment. Anyone who worships the beast will "drink of the wine of the wrath of God . . . and he will be tormented with fire and brimstone in the presence . . . of the Lamb. And the smoke of their torment goes up forever and ever; and they have no rest day and night" (Rev 14:10-11 NASB). The beast, Satan and all the unrighteous from the beginning of time will be thrown into this pit of eternal torment as a final judgment on their sins. Thus Revelation concludes that though the peoples of the earth have inflicted incredible torture on each other, the ultimate torment of the wicked will be even more severe—worse than any human has ever attempted or imagined.

See also END TIMES; HELL; MARTYR; PAIN; PERSECUTION; SUFFERING; TORMENT.

TOUCH

Throughout the Bible is a recognition of the importance of touch to human beings—both the pleasure and reassurance and the sin and pain it can bring. Because God knows us to be material creatures, he communicates himself to us in concrete ways, but he also demands that we recognize the limitations and pitfalls of our temporal senses. Both positive and negative images of touch pervade the Bible.

Untouchableness as a Protection of the Holy.

The vocabulary of touching figures prominently in the OT Mosaic law (forty references in Leviticus, Numbers and Deuteronomy). In Israel's legal system the outward *purity of touch becomes a symbol for the moral purity of the heart which God greatly desires. God accordingly designates certain objects as *holy and other objects as unholy or unclean to the touch. Among the holy objects are the *altar and God's *sacrificial meats (Ex 29:37; Lev 6:27). God intends this material holiness to be so real to his people that he declares that "whatever touches the altar becomes holy" (Ex 29:37 NRSV). Equally powerful is physical contact with anything that God terms unclean: if any Israelites touched any of these objects, they must ritually purify themselves (Lev 5:2-3; 7:19, 21). Among unclean objects are carcasses, people with *diseases or discharge, certain *animals and anything sacrificed to *idols. The extent of these objects' uncleanness is demonstrated by the detail of instructions given in Leviticus. For instance, any person who has physical contact with a man with discharge, his bed or anything that is under him must "wash their clothes, and bathe in water, and be unclean until the evening" (see Lev 15:5-11 NRSV). Even an earthen vessel that he has touched must be broken due to the uncleanness it received from him (Lev 15:12).

Clearly many of these injunctions relate to sanitation and protection from disease. However, the detail of God's instructions about physical contact demonstrates how highly he values the internal holiness that these acts represented.

The Untouchableness of Deity. Deity is completely untouchable (even unviewable) in the OT. In the rituals of separation that are enacted before Moses ascends Mount *Sinai to meet *God, *Moses sets bounds for the people around the mountain, commanding them, "Be careful not to go up the mountain or to touch the edge of it. Any who touch the mountain shall be put to death. No hand shall touch them" (Ex 19:12-13 NRSV). When the *ark of the covenant is being transported and Uzzah extends his hand to steady it when the oxen stumble, God strikes him dead, frightening David so much that the ark remains stranded for three months (2 Sam 6:6-11).

External Touch Versus Internal Spiritual Reality. The overriding purpose of law in the OT is not physical purity so much as purity of the heart. God condemns his people for not understanding that just as they are unclean when they touch a corpse, so "every other work of their hands" is unclean (Hag 2:14 NRSV). In fact, God sees human sin as so serious that people are tangibly marked by it: "Blindly they wandered through the streets, so defiled with blood that no one was able to touch their garments" (Lam 4:14 NRSV).

In the NT, Christ establishes a new *covenant requiring purity of the *heart. Paul considers the old injunctions "Do not handle, do not taste, do not touch" to be superficial, "regulations [referring] to

things that perish with use," which have "no value in checking self-indulgence" (Col 2:21-23). To Paul the real problem is not the senses themselves but the human heart, which causes us to follow "the desires of flesh and senses" (Eph 2:3 NRSV). Therefore Paul calls Christians not to asceticism—the regulation of what can be touched—but to a regulation of the heart and its desires. However, he does not negate the power of touch.

The New Testament Reversal. Given the OT prohibition of touching the holy, one can scarcely imagine a more shocking reversal than we find with the incarnation of Christ in the NT. John tells his audience that he proclaimed to them "what was from the beginning, what we have heard, what we have seen with our eyes, what we have looked at and touched with our hands, concerning the word of life" (1 Jn 1:1 NRSV). When Christ rises from the dead, he offers his followers concrete evidence of the resurrection, asking them to "touch me and see; for a ghost does not have flesh and bones as you see that I have" (Lk 24:39 NRSV). Thus Christ is the meeting ground of the ethereal and the concrete.

The importance of touch is also seen in the performance of miracles, for often a miracle in the Bible is performed only by physical contact. This is not meant to demonstrate that touch is the only mechanism by which miracles can be performed or that this touch is "magical" in an automatic sense. Jesus performs numerous miracles from a distance. However, physical contact clearly identifies the agent of God's power, and the examples of this are numerous. In an unusual instance, even contact with the dead body of a prophet transmits miraculous power: when a dead man was thrown into Elisha's tomb, "as soon as the man touched the bones of Elisha, he came to life and stood on his feet" (2 Kings 13:21 NRSV).

The NT examples of touch are usually instances of healing and therefore suggest the individuals' being made clean in the OT sense of the word. The physical contact is one method by which Jesus and his disciples heal people, echoing the OT idea that anything that touches something holy, like the altar, becomes holy itself. Jesus performs several miracles by touch, among them cleansing a man from *leprosy, opening the eyes of the *blind and healing the guard's *ear which Peter had cut off (Mt 8:3; 9:29; 20:34; Lk 22:51). In fact, simply touching Jesus' clothing is enough to bring healing. A woman long suffering from hemorrhages has the faith to discover this, and subsequently all who touch the fringe of Jesus' cloak are healed (Mt 9:20; 14:36). The same thing happens with the disciples: "God did extraordinary miracles through Paul, so . . . handkerchiefs and aprons that had touched his skin" were used to heal the sick (Acts 19:11-12 NRSV). In both OT and NT, touch is an important method by which God uses his servants to heal and restore life.

Despite the emphasis on the accessibility of the holy, the NT does not, of course, eliminate the essential spirituality of life in Christ. The book of

Hebrews declares that despite the tangibility of Christ's coming, he is concerned with offering the spiritual reality of grace rather than the legal and outward law given at Mount Sinai. The author declares that the NT believer has "not come to something that can be touched, a blazing fire, and darkness," and a startling voice from the mountain which made even Moses tremble with fear and which prevented all from touching the mountain on fear of death (Heb 12:18-21 NRSV). Instead the believer has "come to Mount Zion and to the city of the living God, the heavenly Jerusalem . . . and to Jesus, the mediator of the new covenant" (Heb 12:22, 24 NRSV). While God's voice had shaken the whole earth before, his voice will now shake " 'not only the earth but also the heaven' . . . so that what cannot be shaken may remain" (Heb 12:26-27 NRSV).

The Touch of God. Having made touch an important element of communication of human beings' lives, God often uses it as a method of communication or comfort for his people. This touching takes both literal and spiritual forms. 1 Samuel 10:26 speaks of those who knew God as those "whose hearts God had touched" (NRSV). Jeremiah says that when he began his ministry, God "put out his hand and touched my mouth" to tell him, "Now I have put my words in your mouth" (Jer 1:9 NRSV). Several times when an angel appears to Daniel, he touches Daniel to give him strength after the burden of the vision, to enable him to speak and to stand (Dan 10:10, 16, 18). In a similar way God promises spiritual comfort to his own people and describes it in the tangible terms of touch: "I am the LORD, your God, who takes hold of your right hand and says to you, Do not fear; I will help you" (Is 41:13 NIV). Thus although many of the biblical reassurances speak in fact of spiritual comforts that God offers us, these comforts are so real that they are described in terms of touch.

God's closeness to his creation is described in similarly concrete terms. His might is expressed in terms of his power to make *mountains smoke at his touch and the earth melt beneath his fingertips (Ps 104:32; Amos 9:5). Indeed, God created all things, and the heavens and the earth are "the work of [his] *fingers" (Ps 8:3 NRSV). God was equally close to the creation of people. The psalms describe him as knitting the psalmist together in his mother's *womb, and Isaiah calls God the potter who is molding the *clay of his nation Israel into a work of his own design (Ps 139:13; Is 45:9; 63:8). Thus God describes himself as being so intimately involved with the workings of creation that he metaphorically touches it at all times.

Human Touch. Touch can be a great source of pleasure to people. Among other sensuous pleasures is sexual intimacy, a pleasure that the Song of Songs celebrates in vivid, poetic terms. The lover takes delight in his bride's *breasts, which are as *soft and symmetrical as "two fawns, twins of a gazelle," and in her luxuriant *hair, which captivates him like

purple threads (Song 4:5 NRSV; 7:5). In turn, she praises his solidity and muscularity, comparing various portions of his anatomy with ivory, alabaster and rods of gold (Song 5:10-16). They take delight in each other's touch: the bride enjoys "the kisses of his mouth"; the lover compares her to a *palm tree, whose clusters are her breasts; he delights to climb the tree and "lay hold of its branches" (Song 1:2; 7:7-8 NRSV). Joy in sensuous touch is an integral element of their relationship.

See also FINGER; HAND; HARD, HARDEN, HARDNESS; PURITY; SOFT, SOFTNESS.

TOWER

Although in literature generally the tower can be an image of intellectual contemplation and spiritual aspiration, the fifty references to towers in the Bible are virtually all to parts of a military *fortress. The main exception is the tower of Babel, which is less a defensive structure than a symbol of human aspiration beyond the limits God has imposed on the human race. In biblical times, four kinds of towers were used for defense, two associated with cities and two in the hinterlands. In the Bible we mainly find literal references to such towers, which occasionally become metaphoric for God and the protection that believers find in him.

A tower that was incorporated into a city *wall projected out from the line of the wall so that defenders could direct arrows and other projectiles at attackers along the base of the wall. Referred to as a "projecting tower" (Neh 3:26-27 NRSV), such a tower also served to strengthen the wall at intervals and at corners. The Israelites took satisfaction in counting the towers in the wall surrounding *Jerusalem and considered them testimony "that this is God, our God forever and ever" (Ps 48:12-14 NRSV).

The second kind of tower associated with cities was an inner citadel or fortress at the center of the *city and at its highest point (Judg 9:51). This was both a governmental building, such as a governor's palace, and a refuge of last resort to which the city's rulers, and perhaps the whole surviving citizenry, could flee when the city walls had been breached. It contained *storehouses (1 Chron 27:25) of provisions for withstanding a siege. No wonder David's Song began, "The LORD is my rock, my fortress, and my deliverer," and ended, "He is a tower of salvation for his king" (2 Sam 22:2, 51 NRSV).

Both kinds of city towers were topped by battlements such as those pictured on Assyrian reliefs, for example, of the siege of Lachish. Originally these were *shields lashed into place atop the wall, behind which a defender could take cover. Later they evolved into wooden structures and eventually crenelated masonry. The battlements probably gave the appearance of adornment to the walls and thus inspired pride and confidence in the citizens who looked to these towers and walls for their personal and corporate protection. During times of hostility and attack, the people must have frequently cast glances over their shoulder at their tower while going about daily

A thirty-six-foot-high stone tower discovered at Jericho.

routines. Its appearance brought a feeling of security and well-being. Similarly, in a world filled with both spiritual and physical peril, the psalmist could look to God as "my refuge, a strong tower against the enemy" (Ps 61:3 NRSV). Fleeing to a tower in time of terror provides the metaphor in Proverbs: "The name of the LORD is a strong tower; the righteous run into it and are safe" (Prov 18:10 NRSV).

But defensive towers can also be a negative image. Along with cedars of *Lebanon, high hills, fortified walls and trading ships, the "lofty tower" is a symbol of human arrogance and pride in Isaiah 2:12-18. All such high things will be brought low in the day when the Lord alone will be exalted.

Outside the cities, two types of watchtowers were employed, one domestic and one military. A domestic tower was built on a family farmstead (Is 5:2; Mt 21:33) or in a cultivated field. Jesus used this as an image in cautioning potential disciples to consider the cost of following him: "Which one of you, intending to build a tower, does not first sit down and estimate the cost?" (Lk 14:28 NRSV). In addition, military watchtowers or small fortresses were built at strategic points of land between cities and overlooking travel routes, primarily to warn of approaching enemies (2 Kings 9:17). In Roman times they were positioned at intervals along roads the army had constructed, to monitor traffic and flash signals up and down a line of defense.

In addition to the four types of defensive towers was an offensive tower, the siege tower, referred to in Isaiah 23:13 and 29:3. Developed by the Assyrians, the mobile battering ram and mobile attack tower were used in concert to try to breach the wall of a city under siege. Ramps of soil and stone were built by attackers to span moats in front of city walls; on these ramps the battering rams and mobile towers would be pushed up to the city wall (Ezek 21:22). Defenders who had placed their trust in the towers of their city would be a spectacle of helplessness on such occasions.

A perusal of the fifty biblical references to towers gives a picture of how central the building of towers was to OT city planning. Nearly all the references are literal, picturing physical means of protection. The physical image is itself double in meaning. On the one hand, "strong tower" (Ps 61:3; Prov 18:10) and "security within your towers" (Ps 122:7 NRSV) is a picture of protection that elicits a feeling of safety. But mention of towers falling (Is 30:25) and being broken down (Ezek 26:4; 26:9) makes us aware that towers are susceptible to attack, becoming images of human helplessness, vulnerability and misplaced trust.

In addition to the literal references to towers, the Song of Songs uses the image metaphorically. The woman's *neck is said to be "like the tower of David, . . . on it hang a thousand bucklers, all of them shields of warriors" (Song 4:4 NRSV). The point of the simile is not visual correspondence but a transfer of value: the beloved's neck is the best of its kind, raised to transcendent value by being surrounded with glorious national associations. The same principle underlies the comparison of the beloved's neck to "an ivory tower" and her *nose to "a tower of Lebanon" (Song 7:4 NRSV). At the end of the book, the bride, recalling her younger years, discounts her brothers' offer to protect her chastity (Song 8:8-9) by asserting, "I was a wall, and my breasts were like towers" (Song 8:10 NRSV). In other words, now that she is mature she has proved her ability to protect herself and even find a husband.

See also CITY; FORTRESS, STRONGHOLD; REFUGE, RETREAT, SAFE PLACE; WALL.

TOWER OF BABEL. *See* BABEL, TOWER OF.

TOWN. *See* VILLAGE.

TRAGEDY AS PLOT MOTIF

A tragic plot moves from prosperity to calamity. As a change-of-fortune story it must be differentiated from pathos, which depicts unmitigated suffering from start to finish. Tragedy, moreover, is a story of exceptional calamity, not commonplace misfortune. It focuses on what we most fear and wish to avoid facing—the destructive potential of evil.

While the lowest common denominator of tragedy is that it is the story of a fall, further elements are usually considered essential for a plot to be labeled a tragedy. Tragedy focuses on a protagonist—the tragic hero—in contrast to comedy's more social or communal emphasis. The tragic hero is typically a person of exalted social rank, like a king or ruler—someone greater than common humanity, though at the same time representative of people generally. The tragedy itself is always caused by something the tragic hero does. Aristotle called it *hamartia*—a tragic flaw of character that makes the tragic victim not only responsible for the downfall but also to some extent deserving of it. Tragedy thus bases itself on the bedrock of human error or frailty, and it highlights human choice as opposed to determinism. All biblical tragedies are variations on the theme of human disobedience to God. Often the tragic hero comes to a moment of perception, usually an insight into what he or she has done wrong to set the forces of retribution in motion. As the tragic plot unfolds, the tragic hero becomes gradually isolated from society. Tragedies typically end with the death of the hero.

The prototypical biblical tragedy is the *fall from innocence in Genesis 3. It is a story of wrong choice in the form of disobedience to God's command, and of *crime and punishment. The grand masterpiece of tragedy in the Bible is the story of King Saul in 1 Samuel, which turns on Saul's failure as a leader. Of similar import is the tragedy of *Samson (Judg 13—16), where the hero is guilty of a host of sins, including violation of a Nazirite vow and squandering of God's gifts. In keeping with tragedy's tendency to assign a specific cause to the hero's downfall, the story of *David as narrated in 1 and 2 Samuel is a tragedy, inasmuch as it is a success story until the *Bathsheba/Uriah episode, after which the hero's suffering sets in.

OT historical chronicles also contain stories of tragedy. Numerous characters cast their lot with evil rather than good and display character flaws in the process. The cause-effect link between *sin and *suffering runs strong throughout these individual and national histories. *Cain commits a murder and dooms himself to a life of *wandering (Gen 4:1-16). Achan hides the spoil of silver and gold in his tent and dies for it (Josh 7). Korah, Dathan and Abiram rebel against the authority of Moses and Aaron, and the earth swallows them and their households (Num 16). The nation of Israel resorts to *idolatry and fails to live up to its *covenant responsibilities, and it is carried into *exile. These are only specimens of the tragic narratives that we encounter in biblical narrative.

OT *wisdom literature also has a tragic thread. Here we find portraits of the self-destruction of people who live by *violence (Prov 1:10-19) or who are ensnared by the toils of sin or who die for lack of discipline (Prov 5:22-23). Succumbing to the *temptation of a *seductress leads to a metaphoric slaughter—a victim laid low (Prov 7:21-27; see also Prov 2:16-19; 5:3-6; 22:14).

The parables of Jesus are another source of tragedies. In these dramas of the soul's choice we see the inevitable potential for either tragedy or comedy. The gallery of tragic figures is impressive: the slothful *servant who hides his master's money, the five foolish *virgins, the *wedding guests who refuse the invitation, the elder brother who *refuses the festivities of forgiveness, the rich man who ignores the beggar and finds his fortune reversed in the afterlife, the self-righteous *Pharisee who goes home from his temple *prayer condemned, the wealthy *farmer who complacently plans for his retirement.

Yet despite the tragic thread in the Bible, tragedy is not the dominant biblical form. Biblical narrative is full of incidents that are potentially tragic but in which tragedy is averted through the protagonist's repentance and God's forgiveness. David's repentance after his sin with Bathsheba (and Uriah) is the paradigm. The world of literary tragedy is a closed world, with no escape after the hero makes the tragic mistake. But the world of biblical religion is always open to God's *forgiveness, even after a tragic mistake has been made. The Bible is preoccupied with human waywardness but also with the *redemptive potential of tragedy—with what is more than tragic.

See also CHARACTER TYPES; COMEDY AS PLOT MOTIF; FALL FROM INNOCENCE; PLOT MOTIFS.

TRAMPLE. *See* TRIUMPH; UNDER THE FEET.

TRANSFORMATION

The transformation motif looms large in the stories of the world, if for no other reason than that stories are built around the principle of character development. If the development is sufficiently drastic, we experience the account as a transformation. In mythical literature, too, stories of transformation—trees becoming people, people becoming animals or statues—are prominent (with Ovid's *Metamorphoses* the chief monument). But the transformation motif assumes spiritual depth in the Bible, with its sense of the momentous possibilities for good or ill that characterize human life.

In the Bible, characters are transformed through their own choices, usually occasioned by some ordeal. The conditions of human life in this world are transformed by *Adam and *Eve's choice to disobey, with nature now bringing forth *thorns and thistles (Gen 3:18). The first chapter of the epistle of Romans traces the downward spiral of the human race after the Fall, and it is a story of transformation from true human dignity and pure *worship into perverse behavior and false worship, as people "exchanged" the true and the moral for their opposites, and as people themselves are transformed from reflecting divine qualities of *glory and immortality to engaging in *shameful and beastly behavior. In effect, people are transformed into animals.

OT narrative is replete with stories of transformation. *Cain, the first murderer, is transformed into a moral monster when he fails to heed God's warning to "do well" and foil the monster sin that is crouching at the door (Gen 4:7 RSV). Lot's materialistic lifestyle is transformed when the region surrounding *Sodom is turned from a well-watered plain into a *wasteland and his wife is transformed into a pillar of salt (Gen 19:26). Transformation can be conveyed by more subtle means as well, as when in Genesis 17 four characters are given new names symbolic of changes that are occurring in the action—God as "Overpowerer," Abraham ("father of a multitude"), Sarah ("princess") and Isaac (here named for the first time). Jacob too receives a new name when he wrestles with God's angel, symbolic of a new life as he enters a new spiritual era.

It is common in the OT for characters to be transformed gradually through life's experiences. *Joseph moves from being an outcast younger son to a leader of international importance. *Moses grows from a reluctant leader to an unusually seasoned and strong leader, a process paralleled in the life of Gideon. Saul is transformed from a promising king to a tragic failure. *David the adulterer reaches a state of old age in which a beautiful young woman served as a body warmer, "but the king knew her not" (1 Kings 1:3 RSV). *Job is transformed from prosperous citizen to social outcast back to prosperous citizen. The haunting metaphoric portrait of old age near the end of *Ecclesiastes pictures the gradual transformation of life by a process of physiological symptoms and diminished desire, finally ending in death as "the dust returns to the earth as it was, and the spirit returns to God who gave it" (Eccles 12:7 RSV).

Other transformations are more dramatic. Enoch (Gen 5:24) and Elijah (2 Kings 2:1-12) are translated from earth to heaven without death. Self-indulgence and sensuality bring a sudden change in Samson's life, as his eyes are gouged out and he is reduced to a prisoner. Some characters are transformed into instantaneous lepers (Num 12:9-16; 2 Kings 5:19-27; 2 Chron 26:16-21), while lepers are miraculously healed (2 Kings 5:14). Haman goes from king's favorite to king's enemy in a matter of seconds (Esther 7). The Song of Songs shows us the world transformed by the heightened emotions of romantic love.

The psalms have their own slant on transformation, as we move in a world of human emotions with their highs and lows. This is most evident in the psalms of lament, which nearly always include a recantation: the speaker's plight, which had been portrayed as hopeless, is suddenly transformed as he expresses confidence in God and vows to praise God. Psalms of praise and deliverance often portray a sudden transformation of the speaker's fortunes, and the penitential psalms speak of a sudden transformation effected by *repentance and *forgiveness (Ps 32:3-5; 51:10-14).

OT prophetic books, too, give us variations on the transformation motif. One thrust is to predict a transformation of existing conditions into their opposite, as those who are now prosperous will be destroyed. But interspersed through prophetic books, or concluding them, is a vision of desolation transformed into blessing and prosperity. The transformation is personal as well as national; for example, God exchanges a *heart of *stone for a heart of flesh (Ezek 11:19; 36:26).

NT manifestations take us to quite a different world. An important premise of the NT, signaled by its very title, is that old things are being transformed into something new. OT forms of worship give way to more spiritual forms. External trappings are transformed into internal qualities. OT prefigurings, including even the ceremonial laws, are understood to be fulfilled in Christ, with a resultant transformation of religious life. Israel as a political entity is transformed in NT theology into a spiritual phenomenon (Rom 9). In the transforming world of the NT, conventional expectations are transformed, so that (for example) "the very stone which the builders rejected has become the head of the corner" (Mk 12:10 RSV).

A second NT repository of transformations is the numerous miracles that Jesus performs. Here people's situations transformed in a moment—the *blind see, the lame walk, the *leprous are healed, the *demon possessed are delivered, the dead are even brought back to life.

The transformed life of those who are regenerated into life in Christ is a main motif in the book of Acts and in the epistles. Acts gives us repeated conversions, most notably that of Paul, who is transformed from a zealous persecutor of followers of the Way to a zealous proclaimer of the Christian faith (Gal 1:23). The *Holy Spirit falls suddenly on characters in Acts, with accompanying signs like speaking in *tongues. In the Epistles the transformation is moral as well as spiritual, taking as its point of departure the fact that "if any one is in Christ, he is a new creation; the old has passed away, behold, the new has come" (2 Cor 5:17 RSV), as those who are in Christ experience the first signs of the transformation that will one day envelop the cosmos. The imagery of old and new, "then" (or "once") and "now," supports this theme of transformation, as does the motif of "former" or "formerly." "Once you were no people," writes Peter, "but now you are God's people" (1 Pet 2:10 RSV). Part of the moral appeal of the Epistles is to call people to live up to the expectations of the transformed life.

Some of the most dramatic transformations of the Bible come in the book of Revelation, where the whole earthly order is being transformed before our eyes in a pageant of visions. Part of the transformation is downward, toward a *decay and cataclysmic destruction of the earthly order. But the transformed cosmos of Revelation also includes the motif of renewal, especially in the creation of a new heaven and a new earth. "The former things have passed away," God says. "Behold, I make all things new" (Rev 21:4-5 RSV). Life will be completely transformed in the world to come. At the final resurrection, moreover, the transformation of individual believers will be instantaneous: "We shall all be changed, in a moment, in the twinkling of an eye, at the last trumpet" (1 Cor 15:51-52 RSV).

The archetypal pattern of transformation in the Bible signals an important part of the biblical message. At the most elementary level, the motif captures the dynamic nature of human life, in which things never stay the same but always change into something better or worse, or at least different. Another theme is the transformation of life and character that is expected to occur in all who are reborn in Christ and choose to follow the life of faith. A third dimension is the cosmic transformation that will accompany the end.

See also CREATION; DECAY; REPENTANCE; RESTORE, RESTORATION; RESURRECTION; REVERSAL.

TRANSIENCE

Along with the heavenly bodies and the material world, people's bodies are transient, as Paul writes in 2 Corinthians 4:18. The imagery used by biblical writers to express the quality of transience falls mainly into four categories: the imagery of *plants, *shadows, air and *numbers.

Vegetation. The botanical images for transience are simple and powerful. Human beings and their glory are like *grass, like *flowers—living briefly and passing quickly—in contrast to God or his characteristics. People are compared to fading flowers and grass (Job 14:2; Ps 1; 2:11; 90:5-6; 103:15). In more extended pictures the writer heightens the effect with vivid descriptive detail and with a foil (a contrast introduced to "set off" a subject), usually the permanence of God or his word. Isaiah 10:6-8 (to which 1 Pet 1:24-25 alludes) illustrates the practice:

All flesh is grass,
and all its beauty is like the flower of the field.
The grass withers, the flower fades,
when the breath of the LORD blows upon it;
surely the people is grass.
The grass withers, the flower fades;
but the word of our God will stand for ever.
(Is 40:6-8 RSV)

Similarly, in Psalm 103:15-17 human beings are like grass and flowers, subject to the destroying wind, while "the steadfast love of the LORD" for his followers has neither beginning nor end.

Although all flesh is transient, that of the wicked should be most notably so; and here the image of grass appears again, as in Psalm 129:6-7, which inveighs against the enemies of Israel:

Let them be like the grass on the housetops,
which withers before it grows up,
with which the reaper does not fill his hand
or the binder of sheaves his bosom. (RSV)

Vegetation serves not only to suggest the transience of human life but also, through an a fortiori ("how much more") argument, to show the foolishness of human anxiety. Without working, the "lilies of the field" grow more glorious than Solomon ever was; like the other "grass of the field," though, they soon perish and are "thrown into the oven." If God provides such clothes for short-lived plants, he will all the more provide clothes for those who trust him (Mt 6:28-30 RSV; also Lk 12:27-28).

Yet another botanical image of transience depicts the brevity of dedication among some who hear God's word. In the parable of the sower, some seed falls on "rocky ground" and grows fast, only to wither and die for lack of a root. Jesus explains to the twelve disciples that, by analogy, such withering plants are those persons who receive the message of the kingdom joyfully but "fall away" when they encounter "tribulation or persecution" (Mk 4:1-20 RSV; also Mt 13:1-23, Lk 8:4-15).

Shadow Images. The Bible's main optical image of transience is as simple and powerful as those drawn from crops and wild plants: human beings are like fleeting shadows. According to the Chronicler, David, nearing death in his old age, gives thanks for the wealth God has given and remarks on Israel's unworthiness: "For we are strangers before thee, and sojourners, as all our fathers were; our days on the earth are like a shadow, and there is no abiding" (1 Chron 29:15 RSV).

Sometimes shadow imagery is joined to other kinds of imagery to indicate the brevity of human life. For instance, in lamenting the human condition, Job asserts,

Man that is born of a woman is of few days. . . .
He flees like a shadow, and continues not. . . .
As waters fail from a lake,
and a river wastes away and dries up,
so man lies down and rises not again.
(Job 14:1-2, 11-12 RSV)

The psalmist in his complaint says that his "days are like an evening shadow" (Ps 102:11 RSV).

Breath, Wind and Cloud. Besides being like ephemeral plants and shadows, humans in the brevity of their lives are like breath or wind (Ps 146:4). Indeed, the Hebrew noun *rûaḥ* fundamentally means "moving air," and among its English translations are "breath" and "wind." Job calls on God to remember that his "life is a breath" and like "the cloud [that] fades and vanishes" (Job 7:7, 9 RSV). Similarly, the psalmist recalls God's restraint of his wrath against the Israelites: "He remembered that they were but flesh, a wind that passes and comes not again" (Ps 78:39 RSV). Psalm 144:4 presents the images of both "breath" and "a passing shadow" to express human mutability (RSV). Even when another Hebrew noun, *hebel*, is used, the suggestion of transience, as well as emptiness, remains, as when the psalmist observes that "surely every man is a mere breath" (Ps 39:11 RSV).

The disappearance of moisture also suggests transience. James 4:14 contains a warning against people's confidence in their own plans: "You do not know about tomorrow. What is your life? For you are a mist that appears for a little time and then vanishes" (RSV). Hosea presents a similar image in describing the transience of Israel's devotion: "Your love is like a morning cloud, like the *dew that goes early away" (Hos 6:4 RSV). Later in his book the prophet describes the idolatry in the Northern Kingdom; then, piling on images of vapor and wind, he depicts how fleeting the existence of its inhabitants will be:

Therefore they shall be like the morning mist
or like the dew that goes early away,
like the chaff that swirls from the threshing floor
or like smoke from a window. (Hos 13:3 RSV)

Number Imagery. A clear indication of the transience of human life is that it is measurable. In Genesis 6:3 the Lord says, "My spirit shall not abide in man for ever, for he is flesh, but his days shall be a hundred and twenty years" (RSV). The psalmist arrives at smaller figures, and therefore the related ideas of finitude and transience are more striking:

The years of our life are threescore and ten,
or even by reason of strength fourscore;
yet their span is but toil and trouble;
they are soon gone, and we fly away.
(Ps 90:10 RSV)

Elsewhere in Psalms there appears a linear measuring of human life: "Behold, thou hast made my days a few handbreadths, and my lifetime is as nothing in thy sight" (Ps 39:5 RSV). Even in the *restoration that Isaiah prophesies, life will be finite and thus transient. An index to the superiority of life in the New Jerusalem is that infants will no longer die young, nor will adults die in their prime: "for the child shall die a hundred years old, and the sinner a hundred years old shall be accursed" (Is 65:20 RSV).

The more common idea in the OT, however, is that great sinners will die prematurely as God cuts short their years. One such example is King Belshazzar of Babylon, who has *wine for his *feast served in vessels his father brought from the Lord's temple in Jerusalem. Daniel interprets the first word written on the palace wall by a mysterious hand as "MENE" (meaning either the infinitive "to number" or the unit of weight a "mina") and adds, "God has numbered the days of your kingdom and brought it to an end" (Dan 5:26 RSV). As the author says several verses later, Belshazzar was killed that night, and Darius the Mede ruled in his place.

Other Images. A few other images of transience are notable. Psalm 102:25-26 uses the imagery of a cloth *garment that wears out and needs changing to picture the mutability of created nature. Psalm 90:5 pictures God as sweeping people away, with the result that they are as fleeting as a *dream. The book of Job contains numerous images of transience; for example, Job complains, "My days are swifter than a runner; they flee away, they see no good. They go by like skiffs of reed, like an eagle swooping on the prey" (Ps 9:25-26 RSV). Job also uses an analogy from weaving to convey the speed of time's passage: "My days are swifter than a weavers shuttle, and come to their end without hope" (Job 7:6 RSV). After his recovery from illness, Hezekiah uses another image from weaving, combined with an image from shepherding, to show the feeling of life's brevity he had while sick:

My dwelling is plucked up and removed from me
like a shepherd's tent;
like a weaver I have rolled up my life;
he cuts me off from the loom. (Is 38:12 RSV)

The transience of wealth is expressed in a memorable metaphor in Proverbs 23:5: "When your eyes light upon it, it is gone; for suddenly it takes to itself wings, flying like an eagle toward heaven" (RSV).

The Sudden Downfall of the Wicked. Note can also be made of the biblical motif of the sudden downfall of the prosperous wicked. Psalm 73:18-20

paints a portrait of them as "set . . . in slippery places," falling to ruin, "destroyed in a moment, swept away utterly by terrors," vanishing as quickly as "a dream when one awakes" (RSV). The book of Proverbs variously describes the wicked as being "cut off" and "rooted out" (Prov 2:22 RSV), being subject to calamity that will come upon them "suddenly" (Prov 6:15) and as being "but for a moment" (Prov 12:19 RSV). Dishonestly gotten riches are "a fleeting vapor" (Prov 21:6 RSV).

Conclusion. According to 1 Peter 1:18-19, even *silver and *gold are "perishable things" when contrasted with "the precious blood of Christ" (RSV). Yet in the "resurrection of the dead," writes Paul, the impermanent becomes permanent: "What is sown is perishable, what is raised is imperishable. It is sown in dishonor, it is raised in glory" (1 Cor 15:42-43 RSV). For Christians there is first that great change, Paul remarks a few verses later, and then immortality.

See also DEATH; DECAY; DEW; MORTALITY; NUMBERS IN THE BIBLE; PLANTS; SHADOW; SMOKE.

TRAP

The image of trapping occurs often in the Bible and is linked with both physical and spiritual peril. Images accompanying it include snares, nets and *pits. The image itself comes primarily from *hunting and may include the killing of *birds, wild *animals such as deer or antelope, or *fish. The traps used in the ancient Near East were often pits covered with camouflaged nets, and this was one of the chief methods of hunting at the time. Job 18:8-10, a passage in which Bildad waxes eloquent on his favorite sermon topic—the calamity that the wicked bring upon themselves—employs the sequence "net," "pitfall," "trap," "snare" and "rope" (NRSV). Psalm 140:5 also contains terms that appear as synonyms for trapping in the Bible: a "trap" that is hidden for a victim, "cords" in the form of a "spread . . . net," and "snares" set "along the road" (NRSV).

Many Mesopotamian kings described battles as hunting scenes in which their armies successfully cast the hunting net to entrap their captors. Thus the act of hunting something demonstrated their complete mastery over their inferiors, a motif repeated in accounts of the Egyptian gods and pharaohs, who were said to cast their net over all the earth's living things. The Bible picks up these Mesopotamian themes; most often the image of a trap is used to show the dominion of the one who casts the net or sets it, accompanied by the powerlessness of the one who is caught in it.

The Bible refers most often to unrighteous practices as a snare to those who practice them. We have, for example, God's warning to the Israelites concerning the Canaanites. In Exodus and Joshua, God told them repeatedly that they must kill all the people and not intermarry with them lest their gods become a snare (Ex 23:33; 34:12; Deut 7:6; Josh 23:13; Ps 106:36). However, by the beginning of Judges, Israel had already disobeyed, so God promised a fulfillment of his earlier prophecy: "They shall become adversaries to you, and their gods shall be a snare to you" (Judg 2:3 NRSV). Idolatry was thus one of the chief sins that trapped God's people.

Other sins are also portrayed as an entrapment. The wise man of Proverbs furnishes his pupils with a long list of such evil entanglements. Among them are the "mouths of fools," rash *vows, the gain of riches by deception, the ways of a hot-tempered person, the misleading of the upright into evil, the flattery of a neighbor, and "the fear of others" instead of trust in God (Prov 18:7; 20:25; 21:6; 22:25; 28:10; 29:5; 29:25). One of the chief images of entrapment in Proverbs is the man ensnared by *adultery. He is elaborately described as one who "goes like an ox to the slaughter, or bounds like a stag to the trap until an arrow pierces its entrails. He is like a bird rushing into a snare, not knowing that it will cost him his life" (Prov 7:22-23 NRSV). Ecclesiastes seconds this warning against evil women: "More bitter than death [is] the woman who is a trap, whose heart is snare

A ingenious bird snare has snapped shut on its prey. Two bows covered with netting (not depicted) spring shut when the bird attempts to take the bait.

and nets, whose hands are fetters" (Eccles 7:26 NRSV). The advice of both teachers is that the godly man should avoid becoming entrapped by the loose woman.

For biblical writers, sin in general is a snare to the sinner. Proverbs declares that "the iniquities of the wicked ensnare them, and they are caught in the toils of their sin" (Prov 5:22 NRSV). Such a theme presents two distinct ways of looking at the immoral person's inevitable punishment. It is a product of God's righteous *judgment on sin and his ultimate authority to judge the earth. However, the Bible also presents it as an inevitable and entirely natural consequence of sin: sin blinds and weighs down sinners until they are so vulnerable and weakened that they essentially self-destruct. This latter perspective is expressed in Ecclesiastes: "Whoever digs a pit will fall into it; and whoever breaks through a wall will be bitten by a snake" (Eccles 10:8 NRSV). Repeatedly the psalms express the same theme, that the wicked will fall into their own pit or net (Ps 7:15; 9:15; 35:8;

57:6; 59:12). Just as breaking a wall puts a person at great risk for being bitten by any snakes resident in it, so digging a pit (a metaphor used throughout Scripture for sin) puts one at a great risk for falling into that pit. This is partly because sin can be distracting and can blur one's judgment, just as Saul hoped to distract or ensnare David from his war against the Philistines by giving him one of his beautiful daughters as a wife (1 Sam 18:21). Thus sin may be a snare merely because it distracts people from more sensible and righteous pursuits.

The NT warnings about sin are in a similar tone. Jesus calls sin *blindness, saying that this is the reason a sinner is more likely to "fall into a pit" (Lk 6:39 NRSV). He also describes the day of judgment as a trap into which those who "are weighed down with dissipation and drunkenness and the worries of this life" will inevitably and unexpectedly fall (Lk 21:34-35 NRSV). Paul describes the desire for riches as an entrapping temptation, one of the "many senseless and harmful desires that plunge people into ruin and destruction" (1 Tim 6:9 NRSV). It is clear that God views sin as an encumbrance that leads people to fall into the trap of natural consequences of their actions.

However, God's judgment of sin is also a central element of this entrapment. Like the Mesopotamian kings and gods, God declares his sovereignty through his power to throw nets over the peoples, to set traps for those who displease him. In his judgment of Egypt, God declares, "I will throw my net over you; and I will haul you up in my dragnet" (Ezek 32:3 NRSV). To Israel he declared that he himself was the trap and snare that would catch them, metaphorically expressing the fact that their disobedience of his commands would result in their destruction (Is 8:14-15). Isaiah describes these punished Israelites like helpless prey, "like an antelope in a net" (Is 51:20 NRSV). They are so helpless that "all of them are trapped in holes and hidden in prisons; they have become a prey with no one to rescue, a spoil with no one to say, 'Restore!' " (Is 42:22 NRSV). Any godly person in a difficult situation perceives himself or herself as perhaps displeasing God. Job laments, "God has put me in the wrong, and closed his net around me" (Job 19:6 NRSV).

Another leading cluster of trapping images revolves around the oppression that the wicked powerful inflict on the weak. The psalmists beg God to save them from the wicked, who are described as preying on the righteous like cruel hunters. The wicked "seize the poor and drag them off in their net," and "without cause" the arrogant dig a pit for the psalmist (Ps 10:9 NRSV; 35:7; 119:85; 140:5). They also "set a net" for the psalmist's steps (Ps 57:6 NRSV). Jeremiah describes the wicked as being like fowlers who set traps to "catch human beings" (Jer 5:26 NRSV). Perhaps the most colorful description of the wicked as hunters is the depiction of the Chaldeans in Habakkuk. Because Israel disobeyed, God turned them over to their enemies and "made the people like the fish of the sea" (Hab 1:14 NRSV).

In their great power the Chaldeans began to conquer the earth, bringing "all of them up with a hook; he drags them out with his net, he gathers them in his seine" and then enjoying the spoils of war by endlessly consuming the peoples like fish (NRSV).

Of the wicked, *Satan is seen as the most wicked predator, and his temptations are described in the New Testament as the "snare of the devil" (1 Tim 3:7 NRSV; 2 Tim 2:26). Thus the wicked are often painted as wily hunters with an insatiable appetite to destroy and consume anyone weaker.

However, God sees the cruelty of the wicked and thus justly causes the traps they set for the righteous to spring on them. Psalm 69 describes their own plentiful *table as a snare that will close upon them, using the image of a typical Mesopotamian trap in which the net is spread flat and is sprung closed by two lever arms that snap together (Ps 69:22). God also declares that he has his own judgment for these persons. Of the "bloodthirsty and treacherous," he threatens, "I will cast then down into the lowest pit" (Ps 55:23 NRSV). Moreover, Satan himself and all who have sinned will ultimately be cast into "the bottomless pit" of burning *fire (Rev. 17:8; 20:1, 10). Thus God promises that just punishment will come to those who delight in tormenting others; the wicked themselves will become the conquered prey.

In addition to punishing the wicked, God systematically saves the righteous from them. The psalms are full of images of deliverance for those who call on God. When the righteous become entangled, God "will pluck [their] feet out of the net" (Ps 25:15 NRSV). Moreover, God breaks the traps which the wicked set, so that the righteous can rejoice: "We have escaped like a bird from the snare of the fowlers; the snare is broken, and we have escaped" (Ps 124:7 NRSV). God may even prevent the righteous from falling into the trap in the first place. In Psalm 142 the psalmist prays that God will do this, acknowledging the sovereignty of a God who "know[s] my way" and who knows where "they have hidden a trap for me" (Ps 142:3 NRSV). Thus God delivers the hunted and traps the hunters.

Although most biblical images of entrapment involve sin or the cruel exercise of power, one NT image is positive. In the Gospels, Jesus compares the recruitment of new people for his kingdom to *fishing. Among his disciples are several former fishermen, and when he calls Peter and Andrew he promises, "I will make you fish for people" (Mt 4:18-19 NRSV). He continues this metaphor in a parable in which he compare the kingdom of heaven to "a net that was thrown into the sea and caught fish of every kind" (Mt 13:47 NRSV); then the bad fish were sifted out from among the good fish and thrown back into the sea. Thus the fishing metaphor conveys selectivity. It also, however, conveys the necessity of God's miraculous involvement in this process. In the Gospel of John the disciples are taught this through a symbolic miracle: they were unable to catch any fish after a long night of work, but at Jesus'

command they cast down their net, which instantly filled with catch (Jn 21:1-14). The net was so full that it was bulging, but surprisingly, "though there were so many, the net was not torn" (Jn 21:11 NRSV).

In the ancient world trapping was a condition of life, both as a source of food and as protection. The imagery of trapping is applied in the Bible mainly in metaphoric ways.

See also ANIMALS; BIRDS; FISH, FISHING; HUNTING; PIT.

TRAVEL STORIES

Travel stories have always been popular. Their virtues as stories are obvious. They provide variety of both *adventure and locale. They almost inevitably involve *danger, *risk, suspense and *testing. Travel stories bring the traveler into encounters with unknown characters and customs. In ancient literature, including the Bible, travel usually brings a traveler into an encounter with *God or other supernatural beings. Travel also produces change and growth in character, and physical movement often provides new revelation; this perhaps explains why travel stories are prominent in religious narratives of many traditions. Subgenres within the category of travel stories include *quest stories (including stories of *pilgrimage), stories of *wandering, stories of *flight and stories of *exile.

It is no exaggeration to call the Bible an anthology of travel stories. Wherever we turn in the narrative sections of the Bible we are likely to observe characters in transit, either locally or internationally. A host of minitravel stories exist in addition to the major ones. *Adam and *Eve make the short journey from paradise to the wasteland beyond it, and their son *Cain becomes the prototypical *wanderer in the land of Nod ("Wandering"). Noah travels by boat. *Abraham's servant travels by camel to find a wife for Isaac. Hagar journeys on foot into the wilderness and back, while *Joseph's brothers journey on donkeys back and forth between home and Egypt (as well as to closer places like Dothan). Most of the judges move about their regions, and prophets like Elijah and Elisha crisscross the nation. *David is constantly on the run during his years as a fugitive. People also travel internationally—Moses from Egypt to Midian, Ruth from Moab to Bethlehem, the queen of Sheba to Solomon's court, Naaman to Elijah's home, *Jonah to Nineveh, Ezra from Babylon to Jerusalem. The apostles are pictured as traveling more than a dozen times in the book of Acts, and the Epistles confirm the traveling lives of the apostles.

Of course danger is always a threat in journeys. For the traveler in Jesus' parable of the good Samaritan, the danger comes from robbers on a road down to Jericho that was notorious for robbers (the equivalent in danger to our inner-city alley). During certain eras of Israelite history, travel was so dangerous that people avoided it (2 Chron 15:5; Is 33:8), and in the days of the judge Shamgar "travelers kept to the byways" (Judg 5:6 NRSV). Most pathetic of all is the story of the Levite and his concubine who meet with disaster as they travel (Judg 19).

In the anthology of travel stories that make up the Bible, the main chapters are devoted to the patriarchs Abraham, Jacob and Joseph; the nation of Israel during the exodus; the itinerant teacher and miracle worker Jesus; and the missionary Paul. But travel on a smaller scale is nearly always occurring in any of the Bible's narrative parts.

Abraham is the first traveler whose story is told in full detail. It is both a quest story (never fulfilled in his lifetime) and a story of wandering. The journeys of Abraham, moreover, are tied up with the *covenant, which begins with the command from God to "go from your country and your kindred and your father's house to the land that I will show you" (Gen 12:1 RSV). "So Abram went" (Gen 12:4), and thereafter his story is a continuing travel story, spanning the entire Fertile Crescent, from Haran to Canaan to the Negev to Egypt, returning at the end to Canaan. Abraham's travels are punctuated by encounters with God and a range of human beings. There are interludes of danger and run-ins with various natives, and we can infer a continuous testing of faith as the fulfillment of the covenant promises is delayed. The most memorable chapter in the saga is Abraham's three-day journey to Mount Moriah to sacrifice Isaac. Overall, this travel story is a story of growth, as Abraham moves from being childless to becoming a father, in the process growing "strong in his faith" (Rom 4:20).

The travels of Jacob and Joseph run along parallel lines. Both are stories of *initiation in which young men are thrust out of their parental home to seek their fortune in a distant land. The travels of both are stories of *ordeal and temporary defeat followed by

A group of Asians traveling to Egypt (from a wall painting at Beni Hasan).

eventual triumph and family reunions. Jacob encounters God at several memorable moments in his odyssey, while Joseph encounters a series of hostile natives in the land of Egypt. Both are stories of destiny in which young men lose everything to gain material and spiritual prosperity.

The *exodus is a travel story par excellence—the story of a traveling community in which everything is "writ large" because it involves a group rather than an individual. It is, in fact, an epic journey, eventuating in the founding of a nation in a promised land. The journey begins as a *rescue from oppression. Testing is a primary feature of the story—not simply God's testing of the loyalty of his people but an ignominious, tenfold testing of God by the people (Num 14:22). The journey begins and ends with a crossing (of the Red Sea and Jordan River, respectively). Life for the traveling community is a continual narrow escape, punctuated by God's miraculous rescues, and an ongoing adventure story comprising ordeals, defeats, triumphs and encounters with God (most notably at Sinai). Conflicts include the struggle for survival against the environment, run-ins with neighboring nations and tensions within the traveling community (most notably the people's murmuring against God and his chosen leader Moses). A pattern of *death and *rebirth comes to dominate the journey, as the disobedient generation is purged before its successors enter the Promised Land.

*Jesus is also the archetypal traveler during his three-year earthly ministry. His itinerant life is a continual movement from one locale to another, with place names scattered throughout the Gospels. Jesus' travel is by foot and is accordingly limited to Palestine. He lacks a rooted place of residence and is pictured as a frequent visitor in homes. The natural landscape is a customary setting for events in this travel story. The continuous-travel motif in the Gospels produces a gallery of memorable encounters with a wide range of characters. The Gospels (Mark most notably) also wind their way to the final, self-conscious journey to Jerusalem, where Jesus knows he will face persecution and death. A story of geographical travel thus also becomes a spiritual journey of salvation for the human race, the culmination of God's history of salvation through the centuries.

The missionary travels of Paul are the last of the major travel stories in the Bible. Paul's is a story of international travel, for he and his companions visit nearly all the major cities of the Greco-Roman world of the time. The narrative has virtually all the ingredients that are possible in a travel story: adventure, excitement, suspense, danger, *shipwreck, the exotic appeal of faraway places, memorable encounters with individuals and groups, riots, arrests, imprisonments, *trials, *escapes, *rescues. The travelogue genre provides structure for the second half of the book of Acts.

Several conclusions can be drawn from the presence of travel stories in the Bible. The prevalence of traveling reinforces the active nature of the world of the Bible—a world in which people exert themselves energetically in daily pursuits. The world of the Bible is a realistic world, thoroughly rooted in life as we know it, a quality that the travel stories highlight. The emphasis on people busily traveling also lends a supreme narrative quality to the Bible, and the spectacle of purposeful movement shows that life never stands still but is progressive even in its physical dimension. The biblical travel stories also take on an incipient symbolic and spiritual meaning. Where, how and why people travel is an index to their spiritual state. Most biblical travelers are in transit for spiritual reasons, most notably obedience to a call from God. In some measure, therefore, the travel stories of the Bible send the message that everyone is a traveler in this world.

See also ADVENTURE STORY; FLEE, FLIGHT; JOURNEY; PATH; PILGRIM, PILGRIMAGE; QUEST; SHIP, SHIPWRECK; WANDERER, WANDERING.

TREAD. *See* TRIUMPH; UNDER THE FEET.

TREASURE
In the ancient world, treasure spoke of wealth, one's accumulation of valuable possessions. For example, King Hezekiah displayed what he possessed in his treasure house: *silver, *gold, spices, fine *oil, his armory and other treasures (2 Kings 20:13; Is 39:2). The quantity of his treasure proved his prosperity and God's *blessing on his reign. This use of treasure to represent physical wealth is common and extensive (e.g., Gen 43:23; 1 Chron 29:3; Prov 15:16; Eccles 2:8; Nahum 2:9; Mt 13:44; Lk 12:21; Acts 8:27).

Often physical treasure was seen as the outcome of moral or spiritual virtue. In proverbial language, the possession of *wisdom or righteousness assured one of treasure, while the foolish or the wicked could anticipate trouble or poverty (Prov 15:6; 21:20).

Treasure symbolizes what is of great value. God calls Israel his treasured possession (Ex 19:5; cf. Ps 135:4). At the same time, God gives to his people great treasures if they will obey his commands (Deut 28:8-14; *see* Obedience). Given the natural human tendency to desire, pursue and hoard material wealth, treasure comes to symbolize what people consider truly valuable, worth possessing and pursuing. As a symbol then of value and significance, the kind of treasure a person seeks indicates what he or she esteems as most important. And what people treasure (value in their *hearts) determines how they live (Mt 12:35; Lk 6:45).

People pursue either earthly or *heavenly treasure. From God's perspective, heavenly treasure has far more value than earthly, material wealth (Lk 12:21). This implies, for example, that an astute son will treasure wise words and godly commandments (Prov 2:1; 7:1). Likewise, the godly will treasure the *fear of the Lord (Is 33:6). As incredible as it sounds to modern ears (and ancient ears as well, no doubt), a person is better off disposing of this world's wealth if that is what it takes to gain God's *kingdom. That is, to embrace God's rule in one's life is a far greater treasure than all the material wealth and possessions one can accumulate. In fact, the kingdom of God itself is compared to an immense treasure that is worth securing at all costs (Mt 13:44). It is the mark of a fool to lay up treasure only on this earth (Lk 12:20-21). For this reason Jesus challenged the

wealthy young man to dispose of his material wealth and follow him (Mk 10:21 and par.). Paul considered the gospel, the message of *salvation that God entrusted to him and that he proclaimed, as a treasure in *clay jars (2 Cor 4:6-7). God chose to use fallible people like Paul to transmit this most valuable of all entities, eternal life in Christ. Indeed, in Christ reside all the treasures of wisdom and knowledge (Col 2:3).

Therefore, how people act displays what they treasure, what is really important to them on the deepest level (Mt 12:35). Living according to kingdom principles, Jesus taught, amounts to withdrawing riches from a treasury containing true riches as God values treasure (Mt 13:52). If disciples truly treasure God's reign in their lives, their heart's devotion will focus on godly values as well (Mt 6:21). One accumulates heavenly treasure—achieves what God desires—through righteous acts on the earth (Lk 12:33; cf. Tobit 12:8; Sirach 29:11). In contrast, wicked deeds accumulate a "treasure" too, but that treasure equals an inheritance of judgment (Jas 5:3; cf. Rom 2:5).

See also GOLD; JEWELS AND PRECIOUS STONES; PROSPERITY; SILVER; STOREHOUSE; STORING UP.

TREE OF LIFE
The tree of life is an image of life and immortality, but also of irretrievable loss. Except for four metaphoric references in Proverbs, references to the tree of life occur only in Genesis and Revelation. The tree of life thus connects the creation of the world to the re-created world that is to come.

The tree of life is one of two named trees in the *Garden of Eden. We first read about these *trees together in Genesis 2:9, where the tree of life is said to be "in the midst of the garden" (RSV). Although the two trees are mentioned together, they are essentially distinct. The prohibition against eating the fruit did not extend to the tree of life. We read about the tree of life again after the Fall has occurred, when the man and woman are expelled from the Garden (Gen 3:22-24). The name of the tree tells us its essential meaning: it is an image of eternal or unending life. After *Adam and *Eve sinned, God barred their access to the tree of life, not as a punishment but as an act of mercy, lest they doom themselves to endless physical life in a fallen world. Alternately, or as a complementary interpretation, being barred from the tree of life pictures the perfection and bliss that the human race lost through its sinfulness. By definition, the death that God prophesied as the penalty for eating from the forbidden tree (Gen 2:15) precludes the immortality represented by the tree of life. The tree of life is a supreme image at once of edenic splendor and of paradise lost—an image of nostalgia and longing for a lost perfection.

But if the tree of life is an image of loss and nostalgia to which we look back, it is also an image of hope to which the Bible looks forward. It reappears at the end of the Bible in the visions of Revelation. In one of the letters to the seven churches, the

Spirit promises, "To him who conquers I will grant to eat of the tree of life, which is in the paradise of God" (Rev 2:7 RSV). It is an image of immortality and eternal life in *heaven, a reward for those who have their robes washed in the *blood of the *Lamb (Rev 22:14; see also Rev 7:14) and something denied to any who take away from "this prophecy" (Rev 22:19).

In Revelation the tree of life is the supreme image of future splendor and paradise regained. Its final appearance in the Bible occurs in the last chapter, as part of the combined city and garden that climaxes the heavenly vision: "Then he showed me the river of the water of life, bright as crystal, flowing . . . through the middle of the street of the city; also, on either side of the river, the tree of life with its twelve kinds of fruit, . . . and the leaves of the tree were for the healing of the nations" (Rev 22:1-2 RSV; cf. Ezek 47:12). With the death of death, access to the tree of life is restored.

Between the enveloping references in Genesis and Revelation to the tree of life are several evocative metaphoric references in the book of Proverbs. Here we read that wisdom "is a tree of life to those who lay hold of her" (Prov 3:18 RSV), that "the fruit of the righteous is a tree of life" (Prov 11:30 RSV), that "a desire fulfilled is a tree of life" (Prov 13:12 RSV) and that "a gentle tongue is a tree of life" (Prov 15:4 RSV). Here the tree of life becomes a general image of blessing and fulfillment, a touchstone for what one would desire. Some have also identified the golden *lampstand of the tabernacle as a representation of the tree of life. With its vertical shaft, its three branches on each side and its cups "shaped like almond flowers with buds and blossoms" (Ex 25:34 NIV), it gives the impression of a stylized tree and seems to complement other Edenic imagery within the *tabernacle and *temple (see Adam).

See also GARDEN; LAMP, LAMPSTAND; LEAF; MORTALITY; TREE.

TREE, TREES

The special status of trees (even individual trees) in the Bible is explainable partly by the fact that the Palestinian world is arid, with trees scarce. Buildings made from wood are not the norm (as in the Western world) but a luxury. In such a world, even the planting of a single tree (Gen 21:33) or the burial of someone under an oak tree (Gen 35:8) might merit mention. If *wood as a building material is scarce, it becomes a mark of superiority if a royal bower boasts a house with beams of cedar and rafters of pine (Song 1:17). The 250 generic references to trees in the Bible are thus not to be interpreted as evidence of their abundance (with the exception of the common olive tree) but of the special status of trees in a world where they are scarce.

Images of Nature and Abundance. In the Bible, trees are first of all images of nature. They are mentioned eight times in the creation story, where they stand out prominently as evidence of the vital life force that energizes this account. They retain this meaning in subsequent parts of the Bible, as in the picture of the well-watered tree planted by streams of water, whose *leaves remain green even in *drought (Ps 1:3; Jer 17:8). The ultimate image of the tree as a life force is the one that appears in the apocalyptic visions of Ezekiel (Ezek 47:12) and Revelation (Rev 22:2), which picture trees so abundant that they monthly produce a different kind of fruit, whose leaves are "for the healing of the nations."

As objects of nature, trees are also images of providence, in a twofold sense. They are themselves the objects of God's provision: "The trees of the LORD are watered abundantly" (Ps 104:16 RSV). And trees in turn are means by which God provides for people and *animals: in trees watered by God "the birds build their nests; the stork has her home in the fir trees" (Ps 104:17 RSV). Trees can be an image of abundance, as in pictures of fruit trees that produce in their season (Ps 1:3) and do "not cease to bear fruit" (Jer 17:8 RSV). The *fig tree (three dozen references) and the olive tree (twenty) represent staples in the subsistence economy that prevailed in the biblical world.

Symbolism. The Bible's story of salvation history begins and ends with references to symbolic trees. We find the *tree of life and the tree of the knowledge of good and evil in the Garden of Eden (Gen 2:9). In the book of Revelation we find the tree of life again in the final eschatological vision of the New Jerusalem (Rev 22:2); its leaves are for the healing of the nations, and there will no longer be any *curse. The tree of life may be symbolized by the golden lampstand in the tabernacle. The vertical shaft, with its three branches on each side and its cups "shaped like almond flowers with buds and blossoms" (Ex 25:34 NIV) gives the impression of a stylized tree (see Lamp, Lampstand). The trees in the Garden of Eden have the potential for both *blessing (immortality) and cursing (the fruit that leads to death). Thus we can see the ambiguity of the symbolism of trees in the Bible.

Sandwiched between Genesis and Revelation is *the* tree, the *cross of salvation, which is the ultimate ground of both curse and blessing, judgment and healing. The apostle Paul (Gal 3:13) speaks of the curse on the sin-bearing Savior who hung on the tree, a theme picked up again by the apostle Peter (1 Pet 2:24). These draw upon the OT tradition (Deut 21:23) that an executed person who is hung on a tree is under God's curse. The cursing of Christ brought about both the destruction of *death and the renewal of life and immortality through the gospel; all this came through the tree.

The whole range of biblical symbolism relating to trees can be found in the representation of Assyria and Egypt as a cedar of *Lebanon (Ezek 31). Here we have images of majesty (Ezek 31:2), *beauty (Ezek 31:3), dependency (Ezek 31:4) and protection (Ezek 31:6). In contrast to these positive features, the tree here also symbolizes *pride (Ezek 31:10) and *judgment (Ezek 34:12, 18).

Images of Blessing, Goodness and Wholesomeness. The aesthetic qualities of trees are occasionally mentioned in the Bible. Genesis 2:9 speaks of "trees that were pleasing to the eye" (NIV). The cedar in Lebanon has "beautiful branches" (Ezek 31:3 NIV). The lover in the Song of Songs compares his beautiful beloved with the stately palm tree (Song 7:7).

The *protective shade of a leafy tree is a place of security and *rest. The beloved delights to sit in the shade of her lover, who is likened to a fruit-laden apple tree (Song 2:3). Nebuchadnezzar was described in Daniel's interpretation of the king's vision as an enormous tree, whose branches had beautiful leaves, and which bore abundant fruit and gave shelter to the beasts of the field and nesting places for the *birds (Dan 4). Similar imagery is seen when the growth of the kingdom of heaven is likened to that of a *mustard seed, which from tiny beginnings rapidly shoots up into a great tree that provides shelter for the birds (Mt 13:31).

A tree of life is a symbol of happiness and well-being. An evocative and metaphoric "tree of life" makes four appearances in Proverbs—as *wisdom (Prov 3:18), the *fruit of righteousness (Prov 11:30), desire fulfilled (Prov 13:12) and a gentle *tongue (Prov 15:4). Longevity and indestructibility are attributes characteristic of a tree: "As the days of a tree, so will be the days of my people" (Is 65:22 NIV). Job contrasts what he sees as the hopelessness of humankind in the face of death with the remarkable capacity of a dried-up stump of a felled tree to sprout at the scent of water (Job 14:7-10). A tree also figures in the OT counterpart of the American dream of a car in every garage and a chicken in every oven: "Every one of you will invite his neighbor under his vine and fig tree" (Zech 3:10 NIV).

The tree that continues to thrive even in a season of drought because of its deep *roots is an apt illustration of the constancy of the walk of a believer in every circumstance, both good and ill. The person who trusts in the Lord is "like a tree planted by the water that sends out its roots by the stream. It does not fear when heat comes; its leaves are always green" (Jer 17:7-8 NIV; cf. Ps 1). The psalmist also pictures the godly person as a tree: "I am like an olive tree flourishing in the house of God. I trust in God's unfailing love for ever and ever" (Ps 52:8 NIV). Renewed Israel under God's blessing is likened to a fruitful tree: "Like a cedar of Lebanon he will send down his roots; his young shoots will grow. His splendor will be like an olive tree, his fragrance like a cedar of Lebanon. Men will dwell again in his shade" (Hos 14:5-7 NIV).

God himself is pictured as a tree in Hosea 14:8: "I am like a green pine tree; your fruitfulness comes from me" (NIV). The covenant God of Israel is the source of all fertility, both physical and spiritual. Trees play an important role in the glorious *eschato-logical blessings at the end of the age. They are representatives of the whole of the renewed created order, praising the Lord for his righteous judgments: "Then all the trees of the forest will sing for joy . . . before the LORD, for he comes . . . to judge the earth" (Ps 96:12-13 NIV). The desert will be replanted with the cedar, the acacia, the myrtle, the olive, the pine, the fir and the cypress (Is 41:19). All the trees of the field will clap their hands when the *thorns and brambles are replaced by the pine trees and the myrtle (Is 55:12-13). This personification of the natural order is a stimulus for all humankind to respond to the glorious revelation of the Lord.

Images of Judgment, Pride and Curse. Yet the qualities symbolized by trees—strength, power, glory, wealth, honor—are the very qualities that are easily abused by sinful rebellious humanity. So it is no surprise to find that this dark side of humanity, and all the consequences flowing from it, should be readily portrayed through the figure of the tree.

One of the more catastrophic results of the Fall is the confusion of the Creator with the creation. The divinization of the natural order by humankind's perverse religious instincts led to the abominable orgies of a nature religion that violated every tenet of Israel's revealed religion. The prophets condemned Israel for worshiping their *idols under every spreading tree and every oak (Ezek 6:13). "Every high hill and every spreading tree" became a stereotyped phrase to indicate the Israelite *abominations (1 Kings 14:23).

Human self-exaltation and arrogance is illustrated by the proud and lofty trees: "all the cedars of Lebanon, tall and lofty, and all the oaks of Bashan" (Is 2:13 NIV). The powerful Ammonites were destroyed by the Lord even though they were "tall as the cedars and strong as the oaks" (Amos 2:9 NIV). The metaphor is extended further in the imagery of cutting down trees as an act of judgment. John the Baptist spoke of an ax already at the root of the tree (Mt 3:10); the fruitless tree was to be cut down and destroyed. Fruitlessness was one of the curses of the covenant (Lev 26:20), and godless people are described by Jude as "autumn trees, without fruit and uprooted—twice dead" (Jude 12 NIV).

This judgment is applied at a corporate national level as well as at an individual level, and the imagery of the tree applies here also. Pharaoh, king of Egypt, and his hordes are represented by the cedar of Lebanon (Ezek 31) that the Lord cast down. Nebuchadnezzar's kingdom is to be cut down, signified by the tree that is to be hewn down but left with its stump in the ground, indicating the hope of possible restoration (Dan 4). The destruction of the armies of Assyria is likened to the conflagration of a mighty forest fire, with only a few tree stumps surviving. The Assyrian destruction is also described by the Almighty's wreaking havoc on the forests with his powerful ax. "He will cut down the forest thickens with an ax; Lebanon will fall before the Mighty One" (Is 10:34 NIV). A generalized prophecy of judgment against the enemies of Israel is found in Zechariah 11:1-2: "Open your doors, O Lebanon, so that fire may devour your cedars! Wail, O pine tree, for the cedar has fallen; the stately trees are ruined! Wail, oaks of Bashan; the dense forest has been cut down!" (NIV).

Trees appear as personifications in the fables of Jotham (Judges 9:15) and Amaziah (2 Kings 14:9). The main thrust of these fables lies in the inappropriate interaction between the thistle or thornbush and the vine, the olive, the fig tree and the cedar. Wrong choices lead only to strife. Thus we see the glory and shame of humankind, the blessing of God and the curses of his covenant, all mirrored in various ways in this very flexible metaphor of the tree.

See also ADAM; FIG, FIG TREE; LEBANON; PALM TREE; TREE OF LIFE; WOOD.

TREMBLING, SHAKING, BODILY ANGUISH

The Bible frequently uses the imagery of shaking or trembling to picture the intense *fear, terror or panic that sweeps over those who suddenly realize their lives are in danger. Such a response is both a physical and an emotional reaction to realized or pending *sorrow, *suffering or loss. Typically it is the news of an approaching *army or impending military defeat that causes such trembling (e.g., Ex 15:14; Deut 2:25; 2 Sam 22:46; Is 14:16; 15:4; 41:5; Jer 49:21; 50:46; Ezek 26:16; 32:10; Hos 5:8; Nahum 2:10).

References to the trembling of *nature and *enemies were a common feature in ancient Near Eastern *battle accounts. These texts often depict warrior-kings, both divine and human, as shaking the earth with their battle cry and terrorizing their trembling enemies. In similar fashion God's self-revelation as a powerful *divine warrior produces mass terror, often on a universal scale. At *Sinai, where the Lord revealed himself as a victorious warrior who claimed the allegiance of the people he had delivered from *slavery, his frightful appearance caused both the *mountain and the Israelites to tremble in fear (Ex 19:16-18; 20:18; Heb 12:21).

Throughout Israel's early history God intervened in its battles, striking the enemy with terror and panic. 1 Samuel 14:15 describes one such occasion: "Then panic [or trembling] struck the whole army . . . and the ground shook. It was a panic [or trembling] sent by God" (NIV). According to Hebrew poets, the divine warrior's appearance in a *storm causes the earth to shake (Judg 5:4; 2 Sam 22:8; Ps 18:7; 29:8; 77:18; 97:4; 104:32; 114:7; Is 13:13; 19:1; 24:18-19; Joel 2:10; 3:16; Hab 3:7) and its inhabitants to tremble (Is 19:16; 33:14; 64:2; Joel 2:1) at the prospect of divine *judgment. The mountains, which appear to be stable and immovable, shake violently before him (Ps 29:6; 114:6). The unruly *chaos waters, symbolic of earthly forces that oppose God, writhe in fear at his appearance (Ps 77:16). He shakes even the heavenly bodies, which seem so fixed in their courses (Is 13:13).

It is not only God's self-revelation as warrior that causes people to tremble before him. His prophets often responded in fear when he revealed his presence or word to them. *Moses trembled before the *burning bush when he realized he was speaking with the God of the patriarchs (Acts 7:32). When Jeremiah received the Lord's word to preach, his whole physical frame shook, for he realized its dreadful implications for his sinful generation (Jer 23:9). Daniel's vision of a fiery-looking man dressed in linen robbed him of his *strength and left him trembling before his *angelic visitor (Dan 10:10-11). Even those nearby, though they had not actually seen the vision, trembled and ran away (Dan 10:7). The prophet Habakkuk, after seeing a vision of the Lord coming in judgment, felt his *legs tremble, for the vivid images of divine power and *anger overwhelmed him emotionally (Hab 3:16).

Fearful trembling is sometimes viewed as a positive sign of *humility and submissiveness. The author of Psalm 2 exhorts the rebellious kings of the earth to wisely submit to God's *authority with genuine fear and trembling (Ps 2:11). When the postexilic community heard the reading of God's Word and realized their marriages with foreign women violated the law, they trembled in fear and committed themselves to follow God's commandments (Ezra 9:4; 10:3, 9). The apostle Paul urged the Philippian Christians to demonstrate humility and in so doing to "work out" their "salvation with fear and trembling" (Phil 2:12 NIV). The Lord esteems, or responds favorably to, those who humbly tremble before his word (Is 66:2). Such a response is only proper, for he is the sovereign Creator of all things (Jer 5:22; Dan 6:26). God's *holiness, anger and goodness toward his people should fill them with such awe, humility and gratitude that they tremble before him (Jer 33:9; Hos 11:10).

See also BATTLE STORIES; DIVINE WARRIOR; ENEMY; FEAR; FEAR OF GOD.

TRIAL

The purpose of a trial is to reveal what is genuine, to prove what is true and expose what is false. Such trial is key to the verification of God's Word, reality and very nature (Ps 12:6; Is 43:26). The image of trial in the Bible is richly multifaceted, encompassing the "trials of life" and the legal courts of societies ultimately established by God. Particularly central to a biblical use of such ordeal is trial by *water and by *fire. 2 Peter 3:10 combines the motifs in its picture of a world once drowned that is to be finally dissolved by fire. The most explicit picture of trial by water and fire occurs in Isaiah 43:2: "When you pass through the waters, I will be with you; and through the rivers, they shall not overwhelm you; when you walk through fire you shall not be burned, and the flame shall not consume you" (NRSV).

Trial by Water. The context of all trial by water (and indeed all trial) is God's sovereignty. In the psalmist's vivid phrase, God rules "the raging of the sea; when its waves rise, you still them" (Ps 89:9 NRSV). *Seas, lakes, *rivers—bodies of water traditionally symbolic of *chaos and misrule—are in God's hand (e.g., Jer 5:22). Jesus dramatically signaled his cosmic lordship by stilling the stormy waters of Galilee (Mt 8:26).

To survive the ordeal of water was, in the ancient Near East, a sign of innocence vindicated, whereas the wicked are overwhelmed in such a trial. In the momentous events of the *exodus, the Israelites crossed the Red Sea; its waters miraculously held back, but the pursuing Egyptians were engulfed by the flood of the returning waters. This saving event, with its motif of trial by water, was deeply embedded in the Hebrew consciousness (Ps 66). Of similar import is the *flood (Gen 7), in which a faithful remnant was preserved in a cataclysmic judgment by water. God is here both Judge and Savior, and a harrowing trial plays a central role in his dual activity.

The crossing of the Jordan in order to enter the *Promised Land (Josh 3) further signifies God's control over the waters of trial and his preservation of his faithful people. It is yet another proof of his character and trustworthiness, his promise keeping. Trial by water also has a central place as a motif in the narrative of the prophet *Jonah. The horrors of the overwhelming waters are vividly captured in Jonah's anguished prayer from the belly of the great fish (Jon 2). The lyrical prayer ends in triumphant hope in God's deliverance of the faithful (Jon 2:9). Jonah's prayer evokes the poignant prayer of David in Psalm 69, a prayer full of messianic anticipation of Christ's own harrowing trials centuries later (cf. Lk 11:29-32).

Trial by water also appears in the NT. In the parable with which Jesus closes his Sermon on the Mount, an overpowering rainstorm and flood puts two houses to the test, with the house built on a rock withstanding the flood while the house built on sand collapses (Mt 7:24-27). In several narratives in the Gospels (Mt 8:23-27; Mk 4:35-41; Lk 8:22-25) the disciples' faith is tested when they are threatened in a boat while with Jesus on the Sea of Galilee; in all three passages Jesus indicts them for lack of faith. In an additional incident, Peter's faith is tested when he walks on the water toward Jesus, only to sink when he looks at the sea instead of Jesus, and here too Jesus' epithet "you of little faith" confirms that the experience has been a trial of faith (Mt 14:22-33).

Trial by Refining Fire. The trial and proving of faith in God is imaged throughout the Bible in the refining fire. God's vigorous trial of the human heart is compared to a crucible and furnace (Prov 17:3). This trial can be very subtle; the person under trial may not realize that his or her soul is being searched by God (see Prov 27:21; cf. 1 Sam 18:7 and its effects on Saul). Jeremiah vividly describes the work of refining and smelting (Jer 6:29). If the apparent "silver" fails to refine, it is rejected (Jer 6:30).

Trial by fire, smelting or refining refers not only to the testing of the human heart but also to God's

*judgment (Is 1:25) and the purpose of *suffering (Ps 66:10-12). Those who are purified by suffering and trial are then blessed by God's acknowledgment of them as his people (Zech 13:9). The image of refining is boldly applied to the coming and work of the future Messiah in Malachi 3:1-4, where the Messiah is pictured as a gold- and silversmith, a master craftsman. Even more boldly, the very word of God is spoken of as being well tried (Ps 119:140; cf. Ps 18:30; Prov 30:5).

Trial by fire occurs as a dramatic motif in the ordeal of Daniel's friends in the fiery furnace (Dan 3). Their survival was a proof of their faith in the living God, in his utter reality.

Trial by fire receives an eschatological meaning in a NT passage that discusses the range of ways believers build on the foundation of Christ (1 Cor 3:13-17). Writes Paul, "The work of each builder will become visible, for the Day will disclose it, because it will be revealed with fire, and the fire will test what sort of work each has done. If what has been built on the foundation survives, the builder will receive a reward" (NRSV).

The Trial of Love. Trial as a period of difficulty and suffering is not always accompanied by imagery of fire or water; Job's trial is such an exception. Deuteronomy 7:17-19 links periods of trial with God's judgment and his public vindication of his chosen people caught up in suffering. God uniquely used trials in the establishment of his nation (Deut 4:34), but they can also be intensely personal, as in a love relationship.

A recurrent motif in the biblical narratives is the trial of love, whether *friendship or *sexual love. This may be seen, for instance, in the trial of the love of Jacob and Rachel (Gen 29), the lovers in the Songs of Songs (as in Song 5:2-8), the wrong love made right in the relationship of David and Bathsheba (2 Sam 11—12) and Hosea's love for the unfaithful Gomer (Hos 1—3). The trial of friendship is particularly seen in the love of David and Jonathan (1 Sam 19—20), Ruth and Naomi (Ruth 1), and Peter and our Lord, where restoration succeeds betrayal (Jn 21).

Trial by Ordeal. The Mosaic law contains a single prescription for determining innocence or *guilt by ritual trial by *ordeal. A woman whose husband suspected her of unfaithfulness was subject to an elaborate trial through the ingestion of holy water (Num 5:11-31). The NT gives us a spiritualized version of trial by ordeal: James encourages his readers to rejoice "whenever you face trials of any kind," because "the testing of your faith produces endurance, . . . so that you may be mature and complete, lacking in nothing" (Jas 1:2-4 NRSV). This trial is part of the goal toward which the life of faith is oriented: anyone who "has stood the test . . . will receive the crown of life that the Lord has promised to those who love him" (Jas 1:12 NRSV).

Trial by the Legal System. Trial within the legal system as a proof of faith and truth frequently occurs as a motif in NT events, most notably in the trial and wrongful punishment of Jesus. Here, in historical perspective, the tables are turned: the accused and condemned man is, ironically, the judge. In the book of Acts the portrayal of a number of trials of believers builds on this patent innocence of Christ in his trial, symbolized by Pilate's threefold declaration that he finds in Jesus no wrongdoing. So far as the Roman governor is concerned, Christ is emphatically innocent (Lk 23:4, 14, 22). Luke employs the trials in Acts as a political apologetic for Christianity. Part of his case is that the Roman authorities could find no guilt in either Jesus or his apostles. Tried by the highest law of the world at the time, the integrity of Christ and his followers was vindicated. John Stott comments,

> Jesus had been accused of sedition, but neither Herod nor Pilate could discover any basis for the accusation. As for Paul, in Philippi the magistrates apologized to him, in Corinth the proconsul Gallio refused to adjudicate, and in Ephesus the town clerk declared Paul and his friends to be innocent. Then Felix, Festus and Agrippa all failed to convict him of any offence—three acquittals corresponding to the three times Luke says Pilate had declared Jesus innocent. (Stott, 26)

In the OT the trials of history vindicated God's choice of a people upon whom to bestow his means and grace of salvation. In the NT, similarly, any trial could be thrown at the church of Christ; in fact, this is the expectation running through the NT letters. Revelation is a book of consolation for a suffering church. Though it passed through the waters, though it was purged in the refining process, the church emerged as a clear and undeniable testimony to God's Word and the truth and worth of the gospel. Again, as in the OT, history itself was the crucible.

See also FIRE; LEGAL IMAGES; ORDEAL, STORIES OF; TEST, TESTING.

BIBLIOGRAPHY. J. R. W. Stott, *The Message of Acts* (Downers Grove, IL: InterVarsity Press, 1990).

TRICKSTER

A trickster is a person who attempts to improve his or her situation or simply to survive by tricking others. The type is common in folklore and is represented in ancient Greek literature by the Trojan horse that turned the tide of battle in the Trojan War, and by Odysseus, famous for his wily escapes and outwitting of his antagonists on his ten-year journey home from that war. The Bible likewise features some famous tricksters. In literature generally, the trickster is either a comic figure who breaks the rigidity of the fixed social order with the audience's applause or a heroic figure who defeats forces of oppression. While this image of the sympathetic trickster is present in Scripture, the Bible also gives prominence to the opposing motif, in which divine punishment is meted out to the trickster for evil conduct.

*Jacob is the prime trickster in the Bible. His trickery is first seen when he takes advantage of his brother's hunger and buys his birthright for a bowl of soup (Gen 25:33). Then he cooperates with his domineering mother to deceive the blind Isaac and steal the blessing intended for *Esau (Gen 27:28-29). Fleeing the wrath of his understandably angry brother, Jacob goes to Haran, the ancestral homeland, where he falls in love with Rachel, daughter of his uncle Laban, who proves a worthy opponent for him. In the incident of the substitute bride, Laban tricks Jacob into thinking he is marrying Rachel, only to find in the morning light that he has married Leah instead (Gen 29:25). We are to see in this an element of justice for Jacob's earlier exploiting a family member's appetite for his own advantage. The duel between the two tricksters continues when they agree that Jacob is to receive the less common speckled or striped animals from the *flock for his wages, only to have Laban send all such animals away. In retaliation, Jacob resorts to some quack animal husbandry in an effort to increase the offspring of speckled and striped animals (Gen 30:37-43). The final trick he plays on his father-in-law is to steal away with his family and possessions while Laban is gone shearing *sheep (Gen 31:17-21). We need not suppress the latent humor in this story of tricksters who try to outwit each other and who richly deserve each other.

Other tricksters also populate the pages of Genesis, though some of them fare less well than Jacob. The trick of a patriarch's claiming to a foreign king that his wife is his sister is tried twice by *Abraham (Gen 12:10-20; 20) and once by Isaac (Gen 26:6-11). In the cases involving Abraham, God brings calamity on the king, and in all three cases the king justly rebukes the trickster. On a happier note, after the pathetic tricking of Jacob by his sons (who claim that an animal has devoured Joseph), *Joseph tricks his brothers by concealing his identity and manipulating them, all for the redemptive purpose of bringing the family (including Benjamin) together again. On the sordid side, the brothers of Dinah revenge her rape by tricking the men of Shechem into undertaking wholesale circumcision and then attacking them while they recover from the surgery (Gen 34).

The book of Judges furnishes further examples of the type. The crafty Ehud is a case study in trickery in his assassination of the oppressive foreign king Eglon (Judg 3:15-25). Ehud is resourceful in preparing a homemade sword at a time when Israelites were forbidden to fashion metal objects, in managing to gain a private audience with the king, in concealing his weapon by carrying it on the unexpected right side (he being a left-hander), in making his weapon disappear into the fat belly of Eglon, in locking the doors to the king's chamber to allow time to make a getaway while the attendants waited in consternation, and in summoning an army to capitalize on the escapade. *Samson too has a lot of the trickster in him as he uses his strength to play games against the Philistines (Judg 14—16), though he has his comeuppance when Delilah tricks him into divulging the secret of his strength. In the book of Judges, replete as it is with stories of deliverance, trickery is part of the military arsenal by which the Israelites defend themselves against their enemies.

OT history is interspersed with additional examples of trickery. When the people of Gibeon hear of Joshua's success at Jericho and Ai, they trick Joshua into thinking they are people from a distant country who desire a covenant of peace (Josh 9). *David has a checkered career as a trickster. He nettles Saul's self-confidence when he trims Saul's cape and steals his jug and spear while sparing his life (1 Sam 24; 26). He escapes from Saul's siege when Michal puts an image with goats' hair in his bed (1 Sam 19:11-17), and he successfully convinces the king of Gath that he is a madman by letting spit run down his beard (1 Sam 21:10-15). But David's attempt to get Uriah to spend the night with Bathsheba fails (2 Sam 11:6-13), and his cleverness in sending Uriah to his death in frontline duty (2 Sam 11:14-25) delivers him into God's judgment, climaxed by Nathan's tricking him into rendering a civil judgment against himself (2 Sam 12:1-15).

Stories of feminine tricksters also abound. The widowed Tamar tricks Judah into sexual union with her as a way of raising up offspring (Gen 38). The midwives trick *Pharaoh in sparing the Hebrew male infants (Ex 1:15-21), and *Moses' mother (aided by her daughter) tricks him into paying her to care for her own infant son (Ex 2:1-9). Jael uses lavish hospitality to lure the fleeing Sisera to his death (Judg 4—5). *Ruth springs a surprise on Boaz by sneaking up on him on the threshing floor and, when he awakens at midnight, telling him to propose to her (Ruth 3:6-13). We might note in passing that Boaz steals a page from Ruth and Naomi's book at the village gate the next morning, forcing his rival into a decision on the spur of the moment and making marriage to Ruth appear to be a financial transaction that he cannot possibly afford (Ruth 4:1-6).

While we might hesitate to place *Jesus among the tricksters of the Bible, he has affinities with the type, and the aura of stories of trickery hovers over some places in the Gospels. Herod tries to trick the wise men into disclosing the newborn king's identity, but they in turn trick him by returning to their native land by an alternate route (Mt 2:1-12). In the *temptation in the wilderness, *Satan and Jesus engage in a riddling battle of wits based on the use of passages from the OT Scripture (Mt 4:1-11; Lk 4:1-13). Jesus' exchanges with the Pharisees also sometimes are a battle of wits in which the two try to trap each other and in which Jesus invariably thwarts his antagonists, even to the point of silencing them. Jesus' enemies mock him in temporary triumph at the cross, but by his resurrection Jesus tricks Satan and all the forces of evil that seek to defeat his redemptive purposes for history.

In fact, there is more trickery going on the Bible than we may customarily notice. Some of it is heroic, used of God to defeat *villains and achieve good. Some of it is self-seeking and therefore self-defeating in a world governed by a God who cannot be tricked by human craftiness.

See also DECEPTION, STORIES OF; JACOB; REVERSAL.

BIBLIOGRAPHY. S. Niditch, *Underdogs and Tricksters: A Prelude to Biblical Folklore* (San Francisco: Harper & Row, 1990).

TRIUMPH

The Bible may be read as a book of the triumph of God the *divine warrior. Broadly speaking, it is a book in which God is at war against evil. The climax of the battle comes at the cross of Christ. But a final victory is yet to come, when Christ the divine warrior returns to finally overthrow death and seal his conquest over the powers of this age. The Bible is also a book of many *battles, defeats and triumphs, some of which are central to the plot line of the larger story. It is no surprise then that we encounter a number of images of triumph, and that they are used of both human and divine victories. Nearly every image of triumph owes something to the broader cultural background in which the biblical story takes place.

The Enemy Struck Down, Shattered, Crushed and Chained. In the OT we find numerous references to striking, smiting, crushing or shattering the *enemy. In some cases the action is clearly directed toward the head of the enemy. In Psalm 68:21 we read, "Surely God will crush the heads of his enemies, the hairy crowns of those who go on in their sins" (NIV). In the so-called star and scepter messianic text of Numbers 24:17, the future ruler of Israel's conquest over his enemies is vividly pictured by this image of conquest: "A star will come out of Jacob; a scepter will rise out of Israel. He will crush the foreheads of Moab, the skulls of all the sons of Sheth" (NIV). These and the numerous other biblical examples are variations on an image of kingly triumph over enemies that is well illustrated from Egyptian iconography. In these pictures the *pharaoh is represented as grasping with his *left hand the *hair of the enemy (who is squatting or on his knees) and, with mace or scimitar lifted up in his right hand, preparing to smite the enemy's skull (in a similar image from Ugarit, in northern Syria, the king's right hand holds a sword to the enemy's head, as if to pierce it). The scene, though closely tied to the battlefield, is probably a sacred execution of the enemy (see Keel, 292-93).

The story of Joshua's victory over the five Canaanite kings, followed by their public execution and the exposure of their bodies (Josh 10:26, "then Joshua struck and killed the kings and hung them on five trees" NIV; cf. Judg 5:26) is a historical depiction of this image of triumph. The numerous instances of this image (from monuments to scarabs) demonstrates that it was a stock image of triumph at least for cultures within the sphere of Egyptian influence. It was a public reminder, a mass-media image of the sovereign conquering power and authority of the king, the one who maintained the order of the kingdom against all threats of danger. And it becomes a well-used image in the OT, particulary in the psalms and prophets (e.g., Is 30:31). Perhaps we should understand the images of "breaking the teeth" and "smiting the jaw" of the enemy as variations on this image (e.g., Ps 3:7; 58:6).

We also find numerous instances of "shattering" the enemy in a manner that sometimes evokes the picture of a shattered pottery vessel (Jer 25:34). This is another image of triumph (Judg 10:8; Is 8:9; Jer 48:1, 20, 39; 50:23), but its relationship to the image of shattering the head is not clear, for "shattering" is a stock image of Yahweh's power over an object or a foe (e.g., Ex 15:6; 1 Sam 2:10; Ps 48:7; Nahum 1:6).

The imagery of lifting the hand over the enemy bears some resemblance to the image of striking the head of the enemy. In Micah 5:9 we find this image of Israel's triumph: "Your hand will be lifted up in triumph over your enemies, and all your foes will be destroyed" (NIV). In Psalm 21:8 the king uses a related image to speak of God's victory over the enemy: "Your hand will lay hold on all your enemies; your right hand will seize your foes" (NIV).

An effective image of triumph is the trampling, or crushing, of enemies underfoot. In Isaiah 14:25 Yahweh swears, "I will break the Assyrian in my land, and on my mountains trample him under foot" (NRSV). In Lamentations 1:15, where Jerusalem mourns its judgment under the hand of Yahweh, we read that Yahweh himself has "summoned an army against me to crush my young men" (NIV; cf. Amos 2:13). And in Psalm 91:13 the enemy is transposed into dangerous beasts: "You will tread on the lion and the adder, the young lion and the serpent you will trample under foot" (NRSV). This image is used by Jesus as he celebrates the return of the *Seventy and his vision of *Satan's fall from heaven: "See, I have given you authority to tread on snakes and scorpions, and over all the power of the enemy" (Lk 10:19 NRSV). And Paul tells the Romans that God will "soon crush Satan under your feet" (Rom 16:20), an allusion to divine triumph in which he incorporates *Adamic imagery (cf. Gen 3:16; Ps 8:6) and the hope of a new *creation.

Finally, the image of an enemy bound or chained, or even caught in a net, is an image of triumph. Numerous examples of Egyptian and Mesopotamian iconography depict conquered warriors and kings bound and tethered by a rope or held captive in a net (Keel, 299-303). In some cases the rope is held by a god, since a victory of the king is also a divine victory. This ancient Near Eastern imagery richly illuminates the scene of Psalm 2, where the action moves between two stages, the *throne rooms of heaven and of Mount Zion, between the heavenly *king and the Davidic king. The kings of the earth, who are bound in subjection, are conspiring to revolt: "The kings of the earth take their stand and the rulers gather together against the LORD and against his Anointed One. 'Let us break their chains,' they say, 'and throw off their fetters.' The One enthroned in heaven

laughs; the Lord scoffs at them" (Ps 2:2-4 NIV). In Psalm 149:8 Israel's triumph over her enemies is depicted as binding "their kings with fetters, their nobles with shackles of iron" (NIV). And we find numerous instances of the imagery of people being caught in a net, an instrument not only of the *hunt but of warfare (e.g., Ps 9:15; Ezek 17:20; Hos 5:1; Hab 1:15-17). In the psalms it is a frequent image of the hostility of the foes of an individual (e.g., Ps 10:9; 35:7-8; 57:6). Jesus speaks of "binding the strong man" (Mt 12:29; Mk 3:27) and in Revelation 20:2 Satan, the great enemy, is bound "for a thousand years."

Triumphal Procession. In the world of the OT a triumph over enemies had two aspects: the triumph of a god and the triumph of a human king. "Religion" and warfare were interwoven, and the celebration of a triumph was as much a celebration of divine triumph as it was a celebration of kingly triumph. The archetypal pattern of divine warfare and triumph was fivefold: (1) a *god battled against an enemy god (of monstrous proportions, such as *Sea) and was (2) victorious over the enemy; this was followed by (3) the enthronement of the god as king, (4) the building of his house (temple) and (5) a great banquet of celebration. The pattern is one that leads from the battlefield to the *city and *temple. In the OT we observe this general pattern in the Song of Moses (Ex 15:1-18), where Yahweh, "a warrior" (Ex 15:3; see Divine Warrrior), is victorious over Pharaoh and his army (and by implication, over Egypt's gods). The kingship of Yahweh and the building of his temple is described in the final lines of this hymn, which suggest a procession of God and people to "the mountain [Zion] of your own possession, the place that you made your abode, the sanctuary, O Lord, that your hands have established. The LORD will reign forever and ever" (Ex 15:17-18). In this case the hymn itself is a celebration of the progression through the first four phases of the pattern.

Segments of this triumphal march of Yahweh may also be observed in various poetic renderings of his march from the region of Sinai or his approaching the *gates of Jerusalem:

The LORD came from Sinai,
and dawned from Seir upon us;
he shone forth from Mount Paran.
With him were myriads of holy ones;
at his right, a host of his own.
(Deut 33:2 NRSV)

With mighty chariotry, twice ten thousand,
thousands upon thousands,
the Lord came from Sinai into the holy place.
You ascended the high mount,
leading captives in your train
and receiving gifts from people,
even from those who rebel against the
LORD God's abiding there.
(Ps 68:17-18 NRSV)

The same pattern may be observed in the stirring hymn of the divine warrior in Habakkuk 3:2-19. And it is this pattern of triumphal march that lies behind the familiar words of Isaiah 40:3-5: "A voice cries out: 'In the wilderness prepare the way of the LORD, make straight in the desert a highway for our God. . . . Then the glory of the LORD shall be revealed' " (NRSV). This is a preparation for Yahweh's return to Zion as the divine warrior who now liberates Israel from Exile in a second exodus (*see* Exodus, Second Exodus). Within Isaiah 40—66 the motif resurfaces in passages such as Isaiah 52:7-12, where heralds of peace appear on the mountains of Judah and declare to Zion, "Your God reigns." Zion's sentinels cry out as they see "the return of the LORD to Zion." Yahweh the divine warrior is returning in his victory procession: "The LORD has bared his holy arm before the eyes of all the nations; and all the ends of the earth shall see the salvation of our God" (Is 52:10 NRSV).

There is some evidence that during the kingdom period Israel celebrated the kingship and victories of Yahweh (in a New Year's festival) by reenacting his march to Jerusalem and his entrance into his temple (see, e.g., Cross, 91-111). The *ark of the covenant, the symbolic palladium of the divine warrior (cf. Num 10:35-36), may have played an important role in this procession to the temple mount. We catch a glimpse of this in the story of *David bringing the ark into *Jerusalem in the midst of great celebration (2 Sam 6). This type of celebration may have been the occasion for psalms celebrating the kingship of God (e.g., Ps 47, 95, 96, 98, 99), and the procession of Yahweh to Zion may well lie behind the repeated refrain in Psalm 24:7, 9: "Lift up your head, O gates! and be lifted up, O ancient doors! that the King of glory may come in." The "King of glory" is identified as "The LORD, strong and mighty, the LORD, mighty in battle" (Ps 24:8 NRSV).

The triumphal entry of Jesus into Jerusalem should be viewed against the background of this *processional motif (*see* Procession, Triumphal Procession). Jesus comes riding on a *donkey, and so fulfills Zechariah's prophecy of a king who would come to Zion riding "a colt, the foal of a donkey" (Zech 9:9) and proclaim peace to the nations (Zech 9:10). Jesus is greeted as a Davidic Messiah, with crowds shouting the words of Psalm 118:25-26. They spread cloaks and branches on the road before him (Mk 11:8-10) in a manner reminiscent of Jehu being declared king (2 Kings 9:13). But more than that, the Synoptic Gospels point out that Jesus has been making his way to Jerusalem with numerous signs that he is enacting this great return of Yahweh to Zion (see Wright, 612-53). Mark makes this evident by opening his Gospel (Mk 1:2-3) with fulfillment of Isaiah 40:3—"Prepare the way for the LORD"—and then showing Jesus progressively moving along the "way" (particularly in Mark 8:22—11:1) to Jerusalem. Jesus is enacting the role of the divine warrior who makes his way to his holy mount and temple. But the story takes an unusual turn: he inspects the temple, departs and then returns to symbolically enact its destruction (Mk 11:15-17). This prediction of *judgment brings about his own destruction (Mk 11:18), which in fact proves to be his victory. It is through the destruction of "this temple," "his body" (Jn 2:18-22), that he will build his new temple, the church (cf. Mk 14:57-58; 15:29-30; Mt 26:61; 27:40; Eph 2:19-22).

In the NT world the triumphal procession was developed by the Romans to celebrate the occasion of a major victory. The victorious general or ruler in ceremonial dress would drive his captives—usually those of highest status—and the spoils of war before him into Rome. When he arrived at the god's temple, the prisoners, or representatives of their number, would be executed. In this processional the glory and power of the Roman *imperium* was celebrated, with the triumphant general playing the role of Jupiter, the god who had blessed the warrior with victory in battle (cf. Josephus *J.W.* 7.5.6 §§153-55). Paul employs the image of the Roman triumphal procession to depict the victory of Christ on the *cross.

In 1 Corinthians 2:6-8 Paul alludes to the story behind the scene of the victory at the cross: the "rulers of this age" did not comprehend the mystery of the divine *wisdom of the cross, "for if they had, they would not have crucified the Lord of glory." These rulers are spiritual, cosmic powers who are hostile and oblivious to the wisdom of God's plan for the ages (cf. Eph 3:10), and so they have crucified the Lord of glory. But this was their monumental folly, for they did not understand that God's strategy of triumph was a deeply paradoxical one and utterly contradictory to the strategies of this age. Colossians 2:15 alludes to the circumstances of the defeat of these powers. The powers unleashed their assault on Christ, in a climactic expression of the nations attacking *Zion, and on the cross they destroyed his "body of flesh" (Col 2:11). But this was only a pyrrhic victory. Christ absorbed and exhausted their fury in his death (with his vindication in the resurrection implied) and so he triumphed over the powers (Col 2:15). On the cross Christ marched them in his own triumphal procession, publicly displaying their defeat and exposing them to shame. J. B. Lightfoot elegantly summed it up: "The paradox of the crucifixion is thus placed in its strongest light—triumph in helplessness and glory in shame. The convict's gibbet is the victor's car."

The metaphor of victory is, at its heart, not simply the victory of a superior power but the triumph of God's holy, righteous and creative love over the destructive forces of evil, the reclaiming of a creation gone astray. Paul elsewhere makes plain that the cross is not the last chapter in the warfare against the powers of this age. The enemy is still hostile and active, posing a threat to the church (Eph 6:10-18). On the final day this battle will reach its resolution when "every dominion, and every authority and power will be destroyed," along with the final enemy, death (1 Cor 15:24, 26; cf. 2 Tim 1:10).

In 2 Corinthians 2:14 Paul speaks of himself as being led in the triumphal procession of Christ. Paul is not portraying himself as one of the high-ranking officers in Christ's army but as a former enemy and persecutor of Christ, who has been conquered and is now marched as a captive, constantly being led to his death (cf. 2 Cor 4:10). By this metaphor he sets forth the paradox of his apostolic ministry: in his *weakness and cruciform suffering the power of the triumphant Christ is made manifest (2 Cor 12:10). The triumph of God in Christ is not the triumph of brute force, as if to assert a cosmic principle of "might is right." It is a triumph of grace in which divine love goes forth in sacrifice.

Triumph at the End of the Age. When Paul speaks of the *Day of the Lord (e.g., 1 Cor 5:5; 1 Thess 5:2, 4; 2 Thess 1:10; 2:2) he quite naturally uses the imagery of the divine warrior's day of triumph. The parousia, or arrival, of Christ is a christological interpretation of the coming of the divine warrior. The overall impression is of the Lord Jesus acting as the eschatological agent of God the Father (cf. 1 Cor 15:23-28; 1 Thess 1:10; 4:14, 16; 5:9; but cf. Tit 2:13). God acts in Christ, and so Paul can readily ascribe the imagery of the divine warrior to the coming of Christ. The visual imagery includes *fire (2 Thess 1:7; cf. Ps 104:4; Is 29:6; 30:30; 66:15-16; Dan 7:9); *angels, or "holy ones" (1 Thess 3:13; 2 Thess 1:7; cf. Deut 33:2; Zech 14:5; *1 Enoch* 1:9; Jude 14); and *clouds, most likely an oblique reference to the cloud chariot of the divine warrior (Ps 68:4; Dan 7:13; Mk 13:26; cf. 2 Kings 2:11-12; see 1.1 above). The event of "meeting" (*apantēsin*) the Lord in the air (1 Thess 4:16-17) is the equivalent of dignitaries and citizens of a city going out to greet an approaching ruler or deliverer

A Pharaoh tirumphs over his enemies, trampling and smiting them.

to escort him into the city. Paul has tilted the scene on a vertical axis with believers going forth to greet Christ, the arriving victorious warrior, to welcome and escort him in his triumphal approach (cf. Ps 68:24-35; Mt 25:6). It is a sort of reprise of Jesus' triumphal entry into Jerusalem. The "loud command," the "call" of the archangel (1 Thess 4:16;

cf. Josh 6:5; Judg 7:20; Zeph 1:16; 1 Macc 3:54) and the "trumpet call of God" (1 Cor 15:52; 1 Thess 4:16; cf. Num 10:9; Josh 6:5; Zeph 1:16; 1 Macc 3:54) all reflect a summons to battle. The cumulative picture recalls the processional of the divine warrior to his holy mountain and temple to reclaim his territory.

If we understand 2 Thessalonians 2:3-12 as a continuation or enlargement of this story, Christ finds on his arrival a usurping power seated in the "temple of God" (2 Thess 2:3-4). This "man of lawlessness," who has led many astray by his counterfeit parousia and is inspired by Satan (2 Thess 2:9-10), is overthrown at the parousia of Christ the divine warrior (2 Thess 2:8; cf. Is 66:6). This compressed episode in which the enemy is "destroyed" by Christ's *breath/spirit and "annihilated" by his splendor recalls the victory of the messianic conqueror of Isaiah 11:4 and is replete with images of divine warfare.

Dividing the Spoils. "To the victor go the spoils" is a fundamental rule of warfare. In the Song of Moses we overhear the boast of the enemy, "I will divide the spoil, my desire shall have its fill of them" (Ex 15:9 NRSV). In the Song of Deborah the Canaanite women await the return of their warrior Sisera, unaware that he has been slain by Jael. The "wisest lady's" imaginary depiction of the victor dividing spoils after battle offers a glimpse of a classic scene repeated after many an ancient battle: "Are they not finding and dividing the spoil?—A girl or two for every man; spoils of dyed stuffs for Sisera, spoil of dyed stuffs embroidered, two pieces of dyed work embroidered for my neck as spoil?" (Judg 5:30 NRSV). This scene offers a sharp contrast with the noble Abraham who will take no spoil after his defeat of Chedorlaomer and his coalition of kings. To the king of Sodom, Abraham says, "I have sworn . . . that I would not take a thread or a sandal-thong or anything that is yours, so that you might not say, 'I have made Abram rich' " (Gen 14:22-23 NRSV; cf. 14:24).

The taking of a trophy from the enemy had ceremonial significance. It might consist of armor or a head or even the living leader of the rival army brought back for public display. But in Israel's "holy warfare," all adult males were to be slaughtered (Deut 20:13-14) and women, children, livestock and everything else could be taken as plunder. But in some instances much more is to be "devoted" to the Lord in a sacrificial slaughter and burning (e.g., Josh 6:24). David is remembered in 1 Samuel 30:23-25 for laying down the principle of distributing the war booty evenly between those who stayed with the supplies and those who fought on the front lines, for the Lord has given them the spoils (1 Sam 30:23).

Holy warfare in Israel is classically defined as the wars of conquest, the taking of Canaan. Here the *land is the primary "plunder," though in the truest sense the battles of conquest in the Book of Joshua are Yahweh's battles and Yahweh's victories (e.g., Josh 10:42). The land belongs to Yahweh and it is given to Israel as a trust. These battle stories are capped with a careful survey and allotment of the spoils of war—the land—to the tribes of Israel (Josh 13—21). Psalm 60:6-8 captures the spirit of divine triumph and the land as the booty of war:

> God has spoken from his sanctuary:
> "In triumph I will parcel out Shechem
> and measure off the Valley of Succoth.
> Gilead is mine, and Manasseh is mine;
> Ephraim is my helmet,
> Judah my scepter.
> Moab is my washbasin,
> upon Edom I toss my sandal;
> over Philistia I shout in triumph."
> (NIV; cf. Ps 108:7-9)

Even Isaiah's *suffering servant is essentially a warrior figure who will be "exalted and lifted up" (Is 52:13 NRSV). God declares, "Therefore I will allot him a portion with the great, and he shall divide the spoil with the strong" (Is 53:12 NRSV). Jesus refers to his own triumph over demonic powers when he speaks of defeating the "strong man," Satan, and dividing up the spoils (Lk 11:21-22). In Ephesians 4:8 Paul echoes the picture of a triumphant warrior in Psalm 68:18. But whereas in the psalm the victor receives gifts from his people, Paul says, "When he ascended on high he made captivity itself a captive; he *gave* gifts to his people" (NRSV). These gifts are the apostles, prophets, evangelists, pastors and teachers given to the church "to equip the saints" (Eph 4:11-12)

Enthroned with Enemies Under the Feet. In the ancient Near East a pervasive image of triumph over an enemy is the positioning of the enemy *under the feet of the conqueror. In Joshua 10:24 Joshua commands the "chiefs of the warriors" to come forward and place their feet on the *necks of the five Canaanite kings Israel has just conquered. After this symbolic act of triumph, the kings are killed, their bodies hung on *trees and then sealed in a *cave. In ancient Near Eastern iconography we find images of enemies under a footstool, beneath the feet of the reigning king (Keel, 253-55). This image seems to carry the connotation of shaming the enemy (to direct the sole of the foot toward someone is a shaming action) and treading on them in a manner that lays claim to them, perhaps analogous to walking over their territory (Josh 1:3; 14:9; Ps 8:6). We find the image in Psalm 47:3: "He subdued nations under us, peoples under our feet" (NIV; cf. 1 Kings 5:3; Mal 4:3). This image comes to the fore in Psalm 110:1, where the coming Davidic king is commanded by God to "sit at my right hand until I make your enemies a footstool for your feet" (NRSV). The imagery of enemies under the feet (particularly the language of Ps 110:1) becomes a favorite image of NT writers for depicting the *ascended and triumphant Christ, sometimes with the emphasis on the spiritual enemies (e.g., principalities and powers) that

Christ has conquered. Thus Paul speaks of Christ reigning "until he has put all his enemies under his feet. The last enemy to be destroyed is death. For 'God has put all things in subjection under his feet' " (1 Cor 15:25-27 NRSV; cf. Acts 2:35; Eph 1:22; Heb 1:13; 2:8; 10:13). And in Romans 16:20 Paul speaks of a coming victory: "the God of peace will shortly crush Satan under your feet" (NRSV; cf. Gen 3:15). Finally, in Revelation 4—5 we have a heavenly throne room scene in which "the Lord God the Almighty" is enthroned and the conquering *"Lamb," who is "the Lion of the tribe of Judah, the Root of David" is beside the throne (Rev 5:5-6 NRSV).

Victory Banquet. Victory celebrations are one image of triumph, and we catch a first glimpse of one in the first story of triumph in the Bible in Genesis 14. There Abraham is victorious over Chedorlaomer and his coalition of kings. When Abraham returns from battle he brings back all of the goods that had been taken and the people who had been captured. Abraham takes nothing for himself, but Melchizedek, king of Salem, comes forth to bless Abraham and share bread and wine with him. From a later period, Psalm 118:15-16 captures the scene of a triumph in Israel:

> Shouts of joy and victory
> resound in the tents of the righteous:
> "The LORD's right hand has done mighty things!
> The LORD's right hand is lifted high;
> the LORD's right hand has done mighty things!"
> (NIV)

One of the most memorable images of a victory banquet celebration comes in Isaiah 25:6-10, where the Lord finally triumphs over death and "makes for all peoples a feast of rich food, a feast of well-aged wines, of rich food filled with marrow, of well-aged wines strained and clear" (NRSV). Jesus alludes to this eschatological banquet when at the last supper he tells his disciples, "I will not drink again of the fruit of the vine until that day when I drink it again in the kingdom of God" (Mk 14:25 NIV). The book of Revelation caps the theme of triumph with a variety of scenes of celebration. The vision of the Lamb who has conquered (Rev 5:5-6) is followed by an awesome chorus sung by the hosts of heaven celebrating the victory of the Lamb (Rev 5:9-14), and worship is offered to "the one seated on the throne and to the Lamb" (Rev 5:13 NRSV). The theme of celebration swells to a climax in the appearance of the "new heaven and a new earth" and the New Jerusalem, the city of the victorious King and the Lamb (Rev 21—22). In this city there is no temple, "for its temple is the Lord God the Almighty and the Lamb" (Rev 21:22). The banquet of victory is the "water of life" (Rev 21:6) and the twelve fruits of the "tree of life" (Rev 22:2).

See also ARK OF THE COVENANT; ARMOR; ARMY, ARMIES; BANQUET; BATTLE STORIES; CROSS; DAY, DAY OF THE LORD; DIVINE WARRIOR; ENEMY; KING, KING-

899

SHIP; PROCESSION, TRIUMPHAL PROCESSION; UNDER THE FEET; WEAPONS.

BIBLIOGRAPHY. F. M. Cross, *Canaanite Myth and Hebrew Epic* (Cambridge, MA: Harvard University Press, 1973); O. Keel, *The Symbolism of the Biblical World* (Winona Lake, IN.: Eisenbrauns, 1997) 291-306; T. Longman III and D. G. Reid, *God Is a Warrior* (SOTBT; Grand Rapids: Zondervan, 1995); N. T. Wright, *Jesus and the Victory of God* (Minneapolis: Fortress, 1996).

TRIUMPHAL PROCESSION. *See* PROCESSION, TRIUMPHAL PROCESSION; TRIUMPH.

TRUMPET

In the Bible the word *trumpet* generally refers to ram's *horns used as sound makers. The trumpets commissioned by Moses, however, were probably straight metal instruments (Num 10:10). All were used for a variety of proclamatory and signaling purposes.

Probably none of the biblical trumpets were primarily *musical* instruments. Their short air column meant the number of pitches available was very limited. Also, whether a trumpet could be tuned is doubtful, although 2 Chronicles 5:12 refers to 120 trumpets sounding "in unison," and the Dead Sea scroll known as the *War Scroll* (1QM) indicates that trumpets were used musically in *worship. In any case, the trumpet was principally marked not by musical tones but by loudness; it was primarily an announcement device (the terrifyingly loud *voice of the Lord at *Sinai was said to be like a trumpet; Ex 19—20). Its symbolic value was to stress the publicness of an event.

The trumpet's most common use was in *war making: as a summons to war (Job 39:24; Jer 4:19), to mark the commencement of an attack (Judg 3:27; 6:34), to signal the end of an attack (2 Sam 2:28; 18:16; 20:22), to warn of coming attack (Jer 6:1, 17; Ezek 33:3-6; Hos 5:8; Joel 2:1) or to proclaim military victory (1 Sam 13:3). Hence in Jeremiah 4:21 the sound of the trumpet is a metonym for war itself.

Trumpets also called public attention to other events: claims to *kingship (2 Sam 5:10; 1 Kings 1:34, 39; 2 Kings 9:13), public disavowals (2 Sam 20:1) or *oath takings (2 Chron 15:14). They marked special celebrations (Ps 81:3; Joel 2:15) and rejoicing (2 Sam 6:15). Thus the trumpet was also an instrument of civic ritual.

Consequently, trumpets were appropriate for certain acts of worship. Trumpets could announce the time of worship (Is 27:13) and accompanied public adulation and praise (1 Chron 15:28; 2 Chron 15:12-13; Ps 98:6; 150:3). There was even a special *feast day marked by trumpets (Lev 23:23-25). But the trumpet's most abiding function in worship was on the Day of Atonement. The trumpet was to be blown at Yom Kippur in the year of Jubilee to announce liberation and *restoration (Lev 25:9).

Later Jewish worship applied this mandate to every Yom Kippur, to symbolize the substitution of the ram for Isaac in Genesis 22:13.

Public announcement or summons is the function of trumpets in the NT. Paul observes in 1 Corinthians 14:8 that "if the trumpet does not sound a clear call, who will get ready for battle?" (NIV). Jesus uses trumpet blowing as a metaphor for ostentation in Matthew 6:2. Probably no one literally blew a trumpet when they gave alms—but some people make such a show of their piety that they might as well have.

In the NT a trumpet serves in particular as an eschatological image to declare the coming of Christ in *judgment. This appears to combine a number of the trumpet functions: summoning, warning, call to arms and announcement of *kingship. In Matthew 24:31 the *angels are sent out "with a loud trumpet call" (NIV) to gather the elect. Paul extends the image to include a summoning of the dead to life (1 Cor 15:52; 1 Thess 4:16). The trumpet ensures that these events are extremely and unambiguously public. The book of Revelation depicts a series of *seven trumpets, six of which announce various disasters and judgments (the onset of spiritual battles) coming upon the earth. The seventh, climactic trumpet (Rev 11:15) signals the complete investiture of Christ and the beginning of his total and eternal dominion of the world (the end of the battle and recall of troops).

Revelation 1:10-13 and 4:1 indicate that the One "like a son of man" (Jesus) speaks with a voice that sounds like a trumpet. This of course picks up on the fact that the Lord's voice on Mount Sinai sounded like a trumpet (Ex 19—20). It is one of the many OT depictions of YHWH that are applied to Jesus in Revelation.

See also HORN; MUSIC.

TUTOR. *See* TEACHER, TEACHING.

TWELVE

As a symbol, twelve is one of the most important numbers in the Bible. The importance of the number twelve arose, in part, from the culture of the ancient Near East, where there were twelve months in the lunar calendar and twelve was prominent in the number system. However, in the Bible the importance of this number derives from the emergence of the twelve tribes of *Israel (Gen 49:28).

Following the *exodus, Moses built twelve *pillars on Mount *Sinai, according to the twelve tribes (Ex 24:4). In anticipation of the conquest of the *Promised Land, twelve spies were sent to spy out the land (Num 13:1-16; Deut 1:23). When Joshua led the people of Israel across the *Jordan River, twelve men, one from each tribe, were commanded to gather twelve *stones as a memorial of the crossing (Josh 3—4). Twelve stones were attached to the breastpiece of the priestly vestments, bearing the names of the twelve tribes (Ex 39:8-14). Solomon's various building projects, including the *temple, involved numbers and measurements of twelve (twelve district governors, 1 Kings 4:7; twelve thousand *horses, 1 Kings 4:26; two bronze pillars, each eighteen cubits high and twelve cubits around by line, 1 Kings 7:15; the *Sea stood on twelve bulls, 1 Kings 7:25; twelve *lions stood on the six steps, one at either end of each step, 1 Kings 10:20). In his contest with the *prophets of Baal, Elijah built an *altar with twelve stones (1 Kings 18:31-32).

The significance of twelve carries over into the NT. Jesus appointed twelve apostles (Mk 3:14), probably as a symbol of the *restoration of Israel. Similar symbolism is probably intended in the gathering up of the twelve baskets of fragments following the feeding of the five thousand (Mk 6:43; 8:19). Jesus' promise that the Twelve would someday sit on twelve *thrones judging the twelve tribes of Israel (Mt 19:28; Lk 22:30) probably had to do with his desire to restore Israel. James's reference to the twelve tribes of the Dispersion (Jas 1:1) in all probability reflects similar thinking.

The symbolism of twelve appears frequently in the book of Revelation. Twelve thousand persons from each of the twelve tribes of Israel are sealed, totaling 144,000 in all (Rev 7:5-8). The woman (= Israel) who gives birth to the child (= Jesus) is *crowned with "twelve stars," probably an allusion to the twelve tribes (Rev 12:1-2). The new *Jerusalem, which will descend from heaven (Rev 21:1-4), is rich with symbolism, much of which revolves around the number twelve. The eschatological city will have twelve *gates, twelve angels as gatekeepers, and the names of the twelve tribes written on the gates (Rev 21:12). We are told that these gates are twelve *pearls (Rev 21:21). The *wall of the city will rest on twelve *foundations, on which will be inscribed the names of the twelve apostles (Rev 21:14). The city will be twelve thousand stadia square (Rev 21:16). Finally, the *tree of life, an image that surely is meant to recall the tree of life that once stood in the Garden of Eden (Gen 2:9; 3:22), will stand in the city and bear twelve kinds of *fruit every month, for the healing of the nations (Rev 22:2).

The NT's adoption of symbolism of twelve is testimony to the enduring power of this OT image. Underlying this interest in the number twelve is the conviction that ultimately God will fulfill his promises of redemption. It is a number that clearly is associated with the twelve tribes and thus with divine election.

See also DISCIPLE, DISCIPLESHIP; FIFTY; FIVE; FORTY; FOUR; HUNDRED; ISRAEL; NUMBERS IN THE BIBLE; ONE; SEVEN; SEVENTY; TEN; THOUSAND; THREE; TWO.

BIBLIOGRAPHY. E. Best, "Mark's Use of the Twelve," *ZNW* 69 (1978) 11-35; R. P. Meye, *Jesus and the Twelve* (Grand Rapids: Eerdmans, 1968).

TWILIGHT

Technically twilight is the time between sunset and *night, though the ancient Hebrews extended the time beyond that. In the Bible, twilight is above all a transition time in the daily cycle. It brings daytime to a close and ushers in the night. In the nature-dominated world of the Bible, the normal human rhythm is that in the morning "man goes forth to his work and to his labor until the evening" (Ps 104:23 RSV). In Jesus' parable of the *workers in the *vineyard, too, the laborers work until evening, when they receive their payment (Mt 20:8). Evening here has associations of rest and reward after the laboring day.

It is inherent in human experience that some activities are performed in the *morning and again in the evening. The OT is replete with references to *sacrifices and *offerings that were performed in the evening as well as the morning. The most important twilight ritual was doubtless the slaughter of a sacrificial *Passover *lamb at twilight (Ex 12:6; Lev 23:5; Num 9:3, 5 NRSV). In such cases, evening or twilight assumes a sacral significance. Elsewhere the rhythm of morning and evening exists without such associations. The giant Goliath came out to chant his ritual *taunt "morning and evening" (1 Sam 17:16). In a psalm that praises God's control of nature, the poet asserts that God makes "the outgoings of the morning and the evening to shout for joy" (Ps 65:8 RSV).

*Days in biblical cultures were numbered from sunset to sunset, and the *sabbath and religious festivals began and ended at twilight. Here too twilight possesses a sacral significance, the beginning of a religious exercise. Certain forms of ceremonial uncleanness also ended in the evening. It is easy to imagine that evening would connote release for people who waited for the end of day to complete their time of uncleanness.

In human experience twilight is a mysterious and pensive time. In some pagan religions and mythologies, the threshold between the natural and supernatural realms was less clearly defined at twilight. We find virtually no such images of twilight in the Bible, where it is *morning that is more typically infused with spiritual significance. The exception is the evocative picture of Isaac going "out to meditate in the field in the evening," on which occasion he met his bride for the first time (Gen 24:63 RSV).

The settling of dusk can also be a time for people to engage in illicit activities. Proverbs 7:9 gives us a memorable picture of the sexual adventuress (*see* Seduction) who meets her naive young victim on the street "in the twilight, in the evening, at the time of night and darkness" (RSV). In similar fashion, Job's portrait of the wicked includes the detail "The eye of the adulterer also waits for the twilight, saying, 'No eye will see me' " (Job 24:15 RSV). And Isaiah pictures twilight as a time of literal and metaphoric stumbling (Is 59:10).

See also DAY; MORNING; NIGHT; NOON; SUN.

TWO

While lacking the obvious symbolic and sacral significance of numbers like *seven, *ten and *twelve, two has a high incidence in the Bible, showing that no number is more important, as even a word search indicates (NIV 559 references; NRSV 645). From the very start, the image of two is essential in Scripture. Inherent in the created order is the fact of two genders, and virtually the entire Bible presupposes an awareness of them. Equally pervasive is the conflict between good and *evil, *light and *darkness, as the Bible repeatedly employs the motif of two sides in the cosmic *battle. Still, the Bible rejects the dualism that characterizes many other religions. In the Bible the cosmos is not the result of a battle between two conflicting powers or deities. Every biblical image of two has to be seen as second to the sentence "Hear, O Israel: The LORD our God, the LORD is one" (Deut 6:4 NIV; cf. Eph 4:4-6).

Following that fundamental creed, the number two refers to powers, persons, experiences and facts within the cosmos. In many ways two encompasses the basic structure of all relationships, such as love or hatred, prosperity or deprivation, *obedient or disobedient to God. The image of two is thus part of the biblical superstructure of human choice between contrary possibilities. Within the general principle various categories can be discerned.

Complementary pairs are part of the created order, as evidenced already in the *creation story: "In the beginning God created the heaven and the earth" (Gen 1:1), day and night, land and sea, and "two great lights" (Gen 1:16 NIV). The concept of two also becomes an experience of human life and society when God creates humankind as male and female (Gen 1:27). So the primordial principle of human life is to be coexistent with an "other," as a pair (Gen 2:24; Mt 19:5-6). This does not refer only to man and woman, as Ecclesiastes points out: "Two are better than one, because they have a good return for their work: if one falls down, his friend can help him up" (Eccles 4:9-10 NIV).

From the origin of two, new life comes into being. Most of the patriarchal offspring come in significant pairs: *Cain and *Abel (Gen 4), Ishmael and Isaac (Gen 16; 21), *Jacob and *Esau (Gen 25). They are of importance not as individuals but as types of humans with different ways of living: Abel keeps flocks, Cain works the soil. Or they are regarded as origins of different people: the Lord said to Rebekah, "Two nations are in your womb, and two peoples from within you will be separated" (Gen 25:23 NIV).

Or we might consider the motif of the *covenant. When God makes the covenant with Israel at Mt. *Sinai, he gives Moses "two tablets . . . of stone inscribed by the finger of God" (Ex 31:18 NIV), indicating that relationships to God and to fellow humans are inseparable. Jesus is very clear about on the matter: " 'Love the Lord your God.' . . . This is the first and greatest commandment. And the second is like it: 'Love your neighbor as yourself.' All the Law and the Prophets hang on these two commandments" (Mt 22:37-40 NIV). Again, the two options of obedience and disobedience are inherent in the covenant. Moses highlights the contrast between the

two in his *farewell discourse: "See, I set before you today life and prosperity, death and destruction, . . . blessings and curses. Now choose life" (Deut 30:15, 19 NIV). Even more foundational to the Bible is the motif of two covenants or two testaments, with the one anticipating its fulfillment in the other.

The NT anchors the call for decision in the image of two possibilities: "For wide is the gate . . . that leads to destruction. . . . But small is the gate . . . that leads to life" (Mt 7:13-14 NIV). Again, "No one can serve two masters" (Mt 6:24 NIV). Many of Jesus' parables show two types of behavior and therefore two alternative choices about one's life, including the parables about the *younger and *elder sons, the *Pharisee and tax collector, good and bad stewards, wise and unwise virgins, wheat and weeds, the passersby and the good Samaritan, the two sons of the father with the vineyard.

OT wisdom literature adds to the "literature of two" with the motif of the two *paths or ways. Psalm 1, for example, is structured as a prolonged contrast between "the way of the righteous" and "the way of the wicked." Passages early in Proverbs contrast "the way of evil" and "the paths of uprightness" (Prov 2:12-15 RSV), "the way of evildoers" and "the path of the righteous" (Prov 4:14-19 RSV). Psalm 139 ends with a contrast between the "wicked way" and "the way everlasting" (Ps 139:24 RSV).

On a more mundane level, in the OT two is the minimum number of people to be sent on an important assignment. For instance, two *angels are sent to Sodom (Gen 19:1) and two *spies to Jericho (Josh 2:1). When Jesus called the *Twelve to him, "he sent them out two by two" (Mk 6:7 NIV; cf. Mt 21:1). The minimum number of two also appears in an ancient rule of jurisdiction that asks for two *witnesses (Deut 17:6; Mt 18:16; Rev 11:3). The Gospel of John depicts two witnesses on Easter morning (Jn 20:3). And the most important exemplary story of encountering the risen Jesus calls two disciples as witnesses on their way to Emmaus (Lk 24:13; cf. Mk 16:12).

While some of the references to two are devoid of inherent significance (such as references to two days), most of the references suggest something elemental to the number, perhaps implying completeness (on the principle of two halves making a whole, or two providing a balance, or two serving as foils to each other). The OT ceremonial laws, as well as the details of the construction and rituals of the *tabernacle and *temple, ring the changes on the number two (the NIV lists nearly 150 references in the last four books of the Pentateuch). In addition, the list of paired characters extends almost indefinitely: Adam and Eve, Cain and Abel, Abraham and Sarah, Rachel and Leah, Jacob and Esau, Joseph and Benjamin, Moses and Aaron, Joshua and Caleb, Deborah and Barak, David and Jonathan, Mary and Martha.

In summary, the motif of two appears in creation, in the procreation of people and *animals, in *marriage, in the moral choice confronting everyone in the "two ways." Two is a fundamental biblical image. Even the biblical worldview divides reality into a great duality of God versus *Satan, obedience versus disobedience to God's law, heaven versus hell, good versus evil, a giving spirit versus self-centeredness, heavenly mindedness versus worldly mindedness.

See also FIFTY; FIVE; FORTY; FOUR; HUNDRED; NUMBERS IN THE BIBLE; ONE; SEVEN; SEVENTY; TEN; THOUSAND; THREE; TWELVE.

TWO WAYS. *See* PATH.

TYRANNICAL FATHER, HUSBAND

The tyrannical and obtuse father is a stock figure in classical and Shakespearean romantic comedy, where he serves the role of blocking character whom the young couple outwit en route to the happy conclusion of their romance. Biblical examples of the archetype are more far-ranging, and they give us a figure who is repulsive rather than a laughingstock.

The Bible's "book of beginnings" gives us some early examples. The archetype is latent in the blustering, mean-hearted braggart Lamech, who parades his bullying before his wives in a litany of his vengeful exploits (Gen 4:23-24). The motif is also latent in *Abraham's telling his wife that a "kindness" she "must do" him as they travel in potentially hostile lands is to claim that he is her brother rather than her husband (Gen 20:13 RSV), a ploy that twice lands her in a foreign king's harem and occasions the first moral sermon in the Bible—directed by *Pharaoh to the patriarch! Laban too fills the role of a domineering father and father-in-law in his substitution of Leah for Rachel on the wedding night and in his business dealings with Jacob.

The book of *Judges, a veritable gallery of strong-willed males, furnishes further instances. The daughter of the impulsive Jephthah pays the price for his rash vow (Judg 11). The *trickster *Samson manipulates Delilah until she turns the tables on him (Judg 16). The man of Bethlehem, like Lot on a similar occasion (Gen 19:8), offers his virgin daughter and the Levite's concubine to lustful men prowling about his house, finally thrusting the concubine out of his house to be abused to death (Judg 19:22-26).

In the book of *Esther the Persian king Ahasuerus is a stock tyrannical husband. As part of the entertainment at his stag party, he orders his queen Vashti to make a public display of her physical *beauty. When she refuses, he erupts in rage, finally deposing her and bringing the vaunted Persian postal system into action to publish an edict that "all women . . . give honor to their husbands, high and low" (Esther 1:20 RSV).

Perhaps the clearest biblical example of the exasperating father is King Saul, whose volatile temper frightens both his children and their best friends (1 Sam 19—20). Saul tries to bully his son Jonathan into taking his side against David, even hurling his spear at Jonathan in an attempt to kill him when he resists (1 Sam 20). Earlier Saul had been ready to kill Jonathan for unwittingly eating honey when it had been prohibited, with Saul's soldiers finally rescuing his son from the unreasonable wrath of a misguided father (1 Sam 14). When Michal ridicules her husband, *David, for his abandoned dancing before the transported *ark of God, David responds in heavy-handed fashion and cuts off sexual relations with her (1 Sam 6:20-23). Mordecai seems to pull the strings on his niece Esther, treating her almost like a perpetual child.

Two husbands in the OT annals are not so much tyrannical as obtuse and insensitive. One is Elkanah, who at the annual pilgrimage to Shiloh gave multiple portions of food to his productive wife and her offspring but only a single portion to the barren Hannah, and who asked the weeping Hannah, "Am I not more to you than ten sons?" (1 Sam 1:8 RSV). One can almost hear Hannah's unspoken response: *No way.* And the wise and beautiful Abigail has to compensate for the foolishness of her husband Nabal, who is "churlish and ill-behaved" in his dealings with David (1 Sam 25:3 RSV).

The domineering husband and father also lurks in the background of several NT passages. Jesus' interpretation of the Mosaic rules governing a man's divorcing of his wife is that the rules were necessary to protect the rights of wives from the hardness of their husbands' heart (Mk 10:2-12). And Paul's injunctions that husbands must love their wives and "not be harsh with them" (Col 3:19 RSV; cf. Eph 5:25), and that fathers must "not provoke" their children "to anger" (Eph 6:4 RSV) or discouragement (Col 3:21) evoke the contrary picture of tyrannical husbands and fathers.

See also CHARACTER TYPES; DOMINEERING MOTHER, WIFE; FATHER, FATHERHOOD; HUSBAND; MAN, IMAGES OF; TYRANT, TYRANNY.

TYRANNY. *See* TYRANT, TYRANNY.

TYRANT, TYRANNY

Although the terms *tyrant* and *tyranny* rarely appear in English translations of the Bible, the image of one who seizes power unconstitutionally and then exploits and oppresses subject people is common in the biblical text. Much of the OT is *slave literature, arising from a culture oppressed by foreign tyrants. As in other slave literature, a mocking tone is often discernible, accompanied by a pervasive *fear based on an awareness of how miserable life under a tyrant can be. In the Bible the power that a tyrant seizes belongs rightfully only to God. The *sin of the tyrant is the refusal to confess and live under God's sovereignty. Accompanying themes include justice and God's impending judgment against tyrants and tyranny.

The history of tyranny in the Bible goes all the way back to the *Fall (Gen 3). *Satan is the original usurper who seizes what is not legitimately his and then exploits the human race. Once human beings fall into sin, the tendency to tyranny characterizes human life in the world. We see this tendency in the problematic Genesis 6:1-4. Whatever the identity of the "sons of God" in Genesis 6:2 (NASB), the focus is on the hubris of the *"sons," who strive for fame and fertility. As a symbol of how corrupt the world had become, these "sons" sexually exploit the "daughters of men." The result of the union is a race of "mighty men of renown," a reference to the use of political power to exploit.

Nimrod is another tyrannical figure. Because his name seems to be connected with the Hebrew verb "to rebel" *(mārad)*, tradition has identified him with tyrannical power. He founded the earliest imperial world powers, *Babylon and Assyria (Gen 10:10-11). In Genesis 10:9 he is identified as a "mighty hunter" (NASB), a trait characteristic of the ruthless, tyrannical Assyrian kings. In postbiblical literature (e.g., the Jewish Haggadah and Muslim texts), Nimrod is singled out as the greatest sinner since the flood, whose crowning evils were his claim to be divine and his willingness to sponsor the Tower of *Babel, the very symbol of human *rebellion against God.

There is no more famous human tyrant in the Bible than *Pharaoh and by extension the Egyptians, who made *Egypt a house of *bondage for the fledgling Israelite nation (Ex 1), withstood the plans of God for his chosen nation (Ex 5—12) and pursued the Israelites with intent to enslave them anew (Ex 14). While never minimizing the terror represented by such tyranny, the narrative is told in such a way as to mock the tyrant, showing his efforts to be futile and satirizing him by recounting his unwitting contribution to his own downfall by preserving the future leader Moses and even paying his mother to care for her own infant (Ex 2:1-10). A similar tone pervades the story of Ehud's assassination of Eglon (Judg 3:15-30). It is evident also in the story of the NT counterpart to Pharaoh, Herod, who does horrible things in the slaughter of the innocents (Mt 2:1-18) and the beheading of John the Baptist (Mt 14:1-12) but is ultimately outwitted by the wise men, who return home by a different route, and by the *flight into Egypt of Jesus' parents.

Another powerful image of the hubris of tyranny is Nebuchadnezzar, who boasted that Babylon was built "by the might of my power and for the glory of my majesty" (Dan 4:30 NASB). In keeping with the ever-present motif of God's judgment against human tyranny, God promptly punished Nebuchadnezzar with mental illness. The point of the narrative is that Nebuchadnezzar, and all rulers, are to learn that God is "ruler over the realm of mankind, and bestows it on whomever He wishes" (Dan 4:25 NASB). Tyrannical power cannot ultimately usurp God's sovereignty.

Not all OT tyrants are foreign kings. Solomon seemed a tyrant in the eyes of the northern tribes (1 Kings 12:4, 14; 2 Chron 10:4, 10, 14). Ahab preyed upon his own subjects (1 Kings 21), and even worse was his queen wife Jezebel, killer of the prophets of God, engineer of Naboth's death on false charges and recipient of God's swift judgment as her body was eaten by *dogs (1 Kings 16—21; 2 Kings 9:30-37). In the book of Ezekiel, God charges that the leaders of Israel have ruled "with force and with severity" as they "have dominated" their charges (Ezek 34:4 NASB).

The archtyrant in the Bible is *Satan, or the devil, who epitomizes the spirit of tyranny. Depicted in Ezekiel 28:12-19 (and possibly Is 14:12-21) as the energizer of powerful earthly kings, he attempts to usurp God's position as ruler of the universe. He bears the NT titles "ruler of this world" (Jn 12:31; 14:30; 16:11) and "god of this age" (2 Cor 4:4). Motivated by pride (1 Tim 3:6), he and his demonic hosts accuse, tempt, exploit, manipulate and terrorize human beings as they seek to thwart God's sovereign rule. In the same category is the NT figure of *antichrist, who denies Christ's deity and is already present in the world (1 Jn 4:3; 2:18; 2 Jn 7). Tyranny of this type is a coming apocalyptic reality, the opponent of Christ whose power and tyranny increase prior to the eschaton (cf. the dragon of Revelation).

But in all cases the Bible affirms the defeat of tyranny. Tyrannical power violates God's justice and sovereignty and always meets with judgment and destruction. Therefore the NT depicts the archtyrant—Satan—as already defeated at the *cross (Lk 10:18; Jn 12:31; 16:11; Rom 16:20). His ultimate doom is judgment in the lake of fire (Rev 20:10). The tyranny that exploits will then be replaced by the benevolent, just rule of the *kingdom of God.

See also ANTICHRIST; BABYLON; BONDAGE AND FREEDOM; EGYPT; PHARAOH; KING, KINGSHIP; SATAN; TYRANNICAL FATHER, HUSBAND.

U

UNBIND. *See* LOOSE, LOOSEN.

UNDER

Being under something is an image that functions in a variety of ways in the Bible, from characterizing individual relationships to outlining the shape of God's *creation. The relationship of under/over plays a significant role in Hebrew cosmology. In the creation narrative God separates the *waters above from those below, making space in between for the sky and *land to appear (Gen 1:6-9 NIV). Here the image is of a great cosmic sandwich, wherein the earth and sky exist beneath a vast expanse of water with yet another expanse of water under them. This image suggests vulnerability and dependence: all creation depends on God to continue to hold the waters back. Otherwise water would cover the whole earth, as it does during the *flood (Gen 7:19).

The Bible employs similar imagery to locate the earth between God's dwelling and the dwelling place of the dead. Declaring that nothing escapes God's notice, Job identifies the very "ends of the earth" (and all that lies between) with "everything under the heavens" (Job 28:24 NIV). Just as the *earth is under the *heavens, so also Sheol, the place of the dead, is under the earth: when Israel turns to *idolatry, the Lord's wrath "burns to the realm of death [literally, Sheol] below" (Deut 32:22 NIV). Job muses on the permanence of death, declaring, "He who goes down to the grave [Sheol] does not return" (Job 7:9 NIV). In these contexts the image of being under reflects a cosmic hierarchy: the dead exist under the earth because they are now *weak and powerless (Is 14:9-10), but all the earth, living and dead alike, exist under the heavens before the eyes of God.

More frequently *under* illustrates the nature of a relationship at the personal level. Because it is a relational image, it always describes one thing with reference to another. For example, Nathanael is the one who was "under the fig tree" when Jesus saw him (Jn 1:48 NIV). But "under" does not merely serve to distinguish one person from another; rather, the Bible often describes an important relationship in terms of a person's being under something. Though the precise import of the image may vary with context, a common feature remains: being under something entails being affected by it in a significant way.

In some contexts, being under describes a relationship of influence, as with *blessings and *curses. For example, Abraham pleads with God in order that Ishmael "might live under [God's] blessing" (Gen 17:18 NIV). Following Abel's murder, God declares to *Cain, "Now you are under a curse.... You will be a restless wanderer on the earth" (Gen 4:11-12 NIV). Whether referring to a blessing or to a curse, the image of being under denotes a relationship of thoroughgoing, unavoidable influence. The spatial element of the image lends it power: no matter how far Cain may wander, he cannot escape being "under" the curse.

Under can also portray a relationship of *protection, as when the psalmist declares of the Lord, "Under his wings you will find refuge" (Ps 91:4 NIV). Here the image is of God providing shelter and safety like a bird protecting its young. However, in a context of divine *judgment, being under becomes a very different image—one of *nakedness and vulnerability. The prophet calls Edom "a people always under the wrath of the LORD" (Mal 1:4 NIV). Speaking to an *exiled Israel, the Lord proclaims, "I will take note of you as you pass under my rod.... I will purge you of those who revolt and rebel against me" (Ezek 20:37-38 NIV). Passing under God's rod is a vivid picture of judgment in which one will be either accepted into the *covenant or swept aside. In each of these instances, being under means being subject to God's sovereignty, whether for protection or for judgment.

Being under can also denote a relationship characterized by power and dominion. The psalmist describes the coming of the Lord from heaven in the midst of a thunderstorm, in which "dark clouds were under his feet" (Ps 18:9 NIV). To have something under one's *feet is to control it completely; thus all the raging of the elements is subject to God's command. Likewise in the NT Paul declares of Jesus, "God placed all things under his feet and appointed him to be head over everything" (Eph 1:22 NIV). Here Jesus, the *head of the church, exercises power and dominion where *sin had reigned previously. Speaking of dominion of a different sort, Paul employs a similar image to describe the human state apart from Christ: "Jews and Gentiles alike are all under sin" (Rom 3:9 NIV). In this instance sinners are most immediately controlled by the power of sin rather than by the power of God, but the image of dominion remains the same.

Closely related to the relationship of dominion, the image of being under also serves to describe a relationship of obligation or subjection. One example is the taking of an *oath: when the high priest says to Jesus, "I charge you under oath by the living God: Tell us if you are the Christ" (Mt 26:63 NIV), Jesus accepts the obligation of the charge and confirms that he is. To be under an oath is to be compelled to a particular action. Paul uses the image in a similar fashion when he compares life "under law" with life "under grace" (Rom 6:14). Those under the *law are obligated to keep it, but failing to do so, they subsequently become subject to sin. In contrast, those under grace are subject to the One who extends grace to them; thus they must avoid any obligation or subjection to sin. Here the image of being under is not only descriptive but prescriptive as well; it underscores the obligation to live and make choices according to the grace that God has extended.

While the biblical image of being under conveys a variety of ideas ranging from the structure of creation to the nature of grace, many instances pertain to human relationships, whether individual or collective. Among all the various ways that being under characterizes relationships, the common element is that one is always significantly affected by that which one comes under; a person *under* another is defined and identified by the relationship.

See also UNDER THE FEET.

UNDER THE FEET

The literal trampling of *enemies in *warfare accounts for the use of "trampling under the feet" as an image for any victory over one's enemies (e.g., Judg 20:43; Ps 18:38; Is 14:25; 41:2; Dan 8:7), including the victory of believers over *Satan (Rom 16:20) and the eschatological victory of Christ (1 Cor 15:25). Yahweh even tramples Israel's *sins underfoot (Mic 7:19).

To place "under one's feet" also implies dominion and rule. Yahweh's primeval victory over the *sea is depicted as a trampling (*dārak*) of the "waves (*bāmâ*) of the Sea" (Job 9:8 NRSV; cf. Hab 3:15); his judgment in history is correlatively a treading (*dārak*) on the "high places (*bāmâ*) of the earth" (Micah 1:3 NRSV; cf. Amos 4:13). Such actions portray Yahweh's cosmic dominion, in which humans participate by having all things put "under their feet" (Ps 8:6 NRSV). But this cosmic dominion is especially realized in Christ as the perfect human (1 Cor 15:24-28; Heb 2:5-9), as head of the church (Eph 1:22) and as the victorious Messiah (Ps 110:1; cf. Mk 12:36; Lk 20:43; Acts 2:35; Heb 1:13; 10:13). Perhaps this sense of dominion also underlies references to *earth (Is 66:1) and the *temple (Ps 99:5; 132:7) as the footstool of Yahweh.

The imagery of "under the feet" can also connote possession. Exclusively in Deuteronomy, the *land

that the Israelites will possess is defined as that "on which the sole of your foot treads" (Deut 11:24 passim), a natural extension of the "under the foot" image from the conquest and dominion of the land to the possession of land. Conversely, finding "no rest for the sole of your foot" (Deut 28:65) may signify not owning any land (*see* Place, No Abiding).

Additional meanings of the imagery of being under the feet include disdain, defilement and judgment. Disdain, especially for despised persons such

A young Pharaoh sitting on his nurse's lap is symbolically depicted as already having his enemies bound and under his feet.

as Jezebel (2 Kings 9:33; cf. 2 Kings 7:17, 20; Is 14:19), is shown by trampling their corpses underfoot. Seating the poor at one's footstool is likewise an act of disdain (Jas 2:3), as is shaking off the dust of one's *feet (Mk 6:11). *Pearls are defiled under the feet of swine (Mt 7:6); *foreigners defile the land of Israel (Micah 5:5-6), the city of Jerusalem (Lk 21:24) and especially the *temple (Is 63:10; Dan 8:13; Rev 11:2) by trampling it underfoot (cf. the removal of shoes on holy ground in Ex 3:5 and 1 Sam 5:5). Treading the *winepress is an image of divine judgment (Jer 25:30; Lam 1:15; Joel 3:13; Rev 19:15; cf. treading grain in Jer 51:33), the juice of the grapes vividly suggesting the blood of the slain (Is 63:1-4; Rev 14:20).

Oppression and *persecution are also pictured by the image of the foot. In Psalms, ongoing persecution is described as being trampled by one's foes (Ps 56:1-2; 57:3), and Amos characterizes social oppression as a trampling on the poor (Amos 2:7; 8:4). In all these cases the verb is *'apar,* which connotes a crushing underfoot, rather than the more common words for trampling and treading. See also the use of *dārak* to express oppressive crushing under foot in Lamentations 3:34 (cf. Ps 74:21).

See also FEET; TRIUMPH; UNDER.

UNDERDOG

The archetypal triumph of the underdog is a favorite of the human race, appealing perhaps to the self-concept that most people have as being less qualified than the great of their society, combined with a degree of resentment at the "top dog." Stories of the triumph of the underdog also possess the appeal of such *plot motifs as *surprise, *reversal and (sometimes) *poetic justice (based on the premise that the underdog really deserves victory).

Given the Bible's fondness for reversing human conventions and substituting spiritual standards for them, it is no surprise that we find stories of underdogs in it. Usually these underdogs are prime specimens of God's grace. The nation of *Israel is a chief example, being essentially an underdog nation. God explains to them, "It was not because you were more in number than any other people that the LORD set his love upon you and chose you, for you were the fewest of all peoples " (Deut 7:7 RSV). It is as though God chose the *least* likely to succeed. The mission of the Israelites when they entered the *Promised Land was that of an underdog—"to dispossess nations greater and mightier than yourselves, cities great and fortified up to heaven, a people great and tall" (Deut 9:1-2 RSV). In Joshua we read that the Canaanite army was "a great host, in number like the sand that is upon the seashore, with very many horses and chariots" (Josh 11:4 RSV).

In addition to choosing a people who were underdogs among the nations, God chose leaders for that nation who were equally underdogs. *Moses, the greatest Hebrew leader, was a poor speaker, lacking eloquence; Gideon was the youngest member of the least important family in Manasseh, the smallest tribe in Israel (Judg 6:15); Jephthah was an outcast from his family, who was denied an inheritance because he was illegitimate; Deborah, one of Israel's judges, was a woman. Thus God equipped many underdogs with his own might to become effective judges and leaders of Israel.

The greatest of the Bible's underdog stories is the David-Goliath story (1 Sam 17). To this day we speak of underdogs metaphorically as "little Davids." Goliath himself is the archetypal "top dog"—nine feet, nine inches tall, clothed in 125-pound scale armor, carrying a bronze javelin with a sixteen-pound warhead, and protected by shield bearers. All the Israelite men "were dismayed and greatly afraid" (1 Sam 17:11 RSV), but a young boy was not. *David was the youngest member of his family, yet he feared God and believed in his promise of protection. With only a slingshot, the boy hero defeated the mighty warrior whom no one else in the army had dared to face, demonstrating once again that God supported Israel, his underdog nation, by his grace and might alone.

In the NT, God indicates that those he saves are no less underdogs than the Israelites had been among the nations. Jesus himself associated with the underdogs of his society—tax collectors, *prostitutes and the poor—more than with the rich and prestigious. Paul paints a similar pictures of the early church believers:

For consider your call, brethren; not many of you were wise according to worldly standards, not many were powerful, not many were of noble

birth; but God chose what is foolish in the world to shame the wise, God chose what is weak in the world to shame the strong, God chose what is low and despised in the world . . . so that no human being might boast in the presence of God. (1 Cor 1:26-29 RSV)

Here is the NT counterpart to the lowly nation of Israel in the OT.

A related cluster of underdog images converges in the OT motif of the *younger sibling who supplants the older. Given ancient patterns of preference and primogeniture, these younger siblings are underdogs who triumph. Examples include Abel who is favored by God over Cain, Isaac who receives advancement over Ishmael, Jacob who triumphs over Esau, Rachel who is preferred before Leah, Joseph who rises over his older brothers and Moses who becomes leader of a nation rather than Aaron.

See also POETIC JUSTICE; REVERSAL, STORIES OF; SURPRISE, STORIES OF; WEAK, WEAKNESS; YOUNGER CHILD.

UNFADING. *See* FADE, FADING; PERMANENCE.

UNKNOWN GOD. *See* GODS, GODDESSES.

UNLEAVENED

Unleavened *bread is an image both of *pilgrimage and *corruption. As an image of pilgrimage, unleavened bread is associated with the *exodus. The Israelites, hurrying to leave Egypt, "took their dough before the yeast was added, and carried it on their shoulders in kneading troughs wrapped in clothing" (Ex 12:34 NIV), departing from the land of *slavery as a pilgrim people. Thereafter only unleavened bread was eaten during the yearly *Passover (Ex 12:8), a reminder to Israel that even when settled in Canaan they remained a pilgrim people.

The *Feast of Unleavened Bread, which took place immediately after the Passover (Ex 12:17-20), also served to remind Israel of its pilgrim character: "Eat nothing made with yeast. Wherever you live, you must eat unleavened bread" (Ex 12:20 NIV).

Unleavened bread was prescribed for the *offering made at the consecration of priests (Lev 8:2) and Nazirites (Num 6:15) and for the *grain offering (Lev 10:12). Leaven, which causes fermentation and disintegration, would be associated with *evil and corruption, thus making the offering impure. Unleavened bread therefore would be the only kind of offering worthy of a holy God (but note the exceptions, Lev 7:13; 23:17-20).

In rabbinical writings, leaven was often used figuratively of evil and human corruption, a view that is also found in the NT. Jesus warns his disciples against the yeast of the *Pharisees and Sadducees (Mt 16:6; Mk 8:15), meaning the *hypocrisy of their outward show of religious devotion and inner corruption (Mt 23:25-26). As yeast works through the whole batch of dough, the yeast of the Pharisees and Sadducees is able to work its way through the whole person, corrupting him or her entirely. In contrast, Jesus' disciples are to live with integrity, uncorrupted by the desire to impress others by their performance of religious ritual.

The apostle Paul draws the same contrast in 1 Corinthians 5:6-8 when he appeals for the exercise of church discipline against the incestuous brother. The festival of Christ, the Passover *Lamb, must be kept "not with the old yeast . . . of malice and wickedness, but with bread without yeast, the bread of sincerity and truth" (1 Cor 5:8 NIV). By employing the exodus motif and connecting it with behavior expressive of new existence in Christ, the apostle unites the figures of pilgrimage and influence: Christian pilgrims are to live lives in which the old leaven has no place whatsoever (cf. Gal 5:9).

See also BREAD; LEAVEN, LEAVENING; PASSOVER.

UNTOUCHABLE. *See* TOUCH.

UPSTART

The archetypal upstart is a person who usurps a position that does not properly belong to him or her. Such presumption is akin to *pride, greed, ambition and a thirst for power. It may be motivated by discontent with one's present lot.

*Eve is the first upstart in the Bible as she attempts to "be like God, knowing good and evil" (Gen 3:5 RSV). The human race at *Babel suffers from similar illusions of deity, thinking to build a *tower that will reach to heaven (Gen 11:4). *Jacob, the younger sibling, has something of the upstart in him when he successfully manipulates his older brother in a scheme to supplant him. The youthful *Joseph's family falsely accuses him of being an upstart when he shares his dreams of a glorious destiny. When the youthful *David arrives at the battlefront as the family's "gofer boy," his older brothers indignantly treat him as an upstart (1 Sam 17:26-30).

The motif can be present in less obvious ways as well. Saul is impatient with Samuel's late arrival and therefore presumes to perform the priestly duties himself (1 Sam 13), and later he decides to ignore God's command to annihilate the Amalekites (1 Sam 15). Characters who believe they can successfully ignore a command from God also fit the type (*see* Cheat the Oracle): such are the cases of the band of Israelites who try to march directly to the Promised Land after God has doomed them to wander in the wilderness (Num 14:39-45), Ahab when he ignores the counsel of the prophet Micaiah (2 Chron 18:1-27) and Jonah in his futile attempt to flee from God (Jon 1).

A further category of upstarts is people who try to grab a position of leadership to which they are not entitled. Aaron's behavior on the occasion of the golden calf is an example (Ex 32:1-24). So are the attempts by Aaron and Miriam and by Korah, Dathan and Abiram to usurp authority (Numb 12; 16). Adonijah tries to become king when God has chosen Solomon (1 Kings 1:5-9). Absalom becomes an upstart son and temporarily dislodges David from the kingship. "The nations" plot against God and his anointed and are treated derisively by God (Ps 2), while the king of Assyria exerts himself against God as though he were an ax vaunting itself over the person who wields it (Is 10:15).

In other cases the upstart seems simply to suffer from youthful indiscretion. Rehoboam, for example, foolishly listens to his young advisers' counsel to adopt an oppressive stance when he becomes king (1 Kings 12:25-33; 2 Chron 10:1-16). *Samson behaves presumptuously, like a permanently immature juvenile delinquent—bossing his parents, muscling his way around, thinking he can violate his vow to God with impunity (Judg 14—16). The *prodigal of Jesus' parable, who presumptuously asks for his inheritance before his father is dead, reenacts the archetype as well (Lk 15:11-12).

Other upstarts are victims of their own pride and presumed self-sufficiency. Examples include the history of Judah narrative in Ezekiel 16:8-34, as the nation beautified by God decides to trust in itself rather than God; the king of Tyre who becomes overly impressed with his power (Ezek 28); Nebuchadnezzar (Dan 4:28-33); and Darius (Dan 5:17-29). Perhaps too we can include various evildoers who are pictured as thinking that God cannot see their evil and who therefore decide to go all out in oppressing the poor and exalting themselves (Ps 10:3-6; 73:8-11). We think too of Peter—impulsively walking on the water, striking off a soldier's ear, claiming he will never deny his Savior.

See also CHARACTER TYPES.

URBAN IMAGERY. *See* CITY.

URIM AND THUMMIM. *See* ORACLE.

V

VALE OF TEARS. *See* TEARS.

VALLEY

Like the land of Palestine, the topography of Scripture is marked by numerous valleys large and small, named and unnamed. These references are almost exclusively found in the OT. For the most part the Israelites were inhabitants of the hill country and seldom gained control of all of the great valleys of the land of promise. So much was this the case that a man of God could say to the king of Israel, "the Arameans think the LORD is a god of the hills and not a god of the valleys" (1 Kings 20:28 NIV). George Adam Smith captured a sense of the OT descriptions and imagery of the land:

> By numerous little tokens, we feel that this is scenery described by Highlanders: by men who, for the most part, looked down upon their prospects and painted their scenes from above. Their usual word for valley is depth—something below them. (Smith, 87)

Valleys of Fertility. In considering the image of a valley in the Bible, we must keep in mind that valley bottoms frequently (there are notable exceptions such as the "Valley of Siddim") have deep soil and make the best and most natural farm land. Many of the larger valleys in Palestine were created by faults, breaks in the earth's crust where springs of water naturally occur. Although the hill country is productive, fed by springs and well-developed agriculturally, a valley is a ready and universal image of fertility.

In Deuteronomy the "good land" is described as possessing "springs flowing in the valleys and hills" (Deut 8:7) and "a land of mountains and valleys that drinks rain from heaven" (Deut 11:11). The latter expression is a merism, a statement of the two extremes in topography which bracket the whole and thus portray a well-watered *land. In Numbers we learn of the Valley of Eshcol, where the Israelite spies acquire the stupendous fruits of the land, a massive cluster of grapes along with pomegranates and figs (Num 13:23-24). Later, as Balaam views the children of Israel from the heights, his vision of a divinely blessed people attracts the imagery of the verdant valleys they are destined to inherit: "Like valleys they spread out, like gardens beside a river, like aloes planted by the

Lord, like cedars beside the waters" (Num 24:6).

The fertility of a valley is evoked in Psalm 65:13, where "the meadows are covered with flocks and the valleys are mantled with grain; they shout for joy and sing" (Ps 65:13 NIV). Elsewhere the psalmist addresses the Lord as the One who makes "springs gush forth in the valleys; they flow between the hills" (Ps 104:10 NRSV). The lover of Song of Songs even identifies herself as "a rose of Sharon, a lily of the valleys" (Song 2:1 NIV). And the imagery of a fecund valley is lushly intertwined with human sexuality as later she goes down "to the grove of nut trees to look at the new growth in the valley, to see if the vines had budded or the pomegranates were in bloom" (Song 6:11 NIV).

Valleys of Battle. Although valleys frequently evoke the ideals of fertility, *beauty and *peace, they are more often associated with warfare and *judgment. Because battles are more easily fought on an open plain or in a broad valley than in the hill country of Judah or Galilee, the valley becomes a stock image of human and divine warfare. While David and his band of men can carry out effective guerilla warfare in the rugged hill country of Judah, the full dress battles of infantry, cavalry and *chariots require broad, open spaces. Thus Isaiah, alluding to Elam and Kir prepared for battle, says, "Your choicest valleys are full of chariots" (Is 22:7 NIV). When the Arameans consider the Lord of Israel "a god of the hills and not of the valleys," they surmise that they will have the advantage in battle. But the Lord will prove himself as much the God of the valleys as of the hills and deliver the vast Aramean army into Israel's hand (1 Kings 20:28). We find numerous biblical battles fought in valleys, some of which are remembered by name.

The first battle in Scripture takes place in the Valley of Siddim, in the region of the "Salt Sea." This valley is pocked with tar pits which trap some of the fleeing armies of *Sodom and Gomorrah (Gen 14:3-10). When Israel enters the land, the Amalekites and Canaanites are living in the valleys (Num 14:25). It is no wonder then that many battles take place in valleys. Joshua's memorable battle against the Amorites, in which the sun and moon "stood still," culminates in the valley of Aijalon (Josh 10:12). The accounts of warfare under Joshua include the Valley of Mizpah (Josh 11:8) and the Valley of Lebanon

(Josh 11:17), and the boundaries of tribal inheritances run through a catalog of Israel's valleys, including the valleys of Achor, Ben Hinnom, Rephaim, Jezreel and Iphtah El. In Judges we read of armies camped and battles waged in the Valley of Jezreel (Judg 6:33) and the valley near the hill of Moreh (Jud 7:1, 8, 12), and in the Books of Samuel (and parallel passages in Chronicles) we encounter warfare in the Valley of Elah (1 Sam 17:2-3, 19), where Goliath was slain; the Valley of Rephaim (2 Sam 5:18, 22; 23:13); and the Valley of Salt (2 Sam 8:13). Later we read of King Amaziah of Judah who "killed ten thousand Edomites in the Valley of Salt" (2 Kings 14:7). These and other texts (e.g., 2 Chron 18:12; 25:11; Ps 60:1) form a collective image of valleys soaked and flowing with blood instead of water. And that is precisely the illusion created by the flash-flood waters that spill into a valley and reflect the blood-red dawn, fooling the Moabites into thinking that a great battle has taken place (2 Kings 4:16-24).

Valleys of Judgment. Closely akin to these images of battle are the judgments against *idolatry in valleys. Elijah slaughters the prophets of Baal in the Kishon Valley (1 Kings 18:40). And two valleys bordering Jerusalem, the Hinnom and the Kidron, are the sites of judgment against idolatry. In the Kidron Valley, Asa burns the Asherah, pole (2 Chron 15:16). Under Hezekiah's reforms the Kidron becomes a dumpsite for unclean things found in the temple (2 Chron 29:16; 30:14). And under Josiah all the articles of the *gods Baal and Asherah and of "all the starry hosts" are burned in the Kidron Valley, and the rubble of idolatrous *altars are thrown there (2 Kings 23:4, 6, 12).

But the Valley of (Ben) Hinnom becomes synonymous with idolatry and judgment against idolatry. There Kings Ahaz and Manasseh indulged in idolatry and *sacrificed their sons to Canaanite gods (2 Chron 28:3; 33:6). For Jeremiah, the idolatry and human sacrifices in the Valley of Ben Hinnom is emblematic of Israel's great sin: "See how you have behaved in the valley . . . they have built the high places of Topheth in the Valley of Ben Hinnom to burn their sons and daughters in the fire . . . to sacrifice their sons and daughters to Molech" (Jer 2:23; 7:32; 32:35; cf. 31:40). The image of idolatry taking place in a valley overshadowed by *Jerusalem is set in sharp contrast with the powerful biblical image of *worship offered to Yahweh on his high *temple mount. The bloodshed of idolatrous sacrifice in the valley will recoil in judgment on its practitioners when God executes judgment against them: "people will no longer call it Topheth or the Valley of Ben Hinnom, but the Valley of Slaughter, for they will bury the dead in Topheth until there is no more room" (Jer 7:32 NIV; cf. Jer 19:6). The valley of idolatry will become one with the valleys of battle, where Yahweh defeats his enemies, in this case Israel. The Valley of Hinnom, *gê hinnōm* in Hebrew, became *geenna* in Greek, and *Gehenna* in Latin and English. In

later Jewish thought it became an image of the judgment of the wicked by *fire, *darkness and gnashing of *teeth. In this sense it is used as a synonym for *hell, or hades, in the Gospels (cf. Mt 5:22, 29, 30; 10:28; 18:9; 23:15; Mk 9:43, 45, 47; Lk 12:5). The valley of Israel's sin and judgment is the very gate of hell.

Ezekiel's oracles of judgment repeat the refrain of "hills and valleys" that will not escape the Lord's judgment. There will be valleys of gore and Yahweh promises to "fill the valleys with your remains" (Ezek 32:5; cf 6:3; 35:8; 36:4, 6) Whether Ezekiel has in mind Ben Hinnom or another valley, he envisions the *resurrection of Israel after the *exile as the reanimation of a valley of dry *bones (Ezek 37).

The memory of historical battles fought in Israel's valleys informs the imagery of the prophets. God will "break Israel's bow in the Valley of Jezreel" (Hos 1:5 NIV), he will "gather all nations and bring them down to the Valley of Jehoshaphat" and "enter into judgment against them" (Joel 3:2; cf. 3:12 NIV):

Multitudes, multitudes
   in the valley of decision!
For the day of the Lord is near
   in the valley of decision. (Joel 3:14 NIV)

The valley of decision resonates with the scene of Israel's *covenant renewal ceremony at Shechem, situated between Mounts Ebal and Gerizim. Between these mountains echoed the words of the *law with its *blessings and *curses (Josh 8:30-35; Deut 27—28), *salvation and *judgment hinging on Israel's decision for or against obedience to the covenant.

Amos also envisions valleys of judgment for Damascus (1:5) and for Israel (Amos 6:14), and Micah speaks of Samaria being reduced to "a heap of rubble," her stones poured into a valley (Mic 1:6). Jeremiah addresses the Ammonites: "Why do you . . . boast of your valleys so fruitful?" (Jer 49:4). The tables will soon be turned on them. When Yahweh, the *divine warrior, marches forth, all creation responds in terror: "the mountains melt beneath him and the valleys split apart, like wax before the fire, like water rushing down a slope" (Mic 1:4 NIV). This imagery of splitting valleys carries positive benefit in Zechariah 14:4-5, where "the Mount of Olives will be split in two from east to west, forming a great valley" for Israel's escape. Isaiah memorably envisions a highway miraculously formed before the divine warrior as he marches forth to bring deliverance to Israel: "Every valley shall be raised up, every mountain and hill made low" (Is 40:4 NIV). And Luke sees this scene fulfilled in John as he baptizes repentant Israelites in advance of the Coming One who will bring judgment and salvation (Lk 3:5).

Valleys of Renewed Fertility. On the far side of divine warfare and judgment, the vision of the prophets returns to valleys of fertility and peace evoking scenes of Eden. Isaiah's vision of the new creation draws on a rich store of nature imagery. Yahweh will make *springs flow within the valleys (Is 41:18). For Isaiah "the Valley of Achor," so named for the judgment that fell upon Achan's household (Josh 7:24, 26; Achor being a play on the word meaning "to bring disaster"), will become "a resting place for herds" (Is 65:10). For Hosea, Yahweh "will make the Valley of Achor a door of hope" (Hos 2:15 NIV). Joel's day of redemption dawns with the *mountains dripping with new *wine, hills flowing with *milk, ravines running with *water, and a *fountain flowing from the house of the Lord to "water the valley of acacias" (Joel 3:18). Here the image of the valley is clearly imbued with Edenic overtones, leveraged on ancient Near Eastern mythic conceptions in which temple, river and paradise are closely joined (see Adam). By the Creator God's providence and plan, the image of an idyllic and fertile valley will prevail in the end. God the *shepherd leads his people through the "valley of the shadow of death" to the green *pastures and still waters (Ps 23).

See also IDOLATRY; MOUNTAIN; PASTURE; RIVER; SPRING OF WATER.

BIBLIOGRAPHY. G. A. Smith, *The Historical Geography of the Holy Land* (New York: Harper, 1966 [1894]).

VALUING. *See* MISPRIZING, MISVALUING.

VAPOR. *See* MIST.

VEIL

Veil in the Bible, sometimes called "curtain," refers either to a part of a person's attire or to a piece of hanging cloth that serves as a barrier between parts of a space. The primary connotation of the veil or curtain in the Bible is that it conceals something, usually something sacred but sometimes something *shameful.

A whole category of images arises from the ancient practice of women's going about with their faces veiled. Some of the contexts are ignominious, such as a *prostitute's wearing a veil (Gen 38;14, 19) and false female *prophets' wearing a veil as part of their magical regalia (Ezek 13:17-21).

In other instances the veiled face is a strongly positive image. The veil becomes an image of the numinous in the case of *Moses' face, which shone so brightly after his meetings with God that he had to veil it as he moved about the community (Ex 34:29-35). In a similar vein, we find references to *brides-to-be who keep their faces veiled until *marriage (Gen 24:65; Song 4:1, 3; 6:7). Perhaps modesty is also part of the meaning here. In the NT, Paul commands the veiling of women as their honorable attire in public *worship (1 Cor 11:2-10).

The veil or curtain was also an image of the numinous in the synagogue and *temple, where it protected the sanctity of the *ark of the covenant and holy of holies from common view (Ex 26:31-35; 2 Chron 3:14). In fact, only the high *priest could go beyond the veil, and he did so only on the Day of Atonement (Lev 16; Heb 9:7). The symbolism of the rent temple curtain at Christ's crucifixion (Mt 27:51; Mk 15:38; Lk 23:45) is the directness of access of the believer to God in the NT era, with the OT prefigurings now fulfilled and abrogated (Heb 6:19-20; 10:19-20). In the new dispensation, believers can behold the *glory of God with unveiled face (2 Cor 3:18).

As an image of concealment, the veil also has the negative meaning of a mind that is cut off from the truth. Paul pictures the unbelieving mind as having a veil over it (2 Cor 3:12-16) and the gospel as being veiled to people who disbelieve it (2 Cor 4:3).

See also FACE, FACIAL EXPRESSIONS; GLORY.

VENGEANCE/REVENGE, STORIES OF

Before the human race developed the civilized institution of the court of *justice, people attempted to settle questions of retribution by means of private revenge. The danger of this system of justice is that the aggrieved party is generally too subjectively involved to be a fair-minded agent of justice. Still, in the ancient world the concept of revenge might not always be tied to our more modern connotations of retaliation in *anger. In any case, in certain eras of the past revenge stories have been very popular with readers and audiences. The genre of revenge stories is represented in the Bible, but not extravagantly so.

Wrongs done within a family spark one cluster of biblical revenge stories. Dinah's *brothers avenge Shechem's defilement of their *sister by requiring the men from Shechem's tribe to be *circumcised and then annihilating them on the third day, when they were incapacitated by pain (Gen 34). Such stories include an element of a grim wink exchanged with the audience. *Esau's threatened revenge necessitates *Jacob's twenty-year exile in Paddanaram. Potiphar's wife gets even with *Joseph for his repulsion of her *sexual advances by falsely and successfully accusing him (Gen 39:6-20), and *Moses avenges an Egyptian's *beating of a Hebrew *slave (Ex 2:11-12).

Military action shades off imperceptibly into revenge, so that it is hard to know where to draw the distinction between the ethics of *battle and the administration of revenge. Retributive *warfare underlies God's commands that vengeance be taken on the Midianites (Num 31:3), Amalekites (1 Sam 15:2-3) and *Philistines (Ezek 25:15-17). Within a holy war context in which the people of God are viewed as being in the right, victory over pagan *enemies is sometimes viewed as just revenge, as in David's song of victory (2 Sam 22:48; Ps 18:47 NRSV). Viewed as following the tradition of slave literature, the story of Ehud's assassination of Eglon has an element of the revenge story in it (Judg 3:12-30). Gideon gets even with people who taunted him instead of helping him when he was chasing the Midianite army (Judg 8). Abimelech avenges Gaal's revolt against him (Judg 9:26-41), but when Abimelech in turn is mortally wounded by a millstone pushed on him from a city *wall by a woman, the biblical author views that event as God's requiting of Abimelech's crime of killing seventy of his brothers (Judg 9:50-57).

*Samson's exploits against the Philistines seem at times to be viewed by the author as a form of vengeance against a troublesome *neighbor (Judg 14:4; 16:30), and certainly there is an element of personal revenge when Samson kills thirty Philistines after he loses his bet regarding his riddle (Judg 14:10-19) and his burning of the Philistines' grain fields when his bride is given to his best man (Judg 15:1-8). The Philistines get their revenge on Samson through Delilah (Judg 16:4-27), but Samson in turn gets his revenge on them when God answers his prayer to be "avenged upon the Philistines for one of my two eyes" (Judg 16:28 RSV).

The revenge motif is prominent in the story of Saul and David (as Thomas Hardy sensed when he wrote *The Mayor of Casterbridge*). Saul futilely tries to retaliate against David for the latter's popularity as a warrior. Saul also enlists Doeg the Edomite to kill eighty-five priests in revenge for the high priest's aid to David (1 Sam 22:11-19). For his part, David often suppresses revenge—in his refusal to kill Saul when he has opportunity (1 Sam 24; 26), in refraining from revenge against Nabal after Abigail's intervention (1 Sam 25), in his restraining an eager ally from taking vengeance on the taunting Shimei (2 Sam 16:5-14), in his command to "deal gently" with *Absalom during the civil war (2 Sam 18:5).

The imprecatory psalms that call down curses on the poet's enemies present a variation on the revenge motif. The very fact that the speaker invokes God to perform the vengeance reflects the omnipresent biblical premise that vengeance belongs to God (Prov 20:22; Rom 12:19; Heb 10:30), yet the vividness with which the poet prays for vengeance shows that the wished-for revenge has a human component as well (Ps 28:4; 41:10; 54:5; 56:7; 58:10; 94:1, 23; 137:8-9).

The most extended revenge story in the Bible emerges from *apocalyptic visions of God's future *judgment against *evil. "For the LORD has a day of vengeance," we read in Isaiah 34:8 (RSV). And again, "Your God will come with vengeance, with the recompense of God" (Is 35:4 RSV). We find approximately thirty references to God's vengeance in the OT Prophets, buttressed by similar references in the eschatological passages of the NT (Mt 16:27; Lk 21; 22; 2 Thess 1:8; Rev 18:6).

See also ANGER; AVENGER; JUDGMENT; MURDER STORIES.

VILLAGE

There are nearly 450 references to towns and villages in the English Bible. Towns and villages were made up of a small group of dwelling places and other buildings. Whether walled or not, these communities were distinct from *cities, which were larger and more elaborately fortified (Lev 25:29, 31; Deut 3:5; 1 Sam 6:18). A town or village was a miniature city. Like a city, it was a communal settlement, but it was distinctly "homey" and "small-time" compared with cities. In some cases the distinction between town and village is not clear. For example, Bethlehem is called both town *(polis)* in Luke 2:4 and village *(komē)* in John 7:42. Some villages eventually grew into cities (1 Sam 23:7)—hence Capernaum ("village of Nehum") and Hazar-addar ("village of Addar").

A biblical village was dominated by simple one-room houses, mud huts and tents, and its administration and organization were simpler than those of cities. In contrast to cities, villages had no elaborate defensive features like *walls, moats, *towers or fortified *gates (Ezek 38:11). Because of this the inhabitants of a village depended on the nearby city for protection, as well as other political and economic needs (Josh 15:20-63). This dependency goes back to the distribution of land under Joshua; cities were allotted to each tribe "with their villages" (Josh 15:32-62; 1 Chron 6:54). For all their simplicity, towns and villages share an important quality with cities: they are an image of community and civilization. They represent a bonding together of people to meet mutual needs. Accompanying associations include interdependence, social interaction and joint security.

The Bible gives us no extended pictures of its towns and villages, but reconstructing their milieu from extrabiblical sources will help us to picture what lies behind the numerous biblical references to them. The abundance of unadorned references to towns and villages in the Bible does hint at one of their qualities: they are prosaic, mundane, unpretentious places. There is nothing distinguished about them, as there is about large cities. One village is much like another. Yet the very number of towns and villages in the world of the Bible shows us that this is where most people lived. Towns and villages are an image of the commonplace.

Villages were settled by extended family units, "clan by clan," with common genealogy (Josh 13:23, 28). In fact, the 212 gatekeepers of the Solomonic *temple were registered by genealogy in their villages (1 Chron 9:22). Regarding their duties, we read that "their brothers in their villages had to come from time to time and share their duties for seven-day periods" (1 Chron 9:25 NIV). Hence most OT village dwellers had some genealogical family connections with others in the settlement.

Towns and villages of the Bible are primarily rural. Agriculture was the main occupation of village dwellers, who were mostly *farmers and *shepherds. Although their work took them to the countryside by day, by night they congregated in villages for safety. Nehemiah 11:25 speaks of "the villages with their fields" (NIV), while the Levitical law stipulates that "houses in villages without walls around them are to be considered as open country" (Lev 25:31 NIV). For city dwellers such villages possessed the charm of a rustic escape already back in biblical times, as witnessed by the lover's invitation in Song of Songs 7:11: "Come, my lover, let us go to the countryside, let us spend the night in the villages" (NIV). Here too is an image of the village as part of *nature, free from the clutter and crowdedness of the city.

Life in these agrarian rural villages was simpler than it was for city dwellers, even in matters of worship. In Talmudic times a village was defined as a place without a synagogue. Although Jesus was not exempt from opposition and rejection anyplace during his earthly ministry, the Gospels nonetheless manifest a general dichotomy between the city and the village. The city of Jerusalem, dominated by the religious establishment, represents hostility to Jesus, being the place where Jesus was finally condemned and executed. The nearly eighty references to towns and villages in the Gospels, on the other hand, suggest that they are the home of ordinary people, with their ordinary needs and subsistence living, open to hear Jesus' claims and in many cases to believe on him as Savior.

To sum up, towns and villages in the Bible represent civilized community; of the commonplace, domestic and rural; and of prevailing (though not uniform) religious piety. The village is a universal and timeless image, and anyone today who has lived in a genuinely small town is likely to find the picture familiar.

See also CITY.

VILLAIN

The archetypal villain is characterized chiefly by evil. Because the forms of evil in a fallen world are numerous, the list of specific villains keeps expanding. Villains can be bullies, *prostitutes, *adulterers, *seducers or *rapists. They can be *tempters, traitors, *thieves, *murderers, *torturers and *tricksters. Or they can be blasphemers, cowards, *sluggards, *hypocrites, *drunkards, churls, braggarts, *prodigals and *taunters. One soon gets the impression that it is easy to be bad without really trying. To rank as a villain, one's character must be dominated by a form of evil; moral lapses by predominantly virtuous people are not enough to turn them into villains. The term *villain* also designates a function that a character might play in a story as the one who opposes the good characters and does the most mischief.

While most villains represent specific character types, some biblical characters are known to us simply as generic villains. Among these are *Cain, *Joseph's brothers, the men of *Sodom and the *pharaoh of *the exodus, along with Haman, Goliath, Ahab and Jezebel as well as Judas Iscariot, Herod, the *Pharisees and the figures of evil in the book of Revelation. Beyond these generic villains we can devise various organizing schemes, much as Dante does in the *Inferno.*

One group's villainy is expressed mainly in sexual behavior. Here we find harlots like Rahab, Delilah and the "loose woman" of Proverbs 1—9 (*see* Prostitute) as well as the seductress (*see* Seduction), such as Potiphar's wife (Gen 39:7-17) and the wily woman who entices a naive young man in Proverbs 7, or instigators of incest like the daughters of Lot, who make their father drunk to have sex with him (Gen 19:30-38). The male counterparts are adulterers like *David (2 Sam 11:2-5) and the man who waits for twilight and disguises himself before going out (Job 24:15), men like Judah (Gen 38:12-19) and Amnon (2 Sam 13) who prey on women, perverts like the men of Sodom (Gen 19:4-10), and men like *Samson (Judg 16:1) who solicit the services of prostitutes. A bad lot, to be sure.

Traitors have also been regarded as especially villainous. The most famous traitor in history is Judas Iscariot. Absalom's wresting the kingship from his father is similar in nature (2 Sam 15:1-12), and in its wake other erstwhile friends of David prove treacherous to him (2 Sam 15:30-31; 16:5-14). Small wonder that in Psalm 41:9 David is particularly devastated by the treachery of "my bosom friend in whom I trusted, who ate of my bread" (RSV).

Equally heinous in the eyes of the world are murderers. Not only is their sin in a category by itself; murderers themselves are noteworthy for their callousness. Examples include Cain (Gen 4:1-16), David (2 Sam 11:14-25), Jael (Judg 5:24-27), the men of Gibeah who abuse the Levite's concubine to the point of death (Judg 19:22-28), Jezebel and Ahab (1 Kings 21). Such cruelty becomes intensified in stories of multiple murders, as when Samson murders thirty Philistines to get their garments (Judg 14:19), Abimelech murders his seventy brothers (Judg 9:5) and Jehoram kills all his brothers (2 Chron 21:4).

Cut from the same cloth as murderers are *persecutors and *torturers. The leading torturers in the Bible are the soldiers and Jews who torment Christ during the trial process and during the crucifixion (*see* Cross; Passion of Christ). *Persecution is also a prominent feature of the history of the early Christian church, where Paul is public enemy number one, but the Jews in the book of Acts swell the ranks. In Jesus' eschatological discourses, villainous persecutors loom large as well. In the OT persecutors include Pharaoh and the taskmasters of the exodus, along with kings who manhandle prophets. Persecution in its extreme form produces murder, as in the case of Pharaoh's edict against newborn Hebrew males, Herod's slaughter of the innocents and the stoning of Stephen.

Only slightly less repulsive are other types of domineering persons who bully or *oppress weaker people. Here are the *tyrant, *tyrannical father/husband and *domineering mother/wife. The *lament psalms paint vivid pictures, partly hyperbolic and metaphoric, of oppressors who hunt down their victims for destruction (e.g., Ps 10:3-11; 94:4-7). The archetypal tempter or temptress (*see* Temptation, Tempter) also seeks to dominate a victim.

Another cluster of villainous behaviors turns on

various forms of dishonesty. Here we can place the *thief, *trickster, *robber, *hypocrite, deceiver (Abraham and Isaac deceiving a foreign king about the identity of their wives, Jacob deceiving Isaac to receive a blessing, Joseph's brothers telling their father that a wild animal has killed Joseph) and liar (Prov 6:17; 12:22). The false *witness is particularly criticized in the Bible (Ex 23:1; Deut 19:18; Prov 6:19; 12:17; 14:5, 25; 19:5, 9; 21:28; 25:18); narrative examples of the type appear in the fraudulent trials of Naboth (1 Kings 21) and Jesus (Mt 29:59-60; Mk 14:57). False judges, including those who accept a bribe (two dozen references), are villainous, especially to the OT prophets (Is 5:23; Ezek 22:12; Amos 5:12; Mic 7:3). If the essential trait of these deceivers is their urge to get something for themselves by invalid means, we can put in the same family the rebel of OT history who usurps something that is not his by right (see Rebellion).

Another category focuses on characters guilty of sins of speech. This includes the person of "perverse" *mouth or *tongue (Prov 10:31-32), the flatterer (2 Sam 15:4-5; Ps 5:9; Prov 27:6; 26:28; Ezek 33:31; Rom 16:18), and the smooth talker whose speech is "smoother than butter" and whose words are "softer than oil" (Ps 55:21 RSV). Here we can also put braggarts or *boasters (approximately twenty-five references to boasting in the negative sense, with Goliath in a category by himself), as well as blasphemers (approximately three dozen references), slanderers (several psalms of lament; Prov 10:19), gossips (Prov 20:19) and the nagging spouse (Prov 19:13; 21:9, 19; 25:24; 27:15-16).

Villains can be identified by sins of omission as well as commission. The coward is an example. Cowards of the Bible include Abraham when he shrank from acknowledging Sarah as his wife, twenty-two thousand men who left Gideon's army when given the chance (Judg 7:3), the ten spies who were intimidated by the inhabitants of Canaan (Num 13:27-33), Barak in his fear to go into battle as sole leader (Judg 4:8-9), reluctant leaders like Moses and Gideon (Ex 3—4; Judg 6:11-40), Peter in his denial of Jesus, Pilate in his sanctioning a false conviction because he was too weak to resist it, and the slothful steward of Jesus' parable of the talents (Mt 25:24-26). The *sluggard or slothful person, object of such scorn in the book of Proverbs, is also defined by action withheld (Prov 6:6-11; 13:4; 19:15, 24; 20:4; 24:30-34; 26:13-16). The ignoramus or simpleton is similar (Prov 1:24-32; 14:15; 22:3; 27:12). The composite biblical portrait of the fool (see Folly) is drawn so fully that the figure emerges in our imagination as particularly loathsome, yet the figure is essentially an empty shell—a kind of nonentity rather than an assertion of active evil. The archetypal unbeliever of the Bible, as well as a doubter like Thomas (Jn 20:24-29), is likewise guilty for lack of response to a message that calls for faith.

A further class of villains is defined by physical behavior. The *drunkard belongs here, as imaged in such examples as the character sketch of Proverbs 23:29-35, Noah lying drunk in his tent (Gen 9:20), the drunken Lot committing incest with his daughters (Gen 19:30-38), and Nabal and Ahasuerus losing their judgment while drunk (1 Sam 25:36; Esther 1:10-12). The brawler is similar; examples include Goliath and Samson.

A final category of biblical villains are people whose sin is a failure to live up to obligations of their position. The wayward *child, for example—an aversion in the book of Proverbs and pictured most memorably in the *prodigal of Jesus' parable— fails to live up to a parent's values and instruction. The *hireling or false shepherd runs when his presence is particularly required (Jn 10:12-13). Few biblical villains are excoriated so severely as false or ignoble religious leaders who abdicate their spiritual responsibilities, as typified by the false shepherds of Ezekiel 34 and the Pharisees of the Gospels (see especially Mt 23; see also numerous NT references to "false teachers").

Underlying all these specific types of villain is a single figure—the archetypal sinner. In Christian theology, as well as in the literary and popular imaginations, *Adam and *Eve are the prototypes—the people who disobey what God told them not to do. The villains of the Bible are variations on the original text.

The character type of the villain is prominent in the Bible for at least two reasons. Stories require an antagonist who opposes the protagonist, and since most protagonists are in some sense *heroic, it is inevitable that a book where narrative predominates as it does in the Bible would contain a memorable gallery of villains. Second, the Bible is a book preoccupied with human sinfulness, and when projected in concrete form human sinfulness takes the form of the villain. For a quick gallery of ways to be villainous, several lists in the Epistles will suffice (Rom 1:30-31; Col 3:5-9; 2 Tim 3:2-9).

See also ADULTERY; CHARACTER TYPES; DOMINEERING MOTHER, WIFE; DRUNKARD; DRUNKENNESS; HYPOCRITE; MURDER STORIES; PERSECUTION; PHARAOH; PRODIGAL SON; PROSTITUTE, PROSTITUTION; RAPE, SEXUAL VIOLENCE; ROB, ROBBER; SATAN; SEDUCTION, SEDUCER, SEDUCTRESS; SLUGGARD; TAUNT; TEMPTATION, TEMPTER; THIEF; TORTURE; TRICKSTER; TYRANNICAL FATHER, HUSBAND; TYRANT, TYRANNY.

VINE, VINEYARD

Israel was a land of vineyards. Even today, traveling through the central hill country of Israel during the right season, one can see abundant evidence of fruitful vines. The fruit of the vine, of course, is the *grape, whose juice, when fermented, produces *wine.

Perhaps then it is not surprising that the vine and the vineyard, so characteristic of this country's agricultural fertility, serve as potent images for the *land itself. For good reason most discussions of the biblical image of the vineyard begin with Isaiah 5:1-7:

I will sing for the one I love
a song about his vineyard:
My loved one had a vineyard
on a fertile hillside.
He dug it up and cleared it of stones
and planted it with the choicest vines.
He built a watchtower in it
and cut out a winepress as well.
Then he looked for a crop of good grapes.
(Is 5:1-2 NIV)

The parable of the vineyard, as this text is often called, describes Israel as God's vineyard. It is God's not only because God loves it, but because he painstakingly prepared the land and planted it. He also carefully protected it. In this way the parable describes God's election of Israel as a nation (Deut 7:7-11) and his providential care of it. As with any vineyard, the vinedresser does all this work with the expectation of a fruitful and bountiful *harvest.

Psalm 80 is a notable example of other biblical passages that share this theme. The psalmist describes the exodus in the language of a vineyard:

You brought a vine out of Egypt;
you drove out the nations and planted it.
You cleared the ground for it,
and it took root and filled the land.
(Ps 80:8-9 NIV)

Israel, the vine, was transplanted from Egypt to the *Promised Land, where it spread quickly and over a vast space (Ps 80:10-11).

The rapid growth and fertile bounty of the vine accentuate the blessing God placed on his people. We can see this developed in Jacob's *blessings on the descendants of two of his sons, Judah and Joseph:

[Judah] will tether his donkey to a vine,
his colt to the choicest branch;
he will wash his garments in wine,
his robes in the blood of grapes.
His eyes will be darker than wine,
his teeth whiter than milk. . . .
Joseph is a fruitful vine,
a fruitful vine near a spring,
whose branches climb over a wall.
(Gen 49:11-12, 22 NIV)

The Vine Turns Bad. Isaiah's parable of the vine, after stating that the divine vinedresser looked for good grapes, sadly declares, "But it yielded only bad fruit" (Is 5:2).

In spite of God's efforts, Israel turns bad. Other prophets share Isaiah's perspective on the incredible perversity of Israel:

I had planted you like a choice vine
of sound and reliable stock.
How then did you turn against me
into a corrupt, wild vine? (Jer 2:21 NIV)

Hosea describes how it was Israel's penchant for the worship of *idols that led to the rotten fruit of the vine (Hos 10:1).

The bad fruit is not the responsibility of the vinedresser, who took careful pains to plant and take care of the vine (Ezek 17:5-6). It is the vine itself that

is at fault. It produced bad grapes in spite of all the advantages it had. As a result, the vines will be destroyed.

Judgment: The Destruction of the Vineyard. Isaiah's parable identifies Israel with the vineyard God planted. The fruit that vineyard produced was not good, so God will take the following steps:

Now I will tell you
what I am going to do to my vineyard:
I will take away its hedge,
and it will be destroyed;
I will break down its wall,
and it will be trampled.
I will make it a wasteland,
neither pruned nor cultivated,
and briers and thorns will grow there.
I will command the clouds
not to rain on it.
The vineyard of the LORD Almighty
is the house of Israel,
and the men of Judah
are the garden of his delight.
And he looked for justice, but saw bloodshed;
for righteousness, but heard cries of distress.
(Is 5:5-7 NIV)

In other words, God will come in judgment and destroy the vineyard. The destruction of the vineyard is a frequent motif in the Prophets (e.g., Is 16:8; Jer 5:10, 17; 12:10; Hos 2:12; Amos 4:10).

Foretelling the vineyard's destruction is just one way the vineyard image is used in judgment contexts. In an oracle against *Jerusalem, God says:

Let them glean the remnant of Israel
as thoroughly as a vine;
pass your hand over the branches again,
like one gathering grapes. (Jer 6:9 NIV)

The picture of a vine being plucked clean is a vivid one for the total destruction of the city.

Micah also varies the theme when he describes the destruction of Samaria as so thorough that vineyards could be planted in the empty spaces that remain: "Therefore I will make Samaria a heap of rubble, a place for planting vineyards" (Mic 1:6 NIV).

In one of his judgment speeches Zephaniah allows that vineyards will be planted and perhaps even produce fruit, but even after all the labor, the people of God, because of their sin, will not enjoy the fruit of their labor. In reference to Judah, he proclaims:

Their wealth will be plundered,
their houses demolished.
They will build houses
but not live in them;
they will plant vineyards
but not drink the wine. (Zeph 1:13 NIV)

In one of the more interesting biblical uses of the vineyard image, Deuteronomy emphasizes not only judgment but also the organic connection between the sins of God's people and those of the notorious city of Sodom:

Their vine comes from the vine of Sodom

and from the fields of Gomorrah.
Their grapes are filled with poison,
and their clusters with bitterness.
      (Deut 32:32 NIV)

The lamentation that judgment arouses is pictured as people crying in a vineyard. According to Isaiah 16:10, "Joy and gladness are taken away from the orchards; no one sings or shouts in the vineyards" (NIV; see also Amos 5:17). The irony is that a place where one normally finds joy has become a place of weeping.

These passages illustrate the use of the vineyard image in contexts of judgment. Prophetic judgment speeches often derive from covenant *curses, and Deuteronomy 28 shows that this is the case with this image as well. After recounting Israel's relationship with God and their responsibility to follow his law, Deuteronomy concludes with a series of blessings and curses attendant upon obedience or disobedience of the law. Two passages mention the vineyard. According to Deuteronomy 28:30, those who break the law of God "will plant a vineyard, but . . . will not even begin to enjoy its fruit" (NIV). The same thought is repeated in Deuteronomy 28:39.

The image of the destroyed vineyard, of course, flowed from the fact that military intrusion often entailed disruption of agricultural production. In other words, God's judgment often included the literal devastation of vineyards (Ps 78:47).

Blessing and Restoration: The Fertility of the Vine. If God's *anger and *judgment is represented by the destroyed vineyard, it is not surprising that God's *blessing and *restoration are expressed through the image of the fertile vineyard. The prophets looked beyond God's judgment to the restoration and envisioned healthy and productive vineyards. In the so-called Book of Consolation (Jeremiah 31—33), the prophet tells the people of God:

Again you will plant vineyards
  on the hills of Samaria;
the farmers will plant them
  and enjoy their fruit.
      (Jer 31:5 NIV; cf. Jer 32:15)

After delivering hard-hitting judgment speeches against Israel, Amos concludes with this promising picture:

I will bring back my exiled people Israel;
  they will rebuild the ruined cities and live in
    them.
They will plant vineyards and drink their wine;
  they will make gardens and eat their fruit.
      (Amos 9:14 NIV)

A particularly memorable biblical phrase uses the vine image to describe the prosperity of those whom God blesses: "each man [lived] under his own vine and fig tree" (1 Kings 4:25; 2 Kings 18:31; Is 36:16). The picture is of security and *peace. One does not have to go any distance to have the finest delicacies.

The Vineyard in the Song of Songs. Fertile vines produced luscious grapes, pleasing to the taste and, when fermented, intoxicating. It is not surpris-

ing, considering the general use of agricultural images for *sexuality, that the vine is frequently employed in that most sensual of all biblical poems, the *Song of Songs. What is perhaps somewhat unexpected is the variety of ways the poet uses the image.

In the first place, the vine and its fruit describe the woman's body. In Song of Songs 1:14 the man describes his beloved as a cluster of henna blossoms from the oasislike vineyards of En-Gedi. In a poem that describes the physical beauty of the woman's body, the man anticipates the *touch and taste of the her *breasts by his exuberant blessing "May your breasts be like the clusters of the vine" (Song 7:8 NIV).

The vineyard as a metaphor of a woman's body is likely behind two passages that are at first enigmatic. In Song of Songs 1:6 the woman asks the daughters of Jerusalem not to look at her, for "my own vineyard I have neglected" (NIV). Then at the end of the book there is talk of "Solomon's vineyard," while the woman asserts, "My own vineyard is mine to give" (Song 8:11-12 NIV). Most commentators today take this as the woman arguing that she is the only one who can give herself sexually to another.

Elsewhere in the Song, however, the vineyard is not the woman's body but the place where the man and the woman will share their love. The vineyard, along with the *garden, the orchard and the nut grove, is the setting for passion (Song 6:11; 7:12). And further, the fragrant, blossoming vineyard is a sign of the coming of spring, a particularly appropriate time for erotic love (Song 2:13, 15).

Other Uses in the Old Testament. The vineyard is a place of excess in the account of Noah's *drunkenness. After the flood, Noah, "a man of the soil, proceeded to plant a vineyard" (Gen 9:20 NIV). His overuse of the fruit of his labors resulted in his drunken state, giving Ham, his youngest son, the opportunity to sin against him. This led to Noah's curse on Canaan, Ham's son, which was borne out in the subjugation of the Canaanites to the descendants of Ham's brother Shem, the Israelites.

In the book of Proverbs the condition of a vineyard is a sign of laziness or industriousness. The former is illustrated by Proverbs 24:30-34, in which the sluggard's vineyard is described as unkept, while the noble woman of Proverbs 31 "plants a vineyard" through her hard work (Prov 31:16 NIV).

In Judges 9 Abimelech succeeds in killing all his brothers except for Jotham, who escapes. Abimelech then sets himself up as king. Jotham reappears to tell a parable in which all productive plants, including the vine (whose positive trait is the production of wine, Judg 9:13), turn down an offer to be king of the plant world. Only the useless thornbush agrees to rule. After that plant assumes rulership, it thinks itself productive and superior to even the mighty cedar.

Vineyard Imagery in the New Testament. The NT continues the use of the vineyard theme that began in the OT, but with a twist. It is no longer ethnic Israel that is God's vineyard, but the *kingdom of God. This may be seen in Jesus' parables of the vineyard (Mt 20:1-11; 21:33-43). The parable of the tenants (Mt 21:33-43) has the closest similarity to Isaiah 5. The landowner, who is surely meant to represent God, plants and protects a vineyard and then rents it to tenants who end up abusing his servants. The parable concludes with a threat against those who misuse the vineyard.

Revelation 14:18-20 shows that even at the end of the canon the vineyard image can be used to picture the judgment coming on those who resist God. The passage describes an *angel who gathers "the clusters of grapes from the earth's vine" and throws them into the "great *winepress of God's wrath," with the result that "*blood flowed out of the press, rising as high as the horses' bridles for a distance of 1,600 stadia" (NIV).

Perhaps the most striking of all NT uses of the image occurs in association with Jesus. Speaking to the disciples, Jesus proclaims, "I am the vine; you are the branches" (Jn 15:5 NIV). By identifying himself as the vine he claims that participation in the kingdom is possible only for those who "remain in" him. Those disciples who do will bear much fruit.

In the light of this passage, how fitting it is that the ritual of the *supper that Jesus institutes on the eve of his death involves drinking the "fruit of the vine" (Mt 26:29; cf. Mk 14:25; Lk 22:18).

See also BLOOD; CUP; DRUNKENNESS; FARMING; GRAPES; HARVEST; PRUNING; WINE; WINEPRESS.

VIOLENCE, STORIES OF

Stories of violence are part of every branch of realistic literature, and the Bible is a realistic book that sometimes looks at life at its worst. Acts of violence in the Bible are prompted by bravado, *anger, revenge, *judgment and (most of all) degeneration.

Acts of reprobate violence explode from the pages of the Bible as evil people perform unspeakable acts. We read about *children cannibalized (2 Kings 6:28-29; Ezek 5:10; Lam 2:20), boiled (Lam 4:10) and dashed against a rock (Ps 137:9). During the Babylonian invasion, Zedekiah is forced to watch his *sons slaughtered, after which his own eyes are gouged out (Jer 52:10-11). Pregnant *women are ripped open (2 Kings 15:16; Amos 1:13). Other women are *raped (Gen 34:1-5; 1 Sam 13:1-15; Ezek 22:11); one of them is gang raped to the point of death (Judg 19:22-30).

Military atrocities are equally shocking. We read about stabbings (Judg 3:12-20; 2 Sam 2:23; 20:10) and beheadings (1 Sam 17:54; 2 Sam 4:7-9). These are normal military atrocities. More extraordinary cases involve *torture and mutilation: limbs are cut off (Judg 1:6-7), bodies hewed in pieces (1 Sam 15:33), *eyes gouged out (Judg 16:21; 2 Kings 25:7), skulls punctured (Judg 4:12-23; 5:26-27) or crushed by a millstone pushed from a city wall (Judg 9:53). Two hundred foreskins are collected (1 Sam 18:27), seventy heads gathered (2 Kings 10:7-8), thirty men killed for their clothing (Judg 14:19). Bodies are hanged (Josh

8:29), mutilated and displayed as trophies (1 Sam 31:9-10), trampled beyond recognition (2 Kings 9:30-37), destroyed by wild beasts (Josh 13:8; 2 Kings 2:23-24) or flailed with *briers (Judg 8:16). Entire groups are massacred (1 Sam 22:18-19; 1 Kings 16:8-14) or led into captivity strung together with hooks through their lips (Amos 4:2).

In the NT the violence takes the specific form of persecution of *martyrs. The *passion of Christ is the supreme example. The beheading of John the Baptist (Mt 14:1-12; Mk 6:14-29; Lk 9:7-9), though narrated more summarily, is no less gruesome. And the honor roll of faith in Hebrews 11 concludes not with stories of survival and triumph but with an ever-expanding vision of violence against the innocent: "They were stoned, they were sawn in two, they were killed with the sword; they went about in skins of sheep and goats, destitute, afflicted, ill-treated" (Heb 11:37 RSV).

What are we to make of this violence in the Bible? An obvious answer is that the Bible is not a "nice" book that hides the sordid side of life. The Bible is a book of thoroughgoing realism. The Bible's stories of violence demonstrate the depths of depravity to which the human race descends. Paradoxically, though, the nadir of depravity represented by biblical stories of violence is also the climax of the Bible's story of redemption. The violence of the *cross is the pivot point of redemption. The song of the *suffering servant in Isaiah 53 hints at this paradox: written in a highly stylized poetic form replete with parallelism and an unusually high degree of patterning, this song uses the resources of artistic form to beautify its portrait of a person subjected to unfair violence for the sake of others.

See also ANGER; BATTLE STORIES; CROSS; MURDER STORIES; RAPE, SEXUAL VIOLENCE; TORTURE; VENGEANCE, REVENGE.

VIRGIN, VIRGINITY

The idea of virginity, referring generally to any young unmarried person and specifically to those who have not yet experienced *sexual intercourse, is commonly used in both a literal and a metaphorical sense in Scripture. There is something of an equivocal attitude toward virginity. On the one hand, it is something to be prized, indicating *purity and *newness (Gen 24:16; Esther 2:2; Song 6:8). On the other hand, it is seen as something of a *shame or a sadness, indicating lack of fulfillment or incompletion.

Virgins are to be *protected. Israel had legislation concerning sexual abuse, and the *rape of a virgin is seen as particularly heinous (Ex 22:16; Lam 5:11). Virgin *brides are particularly valued; indeed, the high *priest is allowed to marry only a virgin (Lev 21:13-14). Virgin princesses appear to have had a special role (2 Sam 13:18); hence the tragedy for Tamar when she had this status taken away from her (2 Sam 13:2, 14).

The sense of sadness at the prospect of continuing virginity, or of never experiencing sex or perhaps more particularly childbirth, is shown by the attitude of Lot's *daughters (Gen 19:8) and that of Jephthah's daughter, who asked for her death to be postponed for two months so that she might "bewail" her virginity (Judg 11:37 NRSV).

The concept of purity and freshness, allied with a sense of looking forward to something more to come and moving on to a greater maturity, made it appropriate to refer to *Israel as a virgin, prized by God and yet looking forward to future *blessings.

Again I will build you, and you shall be built,
    O virgin Israel!
Again you shall take your tambourines,
    and go forth in the dance of the merrymakers.
        (Jer 31:4 NRSV)

A sense of helplessness, lack of power and sometimes abuse or a fallen condition comes across in references to both Israel and other nations: "Come down and sit in the dust, virgin daughter Babylon!" (Is 47:1 NRSV). "The virgin Israel has done a most horrible thing" (Jer 18:13 NRSV). "Fallen, no more to rise, is maiden Israel" (Amos 5:2 NRSV).

In the NT, 2 Corinthians 11:2 sees the *church presented to Christ "as a chaste virgin" (NRSV), again picking up the theme of both purity and expectation. The fact that virgins are without family responsibility and therefore able to devote themselves to serving God is also noted in theory in 1 Corinthians 7 and in practice in the lives of Philip's daughters (Acts 21:9).

Most biblical language of virginity relates to women; the male equivalent in the eunuch does not have quite the same symbolism. However, Isaiah 56:3 stresses that the eunuch is not to be seen as useless; Matthew 19:12 speaks of those who choose to be eunuchs "for the sake of the kingdom of heaven" (NRSV), presumably referring to the *work potential of unmarried men and parallel to 1 Corinthians 7, which refers clearly to both sexes. Revelation 14:4 describes the men who have totally dedicated themselves to God as male virgins—emphasizing both purity and dedication.

The Gospels of Matthew and Luke indicate that *Mary was a virgin (Mt 1:23; Lk 1:27, 34). In this case her virginity does not so much emphasize her freshness or desirability. Rather, it dramatically shows her *Son's special relationship to God. He was not conceived by human means but was born of a woman. Thus the *salvation that God brought to humanity was accomplished not by human ability but by divine intervention.

See also BRIDE, BRIDEGROOM; DAUGHTER; MARY THE MOTHER OF JESUS; PURITY; RAPE, SEXUAL VIOLENCE; SEX; WOMAN, IMAGES OF.

VISIONS. *See* DREAMS, VISIONS.

VOCATION. *See* CALLING, VOCATION.

VOICE

The Bible is not characterized primarily by specifi-

cally visualized descriptions but is rather a book of oral and aural imagery. It is not surprising, then, that the term *voice* appears in English translations between 217 times (NIV) and 325 times (NRSV). A wide range of uses is included, but in every case "voice" implies a spoken utterance, usually in the form of language.

Hearing someone's voice forms a personal connection to him or her. Each person's voice is distinct, unique to that individual. Therefore the lover in *Song of Songs longs to hear his beloved's voice; it is sweet to him and it reflects her qualities (Song 2:14). Jesus' voice is sweet to his followers as well. He says, "My sheep listen to my voice; I know them, and they follow me" (Jn 10:27; also Jn 10:3-5). The Good *Shepherd's voice is unique to him; in it there is safety and security. The sheep know the voice because they know the Shepherd.

A person's voice reveals emotion and character as well. Crying out in a loud voice may indicate desperation (Mt 27:46) or *anger (1 Sam 28:12), while a soft voice may indicate *gentleness or *patience.

However, while a voice may give us more information about someone or bring us closer to him or her, it may also be elusive and stir up uncertainty, especially when it is God's voice. Deuteronomy 4:12 says, "The LORD spoke to you out of the fire. You heard the sound of words but saw no form; there was only a voice" (NIV). Likewise, the voice from *heaven in John 12:28 brings as many questions as it does answers; the unbelieving crowd believes it was *thunder or an *angel's voice (see also Mt 3:17; 17:5-10).

The voice of God is a major biblical motif, mentioned three dozen times (NRSV). Sometimes it signifies God's transcendent power. Psalm 29, "the song of the thunderstorm," *seven times refers to the rushing sound of the *storm as "the voice of the LORD," which is treated as the active agent in the unfolding drama of the storm as it rises in the Mediterranean *Sea and moves eastward onto land.

Because of its mysterious quality and God's transcendence, his voice may stir up great *fear: "What mortal has ever heard the voice of the living God speaking out of fire, as we have, and survived?" (Deut 5:26 NIV; cf. Is 6:8; Ezek 1:24; 43:2; Heb 12:19). His voice connotes his power: it is often identified with thunder (e.g., 2 Sam 22:14; Job 37:2-5; Ps 18:13; Is 30:30) to depict the power of his intervention in human life. Hebrews looks forward to such an intervention: "At that time his voice shook the earth, but now he has promised, 'Once more I will shake not only the earth but also the heavens' " (Heb 12:26 NIV). *Judgment is implicitly associated with his voice here (see also Is 30:31 and Jn 5:25, 28, where the idea is dramatically transferred to Christ).

The voice of God, while enigmatic and terrifying, is also used in Scripture as a metaphor referring to his person. When Moses speaks with God in the tent of meeting, "he heard the voice speaking to him from between the two cherubim above the atonement cover on the ark of the Testimony" (Num 7:89 NIV; cf. 1 Kings 19:13; 2 Pet 1:17). This lies behind the later (Aramaic) Jewish practice of referring to God enigmatically as "the Voice" or "the Word."

Revelation comes through voices: John the Baptist's "voice in the desert" (Is 40:3; Mt 3:3), the voice of the herald proclaiming good news to *Jerusalem (Is 40:2, 9; 52:7), the voice of *wisdom that "calls aloud in the street" (Prov 1:20 NIV) and even the voice of God himself (Deut 5:22; Is 6:8). Often the phrase "loud voice" connotes this kind of prophetic announcement (e.g., Ezek 11:13; Mt 27:46; Lk 1:42; Jn 7:37).

Often the revelatory "voice" is mentioned without specific reference to God yet connoting communication from him. These "voices" fall into three categories. *Heavenly* voices are heard at significant moments when the divine and the world meet—for instance, at Jesus' baptism (Mt 3:17) and transfiguration (Mt 17:5) and at Paul's conversion (Acts 9:4; cf. also Dan 4:13; *see* Divine-Human Encounter). *Apocalyptic* voices are heard by John (Rev 6:1; 10:4; 21:3) with some compelling announcement from heaven. Similarly, *prophetic* voices proclaim God's plans for his people.

See also EAR, HEARING; MOUTH; THUNDER; TONGUE.

VOMIT

Vomiting is one of numerous biblical images of revulsion (*see* Disgust, Revulsion). The image is usually used in relation to sin or its disgraceful punishment. Proverbs 26:11 likens a persistence in sin and folly to "a dog that returns to its vomit" (RSV), and 2 Peter 2:22 compares the *apostate who abandons the Christian faith to a *dog that "turns back to his own vomit" (RSV).

The word is found most often in the OT prophets as a part of God's judgment on the nations. In such passages vomiting is often a natural result of *drunkenness and a sign of defilement and excess that God views as disgraceful. In Jeremiah, God declares that the nations he is judging will be forced to drink a "cup of the wine of wrath" that will cause then to "drink, be drunk and vomit, fall and rise no more, because of the sword" God is sending to destroy them (Jer 25:15, 27 RSV). Similarly, God promises to punish Egypt with a spirit of confusion that will make it "stagger . . . as a drunken man staggers in his vomit" (Is 19:14 RSV), and the drunkards of Ephraim will find that "all tables are full of vomit" (Is 28:8 RSV). God also promises to make Moab drunk to "wallow in his vomit, and . . . be held in derision" (Jer 48:26 RSV). In such prophetic visions of judgment, drunkenness and its attendant vomiting are vividly symbolic of both the depravity into which nations have fallen and the punishment and disgrace to which God appropriately subjects them.

In another type of image, people under *judgment are not pictured as themselves vomiting but as being vomited out, again a picture of revulsion. In

Leviticus, God declares that the *Promised Land vomited up its previous inhabitants because of their depravity (Lev 18:25). God promises similar rejection to the children of Israel if they defile the land with their sins (Lev 18:28; 20:22). When Israel disobeyed God, he allowed King Nebuchadnezzar to devour and crush the nation, so that it lamented, "He has swallowed me like a monster; he has filled his belly with my delicacies, he has spewed me out" (Jer 51:34 NRSV). In Revelation, God threatens a similar judgment to those who refuse to take their faith seriously, declaring that because the Laodiceans are lukewarm, he will spew them out of his *mouth (Rev 3:16). Vomiting is here a gesture of disgust, as when the fish expelled Jonah on the land (Jon 2:11); while the act rescued Jonah from his watery threat, the word used is a term of repulsion that suggests that Jonah was nauseating to the fish.

At times vomiting graphically portrays the biting betrayal of *sin, especially overindulgence in its various forms. Thus the sages promise that the wicked must vomit up the wealth they have swallowed (Job 20:15) and that vomiting is the gruesome penalty for overindulgence (Prov 25:16; 23:8).

See also DISGUST, REVULSION; DUNG; EATING; MOUTH; SPIT.

VOW, OATH

Vows and oaths evoke the idea of a serious setting, such as a court of law (oath) or a *wedding ceremony (vow). That the wedding vow is actually an oath betrays a widespread blurring of the distinction between oaths and vows in the Hebrew Bible. An oath is an abbreviated *covenant (Gen 26:28), a promise between two or more persons in which the name of a deity is invoked as witness and guarantor. The oath is normally represented by the act of "swearing" (making a solemn promise) or by placing oneself under a *curse. In his denial of Jesus, Peter did both (Mk 14:71). By contrast, a vow is a solemn promise made by a person to his or her deity. The vow normally includes an oath formula, but its direction is vertical, not horizontal like the oath. Whereas oaths are between persons, the vow is directed toward God. It always takes place within the context of prayer since it is always addressed to God. Vows are normally made in times of distress, and the supplicant's gift is often contingent upon the granting of his petition (Judg 11:30; 1 Sam 14:24).

The serious nature of all promises and conduct before God is reflected in the taking of oaths and vows. According to Mosaic *law, the Lord's *name was not to be taken lightly in the swearing of oaths (Ex 20:7; Deut 5:11). Yahweh would personally punish the swearer of such a false oath. Sin is not determined by whether a person vows or not. Rather, once uttered, a vow is as binding as an oath (Deut 23:21-23) and should therefore not be made carelessly (Prov 20:25).

Truthfulness as the paragon of all speech is reflected in God's binding of himself by an oath (Heb

6:13-18, cf. Jer 22:5) and by the fact that Christ is the guarantor of all the OT promises. Jesus taught that oaths were binding (Mt 5:33) and that the Christian's daily conversation is considered as sacred as oaths. If, as the obedience of God's kingdom mandates, deeds correspond to words, then oaths will be unnecessary (Mt 5:34-37; Col 3:17; Jas 1:22; 5:12; 1 Jn 3:18).

The *Nazirite vow* symbolized extreme devotion to God. A solemn oath was sworn to separate oneself *from* certain items, such as symbols of *feasting (*grape products) and ritual impurity (dead bodies), as well as *to* Yahweh's unique service (symbolized by letting the hair grow long). At the end of the prescribed period, the Nazirite would offer the symbol of special consecration (the shorn hair) as part of a thank *offering in conclusion of the vow.

Utmost dedication and trust in Yahweh was signified by the *war vow*. This was a more intense type of Nazirite vow in which Yahweh's warriors would not only consecrate themselves as Nazirites, but would also vow to him a particular city as booty (Num 21:2). With this vow, the devotee placed his very life at risk. This is especially true in light of the fact that Israelite holy wars, in human terms, amounted to suicide missions (*see* Battle Stories).

By way of contrast, the *nād⁼bâ vow* (freewill offering) symbolizes a fervent attitude of thankfulness and appreciation toward God. The worshiper would contribute personal items of great value to God's work. The most striking examples are the unusually generous freewill offerings of God's people in the building of the wilderness *tabernacle (Ex 35:21, 29) and the first (2 Chron 29:6ff) and second (Ezra 1:6; 2:68; 7:16) *temples. The magnitude of sacrifice is seen by the fact that the offering greatly exceeded the requirements of the law.

As with *covenants, the keeping of an oath or the completion of a vow is associated with a state of happiness (blessedness), whereas the breaking of it precipitates the curses as consequences. In vowing, a person places him- or herself under solemn obligation by entering into the domain of the promised *offering or *sacrifice. The vower is released only when the sacrifice is made. Fulfillment of this obligation is associated with a state of happiness and answered prayer (Job 22:27, cf. 1 Sam 13:12). On the other hand, a vow could bring down God's curse, especially if blemished animals were substituted to fulfill a vow (Mal 1:14). Both the oath and the vow reflect a profound consciousness that everything a person does in this life is intimately connected with the nature of God as scrutinizing and assessing every action and motive. The two opposite states of happiness and cursedness reflect God's response to these actions and motives with respect to their moral value. God is deeply concerned with the manner in which his people conduct themselves in his limitless presence.

Among Israel's neighbors, oaths and vows were also sealed by appeal to deities and followed by blessings and cursings. The deity called as witness enforced the appropriate consequences on the parties. The curses were believed to be visited on oath breakers by evil powers that were greatly feared and were personified as demons named "Oath." For the Hebrews, to swear by other deities was to ascribe to them the power and position of Yahweh and thus amounted to *idolatry (Josh 23:7; Jer 12:16; Amos 8:14; Zeph 1:5; Jas 5:12).

See also COVENANT; CURSE.

BIBLIOGRAPHY. T. W. Cartledge, *Vows in the Hebrew Bible and the Ancient Near East*, JSOTS (Sheffield: JSOT Press, 1992) 11-14.

VULTURE. *See* BIRDS; EAGLE.

WAGES

In the Bible wages are a comprehensive idea representing compensation for *time, energy or skills invested in a form of service. Wages may satisfy physical, financial, social and political obligations and needs, and may be paid in money (Mk 14:5; cf. Jn 12:5), *food (Num 18:31), possessions (Gen 30:32) or another gift in kind (e.g., *Egypt is described as a wage paid to Nebuchadnezzar, Ezek 29:19-20).

References to wages call attention to different qualities of compensation. First, compensation should be *fair*. The Bible indicates that *work deserves wages (Lk 10:7; Rom 4:4; Phil 4:18; 1 Tim 5:18) and that appropriate regulations should govern their payment in order to protect the worker from exploitation (Lev 19:13; Deut 24:15). Second, compensation is sometimes *inadequate*. The prophets condemn exploitation (Jer 22:13; Mal 3:5), and James deplores it (Jas 5:4). Third, compensation can be *polluted*. An example here is the wages of a *prostitute (Deut 23:18; Mic 1:7), suggesting that *evil activity cannot be *rewarded by that which is wholesome (cf. 2 Pet 2:15, Balaam's love of wicked wages). Israel's love for "the wages of a prostitute" symbolizes its unfaithfulness to God (Hos 9:1 NIV). According to Proverbs 10:16 and 11:18, the quality of compensation has eternal consequences—as exemplified by Judas's payment for *betraying Christ (Mt 26:15).

In the NT the idea of wages has figurative overtones, as when Jesus gives a task to his followers. In John 4:36 Jesus suggests that "the reaper" is involved in work of eternal consequence that will earn "wages." The pictorial language of this passage allows that wages may symbolize eternal rewards, but in *Matthew 20:1-16 the parable of the *vineyard where each worker receives the same wage regardless of *hours worked, it appears that wages are mentioned to affirm the endurance and significance of the work assigned (cf. 1 Cor 3:8-14). NT wages imagery also points to God's gracious dealings with humanity. In Romans 4:4-5 the symbolism contrasts the obligation to pay wages with God's free decision to reward those who trust in him. Finally, God's dealing with *sin is sometimes pictured as the paying of wages. The key verse here is Romans 6:23, where *wages* symbolizes the idea that eternal *death is the appropriate payment for sin, whereas eternal life is simply a gift.

In the Bible as a whole, the requirement of fair compensation for human labor serves only to highlight the spiritual truth that fair compensation for human life always leads to condemnation. God's grace alone can deal with the human condition.

See also REWARD; WORK, WORKER.

WAITING ON GOD

The motif of waiting on God, rendered famous in English literature by the aphoristic last line of Milton's sonnet on his blindness ("They also serve who only stand and wait"), is major in Scripture, encompassing a rich range of specific meanings. Although the modern world has conspired to multiply occasions of our tedious waiting for something or someone, the biblical motif of waiting for God is a strongly positive image. Waiting on God is a biblical virtue, and a large number of passages command such waiting. While the clusters are interrelated, we can discern five main usages.

On the more passive side, waiting on God is associated with patience, resignation, submission, dependence and contentment with a less-than-ideal current state. For example, as the psalmist contemplates his vindication from God against his *enemies (Ps 27:12-13), he enjoins himself to "wait for the LORD; be strong, and let your heart take courage; wait for the LORD" (Ps 27:14 NRSV). Of similar import is "Be still before the LORD, and wait patiently for him" (Ps 37:7 NRSV). And again, "It is good that one should wait quietly for the salvation of the LORD" (Lam 3:26 NRSV).

In some passages, waiting for God to act is an implied withholding of human exertion. Here waiting becomes a venture of faith, a trust in God rather than human means. Hence the proverb "Do not say, 'I will repay evil'; wait for the LORD, and he will help you" (Prov 20:22 NRSV). An oppressed people prays, "O LORD, be gracious to us; we wait for you. Be our . . . salvation in the time of trouble" (Is 33:2 NRSV). Youthful strength is insufficient to ward off weariness, but "those who wait for the LORD shall renew their strength, they shall mount up with wings like eagles, they shall run and not be weary, they shall walk and not faint" (Is 40:31 NRSV).

A third motif joins the virtue of waiting on God with hope and expectancy. To wait is to anticipate the time that God will act. The psalmist asserts, "But it is for you, O LORD, that I wait; it is you, O LORD my God, who will answer" (Ps 38:15 NRSV). "And now, O Lord, what do I wait for? My hope is in you" (Ps 39:7 NRSV). "I wait for the LORD, my soul waits, and in his word I hope" (Ps 130:5 NRSV; see also Is 8:17). "I will wait for the God of my salvation; my God will hear me" (Mic 7:7 NRSV). Part of the hope is that those who wait for God "shall not be put to shame" (Is 49:23 NRSV) and that God "is good to those who wait for him, to the soul that seeks him" (Lam 3:25 NRSV).

A fourth cluster of passages casts waiting for God into an eschatological light, as we are called to wait for the coming redemption. While there is a premonition of the motif in the OT (Zeph 3:8; cf. Ps 37:9, 34, which speak of those who wait for the Lord inheriting the land), it comes to fruition in the NT, where we read about waiting "for the revealing of our Lord Jesus Christ" (1 Cor 1:7 NRSV) and for the "the blessed hope and the manifestation of the glory of our great God and Savior, Jesus Christ" (Tit 2:13 NRSV). Such waiting even has the efficacy of "hastening the coming of the day of God" (2 Pet 3:12 NRSV; see also 2 Pet 3:13-14, which speaks of how "we wait for new heavens and a new earth" and of the need, "while you are waiting for these things," to "strive to be found by him at peace, without spot or blemish" [NRSV]).

Finally, some passages make the act of waiting for God so general as to leave it a virtual picture of the whole life of faith—on a par with being "God-fearing," for example. Here we have references to how "blessed are all those who wait for [God]" (Is 30:18 NRSV) and to people who "wait continually for . . . God" (Hos 12:6 NRSV). In Psalm 31:23-24 the group designated as God's "saints" and "the faithful" is also called "you who wait for the LORD" (NRSV). At times, indeed, waiting on God seems synonymous with the *covenant itself: "From ages past no one has heard, no ear has perceived, no eye has seen any God besides you, who works for those who wait for him" (Is 64:4 NRSV).

See also FAITH; FEAR OF GOD; HOPE; PRAYER.

WAKE UP. *See* AWAKENING.

WALK, WALKING

In biblical times walking was the most common way of going somewhere, even over long distances. It is not surprising, then, that references to walking in the Bible number well over two hundred (and in some versions nearly three hundred). A survey of references to the physical act of walking reveal that Jesus is the most persistent pedestrian in the Bible. Beyond the literal mechanics of movement by *foot, walking at a more figurative level becomes a prime metaphor for two (often related) motifs—interaction with someone else (a companion on a metaphoric walk) or a person's lifestyle (with the image of walking suggesting continuing progress in time and in a chosen direction).

Walking with God. The first occurrence of walking in the Bible is the picture of *God's "walking" in the *Garden of Eden in the cool of the day (Gen 3:8). After the exodus, God promises the nation of Israel, "I will walk among you and be your God" (Lev 26:12 NIV; quoted in 2 Cor 6:16). God also visits and walks around the camp of the Israelites (Deut 23:14). These examples of God's "walking" on the earth picture the active divine presence among the people God has created and called.

The counterpart of God's walking with his people is their walking "with" him or "before" him. Enoch and Noah "walked with God" (Gen 5:22, 24; 6:9). In Malachi 2:6 God pictures the original priesthood as walking with him in peace and uprightness, and in Revelation 3:4 Christ promises that the remnant in Sardis who remain pure "will walk with me, dressed in white, for they are worthy" (NIV). To walk "before" God has the same meaning as walking "with" him: God commanded Abraham to "walk before me and be blameless" (Gen 17:1 NIV) and promised David and his successors favor if they walked before him (1 Kings 8:25; 9:4; 2 Chron 6:16; 7:17; see also 2 Kings 20:3; Is 38:3).

A NT fulfillment of the motif of walking with God is the life Jesus' *disciples led with him. They literally and spiritually walked with Jesus. The most memorable picture is perhaps Jesus walking with the two men to Emmaus, disclosing to them his own mission and identity (Lk 24:13-35).

The Virtuous Life. In the OT, walking is frequently paired with the image of the path or way to picture the lifestyle and choices people should make, as well as the ones they should avoid. The blessed person "does not walk in the counsel of the wicked" (Psalm 1:1 NIV), and the wise person avoids walking "in the way of evil men" (Prov 4:14 NIV). Nebuchadnezzar learned that God will humble "those who walk in pride" (Dan 4:37 NIV). Positively, people should walk *humbly with God (Mic 6:8). In practice this means living in conformity with God's *paths (Is 2:3) or law (Ps 119: 2-3). To obey God's law is to "walk about in freedom" (Ps 119:45 NIV), and "the man of integrity walks securely" (Prov 10:9 NIV). Similarly, "those who walk uprightly enter into peace" (Is 57:2 NIV). Passages such as these use the metaphor of walking to identify a person's conduct of life and the results that flow from it.

References to how people walk yield a composite picture of how the godly person lives. The model person walks in all of God's ways (Deut 8:6 and dozens of additional passages), in the *fear of God (Neh 5:9), in God's truth (Ps 86:11) and in the light of God's presence (Ps 89:15), in the ways of good people (Prov 2:20), in the way of righteousness (Prov 8:20) and understanding (Prov 9:6) and wisdom (Prov 28:26). The ideal person is one "whose walk is blameless" (Ps 15:2 NIV; 84:11). Such a person is also known by the human companions with whom he or she walks—with "the throng at the house of God" (Ps 55:14 NIV) and "with the wise" (Prov 13:20 NIV).

The formula of a *king's "walking in the ways" of a previous king appears repeatedly in the books of Kings and Chronicles. These references either commend a virtuous course of ruling or denigrate a bad one, in both cases by linking it to a predecessor's course. This cluster of images reveals the continuity ancient people experienced in kingly practices in a political system where kingship was hereditary.

Followers of the Way. NT references to walking build on OT motifs. Walking now becomes a metaphor for how Christians are expected to live. John alone among the Gospels portrays Jesus as encouraging his people to walk in the *light rather than in *darkness (Jn 8:12; 11:9). This expression also occurs in John's letters, which are small classics in the literature of how Christians are to live. Believers are not to walk in darkness (1 Jn 1:16; 2 Jn 11) but in the light (1 Jn 1:7); they "must walk as Jesus did" (1 Jn 2:6 NIV), in the truth (2 Jn 4; 3 Jn 3-4), in obedience to God's commands and in love (2 Jn 6).

In Paul's letters the figurative use of walking is primarily drawn from Paul's extensive practice of it. In keeping with his tendency toward heightened contrasts, Paul portrays the Christian life in terms of contrasting walks: Christians are to walk in newness of life rather than *death (Rom 6:4), in good works rather than trespasses and sins (Eph 2:1-2, 10), as children of light instead of darkness (Eph 5:8), with moral self-control rather than in sensuality (Rom 13:13), by faith rather than sight (2 Cor 5:7).

Summary. Walking is one of the Bible's vivid metaphors for how godly people should live, both positively in terms of what to follow and negatively in warnings about what to avoid. Unfortunately, some recent translations tend to replace the concrete vigor of the original with prosaic words like *live, conduct* or *behave*. The result is to diminish a reader's capacity to allow concrete, everyday activities to become windows on divine realities.

See also FEET; OBEDIENCE; PATH; WANDERER, WANDERING.

BIBLIOGRAPHY. R. Banks, " 'Walking' as a Metaphor of the Christian Life: The Origins of a Significant Pauline Usage" in *Perspectives on Language and Text*, ed. E. W. Conrad and E. G. Newing (Winona Lake, IN: Eisenbrauns, 1987) 303-13.

WALL

It is not surprising that walls are mentioned frequently in the Bible. Walls were a dominating and impressive component of ancient Palestinian cities. A *city was usually built on a hill, and from a distance city walls were the most obvious feature to be seen by the ancient Israelites. So massive and strong were city walls, whether of mud *brick or *stone, that they are often among the most prominent remains excavated by archaeologists. In fact, a person of biblical times would find a city without a wall to be an absolute incongruity.

Israelites of the Iron Age (c. 1200-586 B.C.) incorporated many associated structures into their city walls. In the early years casemate walls were most common: two parallel walls (perhaps three to six feet thick and five to eight feet apart) encircling the city were joined at intervals by transverse walls. Later, perhaps in response to the mobile battering ram introduced by the Assyrians, the Israelites began building solid walls, about twelve to eighteen feet thick, with offsets and insets, such as can be seen in the Assyrian drawings of Lachish from the days of Sennacherib. Later still, casemate and solid walls were used contemporaneously.

Additional features enhanced the fortification of walls. A glacis, or plastered surface, was added to the slope at the foot of a wall to thwart tunneling operations and keep attackers at a distance. A small retaining wall was sometimes built at the bottom of the glacis. In front of the retaining wall a dry moat was dug in the soil or bedrock to exaggerate the height of the wall. Although the evidence is sketchy, mud bricks and timbers were likely used in the superstructure of walls. Battlements surmounted the walls to give additional advantage to defenders.

Walls were costly defenses that had to be continually repaired and maintained. The inhabitants of a city were well aware of the great amount of resources and energy required to build its walls, since many of them were taxed or pressed into labor for their construction. City dwellers must have had some emotional attachment to the walls, for they provided security and a sense of well-being in an environment that was frequently hostile and threatening. The writer of Psalm 48 lingers lovingly over the details of the wall of *Jerusalem (Ps 48:12-13).

No doubt much daily activity took place outside city walls: tending livestock, cultivating crops, fetching water, gathering raw materials such as *clay, *stone and *wood, and trading with other towns. Even in peaceful times, coming home to the encircling walls of a city wherein the family gathered, dined and rested must have brought comfort and serenity. When raids or wars threatened, the wall stood between the citizens and the *enemy; it even gave them a height advantage, allowing them to look down on attackers and to hurl projectiles at them. City walls are sites of some vivid scenes in biblical narrative; one thinks of Rahab's house situated on a city wall (Josh 2:15), the body of the dead King Saul fastened to an enemy city's wall (1 Sam 31:10), Abimelech's head crushed by a millstone dropped by a woman from the tower of a wall (Judg 9:52), Queen Jezebel thrown from the wall by three court eunuchs and her blood splattered on the wall (2 Kings 9:30-35), Paul lowered down the wall of Damascus by night on his escape (Acts 9:23-25). In short, a city's wall in the ancient world was a place of significant events.

Because walls defined a city, they became social centers for public and civic activity. The numerous biblical references to city *gates or to "sitting in the gate" highlight the location of the town council immediately inside the entrance to a city. In the book of Proverbs, when Wisdom makes her pronouncements, she does so "at the entrance of the city gates" (Prov 1:21 RSV) and "from the highest places in the town" (Prov 9:3). City gates clearly often functioned as a philosophical think tank and courtroom (Ruth 4; Prov 31:23; Amos 5:10, 15).

In addition to the obvious defensive walls of the ancient cities, the Israelites knew *fences and pens, walls around houses, barriers and walls in *sacred spaces, and *mountains and *rivers that served as effective walls to invaders. Walls in ill repair, bulging or flimsy, are a hazard and cannot be cosmetically concealed by whitewash (Ezek 13:10-15). A *hypocrite is such a "whitewashed wall" (Acts 23:3 RSV). His real character is covered by only a thin surface of respectability.

The Wall as a Positive Image. The most obvious meaning of the image of the wall in the Bible is that of military protection and resulting security. "Peace be within your walls," says one of the pilgrimage psalms, "and security within your towers!" (Ps 122:7

A cutaway view of a fortified town wall such as those used in Palestine.

RSV). Virtually the most important building project for the remnant who returned to Jerusalem after captivity was to rebuild the wall, "to give us protection in Judea and Jerusalem" (Ezra 9:9 RSV).

Because of their usefulness in protecting a city, walls were the visible sign of a city's success and stature. They were a source of *pride and *beauty, and without them a city was incomplete; hence the preoccupation with walls in *apocalyptic visions of Jerusalem (Ezek 40; Rev 21:15-21). The rebuilt wall of Jerusalem was dedicated with full flourish (Neh 12:27-47), while the Israelites' enemies disparaged the effort with the scoffing comment that "if a fox goes up on it he will break down their stone wall" (Neh 4:3 RSV).

In addition to protection, a city's walls carried connotations of civilization as opposed to barbarism, settledness as contrasted to chaos and rootlessness. The Levitical laws for redemption of property contain an evocative picture of "a dwelling house in a walled city," not even to be relinquished in the

Jubilee (Lev 25:29-30).

Walls, of course, define space (personal, communal, social), separating one area from another. Of particular importance is the use of walls to protect sacred space, with the OT *temple being the most notable example (nowhere more elaborately than in the description of the new temple in Ezek 40).

In keeping with the providential view of life found in the OT, city walls are more than a source of security—they are a visible sign of God's blessing. When King Asa purged the land of *idols, he told the nation, " 'Let us build these cities, and surround them with walls and towers, gates and bars; the land is still ours, because we have sought the LORD our God.' . . . So they built and prospered" (2 Chron 14:7 RSV). The walls of Jerusalem were regarded as a testimony to the faithfulness of God to his covenant nation:

> Walk about Zion, go round about her,
>   number her towers,
> consider well her ramparts,
>   go through her citadels;
> that you may tell the next generation
>   that this is God,
> our God for ever and ever.
> He will be our guide for ever.
>   (Ps 48:12-14 RSV)

Carried a step further, walls become a symbol of *salvation itself. Just as a wall could literally provide physical salvation for a people living inside them, so also the Lord's salvation ultimately protects his people.

> We have a strong city;
>   [God] sets up salvation
>   as walls and bulwarks.
> Open the gates,
>   that the righteous nation which keeps faith
>   may enter in. (Is 26:1 RSV)

Again, "You shall call your walls Salvation, and your gates Praise" (Is 60:18 RSV).

Finally, although the wall is preeminently an image of the community, its symbolic meanings are sometimes applied to the individual. Thus God's promises to Jeremiah are couched in terms of making him "bronze walls, against the whole land" (Jer 1:18 RSV) and "a fortified wall of bronze" (Jer 15:20 RSV). In the Song of Songs the imagery of the wall is used for female chastity (Song 4:12; 8:8-9; *garden* in Hebrew means "enclosure"), and the wall, with *window and lattice, is a boundary about to be breached by the beloved (Song 2:8).

The Wall as a Negative Image. While walls were intended to be impenetrable, they of course never were completely exempt from penetration and destruction. They are thus an image of vulnerability as well as security. Enemies sought every means of penetrating cities: scaling the walls (Joel 2:7), tunneling under them, battering through them (2 Sam 20:15; Ezek 26:8-9), breaking them down (2 Kings 14:13) or burning them with fire (Jer 49:27).

Because walls were vulnerable, they become in

the biblical imagination a picture of misplaced trust. The risk of putting confidence in people rather than God is pictured as "a leaning wall, a tottering fence" (Ps 62:3 RSV). The penalty for disobeying God is that Israel's enemies "shall besiege you in all your towns, until your high and fortified walls, in which you trusted, come down throughout all your land" (Deut 28:52 RSV). The walls of Jericho (Josh 6), which were so imposing but could not keep out the Israelites, serve as a symbol of misplaced trust. It is ironic that Rahab, who assists the Israelites, lives inside this supposed source of strength.

A broken wall is a preeminent biblical image for defeat. God's prediction to Joshua regarding the fall of Jericho is that "the wall of the city will fall down flat" (Josh 6:5 RSV). When Joash defeats Amaziah, the key to conquest is that he "broke down the wall of Jerusalem for four hundred cubits" (2 Chron 25:23 RSV), a feat repeated by Nebuchadnezzar on a grand scale when he carries the nation into captivity (2 Chron 36:19).

If the wall is an image of God's *blessing, its destruction is a sign of God's *judgment. When God pronounces judgment against Judah, it is pictured as being "like a break in a high wall, bulging out, and about to collapse" (Is 30:13 RSV). Elsewhere God is pictured as having breached the walls of Israel (Ps 89:40), casting the walls of Moab to the ground (Is 25:12) and breaking down the wall of the *vineyard, symbolic of Judah (Is 5:5).

Just as the positive image of the wall was sometimes applied metaphorically to the individual, so too the negative image. Proverbs 25:28 states, "A man without self-control is like a city broken into and left without walls" (RSV). Similarly, the false optimism of prophets who declare peace where there is none are compared to people who daub a flimsy wall with whitewash that God will destroy (Ezek 13:10-15), and Paul calls the high priest Ananias a whitewashed wall (Acts 23:3).

Finally, a wall that separates one area from another can be a negative as well as positive image. If the walls in the OT temple precinct kept the profane from entering the sacred, in the NT "the law with its commandments and ordinances," the "dividing wall of hostility" separating Jews from Gentiles, is something that Christ has "broken down" and abolished (Eph 2:14).

See also CITY; FENCE, FENCED PLACE; FORTRESS, STRONGHOLD; GATE; TOWER.

WANDERER, WANDERING

Wandering means going from place to place without a settled route or destination. It also implies aimlessness and meandering. Stories of wandering are a category of the journey or *travel story. Their resemblance to stories of *quest is more tenuous: both involve physical travel that brings characters into conflict with a series of obstacles, but quests imply purposeful action toward a goal that is attained, while stories of wandering lack both the sense of purpose

and the attainment of a goal. In conversation or thought, wandering entails incoherence, drifting or disconnectedness.

All these familiar ideas of wandering are present in the Bible. Scripture particularly conveys wandering as straying or deviating from a way, course or *path.

Stories of Wandering. In its more literal sense, *wandering* refers primarily to a nomadic existence, which often carries a metaphoric implication of dislocation. At its most positive, wandering is reflected in the nomadic lives of the patriarchs *Abraham, Isaac and *Jacob. They are all heirs of a homeland by promise, but the promise is never achieved in their lifetimes. Thus while the travels that make up their lives are disjointed and lead to no fixed place of residence, that very wandering becomes an index to the faith of the patriarchs, as Hebrews 11:8-16 notes. This is implied as well by the confession Moses commands the Israelites to make when they present thank offerings upon entering the Promised Land: "A wandering Aramean was my father" (Deut 26:5 RSV).

Wandering first assumes its negative form in early Genesis. Expelled from paradise, *Adam and *Eve are displaced persons as they take up life in a fallen world. Their first son, *Cain, becomes the first archetypal wanderer when God makes him "a fugitive and a wanderer on the earth" as punishment for his murder of Abel; even the name of the land God gives Cain, Nod, means "Wandering" (Gen 4:12-16). The presumptuous people who build the Tower of *Babel, too, become wanderers, "scattered abroad over the face of all the earth" (Gen 11:9 RSV). In all these early stories of wandering we see the strong link between wandering and transgression.

This can be seen as well in the most extended story of wandering in the Bible, the *wilderness wanderings of the fledgling nation of *Israel as it travels from *bondage in Egypt to the *Promised Land. This journey begins as a quest, but it loses much of that quality and becomes a story of wandering when the people test God ten times (cf. Num 14:22) and are punished by having to wander in the wilderness for forty years until the generation of the disobedient dies off. As a travel story the epic of the exodus is ambivalent, demonstrating both positive and negative features of the nomadic existence of the people of God. It is a temporary disinheritance that is both punishment for faithlessness and an opportunity to practice a faith oriented to the future promise of a homeland. The wilderness wanderings become a demonstration of the reality of God's loving and steadfast care, his determination to mold the community into his life-giving ways, and his purging of the nation in punishment. Deuteronomy 8:15-16 provides an apt summary of the Israelites' experience of wandering, as God is said to have "led you through the great and terrible wilderness, with its fiery serpents and scorpions and thirsty ground where there was no water, . . . who fed you in the wilderness with manna . . . , that he might humble you and test you, to do you good in the end" (RSV).

Pictures of Wandering. In addition to full-fledged stories of wandering, the Bible presents some brief snapshots of wandering and wanderers. One of the most haunting is the "lost boy" motif of Genesis 37:15, where a man finds the youthful *Joseph "wandering the fields" far from home and on the verge of being sold into Egypt. Jephthah's doomed daughter wanders on the mountains with her companions for two months, bewailing her virginity (Judg 11:37). In the bitter man's creed that Job voices at a low point of his disillusionment, he claims that God "takes away understanding from the chiefs of the people of the earth, and makes them wander in a pathless waste" (Job 12:24 RSV; cf. Ps 107:40). The distraught speaker of Psalm 55:7 longs to escape from his anguish and "wander afar" in the wilderness (RSV). One of four vivid pictures of rescue in Psalm 107 is that of people who "wandered in desert wastes" until God led them to "a city to dwell in" (Ps 107:4, 7 RSV).

Jeremiah pictures people under God's judgment wandering blind through the streets (Lam 4:14-15), and Ezekiel gives a pastoral version of the same motif with his picture of God's scattered *sheep wandering over the mountains (Ezek 34:6; cf. Zech 10:2). Wandering as an image of people under God's judgment recurs throughout the OT prophetic books (Is 47:15; Jer 49:30; Hos 9:17; Amos 4:8; 8:12). Also evocative are the pathetic martyrs of Hebrews 11:38, who wander "over deserts and mountains, and in dens and caves of the earth" (RSV), Jude's picture of false teachers as "wandering stars for whom the nether gloom of darkness has been reserved for ever" (Jude 13 RSV) and the "wandering of desire" that the book of Ecclesiastes captures (Eccles 6:9 RSV).

At least once, though, wandering pictures a positive experience. In her fantasy, the woman in the Song of Songs wanders about the city streets by night seeking her beloved, whom she finds and claims (Song 3:1-4).

Moral and Spiritual Wandering. The Bible also uses wandering to picture moral and spiritual experience, such as deviating from God's standard of truth and morality. One form of metaphoric wandering is to leave truth for falsehood. Thus we read about a person "who wanders from the way of understanding" and as a result "will rest in the assembly of the dead" (Prov 21:16 RSV) and of people who are "ever learning, and never able to come to the knowledge of the truth" (2 Tim 3:7 KJV). This is buttressed by pictures of people who wander "into vain discussion" (1 Tim 1:6 RSV), "wander into myths" (2 Tim 4:4 RSV) and wander "from the truth" (Jas 5:19 RSV).

Straying from an approved standard can also carry moral and spiritual meanings. Thus we find references to wandering from God's commandments (Ps 119:10, 21) and straying like lost sheep (Ps 119:176; Is 53:6; 1 Pet 2:25). Wandering is also used to picture deviation from faith (1 Tim 6:10), from light (John 8:12), from the Lord (1 Sam 12:20-21; Deut 29:38) and from the path of life available to those who follow *wisdom (Prov 5:6).

See also LOST AND FOUND; PILGRIM, PILGRIMAGE; QUEST; TRAVEL STORY; WILDERNESS.

WARFARE. *See* ARMOR; ARMY; ARMIES; BATTLE STORIES; DIVINE WARRIOR; TRIUMPH; WEAPONS.

WARM. *See* TEMPERATURE.

WARRIOR. *See* ARMOR; ARMY; ARMIES; BATTLE STORIES; DIVINE WARRIOR; TRIUMPH; WEAPONS.

WARRIOR, DIVINE. *See* DIVINE WARRIOR.

WASH, WASHING

"Cleanliness is, indeed, next unto godliness." Although the idea is likely of earlier Hebrew origin, John Wesley's well-known comment about appropriate dress combines two of the central ideas in the biblical usage of *wash* or *washing*. He realized that physical cleanness is in some fashion related to what God is like and that there is a spiritual dimension connected to personal hygiene.

The first use of the term in Scripture, though not the majority usage (Gen 18:4), has to do with physical *cleansing. This is the basis for understanding the large number of references to sacramental washing. Both hygienic and sacramental uses have physical and symbolic meanings.

Hygienic/Refreshment Washings. Although there may have been some sacramental implications in Pharaoh's daughter's bathing in the Nile, her providentially timed physical bath certainly included bodily cleansing and refreshment (Ex 2:5). *Bathsheba's ill-fated bath (2 Sam 11:2), the ending of *David's prayerful *fast for his ill child (2 Sam 12:20), *Ruth's preparation to meet Boaz (Ruth 3:3), Laban's treatment of *Abraham's servants (Gen 24:32) and the beloved's disturbed *dream (Song 5:3) are also illustrative of physical cleansing and refreshment. Abraham's offer of washing for his divine visitors shows that the physical dimension also had the symbolic meaning of *hospitality (Gen 18:4).

Jesus refers to both of these usages in his affirmation of the *faith of the woman who washed (literally, wet) his *feet with her *tears of gratitude (Lk 7:36-50), in contrast to his host (Lk 7:44). In his modeling of *servanthood on the eve of his *death (Jn 13:1-15), he himself washed the feet of his disciples. Thus he elevated the humble physical gesture to express his own servant heart, which would lead him to the cross (Phil 2:7-8) and which he desired to replicate in his followers (Jn 13:15). Later, Paul uses the physical image "washed the feet of the saints" in the symbolic sense of humble servanthood (1 Tim 5:10) to describe the service of a destitute *widow as one of the qualifications for material support from a congregation.

Sacramental Washings. The sacramental meaning of washing goes far beyond the removal of physical uncleanness. It develops most clearly with the establishment of the Mosaic *covenant, which included more than mere verbal acceptance (Ex 19:8) to encompass the terrifying meeting of the people with the holy God (Ex 3:5; 19:9, 11). Preparation for this potentially fatal encounter involved washing one's clothes (Ex 19:10, 12-13), obviously not for hygienic purposes but as a symbolic reminder of the vast separation between people and God. The whole nation was the "treasured possession" (Ex 19:5 NIV) of the infinitely holy God. The varied phenomena (Ex 19:16-25) involved in the communicative work of God and the threefold prohibition (Ex 19:12, 21, 24) accentuated that separation, the difference not only between the Creator and the created but also between the holy and unholy. But of equal importance is the revelation that this God was the covenant-making God of grace and was accessible to them (the priestly *kingdom) and to the whole world through them (Ex 19:5-6). This was later restricted to Aaron and his *family (Num 3:1-4, 10), who were assisted by the remaining Levitical families (Num 3:5-13).

*Israel was to be a "holy nation" (Ex 19:6) separated from other nations because they were especially separated through covenant relationship (Ex 20:2) and holy living (Ex 20:4-17; Lev 19). Washing their clothes and sexual abstinence (Ex 19:15) indicated the inner and external *holiness God required of them to serve him.

As the revelation from God became more complete, ceremonial washings included parts of sacrificial *animals (Ex 29:17; Lev 1:9, 13), *blood-spattered priestly *garments (Lev 6:27), the *hands and *feet of the *priests (Ex 30:1-21), those who made contact with *death (Lev 11:25, 39-40), and situations involving *leprosy (Lev 13:53-59; 14:8, 9, 47) and male and female bodily discharges (Lev 15). Although some of these washings were especially hygienic, the deeper significance had to do with ritual *purity and inner purity. Physical washing became associated with the need for cleansing of the sinful soul (Job 9:28-31; Ps 51:2, 7; Jer 2:22; 4:14; Is 1:16; 4:3-4).

One of the great tragedies of the covenant people was that the external symbol of washing became the actual substance or reality in their eyes. Sacramental cleansing was assumed effective as long as they followed the ritual precisely as prescribed. Jesus confronted this on numerous occasions (Mt 15:2; Lk 11:38). Pilate tried to assuage his conscience by practicing the empty ritual (Mt 27:24; see also Ps 26:6). Yet Peter's image of an externally washed sow demonstrates that the internal washing that brings about a changed *heart is more costly and rare (2 Pet 2:22).

The Washing of Christ's Work. The ending of all physical and sacramental washings is located in the work of Christ (Jn 1:20; Acts 22:16; Heb 9:6-14;

10:1-22; 1 Jn 1:7, 9). Through his work, believers are "bathed" once and for all (Jn 13:10; 1 Cor 6:11; Heb 10:10) when the regenerating work of the *Holy Spirit (Tit 3:5) and the Word of God (1 Pet 1:2-3, 22-23) gives them divine life and *forgiveness.

The work of the Spirit and the Word of God also includes renewing life in the process of developing increasing levels of holiness (Rom 12:1-2; 2 Cor 3:18; Eph 5:26; Tit 3:5-9). The initial washing or bathing at the time of *new *birth is followed by daily "root washings" (see Jn 13:8-10). As priests in the Mosaic covenant had to be bathed to procure forgiveness and continued fellowship and *ministry (Ps 132:9; Heb 7:27-28), so must the believer-priest of the new covenant (1 Pet 2:9-11). The Spirit indicates points of uncleanness that need to be cleansed (2 Cor 7:10) to permit uninterrupted fellowship with the Savior and continued ministry and growth (1 Jn 1:7-9).

The final statements on the sacramental and symbolic uses of washing are recorded by John in Revelation 7:14 and 22:14. Blood, a highly stain-producing substance, is used to wash the robes of tribulation *saints and make them white. This blood is not that of sacrificial animals, which was washed out of priestly garments (Lev 6:27), but of the ultimate *Lamb of God (1 Pet 1:19), who frees us from our sins (Rev 1:5). "Blessed are those who wash their robes, that they may have the right to the tree of life and may go through the gates into the city" (Rev 22:14 NIV).

See also CLEANSING; FORGIVENESS; PURITY; WATER.

WASTE. *See* DUNG.

WASTELAND

While twentieth-century poet T. S. Eliot gave us the term *wasteland,* the image is archetypal and universal. A wasteland is a desolate landscape, usually a hot and arid desert. Associations of *death, *decay and ruin belong to the image, with implications of terror and threat to life. The NRSV uses the specific terminology of *wasteland* or *waste* approximately eighty times, fifteen of them referring to cities' being laid waste. Seventy-five percent of the references occur in the books of Isaiah, Jeremiah and Ezekiel, and all the passages that use the "wasteland" vocabulary are in the OT.

In the Bible the wasteland is characterized by desolation or abandonment, a privation of life, *water, civilization and vegetation. It is a place not for people, who will die there (Job 6:18), but for wild *donkeys (Job 24:5; 39:6; Is 32:14) and desert jackals (Mal 1:3). It is a parched place (Job 38:27; Jer 12:11) of *salt flats and salt pits (Job 39:6; Zeph 2:9). It is a *vineyard left uncultivated (Is 5:6; Jer 12:10-11), the only surviving vegetation being *briers, *thorns and weeds (Is 5:6; Zeph 2:9).

Before we come upon the apocalyptic wastelands, the primary wasteland of the OT is the wilderness through which God led the Israelites. It is described as "a dread and terrible wilderness, an arid wasteland with poisonous snakes and scorpions" (Deut 8:15 NRSV), and as "a howling wilderness waste" (Deut 32:10 NRSV). In the poetic books we read about more generic wastelands—about "the pathless waste" in which God causes leaders to *wander (Job 12:24 NRSV), about God's sending rain to "the waste and desolate land" (Job 38:27 NRSV), about "the owl of the waste places" to which the despondent psalmist compares himself (Ps 102:6 NRSV) and about the fruitful land that God turns "into a salty waste, because of the wickedness of its inhabitants" (Ps 107:34 NRSV).

Above all, though, the Bible reserves the imagery of wasteland for its apocalyptic visions of God's judgment against a sinful world and rebellious covenant nation. Here we have visions of cities that "lie waste without inhabitant" (Is 6:11 NRSV), of lands made "a waste," their cities "in ruins, without inhabitant" (Jer 2:15 NRSV; cf. Jer 4:7; 7:34). God predicts, "I will lay waste mountains and hills, and dry up all their herbage; I will turn the rivers into islands, and dry up the pools" (Is 42:15 NRSV). We also picture pastures "laid waste so that no one passes through, and the lowing of cattle is not heard; both the birds of the air and the animals have fled and are gone" (Jer 9:10 NRSV; cf. Jer 9:12). The book of Ezekiel contains twenty wasteland prophecies, and the minor prophets give us memorable pictures of vineyards and *fig trees laid waste (Hos 2:12; Joel 1:7; Amos 4:9).

While concordances do not list NT references under the heading "wasteland," the idea of the wasteland may reasonably be inferred in the Greek *erēmos*, "desert place," or its relative *erēmōsis*. The latter appears in the prophetic Luke 21:20, a plausible translation of which might be "You know that the time of its [Jerusalem's] becoming a wasteland is near" (cf. the parallel passages Mt 24:15 and Mk 13:14). Further, the idea may be construed (in verb form) in some apocalyptic texts (e.g., Mt 12:25; Lk 11:17; Rev 17:16; 18:17, 19). Revelation expands on the idea in the middle chapters, although the word does not appear. In sum, the NT conveys the notion of wasteland not so much through particular vocabulary as through *apocalyptic imagery.

The wasteland is an evocative biblical image of desolation and emptiness. The image takes its origin from actual wilderness landscapes and military practices. Building on those literal images, biblical writers transform the archetype into a prophetic vision of coming judgment and a symbolic vision of spiritual emptiness or deprivation. In literature generally, the wasteland is either an existing place of *ordeal where the *hero proves his or her prowess or (in modern literature) the state to which a degenerate culture has reduced itself. In the Bible, God is usually the One who produces a wasteland as a judgment against sinful humanity.

See also GARDEN; PROMISED LAND; WILDERNESS.

WATCH, WATCHMAN

"The God who sees me" (Gen 16:13 NIV) is the watchman over his people. His watching is not idle observation, but entails his active presence (Gen 28:15), provision of food and clothing (Gen 28:20; *see* Providence), deliverance from *slavery (Ex 3:16), safe passage in the *wilderness (Deut 2:7) and protection from *enemies (Ezra 5:5). God watches over his people for nurture as well, as a gardener sees to a *vine (Is 27:3) or as a shepherd watches his *flock (Jer 31:10; *see* Sheep, Shepherd). His all-seeing *eye enables him to save his people in every extremity (Ps 34:12-19). Nor does God need periodic relief from his watchpost, for "he who watches over Israel will neither slumber nor sleep" (Ps 121:3-4 NIV).

Although "the LORD watches over the way of the righteous," the "way of the wicked will perish" (Ps 1:6 NIV). His *watching over* the godly is thus often contrasted to his *keeping a watch on* the ungodly. The Lord watches the wicked "for harm, not for good" (Jer 44:27 NIV). Job is tempted to servile fear of God because he knows that the "watcher of men" (Job 7:20) has ways of following the tracks of the unrighteous, to their dismay: "you keep close watch on all my paths by putting marks on the soles of my feet" (Job 13:27 NIV).

Since the "eyes of the LORD are everywhere, keeping watch on the wicked and the good" (Prov 15:3 NIV), the people of God are commanded to "watch yourselves closely" (Deut 4:9 NIV; cf. Lk 17:3; Gal 6:1). This metaphor is sometimes used in the context of a holy pilgrimage in which the *pilgrim must "watch his ways" (Ps 39:1 NIV). The protective stance of God in *watching over* his people (Ps 121:7-8) does not obviate the need for them to adopt the defensive posture of *watching out for* sin (Lk 12:15), or for the ferocity of false teaching (Mt 7:15; cf. Phil 3:2). The disciples are rebuked for not keeping watch with Jesus in the *garden because they are thereby exposing themselves to temptation (Mt 26:41, 69-75).

The wicked are keeping watch as well, but they are watching for opportunities to do evil. "The eye of the adulterer watches for dusk" (Job 24:15 NIV). The *murderer lies in wait, "watching in secret for his victims" (Ps 10:8 NIV). Not surprisingly, Judas "watched for an opportunity to hand [Jesus] over" (Mk 14:11 NIV).

Believers are to *watch for* as well as *watch out*, watching and waiting for the Lord. They are to linger near the doorway of divine *wisdom like a pupil waiting at the door of the schoolmaster (Prov 8:34). The psalmist uses repetition both to capture the tedium of the watchman's task and to heighten the urgency of his longing for a new dawn in his relationship with the Lord: "My soul waits for the Lord more than watchmen wait for the morning, more than watchmen wait for the morning" (130:6 NIV).

The prophet is "a watchman for the house of Israel" (Ezek 3:17 NIV; Acts 20:28). His calling includes both *watching out for* the dangers of *sin

(Hos 9:8) and *watching for* signs of divine deliverance (Mic 7:7). Like God himself, those who watch over Israel are to give themselves no *rest (Is 62:6), suggesting that they are in perpetual *prayer for God's people. Isaiah portrays a faithfully persistent watchman even when nothing but the routine seems to be taking place: " 'Watchman, what is left of the night? Watchman, what is left of the night?' The watchman replies, 'Morning is coming, but also the night' " (Is 21:11-12 NIV). When deliverance does come, the prophetic watchmen will be the first to "lift up their voices" and "shout for joy" (Is 52:8 NIV) as they proclaim *salvation to the people of God. If the prophets are mute (Ezek 33:6), *blind, asleep at their posts (Is 56:10) or simply ignored (Jer 6:17), then the Lord's people are vulnerable to spiritual or military attack. The bleak silhouette of an abandoned watchtower (Is 32:14) is a symbol of spiritual abandonment and vulnerability to attack. But even diligent watchmen do not guarantee security, for "unless the LORD watches over the city, the watchmen stand guard in vain" (Ps 127:1 NIV; cf. Lam 4:16-17).

Watching takes on eschatological overtones in the NT. Like the homeowner who watches for the *thief, or the servant who watches for the master, or the *virgins who watch for the *bridegroom, the followers of Christ must be ready perpetually for the unpredictable return of the Son of Man (Mt 24:42—25:13). The diligent urgency of life in Christ in the present age is thus captured in the single command Jesus gives his disciples: "Watch!" (Mk 13:32-37; cf. Mk 14:32-42).

See also FORTRESS; ROB, ROBBER; THIEF; TOWER.

WATER

Because water is an element essential to life, its meaning and evocativeness are universal. Yet the significance of water was heightened for biblical writers, who lived in a region where water was scarce and drought (*see* Dry, Drought) a constant threat to life. Water figures in the Bible in three main ways—as a cosmic force that only God can control and govern, as a source of life, and as a *cleansing agent. We can also detect a polarity at work in the six hundred biblical references to water: water can mean both life and *death, *blessing and *affliction, *order and *chaos.

Cosmic Waters. Water was important in the cosmology of the ancient world, where the sea was associated with the primal waters, or the waters of chaos, suggested in Genesis 1:2 by the term *deep.* The Hebrew word *ťhôm* here is etymologically related to the *Tiamat,* the name of the sea monster from whose carcass the world was carved according to the Babylonian cosmogony (*see* Cosmology). The Genesis account acknowledges no trace of resistance to God's purpose from his materials, and one does not need to assume that the deep is a kind of reservoir of raw materials. Even so, biblical poetry makes occasional reference to a cosmic battle between God and the *monster of the *sea, or chaos, variously identified

as Leviathan, Rahab, serpent and dragon (Ps 74:13-14; 89:10; Is 27:1).

In the biblical vision the original creation and God's continuing providential oversight of his world are presented in terms of the mastery of water by the divine word. The original creation has the creatures called into existence by divine fiat or utterance. This created order is preserved as God maintains the sea within bounds (Job 38:11) and so, by implication, restrains the background threat of chaos. Though storms may appear to threaten cosmic order, God is himself the Lord of the *storm, with all the elements of *nature, water in particular, firmly under his sovereign control (cf. Ps 29).

Noah's *flood at several points reflects the ancient understanding of the cosmic waters. The flood is the return of the waters of chaos, with the creation in a sense undone, making way for the *new creation—the world renewed after judgment and the preservation of righteous Noah with his family. In the references to the *windows of heaven being opened and the *fountains of the deep breaking forth (Gen 7:11), we are to understand that the waters of chaos encompass the created order, ordinarily restrained overhead by the crystalline dome of the firmament and sealed off underfoot by dry land.

The rich ambiguity of the waters of chaos or the deep is apparent on other biblical occasions. The common background belief was that a great reservoir of primal water lay beneath the earth (indeed the conviction that the water cycle included such a central abyss of subterranean water, common to classical culture as well as the Near East, did not begin to fade in Europe until late in the seventeenth century). When *Jacob blesses his sons on his deathbed, he assures Joseph of "the blessings of the deep that lies beneath" (Gen 49:25 NRSV, cited again in Deut 33:13). Here the deep is the grand reservoir of water that supplies the springs of surface water, including, presumably, even the fountain of Eden's *garden. This positive valence for the primal waters is assumed by the psalmist when sea monsters and all deeps are invited to praise the Creator (Ps 148:7). The injunction is also extended to the "waters above the heavens" (Ps 148:4 NRSV).

The cosmic waters loom large in 2 Peter, a letter notable for its diversity of water imagery. The encouragement to believers stresses the divine word which has always ruled the waters of contingency and chaos. Scoffers foolishly ignore the fact that "by the word of God heavens existed long ago and an earth was formed out of water and by means of water, through which the world of that time was deluged with water and perished" (2 Pet 3:5-6 NRSV).

Water in the Landscape of the Holy Land. The geography (or hydrology) of the Holy *Land is rich with figurative significance. As a semiarid landscape with marginal *rainfall in many sectors, the Holy Land is typified by careful exploitation of water both stored and free-flowing ("living"). The Sea of Galilee (or Tiberias), thirteen miles by eight at its maxima, lying in a heart-shaped bowl dating from volcanic activity in the Cenozoic era, is a fresh-water reservoir without which the culture of the area is scarcely imaginable. The *Jordan River flows from its southern edge and nourishes the countryside all the way to the Dead Sea in Judea. The river is today the feeder for extensive drip-irrigation projects, which involve a technology shared by Israel with neighboring Jordan.

Apart from the environs of the Sea of Galilee and the Jordan River, and a few fertile plains, the Holy Land is dependent on *springs, *wells and *cisterns. The frequent experience of *thirst and the anticipation of water (Ps 42:1-2), the need to husband water resources, the labor of drawing and carrying water, the contrast of fresh and long-stored water—all these are recurrent features of biblical experience.

While strategically placed wells and springhouses could provide continually renewed water, cisterns captured and stored run-off water. The latter was usually used for livestock and domestic utilities. Jeremiah draws on this contrast to distinguish true *worship from *idolatry. The former acknowledges God as the fountain of living water, while the latter relies on one's own cisterns, which in fact do not even hold water (Jer 2:13). Since the drawing of well water was a laborious task usually reserved for women, we are not surprised to learn that the Samaritan woman whom Jesus meets at Jacob's well (*see* Well, Meeting at the) is responsive to Jesus' offer of a living water that carries the promise of being miraculously replenished (Jn 4).

In the Israelites' wanderings in the wilderness, they made extensive use of famous springs such as the one at Kadesh-Barnea, and the victory at Jericho involved the capture of one of the great oases of the ancient Near East. Jericho may be the oldest city on the planet, twice as ancient as the pyramids of *Egypt. Known from early times as a city of *palm trees, it is situated well below sea level around a massive natural spring.

When finally in possession of the city of *Jerusalem, the Israelites undertook repeated and ingenious efforts to ensure adequate fresh water for the central fortress (*Zion's hill). The future providence that will eternally transcend such precarious dependency is celebrated by both Ezekiel and Zechariah in their prophecies that Zion and its *temple will miraculously become water sources. Ezekiel even has the Dead Sea being freshened as living water from the city produces a paradise on earth: "Wherever the river goes every living creature that swarms will live, and there will be very many fish, once these waters reach there. It will become fresh; and everything will live where the river goes" (Ezek 47:9 NRSV). The striking images of fecundity, strongly reminiscent of the swarming waters described in Genesis 1, imply nothing less than a new creation, perpetually nourished out of Zion. When Zechariah adds to this picture the details that the miraculous fresh waters will flow *west as well as *east, we glimpse the

promise that the great deeps (seas) of the whole earth will be freshened as part of the ultimate taming of nature by God's providence.

Water and Weather. *Rains in the Holy Land are seasonal, with light rains coming in fall and spring and the bulk of the precipitation falling in the months of December through February. Summers are extremely *dry. Rain is commonly seen by biblical writers as evidence of special *providence, with the return of rains after a prolonged dry spell associated with God's new advent and the withholding of rains a sign of divine displeasure (1 Kings 8:35; Amos 4:7). Hosea urges a diligent quest for God, certain that "he will come to us like the showers, like the spring rains that water the earth" (Hos 6:3 NRSV).

The seasonal nature of the rains was in part responsible for the long-term seductiveness of Canaanite religion for the people of God. The Israelites arriving from the wilderness were nomadic herdspeople, while the resident Canaanites were experts in settled agriculture, an expertise couched in the practices of Baal-worship. In Canaanite myth Baal had vanquished the fractious power Sea-and-River and so became the dispenser of the tamed waters vital to agriculture. By the time of the exodus Baal was firmly established in Canaan as the god of the winter rains and *storms and hence of the primary rainfalls of the countryside. In biblical faith the Lord of Israel is resolutely honored as the God of storms and rains (Ps 29; Jer 10:13; Zech 10:1), but the magical practices of Baal worshipers were a persisting temptation to the Israelites as they came late to settled agriculture.

In the NT, Jesus discounts any strict equating of the supply of rain with people's moral state. In keeping with the Sermon on the Mount's stress on the fullness of providence—one that is primordial, continuing, responsive and perfecting of the recipient—Jesus urges his listeners to be unstinting in their love and giving, "so that you may be children of your Father in heaven; for he . . . sends rain on the righteous and on the unrighteous" (Mt 5:45 NRSV).

Waters of Affliction. Notwithstanding Jesus' words about the Father's gracious supply of rain, in the OT it is common for divine *judgment to involve the withholding of rain. God's sovereignty over life and death is implicit as well in the allotting of the waters of affliction, ordinarily pictured as the destructive waters of the sea which threaten to inundate. God's waves have gone over him, *laments the psalmist (Ps 42:7). In one of the more vivid images of Scripture, *Jonah describes from the whale's belly how the waters have closed in over his head: "The deep surrounded me; weeds were wrapped around my head at the roots of the mountains" (Jon 2:5-6 NRSV). Jonah of course experiences a kind of death, immersed as he is in the destructive element, which he identifies with Sheol or the *grave (Jon 2:2). Yet in the Hebrew vision there are not separate powers which preside over life and death, as is the case with Egyptian, Greek and Roman pantheons. One God is

Lord over all the powers. Isaiah presents the divine pronouncement, "I form light and create darkness, I make weal and create woe; I the LORD do all these things" (Is 45:7 NRSV). Included in the divine dispensation of water is the meting out of affliction and judgment.

Ceremonial Water. In the holiness code of Israel, water was an essential means of *cleansing, since defilement could come in a host of ways: through contact with the dead or with one of the body fluids, or by the eating of forbidden *foods, or by contact with *lepers. The Mosaic rituals prescribed in the Pentateuch are a veritable handbook of how to use water in washing food, utensils and clothing, as well as in bathing. Jesus' studied neglect of such rituals as washing before eating brought down on him the wrath of the Pharisees, whose earnest perfectionism found it easier to monitor externals than attitudes (Lk 11:37-41). Jesus' emphasis on the inclusiveness of the divine invitation created conflict with a code that stressed careful segregation and quarantines to avoid superficial contamination. Reflecting his attention to motives—the inward reality—Jesus asks, "Did not the one who made the outside make the inside also?" (Lk 11:40 NRSV). Cleaning the outside is inadequate.

The most significant form of ceremonial cleansing was of course *baptism. Jesus' cousin John came out of the wilderness preaching a message of baptism unto *repentance. In Christian baptism the immersion in water symbolizes both cleansing and a passage from death to life (Col 2:12). Perhaps the equation of descent into water with death is based on the premise of reversion to watery chaos (a form of dissolution) that precedes the new creation and new life (echoing the imagery of the creation story). Jesus tells Nicodemus that spiritual birth involves both water and the Spirit, implying a role for baptism and also for the explicit agency of the Holy Spirit. Jesus' words to Nicodemus imply a necessary conjunction of natural and supernatural, of physical water and the invisible work of God Himself cleansing the heart unto new life in the Spirit.

Water and the Spirit. John 7 records the appearance of Jesus at the temple during the *Feast of Tabernacles, an annual celebration that included the transportation of water over a period of seven days from the Pool of Siloam to the temple, in commemoration of the miraculous waters of Meribah provided in Israel's wilderness experience (Num 20:2-13). Against the backdrop of that richly significant ritual, Jesus announces that anyone who is truly thirsty should come to him and drink (Jn 7:37). Moreover, believers in Jesus will find that *rivers of living water will flow out of their own heart (Jn 7:38). This water, the writer is careful to explain, is the promised Holy Spirit.

This passage draws on two strands of traditional symbolism. The first is of miraculous *spring or *fountain as a special providence for the community. The second is of inner fountain as the movement of God in the personal depths. Fresh (living) water is miraculously provided notably at the *rock of Horeb, where Moses strikes the rock and taps into a spring. God supplies living water even though the murmuring Israelites have complained bitterly about the rigors of their *exodus. The Sinai region, like much of Greece, is characterized by a layer of limestone that allows for underground water to issue in springs. If in Greek tradition springs became associated with the inspirations behind the arts, in Hebrew tradition springs issuing in the desert became the sign and symbol of special divine help for God's wayfaring people. Isaiah, rejoicing in the prospect of the return from exile, presents God saying, "I will open rivers on the bare heights, and fountains in the midst of the valleys . . . so that all may see and know, all may consider and understand, that the hand of the LORD has done this, the Holy One of Israel has created it" (Is 41:18, 20 NRSV). Characteristically, Isaiah sees the miracle-working power of God as one with his creative power, and this power creates and sustains an ever more inclusive community.

Fountains and springs also provide a traditional language for the movement of God's Spirit within the individual. The refreshment of one's spirit, the surge of new strength, the impulse of joy are all evidences of God's effectual presence. Isaiah offers the powerful assurance that those who pour themselves out for the *hungry and *afflicted will be satisfied with good things, with renewal of *strength and *joy: "The LORD will . . . make your bones strong; and you shall be like a watered garden, like a spring of water, whose waters never fail" (Is 58:11 NRSV). The prophet had earlier conjoined new strength with God's presence and salvation. The comforted ones will say, "The LORD God is my strength and my might; he has become my salvation. With joy you will draw water from the wells of salvation" (Is 12:2-3 NRSV). Spiritual life and inner fountain are also identified in Jesus' offer to the Samaritan woman: "The water that I give will become . . . a spring of water gushing up to eternal life" (Jn 4:14 NRSV). The assurance in all this is that God's Spirit within is experienced as a mysterious ever-renewed source, upwelling in fullness of life.

Jesus as Lord of Waters. In the NT's affirming of Jesus as Lord and Messiah, a notable claim is the ascription to him of the same divine power over water that the OT had reserved for God alone. In commanding the raging sea to be still (Lk 8:22-25), Jesus exercises a power akin to that displayed in the original taming of the waters of the deep, the power that later miraculously delivered the Israelites at the edge of the Red Sea. It is no wonder that the disciples ask, "Who then is this, that he commands even the winds and the water, and they obey him?" (Lk 8:25 NRSV). John Milton reflects this equivalence in the creation scene of *Paradise Lost* when he has the preincarnate Son of God command the tempestuous chaos, "Silence, ye troubl'd waves, and thou Deep, peace" (8.216). A similar event is described in Matthew's account of Jesus' walking on the water of the Sea of Galilee (Mt 14:22-33). After Jesus gets into the disciples' *boat, the wind ceases, and they worship him, saying, "Truly you are the Son of God" (Mt 14:33 NRSV).

In a culture steeped in centuries of associating divinity with power over water, it was inevitable that Jesus' mastery of the element would imply divine status, including elements of omniscience. A minor miracle recorded by Matthew (Mt 17:24-27) suggests that Jesus has intimate knowledge of both the sea and its contents. When a coin is needed to pay the temple tax, Jesus gives instructions on catching a *fish that will have the needed coin in its mouth. A more fully developed miracle implying mastery of water is descried by John at the close of his narrative. The risen Christ finds several of the disciples back at their fishing and prepares a charcoal fire on the shore. Jesus instructs them to cast their net on the right side of the boat, and the catch all but breaks the net. Here the sea is associated with bounty rather than with destruction and chaos, and the risen Christ knows and is free to dispense this bounty. In keeping with John's emphasis on Jesus as the very wellspring of life and goodness, it is appropriate that Jesus provide a *resurrection breakfast in the way he does.

In John's Revelation, Jesus is again closely associated with water. When John sees the exalted Christ standing among the seven golden lampstands, he hears a voice "like the sound of many waters" (Rev 1:15 NRSV). The simile suggests the mighty roar of confluent streams, but in this joining of utterance with the imagery of water a profound resolution is effected. Again and again in Scripture, word and water are in tension, with the divine word quelling and taming water. But just as the waters of the deep are tamed as they flow from the throne of God in the New Jerusalem as a resource for eternal life, so here the subliming of water is implicit in the voice of the heavenly Christ. His word forever vivifies, like life-giving streams.

Summary. The richness and multiplicity of meanings inherent in the Bible's imagery of water can be brought into focus if we simply catalog some of the most memorable references to water: the fertile waters that swarm with living creatures in the creation story (Gen 1:20-21); the stream that waters the face of the ground in Eden (Gen 2:6, 10); the flood of waters that destroys life in Noah's time (Gen 7); the plain of the Jordan that "was well watered everywhere like the garden of the LORD," which Lot chose (Gen 13:10 NRSV); Rebekah's watering the camels of Abraham's servant (Gen 24); the water of the Nile turned to blood (Ex 7); the Israelites' dry land passage through the Red Sea, in which the Egyptian army drowned (Ex 14); the miraculous water from a rock during Israel's wilderness wanderings (Ex 17:6; Num 20:11); the streams of water that nourish the productive tree to which the godly person is compared (Ps 1:3); the evocative "still waters" of Psalm 23:2, the "deep waters" of the lament psalms (e.g.,

Ps 69:1-2, 14); God as cosmic gardener watering his creation (Ps 104:13-16); the stolen water of the temptress in Proverbs 9:17, the "cold water to a thirsty soul" to which good news from a far country is compared (Prov 25:25); drawing water from the wells of salvation (Is 12:3); the water gushing from the temple in Ezekiel's vision (Ezek 47); Amos's picture of justice rolling down "like waters"; and "righteousness like an everflowing stream" (Amos 5:24 NRSV).

Add to these the *cup of cold water offered in the name of a disciple (Mt 10:42); the "spring of water gushing up to eternal life" that Jesus offers to the woman at the well (Jn 4:14 NRSV); the contaminated water described in the apocalypse (Rev 8:10-11; 11:6); the "river of the water of life, bright as crystal, flowing from the throne of God and of the Lamb" (Rev 22:1 NRSV); the water of life that anyone who is thirsty may take as a gift (Rev 22:17).

See also BAPTISM; BROOK; CISTERN; COSMOLOGY; DEEP; DEW; DRY, DROUGHT; FLOOD; RAIN; RIVER; SEA; SPRING OF WATER; STORM; THIRST; WELL; WELL, MEETING AT THE.

WAVES. *See* COSMOLOGY; STORM.

WAX. *See* MELT.

WAY, TWO WAYS. *See* PATH; PROVERBS, BOOK OF; WALK, WALKING.

WEAK, WEAKNESS

Weakness is a prominent image in the Bible, for weakness stands in contrast with the surpassing *strength of the principal character of the biblical story, *God.

Old Testament Images of Weakness. *Samson's taunting refrain to Delilah, "I'll become as weak as any other man" (Judg 16:7, 11, 13, 17 NIV), underscores Samson's superhuman strength. But compared with God's power, even the strongest man is weak. When Jesus warns his disciples that "the spirit is willing but the flesh is weak" (Mk 14:38), he is echoing an OT image of the weakness of human "flesh" in contrast with God who is powerful. In the face of his *enemies the psalmist reflects, "In God I trust; I am not afraid; what can flesh do to me?" (Ps 56:4 NRSV). King Hezekiah of Jerusalem considers the ultimate weakness of the great Assyrian king Sennacherib and then encourages the Jerusalemites with the reminder, "With him is an arm of flesh; but with us is the LORD our God" (2 Chron 32:8 NRSV). And when the wilderness generation of Israel was deserving punishment, God restrained his anger because "he remembered that they were but flesh" (Ps 78:38-39).

The OT projects a pattern of the God of Israel caring for the weak and the helpless. These are the ones who, pressed to the margins of life and unable to care for themselves, cry out to the Lord in their *affliction. We see this in God's choosing Israel from among the nations, in God's dealing with individuals within Israel, and in God's covenantal commands to care for the weak and afflicted, most notably the *widows and *orphans. The psalmist speaks of God taking pity on the "weak and needy" (Ps 72:13). The oppression of the weak and needy causes God to arise and declare, "I will protect them from those who malign them" (Ps 12:5 NIV). And *exiled Israel, having paid the penalty for her *sin, will find that God "gives strength to the weary and increases the power of the weak" (Is 40:29 NIV).

The world is a harsh place for the weak. Weakness can symbolize helplessness in the face of society's predators. The arrogant and wicked man "hunts down the weak, who are caught in the schemes he devises" (Ps 10:2 NIV). Who on earth can they turn to if not to the righteous? And God in turn promises to bless the righteous person who has regard for the weak and "delivers him in times of trouble" (Ps 41:1 NIV).

Because of God's concern for the weak, he will not tolerate leaders who oppress the weak. This is dramatically enacted in the words of Psalm 82, where the cosmic powers, the *"gods" of the nations, are hauled onto the celestial carpet and condemned for their failure to "defend the cause of the weak and fatherless; maintain the rights of the poor and oppressed" (Ps 82:3 NIV). The divine injunction rings out: "Rescue the weak and needy; deliver them from the hand of the wicked" (Ps 82:3-4 NIV). Ezekiel, as a prophetic spokesperson of the heavenly king, likewise condemns the "shepherds of Israel," Israel's royal leaders, who have not cared for the *flock and have not "strengthened the weak or healed the sick" (Ezek 34:4 NIV). Now God himself, the great Shepherd of Israel, will directly care for the flock and "strengthen the weak" (Ezek 34:16 NIV).

In contrast we find a recurring image of the high and mighty being made low, the strong king or nation being reduced to weakness by God. Isaiah pictures the underworld astir as the former great ruler of Babylon makes his entrance: the kings of the earth greet him, "You also have become weak, as we are" (Is 14:10 NIV). Death is the great equalizer of those who strive after power.

In the OT we sometimes find weakness as an image of psychological distress. The psalmist captures a universal human experience in confession before God: "My eyes grow weak with sorrow, . . . my strength fails because of my affliction, and my bones grow weak" (Ps 31:9 NIV; cf. Ps 6:7). More striking is the image of weakness that overcomes an enemy of God. Even Israel withers in weakness before the judgment of God: "Every hand will go limp, and every knee will become as weak as water" (Ezek 7:17; 21:7 NIV). In these contexts weakness is an image of the inevitable result of sin and rebellion, a dissolution of strength in the face God's wrath.

A special idiom of weakness has to do with the *eyes. The eyes were regarded by the ancients as an indicator of vigor and *beauty. The weak eyes of the aged are an image of decline in vital powers. Old Isaac's eyes are so weak that he can no longer distinguish *Jacob from *Esau (Gen 27:1; cf. 1 Sam 3:2), but Moses' unnatural death at 120 years is underscored by the note that "his eyes were not weak nor his strength gone" (Deut 34:7 NIV). The afflictions of life can also sap vitality, so that the psalmist laments "my eyes grow weak with sorrow" (Ps 6:7; 31:9 NIV). But Leah's "weak" eyes do not signify old age, poor eyesight or homeliness. It is an image of a delicate and tender loveliness, though no match for her sister Rachel's ravishing beauty (Gen 29:17).

New Testament Images of Weakness. *Jesus is the incarnate expression of God's care for the weak. The *mercy of God is embodied in the one truly righteous man. Although the *Beatitudes do not mention the weak per se, the poor in spirit, the *mourners, the meek and the persecuted all share in a weakness that qualifies them for the blessing of the *kingdom of God. The Gospels are populated by the weak, the little people of Israel who are powerless in the face of Roman, Herodian and Sadducean politics and the demands of wealthy landlords. The stories of the *birth of Jesus provide vivid profiles of the pious weak of Israel, such as Anna, a widow of great age, who is "looking for the redemption of Jerusalem" (Lk 2:38). The song of *Mary (Lk 1:46-55) dwells on the theme of God's overthrow of the mighty and his care for the lowly ones in Israel. Mary considers herself a lowly *servant who is now exalted (Lk 1:48). The prophecy of Zechariah (Lk 1:68-79) pictures Israel as languishing in *bondage and awaiting God's *rescue, his dawning *light to illumine "those who sit in darkness and in the shadow of death" (Lk 1:79 NIV). Throngs of weak gather around Jesus and receive the blessings of God's new age. The *blind, the *deaf, the sick, the *leprous, the *demon possessed, all present us with concrete images of weakness. *Women, particularly widows, and little *children also epitomize the weak in Israel. But they are also apertures into the weakness and neediness of Israel as a whole.

The entire Gospel story can be viewed as Jesus taking on weakness for the sake of Israel and of the world. In the *passion narratives we arrive at the climax of the God of Israel's mercy toward the weak. The narrative reverberates with the imagery of the weak and *Suffering Servant of Isaiah 52:13—53:12 and the suffering righteous one of Psalm 22. Both of these OT texts are finely drawn images of the profile and mission of righteous Israel in and for the world. But whereas Israel had lost its way in the drama of redemptive weakness, God in Christ assumes Israel's weakness and carries the story through the *cross to its powerful resolution. The utter and shameful weakness of Jesus dying naked on the cross is the emblem of the heart of God who redemptively bears in himself the weakness of the world.

What the Gospels embed in narrative Paul formulates in life and letters. Perhaps no biblical writer uses the imagery of weakness more effectively than Paul. Jesus himself "was crucified in weakness, yet he lives by God's power" (2 Cor 13:4 NIV). But this image is pressed further as Paul ironically attributes weakness to God: the cross stunningly exhibits that "God's foolishness is wiser than human wisdom, and God's weakness is stronger than human strength" (1 Cor 1:25 NRSV). What the world regards as weakness is for Paul a subversive symbol of divine power, an encrypted image of God's triumph.

Christians are to pattern their lives after this image of power in weakness (2 Cor 13:4), and Paul leads the way. In fact the image of weakness becomes the logo of Paul's apostolic ministry, and he delights in its irony. The cross has revealed the strategy of God's ways: "God chose the weak things of the world to shame the strong. He chose the lowly things of this world and the despised things—and the things that are not—to nullify the things that are" (1 Cor 1:27-28 NIV). So the chief of apostles is the least of apostles, who admits that he came to the Corinthians "in weakness and fear, and with much trembling" (1 Cor 2:3 NIV). But he can also say that "for Christ's sake, I delight in weaknesses, in insults, in hardships, in persecutions, in difficulties. For when I am weak, then I am strong" (2 Cor 12:10 NIV). In the midst of his afflictions Paul has heard the divine voice say, "My grace is sufficient for you, for my power is made perfect in weakness" (2 Cor 12:9 NIV). For this reason, in a Hellenistic world where weakness is an image of shame, Paul can "boast all the more gladly about my weaknesses, so that Christ's power may rest on me" (2 Cor 12:9 NIV; cf. 2 Cor 11:30). And to the Romans he can speak assuringly that "the Spirit helps us in our weakness" (Rom 6:26 NIV). If Christ "was crucified in weakness," he now "lives by God's power," and so he "is not weak in dealing with you, but is powerful among you" (2 Cor 13:3 NIV).

Weakness is an image of life in the footsteps of Jesus, and like their master his followers must make the final descent through weakness to reach higher ground. The paradoxical pattern of strength through weakness leads through death: The body "is sown in dishonor, it is raised in glory; it is sown in weakness, it is raised in power" (1 Cor 15:43 NIV).

Christlike weakness brings with it a sensitivity to the weak. Paul reminds the Ephesian elders of his own example of pastoral concern: "In everything I did, I showed you that by this kind of hard work we must help the weak" (Acts 20:35 NIV; cf. 1 Thess 5:14). The "strong" in the church at Rome are to accept their fellow believers whose faith or conscience is "weak" (Rom 14:1), to "bear with the failings of the weak" (Rom 15:1 NIV) and "not become a stumbling block to the weak" (1 Cor 8:9 NIV). Following Christ, whose weakness was a partaking of the weakness of humankind, Paul can say "Who is weak, and I do not feel weak?" (2 Cor 11:29 NIV). Indeed, as a principle, he carries the image of weakness to the forefront of ministry: "To the weak I became weak, to win the weak" (1 Cor 9:22 NIV).

Paul nowhere condones weakness of character, however. Weakness can be an image of crippling by sin, a weakness that leads to sickness and even death (1 Cor 11:30). And we read of "weak-willed women who are loaded down with sins and are swayed by all kinds of evil desires" and are easy prey for false teachers (2 Tim 3:6).

In some contexts weakness is an image of the general human condition. Jesus warns his disciples in Gethsemane that "the spirit indeed is willing but the flesh is weak." The antidote to succumbing to the coming "time of trial" was the spiritual discipline of wakefulness and prayer (Mt 26:41 NIV; cf. Mk 14:38). Paul even shapes metaphors in Romans 6:19 to accommodate those who are "weak in the flesh." The image of human weakness is taken up by the author of Hebrews, who contrasts the risen *priest, Christ, with a human priest who deals gently with human ignorance and waywardness "since he himself is subject to weakness." (Heb 5:2 NIV; cf. Heb 7:28). Christ too has partaken of human weakness but without sin, and his perfect ministry is not without a loving discipline that calls out to "strengthen your feeble arms and weak knees" (Heb 12:12 NIV). Weakness can be transformed by faith like that modeled by their Hebrew ancestors "whose weakness was turned to strength; and who became powerful in battle and routed foreign armies" (Heb 11:34 NIV). Weakness in this case images an opportunity for *faith, not for self-pity and a victim mentality.

See also Affliction; Cross; Low; Orphan; Shame; Strong, Strength; Suffering; Suffering Servant; Widow.

WEALTH. *See* Prosperity; Rags to Riches.

WEAPONS

Military language fills the pages of the Bible. The sounds of war reverberate from Genesis to Revelation. Thus throughout the Scriptures weapons play a major role.

This dictionary contains numerous articles on individual weapons (*see* Armor; Army; Arrow; Chariot; Shield; Sword), as well as a major article on the *divine warrior that gives a canonical overview of the transformation of the theme of warfare in the Bible from the beginning of the OT to the end of the NT. But how are weapons generally used as literary images in the Scriptures?

Many mentions of weapons in the Bible refer to literal tools of warfare, whether defensive like a shield or offensive like a sword. But even in many of these contexts we observe that weapons stand for more than a struggle for political and military power; they are tools in the *battle of God against the forces of *evil.

The famed battle of *David and Goliath provides an impressive example of human weapons in the service of God's cosmological battle against the forces of evil. In a rare biblical description, Goliath, the *Philistine professional soldier, is pictured as outfitted in the most advanced and terrifying weaponry available at the time: "He had a bronze helmet on his head and wore a coat of scale armor of bronze

A line of archers prepares to shoot.

weighing five thousand shekels; on his legs he wore bronze greaves, and a bronze javelin was slung on his back. His spear shaft was like a weaver's rod, and its iron point weighed six hundred shekels. His shield bearer went ahead of him" (1 Sam 17:5-7 NIV).

On the other side stood young David. Not a professional soldier, he entered the fray by happening upon the scene while bringing supplies from home to his brothers who were in the *army. So small that he could not wear *armor, he carried a simple slingshot into the combat.

The weapons take on literary and theological significance in the light of David's prefight speech in 1 Samuel 17:45-47 (NIV):

You come against me with sword and spear and javelin, but I come against you in the name of the LORD Almighty, the God of the armies of Israel, whom you have defied. This day the LORD will hand you over to me, and I'll strike you down and cut off your head. Today I will give the carcasses of the Philistine army to the birds of the air and the beasts of the earth, and the whole world will know that there is a God in Israel. All those gathered here will know that it is not by sword or spear that the LORD saves; for the battle is the LORD's, and he will give all of you into our hands.

David does use a weapon, a slingshot, but it is observably much less powerful than the weapons of his adversary. The principle illustrated is that God's *strength works through his human agents' *weakness. As a result, they cannot boast in themselves but only in God, who provides the victory.

But God's weapons are not limited even in the OT to those borne by his willing servants. When Israel turns against the Lord, he uses even the pagan armies that defeat them as a weapon. The prophet Jeremiah employs this language when he refers to *Babylon as God's "war club" with which he shatters nations (Jer 51:20 NIV). The Lord states his intention to destroy this weapon that he used without their knowledge. Earlier the prophet reports God as opening "his arsenal" and bringing out the "weapons of his wrath" (Jer 50:25).

In fact, God's arsenal is not restricted to his human creatures. When God goes to war, he has all the resources of his *creation to use as weapons. Against the *Egyptians at the Red Sea, God uses the *wind to part the sea, which, after the Israelites cross safely, envelops *Pharaoh's troops and destroys them (Ex 14). In a battle against a coalition of southern Canaanite kings, God hurls hailstones down on the *enemy and allows a greater slaughter by making the *sun and the *moon stand still in the sky (Josh 10:9-15).

A significant transition point in God's warfare occurs during Jesus' arrest. When the mob arrived to arrest Jesus, the Gospels report, Peter stepped forward to resist the arrest. With drawn sword, he struck one of the high priest's servants, severing his ear. Jesus responds by saying, "Put your sword back in its place, . . . for all who draw the sword will die by the sword. Do you think I cannot call on my Father, and he will at once put at my disposal more than twelve legions of angels? But how then would the Scriptures be fulfilled that say it must happen in this way?" (Mt 26:52-54 NIV). Jesus then goes to the *cross, where he defeats *Satan not by killing him but by dying (Col 2:13-15).

In the NT, in other words, we have a transition from physical warfare to spiritual. This results in the extensive use of weapon imagery for the spiritual power that God gives his people.

Ephesians 6:10-20 is the most developed example of this imagery. Paul admonishes his Christian readers to "stand firm then, with the belt of truth buckled around your waist, with the breastplate of righteousness in place, and with your feet fitted with the readiness that comes from the gospel of peace. In addition to all this, take up the shield of faith, with which you can extinguish all the flaming arrows of the evil one" (Eph 6:14-16 NIV). Other comparable passages may be found in Romans 13:12; 2 Corinthians 6:7; 10:4; and 1 Thessalonians 5:8.

Finally, weapons have a role in the concluding scene of the history of redemption in the Bible. The final *judgment against human and spiritual forces of evil is described as a great battle. The most extensive description of this final battle is found in the book of Revelation, an *apocalyptic work that contains extensive imagery. Not surprising, considering the subject matter and the genre, weapons find frequent mention in this book. They are the tools of God and his servants (e.g., Rev 19:11-16).

See also ARMOR; ARMY, ARMIES; ARROW, ARROW OF GOD; BATTLE STORIES; CHARIOT; DIVINE WARRIOR; HUNTING; SHIELD; SWORD.

WEATHER

The Bible does not refer to the weather in general,

but it frequently speaks of weather phenomena. These include *rain, *mist, *hail, *snow, *storm, *cloud, *lightning, *thunder, *wind and *whirlwind, all of which make up important biblical images. These weather phenomena play a role in the narrative, poetry, proverbs, prophecy parables and apocalyptic visions of Scripture.

We find some references to popular weather lore, such as in Jesus' reply to those who request a sign from heaven: "When evening comes, you say, 'It will be fair weather, for the sky is red,' and in the morning, 'Today it will be stormy, for the sky is red and overcast.' You know how to interpret the appearance of the sky, but you cannot interpret the signs of the times" (Mt 16:2-3 NIV). Or a proverb can draw on the analogy of weather: "As a north wind brings rain, so a sly tongue brings angry looks" (Prov 25:23 NIV).

Weather rarely if ever forms the aesthetic backdrop of biblical scenes. We do not read of early morning mist giving way to midday sun as Abraham and Isaac ascend Mount Moriah. When we read of Abraham sitting at the entrance to his tent "in the heat of the day," it is to set the time of day and underscore the need to offer hospitality to the travelers who appear before him (Gen 18:1 NIV). Never do the Gospels even hint at the midsummer heat of Galilee's shore (695 feet below sea level). In Acts 28:2 we read that the natives of Malta "built a fire and welcomed us all because it was raining and cold." But this points out the islanders' kindness and sets the scene for the story of the viper that emerges from the firewood and bites Paul (Acts 28:3-6).

Weather as the Medium of God. When weather does appear in the biblical narratives, it is frequently a powerful actor. The *cloud rising from the sea, at first no larger than a *hand, swells and spreads until "the heavens grew black with clouds and wind, and there was heavy rain" (1 Kings 18:44-45). But this gathering *storm lies at the center of the narrative, for it is a dramatic, drought-breaking fulfillment of Elijah's prophetic word to Ahab: "There is the sound of rushing rain" (1 Kings 18:41). It portrays the power of Yahweh and his true prophet in contrast with the false prophets of the purported *storm deity Baal.

In the Bible, weather imagery forms a ready means of evoking the power of God. Even in a day when our understanding of weather is detailed and finely tuned, and the science of forecasting is remarkably advanced, the weather still evades our grasp and stands as a ready metaphor for power, beauty and wonder. A secularized worldview still finds room for "acts of God" when faced with the destructive power of a hurricane or tornado. If convergence zones, lake effects and down drafts help us explain the "how," the "what" nevertheless shocks and amazes. But in their prescientific worldview the ancients perhaps more readily perceived the wonder of weather, and this perception frequently shapes the imagery of weather on the biblical page. It can only and ever be controlled by God or some other powerful spiritual being. Of this the ancient Israelites were absolutely certain. Thus weather imagery is a ready expression of divine qualities, attitudes and actions. While weather inspired the pagan worship of nature's forces, the Bible redirects this awe to the worship of the Lord of all weather.

As images of awesome, terror-inducing power, *thunder and *lightning are sovereign. Jeremiah traces the power of God in these phenomena: "When he thunders, the waters in the heavens roar. . . . He sends lightning with the rain and brings out the wind from his storehouses" (Jer 10:13 NIV; cf. Jer 51:16). As in other ancient Near Eastern cultures, lightning is imaged as the *arrow of God (Ps 18:14) and thunder as his voice that "thunders . . . upon many waters" (Ps 29:3-4 RSV).

God's ability to create and orchestrate weather is a sure sign of his power: "He makes clouds rise from the ends of the earth; he sends lightning with the rain and brings out the wind from his storehouses" (Ps 135:7 NIV). "His way is in the whirlwind and the storm" (Nahum 1:3 NIV). His providential care is written in the good gift of *rain: "He covers the sky with clouds; he supplies the earth with rain and makes grass grow on the hills" (Ps 147:8 NIV). God's mastery over the weather sometimes brings about dramatic provision for the people of God, as in the wilderness when the "wind went out from the LORD and drove quail in from the sea" (Num 11:31 NIV). In other instances we find images of God's mastery of the stormy *sea (Is 51:15; Jer 31:35). This motif lies behind the story of Jesus and disciples in a storm-tossed *boat on Galilee. As the storm wailed and the disciples cried out in fear, Jesus "rebuked the wind and said to the waves, 'Quiet! Be still!' Then the wind died down and it was completely calm" (Mk 4:37-41 NIV).

Weather as the smiling providence of God is perhaps not as memorable a biblical image as weather delivering divine *judgment. The first rainfall we encounter in the biblical story (cf. Gen 2:5) is a destructive force that results in the great *flood: the "windows of the heavens were opened and rain fell on the earth forty days and forty nights" (Gen 7:11-12 NIV). But God's mercy is evident as the "rain from the heavens was restrained" (Gen 8:2 NIV) and the *rainbow is set in the clouds to remind God of his covenant with Noah (Gen 9:12-15). In the *exodus event the *plagues on *Egypt include "the worst hailstorm that has ever fallen on Egypt, from the day it was founded till now" (Ex 9:18-35 NIV). And in a subsequent plague we find the east wind blowing all day and night and bringing a mass of destructive *locusts from the east (Ex 10:13). Amos opens his prophecy with an image of a blasting wind of Yahweh that desiccates everything in its path: "The LORD roars from Zion and thunders from Jerusalem; the pastures of the shepherds dry up, and the top of Carmel withers" (Amos 1:2 NIV).

Weather also provides metaphors for Israel's *restoration after the judgment of *exile. Isaiah speaks of the Creator's hand in bringing "the rain and snow" down from heaven and its not returning "without watering the earth and making it bud and flourish"; the same God will not allow his word to go forth without accomplishing his redemptive purpose (Is 55:10-11 NIV). A similar analogy between *creation and *salvation as a new creation is employed in Isaiah 45:8 (NIV): "You heavens above, rain down righteousness; let the clouds shower it down. Let the earth open wide, let salvation spring up, let righteousness grow with it; I, the LORD, have created it." Only the God who forms and moves the weather can convincingly claim of Israel's forgiveness, "I have swept away your offenses like a cloud, your sins like the morning mist" (Is 44:22 NIV).

Weather and Life. Unlike Egypt, where the Nile watered the crops, Palestine depended on the rain for the maintenance of agriculture (*see* Farming) and life. For the pre-Israelite population of Canaan, the storm god Baal assured the seasonal rains and the fertility of the soil. No doubt the perceived power of this god was a significant factor in seducing Israelites to the worship of Baal. Briefly put, the question was whether Yahweh, the God of Israel, who was associated with *Sinai and the *wilderness, was capable of meeting the needs of agrarian life in the *Promised Land. Could Yahweh provide the autumn ("early" KJV) and spring ("latter" KJV) rains (cf. Deut 11:14; Joel 2:23) that were needed to support the cycle of planting and harvesting? Does he have power over the clouds and storm? For Israel's leaders and for the writers of Israel's Scripture, the answer came as a "yes" clothed in a host of storm imagery attributed to Yahweh. From Elijah's bout with the prophets of Baal on Mount Carmel (1 Kings 18) to the sevenfold thunder of Psalm 29 to the imagery of shaking earth and pouring rain accompanying Yahweh's march from Sinai (Ps 68:7-9), Israel's prophets, poets and chroniclers affirmed Yahweh as a master of the mighty storm, one who would bring the rains in their season.

Long range forecasts and close observation of regional and hemispheric weather movements (e.g., El Niño)—which we take for granted—were inconceivable to the ancients (and to our great-grandparents). The ancients would have maintained that weather comes and goes; how and when God only knows. In the biblical metaphor, God calls for the wind and hail from his storehouse (Job 38:22). Seasons are marked by regular weather patterns that shape the traditional cycles of planting and harvesting, grazing and shearing, warring and celebrating. But weather is also full of surprises that break the rules, *drought being the most dreaded of these suprises.

Weather affects land and sea *travel, making roads and rivers impassable and seas treacherously dangerous. The passing notation at the beginning of the story of David and Bathsheba—"In the spring, at the time when kings go off to war" (2 Sam 11:1 NIV)—assumes a reality of ancient warfare: the rains of winter, which swelled streams and rivers, and soaked the soil, could make travel and warfare difficult, particularly in the case of heavy-wheeled chariots attempting to maneuver in the open plains and valleys. And in the NT we can assume that weather stands behind some of the apostolic trials and afflictions Paul recites in 2 Corinthians 1:23-29: "three times shipwrecked, . . . a night and a day in the open sea, . . . in danger from rivers, . . . in danger at sea, . . . cold and naked (NIV). When Paul instructs Timothy to hasten and "do your best to get here before winter" (2 Tim 4:21 NIV)—and "bring the cloak that I left with Carpus at Troas (2 Tim 4:13 NIV)—he has in mind the onset of winter and the closing down of the Mediterranean shipping lanes.

We commonly think of weather affecting our moods. Those who live in cold northern climates associate winter weather and shortened hours of daylight with melancholy and depression, no doubt exacerbated by the modern possibility of fleeing to the south and the constant reminder through travel advertising that warmth persists in tropical climes. But in the Bible there is scant evidence of the psychological wear of weather, neither cold nor heat. Admittedly, winter does not so harshly assert itself in Palestine, but we sense an attitude that since weather is something that cannot be changed and few can escape it (a Jerusalemite of means could spend the winter in lower elevations of the rift valley). It is to be accepted in its seasons. The rhythm of creation—"seedtime and harvest, cold and heat, summer and winter, day and night" (Gen 8:22 NIV)—is a gift from the God of order. Perhaps the closest we come to a biblical registry of the annoyance of weather is the proverb likening a nagging wife to a persistent drip on a rainy day (Prov 27:15; cf. 19:13).

Weather also provides a variety of biblical images having to do with human behavior. The book of Proverbs warns us of the nature of the fool: "Like snow in summer or rain in harvest, honor is not fitting for a fool" (Prov 26:1 NIV). Rain provides both positive and negative images of *kingship. On the one hand, the good king is "like rain falling on a mown field, like showers watering the earth. In his days the righteous will flourish" (Ps 72:6-7 NIV). On the other hand, "A ruler who oppresses the poor is like a driving rain that leaves no crops" (Prov 28:3 NIV). God can speak of the unfaithfulness of Judah and Ephraim in weather-related imagery: "Your love is like the morning mist, like the early dew that disappears" (Hos 6:4 NIV). And James reminds his readers of the shortness of life: "You are a mist that appears for a little while and then vanishes" (Jas 4:14 NIV).

See also CLOUD; HAIL; LIGHTNING; MIST; RAIN; SEASONS; SNOW; STORM; SUN; TEMPERATURE; THUNDER; WHIRLWIND; WIND.

BIBLIOGRAPHY. F. S. Frick, "Palestine, Climate of," *ABD* 5:119-26.

WEDDING

The Bible abounds in images of marriage, but pictures of weddings are relatively sparse (though *see* Bride, Bridegroom). The two obvious exceptions are the two epithalamia (wedding songs) in the Bible—Psalm 45 and the *Song of Songs—and these are a good starting point for considering the biblical imagery of wedding.

Two Royal Epithalamia. The most obvious qualities of a wedding as portrayed in Psalm 45, an epithalamion in honor of a royal wedding, are extravagant joy and sensory richness. The poet sets the tone at the outset when he asserts, "My heart overflows with a goodly theme" (Ps 45:1 RSV). The couple stand at the center of the event, and both appear at their best. The king is "fairest of the sons of men" (Ps 45:2 RSV), girded with his sword, in "glory and majesty" (Ps 45:3). He is anointed with "the oil of gladness," and his robes "are all fragrant with myrrh and aloes and cassia" (Ps 45:7-8 RSV). The princess, for her part, "is decked in her chamber with gold-woven robes" (Ps 45:13) and then led to the king "in many-colored robes . . . with her virgin companions" (Ps 45:14 RSV). The whole procession enters the palace of the king "with joy and gladness" (Ps 45:15 RSV).

A wedding ceremony occupies the very center of the Song of Songs (Song 3:6—5:1), flanked on both sides by courtship lyrics. In the bride's anticipation of the event, she fantasizes about her groom's arrival to claim her in hyperbolic images of eagerness (Song 2:8-9). When the groom does actually arrive in process, it is an extravagant picture, replete with sensory richness that becomes metaphoric for emotional fullness as well as a literal picture of a royal entourage. The sexual consummation that comes as part of the wedding is portrayed in the imagery of an Oriental spice and fruit *garden that the beloved claims (Song 4:9—5:1).

Images of Extravagance. Other scattered wedding images in the Bible ring the changes on the motifs of heightened celebration, joy and ceremony. To express the sheer rapture of a sunrise, the nature poet in Psalm 19:5 claims that the sun "comes forth like a bridegroom leaving his chamber" (RSV). In the story of Jesus' turning *water into *wine to keep a wedding party going (Jn 2:1-11), we look in on an extravagant celebration, carried out according to prescribed protocol. Similar luxuriance of celebration and prescribed etiquette emerge from Jesus' parables of marriage feasts, where we read about formal invitations to guests, preparation of an elaborate *banquet of wine and choice *food, and the need to attend in an appropriate (presumably festive and formal) wedding *garment (Mt 22:1-14; Lk 14:7-24). The actual arrangements of a wedding were the particular responsibility of the groom (Jn 2:9) and his *father (Judg 13:3, 10; Mt 22:2).

The picture of adorning the couple in their chambers before the wedding that has already emerged from the epithalamia noted earlier is extended in several other passages. Isaiah gives us a typical picture when he compares the God-bequeathed "garments of salvation" and "robe of righteousness" to the manner in which "a bridegroom decks himself with a garland, and . . . a bride adorns herself with her jewels" (Is 61:10 RSV). Joel 2:16 gives us a picture of the bridegroom and bride leaving their respective chambers, apparently a regular ceremony on wedding days. A bride's *jewelry represents her readiness for the groom: "Does a maiden forget her jewelry, a bride her wedding ornaments?" (Jer 2:32 NIV). The *veil is important to the bride; indeed, Leah hid behind it in her wedding.

Gladness of heart marked a wedding day (Song 3:11). It was against custom to *mourn or *fast on the day of the wedding (Mt 9:15). *Music and *dancing were an important part of the feast (Jer 7:34). Gifts were given (1 Kings 9:16), and special wedding songs were sung (Ps 45; 78:63). Joy is symbolized by "the voices of bride and bridegroom" (Jer 16:9 NIV; 25:10; 33:11). Rejoicing and gladness overflowed from the hearts of people attending (Rev 19:7).

For all the changing customs of weddings through the centuries, the emotions surrounding them are universal. The emotional intoxication of the lovers in Song of Songs is that of any couple in love, even though the literary expression of those feelings is partly rooted in ancient love poetry. One of the realistic touches of the Song of Songs is the anticipation of the couple as they think about the upcoming wedding day. Numerous lyrics in the collection express their eagerness and the perfection they see in their beloved. The bride is so eager that she introduces a refrain of self-rebuke, asserting the need to restrain her emotions and let love run its course (Song 2:7; 3:5).

The charged atmosphere of weddings is also captured in several apocalyptic visions of the future. Isaiah gives us the picture of God's rejoicing over redeemed *Zion "as the bridegroom rejoices over the bride" (Is 62:5 RSV). Similarly, Jeremiah pictures the coming golden age with its joyful new beginning as a time when "there shall be heard again the voice of mirth and the voice of gladness, the voice of the bridegroom and the voice of the bride, the voices of those who sing" (Jer 33:10-11 RSV).

These customs were metaphors of *salvation. As God is pictured as a husband, the OT redemption at *Sinai is portrayed as a wedding ceremony. The *seventy Israelite leaders who go up the *mountain with Moses *eat and *drink as God gives the law to him (Ex 24:9-11).

Ceremony of Devotion. Along with feast and celebration, a wedding was a ceremony that signaled the blessing of the community, the legal union in covenant before God and a public profession of devotion. Blessings were given, especially to the bride, who would hence identify wholly with the groom's family. Laban and his family blessed Rebekah to be the mother of "thousands of ten thousands" of successful descendants (Gen 24:59-60 RSV). Those witnessing Boaz's decision for Ruth likewise blessed her (Ruth 4:11-12).

From the first joining of *woman to *man, a wedding is a covenant before God (Prov 2:17; Ezek 16:8; Mal 2:14). At the original wedding in paradise it is God himself who brings the woman to the man (Gen 2:23). In Hebrew culture, God's presence lends definitive legal force to the union. Malachi pictures God as being "witness to the covenant between you and the wife of your youth, . . . your companion and your wife by covenant" (Mal 2:14 RSV). He adds, "Has not the LORD made them one? In flesh and spirit they are his" (Mal 2:15 NIV). Jesus also reflects the impact: "What therefore God has joined together, let no man separate" (Mk 10:9 NASB).

Weddings are public professions of loyal devotion. The first joyful profession is given by *Adam before God to *Eve (Gen 2:22-24); his commitment resounds in Paul's command that *husbands love their *wives as themselves (Eph 5:28-30). The promised union of Adam and Eve as "one flesh" before God is echoed and imitated in every wedding by these mutual professions.

Metaphor of Salvation. Like almost every other image in the Bible, the wedding is turned to profound spiritual use, becoming a metaphor for the relationship between God and his people. In this motif, God is the One who chooses believers to be his wife.

Jesus is repeatedly called a bridegroom. John the Baptist calls himself the friend of the groom (Jn 3:22-30). Jesus explains his disciples' lack of fasting by saying, "Can the wedding guests fast while the bridegroom is with them? As long as they have the bridegroom with them, they cannot fast" (Mk 2:19 RSV; cf. Mt 9:14-15; Lk 5:33-35). Jesus's earthly ministry is likened to a wedding feast. The parable of the king's wedding feast for his son, dedicated to the *Pharisees, understands Jesus as the son/groom and a rejection of the invitation as a rejection of Jesus himself (Mt 22:14).

Christ's second coming is strongly described as a feast as well. Though Jesus feasted with his followers as a human, the consummation of Jesus with his saints at the parousia (second coming) is described as a wedding banquet between the *Lamb of God, an epithet for Jesus, and his bride, the *church (Rev 19:6-9). Near its closing, Scripture anticipates the joyous celebration of union between an arrived groom and a ready bride: "Let us rejoice and be glad and give the glory to [God], for the marriage of the Lamb has come and His bride has made herself ready" (Rev 19:7 NASB). As salvation is extended in the metaphor of this marriage, the words of the angel ring true: "Blessed are those who are invited to the wedding supper of the Lamb" (Rev 19:9 NASB).

See also BANQUET; BRIDE, BRIDEGROOM; HUSBAND; LOVE STORY; MARRIAGE; WIFE.

BIBLIOGRAPHY. G. P. Hugenberger, *Marriage as a Covenant: A Study of Biblical Law and Ethics Covering Marriage, Developed from the Perspective of Malachi* (Leiden: E. J. Brill, 1994); G. L. Scheper, "Bride, Bridegroom," *DBTEL* 106-12; S.-T. Sohn, *The Divine Election of Israel* (Grand Rapids: Eerdmans, 1991).

WEEDS. *See* PLANTS.

WEEPING

Weeping is an expression of *sorrow, a reaction to being wronged or to having committed a wrong, or to the experience of loss. Scripture frequently portrays weeping as corporate and public.

In the Bible, weeping is most frequently audible and thus involves more than *tears. It is outright bawling or a culturally shaped expression of *grief or sorrow. When *Joseph retreats to a private room to weep, he vocalizes so loudly that the Egyptians hear him (Gen 43:30). Weeping in ancient cultures is thus more than the moist *eye or a tear quietly running down the cheek; it includes *facial contortions, shortness of *breath and feelings of angst.

Weeping in the presence of someone, particularly God, is notably common in the Bible. Sometimes it is associated with *temple scenes (Ezra 3:12; 10:1; Joel 2:17; Mal 2:13). Weeping is regularly associated with the plight of *Israel or *Jerusalem (judgment and *exile). Thus Jesus' weeping in Luke 19:41 (cf. Lk 23:28, also probably referring to the coming judgment on Jerusalem) is all the more poignant as the christological culmination of this motif. The city did not recognize the time of God's visitation (in Jesus) and now faces certain and irrevocable judgment.

With the exception of the much-vaunted shortest verse in the Bible, where Jesus weeps (Jn 11:35), weeping is not a display of emotion by God. Emotions such as *joy, *anger and passion are associated with God, but not weeping. However, there are numerous occasions when God's people are depicted with tears in their eyes, usually for quite specific reasons.

Very often people weep because of intense personal loss. Thus Abraham weeps over the death of Sarah (Gen 23:2) and David over the death of Jonathan (2 Sam 1). Hannah weeps in mourning over her infertility. In Acts 20 we see a rare display of outward emotion from the apostle Paul, when he takes his leave of the elders in Ephesus. Tears can also be triggered by a sense of spiritual loss or hunger, as when the psalmist speaks of his tears flowing "day and night" when he is kept from worshiping at the temple (Ps 42:3 NIV).

On other occasions weeping is a sign not of sorrow but of joy. The tears flow when Jacob and Esau are reunited in Genesis 33:4, and again when Joseph is reunited with his brothers after much sorrow (Gen 45:15). The tears of the sinful woman in Luke 7 may be tears of joy too. Although they express her sorrow and contrition, they are also the free-flowing tears of one who knows herself to be forgiven.

The most poignant OT instances are found in the prophets as they weep over the sins of the people. After describing the fate of his people, Jeremiah laments that "this is why I weep and my eyes overflow with tears" (Lam 1:16 NIV). He is so tied to the fate of his people that he weeps even in anticipation of their suffering and feels their sorrow as his own. Unlike the crocodile tears of official mourners, these tears are genuine and heartfelt.

The most striking NT image is in Matthew and Luke's eschatological phrase "the weeping and gnashing of teeth." Here the tears are genuine, but their effect on the wrath of God is nil, as it is too late for those who shed them. The image is of utter hopelessness and is intended as a warning to those who read or hear.

See also FACE, FACIAL EXPRESSIONS; GRIEF; MOURN, MOURNING; SORROW; SUFFERING; TEARS, VALE OF TEARS.

WELL

Wells in the biblical world must be understood in context of the aridity of the land. In such a climate and geographical locale, water is both essential to life and scarce. The well thus becomes an image of life and value. In addition, because wells were scarce (perhaps one to a community), wells were where people congregated and social contacts were made. Of special importance in the Bible is the "type scene" in which a traveling male (or his surrogate) meets his future betrothed at a well (*see* Well, Meeting at the).

Physical Wells. Simply at a physical level, the well means life for the agrarian society of the OT. As something that people dig, it represents an imposition of human civilization on the recalcitrance of nature (Gen 26:15-32; Num 21:18). As the key to life, the well becomes a thing of value over which clan leaders contend (Gen 26:15-32). Some wells became so prominent that as late as the time of Jesus the well outside Samaria was still known as "Jacob's well" (Jn 4:6).

Although people go to the well to draw *water for their own *drinking and *washing (Gen 24:11; 2 Sam 23:15-16), a more familiar picture from the pages of the OT is of flocks gathering at the community well (Gen 29:3; Ex 2:16-17; Jn 4:12). A well was sometimes protected by a huge stone that only multiple shepherds could move, so that no one could steal a disproportionate share of the water (Gen 29:10).

Metaphoric Wells. Based on the life-giving properties of physical wells, the Bible also uses the well as a metaphor. The spiritual refreshment of the *pilgrimage journey to Jerusalem, for example, is pictured as the pilgrims' making the arid valley of Baca "a place of springs" (Ps 84:6 RSV) or "a well" (KJV). Equally evocative is Isaiah's exuberant picture of drawing "water from the wells of salvation" with joy (Is 12:3). Here the life-giving quality of water becomes a symbol of *salvation.

Other metaphoric uses appear elsewhere in the OT. Elaborating the metaphor of the *garden as a locus of the value the lover attaches to his beloved, the speaker in the Song of Songs calls his *bride "a garden fountain, a well of flowing water" (Song 4:15 NIV). The image of the fountain (RSV) or well is a favorite archetype of the wisdom teachers as well. Proverbs makes the well an image of personal character. The positive image is clear: "The mouth of a righteous man is a well of life" (Prov 10:11 KJV). On the negative side, "a righteous man who gives way to the wicked" is like a "a muddied spring or a polluted well" (Prov 25:26 NIV), while a sexual adventuress is "a narrow well" (Prov 23:27 NIV). In the Prophets a well that dries up is used to picture God's impending judgment (Hos 13:15 NIV), and in a paradoxical assertion Jeremiah states, "As a well keeps its water fresh, so she keeps fresh her wickedness" (Jer 6:7 RSV).

Jesus at the Well. The Bible's last story of a well (Jn 4:1-42) is a fitting summary of the Bible's range of uses for well imagery. In a spiritualized version of meeting one's future betrothed at a well, Jesus meets a Samaritan woman as the archetypal *outcast, who comes to the well at noon to avoid being present when the community gathers at the well. Jesus infuses new life into the image of a well as he ministers to the Samaritan woman outside her town. As the story unfolds, we are reminded of the political, social and historical significance of wells by John's careful identification of the well as Jacob's (Jn 4:6). Here the pride of generations is embodied in the Samaritans' ownership (Jn 4:12). Second, Jesus arrives there as a tired traveler, seeking refreshment (Jn 4:6) as Eliezer, Jacob and Moses had done before him (and like Moses, Jesus is in hostile land). The economic necessity of the well is evident: its depth requires the use of special tools (Jn 4:11), and when offered the prospect of water that does not need to be drawn daily, the woman is eager at the prospect of escape from the onerous ongoing task (Jn 4:15).

While Eliezer, Jacob and Moses found wives at the well, Jesus seeks a different bride, those who will "worship the Father in spirit and in truth" (Jn 4:23 NIV). Amidst a poignant knowledge of the woman's history of unfaithfulness, he reveals that he is the One for whom she has been waiting—the Bridegroom— the Messiah "who will explain everything to us" (Jn 4:25 NIV). Jesus also turns the water-giving well into a full-fledged symbol of salvation. In sum, in the Bible's last well scene Jesus visits this common setting of opportunity and blessing and reveals its transformation into a metaphor of redemption, as we are reminded how the incarnation changes everyday life.

See also CISTERN; SPRING OF WATER; WATER; WELL, MEETING AT THE.

WELL, MEETING AT THE

In the arid landscape of the Near East, wells have long been natural meeting places. The Bible presents them as accommodating three sorts of encounter: human beings with the supernatural; clan with clan (or culture with culture); and *man with *woman, often in a betrothal scene. As examples of the first, one may cite the account in Genesis 16 of Hagar's epiphany at Beerlahairoi (the "well of the living one that beholds me," or the "well of the one who sees and lives") and the account of the disclosure of Jesus as the Christ to the Samaritan woman at Jacob's well in John 4. This latter passage also illustrates the encounter of clans or cultures at well sites, for Jews and Samaritans did not ordinarily mix.

An earlier case of such an encounter involves *Moses after he has fled Egypt upon killing a man. He comes into the land of Midian and finds the seven daughters of the local priest being harassed by *shepherds at a well. He *rescues them and draws water for them. Conflict of more than one sort is present here, for it is not only the daughters of Jethro the priest confronting a neighboring clan, but also Moses, who to this point had known nothing but the life in *Egypt, confronting the exigencies of the new culture. So begins his long rustication, which is training for his later leading of the Israelites in their wanderings.

The third sort of encounter is the one developed most fully in the Bible. The well provides the site for men to meet women, and often a betrothal is arranged or soon follows the encounter. As a type scene, the meeting of one's future betrothed at a well has a set of conventional ingredients, including the arrival after journey of the man (or his surrogate) from a distant land, meeting the future bride at the well, the girl's rushing home to announce the event, the inviting of the stranger into the parental home (usually for a meal) and the conclusion of the visit with betrothal. Such are the stories of Abraham's servant and Rebekah (Gen 22), Jacob and Rachel (Gen 29:1-14), Moses and Zipporah (Ex 2:15-22). Although the initial meeting between Ruth and Boaz occurs in a field rather than at a well, it reenacts a similar sequence.

There is no need to attribute fiction to the recurrent presence of conventional motifs: the well was simply the place where social meetings occurred. The equivalent today would be a couple's meeting at college or church. The incipient symbolism of the romantic meeting at the well is easy to see: the arrival of the man from a distant land represents the "otherness" of the relationship, the drawing of the water establishes a bond (the first rite of romance, in effect) and the gesture of hospitality in the parental home represents acceptance in a broader family context.

Perhaps an additional level of symbolic overtones can also be seen in the motif, which brings together two of the most important ingredients in the survival of any man in the ancient Near East—water and woman. Meeting one's future betrothed at a well brings the two together.

Isaac's history, as it happens, is intertwined with well encounters of all three kinds listed above. He is associated with Beerlahairoi (Gen 24:6) and with three other wells whose names record his ongoing strife with the herdsmen of Gerar: (Esek [i.e., contention] in Genesis 26:17-20, Sitnah [i.e., enmity] in Genesis 26:21 and Rehoboth [i.e., broad places] in Genesis 26:22.

In the NT it is Jesus' encounter with the Samaritan woman that pulls together the three significant sorts of meeting associated with such sites. In the theological disputation over the proper place to worship (4:20-23), we see the clash of Jewish and Samaritan cultures. In Jesus' explicit announcement to the woman that he is the Messiah who will make all things plain, we have an epiphany reminiscent of Beerlahairoi. As encounter of man and woman, the narration presents a dramatic conversation, rich in double entendre, which sets the woman's flirtation over against Jesus' altogether more spiritual grasp of the situation.

Jesus is, of course, unconventional on at least three counts in initiating conversation with the woman. She is, first of all, a woman; she is, moreover, a Samaritan woman; and Jesus is aware that she is a person of loose morals. We can suppose that, in her somewhat limited framework, Jesus' opening words are heard as a carnal overture. Behind the exchange that follows there stands not only the precedent for well as betrothal site, but also the rich biblical language of well, *spring, *fountain and living water as terms implying to *sexual congress (cf. Prov 5:15-18; Song 4:15; Jer 2:13).

Yet at the crucial point in the dialogue between Jesus and the worldly woman, who has presumably taken at its basest possible meaning Jesus' discussion of water and thirst, Jesus abruptly says, "Go, call your husband, and come back" (Jn 4:16 NRSV). Her flirtation dismissed, the woman at once turns to theological dispute. Is Jerusalem or Mount Gerizim the proper place to *worship? She, or course, has a strong opinion on this, but Jesus is not to be deflected. His discourse on God as spirit makes clear the final irrelevance of where one worships, and when the woman ends by saying that in any case the Messiah will clear up all theological disputes, Jesus declares his identity to her.

In John's telling, this encounter at the well is by far the most highly crafted account of its kind in the Bible. John's presentation of Jesus stresses the manifold difficulties in understanding his person and true significance. The Samaritan woman is only one among many of Jesus' interlocutors who begin by misunderstanding him. Framing the Samaritan woman's dialogue with Jesus is the typology of the well as the perennial site for epiphany, conflict of clans and the encounter of man and woman.

See also BRIDE, BRIDEGROOM; FOUNTAIN; LOVE STORY; SPRING OF WATER; WATER; WELL.

BIBLIOGRAPHY. L. Enslinger, "The Wooing of the Woman at the Well: Jesus, the Reader and Reader-Response Criticism," *Literature & Theology* 1 (1987-1988) 167-83.

WEST

In the Bible west is the most ominous of the *four directions. The broad expanse of the Mediterranean *Sea was the only geographical feature immediately to the west of ancient Israel (Num 34:6), and so imposing was the sea's physical presence that "west" is often indicated by the term *sea(ward)* (Ex 26:22; Num 3:23). Since the sea was one of the primary symbols associated with *chaos, *evil and *death, these associations are inevitable for the west. The merisms of Psalm 139:8-10 capture nicely both the moral and spatial dimensions of the contrast between *east (poetically parallel to *heaven) and west (poetically parallel to Sheol; *see* Hell): "If I ascend to heaven . . . if I make my bed in Sheol . . . if I take the wings of the dawn, if I dwell in the remotest part of the sea" (NASB).

The ancient Semitic orientation toward the east ("forward") meant that the west was *"behind" (Is 9:12). Thus *behind* is another designation for the west in the Bible, conjuring up notions of that which is to be discarded, irrelevant, lacking in priority and not requiring attention. The Mediterranean is the sea that is "behind" (Deut 11:24; 34:2; Joel 2:20; Zech 14:8), a fact that correlates with the dearth of biblical accounts dealing with Israelite maritime activity: the Israelites literally turned their back on the west.

"The setting of the sun" is yet a further designation of the west that reinforces with a different image the unattractive connotations of this direction. The frequently articulated contrast "from the rising to the setting of the sun" is a merism that encompasses all the *earth (Is 45:6 NASB; 59:19; also Ps 113:3; Mal 1:11), but one must not overlook the moral overtones implicit in the image. In contrast to the *joyous response of life to the *light of the rising *sun, *darkness and the cessation of human activity result when the sun sets in the west (Ps 104:19-23). The west is the place where the sun ceases to provide its light, and Joshua once successfully persuaded God to postpone sunset to allow him time to complete a task (Josh 10:12-13).

The presence of the *foreign, uncircumcised *Philistines along Judah's western border probably reinforced the perception of the west as an unattractive direction (Is 11:14). Yet perhaps because of the need to extend God's *kingdom to the realms of chaos (i.e., westward), there is a strong awareness in many biblical texts that movement toward the west is actually a favorable enterprise, in contrast to the negative associations of movement toward the east. The catastrophes of the opening chapters of Genesis, where eastward movement predominates, are followed by the first movement that brings promise, and that is to the west: *Abraham obeys God in leaving Ur to go to Canaan (Gen 11:31).

Once God's people are in Canaan, moving west means *prosperity and *blessing, in contrast to a retrograde movement eastward (Gen 13:11-13), which Abraham expressly forbids (Gen 24:6). Both the *tabernacle and the *temple require *worshipers to approach the sacred area by walking west in the *sacred precincts. The Israelite tribes conquer Canaan by entering the *land in a westward movement (Judg 11:18). The summons to *return from *exile in *Babylon requires a move westward. In the NT the *journeys of Paul represent a progressive move to the west as Christianity spreads: Galatia, then Greece, then Rome and ultimately perhaps even Spain (Rom 15:24). At the *birth of Christ, magi from the east follow the *star westward (Mt 2:1-9), echoing the prophecy of Ezekiel that God's *glory would one day return from the east to dwell in Israel (Ezek 43:2-5).

See also BEHIND; EAST; NORTH; SEA; SOUTH; SUN.

WHEAT

In the world of the ancient Near East, wheat was an important dietary staple; moreover, it carried significant value for trade. When King Solomon purchases cedars from *Lebanon to build a *temple for the Lord, he pays in part with wheat (1 Kings 5:11). While its functions range from *food to wealth, wheat's availability always depends on a good *harvest, which is a gift from God (Ps 85:12). It is no wonder that the biblical image of wheat carries a variety of connotations.

At the most concrete level, wheat is an image of plenty—the bountiful *blessings of God upon his people. When Moses speaks of the *Promised Land of Canaan, Israel's inheritance, he describes a *land filled "with wheat and barley, vines and fig trees," and other good things (Deut 8:8 NIV). The image of wheat also plays an important role in Israel's thanksgiving to God for a good harvest. Through Moses, God instructs Israel to observe the *Feast of Weeks, during which the people offer the firstfruits of the wheat harvest to God (Ex 34:22); here the thanksgiving offering of wheat is a token of the vast bounty God has showered upon Israel. Likewise, in examining his past deeds for any wrongdoing, Job likens the contrast between blessing and *judgment to the contrast between wheat and briers (Job 31:40).

Even as wheat can represent that which supports life, it can also serve as a metaphor for life itself. The psalmist declares that God will feed an obedient Israel with the finest wheat and *honey (Ps 81:16). Wheat here does not merely represent bounty; the full import of the image becomes clearer by the contrast of the previous verse, in which "those who hate the LORD would cringe before him, and their punishment would last forever" (Ps 81:15 NIV). These two very different possibilities appear side by side; in contrast to everlasting punishment, feeding on wheat and honey conveys the notion of a life that is sustained and nurtured by God himself.

Further uses of wheat imagery are closely wrapped up with another agricultural image: the threshing of *grain. In the Prophets, threshing is often a symbol of judgment, with God as the thresher; Hosea likens an *idolatrous Israel to "chaff swirling from a threshing floor" (Hos 13:3 NIV), with little substance before the judgment of God. God's judgment on *Babylon leads the prophet Jeremiah to describe that fallen empire as a trampled threshing floor (Jer 51:33).

But because God also intends to *restore Israel from *exile, Isaiah declares, "the LORD will thresh . . . and you, O Israelites, will be gathered up one by one" (Is 27:12 NIV). Here the key element of the image is the action of sorting, by which God once again brings Israel into being out of an existing nation. Although these images do not deal with wheat directly, the natural association between threshing and wheat fosters a parallel association between their respective images that is developed more fully in the Gospels, where wheat figures prominently in a number of contexts relating to the sorting action of judgment.

In the Gospels of both Matthew and Luke, the writers preface the beginning of Jesus' public ministry with John the Baptist's words concerning him: "He will clear his threshing floor, gathering his wheat into the barn and burning up the chaff with unquenchable fire" (Mt 3:12 NIV). With this statement the Baptist points beyond himself to the coming of Christ, the judge who will sort out the wheat from the *chaff—a most powerful and evocative introduction to the public ministry of Jesus. Here wheat stands in contrast with chaff, in a double metaphor that conveys the distinction between value and worthlessness; but given the association of *threshing with *judgment, John the Baptist's words invite his hearers to understand wheat and chaff as images of the righteous and the *wicked, respectively.

Jesus further develops the association of wheat with righteous people in his parable of the weeds (Mt 13:24-30). The picture is similar: wheat and weeds grow together until the harvest; then they are separated—the weeds to be burned, the wheat to be gathered into the *barn. But the imagery Jesus uses has a very explicit meaning; in his explanation of the parable he identifies citizens of the kingdom of heaven with the good *seed and the wheat that *grows from it (Mt 13:38). Moreover, the image of sorting does not suggest a fleeting or partial judgment; rather, it is the final and comprehensive judgment by the Son of Man. The parable is Jesus' description of the kingdom of heaven coming upon the world. Here the image of wheat being sorted moves into an eschatological framework; it is a picture of God's creating a new people for himself through the work of Christ.

See also BARN; BREAD; CHAFF; FARMING; GRAIN; HARVEST; SEED; THRESHING, THRESHING FLOOR.

WHIRLWIND

*Wind is one of the most powerful forces in nature. While humans have at times harnessed and converted its power for useful purposes, the mere mention of a mighty windstorm usually brings to mind images of destruction and stirs up feelings of helplessness and even terror. It is no surprise, then, that the OT uses the imagery of a powerful windstorm to picture calamity and irresistible divine judgment.

The Hebrew terms translated "whirlwind" (sāʿar, sᵉʿārâ and sûpâ) refer generally to high winds (Ps 55:8; Hos 8:7), such as a tornado-like whirlwind (Jer 23:19), the powerful winds that accompany *storms at sea (Ps 107:25, 29; Jon 1:4, 11-13) or a destructive thunderstorm (Job 27:20; Ezek 13:11, 13). In several cases the terms, especially sûpâ, appear to refer to the hot sirocco or khamsin windstorms that sweep into Israel from the southern or eastern deserts at the beginning or end of summer. This wind can raise the temperature to unbearable limits, while nearly eliminating any humidity in the air (see Stadelmann, 105-7).

The prophets, because of their thematic emphasis on judgment, frequently use the whirlwind as a metaphor. They picture the Lord as coming in the midst of a windstorm to do *battle against his *enemies. Isaiah announced that the sovereign Lord would attack Jerusalem (Is 29:6). His appearance would be accompanied by "thunder, earthquake and great noise," as well as a "windstorm and tempest and flames of a devouring fire." This *theophanic *divine warrior imagery is stereotypical, being attested elsewhere in the OT (Nahum 1:3; Zech 9:14) and in ancient Near Eastern literature. For example, the Assyrian king Adad-nirari II boasted, "I blow like the onslaught of the wind, I rage like the gale" (A. K. Grayson, Assyrian Royal Inscriptions, 2: sect. 418). The prophets depict the windstorm as one of the Lord's instruments of destructive judgment against the wicked (Jer 23:19; 30:23; Ezek 13:11, 13; Amos 1:14; Zech 7:14) or liken his *chariots to a whirlwind (Is 66:15). The quickly revolving wheels of speeding chariots would produce a great cloud of dust, like a whirlwind or dust storm (see Is 5:28; Jer 4:13). God's whirlwind of judgment blows away rulers like uprooted plants (Is 40:24) and hostile nations like *chaff (Is 17:13; 41:16).

Like the prophets, OT wisdom literature employs the image of the whirlwind or windstorm when speaking of the destiny of the wicked. Job knew that the wicked typically do not survive calamity, which sweeps them away like *straw or chaff before a powerful wind (Job 21:18; 27:20-21). Lady *Wisdom warns the fool that she will mock him in the day of calamity, for disaster will blow him away like a windstorm (Prov 1:27). In a similar vein, one of Solomon's proverbs observes, "When the storm (= calamity) has swept by, the wicked are gone" (Prov 10:25).

See also EARTHQUAKE; STORM; THEOPHANY; THUNDER; WEATHER; WIND.

BIBLIOGRAPHY. R. B. Y. Scott, "Meteorological Phenomena and Terminology in the Old Testament," ZAW 64 (1952) 11-25; L. I. J. Stadelmann, The Hebrew Conception of the World (Rome: Biblical Institute Press, 1970) 105-9.

WHITE

White appears more than fifty times in the Bible, both as a color and as a description of the radiance of *light. Scenes of transcendent *glory and redemption are painted in strokes of white, but so are the telltale signs of *leprosy. References can be divided between the color of earth and the *color of heaven.

Sometimes *white* denotes the physical color of objects. Examples of such a neutral use include references to *goats (Gen 30:35), *teeth and *milk (Gen 49:12), *snow (Dan 7:9), the rods Jacob used in his ridiculous attempt at animal husbandry (Gen 30:37), *manna (Ex 16:31), *wool (Ezek 27:18), the stripped branches of *trees (Joel 1:7), *grain that is ready for *harvest (Jn 4:35 RSV) and *hair (Mt 5:36).

Two categories of white as an earthly color go beyond the merely denotative level. More than a dozen times in Leviticus, white is strongly negative in connotation; here it is the color of leprosy and is accompanied by repulsive and terrifying images of raw flesh, boils and swelling. On the other hand, white sometimes has associations of festivity and privileged power, including royalty. In the song of Deborah those who sit on rich carpets are said to ride on white *donkeys (Judg 5:10). When Ahasuerus shows off his royal splendor, the adornments at the seven-day *banquet include white cotton curtains (Esther 1:6), and when Mordecai is honored, he wears royal robes of blue and white (Esther 8:15). Employing conventional images of festivity, the writer of Ecclesiastes urges, "Let your garments always be white" (Eccles 9:8 NRSV).

The voltage rises as we move to biblical scenes of heavenly or transcendent reality. White suggests a supernatural brilliance beyond the earthly in descriptions of the Ancient One seated on the throne, whose "clothing was white as snow, and the hair of his head like pure wool; his throne was fiery flames, and its wheels were burning fire" (Dan 7:9 NRSV). At the transfiguration Jesus' appearance "shone like the sun" (Mt 17:2 NRSV), and his clothes "became dazzling white, such as no one on earth could bleach them" (Mk 9:3 NRSV; see also Lk 9:29). Similar images of transcendent brilliance characterize the *angels who appeared at the *resurrection (Mt 28:3; Mk 16:5; Jn 20:12) and the *ascension (Acts 1:10).

Not surprisingly, therefore, the writers who gravitate most to the color white are the apocalyptic visionaries (with fifteen references in the book of Revelation alone). In these visions we find white *horses (Zech 1:8; 6:3, 6; Rev 6:2; 19:11, 14). The glorified saints and angels in heaven wear white robes (Rev 3:4-5, 18; 4:4; 6:11; 7:9, 13-14; 19:14). Our imaginations are similarly fired by the famous images of the white *stone with a name written on it that believers receive in heaven (Rev 2:17), a white *cloud surrounding the "one like the Son of Man" as he comes to harvest the earth (Rev 14:14 NRSV), and God's "great white throne" of judgment (Rev 20:11).

To our surprise, in the symbolism of the Bible white is not set against *black (the great biblical antithesis is light versus darkness). And only once is it set in contrast with red—in the famous verse in which Isaiah quotes God as offering to turn the scarlet of sins into the whiteness of snow and wool (Is 1:18).

See also BLACK; CLEANSING; CLOUD; COLORS; GREEN; LIGHT; MILK; PURITY; SNOW; TEETH; WOOL.

WHITEWASHED TOMBS. *See* PHARISEE.

WHOLE, WHOLENESS

Biblical uses of *whole* and related words number over three hundred, the vast majority of them reflecting simply the idea of "all" or "complete." Most are translations of the Hebrew *kōl* and *šālēm* (which is related to the oft-used Hebrew word for peace, *šālôm*) and the Greek *holos, pas, hygiēys* and *sōdzō*. Wholeness refers to such things as the whole of the burnt *offering (Lev 1:13), all of a group of people (Num 1:2), the *covenant-making God's ownership of the totality of the earth (Ex 19:5), the uncompromised heart's *obedient seeking for God (Ps 119:2, 10), the provision of Christ's *death (Is 53:5), the restoration of physical health (Mt 9:22), the universal impact of the *Fall (Rom 8:18) and the corruption and culpability of all humankind (Rom 3:19). Often the implied context is the fracture of wholeness occasioned by the Fall and the longing for a future *redemption that will restore wholeness to human existence.

The Wholeness of God and People. Ideal human wholeness must be understood in light of the infinite God, who is imaged in his finite human creation (Gen 1:26-31). The one and only God (Deut 6:4; 1 Tim 2:5) is a triune being (Mt 28:19). God is consistent (Jas 1:17). His perfections are expressed coherently, never antagonistically (Jn 3:16; Rom 3:25-26; 1 Cor 2:24; Tit 2:11). Although God experiences various emotions, such as satisfaction (Gen 1:31), compassion (Gen 4:6-7, 15), grief (Gen 6:6-7), jealousy (Ex 20:5), delight (Jer 9:27), anger (Num 14:12, 18), joy (Jn 15:12) and peace (Rom 16:20), he is never unbalanced or controlled by irrational emotions as humans can be (Num 14:18; Prov 25:28). The triune God is the embodiment of self-sufficient (Acts 17:25) wholeness. His actions express perfect balance, the infinite beauty and symmetry of his person.

In contrast to God's wholeness, creatureliness as we know it is inherently lacking in itself, in at least two dimensions. The first is cogently expressed by Augustine's aphorism (addressed to God) that "you made us for yourself, and our hearts are restless till they rest in you." People are whole only in relationship with God. God's moral directive (Gen 2:17), his cultural mandate (Gen 1:26-28), his establishment of *marriage (Gen 2:18-25), the implications of "walking in the garden in the cool of the day" (Gen 3:8 RSV) and the emotional alienation included in human *shame, *fear and *guilt (Gen 3:7-11) all indicate that God created human beings with a need for important relationship with himself. After the Fall this need for relationship to God is intensified (Ps 16:1-2, 5; 73:25; Jer 9:23-24). The exhortation to love God wholly (Mk 12:28-30) underscores that we are image-bearers of the God who also thinks (Rom 11:33-36), feels (Gen 3:9; Lk 15:22-25) and chooses (Gen 1:26). In his grace he has provided the vehicle and the opportunity for meeting this need, in making himself accessible (Gen 3:9; Ex 29:45-46; Lev 1:1-2; Ps 91:14-15; Mt 11:28-29; Heb 10:19-22).

The second creaturely need for wholeness is horizontal: the need for human companionship and community, without which people remain lacking. This human need too is rooted in God's creation of people, with God creating Eve because "it is not good that the man should be alone" (Gen 2:18 NRSV). Confirmation can be found in *Adam's enthusiastic response to the creation of *Eve (Gen 2:23), the second half of the great commandment (Mk 12:28-30), the interdependence of members of the body of Christ (1 Cor 12:7, 24-27) and the multitude of passages that exhort us to pursue healthy interpersonal relationships (Jn 13:35; Gal 6:1-10; Eph 4:25—5:2, 21). The Bible never considers the possibility that people can be whole as isolated individuals; that is possible only in relationship. The master image in this regard is Paul's detailed elaboration of the analogy between the *church and the human *body (1 Cor 12).

After the Fall. The Fall compounds and twists the legitimate twofold need for wholeness and creates a threefold hindrance to it. The essential relationship with the Creator changes from tilling the *garden to hiding in the garden (Gen 2:15; 3:8), from worship and joy to shame and fear (Gen 2:23; 3:10) and from acceptance of responsibility to its rejection (Gen 2:15-20; 3:12). Into this state of alienation the God of grace calls, inviting Adam and Eve to realize that their *fig leaves will never compensate for the loss of intimacy with him and consequent loss of wholeness.

The second area of diminished wholeness occurs between people. The joy of equality (Gen 2:23-25) is replaced with superiority (Gen 3:12) and competition (Gen 3:16); the joy of intimacy is replaced with alienation (3:7); the privilege of sharing in the work of dominion (Gen 1:26-28) is replaced with individualism (Gen 3:12-13) and ultimately domination (Gen 4:8, 23-24), and words of affirmation become words of criticism (Gen 3:12).

Alienation is also seen in the internal disequilibrium that issues from fractured relationships. Fear and shame lead to misdirected creativity when Adam and Eve make loincloths (Gen 3:7). Recognition of moral accountability (Gen 2:17; 3:2-3) is replaced with denial of accountability (Gen 3:12). The mind is darkened; the emotions are degraded; the will is deadened (Rom 1:18-32; Eph 4:17-19). Internal peace is absent; anxiety is present (Gen 4:5; Is 57:16,

20-21). Before the Fall the experience of wholeness flowed naturally from unhindered fellowship between Adam and Eve and between them and God. Afterward the experience of wholeness with God requires the grace of God, accompanied by personal humility and discipline, because of violence within and without.

The dominant picture of human wholeness in a fallen world is that it requires struggle and is always precarious, in constant danger of being lost. Paul's benedictory prayer that the God of peace might "sanctify you wholly; and may your spirit and soul and body be kept sound and blameless at the coming of our Lord Jesus Christ. He who calls you is faithful, and he will do it" (1 Thess 5:23-24 RSV) is hopeful but realistic: it takes the power of the God of peace to effect our wholeness and to keep us until Christ's coming. Although we are complete in Christ, having come "to fulness of life" in him (Col 2:10 RSV), and are restored as friends and family (Gal 4:4-7; Col 1:21-22), we limit intimacy by disobedience (Jn 14:21) and by lack of discipline (1 Cor 9:27), lack of faith (Heb 11:6) and lack of endurance (Heb 10:32-36).

The Coming Age. A leading ingredient in the Bible's *eschatological images of the future age is the restored wholeness that glorified saints will finally enjoy in perpetuity. The book of Revelation contains all the important biblical motifs (which can be found scattered through OT apocalyptic visions as well). One is the union of people with God and Christ, pictured as a marriage (Rev 19:7; 21:2, 9) and as an existence in which the redeemed "follow the Lamb wherever he goes" (Rev 14:4 RSV). To be whole is to be one with the God whose "dwelling . . . is among mortals" (Rev 21:3 NRSV). Social wholeness is also present, imaged in the single city where all the redeemed will reside through all eternity (cf. Jesus' homey image of *heaven as a stately house with many rooms [Jn 14:2]). Inner wholeness is marked by the true shalom of God, which replaces *pain and *tears with healing and compassion (Rev 21:4). Feelings of insecurity and alienation will be replaced with security and intimacy (Rev 21:3). Here is the ultimate fulfillment of Isaiah's prophecy regarding the *suffering servant, that "upon him was the chastisement that made us whole" (Is 53:5 RSV).

See also APOCALYPTIC VISIONS OF THE FUTURE; END TIMES; ONE; PEACE; RESTORE, RESTORATION; REUNION, RECONCILIATION; TRANSFORMATION.

WHORE. *See* PROSTITUTE, PROSTITUTION.

WIDE, WIDENESS

Wideness has both negative and positive meanings in Scripture. First, wideness pictures in several ways the activity of people opposed to God. Sometimes they open themselves up to embrace *evil, as did the idolatrous people of Isaiah's time. "Forsaking me, you uncovered your bed," God accuses them, "you climbed into it and opened it wide" (Is 57:8 NIV).

The picture suggests an unfaithful wife opening herself up to the embraces of many others. Sometimes the wicked one himself is pictured as opening up to engulf another. The writer of Lamentations tells God's conquered people: "All your enemies open their mouths wide against you; they scoff and gnash their teeth and say, 'We have swallowed her up' " (Lam 2:16 NIV; cf. 3:46).

Rather than still portraits of evil, both of these pictures show little mini-dramas, with progressive action sketched rapidly but vividly. The *adulterous woman throws back the covers, climbs into the *bed and calls an open invitation. The *enemies' faces have open *mouths, then wide open mouths, then violently moving mouths. And the next minute the prey is chewed and gulped. Widening happens, ominously, almost as we read.

A wide bed, wide mouths and a wide *gate all lead away from God. Jesus warned his disciples against that wide gate and broad road that lead to destruction (Mt 7:13). The wideness of the way gives a sense of so many, so easily traveling that smooth road away from God.

The way toward God is *narrow, and the gate is small, but it opens up onto its own wide vistas farther on. In contrast to the faithless woman opening her bed, Isaiah offers another picture, this time of a *barren woman, representing God's conquered, *exiled people waiting to be *restored. God promises whole generations of children to this poor barren woman, who must open wide her *house to get ready for them: "Enlarge the place of your tent, stretch your tent curtain wide, do not hold back" (Is 54:2 NIV).

Positive images of wideness often involve such opening up to receive all the blessings God will give. Isaiah 45:8 calls for the earth to open wide to receive God's righteousness like the *rain, so that *salvation can spring up. In its most exalted pictures, wideness points to the nature of God himself, whose limits cannot be measured, being "wider than the sea" (Job 11:9 NIV). Paul prays that believers might grasp how "wide and long and high and deep is the love of Christ," but immediately admits this love "surpasses knowledge" (Eph 3:18-19 NIV). The tent of the barren woman, the whole earth and the believer's own heart will be stretched wide indeed to receive a love of such dimensions.

See also NARROW, NARROWNESS.

WIDOW

Mentioned nearly a hundred times in the Bible, the widow is an archetypal image of affliction and desolation. The writer of Lamentations, for example, begins his lament over the destruction of *Jerusalem by comparing the city to a widow:

How deserted lies the city,
 once so full of people!
How like a widow is she,
 who once was great among the nations! . . .
Bitterly she weeps at night,

tears are upon her cheeks. (Lam 1:1-2 NIV)
Lonely, with no one to *comfort her, she grieves bitterly. Jerusalem's *sin has provoked God's *anger and *judgment.

The low social standing of widows is suggested by other classes with whom they are mentioned in the Bible, such as the *orphan and the stranger. *Marriage is an image of domestic fullness in Scripture; widowhood is an image of loss and emptiness.

The same image recurs in Isaiah, and the book of Revelation, in the judgment of *Babylon:

In her heart she boasts,
 "I sit as queen; I am not a widow,
 and I will never mourn."
Therefore in one day her plagues will overtake
 her:
 death, mourning and famine.
She will be consumed by fire,
 for mighty is the Lord God who judges her.
 (Rev 18:7-8 NIV; cf. Is 47:8-9)
Judgment, bereavement, widowhood fall swiftly on Babylon.

Yet the widow image is not necessarily associated with judgment. God defends the cause of the widow and has a special concern for her welfare (Deut 10:18; Ps 146:9). This concern is concretized in several *laws: Israel is commanded, "Do not . . . take the cloak of the widow as a pledge," and is told to leave what remains from harvesting *grain, olives and *vines for the alien, the fatherless and the widow (Deut 24:17-22 NIV).

Isaiah uses the metaphor of Israel as a widow very positively to illustrate how God relieves the widow's *suffering and redeems his people. He consoles Israel and encourages her to forget the past, including the reproach of widowhood:

Do not be afraid; you will not suffer shame.
 Do not fear disgrace; you will not be humiliated.
You will forget the shame of your youth
 and remember no more the reproach of your
 widowhood.
For your Maker is your husband—
 the LORD Almighty is his name—
the Holy One of Israel is your Redeemer.
 (Is 54:4-5 NIV)
Shame, disgrace, humiliation and reproach are forgotten as Israel enjoys the unfailing love of the Lord.

The book of *Ruth illustrates beautifully in a more concrete fashion how the emptiness of widowhood may be turned to joy and life. It is a picture of *redemption.

The opening scene is bleak and desolate. The Israelite Naomi and her Moabite daughter-in-law, Ruth, return to *Bethlehem from the land of Moab, where they have endured *famine and have both been widowed. Naomi expresses her feelings on returning in her lament: "Don't call me Naomi. . . . Call me Mara, because the Almighty has made my life very bitter. I went away full, but the LORD has brought me back empty" (Ruth 1:20 NIV).

They arrive in Bethlehem as the barley *harvest

is beginning. Ruth *gleans leftover grain and, as it turns out, finds herself in the fields of Boaz, a kinsman. He shows kindness to her and prays, "May you be richly rewarded by the LORD, the God of Israel, under whose wings you have come to take refuge" (Ruth 2:12 NIV). The rest of the book narrates how Boaz proves to be the fulfillment of his own prayer. In a dramatic encounter with Ruth on the *threshing floor, Boaz agrees to do the duty of a kinsman-redeemer under the levirate law (Deut 25:5-10); to buy the property of the dead men and to marry Ruth, "to maintain the name of dead with his property, so that his name will not disappear" (Ruth 4:10 NIV).

The story ends with *restoration, renewal and *hope for the women and for Israel. Ruth gives *birth to a son, Obed, of whom the women say to Naomi, "He will renew your life and sustain you in your old age" (Ruth 4:15 NIV). Obed grew up to become the father of Jesse, and Jesse the father of David, from whose line Christ our redeemer was born (Mt 1:5-6).

See also BARRENNESS; HUSBAND; MARRIAGE; ORPHAN; TIMOTHY, FIRST LETTER TO; WIFE; WOMAN, IMAGES OF.

WIFE

In the biblical world the essential role of a wife is consort and companion to her *husband, just as the essential role of a husband is defined in terms of his relationship to his wife. While the creation account in Genesis 2 actually depicts a dual relationship—man and woman as well as husband and wife—it is clear that later passages in the Bible accept the account as a picture of the origin of the *marriage relationship, with *Adam and *Eve as prototypical husband and wife.

Wives in the Bible. The first wife, Eve, was formed from her husband. She was constructed from his rib, or side. The very name *woman* is a play on the double meaning for the word *rib,* which carries with it the idea of "side" or even "alter ego" (Gen 2:21-25). The basic role of wife in the Bible is epitomized here at the outset. Eve was created to be "a helper fit" for Adam (Gen 2:20 RSV), or in the quaint phrase bequeathed by the KJV, a "help meet." Adam is incomplete until his wife comes into his life. He is therefore rapturous in his lyrical declaration that "this at last is bone of my bones and flesh of my flesh" (Gen 2:23 RSV), suggesting the basic unity and identity of husband and wife. Because of this unity "a man leaves his father and his mother and cleaves to his wife" (Gen 2:24 RSV). The image of *sexual union completes the picture, as husband and wife "become one flesh" (Gen 2:24; see 1 Cor 6:16 for confirmation that this phrase denotes sexual union).

While wife and husband share their essential human identity and by implication have the same potential for spiritual good or *evil, the story of *creation and *Fall in early Genesis implies a differentiation of role. Both man and woman, created in God's image, are given the mandate to "have dominion over" the created order (Gen 1:26, 28 RSV), but the specifically marital picture that emerges in the story of Adam and Eve shows the wife in the role of childbearer (Gen 3:16) and Adam as a "breadwinner" who toils to produce food for the family (Gen 3:17-19; cf. Gen 18:6-7 for a somewhat similar division of duties when Abraham and Sarah serve as hosts to three heavenly visitors). Accordingly, one of the primary wifely roles throughout the Bible is to give *birth to a couple's children, and the roll call of well-known wives in the Bible is at the same time a catalog of mothers.

Implicit in this role too is the wife as a sexual partner, a role that Paul elaborates in a famous passage on the needs for husband and wife to meet each other's sexual needs (1 Cor 7:1-7), and we might note in passing that in this passage neither wife nor husband is viewed more than the other as a source of sexual pleasure. An OT counterpart is a passage in Proverbs 5:15-19 enjoining a husband to find sexual satisfaction "in the wife of your youth, a lovely hind, a graceful doe" (RSV). Still, the Bible does not highlight sexual attractiveness as a trait of a good wife (though the Song of Songs cautions us not to disparage the normal attractiveness men and women find in each other). The portrait of the ideal wife that concludes the book of Proverbs positively warns against putting much value on feminine beauty as a wifely virtue (Prov 31:30). And the wives who emerge as ideal consorts in the Bible—Sarah, Rachel, *Ruth, *Mary—are known to us solely by their godly and virtuous character, and not at all by physical appearance.

What does the image of a "help meet" actually entail when fleshed out? A companionable wife is a literal (as the occasion arises) and metaphoric fellow traveler who accompanies her husband on the journeys of life. She shares in the moral and religious instruction of children (Prov 1:8; 6:20). A good wife supports her husband, doing "him good, and not harm, all the days of her life" (Prov 31:12 RSV). Wifely virtues also include submissiveness to a husband (Eph 5:22; Col 3:18; 1 Pet 3:1, 5-6). The image of the wife as "weaker" than her husband (1 Pet 3:7) is doubtless a comment on physical strength and constitution, yet the physical stamina of wives like Rebekah (who displays physical strength in drawing water for the camels of Abraham's servant [Gen 24:17-20]), Ruth (who *gleans from early morning until noon "without resting even for a moment" [Ruth 2:7 RSV]) and the wife of Proverbs 31 are an obvious asset to their husbands.

The ideal wife emerges more clearly when set against her foil. Instead of doing her husband "good, and not harm," a wife like Rebekah enters into a prolonged competition with her husband (and he, no doubt, with her) to subvert his intentions and outmaneuver him as she pursues her personal vision for her favored son's destiny. The *adulterous wife of Proverbs 7:10-27 pursues extramarital liaisons when her husband is absent on a business trip. Wifely vices include nagging (Prov 19:13; 27:15) and disparagement of one's husband (as in Michal's putdown of David for his religious fervor in 2 Sam 6:20-23). The worst wife of all is Jezebel, who dominates her husband and secures his earthly and spiritual downfall as she opposes the cause of God.

For a composite and hyperbolic picture of the ideal wife, we can turn to the encomium in praise of the virtuous wife that concludes the book of Proverbs (Prov 31:10-13). We should note first that the portrait itself begins and ends by placing the wife into her marital role as spouse to her husband (Prov 31:11-12, 28), buttressed by a reference to her maternal role (Prov 31:28). This human dynamo not only supports her husband in his public success (Prov 31:23) but also sews (Prov 31:13, 19), buys food and provides food for her family (Prov 31:14-15), buys and plants a *vineyard (Prov 31:16), sells merchandise (Prov 31:18), is physically strong and energetic (Prov 31:15, 17-18), extends deeds of mercy to the poor of the community (Prov 31:20), provides clothing for her family (Prov 31:21), is herself well dressed (Prov 31:22), conducts a cottage industry of making and selling clothes (Prov 31:24), teaches (Prov 31:26), governs the household (Prov 31:27) and works hard (Prov 31:27, which climaxes the catalog of the wife's activity with the laconic understatement that she "does not eat the bread of idleness" [RSV]). The climactic praise for such a wife comes from her family (Prov 31:28), who praise not only her excellence (Prov 31:29) but also her godliness (Prov 31:30).

In sum, wives (like husbands) can be either very good or very bad. Priscilla is coworker with her husband in the work of the church (Acts 18:26; Rom 16:3; 1 Cor 16:19). Ruth and Mary are loyal companions with their husbands on the journey of life. Abigail takes the initiative in overriding the effect of her husband's foolish behavior (1 Sam 25). The wives of some very bad husbands try to counsel them wisely at breaking points in their lives, such as the wives of Belshazzar (Dan 5:10-12) and Pilate (Mt 27:19), or to dissuade them from foolish behavior, as Vashti does (Esther 1:12). But wives can also trick their husbands, as do Rebekah, Potiphar's wife and Delilah, or be unfaithful, as Hosea's wife is (Job 2:9), or become an ungodly influence, as Solomon's wives do (1 Kings 11:4), or support their husband in an immoral act, as Sapphira does (Acts 5:1-11).

Metaphoric Extensions. Such is the image of the wife as she exists in the pages of the Bible. Given the closeness of the union between husband and wife, it was inevitable that biblical writers would evoke the intimacy of the marriage relationship between God and his people, and that God himself speaks of a metaphoric marriage in which believers are pictured as God's wife. *Hosea portrays the vicissitudes in the relationship between Yahweh and his adulterous wife, Israel. Hosea's own wife Gomer has deserted

him in the same way that Israel has deserted the Lord, her husband, for spiritual adultery and the *idolatrous *worship of the Baals. Hosea vividly depicts the consequences of Israel's faithlessness: "There is no faithfulness or kindness, and no knowledge of God " (Hos 4:1 RSV). In heart-rending passages Hosea conveys the overwhelming love of Yahweh for his people. They are determined to turn away from him, but he expresses his deep longing for them: "How can I give you up, O Ephraim!" (Hos 11:8 RSV). The concluding section of the prophecy becomes a love song reminiscent of the Song of Songs. Yahweh, the husband, promises to "heal their faithlessness" and "love them freely" (Hos 14:4 RSV).

Jeremiah employs the same metaphor of Israel as wife as he urges the nation to remember its youthful devotion and to renew the covenant with its husband, Yahweh (Jer 2:2; 3:14; 31:32). Isaiah too communicates God's passionate, unfailing love and delight in his people through nuptial imagery. He declares God's intentions in majestic language: "For your Maker is your husband. . . . The LORD has called you like a wife forsaken and grieved in spirit, like a wife of youth when she is cast off" (Is 54:5-6 RSV). Again, in the redeemed future, Zion "shall no more be termed Forsaken," but "you shall be called My delight is in her, and your land Married; for the LORD delights in you, and your land shall be married" (Is 62:4 RSV).

The marriage metaphor is carried into the NT, where the *church is portrayed as the spouse of Christ. Writing to the church in Ephesus on the subject of Christian marriage, the apostle Paul instructs husbands to "love your wives, as Christ loved the church and gave himself up for her, that he might sanctify her, . . . that he might present the church to himself in splendor" (Eph 5:25-27 RSV). Paul concludes by echoing Genesis 2:24 (with its assertion that "the two shall become one flesh"), making explicit that he is actually speaking of Christ and the church: "This mystery is a profound one, and . . . it refers to Christ and the church" (Eph 5:32 RSV). The biblical imagery of God people's as wife culminates in the book of Revelation, which provides us with glimpses of the "wife of the Lamb," "prepared as a bride adorned for her husband" (Rev 21:2, 9 RSV), who lives happily ever after with her husband in a palace glittering with *jewels.

See also CHILD, CHILDREN; DOMINEERING WIFE; MOTHER; FAMILY; HOME, HOUSE; HUSBAND; MARRIAGE; SEX; TYRANNICAL FATHER, HUSBAND; WIDOW; WOMAN, IMAGES OF.

WILDERNESS

The English word *wilderness* serves to translate various Hebrew (and also Greek) words: among others, *midbār,* "a place for the driving of cattle," designating steppe, land burned by summer heat, generally wasted rocky and sandy land with minimal rainfall, in which only nomadic settlements were found; *jeschimon,* primarily the uninhabited land on both sides of the *Jordan north of the Dead Sea; and *arabah,* which when used with an article refers to the land on both sides of the Jordan on its further way to the Gulf of Aqaba, but also to any dry stretch of land. *Wilderness* in the Bible thus designates both mountainous regions and plains that after rainfall can be used as *pastures.

Though it is often claimed that "wilderness" as a geographical region, a biological phenomenon and an image has a purely negative meaning throughout the Bible, the connotations of nonfigurative references to wilderness range from a relatively neutral use as a topographical identification of *travel routes, towns and *battle sites to pronouncedly negative implications as a site of danger and *death, *rebellion, *punishment and *temptation, and as the dwelling place of evil spirits, but also to positive memories of God's guidance and help, his miracles and the revelation of his will and commandments. Some biblical characters experience the wilderness as a place of *refuge, while others are driven there against their will. The figurative use of the term mirrors both negative and positive connotations: similes and metaphors are employed to show a reversal of fortunes in both directions.

Old Testament Uses. Many of the references to wilderness in the OT naturally are indications of geographical locations or travel routes and, as such, lack any positive or negative evaluation. Sometimes, however, such a topographical indication is related to a land promise—as in Deuteronomy 11:24 ("Every place whereon the soles of your feet shall tread shall be yours: from the wilderness and Lebanon, from the river, the river Euphrates, even to the uttermost sea shall your coast be," KJV; cf. also Josh 15—20). Elsewhere wilderness regions are the sites of battles between the Israelites and their enemies, as in Joshua 8, Judges 20 and 2 Chronicles 20.

Danger and death. The negative connotations are partly rooted in the poor living conditions the wilderness offered. On their way from *Egypt to Canaan, the people of Israel wandered through "that great and terrible wilderness, wherein were fiery serpents, and scorpions, and drought, where there was no water" (Deut 8:15 KJV)—a place full of dangers that contrasted sharply to their life in Egypt, where they thought they had enjoyed relative wellbeing: "when we sat by the flesh pots, and when we did eat bread to the full" (Ex 16:3 KJV). But also in other instances the wilderness bodes destruction and death: from the wilderness comes the strong *wind that destroys the house of Job's children (Job 1:19).

Rebellion and punishment. In a number of instances this deprivation led the Israelites to rebel against God and the leaders he had appointed for them. In tones of irony, they play off one evil against the other: "Is it because there were no graves in Egypt that you have taken us away to die in the wilderness?" (Ex 14:11 NASB). To that extent the wilderness appears as a place of political revolt, often described as "murmuring" (Ex 16:2) but implying

an active *rebellion against God's commandments (Num 27:14) and provoking his wrath. This is recalled by the prophets (e.g., Ezek 20:13, 21).

As a punishment for such faithlessness, God declares that they must wander through the wilderness for forty years—"until the last of our dead bodies lies in the wilderness" (see Num 14:32-33; Deut 9:28). This wilderness wandering becomes one of the central themes of Jewish history; it is later alluded to in the book of Job (Job 12:24), in Psalms (Ps 106:26) and in the Prophets (Ezek 20).

Evil and temptation. That the wilderness was also considered a place where evil spirits abide becomes apparent in the ritual of the *scapegoat, over which all the sins of the people are confessed and which is to "bear upon him all their iniquities to a land not inhabited" (Lev 16:22 KJV). Satyrs are dancing there (Is 13:21; 34:14). In other instances the wilderness appears as a place of immorality (see Jer 3:2).

The evil dwelling in the wilderness occasions the people's temptation, and God himself humbles them there, "testing you to know what was in your heart, whether you would keep his commandments, or not," but always with the plan "to do you good in the end" (Deut 8:2, 16 RSV). This day of temptation in the wilderness (Ps 95:8-9) and its consequences serve as a warning to future generations.

Sanctuary and guidance. The various wilderness regions turn up as places of refuge—the Israelites' escape from Egypt into the wilderness being the most prominent one. But it is by placing Joseph in a *pit in the wilderness that Reuben saves his brother's life (Gen 37:2); David escapes to a stronghold in the wilderness during his flight from Saul (1 Sam 23:14; 26:2-3)—which he makes the subject of a psalm (Ps 55:7). Jeremiah wants to leave his sinful people for a "wayfarers' lodging place" in the wilderness (Jer 9:2 RSV) and warns them to save their lives and be like a bush in the wilderness (Jer 48:6).

When Elijah flees into the wilderness from Jezebel (1 Kings 19:4), it becomes much more than a place of refuge: God saves the prophet from starvation and despair there. Earlier, in the time of the exodus, the poor living conditions in the wilderness had occasioned many of the miracles that made the wanderings of the Israelites an experience of God's glory and divine help and guidance (Num 14:22). It was the place where they were given *manna—"upon the face of the wilderness . . . a small round thing" (Ex 16:14 KJV)—*water and quail. This experience of being saved in the "waste howling wilderness" (Deut 32:10 KJV) reverberates throughout the OT—from Moses' speech ("For the LORD thy God hath blessed thee in all the works of thy hand: he knoweth thy walking through this great wilderness: these forty years the LORD thy God hath been with thee; thou hast lacked nothing" [Deut 2:7 KJV]) to David's psalms (Ps 68:7) and Isaiah's simile that God led Israel like a *horse in the wilderness. The Feast of Tabernacles (still today celebrated by the Jews as the Feast of Sukkot) is a remembrance of the people's existence in the wilderness (Lev 23:34-36).

Worship and covenant. The exodus of the Israelites from Egypt begins with their requesting permission to hold a religious *festival in the wilderness—a request repeatedly denied by Pharaoh (Ex 3:18; 5:1; 7:16; 8:27). This practice of *sacrificing and keeping the *Passover in the wilderness becomes a habit (e.g., Num 9:5). Likewise, the *tabernacle and the *altar of the burnt offering are usually associated with the wilderness (e.g., 1 Chron 21:29; 2 Chron 1:3). One of its most important positive connotations is that there God reveals himself to people—at the Horeb (Ex 3) and the *Sinai (Ex 19), where he enters into a *covenant with them and gives them his commandments (Ex 20), a fact that firmly connects the Mosaic law with the wilderness experience (Ex 24:9). The messianic dimension of the wilderness is opened in Hosea 11:1, where God calls Israel, his *son, from Egypt (which in Tobit 8:3 is identified as a wilderness). Matthew 2:15 applies this to Jesus, who returns from Egypt, where he had to flee with Mary and Joseph.

New Testament Uses. NT views of the wilderness run the whole gamut of connotations found in the OT. The memory of the Israelites' wilderness wanderings is found in Jesus' dealing with the *Pharisees (Jn 6:31-32, 49), Peter's speech before the Sanhedrin (Acts 7), Paul's warning to the Corinthians not to become *idolaters (1 Cor 10:31) and the epistle to the Hebrews (Heb 3:8-11).

The OT view of the wilderness as a dwelling place of evil also looms large in the NT—a possessed man is driven by a demon into the wilderness (Lk 15:4); Jesus lives and fasts in the wilderness with the wild beasts and is tempted by the devil (Mt 4:1-11). But he is led there by the Spirit, and with him are also the angels who minister to him. Paul has to face danger in the wilderness (2 Cor 11:26). And John is carried into the wilderness and sees a woman on a scarlet beast, "full of names of blasphemy" (Rev 17:3 KJV). But the wilderness is also a sanctuary for the woman in the Apocalypse who flees there and is saved from the dragon (Rev 12:6, 14). Evil can be overcome by prayer and the power of God: Jesus withdraws into the wilderness in order to pray (Mk 1:35; Lk 5:16), and he does some of his miracles in the wilderness, such as the feeding of the multitudes (Mt 14:21; 15:32-39).

In the NT the wilderness is also the place of revelation and proclamation of the good news. As prophesied by Isaiah (Is 40:3), John the Baptist lives in the wilderness (Lk 1:80); there the word of God comes to him (Lk 3:2), and he preaches and baptizes (Mk 1:3-5). Philip's missionary outreach to the Ethiopian takes place in the desert between Jerusalem and Gaza (Acts 8).

Figurative Meanings. In biblical writings as early as Psalms, wilderness is used in metaphors, similes and metonymies. The aridity of the wilderness surrounding David's hideout moves him to express his longing for God metaphorically: "My soul thirsteth for thee in a dry and thirsty land, where no water is" (Ps 63:1 KJV).

The Bible's most pronounced figurative use of wilderness is in contrast to fertile ground, and God's power is frequently described as being able to turn the one into the other. Thus the psalmist describes God's "wonderful works" in terms of a just reversal of fortunes:

> He turneth rivers into a wilderness, and the watersprings into dry ground; A fruitful land into barrenness, for the wickedness of them that dwell therein. He turneth the wilderness into a standing water, and dry ground into watersprings. And there he maketh the hungry to dwell, that they may prepare a city for habitation. (Ps 107:33-36 KJV; cf. also Is 50:2)

Many eschatological pronouncements in the Prophets make use of the same image, as when Isaiah says that with the outpouring of the Spirit the wilderness is turned into a fruitful field (Is 32:15) or even that Zion's wilderness will be made like Eden (Is 50:2; *see* Garden). Conversely, God's judgments are described as the laying to waste of fruitful places (Jer 4:26) and his wrath as "the wind of the wilderness" (Jer 13:24 KJV). Of course for a people living in or close to the wilderness, these images had a strong metonymic quality; they experienced *drought and destruction, *rainfall and good crops as the acts of God.

But the figurative use of wilderness goes beyond metonymy: the wilderness is compared to Israel (Hos 2:3) or—in ironic reversal—even to God, who asks, "Have I been a wilderness unto Israel?" (Jer 2:31 KJV). In the NT this occurs in the context of antitypical references—as when Jesus compares himself (Jn 3:14) to the *serpent of bronze that Moses raised in the wilderness in order to save the people from the bites of the fiery serpents God had sent as a punishment for their sins (Num 21).

Jesus' parables abound in allusions to wilderness, usually as representing evil and danger, lostness and spiritual decline. It is the setting of the *robbery that occasions the good Samaritan's charitable act (Lk 10:25-37) and of the search for the lost *sheep (Lk 15:4), and it characterizes the area beyond the fruitful field in the parable of the *sower (Mt 13:1-8).

Having adopted a typological view of themselves as the new people of Israel, the American Puritans equated the New England wilderness around them—in spite of the obvious differences—with its biblical counterpart and considered it to be the realm of the devil and his *demons. A thoroughly positive view of the wilderness and its inhabitants was introduced by the Enlightenment, but celebration of the "virgin land" and the "noble savage" took place largely without *theophanies or memories of divine guidance. The materialism of later Western civilization replaced this idealistic view with a positive vision of another kind: it saw wilderness regions in terms of their potential resources, but equally without any of the spiritual connotations of the OT and NT. Even the countermovement to this—the twentieth century's ecological movement—mostly values the wilderness not in terms of possible theophanies but as a repository of wildlife worthy of being saved for future generations. In contemporary culture no rediscovery of the biblical dimensions of the wilderness is yet in sight.

In summary, the wilderness is an ambivalent image in the Bible. If it is a place of deprivation, danger, attack and punishment, it is also the place where God delivers his people, provides for them and reveals himself.

See also EXODUS, SECOND EXODUS; JORDAN RIVER; LAND; LAND FLOWING WITH MILK AND HONEY; PROMISED LAND; SINAI; WASTELAND.

BIBLIOGRAPHY. O. Böcher, "Wilderness etc.," *NIDNTT* 3:1004-15; R. Nash, *Wilderness and the American Mind* (3d ed.; New Haven, CT: Yale University Press, 1982); M. D. Howe, *The Garden and the Wilderness: Religion and Government in American Constitutional History* (Chicago: Chicago University Press, 1965).

WIND

Wind in Scripture can picture lack of substance and meaning, adversity or changeableness. Only when the pictures of wind connect to the person of God do we find more positive meanings: winds can picture God's supremacy, his *authority over his *creation, his *judgment on that creation, and the very Spirit that breathes new life into a human soul.

Wind as Nothingness. Ecclesiastes offers one of the most memorable series of wind images, as the Preacher pronounces one after another sphere of human activity meaningless, a mere "chasing after the wind." The image, used repeatedly in a kind of refrain (Eccles 1:14, 17 NIV, etc.), expresses the monotonous futility of going after something and finding it to be nothing after all—like trying to capture the wind in one's *hands. What does any human being gain, the Preacher asks, "since he toils for the wind?" (Eccles 5:16 NIV).

Wind in other biblical passages pictures the nothingness at the end of an effort or a life. Those who bring trouble on their *families, for example, will "inherit only wind": nothing, that is, rather than the expected substantial *inheritance (Prov 11:29 NIV). Isaiah compares the *sufferings and punishments of God's people to the labor pains of a *woman who gives *birth only to wind (Is 26:18). In their disobedience they brought no life, no *salvation to the earth, Isaiah says.

The book of Job offers several pictures of the wind, pictures that suggest meaninglessness specifically in relation to words. The wind from human lungs can be as meaningless—or as hurtful—as the wind in the sky. Arguing with "empty notions" and useless words, Eliphaz suggests, is like filling one's *belly with the hot *east wind: there is sound there, but no substance—in fact, only the destructiveness of a scorching desert wind (Job 15:2). Bildad as well calls Job's words "a blustering wind" (Job 8:2 NIV).

Job marvels that his friends would "treat the words of a despairing man as wind" (Job 6:26 NIV). When God speaks, in the end, all the previous speeches seem by contrast a kind of desert wind, and finally Job must put his *hand over his *mouth and simply bow in hushed *repentance before his Creator God (Job 40:1-5; 42:1-6).

Jeremiah calls the false *prophets "but wind": "the word is not in them" (Jer 5:13 NIV). Their *breath which comes out in words is indeed but a little bit of air, with no true meaning.

Wind as Adversary. Wind can picture adverse forces of many kinds. Job, trying to articulate his sense of the disaster that has so quickly overtaken him, describes a *storm suddenly arising in the *night, an east wind that snatches up and sweeps off a man who had gone to bed wealthy and happy. Anyone who has struggles against literal storm winds knows this malicious wind that "hurls itself against him without mercy . . . claps its hands in derision . . . hisses him out of his place" (see Job 27:19-23 NIV). The wind becomes personified here as a cruel *enemy intent on destruction.

Winds can picture many kinds of adversity: an *army of *horsemen that advances "like a desert wind" (Hab 1:9, 11 NIV); *sins, which sweep us away like the wind (Is 64:6); any kind of adversity tempting us to disobedience and disbelief, as in Jesus' story of the wise and foolish *builders who build their *houses on the *rock and on the sand. The storm, with its winds that blow and beat against those houses, symbolizes adversity that would spiritually uproot the foolish person who does not hear and obey the Word of God (Mt 7:24-27).

Sometimes a house does not fall with a great crash; sometimes it just shifts with the wind. The wind by nature comes and goes, first from one direction and then from another. Its variability suggests the changeableness of ideas and people not rooted in the Word of God. Paul longs for the Ephesian Christians to be no longer infants "blown here and there by every wind of teaching" (Eph 4:14 NIV). James compares the one who doubts to "a wave of the sea, blown and tossed by the wind" (Jas 1:6 NIV). According to Jude, false *teachers in the *church are "clouds without rain, blown along by the wind" (Jude 12): unstable and unsatisfying, they will bring no good. Back in the OT, the prophet Hosea describes changeable *Israel as feeding on the wind (Hos 12:1): first it tried to please Assyria, and then *Egypt, instead of staying true to its God.

Positive Images. Winds in Scripture are more positively portrayed in pictures relating to God, the One who made and rules the winds. The power and supremacy of God emerge in the picture of him soaring on the *wings of the wind (2 Sam 22:11; Ps 18:10; 104:3). The wind here appears as one of God's creatures, perhaps a great *bird with wings that can reach across the sky, but in any case one made to serve at the command of its Creator. The Bible pictures God as the Master of the winds: he keeps them in his "storehouse," and only by his *authority do they emerge and blow where he sends them (Ps 135:7; Jer 10:13; 51:16). The winds again take living shape and become "messengers" sent out by God to "do his bidding" (Ps 104:4; 148:8).

God's bidding is often *punishment and destruction. Jeremiah prophesies the coming *judgment for *Jerusalem as "a scorching wind from the barren heights in the desert" sent from God, who now pronounces his judgment against them (Jer 4:11-12 NIV). In fact, Jeremiah looks up and catches a vision of God himself advancing like the *clouds: "his chariots come like a whirlwind" (Jer 4:13 NIV). In many passages the wind becomes a vivid image of God's wrath (Ps 11:6; Jer 18:17; 30:22; Ezek 13:13).

Winds also picture the comprehensiveness of God's judgment and supremacy. The Bible contains references to *four different winds: *north, *south, *east and *west. Each has certain distinct characteristics. The east wind, for example, as we have seen, most often blows a *dry, scorching wind from the desert. But to picture all the winds together emphasizes the totality of God's sovereign dominion. When God announces through Jeremiah, "I will bring against Elam the four winds from the four quarters of the heavens," he is announcing the comprehensiveness of his power and of the punishment he is delivering (Jer 49:36 NIV). When God promises to scatter his enemies "to the winds," he means to show the wideness and completeness of that scattering (Jer 49:36; Ezek 5:12; Zech 2:6). When Jesus speaks of gathering his elect "from the four winds, from the ends of the earth to the ends of the heavens" (Mk 13:27 NIV), we can be certain that in his comprehensive *wisdom and power he will not overlook one of his own, in all the realm of the living and the dead. When Ezekiel prophetically announces the word of the "Sovereign LORD" in the *valley of dry *bones, he announces God's comprehensive power over death and life, the very *breath* (the Hebrew word can also mean *wind*) of life: "Come from the four winds, O breath, and breathe into these slain, that they may live" (Ezek 37:9 NIV).

Jesus taught that the Spirit of God gives life, spiritual life. "Flesh gives birth to flesh, but the Spirit gives birth to spirit" (Jn 3:6 NIV). Using a metaphor full of *beauty and mystery, Jesus went on to picture this Spirit in terms of the wind, which blows where it pleases, unpredictably, according to the hidden plan of God. He comprehensively controls the four winds, even bringing through them the breath of life. He comprehensively controls the wind of his Spirit as well, bringing new life to "everyone born of the Spirit" (Jn 3:8).

See also BREATH; CLOUD; HOLY SPIRIT; STORM; WEATHER; WHIRLWIND.

WINDOW

Windows are mentioned in the Bible relatively few times. As openings in *houses from which people see out and view the world, windows connote knowl-

edge and vision, as well as an avenue of contact with the world beyond one's house. When set in the outer *walls of a *city, they present a way of *escape from danger.

The Bible speaks of windows incidentally as people look out of them and interpret what they see. For Noah, opening the window of the *ark at the end of forty days represents a reestablishment of contact with the outside world of nature (Gen 8:6). Abimelech, king of the *Philistines, looks down from a window and sees that Isaac is not Rebekah's brother (Gen 26:8). Having watched David through a window as he *dances before the *ark of the covenant, Michal despises him (2 Sam 6:16). In Proverbs the narrator pictures himself as looking out a window and observing the *seduction of a naive young man by a sexual adventuress (Prov 7:6-7).

In other passages, looking out of windows implies eagerness to receive an expected piece of news from the outside world. A motif in ancient martial literature is women's looking out a window in anticipation of the *return of their warriors with spoils (Judg 5:28; cf. 2 Kings 9:30). Looking *in* through a window can also be a picture of eager anticipation: as the *bride in *Song of Songs fantasizes about the arrival of her groom for the *wedding, she imagines him as gazing in the windows of her house in eagerness (Song 2:9).

Another cluster of images makes the window a vehicle of stealth and the intrusion of unwelcome visitors. Joel describes an *army of *locusts coming "like thieves" through windows (Joel 2:9). "Death," the prophet laments, "has climbed in through our windows" (Jer 9:21 NIV). Perhaps this last reference reflects a well-known scene in an Ugaritic religious text. The god Baal fears his rival Mot (Death) and so instructs the divine craftsman, Kothar-waHasis, not to place windows in his new house. The latter apparently does not follow these instructions, because Mot captures and destroys Baal in this version of the dying-and-rising-god myth.

Windows that offer a way of escape from danger represent God's deliverance of his people. Rahab helps the spies escape from Jericho by a rope from her window. The scarlet cord in the window saves her life (Josh 2:15, 18, 21) and recalls the *Passover blood on Israelite *doors in Egypt (Ex 12:7). Michal helps David escape from Saul by letting him down through a window (1 Sam 19:12). Such stories reveal how completely those who escape must depend on help from another. Paul tells how he was "lowered in a basket from a window in the wall and slipped through [the governor's] hands" (2 Cor 11:33 NIV) as an example of God's power in his *weakness. The window of escape symbolizes human dependence on God's grace and *salvation.

Elsewhere movement out of a window is a picture of *death. The lavishly adorned Queen Jezebel, probably dressing (like Cleopatra) for her death, looks out her window at the arrival of the new *king (her *enemy) Jehu, who asks her eunuchs to throw her through the window to her death (2 Kings 9:30-33). The window is also an image of hazard for Eutychus, who sinks into a deep sleep and falls from the third story while Paul is preaching (Acts 20:9). Paul is able to restore him and comfort the people who picked him up dead.

Windows open toward *Jerusalem demonstrate *Daniel's *faith in the God of Israel and prove his defiance of Darius's decree. Risking the den of *lions, Daniel goes to "his upstairs room where the windows opened toward Jerusalem" and *prays (Dan 6:10 NIV). Daniel's prayer conforms to Solomon's petition at the *temple dedication: "if they . . . pray to you toward the land you gave their fathers, toward the city you have chosen and the temple I have built for your Name; then from heaven, your dwelling place, hear their prayer and their plea, and uphold their cause" (1 Kings 8:48-49 NIV). Daniel's windows point toward the *city central to Israel's faith and hope (Ps 137:5).

In some passages windows imply luxurious *beauty of architecture. Jeremiah pronounces woe against wealthy kings who build a great house with spacious upper rooms and have windows cut for them (Jer 22:14). More positively, windows appear repeatedly in Ezekiel's vision of the restored temple (Ezek 40-41).

Figuratively, the *eyes are the windows of the soul, and so the Teacher describes one trait of old age: "Those looking through the windows grow dim" (Eccles 12:3 NIV). A window is part of the pattern of symbolism when Elisha, on his deathbed, orders Jehoash to open the *east window and shoot his arrows, each a victory over his enemies (2 Kings 13:17).

A final motif is the mysterious windows of *heaven, lost in many modern translations to "floodgates of heaven." In the KJV the "windows of heaven" open so God can pour out *rain (Gen 7:11) or a *blessing that there is not room enough to receive (Mal 3:10). During a siege, a skeptical lord questions Elisha's *prophecy of *food: "if the LORD would make windows in heaven, might this thing be?" (2 Kings 7:2 KJV). The reference in the flood story may have a cosmological backdrop (see Cosmology). The ancients pictured the firmament as a vast, hard-shelled dome with openings through which God's benevolent *providence allowed fructifying waters to drip or (as on the occasion of the flood) pour (see Cosmology).

See also DOOR; GATE; HEAVEN; HOME, HOUSE; WALL.

WINDSTORM. See WHIRLWIND; WIND.

WINE

In the ancient Near East, with its scarcity of *water, wine was a necessity rather than a luxury. It therefore easily became an image of sustenance and life. Isaac's *blessing over Jacob is that God may "give you of heaven's dew and of earth's richness—an abundance of grain and new wine" (Gen 27:28 NIV). The lover of Solomon's song uses this sustaining nature of wine as a foil for her declaration that "your love is better than wine," with the additional connotation that the beloved's *kisses are more intoxicating (emotionally) than wine (Song 1:1-2 RSV).

Due to its close relationship to the ongoing life of the community, *wine* becomes, in association with *grain* and *oil*, a technical term for the *covenant blessings promised by God to Israel for *obedience and withheld by God for disobedience. These terms will often be found linked in texts relating their presence or absence to God's provision or punishment and to Israel's obedience or covenant breaking. The basis for this is found in the covenant blessings and *cursings of Deuteronomy 28—29. If Israel breaks covenant, they "will plant vineyards and cultivate them but . . . not drink the wine"; nations will be sent who will "leave you no grain, new wine or oil" (Deut 28:39, 51 NIV). The prophets continue the theme of wine as a sign of covenant blessing, in both its presence and its absence. Joel proclaims the *locust *plague a covenant curse with this phrase: "The fields are ruined, the ground is dried up; the grain is destroyed, the new wine is dried up, the oil fails" (Joel 1:10). God complains through Hosea that Israel "does not know that it was I who gave her the grain, the wine, and the oil" (Hos 2:8 RSV) and proclaims that as punishment "threshing floors and winepresses will not feed the people; the new wine will fail them" (Hos 9:2) but that upon *repentance he "will respond to the skies, and they will respond to the earth; and the earth will respond to the grain, the new wine and oil" (Hos 2:21-22 NIV).

It is not a surprising extension that wine as covenant blessing takes on eschatological imagery as well. *Abundance of wine becomes a stock prophetic image of eschatological blessing: "in that day the mountains will drip new wine" (Joel 3:18 NIV); "new wine will drip from the mountains and flow from all the hills" (Amos 9:13 NIV); "the LORD Almighty will prepare a feast of rich food for all peoples, a banquet of aged wine" (Is 25:6).

Alternately, wine also takes on the image of eschatological *judgment as a *cup poured out on God's *enemies or forced to be *drunk by them. Thus the image of God's blessing takes on also the imagery of wrath. To Jeremiah God says, "Take from my hand this cup filled with the wine of my wrath and make all the nations to whom I send you drink it" (Jer 25:15 NIV). Isaiah describes God's judgment as God making people drunk in his wrath (Is 63:6).

The fermentation of the wine opens the way for both positive and negative imagery. Negatively, wine can be abused and become a means to loss of *self-control. "Wine is a mocker and beer a brawler; whoever is led astray by them is not wise" (Prov 20:1 NIV); "old wine and new . . . take away the understanding of my people" (Hos 4:11-12 NIV); "do not get drunk on wine" (Eph 5:18).

Positively, wine becomes an important image of

*joy, celebration and festivity, often expressive of the abundant blessing of God. The presence of wine at the *wedding at Cana in John 4 is well known. The psalmist declares, "You have filled my heart with greater joy than when their grain and new wine abound" (Ps 4:7 NIV). The Preacher of Ecclesiastes encourages his readers, "Go, eat your food with gladness, and drink your wine with a joyful heart" (Eccles 9:7 NIV). Such imagery, along with that of eschatological blessing, informs Jesus' statement at the *Passover meal that "I will not drink again from the fruit of the vine until the kingdom of God comes" (Lk 22:18 NIV).

See also BANQUET; CUP; DRINKING; DRUNKENNESS; GRAPES; VINE, VINEYARD; WINEPRESS.

WINEPRESS

With fewer than two dozen references, the winepress is an evocative biblical image but not a major one. Physically, winepresses were *pits (Mt 21:33; Mk 12:1), either hewn out of *rock (Is 5:2) or lined with plaster, into which harvested *grapes were thrown and trampled to squeeze the juice out. The winepress was a place of *joy and singing, and God's silencing of this song is an evocative picture of his *judgment (Is 16:10; Jer 48:33). The winepress is also an image of *abundance, sometimes paired with the supreme archetype of abundance in the Bible—the *threshing floor (Num 18:27, 30; Deut 15:14; 16:13; 2 Kings 6:27; Hos 9:2; Joel 2:14). The person who treads the winepress but is not allowed to drink (Job 24:11; Mic 6:15) is a picture of pathetic deprivation.

The winepress sometimes becomes the site of an event or activity unrelated to the making of wine. During a time of oppression by the Midianites, Gideon beat out *wheat in a winepress to conceal what he was doing (Judg 6:11). As the Israelites pursued the Midianites, they killed the enemy captain Zeeb at a winepress (Judg 7:25).

As a metaphor (in contrast to the physical image) the winepress is a negative image in the Bible. Instead of accentuating the motif of *harvest, writers seize upon the trampling of the grapes that went on inside the winepress and associate it with destruction and judgment. Thus an invading army is compared to grape treaders in a winepress (Lam 1:15). Elsewhere the overflowing wine vat becomes a picture of a nation whose wickedness overflows (Joel 3:13).

All the foregoing references to the winepress pale when put alongside the terrifying winepress of God's wrath—his final destruction of evil and punishment of evildoers. We read about this in the *apocalyptic visions of the Bible, first in Isaiah 63:3, where God is pictured as treading the winepress alone in anger, trampling the wicked in wrath and staining his robes in the process. The climactic pictures are in the book of Revelation (Rev 14:19-20; 19:15), where the winepress is strongly identified with God's *anger against *sin and where in a surrealistic vision the wine vat flows with *blood instead of wine (Rev 14:20).

See also ABUNDANCE; BLOOD; GRAPES; HARVEST; JUDGMENT; THRESHING, THRESHING FLOOR; WINE.

WING

The ancient Near Eastern imagination was fascinated with winged creatures, as evidenced by examples in art and statuary of winged deities, monsters, sphinxes, humans and disks. Some of the same fascination is reflected in the Bible, where the primary meanings of the image are protection (based on wings' ability to cover), escape (based on the flight of birds) and spirit (inasmuch as winged creatures are beyond the limitations of gravity).

Literal and Figurative Meanings. The imagery of wings in the Bible is primarily figurative; in fact, references to the literal wings of *birds are striking for their scarcity. The creation account refers to "every winged bird" (Gen 1:21 NIV), and the story of the flood speaks of "every bird . . . with wings" (Gen 7:14 NIV). Similarly, the Mosaic laws regarding *sacrifices (Lev 1:17) and diet (Lev 11:21, 23; Deut 14:20) speak of winged creatures with technical precision. The Hebrew imagination was captivated by the spectacle of *eagle parents catching their young on their wings (Ex 19:4; Deut 32:11), the ease with which *doves can fly (Ps 55:6), the sheer strength and endurance represented by the wings of such birds as the ostrich and stork (Job 39:13), the hawk (Job 39:26) and the eagle (Is 40:31; Ezek 17:3, 7), and the domestic tenderness of mother hens protecting their young (Mt 23:37; Lk 13:34). All these references are based on close observation of nature that is a hallmark of the Bible throughout.

From time immemorial, time has been pictured as being winged, as have natural phenomena that move fast. Thus in the Bible we find references to "the wings of the wind" (2 Sam 22:11 NIV; Ps

Two men treading grapes in a winepress.

18:10; 104:3) and to "the wings of the dawn" (Ps 139:9 NIV), based on the sun's properties of "rising" from the horizon and moving across the sky during its daily cycle (alternately, the sun's rays make it "winged"). Again, if birds with wings can depart quickly, the wing becomes a natural metaphor for the transience of riches (Prov 23:5) and the human inability to recapture words that have been spoken (Eccles 10:20, reminiscent of Homer's "winged words").

The ability of birds to soar above earthly danger makes them an apt symbol of escape. The psalmist wishes for "the wings of a dove" that would allow him to "fly away and be at rest" (Ps 55:6 NIV), and the woman who gives birth to Christ in Revelation 12:14 is "given the two wings of a great eagle, so that she might fly to the place prepared for her in the desert, . . . out of the serpent's reach" (NIV).

Biblical prophets love to work with irony and parody, and we can see the impulse at work in references to wings. The way a mother bird uses her wings to cover her young—a positive quality—becomes an image of suffocation and involuntary containment in Jeremiah's picture of an eagle "swooping down, spreading its wings over Moab" (Jer 48:40 NIV) and over Bozrah (Jer 49:22). Isaiah has a similar prophecy of doom against Judah (Is 8:8). Usually the wing is an image of escape from earthly restraints; in this satiric parody the covering wing prevents escape.

The Wings of God. As we move beyond the world of nature, wing imagery becomes decidedly spiritual and otherworldly in import, beginning with the wings of God. The first reference is Genesis 1:2, where God is pictured as "hovering over the waters"; although wings are not specifically named, they are implied (as in Milton's famous image of God the Creator "brooding on the vast abyss / with mighty wings outspread" [*Paradise Lost* 1.20-21]). The primary meaning here might be fertility, based on the way mother birds keep eggs warm during gestation.

Elsewhere the wings of God are primarily an image of protection. Thus we find numerous references to being in "the shelter" of God's wings (Ps 17:8; 36:7; 57:1; 61:4; 63:7; Is 34:15), an image that no doubt arises from the familiar sight of mother birds protecting their young from the elements. Jesus picked up on the image to express his longing to save his Jewish compatriots (Mt 23:37; Lk 13:34). Even when God is not pictured as actually having wings, his protection and care are compared in simile to the protection of eagles' wings (Ex 19:4; Deut 32:11) or the wings of an unidentified parent bird (Ps 91:4).

In a category by themselves are two evocative references in the book of Ruth. Before Boaz realizes the role he will play in the redemption of Ruth's life, he expresses the sentiment "May you be richly rewarded by the LORD, . . . under whose wings you have come to take refuge" (Ruth 2:12 NIV). But the same root word appears when Ruth encounters Boaz at midnight on the threshing floor and urges him to claim her in marriage: "Spread your wing over your maid-servant" (Ruth 3:9 Anchor Bible; cf. Ezek 16:8, where the same image is used to signify God's betrothal to Israel). Here we get a glimpse into the range of meanings that cluster in the image of God's wings over his people, including *protection, redemption, favor and love.

A final cluster of images for the wings of God appears in connection with the two statuesque cherubim that hovered over the *ark of the covenant in the *tabernacle (Ex 25:20; 37:9) and the *temple (1 Kings 6:24, 27; 8:6-7; 1 Chron 28:18; 2 Chron 3:11-13; 5:7-8). Why wings? Probably because the more-than-earthly quality of birds in flight made the wing a symbol in ancient iconography for the spiritual, the numinous, the transcendent. A winged being is a spiritual being. In the NT the *Holy Spirit descended on Christ at his *baptism in the form of a dove (Mt 3:16; Jn 1:32).

The Wings of Spiritual Beings. The most numerous references to wings occur in the apocalyptic visions of the Bible, which sometimes are a virtual riot of the motion of winged creatures. We read about seraphs with wings (Is 6:2), cherubim with wings (Ezek 10:5, 8, 12, 16, 19), apocalyptic "beasts" with wings (Dan 7:4, 6), two mysterious women with "wings like those of a stork" (Zech 5:9 NIV) and "four living creatures" with six wings (Rev 4:8). Most impressive of all is the spectacle we find in Ezekiel's vision of "four living creatures" whose arrangement of wings is elaborately described (Ezek 1). The best thing to do with these references is simply accept them as pictures of supernatural reality, full of mystery and the otherworldly.

See also BIRDS; DOVE; EAGLE; MYTHICAL ANIMALS; PROTECTION.

WINTER. *See* SEASONS.

WISDOM

While the word wisdom strikes moderns as an abstraction, there is evidence that it was a living and palpable reality for the ancient imagination. Biblical wisdom is definable as skill for living, but by the time biblical wisemen have transformed it into images, it is more concrete than conceptual.

Old Testament Images of Wisdom. On the strength of some magnificent pictures in Proverbs 1—9, the most familiar picture of wisdom is probably that of the personified woman Wisdom. She is a commanding presence who summons people boldly and loudly in the most public places of a city—the *street, the *market, on top of the *walls, and at the city *gates (Prov 1:20-21). She is an alluring woman who builds a house and invites people to a lavish *banquet of food and wine (Prov 9:1-12). As an extension of this evocative feminine imagery, the "son" to whom the speaker in the book of Proverbs repeatedly addresses his instruction is urged to have a love affair with wisdom: "do not forsake her . . . love her . . . prize her highly . . . embrace her" (Prov 4:6-9, RSV).

Equally impressive is the imagery of the ancient and even divine origin by which wisdom is portrayed. The magnificent poem on wisdom in Job 28 highlights the motif. The poem unfolds in three parts: people's ability to find virtually everything that the earth contains (Job 28:1-11); contrastingly, the human inability to find the place of wisdom (Job 28:12-22); and, again in contrast, the ability of God to know the place of wisdom, with the logical result that the fear of God is wisdom (Job 28:23-28). The *encomium in praise of wisdom in Proverbs 8 reinforces the divine origin of wisdom by picturing it as a companion of God at the very creation of the world (Job 28:22-31).

In terms of sheer quantity of imagery, the dominant motif is value terms such as *jewelry and *wealth associated with wisdom. Sometimes the superior value of wisdom is directly asserted: "the gain from it is better than gain from silver and its profit better than gold" (Prov 3:14 RSV); "she is more precious than jewels" (Prov 3:15 RSV); "my fruit is better than gold, even fine gold, and my yield than choice silver" (Prov 8:19 RSV). Elsewhere the value of wisdom is pictured metaphorically as jewelry: it is an "adornment for your neck" (Prov 3:22 RSV), "a fair garland for your head, and pendants for your neck" (Prov 1:9 RSV), "a beautiful crown" (Prov 4:9 RSV) and "a precious jewel" (Prov 20:15 RSV).

Another pattern combines the motifs of success and *reward to convey a sense of the present benefits of wisdom in a person's life. We might note here a contrast to the imagery that is characteristically associated with *folly in the wisdom literature of the Bible, which pictures folly in terms of its destructive end or destiny: folly causes a person to be *lost (Prov 5:23), to end in *death (Prov 14:12; 16:25), to go like an *ox to its slaughter (Prov 7:22), to end up as a guest in the depths of Sheol (Prov 9:18), to be caught in a *trap (Eccles 7:26), to end up with a *thorn infested field (Prov 24:31) or a leaking roof (Eccles 10:18). These melancholy pictures of a self-destructive end are a foil to the robustly positive rewards of wisdom—rewards like "abundant welfare" (Prov 3:2 RSV), "vats . . . bursting with wine" (Prov 3:10 RSV) and "riches and honor" (Prov 3:16 RSV). Stated as a formula, "wisdom helps one to succeed" (Eccles 10:10 RSV). Whereas the path of folly is a downward slide toward destruction, the progress of wisdom is toward something better and better, as encapsulated in the proverb that "the path of the righteous is like the light of dawn, which shines brighter and brighter until full day" (Prov 4:18 RSV).

Another leading motif is the contrast between wisdom and folly. The motif of the two ways, for example, is an archetype in wisdom literature (see Path). Nearly three dozen proverbs in the book of Proverbs are comparative proverbs that contrast wise and foolish behavior. Within an implied context of conflict with its opposite, wisdom's role is to guard (Prov 2:11), deliver (Prov 2:12), save (Prov 2:16) and protect (Eccles 7:12) a person from folly and its destructiveness.

Another motif associated with wisdom is the need to *search for it and obtain it. We need to distinguish here between a pessimistic tradition within the Hebrew wisdom literature and an optimistic tradition.

The narrator in Ecclesiastes pictures the futility of searching for wisdom by purely human means. When he makes the attempt, he finds only vexation and sorrow (Eccl 1:12-18), and he discovers the elusiveness of wisdom, so that "however much man may toil in seeking, he will not find it out" (Eccl 8:16-17 RSV). But the book of Proverbs, which locates the beginning point of wisdom as fearing the Lord (Prov 1:7), is optimistic about the quest for wisdom, promising that those who search long enough will "find the knowledge of God" (Prov 2:1-5 RSV).

An additional feature of the imagery associated with wisdom is that the imagery roots wisdom thoroughly in the everyday, practical world of actual life. In the book of Ecclesiastes, wisdom and its rewards are located in the world of *eating, *drinking, toil, *marriage, *authority structures, log splitting, planting and investment. The book of Proverbs covers even more areas of life, from *farming to household management to the professions to finances to *sex to a *toothache. Again, therefore, we can see the resistance of the biblical imagination to reducing wisdom to an abstraction.

Christ as Wisdom. The imagery of wisdom plays an important role in the NT's depiction of *Jesus. The primary motif developed is that of God's wisdom personified, beginning with Proverbs 8, where Lady Wisdom calls out and speaks of herself as the one who was created by God at the beginning of his work (Prov 8:22), as his master *worker, present at God's side at the *creation of the world (Prov 8:30-31). This motif passes through later Jewish wisdom literature, particularly the Wisdom of Solomon and the Book of Sirach, before it finds its way into the NT. These apocryphal books develop the motif with the imagery of wisdom present at God's side, active in creation and taking up residence in Israel (closely associated with the law given at Sinai).

Jesus associates himself with divine wisdom in several passages in the Synoptic Gospels, and the theme is developed in the Fourth Gospel and epistles. When Jesus declares that "something greater than Solomon is here" (Mt 12:42; Lk 11:31), he is claiming to possess wisdom greater than *Solomon's. But the image of Jesus as a wise man is transcended when he says "wisdom is vindicated by her deeds," in apparent reference to himself (Mt 11:16-19; Lk 7:31-35). When Jesus identifies himself, along with the prophets and "apostles," as one of wisdom's envoys sent to Israel and met with hostile reception (Lk 11:49-51; Mt 23:34-36; cf. Prov 9:3-6; Wis 7:27), he is closely identifying himself with the very wisdom of God. A similar image of wisdom is evoked in Jesus' lament over *Jerusalem (Mt 23:37-39; Lk 13:34-35). And in Jesus' beckoning to the weary and heavy laden to come and take his yoke upon them (Mt 11:25-30), the imagery of wisdom lies close to the surface. The book of Sirach closes with wisdom beckoning the "uneducated" to "draw near to me . . . acquire wisdom. . . . Put your neck under her yoke and let your souls receive instruction" (Sir 51:23-27

NRSV). Jesus, in comparison with the burdens of the law codified in the "traditions of men," offers a *yoke that is "easy" and a burden that is "light." Heavenly wisdom is imaged as coming from above in Jesus' thanksgiving to God: "All things have been delivered to me by my Father; and no one knows the Son except the Father, and no one knows the Father except the Son and any one to whom the Son chooses to reveal him" (Mt 11:27; Lk 10:22 RSV). In the apocryphal book of Wisdom the wise man "professes to have knowledge of God and calls himself a child of the Lord . . . and boasts that God is his father" (Wis 2:13-16 NRSV). The context suggests an identification with divine wisdom, entrusted with the secret things of God and the task of revealing them (Prov 8:14-36; Wis 2:13, 16; 4:10-15).

In the prologue of the Gospel of John, Jesus is identified as the Word, the *logos*, that was "with God . . . was God . . . was in the beginning with God" and was active in creation (Jn 1:1-3 NRSV). For those attuned to the imagery of wisdom, the evocation could not be more forthright, and the well-known scene of wisdom choosing Israel from among all of the nations as her dwelling place is replayed as "the Word became flesh and dwelt among us" (Jn 1:14 NRSV). In Sirach 24 wisdom, who "came forth from the mouth of the Most High" and sought a resting place among the nations, is commanded, "Make your dwelling in Jacob, and in Israel receive your inheritance" (Sir 24:3, 8 NRSV). Wisdom obeys and takes up her dwelling in the "holy tent" and is "established in Zion" (Sir 24:10-12). But Jesus, the wisdom of God incarnate, is not known or recognized by "the world" or by "his own people" (Jn 1:10-11 NRSV).

Jesus as wisdom appears again in Paul, in an image spawned by Israel's wisdom tradition. When Paul writes that Christ is "the image of the invisible God, the firstborn of all creation" (Col 1:15 NRSV), he is clothing Christ with the imagery of a preexistent *Adam and of wisdom. In Sirach 24:3-4 wisdom is said to have "come forth from the mouth of the Most High" and "dwelt in the highest heavens" (NRSV), and in Wisdom of Solomon 7:25, wisdom is the "pure emanation of the glory of the Almighty . . . a reflection of eternal light, a spotless mirror of the working of God, and an image of his goodness" (NRSV). This imagery is picked up even more eloquently in Hebrews 1:2-3, where Christ is the one "through whom he also created the worlds. He is the reflection of God's glory and the exact imprint of God's very being, and he sustains all things by his powerful word" (NRSV). The motif of wisdom and its associated imagery was employed by Israel's sages and poets to search out the nature of the inner life of God and his powerful and eternal word. In the NT the story and imagery of wisdom is discovered as a garment ready made for the figure of Jesus.

See also ECCLESIASTES, BOOK OF; FOLLY; PATH; PROVERB AS LITERARY FORM; PROVERBS, BOOK OF; SOLOMON.

WIT. *See* HUMOR.

WITCH

The modern concept behind the English word *witch* does not entirely correspond to the practice of witchcraft in the ancient Near East. The modern concept has to do with a woman who gains power through a compact with the devil in order to cause injury to others. The point of correspondence between the ancient Near East and the English concept is the malevolence and the antisocial intent. Whereas religion—be it pagan, OT cultic or Christian—emphasizes group goals and sustenance of the whole community, *magic, in general, is individualistic. In the specific case of witchcraft it is explicitly antisocial in that it empowers and advances one individual at the expense of other individuals and of the community as a whole. Simon the magician was cursed by Peter because he was esteeming power for himself higher than the good of the people and the *glory of God (Acts 8:9-24).

The witch is one type of practitioner of magic. Magic differs from religion in that magic is manipulative while religion is supplicative. Magic might involve an appeal to God, but in a deviant way—being selfish, not being dependent, not making a humble entreaty. On the other hand, the practitioner might be directly violating the first commandment in one of two ways: (1) by making an appeal to another *god, acting on the assumption of pantheism or polytheism, or (2) by making a conscious appeal to *Satan or his *demons, which is treason—trafficking with the *enemy.

Paul says the Galatians were bewitched by someone (the Judaizers) and led away from the truth (Gal 3:1). Paul is saying that they were enticed by a perversion of the true gospel. Witchcraft advocates perverted *worship; witchcraft therefore is a direct affront to God. It is condemned along with *rebellion (1 Sam 15:23) and *idolatry (2 Chron 33:6; Mic 5:12; Gal 5:20; Rev 21:8). Jehu accused Jezebel of "harlotries and witchcraft," that is, of enticing Israel into idolatry and perverted religion (2 Kings 9:22). Through the prophet Nahum, God charged *Nineveh, the oppressor of his people, with the same crimes (Nahum 3:4).

In general, then, witchcraft represents a selfish lust for power, social malevolence and deviance from biblical worship. For this reason Exodus 22:18 tersely prescribes the death penalty for witches.

Incidentally, the woman of Endor is not called a witch in the text of the Bible. The title is used only in the headings and summaries of some versions, and it is as a result of these that the phrase "the witch of Endor" has entered into literature and common parlance. She is in fact a necromancer, one who specifically consults the spirits of the dead in order to predict the future, and not a witch in the broader sense of the term.

See also DEMONS; IDOL, IDOLATRY; MAGIC; SATAN.

WITCHCRAFT. *See* MAGIC; WITCH.

WITHIN. *See* INNER, INSIDE, WITHIN.

WITNESS

In modern Western societies there are three types of "witness": (1) a witness to a signature on a will or other document, (2) a witness to a crime or a major event and (3) a religious witness, someone who "testifies" to the truth he or she holds. All three senses are present in the biblical understanding of "witness," but they converge much more closely with each other.

The first (and basic) sense appears in the many passages in which God, other people, written documents, *heaven and *earth, and a whole range of objects are "called to witness" a commitment or agreement. Human witnesses observe Boaz's commitment to Ruth (Ruth 4:9-11) and Jeremiah's purchase of a field (Jer 32:10-12). Similarly, a small *flock (Gen 21:30), a heap of *stones (Gen 31:48), a specially constructed *altar (Josh 22:27-28), a large stone (Josh 24:27; 1 Sam 6:18) or heaven and earth (Deut 4:26; 30:19) can be summoned as "witnesses" to a commitment between people or between God and human beings. *God himself is frequently so summoned (e.g., Gen 31:50; Judg 11:10; 1 Sam 12:5; 20:23; Jer 42:5).

In all these cases, those summoned are witnesses to a possible *future* crime of noncompliance with the agreement: "May the LORD be a true and faithful witness against us if we do not act according to everything the LORD your God sends you to tell us" (Jer 42:5 NIV). The thought behind calling an inanimate object (usually something very long-lasting) to witness is that it *stands for* God's permanent memory of the words spoken (see Gen 31:48-50).

In his relation with Israel, God too calls things to witness: the Song of Moses (Deut 31:19) and supremely the *law (Deut 31:26), which was deposited in the "*ark of the testimony" as a permanent witness of the commitment Israel had made to obey it (Ex 25:16; 31:18; 40:21-22).

Under Israelite law witnesses were obliged to act if they saw a crime being committed. Here we move to the second meaning: the potential future crime is now a past reality. Because the whole nation was party to the agreement to obey the law, they were all technically "witnesses" and thus had to "bear witness" to the crime (e.g., Deut 13:8-9). Great emphasis is laid on the necessity of truthfulness (Deut 19:16-19; Ps 27:12).

*Israel the nation is thus a standing "witness" to the *covenant. Here we move toward the third meaning: " 'I have revealed and saved and proclaimed—I, and not some foreign God among you. You are my witnesses,' declares the LORD, 'that I am God' " (Is 43:12 NIV; cf. Is 44:8; 55:4). Here the thought is that Israel—like a long-lasting *rock—bears automatic testimony to the power and reality of the Lord.

All these thoughts come together in the NT concept of witness. John the Baptist bears witness to Christ (Jn 1:15, 19, 32-34). Those who simply benefit from the work of Christ become witnesses de facto, because they are filled with the Spirit (Jn 15:26-27; Acts 5:32). But the *disciples who actually saw the resurrection have a special status as witnesses, like the direct signatories to a will (e.g., Acts 1:22; 10:41; 22:15). Either way, such testimony may mean martyrdom: in the book of Revelation the Greek word for "witness," *martys*, is already taking on this further significance. The witnesses who testify to the saving death of Jesus may seal that testimony with their own death (e.g., Rev 6:9; 12:11; 17:6).

See also COVENANT; LEGAL IMAGES; MARTYR.

WOLF

Every locale, and therefore every people's literature, has its terrifying predators. Chief among them in the Bible is the wolf, which emerges from a dozen references as an *animal of particular ferocity. These terrifying creatures are "ravenous" (Gen 49:27 NRSV; Mt 7:15) and "savage" (Acts 20:29 NRSV). They devour (Gen 49:27), tear (Ezek 22:27) and "destroy" (Jer 5:6 NRSV) their prey, especially helpless *sheep (Mt 10:16; Lk 10:3; Jn 10:12; Acts 20:29). In real life these nocturnal predators lie low during the day and begin to prowl at evening (Hab 1:8; Zeph 3:3), and they have a reputation for gorging themselves (Zeph 3:3). These literal details present a heightened picture of *terror and ferocity, which provides the context for the revulsion that biblical writers and Jesus have toward evil people and institutions that they compare to wolves.

Who evokes these feelings of revulsion? Dishonest public officials do (Ezek 22:27; Zeph 3:3), so do false *prophets and false *teachers (Mt 7:15; Acts 20:29) as well as selfish religious leaders (Jn 10:12). The unbelieving world itself is like a wolf in its hostility to disciples of Jesus (Mt 7:15; 10:16; Lk 10:3). In all these instances the literal image helps to define the persons who are compared to wolves.

The heightened ferocity of the wolf in the Bible also informs the apocalyptic pictures of transformation in which the no-longer-predatory wolf lives with the *lamb, with both of them led by a *child (Is 11:6). Similarly, Isaiah pictures the wolf and lamb as feeding together, not hurting or destroying any creature on God's holy mountain (Is 65:25). The general import of these pictures is that in the coming millennium even the most ferocious and repulsive of predators will revert to the peaceful world of original innocence (Gen 1:30).

See also ANIMALS; LAMB; LION.

WOMAN, IMAGES OF

From the first chapter of Genesis to the final verses of Revelation, the Bible is filled with images of woman. At creation she shares the image of God. At the brink of the second coming she is the bride of the Spirit who joins in the invitation to the "come." From alpha to omega, the feminine in Judeo-Christian tradition is a high and holy concept, though no more so than its masculine counterpart. Some of the Bible's images of woman focus on her roles, and in this dictionary these are treated in separate articles on *wife, *mother, *daughter, *sister and *widow.

The background against we must understand biblical images of woman is that in the Bible, especially the OT, women do not have the same social rights and advantages as men. Property was inherited by *sons rather than daughters. Women had little legal power, and they were not allowed to divorce their *husbands. Women are mentioned in biblical genealogies only sometimes, and then only as sisters to the already-mentioned sons. Women are also given as wives to whomever their *fathers desired. For example, after an absence Samson returns to find that the father of his Philistine bride has given her to one of his friends; in compensation the father offers Samson her younger sister (Judg 15:2).

However, in God's economy women are treated with respect. In fact, when no sons are available to inherit their father's property, daughters are the next in line, as seen when God commands Moses to give Zelophehad's five daughters his *inheritance since they had no brothers (Num 27:1-11).

Woman in the Creation and Fall. In Genesis 1 the creation of humankind in the image of God is both male and female. Woman therefore at the very core of her being has the same spiritual essence as man, with the same potential for good or evil and equal dignity with man. Woman's being made in the image of God is reflected in the fact that later in the Bible God is sometimes portrayed as having qualities of woman as well as man. God carries Israel in his bosom "as a nurse carries the sucking child" (Num 11:12 RSV). Elsewhere God is portrayed metaphorically as midwife, seamstress, housekeeper, *nurse and mother (Ps 22:9-10; 71:6; 139:13; Is 49:15; 66:9, 13).

Genesis 2 presents a more elaborate narrative of the creation of *Eve, the "mother of all living." Eve was created as a companion to man, to share his work in the *Garden. This prelapsarian woman was a helper to *Adam, a creature of free will and responsibility, with the same obligations that fell on man. Made from Adam, Eve is "a helper fit for him" (Gen 2:18) and a wife who becomes "one flesh" with her husband (Gen 2:24), confirming one of the most basic of all facts regarding both woman and man—that they complement each other and are in some sense incomplete alone. The duality of humankind—its constitution as two sexes—is inherent in virtually everything that can be said about women and men.

Because of the first woman's susceptibility to the temptation of the *serpent, woman is often portrayed in the postbiblical tradition as more vulnerable than man. Her readiness to eat of the *fruit—because it was lovely to look at, good to *eat and the path to knowledge like God's—marked her in human thought as the means of man's fall and the source of the expulsion from the Garden. Out of that role came a path marked for her daughters for centuries—submission in *marriage and *pain in childbearing (Gen 3:16; 1 Cor 11:3; 14:34; Eph 5:22-23; Col 3:18; 1 Tim 2:11-14; 1 Pet 3:1-6). In the Bible, however, woman's picture is far from unrelieved bleakness: her love of *beauty, *food and knowledge did not disappear with the Fall. Though tainted, her delights continue to mark womankind.

The Virtuous Woman. The young girl, the unmarried woman or the virgin is usually pictured in the Bible as a particularly vulnerable creature. The *law of Moses protected her against *rape but not against sale into *slavery. Because women were not autonomous beings, every young woman was seen as a potential wife or *maidservant. The pictures of female beauty in the *Song of Songs testify to the very real love of physical beauty, but this is a rare case of such celebration (though a picture of resplendent feminine beauty emerges from the psalmist's prayer that the young women of Israel might be "like corner pillars cut for the structure of a palace" [Ps 144:12 RSV]). The physical appearance of most young women in the Bible is not subject to the kind of detailed attention we find in romantic tales, especially those of the Western tradition. Like the wife and mother, the young woman was cherished for her beauty, virtue and fidelity, as the example of *Ruth perhaps demonstrates most vividly.

A good wife, like Sarah, follows her husband, obeys and reveres him (1 Pet 3:6), bears his *child (though sometimes late and with angelic help) and proves a good *friend (perhaps even a *sister). *Mary the mother of Jesus adds to the picture: a godly woman, a devoted mother, a literal and metaphoric traveling companion to her husband. The most explicit portrait the Bible gives us of the ideal wife is the *encomium that concludes the book of Proverbs (Prov 31:10-31). Here we find a woman who is honored for her worthiness by her husband and children, supports her husband, governs household matters, is a tireless worker, is active in economic affairs, provides for the physical needs of the household, is active on behalf of the underprivileged of the community, is wise in her teaching and is "a woman who fears the LORD" (RSV).

These biblical images of the good wife have as their foil interspersed glimpses of the bad wife. A bad wife, like Rebekah, betrays her husband, plots against him and *tricks him into acting against his will. These subversive maneuvers are the actions of an angry subordinate with a rebellious spirit. The very worst kind of wife is Jezebel, a woman without scruples who leads her country and her husband into the worship of foreign gods; she fully deserves her violent death.

Because woman is the receiver of the seed and the nurturer of the child who provides the Jew much of his promise of immortality, the woman is cherished especially for her *purity and her fecundity. The patriarch's selection of a *bride and her fidelity to her husband are keys to her value. The greatest curse she can know is the *barren *womb. Realistically, her sons were to provide for her old age; without progeny she faced a destitute old age (Naomi, a widow who lost her sons, had reason to call herself "bitter").

Because women in biblical times were subordinate to men in power and economically dependent on them, the women whose portraits emerge most strongly are those who display unusual courage in rising above conventional roles. Paragons of courage include Jochebed (mother of Moses), Deborah, Jael, Ruth, Esther, Abigail (1 Sam 25) and Mary the mother of Jesus. The same social structure that made women less powerful than men also produced the archetype of the woman as sympathetic victim of male chauvinism. One thinks of Sarah's use as a pawn to protect Abraham's life as a traveler in foreign realms, the Levite's concubine abused to death (Judg 19:22-30), Hannah's trials as the barren wife of Elkanah (1 Sam 1) and Jephthah's daughter, made to suffer for her father's rash vow (Judg 11).

When considering the Bible's images of woman and man, we need constantly to remind ourselves that the conditions of ultimate spiritual worth are the same regardless of one's gender. The virtuous woman, whatever her female beauty and womanly roles, is virtuous primarily because she is godly. Biblical writers therefore warn against external beauty as a touchstone for womanly excellence (Prov 31:30; 1 Pet 3:3) and commend as the true standard "a woman who fears the LORD" (Prov 31:30) and "the hidden person of the heart with the imperishable jewel of a gentle and quiet spirit, which in God's sight is very precious" (1 Pet 3:4 RSV).

Wicked Women. The most frequently mentioned women in the OT are those who break the rules in some way, in either a positive or a negative sense. On the negative side we find women who tempt their husbands or lovers to do evil. Jezebel, whose name becomes synonymous with evil, is a powerful image of the woman without scruples, a prototype for Revelation's whore of Babylon. Usually the wayward woman is a foreigner who seeks to corrupt the Hebrew. Potiphar's wife, for example, tries to seduce the upright Joseph. Delilah, a *Philistine temptress, becomes a symbol of the corrupting power of lust. In the prophecy of Hosea the wicked wife who whores after foreign gods and foreign men becomes a symbol of the wayward Israelites. The writer of Ecclesiastes laments "the woman whose heart is snares and nets, and whose hands are fetters," claiming that he has not found a guiltless woman on this score among a thousand (Eccles 7:26-28 RSV; according to Eccles 7:28, men are only one-tenth of one percent better in this regard). In the book of Proverbs too, folly is sometimes personified as a loose woman who tempts men.

A major biblical archetype of the evil woman is the *adulteress, most vividly portrayed in the early chapters of Proverbs (Prov 2:16-19; 6:24-26; 7:5-27; 9:13-18). Yet the Bible springs some surprises on us even here. Hosea's wife Gomer is remembered less for her adulterous abandonment of her husband than for his redemption of her. Although the Mosaic law prescribed death by stoning for adulteresses, Jesus forgave a woman caught in adultery (Jn 8:1-11). The OT even contains an occasional positive portrayal of the adulteress. Examples include Tamar, who tricks her delinquent kinsman into marriage by disguising herself as a prostitute (Gen 38) and Rahab the prostitute who helped the Israelites enter Jericho (Josh 2). Modifications occur in the stories of Esther (who bathes and dresses up to change the king's mind) and *Ruth (who encounters Boaz on the threshing floor in a situation that is sexually charged, even though Ruth and Boaz behave themselves with romantic restraint). Even *Bathsheba, the very image of beauty and temptation, is not judged as evil. She is the reason that *David lied and murdered and wept. David is perceived as the guilty party and Bathsheba a lovely pawn in this tragic masculine game of lust and power. She wept with David at the death of their child and subsequently gathered herself together, married the king and pressured him to put her next son, *Solomon, in line as his heir. In the law of Moses adulteresses were to be stoned to death, but here we see one crowned queen.

A final category of wicked women is the domineering mother and shrewish wife (see Domineering Mother, Wife). The list of such females includes Sarah, Rebekah, the nagging wife of Proverbs, Job's wife, Jezebel and Herodias (Mk 6:14-29).

Warriors and Leaders. Warfare in the ancient world was a rather solidly man's world, but not without exception. Classical literature has its Amazons—martial women known for their physical strength and military prowess. The OT gives us a variation on the theme. Deborah leads an army (and a man) into a *battle whose most decisive feat is performed by another woman, Jael, who pounds a tent peg through the skull of the fleeing enemy captain (Judg 4—5). Jael does not win simply through superior physical strength (as male warriors typically do) but through *trickery (Judg 5:24-27), rather like Delilah's use of trickery to subdue a strong man while he slept.

Book 1 of Virgil's *Aeneid* includes an evocative scene of Queen Dido's masterful government of the nation of Carthage. While the Bible gives us no extended portraits of women as rulers, there are moments when we catch glimpses of a similar role for biblical women. The clearest example is Deborah, "a prophetess" who "used to sit under the palm of Deborah" as "the people of Israel came up to her for judgment" (Judg 4:4-5 RSV). Her wicked counterpart is Jezebel, the *queen wife of Ahab who wields inordinate power at court (1 Kings 16—21). Miriam the sister of Moses also fits the image of the strong woman who moves into a role generally reserved for men when she leads women in a victory song following battle (Ex 15:20-21). Miriam later grew weary of her role as follower and leader of the women, joining her brother Aaron as a rebel against the established authority of Moses, for which she was punished with temporary *leprosy (Num 12).

While the OT shows a patriarchal bias—a preponderance of space is allotted to the deeds of men rather than women—women are recorded, even if only once, as holding virtually every position that OT society afforded: prophet (2 Kings 22:14; Neh 6:14), judge (Judg 4:4), ruler (2 Kings 11:3), military deliverer (Judg 4—5), wise person and teacher (repeatedly in Prov 1—9).

Women as Lovers. One of the most prevalent images of women in the literature of the world is the romantic lover—sometimes the one who loves a man but more often the attractive subject of a man's affection. The example par excellence in the Bible is the Shulammite woman of the Song of Songs—ideally ardent in her love of her man, and herself "fairest among women." In another epithalamion the court poet says regarding the *bride that "the king will desire your beauty" as she is led to the king on the wedding day "decked . . . in many-colored robes" (Ps 45:11-14 RSV).

We catch glimpses of other beautiful women as well. *Esther was a beauty queen, taken into the king's harem as a candidate for queenship because she belonged to the category of "beautiful young virgins" (Esther 2:2 RSV), and after she had undergone a whole year of beautifying (Esther 2:12), "the king loved Esther more than all the women" (Esther 2:17 RSV). Esther's predecessor as queen was renowned for her beauty and "fair to behold" (Esther 1:11). Other women too are objects of male affection partly because of their physical beauty; examples include Sarah (Gen 12:14), Rebekah (Gen 24:16), Rachel (Gen 29:17) and Abigail (1 Sam 25:3). Bathsheba, object of David's sexual desire, was "very beautiful" (2 Sam 11:2).

Women as Contemplatives and Disciples. The Bible also gives us an image of women as people of superior spiritual depth and insight. The book of Proverbs portrays *Wisdom as a woman—Lady Knowledge, we might call her, sometimes portrayed as a strikingly attractive woman pursued with romantic ardor. Elsewhere in Proverbs the command to listen to a father's instruction is complemented by similar commands to heed a mother's instruction (Prov 1:8; 6:20).

Related to the wise woman is the contemplative. Anna is called a *prophetess, and it is said that she "did not depart from the temple, worshiping with fasting and prayer night and day"; when the infant Jesus was brought to the *temple, she recognized him as the promised Messiah (Lk 2:36-38 RSV). The contemplative Mary the mother of Jesus "kept all these things in her heart" when she saw and heard her youthful son's wisdom displayed in the temple (Lk 2:51 RSV). Mary the sister of Martha "sat the Lord's feet and listened to his teaching" (Lk 10:39 RSV).

In the NT a new image emerges with women as disciples of Jesus. We might note that in the days of Jesus and the early church, the roles and images of women changed from OT practices. Mary the mother of Jesus is portrayed as both mother and disciple, as Jesus rejects the simple blood relationship that would have kept his mother always in a maternal relationship to him. Thus when Mary continues to follow Christ to the foot of the *cross, then to the tomb and finally to the upper room after the ascension (where she is accompanied by "the women," Acts 1:14), we realize she has become more than a mother: she is a *disciple.

Mary and Martha, who appear to be single or widowed, are both disciples and friends of Jesus, eager to entertain him at Bethany, ready to discuss the afterlife with him, quick to seek his help when their brother dies. Here women are no longer valued for their beauty or their fertility. They are sisters of Christ. Jesus, who sought neither lover nor wife, allowed women to become his followers and helpers. The woman's body is not an object of horror for Christ (as it was in some forms of Judaism); he has no fear of touching and healing the hemorrhaging woman or defending the woman caught in adultery. Jesus knows the history of the woman at the *well (*see* Well, Meeting at the) but does not hesitate to instruct her in the faith (in the process breaking the taboo not only against a Jew's conversing with a Samaritan but also against a man's conversing with a woman in public). Jesus' imagery of women is consistently ennobling and affectionate, as in the incident of the *widow's mite (Mk 12:41-44) and his parables of the woman who finds a lost coin (Lk 15:8-10), the wise virgins who attend the messianic *banquet (Mt 25:1-13) and the widow whose persistence is rewarded (Lk 18:1-8). Jesus does not hesitate to compare himself to a woman when he weeps for Jerusalem (Mt 23:37), nor does he think the image of the bride too lowly to picture his union with his church.

The heroism of women in the passion narratives is noteworthy. Women followed Jesus to the cross and suffered alongside him. They accompanied the corpse to the tomb and prepared spices for embalming. They were both disciples (followers) and witnesses of the crucifixion. Women were also the first witnesses of the *resurrection.

Images of Women in the Early Church. Paul sees women as individuals—individuals who helped him or hindered him in the Lord's work, who sheltered him and counseled him. He also uses female imagery in his epistles, where he builds on the traditional marriage imagery that pictures the church as a kind of family, with Christ as the head and the church as his *bride. Paul also revisits OT female imagery, noting that much of the older Scripture points to the new revelation of truth in Christ. While noting that humankind's fall came by means of one woman—Eve—he also shows that humankind's redemption is possible through the woman Mary (Gal 4:4). And he proclaims that all are one in Christ, in whom "there is neither male nor female" (Gal 3:28 RSV). The author of Hebrews includes Sarah, Rahab and unnamed women in his roll call of faith (Heb 11).

Although Paul criticizes women in some of the churches (especially Corinth) for their behavior and dress, recommending greater decorum, his female correspondents are approached as fellow workers for the Lord, loved for their service, not for their roles as mothers or grandmothers. He calls them "helpers." In Romans 16 he mentions Phoebe, Prisca and Mary as "helpers" and "fellow workers." Priscilla is mentioned as both host and missionary (Acts 18:1-3, 18), as well as someone who took initiative (along with her husband) in correcting the theological errors of Apollos (Acts 18:26). Phoebe is a deacon (Rom 16:1), and Lydia a "seller of purple" who brought her household to Christ (Acts 16:14-15). Paul addresses them all as friends whom he admires. Paul also endorses the "Jesus tradition" of full equality in Christ (Gal 3:28), though his comments about the headship of the husband and submission of wives (Eph 5:22-23; Col 3:18) shows that spiritual standing does not obliterate gender and institutional differences between men and women.

Summary. The book of Revelation sums up the ambivalent image of woman found elsewhere in the Bible. On the one hand, we have woman as the mother of the Messiah (Rev 12:1-5) and the church (Rev 12:17). She is herself the spotless church, the bride of Christ (Rev 19:7-8; 21:2), the queen of heaven. But if woman is thus the image of humankind at its best, she is also an emblem of evil in the form of the terrifying whore of Babylon, drunk with the blood of the saints and martyrs, defiant against Christ (Rev 17—18). She is also Jezebel, calling herself a prophetess and beguiling Christ's servants to practice immorality (Rev 2:20-23). Much of the Bible's picture of women converges here—woman as mother, bride, temptress to apostasy, the figure of what is both best and worst in God's creatures. While some biblical images of women are gender-specific, the spiritual potential of women for good or evil is the same as it is for men.

See also BARRENNESS; BATHSHEBA; BIRTH; BIRTH STORY; DAUGHTER; DOMINEERING MOTHER, WIFE; ENDANGERED ANCESTRESS; ESTHER, BOOK OF; EVE; MAID, MAIDEN; MARY THE MOTHER OF JESUS; MOTHER, MOTHERHOOD; NURSE; PROSTITUTE; QUEEN; RAPE, SEXUAL VIOLENCE; RUTH, BOOK OF; SEDUCTION, SEDUCER, SEDUCTRESS; SISTER; VIRGIN, VIRGINITY; WIDOW; WIFE; WOMB.

WOMB

Womb in Scripture can refer to any place of origin, as in the psalmist's "womb of the dawn" which brings forth the *dew (Ps 110:3 NIV). The Lord asks Job, "From whose womb comes the ice?" (Job 38:29 NIV). The question means "Where did the ice come from originally?" and implies that no human process of reproduction could ever attain to the awesome,

original *creation of God, whose womb, figuratively speaking, brought forth our whole world.

Most often in the Bible *womb* refers to that place inside a *woman where a *child originates and develops. Most often as well, references to the womb involve the power of God at work in that unseen, mysterious place. The womb is the place of God's originating or not originating life, the secret workplace of the Almighty. It is God who knit him together in his mother's womb, the psalmist declares (Ps 139:13). And Isaiah calls the Lord, "your Redeemer, who formed you in the womb" (Is 44:24). The language brings to mind a picture of the Almighty God reaching down from heaven and with his own *fingers reaching into a womb to knit and delicately shape a new life into the form he desires.

It is God as well who denies life in the womb. The Lord had "closed" Hannah's womb, we read in 1 Samuel 1:5. This image of opening and closing comes often in relation to the womb, as if it were a room with a *door or a place that could be closed off. In Job's *suffering, he wishes that the "doors of the womb" had shut on him (Job 3:10 NIV). God sometimes closed wombs en masse, as in Abimelech's household (Gen 20:18). And only he can open, as when he remembered Rachel and "listened to her and opened her womb" (Gen 30:22). Such images of opening and closing communicate the inaccessibility of the place and power of creation. They give a glimpse of God's sovereignty and God's involvement with us as our Creator.

The other image often associated with the womb is *fruit, as in Deuteronomy, when Moses tells the people that the fruit of the womb will be *blessed if they obey and *cursed if they do not (Deut 28:4, 18). The image communicates first of all the process of *growth that culminates in maturity and separation from the source of life. But *fruit* also bears witness to the goodness and sweetness of life itself, a gift of God to be relished and enjoyed to the full. One of the evocative passages in the Bible is the statement that "the fruit of the womb" is God's *reward to people (Ps 127:3 RSV).

See also BARRENNESS; BIRTH; BIRTH STORY; ENDANGERED ANCESTRESS; MOTHER.

WOOD

It is difficult to imagine a world without wood. It is one of the most useful natural materials available to humankind. Except in the most arid deserts, wood is widely available. It is a material that can be used to fuel a *fire, to build a house or to make a variety of furnishings, tools, implements, *weapons, water craft, land vehicles, musical instruments and objects of *beauty. Depending on the quality of the wood, it can be cut, chopped, split, hollowed, angled, joined, pierced, carved, drilled, beveled, grooved, rounded, planed, sharpened, smoothed and polished. Today these and other tasks are frequently carried out with power tools, and wooden products appear without a trace of origin in our stores. We easily forget that although wood yields itself to many shapes and uses, for most of human history wooden products have represented not only sharp tools, skill and ingenuity, but also muscle, sweat, time and patience.

In the Bible we encounter the names of various *trees known for the quality of their wood. The cedar, cypress, juniper, oak, pine, poplar tamarisk, willow, myrtle and olive all had distinct properties and values, some for rough timber and some for more specialized uses. The fragrant and durable cedar was used extensively in Solomon's *temple. Cypress wood was prized for construction, shipbuilding, *idols, furniture and doors. The rapidly growing poplar was used for roofing and timber, the tamarisk for charcoal, the willow for practical but simple objects such as troughs, sieves and handles, and the richly grained olive for construction, household utensils and polished ornaments. This is but a sampling of the variety and uses of wood in the biblical world. The imagery of wood in the Bible builds on its varied uses and values. Several fields of imagery are dominant.

Tabernacle and Temple. Wood is a prominent building material in the plan and construction of the *tabernacle and the articles associated with it. The frames, crossbars and posts of the tabernacle are made of acacia ("shittim," KJV) wood, as were the *ark, the *altar for offering, the altar for *incense, and the *table for bread. Israelites who have acacia wood (as well as other materials for construction) donate them to the tabernacle (Ex 35:24), and artisans in *stone and wood are engaged in work on the Tabernacle and its furnishings (Ex 31:5; 35:33). Wood is one material called for by the heavenly blueprint given on *Sinai. It supports the superstructure of the tabernacle and forms the contours of its furnishings. Wood and worship are joined again in the construction of *Solomon's *temple, where choice woods are employed (Is 60:13). We read of cherubim (1 Kings 6:23), *doors (1 Kings 6:31) and door jambs (1 Kings 6:33) crafted from olive wood, flooring laid in planks of pine (1 Kings 6:15), and beams, roofing and paneling constructed of cedar from Lebanon.

So extensively is wood employed in the temple that it is proudly noted that "no stone was to be seen" (1 Kings 6:8-20). The quality and quantity of these woods is described in a manner suggesting richness befitting the palace of the King of Heaven (cf. 1 Chron 22:14; 29:2). The choice and aromatic wood of the cedar of Lebanon is so synonymous with the Solomonic temple that "Lebanon" becomes a metaphor for the temple and its glory (Ps 92:12-13; Is 60:13; Jer 22:23; Ezek 17:3, 12; cf. Sir 50:12). So it is no surprise that Ezekiel envisions the new temple with thresholds, *windows, galleries—everything—covered with wood (Ezek 41:16) and furnished with a wooden altar (Ezek 41:22).

Wood and Offerings. Wood is associated not only with the architecture and furnishings of worship but with the *fire of sacrifice. In the story of *Abraham and the sacrifice of Isaac, we find the wood cut by Abraham and carried by Isaac. And when Isaac is placed on top of the wood and the knife is in Abraham's hand, the tension of the story reaches its climax (Gen 22). Wood is a vital part of the sacrificial imagery of the OT, and the wood burned on the altar is repeatedly mentioned in Leviticus, though it is not described. We can well imagine the great quantities of wood that were cut, hauled, stacked and kindled during temple festivals, though the OT barely alludes to this reality (Neh 10:34; 13:31).

In a few OT stories the wood for a sacrifice is an object of interest: the wooden Asherah pole cut down by Gideon (Judg 6:26), the wood of the cart bearing the ark of the covenant (1 Samuel 6:14), the wood of the *threshing sledges and the *yokes of oxen used for the burnt offerings on the threshing floor of Araunah (2 Sam 24:22; 1 Chron 21:23), the wood arranged on Elijah's altar on Mt. Carmel, drenched with water and then consumed by fire (1 Kings 18). Wood is consumed by fire along with the sacrifice. It is the divinely appointed fuel for sacrifices and offerings that are to be burned before God, the catalyst and propellant for the sweet savor that ascends to heaven. It is an agent of the symbolic reversal of the human condition of *sin, *guilt and an unthankful heart.

Within the pages of the OT, wood is an ordinary material, a resource of the natural world that is put to holy purpose with little attention to its source or type. As to its purity or impurity, we only read that wood, along with cloth, leather and sackcloth, is rendered unclean by contact with a corpse (Lev 11:32) and must be purified (Num 31:20). Only cedar wood, along with scarlet yarn, hyssop and birds, is specially prescribed for a sacred rite, the cleansing of a *leper (Lev 14:4-6) or a "leprous house" (Lev 14:48-57).

Wooden Idols. If wood takes an honored place in the sanctuary and on the altar, and is even covered with *gold, it is never to be carved into the image of a *god and worshiped. In the context of Israel's worship, artistry and craftsmanship in wood is only for directing human hearts to worship God in his sovereign majesty and *glory. Like the trees of the field that clap their hands and sing, wood is to celebrate God's glory and not receive it.

The OT roundly condemns and ridicules wooden idols as the epitome of human *folly. The trajectory of this biblical *satire begins with Deuteronomy's warning against falling into idolatry and worshiping "gods of wood and stone, which cannot see or hear or eat or smell" (Deut 4:28 NIV; cf. Deut 28:36, 64; 29:17). The living, merciful and powerful God of Israel who has delivered his people from *Egypt is contrasted with pagan idols shaped of lifeless, dense, obtuse material, unresponsive to prayer and sacrifice. This satiric imagery has no time for whatever theology may have informed the pagan understanding of the relation between the idol and its spiritual reality.

It fastens its ridicule on the observable phenomena.

The imagery echoes in Hezekiah's prayer: the gods of the nations overthrown by the Assyrians were cast into the fire and consumed "for they were not gods but only wood and stone, fashioned by men's hands" (2 Kings 19:18 NIV; cf. Is 37:19). But Yahweh is the living God who will deliver. The prophets, particularly Isaiah, most memorably develop the imagery of a wooden idol. A man "selects wood that will not rot" (NIV) and looks for a craftsman to make an idol that will not topple (Is 40:20). A man cuts down a cedar or cypress or oak or pine. Half the wood he burns in a fire, preparing a *meal, roasting his meat, warming himself—all of these are good and fitting uses of wood—but the remainder is used for an idol! (Is 44:13-20). To the wooden god he bows down and says, "Save me; you are my god" (Is 44:17). "No one stops to think . . . 'Shall I bow down to a block of wood?' " (Is 44:19 NIV).

The irony is shocking if not comical and echoes through the prophetic texts, spinning off fresh nuances. "They say to wood, 'You are my father,' and to stone, 'You gave me birth' " (Jer 2:27 NIV). Israel has "committed adultery with stone and wood" (Jer 3:9 NIV). Israel wants to be like the nations, "who serve wood and stone" (Ezek 20:32 NIV). Belshazzar praises "gods of silver and gold, of bronze, iron, wood and stone, which cannot see or hear or understand" (Dan 5:4, 23 NIV). The wayward people of God "consult a wooden idol and are answered by a stick of wood" (possibly an oracular device such as lots; Hos 4:12 NIV). Israel's *apostasy is epitomized in the one "who says to wood, 'Come to life!' Or to lifeless stone, 'Wake up!' " (Hab 2:19 NIV). And the prophetic imagery is reborn in Revelation as the survivors of the sixth trumpet judgment are unrepentant and continue to worship "idols of gold, silver, bronze, stone and wood—idols that cannot see or hear or walk" (Rev 9:20 NIV), let alone save them from destruction.

Judgment. Wood with fire can also form an image of judgment. Isaiah speaks of Topheth, an idolatrous high place in the Valley of Hinnom outside Jerusalem, as a fire pit with abundant wood ready to be set ablaze by the Lord as the funeral pyre of the king of Assyria (Is 30:33). Or God can promise Jeremiah, "I will make my words in your mouth a fire and these people the wood it consumes" (Jer 5:14 NIV). For Ezekiel the people of Jerusalem are as a vine to any other wood, good only for the fire:

> How is the wood of the vine better than that of a branch on any of the trees of the forest? Is wood ever taken from it to make anything useful? Do they make pegs from it to hang things on? . . . As I have given the wood of the vine among the trees of the forest as fuel for the fire, so will I treat the people living in Jerusalem. (Ezek 15:2-6 NIV)

Ezekiel is to pile wood beneath a pot, heap it on and kindle the fire to cook the bones of a *sheep, for Yahweh too piles the wood high for the city of bloodshed, Jerusalem (Ezek 24:5-10).

For Isaiah, Assyria is only a wooden weapon of judgment in God's hand. Once God has accomplished his work in Jerusalem, he will do with Assyria as he pleases, and Assyria will not control God. An ax or rod or club does not wield or brandish the arm that swings it, and neither will Assyria swing the arm of God "who is not wood" (Is 10:15)

Gathering Firewood. Cutting and collecting firewood is a toilsome task even when wood is abundant. Viewed over the full course of biblical narrative, the *Sabbath is a day of rest that foreshadows the final day of rest when the toil of gathering wood will be no more. Its sanctity is shockingly underscored when a man found gathering wood on the Sabbath is put to death (Num 15:32-36). The image of an "alien" serving in Israel as a domestic servant is memorably evoked in the KJV wording of "the hewer of thy wood" and "the drawer of thy water" (Deut 29:11). The poverty and vulnerability of a *widow is epitomized as she gathers a few sticks to cook the last of her food (1 Kings 17:10-12). The good days, when families of means had domestic servants and when fuel wood was in plenty, serve as a backlight for images of judgment and affliction in which "wood can be had only at a price" (Lam 5:4 NIV), "boys stagger under loads of wood" (Lam 5:13 NIV) and children gather wood while fathers light the fire (Jer 7:18). But on the far side of judgment, Ezekiel envisions a day when Israel will have no need to gather wood from the fields or cut it from the forests, because abandoned and useless wooden weapons—shields, bows, arrows, war clubs and spears—will serve as fuel (Ezek 39:10).

Various Images. An assortment of images of wood is also found in the Bible. Leviathan (see Monster) is so mighty and awesome that he treats *iron like straw and bronze like rotten wood (Job 41:27). The everyday reality of wood fueling flames informs two proverbs on quarrelsomeness: "Without wood a fire goes out; without gossip a quarrel dies down" (Prov 26:20 NIV); "As charcoal to embers and as wood to fire, so is a quarrelsome man for kindling strife" (Prov 26:21 NIV). Particular woods evoke wealth and power. Cedar is a wood fit for kings, and so in the Song of Songs the lover sees her beloved splendidly escorted in a carriage of wood from Lebanon (Song 3:9). Tyre is imaged as a magnificent *ship constructed of the best woods: pine for timbers, cedar for mast, oak for oars and cypress for decking (Ezek 27:6).

But in the grading of material for building and craftsmanship, wood takes a place in the lower echelon. In Isaiah's vision of the new creation, the nations will bring to *Zion *gold instead of *bronze, *silver in place of iron, bronze instead of wood, iron in place of *stones (Is 60:17). Paul sees disreputable contractors building on the foundation for God's new temple; the work of those who build with gold, silver, costly stones, wood, hay or *straw will be revealed on the last day (1 Cor 3:12). In the context of a household, and in the household of God, wood is useful but common: there are vessels of gold and silver, but also wood and *clay; some for noble purposes and some for ordinary purposes (2 Tim 2:20).

Wood participates in an image of salvation when Noah's *Ark, constructed of gopher wood, saves his family and creatures from the Flood. Wood also serves as an image of reversal when *Moses casts wood into bitter water and makes it sweet (Ex 15:25), and when Elijah throws a branch into the Jordan and a lost axhead floats to the surface (2 Kings 6:1-7). In the prophecy of Ezekiel, Ephraim and Judah are represented by two sticks of wood that are miraculously joined into one stick representing the restoration of Israel. And although the NT does not overtly underscore the image of a carpenter's son dying on a wooden cross, it does present us with the image of Christ dying on a *xylon*, a word that can mean either "tree" or "wood" (Acts 5:30; Gal 3:13; 1 Pet 2:24). Christian tradition has rightly perceived and elaborated the image of "the wood" as a cruciform symbol of redemption but also of judgment.

See also ARK; BUILD, BUILDING; CROSS; FIRE; GOLD; IDOL, IDOLATRY; SACRIFICE; SILVER; STONE; TABERNACLE; TEMPLE; TREE.

WOOL

In view of the prominence of *sheep in biblical societies, the scarcity of scriptural references to wool (fewer than twenty) comes as a surprise. Three main categories can be found among these references.

It is obvious, first, that the chief use of wool was to make *cloth for *garments. In this regard it is regularly paired with *linen (Lev 13:48, 59; Deut 22:11) and flax (Prov 31:13; Hos 2:5, 9). Cloth made from wool gets a divided verdict in the Bible. On the one hand, the celebrated wife of Proverbs 31 makes garments from wool (as well as flax) for her family (Prov 31:13), and wool is an image of wealth to nations who have an abundance of it (1 Kings 3:4; Ezek 27:18). But garments made from wool are also a symbol of the transience of earthly securities (Is 51:8), and in Ezekiel's vision of reconstituted temple worship the vestments of the priests "shall have nothing of wool on them" (Ezek 44:17 RSV).

Wool is used, second, as a touchstone of *whiteness, sometimes with associations of transcendence. As something white, wool is paired with *snow three times: it is a picture of the purity that remains after God has cleansed the "crimson" of sin from a person (Is 1:18); as the color of the *hair of the Ancient of Days in Daniel's vision, it suggests age as well as purity (Dan 7:9); and it is part of the dazzling effect of Christ as envisioned by John (Rev 1:14).

There is, finally, a miscellaneous category of references. Gideon's fleece of wool (Judg 6:37) used to elicit a sign from God is proverbial to this day; his choice of wool for this supernatural sign was based on wool's absorbent quality. The whiteness of wool makes it an apt simile for the color of the snow that God sends (Ps 147:16). And we look on with admiration as the industrious wife of Proverbs 31 "works with willing hands" as she weaves cloth from wool (Prov 31:13).

See also CLOTH; LINEN; SHEEP, SHEPHERD; SNOW; WHITE.

WORD. *See* BIBLE; WISDOM.

WORK, WORKER

Paul Minear once wrote that the Bible is "an album of casual photographs of laborers. . . . A book by workers, about workers, for workers—that is the Bible" (Minear, 33). This is an apt summary of the images of work and worker and we find in the Bible.

God as Worker. In contrast to Greek mythology, where the gods live a life of celestial loafing, the Bible pictures God himself as a ceaseless worker. His first great work was the work of *creation (Gen 1). Although that work exudes the delight of the creative artist in doing what he enjoys, it is nonetheless work rather than *leisure, as suggested by Genesis 2:2, which tells us that "God finished his work which he had done, and he rested on the seventh day from all his work which he had done" (RSV). The concept of work that emerges from Genesis 1 is that it is purposeful, creative and above all "good." God's work of creation provides a model and sanction for human work, and by involving the material world it leads us to understand that human work in the physical sphere is likewise good.

God's work as Creator is extended in Genesis 2 to a more *providential plane. Here God "formed man of dust from the ground" (Gen 2:7 RSV), planted a *garden for him (Gen 2:8), watered the garden (Gen 2:6) and fashioned a *wife for the man (Gen 2:21-22). In short, God, the provider for human life, works incessantly. So too in later times: Psalm 104:10-22 gives us a picture of God as cosmic caretaker of the creation; Psalm 121 tells us that God neither slumbers nor *sleeps but is always busy protecting people; Psalm 107, a psalm that catalogs some of God's acts of *rescue, claims that God is known "for his wonderful works to the sons of men" (Ps 107:8, 15, 21, 31 RSV). The psalms of praise ring the changes on the extent of God's praiseworthy work in the world—work that occurs chiefly in the four arenas of *creation, *providence, *judgment and *redemption.

In the NT, Christ too is a worker. He is a carpenter until the age of thirty. During his public ministry he speaks repeatedly of his work. His *food, he tells his disciples, was "to do the will of him who sent me, and to accomplish his work" (Jn 4:34 RSV). On another occasion he says, "We must work the works of him who sent me" (Jn 9:4 RSV). He tells the Jews, "My Father is working still, and I am working" (Jn 5:17 RSV).

"The God of the Bible," Minear aptly notes, "is preeminently a worker" (Minear, 44). Robert Banks explores some of the specific images of God, including composer and performer, metalworker and potter, *garment maker, gardener, *farmer, *shepherd, tentmaker and *builder.

As an extension of the picture of God as solitary worker, we have pictures of God as coworker with people. A key text is Psalm 127:1: "Unless the LORD builds the house, those who build it labor in vain" (RSV). Implied is that God works through the human worker. A similar picture emerges in Psalm 90:16-17, which combines the prayer that God's work will "be manifest to thy servants" and the wish that God will "establish . . . the work of our hands" (RSV). When the *wall of *Jerusalem was rebuilt under Nehemiah's direction, Nehemiah offered a double assessment of his success: the work was accomplished with dispatch because the people "had a mind to work" (Neh 4:6 RSV), but the work was also "accomplished with the help of our God" (Neh 6:16 RSV).

Human Work. The first image of human work

Two Egyptian women at work weaving (c. 2000 B.C.).

in the Bible stresses its perfection. Work existed in the time of human innocence in paradise, as the Protestant Reformers never tired of pointing out. The notion of work as part of God's perfect design for human life is captured in the majestic simplicity of Genesis 2:15: "The LORD God took the man and put him in the garden of Eden to till it and keep it" (RSV). Here human work is shown to have worth and dignity as a service to God and as something that gives purpose to human life. Work is here a creation ordinance, a God-appointed necessity for human life. This view of work as part of natural law is implied also in Psalm 104, where in a celebration of the natural rhythm of day and night we read that by day "man goes forth to his work and to his labor until the evening" (Ps 104:23 RSV). Work, in other words, is much a part of the natural order as the rising and setting of the *sun.

The second concept of human work that we encounter in the Bible is work as toil, the result of the Fall. This picture of work emerges from the very curse that God pronounces on Adam in Genesis 3:17-19, where the dominant images are a ground that is cursed, *thorns and thistles as something with

which people have to contend, and the *sweat with which one must perform labor in a fallen world. Several motifs are important here. We note first that work does not originate with the Fall, as is often and erroneously claimed. The Fall neither cancels God's command to work nor does it introduce work into the world. What is new is work as a curse and as toil—something that must be accomplished against the hostility of the environment. W. R. Forrester's formula is that "man was meant to be a gardener, but by reason of his sin he became a farmer" (Forrester, 130).

The image of thorns and thistles suggests a further dimension of the curse of work—that in a fallen world a lot of work consists of undoing rather than creating and constructing. Part of the curse of work in a fallen world is its frequent fruitlessness (see Deut 28 for an extended portrait of the curse of fruitless work). Finally, we should note that in the story of the Fall *woman's *pain in giving *birth (Gen 3:16) parallels the curse on work (Gen 3:17). The Hebrew word for toil and pain in these verses is the same, and Forrester notes that "in language after language the same word is used for toil and child-bearing, e.g., 'labour' and 'travail' " (Forrester, 129).

A third idea of work in the Bible is the redemption of work in a fallen world. Here we find pictures of work as having some of the qualities that it possessed in its unfallen state. The prophecy of Isaiah, for example, paints a picture of a coming golden age in which work will have the fruitfulness and enjoyment it possesses in its ideal state (Is 65:21-13). Among the details in the vision are people's enjoying "the work of their hands" and not laboring "in vain" (RSV).

The book of Ecclesiastes can serve as a fitting summary for biblical images of human work. If life is lived only at ground level ("under the sun"), work is a terrible toil, "vain" and empty, a mere striving after wind (Eccles 2:18-23; 5:16-17; 6:7). But in the God-centered passages, which offer a blueprint for finding enjoyment in life, one of the repeated images of enjoyment is human work, accepted as a gift from God (Eccles 2:24; 5:18-19; 8:15; 9:10).

People as Workers. The foregoing section has explored how the Bible pictures work itself. Here we find the principles underlying human work in the world. A remaining topic is the worker—people who work.

The primary biblical image for the person who works is the steward—someone who works with possessions that a master has entrusted to him or her. In the background is the biblical doctrine of *calling or vocation. On this understanding, God is the One who calls people to their tasks and roles in life. To follow God's call to labor in the ordinary tasks of life is to serve him. The classic passage on workers as stewards of God is Jesus' parable of the talents (Mt 25:14-30), but the image itself aptly summarizes a general tenor of scriptural teaching about people as workers for God. An important aspect of the biblical image of workers as stewards is that ultimately they are working for God rather than people (Eph 6:5-7; Col 3:23-24).

Related to workers as stewards is the biblical rejection of any sacred-secular dichotomy for work. All work is potentially sacred in the sense that people can serve God through it (and not simply *in* it, incidentally). Although Paul is called to be an apostle, he remains a tentmaker to earn his livelihood. Paul could have become a professional cleric but refused to do so (1 Cor 9:3-18; 2 Thess 3:7-9). Alan Richardson notes that in the Bible "daily work, so far from being a hindrance to Christian living, is a necessary ingredient of it" (Richardson, 36-37).

Workers, on such a view, hold an honorable position. The dignity of common work in the Bible is established not so much by specific proof texts as by the general picture of life that emerges. As we read the Bible we find a veritable gallery of people engaged in the ordinary work of life. Many biblical characters are known to us by their occupations. We read about soldiers, *chariot drivers, *garment makers, *farmers, merchants, homemakers and judges. We see King Saul not only as a *king but also as a farmer plowing with his *oxen in the field (1 Sam 11:5). His successor, David, begins life as a *shepherd (Ps 78:70-72) and never fully outgrows his agrarian roots (Ps 23; 144:12-15). Abraham is a nomadic shepherd as well as a spiritual pilgrim. We find lists of people who mix the spices and make the flat cakes for worship in the temple (1 Chron 9). Jesus' parables are a virtual survey of occupations in his society.

In the Bible no stigma is attached to being a worker. On the contrary, it is an expected part of life. Hence we find Paul's injunction that Christians should "be ready for any honest work" (Tit 3:1 RSV). The Bible presents no hierarchy of occupation.

Summary. The Bible's images of work and workers show a noteworthy range. Overshadowing them is the twofold image of God as himself a worker and as the Master of the world who delegates work to people as his stewards. For people, work is a paradox. It is good in principle, as well as a necessity of life. In its most positive forms it is creative, enjoyable and purposeful. But it is also toilsome, often unproductive and a curse. In either case, though, it is the arena within which the worker serves God.

See also FARMING; LEISURE; MARKETPLACE; SABBATH; SWEAT.

BIBLIOGRAPHY. R. Banks, *God the Worker* (Sutherland, Australia: Albatross, 1992); W. R. Forrester, *Christian Vocation* (New York: Scribner's, 1953); P. S. Minear, "Work and Vocation in Scripture" in *Work and Vocation,* ed. J. O. Nelson (New York: Harper & Brothers, 1954) 32-81; A. Richardson, *The Biblical Doctrine of Work* (London: SCM Press, 1952); L. Ryken, *Redeeming the Time: A Christian Approach to Work and Leisure* (Grand Rapids: Baker, 1995).

WORLD

The NT writers build on both Jewish and Greek language traditions when writing of the world. The Greeks provided the word *kosmos,* which has become a technical term in Western tradition. By the first century this word was used to convey a complex range of meaning. The dominant sense of an ordered system had applications to areas other than *cosmology. In the NT the *kosmos* is sometimes understood as planet earth but also, in a wider sense, as the universe. In this latter sense it has the same meaning as the OT "*heaven and *earth" (Hebrew, *haššāā̄mayim wᵉhā'areṣ*), meaning the *creation. Translators of the Greek version of the OT (LXX) had no cause to use the term *kosmos* because the natural translation for the Hebrew of "heaven and earth" is *ouranos kai gē,* and the OT has no single word which covers the same semantic area as *kosmos.* The Synoptic Gospels show a preference for the use of *gē* ("earth"), while in the Gospel of John *kosmos* is the preferred term (78 times).

Two other expressions relate to what we mean by "world" and overlap the Greek use of *kosmos.* The first of these is *oikoumenē,* which is short for *oikoumenē gē* and was used in the LXX to translate Hebrew *tēbēl.* In the poetic works of the OT, *tēbēl* is frequently used in parallel with *'ereṣ* ("earth"). By the time the Gospels were written, *oikoumenē* had come to mean "the inhabited world" which was sometimes considered to be coterminus with the Roman empire (*see* Rome). The second word is *aiōn,* which was used to translate the Hebrew *'ōlām.* Both the Hebrew and the Greek words have a reference to *time, but when used in the expression "this age" they have substantially the same meaning as "this world."

World as "Age" (Gk *aiōn;* Heb *'ōlām*). In the Synoptic Gospels the world is conceived as a temporal reality with beginning and end. Beyond that it can also be a new world, "the age to come" in contrast with "this age," expressions that are found on the lips of Jesus. In Paul the present age is *evil (Gal 1:4), being ruled by the "elemental spirits of the world" (Gal 4:3, 9; Col 2:8, 20), "the rulers of this age" (1 Cor 2:6; cf. Jn 12:31), "the god of this age" (2 Cor 4:4), "the prince of the power of the air, of the spirit now working in the sons of disobedience" (Eph 2:2), the "devil," "rulers," "powers," the "world rulers of this darkness," the evil spiritual powers in heavenly places (Eph 6:11-12). "This age" may also have the sense of "the present time" (Rom 3:26; 8:18; 11:5; 2 Cor 6:2; 8:13) and "the present age" (1 Tim 6:17; 2 Tim 4:10; Tit 2:12). This age/world is evil and opposed to God. It has a hostile character. It is opposed to God just as the *wisdom of the world is opposed to the wisdom of God. God chose the *foolish, the *weak and the despised, and even those considered non-entities according to this world, which turn out to be the wisdom and power of God in the fulfillment of his purpose (1 Cor 1:18-28; 2:6-13; 3:18-19; 4:9, 13). This age is ruled by spiritual powers, and to it, fallen, unredeemed humanity belongs (1 Cor 1:20, 21, 27, 28; 2:12; 3:19;

5:10; 6:2; 11:32; 2 Cor 7:10; Gal 4:3; 6:14; Eph 2:2; Col 2:8, 20) and needs to be *redeemed (Rom 3:6, 19; 2 Cor 5:19).

For Paul the notion of the coming age, explicit in Ephesians 1:21; 2:7 and implicit in Romans 8:18-25 and 1 Corinthians 15:20-28, implies the fulfillment of God's purpose in creation when evil and corruption will be overcome. Christ is present and active in both the *creation and *reconciliation of "all things" (Col 1:16, 20.).

World as "Earth" (Gk *gē*; Heb *ēre*). Each of the four Gospels uses the word *earth* to mean "soil," a particular *"land" and planet "earth," though the latter sense is rarely found in John. It is evident in the phrase "heaven and earth," in which the OT spoke of creation, an idiom familiar to Jesus and found in each of the Synoptics but not in John. Sayings which have reference only to the earth can be ambiguous because the word can mean "soil" and "land" as well as "planet earth." Paul in Romans 9:17 (Ex 9:16) uses *gē* ethnically, not of planet earth (cf. Rom 9:28; Is 1:9) as it is in the phrase "heaven and earth" (1 Cor 8:5; Eph 1:10; 3:15; Phil 2:10; Col 1:16, 20; implied in Col 3:2, 5), the Jewish idiom for the whole creation. Heaven represents the realm of God and earth the sphere of human activity.

World as the "Inhabited World" (Gk *oikoumenē*; Heb *tēbēl*). *Oikoumenē* is used only fifteen times in the NT of which Luke is responsible for eight (five in Acts and three in the Gospel). It is used once in Matthew 24:14 in the context of the Markan apocalyptic discourse to assert that before the end comes this gospel of the kingdom must first be preached in the whole inhabited world. Here Matthew's use of *oikoumenē* is an interpretation of Mark's "all the nations" (*ta ethnē*, Mk 13:10). In the *temptation of Jesus, where Jesus is shown all the kingdoms of the world, Luke uses *oikoumenē* (Lk 4:5) to bring out the political sense in a way that Matthew's use of *kosmos* (Mt 4:8) does not. Luke 2:1 refers to the decree to tax "the whole world," in other words, "the entire Roman empire." And in Luke's version of Jesus' apocalyptic discourse, Jesus warns of men fainting with fear and foreboding of what is coming on the inhabited world (*oikoumenē*, Lk 21:26). In Paul's letters the extensive nature of the world is expressed in Romans 10:18 (Ps 19:4) where "to the ends of the world [*oikoumenēs*]" is a parallel image of "to every land [*gē*]."

World as "Cosmos" (Gk *kosmos*). In John's Gospel and first letter of John we find more than half of the uses of the Greek term *kosmos* in the NT. Paul uses *kosmos* forty-seven times, of which twenty-one uses occur in 1 Corinthians. In the Synoptic Gospels we find Jesus asking what value there is in gaining the whole world and losing life itself (Mk 8:36 par. Mt 16:26 and Lk 9:25). Jesus says that wherever the gospel is preached in the whole world the details of his anointing will be spoken of (Mk 14:9 par. Mt 26:13).

The foundation of the world (katabolēs tou kosmou)

or *beginning of the world (archē tou kosmou)*. Jesus speaks of "the blood of all the prophets shed from the foundation of the world" (Lk 11:50; cf. Mt 23:35). And in the Fourth Gospel, Jesus asserts the Father's love for him "before the foundation of the world" (Jn 17:24; cf. Jn 17:5; *see* Foundation). In the parable of the great *judgment the king tells those on his right hand, "inherit the kingdom prepared for you from the foundation of the world" (Mt 25:34). The "beginning of the world" (*archē tou kosmou*) has the same meaning (Mt 24:21). The Markan parallel has, "from the beginning of the creation" (*ap archēs ktiseōs*, 13:19). In Ephesians 1:4 the plan and action of God is envisioned "before the foundation of the world" (*pro katabolēs kosmou*).

The world of humanity. The expressions "nations of the world" (*ta ethnē tou kosmou*, Lk 12:30; *see* Gentiles) and the "kingdoms of the world" (*hai basileiai tou kosmou*, Mt 4:8), like the references to the *kings of the earth and the tribes of the earth (Mt 17:25; 24:30), refer to the world of humanity. The disciples are told by Jesus, "you are the salt of the earth" (Mt 5:13) and "you are the light of the world" (Mt 5:14). In Hebrew this parallelism might have been expressed using *ere* and *ēbēl*. And in John's Gospel, Jesus claims, "I am the light of the world [*kosmou*]" (Jn 8:12; 9:5). In the parable of the tares it is explained that the field is the world (Mt 13:38). Woe is pronounced on the world of humanity (Mt 18:7). This reminds us that this world, though the creation of God, is dominated by the demonic (*see* Demons). The world is under the power of evil and needs to be liberated by God, and so Jesus' inaugurates the kingdom of God through exorcisms (*see* Demons): here is the evidence that the present world ruler has been overthrown and that the kingdom of God is already dawning (Mk 3:20-30; Mt 12:2 par. Lk 11:20).

James, 2 Peter and 1 John identify the world (*kosmos*) as people at enmity with God, those who oppose God's will and purpose. James asks, "Do you not know that friendship with the world is enmity with God?" (Jas 4:4). Therefore a Christian is "to keep oneself unstained from the world" (Jas 1:27). 2 Peter describes the world as the place where antagonism toward God dwells, and believers must escape its "defilements" (2 Pet 2:20).

Distinctive usages in John's Gospel and Letters. John's prologue (Jn 1:1-18) provides a detailed reinterpretation of the Genesis creation story. A Jewish understanding of creation is daringly reinterpreted in the light of faith in Jesus as the Savior of the world. Here the *kosmos* is first the universe, the totality of the creation: "All things were made by him and without him was not anything made that was made" (Jn 1:3). There is a notable dualistic framework in John, with references to "this world" (planet earth) and "the judgment of the prince of this world" (Jn 12:31; 14:30; 16:11). This world is not contrasted with some future world. Rather, the world below is contrasted with the world above, the world of *darkness with the world of *light. This world, though created by the Word, is ruled by the prince of this world. Even though the Fourth Gospel does not show Jesus exorcizing demons, Jesus' struggle with the prince of this world is a central feature further accentuated by the prominent antithesis of light and darkness in this Gospel.

Jesus, the emissary from above, has come into this world (Jn 1:9, 10; 3:16, 17, 19; 6:14; 10:36; 11:27; 12:46; 16:28; 17:18, 21, 23; 18:37). His mission is an expression of God's love for the world (Jn 3:16). This world is dominated by darkness and the prince of this world. And the world in view is humanity. The coming of the emissary was to save, not to condemn the world (Jn 3:17; 4:42; 6:33, 51; 12:47), but condemnation is inevitable where the saving mission is rejected (Jn 9:39). The coming of the emissary is expressed in terms of the coming of the light into the world as the light of the world (Jn 3:19; 8:12; 9:5; 12:46). The light does not belong to the world (Jn 8:23; 17:16; 18:36) but has come to reveal the Father and his love for the world (Jn 14:31; 17:21, 23, 24). His coming was to bring life to the world (Jn 6:33) by giving his life for the world (Jn 1:29; 6:51). Having entered the world and completed his mission, the emissary departs from it (Jn 13:1; 14:19; 16:28). But first he commissions his disciples to continue his mission to the world (Jn 17:21, 23). Those who are called out from the world (by the emissary) and no longer belong to it (Jn 15:19; 17:6, 11, 14, 16) are consequently hated by it, as the emissary himself was hated (Jn 15:18, 19; 17:14). The mission was made possible by the coming of the Paraclete/Spirit of Truth (*see* Holy Spirit) to expose the world to the truth revealed by the light (Jn 3:19-21; 16:8). Yet the world does not recognize the Spirit, just as it did not recognize the emissary. It knows only the mission of Jesus and those who continue his mission. Only those who believe perceive the light of the world which has the power to transform those who belong to the world so that their lives are shaped by the light from above.

In John the focus moves from the world perceived as creation to the world of humanity dominated by the darkness of false loves, false values, false knowledge and to the mission to save the world. Much of this interpretation of the world is given in the words of the narrator (Jn 1:9, 10; 3:16, 17, 19) or other characters such as John the Baptist (Jn 1:29), the Samaritans (Jn 4:42) and the crowd (Jn 6:14) in addition to Jesus himself.

In 1 John we also find a sharp dichotomy between two sides. God and the world are diametrically opposed, and believers must choose between them. The world is apostate from God, and John urges full loyalty to God: "We know that we are of God, and the whole world is in the power of the evil one" (1 Jn 5:19); "they are of the world, therefore what they say is of the world and the world listens to them" (1 Jn 4:5). Believers are not to "love the world or the things in the world. If anyone loves the world, love

for the Father is not in him" (1 Jn 2:15). They sho not be perplexed that the world "hates" them (1 3:13). Sinfulness originates from and belongs to this world and is to be avoided (1 Jn 2:16-17; cf. 1 Jn 4:3-5, 9).

But as in the Fourth Gospel, there is hope for the world because Christ was sent "as the savior of the world" (1 Jn 4:14), and whoever has faith in him will be victorious in overcoming the opposition of the world (1 Jn 5:4-5). 1 John uses "world" sometimes in a sense that encompasses the entire sphere of people outside the church. This is how false teachers can be identified: they no longer side with the church but "have gone out into the world" (1 Jn 4:1). Since they are "of the world" they no longer should be heeded or trusted (1 Jn 4:5; cf. 2 Jn 7).

See also COSMOLOGY; EARTH; KINGDOM OF GOD.

WORM

It is hard to put a good face on a worm. Throughout history and across cultures this creature has been quite consistent in its ability to stir up emotions of disgust. Biblical references are uniformly negative, as the worm appears in contexts of *disease, *decay, *torture and the dehumanizing of people.

As an image of decay, worms are linked with putrid materials. When some of the Israelites disobeyed the command not to leave any *manna overnight, the manna thus stored "bred worms and became foul" (Ex 16:20 NRSV). There is no more repulsive *death recorded in the Bible than that of the arrogant Herod, struck by an *angel of the Lord and "eaten by worms" (Acts 12:23 NRSV). Job in his desolation claims that his flesh "is clothed with worms and dirt" (Job 7:5 NRSV). To render the decay of corpses in the earth vivid, several passages include the detail of worms feeding on the flesh (Job 21:26; Is 14:11; 51:8). In another form of destruction, worms destroy *trees or *vines (Deut 28:39; Jon 4:7).

As image of minimal life, the worm sometimes represents people reduced to something less than human (Job 25:6; Ps 22:6; Is 41:14). *Wormwood* is also synonymous in the Bible not only with decay but also with bitterness (approximately ten references). Finally, the worm that never dies is an image for the *torment of *hell (Is 66:24; Mk 9:48).

See also DEATH; DECAY; HELL.

WORMWOOD. *See* WORM.

WORSHIP

Worship is homage; it is an attitude and activity designed to recognize and describe the worth of a person. In Jewish and Christian practice, worship is properly reserved for the divine person revealed in the canonical Scriptures. There is, however, an inescapable tension in worshiping the God revealed in the Hebrew Scriptures. *God is transcendent and cannot be seen (Ex 33:17-23); he has no form that can be represented in physical terms (Deut 4:11-19), and his majesty is such that one may not approach him (Ex 19:12-13, 21-22, 24). Yet this transcendent God desires to be intimate with his people, both collectively and individually. The worship of such a God requires an understanding of how such intimacy may be possible; the essence of theology is to know God, while the forms and activity of the worship of this God are expressions of that theology. The imagery of worship must express both holiness and intimacy. For so large a task, the imagery encompasses movement and setting in worship.

The Goal of Liberation. There is a second tension in worship images: between worship of the true God and *idolatry, or worship of false *gods. The forms of worship are the same in both cases, and we might say that the desire to worship stems from a shared conviction regarding the power of the forms of worship. But worship of the true God requires freedom from dependency on other gods. In order to serve God in worship, one must be free from service to other things.

This motif can be traced if we observe the use of the Hebrew '$\bar{a}bad$/$^{a}\underline{b}\bar{o}d\hat{a}$, or "worship"/"serve" vocabulary in the English Bible. The theme of Israel's going out into the wilderness to worship ($^{c}\bar{a}bad$) God appears in one way or another in Exodus 3:12; 4:23; 7:16; 8:1, 20; 19:1, 13; 10:3, 7, 11, 24, 26; 12:31. This is in contrast with the Israelites' condition in Egypt—slavery ($^{a}\underline{b}\bar{o}d\hat{a}$, Ex 2:23) in the "house of slavery" ($b\hat{e}t$ $^{a}\underline{b}\bar{o}d\hat{a}$, Ex 13:3, 14; 20:2). This small-scale example demonstrates the link between freedom from slavery and the ability to worship. On a larger scale, liberty is promised where the Spirit of the Lord resides (2 Cor 3:17), so that believers are free to offer themselves in service to God (Rom 12:1). Thus the proper motivation for freedom is to be able to worship God.

The Movement of Worship. *Worship* is first and foremost a verb, an action. It is motivated by a desire to honor another. The Bible includes a wide range of physical movement and expression in its images of worship, including bowing down, lifting hands, clapping hands, dancing, processions and singing.

In keeping with the idea of worship as homage, we find that *bowing low is a prominent indicator of worship. Bowing down is equated with worship in the Ten Commandments and other places (Ex 20:5; 23:24; Lev 26:1; Deut 5:9). Bowing to other gods, to nature or to "the work of your hands" is punished as idolatry (Mic 5:13; Zeph 1:5). Bowing down is a part of the ritual of *sacrifice (Deut 26:10; 2 Kings 17:36). It is a position of listening, of ready *obedience. Holy ones bow down at the feet of God and receive instruction (Deut 33:3). Enjoined as part of the invitation to worship (Ps 95:9), bowing down is a position proper to entering the house of God (Ps 5:7; 138:2). The instruction passages of Scripture clearly commend the posture.

Stories couple *kneeling with verbal confession in worship. When David knew that Solomon had become king, in thanksgiving he "bowed in worship on his bed" (1 Kings 1:47 NIV). Job responds to news of his family's death by "[falling] to the ground in worship" and confessing the sovereignty of God to give and take away (Job 1:20 NIV). Daniel and his three friends are commanded to "fall down and worship" the image of Nebuchadnezzar; their silence and refusal to bow are punished by furnace fire, though to no avail (Dan 3:11). The apostle Paul includes a speech confession with physical kneeling in worship (Rom 14:11; Phil 2:10). Finally, the Bible tells stories about a future day when all the world's nations will recognize God's rule; at this time "every knee will bow" (Ps 22:27; 72:9, 11; Is 45:14, 23; Is 46:2, 6-7, 23; Rom 14:11; Phil 2:10). Reverence appropriate to the majesty of God is expressed in this action.

Jubilation joins reverence in other actions of worship. Miriam and the Israelite women worship God for his faithful deliverance at the Red Sea by *dancing before him (Ex 15:20); David likewise celebrates the return of the ark (2 Sam 6:16). The psalmist leads worship by instructing the people to "praise his name with dancing" (Ps 149:3 NIV) and to "praise him with tambourine and dancing" (Ps 150:4 NIV). Clapping hands indicates great joy at the blessings and provision of God (Ps 47:1; 98:8; Is 55:12). Lifting one's hands is recommended in the worship of God: "lift up your hands in the sanctuary and praise the LORD" (Ps 134:2 NIV; also Ps 28:2; 119:48; Lam 2:19; 1 Tim 2:8). The psalmists' Songs of Ascent (Ps 120—34) join other instances of processions in worship (Neh 12; Ps 24; 68). Musicians, singers and choirs also contribute to the worship of God (Neh 12; Ps 150). Even *eating can be part of expressing reverence for God, as in the case of observing *Passover (Ex 12:18). These actions make up part of the worship of God; they symbolize externally an internal attitude of devotion and enthusiasm to honor God.

Finally, the action of extravagant sacrifice and the burning of *incense are integrally linked to worship. At the dedication of the temple "twenty thousand cattle and a hundred and twenty thousand sheep and goats" were offered to God (1 Kings 8:63). Many instructions are given concerning the symbolic sacrifices of *animals in the OT *tabernacle, as well as the constant fragrant offering of burned incense.

But it is the obedient sacrifice of human lives to the purposes of God that stands out as the pinnacle of worship through sacrifice. *Abraham foreshadows God's sacrifice by being willing to sacrifice his *son Isaac to honor God; he is credited with great faith for it (Heb 11:17). NT believers are instructed to model the temple by sacrificing all of themselves as an act of worship to God (Rom 12:1). But in this they only follow Christ's example as a sacrifice for the whole world; his extravagant sacrifice remains prominent throughout the NT (Rom 3:5; Eph 3:2; Heb 9:26, 10:5-10; 1 Jn 2:2; 4:10). Paul rejoices to be a scant addition to the sacrifice of Christ, to be "poured out like a drink offering on the sacrifice"

(Phil 2:17 NIV). The pulse of worship for the church consists of sacrifice as well, "a sacrifice of praise—the fruit of lips that confess his name" (Heb 13:15 NIV). Sacrifice bridges the important space between actions of worship and their setting because it is both. Like other actions, it indicates a willing *heart, and with the temple details it pictures active obedience.

Settings for Worship: Temple and Sacrifice. There is a central imagery of worship within the progression of worship forms in the Hebrew Scriptures. This imagery concerns the way the presence of God is understood and how the approach to him is expressed. The central revelatory event concerning the proper worship of God is in the *theophany at Mt. *Sinai; here the relationship with God is established in the *covenant, which shows how the presence of God is known and by which forms he may be approached in worship. This revelation of God is anticipated in the story of the patriarchs; the presence of God is experienced in theophanies in which God makes his covenant promise (Gen 15:1-21) or affirms it (Gen 18:1-18; 28:10-21), and the altar serves as the means of expressing worship to God (Gen 12:7-8; 13:3-4; 26:24-25; 35:1-7).

The theophany at Mt. Sinai fulfills the covenant promise God made to the patriarchs, and it reveals the theological significance of the name Yahweh (Ex 6:3-4). The fundamental significance of this name is to be found in the continual presence of God established in the covenant at Sinai (Ex 3:12-14). This covenant provides for the perpetual representation of the presence of God and develops the forms of his worship, particularly the significance of the altar. This is continued in the eventual building of the temple as a permanent structure representing the presence of God in the nation. It is continued further in the postexilic period with the rebuilding of the temple and its function in a totally different social and political circumstance. These vast differences in the circumstances of worship are presented in the Scriptures as having a theological continuity in the provisions for approaching a holy God.

The theophany of God at Mt. Sinai is manifested in the *glory *cloud that appeared as a *storm with *thunder and *lightning (Ex 19:16). This revelatory event and the ceremony of the covenant is related in Exodus 19:1—24:8; however, the revelation is continued at length in the making of provisions for the continual representation of the presence of God. This presence is to be represented in the tabernacle. The instructions for the *priests (Ex 25:1—31:11) conclude with the *sabbath as a sign of the covenant (Ex 31:12-17) and the statement that all these things were revealed when God wrote the tablets of stone (Ex 31:18).

The tabernacle structure is completed according to the instructions (Ex 35:1—40:33), and the glory cloud seen at the *mountain descends upon it (Ex 40:34-35); it is the sign of the presence of God with the people always (Ex 40:36-38). The sacrifices for the function of the tabernacle are then described (Lev 1:1—7:38), and in conclusion it is noted that this was a part of the revelation of Sinai (Lev 7:37-38). The book of Leviticus continues with other elements of the tabernacle function, such as the ordination and function of priests (Lev 8:1—10:20), the symbolism of holiness in regulations of *purity (Lev 11:1—16:34) and regulations for practical *holiness (Lev 17:1—27:34). In each of these units "that which Yahweh commanded Moses" (cf. Lev 7:38) is a repeated refrain, especially at the beginning or the conclusion of a key section (Lev 8:4-5, 36; 16:34; 17:2). Leviticus concludes with references to the forty days at Mt. Sinai in the development of the sign of the sabbath (Lev 25:1), in the conclusion of covenant blessings and cursings (Lev 26:46) and in the conclusion of the final chapter on the redemption of votive gifts (Lev 27:34).

The whole of the tabernacle and its function, both the forms and the times of worship, are integrated as part of the covenant at Sinai in prescribing the continued worship of God. Each part of the ritual has significance only as a part of the whole; the whole is an expression of the presence of God as experienced at Mt. Sinai. It expresses majesty and power like that in the storm at Sinai and testifies to the presence of God in the midst of an unholy people.

The tabernacle and the rituals of homage express the holy transcendence of God and the need for cleansing for those who worship him. The significance of these is not explicit in the lengthy details of the covenant instructions.

The tabernacle or temple structure has the general features of temples in Egypt, Mesopotamia and Canaan. Courtyard temples as that of Arad (tenth to eighth century B.C.) are similar to those of the Ur III period of Mesopotamia (c. 2050-1950 B.C.), consisting of an interior courtyard and a broad room. Within the latter was a niche in which a symbol of the deity was kept, which served as a holy of holies. This type is still found in the Ninmach Temple of Nebuchadnezzar in Babylon (604-562 B.C.). In the Jerusalem temple the forecourt extended in front of the temple proper, forming a series of increasingly holy precincts. In this respect it bears a certain resemblance to the Egyptian temples such as that of Amenhotep III (1404-1366 B.C.), consisting essentially of an open forecourt, a covered hall of columns and the holy of holies, which is surrounded by various chapels. The Baal temple at Ugarit has the same features but is distinct in that the cella is not in line with the axis of the forecourt and vestibule. The main furnishing of the court was the altar that facilitated offerings made to the god. Temples represented the palace of the ruling god, and the rituals were part of the service performed for the god. The structure served both to create distance from the deity and to provide access to him.

The tabernacle or temple is the palace of Yahweh. The Hebrew word translated "temple" (*hêkāl*) simply means "palace"; the distinct meaning "temple" comes with a designation of the occupant. The palace of Yahweh is particularly distinct in the holy of holies, which is an enclosed cube at the far end of the principal chamber. In it we do find the features of a royal dais in the cherubim *throne, which was popular in Canaan and Phoenicia during the Late Bronze and Early Iron ages. The cherubim constitute the base and back of the throne, or even the entire structure; their composition of a *lion's body, *eagle's wings and a human head points to a union of the highest powers. Yahweh is said to be enthroned upon the cherubim (2 Kings 19:14-15; Ps 82:1; 99:1), who represent the throne of the formless God. The holy of holies, however, is enveloped in complete *darkness to shield the worshipers from the glory of the King (1 Kings 8:10-13).

The ark of the covenant constitutes the footstool of the throne (Ps 99:5; 132:7-8; 1 Chron 28:2), a constant reminder that access to God's presence in worship is possible only through the terms of the covenant. The holiness of God is further indicated in the tabernacle structure, which has a carefully itemized gradation of the worth of materials, the most precious representing the sanctity of the holy of holies. The furnishings of the throne room are of the finest metals, and the cherubim of the curtains are made in a special weave. These unique features of the palace give testimony to the holiness and majesty of the God revealed at Sinai.

Sacrifice is the central ritual associated with the temple. In other ancient temples the sacrifice represented a *meal or gift for the deity, so the altar was also a type of table. In Israel sacrifice serves instead to restore proper *order within the creation and to make worship possible. God and life are represented by the temple, while the Gentiles live outside in the arena of death and nothingness. The people of the covenant, who maintain the rules of purity which signify life and order (Lev 11:1—15:33), are the ones who may approach God. However, they may not approach him apart from the recognition that they also belong in the realm of death. The key element of sacrifice is the shedding of the blood by which offerers may make *atonement *(kipper)* for their lives (Lev 1:4; 4:20); the *ransom *(kōper)* appears to be a substitute for the endangered life (cf. Ex 21:30). Sacrifice is the means by which one may move toward life and holiness from the realm of death; it symbolizes restoration to a proper state of life in dependence on God. Direct contact of the mortal with the holy results in death; through the mediation of priest and sacrifice, however, there may be life. As part of an act of worship, sacrifice confesses both the holiness and the grace of the life-giving God.

The OT clearly recognizes that temple, sacrifice and all the special times of worship at the temple that give testimony to redemptive events (Ex 23:14-19) are images that express the worshiper's faith in giving homage to the sovereign God. What is required in worship is not sacrifice but obedience, the performance of the will of God (Ps 40:6-8) that men and women may be in right relationship with him. Obedience is the requisite for true worship, but not a substitute, for the rituals declare who people are in relation to God.

Worship Through the Incarnation. Jesus declares that he is the divine presence who takes the place of the symbolism of the temple. In declaring his authority over the temple, he responds to his challengers with the words "Destroy this temple, and I will raise it again in three days" (Jn 2:19 NIV). This enigmatic saying was understood after the resurrection to be referring to the temple of his *body (Jn 2:20-22). Jesus would then invite the worship of his *disciples (Jn 20:28-29). This would be the time when neither Samaria nor Jerusalem would be appropriate for worship, but proper worship of the transcendent God would be "in spirit and in truth" (Jn 4:23-24).

Jesus is recognized as being both the priest and the sacrifice (Heb 4:14-16; 10:1-10). Through the "veil" of his flesh we enter into the very presence of the throne room by means of the life-giving power of his blood (Heb 10:19-22). This is the worship of the new covenant, which renders that of the Sinai covenant old and obsolete (Heb 8:7-13). Christian worship is not that of Mt. Sinai but of Mt. *Zion, the city of the living God, the heavenly Jerusalem (Heb 12:18-24). The person of Christ, the redemption of his death and the worship of him are all expressed in terms of the familiar images of worship of the Sinai covenant; these vehicles reveal the significance of the person and work of Christ, whose redemption provides access to the worship of the God no one has seen or can see.

Christian worship expresses homage in terms of the redemption and divine presence of Christ. *Baptism, Lord's *Supper and prayer are the primary means by which this relationship to God is expressed. All of these have their roots in the former worship of the OT, but they have taken on a distinct significance. The water of purification had already been used by Ezekiel to signify renewal from sin and death, and the sign that God would instill his will within his people (Ezek 36:25-27). For the Christian, baptism becomes the sign of cleansing and a new life that makes possible the worship of God (Rom 6:3-9). Communion not only recalls the redemption of the Passover but gives testimony to life under the new covenant (Lk 22:19-20). Prayer is now made to Jesus, for he is one with the Father and does his works (Jn 14:9-12). He instructs his disciples to make petition in his name (Jn 14:13-14). The presence of Jesus will abide with his followers in the Spirit, who will continue the work of Jesus in the new age (Jn 14:25-26; 16:12-14). The presence of God abides, but without the old symbols; the worship of God is now in spirit and in truth.

The elements of worship, such as baptismal liturgies, the celebration of Communion, *hymns and prayers are preserved in the NT, but there is little indication of their liturgical setting—that is, the way these might form a worship service. The structure of worship services had little uniformity in early Christian worship. The concept that the temple represents God's presence as the body of the Lord Jesus was extended to include the gathered *church as his body, the temple of God. We are living *stones built up into a spiritual house, a holy priesthood, offering spiritual sacrifices pleasing to God (1 Pet 2:4-5). The gathering for worship is of the very essence of Christian faith and the representation of the presence of God. Those who may with boldness enter through the flesh of Christ into the holy of holies (Heb 10:20) must not neglect meeting together but must gather in worship in anticipation of the consummation of the *hope of being with Christ in inseparable glory (Heb 10:24-25). Worship will then have achieved its ultimate goal.

Heavenly Worship. A final repository of imagery of worship is the book of *Revelation, where worship is perhaps the central ingredient in heavenly ritual. Revelation 4 is an entire chapter devoted to the portrayal of worship. Elaborate attention is devoted to the transcendent setting of the worship and to the strange beings who conduct it. Worship occurs around the throne of God, and its keynote is praise of God's worthiness. Thereafter we find interspersed scenes that resemble this opening scene (Rev 5:6-14; 7:9-12; 11:16-19; 15:2-8). Much of the worship imagery in the Apocalypse draws upon OT references to temple worship and the theophanies of God (with imagery of thunder and lightning).

See also ALTAR; BOWING; CHRIST HYMN; FEAR OF GOD; FESTIVAL; GOD; IDOL, IDOLATRY; INCENSE; KNEE, KNEEL; LAMP, LAMPSTAND; MUSIC; OFFERING; PRAISE PSALMS; PRAYER; PRIEST; PURITY; SABBATH; SACRED SPACE; SACRIFICE; TABERNACLE; TEMPLE; THEOPHANY; WORSHIP PSALMS.

BIBLIOGRAPHY. D. Davies, "An Interpretation of Sacrifice in Leviticus," *ZAW* 89 (1977) 387-99; M. Douglas, *Purity and Danger: An Analysis of the Concepts of Pollution and Taboo* (London: Ark, 1984) 7-57; M. Haran, *Temples and Temple-Service in Ancient Israel* (Winona Lake, IN: Eisenbrauns, 1985); O. Keel, *The Symbolism of the Biblical World: Ancient Near Eastern Iconography and the Book of Psalms* (New York: Crossroad, 1985) 111-356; R. P. Martin, *Worship in the Early Church* (Grand Rapids: Eerdmans, 1975).

WORSHIP PSALMS

Worship psalms, also known as songs of *Zion (Ps 46, 48, 76, 84, 87, 121, 122), are defined by their context and content. They are occasional poems that celebrate various aspects of public *worship at the *temple—the Psalter itself is a temple collection—and their content accordingly focuses on the rituals of worship and the emotions of the worshiper.

The background against which the psalms of worship must be viewed is the pervasive awareness of the Israelites that God dwelt in the temple in Jerusalem. The *glory of God rested in visible form over the *ark of the covenant, and the Psalms have nu-

merous references to God's dwelling in the temple. Because of the presence of God in Jerusalem, the songs of Zion place conspicuous emphasis on the place of worship.

Another factor that helps to explain references in the psalms of worship is the institution of the *pilgrimage. Hebrew males were to go to Jerusalem a minimum of three times each year to worship. In fact, a grouping of fifteen psalms (Ps 120—134) bear the common heading "A Song of Ascents," meaning that these psalms were pilgrim songs sung or chanted en route to worship God in the temple.

The overall logic of the worship psalm is twofold: to express and awaken human longing to worship God at the temple, and to celebrate the joys of performing such worship. The songs of Zion paint minute pictures of the physical details of either the pilgrimage or the temple worship. A strong sense of place pervades these pictures (with God's miraculous protection of the holy city a motif in several of the psalms). God himself is exalted in these psalms, with stately epithets (titles) for God a common feature of this exaltation.

See also ENCOMIUM; LAMENT PSALMS; NATURE PSALMS; PRAISE PSALMS; PSALMS, BOOK OF; WORSHIP.

WOUND

Wound in the Bible usually refers to a bodily injury. Such injury may be received in combat (2 Kings 2:28-29) or be the direct result of the *judgment of God (Ps 38:5). Job's declaration that "the souls of the wounded cry out for help" (Job 24:12 NIV) encompasses the mental and emotional aspects of wounds. Whether external or internal, a wound is a hurt that needs relief and tender care.

The use of the image in Scripture focuses for the most part on wounds inflicted by God rather than borne by him. Thus Job believes that God is responsible for his wounds (Job 9:17), Jeremiah identifies God as the one who inflicts a grievous wound on *Jerusalem (Jer 51:52; Lam 2:12), and Isaiah indicates that the Lord who heals is the same one who wounds. These examples speak of God's fearsome judgment on those who bear his name.

The most sensitive of the *prophets find themselves bearing the people's wounds as their own, often in anticipation. They experience the blow dealt by God's hand long before it falls on the people (Jer 10:19; Mic 1:8-9). Thus theirs is a double agony, for they suffer both in themselves and on behalf of others. Their wounds are an image of the price of prophetic *leadership.

Wounds speak not only of God's judgment but also of his sovereign power. The writers of the OT make plain that any wounds God inflicts he can also bind up (Job 5:18; Hos 6:1). They serve as a reminder of our contingent existence in his hands. In his sovereign plan they are "wounds from a friend" (Prov 27:6 NIV), for their purpose is redemptive.

Ultimately, for the believer the image of the wound speaks most powerfully in the wounds of

Christ, foreshadowed in the Isaianic *suffering servant who was "wounded for our transgressions . . . and by his bruises we are healed" (Is 53:5 NRSV). In them we see both the measure of his love and the source of our healing (1 Pet 2:24). They are redemptive because they are God's wounds (Is 53:5).

See also BRUISE; SUFFERING SERVANT.

WRATH. *See* ANGER.

WRESTLING

Wrestling was a popular sporting activity in the ancient world. This was particularly true of Hellenistic civilization, which featured wrestling as one of the key events at the Olympic Games and in various local games. Although rules varied depending on time and locale, the basic idea of wrestling remained unchanged. The event involved two people in a weaponless hand-to-hand struggle.

Quite naturally, then, wrestling became a symbol for struggle. Rachel, the wife of Jacob, once said, "With mighty wrestlings I have wrestled with my sister, and have prevailed" (Gen 30:8 RSV). Her remark characterized the intense rivalry between her and Leah, spurred on by Rachel's barrenness while Leah was able to bear four children.

In a well-known story shrouded with much mystery, *Jacob is portrayed as wrestling with a man throughout the *night till dawn (Gen 32:24). The angelic wrestler was never able to overpower Jacob, though he did wrench Jacob's hip at the sciatic muscle (Gen 32:25, 32). Though the identity of this adversary is never revealed, he is more than a human opponent, exhibiting divine characteristics. The stranger announced to Jacob that he was changing his name to *Israel, meaning "he struggles with God" (Gen 32:28). Jacob apparently believed his opponent to be divine, since he named the place Peniel, on the rationale "I have seen God face to face" (Gen 32:30 RSV). Most interpreters throughout the history of the church have therefore suggested that Jacob's opponent was an angelic emissary, an interpretation confirmed by the statement in Hosea that Jacob "strove with God. He strove with the angel and prevailed" (Hos 12:3-4 RSV). To this day the idea of "wrestling with God" persists in Christian thought and experience, imaging human tenacity in claiming a blessing from God.

In the only occurrence of the term *wrestling* in the NT, Paul describes the nature of the Christian life as a wrestling match *(palē)* with hostile evil spirits intent on perpetrating the fall of God's people (Eph 6:12). He then mixes his metaphors by quickly shifting to warfare imagery and calling for the believer to don protective pieces of *armor.

Paul more often uses the terms *struggle (agōnizō)* and *strive (athleō)*—derived from the context of *athletic events—to symbolically represent the efforts of Christians on behalf of the gospel. He tells the Colossians that he labors for the gospel, "struggling with all his energy, which so powerfully works in me" (Col 1:29 NIV). He also commends Epaphras to the Colossians as one who "is always wrestling *(agōnizō)* in prayer for you" (Col 4:12 NIV).

See also ATHLETICS; RACE; RUNNING; STRIFE.

ϒ

YEAR. *See* TIME.

YEAST. *See* BREAD; LEAVEN; LEAVENING.

YOKE

The more then fifty references to the yoke in the Bible speak of the wooden bar or frame used to join animals to enable them to pull a load. Two aspects of a yoke are important in these references: the yoke is an image of subjection, service or *bondage (just as a yoked *donkey or *ox is in service to its owner) or an image of joining (just as two animals are joined together by means of a yoke).

Literal references to yokes are relatively rare in the Bible. Some of them occur in the ceremonial laws, where (for example) we read about using a previously unyoked heifer as a *sacrifice (Num 19:2) or in a ritual of innocence (Deut 21:1-9) and about not yoking an ox and donkey together (Deut 22:10). Yoking here assumes a ceremonial aura, as something with religious meaning. This was also the case when Saul cut a yoke of oxen in pieces and sent the pieces throughout the land of Israel as a symbolic statement (1 Sam 11:7). Other literal images of yoked animals simply reinforce the down-to-earth realism of the Bible. We have a picture of yoking two cows to pull the cart carrying the ark of the Lord and shutting up their calves at home (1 Sam 6:10), or the spectacle of the most impressive farmer in the neighborhood—Elisha—plowing with twelve yoke of oxen (1 Kings 19:19). In Jesus' parable of the banquet, one of the everyday excuses an invited guest uses is that he has bought five yoke of oxen and wants to try them out (Lk 14:19).

Most biblical references are figurative, and the largest category is the yoke as a symbol of political slavery to a foreign king (Deut 28:48; Jer 27:8-12) or oppressive subservience to one's own king (1 Kings 12:4-14). Correspondingly, an evocative image of freedom is breaking loose from the yoke of servitude (e.g., Gen 27:40; Is 9:4; 10:27; Jer 28:2, 4; Ezek 34:27). As a demonstration that Judah and surrounding nations should submit to Nebuchadnezzar, God instructed Jeremiah to wear a yoke around his neck (Jer 27).

Other meanings also inhere in the yoke as an image of bondage. *Sin is a yoke around a person's neck (Lam 1:14), and to require Gentile Christians to submit to the Jewish ceremonial code would be an unwelcome yoke (Acts 15:10), as it is for Christians who return to the *law (Gal 5:1).

Because yoking joins two animals together, it also becomes a symbol of close alliance or union. Israel's dabbling in pagan practices is pictured as a yoking of itself to Baal (Num 25:3, 5). Paul's warning against a Christian's marrying an unbeliever is expressed in the command "Do not be yoked together with unbelievers" (2 Cor 6:14 NIV), perhaps an allusion to the prohibition against yoking an ox and donkey together (Deut 22:10).

In most of the references noted thus far, the yoke is a negative image—something a person would do virtually anything to avoid. But the image can also have positive meanings. As a symbol of legitimate discipline in a person's life, bearing the yoke in one's youth "is good," on a par with waiting quietly for the salvation of the Lord (Lam 3:26-27). The supreme example is Jesus' turning his paradoxical rhetoric to the yoke as a form of good subjection to him: "Take my yoke upon you and learn from me, . . . and you will find rest for your souls. For my yoke is easy and my burden is light" (Mt 11:29-30 NIV).

See also BONDAGE AND FREEDOM; DONKEY, ASS; OX, OXEN.

YOUNG, YOUTH

A majority of the Bible's more than three hundred references to *young* or *youth* use the term in a neutral sense to designate age or a grouping within society. Poetic writers of the OT often use the words *children* and *youth* synonymously. The stock phrase "young and old" is a Hebrew merism—naming opposites with the implication that everything between is also included. We move in the direction of symbolic meanings with the stock phrase "from my youth" (or variants "from his youth" or "from youth"), where youth designates a starting point—the beginning of either life or adult accountability. Yet we should not limit the status of being "young" to the pretwenty segment of society; sometimes the term is extended to cover a large span of the population between children and *old people. One may be *married (Prov 5:18) or a *father (Ps 127:4) and still considered a youth. Or consider the age categories in the following passages: "old men, . . . young men and maidens, little children and women" (Ezek 9:6 RSV).

In the realm of more overtly symbolic meanings, three uses can be discerned. One category treats youthfulness as a time of promise—early adulthood at its most pristine, just waiting for fulfillment. The young are virile, possessing a future, laden with potential, brimming with promise. Three dozen references to young women or young *virgins, for example, hint at feminine attractiveness at its most resplendent. References to young men are much more numerous, and usually we can infer that young men are the prime physical specimens of society. The evocative phrase "the wife of your youth" (Prov 5:18 RSV; Mal 2:14) speaks of the era when romantic devotion between a couple burns most brightly. In a similar vein, "the sons of one's youth" (Ps 127:4 RSV) pictures early parenthood, when the venture is new and filled with optimistic energy. Daniel and his compatriots are sketched as "youths without blemish, handsome and skillful in all wisdom, endowed with knowledge, understanding learning, and competent to serve in the king's palace" (Dan 1:4 RSV)—in short, the best one can imagine.

Physical *strength and vigor are a special attribute of the young. One of the proverbs asserts that "the glory of young men is their strength" (Prov 20:29 RSV). When Isaiah 40:30-31 promises that those who wait on God will renew their strength, it prefaces the assertion with the comment that "even youths shall faint and be weary, and young men shall fall exhausted" (RSV), with the implication that these are the most vigorous members of society and the last group to succumb to weariness.

A second, contrasting motif pictures youth as a time (or a segment of the population) characterized by waywardness of one sort or another, along the lines of our proverbial "misspent youth." Here youth is a time when people do things that they regret later in life, as captured especially in the phrase "the sins of my youth" (Ps 25:7 RSV; Job 13:26). The implied contrast is between mature experience and responsibility on one side and the careless, unfettered behavior of youth on the other. Thus youth is linked with acts of *shame (Is 54:4), disgrace (Jer 31:13) and lewdness (Ezek 23:21). In the seduction story of Proverbs 7:6-27, it is "among the youths" that the seductress finds "a young man without sense" (Prov 7:7 RSV). When mature adults look back on these youthful indiscretions and follies, they do so with a tone of chagrin (Ps 25:7). As the writer of Ecclesiastes looks back at his misspent years, his conclusion is that "youth and the dawn of life are vanity" (Eccles 11:10 RSV).

The biblical concept of youth here should not be confused with twentieth-century adolescence; biblically, *youth* refers to a condition of life and is symbolic of one's moral, spiritual and social state. The definitive image of this is the *prodigal of Jesus' parable, a figure of youth with its thirst for life, its indulgence of forbidden appetites (including the sexual), the breaking of taboos, abandoning of restraint, and the impulse to leave the domestic, the secure and the morally governed in favor of the distant and adventurous.

Third, with the image of misspent youth serving as a foil, youth is also treated as the time of establishing a positive pattern for life. Obadiah captures the ideal when he speaks of himself as someone who has "revered the LORD from my youth" (1 Kings 18:12 RSV; cf. Ps 71:5, 17). Sometimes in the Bible, youthful years are pictured as a formative time of commitment that sets the tenor for the adult life to come. Often these pictures emerge from the earnest exhortations and commands of adults to young people, as in the repeated addresses to "my son" in the book of Proverbs. As the writer of Ecclesiastes nears the climax of his reminiscence about having looked for satisfaction in all the wrong places, he advises his youthful readers to be spared the dead ends he pursued and instead to live life in the double awareness of God as Creator and Judge, beginning and end:

> Rejoice, O young man, in your youth, and let your heart cheer you in the days of your youth; walk in the ways of your heart and the sight of your eyes. But know that for all these things God will bring you into judgment. . . .
> Remember also your Creator in the days of your youth." (Eccles 11:9; 12:1 RSV)

The psalmist offers this advice to a novice: "How can a young man keep his way pure? By guarding it according to thy word" (Ps 119:9 RSV).

NT references continue such exhortations to the young to be models of piety. Paul exhorts Timothy to "shun youthful passions and aim at righteousness, faith, love, and peace" (2 Tim 2:22 RSV). And again, "Let no one despise your youth, but set the believers an example in speech and conduct, in love, in faith, in purity" (1 Tim 4:12 RSV). In the book of Titus the writer offers moral advice to various groups, with the advice apparently matching the besetting sins of that group; in this catalog appears the advice "Likewise urge the younger men to control themselves" (Tit 2:6 RSV). When speaking of youth as a time of godly commitment, the biblical writers generally treat it as the time of laying an adequate foundation for life and serving as an example to others.

Overall, youth is an ambivalent image in the Bible. At a natural level it is a time of strength and promise. But this very energy can lead the young into moral waywardness and immature behavior that they will later regret. The antidote is consciously to set one's youthful life in a direction of godliness and moral rectitude. Modern poet William Butler Yeats lamented that human life seems to be structured in such a way as to make it impossible for strength and wisdom to reside in the same person. The Bible acknowledges the problem but also holds the possibility of a solution.

See also CHILD, CHILDREN; DAUGHTER; ELDER CHILD, SIBLING; OLD, OLD AGE; SON; STRONG, STRENGTH; VIRGIN; YOUNGER CHILD, SIBLING.

YOUNGER CHILD, YOUNGER SIBLING

Despite the law of primogeniture (*see* Elder Child), the Bible consistently reverses our expectations that the eldest child will receive a double inheritance and greater blessings. From the first trio of brothers—*Cain, *Abel and Seth—God marks out the youngest for special favor, as if to confirm that "my thoughts are not your thoughts, neither are your ways my ways" (Is 55:8 RSV).

This reversal of expectations is firmly established in the Genesis narratives. First Abel, and then Seth, receive God's mark of approval over their elder brother, Cain (Gen 4:4, 25). Ishmael is displaced by Isaac, the son of laughter (Gen 21:12-13). God's choice of the younger *Jacob over the elder *Esau, even before *birth, becomes the primary example of mysterious election as both prophets and NT writers reflect on the story (Mal 1:2, 3; Rom 9:13). The three eldest sons of Jacob—Reuben, Simeon and Levi—are passed over in favor of Judah with another double blessing devoted to Joseph's two sons, again with the younger (Ephraim) receiving more than the elder (Mannaseh; Gen 49:8-12; 48:19-20).

Although we never again see such a concentrated effort to upset the law of primogeniture, the pattern of funneling God's promises through the younger rather than the elder child continues with some exceptions. It is *Moses, not Aaron or Miriam, who leads the people out of Egypt; *David not Eliab who becomes the *king after God's own heart; *Solomon, not Absalom who builds the *temple.

Given the reversal of expectations, we are not surprised to find that this preferential treatment of the younger child produces burning jealousy among the older siblings. From Cain's murderous rage (Gen 4:8) to Leah's unhappy marriage (Gen 29:31) to Eliab's snide dismissal of his sheep-herding brother (1 Sam 17:28), elder children are disconcerted to find themselves displaced by *upstart youngsters. The archetypal example of such *sibling rivalry, of course, is the relationship between *Joseph and his brothers, who sell him into slavery (Gen 37).

That image of intrafamilial strife works its way into the NT in the portrayal of Jesus with the scribes and Pharisees. Although Jesus is designated as the firstborn in the Epistles (*see* Elder Child), in the Gospels he is clearly the younger upstart. Although he is "before Abraham" (Jn 8:58 RSV), in the eyes of the leaders he is the promoter of new doctrines, the child sitting in the temple correcting his elders (Lk 2:46-47).

The image of the freshness of the gospel and the mysterious election of younger siblings continues into the establishment of the church. Although the gospel comes first to the Jews, God's firstborn (Ex 4:22; Jer 31:9), it is soon offered as well to the Gentiles, including the Syrophoenician woman who, below even the level of younger children, is merely a *"dog" in the household (Mk 7:28). And although elders are given authority in the church, the apostle Paul reminds Timothy to "let no one despise your youth" (1 Tim 4:12 RSV). The preference given to the younger over the elder becomes, in the pattern of biblical imagery, another reminder that in the *kingdom of God, the lesser receive precedence over the greater.

See also BIRTHRIGHT; ELDER CHILD, SIBLING; FAMILY; FIRST; SIBLING RIVALRY.

YOUTH. *See* YOUNG, YOUTH.

Z

ZECHARIAH, BOOK OF

Zechariah is the longest work among the collection of the twelve Minor Prophets. The book shimmers with *apocalyptic hues and discloses a future horizon where the Lord of Hosts, the *King, will establish his universal reign. Zechariah foresees the *worship of God by both Jew and *Gentile in a *kingdom where his *holiness is pervasive. The book of Zechariah is eclipsed only by Isaiah in pronouncements foreshadowing the Messiah. It is also noteworthy for its influence on the NT writings, especially the Gospel accounts (e.g., Mt 9:6; 26:15, 28) and the book of Revelation (e.g., Rev 6:2, 4-5; 11:4; 19:11).

Like Jeremiah (Jer 1:1) and Ezekiel (Ezek 1:3) before him, Zechariah was a *priest by descent and a *prophet by divine commission. The name Zechariah means "Yahweh has remembered," the essence of his message to *Jerusalem after the *exile. God intends to honor his *covenant agreement and *restore his people in the *land of covenant promise (Zech 2:10-12). Zechariah's priestly lineage helps explain his knowledge of the Mosaic *law (Zech 7:8-10; 8:14-17) and fasting (Zech 8:18-19) and his careful descriptions of priestly dress (Zech 3:1-5), *temple vessels like *bowls and *lampstands (Zech 4:2-3) and even the coronation of the "Branch" (Zech 6:9-14).

Zechariah's message may be dated to the reign of King Darius I of Persia (521-485 B.C.). In fact, three of the prophet's oracles include date formulas indicating precisely the day, month and year he prophesied (Zech 1:1-6 [Oct./Nov. 520 B.C.], 1:7 [Feb. 15, 519 B.C.] and 7:1 [Dec. 7, 518 B.C.]). The book naturally divides into two sections: the visions (Zech 1—8) and the (undated) oracles (Zech 9—14). The lapse of time separating the writing of the two halves of the book (perhaps two or three decades) explains the difference in language, style and theme between the earlier visions and the later oracles.

Zechariah's message was essentially a tract for troubled times. First, the prophet rebukes the postexilic community and calls them to *repentance because they persist in the evil deeds of their ancestors (Zech 1:3-5; cf. 7:8-14). Next, Zechariah exhorts the people "to do good," to act in accordance with the laws of God (Zech 1:13-17). God can "do good" to Israel only as they reciprocate by obeying the stipulations of covenant relationship (Zech 7:8-14; 8:14-17). Finally, God's servant encourages his compatriots by assuring them that the words of the "former prophets" are still valid (Zech 1:4; 7:7, 12) and that God intends to *bless and restore his people (Zech 8:1- 8).

Much of the imagery contained in Zechariah relates directly to the prophet's historical setting. The book highlights several themes, including the migration of Hebrews back to the land of Israel, the restoration of temple *worship, the anointing of local leaders and the visions of *glory and splendor for Israel among the nations. Each one depicts the reversal of conditions encountered by the first waves of Israelites reentering a homeland lying in ruins.

The book is cast in the literary form of "oracular prose," a blend of prose and poetry characteristic of OT prophetic literature (except for Zech 9, which is entirely poetic material). Zechariah may also be classified as prophetic-apocalyptic literature, since the book contains numerous apocalyptic features and motifs, including narrative in the form of a vision (Zech 1:7—6:8), prediction with revelation and interpretation formulas (e.g., Zech 5:1-4), extensive *angelic activity (e.g., Zech 5:5; 6:4), bold and at times cryptic symbolism (in both language and actions, Zech 6:9-15), and themes of divine *judgment and the triumph of the kingdom of God in history (Zech 12—14).

The most striking literary feature of Zechariah is the "vision." The OT vision is an unusual revelatory experience in which the recipient privately sees and experiences the word of divine truth sent from God—a "virtual reality" encounter of sorts for the prophet. The prophet's eight visions are characterized by a high frequency of revelatory language and rich symbolism. Each vision is introduced by a formula such as "And I looked up and saw . . ." (see Zech 1:8, 18; 2:1; 5:1; 6:1) or by the angelic messenger's inviting Zechariah to "look up and see" (see Zech 3:1; 4:2; 5:5). The "visionary" format of the book helps explain Zechariah's vivid and colorful language, as he actually viewed the revelation God gave to him. Zechariah's repeated inquiries as to the meaning of the various symbols and images shed light on what might otherwise be considered an unintelligible message from God (Zech 1:9, 19, 21; 2:2, 4, 11-12; 5:6, 10; 6:4).

God resorts to the vision as a means for revelation for a variety of reasons, chief among them being that (1) visions tend to be cosmic and universal in nature; (2) often the symbolism characteristic of *dreams and visions is required to convey a "history" that has not yet occurred; (3) dreams and visions help maintain the mystery of divine revelation; (4) at times the dream or vision is necessary "shock treatment" for a hardhearted audience; and (4) the unusual nature of the dream and vision functions as surety—guaranteeing the certain fulfillment of the divine word. The latter is probably the case for Zechariah, since his ministry to postexilic Jerusalem was largely one of encouragement and exhortation.

Zechariah appeals to a wide array of biblical images and symbols in his visions and oracles, rivaling the literary artistry of the major prophets Isaiah, Jeremiah and Ezekiel. The following catalog is merely representative of the abundant symbolism contained in the book of Zechariah.

The "horns" mentioned in the second vision (Zech 2:18-21) are a frequent apocalyptic motif and represent nations or kings, at times with specific reference (e.g., the single horn of the goat as a figure for Alexander the Great, Dan 8:5, 8) but here only a general reference to ancient "superpowers."

The "measuring line" cited in the third vision (Zech 2:1-5; cf. 1:16) signifies the blessing of God in the enlargement of Jerusalem, perhaps an allusion to the promise of such enlargement in the new covenant pronouncement of Jeremiah (Jer 31:39; cf. Rev 21:15-17, where the angel with a measuring rod surveys the new Jerusalem).

Zechariah makes mention of two important biblical symbols of spiritual *cleansing, the change of clothing in the fourth vision (Zech 3:1-5; cf. Is 61:10; cf. Rev 6:11; 7:9, 13-14) and the *fountain (Zech 13:1; cf. Ps 36:9; 68:26; Jer 2:13; 17:13; Rev 21:6).

Zechariah's series of visions begins (Zech 1:7-17) and concludes (Zech 6:1-8) with reference to *horses of assorted colors traversing the earth. These heavenly messengers patrol the earth and report to God, a graphic symbol of his sovereignty (cf. Rev 6:2, 4-5, 8, where the military motif of divine judgment is associated with these horsemen).

The *crown is a symbol of royal *authority in the Bible (e.g., Ps 89:19-20) or even an emblem of redemption (Is 62:3; Jas 1:12; 1 Pet 5:4; Rev 2:10), but in Zechariah 6:11, 14 the crown is given to the high priest Joshua—a metaphorical merging of offices of king and priest in postexilic Judaism and a foreshadowing of the ministry of Messiah (Ps 110:4; cf. Heb 7:11-28).

A rather unusual symbolic action, the grasping of a *garment (Zech 8:23), is a gesture of utter dependence and often an act of desperation on the part of the one laying hold of another's clothing (Is 4:1; cf. the poignant story of the ailing woman who rashly touched the fringe of Jesus' cloak hoping for a remedy for her chronic hemorrhaging, Mt 9:19-22).

One of the best known of Zechariah's messianic images is that of Jerusalem's king riding triumphantly into the city on a *donkey, a symbol of *humility and *peace in the biblical world (cf. Mt 21:2, 5, 7; Jn 12:15).

The imagery of *shepherd and *flock, a pervasive motif in the OT Prophets, dominates the oracles of Zechariah (Zech 9—13). Especially significant is the reference to the striking of the shepherd and the scattering of the sheep, another of the messianic passages in Zechariah fulfilled in the life of the "good shepherd" Jesus (Jn 10:11; Heb 13:20; Rev 7:17; cf. Mt 26:31; Mk 14:27).

The most graphic among Zechariah's messianic portraits is the prediction that the *house of *David will one day recognize "the one they have pierced" (Zech 12:10 NIV)—an allusion to the crucifixion of Jesus, according to the NT (Jn 19:37; Rev 1:7), and a metaphor for saving *faith in that only those who confess their part in "piercing" Christ by their own *sin can be reconciled to God (Rom 5:6-11).

The closing chapter, Zechariah 14, includes a range of imagery, especially the kingship of God—the closing theme of the old and new covenants (Zech 14:16; Rev 22:3)—and the figure of *light, the symbol of God's numinous presence with his people throughout the Bible (Zech 14:7; Rev 21:5; cf. Ps 27:1; 36:9; Jn 8:12; 1 Jn 1:5).

*Haggai and Zechariah were complementary postexilic prophets. Haggai was commissioned to call the people of God to rebuild the Jerusalem temple. Zechariah summoned the community to repentance and spiritual renewal. His primary task was to prepare the people spiritually for proper worship and temple service once the building project was completed. After careful reading of Zechariah's visions, it is apparent that his message is more than the rehashing of themes already introduced by Haggai. As Baldwin (59) notes, "If Haggai was the builder, responsible for the solid structure of the new Temple, Zechariah was more like the artist, adding colourful windows with their symbolism, gaiety and light."

See also HAGGAI, BOOK OF; PROPHECY, GENRE OF.

BIBLIOGRAPHY. J. Baldwin, "Zechariah" in *Haggai, Zechariah, Malachi* (TOTC; Downers Grove, IL: InterVarsity Press, 1972) 59-208.

ZEPHANIAH, BOOK OF

Like *Joel, the book of Zephaniah focuses on the theme of the *Day of the Lord. The message is twofold: (1) the coming day is one of *judgment for *sins against God and humankind, a judgment that encompasses all nations, including God's own *covenant people; and (2) there will be purification for sin when the redeemed of all nations join a regathered *Israel in serving God and enjoying his *blessings.

Zephaniah's indebtedness to Joel is evident, not only in basic theme but in details relative to the coming judgment (e.g., cf. Zeph 1:14-18 with Joel 2:1-11). Like Joel, Zephaniah is at home with subject matter admirably suited to the Day of the Lord theme: the hopeless corruption of society (Zeph 1:8, 10-13, 18; 3:5), false *worship practices (Zeph 1:4-6, 9; 3:2, 4), the need for *repentance (Zeph 1:10; 2:1-3) and a reminder of God's love for his own (Zeph 3:14-17) that calls for *humility, *faith and faithfulness (Zeph 2:3; 3:12). For a repentant people there is a fond hope of *restoration (Zeph 3:8-10) and everlasting felicity (Zeph 3:13-20).

While not displaying the literary sophistication of some other prophets (e.g., Isaiah, Nahum), Zephaniah's artistry is not lacking. In addition to oracles of judgment, *salvation oracles and instructional prophecies, we encounter woe oracles (Zeph 2:5-7; 3:1-7), a lament (Zeph 1:10-11) and even a pun accomplished through paronomasia: Gaza (*'azzâ*) will be abandoned (*''zûbâ*) and Ekron (*'eqrôn*) will be uprooted (*tē 'āqēr;* Zeph 2:4). Several literary figures are also present, including anthropopoeia (Zeph 1:4, 12-13), merismus (Zeph 1:12), metaphor and simile (Zeph 1:7; 2:2, 9; 3:3, 13), and synecdoche (Zeph 1:16; 3:16). Particularly picturesque is the description of God, like an ancient Diogenes, walking through *Jerusalem with *lamp in hand, searching for those who live with the sense of false security (Zeph 1:12).

Zephaniah is most remembered, however, for his graphic description of the Day of the Lord in Zephaniah 1:14-18. An oracle with eschatological implications, this pericope has often been cited for its *apocalyptic qualities: cosmic setting, divine intervention with cataclysmic effects on earth and hyperbolic language. Although Zephaniah does write in a style that anticipates the full-blown apocalypses of later Judaism, he lacks the fervor and excessive language and imagery of those later writers. Moreover, his subject matter and vocabulary frequently occur elsewhere in prophetic eschatology. Zephaniah is not so much concerned with a future that breaks into the present as with the unfolding of God's sovereign and ordered arrangement of history so as to bring it to its intended culmination.

Perhaps the most distinctive trait of Zephaniah's prophecy, however, is his penchant for repetition and wordplay and his use of allusions. The latter are particularly significant. Zephaniah likens the coming judgment to the sweeping away of all life in the days of the great *flood (Zeph 1:2-3). The catalog of *death mentioned here is arranged in inverse order to God's original *creation: humankind, beasts, the creatures of the air, those of the *sea (cf. Gen 1:20-27). In depicting the destruction of the *Philistine cities (Zeph 2:4-7), Zephaniah combines wordplay with the metaphor of a deserted woman, thus dramatically portraying their sure demise.

The boldest stroke of all comes in Zephaniah 3:9-10. Here the prophet draws on an earlier Canaanite tradition telling of a time when Baal was to be handed over to Yamm both as *servant and as tribute:

Thy slave is Baal, O Yamm,
    Thy slave is Baal for[eve]r,

Dagon's Son is thy captive;
    He shall be brought as thy tribute.

The allusion is made certain by Zephaniah's choice of vocabulary drawn from the Ugaritic epic: *servant/slave, bring* and *tribute/offering.* Even as Baal was to be Yamm's servant and was sent as tribute to him, so converted *Gentiles who "call on the name of the LORD" and "serve him shoulder to shoulder" are "my worshipers" who will "bring my scattered ones" (the Jews) as "my tribute."

See also DAY OF THE LORD; PROPHECY, GENRE OF.

ZEUS. *See* GODS, GODDESSES.

ZION
Zion is a symbol or metaphor for the historical *city of *Jerusalem. But behind this metaphor lies a complex cluster of interlocking themes of immense theological significance. In various parts of the Scriptures we find the following concepts associated with the city of Zion: the *temple as Yahweh's dwelling place; the covenant people of God, both as the apostate *Israel under *judgment and the purified *remnant who inherit God's *blessings; the royal *Davidic *kingship leading to the idea of the Messiah; the world center from which God's *law will be promulgated and to which the *Gentile nations of the world will flow; the renewed *heavens and earth, where *peace and *prosperity will reign. We will look only very briefly at some of the images generated by these themes.

Our starting point is the historical city of Jerusalem, the Canaanite city captured by David (2 Sam 5:6), who made it his political and religious capital. He installed the *ark of the covenant there (2 Sam 6), but it was his son *Solomon who built the temple. Yahweh made his dwelling there and chose Zion for himself, though it was recognized that even the heaven of heavens cannot contain the presence of the infinite God (1 Kings 8:27).

In both OT and NT, the city stands for the people of God. In Revelation 21:9 the Holy City is the *bride, the wife of the *Lamb. In the OT what happens to Zion, in blessing or *cursing, is a microcosm of Yahweh's purposes for his people. In Isaiah's day, at the time of the eighth-century B.C. Assyrian crisis, the city was left like a shelter in a *vineyard, like a hut in a field of melons (Is 1:8), totally surrounded but not captured. This led to the false ideology of the inviolability of Zion. The prophetic word for Hezekiah and Ahaz did not have eternal validity. Jeremiah rebuked those who trusted with facile optimism in the words "This is the temple of the LORD, the temple of the LORD, the temple of the LORD" (Jer 7:4). And God's judgment fell on the city, and it was captured and desecrated by the Babylonians.

It is characteristic of the prophets that they oscillate rapidly between references to historical Zion under judgment and references to the glorified Zion in the last days. In Isaiah 2:2-4 (par. Mic 4:1-3), Mt.

Zion is portrayed as the seat of Yahweh's world government; peace will prevail, Yahweh's word will issue from it, and all the Gentile nations will flow to it. Yahweh will reign from there, the city of the Great King (Ps 48:1-8). It is like Mt. Zaphon in the far north, the mythological *mountaintop, the dwelling of the Canaanite pantheon of *gods. But those who inhabit this eschatological Zion will be the saved remnant (Is 4:2-6), who have been purged by *fire and washed clean (see Cleansing) so as to be perfectly consecrated to the Lord. The symbol here of the *Branch, later to become a technical term for the Messiah (Jer 23:5), probably refers to this elect remnant.

Yahweh himself is the King who reigns from Zion (Ps 132:13). But he has installed his own king on Zion, his holy hill (Ps 2:6). The continuing Davidic dynasty is a result of the promise to David through Nathan's oracle (2 Sam 7). But the failure of the historical kings of Judah led to the projection of the ideal Davidic king into the future concept of the Messiah.

The ideas of a gloriously renewed creation, centered on the exalted city of Zion, presided over by the messianic King, are found linked together in Isaiah 11. Similar passages are found in Isaiah 66. "They will neither harm nor destroy in all my holy mountain" (Is 65:25 NIV), and the land will be irrigated by a supernatural stream flowing from Mt. Zion (Ps 46:4; Ezek 47:1-12; see Water).

Perhaps the most striking image used to describe Zion is the metaphor of a woman. She is the *daughter of Zion, that is, the Lady Zion (Is 1:8). Even here there is a wide range of connotations, with different nuances appropriate to differing historical and theological contexts. Isaiah uses the covenantal concept of *marriage (Is 1:21). She is the faithful city, loyal to her covenant partner Yahweh, bound to her husband by ties of loving obligation; but she has become unfaithful, a *prostitute, with all the connotations of degradation, disloyalty, impurity and judgment.

In the later context of the Babylonian exile, Zion likens herself to an abandoned wife (Is 49:14). She is like a bereaved and *barren mother (Is 49:20-21) who stands amazed in incomprehension at her spiritual offspring. This theme is repeated in Isaiah 54:1, 6—a wife deserted, distressed in spirit, a wife who married young only to be rejected. But abandonment is not to be the last word, for she will be no longer called deserted but will be given a new name, Hephizbah, "my delight is in her" (Is 62:4).

Finally, in Isaiah 66:7-9 Zion is pictured as a pregnant woman in labor and then as a nursing mother, giving suck and dandling her infant on her knees. This miraculous *birth—no labor pains—portrays the rebirth of the nation after the *exile. Nothing like this has ever happened before—a picture of the *curse removed in the new Eden (see Garden). So will Zion's spiritual offspring inhabit the earth.

Perhaps one of the most dramatic uses of Zion imagery appears in Hebrews 12. Here Zion is contrasted with that other theologically significant mountain, *Sinai. The latter represents a formal, legal relationship with God, while Zion stands for a relationship of grace. The author encourages his readers to come to Zion to join the fellowship of other saints and the worship of the living God: "You have come to Mount Zion and to the city of the living God, the heavenly Jerusalem, and to innumerable angels in festal gathering, and to the assembly of the first-born who are enrolled in heaven" (Heb 12:22-23 RSV).

See also DAVID; JERUSALEM; KING, KINGSHIP; MOUNTAIN; SINAI; TEMPLE.

37, *175, 320, 432,*
  460, 977
37:1, *871*
37:2, *949*
37:3, *320*
37:3-4, *63, 274*
37:5-11, *477, 799*
37:6, *353*
37:7, *92, 347*
37:8, *217, 347*
37:9, *173, 828*
37:11, *789*
37:12, *782*
37:12-28, *855*
37:15, *926*
37:19, *799*
37:19-20, *219*
37:19-30, *706*
37:20, *646*
37:22, *646, 710*
37:23, *320*
37:24, *150, 204*
37:25, *210, 604, 634*
37:25-28, *250*
37:28, *791, 797*
37:29, *319, 320, 351*
37:31-33, *320*
37:31-35, *274*
37:34, *318, 351, 574*
37:34-35, *129*
38, *200, 222, 304,*
  410, 501, 852,
  895, 960
38:1-30, *829*
38:6, *289*
38:6-24, *676*
38:8, *805*
38:12-19, *913*
38:14, *318*
38:18, *620, 766*
38:19, *318*
38:21, *418*
38:24, *287*
38:25, *620*
38:26, *778*
38:28, *289, 571*
38:29-30, *125*
39, *229, 706*
39:1-6, *706*
39:1-19, *797*
39:3, *675, 681*
39:6, *104, 381*
39:6-20, *214, 852,*
  911
39:7, *85*
39:7-17, *913*
39:9, *773*
39:12, *85, 320, 773*
39:12-18, *320*
39:19, *25*
39:20, *112, 663*
40:5, *217*
40:5-19, *217*
40:6, *567*
40:9, *651*
40:10, *116, 866*
40:13, *710*
40:15, *150*
40:16-22, *799*
40:20, *71*
40:21, *710*
41, *217, 221, 273,*
  366, 621, 706
41:1-8, *800*
41:1-18, *730*
41:1-40, *207*
41:4, *64*
41:5-7, *347*
41:7, *284*
41:7-11, *366*
41:8, *524, 525, 555,*
  567
41:11, *217*
41:14, *320, 781*
41:18, *650*
41:24, *524, 525*
41:25, *366*

41:26, *27, 347*
41:27, *347, 348*
41:29-31, *267*
41:33, *207*
41:39, *207*
41:39-44, *742*
41:40, *348, 868*
41:41-43, *397*
41:42, *286, 320,*
  341, 361, 451,
  513, 557, 591,
  728, 766, 791
41:43, *787*
41:45, *583*
41:49, *6, 348, 816,*
  817
41:56, *348, 816*
41:57, *267*
42, *200, 229*
42:6, *348*
42:7, *403*
42:9, *581*
42:9-11, *809*
42:9-16, *812*
42:18, *278, 864*
42:24, *256*
42:26, *215*
42:27, *575*
42:28, *176*
42:30-34, *812*
42:36, *142*
42:38, *360, 605,*
  606, 807
43:11, *396, 634*
43:14, *548*
43:15, *87*
43:16, *403, 596*
43:23, *889*
43:24, *403*
43:28, *519*
43:30, *846, 939*
43:31, *259, 846*
43:31-34, *71, 840*
43:32-34, *840*
43:34, *87, 291*
44:2, *791*
44:5, *609*
44:13, *351*
44:15, *609*
44:21, *256*
44:29, *350, 360, 606*
44:31, *360, 605, 606*
44:33, *824*
45:1-15, *242, 716,*
  829
45:5-8, *789, 826*
45:6, *271*
45:7-8, *140, 682*
45:15, *327, 482, 939*
45:17, *27*
45:18, *273*
45:22, *291, 320*
45:26, *830*
46, *775*
46:1, *713*
46:2, *217*
46:3, *348, 358*
46:8, *251*
46:26, *251*
46:27, *775*
46:33-34, *2, 151*
47:1-6, *267*
47:4, *644*
47:9, *300, 463, 644*
47:11, *300*
47:18, *382*
47:19, *770*
47:20-26, *229*
47:23-24, *770*
47:24, *142*
47:27, *11*
47:29, *519, 778*
48, *98, 268*
48:1-20, *362*
48:3-4, *11*
48:4, *310*
48:6, *142, 582*

48:10, *327, 373, 605*
48:11, *142*
48:12, *483, 522*
48:13-14, *290, 500*
48:13-17, *362*
48:13-18, *361*
48:14, *367*
48:15, *151*
48:15-16, *606*
48:16, *582*
48:17-20, *727*
48:19-20, *977*
48:22, *41*
49, *462, 529*
49:1, *225, 609*
49:1-28, *606*
49:3, *805*
49:3-4, *97, 229*
49:4, *85, 471*
49:6-7, *25*
49:8, *361, 591*
49:8-12, *477, 977*
49:9, *30, 448, 514,*
  515
49:10, *215, 477, 764*
49:11, *92, 101, 215*
49:11-12, *915*
49:12, *551, 944*
49:17, *31, 376, 773*
49:17-18, *229*
49:19, *376*
49:22, *116, 811, 915*
49:24, *332, 556,*
  584, 620, 784, 815
49:25, *201, 929*
49:27, *88, 958*
49:28, *900*
49:29-32, *135, 568*
49:31, *129*
50, *129*
50:1, *327*
50:3, *129, 776*
50:10, *129, 776*
50:12-13, *300*
50:13, *129, 135*
50:18, *326, 522*
50:20, *90, 140, 344,*
  348, 789, 826
50:23, *15*
50:24, *300*
50:25, *113, 114*

Exodus
1, *120, 222, 229,*
  251, 408, 420,
  607, 904
1:1, *251*
1:1-14, *797*
1:5, *775*
1:7, *6, 42, 252, 420*
1:7-20, *140*
1:8, *189, 252, 300,*
  420
1:8-14, *151*
1:12, *140, 408, 420,*
  717
1:14, *162*
1:15-21, *200, 571,*
  895
1:15-22, *68, 154,*
  617
1:16, *408, 717*
1:19, *409*
1:22, *586, 731*
2, *570*
2:1-3, *42*
2:1-9, *895*
2:1-10, *67, 96, 154,*
  189, 200, 617,
  706, 795, 830, 904
2:2, *42*
2:2-3, *142*
2:3-5, *731*
2:4, *528*
2:4-8, *227*
2:5, *102, 193, 362,*
  926

2:7, *600*
2:10, *15*
2:11, *81*
2:11-12, *154, 911*
2:11-14, *706*
2:11-15, *744*
2:14, *277*
2:14-15, *570*
2:15, *250, 783*
2:15-19, *706*
2:15-22, *941*
2:16, *782*
2:16-17, *940*
2:20, *402*
2:22, *251, 300, 463*
2:23, *112, 790, 970*
2:23-24, *236*
2:23-25, *608, 825*
2:24, *3, 4, 790*
3, *24, 34, 133, 335,*
  389, 422, 492,
  570, 829, 914, 950
3:1, *130, 230, 661,*
  782, 794
3:1-2, *573*
3:1-6, *716, 748*
3:2, *23, 287, 634*
3:2-4, *650, 858*
3:4, *582*
3:5, *74, 130, 280,*
  389, 781, 787,
  794, 906, 927
3:6, *4, 130, 259,*
  276, 277, 382, 584
3:7, *223, 661, 706,*
  797
3:7-9, *608*
3:7-10, *251*
3:8, *6, 204, 270,*
  297, 310, 396,
  488, 551, 691, 706
3:8-9, *675*
3:10, *706*
3:12, *358, 706, 794,*
  970
3:12-14, *971*
3:14, *130, 583*
3:15, *4, 584*
3:16, *3, 4, 928*
3:17, *270, 396, 551,*
  665
3:18, *950*
3:19-20, *361*
3:22, *318*
4, *639*
4:3, *527*
4:5, *4*
4:6, *802*
4:7, *710*
4:9, *100*
4:10, *373, 380*
4:11, *197*
4:13-15, *25*
4:14, *25, 369, 377*
4:14-15, *575*
4:15, *334*
4:19-20, *543*
4:20, *1, 215*
4:21, *369*
4:21-23, *97*
4:22, *229, 443, 530,*
  736, 754, 977
4:22-23, *446, 501,*
  805
4:23, *970*
4:24-26, *149*
4:25, *426, 556*
5, *471, 493, 820, 904*
5:1, *950*
5:2, *822*
5:5-21, *151*
5:12, *136*
5:14, *81*
5:16, *81*
5:23, *585*
6, *155*
6:1, *361*

6:1-13, *230*
6:3, *3, 4, 584*
6:3-4, *971*
6:4, *462, 644*
6:6, *43, 699*
6:8, *3*
6:12, *421*
6:20, *796*
6:26, *373*
7, *832, 855, 932*
7:1, *584*
7:3, *369*
7:4, *373*
7:4-5, *361*
7:8, *230*
7:8-12, *1*
7:8-13, *62*
7:9-10, *565, 580*
7:11, *524, 525, 649,*
  741
7:12, *527, 565, 580*
7:14, *230*
7:14-23, *1*
7:15, *567*
7:15-25, *731*
7:16, *950, 970*
7:17, *100, 290*
7:18, *802*
7:19, *230*
7:21, *290, 802*
7:22, *525, 649*
8:1, *970*
8:1-5, *1, 230*
8:3, *525*
8:7, *524, 649*
8:14, *802*
8:14-15, *525*
8:15, *369*
8:16-19, *1*
8:18-19, *649*
8:19, *286, 513*
8:20, *567, 970*
8:22-23, *473*
8:27, *950*
9:3, *648*
9:11, *524, 525, 649*
9:13, *567*
9:13-35, *359, 869*
9:14, *648*
9:15, *648*
9:16, *639, 968*
9:18-35, *936*
9:19-20, *394*
9:24, *288*
9:27, *648*
9:29, *326, 869*
9:30, *278*
9:33, *326*
10, *639*
10:1-20, *516*
10:3, *407, 639, 970*
10:7, *970*
10:11, *970*
10:13, *634, 936*
10:15, *310*
10:21-23, *193*
10:23, *509*
10:24, *970*
10:26, *558, 970*
11, *473*
11:2, *451, 791*
11:4, *550*
11:5, *868*
11:7, *29*
11:8, *25*
12, *28, 299, 629,*
  662, 828
12:1-28, *117, 473*
12:1-30, *55*
12:3, *265*
12:5, *810*
12:6, *901*
12:7, *952*
12:8, *70, 286, 907*
12:9, *500*
12:10, *567*
12:11, *733, 787*

12:12, *639, 648*
12:14, *703*
12:15, *498*
12:17-20, *907*
12:18, *567, 970*
12:19, *498, 502*
12:20, *907*
12:21, *288*
12:22-23, *216*
12:23, *100, 649*
12:26, *844*
12:29, *550, 646, 868*
12:29-30, *229*
12:29-36, *242*
12:31, *493, 970*
12:34, *70, 498, 907*
12:35, *318*
12:37, *865*
12:39, *498*
12:41, *58*
12:44, *797*
12:45, *92, 385*
12:46, *114, 630*
12:48, *421*
12:51, *373*
13:2, *28, 289*
13:2-16, *310*
13:3, *394, 970*
13:5, *551*
13:7, *498*
16, *299*
13:9, *361, 515, 703,*
  821
13:11-16, *229*
13:12, *289, 531*
13:13, *28, 289, 591,*
  698
13:14, *361, 970*
13:14-15, *571*
13:15, *289, 396*
13:16, *361*
13:17, *118*
13:18, *251*
13:19, *113, 114*
13:20, *854*
13:21, *354, 510,*
  512, 631, 682, 780
13:21-22, *634, 646*
14, *155, 211, 461,*
  683, 818, 904,
  932, 935
14:9, *400*
14:10-14, *251*
14:10-18, *252*
14:11, *949*
14:14, *251*
14:15-20, *251*
14:21, *119, 225, 821*
14:23, *400*
14:24, *512*
14:25, *28, 138*
14:27, *568*
14:30-31, *252*
14:31, *570*
15, *142, 707, 765,*
  818, 832
15:1, *400*
15:1-18, *78, 479,*
  841, 896
15:2, *577*
15:3, *47, 80, 210,*
  251, 333, 479, 896
15:5, *201, 556*
15:6, *361, 362, 728,*
  896
15:7, *136, 335*
15:8, *201, 597*
15:9, *101, 234, 832,*
  898
15:10, *119, 492, 555*
15:11, *276, 337*
15:12, *198, 361,*
  728, 832
15:13, *355, 821*
15:14, *892*
15:15, *276, 277*
15:16, *276, 277,*

ISAIAH

133, 211, 230,
277, 287, 382,
389, 488, 573,
650, 665, 691,
716, 748, 752,
858, 865, 892,
949

butter, 27, **130,**
621, 914

buying, 31, 110,
112, 202, 298,
341, 410, 411,
436, 443, 451,
497, 501, 502,
503, 504, 518,
537, 582, 633,
673, 679, 681,
698, 699, 705,
754, 791, 797,
805, 865, 894,
947, 948, 975

buzzard, 93, 130

Cain, 1, 2, 10, 11,
20, 67, 100, 125,
131-32, 137,
144, 150, 151,
182, 187, 216,
225, 229, 230,
244, 247-50,
263, 264, 270,
271, 275, 287,
292, 300, 323,
324, 383, 393,
422, 467, 470,
576, 593, 602,
615, 617, 647,
656, 696, 717,
721, 775, 789,
792-94, 793,
796, 829, 855,
882, 887, 902,
905, 907, 913,
925, 977

calf, calves, 27, 31,
62, 63, 75, 88,
111, 115, **132,**
135, 142, 167,
181, 188, 226,
251, 253, 273,
326, 338, 349,
371, 375, 403,
408, 410, 417,
449, 483, 493,
531, 564, 580,
603, 651, 718,
728, 794, 837,
849, 908, 975

camel, 3, 28, 40,
134, 168, 222,
226, 256, 324,
329, 410, 435,
591, 630, 634,
640, 677, 887,
932, 947

captive, captives,
18, 49, 56, 112,
113, 132, 134,
166, 213, 237,
238, 241, 304,
318, 340, 357,
441, 475, 502,
517, 575, 664,
665, 695, 709,
770, 787, 810,
875, 896-99, 980

catalog, catalogs,
17, 25, 49, 83,
106, 134, 135,
139, 166, 189,
192, 201, 230,
271, 276, 316,
328, 342, 344,
376, 399, 420,
438, 451, 470,
506, 523, 538,
558, 588, 620,
625, 638, 651,

652, 658, 662,
678, 681, 684,
696, 703, 704,
722, 724, 729,
731, 784, 796,
826, 829, 841,
842, 855, 856,
910, 948, 965,
976, 979, 980

cave, 129, **135**-36,
155, 197, 204,
208, 231, 382,
410, 411, 493,
494, 568, 572,
575, 587, 608,
609, 616, 620,
645, 646, 647,
673, 701, 769,
822, 899, 926

cedar, 12, 103, 116,
294, 302, 352,
499, 499, 622,
669, 686, 741,
780, 838, 868,
881, 890-92,
891, 892, 909,
916, 942, 963,
964

center, centered, 7,
20, 39, 41, 50,
58, 76, 105, 134,
146, 150, 152,
153, 161, 180,
191, 201, 211,
227, 228, 233,
242, 246, 247,
251, 256, 257,
258, 276, 296,
299, 306, 313,
324, 340, 343,
345, 346, 358,
361, 364, 367,
388, 423, 428,
435-40, 446,
453, 455, 457,
461, 464, 479,
482, 485, 495,
503, 535, **549**-
50, 554, 556,
558, 573, 587,
589, 592, 602,
612, 616, 637,
643, 644, 647,
651, 661, 671,
672, 677, 708,
711, 712, 714,
721, 758, 760,
814, 841, 843,
845, 849, 850,
865, 874, 880,
923, 936, 938,
966, 980, 981

chaff, 68, 75, **136,**
190, 207, 213,
236, 288, 352,
366, 367, 442,
473, 668, 818,
819, 867, 884,
942, 943

chaos, 11, 38, 58,
102, **136**-37,
169-71, 180,
191, 201, 202,
239, 256, 290,
293, 377, 391,
435, 442, 453,
466, 508-10,
524, 527, 547,
562-64, 569,
579, 589, 592,
598, 613, 668,
688, 765, 767,
773, 786, 817,
850, 851, 892,
893, 924, 929,
931, 932, 942

character type, 79,

81, **137**-38, 144,
220, 222, 230,
250, 274, 323,
343, 381, 587,
615, 679, 680,
684, 724, 750,
751, 800, 913

chariot, 28, 37, 47,
52, 54, 77, 78,
98, 106, 134,
138-39, 157,
172, 183, 212,
242, 262, 287,
293, 362, 371,
400, 401, 426,
436, 447, 454,
511, 513, 516,
526, 549, 568,
569, 589, 607,
620, 671, 674,
679, 682, 708,
744, 745, 813,
898, 907, 909,
937, 943, 952,
967

charm, 84, 104,
315, 525-28,
773, 912

chase and flight,
291, 292

cheating the oracle,
139, 561

Chemosh, 339

cherub, cherubim,
11, 43, 58, 64,
139, 173, 179,
223, 256, 287,
291, 294, 417,
428, 562, 575,
579, 651, 743,
762, 779, 838,
850, 858, 918,
955, 963, 972

child, 1, 5, 9, 12,
15, 32-34, 42,
55, 57, 63, 68,
73, 75, 83, 92,
95, 96, 100, 107,
113, 118, 119,
125, 137, 138,
141-43, 160,
161, 168, 182,
194, 195, 198,
214, 224, 229,
244, 261, 266,
267, 274, 275,
289, 306, 313,
342, 363, 369,
376, 377, 380,
397, 413, 427,
432, 438, 439,
441, 445, 446,
457, 502, 503,
519, 529, 537,
541, 543, 549,
550, 553, 565,
571, 572, 574,
583, 587, 600,
607, 612, 614,
615, 620, 622,
633, 651, 658-
661, 666, 686,
696, 699, 715,
723, 724, 726,
745, 751, 754,
759, 790, 792,
812, 816, 829-
31, 844, 850,
873, 885, 901,
903, 914, 926,
957-60, 962,
966, 977

childlessness, 119,
142, 435, 610,
731, 888

childlikeness, 38,
141, 259, 480,

581, 667, 686

children, 4, 6, 7,
14, 15, 17, 21,
24-27, 29, 30,
39, 55, 58, 59,
62, 63, 67, 68,
72, 75, 76, 81,
82, 86, 89, 95,
113, 119, 121,
126, 137, **141**-
43, 151, 153,
154, 157, 160-
63, 166, 168,
173, 174, 181,
183, 192, 193,
195, 198, 203,
206, 207, 214,
229, 230, 240,
241, 247, 248,
258, 262, 264-
67, 271, 273-75,
282, 284, 287,
289, 303, 310,
312, 314, 315,
322-24, 326,
337, 340, 342,
343, 345, 352,
358, 359, 362,
375, 389, 391,
395-398, 401,
402, 406, 420,
421, 426, 428,
433, 438, 457,
458, 465, 470,
483, 486, 489,
494, 495, 497,
501, 502, 506,
511, 512, 515,
528, 532, 534,
537, 538, 543,
557, 568, 571,
572, 583, 600,
602, 614, 615,
618, 628, 635,
637, 642, 650-
52, 659-61, 668,
673, 675, 685,
696, 702, 706,
714, 719, 720,
734, 736, 738,
751, 752, 755,
772, 778, 789,
791, 793, 795,
796, 798, 801,
804, 805, 808,
817, 818, 825,
834, 844, 846,
858, 861, 864,
874, 898, 903,
909, 917, 919,
923, 930, 933,
946, 947, 949,
959, 964, 974,
975, 977

choice, 33, 88, 91,
92, 119-21, 124,
131, 141, **143**-
44, 151, 178,
215, 219, 245,
246, 263, 264,
282, 302, 316,
341, 346, 352,
360, 381, 389,
403, 426, 435,
499, 500, 505,
513, 550, 559,
561, 576, 610,
655, 660, 676,
677, 682, 691,
702, 713, 763,
777, 779, 798,
824, 828, 831,
842, 853, 856,
864, 882, 894,
902, 903, 915,
938, 956, 963,
965, 977, 980

Christ hymn, **144,**
159, 179, 230,
396, 456, 602,
716

Christlikeness, 168,
697, 751, 754,
758, 934

Christus victor,
442, 699, 773

churl, churlish, 72,
138, 381, 403,
410, 414, 701,
729, 789, 903,
913

circumcision, 4, 14,
72, 73, 101, 106,
148-49, 160,
163, 164, 178,
200, 222, 239,
312-14, 324,
368, 421, 422,
430, 431, 461,
491, 492, 504,
531, 571, 594,
611, 618, 642,
737, 738, 739,
758, 765, 863,
864, 894, 911

cistern, **149**-50,
204, 220, 283,
412, 435, 436,
620, 646, 673,
706, 811, 865,
930

citizen, citizens, 62,
114, 134, 147,
153, 154, 194,
198, 239, 300,
325, 341, 423,
461, 480, 497,
501, 505, 514,
542, 552, 609,
628, 639, 642,
647, 669, 725,
728, 743, 751,
796, 822, 857,
880, 883, 898,
923, 943

city, cities, 3, 7-9,
22-25, 27, 30,
34, 45, 46, 50,
51, 54, 59, 64,
66, 67, 68, 76-
78, 80, 82, 85,
88, 89, 92, 95,
100, 106, 111,
114, 118, 119,
120, 124, 126,
128, 129, 131,
149, **150**-55,
159, 163, 169,
174, 175, 176,
185, 189, 194,
203-5, 211, 212,
214, 215, 232,
234, 236, 241,
243, 257, 259,
265, 269, 270,
279, 280, 282,
284, 285, 287,
291, 301, 302,
304-7, 311, 315,
317, 321, 322,
324, 325, 327-
31, 333, 339-41,
353, 371, 372,
375, 376, 378,
382, 395, 402,
408, 417, 418,
427-29, 436-38,
441, 452, 458,
459, 461, 462,
464, 469, 473,
478, 485, 488,
492, 501, 510,
512, 513, 518,
519, 522, 549,

550, 552, 553,
566, 567, 572,
574, 580-83,
586, 592, 593,
595, 596, 605,
608, 615-17,
622, 624, 626,
630, 632, 633,
635, 636, 641,
642, 645, 647,
648, 656, 663-
65, 667, 669,
670, 673, 674,
678, 679, 685,
697, 701-04,
710, 713, 714,
718, 719, 721,
723, 725, 729,
730, 732, 733,
740, 745, 748,
749, 752, 757,
764, 769, 776,
779, 786, 788,
791, 792, 796,
802, 803, 807-9,
820-23, 830,
834, 835, 845,
847, 857-60,
877, 880, 881,
887, 888, 890,
896, 898, 899,
901, 906, 907,
912, 913, 915-
17, 920, 923-30,
939, 945, 946,
950, 952, 953,
955, 964, 972,
973, 979-81

civil disobedience,
154-55

clay, 57, 82, 103,
114, 120, **155,**
199, 257, 307,
341, 485, 555,
684, 686, 738,
764, 765, 792,
817, 874, 875,
880, 889, 923,
965

clean, cleansing, 12,
40, 50, 56, 74,
81, 106, 108,
127, **156**-58,
163, 164, 167,
168, 182, 196,
206, 216, 240,
257, 258, 281,
289, 290, 298,
302, 307, 326,
331, 356, 361-
63, 373, 375,
390, 415, 424,
425, 427-29,
434, 439, 489-
91, 495, 504,
508, 509, 514,
515, 516, 530,
539, 554, 575,
580, 594, 611,
616, 638, 667,
688, 689, 704,
727, 730, 731,
749, 750, 752,
754, 758, 759,
764, 781, 792,
800, 810, 811,
812, 815, 832,
835, 843, 850,
874, 875, 879,
915, 926, 927,
929, 931, 963,
971, 972, 979,
981

clean and unclean,
156, 257, 258,
290, 489, 850

close, 2, 3, 8, 23,

453, 457, 458,
460, 461-63,
469, 470, 473,
480, 482, 487,
488, 492-94, 501-
3, 505, 517-19,
521, 532, 533,
537, 538, 540,
541, 544-46,
558, 572, 582,
583, 595, 600,
602, 610, 612,
614-16, 619,
643, 620, 623,
629, 637, 638,
642, 644, 650,
652, 655, 656,
658, 662, 665,
676, 681-83,
687, 695, 696,
698, 706, 710,
713, 717, 719,
721, 722, 726,
736, 738, 740,
744, 746, 749,
754, 757, 766,
770, 775, 786,
788, 789, 791,
795-98, 805,
807, 816, 826,
828, 829, 835,
844, 861, 862,
864, 867, 872-
74, 877, 881,
888, 894, 907,
908, 911, 912,
914, 918, 923,
927, 929, 938,
941, 945, 947,
948, 951, 961,
964, 965, 970
famine, 22, 36, 37,
38, 41, 48, 59,
69, 78, 93, 98,
183, 196, 221,
227-29, 231,
232, **267-68**,
276, 297, 300,
339, 347, 348,
374, 380, 401,
403, 411, 453,
460, 471, 472,
517, 619, 667,
682, 697, 706,
708, 715, 739,
741, 745, 763,
770, 814, 816-
18, 826, 855,
867, 946
far, farness, 1, 7, 9,
17, 22, 28, 34,
49, 51, 53, 61,
81, 84, 86, 90,
97, 126, 140,
148, 152, 158,
162, 164, 175,
180, 185, 197,
200, 203-5, 210,
220, 225, 228,
238, 239, 241,
245, 247, 261,
266, **268**, 293,
296, 303, 325,
331, 335, 342,
360, 371, 376,
378, 391, 393-
95, 402, 410,
415, 423, 429,
437, 438, 449,
450, 462, 477,
481, 482, 489,
493, 502, 507,
508, 515, 525,
538, 541, 556,
575, 589, 591,
596, 597, 599,
604, 605, 609,

615, 638, 642,
652, 654, 657,
659, 669, 672,
678, 680, 684,
685, 690, 694,
697, 699, 702,
703, 706, 712,
717, 719, 729,
736, 737, 750,
751, 753, 755,
763, 781, 786,
792, 793, 796,
803, 813, 816,
832, 848, 869,
872, 878, 889,
894, 903, 905,
910, 926, 927,
932, 941, 959,
964, 967, 972,
975, 981
farewell discourse,
133, 178, 253,
268-69, 274,
299, 550, 606,
627, 631, 638,
691, 696, 814,
817, 869, 902
farm, farming, 27,
28, 74, 76, 79,
148, 165, 175,
269-71, 281,
316, 324, 334,
365, 367, 379,
453, 488, 553,
558, 559, 588,
623, 733, 741,
870, 909, 956
fast, fasting, 5, 72,
113, 130, 164,
178, 201, 226,
246, **272**-73,
278, 279, 305,
306, 307, 329,
415, 439, 440,
450, 459, 480,
535, 536, 543,
574, 592, 631,
640, 650, 680,
698, 704, 814,
704, 731, 744,
747, 755, 788,
813, 853, 856,
864, 884, 926,
938, 939, 950,
954, 961, 978
fat, fatness, 31, 105,
131, 132, 206,
207, 222, **273**,
287, 405, 408,
410, 425, 554,
576, 602, 604,
718, 750, 894
father, fatherhood,
3-6, 10, 13-15,
17, 23, 24, 46,
49, 52, 57-61,
63, 64, 69, 72,
73, 85, 88, 93,
96, 97, 107, 114,
115, 118, 125,
126, 133, 135,
137, 138, 142,
143, 150, 152,
161, 162, 163,
166, 170, 174,
177, 179, 186,
188, 193-95,
200, 204, 206,
208, 212, 214,
215, 219, 220,
227, 229, 233,
237, 241, 244,
245, 264, 265,
266-69, **273**-75,
284, 286, 289,
300, 302-4, 306,
312-14, 319,

320, 324, 327,
331-33, 335,
336, 339, 342,
343, 352, 361,
363, 364, 374,
376, 378, 381,
385, 386, 388,
391-93, 395-98,
402, 405-7, 409,
412, 419, 420,
422, 424, 432-
34, 437, 439,
440, 445-47,
449, 450, 456-
58, 460, 462-65,
468, 471, 480,
481, 483, 486,
494, 502, 503,
506, 511, 512,
517, 518, 520,
521, 530-34,
537, 538, 540,
541, 546, 548,
569, 571, 572,
584, 587, 593,
602, 606, 607,
614-16, 620,
623, 624, 631,
637, 641, 643,
644, 650, 656,
659, 660, 665-
67, 670, 674,
680, 681, 686,
697, 698, 700,
707, 709, 710,
712, 717, 720,
723, 726, 728,
729, 733, 736-
39, 744-46, 749,
750, 755, 756,
765, 766, 776,
778, 784, 789,
796, 799, 801,
805-7, 830, 832,
835, 839, 841,
845, 853, 857,
858, 861, 872,
882, 885, 888,
894, 898, 902,
903, 908, 913,
914, 925, 930,
935, 938, 940,
947, 957, 959-
61, 964, 965,
968, 969, 972,
975
favored child, 137,
275
fear, 11, 15, 16, 24,
25, 29, 32, 48,
50, 52, 53, 55,
61-63, 66, 74,
78, 84, 86, 100,
102, 103, 107,
104, 109, 118,
130, 150, 151,
154, 155, 162,
172, 174, 177,
179, 183, 189,
196, 198, 204,
207, 212, 218,
219, 221, 228,
234, 237, 242,
255, 263, 265,
268, **275**-78,
290, 293, 296,
298, 301, 305,
307, 308, 319,
326, 328, 330,
337, 343, 344,
351, 359, 366,
369, 375, 380,
389, 395, 398,
400, 403, 407,
412, 429, 441,
470, 472, 473,
483, 493, 497,

500, 512, 514,
520, 522, 524,
526, 541, 536,
540, 547, 578,
579, 581, 584,
605, 608, 609,
615, 618, 622,
624, 636, 649,
654, 678, 682,
683, 692, 695,
702, 711, 717,
719, 734, 742,
751, 763, 767,
768, 773, 783,
785, 790, 791,
797, 804, 818,
824, 825, 832,
842, 853, 855-
57, 859, 862,
880, 881, 886,
889, 891, 892,
903, 907, 914,
918, 922, 920,
928, 934, 936,
945, 946, 952,
956, 959, 960,
961, 968
fear of God, 25, 50,
86, 151, 154,
207, 242, 265,
275, 277-78,
296, 343, 615,
702, 717, 767,
804, 922, 928,
956
feast, feasting, 23,
26, 31, 37, 41,
56, 70-72, 78,
88, 116, 121,
132, 135, 138,
160, 170, 183,
188, 191, 220,
222, 246, 247,
258, 270, **278**-
83, 299, 358,
359, 365, 366,
403-7, 440, 444,
453, 456, 480,
456, 466, 480,
495, 544, 505,
535, 536, 545,
552, 574, 603,
616, 623, 624,
629, 633, 653,
658, 663, 668,
679, 698, 702,
715, 729, 747,
750, 795, 828,
844, 857, 885,
899, 900, 907,
920, 931, 938,
939, 942, 949,
953
fence, 239, **280**-81,
305, 687, 924,
925
fenced place, **280**
festival, 23, 70,
246, 257, 258,
270, 279, **281**-
82, 289, 342,
348, 358, 359,
365, 366, 407,
408, 417, 505,
565, 566, 574,
623, 629, 633,
643, 644, 647,
652, 702, 664,
709, 747, 758,
844, 854, 870,
897, 901, 908,
950, 963
festivities, 72, 83,
138, 148, 216,
279, 282, 405,
459, 701, 702,
882

field, fields, 6, 9,
20, 29, 44, 46,
58, 68, 74, 77,
83, 89, 104, 116,
131, 132, 148,
165, 175, 176,
178, 182, 197,
215, 222, 224,
236, 244, 269-
71, 286, 294,
295, 302, 304,
313, 314, 318,
325, 329, 330,
334, 348, 349,
352, 353, 357,
363, 365, 366,
367, 377, 379,
382, 391, 397,
402, 408, 423,
430, 432, 434,
436, 451, 479,
472, 480, 497,
499, 504, 506,
516, 524, 533,
536, 542, 549,
552, 559, 561,
574, 576, 587,
588, 589, 590,
611, 614, 618,
628, 650, 658,
673, 694, 703,
740, 741, 749,
756, 764, 771,
780, 784, 800,
805, 831, 858,
881, 884, 891,
901, 912, 916,
926, 937, 941,
947, 950, 956,
953, 958, 963,
964, 967, 968,
980
fifty, 90, 111, 128,
139, 162, 163,
189, 204, **283**,
291, 292, 330,
349, 384, 483,
530, 531, 599,
605, 630, 633,
634, 659, 674,
701, 744, 748,
770, 773, 810,
822, 837, 880,
881, 944, 975
fig, fig tree, 6, 12,
103, 116, 146,
269, 270, **283**-
84, 297, 305,
311, 320, 350,
357, 363, 433,
465, 482, 488,
497, 498, 521,
537, 549, 581,
588, 596, 612,
620, 650, 665,
666, 667, 670,
671, 673, 675,
741, 833, 843,
865, 890-92,
905, 909, 916,
928, 942, 945
fill, filling, 6, 9-11,
18, 31, 42, 49,
56, 64, 104, 107,
134, 138, 147,
159, 160, 180,
214, 220, 227,
232, 233, 238,
247, 252, 256,
261, 264, 269,
284-85, 310,
330, 340, 341,
362, 369, 371,
378, 392, 434,
487, 467, 489,
493, 498, 531,
534, 535, 554,

567, 612, 644,
651, 653, 708,
742, 746, 765,
783, 803, 814,
815, 846-48,
850, 852, 865,
884, 892, 898,
910, 951
filth, filthiness, 29,
74, 167, 221,
320, 325, 370,
415, 696
finger, fingers, 12,
104, 173, 180,
190, 191, **286**,
291, 328, 361,
513, 542, 566,
587, 663, 728,
765, 811, 766,
787, 811, 813,
875, 878, 880,
902, 962
fire, 8, 19, 20, 22,
23, 25, 30, 36,
38, 40, 42, 46,
50, 52, 57, 59,
66, 68, 73, 75,
84, 88, 93, 114,
117, 123, 126,
130, 136, 139,
157, 159, 160,
169, 172, 173,
182, 183, 189,
193, 196, 199,
201, 206, 212,
213, 221, 225,
227, 232, 233,
236, 242, 249,
251, 253, 260,
261, 281, **286**-
88, 302, 321,
325, 330, 334,
344, 354, 356,
359, 366, 371,
374, 376, 377,
389, 390, 393,
401, 405, 410,
418, 428, 429,
433, 442, 449,
452, 467, 468,
471-73, 486,
499, 500, 508,
509, 511-13,
516, 525, 530,
547, 554, 564,
568-70, 573,
592, 595, 601,
607, 615, 616,
634, 635, 639,
646, 667-72,
674, 679, 682,
685, 686, 688,
689, 694, 700,
708, 715, 726,
729, 745, 748,
749, 762, 765,
785, 792, 794,
801-3, 820, 832,
844, 848, 849,
857-61, 865,
866, 869, 876,
878, 880, 887,
891-93, 898,
904, 910, 918,
924, 932, 936,
943, 944, 946,
962-64, 970, 981
firewood, 466, 673,
936, 964
firmament, 169,
170, 172, 201,
370, 611, 657,
765, 819, 828,
929, 953
first, **289**-91
firstborn, 14, 28,
96, 97, 126, 131,

135, 150, 227,
229, 244, 248,
253, 289-91,
339, 376, 400,
435, 440, 446,
447, 473, 492,
500, 507, 530-
33, 541, 571,
574, 618, 629,
649, 662, 698,
699, 805, 829,
957, 977
firstborn child, 229,
699
firstborn son, 97,
150, 227, 339,
435, 446, 530,
574
firstfruits, 70, 95,
97, 100, 278,
283, 289, 347,
434, 435, 463,
740, 750, 799,
942
fish, 7, 10, 31, 32,
87, 102, 105,
117, 118, 179,
224, 245, 257,
290, 298, 321,
329, 357, 405,
420, 434, 444,
458, 459, 480,
488, 489, 494,
534, 537, 574,
587, 702, 707,
801, 815, 830,
864, 866, 885-
87, 893, 919,
930, 932
fisher, 138, **290**,
533, 772
fishing, 31, 32, 290,
385, 489, 843,
887, 932
five, **291**
flag, 70
flame, 8, 25, 84,
130, 172, 233,
260, 287, 393,
509, 818, 858,
859, 869, 878,
892, 943
flee, flight, 30, 42,
49, 76, 77, 79,
80, 89, 93, 94,
96, 107, 139,
170, 197, 204,
208, 211, 212,
217, 229, 235,
237, 245, 248,
250, 276, 277,
291, 278, **291**-
92, 309, 386,
409, 413, 436,
439, 458, 459,
462, 468, 497,
519, 535, 541,
550, 551, 572,
580, 627, 629,
701, 706, 712,
714, 743, 744,
786, 823, 790,
800, 801, 803,
825, 838, 873,
869, 880, 885,
887, 904, 908,
928, 941, 949,
950, 954, 955
flesh, fleshly, 9, 10,
17, 18, 20, 23,
32, 34, 36, 56,
72, 86, 87, 91,
93, 95, 100, 101,
103-13, 118,
120, 123, 124,
126, 129, 141,
144, 160, 163,

168, 177, 178,
198, 202, 203,
209, 211, 213,
227, 233, 235-
37, 239, 240,
247, 250, 257,
264, 266, 274,
279, 288, 290,
291, 295, 299,
301, 311, 314,
330, 349, 368,
377, 391-94,
400, 405, 408,
413, 418, 431,
434, 441, 443-
46, 453, 455,
464, 466, 468,
469, 503, 506-8,
514, 527, 532,
538, 542, 545,
551, 554, 555,
557, 568, 569,
570, 571, 572,
587, 608, 614,
638, 641, 642,
650, 662, 669,
684, 731, 736,
737, 738, 745,
750, 761, 777,
778, 796, 810,
815, 826, 838-
40, 847, 858,
859, 865, 873,
879, 883-85,
897, 932, 934,
939, 944, 947-
49, 952, 957,
959, 969, 972,
973,
flint, 148, 436, 461,
556, 804, 821
flock, flocks, 3, 22,
29, 30, 32, 39,
41, 44, 60, 68,
75, 77, 82, 131,
148, 185, 208,
212, 216, 218,
226, 269, 270,
288, **292-93**,
331, 332, 344,
357, 359, 386,
392, 433, 435,
489, 522, 497,
514, 536, 549,
552, 553, 554,
561, 596, 619,
630, 632, 637,
669, 671, 676,
708, 733, 734,
782, 783, 784,
830, 863, 894,
902, 909, 928,
933, 940, 958,
979
flood, 10, 20, 42,
48, 58, 73, 77,
98, 101, 119,
140, 150, 157,
158, 167, 170,
172, 175, 177,
182, 201, 230,
245, 256, 263,
265, **293-95**,
297, 298, 305,
323, 329, 330,
350, 369, 387,
395, 400, 412,
458, 460, 471,
473, 482, 504,
513, 547, 588,
589, 590, 601,
602, 611, 614,
638, 639, 654,
656, 664, 682,
694-96, 703,
706, 729, 765,
786, 808, 818,

819, 855, 893,
904, 905, 910,
916, 929, 932,
936, 953, 954,
965, 980
flower, flowers, 11,
83, 84, 104, 261,
294-96, 349,
434, 450, 479,
486, 587, 588,
604, 650, 651,
806, 833, 884,
890
fly, flying, 30, 37,
48, 93, 94, 281,
408, 428, 432,
516, 579, 580,
670, 671, 707,
708, 724, 738,
808, 855, 885,
954, 955
follower, followers,
26, 38, 39, 44,
48, 53, 59, 61,
64, 73, 82, 86,
99, 102, 109,
115, 116, 118,
144, 147, 148,
159, 160, 183,
184, 186, 212,
223, 230, 232,
238, 243, 245,
266, 268, 277,
280, 298, 299,
301, 339, 340,
345, 371, 373,
374, 379, 395,
396, 404, 411,
426, 439, 442,
444, 449, 457,
463, 464, 465,
479, 486, 491,
493, 494, 496-
498, 497, 534,
543, 546, 551,
558, 559, 572,
586, 600, 607,
635, 643, 664,
665, 673, 682,
699, 707, 709,
711, 713, 718,
729, 745, 749,
752, 761, 764,
766, 768, 769,
772, 798, 832,
834, 841, 846,
852, 859, 861,
863, 865, 877,
879, 883, 884,
894, 918, 921,
923, 926, 929,
934, 939, 961,
972
folly, foolishness,
16, 87, 92, 101,
107, 117, 127,
141, 168, 184,
192, 219, 227,
264, **296**-97,
337, 349, 353,
399, 404, 408,
409, 410, 500,
524, 531, 575,
601, 605, 610,
612, 653, 679-
81, 723, 762,
779, 810, 792,
823, 831, 832,
845, 852, 853,
884, 897, 903,
919, 934, 956,
960, 963
food, 2, 5-7, 9, 16,
21, 26, 29, 31,
40, 60, 64, 71,
74, 75, 81, 87,
88, 93, 94, 102,

103, 105, 117,
132, 155, 156,
165, 171, 175,
180, 184, 190,
198, 210, 212,
214, 221, 224,
226, 227, 231,
236, 237, 249,
252, 257, 258,
267, 270, 272,
276, 278, 279,
281, 282, 284,
286, 290, 291,
297-99, 304,
307, 310, 312,
315, 316, 318,
325, 332, 342,
349-51, 357,
366, 375, 402-6,
411, 412, 419,
420, 422, 423,
433-35, 443,
444, 461, 479,
482, 488, 492,
494, 495, 498,
507, 508, 515,
525, 527, 534,
536, 537, 544,
545, 551, 565,
588, 590, 598,
603, 604, 607,
610, 611, 622,
632, 636, 650,
651, 656, 658,
662, 672, 673,
677, 682, 683,
687, 693, 694,
698, 702, 704,
707, 722, 723,
739, 745, 752,
766, 770, 779,
782, 784, 794,
800, 803, 807,
814, 815, 817,
820, 824, 828,
834, 840, 846,
847, 865, 867,
874, 887, 899,
903, 921, 928,
931, 938, 942,
947, 948, 953-
55, 959, 964, 965
fool, 2, 25, 87, 111,
117, 138, 162,
169, 222, 255,
264, 296, 337,
341, 362, 366,
398, 401, 409,
410, 465, 496,
500, 515, 521,
524, 534, 575,
612, 650, 654,
679, 680, 734,
865, 886, 889,
914, 937, 943
foot, feet, 8, 11, 13,
16, 20, 37, 42,
44, 49, 50, 57,
61, 74, 77, 78,
82, 84, 85, 92,
98, 103-7, 115,
124, 130, 132,
155, 157, 159,
162, 179, 183,
188, 190, 223,
236-38, 247,
250, 257, 264,
269, 280, 295,
294, 326, 296,
314, 327, 328,
329, 337, 341,
354, 355, 358-
60, 371, 374,
375, 376, 377,
380, 391, 394,
399, 403, 406,
407, 408, 409,

442, 461, 486,
496, 499, 511,
530, 540, 544,
550, 561, 562,
566, 572, 578,
581, 591, 605,
618, 619, 633,
627, 631, 633,
644, 650, 662,
671, 678, 680,
681, 708, 717,
724, 727, 728,
733, 739, 744,
745, 748, 764,
774, 777, 778,
781, 786, 787,
793, 795, 798,
802, 812, 815,
822, 823, 828,
835, 841, 843,
846, 859, 874,
875, 879, 887,
896, 888, 896,
899, 905-907,
922, 923, 926-
928, 935, 936,
949, 961, 970
footstool, 43, 77,
78, 224, 236,
238, 374, 394,
419, 437, 442,
743, 838, 849,
899, 906, 972
forehead, 50, 85,
206, **299**-300,
364, 591, 703,
878, 895
foreigner, 138, 144,
217, 254, 279,
300-301, 303,
324, 325, 330,
334, 338, 370,
409, 421, 477,
506, 553, 614,
637, 643, 644,
645, 657, 693,
743, 746, 797,
798, 906, 960
forest, 29, 30, 46,
116, 175, 182,
224, 288, **302**,
433, 465, 472,
479, 499, 573,
618, 686, 623,
726, 806, 891,
892, 964
forgiveness, 2, 17,
25, 51, 54, 69,
114, 127, 128,
156, 158, 161,
163, 167, 186,
195, 200, 209,
299, 237, **302-3**,
320, 331, 332,
334, 342, 344,
346, 347, 352,
355, 373, 436,
440, 441, 446,
450, 458, 459,
461, 491, 492,
508, 522, 527,
535, 542, 546,
548, 549, 585,
605, 628, 632,
641, 678, 687,
692, 697, 699,
700, 702, 704,
705, 713, 750,
751, 755, 765,
775, 780, 781,
793, 802, 820,
837, 843, 882,
883, 927, 937,
960
forsake, forsaken,
22, 39, 40, 94,
115, 168, 192,

237, **303**-4, 322,
349, 414, 435,
438, 491, 522,
538, 545, 601,
616, 712, 745,
816, 821, 865,
948, 955
fortress, 5, 14, 22,
31, 45, 46, 111,
120, 128, 132,
184, 196, 199,
244, 286, **304**-5,
315, 334, 369,
383, 390, 395,
399, 404, 451,
464, 537, 555,
570, 572, 586,
596, 606, 638,
641, 674, 678,
684, 685, 701,
725, 733, 740,
822, 845, 854,
868, 880, 881,
900, 930
forty, 25, 76, 111,
129, 157, 166,
182, 200, 249,
253, 254, 272,
283, **305-6**, 318,
347, 393, 460,
462, 463, 467,
471, 497, 530,
543, 572, 583,
599, 615, 630,
632, 636, 647,
666, 691, 694,
704, 722, 767,
776, 794, 801,
814, 825, 841,
879, 925, 936,
949, 952, 968,
971
foundation, 4, 7,
60, 61, 84, 114,
128, 129, 151,
154, 165, 166,
169, 181, 194,
206, 224, 229,
239, 240, 294,
299, 304-5, **306**-
7, 335, 358, 374,
398, 375, 398,
428, 437, 446,
449, 451, 452,
496, 537, 538,
556, 559, 573,
587, 602, 626,
637, 646, 645,
687, 713, 717,
720, 723, 725,
732, 733, 738,
751, 759, 765,
782, 792, 806,
816, 819, 820,
823, 845, 858,
873-75, 893,
901, 964, 968,
976
fountain, 12, 41,
150, 201, **307**,
315, 371, 413,
538, 594, 665,
681, 694, 725,
777, 793, 806,
810, 811, 819,
842, 846, 847,
911, 929, 930,
931, 940, 941,
979
four, **307-8**
fox, 30, 851, 924
freedom, 59, 70,
90, 103, 104,
112, 113, 141,
160, 168, 181,
187-89, 236,
253, 276, 283,

691, 696, 698,
699, 701, 703,
705-9, 711, 716,
719, 720, 724,
726-28, 731-35,
739, 742, 743,
760, 749, 757,
763, 764, 768,
769, 776, 777,
779-81, 783,
786, 787, 796-
98, 800, 801,
803, 805, 807-9,
813, 815-21,
825, 830-32,
840, 842, 843,
845, 849, 851,
852, 854, 857,
859-61, 862,
863, 865, 867,
869, 871, 872,
875, 876, 877,
879-81, 884-86,
891, 893, 895,
896, 899, 909,
913, 915, 917,
920, 927, 928,
931, 933, 935-
37, 944, 949,
951, 952, 953,
957, 960, 962-
66, 968, 970,
973, 974, 980
hand over, 361,
896, 915, 951
hand washing, 72,
362-63, 544
hang, hanging, 5,
46, 48, 103, 108,
184, 313, **363**,
425, 462, 500,
881, 902, 911,
964
happy, happiness, 6,
42, 75, 81, 121,
122, 139, 140,
160, 161, 200,
221, 246, 262,
274, 284, 318,
327, 343, **363-
64**, 406, 364,
432, 440, 464,
473, 495, 569,
618, 631, 644,
652, 653, 657,
673, 702, 730,
745, 831, 850,
891, 903, 920,
951
hard, hardness, 26,
27, 33, 47, 54,
105, 112, 120,
123, 124, 143,
163, 170, 184,
198, 201, 223,
224, 273, 299,
314, 315, 322,
333, 342, 360,
364-65, 369,
385, 417, 443,
463, 536, 537,
547, 554, 556,
557, 579, 638,
639, 641, 642,
649, 658, 666,
675, 679, 680,
687, 723, 736,
740, 787, 788,
790, 796, 804,
811, 815, 832,
844, 862, 867,
911, 916, 934,
948, 953, 969
harden, hardening,
364, 373, 809
harp, 19, 48, 54,
72, 83, **364-65**,

419, 560, 578,
652, 834, 834
harvest, harvesting,
6, 7, 22, 32, 37,
53, 68, 70, 71,
81, 86, 102, 106,
136, 157, 175,
228, 267, 270,
271, 278, 281,
283, 289, 290,
298, 310, 311,
314, 334, 342,
347, 348, 358,
365-67, 392,
398, 402, 411,
420, 434, 435,
454, 455, 465,
473, 480, 488,
497, 498, 515,
553, 563, 587-
89, 588, 623,
624, 633, 668,
681, 694, 697,
713, 719, 745,
746, 767, 768,
772, 800, 818,
809, 819, 848,
860, 864, 867,
869, 870, 915,
937, 942-44,
946, 954
head, 5, 8, 10, 14,
20, 23, 28, 44,
45, 49, 52, 60,
62, 70, 71, 77,
78, 80, 81, 84,
100, 103, 104,
109, 122-24,
126, 128-30,
132, 135, 148,
165, 166, 179,
185, 187, 188,
192, 212, 236-
38, 240, 246,
251, 265, 266,
272, 280, 295,
296, 301, 307,
318, 326-28,
331, 337, 339,
341, 348, 351,
359-61, **367-68**,
376, 379, 395,
403-5, 407-9,
414, 415, 420,
440, 444, 451,
453, 463, 494,
502, 506, 508,
511, 532, 534,
536, 538, 540,
551, 554, 555,
574, 598, 604,
605, 612, 615,
616, 619, 623,
627, 641, 648,
650, 659, 672,
680, 687, 695,
698, 704, 739,
752, 753, 764,
768, 774, 775,
777, 781, 782,
787, 790, 807,
813, 816, 820,
828, 858, 859,
865, 872, 874,
877, 883, 895-
98, 905, 906,
923, 930, 935,
944, 956, 961,
972
healed, healing, 20,
27, 34, 36, 48,
58, 73, 86, 94,
99, 107, 123,
128, 143, 155,
163, 164, 166,
174, 194, 197,
202, **209**-10,

213, 227, 243,
256, 303, 310,
315, 320, 326,
334, 340, 351,
362, 364, 380,
382, 390, 407,
410, 415, 423,
427-29, 437,
439, 441, 443,
444, 446, 450,
455, 456, 460,
483, 496, 526,
498, 507, 520,
521, 522, 525-
29, 531, 535,
537, 544, 548,
568, 598, 603,
605, 614, 621,
632, 640, 658,
667, 683, 697,
702, 718, 748,
751, 753-56,
780, 810, 783,
787, 788, 845,
790, 795, 827,
846, 849, 864,
876, 878, 879,
883, 890, 901,
933, 945, 948,
961, 973, 974
hear, hearing, 18,
46, 80, 91, 95,
96, 108, 117,
120, 128, 136,
142, 149, 157,
163, 164, 177,
197, 198, 206,
199, 208, 215,
217, 223, 224,
227, 228, 249,
254, 268, 271,
276, 277, 299,
324, 326, 332,
337, 351, 363,
364, 441, 367,
401, 410, 432,
434, 435, 439,
450, 454, 456,
457, 462, 463,
465, 467, 470,
477, 479, 492,
495, 504, 534-
37, 539, 545,
549, 568, 569,
573, 586, 592,
594, 606, 605,
607, 614, 626,
627, 632, 659,
665, 668-74,
677, 679, 687,
696, 704, 710,
714, 716, 717,
719, 726, 727,
739, 740, 742,
746, 747, 767,
788, 801, 794,
802, 804, 820,
841, 850, 865,
866, 876, 884,
895, 902, 903,
913, 918, 922,
939, 940, 951,
953, 963, 964
heart, hearts, 4, 6,
14, 16, 19, 33,
38-41, 45, 47,
52, 62, 72, 73,
80, 82, 83, 85,
86, 88, 91, 92,
99, 102, 104-7,
112, 117, 120,
123, 124, 127,
130, 133, 141,
149, 156, 157,
159-61, 162,
164, 167, 168,
173, 175, 176,

178, 183, 189,
195, 200, 202,
206, 207, 214,
216, 223, 231,
235, 241, 245,
248-50, 252,
255, 257, 260,
265, 266, 268,
275-77, 279,
282, 285, 293,
296, 298, 299,
301-3, 309, 314,
325-27, 331, 335-
37, 341, 344,
351, 352, 353,
355, 362-64,
368-70, 371,
373, 375, 376,
380, 382, 390-
92, 395, 403-5,
408, 415, 420,
421, 424-26,
428, 431, 434-
36, 438, 440,
459, 463, 465,
469, 470, 477,
479-81, 483,
487, 489-91, 493-
97, 509, 511,
512, 515, 533,
534, 536, 537,
541, 545-49,
554, 555, 558,
560, 561, 566,
568, 574-78,
587, 591, 594,
595, 602, 603,
606-8, 611, 614,
618, 625, 633,
634, 639-41,
644, 652-55,
660, 662, 665,
670, 672, 673,
676-78, 682,
687, 688, 690,
697, 698, 700,
704, 712, 720,
721, 728, 730,
731, 737-39,
745, 748, 750,
751, 754-56,
761, 766, 767,
777, 783-85,
788, 791, 792,
794, 800, 804,
805, 807-9, 811,
812, 814, 815,
825, 817, 823,
829-33, 836,
842, 846, 852,
853, 854, 858,
860, 868, 871,
874, 876, 879,
880, 883, 886,
889, 893, 897,
921, 926, 927,
930, 931, 933,
938, 944, 946,
948, 949, 954,
960, 961, 963,
971, 976, 977
heat, 24, 38, 40,
41, 74, 157, 168,
221, 232, 260,
276, 295, 298,
312, 313, 349,
372, 377, 401,
402, 434, 435,
455, 490, 513,
530, 535, 547,
562, 563, 589,
610, 632, 649,
650, 670, 677,
700, 701, 767,
779, 808, 827,
838, 848, 849,
862, 864, 878,

891, 936, 937,
948
heaven, 5-8, 12-15,
17-20, 23, 24, 35-
38, 40, 43, 47-
52, 49, 54,
56-58, 66, 68,
70, 74, 82, 84-
89, 92, 94, 96,
98, 99, 113, 117-
120, 126, 128,
131, 139, 141,
144, 151, 153,
154, 157, 159,
163-65, 169, 170-
75, 177, 181,
182, 190, 191,
196, 198, 201-7,
213, 217, 224,
220, 224-26,
228, 231-33,
236, 238, 241,
242, 245, 253,
255, 261-63,
266, 267, 273,
286-88, 293,
294, 297-303,
306, 307, 313,
315, 316, 318-
20, 322, 326,
329-31, 339,
341, 343, 347,
349, 352, 354,
358, 364, 370-
73, 375, 376,
378, 381, 382,
384, 385, 391,
392, 394-97,
399, 401, 404,
405, 407, 411,
415, 419, 421,
427-29, 433,
437, 440, 444-
47, 449-52, 456,
460, 464-67,
472, 476, 478-
83, 486, 488,
489, 494, 495,
497, 506, 510-
12, 514, 517,
521, 525, 526,
534, 535, 540,
541, 543, 547,
561, 555, 563,
565, 566, 569,
570, 573, 574,
578, 582, 585,
587, 589, 590,
594, 596, 598,
606, 607, 612,
608, 611, 619,
620, 623, 624,
627, 632-35,
643, 644, 645,
671, 653, 654,
663-65, 668,
671, 672, 674,
682, 685, 686,
690-92, 694,
696, 707, 709,
710, 713-16,
720, 721, 723-
25, 730, 735,
739, 743, 745,
747-49, 751,
755, 756, 761,
762, 763, 765,
767-69, 771,
776, 788-91,
794, 796, 802,
804, 805, 811,
813, 814, 817,
819, 820, 825,
827, 828, 837-
39, 844, 841,
849, 850, 854,
857, 859-61,

863, 865, 867,
869, 873, 878,
880, 883, 885,
887, 890, 891,
896, 899, 901-3,
905, 907-9, 918,
919, 922, 929,
936, 930, 936,
937, 942-45,
952, 953, 957,
958, 962, 963,
967, 968, 980,
981
heavenlies, 59, 238,
241
heavenly
army/hosts, 23,
24, 47, 48, 54,
58, 172, 211,
212, **372**-73,
401, 467, 479,
526, 674, 860,
899
heavy, heaviness,
30, 52, 99, 107,
207, 223, 356,
361, **373**-74,
388, 392, 444,
445, 452, 476,
494, 499, 534,
574, 621, 685,
710, 715, 787,
797, 800, 807,
834, 903, 936,
937, 956
hedge, 280, 281,
683, 865, 872,
874, 915
heel, 128, 218,
376, 432, 583,
675, 752
height, heights, 3,
12, 20, 49, 103,
104, 116, 129,
135, 151, 152,
200, 226, 234,
238, 295, 328,
335, 344, 383,
384, 385, 397,
499, 578, 596,
601, 706, 714,
794, 801, 909,
923, 931, 952
heir, heirs, 14, 59,
75, 97, 121, 141,
145, 184, 194,
240, 241, 267,
301, 312, 313,
374, 375, 408,
412, 414, 421,
434, 448, 464,
503, 618, 631,
738, 754, 757,
771, 805, 806,
826, 872, 925,
960
hell, 1, 5, 17-19,
31, 49, 107, 173,
182, 193, 201,
204, 231, 232,
238, 276, 288,
363, 371, **376**-
77, 415, 433,
473, 528, 615,
639, 647, 653,
657, 664, 715,
745, 847, 876,
878, 903, 910,
969
helmet, 44-47, 124,
240, 367, 377,
399, 755, 860,
861, 899, 935
help, helper, 10, 24,
27, 30, 31, 40,
45, 59, 76, 77,
86, 112, 120,

346, 355, 369, 382, 415, **423**-25, 441, 446, 449, 459, 464, 486, 494, 506, 547, 553, 575, 584, 616, 624, 640, 662, 692, 720, 732, 738-40, 745, 754, 758, 759, 781, 811, 815, 846, 848-50, 852, 853, 880, 887, 907, 927, 931, 945, 957

inner part, **424**-25, 459

innocence, innocent, 62, 91, 141, 143, 169, 192, 255, 259, 262, 263, 283, 303, 319, 320, 323, 326, 342, 357, 361, 362, 423, **425**-26, 452, 453, 470, 484, 517, 566, 581, 588, 615, 627, 628, 655, 701, 748, 782, 858, 882, 893, 894, 958, 966, 975

inside, 42, 43, 78, 100, 120, 194, 215, 299, 321, 399, 410, 415, **423**-24, 463, 492, 515, 616, 617, 640, 646, 647, 737, 757, 764, 788, 796, 840, 850, 851, 923-25, 931, 954, 962

instruction, 131, 133, 147, 205, 237, 256, 264, 267, 273, 274, 299, 313, 333, 343, 362, 375, 380-82, 437, 442, 444, 445, 464, 489, 492, 494, 515, 538, 540, 542, 591, 595, 600, 680, 683, 765, 816, 842-44, 850, 853, 862, 914, 947, 955, 956, 961, 970

invective, 22, 575, 667, 669, 801

iron, 8, 85, 124, 128, 138, 148, 236, 239, 286, 309, 328, 360, 367, 397, 400, **426**-27, 436, 492, 507, 516, 547, 553, 555, 557, 558, 670, 704, 734, 745, 764, 821, 847, 867, 875, 877, 896, 923, 935, 964, 972

irony, 2, 8, 22, 36, 43, 67, 76, 88, 94, 99, 101, 115, 123, 151, 200, 237, 248, 279, 285, 291, 330, 337, 363, 404, 407, 409, 410,

416, 423, 427, 450, 453, 459, 462, 469, 482, 520, 529, 542, 583, 601, 629, 726, 651, 670, 726, 727, 736, 763, 801, 809, 825, 833, 834, 843, 916, 925, 934, 949, 950, 955, 964

Isaac, 3, 4, 21, 24, 63, 67, 71, 92, 95, 96, 98, 99, 122, 125, 129, 140, 161, 175, 177, 189, 193, 207, 221, 222, 227, 229, 230, 233, 242, 264, 266, 273-75, 278, 290, 300, 323, 347, 352, 353, 355, 366, 375, 379, 380, 386, 391, 403, 410, 411, 412, 413, 432, 436, 440, 451, 463, 464, 471, 506, 510, 518, 519, 533, 537, 533, 567, 568, 573, 583, 588, 602, 605, 606, 615, 617, 632, 675, 682, 696, 698, 716, 726, 738, 748, 749, 752, 771, 782, 789, 790, 814, 824, 825, 829, 855, 856, 864, 882, 887, 888, 894, 900-902, 907, 914, 925, 933, 936, 941, 952, 953, 963, 970, 977

island, 102, 232, 406, **429**-30, 475, 679, 715, 928, 936

Israel, 4, 6, 12, 15, 17, 20, 23, 28, 39, 43, 47, 50, 52, 55, 58, 72, 76, 77, 79, 86, 96, 105, 107, 108, 112, 120, 129, 131, 141, 145, 147, 149, 152, 167, 172, 179, 181, 187, 196, 203, 206, 208, 211, 217, 221, 222, 229, 234-39, 251, 252, 254, 257-59, 266, 271, 276, 281, 289, 292, 303, 307, 310, 312, 325, 327, 333, 338, 340, 348, 361, 363, 364, 367, 369, 383-90, 392, 393, 395, 397, 398, 400-404, 411-14, 419-22, **430**, 436, 437, 440-43, 446, 448-50, 463, 470, 474, 479, 481, 483, 488, 489, 492,

494, 508, 514, 517, 521, 526, 530, 536, 537, 539, 549, 552, 561, 569, 570, 597, 602, 606, 616, 618, 619, 637, 648, 651, 673-75, 677, 685, 703, 706, 707, 728, 736, 738, 740, 746, 753, 763, 775, 776, 787, 791, 795, 803, 808, 823, 834, 837, 842-44, 851, 863, 891, 902, 909, 914, 915, 920, 928, 931, 933, 942, 948

jackal, 30, 126, 203, 204, 549, 562, 563, 580, 630, 773, 927

Jacob, 4, 25, 33, 63, 67, 70, 87, 88, 95-98, 104, 121, 122, 125, 126, 129, 131, 137, 140, 144, 163, 173, 174, 177, 182, 189, 193, 200, 204, 205, 207, 214, 218, 221, 222, 225, 227, 229, 230, 242, 244, 245, 250, 260, 263, 264, 268-70, 273-75, 277, 290-92, 300, 302, 318-20, 322, 323, 332, 338, 342, 347-49, 351, 367, 369, 370, 375, 376, 379, 380, 395, 397, 407-414, 417, 418, 422, 426, 429, 430, **432**-33, 440, 444-46, 462, 463, 464, 477, 482, 498, 499, 512, 513, 520, 521, 529, 530, 531, 535, 536, 539, 541-44, 550-52, 554, 557, 568, 570-74, 579, 583, 585, 586, 591-94, 593, 596, 601, 603, 607, 608, 615, 616, 623, 624-26, 628, 633, 637, 643-49, 651, 652, 654, 663-65, 667, 669, 670, 672, 673, 676, 686, 691, 692, 696, 702, 703, 705, 708, 712, 713, 724, 730, 732, 733, 740, 743, 748, 749, 755, 757, 759, 765, 768, 786-88, 791, 793, 794, 802, 803, 812, 815, 816, 820, 822, 823, 825, 827, 840, 845-48, 850, 851, 855, 857, 867, 875, 880, 885, 887, 888, 890, 896-99, 901, 910, 913, 915, 916, 919, 923-25, 930, 932, 933, 936, 939-41, 943, 946, 950, 952, 953, 956, 961, 964, 966, 971-73, 978-81

953, 957, 974, 977

Jacob's ladder, **433**, 716

Jerusalem, 3, 5, 7-9, 11, 20, 21, 29, 30, 36, 37, 41, 43, 45, 50, 51, 59, 61-63, 67-69, 72, 75, 78, 80, 84, 88, 89, 92, 98, 105, 108, 112, 113, 116, 119, 122, 123, 126, 128, 129, 146, 147, 149-54, 169, 185, 187, 188, 191, 194, 205, 208, 210, 215, 222, 229, 234, 236, 239, 240, 251, 257, 271, 272, 278, 279, 281, 282, 293, 305-7, 310, 312-15, 317, 319, 322, 325, 326, 330, 336-38, 340, 341, 343, 346, 354, 358, 365, 370-72, 376, 377, 382, 384, 388, 393, 394, 398, 401, 406, 409, 410, 429, 430, 435, **436**-38, 440-42, 445, 448, 450-52, 455, 463, 464-66, 476, 477, 481, 486, 487, 498, 499, 512, 513, 520, 521, 529, 530, 531, 535, 536, 539, 541-44, 550-52, 554, 557, 568, 570-74, 579, 583, 585, 586, 591-94, 593, 596, 601, 603, 607, 608, 615, 616, 623, 624-26, 628, 633, 637, 643-49, 651, 652, 654, 663-65, 667, 669, 670, 672, 673, 676, 686, 691, 692, 696, 702, 703, 705, 708, 712, 713, 724, 730, 732, 733, 740, 743, 748, 749, 755, 757, 759, 765, 768, 786-88, 791, 793, 794, 802, 803, 812, 815, 816, 820, 822, 823, 825, 827, 840, 845-48, 850, 851, 855, 857, 867, 875, 880, 885, 887, 888, 890, 896-99, 901, 910, 913, 915, 916, 919, 923-25, 930, 932, 933, 936, 939-41, 943, 946, 950, 952, 953, 956, 961, 964, 966, 971-73, 978-81

jewel, jewels, 6, 37, 84, 104, 147, 159, 161, 185, 196, 317, 371, 418, **451**-52, 500, 511, 512, 633, 635, 680, 713, 715, 714, 807, 938, 948, 956, 960

John the Baptist, 26, 53, 56, 67, 72-74, 96, 107, 111, 134, 136, 156, 188, 208, 213, 215, 242, 254, 272, 284, 288, 311, 367, 379, 385, 393, 397, 410, 419, 422, 439, 441, 442, 443, 449, 456, 460, 481, 486, 495, 512, 516, 534-36, 543, 571, 572, 587, 631, 633, 651, 666, 667, 674, 716, 731, 752, 764, 787, 804, 855, 867, 891, 904, 917, 919, 939, 943, 950, 958, 969

Jordan River, 73, **459**-60, 461, 462, 535, 560, 598, 683, 717, 730, 748, 859, 888, 930

journey, journeying, 3, 7, 9, 16, 29, 36, 38, 39, 59, 117, 120, 157, 183, 197, 198, 206, 248, 250-53, 251, 262, 278, 279, 281, 301, 323, 329, 342, 378, 394, 396, 403, 409, 411, 417, 422, 438, 450, 453, 459, **462**-64, 501, 519, 520, 542, 567, 572, 598, 611, 624, 626, 630, 631, 643-45, 647, 654, 655, 665, 666, 675, 682, 690, 700, 690, 691, 692, 712, 731, 729, 733, 744, 769, 785-87, 809, 827, 832, 837, 841, 854-56, 859, 864, 887, 888, 894, 925, 940, 941, 942, 947, 948

joy, joyousness, 7, 18-20, 33, 51, 59, 62, 67, 68, 72, 75, 95, 107, 120-22, 142, 147, 162, 173, 180, 182, 185, 188, 189, 195, 199, 224, 241, 246, 271, 279, 280, 283, 292, 297, 299, 303, 327, 329, 337, 343, 350, 352, 357, 361, 365-

67, 369, 372, 378, 392, 393, 395, 396, 399, 400, 413, 421, 427, 428, 434, **464**-66, 475, 479, 509, 511, 541, 545, 553, 554, 568, 573, 575, 577, 587, 589, 593, 596, 642, 650, 652-54, 668, 672, 693, 697, 702, 705, 710, 711, 713, 720, 728, 733, 744, 745, 751, 769, 787, 789, 790, 809, 820, 846, 856, 858, 859, 862, 880, 891, 899, 901, 909, 916, 929, 931, 938-40, 942, 944, 945, 954, 970, 973

jubilee, 61, 270, 283, 502, 611, 619, 698, 900, 924

judgment, 2, 7, 11, 13, 18, 21-26, 32, 35-38, 40-43, 48, 51-56, 60, 63, 65, 67, 68, 69, 70, 72, 73, 75, 76, 78, 80, 84, 91-93, 95, 97-99, 101-3, 105-8, 110, 111, 113, 114, 116, 117, 119, 120, 123, 124, 127-29, 131, 135, 136, 138-42, 145, 147, 152, 155, 157, 159, 161, 165, 169, 172, 173, 179, 181, 183, 186, 187, 189-91, 193, 195-200, 204-6, 209, 210, 217, 219-25, 227, 229-33, 235, 246, 247, 249, 250, 252, 255-57, 262, 263, 265, 267, 268, 271, 276, 278-80, 283-86, 288, 290-95, 301, 302, 305, 306, 308, 310, 311, 316, 319, 323, 328-32, 338, 340, 343, 346-52, 354, 356-62, 365-68, 370, 373, 376, 377, 379, 380, 384, 385, 387-90, 393, 397, 401, 402, 406, 413, 427, 428, 434-37, 439, 441, 449, 451, 454, 455, 457, 459, 461, 465-67, **470**-74, 476, 479, 480, 481, 485, 487, 489, 491, 492, 494, 495, 496, 498-500, 504, 505, 509, 511, 512, 516, 517, 521,

212, 222, 223,
225, 226, 254,
265, 270, 275,
277, 278, 280,
286, 292-94,
297, 300, 298,
308-10, 313,
316, 323, 325,
364, 343, 348,
364, 365-67,
373, 374, 379,
381, 387, 388,
392, 397, 398,
411, 421, 434,
435, 438, 442,
447, 463, 465,
473, 477, 487,
490, 491, 497,
506, 513, 515,
518, 524, 533,
550, 558, 559,
561, 567, 590,
597, 601-2, 610,
625, 656, 632,
639, 643, 654,
659, 660, 661,
665, 673, 675,
677, 691, 694,
696, 702, 708,
713, 717, 719,
727, 734, 736,
737, 750, 737,
751, 758, 759,
766, 767, 768,
771, 772, 774,
780, 786, 797,
798, 803, 805,
810, 812, 826,
827, 855, 863,
889, 902, 889,
902, 903, 910,
916, 920, 922,
923, 931, 942,
944, 951, 953,
958, 962, 970-72
odor, 282, 377,
534, 654, 801,
802, 834
offering, 2, 3, 20,
21, 23, 24, 27,
28, 31, 55, 56,
61-63, 70, 72,
100, 103, 110,
118, 120, 128,
129, 131, 132,
175, 187, 216,
242, 260, 279,
281-283, 286,
287, 298, 299,
306, 324, 327,
331, 337, 338,
344, 347, 354,
356, 368, 370,
375, 384, 405,
407, 411, 420,
424, 428, 443,
463, 470, 496,
498, 499, 508,
509, 520, 530,
544, 557, 567,
557, 559, 560,
571, 580, 593,
602-4, 607, 616,
619, 624, 630,
633, 640, 654,
663, 682, 702,
728, 732, 740,
749, 750, 752,
763, 764, 776,
793, 799, 801,
811, 820, 826,
828, 832, 834,
837, 838, 838,
840, 843, 844,
855, 864, 872,
880, 901, 907,
920, 925, 942,

944, 950, 963,
970, 963, 971,
973, 980
offspring, 10, 17,
28, 67, 127, 162,
168, 169, 200,
215, 221, 225,
232, 265, 267,
310, 312, 313,
315, 333, 349,
367, 376, 388,
392, 398, 418,
436, 448, 458,
615, 644, 645,
649, 666, 734,
746, 771, 776,
857, 874, 894,
895, 902, 903,
981
oil, oils, 27, 33, 34,
46, 70, 71, 74,
81, 105, 122,
126, 130, 209,
215, 259, 280,
281, 286, 294,
296, 297, 298,
310, 318, 344,
360, 367, 390,
392, 400, 402-4,
410, 420, 455,
465, 486, 488,
510, 525, 528,
534, 544, 551-
53, 575, 587,
603-5, 634, 652,
663, 669, 677,
682, 683, 687,
719, 749, 750,
768, 770, 792,
801, 804, 807,
811, 833, 875,
889, 914, 938,
953
ointment, 448, 603,
604-5, 604, 634,
802, 832, 833
old, 3, 13-15, 17,
20, 25, 29, 31,
40, 54, 67, 70,
83, 85, 90, 94,
95, 100, 108,
111, 112, 115,
120, 126, 131,
132, 138, 142,
147-49, 152,
165, 166, 168,
174, 199, 205,
209, 215, 219,
228, 233, 240,
247, 248, 253,
257, 261, 274,
281, 283, 284,
286, 295, 300,
301, 304, 312,
314, 319, 322,
336, 339, 342,
347, 351, 360,
363, 364, 369,
374, 380, 383,
384, 387, 388,
390, 393, 397,
401, 410, 411,
421, 429, 431,
437, 440, 449,
451, 454-56,
459, 469, 479,
481, 488, 491,
492, 507, 535,
549, 552, 553,
555, 564, 568,
569, 577, 583,
586, 587, 592,
594, 597, 598,
605-6, 620, 628,
629, 637, 638,
641, 647, 651,
652, 656, 662,

668, 674, 675,
684, 691, 695,
719, 721, 723,
727, 733, 736,
737, 754, 758,
759, 770, 778,
780, 787, 794,
799-801, 805,
820, 833, 838,
840, 847, 854,
857, 861, 865,
868, 871, 874,
879, 883-85,
908, 916, 932,
933, 943, 947,
949, 953, 955,
960, 972, 975,
979
old age, 94, 108,
115, 142, 199,
228, 322, 351,
360, 410, 568,
569, 605-6, 652,
723, 805, 820,
883, 884, 933,
947, 953, 960
olive, olive tree, 12,
34, 36, 42, 81,
83, 116, 117,
216, 269-71,
273, 274, 294,
304, 310, 324,
324, 325, 325,
347, 351, 352,
357, 359, 363,
392, 431, 433,
486, 488, 497,
510, 520, 549,
551, 573, 603,
604, 612, 622,
632, 626, 633,
650, 652, 665,
684, 686, 738,
740, 890, 749,
757, 859, 890-
892, 910, 946,
963
oneness, 241, 293,
392, 606, 612,
738, 838
open, opening, 6, 8,
12, 18, 20, 22,
31, 36, 37, 49,
52, 72, 80, 85,
86, 89, 93, 95,
104, 117, 127,
145, 171, 174,
175, 191, 210,
215, 216, 218,
221, 227, 236,
237, 240, 244,
256, 262, 265,
272, 277, 282,
285, 294, 297,
305, 316, 317,
322, 326, 327,
336, 346, 349,
357, 361, 371,
377, 384, 389,
392, 402, 407,
408, 412, 424,
425, 436, 441,
453, 456, 471,
476, 480, 482,
486, 497, 499,
503, 506, 512,
515, 521, 526,
537, 541, 553,
556, 575, 577,
593, 606-7, 629,
631, 636, 646,
658, 660, 664,
666, 672, 682,
687, 699, 708,
714, 715, 721,
726, 729, 732,
743, 745, 760,

761, 763, 765,
767, 777, 787-
89, 792, 817,
820, 823, 828,
829, 843, 854,
879, 867, 868,
877, 882, 892,
897, 909, 912,
913, 917, 924,
931, 935, 937,
941, 942, 945,
946, 952, 953,
962, 971, 973
oppression, 54, 81,
86, 87, 135, 161,
229, 236, 253,
254, 281, 286,
349, 357, 430,
441, 447, 467,
492, 537, 553,
578, 596, 607-8,
615, 655, 658,
662, 694, 707,
734, 753, 790,
800, 803, 824-
26, 886, 888,
894, 906, 933,
954
oracle, oracles, 21-
23, 30, 49, 75,
79, 84, 90, 98,
107, 116, 117,
128, 135, 139-
41, 172, 173,
203, 209, 217-
19, 230, 244,
237, 242, 262,
271, 302, 316,
307, 318, 319,
348, 349, 357,
358, 365, 401,
402, 417, 429,
432, 435, 436,
449, 454, 525,
530, 525, 549,
561, 566, 590,
598, 599, 601-3,
608-10, 614,
647, 656, 658,
662, 668-70,
672, 674, 697,
717, 718, 726,
731, 738, 762,
785, 796, 845,
910, 915, 978-81
ordeal, ordeals, 185,
186, 246, 252,
269, 287, 342,
381, 446, 469,
610-11, 648,
655, 691, 696,
710, 867, 878,
882, 888, 892,
893, 928
orderliness, 180,
347, 455, 485,
520, 521, 542,
590, 592, 611,
612, 613, 742,
870
ordinance, ordi-
nances, 94, 205,
239, 362, 490,
616, 925, 966
origin, origins, 5,
35, 67, 90, 145,
153, 171, 174,
181, 197, 198,
202, 209, 211,
225, 246, 248,
253, 264, 267,
273, 275, 287,
300, 301, 307,
323, 340, 393,
418, 422, 426,
432, 436, 462,
505, 509, 510,

524, 525, 543,
551, 556, 588,
589, 595, 604,
612-15, 688,
703, 712, 718,
764, 775, 777,
781, 792, 844,
851, 902, 923,
926, 928, 947,
955, 956, 962
orphan, orphaned,
15, 63, 246, 301,
304, 403, 428,
430, 608, 615,
619, 677, 690,
693, 861, 946
outcast, outcasts,
67, 96, 138, 156,
209, 301, 303,
346, 350, 460,
482, 521, 529,
536, 541, 615-
16, 624, 636,
642, 744, 883,
828, 907, 940
outer, 11, 14, 83,
92, 107, 158,
176, 183, 318,
424, 466, 515,
615, 616, 667,
739, 776, 796,
813, 837, 876,
878, 952
outside, 4, 17, 36,
42, 55, 76, 89,
92, 100, 102,
103, 107, 108,
121, 126, 129,
131, 156, 161,
174, 175, 194,
203, 205, 209,
215, 216, 218,
221, 222, 225,
239, 245, 248,
251, 257, 259,
264, 275, 278,
304, 312, 324,
331, 336, 339,
375, 377, 399,
408-10, 415,
424, 426, 427,
429, 434, 440,
445, 462, 473,
474, 481, 502,
508, 512, 519,
558, 562, 572,
598, 600, 609-
11, 616-17, 640,
642, 666, 673,
688, 701, 735,
737, 764, 775,
788, 794, 795,
820, 825, 840,
859, 881, 923,
931, 940, 952,
964, 969, 972
outwitting, 408,
617-18, 655,
773, 894
overhearing, 66,
227, 314, 449,
522, 898
overseer, oversee-
ing, 60, 81, 275,
323, 385, 414,
422, 470, 495,
542, 589, 700,
774, 797, 874,
875
owl, 27, 94, 203,
528, 549, 580,
687, 773, 928
owner, ownership,
3, 27, 60, 112,
135, 138, 150,
166, 168, 281,
283, 286, 362,

363, 392, 480,
502-4, 532, 618-
20, 624, 668,
698, 710, 728,
754, 766, 774,
797, 806, 874,
940, 944, 975
ox, oxen, 6, 16, 26-
28, 31, 40, 72,
88, 100, 139,
142, 168, 191,
223, 269, 270,
291, 308, 327,
349, 379, 400,
410, 469, 508,
564, 580, 592,
618-19, 620-21,
654, 672, 676,
686, 695, 698,
707, 754, 773,
787, 820, 821,
852, 853, 867,
874, 879, 963,
886, 956, 967,
975
pain, 10, 14, 44,
72, 75, 81, 85,
95, 107, 113,
122, 123, 127,
141, 184, 224,
232, 279, 293,
298, 310, 313-
15, 351, 361,
377, 397, 427,
439, 443, 453,
472, 512, 541,
571, 589, 616,
622, 628, 657,
677, 727, 733,
736, 745, 790,
808, 824, 825,
855, 860, 864,
877, 915, 951,
945, 959, 981
palm tree, 294,
352, 622-23,
686, 775, 777,
806, 880, 891,
930
pangs, 14, 95, 107,
221, 277, 315,
622, 815, 860
parable, parables, 5,
7, 18, 26, 27, 39,
44, 59, 60, 64,
70, 71, 72, 74,
81, 86, 87, 92,
117, 118, 122-
24, 128, 132,
135, 160-62,
164, 166, 175,
182, 186, 196-
98, 204, 210,
221, 222, 224,
227, 229, 232,
235, 255, 263,
268, 269, 271,
279, 281, 285,
286, 291, 294,
296, 302, 318,
331, 332, 335,
345, 346, 348,
350, 352, 366,
367, 371, 372,
377, 379, 380,
383, 405, 385,
394, 405, 411,
420, 422, 423,
439, 449, 450,
451, 462, 464,
474, 480, 481,
484, 489, 494-
96, 498, 499,
501, 504, 506,
507, 517, 520,
521, 528, 529,
535, 536, 542,